An Introduction to

Statistical Concepts

The new edition of *An Introduction to Statistical Concepts* is designed to help students really understand statistical concepts, the situations in which they can be used, and how to apply them to data.

Hahs-Vaughn and Lomax discuss the most popular, along with many of the lesser-known, procedures and models, while also exploring nonparametric procedures used when standard assumptions are violated. They provide in-depth coverage of testing assumptions and highlight several online tools for computing statistics (e.g., effect sizes and their confidence intervals and power). This comprehensive, flexible, and accessible text includes a new chapter on mediation and moderation; expanded coverage of effect sizes; and discussions of sensitivity, specificity, false positive, and false negative, along with using the receiver operator characteristic (ROC) curve.

This book, noted for its crystal-clear explanations, and its inclusion of only the most crucial equations, is an invaluable resource for students undertaking a course in statistics in any number of social science and behavioral disciplines—from education, business, communication, exercise science, psychology, sociology and more.

Debbie L. Hahs-Vaughn is Professor of Methodology, Measurement, and Analysis at the University of Central Florida, US. Her primary research interest relates to methodological issues associated with applying quantitative statistical methods to survey data obtainec under complex sampling designs and using complex survey data to answer substantiv research questions.

Richard G. Lomax is Professor Emeritus of Educational and Human Ecology at the Oh State University, US, and former Associate Dean for Research and Administration. I research primarily focuses on early literacy and statistics.

An Introduction to Statistical Concepts

Fourth Edition

Debbie L. Hahs-Vaughn
University of Central Florida

Richard G. Lomax
The Ohio State University

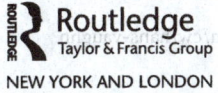

Routledge
Taylor & Francis Group
NEW YORK AND LONDON

Fourth edition published 2020
by Routledge
52 Vanderbilt Avenue, New York, NY 10017

and by Routledge
2 Park Square, Milton Park, Abingdon, Oxon, OX14 4RN

Routledge is an imprint of the Taylor & Francis Group, an informa business

First edition published by Psychology Press 2000

Third edition published by Routledge 2012

Library of Congress Cataloging-in-Publication Data
A catalog record for this book has been requested

ISBN: 978-1-138-65055-8 (hbk)
ISBN: 978-1-315-62435-8 (ebk)

Typeset in Palatino
by Apex CoVantage, LLC

Visit the companion website: www.routledge.com/cw/hahs-vaughn

This book is dedicated to our families and to all our former students.

You are statistically significant.

Contents

Preface

Approach

Many individuals have an aversion to statistics, which is quite unfortunate. Statistics is a tool that unleashes great power to the user—the potential to *really* make a difference. Being able to *understand* statistics means that you can critically evaluate empirical research conducted by others and thus better apply what others have found. Being able to *do* statistics means that you contribute to solving problems. We approach the writing of this text with the mindset that we want this text to be an instrument that contributes to your success as a researcher. With the help of this text, you will gain tools that can be used to make a positive contribution in your discipline. Perhaps this is the moment for which you have been created (Esther 4:14)! Consider the use of text as moving one step closer to making the world a better place.

This text is designed for a course in statistics for students in any number of social science and behavioral disciplines—from education to business to communication to exercise science to psychology to sociology and more. The text begins with the most basic introduction to statistics in the first chapter and then proceeds through intermediate statistics. The text is designed for you to become a better prepared researcher and a more intelligent consumer *and* producer of research. We do not assume that you have extensive or recent training in mathematics. Perhaps you have only had algebra, and perhaps that was some time ago. We also do not assume that you have ever had a statistics course. Rest assured; you will do fine.

We believe that a text should serve as an effective instructional tool. You should find this text to be more than a reference book. It is designed to help those who read it really understand statistical concepts, in what situations they can be applied, and how to apply them to data. With that said, there are several things that this text is *not*. This text is not a theoretical statistics book, nor is it a cookbook on computing statistics, nor a statistical software manual. Recipes suggest that there is one effective approach in all situations, and following that approach will produce the same results always. Additionally, recipes tend to be a crutch—followed without understanding how or why you obtain the desired product. As well, knowing how to run a statistics package without understanding the concepts or the output is not particularly useful. Thus, concepts drive the field of statistics, and that is the framework within which this text was approached.

Goals and Content Coverage

Our goals for this text are lofty, but the effort that you put forth in using it and its effects on your learning of statistics are more than worthwhile. First, the text provides comprehensive coverage of topics that could be included in an undergraduate or graduate one- or two-course sequence in statistics. The text is flexible enough so that instructors can select those topics that they desire to cover as they deem relevant in their particular discipline. In other words, chapters and sections of chapters from this text can be included in a statistics course as the instructor sees fit. Most of the popular, as well as many of the lesser-known procedures and models, are described in the text. A particular feature is a thorough discussion of assumptions, the effects of their violation, and how to deal with their violation.

The first five chapters of the text cover basic descriptive statistics, including ways of representing data graphically, statistical measures that describe a set of data, the normal distribution and other types of standard scores, and an introduction to probability and sampling. The remainder of the text covers different inferential statistics. In Chapters 6 through 10 we deal with different inferential tests involving means (e.g., t tests), proportions, variances, and correlations. In Chapters 11 through 16, all of the basic analysis of variance (ANOVA) models are considered. Finally, in Chapters 17 through 20 we examine various regression models.

This text also communicates a *conceptual, intuitive* understanding of statistics, which requires only a rudimentary knowledge of basic algebra, and emphasizes the important concepts in statistics. The most effective way to learn statistics is through the conceptual approach. Statistical concepts tend to be easy to learn because (a) concepts can be simply stated, (b) concepts can be made relevant through the use of real-life examples, (c) the same concepts are shared by many procedures, and (d) concepts can be related to one another. This is not to say that the text is void of mathematics, as understanding the math behind the technique blows apart the "black box" of statistics, particularly in a world where statistical software is so incredibly powerful. However, understanding the concepts is the first step in advancing toward a true understanding of statistics.

This text will help you to reach the goal of being a better consumer and producer of research. The following indicators may provide some feedback as to how you are doing. First, there will be a noticeable change in your attitude toward statistics. Thus, one outcome is for you to feel that "Statistics is not half bad" or "This stuff is OK." Second, you will feel comfortable using statistics in your own work. Finally, you will begin to "see the light." You will know when you have reached this highest stage of statistics development when suddenly in the middle of the night you wake up from a dream and say, "Now I get it!" In other words, you will begin to *think* statistics rather than think of ways to get out of doing statistics.

Pedagogical Tools

The text contains several important pedagogical features to allow you to attain these goals. First, each chapter begins with a list of key concepts, which provide helpful landmarks within the chapter. Second, realistic examples from education and the behavioral sciences are used to illustrate the concepts and procedures covered in each chapter. Each example includes an initial vignette, an examination of the relevant procedures and necessary assumptions, how to run SPSS and **R** and develop an APA-style write-up, as well as tables, figures, and annotated SPSS and **R** output to assist you. Third, the text is based on the conceptual approach; that is, material is presented so that you obtain a good understanding of statistical concepts. *If you know the concepts, then you know statistics.* Finally, each chapter ends with three sets of problems—computational, conceptual, and interpretive. Pay particular attention to the conceptual problems as they provide the best assessment of your understanding of the concepts in the chapter. We strongly suggest using the example datasets and the computational and interpretive problems for additional practice through available statistical software. This will serve to reinforce the concepts covered. Answers to the odd-numbered problems are given at the end of each chapter.

Important Features in This Edition

A number of changes have been made in this edition based on the suggestions of reviewers, instructors, teaching assistants, and students. These improvements have been made in order to better achieve the goals of the text. The changes include the following:

1. The content has been updated and numerous additional references have been provided.
2. The final chapter on mediation and moderation has been added for a more complete presentation of regression models.
3. To parallel the generation of statistics using SPSS (version 25), script and annotated output using **R** have been included to assist in the generation and interpretation of statistics.
4. Coverage of effect sizes has been expanded, including the use of online tools for computing effect sizes.
5. A discussion of sensitivity, specificity, false positive, and false negative has been included in the logistic regression chapter, along with using the receiver operator characteristic (ROC) curve to determine classification accuracy.
6. A discussion of the general linear model has been folded into the analysis of variance (ANOVA) chapter to help readers understand how ANOVA and regression models are connected.
7. An expanded discussion of testing, and illustration of how to test for, interactions in factorial ANOVA is now provided.
8. More organizational features (e.g., boxes, tables, figures) have been included to summarize concepts and/or increase understanding of the material.
9. Additional end-of-chapter problems have been included.
10. A website for the text provides instructor-only access to a test bank (the website continues to offer the datasets, chapter outline, answers to the even-numbered problems, and PowerPoint slides for each chapter, with students granted access to the appropriate elements).

Acknowledgments

We have been blessed beyond measure, and are thankful for so many individuals who have played an important role in our personal and professional lives and, in some way, have shaped this text. Rather than include an admittedly incomplete listing, we just say "thank you" to all of you. A special thank you to all of the terrific students that we have had the pleasure of teaching at the University of Pittsburgh, the University of Illinois at Chicago, Louisiana State University, Boston College, Northern Illinois University, the University of Alabama, The Ohio State University, and the University of Central Florida. For all of your efforts, and the many lights that you have seen and shared with us, this book is for you.

Thanks also to so many wonderful publishing staff that we've had the pleasure of working along the way, first at Lawrence Erlbaum Associates and now at Routledge/Taylor & Francis. Additionally, we are most appreciative of the insightful suggestions provided by the reviewers of this text over the years.

For the users of this text, *you are the reason we write*. Thank you for bringing us along in your research and statistical journey. To those that have contacted us with questions, comments, and suggestions, we are very appreciative. We hope that you will continue to contact us to offer feedback (good and bad).

Last but not least, we extend gratitude to our families, in particular, to Lea and Kristen, and to Mark and Malani. Your unfailing love, understanding, and tolerance during the writing of this text allowed us to cope with such a major project. *You are statistically significant!* Thank you one and all.

DLHV & RGL

1

Introduction

Chapter Outline

Key Concepts

1. *General statistical concepts*
   - Population
   - Parameter
   - Sample
   - Statistic
   - Descriptive statistics
   - Inferential statistics
2. *Variable-related concepts*
   - Variable
   - Constant

Categorical variables
Dichotomous variables
Numerical variables
Discrete variables
Continuous variables

3. Measurement scale concepts
Measurement
Nominal scale
Ordinal scale
Interval scale
Ratio scale

Welcome to the wonderful world of statistics! More than ever, statistics are everywhere. Listen to the weather report and you hear about the measurement of variables such as temperature, rainfall, barometric pressure, and humidity. Watch a sporting event and you hear about batting averages, percentage of free throws completed, and total rushing yardage. Read the financial page and you can track the Dow Jones average, the gross national product (GNP), and bank interest rates. Turn to the entertainment section to see movie ratings, movie revenue, or the top 10 best-selling novels. These are just a few examples of statistics that surround you in every aspect of your life. This is not to mention the way statistics have, probably unnoticeably, influenced our everyday lives—just consider the impact that statistics have had the next time you buckle your seatbelt or help a child into their booster seat.

Although you may be thinking that statistics is not the most enjoyable subject on the planet, by the end of this text you will (a) have a more positive attitude about statistics; (b) feel more comfortable using statistics, and thus be more likely to perform your own quantitative data analyses; and (c) certainly know much more about statistics than you do now. In other words, our goal is to equip you with the skills you need to be both a better consumer and producer of research. But be forewarned; the road to statistical independence is not easy. However, we will serve as your guides along the way. When the going gets tough, we will be there to provide you with advice and numerous examples and problems. Using the powers of logic, mathematical reasoning, and statistical concept knowledge, we will help you arrive at an appropriate solution to the statistical problem at hand.

Some students begin statistics courses with some anxiety, or even much anxiety. This could be the result of not having had a quantitative course for some time, apprehension built up by delaying taking statistics, a poor past instructor or course, or less than adequate past success, among other possible reasons. We hope this text will help alleviate any anxiety you may have. This is a good segue to discuss what this text is and what it is not. First, this is not a textbook on only one statistical procedure. This is a text on the application of *many different types of statistics* to a variety of disciplines. If you are looking for a text that goes very deep and into the weeds, so to speak, into just one area of statistics, then please review the Additional Resources sections at the conclusion of the respective chapters of interest. Although we feel we have provided a very comprehensive overview of and introduction into many types of statistics that are covered in the first few statistics courses, we do not pretend to suggest that everything you need to know about any one procedure will be covered in our book. Indeed, we do not know of any text that can make that claim! We do anticipate you will find the text is an excellent starting point, and should you desire to delve deeper, we have offered resources to assist in that endeavor.

Second, the philosophy of the text is on the *understanding of concepts* rather than on the derivation of statistical formulas. In other words, this is not a mathematical statistics textbook. We have written the book with the perspective that it is more important to understand concepts than to solve theorems and derive or memorize various and sundry formulas. If you understand the concepts, you can always look up the formulas if need be. If you do not understand the concepts, then knowing the formulas will only allow you to operate in a cookbook mode without really understanding what you are doing.

Third, the calculator and computer are your friends. These devices are tools that allow you to complete the necessary computations and obtain the results of interest. There is no need to compute equations by hand (another reason why we concentrate on the concepts rather than formulas). If you are performing computations by hand, find a calculator that you are comfortable with; it need not have 800 functions, as the four basic operations, sum, and square root functions are sufficient (one of our personal calculators is one of those little credit card calculators, although we often use the calculator on our computers). If you are using a statistical software program, find one that you are comfortable with (most instructors will have you use a program such as **R**, SPSS, or SAS). In this text, we do walk through basic formulas by hand so that you become acquainted with how the statistical program works and the numbers that are used in it. However, we don't anticipate (nor do we encourage) that you make a practice of working statistics by hand. Throughout the text, we use SPSS and **R** to illustrate statistical applications. Although this book is *not* a guide on all things SPSS and **R**, we do try to provide the tools you need to compute the various statistics. We hope that you will supplement what we provide with your own motivation to learn more about software that can assist you in computing statistics.

Finally, this text will take you from raw data to results using realistic examples. The examples may not always be from a discipline that is like the one you are in, but we hope that you are able to transfer or generalize the illustration to an area in which you more comfortable. These examples can then be followed up using the problems at the end of each chapter. Thus, you will not be on your own, but will have the text, a computer/calculator, as well as your course and instructor, to help guide you.

The intent and philosophy of this text is to be conceptual and intuitive in nature. We have written the text so that students who have completed basic mathematical requirements in high school can be comfortable reading the text. Thus, the text does not require a high level of mathematics, but rather emphasizes the important concepts in statistics. Most statistical concepts really are fairly easy to learn because (a) concepts can be simply stated, (b) concepts can be related to real-life examples, (c) many of the same concepts run through much of statistics, and therefore (d) many concepts can be related.

In this introductory chapter, we describe the most basic statistical concepts. We begin with the question, "What is the value of statistics?" We then look at a brief history of statistics by mentioning a few of the more important and interesting statisticians. Then we consider the concepts of population, parameter, sample, statistic, descriptive and inferential statistics, types of variables, and scales of measurement. Our objectives are that by the end of this chapter you will (a) have a better sense of why statistics are necessary, (b) see that statisticians are an interesting group of people, and (c) have an understanding of several basic statistical concepts.

1.1 What Is the Value of Statistics?

Let us start off with a reasonable rhetorical question: "Why do we need statistics?" In other words, what is the value of statistics, either in your research or in your everyday life? As a way of thinking about these questions, consider the following headlines, which have probably appeared in your local newspaper.

Cigarette Smoking Causes Cancer—Tobacco Industry Denies Charges

A study conducted at Ivy-Covered University Medical School recently published in the *New England Journal of Medicine* has definitively shown that cigarette smoking causes cancer. In interviews with 100 randomly selected smokers and nonsmokers over 50 years of age, 30% of the smokers have developed some form of cancer, while only 10% of the nonsmokers have cancer. "The higher percentage of smokers with cancer in our study clearly indicates that cigarettes cause cancer," said Dr. Jason P. Smythe. On the contrary, "this study doesn't even suggest that cigarettes cause cancer," said tobacco lobbyist Cecil B. Hacker. "Who knows how these folks got cancer; maybe it is caused by the aging process or by the method in which individuals were selected for the interviews," Mr. Hacker went on to say.

North Carolina Congressional Districts Gerrymandered—African Americans Slighted

A study conducted at the National Center for Legal Research indicates that congressional districts in the state of North Carolina have been gerrymandered to minimize the impact of the African American vote. "From our research, it is clear that the districts are apportioned in a racially biased fashion. Otherwise, how could there be no single district in the entire state which has a majority of African American citizens when over 50% of the state's population is African American? The districting system absolutely has to be changed," said Dr. I. M. Researcher. A spokesman for the American Bar Association countered with the statement, "according to a decision rendered by the U.S. Supreme Court in 1999 (No. 98–85), intent or motive must be shown for racial bias to be shown in the creation of congressional districts. The decision states a 'facially neutral law . . . warrants strict scrutiny only if it can be proved that the law was motivated by a racial purpose or object.' The data in this study do not show intent or motive. To imply that these data indicate racial bias is preposterous."

Global Warming—Myth According to the President

Research conducted at the National Center for Global Warming (NCGW) has shown the negative consequences of global warming on the planet Earth. As summarized by Dr. Noble Pryze, "our studies at NCGW clearly demonstrate that if global warming is not halted in the next 20 years, the effects on all aspects of our environment and climatology will be catastrophic." A different view is held by U.S. President Harold W. Tree. He stated in a recent address that "the scientific community has not convinced him that global warming even exists. Why should our administration spend millions of dollars on an issue that has not been shown to be a real concern?"

How is one to make sense of the studies described by these headlines? How is one to decide which side of the issue these data support, so as to take an intellectual stand? In other words, do the interview data clearly indicate that cigarette smoking causes cancer? Do the congressional district percentages of African Americans necessarily imply that there is racial bias? Have scientists convinced us that global warming is a problem? These studies are examples of situations where the appropriate use of statistics is clearly necessary. *Statistics will provide us with an intellectually acceptable method for making decisions in such matters.* For instance, a certain type of research, statistical analysis, and set of results are all necessary to make causal inferences about cigarette smoking. Another type of research, statistical analysis, and set of results are all necessary to lead one to confidently state that the districting system is racially biased or not, or that global warming needs to be dealt with. *The bottom line is that the purpose of statistics, and thus of this text, is to provide you with the tools to make important decisions in an appropriate and confident manner using data.* W. Edwards Deming has been credited with bringing quality to manufacturing (e.g., Gabor, 1990), and he once stated, "In God we trust. All others must have data." These are words to live by! After reading this text, you will not have to trust a statement made by some so-called expert on an issue, which may or may not have any empirical basis or validity; you can make your own judgments based on the statistical analyses of data. For you, the value of statistics can include (a) the ability to read and critique articles in both professional journals and in the popular press, and (b) the ability to conduct statistical analyses for your own research (e.g., thesis or dissertation). We hope that this text will guide you in becoming both a better consumer and better producer of statistics. You are gaining skills that you can use to make a contribution to your field and, more important, make the world a better place. The statistical skills you are gaining through this text are powerful. Use them—wisely!

1.2 Brief Introduction to the History of Statistics

As a way of getting to know the topic of statistics, we want to briefly introduce you to a few famous statisticians. The purpose of this section is not to provide a comprehensive history of statistics, as those already exist (e.g., Heyde, Seneta, Crepel, Feinberg, & Gain, 2001; Pearson, 1978; Stigler, 1986). Rather, the purpose of this section is to show that famous statisticians are not only interesting, but are human beings just like you and me.

One of the fathers of probability (see Chapter 5) is acknowledged to be Blaise Pascal from the late 1600s. One of Pascal's contributions was that he worked out the probabilities for each dice roll in the game of craps, enabling his friend, a member of royalty, to become a consistent winner. He also developed Pascal's triangle, which you may remember from your early mathematics education. The statistical development of the normal or bell-shaped curve (see Chapter 4) is interesting. For many years, this development was attributed to Karl Friedrich Gauss (early 1800s), and was actually known for some time as the Gaussian curve. Later historians found that Abraham DeMoivre actually developed the normal curve in the 1730s. As statistics was not thought of as a true academic discipline until the late 1800s, people like Pascal and DeMoivre were consulted by the wealthy on odds about games of chance and by insurance underwriters to determine mortality rates.

Karl Pearson is one of the most famous statisticians to date (late 1800s to early 1900s). Among his many accomplishments is the Pearson product-moment correlation coefficient still in use today (see Chapter 10). You may know of Florence Nightingale (1820–1910) as an important figure in the field of nursing. However, you may not know of her importance in the field of statistics. Nightingale believed that statistics and theology were linked and that by studying statistics we might come to understand God's laws.

A quite interesting statistical personality is William Sealy Gossett, who was employed by the Guinness Brewery in Ireland. The brewery wanted to select a sample of people from Dublin in 1906 for purposes of taste testing. Gossett was asked how large a sample was needed in order to make an accurate inference about the entire population (see next section). The brewery would not let Gossett publish any of his findings under his own name, so he used the pseudonym of Student. Today the t distribution is still known as Student's t distribution. Sir Ronald A. Fisher is another of the most famous statisticians of all time. Working in the early 1900s Fisher introduced the analysis of variance (see Chapters 11–16) and Fisher's z transformation for correlations (see Chapter 10). In fact, the major statistic in the analysis of variance is referred to as the F ratio in honor of Fisher. These individuals represent only a fraction of the many famous and interesting statisticians over the years. For further information about these and other statisticians, we suggest you consult the references noted previously (e.g., Heyde et al., 2001; Pearson, 1978; Stigler, 1986), which provide many interesting stories about statisticians.

1.3 General Statistical Definitions

In this section we define some of the most basic concepts in statistics. Included here are definitions and examples of the following concepts: population, parameter, sample, statistic, descriptive statistics, and inferential statistics.

The first four concepts are tied together, so we discuss them together. A **population** is defined as *all members of a well-defined group*. A population may be large in scope, such as when a population is defined as all of the employees of IBM worldwide. A population may be small in scope, such as when a population is defined as all of the IBM employees at the building on Main Street in Atlanta. *The key is that the population is well defined* such that one could determine specifically who all of the members of the group are and then information or data could be collected from all such members. Thus, if our population is defined as all members working in a particular office building, then our study would consist of collecting data from all employees in that building. It is also important to remember that *you*, the researcher, define the population.

A **parameter** is defined as a *characteristic of a population*. For instance, parameters of our office building example might be the number of individuals who work in that building (e.g., 154), the average salary of those individuals (e.g., $49,569), and the range of ages of those individuals (e.g., 21 to 68 years of age). When we think about characteristics of a population we are thinking about **population parameters**. The two terms are often linked together.

A **sample** is defined as a *subset of a population*. A sample may be large in scope, such as when a population is defined as all of the employees of IBM worldwide and 20% of those individuals are included in the sample. A sample may be small in scope, such as when a population is defined as all of the IBM employees at the building on Main Street in Atlanta and 10% of those individuals are included in the sample. Thus, a sample could be large or small in scope and consist of any portion of the population. *The key is that the sample consists of some, but not all, of the members of the population*; that is, anywhere from one individual to all but one individual from the population is included in the sample. Thus, if our population is defined as all members working in the IBM building on Main Street in Atlanta, then our study would consist of collecting data from a sample of some of the employees in that building. It follows that if we, the researchers, define the population, then we also determine what the sample will be.

A **statistic** is defined as a *characteristic of a sample*. For instance, statistics of our office building example might be the number of individuals who work in the building that we sampled (e.g., 77), the average salary of those individuals (e.g., $54,022), and the range of ages of those individuals (e.g., 25 to 62 years of age). Notice that the statistics of a sample need not be equal to the parameters of a population (more about this in Chapter 5). When we think about characteristics of a sample we are thinking about **sample statistics**. The two terms are often linked together. Thus, we have *population parameters* and *sample statistics*, but no other combinations of those terms exist. The field has become known as "statistics" simply because we are almost always dealing with sample statistics because population data are rarely obtained.

The final two concepts are also tied together, and thus are considered together. The field of statistics is generally divided into two types of statistics: descriptive and inferential. **Descriptive statistics** are defined as *techniques that allow us to tabulate, summarize, and depict a collection of data in an abbreviated fashion*. In other words, the purpose of descriptive statistics is to allow us to talk about (or describe) a collection of data without having to look at the entire collection. For example, say we have just collected a set of data from 100,000 graduate students on various characteristics (e.g., height, weight, gender, grade point average, aptitude test scores). If you were to ask us about the data, we could do one of two things. On the one hand, we could carry around the entire collection of data everywhere we go and when someone asks us about the data simply say, "Here is the data; take a look at them yourself." On the other hand, we could summarize the data in an abbreviated fashion and when someone asks us about the data simply say, "Here is a table and a graph about the data; they summarize the entire collection." So, rather than viewing 100,000 sheets of paper, perhaps we would only have to view two sheets of paper. Because statistics is largely a system of communicating information, descriptive statistics are considerably more useful to a consumer than an entire collection of data. Descriptive statistics are discussed in Chapters 2 through 4.

Inferential statistics are defined as *techniques that allow us to employ inductive reasoning to infer the properties of an entire group or collection of individuals, a population, from a small number of those individuals, a sample*. In other words, the purpose of inferential statistics is to allow us to collect data from a sample of individuals and then infer the properties of that sample back to the population of individuals. In case you have forgotten about logic, inductive reasoning is where you infer from the specific (here the sample) to the general (here the population). For example, say we have just collected a set of sample data from 5000 of the population of 100,000 graduate students on various characteristics (e.g., height, weight, gender, grade point average, aptitude test scores). If you were to ask us about the data, we could compute various sample statistics and then infer with some confidence that these would be similar to the population parameters. In other words, this allows us to collect data from a subset of the population, yet still make inferential statements about the population without collecting data from the entire population. So, rather than collecting data from all 100,000 graduate students in the population, we could collect data on a sample of say 5000 students.

As another example, Gossett (aka Student) was asked to conduct a taste test of Guinness beer for a sample of Dublin residents. Because the brewery could not afford to do this with the entire population of Dublin, Gossett collected data from a sample of Dublin and was able to make an inference from these sample results back to the population. A discussion of inferential statistics begins in Chapter 5. In summary, the field of statistics is roughly divided into descriptive statistics and inferential statistics. Note, however, that many further distinctions are made among the types of statistics, but more about that later.

1.3.1 Statistical Notation

Statistics can be denoted in words or in symbols. Statistical notation that refers to the *population* uses Greek symbols. Statistical notation that refers to the *sample* uses upper- and lowercase letters. Table 1.1 provides a handy reference for the upper and lowercase Greek

TABLE 1.1

Statistical Notation

Uppercase Letter	Lowercase Letter	Symbol Name	Definition and/or What the Symbol Denotes
Greek Alphabet			
Α	α	Alpha	Type I error rate (also known as level of significance or significance level)
Β	β	Beta	Type II error rate; regression coefficient
Γ	γ	Gamma	Correlation coefficient for ordinal data
Δ	δ	Delta	Standardized effect size
Ε	ε	Epsilon	Random residual error
Ζ	ζ	Zeta	Discrete probability distribution
Η	η	Eta	When squared, a proportion of variance explained effect size
Θ	θ	Theta	General population parameter
Ι	ι	Iota	
Κ	κ	Kappa	A measure of interrater reliability (as in Cohen's kappa)
Λ	λ	Lambda	Probability distribution (as in Wilks' lambda)
Μ	μ	Mu	Mean
Ν	ν	Nu	Degrees of freedom
Ξ	ξ	Xi	
Ο	ο	Omicron	
Π	π	Pi	Population proportion
Ρ	ρ	Rho	Population correlation coefficient
Σ	σ	Sigma	Population standard deviation
Τ	τ	Tau	Correlation coefficient for ordinal data (as in Kendall's tau); in multilevel modeling, the intercept variance
Υ	υ	Upsilon	Effect size for mediation models
Φ	ϕ, φ	Phi	Correlation coefficient for binary variables
Χ	χ	Chi	When squared, a probability distribution
Ψ	ψ	Psi	
Ω	ω	Omega	When squared, a proportion of variance explained effect size
Select Additional Notation			
N	n		Population and sample size, respectively
	p		Observed probability
	r		Sample correlation coefficient
	s		Sample standard deviation
	t		Student's t
$\bar{X}$		X bar	Sample mean

alphabet, the name of the symbol, and how the symbol is commonly used in statistics. The table also includes additional notation commonly used to denote statistics. We will use many of these symbols throughout the text. This table is provided with a caveat. Unfortunately, statistical notation is not standardized. Should you pick up a different text, it's likely that the authors have used at least some different notation than what has been used in this text. (Argh! How frustrating, right?) Thus, throughout the text we have attempted to clearly indicate what the notation means as it is used.

1.4 Types of Variables

There are several terms we need to define about variables. First, it might be useful to define the term variable. A **variable** is defined as *any characteristic of persons or things that is observed to take on different values*. In other words, the values for a particular characteristic vary across the individuals observed. For example, the annual salary of the families in your neighborhood varies because not every family earns the same annual salary. One family might earn $50,000 while the family right next door might earn $65,000. Thus, the annual family salary is a *variable* because it *varies* across families.

In contrast, a **constant** is defined as *any characteristic of persons or things that is observed to take on only a single value*. In other words, the values for a particular characteristic are the *same* for all individuals or units observed. For example, say every family in your neighborhood has a lawn. Although the nature of the lawns may vary, everyone has a lawn. Thus, whether a family has a lawn in your neighborhood is a constant and therefore would not be a very interesting characteristic to study. *When designing a study, you (i.e., the researcher) can determine what is a constant*. This is part of the process of *delimiting*, or narrowing the scope of, your study. As an example, you may be interested in studying career paths of girls who complete AP science courses. In designing your study, you are only interested in girls, and thus sex would be a constant—you would be delimiting your study to girls. This is not to say that the researcher wholly determines when a characteristic is a constant. It is sometimes the case that we find that a characteristic is a constant *after* we conduct the study. In other words, one of the measures has no variation—everyone or everything scored or remained the same on that particular characteristic.

A number of different typologies are available for describing variables. One typology is categorical (or qualitative) versus numerical (or quantitative), and within numerical, discrete and continuous. A **categorical variable** is a *qualitative variable that describes categories of a characteristic or attribute*. Examples of categorical variables include political party affiliation (Republican = 1, Democrat = 2, Independent = 3), religious affiliation (e.g., Methodist = 1, Baptist = 2, Roman Catholic = 3, etc.), and course letter grade (A = 4, B = 3, C = 2, D = 1, F = 0). A **dichotomous variable** (also known as a *binary variable*) is a special, restricted type of categorical variable and is defined as a *variable that can take on only one of two values*. For example, sex at birth is a variable that can take on the values of male or female and is often coded numerically as 0 (e.g., for males) or 1 (e.g., for females). Other dichotomous variables include pass/fail, true/false, living/dead, and smoker/non-smoker. Dichotomous variables will take on special importance as we later study binary logistic regression (Chapter 19).

A **numerical variable** is a quantitative variable. Numerical variables can further be classified as either discrete or continuous. A **discrete variable** is defined as a *variable that can* *only take on certain values*. For example, the number of children in a family can only take on certain values. Many values are not possible, such as negative values (e.g., the Joneses cannot have –2 children) or decimal values (e.g., the Smiths cannot have 2.2 children). In contrast, a **continuous variable** is defined as a *variable that can take on any value within a certain range, given a precise enough measurement instrument*. For example, the distance between two cities can be measured in miles, with miles estimated in whole numbers. However, given a more precise instrument with which to measure, distance can even be measured down to the inch or millimeter. When considering the difference between a discrete and continuous variable, keep in mind that *discrete variables arise from the counting process* and *continuous variables arise from the measuring process*. For example, the number of students enrolled in your statistics class is a discrete variable. If we were to measure (i.e., count) the number of students in the class, it would not matter if we counted first names alphabetically from A to Z or if we counted beginning with the person sitting in the front row to the last person sitting in the back row—either way, we would arrive at the same value. In other words, how we "measure" (again, in this instance, how we count) the students in the class does not matter—we will always arrive at the same result. In comparison, the value of a continuous variable is dependent on how precise the measuring instrument is. Weighing yourself on a scale that rounds to whole numbers will give us one measure of weight. However weighing on another, more precise, scale that rounds to three decimal places will provide a more precise measure of weight.

Here are a few additional examples. Other discrete variables include number of books owned, number of credit hours enrolled, and number of teachers employed at a school. Other continuous variables include salary (from zero to billions in dollars and cents), age (from zero up, in millisecond increments), height (from zero up, in increments of fractions of millimeters), weight (from zero up, in increments of fractions of ounces), and time (from zero up, in millisecond increments). Variable type is a very important concept in terms of selecting an appropriate statistic, as will be shown later.

1.5 Scales of Measurement

Another concept useful for selecting an appropriate statistic is the scale of measurement of the variables. First, however, we define **measurement** as the *assignment of numerical values to persons or things according to explicit rules*. For example, how do we measure a person's weight? Well, there are rules that individuals commonly follow. Currently weight is measured on some sort of balance or scale in pounds or grams. In the old days weight was measured by different rules, such as the number of stones or gold coins. These explicit rules were developed so that there was a standardized and generally agreed upon method of measuring weight. Thus, if you weighted 10 stones in Coventry, England, then that meant the same as 10 stones in Liverpool, England.

In 1951 the psychologist S.S. Stevens developed four types of measurement scales that could be used for assigning these numerical values. In other words, the type of rule used was related to the measurement scale. The four types of measurement scales are the nominal, ordinal, interval, and ratio scales. They are presented in order of increasing complexity (i.e., *nominal is the simplest* and *ratio is the most complex*) and of increasing information (i.e., *nominal provides the least information* and *ratio provides the most information*) (remembering the mnemonic NOIR might be helpful). It is worth restating the importance of understanding

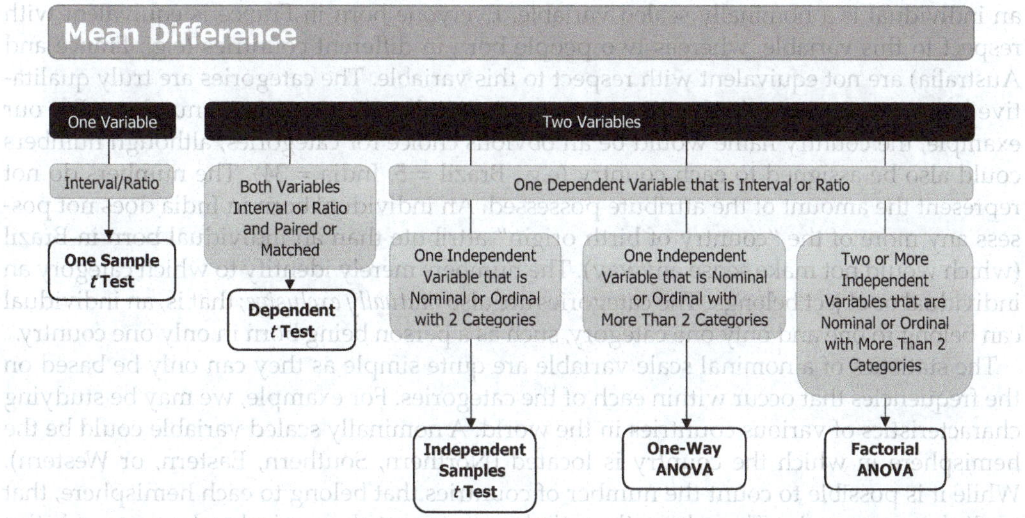

FIGURE 1.1
Flow chart for mean difference tests.

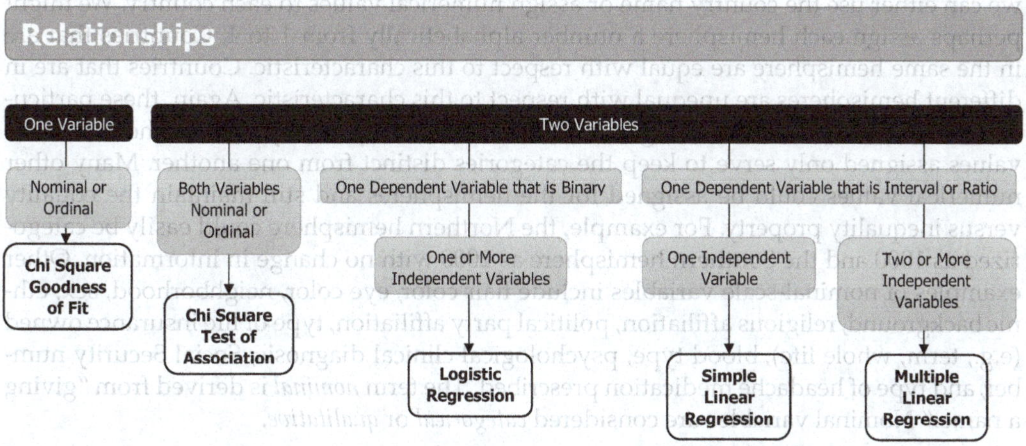

FIGURE 1.2
Flow chart for relationship tests.

the measurement scales of variables as the measurement scale will dictate what statistical procedures can be performed with the data. While we recommend approaching your analysis by first defining your research question *and then* determining the requisite data and statistical procedure needed, Figures 1.1 and 1.2 may be helpful in understanding how a variable's measurement scale relates to some of the more basic statistical procedures that will be covered in the text.

1.5.1 Nominal Measurement Scale

The simplest scale of measurement is the **nominal scale**. Here, the units (e.g., individuals or objects) are classified into categories so that all of those in a single category are equivalent with respect to the characteristic being measured. For example, the country of birth of an individual is a nominally scaled variable. Everyone born in France is equivalent with respect to this variable, whereas two people born in different countries (e.g., France and Australia) are not equivalent with respect to this variable. The categories are truly qualitative in nature, not quantitative. Categories are typically given names or numbers. For our example, the country name would be an obvious choice for categories, although numbers could also be assigned to each country (e.g., Brazil = 5, India = 34). The numbers do not represent the amount of the attribute possessed. An individual born in India does not possess any more of the "country of birth origin" attribute than an individual born in Brazil (which would not make sense anyway). The numbers merely identify to which category an individual or object belongs. The categories are also *mutually exclusive*; that is, an individual can belong to one and only one category, such as a person being born in only one country.

The statistics of a nominal scale variable are quite simple as they can only be based on the frequencies that occur within each of the categories. For example, we may be studying characteristics of various countries in the world. A nominally scaled variable could be the hemisphere in which the country is located (Northern, Southern, Eastern, or Western). While it is possible to count the number of countries that belong to each hemisphere, that is all that we can do. *The only mathematical property that the nominal scale possesses is that of equality versus inequality*. In other words, two individuals or objects are either in the same category (equal) or in different categories (unequal). For the hemisphere variable, we can either use the country name or assign numerical values to each country. We might perhaps assign each hemisphere a number alphabetically from 1 to 4. Countries that are in the same hemisphere are equal with respect to this characteristic. Countries that are in different hemispheres are unequal with respect to this characteristic. Again, these particular numerical values are meaningless and could arbitrarily be any values. The numerical values assigned only serve to keep the categories distinct from one another. Many other numerical values could be assigned for the hemispheres and still maintain the equality versus inequality property. For example, the Northern hemisphere could easily be categorized as 1000 and the Southern hemisphere as 2000 with no change in information. Other examples of nominal-scale variables include hair color, eye color, neighborhood, sex, ethnic background, religious affiliation, political party affiliation, type of life insurance owned (e.g., term, whole life), blood type, psychological clinical diagnosis, Social Security number, and type of headache medication prescribed. The term *nominal* is derived from "giving a name." Nominal variables are considered *categorical* or *qualitative*.

1.5.2 Ordinal Measurement Scale

The next most complex scale of measurement is the **ordinal scale**. Ordinal measurement is determined by the relative size or position of individuals or objects with respect to the characteristic being measured. That is, the units (e.g., individuals or objects) are *rank ordered* according to the amount of the characteristic that they possess. For example, say a high school graduating class had 250 students. Students could then be assigned class ranks according to their academic performance (e.g., grade point average) in high school. The student ranked 1 in the class had the highest relative performance and the student ranked 250 had the lowest relative performance.

However, equal differences between the ranks do not imply equal distance in terms of the characteristic being measured. For example, the students ranked 1 and 2 in the class may have a different distance in terms of actual academic performance than the students ranked 249 and 250, even though both pairs of students differ by a rank of 1. In other words, here a rank difference of 1 does not imply the same actual performance distance. The pairs of students may be very, very close or may be quite distant from one another. As a result of *equal differences* not implying *equal distances,* the statistics that we can use are limited due to these unequal intervals. *The ordinal scale then, consists of two mathematical properties: equality versus inequality; and if two individuals or objects are unequal, then we can determine greater than or less than.* That is, if two individuals have different class ranks, then we can determine which student had a greater or lesser class rank. Although the greater than or less than property is evident, an ordinal scale cannot tell us how much greater than or less than because of the unequal intervals. Thus, the student ranked 250 could be farther away from student 249 than the student ranked 2 from student 1.

When we have *untied ranks,* as shown on the left side of Table 1.2, assigning ranks is straightforward. What do we do if there are *tied ranks*? For example, suppose there are two students with the same grade point average of 3.8 as given on the right side of Table 1.1. How do we assign them into class ranks? It is clear that they have to be assigned the same rank, as that would be the only fair method. However, there are at least two methods for dealing with tied ranks. One method would be to assign each of them a rank of 2, as that is the next available rank. However, this method has two problems. First, the sum of the ranks for the same number of scores would be different depending on whether there were ties or not. Statistically, this is not a satisfactory solution. Second, what rank would the next student having the 3.6 grade point average be given, a rank of 3 or 4?

The second and preferred method is to take the average of the available ranks and assign that value to each of the tied individuals. Thus, the two persons tied at a grade point average of 3.8 have as available ranks 2 and 3. Both would then be assigned the average rank of 2.5. Also the three persons tied at a grade point average of 3.0 have as available ranks 5, 6, and 7. These all would be assigned the average rank of 6. You also see in the table that with this method the sum of the ranks for 7 scores is always equal to 28, regardless of the number of ties. Statistically this is a satisfactory solution and the one we prefer whether we are using a statistical software package or hand computations. Other examples of ordinal scale variables include course letter grades (e.g., A, B, C, . . .), order of finish in the Boston Marathon (e.g., 1st, 2nd, 3rd, . . .), socioeconomic status (e.g., low, middle, high), hardness of minerals (1 = softest to 10 = hardest), faculty rank (assistant, associate, and full professor), student class (freshman, sophomore, junior, senior, graduate student), ranking on a personality trait (e.g., extreme intrinsic to extreme extrinsic motivation), and military rank (e.g., E-1, E-2, E-3, . . .). The term *ordinal* is derived from "ordering" individuals or objects. Ordinal variables

TABLE 1.2

Untied Ranks and Tied Ranks for Ordinal Data

Untied Ranks		Tied Ranks	
Grade Point Average	**Rank**	**Grade Point Average**	**Rank**
4.0	1	4.0	1
3.9	2	3.8	2.5
3.8	3	3.8	2.5
3.6	4	3.6	4
3.2	5	3.0	6
3.0	6	3.0	6
2.7	7	3.0	6
	Sum = 28		Sum = 28

are most often considered *categorical* or *qualitative*. We say "most often" because ordinal items are sometimes considered quantitative. In our professional opinion, ordinal items are categorical or qualitative. However, researchers in some disciplines treat ordinal items as quantitative and use them as they would an interval or ratio variable (this won't make much sense yet, but it will soon). We strongly discourage that practice. The only exception may be a situation where an ordinal item has many categories or levels, such as more than 10. In those instances, treating an ordinal item as interval or ratio *may* make sense.

1.5.3 Interval Measurement Scale

The next most complex scale of measurement is the **interval scale**. An interval scale is one where units (e.g., individuals or objects) can be ordered, and equal differences between the values do imply equal distance in terms of the characteristic being measured. That is, *order and distance relationships are meaningful. However, there is no absolute zero point*. Absolute zero, if it exists, implies the total absence of the property being measured. The zero point of an interval scale, if it exists, is arbitrary and does not reflect the total absence of the property being measured. Here, the *zero point merely serves as a placeholder*. For example, suppose that we gave you the final exam in advanced statistics right now. If you were to be so unlucky as to obtain a score of 0, this score does not imply a total lack of knowledge of statistics. It would merely reflect the fact that your statistics knowledge is not that advanced yet (or perhaps the questions posed on the exam just did not capture those concepts that you do understand). You do have some knowledge of statistics, but just at an introductory level in terms of the topics covered so far. Take as an example the Fahrenheit temperature scale, which has a freezing point of 32 degrees. A temperature of zero is not the total absence of heat, just a point slightly colder than 1 degree and slightly warmer than −1 degree.

In terms of the *equal distance* notion, consider the following example. Say that we have two pairs of Fahrenheit temperatures, the first pair being 55 and 60 degrees and the second pair being 25 and 30 degrees. The difference of 5 degrees is the same for both pairs, and is also the same everywhere along the Fahrenheit scale if you are moving in 5 degree intervals. Thus, every 5-degree interval is an equal interval. However, we cannot say that 60 degrees is twice as warm as 30 degrees, as there is no absolute zero. In other words, *we cannot form true ratios of values* (i.e., 60/30 = 2). This property only exists for the ratio scale of measurement. The interval scale has the following mathematical properties: (a) equality versus inequality, (b) greater than or less than if unequal, and (c) equal intervals. Other examples of interval scale variables include the Celsius temperature scale, year (since 1 AD), and arguably, many educational and psychological assessments (both cognitive and noncognitive) (although statisticians have been debating this one for many years; for example, on occasion there is a fine line between whether an assessment is measured along the ordinal or the interval scale, as mentioned previously). Interval variables are considered *numerical* and primarily *continuous*.

1.5.4 Ratio Measurement Scale

The most complex scale of measurement is the **ratio scale**. *A ratio scale has all of the properties of the interval scale, plus an absolute zero point exists*. Here a measurement of 0 indicates a total absence of the property being measured. Due to an absolute zero point existing, true ratios of values can be formed that actually reflect ratios in the amounts of the characteristic being measured. Thus, if concepts such as "one-half as big" or "twice as large" make sense, then that may be a good indication that the variable is ratio in scale.

For example, the height of individuals measured in inches is a ratio-scale variable. There is an absolute zero point of zero height. We can also form ratios such that 6′0″ Mark is twice as tall as his 3′0″ daughter Malani. The ratio scale of measurement is not observed frequently in education and the behavioral sciences, with certain exceptions. Motor performance variables (e.g., speed in the 100-meter dash as measured in seconds, distance driven in 24 hours as measured in miles or kilometers), elapsed time measured in seconds, calorie consumption, and physiological characteristics (e.g., weight measured in pounds and ounces, height measured in inches, age measured in years and months, and blood pressure measured using a **sphygmomanometer)** are ratio-scale measures. These are all also examples of continuous variables. Discrete variables, those that arise from the counting process, are also examples of ratio variables, because zero indicates an absence of what is measured (e.g., the number of children in a family, the number of trees in a park, pulse rate measured as the number of beats per second). A summary of the measurement scales, their characteristics, and some examples are given in Table 1.3. Ratio variables are considered numerical and can be either discrete or continuous.

TABLE 1.3
Summary of the Scales of Measurement

Scale	Characteristics	Mathematical Property	Examples
Nominal	Classify into categories; categories are given names or numbers, but the numbers are arbitrary.	Equality versus inequality	Hair or eye color, ethnic background, neighborhood (e.g., subdivision name), sex, country of birth, Social Security number, type of life insurance, religious or political affiliation, blood type
Ordinal*	Rank-ordered according to relative size or position	Equality versus inequality Greater or less than if unequal	Letter grades (e.g., A, B, C), order of finish in race (e.g., 1st, 2nd, 3rd), class rank (e.g., freshman, sophomore, junior, senior), socioeconomic status (e.g., low, middle, high), hardness of minerals (e.g., Moh's scale of hardness, 1–10), faculty rank (e.g., assistant, associate, professor), military rank (e.g., E-7, E-8, etc.)
Interval*	Rank-ordered and equal differences between values imply equal distances in the attribute	Equality versus inequality Greater or less than if unequal Equal intervals	Temperature on Fahrenheit scale, most assessment devices (e.g., cognitive or psychological tests)
Ratio*	Rank-ordered, equal intervals, absolute zero allows ratios to be formed	Equality versus inequality Greater or less than if unequal Equal intervals Absolute zero	Speed in 100-meter dash measured in seconds, height measured in inches, weight measured in pounds and ounces, age measured in months, distance driven, elapsed time measured in seconds, pulse rate, blood pressure, calorie consumption

**Note: The response scale for an ordinal, interval, or ratio variable can always be collapsed so that it takes on the properties of the measurement scale below it.* For example, the responses for an ordinal variable can be collapsed into a binary variable, which then takes on the properties of a nominal variable. The values of an interval or ratio variable can be collapsed into an ordinal variable by grouping the values or further collapsed into a binary variable, which would then take on the properties of an ordinal variable. *Takeaway tip:* Look at the response scale of the variable before making judgment on the variable's measurement scale. Only then will you truly know the measurement scale.

1.5.5 Summary of Terms

We have defined a number of variable-related terms, including variable, constant, categorical variable, and continuous variable. For a summary of these definitions, see Box 1.1.

BOX 1.1 Summary of Definitions

Term	Definition	Example(s)
Categorical variable	A qualitative variable	Political party affiliation (e.g., Republican, Democrat, Independent)
Constant	Any characteristic of persons or things that is observed to take on only a single value	*Every* unit measured shares the characteristic (this could be any number of examples, but the key is that of all units that are measured, *all* units have the same value on what has been measured; e.g., consider a sample that includes only dancers from the American Ballet Theater—asking whether the participant is a dancer would produce a constant as the only individuals in the sample are dancers)
Continuous variable	A numerical variable that can take on any value within a certain range, given a precise enough measurement instrument	Distance between two cities measured in miles
Descriptive statistics	Techniques that allow us to tabulate, summarize, and depict a collection of data in an abbreviated fashion	Table or graph summarizing data
Dichotomous variable	A categorical variable that can take on only one of two values	Sex defined at birth (male, female); questions that require a 'yes' or 'no' response
Discrete variable	A numerical variable that arises from the counting process that can take on only certain values	Number of children in a family (e.g., 0, 1, 2, 3, 4, . . .)
Inferential statistics	Techniques that allow us to employ inductive reasoning to infer the properties of a population from a sample	One-sample *t* test, independent *t* test, chi square test of association
Numerical variable	A quantitative variable that is either discrete or continuous	Number of children in a family (e.g., 0, 1, 2, 3, 4, . . .); the distance between two cities measured in miles
Parameter	A characteristic of a population	Average salary of a population of individuals
Population	All members of a well-defined group	*All* employees of a particular group
Sample	A subset of a population	*Some* employees of a particular group
Statistic	A characteristic of a sample	Average salary of a sample of individuals
Variable	Any characteristic of persons or things that is observed to take on different values	*Not every* unit measured shares the characteristic (this could be any number of examples, but the key is that of all units that are measured, at least *one* has a different measurement than the others in the sample)

1.6 Additional Resources

A number of excellent resources are available for learning statistics. Throughout the text, we will introduce you to many related to the respective topics for the concepts studied in the individual chapters. Here we offer recommendations for resources that are a bit more general in nature for learning, understanding, and appreciating statistics:

- Designed as a reference tool for manuscript and proposal reviewers, this is a great tool for researchers learning about statistics and wanting to learn more about quantitative data analysis (Hancock & Mueller, 2010)
- A resource that introduces readers to statistical concepts through verse, graphics, and text, with no equations (Keller, 2006)
- An edited text whose contributions from authors address statistical issues (e.g., mediation), methodological issues (e.g., qualitative research, sample size practices), and more (Lance & Vandenberg, 2009)
- Statistical misconceptions related to, among others, probability, estimation, hypothesis testing, ANOVA, and regression are discussed and discarded (Huck, 2016)
- A great additional resource that explains statistics in plain language (Huck, 2012)
- Common statistical conventions, ranging from sample size to bootstrapping to transformations and just about everything in between (Van Belle, 2002)
- A dictionary of statistics and related terms (Vogt, 2005)

Problems

Conceptual Problems

1. A mental health counselor is conducting a research study on satisfaction that married couples have with their marriage. In this scenario, "Marital status" (e.g., single, married, divorced, widowed) is which of the following?
   a. Constant
   b. Variable
2. Belle randomly samples 100 library patrons and gathers data on the genre of the "first book" that they checked out from the library. She finds that 85 library patrons checked out a fiction book and 15 library patrons checked out a nonfiction book. Which of the following best characterizes the type of "first book" checked out in this study?
   a. Constant
   b. Variable
3. For interval-level variables, which of the following properties does *not* apply?
   a. A is two units greater than B.
   b. A is greater than B.
   c. A is twice as good as B.
   d. A differs from B.

4. Which of the following properties is appropriate for ordinal, but not for nominal variables?
   a. A differs from B.
   b. A is greater than B.
   c. A is 10 units greater than B.
   d. A is twice as good as B.
5. Which scale of measurement is implied by the following statement: "JoAnn's score is three times greater than Oscar's score?"
   a. Nominal
   b. Ordinal
   c. Interval
   d. Ratio
6. Which scale of measurement is produced by the following survey item: "Which season is your favorite, spring, summer, fall, or winter?"
   a. Nominal
   b. Ordinal
   c. Interval
   d. Ratio
7. A band director collects data on the number of years in which students in the band have played a musical instrument. Which scale of measurement is implied by this scenario?
   a. Nominal
   b. Ordinal
   c. Interval
   d. Ratio
8. Kristen has an IQ of 120. I assert that Kristen is 20% more intelligent than the average person having an IQ of 100. Am I correct?
9. True or false? Population is to parameter as sample is to statistic.
10. True or false? A dichotomous variable is also a categorical variable.
11. True or false? The amount of time spent studying in one week for a population of students is an inferential statistic.
12. A sample of 50 students take an exam and the instructor decides to give the top five scores a bonus of 5 points. Compared to the original set of scores (no bonus), will the ranks of the new set of scores (including the bonus) be exactly the same?
13. Malani and Laila have class ranks of 5 and 6. Ingrid and Toomas have class ranks of 55 and 56. Will the GPAs of Malani and Laila be the same distance apart as the GPAs of Ingrid and Toomas?
14. Aurora is studying sleep disorders in adults. She gathers data on whether they take medication to assist their sleep. Aurora finds that one-third of the adults take medication, and two-thirds do not. Which of the following best characterizes "whether or not medication is taken"?
    a. Constant
    b. Variable

15. A researcher has collected data that compares an intervention program to a comparison program. The researcher finds that the intervention program produces results that are four times better than the comparison program. Which measurement scale is implied and that will allow the researcher to make this type of interpretation? Select all that apply.

a. Nominal

b. Ordinal

c. Interval

d. Ratio

16. A researcher has access to 22 local health clinics that are part of a network of 56 health clinics in the state. The researcher conducts a study that includes the 22 regional health clinics. In this scenario, the 22 local health clinics are which of the following?

a. Dichotomous

b. Interval

c. Sample

d. Population

17. A researcher has access to 22 regional health clinics that are part of a network of 56 health clinics in the state. The researcher conducts a study that includes the 22 regional health clinics. In this scenario, the 56 health clinics in the state are which of the following?

a. Dichotomous

b. Interval

c. Sample

d. Population

18. Which of the following is an example of a dichotomous variable?

a. Dance type (ballet, contemporary, jazz, lyrical, tap)

b. Interest (no interest, somewhat interested, much interest)

c. Total cost (measured in whole dollars ranging from $0 to infinity)

d. Age (ages < 40 and ages 40+)

19. Which of the following is an example of an ordinal variable?

a. Dance type (ballet, contemporary, jazz, lyrical, tap)

b. Interest (no interest, somewhat interested, much interest)

c. Total cost (measured in whole dollars ranging from $0 to infinity)

d. Age (ages < 40 and ages 40+)

20. Which of the following is an example of a ratio variable?

a. Scores on the Myers-Briggs Type Indicator (MBTI) personality inventory

b. Number of pieces of cake eaten at birthday parties (measured in whole numbers)

c. Pleasure experienced on vacation (none, some, much)

d. Types of plants preferred by homeowners (bushes, flowers, grasses, trees)

Answers to Conceptual Problems

1. **a** (All individuals in the study are married, thus the marital status will be "married" for everyone participating; in other words, there is no variation in "marital status" for this particular scenario.)
3. **c** (True ratios cannot be formed with interval variables.)
5. **d** (True ratios can only be formed with ratio variables.)
7. **d** (An absolute value of zero would indicate an absence of what was measured—that is, the number of years playing in a band—and thus ratio is the scale of measure; although an answer of zero is not likely given that the students in the band are those being measured, *if* someone were to respond with an answer of zero, that value would truly indicate "no years playing an instrument.")
9. **True** (There are only population parameters and sample statistics; no other combinations exist.)
11. **False** (Given that this is a population parameter, no inference need be made.)
13. **No** (Class rank is ordinal, and equal intervals are not a characteristic of ordinal variables.)
15. **d** (Ratio variables will allow interpretations such as "four times greater" to be made from the data as they have equal intervals and a true zero point.)
17. **d** (The total population is 56.)
19. **b** (This is a three-point scale, ranked from least to greatest interest, thus it is ordinal; because we cannot tell the distance between each category, it is not interval.)

Computational Problems

1. Rank the following values of the number of books owned, assigning rank 1 to the largest value:

   10 15 12 8 20 17 5 21 3 19

2. Rank the following values of the number of credits earned, assigning rank 1 to the largest value:

   10 16 10 8 19 16 5 21 3 19

3. Rank the following values of the number of pairs of shoes owned, assigning rank 1 to the largest value:

   8 6 3 12 19 7 10 25 4 42

4. A researcher is assisting a colleague with data analysis from a survey. One of the questions asked respondents to indicate the frequency in which they laughed during an average day. In which order should the following responses be ranked, assuming this is an ordinal item and the researcher desires the frequency to be in ascending order?

   o 1–2 times

   o 9 or more times

   o 3–4 times

   o 5–6 times

- o Never
- o 7–8 times

Answers to Computational Problems

1.

Value	Rank
10	7
15	5
12	6
8	8
20	2
17	4
5	9
21	1
3	10
19	3

3.

Value	Rank
8	6
6	8
3	10
12	4
19	3
7	7
10	5
25	2
4	9
42	1

Interpretive Problems

1. Consider the following survey:
   - a. What sex was listed on your birth certificate? Male or female?
   - b. What is your height in inches?
   - c. What is your shoe size (length)?
   - d. Do you smoke cigarettes?
   - e. Are you left- or right-handed?
   - f. Is your mother left- or right-handed?
   - g. Is your father left- or right-handed?
   - h. How much did you spend at your last hair appointment (in whole dollars, including tip)?

i. How many songs are downloaded on your phone?
j. What is your current GPA on a 4.00 scale?
k. What is your current GPA letter grade (e.g., B, B+, A−, A)?
l. On average, how much exercise do you get per week (in hours)?
m. On average, how much exercise do you get per week (no exercise; 1–2 hours; 3–4 hours, 5–6 hours, 7+ hours)?
n. On a 5-point scale, what is your political view (1 = very liberal, 3 = moderate, 5 = very conservative)?
o. On average, how many hours of TV do you watch per week?
p. How many cups of coffee did you drink yesterday?
q. How many hours did you sleep last night?
r. On average, how many alcoholic drinks do you have per week?
s. Can you tell the difference between Pepsi and Coke? Yes or no?
t. What is the natural color of your hair (black, blonde, brown, red, other)?
u. What is the natural color of your eyes (black, blue, brown, green, other)?
v. How far do you live from this campus (in miles)?
w. How far do you live from this campus (less than 10 miles; 10–70 miles, 71+ miles)?
x. On average, how many books do you read for pleasure each month?
y. On average, how many hours do you study per week?
z. On average, how many hours do you study per week (0–5; 6–10; 11–15; 16–20; 21+)?
aa. Which question on this survey is the most interesting to you?
bb. Which question on this survey is the least interesting?

Possible activities:

i. For each item, determine the most likely scale of measurement (nominal, ordinal, interval, or ratio) and the type of variable [categorical or numerical (if numerical, discrete or continuous)].

ii. Create scenarios in which one or more of the variables in this survey would be a constant, given the delimitations that you define for your study. For example, we are designing a study to measure study habits (as measured by question *y*) for students who *do not* exercise (question *l*). In this sample study, our constant is the number of hours per week that a student exercises (in this case, we are delimiting that to be zero—and thus question *l* will be a constant; all students in our study will have answered question *l* as "zero" indicating that they did not exercise).

iii. Collect data from a sample of individuals. In subsequent chapters you will be asked to analyze this data for different procedures.

Note: An actual sample dataset using this survey is contained on the website (survey1.sav or survey1.csv) and is utilized in later chapters. If you are using the SPSS file, please note that all the variables in the survey1 datafile have been coded as having a measurement scale of "scale" (i.e., interval or ratio). This is not correct, and you will need to determine the most likely scale of measurement of each.

2. The Integrated Postsecondary Education Data System (IPEDS) is just one of many, many public secondary data sources available to researchers. Using 2017 IPEDS dataset (see https://nces.ed.gov/ipeds/use-the-data; accessible from the text website as IPEDS2017.sav), consider the following possible activities:

  i. For each item, determine the most likely scale of measurement (nominal, ordinal, interval, or ratio) and the type of variable (categorical or numerical; if numerical, discrete or continuous). *Note: If you are using the SPSS file, please note that all the variables in IPEDS2017.sav datafile have been coded as having a measurement scale of "scale" (i.e., interval or ratio). This is not correct, and you will need to determine the most likely scale of measurement of each.*

  ii. Create scenarios in which one or more of the variables in this survey would be a constant, given the delimitations that you define for your study. For example, we are designing a study to examine institutions who are NCAA/NAIA members for football. In this sample study, our constant is institutional members in NCAA/NAIA for football (in this case, we are delimiting the variable "NCAA/NAIA member for football" [*sport1*] to "yes," which is coded as "1" in the datafile—and thus the "NCAA/NAIA member for football" question will be a constant; all institutions in our study will have answered "NCAA/NAIA member for football" as "yes").

3. The National Health Interview Survey (NHIS*; https://www.cdc.gov/nchs/nhis/) is just one of many, many public secondary data sources available to researchers. Using data from the 2017 NHIS family file (see https://www.cdc.gov/nchs/nhis/nhis_2017_data_release.htm; accessible from the text website as *NHIS_family2017.sav*), consider the following possible activities:

  i. For each item, determine the most likely scale of measurement (nominal, ordinal, interval, or ratio) and the type of variable (categorical or numerical; if numerical, discrete or continuous). *Note: If you are using the SPSS file, please note that all the variables in the NHIS_family2017.sav datafile have been coded as having a measurement scale of "scale" (i.e., interval or ratio). This is not correct, and you will need to determine the most likely scale of measurement of each.*

  ii. Create scenarios in which one or more of the variables in this survey would be a constant, given the delimitations that you define for your study. For example, we are designing a study to examine individuals who are living alone. In this sample study, our constant is "family structure." In this case, we are delimiting the variable "family structure" (*FM_STRCP* or *FM_STRP*) to "living alone," which is coded as "11" in the datafile—and thus the family structure question will be a constant; all individuals in our study will have answered family structure as "living alone."

*Should you desire to use the NHIS data for your own research, please access the data directly here as updates to the data may have occurred: https://www.cdc.gov/nchs/nhis/data-questionnaires-documentation.htm. Also, it is important to note that the NHIS is a *complex sample* (i.e., not a simple random sample). We won't get into the technical aspects of this, but when the data are analyzed to adjust for the sampling design (including nonsimple random sampling procedure and disproportionate sampling) the end results are then representative of the intended population. The purpose of the text is not to serve as a primer for understanding complex samples, and thus readers interested in learning more about complex survey designs are referred to any number of excellent resources (Hahs-Vaughn, 2005; Hahs-Vaughn, McWayne, Bulotskey-Shearer, Wen, & Faria, 2011a, 2011b; Lee, Forthofer, & Lorimor, 1989; Skinner, Holt, & Smith, 1989). Additionally, so as to not complicate matters any more than necessary, the applications in the textbook do not illustrate how to adjust for the complex sample design. As such, if you do not adjust for the complex sampling design, the results that you see should not be interpreted to represent any larger population but only that select sample of individuals who actually completed the survey. I want to stress that the reason why the sampling design has not been illustrated in the textbook applications is because the point of this section of the textbook is to illustrate how to use statistical software to generate various procedures and how to interpret the output and not to ensure the results are representative of the intended population. Please do not let this discount or diminish the need to apply this critical step in your own analyses when using complex survey data as there is quite a large body of research that describes the importance of effectively analyzing complex samples as well as provides evidence of biased results when the complex sample design is not addressed in the analyses (Hahs-Vaughn, 2005, 2006a, 2006b; Hahs-Vaughn et al., 2011a, 2011b; Kish & Frankel, 1973, 1974; Korn & Graubard, 1995; Lee et al., 1989; Lumley, 2004; Pfeffermann, 1993; Skinner et al., 1989).

2

Data Representation

Chapter Outline

Key Concepts

1. Frequencies, cumulative frequencies, relative frequencies, and cumulative relative frequencies
2. Ungrouped and grouped frequency distributions
3. Sample size
4. Real limits and intervals
5. Frequency polygons
6. Normal, symmetric, and skewed frequency distributions
7. Percentiles, quartiles, and percentile ranks

In the first chapter we introduced the wonderful world of statistics. We discussed the value of statistics, met a few of the more well-known statisticians, and defined several basic statistical concepts, including population, parameter, sample, statistic, descriptive and inferential statistics, types of variables, and scales of measurement. In this chapter we begin our examination of descriptive statistics, which we previously defined as techniques that allow us to tabulate, summarize, and depict a collection of data in an abbreviated fashion. We used the example of collecting data from 100,000 graduate students on various characteristics (e.g., height, weight, sex, grade point average, aptitude test scores). Rather than having to carry around the entire collection of data in order to respond to questions, we mentioned that you could summarize the data in an abbreviated fashion through the use of tables and graphs. This way we could communicate features of the data through a few tables or figures without having to carry around the entire dataset.

This chapter deals with the details of the construction of tables and figures for purposes of describing data. Specifically, we first consider the following types of tables: frequency distributions (ungrouped and grouped), cumulative frequency distributions, relative frequency distributions, and cumulative relative frequency distributions. Next we look at the following types of figures: bar graphs, histograms, frequency polygons (or line graphs), cumulative frequency polygons, and stem-and-leaf displays. We also discuss common shapes of frequency distributions. Then we examine the use of percentiles, quartiles, percentile ranks, and box-and-whisker plots. Finally, we look at the use of SPSS and **R** and develop an APA-style paragraph of results. Concepts to be discussed include frequencies, cumulative frequencies, relative frequencies, and cumulative relative frequencies; ungrouped and grouped frequency distributions; sample size; real limits and intervals; frequency polygons; normal, symmetric, and skewed frequency distributions; and percentiles, quartiles and percentile ranks. Our objectives are that by the end of this chapter, you will be able to (a) construct and interpret statistical tables, (b) construct and interpret statistical graphs, and (c) determine and interpret percentile-related information.

2.1 Tabular Display of Distributions

Throughout this text, we will be following a group of superbly talented, creative, and energetic graduate research assistants (Challie Lenge, Ott Lier, Addie Venture, and Oso Wyse) working in their institution's statistics and research lab, fondly known as CASTLE

(Computing and Statistical Technology Laboratory). The students are supervised and mentored by a research methodology faculty member who empowers the group to lead their projects to infinity and beyond, so to speak. With each chapter, we will find the group, or a subset of members thereof, delving into a fantastical statistical journey.

The statistics and research lab at the university serves clients within the institution, such as faculty and staff, and outside the institution, including a multitude of diverse community partners. The lab is supervised by a research methodology faculty member and is staffed by the institution's best and brightest graduate students. The graduate students, Addie Venture, Oso Wyse, Challie Lenge, and Ott Lier, have been assigned their first task as research assistants. Dr. Debhard, a statistics professor, has given the group of students quiz data collected from 25 students enrolled in an introductory statistics course and has asked the group to summarize the data. We find Addie taking lead on this project. Given the discussion with Dr. Debhard, Addie has determined that the following four research questions should guide the analysis of the data:

1. What interpretations can be made from the frequency table of quiz scores from students enrolled in an introductory statistics class?
2. What interpretations can be made from graphical representations of quiz scores from students enrolled in an introductory statistics class?
3. What is the distributional shape of the statistics quiz scores?
4. What is the 50th percentile of the quiz scores?

In this section we consider ways in which data can be represented in the form of tables. More specifically, we are interested in how the data for a single variable can be represented (the representation of data for multiple variables is covered in later chapters). The methods described here include frequency distributions (both ungrouped and grouped), cumulative frequency distributions, relative frequency distributions, and cumulative relative frequency distributions.

2.1.1 Frequency Distributions

Let us use an example set of data in this chapter to illustrate ways in which data can be represented. We have selected a small dataset for purposes of simplicity, although datasets are typically larger in size. Note that there is a larger dataset (based on the survey from the Chapter 1 interpretive problem) utilized in the end-of-chapter problems and available on our website as "survey1." As shown in Table 2.1, the smaller dataset consists of a sample of 25 student scores on a statistics quiz, where the maximum score is 20 points. If a colleague asked a question about this data, again a response could be, "Take a look at the data yourself." This would not be very satisfactory to the colleague, as the person would have to eyeball the data to answer the question. Alternatively, one could present the data in the form of a table so that questions could be more easily answered. One question might be: Which score occurred most frequently? In other words, what score occurred more than any other score? Other questions might be: Which scores were the highest and lowest scores in the class? Where do most of the scores tend to fall? In other words, how well did the students tend to do as a class? These and other questions can be easily answered by looking at a **frequency distribution**.

TABLE 2.1
Statistics Quiz Data

9	11	20	15	19	10	19	18	14	12	17	11	13
16	17	19	18	17	13	17	15	18	17	19	15	

TABLE 2.2
Ungrouped Frequency Distribution of Statistics Quiz Data

X	f	cf	rf	crf
9	1	1	$f/n = 1/25 = .04$	.04
10	1	2	.04	.08
11	2	4	.08	.16
12	1	5	.04	.20
13	2	7	.08	.28
14	1	8	.04	.32
15	3	11	.12	.44
16	1	12	.04	.48
17	5	17	.20	.68
18	3	20	.12	.80
19	4	24	.16	.96
20	1	25	.04	1.00
	$n = 25$		1.00	

Let us first look at how an **ungrouped frequency distribution** can be constructed for these and other data. By following these steps, we develop the ungrouped frequency distribution as shown in Table 2.2. The first step is to arrange the unique scores on a list from the lowest score to the highest score. The lowest score is 9 and the highest score is 20. Even though scores such as 15 were observed more than once, the value of 15 is only entered in this column once. This is what we mean by unique. Note that if the score of 15 was not observed, it could still be entered as a value in the table to serve as a placeholder within the distribution of scores observed. We label this column as "raw score" or "X," as shown by the first column in the table. **Raw scores** are a set of scores in their original form; that is, the scores have not been altered or transformed in any way. X is often used in statistics to denote a variable, so you see X quite a bit in this text. (As a side note, whenever upper- or lowercase letters are used to denote statistical notation, the letter is always italicized.)

The second step is to determine for each unique score the number of times it was observed. We label this second column as "frequency" or by the abbreviation "f." *The frequency column tells us how many times or how frequently each unique score was observed.* In other words, the **frequency** (f) is simply *count* data. For instance, the score of 20 was only observed one time whereas the score of 17 was observed five times. Now we have some information with which to answer our colleague's question. The most frequently observed score is 17, the lowest score is 9, and the highest score is 20. We can also see that scores tended to be closer to 20 (the highest score) than to 9 (the lowest score).

Two other concepts need to be introduced that are included in Table 2.2. The first concept is **sample size**. At the bottom of the second column you see $n = 25$. From now on, n will be used to denote sample size, that is, the total number of scores obtained for the sample. Thus, because 25 scores were obtained here, then $n = 25$.

The second concept is related to real limits and intervals. Although the scores obtained for this dataset happened to be whole numbers, not fractions or decimals, we still need a system that will cover that possibility. For example, what would we do if a student obtained a score of 18.25? One option would be to list that as another unique score, which would probably be more confusing than useful. A second option would be to include it with one of the other unique scores somehow; this is our option of choice. All researchers use the concepts of **real limits** and **intervals** to cover the possibility of any score being obtained. Each value of X in Table 2.2 can be thought of as being the **midpoint** of an interval. Each interval has an upper and a lower real limit. The **upper real limit** of an interval is halfway between the midpoint of the interval under consideration and the midpoint of the next larger interval. For example, the value of 18 represents the midpoint of an interval. The next larger interval has a midpoint of 19. Therefore the upper real limit of the interval containing 18 would be 18.5, halfway between 18 and 19. The **lower real limit** of an interval is halfway between the midpoint of the interval under consideration and the midpoint of the next smaller interval. Following the example interval of 18 again, the next smaller interval has a midpoint of 17. Therefore, the lower real limit of the interval containing 18 would be 17.5, halfway between 18 and 17. Thus, the interval of 18 has 18.5 as an upper real limit and 17.5 as a lower real limit. Other intervals have their upper and lower real limits as well.

Notice that adjacent intervals (i.e., those next to one another) touch at their respective real limits. For example, the 18 interval has 18.5 as its upper real limit and the 19 interval has 18.5 as its lower real limit. This implies that any possible score that occurs can be placed into some interval and no score can fall between two intervals. If someone obtains a score of 18.25, that will be covered in the 18 interval. The only limitation to this procedure is that because adjacent intervals must touch in order to deal with every possible score, what do we do when a score falls precisely where two intervals touch at their real limits (e.g., at 18.5)? There are two possible solutions. The first solution is to assign the score to one interval or another based on some rule. For instance, we could randomly assign such scores to one interval or the other by flipping a coin. Alternatively, we could arbitrarily assign such scores always into either the larger or smaller of the two intervals. The second solution is to construct intervals such that the number of values falling at the real limits is minimized. For example, say that most of the scores occur at .5 (e.g., 15.5, 16.5, 17.5, etc.). We could construct the intervals with .5 as the midpoint and .0 as the real limits. Thus, the 15.5 interval would have 15.5 as the midpoint, 16.0 as the upper real limit, and 15.0 as the lower real limit. It should also be noted that, strictly speaking, *real limits are only appropriate for continuous variables, but not for discrete variables*. That is, because discrete variables can only have limited values, we probably don't need to worry about real limits (e.g., there is not really an interval for two children). The concept of discrete variables was introduced in Chapter 1. Discrete variables are variables that arise from the counting process.

Finally, the **width** of an interval is defined as the *difference between the upper and lower real limits of an interval*. We can denote this as $w = URL - LRL$, where w is interval width, and URL and LRL are the upper and lower real limits, respectively. In the case of our example interval, we see that $w = URL - LRL = 18.5 - 17.5 = 1.0$. For Table 2.2, then, all intervals have the same interval width of 1.0. For each interval we have a midpoint, a lower real limit that is one-half unit below the midpoint, and an upper real limit that is one-half unit above the midpoint. In general, we want all of the intervals to have the same width for consistency as well as for equal interval reasons. The only exception might be if the largest or smallest intervals were above a certain value (e.g., greater than 20) or below a certain value (e.g., less than 9), respectively.

A frequency distribution with an interval width of 1.0 is often referred to as an **ungrouped frequency distribution**, as the intervals have not been grouped together. Does the interval width always have to be equal to 1.0? The answer, of course, is no. We could group intervals together and form what is often referred to as a **grouped frequency distribution**. For our example data, we can construct a grouped frequency distribution with an interval width of 2.0, as shown in Table 2.3. The largest interval now contains the scores of 19 and 20, the second largest interval the scores of 17 and 18, and so on, down to the smallest interval with the scores of 9 and 10. Correspondingly, the largest interval has a frequency of 5, the second largest interval a frequency of 8, and the smallest interval a frequency of 2. All we have really done is collapse the intervals from Table 2.2, where the interval width was 1.0, into the intervals of width 2.0, as shown in Table 2.3. If we take, for example, the interval containing the scores of 17 and 18, then the midpoint of the interval is 17.5, the *URL* is 18.5, the *LRL* is 16.5, and thus $w = 2.0$. The interval width could actually be any value, including .20 or 100, among other values, depending on what best suits the data.

How does one determine what the proper interval width should be? If there are many frequencies for each score and fewer than 15 or 20 intervals, then an *ungrouped frequency distribution* with an interval width of 1 is appropriate (and this is the default in SPSS for computing frequency distributions). If there are either minimal frequencies per score (say 1 or 2) or a large number of unique scores (say more than 20), then a *grouped frequency distribution* with some other interval width is appropriate. For a first example, say that there are 100 unique scores ranging from 0 to 200. An ungrouped frequency distribution would not really summarize the data very well, as the table would be quite large. The reader would have to eyeball the table and actually do some quick grouping in his or her head so as to gain any information about the data. An interval width of perhaps 10 to 15 would be more useful. In a second example, say that there are only 20 unique scores ranging from 0 to 30, but each score occurs only once or twice. An ungrouped frequency distribution would not be very useful here either, as the reader would again have to collapse intervals in his or her head. Here an interval width of perhaps 2 to 5 would be appropriate.

Ultimately, deciding on the interval width, and thus the number of intervals, becomes a trade-off between good communication of the data and the amount of information contained in the table. As interval width increases, more and more information is lost from

TABLE 2.3
Grouped Frequency Distribution of Statistics Quiz Data

X	*f*
9–10	2
11–12	3
13–14	3
15–16	4
17–18	8
19–20	5
	$n = 25$

the original data. For the example where scores range from 0 to 200 and using an interval width of 10, some precision in the 15 scores contained in the 30–39 interval is lost. In other words, the reader would not know from the frequency distribution where in that interval the 15 scores actually fall. If you want that information (you may not), you would need to return to the original data. At the same time, an ungrouped frequency distribution for that data would not have much of a message for the reader. Ultimately, the decisive factor is the adequacy with which information is communicated to the reader. There are no absolute rules on how to best group values into intervals. The nature of the interval grouping comes down to whatever form best represents the data. With today's powerful statistical computer software, it is easy for the researcher to try several different interval widths before deciding which one works best for a particular set of data. Note also that the frequency distribution can be used with variables of any measurement scale, from nominal (e.g., the frequencies for eye color of a group of children) to ratio (e.g., the frequencies for the height of a group of adults).

2.1.2 Cumulative Frequency Distributions

A second type of frequency distribution is known as the **cumulative frequency distribution** (*cf*). For the example data, this is depicted in the third column of Table 2.2 and labeled as "*cf*." To put it simply, *the number of cumulative frequencies for a particular interval is the number of scores contained in that interval and all of the smaller intervals*. Thus, the 9 interval contains one frequency and there are no frequencies smaller than that interval, so the cumulative frequency is simply 1. The 10 interval contains one frequency and there is one frequency in a smaller interval, so the cumulative frequency is 2 (i.e., 1 + 1). The 11 interval contains two frequencies and there are two frequencies in smaller intervals; thus the cumulative frequency is 4 (i.e., 2 + 2). Then, four people had scores in the 11 interval and smaller intervals. One way to think about determining the cumulative frequency column is to take the frequency column and accumulate downward (i.e., from the top down, yielding 1; 1 + 1 = 2; 1 + 1 + 2 = 4; etc.). Just as a check, the *cf* in the largest interval (i.e., the interval largest in value) should be equal to *n*, the number of scores in the sample, 25 in this case. Note also that the cumulative frequency distribution can be used with variables of measurement scales from ordinal (e.g., with grade level, the cumulative frequency could tell us, among other things, the number of students receiving a B or lower) to interval and ratio (e.g., the number of adults who are 5′7″ or shorter), but cannot be used with nominal as there is not at least rank order to nominal data (and thus accumulating information from one nominal category to another does not make sense).

2.1.3 Relative Frequency Distributions

A third type of frequency distribution is known as the relative frequency distribution. For the example data, this is shown in the fourth column of Table 2.2 and labeled as "*rf*." **Relative frequency (*rf*)** is simply *the percentage of scores contained in an interval; it is also known as a proportion or percentage*. Computationally, $rf = f/n$. For example, the percentage of scores occurring in the 17 interval is computed as $rf = f/n = 5/25 = .20$. Relative frequencies take sample size into account, allowing us to make statements about the number of individuals in an interval relative to the total sample. Thus, rather than stating that five individuals had scores in the 17 interval, we could say that 20% of the scores were in that interval. In the popular press, relative frequencies are quite often reported in tables without the frequencies (e.g., "56% of voters agreed with . . ."). Note that the sum of the relative frequencies should be 1.00 (or 100%) within rounding error. Also note that the *relative frequency distribution can be used with variables of all measurement scales*, from nominal (e.g., the percent of children with blue eye color) to ratio (e.g., the percent of adults who are 5′7″).

2.1.4 Cumulative Relative Frequency Distributions

A fourth and final type of frequency distribution is known as the cumulative relative frequency distribution. For the example data this is depicted in the fifth column of Table 2.2 and labeled as "*crf*." The number of **cumulative relative frequencies** (*crf*) for a particular interval *is the percentage of scores in that interval and smaller*. Thus, the 9 interval has a relative frequency of .04, and there are no relative frequencies smaller than that interval, so the cumulative relative frequency is simply .04. The 10 interval has a relative frequency of .04 and the relative frequencies less than that interval are .04, so the cumulative relative frequency is .08. The 11 interval has a relative frequency of .08 and the relative frequencies less than that interval total .08, so the cumulative relative frequency is .16. Thus, 16% of the people had scores in the 11 interval and smaller. In other words, *16% of people scored 11 or less.* One way to think about determining the cumulative relative frequency column is to take the relative frequency column and accumulate *downward* (i.e., from the top down, yielding .04; .04 + .04 = .08; .04 + .04 + .08 = .16; etc.). Just as a check, the *crf* in the largest interval should be equal to 1.0, within rounding error, just as the sum of the relative frequencies is equal to 1.0. Also note that the cumulative relative frequency distribution can be used with variables of measurement scales from ordinal (e.g., the percent of students receiving a B or less) to interval and ratio (e.g., the percent of adults who are 5′7″ or shorter). As with relative frequency distributions, cumulative relative frequency distributions cannot be used with nominal data.

2.2 Graphical Display of Distributions

In this section we consider several types of graphs for viewing a distribution of scores. Again, we are still interested in how the data for a single variable can be represented, but now in a graphical display rather than a tabular display. The methods described here include the bar graph; histogram; frequency, relative frequency, cumulative frequency and cumulative relative frequency polygons (or line graphs); and stem-and-leaf display. Common shapes of distributions will also be discussed.

2.2.1 Bar Graph

A popular method used for displaying nominal scale data in graphical form is the **bar graph**. As an example, say that we have data on the eye color of a sample of 20 children. Ten children are blue-eyed, six are brown-eyed, three are green-eyed, and one is black-eyed. Note that this is a *discrete* variable rather than a continuous variable. A bar graph for this data is shown in Figure 2.1 (generated using the default options in SPSS). The **horizontal axis**, going from left to right on the page, is often referred to in statistics as the ***X* axis** (for variable X, in this example our variable is *eye color*). On the X axis of Figure 2.1, we

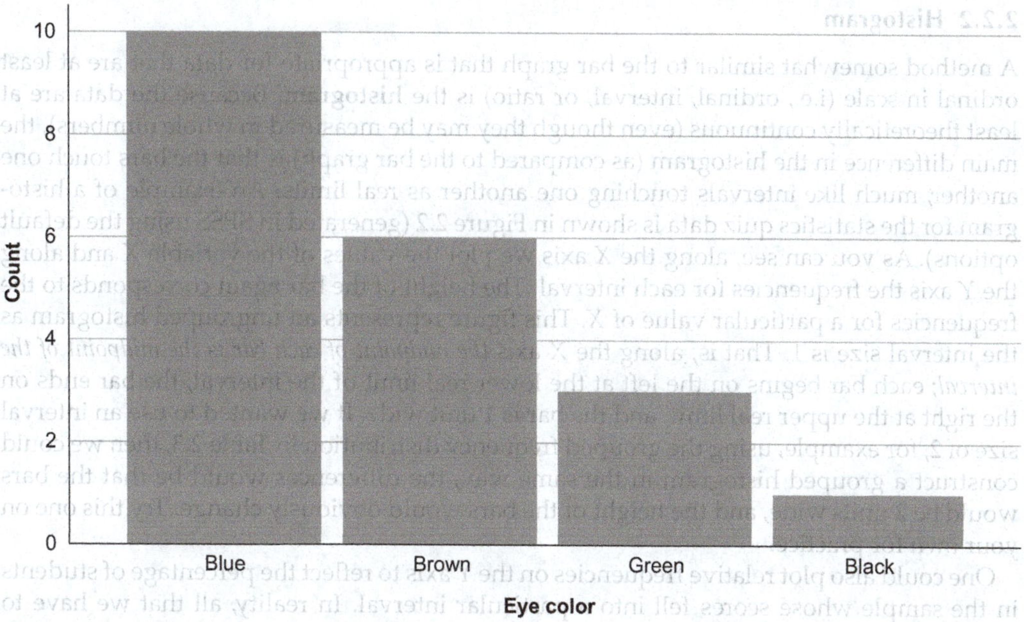

FIGURE 2.1
Bar graph of eye-color data.

have labeled the different eye colors that were observed from individuals in our sample. The order of the colors is not relevant (remember, this is nominal data, so order or rank is irrelevant), but the default happens to be ascending order of how they are labeled in the dataset. In this case, 1 refers to "blue," 2 refers to "brown," 3 refers to "green," and 4 refers to "black." The **vertical axis,** going from bottom to top on the page, is often referred to in statistics as the ***Y* axis** (the *Y* label will be more relevant in later chapters when we have a second variable *Y*). On the *Y* axis of Figure 2.1, we have labeled the frequencies or the counts. In other words, the number of children who have each eye color is represented on the *Y* axis. Finally, a bar is drawn for each eye color where the height of the bar denotes the number of frequencies for that particular eye color (i.e., the number of times that particular eye color was observed in our sample). For example, the height of the bar for the blue-eyed category is 10 frequencies. Thus, we see in the graph which eye color is most popular in this sample (i.e., blue) and which eye color occurs least (i.e., black).

Note that the bars are separated by some space and do not touch one another, reflecting the nature of nominal data being discrete. Because there are no intervals or real limits here, we do not want the bars to touch one another, as we will see in a histogram. One could also plot relative frequencies on the *Y* axis to reflect the percentage of children in the sample who belong to each category of eye color. Here we would see that 50% of the children had blue eyes, 30% brown eyes, 15% green eyes, and 5% black eyes. Another method for displaying nominal data graphically is the pie chart, where the pie is divided into slices whose sizes correspond to the frequencies or relative frequencies of each category. However, for numerous reasons (e.g., contains little information when there are few categories; is unreadable when there are many categories; visually assessing the sizes of each slice is difficult at best), the pie chart is statistically problematic such that Tufte (2001) asserts that the only thing worse than a pie chart is a lot of them. *The bar graph is the recommended graphic for nominal data.*

2.2.2 Histogram

A method somewhat similar to the bar graph that is appropriate for data that are at least ordinal in scale (i.e., ordinal, interval, or ratio) is the **histogram.** Because the data are at least theoretically continuous (even though they may be measured in whole numbers), the main difference in the histogram (as compared to the bar graph) is that the bars touch one another, much like intervals touching one another as real limits. An example of a histogram for the statistics quiz data is shown in Figure 2.2 (generated in SPSS using the default options). As you can see, along the *X* axis we plot the values of the variable *X* and along the *Y* axis the frequencies for each interval. The height of the bar again corresponds to the frequencies for a particular value of X. This figure represents an ungrouped histogram as the interval size is 1. That is, along the *X* axis *the midpoint of each bar is the midpoint of the interval*; each bar begins on the left at the lower real limit of the interval, the bar ends on the right at the upper real limit, and the bar is 1 unit wide. If we wanted to use an interval size of 2, for example, using the grouped frequency distribution in Table 2.3, then we could construct a grouped histogram in the same way; the differences would be that the bars would be 2 units wide, and the height of the bars would obviously change. Try this one on your own for practice.

One could also plot relative frequencies on the *Y* axis to reflect the percentage of students in the sample whose scores fell into a particular interval. In reality, all that we have to change is the scale of the *Y* axis. The height of the bars would remain the same regardless of plotting frequencies or relative frequencies. For this particular dataset, each frequency corresponds to a relative frequency of .04.

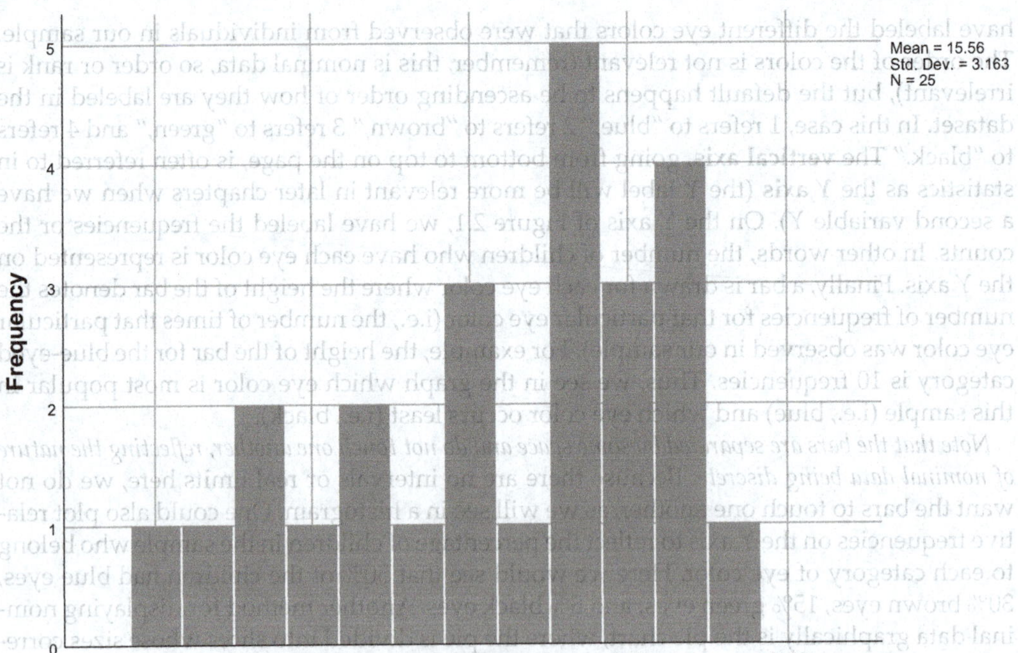

FIGURE 2.2
Histogram of statistics quiz data.

2.2.3 Frequency Polygon (Line Graph)

Another graphical method appropriate for data that have at least some rank order (i.e., ordinal, interval, or ratio) is the **frequency polygon** (i.e., **line graph**). A polygon is a many-sided figure. The frequency polygon is set up in a fashion similar to the histogram. However, rather than plotting a bar for each interval, points are plotted for each interval and then connected together as shown in Figure 2.3 (generated in SPSS using the default options). The *X* and *Y* axes are the same as with the histogram. A point is plotted at the intersection (or coordinates) of the midpoint of each interval along the *X* axis and the frequency for that interval along the *Y* axis. Thus, for the 15 interval, a point is plotted at the midpoint of the interval 15.0 and for three frequencies. Once the points are plotted for each interval, we "connect the dots."

One could also plot relative frequencies on the *Y* axis to reflect the percentage of students in the sample whose scores fell into a particular interval. This is known as the **relative frequency polygon**. As with the histogram, all we have to change is the scale of the *Y* axis. The position of the polygon would remain the same. For this particular dataset, each frequency corresponds to a relative frequency of .04.

Note also that because the histogram and frequency polygon/line graph each contain the exact same information, Figures 2.2 and 2.3 can be superimposed on one another. If you did this, you would see that the points of the frequency polygon are plotted at the top of each bar of the histogram. There is no advantage of the histogram or frequency polygon over the other; however, the histogram is used more frequently, perhaps because it is a bit easier to visually interpret.

2.2.4 Cumulative Frequency Polygon

Cumulative frequencies of data that have at least some rank order (i.e., ordinal, interval, or ratio), can be displayed as a **cumulative frequency polygon** (sometimes referred to as the **ogive curve**). As shown in Figure 2.4 (generated in SPSS using the default options), the

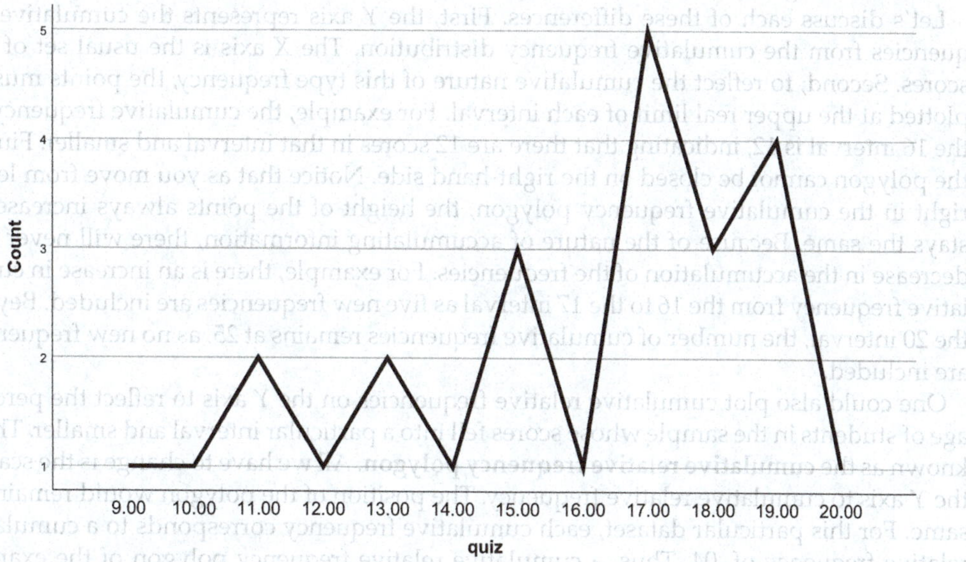

FIGURE 2.3
Frequency polygon (line graph) of statistics quiz data.

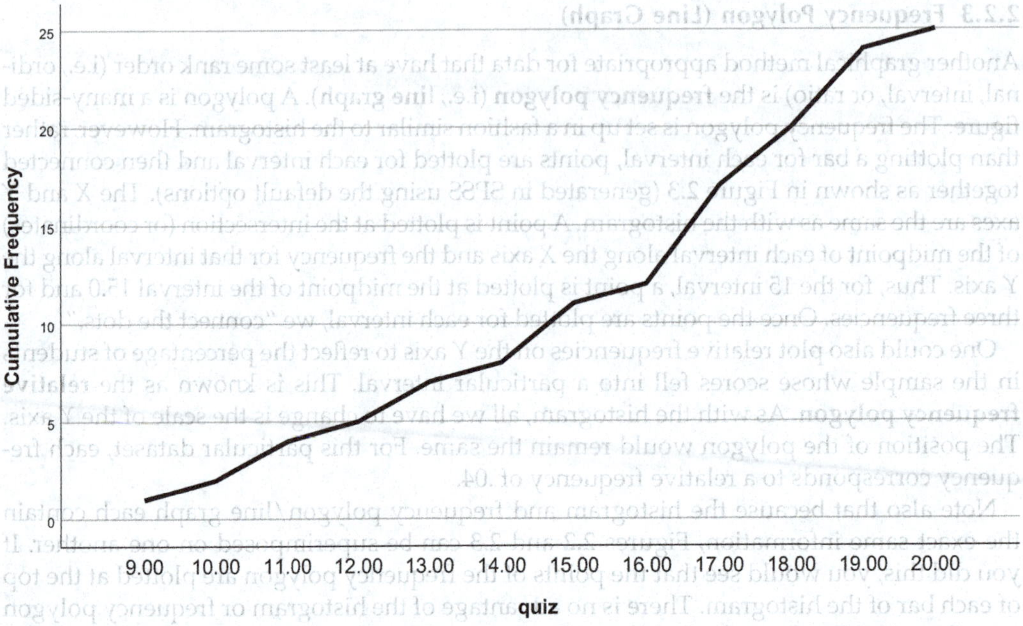

FIGURE 2.4
Cumulative frequency polygon (ogive curve) of statistics quiz data.

differences between the frequency polygon and the cumulative frequency polygon are that the cumulative frequency polygon (a) involves plotting cumulative frequencies along the *Y* axis, (b) the points should be plotted at the upper real limit of each interval (although SPSS plots the points at the interval midpoints by default), and (c) the polygon cannot be closed on the right-hand side.

Let's discuss each of these differences. First, the *Y* axis represents the cumulative frequencies from the cumulative frequency distribution. The *X* axis is the usual set of raw scores. Second, to reflect the cumulative nature of this type frequency, the points must be plotted at the upper real limit of each interval. For example, the cumulative frequency for the 16 interval is 12, indicating that there are 12 scores in that interval and smaller. Finally, the polygon cannot be closed on the right-hand side. Notice that as you move from left to right in the cumulative frequency polygon, the height of the points always increases or stays the same. Because of the nature of accumulating information, there will never be a decrease in the accumulation of the frequencies. For example, there is an increase in cumulative frequency from the 16 to the 17 interval as five new frequencies are included. Beyond the 20 interval, the number of cumulative frequencies remains at 25, as no new frequencies are included.

One could also plot cumulative relative frequencies on the *Y* axis to reflect the percentage of students in the sample whose scores fell into a particular interval and smaller. This is known as the **cumulative relative frequency polygon**. All we have to change is the scale of the *Y* axis to cumulative relative frequency. The position of the polygon would remain the same. For this particular dataset, each cumulative frequency corresponds to a cumulative relative frequency of .04. Thus, a cumulative relative frequency polygon of the example data would look exactly like Figure 2.4, except on the *Y* axis we plot cumulative relative frequencies ranging from 0 to 1.

2.2.5 Shapes of Frequency Distributions

You will likely encounter several common shapes of frequency distributions, as shown in Figure 2.5. These are briefly described here and more fully in later chapters. Figure 2.5(a) is a **normal distribution** (or bell-shaped curve) where most of the scores are in the center of the distribution, with fewer higher and lower scores. The normal distribution plays a large role in statistics, both for descriptive statistics (as we show beginning in Chapter 4), and particularly as an assumption for many inferential statistics (as we show beginning in Chapter 6). This distribution is also known as **symmetric**, because if we divide the distribution into two equal halves vertically, the left half is a mirror image of the right half (see Chapter 4).

Skewed distributions are not symmetric, as the left half is not a mirror image of the right half. Figure 2.5b is a **positively skewed** distribution, where most of the scores are fairly low and there are a few higher scores (see Chapter 4). Figure 2.5c is a **negatively skewed** distribution, where most of the scores are fairly high and there are a few lower scores (see Chapter 4).

2.2.6 Stem-and-Leaf Display

A refined form of the grouped frequency distribution is the **stem-and-leaf display**, developed by Tukey (1977). This is shown in Figure 2.6 (generated in SPSS using the default options in "Explore") for the example statistics quiz data. The stem-and-leaf display was originally developed to be constructed on a typewriter using lines and numbers in a minimal amount of space. In a way, the stem-and-leaf display looks like a grouped type of histogram on its side. The vertical value on the left is the **stem** and, in this example, represents all but the last digit (i.e., the tens digit). The **leaf** represents, in this example, the remaining

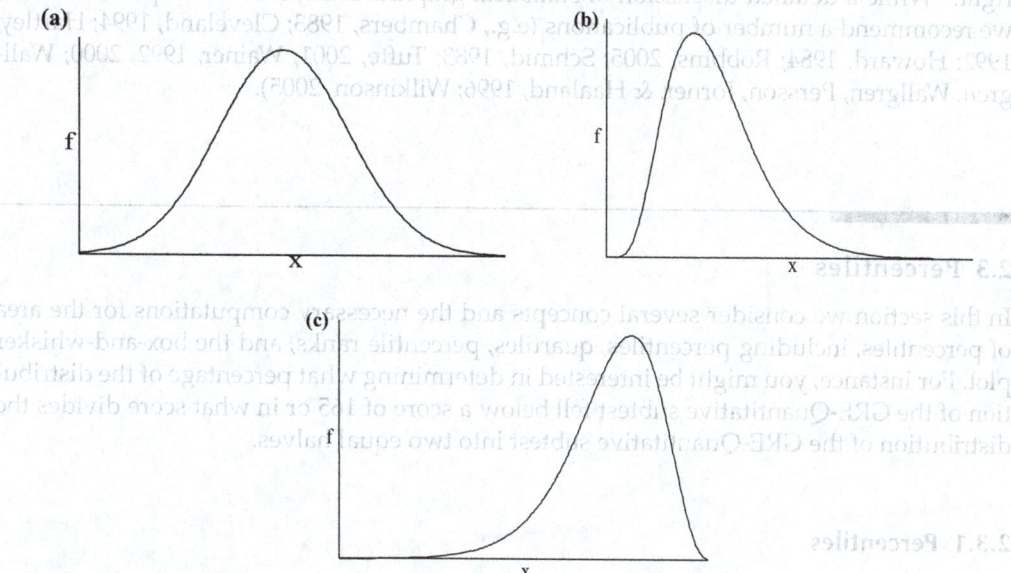

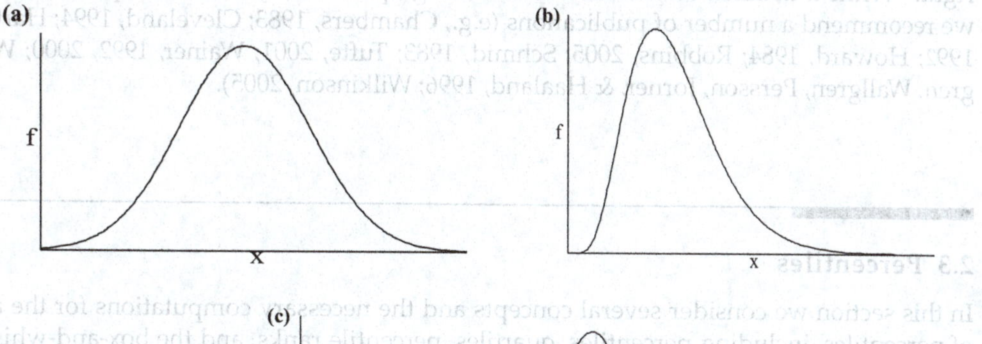

FIGURE 2.5
Common shapes of frequency distributions: (a) normal, (b) positively skewed, and (c) negatively skewed.

```
quiz Stem-and-Leaf Plot

 Frequency    Stem &  Leaf

     1.00        0 .  9
     7.00        1 .  0112334
    16.00        1 .  5556777778889999
     1.00        2 .  0

 Stem width:    10.00
 Each leaf:      1 case(s)
```

FIGURE 2.6
Stem-and-leaf display of statistics quiz data.

digit of each score (i.e., the unit's digit). Note that SPSS has grouped values in increments of five. For example, the second line ("1 . 0112334") indicates that there are seven scores from 10 to 14; thus, "1 . 0" means that there is one frequency for the score of 10. The fact that there are two values of "1" that occur in that stem indicates that the score of 11 occurred twice. Interpreting the rest of this stem, we see that 12 occurred once (i.e., there is only one 2 in the stem), 13 occurred twice (i.e., there are two 3s in the stem), and 14 occurred once (i.e., only one 4 in the stem). From the stem-and-leaf display, one can determine every one of the raw scores; this is not possible with a typical grouped frequency distribution (i.e., no information is lost in a stem-and-leaf display). However, with a large sample the display can become rather unwieldy. Consider what a stem-and-leaf display would look like for 100,000 values!

In summary, this section included the most basic types of statistical graphics, although more advanced graphics are described in later chapters. Note, however, that there are a number of publications on how to properly display graphics; that is, "how to do graphics right." While a detailed discussion of statistical graphics is beyond the scope of this text, we recommend a number of publications (e.g., Chambers, 1983; Cleveland, 1994; Hartley, 1992; Howard, 1984; Robbins, 2005; Schmid, 1983; Tufte, 2001; Wainer, 1992, 2000; Wallgren, Wallgren, Persson, Jorner, & Haaland, 1996; Wilkinson, 2005).

2.3 Percentiles

In this section we consider several concepts and the necessary computations for the area of percentiles, including percentiles, quartiles, percentile ranks, and the box-and-whisker plot. For instance, you might be interested in determining what percentage of the distribution of the GRE-Quantitative subtest fell below a score of 165 or in what score divides the distribution of the GRE-Quantitative subtest into two equal halves.

2.3.1 Percentiles

Let us define a **percentile** as that score below which a certain percentage of the distribution lies. For instance, you may be interested in that score below which 50% of the distribution of the GRE-Quantitative subtest lies. Say that this score is computed as 150; this would mean that 50% of the scores fell below a score of 150. Because percentiles are scores, they are continuous values, and can take on any value of those possible. The 30th percentile could be, for example, the score of 145. For notational purposes, a percentile will be known as P_i, where the *i* subscript denotes the particular percentile of interest, between 0 and 100. Thus the 30th percentile for the previous example would be denoted as $P_{30} = 145$.

Let us now consider how percentiles are computed. The formula for computing the P_i percentile is

$$P_i = LRL + \left(\frac{(i\%)(n) - cf}{f}\right)(w)$$

where *LRL* is the lower real limit of the interval containing P_i, *i*% is the percentile desired (expressed as a proportion from 0 to 1), *n* is the sample size, *cf* is the cumulative frequency less than but not including the interval containing P_i (known as "*cf* below"), *f* is the frequency of the interval containing P_i, and *w* is the interval width.

As an example, consider computing the 25th percentile of our statistics quiz data. This would correspond to that score below which 25% of the distribution falls. For the example data in the form presented in Table 2.2, we can compute P_{25} as follows:

$$P_i = LRL + \left(\frac{(i\%)(n) - cf}{f}\right)(w)$$

$$P_{25} = 12.5 + \left(\frac{(25\%)(25) - 5}{2}\right)(1) = 12.5 + 0.625 = 13.125$$

Conceptually, let us discuss how the equation works. First we have to determine what interval contains the percentile of interest. This is easily done by looking in the *crf* column of the frequency distribution for the interval that contains a *crf* of .25 somewhere within the interval. We see that for the 13 interval the *crf* = .28, which means that the interval spans a *crf* of .20 (the *URL* of the 12 interval) up to .28 (the *URL* of the 13 interval), and thus contains .25. The next largest interval of 14 takes us from a *crf* of .28 up to a *crf* of .32, and thus is too large for this particular percentile. The next smallest interval of 12 takes us from a *crf* of .16 up to a *crf* of .20, and thus is too small. The *LRL* of 12.5 indicates that P_{25} is at least 12.5. The rest of the equation adds some positive amount to the *LRL*.

Next we have to determine how far into that interval we need to go in order to reach the desired percentile. We take *i* percent of *n*, or in this case 25% of the sample size of 25, which is 6.25. So we need to go one-fourth of the way into the distribution, or 6.25 scores, to reach the 25th percentile. Another way to think about this is that because the scores have been rank-ordered from lowest or smallest (top of the frequency distribution) to highest or largest (bottom of the frequency distribution), we need to go 25%, or 6.25 scores, into the distribution from the top (or smallest value) to reach the 25th percentile. We then subtract out all cumulative frequencies smaller than (or below) the interval we are looking in, where *cf* below = 5. Again we just want to determine how far into this interval we need to go, and thus we subtract out all of the frequencies smaller than this interval, or *cf* below. The numerator then becomes 6.25 − 5 = 1.25. Then we divide by the number of frequencies in the interval containing the percentile we are looking for. This forms the ratio of how far into the interval we go. In this case, we needed to go 1.25 scores into the interval and the interval contains two scores; thus the ratio is 1.25 / 2 = .625. In other words, we need to go .625 units into the interval to reach the desired percentile. Now that we know how far into the interval to go, we need to weigh this by the width of the interval. Here we need to go 1.25 scores into an interval containing two scores that is 1 unit wide, and thus we go .625 units into the interval [(1.25 / 2) 1 = .625]. If the interval width was instead 10, then 1.25 scores into the interval would be equal to 6.25 units.

Consider two more worked examples to try on your own, either through statistical software or by hand. The 50th percentile, P_{50}, is

$$P_{50} = 16.500 + \left(\frac{(50\%)(25) - 12}{5}\right)(1) = 16.500 + 0.100 = 16.600$$

and the 75th percentile, P_{75}, is

$$P_{75} = 17.500 + \left(\frac{(75\%)(25) - 17}{3}\right)(1) = 17.500 + 0.583 = 18.083$$

We have only examined a few example percentiles of the many possibilities that exist. For example, we could also have determined $P_{55.5}$ or even $P_{99.5}$. Thus, we could determine any percentile, in whole numbers or decimals, between 0 and 100. Next we examine three particular percentiles that are often of interest, the quartiles.

2.3.2 Quartiles

One common way of dividing a distribution of scores into equal groups of scores is known as **quartiles.** This is done by dividing a distribution into fourths or quartiles where there are four equal groups, each containing 25% of the scores. In the previous examples, we determined P_{25}, P_{50}, and P_{75}, which divided the distribution into four equal groups, from 0 to 25, from 25 to 50, from 50 to 75, and from 75 to 100. *Thus the quartiles are special cases of percentiles.* A different notation, however, is often used for these particular percentiles, where we denote P_{25} as Q_1, P_{50} as Q_2, and P_{75} as Q_3. *The Qs represent the quartiles.*

An interesting aspect of quartiles is that they can be used to determine whether a distribution of scores is positively or negatively skewed. This is done by comparing the values of the quartiles as follows. If $(Q_3 - Q_2) > (Q_2 - Q_1)$, then the distribution of scores is *positively skewed* as the scores are more spread out at the high end of the distribution and more bunched up at the low end of the distribution (remember the shapes of the distributions from Figure 2.5). If $(Q_3 - Q_2) < (Q_2 - Q_1)$, then the distribution of scores is negatively skewed as the scores are more spread out at the low end of the distribution and more bunched up at the high end of the distribution. If $(Q_3 - Q_2) = (Q_2 - Q_1)$, then the distribution of scores is obviously not skewed, but is *symmetric* (see Chapter 4). For the example statistics quiz data $(Q_3 - Q_2) = 1.4833$ and $(Q_2 - Q_1) = 3.4750$; thus $(Q_3 - Q_2) < (Q_2 - Q_1)$ and we know that the distribution is negatively skewed. This should already have been evident from examining the frequency distribution in Figure 2.3 as scores are more spread out at the low end of the distribution and more bunched up at the high end. Examining the quartiles is a simple method for getting a general sense of the skewness of a distribution of scores.

2.3.3 Percentile Ranks

Let us define a **percentile rank** as the *percentage of a distribution of scores that falls below (or is less than) a certain score*. For instance, you may be interested in the percentage of scores of the GRE-Quantitative Reasoning subscale that falls below the score of 150. Say that the percentile rank for the score of 150 is computed to be 50; then this would mean that 50% of the scores fell below a score of 150. If this sounds familiar, it should. The 50th percentile was previously stated to be 150. Thus we have logically determined that the percentile rank of 150 is 50. *This is because percentile and percentile rank are actually opposite sides of the same coin.* Many are confused by this and equate percentiles and percentile ranks; however, they are related but different concepts. Recall earlier we said that percentiles are scores. *Percentile ranks are percentages* because they are continuous values and can take on any value from 0 to 100. For notational purposes, a percentile rank will be known as $PR(P_i)$, where P_i is the particular score whose percentile rank, PR, you wish to determine. Thus, the percentile rank of the score 150 would be denoted as $PR(150) = 50.00$. In other words, about 50% of the distribution falls below the score of 150.

Let us now consider how percentile ranks are computed. The formula for computing the $PR(P_i)$ percentile rank is

$$PR(P_i) = \left(\frac{cf + \frac{f(P_i - LRL)}{w}}{n} \right)(100\%)$$

where $PR(P_i)$ indicates that we are looking for the percentile rank PR of the score P_i, cf is the cumulative frequency up to but not including the interval containing $PR(P_i)$ (again known as "*cf* below"), f is the frequency of the interval containing $PR(P_i)$, LRL is the lower real limit of the interval containing $PR(P_i)$, w is the interval width, n is the sample size, and finally we multiply by 100% to place the percentile rank on a scale from 0 to 100 (and also to remind us that the percentile rank is a percentage).

As an example, consider computing the percentile rank for the score of 17. This would correspond to the percentage of the distribution that falls below a score of 17. For the example data again, using the percentile rank equation we compute $PR(17)$ as follows:

$$PR(17) = \left(\frac{12 + \frac{5(17 - 16.5)}{1}}{25} \right)(100\%) = \left(\frac{12 + 2.5}{25} \right)(100\%) = 58.00\%$$

Conceptually, let us discuss how the equation works. First we have to determine what interval contains the percentile rank of interest. This is easily done because we already know the score is 17, and we simply look in the interval containing 17. The *cf* below the 17 interval is 12 and n is 25. Thus we know that we need to go at least 12/25, or 48%, of the way into the distribution to obtain the desired percentile rank. We know that $P_i = 17$ and the LRL of that interval is 16.5. The interval has five frequencies, so we need to go 2.5 scores into the interval to obtain the proper percentile rank. In other words, because 17 is the midpoint of an interval with width of 1, we need to go halfway, or 2.5/5, of the way into the interval to obtain the percentile rank. In the end, we need to go 14.5/25 (or .58) of the way into the distribution to obtain our percentile rank, which translates to 58%.

As another example, we have already determined that P_{50} = 16.6000. Therefore, you should be able to determine on your own that *PR*(16.6000) = 50%. This verifies that percentiles and percentile ranks are two sides of the same coin. The computation of percentiles identifies a specific score, and you start with the score to determine the score's percentile rank. You can further verify this by determining that *PR*(13.1250) = 25.00% and *PR*(18.0833) = 75.00%. Next we consider the box-and-whisker plot, where quartiles and percentiles are used graphically to depict a distribution of scores.

2.3.4 Box-and-Whisker Plot

A simplified form of the frequency distribution is the **box-and-whisker plot** (often referred to simply as a **box plot**), developed by Tukey (1977). This is shown in Figure 2.7 (generated in SPSS using the default options) for the example data. The box-and-whisker plot was originally developed to be constructed on a typewriter using lines in a minimal amount of space. The **box** in the center of the figure displays the middle 50% of the distribution of scores with the thick black line representing the median. The bottom edge or hinge of the box represents the 25th percentile (or Q_1) (i.e., the bottom or lowest 25% of values). The top edge or hinge of the box represents the 75th percentile (or Q_3) (i.e., the top or highest 25% of values). The middle thick vertical line in the box represents the 50th percentile (also known as Q_2 or the median). The lines extending from the box are known as the **whiskers**. The purpose of the whiskers is to display data outside of the middle 50%. The *bottom whisker* can extend down to the lowest score (as is the case with SPSS using default options), or to the 5th or the 10th percentile (by other means), to display more extreme low scores, and the *top whisker* correspondingly can extend up to the highest score (again, as is the case

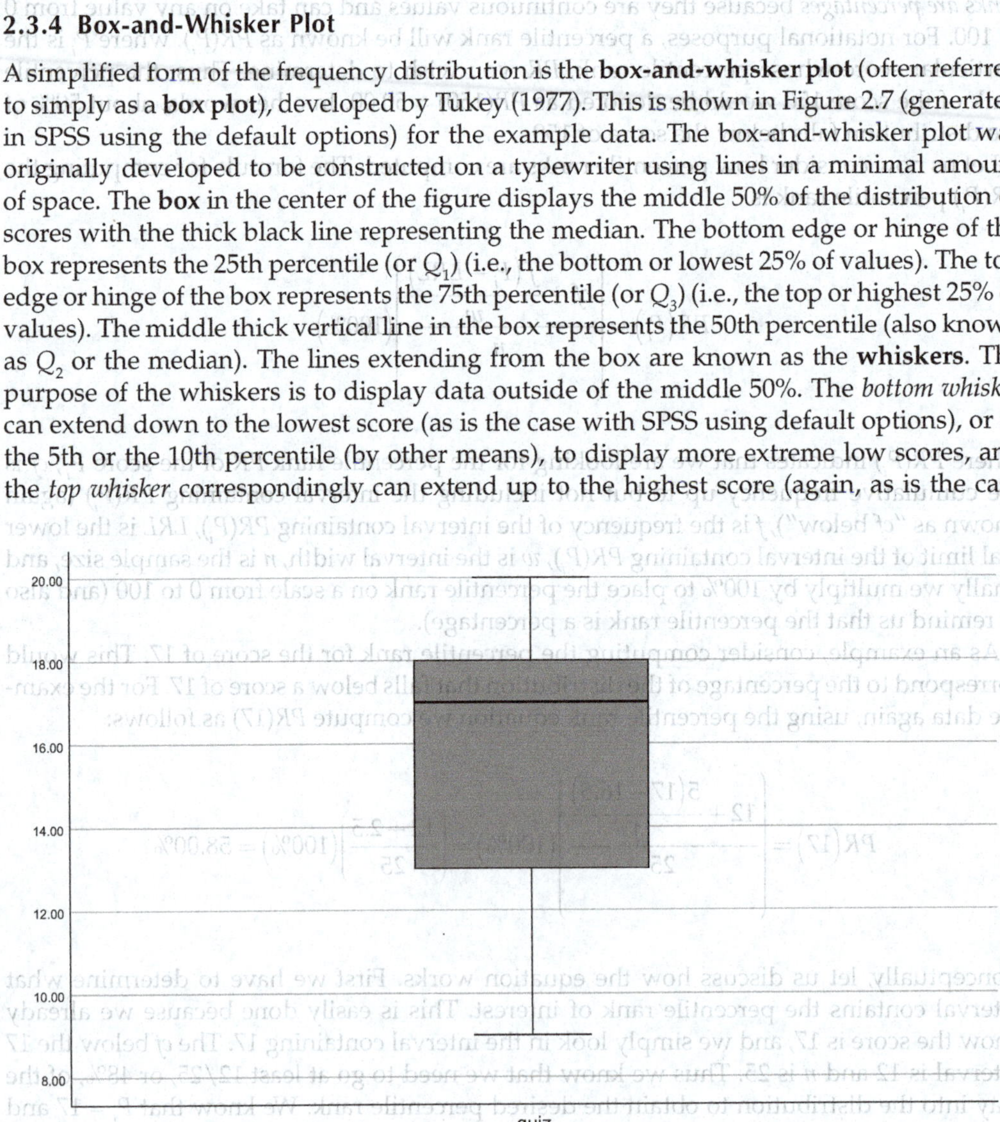

FIGURE 2.7
Box-and-whisker plot of statistics quiz data.

with SPSS using default options), or to the 95th or 90th percentile (elsewhere), to display more extreme high scores. The choice of where to extend the whiskers is the preference of the researcher and/or the software. Scores that fall beyond the end of the whiskers, known as **outliers** due to their extremeness relative to the bulk of the distribution, are often displayed by dots and/or asterisks. Box-and-whisker plots can be used to examine such things as skewness (through the quartiles), outliers, and where most of the scores tend to fall. *If you turn the boxplot clockwise and compare to the histogram, you'll see similar displays of the distribution*—simply with fewer elements in the boxplot.

Let's talk specifically about some of the elements displayed in Figure 2.7. We see, for example, that the bottom 25% of the distribution (i.e., from the bottom of the box to the bottom whisker) is more spread out than the top 25% of the distribution (i.e., from the top of the box to the top whisker). This indicates that there is more variation in the bottom 25% of values than in the top 25% of values. We can make similar interpretations about the spread of the data comparing area inside the box. For example, there is more variation between Q_1 (i.e., the bottom of the box) and the median (i.e., Q_2) than between the median and Q_3 (i.e., the top of the box). We know this because the space between the median and Q_1 is much more condensed as compared to the space between Q_1 and the median.

Keep the following point in mind when interpreting boxplots: *don't confuse the variation or spread of the data with the percentage of points between the elements of the box*. There is *always* 25% of the distribution between each quartile (e.g., from Q_1 to Q_2 or from Q_2 to Q_3), regardless of how spread out or condensed that area is. Sometimes you may find a quirky boxplot. For example, you might find a boxplot with two whiskers but just one line between them (i.e., no real "box"). This would indicate that there is no variation in the middle 50% of the data; that is, all values, from the 25th to 75th percentile, are the same. As another example, you might find a boxplot where the median is setting on the top of the box. This would indicate that the median and the 75th percentile, all values between, are the same value. In those instances of quirkiness, stay true to what you understand about the boxplot and apply accordingly to your interpretations.

2.4 Recommendations Based on Measurement Scale

We cannot stress enough how important it is that you understand the measurement scale of the variable(s) with which you are working, as that will dictate what statistics can (and cannot) be computed using them. You will use the knowledge of measurement scale in every statistic that you compute. To help in this endeavor, we include Box 2.1 as a summary of which data representation techniques are most appropriate for each type of measurement scale.

BOX 2.1 Appropriate Data Representation Techniques Given the Measurement Scale of the Variable

Measurement Scale	Tables	Figures
Nominal	Frequency distribution	Bar graph
	Relative frequency distribution	

(continued)

(continued)

Measurement Scale	Tables	Figures
Ordinal, interval, or ratio	Frequency distribution	Histogram
	Cumulative frequency distribution	Frequency polygon
	Relative frequency distribution	Relative frequency polygon
	Cumulative relative frequency distribution	Cumulative frequency polygon
		Cumulative relative frequency polygon
		Stem-and-leaf display
		Box-and-whisker plot

2.5 Computing Tables, Graphs, and More Using SPSS

The purpose of this section is to briefly consider applications of SPSS for the topics covered in this chapter (including important screenshots). We will begin with a brief introduction to SPSS and then demonstrate SPSS procedures for generating frequencies and graphs.

2.5.1 Introduction to SPSS

Before we get into using SPSS, let's go over a few basics. SPSS is one of the most common standard statistical software programs available. Among other nice features of SPSS is that it is user-friendly, particularly compared to many other standard statistical software. Most SPSS users take advantage of the point-and-click interface of SPSS, although you can also use syntax to run statistics in SPSS. While the graphical user interface makes generating statistics in SPSS pretty easy, you need to be aware of a few nuances when working with the program.

If you use the point-and-click interface (which will be illustrated throughout the text using version 25), then it's important to understand the SPSS environment in which you'll be working. SPSS has two "environments": **Data View** and **Variable View**. Figure 2.8 illustrates what the user sees in *Data View*, which is essentially a spreadsheet with rows (which usually represent individual cases) and columns (which usually represent unique variables). If you were entering data, you would do that in Data View. Even if you haven't used SPSS, Data View probably seems familiar because it's very similar to what you've encountered if you've ever used Excel or a similar spreadsheet.

The second environment in SPSS is Variable View. Figure 2.9 illustrates what the user sees in *Variable View*. Variable View is probably dissimilar to any other software program with which you've worked. This is the environment in SPSS that allows you to refine how your variable(s) are displayed and operationalized. Many options are available in Variable View, and the illustrations in this text don't cover all of them. This isn't to say that you won't need one or more of these options in the future. However, for purposes of the illustrations in the text, we will examine some of the most common options in Variable View: (a) **name**, which is simply the column header that appears in Data View; (b) **label**, which

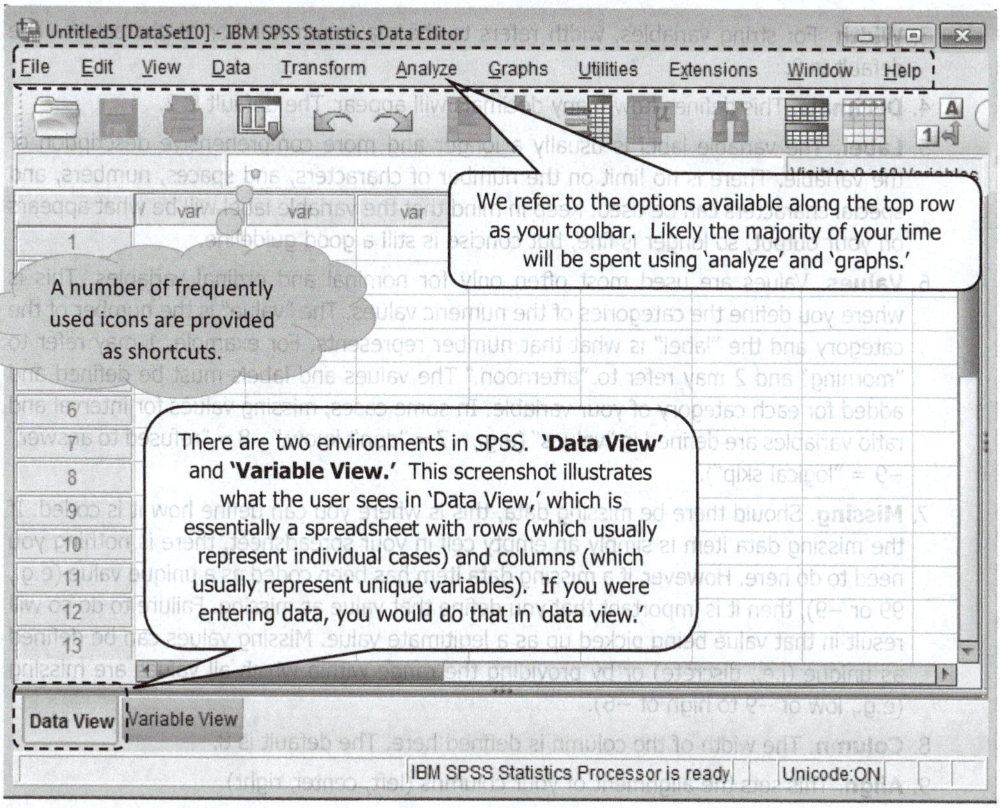

FIGURE 2.8
SPSS Data View interface.

is a longer name that can be provided to better define the variable; and (c) **values**, which connect the numbers assigned to categories with the respective categories for nominal and ordinal variables (e.g., 1 = "morning," 2 = "afternoon").

Variable View offers many options for defining and working with your data:

1. **Name**. This is the column header that will appear in Data View. The name cannot begin with a number or special character, and names cannot include spaces. The name is not limited to a particular length; however, we recommend keeping the name to eight or fewer characters so that it's more efficient to transfer your data into programs that do have limitations on length for column headers. If you haven't defined the variable label, then the name will be what appears on your output.
2. **Type**. This defines the type of variable. Variables that are alphanumeric will be "string." Most variables that we will use in the illustrations in the text are "numeric."

3. **Width**. For string variables, width refers to the maximum number of characters. The default is 8.
4. **Decimals**. This defines how many decimals will appear. The default is 2.
5. **Label**. The variable label is usually a longer and more comprehensive description of the variable. There is no limit on the number of characters, and spaces, numbers, and special characters can be used. Keep in mind that the variable label will be what appears on your output, so longer is fine, but concise is still a good guideline.
6. **Values**. Values are used most often only for nominal and ordinal variables. This is where you define the categories of the numeric values. The "value" is the number of the category and the "label" is what that number represents. For example, 1 may refer to "morning" and 2 may refer to "afternoon." The values and labels must be defined and added for each category of your variable. In some cases, missing values for interval and ratio variables are defined in "values" (e.g., −7 = "don't know," −8 = "refused to answer," −9 = "logical skip").
7. **Missing**. Should there be missing data, this is where you can define how it is coded. If the missing data item is simply an empty cell in your spreadsheet, there is nothing you need to do here. However, if a missing data item has been coded as a unique value (e.g., 99 or −9), then it is important that you define that value as missing. Failure to do so will result in that value being picked up as a legitimate value. Missing values can be defined as unique (i.e., discrete) or by providing the range within which all values are missing (e.g., low of −9 to high of −6).
8. **Column**. The width of the column is defined here. The default is 8.
9. **Align**. This sets the alignment of your columns (left, center, right).
10. **Measure**. The measurement scale of your variable is defined here. Interval and ratio are defined as "scale," with options for nominal and ordinal as well.
11. **Role**. The role is how the variable will be used. The default is "input," which refers to an independent variable. "Target" is a dependent variable. "Both" indicates the variable can be used as either an independent or a dependent variable. Defining the role is not required. However, some dialogs in SPSS support predefined roles. When using those dialog menus, variables that meet the requisite role are automatically displayed in the destination list.

An additional feature of SPSS that is important to know is how the datafiles and output operate. The *datafile* (or *dataset* as we often call it) is the actual raw data—those rows and columns of data in spreadsheet form. Datasets in SPSS are saved as **.sav** files. Once you have data (i.e., a .sav file) and generate a statistic using that data, a new page will appear, and that is your output. *If you want to save your output (and we recommend doing that!), then you must save your output page separately from your dataset.* Saving the dataset does *not* save your output, and saving your output does *not* save your dataset. Output files have an extension of **.spv**. We will repeat this because it's that important—*saving your dataset file does not save your output in SPSS.* In SPSS, the data exist independent of any output that is generated using it. Don't know whether you need to save your output? Our best recommendation is this: If in doubt, just save it! Err on the side of caution. You can always delete the file later.

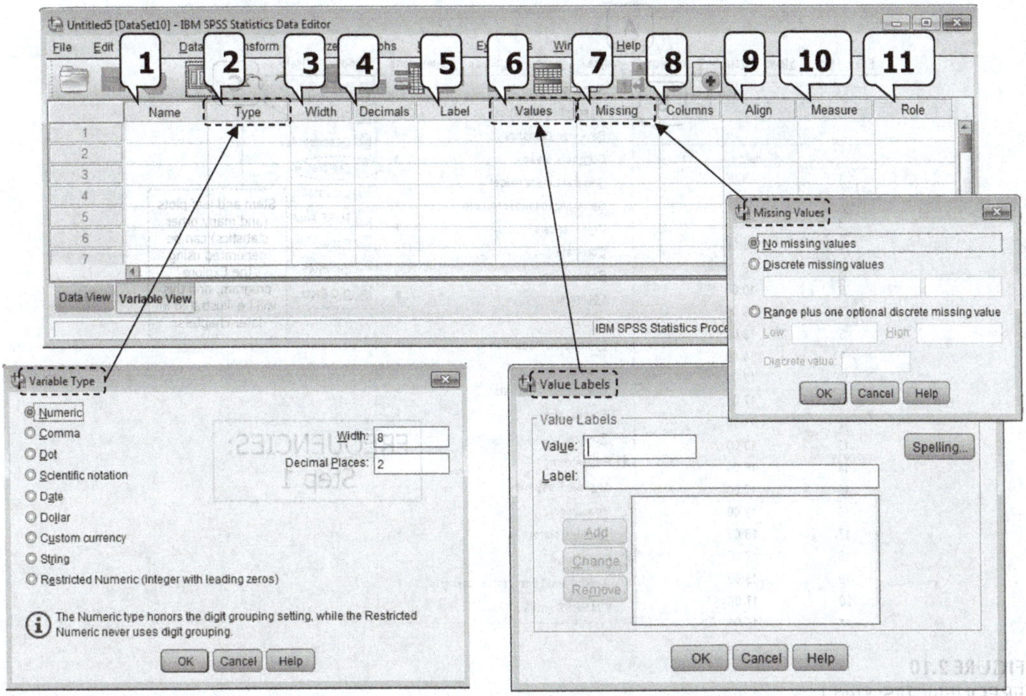

FIGURE 2.9
SPSS Variable View interface.

Referring back to Figure 2.8, it is also important to know that you can use the options in the top toolbar regardless of which environment you are in (Data View or Variable View), and even if you are on the output page. SPSS offers quite a bit of flexibility in being able to access and use the toolbar from any view.

These are just a few tips on the nuances of using SPSS. The more you use SPSS, as with any software, the better you will understand the functionalities, shortcuts, and more. We encourage you to experiment in SPSS. You can't break it, so to speak, so explore what it has to offer. The illustrations in the text are just a starting point but will hopefully whet your appetite to learn more about the software to allow you to become a better researcher.

2.5.2 Frequencies

Step 1. For the types of tables discussed in this chapter, in SPSS go to "Analyze" in the top pulldown menu, then "Descriptive Statistics," and then select "Frequencies." Following the steps (A–C) in the screenshot for "FREQUENCIES: Step 1" in Figure 2.10 will produce the "Frequencies" dialog box.

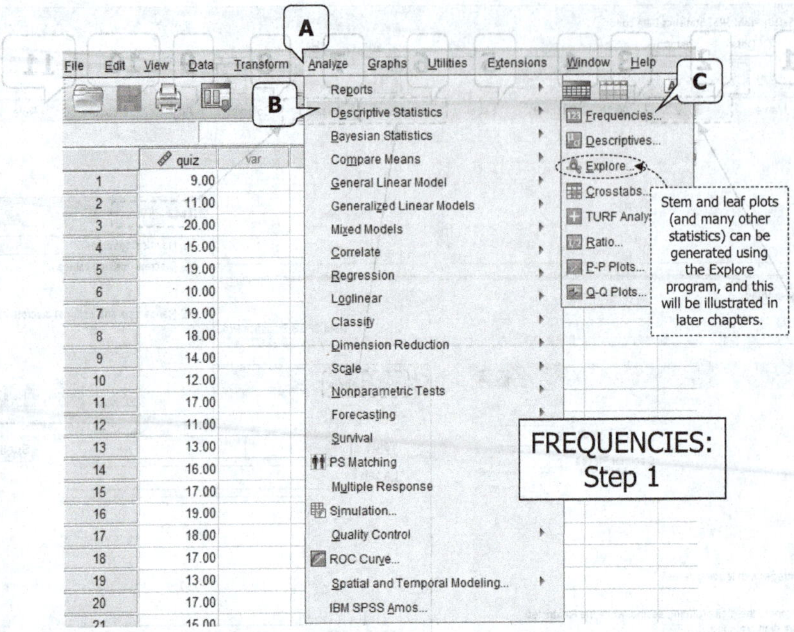

FIGURE 2.10
FREQUENCIES: Step 1.

Step 2. The Frequencies dialog box will open (see screenshot for "FREQUENCIES: Step 2" in Figure 2.11). From this main Frequencies dialog box, click the variable of interest from the list on the left (e.g., "quiz") and move it into the "Variables" box by clicking the arrow button. By default, there is a checkmark in the box "Display frequency tables," and we will keep this checked; this will generate a table of frequencies, relative frequencies, and cumulative relative frequencies. Four buttons are listed on the right side of the Frequencies dialog box: "Statistics," "Charts," "Format," and "Style." Let's first talk about options available through Statistics and then about Charts. Format and Style provide options for aesthetics (e.g., ordering by ascending or descending values, formatting the cell background and text), and we won't go into detail on those (however, you are encouraged to explore these on your own).

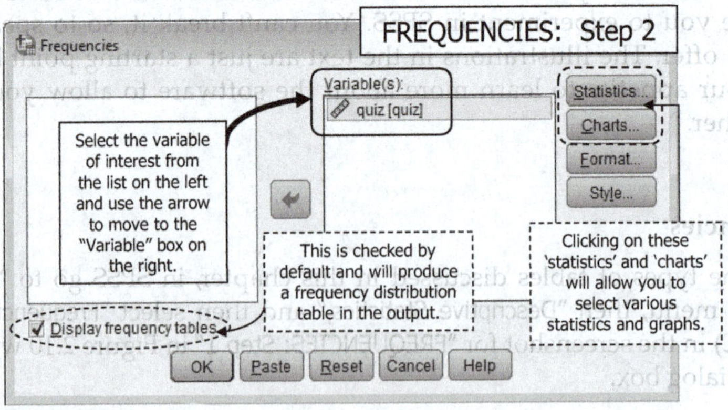

FIGURE 2.11
FREQUENCIES: Step 2.

Step 3a. If you click on the Statistics button from the main Frequencies dialog box, a new box labeled "Frequencies: Statistics" will appear (see the screenshot for "FREQUENCIES: Step 3a" in Figure 2.12). From here, you can obtain quartiles and selected percentiles as well as numerous other descriptive statistics simply by placing a checkmark in the boxes for the statistics that you want to generate. For better accuracy when generating the median, quartiles and percentiles, check the box "Values are group midpoints." However, note that these values are not always as precise as those from the formula given earlier in this chapter and *not* taking this step doesn't mean your results will be incorrect.

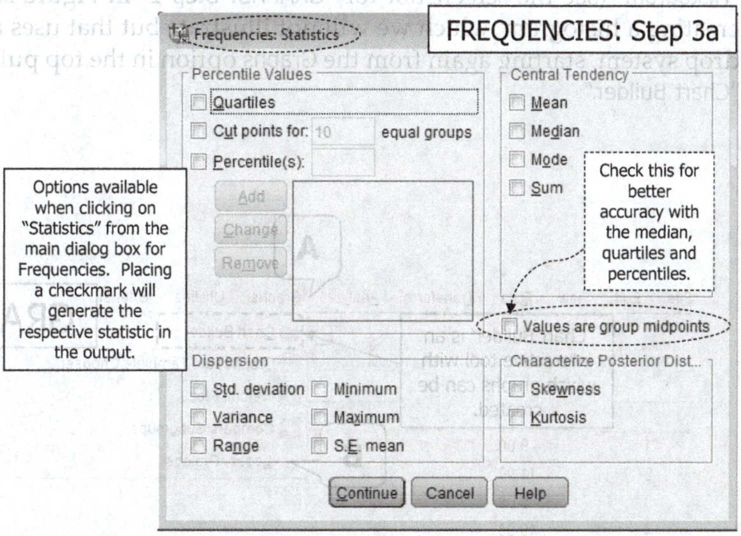

FIGURE 2.12
FREQUENCIES: Step 3a.

Step 3b. If you click on the Charts button from the main Frequencies dialog box, a new box labeled "Frequencies: Charts" will appear (see the screenshot for "FREQUENCIES: Step 3b" in Figure 2.13). From here, you can select options to generate bar graphs, pie charts, or histograms. If you select bar graphs or pie charts, you can plot either frequencies or percentages (relative frequencies). Thus the Frequencies program enables you to do much of what this chapter has covered. In addition, stem-and-leaf plots are available in the Explore program (see "Frequencies: Step 1" for a screenshot on where the Explore program can be accessed).

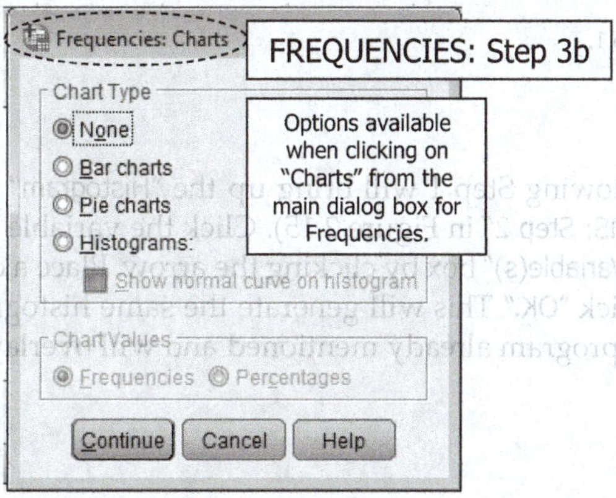

FIGURE 2.13
FREQUENCIES: Step 3b.

2.5.3 Graphs

SPSS can generate multiple types of graphs. We will examine how to generate histograms, boxplots, bar graphs, and more using the Graphs procedure in SPSS.

2.5.3.1 Histograms

Step 1. For other ways to generate the types of graphical displays covered in this chapter, go to "Graphs" in the top pulldown menu. From there, select "Legacy Dialogs," then "Histogram" (see the screenshot for "GRAPHS: Step 1" in Figure 2.14). Another option for creating a histogram, which we will not illustrate but that uses an interactive drag-and-drop system, starting again from the Graphs option in the top pulldown menu, is to select "Chart Builder."

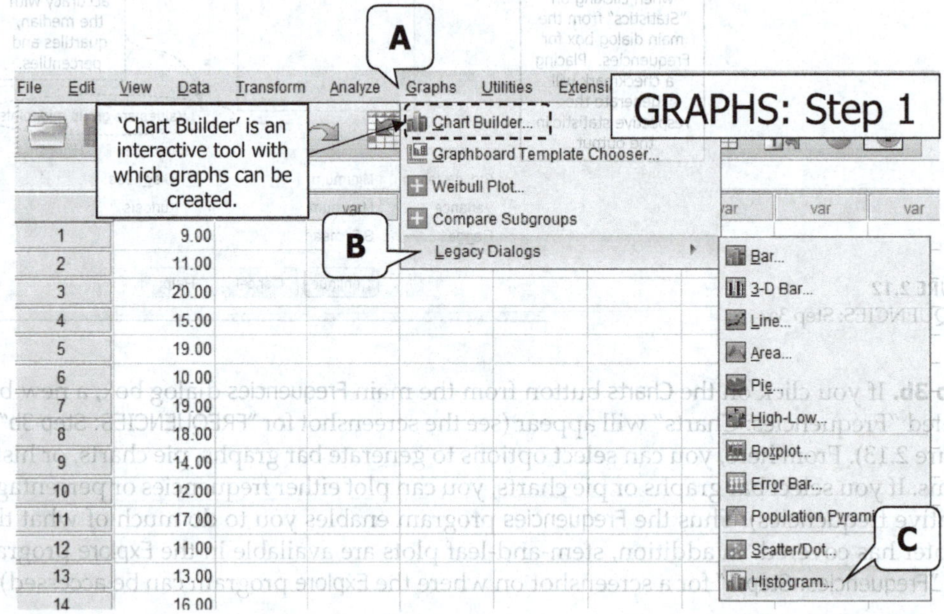

FIGURE 2.14
GRAPHS: Step 1.

Step 2. Following Step 1 will bring up the "Histogram" dialog box (see the screenshot for "HISTOGRAMS: Step 2" in Figure 2.15). Click the variable of interest (e.g., "quiz") and move it into the "Variable(s)" box by clicking the arrow. Place a checkmark in "Display normal curve," and then click "OK." This will generate the same histogram as was produced through the Frequencies program already mentioned and will overlay a normal curve.

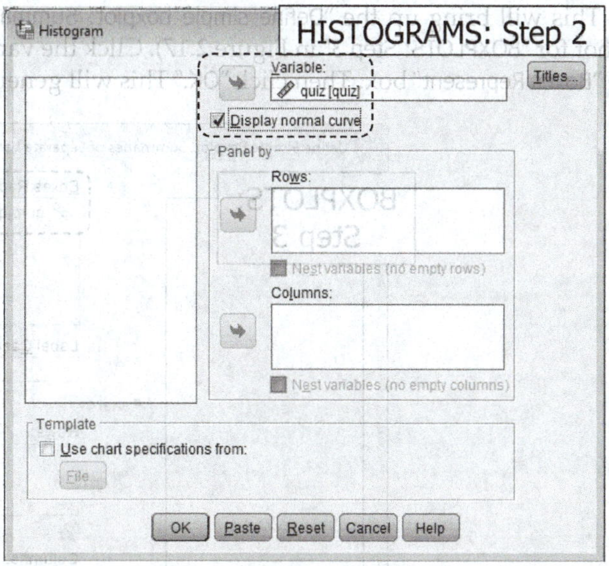

FIGURE 2.15
HISTOGRAMS: Step 2.

2.5.3.2 Boxplots

Step 1. To produce a boxplot for individual variables, click "Graphs" in the top pulldown menu. From there, select "Legacy Dialogs," then "Boxplot" (see "GRAPHS: Step 1," Figure 2.14, for a screenshot of this step). Another option for creating a boxplot, which we will not illustrate but uses an interactive drag-and-drop system, starting again from the "Graphs" option in the top pulldown menu, is to select "Chart Builder."

Step 2. This will bring up the "Boxplot" dialog box (see the screenshot for "BOXPLOTS: Step 2" in Figure 2.16). Select the "Simple" option (this will already be selected by default). To generate a separate boxplot for individual variables, click the "Summaries of separate variables" radio button, then click "Define."

FIGURE 2.16
BOXPLOTS: Step 2.

Step 3. This will bring up the "Define simple boxplot: Summaries . . ." dialog box (see the screenshot for "BOXPLOTS: Step 3" in Figure 2.17). Click the variable of interest (e.g., "quiz") into the "Boxes Represent" box. Then click "OK." This will generate a boxplot.

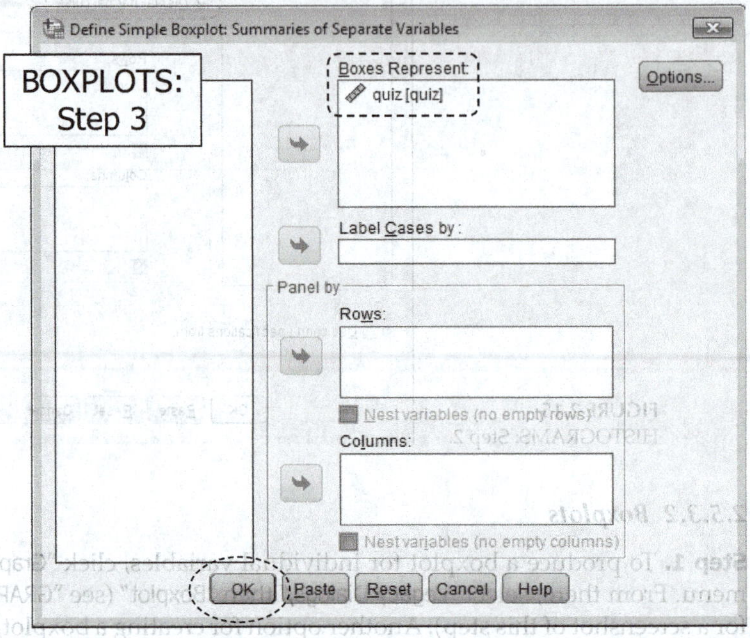

FIGURE 2.17
BOXPLOTS: Step 3.

2.5.3.3 Bar Graphs

Step 1. To produce a bar graph for individual variables, select "Graphs" from the top pull-down menu. From there, select "Legacy Dialogs," then "Bar" (see "GRAPHS: Step 1" in Figure 2.14 for a screenshot of this step).

Step 2. From the main "Bar Chart" dialog box, select "Simple" (which will be selected by default), and click the "Summaries for groups of cases" radio button (see "BAR GRAPHS: Step 2" in Figure 2.18 for a screenshot of this step).

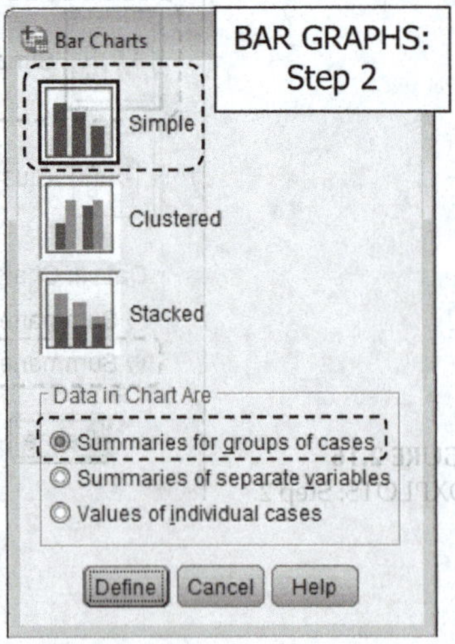

FIGURE 2.18
BAR GRAPHS: Step 2.

Step 3. A new box labeled "Define Simple Bar: Summaries . . ." will appear. Click the variable of interest (e.g., "eye color") and move it into the "Variable" box by clicking the arrow button. Then a decision must be made for how the bars will be displayed. Several types of displays for bar graph data are available, including "N of cases" for frequencies, "Cum. N" for cumulative frequencies, "% of cases" for relative frequencies, and "Cum. %" for cumulative relative frequencies (see the screenshot for "BAR GRAPHS: Step 3" in Figure 2.19). The most common bar graph is one that simply displays the frequencies (i.e., selecting the radio button for "N of cases"). Once your selections are made, click "OK." This will generate a bar graph.

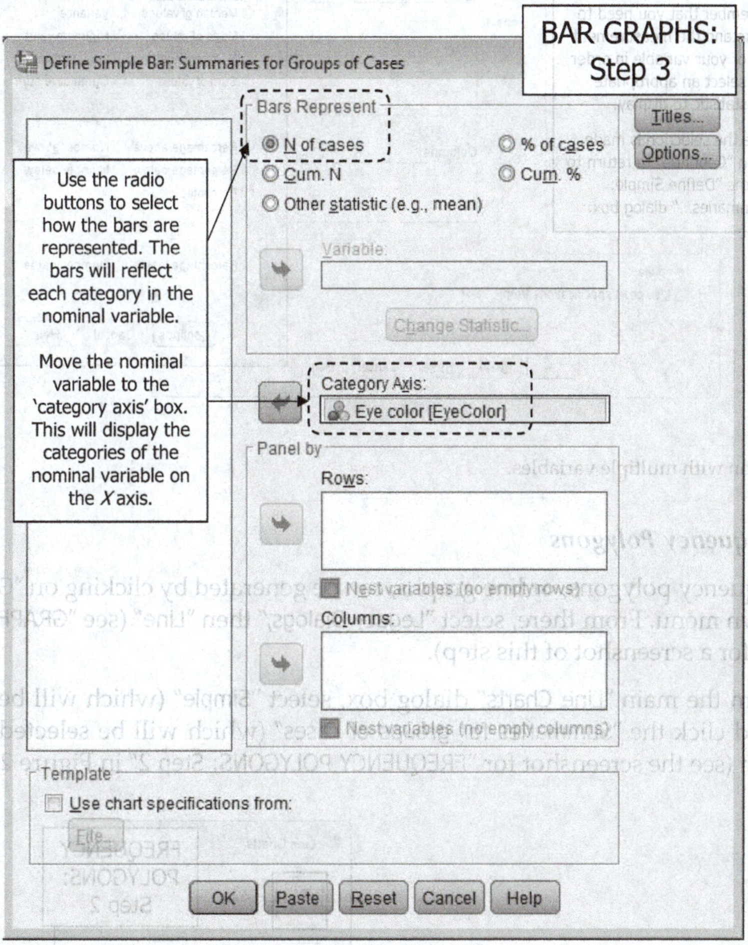

FIGURE 2.19
BAR GRAPHS: Step 3.

Additionally, if you have more than one variable, more complex bar graphs can be created. The categories can continue to appear on the X axis; however, the bars can represent other statistics using the "Other statistic (e.g., mean)" option (Figure 2.20). *Keep in mind that the measurement scale of the variable needs to be appropriate for the statistic that you are computing*. Thus, for example, if you want the bars to represent the mean of a second variable, the second variable should be at least interval in scale.

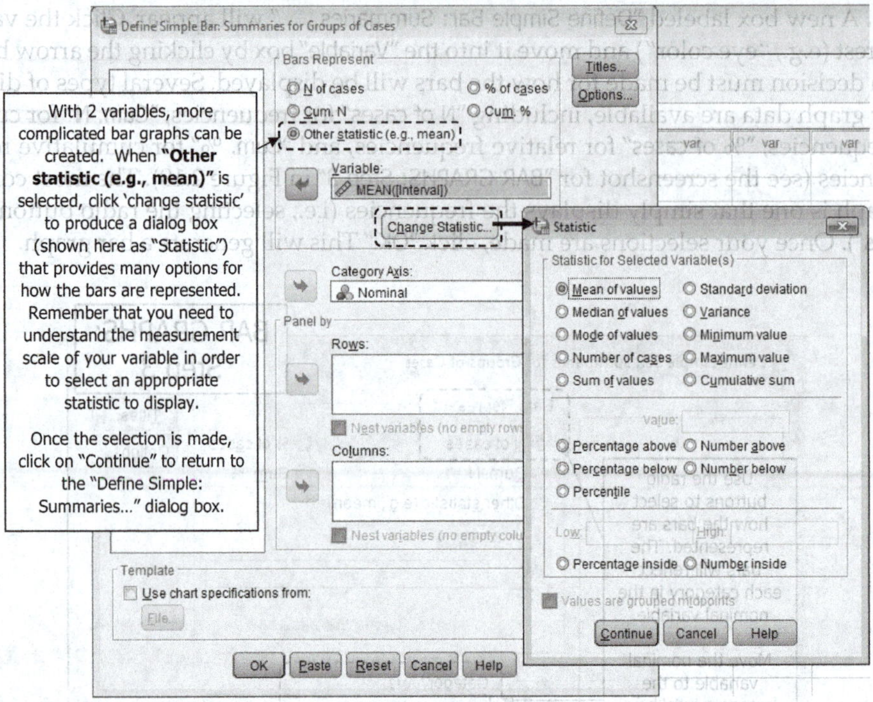

FIGURE 2.20
Bar graph option with multiple variables.

2.5.3.3 Frequency Polygons

Step 1. Frequency polygons, or line graphs, can be generated by clicking on "Graphs" in the top pulldown menu. From there, select "Legacy Dialogs," then "Line" (see "GRAPHS: Step 1" in Figure 2.14 for a screenshot of this step).

Step 2. From the main "Line Charts" dialog box, select "Simple" (which will be selected by default), and click the "Summaries for groups of cases" (which will be selected by default) radio button (see the screenshot for "FREQUENCY POLYGONS: Step 2" in Figure 2.21).

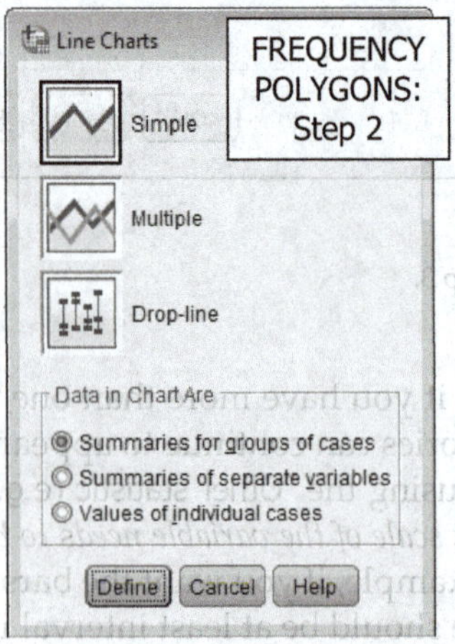

FIGURE 2.21
FREQUENCY POLYGONS: Step 2.

Step 3. A new box labeled "Define Simple Line: Summaries . . ." will appear. Click the variable of interest (e.g., "quiz") and move it into the "Variable" box by clicking the arrow button. Then a decision must be made for how the lines will be displayed. Several types of displays for line graph (i.e., frequency polygon) data are available, including "N of cases" for frequencies, "Cum. N" for cumulative frequencies, "% of cases" for relative frequencies, and "Cum. %" for cumulative relative frequencies (see the screenshot for "FREQUENCY POLYGONS: Step 3" in Figure 2.22). Additionally, other statistics can be selected through the "Other statistic (e.g., mean)" option (similar to what was illustrated with the bar graphs). The most common frequency polygon is one that simply displays the frequencies or counts for the values in the variable (i.e., selecting the radio button for "N of cases"). Once your selections are made, click "OK." This will generate a frequency polygon.

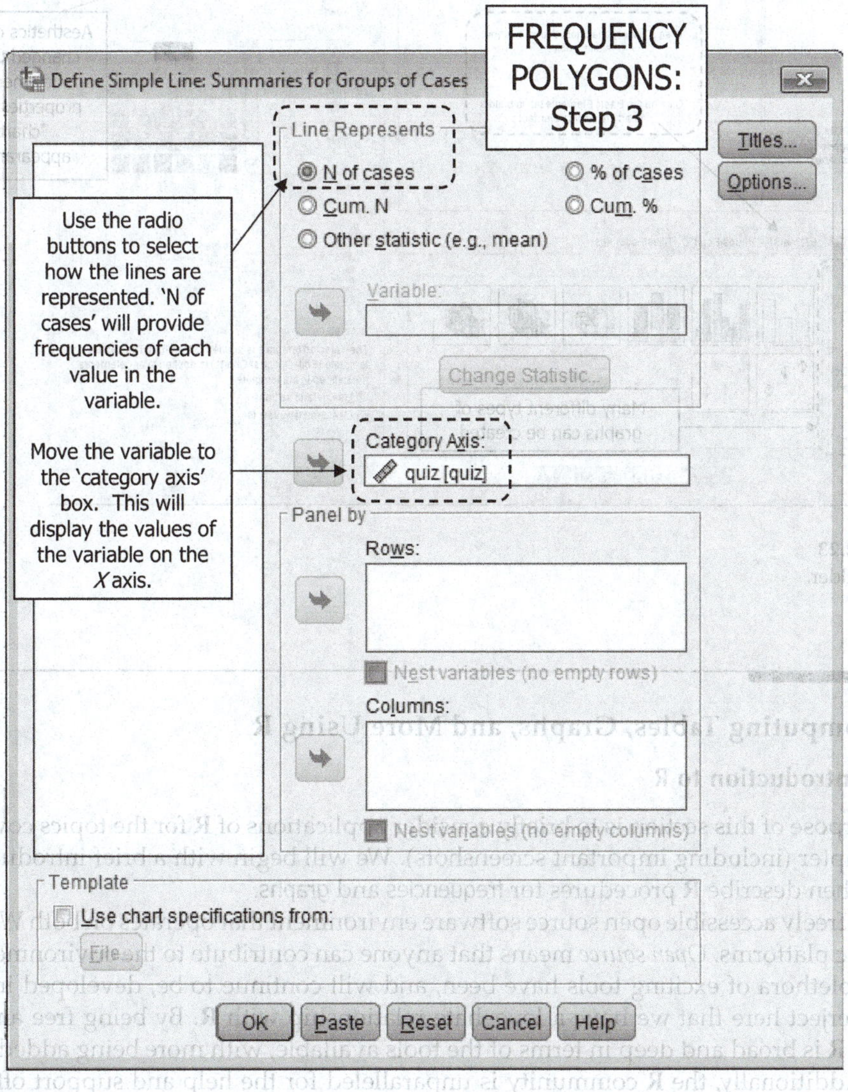

FIGURE 2.22
FREQUENCY POLYGONS: Step 3.

Graphs can also be generated in SPSS using Chart Builder (click on "Graphs" in the top pulldown menu and then go to "Chart Builder"). This is an interactive tool that allows researchers to drag and drop variables and types of graphs (e.g., bar, line, boxplots, and more) to build the figure. On the right side, "Element Properties" and "Chart Appearance" provide researchers with aesthetic options. Should you not choose to use Chart Builder to create your graph, you still have the ability to adapt the look of your graph by double-clicking on the graph in your output. This will allow you to access Chart Editor and make aesthetic alterations to your figure.

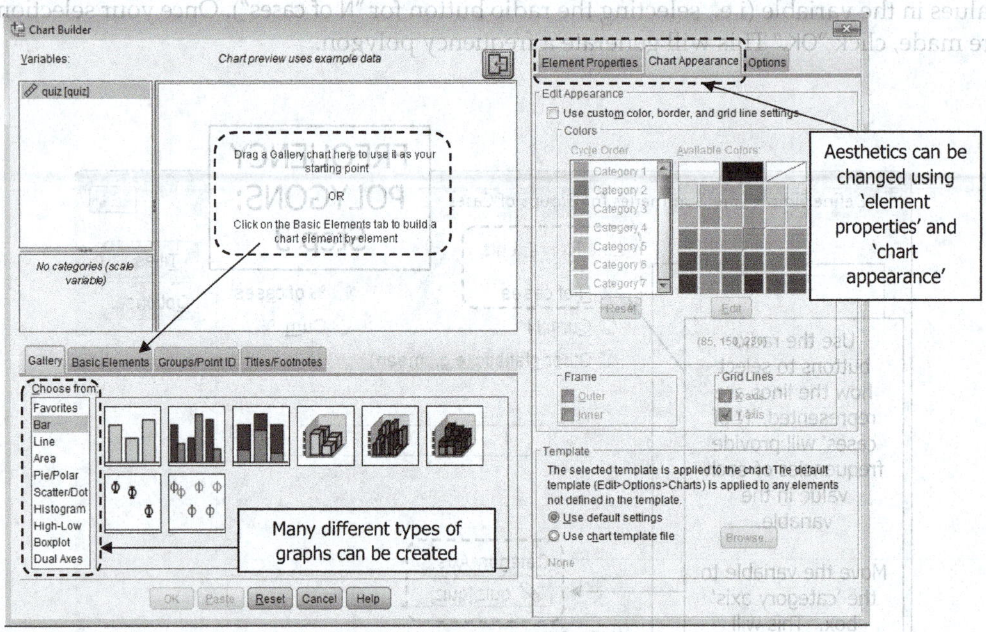

FIGURE 2.23
Chart Builder.

2.6 Computing Tables, Graphs, and More Using R

2.6.1 Introduction to R

The purpose of this section is to briefly consider applications of **R** for the topics covered in this chapter (including important screenshots). We will begin with a brief introduction to **R** and then describe **R** procedures for frequencies and graphs.

R is a freely accessible open source software environment that operates on both Windows and Mac platforms. *Open source* means that anyone can contribute to the environment, and thus a plethora of exciting tools have been, and will continue to be, developed in **R**. We will interject here that we have a love–hate relationship with **R**. By being free and open source, **R** is broad and deep in terms of the tools available, with more being added almost daily. Additionally, the **R** community is unparalleled for the help and support offered to users. On the other hand, **R** does not operate in a point-and-click environment. Rather, **R**

operates using command language and users have to write "scripts" (i.e., code or syntax) to *tell* **R** what to do, and **R** is very finicky in its prose. At this point, you may be asking: "Why in the world would I want to subject myself to the torture of having to write commands to generate statistics when just learning statistics is hard enough?" Great question, and we've asked ourselves the same question! If you ask around to a few **R** users, what you'll often find is that many **R** users avoided **R** for as long as they could, but when they finally gave it a shot (or perhaps *had* to give it a shot as the **R** environment was the only tool accessible for a particular statistic needed), were actually quite pleased—or at least were able to endure **R** sufficiently so that they saw the value in it and continued to use it. We've already mentioned a few benefits of **R**, and the fact that it's free, extremely powerful, open source, and overflowing with helpful users just waiting to lend support are really all that should be needed to convince you that **R** is a tool that you need in your toolkit. You may have heard the assertion, "Do something for 21 days and it becomes a habit." (Pardon us for a momentary detour: This assertion came from a book published in 1960 by Dr. Maxwell Maltz, a plastic surgeon, who studied the number of days it took amputees to adjust to losing a limb. Dr. Maltz generalized these results to other major life events, and the assertion of 21 days for a habit was almost set in stone. More recently, research suggests that habit formation takes much longer than 21 days, and is quite varied depending on the task. For our purposes, we're going with Dr. Maltz! Now let's get back on track!) We apply this principle to **R** and say, "Use **R** for 9 chapters and it becomes a habit" (okay, it's not 21, but 19 of the 20 chapters use **R**!). We encourage you to give **R** a shot throughout the text. By the time you've finished the text, or even sooner, we think you'll be an **R** convert. At the very least, you'll be able to say that you have used **R** and it is in your toolkit! That is no small feat!

All that being said, we're not necessarily saying that **R** will be easy to learn. Again, ask around to a few **R** users and you'll most likely quickly come to understand that there is a learning curve to **R**, one that is steeper for some than others (we've ourselves experienced points at which it was nearly vertical). If you can get over the hump, so to speak, in using **R**, however, you're home free (remember our suggestion to try **R** for 19 chapters?). Thus, just when you feel like throwing in the towel on **R**, don't do it. Stick with it. Take the hurdles in learning **R** as opportunities to connect with the **R** help community, and keep going. We have offered a number of excellent resources at the end of the chapter to help in learning more about **R**. We hope that the **R** sections in this textbook will provide a smooth transition into the **R** environment and will whet your appetite to learn more about **R**. We want to remind you that what we have provided is an introduction to **R** for the various statistics generated in the text. Keep in mind that this text is *not* meant to serve as a comprehensive resource for all things **R**. There *are* resources that serve in that capacity, and we will offer a few of those at the conclusion of this chapter. However, this textbook is first and foremost a resource for learning about statistical concepts, which is supplemented with resources for computing statistics using both SPSS and **R**. With that introduction, let's get rolling in **R**!

2.6.1.1 R Basics

You need to understand a few basic things about **R** before we delve into writing commands. **R** is a base package. Similar to SPSS, Mplus, and many other software programs, there is a base package **R**, to which additional modules (called *packages* in the **R** environment) can be added. The packages written for **R** are stored in the Comprehensive **R** Archive Network (CRAN). There are identical versions of CRAN, called CRAN "mirrors," all around the world. Thus, when you first download **R**, you have to select from which mirror you want to download. What most **R** users do is to select a CRAN location that is geographically close to them, or at least in their same time zone.

2.6.1.2 Downloading R and RStudio

R can be downloaded from https://www.r-project.org. When you click "download **R**," you will be asked from which CRAN mirror you want to download. Many **R** users work directly from the original **R** environment. We prefer using **R** from **RStudio**. The makers of RStudio claim that it "makes **R** easier to use" by providing a console within which to work, visualization space, debugging, and more—and we agree. We have used **R** (version 3.5.1) through RStudio (version 1.1.456) in a Windows platform throughout the text. To download RStudio, download **R** first and then visit http://www.rstudio.com and click "download." The RStudio Desktop open source license can be downloaded for free. That is the version that has been used throughout the text.

When you use **R** through RStudio, you'll see that you will have access to four quadrants (see Figure 2.24). The top-left quadrant is the **source editor window**. This is where you will write and execute scripts or commands (i.e., syntax or code). The bottom-left quadrant is the **console**, and this is where the output will appear once you run a command (the exceptions are graphs and figures, which display in the bottom-right quadrant). When you open

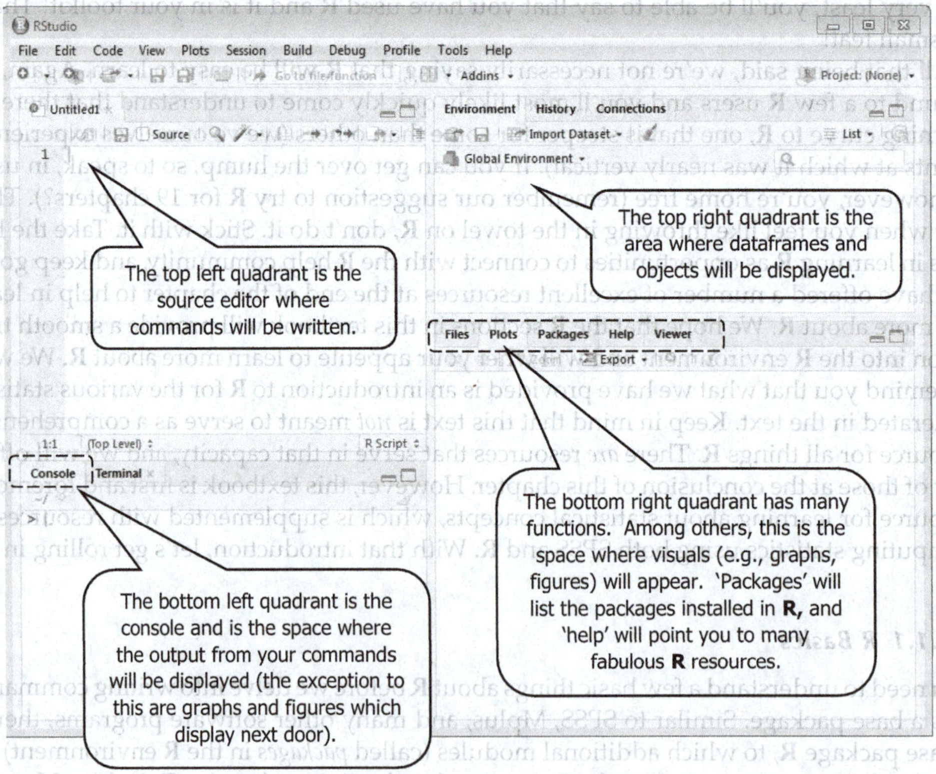

FIGURE 2.24
RStudio.

RStudio, the console will autopopulate with information—one very important piece of information is contained within the first line, and that is the version of **R** that is being used by RStudio. In Windows, the current version is the default. However, you may find yourself in a situation where you want to run an older version of **R**, as not all packages run in all versions of **R**. To override which version of **R** is being used, go to "Tools" in RStudio's top toolbar and select "Global options." If not already selected, click "general" in the left navigational menu. The version of **R** that is being used is displayed. Click the button labeled "change" to display other options of **R** available on your computer and to select the specific version of **R** that you want to work with. You can install previous released of **R** by visiting the CRAN project website (https://cran.r-project.org/bin/windows/base/old/). The top-right quadrant is where you will see the list of dataframes and objects (you'll learn about these soon) that you have called up to work with. The bottom-right quadrant is the visualization space (i.e., graphs and plots that are generated will appear in this quadrant), and also where you can find the list of **R** packages installed, update packages, and link to various help tools.

2.6.1.3 Packages

Again, base **R** has a number of functionalities in it ready to use, but there are lots of great packages available that provide additional functionality. Accessing and using a package is a two-step process. The package has to first be installed (using the *install.packages("PackageNameHere")* command), and then the package has to be called into the library (using the *library(PackageNameHere)* command). Packages only need be installed once (i.e., once installed, always installed). However, they have to be called into the library each time they are used. Throughout the text, as a package is needed, we will provide the commands to both install it and call it into the library. It's not uncommon to get a warning when you install a package that it was created under an earlier version of **R**. Only in a rare instance will you encounter problems in continuing to use the package, so don't be too worried if you encounter this warning. Remember that packages, just like software, get updated from time to time. This is easy to do in RStudio using the *update* icon. **R** also gets updated from time to time. You can efficiently, and painlessly, update **R** by running the following script. You will want to copy all your packages to the new version of **R**.

```
install.packages("installr")
library(installr)
updateR()
```

Let us digress for a moment. Previously we mentioned that **R** can be quite persnickety. Notice that quotation marks are used to enclose the name of the package in the command for installing the package but not in the command for calling it into the library. Yes, that's correct—you have to pay close attention to little details in **R** like quotation marks, commas, capitalization, etc.

2.6.1.4 Working in R

There are different ways to work in **R**, none of which are necessarily right or wrong, and different users have different preferences. However, throughout the text we have guided your work in **R** so that you begin your work by establishing a **working directory**. Within that working directory, your files and scripts will be stored. We have found that to be the easiest way to keep track of your files and stay organized.

Throughout the text, we will refer to objects and functions. An **object** is something created from a **function.** Many times, a function will be running a statistical procedure (e.g., generating an ANOVA or a regression model), but a function could also be generating a table or creating a variable or more. An object is what results from that function (e.g., the results of the ANOVA model, the table, or the variable). Throughout the text, we will try to remind you what is the object versus the function but generally this takes the form in **R** command language as the following: *object <- function*, where the object appears to the left of <- and the function appears to the right of <-. You might be wondering why this is important. Creating objects from functions is not necessarily a requirement, but it can make life much easier when you want to extend the results from your function to something else. This is because rather than writing the entire function again (e.g., an entire ANOVA or regression model), you simply have to write the name of your object. As you will see, some functions are short and sweet, whereas others are long and tedious. Naming your function as an object is particularly helpful in the case of the latter!

Although data can be created in **R**, the data examples provided in the text use comma-separated (.csv) files. Command language is provided in the illustrations to bring the .csv file into the **R** environment. We have done this because it is usually the case that the data that we work with already exist in spreadsheet form (e.g., Excel, SPSS, SAS). And if the data do not already exist, we encourage you to use a spreadsheet tool to create the dataset and then bring it into the **R** environment. Once the data are brought into **R**, it is called a **dataframe**. There are lots of ways to work with data in dataframes (e.g., recoding variables, creating new variables), and you'll be introduced to quite a few of those in the examples throughout the text. If you manipulate your dataframe, you may want to save it and export it out of the **R** environment. That's easy to do using the *write.csv(DataframeName, "FileName.csv")* command. This command, along with a few other "staples," are provided in Box 2.2. RStudio has a number of time-saving shortcuts. You can access these directly in RStudio by going to "Tools" in the top menu, and then selecting "keyboard shortcuts help." You'll find that some are the same as what you're accustomed in other environments (e.g., in Windows, Ctrl+O to open, Ctrl+S to save).

BOX 2.2 Need-to-Know Commands in R

Command	Functionality
install. packages("PackageNameHere")	Installs a package into **R**. Once a package is installed, it remains installed in **R**. However, each time it is used, the user needs to call it in using the library command. *(Note: Quotation marks around the package name are required.)*
library(PackageNameHere)	Calls a package into **R** so that it can be used. Each time a package is used, it must be called into the **R** environment using the library command.
getwd()	**R** is always directed to a directory on your computer. To find out which directory it is pointed to, run this "get working directory" command. We will assume that we need to change the working directory, and will use the next line of code to set the working directory to the desired path.

Command	Functionality
setwd("E:/Folder")	Establishes a working directory that points to a specific folder that is designated by the user. (Momentary detour: If you don't know where a file is located, right-click on the file and go to "properties." The "location" in properties will provide the specific file location.) *(Note: Quotation marks around the folder are required.)*
DataframeName <- read.csv ("DatasetName.csv")	Renames the dataset to whatever is designated to the left of the <-. *(Note: Quotation marks around the file name are required.)*
names(DataframeName)	Lists the names of the variables in the dataframe (this output is provided in the console).
View(DataframeName)	Calls the dataframe into RStudio (i.e., creates a tab in the source editor where the user can see the actual spreadsheet view of the data).
write.csv(DataframeName, "FileName.csv")	Exports the dataframe from **R** into a comma separated file.

Now that you've been provided the basics of **R**, let's dive in! Next we consider **R** for various tables, graphs, and more. The **R** code is only those lines of text that are included in the boxes. The remainder is annotation, provided here to help you understand what the various lines of code are doing. We will preface this by reading in our data. We will be using both the quiz data and the eye color data. These reside in two separate data files, so we will read them in separately using the following code (Figure 2.25). One additional tip as we're getting started. . . . When you run script in **R**, do *not* highlight the command and then hit run. *Rather, simply place your cursor anywhere in the command that you want to run and then hit the run icon (or Ctrl+Enter)*. This is especially helpful when you have very long lines of code, and it will prevent you from failing to highlight parts of it.

```
getwd()
```

R is always directed to a directory on your computer. To find out which directory it is pointed to, run this "get working directory" command. We will assume that we need to change the working directory, and will use the next line of code to set the working directory to the desired path.

```
setwd("E:/Folder")
```

Change what is in parentheses to your file location. Also, if you are copying the directory name, it will copy in slashes. You will need to change the slash (i.e., \) to a forward slash (i.e., /). Additionally, note that you need the name of your folder location in quotation marks.

```
Ch2_quiz <- read.csv("Ch2_quiz.csv")
Ch2_eye <- read.csv("Ch2_eye.csv")
```

This command reads your data into **R**. What's to the left of the <- will be what you want to call the dataframe in **R**. In this example, we're calling the first **R** dataframe "Ch2_quiz." What's to the right of the <- tells **R** to find

FIGURE 2.25
Getting started in **R**.

this particular .csv file. In this example, our file is called "Ch2_quiz.csv." Make sure the extension (i.e., .csv) is there. Also note that you need this in quotation marks. We are reading in the eye color data similarly.

```
names(Ch4_quiz)
names(Ch2_eye)
```

This command will display in the console a list of variable names for each dataframe as follows:

```
# names(Ch2_quiz)
[1] "quiz"

# names(Ch2_eye)
[1] "EyeColor"
```

This is a good check to make sure your data have been read in correctly.

```
View(Ch2_quiz)
View(Ch2_eye)
```

This command will let you view the dataset in spreadsheet format in R Studio. It will set as an additional tab in the upper-left quadrant in RStudio so you can toggle to it from any other open file.

```
Ch2_eye$color <- factor(Ch2_eye$EyeColor,
                        labels = c("blue",
                                   "brown",
                                   "green",
                                   "black"))
```

This will create a new variable in our dataframe named "color" that is a nominal variable with four categories with labels of the eye colors. The colors are listed in order of their values. For example, "blue" is 1 and "brown" is 2.

```
summary(Ch2_quiz)
```

The *summary* command will produce basic descriptive statistics on all the variables in our dataframe. This is a great way to quickly check to see if the data have been read in correctly and get a feel for your data, if you haven't already. The output from the summary statement for this dataframe looks like this:

```
     quiz
Min.   : 9.00
1st Qu.:13.00
Median :17.00
Mean   :15.56
3rd Qu.:18.00
Max.   :20.00
```

```
levels(Ch2_eye$color)
```

This command will output the categories in our nominal variable as follows:

```
[1] "blue"  "brown" "green" "black"
```

FIGURE 2.25 (continued)
Getting Started in R.

2.6.2 Frequencies

```
install.packages("plyr")
```

Frequencies can be generated using many different packages in **R**. This command will install the *plyr* package that we can use to generate frequencies.

```
library(plyr)
```

This command will load the *plyr* package.

```
count(Ch2_eye$color)
```

The *count* function will generate a frequency table for the variable "color" in our dataframe "Ch2_eye."

```
      x freq
1  blue   10
2 brown    6
3 green    3
4 black    1
```

FIGURE 2.26
Frequencies.

2.6.3 Graphs

2.6.3.1 Histograms

```
hist(Ch2_quiz$quiz,
     main = "Histogram of Quiz Scores",
     xlab = "Quiz Score", ylab = "Frequency")
```

The *hist* function will produce a histogram using the variable "quiz" from the "Ch4_quiz" dataframe (i.e., "ch2_quiz$quiz"). The histogram will include "Histogram of Quiz Scores" as the title (i.e., main = "Histogram of Quiz Scores"), with the *X* axis being labeled "Quiz Score" (i.e., *xlab = "Quiz Score"*) and the *Y* axis being labeled "Frequency" (i.e., *ylab = "Frequency"*).

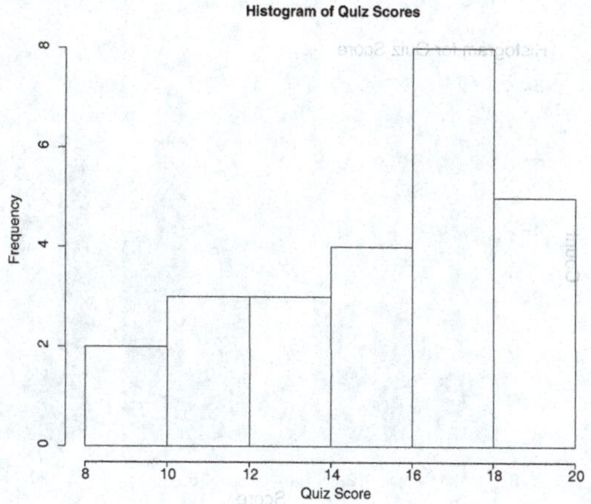

FIGURE 2.27
Histograms.

```
install.packages("ggplot2")
```

Histograms can be made using many different packages in **R**. This command will install the *ggplot2* package that we can use to create various graphs and plots, including a histogram.

```
library(ggplot2)
```

This command will load the *ggplot2* package.

```
qplot(Ch2_quiz$quiz, geom="histogram")
```

We can generate a very simple histogram using this command.

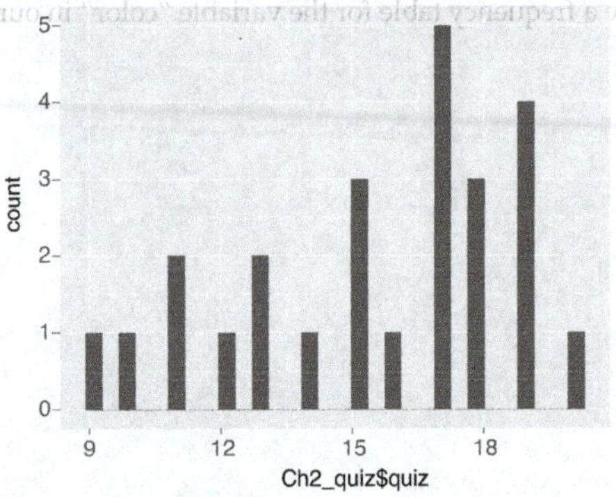


```
qplot(Ch2_quiz$quiz, geom="histogram",
      binwidth=0.8,
            main = "Histogram for Quiz Score",
      xlab = "Score", ylab = "Count",
      fill=I("gray"),
      col=I("white"))
```

We can add a few commands to change the width of the bars (i.e., *binwidth = 0.8*), color of the bars (i.e., *fill = I("gray")*), and outline of the bars (i.e., *col = I("white")*). We can also add a title (i.e., *main = "Histogram for Quiz Score"*) and change the *X* and *Y* axes (*xlab = "Score," ylab = "Count"*).

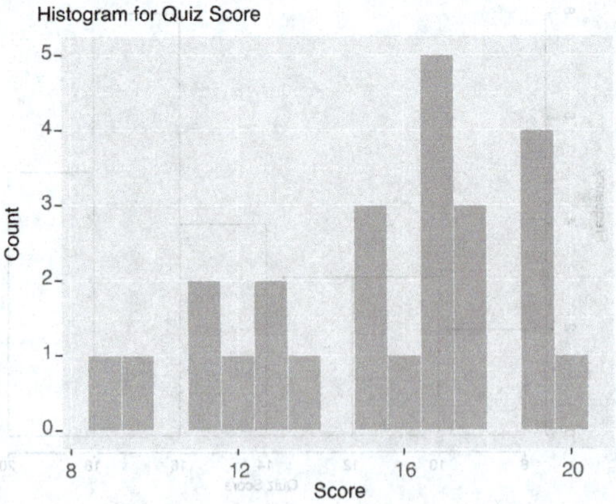

FIGURE 2.27 (continued)
Histograms.

2.6.3.2 Boxplots

```
boxplot(Ch2_quiz$quiz,ylab="Score")
```

The *boxplot* function can be used to generate a boxplot. In parentheses, we tell **R** which variable in our dataframe to compute the boxplot (i.e., "Ch2_quiz$quiz") and we label the *Y* axis as "Score."

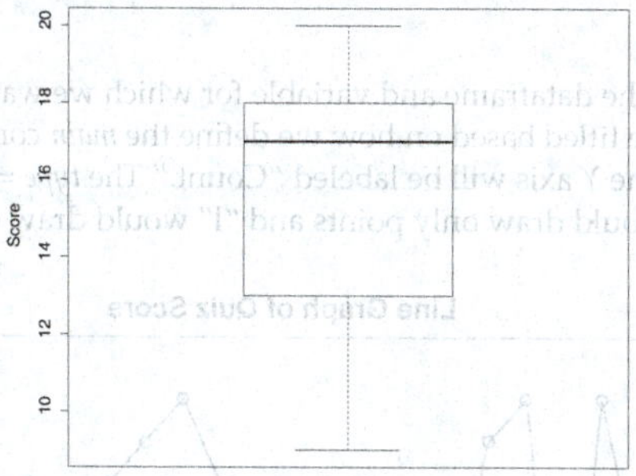

FIGURE 2.28
Boxplots.

2.6.3.3 Bar Graphs

```
eyecounts <- table(Ch2_eye$color)
```

To generate a bar graph, we first need to create a table of counts of our variable. We do this using the *table* function. If we run only the command, *table(Ch2_eye$color)*, we see the counts for the categories in our variable, but we are not creating an object:

```
blue brown green black
  10     6     3     1
```

By adding "eyecounts <-" to the command, we are creating an object called "eyecounts" that we can use to create our bar graph in the following command.

```
barplot(eyecounts,
        main= "Bar Graph of Eye Color",
        xlab = "Eye Color",
        ylab = "Count",
        col = "gray")
```

This command will create a bar graph using the counts from "eyecounts." The graph will be titled based on the *main* command (i.e., "Bar Graph of Eye Color"). The X axis will be labeled "Eye Color," and the *Y* axis will be labeled "Count." The color of the bars will be gray.

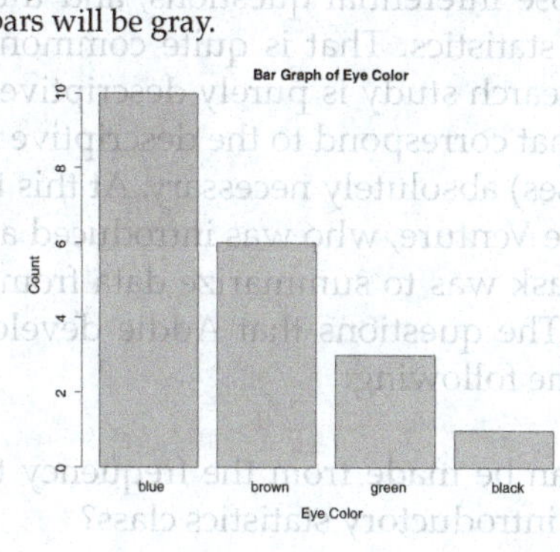

FIGURE 2.29
Bar graphs.

2.6.3.4 Frequency Polygons

```
plot(Ch2_quiz$quiz,
     type = "o",
     xlab = "Score",
     ylab = "Count",
     main = "Line Graph")
```

We use the *plot* function and define the dataframe and variable for which we want to create the line graph (i.e., "Ch2_quiz$quiz"). The graph will be titled based on how we define the *main* command (i.e., "Line Graph"). The *X* axis will be labeled "Score," and the *Y* axis will be labeled "Count." The *type* = "o" tells **R** to draw both the lines and points in the graph ("p" would draw only points and "l" would draw only lines).

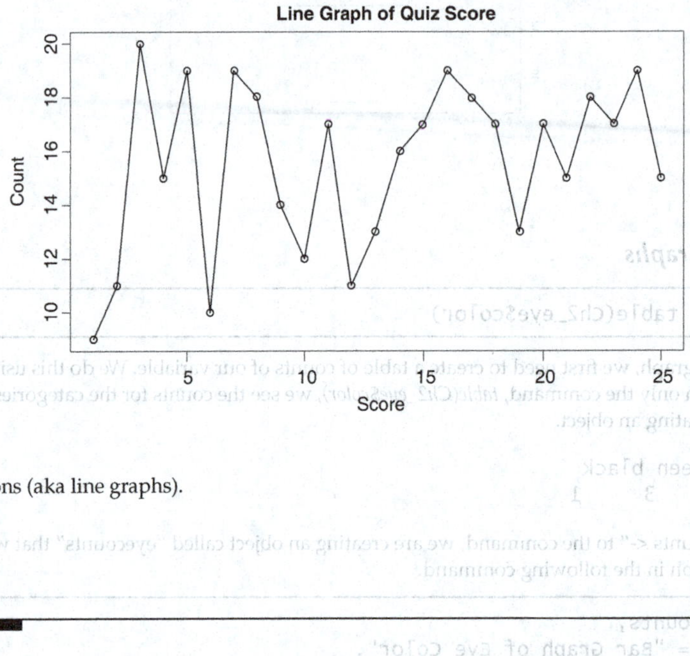

FIGURE 2.30
Frequency polygons (aka line graphs).

2.7 Research Question Template and Example Write-Up

Depending on the purpose of your research study, you may or may not write a research question that corresponds to your descriptive statistics. If the end result of your research paper is to present results from inferential statistics, it may be that your research questions correspond only to those inferential questions, and thus no question is presented to represent the descriptive statistics. That is quite common. On the other hand, if the ultimate purpose of your research study is purely descriptive in nature, then writing one or more research questions that correspond to the descriptive statistics is not only entirely appropriate, but (in most cases) absolutely necessary. At this time, let us revisit our graduate research assistant, Addie Venture, who was introduced at the beginning of the chapter. As you may recall, her task was to summarize data from 25 students enrolled in Dr. Debhard's statistics course. The questions that Addie developed based on consultation with Dr. Debhard included the following:

1. What interpretations can be made from the frequency table of quiz scores from students enrolled in an introductory statistics class?

2. What interpretations can be made from graphical representations of quiz scores from students enrolled in an introductory statistics class?
3. What is the distributional shape of the statistics quiz scores?
4. What is the 50th percentile of the quiz scores?

A template for writing descriptive research questions for summarizing data follows. Note that these are just a few examples. Given the multitude of descriptive statistics that can be generated, these are not meant to be exhaustive:

What interpretations can be made from the table of [variable]? What interpretations can be made from the graphical representation of [variable]? What is the distributional shape of the [variable]? What is the 50th percentile of [variable]?

Next, we present an APA-like paragraph summarizing the results of the statistics quiz data example:

As shown in Table 2.2 and Figure 2.2, scores ranged from 9 to 20, with more students achieving a score of 17 than any other score (20%). From Figure 2.2 we also know that the distribution of scores was negatively skewed, with the bulk of the scores being at the high end of the distribution. Skewness was also evident as the quartiles were not equally spaced, as shown in Figure 2.7. Thus, overall the sample of students tended to do rather well on this particular quiz, although a few low scores should be troubling (as 20% did not pass the quiz and suggest the need for some remediation).

2.8 Additional Resources

Throughout the chapter, we've shared a number of resources related to graphing. As you step into learning statistical software, a number of excellent tools are available to help you:

- An increasing number of books are available for learning **R** (e.g., Crawley, 2013; Rahlf, 2017; Wickham & Grolemund, 2017). Wickham and Grolemund (2017) is also available online at https://r4ds.had.co.nz.
- As mentioned in the text, the **R** user community is both large and immensely helpful. The following websites are a few places you can start when you need **R** support:
    - **R** cookbook: http://www.cookbook-r.com
    - Datacamp: https://www.datacamp.com
    - Stackoverflow: https://stackoverflow.com/questions/tagged/r
    - Comprehensive **R** Archive Network (CRAN): https://cran.r-project.org
    - Learning **R** in **R**: https://swirlstats.com
- Discussion lists are one of the quickest ways to find support; users of SPSS can join the SPSS listserv to post questions or search the archives (https://listserv.uga.edu/cgi-bin/wa?A0=SPSSX-L).

Problems

Conceptual Problems

1. For a distribution where the 50th percentile is 100, what is the percentile rank of 100?
   a. 0
   b. .50
   c. 50
   d. 100
2. Which of the following frequency distributions will generate the same relative frequency distribution?

X	f	Y	f	Z	f
100	2	100	6	100	8
99	5	99	15	99	18
98	8	98	24	98	28
97	5	97	15	97	18
96	2	96	6	96	8

   a. *X* and *Y* only
   b. *X* and *Z* only
   c. *Y* and *Z* only
   d. *X*, *Y*, and *Z*
   e. None of the above
3. Which of the following frequency distributions will generate the same cumulative relative frequency distribution?

X	f	Y	f	Z	f
100	2	100	6	100	8
99	5	99	15	99	18
98	8	98	24	98	28
97	5	97	15	97	18
96	2	96	6	96	8

   a. *X* and *Y* only
   b. *X* and *Z* only
   c. *Y* and *Z* only
   d. *X*, *Y*, and *Z*
   e. None of the above

4. True or false? In a histogram, 48% of the area lies below the score whose percentile rank is 52.
5. Which of the following would be the preferred method of graphing data pertaining to the ethnicity of a sample?
   a. Histogram
   b. Frequency polygon
   c. Cumulative frequency polygon
   d. Bar graph
6. True or false? The proportion of scores between Q_1 and Q_3 may be less than .50.
7. The values of Q_1, Q_2, and Q_3 in a positively skewed population distribution are calculated. What is the expected relationship between $(Q_2 - Q_1)$ and $(Q_3 - Q_2)$?
   a. $(Q_2 - Q_1)$ is greater than $(Q_3 - Q_2)$.
   b. $(Q_2 - Q_1)$ is equal to $(Q_3 - Q_2)$.
   c. $(Q_2 - Q_1)$ is less than $(Q_3 - Q_2)$.
   d. Cannot be determined without examining the data.
8. True or false? If the percentile rank of a score of 72 is 65, we can say that 35% of the scores exceed 72.
9. True or false? In a negatively skewed distribution, the proportion of scores between Q_1 and Q_2 is less than .25.
10. A group of 200 sixth-grade students was given a standardized test and obtained scores ranging from 42 to 88. If the scores tended to "bunch up" in the low 80s, the shape of the distribution would be which of the following?
   a. Symmetrical
   b. Positively skewed
   c. Negatively skewed
   d. Normal
11. Which of the following is the preferred method of graphing data on the eye color of a sample?
   a. Bar graph
   b. Frequency polygon
   c. Cumulative frequency polygon
   d. Relative frequency polygon
12. If $Q_2 = 60$, then what is P_{50}?
   a. 50
   b. 60
   c. 95
   d. Cannot be determined with the information provided.
13. True or false? With the same data and using an interval width of 1, the frequency polygon and histogram will display the same information.

14. A researcher develops a histogram based on an interval width of 2. Can she reconstruct the raw scores using only this histogram? Yes or No?

15. True or false? $Q_2 = 50$ for a positively skewed variable and $Q_2 = 50$ for a negatively skewed variable. Given this, Q_1 will be the same for both variables.

16. Which of the following statements is *correct* for a continuous variable?
    a. The proportion of the distribution below the 25th percentile is 75%.
    b. The proportion of the distribution below the 50th percentile is 25%.
    c. The proportion of the distribution above the third quartile is 25%.
    d. The proportion of the distribution between the 25th and 75th percentile is 25%.

17. For a dataset with four unique values (55, 70, 80, and 90), the relative frequency for the value 55 is 20%, the relative frequency for 70 is 30%, the relative frequency for 80 is 20%, and the relative frequency for 90 is 30%. What is the cumulative relative frequency for the value 70?
    a. 20%
    b. 30%
    c. 50%
    d. 100%

18. In examining data collected over the past 10 years, researchers at a theme park find the following for 5000 first-time guests: 2250 visited during the summer months; 675 visited during the fall; 1300 visited during the winter; and 775 visited during the spring. What is the relative frequency for guests who visited during the spring?
    a. .135
    b. .155
    c. .260
    d. .450

19. A researcher is analyzing student enrollment data for the last academic year for all public postsecondary institutions in the United States. The researcher has data on the number of graduate students enrolled in at least six credit hours per semester, a variable measured in whole numbers. Which of the following graphs would be appropriate to use to graph this variable? Select all that apply.
    a. Bar graph
    b. Boxplot
    c. Histogram
    d. Stem-and-leaf plot

20. Data have been collected on how often adults feel they "eat healthy" during an average week. Responses include: "all the time," "most of the time," "sometimes," and "never." Which of the following graphs would be appropriate to use to graph this variable? Select all that apply.
    a. Bar graph
    b. Boxplot
    c. Histogram
    d. Stem-and-leaf plot

21. Your statistics professor requires you to submit a report that includes a boxplot. The following variables are available in your dataset. Which of the following would be appropriate for graphing a boxplot? Select all that apply.
    a. Dollar amount of donations to charitable organizations reported on last year's taxes (measured in whole dollars)
    b. Favorite vacation destination (responses of "beach," "mountain," "city," "other")
    c. Home ownership (responses of "own," "rent," "other")
    d. Number of days per week that at least 30 minutes of exercise is achieved (responses of 0, 1, 2, 3, 4, 5, 6, 7)
22. Your statistics professor requires you to submit a report that includes a boxplot. The following variables are available in your dataset. Which of the follwoing would be appropriate for computing a relative frequency distribution? Select all that apply.
    a. Dollar amount of donations to charitable organizations reported on last year's taxes (measured in whole dollars)
    b. Favorite vacation destination (responses of "beach," "mountain," "city," "other")
    c. Home ownership (responses of "own," "rent," "other")
    d. Number of days per week that at least 30 minutes of exercise is achieved (responses of 0, 1, 2, 3, 4, 5, 6, 7)
23. Which of the following is a correct interpretation of the 30th percentile?
    a. The value at which 30% of the distribution is above.
    b. The value at which 30% of the distribution is below.
    c. The value at which 70% of the distribution is above.
    d. Two values, between which 70% of the distribution falls.

Answers to Conceptual Problems

1. **c** (Percentile and percentile rank are two sides of the same coin; if the 50th percentile = 100, then *PR*(100) = 50.)
3. **a** (For 96, *crf* = .09 for both *X* and *Y* and *crf* = .10 for Z.)
5. **d** (Ethnicity is not continuous, so only a bar graph is appropriate.)
7. **c** (See Section 2.2.3.)
9. **False** (The proportion is .25 by definition.)
11. **a** (Eye color is nominal and not continuous.)
13. **True** (With the same interval width, each is based on exactly the same information.)
15. **False** (It is most likely that Q_1 will be *smaller* for the negatively skewed variable.)
17. **c** (If the relative frequency for the value 55 is 20% and for 70 is 30%, the cumulative relative frequency for the value 70 is 50%.)
19. **b, c, d** (Graduate student enrollment, measured in whole numbers, is a ratio variable; thus all graphs listed except bar graphs can be applied.)
21. **a, d** (Dollar amount donated to charity and number of days exercised are both ratio variables, thus boxplots can be computed using them.)
23. **b** (30% of the distribution is below the value reflected in the 30th percentile.)

Computational Problems

1. The following scores were obtained from a statistics exam.

50.00	44.00	41.00	43.00	43.00
47.00	49.00	49.00	47.00	42.00
45.00	48.00	41.00	45.00	46.00
44.00	46.00	46.00	46.00	49.00
47.00	50.00	47.00	47.00	44.00
47.00	48.00	45.00	46.00	48.00
45.00	46.00	43.00	44.00	47.00
43.00	45.00	47.00	49.00	45.00
44.00	47.00	50.00	48.00	46.00

Using an interval size of 1, construct or compute each of the following:

a. Frequency distribution
b. Relative frequency distribution
c. Cumulative relative frequency distribution
d. Histogram
e. Frequency polygon
f. Cumulative frequency polygon
g. Quartiles
h. P_{10} and P_{90}
i. Box-and-whisker plot
j. Stem-and-leaf display

2. The following data were obtained from classroom observations and reflect the number of times that preschool children shared during an 8-hour period.

4	8	10	5	12	10	14	5
10	14	12	14	8	5	0	8
12	8	12	5	4	10	8	5

Using an interval size of 1, construct or compute each of the following:

a. Frequency distribution
b. Cumulative frequency distribution
c. Relative frequency distribution
d. Cumulative relative frequency distribution
e. Histogram and frequency polygon
f. Cumulative frequency polygon
g. Quartiles
h. P_{10} and P_{90}

i. $PR(10)$
j. Box-and-whisker plot
k. Stem-and-leaf display

3. A sample distribution of variable X is as follows:

X	f
2	1
3	2
4	5
5	8
6	4
7	3
8	4
9	1
10	2

Calculate or draw each of the following for the sample distribution of X:

a. Q_1
b. Q_2
c. Q_3
d. $P_{44.5}$
e. Box-and-whisker plot
f. Histogram (ungrouped)

4. A sample distribution of aptitude scores is as follows:

X	f
70	1
75	2
77	3
79	2
80	6
82	5
85	4
90	4
96	3

Calculate or draw each of the following for the sample distribution of X:

a. Q_1
b. Q_2
c. Q_3

d. $P_{44.5}$
e. $PR(82)$
f. Box-and-whisker plot
g. Histogram (ungrouped)

5. Using the rollercoaster data (ch2_rollercoaster.sav or ch2_rollercoaster.csv), drawn from the Roller Coaster Database (https://rcdb.com/), compute the following for the variable "number of steel sit down rollercoasters" ("SteelSitDown") using statistical software.

a. Frequency distribution
b. Relative frequency distribution
c. Cumulative relative frequency distribution
d. Histogram
e. Quartiles
f. P_{10} and P_{90}
g. Box-and-whisker plot
h. Stem-and-leaf display

Selected Answers to Computational Problems

1. a–c. Frequency distributions, relative frequency distribution, and cumulative relative frequency distribution

Using SPSS, your frequency distribution (labeled "frequency"), relative frequency distribution (labeled "percent"), and cumulative relative frequency (labeled "cumulative percent") would appear like this:

Score					
		Frequency	Percent	Valid Percent	Cumulative Percent
Valid	41.00	2	4.4	4.4	4.4
	42.00	1	2.2	2.2	6.7
	43.00	4	8.9	8.9	15.6
	44.00	5	11.1	11.1	26.7
	45.00	6	13.3	13.3	40.0
	46.00	7	15.6	15.6	55.6
	47.00	9	20.0	20.0	75.6
	48.00	4	8.9	8.9	84.4
	49.00	4	8.9	8.9	93.3
	50.00	3	6.7	6.7	100.0
	Total	45	100.0	100.0	

d. Histogram

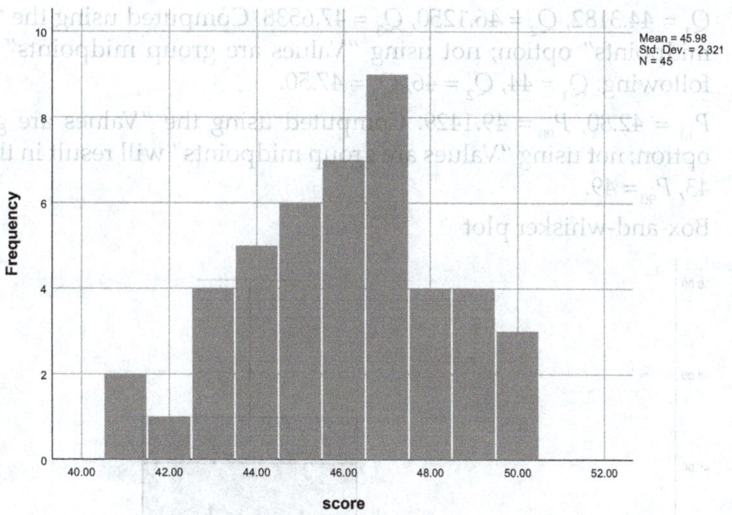

e. Frequency polygon

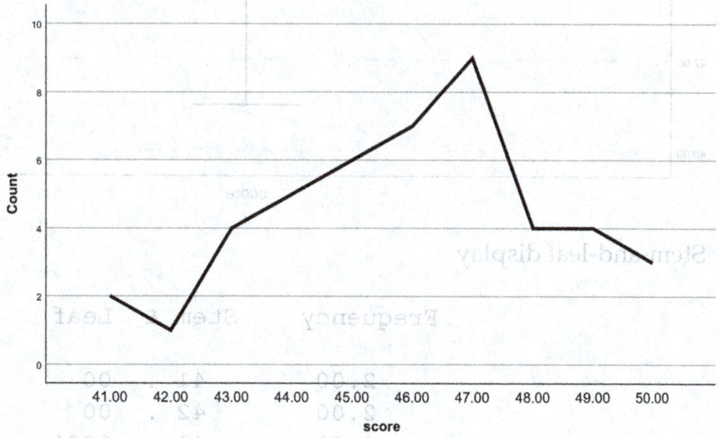

f. Cumulative frequency polygon

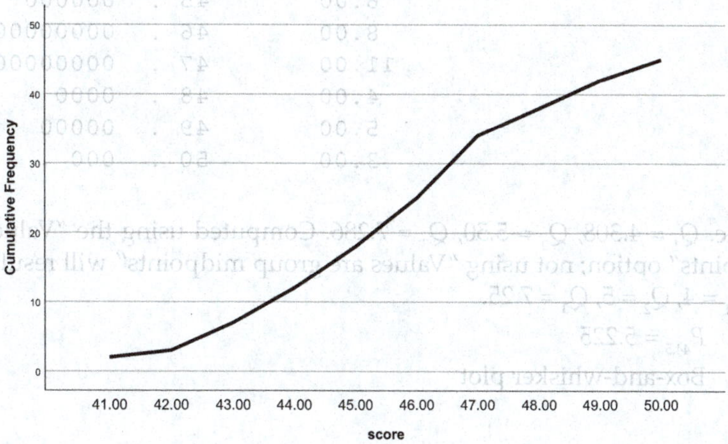

g. $Q_1 = 44.3182$, $Q_2 = 46.1250$, $Q_3 = 47.6538$. Computed using the "Values are group midpoints" option; not using "Values are group midpoints" will result in the following: $Q_1 = 44$, $Q_2 = 46$, $Q_3 = 47.50$.

h. $P_{10} = 42.80$, $P_{90} = 49.1429$. Computed using the "Values are group midpoints" option; not using "Values are group midpoints" will result in the following: $P_{10} = 43$, $P_{90} = 49$.

j. Box-and-whisker plot

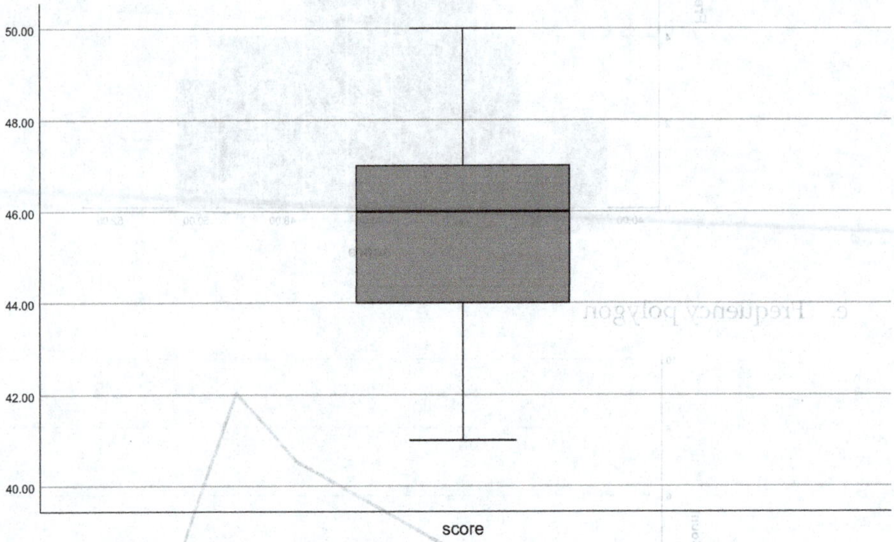

k. Stem-and-leaf display

Frequency	Stem &	Leaf
2.00	41 .	00
2.00	42 .	00
4.00	43 .	0000
5.00	44 .	00000
6.00	45 .	000000
8.00	46 .	00000000
11.00	47 .	00000000000
4.00	48 .	0000
5.00	49 .	00000
3.00	50 .	000

3. a–c. $Q_1 = 4.308$, $Q_2 = 5.50$, $Q_3 = 7.286$. Computed using the "Values are group midpoints" option; not using "Values are group midpoints" will result in the following: $Q_1 = 4$, $Q_2 = 5$, $Q_3 = 7.25$.

d. $P_{44.5} = 5.225$

e. Box-and-whisker plot

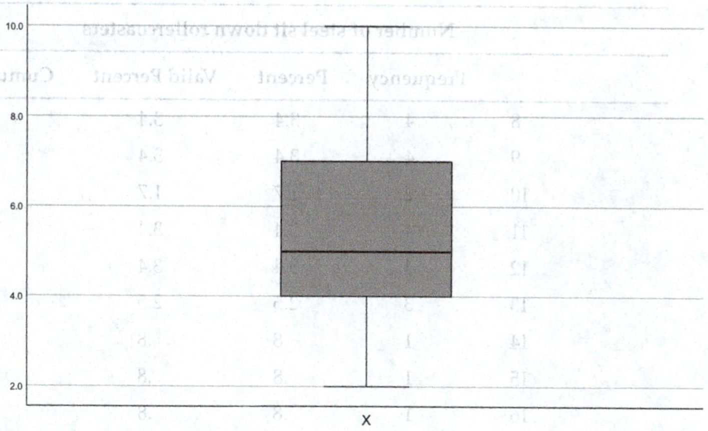

g. Histogram

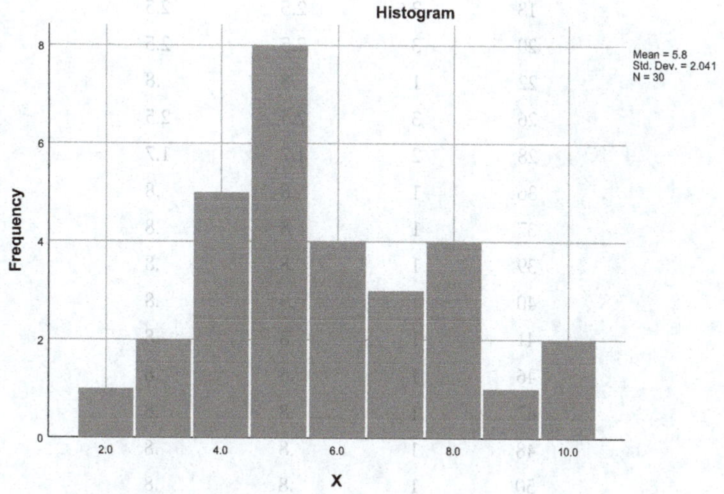

5. Given the Ch2_rollercoaster data, we find:

a. Frequency distribution (column labeled "frequency")

b. Relative frequency distribution (column labeled "percent")

c. Cumulative relative frequency distribution (column labeled "cumulative relative frequency")

Number of steel sit down rollercoasters

		Frequency	Percent	Valid Percent	Cumulative Percent
Valid	1	21	17.6	17.6	17.6
	2	10	8.4	8.4	26.1
	3	3	2.5	2.5	28.6
	4	12	10.1	10.1	38.7
	5	3	2.5	2.5	41.2
	6	8	6.7	6.7	47.9
	7	1	.8	.8	48.7

(continued)

Number of steel sit down rollercoasters				
	Frequency	Percent	Valid Percent	Cumulative Percent
8	4	3.4	3.4	52.1
9	4	3.4	3.4	55.5
10	2	1.7	1.7	57.1
11	4	3.4	3.4	60.5
12	4	3.4	3.4	63.9
13	3	2.5	2.5	66.4
14	1	.8	.8	67.2
15	1	.8	.8	68.1
16	1	.8	.8	68.9
17	1	.8	.8	69.7
18	3	2.5	2.5	72.3
20	3	2.5	2.5	74.8
22	1	.8	.8	75.6
26	3	2.5	2.5	78.2
28	2	1.7	1.7	79.8
36	1	.8	.8	80.7
37	1	.8	.8	81.5
39	1	.8	.8	82.4
40	1	.8	.8	83.2
41	1	.8	.8	84.0
46	1	.8	.8	84.9
47	1	.8	.8	85.7
48	1	.8	.8	86.6
50	1	.8	.8	87.4
51	1	.8	.8	88.2
53	1	.8	.8	89.1
61	1	.8	.8	89.9
72	1	.8	.8	90.8
81	1	.8	.8	91.6
89	1	.8	.8	92.4
94	1	.8	.8	93.3
115	1	.8	.8	94.1
145	1	.8	.8	95.0
158	1	.8	.8	95.8
165	1	.8	.8	96.6
184	1	.8	.8	97.5
204	1	.8	.8	98.3
575	1	.8	.8	99.2
1176	1	.8	.8	100.0
Total	119	100.0	100.0	

d. Histogram

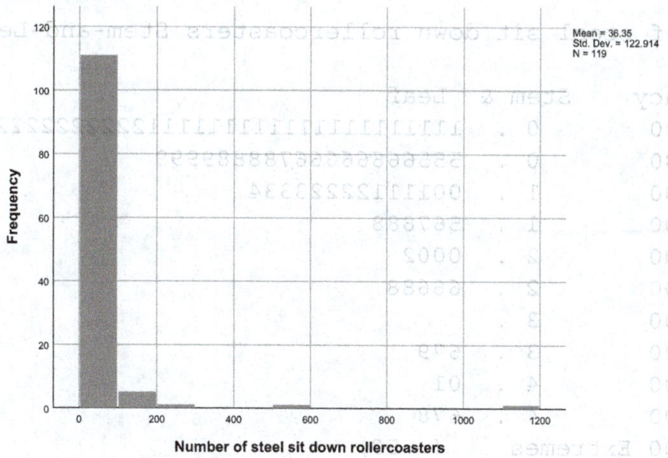

e. Quartiles (noted as 25th, 50th, and 75th percentiles)

f. P_{10} and P_{90}

Statistics

Number of steel sit down rollercoasters

N	Valid	119
	Missing	0
Percentiles	10	1.00
	25	2.00
	50	8.00
	75	22.00
	90	72.00

g. Box-and-whisker plot

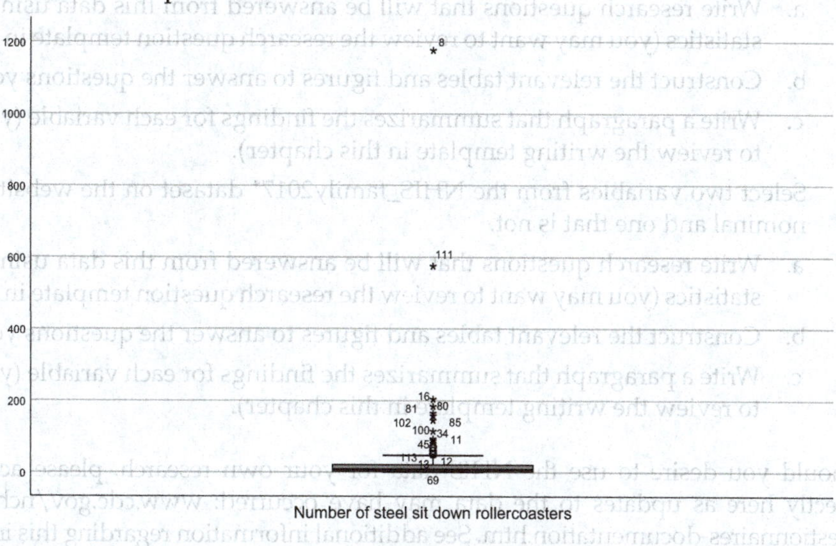

h. Stem-and-leaf display

```
Number of steel sit down rollercoasters Stem-and-Leaf Plot

 Frequency    Stem &  Leaf
    46.00        0 .  1111111111111111111122222222223334444444444
    20.00        0 .  55566666666788889999
    14.00        1 .  00111122223334
     6.00        1 .  567888
     4.00        2 .  0002
     5.00        2 .  66688
      .00        3 .
     3.00        3 .  679
     2.00        4 .  01
     3.00        4 .  678
    16.00 Extremes      (>=50)

 Stem width:       10
 Each leaf:         1 case(s)
```

Interpretive Problems

1. Select two variables from the survey1 dataset on the website, one that is nominal and one that is not.
   a. Write research questions that will be answered from this data using descriptive statistics (you may want to review the research question template in this chapter).
   b. Construct the relevant tables and figures to answer the questions you posed.
   c. Write a paragraph that summarizes the findings for each variable (you may want to review the writing template in this chapter).
2. Select two variables from the Integrated Postsecondary Education Data System dataset (IPEDS2017) on the website, one that is nominal and one that is not.
   a. Write research questions that will be answered from this data using descriptive statistics (you may want to review the research question template in this chapter).
   b. Construct the relevant tables and figures to answer the questions you posed.
   c. Write a paragraph that summarizes the findings for each variable (you may want to review the writing template in this chapter).
3. Select two variables from the NHIS_family2017* dataset on the website, one that is nominal and one that is not.
   a. Write research questions that will be answered from this data using descriptive statistics (you may want to review the research question template in this chapter).
   b. Construct the relevant tables and figures to answer the questions you posed.
   c. Write a paragraph that summarizes the findings for each variable (you may want to review the writing template in this chapter).

*Should you desire to use the NHIS data for your own research, please access the data directly here as updates to the data may have occurred: www.cdc.gov/nchs/nhis/data-questionnaires-documentation.htm. See additional information regarding this in chapter one.

3

Univariate Population Parameters and Sample Statistics

Chapter Outline

Key Concepts

1. Summation
2. Central tendency
3. Outliers
4. Dispersion

5. Exclusive versus inclusive range
6. Deviation scores
7. Bias

In Chapter 2, we began our discussion of descriptive statistics, previously defined as techniques that allow us to tabulate, summarize, and depict a collection of data in an abbreviated fashion. We considered various methods for representing data for purposes of communicating something to the reader or audience. In particular, we were concerned with ways of representing data in an abbreviated fashion through both tables and figures.

In this chapter, we delve more into the field of descriptive statistics in terms of three general topics. First, we examine **summation notation**, which is important for much of the chapter, and to some extent, the remainder of the text. Second, *measures of central tendency* allow us to boil down a set of scores into a single value, a point estimate, which somehow represents the entire set. The most commonly used measures of central tendency are the mode, median, and mean. Finally, *measures of dispersion* provide us with information about the extent to which the set of scores varies—in other words, whether the scores are spread out quite a bit or are pretty much the same. The most commonly used measures of dispersion are the range (exclusive and inclusive ranges), *H* spread, and variance and standard deviation. In summary, concepts to be discussed in this chapter include summation, central tendency, and dispersion. Within this discussion, we also address outliers and bias. Our objectives are that by the end of this chapter, you will be able to do the following: (a) understand and utilize summation notation, (b) determine and interpret the three commonly used measures of central tendency, and (c) determine and interpret commonly used measures of dispersion.

3.1 Summation Notation

A superbly talented and motivated group of graduate students are working in the statistics lab. We now find Oso Wyse tasked with his first lead role.

The graduate students in the statistics lab, Addie Venture, Oso Wyse, Challie Lenge, and Ott Lier, have been assigned their first task as research assistants. Dr. Debhard, a statistics professor, has given the group of students quiz data collected from 25 students enrolled in an introductory statistics course and has asked the group to summarize the data. Dr. Debhard was pleased with the descriptive analysis and presentation of results previously shared and is now working with Oso Wyse to conduct additional analyses related to the following research questions: *How can quiz scores of students enrolled in an introductory statistics class be summarized using measures of central tendency? How can quiz scores of students enrolled in an introductory statistics class be summarized using measures of dispersion?*

Many areas of statistics, including many methods of descriptive and inferential statistics, require the use of summation notation. Say we have collected heart rate scores from 100 students. Many statistics require us to develop "sums" or "totals" in different ways. For example, what is the simple sum, or total, of all 100 heart rate scores? **Summation** (i.e., addition) is not only quite tedious to do computationally by hand, but we also need a system of notation to communicate how we have conducted this summation process. This section describes such a notational system.

For simplicity let us utilize a small set of scores, keeping in mind that this system can be used for a set of numerical values of any size. In other words, while we speak in terms of "scores," this could just as easily be a set of heights, distances, ages, or other measures. Specifically, in this example we have a set of five ages: 7, 11, 18, 20, and 24. Recall from Chapter 2 the use of X to denote a variable. Here we define X_i as the score for variable *X* (in this example, age) for a particular individual or object *i*. The subscript *i* serves to identify one individual or object from another. These scores would then be denoted as follows: $X_1 = 7$, $X_2 = 11$, $X_3 = 18$, $X_4 = 20$, and $X_5 = 24$. To interpret $X_1 = 7$ means that for variable X and individual 1, the value of the variable "age" is 7. In other words, individual 1 is 7 years of age. With five individuals measured on age, then $i = 1, 2, 3, 4$, or 5. However, with a large set of values this notation can become quite unwieldy, so as shorthand we abbreviate this as $i = 1, \ldots, 5$, meaning that X ranges or goes from $i = 1$ to $i = 5$.

Next we need a system of notation to denote the summation or total of a set of scores. The standard notation used is $\sum_{i=a}^{b} X_i$ where $\sum$ is the Greek capital letter sigma and means "the sum of," X_i is the variable we are summing across for each of the *i* individuals, $i = a$ indicates that *a* is the lower limit (or beginning) of the summation (i.e., the first value with which we begin our addition), and *b* indicates the upper limit (or end) of the summation (i.e., the last value added). For our example set of ages, the sum of all of the ages would be denoted as $\sum_{i=1}^{5} X_i$ in shorthand version and as follows in longhand version:

$$\sum_{i=1}^{5} X_i = X_1 + X_2 + X_3 + X_4 + X_5$$

In narrative, this is simply saying "sum all five Xs, from X_1 to X_5." For the example data, the sum of all of the ages is computed as follows:

$$\sum_{i=1}^{5} X_i = X_1 + X_2 + X_3 + X_4 + X_5 = 7 + 11 + 18 + 20 + 24 = 80$$

Thus, the sum of the age variable across all five individuals is 80.

For large sets of values, the longhand version is rather tedious, and thus the shorthand version is almost exclusively used. A general form of the longhand version is as follows:

$$\sum_{i=a}^{b} X_i = X_a + X_{a+1} + \ldots + X_{b-1} + X_b$$

The ellipse notation (i.e., . . .) indicates that there are as many values in between the two values on either side of the ellipse as are necessary. The ellipse notation is then just shorthand for "there are some values in between here." The most frequently used values for *a* and *b* with sample data are $a = 1$ and $b = n$ (as you may recall, *n* is the notation used to represent our sample size). *Thus, the most frequently used summation notation for sample data is* $\sum_{i=1}^{n} \boldsymbol{X_i}$. Reading this, we can say that we are summing all X_i from 1 to *n*, where *n* denotes the sample size. Thus, we are summing all X_i in the entire dataset.

3.2 Measures of Central Tendency

One method for summarizing a set of scores is to construct a single index or value that can somehow be used to represent the entire collection of scores. In this section we consider the three most popular indices, known as **measures of central tendency**. Although other indices exist, the most popular ones are the mode, the median, and the mean.

3.2.1 The Mode

The simplest method to use for measuring central tendency is the mode. The **mode** is defined as *that value in a distribution of scores that occurs most frequently*. An easy way to remember the definition of the mode is to associate "mode" with "most," as that what the mode represents—the value or category (in the case of nominal or ordinal variables) that occurs most often. Consider the example frequency distributions of the number of hours of TV watched per week, as shown in Table 3.1. In distribution *f*(a) the mode is easy to determine, as the interval for value 8 contains the most scores, three (i.e., the mode number of hours of TV watched is 8). In distribution *f*(b) the mode is a bit more complicated as two adjacent intervals each contain the most scores; that is, the 8- and 9-hour intervals each contain three scores. Strictly speaking, this distribution is *bimodal*, that is, containing two modes, one at 8 and one at 9. This is our personal preference for reporting this particular situation. However, because the two modes are in adjacent intervals, some individuals make an arbitrary decision to average these intervals and report the mode as 8.5.

Distribution *f*(c) is also bimodal; however, here the two modes at 7 and 11 hours are not in adjacent intervals. Thus, one cannot justify taking the average of these intervals, as the average of 9 hours, $7+11)/2$, is not representative of the most frequently occurring score. The score of 9 occurs less than any other score observed. We recommend reporting both modes here as well. Obviously, there are other possible situations for the mode (e.g., trimodal distribution), but these examples cover the basics. As one further example, the example data on the statistics quiz from Chapter 2 are shown in Table 3.2 and are used to illustrate the methods in this chapter. The mode is equal to 17 because that interval contains more scores (five) than any other interval. Note also that the mode is determined in precisely the same way whether we are talking about the population mode (i.e., the population parameter) or the sample mode (i.e., the sample statistic).

TABLE 3.1
Example Frequency Distributions

X	*f*(a)	*f*(b)	*f*(c)
6	1	1	2
7	2	2	3
8	3	3	2
9	2	3	1
10	1	2	2
11	0	1	3
12	0	0	2

TABLE 3.2

Frequency Distribution of Statistics Quiz Data

X	*f*	*cf*	*rf*	*crf*
9	1	1	.04	.04
10	1	2	.04	.08
11	2	4	.08	.16
12	1	5	.04	.20
13	2	7	.08	.28
14	1	8	.04	.32
15	3	11	.12	.44
16	1	12	.04	.48
17	5	17	.20	.68
18	3	20	.12	.80
19	4	24	.16	.96
20	1	25	.04	1.00
	$n = 25$		1.00	

Let's turn to a discussion of the general characteristics of the mode, as well as whether a particular characteristic is an advantage or a disadvantage in a statistical sense. The first characteristic of the mode is *it is simple to obtain*. The mode is often used as a quick-and-dirty method for reporting central tendency. This is an obvious advantage.

The second characteristic is that the mode *does not always have a unique value*. We saw this in distributions *f*(b) and *f*(c) of Table 3.1. This is generally a disadvantage, as we initially stated we wanted a single index that could be used to represent the collection of scores. The mode cannot guarantee a single index.

Third, the mode is *not a function of all of the scores in the distribution*, and this is generally a disadvantage. The mode is strictly determined by which score or interval contains the most frequencies. In distribution *f*(a), as long as the other intervals have fewer frequencies than the interval for value 8, then the mode will always be 8. That is, if the interval for value 8 contains three scores and all of the other intervals contain less than three scores, then the mode will be 8. The number of frequencies for the remaining intervals is not relevant as long as it is less than three. Also, the location or value of the other scores is not taken into account.

The fourth characteristic of the mode is that it is *difficult to deal with mathematically*. For example, the mode is not very stable from one sample to another, especially with small samples. We could have two nearly identical samples except for one score, which can alter the mode. For example, in distribution *f*(a) if a second similar sample contains the same scores except that an 8 is replaced with a 7, then the mode is changed from 8 to 7. Thus changing a single score can change the mode, and this is considered to be a disadvantage.

A fifth and final characteristic is the mode *can be used with a variable of any type of measurement scale*, from nominal to ratio, and *is the only measure of central tendency appropriate for nominal data*.

3.2.2 The Median

A second measure of central tendency represents a concept that you are already familiar with. *The **median** is that score which divides a distribution of scores into two equal parts.* In other words, one-half of the scores fall below the median and one-half of the scores fall above the median. We already know this from Chapter 2 as the 50th percentile or Q_2. In other words, the 50th percentile, or Q_2, represents the median value. The formula for computing the median is

$$Median = LRL + \left(\frac{50\%(n) - cf}{f}\right)(w)$$

where the notation is the same as previously described in Chapter 2. Just as a reminder, *LRL* is the lower real limit of the interval containing the median, 50% is the percentile desired, *n* is the sample size, *cf* is the cumulative frequency of all intervals less than but not including the interval containing the median (*cf* below), *f* is the frequency of the interval containing the median, and *w* is the interval width. For the example quiz data, the median is computed as follows:

$$Median = 16.5 + \left(\frac{50\%(25) - 12}{5}\right)(1) = 16.5 + 0.10 = 16.60$$

Occasionally, you will run into simple distributions of scores where the median is easy to identify. *If you have an odd number of untied scores, then the median is the middle-ranked score.* For an example, say we have measured individuals on the number of autographed jerseys owned and find values of 1, 3, 7, 11, and 21. For this data, the median is 7 (e.g., 7 autographed jerseys is the middle-ranked value or score). *If you have an even number of untied scores, then the median is the average of the two middle-ranked scores.* For example, a different sample reveals the following number of autographed jerseys owned: 1, 3, 5, 11, 21, and 32. The two middle scores are 5 and 11, and thus the median is the average of 8 autographed jerseys owned; that is, $(5+11)/2$. *In most other situations where there are tied scores, the median is not as simple to locate and first equation is necessary.* Note also that the median is computed in precisely the same way whether we are talking about the population median (i.e., the population parameter) or the sample median (i.e., the sample statistic).

The general characteristics of the median are as follows. First, *the median is not influenced by extreme scores* (scores far away from the middle of the distribution are known as **outliers**). Because the median is defined conceptually as the middle score, the actual size of an extreme score is not relevant. For the example statistics quiz data, imagine that the extreme score of 9 was somehow actually 0 (e.g., incorrectly scored). The median would still be 16.6, as half of the scores are still above this value and half below. Because the extreme score under consideration here still remained below the 50th percentile, the median was not altered. This characteristic is an advantage, particularly when extreme scores are observed. As another example using salary data, say that all but one of the individual salaries is below $100,000 and the median is $50,000. The remaining extreme observation has a salary of $5,000,000. The median is not affected by this millionaire—the extreme individual is simply treated as every other observation above the median, no more or no less than, say, the salary of $65,000.

A second characteristic is that *the median is not a function of all of the scores.* Because we already know that the median is not influenced by extreme scores, we know that the median does not take such scores into account. Another way to think about this is to examine the first equation for the median. The equation only deals with information for the interval containing the median. The specific information for the remaining intervals is not relevant so long as we are looking in the median-contained interval. We could, for instance, take the top 25% of the scores and make them even more extreme (say we add 10 bonus points to the top quiz scores). The median would remain unchanged. As you have probably surmised, this characteristic is generally thought to be a disadvantage. If you really think about the first two characteristics, no measure could possibly possess both. That is, if a measure is a function of all of the scores, then extreme scores must also be taken into account. If a measure does not take extreme scores into account, like the median, then it cannot be a function of all of the scores.

A third characteristic is that *the median is difficult to deal with mathematically,* a disadvantage as with the mode. The median is somewhat unstable from sample to sample, especially with small samples.

As a fourth characteristic, *the median always has a unique value,* another advantage. This is unlike the mode, which does not always have a unique value.

Finally, the fifth characteristic of the median is that *it can be used with all types of measurement scales except the nominal.* Nominal data cannot be ranked, and thus percentiles (including the 50th percentile, i.e., the median) are inappropriate.

3.2.3 The Mean

The final measure of central tendency to be considered is the mean, also known as the *arithmetic mean* or *average* (although the term "average" is used rather loosely by laypeople). Note that there are different types of means; we will generally be concerned only with the arithmetic mean. Statistically, we define the **mean** as *the sum of all of the scores divided by the number of scores.* Thought of in those terms, you may have been computing the mean for many years, and may not have even known it.

The **population mean** is denoted by μ (lowercase Greek mu) and computed as follows:

$$\mu = \frac{\sum_{i=1}^{N} X_i}{N}$$

For sample data, the **sample mean** is denoted by $\bar{X}$ (read "X bar") and computed as follows:

$$\bar{X} = \frac{\sum_{i=1}^{n} X_i}{n}$$

For the example quiz data, the sample mean is computed as follows:

$$\bar{X} = \frac{\sum_{i=1}^{n} X_i}{n} = \frac{389}{25} = 15.56$$

Here are the general characteristics of the mean. First, *the mean is a function of every score,* which is a definite advantage in terms of a measure of central tendency representing all of the data. If you look at the numerator of the mean, you see that all of the scores are clearly taken into account in the sum.

The second characteristic of the mean is that *it is influenced by extreme scores.* Because the numerator sum takes all of the scores into account, it also includes the extreme scores, which is (or at least can be) a disadvantage. Let us return for a moment to a previous example of salary data where all but one of the individuals has an annual salary under $100,000, and the one outlier is making $5,000,000. Because this one outlying value is so extreme, the mean will be greatly influenced. In fact, the mean could easily fall somewhere between the second highest salary and the millionaire, which does not represent well the collection of scores.

Third, *the mean always has a unique value*, another advantage. As we will see, many inferential statistics use the mean in their calculation. Thus, since the mean generates a unique value, we are able to use that value as both a way to summarize data but also to make inferences to a larger population.

Fourth, *the mean is easy to deal with mathematically*. The mean is the most stable measure of central tendency from sample to sample, and because of that is the measure most often used in inferential statistics (as we show in later chapters).

Finally, the fifth characteristic of the mean is that *it is only appropriate for interval and ratio measurement scales*. This is because the mean implicitly assumes equal intervals, which of course the nominal and ordinal scales do not possess.

3.2.4 Summary of Measures of Central Tendency

To summarize, some of the distinguishing features of the measures of central tendency are as follows:

1. The mode is the only appropriate measure for nominal data.
2. The median and mode are both appropriate for ordinal data (and conceptually the median fits the ordinal scale as both deal with ranked scores).
3. All three measures (mode, median, and mean) are appropriate for interval and ratio data.

As discussed, each measure of central tendency has advantages and disadvantages. A summary of the advantages and disadvantages of each measure is presented in Box 3.1.

BOX 3.1 Advantages and Disadvantages of Measures of Central Tendency

Measure of Central Tendency	Advantages	Disadvantages
Mode	• Quick and easy method for reporting central tendency • Can be used with any measurement scale of variable	• Does not always have a unique value • Not a function of all scores in the distribution • Difficult to deal with mathematically due to its instability
Median	• Not influenced by extreme scores • Has a unique value • Can be used with ordinal, interval, and ratio measurement scales of variables	• Not a function of all scores in the distribution • Difficult to deal with mathematically due to its instability • Cannot be used with nominal data
Mean	• Function of all scores in the distribution • Has a unique value • Easy to deal with mathematically • Can be used with interval and ratio measurement scales of variables	• Influenced by extreme scores • Cannot be used with nominal or ordinal variables

We began our discussion of measures of central tendency by stating that *other indices exist*; however, the most popular ones are the mode, the median, and the mean. You may be wondering what those other indices are! While the *arithmetic mean* is the most common mean, and the one with which we are generally concerned, it is not the only mean, and it should not be confused with other types of means. Other means that you may encounter include the harmonic mean, trimmed mean, winsorized mean, and more. Huck (2016) provides a concise discussion on understanding the most common measures of central tendency relative to other statistics you may encounter.

3.3 Measures of Dispersion

In the previous section, we discussed one method for summarizing a collection of scores, the measures of central tendency. Central tendency measures are useful for describing a collection of scores in terms of a single index or value (with one exception: the mode for distributions that are not unimodal). However, what do they tell us about the distribution of scores? Consider the following example. If we know that a sample has a mean of 50, what do we know about the distribution of scores? Can we infer from the mean what the distribution looks like? Are most of the scores fairly close to the mean of 50, or are they spread out quite a bit? Perhaps most of the scores are within 2 points of the mean. Perhaps most are within 10 points of the mean. Perhaps most are within 50 points of the mean. Do we know? The answer, of course, is that the mean provides us with no information about what the distribution of scores looks like, and any of the possibilities mentioned, and many others, can occur. The same goes if we only know the mode or the median.

Another method for summarizing a set of scores is to construct an index or value that can be used to describe the amount of *spread* amongst the collection of scores. In other words, we need measures that can be used to determine whether the scores fall fairly close to the central tendency measure, are fairly well spread out, or are somewhere in between. In this section we consider the four most popular such indices, which are known as **measures of dispersion** (i.e., the extent to which the scores are dispersed or spread out). Although other indices exist, the most popular ones are the range (exclusive and inclusive), *H* spread, variance, and standard deviation.

3.3.1 The Range

The simplest measure of dispersion is the **range**. The term *range* is one that is in common use outside of statistical circles, so you have some familiarity with it already. For instance, say you are at the mall shopping for a new pair of shoes. You find six stores have the same pair of shoes that you really like, but the prices vary somewhat. At this point you might actually make the statement "the price for these shoes ranges from $59 to $75." In a way you are talking about the range.

Let us be more specific as to how the range is measured. In fact, there are actually two different definitions of the range, exclusive and inclusive, which we consider now. The **exclusive range** is defined as *the difference between the largest and smallest scores in a collection of scores*. For notational purposes, the exclusive range (*ER*) is shown as $ER = X_{max} - X_{min}$, where X_{max} is the largest or maximum score obtained, and X_{min} is the smallest or minimum score obtained. For the shoe example then, $ER = X_{max} - X_{min} = 75–59 = 16$. In other words, the actual exclusive range of the scores is 16 because the price varies from 59 to 75 (in dollar units).

A limitation of the exclusive range is that it fails to account for the width of the intervals being used. For example, if we use an interval width of one dollar, then the 59 interval really has 59.5 as the upper real limit and 58.5 as the lower real limit. If the least expensive shoe is $58.95, then the exclusive range covering from $59 to $75 actually *excludes* the least expensive shoe. Hence, the term exclusive range means *that scores can be excluded from this range*. The same would go for a shoe priced at $75.95, as it would fall outside of the exclusive range at the high end of the distribution.

Because of this limitation, a second definition of the range was developed, known as the *inclusive range*. As you might surmise, the inclusive range takes into account the interval width so that all scores are *included* in the range. The **inclusive range** is defined as *the difference between the upper real limit of the interval containing the largest score and the lower real limit of the interval containing the smallest score in a collection of scores*. For notational purposes, the inclusive range (*IR*) is shown as $IR = URL$ of $X_{max} - LRL$ of X_{min}. If you think about it, what we are actually doing is extending the range by one-half of an interval at each extreme, one-half an interval width at the maximum value and one-half an interval width at the minimum value. In notational form $IR = ER + w$. For the shoe example, using an interval width of 1, then $IR = URL$ of $X_{max} - LRL$ of $X_{min} = 75.5 - 58.5 = 17$. In other words, the actual inclusive range of the scores is 17 (in dollar units). If the interval width was instead 2, then we would add 1 unit to each extreme rather than the .5 unit that we previously added to each extreme. The inclusive range would instead be 18. For the example quiz data (presented in Table 3.2), note that the exclusive range is 11 and the inclusive range is 12 (as interval width is 1).

Finally, we need to examine the general characteristics of the range (they are the same for both definitions of the range). First, *the range is simple to compute*, which is a definite advantage. One can look at a collection of data and almost immediately, even without a computer or calculator, determine the range.

The second characteristic is that *the range is influenced by extreme scores*, a disadvantage. Because the range is computed from the two most extreme scores, this characteristic is quite obvious. This might be a problem, for instance, if all of the salary data range from $10,000 to $95,000 except for one individual with a salary of $5,000,000. Without this outlier the exclusive range is $85,000. With the outlier the exclusive range is $4,990,000. Thus, the millionaire's salary has a drastic impact on the range.

Third, *the range is only a function of two scores*, another disadvantage. Obviously the range is computed from the largest and smallest scores, and thus is only a function of those two scores. The spread of the distribution of scores between those two extreme scores is not at all taken into account. In other words, for the same maximum ($5,000,000) and minimum ($10,000) salaries, the range is the same whether the salaries are mostly near the maximum salary, mostly near the minimum salary, or spread out evenly.

The fourth characteristic is that *the range is unstable from sample to sample*, another disadvantage. Say a second sample of salary data yielded the exact same data except for the maximum salary now being a less extreme $100,000. The range is now dramatically different. Also, in statistics we tend to worry about measures that are not stable from sample to sample, as this implies that the results are not very reliable.

Finally, the range is appropriate for *data that are ordinal, interval, or ratio in measurement scale*.

3.3.2 *H* Spread

The next measure of dispersion is *H* spread, a variation on the range measure with one major exception. Although the range relies upon the two extreme scores, resulting in certain disadvantages, *H* spread relies upon the difference between the third and first quartiles. To be more specific, ***H* spread** is defined as $Q_3 - Q_1$, *the simple difference between the third and first quartiles*. The term *H* spread was developed by Tukey (1977), *H* being short for "hinge" from the box-and-whisker plot; it is also known as the **interquartile range**.

For the example statistics quiz data (presented in Table 3.2), we already determined in Chapter 2 that $Q_3 = 18.0833$ and $Q_1 = 13.1250$. Therefore, $H = Q_3 - Q_1 = 18.0833 - 13.1250 = 4.9583$. *H* measures the range of the middle 50% of the distribution. *The larger the value, the greater the spread in the middle of the distribution*. The size or magnitude of any of the range measures takes on more meaning when making comparisons across samples. For example, you might find with salary data that the range of salaries for middle management is smaller than the range of salaries for upper management. As another example, we might expect the salary range to increase over time.

What are the characteristics of *H* spread? The first characteristic is that *H is unaffected by extreme scores*, an advantage. Because we are looking at the difference between the third and first quartiles, extreme observations will be outside of this range. Second, *H is not a function of every score*, a disadvantage. The precise placement of where scores fall above Q_3, below Q_1, and between Q_3 and Q_1 is not relevant. All that matters is that 25% of the scores fall above Q_3, 25% fall below Q_1, and 50% fall between Q_3 and Q_1. Thus, *H* is not a function of very many of the scores at all, just those around Q_3 and Q_1. Third, *H is not very stable from sample to sample*, another disadvantage, especially in terms of inferential statistics and one's ability to be confident about a sample estimate of a population parameter. Finally, *H is appropriate for all scales of measurement except for nominal*.

3.3.3 Deviational Measures

In this section we examine deviation scores, population variance and standard deviation, and sample variance and standard deviation, all methods that deal with deviations from the mean.

3.3.3.1 Deviation Scores

In the last category of measures of dispersion are those that utilize deviations from the mean. Let us define a **deviation score** as the *difference between a particular raw score and the mean of the collection of scores* (population or sample, either will work). For *population data* we define a deviation as $d_i = X_i \mu$. In other words, we can compute the deviation from the mean for each individual or object. Consider the credit card dataset as shown in Table 3.3. To make matters simple, we only have a small population of data, five values to be exact. The first column lists the raw scores, which are in this example the number of credit cards owned for five individuals and, at the bottom of the first column, indicates the sum ($\Sigma = 30$), population size ($N = 5$), and population mean ($\mu = 6.0$). The second column provides the deviation scores for each observation from the

TABLE 3.3

Credit Card Dataset

X	$X-\mu$	$(X-\mu)^2$
1	-5	25
5	-1	1
6	0	0
8	2	4
10	4	16
$\Sigma = 30$	$\Sigma = 0$	$\Sigma = 46$
$N = 5$		
$\mu = 6$		

population mean and, at the bottom of the second column, indicates the sum of the deviation scores, denoted by

$$\sum_{i=1}^{N}(X_i - \mu)$$

From the second column we see that two of the observations have positive deviation scores as their raw score is above the mean, one observation has a zero deviation score as that raw score is at the mean, and two other observations have negative deviation scores as their raw score is below the mean. However, when we sum the deviation scores, we obtain a value of zero. This will always be the case, as follows:

$$\sum_{i=1}^{N}(X_i - \mu) = 0$$

The positive deviation scores will exactly offset the negative deviation scores. *Thus, any measure involving simple deviation scores will be useless in that the sum of the deviation scores will always be zero, regardless of the spread of the scores.*

What other alternatives are there for developing a deviational measure that will yield a sum other than zero? One alternative is to take the absolute value of the deviation scores (i.e., where the sign is ignored). Unfortunately, however, this is not very useful mathematically in terms of deriving other statistics, such as inferential statistics. As a result, this deviational measure is rarely used in statistics.

3.3.3.2 Population Variance and Standard Deviation

So far we found the sum of the deviations and the sum of the absolute deviations not to be very useful in describing the spread of the scores from the mean. What other alternative might be useful? As shown in the third column of Table 3.3, one could square the deviation scores to remove the sign problem. The sum of the squared deviations is shown at the bottom of the column as $\Sigma = 46$ and denoted as

$$\sum_{i=1}^{N}(X_i - \mu)^2$$

As you might suspect, with more scores, the sum of the squared deviations will increase. So we have to weigh the sum by the number of observations in the population. This yields a deviational measure known as the **population variance**, which is denoted as σ^2 (sigma squared) and computed by the following formula:

$$\sigma^2 = \frac{\sum_{i=1}^{N} (X_i - \mu)^2}{N}$$

For the credit card example, $\sigma^2 = (46/5) = 9.2$. We refer to this particular formula for the population variance as the **definitional formula**, as conceptually that is how we define the variance. *Conceptually, the variance is a measure of the area of a distribution, and, more specifically, the spread of the distribution from the mean.* That is, the more spread out the scores, the more area or space the distribution takes up and the larger the variance. *The variance may also be thought of as an average distance from the mean.* The variance has nice mathematical properties and is useful for deriving other statistics, such as inferential statistics.

The **computational formula** for the population variance is

$$\sigma^2 = \frac{(N)\left(\sum_{i=1}^{N} X_i^2\right) - \left(\sum_{i=1}^{N} X_i\right)^2}{N^2}$$

This method is computationally easier to deal with than the definitional formula. Imagine if you had a population of 100 scores. Using hand computations, the definitional formula would take considerably more time than the computational formula. With the computer this is a moot point, obviously. But, if you do have to compute the population variance by hand, then the easiest formula to use is the computational one.

Exactly how does this formula work? The numerator is three basic terms: (a) the population size (N), (b) the sum of all X_i^2 (i.e., square each X_i and then sum those squared values), and (c) the squared sum of all X_i (i.e., sum all the X_i and then square that summed value). The denominator is simply the squared population size.

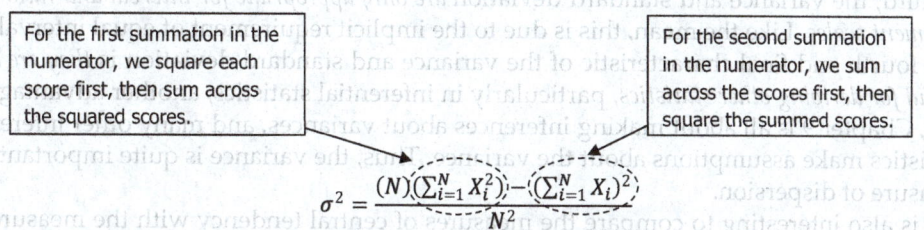

Let's look at this again. For the first summation in the numerator, we square each score first, then sum all the squared scores. This value is then multiplied by the population size. For the second summation in the numerator, we sum all the scores first, then square the summed scores. After subtracting the values computed in the numerator, we divide by the squared population size.

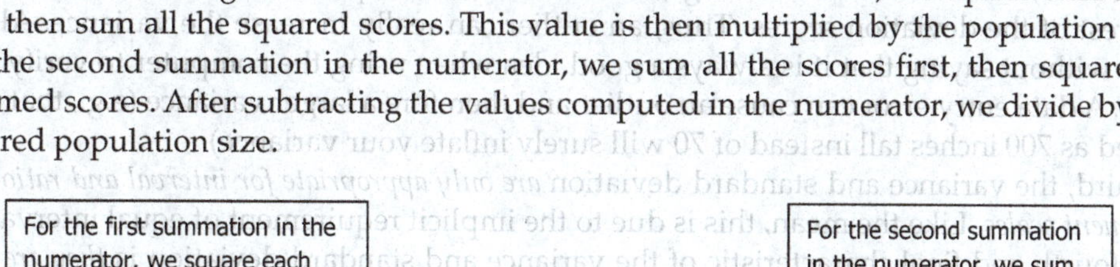
For the first summation in the numerator, we square each score first, then sum across the squared scores.
For the second summation in the numerator, we sum across the scores first, then square the summed scores.

$$\sigma^2 = \frac{(N)(\sum_{i=1}^{N} X_i^2) - (\sum_{i=1}^{N} X_i)^2}{N^2}$$

The two quantities derived by the in summation operations the numerator are computed in much different ways and generally yield different values.

Let us return to the credit card dataset and see if the computational formula actually yields the same value for σ^2 as the definitional formula did earlier ($\sigma^2 = 9.2$). The computational formula shows σ^2 to be:

$$\sigma^2 = \frac{(N)\left(\sum_{i=1}^{N} X_i^2\right) - \left(\sum_{i=1}^{N} X_i\right)^2}{N^2} = \frac{(5)(226) - (30)^2}{(5)^2} = \frac{1130 - 900}{25} = 9.20$$

which is precisely the value we computed previously.

A few individuals (none of us, of course) are a bit bothered about the variance for the following reason. Say you are measuring the height of children in inches. The raw scores are measured in terms of inches, the mean is measured in terms of inches, but the variance is measured in terms of inches squared. *Squaring the scale is bothersome to some as the scale is no longer in the original units of measure, but rather a squared unit of measure*—making interpretation a bit difficult. To generate a deviational measure in the original scale (i.e., inches), we can take the square root of the variance. This is known as the **standard deviation**, and it is the final measure of dispersion we discuss. The **population standard deviation** is defined as the *positive square root of the population variance* and is denoted by sigma, σ *i.e.*, $\sigma = \sqrt{\sigma^2}$. The standard deviation, then, is measured *in the original scale* (i.e., in this example, inches). For the credit card data, the standard deviation is computed as follows:

$$\sigma = \sqrt{\sigma^2} = \sqrt{9.2} = 3.0332$$

What are the major characteristics of the population variance and standard deviation? First, the variance and standard deviation *are a function of every score*, an advantage. An examination of either the definitional or computational formula for the variance (and standard deviation as well) indicates that all of the scores are taken into account, unlike the range or H spread.

Second, therefore, the variance and standard deviation *are affected by extreme scores*, a disadvantage. As we said earlier, if a measure takes all of the scores into account, then it must take into account the extreme scores as well. Thus, a child much taller than all of the rest of the children will dramatically increase the variance, as the area or size of the distribution will be much more spread out. Another way to think about this is the size of the deviation score for such an outlier will be large, and then it will be squared, and then summed with the rest of the deviation scores. Thus, an outlier can really increase the variance. Also, it goes without saying that it is always a good idea when using the computer to verify your data. A data entry error can cause an outlier and therefore a larger variance (e.g., that child coded as 700 inches tall instead of 70 will surely inflate your variance).

Third, the variance and standard deviation *are only appropriate for interval and ratio measurement scales*. Like the mean, this is due to the implicit requirement of equal intervals.

A fourth and final characteristic of the variance and standard deviation is *they are quite useful for deriving other statistics*, particularly in inferential statistics, another advantage. In fact, Chapter 9 is all about making inferences about variances, and many other inferential statistics make assumptions about the variance. Thus, the variance is quite important as a measure of dispersion.

It is also interesting to compare the measures of central tendency with the measures of dispersion, as they do share some important characteristics. *The mode and the range share certain characteristics*. Both only take some of the data into account, are simple to compute, and are unstable from sample to sample. *The median shares certain characteristics with H spread.*

These are not influenced by extreme scores, are not a function of every score, are difficult to deal with mathematically due to their instability from sample to sample, and can be used with all measurement scales except the nominal scale. *The mean shares many characteristics with the variance and standard deviation.* These all are a function of every score, are influenced by extreme scores, are useful for deriving other statistics, and are only appropriate for interval and ratio measurement scales.

To complete this section of the chapter, we take a look at the sample variance and standard deviation and how they are computed for large samples of data (i.e., larger than our credit card dataset).

3.3.3.3 Sample Variance and Standard Deviation

Most of the time we are interested in computing the sample variance and standard deviation; we also often have large samples of data with multiple frequencies for many of the scores. Here we consider these last aspects of the measures of dispersion. Recall when we computed the sample statistics of central tendency. The computations were exactly the same as with the population parameters (although the notation for the population and sample means was different). There are also no differences between the sample and population values for the range, or H spread. However, there *is* a difference between the sample and population values for the variance and standard deviation, as we see next.

Recall the definitional formula for the population variance:

$$\sigma^2 = \frac{\sum_{i=1}^{N}(X_i - \mu)^2}{N}$$

Why not just take this equation and convert everything to sample statistics? In other words, we could simply change N to n and μ to $\bar{X}$. What could be wrong with that? The answer is that there is a problem that prevents us from simply changing the notation in the formula from population notation to sample notation.

Here is the problem. First, the sample mean, $\bar{X}$, may not be exactly equal to the population mean, μ. In fact, for most samples, the sample mean will be somewhat different from the population mean. Second, we cannot use the population mean because it is unknown (in most instances anyway). Instead, we have to substitute the sample mean into the equation (i.e., the sample mean, $\bar{X}$, is the sample estimate for the population mean, μ). Because the sample mean is different from the population mean, the deviations will all be affected. Also, the sample variance that would be obtained in this fashion would be a biased estimate of the population variance. In statistics, **bias** means that *something is systematically off*. In this case, the sample variance obtained in this manner would be systematically too small.

In order to obtain an unbiased sample estimate of the population variance, the following adjustments have to be made in the definitional and computational formulas, respectively:

$$s^2 = \frac{\sum_{i=1}^{n}(X_i - \bar{X})^2}{n-1}$$

$$s^2 = \frac{(n)\left(\sum_{i=1}^{n} X_i^2\right) - \left(\sum_{i=1}^{n} X_i\right)^2}{n(n-1)}$$

In terms of the notation, s^2 is the **sample variance**, n has been substituted for N, and $\bar{X}$ has been substituted for μ. These changes are relatively minor and expected. The major change is in the denominator, where instead of N for the definitional formula we have $n - 1$, and instead of N^2 for the computational formula we have $n(n - 1)$. *This turns out to be the correction that early statisticians discovered was necessary to obtain an unbiased estimate of the population variance.*

The following two points should be noted: (a) when sample size is relatively large (e.g., $n = 1000$), the correction will be quite small; and (b) when sample size is relatively small (e.g., $n = 5$), the correction will be quite a bit larger. One suggestion is that when computing the variance on a calculator or computer, you might want to be aware of whether the sample or population variance is being computed, as it can make a difference (typically the sample variance is computed). The sample standard deviation is denoted by s and computed as the positive square root of the sample variance, s^2 (i.e., $s = \sqrt{s^2}$).

For our example statistics quiz data (presented in Table 3.2), we have multiple frequencies for many of the raw scores that need to be taken into account. A simple procedure for dealing with this situation when performing hand computations is shown in Table 3.4. Here we see that in the third and fifth columns the scores and squared scores are multiplied by their respective frequencies. This allows us to take into account, for example, that the score of 19 occurred four times. Note for the fifth column that the frequencies are not squared; only the scores are squared. At the bottom of the third and fifth columns are the sums we need to compute the parameters of interest.

We compute the **sample mean** as follows:

$$\bar{X} = \frac{\sum_{i=1}^{n} fX_i}{n} = \frac{389}{25} = 15.5600$$

TABLE 3.4

Sums for Statistics Quiz Data

X	f	fX	X^2	fX^2
9	1	9	81	81
10	1	10	100	100
11	2	22	121	242
12	1	12	144	144
13	2	26	169	338
14	1	14	19	196
15	3	45	225	675
16	1	16	256	256
17	5	85	289	1445
18	3	54	324	972
19	4	76	361	1444
20	1	20	400	400
	$n = 25$	$\sum = 389$		$\sum = 6293$

The **sample variance** is computed to be:

$$s^2 = \frac{(n)\left(\sum_{i=1}^{n} fX_i^2\right) - \left(\sum_{i=1}^{n} fX_i\right)^2}{n(n-1)}$$

$$s^2 = \frac{(25)(6293)-(389)^2}{25(25-1)} = \frac{157,325-151,321}{600} = \frac{6004}{600} = 10.0067$$

Therefore, the **sample standard deviation** is

$$s = \sqrt{s^2} = \sqrt{10.0067} = 3.1633$$

One concluding thought related to our discussion of variance is that it is common to want to interpret the value of the variance as "large" or "small." Keep in mind that the spread of the distribution is only large or small relative to the size of the mean, for example. A standard deviation of 1 sounds tiny, however relative to a mean of .05 it's huge! There are no conventions on interpreting the size of a variance or standard deviation. Rather, report these values as descriptive statistics in connection with the mean and do not try to interpret the magnitude of the dispersion.

3.3.4 Summary of Measures of Dispersion

To summarize the measures of dispersion then:

1. The range and *H* spread are the only appropriate measures for ordinal data.
2. The range, *H* spread, variance, and standard deviation can be used with interval or ratio measurement scales.
3. There are no measures of dispersion appropriate for nominal data.

A summary of the advantages and disadvantages of each measure is presented in Box 3.2.

BOX 3.2 Advantages and Disadvantages of Measures of Dispersion

Measure of Dispersion	Advantages	Disadvantages
Range	• Simple to compute • Can be used with ordinal, interval and ratio measurement scales of variables	• Influenced by extreme scores • Function of only two scores • Unstable from sample to sample • Cannot be used with nominal data
H spread	• Unaffected by extreme scores • Can be used with ordinal, interval, and ratio measurement scales of variables	• Not a function of all scores in the distribution • Difficult to deal with mathematically due to its instability • Cannot be used with nominal data
Variance and standard deviation	• Function of all scores in the distribution • Useful for deriving other statistics • Can be used with interval and ratio measurement scales of variables	• Influenced by extreme scores • Cannot be used with nominal or ordinal variables

3.3.5 Recommendations Based on Measurement Scale

A summary of when these descriptive statistics are most appropriate for each of the scales of measurement is shown in Box 3.3. Throughout the text we emphasize that it is the researcher's responsibility to understand the data and its measurement scale so that the appropriate statistics can be generated given the measurement scale of the data.

BOX 3.3 Appropriate Descriptive Statistics

Measurement Scale	Measure of Central Tendency	Measure of Dispersion
Nominal	Mode	
Ordinal	Mode Median	Range *H* spread
Interval/ratio	Mode Median Mean	Range *H* spread Variance and standard deviation

3.4 Computing Sample Statistics Using SPSS

The purpose of this section is to see what SPSS has to offer in terms of computing measures of central tendency and dispersion. In fact, SPSS provides us with many different ways to obtain such measures. The three tools that we have found to be most useful for generating descriptive statistics covered in this chapter are Explore, Descriptives, and Frequencies.

3.4.1 Explore

Step 1. The first tool, Explore, can be invoked by clicking "Analyze" in the top pulldown menu, then "Descriptive Statistics," and then "Explore." Following the screenshot in Figure 3.1 will produce the Explore dialog box. For brevity, we have not reproduced this initial screenshot when we discuss the Descriptives and Frequencies programs; however, you can see in Figure 3.1 where they can be found on the pulldown menus.

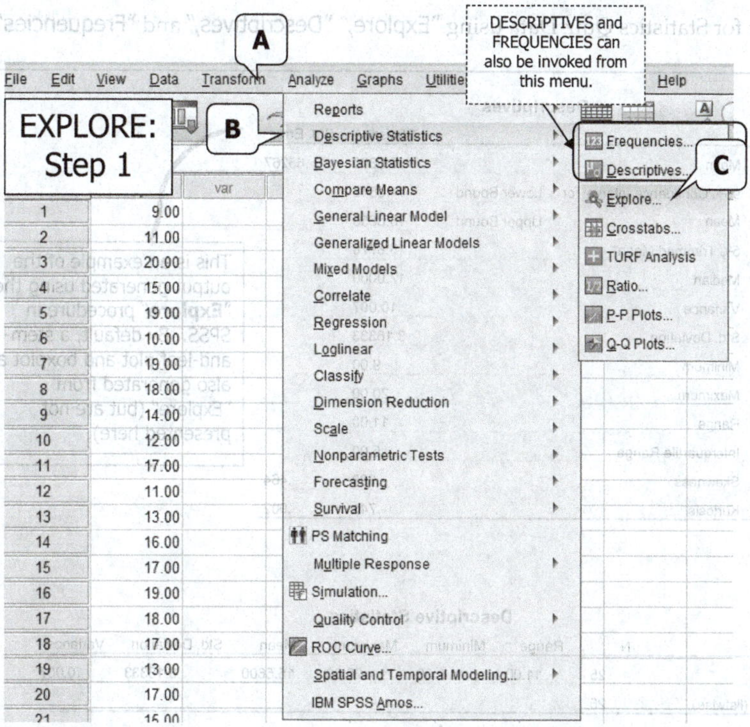

FIGURE 3.1
EXPLORE: Step 1.

Step 2. Next, from the main Explore dialog box, click the variable of interest from the list on the left (e.g., "quiz"), and move it into the "Dependent List" box by clicking the arrow button (see screenshot for "EXPLORE: Step 2" in Figure 3.2). Then click the "OK" button.

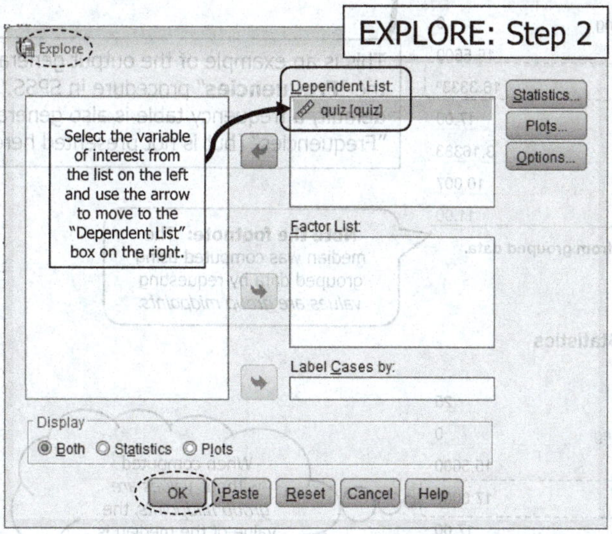

FIGURE 3.2
EXPLORE: Step 2.

TABLE 3.5

Select Output for Statistics Quiz Data using "Explore," "Descriptives," and "Frequencies" Options in SPSS

Descriptives

			Statistic	Std. Error
quiz	Mean		15.5600	.63267
	95% Confidence Interval for Mean	Lower Bound	14.2542	
		Upper Bound	16.8658	
	5% Trimmed Mean		15.6778	
	Median		17.0000	
	Variance		10.007	
	Std. Deviation		3.16333	
	Minimum		9.00	
	Maximum		20.00	
	Range		11.00	
	Interquartile Range		5.00	
	Skewness		-.598	.464
	Kurtosis		-.741	.902

This is an example of the output generated using the "**Explore**" procedure in SPSS. By default, a stem-and-leaf plot and boxplot are also generated from "Explore" (but are not presented here).

Descriptive Statistics

	N	Range	Minimum	Maximum	Mean	Std. Deviation	Variance
quiz	25	11.00	9.00	20.00	15.5600	3.16333	10.007
Valid N (listwise)	25						

This is an example of the output generated using the "**Descriptives**" procedure in SPSS.

Statistics

quiz

N	Valid	25
	Missing	0
Mean		15.5600
Median		16.3333[a]
Mode		17.00
Std. Deviation		3.16333
Variance		10.007
Range		11.00

a. Calculated from grouped data.

This is an example of the output generated using the "**Frequencies**" procedure in SPSS. By default, a frequency table is also generated from "Frequencies" (but is not presented here).

Note the footnote: The median was computed using grouped data by requesting *values are group midpoints.*

Statistics

quiz

N	Valid	25
	Missing	0
Mean		15.5600
Median		17.0000
Mode		17.00
Std. Deviation		3.16333
Variance		10.007
Range		11.00

When computed without *values are group midpoints,* the value of the median is slightly different.

This will automatically generate the mean, median (approximate), variance, standard deviation, minimum, maximum, exclusive range, and interquartile range (H), as well as many other statistics, some of which will be covered in later chapters. The SPSS output from Explore is shown in the top panel of Table 3.5.

3.4.2 Descriptives

Step 1. The second tool we consider is Descriptives. It can also be accessed by going to "Analyze" in the top pulldown menu, then selecting "Descriptive Statistics," and then "Descriptives" (see Figure 3.1, "EXPLORE: Step 1," for a screenshot of this step).

Step 2. This will bring up the Descriptives dialog box (see the "Descriptives: Step 2" screenshot in Figure 3.3). From the main Descriptives dialog box, click the variable of interest (e.g., "quiz") and move into the "Variable(s)" box by clicking on the arrow. Next, click the "Options" button.

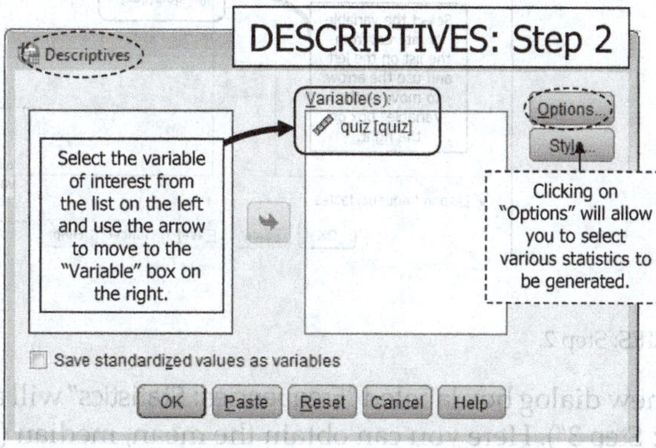

FIGURE 3.3
DESCRIPTIVES: Step 2.

Step 3. A new box called "Descriptives: Options" will appear (see the "DESCRIPTIVES: Step 3" screenshot in Figure 3.4), and you can simply place a checkmark in the boxes for the statistics that you want to generate. By default, the mean, standard deviation, minimum, and maximum are selected. From illustrative purposes, we will also select the variance and range. After making your selections, click "Continue." You will then be returned to the main Descriptives dialog box. From there, click "OK." The SPSS output from the Descriptives tool is shown in the middle panel of Table 3.5.

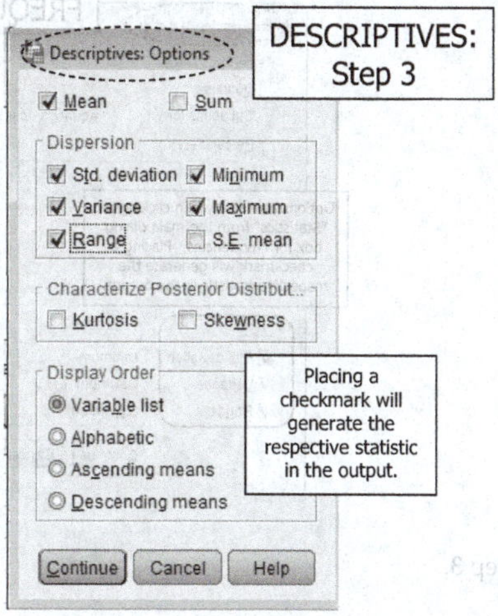

FIGURE 3.4
DESCRIPTIVES: Step 3.

3.4.3 Frequencies

Step 1. The final program to consider is Frequencies. Go to "Analyze" in the top pulldown menu, then "Descriptive Statistics," and then select "Frequencies" (see Figure 3.1, "EXPLORE: Step 1," for a screenshot of this step).

Step 2. The Frequencies dialog box will open (see the screenshot for "FREQUENCIES: Step 2" in Figure 3.5). From this main Frequencies dialog box, click the variable of interest from the list on the left (e.g., "quiz") and move it into the "Variables" box by clicking on the arrow button. By default, there is a checkmark in the box for "Display frequency tables," and we will keep this checked. Selecting "Display frequency tables" will generate a table of frequencies, relative frequencies, and cumulative relative frequencies. Then click on "Statistics" located in the top-right corner.

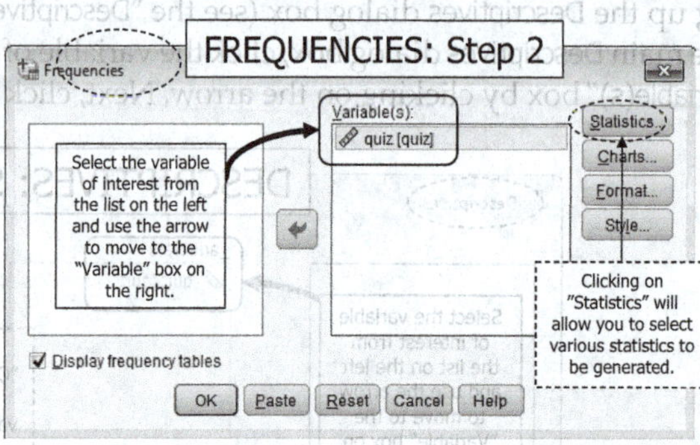

FIGURE 3.5
FREQUENCIES: Step 2.

Step 3. A new dialog box labeled "Frequencies: Statistics" will appear (see screenshot for "FREQUENCIES: Step 3"). Here you can obtain the mean, median (approximate), mode, variance, standard deviation, minimum, maximum, and exclusive range (among others). In order to obtain the closest approximation to the median, check the "Values are group midpoints" box, as shown. However, it should be noted that these values are not always as precise as those from the formula given earlier in this chapter, and your results will not be incorrect should you not select values at group midpoint. After making your selections, click "Continue." You will then be returned to the main Frequencies dialog box. From there, click "OK." The SPSS output from the Frequencies tool is shown in the bottom panel of Table 3.5.

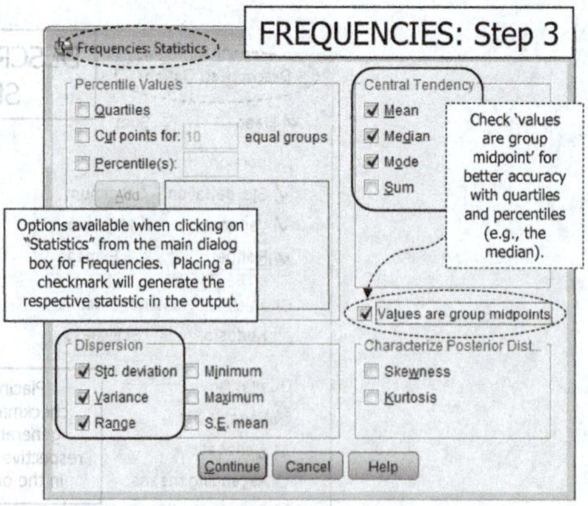

FIGURE 3.6
FREQUENCIES: Step 3.

3.5 Computing Sample Statistics Using R

Next we consider **R** for computing the mean, median, mode, standard deviation, variance, range, minimum, and maximum. The commands are provided within the blocks with additional annotation to assist you in understanding how each command works. Should you want to write reminder notes and annotation to yourself as you write the commands in **R** (and we highly encourage doing so), remember that any text that follows a hashtag (i.e., #) is annotation only and not part of the **R** code. Thus, you can write annotations directly into **R** with hashtags. We encourage this practice so that when you call up the commands in the future you'll understand what the various lines of code are doing. You may think you'll remember what you did. However, trust us. There is a good chance that you won't. Thus, consider it best practice when using **R** to annotate heavily!

3.5.1 Reading Data into R

We will first read in our data (Figure 3.7). We will be using the quiz data that we have used previously.

```
getwd()
```

R is always pointed to a directory on your computer. To find out which directory it is pointed to, run this "get working directory" command. We will assume that we need to change the working directory, and will use the next line of code to point the working directory to the desired path.

```
setwd("E:/Folder")
```

To set the working directory, use the *setwd* function and change what is in quotation marks here to your file location. Also, if you are copying the directory name, it will copy in slashes. You will need to change the slash (i.e., \) to a forward slash (i.e., /). Note that you need your destination name within quotation marks in the parentheses.

```
Ch3_quiz <- read.csv("Ch3_quiz.csv")
```

The *read.csv* function reads your data into **R**. What's to the left of the <- will be what you want to call the data in **R**. In this example, we're calling the dataframe "Ch3_quiz." What's to the right of the <- tells **R** to find this particular .csv file. In this example, our file is called "Ch3_quiz.csv." Make sure the extension (i.e., .csv) is included in your script. Also note that you need the name of your file in quotation marks within the parentheses.

```
names(Ch3_quiz)
```

The *names* function will produce a list of variable names for each dataframe as follows. This is a good check to make sure your data have been read in correctly.

```
[1] "quiz"
```

```
View(Ch3_quiz)
```

The *View* function will let you view the dataset in spreadsheet format in RStudio.

FIGURE 3.7
Reading data into **R**.

3.5.2 Generating Sample Statistics

Similar to SPSS, statistics can be generated in **R** in a number of different ways. The *summary* function will produce a number of helpful statistics, including the mean, median, minimum, and maximum, as well as the 1st and 3rd quartiles (which we will learn about soon) (Figure 3.8).

```
summary(Ch3_quiz)
```

The *summary* function will produce basic descriptive statistics on all the variables in your dataframe. This is a great way to quickly check to see if the data have been read in correctly and get a feel for your data, if you haven't already. The output from the summary statement for this dataframe looks like this:

```
     quiz
Min.   : 9.00
1st Qu.:13.00
Median :17.00
Mean   :15.56
3rd Qu.:18.00
Max.   :20.00
```

FIGURE 3.8
Summary function in **R**.

We can also use the *pastecs* package to generate similar statistics (Figure 3.9).

```
install.packages("pastecs")
library(pastecs)
```

To use a package in **R**, we first have to install the package using the *install.package* function. The name of the package is placed in quotation marks within parentheses. Once the package is installed, we call it into our **R** library so we can access its functionalities using the *library* function.

```
stat.desc(Ch3_quiz$quiz)
```

The function we will use is *stat.desc*, and we define, within parentheses, the dataframe (i.e., "Ch3_quiz") and variable (i.e., "quiz") for which we want to generate the descriptive statistics. The script *Ch3_quiz$quiz* tells **R** to use the variable "quiz" from the "Ch3_quiz" dataframe. The output from this function includes the number of cases in our dataframe (i.e., sample size; *nbr.val*), the number of null values (*nbr.null*), the number of missing values (*nbr.na*), the minimal value (*min*), the maximal value (*max*), the range (*range*, which is computed as max-min), and the sum of all nonmissing values (*sum*). What we are most likely interested in are the values of the median (*median*), mean (*mean*), standard error of the mean (*SE.mean*; we will learn about this in an upcoming chapter), 95% confidence interval of the mean (*CI.mean.0.95*), variance (*var*), standard deviation, (*std.dev*), and coefficient of variation (*coef.var*).

```
     nbr.val     nbr.null       nbr.na
  25.0000000    0.0000000    0.0000000

         min          max        range
   9.0000000   20.0000000   11.0000000

         sum       median         mean
 389.0000000   17.0000000   15.5600000

     SE.mean CI.mean.0.95          var
   0.6326663    1.3057591   10.0066667

     std.dev     coef.var
   3.1633316    0.2032989
```

FIGURE 3.9
Summary statistics using the *pastecs* package.

If we want to produce just one statistic, such as the mean, standard deviation, or variance, we can generate those values with the following scripts (Figure 3.10). The first part of the script defines the function (i.e., *mean, sd, var*) to compute the mean, standard deviation, or variance, respectively. What is enclosed in parentheses tells **R** which dataframe (i.e., "Ch3_quiz") and which variable within that dataframe (i.e., "quiz") to use to compute the statistics. These terms are separated by a $.

```
mean(Ch3_quiz$quiz)
sd(Ch3_quiz$quiz)
var(Ch3_quiz$quiz)
```

The *mean, sd*, and *var* functions can be used to generate, respectively, the mean, standard deviation, and variance. The script *Ch3_quiz$quiz* tells **R** to use the variable "quiz" from the "Ch3_quiz" dataframe. The output follows.

```
# mean(Ch3_quiz$quiz)
[1] 15.56

# sd(Ch3_quiz$quiz)
[1] 3.163332

# var(Ch3_quiz$quiz)
[1] 10.00667
```

FIGURE 3.10
Sample statistics.

3.6 Research Question Template and Example Write-Up

As we stated in Chapter 2, depending on the purpose of your research study, you may or may not write a research question that corresponds to your descriptive statistics. If the end result of your research paper is to present results from inferential statistics, it may be that your research questions correspond only to those inferential questions, and thus no question is presented to represent the descriptive statistics. That is quite common. On the other hand, if the ultimate purpose of your research study is purely descriptive in nature, then writing one or more research questions that correspond to the descriptive statistics is not only entirely appropriate but (in most cases) absolutely necessary. At this time, let us revisit our graduate research assistant, Oso Wyse, who was working with Dr. Debhard. As you may recall, his task was to summarize data from 25 students enrolled in a statistics course. The questions with which Oso was assisting Dr. Debhard were as follows: *How can quiz scores of students enrolled in an introductory statistics class be summarized using measures of central tendency? How can quiz scores of students enrolled in an introductory statistics class be summarized using measures of dispersion?*

The following is a template for writing descriptive research questions for summarizing data with measures of central tendency and dispersion:

How can [variable] be summarized using measures of central tendency? How can [variable] be summarized using measures of dispersion?

Next, we present an APA-like paragraph summarizing the results of the statistics quiz data example answering the questions posed to Marie.

As shown in Table 3.5, scores ranged from 9 to 20. The mean was 15.56, the approximate median was 17.00 (or 16.33 when calculated from grouped data), and the mode was 17.00. Thus, the scores tended to lump together at the high end of the scale. A negatively skewed distribution is suggested given that the mean was less than the median and mode. The exclusive range was 11, *H* spread (interquartile range) was 5.0, variance was 10.007, and standard deviation was 3.1633. From this we can tell that the scores tended to be quite variable. For example, the middle 50% of the scores had a range of 5 (*H* spread), indicating that there was a reasonable spread of scores around the median. Thus, despite a high "average" score, there were some low-performing students as well. These results are consistent with those described in Section 2.4.

3.7 Additional Resources

In the previous chapters, we have mentioned a number of excellent resources for learning statistics. As we are still in the early stages of learning statistics, there are no additional resources that we suggest here. Rather, we refer you back to those chapters for supplemental resources for statistics as well as statistical software.

Problems

Conceptual Problems

1. Adding just one or two extreme scores to the low end of a large distribution of scores will have a greater effect on:
   a. *Q* than on the variance.
   b. the variance than on *Q*.
   c. the mode than on the median.
   d. none of the above
2. Which of the following is true of the variance of a distribution of scores?
   a. It is always 1.
   b. It can be any number—negative, zero, or positive.
   c. It can be any number greater than zero.
   d. It can be any number equal to or greater than zero.
3. A 20-item statistics test was graded using the following procedure: a correct response is scored +1, a blank response is scored 0, and an incorrect response is scored −1. The highest possible score is +20; the lowest score possible is −20. Because the variance of the test scores for the class was −3, we can conclude which of the following?

a. The class did very poorly on the test.
b. The test was too difficult for the class.
c. Some students received negative scores.
d. A computational error was made.

4. Adding just one or two extreme scores to the high end of a large distribution of scores will have a greater effect on:

a. the mode than on the median.
b. the median than on the mode.
c. the mean than on the median.
d. none of the above

5. True or false? In a negatively skewed distribution, the proportion of scores between Q_1 and the median is less than .25.

6. True or false? Median is to ordinal as mode is to nominal.

7. I assert that it is appropriate to utilize the mean in dealing with class-rank data. Am I correct?

8. For a perfectly symmetrical distribution of data, the mean, median, and mode are calculated. I assert that the values of all three measures are necessarily equal. Am I correct?

9. In a distribution of 100 scores, the top 10 examinees received an additional bonus of 5 points. Compared to the original median, I assert that the median of the new (revised) distribution will be the same value. Am I correct?

10. A set of eight scores was collected and the variance was found to be zero. I assert that a computational error must have been made. Am I correct?

11. For a set of 10 test scores, which of the following values will be different when computing the sample statistic as compared to the population parameter?

a. Mean
b. *H*
c. Range
d. Variance

12. True or false? The inclusive range will be greater than the exclusive range for any dataset.

13. For a set of IQ test scores, the median was computed to be 95 and Q_1 to be 100. I assert that the statistician is to be commended for her work. Am I correct?

14. A physical education teacher is conducting research related to elementary children's time spent in physical activity. As part of his research, he collects data from schools related to the number of minutes that they require children to participate in physical education classes. She finds that the most frequently occurring number of minutes required for children to participate in physical education classes is 22.00 minutes. Which measure of central tendency does this statement represent?

a. Mean
b. Median
c. Mode
d. Range
e. Standard deviation

15. A physical education teacher is conducting research related to elementary children's time spent in physical activity. As part of his research, he collects data from schools related to the number of minutes that they require children to participate in physical education classes. He finds that the fewest number of minutes required per week is 15 minutes and the maximum number of minutes is 45. Which measure of dispersion do these values reflect?

a. Mean
b. Median
c. Mode
d. Range
e. Standard deviation

16. A physical education teacher is conducting research related to elementary children's time spent in physical activity. As part of his research, he collects data from schools related to the number of minutes that they require children to participate in physical education classes. He finds that 50% of schools required 20 or more minutes of participation in physical education classes. Which measure of central tendency does this statement represent?

a. Mean
b. Median
c. Mode
d. Range
e. Standard deviation

17. One item on a survey of incoming college students asks students to indicate if they plan to live within a 50-mile radius of the university. Responses to the question include "yes," "maybe," or "no." The researcher who gathers this data computes the variance of this variable. Is this appropriate given the measurement scale of this variable? Yes or no?

18. A marriage and family counselor randomly samples 250 clients and collects data on the number of hours they spent in counseling during the past year. What is the most stable measure of central tendency to compute given the measurement scale of this variable?

a. Mean
b. Median
c. Mode
d. Range
e. Standard deviation

19. A report issued by a research think tank states that the average teenager spends 9 hours per day on social media. Which measure is reflected in this statement?

a. Mean
b. Median
c. Mode
d. Range
e. Standard deviation

20. A researcher is analyzing data from a patient registry. One of the variables is patient response to the question, "Does your family have a history of this disease?" Responses are "yes" or "no." Which measure of central tendency can the researcher use to analyze data from this question? Select all that apply.

a. Median

b. Mean

c. Mode

d. None of the above

21. A researcher has collected survey data from adults who have visited the Maldives. One of the items asked is, "How many vacations do you take per year?" Responses included: 0–1, 2–3, 4–5, 6 or more. Which of the following measures of central tendency and dispersion would be appropriate given the measurement scale of this variable? Select all that apply.

a. Mean

b. Median

c. Mode

d. Range

e. Standard deviation

22. A researcher is examining the relationship between daytime light exposure and energy expenditure. Subjects are randomly assigned to three light conditions (continuous warm white light, continuous blue-enriched white light, or intermittent warm white and blue-enriched white light). Energy expenditure is measured using indirect calorimetry (i.e., the amount of oxygen consumed and carbon dioxide produced), with values recorded to the third decimal place. The researcher wishes to compute measures of central tendency and dispersion on energy expenditure. Which of the following measures of central tendency and dispersion would be appropriate given the measurement scale of this variable? Select all that apply.

a. Mean

b. Median

c. Mode

d. Range

e. Standard deviation

23. A researcher is examining the relationship between tourism development and economic growth. Economic growth is measured by a country's gross domestic product (GDP) (measured in whole numbers). The researcher wishes to compute measures of central tendency and dispersion on GDP. Which of the following measures of central tendency and dispersion would be appropriate given the measurement scale of this variable? Select all that apply.

a. Mean

b. Median

c. Mode

d. Range

e. Standard deviation

Answers to Conceptual Problems

1. **b** (It will affect variance the most.)
3. **d** (The variance cannot be negative.)
5. **False** (That proportion is always .25.)
7. **No** (Class rank is ordinal, so the mean is inappropriate.)
9. **Yes** (Middle score is still the same.)
11. **d** (Variance has two different formulas.)
13. **No** (By nature of the median being the second quartile, the median must be larger than the first quartile; fire the statistician.)
15. **d** (Range, as it is computed as the difference between the two extreme values in the data.)
17. **No** (Interval or ratio data must be used to compute the variance.)
19. **a** (The average is also the mean.)
21. **b, c, d** (With responses of 0–1, 2–3, 4–5, 6 or more, this is an ordinal measurement scale, and thus mean and standard deviation are not appropriate.)
23. **a, b, c, d, e** (Given the continuous scale of GDP in this example, suggesting a ratio variable, all measures of central tendency and dispersion can be computed.)

Computational Problems

1. The following scores were obtained from a statistics exam.

50.00	47.00	45.00	44.00	47.00
47.00	45.00	43.00	44.00	44.00
49.00	48.00	46.00	50.00	48.00
46.00	45.00	47.00	41.00	49.00
41.00	46.00	47.00	45.00	43.00
47.00	50.00	43.00	47.00	45.00
46.00	47.00	46.00	44.00	49.00
48.00	43.00	42.00	46.00	49.00
44.00	48.00	47.00	45.00	46.00

Assuming an interval width of 1, compute the following:

a. Mode
b. Median
c. Mean
d. Interquartile range
e. Variance
f. Standard deviation

2. Given a negatively skewed distribution with a mean of 10, a variance of 81, and N = 500, what is the numerical value of the following?

$$\sum_{i=1}^{N}(X_i - \mu)$$

3. The following data were obtained from classroom observations and reflect the number of times that preschool children shared during an 8-hour period.

4	8	10	5	12	10	14	5
10	14	12	14	8	5	0	8
12	8	12	5	4	10	8	5

Assuming an interval width of 1, compute the following:

a. Mode
b. Median
c. Mean
d. Interquartile range
e. Variance
f. Standard deviation

4. A sample distribution of aptitude scores is as follows:

X	*f*
70	1
75	2
77	3
79	2
80	6
82	5
85	4
90	4
96	3

Assuming an interval width of 1, compute the following:

a. Mode
b. Median
c. Mean
d. Interquartile range
e. Variance
f. Standard deviation

5. A sample of 30 test scores are as follows:

X	*f*	*X*	*f*
8	1	15	3
9	4	16	0
10	3	17	0
11	7	18	2
12	9	19	0
13	0	20	1
14	0		

Compute each of the following statistics.

a. Mode
b. Median
c. Mean
d. Interquartile range
e. Variance
f. Standard deviation

6. Without doing any computations, which of the following distributions has the largest variance?

X	*f*	*Y*	*f*	*Z*	*f*
15	6	15	4	15	2
16	7	16	7	16	7
17	9	17	11	17	13
18	9	18	11	18	13
19	7	19	7	19	7
20	6	20	4	20	2

7. Without doing any computations, which of the following distributions has the largest variance?

X	*f*	*Y*	*f*	*Z*	*f*
5	3	5	1	5	6
6	2	6	0	6	2
7	4	7	4	7	3
8	3	8	3	8	1
9	5	9	2	9	0
10	2	10	1	10	7

8. A researcher has pulled data from the National Oceanic and Atmospheric Administration's (NOAA) Significant Volcanic Eruption Database (https://www.ngdc.noaa.gov/nndc/servlet/ShowDatasets?dataset=102557&search_look=50&display_look=50) and is examining volcanos that occurred between 2000 and 2018. Using the Ch2_volcano.sav data, answer the following questions.

a. What type of volcano occurred most often (use "VolcanoType")?
b. How many deaths occurred most often (use "Deaths")?
c. What was the range, standard deviation, and average elevation of the volcanos that erupted (use "VolcanoElevation")?

9. A researcher has pulled country-level data from the rollercoaster census report (https://rcdb.com/census.htm) and is examining rollercoasters within North American countries. Using the Ch2_rollercoaster.sav data, answer the following questions.

a. What is the range, standard deviation, and average number of sit-down rollercoasters (use "SitDown")?
b. What is the mean, median, and standard deviation for steel rollercoasters (use "Steel")?
c. How can the median number of steel rollercoasters be interpreted?

Answers to Computational Problems

1. Mode = 47, median = 46.00 (46.125 if computed using "values at group midpoints"), mean = 45.9778, interquartile range = 3.50 variance = 5.386, standard deviation = 2.32075.

3. Mode = multiple modes exist, 5 is the smallest mode; median = 8.0 (8.6667 if calculated using "values at group midpoint"), mean = 8.4583, interquartile range = 7.0, variance = 14.085, standard deviation = 3.75302.

5. Mode = 12, median = 11.5 (11.4375 if computed using "values at group midpoint"), mean = 12, interquartile range = 13, variance = 8.0690, standard deviation = 2.8406.

7. Distribution Z. It has more extreme scores than the other distributions.

   a. Stratovolcano occurred most often (mode = 5, which refers to "stratovolcano"; 82 stratovolcanoes occurred).

   b. "Few (1–50 deaths)" occurred most often (mode = 1, which refers to the category "few"; there were 53 in this category.

   c. The average elevation of the volcanoes was 2298.57, *SD* = 1251.615, with a range of 5428.

9. Using the Ch2_rollercoaster.sav data, we find:

   a. The range is 574, *SD* = 187.717, and the average number of sit-down rollercoasters is 77.00.

   b. Mean = 86.56; median = 5; standard deviation = 213.429.

   c. The median is 5. This indicates that one-half of the countries in North America have fewer than five steel rollercoasters and one-half have more than five steel rollercoasters.

Interpretive Problem

1. Select one interval or ratio variable from the survey1 sample dataset on the website.

   a. Calculate all of the measures of central tendency and dispersion discussed in this chapter that are appropriate for this measurement scale.

   b. Write an APA-style paragraph that summarizes the findings.

2. Select one ordinal variable from the survey1 sample dataset on the website.

   a. Calculate the measures of central tendency and dispersion discussed in this chapter that are appropriate for this measurement scale.

   b. Write an APA-style paragraph that summarizes the findings.

4

The Normal Distribution and Standard Scores

Chapter Outline

Key Concepts

1. Normal distribution (family of distributions, unit normal distribution, area under the curve, points of inflection, asymptotic curve)
2. Standard scores (z, T, IQ)
3. Symmetry
4. Skewness (positively skewed, negatively skewed)

5. Kurtosis (leptokurtic, platykurtic, mesokurtic)
6. Moments around the mean

In Chapter 3, we continued our discussion of descriptive statistics, which were defined as techniques that allow us to tabulate, summarize, and depict a collection of data in an abbreviated fashion. We considered the following three topics: summation notation (method for summing a set of scores), measures of central tendency (measures for boiling down a set of scores into a single value used to represent the data), and measures of dispersion (measures dealing with the extent to which a collection of scores vary).

In this chapter, we delve more into the field of descriptive statistics in terms of three additional topics. First, we consider the most commonly used distributional shape, the normal distribution. Although in this chapter we discuss the major characteristics of the normal distribution and how it is used descriptively, in later chapters we see how the normal distribution is used inferentially as an assumption for certain statistical tests. Second, several types of standard scores are considered. To this point we have looked at raw scores and deviation scores. Here we consider scores that are often easier to interpret, known as *standard scores*. Third, we examine two other measures useful for describing a collection of data, namely skewness and kurtosis. As we show shortly, *skewness* refers to the lack of symmetry of a distribution of scores and kurtosis refers to the *peakedness* of a distribution of scores. Finally, we provide a template for writing research questions, develop an APA-style paragraph of results for an example dataset, and also illustrate the use of SPSS and **R**. Concepts to be discussed include the normal distribution (i.e., family of distributions, unit normal distribution, area under the curve, points of inflection, asymptotic curve), standard scores (e.g., z, T, IQ), symmetry, skewness (positively skewed, negatively skewed), kurtosis (leptokurtic, platykurtic, mesokurtic), and moments around the mean. Our objectives are that by the end of this chapter, you will be able to (a) understand the normal distribution and utilize the normal table; (b) determine and interpret different types of standard scores, particularly z scores; and (c) understand and interpret skewness and kurtosis statistics.

4.1 The Normal Distribution and How It Works

You may remember the following research scenario that was first introduced in Chapter 2. We will revisit our talented group of graduate students in this chapter as they continue to explore the data.

The graduate students in the statistics lab, Addie Venture, Oso Wyse, Challie Lenge, and Ott Lier, have been assigned their first task as research assistants. Dr. Debhard, a statistics professor, has given the group of students quiz data collected from 25 students enrolled in an introductory statistics course and has asked the group to summarize the data. Working now with Challie Lenge, Dr. Debhard has asked Challie to revisit the following research question related to distributional shape: *What is the distributional shape of the statistics quiz score?* Additionally, Dr. Debhard has asked Challie to standardize the quiz score and compare student 1 to student 3 relative to the mean. The corresponding research question that Challie is provided for this analysis is as follows: *In standard deviation units, what is the relative standing to the mean of student 1 compared to student 3?*

Recall from Chapter 2 that there are several commonly seen distributions. The most commonly observed and used distribution is the *normal distribution*. It has many uses, both in descriptive and inferential statistics, as we will show. In this section, we discuss the history of the normal distribution and the major characteristics of the normal distribution.

4.1.1 History

Let us first consider a brief history of the normal distribution. From the time that data were collected and distributions examined, a particular bell-shaped distribution occurred quite often for many variables in many disciplines (e.g., many physical, cognitive, physiological, and motor attributes). This has come to be known as the **normal distribution**. Back in the 1700s, mathematicians were called on to develop an equation that could be used to approximate the normal distribution. If such an equation could be found, then the probability associated with any point on the curve could be determined, and the amount of space or area under any portion of the curve could also be determined. For example, one might want to know what the probability of being taller than 6′2″ would be for a male, given that height is normally shaped for each gender. Until the 1920s the development of this equation was commonly attributed to Karl Friedrich Gauss. Until that time this distribution was known as the *Gaussian curve*. However, in the 1920s, Karl Pearson found this equation in an earlier article written by Abraham DeMoivre in 1733 and renamed the curve as the "normal distribution." Today the normal distribution is obviously attributed to DeMoivre. The history of statistics is quite fascinating, and we encourage those interested to explore any number of resources to learn more (e.g., Koren, 1970; Stigler, 1986).

4.1.2 Characteristics

The normal distribution has seven important characteristics. Because the normal distribution occurs frequently, features of the distribution are standard across all normal distributions. This **standard curve** allows us to make comparisons across two or more normal distributions as well as look at areas under the curve, as becomes evident.

4.1.2.1 Standard Curve

First, the normal distribution is a standard curve because *it is always (a) symmetric around the mean, (b) unimodal, and (c) bell-shaped*. As shown in Figure 4.1, if we split the distribution in one-half at the mean (μ), the left-hand half (below the mean) is the mirror image of the right-hand half (above the mean). Also, the normal distribution has only one mode (i.e., unimodal), and the general shape of the distribution is bell shaped (some even call it the *bell-shaped curve*). Given these conditions, the mean, median, and mode will always be equal to one another for any normal distribution. (We will see later, however, that rarely do we encounter *perfectly* normal distributions where the mean, median, and mode are exactly equal to each other. Indeed, in our many combined years of generating statistics, we cannot necessarily recall a time when that happened! Rather, we will examine the range in which a distribution can be considered normal.)

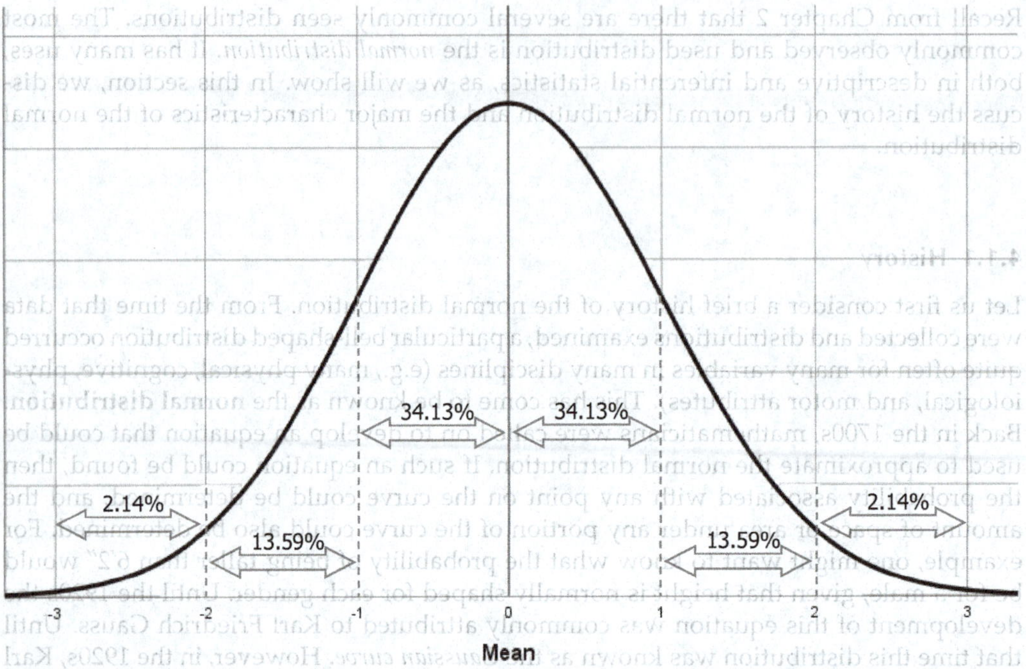

FIGURE 4.1
The normal distribution.

4.1.2.2 Family of Curves

Second, there is no single normal distribution, but rather *the normal distribution is a family of curves*. For instance, one particular normal curve has a mean of 100 and a variance of 225 (recall that the standard deviation is the square root of the variance, thus the standard deviation in this instance is 15). This normal curve is exemplified by the Wechsler Intelligence Scales. Another specific normal curve has a mean of 50 and a variance of 100 (and thus a standard deviation of 10). This normal curve is used with most behavior rating scales. *In fact, there are an infinite number of normal curves, one for every distinct pair of values for the mean and variance*. Every member of the family of normal curves has the same characteristics; however, the scale of X, the mean of X, and the variance (and standard deviation) of X can differ across different variables and/or populations.

To keep the members of the family distinct, we use the following notation. If the variable X is normally distributed, we write $X \sim N(\mu, \sigma^2)$. This is read as, "X is distributed normally with population mean μ and population variance σ^2." This is the general notation; for notation specific to a particular normal distribution, the mean and variance values are given. For our examples, the Wechsler Intelligence Scales are denoted by $X \sim N(100,225)$, whereas the behavior rating scales are denoted by $X \sim N(50,100)$. Narratively speaking, therefore, the Wechsler Intelligence Scale is distributed normally with a population mean of 100 and population variance of 225. A similar interpretation can be made on the behavior rating scale.

4.1.2.3 Unit Normal Distribution

Third, there is one particular member of the family of normal curves that deserves additional attention. This member has a mean of 0 and a variance (and standard deviation) of 1, and thus is denoted by $X \sim N(0,1)$. This is known as the **unit normal distribution** ("unit" referring to the variance of 1) or as the **standard unit normal distribution**. On a related matter, let us define a *z* score as follows:

$$z_i = \frac{(X_i - \mu)}{\sigma}$$

The numerator of this equation is actually a deviation score, previously described in Chapter 3, and indicates how far above or below the mean an individual's score falls. *When we divide the deviation from the mean (i.e., the numerator) by the standard deviation (i.e., denominator), the value derived indicates how many deviations above or below the mean a unit's score falls.* If one individual has a *z* score of +1.00, then the person falls one standard deviation above the mean on that particular measure. If another individual has a *z* score of −2.00, then that person falls two standard deviations below the mean on that particular measure. There is more to say about this as we move along in this section.

4.1.2.4 Area

The fourth characteristic of the normal distribution is the ability to determine any area under the curve. *Specifically, we can determine the area above any value, the area below any value, or the area between any two values under the curve.* Let us chat about what we mean by *area*. If you return to Figure 4.1, areas for different portions of the curve are listed. Here, **area** is defined as *the percentage or amount of space of a distribution, either above a certain score, below a certain score, or between two different scores*. For example, we see that the area between the mean and one standard deviation above the mean is 34.13%. In other words, roughly one-third of the entire distribution falls into that region. The entire area under the curve then represents 100%, and smaller portions of the curve represent somewhat less than that.

For example, say you wanted to know what percentage of adults had an IQ score greater than 120, or what percentage of adults had an IQ score less than 107, or what percentage of adults had an IQ score between 107 and 120. How can we compute these areas under the curve? A table of the unit normal distribution has been developed for this purpose. Although similar tables could also be developed for every member of the normal family of curves, these are unnecessary, as any normal distribution can be converted to a unit normal distribution. The **unit normal table** is given in Table A.1 in the Appendix.

Turn to Appendix Table A.1 now and familiarize yourself with its contents. To help illustrate, a portion of the table is presented in Figure 4.2. The first column simply lists the values of *z*. These are standardized scores on the X axis. Note that the values of *z* only range from 0 to 4.0. There are two reasons for this. First, values above 4.0 are rather unlikely, as the area under that portion of the curve is negligible (less than .003%). Second, values below 0 (i.e., negative *z* scores) are not really necessary to present in the table, as the normal distribution is symmetric around the mean of 0. Thus, that portion of the table would be redundant and is not shown here (we show how to deal with this situation for some example problems in a bit).

The second column, labeled $P(z)$, gives the area below the respective value of *z*. In other words, the area between that value of *z* and the most extreme left-hand portion of the curve

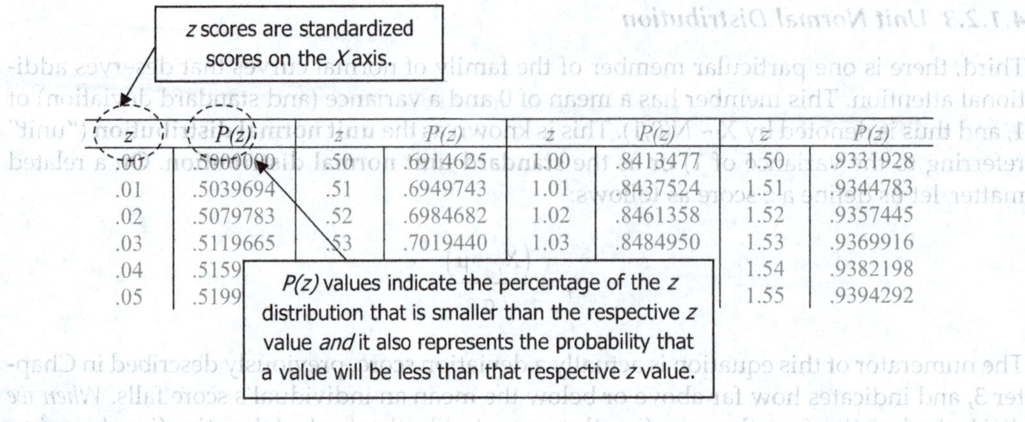

FIGURE 4.2
Portion of z table.

(i.e., $-\infty$ or negative infinity, on the far negative or left-hand side of zero). So if we wanted to know what the area was below $z = +1.00$, we would look in the first column under $z = 1.00$ and then look in the second column, $P(z)$, to find the area of .8413. *This value, .8413, represents the percentage of the distribution that is smaller than z of +1.00. It also represents the probability that a score will be smaller than z of +1.00.* In other words, about 84% of the distribution is less than z of +1.00 *and* the probability that a value will be less than z of +1.00 is about 84%. More examples are considered later in this section.

4.1.2.5 Transformation to Unit Normal Distribution

A fifth characteristic is that *any normally distributed variable, regardless of the mean and variance, can be converted into a unit normally distributed variable.* Thus, our Wechsler Intelligence Scales, as denoted by $X \sim N(100,225)$, can be converted into $z \sim N(0,1)$. Conceptually this transformation is done by moving the curve along the X axis until it is centered at a mean of 0 (by subtracting out the original mean) and then by stretching or compressing the distribution until it has a variance of 1 (remember, however, that the shape of the distribution does not change during the standardization process, only those values on the X axis). This allows us to make the same interpretation about any individual's score on any normally distributed variable. If $z = +1.00$, then for *any* variable this implies that the individual falls one standard deviation above the mean.

This also allows us to make comparisons between two different individuals or cases or across two different variables. If we wanted to make comparisons between two different individuals on the same variable X, then rather than comparing their individual raw scores, X_1 and X_2, we could compare their individual z scores, z_1 and z_2, where

$$z_1 = \frac{(X_1 - \mu)}{\sigma}$$

and

$$z_2 = \frac{(X_2 - \mu)}{\sigma}$$

This is the reason we only need the unit normal distribution table to determine areas under the curve rather than a table for every member of the normal distribution family. In another situation we may want to compare scores on the Wechsler Intelligence Scales, $X \sim N(100,225)$, to scores on behavior rating scales, $X \sim N(50,100)$, for the same individual. We would convert to z scores again for two variables, and then direct comparisons could be made.

It is important to note that in standardizing a variable, it is only the values on the X axis that change. The shape of the distribution (e.g., skewness and kurtosis) remains the same.

4.1.2.6 Constant Relationship With the Standard Deviation

The sixth characteristic is that *the normal distribution has a constant relationship with the standard deviation.* Consider Figure 4.1 again. Along the X axis we see values represented in standard deviation increments. In particular, from left to right, the values shown are three, two, and one standard deviation units below the mean; the mean; and one, two, and three standard deviation units above the mean. Under the curve, we see the percentage of scores that are under different portions of the curve. For example, the area between the mean and one standard deviation above or below the mean is 34.13%. The area between one standard deviation and two standard deviations on the same side of the mean is 13.59%, the area between two and three standard deviations on the same side is 2.14%, and the area beyond three standard deviations is .13%.

In addition, three other areas are often of interest. The area within one standard deviation of the mean, from one standard deviation below the mean to one standard deviation above the mean, is approximately 68% (or roughly two-thirds of the distribution). The area within two standard deviations of the mean, from two standard deviations below the mean to two standard deviations above the mean, is approximately 95%. The area within three standard deviations of the mean, from three standard deviations below the mean to three standard deviations above the mean, is approximately 99%. In other words, nearly all of the scores will be within two or three standard deviations of the mean for any normal curve.

4.1.2.7 Points of Inflection and Asymptotic Curve

The seventh and final characteristic of the normal distribution is as follows. *The points of inflection are where the curve changes from sloping down (concave) to sloping up (convex).* These **points of inflection** occur precisely at one standard deviation unit *above* and *below* the mean. This is more a matter of mathematical elegance than a statistical application. The curve also never touches the X axis. This is because with the theoretical normal curve, all values from negative infinity to positive infinity have a nonzero probability of occurring. Thus, while the curve continues to slope ever-downward toward more extreme scores, it approaches, but never quite touches, the X axis. The curve is referred to here as being **asymptotic**. This allows for the possibility of extreme scores.

4.1.2.8 Examples

Now for the long-awaited examples for finding area using the unit normal distribution. These examples require the use of Table A.1 in the Appendix, the z table. Our personal preference is to start by drawing a picture of the normal curve so that the proper area is visualized. Let us consider four examples of finding the area below a certain value of z: (a) below z = –2.50; (b) below z = 0; (c) below z = 1.00; and (d) between z = –2.50 and z = 1.00.

To determine the value below z = –2.50, we draw a picture as shown in Figure 4.3a. We draw a vertical line at the value of z, then shade in the area we want to find. In this example, that represents z ≤ –2.50. Because the shaded region is relatively small, we know the area must be considerably smaller than .50. In the unit normal table we already know negative values of z are not included. However, because the normal distribution is symmetric, we know the area *below* –2.50 is the same as the area *above* +2.50. Thus, we look up the area below +2.50 and find the value of .9938. This indicates that about 99.38% of the distribution is below z = +2.50 and what remains in the distribution z ≥ +2.50. Thus, we can subtract .9938 from 1.0000 and find the value of .0062, or .62%, very small area indeed, which represents the area of the distribution where z ≥ +2.50 as well as z ≤ –2.50.

How do we determine the area *below* z = 0 (i.e., the mean)? As shown in Figure 4.3b, we already know from reading this section that the area has to be .5000, or one-half of the total area under the curve. However, looking in the table again for the area below z = 0, we find the area is .5000. How do we determine the area below z = 1.00? As shown in Figure 4.3c, this region exists on both sides of zero and actually constitutes two smaller areas, the first area below 0 and the second area between 0 and 1. For this example we use the table directly and find the value of .8413. We leave you with two other problems to solve on your own. First, what is the area below z = 0.50 (answer: .6915)? Second, what is the area below z = 1.96 (answer: .9750)?

Because the unit normal distribution is symmetric, finding the area *above* a certain value of z is solved in a similar fashion as the area *below* a certain value of z. We need not devote any further attention to that particular situation. However, how do we determine the area

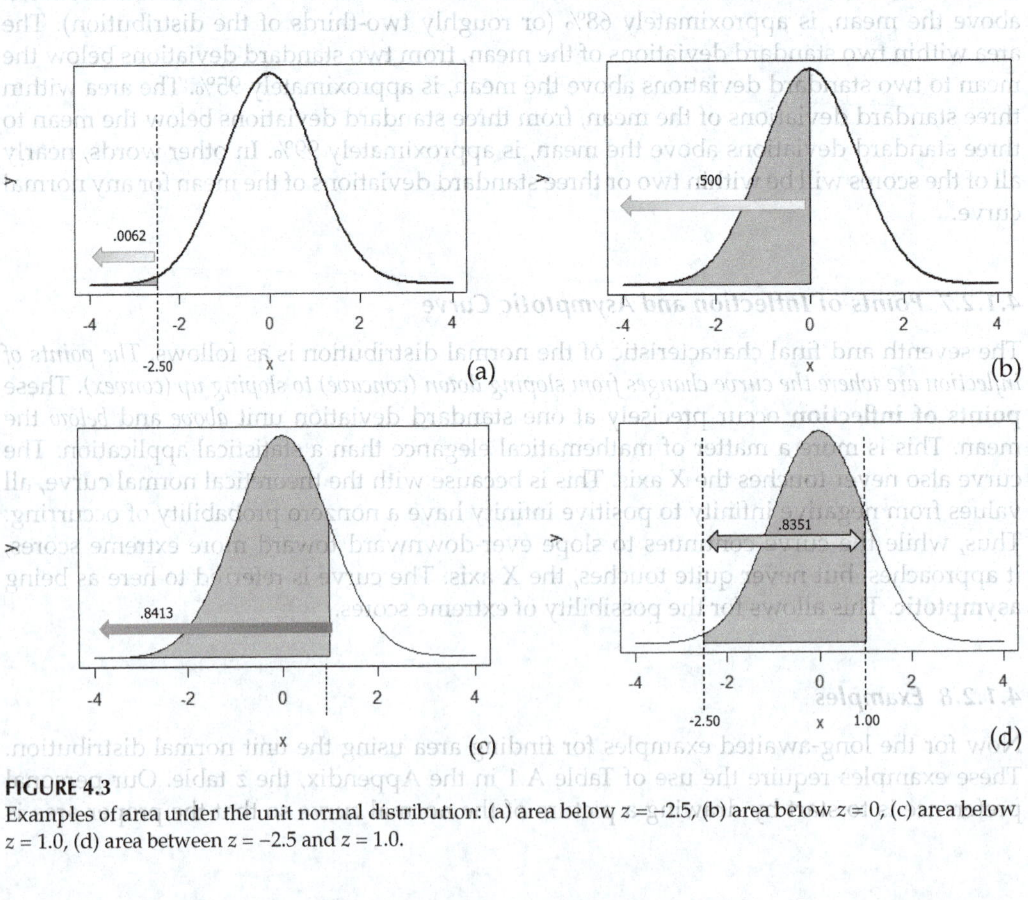

FIGURE 4.3
Examples of area under the unit normal distribution: (a) area below z = –2.5, (b) area below z = 0, (c) area below z = 1.0, (d) area between z = –2.5 and z = 1.0.

between two values of z? This is a little different and needs some additional discussion. Consider as an example finding the area between $z = -2.50$ and $z = 1.00$, as depicted in Figure 4.3 (d). Here we see that the shaded region consists of two smaller areas, the area between the mean ($z = 0$) and −2.50 and the area between the mean ($z = 0$) and 1.00. Using the table again, we find the area *below* 1.00 is .8413 and the area *below* −2.50 is .0062. Thus, the shaded region is the difference, as computed by .8413 − .0062 = .8351. Thus, the area between $z = -2.50$ and $z = 1.00$ is about 83.51% of the distribution. On your own, determine the area between $z = -1.27$ and $z = 0.50$ (answer: .5895).

Finally, what if we wanted to determine areas under the curve for values of X rather than z? The answer here is simple, as you might have guessed. First, we convert the value of X to a z score, and then we use the unit normal table to determine the area. Because the normal curve is standard for all members of the family of normal curves, the scale of the variable, X or z, is irrelevant in terms of determining such areas. In the next section we deal more with such transformations.

4.2 Standard Scores and How They Work

We have already devoted considerable attention to z scores, which are one type of standard score. In this section we describe an application of z scores leading up to a discussion of other types of standard scores. As we show, the major purpose of standard scores is to place scores on the same standard scale so that comparisons can be made across individuals and/or variables. Without some standard scale, comparisons across individuals and/or variables would be difficult to make. Examples are coming right up.

4.2.1 *z* Scores

You have just interviewed for your dream job. As part of your interview, you completed a cognitive ability assessment (which measured problem-solving skills and ability to learn and understand instructions) and a motivation index (designed to measure work engagement motivation). On the cognitive ability assessment, you receives a score of 75 and on the motivation index you receive a score of 60. The natural question to ask is, "Which performance was the stronger one?" The suspense is killing you! No information about any of the following is available: maximum score possible, mean of the candidates who were interviewed (or any other central tendency measure), or standard deviation of the candidates who were interviewed (or any other dispersion measure). It is possible, and quite likely, that the two assessments had a different number of possible points, different means, and/or different standard deviations. How can we possibly answer our question?

The answer, of course, is to use z scores if the data are assumed to be normally distributed, once the relevant information is obtained. Let us take a minor digression before we return to answer our question in more detail. Recall the formula for standardizing variable X into a z score:

$$z_i = \frac{(X_i - \mu_X)}{\sigma_X}$$

where the X subscript has been added to the mean and standard deviation for purposes of clarifying which variable is being considered. If variable X is the number of items correct on a test, then the numerator is the deviation of the student's raw score from the class mean (i.e., the numerator is a deviation score as previously defined in Chapter 3), measured in terms of items correct, and the denominator is the standard deviation of the class, measured in terms of items correct. Because both the numerator and denominator are measured in terms of items correct, the resultant z score is measured in terms of no units (as the units of the numerator and denominator essentially cancel out). *Given that z scores have no units (i.e., the z score is interpreted as the number of standard deviation units above or below the mean), this allows us to compare two different raw score variables with different scales, means, and/or standard deviations.* By converting our two variables to z scores, the transformed variables are now on the same z score scale with a mean of 0 and a variance and standard deviation of 1.

Let us return to our previous situation where the cognitive ability score is 75 and the motivation index score is 60. In addition, we are provided with information that the standard deviation for the cognitive ability is 15 and the standard deviation for the motivation index is 10. Consider the following three examples. In the first example, the means are 60 for the cognitive ability assessment and 50 for the motivation index. The z scores are then computed as follows:

$$z_i = \frac{(X_i - \mu)}{\sigma}$$

$$z_{cognitive\ ability} = \frac{(75-60)}{15} = 1.0$$

$$z_{motivation} = \frac{(60-50)}{10} = 1.0$$

The conclusion for the first example is that the performance on both instruments is the same; that is, you scored one standard deviation above the mean on both assessments.

In the second example, the means are 60 for the cognitive ability assessment and 40 for the motivation index. The z scores are then computed as follows:

$$z_{cognitive\ ability} = \frac{(75-60)}{15} = 1.0$$

$$z_{motivation} = \frac{(60-40)}{10} = 2.0$$

The conclusion for the second example is that performance is better on the motivation index; that is, you scored two standard deviations above the mean for the motivation index and only one standard deviation above the mean for the cognitive ability assessment.

In the third example, the means are 60 for the cognitive ability assessment and 70 for the motivation index. The z scores are then computed as follows:

$$z_{cognitive\ ability} = \frac{(75-60)}{15} = 1.0$$

$$z_{motivation} = \frac{(60-70)}{10} = -1.0$$

The conclusion for the third example is that performance is better on the cognitive ability assessment; that is, you scored one standard deviation above the mean for the cognitive ability assessment and one standard deviation below the mean for the motivation index. These examples serve to illustrate a few of the many possibilities, depending on the particular combinations of raw score, mean, and standard deviation for each variable.

Let us conclude this section by mentioning the major characteristics of z scores. The first characteristic is that *z* scores provide us with *comparable distributions*, as we just saw in the previous examples. Second, *z* scores take into account *the entire distribution of raw scores*. All raw scores can be converted to *z* scores such that every raw score will have a corresponding *z* score. Third, we can evaluate an individual's performance *relative to the scores in the distribution*. For example, saying that an individual's score is one standard deviation above the mean is a measure of relative performance. This implies that approximately 84% of the scores will fall below the performance of that individual. Finally, *negative values* (i.e., below 0) and *decimal values* (e.g., $z = 1.55$) *are obviously possible* (and will most certainly occur) with *z* scores. On the average, about one-half of the *z* scores for any distribution will be negative and some decimal values are quite likely. This last characteristic is bothersome to some individuals and has led to the development of other types of standard scores, as described in the next section.

4.2.2 Other Types of Standard Scores

Over the years, other standard scores besides *z* scores have been developed, either to alleviate the concern over negative and/or decimal values associated with *z* scores or to obtain a particular mean and standard deviation. Let us examine some common examples. The first additional standard score is known as the *T* score and is used in tests such as most behavior rating scales, as previously mentioned. The ***T* scores** have a mean of 50 and a standard deviation of 10. A second additional standard score is known as the **IQ score** and is used in the Wechsler Intelligence Scales. The IQ score has a mean of 100 and a standard deviation of 15 (the Stanford-Binet Intelligence Scales have a mean of 100 and a standard deviation of 16). Entrance exams are also standardized scores but with means and standard deviations that differ from 0 and 1, respectively.

Say we want to develop our own type of standard score, where we determine in advance the mean and standard deviation that we would like to have. How would that be done? Given that the equation for *z* scores is as follows:

$$z_i = \frac{(X_i - \mu_X)}{\sigma_X}$$

then algebraically the following can be shown:

$$X_i = \mu_X + \sigma_X z_i$$

If, for example, we want to develop our own "stat" standardized score, then the following equation would be used:

$$stat_i = \mu_{stat} + \sigma_{stat} z_i$$

where $stat_i$ is the "stat" standardized score for a particular individual *i*, μ_{stat} is the desired mean of the "stat" distribution, and σ_{stat} is the desired standard deviation of the "stat" distribution. If we want to have a mean of 10 and a standard deviation of 2, then our equation becomes

$$stat_i = 10 + 2z_i$$

We would then have the computer simply plug in a z score and compute an individual's "stat" score. Thus, a z score of 1.0 would yield a "stat" standardized score of 12.0.

Consider a realistic example where we have a raw score variable we want to transform into a standard score, and we want to control the mean and standard deviation. For example, we have statistics midterm raw scores with 225 points possible. We want to develop a standard score with a mean of 50 and a standard deviation of 5. We also have scores on other variables that are on different scales with different means and different standard deviations (e.g., statistics final exam scores worth 175 points, a set of 20 lab assignments worth a total of 200 points, a statistics performance assessment worth 100 points). We can standardize each of those variables by placing them on the same scale with the same mean and same standard deviation, thereby allowing comparisons across variables. This is precisely the rationale used by testing companies and researchers when they develop standard scores. In short, from z scores we can develop a T, IQ, "stat," or any other type of standard score. Examples of types of standard scores are summarized in Box 4.1.

BOX 4.1 Examples of Types of Standard Scores

Standard Score	Distribution*
Z (unit normal)	$N(0,1)$
College Entrance Examination Board (CEEB) score	$N(500,10{,}000)$
T score	$N(50,100)$
Weschler intelligence scale	$N(100,225)$
Stanford-Binet intelligence scale	$N(100,256)$

$^*N(\mu, \sigma^2)$

4.3 Skewness and Kurtosis Statistics

In previous chapters we discussed the distributional concepts of symmetry, skewness, central tendency, and dispersion. In this section we more closely define symmetry as well as the statistics commonly used to measure skewness and kurtosis.

4.3.1 Symmetry

Conceptually, we define a distribution as being **symmetric** *if when we divide the distribution precisely in one-half, the left-hand half is a mirror image of the right-hand half.* That is, the distribution above the mean is a mirror image of the distribution below the mean. To put it another way, a distribution is **symmetric around the mean** if for every score that is q units below the mean, there is a corresponding score that is q units above the mean.

Two examples of symmetric distributions are shown in Figure 4.4. In Figure 4.4a, we have a normal distribution, which is clearly symmetric around the mean. In Figure 4.4b, we have

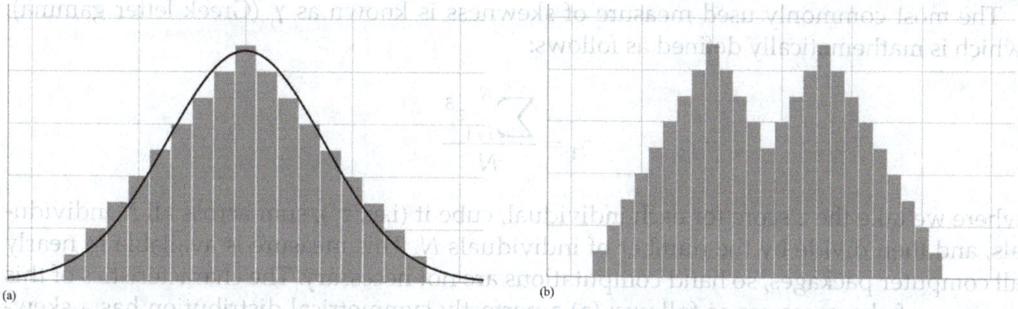

FIGURE 4.4
Symmetric distributions: (a) normal distribution and (b) bimodal distribution.

a symmetric distribution that is bimodal, unlike the previous example. From these and other numerous examples, we can make the following two conclusions. First, if a distribution is *symmetric*, then the mean is equal to the median. Second, if a distribution is *symmetric and unimodal*, then the mean, median, and mode are all equal. This indicates we can determine whether a distribution is symmetric by simply comparing the measures of central tendency.

4.3.2 Skewness

We define **skewness** as *the extent to which a distribution of scores deviates from perfect symmetry*. This is important because perfectly symmetrical distributions rarely occur with actual sample data (i.e., "real" data). A skewed distribution is known as being **asymmetrical**. As shown in Figure 4.5, there are two general types of skewness, distributions that are negatively skewed, as in Figure 4.5a, and those that are positively skewed, as in Figure 4.5b. *Negatively skewed distributions, which are skewed to the left, occur when most of the scores are toward the high end of the distribution and only a few scores are toward the low end*. If you make a fist with your thumb pointing to the left (skewed to the left), you have graphically defined a negatively skewed distribution. For a negatively skewed distribution, we also find the following: mode > median > mean. This indicates that we can determine whether a distribution is negatively skewed by simply comparing the measures of central tendency.

Positively skewed distributions, which are skewed to the right, occur when most of the scores are toward the low end of the distribution and only a few scores are toward the high end. If you make a fist with your thumb pointing to the right (skewed to the right), you have visually defined a positively skewed distribution. For a positively skewed distribution, we also find the following: mode < median < mean. This indicates that we can determine whether a distribution is positively skewed by simply comparing the measures of central tendency.

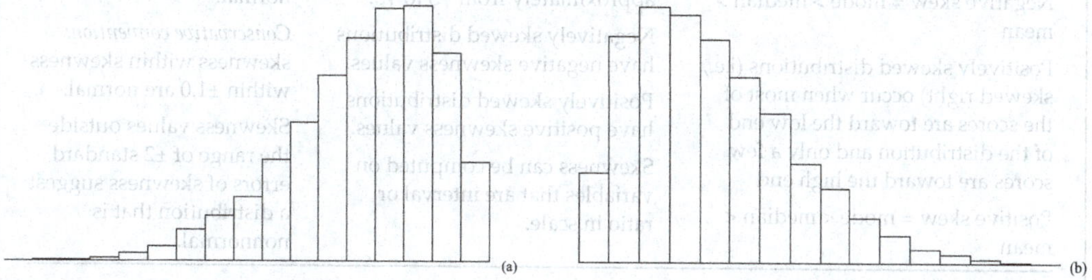

FIGURE 4.5
Skewed distributions: (a) negatively skewed distribution and (b) positively skewed distribution.

The most commonly used measure of skewness is known as γ_1 (Greek letter gamma), which is mathematically defined as follows:

$$\gamma_1 = \frac{\sum_{i=1}^{N} z_i^3}{N}$$

where we take the z score for each individual, cube it (i.e., z_i^3), sum across all N individuals, and then divide by the number of individuals N. This measure is available in nearly all computer packages, so hand computations are not necessary. The characteristics of this measure of skewness are as follows: (a) a perfectly symmetrical distribution has a skewness value of 0, (b) the range of values for the skewness statistic is approximately from −3 to +3, (c) negatively skewed distributions have negative skewness values, and (d) positively skewed distributions have positive skewness values.

You will rarely, if ever, find a distribution that has a skewness statistic that is exactly equal to zero. In other words, most distributions have some degree of skew. Different conventions are available for determining how extreme skewness can be and still retain a relatively normal distribution. One simple guideline is that skewness values within ±2.0 are considered relatively normal, with more liberal researchers applying a ±3.0 guideline, and more conservative researchers using ±1.0. Another recommendation for determining how extreme a skewness value must be for the distribution to be considered nonnormal is as follows: Skewness values outside the range of plus or minus two standard errors of skewness suggest a distribution that is nonnormal. Applying this suggestion, if the standard error of skewness is .85, then anything outside of −2(.85) to +2(.85), or −1.7 to +1.7, would be considered nonnormal. It is important to note that this second recommendation is sensitive to small sample sizes and should only be considered as a general guide. When we delve into inferential statistics (see Chapter 6), we will discuss how we can use skew and kurtosis divided by their standard errors to determine what is statistically significantly different from normal—but we'll save that conversation for a few more chapters! ☺ A summary of items related to skewness is provided in Box 4.2.

BOX 4.2 Summary of Skewness

Property	Characteristic	Conventions
Negatively skewed distributions (i.e., skewed left) occur when most of the scores are toward the high end of the distribution and only a few scores are toward the low end/ Negative skew = mode > median > mean Positively skewed distributions (i.e., skewed right) occur when most of the scores are toward the low end of the distribution and only a few scores are toward the high end Positive skew = mode < median < mean	A perfectly symmetrical distribution has a skewness value of 0. The range of values for the skewness statistic is approximately from −3 to +3. Negatively skewed distributions have negative skewness values. Positively skewed distributions have positive skewness values. Skewness can be computed on variables that are interval or ratio in scale.	*Liberal convention:* skewness within ±3.0 are normal *Moderate convention:* skewness within ±2.0 are normal. *Conservative convention:* skewness within skewness within ±1.0 are normal. Skewness values outside the range of ±2 standard errors of skewness suggest a distribution that is nonnormal.

4.3.3 Kurtosis

Kurtosis is the fourth and final property of a distribution (often referred to as the **moments around the mean**). *These four properties are central tendency (first moment), dispersion (second moment), skewness (third moment), and kurtosis (fourth moment).* **Kurtosis** is conceptually defined as the "peakedness" of a distribution (*kurtosis* is Greek for "peakedness"). Some distributions are rather flat and others have a rather sharp peak. Specifically, the three general types of peakedness are shown in Figure 4.6. A distribution that is very peaked is known as being **leptokurtic** (*lepto* meaning "slender" or "narrow"; Figure 4.6a). A distribution that is relatively flat is known as being **platykurtic** (*platy* meaning "flat" or "broad"; Figure 4.6b). A distribution that is somewhere in between, such as a normal distribution, is known as being **mesokurtic** (*meso* meaning "intermediate"; Figure 4.6c).

The most commonly used measure of kurtosis is known as γ_2, which is mathematically defined as

$$\gamma_2 = \frac{\sum_{i=1}^{N} z_i^4}{N} - 3$$

where we take the *z* score for each unit, take it to the fourth power (being the fourth moment), sum across all *N* individuals, divide by the number of individuals *N*, and then subtract 3. This measure is available in nearly all computer packages, so hand computations are not necessary. The characteristics of this measure of kurtosis are as follows: (a) a perfectly mesokurtic distribution, which would be a normal distribution, has a kurtosis value of 0; (b) platykurtic distributions have negative kurtosis values (being flat rather than peaked); and (c) leptokurtic distributions have positive kurtosis values (being peaked).

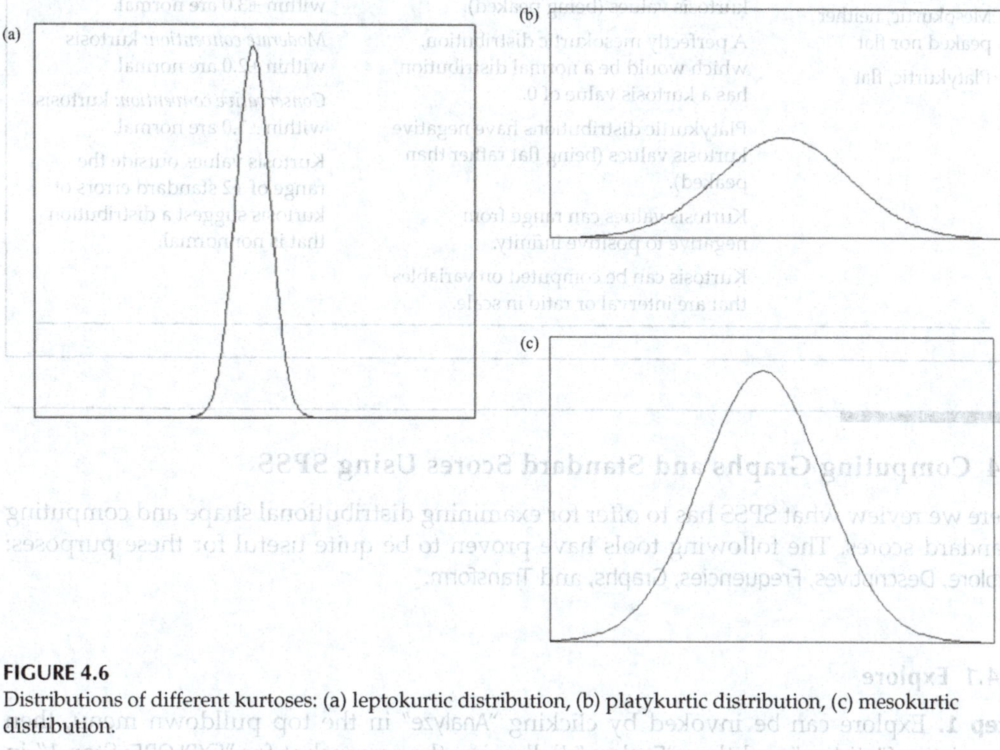

FIGURE 4.6
Distributions of different kurtoses: (a) leptokurtic distribution, (b) platykurtic distribution, (c) mesokurtic distribution.

Kurtosis values can range from negative to positive infinity, and kurtosis can be computed on variables that are interval or ratio in scale.

Similar to skewness, you will rarely, if ever, find a distribution that has a kurtosis statistic that is exactly equal to zero. In other words, most distributions have some degree of kurtosis. Different conventions are available for determining how extreme kurtosis can be and still retain a relatively normal distribution. One simple guideline is that kurtosis values within ±2.0 are considered relatively normal, with more conservative researchers applying a ±3.0 guideline, and more stringent researchers using ±1.0. A suggestion for determining how extreme a kurtosis value may be for the distribution to be considered nonnormal is as follows: Kurtosis values outside the range of ±2.0 standard errors of kurtosis suggest a distribution that is nonnormal. Applying this criteria, if the standard error of kurtosis is 1.20, then anything outside of (−2.00) (1.20) to (+2.00)(1.20), or −2.40 to +2.40, would be considered nonnormal. It is important to note that this second guideline (i.e., ±2.0 *SE*) is sensitive to small sample sizes and should only be considered as a general guide.

Skewness and kurtosis statistics are useful for the following two reasons: (a) as descriptive statistics used to describe the shape of a distribution of scores, and (b) in inferential statistics, which often assume a normal distribution, so the researcher has some indication of whether the assumption has been met (more about this beginning in Chapter 6). Skewness and kurtosis are appropriate to compute only on variables that are interval or ratio in scale. A summary of items related to kurtosis is provided in Box 4.3.

BOX 4.3 Summary of Kurtosis

Property	Characteristics	Conventions
Leptokurtic, peaked Mesokurtic, neither peaked nor flat Platykurtic, flat	Leptokurtic distributions have positive kurtosis values (being peaked). A perfectly mesokurtic distribution, which would be a normal distribution, has a kurtosis value of 0. Platykurtic distributions have negative kurtosis values (being flat rather than peaked). Kurtosis values can range from negative to positive infinity. Kurtosis can be computed on variables that are interval or ratio in scale.	*Liberal convention:* kurtosis within ±3.0 are normal. *Moderate convention:* kurtosis within ±2.0 are normal. *Conservative convention:* kurtosis within ±1.0 are normal. Kurtosis values outside the range of ±2 standard errors of kurtosis suggest a distribution that is nonnormal.

4.4 Computing Graphs and Standard Scores Using SPSS

Here we review what SPSS has to offer for examining distributional shape and computing standard scores. The following tools have proven to be quite useful for these purposes: Explore, Descriptives, Frequencies, Graphs, and Transform.

4.4.1 Explore

Step 1. Explore can be invoked by clicking "Analyze" in the top pulldown menu, then "Descriptive Statistics," and then "Explore." Following the screenshot for "EXPLORE: Step 1" in

Figure 4.7 produces the Explore dialog box. For brevity, we have not reproduced this initial screenshot when we discuss the Descriptives and Frequencies tools; however, you see here where they can be found from the pulldown menus.

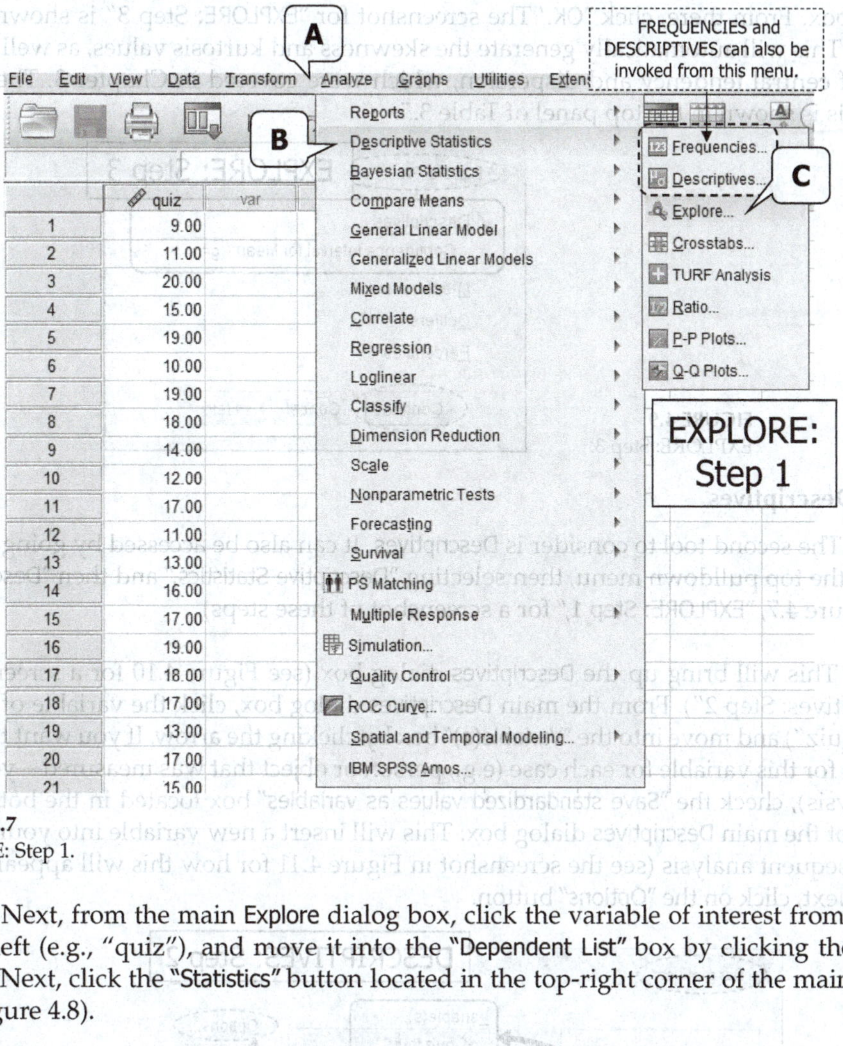

FIGURE 4.7
EXPLORE: Step 1.

Step 2. Next, from the main Explore dialog box, click the variable of interest from the list on the left (e.g., "quiz"), and move it into the "Dependent List" box by clicking the arrow button. Next, click the "Statistics" button located in the top-right corner of the main dialog box (Figure 4.8).

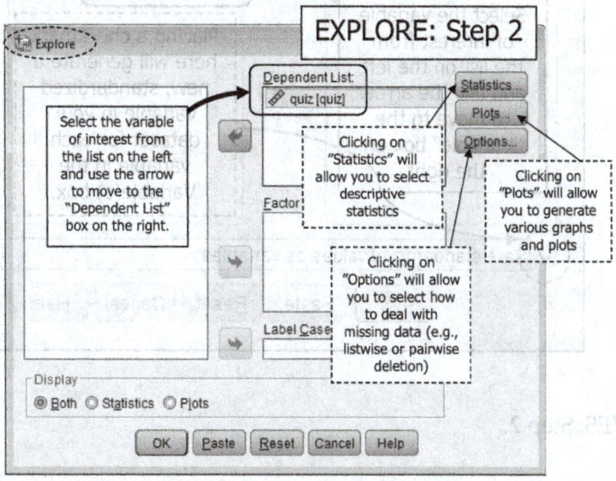

FIGURE 4.8
EXPLORE: Step 2.

Step 3. A new box labeled "Explore: Statistics" will appear. Simply place a checkmark in the "Descriptives" box. Should you desire to use an alpha other than .05 (i.e., 95% confidence interval for the mean), then that change can be made here. For this illustration, we will keep the default 95%. Next click "Continue." You will then be returned to the main Explore dialog box. From there, click "OK." The screenshot for "EXPLORE: Step 3" is shown in Figure 4.9. This will automatically generate the skewness and kurtosis values, as well as measures of central tendency and dispersion, which were covered in Chapter 3. The output from this is shown in the top panel of Table 3.5.

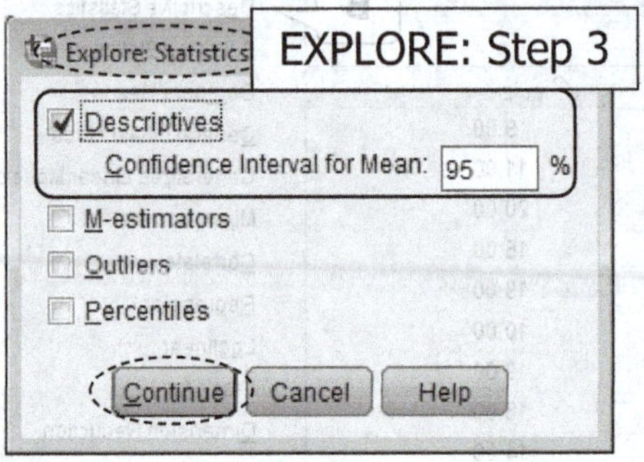

FIGURE 4.9
EXPLORE: Step 3.

4.4.2 Descriptives

Step 1. The second tool to consider is Descriptives. It can also be accessed by going to "Analyze" in the top pulldown menu, then selecting "Descriptive Statistics," and then "Descriptives" (see Figure 4.7, "EXPLORE: Step 1," for a screenshot of these steps).

Step 2. This will bring up the Descriptives dialog box (see Figure 4.10 for a screenshot of Descriptives: Step 2"). From the main Descriptives dialog box, click the variable of interest (e.g., "quiz") and move into the "Variable(s)" box by clicking the arrow. If you want to obtain *z* scores for this variable for each case (e.g., person or object that was measured—your unit of analysis), check the "Save standardized values as variables" box located in the bottom-left corner of the main Descriptives dialog box. This will insert a new variable into your dataset for subsequent analysis (see the screenshot in Figure 4.11 for how this will appear in Data View). Next, click on the "Options" button.

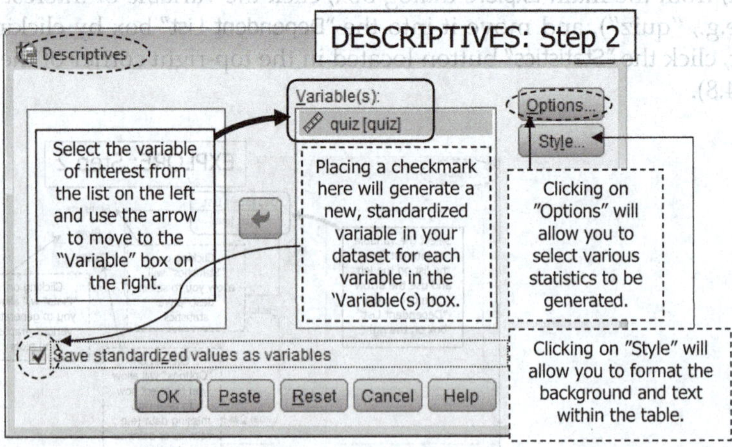

FIGURE 4.10
DESCRIPTIVES: Step 2.

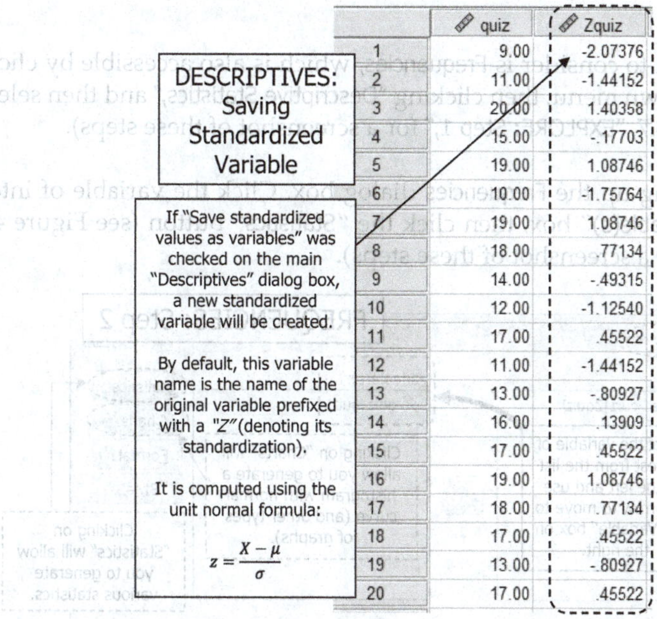
DESCRIPTIVES: Saving Standardized Variable
quiz
Zquiz
1 9.00 -2.07376
2 11.00 -1.44152
3 20.00 1.40358
4 15.00 -.17703
5 19.00 1.08746
6 10.00 -1.75764
7 19.00 1.08746
8 18.00 .77134
9 14.00 -.49315
10 12.00 -1.12540
11 17.00 .45522
12 11.00 -1.44152
13 13.00 -.80927
14 16.00 .13909
15 17.00 .45522
16 19.00 1.08746
17 18.00 .77134
18 17.00 .45522
19 13.00 -.80927
20 17.00 .45522
If "Save standardized values as variables" was checked on the main "Descriptives" dialog box, a new standardized variable will be created.
By default, this variable name is the name of the original variable prefixed with a "Z" (denoting its standardization).
It is computed using the unit normal formula:
z = (X − μ) / σ

FIGURE 4.11
Standardized variable (first 20 cases).

Step 3. A new box called "Descriptives: Options" will appear (see Figure 4.12 for the screenshot of "DESCRIPTIVES: Step 3"), and you can simply place a checkmark in the boxes for the statistics that you want to generate. This will allow you to obtain the skewness and kurtosis values, as well as measures of central tendency and dispersion discussed in Chapter 3. After making your selections, click on "Continue." You will then be returned to the main Descriptives dialog box. From there, click "OK."

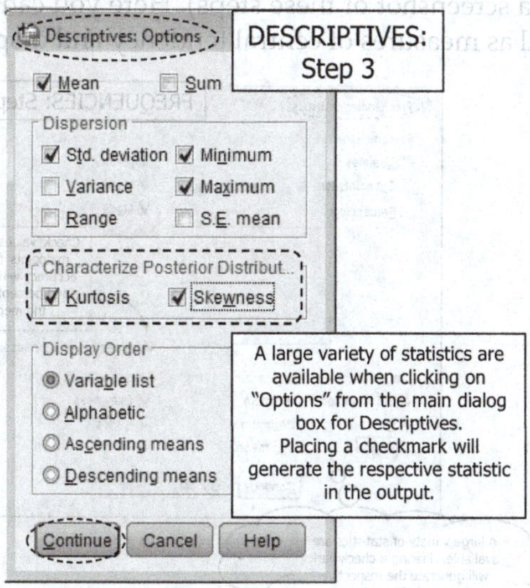

FIGURE 4.12
DESCRIPTIVES: Step 3.

4.4.3 Frequencies

Step 1. The third tool to consider is Frequencies, which is also accessible by clicking "Analyze" in the top pulldown menu, then clicking "Descriptive Statistics," and then selecting "Frequencies" (see Figure 4.7, "EXPLORE: Step 1," for a screenshot of these steps).

Step 2. This will bring up the Frequencies dialog box. Click the variable of interest (e.g., "quiz") into the "Variable(s)" box, then click the "Statistics" button (see Figure 4.13, "FREQUENCIES: Step 2," for a screenshot of these steps).

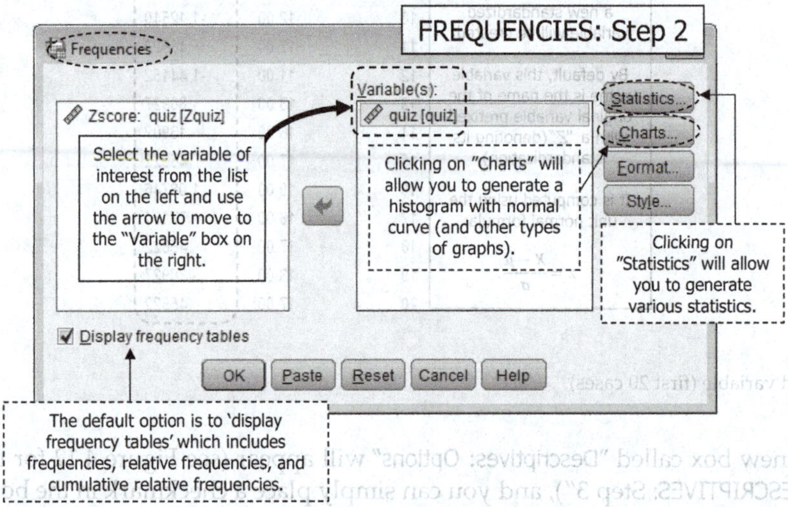

FIGURE 4.13
FREQUENCIES: Step 2.

Step 3. A new box labeled "Frequencies: Statistics" will appear. Again, you can simply place a checkmark in the boxes for the statistics that you want to generate (see Figure 4.14, "FREQUENCIES: Step 3," for a screenshot of these steps). Here you can obtain the skewness and kurtosis values, as well as measures of central tendency and dispersion from Chapter 3.

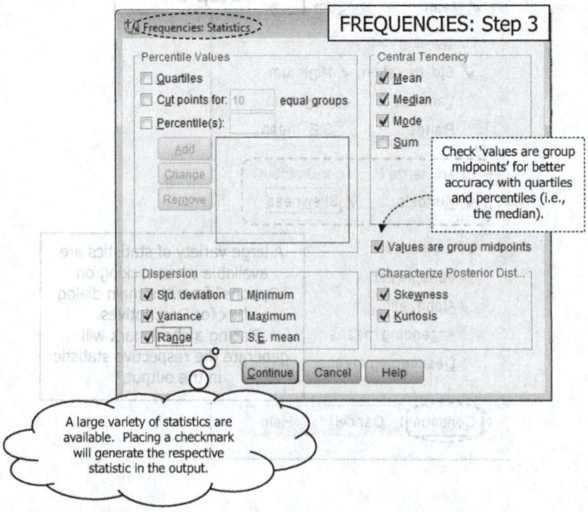

FIGURE 4.14
FREQUENCIES: Step 3.

If you click the "Charts" button, you can also obtain a histogram with a normal curve overlay by clicking the "Histogram" radio button and checking the "With normal curve" box. This histogram output is shown in Figure 4.15. After making your selections, click "Continue." You will then be returned to the main Frequencies dialog box. From there, click "OK."

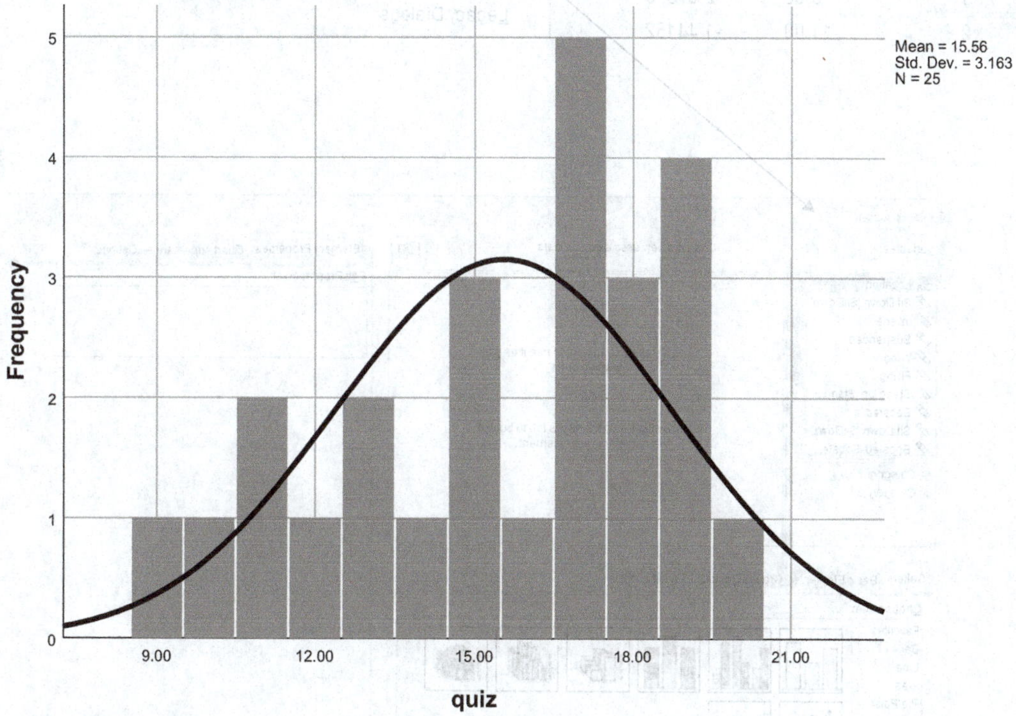

FIGURE 4.15
Histogram of statistics quiz data with normal distribution overlay.

4.4.4 Graphs

Two other tools also yield a histogram with a normal curve overlay. Both can be accessed by first going to "Graphs" in the top pulldown menu. From there, select "Legacy Dialogs," then "Histogram." Simply move the variable of interest into the "variable" box and place a check in the appropriate box if you want to display a normal curve.

Another option for creating a histogram, starting again from the "Graphs" option in the top pulldown menu, is to select "Chart Builder." Chart Builder allows researchers to drag and drop variable(s) and select the type of graph from a menu, with options for defining the elements of the graph (such as displaying the normal curve) (see Figure 4.16, "GRAPHS: Step 1," for a screenshot of these steps).

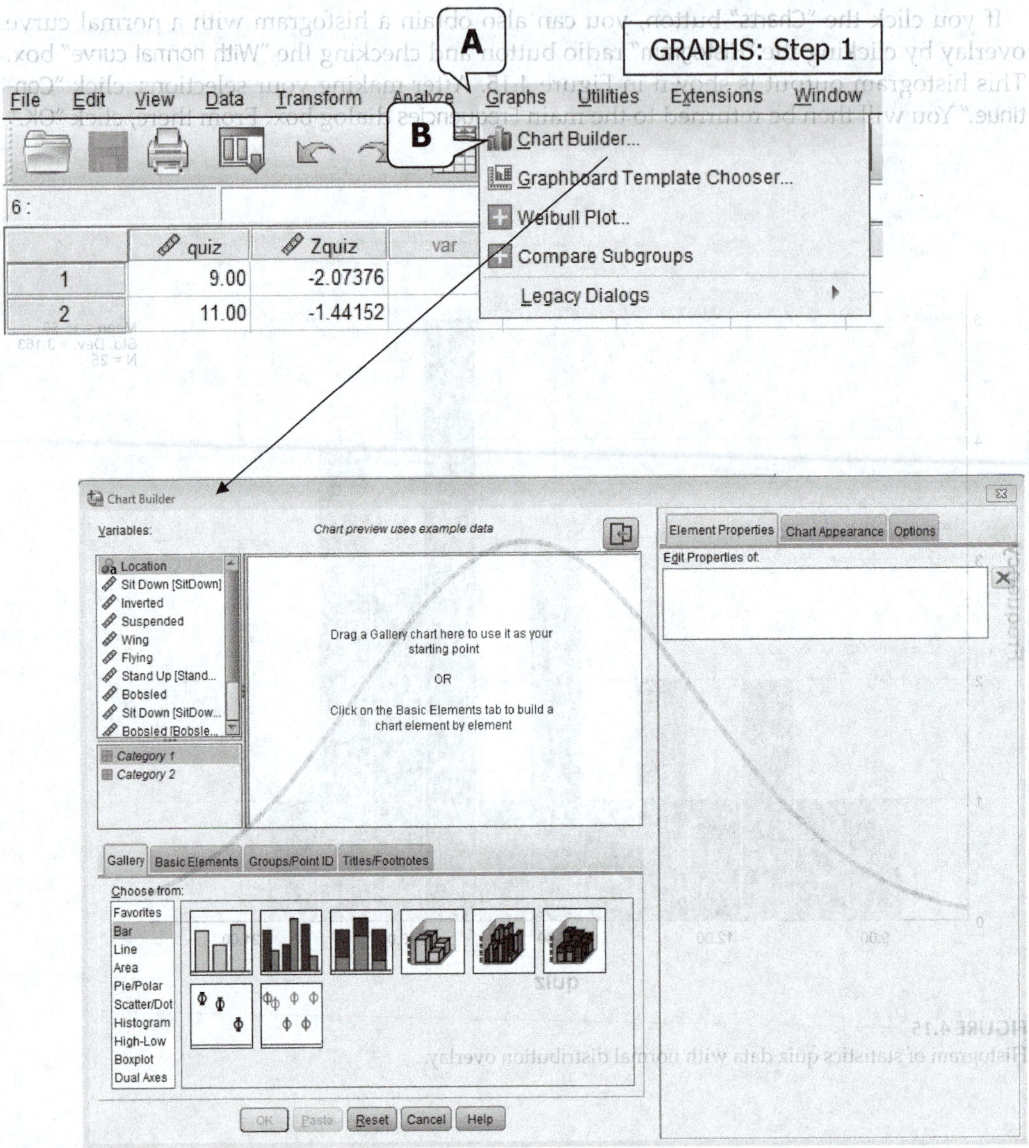

FIGURE 4.16
GRAPHS: Step 1.

4.4.5 Transform

Step 1. A final tool that comes in handy is for transforming variables, such as creating a standardized version of a variable (most notably standardization *other* than the application of the unit normal formula, where the unit normal standardization can be easily performed as seen previously by using Descriptives). Go to "Transform" from the top pulldown menu, and then select "Compute Variables." A dialog box labeled "Compute Variables" will appear (see Figure 4.17, "TRANSFORM: Step 1," for a screenshot of these steps). SPSS offers a number of different mathematical formulas, and researchers can also write their own equation.

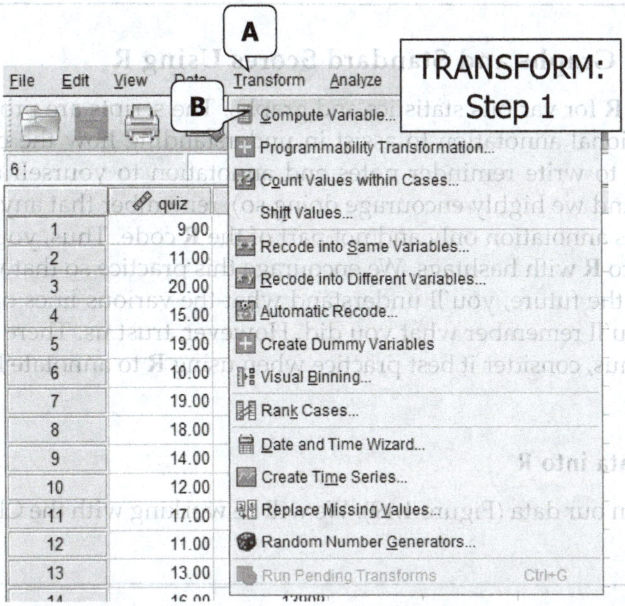

FIGURE 4.17
TRANSFORM: Step 1.

Step 2. The "Target Variable" is the name of the new variable you are creating and the "Numeric Expression" box is where you insert the commands of which original variable to transform and how to transform it (e.g., "stat" variable). When you are done defining the formula, simply click "OK" to generate the new variable in the datafile (see Figure 4.18, "TRANSFORM: Step 2," for a screenshot of these steps).

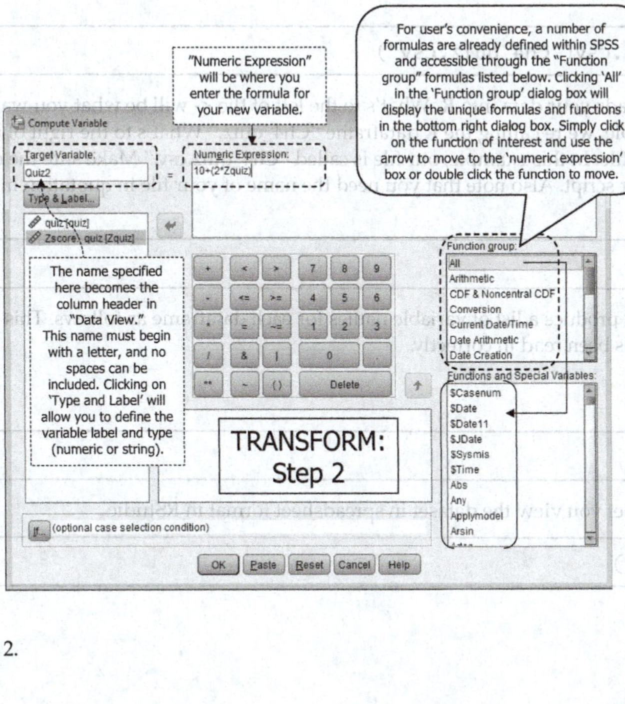

FIGURE 4.18
TRANSFORM: Step 2.

4.5 Computing Graphs and Standard Scores Using R

Next we consider **R** for various statistics and graphs. The scripts are provided within the blocks with additional annotation to assist in understanding how the commands work. Should you want to write reminder notes and annotation to yourself as you write the commands in **R** (and we highly encourage doing so), remember that any text that follows a hashtag (i.e., #) is annotation only and not part of the **R** code. Thus, you can write annotations directly into **R** with hashtags. We encourage this practice so that when you call up the commands in the future, you'll understand what the various lines of code are doing. You may think you'll remember what you did. However, trust us. There is a good chance that you won't. Thus, consider it best practice when using **R** to annotate heavily!

4.5.1 Reading Data into R

We will first read in our data (Figure 4.19). We will be working with the Ch4_quiz.csv data.

```
getwd()
```

R is always pointed to a directory on your computer. To find out which directory it is pointed to, run this "get working directory" command. We will assume that we need to change the working directory, and will use the next line of code to set the working directory to the desired path.

```
setwd("E:/Folder")
```

To set the working directory, use the *setwd* function and change what is in quotation marks here to your file location. Also, if you are copying the directory name, it will copy in slashes. You will need to change the slash (i.e., \) to forward slash (i.e., /). Note that you need your destination name within quotation marks in the parentheses.

```
Ch4_quiz <- read.csv("Ch4_quiz.csv")
```

The *read.csv* function reads your data into **R**. What's to the left of the <- will be what you want to call the data in **R**. In this example, we're calling the **R** dataframe "Ch4_quiz." What's to the right of the <- tells **R** to find this particular csv file. In this example, our file is called "Ch4_quiz.csv." Make sure the extension (i.e., .csv) is included in your script. Also note that you need the name of your file in quotation marks within the parentheses.

```
names(Ch4_quiz)
```

The *names* function will produce a list of variable names for each dataframe as follows. This is a good check to make sure your data has been read in correctly.

```
[1] "quiz"
```

```
View(Ch4_quiz)
```

The *View* function will let you view the dataset in spreadsheet format in RStudio.

```
summary(Ch4_quiz)
```

FIGURE 4.19
Reading data into **R**.

The *summary* function will produce basic descriptive statistics on all the variables in your dataframe. This is a great way to quickly check to see if the data have been read in correctly and get a feel for your data, if you haven't already. The output from the summary statement for this dataframe looks like this:

```
      quiz
 Min.    : 9.00
 1st Qu.:13.00
 Median :17.00
 Mean   :15.56
 3rd Qu.:18.00
 Max.   :20.00
```

FIGURE 4.19 (continued)
Reading data into **R**.

4.5.2 Generating Skewness and Kurtosis

```
install.packages("e1071")
```

The *install.packages* function will install the *e1071* package that we will use to generate skewness and kurtosis. Note that the name of the package needs to be placed within quotation marks in the script.

```
library(e1071)
```

We only need to install the package once; however, we need to call it into our library each time we use it. The *library* function will load the *e1071* package into our library.

```
skewness(Ch4_quiz$quiz, type=3)
skewness(Ch4_quiz$quiz, type=2)
skewness(Ch4_quiz$quiz, type=1)
```

The *skewness* command will generate skewness statistics on the variable(s) we specify. In this example, we are using the variable "quiz" from the dataframe "Ch4_quiz," and we indicate this in **R** by the script *Ch4_quiz$quiz*. The *type=script* defines how skewness is calculated. Specifying *type=2* will use the algorithm that is used by SPSS. Readers interested in learning more, including the algorithms for each of the three methods, are encouraged to review Joanes and Gill (1998). We see that using *type=2* our skew is –.598.

```
# skewness(Ch4_quiz$quiz, type=3)
[1] -0.5280266

# skewness(Ch4_quiz$quiz, type=2)
[1] -0.5978562

# skewness(Ch4_quiz$quiz, type=1)
[1] -0.5613697
```

```
kurtosis(Ch4_quiz$quiz, type=3)
kurtosis(Ch4_quiz$quiz, type=2)
kurtosis(Ch4_quiz$quiz, type=1)
```

FIGURE 4.20
Generating skewness and kurtosis.

The *kurtosis* function will generate kurtosis statistics on the variable(s) we specify. In this example, we are using the variable "quiz" from the dataframe "Ch4_quiz," and we indicate this in **R** by the script *Ch4_quiz$quiz*. The "type=script" defines how kurtosis is calculated. Specifying "type=2" will use the algorithm that is used by SPSS. Readers interested in learning more, including the algorithms for each of the three methods, are encouraged to review Joanes and Gill (1998). We see that using *type=2* our kurtosis is −.741.

```
# kurtosis(Ch4_quiz$quiz, type=3)
[1] -1.002001

# kurtosis(Ch4_quiz$quiz, type=2)
[1] -0.741478

# kurtosis(Ch4_quiz$quiz, type=1)
[1] -0.8320318
```

FIGURE 4.20 (continued)
Generating skewness and kurtosis.

4.5.3 Generating a Histogram

```
hist(Ch4_quiz$quiz,
     main = "Histogram of Quiz Scores",
     xlab ="Quiz Score", ylab = "Frequency")
```

The *hist* function will produce a histogram using the variable "quiz" from the "Ch4_quiz" dataframe. The histogram will include "Histogram of Quiz Scores" as the title (generated based on main = "Histogram of Quiz Scores"), with the *X* axis being labeled "Quiz Score" (i.e., *xlab* = *"Quiz Score"*) and the *Y* axis being labeled "Frequency" (i.e., *ylab* = *"Frequency"*).

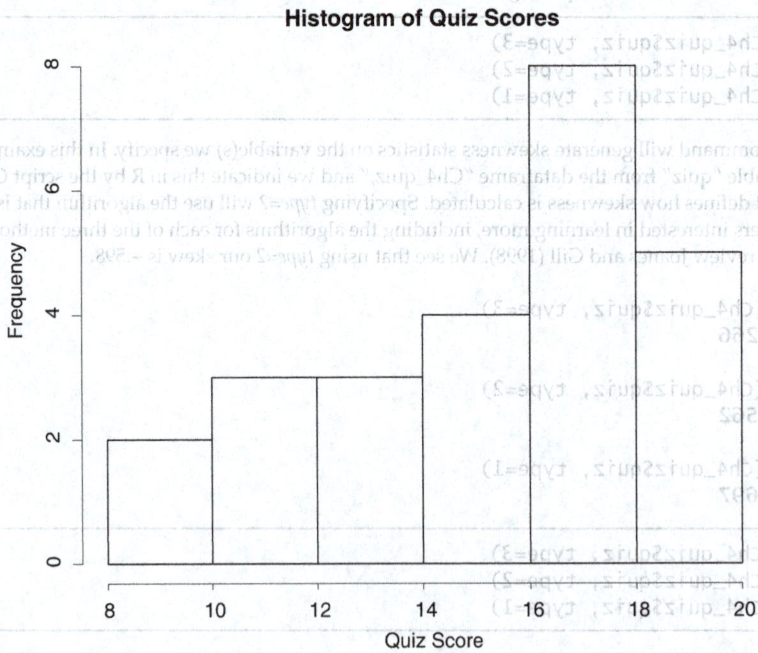

FIGURE 4.21
Generating a histogram.

4.5.4 Creating a Standardized Variable

```
Ch4_quiz$Zquiz <- scale(Ch4_quiz$quiz)
```

To create a new standardized variable in our dataframe, we use the *scale* function. The script to the left of <- (i.e., "Ch4_quiz$Zquiz") tells **R** to create a new variable in the dataframe "Ch4_quiz" that is called "Zquiz." In parentheses, we are telling **R** to use the variable "quiz" from our dataframe "Ch4_quiz" to create the standardized variable (i.e., "Ch4_quiz$quiz").

```
View(Ch4_quiz)
```

We use the *View* function to confirm that our new variable has been created and added to our dataframe by displaying the dataframe in RStudio.

```
summary(Ch4_quiz)
```

We use the *summary* function to generate basic descriptive statistics on our variable. We see that the mean of our new standardized variable, "Zquiz.v1," is 0, which is expected!

```
      quiz            Zquiz.V1
 Min.   : 9.00   Min.   :-2.0737630
 1st Qu.:13.00   1st Qu.:-0.8092734
 Median :17.00   Median : 0.4552163
 Mean   :15.56   Mean   : 0.0000000
 3rd Qu.:18.00   3rd Qu.: 0.7713387
 Max.   :20.00   Max.   : 1.4035835
```

FIGURE 4.22
Creating a standardized variable.

4.6 Research Question Template and Example Write-Up

As stated in the previous chapter, depending on the purpose of your research study, you may or may not write a research question that corresponds to your descriptive statistics. If the end result of your research paper is to present results from inferential statistics, it may be that your research questions correspond only to those inferential questions, and thus no question is presented to represent the descriptive statistics. That is quite common. On the other hand, if the ultimate purpose of your research study is purely descriptive in nature, then writing one or more research questions that correspond to the descriptive statistics is not only entirely appropriate, but (in most cases) absolutely necessary.

It is time again to revisit our graduate research assistant, Challie Lenge, who was reintroduced at the beginning of the chapter. As a reminder, Challie was working with Dr. Debhard, a statistics professor. Challie's task was to continue to summarize data from 25 students enrolled in a statistics course, this time paying particular attention to distributional shape and standardization. The questions posed this time by Dr. Debhard were as follows: *What is the distributional shape of the statistics quiz score? In standard deviation units, what is the relative standing to the mean of student 1 compared to student 3?* The following is a template for writing a descriptive research question for summarizing distributional shape (this may sound familiar as this was first presented in Chapter 2 when we initially discussed distributional shape). This is followed by a template for writing a research question related to standardization.

What is the distributional shape of the [variable]? In standard deviation units, what is the relative standing to the mean of [unit 1] compared to [unit 3]?

Next, we present an APA-style paragraph summarizing the results of the statistics quiz data example answering the questions posed to Marie.

The skewness value is –.598 (*SE* = .464) and the kurtosis value is –.741 (*SE* = .902). Skewness and kurtosis values within the range of ±2 (*SE*) are generally considered normal. Given our values, skewness is within the range of –.928 to +.928 and kurtosis is within the range of –1.804 and +1.804, and these would be considered normal. Another convention is that the skewness and kurtosis values should fall within an absolute value of 2.0 to be considered normal. Applying this rule, normality is still evident. The histogram with a normal curve overlay is depicted in Figure 4.15. Taken with the skewness and kurtosis statistics, these results indicate that the quiz scores are reasonably normally distributed. There is a slight negative skew such that there are more scores at the high end of the distribution than a typical normal distribution. There is also a slight negative kurtosis indicating that the distribution is slightly flatter than a normal distribution, with a few more extreme scores at the low end of the distribution. Again, however, the values are within the range of what is considered a reasonable approximation to the normal curve.

Prior to standardization, student 1 had a score of 9 and student 3 had a score of 20. The quiz score data were standardized using the unit normal formula. After standardization, student 1's score was –2.07 and student 3's score was 1.40. This suggests that student 1 was slightly more than two standard deviation units below the mean on the statistics quiz score while student 3 was nearly 1.5 standard deviation units above the mean.

4.7 Additional Resources

In the previous chapters, we have mentioned a number of excellent resources for learning statistics. As we are still in the early stages of learning statistics, there are no additional resources that we suggest that are specifically related to normal distributions and standard scores. Rather, we refer you back to earlier chapters for supplemental resources for statistics as well as statistical software.

Problems

Conceptual Problems

1. For which of the following distributions will the skewness value be zero?
   a. $N(0,1)$
   b. $N(0,2)$

c. $N(10,50)$

d. All of the above

2. For which of the following distributions will the kurtosis value be zero?

a. $N(0,1)$

b. $N(0,2)$

c. $N(10,50)$

d. All of the above

3. A set of 400 scores is approximately normally distributed with a mean of 65 and a standard deviation of 4.5. Approximately 95% of the scores would fall between which range of scores?

a. 60.5 and 69.5

b. 56 and 74

c. 51.5 and 78.5

d. 64.775 and 65.225

4. What is the percentile rank of 60 in the distribution of $N(60,100)$?

a. 10

b. 50

c. 60

d. 100

5. The skewness value is calculated for a set of data and is found to be equal to +2.75. This indicates that the distribution of scores is which of the following?

a. Highly negatively skewed

b. Slightly negatively skewed

c. Symmetrical

d. Slightly positively skewed

e. Highly positively skewed

6. The kurtosis value is calculated for a set of data and is found to be equal to +2.75. This indicates that the distribution of scores is which of the following?

a. Mesokurtic

b. Platykurtic

c. Leptokurtic

d. Cannot be determined

7. True or false? For a normal distribution, all percentiles above the 50th must yield positive *z* scores.

8. True or false? If one knows the raw score, the mean, and the *z* score, then one can calculate the value of the standard deviation.

9. True or false? In a normal distribution, a *z* score of 1.0 has a percentile rank of 34.

10. True or false? The mean of a normal distribution of scores is always 1.

11. If in a distribution of 200 IQ scores, the mean is considerably above the median, then the distribution is which of the following?

a. Negatively skewed
b. Symmetrical
c. Positively skewed
d. Bimodal

12. Which of the following is indicative of a distribution that has a skewness value of −3.98 and a kurtosis value of −6.72?
a. A left tail that is pulled to the left and a very flat distribution
b. A left tail that is pulled to the left and a distribution that is neither very peaked nor very flat
c. A right tail that is pulled to the right and a very peaked distribution
d. A right tail that is pulled to the right and a very flat distribution

13. Which of the following is indicative of a distribution that has a kurtosis value of +4.09?
a. Leptokurtic distribution
b. Mesokurtic distribution
c. Platykurtic distribution
d. Positive skewness
e. Negative skewness

14. For which of the following distributions will the kurtosis value be greatest?

A	*f*	B	*f*	C	*f*	D	*f*
11	3	11	4	11	1	11	1
12	4	12	4	12	3	12	5
13	6	13	4	13	12	13	8
14	4	14	4	14	3	14	5
15	3	15	4	15	1	15	1

a. Distribution A
b. Distribution B
c. Distribution C
d. Distribution D

15. The distribution of variable *X* has a mean of 10 and is positively skewed. The distribution of variable *Y* has the same mean of 10 and is negatively skewed. I assert that the medians for the two variables must also be the same. Am I correct?

16. True or false? The variance of *z* scores is always equal to the variance of the raw scores for the same variable.

17. True or false? The mode has the largest value of the central tendency measures in a positively skewed distribution.

18. Which of the following represents the highest performance in a standard normal distribution?
a. P_{90}
b. $z = +1.00$
c. Q_3
d. IQ = 115

19. A student came home with two test scores, $z = +1$ in math and $z = -1$ in biology. For which test did the student perform better?

20. A psychologist analyzing data from creative intelligence scores finds a relatively normal distribution with a population mean of 100 and population standard deviation of 10. When standardized into a unit normal distribution, what is the mean of the (standardized) creative intelligence scores?

a. 0

b. 70

c. 100

d. Cannot be determined from the information provided

21. A distribution has the following parameters: mean = 6, median = 4, mode = 2. Which of the following is suggested?

a. Negatively skewed distribution

b. Normal distribution

c. Positively skewed distribution

d. Cannot be determined from these values

22. A distribution has the following parameters: mean = 10, median = 16, mode = 20. Which of the following is suggested?

a. Negatively skewed distribution

b. Normal distribution

c. Positively skewed distribution

d. Cannot be determined from these values

23. What is the percentile rank of a standardized normal score of 2.0?

a. 2nd percentile

b. 34th percentile

c. 50th percentile

d. 98th percentile

24. What is the percentile rank of a standardized normal score of −2.0?

a. 2nd percentile

b. 34th percentile

c. 50th percentile

d. 98th percentile

25. Which of the following graphs reflects a negatively skewed distribution?

a.

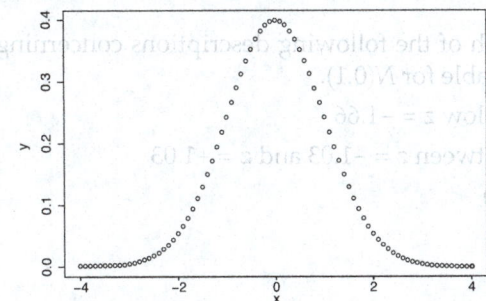

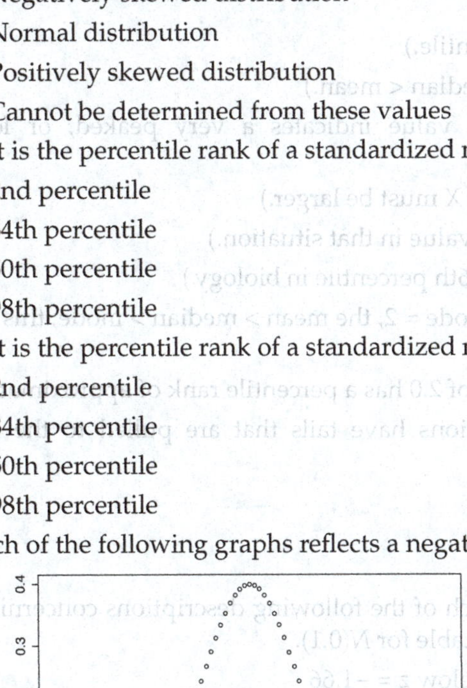

b.

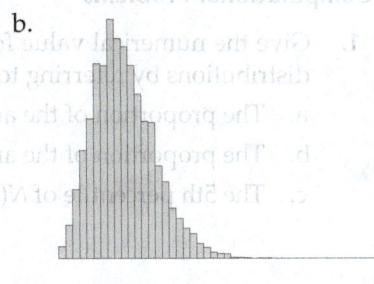

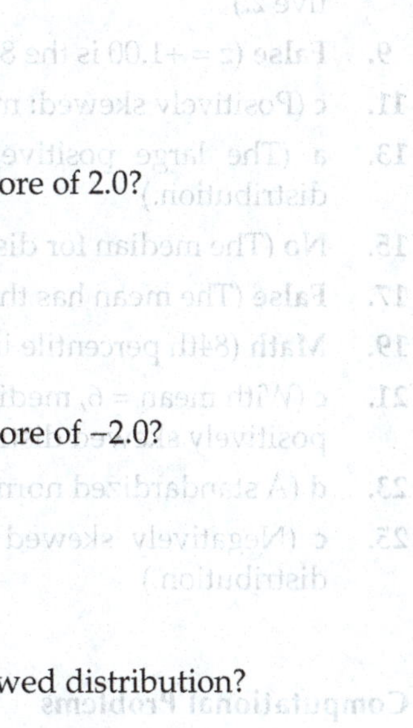

c.

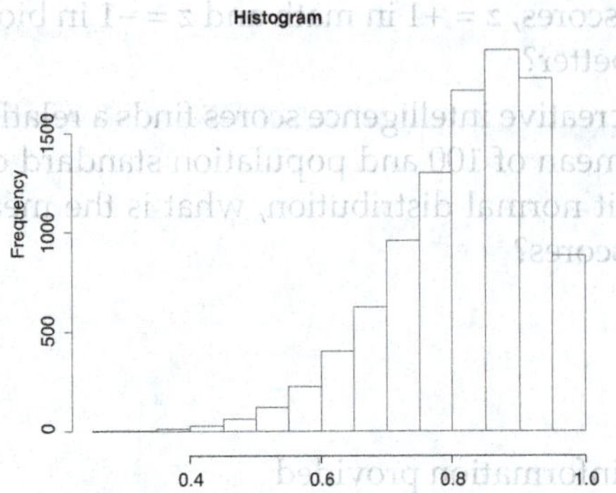

d.

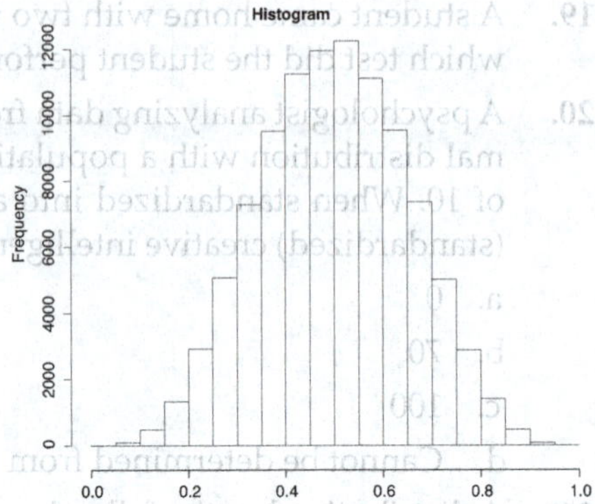

Answers to Conceptual Problems

1. **d** (Skewness is zero for normal.)
3. **b** (±2.0 standard deviations.)
5. **e** (High positive value = high positive skew.)
7. **True** (Mean = median for a normal distribution, so above the 50th percentile = positive z.)
9. **False** ($z = +1.00$ is the 84th percentile.)
11. **c** (Positively skewed: mode < median < mean.)
13. **a** (The large positive kurtosis value indicates a very peaked, or leptokurtic, distribution.)
15. **No** (The median for distribution X must be larger.)
17. **False** (The mean has the largest value in that situation.)
19. **Math** (84th percentile in math, 16th percentile in biology.)
21. **c** (With mean = 6, median = 4, mode = 2, the mean > median > mode; this suggests a positively skewed distribution.)
23. **d** (A standardized normal score of 2.0 has a percentile rank of approximately 98.)
25. **c** (Negatively skewed distributions have tails that are pulled to the left of the distribution.)

Computational Problems

1. Give the numerical value for each of the following descriptions concerning normal distributions by referring to the table for $N(0,1)$.
   a. The proportion of the area below $z = -1.66$
   b. The proportion of the area between $z = -1.03$ and $z = +1.03$
   c. The 5th percentile of $N(20,36)$

d. The 99th percentile of $N(30,49)$
e. The percentile rank of the score 25 in $N(20,36)$
f. The percentile rank of the score 24.5 in $N(30,49)$
g. The proportion of the area in $N(36,64)$ between the scores of 18 and 42

2. Give the numerical value for each of the following descriptions concerning normal distributions by referring to the table for $N(0,1)$.
a. The proportion of the area below $z = -.80$
b. The proportion of the area between $z = -1.49$ and $z = +1.49$
c. The 2.5th percentile of $N(50,81)$
d. The 50th percentile of $N(40,64)$
e. The percentile rank of the score 45 in $N(50,81)$
f. The percentile rank of the score 53 in $N(50,81)$
g. The proportion of the area in $N(36,64)$ between the scores of 19.7 and 45.1

3. Give the numerical value for each of the following descriptions concerning normal distributions by referring to the table for $N(0,1)$.
a. The proportion of the area below $z = +1.50$
b. The proportion of the area between $z = -.75$ and $z = +2.25$
c. The 15th percentile of $N(12,9)$
d. The 80th percentile of $N(100{,}000,5000)$
e. The percentile rank of the score 300 in $N(200,2500)$
f. The percentile rank of the score 61 in $N(60,9)$
g. The proportion of the area in $N(500,1600)$ between the scores of 350 and 550

4. Using the Ch6.HW4.sav data, compute and interpret the distributional shape for the variables "learning strategies" and "coping strategies" based on mean, median, mode, skew, kurtosis, and histograms.

Answers to Computational Problems

1. a = .0485; b = .6970; c = 10.16; d = 46.31; e = approximately 79.67%; f = approximately 21.48%; g = 76.12%

3. a = .9332; b = .7611; c = 8.91; d = 100059.40; e = approximately 97.72%; f = approximately 62.93%; g = 20%

Interpretive Problems

1. Select one interval or ratio variable from the survey1 dataset on the website (e.g., one idea is to select the same variable you selected for the interpretive problem from Chapter 3).
a. Determine the measures of central tendency, dispersion, skewness, and kurtosis.

b. Write a paragraph that summarizes the findings, particularly commenting on the distributional shape.

2. Use the same variable selected in the previous problem, and standardize it.
   a. Determine the measures of central tendency, dispersion, skewness, and kurtosis for the standardized variable.
   b. Compare and contrast the differences between the standardized results and unstandardized results.

5

Introduction to Probability and Sample Statistics

Chapter Outline

Key Concepts

1. Probability
2. Inferential statistics
3. Simple random sampling (with and without replacement)
4. Sampling distribution of the mean
5. Variance and standard error of the mean (sampling error)
6. Confidence intervals (point vs. interval estimation)
7. Central limit theorem

In Chapter 4 we extended our discussion of descriptive statistics. We considered the following three general topics: the normal distribution, standard scores, and skewness and kurtosis. In this chapter we begin to move from descriptive statistics into inferential statistics (in which normally distributed data plays a major role). The two basic topics described in this chapter are (a) probability and (b) sampling and estimation. First, as a brief introduction to probability, we discuss the importance of probability in statistics, define probability in a conceptual and computational sense, and discuss the notion of intuition versus probability. Second, under sampling and estimation, we formally move into inferential statistics by considering the following topics: simple random sampling (and briefly other types of sampling), and estimation of population parameters and sampling distributions. Concepts to be discussed include probability, inferential statistics, simple random sampling (with and without replacement), sampling distribution of the mean, variance and standard error of the mean (sampling error), confidence intervals (point vs. interval estimation), and central limit theorem. Our objectives are that by the end of this chapter, you will be able to (a) understand the most basic concepts of probability; (b) understand and conduct simple random sampling; and (c) understand, determine, and interpret the results from the estimation of population parameters via a sample.

5.1 Brief Introduction to Probability

The area of probability became important and began to be developed during the Middle Ages (17th and 18th centuries) when royalty and other well-to-do gamblers consulted with mathematicians for advice on games of chance. For example, in poker if you hold two jacks, what are your chances of drawing a third jack? Or in craps, what is the chance of rolling a 7 with two dice? During that time, probability was also used for more practical purposes, such as to help determine life expectancy to underwrite life insurance policies. Considerable development in probability has obviously taken place since that time. In this section, we discuss the importance of probability, provide a definition of probability, and consider the notion of intuition versus probability. Although there is much more to the topic of probability, here we simply discuss those aspects of probability necessary for the remainder of the text. For additional information on probability, take a look at texts by Rudas (2004) or Tijms (2004).

5.1.1 Importance of Probability

Let us first consider why probability is important in statistics. A researcher is out collecting some sample data from a group of individuals (e.g., students, parents, teachers, voters, corporations, animals, etc.). Some descriptive statistics are generated from the sample data. Say the sample mean, $\bar{X}$, is computed for several variables (e.g., number of hours of study time per week, grade point average, confidence in a political candidate, widget sales, animal food consumption). To what extent can we generalize from these sample statistics to their corresponding population parameters? For example, if the mean amount of study time per week for a given sample of graduate students is $\bar{X} = 10$ hours, to what extent are we able to generalize to the population of graduate students on the value of the population mean, μ?

As we see, beginning in this chapter, inferential statistics involve making an inference about population parameters from sample statistics. We would like to know (a) how much uncertainty exists in our sample statistics, as well as (b) how much confidence to place in our sample statistics. These questions can be addressed by assigning a probability value to an inference. As we show beginning in Chapter 6, probability can also be used to make statements about areas under a distribution of scores (e.g., the normal distribution). First, however, we need to provide a definition of probability.

5.1.2 Definition of Probability

In order to more easily define probability, consider a simple example of rolling a six-sided die (as there are dice with different numbers of sides). Each of the six sides, of course, has anywhere from one to six dots. Each side has a different number of dots. What is the probability of rolling a 4? Technically, there are six possible outcomes or events that can occur. One can also determine how many times a specific outcome or event actually can occur. These two concepts are used to define and compute the probability of a particular outcome or event by

$$p(A) = \frac{S}{T}$$

where $p(A)$ is the probability that outcome or event A will occur, S is the number of times that the specific outcome or event A can occur, and T is the total number of outcomes or events possible. Let us revisit our example, the probability of rolling a 4. A 4 can occur only once, thus $S = 1$; and six possible values can be rolled, thus $T = 6$. Therefore, the probability of rolling a 4 is determined by

$$p(4) = \frac{S}{T} = \frac{1}{6}$$

This assumes, however, that the die is *unbiased*, which means that the die is fair and that the probability of obtaining any of the six outcomes is the same. For a fair, unbiased die, the probability of obtaining any outcome is 1/6. Gamblers have been known to possess an unfair, biased die such that the probability of obtaining a particular outcome is different from 1/6 (e.g., to cheat their opponent by shaving one side of the die).

Consider one other classic probability example. Imagine you have an urn (or other container). Inside of the urn and out of view are a total of nine balls (thus $T = 9$). Six of the balls are red (event A; $S = 6$), and the other three balls are green (event B; $S = 3$). Your task is to draw one ball out of the urn (without looking) and then observe its color. The probability of each of these two events occurring on the *first draw* is as follows:

$$p(A) = \frac{S}{T} = \frac{6}{9} = \frac{2}{3}$$

$$p(B) = \frac{S}{T} = \frac{3}{9} = \frac{1}{3}$$

Thus, the probability of drawing a red ball on the first draw is 2/3 and the probability of drawing a green ball is 1/3.

Two notions become evident in thinking about these examples. *First, the sum of the probabilities for all distinct or independent events is precisely one.* In other words, if we take each distinct event and compute its probability, then the sum of those probabilities must be equal to one so as to account for all possible outcomes. *Second, the probability of any given event (a) cannot exceed one, and (b) cannot be less than zero.* Part (a) should be obvious in that the sum of the probabilities for all events cannot exceed one, and therefore the probability of any one event cannot exceed one either (it makes no sense to talk about an event occurring more than all of the time). An event would have a probability of one if no other event can possibly occur, such as the probability that you are currently breathing. For part (b) no event can have a negative probability (it makes no sense to talk about an event occurring less than never); however, an event could have a zero probability if the event can never occur. For instance, in our urn example, one could never draw a purple ball (as only red and green balls are possibilities).

5.1.3 Intuition vs. Probability

At this point you are probably thinking that probability is an interesting topic. However, without extensive training to think in a probabilistic fashion, people tend to let their intuition guide them. This is all well and good, except that intuition can often guide you to a different conclusion than probability. Let us examine two classic examples to illustrate this dilemma. The first classic example is known as the "birthday problem." Imagine you are in a room of 23 people. You ask each person to write down their birthday (month and day) on a piece of paper. What do you think is the probability that in a room of 23 people at least two will have the same birthday?

Assume first that we are dealing with 365 different possible birthdays, where leap year (February 29) is not considered. Also assume the sample of 23 people is randomly drawn from some population of people. Taken together, this implies that each of the 365 different possible birthdays has the same probability (i.e., 1/365). An intuitive thinker might have the following thought processing. "There are 365 different birthdays in a year and there are 23 people in the sample. Therefore, the probability of two people having the same birthday must be close to zero." We have tried this on our introductory classes often and students' guesses are usually around zero.

Intuition has led us astray and we have not used the proper thought processing. True, there are 365 days and 23 people. However, the question really deals with *pairs of people*. The number of different possible pairs of people is fairly large (i.e., person 1 with 2, 1 with 3, etc.); specifically, the total number of different pairs of people is equal to $n(n - 1)/2 = 23(22)/2 = 253$. But all we need is for one *pair* to have the same birthday. While the probability computations are a little complex (see Appendix 5.A at the end of the chapter), the probability that at least two individuals will have the same birthday in a group of 23 is equal to .507. *That's right, about one-half of the time, a group of 23 people will have 2 or more with the same birthday.* Our introductory classes typically have between 20 and 40 students. More often than not, we are able to find two students with the same birthday. One year one of us wrote each birthday on the board so that students could see the data. The first two students selected actually had the same birthday, so our point was very quickly shown. What was the probability of that event occurring?

The second classic example is the "gambler's fallacy," sometimes referred to as the "law of averages." This works for any game of chance, so imagine you are flipping a coin. Obviously there are two possible outcomes from a coin flip, heads and tails. Assume the coin is fair and unbiased such that the probability of flipping a head is the same as flipping a tail, that is, .5. After flipping the coin nine times, you have observed a tail every time. What is the probability of obtaining a head on the next flip?

An intuitive thinker might have the following thought processing. "I have just observed a tail each of the last nine flips. According to the law of averages, the probability of observing a head on the next flip must be near certainty. The probability must be nearly one." We also try this on our introductory students and their guesses are almost always near one.

Intuition has led us astray once again, as we have not used the proper thought processing. True, we have just observed nine consecutive tails. However, the question really deals with the *probability of the 10th flip being a head*, not the probability of obtaining 10 consecutive tails. The probability of a head is always .5 with a fair, unbiased coin. The coin has no memory; thus, the probability of tossing a head after nine consecutive tails is the same as the probability of tossing a head after nine consecutive heads, .5. In technical terms, *the probabilities of each event (each toss) are independent of one another.* In other words, the probability of flipping a head is the same regardless of the preceding flips. This is not the same as the probability of tossing 10 consecutive heads, which is rather small (approximately .0010). So when you are gambling at the casino and have lost the last nine games, do not believe that you are guaranteed to win the next game. You can just as easily lose game 10 as you did game 1. The same goes if you have won a number of games. You can just as easily win the next game as you did game 1. To some extent, the casinos count on their customers playing the gambler's fallacy to make a profit.

5.2 Sampling and Estimation

In Chapter 3 we spent some time discussing sample statistics, including the measures of central tendency and dispersion. In this section we expand upon that discussion by defining inferential statistics, describing different types of sampling, and then moving into the implications of such sampling in terms of estimation and sampling distributions.

Consider the situation where we have a population of graduate students. **Population parameters** (which are characteristics of a population) could be determined, such as the population size (N), the population mean (μ), the population variance (σ^2), and the population standard deviation (σ). Through some method of sampling, we then take a sample of students from this population. **Sample statistics**, which are just characteristics of a sample, could be determined, such as the sample size (n), the sample mean ($\bar{X}$), the sample variance (s^2), and the sample standard deviation (s).

How often do we actually ever deal with population data? Except when dealing with very small, well-defined populations, we almost never deal with population data. (There are always exceptions; however, our experience dictates that it is almost always the case that we are working with sample data.) The main reason for this is cost, in terms of time, personnel, and economics. *This means then that we are almost always dealing with sample data.* With descriptive statistics, dealing with sample data is very straightforward, and we only need to make sure we are using the appropriate sample statistic equation. However, what if we want to take a sample statistic and make some generalization about its relevant population parameter? For example, you have computed a sample mean on grade point average (GPA) of $\bar{X} = 3.25$ for a sample of 25 graduate students at State University. You would like to make some generalizations from this sample mean to the population mean (m) at State University. How do we do this? To what extent can we make such a generalization? How confident are we that this sample mean actually represents the population mean?

This brings us to the field of inferential statistics. We define **inferential statistics** as *statistics that allow us to make an inference or generalization from a sample to the population.* In terms of reasoning, *inductive reasoning* is used to infer from the specific (the sample) to the general (the population). Thus, inferential statistics is the answer to all of our preceding questions about generalizing from sample statistics to population parameters. *How* the sample is derived, however, is important in determining to what extent the statistical results we derive can be inferred from the sample back to the population. Thus, it is important to spend a little time talking about simple random sampling, the only sampling procedure that directly allows generalizations to be made from the sample to the population. Although there are statistical means to correct for non-simple random samples, they are beyond the scope of this textbook. Researchers may wish to refer to references, such as Skinner, Holt, and Smith (1989). In the remainder of this section, and in much of the remainder of this text, we take up the details of inferential statistics for many different procedures.

5.2.1 Simple Random Sampling

A sample can be drawn from a population in several different ways. In this section we introduce simple random sampling, which is a commonly used type of sampling. It is also assumed for many inferential statistics (beginning in Chapter 6), as it is the only sampling procedure that *directly* allows generalizations to be made from the sample to the population. **Simple random sampling** is defined as the *process of selecting sample observations from a population so that each observation has an equal and independent probability of being selected.* If the sampling process is truly random, then (a) each observation in the population has an equal chance of being included in the sample, and (b) each observation selected into the sample is independent of (or not affected by) every other selection. Thus, a volunteer or "street-corner" sample would not meet the first condition because members of the population who do not frequent that particular street corner have no chance of being included in the sample.

In addition, if the selection of spouses *required* the corresponding selection of their respective mates, then the second condition would not be met. For example, if the selection of Mr. Joe Smith III also required the selection of his wife, then these two selections are not independent of one another. Because we selected Mr. Joe Smith III, we must also therefore select his wife. Note that through independent sampling it is possible for Mr. Smith and his wife to both be sampled, but it is not required. *Thus, independence implies that each observation is selected without regard to any other observation sampled.*

We also would fail to have equal and independent probability of selection if the sampling procedure employed was something other than a simple random sample—because it is only with a simple random sample that we have met the conditions of equal probability and independence. (Although there are statistical means to correct for non-simple random samples, they are beyond the scope of this textbook.) This concept of **independence** is an important assumption that we will become acquainted with more in the remaining chapters. If we have independence, then generalizations from the sample back to the population can be made (you may remember this as *external validity*, which was likely introduced in your research methods course) (see Figure 5.1). Because of the connection between simple random sampling and independence, let us expand our discussion on the two types of simple random sampling.

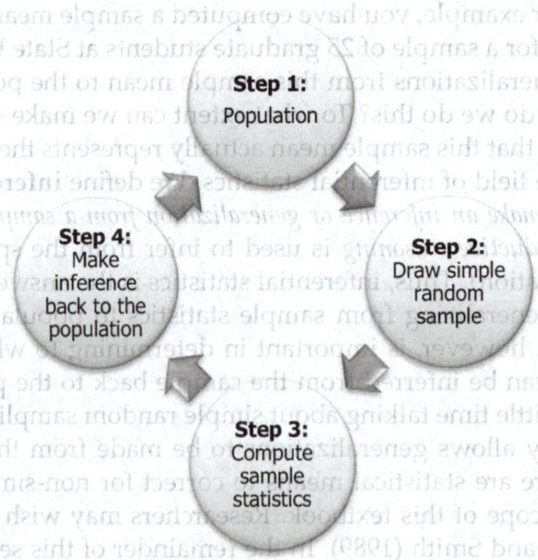

FIGURE 5.1
Cycle of Inference.

5.2.1.1 Simple Random Sampling With Replacement

There are two specific types of simple random sampling. **Simple random sampling with replacement** is conducted as follows. The first observation is selected from the population into the sample, and that observation is then replaced back into the population. The second observation is selected and then replaced in the population. This continues until a sample of the desired size is obtained. *The key here is that each observation sampled is placed back into the population and could be selected again.*

This scenario makes sense in certain applications and not in others. For example, return to our coin-flipping example where we now want to flip a coin 100 times (i.e., a sample size of 100). How does this operate in the context of sampling? We flip the coin (e.g., heads) and record the result. This "head" becomes the first observation in our sample. This observation is then placed back into the population. Then a second observation is made and is placed back into the population. This continues until our sample size requirement of 100 is reached. In this particular scenario we always sample with replacement, and we automatically do so even if we have never heard of sampling with replacement. If no replacement took place, then we could only ever have a sample size of two, one "head" and one "tail."

5.2.1.2 Simple Random Sampling Without Replacement

In other scenarios, sampling with replacement does not make sense. For example, say we are conducting a poll for the next major election by randomly selecting 100 students (the sample) from among all students who attend a local university (the population). As each student is selected into the sample, they are removed and cannot be sampled again. It simply would make no sense if our sample of 100 students only contained 78 different students due to replacement (as some students were polled more than once). Our polling example represents the other type of simple random sampling, this time *without replacement*. **Simple random sampling without replacement** is conducted in a similar fashion except that *once an observation is selected for inclusion in the sample, it is not replaced and cannot be selected a second time.*

5.2.1.3 Other Types of Sampling

Several other types of sampling are possible. These other types of sampling include convenience sampling (i.e., volunteer or "street-corner" sampling previously mentioned), systematic sampling (e.g., select every 10th observation from the population into the sample), cluster sampling (i.e., sample groups or clusters of observations and include all members of the selected clusters in the sample), stratified sampling (i.e., sampling within subgroups or strata to ensure adequate representation of each strata), and multistage sampling (e.g., stratify at one stage and randomly sample at another stage or randomly select clusters, and then within clusters, randomly select individual units). These types of sampling are beyond the scope of this text, and the interested reader is referred to sampling texts (e.g., Fink, 2002; Jaeger, 1984; Kalton, 1983; Levy & Lemeshow, 2011; Sudman, 1976).

5.2.2 Estimation of Population Parameters and Sampling Distributions

Take as an example the situation where we select one random sample of n females (e.g., $n = 20$), measure their weight, and then compute the mean weight of the sample. We find the mean of this first sample to be 102 pounds and denote it by $\bar{X}_1 = 102$, where the subscript identifies the first sample. This one sample mean is known as a **point estimate** of the population mean, μ, as it is simply one value or point. We can then proceed to collect weight data from a second sample of *n* females and find that $\bar{X}_2 = 110$. Next we collect weight data from a third sample of *n* females and find that $\bar{X}_3 = 119$. Imagine that we go on to collect such data from many other samples of size *n* and compute a sample mean for each of those samples.

5.2.2.1 Sampling Distribution of the Mean

At this point we have a *collection of sample means*, which we can use to construct a frequency distribution of sample means. This frequency distribution is formally known as the **sampling distribution of the mean**. To better illustrate this new distribution, let us take a very small population from which we can take many samples. Here we define our population of observations as follows: 1, 2, 3, 5, 9 (in other words, we have five values in our population). As the entire population is known here, we can better illustrate the important underlying concepts. We can determine that the population mean $\mu_X = 4$ and the population variance $\sigma_X^2 = 8$, where *X* indicates the variable we are referring to. Let us first take all possible samples from this population of size 2 (i.e., $n = 2$) with replacement. As there are only five observations, there will be 25 possible samples, as shown in the upper portion of Table 5.1, called "Samples." Each entry represents the two observations for a particular sample. For instance, in row 1 and column 4, we see 1,5. This indicates that the first observation is a 1 and the second observation is a 5. If sampling was done without replacement, then the diagonal of the table from upper left to lower right would not exist. For instance, a 1,1 sample could not be selected if sampling without replacement.

Now that we have all possible samples of $n = 2$, let us compute the sample means for each of the 25 samples. The sample means are shown in the middle portion of Table 5.1, called "Sample means." Just eyeballing the table, we see the means range from 1 to 9 with numerous different values in between. We then compute the mean of the 25 sample means to be 4, as shown in the bottom portion of Table 5.1, called "Mean of the sample means."

This is a matter for some discussion, so consider the following three points. *First, the distribution of $\bar{X}$ for all possible samples of size n is known as the sampling distribution of the mean.* In other words, if we were to take all of the "sample mean" values in Table 5.1 and construct a histogram of those values, then that is what is referred to as a *sampling distribution of the mean*. It is simply the distribution (i.e., histogram) of all the sample mean values. *Second, the mean of the sampling distribution of the mean for all possible samples of size n is equal to $\mu_{\bar{X}}$.* As the mean of the sampling distribution of the mean is denoted by $\mu_{\bar{X}}$ (the mean of the $\bar{X}$s), then we see for the example that $\mu_{\bar{X}} = \mu_X = 4$. In other words, the mean of the sampling distribution of the mean is simply the average of all of the sample means in Table 5.1. The mean of the sampling distribution of the mean will always be equal to the population mean.

Third, we define sampling error in this context as the difference (or deviation) between a particular sample mean and the population mean, denoted as $\bar{X} - \mu_X$. A *positive sampling error* indicates a sample mean greater than the population mean, where the sample mean is known as an *overestimate* of the population mean. A *zero sampling error* indicates a sample mean exactly

TABLE 5.1
All Possible Samples and Sample Means for $n = 2$ From the Population of 1, 2, 3, 5, 9

First Observation	Second Observation				
Samples	**1**	**2**	**3**	**5**	**9**
1	1,1	1,2	1,3	1,5	1,9
2	2,1	2,2	2,3	2,5	2,9
3	3,1	3,2	3,3	3,5	3,9
5	5,1	5,2	5,3	5,5	5,9
9	9,1	9,2	9,3	9,5	9,9
	Sample means				
1	1.0	1.5	2.0	3.0	5.0
2	1.5	2.0	2.5	3.5	5.5
3	2.0	2.5	3.0	4.0	6.0
5	3.0	3.5	4.0	5.0	7.0
9	5.0	5.5	6.0	7.0	9.0
	$\sum \bar{X} = 12.5$	$\sum \bar{X} = 15.0$	$\sum \bar{X} = 17.5$	$\sum \bar{X} = 22.5$	$\sum \bar{X} = 32.5$

Mean of the sample means:

$$\mu_{\bar{X}} = \frac{\sum \bar{X}}{\textit{number of samples}} = \frac{100}{25} = 4.0$$

Variance of the sample means:

$$\sigma_{\bar{X}}^2 = \frac{(\textit{number of samples})\left(\sum \bar{X}^2\right) - \left(\sum \bar{X}\right)^2}{(\textit{number of samples})^2} = \frac{(25)(500) - (100)^2}{(25)^2} = \frac{(25)(500) - 10{,}000}{625} = 4.0$$

equal to the population mean. A *negative sampling error* indicates a sample mean less than the population mean, where the sample mean is known as an *underestimate* of the population mean. As a researcher, *we want the sampling error to be as close to zero as possible to suggest that the sample reflects the population well.*

5.2.2.2 Variance Error of the Mean

Now that we have a measure of the mean of the sampling distribution of the mean, let us consider the variance of this distribution. We define the variance of the sampling distribution of the mean, known as the **variance error of the mean**, as $\sigma_{\bar{X}}^2$. This will provide us with a dispersion measure of the extent to which the sample means vary and will also provide some indication of the confidence we can place in a particular sample mean. The variance error of the mean is computed as

$$\sigma^2_{\bar{X}} = \frac{\sigma^2_X}{n}$$

where σ^2_X is the population variance of X and n is the sample size. For the example, we have already determined that $\sigma^2_X = 8$ and that $n = 2$; therefore,

$$\sigma^2_{\bar{X}} = \frac{\sigma^2_X}{n} = \frac{8}{2} = 4$$

This is verified in the bottom portion of Table 5.1, "Variance of the sample means," where the variance error is computed from the collection of sample means.

What will happen if we *increase* the size of the sample? If we increase the sample size to $n = 4$, then the variance error is reduced to 2. Thus we see that *as the size of the sample* n *increases, the magnitude of the sampling error decreases*. Why? Conceptually, as sample size increases, we are sampling a larger portion of the population. In doing so, we are also obtaining a sample that is likely more representative of the population. In addition, the larger the sample size, the less likely it is to obtain a sample mean that is far from the population mean. Thus, *as sample size increases, we hone in closer and closer to the population mean and have less and less sampling error.*

For example, say we are sampling from a voting district with a population of 5000 voters. A survey is developed to assess how satisfied the district voters are with their local state representative. Assume the survey generates a 100-point satisfaction scale. First we determine that the population mean of satisfaction is 75. Next we take samples of different sizes. For a sample size of 1, we find sample means that range from 0 to 100 (i.e., each mean really only represents a single observation). For a sample size of 10, we find sample means that range from 50 to 95. For a sample size of 100, we find sample means that range from 70 to 80. We see then that *as sample size increases, our sample means become closer and closer to the population mean, and the variability of those sample means becomes smaller and smaller.*

5.2.2.3 Standard Error of the Mean

We can also compute the standard deviation of the sampling distribution of the mean, known as the **standard error of the mean**, by

$$\sigma_{\bar{X}} = \frac{\sigma_X}{\sqrt{n}}$$

Thus, for our example we have

$$\sigma_{\bar{X}} = \frac{\sigma_X}{\sqrt{n}} = \frac{2.8284}{\sqrt{2}} = 2$$

Because the applied researcher typically does not know the population variance, the population variance error of the mean and the population standard error of the mean can be estimated by the following, respectively:

$$s_{\bar{X}}^2 = \frac{s_X^2}{n}$$

and

$$s_{\bar{X}} = \frac{s_X}{\sqrt{n}}$$

5.2.2.4 Confidence Intervals

Thus far we have illustrated how a sample mean is a point estimate of the population mean and how a variance error gives us some sense of the variability among the sample means. Putting these concepts together, we can also build an **interval estimate** for the population mean to give us a sense of how confident we are in our particular sample mean. We can form a **confidence interval** around a particular sample mean as follows. As we learned in Chapter 4, for a normal distribution 68% of the distribution falls within one standard deviation of the mean. A 68% confidence interval (CI) of a sample mean can be formed as follows:

$$68\%CI = \bar{X} \pm (1.00)(\sigma_{\bar{X}})$$

Conceptually, this means that if we form 68% confidence intervals for 100 sample means, then 68 of those 100 intervals would contain or include the population mean (it does *not* mean that there is a 68% probability of the interval containing the population mean—the interval either contains it or does not). Because the applied researcher typically only has one sample mean and does not know the population mean, he or she has no way of knowing if this one confidence interval actually contains the population mean or not. If one wanted to be more confident in a sample mean, then a 90% CI, a 95% CI, or a 99% CI could be formed as follows:

$$90\%CI = \bar{X} \pm (1.645)(\sigma_{\bar{X}})$$

$$95\%CI = \bar{X} \pm (1.96)(\sigma_{\bar{X}})$$

$$99\%CI = \bar{X} \pm (2.5758)(\sigma_{\bar{X}})$$

Thus, for the 90% CI, the population mean will be contained in 90 out of 100 CIs; for the 95% CI, the population mean will be contained in 95 out of 100 CIs; and for the 99% CI, the population mean will be contained in 99 out of 100 CIs. The critical values of 1.645, 1.96, and 2.5758 come from the standard unit normal distribution table (Table A.1 in the Appendix) and indicate the width of the confidence interval. The earlier example of a 68% CI refers to the standard unit normal distribution table as well, with $z \simeq .84$. *Wider confidence intervals, such as the 99% CI, enable greater confidence*. For example, with a sample mean of 70 and a standard error of the mean of 3, the following confidence intervals result: 68% CI = (67, 73) [i.e., ranging from 67 to 73]; 90% CI = (65.065, 74.935); 95% CI = (64.12, 75.88); and 99% CI = (62.2726, 77.7274). We can see here that to be assured that 99% of the confidence intervals contain the population mean, then our interval must be wider (i.e., ranging from about 62.27 to 77.73, or a range of about 15) than the confidence intervals that are lesser (e.g., the 95% confidence interval ranges from 64.12 to 75.88, or a range of about 11).

In general, a confidence interval for any level of confidence (i.e., #% CI) can be computed by the following general formula:

$$\#\%CI = \bar{X} \pm (z_{CV})(\sigma_{\bar{X}})$$

where z_{cv} is the critical value taken from the standard unit normal distribution table for that particular level of confidence, and the other values are as before.

5.2.2.5 Central Limit Theorem

In our discussion of confidence intervals, we used the normal distribution to help determine the width of the intervals. Many inferential statistics assume the population distribution is normal in shape. Because we are looking at sampling distributions in this chapter, does the shape of the original population distribution have any relationship to the sampling distribution of the mean we obtain? For example, if the population distribution is nonnormal, what form does the sampling distribution of the mean take (i.e., is the sampling distribution of the mean also nonnormal)? There is a nice concept, known as the central limit theorem, to assist us here. The **central limit theorem** *states that as sample size* n *increases, the sampling distribution of the mean from a random sample of size* n *more closely approximates a normal distribution. If the population distribution is normal in shape, then the sampling distribution of the mean is also normal in shape. If the population distribution is not normal in shape, then the sampling distribution of the mean becomes more nearly normal as sample size increases*. This concept is graphically depicted in Figure 5.2.

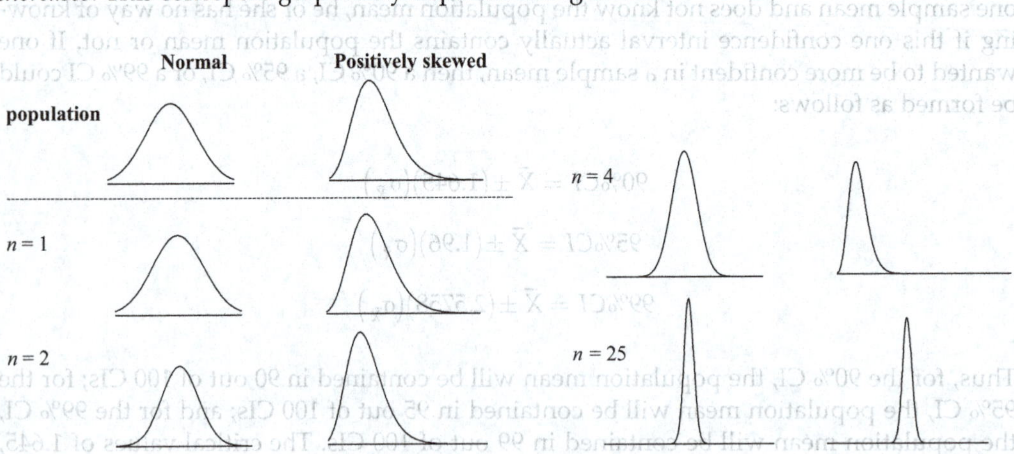

FIGURE 5.2
Central limit theorem for normal and positively skewed population distributions.

The top row of Figure 5.2 depicts two population distributions, the left one being normal and the right one being positively skewed. The remaining rows are for the various sampling distributions, depending on the sample size. The second row shows the sampling distributions of the mean for $n = 1$. Note that these sampling distributions look precisely like the population distributions, as each observation is literally a sample mean. The next row gives the sampling distributions for $n = 2$; here we see for the skewed population that the sampling distribution is slightly less skewed. This is because the more extreme observations are now being averaged in with less extreme observations, yielding less extreme means. For $n = 4$ the sampling distribution in the skewed case is even less skewed than for $n = 2$. Eventually we reach the $n = 25$ sampling distribution, where the sampling distribution for the skewed case is nearly normal and nearly matches the sampling distribution for the normal case. This phenomenon will occur for other nonnormal population distributions as well (e.g., negatively skewed). The moral of the story here is a good one. *If the population distribution is nonnormal, then this will have minimal effect on the sampling distribution of the mean except for rather small samples.* This can come into play with inferential statistics when the assumption of normality is not satisfied, as we see in later chapters.

5.3 Additional Resources

This chapter is meant to serve as a concise and general introduction to probability, sampling, and related concepts. For readers who want more in-depth and comprehensive coverage, numerous superb references are available to assist in learning more about concepts introduced in this chapter. A number of these have already been cited. Additional resources you may wish to consider include the following:

- Probabilities in the context of everyday examples (Olofsson, 2007).
- A general introduction to probability and statistics (Kinney, 2015).
- An edited work that is a compilation of papers related to teaching and learning probability, valuable both to those teaching probability as well as those learning probability (Batanero & Chernoff, 2018).

Appendix: Probability that at Least Two Individuals Have the Same Birthday

This probability can be shown by either of the following equations. Note that there are $n = 23$ individuals in the room. One method is as follows:

$$1-\left(\frac{(365)(364)(363)\ldots(365-n+1)}{365^{n}}\right)=1-\left(\frac{(365)(364)(363)\ldots(343)}{365^{23}}\right)=.507$$

An equivalent method is as follows:

$$1-\left[\left(\frac{365}{365}\right)\left(\frac{364}{365}\right)\left(\frac{363}{365}\right)\cdots\left(\frac{365-n+1}{365}\right)\right]=1-\left[\left(\frac{365}{365}\right)\left(\frac{364}{365}\right)\left(\frac{363}{365}\right)\cdots\left(\frac{343}{365}\right)\right]=.507$$

Problems

Conceptual Problems

1. The standard error of the mean is which of the following?
   a. Standard deviation of a sample distribution
   b. Standard deviation of the population distribution
   c. Standard deviation of the sampling distribution of the mean
   d. Mean of the sampling distribution of the standard deviation
2. An unbiased six-sided die is tossed on two consecutive trials and the first toss results in a "2." What is the probability that a "2" will result on the second toss?
   a. Less than 1/6
   b. 1/6
   c. Greater than 1/6
   d. Cannot be determined
3. An urn contains 9 balls: 3 green, 4 red, and 2 blue. What is the probability that a ball selected at random is blue?
   a. 2/9
   b. 5/9
   c. 6/9
   d. 7/9
4. Sampling error is which of the following?
   a. The amount by which a sample mean is greater than the population mean
   b. The amount of difference between a sample statistic and a population parameter
   c. The standard deviation divided by the square root of n
   d. When the sample is not drawn randomly
5. What does the central limit theorem state?
   a. The means of many random samples from a population will be normally distributed.
   b. The raw scores of many natural events will be normally distributed.
   c. z scores will be normally distributed.
   d. None of the above
6. True or false? For a normal population, the variance of the sampling distribution of the mean increases as sample size increases.

7. True or false? All other things being equal, as the sample size increases, the standard error of a statistic decreases.
8. I assert that the 95% CI has a larger (or wider) range than the 99% CI for the same parameter using the same data. Am I correct?
9. I assert that the 90% CI has a smaller (or more narrow) range than the 68% CI for the same parameter using the same data. Am I correct?
10. I assert that the mean and median of any random sample drawn from a symmetric population distribution will be equal. Am I correct?
11. A random sample is to be drawn from a symmetric population with mean 100 and variance 225. I assert that the sample mean is more likely to have a value larger than 105 if the sample size is 16 than if the sample size is 25. Am I correct?
12. A gambler is playing a card game where the known probability of winning is .40 (win 40% of the time). The gambler has just lost 10 consecutive hands. What is the probability of the gambler winning the next hand?
    a. Less than .40
    b. Equal to .40
    c. Greater than .40
    d. Cannot be determined without observing the gambler
13. On the evening news, the anchorwoman announces that the state's lottery has reached $72 billion and reminds the viewing audience that there has not been a winner in over 5 years. In researching lottery facts, you find a report that states the probability of winning the lottery is 1 in 2 million (i.e., a very, very small probability). What is the probability that you will win the lottery?
    a. Less than 1 in 2 million
    b. Equal to 1 in 2 million
    c. Greater than 1 in 2 million
    d. Cannot be determined without additional statistics
14. True or false? The probability of being selected into a sample is the same for every individual in the population for the convenient method of sampling.
15. Malani is conducting research on elementary teacher attitudes toward changes in mathematics standards. Malani's population consists of all elementary teachers within one district in the state. Malani wants her sampling method to be such that every teacher in the population has an equal and independent probability of selection. Which of the following is the most appropriate sampling method?
    a. Convenience sampling
    b. Simple random sampling with replacement
    c. Simple random sampling without replacement
    d. Systematic sampling
16. True or false? Sampling error increases with larger samples.
17. If a population distribution is highly positively skewed, then the distribution of the sample means for samples of size 500 will be:
    a. highly negatively skewed.
    b. highly positively skewed.

c. approximately normally distributed.
d. Cannot be determined without further information

18. A dance studio has 35 competitive dancers and four competition teams with the following numbers of dancers on each team: mini troupe, 6; junior company, 9; apprentice, 8; and senior, 12. The probability that one dancer selected at random will be from junior company is equal to which of the following?
a. 6/35
b. 8/35
c. 9/35
d. 12/35

19. Mark is conducting research on the effects of the concussion protocol in professional football. Mark's population consists of all active professional football players in the National Football League (NFL). He wants to make sure that football players in both the the NFL's conferences (AFC and NFC) are proportionally represented. Which of the following sampling methods would be most appropriate?
a. Convenience sampling
b. Simple random sampling without replacement
c. Stratified sampling
d. Systematic sampling

20. A game of chance is offered at a fall festival with multiple prizes available, including the grand prize, a 7-day Caribbean cruise on the Disney Cruise Line. To enter to win, adults filled out an entry form with their name and contact information. The entry forms were dropped into container. Once a winning entry was selected, it was returned to the container. Which type of sampling methods is suggested by this example?
a. Convenience sampling
b. Simple random sampling with replacement
c. Simple random sampling without replacement
d. Systematic sampling

21. The previous football season's average number of points scored per game is computed for each college in the Southeastern Conference (SEC). A sports analyst computes a frequency distribution of these mean values. Which of the following has the sports analyst computed?
a. Confidence interval
b. Sampling distribution of the mean
c. Sampling error
d. Standard error of the mean

22. Probability is important to statistics because it enables which of the following?
a. To describe a sample
b. To generalize from a sample to a population
c. To infer from a group to an individual
d. To prove an idea is correct

Answers to Conceptual Problems

1. c (See definition in Section 5.2.2.)
3. a (2 out of 9.)
5. a (See Section 5.2.2.)
7. **True** (Less sampling error as *n* increases.)
9. **False** (90% CI has a wider range than 68% CI.)
11. **Yes** (An extreme mean is more likely with smaller *n*.)
13. b (Probability of winning the lottery is the same for each attempt, regardless of how long it has been since a winner was announced.)
15. c (For all teachers to have an equal and independent probability of being selected, the sampling procedure must be a type of simple random sampling; the nature of Malani's research is such that this should be done without replacement, as she would not want to survey the same teacher twice.)
17. c (Due to the central limit theorem with large size samples.)
19. c (To ensure that football players in both the NFL's conferences, the AFC and the NFC, are proportionally represented, stratified sampling can be used where the conference—AFC and NFC—is the strata, within which the sampling would occur.)
21. b (The sampling distribution of the mean is the frequency distribution of the sample means; in this case, the frequency distribution of the average number of points scored for all football games for SEC teams during the past season.)

Computational Problems

1. The population distribution of variable X, the number of pets owned, consists of the five values of 1, 4, 5, 7, and 8.
   a. Calculate the values of the population mean and variance.
   b. List all possible samples of size 2 where samples are drawn with replacement.
   c. Calculate the values of the mean and variance of the sampling distribution of the mean.
2. The following is a random sampling distribution of the mean number of children for samples of size 3, where samples are drawn with replacement.

Sample mean	f
1	1
2	2
3	4
4	2
5	1

   a. What is the population mean?
   b. What is the population variance?
   c. What is the mean of the sampling distribution of the mean?
   d. What is the variance error of the mean?

3. In a study of the entire student body of a large university, if the standard error of the mean is 20 for $n = 16$, what must the sample size be to reduce the standard error to 5?
4. A random sample of 13 statistics texts had a mean number of pages of 685 and a standard deviation of 42. Calculate the standard error of the mean, then calculate the 95% CI for the mean length of statistics texts.
5. A random sample of 10 high schools employed a mean number of guidance counselors of 3 and a standard deviation of 2. Calculate the standard error of the mean, then calculate the 90% CI for the mean number of guidance counselors.
6. A random sample of average systolic blood pressure from patients at 10 general practitioners were recorded as follows. Calculate the standard error of the mean given the following data:

115	120	122	118	125
130	126	112	117	124

Selected Answers to Computational Problems

1. a. Population mean = 5; population variance = 6;
   b. Construct table of possible sample means as in Table 5.1.
   c. Mean of the sampling distribution of the mean = 5; variance of the sampling distribution of the mean = 3.
3. a. 3
   b. 3.6
   c. 3
   d. 1.2
5. If the standard error of the mean is 20 and we want to reduce it to 5, that means we are reducing the standard error of the mean by 1/4 but holding the standard deviation of X constant. Our equation is $s_{\bar{X}} = s_X / \sqrt{n}$. Thus, $20 = s_X / \sqrt{16}$, and therefore $s_X = 80$. When the standard error of the mean if 5, given $s_X = 80$, we have: $5 = 80 / \sqrt{n}$, which is $5\sqrt{n} = 80$. Dividing each side by 5 and squaring to remove the square root, that is, $\left(\sqrt{n}\right)^2 = (80/5)^2$, we need a sample size of 256 to reduce the standard error to 5, holding the standard deviation of X constant at 80.
7. Standard error of the mean = 11.6487; 95% CI = 662.1685 to 707.74.
9. Standard error of the mean = .6325; 90% CI = 1.9595 to 4.0405.
11. With a sample size of 10 and standard deviation of X of 5.5267, the standard error of the mean is $s_{\bar{X}} = 5.5267 / \sqrt{10} = 1.7477$.

Interpretive Problems

1. Take a six-sided die, where the population values are obviously 1, 2, 3, 4, 5, and 6. Take 20 samples, each of size 2 (e.g., every two rolls is one sample). For each sample calculate the mean. Then determine the mean of the sampling distribution of the mean and the variance error of the mean. Compare your results to those of your colleagues.

2. You will need 20 plain M&M candy pieces and one cup. Put the candy pieces in the cup and toss them onto a flat surface. Count the number of candy pieces that land with the "M" facing up. Write down that number. Repeat these steps five times. These steps will constitute *one sample*. Next, generate four additional samples (i.e., repeat the process of tossing the candy pieces, counting the "Ms," and writing down that number). Then determine the mean of the sampling distribution of the mean and the variance error of the mean. Compare your results to those of your colleagues.

6

Introduction to Hypothesis Testing: Inferences About a Single Mean

Chapter Outline

Key Concepts

1. Null or statistical hypothesis versus scientific or research hypothesis
2. Type I error (α), type II error (β), and power ($1 - \beta$)
3. Two-tailed versus one-tailed alternative hypotheses
4. Critical regions and critical values
5. *z* test statistic
6. Confidence interval around the mean
7. *t* test statistic
8. *t* distribution, degrees of freedom, and table of *t* distributions

In Chapter 5 we began to move into the realm of inferential statistics. There we considered the following general topics: probability, sampling, and estimation. In this chapter we move totally into the domain of inferential statistics, where the concepts involved in probability, sampling, and estimation can be implemented. The overarching theme of the chapter is the use of a statistical test to make inferences about a single mean. In order to properly cover this inferential test, a number of basic foundational concepts are described in this chapter. Many of these concepts are utilized throughout the remainder of this text. Thus, even though there are likely lots of new concepts introduced in this chapter, a large portion of them will resurface in the remaining chapters (i.e., you'll be able to continue to apply what you learn in this chapter).

The topics described in the chapter include the following: types of hypotheses; types of decision errors; level of significance (α); overview of steps in the decision-making process; inferences about μ when σ is known; Type II error (β) and power ($1 - \beta$); statistical versus practical significance; and inferences about μ when σ is unknown. Concepts to be discussed include the following: the null or statistical hypothesis versus the scientific or research hypothesis; Type I error (α), Type II error (β), and power ($1 - \beta$); two-tailed versus one-tailed alternative hypotheses; critical regions and critical values; the z test statistic; the confidence interval around the mean; the t test statistic; and the t distribution, degrees of freedom, and table of t distributions. Our objectives are that by the end of this chapter, you will be able to (a) understand the basic concepts of hypothesis testing; (b) utilize the normal and t tables; and (c) understand, determine, and interpret the results from the z test, t test, and confidence interval procedures.

6.1 Inferences About a Single Mean and How They Work

6.1.1 Characteristics

You may remember Ott Lier and his graduate student colleagues from previous chapters as they have assisted in solving various statistical dilemmas. We see Ott has now been tasked with quite an interesting project.

Ott Lier has greatly enjoyed working with his colleagues on various statistical projects in which they have been involved through the stats lab. Ott and his group completed their first tasks as research assistants—determining a number of descriptive statistics on data. The faculty advisor for the statistical lab has been contacted by a community partner, Coach Wesley, the local hockey coach, who is interested in examining team skating performance. Ott has been assigned to the project. After consulting with Coach Wesley, Ott determines the most appropriate research question to be the following: *Is the mean skating speed of the hockey team different from the league mean speed of 12 seconds?* Ott suggests a one-sample test of means as the test of inference. His task is to assist Coach Wesley in generating the test of inference to answer his research question.

6.1.1.1 Types of Hypotheses

Hypothesis testing is a decision-making process where two possible decisions are weighed in a statistical fashion. In a way, this is much like any other decision involving two possibilities, such as whether to carry an umbrella with you today or not. In statistical decision-making, the two possible decisions are known as **hypotheses**. Sample data are then used to help us select one of these decisions. The two types of hypotheses competing against one another are known as the **null** or **statistical hypothesis**, denoted by H_0, and the **scientific, alternative,** or **research hypothesis**, denoted by H_1.

The null or statistical hypothesis is *a statement about the value of an unknown population parameter*. Considering the statistical procedure we are discussing in this chapter, the one-sample mean test, one example null hypothesis, H_0, might be that the population mean IQ score is 100, which we denote as

$$H_0\colon \mu = 100 \quad \text{or} \quad H_0\colon \mu - 100 = 0$$

Mathematically, both of these equations say the same thing. The version on the left is the more traditional form of the null hypothesis involving a single mean. However, the version on the right makes clear to the reader why the term "null" is appropriate; that is, there is no difference, or a "null" difference, between the population mean and the hypothesized mean value of 100. In general, the **hypothesized mean value** is denoted by μ_0 (here $\mu_0 = 100$). Another H_0 might be that statistics exam population means are the same for male and female students, which we denote as

$$H_0\colon \mu_1 - \mu_2 = 0$$

where μ_1 is the population mean for males and μ_2 is the population mean for females. Here there is no difference, or a "null" difference, between the two population means. The test of the difference between two means is presented in Chapter 7. As we move through subsequent chapters, we become familiar with null hypotheses that involve other population parameters such as proportions, variances, and correlations.

The null hypothesis is basically set up by the researcher in an attempt to reject the null hypothesis in favor of our own personal scientific, alternative, or research hypothesis. In other words, the scientific hypothesis is what we believe the outcome of the study will be, based on previous theory and research. *Thus, we are trying to reject the null hypothesis and find evidence in favor of our scientific hypothesis.* The scientific hypotheses (alternative hypotheses) H_1, for our two examples are:

$$H_1\colon \mu \neq 100 \quad \text{or} \quad H_1\colon \mu - 100 \neq 0$$

and

$$H_1\colon \mu_1 - \mu_2 \neq 0 \quad \text{or} \quad H_1\colon \mu_1 \neq \mu_2$$

Based on the sample data, *hypothesis testing involves making a decision as to whether the null or the research hypothesis is supported*. Because we are dealing with sample statistics in our decision-making process, and trying to make an inference back to the population parameter(s), *there is always some risk of making an incorrect decision*. In other words, the sample data might lead us to make a decision that is not consistent with the population. We might decide to take an umbrella and it does not rain, or we might decide to leave the umbrella at home and it rains. Thus, as in any decision, the possibility always exists that an incorrect decision may be made. *This uncertainty is due to sampling error*, which we will see can be described by a probability statement. That is, because the decision is made based on sample data, the sample may not be very representative of the population, and therefore leads us to an incorrect decision. If we had population data, we would always make the correct decision about a population parameter. Because we usually do not, we use inferential statistics to help make decisions from sample data and infer those results back to the population. The nature of such decision errors and the probabilities we can attribute to them are described in the next section.

6.1.1.2 *Types of Decision Errors*

In this section we consider more specifically the types of decision errors that might be made in the decision-making process. First an example decision-making situation is presented. This is followed by a decision-making table whereby the types of decision errors are easily depicted.

6.1.1.2.1 Example Decision-Making Situation

Let us propose an example decision-making situation using an instrument that measures adult intelligence. It is known somehow that the population standard deviation of the instrument is 15 (i.e., $\sigma^2 = 225$, $\sigma = 15$). (In the real world it is rare that the population standard deviation is known, and we return to reality later in the chapter when the basic concepts have been covered. But for now, assume that we know the population standard deviation.) Our null and alternative hypotheses, respectively, are as follows:

$$H_0: \mu = 100 \quad \text{or} \quad H_0: \mu - 100 = 0$$

$$H_1: \mu \neq 100 \quad \text{or} \quad H_1: \mu - 100 \neq 0$$

Thus, we are interested in testing whether the population mean for the intelligence instrument is equal to 100, our hypothesized mean value, or not equal to 100.

Next we take several random samples of individuals from the adult population. We find for our first sample $\bar{Y}_1 = 105$ (i.e., denoting the mean for sample 1). Eyeballing the information for sample 1, the sample mean is one-third of a standard deviation above the hypothesized value, which we determine by computing a *z* score of $(105 - 100)/15 = .3333$, so our conclusion would probably be that we fail to reject H_0. In other words, if the population mean actually is 100, then we believe that one is quite likely to observe a sample mean of 105. Thus, our decision for sample 1 is that we fail to reject H_0; however, there is some likelihood or probability that our decision is incorrect.

We take a second sample and find $\bar{Y}_2 = 115$ (i.e., denoting the mean for sample 2). Eyeballing the information for sample 2, the sample mean is one standard deviation above the hypothesized value, based on $z = (115 - 100)/15 = 1.0000$, so our conclusion would probably be that we fail to reject H_0. In other words, if the population mean actually is 100, then we believe that it is somewhat likely to observe a sample mean of 115. Thus, our decision for sample 2 is that we fail to reject H_0. However, there is an even greater likelihood or probability that our decision is incorrect than was the case for sample 1; this is because the sample mean is further away from the hypothesized value.

We take a third sample and find $\bar{Y}_3 = 190$ (i.e., denoting the mean for sample 3). Eyeballing the information for sample 3, the sample mean is six standard deviations above the hypothesized value, based on $z = (190 - 100)/15 = 6.0000$, so our conclusion would probably be to reject H_0. In other words, if the population mean actually is 100, then we believe that it is quite unlikely to observe a sample mean of 190. Thus our decision for sample 3 is to reject H_0; however, there is some small likelihood or probability that our decision is incorrect.

6.1.1.2.1 Decision-Making Table

Let us consider Table 6.1 as a mechanism for sorting out the possible outcomes in the statistical decision-making process. The table consists of the general case and a specific case. First, in part (a) of the table, we have the possible outcomes for the general case. For the state of nature or reality (i.e., how things really are in the population), there are two distinct possibilities, as depicted by the rows of the table: either H_0 is *indeed true* or H_0 is *indeed false*. In other words, according to the real-world conditions in the population, either H_0 is actually true or H_0 is actually false. Admittedly, we usually do not know what the state of nature truly is; however, it does exist in the population data. It is the state of nature that we are trying to best approximate when making a statistical decision based on sample data.

For our statistical decision, there are two distinct possibilities, as depicted by the columns of the table: either we *fail to reject* H_0 or we *reject* H_0. In other words, based on our sample data, we either fail to reject H_0 or reject H_0. As our goal is *usually* to reject H_0 in favor of our research hypothesis, we prefer to say "fail to reject" rather than "accept." "Accept" implies you are willing to throw out your research hypothesis and admit defeat based on one sample (i.e., this is the absolute and final truth). "Fail to reject" implies you still have some hope for your research hypothesis, despite evidence from a single sample to the contrary (i.e., there is some evidence that supports the null but you are not assuming this is the absolute and final truth).

If we look inside of the table, we see four different outcomes based on a combination of our statistical decision and the state of nature. Consider the first row of the table where H_0 is in actuality true. First, if H_0 is true and we fail to reject H_0, then we have made a correct decision; that is, we have *correctly failed to reject a true* H_0. The probability of this first outcome is known as $1 - \alpha$, where α represents alpha. Second, if H_0 is true and we reject H_0, then we

TABLE 6.1

Statistical Decision Table

	Decision	
State of nature (reality)	**Fail to reject H_0**	**Reject H_0 (reality)**
(a) General Case		
H_0 is true	Correct decision: $(1 - \alpha)$	Type I error: a
H_0 is false	Type II error: β	Correct decision: $(1 - \beta)$ = power
(b) Example Rain Case		
H_0 is true (no rain)	Correct decision (do not take umbrella and no umbrella needed): $(1 - \alpha)$	Type I error (take umbrella but umbrella not needed): α
H_0 is false (rains)	Type II error (do not take umbrella and get wet): β	Correct decision (take umbrella and stay dry): $(1 - \beta)$ = power

have made a decision error known as a **Type I error**. That is, we have *incorrectly rejected a true* H_0; this is also referred to as a **false positive**. Our sample data has led us to a different conclusion than the population data would have. The probability of this second outcome is known as alpha (α). Therefore, if H_0 is actually true, then our sample data lead us to one of two conclusions: either we correctly fail to reject H_0 or we incorrectly reject H_0. The sum of the probabilities for these two outcomes when H_0 is true is equal to 1; that is, $(1 - \alpha) + \alpha = 1$.

Consider now the second row of the table where H_0 is in actuality false. First, if H_0 is really false and we fail to reject H_0, then we have made a decision error known as a **Type II error**. That is, we have *incorrectly failed to reject a false* H_0, also referred to as a **false negative**. Our sample data has led us to a different conclusion than the population data would have. The probability of this outcome is known as beta (β). Second, if H_0 is really false and we reject H_0, then we have made a correct decision; that is, we have *correctly rejected a false* H_0. The probability of this second outcome is known as $1 - \beta$, or power (to be more fully discussed later in this chapter). Therefore, if H_0 is actually false, then our sample data lead us to one of two conclusions: either we incorrectly fail to reject H_0 or we correctly reject H_0. The sum of the probabilities for these two outcomes when H_0 is false is equal to 1; that is, $\beta + (1 - \beta) = 1$.

Consider the following specific case, as shown in part (b) of Table 6.1. We wish to test the following hypotheses about whether it will rain tomorrow:

$$H_0\text{: no rain tomorrow}$$
$$H_1\text{: rains tomorrow}$$

We collect some sample data from prior years for the same month and day, and go to make our statistical decision. Our two possible statistical decisions are (a) we do not believe it will rain tomorrow, and therefore do not bring an umbrella with us, or (b) we do believe it will rain tomorrow, and therefore do bring an umbrella.

Again, there are four potential outcomes. First, if H_0 is really true (no rain) and we do not carry an umbrella, then we have made a correct decision as no umbrella is necessary (probability $= 1 - \alpha$). Second, if H_0 is really true (no rain) and we carry an umbrella, then we have made a Type I error, and we carry an umbrella around all day when we do not need to (probability $= \alpha$). Third, if H_0 is really false (rains) and we do not carry an umbrella, then we have made a Type II error and we get wet (probability $= \beta$). Fourth, if H_0 is really false (rains) and we carry an umbrella, then we have made the correct decision, as the umbrella keeps us dry (probability $= 1 - \beta$).

Let us make two concluding statements about the decision table. First, one can never prove the truth or falsity of H_0 in a single study. One only gathers evidence in favor of or in opposition to the null hypothesis. Something is proven in research when an entire collection of studies or evidence reaches the same conclusion time and time again. Scientific proof is difficult to achieve in the social and behavioral sciences, and we should not use the terms "prove" or "proof" loosely. As researchers, we gather multiple pieces of evidence that eventually lead to the development of one or more theories. When a theory is shown to be unequivocally true (i.e., in all cases), then proof has been established.

Second, let us consider the decision errors in a different light. One can totally eliminate the possibility of a Type I error by deciding to *never* reject H_0. That is, if we always fail to reject H_0 (do not ever carry an umbrella), then we can never make a Type I error (carry an unnecessary umbrella). Although this strategy sounds fine, it totally takes the decision-making power out of our hands. With this strategy we do not even need to collect any sample data, as we have already decided to never reject H_0.

One can totally eliminate the possibility of a Type II error by deciding to *always* reject H_0. That is, if we always reject H_0 (always carry an umbrella), then we can never make a Type II error (get wet without an umbrella). Although this strategy also sounds fine, it totally takes the decision-making power out of our hands. With this strategy we do not even need to collect any sample data as we have already decided to always reject H_0. Taken together, one can never totally eliminate the possibility of both a Type I and a Type II error. No matter what decision we make, there is always some possibility of making a Type I and/or Type II error. Therefore as researchers, our job is to make conscience decisions in designing and conducting our study and in analyzing the data so that the possibility of decision error is minimized. And, as we will see in the next section, it is the researcher's judgment on how to balance Type I versus Type II errors.

6.1.1.2.2 A Little History

Neyman and Pearson (1933) presented the term "hypothesis testing" as a contrast with "significance testing," which was coined by Fisher (thus, referring to "significance level" as "Type I error" actually has mixed these two approaches, among other ways the two have mixed). The approach by Neyman and Pearson includes two competing hypotheses, the null *and* the alternative hypotheses, whereas the approach by Fisher includes *just* the null hypothesis. This explicit specification of an alternative hypothesis distinguishes the approaches of Fisher and Neyman and Pearson and, more important, introduced probabilities associated with committing two kinds of errors related to the null hypothesis (i.e., Type I and Type II). The approach by Neyman and Pearson also introduced the concept of statistical power. Because Fisher's approach has no alternative hypothesis, Type II error and power are irrelevant. As stated by Fisher (1935, p. 474), "'Errors of the second kind' are committed only by those who misunderstand the nature and application of tests of significance."

Fisher and Neyman and Pearson also viewed inductive reasoning differently. Fisher was centered on rejection of the null hypothesis, whereas Neyman and Pearson conceptualized inductive behavior, which was irrespective of the beliefs in either the null or alternative hypothesis. Rather, establishing rules for making decisions between the two hypotheses was their focus: "To accept a hypothesis *H* means only to decide to take action *A* rather than action *B*. This does not mean that we necessarily believe that the hypothesis *H* is true . . . [Rejecting *H*] . . . means only that the rule prescribes action *B* and does not imply that we believe that *H* is false" (Neyman, 1950, pp. 259–260). The Neyman–Pearson approach recognizes the costs of committing a Type I or Type II error when accepting or rejecting the null hypothesis, with these costs being context dependent, and thus based on the judgment of the researcher. At the same time, they noted that control of Type I errors was most important (Neyman, 1950). Balancing between Type I and Type II error was critical to Neyman and Pearson (1933), and they provided an example to illustrate:

> In a scientific investigation we may be testing some new hypothesis H_0 . . . The hypothesis is perhaps novel and important, and we do not wish to throw it aside lightly. . . . [W]e shall therefore be inclined to give H_0 the benefit of the doubt, and fix the level of rejection low . . . perhaps .01 or less. On the other hand we may be analyzing the results of a series of experiments designed to detect possible factors which may modify the working of a standard law. In this case we shall be watching carefully for any signs of divergence from the standard hypotheses H_0, and shall allow [Type I error] to be

large—perhaps .10—in order than the risk of error II may be reduced. The importance of finding some new line of development here outweighs any loss due to certain waste of effort in starting on a false trail.

(pp. 497–498)

6.1.1.3 Level of Significance (α)

We have already stated that a Type I error occurs when the decision is to reject H_0 when in fact H_0 is actually true. We defined the probability of a Type I error as α, which is also known as the *level of significance* or *significance level*. We now examine α as a basis for helping us make statistical decisions. Recall from a previous example that the null and alternative hypotheses, respectively, are as follows:

$$H_0: \mu = 100 \quad \text{or} \quad H_0: \mu - 100 = 0$$

$$H_1: \mu \neq 100 \quad \text{or} \quad H_1: \mu - 100 \neq 0$$

Thus, we need a mechanism for deciding how far away a sample mean needs to be from the hypothesized mean value of $\mu_0 = 100$ in order to reject H_0. In other words, at a certain point or distance away from 100, we will decide to reject H_0. We use α to determine that point for us, where in this context α is known as the **level of significance**. Figure 6.1a

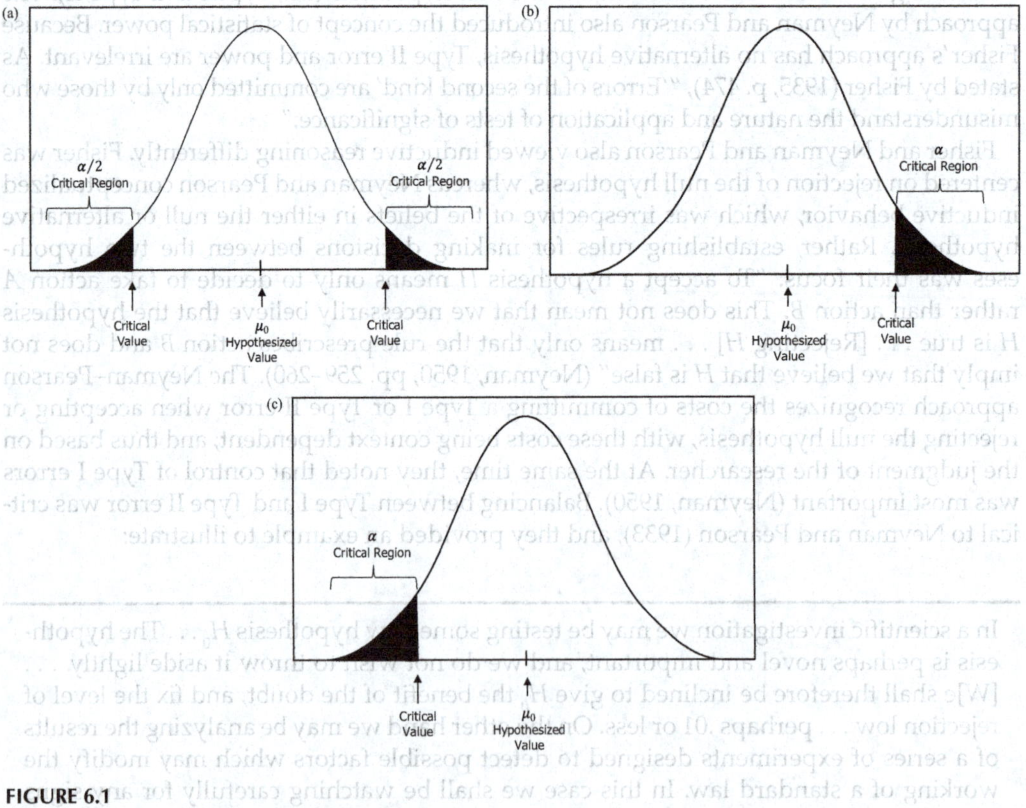

FIGURE 6.1
Alternative hypotheses and critical regions.

shows a sampling distribution of the mean where the hypothesized value μ_0 is depicted at the center of the distribution. Toward both tails of the distribution, we see two shaded regions known as the **critical regions**, or regions of rejection. The combined area of the two shaded regions is equal to α, and thus the area of either the upper or the lower tail critical region is equal to a/2 (i.e., we split α into one-half by dividing by 2). If the sample mean is far enough away from the hypothesized mean value, μ_0, that it falls into either critical region, then our statistical decision is to *reject* H_0. In this case our decision is to reject H_0 at the α level of significance. If, however, the sample mean is close enough to μ_0 that it falls into the unshaded region (i.e., not into either critical region), then our statistical decision is to *fail to reject* H_0. The **critical values** are the *precise points on the X axis at which the critical regions are divided from the unshaded region*. Determining critical values is discussed later in this chapter.

Note that under the alternative hypothesis, H_1, we are willing to reject H_0 when the sample mean is either significantly greater than or significantly less than the hypothesized mean value μ_0. This particular alternative hypothesis is known as a *nondirectional alternative hypothesis*, as no direction is implied with respect to the hypothesized value; that is, *we will reject the null hypothesis in favor of the alternative hypothesis in either direction, either above or below the hypothesized mean value*. This also results in what is known as a *two-tailed test of significance* in that we are willing to reject the null hypothesis in either tail or critical region.

Two other alternative hypotheses are also possible, depending on the researcher's scientific hypothesis, which are known as *directional alternative hypotheses*. One directional alternative is that the *population mean is greater than the hypothesized mean value*, also known as a *right-tailed test*, as denoted by:

$$H_1\colon \mu > 100 \quad \text{or} \quad H_1\colon \mu - 100 > 0$$

Mathematically, both of these equations say the same thing. With a right-tailed alternative hypothesis, the entire region of rejection is contained in the upper tail, with an area of α, known as a one-tailed test of significance (and specifically the right tail). If the sample mean is significantly greater than the hypothesized mean value of 100, then our statistical decision is to reject H_0. If, however, the sample mean falls into the unshaded region, then our statistical decision is to fail to reject H_0. This situation is depicted in Figure 6.1b.

A second directional alternative is that the *population mean is less than the hypothesized mean value*, also known as a left-tailed test, as denoted by:

$$H_1\colon \mu < 100 \quad \text{or} \quad H_1\colon \mu - 100 < 0$$

Mathematically, both of these equations say the same thing. With a left-tailed alternative hypothesis, the entire region of rejection is contained in the lower tail, with an area of α, also known as a one-tailed test of significance (and specifically the left tail). If the sample mean is significantly less than the hypothesized mean value of 100, then our statistical decision is to reject H_0. If, however, the sample mean falls into the unshaded region, then our statistical decision is to fail to reject H_0. This situation is depicted in Figure 6.1c.

The potential for misuse exists for the different alternatives, which we consider to be an ethical matter. For example, say that a researcher conducts a one-tailed test with an upper-tail critical region and fails to reject H_0. However, the researcher notices that the sample mean is considerably below the hypothesized mean value and then decides to change the alternative hypothesis to either a nondirectional test or a one-tailed test in the other tail. This is unethical, as the researcher has examined the data and changed the alternative hypothesis. The moral of the story is this: *If there is previous and consistent empirical evidence to use a specific directional alternative hypothesis, then you should do so. If, however, there is minimal or inconsistent empirical evidence to use a specific directional alternative, then you should not. Instead, you should use a nondirectional alternative.* Once you have decided which alternative hypothesis to go with, then you need to stick with it for the duration of the statistical decision. If you find contrary evidence, then report it, as it may be an important finding, but do not change the alternative hypothesis in midstream.

6.1.1.4 Overview of Steps in the Decision-Making Process

Before we get into the specific details of conducting the test of a single mean, we want to discuss the basic steps for hypothesis testing of any inferential test:

1. State the null and alternative hypotheses.
2. Select the level of significance (i.e., alpha, α).
3. Calculate the test statistic value.
4. Make a statistical decision (reject or fail to reject H_0).

Step 1: State the null and alternative hypotheses. Recall from our previous example that the null and nondirectional alternative hypotheses, respectively, for a two-tailed test are as follows:

$$H_0\colon \mu = 100 \quad \text{or} \quad H_0\colon \mu - 100 = 0$$

$$H_1\colon \mu \neq 100 \quad \text{or} \quad H_1\colon \mu - 100 \neq 0$$

One could also choose one of the other directional alternative hypotheses described previously.

If we choose to write our null hypothesis as $H_0\colon \mu = 100$, we would want to write our research hypothesis in a consistent manner: $H_1\colon \mu \neq 100$ (rather than $H_1\colon \mu - 100 \neq 0$). In publication, many researchers opt to present the hypotheses in narrative form (e.g., "the null hypothesis states that the population mean will equal 100, and the alternative hypothesis states that the population mean will not equal 100"). How you present your hypotheses (mathematically or using statistical notation) is up to you.

Step 2: Select a level of significance, α. Two things must be taken into consideration when selecting a level of significance. The first is the cost associated with making a Type I error, which is what α really is. Recall that alpha is the probability of rejecting the null hypothesis if in reality the null hypothesis is true. When a Type I error is made, that means evidence is building in favor of the research hypothesis (which is actually false). Let us take an example of a new drug. To test the efficacy of the drug, an experiment is conducted where some individuals take the new drug, whereas others receive a placebo. The null hypothesis, stated nondirectionally, would essentially indicate that the effects of the drug and placebo are the same. Rejecting that null hypothesis would mean that the effects are not equal—suggesting that perhaps this new drug, which in reality is not any better than a placebo, is being touted as effective medication. That is obviously problematic and potentially very hazardous!

Thus, if there is a relatively high cost associated with a Type I error—for example, such that lives are lost, as in the medical profession—then one would want to select a relatively small level of significance (e.g., .01 or smaller). A small alpha would translate to a very small probability of rejecting the null if it were really true (i.e., a small probability of making an incorrect decision). If there is a relatively low cost associated with a Type I error—for example, such that children have to eat the second-rated candy rather than the first—then selecting a larger level of significance may be appropriate (e.g., .05 or larger). Costs are not always known, however. A second consideration is the level of significance commonly used in your field of study. In many disciplines the .05 level of significance has become the standard (although no one seems to have a really good rationale). This is true in many of the social and behavioral sciences. Thus, you would do well to consult the published literature in your field to see if some standard alpha is commonly used and to consider it for your own research.

Here is a good point to interject a little history as well as new developments. We just stated that .05 is the standard alpha in many disciplines, and this is generally attributed to Fisher (1925) when he developed analysis of variance procedures. Later, Fisher (1926), acknowledged the use of other alpha levels, stating,

> If one in twenty does not seem high enough odds, we may, if we prefer it, draw the line at one in fifty (the 2 per cent point), or one in a hundred (the 1 per cent point). Personally, the writer prefers to set a low standard of significance at the 5 per cent point, and ignore entirely all results which fail to reach this level. A scientific fact should be regarded as experimentally established only if a properly designed experiment rarely fails to give this level of significance.
>
> (p. 504)

Many scholars who have studied the history of probability feel the selection of an alpha of .05 as the cutoff is arbitrary (Cowles & Davis, 1982). Cowles and Davis (1982) argue that the reason why the adoption of .05 was appropriate to early statisticians and why it prevailed was due to its consideration as a concept of probability. Alpha of .05 was justified as a criterion for judging outcomes, as generally, people feel that an event that occurs 5% of the time is a rare event *and* they are comfortable assigning a nonchance cause to an event that occurs that infrequently (Cowles & Davis, 1982).

Approaching 100 years in use, there is obviously a long history in the application of an alpha of .05. However, a number of scholars argue that the threshold should be changed from .05 to .005, claiming that "statistical standards of evidence for claiming new discoveries in many fields of science are simply too low. Associating 'statistically significant' findings with $p < .05$ results in a high rate of false positives even in the absence of other experimental, procedural and reporting problems" (Benjamin et al., 2018, p. 5). Others argue that simply adjusting the alpha level will not solve the problem but may actually have adverse effects (Crane, 2018). Some scholars argue that getting rid of significance testing altogether is needed (Trafimow et al., 2018). Bayesian methods are one attractive alternative to null hypothesis significance testing (Cristea & Ioannidis, 2018). Still others suggest using probability values (i.e., p) on a scale of 0 (completely incompatible) to 1 (completely compatible) or replacing the p value with a scale that is more intuitive, such as a likelihood ratio (Amrhein & Greenland, 2018).

This is just a tip of the iceberg. As this likely illustrates, there is quite a robust discussion in the research community on this topic. Our philosophy is that your research question should *always* guide your statistical approach and analysis. In some instances, a frequentist perspective, which applies parametric inference and within which this text is framed, is needed. In other instances, Bayesian statistics are more appropriate. In still other instances, neither is needed. This text provides many useful tools for conducting statistics. However, we do not claim these to be the only tools you will ever need. Rather, we hope that this text whets your appetite to learn other approaches, such as Bayesian statistics, so that you can make informed decisions on how best to approach a particular research problem.

Step 3: Calculate the test statistic. For the one-sample mean test, we will compute the sample mean $\bar{Y}$ and compare it to the hypothesized value μ_0. This allows us to determine the size of the difference between $\bar{Y}$ and μ_0, and subsequently the probability associated with the difference. The larger the difference, the more likely it is that the sample mean really differs from the hypothesized mean value and the larger the probability associated with the difference.

Step 4: Make a statistical decision regarding the null hypothesis, H_0. That is, a decision is made whether to reject H_0 or to fail to reject H_0. If the difference between the sample mean and the hypothesized value is large enough relative to the critical value (we will talk about critical values in more detail later), then our decision is to reject H_0. If the difference between the sample mean and the hypothesized value is not large enough relative to the critical value, then our decision is to fail to reject H_0. This is the basic four-step process for hypothesis testing of any inferential test. The specific details for the test of a single mean are given in the following section.

6.1.1.5 *Inferences About μ When σ Is Known*

In this section we examine how hypotheses about a single mean are conducted when the population standard deviation is known. Specifically we consider the *z* test, an example illustrating use of the *z* test, and how to construct a confidence interval around the mean.

6.1.1.5.1 The *z* Test

Recall from Chapter 4 the definition of a *z* **score** as

$$z = \frac{Y_i - \mu}{\sigma_Y}$$

where Y_i is the score on variable Y for individual i, μ is the population mean for variable Y, and σ_Y is the population standard deviation for variable Y. The *z* score is used to tell us how many standard deviation units an individual's score is from the mean.

In the context of this chapter, however, we are concerned with the extent to which a sample mean differs from some hypothesized mean value. We can construct a variation of the *z* score for testing hypotheses about a single mean. In this situation we are concerned with the sampling distribution of the mean (introduced in Chapter 5), so the equation must reflect means rather than raw scores. Our *z* score equation for testing hypotheses about a single mean becomes the following:

$$z = \frac{\bar{Y} - \mu_0}{\sigma_{\bar{Y}}}$$

where $\bar{Y}$ is the sample mean for variable Y, μ_0 is the hypothesized mean value for variable Y, and $\sigma_{\bar{Y}}$ is the population standard error of the mean for variable Y. From Chapter 5, recall that the population standard error of the mean $\sigma_{\bar{Y}}$ is computed by

$$\sigma_{\bar{Y}} = \frac{\sigma_Y}{\sqrt{n}}$$

where σ_Y is the population standard deviation for variable Y and n is sample size. Thus, the numerator of the z score equation is the difference between the sample mean and the hypothesized value of the mean, and the denominator is the standard error of the mean. *What we are really determining here is how many standard deviation (or standard error) units the sample mean is from the hypothesized mean.* Henceforth, we call this variation of the z score the **test statistic for the test of a single mean**, also known as the **z test**. This is the first of several test statistics we describe in this text; every inferential test requires some test statistic for purposes of testing hypotheses.

We need to make a statistical assumption regarding this hypothesis-testing situation. We assume that z is normally distributed with a mean of 0 and a standard deviation of 1. This is written statistically as $z \sim N(0,1)$ following the notation we developed in Chapter 4. Thus, the assumption is that z follows the unit normal distribution (in other words, the shape of the distribution is approximately normal). An examination of our test statistic z reveals that only the sample mean can vary from sample to sample. The hypothesized value and the standard error of the mean are constant for every sample of size n from the same population.

In order to make a statistical decision, the critical regions need to be defined. Because the test statistic is z and we have assumed normality, then the relevant theoretical distribution we compare the test statistic to is the *unit normal distribution*. We previously discussed this distribution in Chapter 4, and the table of values is given in Table A.1 in the Appendix. If the alternative hypothesis is nondirectional, then there would be two critical regions—one in the upper tail and one in the lower tail. Here we would split the area of the critical region, known as α, in two. If the alternative hypothesis is directional, then there would only be one critical region, either in the upper tail or in the lower tail, depending on which direction one is willing to reject H_0.

6.1.1.5.2 An Example

Let us illustrate use of this inferential test through an example. We are interested in testing whether the population of undergraduate students from Awesome State University (ASU) have a mean intelligence test score different from the hypothesized mean value of $\mu_0 = 100$. (Remember that the hypothesized mean value does not come from our sample, but from another source; in this example, let us say that this value of 100 is the national norm as presented in the technical manual of this particular intelligence test.)

Our first step in hypothesis testing is to state the hypothesis. A nondirectional alternative hypothesis is of interest as we simply want to know if this population has a mean intelligence different from the hypothesized value, either greater than or less than. Thus, the null and alternative hypotheses can be written, respectively, as follows:

$$H_0: \mu = 100 \quad \text{or} \quad H_0: \mu - 100 = 0$$

$$H_1: \mu \neq 100 \quad \text{or} \quad H_1: \mu - 100 \neq 0$$

A sample mean of $\bar{Y} = 103$ is observed for a sample of $n = 100$ ASU undergraduate students. From the development of this intelligence test, we know that the theoretical population standard deviation is $\sigma_Y = 15$ (again, for purposes of illustration, let us say that the population standard deviation of 15 was noted in the technical manual for this test).

Our second step is to select a level of significance. The standard level of significance in this field is the .05 level; thus, we perform our significance test at $\alpha = .05$.

The third step is to compute the test statistic value. To compute our test statistic value, first we compute the standard error of the mean (the denominator of our test statistic formula) as follows with the population standard deviation of 15 and a sample size of 100 (values of which were given previously):

$$\sigma_{\bar{Y}} = \frac{\sigma_Y}{\sqrt{n}} = \frac{15}{\sqrt{100}} = 1.50$$

Then we compute the test statistic z, where the numerator is the difference between the mean of our sample $(\bar{Y} = 103)$ and the hypothesized mean value ($\mu_0 = 100$) and the denominator is the standard error of the mean:

$$z = \frac{\bar{Y} - \mu_0}{\sigma_{\bar{Y}}} = \frac{103 - 100}{1.50} = 2.00$$

Finally, in the last step we make our statistical decision by comparing the test statistic z to the critical values. To determine the critical values for the z test, we use the unit normal distribution in Table A.1 in the Appendix. Because $\alpha = .05$ and we are conducting a nondirectional test, we need to find critical values for the upper and lower tails, where the area of each of the two critical regions is equal to .025 (i.e., splitting alpha in half: $\alpha/2$ or $.05/2 = .025$). From the unit normal table we find these critical values to be +1.96 (the point on the X axis where the area above that point is equal to .025) and −1.96 (the point on the X axis where the area below that point is equal to .025). As shown in Figure 6.2, the test statistic $z = 2.00$ falls into

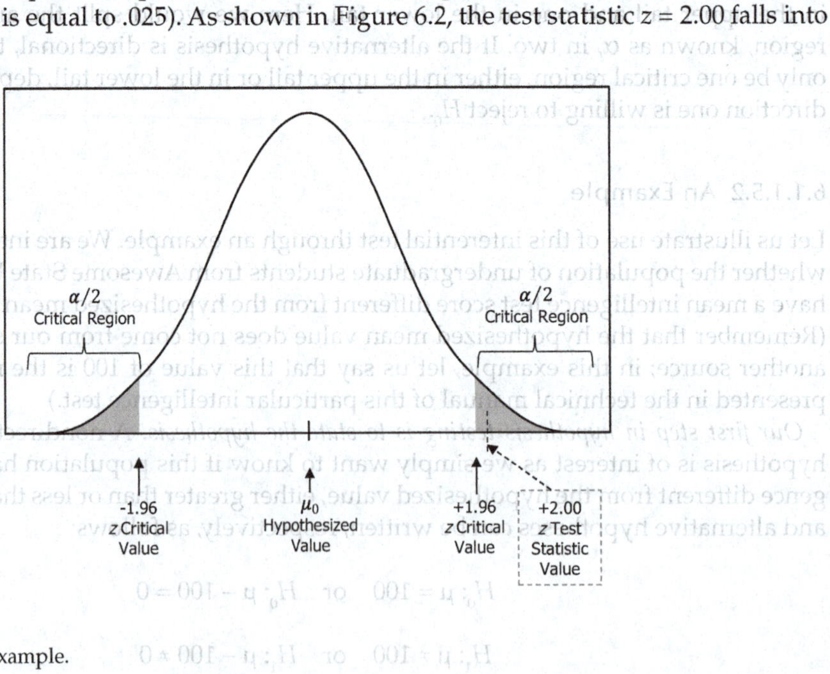

FIGURE. 6.2
Critical regions for example.

the upper-tail critical region, just slightly larger than the upper-tail critical value of +1.96. Our decision is to reject H_0 and conclude that the ASU population from which the sample was selected has a mean intelligence score that is statistically significantly different from the hypothesized mean of 100 at the .05 level of significance.

A more precise way of thinking about this process is to determine the **exact probability** of observing a sample mean that differs from the hypothesized mean value. From the unit normal table, the area above $z = 2.00$ is equal to .0228. Therefore, the area below $z = -2.00$ is also equal to .0228. Thus, the probability, p, of observing, by chance, a sample mean of 2.00 or more standard errors (i.e., $z = 2.00$) from the hypothesized mean value of 100, in either direction, is two times the observed probability level, or $p = (2)(.0228) = .0456$. To put this in the context of the values in this example, there is a relatively small probability (less than 5%) of observing a sample mean of 103 just by chance if the true population mean is really 100. As this exact probability ($p = .0456$) is smaller than our level of significance $\alpha = .05$, we reject H_0. Thus, there are two approaches to dealing with probability. One approach is a decision based solely on the critical values. We reject or fail to reject H_0 at a given α level, but no other information is provided. The other approach is a decision based on comparing the exact probability to the given α level. We reject or fail to reject H_0 at a given α level, but we also have information available about the closeness or confidence in that decision.

For this example, the findings in a publication would be reported based on comparing the p value to alpha and reported either as $z = 2$ ($p < .05$) or as $z = 2$ ($p = .0456$). (You may want to refer to the style manual relevant to your discipline, such as the *Publication Manual for the American Psychological Association* (2010), for information on which is the recommended reporting style.) Obviously, the conclusion is the same with either approach; it is just a matter of how the results are reported. Most statistical computer programs, including SPSS, report the exact probability so that the readers can make a decision based on their own selected level of significance. These programs do not provide the critical value(s), which are only found in the appendices of statistics textbooks.

6.1.1.5.3 Constructing Confidence Intervals Around the Mean

Recall our discussion from Chapter 5 on confidence intervals (CI). Confidence intervals are often quite useful in inferential statistics for providing the researcher with an interval estimate of a population parameter. Although the sample mean gives us a point estimate (i.e., just one value) of a population mean, a confidence interval *gives us an interval estimate of a population mean and allows us to determine the accuracy or precision of the sample mean.* For the inferential test of a single mean, a confidence interval around the sample mean $\bar{Y}$ is formed from

$$\bar{Y} \pm z_{cv}\sigma_{\bar{Y}}$$

where z_{cv} is the critical value from the unit normal distribution and $\sigma_{\bar{Y}}$ is the population standard error of the mean.

Confidence intervals are typically formed for nondirectional or two-tailed tests, as shown in the equation. *A confidence interval will generate a lower and an upper limit.* If the hypothesized mean value falls within the lower and upper limits, then we would fail to reject H_0. In other words, if the hypothesized mean is contained in (or falls within) the confidence interval around the sample mean, then we conclude that the sample mean and the hypothesized mean are not significantly different and that the sample mean could have come from a population with the hypothesized mean; that is, we *fail to reject* H_0. If the hypothesized mean value falls outside the limits of the interval, then we would *reject* H_0. Here we conclude that it is unlikely that the sample mean could have come from a population with the hypothesized mean.

One way to think about CIs is as follows. Imagine we take 100 random samples of the same sample size *n*, compute each sample mean, and then construct each 95% confidence interval. Then we can say that 95% of these CIs will contain the population parameter and 5% will not. In short, 95% of similarly constructed CIs will contain the population parameter. It should also be mentioned that at a particular level of significance, one will always obtain the same statistical decision with both the hypothesis test and the confidence interval. The two procedures use precisely the same information. The hypothesis test is based on a point estimate; the CI is based on an interval estimate, providing the researcher with quite a bit more information.

For the ASU example situation, the 95% CI would be computed by

$$\bar{Y} \pm z_{cv}\sigma_{\bar{Y}} = 103 \pm (1.96)(1.50) = 103 \pm 2.94 = (100.06, 105.94)$$

Thus, the 95% confidence interval ranges from 100.06 to 105.94. Because the interval does not contain the hypothesized mean value of 100, we reject H_0 (the same decision we arrived at by walking through the steps for hypothesis testing). Thus, it is quite unlikely that our sample mean could have come from a population distribution with a mean of 100.

6.1.1.8 Inferences About μ When σ Is Unknown

We have already considered the inferential test involving a single mean when the population standard deviation σ is known. However, rarely is σ known to the applied researcher. When σ is unknown, then the *z* test is no longer appropriate. In this section we consider the following: the test statistic for inferences about the mean when the population standard deviation is unknown, the *t* distribution, the *t* test, and an example using the *t* test.

6.1.1.8.1 A New Test Statistic, *t*

What is the applied researcher to do then when σ is unknown? The answer is to estimate σ by the sample standard deviation *s*. This changes the standard error of the mean to be

$$s_{\bar{Y}} = \frac{s_Y}{\sqrt{n}}$$

Now we are estimating two population parameters: (1) the population mean, μ_Y, is being estimated by the sample mean, $\bar{Y}$; and (2) the population standard deviation, σ_Y, is being estimated by the sample standard deviation, s_Y. Both $\bar{Y}$ and s_Y can vary from sample to sample. Thus, although the sampling error of the mean is taken into account explicitly in the *z* test, we also need to take into account the sampling error of the standard deviation, which the *z* test does not at all consider.

We now develop a new inferential test for the situation where σ is unknown. The test statistic is known as the ***t* test** and is computed as follows:

$$t = \frac{\bar{Y} - \mu_0}{s_{\bar{Y}}}$$

The t test was developed by William Sealy Gossett, also known by the pseudonym Student, mentioned in Chapter 1. The unit normal distribution cannot be used here for the unknown σ situation. A different theoretical distribution must be used for determining critical values for the t test, known as the ***t* distribution**.

6.1.1.8.2 The t Distribution

The t distribution is the theoretical distribution used for determining the critical values of the t test. Like the normal distribution, the t distribution is actually a *family of distributions*. A different t distribution exists for each degrees of freedom. However, before we look more closely at the t distribution, some discussion of the **degrees of freedom** concept is necessary.

As an example, say we know a sample mean $\bar{Y} = 6$ for a sample size of $n = 5$. How many of those five observed scores are free to vary? The answer is that four scores are free to vary. If the four known scores are 2, 4, 6, and 8 and the mean is 6, then the remaining score must be 10. The remaining score is not free to vary, but is already totally determined. We see this in the following equation where, to arrive at a solution of 6, the sum in the numerator must equal 30, and Y_5 must be 10.

$$\bar{Y} = \frac{\sum_{i=1}^{n} Y_i}{n} = \frac{\sum_{i=1}^{5} Y_i}{5} = \frac{2+4+6+8+Y_5}{5} = 6$$

Therefore, the number of degrees of freedom is equal to 4 in this particular case, and $n - 1$ in general. For the t test being considered here, we specify the degrees of freedom as $\nu = n - 1$ (where ν is the Greek letter nu). We use ν often in statistics to denote some type of degrees of freedom.

Another way to think about degrees of freedom is that we know the sum of the deviations from the mean must equal zero (recall the unsquared numerator of the variance conceptual formula). For example, if $n = 10$, there are 10 deviations from the mean. Once the mean is known, only 9 of the deviations are free to vary. A final way to think about this is that, in general, $df = (n - \text{number of restrictions})$. For the one-sample t test, because the population variance is unknown, we have to estimate it resulting in one restriction. Thus, $df = (n - 1)$ for this particular inferential test.

Several members of the family of t distributions are shown in Figure 6.3. The distribution for $\nu = 1$ has thicker tails than the unit normal distribution and a shorter peak. This

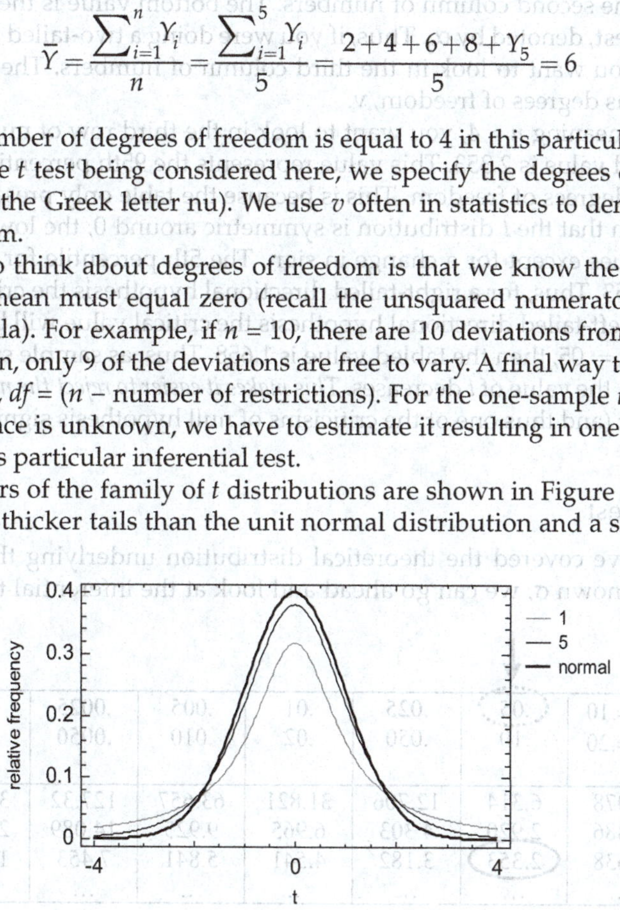

FIGURE 6.3
Several members of the family of t distributions.

indicates that there is considerable sampling error of the sample standard deviation with only 2 observations (as $\nu = 2 - 1 = 1$). For $\nu = 5$, the tails are thinner and the peak is taller than for $\nu = 1$. As the degrees of freedom increase, the t distribution becomes more nearly normal. For $\nu = 4$ (i.e., infinity), the t distribution is precisely the unit normal distribution.

A few important characteristics of the t distribution are worth mentioning. First, like the unit normal distribution, the mean of any t distribution is 0, and the t distribution is symmetric around the mean and unimodal. Second, unlike the unit normal distribution, which has a variance of 1, the variance of a t distribution is equal to

$$\sigma^2 = \frac{\nu}{\nu - 2} \text{ for } \nu > 2$$

Thus, the variance of a t distribution is somewhat greater than 1, but approaches 1 as ν increases.

The table for the t distribution is given in Table A.2 in the Appendix, and a snapshot of the table is presented in Figure 6.4 for illustration purposes. In looking at the table, each column header has two values. The top value is the significance level for a **one-tailed test**, denoted by α_1. Thus, if you were doing a one-tailed test at the .05 level of significance, you want to look in the second column of numbers. The bottom value is the significance level for a **two-tailed test**, denoted by α_2. Thus, if you were doing a two-tailed test at the .05 level of significance, you want to look in the third column of numbers. The rows of the table denote the various degrees of freedom, ν.

Thus, if $\nu = 3$, meaning $n = 4$, you want to look in the third row of numbers. If $\nu = 3$ for $\alpha_1 = 05$, the tabled value is 2.353. This value represents the 95th percentile point in a t distribution with 3 degrees of freedom. This is because the table only presents the upper tail percentiles. Given that the t distribution is symmetric around 0, the lower-tail percentiles are the same values except for a change in sign. The 5th percentile for 3 degrees of freedom then is −2.353. Thus, for a right-tailed directional hypothesis the critical value will be +2.353 and for a left-tailed directional hypothesis the critical value will be −2.353.

If $\nu = 120$ for $\alpha_1 = .05$, then the tabled value is 1.658. Thus, as sample size and degrees of freedom increase, the value of t decreases. *This makes it easier to reject the null hypothesis when sample size is large* (and thus one of the criticisms of null hypothesis significance testing).

6.1.1.8.3 The *t* Test

Now that we have covered the theoretical distribution underlying the test of a single mean for an unknown σ, we can go ahead and look at the inferential test. First, the null

ν	α_1=.10 α_2=.20	.05 .10	.025 .050	.01 .02	.005 .010	.0025 .0050	.001 .002	.0005 .0010
1	3.078	6.314	12.706	31.821	63.657	127.32	318.31	636.62
2	1.886	2.920	4.303	6.965	9.925	14.089	22.327	31.598
3	1.638	2.353	3.182	4.541	5.841	7.453	10.214	12.924
…	…	…	…	…	…	…	…	…

FIGURE 6.4
Snapshot of t distribution table.

and alternative hypotheses for the t test are written in the same fashion as for the z test presented earlier. Thus, for a two-tailed test we have the same notation as previously presented:

$$H_0: \mu = 100 \quad \text{or} \quad H_0: \mu - 100 = 0$$

$$H_1: \mu \neq 100 \quad \text{or} \quad H_1: \mu - 100 \neq 0$$

The test statistic t is determined as follows:

$$t = \frac{\bar{Y} - \mu_0}{s_{\bar{Y}}}$$

The critical values for the t distribution are obtained from the t table in Table A.2 in the Appendix, where you take into account the α level, whether the test is one or two tailed, and the degrees of freedom ($\nu = n - 1$). If the test statistic falls into a critical region, as defined by the critical values, then our conclusion is to *reject* H_0. If the test statistic does not fall into a critical region, then our conclusion is to *fail to reject* H_0. For the t test the critical values depend on the sample size, whereas for the z test the critical values do not.

As was the case for the z test, for the t test a confidence interval for μ_0 can be developed. The $(1 - \alpha)\%$ confidence interval is formed from

$$\bar{Y} \pm t_{cv} s_{\bar{Y}}$$

where t_{cv} is the critical value from the t table. If the hypothesized mean value m_0 is not contained in the interval, then our conclusion is to *reject* H_0. If the hypothesized mean value μ_0 is contained in the interval, then our conclusion is *fail to reject* H_0. The confidence interval procedure for the t test then is comparable to that for the z test.

6.1.1.8.4 An Example

Let us consider the entire t test process using the example that we saw earlier with Ott Lier in the opening scenario. A hockey coach wanted to determine whether the mean skating speed of his team differed from the hypothesized league mean speed of 12 seconds. The hypotheses are developed as a *two-tailed test* and written as follows:

$$H_0: \mu = 12 \text{ or } H_0: \mu - 12 = 0$$

$$H_1: \mu \neq 12 \text{ or } H_1: \mu - 12 \neq 0$$

Skating speed around the rink was timed for each of 16 players (data are given in Table 6.2 and on the website as "ch6skatingtime"). The mean speed of the team was $\bar{Y} = 10$ seconds with a standard deviation of $s_Y = 1.7889$ seconds. The standard error of the mean is then computed as follows:

$$s_{\bar{Y}} = \frac{s_Y}{\sqrt{n}} = \frac{1.7889}{\sqrt{16}} = 0.4472$$

TABLE 6.2
SPSS Output for Skating Example

Raw data:	8, 12, 9, 7, 8, 10, 9, 11, 13.5, 8.5, 10.5, 9.5, 11.5, 12.5, 9.5, 10.5

We wish to conduct a *t* test at a = .05, where we compute the test statistic *t* as

$$t = \frac{\bar{Y} - \mu_0}{s_{\bar{Y}}} = \frac{10 - 12}{0.4472} = -4.4722$$

We turn to the *t* table in Table A.2 in the Appendix and determine the critical values based on $\alpha_2 = .05$ and $\nu = 15$ degrees of freedom. The critical values are +2.131, which defines the upper-tail critical region, and −2.131, which defines the lower-tail critical region. Given that the test statistic *t* (i.e., −4.4722) falls into the lower-tail critical region (i.e., the test statistic is less than the lower-tail critical value), our decision is to *reject* H_0 and conclude that the mean skating speed of this team is statistically significantly different from the hypothesized league mean speed at the .05 level of significance. A **95% confidence interval** can be computed as follows:

$$\bar{Y} \pm t_{cv} s_{\bar{Y}} = 10 \pm (2.131)(0.4472) = 10 \pm .9530 = (9.0470, 10.9530)$$

As the confidence interval does not contain the hypothesized mean value of 12, our conclusion is again to reject H_0. Thus, there is evidence to suggest that the mean skating speed of the team differs from the hypothesized league mean speed of 12 seconds.

6.1.2 Sample Size

We will start our discussion of sufficient sample size for the one-sample *t* test by noting that there is a difference in having a sample size that produces *sufficiently powered results* as compared to a sample size that will produce *robust results*. **Robust results** mean that the results are still relatively accurate even if there are some violations of assumptions. Having robust results does *not* equate, necessarily, to having a sufficiently powered test (i.e., being able to detect a statistically significant difference if it exists). It is possible to have robust results for an underpowered test (i.e., assumptions are met, but the sample size is not large enough for detecting a difference if it is there). And it is also possible to have a sufficiently powered test that does not produce robust results (i.e., sample size is sufficient for detecting a difference if it is there, but assumptions have been violated). It is a common myth that a sample size of 30 is sufficient for conducting a one-sample *t* test (or generally any of the three *t* tests). We have also seen researchers say that a sample size of 20 is sufficient. Other researchers say that as long as the normality assumption is met, regardless of the sample size, the results will be robust. *We do not condone going by any of these suggested guidelines for determining sample size.* There are no conventions that we recommend for sample size. Rather, we encourage researchers to conduct a power analysis to determine the sample size needed for sufficient power.

6.1.3 Power

In this section we complete our discussion of Type II error (β) and power (1 − β). First, we return to our rain example and discuss the entire decision-making context. Then we describe the factors that determine power.

6.1.3.1 The Full Decision-Making Context

Previously, we defined Type II error as the probability of failing to reject H_0 when H_0 is really false. In other words, in reality H_0 is false, yet we made a decision error and did not reject H_0. The probability associated with a Type II error is denoted by β. **Power** is a related concept and is defined as the *probability of rejecting* H_0 *when* H_0 *is really false*. In other words, in reality H_0 is false, and we made the correct decision to reject H_0. The probability associated with power is denoted by (1 – b). Let us return to our "rain" example to describe Type I and Type II errors and power more completely.

The full decision-making context for the rain example is given in Figure 6.5. The distribution on the left-hand side of the figure is the sampling distribution when H_0 is true, meaning in reality it does not rain. The vertical line represents the critical value for deciding whether to carry an umbrella or not. To the left of the vertical line we do not carry an umbrella, and to the right side of the vertical line we do carry an umbrella. For the no-rain sampling distribution on the left, there are two possibilities. *First, we do not carry an umbrella and it does not rain.* This is the *unshaded* portion under the no-rain sampling distribution to the left of the vertical line. This is a *correct decision*, and the probability associated with this decision is 1 – α. *Second, we do carry an umbrella and it does not rain.* This is the *shaded* portion under the no-rain sampling distribution to the right of the vertical line. This is an *incorrect decision*, a Type I error, and the probability associated with this decision is α/2 in either the upper or lower tail, and α collectively.

The distribution on the right-hand side of the figure is the sampling distribution when H_0 is false, meaning in reality it does rain. For the rain sampling distribution, there are two possibilities. *First, we do carry an umbrella and it does rain.* This is the *unshaded* portion under the rain sampling distribution to the right of the vertical line. This is a *correct decision* and the probability associated with this decision is 1 – β, or power. *Second, we do not carry an umbrella and it does rain.* This is the *shaded* portion under the rain sampling distribution to the left of the vertical line. This is an *incorrect decision*, a Type II error, and the probability associated with this decision is β.

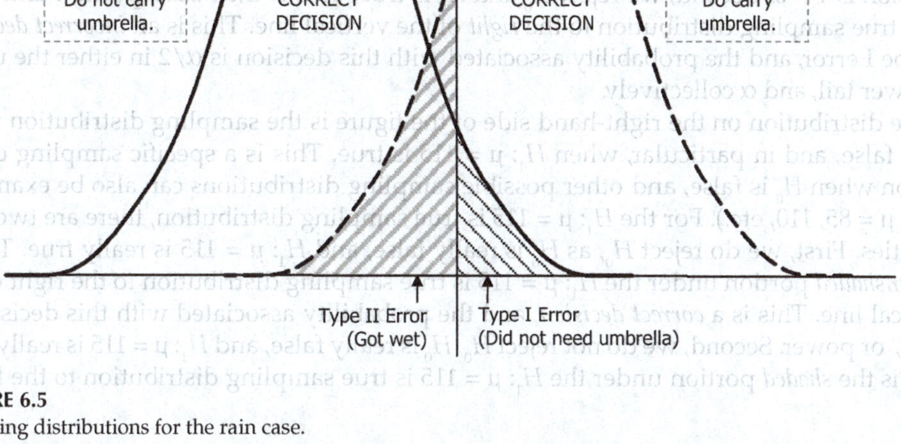

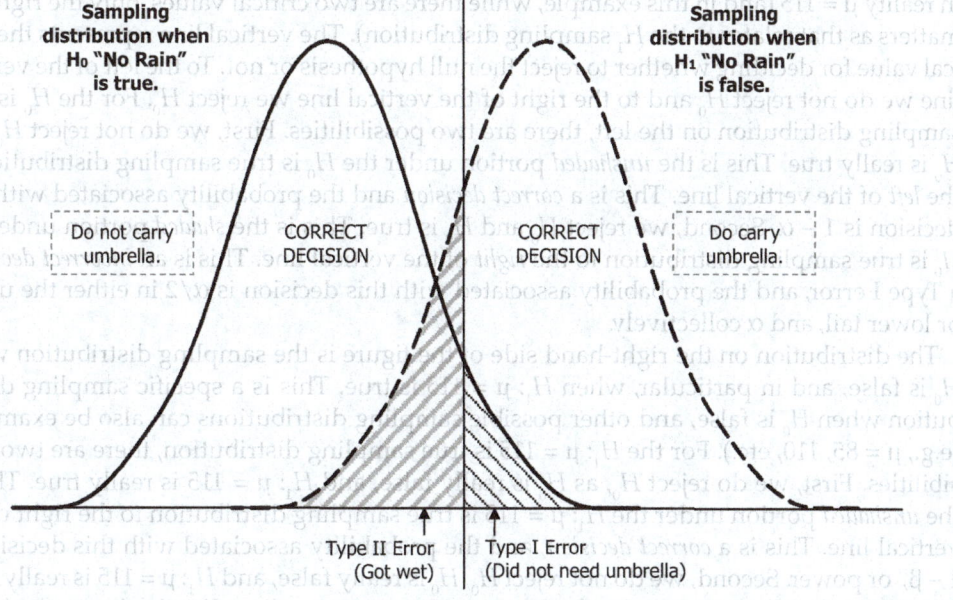

FIGURE 6.5
Sampling distributions for the rain case.

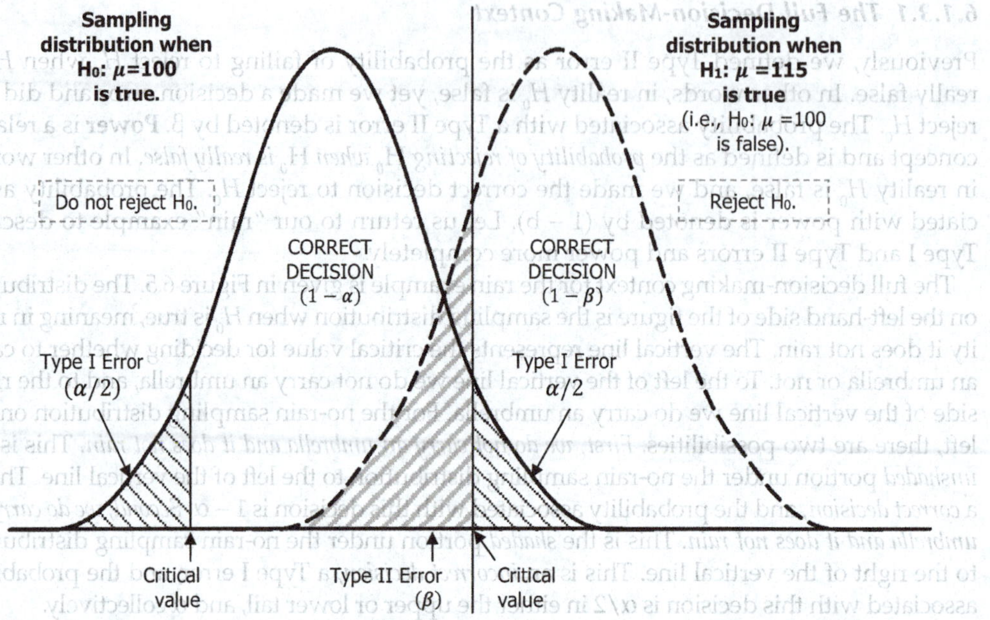

FIGURE 6.6
Sampling distributions for the intelligence test case.

As a second illustration, consider again the example intelligence test situation. This situation is depicted in Figure 6.6. The distribution on the left-hand side of the figure is the sampling distribution of $\bar{Y}$ when H_0 is true, meaning in reality μ = 100. The distribution on the right-hand side of the figure is the sampling distribution of $\bar{Y}$ when H_1 is true, meaning in reality μ = 115 (and in this example, while there are two critical values, only the right tail matters as that relates to the H_1 sampling distribution). The vertical line represents the critical value for deciding whether to reject the null hypothesis or not. To the left of the vertical line we do not reject H_0 and to the right of the vertical line we reject H_0. For the H_0 is true sampling distribution on the left, there are two possibilities. First, we do not reject H_0 and H_0 is really true. This is the *unshaded* portion under the H_0 is true sampling distribution to the *left* of the vertical line. This is a *correct decision* and the probability associated with this decision is 1 − α. Second, we reject H_0 and H_0 is true. This is the *shaded* portion under the H_0 is true sampling distribution to the *right* of the vertical line. This is an *incorrect decision*, a Type I error, and the probability associated with this decision is α/2 in either the upper or lower tail, and α collectively.

The distribution on the right-hand side of the figure is the sampling distribution when H_0 is false, and in particular, when H_1: μ = 115 is true. This is a specific sampling distribution when H_0 is false, and other possible sampling distributions can also be examined (e.g., μ = 85, 110, etc.). For the H_1: μ = 115 is true sampling distribution, there are two possibilities. First, we do reject H_0, as H_0 is really false, and H_1: μ = 115 is really true. This is the *unshaded* portion under the H_1: μ = 115 is true sampling distribution to the right of the vertical line. This is a *correct decision*, and the probability associated with this decision is 1 − β, or power. Second, we do not reject H_0, H_0 is really false, and H_1: μ = 115 is really true. This is the *shaded* portion under the H_1: μ = 115 is true sampling distribution to the left of the vertical line. This is an *incorrect decision,* a Type II error, and the probability associated with this decision is β.

6.1.3.2 Power Determinants

Power is determined by five different factors: (1) level of significance, (2) sample size, (3) population standard deviation, (4) difference between the true population mean μ and the hypothesized mean value μ_0, and (5) directionality of the test (i.e., one- or two-tailed test). Let us talk about each of these factors in more detail.

First, power is determined by the level of significance, α. As α increases, power increases. Thus, if α increases from .05 to .10, then power will increase. This would occur in Figure 6.5 if the vertical line were shifted to the left (thus creating a larger critical region and thereby making it easier to reject the null hypothesis). This would increase the alpha level and also increase power. This factor is under the control of the researcher as the researcher is the one to establish α.

Second, power is determined by sample size. As sample size *n* increases, power increases. Thus, if sample size increases, meaning we have a sample that consists of a larger proportion of the population, this will cause the standard error of the mean to decrease, as there is less sampling error with larger samples. In our figure, this would also result in the vertical line being moved to the left (again thereby creating a larger critical region and thereby making it easier to reject the null hypothesis). In addition, because a larger sample yields a smaller standard error, it will be easier to reject H_0 (all else being equal) as sample size increases, and the confidence intervals generated will also be narrower. This factor is *theoretically* under the control of the researcher. In theory, researchers have access to populations that are sufficient for drawing the sample size needed for sufficient power. In practice, researchers may have access to populations that are limited in size, and thus regardless of what sample size is needed for sufficient power, they simply don't have a population that meets that requirement. In the latter situation, the researcher may consider adjustments on other factors that influence power so that they can still have a sufficiently powered test.

Third, power is determined by the size of the population standard deviation, σ. Although not under the researcher's control, as the population standard deviation increases, power decreases. Thus, if the population standard deviation *increases,* meaning the variability in the population is larger, this will cause the standard error of the mean to increase as there is more sampling error with larger variability. In our figure, this would result in the vertical line being moved to the right . If the population standard deviation *decreases,* meaning the variability in the population is smaller, this will cause the standard error of the mean to decrease as there is less sampling error with smaller variability. This would result in the vertical line in our figure being moved to the left. Considering, for example, the one-sample mean test, the standard error of the mean is the denominator of the test statistic formula. When the standard error term decreases, the denominator is smaller, and thus the test statistic value becomes larger (and thereby easier to reject the null hypothesis).

Fourth, power is determined by the difference between the true population mean, μ, and the hypothesized mean value, μ_0. Although not always under the researcher's control (only in true experiments, as described in Chapter 14), as the difference between the true population mean and the hypothesized mean value increases, power increases. Thus, if the difference between the true population mean and the hypothesized mean value is large, it will be easier to correctly reject H_0. This would result in greater separation between the two sampling distributions. In other words, the entire H_1 is true sampling distribution would be shifted to the right. Consider, for example, the one-sample mean test. The numerator is the difference between the means. The larger the numerator (holding the denominator constant), the more likely it will be to reject the null hypothesis.

Finally, power is determined by directionality and type of statistical procedure—whether we conduct a one- or a two-tailed test as well as the type of test of inference. There is greater power in a one-tailed test, such as when $\mu > 100$, than in a two-tailed test. In a one-tailed test the vertical line in our figure will be shifted to the left, creating a larger rejection region. This factor is *theoretically* under the researcher's control, however it may be hard to justify a one-tailed test if there is a complete absence of theory to support directionality. There is also often greater power in conducting parametric as compared to nonparametric tests of inference (we will talk more about parametric vs. nonparametric tests in later chapters). This factor is under the researcher's control to some extent depending on the scale of measurement of the variables and the extent to which the assumptions of parametric tests are met.

Power has become of much greater interest and concern to the applied researcher in recent years. We begin by distinguishing between ***a priori* power**, when power is determined as a study is being planned or designed (i.e., prior to the study), and **post hoc power**, when power is determined after the study has been conducted and the data analyzed.

For *a priori* power, if you want to ensure a certain amount of power in a study, then you can determine what sample size would be needed to achieve such a level of power. This requires the input of characteristics such as alpha level; the estimated effect size, which requires knowledge of difference between the true population mean (μ) and the hypothesized mean value (μ_0), as well as the standard deviation; and one- versus two-tailed test. Alternatively, one could determine power given each of those characteristics. This can be done by either using statistical software (e.g., G*Power), or by using tables, with the most definitive collection of tables being in Cohen (1988).

For post hoc power (also called *observed power*), most statistical software packages (e.g., SPSS, SAS) will compute this as part of the analysis for many types of inferential statistics (e.g., analysis of variance). However, even though post hoc power is routinely reported in some journals, it has been found to have some flaws. For example, Hoenig and Heisey (2001) concluded that it should not be used to aid in interpreting nonsignificant results. They found that low power may indicate a small effect (e.g., a small mean difference) rather than an underpowered study. Thus, increasing sample size may not make much of a difference. Yuan and Maxwell (2005) found that observed power is almost always biased (too high or too low), except when true power is .50. Therefore, we do not recommend the sole use of post hoc power to determine sample size in the next study; rather, we recommended that CIs be used in addition to post hoc power. (An example presented later in this chapter will use G*Power to illustrate both *a priori* sample size requirements given desired power and post hoc power analysis.)

6.1.4 Effect Size

We have discussed the inferential test of a single mean in terms of statistical significance. However, are statistically significant results always *practically* (or *clinically*) *important*? In other words, if a result is statistically significant, should we make a big deal out of this result in a practical or clinical sense? Regardless of the results of the null hypothesis significance test, are the results clinically important such that they make a difference? Consider again the simple example where the null and alternative hypotheses are as follows.

$$H_0: \mu = 100 \quad \text{or} \quad H_0: \mu - 100 = 0$$

$$H_1: \mu \neq 100 \quad \text{or} \quad H_1: \mu - 100 \neq 0$$

A sample mean intelligence test score of $\bar{Y} = 101$ is observed for a sample size of $n = 2000$ and a known population standard deviation of $\sigma_Y = 15$. If we perform the test at the .01 level of significance, we find we are able to reject H_0 even though the observed mean is only 1 unit away from the hypothesized mean value. The reason is, because the sample size is rather large, a rather small standard error of the mean is computed $(\sigma_{\bar{Y}} = 0.3354)$, and we thus reject H_0 because the test statistic ($z = 2.9815$) exceeds the critical value ($z = 2.5758$). Holding the mean and standard deviation constant, if we had a sample size of 200 instead of 2000, the standard error becomes much larger $(\sigma_{\bar{Y}} = 1.0607)$, and we thus fail to reject H_0 because the test statistic ($z = 0.9428$) does not exceed the critical value ($z = 2.5758$). From this example we can see how the sample size can drive the results of the hypothesis test, and how it is possible that statistical significance can be influenced simply as an artifact of sample size.

Should we make a big deal out of an intelligence test sample mean that is 1 unit away from the hypothesized mean intelligence? In other words, does this difference have practical significance—is it clinically important? The answer is "maybe not." If we gather enough sample data, any small difference, no matter how small, can wind up being statistically significant. Larger samples are simply more likely to yield statistically significant results. On the other hand, *practical or clinical significance is not entirely a statistical matter*. It is also a matter for the substantive field under investigation. Thus, the meaningfulness of a "small difference" (or a moderate or large one) is for the substantive area to determine. All that inferential statistics can really determine is statistical significance. However, we should always keep practical or clinical significance in mind when interpreting our findings.

As we have already noted, in recent years, a major debate has been ongoing in the statistical community about the role of significance testing. The debate centers on whether null hypothesis significance testing (NHST) best suits the needs of researchers. At one extreme, some argue that NHST is fine as is. At the other extreme, others argue that NHST should be totally abandoned. In the middle, yet others argue that NHST should be supplemented with measures of effect size, which are metrics for practical or clinical significance. In this text we have taken the middle road believing that more information is a better choice. Many other researchers agree with this, and if you follow the American Psychological Association (APA) style guide (2020), you'll find that they agree as well:

> APA, for example, stresses that *NHST is but a starting point* and that additional reporting elements, such as effect sizes, confidence intervals, and extensive description are needed to convey the most complete meaning of the results.... [C]omplete reporting of all tested hypotheses and estimates of appropriate effect sizes and confidence intervals are the *minimum expectations* for all APA journals.
>
> (p. 87, italics added for emphasis)

6.1.4.1 Cohen's Delta

Let us now formally introduce the notion of **effect size**, which again *are metrics for practical or clinical significance*. While there are a number of different measures of effect size, the most commonly used measure is **Cohen's delta (δ)** for population data or **d** for sample data (Cohen, 1988). For the *population case* of the one-sample mean test, Cohen's δ is computed as follows:

$$\delta = \frac{\mu - \mu_0}{\sigma}$$

For the corresponding *sample case*, **Cohen's d** is computed as follows:

$$d = \frac{\bar{Y} - \mu_0}{s}$$

Using the skating time example presented earlier, we find the following:

$$d = \frac{10 - 12}{1.7889} = -1.118$$

For the one-sample mean test, d indicates how many standard deviations the sample mean is from the hypothesized mean. Thus, if $d = 1.0$, the sample mean is one standard deviation away from the hypothesized mean. In this example, d indicates that there is slightly more than one standard deviation difference between our sample mean skating speed and the hypothesized mean value. The negative value for d is simply a reflection of the fact that our sample skating speed is less than what we hypothesized and that our sample is about one standard deviation quicker than what was hypothesized.

Cohen has proposed the following subjective standards for the social and behavioral sciences as a convention for interpreting d: small effect size, $d = .2$; medium effect size, $d = .5$; large effect size, $d = .8$. Applying Cohen's subjective standards for interpreting the size of your effect should always be a last resort. Rather, a good starting place for interpreting the size of an effect is to translate that effect back into a comparison within your study. In other words, contextualize the effect with your own sample. For example, if you find an effect size of 1.0, you can say that there is one standard deviation difference between your sample mean and the hypothesized mean value. More specifically, you can say that 84% of the cases in your sample will be above the hypothesized mean (recall the normal distribution and when $z = 1.0$, 84% of the distribution is below that value?). Researchers may want to review online resources for interpreting Cohen's d (e.g., http://rpsychologist.com/d3/cohend/, an interactive tool that provides multiple types of interpretation given d). Interpretation of effect size can also be made based on a comparison to similar studies; what is considered a "small" effect using Cohen's rule of thumb may actually be quite large in comparison to other related studies that have been conducted. In lieu of a comparison to other studies, such as in those cases where there are no or minimal related studies, then Cohen's subjective standards may be considered.

6.1.4.2 Confidence Intervals for Cohen's Delta

Computing **confidence intervals for effect sizes** is also valuable. The benefit in creating confidence intervals for effect size values is similar to that of creating confidence intervals for parameter estimates—*confidence intervals for the effect size provide an added measure of precision that is not obtained from knowledge of the effect size alone.* Computing confidence intervals for effect size indices, however, is not as straightforward as simply plugging in known values into a formula. This is because *d* is a function of both the population mean and population standard deviation (Finch & Cumming, 2009), and the noncentrality parameter comes into play. Without going deep into the weeds, we'll provide an overview into the noncentrality parameter and what it means in relation to confidence intervals for effect sizes [readers who wish to learn more may want to consult Smithson (2003)]. A central *t* distribution occurs when we subtract the true population mean from the sample mean. A **noncentral *t* distribution** is not distributed around zero but around some other point, which is referred to as the **noncentrality parameter (*ncp*)**. If $\mu = m_0$, then *ncp* is 0 and the distribution is a central *t*. Effect size *d* is a linear function of the noncentrality parameter, and thus putting confidence limits on *ncp* will allow us to compute confidence intervals for effect size *d*.

A nice online calculator for computing the one-sample *t* test confidence interval for effect size *d* using the noncentrality parameter is available at https://effect-size-calculator.herokuapp.com (Uanhoro, 2017). As we see in Figure 6.7, five inputs are required: sample mean, population mean (where the population mean is the hypothesized mean value), sample standard deviation, sample size, and confidence interval (i.e., the complement of alpha). Cohen's *d* is −1.118, as noted previously as well, with confidence intervals of −1.734 and −.477. Putting this in context of our skating example, if multiple random samples were drawn from the population, 95% of the samples could expect, at minimum, about one-half

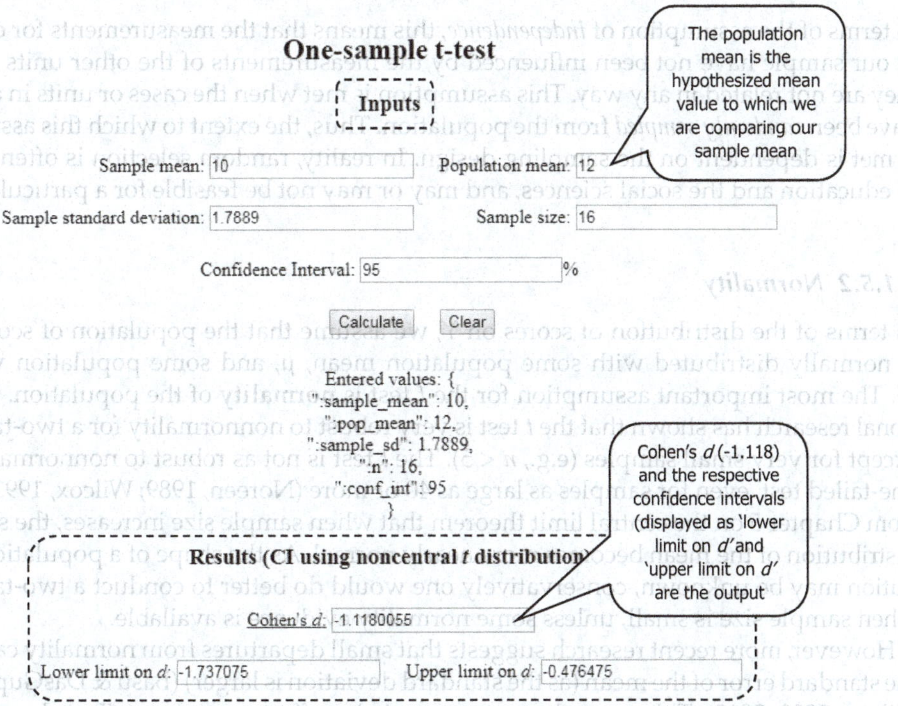

FIGURE 6.7
Effect size *d* and confidence interval of *d*.

and, at maximum, up to nearly 2 standard deviation units quicker skating speed relative to the hypothesized mean of 12.

Interested readers are referred to appropriate sources to learn more about confidence intervals for d (e.g., Algina & Keselman, 2003; Algina, Keselman, & Penfield, 2005; Cumming & Calin-Jageman, 2017; Cumming & Finch, 2001).

While a complete discussion of issues discussed in this section is beyond this text, further information on effect sizes can be seen in special sections of *Educational and Psychological Measurement* (April 2001; August 2001), Grissom and Kim (2005), and Grissom and Kim (2012), among many other resources, while additional material on NHST can be viewed in Harlow, Mulaik, and Steiger (1997) and a special section of *Educational and Psychological Measurement* (October 2000). Additionally, style manuals (e.g., American Psychological Association, 2020) often provide useful guidelines on reporting effect size.

6.1.5 Assumptions

In order to use the theoretical t distribution to determine critical values, we must assume that $Y_i \sim N(\mu, \Sigma^2)$ (i.e., Y is approximately normally distributed with a population mean, μ, and population variance, σ^2) and that the observations are independent of each other (also referred to as being "independent and identically distributed," or IID). Thus, there are two assumptions for the one-sample t test: independence and normality.

6.1.5.1 Independence

In terms of the assumption of *independence*, this means that the measurements for each unit in our sample have not been influenced by the measurements of the other units and that they are not related in any way. This assumption is met when the cases or units in a sample have been *randomly sampled* from the population. Thus, the extent to which this assumption is met is dependent on the sampling design. In reality, random selection is often difficult in education and the social sciences, and may or may not be feasible for a particular study.

6.1.5.2 Normality

In terms of the distribution of scores on Y, we assume that the population of scores on Y is normally distributed with some population mean, μ, and some population variance, σ^2. The most important assumption for the t test is **normality** of the population. Conventional research has shown that the t test is very robust to nonnormality for a two-tailed test except for very small samples (e.g., $n < 5$). The t test is not as robust to nonnormality for a one-tailed test, even for samples as large as 40 or more (Noreen, 1989; Wilcox, 1993). Recall from Chapter 5 on the central limit theorem that when sample size increases, the sampling distribution of the mean becomes more nearly normal. As the shape of a population distribution may be unknown, conservatively one would do better to conduct a two-tailed test when sample size is small, unless some normality evidence is available.

However, more recent research suggests that small departures from normality can inflate the standard error of the mean (as the standard deviation is larger) (Basu & DasGupta, 1995; Wilcox, 2003, 2012). This can reduce power and also affect control over Type I error. Thus, a cavalier attitude about ignoring nonnormality may not be the best approach, and if nonnormality *is* an issue, other procedures, such as the nonparametric Kolmogorov-Smirnov one-sample test, should be considered.

Many different tools can be used for testing the assumption of normality, and researchers should approach testing this assumption as collecting multiple forms of evidence to best understand the extent to which the assumption was met. Sample statistics, such as skewness and kurtosis, can be reviewed. Values within an absolute value of 2.0 suggest evidence of normality. We can also divide the skew and kurtosis values by their standard errors to get *standardized skew and kurtosis* values. We can compare those values to a critical value (e.g., ±1.65 if $\alpha = .10$; ±1.96 if $\alpha = .05$; ±2.06 if $\alpha = .01$) and determine if there is statistically significant skew and/or kurtosis. **D'Agostino's test** (D'Agostino, 1970) can be used to examine the null hypothesis that skewness equals zero, with a statistically significant D'Agostino's test indicating that there is statistically significant skewness. For kurtosis, we can use the **Bonett-Seier test for Geary's kurtosis** (Bonett & Seier, 2002). The null hypothesis states that data should have a Geary's kurtosis value equal to $\sqrt{2/\pi} = .7979$. Thus, a statistically significant Bonett-Seier test for Geary's kurtosis would indicate that there is statistically significant kurtosis. Thus, with these tests, as with the Kolmogorov-Smirnov (K-S) and the Shapiro-Wilk (S-W), we do *not* want to find statistically significant results.

A few other statistics can be used to gauge normality as well. Quantile-quantile (Q-Q) plots are also often examined to determine evidence of normality. Q-Q plots are graphs that depict quantiles of the sample distribution to quantiles of the theoretical normal distribution. Points that fall on or closely to the diagonal line of the Q-Q plot suggest evidence of normality. The detrended normal Q-Q plot is another graph that can be reviewed. This plot provides evidence of normality when the points exhibit little or no pattern around zero (the horizontal line); however, due to subjectivity in determining the extent of a pattern, this graph can often be difficult to interpret. Thus, in many cases, you may wish to rely more heavily on the other forms of evidence of normality. A summary of several different types of evidence for examining normality is provided in Box 6.1.

BOX 6.1 Evidence for Testing the Assumption of Normality

Evidence	Interpretation for Providing Evidence of Normality
Boxplot	Normality suggested when the quartiles are relatively evenly distributed with no outliers
Histogram	Normality suggested with a relatively bell-shaped curve
Skewness	Values within an absolute value of 2.0 suggest evidence of normality
Kurtosis	Values within an absolute value of 2.0 suggest evidence of normality
Standardized skew and standardized kurtosis	Divide the skew and kurtosis values by their standard errors to get *standardized skew* and *kurtosis* values. Compare those values to a critical value (e.g., ±1.65 if $\alpha = .10$; ±1.96 if $\alpha = .05$; ±2.06 if $\alpha = .01$). Standardized skew and kurtosis that are less than the critical value suggest evidence of normality
D'Agostino's test	Tests the null hypothesis that skewness equals zero, with a statistically significant D'Agostino's test indicating that there is statistically significant skewness
Bonett-Seier test for Geary's kurtosis	Tests the null hypothesis that data should have a Geary's kurtosis value equal to $\sqrt{2/\pi} = .7979$. A statistically significant test indicates that there is statistically significant kurtosis
Quantile-quantile (Q-Q) plots	Plots that depict quantiles of the sample distribution to quantiles of the theoretical normal distribution. Points that fall on or closely to the diagonal line of the Q-Q plot suggest evidence of normality

(continued)

Detrended quantile-quantile plot	Evidence of normality is provided when the points exhibit little or no pattern around zero (the horizontal line).
Kolmogorov-Smirnov (K-S) and Shapiro-Wilk (S-W) tests	K-S and S-W are formal tests of normality. K-S is conservative; S-W test is usually considered more powerful and is recommended for use with small sample sizes ($n < 50$). Non-statistically significant K-S and S-W results are interpreted to say that our distribution is *not* statistically significantly different than a normal distribution

6.2 Computing Inferences About a Single Mean Using SPSS

Here we consider what SPSS has to offer in the way of testing hypotheses about a single mean. As with most statistical software, the *t* test is included as an option in SPSS, but the *z* test is not. Thus, instructions for determining the one-sample *t* test using SPSS are presented first.

Step 1. To conduct the one-sample *t* test, go to "Analyze" in the top pulldown menu, then select "Compare Means," and then select "One-Sample T Test." Following the steps in the screenshot shown in Figure 6.8 produces the "One-Sample T Test" dialog box.

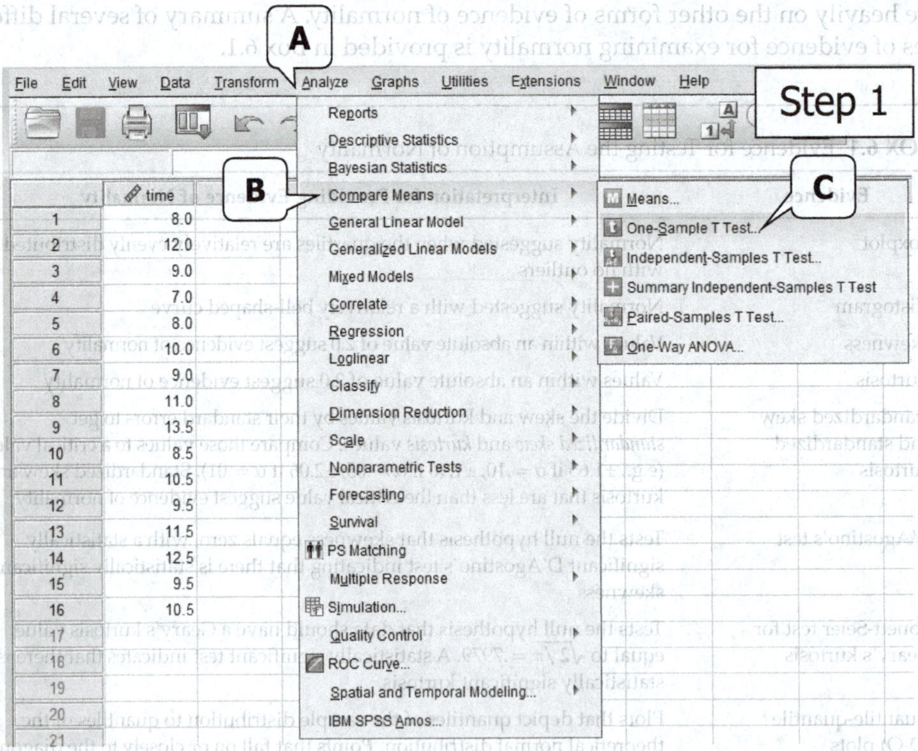

FIGURE 6.8
Step 1: One-sample *t* test.

Step 2. Next, from the main "One-Sample T Test" dialog box, click the variable of interest from the list on the left (e.g., "time"), and move it into the "Test Variable" box by clicking the arrow button. At the bottom right of the screen is a box for "Test Value," where you indicate the hypothesized value (e.g., "12") (see the screenshot in Figure 6.9). It's obviously very important not to fail to input your hypothesized value as doing so will test against the default, which is zero!

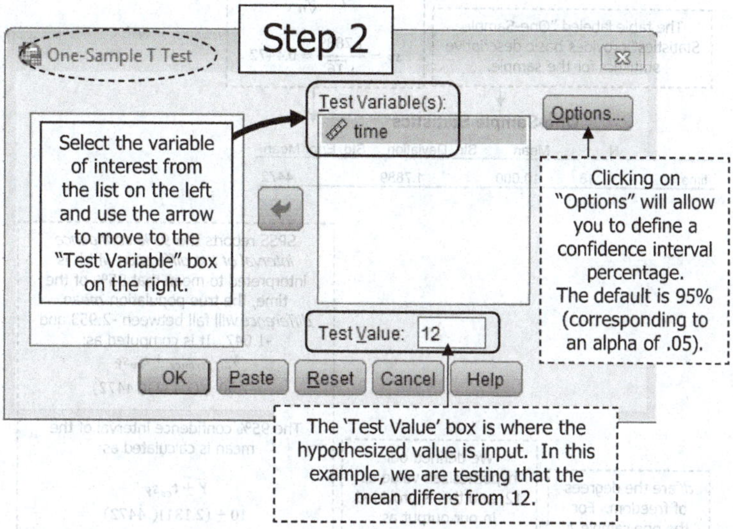

FIGURE 6.9
Step 2: One-sample *t* test.

Step 3 (optional). The default alpha level in SPSS is .05, and thus the default corresponding confidence interval is 95%. If you wish to test your hypothesis at an alpha level other than .05 (and thus obtain confidence intervals other than 95%), then click the "Options" button located in the top-right corner of the main dialog box. From here, the confidence interval percentage can be adjusted to correspond to the alpha level at which your hypothesis is being tested (see the screenshot in Figure 6.10). For purposes of this example, the test has been generated using an alpha level of .05.

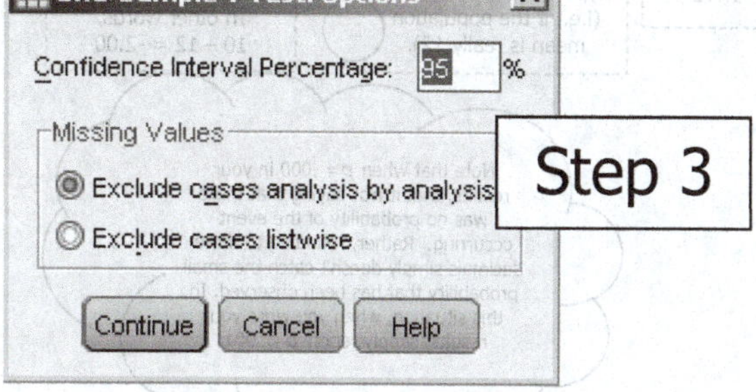

FIGURE 6.10
Step 3: One-sample *t* test.

The one-sample t test output for the skating example is provided in Table 6.3.

TABLE 6.3
SPSS Output for Skating Example

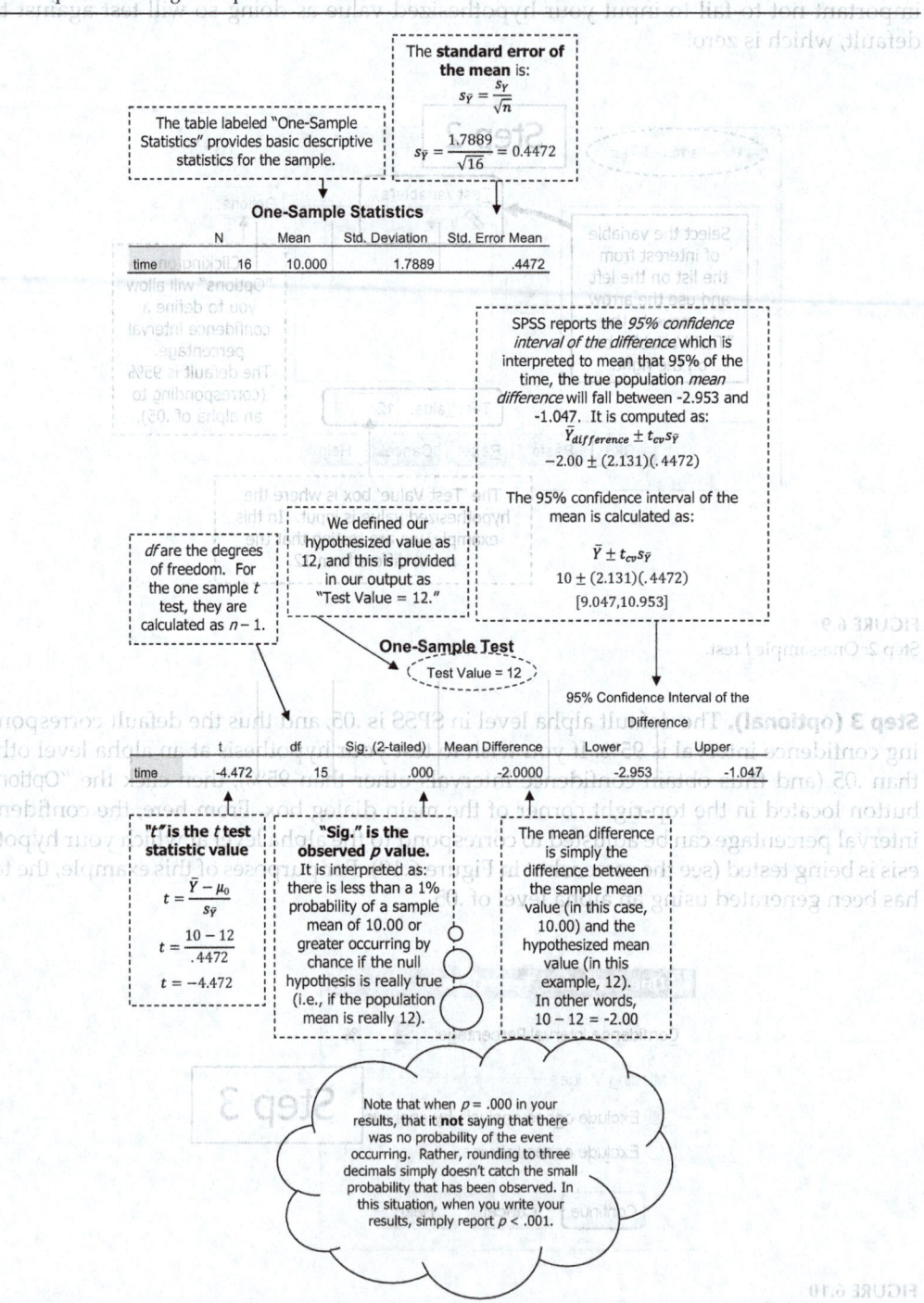

The **standard error of the mean** is:

$$s_{\bar{Y}} = \frac{s_Y}{\sqrt{n}}$$

$$s_{\bar{Y}} = \frac{1.7889}{\sqrt{16}} = 0.4472$$

The table labeled "One-Sample Statistics" provides basic descriptive statistics for the sample.

One-Sample Statistics

	N	Mean	Std. Deviation	Std. Error Mean
time	16	10.000	1.7889	.4472

SPSS reports the *95% confidence interval of the difference* which is interpreted to mean that 95% of the time, the true population *mean difference* will fall between -2.953 and -1.047. It is computed as:

$$\bar{Y}_{difference} \pm t_{cv} s_{\bar{Y}}$$

$$-2.00 \pm (2.131)(.4472)$$

The 95% confidence interval of the mean is calculated as:

$$\bar{Y} \pm t_{cv} s_{\bar{Y}}$$

$$10 \pm (2.131)(.4472)$$

$$[9.047, 10.953]$$

df are the degrees of freedom. For the one sample t test, they are calculated as $n - 1$.

We defined our hypothesized value as 12, and this is provided in our output as "Test Value = 12."

One-Sample Test

Test Value = 12

	t	df	Sig. (2-tailed)	Mean Difference	95% Confidence Interval of the Difference	
					Lower	Upper
time	-4.472	15	.000	-2.0000	-2.953	-1.047

"*t*" is the *t* test statistic value

$$t = \frac{\bar{Y} - \mu_0}{s_{\bar{Y}}}$$

$$t = \frac{10 - 12}{.4472}$$

$$t = -4.472$$

"Sig." is the observed *p* value. It is interpreted as: there is less than a 1% probability of a sample mean of 10.00 or greater occurring by chance if the null hypothesis is really true (i.e., if the population mean is really 12).

The mean difference is simply the difference between the sample mean value (in this case, 10.00) and the hypothesized mean value (in this example, 12). In other words, 10 – 12 = -2.00

Note that when $p = .000$ in your results, that it **not** saying that there was no probability of the event occurring. Rather, rounding to three decimals simply doesn't catch the small probability that has been observed. In this situation, when you write your results, simply report $p < .001$.

6.3 Computing Inferences About a Single Mean Using R

Next we consider **R** for the one-sample *t* test. The scripts are provided within the blocks with additional annotation to assist in understanding how the commands work. Should you want to write reminder notes and annotation to yourself as you write the commands in **R** (and we highly encourage doing so), remember that any text that follows a hashtag (i.e., #) is annotation only and not part of the **R** script. Thus, you can write annotations directly into **R** with hashtags. We encourage this practice so that when you call up the commands in the future, you'll understand what the various lines of code are doing. You may think you'll remember what you did. However, trust us. There is a good chance that you won't. Thus, consider it best practice when using **R** to annotate heavily!

6.3.1 Reading Data into R

```
getwd()
```

R is always pointed to a directory on your computer. To find out which directory it is pointed to, run this "get working directory" command. We will assume that we need to change the working directory, and will use the next line of code to set the working directory to the desired path.

```
setwd("E:/Folder")
```

To set the working directory, use the *setwd* function and change what is in quotation marks here to your file location. Also, if you are copying the directory name, it will copy in slashes. You will need to change the slash (i.e., \) to forward slash (i.e., /). Note that you need your destination name within quotation marks in the parentheses.

```
Ch6_skate <- read.csv("Ch6_skate.csv")
```

The *read.csv* function reads your data into **R**. What's to the left of the <- will be what the data will be called in **R**. In this example, we're calling the **R** dataframe "Ch6_skate." What's to the right of the <- tells **R** to find this particular .csv file. In this example, our file is called "Ch6_skate.csv." Make sure the extension (i.e., .csv) is included in your script. Also note that the name of your file should be in quotation marks within the parentheses.

```
names(Ch6_skate)
```

The *names* function will produce a list of variable names for each dataframe as follows. This is a good check to make sure your data have been read in correctly.

```
[1] "time"
```

```
View(Ch6_skate)
```

The *View* function will let you view the dataset in spreadsheet format in RStudio.

```
summary(Ch6_skate)
```

The *summary* function will produce basic descriptive statistics on all the variables in your dataframe. This is a great way to quickly check to see if the data have been read in correctly and get a feel for your data, if you haven't already. The output from the summary statement for this dataframe looks like this:

FIGURE 6.11
Reading data into **R**.

```
       time
 Min.    : 7.000
 1st Qu.: 8.875
 Median : 9.750
 Mean   :10.000
 3rd Qu.:11.125
 Max.   :13.500
```

FIGURE 6.11 (continued)
Reading data into **R**.

6.3.2 Generating the One-Sample *t* Test

```
install.packages("devtools")
```

We will use the *devtools* package in **R** to compute our one-sample *t* test. The *install.packages* function will install the package. We only need to install the package once.

```
library(devtools)
```

Once the package is installed, we load it into our library using the *library* function, and we will need to load it into the library whenever we start a new session in **R**.

```
Ch6_onet <- t.test(Ch6_skate$time,
                   mu = 12,
                   alternative = "two.sided")
```

We use the *t.test* function to generate the one-sample *t* test. We use the variable "time" from our dataframe, "Ch6_skate." We are testing our sample mean to a hypothesized mean of 12 (i.e., *mu = 12*). And we are conducting a two-tailed test (i.e., *alternative = "two.sided"*). We are creating an object named "Ch6_onet" from the model we generate.

```
Ch6_onet
```

This script will output the results from our one sample *t* test into the RStudio console. We see our test statistic value, $t = -4.4721$, with 15 degrees of freedom, and a p value of $< .001$. The 95% confidence interval of the mean is 9.05 to 10.95. The mean of our variable is 10 and is provided in the "sample estimates" output.

```
        One Sample t-test

data:  Ch6_skate$time

t = -4.4721, df = 15, p-value = 0.0004475

alternative hypothesis: true mean is not equal to 12

95 percent confidence interval:
  9.046787 10.953213

sample estimates:
mean of x
       10
```

FIGURE 6.12
Generating the one-sample *t* test.

6.4 Data Screening

Recall that the one-sample t test rests on two assumptions: independence of observations and normality. In terms of data screening to examine the extent to which assumptions were met, we will focus on normality, as independence is a matter of sampling method.

6.4.1 Generating Normality Evidence

As alluded to earlier in the chapter, understanding the distributional shape of your variable, specifically the extent to which normality is a reasonable assumption, is important. In earlier chapters, we saw how we could use the Explore tool in SPSS to generate a number of useful descriptive statistics. In conducting our one-sample t test, we can again use Explore to examine the extent to which the assumption of normality is met for our sample distribution. As the general steps for accessing Explore from the top toolbar in SPSS have been presented in previous chapters (e.g., Chapter 4), they will not be reiterated here. Thus, we will begin from the main dialog box. We first move the variable of interest to the "Dependent List" box in the main Explore dialog box. Next, click "Plots" in the upper-right corner. Place a checkmark in the boxes for "Normality plots with tests" and also for "Histogram" (see the screenshot in Figure 6.13a).

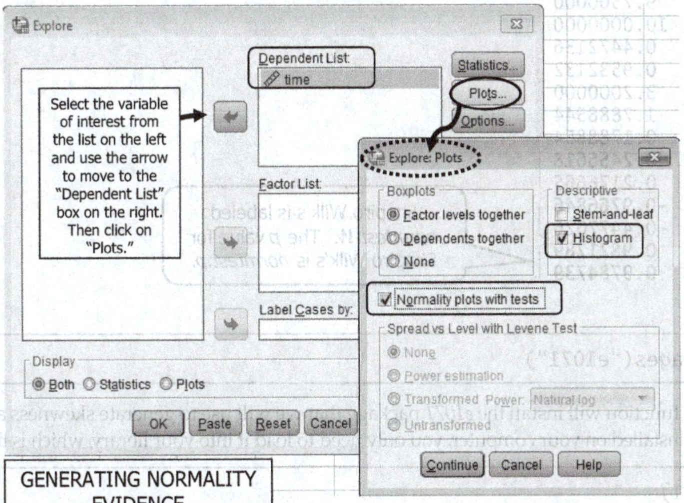

GENERATING NORMALITY EVIDENCE

Working in **R**, we can generate normality evidence as well.

```
install.packages("pastecs")
```

The *install.packages* function will install the *pastecs* package, which we will use to generate various forms of normality evidence.

```
library(pastecs)
```

The *library* function will load the *pastecs* package.

FIGURE 6.13
Generating normality evidence.

```
stat.desc(Ch6_skate,
          norm = TRUE)
```

The *stat.desc* function will generate normality indices on all variables in the dataframe as follows (had we wanted to generate for specific variables, rather than "Ch6_skate," our script would have read "Ch6_skate$VariableName"). We see skew (.25) and kurtosis (−.98) *(wait—these aren't the same values as what we found with SPSS; if that's what you're thinking, hold that thought!)*, along with $SW = .98$, $p = .98$ for the "time" variable. All indicate that the assumption of normality has been met. As we will see later, we can divide the skew and kurtosis values by their standard errors to get a standardized value that can be used to determine if the skew and/or kurtosis is statistically different from zero. Because this output provides "2SE," we would simply divide this value by 2 to arrive at the standard error.

Note: You may have noticed that the skewness and kurtosis values that we've just generated differ from what we found in SPSS, which was skew = .299 and kurtosis = −.483. *This is because there are different ways to calculate skewness and kurtosis.*

Let's use another package in R to calculate these statistics with different algorithms.

```
                    time
nbr.val       16.0000000
nbr.null       0.0000000
nbr.na         0.0000000
min            7.0000000
max           13.5000000
range          6.5000000
sum          160.0000000
median         9.7500000
mean          10.0000000
SE.mean        0.4472136
CI.mean.0.95   0.9532132
var            3.2000000
std.dev        1.7888544
coef.var       0.1788854
skewness       0.2456618
skew.2SE       0.2176665
kurtosis      -0.9766846
kurt.2SE      -0.4477026
normtest.W     0.9821789
normtest.p     0.9784739
```

Shapiro Wilk's is labeled *normtest.W.* The *p* value for Shapiro Wilk's is *normtest.p.*

```
install.packages("e1071")
```

The *install.packages* function will install the *e1071* package that we will use to generate skewness and kurtosis. (If this package is already installed on your computer, you only need to load it into your library, which is the next command.)

```
library(e1071)
```

The *library* function will load the *e1071* package.

```
skewness(Ch4_quiz$quiz, type=3)
skewness(Ch4_quiz$quiz, type=2)
skewness(Ch4_quiz$quiz, type=1)
```

The *skewness* function will generate skewness statistics on the variable(s) we specify. The *type=* script defines how skewness is calculated. Specifying *type=2* will use the algorithm that is used by SPSS. Readers interested in learning more, including the algorithms for each of the three methods, are encouraged to review Joanes and Gill (1998). We see that using *type=2*, our skew is .299, the same value as generated using SPSS.

FIGURE 6.13 (continued)
Generating normality evidence.

```
# skewness(Ch6_skate$time, type=3)
[1] 0.2456618

# skewness(Ch6_skate$time, type=2)
[1] 0.2994734

# skewness(Ch6_skate$time, type=1)
[1] 0.2706329
```

```
kurtosis(Ch6_skate$time, type=3)
kurtosis(Ch6_skate$time, type=2)
kurtosis(Ch6_skate$time, type=1)
```

The *kurtosis* function will generate kurtosis statistics on the variable(s) we specify. The *type=* script defines how kurtosis is calculated. Specifying *type=2* will use the algorithm that is used by SPSS. Readers interested in learning more, including the algorithms for each of the three methods, are encouraged to review Joanes and Gill (1998). We see that using *type=2*, our kurtosis is −.483, the same value as generated using SPSS.

```
# kurtosis(Ch6_skate$time, type=3)
[1] -0.9766846

# kurtosis(Ch6_skate$time, type=2)
[1] -0.4833448

# kurtosis(Ch6_skate$time, type=1)
[1] -0.6979167
```

FIGURE 6.13 (continued)
Generating normality evidence.

6.4.2 Interpreting Normality Evidence

We have already developed a good understanding of how to interpret some forms of evidence of normality, including skewness and kurtosis, histograms, and boxplots. Using data from the hockey team, the histogram suggests relative normality (see Figure 6.14).

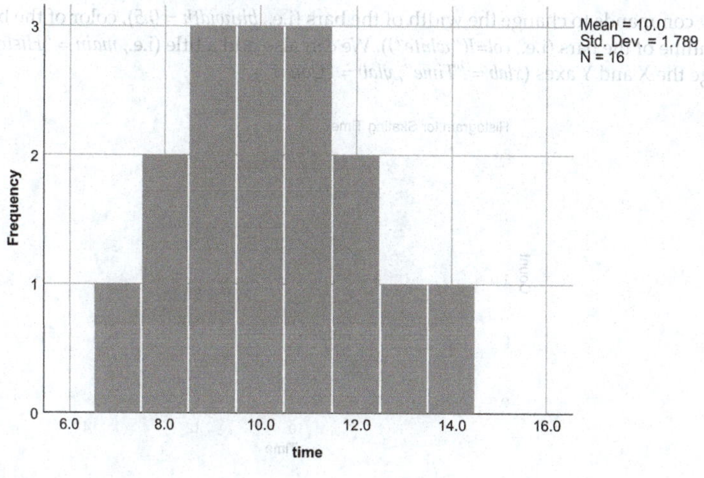

FIGURE 6.14
Histogram and boxplot.

Working in **R**, we can use the *ggplot2* package to produce a histogram.

```
install.packages("ggplot2")
```

The *install.packages* function will install the *ggplot2* package that we can use to create various graphs and plots. If this package is already installed on your computer, you can skip this step and just load it into your library (if not already loaded!).

```
library(ggplot2)
```

The *library* function will load the *ggplot2* package.

```
qplot(Ch6_skate$time, geom="histogram")
```

We can generate a very simple histogram, as seen in Figure 6.14b, using the *qplot* function, where "Ch6 skate$time" represents the variable "time" from our dataframe "Ch6_skate." The command *geom=histogram* tells R to generate a histogram.

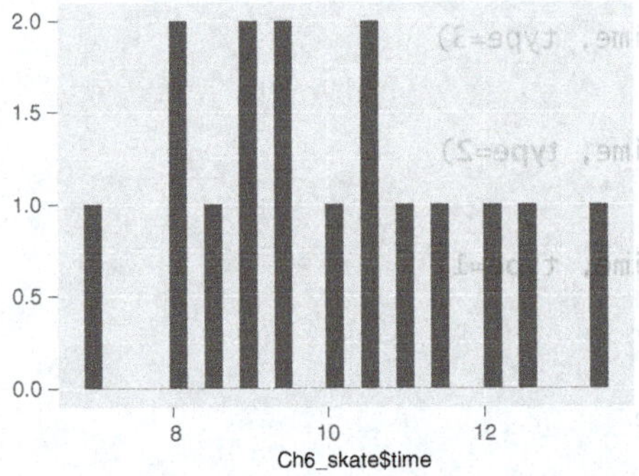


```
qplot(Ch6_skate$time, geom="histogram",
      binwidth=0.5,
        main = "Histogram for Skating Time",
        xlab = "Time", ylab = "Count",
        fill=I("gray"),
        col=I("white"))
```

We can add a few commands to change the width of the bars (i.e., *binwidth = 0.5*), color of the bars (i.e., *fill = I("gray")*), and outline of the bars (i.e., *col=I("white")*). We can also add a title (i.e., *main = "Histogram for Skating Time"*) and change the X and Y axes (*xlab = "Time", ylab = "Count"*).

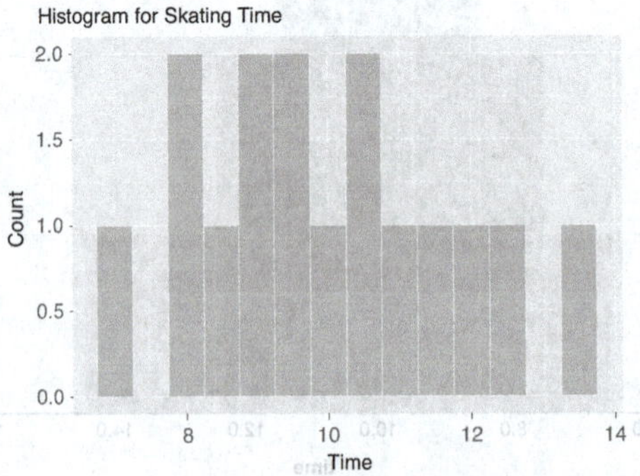

FIGURE 6.14 (continued)
Histogram and boxplot.

```
boxplot(Ch6_skate$time,ylab="Time")
```

We can also generate a boxplot of the "time" variable from the "Ch6_skate" dataframe using the *boxplot* function. We change the Y axis with the script *ylab = "Time."*

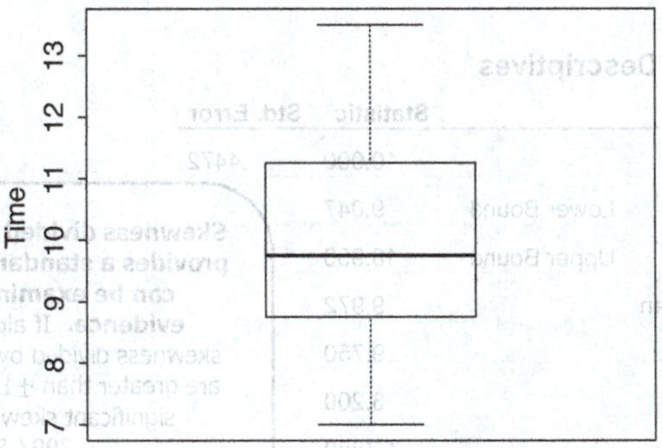

FIGURE 6.14 (continued)
Histogram and boxplot.

The skewness statistic is .299 and kurtosis is −.483—both within the range of an absolute value of 2.0, suggesting some evidence of normality. We can divide the skew and kurtosis values by their standard errors to get standardized skew and kurtosis values. We can review those values to a critical value (e.g., ±1.65 if alpha = .10; ±1.96 if alpha = .05; ±2.06 if alpha = .01) and determine if there is statistically significant skew and/or kurtosis. In this example, the standardized skew and kurtosis values are .530 and −.443, respectively. Both are well under ±1.96 (given alpha = .05), suggesting normality.

A few other statistics can be used to gauge normality as well. Using SPSS, we can obtain two statistical tests of normality. The **Kolmogorov-Smirnov (K-S)** (Chakravart, Laha, & Roy, 1967) with Lilliefor's significance (Lilliefors, 1967) and the **Shapiro-Wilk (S-W)** (Shapiro & Wilk, 1965) are tests that provide evidence of the extent to which our sample distribution is statistically different from a normal distribution. The K-S test tends to be conservative and lacks power for detecting nonnormality; thus, it is is not recommended (D'Agostino, Belanger, & D'Agostino, 1990). The S-W test is considered the more powerful of the two for testing normality and is recommended for use with small sample sizes ($n < 50$) (D'Agostino et al., 1990). Both of these statistics are generated from the selection of "Normality plots with tests." The output for the K-S and S-W tests is presented in Figure 6.15. As we have learned in this chapter, when the observed probability (i.e., p value which is reported in SPSS as "Sig.") is less than our stated alpha level, then we reject the null hypothesis. We follow those same rules of interpretation here. When testing the K-S and S-W for normality, we do *not* want to find statistically significant results. Nonstatistically significant K-S and S-W results are interpreted to say that our distribution is *not* statistically significantly different than a normal distribution. Thus, regardless of which test (K-S or S-W) we examine, both provide the same evidence—our sample distribution is not statistically significantly different than what would be expected from a normal distribution.

Working in **R, D'Agostino's test** (D'Agostino, 1970) can be used to examine the null hypothesis that skewness equals zero. Thus, a statistically significant D'Agostino's test would indicate that there is statistically significant skewness. For kurtosis, we can use the **Bonett-Seier test for Geary's kurtosis** (Bonett & Seier, 2002) for data that are normally distributed. The null hypothesis states that data should have a Geary's kurtosis value equal to

$\sqrt{2/\pi} = .7979$. Thus, a statistically significant Bonett-Seier test for Geary's kurtosis would indicate that there is statistically significant kurtosis. Thus, with these tests, as with K-S and S-W, we do *not* want to find statistically significant results.

Descriptives

			Statistic	Std. Error
time	Mean		10.000	.4472
	95% Confidence Interval for Mean	Lower Bound	9.047	
		Upper Bound	10.953	
	5% Trimmed Mean		9.972	
	Median		9.750	
	Variance		3.200	
	Std. Deviation		1.7889	
	Minimum		7.0	
	Maximum		13.5	
	Range		6.5	
	Interquartile Range		2.8	
	Skewness		.299	.564
	Kurtosis		-.483	1.091

Skewness divided by its standard error provides a standardized value that also can be examined for normality evidence. If alpha = .05, values of skewness divided by its standard error that are greater than ±1.96 indicate statistically significant skew. For skew we see: $.299/.564 = .530$

We can apply this to kurtosis and the standard error of kurtosis as well. For kurtosis we see: $-.483/1.091 = -.443$

Tests of Normality

	Kolmogorov-Smirnov[a]			Shapiro-Wilk		
	Statistic	df	Sig.	Statistic	df	Sig.
time	.110	16	.200*	.982	16	.978

*. This is a lower bound of the true significance.

a. Lilliefors Significance Correction

Working in **R**, we saw in Figure 6.13 how we could generate Shapiro-Wilk's test using the *stat.desc* function from the *pastecs* package. Should we want to generate *just* the S-W test, we can run the following script.

```
shapiro.test(Ch6_skate$time)
```

```
	Shapiro-Wilk normality test

data: Ch6_skate$time
W = 0.98218, p-value = 0.9785
```

Normality can also be tested in **R** using Agostino's test for skewness and the Bonett-Seier test for Geary's kurtosis.

```
install.packages("moments")
library(moments)
```

To conduct Agostino's test, we first have to install the *moments* package and then load it into our library. The null hypothesis for this test is that skewness equals zero. Thus, a statistically significant Agostino's test would indicate that there is statistically significant skewness.

FIGURE 6.15
Skewness and kurtosis and Shapiro-Wilk's test of normality.

```
agostino.test(Ch6_skate$time)
```

The function *agostino.test* is generated using the variable "time" from our "Ch6_skate" dataframe. The results suggest evidence of normality as $p = .5762$, greater than alpha.

```
        D'Agostino skewness test

data: Ch6_skate$time
skew = 0.2706, z = 0.5590, p-value = 0.5762
alternative hypothesis: data have a skewness
```

```
bonett.test((Ch6_skate$time))
```

The *bonett.test* function, using the "time" variable from our "Ch6_skate" dataframe, performs the Bonett-Seier test for Geary's kurtosis for data that are normally distributed. The null hypothesis states that data should have a Geary's kurtosis value equal to $\sqrt{2/\pi} = .7979$. The results suggest evidence of normality as $p = .531$, greater than alpha.

```
        Bonett-Seier test for Geary kurtosis

data: (Ch6_skate$time)
tau = 1.4375, z = -0.6265, p-value = 0.531
alternative hypothesis: kurtosis is not equal to sqrt(2/pi)
```

FIGURE 6.15
Skewness and kurtosis and Shapiro-Wilk's test of normality.

Quantile-quantile (Q-Q) plots are also often examined to determine evidence of normality. Q-Q plots are graphs that depict quantiles of the sample distribution to quantiles of the theoretical normal distribution. Points that fall on or closely to the diagonal line suggest evidence of normality. The Q-Q plot of our hockey skating time provides another form of evidence of normality (see Figure 6.16).

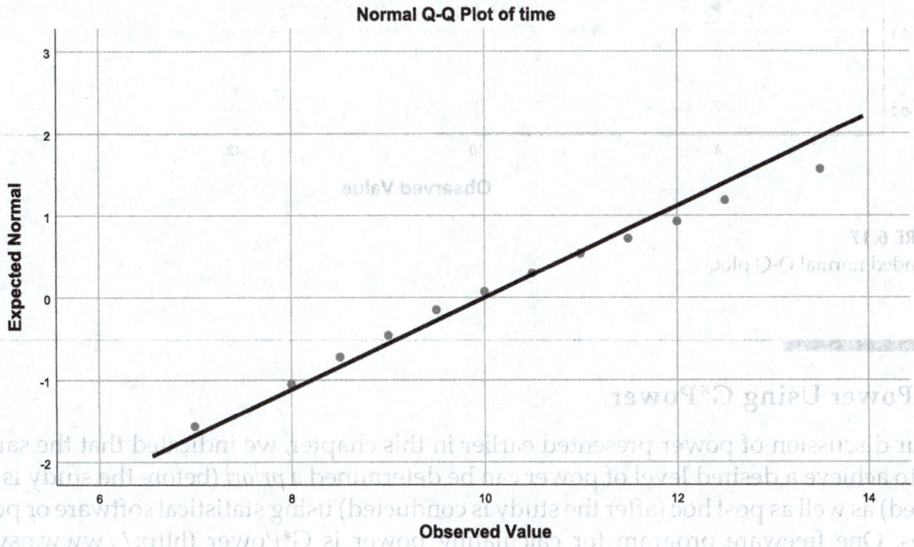

FIGURE 6.16
Q-Q plot.

Working in **R**, we can generate a Q-Q plot with the following script, again using the *ggplot2* package.

```
qplot(sample=time, data = Ch6_skate)
```

The *qplot* function will generate a Q-Q plot using our variable "time" (i.e., using the script *sample=time*) from the dataframe "Ch6_skate" (i.e., *data = Ch6_skate*).

FIGURE 6.16 (continued)
Q-Q plot.

The detrended normal Q-Q plot shows deviations of the observed values from the theoretical normal distribution. Evidence of normality is suggested when the points exhibit little or no pattern around zero (the horizontal line); however, due to subjectivity in determining the extent of a pattern, this graph can often be difficult to interpret. Thus, in many cases you may wish to rely more heavily on the other forms of evidence of normality. For a summary of normality evidence, please see Box 6.1.

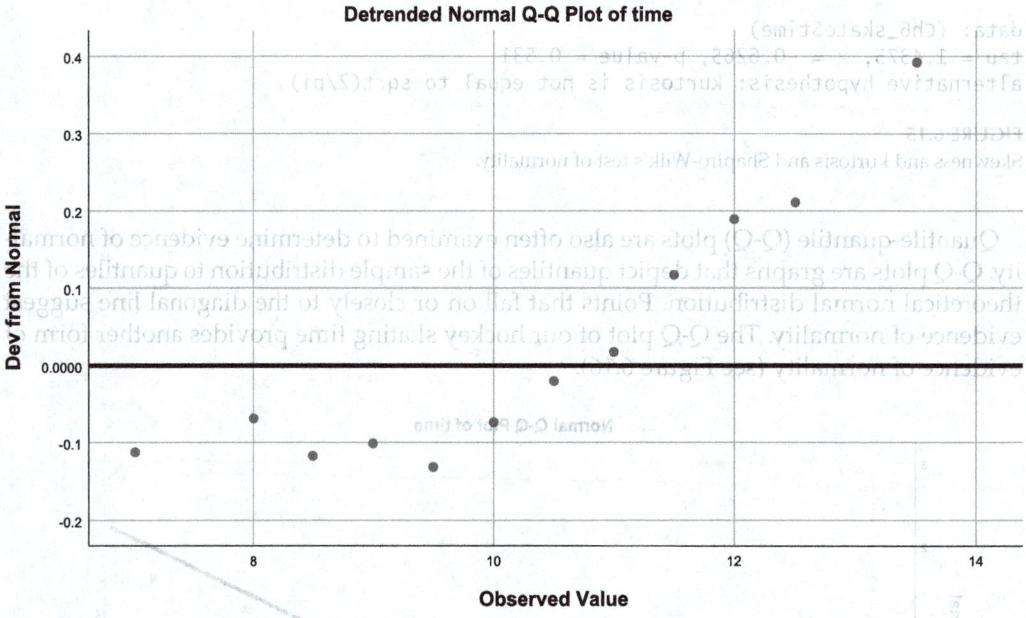

FIGURE 6.17
Detrended normal Q-Q plot.

6.5 Power Using G*Power

In our discussion of power presented earlier in this chapter, we indicated that the sample size to achieve a desired level of power can be determined *a priori* (before the study is conducted) as well as post hoc (after the study is conducted) using statistical software or power tables. One freeware program for calculating power is G*Power (http://www.psycho.uni-duesseldorf.de/abteilungen/aap/gpower3/) which can be used to compute both *a priori* sample size and post hoc power analyses (among other things). Using the results of the one-sample *t* test just conducted, let us utilize G*Power to first determine the required sample size given various estimated parameters and then compute the post hoc power of our test.

6.5.1 *A Priori* Power

Step 1. As shown in the screenshot for Step 1 in Figure 6.18, several decisions need to be made from the initial G*Power screen. First, the correct test family needs to be selected. In our case, we conducted a one-sample *t* test; therefore, the default selection of "t tests" is the correct test family. Next, we need to select the appropriate statistical test. We use the arrow to toggle to "Means: Difference from constant (one sample case)."

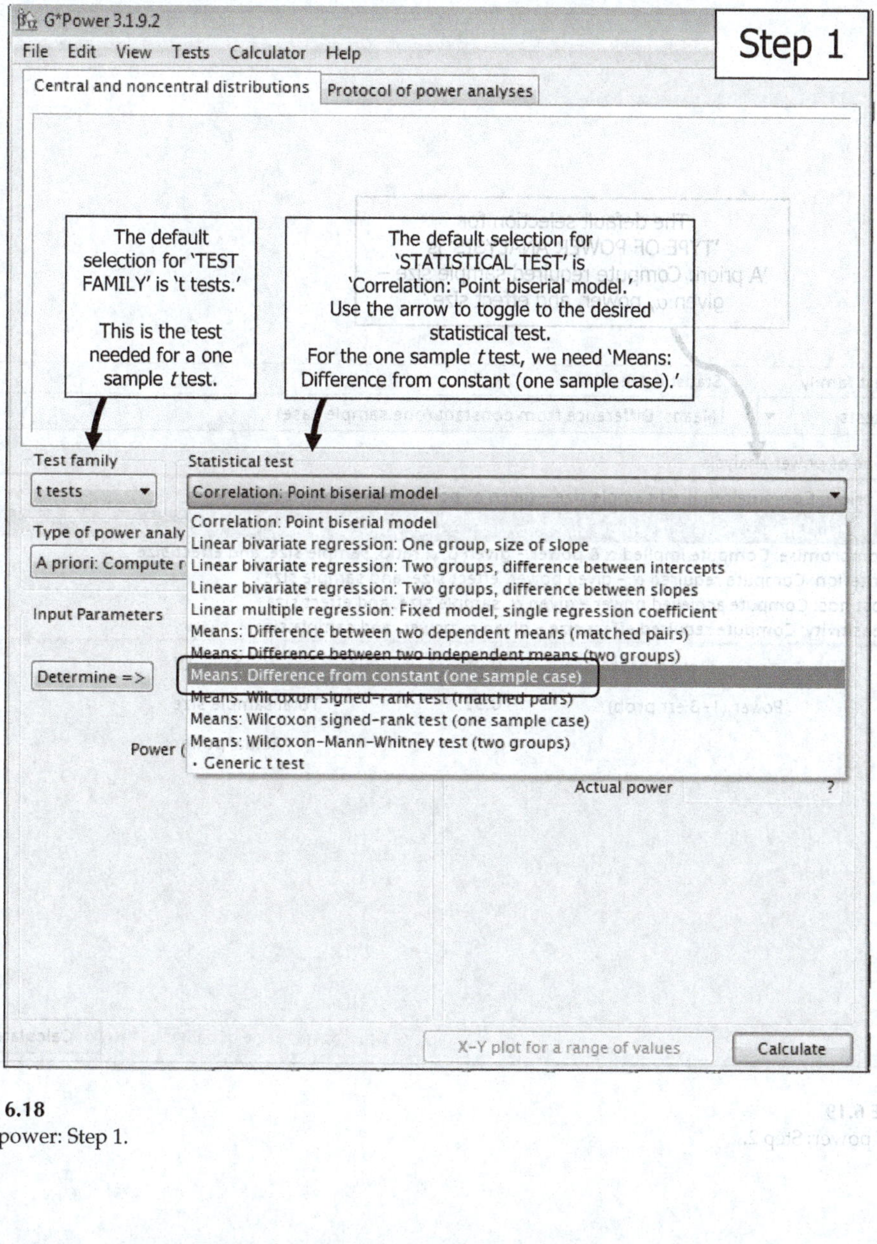

FIGURE 6.18
A priori power: Step 1.

Step 2. The type of power analysis is selected. As shown in the screenshot in Figure 6.19, the options for the type of power analysis are shown in the drop-down menu "Type of power analysis." The default is "A priori: Compute required sample size—given α, power, and effect size." For this example, we will first compute the *a priori* sample size (i.e., the default option), and then we will compute post hoc power. Note that there are three additional forms of power analysis that can be conducted using G*Power: "Compromise," "criterion," and "sensitivity."

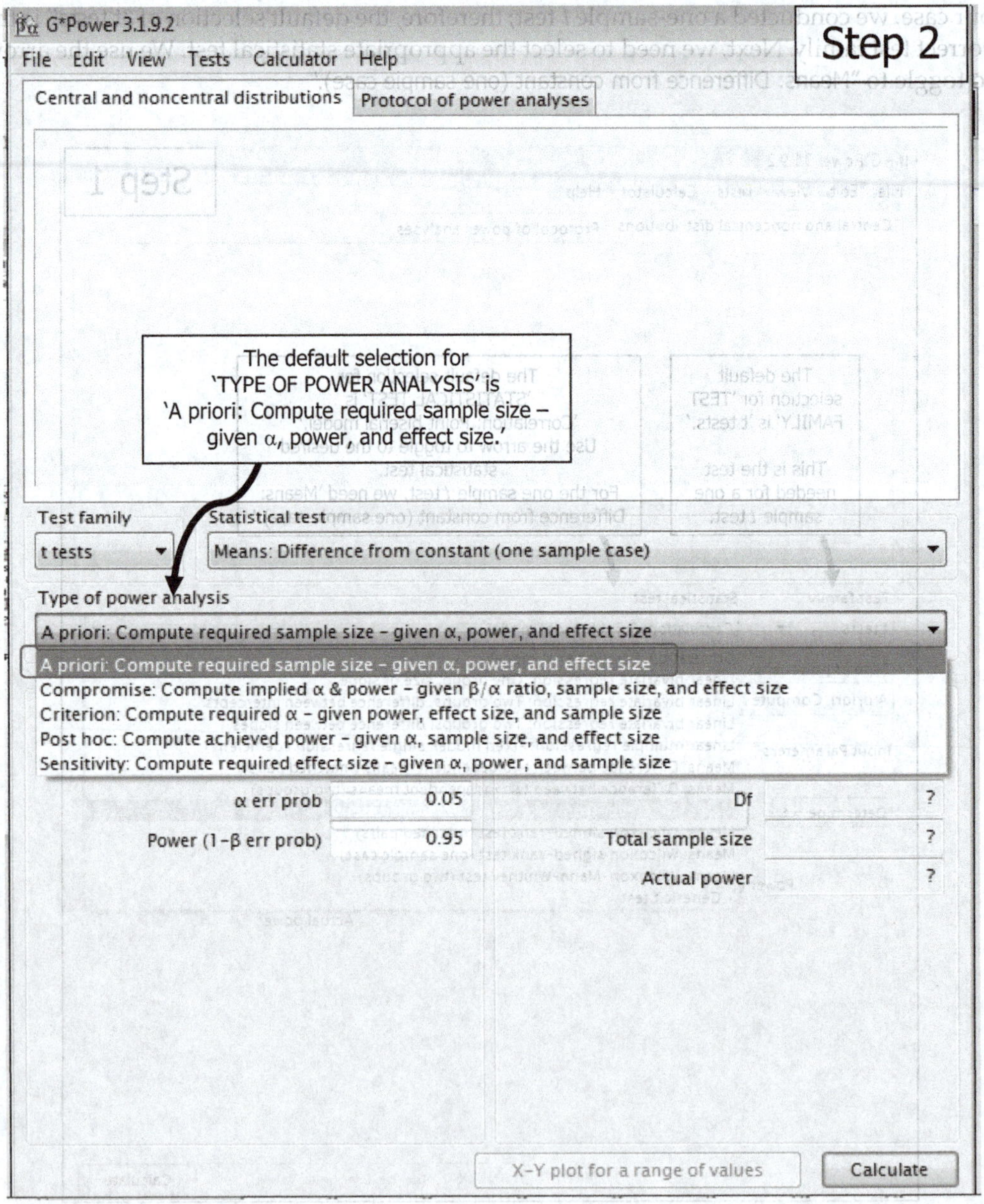

FIGURE 6.19
A priori power: Step 2.

Step 3. The input parameters are specified in the "Input Parameters" box shown in the screenshot in Figure 6.20. The first parameter is whether your test is one tailed (i.e., directional) or two tailed (i.e., nondirectional). In this example we have a two-tailed test, so we use the arrow to toggle "Tail(s)" to "Two." For *a priori* power, we have to indicate the anticipated effect size. The best estimate of effect size that you can anticipate on achieving is usually to rely on previous studies that have been conducted that are similar to yours. In G*Power, the default effect size is d = .50. For the purposes of this example, we will use the default. The alpha level must also be defined. The default significance level in G*Power is .05, which is the alpha level we will be use for our example. The desired level of power must also be defined. The G*Power default for power is .95. Many researchers in the social sciences indicate that a desired power of .80 or above is usually desired. Thus .95 may be higher than what many would consider sufficient power. For purposes of this example, however, we will use the default power of .95. Once the parameters are specified, simply click on "Calculate" to generate the *a priori* power statistics.

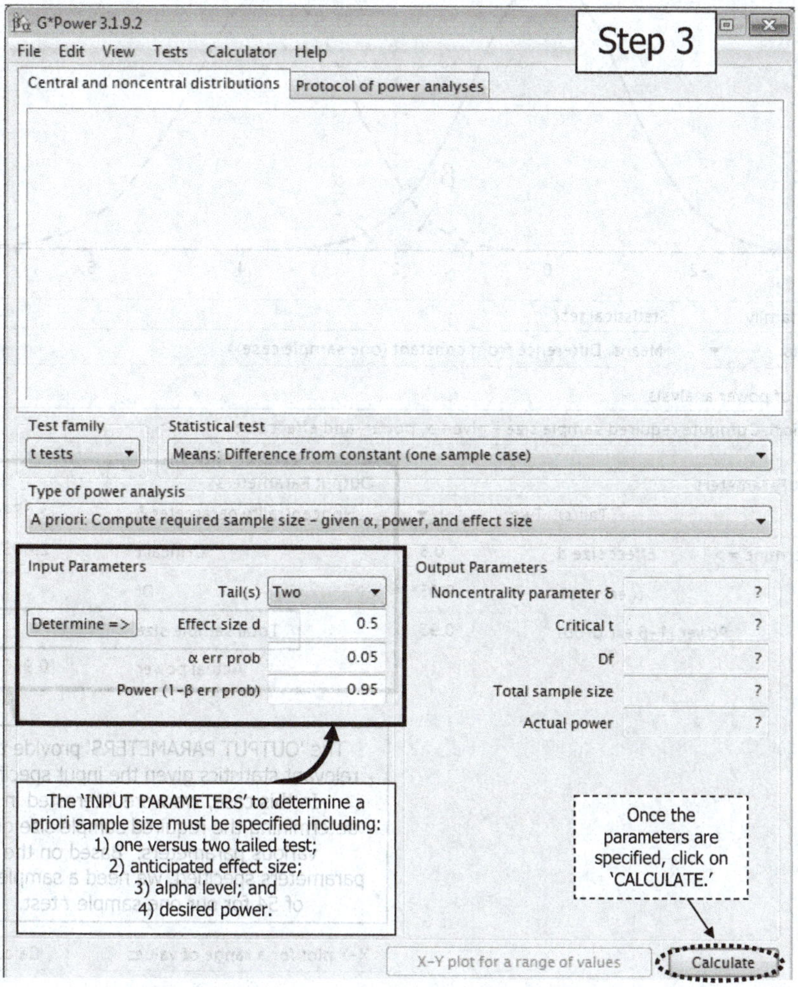

FIGURE 6.20
A priori power: Step 3.

Step 4. The output parameters provide the relevant statistics given the input specified (see the screenshot in Figure 6.21). In this example, we were interested in determining the *a priori* sample size given a two-tailed test, with an anticipated effect size of .50, an alpha level of .05, and desired power of .95. *Based on those criteria, the required sample size for our one-sample* t *test is 54.* In other words, if we have a sample size of 54 individuals or cases in our study, testing at an alpha level of .05, with a two-tailed test, and achieving a moderate effect size of .50, then the power of our test will be .95—the probability of rejecting the null hypothesis when it is really false will be 95%.

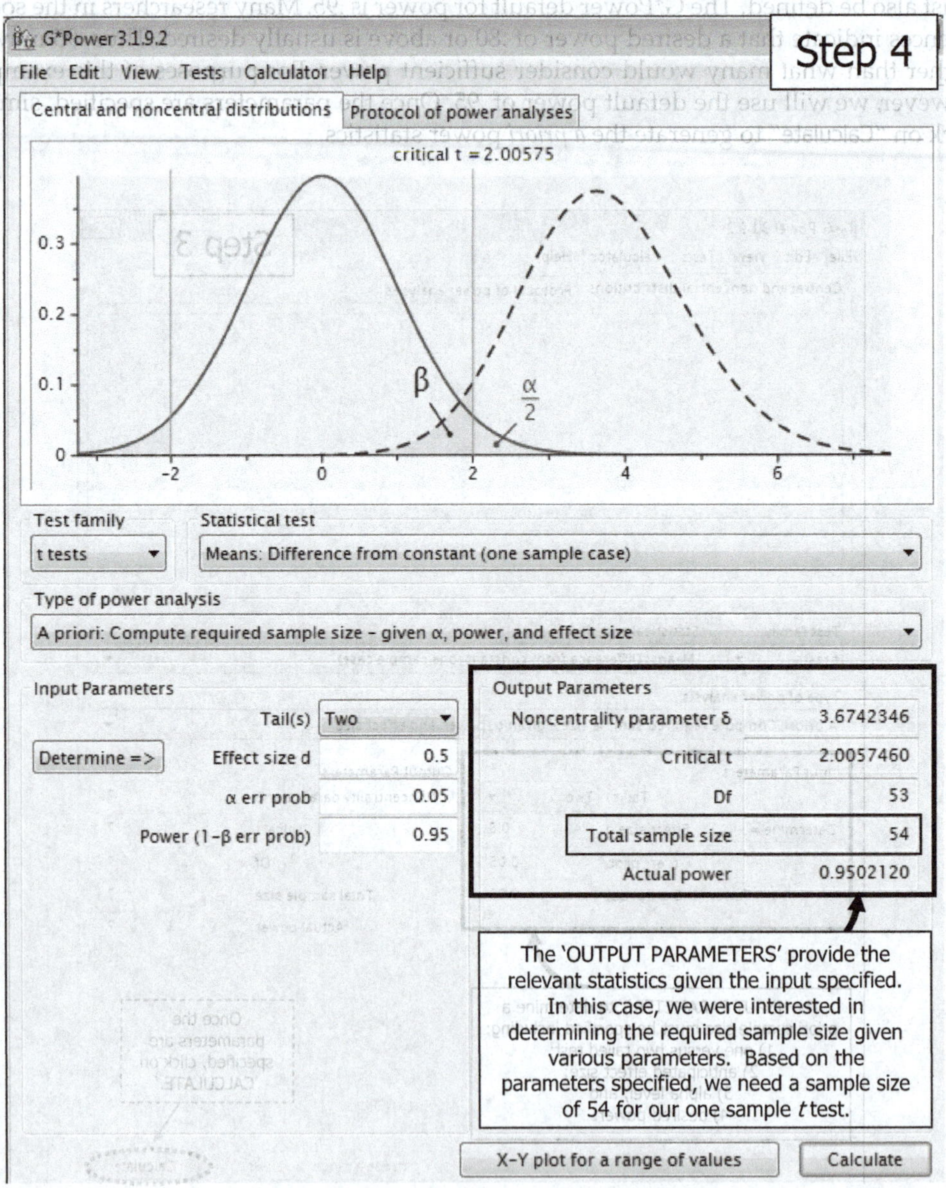

FIGURE 6.21
A priori power: Step 4.

If we had anticipated a smaller effect size, say .20 rather than .50, but left all of the other input parameters the same, the required sample size needed to achieve a power of .95 increases greatly—from 54 to 327 (see the screenshot in Figure 6.22). This demonstrate that there is less power with smaller effect sizes.

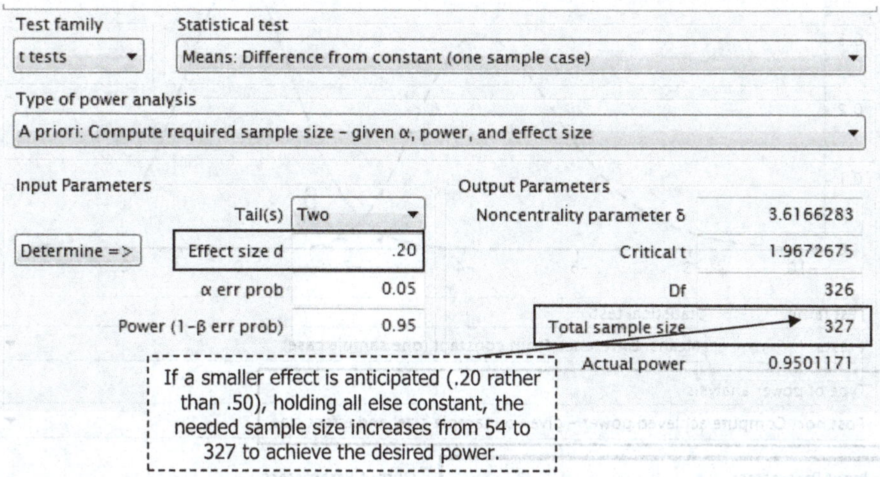

FIGURE 6.22
Change in power based on size of effect.

6.5.2 Post Hoc Power

Now, let us use G*Power to compute post hoc power. Step 1, as presented earlier for *a priori* power, remains the same; thus we will start from Step 2. See the screenshots in Figure 6.23.

Step 2. The type of power analysis needs to be selected from the "Type of power analysis" menu. In this case, you would select "Post hoc: Compute achieved power—given α, sample size, and effect size."

Step 3. You specify the input parameters. The first parameter is the selection of whether your test is one tailed (i.e., directional) or two tailed (i.e., nondirectional). In this example, we have a two-tailed test so we use the arrow to toggle to "Tail(s) to "Two." The achieved or observed effect size was −1.118. The alpha level we tested at was .05, and the actual sample size was 16. Once the parameters are specified, simply click on "Calculate" to generate the achieved power statistics.

Step 4. The output parameters provide the relevant statistics given the input specified. In this example, we were interested in determining post hoc power given a two-tailed test, with an observed effect size of −1.118, an alpha level of .05, and sample size of 16. Based on those criteria, the post hoc power is .986. In other words, with a sample size of 16 skaters in our study, testing at an alpha level of .05, with a two-tailed test, and observing a large effect size of −1.118, then the power of our test is .986—the probability of rejecting the null hypothesis when it is really false is about 99%, an excellent level of power. Keep in mind that conducting power analysis *a priori* is highly recommended so that you avoid a situation where, post hoc, you find that the sample size was not sufficient to reach the desired power (given the observed effect size and alpha level).

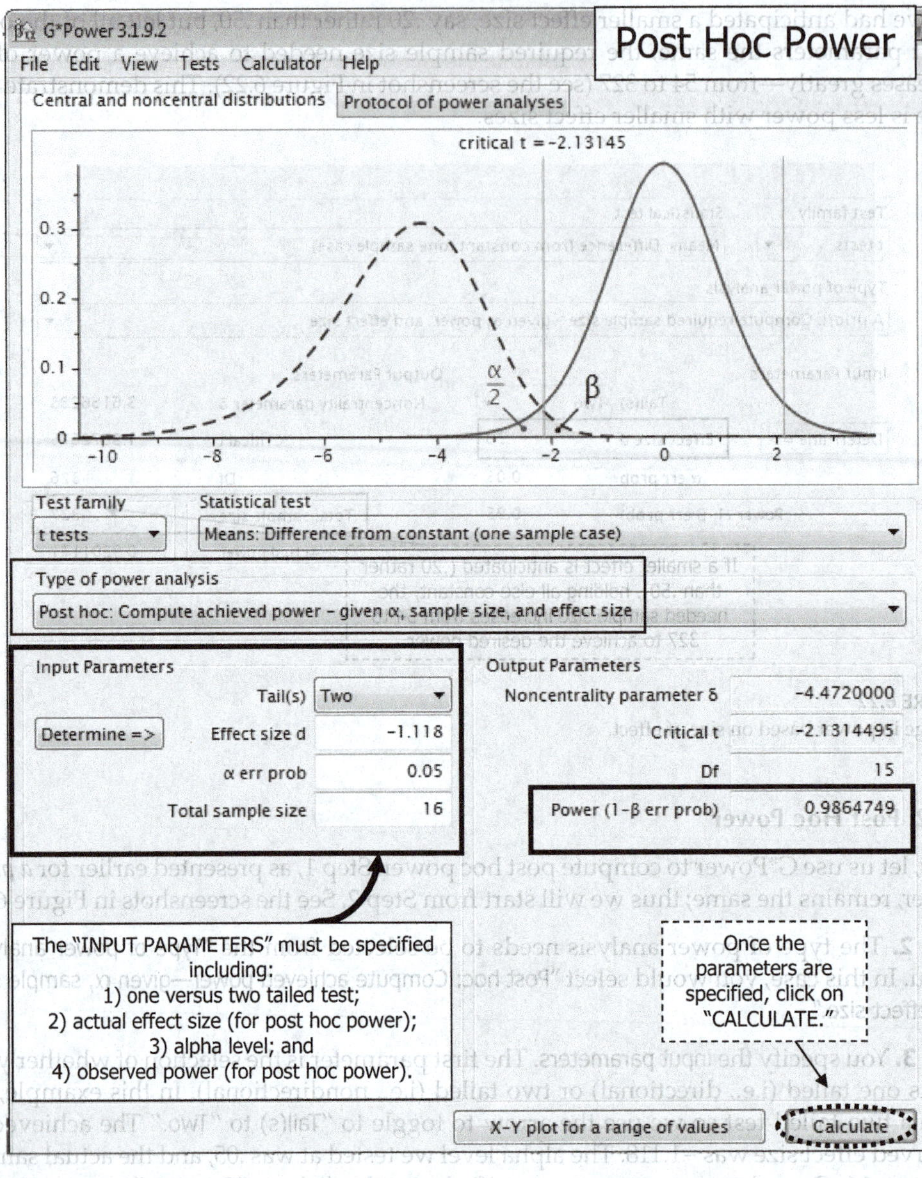

FIGURE 6.23
Post hoc power.

6.6 Research Question Template and Example Write-Up

Let us revisit our graduate research assistant, Ott Lier, who was working with Coach Wesley, a local hockey coach, to assist in analyzing his team's data. As a reminder, Ott's task was to assist Coach Wesley in generating the test of inference to answer the following research question: *Is the mean skating speed of our hockey team different from the league mean speed of 12 seconds?* Ott suggested a one-sample test of means as the test of inference. A template for writing a research question for a one-sample test of inference (i.e., one-sample *t* test) follows:

Is the mean of [sample variable] different from [hypothesized mean value]?

It may be helpful to preface the results of the one-sample *t* test with information we gathered to examine the extent to which the assumption of normality was met. This assists the reader in understanding that you were thorough in data screening prior to conducting the test of inference.

The distributional shape of skating speed was examined to determine the extent to which the assumption of normality was met. Skewness (.299, SE = .564) and kurtosis (−.483, SE = 1.091) were within the range of an absolute value of 2, suggesting evidence of normality. Standardized skew and kurtosis (.530 and −.443, respectively, calculated as skew or kurtosis divided by their standard errors) were not statistically significant, providing further evidence of normality. The Shapiro-Wilk test of normality (W = .982, df = 16, p = .978) suggests that normality is a reasonable assumption. Additional tests, including D'Agostino's test for skewness (z = .559, p = .576) and the Bonett-Seier test for Geary's kurtosis (z = −.627, p = .531) suggested evidence of normality. Visually, a relatively bell-shaped distribution displayed in the histogram (reflected similarly in the boxplot) as well as a Q-Q plot with points adhering closely to the diagonal line also suggest evidence of normality. Additionally, the boxplot did not suggest the presence of any potential outliers. These indices suggest evidence that the assumption of normality was met.

An additional assumption of the one sample *t* test is the assumption of independence. This assumption is met when the cases in our sample have been randomly selected from the population. This is an often overlooked, but important, assumption for researchers when presenting the results of their test. One or two sentences are usually sufficient to indicate if this assumption was met.

Because the skaters in this sample represented a random sample, the assumption of independence was met.

It is also desirable to include a measure of effect size. Recall our formula for computing the effect size, *d*, presented earlier in the chapter. Plugging in the values for our skating example, we find an effect size of −1.118, interpreted according to Cohen's (1988) guidelines as a large effect.

$$d = \frac{\bar{Y} - \mu_0}{s} = \frac{10 - 12}{1.7889} = -1.118$$

Remember that for the one-sample mean test, *d* indicates how many standard deviations the sample mean is from the hypothesized mean. Thus with an effect size of −1.118, there are nearly one and one-quarter standard deviation units between our sample mean and the hypothesized mean. The negative sign simply indicates that our sample mean was the smaller mean (as it is the first value in the numerator of the formula). In this particular example, the negative effect is desired as it suggests the team's average skating time is quicker than the league mean. Using Uanhoro's online calculator (Uanhoro, 2017), we find the confidence interval for the effect size of (−1.7371,−0.4765).

Here is an example APA-style paragraph of results for the skating data (remember that this will be prefaced by the paragraph reporting the extent to which the assumptions of the test were met).

A one sample t test was conducted at an alpha level of .05 to answer the research question: *Is the mean skating speed of a hockey team different from the league mean speed of 12 seconds?* The null hypothesis stated that the team mean speed would not differ from the league mean speed of 12. The alternative hypothesis stated that the team average speed would differ from the league mean. Based on a random sample of 16 skaters, there was a mean time of 10 seconds and a standard deviation of 1.7889 seconds. When compared against the hypothesized mean of 12 seconds, the one-sample t test was shown to be statistically significant ($t = -4.472$, $df = 15$, $p < .001$). Therefore, the null hypothesis that the team average time would be 12 seconds was rejected. This provides evidence to suggest that the sample mean skating time for this particular team was statistically different from the hypothesized mean skating time of the league. Additionally, the effect size d was −1.118 (*CI* −1.7371,−0.4765), generally interpreted as a large effect (Cohen, 1988), and indicating that there is more than a one standard deviation difference between the team and league mean skating times, with the team speed quicker than the league speed. The post hoc power of the test, given the sample size, two-tailed test, alpha level, and observed effect size, was .986.

6.7 Additional Resources

A number of resources are available for learning more about statistics and how to interpret statistics. In addition to those already cited, Huck (2000) is an excellent general resource to assist in learning more about statistics and how to interpret statistics

Problems

Conceptual Problems

1. In hypothesis testing, the probability of failing to reject H_0 when H_0 is false is denoted by which of the following?

   a. α

   b. $1 - \alpha$

   c. β

   d. $1 - \beta$

2. The probability of observing the sample mean (or some value greater than the sample mean) by chance if the null hypothesis is really true is denoted by which of the following?
   a. a
   b. Level of significance
   c. *p* value
   d. Test statistic value
3. When testing the following hypothesis at a .05 level of significance with the *t* test, where is the rejection region?

$$H_0: \mu \geq 100$$
$$H_1: \mu < 100$$

   a. Upper tail
   b. Lower tail
   c. Both the upper and lower tails
   d. Cannot be determined
4. A research question asks, "Is the mean age of children who enter preschool different from 48 months?" Which of the following is implied?
   a. Left-tailed test
   b. Right-tailed test
   c. Two-tailed test
   d. Cannot be determined based on this information
5. If the 90% CI does not include the value for the parameter being estimated in H_0, then which of the following is a correct statement?
   a. H_0 cannot be rejected at the .10 level
   b. H_0 can be rejected at the .10 level
   c. A Type I error has been made
   d. A Type II error has been made
6. Other things being equal, which of the following values of *t* is least likely to result for a two-tailed test when H_0 is true?
   a. 2.67
   b. 1.00
   c. 0.00
   d. −1.96
   e. −2.70
7. Which of the following is the fundamental difference between the *z* test and the *t* test for testing hypotheses about a population mean?
   a. Only *z* assumes the population distribution be normal.
   b. *z* is a two-tailed test whereas *t* is one-tailed.
   c. Only *t* becomes more powerful as sample size increases.
   d. Only *z* requires the population variance be known.

8. True or false? If one fails to reject a true H_0, one is making a Type I error.
9. Which of the following is a correct interpretation of *d*?
   a. Alpha level
   b. Confidence interval
   c. Effect size
   d. Observed probability
   e. Power
10. A one-sample *t* test is conducted at an alpha level of .10. The researcher finds a *p* value of .08 and concludes that the test is statistically significant. Is the researcher correct?
11. When testing the following hypothesis at the .01 level of significance with the *t* test a sample mean of 301 is observed. I assert that if I calculate the test statistic and compare it to the *t* distribution with $n - 1$ degrees of freedom, then it is possible to reject H_0. Am I correct?

$$H_0: \mu \geq 295$$
$$H_1: \mu < 295$$

12. I assert that H_0 can be rejected with 100% confidence if the sample consists of the entire population. Am I correct?
13. I assert that the 95% CI has a larger width than the 99% CI for a population mean using the same data. Am I correct?
14. True or false? A 90% CI will have a smaller width than a 95% CI for a population mean using the same data.
15. I assert that the critical value of *z* for a test of a single mean will increase as the sample size increases. Am I correct?
16. True or false? The mean of the *t* distribution increases as degrees of freedom increase.
17. True or false? It is possible that the results of a one-sample *t* test and for the corresponding CI will differ for the same dataset and level of significance.
18. True or false? The width of the 95% CI does not depend on the sample mean.
19. The null hypothesis is a numerical statement about which of the following?
   a. An unknown parameter
   b. A known parameter
   c. An unknown statistic
   d. A known statistic
20. A research question asks, "To what extent does the average aptitude for success onboarding employees higher than 78?" Which of the following is implied?
   a. Left-tailed test
   b. Right-tailed test
   c. Two-tailed test
   d. Cannot be determined based on this information

21. In hypothesis testing, the probability of rejecting H_0 when H_0 is true is denoted by which of the following?

a. α

b. 1 – α

c. β

d. 1 – β

22. A one-sample *t* test is conducted at an alpha level of .05. The researcher finds a *p* value of .10. Which of the following is a correct interpretation of these results?

a. Results are not statistically significant.

b. Results are statistically significant.

c. Cannot be determined without additional information.

d. Both a and b, depending on the situation.

23. A one-sample *t* test is conducted at an alpha level of .01. The researcher finds a *p* value of .05. Which of the following is a correct interpretation of these results?

a. Results are not statistically significant.

b. Results are statistically significant.

c. Cannot be determined without additional information.

d. Both a and b, depending on the situation.

24. Effect size measures provide which of the following?

a. Inferences from the sample to population

b. Level of confidence

c. Practical significance

d. Probability of rejecting the null hypothesis when it is false

25. A researcher computes a one-sample *t* test and finds an effect size $d = .75$. Which of the following is a correct interpretation of this effect?

a. About 75% of the sample means will fall between the lower and upper levels.

b. The probability of rejecting the null hypothesis is about 75%.

c. There is evidence of normality.

d. There is three-quarter of one standard deviation between the sample and hypothesized means.

Answers to Conceptual Problems

1. **c** (Beta is the probability of failing to reject the null hypothesis when the null hypothesis is false.)

3. **b** (Willing to reject only if sample mean is less than 100.)

5. **b** (Reject when CI does not contain parameter value.)

7. **d** (*z* is based on known population variance, *t* is not.)

9. **c** (*d* is an effect size index, a measure of practical significance.)

11. **No** (Cannot reject when sample mean is in opposite direction of region of rejection.)

13. **No** (The range will be wider for the 99% CI.)

15. **No** (The critical value of z does not depend on sample size.)
17. **False** (They will always agree.)
19. **a** (The null hypothesis is always about an unknown population parameter, hence the term inferential statistics.)
21. **a** (Alpha, α, is the probability of falsely rejecting the null hypothesis when it is really true.)
23. **b** ($p <$ alpha so reject the null hypothesis.)
25. **d** (d is a standardized mean difference effect size, and a d of .75 indicates three-quarters of one standard deviation between the sample and hypothesized means.)

Computational Problems

1. Using the same data and the same method of analysis, the following hypotheses are tested about whether mean height is 72 inches. Researcher A uses the .05 level of significance, and Researcher B uses the .01 level of significance.

$$H_0: \mu = 72$$
$$H_1: \mu \neq 72$$

   a. If Researcher A rejects H_0, what is the conclusion of Researcher B?
   b. If Researcher B rejects H_0, what is the conclusion of Researcher A?
   c. If Researcher A fails to reject H_0, what is the conclusion of Researcher B?
   d. If Researcher B fails to reject H_0, what is the conclusion of Researcher A?
2. Give a numerical value for each of the following descriptions by referring to a t table.
   a. Percentile rank of $t_5 = 1.476$
   b. Percentile rank of $t_{10} = 3.169$
   c. Percentile rank of $t_{21} = 2.518$
   d. Mean of the distribution of t_{23}
   e. Median of the distribution of t_{23}
   f. Variance of the distribution of t_{23}
   g. 90th percentile of the distribution of t_{27}
3. Give a numerical value for each of the following descriptions by referring to a t table.
   a. Percentile rank of $t_5 = 2.015$
   b. Percentile rank of $t_{20} = 1.325$
   c. Percentile rank of $t_{30} = 2.042$
   d. Mean of the distribution of t_{10}
   e. Median of the distribution of t_{10}
   f. Variance of the distribution of t_{10}
   g. 95th percentile of the distribution of t_{14}

4. The following random sample of weekly student expenses is obtained from a normally distributed population of undergraduate students with unknown parameters:

68	56	76	75	62	81	72	69	91	84
49	75	69	59	70	53	65	78	71	87
71	74	69	65	64					

a. Test the following hypothesis at the .05 level of significance:

$$H_0: \mu = 74$$
$$H_1: \mu \neq 74$$

b. Construct a 95% confidence interval.

5. The following random sample of hours spent per day answering email is obtained from a normally distributed population of community college faculty with unknown parameters:

2	3.5	4	1.25	2.5	3.25	4.5	4.25	2.75	3.25
1.75	1.5	2.75	3.5	3.25	3.75	2.25	1.5	1.25	3.25

a. Test the following hypothesis at the .05 level of significance:

$$H_0: \mu = 3.0$$
$$H_1: \mu \neq 3.0$$

b. Construct a 95% confidence interval.

6. In the population it is hypothesized that flags have a mean usable life of 100 days. Twenty-five flags are flown in the city of Tuscaloosa and are found to have a sample mean usable life of 200 days with a standard deviation of 216 days. Does the sample mean in Tuscaloosa differ from that of the population mean?
   a. Conduct a two-tailed t test at the .01 level of significance.
   b. Construct a 99% confidence interval.

7. A researcher is examining IPEDS data (https://nces.ed.gov/ipeds/use-the-data). The researcher is interested in knowing if the mean number of students enrolled exclusively in distance education courses in 2016 differs from 600. Use the Ch6_IPEDS data with the variable "DE2016." Using statistical software, test at alpha = .05 and report the appropriate test results.

8. A researcher is examining IPEDS data (https://nces.ed.gov/ipeds/use-the-data) from land grant institutions. The researcher is interested in knowing if the mean number of students enrolled exclusively in distance education courses in 2012 differs from 350. Use the Ch6_IPEDS data with the variable "DE2012." Using statistical software, test at alpha = .05 and report the appropriate test results.

Answers to Computational Problems

1. a. B may or may not reject as B's level of significance is more stringent than A's.
   b. A also rejects as A's level of significance is more liberal than B's.

c. B also fails to reject. If it's not significant at .05, it won't be significant at a smaller alpha.

d. A may or may not fail to reject as A's alpha level is more liberal than B's.

3. a. 95th

b. 90th

c. 97.5th

d. 0

e. 0

f. 1.25

g. 1.761

5. a. $t = -.884$, critical values = -2.093 and $+ 2.093$, and thus fail to reject H_0.

b. (2.3265, 3.2735) includes hypothesized value of 3.0, and thus fail to reject H_0.

7. The mean number of students at land grant institutions who were enrolled exclusively in distance education courses in 2016 was 678.73 ($SD = 758.233$). This value is not statistically significantly different than the hypothesized value of 600, $t = .893$, $df = 73$, $p = .375$.

Interpretive Problem

1. Using the survey1 data (accessible from the website) and SPSS or **R**, conduct a one-sample *t* test to determine whether the mean number of songs downloaded to a phone [SONGS] significantly differs from 25 at the .05 level of significance. Test for the extent to which the assumption of normality has been met. Calculate an effect size as well as post hoc power. Then write an APA-style paragraph reporting your results.
2. Using the survey1 data (accessible from the website) and SPSS or **R**, conduct a one-sample *t* test to determine whether the mean number of hours slept [SLEEP] is significantly different from 8 at the .05 level of significance. Test for the extent to which the assumption of normality has been met. Calculate an effect size as well as post hoc power. Then write an APA-style paragraph reporting your results.
3. A researcher has pulled country-level data from the rollercoaster census report (https://rcdb.com/census.htm) and is examining rollercoasters within North American countries. Using the Ch2_rollercoaster data (accessible from the website) and SPSS or **R**, conduct a one-sample *t* test to determine whether the mean number of steel rollercoasters [STEEL] is significantly different from 50 at the .05 level of significance. Test for the extent to which the assumption of normality has been met. Calculate an effect size as well as post hoc power. Then write an APA-style paragraph reporting your results.

7

Inferences About the Difference Between Two Means

Chapter Outline

Key Concepts

1. Independent versus dependent samples
2. Sampling distribution of the difference between two means
3. Standard error of the difference between two means
4. Parametric versus nonparametric tests

In Chapter 6 we introduced hypothesis testing and ultimately considered our first inferential statistic, the one-sample t test. There we examined the following general topics: types of hypotheses, types of decision errors, level of significance, steps in the decision-making process, inferences about a single mean when the population standard deviation is known (the z test), power, statistical versus practical significance, and inferences about a single mean when the population standard deviation is unknown (the t test).

In this chapter we consider inferential tests involving the difference between two means. In other words, our research question is the extent to which two sample means are statistically different and, by inference, the extent to which their respective population means are different. Several inferential tests are covered in this chapter, depending on whether the two samples are selected in an independent or dependent manner, and on whether the statistical assumptions are met. More specifically, the topics described include the following inferential tests: for two independent samples, the independent t test, the Welch t' test, and the Mann-Whitney-Wilcoxon test; for two dependent samples, the dependent t test and the Wilcoxon signed ranks test. We use many of the foundational concepts covered in Chapter 6. New concepts to be discussed include the following: independent versus dependent samples; the sampling distribution of the difference between two means; and the standard error of the difference between two means. Our objectives are that by the end of this chapter, you will be able to: (a) understand the basic concepts underlying the inferential tests of two means, (b) select the appropriate test, and (c) determine and interpret the results from the appropriate test.

7.1 Inferences About Two Independent Means and How They Work

Remember our very capable quad of graduate students who work in the stats lab? Let's see what Oso Wyse and Addie Venture have in store now . . .

The stats lab has been humming with research project requests from faculty and the community. The latest request comes from Dr. Nightingale, a local nurse practitioner, who is studying cholesterol levels of adults and how they differ based on sex. Oso Wyse has been assigned to the project and suggests the following research question: *Is there a mean difference in cholesterol level between males and females?* Oso suggests an independent samples t test as the test of inference. His task is then to assist Dr. Nightingale in generating the test of inference to answer the research question.

Addie Venture has been asked to consult with the institution's swimming coach, Coach Bryant, who works with the community and various swimming programs that are offered through their local Parks & Recreation Department. Coach Bryant has just conducted an intensive 2-month training program for a group of 10 swimmers. He wants to determine if, on average, their time in the 50-meter freestyle event is different after the training. The following research question is suggested by Addie: *Is there a mean difference in swim time for the 50-meter freestyle event before participation in an intensive training program as compared to swim time for the 50-meter freestyle event after participation in an intensive training program?* Addie suggests a dependent samples *t* test as the test of inference. Her task is then to assist Coach Bryant in generating the test of inference to answer his research question.

Before we proceed to inferential tests of the difference between two means, a few new concepts need to be introduced. The new concepts are the difference between the selection of independent samples and dependent samples, the hypotheses to be tested, and the sampling distribution of the difference between two means.

7.1.1 Independent vs. Dependent Samples

The first new concept to address is to make a distinction between the selection of **independent samples** and **dependent samples**. *Two samples are independent when the method of sample selection is such that those individuals selected for sample 1 do not have any relationship to those individuals selected for sample 2.* In other words, the selection of individuals to be included in the two samples are unrelated or uncorrelated such that they have absolutely nothing to do with one another. You might think of the samples as being selected totally separate from one another. Because the individuals in the two samples are independent of one another, their scores on the dependent variable, *Y*, should also be independent of one another. The independence condition leads us to consider, for example, the **independent samples *t* test**. (This should not, however, be confused with the assumption of independence, which was introduced in the previous chapter. The assumption of independence still holds for the independent samples *t* test, and we will talk later about how this assumption can be met with this particular procedure.)

Two samples are dependent when the method of sample selection is such that those individuals selected for sample 1 do have a relationship to those individuals selected for sample 2. In other words, the selections of individuals to be included in the two samples *are* related or correlated. You might think of the samples as being selected simultaneously such that there are actually pairs of individuals. Consider the following two typical examples. First, if the same individuals are measured at two points in time, such as during a pretest and a posttest, then we have two dependent samples. The scores on *Y* at time 1 will be correlated with the scores on *Y* at time 2 because the same individuals are assessed at both time points. *Second, if units are selected that are paired or matched in some way such that measurements will be matched (e.g., husband–wife pairs, twins), then we have two dependent samples.* For example, if a particular wife is selected for the study, then her corresponding husband is also automatically selected—this is an example where individuals are paired or matched in some way such that they share characteristics that makes the score of one person related to (i.e., dependent on) the score of the other person. In both examples we have natural pairs of individuals or scores. The dependence condition leads us to consider the **dependent samples *t* test**, alternatively known as the **correlated samples *t* test** or the **paired samples *t* test**. As we show in this chapter, whether the samples are independent or dependent determines the appropriate inferential test.

7.1.2 Hypotheses

The hypotheses to be evaluated for detecting a difference between two means are as follows. The null hypothesis, H_0, for a *nondirectional* test is that there is no difference between the two population means, which we denote as the following:

$$H_0: \mu_1 - \mu_2 = 0 \text{ or } H_0: \mu_1 = \mu_2$$

where μ_1 is the population mean for sample 1 and μ_2 is the population mean for sample 2. Mathematically, both equations say the same thing. The version on the left makes it clear to the reader why the term "null" is appropriate; that is, there is no difference, or a "null" difference, between the two population means. The version on the right indicates that the population mean of sample 1 is the same as the population mean of sample 2, which is another way of saying that there is no difference between the means (i.e., they are the same). The *nondirectional* scientific or alternative hypothesis, H_1, is that there is a difference between the two population means, which we denote as follows:

$$H_1: \mu_1 - \mu_2 \neq 0 \text{ or } H_1: \mu_1 \neq \mu_2$$

The null hypothesis, H_0, will be rejected here in favor of the alternative hypothesis, H_1, if the population means are different. As we have not specified a direction on H_1, we are willing to reject either if μ_1 is greater than μ_2 or if μ_1 is less than μ_2. This alternative hypothesis results in a two-tailed test.

Directional alternative hypotheses can also be tested if we believe μ_1 is greater than μ_2, denoted as follows:

$$H_1: \mu_1 - \mu_2 > 0 \text{ or } H_1: \mu_1 > \mu_2$$

In this case, the equation on the left tells us that when μ_2 is subtracted from μ_1, a positive value will result (i.e., μ_1 is larger in value than μ_2, and thus results in some value greater than zero). The equation on the right makes it somewhat clearer what we hypothesize.

Or if we believe μ_1 is less than μ_2, the directional alternative hypotheses will be denoted as we see here:

$$H_1: \mu_1 - \mu_2 < 0 \text{ or } H_1: \mu_1 < \mu_2$$

In this case, the equation on the left tells us that when μ_2 is subtracted from μ_1, a negative value will result (i.e., μ_1 is smaller in value than μ_2, and thus results in some value less than zero). The equation on the right makes it somewhat clearer what we hypothesize. Regardless of how they are denoted, directional alternative hypotheses result in a one-tailed test.

The underlying sampling distribution for these tests is known as the *sampling distribution of the difference between two means*. This makes sense, as the hypotheses examine the extent to which two sample means differ. The mean of this sampling distribution is zero, as that is the hypothesized difference between the two population means $\mu_1 - \mu_2$. The more the two sample means differ, the more likely we are to reject the null hypothesis. As we show later, the test statistics in this chapter all deal in some way with the difference between the two means and with the standard error (or standard deviation) of the difference between two means.

7.1.3 Characteristics of Tests of Difference Between Two Independent Means

In this section, three inferential tests of the difference between two independent means are described: the independent t test, the Welch t' test, and the Mann-Whitney-Wilcoxon test. The section concludes with a list of recommendations.

7.1.3.1 The Independent t Test

The test statistic for the **independent t test** is known as t and is denoted by the following formula:

$$t = \frac{\bar{Y}_1 - \bar{Y}_2}{s_{\bar{Y}_1 - \bar{Y}_2}}$$

where $\bar{Y}_1$ and $\bar{Y}_2$ are the means for sample 1 and sample 2, respectively, and $s_{\bar{Y}_1 - \bar{Y}_2}$ is the *standard error of the difference between two means*. This standard error is the *standard deviation of the sampling distribution of the difference between two means* and is computed as follows:

$$s_{\bar{Y}_1 - \bar{Y}_2} = s_p \sqrt{\frac{1}{n_1} + \frac{1}{n_2}}$$

where s_p is the *pooled standard deviation* computed as

$$s_p = \sqrt{\frac{(n_1 - 1)(s_1^2) + (n_2 - 1)(s_2^2)}{n_1 + n_2 - 2}}$$

and where s_1^2 and s_2^2 are the sample variances for groups 1 and 2, respectively, and n_1 and n_2 are the sample sizes for groups 1 and 2, respectively. Conceptually, the standard error $s_{\bar{Y}_1 - \bar{Y}_2}$ is a pooled standard deviation weighted by the two sample sizes; more specifically, the two sample variances are weighted by their respective sample sizes and then pooled. This is conceptually similar to the standard error for the one-sample t test, which you will recall from Chapter 6 as

$$s_{\bar{Y}} = \frac{s_Y}{\sqrt{n}}$$

where we also have a standard deviation weighted by sample size. If the sample variances are not equal, as the test assumes, then you can see why we might not want to take a pooled or weighted average (i.e., as it would not represent well the individual sample variances).

The test statistic t is then compared to a critical value(s) from the t distribution. For a two-tailed test, from Table A.2 in the Appendix we would use the appropriate α_2 column depending on the desired level of significance and the appropriate row depending on the degrees of freedom. The *degrees of freedom* for this test are $n_1 + n_2 - 2$. Conceptually, we lose one degree of freedom from each sample for estimating the population variances (i.e., there are two restrictions along the lines of what was discussed in Chapter 6). The *critical values* are denoted as $\pm_{\alpha_2} t_{n_1+n_2-2}$. The subscript α_2 of the critical values reflects the fact that this is a two-tailed test, and the subscript $n_1 + n_2 - 2$ indicates this particular degrees of freedom. (Remember that the critical value can be found based on the knowledge of the degrees of freedom and whether it is a one- or two-tailed test.) If the test statistic falls into either critical region, then we reject H_0; otherwise, we fail to reject H_0.

For a one-tailed test, from Table A.2 in the Appendix we would use the appropriate α_1 column depending on the desired level of significance and the appropriate row depending on the degrees of freedom. The degrees of freedom are again $n_1 + n_2 - 2$. The critical value is denoted as $+_{\alpha_1}t_{n_1+n_2-2}$ for the alternative hypothesis H_1: $\mu_1 - \mu_2 > 0$ (i.e., right-tailed test, so the critical value will be positive), and as $-_{\alpha_1}t_{n_1+n_2-2}$ for the alternative hypothesis H_1: $\mu_1 - \mu_2 < 0$ (i.e., left-tailed test, and thus a negative critical value). If the test statistic t falls into the appropriate critical region, then we reject H_0; otherwise, we fail to reject H_0.

7.1.3.1.1 Confidence Interval

For the two-tailed test, a $(1 - \alpha)$% confidence interval can also be examined. The confidence interval is formed as follows:

$$(\bar{Y}_1 - \bar{Y}_2) \pm ({}_{\alpha_2}t_{n_1+n_2-2})(s_{\bar{Y}_1-\bar{Y}_2})$$

If the confidence interval contains the hypothesized mean difference of 0, then the conclusion is to *fail to reject* H_0; otherwise, we *reject* H_0. The interpretation and use of CIs is similar to that of the one-sample test described in Chapter 6. Imagine we take 100 random samples from each of two populations and construct 95% CIs. Then 95% of the CIs will contain the true population mean difference $\mu_1 - \mu_2$ and 5% will not. In short, 95% of similarly constructed CIs will contain the true population mean difference.

7.1.3.1.2 Example of the Independent *t* Test

Let us now consider an example where the independent *t* test is implemented. Recall from Chapter 6 the basic steps for hypothesis testing for any inferential test: (1) State the null and alternative hypotheses; (2) select the level of significance (i.e., alpha, α); (3) calculate the test statistic value; and (4) make a statistical decision (reject or fail to reject H_0). We will follow these steps again in conducting our independent *t* test.

In our example, samples of 8 female and 12 male middle-age adults are randomly and independently sampled from the populations of female and male middle-age adults, respectively. Each individual is given a cholesterol test through a standard blood sample. *The null hypothesis to be tested is that males and females have equal cholesterol levels. The alternative hypothesis is that males and females will not have equal cholesterol levels,* thus necessitating a *nondirectional* or *two-tailed test*. We will conduct our test using an alpha level of .05. The raw data and summary statistics are presented in Table 7.1. For the female sample (sample 1) the mean and variance are 185.0000 and 364.2857, respectively, and for the male sample (sample 2) the mean and variance are 215.0000 and 913.6363, respectively.

In order to compute the test statistic t, we first need to determine the standard error of the difference between the two means. The pooled standard deviation is computed as

$$s_p = \sqrt{\frac{(n_1-1)(s_1^2)+(n_2-1)(s_2^2)}{n_1+n_2-2}}$$

$$s_p = \sqrt{\frac{(8-1)(364.2857)+(12-1)(913.6363)}{8+12-2}} = 26.4575$$

TABLE 7.1

Cholesterol Data for Independent Samples

Female (Sample 1)	Male (Sample 2)
205	245
160	170
170	180
180	190
190	200
200	210
210	220
165	230
	240
	250
	260
	185
$\bar{Y}_1 = 185.0000$	$\bar{Y}_2 = 215.0000$
$s_1^2 = 364.2857$	$s_2^2 = 913.6363$

and the standard error of the difference between two means is computed as

$$s_{\bar{Y}_1-\bar{Y}_2} = s_p\sqrt{\frac{1}{n_1}+\frac{1}{n_2}} = 26.4575\sqrt{\frac{1}{8}+\frac{1}{12}} = 12.0752$$

The test statistic t can then be computed as

$$t = \frac{\bar{Y}_1-\bar{Y}_2}{s_{\bar{Y}_1-\bar{Y}_2}} = \frac{185-215}{12.0752} = -2.4844$$

The next step is to use Table A.2 in the Appendix to determine the critical values. As there are 18 degrees of freedom $(n_1 + n_2 - 2) = 8 + 12 - 2 = 18$, using $\alpha = .05$ and a two-tailed or nondirectional test, we find the critical values using the appropriate α_2 column to be +2.101 and −2.101. Because the test statistic falls beyond the critical values as shown in Figure 7.1, we therefore *reject the null hypothesis* that the means are equal in favor of the nondirectional alternative that the means are not equal. Thus, we conclude that the mean cholesterol levels for males and females are *not* equal at the .05 level of significance (denoted by $p < .05$).

The 95% confidence interval can also be examined. For the cholesterol example, the confidence interval is formed as follows:

$$\left(\bar{Y}_1-\bar{Y}_2\right) \pm \left({}_{\alpha_2}t_{n_1+n_2-2}\right)\left(s_{\bar{Y}_1-\bar{Y}_2}\right) = (185-215) \pm (2.101)(12.0752)$$
$$= (-30) \pm (25.3700) = (-55.3700, -4.6300)$$

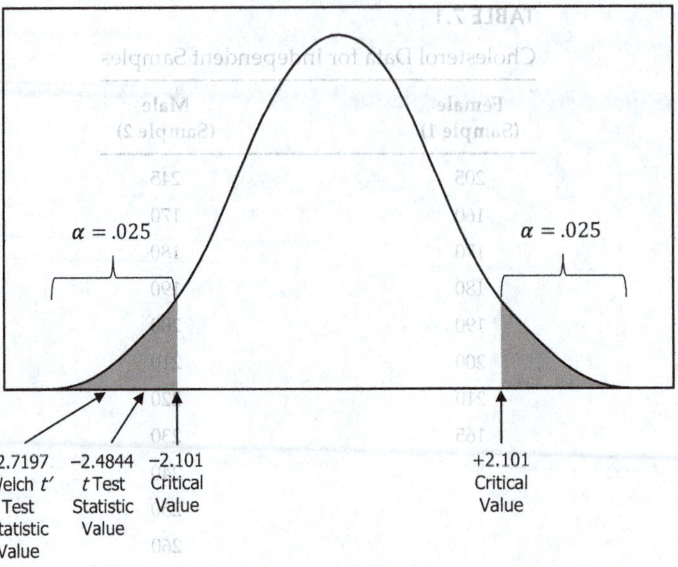

FIGURE 7.1
Critical regions and test statistics for the cholesterol example.

Because the confidence interval does not contain the hypothesized mean difference value of zero, then we would again reject the null hypothesis and conclude that the mean difference in cholesterol levels was not equal to zero at the .05 level of significance ($p < .05$) for males and females. In other words, there is evidence to suggest that the males and females differ, on average, on cholesterol level. More specifically, the mean cholesterol level for males is greater than the mean cholesterol level for females.

7.1.3.2 The Welch t′ Test

The **Welch *t*′ test** is usually appropriate when the population variances are unequal and the sample sizes are unequal. The Welch *t*′ test assumes that the scores on the dependent variable *Y* are normally distributed in each of the two populations and are independent.

The test statistic is known as *t*′ and is denoted by

$$t' = \frac{\bar{Y}_1 - \bar{Y}_2}{s_{\bar{Y}_1 - \bar{Y}_2}} = \frac{\bar{Y}_1 - \bar{Y}_2}{\sqrt{s^2_{\bar{Y}_1} + s^2_{\bar{Y}_2}}} = \frac{\bar{Y}_1 - \bar{Y}_2}{\sqrt{\frac{s_1^2}{n_1} + \frac{s_2^2}{n_2}}}$$

where $\bar{Y}_1$ and $\bar{Y}_2$ are the means for samples 1 and 2, respectively, and $s^2_{\bar{Y}_1}$ and $s^2_{\bar{Y}_2}$ are the variance errors of the means for samples 1 and 2, respectively. Here we see that the denominator of this test statistic is conceptually similar to the one-sample *t* and the independent *t* test statistics. The *variance errors of the mean* are computed for each group by

$$s^2_{\bar{Y}_1} = \frac{s_1^2}{n_1}$$

$$s_{\bar{Y}_2}^2 = \frac{s_2^2}{n_2}$$

where s_1^2 and s_2^2 are the sample variances for groups 1 and 2, respectively. The square root of the variance error of the mean is the standard error of the mean (i.e., $s_{\bar{Y}_1}$ and $s_{\bar{Y}_2}$). *Thus we see that rather than take a pooled or weighted average of the two sample variances as we did with the independent* t *test, the two sample variances are treated separately.*

The test statistic t' is then compared to a critical value(s) from the t distribution in Table A.2 in the Appendix. We again use the appropriate α column depending on the desired level of significance and whether the test is one- or two-tailed (i.e., α_1 and α_2), and the appropriate row for the degrees of freedom. The degrees of freedom for this test are a bit more complicated than for the independent t test. The degrees of freedom are adjusted from $n_1 + n_2 - 2$ for the independent t test to the following value for the Welch t' test:

$$\nu = \frac{\left(s_{\bar{Y}_1}^2 + s_{\bar{Y}_2}^2\right)^2}{\dfrac{\left(s_{\bar{Y}_1}^2\right)^2}{n_1 - 1} + \dfrac{\left(s_{\bar{Y}_2}^2\right)^2}{n_2 - 1}}$$

The degrees of freedom, ν, are approximated by rounding to the nearest whole number prior to using the table. If the test statistic falls into a critical region, then we reject H_0; otherwise, we fail to reject H_0.

For the two-tailed test, a $(1 - \alpha)\%$ confidence interval can also be examined. The confidence interval is formed as follows:

$$\left(\bar{Y}_1 - \bar{Y}_2\right) \pm {}_{\alpha_2}t_{\nu}\left(s_{\bar{Y}_1 - \bar{Y}_2}\right)$$

If the confidence interval contains the hypothesized mean difference of zero, then the conclusion is to *fail to reject* H_0; otherwise, we *reject* H_0. Thus, interpretation of this CI is the same as with the independent t test.

Consider again the example cholesterol data where the sample variances were somewhat different and the sample sizes were different. The *variance errors of the mean* are computed for each sample as follows:

$$s_{\bar{Y}_1}^2 = \frac{s_1^2}{n_1} = \frac{364.2857}{8} = 45.5357$$

$$s_{\bar{Y}_2}^2 = \frac{s_2^2}{n_2} = \frac{913.6363}{12} = 76.1364$$

The t' test statistic is computed as

$$t' = \frac{\bar{Y}_1 - \bar{Y}_2}{s_{\bar{Y}_1 - \bar{Y}_2}} = \frac{185 - 215}{\sqrt{45.5357 + 76.1364}} = \frac{-30}{11.0305} = -2.7197$$

Finally, the degrees of freedom, v, are determined to be

$$v = \frac{\left(s_{\bar{Y}_1}^2 + s_{\bar{Y}_2}^2\right)^2}{\frac{\left(s_{\bar{Y}_1}^2\right)^2}{n_1 - 1} + \frac{\left(s_{\bar{Y}_2}^2\right)^2}{n_2 - 1}} = \frac{(45.5357 + 76.1364)^2}{\frac{(45.5357)^2}{8-1} + \frac{(76.1364)^2}{12-1}} = 17.9838$$

which is rounded to 18, the nearest whole number. The degrees of freedom remain 18 as they were for the independent t test, and thus the critical values are still +2.101 and −2.101. Because the test statistic falls beyond the critical values shown in Figure 7.1, we therefore reject the null hypothesis that the means are equal in favor of the alternative that the means are not equal. Thus, as with the independent t test, with the Welch t' test we conclude that the mean cholesterol levels for males and females are not equal at the .05 level of significance. In this particular example, then, we see that the unequal sample variances and unequal sample sizes did not alter the outcome when comparing the independent t test result with the Welch t' test result. However, note that the results for these two tests may differ with other data.

Finally, the 95% confidence interval can be examined. For the example, the confidence interval is formed as follows:

$$\left(\bar{Y}_1 - \bar{Y}_2\right) \pm {}_{\alpha_2}t_v\left(s_{\bar{Y}_1 - \bar{Y}_2}\right) = (185 - 215) \pm (2.101)(11.0305) =$$
$$= (-30) \pm (23.1751) = (-53.1751, -6.8249)$$

Because the confidence interval does not contain the hypothesized mean difference value of zero, then we would again reject the null hypothesis and conclude that the mean gender difference was not equal to zero at the .05 level of significance ($p < .05$).

7.1.3.3 Recommendations

The following four recommendations are made regarding the two independent samples case. Although there is not total consensus in the field, our recommendations take into account, as much as possible, the available research and statistical software.

First, if the *normality assumption is satisfied*, the following recommendations are made: (a) the independent t test is recommended when the homogeneity of variance assumption is met (i.e., equal variance assumption is met and there is either an equal, balanced or unequal, unbalanced number of observations in the sample); (b) the independent t test is recommended when the homogeneity of variance assumption is not met and when there are an equal number of observations in the samples (i.e., balanced design but equal variance assumption is violated); and (c) the Welch t' test is recommended when the homogeneity of variance assumption is not met and when there are an unequal number of observations in the samples (i.e., unbalanced design and equal variance assumption is violated).

Second, if the *normality assumption is not satisfied*, the following recommendations are made: (a) if the homogeneity of variance assumption is met, then the independent t test using ranked scores (Conover & Iman, 1981), rather than raw scores, is recommended; and (b) if homogeneity of variance assumption is *not* met, then the Welch t' test using ranked scores is recommended, regardless of whether there are an equal number of observations in the samples. Using ranked scores means you rank order the observations from highest to lowest regardless of group membership, then conduct the appropriate t test with ranked scores rather than raw scores.

Third, the dependent t test is recommended when there is some dependence between the groups (e.g., matched pairs or the same individuals measured on two occasions), as described later in this chapter.

Fourth, the nonparametric Mann-Whitney-Wilcoxon test is *not* recommended under any circumstances. Among the disadvantages of this test are that (a) the critical values are not extensively tabled, (b) tied ranks can affect the results and no optimal procedure has yet been developed (Wilcox, 1986), and (c) Type I error appears to be inflated regardless of the status of the assumptions (Zimmerman, 2003). For these reasons the Mann-Whitney-Wilcoxon test is not further described here. Note that most major statistical packages, including SPSS, have options for conducting the independent t test, the Welch t' test, and the Mann-Whitney-Wilcoxon test. Alternatively, one could conduct the Kruskal-Wallis nonparametric one-factor analysis of variance, which is also based on ranked data, and which is appropriate for comparing the means of two or more independent groups. This test is considered more fully in Chapter 11. These recommendations are summarized in Box 7.1.

BOX 7.1 Recommendations for the Independent and Dependent Samples Tests Based on Meeting or Violating the Assumption of Normality

Assumption	Independent Samples Tests	Dependent Samples Tests
Normality is met.	Use the independent t test when homogeneity of variances is met. Use the independent t test when homogeneity of variances is *not* met, but there are equal sample sizes in the groups. Use the Welch t' test when homogeneity of variances is *not* met and there are unequal sample sizes in the groups.	Use the dependent t test.
Normality is *not* met.	Use the independent t test with ranked scores when homogeneity of variances is met. Use the Welch t' test with ranked scores when homogeneity of variances is *not* met, regardless of equal or unequal sample sizes in the groups. Use the Kruskal-Wallis nonparametric procedure.	Use the dependent t test with ranked scores or alternative procedures, including bootstrap methods, trimmed means, medians, or Stein's method. Use the Wilcoxon signed ranks test when data are both nonnormal and have extreme outliers. Use the Friedman nonparametric procedure.

7.1.4 Sample Size of the Independent *t* Test

We will start our discussion of sufficient sample size for the independent t test with the same thing that we began the discussion in Chapter 6: Remember that there is a difference in having a sample size that produces *sufficiently powered results* as compared to a sample size that will produce *robust results*. **Robust results** mean that the results are still relatively accurate even if there are some violations of assumptions. Having robust results does *not* equate, necessarily, to having a sufficiently powered test (i.e., being able to detect a statistically significant difference if it exists). It's possible to have robust results for an underpowered test (i.e., assumptions are met, but the sample size is not large enough for detecting a difference if it's there). And it's also possible to have a sufficiently powered test that does not produce robust results (i.e., sample size is sufficient for detecting a difference if it's there, but assumptions have been violated). A common myth is that a sample size of 30 is sufficient for conducting an independent t test (or generally any of the three t tests). We've also seen researchers say that a sample size of 20 is sufficient. Other researchers say that as long as the normality assumption is met, regardless of the sample size, the results will be robust. *We do not condone going by any of these suggested guidelines for determining sample size.* There are no conventions that we recommend for sample size. Rather, we encourage researchers to conduct a power analysis to determine the sample size needed for sufficient power.

7.1.5 Power of the Independent *t* Test

Power for the independent t test can be determined based on reviewing power tables or using statistical software (e.g., G*Power).

7.1.6 Effect Size of the Independent *t* Test

Several effect size indices can be computed for the independent t test. We will examine standardized mean difference effects and proportion of variance accounted for.

7.1.6.1 Standardized Mean Difference

We extend Cohen's (1988) sample measure of effect size, *delta* or d, from Chapter 6 to the two independent samples situation. Here we compute the **standardized mean difference**, d, as follows:

$$d = \frac{\bar{Y}_1 - \bar{Y}_2}{s_p}$$

The numerator of the formula is the difference between the two sample means. The denominator is the pooled standard deviation, for which the formula was presented previously. Cohen (1988) originally used n_1 and n_2 to compute s_p. However, Hedges and Olkin (1985) used $n_1 - 1$ and $n_2 - 1$ to compute s_p, as we have done.

A **bias corrected effect size** (Hedges, 1981) for small sample sizes (e.g., $n < 50$) is computed as follows, where $df = n_1 + n_2 - 2$.

$$g = \left(\frac{\bar{Y}_1 - \bar{Y}_2}{s_p}\right)\left(1 - \frac{3}{(4)(df) - 1}\right)$$

The correction factor, $\left(1 - \frac{3}{(4)(df) - 1}\right)$, will always less than 1.0. Thus, the **sample size adjusted Hedge's *g*** will always be less than d. The correction factor will always be close to 1.0 unless the df are very small (e.g., < 10) (Hedges, 1981).

The effect size d is measured in standard deviation units, and again we use Cohen's proposed subjective standards for interpreting d: small effect size, $d = .2$; medium effect size, $d = .5$; large effect size, $d = .8$. Conceptually, this is similar to d in the one-sample case from Chapter 6. The effect size d is considered a standardized group difference type of effect size (Huberty, 2002).

Alternative methods are available for computing the standardizer (i.e., the denominator). Rather than the pooled standard deviation, the standard deviation of just one of the groups (typically the control group) can be used as the denominator (Glass, 1976), and this is often referred to as Glass's d, or d_G. Glass's d has been recommended when the homogeneity of variance assumption is not met (Olejnik & Algina, 2000). As noted by Olejnik and Algina (2000, p. 246), when the equal variances assumption is violated, *the researcher will have to select one standard deviation that expresses the contrast on the scale the researcher thinks is most important or will have to report the mean difference standardized by several standard deviations and discussion the implications of these figures.*

7.1.6.2 Strength of Association

Other types of effect sizes can be computed for independent t test results. One such effect size index measures strength of association; that is, the amount of variation in the dependent variable that can be explained or accounted for by the independent variable. For the independent t test, we will examine **eta squared (η^2)** and **omega squared (ω^2)**.

For the independent t test, **eta squared (η^2)** can be calculated as follows:

$$\eta^2 = \frac{t^2}{t^2 + df} = \frac{t^2}{t^2 + (n_1 + n_2 - 2)}$$

The numerator is the squared t test statistic value and the denominator is the sum of the squared t test statistic value and the degrees of freedom. Values for eta squared range from 0 to +1.00, where values closer to one indicate a stronger association. In terms of what this effect size tells us, as noted earlier, eta squared is interpreted as the *proportion of variance accounted for in the dependent variable by the independent variable* and indicates the degree of the relationship between the independent and dependent variables. If we use Cohen's (1988) metric for interpreting eta squared: small effect size, $\eta^2 = .01$; moderate effect size, $\eta^2 = .06$; large effect size, $\eta^2 = .14$.

Omega squared (ω^2) can be computed for the independent t test as follows:

$$\omega^2 = \frac{t^2 - 1}{t^2 + N - 1}$$

The interpretation for omega squared is the same as for eta squared: The *proportion of variance accounted for in the dependent variable by the independent variable* and indicates the degree of the relationship between the independent and dependent variables. If we use Cohen's (1988) metric for interpreting omega squared: small effect size, $\omega^2 = .01$; moderate effect size, $\omega^2 = .06$; large effect size, $\omega^2 = .14$.

7.1.6.3 An Example

The effect size, *d*, using the pooled standard deviation for the standardizer for the example examined previously is computed as follows:

$$d = \frac{\bar{Y}_1 - \bar{Y}_2}{s_p} = \frac{185 - 215}{26.4575} = -1.1339$$

Computing the sample size adjusted Hedge's *g*, we find:

$$g = \left(\frac{\bar{Y}_1 - \bar{Y}_2}{s_p}\right)\left(1 - \frac{3}{(4)(df) - 1}\right) = \left(\frac{185 - 215}{26.4575}\right)\left(1 - \frac{3}{(4)(18) - 1}\right) = (-1.1339)(.9577)$$

$$g = -1.0860$$

According to Cohen's recommended subjective standards, this would certainly be a rather large effect size, as the difference between the two sample means is larger than one standard deviation. Rather than *d*, had we wanted to compute eta squared or omega squared, we would have also found a large effect:

$$\eta^2 = \frac{t^2}{t^2 + df} = \frac{(-2.4844)^2}{(-2.4844)^2 + 18} = .2553$$

$$\omega^2 = \frac{t^2 - 1}{t^2 + N - 1} = \frac{(-2.4844)^2 - 1}{(-2.4844)^2 + 20 - 1} = .2055$$

An eta squared value of .26 and omega squared of .21 both indicate a large relationship between the independent and dependent variables, with eta squared suggesting that 26% of the variance in the dependent variable (i.e., cholesterol level) accounted for by the independent variable (i.e., sex) and omega squared indicating that about 21% of the variance is accounted for.

7.1.6.4 Confidence Intervals for Cohen's Delta

As we learned in the previous chapter, computing confidence intervals for effect sizes is also valuable. The benefit in creating confidence intervals for effect size values is similar to that of creating confidence intervals for parameter estimates—*confidence intervals for the effect size provide an added measure of precision that is not obtained from knowledge of the effect size alone.* Computing confidence intervals for effect size indices, however, is not as straightforward as simply plugging in known values into a formula. This is because *d* is a function of both the population mean and population standard deviation (Finch & Cumming, 2009), and the noncentrality parameter comes into play. We refer you back to Chapter 6 for a refresher on this.

A nice online calculator for computing the independent *t* test confidence interval for effect size *d* using the noncentrality parameter is available at https://effect-size-calculator.herokuapp.com (Uanhoro, 2017). As we see in Figure 7.2, seven inputs are required: sample mean for each group, sample standard deviation for each group, sample size for each group, and confidence interval (i.e., the complement of alpha). Cohen's *d* (in absolute value terms; note that we input the larger mean as sample 1 in the online calculator, resulting in a positive effect size but we could have just as easily input the smaller mean as sample 1 and we'll see the effect of this using the Campbell online calculator) is 1.139, as noted previously as well, with confidence intervals of .1533 and 2.0877. Putting this in context of our cholesterol example, if multiple random samples were drawn from the population, 95% of the samples could expect males to have, at minimum, about .15 and, at maximum, over 2 standard deviation units higher cholesterol as compared to females.

Note that while we are provided the additional effect size measure, $r_{equivalent}$, on our output, Rosenthal and Rubin (2003, p. 496) provide a number of limitations to consider when using this effect and refer to it as a "first-aid kit" rather than ideal. Specifically, $r_{equivalent}$ is

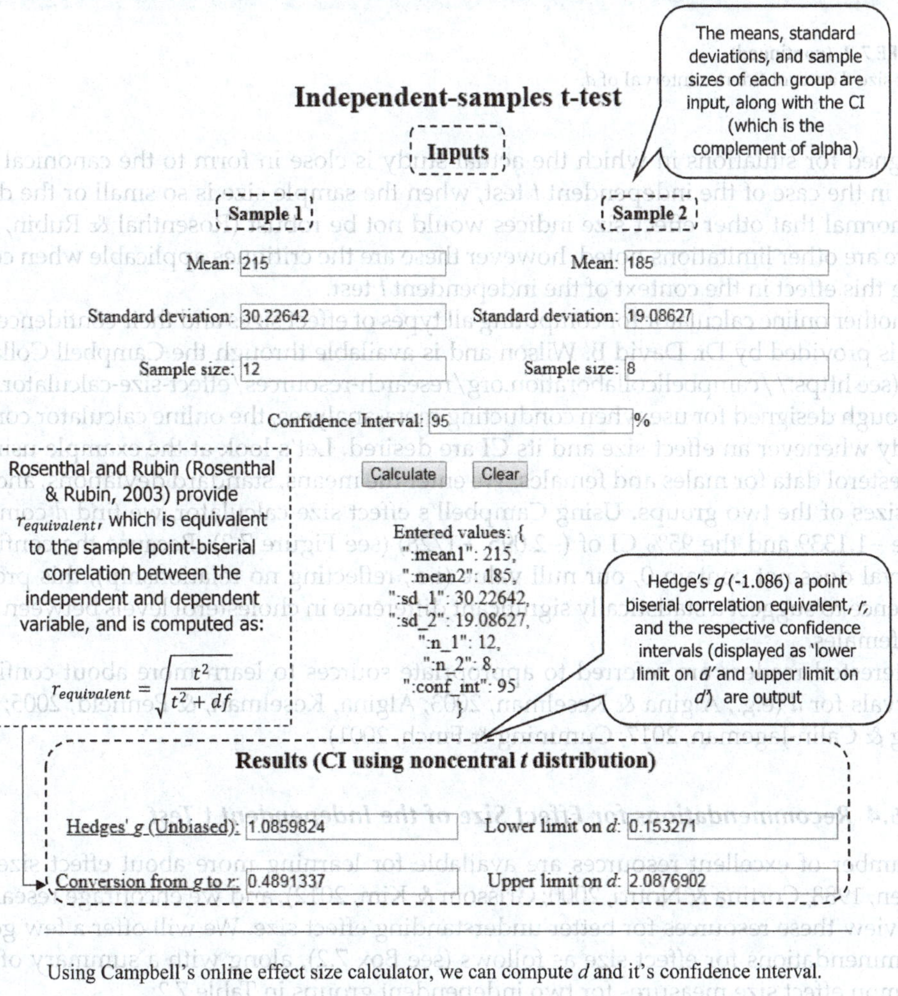

FIGURE 7.2
Effect size *d* and confidence interval of *d*.

Source: R. Rosenthal & D. B. Rubin. (2003). r-sub(equivalent): A simple effect size indicator. *Psychological Methods*, *8*(4), 492–496.

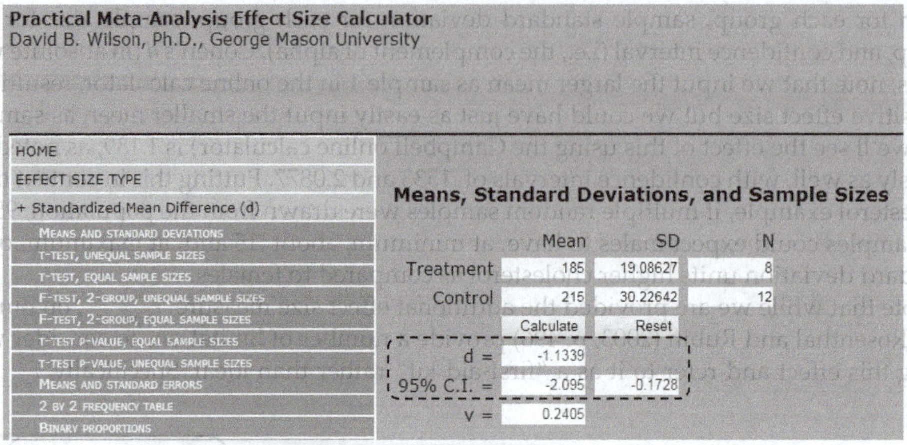

FIGURE 7.2 (continued)
Effect size *d* and confidence interval of *d*.

designed for situations in which the actual study is close in form to the canonical study and, in the case of the independent *t* test, when the sample size is so small or the data so nonnormal that other effect size indices would not be robust (Rosenthal & Rubin, 2003). There are other limitations noted, however these are the critiques applicable when considering this effect in the context of the independent *t* test.

Another online calculator for computing all types of effect sizes and their confidence intervals is provided by Dr. David B. Wilson and is available through the Campbell Collaboration (see https://campbellcollaboration.org/research-resources/effect-size-calculator.html). Although designed for use when conducting meta-analyses, the online calculator comes in handy whenever an effect size and its CI are desired. Let's look at the example using the cholesterol data for males and females. We enter the means, standard deviations, and sample sizes of the two groups. Using Campbell's effect size calculator, we find *d* computed to be −1.1339 and the 95% CI of (−2.095, −1728) (see Figure 7.2). Because the confidence interval does not contain 0, our null value (i.e., reflecting no relationship), this provides evidence to suggest a statistically significant difference in cholesterol levels between males and females.

Interested readers are referred to appropriate sources to learn more about confidence intervals for *d* (e.g., Algina & Keselman, 2003; Algina, Keselman, & Penfield, 2005; Cumming & Calin-Jageman, 2017; Cumming & Finch, 2001).

7.1.6.4 Recommendations for Effect Size of the Independent t *Test*

A number of excellent resources are available for learning more about effect size (e.g., Cohen, 1988; Cortina & Nouri, 2000; Grissom & Kim, 2012), and we encourage researchers to review these resources for better understanding effect size. We will offer a few general recommendations for effect size as follows (see Box 7.2), along with a summary of some common effect size measures for two independent groups in Table 7.2:

1. If you are reporting a standardized mean difference, always report the standardizer with which you have computed the effect size (or better yet, just include the formula for your effect size). There is not a consensus in the field on notation for effect size, and thus reporting *d* may imply different calculations to different researchers.

2. For very small samples, use sample size corrected Hedge's *g*.
3. When the assumption of equal variances is met, report *d* or Hedge's *g* that is corrected for small sample sizes.
4. When the assumption of equal variances is *not* met, do not use the pooled standard deviation. Rather, adhere to the recommendation of Glass (1976) and select the standard deviation for one of the groups as the standardizer.
5. Because nonnormality can unduly influence standardized mean difference effect size estimates, selecting an effect size index that does not require normality is recommended in cases where the assumption of normality is violated (Grissom & Kim, 2012).

TABLE 7.2
Independent *t* Test Effect Sizes and Interpretations

Effect Size	Interpretation
Omega squared (ω^2) and eta squared (η^2)	Proportion of total variability in the dependent variable that is accounted for by the factor (i.e., independent variable) • Small effect = .01 • Medium effect = .06 • Large effect = .14
Cohen's *d* and Hedge's *g* for small samples	The number of standard deviation units for which the groups differ • Small effect = .20 • Medium effect = .50 • Large effect = .80

BOX 7.2 Recommendations for Reporting Effect Size with the Independent *t* Test

Condition	Recommendation
Reporting standardized mean difference	Always report the standardizer (i.e., denominator) with which you have computed the effect size or, even better, include the formula for your effect size.
Very small samples	Report sample size corrected Hedge's *g*.
Assumption of equal variances is met	Report *d* or sample size corrected Hedge's *g*.
Assumption of equal variances is *not* met	Report *d* using the standard deviation for one of the groups as the standardizer (not the pooled standard deviation).
Assumption of normality is *not* met	Select an effect size index that does not require normality.

7.1.7 Assumptions of the Independent *t* Test

The assumptions of the independent *t* test are that the scores on the dependent variable *Y* (a) are *normally distributed* within each of the two populations, (b) are *independent*, and (c) have *equal population variances* (known as *homogeneity of variance* or *homoscedasticity*). (The assumptions of normality and independence should sound familiar as they were introduced as we learned about the one-sample *t* test.) When these assumptions are not met, other procedures may be more appropriate, as we also show later.

7.1.7.1 Normality

Let us being with a discussion of normality. The normality assumption is made because we are dealing with a *parametric inferential test*. **Parametric tests** assume a particular underlying theoretical population distribution, in this case, the normal distribution. **Nonparametric tests** do not assume a particular underlying theoretical population distribution. For the independent *t* test, *the assumption of normality is met when the dependent variable is normally distributed for each sample (i.e., each category or group) of the independent variable.* Conventional wisdom tells us the following about nonnormality. When the normality assumption is violated with the independent *t* test, the effects on Type I and Type II errors are minimal when using a two-tailed test (e.g., Glass, Peckham, & Sanders, 1972; Sawilowsky & Blair, 1992). When using a one-tailed test, violation of the normality assumption is minimal for samples larger than 10 and disappears for samples of at least 20 (Sawilowsky & Blair, 1992; Tiku & Singh, 1981). However, more recent research in situations where the groups have unequal sample sizes and the distributions for the groups differ in skewness, *t* is not asymptotically correct.(Cressie & Whitford, 1986). Additionally, Wilcox (2003) indicates that power for both the independent *t* and Welch *t′* can be reduced even for slight departures from normality, with outliers also contributing to the problem. Wilcox recommends several procedures not readily available and beyond the scope of this text (such as bootstrap methods, trimmed means, medians). Keep in mind, though, that the independent *t* test is fairly robust to nonnormality in most situations. Additionally, Wilcox (2017) suggests that *t* is robust to Type I errors when the group distributions are equal (e.g., the same skew across all groups).

The simplest methods for detecting violation of the normality assumption are graphical methods, such as stem-and-leaf plots, box plots, histograms, or Q-Q plots, as well as statistical procedures such as the Shapiro-Wilk test (1965) and skewness and kurtosis statistics.

7.1.7.2 Independence

The independence assumption is also necessary for the independent *t* test. *The assumption of independence is met when there is random assignment of individuals to the two groups or categories of the independent variable.* Random assignment to the two samples being studied provides for greater internal validity—the ability to state with some degree of confidence that the independent variable caused the outcome (i.e., the dependent variable). If the independence assumption is *not* met, then probability statements about the Type I and Type II errors will not be accurate; in other words, the probability of a Type I or Type II error may be increased as a result of the assumption not being met. Zimmerman (1997) found that Type I error was affected even for relatively small relations or correlations between the samples (i.e., even as small as .10 or .20).

In general, the assumption can be met by (a) keeping the assignment of individuals to groups separate through the design of the experiment (specifically random assignment—not to be confused with random selection), and (b) keeping the individuals separate from one another through experimental control so that the scores on the dependent variable *Y* for sample 1 do not influence the scores for sample 2. Zimmerman also stated that independence can be violated for supposedly independent samples due to some type of matching in the design of the experiment (e.g., matched pairs based on sex, age, and weight). If the observations are not independent, then the dependent *t* test, discussed later in the chapter, may be appropriate.

When considering random assignment to groups, it is important to consider the size of the sample that is being randomized. Hsu (1989) identified conditions under which equivalence is likely to be attained with random assignment. In particular, Hsu noted that the probability of groups being *nonequivalent* after random assignment increases as the number of nuisance variables increase and generally decreases as total sample size increases. For example, with a sample size of 24, the probability of nonequivalence for two groups randomly assigned is about 22% with one nuisance variable but increases to 53% with three nuisance variables. It is only at samples of about 40 in size that randomization appears to be an effective method of creating equivalent groups considering the maximum number of nuisance variables examined by Hsu (1989). The take-home message from this is the following: *Don't assume that random assignment to groups will achieve equivalence with samples of less than 40.*

7.1.7.3 Homogeneity of Variance

Of potentially more serious concern is violation of the homogeneity of variance assumption. Homogeneity of variance is met when the variances of the dependent variable for the two samples (i.e., the two groups or categories of the independent variables) are the same. Research has shown that the effect of heterogeneity (i.e., unequal variances) is minimal when the sizes of the two samples, n_1 and n_2, are equal *and* the assumption of normality holds; this is not the case when the sample sizes are not equal. When the larger variance is associated with the smaller sample size (e.g., group 1 has the larger variance and the smaller n), then the actual (i.e., observed) α level is larger than the nominal (i.e., stated) α level. In other words, if you set alpha at .05, then you are not really conducting the test at the .05 level, but at some larger value. When the larger variance is associated with the larger sample size (e.g., group 1 has the larger variance and the larger n), then the actual alpha level is smaller than the nominal alpha level. In other words, if you set alpha at .05, then you are not really conducting the test at the .05 level, but at some smaller value. When there are equal sample sizes and the assumption of normality is violated, the results from a t test will not be robust unless the distributions of the group are equal (e.g., each group has the same degree of skew) (Wilcox, 2017). One can use statistical tests to detect violation of the homogeneity of variance assumption, although the most commonly used tests are somewhat problematic. These tests include Hartley's F_{max} test (for equal *ns*, but sensitive to nonnormality; it is the unequal *ns* situation that we are concerned with anyway), Cochran's test (for equal *ns*, but even more sensitive to nonnormality than Hartley's test; concerned with unequal *ns* situation anyway), Levene's test, which is provided by default in SPSS (for equal *ns*, but sensitive to nonnormality; concerned with unequal *ns* situation anyway), the Bartlett test (for unequal *ns*, but very sensitive to nonnormality), the Box-Scheffé-Anderson test (for unequal *ns*, fairly robust to nonnormality), and the Browne-Forsythe test (for unequal *ns*, more robust to nonnormality than the Box-Scheffé-Anderson test and therefore recommended). When the variances are unequal and the sample sizes are unequal, the usual method is to use the Welch t' test as an alternative to the independent t test, as described in the next section. Inferential tests for evaluating homogeneity of variance are more fully considered in Chapter 9.

7.1.7.4 Conditions of the Independent *t* Test

In addition to meeting the assumptions of the test, we also must consider the measurement scales of the variables used as they must also be appropriate for the statistical procedure to which they are applied. Because this is a test of means, the *dependent variable* must be measured on an *interval or ratio scale*. The *independent variable*, however, must be *nominal or ordinal*, and only two categories or groups of the independent variable can be used with the independent t test. (If you continue your statistical journey, you will likely learn about analysis of variance, which can accommodate an independent variable with *more* than two categories.) It is *not* a condition of the independent t test that the sample sizes of the two groups be the same. *An unbalanced design (i.e., unequal sample sizes) is perfectly acceptable*. An unbalanced design is only a concern in the event that the assumption of homogeneity is violated. If you find yourself in that situation, please refer to the previous discussion on measures that can be taken.

7.2 Inferences About Two Dependent Means and How They Work

In this section, two inferential tests of the difference between two dependent means are described, the dependent t test and briefly the Wilcoxon signed ranks test. The section concludes with a list of recommendations.

7.2.1 Characteristics of the Dependent *t* Test

As you may recall, the **dependent *t* test** is appropriate to use when there are two samples that are dependent; that is, the individuals in sample 1 have some relationship to the individuals in sample 2. Although there are several methods for computing the test statistic t, the most direct method and the one most closely aligned conceptually with the one-sample t test is as follows:

$$t = \frac{\bar{d}}{s_{\bar{d}}}$$

where $\bar{d}$ is the **mean difference**, and $s_{\bar{d}}$ is the **standard error of the mean difference**. Conceptually, this test statistic looks just like the one-sample t test statistic, except now the notation has been changed to denote that we are dealing with *difference scores* rather than raw scores.

The **standard error of the mean difference** is computed by

$$s_{\bar{d}} = \frac{s_d}{\sqrt{n}}$$

where s_d is the standard deviation of the difference scores (i.e., like any other standard deviation, only this one is computed from the difference scores rather than raw scores), and n is the total number of pairs. Conceptually, this standard error looks just like the standard error for the one-sample t test. If we were doing hand computations, we would compute a difference score for each pair of scores (i.e., $Y_1 - Y_2$). For example, if sample 1 were wives and sample 2 were their husbands, then we calculate a difference score for each couple. From this set of difference scores, we then compute the mean of the difference scores $\bar{d}$ and standard deviation of the difference scores, s_d. This leads us directly into the computation of the t test statistic. Note that although there are n scores in sample 1, n scores in sample 2, and thus $2n$ total scores, there are only n difference scores, which is what the analysis is actually based upon.

The test statistic t is then compared with a critical value(s) from the t distribution. For a two-tailed test, from Table A.2 in the Appendix we would use the appropriate α_2 column depending on the desired level of significance and the appropriate row depending on the degrees of freedom. The *degrees of freedom for this test are n* − 1, where n represents the difference score. Conceptually, we lose one degree of freedom from the number of differences (or pairs) because we are estimating the population variance (or standard deviation) of the difference. Thus, there is one restriction along the lines of our discussion of degrees of freedom in Chapter 6. The critical values are denoted as $\pm_{\alpha_2} t_{n-1}$. The subscript, α_2, of the critical values reflects the fact that this is a two-tailed test, and the subscript $n - 1$ indicates the degrees of freedom. If the test statistic falls into either critical region, then we reject H_0; otherwise, we fail to reject H_0.

For a one-tailed test, from Table A.2 in the Appendix we would use the appropriate α_1 column depending on the desired level of significance and the appropriate row depending on the degrees of freedom. The degrees of freedom are again $n - 1$. The critical value is denoted as $+_{\alpha_1} t_{n-1}$ for the alternative hypothesis where the difference in means is greater than zero, that is, H_1: $\mu_1 - \mu_2 > 0$, and as $-_{\alpha_1} t_{n-1}$ for the alternative hypothesis where the difference in means is less than zero, that is, H_1: $m_1 - \mu_2 < 0$. If the test statistic t falls into the appropriate critical region, then we reject H_0; otherwise, we fail to reject H_0.

7.2.1.1 Confidence Interval for the Dependent t Test

For the two-tailed test, a $(1 - \alpha)\%$ confidence interval can also be examined. The confidence interval is formed as follows:

$$\bar{d} \pm \left({}_{\alpha_2} t_{n-1}\right)\left(s_{\bar{d}}\right)$$

If the confidence interval contains the hypothesized mean difference of 0, then the conclusion is to fail to reject H_0; otherwise, we reject H_0. The interpretation of these confidence intervals is the same as those previously discussed for the one-sample t test and the independent t test.

7.2.1.2 Example of the Dependent t Test

Let us consider an example for purposes of illustrating the dependent t test. Ten young swimmers participated in an intensive 2-month training program. Prior to the program, each swimmer was timed during a 50-meter freestyle event. Following the program, the same swimmers were timed in the 50-meter freestyle event again. This is a classic pretest–posttest design. For illustrative purposes, we will conduct a two-tailed test. However, a case might also be made for a one-tailed test as well, in that the coach might want to see improvement only. However, conducting a two-tailed test allows us to examine the confidence interval for purposes of illustration. The raw scores, the difference scores, and the mean and standard deviation of the difference scores are shown in Table 7.3. The pretest mean time was 64 seconds, and the posttest mean time was 59 seconds.

TABLE 7.3
Swimming Data for Dependent Samples

Swimmer	Pretest Time (in seconds)	Posttest Time (in seconds)	Difference (d)
1	58	54	(58 − 54) = 4
2	62	57	5
3	60	54	6
4	61	56	5
5	63	61	2
6	65	59	6
7	66	64	2
8	69	62	7
9	64	60	4
10	72	63	9
			$\bar{d}$ = 5.0000
			s_d = 2.1602

To determine our test statistic value, t, first we compute the standard error of the mean difference as follows:

$$s_{\bar{d}} = \frac{s_d}{\sqrt{n}} = \frac{2.1602}{\sqrt{10}} = 0.6831$$

Next, using this value for the denominator, the test statistic t is then computed as follows:

$$t = \frac{\bar{d}}{s_{\bar{d}}} = \frac{5}{0.6831} = 7.3196$$

We then use Table A.2 in the Appendix to determine the critical values. Because there are 9 degrees of freedom ($n - 1 = 10 - 1 = 9$), using $\alpha_2 = .05$ and a two-tailed or nondirectional test we find the critical values using the appropriate α column to be +2.262 and −2.262. Because the test statistic falls beyond the critical values, as shown in Figure 7.3, we reject the null hypothesis that the means are equal in favor of the nondirectional alternative that the means are not equal. Thus, we conclude that the mean swimming performance changed from pretest to posttest at the .05 level of significance (observed $p <$ nominal alpha of .05).

The 95% confidence interval is computed to be the following:

$$\bar{d} \pm \left({}_{\alpha_2}t_{n-1}\right)\left(s_{\bar{d}}\right) = 5 \pm (2.262)(0.6831) = 5 \pm (1.5452) = (3.4548, 6.5452)$$

Because the confidence interval does not contain the hypothesized mean difference value of zero, we would again reject the null hypothesis and conclude that the mean pretest–postttest difference was not equal to zero at the .05 level of significance (observed $p <$ nominal alpha of .05).

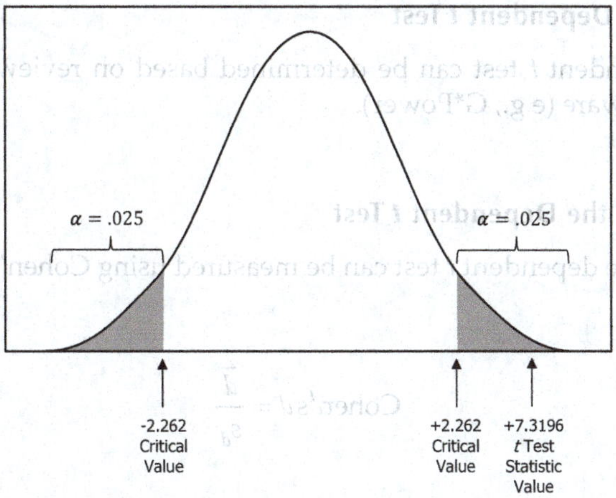

FIGURE 7.3
Critical regions and test statistic for the swimming example.

7.2.1.3 Recommendations

The following three recommendations are made regarding the two dependent samples case. First, the dependent *t* test is recommended when the normality assumption is met.

Second, the dependent *t* test using ranks (Conover & Iman, 1981) is recommended when the normality assumption is not met. Here you rank order the difference scores from highest to lowest, then conduct the test on the ranked difference scores rather than on the raw difference scores. However, more recent research by Wilcox (2003) indicates that power for the dependent *t* can be reduced even for slight departures from normality. Wilcox recommends several procedures beyond the scope of this text (bootstrap methods, trimmed means, medians, Stein's method). Keep in mind, though, that the dependent *t* test is fairly robust to nonnormality in most situations.

Third, the nonparametric Wilcoxon signed ranks test is recommended when the data are nonnormal with extreme outliers (one or a few observations that behave quite differently from the rest). However, among the disadvantages of this test are that (a) the critical values are not extensively tabled and two different tables exist depending on sample size, and (b) tied ranks can affect the results and no optimal procedure has yet been developed (Wilcox, 1995). For these reasons the details of the Wilcoxon signed ranks test are not described here. Note that most major statistical packages, including SPSS, include options for conducting the dependent *t* test and the Wilcoxon signed ranks test. Alternatively, one could conduct the Friedman nonparametric one-factor analysis of variance, also based on ranked data, and which is appropriate for comparing two or more dependent sample means. This test is considered more fully in Chapter 15. These recommendations are summarized in Box 7.1.

7.2.2 Sample Size of the Dependent *t* Test

A common myth is that a sample size of 30 is sufficient for conducting a dependent *t* test (or generally any of the three *t* tests). *We do not condone going by this rule.* Rather, we encourage researchers to conduct a power analysis to determine the sample size needed for sufficient power.

7.2.3 Power of the Dependent *t* Test

Power for the dependent *t* test can be determined based on reviewing power tables or using statistical software (e.g., G*Power).

7.2.4 Effect Size of the Dependent *t* Test

The effect size for the dependent *t* test can be measured using Cohen's (1988) *d*, computed as follows:

$$\text{Cohen's}\,d = \frac{\bar{d}}{s_d}$$

where Cohen's *d* is simply used to distinguish among the various uses and slight differences in the computation of *d*. Interpretation of the value of *d* would be the same as for the one-sample *t* and the independent *t* tests discussed earlier—specifically, the number of standard deviation units for which the mean(s) differ(s).

The effect size for the example examined previously is computed to be the following:

$$\text{Cohen's}\,d = \frac{\bar{d}}{s_d} = \frac{5}{2.1602} = 2.3146$$

which is interpreted as there is approximately a two and one-third standard deviation difference between the pretest and posttest mean swimming times, a very large effect size according to Cohen's subjective standard. See Table 7.4 for guidelines on interpreting Cohen's *d*.

7.2.4.1 Confidence Intervals for Cohen's Delta

As we learned in the previous chapter, computing *confidence intervals for effect sizes* is also valuable. The benefit in creating confidence intervals for effect size values is similar to that of creating confidence intervals for parameter estimates—*confidence intervals for the effect size provide an added measure of precision that is not obtained from knowledge of the effect size alone*. Computing confidence intervals for effect size indices, however, is not as straightforward as simply plugging in known values into a formula. This is because *d* is a function of both the population mean and population standard deviation (Finch & Cumming, 2009),

TABLE 7.4

Dependent *t* Test Effect Size and Interpretation

Effect Size	Interpretation
d	Standard deviation units in which the groups differ • Small effect = .20 • Medium effect = .50 • Large effect = .80

and the noncentrality parameter comes into play. We refer you back to Chapter 6 for a refresher on this.

A nice online calculator for computing the dependent *t* test confidence interval for effect size *d* using the noncentrality parameter is available at https://effect-size-calculator.herokuapp.com (Uanhoro, 2017). As shown in Figure 7.4, seven inputs are required: sample mean for each group, sample standard deviation for each group, number of pairs (i.e., sample size), the bivariate correlation between measures (*r*, which we will learn about in more detail in an upcoming chapter), and confidence interval (i.e., the complement of alpha). Hedge's *g* is 1.1632, with confidence intervals for *d* of .5935 and 1.9345. Putting this in context of our swimming example, if multiple random samples were drawn from the population, 95% of the samples could expect the posttest swimming speed to have, at minimum, about .60 and, at maximum, nearly two standard deviation units faster swim time as compared to speed at pretest.

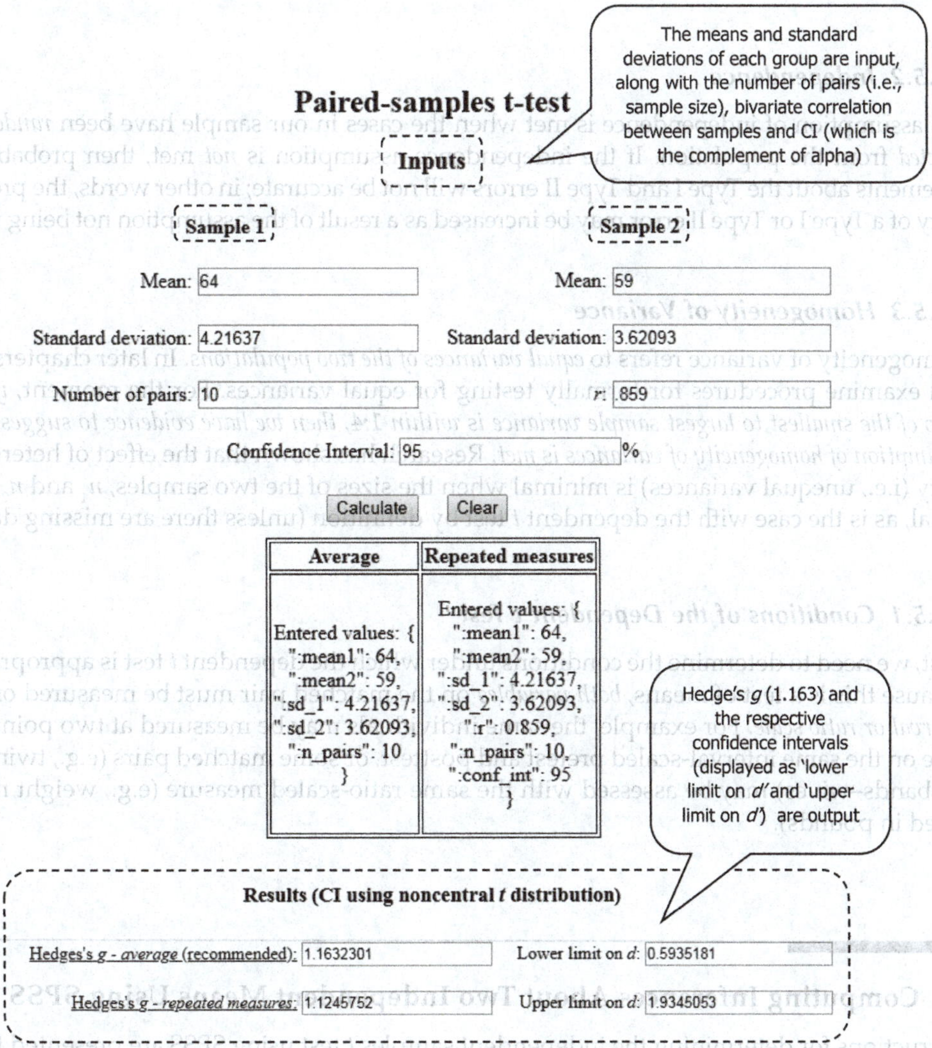

FIGURE 7.4
Effect size *d* and confidence interval of *d*.

7.2.5 Assumptions of the Dependent *t* Test

The assumptions of the dependent *t* test include: normality, independence, and homogeneity of variance. These should sound familiar as they are the same assumptions as those for the independent *t* test. As you will see, however, how we approach estimating evidence of these assumptions differs.

7.2.5.1 Normality

For the dependent *t* test, the assumption of normality is met when the *difference scores* are normally distributed. Normality of the difference scores can be examined as discussed previously—graphical methods (such as stem-and-leaf plots, box plots, histograms, and/or Q-Q plots), statistical procedures such as the Shapiro-Wilk test (1965), and skewness and kurtosis statistics.

7.2.5.2 Independence

The assumption of independence is met when the cases in our sample have been *randomly selected* from the population. If the independence assumption is *not* met, then probability statements about the Type I and Type II errors will not be accurate; in other words, the probability of a Type I or Type II error may be increased as a result of the assumption not being met.

7.2.5.3 Homogeneity of Variance

Homogeneity of variance refers to *equal variances of the two populations*. In later chapters we will examine procedures for formally testing for equal variances. For the moment, *if the ratio of the smallest to largest sample variance is within 1:4, then we have evidence to suggest the assumption of homogeneity of variances is met*. Research has shown that the effect of heterogeneity (i.e., unequal variances) is minimal when the sizes of the two samples, n_1 and n_2, are equal, as is the case with the dependent *t* test by definition (unless there are missing data).

7.2.5.1 Conditions of the Dependent t Test

First, we need to determine the conditions under which the dependent *t* test is appropriate. Because this is a test of means, *both variables* on the matched pair must be measured on an *interval or ratio scale*. For example, the same individuals may be measured at two points in time on the same interval-scaled pretest and posttest, or some matched pairs (e.g., twins or husbands–wives) may be assessed with the same ratio-scaled measure (e.g., weight measured in pounds).

7.3 Computing Inferences About Two Independent Means Using SPSS

Instructions for determining the independent samples *t* test using SPSS are presented first. The data-screening section provides additional steps for examining the assumption of normality for the independent *t* test.

Step 1. In order to conduct an independent *t* test, your dataset needs to include one dependent variable *Y* that is measured on an interval or ratio scale (e.g., "cholesterol") as well as a grouping variable *X* that is measured on a nominal or ordinal scale (e.g., "gender"). For the grouping variable, if there are more than two categories available, only two categories can be selected (or multiple categories must be collapsed so there are only two categories) when running the independent *t* test (the analysis of variance is required for examining more than two categories). To conduct the independent *t* test, go to the "Analyze" in the top pulldown menu, select "Compare Means," and then select "Independent-Samples T Test." Following the steps in the screenshot in Figure 7.5 produces the "Independent-Samples T Test" dialog box.

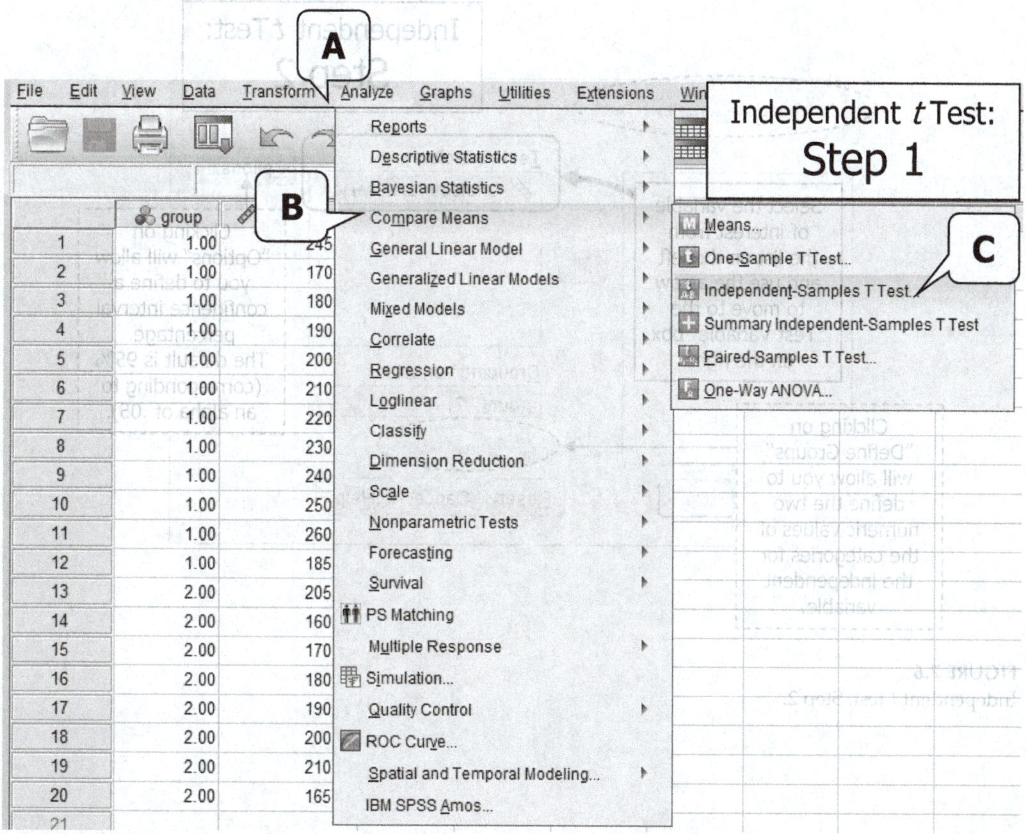

FIGURE 7.5
Independent *t* test: Step 1.

Step 2. Next, from the main "Independent-Samples T Test" dialog box, click the dependent variable (e.g., "cholesterol") and move it into the "Test Variable" box by clicking the arrow button. Next, click the grouping variable (e.g., "gender") and move it into the "Grouping Variable" box by clicking the arrow button. You will notice that there are two question marks next to the name of your grouping variable. This is SPSS letting you know that you need to define (numerically) which two categories of the grouping variable you want to include in your analysis. To do that, click "Define Groups."

Note on changing the alpha level. The default alpha level in SPSS is .05, and thus the default corresponding confidence interval is 95%. If you wish to test your hypothesis at an alpha level other than .05 (and thus obtain confidence intervals other than 95%), click the "Options" button located in the top-right corner of the main dialog box (see Step 2 in the screenshot in Figure 7.6). From here, the confidence interval percentage can be adjusted to correspond to the alpha level at which you wish your hypothesis to be tested (see Step 3 in the screenshot in Figure 7.7). (For purposes of this example, the test has been generated using an alpha level of .05.)

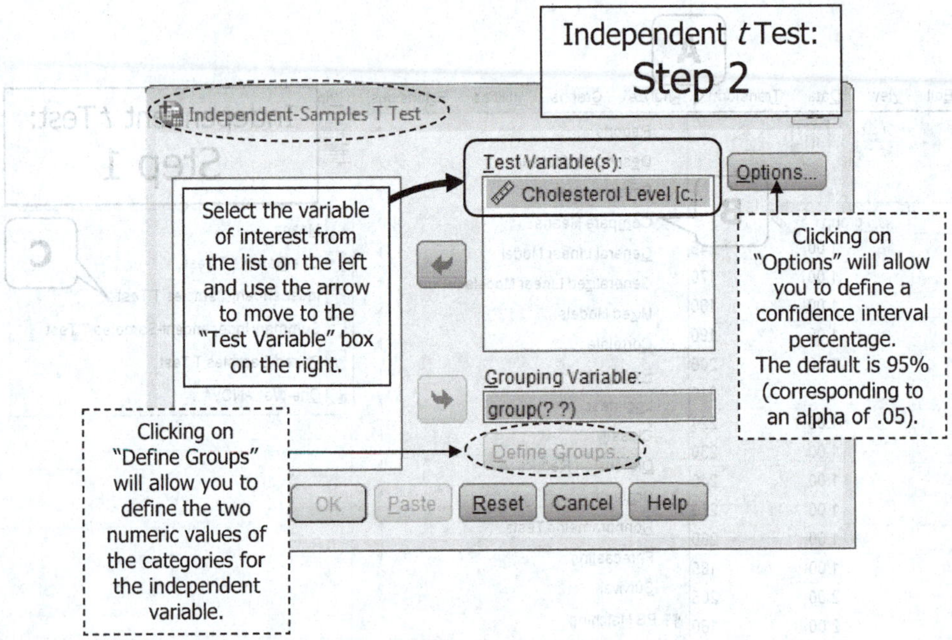

FIGURE 7.6
Independent *t* test: Step 2.

Step 3. From the "Define Groups" dialog box, enter the numeric value designated for each of the two categories or groups of your independent variable. Where it says "Group 1," type in the value designated for your first group (e.g., 1, which in our case indicated that the individual was a female), and where it says "Group 2" type in the value designated for your second group (e.g., 2, in our example, a male) (see Step 3 in the screenshot in Figure 7.7).

Click "Continue" to return to the original dialog box (see the screenshot in Figure 7.6) and then click "OK" to run the analysis.

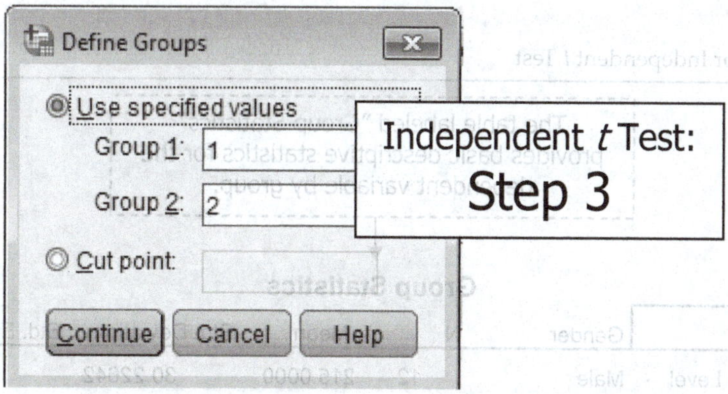

FIGURE 7.7
Independent t test: Step 3.

7.3.1 Interpreting the Output for Inferences About Two Independent Means

The first portion of Table 7.5 provides various descriptive statistics for each group, while the bottom box gives the results of the requested procedure. The following three different inferential tests are automatically provided: (1) Levene's test of the homogeneity of variance assumption (the first two columns of results), (2) the independent t test (which SPSS calls "Equal Variances Assumed"; the top row of the remaining columns of results), and (3) the Welch t' test (which SPSS calls "Equal Variances Not Assumed"; the bottom row of the remaining columns of results).

The first interpretation that must be made is for *Levene's test of equal variances*. We must interpret Levene's test first as the results for Levene's dictates whether the t test results are based on equal variances or unequal variances (which is the Welch t' test). The assumption of equal variances is met when Levene's test is *not* statistically significant, which is interpreted as the variances of the two groups are equal. We can determine statistical significance for Levene's test by reviewing the p value for the F test. In this example, the p value is .090, greater than our alpha level of .05, and thus not statistically significant. *Thus, Levene's test tells us that the variance for cholesterol level for males is not statistically significantly different than the variance for cholesterol level for females, and this provides evidence of meeting the assumption of equal variances.* Having met the assumption of equal variances, the values in the rest of the table will be drawn from the row labeled "Equal Variances Assumed." Had we *not* met the assumption of equal variances ($p <$ alpha for Levene's test), we would report Welch t' results for which the statistics are presented on the row labeled "Equal Variances Not Assumed."

After determining that the variances are equal, the next step is to examine the results of the independent t test. The t test statistic value is 2.484 and the associated p value is .023. *Because the observed probability, p, is less than our nominal alpha of .05, we reject the null hypothesis.* There is a statistically significant difference between groups, and there is evidence to suggest that the mean cholesterol level for males is different than the mean cholesterol level for females.

TABLE 7.5

SPSS Results for Independent t Test

The table labeled "Group Statistics" provides basic descriptive statistics for the dependent variable by group.

Group Statistics

	Gender	N	Mean	Std. Deviation	Std. Error Mean
Cholesterol Level	Male	12	215.0000	30.22642	8.72562
	Female	8	185.0000	19.08627	6.74802

The *F* test (and *p* value) of Levene's Test for Equality of Variances is reviewed to determine if the equal variances assumption has been met. The result of this test determines which row of statistics to utilize. In this case, we meet the assumption and use the statistics reported in the top row.

Had equal variances *not* been met, we would have reported Welch *t'* results, which are provided in the row labeled 'equal variance not assumed.'

"Sig." is the observed *p* value for the independent *t* test. It is interpreted as: there is about a 2% probability of a sample mean difference of -30 or greater occurring by chance if the null hypothesis is really true (i.e., if the population mean difference is 0).

SPSS reports the *95% confidence interval of the difference*. This is interpreted to mean that 95% of the CIs generated across samples will contain the true population *mean difference* of 0.

Independent Samples Test

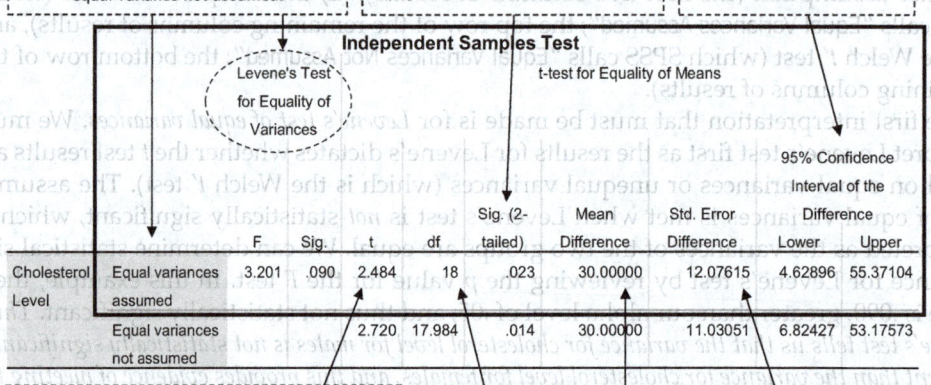

		Levene's Test for Equality of Variances		t-test for Equality of Means						
									95% Confidence Interval of the Difference	
		F	Sig.	t	df	Sig. (2-tailed)	Mean Difference	Std. Error Difference	Lower	Upper
Cholesterol Level	Equal variances assumed	3.201	.090	2.484	18	.023	30.00000	12.07615	4.62896	55.37104
	Equal variances not assumed			2.720	17.984	.014	30.00000	11.03051	6.82427	53.17573

"*t*" is the *t* test statistic value. The *t* value in the top row is used when the assumption of equal variances has been met and is calculated as:

$$t = \frac{\bar{Y}_1 - \bar{Y}_2}{s_{\bar{Y}_1 - \bar{Y}_2}} = \frac{215 - 185}{12.0752} = 2.4844$$

The *t* value in the bottom row is the Welch *t'* and is used when the assumption of equal variances has *not* been met and is calculated as Welch t':

$$t' = \frac{\bar{Y}_1 - \bar{Y}_2}{s_{\bar{Y}_1 - \bar{Y}_2}} = \frac{215 - 185}{\sqrt{45.5357 + 76.1364}}$$

$$t' = \frac{30}{11.0305} = 2.7197$$

df are the degrees of freedom. For the independent samples *t* test, they are calculated as $n_1 + n_2 - 2$, thus in this example $12 + 8 - 2$.

The mean difference is simply the difference between the sample mean cholesterol values. In other words, 215-185 = 30.

The standard error of the mean difference is calculated as:

$$s_{\bar{Y}_1 - \bar{Y}_2} = s_p \sqrt{\frac{1}{n_1} + \frac{1}{n_2}}$$

7.4 Computing Inferences About Two Dependent Means Using SPSS

Next, instructions for determining the dependent samples t test using SPSS are presented. The data-screening section provides additional steps for examining the assumptions of normality and homogeneity for the dependent t test.

Step 1. To conduct a dependent t test, your dataset needs to include the two variables (i.e., for the paired samples) whose means you wish to compare (e.g., pretest and posttest). To conduct the dependent t test, go to the "Analyze" in the top pulldown menu, then select "Compare Means," and then select "Paired-Samples T Test." Following the steps in the screenshot in Figure 7.8 produces the "Paired-Samples T Test" dialog box.

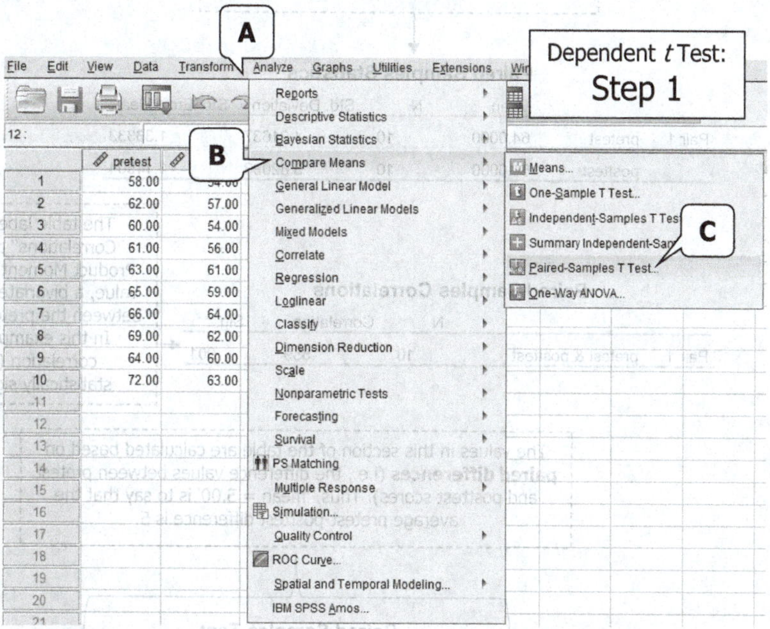

FIGURE 7.8
Dependent t test: Step 1.

Step 2. Click both variables (e.g., pretest and posttest as Variable 1 and Variable 2, respectively) and move them into the "Paired Variables" box by clicking the arrow button. Both variables should now appear in the box, as shown in the screenshot for Step 2 in Figure 7.9. Then click "OK" to run the analysis and generate the output.

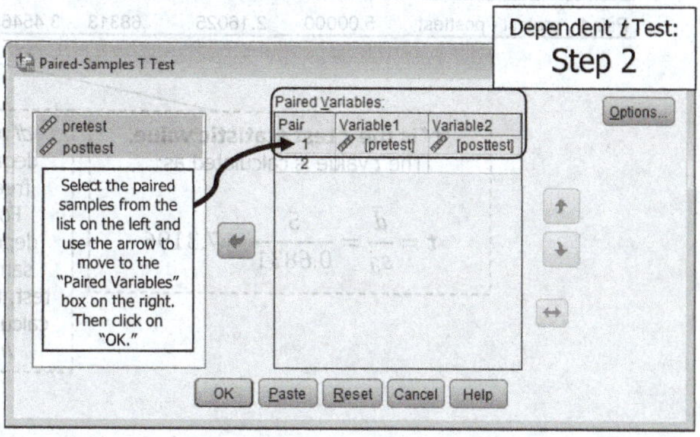

FIGURE 7.9
Dependent t test: Step 2.

7.4.1 Interpreting the Output for Inferences About Two Dependent Means

The output appears in Table 7.6, where again the top box provides descriptive statistics, the middle box provides a bivariate correlation coefficient for the two variables, and the bottom box gives the results of the dependent t test procedure. In terms of our test of inference, with a test statistic value of 7.319 and a probability value of .000, we reject the null hypothesis. There is a statistically significant pre- to post-mean swim time.

TABLE 7.6
SPSS Results for Dependent t Test

The table labeled "Paired Samples Statistics" provides basic descriptive statistics for the paired samples.

Paired Samples Statistics

		Mean	N	Std. Deviation	Std. Error Mean
Pair 1	pretest	64.0000	10	4.21637	1.33333
	posttest	59.0000	10	3.62093	1.14504

Paired Samples Correlations

		N	Correlation	Sig.
Pair 1	pretest & posttest	10	.859	.001

The table labeled "Paired Samples Correlations" provides the Pearson Product Moment Correlation Coefficient value, a bivariate correlation coefficient, between the pretest and posttest values. In this example, there is a strong correlation (r = .859) and it is statistically significant (p = .001).

The values in this section of the table are calculated based on **paired differences** (i.e., the difference values between pretest and posttest scores). Thus, 'mean = 5.00' is to say that the average pretest-posttest difference is 5.

Paired Samples Test

		Paired Differences					t	df	Sig. (2-tailed)
		Mean	Std. Deviation	Std. Error Mean	95% Confidence Interval of the Difference Lower	Upper			
Pair 1	pretest - posttest	5.00000	2.16025	.68313	3.45465	6.54535	7.319	9	.000

"t" is the t test statistic value. The t value is calculated as:

$$t = \frac{\bar{d}}{s_{\bar{d}}} = \frac{5}{0.6831} = 7.3196$$

df are the degrees of freedom. For the dependent samples t test, they are calculated as $n - 1$.

"Sig." is the observed p value for the dependent t test. It is interpreted as: there is less than a 1% probability of a sample mean difference of 5 or greater occurring by chance if the null hypothesis is really true (i.e., if the population mean difference is 0).

7.5 Computing Inferences About Two Independent Means Using R

Next we consider **R** for the dependent *t* test. The scripts are provided within the blocks with additional annotation to assist in understanding how the commands work. Should you want to write reminder notes and annotation to yourself as you write the commands in **R** (and we highly encourage doing so), remember that any text that follows a hashtag (i.e., #) is annotation only and not part of the **R** script. Thus, you can write annotations directly into **R** with hashtags. We encourage this practice so that when you call up the commands in the future, you'll understand what the various lines of code are doing. You may think you'll remember what you did. However, trust us. There is a good chance that you won't. Thus, consider it best practice when using **R** to annotate heavily!

7.5.1 Reading Data into R

```
getwd()
```

R is always pointed to a directory on your computer. To find out which directory it is pointed to, run this "get working directory" function. We will assume that we need to change the working directory, and will use the next line of code to set the working directory to the desired path.

```
setwd("E:/Folder")
```

To set the working directory, use the *setwd* function and change what is in quotation marks here to your file location. Also, if you are copying the directory name, it will copy in slashes. You will need to change the slash (i.e., \) to a forward slash (i.e., /). Note that you need your destination name within quotation marks in the parentheses.

```
Ch7_cholesterol <- read.csv("Ch7_cholesterol.csv")
```

The *read.csv* function reads our data into **R**. What's to the left of the <- will be what the data will be called in **R**. In this example, we're calling the **R** dataframe "Ch7_cholesterol." What's to the right of the <- tells **R** to find this particular .csv file. In this example, our file is called "Ch7_cholesterol.csv." Make sure the extension (i.e., .csv) is included in your script. Also note that the name of your file should be in quotation marks within the parentheses.

```
names(Ch7_cholesterol)
```

The *names* function will produce a list of variable names for each dataframe as follows. This is a good check to make sure your data have been read in correctly.

```
[1] "group"        "cholesterol"
```

```
View(Ch7_cholesterol)
```

The *View* function will let you view the dataset in spreadsheet format in RStudio.

```
Ch7_cholesterol$group <- factor(Ch7_cholesterol$group,
                                labels = c("male",
                                           "female"))
```

FIGURE 7.10
Reading data into **R**.

The *factor* function renames our "group" variable as nominal (i.e., "factor") with two groups or categories with labels of "male" and "female." Had we wanted to create a new variable rather than rename our variable, we would have defined "Ch7_cholesterol$NewName" rather than "Ch7_cholesterol$group" to the left of <- (i.e., as the first portion of this script).

```
levels(Ch7_cholesterol$group)
```

The *levels* function will output the categories in our "group" variable as follows:

```
[1] "male"  "female"
```

```
summary(Ch7_cholesterol)
```

The *summary* function will produce basic descriptive statistics on all the variables in our dataframe. This is a great way to quickly check to see if the data have been read in correctly and to get a feel for your data, if you haven't already. The output from the summary statement for this dataframe looks like this. Because the variable "group" is nominal, our output includes only the frequencies of cases within the categories.

```
   group      cholesterol
 male   :12   Min.   :160.0
 female: 8    1st Qu.:180.0
              Median :200.0
              Mean   :203.0
              3rd Qu.:222.5
              Max.   :260.0
```

FIGURE 7.10 (continued)
Reading data into **R**.

7.5.2 Generating the Independent *t* and Welch *t*′ Tests

Working in **R**, we will first generate the independent *t* test assuming equal variances.

```
Ch7_indT <- t.test(cholesterol ~ group,
                   data=Ch7_cholesterol,
                   conf.level = .95,
                   var.equal=TRUE)
```

The *t.test* function will generate the independent *t* test with "cholesterol" as the dependent variable and "group" as the independent variable from the dataframe "Ch7_cholesterol." We are testing to an alpha of .05 (i.e., "conf.level = .95") and assuming the variances are equal (i.e., "var.equal = TRUE"). Based on the results of Levene's test (see data-screening section), we have met this assumption. We are creating an object from the results of this test, and we're naming that object "Ch7_indT."

```
Ch7_indT
```

This script will generate the output from the test we just conducted. We see our test statistic is 2.4842, with 18 degrees of freedom, and *p* value of .02. The 95% confidence interval of the mean difference is 4.63 to 55.37. The averages for both male ($M = 215$) and female ($F = 185$) are also presented, labeled "sample estimates."

```
        Two Sample t-test
data:  cholesterol by group
t = 2.4842,  df = 18, p-value = 0.02305
```

FIGURE 7.11
Generating the independent *t* and Welch *t*′ tests.

```
alternative hypothesis: true difference in means is not equal to 0

95 percent confidence interval:
  4.628956 55.371044

sample estimates:
  mean in group male    mean in group female
                 215                     185
```

Next, let's generate results of the Welch t' test.

```
Ch7_indT2 <- t.test(cholesterol ~ group,
                    data=Ch7_cholesterol,
                    conf.level = .95,
                    var.equal=FALSE)
```

The *t.test* function with "var.equal = FALSE" will generate the Welch t' test with "cholesterol" as the dependent variable, "group" as the independent variable, and an alpha of .05 (i.e., "conf.level = .95"). This test assumes the variances are *not* equal (i.e., "var.equal = FALSE"). For illustrative purposes, we will generate these results. However, we met the assumption of equal variances, and thus do not need the results from Welch t'.

```
Ch7_indT2
```

This script will generate output from the test we just conducted as follows using Welch t'. We see that our test statistic is 2.7197, with 18 degrees of freedom, and p value of .014. The 95% confidence interval of the mean difference is 6.824 to 53.176. The averages for both male (M = 215) and female (F = 185) are also presented.

```
Welch Two-Sample t Test

data: cholesterol by group
t = 2.7197, df = 17.984, p-value = 0.01406

alternative hypothesis: true difference in means is not equal to 0

95 percent confidence interval:
6.824267 53.175733

sample estimates:
  mean in group male mean in group female
                 215                  185
```

Finally, let's generate effect size indices.

```
install.packages("compute.es")
```

The *install.packages* function will install the *compute.es* package that will be used to generate various effect size values.

```
library(compute.es)
```

The *library* function will load the *compute.es* package.

FIGURE 7.11 (continued)
Generating the independent t and Welch t' tests.

```
compute.es::tes(2.484236, n.1 =12,
                n.2 =8,
                level=95)
```

We will compute the effect size using the value of the t test statistic, sample size of each group, and confidence level. In parentheses, we enter the test statistic value from the independent t test that we just generated (i.e., 2.48236), along with sample sizes of the groups using the *n.1* and *n.2* script (male $n = 12$; female $n = 8$), and the alpha level ("level = 95" for an alpha of .05). A lot of information is provided, but we are most interested in the effect size estimate and their confidence intervals (provided in brackets). We are provided a number of different effect size estimates, but we are primarily interested in Cohen's d (the first estimate, 1.13) and Hedge's g (the second estimate, 1.09). Both of these estimates also include the confidence intervals for the respective effect size.

```
Mean Differences ES:

 d [ 95 %CI] = 1.13 [ 0.1 , 2.16 ]
  var(d) = 0.24
  p-value(d) = 0.03
  U3(d) = 87.16 %
  CLES(d) = 78.87 %
  Cliff's Delta = 0.58

 g [ 95 %CI] = 1.09 [ 0.1 , 2.07 ]
  var(g) = 0.22
  p-value(g) = 0.03
  U3(g) = 86.13 %
  CLES(g) = 77.87 %

 Correlation ES:

 r [ 95 %CI] = 0.51 [ 0.05 , 0.79 ]
  var(r) = 0.03
  p-value(r) = 0.03

 z [ 95 %CI] = 0.56 [ 0.05 , 1.07 ]
  var(z) = 0.06
  p-value(z) = 0.03

 Odds Ratio ES:

 OR [ 95 %CI] = 7.82 [ 1.21 , 50.67 ]
  p-value(OR) = 0.03

 Log OR [ 95 %CI] = 2.06 [ 0.19 , 3.93 ]
  var(lOR) = 0.79
  p-value(Log OR) = 0.03

 Other:

 NNT = 2.41
 Total N = 20
```

FIGURE 7.11 (continued)
Generating the independent t and Welch t' tests.

7.6 Computing Inferences About Two Dependent Means Using R

Next we consider **R** for the dependent *t* test. As noted previously, the scripts are provided within the blocks with additional annotation to assist in understanding how the commands work.

7.6.1 Reading Data Into R

```
getwd()
```

R is always pointed to a directory on your computer. To find out which directory it is pointed to, run this "get working directory" function. We will assume that we need to change the working directory, and will use the next line of code to set the working directory to the desired path.

```
setwd("E:/Folder")
```

To set the working directory, use the *setwd* function and change what is in quotation marks here to your file location. Also, if you are copying the directory name, it will copy in slashes. You will need to change the slash (i.e., \) to a forward slash (i.e., /). Note that you need your destination name within quotation marks in the parentheses.

```
Ch7_swim <- read.csv("Ch7_swim.csv")
```

The *read.csv* function reads our data into **R**. What's to the left of the <- will be what the data will be called in **R**. In this example, we're calling the **R** dataframe "Ch7_swim." What's to the right of the <- tells **R** to find this particular .csv file. In this example, our file is called "Ch7_swim.csv." Make sure the extension (i.e., .csv) is included in your script. Also note that the name of your file should be in quotation marks within the parentheses.

```
names(Ch7_swim)
```

The *names* function will produce a list of variable names for each dataframe as follows. This is a good check to make sure your data have been read in correctly.

```
[1] "pretest" "posttest"
```

```
View(Ch7_swim)
```

The *View* function will let you view the dataset in spreadsheet format in RStudio.

```
summary(Ch7_swim)
```

The *summary* function will produce basic descriptive statistics on all the variables in our dataframe. This is a great way to quickly check to see if the data have been read in correctly and to get a feel for your data, if you haven't already. The output from the summary statement for this dataframe looks like this.

FIGURE 7.12
Reading data into **R** for the dependent *t* test.

```
   pretest         posttest
 Min.   :58.00   Min.   :54.00
 1st Qu.:61.25   1st Qu.:56.25
 Median :63.50   Median :59.50
 Mean   :64.00   Mean   :59.00
 3rd Qu.:65.75   3rd Qu.:61.75
 Max.   :72.00   Max.   :64.00
```

```
Ch7_swim$differ <- Ch7_swim$pretest-Ch7_swim$posttest
```

We can write a script to create a new variable computed as the difference between the pretest and posttest. In our script, what's to the left of <- tells **R** to create a new variable, "differ," and place it into our dataframe, "Ch7_swim." This variable, "differ," is computed as the pretest minus the posttest (i.e., "Ch7_swim$pretest—Ch7_swim$posttest"). In other words, what's the right of <- is the formula for computing the difference score.

```
View(Ch7_swim)
```

The *View* function will let us view the dataset in spreadsheet format in RStudio.

FIGURE 7.12 (continued)
Reading data into **R** for the dependent *t* test.

7.6.2 Generating the Dependent *t* Test

```
Ch7_depT <- t.test(Ch7_swim$pretest, Ch7_swim$posttest,
                paired=TRUE)
```

The *t.test* function with "paired=TRUE" will generate the dependent *t* test, pairing the pretest and posttest variables from the "Ch7_swim" dataframe. It will call the object "Ch7_depT."

```
Ch7_depT
```

This script will generate output from the test we just conducted. We see that our test statistic is 7.3193, with 9 degrees of freedom, and p value of < .001. The 95% confidence interval of the mean difference is 3.45 to 6.54. The mean of the differences is 5.

```
        Paired t-test

data:  Ch7_swim$pretest and Ch7_swim$posttest
t = 7.3193, df = 9, p-value = 4.472e-05
alternative hypothesis: true difference in means is not equal to 0
95 percent confidence interval:
 3.454652    6.545348
sample estimates:
mean of the differences
                      5
```

FIGURE 7.13
Generating the dependent *t* test.

7.7 Data Screening

We will begin data screening with examining the extent to which the assumptions of the independent t test were met. This will be following by data screening for the assumptions of the dependent t test.

7.7.1 Data Screening for the Independent *t* Test

The assumptions for the independent t test that we need to examine via data screening include the *normality* of the distribution of the dependent variable by categories of the independent variable and *homogeneity of variances*. Recall that the assumption of independence is required as well; however, as noted earlier, that is not an assumption with which data will be used to assess the extent to which the assumption is met.

7.7.1.1 Normality for the Independent t Test

Let's first examine the assumption of normality of the distribution of the dependent variable by categories of the independent variable. As alluded to earlier in the chapter, understanding the distributional shape, specifically the extent to which normality is a reasonable assumption, is important. *For the independent* t *test, the distributional shape for the dependent variable should be normally distributed for each category/group of the independent variable.* As with our one-sample t test, we can again use Explore to examine the extent to which the assumption of normality is met.

The general steps for accessing Explore have been presented in previous chapters (e.g., Chapter 4), and they will not be reiterated here. Normality of the dependent variable must be examined for each category of the independent variable, so we must tell SPSS to split the examination of normality by group. Click the dependent variable (e.g., cholesterol) and move it into the "Test Variable" box by clicking on the arrow button. Next, click the grouping variable (e.g., gender) and move it into the "Factor List" box by clicking on the arrow button. The procedures for selecting normality statistics were presented in Chapter 6, and they remain the same here: click "Plots" in the upper-right corner. Place a checkmark in the boxes for "Normality plots with tests" and also for "Histogram." Then click "Continue" to return to the main Explore dialog screen. From there, click "OK" to generate the output.

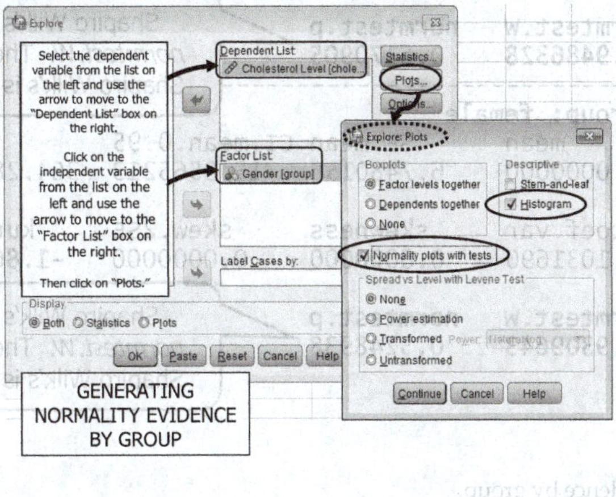

FIGURE 7.14
Generating normality evidence by group.

Working in **R**, we can generate similar normality evidence.

```
install.packages("pastecs")
```

The *install.packages* function will install the *pastecs* package which we will use to generate various forms of normality evidence.

```
library(pastecs)
```

The *library* function will load the *pastecs* package.

```
by(Ch7_cholesterol$cholesterol, Ch7_cholesterol$group,
  stat.desc,
  basic = FALSE,
  norm=TRUE)
```

The *by* function will generate descriptive statistics (i.e., "stat.desc") for our dependent variable, "cholesterol," split by our independent variable, "gender" (i.e., "by(Ch7_cholesterol$cholesterol, Ch7_cholesterol$group"). The command *basic=FALSE* will remove a lot of descriptive statistic estimates that we won't use for examining normality. We could have easily said *basic=TRUE* and generated what we needed plus a lot more. The command *norm=TRUE* will generate statistics related to normality.

Skew and kurtosis are both within the range of normal for both males and females. We see our output as follows, where we have skew and kurtosis along with its standard error. Skew and kurtosis divided by its standard error can be reviewed to a critical value of 1.96 (alpha = .05) to determine statistical significance (where values greater than about 2 indicate statistically significant nonnormality). ***Note:*** You may have noticed that the skewness and kurtosis value that we've just generated differs from what we found in SPSS. *This is because there are different ways to calculate skewness and kurtosis.* Let's use another package in **R** to calculate these statistics with different algorithms.

Shapiro-Wilk's test statistic is labeled "normtest.W" in the output. The *p* value for Shapiro-Wilk's is labeled "normtest.p." For both males and females, the results are not statistically significant.

```
Ch7_cholesterol$group: male
     median        mean     SE.mean CI.mean.0.95          var
215.0000000 215.0000000   8.7256154   19.2049499  913.6363636

    std.dev    coef.var    skewness     skew.2SE     kurtosis
 30.2264183   0.1405880   0.0000000    0.0000000   -1.6316706

   kurt.2SE  normtest.W  normtest.p
 -0.6620715   0.9486328   0.6170905
------------------------------------------------------------
Ch7_cholesterol$group: female
     median        mean     SE.mean CI.mean.0.95          var
185.0000000 185.0000000   6.7480156   15.9565213  364.2857143

    std.dev    coef.var    skewness     skew.2SE     kurtosis
 19.0862703   0.1031690   0.0000000    0.0000000   -1.8661332

   kurt.2SE  normtest.W  normtest.p
 -0.6300756   0.9309643   0.5248938
```

Shapiro Wilk's is labeled *normtest.W*. The *p* value for Shapiro Wilk's is *normtest.p.*

Shapiro Wilk's is labeled *normtest.W*. The *p* value for Shapiro Wilk's is *normtest.p.*

FIGURE 7.14 (continued)
Generating normality evidence by group.

```
install.packages("e1071")
```

The *install.packages* function will install the *e1071* package which we will use to generate skewness and kurtosis.

```
library(e1071)
```

The *library* function will load the *e1071* package.

```
Ch7_female <-Ch7_cholesterol[ which(Ch7_cholesterol$group=='female'), ]
Ch7_female
Ch7_male <- Ch7_cholesterol[ which(Ch7_cholesterol$group=='male'), ]
Ch7_male
```

With this script, we split our dataframe by "group" and create new dataframes consisting of observations of only females or males, respectively, "Ch7_female" and "Ch7_male."

```
skewness(Ch7_female$cholesterol, type=3)
skewness(Ch7_female$cholesterol, type=2)
skewness(Ch7_female$cholesterol, type=1)
```

The *skewness* function will generate skewness statistics on the variable(s) we specify. The *type=* script defines how skewness is calculated. Specifying *type=2* will use the algorithm that is used by SPSS. Readers interested in learning more, including the algorithms for each of the three methods, are encouraged to review Joanes and Gill (1998). We see that using *type=2*, our skew is the same value as generated using SPSS.

```
# skewness(Ch7_female$cholesterol, type=3)
[1] 0

# skewness(Ch7_female$cholesterol, type=2)
[1] 0

# skewness(Ch7_female$cholesterol, type=1)
[1] 0
```

```
kurtosis(Ch7_female$cholesterol, type=3)
kurtosis(Ch7_female$cholesterol, type=2)
kurtosis(Ch7_female$cholesterol, type=1)
```

The *kurtosis* function will generate kurtosis statistics on the variable(s) we specify. The *type=* script defines how kurtosis is calculated. Specifying *type=2* will use the algorithm that is used by SPSS. Readers interested in learning more, including the algorithms for each of the three methods, are encouraged to review Joanes and Gill (1998). We see that using *type=2*, our kurtosis is the same value as generated using SPSS.

```
# kurtosis(Ch7_female$cholesterol, type=3)
[1] -1.866133

# kurtosis(Ch7_female$cholesterol, type=2)
[1] -1.789965

# kurtosis(Ch7_female$cholesterol, type=1)
[1] -1.519031
```

FIGURE 7.14 (continued)
Generating normality evidence by group.

7.7.1.1.1 Interpreting Normality Evidence

We have already developed a good understanding of how to interpret some forms of evidence of normality, including skewness and kurtosis, histograms, and boxplots. As we examine the "Descriptives" table (see Figure 7.15), we see the output for the cholesterol statistics is separated for male (top portion) and female (bottom portion). The skewness statistic of cholesterol level for the males is .000 and kurtosis is −1.446—both within the range of an absolute value of 2.0, suggesting some evidence of normality of the dependent variable for males. Evidence of normality for the distributional shape of cholesterol level for females is also present: skewness = .000 and kurtosis is −1.790. For illustrative purposes, let's take the largest skew or kurtosis value and divide by the standard error. This would be kurtosis for females: −1.790/1.481 = −1.21. This is a standardized value that can be used

Descriptives

	Gender			Statistic	Std. Error
Cholesterol Level	Male	Mean		215.0000	8.72562
		95% Confidence Interval for Mean	Lower Bound	195.7951	
			Upper Bound	234.2049	
		5% Trimmed Mean		215.0000	
		Median		215.0000	
		Variance		913.636	
		Std. Deviation		30.22642	
		Minimum		170.00	
		Maximum		260.00	
		Range		90.00	
		Interquartile Range		57.50	
		Skewness		.000	.637
		Kurtosis		-1.446	1.232
	Female	Mean		185.0000	6.74802
		95% Confidence Interval for Mean	Lower Bound	169.0435	
			Upper Bound	200.9565	
		5% Trimmed Mean		185.0000	
		Median		185.0000	
		Variance		364.286	
		Std. Deviation		19.08627	
		Minimum		160.00	
		Maximum		210.00	
		Range		50.00	
		Interquartile Range		37.50	
		Skewness		.000	.752
		Kurtosis		-1.790	1.481

FIGURE 7.15
Normality evidence.

to determine if the kurtosis is statistically different from zero. Relative to a critical value of ± 1.96, −1.21 does not fall in the rejection region, thus kurtosis is not statistically significantly different from zero. Because all other skew and kurtosis values were less than −1.790, we know that all skew and kurtosis statistics provide evidence of normality.

The histogram of cholesterol level for males is not exactly what most researchers would consider a classic normally shaped distribution (see Figure 7.16). Although the histogram of cholesterol level for females is not presented here, it follows a similar distributional shape.

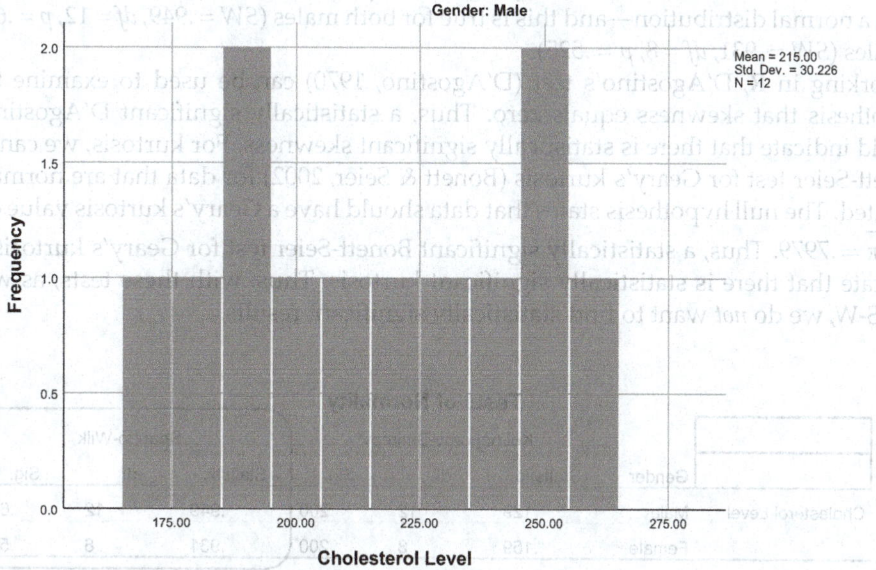

Working in **R**, we can compute histograms for each group.

```
Ch7_female <-Ch7_cholesterol[ which(Ch7_cholesterol$group=='female'), ]
Ch7_female

Ch7_male <- Ch7_cholesterol[ which(Ch7_cholesterol$group=='male'), ]
Ch7_male
```

First, we split our data by the grouping variable, "group," and create two new dataframes to work with, "Ch7_female" and "Ch7_male."

```
hist(Ch7_female$cholesterol)
hist(Ch7_male$cholesterol)
```

The *hist* function will compute a histogram for the variable "cholesterol" from each of the new dataframes.

FIGURE 7.16
Histogram of cholesterol level for males.

A few other statistics can be used to gauge normality as well, providing evidence of the extent to which our sample distribution is statistically different from a normal distribution. As we learned previously, the Kolmogorov-Smirnov (K-S) (Chakravart, Laha, & Roy, 1967) with Lilliefor's significance (Lilliefors, 1967) and the Shapiro-Wilk (S-W) (Shapiro & Wilk,

1965) are tests that provide evidence of the extent to which our sample distribution is statistically different from a normal distribution. The K-S test tends to be conservative and lacks power for detecting nonnormality, so it is not recommended (D'Agostino, Belanger, & D'Agostino, 1990). The S-W test is considered the more powerful of the two for testing normality and is recommended for use with small sample sizes ($n < 50$) (D'Agostino et al., 1990). Nonstatistically significant K-S and S-W results are interpreted to say that our distribution is *not* statistically significantly different than a normal distribution. The output for the Shapiro-Wilk test is presented in Figure 7.17 and suggests that our sample distribution for cholesterol level is not statistically significantly different than what would be expected from a normal distribution—and this is true for both males ($SW = .949$, $df = 12$, $p = .617$) and females ($SW = .931$, $df = 8$, $p = .525$).

Working in **R**, D'Agostino's test (D'Agostino, 1970) can be used to examine the null hypothesis that skewness equals zero. Thus, a statistically significant D'Agostino's test would indicate that there is statistically significant skewness. For kurtosis, we can use the Bonett-Seier test for Geary's kurtosis (Bonett & Seier, 2002) for data that are normally distributed. The null hypothesis states that data should have a Geary's kurtosis value equal to $\sqrt{2/\pi} = .7979$. Thus, a statistically significant Bonett-Seier test for Geary's kurtosis would indicate that there is statistically significant kurtosis. Thus, with these tests, as with K-S and S-W, we do *not* want to find statistically significant results.

Tests of Normality

		Kolmogorov-Smirnov[a]			Shapiro-Wilk		
	Gender	Statistic	df	Sig.	Statistic	df	Sig.
Cholesterol Level	Male	.129	12	.200*	.949	12	.617
	Female	.159	8	.200*	.931	8	.525

*. This is a lower bound of the true significance.

a. Lilliefors Significance Correction

Working in **R**, we saw in Figure 7.14 how we could generate the Shapiro-Wilk test using the *stat.desc* function in the *pastecs* package. Another way to test for normality is D'Agostino's test for skewness and the Bonett-Seier test for Geary's kurtosis.

```
install.packages("moments")
library(moments)
```

To conduct D'Agostino's test, we first have to install the *moments* package and then load it into our library. The null hypothesis for this test is that skewness equals zero. Thus, a statistically significant Agostino's test would indicate that there is statistically significant skewness.

```
agostino.test(Ch7_male$cholesterol)
agostino.test(Ch7_female$cholesterol)
```

The function *agostino.test* is generated using the variable "cholesterol" from our split files, "Ch7_male" and "Ch7_female." The results suggest evidence of normality as $p = 1.00$, greater than alpha.

FIGURE 7.17
Shapiro-Wilk test of normality results.

```
# agostino.test(Ch7_male$cholesterol)

        D'Agostino skewness test

data: Ch7_male$cholesterol
skew = 0, z = 0, p-value = 1
alternative hypothesis: data have a skewness

# agostino.test(Ch7_female$cholesterol)

        D'Agostino skewness test

data: Ch7_female$cholesterol
skew = 0, z = 0, p-value = 1
alternative hypothesis: data have a skewness
```

```
bonett.test((Ch7_male$cholesterol))
bonett.test((Ch7_female$cholesterol))
```

The *bonett.test* function, using the "cholesterol" variable from our split files, "Ch7_male" and "Ch7_female," performs the Bonett-Seier test for Geary's kurtosis for data that are normally distributed. The null hypothesis states that data should have a Geary's kurtosis value equal to $\sqrt{2/\pi} = .7979$. The results suggest evidence of normality for the distribution of males and females as $p = .115$ and $p = .1181$, respectively, both greater than alpha.

```
# bonett.test((Ch7_male$cholesterol))

        Bonett-Seier test for Geary kurtosis

data: (Ch7_male$cholesterol)
tau = 25.8333, z = -1.5759, p-value = 0.115
alternative hypothesis: kurtosis is not equal to sqrt(2/pi)

# bonett.test((Ch7_female$cholesterol))

        Bonett-Seier test for Geary kurtosis
data: (Ch7_female$cholesterol)
tau = 16.2500, z = -1.5626, p-value = 0.1181
alternative hypothesis: kurtosis is not equal to sqrt(2/pi)
```

FIGURE 7.17 (continued)
Shapiro-Wilk test of normality results.

Quantile-quantile (Q-Q) plots are also often examined to determine evidence of normality. Q-Q plots are graphs that plot quantiles of the theoretical normal distribution against quantiles of the sample distribution. Points that fall on or close to the diagonal line suggest evidence of normality. Similar to what we saw with the histogram, the Q-Q plot of cholesterol level for both males and females (although the latter is not shown here) suggests some nonnormality. Keep in mind that we have a relatively small sample size. Thus interpreting the visual graphs (e.g., histograms and Q-Q plots) can be challenging, although we have plenty of other evidence for normality.

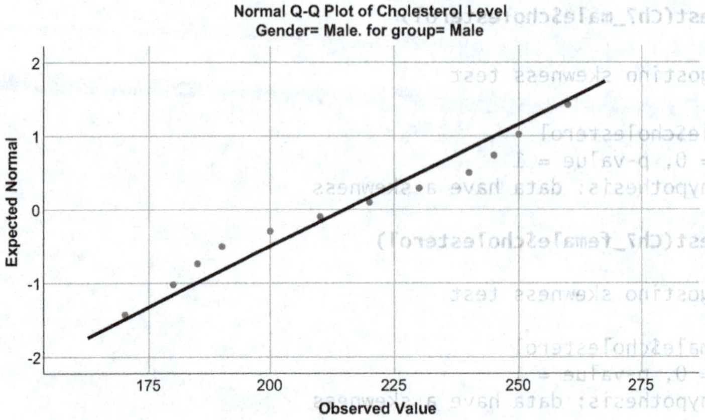

Working in **R**, we can use the *ggplot2* package to produce the Q-Q plot.

```
install.packages("ggplot2")
```

The *install.packages* function will install the *ggplot2* package that we can use to create various graphs and plots.

```
library(ggplot2)
```

The *library* function will load the *ggplot2* package.

```
qplot(sample=cholesterol, data = Ch7_female)
qplot(sample=cholesterol, data = Ch7_male)
```

The *qplot* function will generate a Q-Q plot using the variable "cholesterol" from the dataframes specified in "data =" which correspond to data from females and males, respectively.

FIGURE 7.18
Q-Q plot of cholesterol level for males.

Examination of the boxplots suggests a relatively normal distributional shape of cholesterol level for both males and females and no outliers for either group.

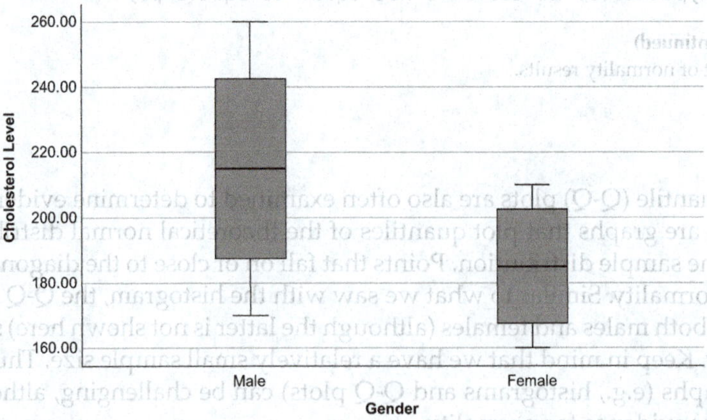

FIGURE 7.19
Boxplot of cholesterol level by gender.

Working in **R**, we can generate a boxplot by groups using the following script.

```
boxplot(Ch7_cholesterol$cholesterol~Ch7_cholesterol$group)
```

The *boxplot* function can be used to generate a boxplot. In parentheses, we tell **R** which variable in our dataframe to use to compute the boxplot (i.e., "Ch7_cholesterol$cholesterol") and to split the boxplot by our grouping variable, "Ch7_cholesterol$group."

FIGURE 7.19 (continued)
Boxplot of cholesterol level by gender.

Considering the forms of evidence we have examined, skewness and kurtosis statistics, the Shapiro-Wilk test, and the boxplots, all suggest normality is a reasonable assumption. Although the histograms and Q-Q plots suggest some nonnormality, this is somewhat expected given the small sample size. Generally, we can be reasonably assured we have met the assumption of normality of the dependent variable for each group of the independent variable. Additionally, recall that when the assumption of normality is violated with the independent *t* test, the effects on Type I and Type II errors are minimal when using a two-tailed test, as we are conducting here (e.g., Glass et al., 1972; Sawilowsky & Blair, 1992).

7.7.1.2 Homogeneity of Variance for the Independent t Test

Testing for the assumption for equal variances is provided by default with the independent *t* test. More specifically, it is provided as "Levene's Test for Equality of Variances" in the output. See Table 7.3.

```
install.packages(car)
```

We use the *install.packages* function to install the *car* package, which we will use to generate Levene's test.

```
library(car)
```

The *library* function will load the *car* package into our library.

```
leveneTest(Ch7_cholesterol$cholesterol,
           Ch7_cholesterol$group)
```

The *leveneTest* function is used to generate Levene's test by variable "group" on the variable "cholesterol."

```
Levene's Test for Homogeneity of Variance (center = mean)
      Df F value  Pr(>F)
group  1  3.2007 0.09045 .
      18
---
Signif. codes:  0 '***' 0.001 '**' 0.01 '*' 0.05 '.' 0.1 ' ' 1
```

We read this output as $F(1,18) = 3.20$, $p = .09$, indicating that we have met the assumption of equal variances. Thus, we can generate the independent *t* test assuming the variances of the groups are equal.

FIGURE 7.20
Generating Levene's test for equal variances in **R**.

7.7.2 Data Screening for the Dependent *t* Test

The assumptions for the dependent *t* test that we need to examine include normality of the distribution of the difference scores and homogeneity of variances. Recall that the assumption of independence is required as well; however, as noted earlier, that is not an assumption with which data will be used to assess the extent to which the assumption is met.

7.7.2.1 Normality for the Dependent t Test

Let's start with using the Explore option to examine normality of the distribution of the difference scores. As with the other *t* tests we have studied, understanding the distributional shape and the extent to which normality is a reasonable assumption is important. For the dependent *t* test, the distributional shape for the *difference scores* should be normally distributed. Thus, we first need to create a new variable in our dataset to reflect the difference scores (in this case, the difference between the pre- and posttest values). To do this, go to "Transform" in the top pulldown menu, then select "Compute Variable." Following the screenshot of Step 1 in Figure 7.21 produces the "Compute Variable" dialog box.

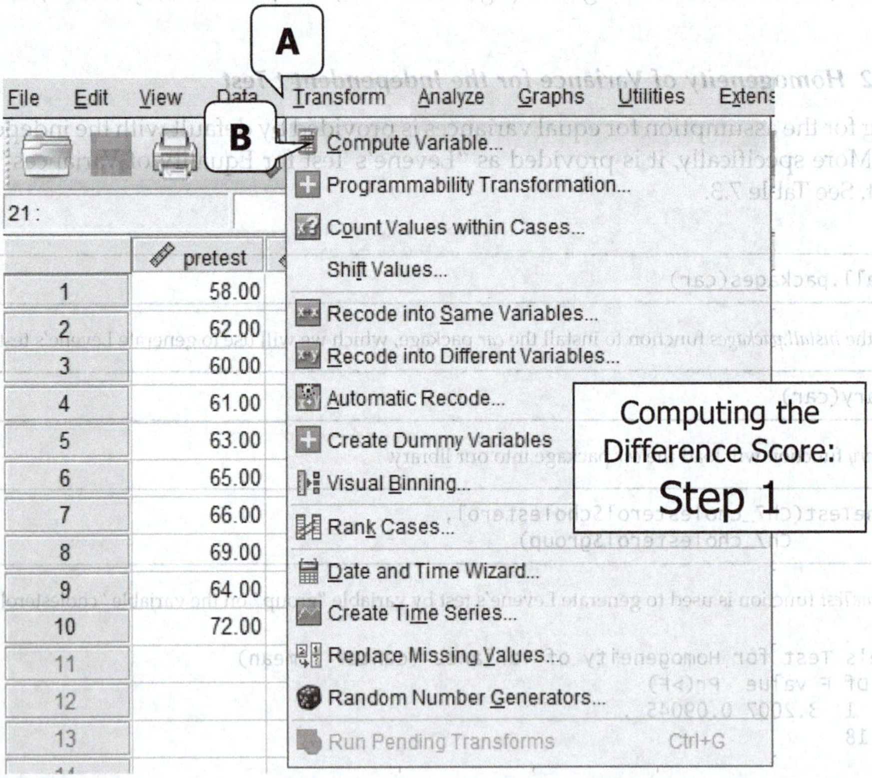

FIGURE 7.21
Computing the difference score: Step 1.

From the "Compute Variable" dialog screen, we can define the column header for our variable by typing in a name in the "Target Variable" box (no spaces, no special characters, and cannot begin with a numeric value). The formula for computing our difference score is inserted in the "Numeric Expression" box. To create this formula: (1) click "pretest" in the left list of variables and use the arrow key to move it into the "Numeric Expression" box; (2) use your keyboard or the mathematical operators within the dialog box to insert a minus sign (i.e., dash) after "pretest" in the "Numeric Expression" box; (3) click "posttest" in the left list of variables and use the arrow key to move it into the "Numeric Expression" box; and (4) click "OK" to create the new difference score variable in your dataset.

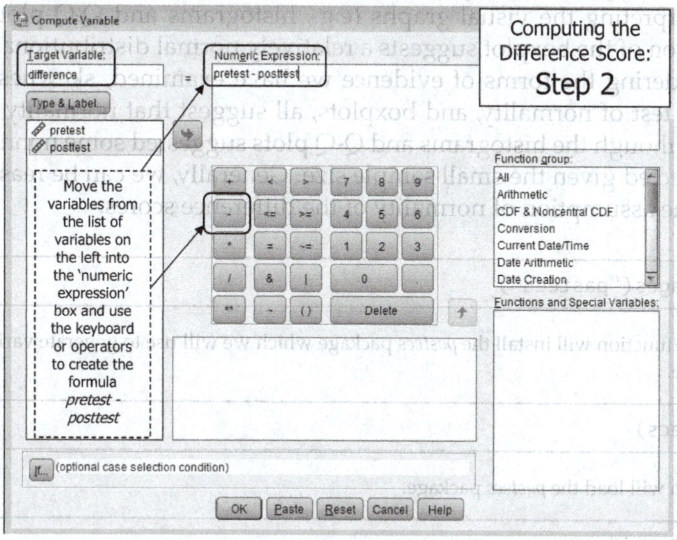

Working in **R**, we can create a new variable in our dataset that reflects the difference score.

```
Ch7_swim$differ <- Ch7_swim$pretest-Ch7_swim$posttest
```

This script will create a new variable named "differ" in the "Ch7_swim" dataframe. This variable, "differ," is computed as the pretest minus the posttest (i.e., "Ch7_swim$pretest—Ch7_swim$posttest").

```
View(Ch7_swim)
```

The *View* function will let us view the dataframe and see the new variable that was created.

FIGURE 7.22
Computing the difference score: Step 2.

We can again use Explore to examine the extent to which the assumption of normality is met for the distributional shape of our newly created difference score. The general steps for accessing Explore (see, for example, Chapter 4) and for generating normality evidence for one variable (see Chapter 6) have been presented in previous chapters, and they will not be reiterated here.

7.7.2.1.1 Interpreting Normality Evidence for the Dependent *t* Test

We have already developed a good understanding of how to interpret some forms of evidence of normality, including skewness and kurtosis, histograms, and boxplots. The skewness statistic for the difference score is .248 and kurtosis is .050—both within the range of an absolute value of 2.0, suggesting one form of evidence of normality of the differences.

The histogram for the difference scores (not presented here) is not necessarily what most researchers would consider a normally shaped distribution. Our formal test of normality, the Shapiro-Wilk (SW) test (Shapiro & Wilk, 1965) suggests that our sample distribution for differences is not statistically significantly different than what would be expected from a normal distribution ($W = .956$, $df = 10$, $p = .734$). Similar to what we saw with the histogram, the Q-Q plot of differences suggests some nonnormality in the tails (as the farthest points are not falling on the diagonal line). Keep in mind that we have a small sample size. Thus interpreting the visual graphs (e.g., histograms and Q-Q plots) can be difficult. Examination of the boxplot suggests a relatively normal distributional shape with no outliers. Considering the forms of evidence we have examined, skewness and kurtosis, Shapiro-Wilk's test of normality, and boxplots, all suggest that normality is a reasonable assumption. Although the histograms and Q-Q plots suggested some nonnormality, this is somewhat expected given the small sample size. Generally, we can be reasonably assured we have met the assumption of normality of the difference scores.

```
install.packages("pastecs")
```

The *install.packages* function will install the *pastecs* package which we will use to generate various forms of normality evidence.

```
library(pastecs)
```

The *library* function will load the *pastecs* package.

```
stat.desc(Ch7_swim,
norm = TRUE)
```

The *stat.desc* function will generate normality indices on all variables in the dataframe as follows. We see skew (.18) and kurtosis (–.99), along with $SW = .96$, $p = .73$ for the difference score. All indicate the assumption of normality has been met. We review the ratio of the variances of the pretest (17.78) and posttest (13.11) to determine that we have met the assumption of equal variances.

```
                 pretest      posttest      differ
nbr.val      10.00000000   10.00000000 10.0000000
nbr.null      0.00000000    0.00000000  0.0000000
nbr.na        0.00000000    0.00000000  0.0000000
min          58.00000000   54.00000000  2.0000000
max          72.00000000   64.00000000  9.0000000
range        14.00000000   10.00000000  7.0000000
sum         640.00000000  590.00000000 50.0000000
median       63.50000000   59.50000000  5.0000000
mean         64.00000000   59.00000000  5.0000000
SE.mean       1.33333333    1.14503760  0.6831301
CI.mean.0.95  3.01620955    2.59025501  1.5453475
var          17.77777778   13.11111111  4.6666667
std.dev       4.21637021    3.62092683  2.1602469
coef.var      0.06588078    0.06137164  0.4320494
skewness      0.44024834   -0.12638397  0.1785510
skew.2SE      0.32039363   -0.09197677  0.1299417
kurtosis     -0.97879688   -1.64689744 -0.9887755
kurt.2SE     -0.36679699   -0.61716281 -0.3705364
normtest.W    0.97233926    0.93703314  0.9555691
normtest.p    0.91164605    0.52049701  0.7344122
```

Shapiro Wilk's is labeled *normtest.W*. The *p* value for Shapiro Wilk's is *normtest.p*.

FIGURE 7.23
Generating and interpreting normality evidence for the dependent *t* test in R.

Note: You may have noticed that the skewness and kurtosis value that we've just generated differs from what we found in SPSS. *This is because there are different ways to calculate skewness and kurtosis.* Let's use another package in **R** to calculate these statistics with different algorithms.

```
install.packages("e1071")
```

The *install.packages* function will install the *e1071* package that we will use to generate skewness and kurtosis.

```
library(e1071)
```

The *library* function will load the *e1071* package.

```
skewness(Ch7_swim$differ, type=3)
skewness(Ch7_swim$differ, type=2)
skewness(Ch7_swim$differ, type=1)
```

The *skewness* function will generate skewness statistics on the variable(s) we specify. The *type=* defines how skewness is calculated. Specifying *type=2* will use the algorithm that is used by SPSS. Readers interested in learning more, including the algorithms for each of the three methods, are encouraged to review Joanes and Gill (1998). We see that using *type=2*, our skew is the same value as generated using SPSS.

```
# skewness(Ch6_skate$time, type=3)
[1] 0.2456618

# skewness(Ch6_skate$time, type=2)
[1] 0.2994734

# skewness(Ch6_skate$time, type=1)
[1] 0.2706329
```

```
kurtosis(Ch7_swim$differ, type=3)
kurtosis(Ch7_swim$differ, type=2)
kurtosis(Ch7_swim$differ, type=1)
```

The *kurtosis* function will generate kurtosis statistics on the variable(s) we specify. The *type=* defines how kurtosis is calculated. Specifying *type=2* will use the algorithm that is used by SPSS. Readers interested in learning more, including the algorithms for each of the three methods, are encouraged to review Joanes and Gill (1998). We see that using *type=2*, our kurtosis is the same value as generated using SPSS.

```
# kurtosis(Ch6_skate$time, type=3)
[1] -0.9766846

# kurtosis(Ch6_skate$time, type=2)
[1] -0.4833448

# kurtosis(Ch6_skate$time, type=1)
[1] -0.6979167
```

We saw in Figure 7.17 how we could generate additional tests for normality, including D'Agostino's test for skewness and the Bonett-Seier test for Geary's kurtosis.

```
install.packages("moments")
library(moments)
```

FIGURE 7.23 (continued)
Generating and interpreting normality evidence for the dependent *t* test in **R**.

To conduct D'Agostino's test, we first have to install the *moments* package and then load it into our library. (Remember that a package needs to be installed only once but loaded when you start a new session in **R**.) The null hypothesis for this test is that skewness equals zero. Thus, a statistically significant Agostino's test would indicate that there is statistically significant skewness.

```
agostino.test(Ch7_swim$differ)
```

The function *agostino.test* is generated using the variable *differ* from our dataframe, "Ch7_swim." The results suggest evidence of normality of the difference score as $p = .7087$, greater than alpha.

```
# agostino.test(Ch7_swim$differ)

        D'Agostino skewness test

data: Ch7_swim$differ
skew = 0.2091, z = 0.3737, p-value = 0.7087
alternative hypothesis: data have a skewness
```

```
bonett.test((Ch7_swim$differ))
```

The *bonett.test* function, using the "differ" variable from our dataframe, "Ch7_swim," performs the Bonett-Seier test for Geary's kurtosis for data that are normally distributed. The null hypothesis states that data should have a Geary's kurtosis value equal to $\sqrt{2/\pi} = .7979$. The results suggest evidence of normality for the distribution of the difference score as $p = .7767$, greater than alpha.

```
# bonett.test((Ch7_swim$differ))

        Bonett-Seier test for Geary kurtosis

data: (Ch7_swim$differ)
tau = 1.6000, z = 0.2836, p-value = 0.7767
alternative hypothesis: kurtosis is not equal to sqrt(2/pi)
```

FIGURE 7.23 (continued)
Generating and interpreting normality evidence for the dependent *t* test in **R**.

7.7.2.2 Homogeneity of Variance for the Dependent t Test

We also need to examine evidence for meeting equal variances, or more specifically homogeneity of variance of the difference scores. Without conducting a formal test of equality of variances (as we do in Chapter 9), a rough benchmark for having met the assumption of homogeneity of variances when conducting the dependent *t* test is that the *ratio of the smallest to largest variance of the paired samples is no greater than 1:4 to decrease the chance of a Type I error. Recent research suggests that a variance ratio lower than 1.5 should be used as convention in the presence of heterogeneity with unequal sample sizes* (Blanca, Alarcón, Arnau, Bono, & Bendayan, 2018). The variance can be computed easily by any number of procedures in SPSS (refer back to Chapter 3, for example), and these steps will not be repeated here. For our paired samples, the variance of the pretest score is 17.778 and the variance of the posttest score is 13.111—well within the range of 1:4 suggesting that homogeneity of variances is reasonable.

7.8 G*Power

Using the results of the independent samples t test just conducted, let's use G*Power to compute the post hoc power of our test.

7.8.1 Post Hoc Power for the Independent *t* Test Using G*Power

The first thing that must be done when using G*Power for computing post hoc power is to select the correct test family. In our case, we conducted an independent samples t test, therefore the default selection of "t tests" is the correct test family. Next, we need to select the appropriate statistical test. We use the arrow to toggle to "Means: Difference between two independent means (two groups)." The "Type of power analysis" then needs to be selected. To compute post hoc power, we need to select "Post hoc: Compute achieved power—given α, sample size, and effect size."

The "Input Parameters" must then be specified. The first parameter is the selection of whether the test is one tailed (i.e., directional) or two tailed (i.e., nondirectional). In this example, we have a two-tailed test, so we use the arrow to toggle to "Two." We can input our observed effect size, d, or we can also use the pop-out calculator to compute the effect size d. Using the pop-out calculator, our effect size is 1.18 (note that the pop-out calculator does not use the pooled standard deviation as the standardizer). The alpha level we tested at was .05, and the sample size for females was 8 and for males, 12. Once the parameters are specified, simply click "Calculate" to generate the achieved power statistics.

The "Output Parameters" provide the relevant statistics given the input just specified. In this example, we were interested in determining post hoc power given a two-tailed test, with an observed effect size of 1.18, an alpha level of .05, and sample sizes of 8 (females) and 12 (males). Based on those criteria, the post hoc power was .69. In other words, with a sample size of 8 female and 12 males in our study, testing at an alpha level of .05 and observing a large effect of 1.18, then the power of our test was .69—the probability of rejecting the null hypothesis when it is really false will be 69%, which is only moderate power (minimally acceptable power is generally about 80%). Keep in mind that conducting power analysis *a priori* is recommended so that you avoid a situation where, post hoc, you find that the sample size was not sufficient to reach the desired power (given the observed effect size and alpha level). We were fortunate in this example in that we were still able to detect a statistically significant difference in cholesterol levels between males and females; however, we will likely not always be that lucky!

How does power change if a different effect size value is input? We know that power is a function of many elements, one of which is effect size. More specifically, holding all else constant in the power calculation, larger effect sizes will produce greater power. Let's look at this in the context of the example illustrated in this chapter. Recall that the achieved or observed effect size calculated using the *pooled standard deviation* (as computed via Hedges and Olkin (1985) using n_1-1 and n_2-1 to compute s_p) as the standardizer was −1.1339. In computing post hoc power, had we used the pooled standard deviation via Hedges and Olkin as the standardizer in our effect size input (i.e., an observed effect size of −1.1339), our post hoc power would be .65, slightly less than what we obtained when we used Cohen's pooled standard deviation formula (i.e., using n_1 and n_2 to compute s_p). The observed Hedge's g with bias correction for small samples was −1.0860. Had we used the

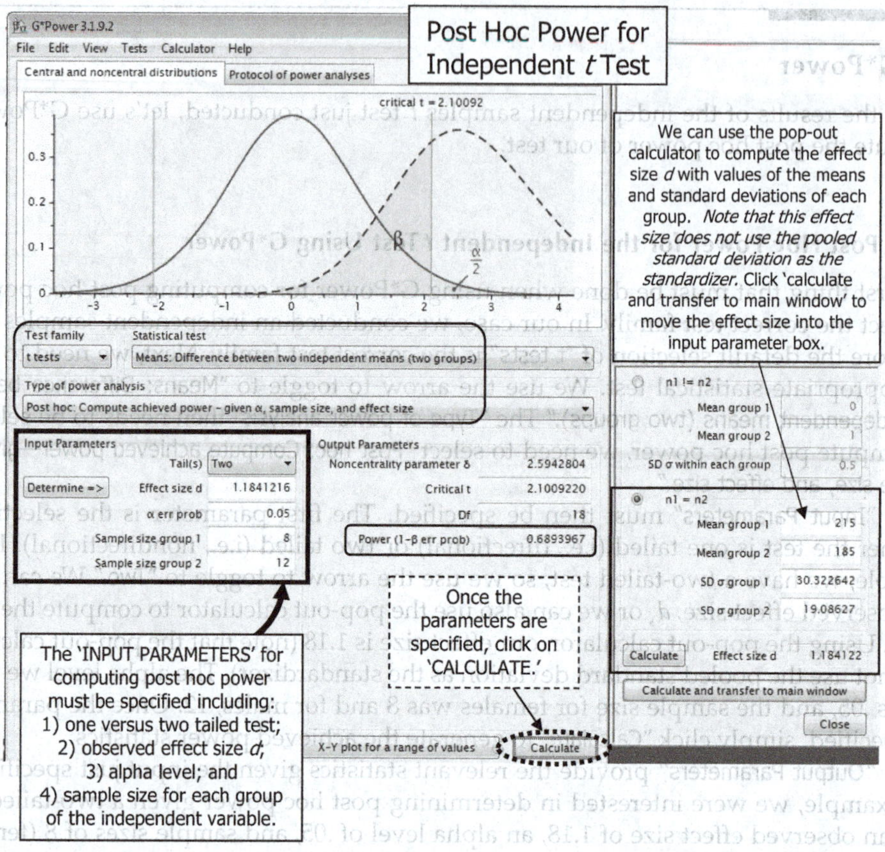

FIGURE 7.24
Independent *t* test: *Post hoc* power.

bias corrected effect size *g*, our post hoc power would be only about .61. Thus, we see that larger effects produce greater power!

7.8.2 Post Hoc Power for the Dependent *t* Test Using G*Power

Now, let us use G*Power to compute post hoc power for the dependent *t* test. First, the correct test family needs to be selected. In our case, we conducted an dependent samples *t* test, therefore the default selection of "t tests" is the correct test family. Next, we need to select the appropriate statistical test. We use the arrow to toggle to "Means: Difference between two dependent means (matched pairs)." The "Type of power analysis" desired then needs to be selected. To compute post hoc power, we need to select "Post hoc: Compute achieved power—given α, sample size, and effect size."

The "Input Parameters" must then be specified. The first parameter is the selection of whether your test is one tailed (i.e., directional) or two tailed (i.e., nondirectional). In this example, we have a two-tailed test, so we use the arrow to toggle to "Two." The achieved or observed effect size was 2.3146. The alpha level we tested at was .05, and the total sample size was 10. Once the parameters are specified, simply click "Calculate" to generate the achieved power statistics.

The "Output Parameters" provide the relevant statistics given the input specified. In this example, we were interested in determining post hoc power given a two-tailed test, with an observed effect size of 2.3146, an alpha level of .05, and total sample size of 10. Based on those criteria, the post hoc power was .99. In other words, with a total sample size of 10, testing at an alpha level of .05 and observing a large effect of 2.3146, then the power of our test was greater than .99—the probability of rejecting the null hypothesis when it is really false will be greater than 99%, about the strongest power that can be achieved. Again, conducting power analysis *a priori* is recommended so that you avoid a situation where, post hoc, you find that the sample size was not sufficient to reach the desired power (given the observed effect size and alpha level).

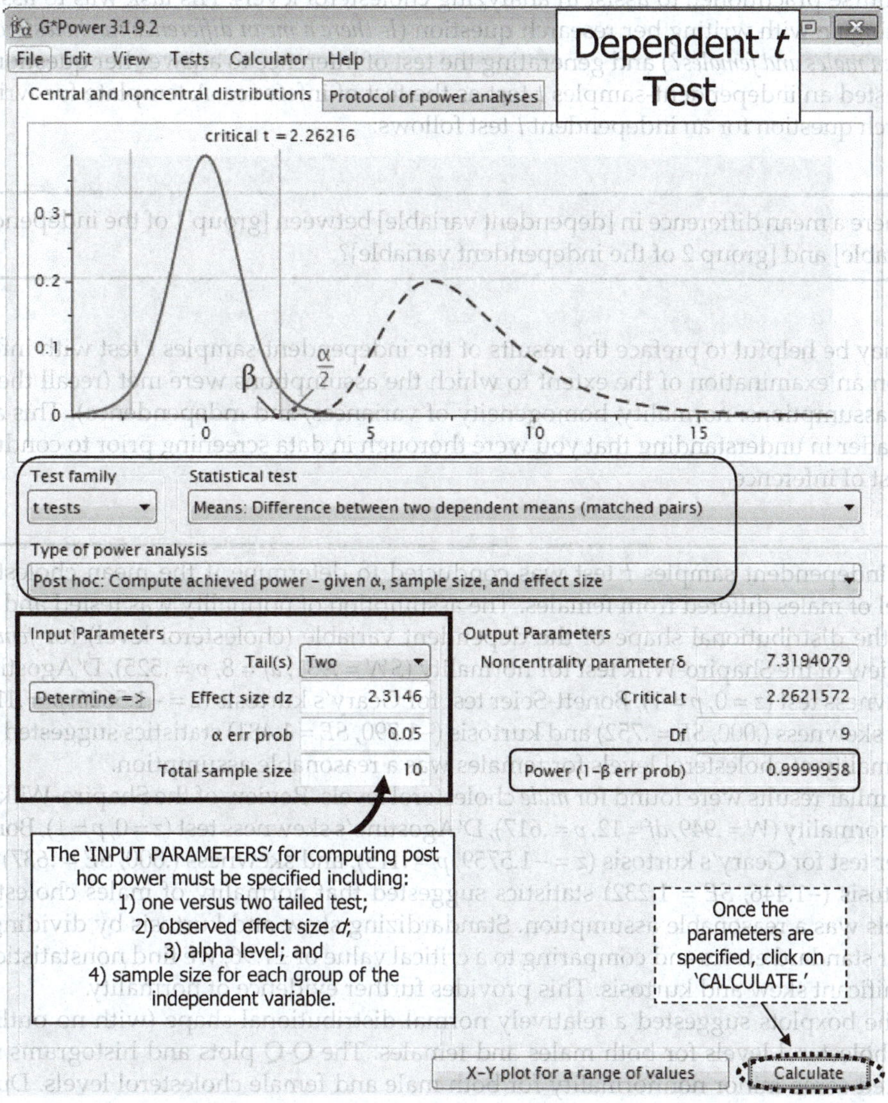

FIGURE 7.25
Dependent *t* test: *Post hoc* power.

7.9 Research Question Template and Example Write-Up

Next we develop APA-style paragraphs describing the results for both examples. First is a paragraph describing the results of the independent t test for the cholesterol example, followed by dependent t test for the swimming example.

7.9.1 Research Question Template and Example Write-Up for the Independent *t* Test

Recall that our graduate research assistant, Oso, was working with Dr. Nightingale, a local nurse practitioner, to assist in analyzing cholesterol levels. His task was to assist Dr. Nightingale with writing her research question (*Is there a mean difference in cholesterol level between males and females?*) and generating the test of inference to answer her question. Oso suggested an independent-samples t test as the test of inference. A template for writing a research question for an independent t test follows:

Is there a mean difference in [dependent variable] between [group 1 of the independent variable] and [group 2 of the independent variable]?

It may be helpful to preface the results of the independent-samples t test with information on an examination of the extent to which the assumptions were met (recall there are three assumptions: normality, homogeneity of variances, and independence). This assists the reader in understanding that you were thorough in data screening prior to conducting the test of inference.

An independent samples t test was conducted to determine if the mean cholesterol level of males differed from females. The assumption of normality was tested and met for the distributional shape of the dependent variable (cholesterol level) for *females*. Review of the Shapiro-Wilk test for normality ($SW = .931$, $df = 8$, $p = .525$), D'Agostino's skewness test ($z = 0$, $p = 1$), Bonett-Seier test for Geary's kurtosis ($z = -1.5626$, $p = .1181$), and skewness (.000, $SE = .752$) and kurtosis (−1.790, $SE = 1.481$) statistics suggested that normality of cholesterol levels for females was a reasonable assumption.

Similar results were found for *male* cholesterol levels. Review of the Shapiro-Wilk test for normality ($W = .949$, $df = 12$, $p = .617$), D'Agostino's skewness test ($z = 0$, $p = 1$), Bonett-Seier test for Geary's kurtosis ($z = -1.5759$, $p = .115$), and skewness (.000, $SE = .637$) and kurtosis (−1.446, $SE = 1.232$) statistics suggested that normality of males cholesterol levels was a reasonable assumption. Standardizing skew and kurtosis by dividing by their standard errors and comparing to a critical value of ±1.96, we find nonstatistically significant skew and kurtosis. This provides further evidence of normality.

The boxplots suggested a relatively normal distributional shape (with no outliers) of cholesterol levels for both males and females. The Q-Q plots and histograms suggested some minor nonnormality for both male and female cholesterol levels. Due to the small sample, this was anticipated. Although normality indices generally suggest the assumption is met, even if there are slight departures from normality, the effects on Type I and Type II errors will be minimal given the use of a two-tailed test (Glass et al., 1972; Sawilowsky & Blair, 1992). According to Levene's test, the homogeneity of variance assumption was satisfied ($F = 3.2007$, $p = .090$). Because there was not random assignment of the individuals to gender, the assumption of independence was not met creating a potential for an increased probability of a Type I or Type II error.

It is also desirable to include a measure of effect size. Recall our formula for computing the effect size, *d*, presented earlier in the chapter. Plugging in the values for our cholesterol example, we find an effect size *d* of −1.1339 and Hedge's *g* of −1.0860, both of which are interpreted according to Cohen's (1988) guidelines as a large effect. Given the small sample size, we will report Hedge's *g*, as calculated here, along with the respective confidence intervals that were found earlier using the online calculator. (Remember that the sign for the effect size is simply an artifact of which group is entered into the numerator equation first; had the cholesterol level for males been entered as $\bar{Y}_1$, the effect size would be positive. The sign of the effect doesn't change the interpretation; it only reflects which group happens to be larger or smaller.)

$$g = \left(\frac{\bar{Y}_1 - \bar{Y}_2}{s_p}\right)\left(1 - \frac{3}{(4)(df) - 1}\right) = \left(\frac{185 - 215}{26.4575}\right)\left(1 - \frac{3}{(4)(18) - 1}\right) = (-1.1339)(.9577)$$

$$g = -1.0860$$

Keep in mind that for the two-sample mean test, standardized mean difference effects indicates how many standard deviations the mean of sample 1 is from the mean of sample 2. Thus, with an effect size *g* of −1.0860, there is more than one standard deviation unit between the mean cholesterol levels of males as compared to females. The negative sign simply indicates that group 1 (i.e., females) has the smaller mean (as it is the first value in the numerator of the formula; in our case, the mean cholesterol level of females). We will report the effect size in absolute value terms to align with the computation of the t statistic (i.e., numerator being males minus females).

Here is an APA-style example paragraph of results for the cholesterol level data (remember that this will be prefaced by the paragraph reporting the extent to which the assumptions of the test were met).

Cholesterol data were gathered from samples of 12 males and 8 females, with a female sample mean of 185 ($SD = 19.09$) and a male sample mean of 215 ($SD = 30.22$). The independent *t* test indicated that the cholesterol means were statistically significantly different for males and females ($t = 2.48$, $df = 18$, $p = .02$). Thus, the null hypothesis that the cholesterol means were the same by gender was rejected at the .05 level of significance. The effect size *g* (Hedge's sample size adjusted effect size) was 1.09 (CI .15, 2.09) and *d* was 1.13 (CI .17, 2.10). Using Cohen's (1988) guidelines, this is interpreted as a large effect. The results provide evidence to support the conclusion that males and females differ in cholesterol levels, on average. More specifically, males were observed to have higher cholesterol levels, on average, than females.

Parenthetically, notice that the results of the Welch *t*′ test were the same as for the independent *t* test (Welch $t' = 2.720$, rounded $df = 18$, $p = .014$). Thus any deviation from homogeneity of variance did not affect the results.

7.9.2 Research Question Template and Example Write-Up for the Dependent *t* Test

Addie, as you recall, was also working with Coach Bryant, a local swimming coach, to assist in analyzing freestyle swimming time before and after swimmers participated in an intensive training program. Addie suggested a research question (*Is there a mean difference in swim time for the 50-meter freestyle event before participation in an intensive training program as compared to swim time for the 50-meter freestyle event after participation in an intensive training program?*) and assisted in generating the test of inference (specifically the dependent *t* test) to answer her question. A template for writing a research question for a dependent *t* test follows:

Is there a mean difference in [paired sample 1] as compared to [paired sample 2]?

It may be helpful to preface the results of the dependent samples *t* test with information on the extent to which the assumptions were met (recall there are three assumptions: normality, homogeneity of variance, and independence). This assists the reader in understanding that you were thorough in data screening prior to conducting the test of inference.

A dependent samples *t* test was conducted to determine if there was a difference in the mean swim time for the 50-meter freestyle before participation in an intensive training program as compared to the mean swim time for the 50-meter freestyle after participation in an intensive training program. The assumption of normality was tested and met for the distributional shape of the paired differences. Review of the Shapiro-Wilk test for normality ($SW = .956$, $df = 10$, $p = .734$) and skewness (.248, $SE = .687$) and kurtosis (.050, $SE = 1.334$) statistics suggested that normality of the paired differences was reasonable. Standardizing skew and kurtosis by dividing by their standard errors and comparing to a critical value of ±1.96, we find nonstatistically significant skew and kurtosis. Additional tests, including D'Agostino's test for skewness ($z = .3737$, $p = .7087$) and the Bonett-Seier test for Geary's kurtosis ($z = .2836$, $p = .7767$) suggested further evidence of normality.

The boxplot suggested a relatively normal distributional shape and there were no outliers present. The Q-Q plot and histogram suggested minor nonnormality. Due to the small sample, this was anticipated. Homogeneity of variance was tested by reviewing the ratio of the raw score variances. The ratio of the smallest (posttest = 13.111) to largest (pretest = 17.778) variance was less than 1:4 therefore there is evidence of the equal variance assumption. The individuals were not randomly selected, therefore the assumption of independence was not met creating a potential for an increased probability of a Type I or Type II error.

It is also important to include a measure of effect size. Recall our formula for computing the effect size, *d*, presented earlier in the chapter. Plugging in the values for our swimming example, we find an effect size *d* of 2.3146, which is interpreted according to Cohen's (1988) guidelines as a large effect.

$$\text{Cohen's } d = \frac{\bar{d}}{s_d} = \frac{5}{2.1602} = 2.3146$$

With an effect size of 2.3146, there are about two and a third standard deviation units between the pretraining mean swim time and the posttraining mean swim time. Using Uanhoro's online calculator (Uanhoro, 2017), we find Hedge's g to be 1.1632 with a confidence interval of (.5935, 1.9345).

Here is an APA-style example paragraph of results for the swimming data (remember that this will be prefaced by the paragraph reporting the extent to which the assumptions of the test were met).

The pretest and posttest data were collected from a sample of 10 swimmers, with a pretest mean of 64 seconds ($SD = 4.22$) and a posttest mean of 59 seconds ($SD = 3.62$). Thus, swimming times decreased from pretest to posttest. The dependent t test was conducted to determine if this difference was statistically significantly different from zero, and the results indicate that the pretest and posttest means were statistically different ($t = 7.32$, $df = 9$, $p < .001$). The null hypothesis that the freestyle swimming means were the same at both points in time was rejected at the .05 level of significance. The effect size d (calculated as the mean difference divided by the standard deviation of the difference) was 2.3146. Hedge's g was computed to be 1.16 (CI .59, 1.93). Using Cohen's (1988) guidelines, this is interpreted as a large effect. The results provide evidence to support the conclusion that the mean 50-meter freestyle swimming time prior to intensive training is different than the mean 50-meter freestyle swimming time after intensive training. The effect size suggests almost a 2 1/2 standard deviation unit difference between pre and post (i.e., post swim time was nearly 2 1/2 standard deviation units quicker than pre swim time).

7.10 Additional Resources

A number of resources are available for learning more about statistics and how to interpret statistics. In addition to those already cited, Huck (2000) is an excellent general resource to assist in learning more about statistics and how to interpret statistics.

Problems

Conceptual Problems

1. When H_0 is true, the difference between two independent sample means is a function of which of the following?

a. Degrees of freedom

b. Standard error

c. Sampling distribution

d. Sampling error

2. The denominator of the independent t test is known as the standard error of the difference between two means, and may be defined as which of the following?

a. The difference between the two group means
b. The amount by which the difference between the two group means differs from the population mean
c. The standard deviation of the sampling distribution of the difference between two means
d. All of the above
e. None of the above

3. In the independent t test, what does the homoscedasticity assumption state?
   a. The two population means are equal
   b. The two population variances are equal
   c. The two sample means are equal
   d. The two sample variances are equal
4. True or false? Sampling error increases with larger samples.
5. True or false? At a given level of significance, it is possible that the significance test and the confidence interval results will differ for the same dataset.
6. I assert that the critical value of t required for statistical significance is smaller (in absolute value) when using a directional rather than a nondirectional test. Am I correct?
7. If a 95% CI from an independent t test ranges from −.13 to +1.67, I assert that the null hypothesis would not be rejected at the .05 level of significance. Am I correct?
8. The mathematic ability of 10 preschool children was measured when they entered their first year of preschool and then again in the spring of their kindergarten year. To test for pre to post mean differences, which of the following tests would be used?
   a. Independent t test
   b. Dependent t test
   c. z test
   d. None of the above
9. A researcher collected data to answer the following research question: Are there mean differences in science test scores for middle school students who participate in school-sponsored athletics as compared to students who do not participate? Which of the following tests would be used to answer this question?
   a. Independent t test
   b. Dependent t test
   c. z test
   d. None of the above
10. True or false? The number of degrees of freedom for an independent t test with 15 females and 25 males is 40.
11. I assert that the critical value of t, for a test of two dependent means, will increase as the samples become larger. Am I correct?
12. Which of the following is NOT an assumption of the independent t test?
    a. Normality
    b. Independence

c. Equal sample sizes
d. Homogeneity of variance

13. For which of the following assumptions of the independent t test is evidence provided in the SPSS output by default?
    a. Normality
    b. Independence
    c. Equal sample sizes
    d. Homogeneity of variance
14. A researcher conducts an independent t test with balanced samples, equal variances, and a total sample size of 12. Which of the following standardized mean differences measures of effect is recommended?
    a. Cohen's d
    b. Eta squared
    c. Glass's d
    d. Hedge's g
15. A researcher is computing a dependent t test to examine the difference between a pre- and post-assessment. Which of the following is used to examine the assumption of normality with the dependent t test?
    a. Both variables (i.e., pre- and post-assessment)
    b. The dependent variable
    c. The dependent variable by each category of the independent variable
    d. The pre- to post-assessment difference score
16. The denominator of the dependent t test is known as the standard error of the mean difference, and may be defined as which of the following?
    a. The difference between the two group means
    b. The amount by which the difference between the two group means differs from the population mean
    c. The standard deviation of the sampling distribution of the mean difference
    d. All of the above
    e. None of the above
17. True or false? The degrees of freedom lost with a dependent t test are greater than the degrees of freedom lost with an independent t test.

Answers for Conceptual Problems

1. **d** (If the population means are equal, then the difference between the two sample means is only due to sampling error)
3. **b** (The assumption of equal variances stated that the variances of the populations are equal)
5. **False** (They will always agree for constant alpha)
7. **Yes** (The CI contains zero)
9. **a** (The independent t test is appropriate to use for testing mean differences between groups, as is the case here)

11. **No** (It will decrease, as shown in Table A.2 in the Appendix)
13. **d** (Homogeneity of variances, via Levene's test, is provided by default in SPSS when conducting the independent t test)
15. **d** (The assumption of normality with the dependent t test can be examined using the difference score; in this example, that would be the pre- to post-assessment difference)
17. **False** (The degrees of freedom lost with a dependent t test (i.e., $n-1$), are *less* than the degrees of freedom lost with an independent t test, (i.e., $n_1 + n_2 - 2$))

Computational Problems

1. The following two independent samples of older and younger adults were measured on an attitude towards violence test:

Sample 1 (Older Adult) Data			Sample 1 (Younger Adult) Data		
42	36	47	45	50	57
35	46	37	58	43	52
52	44	47	43	60	41
51	56	54	49	44	51
55	50	40	49	55	56
40	46	41			

a. Test the following hypothesis at the .05 level of significance.

$$H_0: \mu_1 - \mu_2 = 0$$
$$H_1: \mu_1 - \mu_2 \neq 0$$

b. Construct a 95% CI.

2. The following two independent samples of male and female undergraduate students were measured on an English literature quiz:

Sample 1 (Male) Data			Sample 1 (Female) Data		
5	7	8	9	9	11
10	11	11	13	15	18
13	15		19	20	

a. Test the following hypothesis at the .05 level of significance.

$$H_0: \mu_1 - \mu_2 = 0$$
$$H_1: \mu_1 - \mu_2 \neq 0$$

b. Construct a 95% CI.

3. The following two independent samples of preschool children (who were demographically similar but differed in Head Start participation) were measured on teacher-reported social skills during the spring of kindergarten.

Sample 1 (Head Start) Data			Sample 1 (Non–Head Start) Data		
18	14	12	15	12	9
16	10	17	10	18	12
20	16	19	11	8	11
15	13	22	13	10	14

a. Test the following hypothesis at the .05 level of significance.

$$H_0: \mu_1 - \mu_2 = 0$$
$$H_1: \mu_1 - \mu_2 \neq 0$$

b. Construct a 95% CI.

4. The following is a random sample of paired values of weight measured before (time 1) and after (time 2) a weight-reduction program:

Pair	1	2
1	127	130
2	126	124
3	129	135
4	123	127
5	124	127
6	129	128
7	132	136
8	125	130
9	135	131
10	126	128

a. Test the following hypothesis at the .05 level of significance.

$$H_0: \mu_1 - \mu_2 = 0$$
$$H_1: \mu_1 - \mu_2 \neq 0$$

b. Construct a 95% CI.

5. Individuals were measured on the number of words spoken during the 1 minute prior to exposure to a confrontational situation. During the 1 minute after exposure, the individuals were again measured on the number of words spoken. The data are as follows:

Person	Pre	Post
1	60	50
2	80	70
3	120	80
4	100	90
5	90	100
6	85	70
7	70	40
8	90	70
9	100	60
10	110	100
11	80	100
12	100	70
13	130	90
14	120	80
15	90	50

a. Test the following hypothesis at the .05 level of significance.

$$H_0: \mu_1 - \mu_2 = 0$$
$$H_1: \mu_1 - \mu_2 \neq 0$$

b. Construct a 95% CI.

6. The following is a random sample of scores on an attitude toward family planning scale for husband (sample 1) and wife (sample 2) pairs:

Pair	1	2
1	1	3
2	2	3
3	4	6
4	4	5
5	5	7
6	7	8
7	7	9
8	8	10

a. Test the following hypothesis at the .05 level of significance.

$$H_0: \mu_1 - \mu_2 = 0$$
$$H_1: \mu_1 - \mu_2 \neq 0$$

b. Construct a 95% CI.

7. For two dependent samples, test the hypothesis below at the .05 level of significance. Sample statistics: $n = 121$; $\bar{d} = 10$; $s_d = 45$.

$$H_0: \mu_1 - \mu_2 \leq 0$$
$$H_1: \mu_1 - \mu_2 > 0$$

8. For two dependent samples, test the hypothesis below at the .05 level of significance. Sample statistics: $n = 25$; $\bar{d} = 25$; $s_d = 14$.

$$H_0: \mu_1 - \mu_2 \leq 0$$
$$H_1: \mu_1 - \mu_2 > 0$$

9. Use the Ch7_ER.sav data to test the hypothesis that the anxiety of emergency room doctors differs from the anxiety of doctors who work in other areas of the hospital. Test at alpha = .05 and report the appropriate test results based on the extent to which the assumption of equal variances is met.

10. A researcher is examining IPEDS data (https://nces.ed.gov/ipeds/use-the-data) from land grant institutions. The researcher is interested in knowing if the mean number of students enrolled exclusively in distance education courses between 2012 and 2016 has changed. Use the Ch7_IPEDS.sav data. Test at alpha = .05 and report the appropriate test results.

Answers to Computational Problems

1. **a.** $t = -2.110$, critical values are approximately -2.041 and $+2.041$, reject $H_{0.}$

b. (-9.24377, $-.15623$), does not include hypothesized value of 0, reject H_0.

3. **a.** $t = -3.185$, critical values are -2.074 and $+2.074$, reject $H_{0.}$

b. (-6.742, -1.4248), does not include hypothesized value of 0, reject $H_{0.}$

5. **a.** $t = 4.117$, critical values are -2.145 and $+2.145$, reject $H_{0.}$

b. (9.7396, 30.9271), does not include hypothesized value of 0, reject $H_{0.}$

7. $t = 2.4444$, critical value is 1.658, reject $H_{0.}$

9. The assumption of equal variances is violated, $F = 9.39$, $p = .002$, thus we report Welch t'. There is a statistically significant difference in mean anxiety for doctors in the ER ($M = 26.63$, $SD = 4.41$) as compared to doctors who do not teach in the ER ($M = 24.13$, $SD = 5.48$), Welch $t' = -3.511$, $df = 174.20$, $p < .001$.

Interpretive Problems

1. Using the survey1 dataset from the website, use SPSS or **R** to conduct an independent t test, where gender is the grouping variable and the dependent variable is a continuous variable of interest to you. Test for the extent to which the assumptions have been met. Calculate an effect size as well as post hoc power. Then write an APA-style paragraph describing the results.

2. Using the survey1 dataset accessible from the website, use SPSS or **R** to conduct an independent t test, where the grouping variable is whether or not the person could tell the difference between Pepsi and Coke and the dependent variable is a continuous variable of interest to you. Test for the extent to which the assumptions have been met. Calculate an effect size as well as post hoc power. Then write an APA-style paragraph describing the results.

3. Using the Ch2_volcano dataset accessible from the website, use SPSS or **R** to conduct an independent t test, where the grouping variable is "stratovolcano" and the dependent variable is a continuous variable of interest to you. Test for the extent to which the assumptions have been met. Calculate an effect size as well as post hoc power. Then write an APA-style paragraph describing the results.

8

Inferences About Proportions

Chapter Outline

Key Concepts

1. Proportion
2. Sampling distribution and standard error of a proportion
3. Contingency table
4. Chi-square distribution
5. Observed versus expected proportions

In Chapters 6 and 7 we considered testing inferences about means, first for a single mean (Chapter 6) and then for two means (Chapter 7). The major concepts discussed in those chapters that are applicable throughout the rest of the text include the following: types of hypotheses, types of decision errors, level of significance, power, confidence intervals, effect sizes, sampling distributions, and standard errors. While we previously examined inferences about a single mean, inferences about the difference between two independent means, and inferences about the difference between two dependent means, in this chapter we consider inferential tests involving proportions. We define a *proportion* as the percentage of scores falling into particular categories. Thus, the tests described in this chapter deal with variables that are categorical in nature and thus are *nominal* or *ordinal* in terms of measurement scale (see Chapter 1), or have been collapsed from higher level variables into nominal or ordinal variables (e.g., high and low scorers on an achievement test; although, generally, collapsing interval or ratio into categorical is not good practice as much information is lost in the process).

The tests that we cover in this chapter are considered ***nonparametric*** procedures, also sometimes referred to as *distribution-free* procedures, as there is no requirement that the data adhere to a particular distribution (e.g., normal distribution). Nonparametric procedures are often *less preferable* than parametric procedures (e.g., *t* tests, which assume normality of the distribution) for the following reasons: (a) parametric procedures are often robust to assumption violations, in other words, the results are often still interpretable even if there may be assumption violations; (2) nonparametric procedures have lower power relative to sample size, in other words, rejecting the null hypothesis if it is false requires a larger sample size with nonparametric procedures; and (3) the types of research questions that can be addressed by nonparametric procedures are often quite simple (e.g., while complex interactions of many different variables can be tested with parametric procedures such as factorial analysis of variance, this cannot be done with nonparametric procedures). Nonparametric procedures can still be valuable to use given the measurement scale(s) of the variable(s) and the research question. However, at the same time it is important that researchers recognize the limitations in using these types of procedures.

Research questions to be asked of proportions include the following examples:

1. Is the quarter in my hand a fair or biased coin; in other words, over repeated samples, is the proportion of heads equal to .50 or not?
2. Is there a difference between the proportions of Republicans and Democrats who support the local school bond issue?
3. Is there a relationship between education level (e.g., less than high school diploma, high school graduate, some college, college graduate) and type of criminal offense

(e.g., petty theft, rape, murder); in other words, is the proportion of one education level different from another in terms of the types of crimes committed?

Several inferential tests are covered in this chapter, depending on (a) whether there are one or two samples, (b) whether the two samples are selected in an independent or dependent manner, and (c) whether there are one or more categorical variables. More specifically, the topics described include the following inferential tests: testing whether a single proportion is different from a hypothesized value; testing whether two independent proportions are different; testing whether two dependent proportions are different; and the chi-square goodness-of-fit test and chi-square test of association. We use many of the foundational concepts previously covered in Chapters 6 and 7. New concepts to be discussed include the following: proportion; sampling distribution and standard error of a proportion; contingency table; chi-square distribution; and observed versus expected frequencies. Our objectives are that by the end of this chapter, you will be able to (a) understand the basic concepts underlying tests of proportions, (b) select the appropriate test, and (c) determine and interpret the results from the appropriate test.

8.1 Inferences About Proportions Involving the Normal Distribution and How They Work

A superbly talented set of four graduate students have been expertly completing research projects through their work in the statistics lab. We find the group, once again, ready for a challenge!

The statistics lab has been contracted to work with Dr. Senata, the Director of the Undergraduate Services Office at Ivy Covered University, and Dr. Walnut, a lobbyist from a state that is considering legalizing gambling. Challie Lenge will be advising Dr. Senata, and Addie Venture will be working with Dr. Walnut.

In conversation with Challie, Dr. Senata shares that she recently read a report that provided national statistics on the proportion of students that major in various disciplines. Dr. Senata wants to know if there are similar proportions at their institution. Dr. Senata suggests the following research question: *Are the sample proportions of undergraduate student college majors at Ivy Covered University in the same proportions of those nationally?* Challie suggests a chi-square goodness of fit test as the test of inference. Her task is then to assist Dr. Senata in generating the test of inference to answer her research question.

Addie is consulting with Dr. Walnut, a lobbyist who is lobbying against legalizing gambling in his state. Dr. Walnut wants to determine if there is a relationship between level of education and stance on a proposed gambling amendment. Addie suspects that the proportions supporting gambling vary as a function of their education level. The following research question is suggested by Addie: *Is there an association between level of education and stance on gambling?* Addie suggests a chi-square test of association as the test of inference. Her task is then to assist Dr. Walnut in generating the test of inference to answer the research question.

This section deals with concepts and procedures for testing inferences about proportions that involve the normal distribution. Following a discussion of the concepts related to tests of proportions, inferential tests are presented for situations when there is a single proportion, two independent proportions, and two dependent proportions.

8.1.1 Characteristics

Let us examine in greater detail the concepts related to tests of proportions. First, a **proportion** represents *the percentage of individuals or objects that fall into a particular category*. For instance, the proportion of individuals who support a particular political candidate might be of interest. Thus the variable here is a dichotomous, categorical, nominal variable, as there are only two categories represented, support or do not support the candidate.

For notational purposes, we define the **population proportion**, π (pi), as

$$\pi = \frac{f}{N}$$

where f is the *number of frequencies in the population who fall into the category of interest* (e.g., the number of individuals in the population who support the candidate), and N is the total number of units (e.g., individuals) in the population. For example, if the population consists of 100 individuals and 58 support the candidate, then $\pi = .58$ (i.e., 58/100). If the proportion is multiplied by 100%, this yields the percentage of individuals in the population who support the candidate, which in the example would be 58%. At the same time, $1 - \pi$ represents the population proportion of individuals who do *not* support the candidate, which for this example would be $1 - .58 = .42$. If this is multiplied by 100%, this yields the percentage of individuals in the population who do not support the candidate, which in the example would be 42%.

In a fashion, the population proportion is conceptually similar to the population mean if the category of interest (support of candidate) is coded as 1 and the other category (not support) is coded as 0. In the case of the example with 100 individuals, there are 58 individuals coded 1, 42 individuals coded 0, and therefore the mean (i.e., the proportion of cases coded as 1) would be .58. To this point then we have π representing the population proportion of individuals *supporting* the candidate and $1 - \pi$ representing the population proportion of individuals *not supporting* the candidate.

The **population variance of a proportion** can be determined by $\sigma^2 = \pi(1 - \pi)$. Thus, the **population standard deviation of a proportion** is $\sigma = \sqrt{\pi(1-\pi)}$. These provide us with *measures of variability* that represent the extent to which the individuals in the population vary in their support of the candidate. For the example population then, the variance is computed to be $\sigma^2 = \pi(1 - \pi) = .58(1 - .58) = .58(.42) = .2436$ and the standard deviation is $\sigma = \sqrt{\pi(1-\pi)} = \sqrt{.58(1-.58)} = \sqrt{.58(.42)} = .4936$.

For the *population parameters*, we now have the population proportion (or mean), the population variance, and the population standard deviation. The next step is to discuss the corresponding *sample statistics* for the proportion. The **sample proportion**, p, is defined as

$$p = \frac{f}{n}$$

where f is the *number of frequencies in the sample that fall into the category of interest* (e.g., the number of individuals who support the candidate), and n is the *total number of units* (e.g., individuals) in the sample. The sample proportion p is thus a *sample estimate* of the population proportion, π. One way we can estimate the population variance is by the sample variance $s^2 = p(1 - p)$ and the population standard deviation of a proportion can be estimated by the sample standard deviation $s = \sqrt{p(1-p)}$.

The next concept to discuss is the sampling distribution of the proportion. This is comparable to the sampling distribution of the mean discussed in Chapter 5. If one were to take many samples, and for each sample compute the sample proportion p, then we could generate a distribution of p. This is known as the **sampling distribution of the proportion**. For example, imagine that we take 50 samples of size 100 and determine the proportion for each sample. That is, we would have 50 different sample proportions each based on 100 observations. If we construct a frequency distribution of these 50 proportions, then this is actually the sampling distribution of the proportion.

In theory, the sample proportions for this example could range from .00 ($p = 0/100$) to 1.00 ($p = 100/100$), given that there are 100 observations in each sample. One could also examine the variability of these 50 sample proportions. That is, we might be interested in the extent to which the sample proportions vary. We might have, for one example, most of the sample proportions falling near the mean proportion of .60. This would indicate for the candidate data that (a) the samples generally support the candidate, as the average proportion is .60, and (b) the support for the candidate is fairly consistent across samples, as the sample proportions tend to fall close to .60. Alternatively, in a second example, we might find the sample proportions varying quite a bit around the mean of .60, say ranging from .20 to .80. This would indicate that (a) the samples generally support the candidate again, as the average proportion is .60, and (b) the support for the candidate is not very consistent across samples, leading one to believe that some groups support the candidate and others do not.

The variability of the sampling distribution of the proportion can be determined as follows. The *population variance of the sampling distribution of the proportion* is known as the **variance error of the proportion**, denoted by σ_p^2. The **variance error** is computed as

$$\sigma_p^2 = \frac{\pi(1-\pi)}{n}$$

where π is again the population proportion and n is sample size (i.e., the number of observations in a single sample).

The *population standard deviation of the sampling distribution of the proportion* is known as the **standard error of the proportion**, denoted by σ_p. The **standard error** is an index of how variable a sample statistic (in this case, the sample proportion) is when multiple samples of the same size are drawn, and is computed as follows:

$$\sigma_p = \sqrt{\frac{\pi(1-\pi)}{n}}$$

This situation is quite comparable to the sampling distribution of the mean discussed in Chapter 5. There we had the variance error and standard error of the mean as measures of the variability of the sample means.

Technically speaking, the binomial distribution is the exact sampling distribution for the proportion; **binomial** here refers to a categorical variable with two possible categories, which is certainly the situation here. *However, except for rather small samples, the normal distribution is a reasonable approximation to the binomial distribution and is therefore typically used.* The reason we can rely on the normal distribution is due to the *central limit theorem*, previously discussed in Chapter 5. For proportions, the central limit theorem states that as sample size n increases, the sampling distribution of the proportion from a random sample of size n more closely approximates a normal distribution. If the population distribution is normal in shape, then the sampling distribution of the proportion is also normal in shape. If the population distribution is not normal in shape, then the sampling distribution of the proportion becomes more nearly normal as sample size increases. As previously shown in Figure 5.2 in the context of the mean, *the bottom line is that if the population is nonnormal, this will have a minimal effect on the sampling distribution of the proportion except for rather small samples.*

Because nearly always the applied researcher only has access to a single sample, the population variance error and standard error of the proportion must be estimated. The sample variance error of the proportion is denoted by s_p^2 and computed as

$$s_p^2 = \frac{p(1-p)}{n}$$

where p is again the sample proportion and n is sample size. The sample standard error of the proportion is denoted by s_p and computed as

$$s_p = \sqrt{\frac{p(1-p)}{n}}$$

8.1.1.1 Inferences About a Single Proportion

In the first inferential testing situation for proportions, the researcher would like to know whether the population proportion is equal to some hypothesized proportion or not. This is comparable to the one-sample t test described in Chapter 6 where a population mean was compared against some hypothesized mean. Now, we are examining a population proportion compared to some hypothesized proportion.

First, the hypotheses are stated. The hypotheses to be evaluated for detecting whether a population proportion differs from a hypothesized proportion are as follows. The *null hypothesis*, H_0, is that there is no difference between the population proportion, π, and the hypothesized proportion, π_0, which we denote as

$$H_0: \pi = \pi_0$$

Here there is no difference, or a "null" difference, between the population proportion and the hypothesized proportion. For example, if we are seeking to determine whether the quarter you are flipping is a biased coin or not, then a reasonable hypothesized value would be .50, as an unbiased coin should yield "heads" about 50% of the time.

The *nondirectional, scientific, or alternative hypothesis*, H_1, is that there *is* a difference between the population proportion, π, and the hypothesized proportion, π_0, which we denote as

$$H_1: \pi \neq \pi_0$$

The null hypothesis, H_0, will be rejected here in favor of the alternative hypothesis, H_1, if the population proportion is different from the hypothesized proportion. As we have not specified a direction on H_1, we are willing to reject H_0 either if π is greater than π_0 or if π is less than π_0. This alternative hypothesis results in a two-tailed test. Directional (or one-tailed) alternative hypotheses can also be tested if we believe either that π is greater than p_0 or that π is less than π_0. In either case, the more the resulting sample proportion differs from the hypothesized proportion, the more likely we are to reject the null hypothesis.

Second, we then compute the test statistic z as

$$z = \frac{p - \pi_0}{s_{\hat{p}}} = \frac{p - \pi_0}{\sqrt{\dfrac{\pi_0(1 - \pi_0)}{n}}}$$

Where $s_{\hat{p}}$ is estimated based on the hypothesized proportion π_0.

Third, the test statistic z is then compared to a critical value(s) from the unit normal distribution. For a two-tailed test, the critical values are denoted as $\pm_{\alpha/2}z$ and are found in Table A.1 in the Appendix. If the test statistic z falls into either critical region, then we reject H_0; otherwise, we fail to reject H_0. For a one-tailed test, the critical value is denoted as $+_{\alpha}z$ for the alternative hypothesis H_1: $\pi > \pi_0$ (i.e., a right-tailed test) and as $-_{\alpha}z$ for the alternative hypothesis H_1: $\pi < \pi_0$ (i.e., a left-tailed test). If the test statistic z falls into the appropriate critical region, then we reject H_0; otherwise, we fail to reject H_0.

For the two-tailed test, a $(1 - \alpha)$% confidence interval can also be examined. The confidence interval is formed as follows:

$$p \pm {}_{\alpha/2}z\left(s_{\hat{p}}\right)$$

where p is the observed sample proportion, $\pm_{\alpha/2}z$ is the tabled critical value, and $s_{\hat{p}}$ is the sample standard error of the proportion. If the confidence interval contains the hypothesized proportion π_0, then the conclusion is to fail to reject H_0; otherwise, we reject H_0. The interpretation of confidence intervals described in this chapter is the same as those in Chapter 7.

Simulation research has shown that this confidence interval procedure works fine for small samples when the sample proportion is near .50; that is, the normal distribution is a reasonable approximation in this situation. However, as the sample proportion moves closer to 0 or 1, larger samples are required for the normal distribution to be reasonably approximate. Alternative approaches have been developed that appear to be more widely applicable. The interested reader is referred to Ghosh (1979) and Wilcox (1996).

8.1.1.1.1 An Example

Let us consider an example to illustrate use of the test of a single proportion. We follow the basic steps for hypothesis testing that we applied in previous chapters. These steps include:

1. State the null and alternative hypotheses.
2. Select the level of significance (i.e., alpha, α).
3. Calculate the test statistic value.
4. Make a statistical decision (reject or fail to reject H_0).

Suppose a researcher conducts a survey in a city that is voting on whether or not to have an elected school board. Based on informal conversations with a small number of influential citizens, the researcher is led to hypothesize that 50% of the voters are in favor of an elected school board. Through use of a scientific poll, the researcher would like to know whether the population proportion is different from this hypothesized value; thus, a nondirectional, two-tailed alternative hypothesis is utilized. The null and alternative hypotheses are denoted as follows:

$$H_0: \pi = \pi_0$$

$$H_1: \pi \neq \pi_0$$

If the null hypothesis is *rejected*, this would indicate that scientific polls of larger samples yield different results than what was anticipated based on informal conversations and are important in this situation. If the null hypothesis is *not rejected*, this would indicate that informal conversations with a small sample are just as accurate as a scientific larger-sized sample.

A random sample of 100 voters is taken and 60 indicate their support of an elected school board (i.e., $p = .60$). In an effort to minimize the Type I error rate, the significance level is set at $\alpha = .01$. The test statistic z is computed as

$$z = \frac{p - \pi_0}{\sqrt{\frac{\pi_0(1-\pi_0)}{n}}} = \frac{.60 - .50}{\sqrt{\frac{.50(1-.50)}{100}}} = \frac{.10}{\sqrt{\frac{.50(.50)}{100}}} = \frac{.10}{.05} = 2.00$$

Note that the final value for the denominator is the standard error of the proportion (i.e., $s_{\hat{p}} = .0500$), which we will need for computing the confidence interval. From Table A.1 in the Appendix, we determine the critical values to be $\pm_{\alpha/2} z = \pm_{.005} z = \pm 2.58$, in other words, the z value that corresponds to the $P(z)$ value closest to .995 is when z is equal to 2.58. As the test statistic (i.e., $z = 2.000$) does not exceed the critical values (i.e., ± 2.58) and thus fails to fall into a critical region, our decision is to *fail to reject* H_0. Our conclusion then is that the accuracy of the scientific poll is not any different from the hypothesized value of .50 as determined informally. In other words, the proportion of individuals who stated during informal conversations that they would be in favor of an elected school board is similar to the proportion of individuals who would be in favor in the sample.

The 99% confidence interval for the example would be computed as follows:

$$p \pm {}_{\alpha/2} z(s_{\hat{p}}) = .60 \pm (2.58)(.05) = .60 \pm .129 = (.471, .729)$$

Because the confidence interval contains the hypothesized value of .50, our conclusion is to fail to reject H_0 (the same result found when we conducted the statistical test). The conclusion derived from the test statistic is always consistent with the conclusion derived from the confidence interval. We can interpret the confidence interval as follows: 99% of similarly constructed CIs will contain the hypothesized value of .50.

8.1.1.2 Inferences About Two Independent Proportions

In our second inferential testing situation for proportions, the researcher would like to know whether the population proportion for one group is different from the population proportion for a second independent group. This is comparable to the independent *t* test described in Chapter 7 where one population mean was compared to a second independent population mean. Once again we have two independently drawn samples, as discussed in Chapter 7.

First, the hypotheses to be evaluated for detecting whether two independent population proportions differ are as follows. The *null hypothesis*, H_0, is that there is no difference between the two population proportions, π_1 and π_2, which we denote as

$$H_0: \pi_1 - \pi_2 = 0$$

Here there is no difference, or a "null" difference, between the two population proportions. For example, a researcher wants to determine how shift work (i.e., working outside traditional 9 a.m. to 5 p.m. hours, such as an afternoon shift, 3 p.m. to 11 p.m., or a night shift, 11 p.m. to 7 a.m.) may impact sleep. Thus, we may be seeking to determine whether the proportion of adults who work in shifts (relative to those that don't work in shifts) who have sleep disorders (relative to not having a sleep disorder) is equal to the proportion of adults who work in shifts (relative to those that don't work in shifts) who *do not* have sleep disorders. In this example, we have two variables, each with two categories: shift work status (job requires shift work, job does not require shirt work) and sleep disorder status (has sleep disorder, does not have sleep disorder). As we will see later, this tests of proportions for independent samples can be conducted with categorical variables with more than two categories or levels.

The *nondirectional, scientific, or alternative hypothesis*, H_1, is that there is a difference between the population proportions, π_1 and π_2, which we denote as

$$H_1: \pi_1 - \pi_2 \neq 0$$

The null hypothesis, H_0, will be rejected here in favor of the alternative hypothesis, H_1, if the population proportions are different. As we have not specified a direction on H_1, we are willing to reject either if π_1 is greater than π_2 or if π_1 is less than π_2. This alternative hypothesis results in a two-tailed test. Directional alternative hypotheses can also be tested if we believe either that π_1 is greater than π_2 or that π_1 is less than p_2. In either case, the more the resulting sample proportions differ from one another, the more likely we are to reject the null hypothesis.

It is assumed that the two samples are independently and randomly drawn from their respective populations (i.e., the assumption of independence) and that the normal distribution is the appropriate sampling distribution. The next step is to compute the test statistic *z* as

$$z = \frac{p_1 - p_2}{s_{p_1 - p_2}} = \frac{p_1 - p_2}{\sqrt{(p)(1-p)\left(\frac{1}{n_1} + \frac{1}{n_2}\right)}}$$

where n_1 and n_2 are the sample sizes for samples 1 and 2 respectively, and

$$p = \frac{f_1 - f_2}{n_1 + n_2}$$

where f_1 and f_2 are the number of observed frequencies for samples 1 and 2 respectively. The denominator of the z test statistic $s_{p_1-p_2}$ is known as the **standard error of the difference between two proportions** and provides an index of how variable the sample statistic (in this case, the sample proportion) is when multiple samples of the same size are drawn. This test statistic is conceptually similar to the test statistic for the independent t test.

The test statistic z is then compared to a critical value(s) from the unit normal distribution. For a two-tailed test, the critical values are denoted as $\pm_{\alpha/2}z$ and are found in Table A.1 in the Appendix. If the test statistic z falls into either critical region, then we reject H_0; otherwise, we fail to reject H_0. For a one-tailed test, the critical value is denoted as $+_{\alpha}z$ for the alternative hypothesis H_1: $\pi_1 - \pi_2 > 0$ (i.e., a right-tailed test) and as $-_{\alpha}z$ for the alternative hypothesis H_1: $\pi_1 - \pi_2 < 0$ (i.e., a left-tailed test). If the test statistic z falls into the appropriate critical region, then we reject H_0; otherwise, we fail to reject H_0. It should be noted that other alternatives to this test have been proposed (e.g., Storer & Kim, 1990).

For the two-tailed test, a $(1 - \alpha)$% confidence interval can also be examined. The confidence interval is formed as follows:

$$(p_1 - p_2) \pm {}_{\alpha/2}z\left(s_{p_1-p_2}\right)$$

If the confidence interval contains zero, then the conclusion is to fail to reject H_0; otherwise, we reject H_0. Alternative methods are described by Beal (1987) and Coe and Tamhane (1993).

8.1.1.2.1 An Example

Let us consider an example to illustrate use of the test of two independent proportions. Suppose a researcher is taste-testing a new chocolate candy ("chocolate yummies") and wants to know the extent to which individuals would likely purchase the product. As taste in candy may be different for adults versus children, a study is conducted where independent samples of adults and children are given "chocolate yummies" to eat and asked whether they would buy them or not. The researcher would like to know whether the population proportion of individuals who would purchase "chocolate yummies" is different for adults and children. Thus, a nondirectional, two-tailed alternative hypothesis is utilized. The null and alternative hypotheses are denoted as follows:

$$H_0: \pi_1 - \pi_2 = 0$$
$$H_1: \pi_1 - \pi_2 \neq 0$$

If the null hypothesis is rejected, this would indicate that interest in purchasing the product is different in the two groups, and this might result in different marketing and packaging strategies for each group. If the null hypothesis is not rejected, then this would indicate the product is equally of interest to both adults and children, and different marketing and packaging strategies are not necessary.

A random sample of 100 children (sample 1) and a random sample of 100 adults (sample 2) are independently selected. Each individual consumes the product and indicates whether or not he or she would purchase it. Sixty-eight of the children and 54 of the adults state they would purchase "chocolate yummies" if they were available. The level of significance is set at $\alpha = .05$.

The test statistic z is computed as follows. We know that $n_1 = 100$, $n_2 = 100$, $f_1 = 68$, $f_2 = 54$, $p_1 = .68$, and $p_2 = .54$. We compute the sample proportion, p, to be

$$p = \frac{f_1 + f_2}{n_1 + n_2} = \frac{68 + 54}{100 + 100} = \frac{122}{200} = .61$$

This allows us to compute the test statistic z as

$$z = \frac{p_1 - p_2}{\sqrt{(p)(1-p)\left(\frac{1}{n_1} + \frac{1}{n_2}\right)}} = \frac{.68 - .54}{\sqrt{(.61)(1-.61)\left(\frac{1}{100} + \frac{1}{100}\right)}} =$$

$$z = \frac{.14}{\sqrt{(.61)(.39)(.02)}} = \frac{.14}{.069} = 2.0290$$

The denominator of the z test statistic, $s_{p1-p2} = .0690$, is the standard error of the difference between two proportions, which we will need for computing the confidence interval.

The test statistic z is then compared to the critical values from the unit normal distribution. As this is a two-tailed test, the critical values are denoted as $\pm_{\alpha/2}z$ and are found in Table A.1 of the Appendix to be $\pm_{\alpha/2}z = \pm_{.025}z = \pm 1.96$. In other words, this is the z value that is closest to a $P(z)$ of .975. As the test statistic z falls into the upper-tail critical region, we reject H_0 and conclude that the proportion of adults and children are *not* equally interested in the product.

Finally, we can compute the 95% confidence interval as follows:

$$(p_1 - p_2) \pm \left({}_{\alpha/2}z\right)\left(s_{p_1-p_2}\right) = (.68 - .54) \pm (1.96)(.0690) =$$

$$= (.14) \pm (.1352) = (.0048, .2752)$$

Because the confidence interval does not include zero, we would again reject H_0 and conclude that the proportion of adults and children are not equally interested in the product. As previously stated, the conclusion derived from the test statistic is always consistent with the conclusion derived from the confidence interval at the same level of significance. We can interpret the confidence interval as follows: for 95% of similarly constructed CIs, the true population proportion difference will not include zero.

8.1.1.3 Inferences About Two Dependent Proportions

In our third inferential testing situation for proportions, the researcher would like to know whether the population proportion for one group is different from the population proportion for a second dependent group. This is comparable to the dependent t test described in Chapter 7 where one population mean was compared to a second dependent population mean. Once again we have two dependently drawn samples as discussed in Chapter 7. For example, we may have a pretest–posttest situation where a comparison of proportions over time for the same individuals is conducted. Alternatively, we may have pairs of matched individuals (e.g., spouses, twins, brother–sister) for which a comparison of proportions is of interest.

First, the hypotheses to be evaluated for detecting whether two dependent population proportions differ are as follows. The *null hypothesis*, H_0, is that there is no difference between the two population proportions π_1 and π_2, which we denote as

$$H_0: \pi_1 - \pi_2 = 0$$

Here there is no difference, or a "null" difference, between the two population proportions. For example, a political analyst may be interested in determining whether the approval rating of the president is the same just prior to and immediately following his annual State of the Union address (i.e., a pretest–posttest situation). As a second example, a marriage counselor wants to know whether husbands and wives equally favor a particular training program designed to enhance their relationship (i.e., a couple situation).

The *nondirectional, scientific, or alternative hypothesis*, H_1, is that there is a difference between the population proportions, π_1 and π_2, which we denote as follows:

$$H_1: \pi_1 - \pi_2 \neq 0$$

The null hypothesis, H_0, will be rejected here in favor of the alternative hypothesis, H_1, if the population proportions are different. As we have not specified a direction on H_1, we are willing to reject either if π_1 is greater than π_2 or if π_1 is less than π_2. This alternative hypothesis results in a two-tailed test. Directional alternative hypotheses can also be tested if we believe either that π_1 is greater than π_2 or that π_1 is less than π_2. The more the resulting sample proportions differ from one another, the more likely we are to reject the null hypothesis.

Before we examine the test statistic, let us consider a table in which the proportions are often presented. As shown in Table 8.1, the **contingency table** lists proportions for each of the different possible outcomes. *The columns indicate the proportions for sample 1.* The left column contains those proportions related to the "unfavorable" condition (or disagree or no, depending on the situation), and the right column those proportions related to the "favorable" condition (or agree or yes, depending on the situation). At the bottom of the columns are the marginal proportions shown for the "unfavorable" condition, denoted by $1 - p_1$, and for the "favorable" condition, denoted by p_1. *The rows indicate the proportions for sample* 2. The top row contains those proportions for the "favorable" condition, and the bottom row contains those proportions for the "unfavorable" condition. To the right of the rows are the marginal proportions shown for the "favorable" condition, denoted by p_2, and for the "unfavorable" condition, denoted by $1 - p_2$.

TABLE 8.1

Contingency Table for Two Samples

	Sample 1		
Sample 2	**"Unfavorable"**	**"Favorable"**	**Marginal Proportions**
"Favorable"	a	b	p_2
"Unfavorable"	c	d	$1 - p_2$
Marginal proportions	$1 - p_1$	p_1	

Within the box of the table are the proportions for the different combinations of conditions across the two samples. The *upper left-hand cell* is the proportion of observations that are "unfavorable" in sample 1 and "favorable" in sample 2 (i.e., dissimilar across samples), denoted by *a*. The *upper right-hand cell* is the proportion of observations who are "favorable" in sample 1 and "favorable" in sample 2 (i.e., similar across samples), denoted by *b*. The *lower left-hand cell* is the proportion of observations who are "unfavorable" in sample 1 and "unfavorable" in sample 2 (i.e., similar across samples), denoted by *c*. The *lower right-hand cell* is the proportion of observations who are "favorable" in sample 1 and "unfavorable" in sample 2 (i.e., dissimilar across samples), denoted by *d*.

The next step is to compute the test statistic *z* as

$$z = \frac{p_1 - p_2}{s_{p_1 - p_2}} = \frac{p_1 - p_2}{\sqrt{\dfrac{d + a}{n}}}$$

where *n* is the total number of pairs. The denominator of the *z* test statistic, $s_{p_1-p_2}$, is again known as the **standard error of the difference between two proportions** and provides an index of how variable the sample statistic (i.e., the difference between two sample proportions) is when multiple samples of the same size are drawn. This test statistic is conceptually similar to the test statistic for the dependent *t* test.

The test statistic *z* is then compared to a critical value(s) from the unit normal distribution. For a two-tailed test, the critical values are denoted as $\pm_{\alpha/2}z$ and are found in Table A.1 in the Appendix. If the test statistic *z* falls into either critical region, then we reject H_0; otherwise, we fail to reject H_0. For a one-tailed test, the critical value is denoted as $+_{\alpha}z$ for the alternative hypothesis H_1: $\pi_1 - \pi_2 > 0$ (i.e., right-tailed test) and as $-_{\alpha}z$ for the alternative hypothesis H_1: $\pi_1 - \pi_2 < 0$ (i.e., left-tailed test). If the test statistic *z* falls into the appropriate critical region, then we reject H_0; otherwise, we fail to reject H_0. It should be noted that other alternatives to this test have been proposed (e.g., the chi-square test as described in the following section). Unfortunately, the *z* test does not yield an acceptable confidence interval procedure.

8.1.1.3.1 An Example

Let us consider an example to illustrate use of the test of two dependent proportions. Suppose a medical researcher is interested in whether husbands and wives agree on the effectiveness of a new headache medication "No-Ache." A random sample of 100 husband–wife couples were selected and asked to try "No-Ache" for 2 months. At the end of 2 months, each individual was asked whether the medication was effective or not at reducing headache pain. The researcher wants to know whether the medication is differentially effective for husbands and wives. Thus, a nondirectional, two-tailed alternative hypothesis is utilized.

The resulting proportions are presented as a contingency table in Table 8.2. The level of significance is set at $\alpha = .05$. The test statistic *z* is computed as follows:

$$z = \frac{p_1 - p_2}{s_{p_1 - p_2}} = \frac{p_1 - p_2}{\sqrt{\dfrac{d + a}{n}}} = \frac{.40 - .65}{\sqrt{\dfrac{.15 + .40}{100}}} = \frac{-.25}{.0742} = -3.3693$$

TABLE 8.2
Contingency Table for Headache Example

	Husband Sample		
Wife Sample	**Ineffective**	**Effective**	**Marginal Proportions**
Effective	$a = .40$	$b = .25$	$p_2 = .65$
Ineffective	$c = .20$	$d = .15$	$1 - p_2 = .35$
Marginal proportions	$1 - p_1 = .60$	$p_1 = .40$	

The test statistic z is then compared to the critical values from the unit normal distribution. As this is a two-tailed test, the critical values are denoted as $\pm_{\alpha/2}z$ and are found in Table A.1 in the Appendix to be $\pm_{\alpha/2}z = \pm_{.025}z = \pm 1.96$ In other words, this is the z value that is closest to a $P(z)$ of .975. As the test statistic z falls into the lower-tail critical region, we *reject* H_0 and conclude that the husbands and wives do not believe equally in the effectiveness of "No-Ache." In other words, there are dissimilar proportions of husbands and wives who believe in the effectiveness of "No-Ache."

8.1.2 Power

As stated elsewhere, in general, nonparametric procedures have lower power relative to sample size, in other words, rejecting the null hypothesis if it is false requires a larger sample size with nonparametric procedures. We encourage researchers to examine power prior, such as power tables or software (e.g., G*Power), to conducting their study so that the study is sufficiently powered to detect an effect.

8.1.3 Effect Size

Cohen's (1988) measure of effect size for proportion tests using z is known as h; thus, h is the effect size index for a difference in proportions. Unfortunately, h involves the use of arcsin transformations of the proportions, which is beyond the scope of this text. In addition, standard statistical software, such as SPSS, does not provide measures of effect size for any of these tests. Using **R**, however, we can compute h, as shown in Figure 8.1. Using Cohen's (1988) conventions, a small difference between proportions is $h = 20$, medium effect is $h = 50$, and large effect is $h = .80$.

Working in **R**, we can compute the effect size *h* using the *pwr* package.

```
install.packages("pwr")
library(pwr)
```

With the *install.packages* function, we install the *pwr* package. Using the *library* function, we then load *pwr* into our library.

```
h<-ES.h(0.40,.65)
h
```

FIGURE 8.1
Computing effect size *h* in **R**.

We use the *ES.h* function and include our proportions in parentheses, where the first value represents p_1 and the second value represents p_2 Using the data from the headache example, our proportions are .40 and .65. From the results, we create an object named "h." The second line of script is simply telling **R** to output the results, which we see here. Thus, $h = -.51$. Using Cohen's conventions, this represents a moderate effect.

```
[1] -0.5060506
```

```
pwr.p.test(h=h,n=100,sig.level=0.05,
           alternative="two.sided")
```

The *pwr.p.test* function can be used to compute observed power given the observed *h*, sample size (i.e., "n=100"), alpha level ("sig.level=0.05"), and two-sided test (alternative = "two.sided"). In this example, we find power to be .999, which indicates very high power.

```
roportion power calculation for binomial distribution (arcsine transformation)
              h = 0.5060506
              n = 100
      sig.level = 0.05
          power = 0.9990342
    alternative = two.sided
```

FIGURE 8.1 (continued)
Computing effect size *h* in **R**.

8.1.4 Assumptions

For inferences about proportions assuming the normal distribution, it is assumed that the sample (in the case of a single proportion) or samples (in the case of independent and dependent proportions) have been randomly selected from the population (i.e., the assumption of independence) and that the normal distribution is the appropriate sampling distribution.

8.2 Inferences About Proportions Involving the Chi-Square Distribution and How They Work

This section deals with concepts and procedures for testing inferences about proportions that involve the chi-square distribution. Following a discussion of the chi-square distribution relevant to tests of proportions, inferential tests are presented for the chi-square goodness-of-fit test and the chi-square test of association.

8.2.1 Characteristics

The previous tests of proportions in this chapter were based on the *unit normal distribution*, whereas the tests of proportions in the remainder of the chapter are based on the **chi-square distribution**. Thus, we need to become familiar with this new distribution. Like the normal and *t* distributions, the chi-square distribution is really a *family of distributions*. Also, like the *t* distribution, the chi-square distribution family members depend on the number of degrees of freedom represented. As we shall see, the *degrees of freedom* for the chi-square

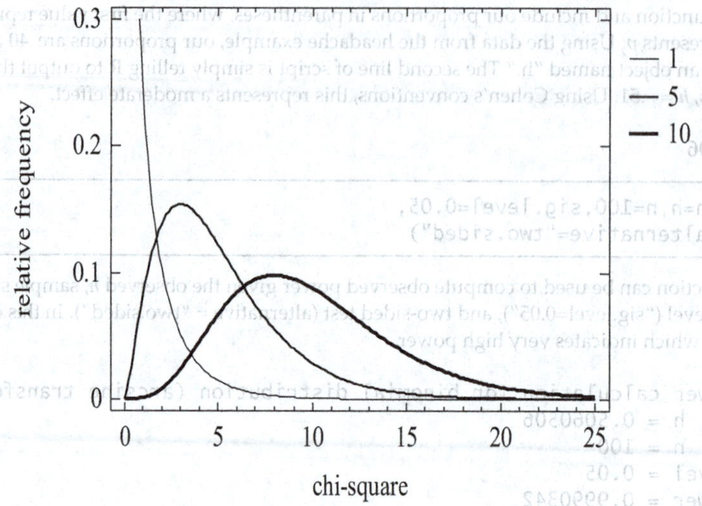

FIGURE 8.2
Several members of the family of the chi-square distribution.

goodness-of-fit test are calculated as *the number of categories (denoted as J) minus 1*. For example, the chi-square distribution for one degree of freedom (i.e., for a variable that has two categories) is denoted by χ_1^2, as shown in Figure 8.2. This particular chi-square distribution is especially positively skewed and leptokurtic (sharp peak).

Figure 8.2 also describes graphically the distributions for χ_5^2 and χ_{10}^2. As you can see in the figure, as the degrees of freedom increase, the distribution becomes less skewed and less leptokurtic; in fact, *the distribution becomes more nearly normal in shape as the number of degrees of freedom increase*. For extremely large degrees of freedom, the chi-square distribution is approximately normal. In general we denote a particular chi-square distribution with ν degrees of freedom as χ_ν^2. The *mean* of any chi-square distribution is ν, the *mode* is ν − 2 when ν is at least 2, and the *variance* is 2ν. The value of chi-square can range from zero to positive infinity. A table of different percentile values for many chi-square distributions is given in Table A.3 in the Appendix. This table is utilized in the following two chi-square tests.

One additional point that should be noted about each of the chi-square tests of proportions developed in this chapter is that there are *no confidence interval procedures* for either the chi-square goodness-of-fit test or the chi-square test of association.

8.2.1.1 The Chi-Square Goodness-of-Fit Test

The first test to consider is the **chi-square goodness-of-fit test**. This test is used to determine whether the observed proportions in two or more categories of a categorical variable differ from what we would expect *a priori*. For example, a researcher is interested in whether the current undergraduate student body at Ivy-Covered University (ICU) is majoring in disciplines according to an *a priori* or expected set of proportions. Based on research at the national level, the expected proportions of undergraduate college majors are as follows: .20 Education; .40 Arts and Sciences; .10 Communications; and .30 Business.

In a random sample of 100 undergraduates at ICU, the observed proportions are as follows: .25 Education, .50 Arts and Sciences, .10 Communications, and .15 Business. Thus, the researcher would like to know whether the sample proportions observed at ICU fit the expected national proportions. In essence, the chi-square goodness-of-fit test is used to test proportions for a single categorical variable (i.e., nominal or ordinal measurement scale) and in this way is akin to a one-sample *t* test.

The **observed proportions** are denoted by p_j, where p represents a sample proportion and j represents a particular category (e.g., Education majors), where $j = 1, \ldots, J$ categories. The **expected proportions** are denoted by π_j, where π represents an expected proportion and j represents a particular category. The null and alternative hypotheses are denoted as follows, where the null hypothesis states that the difference between the observed and expected proportions is zero for all categories.

$$H_0: (p_j - \pi_j) = 0 \, for \, all \, j$$

$$H_1: (p_j - \pi_j) \neq 0 \, for \, all \, j$$

The test statistic is a chi-square and is computed by

$$\chi^2 = n\sum_{j=1}^{J}\frac{(p_j - \pi_j)^2}{\pi_j}$$

where n is the size of the sample. The test statistic is compared to a critical value from the chi-square table (Table A.3 in the Appendix) ${}_{\alpha}\chi^2_{\nu}$, where $\nu = J - 1$. The degrees of freedom are one less than the total number of categories J, because the proportions must total to 1.00; thus, only $J - 1$ are free to vary.

If the test statistic is larger than the critical value, then the null hypothesis is rejected in favor of the alternative. This would indicate that the observed and expected proportions were *not* equal for all categories. The larger the differences are between one or more observed and expected proportions, the larger the value of the test statistic, and the more likely it is to reject the null hypothesis. Otherwise, we would fail to reject the null hypothesis (i.e., the test statistic is smaller than the critical value), indicating that the observed and expected proportions were approximately equal for all categories.

If the null hypothesis is rejected, one may wish to determine which sample proportions are different from their respective expected proportions, and one option is to conduct tests of a single proportion as described in the preceding section. If you would like to control the experiment-wise Type I error rate across a set of such tests, then the Bonferroni method is recommended where the alpha level is divided up among the number of tests conducted. For example, with an overall $\alpha = .05$ and five categories, one would conduct five tests of a single proportion, each at the .01 level of alpha.

Another way to determine which cells are statistically different in observed to expected proportions is to examine the **standardized residuals**, which can be computed as follows:

$$R = \frac{O - E}{\sqrt{E}}$$

Standardized residuals that are greater (in absolute value terms) than 1.96 (when $\alpha = .05$) or 2.58 (when $\alpha = .01$) have different observed to expected frequencies and are contributing to the statistically significant chi-square statistic. The sign of the residual provides information on whether the observed frequency is greater than the expected frequency (i.e., positive value) or less than the expected frequency (i.e., negative value).

Let us return to the example and conduct the chi-square goodness-of-fit test. The test statistic is computed as follows:

$$\chi^2 = n \sum_{j=1}^{J} \frac{\left(p_j - \pi_j\right)^2}{\pi_j}$$

$$\chi^2 = 100 \sum_{j=1}^{4} \left[\frac{(.25-.20)^2}{.20} + \frac{(.50-.40)^2}{.40} + \frac{(.10-.10)^2}{.10} + \frac{(.15-.30)^2}{.30} \right]$$

$$\chi^2 = 100 \sum_{j=1}^{4} \left[.0125 + .0250 + .0000 + .0750 \right] = 100(.1125) = 11.25$$

The test statistic is compared to the critical value from Table A.3 in the Appendix, which is ${}_{.05}\chi^2_3 = 7.8147$. Because the test statistic is larger than the critical value, we *reject the null hypothesis* and conclude that the sample proportions from ICU are different from the expected proportions at the national level. Follow-up tests to determine which cells are statistically different in their observed to expected proportions involve examining the standardized residuals. In this example, the standardized residuals are computed as follows:

$$R_{Education} = \frac{O-E}{\sqrt{E}} = \frac{25-20}{\sqrt{20}} = 1.118$$

$$R_{Arts\ \&\ Sciences} = \frac{O-E}{\sqrt{E}} = \frac{50-40}{\sqrt{40}} = 1.581$$

$$R_{Communication} = \frac{O-E}{\sqrt{E}} = \frac{10-10}{\sqrt{10}} = 0$$

$$R_{Business} = \frac{O-E}{\sqrt{E}} = \frac{15-30}{\sqrt{30}} = \mathbf{-2.739}$$

The standardized residual for Business is greater (in absolute value terms) than 1.96 ($\alpha = .05$), and thus *suggests that there are different observed to expected frequencies for students majoring in Business at ICU compared to national estimates, and that this category is the one which is contributing most to the statistically significant chi-square statistic.*

8.2.1.2 The Chi-Square Test of Association

The second test to consider is the chi-square test of association. This test is equivalent to the chi-square test of independence and the chi-square test of homogeneity, which are not discussed further. The chi-square test of association incorporates both of these tests (e.g., Glass & Hopkins, 1996). The **chi-square test of association** *is used to determine whether there is an association or relationship between two or more categorical (i.e., nominal or ordinal) variables.* Our discussion is, for the most part, restricted to the two-variable situation where each variable has two or more categories. The chi-square test of association is the logical extension to the chi-square goodness-of-fit test, which is concerned with one categorical variable. Unlike the chi-square goodness-of-fit test where the expected proportions are known *a priori*, for the chi-square test of association the expected proportions are not known *a priori*, but must be estimated from the sample data.

For example, suppose a researcher is interested in whether there is an association between level of education and stance on a proposed amendment to legalize gambling. Thus, one categorical variable is level of education with the categories being: (a) less than a high school education, (b) high school graduate, (c) undergraduate degree, and (d) graduate school degree. The other categorical variable is stance on the gambling amendment with the categories being: (a) in favor of the gambling bill and (b) opposed to the gambling bill. The null hypothesis is that there is no association between level of education and stance on gambling, whereas the alternative hypothesis is that there is some association between level of education and stance on gambling. The alternative would be supported if individuals at one level of education felt differently about the bill than individuals at another level of education.

The data are shown in the contingency table (or cross-tabulation table) in Table 8.3. Because there are two categorical variables, we have a two-way, or two-dimensional, contingency table. Each combination of the two variables is known as a **cell**. For example, the cell for row 1, "favor bill," and column 2, "high school graduate," is denoted as *cell 12*; the first value (i.e., 1) refers to the *row* and the second value (i.e., 2) to the *column*. Thus, the first subscript indicates the particular row r and the second subscript indicates the particular column c. The row subscript ranges from $r = 1, \ldots, R$ and the column subscript ranges from $c = 1, \ldots, C$, where R is the last row and C is the last column. This example contains a total of eight cells, two rows multiplied by four columns, denoted by $R \times C = 2 \times 4 = 8$.

Each cell in the table contains two pieces of information: the number (or count or frequencies) of observations in that cell and the observed proportion in that cell. Cell 12 has 13 observations, denoted by $n_{12} = 13$, and an observed proportion of .65, denoted by $p_{12} = .65$. The observed proportion is computed by taking the number of observations in the cell and dividing by the number of observations in the column. Thus for cell 12, 13 of the 20 high school graduates favor the bill, or 13/20 = .6. The column information, known as the **column marginal**, is given at the bottom of each column. Here we are given the number of

TABLE 8.3

Contingency Table for Gambling Example

	Level of Education				
Stance on Gambling	**Less Than High School**	**High School**	**Undergraduate**	**Graduate**	**Row Marginals**
Favor	$n_{11} = 16$ $p_{11} = .80$	$n_{12} = 13$ $p_{12} = .65$	$n_{13} = 10$ $p_{13} = .50$	$n_{14} = 5$ $p_{14} = .25$	$n_{1.} = 44$ $\pi_{1.} = 55$
Opposed	$n_{21} = 4$ $p_{21} = .20$	$n_{22} = 7$ $p_{22} = .35$	$n_{23} = 10$ $p_{23} = .50$	$n_{24} = 15$ $p_{24} = .75$	$n_{2.} = 36$ $\pi_{2.} = .45$
Column marginals	$n_{.1} = 20$	$n_{.2} = 20$	$n_{.3} = 20$	$n_{.4} = 20$	$n = 80$

observations in a column, denoted by $n_{.c}$, where the "." indicates we have summed across rows and c indicates the particular column. For column 2 (reflecting high school graduates), there are 20 observations, denoted by $n_{.c} = 20$.

Row information is also provided at the end of each row, known as the **row marginals**. Two values are listed in the row marginals. First, the number of observations in a row is denoted by $n_{r.}$, where r indicates the particular row and the "." indicates we have summed across the columns. Second, the expected proportion for a specific row is denoted by $\pi_{r.}$, where again r indicates the particular row and the "." indicates we have summed across the columns. The expected proportion for a particular row is computed by taking the number of observations in row $n_{r.}$ and dividing by the number of total observations n. Note that the total number of observations is given in the lower right-hand portion of the figure and denoted as $n. = 80$. Thus for the first row, the expected proportion is computed as $\pi_1 = n_1/n = 44/80 = 55$.

The null and alternative hypotheses can be written as follows:

$$H_0: (p_{rc} - \pi_{r.}) = 0 \; for \; all \; cell$$

$$H_1: (p_{rc} - \pi_{r.}) \neq 0 \; for \; all \; cells$$

The test statistic is a chi-square and is computed by

$$\chi^2 = \sum_{r=1}^{R} \sum_{c=1}^{C} n_{.c} \frac{(p_{rc} - \pi_{r.})^2}{\pi_{r.}}$$

The test statistic is compared to a critical value from the chi-square table (Table A.3 in the Appendix) ${}_{.05}\chi^2_{\nu}$, where $\nu = (R - 1)(C - 1)$. That is, the degrees of freedom are one less than the number of rows multiplied by one less than the number of columns.

If the test statistic is *larger* than the critical value, then the null hypothesis is *rejected* in favor of the alternative. This would indicate that the observed and expected proportions *were not* equal across cells such that the two categorical variables have some association. The larger the differences between the observed and expected proportions, the larger the value of the test statistic, and the more likely it is to reject the null hypothesis. Otherwise, we would fail to reject the null hypothesis, indicating that the observed and expected proportions were approximately equal, such that the two categorical variables have no association.

If the null hypothesis is rejected, then one may wish to determine for which combination of categories the sample proportions are different from their respective expected proportions. One way to do this is to construct 2 × 2 contingency tables as subsets of the larger table and conduct chi-square tests of association. If you would like to control the experiment-wise Type I error rate across the set of tests, then the Bonferroni method is recommended, where the α level is divided up among the number of tests conducted. For example, with $\alpha = .05$ and five 2 × 2 tables, one would conduct five tests each at the .01 alpha level. Another way to do this (i.e., to determine for which combination of categories the sample proportions are different from their respective expected proportions), as with the chi-square goodness of fit test, is to examine the standardized residuals to determine the cells that have statistically significantly different observed to expected proportions. Cells where the standardized residuals are greater (in absolute value terms) than 1.96 (when $\alpha = .05$) or 2.58 (when $\alpha = .01$) are statistically significantly different in observed to expected frequencies.

Finally, it should be noted that we have only considered two-way contingency tables here. Multiway contingency tables can also be constructed and the chi-square test of association utilized to determine whether there is an association among several categorical variables.

8.2.1.2.1 An Example

Let us complete the analysis of the example data. The test statistic is computed as

$$\chi^2 = \sum_{r=1}^{R}\sum_{c=1}^{C}(n_{.c})\left[\frac{(p_{rc}-\pi_{r.})^2}{\pi_{r.}}\right]$$

$$\chi^2 = (20)\left[\frac{(.80-.55)^2}{.55}\right] + (20)\left[\frac{(.20-.45)^2}{.45}\right] + (20)\left[\frac{(.65-.55)^2}{.55}\right] + (20)\left[\frac{(.35-.45)^2}{.45}\right]$$

$$+ (20)\left[\frac{(.50-.55)^2}{.55}\right] + (20)\left[\frac{(.50-.45)^2}{.45}\right] + (20)\left[\frac{(.25-.55)^2}{.55}\right] + (20)\left[\frac{(.75-.45)^2}{.45}\right]$$

$$= 2.2727 + 2.778 + 0.3636 + 0.4444 + 0.0909 + 0.1111 + 3.2727 + 4.0000 = 13.3332$$

The test statistic is compared to the critical value, from Table A.3 in the Appendix, of ${}_{.05}\chi^2_3 = 7.8147$. Because the test statistic is larger than the critical value, we *reject the null hypothesis* and conclude that there is an association between level of education and stance on the gambling bill. In other words, stance on gambling is not the same for all levels of education.

Follow-up tests to determine which cells are statistically different in the observed to expected proportions can be conducted by examining the standardized residuals. As we will see later in Table 8.6, the standardized residual for the cell "do not support" and "graduate level of education" are statistically significant. Thus, this cell is contributing to the statistically significant association between stance on gambling and education level.

8.2.2 Power

As stated elsewhere, in general, nonparametric procedures (compared to parametric procedures) have lower power relative to sample size, in other words, rejecting the null hypothesis if it is false requires a larger sample size with nonparametric procedures. Researchers are encouraged to examine *a priori* power using power tables or software (e.g., G*Power) so that their study is sufficiently powered to detect a meaningful effect.

8.2.3 Effect Size

Different effect size indices can be computed depending on whether you are working with just one categorical variable or a cross-tabulation of two categorical variables. A summary of effect size indices is presented in Table 8.4, with details provided in the following sections.

TABLE 8.4

Effect Sizes Indices for Chi-Square Tests and Interpretations

Chi-Square Test	Effect Size	Interpretation
Chi-square goodness-of-fit test	Cohen's *w*	Ranges from 0 (no difference between the sample and hypothesized proportions, and thus no effect) to +1.0 (maximum difference between the sample and hypothesized proportions and thus a large effect): • Small effect = .10 • Medium effect = .30 • Large effect = .50
Chi-square test of association with one nominal and one ordinal variable *or* two nominal variables	Phi (ρ_ϕ) Cramer's Phi (ϕ_C)	Degree of relationship between two variables. Zero indicates no association; +1.0 indicates a perfect relationship between the variables: • Small effect = .10 • Medium effect = .30 • Large effect = .50
Chi-square test of association with *two ordinal variables*	Spearman's rho (ρ_s) Kendall's tau (τ)	Degree of relationship between two variables. Zero indicates no relationship; +1.0 indicates a perfect relationship between the variables: • Small effect = .10 • Medium effect = .30 • Large effect = .50

8.2.3.1 Chi-Square Goodness-of-Fit Effect Size

An effect size for the chi-square goodness-of-fit test, Cohen's *w* (Cohen, 1988), can be computed as follows:

$$w = \frac{\chi^2}{N(J-1)}$$

where χ^2 is the computed chi-square test statistic value, N is the total sample size, and J is the number of categories in the variable. This effect size statistic, w, can range from 0 to 1, where 0 indicates no difference between the sample and hypothesized proportions (and thus no effect). A value of 1 indicates the maximum difference between the sample and hypothesized proportions (and thus a large effect). Given the range of this value (0 to +1.0) and the similarity to a correlation coefficient, it is reasonable to apply Cohen's interpretations for correlations as a rule of thumb. These include the following: small effect size = .10, medium effect size = .30, and large effect size = .50. For the previous example, the effect size would be calculated as follows and would be interpreted as a small effect:

$$w = \frac{\chi^2}{N(J-1)} = \frac{11.25}{100(4-1)} = \frac{11.25}{300} = .0375$$

8.2.3.2 Chi-Square Test of Association Effect Size

Several measures of effect size, such as correlation coefficients and measures of association, can be requested in SPSS or computed in **R**, and are commonly reported effect size indices for results from chi-square tests of association. Which effect size value is selected depends in part on the measurement scale of the variable. For example, researchers working with nominal data can select a contingency coefficient: phi (for 2 × 2 tables), Cramer's *V* (for tables larger than 2 × 2), lambda, or an uncertainty coefficient. Correlation options available for ordinal data include gamma, Somer's *d*, Kendall's tau-*b*, and Kendall's tau-*c*. From the contingency coefficient, *C*, we can compute Cohen's *w* as follows:

$$w = \sqrt{\frac{C^2}{1 - C^2}}$$

Cohen's recommended subjective standard for interpreting *w* (as well as the other correlation coefficients presented) is as follows: small effect size, $w = .10$, medium effect size, $w = .30$, large effect size, $w = .50$. See Cohen (1988) for further details. We will later review how to compute confidence intervals for *w*.

8.2.4 Assumptions

8.2.4.1 Chi-Square Goodness-of-Fit Assumptions

Two assumptions are made for the chi square goodness-of-fit test: (a) observations are *independent* (which is met when a random sample of the population is selected) and (b) an *expected* frequency of at least five per cell (and in the case of the chi-square goodness-of-fit test, this translates to an expected frequency of at least five per category, as there is only one variable included in the analysis). When the expected frequency is less than five, that particular cell (i.e., category) has undue influence on the chi-square statistic. In other words, the chi-square goodness-of-fit test becomes too sensitive when the expected values are less than five.

8.2.4.1 Chi-Square Test of Association Assumptions

The same two assumptions that apply to the chi-square goodness-of-fit test also apply to the chi-square test of association: (a) observations are independent (which is met when a random sample of the population is selected) and (b) an *expected* frequency of at least five per cell. When the expected frequency is less than five, that particular cell has undue influence on the chi-square statistic. In other words, the chi-square test of association becomes too sensitive when the expected values are less than five.

8.3 Computing Inferences About Proportions Involving the Chi-Square Distribution Using SPSS

Once again we consider the use of SPSS for the example datasets. Although SPSS does not have any of the *z* procedures described in the first part of this chapter, it is capable of conducting both of the chi-square procedures described.

8.3.1 The Chi-Square Goodness-of-Fit Test

Step 1. To conduct the chi-square goodness-of-fit test, you need one variable that is either nominal or ordinal in scale. We will be using the college major data (Ch8_CollegeMajor.

sav) and the nominal variable that represents college major. To conduct the chi-square goodness-of-fit test, go to "Analyze" in the top pulldown menu, then select "Nonparametric Tests," followed by "Legacy Dialogs," and then "Chi-Square." Following the screenshot for Step 1 shown in Figure 8.3 produces the "Chi-Square Goodness-of-Fit" dialog box.

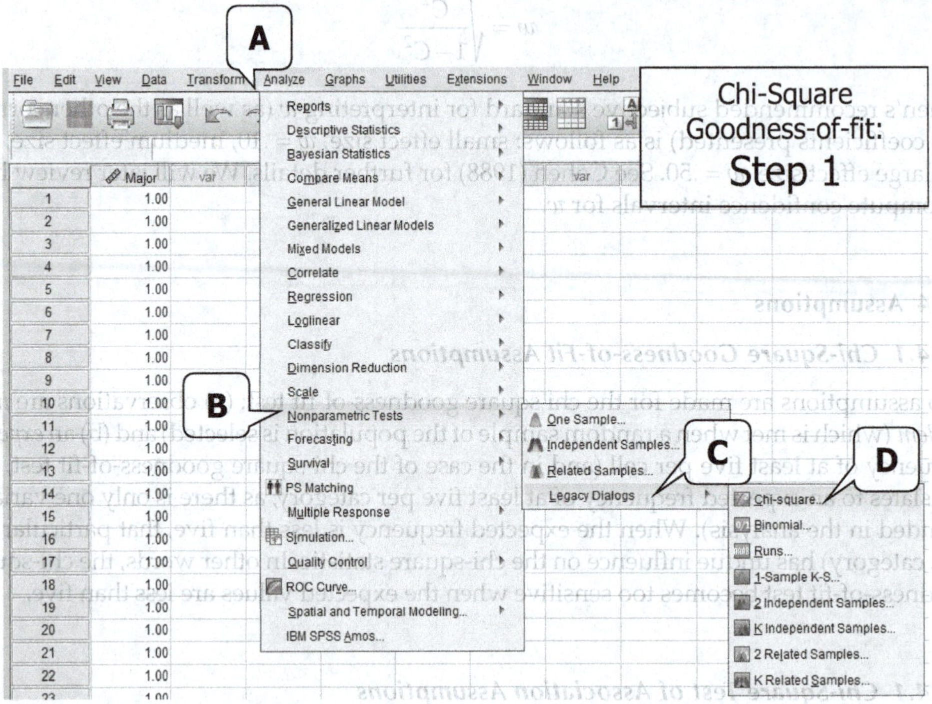

FIGURE 8.3
Chi-square goodness-of-fit test: Step 1.

Step 2. Next, from the main "Chi-Square Goodness-of-Fit" dialog box, click the variable (e.g., "College major") and move it into the "Test Variable List" box by clicking the arrow button. In the lower right-hand portion of the screen is a section labeled "Expected Values." The default is to conduct the analysis with the expected values equal for each category (you will see that the radio button for "All categories equal" is preselected). Much of the time you will want to use different expected values. To define different expected values, click the "Values" radio button (see the screenshot for Step 2a in Figure 8.4). Enter each expected value in the box below "Values," in the same order as the categories (e.g., first enter the expected value for category 1, then the expected value for category 2, etc.), and then click "Add" to define the value in the box. This sets up an expected value for each category. Repeat this process for every category of your variable (see the screenshot for Step 2b in Figure 8.5). Then click on "OK" to run the analysis. The output is shown in Table 8.5

Interpreting the output. The top table provides the frequencies observed in the sample ("Observed *N*") and the expected frequencies based on the values defined by the researcher ("Expected *N*"). The "Residual" is simply the difference between the two *N*s. The chi-square test statistic value is 11.25 and the associated *p* value is .01. Because *p* is less than α, we *reject* the null hypothesis. Let us translate this back to the purpose of our null hypothesis statistical test. *The evidence suggests that the sample proportions observed differ from the proportions of*

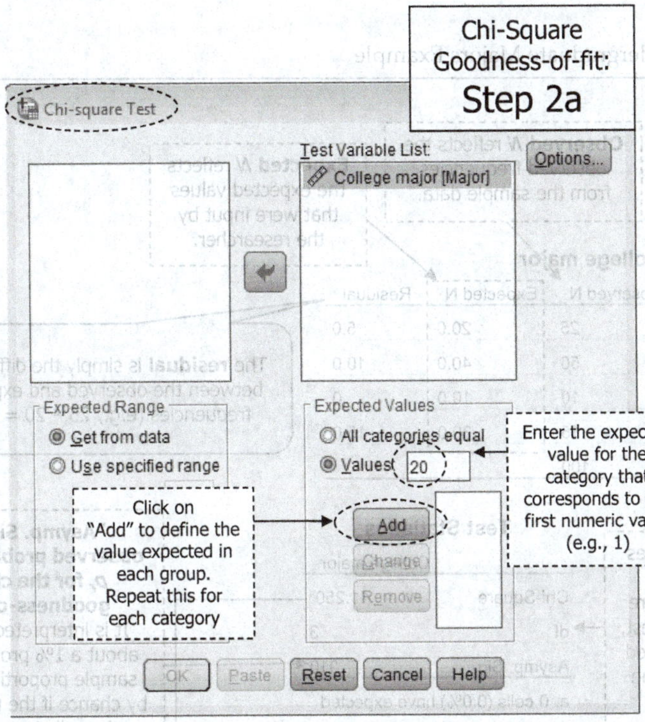

FIGURE 8.4
Chi-square goodness-of-fit test: Step 2a.

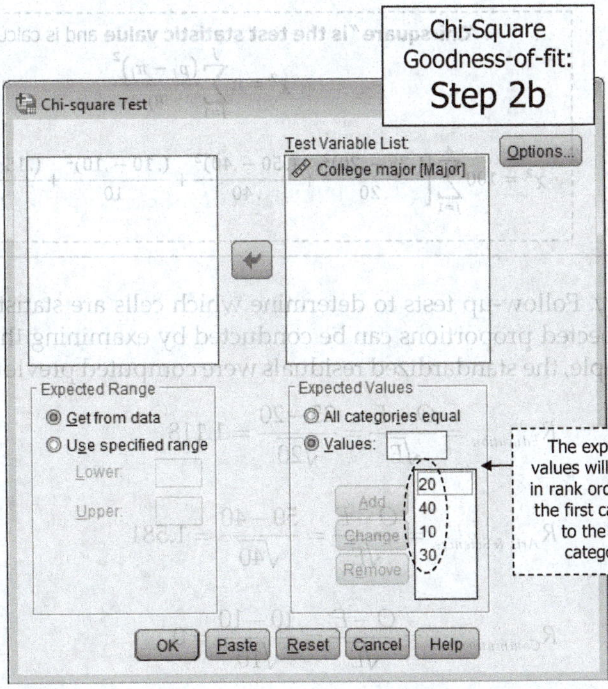

FIGURE 8.5
Chi-square goodness-of-fit test: Step 2b.

TABLE 8.5

SPSS Results for Undergraduate Majors Example

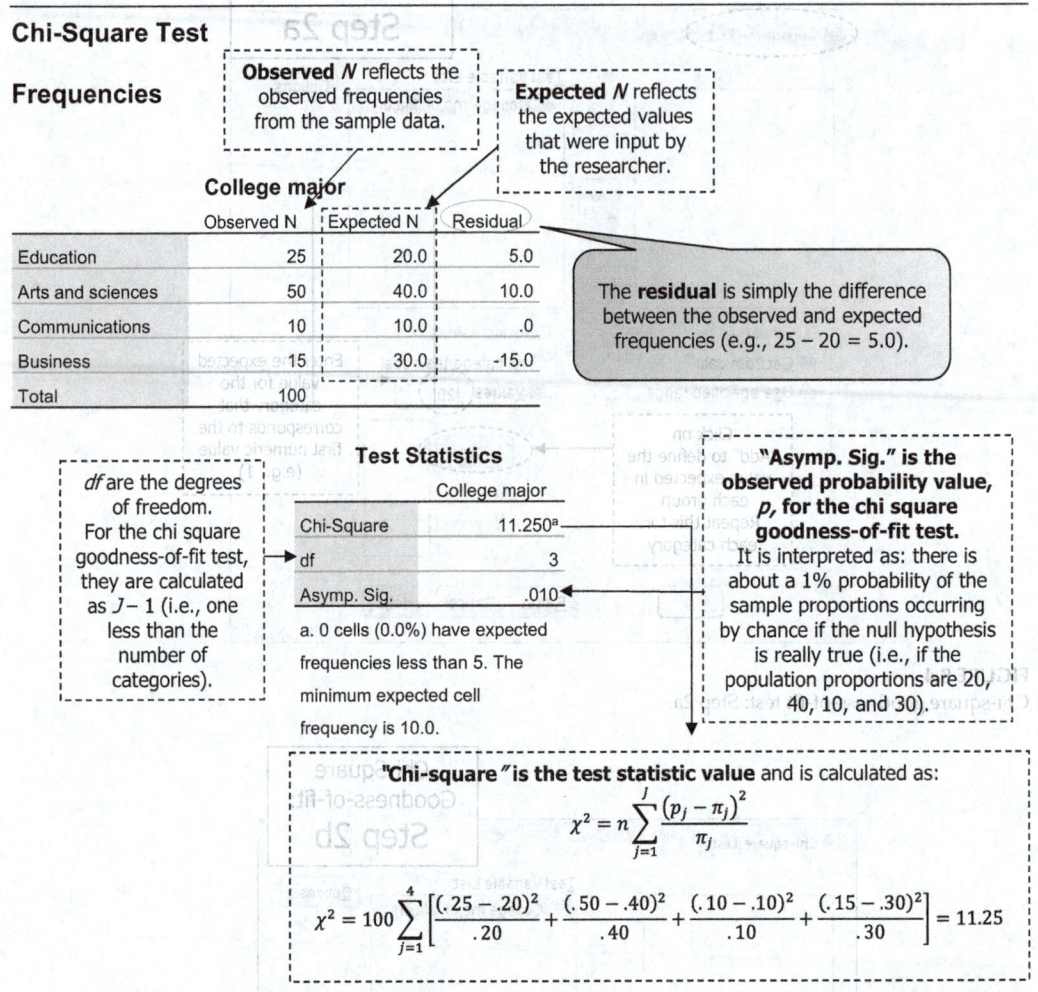

Chi-Square Test

Frequencies

Observed *N* reflects the observed frequencies from the sample data.

Expected *N* reflects the expected values that were input by the researcher.

College major

	Observed N	Expected N	Residual
Education	25	20.0	5.0
Arts and sciences	50	40.0	10.0
Communications	10	10.0	.0
Business	15	30.0	-15.0
Total	100		

The **residual** is simply the difference between the observed and expected frequencies (e.g., 25 – 20 = 5.0).

Test Statistics

	College major
Chi-Square	11.250[a]
df	3
Asymp. Sig.	.010

a. 0 cells (0.0%) have expected frequencies less than 5. The minimum expected cell frequency is 10.0.

df are the degrees of freedom. For the chi square goodness-of-fit test, they are calculated as $J - 1$ (i.e., one less than the number of categories).

"Asymp. Sig." is the observed probability value, *p*, for the chi square goodness-of-fit test. It is interpreted as: there is about a 1% probability of the sample proportions occurring by chance if the null hypothesis is really true (i.e., if the population proportions are 20, 40, 10, and 30).

"Chi-square" is the test statistic value and is calculated as:

$$\chi^2 = n\sum_{j=1}^{J}\frac{(p_j - \pi_j)^2}{\pi_j}$$

$$\chi^2 = 100\sum_{j=1}^{4}\left[\frac{(.25-.20)^2}{.20}+\frac{(.50-.40)^2}{.40}+\frac{(.10-.10)^2}{.10}+\frac{(.15-.30)^2}{.30}\right] = 11.25$$

college majors nationally. Follow-up tests to determine which cells are statistically different in the observed to expected proportions can be conducted by examining the standardized residuals. In this example, the standardized residuals were computed previously as follows:

$$R_{Education} = \frac{O-E}{\sqrt{E}} = \frac{25-20}{\sqrt{20}} = 1.118$$

$$R_{Arts\ \&Sciences} = \frac{O-E}{\sqrt{E}} = \frac{50-40}{\sqrt{40}} = 1.581$$

$$R_{Communication} = \frac{O-E}{\sqrt{E}} = \frac{10-10}{\sqrt{10}} = 0$$

$$R_{Business} = \frac{O-E}{\sqrt{E}} = \frac{15-30}{\sqrt{30}} = -2.739$$

The standardized residual for business is greater (in absolute value terms) than 1.96 (given $\alpha = .05$), and thus suggests that there are different observed to expected frequencies for students majoring in business at ICU compared to national estimates. This category is the one contributing most to the statistically significant chi-square statistic.

The effect size can be calculated as follows and, using Cohen's conventions, is interpreted as a small effect:

$$w = \frac{\chi^2}{N(J-1)} = \frac{11.25}{100(4-1)} = \frac{11.25}{300} = .0375$$

8.3.2 The Chi-Square Test of Association

Step 1. To conduct a chi-square test of association, you need two categorical variables (nominal and/or ordinal) whose frequencies you wish to associate. We will use the Ch8_Gambling.sav data with two nominal variables: education level and stance on gambling. To compute the chi-square test of association, go to "Analyze" in the top pulldown, then select "Descriptive Statistics," and then select the "Crosstabs" procedure (see the screenshot of Step 1 in Figure 8.6).

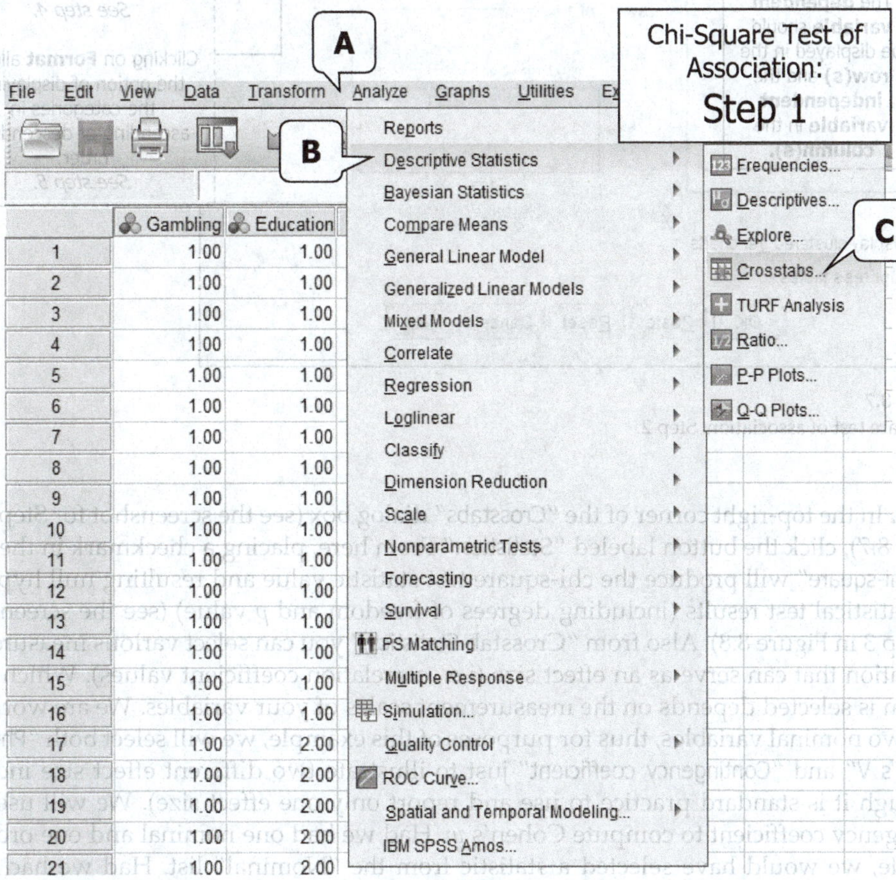

FIGURE 8.6
Chi-square test of association: Step 1.

Step 2. Select the *dependent variable* and move it into the "Row(s)" box by clicking the arrow key. Here we use "Stance on gambling" as the dependent variable (1 = support; 0 = not support). Then select the *independent variable* and move it into the "Column(s)" box. In this example, "Level of education" is the independent variable (1 = less than high school; 2 = high school; 3 = undergraduate; 4 = graduate) (see the screenshot of Step 2 in Figure 8.7).

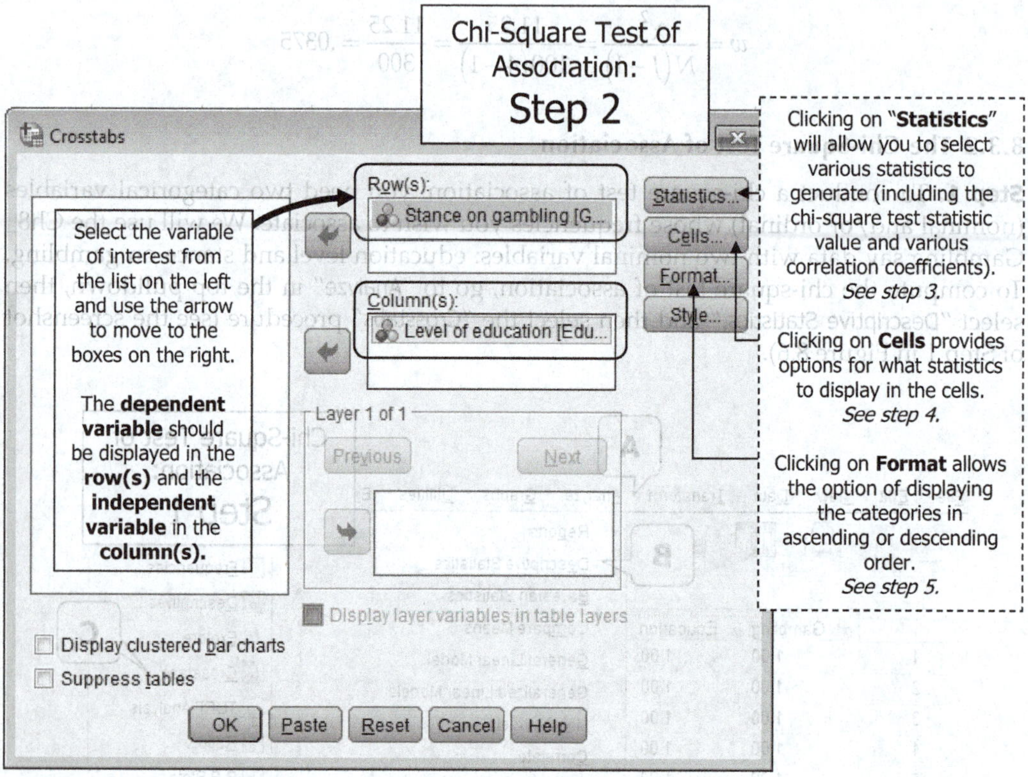

FIGURE 8.7
Chi-square test of association: Step 2.

Step 3. In the top-right corner of the "Crosstabs" dialog box (see the screenshot for Step 2 in Figure 8.7), click the button labeled "Statistics." From here, placing a checkmark in the box for "Chi-square" will produce the chi-square test statistic value and resulting null hypothesis statistical test results (including degrees of freedom and p value) (see the screenshot for Step 3 in Figure 8.8). Also from "Crosstab Statistics," you can select various measures of association that can serve as an effect size (i.e., correlation coefficient values). Which correlation is selected depends on the measurement scales of your variables. We are working with two nominal variables, thus for purposes of this example, we will select both "Phi and Cramer's V" and "Contingency coefficient" just to illustrate two different effect size indices (although it is standard practice to use and report only one effect size). We will use the contingency coefficient to compute Cohen's w. Had we had one nominal and one ordinal variable, we would have selected a statistic from the "Nominal" list. Had we had two

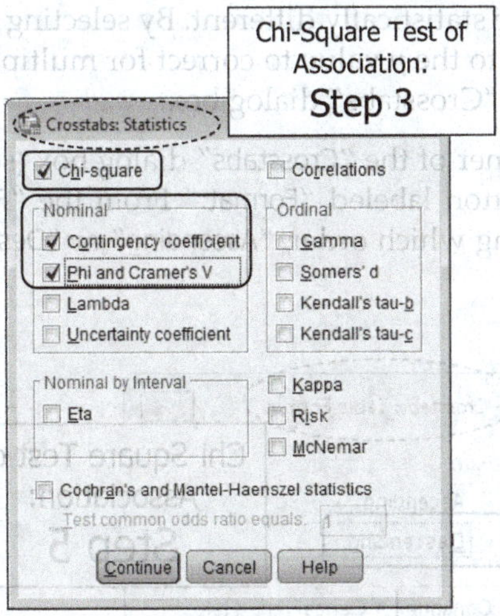

FIGURE 8.8
Chi-square test of association: Step 3.

ordinal variables, we would have selected a statistic from the "ordinal" list (see Chapter 10 for more on this!). Click "Continue" to return to the main "Crosstabs" dialog box.

Step 4. In the top-right corner of the "Crosstabs" dialog box (see the screenshot for Step 2 in Figure 8.7), click the button labeled "Cells." From the "Cells" dialog box, options are available for selecting counts and percentages (see the screenshot for Step 4 in Figure 8.9). We have requested "Observed" and "Expected" counts, "Column" percentages, and "Standardized" residuals. We will review the expected counts to determine if the assumption of five expected frequencies per cell is met. We will use the standardized residuals post hoc if the results of the test are statistically significant to determine which cell(s) are most influencing the chi-square value. We also select the *z* test to "Compare column proportions" and want to "adjust *p* values (Bonferroni method)." Selecting this option will produce pairwise comparisons of the column proportions and provides a subscript to denote which pairs of

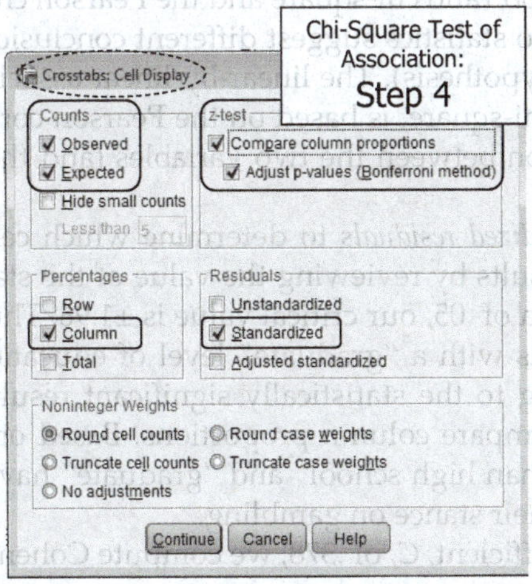

FIGURE 8.9
Chi-square test of association: Step 4.

columns for a given row are statistically different. By selecting to apply the Bonferroni, we are making the adjustment to the p value to correct for multiple comparisons. Click "Continue" to return to the main "Crosstabs" dialog box.

Step 5. In the top-right corner of the "Crosstabs" dialog box (see the screenshot for Step 2 in Figure 8.7), click the button labeled "Format." From the "Format" dialog box, options are available for determining which order, "Ascending" or "Descending," you want the row

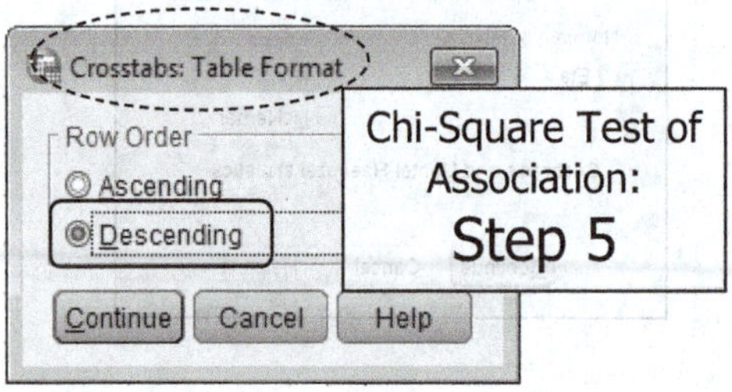

FIGURE 8.10
Chi-square test of association: Step 5.

values presented in the contingency table (we asked for descending in this example, such that row 1 was "gambling = 1" and row 2 was "gambling = 0") (see the screenshot for Step 5 in Figure 8.10). Click "Continue" to return to the main "Crosstabs" dialog box. Then click "OK" to run the analysis.

Interpreting the output. The output appears in Table 8.6 where the top box ("Case Processing Summary") provides information on the sample size and frequency of missing data (if any). The cross-tabulation table is next and provides the contingency table (i.e., counts, percentages, and standardized residuals). The "Chi-Square Tests" box gives the results of the procedure (including chi-square test statistic value labeled "Pearson Chi-Square," degrees of freedom, and p value labeled as "Asymp. Sig."). The likelihood ratio chi-square uses a different mathematical formula than the Pearson chi-square; however, for large sample sizes, the values for the likelihood ratio chi-square and the Pearson chi-square should be similar (and rarely should the two statistics suggest different conclusions in terms of rejecting or failing to reject the null hypothesis). The linear-by-linear association statistic, also known as the Mantel Haenszel chi-square, is based on the Pearson correlation and tests whether there is a linear association between the two variables (and thus should not be used for nominal variables).

We can use the *standardized residuals* to determine which cells are contributing to the statistically significant results by reviewing the value of the standardized residual to the z critical value. With alpha of .05, our critical value is ±1.96. Thus, based on the standardized residuals, individuals with a "graduate" level of education who "do not support" gambling are contributing to the statistically significant results. As you recall, we also requested the z test to compare column proportions. Based on the Bonferroni-corrected z test, we see both "less than high school" and "graduate" have statistically significantly different proportions of their stance on gambling.

For the contingency coefficient, C, of .378, we compute Cohen's w effect size as follows:

TABLE 8.6

SPSS Results for Gambling Example

Case Processing Summary

	Cases					
	Valid		Missing		Total	
	N	Percent	N	Percent	N	Percent
Stance on gambling * Level of education	80	100.0%	0	0.0%	80	100.0%

Review the standardized residuals to determine which cell(s) are contributing to the statistically significant chi-square value. Standardized residuals greater than an absolute value of 1.96 (critical value when alpha = .05) indicate that cell is contributing to the association between the variables. In this case, only one cell, **graduate/do not support,** has a standardized residual of 2.0 and thus is contributing to the relationship. *This is a slightly different result than reviewing the z test for the column comparisons (as denoted by the subscripts).*

Stance on gambling * Level of education Crosstabulation

Observed and expected counts

			Level of education				
			Less than high school	High school	Undergraduate	Graduate	Total
Stance on gambling	Support	Count	16a	13a, b	10a, b	5b	44
		Expected Count	11.0	11.0	11.0	11.0	44.0
		% within Level of education	80.0%	65.0%	50.0%	25.0%	55.0%
		Standardized Residual	1.5	.6	-.3	-1.8	
	Do Not Support	Count	4a	7a, b	10a, b	15b	36
		Expected Count	9.0	9.0	9.0	9.0	36.0
		% within Level of education	20.0%	35.0%	50.0%	75.0%	45.0%
		Standardized Residual	-1.7	-.7	.3	2.0	
Total		Count	20	20	20	20	80
		Expected Count	20.0	20.0	20.0	20.0	80.0
		% within Level of education	100.0%	100.0%	100.0%	100.0%	100.0%

Each subscript letter denotes a subset of Level of education categories whose column proportions do not differ significantly from each other at the .05 level.

When analyzing the percentages in the crosstab table, compare the categories of the dependent variable (rows) across the columns of the independent variable (columns). *For example, of respondents with a high school diploma, 65% support gambling.*

The subscript letters allow us to interpret column comparisons with 'a' denoting 'less than high school' and 'b' denoting 'high school.' (Not seen, but 'c' would be undergraduate and 'd' would be graduate). The column proportions are compared using a *z* test, with Bonferonni adjustment, for each pair of columns. As noted by the footnote, each subscript denotes a subset of education whose column proportion is NOT statistically different. For example, 10ab tells us that the proportion of undergraduates who support versus do not support gambling is *not* statistically significantly different than 'less than high school' and high school'. In other words, there are similar proportions of undergraduates, less than high school, and high school who support and who do not support gambling. As another example, 5b tells us that the proportion of graduates who support versus do not support gambling is not statistically significant different than the proportion of high school (i.e., subscript *b*).

(*continued*)

TABLE 8.6 (continued)

SPSS Results for Gambling Example

Chi-Square Tests

	Value	df	Asymptotic Significance (2-sided)
Pearson Chi-Square	13.333[a]	3	.004
Likelihood Ratio	13.969	3	.003
Linear-by-Linear Association	12.927	1	.000
N of Valid Cases	80		

a. 0 cells (0.0%) have expected count less than 5. The minimum expected count is 9.00.

The probability is less than 1% (see "Asymp. Sig.") that we would see these proportions by random chance if the proportions were all equal (i.e., if the null hypothesis were really true)

Degrees of freedom are computed as: (Rows – 1)(Columns – 1) = (2-1)(4-1) = 3

Zero cells have expected counts less than five, thus we have met this assumption of the chi-square test of association.

"Pearson Chi-square" is the test statistic value and is calculated as:

$$\chi^2 = \sum_{r=1}^{R}\sum_{c=1}^{C} n_c \frac{(p_{rc} - \pi_{r.})^2}{\pi_{r.}}$$

Symmetric Measures

		Value	Approximate Significance
Nominal by Nominal	Phi	.408	.004
	Cramer's V	.408	.004
	Contingency Coefficient	.378	.004
N of Valid Cases		80	

We have a **2 x 4** table thus **Cramer's *V*** is appropriate. It is statistically significant, and using Cohen's interpretations, reflects a moderate to large effect size.

The contingency coefficient can be used to compute Cohen's *w*, a measure of effect size as follows:

$$w = \sqrt{\frac{C^2}{1 - C^2}} = \sqrt{\frac{(.378)^2}{1 - (.378)^2}} = .408$$

$$w = \sqrt{\frac{C^2}{1-C^2}} = \sqrt{\frac{.378^2}{1-.378^2}} = \sqrt{\frac{.143}{1-.143}} = \sqrt{.167} = .408$$

Cohen's w of .408 would be interpreted as a moderate to large effect. Cramer's V, as seen in the output, is .408 and would be interpreted similarly—a moderate to large effect.

8.4 Computing Inferences About Proportions Involving the Chi-Square Distribution Using R

We will illustrate computing both the chi-square goodness-of-fit and chi-square test of association using **R**.

8.4.1 The Chi-Square Goodness-of-Fit Test

Next we consider **R** for the chi-square goodness-of-fit test. The scripts are provided within the blocks with additional annotation to assist in understanding how the commands work. Should you want to write reminder notes and annotation to yourself as you write the commands in **R** (and we highly encourage doing so), remember that any text that follows a hashtag (i.e., #) is annotation only and not part of the **R** script. Thus, you can write annotations directly into **R** with hashtags. We encourage this practice so that when you call up the commands in the future, you'll understand what the various lines of code are doing. You may think you'll remember what you did. However, trust us. There is a good chance that you won't. Thus, consider it best practice when using **R** to annotate heavily!

8.4.1.1 Reading Data Into R

```
getwd()
```

R is always pointed to a directory on your computer. To find out which directory it is pointed to, run this "get working directory" function. We will assume that we need to change the working directory, and will use the next line of code to set the working directory to the desired path.

```
setwd("E:/Folder")
```

To set the working directory, use the *setwd* function and change what is in quotation marks here to your file location. Also, if you are copying the directory name, it will copy in slashes. You will need to change the slash (i.e., \) to a forward slash (i.e., /). Note that you need your destination name within quotation marks in the parentheses.

```
Ch8_CollegeMajor <- read.csv("Ch8_CollegeMajor.csv")
```

The *read.csv* function reads our data into **R**. What's to the left of the <- will be what the data will be called in **R**. In this example, we're calling the R dataframe "Ch8_CollegeMajor." What's to the right of the <- tells **R** to find this particular .csv file. In this example, our file is called "Ch8_CollegeMajor.csv." Make sure the extension (i.e., .csv) is included in your script. Also note that the name of your file should be in quotation marks within the parentheses.

```
names(Ch8_CollegeMajor)
```

The *names* function will produce a list of variable names for each dataframe, as follows. This is a good check to make sure your data have been read in correctly.

```
[1] "Major"
```

```
View(Ch8_CollegeMajor)
```

The *View* function will let you view the dataset in spreadsheet format in RStudio.

```
Ch8_CollegeMajor$Major <- factor(Ch8_CollegeMajor$Major,
                labels = c("education", "A&S",
                "communication", "business"))
```

The *factor* function renames the variable "Major" that is in the "Ch8_CollegeMajor" dataframe as nominal with four groups or categories with labels of "education," "A&S," "communication," and "business."

```
summary(Ch8_CollegeMajor)
```

The *summary* function will produce basic descriptive statistics on all the variables in your dataframe. This is a great way to quickly check to see if the data have been read in correctly and to get a feel for your data, if you haven't already. The output from the summary statement for this dataframe looks like this. Because the variable "Major" is nominal, our output includes only the frequencies of cases within the categories.

```
           Major
education    :25
A&S          :50
communication:10
business     :15
```

FIGURE 8.11
Reading data into R.

8.4.1.2 Generating the Chi-Square Goodness-of-Fit Test

```
install.packages("MASS")
```

The *install.packages* function will install the *MASS* package that will be used to generate our test.

```
library(MASS)
```

Next, we load the *MASS* package into our library using the *library* function.

```
major.freq = table(Ch8_CollegeMajor$Major)
```

We use the *table* function to create a frequency table from our variable "Major" and call this table "major.freq."

```
major.freq
```

This command will let us view the frequency table we just created:

```
  education           A&S communication      business
         25            50            10            15
```

```
major.prob = c(.20,.40,.10,.30)
```

The *major.prob* function creates an object called "major.prob" that defines the hypothesized proportions for the four categories in our variable of 20%, 40%, 10%, and 30%.

```
Chi2_major <- chisq.test(major.freq, p = major.prob)
Chi2_major
```

The *chisq.test* function generates the chi-square goodness-of-fit test using the frequencies in our table (i.e., "major.freq") and the hypothesized values (via the command *p = major.prob*). *Chi2_major* creates an object of the results of our chi-square test. Running the line for *Chi2_major* will present the output in the console in RStudio.

Our output looks like this, where chi-square = 11.25, with 3 degrees of freedom, and a statistically significant finding, $p = .01$.

```
        Chi-squared test for given probabilities

data: major.freq
X-squared = 11.25, df = 3, p-value = 0.01045
```

```
Chi2_major$expected
```

Should we need a reminder on our expected frequencies, we can run this script that uses our chi square results (i.e., *Chi2_major*) and the respective expected frequencies.

```
    education            A&S communication         business
           20                  40          10            30
```

FIGURE 8.12
Generating the chi-square goodness-of-fit test.

8.4.2 The Chi-Square Test of Association

Next we consider **R** for the chi-square test of association. The **R** script includes only those lines of text that are included in the boxes. The remainder is annotation, provided here to help you understand what the various lines of code are doing.

8.4.2.1 Reading Data Into R

```
getwd()
```

R is always pointed to a directory on your computer. To find out which directory it is pointed to, run this "get working directory" function. We will assume that we need to change the working directory, and will use the next line of code to set the working directory to the desired path.

```
setwd("E:/Folder")
```

To set the working directory, use the *setwd* function and change what is in quotation marks here to your file location. Also, if you are copying the directory name, it will copy in slashes. You will need to change the slash (i.e., \) to a forward slash (i.e., /). Note that you need your destination name within quotation marks in the parentheses.

```
Ch8_Gambling <- read.csv("Ch8_Gambling.csv")
```

The *read.csv* function reads our data into **R**. What's to the left of the <- will be what the data will be called in **R**. In this example, we're calling the **R** dataframe "Ch8_Gambling." What's to the right of the <- tells **R** to find this particular .csv file. In this example, our file is called "Ch8_Gambling.csv." Make sure the extension (i.e., .csv) is there. Also note that you need this in quotation marks.

```
names(Ch8_Gambling)
```

The *names* function will produce a list of variable names for each dataframe, as follows. This is a good check to make sure your data have been read in correctly.

```
[1] "Gambling" "Education"
```

```
Ch8_Gambling$Gambling <- factor(Ch8_Gambling$Gambling,
                         labels = c("do not support",
                                    "support"))
```

The *factor* function renames the variable "Gambling" as a categorical variable and defines the levels of gambling within our dataframe as "do not support" and "support."

```
Ch8_Gambling$Education <- factor(Ch8_Gambling$Education,
                          labels = c("less than high school",
                                     "high school",
                                     "undergraduate",
                                     "graduate"))
```

The *factor* function renames the variable "Education" as a categorical variable and defines the four levels of education within our dataframe.

```
View(Ch8_Gambling)
```

The *View* function will let you view the dataset in spreadsheet format in RStudio.

```
levels(Ch8_Gambling$Gambling)
levels(Ch8_Gambling$Education)
```

The *levels* function provides the names of the categories within each of our variables.

```
# levels(Ch8_Gambling$Gambling)
[1] "do not support" "support"

# levels(Ch8_Gambling$Education)
[1] "less than high school" "high school"
[3] "undergraduate"         "graduate"
```

FIGURE 8.13
Reading data into **R**.

8.4.2.2 Generating the Chi-Square Test of Association

```
Chi2_gamble <- chisq.test(Ch8_Gambling$Gambling,
Ch8_Gambling$Education)
```

The *chisq.test* function generates the chi-square test of association with variables "Gambling" and "Education" from the "Ch8_Gambling" dataframe. It will name the object "Chi2_gamble."

```
Chi2_gamble
```

This script will generate the output from the chi-square test of association, which includes the following. We see we have a chi-squared value of 13.33 with 3 degrees of freedom. The *p* value is approximately .004. *Thus, we have a statistically significant relationship between the variables*. In Chapter 10, we will see how to generate measures of the correlation coefficient that can be used as indices of effect size for the chi-square test of association.

```
        Pearson's Chi-squared test

data: Ch8_Gambling$Gambling and Ch8_Gambling$Education
X-squared = 13.3333, df = 3, p-value = 0.003969
```

```
round(Chi2_gamble$residuals,3)
```

We can request standardized residuals to see which cells are contributing to the statistically significant chi-square using this script. *Standardized residuals greater than an absolute value of 1.96 (i.e., the critical value when α = .05) are contributing to the statistically significant chi-square*. The only input that we include in the command is "Chi2gamble" to define the object for which we want the residual values. We see that category 4 ("graduate education") has a standardized residual for stance on gambling of 0 ("do not support") of 2.00, thus is contributing to the association between the variables.

```
                      Ch8_Gambling$Education
Ch8_Gambling$Gambling less than high school   high school
       do not support                -1.667        -0.667
       support                        1.508         0.603
```

```
                        Ch8_Gambling$Education
Ch8_Gambling$Gambling undergraduate              graduate
     do not support          0.333               2.000
     support                -0.302              -1.809
```

```
Chi2_gamble$expected
```

Should we need a reminder on our expected frequencies, we can run this script that uses our chi-square results (i.e., *Chi2_gamble*) and the respective expected frequencies.

```
                        Ch8_Gambling$Education
Ch8_Gambling$Gambling less than high school high school
     do not support                       9           9
     support                             11          11

                        Ch8_Gambling$Education
Ch8_Gambling$Gambling undergraduate graduate
     do not support               9        9
     support                     11       11
```

FIGURE 8.14
Generating the chi-square test of association.

8.5 Data Screening

Because it is a nonparametric procedure, fewer assumptions are associated with chi-square tests, and only one is actually tested when the procedure is generated (that being the assumption of expected frequencies). Examination of the assumptions for the examples have been provided in previous sections and presented with the statistical software computer output.

8.6 Power Using G*Power

A priori power can be determined using specialized software (e.g., Power and Precision, Ex-Sample, G*Power) or power tables (e.g., Cohen, 1988), as previously described. However, because standard statistical software does not provide power information for the results of the chi-square test of association just conducted, let us use G*Power to compute the post hoc power of our test.

8.6.1 Post Hoc Power for the Chi-Square Test of Association Using G*Power

The first thing that must be done when using G*Power for computing post hoc power is to select the correct test family. In our case, we conducted a chi-square test of association; therefore, the toggle button must be used to change the test family to χ^2 (see the screenshot in Figure 8.15). Next, we need to select the appropriate statistical test. We toggle to "Goodness-of-fit tests: Contingency tables." The "Type of power analysis" then needs to be selected. To compute post hoc power, we select "Post hoc: Compute achieved power—given α, sample size, and effect size."

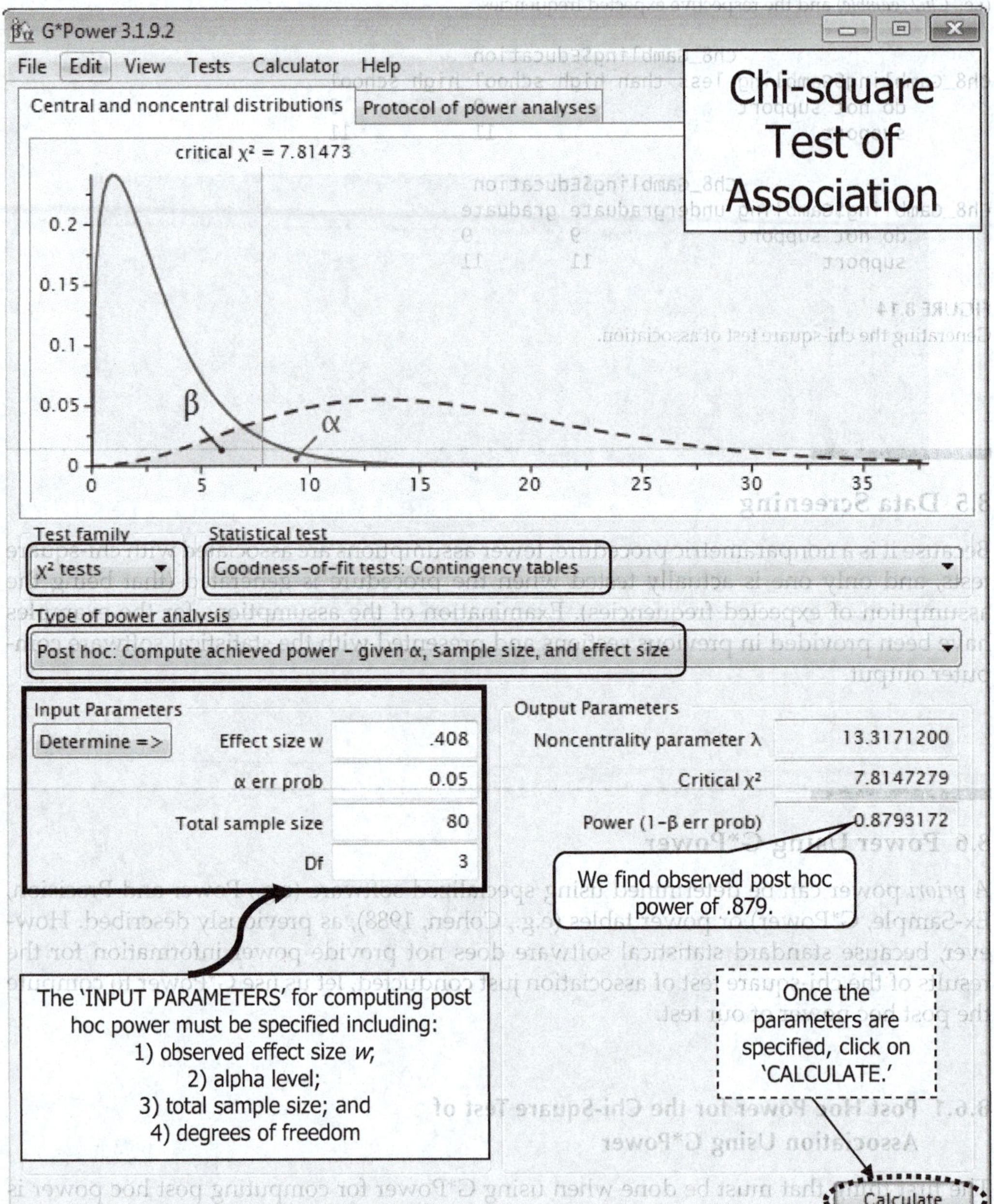

FIGURE 8.15
Chi-square test of association post hoc power.

The "Input Parameters" must then be specified. The first parameter is specification of the effect size w (this was computed by hand from the contingency coefficient and $w = .408$). The alpha level we tested at was .05, the sample size was 80, and the degrees of freedom were 3. Once the parameters are specified, simply click "Calculate" to generate the achieved power statistics.

The "Output Parameters" provide the relevant statistics given the input just specified. In this example, we were interested in determining post hoc power given a two-tailed test, with an observed effect size of .408, an alpha level of .05, and sample size of 80. Based on those criteria, the post hoc power was approximately .88. In other words, with a sample size of 80, testing at an alpha level of .05, and observing a moderate to large effect of .408, the power of our test was .88; thus, the probability of rejecting the null hypothesis when it is really false is 88%, which is very high power. Keep in mind that conducting power analysis *a priori* is recommended so that you avoid a situation where, post hoc, you find that the sample size was not sufficient to reach the desired level of power (given the observed effect size and alpha level).

8.7 Recommendations

Box 8.1 summarizes the tests reviewed in this chapter and the key points related to each (including the distribution involved and recommendations for when to use the test).

BOX 8.1 Characteristics and Recommendations for Inferences About Proportions

Test	Distribution	When to Use
Inferences about a single proportion (akin to a one-sample mean test)	Unit normal, z	• To determine if the sample proportion differs from a hypothesized proportion • One variable, nominal or ordinal in scale
Inferences about two independent proportions (akin to the independent t test)	Unit normal, z	• To determine if the population proportion for one group differs from the population proportion for a second independent group • Two variables, both nominal or ordinal in scale
Inferences about two dependent proportions (akin to the dependent t test)	Unit normal, z	• To determine if the population proportion for one group is different than the population proportion for a second dependent group • Two variables of the same measure, both nominal or ordinal in scale
Chi-square goodness-of-fit test	Chi-square	• To determine if observed proportions differ from what would be expected *a priori* • One variable, nominal or ordinal in scale
Chi-square test of association	Chi-square	• To determine association/relationship between two variables based on observed proportions • Two variables, both nominal or ordinal in scale

8.8 Research Question Template and Example Write-Up

We finish the chapter by presenting templates and example write-ups for our examples. First we present an example paragraph detailing the results of the chi-square goodness-of-fit test and then follow this by the chi-square test of association.

8.8.1 Chi-Square Goodness-of-Fit Test

Recall that our graduate research assistant, Challie Lenge, was working with Dr. Senata, the Director of the Undergraduate Services Office at Ivy Covered University (ICU), to assist in analyzing the proportions of students enrolled in undergraduate majors. Challie's task was to assist Dr. Senata with writing her research question (*Are the sample proportions of undergraduate student college majors at ICU in the same proportions as those nationally?*) and generating the statistical test of inference to answer her question. Challie suggested a chi-square goodness-of-fit test as the test of inference. A template for writing a research question for a chi-square goodness-of-fit test follows:

Are the sample proportions of [units in categories] in the same proportions of those [identify the source to which the comparison is being made]?

It may be helpful to include in the results of the chi-square goodness-of-fit test information on an examination of the extent to which the assumptions were met (recall there are two assumptions: independence and expected frequency of at least five per cell). This assists the reader in understanding that you were thorough in data screening prior to conducting the test of inference.

A chi-square goodness-of-fit test was conducted to determine if the sample proportions of undergraduate student college majors at Ivy Covered University (ICU) were in the same proportions of those reported nationally. The test was conducted using an alpha of .05. The null hypothesis was that the proportions would be as follows: .20 education, .40 arts and sciences, .10 communications, and .30 business. The assumption of an expected frequency of at least five per cell was met. The assumption of independence was met via random selection.

There was a statistically significant difference between the proportion of undergraduate majors at ICU and those reported nationally ($\chi^2 = 11.250$, $df = 3$, $p = .010$). Thus the null hypothesis that the proportions of undergraduate majors at ICU parallel those expected at the national level was rejected at the .05 level of significance. The effect size, w, $\left(\chi^2 / \left[(N)(J-1)\right]\right)$ was .0375, and interpreted using Cohen's guide (1988) as a very small effect.

Follow-up tests were conducted by examining the standardized residuals. The standardized residual for Business was −2.739 and thus suggests that there are different observed to expected frequencies for students majoring in Business at ICU compared to national estimates. Therefore, Business is the college major that is contributing most to the statistically significant chi-square statistic.

8.8.2 Chi-Square Test of Association

Addie Venture, our graduate research assistant, was working with Dr. Walnut, a lobbyist interested in examining the association between education level and stance on gambling. Addie was tasked with assisting Dr. Walnut in writing his research question (*Is there an association between level of education and stance on gambling?*) and generating the test of inference to answer his question. Addie suggested a chi-square test of association as the test of inference. A template for writing a research question for a chi-square test of association follows:

Is there an association between [independent variable] and [dependent variable]?

It may be helpful to include in the results of the chi-square test of association information on the extent to which the assumptions were met (recall there are two assumptions: independence and expected frequency of at least five per cell). This assists the reader in understanding that you were thorough in data screening prior to conducting the test of inference. It is also desirable to include a measure of effect size. Given the contingency coefficient, *C*, of .378, we computed Cohen's *w* effect size to be .408, which would be interpreted as a moderate to large effect.

A chi-square test of association was conducted to determine if there was a relationship between level of education and stance on gambling. The test was conducted using an alpha of .05. It was hypothesized that there was an association between the two variables. The assumption of an expected frequency of at least five per cell was met. The assumption of independence was not met because the respondents were not randomly selected; thus, there is an increased probability of a Type I error.

From Table 8.6 we can see from the row marginals that 55% of the individuals overall support gambling. However, lower levels of education have a much higher percentage of support, while the highest level of education has a much lower percentage of support. Thus, there appears to be an association or relationship between gambling stance and level of education. This is subsequently supported statistically from the chi-square test ($\chi^2 = 13.333$, $df = 3$, $p = .004$). Thus, the null hypothesis that there is no association between stance on gambling and level of education was rejected at the .05 level of significance. Examination of the standardized residuals suggests that respondents who hold a graduate degree are significantly more likely not to support gambling (standardized residual = 2.0) as compared to all other respondents. Further examination of column proportions using a Bonferroni-corrected *z* test suggests that individuals with less than a high school degree are statistically significantly different in proportions relative to all other education levels, proportions of those with a high school degree are also statistically different than undergraduate and graduate, and proportions of undergraduate and graduate also differ. The effect size, Cohen's *w*, was computed to be .408, which is interpreted to be a moderate to large effect (Cohen, 1988).

8.9 Additional Resources

In this chapter we described a third inferential testing situation, testing hypotheses about proportions. A number of resources have been provided throughout. For additional coverage of tests of proportion and analyzing categorical data, you may wish to consider Agresti

(2013), among others. If you are interested in deeper coverage of chi-square, in particular, you may wish to consider Voinov, Balakrishnan, and Nikulin (2013) (which also includes an historical account and many other chi-square tests that are beyond the scope of this text) or Greenwood and Nikulin (1996).

Problems

Conceptual Problems

1. How many degrees of freedom are there in a 5 × 7 contingency table when the chi-square test of association is used?
   a. 12
   b. 24
   c. 30
   d. 35
2. True or false? The more that two independent sample proportions differ, all else being equal, the smaller the z test statistic.
3. True or false? The null hypothesis is a numerical statement about an unknown parameter.
4. True or false? In testing the null hypothesis that the proportion is .50, the critical value of z increases as degrees of freedom increase.
5. When the chi-square test statistic for a test of association is less than the corresponding critical value, I assert that I should reject the null hypothesis. Am I correct?
6. True or false? Other things being equal, the larger the sample size, the smaller the value of s_p.
7. In the chi-square test of association, as the difference between the observed and expected proportions increases:
   a. the critical value for chi-square increases.
   b. the critical value for chi-square decreases.
   c. the likelihood of rejecting the null hypothesis decreases.
   d. the likelihood of rejecting the null hypothesis increases.
8. When the hypothesized value of the population proportion lies outside of the confidence interval around a single sample proportion, I assert that the researcher should reject the null hypothesis. Am I correct?
9. Statisticians at a theme park want to know if the same proportions of visitors select the Jungle Safari as their favorite ride as compared to the Mountain Rollercoaster. They sample 150 visitors and collect data on one variable: favorite ride (two categories: Jungle Safari and Mountain Rollercoaster). Which statistical procedure is most appropriate to use to test the hypothesis?
   a. Chi-square goodness-of-fit test
   b. Chi-square test of association

10. Sophie is a reading teacher. She is researching the following question: Is there a relationship between a child's favorite genre of book and their socioeconomic status? She collects data from 35 children on two variables: (a) favorite genre of book (two categories: fiction, nonfiction) and (b) socioeconomic status (three categories: low, middle, high). Which statistical procedure is most appropriate to use to test the hypothesis?
    a. Chi-square goodness-of-fit test
    b. Chi-square test of association
11. Which of the following are assumptions for the chi-square test of association? Select all that apply.
    a. Balanced design
    b. Expected frequency of 5 per cell
    c. Independence
    d. Normality
12. Which of the following cannot be used when testing inferences about a single proportion?
    a. Counts
    b. Frequencies
    c. Means
    d. Relative frequency
13. After computing a chi-square test of association, the researcher has computed Cohen's w and found $w = .28$. What interpretation can the researcher make based on this using Cohen's subjective standards?
    a. Small effect
    b. Moderate effect
    c. Moderate to large effect
    d. Large effect
14. Which of the following are assumptions for the chi-square goodness-of-fit test? Select all that apply.
    a. Balanced design
    b. Expected frequency of 5 per cell
    c. Independence
    d. Normality

Answers to Conceptual Problems

1. **b** ($4 \times 6 = 24$)
3. **True** (By definition, the null hypothesis is a numerical statement about an unknown parameter.)
5. **No** (Reject when test statistic exceeds critical value.)
7. **d** (As the difference between the observed and expected proportions increases, the chi-square test statistic increases, and thus we are more likely to reject.)
9. **a** (Chi-square goodness-of-fit test given that there is only one variable and the goal is to determine if the proportions within the categories of that variable are the same.)

11. b and c (The two assumptions for chi-square tests are independence of observations and expected frequency of 5 per cell.)
13. b (Cohen's w values around .30 are interpreted to be a medium effect.)

Computational Problems

1. For a random sample of 40 widgets produced by the Acme Widget Company, 30 successes and 10 failures are observed. Test the following hypotheses at the .05 level of significance:

$$H_0: \pi = .60$$
$$H_1: \pi > .60$$

2. The following data are calculated for two independent random samples of male and female teenagers, respectively, on whether they expect to attend graduate school: $n_1 = 48$, $p_1 = 18 / 48$, $n_2 = 52$, $p_2 = 33 / 52$. Test the following hypotheses at the .05 level of significance:

$$H_0: \pi_1 - \pi_2 = 0$$
$$H_1: \pi_1 - \pi_2 \neq 0$$

3. The following frequencies of successes and failures are obtained for two dependent random samples measured at the pretest and posttest of a weight training program:

	Pretest	
Posttest	**Success**	**Failure**
Failure	18	30
Success	33	19

Test the following hypotheses at the .05 level of significance:

$$H_0: \pi_1 - \pi_2 = 0$$
$$H_1: \pi_1 - \pi_2 \neq 0$$

4. A chi-square goodness-of-fit test is to be conducted with six categories of professions to determine whether the sample proportions of those supporting the current government differ from *a priori* national proportions. The chi-square test statistic is equal to 16.00. Determine the result of this test by looking up the critical value and making a statistical decision, using $\alpha = .01$.
5. A chi-square goodness-of-fit test is to be conducted to determine whether the sample proportions of families in Florida who select various schooling options (five categories: "home school," "public school," "public charter school," "private school," and "other") differ from the proportions reported nationally. The chi-square test statistic is equal to 9.00. Determine the result of this test by looking up the critical value and making a statistical decision, using $\alpha = .05$.

6. A random sample of 30 voters was classified according to their general political beliefs (liberal vs. conservative) and also according to whether they voted for or against the incumbent representative in their town. The results were placed into the following contingency table:

	Liberal	Conservative
Yes	10	5
No	5	10

Use the chi-square test of association to determine whether political belief is independent of voting behavior at the .05 level of significance.

7. A random sample of 40 kindergarten children was classified according to whether they attended at least 1 year of preschool prior to entering kindergarten and also according to gender. The results were placed into the following contingency table:

	Boy	Girl
Preschool	12	10
No preschool	8	10

Use the chi-square test of association to determine whether enrollment in preschool is independent of gender at the .05 level of significance.

8. For a random sample of 30 athletes who completed an optional preseason training program, 80% (n = 24) were retained on their team and the rest were released. Test the following hypotheses, that the proportion retained was different than 75%, at the .05 level of significance:

$$H_0: \pi = .75$$
$$H_1: \pi \neq .75$$

9. A researcher followed a sample of 1000 registered nurses after their graduation and collected data on the type of employer and type of position in which they were employed. Using the Ch8_nurses.sav or Ch8-nurses.csv data, compute a chi-square test of association at alpha of .05 to determine the relationship between position and employer.

Answers to Computational Problems

1. $p = .75$, $z = 1.936$, critical values = −1.96 and +1.96, thus fail to reject H_0.
3. $z = -.1644$, critical values = −1.96 and +1.96, thus fail to reject H_0.
5. critical value = 9.48773, fail to reject H_0 as the test statistic does not exceed the critical value.
7. $\chi^2 = .404$, critical value = 3.84, thus fail to reject H_0.
9. Using SPSS, the crosstab of position by employer is:

Position * Employer Crosstabulation

Count

		Employer			
		General practitioner	Hospital	Traveling nurse	Total
Position	General care	190	238	72	500
	Special care	188	238	74	500
Total		378	476	146	1000

The results of the chi-square test are not statistically significant ($\chi^2 = .038$, $df = 2$, $p = .981$). We fail to reject the null hypothesis that there is no association between position and employer.

Chi-Square Tests

	Value	*df*	Asymptotic Significance (2-sided)
Pearson Chi-Square	.038[a]	2	.981
Likelihood Ratio	.038	2	.981
Linear-by-Linear Association	.034	1	.854
N of Valid Cases	1000		

a. 0 cells (0.0%) have expected count less than 5. The minimum expected count is 73.00.

Interpretive Problem

1. The survey1 dataset, which is accessible from the website, can be analyzed in several different ways, as there are several categorical variables. Here are some examples for the tests described in this chapter.
   a. Conduct a test of a single proportion: Is the sample proportion of females equal to .50?
   b. Conduct a test of two independent proportions: Is there a difference between the sample proportion of females who are right-handed and the sample proportion of males who are right-handed?
   c. Conduct a test of two dependent proportions: Is there a difference between the sample proportion of student's mothers who are right-handed and the sample proportion of student's fathers who are right-handed?
   d. Conduct a chi-square goodness-of-fit test: Do the sample proportions for the political view categories differ from their expected proportions (very liberal = .10, liberal = .15, middle of the road = .50, conservative = .15, very conservative = .10)? Determine if the assumptions of the test are met. Determine and interpret the corresponding effect size.
   e. Conduct a chi-square goodness-of-fit test to determine if there are similar proportions of respondents who can (vs. cannot) tell the difference between Pepsi and Coke. Determine if the assumptions of the test are met. Determine and interpret the corresponding effect size.

f. Conduct a chi-square test of association: Is there an association between political view and gender? Determine if the assumptions of the test are met. Determine and interpret the corresponding effect size.

g. Compute a chi-square test of association to examine the relationship between if a person smokes and their political view. Determine if the assumptions of the test are met. Determine and interpret the corresponding effect size.

2. Using the Integrated Postsecondary Education Data System dataset (IPEDS2017), which is accessible from the website, conduct a chi-square test of association to determine if there are similar proportions of institutions by level of institution [LEVEL] and control [CONTROL]. Determine if the assumptions of the test are met. Determine and interpret the corresponding effect size.

3. Using the Integrated Postsecondary Education Data System dataset (IPEDS2017), which is accessible from the website, conduct a chi-square goodness-of-fit test to determine if there are similar proportions of institutions by degree-granting status [DEGGRANT]. Determine if the assumptions of the test are met. Determine and interpret the corresponding effect size.

9

Inferences About Variances

Chapter Outline

Key Concepts

1. Sampling distributions of the variance
2. The *F* distribution
3. Homogeneity of variance tests

In the previous three chapters we looked at testing inferences about means (Chapters 6 and 7) and about proportions (Chapter 8). In this chapter we examine inferential tests involving variances. Tests of variances are useful in two applications: (a) as an inferential test by itself and (b) as a test of the homogeneity of variance assumption for another procedure (e.g., *t* test, analysis of variance).

First, a researcher may want to perform inferential tests on variances for their own sake, in the same fashion that we described for the one- and two-sample *t* tests on means. For example, we may want to assess whether the variance of undergraduates at Ivy-Covered University on an intelligence measure is the same as the theoretically derived variance of 225 (from when the test was developed and normed). In other words, is the variance at a particular university greater than or less than 225? As another example, we may want to determine whether the variances on an intelligence measure are consistent across two or more groups; for example, is the variance of the intelligence measure at Ivy-Covered University different from that at The Greatest University?

Second, for some procedures, such as the independent *t* test (Chapter 7) and the analysis of variance (Chapter 11), it is assumed that the variances for two or more independent samples are equal (known as the homogeneity of variance assumption). Thus, we may want to use an inferential test of variances to assess whether this assumption has been violated or not. The following inferential tests of variance are covered in this chapter: (a) testing whether a single variance is different from a hypothesized value; (b) testing whether two dependent variances are different; and (c) testing whether two or more independent variances are different. We utilize many of the foundational concepts covered in Chapters 6, 7, and 8. New concepts to be discussed include the following: the sampling distributions of the variance, the *F* distribution, and homogeneity of variance tests. Our objectives are that by the end of this chapter, you will be able to (a) understand the basic concepts underlying tests of variances, (b) select the appropriate test, and (c) determine and interpret the results from the appropriate test.

9.1 Inferences About Variances and How They Work

As you remember, Oso Wyse is one of four extraordinarily talented graduate students who is working in the stats lab. Oso and colleagues have had the opportunity to work on quite a number of exciting statistical projects. We revisit the group again, with Oso getting ready to embark on another stats journey.

Another call has been fielded by the stats lab for assistance with statistical analysis. This time, it is Dr. Abraham, an elementary assistant principal within the community. Dr. Abraham shares with Oso that she is conducting a teacher research project related to achievement of first grade students at her school. Dr. Abraham wants to determine if the variances of the achievement scores differ when children begin school in the fall as compared to when they end school in the spring. Oso suggests the following research question: *Are the variances of achievement scores for first grade children the same in the fall as compared to the spring?* Oso suggests a test of variance as the test of inference. His task is then to assist Dr. Abraham in generating the test of inference to answer her research question.

This section deals with concepts for testing inferences about variances, in particular, the sampling distributions underlying such tests. Subsequent sections deal with several inferential tests of variances. Although the sampling distribution of the mean is a normal distribution (Chapters 6 and 7), and the sampling distribution of a proportion is either a normal or chi-square distribution (Chapter 8), the **sampling distribution of a variance** *is a chi-square distribution for a single variance, a t distribution for two dependent variances, or an F distribution for two or more independent variances*. Although we have already discussed the *t* distribution in Chapter 6 and the chi-square distribution in Chapter 8, we need to discuss the *F* distribution (named in honor of the famous statistician Sir Ronald A. Fisher) in some detail here.

9.1.1 Characteristics of the *F* Distribution

Like the normal, *t*, and chi-square distributions, the ***F* distribution** is really a family of distributions. Also, like the *t* and chi-square distributions, the *F* distribution family members depend on the number of degrees of freedom represented. However, unlike any previously discussed distribution, the *F* distribution family members actually depend on a *combination of two different degrees of freedom, one for the numerator and one for the denominator*. The reason is that the *F* distribution is a *ratio of two chi-square variables*. To be more precise, *F* with ν_1 degrees of freedom for the numerator and ν_2 degrees of freedom for the denominator is actually a ratio of the following chi-square variables:

$$F_{\upsilon_1,\upsilon_2} = \frac{\chi^2_{\upsilon_1}/\upsilon_1}{\chi^2_{\upsilon_2}/\upsilon_2}$$

For example, an *F* distribution for a numerator with 1 degree of freedom and a denominator with 10 degrees of freedom is denoted by $F_{1,10}$.

In terms of distributional shape, the *F* distribution is generally positively skewed and leptokurtic in shape (like the chi-square distribution) and has a mean of $\upsilon_2/(\upsilon_2 - 2)$ when $\nu_2 > 2$ (where ν_2 represents the denominator degrees of freedom). A few examples of the *F* distribution are shown in Figure 9.1 for the following pairs of degrees of freedom (i.e., numerator, denominator): $F_{10,10}$, $F_{20,20}$, and $F_{40,40}$.

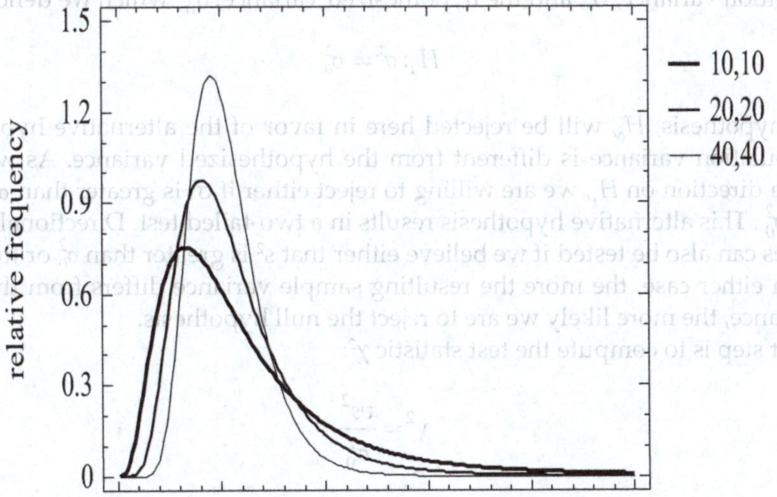

FIGURE 9.1
Several members of the family of *F* distributions.

Critical values for several levels of alpha of the *F* distribution at various combinations of degrees of freedom are given in Table A.4 in the Appendix. The numerator degrees of freedom are given in the *columns* of the table (v_1) and the denominator degrees of freedom are shown in the *rows* of the table (v_2). Only the upper-tail critical values are given in the table (e.g., percentiles of .90, .95, .99 for α = .10, .05, .01, respectively). The reason is that most inferential tests involving the *F* distribution are *one-tailed tests* using the upper-tail critical region. Thus to find the upper-tail critical value for ${}_{.05}F_{1,10}$, look for the α = .05 heading, in the first column of values for that heading for $v_1 = 1$, and where it intersects with the 10th row of values for $v_2 = 10$. There you should find ${}_{.05}F_{1,10} = 4.96$.

9.1.1.1 Inferences About a Single Variance

In our initial inferential testing situation for variances, the researcher would like to know whether the population variance is equal to some hypothesized variance or not—this represents a nondirectional, or two-tailed, test. First, the hypotheses to be evaluated for detecting whether a population variance differs from a hypothesized variance are as follows. The *nondirectional null hypothesis*, H_0, is that there is no difference between the population variance σ^2 and the hypothesized variance σ_0^2, which we denote as

$$H_0: \sigma^2 = \sigma_0^2$$

Here, there is no difference, or a "null" difference, between the population variance and the hypothesized variance. For example, if we are seeking to determine whether the variance on an intelligence measure at Ivy-Covered University is different from the overall adult population, then a reasonable hypothesized value would be 225, as this is the theoretically derived variance for the adult population.

The *nondirectional, scientific, or alternative hypothesis*, H_1, is that there is a difference between the population variance, σ^2, and the hypothesized variance, σ_0^2, which we denote as

$$H_1: \sigma^2 \neq \sigma_0^2$$

The null hypothesis, H_0, will be rejected here in favor of the alternative hypothesis, H_1, if the population variance is different from the hypothesized variance. As we have not specified a direction on H_1, we are willing to reject either if σ^2 is greater than σ_0^2 or if σ^2 is less than σ_0^2. This alternative hypothesis results in a two-tailed test. Directional alternative hypotheses can also be tested if we believe either that s^2 is greater than σ_0^2 or that σ^2 is less than σ_0^2. In either case, the more the resulting sample variance differs from the hypothesized variance, the more likely we are to reject the null hypothesis.

The next step is to compute the test statistic χ^2:

$$\chi^2 = \frac{vs^2}{\sigma_0^2}$$

where s^2 is the sample variance and $\nu = n - 1$. The test statistic χ^2 is then compared to a critical value(s) from the chi-square distribution. For a two-tailed test, the critical values are denoted as ${}_{\alpha/2}\chi_\nu^2$ and ${}_{1-\alpha/2}\chi_\nu^2$ and are found in Table A.3 in the Appendix (recall that unlike *z* and *t* critical values, two unique c^2 critical values must be found from the table because the χ^2 distribution is not symmetric like *z* or *t*). If the test statistic χ^2 falls into either critical region, then we reject H_0; otherwise, we fail to reject H_0. For a one-tailed test, the critical value is denoted as ${}_{\alpha}\chi^2_{\nu}$ for the alternative hypothesis $H_1: \sigma^2 < \sigma_0^2$ and as ${}_{1-\alpha/2}\chi^2_{\nu}$ for the alternative hypothesis $H_1: \sigma^2 > \sigma_0^2$. If the test statistic χ^2 falls into the appropriate critical region, then we reject H_0; otherwise, we fail to reject H_0.

For the two-tailed test, a (1 – α)% confidence interval can also be examined and is formed as follows. The lower limit of the confidence interval is computed as:

$$\frac{\nu s^2}{{}_{1-\alpha/2}\chi^2_{\nu}}$$

The upper limit of the confidence interval is computed as:

$$\frac{\nu s^2}{{}_{\alpha/2}\chi^2_{\nu}}$$

If the confidence interval contains the hypothesized value σ_0^2 then the conclusion is to *fail to reject* H_0; otherwise, we *reject* H_0.

9.1.1.1.1 An Example

Now consider an example to illustrate use of the test of a single variance. We follow the basic steps for hypothesis testing that we applied in previous chapters. These steps include:

1. State the null and alternative hypotheses.
2. Select the level of significance (i.e., alpha, α).
3. Calculate the test statistic value.
4. Make a statistical decision (reject or fail to reject H_0).

A researcher at the esteemed Ivy-Covered University is interested in determining whether the population variance in intelligence at the university is different from the norm-developed hypothesized variance of 225. Thus, a nondirectional, two-tailed alternative hypothesis is utilized. If the null hypothesis is rejected, this would indicate that the intelligence level at Ivy-Covered University is more or less diverse or variable than the norm. If the null hypothesis is not rejected, this would indicate that the intelligence level at Ivy-Covered University is as equally diverse or variable as the norm of 225.

The researcher takes a random sample of 101 undergraduates from throughout the university and computes a sample variance of 149. The test statistic χ^2 is computed as follows:

$$\chi^2 = \frac{\nu s^2}{\sigma_0^2} = \frac{100(149)}{225} = 66.2222$$

From the Table A.3 in the Appendix and using an alpha level of .05, we determine the critical values to be ${}_{.025}\chi^2_{100} = 74.2219$ and ${}_{.975}\chi^2_{100} = 129.561$. Because the test statistic does exceed one of the critical values by falling into the lower-tail critical region (i.e., 66.2222 < 74.2219), our decision is to *reject* H_0. *Our conclusion then is that the variance of the undergraduates at Ivy-Covered University is different from the hypothesized variance value of 225.*

The 95% confidence interval for the example is computed as follows. The lower limit of the confidence interval is computed as:

$$\frac{\nu s^2}{{}_{1-\alpha/2}\chi^2_{\nu}} = \frac{100(149)}{129.561} = 115.0037$$

and the upper limit of the confidence interval is computed as:

$$\frac{vs^2}{{}_{\alpha/2}\chi^2_{\nu}} = \frac{100(149)}{74.2219} = 200.7494$$

As the limits of the confidence interval (i.e., 115.0037, 200.7494) do not contain the hypothesized variance of 225, the conclusion is to *reject* H_0. As always, the confidence interval procedure leads us to the same conclusion as the hypothesis testing procedure for the same alpha level.

9.1.1.2 Inferences About Two Dependent Variances

In our second inferential testing situation for variances, the researcher would like to know whether the population variance for one group is different from the population variance for a second dependent group. This is comparable to the dependent t test described in Chapter 7 where one population mean was compared to a second dependent population mean. Once again we have two dependently drawn samples.

First, the hypotheses to be evaluated for detecting whether two dependent population variances differ (i.e., reflecting a nondirectional, or two-tailed, test) are as follows. The *nondirectional null hypothesis*, H_0, is that there is no difference between the two population variances σ_1^2 and σ_2^2, which we denote as

$$H_0: \sigma_1^2 - \sigma_2^2 = 0$$

Here there is no difference, or a "null" difference, between the two population variances. For example, we may be seeking to determine whether the variance of income of husbands is equal to the variance of their wives' incomes. Thus, the husband and wife samples are drawn as couples in pairs, or dependently, rather than individually, or independently.

The *nondirectional, scientific, or alternative hypothesis*, H_1, is that there is a difference between the population variances σ_1^2 and σ_2^2, which we denote as

$$H_1: \sigma_1^2 - \sigma_2^2 \neq 0$$

The null hypothesis, H_0, is rejected here in favor of the alternative hypothesis, H_1, if the population variances are different. As we have not specified a direction on H_1, we are willing to reject either if σ_1^2 is greater than σ_2^2 or if σ_1^2 is less than σ_2^2. This alternative hypothesis results in a two-tailed test. Directional alternative hypotheses can also be tested if we believe either that σ_1^2 is greater than σ_2^2 or that σ_1^2 is less than σ_2^2. In either case, the more the resulting sample variances differ from one another, the more likely we are to reject the null hypothesis.

The next step is to compute the test statistic t as follows:

$$t = \frac{s_1^2 - s_2^2}{2s_1s_2\sqrt{\frac{1 - r_{12}^2}{\nu}}}$$

where s_1^2 and s_2^2 are the sample variances for samples 1 and 2, respectively; s_1 and s_2 are the sample standard deviations for samples 1 and 2, respectively; r_{12} is the correlation between the scores from sample 1 and sample 2 (which is then squared); and ν is the number of degrees of freedom, $\nu = n - 2$, with n being the number of paired observations (not the number of total observations). Although correlations are not formally discussed until Chapter 10, conceptually the correlation is a measure of the relationship between two variables. This test statistic is conceptually somewhat similar to the test statistic for the dependent t test.

The test statistic t is then compared to a critical value(s) from the t distribution. For a two-tailed test, the critical values are denoted as $\pm\,_{\alpha_2}t_\nu$ and are found in Table A.2 in the Appendix. If the test statistic t falls into either critical region, then we reject H_0; otherwise, we fail to reject H_0. For a one-tailed test, the critical value is denoted as $+\,_{\alpha_1}t_\nu$ for the alternative hypothesis $H_0: \sigma_1^2 - \sigma_2^2 > 0$ and as $-\,_{\alpha_2}t_\nu$ for the alternative hypothesis $H_0: \sigma_1^2 - \sigma_2^2 < 0$. If the test statistic t falls into the appropriate critical region, then we reject H_0; otherwise, we fail to reject H_0. Some of the new procedures can also be used for testing inferences involving the equality of two or more dependent variances. In addition, note that acceptable confidence interval procedures are not currently available.

9.1.1.2.1 An Example

Let us consider an example to illustrate use of the test of two dependent variances. The same basic steps for hypothesis testing that we applied in previous chapters will be applied here as well. These steps include:

1. State the null and alternative hypotheses.
2. Select the level of significance (i.e., alpha, α).
3. Calculate the test statistic value.
4. Make a statistical decision (reject or fail to reject H_0).

A researcher is interested in whether there is greater variation in achievement test scores at the end of the first grade as compared to the beginning of the first grade. Thus, a directional, one-tailed alternative hypothesis is utilized. If the null hypothesis is rejected, this would indicate that first graders' achievement test scores are more variable at the end of the year than at the beginning of the year. If the null hypothesis is not rejected, this would indicate that first graders' achievement test scores have approximately the same variance at both the end of the year and at the beginning of the year.

A random sample of 62 first-grade children is selected and given the same achievement test at the beginning of the school year (September) and at the end of the school year (April). Thus, the same students are tested twice with the same instrument, thereby resulting in dependent samples at time 1 and time 2. The level of significance is set at a = .01. The test statistic t is computed as follows. We determine that $n = 62$, $v = 60$, $s_1^2 = 100$, $s_1 = 10$, $s_2^2 = 169$, $s_2 = 13$, and $r_{12} = .80$ (thus squared = .64). We compute the test statistic t to be

$$t = \frac{s_1^2 - s_2^2}{2s_1s_2\sqrt{\dfrac{1-r_{12}^2}{\nu}}} = \frac{100-169}{(2)(10)(13)\sqrt{\dfrac{1-.64}{60}}} = -3.4261$$

The test statistic t is then compared to the critical value from the t distribution. Because this is a one-tailed test, the critical value is denoted as $-\,_{\alpha_1}t_\nu$ and is determined from Table A.2

in the Appendix to be $-_{.01}t_{60} = -2.390$. The test statistic t falls into the lower-tail critical region, as it is less than the critical value (i.e., $-3.4261 < -2.390$), so we reject H_0 and conclude that the variance in achievement test scores increases from September to April.

9.1.1.3 Inferences About Two or More Independent Variances (Homogeneity of Variance Tests)

In our third and final inferential testing situation for variances, the researcher would like to know whether the population variance for one group is different from the population variance for one or more other independent groups. In this section we first describe the somewhat cloudy situation that exists for the traditional tests. Then we provide details on two recommended tests, the Brown-Forsythe procedure and the O'Brien procedure.

9.1.1.3.1 Traditional Tests

One of the more heavily studied inferential testing situations in recent years has been for testing whether differences exist among two or more independent group variances. These tests are often referred to as **homogeneity of variance tests**. Here we briefly discuss the more traditional tests and their associated problems. In the sections that follow, we then recommend two of the "better" tests. As was noted in the previous procedures, the variable for which the variance(s) is computed must be interval or ratio in scale.

Several tests have traditionally been used to test for the equality of independent variances. An early simple test for two independent variances is to form a ratio of the two sample variances, which yields the following F test statistic:

$$F = \frac{s_1^2}{s_2^2}$$

This F ratio test assumes that the two populations are normally distributed. However, it is known that the F ratio test is not very robust to violation of the normality assumption, except for when the sample sizes are equal (i.e., $n_1 = n_2$). In addition, the F ratio test can only be used for the two-group situation.

Subsequently, more general tests were developed to cover the multiple-group situation. One such popular test is **Hartley's F_{max} test** (developed in 1950), which is simply a more general version of the F ratio test just described. The test statistic for Hartley's F_{max} test is the following:

$$F_{max} = \frac{s_{largest}^2}{s_{smallest}^2}$$

where $s_{largest}^2$ is the largest variance in the set of variances and $s_{smallest}^2$ is the smallest variance in the set. Hartley's F_{max} test assumes normal population distributions and requires equal sample sizes. We also know that Hartley's F_{max} test is not very robust to violation of the normality assumption. **Cochran's C test** (developed in 1941) is also an F test statistic and is computed by taking the ratio of the largest variance to the sum of all of the variances. Cochran's C test also assumes normality, requires equal sample sizes, and has been found to be even less robust to nonnormality than Hartley's F_{max} test. As we see in Chapter 11 for the analysis of variance, *it is when we have unequal sample sizes that unequal variances is a* *problem*; for these reasons none of these tests can be recommended, which is the same situation we encountered with the independent *t* test.

Bartlett's χ^2 test (developed in 1937) does not have the stringent requirement of equal sample sizes; however, it does still assume normality. Bartlett's test is very sensitive to nonnormality, and is therefore not recommended either. Since 1950 the development of homogeneity tests has proliferated, with the goal being to find a test that is fairly robust to nonnormality. Seemingly as each new test was developed, later research would show that the test was not very robust.

Levene's test was developed in 1960 (Levene, 1960) and was developed as an alternative to the *F* test for homogeneity, which was problematic in the presence of nonnormality. Levene's test is essentially an analysis of variance on the transformed variable:

$$Z_{ij} = \left|Y_{ij} - \bar{Y}_{.j}\right|$$

where *ij* designates the ith observation in group *j*, and Z_{ij} is computed for each individual by taking their score *Yij*, subtracting from it the group mean $\bar{Y}_{.j}$ (the "." indicating we have averaged across all *i* observations in group *j*), and then taking the absolute value (i.e., by removing the sign). Unfortunately, Levene's test is not very robust to nonnormality, except when sample sizes are equal. In particular, the nominal alpha is maintained only for symmetric distributions. Thus, kurtosis may not be problematic as long as skew is minimal (i.e., distributions that show nonnormal kurtosis but are still symmetric) (Carroll & Schneider, 1985).

A nonparametric version of Levene's test was developed more recently (Zumbo & Nordstokke, 2010). One of the assumptions of the nonparametric Levene's test is that the samples are drawn from populations with equal means but not necessarily equal variances. However, recent simulation research suggests that sampling from populations with unequal and unknown means can lead to increased or decreased Type I error rates of the nonparametric Levene's test (Shear, Nordstokke, & Zumbo, 2018). Even more recently, Kim and Cribbie (2018) introduced a test for homogeneity of variance that incorporates an equivalence testing approach. Rather than testing the null hypothesis of equal variances, the proposed test examines a null hypothesis that the difference in the variances is beyond or at the border of a predetermined interval (with the alternative hypothesis being that the difference in variances is within the predetermined interval). This aligns the alternative hypothesis with the research hypothesis (i.e., equal variances).

Today, well over 60 such tests are available for examining homogeneity of variance. A recent simulation study by Wang et al. (2017) studied the performance of 14 homogeneity tests on controlling Type I error and power in one-way ANOVA. They found that the Ramsey conditional, O'Brien, Brown-Forsythe, bootstrap Brown-Forsythe, and Levene with squared deviation tests maintained adequate control of Type I errors and performed better than others reviewed, including maintaining acceptable power, across the simulated conditions. Recommendations for selecting a test for homogeneity of variance based on average cell size include the following: (a) when cell size is less than 10, O'Brien is the recommended test for homogeneity of variance as it maintains adequate Type I error control; (b) when cell size is greater than 10 but less than 20, the Ramsey conditional test is recommended as it also maintains adequate Type I error control; and (c) when the cell size is more than 20, the Brown-Forsythe, bootstrap Brown-Forsythe, or Ramsey conditional test are recommended as these tests provide maintains adequate Type I error control and greater power (around .80). Rather than engage in a protracted discussion of these tests and their associated limitations, we simply present a few additional tests that have been shown to be most robust to nonnormality in several recent studies and/or have become more widely available in standard statistical software.

9.1.1.3.2 The Brown-Forsythe Procedure

The Brown-Forsythe procedure is a variation of Levene's test. Developed in 1974, the Brown-Forsythe procedure has been shown to be quite robust to nonnormality in numerous studies (Olejnik & Algina, 1987; Ramsey, 1994). Based on this and other research, the Brown-Forsythe procedure is recommended for leptokurtic distributions (i.e., those with sharp peaks), as it is robust to nonnormality and provides adequate Type I error protection and excellent power. In the next section we describe the O'Brien procedure, which is recommended for other distributions (i.e., mesokurtic and platykurtic distributions). In cases where you are unsure of which procedure to use, Algina, Blair, and Coombs (1995) recommend using a maximum procedure, where both tests are conducted and the procedure with the maximum test statistic is selected.

Let us now examine in detail the Brown-Forsythe procedure. The null hypothesis is that the population variances of the groups are equal, $H_0: \sigma_1^2 = \sigma_2^2 = \cdots = \sigma_J^2$, and the alternative hypothesis is that not all of the population group variances are the same. The Brown-Forsythe procedure is essentially an analysis of variance on the transformed variable

$$Z_{ij} = \left| Y_{ij} - Mdn_{.j} \right|$$

which is computed for each individual by taking their score on the dependent variable, Y_{ij}, subtracting from it the group median, $Mdn_{.j}$, and then taking the absolute value (i.e., by removing the sign). The test statistic is an F and is computed by the following equation:

$$F = \frac{\sum_{j=1}^{J} n_j \left(\bar{Z}_{.j} - \bar{Z}_{..} \right)^2 \Big/ (J-1)}{\sum_{i=1}^{n_j} \sum_{j=1}^{J} \left(Z_{ij} - \bar{Z}_{.j} \right)^2 \Big/ (N-J)}$$

where n_j designates the number of observations in group j, J is the number of groups (where j ranges from 1 to J), $\bar{Z}_{.j}$ is the mean for group j (computed by taking the sum of the observations in group j and dividing by the number of observations in group j, which is n_j), and $\bar{Z}_{..}$ is the overall mean regardless of group membership (computed by taking the sum of all of the observations across all groups and dividing by the total number of observations N). The test statistic F is compared against a critical value from the F table (Table A.4 in the Appendix) with $J - 1$ degrees of freedom in the numerator and $N - J$ degrees of freedom in the denominator, denoted by ${}_{\alpha}F_{J-1,N-J}$. If the test statistic is greater than the critical value, we reject H_0; otherwise, we fail to reject H_0.

An example using the Brown-Forsythe procedure is certainly in order now. Three different groups of children—below-average, average, and above-average readers—play a computer game. The scores on the dependent variable Y are their total points from the game. We are interested in whether the variances for the three student groups are equal or not. The example data and computations are given in Table 9.1. First we compute the median for each group, and then compute the deviation from the median for each individual to obtain the transformed Z values. Then the transformed Z values are used to compute the F test statistic.

TABLE 9.1
Example Using the Brown-Forsythe and O'Brien Procedures

Group 1			Group 2			Group 3		
Y	*Z*	*r*	*Y*	*Z*	*r*	*Y*	*Z*	*r*
6	4	124.2499	9	4	143	10	8	704
8	2	14.2499	12	1	−7	16	2	−16
12	2	34.2499	14	1	−7	20	2	−96
13	3	89.2499	17	4	143	30	12	1104
Mdn	$\bar{Z}$	$\bar{r}$	**Mdn**	$\bar{Z}$	$\bar{r}$	**Mdn**	$\bar{Z}$	$\bar{r}$
10	2.75	65.4999	13	2.50	68	18	6	424
		Overall $\bar{Z}$			Overall $\bar{r}$			
		3.75			185.8333			

Computations for the **Brown-Forsythe** procedure:

$$F = \frac{\left[\sum_{j=1}^{J} n_j\left(\bar{Z}_{.j} - \bar{Z}_{..}\right)^2\right] \Big/ (J-1)}{\left[\sum_{i=1}^{n_j}\sum_{j=1}^{J}\left(Z_{ij} - \bar{Z}_{.j}\right)^2\right] \Big/ (N-J)}$$

$$F = \frac{\left[4(2.75-3.75)^2 + 4(2.50-3.75)^2 + 4(6-3.75)^2\right] \Big/ (2)}{\left[(4-2.75)^2 + (2-2.75)^2 + \ldots + (12-6)^2\right] \Big/ (9)} = 1.6388$$

Computations for the **O'Brien** procedure:

Sample means: $\bar{Y}_1 = 9.75$, $\bar{Y}_2 = 13.0$, $\bar{Y}_3 = 19.0$

Sample variances: $s_1^2 = 10.9167$, $s_2^2 = 11.3333$, $s_3^2 = 70.6667$

Example computation for r_{ij}:

$$r_{ij} = \frac{\left(n_j - 1.5\right)\left(n_j\right)\left(Y_{ij} - \bar{Y}_{.j}\right)^2 - \left(.5s_j^2\right)\left(n_j - 1\right)}{\left(n_j - 1\right)\left(n_j - 2\right)}$$

$$r_{ij} = \frac{(4-1.5)(4)(6-9.75)^2 - (.5)(10.9167)(4-1)}{(4-1)(4-2)} = 124.249$$

Test statistic for the O'Brien:

$$F = \frac{\left[\sum_{j=1}^{J} n_j\left(\bar{r}_j - \bar{r}_{..}\right)^2\right] \Big/ (J-1)}{\left[\sum_{i=1}^{n_j}\sum_{j=1}^{J}\left(r_{ij} - \bar{r}_{.j}\right)^2\right] \Big/ (N-J)}$$

$$F = \frac{\left[(4)(65.4999-185.8333)^2 + (4)(68-185.8333)^2 + (4)(424-185.8333)^2\right] \Big/ (2)}{\left[(124.2499-65.4999)^2 + (14.2499-65.4999)^2 + \ldots + (1{,}104-424)^2\right] \Big/ (9)}$$

$$F = 1.4799$$

The Brown-Forsythe test statistic $F = 1.6388$ is compared against the critical value for $\alpha = .05$ of ${}_{.05}F_{2,9} = 4.26$. As the test statistic is smaller than the critical value (i.e., $1.6388 < 4.26$), we fail to reject the null hypothesis and conclude that the three student groups do not have different variances.

9.1.1.3.3 The O'Brien Procedure

The final test to consider in this chapter is the O'Brien procedure. While the Brown-Forsythe procedure is recommended for leptokurtic distributions, the O'Brien procedure is recommended for other distributions (i.e., mesokurtic and platykurtic distributions). Let us now examine in detail the O'Brien procedure. The null hypothesis is again that the population variances of the groups are equal, $H_0: \sigma_1^2 = \sigma_2^2 = \cdots = \sigma_J^2$, and the alternative hypothesis is that not all of the population group variances are the same.

The O'Brien procedure is an analysis of variance on a *different* transformed variable:

$$r_{ij} = \frac{(n_j - 1.5)(n_j)(Y_{ij} - \bar{Y}_{.j})^2 - (.5)(s_j^2)(n_j - 1)}{(n_j - 1)(n_j - 2)}$$

which is computed for each individual, where n_j is the size of group j, $\bar{Y}_{.j}$ is the mean on the outcome for group j, and s_j^2 is the sample variance for group j.

The test statistic is an F statistic and is computed by the following equation:

$$F = \frac{\sum_{j=1}^{J} n_j (\bar{r}_{.j} - \bar{r}_{..})^2 / (J-1)}{\sum_{i=1}^{n_j} \sum_{j=1}^{J} (r_{ij} - \bar{r}_{.j})^2 / (N-J)}$$

where n_j designates the number of observations in group j, J is the number of groups (where j ranges from 1 to J), $\bar{r}_{.j}$ is the mean for group j (computed by taking the sum of the observations in group j and dividing by the number of observations in group j, which is n_j), and $\bar{r}_{..}$ is the overall mean regardless of group membership (computed by taking the sum of all of the observations across all groups and dividing by the total number of observations N). The test statistic F is compared against a critical value from the F table (Table A.4 in the Appendix) with $J - 1$ degrees of freedom in the numerator and $N - J$ degrees of freedom in the denominator, denoted by ${}_{\alpha}F_{J-1,N-J}$. If the test statistic is greater than the critical value, then we reject H_0; otherwise, we fail to reject H_0.

Let us return to the example in Table 9.1 and consider the results of the O'Brien procedure. From the computations shown in the table, the O'Brien test statistic $F = 1.4799$ is compared against the critical value for $\alpha = .05$ of ${}_{.05}F_{2,9} = 4.26$. Because the test statistic is smaller than the critical value (i.e., $1.4799 < 4.26$), we fail to reject the null hypothesis and conclude that the three student groups do not have different variances.

9.2 Assumptions

9.2.1 Assumptions for Inferences About a Single Variance

It is assumed that the sample is randomly drawn from the population (i.e., the assumption of independence) and that the population of scores is normally distributed. It has been noted by statisticians such as Wilcox (1996) that the chi-square distribution does not perform adequately when sampling from a nonnormal distribution, because the actual Type I error rate can differ greatly from the nominal alpha level (the level set by the researcher).

While not an assumption, because we are testing a variance, a condition of the test is that the variable must be *interval* or *ratio* in scale.

9.2.2 Assumptions for Inferences About Two Dependent Variances

It is assumed that the two samples are dependently and randomly drawn from their respective populations, that both populations are normal in shape, and that the t distribution is the appropriate sampling distribution. It is thought that this test is not particularly robust to nonnormality (Wilcox, 1987). As a result, other procedures have been developed that are thought to be more robust. However, little in the way of empirical results is known at this time.

While not an assumption, because we are testing a variance, a condition of the test is that the variable must be *interval* or *ratio* in scale. Recall that variances can only be computed with data that are interval or ratio in scale.

9.3 Sample Size, Power, and Effect Size

There is really not much we can report on that is available in published in the literature on sample size, power, and effect sizes for tests of variances.

9.4 Computing Inferences About Variances Using SPSS

Unfortunately, there is not much to report on tests of variances for SPSS. There are no unique (i.e., standalone) tests available for inferences about a single variance or for inferences about two dependent variances. For inferences about independent variances, SPSS does provide Levene's test as part of the "Independent t Test" procedure (discussed in Chapter 7) and as part of the "One Way ANOVA" and "Univariate ANOVA" procedures (to be discussed in Chapter 11). While it is commonly reported as evidence for meeting the assumption of equal variances, given our previous concerns with Levene's test, use it with caution.

9.5 Computing Inferences About Variances Using R

Next we consider **R** for computing inferences about variances. We will examine both inferences about a single variance and inferences about two dependent variances. We will review **R** for homogeneity of variances tests as we examine ANOVA in a later chapter, and thus those commands are not presented in this chapter.

Note that the scripts are provided within the blocks with additional annotation to assist in understanding how the command works. Should you want to write reminder notes and annotation to yourself as you write the commands in **R** (and we highly encourage doing so), remember that any text that follows a hashtag (i.e., #) is annotation only and not part of the **R** script. Thus, you can write annotations directly into **R** with hashtags. We encourage this practice so that when you call up the commands in the future, you'll understand what the various lines of code are doing. You may think you'll remember what you did. However, trust us. There is a good chance that you won't. Thus, consider it best practice when using **R** to annotate heavily!

9.5.1 Reading Data Into R for the Test of Inference About a Single Variance

```
getwd()
```

R is always pointed to a directory on your computer. To find out which directory it is pointed to, run this "get working directory" function. We will assume that we need to change the working directory, and will use the next line of code to set the working directory to the desired path.

```
setwd("E:/Folder")
```

To set the working directory, use the *setwd* function and change what is in quotation marks here to your file location. Also, if you are copying the directory name, it will copy in slashes. You will need to change the slash (i.e., \) to a forward slash (i.e., /). Note that you need your destination name within quotation marks in the parentheses.

```
Ch9_psychdistress <- read.csv("Ch9_psychdistress.csv")
```

The *read.csv* function reads our data into **R**. What's to the left of the <- will be what the data will be called in **R**. In this example, we're calling the R dataframe "Ch9_psychdistress." What's to the right of the <- tells **R** to find this particular .csv file. In this example, our file is called "Ch9_psychdistress.csv." Make sure the extension (i.e., .csv) is included in your script. Also note that the name of your file should be in quotation marks within the parentheses.

```
names(Ch9_psychdistress)
```

The *names* function will produce a list of variable names for each dataframe as follows. This is a good check to make sure your data have been read in correctly.

```
[1] "Sport"       "Selection" "Distress"
```

```
Ch9_psychdistress$Sport <- factor(Ch9_psychdistress$Sport,
labels = c("movement", "target", "fielding", "territory"))
```

The *factor* function renames our "Sport" variable (which is in our "Ch9_psychdistress" dataframe) as nominal with four groups or categories with labels of "movement," "target," "fielding," and "territory."

```
View(Ch9_psychdistress)
```

The *View* function will let you view the dataset in spreadsheet format in RStudio.

```
summary(Ch9_psychdistress)
```

The *summary* function will produce basic descriptive statistics on all the variables in your dataframe. This is a great way to quickly check to see if the data have been read in correctly and to get a feel for your data, if you haven't already. The output from the summary statement for this dataframe looks like this. Because the variable "Sport" is nominal, our output includes only the frequencies of cases within the categories.

FIGURE 9.2
Reading data into **R**.

```
      Sport         Selection       Distress
movement :8   deselected:16    Min.   : 3.00
target   :8   selected  :16    1st Qu.:12.00
fielding :8                    Median :20.00
territory:8                    Mean   :18.41
                               3rd Qu.:25.00
                               Max.   :30.00
```

FIGURE 9.2 (continued)
Reading data into **R**.

9.5.2 Generating the Test of Inference About a Single Variance

```
install.packages("EnvStats")
```

The *install.packages* function will be used to install the *EnvStats* package that we will use to test the inference about a single variance. We first install the package using this command. Note that the package name needs to be in quotation marks within the parentheses.

```
library(EnvStats)
```

Now we need to load EnvStats into our library using the *library* function.

```
varTest(Ch9_psychdistress$Distress, alternative = "two.sided",
        conf.level = 0.95,
        sigma.squared = 50)
```

We will use the *varTest* function to test the inference about a single variance. Let's look inside the parentheses. We first define the dataframe (i.e., "Ch9_psychdistress") and variable ("Distress") to compute the test. The *alternative* command specifies the alternative hypothesis that the true variance is different than the hypothesized variance. Had we wanted to test a one-directional hypothesis, we would have had the command *alternative = "greater"* or *alternative = "less,"* respectively. We test at an alpha of .05, so the confidence level is .95 (*conf.level = 0.95*). The command *sigma squared* is the hypothesized value to which we are testing, which is 50 in this example.

Using this script we are provided with the following results. We see that the variance of our variable, "Distress," is 56.44254. The results of the chi-squared test are not statistically significant ($\chi^2 = 34.99$, $df = 31$, $p = .57$).

```
Results of Hypothesis Test
--------------------------

Null Hypothesis:                 variance = 50

Alternative Hypothesis:          True variance is not equal to 50

Test Name:                       Chi-Squared Test on Variance

Estimated Parameter(s):          variance = 56.44254

Data:                            Ch9_distress$Distress

Test Statistic:                  Chi-Squared = 34.99437

Test Statistic Parameter:        df = 31

P-value:                         0.5680487

95% Confidence Interval:         LCL = 36.27722
                                 LCL = 99.76309
```

FIGURE 9.3
Generating a test of inference about a single variance.

9.5.3 Reading Data Into R for the Test of Inference About Two Dependent Variances

```
getwd()
```

R is always pointed to a directory on your computer. To find out which directory it is pointed to, run this "get working directory" function. We will assume that we need to change the working directory, and will use the next line of code to set the working directory to the desired path.

```
setwd("E:/Folder")
```

To set the working directory, use the *setwd* function and change what is in quotation marks here to your file location. Also, if you are copying the directory name, it will copy in slashes. You will need to change the slash (i.e., \) to a forward slash (i.e., /). Note that you need your destination name within quotation marks in the parentheses.

```
Ch9_swimming <- read.csv("Ch9_swimming.csv")
```

The *read.csv* function reads our data into **R**. What's to the left of the <- will be what the data will be called in **R**. In this example, we're calling the dataframe "Ch9_swimming." What's to the right of the <- tells **R** to find this particular .csv file. In this example, our file is called "Ch9_swimming.csv." Make sure the extension (i.e., .csv) is included in your script. Also note that the name of your file should be in quotation marks within the parentheses. Note that this is the same data that we used in our discussion of dependent *t* tests.

```
names(Ch9_swimming)
```

The *names* function will produce a list of variable names for each dataframe as follows. This is a good check to make sure your data have been read in correctly.

```
[1] "pretest" "posttest"
```

```
View(Ch9_swimming)
```

The *View* function will let you view the dataset in spreadsheet format in RStudio.

```
summary(Ch9_swimming)
```

The *summary* function will produce basic descriptive statistics on all the variables in your dataframe. This is a great way to quickly check to see if the data have been read in correctly and to get a feel for your data, if you haven't already. The output from the summary statement for this dataframe looks like this.

```
    pretest          posttest
 Min.   :58.00   Min.   :54.00
 1st Qu.:61.25   1st Qu.:56.25
 Median :63.50   Median :59.50
 Mean   :64.00   Mean   :59.00
 3rd Qu.:65.75   3rd Qu.:61.75
 Max.   :72.00   Max.   :64.00
```

FIGURE 9.4
Reading data into **R** for the test of inference about two dependent variances.

9.5.4 Generating the Test of Inference About Two Dependent Variances

```
var(Ch9_swimming$pretest)
var(Ch9_swimming$posttest)
```

Before we compute the test for the inference about two dependent variances, let's generate the values of the variances for both the pretest and posttest. Using the *var* function for the two variables of interest, the variances are, respectively:

```
[1] 17.77778  #pretest
[1] 13.11111  #posttest
```

```
var.test(Ch9_swimming$pretest, Ch9_swimming$posttest,
        paired=TRUE,
        alternative = "two.sided",
        conf.level = 0.95)
```

We will use the *var.test* function to test the inference about two dependent variances. Let's review what is inside the parentheses. We first define the dataframe ("Ch9_swimming") and variables to compute the test ("Ch9_swimming$pretest" and "Ch9_swimming$posttest). This test is comparable to the dependent *t* test, comparing one population variance to another, and thus we define this as *paired=TRUE*. The *alternative* command specifies the alternative hypothesis the variance for the pretest is different than the variance for the posttest. Had we wanted to test a one-directional hypothesis, we would have had the command *alternative = "greater"* or *alternative = "less,"* respectively. We test at an alpha of .05, so the confidence level is .95 (*conf.level = 0.95*). Using this command, we are provided with the following results. We see the ratio of the variances is about 1.36. The results of the *F* test are not statistically significant ($F = 1.36$, $p = .68$).

```
Results of Hypothesis Test
--------------------------

Null Hypothesis:                 ratio of variances = 1

Alternative Hypothesis:          True ratio of variances is not equal to 1

Test Name:                       F test to compare two variances

Estimated Parameter(s):          ratio of variances = 1.355932

Data:                            Ch9_swimming$pretest and Ch9_swimming$posttest

Test Statistic:                  F = 1.355932

Test Statistic Parameters:       num df   = 9
                                 denom df = 9

P-value:                         0.6574637

95% Confidence Interval:         LCL = 0.3367944
                                 UCL = 5.4589751
```

FIGURE 9.5
Generating a test of inference about two dependent variances.

9.6 Research Question Template and Example Write-Up

Consider an example paragraph for one of the tests described in this chapter, more specifically, testing inferences about two dependent variances. As you may remember, our graduate research assistant, Oso, was working with Dr. Abraham, an assistant principal, to assist in analyzing the variances of first grade students. Oso's task was to assist Dr. Abraham with writing her research question (*Are the variances of achievement scores for first grade children the same in the fall as compared to the spring?*) and generating the test of inference to answer her question. Oso suggested a dependent variances test as the test of inference. A template for writing a research question for the dependent variances follows:

Are the variances of [variable] the same in [time 1] as compared to [time 2]?

The following is an example write-up:

A test of dependent variances was conducted to determine if variances of achievement scores for first grade children were the same in the fall as compared to the spring. The test was conducted using an alpha of .05. The null hypothesis was that the variances would be the same.

There was a statistically significant difference in variances of achievement scores of first grade children in the fall as compared to the spring (t = −3.4261, df = 60, p < .05). Thus the null hypothesis that the variances would be equal at the beginning and end of the first grade was rejected. The variances of achievement test scores significantly increased from September to April.

9.7 Additional Resources

We have offered a number of resources within the chapter and refer readers who are interested in learning more to those resources. Because homogeneity of variance is an integral assumption to tests of means, readers may also find coverage of tests of inference in texts that deal with ANOVA and related designs (e.g., Maxwell, Delaney, & Kelley, 2018).

Problems

Conceptual Problems

1. Which of the following tests of homogeneity of variance is most robust to assumption violations?
   a. F ratio test
   b. Bartlett's chi-square test
   c. O'Brien procedure
   d. Hartley's F_{max} test
2. True or false? Cochran's C test requires equal sample sizes.
3. I assert that if two dependent sample variances are identical, I would not be able to reject the null hypothesis. Am I correct?

4. The 90% CI for a single variance extends from 25.7 to 33.6 and the hypothesized value is 22.0. If the level of significance is .10, do I reject the null hypothesis?
   a. Yes
   b. No
   c. Cannot be determined
5. The 95% CI for a single variance ranges from 82.0 to 93.5, and the hypothesized value is 87.2. If the level of significance is .05, do I reject the null hypothesis?
   a. Yes
   b. No
   c. Cannot be determined
6. If the mean of the sampling distribution of the difference between two variances equals 0, I assert that both samples probably represent a single population. Am I correct?
7. Which of the following is an example of two dependent samples?
   a. Pretest scores of males in one course and posttest scores of females in another course
   b. Husbands and their wives in your neighborhood
   c. Softball players at your school and football players at your school
   d. Professors in education and professors in psychology
8. True or false? The mean of the *F* distribution increases as the degrees of freedom in the denominator (v_2) increase.
9. A researcher is testing whether the population variance for a treatment group differs than the population variance for a control group. The distribution is nonnormal and relatively peaked. Which of the following procedures would you recommend to the researcher?
   a. Brown-Forsythe procedure
   b. Hartley's F_{max} test
   c. O'Brien procedure
   d. Ratio of the sample variances
10. A researcher is testing whether the population variance for a treatment group differs than the population variance for a comparison group. The distribution is nonnormal and relatively flat. Which of the following procedures would you recommend to the researcher?
    a. Brown-Forsythe procedure
    b. Hartley's F_{max} test
    c. O'Brien procedure
    d. Ratio of the sample variances
11. Tests of inferences about variances are appropriate in all but which of the following situations?
    a. To examine linearity between two variances
    b. To examine the extent to which the assumption of equal variances has been met
    c. To determine whether a variance differs from a hypothesized value
    d. To determine whether two variances that are dependent are different from each other

Answers to Conceptual Problems

1. **c** (The O'Brien procedure has been shown to be more robust to nonnormality than the others listed here.)
3. **Yes** (Cannot reject if sample variances are equal.)
5. **b** (The hypothesized value is 87.2 with a 95% CI for a single variance ranging from 82.0 to 93.5, and the level of significance is .05; the hypothesized values falls within the CI, so fail to reject the null hypothesis.)
7. **Yes** (If the mean difference is 0, then there really is only one population.)
9. **False** (The mean decreases as ν_2 increases, as it moves closer and closer to 1.0.)
11. **c** (The O'Brien procedure is recommended for nonnormal distributions that are mesokurtic or platykurtic.)

Computational Problems

1. The following random sample of scores on a preschool ability test is obtained from a normally distributed population of 4-year-olds:

20	22	24	30	18	22	29	27
25	21	19	22	38	26	17	25

   a. Test the following hypotheses at the .10 level of significance:

$$H_0: \sigma^2 = 75$$
$$H_1: \sigma^2 \neq 75$$

   b. Construct a 90% CI.

2. The following two independent random samples of number of books owned are obtained from two populations of undergraduate (sample 1) and graduate students (sample 2), respectively:

Sample 1 data					Sample 2 data				
42	36	47	35	46	45	50	57	58	43
37	52	44	47	51	52	43	60	41	49
56	54	55	50	40	44	51	49	55	56
40	46	41							

   Test the following hypotheses at the .05 level of significance using the Brown-Forsythe and O'Brien procedures:

$$H_0: \sigma_1^2 - \sigma_2^2 = 0$$
$$H_1: \sigma_1^2 - \sigma_2^2 \neq 0$$

3. The following summary statistics are available for two dependent random samples of brothers and sisters, respectively, on their allowance for the past month: $s_1^2 = 49$, $s_2^2 = 25$, $n = 32$, $r_{12} = .60$.

Test the following hypotheses at the .05 level of significance:

$$H_0: \sigma_1^2 - \sigma_2^2 = 0$$
$$H_1: \sigma_1^2 - \sigma_2^2 \neq 0$$

4. The following summary statistics are available for two dependent random samples of first-semester college students who were measured on their high school and first semester college GPAs, respectively: $s_1^2 = 1.56$, $s_2^2 = 4.42$, $n = 62$, $r_{12} = .72$.
Test the following hypotheses at the .05 level of significance:

$$H_0: \sigma_1^2 - \sigma_2^2 = 0$$
$$H_1: \sigma_1^2 - \sigma_2^2 \neq 0$$

5. A random sample of 21 statistics exam scores is collected with a sample mean of 50 and a sample variance of 10. Test the following hypotheses at the .05 level of significance:

$$H_0: \sigma^2 = 25$$
$$H_1: \sigma^2 \neq 25$$

6. A random sample of 30 placement exam scores is collected with a sample mean of 525 and a sample variance of 16900. Test the following hypotheses at the .05 level of significance:

$$H_0: \sigma^2 = 10000$$
$$H_1: \sigma^2 \neq 10000$$

7. An employability assessment was given at the time individuals applied for work (i.e., pre-employment) and after employed for 6 months. The pre-employment variance is 36, the 6-month variance is 64, sample size is 31, and the pre–post correlation is .80. Test the null hypothesis that the two dependent variances are equal against a nondirectional alternative at the .01 level of significance.

8. A random sample of 25 adults completed the Big 5 personality test, and their emotional stability scores are provided here:

2.10	1.80
1.50	4.20
4.50	4.80
1.80	3.70
3.80	3.30
1.80	2.80
4.20	2.70
2.00	3.20
2.60	2.80
3.90	2.20
1.40	3.60
3.60	4.40
2.30	

Test the following hypotheses at the .05 level of significance:

$$H_0: \sigma^2 = 1.25$$
$$H_1: \sigma^2 \neq 1.25$$

9. The following summary statistics are available for two dependent random samples who have been measured on the Big 5 personality test, respectively: $s^2_{conscientiousness} = .503$, $s^2_{imagination} = .427$, $n = 25$, $r_{12} = .10$.

Test the following hypotheses at the .05 level of significance:

$$H_0: \sigma_1^2 - \sigma_2^2 = 0$$
$$H_1: \sigma_1^2 - \sigma_2^2 \neq 0$$

Selected Answers to Computational Problems

1. (a) sample variance = 27.9292, $\chi^2 = 5.5858$, critical values = 7.2609 and 24.9958, thus reject H_0. (b) (16.7603, 57.6978), thus reject H_0 as the interval does not contain 75.
3. $t = 2.3474$, critical values = −2.042 and +2.042, thus reject H_0.
5. $\chi^2 = 8.0$, critical values = 9.59078 and 34.1696, thus reject H_0.
7. $t = -2.6178$, critical values = −2.756 and +2.756, thus fail to reject H_0.
9. Given $s^2_{conscientiousness} = s_1^2 = .50$, $s^2_{imagination} = s_2^2 = .43$, $n = 25$, $r_{12} = .10$.

$$t = \frac{s_1^2 - s_2^2}{2s_1s_2\sqrt{\dfrac{1-r_{12}^2}{\nu}}} = \frac{100-169}{(2)(10)(13)\sqrt{\dfrac{1-.64}{60}}} = -3.4261$$

Interpretive Problem

1. Use the survey1 dataset from the website to determine if there are gender differences among the variances for any items of interest that are at least interval or ratio in scale. Some example items might include the following:
   a. Height in inches [HEIGHT]
   b. Amount spent at last hair appointment [HAIRAPPT]
   c. Number of songs downloaded to your phone [SONGS]
   d. Current GPA [GPA]
   e. Amount of exercise per week [EXERCISE]
   f. Number of alcoholic drinks per week [DRINKS]
   g. Number of hours studied per week [STUDYHRS]

2. Use the survey1 dataset from the website to determine if there are differences between the variances for left- versus right-handed individuals on any items of interest that are at least interval or ratio in scale. Some example items might include the following:

a. Height in inches [HEIGHT]
b. Amount spent at last hair appointment [HAIRAPPT]
c. Number of songs downloaded to your phone [SONGS]
d. Current GPA [GPA]
e. Amount of exercise per week [EXERCISE]
f. Number of alcoholic drinks per week [DRINKS]
g. Number of hours studied per week [STUDYHRS]

10

Bivariate Measures of Association

Chapter Outline

Key Concepts

1. Scatterplot
2. Strength and direction
3. Covariance
4. Correlation coefficient
5. Fisher's *Z* transformation
6. Linearity assumption, causation, and restriction of range issues

We have considered various inferential tests in the last four chapters, specifically those that deal with tests of means, proportions, and variances. In this chapter we examine measures of association as well as inferences involving measures of association. Methods for directly determining the relationship among two variables are known as **bivariate analysis**, rather than **univariate analysis**, which is only concerned with a single variable. The indices used to directly describe the relationship among two variables are known as *correlation coefficients* (in the old days known as co-relation) or as *measures of association*.

These measures of association allow us to determine how two variables are related to one another and can be useful in two applications: (a) as a descriptive statistic by itself and (b) as an inferential test. First, a researcher may want to compute a correlation coefficient for its own sake, simply to tell the researcher precisely how two variables are related or associated. For example, we may want to determine whether there is a relationship between the GRE-Quantitative Reasoning (GRE-Q) subtest and performance on a statistics exam. Do students who score relatively high on the GRE-Q perform higher on a statistics exam than do students who score relatively low on the GRE-Q? In other words, as scores increase on the GRE-Q, do they also correspondingly increase their performance on a statistics exam?

Second, we may want to use an inferential test to assess whether (a) a correlation is significantly different from zero or (b) two correlations are significantly different from one another. For example, is the correlation between GRE-Q and statistics exam performance significantly different from zero? As a second example, is the correlation between GRE-Q and statistics exam performance the same for younger students as it is for older students?

The following topics are covered in this chapter: scatterplot; covariance; Pearson product-moment correlation coefficient; inferences about the Pearson product-moment correlation coefficient; some issues regarding correlations; other measures of association; SPSS and **R**; and power. We utilize some of the basic concepts previously covered in Chapters 6 through 9. New concepts to be discussed include the following: scatterplot, strength and direction, covariance, correlation coefficient, Fisher's Z transformation, linearity assumption, causation, and restriction of range issues. Our objectives are that by the end of this chapter, you will be able to (a) understand the concepts underlying the correlation coefficient and correlation inferential tests, (b) select the appropriate type of correlation, and (c) determine and interpret the appropriate correlation and inferential test.

10.1 What Bivariate Measures of Association Are and How They Work

Challie Lenge, along with her accomplished cohort of graduate research assistants working in the statistics lab, continues to assist with various research projects. We now find her embarking on exciting challenge with a community partner.

The faculty advisor for the stats lab received a telephone call from Dr. Amberly, the director of marketing for the local animal shelter. Based on a recent survey of donors to the shelter, it appears that the donors who contribute the largest donations also have children and pets. In an effort to attract more donors to the animal shelter, Dr. Amberly is targeting select groups—one of which she believes may be families that have children at home and who also have pets. Dr. Amberly believes if there is a relationship between these variables, she can more easily reach the intended audience with her marketing materials, which will then translate into increased donations to the animal shelter. However, Dr. Amberly wants to base her decision on solid evidence and not just a hunch. Having built a good knowledge base with previous consulting work, the faculty advisor puts Dr. Amberly in touch with the graduate students in the statistics lab. After consulting with Dr. Amberly, Challie suggests a Pearson correlation as the test of inference to test her research question: *Is there a correlation between the number of children in a family and the number of pets?* Challie's task is then to assist in generating the test of inference to answer Dr. Amberly's research question.

10.1.1 Characteristics

10.1.1.1 Scatterplot

This section deals with an important concept underlying the relationship among two variables, the scatterplot. Later sections move us into ways of measuring the relationship among two variables. First, however, we need to set up the situation where we have data on two different variables for each of *N* individuals in the population. Table 10.1 displays such a situation. The first column is simply an index of the individuals in the population, from $i = 1, \ldots, N$, where *N* is the total number of individuals in the population. The second column denotes the values obtained for the first variable *X*. Thus, $X_1 = 10$ means that the first individual had a score of 10 on variable X. The third column provides the values for the second variable *Y*. Thus, $Y_1 = 20$ indicates that the first individual had a score of 20 on variable *Y*. In an actual data table, only the scores would be shown, not the X_i and Y_i notation. Thus, we have a tabular method for depicting the data of a two-variable situation in Table 10.1.

A graphical method for depicting the relationship among two variables is to *plot the pair of scores* on *X* and *Y* for each individual on a two-dimensional figure known as a **scatterplot** (or *scattergram*). Each individual has two scores in a two-dimensional coordinate system, denoted by (*X*, *Y*). For example, our individual 1 has the paired scores of (10, 20). An example scatterplot is shown in Figure 10.1. The **X axis** (the *horizontal axis* or *abscissa*) represents the values for variable X, and the **Y axis** (the *vertical axis* or *ordinate*) represents the values for variable Y. Each point on the scatterplot represents a pair of scores (*X*, *Y*) for a particular individual. Thus, individual 1 has a point at $X = 10$ and $Y = 20$ (the circled point). Points for other individuals are also shown. In essence, the scatterplot is actually a bivariate frequency distribution. When there is a moderate degree of relationship, the points may take the shape of an ellipse (i.e., a football shape where the direction of the relationship, positive or negative, may make the football appear to point up to the right—as with a positive relation depicted in this figure), as in Figure 10.1.

TABLE 10.1

Layout for Correlational Data

Individual	*X*	*Y*
1	$X_1 = 10$	$Y_1 = 20$
2	$X_2 = 12$	$Y_2 = 28$
3	$X_3 = 20$	$Y_3 = 33$
.	.	.
.	.	.
.	.	.
N	$X_N = 44$	$Y_N = 65$

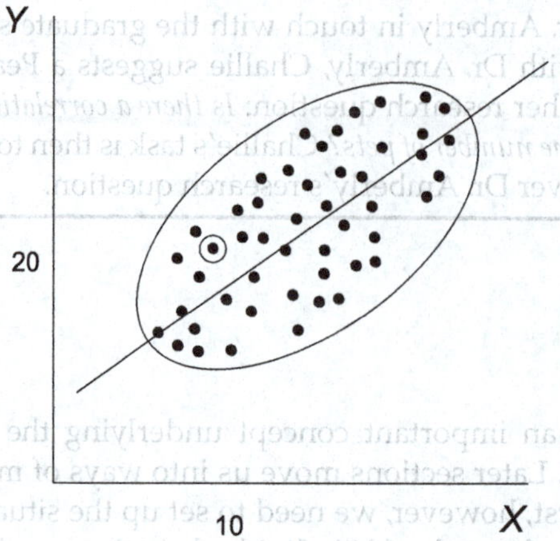

FIGURE 10.1
Scatterplot.

The scatterplot allows the researcher to evaluate both the direction and the strength of the relationship among X and Y. The **direction** of the relationship has to do with whether the relationship is positive or negative. A *positive relationship* occurs when as scores on variable X increase (from left to right), scores on variable Y also increase (from bottom to top). Thus, Figure 10.1 indicates a positive relationship among X and Y. Examples of different scatterplots are shown in Figure 10.2. Figures 10.2a and 10.2d both display positive relationships.

A *negative relationship*, sometimes called an *inverse relationship*, occurs when as scores on variable X increase (from left to right), scores on variable Y decrease (from top to bottom). Figures 10.2b and 10.2e are examples of negative relationships. There is no relationship between X and Y when for a large value of X, a large or a small value of Y can occur, and for a small value of X, a large or a small value of Y can also occur. In other words, X and Y are not related, as shown in Figure 10.2c.

The **strength** of the relationship among X and Y is determined by the scatter of the points (hence the name *scatterplot*). First, we draw a straight line through the points that cuts the bivariate distribution in half, as shown in Figures 10.1 and 10.2. In Chapter 17 we note that this line is known as the **regression line**. If the scatter is such that the points tend to fall close to the line, then this is indicative of a strong relationship among X and Y. Both Figures 10.2a and 10.2b denote strong relationships. If the scatter is such that the points are widely scattered around the line, then this is indicative of a weak relationship among X and Y. Both Figures 10.2d and 10.2e denote weaker relationships. To summarize Figure 10.2, part (a) represents a strong positive relationship, part (b) a strong negative relationship, part (c) no relationship, part (d) a weaker positive relationship, and part (e) a weaker negative relationship. Thus the scatterplot is useful for providing a quick visual indication of the nature of the relationship among variables X and Y.

10.1.1.2 Covariance

The remainder of this chapter deals with statistical methods for measuring the relationship among variables X and Y. The first such method is known as the *covariance*. The **covariance**, conceptually, *is the shared variance (or covariance) among X and Y*. The covariance and

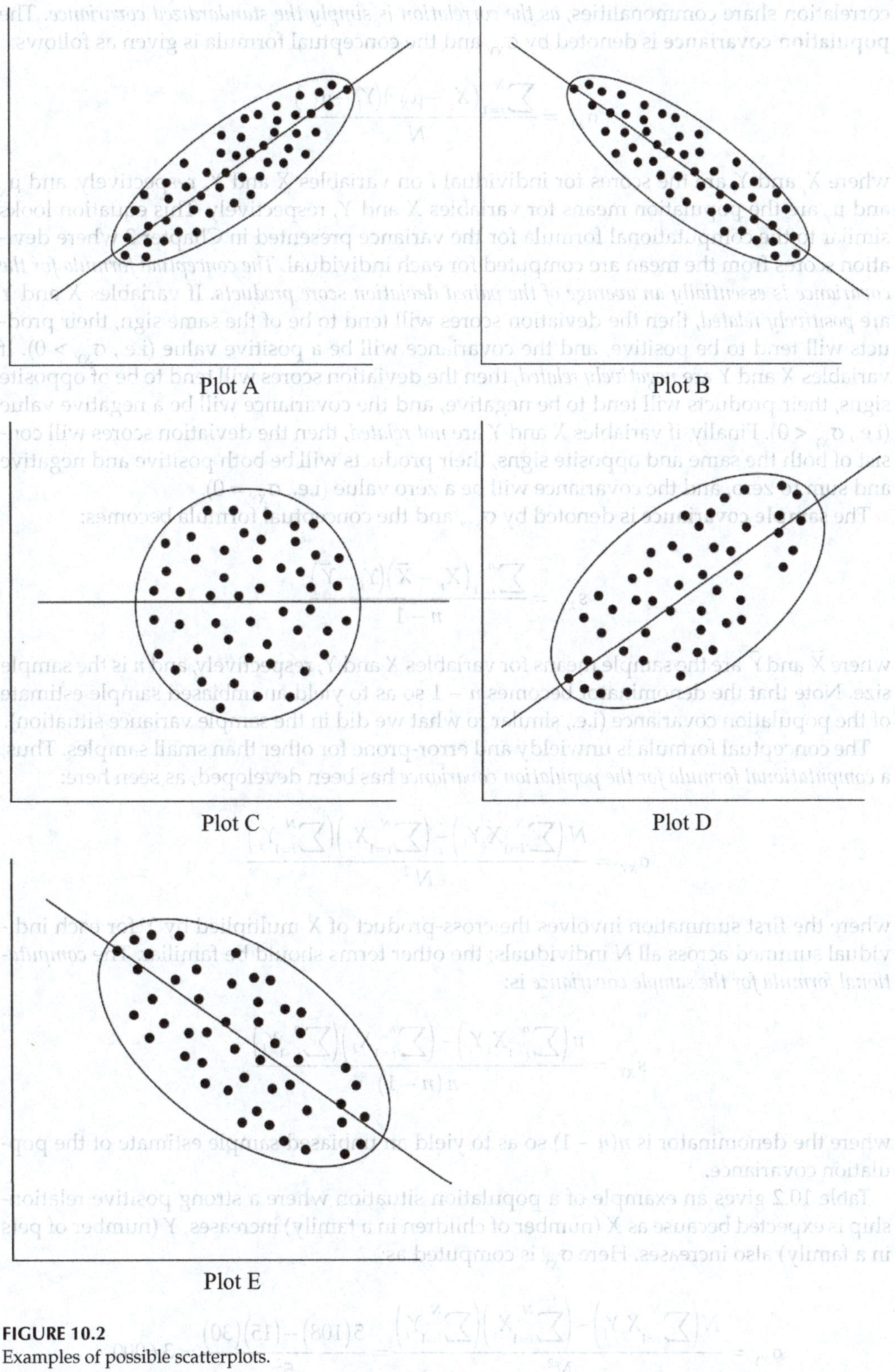

FIGURE 10.2
Examples of possible scatterplots.

correlation share commonalities, *as the correlation is simply the standardized covariance*. The **population covariance** is denoted by σ_{XY} and the conceptual formula is given as follows:

$$\sigma_{XY} = \frac{\sum_{i=1}^{N}(X_i - \mu_X)(Y_i - \mu_Y)}{N}$$

where X_i and Y_i are the scores for individual i on variables X and Y, respectively, and μ_X and μ_Y are the population means for variables X and Y, respectively. This equation looks similar to the computational formula for the variance presented in Chapter 3 where deviation scores from the mean are computed for each individual. *The conceptual formula for the covariance is essentially an average of the paired deviation score products*. If variables X and Y are *positively related*, then the deviation scores will tend to be of the same sign, their products will tend to be positive, and the covariance will be a positive value (i.e., $\sigma_{XY} > 0$). If variables X and Y are *negatively related*, then the deviation scores will tend to be of opposite signs, their products will tend to be negative, and the covariance will be a negative value (i.e., $\sigma_{XY} < 0$). Finally, if variables X and Y are *not related*, then the deviation scores will consist of both the same and opposite signs, their products will be both positive and negative and sum to zero, and the covariance will be a zero value (i.e., $\sigma_{XY} = 0$).

The **sample covariance** is denoted by σ_{XY}, and the conceptual formula becomes:

$$s_{XY} = \frac{\sum_{i=1}^{n}(X_i - \bar{X})(Y_i - \bar{Y})}{n-1}$$

where $\bar{X}$ and $\bar{Y}$ are the sample means for variables X and Y, respectively, and n is the sample size. Note that the denominator becomes $n - 1$ so as to yield an unbiased sample estimate of the population covariance (i.e., similar to what we did in the sample variance situation).

The conceptual formula is unwieldy and error-prone for other than small samples. Thus, a *computational formula for the population covariance* has been developed, as seen here:

$$\sigma_{XY} = \frac{N\left(\sum_{i=1}^{N} X_i Y_i\right) - \left(\sum_{i=1}^{N} X_i\right)\left(\sum_{i=1}^{N} Y_i\right)}{N^2}$$

where the first summation involves the cross-product of X multiplied by Y for each individual summed across all N individuals; the other terms should be familiar. The *computational formula for the sample covariance* is:

$$s_{XY} = \frac{n\left(\sum_{i=1}^{n} X_i Y_i\right) - \left(\sum_{i=1}^{n} X_i\right)\left(\sum_{i=1}^{n} Y_i\right)}{n(n-1)}$$

where the denominator is $n(n - 1)$ so as to yield an unbiased sample estimate of the population covariance.

Table 10.2 gives an example of a population situation where a strong positive relationship is expected because as X (number of children in a family) increases, Y (number of pets in a family) also increases. Here σ_{XY} is computed as:

$$\sigma_{XY} = \frac{N\left(\sum_{i=1}^{N} X_i Y_i\right) - \left(\sum_{i=1}^{N} X_i\right)\left(\sum_{i=1}^{N} Y_i\right)}{N^2} = \frac{5(108) - (15)(30)}{5^2} = 3.6000$$

TABLE 10.2

Example Correlational Data (X = number of children, Y = number of pets)

Individual	X	Y	XY	X^2	Y^2	Rank X	Rank Y	$(\text{Rank X} - \text{Rank Y})^2$
1	1	2	2	1	4	1	1	0
2	2	6	12	4	36	2	3	1
3	3	4	12	9	16	3	2	1
4	4	8	32	16	64	4	4	0
5	5	10	50	25	100	5	5	0
Sums	15	30	108	55	220			2

The sign indicates that the relationship between X and Y is indeed positive; that is, the more children a family has, the more pets they tend to have. However, like the variance, the value of the covariance depends on the scales of the variables involved. Thus, interpretation of the magnitude of a single covariance is difficult, as it can take on literally any value. We see shortly that the correlation coefficient takes care of this problem. For this reason you are only likely to see the covariance utilized in the analysis of covariance (Chapter 14) and advanced techniques such as structural equation modeling and multilevel modeling (beyond the scope of this text).

10.1.1.3 Pearson Product-Moment Correlation Coefficient

Other methods for measuring the relationship among X and Y have been developed that are easier to interpret than the covariance. We refer to these measures as **correlation coefficients**. The first correlation coefficient we consider is the **Pearson product-moment correlation coefficient**, developed by the famous statistician Karl Pearson, and simply referred to as the Pearson here. The Pearson can be considered in several different forms, where the *population value* is denoted by ρ_{XY} (rho) and the *sample* value by r_{XY}. One conceptual form of the Pearson is a product of standardized z scores (previously described in Chapter 4). This formula for the population Pearson is given as:

$$\rho_{XY} = \frac{\sum_{i=1}^{N}(z_X z_Y)}{N}$$

where z_X and z_Y are the z scores for variables X and Y, respectively, whose product is taken for each individual, and then summed across all N individuals.

Because z scores are standardized versions of raw scores, then the Pearson correlation is simply a standardized version of the covariance. The *sign* of the Pearson denotes the direction of the relationship (e.g., positive or negative), and the *value* of the Pearson denotes the strength of the relationship. The Pearson falls on a scale from −1.00 to +1.00, where −1.00 indicates a perfect negative relationship, 0 indicates no relationship, and +1.00 indicates a perfect positive relationship. Values near .50 or −.50 are considered as moderate relationships, values near 0 as weak relationships, and values near +1.00 or −1.00 as strong relationships (although these are subjective terms). Cohen (1988) also offers conventions, which are presented later in this chapter, for interpreting the value of the correlation. As you may see as you read more statistics and research methods textbooks, there are other guidelines offered for interpreting the value of the correlation.

There are other forms of the Pearson. A second conceptual form of the Pearson is in terms of the covariance and the standard deviations, and the *population formula,* denoted by $\rho_{XY,}$ is given as:

$$\rho_{XY} = \frac{\sigma_{XY}}{\sigma_X \sigma_Y}$$

This form is useful when the covariance and standard deviations are already known. A final form of the Pearson is the *computational formula,* written as follows:

$$\rho_{XY} = \frac{N\left(\sum_{i=1}^{N} X_i Y_i\right) - \left(\sum_{i=1}^{N} X_i\right)\left(\sum_{i=1}^{N} Y_i\right)}{\sqrt{\left[N\left(\sum_{i=1}^{N} X_i^2\right) - \left(\sum_{i=1}^{N} X_i\right)^2\right]\left[N\left(\sum_{i=1}^{N} Y_i^2\right) - \left(\sum_{i=1}^{N} Y_i\right)^2\right]}}$$

where all terms should be familiar from the computational formulas of the variance and covariance. This is the formula to use for hand computations, as it is more error-free than the other previously given formulas.

For the example children–pet data given in Table 10.2, we see that the Pearson correlation is computed as follows:

$$\rho_{XY} = \frac{N\left(\sum_{i=1}^{N} X_i Y_i\right) - \left(\sum_{i=1}^{N} X_i\right)\left(\sum_{i=1}^{N} Y_i\right)}{\sqrt{\left[N\left(\sum_{i=1}^{N} X_i^2\right) - \left(\sum_{i=1}^{N} X_i\right)^2\right]\left[N\left(\sum_{i=1}^{N} Y_i^2\right) - \left(\sum_{i=1}^{N} Y_i\right)^2\right]}}$$

$$\rho_{XY} = \frac{5(108) - (15)(30)}{\sqrt{\left[5(55) - (15)^2\right]\left[5(220) - (30)^2\right]}} = .900$$

Thus, there is a very strong positive relationship among variables X (the number of children) and Y (the number of pets).

The **sample correlation** is denoted by r_{XY}. The formulas are essentially the same for the sample correlation, r_{XY}, and the population correlation, ρ_{XY}, except that n is substituted for N. For example, the computational formula for the sample correlation is noted here:

$$r_{XY} = \frac{n\left(\sum_{i=1}^{n} X_i Y_i\right) - \left(\sum_{i=1}^{n} X_i\right)\left(\sum_{i=1}^{n} Y_i\right)}{\sqrt{\left[n\left(\sum_{i=1}^{n} X_i^2\right) - \left(\sum_{i=1}^{n} X_i\right)^2\right]\left[n\left(\sum_{i=1}^{n} Y_i^2\right) - \left(\sum_{i=1}^{n} Y_i\right)^2\right]}}$$

Unlike the sample variance and covariance, the sample correlation has no correction for bias.

10.1.1.4 Inferences about the Pearson Product-Moment Correlation Coefficient

Once a researcher has determined one or more Pearson correlation coefficients, it is often useful to know whether the sample correlations are significantly different from zero. Thus, we need to visit the world of inferential statistics again. In this section we consider two different inferential tests: first for testing *whether a single sample correlation is significantly different from zero,* and second for testing *whether two independent sample correlations are significantly different.*

10.1.1.4.1 Inferences for a Single Sample

Our first inferential test is appropriate when you are interested in determining whether the correlation among variables X and Y for a *single sample* is significantly different from zero. For example, is the correlation between the number of years of education and current income significantly different from zero? The test of inference for the Pearson correlation will be conducted following the same steps as those in previous chapters. The null hypothesis is written as follows:

$$H_0: \rho = 0$$

A nondirectional alternative hypothesis, where we are willing to reject the null if the sample correlation is either significantly greater than or less than zero, is nearly always utilized. Unfortunately, the sampling distribution of the sample Pearson r is too complex to be of much value to the applied researcher. For testing whether the correlation is different from zero (i.e., where the alternative hypothesis is specified as $H_1: \rho \neq 0$), a transformation of r can be used to generate a t distributed test statistic. The test statistic is:

$$t = r\sqrt{\frac{n-2}{1-r^2}}$$

which is distributed as t (i.e., follows a t distribution) with $\nu = n - 2$ degrees of freedom, assuming that both X and Y are normally distributed. Note, however, even if one variable is normal and the other is not, the t distribution may still apply (see Hogg and Craig, 1995).

It should be noted for inferential tests of correlations that sample size plays a role in determining statistical significance. For instance, this particular test is based on $n - 2$ degrees of freedom. If the sample size is small (e.g., 10), then it is difficult to reject the null hypothesis except for very strong correlations. If the sample size is large (e.g., 200), then it is easier to reject the null hypothesis for all but very weak correlations. Thus, the statistical significance of a correlation is definitely a function of sample size, both for tests of a single correlation and for tests of two correlations.

From the example children–pet data, we want to determine whether the sample Pearson correlation is significantly different from zero, with a nondirectional alternative hypothesis and at the .05 level of significance. The test statistic is computed as follows:

$$t = r\sqrt{\frac{n-2}{1-r^2}} = .9000\sqrt{\frac{5-2}{1-.8100}} = 3.5762$$

The critical values from Table A.2 in the Appendix are $\pm_{\alpha_2} t_3 = \pm 3.182$. Thus we would *reject the null hypothesis*, as the test statistic exceeds the critical value, and conclude the correlation among variables X and Y is significantly different from zero. In summary, a strong, positive, statistically significant correlation exists between the number of children and the number of pets.

10.1.1.4.2 Inferences for Two Independent Samples

In a second situation, the researcher may have collected data from two different independent samples. It can be determined whether the correlations among variables X and Y are equal for these two independent samples of observations. For example, is the correlation among height and weight the same for children and adults? Here the null and alternative hypotheses are written as:

$$H_0: \rho_1 - \rho_2 = 0$$

$$H_1: \rho_1 - \rho_2 \neq 0$$

where ρ_1 is the correlation among X and Y for sample 1 and ρ_2 is the correlation among X and Y for sample 2. However, because correlations are not normally distributed for every value of ρ, a transformation is necessary. This transformation is known as **Fisher's Z transformation**, named after the famous statistician Sir Ronald A. Fisher, which is approximately normally distributed regardless of the value of ρ. Table A.5 in the Appendix is used to convert a sample correlation r to a Fisher's Z transformed value. Note that Fisher's Z is a totally different statistic from any z score or z statistic previously covered. The test statistic for this situation is the following:

$$z = \frac{Z_1 - Z_2}{\sqrt{\dfrac{1}{n_1 - 3} + \dfrac{1}{n_2 - 3}}}$$

where n_1 and n_2 are the sizes of the two samples, and Z_1 and Z_2 are the Fisher's Z transformed values for the two samples. The test statistic is then compared to critical values from the z distribution in Table A.1 in the Appendix. For a nondirectional alternative hypothesis where the two correlations may be different in either direction, then the critical values are $\pm_{\alpha_2} z$. Directional alternative hypotheses where the correlations are different in a particular direction can also be tested by looking in the appropriate tail of the z distribution (i.e., either $\pm_{\alpha_2} z$ or $-\pm_{\alpha_2} z$).

Consider the following example. Two samples have been independently drawn of 28 children (sample 1) and 28 adults (sample 2). For each sample, the correlations among height and weight were computed to be $r_{children} = .80$ and $r_{adults} = .40$. A nondirectional alternative hypothesis is utilized where the level of significance is set at .05. From Table A.5 in the Appendix, we first determine the Fisher's Z transformed values to be $Z_{children} = 1.099$ and $Z_{adults} = .4236$. Then the test statistic z is computed as follows:

$$z = \frac{Z_1 - Z_2}{\sqrt{\dfrac{1}{n_1 - 3} + \dfrac{1}{n_2 - 3}}} = \frac{1.099 - .4236}{\sqrt{\dfrac{1}{25} + \dfrac{1}{25}}} = 2.3878$$

From Table A.1 in the Appendix, the critical values are $\pm_{\alpha_2} z = \pm 1.96$. Our decision then is to *reject the null hypothesis* and conclude that height and weight do not have the same correlation for children and adults. In other words, there is a statistically significant difference of the height–weight correlation between children and adults with a strong effect size (as we will see later, the effect size q is computed as $q = Z_1 - Z_2 = 1.099 - .4236 = .6754$). This inferential test assumes both variables are normally distributed for each population and that scores are independent across individuals; however, the procedure is not very robust to nonnormality, because the Fisher's Z transformation assumes normality (Duncan & Layard, 1973; Wilcox, 2003; Yu & Dunn, 1982). Thus, caution should be exercised in using the z test when data are nonnormal (e.g., Yu & Dunn recommend the use of Kendall's τ, as discussed later in this chapter).

10.1.1.5 Issues Regarding Correlations

In the discussion of correlations, there are many concepts that are important, but two in particular that we will note. These include *causality* and *restriction of range*. See Box 10.1 for a summary.

BOX 10.1 Causality and Restriction of Range

Issue	Misinterpretation	Correct Interpretation
Causality	A correlation between X and Y equates to X *causes* Y	A correlation between X and Y equates to evidence of a relationship between X and Y that may be a result of any number of situations including: a. X causing Y b. Y causing X c. A third variable Z causing both X and Y d. Even more variables causing both X and Y
Restriction of range	A weak correlation between X and Y equates to little or no relationship between X and Y	A weak correlation between X and Y *may* equate to little or no relationship between X and Y *or* it may equate to scores on one or both variables being restricted due to the nature of the sample or population

10.1.1.5.1 Correlation and Causality

An important matter to consider is an often-made misinterpretation of a correlation. Many individuals (e.g., researchers, the public, and the media) often infer a causal relationship from a strong correlation. However, a correlation by itself should never be used to infer **causation**. In particular, a high correlation among variables X and Y does not imply that one variable is causing the other; it simply means that these two variables are related in some fashion. Variables X and Y may be highly correlated for a number of different reasons. A high correlation could be the result of (a) X causing Y, or (b) Y causing X, or (c) a third variable Z causing both X and Y, or (d) even more variables being involved in creating the relationship between X and Y. The only methods that can strictly be used to infer cause are experimental methods that employ random assignment where one variable is manipulated by the researcher (the cause), a second variable is subsequently observed (the effect), and all other variables are controlled. Note, however, that there are some excellent quasi-experimental methods—propensity score analysis and regression discontinuity—that can be used in some situations and that mimic random assignment and increase the likelihood of speaking to causal inference (Shadish, Cook, & Campbell, 2002).

10.1.1.5.2 Restriction of Range

A final issue to consider is the effect of **restriction of the range** of scores on one or both variables. For example, suppose that we are interested in the relationship among GRE scores and graduate grade point average (GGPA). In the entire population of students, the relationship might be depicted by the scatterplot shown in Figure 10.3. Say the Pearson correlation is found to be .60 as depicted by the entire sample in the full scatterplot. Now we take a more restricted population of students, those students at highly selective Ivy-Covered University (ICU). ICU only admits students whose GRE scores are above the cutoff score shown in Figure 10.3. Because of restriction of range in the scores of the GRE variable, the strength of the relationship among GRE and GGPA at ICU is reduced to a Pearson correlation of .20, where only the subsample portion of the plot to the right of the cutoff score is involved. Thus, when scores on one or both variables are restricted due to the nature of the sample or population, then the magnitude of the correlation will usually be reduced [although see an exception in Figure 6.3 from Wilcox (2003)].

It is difficult for two variables to be highly related when one or both variables have little variability. This is due to the nature of the formula. Recall that one version of the Pearson formula consisted of standard deviations in the denominator. Remember that the standard deviation measures the distance of the sample scores from the mean. When there is restriction of range, the distance of the individual scores from the mean is minimized. In other words, there is less variation or variability around the mean. This translates to smaller correlations (and smaller covariances). *If the size of the standard deviation for one variable is reduced, everything else being equal, then the size of correlations with other variables will also be reduced.* In other words, we need sufficient variation for a relationship to be evidenced through the correlation coefficient value. Otherwise the correlation is likely to be reduced in magnitude and you may miss an important correlation. If you must use a restrictive subsample, we suggest you choose measures of greater variability for correlational purposes.

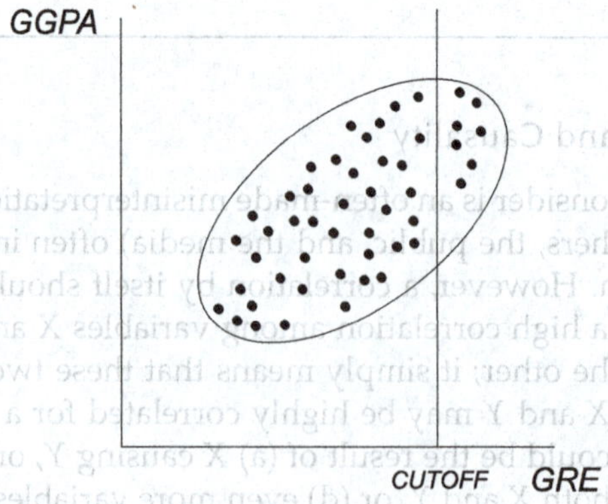

FIGURE 10.3
Restriction of range example.

Outliers, observations that are different from the bulk of the observations, also reduce the magnitude of correlations. If one observation is quite different from the rest such that it fell outside of the ellipse, then the correlation would be smaller in magnitude (e.g., closer to zero) than the correlation without the outlier. We discuss outliers in this context in Chapter 17.

10.1.1.5.3 Confidence Intervals

Confidence intervals for correlation coefficients have been proposed (e.g., Bonett & Wright, 2000) but the computations for such are not as straightforward as the confidence intervals with which we have worked previously given that the sampling distribution of r is not normally distributed. Thus, confidence intervals for Pearson's correlation, for example, require transformation of the correlation coefficient to Fisher's z to obtain the confidence limits and then back transformations to the correlation scale. As such, rather than spend time in hand calculations, we will rely on a number of tools now available that make computing confidence intervals for correlations quite easy. We will later illustrate the use of an online calculator as well as **R** for computing confidence intervals.

10.1.1.6 Other Measures of Association

Thus far we have considered one type of correlation, the Pearson product-moment correlation coefficient. The Pearson is most appropriate when both variables are at least interval level. That is, both variables X and Y are interval and/or ratio level variables. The Pearson is considered a parametric procedure given the distributional assumptions associated with it. If both variables are not at least interval level, then other measures of association, considered *nonparametric procedures*, should be considered because they do not have distributional assumptions associated with them. In this section we examine in detail the Spearman's rho and phi types of correlation coefficients and briefly mention several other types. While a distributional assumption for these correlations is not necessary, the assumption of independence still applies (and thus a random sample from the population is assumed).

10.1.1.6.1 Spearman's Rho

Spearman's rho's rank correlation coefficient is appropriate when *both variables are ordinal in scale*. This type of correlation was developed by Charles Spearman, the famous quantitative psychologist. Recall from Chapter 1 that ordinal data are where individuals have been rank ordered, such as class rank. Thus, for both variables, either the data are already available in ranks, or the researcher (or computer) converts the raw data to ranks prior to the analysis.

The equation for computing Spearman's rho's correlation is:

$$\rho_s = 1 - \frac{6\left[\sum_{i=1}^{N}\left(X_i - Y_i\right)^2\right]}{N\left(N^2 - 1\right)}$$

where ρ_s denotes the population Spearman's rho correlation and $(X_i - Y_i)$ represents the difference between the ranks on variables *X* and *Y* for unit *i*. The sample Spearman's rho correlation is denoted by r_s where *n* replaces *N*, but otherwise the equation remains the same. In case you were wondering where the 6 in the equation comes from, you will find interesting an article by Lamb (1984). Unfortunately, this particular computational formula is only appropriate when there are no ties among the ranks for either variable. An example of a tie in rank would be if two cases scored the same value on either *X* or *Y*. With ties, the formula given is only approximate, depending on the number of ties. In the case of ties, particularly when there are more than a few, many researchers recommend using Kendall's τ (tau) as an alternative correlation (e.g., Wilcox, 1995).

As with the Pearson correlation, Spearman's rho ranges from −1.0 to +1.0. Conventions that we use for interpreting the Pearson correlation (e.g., Cohen, 1988) can be applied to Spearman's rho correlation values as well. The sign of the coefficient can be interpreted as with the Pearson. A *negative sign* indicates that as the values for one variable increase, the values for the other variable decrease. A *positive sign* indicates that as one variable increases in value, the value of the second variable also increases.

As an example, consider the children–pets data again in Table 10.2. To the right of the table, you see the last three columns labeled as rank *X*, rank *Y*, and (*rank X* − *rank Y*)². The raw scores were converted to ranks, where the lowest raw score received a rank of 1. The last column lists the squared rank differences. As there were no ties, the computations are as follows:

$$\rho_s = 1 - \frac{6\left[\sum_{i=1}^{N}(X_i - Y_i)^2\right]}{N(N^2-1)} = 1 - \frac{6(2)}{5(24)} = .9000$$

Thus again there is a strong positive relationship among variables *X* and *Y*. It is a coincidence that $\rho = \rho_s$ for this dataset, but not so for computational problem 1 at the end of this chapter.

To test whether a sample Spearman's rho correlation is significantly different from zero, we examine the following null hypothesis (the alternative hypothesis would be stated as $H_1: \rho_s \neq 0$):

$$H_0 : \rho_s = 0$$

The test statistic is given as follows:

$$t = \frac{r_s\sqrt{n-2}}{\sqrt{1-r_s^2}}$$

which is approximately distributed as a *t* distribution with $\nu = n - 2$ degrees of freedom (Ramsey, 1989). The approximation works best when *n* is at least 10. A nondirectional hypothesis, where we are willing to reject the null if the sample correlation is either significantly greater than or less than zero, is nearly always utilized. From the example, we want to determine whether the sample Spearman's rho correlation is significantly different from zero at the .05 level of significance. For a nondirectional hypothesis, the test statistic is computed as we see here:

$$t = \frac{r_s\sqrt{n-2}}{\sqrt{1-r_s^2}} = \frac{.9000\sqrt{5-2}}{\sqrt{1-.81}} = 3.5762$$

where the critical values from Table A.2 in the Appendix are $\pm_{\alpha_2}t_3 = \pm 3.182$. Given that the test statistic (3.5762) is greater than our critical value (+3.182), we *reject the null hypothesis* and conclude that the correlation is significantly different from zero, *strong in magnitude* (suggested by the value of the correlation coefficient; using Cohen's guidelines for interpretation as an effect size, this would be considered a large effect), and *positive in direction* (evidenced from the sign of the correlation coefficient). The exact sampling distribution for when $3 \le n \le 18$ is given by Ramsey (1989).

10.1.1.6.2 Kendall's Tau

Another correlation that can be computed with ordinal data is Kendall's tau, τ, which also uses ranks of data to calculate the correlation coefficient (and has an adjustment for tied ranks). The ranking for Kendall's tau differs from Spearman's rho in the following way. With Kendall's tau, the values for one variable are rank ordered and then the order of the second variable is examined to see how many pairs of values are out of order. A *perfect positive correlation* (+1.0) is achieved with Kendall's tau when *no* scores are out of order, and a *perfect negative correlation* (−1.0) is obtained when *all* scores are out of order. Values for Kendall's tau range from −1.0 to +1.0. Conventions for interpreting the Pearson correlation (e.g., Cohen, 1988) can be applied to Kendall's tau correlation values as well. The sign of the coefficient can be interpreted as with the Pearson: A *negative sign* indicates that as the values for one variable increase, the values for the second variable decrease. A *positive sign* indicates that as one variable increases in value, the value of the second variable also increases.

While similar in some respects, Spearman's rho and Kendall's tau are based on different calculations and thus finding different results is not uncommon. While both are appropriate when ordinal data are being correlated, it has been suggested that Kendall's tau (rather than Spearman's rho) provides a better estimation of the population correlation coefficient value given the sample data (Howell, 2010), especially with smaller sample sizes (e.g., $n < 10$).

10.1.1.6.3 Phi

The phi coefficient, ρ_ϕ, is appropriate when *both variables are dichotomous in nature* (and is statistically equivalent to the Pearson). Recall from Chapter 1 that a dichotomous variable is one consisting of only two categories (i.e., binary), such as sex, pass/fail, or enrolled/dropped out. Thus, the variables being correlated would be either nominal or ordinal in scale. When correlating two dichotomous variables, one can think of a 2 × 2 contingency table as previously discussed in Chapter 8. For instance, to determine if there is a relationship among gender and whether students are still enrolled since their freshman year, a contingency table like Table 10.3 can be constructed. Here the columns correspond to the two levels of the enrollment status variable, "enrolled" (coded 1) or "dropped out" (0), and the rows correspond to the two levels of the gender variable, "female" (1) or "male" (0). The cells indicate the frequencies for the particular combinations of the levels of the two

TABLE 10.3

Contingency Table for Phi Correlation

	Enrollment Status		
Student Gender	**Dropped Out (0)**	**Enrolled (1)**	
Female (1)	$a = 5$	$b = 20$	$a + b = 25$
Male (0)	$c = 15$	$d = 10$	$c + d = 25$
	$a + c = 20$	$b + d = 30$	$a + b + c + d = 50$

variables. If the frequencies in the cells are denoted by letters, then *a* represents females who dropped out, *b* represents females who are enrolled, *c* indicates males who dropped out, and *d* indicates males who are enrolled.

The equation for computing the phi coefficient is

$$\rho_\phi = \frac{(bc - ad)}{\sqrt{(a+c)(b+d)(a+b)(c+d)}}$$

where ρ_ϕ denotes the population phi coefficient (for consistency's sake, although typically written as ϕ), and r_ϕ denotes the sample phi coefficient using the same equation. Note that the *bc* product involves the *consistent cells*, where both values are the same, either both 0 or both 1, and the *ad* product involves the *inconsistent cells*, where both values are different.

Conventions for interpreting the magnitude of Pearson correlation (e.g., Cohen, 1988) can be applied to the phi coefficient as well. However, given the binary nature of the data, the *sign* of the coefficient *cannot* be interpreted as with the Pearson.

Using the example data from Table 10.3, we compute the phi coefficient to be the following:

$$\rho_\phi = \frac{(bc - ad)}{\sqrt{(a+c)(b+d)(a+b)(c+d)}} = \frac{(300 - 50)}{\sqrt{(20)(30)(25)(25)}} = .4082$$

Thus, there is a moderate, positive relationship between gender and enrollment status. We see from the table that a larger proportion of females than males are still enrolled.

To test whether a sample phi correlation is significantly different from zero, we test the following null hypothesis (the alternative hypothesis would be stated as H_1: $\rho_\varphi \neq 0$):

$$H_0 : \rho_\phi = 0$$

The test statistic is given as:

$$\chi^2 = n r_\phi^2$$

which is distributed as a χ^2 distribution with 1 degree of freedom. From the example, we want to determine whether the sample phi correlation is significantly different from zero at the .05 level of significance. The test statistic is computed as

$$\chi^2 = nr_\phi^2 = (50)(.4082)^2 = 8.3314$$

and the critical value from Table A.3 in the Appendix is ${}_{.05}\chi_1^2 = 3.84$. Thus, we would *reject the null hypothesis* and conclude that the correlation among gender and enrollment status is significantly different from zero.

10.1.1.6.4 Cramer's Phi

When the variables being correlated have more than two categories, Cramer's phi (Cramer's *V* in SPSS) can be computed. Thus, Cramer's phi is appropriate when *both variables are nominal (and at least one variable has more than two categories)* or *when one variable is nominal and the other variable is ordinal (and at least one variable has more than two categories)*. As with the other correlation coefficients that we have discussed, values range from −1.0 to +1.0. Conventions for interpreting the magnitude of Pearson correlation (e.g., Cohen, 1988) can be applied to Cramer's phi coefficient as well. However, given the nominal nature of one or both of the variables being correlated, the *sign* of Cramer's phi coefficient *cannot* be interpreted as with the Pearson.

10.1.1.6.5 Other Correlations

Other types of correlations have been developed for different combinations of types of variables, but these are rarely used in practice and are unavailable in most statistical packages (e.g., rank biserial and point biserial). Table 10.4 provides suggestions for when different types of correlations are most appropriate. We mention briefly the two other types of correlations in the table: the rank biserial correlation is appropriate when one variable is dichotomous and the other variable is ordinal, whereas the point biserial correlation is appropriate when one variable is dichotomous and the other variable is interval or ratio (statistically equivalent to the Pearson, thus the Pearson correlation can be computed in this situation).

TABLE 10.4

Different Types of Correlation Coefficients

	Variable X		
Variable Y	**Nominal**	**Ordinal**	**Interval/Ratio**
Nominal	Phi (when both variables are dichotomous) or Cramer's *V* (when one or both variables have more than two categories)	Rank biserial or Cramer's *V*	Point biserial (Pearson in lieu of point biserial)
Ordinal	Rank biserial or Cramer's *V*	Spearman or Kendall's tau	Spearman or Kendall's tau or Pearson*
Interval/ratio	Point biserial (Pearson in lieu of point biserial)	Spearman or Kendall's tau or Pearson*	Pearson

*See cautionary note in text when using Pearson in this situation.

In reviewing Table 10.4, we see that when one variable is ordinal and the second variable is interval or ratio, researchers may choose Pearson, Spearman, or Kendall's tau. In this situation, a researcher using Pearson with an ordinal item is essentially treating the ordinal item as continuous. *Thus, we caution readers in using Pearson with ordinal variables, particularly if there are a small number of levels within the variable.* Our professional opinion when one variable is ordinal and the second interval/ratio is to use Spearman or Kendall's tau unless you have good evidence to support the case that the ordinal variable has properties of a continuous variable (e.g., skew and kurtosis within normality; bell-shaped histogram) and the assumption of linearity for the Pearson correlation coefficient has been met. An ordinal item with five or fewer categories (and many times more than five categories) will likely *not* provide evidence to support the use of Pearson in this situation.

10.1.2 Power

Cohen (1988) has a nice series of power tables for determining power and sample size when planning a correlational study. We will later illustrate the use of G*Power for conducting power analysis in correlational studies.

10.1.3 Effect Size

We will preface the discussion of effect size as it relates to correlations by saying that correlation coefficients are, by default, effect size indices. A correlation coefficient provides, for example in the case of the Pearson correlation, the strength and direction of a relationship. We can also interpret that correlation coefficient as a measure of effect.

10.1.3.1 Effect Size for Pearson Correlation Coefficient

Effect size and power are always important, particularly here where sample size plays such a large role. Cohen (1988) proposed using r as a measure of effect size, using the subjective standard (ignoring the sign of the correlation) of $r = .1$ as a weak effect, $r = .3$ as a moderate effect, and $r = .5$ as a strong effect. These standards were developed for the behavioral sciences, but other standards may be used in other areas of inquiry.

10.1.3.2 Effect Size for Two Independent Samples

Cohen (1988) proposed a measure of effect size for the difference between two independent correlations as $q = Z_1 - Z_2$. The subjective standards proposed (ignoring the sign) are $q = .1$ as a weak effect, $q = .3$ as a moderate effect, and $q = .5$ as a strong effect (these are the standards for the behavioral sciences, although standards vary across disciplines).

10.1.3.3 Effect Size for Other Correlations

Cohen's guidelines (1988) for interpreting the correlation in terms of effect size can be applied to Spearman's rho, Kendall's tau, phi, and Cramer's phi correlations, as they can with any other correlation examined. These are, where r denotes other correlation coefficient measures: $r = .1$ as a weak effect, $r = .3$ as a moderate effect, and $r = .5$ as a strong effect.

Table 10.5 Correlation Coefficients as Effect Sizes and Interpretations

Effect Size	Interpretation
• Pearson correlation coefficient (r) • Spearman's rho (ρ_s) • Kendall's tau (τ) • Phi (ρ_ϕ) • Cramer's phi (ϕ_c)	Degree of relationship between two variables: • Small effect = .10 • Medium effect = .30 • Large effect = .50
Cohen's q	Standardized difference between Fisher's z_r transformed correlations: • Small effect = .10 • Medium effect = .30 • Large effect = .50

10.1.4 Assumptions

The Pearson correlation has two assumptions. First, the Pearson correlation is appropriate only when there is a linear relationship assumed between the variables (given that both variables are at least interval in scale). Also, and as we have seen with the other inferential procedures discussed in previous chapters, we need to again assume that the scores of the individuals are independent of one another.

First, as mentioned previously, the Pearson correlation assumes that the relationship among X and Y is a *linear relationship*. In fact, the Pearson correlation, as a measure of relationship, is really a *linear* measure of relationship. Recall from earlier in the chapter the scatterplots to which we fit a straight line. The linearity assumption means that a straight line provides a reasonable fit to the data. *If the relationship is not a linear one, then the linearity assumption is violated.* However, these correlational methods can still be computed, fitting a straight line to the data, albeit inappropriately. The result of such a violation is that the strength of the relationship will be reduced. In other words, the linear correlation will be much closer to zero than the true nonlinear relationship.

For example, there is a perfect curvilinear relationship shown by the data in Figure 10.4 where all of the points fall precisely on the curved line. Something like this might occur if you correlate age with time in the mile run, as younger and older folks would take longer to run this distance than others. If these data are fit by a straight line, then the correlation

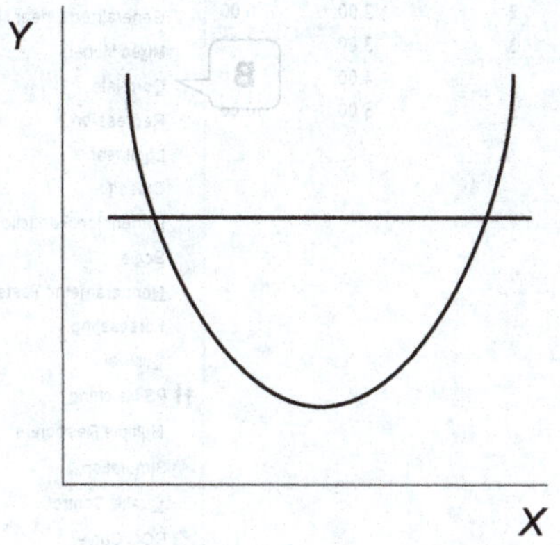

FIGURE 10.4
Nonlinear relationship.

will be severely reduced, in this case, to a value of zero (i.e., the horizontal straight line that runs through the curved line). This is another good reason to always examine your data. The computer may determine that the Pearson correlation among variables X and Y is small or around zero. However, on examination of the data, you might find that the relationship is indeed nonlinear; thus, you should get to know your data. We return to the assessment of nonlinear relationships in Chapter 17.

Second, the assumption of *independence* applies to correlations. This assumption is met when units or cases are randomly sampled from the population.

10.2 Computing Bivariate Measures of Association Using SPSS

Next let us see what SPSS has to offer in terms of measures of association using the children–pets example dataset. SPSS has two tools for obtaining measures of association, dependent on the measurement scale of your variables: the Bivariate Correlation program (for computing the Pearson, Spearman's rho, and Kendall's tau) and the Crosstabs program (for computing the Pearson, Spearman's rho, Kendall's tau, phi, Cramer's phi, and several other types of measures of association).

10.2.1. Bivariate Correlations

Step 1. To locate the Bivariate Correlations program, we go to "Analyze" in the top pulldown menu, then select "Correlate," and then "Bivariate." Following the screenshot of Step 1 in Figure 10.5 produces the "Bivariate" dialog box.

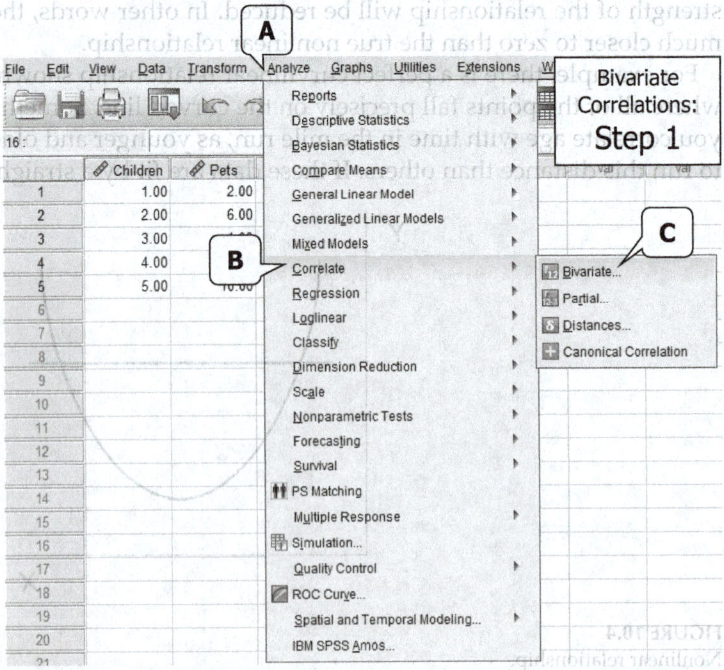

FIGURE 10.5
Bivariate correlations: Step 1.

Step 2. Next, from the main "Bivariate Correlations" dialog box, click the variables to correlate (i.e., "Number of children" and "Number of pets") and move them into the "Variables" box by clicking the arrow button. In the bottom half of this dialog box options are available for selecting the type of correlation (*this is where it's important that you understand the measurement scales of your variables so that you are computing the correct correlation coefficient given the scale of measurement of your variables*), one- or two-tailed test (i.e., directional or nondirectional test), and whether to flag statistically significant correlations. For illustrative purposes, we will place a checkmark to generate the "Pearson," "Kendall's tau-b," and "Spearman's rho" correlation coefficients. We will also select the radio button for a "Two-tailed" test of significance and at the very bottom check "Flag significant correlations" (which simply means an asterisk will be placed next to significant correlations in the output). See the screenshot of Step 2 in Figure 10.6.

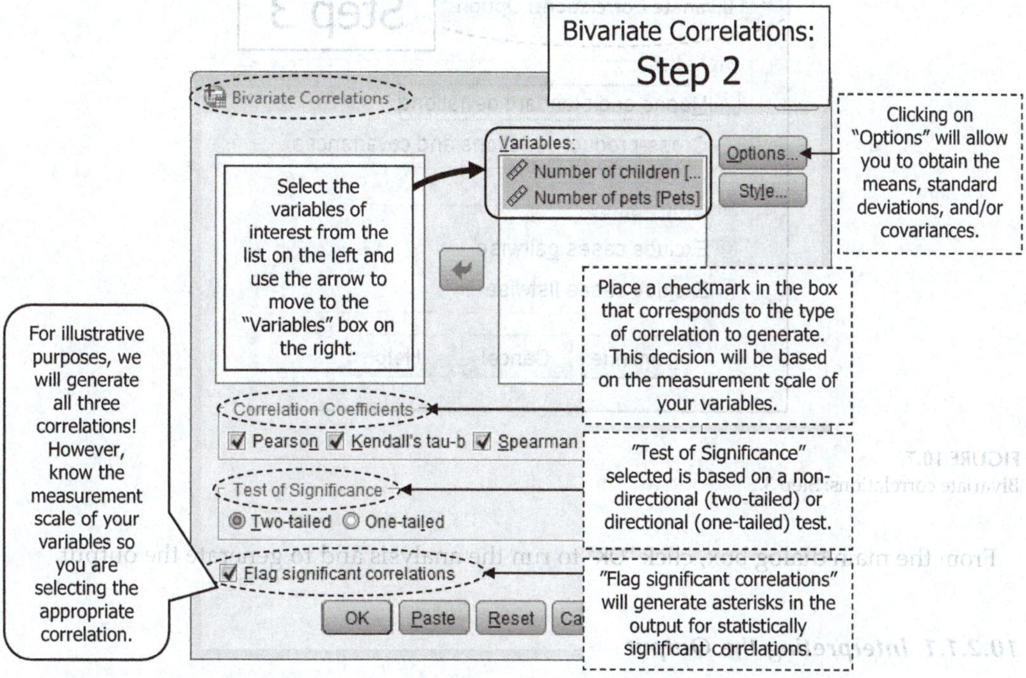

FIGURE 10.6
Bivariate correlations: Step 2.

Step 3 (optional). To obtain means, standard deviations, and/or covariances, as well as options for dealing with missing data (listwise or pairwise deletion), click the "Options" button located in the top-right corner of the main dialog box. Note that the default for dealing with missing values is "Exclude cases pairwise" (see the screenshot of Step 3 in Figure 10.7). This means that all available data are included in the computation for each bivariate correlation, and thus if you are computing more than one correlation, you will end up with varying sample sizes if there is some missing data on one or more variables being correlated.

Listwise deletion means that any case that has missing data is excluded from *all* bivariate correlations that are computed. As an example, let's say we have a total sample size of 10 with three variables (X, Y, and Z) on which we are computing bivariate correlations. Let's also say that we have one case missing a score on X. With pairwise deletion, the correlation between X and Y and the correlation between X and Z will be based on a sample size of 9. However, the correlation between Y and Z will be based on a sample size of 10. This can be quite confusing, particularly if you have quite a bit of missing data and if you are generating quite a few correlations, as the sample for the correlations differs based on the missingness! With listwise deletion, all three correlations will be based on a sample size of 9. In essence, you've completely lost the case that has missing data on variable X with listwise deletion. As a researcher, you need to consider *prior* to generating your correlation coefficients how you want to deal with missing data. Generally, you should deal with missing prior to generating your correlations as neither pairwise or listwise deletion are considered ideal strategies for addressing missing data.

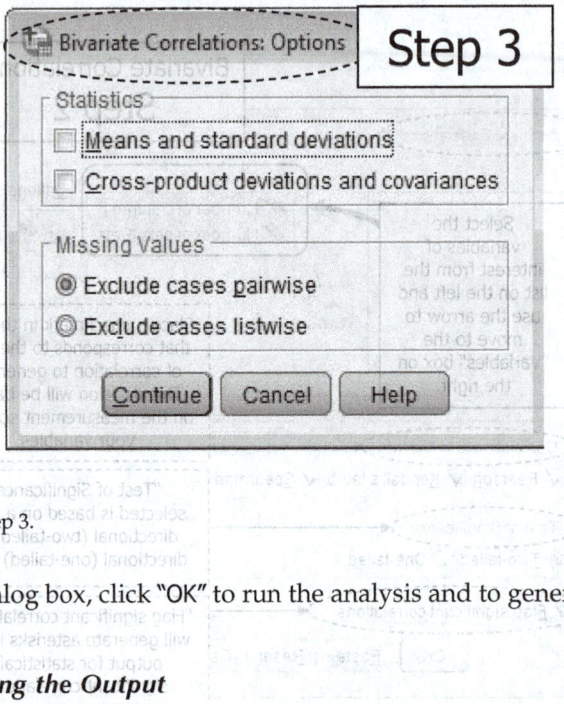

FIGURE 10.7
Bivariate correlations: Step 3.

From the main dialog box, click "OK" to run the analysis and to generate the output.

10.2.1.1 Interpreting the Output

The output for generation of the Pearson and Spearman's rho bivariate correlations between number of children and number of pets appears in Table 10.6. For illustrative purposes, we asked for all three correlations: the Pearson, Kendall's tau-b, and Spearman's rho correlations (although the Pearson is the appropriate correlation given the measurement scales of our variables, we have also generated Kendall's tau-b and Spearman's rho so that the output can be reviewed). Thus, the top Correlations box gives the Pearson results and the bottom Correlations box provides Kendall's tau and Spearman's rho results. In both cases the output presents the correlation, sample size (N in SPSS language, although usually denoted as n by everyone else), observed level of significance, and asterisks denoting statistically significant correlations. In reviewing Table 10.6, we see that SPSS does not provide any output in terms of confidence intervals (illustrated in the next section), power, or effect size. Later in the chapter, we illustrate the use of G*Power for computing power. Effect size is easily interpreted from the correlation coefficient value utilizing Cohen (1988) subjective standards previously described.

TABLE 10.6

SPSS Results for Pearson's Correlation Coefficient

N represents the total sample size.

The results are presented as a matrix. This means that the bottom half of the table presents the same information as that presented in the top half.

Correlations

		Number of children	Number of pets
Number of children	Pearson Correlation	1	.900*
	Sig. (2-tailed)		.037
	N	5	5
Number of pets	Pearson Correlation	.900*	1
	Sig. (2-tailed)	.037	
	N	5	5

*. Correlation is significant at the 0.05 level (2-tailed).

The bivariate Pearson correlations are presented in the top row. The value of '1' indicates the Pearson correlation of the variable with itself. The correlation of interest (relationship of number of children to number of pets) is **.900.** The asterisk indicates the correlation is statistically significant at an alpha of .05.

The probability is less than 4% (see "Sig. (2-tailed)") that we would see this relationship by random chance if the relationship between variables was zero (i.e., if the null hypothesis was really true).

Remember that you will select the correlation to compute based on the measurement scale of the variable. All correlations are computed here simply for illustrative purposes.

Nonparametric Correlations

Correlations

			Number of children	Number of pets
Kendall's tau_b	Number of children	Correlation Coefficient	1.000	.800
		Sig. (2-tailed)	.	.050
		N	5	5
	Number of pets	Correlation Coefficient	.800	1.000
		Sig. (2-tailed)	.050	.
		N	5	5
Spearman's rho	Number of children	Correlation Coefficient	1.000	.900*
		Sig. (2-tailed)	.	.037
		N	5	5
	Number of pets	Correlation Coefficient	.900*	1.000
		Sig. (2-tailed)	.037	.
		N	5	5

*. Correlation is significant at the 0.05 level (2-tailed).

The results for the same data computed with Kendall's tau-b and Spearman's rho are presented here and interpreted similarly. While both correlations are similar in value, Kendall's tau provides a better estimation when sample sizes are smaller (e.g., $n \leq 10$ as seen here).

10.2.1.2 Generating Confidence Intervals for the Effect Size (Pearson Correlation Coefficient)

Confidence intervals (CI) can be computed for correlations. *Larger CI suggest lower precision, and smaller CI reflect higher precision*. An excellent online calculator for computing all types of effect sizes and their confidence intervals is provided by Dr. David B. Wilson and is available through the Campbell Collaboration (see https://campbellcollaboration.org/research-resources/effect-size-calculator.html). Although designed for use when conducting meta-analyses, the online calculator comes in handy whenever an effect size and its CI are desired.

Let's look at the example using the correlation we just generated with children and pets. Correlating the number of children and the number of pets, we find a Pearson correlation

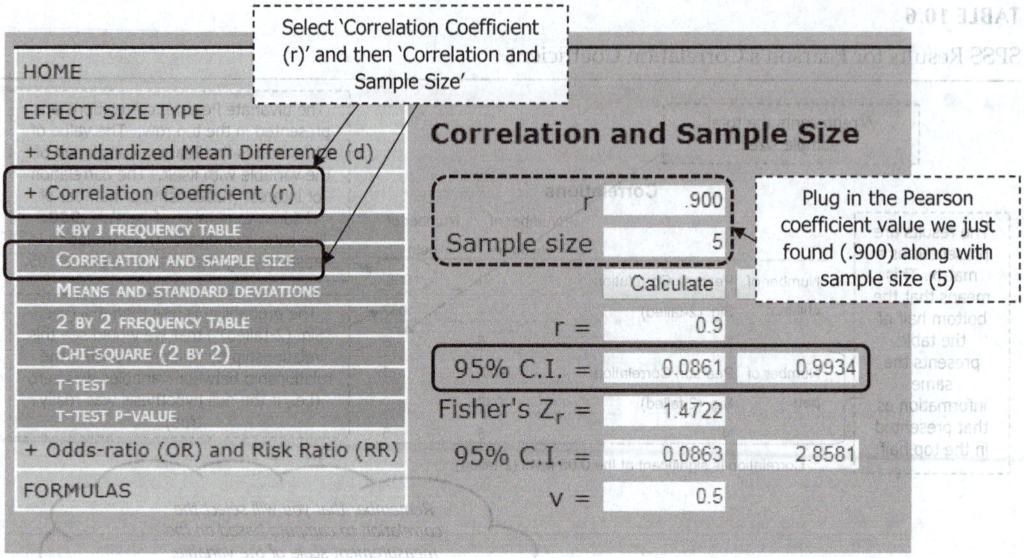

FIGURE 10.8
Confidence interval for the Pearson correlation coefficient.

of .900. Using Campbell's effect size calculator for a correlation, along with the sample size, we find the 95% CI of (.0861, .9934) (see Figure 10.8). Because the confidence interval does not contain 0, our null value (i.e., reflecting no relationship), this provides evidence to suggest a statistically significant relationship between the number of children and the number of pets. Also on the output, we see Fisher's Z_r and its related confidence interval. The sampling distribution of Pearson is not normally distributed. Thus, to compute confidence intervals for a Pearson correlation, r is converted to Fisher's Z_r, the confidence interval using Fisher's Z_r is then computed, and the Fisher's Z_r confidence interval values are then converted back to Pearson's r. Fisher's Z_r may sound familiar as we discussed this in relation to inferences for two independent samples as well!

10.2.2 Using Crosstabs to Compute Correlations

The Crosstabs program has already been discussed in Chapter 8, but it can also be used for obtaining many measures of association (specifically Spearman's rho, Kendall's tau, Pearson, phi and Cramer's phi). We will illustrate the use of Crosstabs for two nominal variables, thus generating phi and Cramer's phi.

Step 1. To compute phi or Cramer's phi correlations, go to "Analyze" in the top pulldown, then select "Descriptive Statistics," and then select the "Crosstabs" procedure. See the screenshot for Step 1 in Figure 10.9.

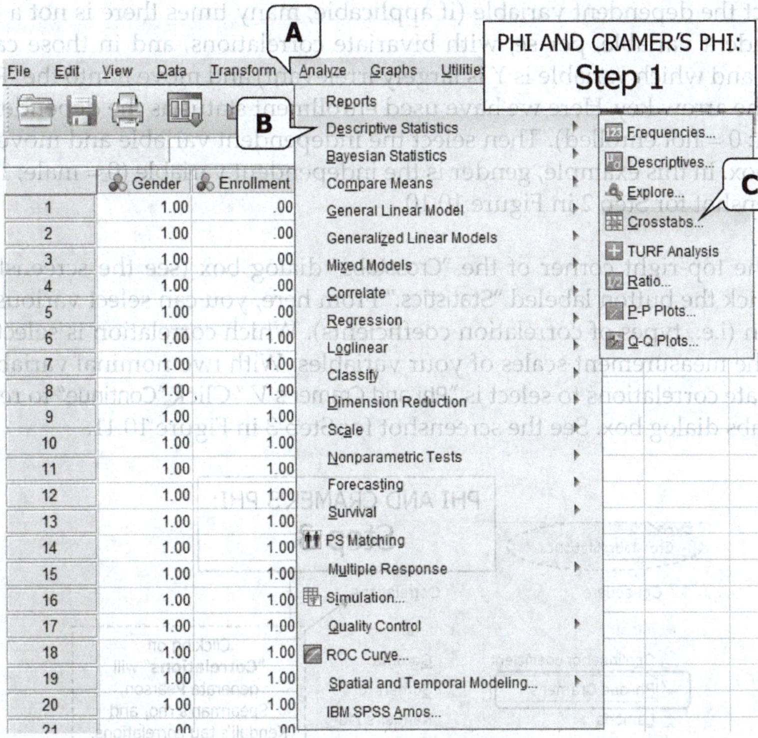

FIGURE 10.9
Phi and Cramer's phi: Step 1.

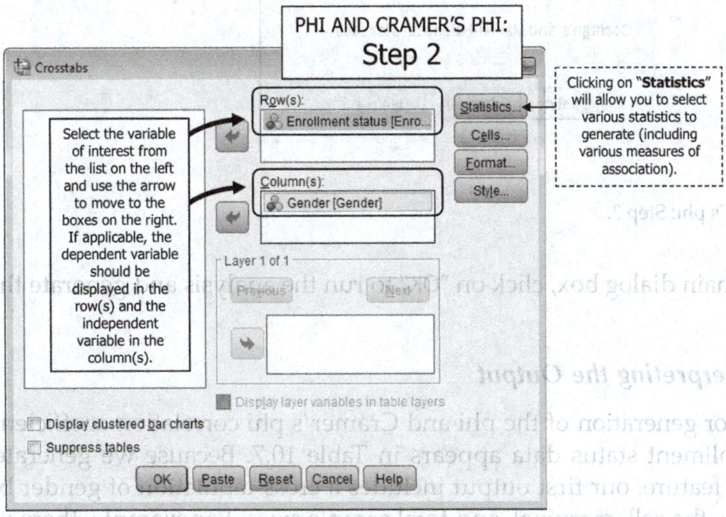

FIGURE 10.10
Phi and Cramer's phi: Step 2.

Step 2. Select the dependent variable (if applicable; many times there is not a dependent and independent variable, per se, with bivariate correlations, and in those cases which variable is *X* and which variable is *Y* is largely irrelevant) and move it into the "Row(s)" box by clicking the arrow key. Here we have used enrollment status as the dependent variable (1 = enrolled; 0 = not enrolled). Then select the independent variable and move it into the "Column(s)" box. In this example, gender is the independent variable (0 = male; 1 = female). See the screenshot for Step 2 in Figure 10.10.

Step 3. In the top-right corner of the "Crosstabs" dialog box (see the screenshot in Figure 10.10), click the button labeled "Statistics." From here, you can select various measures of association (i.e., types of correlation coefficients). Which correlation is selected should depend on the measurement scales of your variables. With two nominal variables, one of the appropriate correlations to select is "Phi and Cramer's *V*." Click "Continue" to return to the main Crosstabs dialog box. See the screenshot for Step 3 in Figure 10.11.

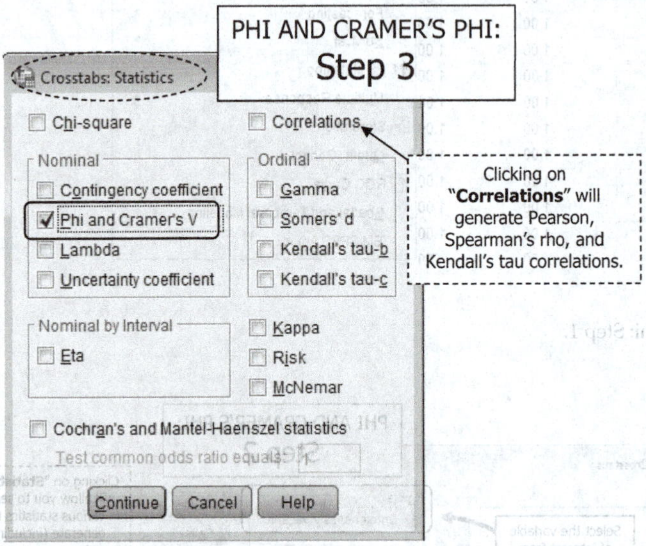

FIGURE 10.11
Phi and Cramer's phi: Step 3.

From the main dialog box, click on "OK" to run the analysis and generate the output.

10.2.2.1 Interpreting the Output

The output for generation of the phi and Cramer's phi correlation coefficients using gender and enrollment status data appears in Table 10.7. Because we generated this using the Crosstab feature, our first output includes a cross-tabulation of gender by enrollment status. We see the cell, marginal, and total sample sizes. For example, there were 15 males who dropped out and 15 females who enrolled. The next table provides the correlation coefficient values. We have a 2 × 2 table, so phi and Cramer's phi results in the same value: .350. At an alpha of .05, this is a statistically significant correlation ($p = .019$). In reviewing Table 10.7, we see that SPSS does not provide any output in terms of confidence intervals (which will be discussed in the next section), power, or effect size. Later in the chapter, we illustrate the use of G*Power for computing power, however G*Power does not have

TABLE 10.7

SPSS Results for Phi and Cramer's Phi Correlations

Enrollment status * Gender Crosstabulation

Count

		Gender		
		Male	Female	Total
Enrollment status	Dropped out	15	5	20
	Enrolled	10	15	25
Total		25	20	45

Since we computed our correlation using the Crosstab feature, we are provided a crosstab of our variables showing the sample sizes per cell as well as marginal and total sample sizes.

Symmetric Measures

		Value	Approximate Significance
Nominal by Nominal	Phi	.350	.019
	Cramer's V	.350	.019
N of Valid Cases		45	

The 'approximate significance' is our *p* value. In this case, we have a 2 x 2 table so phi and Cramer's phi results in the same correlation coefficient value (.350), and this is statistically significant at an alpha of .05 ($p = .019$).

Remember that you will select the correlation to compute based on the measurement scale of the variable and generally will only present results from one procedure. In other words, we would present either phi or Cramer's phi but not generally both.

a direct way to estimate power for phi or Cramer's phi. Effect size is easily interpreted from the correlation coefficient value utilizing Cohen (1988) subjective standards previously described. Remember that the sign for phi and Cramer's phi is irrelevant given the nominal nature of the data.

10.2.2.2 Generating Confidence Intervals for the Effect Size (Phi and Cramer's Phi)

Confidence intervals (CI) can be computed for correlations. *Larger CI suggest lower precision, and smaller CI reflect higher precision.* An excellent online calculator for computing all types of effect sizes and their confidence intervals is provided by Dr. David B. Wilson and is available through the Campbell Collaboration (see https://campbellcollaboration.org/research-resources/effect-size-calculator.html). Although designed for use when conducting meta-analyses, the online calculator comes in handy whenever an effect size and its CI are desired.

Let's look at the example using the correlation we just generated with gender and enrollment. Correlating gender and enrollment, a 2 × 2 table, we find phi and Cramer's phi of .350. Using Campbell's effect size calculator for a correlation, along with the sample size, we find the 95% CI of (.0519, .5908) (see Figure 10.12). Because the confidence interval does not contain 0, our null value (i.e., reflecting no relationship), this provides evidence to suggest a statistically significant relationship between gender and enrollment status. Also on the output, we see Fisher's Z_r and its related confidence interval. As noted previously, Fisher's Z_r transformation is applied so that the confidence interval can be computed.

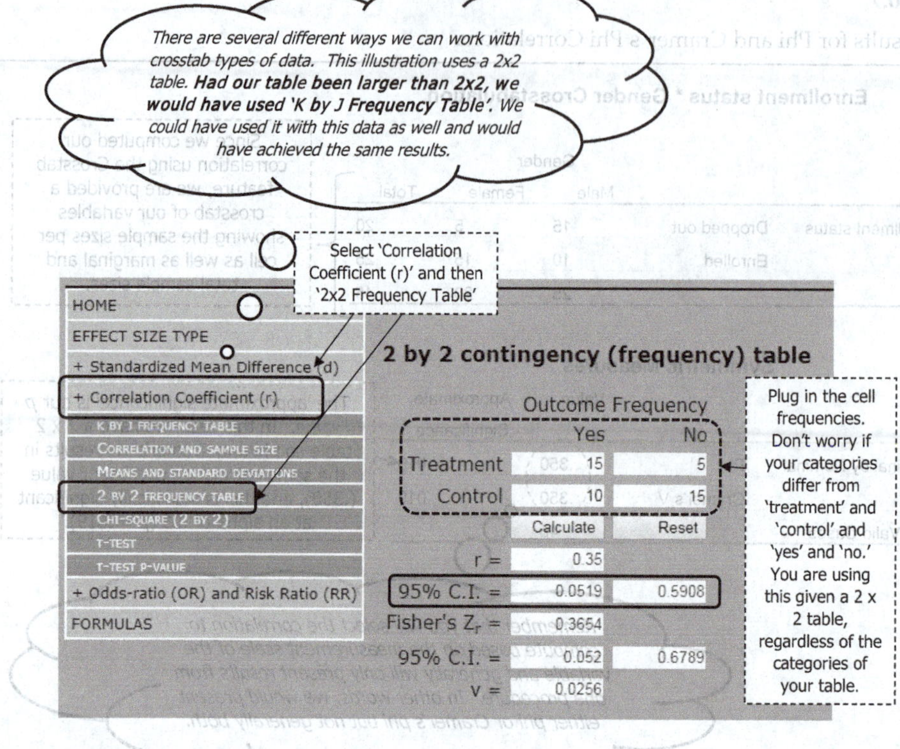

FIGURE 10.12
Confidence interval for phi or Cramer's phi correlation coefficient.

10.3 Computing Bivariate Measures of Association Using R

Next we consider **R** for a bivariate measures of association model. Note that the scripts are provided within the blocks with additional annotation to assist in understanding how the command works. Should you want to write reminder notes and annotation to yourself as you write the commands in **R** (and we highly encourage doing so), remember that any text that follows a hashtag (i.e., #) is annotation only and not part of the **R** script. Thus, you can write annotations directly into **R** with hashtags. We encourage this practice so that when you call up the commands in the future, you'll understand what the various lines of code are doing. You may think you'll remember what you did. However, trust us. There is a good chance that you won't. Thus, consider it best practice when using **R** to annotate heavily!

10.3.1 Reading Data Into R

```
getwd()
```

R is always pointed to a directory on your computer. To find out which directory it is pointed to, run this "get working directory" function. We will assume that we need to change the working directory, and will use the next line of code to set the working directory to the desired path.

FIGURE 10.13
Reading data into R.

```
setwd("E:/FolderName")
```

To set the working directory, change what is in quotation marks to your file location. Also, if you are copying the directory name, it will copy in slashes. You will need to change the slash (i.e., \) to a forward slash (i.e., /). Note that you need your destination name within quotation marks in the parentheses.

```
Ch10_kidspets <- read.csv("Ch10_kidspets.csv")
```

The *read.csv* function reads our data into **R**. What's to the left of the <- will be what the data will be called in **R**. In this example, we're calling the R dataframe "Ch10_kidspets." What's to the right of the <- tells **R** to find this particular .csv file. In this example, our file is called "Ch10_kidspets.csv." Make sure the extension (i.e., .csv) is included in your script. Also note that the name of your file should be in quotation marks within the parentheses.

```
names(Ch10_kidspets)
```

The *names* function will produce a list of variable names for each dataframe as follows. This is a good check to make sure your data have been read in correctly.

```
[1] "Children"     "Pets"
```

```
View(Ch10_kidspets)
```

The *View* function will let you view the dataset in spreadsheet format in RStudio.

```
summary(Ch10_kidspets)
```

The *summary* function will produce basic descriptive statistics on all the variables in your dataframe. This is a great way to quickly check to see if the data have been read in correctly and to get a feel for your data, if you haven't already. The output from the summary statement for this dataframe looks like this.

```
    Children        Pets
 Min.   :1    Min.   : 2
 1st Qu.:2    1st Qu.: 4
 Median :3    Median : 6
 Mean   :3    Mean   : 6
 3rd Qu.:4    3rd Qu.: 8
 Max.   :5    Max.   :10
```

FIGURE 10.13 (continued)
Reading data into **R**.

10.3.2 Generating Correlation Coefficients

```
cor.test(Ch10_kidspets$Children, Ch10_kidspets$Pets,
     use = "everything",
     method = "pearson",
     conf.level = 0.95)
```

FIGURE 10.14
Generating correlation coefficients in **R**.

The *cor.test* function will compute a Pearson (i.e., *method = "pearson"*) correlation coefficient for variables children and pets (i.e., "Ch10_kidspets$Children," "Ch10_kidspets$Pets") and related *p* value using an alpha of .05 (i.e., *conf.level = .95*). The *use = "everything"* command will compute the correlation using all available data ("NA" will be the output if any variables have missing data; we could have used *complete.obs* for listwise deletion or *pairwise.complete.obs* for pairwise deletion, among other options). Because we have no missing data, the method for "use" will not matter; however, if you have missing data, be thoughtful in how you approach this!

Note: To compute Spearman or Kendall's tau, simply change the method (i.e., *method = "pearson"*) to *method = "kendall"* or *method = "spearman,"* using all lowercase letters.

Our output looks like this. We see our observed probability, $p = .037$, which is statistically significant at alpha of .05. We have a 95% confidence interval of the correlation coefficient (.086, .993), and our Pearson correlation coefficient, r, is .90.

```
        Pearson's product-moment correlation
data: Ch10_kidspets$Children and Ch10_kidspets$Pets

t = 3.5762, df = 3, p-value = 0.03739

alternative hypothesis: true correlation is not equal to 0

95 percent confidence interval:
 0.08610194 0.99343752

sample estimates:
cor
0.9
```

FIGURE 10.14 (continued)
Generating correlation coefficients in R.

10.4 Data Screening

As noted previously, the assumptions of the Pearson correlation coefficient are linearity and independence. While the assumption of independence is based on how the data are sampled (with random sampling meeting the assumption of independence), we can use our data to examine the extent to which we meet the assumption of linearity.

10.4.1 Scatterplots to Examine Linearity Using SPSS

Step 1. As alluded to earlier in the chapter, understanding the extent to which linearity is a reasonable assumption is an important first step prior to computing a Pearson correlation coefficient. To generate a scatterplot, go to "Graphs" in the top pulldown menu. From there, select "Legacy Dialogs," then "Scatter/Dot" (see the screenshot for Step 1 in Figure 10.15).

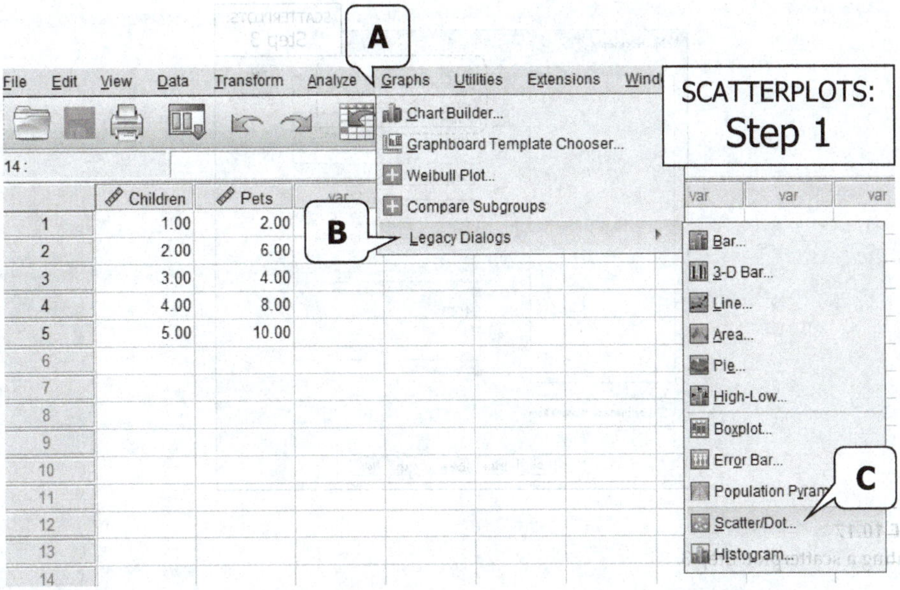

FIGURE 10.15
Generating a scatterplot: Step 1.

Step 2. This will bring up the "Scatter/Dot" dialog box (see the screenshot for Step 2 in Figure 10.16). The default selection is "Simple Scatter," and this is the option we will use. Then click "Define."

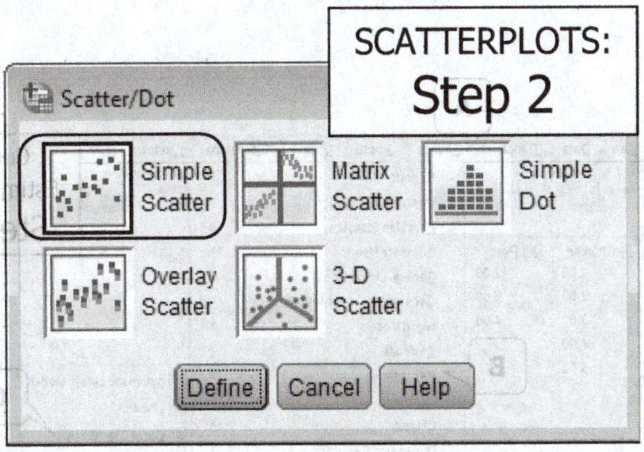

FIGURE 10.16
Generating a scatterplot: Step 2.

Step 3. This will bring up the "Simple Scatterplot" dialog box (see the screenshot for Step 3 in Figure 10.17). Click the dependent variable (e.g., number of pets) and move it into the "Y Axis" box by clicking on the arrow. Click the independent variable (e.g., number of children) and move it into the "X Axis" box by clicking on the arrow. Then click "OK."

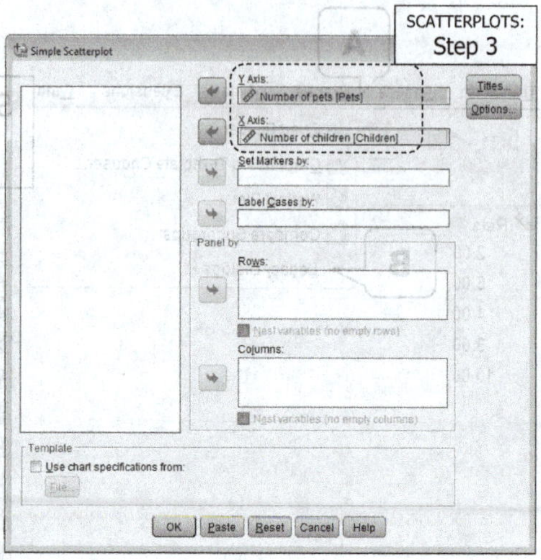

FIGURE 10.17
Generating a scatterplot: Step 3.

10.4.2 Hypothesis Tests to Examine Linearity Using SPSS

Another way to test for linearity is to conduct a hypothesis test using curve estimation to determine if there is a statistically significant linear (versus quadratic or cubic) relationship.

Step 1. To conduct curve estimation, go to "Analyze" in the top pulldown, then select "Regression," and then select the "Curve estimation" procedure (see the screenshot for Step 1 in Figure 10.18).

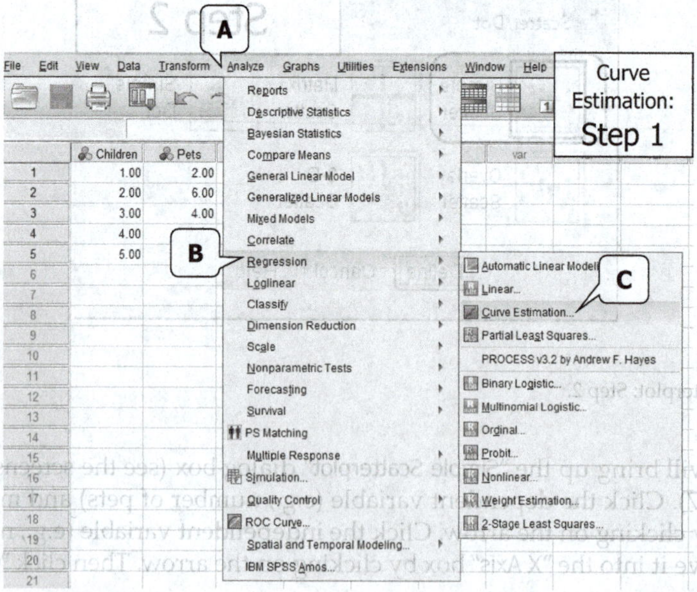

FIGURE 10.18
Hypothesis test for linearity: Step 1.

Step 2. In many cases, there may not be a dependent and independent variable, per se, when conducting a bivariate correlation. In this case, that's fine as we are simply checking the assumption of linearity. Thus, move one variable to the "Dependent(s)" box and the second variable to the "Independent Variable" box. Under "Models," select "Linear," "Quadratic," and "Cubic" (see the screenshot for Step 2 in Figure 10.19).

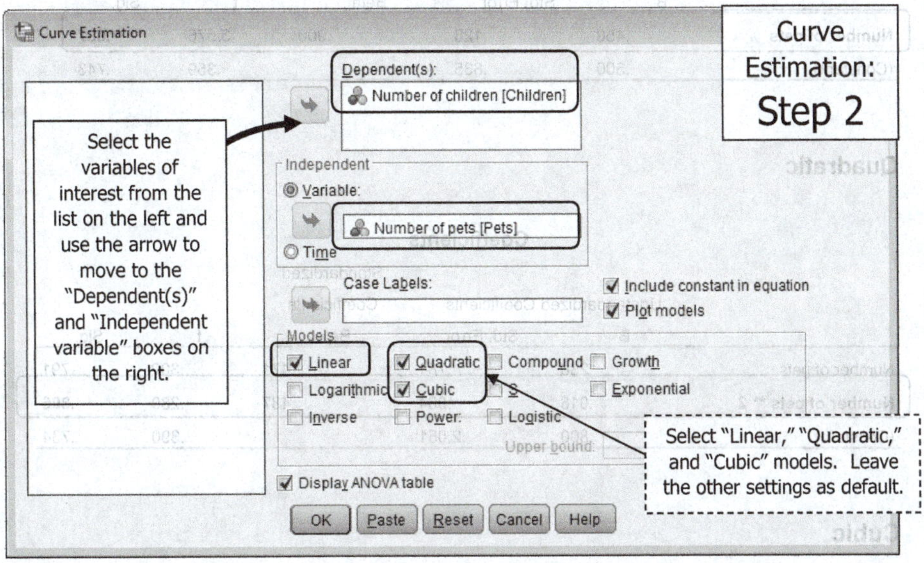

FIGURE 10.19
Hypothesis test for linearity: Step 2.

10.4.2.1 Interpreting Hypothesis Tests to Examine Linearity

For purposes of examining linearity, we are only concerned with the output for the "coefficients" (see Figure 10.20). Each coefficient hypothesis test is estimating whether the standardized coefficient is statistically different from zero. Finding statistical significance for the coefficient in the *linear model* provides evidence to suggest a linear relationship between the variables. For this illustration, we find a statistically significant linear relationship between the number of pets and number of children, $t = 3.576$, $p = .037$.

For the quadratic model, we see we have parameter estimates for number of pets as well as "Number of pets ** 2," where the latter term indicates the number of pets has been squared (i.e., this is the quadratic term). Thus, in the quadratic model, the squared term is of interest. A statistically significant quadratic term indicates that the quadratic trend (i.e., quadratic relationship) is statistically significant beyond the linear relationship. In this illustration, we find a nonstatistically significant quadratic relationship, $t = .280$, $p = .806$, which provides evidence to suggest there is *not* a quadratic relationship between our variables.

Next, we examine the results of the cubic model. We find that a new term has been estimated in this model, specifically "Number of pets ** 3." This term represented the cubic term. This model is estimating the extent to which there is a cubic trend, above and beyond the linear and quadratic relationships. A statistically significant cubic term suggests evidence that there is a cubic relationship between the variables. In this illustration, find a nonstatistically significant relationship, $t = .529$, $p = .690$. Thus, we have evidence to suggest that there is not a cubic relationship between our variables.

Linear

Coefficients

	Unstandardized Coefficients B	Unstandardized Coefficients Std. Error	Standardized Coefficients Beta	t	Sig.
Number of pets	.450	.126	.900	3.576	**.037**
(Constant)	.300	.835		.359	.743

Quadratic

Coefficients

	Unstandardized Coefficients B	Unstandardized Coefficients Std. Error	Standardized Coefficients Beta	t	Sig.
Number of pets	.236	.781	.471	.302	.791
Number of pets ** 2	.018	.064	.437	.280	**.806**
(Constant)	.800	2.051		.390	.734

Cubic

Coefficients

	Unstandardized Coefficients B	Unstandardized Coefficients Std. Error	Standardized Coefficients Beta	t	Sig.
Number of pets	2.202	3.843	4.405	.573	.669
Number of pets ** 2	-.357	.713	-8.737	-.501	.704
Number of pets ** 3	.021	.039	5.372	.529	**.690**
(Constant)	-2.000	5.880		-.340	.791

FIGURE 10.20
Hypothesis test for linearity: Results.

Looking at all three models—linear, quadratic, and cubic—we have evidence to suggest linearity between our variables given the nonstatistically significant nonlinear quadratic and cubic trends.

10.4.3 Scatterplots to Examine Linearity Using R

```
plot(Ch10_kidspets$Children, Ch10_kidspets$Pets,
    xlab = "Number of Children",
    ylab = "Number of Pets",
    main = "Scatterplot")
```

FIGURE 10.21
Generating scatterplots in R.

The *plot* function can be used to generate a scatterplot of the variables "Children" and "Pets" from the "Ch10_kidspets" dataframe (i.e., using the command *Ch10_kidspets$Children, Ch10_kidspets$Pets* will define the variables to plot). We can label the *X* and *Y* axis as "Number of Children" and "Number of Pets," respectively, using the *xlab* and *ylab* commands. Using the *main* command, we can title the graph "Scatterplot."

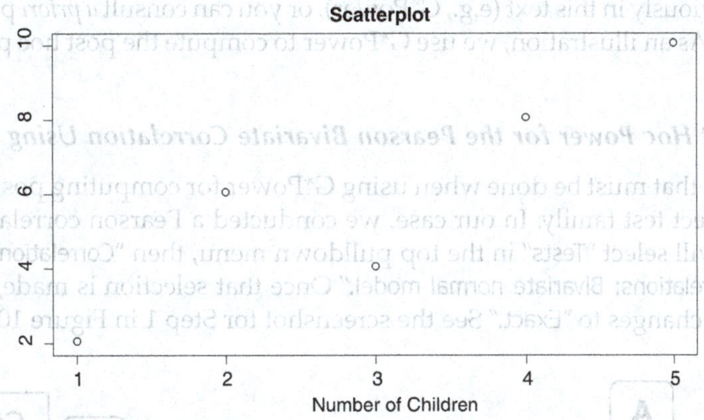

FIGURE 10.21 (continued)
Generating scatterplots in **R**.

10.4.3.1 Interpreting Linearity Evidence

Scatterplots are also often examined to determine visual evidence of linearity prior to computing Pearson correlations. Scatterplots are graphs that depict coordinate values of *X* and *Y*. *Linearity is suggested by points that fall in a straight line or relatively straight line.* This line may suggest a *positive relation* (as scores on *X* increase, scores on *Y* increase, and vice versa), a *negative relation* (as scores on *X* increase, scores on *Y* decrease, and vice versa), *little or no relation* (relatively random display of points), or a *polynomial relation* (e.g., curvilinear). In this example, our scatterplot generally suggests evidence of linearity and, more specifically, a positive relationship between number of children and number of pets (see Figure 10.21, generated in **R,** and Figure 10.22, generated in SPSS). Thus, proceeding to compute a bivariate Pearson correlation coefficient is reasonable.

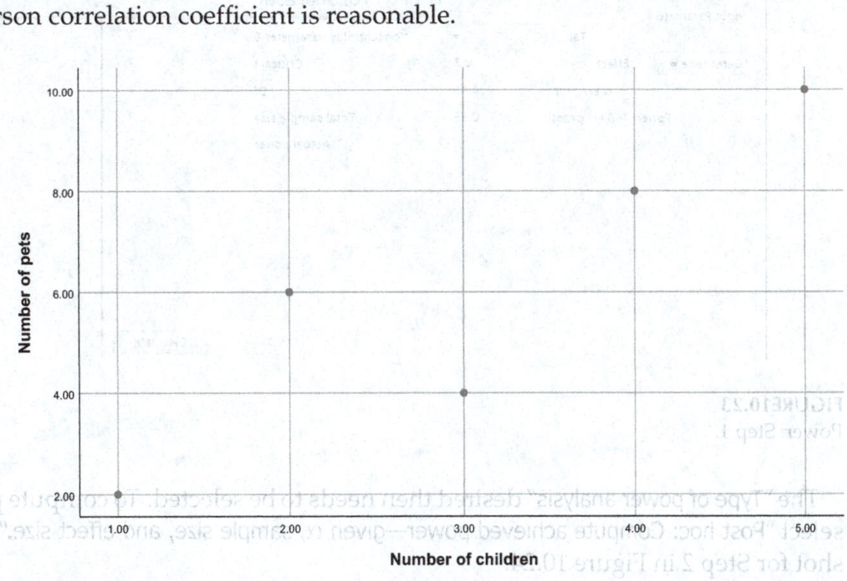

FIGURE 10.22
Scatterplot.

10.5 Power Using G*Power

A priori and post hoc power could again be determined using the specialized software described previously in this text (e.g., G*Power), or you can consult *a priori* power tables (e.g., Cohen, 1988). As an illustration, we use G*Power to compute the post hoc power of our test.

*10.5.1.1 Post Hoc Power for the Pearson Bivariate Correlation Using G*Power*

The first thing that must be done when using G*Power for computing post hoc power is to select the correct test family. In our case, we conducted a Pearson correlation. To find the Pearson, we will select "Tests" in the top pulldown menu, then "Correlations and regression," and then "Correlations: Bivariate normal model." Once that selection is made, the "Test family" automatically changes to "Exact." See the screenshot for Step 1 in Figure 10.23.

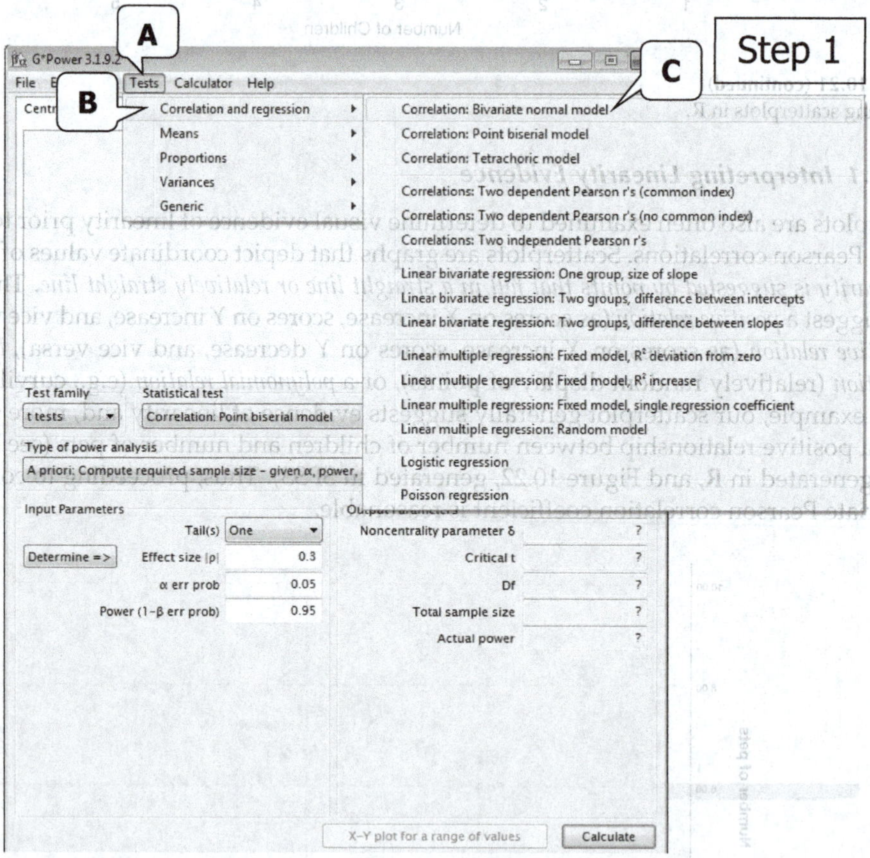

FIGURE10.23
Power: Step 1.

The "Type of power analysis" desired then needs to be selected. To compute post hoc power, select "Post hoc: Compute achieved power—given α, sample size, and effect size." See the screenshot for Step 2 in Figure 10.24.

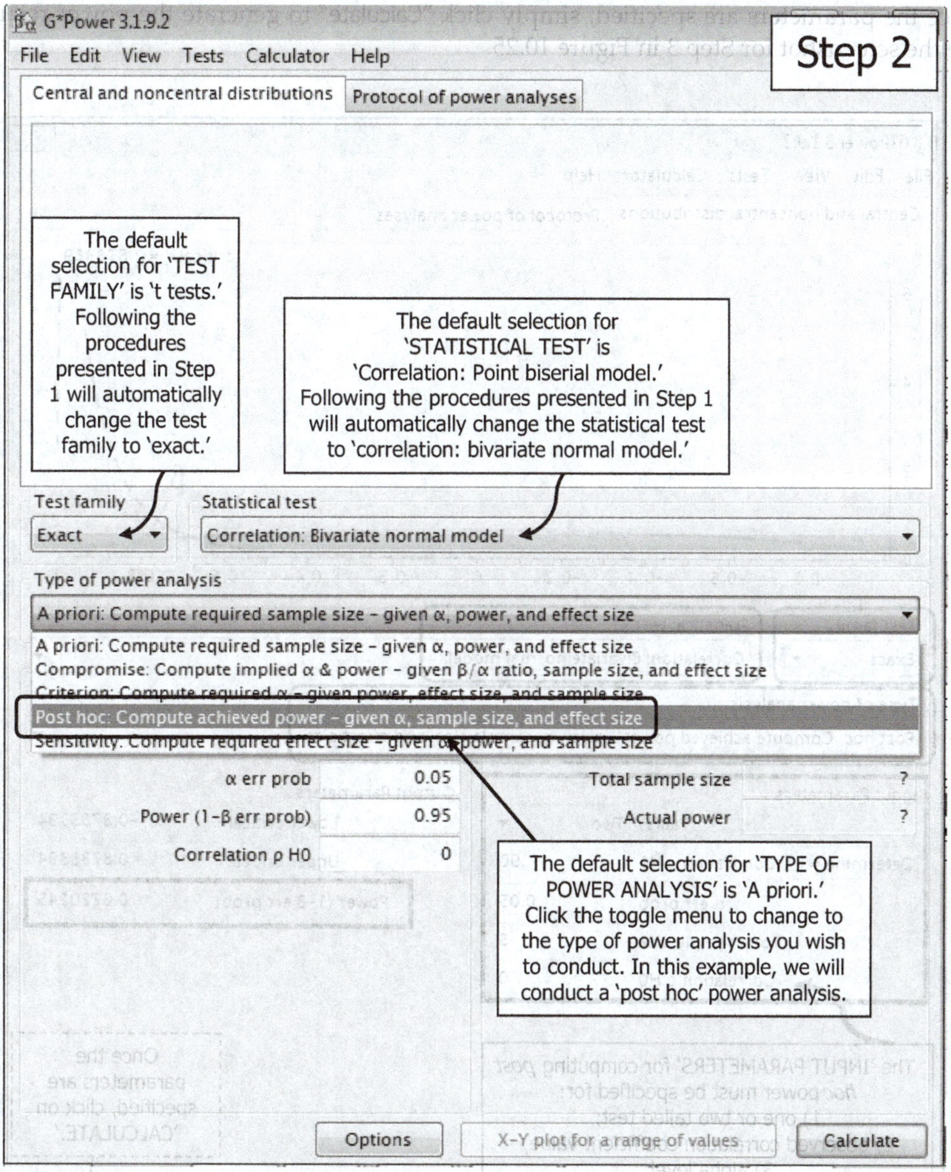

FIGURE 10.24
Power: Step 2.

The "Input Parameters" must then be specified. The first parameter is specification of the number of tail(s). For a directional hypothesis, "One" is selected, and for a nondirectional hypothesis, "Two" is selected. In our example, we chose a nondirectional hypothesis and thus will select "Two" tails. We then input the observed correlation coefficient value in the box for "Correlation ρ H1." In this example, our Pearson correlation coefficient value was .90. The alpha level we tested at was .05, the total sample size was 5, and the "Correlation ρ H0" will remain as the default 0 (this is the correlation value expected if the null hypothesis is true; in other words, there is zero correlation between variables given the null hypothesis).

Once the parameters are specified, simply click "Calculate" to generate the power results. See the screenshot for Step 3 in Figure 10.25.

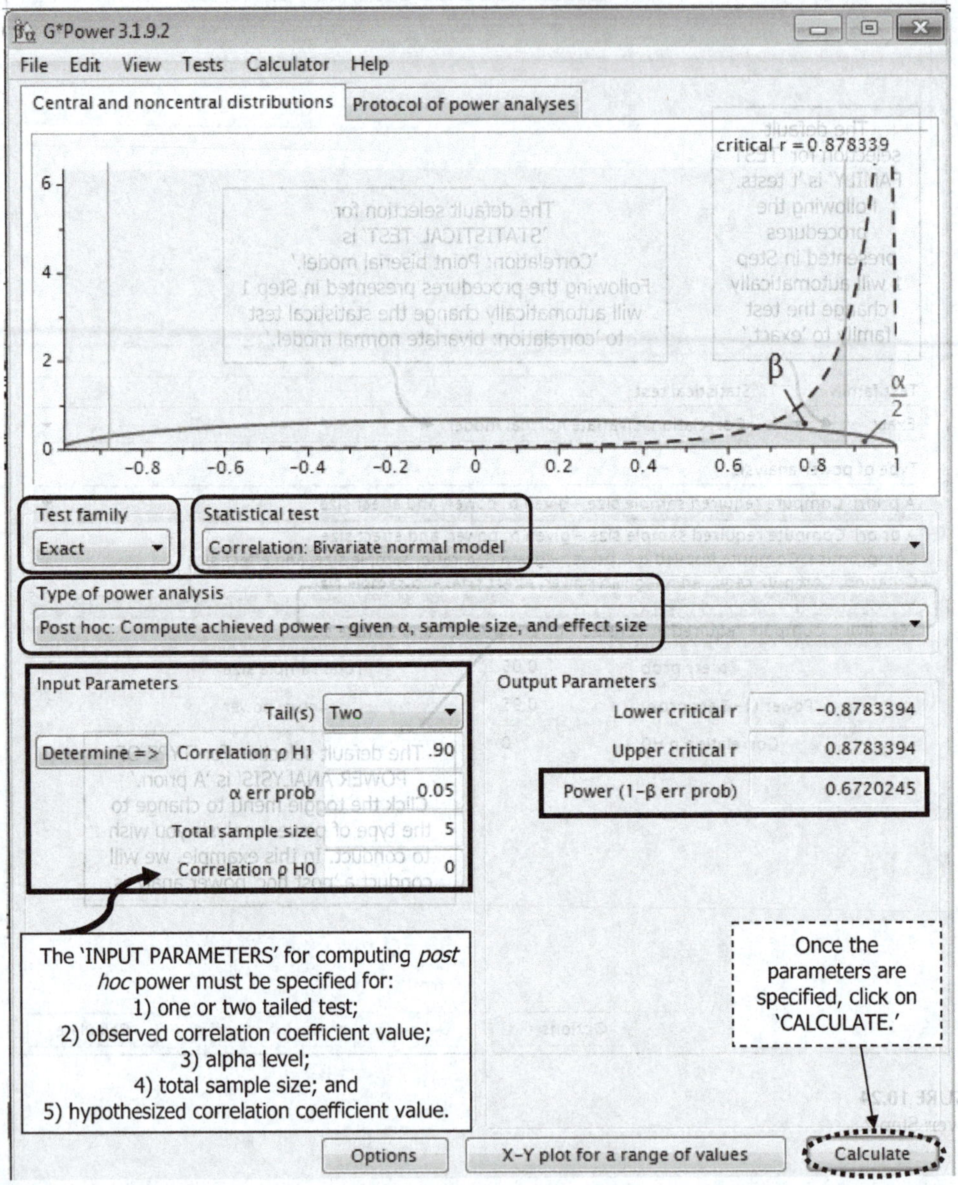

FIGURE 10.25
Post hoc power results.

The "Output Parameters" provide the relevant statistics given the input just specified. In this example, we were interested in determining post hoc power for a Pearson correlation given a two-tailed test, with a computed correlation value of .90, an alpha level of .05, total sample size of 5, and a null hypothesis correlation value of zero.

Based on those criteria, the post hoc power was .67 (see Figure 10.25). In other words, with a two-tailed test, an observed Pearson correlation of .90, an alpha level of .05, sample size of 5, and a null hypothesis correlation value of zero, the power of our test was approximately .67—the probability of rejecting the null hypothesis when it is really false (in this case, the probability that there is *not* a zero correlation between our variables) was 67%, which is slightly less than what would be usually considered sufficient power (sufficient power is often .80 or above). Keep in mind that conducting power analysis *a priori* is recommended so that you avoid a situation where, post hoc, you find that the sample size was not sufficient to reach the desired level of power (given the observed parameters). In our situation, we don't need to worry that post hoc power was less than desirable as we found a statistically significant correlation.

10.6 Research Question Template and Example Write-Up

Finally, we conclude the chapter with a template and an APA-style paragraph detailing the results from an example dataset. As you may recall, our graduate research assistant, Challie Lenge, was working with the marketing director of the local animal shelter, Dr. Amberly. Challie's task was to assist Dr. Amberly in generating the test of inference to answer her research question, "*Is there a relationship between the number of children in a family and the number of pets?*" A Pearson correlation was the test of inference suggested by Challie. A template for writing a research question for a correlation (regardless of which type of correlation coefficient is computed) follows:

Is there a correlation between [variable 1] and [variable 2]?

It may be helpful to include in the results information on the extent to which the assumptions were met (recall there are two assumptions: independence and linearity). This assists the reader in understanding that you were thorough in data screening prior to conducting the test of inference. Recall that the assumption of independence is met when the cases in our sample have been randomly selected from the population. One or two sentences are usually sufficient to indicate if the assumptions are met. It is also important to address effect size in the write-up. Correlations are unique in that they are already effect size measures, so computing an effect size in addition to the correlation value is not needed. However, it is desirable to interpret the correlation value as an effect size. Effect size is easily interpreted from the correlation coefficient value utilizing Cohen's (1988) subjective standards previously described or in comparison to similar studies that have used like variables. Here is an example paragraph of results for the correlation between number of children and number of pets.

A Pearson correlation coefficient was computed to determine if there is a relationship between the number of children in a family and the number of pets in the family. The test was conducted using an alpha of .05. The null hypothesis was that the relationship would be zero. The assumption of independence was met via random selection. The assumption of linearity was reasonable given a visual review of a scatterplot of the variables along with hypothesis tests to examine quadratic and cubic trends (neither of which were statistically significant).

The Pearson correlation coefficient between children and pets is .90 (CI .09, .99), which is positive, is interpreted as a large effect size (Cohen, 1988), and is statistically different from zero ($r = .90, n = 5, p = .037$). Thus, the null hypothesis that the correlation is zero was rejected at the .05 level of significance. There is a strong, positive correlation between the number of children in a family and the number of pets in the family.

10.7 Additional Resources

This chapter has provided an introduction to conducting correlational analysis. However, there are a number of areas related to correlation, particularly as it relates to correlation as a precursor to regression, that space limitations prevent us from delving into. Those who are interested in general coverage of correlation as a precursor to regression may wish to review Sahay (2016).

Problems

Conceptual Problems

1. The variance of X is 9, the variance of Y is 4, and the covariance between X and Y is 2. What is r_{XY}?
   a. .039
   b. .056
   c. .233
   d. .333
2. The standard deviation of X is 20, the standard deviation of Y is 50, and the covariance between X and Y is 30. What is r_{XY}?
   a. .030
   b. .080
   c. .150
   d. .200
3. Which of the following correlation coefficients, each obtained from a sample of 1000 children, indicates the *weakest* relationship?
   a. −.90
   b. −.30
   c. +.20
   d. +.80
4. Which of the following correlation coefficients, each obtained from a sample of 1000 children, indicates the *strongest* relationship?

a. −.90
b. −.30
c. +.20
d. +.80

5. If the relationship between two variables is linear, which of the following is necessarily true?
a. The relation can be most accurately represented by a straight line.
b. All the points will fall on a curved line.
c. The relationship is best represented by a curved line.
d. All the points must fall exactly on a straight line.

6. True or false? In testing the null hypothesis that a correlation is equal to zero, the critical value decreases as α decreases.

7. True or false? If the variances of X and Y are increased, but their covariance remains constant, the value of r_{XY} will be unchanged.

8. We compute $r_{XY} = .50$ for a sample of students on variables X and Y. I assert that if the low-scoring students on variable X are removed, then the new value of r_{XY} would most likely be less than .50. Am I correct?

9. Two variables are linearly related such that there is a perfect relationship between X and Y. I assert that r_{XY} must be equal to either +1.00 or −1.00. Am I correct?

10. True or false? If the number of credit cards owned and the number of cars owned are *strongly positively* correlated, then those with more credit cards tend to own more cars.

11. True or false? If the number of credit cards owned and the number of cars owned are *strongly negatively* correlated, then those with more credit cards tend to own more cars.

12. True or false? If X correlates significantly with Y, then X is necessarily a cause of Y.

13. A researcher wishes to correlate the grade students earned from a pass/fail course (i.e., pass or fail) with their cumulative grade point average. Which of the following is the most appropriate correlation coefficient to examine this relationship?
a. Pearson
b. Spearman's rho or Kendall's tau
c. Phi
d. None of the above

14. True or false? If both X and Y are ordinal variables, then the most appropriate measure of association is the Pearson.

15. A researcher is correlating a 5-point Likert item with a binary variable. Which of the following correlation coefficients is appropriate?
a. Cramer's phi
b. Kendall's tau
c. Pearson
d. Phi

16. A researcher is correlating home ownership (own or do not own) with the number of hours worked per week (measured in whole numbers). Which of the following correlation coefficients is appropriate?

a. Cramer's phi
b. Kendall's tau
c. Pearson
d. Phi

17. True or false? When restriction of range occurs, the strength of the correlation is usually stronger.
18. Which of the following reduce the magnitude of a correlation coefficient? Select all that apply.
a. Outliers
b. Restriction of range
c. Variables that have little variability
d. Variables that are causally related

Answers to Conceptual Problems

1. **d** (2/(3)(2) = .3333)
3. **c** (Weakest relationship means correlation nearest to 0.)
5. **a** (A linear relationship will fall into a reasonably linear scatterplot, although not necessarily a perfectly straight line.)
7. **False** (The correlation will become smaller; see the correlation equation involving covariance.)
9. **Yes** (A perfect relationship implies a perfect correlation, assuming linearity.)
11. **False** (In negative relationships, the *higher* the score on one variable, the *lower* the score on the other variable tends to be.)
13. **a** (The Pearson can be used when one variable is dichotomous, such as pass/fail, and the other variable is at least interval in scale, such as GPA.)
15. **a** (Cramer's phi is appropriate when one variable is nominal, such as a binary variable, and the other variable is ordinal, like a 5-point Likert item.)
17. **False** (When scores on one or both variables that are being correlated are restricted based on the nature of the sample or population, the strength of the correlation is usually decreased.)

Computational Problems

1. You are given the following pairs of sample scores on *X* (number of credit cards in your possession) and *Y* (number of those credit cards with balances):

X	Y
5	4
6	1
4	3
8	7
2	2

e. Graph a scatterplot of the data.

f. Compute the covariance.

g. Determine the Pearson product-moment correlation coefficient.

h. Determine the Spearman's rho correlation coefficient.

2. If $r_{XY} = .17$ for a random sample of size 84, test the hypothesis that the population Pearson is significantly different from 0 (conduct a two-tailed test at the .05 level of significance).

3. If $r_{XY} = .60$ for a random sample of size 30, test the hypothesis that the population Pearson is significantly different from 0 (conduct a two-tailed test at the .05 level of significance).

4. The correlation between vocabulary size and mother's age is .50 for 12 rural children and .85 for 17 inner-city children. Does the correlation for rural children differ from that of the inner-city children at the .05 level of significance?

5. You are given the following pairs of sample scores on *X* (number of coins in possession) and *Y* (number of bills in possession):

X	*Y*
2	1
3	3
4	5
5	5
6	3
7	1

a. Graph a scatterplot of the data.

b. Describe the relationship between *X* and *Y*.

c. What do you think the Pearson correlation will be?

6. Six adults were assessed on the number of minutes it took to read a government report (*X*) and the number of items correct on a test of the content of that report (*Y*). Use the data below to determine the Pearson correlation and the effect size.

X	*Y*
10	17
8	17
15	13
12	16
14	15
16	12

7. Ten kindergarten children were observed on the number of letters written in proper form (given 26 letters) (*X*) and the number of words that the child could read (given 50 words) (*Y*). Use the data below to determine the Pearson correlation and the effect size.

X	Y
10	5
16	8
22	40
8	15
12	28
20	37
17	29
21	30
15	18
9	4

8. Ten adults responded to "I am the life of the party" (*X*) and "I start conversations" (*Y*), both based on 5-point Likert scales. Use the data below to determine Kendall's tau correlation, and the strength of the correlation as an effect size.

X	Y
3	5
1	2
5	5
3	3
4	5
2	4
3	2
1	5
3	4
1	5

9. Ten adults responded to "I pay attention to detail" (*X*) and "I get things done right away" (*Y*), both based on 5-point Likert scales. Use the data below to determine Kendall's tau correlation, and the strength of the correlation as an effect size.

X	Y
4	5
2	1
5	5
5	1
4	3
3	5
3	3
5	5
4	2
4	5

Answers to Computational Problems

1. (a) Scatterplot shown below; (b) covariance = 3.250; (c) r = .631; (d) r = .400.

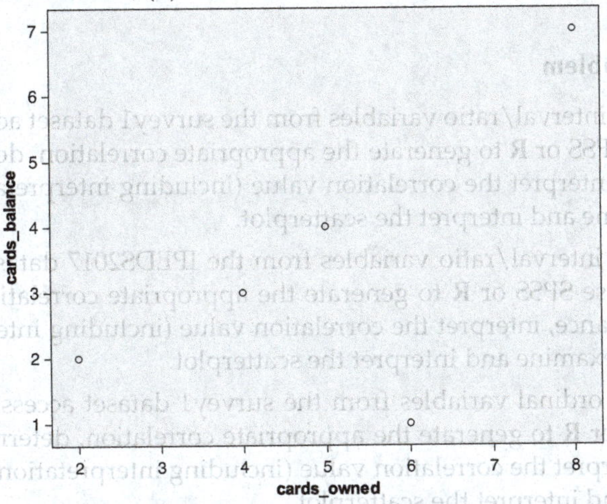

3. t = 3.9686, critical values are approximately −2.048 and +2.048, reject H_0.

5. (a) Scatterplot shown below; (b) nonlinear relationship; (c) r = approximately zero.

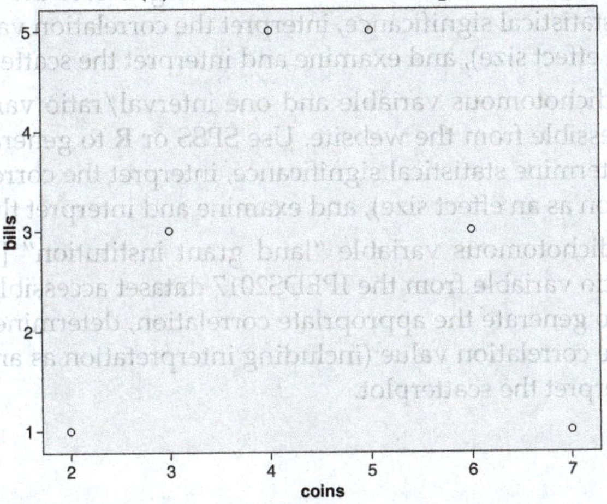

7. (a) r = .78; (b) strong effect.

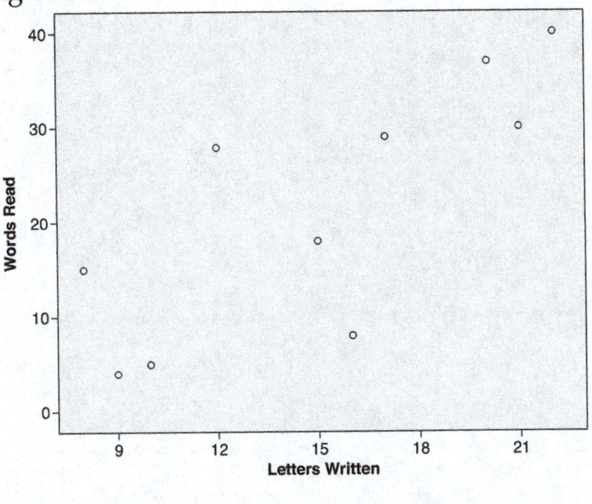

9. Kendall's tau = .206, $p = .475$. This is not a statistically significant correlation. Using Cohen's criteria, this is a weak to moderate relationship.

Interpretive Problem

1. Select two interval/ratio variables from the survey1 dataset accessible from the website. Use SPSS or **R** to generate the appropriate correlation, determine statistical significance, interpret the correlation value (including interpretation as an effect size), and examine and interpret the scatterplot.
2. Select two interval/ratio variables from the IPEDS2017 dataset accessible from the website. Use SPSS or **R** to generate the appropriate correlation, determine statistical significance, interpret the correlation value (including interpretation as an effect size), and examine and interpret the scatterplot.
3. Select two ordinal variables from the survey1 dataset accessible from the website. Use SPSS or **R** to generate the appropriate correlation, determine statistical significance, interpret the correlation value (including interpretation as an effect size), and examine and interpret the scatterplot.
4. Select one ordinal variable and one interval/ratio variable from the survey1 dataset accessible from the website. Use SPSS or **R** to generate the appropriate correlation, determine statistical significance, interpret the correlation value (including interpretation as an effect size), and examine and interpret the scatterplot.
5. Select one dichotomous variable and one interval/ratio variable from the survey1 dataset accessible from the website. Use SPSS or **R** to generate the appropriate correlation, determine statistical significance, interpret the correlation value (including interpretation as an effect size), and examine and interpret the scatterplot.
6. Select the dichotomous variable "land grant institution" [LANDGRNT] and one interval/ratio variable from the IPEDS2017 dataset accessible from the website. Use SPSS or **R** to generate the appropriate correlation, determine statistical significance, interpret the correlation value (including interpretation as an effect size), and examine and interpret the scatterplot.

11

One-Factor Analysis of Variance—Fixed-Effects Model

Chapter Outline

Key Concepts

1. Between- and within-groups variability
2. Sources of variation
3. Partitioning the sums of squares
4. The ANOVA model
5. Expected mean squares

In the last five chapters, our discussion has dealt with various inferential statistics, including inferences about means. The next six chapters are concerned with different analysis of variance (ANOVA) models. In this chapter, we consider the most basic ANOVA model, known as the *one-factor analysis of variance* model. Recall the independent t test from Chapter 7 where the means from two independent samples were compared. What if you wish to compare more than two means? The answer is to use the **analysis of variance**. At this point you may be wondering why the procedure is called the analysis of variance rather than the analysis of means, because the intent is to study possible mean differences. One way of comparing a set of means is to think in terms of the variability among those means. If the sample means are all the same, then the variability of those means would be zero. If the sample means are not all the same, then the variability of those means would be somewhat greater than zero. In general, the greater the mean differences are, the greater is the variability of the means. Thus, mean differences are studied by looking at the variability of the means; hence, the term analysis of variance is appropriate rather than analysis of means (further discussed in this chapter).

We use X to denote our single **independent variable**, which we typically refer to as a **factor**, and Y to denote our **dependent** (or **criterion**) **variable**. *Thus, the one-factor ANOVA is a bivariate, or two variable, procedure.* Our interest here is in determining whether mean differences exist on the dependent variable. Stated another way, the researcher is interested in the influence of the independent variable on the dependent variable (however, be cautious in inferring *causality* unless the design of your study allows that). For example, a researcher may want to determine the influence that method of instruction has on statistics achievement. The independent variable, or factor, would be method of instruction, and the dependent variable would be statistics achievement. Three different methods of instruction that might be compared are large lecture hall instruction, small-group instruction, and computer-assisted instruction. Students would be randomly assigned to one of the three methods of instruction and, at the end of the semester, evaluated as to their level of achievement in statistics. These results would be of interest to a statistics instructor in determining the most effective method of instruction (where "effective" is measured by student performance in statistics). Thus, the instructor may opt for the method of instruction that yields the highest mean achievement.

There are a number of new concepts introduced in this chapter as well as a refresher of concepts that have been covered in previous chapters. The concepts addressed in this chapter include the following: independent and dependent variables; between- and within-groups variability; fixed- and random-effects; the linear model; partitioning of the sums of squares; degrees of freedom, mean square terms, and F ratios; the ANOVA summary table; expected mean squares; balanced and unbalanced models; and alternative ANOVA procedures. Our objectives are that by the end of this chapter, you will be able to (a) understand the characteristics and concepts underlying a one-factor ANOVA, (b) generate and interpret the results of a one-factor ANOVA, and (c) understand and evaluate the assumptions of the one-factor ANOVA.

11.1 What One-Factor ANOVA Is and How It Works

Our very talented group of graduate students has been performing amazing statistical feats that have garnered rave reviews from those with whom they have worked. We now find Ott Lier assisting one of the region's leading sports psychologists in examining elite athletes and vulnerability to psychological distress based on the type of sport in which they participate.

The research lab has been contracted to work with one of the leading sports psychologists in the region, Dr. Rhodes, and Ott Lier has the privilege of being assigned to the project. Dr. Rhodes is examining elite athletes and their vulnerability to psychological distress based on the sport in which they participate. Dr. Rhodes wants to determine if there is a difference in psychological stress based on type of sport (movement, target, fielding, or territory). Ott suggests the following research question is: *Is there a mean difference in psychological distress of elite athletes based on the type of sport in which they participate?* With one independent variable, Ott determines that a one-way ANOVA is the best statistical procedure to use to answer Dr. Rhodes's question. His next task is to collect and analyze the data to address this research question.

11.1.1 Characteristics

This section describes the distinguishing characteristics of the one-factor ANOVA model. Suppose you are interested in comparing the means of two independent samples. Here, the independent t test would be the method of choice (or perhaps Welch's t' test). What if your interest is in comparing the means of more than two independent samples? One possibility is to conduct multiple independent t tests on each pair of means. For example, if you wished to determine whether the means from five independent samples are the same, you could do all possible pairwise t tests. In this case, the following null hypotheses could be evaluated: $\mu_1 = \mu_2$, $\mu_1 = \mu_3$, $\mu_1 = \mu_4$, $\mu_1 = \mu_5$, $\mu_2 = \mu_3$, $\mu_2 = \mu_4$, $\mu_2 = \mu_5$, $\mu_3 = \mu_4$, $\mu_3 = \mu_5$, and $\mu_4 = \mu_5$. Thus, we would have to carry out 10 different independent t tests. The number of possible pairwise t tests that could be done for J means is equal to $[J(J-1)]/2$.

Is there a problem in conducting so many t tests? Yes; the problem has to do with the probability of making a Type I error (i.e., α), where the researcher incorrectly rejects a true null hypothesis. Although the α level for each t test can be controlled at a specified nominal α level that is set by the researcher, say .05, what happens to the overall α level for the entire set of tests? The overall α level for the entire set of tests (i.e., α_{total}), often called the **experiment-wise Type I error rate** (i.e., the Type I error across all experiments), is larger than the α level for each of the individual t tests.

In our example we are interested in comparing the means for 10 pairs of groups (again, these would be $\mu_1 = \mu_2$, $\mu_1 = \mu_3$, $\mu_1 = \mu_4$, $\mu_1 = \mu_5$, $\mu_2 = \mu_3$, $\mu_2 = \mu_4$, $\mu_2 = \mu_5$, $\mu_3 = \mu_4$, $\mu_3 = \mu_5$ and $\mu_4 = \mu_5$). A t test is conducted for each of the 10 pairs of groups at $\alpha = .05$. Although each test controls the α level at .05, the overall α level will be larger because the risk of a Type I error accumulates across the tests. For each test we are taking a risk; the more tests we do, the more risks we are taking. This can be explained by considering the risk you take each day you drive your car to school or work. The risk of an accident is small for any one day; however, over the period of a year, the risk of an accident is much larger.

For C independent (or **orthogonal**) tests the experiment-wise error is as follows.

$$\alpha_{total} = 1 - (1 - \alpha)^C$$

Assume for the moment that our 10 tests are independent (although they are not, because within those 10 tests, each group is actually being compared to another group in four different instances). If we go ahead with our 10 *t* tests at $\alpha = .05$, then the experiment-wise error rate is

$$\alpha_{total} = 1 - (1 - .05)^{10} = 1 - .60 = .40$$

Although we are seemingly controlling our α level at the .05 level, the probability of making a Type I error across all 10 tests is .40. In other words, in the long run, if we conduct 10 independent *t* tests, 4 times out of 10 we will make a Type I error. For this reason we do not want to do all possible *t* tests. Before we move on, the experiment-wise error rate for *C* dependent tests α_{total} (which would be the case when doing all possible pairwise *t* tests, as in our example) is more difficult to determine, so let us just say that

$$\alpha \leq \alpha_{total} \leq C\alpha$$

Are there other options available to us where we can maintain better control over our experiment-wise error rate? The optimal solution, in terms of maintaining control over our overall α level as well as maximizing power, is to conduct *one overall test*, often called an **omnibus test**. Recall that power has to do with the probability of correctly rejecting a false null hypothesis. The omnibus test could assess the equality of all of the means simultaneously and is the one used in the analysis of variance. *The one-factor analysis of variance, then, represents an extension of the independent* t *test for two or more independent sample means, where the experiment-wise error rate is controlled.*

In addition, the one-factor ANOVA has *only one independent variable or factor* with two or more levels. The independent variable is a discrete or grouping variable, where each subject responds to only one level. The levels represent the different samples or groups or treatments whose means are to be compared. In an example, method of instruction is the independent variable with three levels: large lecture hall, small-group, and computer-assisted. There are two ways of conceptually thinking about the selection of levels.

The **fixed-effects model** is one way to conceptualize the levels. *In the fixed-effects model, all levels that the researcher is interested in are included in the design and analysis for the study.* As a result, generalizations can be made only about those particular levels of the independent variable that are actually selected. For instance, if a researcher is interested only in these three methods of instruction—large lecture hall, small-group and computer-assisted—then only those levels are incorporated into the study. Generalizations about other methods of instruction cannot be made because no other methods were considered for selection. Other examples of fixed-effects independent variables might be socioeconomic status, sex, specific types of treatment, age group, weight, or marital status. Not all researchers agree on what constitutes fixed versus random effects, and some would argue that fixed effects are encountered only in experiments in which the researcher can manipulate the independent variable. We err on the side of defining fixed effects in this sense: *In the fixed-effects model, all levels that the researcher is interested in are included in the design and analysis for the study.* Should your independent variable meet this definition, then it is considered a fixed (not random) effect.

The **random-effects model** is the second way to conceptualize the levels. *In the random-effects model, the researcher randomly samples some levels of the independent variable from the population of levels.* As a result, generalizations can be made about *all* of the levels in the population, even those not actually sampled. For instance, a researcher interested in teacher effectiveness may have randomly sampled history teachers from the population of history teachers in a particular school district. Generalizations can then be made about other history teachers in that school district not actually sampled. The random selection of *levels* is much the same as the random selection of individuals or objects in the random sampling process. This is the nature of inferential statistics, where inferences are made about a population (of individuals, objects, or levels) from a sample. Other examples of random-effects independent variables might include randomly selected classrooms or time (e.g., hours, days), among others. The remainder of this chapter is concerned with the fixed-effects model. Chapter 15 discusses the random-effects model in more detail.

In the fixed-effects model, once the levels of the independent variable are selected, subjects (i.e., persons or objects) are randomly assigned to the levels of the independent variable. In certain situations, the researcher does not have control over which level a subject is assigned to. The groups may be preexisting—i.e., already in place when the research commences. For instance, students may be assigned to their classes at the beginning of the year by the school administration. Researchers typically have little input regarding class assignments. In another situation, it may be theoretically impossible to assign subjects to groups. For example, as much as we might like, researchers cannot randomly assign individuals to an age level. Thus, a distinction needs to be made about whether or not the researcher can control the assignment of subjects to groups. Although the analysis will not be altered, the interpretation of the results will differ depending on whether or not there is random assignment to groups. *When researchers have control over group assignments and exercise that control (e.g., in terms of random assignment to groups), the extent to which they can infer causality from their findings is greater than for those researchers who do not have such control.* For further information on the differences between **true experimental designs** (i.e., with random assignment) and **quasi-experimental designs** (i.e., without random assignment), take a look at Campbell and Stanley (1966), Cook and Campbell (1979), and Shadish, Cook, and Campbell (2002).

Moreover, in the model being considered here, each subject is exposed to only one level of the independent variable. Chapter 15 deals with models where a subject is exposed to multiple levels of an independent variable; these are known as **repeated-measures models**. For example, a researcher may be interested in observing a group of young children repeatedly over a period of several years. Thus, each child might be observed every 6 months from birth to 5 years of age. This would require a repeated-measures design because the observations of a particular child over time are obviously not independent observations.

One final characteristic is the **measurement scale** of the independent and dependent variables. In the analysis of variance, because this is a test of means, *a condition of the test is that the scale of measurement on the dependent variable is at the interval or ratio level.* If the dependent variable is measured at the ordinal level, then the nonparametric equivalent, the Kruskal-Wallis test, should be considered (discussed later in this chapter). If the dependent variable shares properties of both the ordinal and interval levels (e.g., grade point average), then both the ANOVA and Kruskal-Wallis procedures could be considered to cross-reference any potential effects of the measurement scale on the results.

As previously mentioned, *the independent variable is a grouping or discrete variable, so it can theoretically be measured on any scale.* However, there is one caveat to the measurement scale of the independent variable. Technically the condition is that the independent variable be a grouping or discrete variable. *Most often, ANOVAs are conducted with independent variables which are categorical—nominal or ordinal in scale.* ANOVAs can also be used in the case of interval or ratio values that are discrete. Recall that discrete variables are variables that can only take on certain values and that arise from the counting process. An example of a discrete variable that could be a good candidate for being an independent variable in an ANOVA model is number of children. What would make this a good candidate? The responses to this variable would likely be relatively limited (in the general population it may be anticipated that the range would be from zero children to five or six, although outliers may be a possibility) and each discrete value would likely have multiple cases (with fewer cases having larger numbers of children). Applying this is obviously at the researcher's discretion; at some point the number of discrete values can become so numerous as to be unwieldy in an ANOVA model. Thus, while at first glance we may not consider it appropriate to use interval or ratio variables as independent variables in ANOVA models, there are situations where it is feasible and appropriate. While the minimum number of levels or categories of the independent variable is two, there is not a maximum number of categories. However, we have found that ANOVA models with independent variables that have more than five or six categories can become unwieldy—particularly in the case of factorial ANOVA, which we will study in a later chapter.

In summary, the characteristics of the one-factor analysis of variance fixed-effects model are as follows (also see Box 11.1):

(a) control of the experiment-wise error rate through an omnibus test;
(b) one independent variable with two or more levels;
(c) the levels of the independent variable are fixed by the researcher;
(d) subjects are randomly assigned to these levels;
(e) subjects are exposed to only one level of the independent variable; and
(f) the dependent variable is measured at least at the interval level, although the Kruskal-Wallis one-factor ANOVA can be considered for an ordinal level dependent variable. In the context of experimental design, the one-factor analysis of variance is often referred to as the **completely randomized design**.

BOX 11.1 Characteristics of the One-Factor Analysis of Variance Fixed Effects

Model Feature	Characteristic
Variables	• One dependent variable • One independent variable
Measurement scale	• Dependent variable: At least interval in scale • Independent variable: Any scale of variable that is grouping (e.g., nominal or ordinal) or discrete (interval or ratio) but caution is given when considering independent variables with a large number of levels
Design features	• Subjects are randomly assigned to the levels of the independent variable • The levels of the independent variable are fixed by the researcher • Subjects are exposed to only one level of the independent variable
Statistical features	The experiment-wise error rate is controlled through an omnibus test

11.1.1.1 The Layout of the Data

Before we get into the theory and analysis of the data, let us examine one tabular form of the data, known as the layout of the data. We designate each observation as Y_{ij}, where the j subscript tells us what group or level the observation belongs to and the i subscript tells us the observation or identification number within that group. For instance, Y_{34} would mean this is the third observation in the fourth group, or level, of the independent variable. The

TABLE 11.1

Layout for the One-Factor ANOVA Model

	Level of the Independent Variable					
	1	**2**	**3**	**...**	**J**	
	Y_{11}	Y_{12}	Y_{13}	...	Y_{1J}	
	Y_{21}	Y_{22}	Y_{23}	...	Y_{2J}	
	Y_{31}	Y_{32}	Y_{33}	...	Y_{3J}	
	.	.	.	.	.	
	Y_{n1}	Y_{n2}	Y_{n3}	...	Y_{nJ}	
Means	$\bar{Y}_{.1}$	$\bar{Y}_{.2}$	$\bar{Y}_{.3}$	...	$\bar{Y}_{.J}$	$\bar{Y}_{..}$

first subscript ranges over $i = 1, \ldots, n$ and the second subscript ranges over $j = 1, \ldots, J$. Thus there are **J levels (or categories or groups) of the independent variable** and **n subjects in each group**, for a total of $Jn = N$ total observations. For now, presume there are n subjects (or cases or units) in each group in order to simplify matters; this is referred to as the **equal n's** or **balanced case**. Later on in this chapter, we consider the **unequal n's** or **unbalanced case**.

The layout of the data is shown in Table 11.1. Here we see that each column represents the observations for a particular group or level of the independent variable. At the bottom of each column are the sample group means $\left(\bar{Y}_{.j}\right)$, with the overall sample mean $\left(\bar{Y}_{..}\right)$ to the far right. In conclusion, the layout of the data is one form in which the researcher can think about the data.

11.1.1.2 ANOVA Theory

This section examines the underlying theory and logic of the analysis of variance, the sums of squares, and the ANOVA summary table. As noted previously, in the analysis of variance mean differences are tested by looking at the variability of the means. Here we show precisely how this is done.

11.1.1.2.1 General Theory and Logic

We begin with the hypotheses to be tested in the analysis of variance. In the two-group situation of the independent t test, the null and alternative hypotheses for a two-tailed (i.e., nondirectional) test are as follows, where the null hypothesis is simply saying that the means of the two groups are the same.

$$H_0: \mu_1 = \mu_2$$
$$H_1: \mu_1 \neq \mu_2$$

In the multiple-group situation (i.e., more than two groups), we have already seen the problem that occurs when multiple independent t tests are conducted for all pairs of population means (i.e., the problem is an increased likelihood of a Type I error). We concluded that the solution was to use an ***omnibus test*** where the equality of all of the means could be assessed simultaneously. The hypotheses for the omnibus analysis of variance test are as follows:

$$H_0: \mu_1 = \mu_2 = \mu_3 = \ldots = \mu_J$$

$$H_1: \textit{not all the } \mu_j \textit{ are equal}$$

Here H_1 is purposely written in a general form to cover the *multitude* of possible mean differences that could arise. These range from only two of the means being different to *all* of the means being different from one another. Thus, because of the way H_0 has been written, only a nondirectional alternative is appropriate. If H_0 were to be rejected, then the researcher might want to consider a multiple comparison procedure so as to determine which means or combination of means are significantly different (we cover this in greater detail in Chapter 12).

As was mentioned in the introduction to this chapter, the analysis of mean differences is actually carried out by looking at variability of the means. At first this seems strange. If one wants to test for mean differences, then do a test of means. If one wants to test for variance differences, then do a test of variances. These statements should make sense because logic pervades the field of statistics. And they do for the two-group situation. For the multiple-group situation, we already know things get a bit more complicated.

Say a researcher is interested in the influence of amount of daily study time on statistics achievement. Three groups were formed based on the amount of daily study time in statistics, 30 minutes, 1 hour, and 2 hours. Is there a differential influence of amount of time studied on subsequent mean statistics achievement (e.g., statistics final exam)? We would expect that the more one studied statistics, the higher the statistics mean achievement would be. *One possible situation in the population is where the amount of study time does not influence statistics achievement; here the population means will be equal.* That is, the null hypothesis of equal group means is actually ***true***. Thus, the three groups are really three samples from the same population of students, with mean μ. The means are equal; thus there is no variability among the three group means. *A second possible situation in the population is where the amount of study time does influence statistics achievement; here the population means will not be equal.* That is, the null hypothesis is actually *false*. Thus, the three groups are not really three samples from the same population of students, but rather, each group represents a sample from a distinct population of students receiving that particular amount of study time, with mean μ_{j}. The means are not equal, so there is variability among the three group means. In summary, the statistical question becomes whether the difference between the sample means is due to the usual sampling variability expected from a single population, or the result of a true difference between the sample means from different populations.

We conceptually define **within-groups variability** *as the variability of the observations within a group combined across groups* (e.g., variability on test scores within children in the same proficiency level, such as low, moderate, and high, and then combined across all proficiency levels), and **between-groups variability** *as the variability between the groups* (e.g., variability among the test scores from one proficiency level to another proficiency level). In Figure 11.1, the columns represent low and high variability *within* the groups. The rows represent low and high variability *between* the groups.

In the upper left-hand plot of Figure 11.1, there is low variability both within and between the groups. That is, performance is very consistent, both within each group as well as across groups. We see that there is little variability *within* the groups since the individual distributions are not very spread out and little variability *between* the groups because the distributions are not very distinct, as they are nearly lying on top of one another. Here within- and between-group variability are both low and it is quite unlikely that one would reject H_0.

In the upper right-hand plot of Figure 11.1, there is high variability within the groups and low variability between the groups. That is, performance is very consistent across groups (i.e., the distributions largely overlap), but quite variable within each group. We see high variability *within* the groups because the spread of each individual distribution is quite large, and low variability *between* the groups because the distributions are lying so closely together. Here within-group variability exceeds between-group variability, and again it is quite unlikely that one would reject H_0.

In the lower left-hand plot of Figure 11.1, there is low variability within the groups and high variability between the groups. That is, performance is very consistent within each group, but quite variable across groups. We see low variability *within* the groups because each distribution is very compact with little spread to the data, and high variability *between* the groups because each distribution is nearly isolated from one another with very little overlap. Here between-group variability exceeds within-group variability, and it is quite likely that one would reject H_0.

In the lower right-hand plot of Figure 11.1, there is high variability both within and between the groups. That is, performance is quite variable within each group, as well as across the groups. We see high variability *within* groups because the spread of each individual distribution is quite large, and high variability *between* groups because of the minimal overlap from one distribution to another. Here within- and between-group variability are both high, and depending on the relative amounts of between- and within-group variability, one may or may not reject H_0. *In summary, the optimal situation when seeking to reject H_0 is the one represented by high variability between the groups and low variability within the groups.*

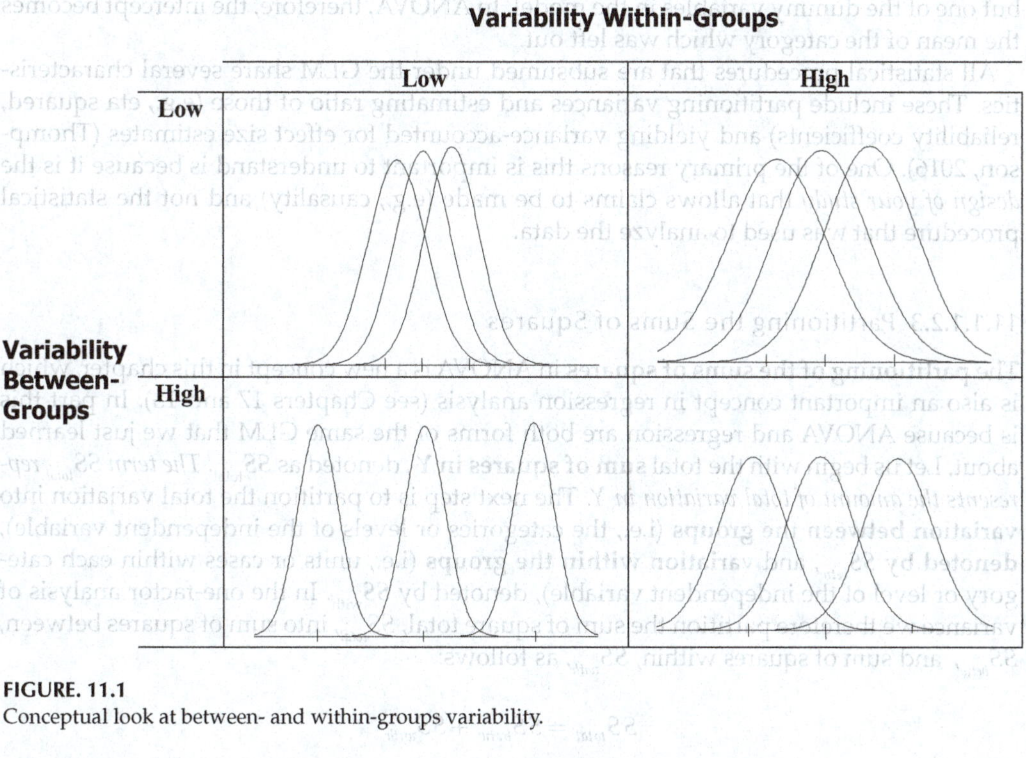

FIGURE. 11.1
Conceptual look at between- and within-groups variability.

11.1.1.2.2 General Linear Model

ANOVA and linear regression are both forms of the same **general linear model (GLM)**. In other words, ANOVA and linear regression are mathematically equal and thus correlational (as we will see later, we are provided ANOVA output when we generate regression). The differences between these methods is largely researcher-created. In practice, historically the methods were used in different disciplines. Multiple regression was used to examine natural variation in the biological and behavioral sciences, while ANOVA was used to study manipulated variation (i.e., experiments) in agricultural science (Cohen, 1968). Different algorithms, terminology, and uses have placed an artificial divide between ANOVA and regression; however, they are mathematically equivalent. Cohen (1968) illustrates the equivalence of the two systems. Thompson (2016) notes how other researchers have shown how other methods are subsumed in GLM. Indeed, most parametric procedures (e.g., *t* test, ANOVA, regression, multivariate ANOVA, structural equation modeling, and more) are part of the general linear model. Given their mathematical equivalence, whether you select ANOVA or regression is largely a consideration of convenience given your data. For example, should all or most of your predictors be continuous, single or multiple regression is more convenient. Should all or more of your predictors be categorical, one-way ANOVA or factorial ANOVA is more convenient.

Let's consider the basic case of the general linear model where one dependent variable is predicted from one or more independent variables. In fitting the linear model, weights or coefficients are computed for each independent variable. The dependent variable is the sum of three elements: the intercept (i.e., a mathematical constant), the sum of the weighted independent variables, and error. In regression, the intercept is the predicted value of the dependent variable when all independent variables have a value of zero. ANOVA in the GLM framework requires dummy coding of the categorical variables and inclusion of all but one of the dummy variables in the model. In ANOVA, therefore, the intercept becomes the mean of the category which was left out.

All statistical procedures that are subsumed under the GLM share several characteristics. These include partitioning variances and estimating ratio of those (e.g., eta squared, reliability coefficients) and yielding variance-accounted for effect size estimates (Thompson, 2016). One of the primary reasons this is important to understand is because it is the *design of your study* that allows claims to be made (e.g., causality) and not the statistical procedure that was used to analyze the data.

11.1.1.2.3 Partitioning the Sums of Squares

The **partitioning of the sums of squares** in ANOVA is a new concept in this chapter, which is also an important concept in regression analysis (see Chapters 17 and 18). In part this is because ANOVA and regression are both forms of the same GLM that we just learned about. Let us begin with the total **sum of squares in *Y***, denoted as SS_{total}. *The term SS_{total} represents the amount of total variation in Y.* The next step is to partition the total variation into **variation between the groups** (i.e., the categories or levels of the independent variable), **denoted by SS_{betw}**, and **variation within the groups** (i.e., units or cases within each category or level of the independent variable), denoted by SS_{with}. In the one-factor analysis of variance we therefore partition the sum of square total, SS_{total}, into sum of squares between, SS_{betw}, and sum of squares within, SS_{with}, as follows:

$$SS_{total} = SS_{betw} + SS_{with}$$

or

$$\sum_{i=1}^{n}\sum_{j=1}^{J}\left(Y_{ij}-\bar{Y}_{..}\right)^2=\sum_{i=1}^{n}\sum_{j=1}^{J}\left(\bar{Y}_{.j}-\bar{Y}_{..}\right)^2+\sum_{i=1}^{n}\sum_{j=1}^{J}\left(Y_{ij}-\bar{Y}_{.j}\right)^2$$

As a side note, algebraically, the sum of squares between can be calculated as follows, where the difference between the group mean and overall mean is weighted by the sample size of the group:

$$\sum_{i=1}^{n}\sum_{j=1}^{J}\left(Y_{ij}-\bar{Y}_{..}\right)^2=\sum_{i=1}^{n}n_j\left(\bar{Y}_{.j}-\bar{Y}_{..}\right)^2+\sum_{i=1}^{n}\sum_{j=1}^{J}\left(Y_{ij}-\bar{Y}_{.j}\right)^2$$

where

- SS_{total} is the total sum of squares due to variation among all of the observations without regard to group membership,
- SS_{betw} is the between-groups sum of squares due to the variation *between* the groups, and
- SS_{with} is the within-groups sum of squares due to the variation *within* the groups combined across groups.

We refer to this particular formulation of the partitioned sums of squares as the **definitional** (or **conceptual**) **formula**, because each term literally defines a form of variation.

Due to computational complexity and the likelihood of a computational error, the definitional formula is rarely used with real data. Instead, a **computational formula** for the partitioned sums of squares is used for hand computations. However, since nearly all data analysis at this level utilizes computer software, we defer to the software to actually perform an analysis of variance (SPSS and **R** examples are provided toward the end of this chapter). A complete example of the one-factor analysis of variance is also considered later in this chapter.

11.1.1.2.4 ANOVA Summary Table

An important result of the analysis is the **ANOVA summary table**. The purpose of the summary table is to literally summarize the analysis of variance. A general form of the summary table is shown in Table 11.2. *The first column lists the sources of variation in the model.* As we already know, in the one-factor model the total variation is partitioned into

TABLE 11.2

Analysis of Variance Summary Table

Source	SS	df	MS	F
Between groups	SS_{betw}	$J-1$	MS_{betw}	MS_{betw}/MS_{with}
Within groups	SS_{with}	$N-J$	MS_{with}	
Total	SS_{total}	$N-1$		

between-groups variation and within-groups variation. *The second column notes the sums of squares terms computed for each source (i.e.,* SS_{betw}*,* SS_{with}*, and* SS_{total}*).*

The third column gives the degrees of freedom for each source. Recall that, in general, the degrees of freedom have to do with the number of observations that are free to vary. For example, if a sample mean and all of the sample observations except for one are known, then the final observation is not free to vary. That is, the final observation is predetermined to be a particular value. For instance, say the mean is 10 and there are three observations, 7, 11, and an unknown observation. Based on that information, first, the sum of the three observations must equal 30 for the mean to be 10. Second, the sum of the known observations is 18. Therefore, the unknown observation must be 12. Otherwise, the sample mean would not be exactly equal to 10.

For the *between-groups source*, the definitional formula is concerned with the deviation of each group mean from the overall mean. There are ***J* group means** (where J represents the number of groups or categories or levels of the independent variable), so the df_{betw} *(also known as the degrees of freedom numerator)* must be $J - 1$. Why? If we have J group means and we know the overall mean, then only $J - 1$ of the group means are free to vary. In other words, if we know the overall mean and all but one of the group means, then the final unknown group mean is predetermined.

For the *within-groups source*, the definitional formula is concerned with the deviation of each observation from its respective group mean. There are ***n* observations** (i.e., cases or units) in each group; consequently, there are $n - 1$ degrees of freedom in each group and J groups. Why are there $n - 1$ degrees of freedom in each group? If there are n observations in each group, then only $n - 1$ of the observations are free to vary. In other words, if we know one group mean and all but one of the observations for that group, then the final unknown observation for that group is predetermined. There are J groups, so the df_{with} *(also known as the degrees of freedom denominator)* is $J(n - 1)$, or more simply as $N - J$. Thus we lose one degree of freedom for each group.

For the **total source**, the definitional formula is concerned with the deviation of each observation from the overall mean. There are N total observations; therefore the df_{total} must be $N - 1$. Why? If there are N total observations and we know the overall mean, then only $N - 1$ of the observations are free to vary. In other words, if we know the overall mean, and all but one of the N observations, then the final unknown observation is predetermined.

Why is the number of degrees of freedom important in the analysis of variance? Suppose two researchers have conducted similar studies, except Researcher A uses 20 observations per group and Researcher B uses 10 observations per group. Each researcher obtains a SS_{with} value of 15. Would it be fair to say that this particular result for the two studies is the same? Such a comparison would be unfair because SS_{with} is influenced by the number of observations per group. A fair comparison would be to weight the SS_{with} terms by their respective number of degrees of freedom. Similarly, it would not be fair to compare the SS_{betw} terms from two similar studies based on different numbers of groups. A fair comparison would be to weight the SS_{betw} terms by their respective number of degrees of freedom. *The method of weighting a sum of squares term by the respective number of degrees of freedom on which it is based yields what is called a* **mean squares** *term.* Thus, $MS_{betw} = SS_{betw} / df_{betw}$ and $MS_{with} = SS_{with} / df_{with}$, as shown in the fourth column of Table 11.2. They are referred to as *mean squares* because they represent a summed quantity that is weighted by the number of observations used in the sum itself, like the mean. *The mean squares terms are also variance estimates* because they represent the sum of the squared deviations from a mean divided by their degrees of freedom, like the sample variance, s^2.

The last column in the ANOVA summary table, the F value (also known as the ***F* ratio** *), is the summary test statistic of the summary table.* The F value is computed by taking the ratio of the two mean squares or variance terms. Thus for the one-factor ANOVA fixed-effects model, the F value is computed as $F = MS_{betw}/MS_{with}$. When developed by Sir Ronald A. Fisher in the 1920s, this test statistic was originally known as the variance ratio because it represents the ratio of two variance estimates. Later the variance ratio was renamed the F ratio by George W. Snedecor (who worked out the table of F values, discussed momentarily) in honor of Fisher (F for Fisher).

The F ratio tells us whether there is more variation *between* groups than there is *within* groups, which is required if we are to reject H_0. Thus, if there is more variation *between* groups than there is *within* groups, then MS_{betw} will be larger than MS_{with}. As a result of this, the F ratio of MS_{betw}/MS_{with} will be greater than 1. If, on the other hand, the amount of variation *between* groups is about the same as there is *within* groups, then MS_{betw} and MS_{with} will be about the same, and the F ratio will be approximately 1. Thus, we want to find large F values in order to reject the null hypothesis.

The F test statistic is then compared with the F critical value so as to make a decision about the null hypothesis. The critical value is found in the F table of Appendix Table A.4 as ${}_{\alpha}F_{(J-1,N-J)}$. Thus the degrees of freedom are $df_{betw} = J - 1$ for the numerator of the F ratio and $df_{with} = N - J$ for the denominator of the F ratio. The significance test is a one-tailed test in order to be consistent with the alternative hypothesis. The null hypothesis is rejected if the F test statistic exceeds the F critical value. This is the **omnibus *F* test** which, again, simply provides evidence of the extent to which there is *at least one* statistically significant mean difference between the groups.

If the F test statistic exceeds the F critical value, and there are more than two groups, then it is not clear where the differences among the means lie. In this case, some **multiple comparison procedure** should be used to determine where the mean differences are in the groups; this is the topic of Chapter 12. When there are only two groups, it is obvious where the mean difference falls, that is, between groups 1 and 2. A researcher can simply look at the descriptive statistics to determine which group had the higher mean relative to the other group. *For the two-group situation*, it is also interesting to note that the F and t test statistics follow the rule of $F = t^2$, for a nondirectional alternative hypothesis in the independent t test. In other words, the one-way ANOVA with two groups and the independent t test will generate the same conclusion such that $F = t^2$. This result occurs when the numerator degrees of freedom for the F ratio is 1. In an actual ANOVA summary table (shown in the next section), except for the source of variation column, it is the values for each of the other entries generated from the data that are listed in the table. For example, instead of seeing SS_{betw} we would see the computed value of SS_{betw}.

11.1.1.3 The ANOVA Model

In this section we introduce the analysis of variance linear model, cover the estimation of parameters of the model, effect size measures, confidence intervals, power, and an example, and finish up with expected mean squares.

11.1.1.3.1 The Model

The one-factor ANOVA fixed-effects model can be written in terms of population parameters as

$$Y_{ij} = \mu + \alpha_j + \varepsilon_{ij}$$

where Y is the observed score on the dependent (or criterion) variable for individual i in group j, μ is the overall or grand population mean (i.e., regardless of group designation), α_j is the group effect for group j, and ε_{ij} is the random residual error for individual i in group j. The residual error can be due to individual differences, measurement error, and/or other factors not under investigation (i.e., other than the independent variable X). The population group effect and residual error are computed as

$$\alpha_j = \mu_{.j} - \mu$$

and

$$\varepsilon_j = Y_{ij} - \mu_{.j}$$

respectively, and $\mu_{.j}$ is the population mean for group j, where the initial dot subscript indicates we have averaged across all i individuals in group j. That is, the group effect is equal to the difference between the population mean of group j and the overall population mean. The residual error is equal to the difference between an individual's observed score and the population mean of the group of which the individual is a member (i.e., group j). The group effect can also be thought of as the average effect of being a member of a particular group. A positive group effect implies a group mean greater than the overall mean, whereas a negative group effect implies a group mean less than the overall mean. Note that in a fixed-effects one-factor model, the population group effects sum to zero. The residual error in the analysis of variance represents that portion of Y not accounted for by X.

11.1.1.3.2 Estimation of the Parameters of the Model

Next we need to estimate the parameters of the model μ, α_j, and ε_{ij}. The sample estimates are represented by $\bar{Y}_{..}$, a_j, and e_{ij}, respectively, where the latter two are computed as

$$a_j = \bar{Y}_{.j} - \bar{Y}_{..}$$

and

$$e_{ij} = Y_{ij} - \bar{Y}_{.j}$$

respectively. Note that $\bar{Y}_{..}$ represents the overall sample mean, where the double dot subscript indicates we have averaged across both the i and j subscripts, and $\bar{Y}_{.j}$ represents the sample mean for group j, where the initial dot subscript indicates we have averaged across all i individuals in group j.

11.1.1.3.3 Confidence Intervals

Confidence interval procedures are often useful in providing an interval estimate of a population parameter (i.e., mean or mean difference); these allow us to determine the accuracy of the sample estimate. One can form confidence intervals around any sample group mean from an ANOVA (provided in software such as SPSS), although confidence intervals for means have more utility for multiple comparison procedures, as discussed in Chapter 12.

Confidence interval procedures have also been developed for several effect size measures (Fidler & Thompson, 2001; Smithson, 2001).

11.1.1.3.4 An Example

Consider now an example problem used throughout this chapter. Our dependent variable is psychological distress (a continuous score), whereas the independent variable is the type of sport in which an elite athlete competes. The researcher is interested in whether the type of sport in which an athlete competes influences their psychological distress. The types of sports are defined as follows:

- Sport 1, movement (e.g., gymnastics, dance);
- Sport 2, target (e.g., golf);
- Sport 3, fielding (e.g., baseball); and
- Sport 4, territory (e.g., football).

There were eight athletes in each sport, for a total of 32. In Table 11.3 we see the raw data and sample statistics (means and variances) for each sport and overall (far right).

The results are summarized in the ANOVA summary table as shown in Table 11.4. The test statistic, F = 6.1877, is compared to the critical value, ${}_{.05}F_{3,28} = 2.95$ obtained from Appendix Table A.4, using the .05 level of significance. To use the *F* table, find the numerator degrees of freedom, df_{betw}, which are represented by the columns, and then the denominator degrees of freedom, df_{with}, which are represented by the rows. The intersection of the two provides the *F* crtical value. The test statistic exceeds the critical value, so we reject H_0 and conclude that type of sport is related to mean differences in psychological distress. The exact probability value (*p* value) given by SPSS is .001.

TABLE 11.3
Data and Summary Statistics for the Elite Athlete Example

	Psychological Distress by Type of Sport				
	Group 1: Movement (e.g., dance)	**Group 2: Target (e.g., golf)**	**Group 3: Fielding (e.g., baseball)**	**Group 4: Territory (e.g., football)**	**Overall**
	15	20	10	30	
	10	13	24	22	
	12	9	29	26	
	8	22	12	20	
	21	24	27	29	
	7	25	21	28	
	13	18	25	25	
	3	12	14	15	
Means	11.1250	17.8750	20.2500	24.3750	18.4063
Variances	30.1250	35.2679	53.0714	25.9821	56.4425

TABLE 11.4

Analysis of Variance Summary Table—Psychological Distress Example

Source	*SS*	*df*	*MS*	*F*
Between groups	738.5938	3	246.1979	6.8177*
Within groups	1,011.1250	28	36.1116	
Total	1,749.7188	31		

* $_{.05}F_{3,28} = 2.95$

Next we examine the group effects and residual errors. The group effects are estimated as follows where the grand mean (irrespective of the group membership; here 18.4063) is subtracted from the group mean (e.g., 11.125 for group 1). The subscript of *a* indicates the level or group of the independent variable (e.g., 1 = movement; 2 = target; 3 = fielding; 4 = territory). A **negative group effect** indicates that group had a larger mean than the overall average and thus exerted a negative effect on the dependent variable (in our case, higher psychological distress). A **positive group effect** indicates that group had a smaller mean than the overall average and thus exerted a positive effect on the dependent variable (in our case, lower psychological distress).

$$a_1 = \bar{Y}_{.1} - \bar{Y}_{..} = 11.125 - 18.4063 = -7.2813$$

$$a_2 = \bar{Y}_{.2} - \bar{Y}_{..} = 17.875 - 18.4063 = -0.5313$$

$$a_3 = \bar{Y}_{.3} - \bar{Y}_{..} = 20.250 - 18.4063 = +1.8437$$

$$a_4 = \bar{Y}_{.4} - \bar{Y}_{..} = 24.375 - 18.4063 = +5.9687$$

Thus group 4 (territory) has the largest *negative* group effect (i.e., highest psychological distress), while group 1 (movement) has the largest *positive* group effect (i.e., lowest psychological distress). In Chapter 12 we use the same data to determine which of these group means, or combination of group means, are statistically different. The residual errors (computed as the difference between the observed value and the group mean) for each individual by group are shown in Table 11.5 and discussed later in this chapter.

TABLE 11.5

Residuals for the Psychological Distress Example by Group

Group 1: Movement (e.g., dance)	Group 2: Target (e.g., golf)	Group 3: Fielding (e.g., baseball)	Group 4: Territory (e.g., football)
3.875	2.125	−10.250	5.625
−1.125	−4.875	3.750	−2.375
0.875	−8.875	8.750	1.625
−3.125	4.125	−8.250	−4.375
9.875	6.125	6.750	4.625
−4.125	7.125	0.750	3.625
1.875	0.125	4.750	0.625
−8.125	−5.875	−6.250	−9.375

11.1.1.3.5 Expected Mean Squares

There is one more theoretical concept called **expected mean squares** to introduce in this chapter. The notion of expected mean squares provides the basis for determining what the appropriate error term is when forming an F ratio (recall this ratio is $F = MS_{betw}/MS_{with}$). That is, when forming an F ratio to test a certain hypothesis, how do we know which source of variation to use as the error term in the denominator? For instance, in the one-factor fixed-effects ANOVA model, how did we know to use MS_{with} as the error term in testing for differences between the groups? There is a good rationale, as becomes evident.

Before we get into expected mean squares, consider the definition of an expected value. *An expected value is defined as the average value of a statistic that would be obtained with repeated sampling*. Using the sample mean as an example statistic, the expected value of the mean would be the average value of the sample means obtained from an infinite number of samples. *The expected value of a statistic is also known as the mean of the sampling distribution of that statistic*. In this case, the expected value of the mean is the mean of the sampling distribution of the mean.

An expected mean square for a particular source of variation represents the average mean square value for that source obtained if the same study were to be repeated an infinite number of times. For instance, the expected value of MS_{betw}, denoted by $E(MS_{betw})$, is the average value of MS_{betw} over repeated samplings. At this point you might be asking, "Why not only be concerned about the values of the mean square terms for my own little study?" Well, the mean square terms from your little study do represent a sample from a population of mean square terms. Thus, sampling distributions and sampling variability are as much a concern in the analysis of variance as they are in other situations previously described in this text.

Now we are ready to see what the expected mean square terms actually look like. Consider the two situations of H_0 actually being true and H_0 actually being false. If H_0 is actually *true*, such that there really are *no* differences between the population group means, then the *expected mean squares* [represented in statistical notation as either $E(MS_{betw})$ or $E(MS_{with})$] are as follows:

$$E(MS_{betw}) = \sigma_\varepsilon^2$$

$$E(MS_{with}) = \sigma_\varepsilon^2$$

and thus the ratio of expected mean squares is:

$$E(MS_{betw}) / E(MS_{betw}) = 1$$

where the expected value of F is then $E(F) = df_{with}/(df_{with}-2)$, and σ_ε^2 is the population variance of the residual errors. This tells us the following: if H_0 is actually true, then each of the J samples really comes from the same population with mean μ.

If H_0 is actually *false*, such that there really *are* differences between the population group means, then the expected mean squares are as follows:

$$E(MS_{betw}) = \sigma_\varepsilon^2 + \left(n\sum_{j=1}^{J} \alpha_j^2\right) / J-1$$

$$E(MS_{with}) = \sigma_\varepsilon^2$$

and thus the ratio of the expected mean squares is as follows:

$$E(MS_{betw})/E(MS_{with}) > 1$$

where $E(F) > df_{with}/(df_{with}-2)$. If H_0 is actually false, then the J samples do really come from different populations with different means μ_j.

There is a difference in the expected mean square between [i.e., $E(MS_{betw})$] when H_0 is actually true as compared to when H_0 is actually false, as in the latter situation there is a second term. The important part of this second term is $\sum_{j=1}\alpha_j^2$ which represents the **sum of the squared group effects**. The larger this part becomes, the larger MS_{betw} is, and thus the larger the F ratio becomes. In comparing the two situations, we also see that $E(MS_{with})$ is the same whether H_0 is actually true or false, and thus represents a reliable estimate of σ_ϵ^2. This term is mean-free because it does not depend on group mean differences. Just to cover all of the possibilities, F could be less than one [or technically less than $df_{with}/(df_{with}-2)$] due to sampling error, nonrandom samples, and/or assumption violations. For a mathematical proof of the $E(MS)$ terms, see Kirk (2013).

Finally, let us try to put all of this information together. In general, the F ratio represents the following:

$$F = (\textit{systematic variability} + \textit{error variability})/\textit{error variability}$$

where, for the one-factor fixed-effects model, *systematic variability* is variability *between* the groups and *error variability* is variability *within* the groups. The F ratio is formed in a particular way because we want to isolate the systematic variability in the numerator. For this model, the only appropriate F ratio is MS_{betw}/MS_{with} because it does serve to isolate the systematic variability (i.e., the variability between the groups). That is, the appropriate error term for testing a particular effect (e.g., mean differences between groups) is the mean square that is identical to the mean square of that effect, except that it lacks a term due to the effect of interest. For this model, the appropriate error term to use for testing differences between groups is the mean square identical to the numerator MS_{betw}, except it lacks a term due to the between-groups effect [i.e., $\left(n\sum_{j=1}^{J}\alpha_j^2\right)/(J-1)$]; this, of course, is MS_{with}. It should also be noted that the F ratio is a ratio of two independent variance estimates, here being MS_{betw} and MS_{with}.

11.1.1.4 The Unequal n's or Unbalanced Procedure

Up to this point in the chapter, we have considered only the equal n's or balanced case where the number of observations is equal for each group. This was done to make things simple for presentation purposes. However, we do not need to assume that the n's must be equal (as some textbooks incorrectly do). This section briefly describes the **unequal *n* 's** or **unbalanced case**. For our purposes, the major statistical software can handle the analysis of this case for the one-factor ANOVA model without any special attention. Thus, interpretation of the analysis, the assumptions, and so forth are the same as with the equal n's case. However, once we get to factorial designs in Chapter 13, things become a bit more complicated for the unequal n's or unbalanced case.

11.1.1.5 Alternative ANOVA Procedures

There are several alternatives to the parametric one-factor fixed-effects ANOVA. These include the Kruskal-Wallis one-factor ANOVA (Kruskal & Wallis, 1952, 1953), the Welch test (Welch, 1951), the Brown-Forsythe procedure (Brown & Forsythe, 1974), and the James procedures (James, 1951). You may recognize the Welch and Brown-Forsythe procedures as similar alternatives to the independent t test.

11.1.1.5.1 Kruskal-Wallis Test

The Kruskal-Wallis test makes no normality assumption about the population distributions, although it assumes similar distributional shapes, but still assumes equal population variances across the groups (although heterogeneity does have some effect on this test, it is less than with the parametric ANOVA). When the normality assumption is met, or nearly so (i.e., with mild nonnormality), the parametric ANOVA is slightly more powerful than the Kruskal-Wallis test (i.e., less likelihood of a Type II error). Otherwise the Kruskal-Wallis test is more powerful.

The Kruskal-Wallis procedure works as follows. First, the observations on the dependent measure are rank ordered, regardless of group assignment (the ranking is done by the computer). That is, the observations are ranked from highest to lowest, disregarding group membership. *The procedure essentially tests whether the mean ranks are different across the groups such that they are unlikely to represent random samples from the same population.* Thus, according to the null hypothesis, the mean rank is the same for each group; whereas for the alternative hypothesis, the mean rank is not the same across groups. The test statistic is denoted by H and is compared to the critical value ${}_{\alpha}\chi^2_{J-1}$. The null hypothesis is rejected if the test statistic H exceeds the χ^2 critical value.

There are two situations to consider with this test. First, the χ^2 critical value is really only appropriate when there are at least three groups and at least five observations per group (i.e., the χ^2 is not an exact sampling distribution of H). The second situation is that when there are tied ranks, the sampling distribution of H can be affected. Typically a midranks procedure is used, which results in an overly conservative Kruskal-Wallis test. A correction for ties is commonly used. Unless the number of ties is relatively large, the effect of the correction is minimal.

Using the elite athlete data as an example, we perform the Kruskal-Wallis analysis of variance. The test statistic $H = 13.0610$ is compared with the critical value ${}_{.05}\chi^2_3 = 7.81$, from Appendix Table A.3, and the result is that H_0 is rejected ($p = .005$). Thus the Kruskal-Wallis result agrees with the result of the parametric analysis of variance. This should not be surprising because the normality assumption apparently was met. Thus, we would probably not have done the Kruskal-Wallis test for the example data. We merely provide it for purposes of explanation and comparison.

In summary, the Kruskal-Wallis test can be used as an alternative to the parametric one-factor analysis of variance under nonnormality and/or when data on the dependent variable are ordinal. Under normality and with interval/ratio dependent variable data, the parametric ANOVA is more powerful than the Kruskal-Wallis test, and thus is the preferred method.

11.1.1.5.2 Welch, Brown-Forsyth, and James Procedures

Next we briefly consider the following procedures for the heteroscedasticity condition: the Welch test (Welch, 1951); the Brown-Forsythe procedure (Brown & Forsythe, 1974); and the James first- and second-order procedures (James, 1951) (more fully desribed in sources such as Coombs, Algina, & Oltman, 1996; Myers, Lorch, & Well, 2010; Wilcox, 1996, 2003). These procedures do not require homogeneity. Research suggests that (a) under homogeneity the F test is slightly more powerful than any of these procedures, and (b) under heterogeneity each of these alternative procedures is more powerful than the F, although the choice among them depends on several conditions, making a recommendation amongst these alternative procedures somewhat complicated (e.g., Clinch & Keselman, 1982; Tomarken & Serlin, 1986; Coombs et al., 1996). The Kruskal-Wallis test is widely available in the major statistical software, and the Welch and Brown-Forsythe procedures are available in the SPSS one-way ANOVA module. Wilcox (1996) and Wilcox (2003) also provide assistance for these alternative procedures.

11.1.2 Power

As for power (the probability of correctly rejecting a false null hypothesis), one can consider either planned power (*a priori*) or observed power (post hoc), as discussed in previous chapters. In the ANOVA context, we know that power is primarily a function of α, sample size, and effect size. For planned power, one inputs each of these components either into a statistical table or power chart (e.g., Cohen, 1988; Murphy, Myors, & Wolach, 2014), or into power software (such as G*Power). Planned power is most often used by researchers to determine adequate sample sizes in ANOVA models, which is highly recommended. Many disciplines recommend a minimum power value, such as .80. Thus, these methods are a useful way to determine the sample size that would generate a desired level of power. Observed power is determined by some statistics software, such as SPSS, and indicates the power that was actually observed in a completed study.

11.1.3 Effect Size

There are various effect size measures to indicate the strength of association between X and Y, that is, the relative strength of the group effect. Let us briefly examine η^2, ω^2, ε^2, and Cohen's (1988) f.

11.1.3.1 Eta Squared

First, η^2 (eta squared), ranging from zero to +1.00, is known as the correlation ratio (generalization of R^2) and represents the proportion of variation in Y explained by the group mean differences in X. An eta squared of zero suggests that *none* of the total variance in the dependent variable is due to differences between the groups. An eta squared of 1.00 indicates that *all* the variance in the dependent variable is due to the group mean differences. We find η^2 to be as follows (Olejnik & Algina, 2000):

$$\eta^2 = \frac{SS_{betw}}{SS_{total}}$$

It is well known that η^2 is a positively biased statistic (i.e., overestimates the association). The bias is most evident for n's (i.e., group sample sizes) less than 30. *In one-way ANOVA, eta squared and partial eta squared (which is reported in SPSS output) will be equal given there is just one independent variable.*

11.1.3.2 Omega Squared and Epsilon Squared

Other effect size measures are ω^2 (omega squared) and ε^2 (epsilon squared). Both are interpreted similarly to eta squared (specifically, the proportion of variation in Y explained by the group mean differences in X) but provide corrections that allow them to be less biased than η^2. Omega squared and epsilon squared will generally differ only slightly (Carroll & Nordholm, 1975). Both can provide negative estimates, and when that happens, the estimate is usually set to zero (Olejnik & Algina, 2000).

We determine **omega squared** through either of the following formulas (the first formula referenced in Olejnik & Algina, 2000):

$$\omega^2 = \frac{(df_{betw})(MS_{betw} - MS_{with})}{SS_{total} + MS_{with}}$$

$$\omega^2 = \frac{SS_{betw} - (J-1)MS_{with}}{SS_{total} + MS_{with}}$$

Epsilon squared is computed as (Olejnik & Algina, 2000):

$$\varepsilon^2 = \frac{(df_{betw})(MS_{betw} - MS_{with})}{SS_{total}}$$

11.1.3.3 Cohen's f

A final effect size measure is f, developed by Cohen (1988). The effect f can take on values from zero (when the means are equal) to an infinitely large positive value. This effect is interpreted as an approximate correlation index but can also be interpreted as the standard deviation of the standardized means (Cohen, 1988). We compute f through the following:

$$f = \sqrt{\frac{\eta^2}{1 - \eta^2}}$$

We can also use f to compute the effect size d, which you recall from the t test is interpreted as the standardized mean difference. The formulas for translating f to d are dependent on whether there is minimum, moderate, or maximum variability between the means of the groups. Interested readers are referred to Cohen (1988).

11.1.3.4 Interpretation of Effect Size Values

Cohen's (1988) subjective standards can be used as follows to interpret these effect size values: small effect, $f = .10$, η^2, ε^2, $\omega^2 = .01$; medium effect, $f = .25$, η^2, ε^2, $\omega^2 = .06$; and large effect, $f = .40$, η^2, ε^2, $\omega^2 = .14$. Note that these are subjective standards developed were for the behavioral sciences; your discipline may use other standards. For further discussion, see O'Grady (1982), Wilcox (1987), Cohen (1988), Keppel and Wickens (2004), and Murphy, Myors, and Wolach (2014).

TABLE 11.6

Effect Sizes and Interpretations

Effect Size	Interpretation
Omega squared (ω^2), **epsilon squared**(ε^2), **and eta squared** (η^2)	Proportion of total variability in the dependent variable that is accounted for by the factor (i.e., independent variable) • Small effect = .01 • Medium effect = .06 • Large effect = .14
Cohen's *f*	Approximate correlation index but can also be interpreted as the standard deviation of the standardized means • Small effect = .10 • Medium effect = .25 • Large effect = .40

11.1.3.5 An Effect Size Example

Let's determine the effect size measures given the data on elite athletes. For illustrative purposes, all effect size measures that were previously discussed have been computed. In practice, only one effect size is usually computed and interpreted. First, eta squared, η^2, is computed as follows. Note that in the one-way ANOVA, eta squared will equal partial eta squared as output in SPSS.

$$\eta^2 = \frac{SS_{betw}}{SS_{total}} = \frac{738.5938}{1749.7188} = .4221$$

Next, omega squared, ω^2, is found to be the following (where either calculation will result in the same value). Note that in the one-way ANOVA, omega squared will equal partial omega squared as output in the online calculator that we will demonstrate shortly.

$$\omega^2 = \frac{(df_{betw})(MS_{betw} - MS_{with})}{SS_{total} + MS_{with}} = \frac{(3)(246.198 - 36.112)}{1749.7188 - 36.1116} = .3529$$

$$\omega^2 = \frac{SS_{betw} - (J-1)MS_{with}}{SS_{total} + MS_{with}} = \frac{738.5938 - (4-1)36.1116}{1749.7188 + 36.1116} = .3529$$

Now we find epsilon squared, ε^2:

$$\varepsilon^2 = \frac{(df_{betw})(MS_{betw} - MS_{with})}{SS_{total}} = \frac{(3)(246.198 - 36.112)}{1749.7188} = .3602$$

Lastly, Cohen's *f* is computed as follows:

$$f = \sqrt{\frac{\eta^2}{1-\eta^2}} = \sqrt{\frac{.4221}{1-.4221}} = .8546$$

Recall Cohen's (1988) subjective standards that can be used to interpret these effect sizes. Based on these effect size measures, all measures lead to the same conclusion: *there is a large effect size for the influence of type of sport on psychological distress.* Examining ω^2, for example, we can also state that about 35% of the variation in Y (psychological distress) can be explained by X (type of sport in which the athlete competes). The other proportion of variance effect size indices provide similar interpretations. The effect f suggests a strong correlation.

In addition, if we rank the group means of the sport from movement (with the lowest mean) to territory (with the highest mean), we see that as physical contact of the sport increases (e.g., from movement to territory), the more psychological distress is reported by the athlete. While visual inspection of the means suggests descriptively there are differences in psychological distress by sport, we examine multiple comparison procedures with this same data in Chapter 12 to determine which groups are statistically significantly different from one another.

11.1.3.6 Confidence Intervals for Effect Size

As we know by this point, computing **confidence intervals** is valuable. The benefit in creating confidence intervals for effect size values is similar to that of creating confidence intervals for parameter estimates—*confidence intervals for the effect size provide an added measure of precision that is not obtained from knowledge of the effect size alone.* Computing confidence intervals for effect size indices, however, is not as straightforward as simply plugging in known values into a formula. Never fear; there are some nice online tools that can be used. One online calculator for computing many types of effect sizes and their confidence intervals is provided by Dr. David B. Wilson and is available through the Campbell Collaboration (see https://campbellcollaboration.org/research-resources/effect-size-calculator.html). In the case of one-way ANOVA, this online calculator can be used with the F test when there are two groups with either a balanced or unbalanced design. Uanhoro's (2017) online calculator (available at https://effect-size-calculator.herokuapp.com/), uses the noncentral F method to compute confidence intervals for partial eta squared in fixed-effects ANOVA models that do not include covariates (i.e., ANCOVA, which we will study in a future chapter). As we see in Figure 11.2, only four inputs are required: F, numerator and denominator degrees of freedom, and confidence interval. Note that the default setting for the 90% confidence interval is equivalent to the 95% two-sided confidence interval since the F cannot be negative (Smithson, 2003)—thus, the recommendation on the site to "use the 90% CI if you have an alpha level of 5%." Partial eta squared is .422 with lower and upper confidence limits of .135 and .548, respectively. Putting this in context of our example, if multiple random samples were drawn from the population, 95% of the samples could expect about 14%, at minimum, and 55%, at maximum, of the proportion of the outcome to be explained by the independent variable.

11.1.3.7 Items to Consider

We will end our discussion on effect size with a few noteworthy items to consider as you compute and interpret effect sizes. Eta squared can be positively biased, overestimating the strength of the population relationship, and thus is best considered a descriptor of proportion of variance in the dependent variable explained for a particular sample (Maxwell,

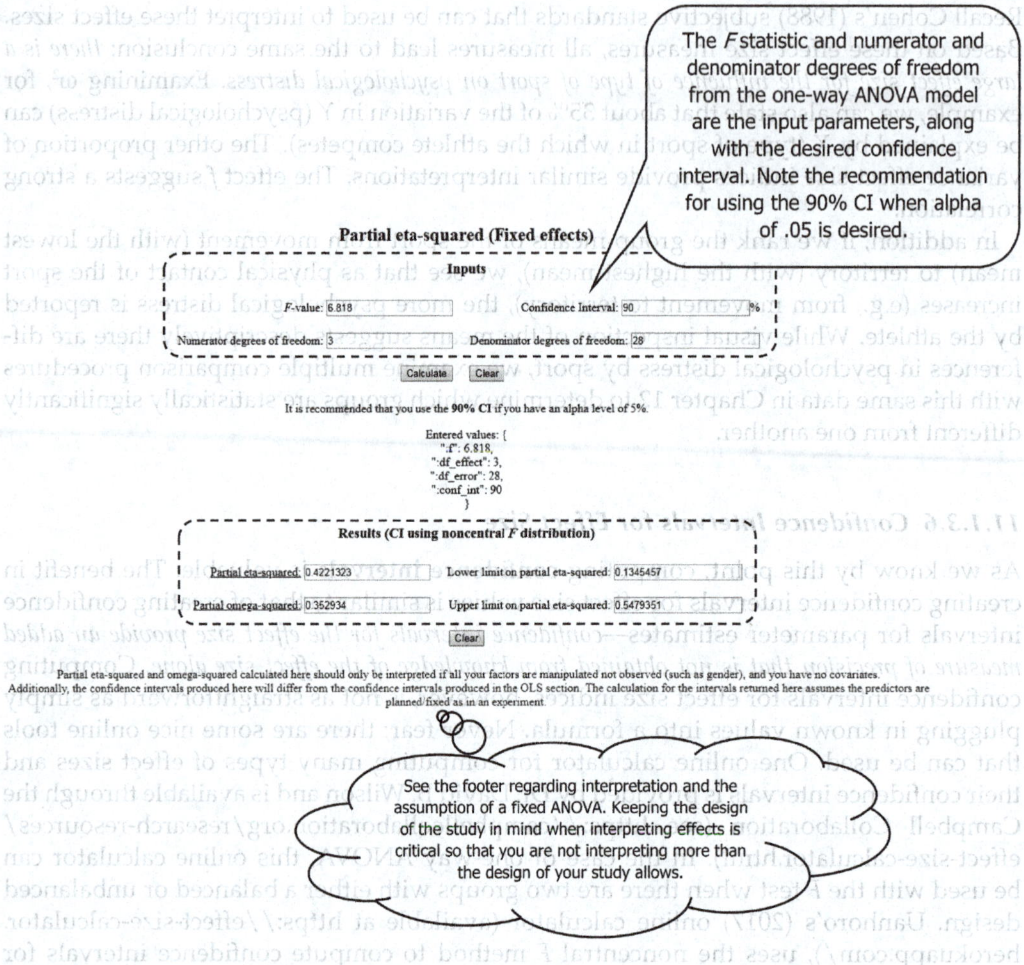

FIGURE 11.2
Confidence Intervals for Effect Size

Arvey, & Camp, 1981). Thus, many researchers discourage reporting eta squared or partial eta squared, although you will still see it widely reported given that it is the only effect size value that is output from SPSS. Both epsilon squared and omega squared introduce a correction to this problem and generally, both will be quite similar in value (Carroll & Nordholm, 1975). If you find yourself in a situation where epsilon squared or omega squared are negative, the standard is simply to set the effect size to zero (Olejnik & Algina, 2000). Proportion of total variance effect size indices are not comparable across studies that incorporate different factors (Olejnik & Algina, 2000) or factors which are theoretically the same but measured differently. This is reasonable given that total variation is influenced by all the factors in the model.

Some researchers find interpreting proportion of variance effect sizes advantageous, as compared to standardized mean differences, given that the index range is from 0 to 1 (Rosenthal, 1994). However, even a large proportion of variance effect size values (e.g., .14+) suggest there is much variance that remains to be explained, and thus even large effects can be perceived as trivial (Rosenthal & Rubin, 1979).

Last but not least, we will touch on general reporting and interpretation considerations. Many researchers encourage interpreting effect size relative to other studies. However, several researchers (e.g., Fern & Monroe, 1996; Maxwell et al., 1981; O'Grady, 1982; Sechrest & Yeaton, 1982) have provided caution in doing this as effect size can be impacted by instrument reliability, heterogeneity of the populations that are compared, the levels or categories of the factors that are modeled, the strength of the treatments, and the range of treatments, all of which can lead to effect size comparisons that are misleading (Olejnik & Algina, 2000).

11.1.4 Assumptions

There are three standard assumptions made in analysis of variance models, which we are already familiar with from the independent *t* test. We see these assumptions often in the remainder of this text. The assumptions are concerned with **independence**, **homogeneity of variance**, and **normality**. We also mention some techniques appropriate to use in evaluating each assumption.

11.1.4.1 Independence

The first assumption is that observations are independent of one another (both within samples and across samples). In general, the assumption of independence for ANOVA designs can be met by (a) keeping the assignment of individuals to groups separate through the design of the experiment (specifically random assignment—not to be confused with random selection), and (b) keeping the individuals separate from one another through experimental control so that the scores on the dependent variable *Y* for group 1 do not influence the scores for group 2 and so forth for other groups of the independent variable. Zimmerman (1997) also stated that independence can be violated for supposedly independent samples due to some type of matching in the design of the experiment (e.g., matched pairs based on gender, age, and weight).

The use of independent random samples is crucial in the analysis of variance. The *F* ratio is very sensitive to violation of the independence assumption in terms of increased likelihood of a Type I and/or Type II error (e.g., Glass, Peckham, & Sanders, 1972). This effect can sometimes even be worse with larger samples (Keppel & Wickens, 2004). A violation of the independence assumption may affect the standard errors of the sample means and thus influence any inferences made about those means. One purpose of random assignment of individuals to groups is to achieve independence. If each individual is observed only once and individuals are randomly assigned to groups, then the independence assumption is usually met. If individuals work together during the study (e.g., through discussion groups or group work), then independence may be compromised. Thus, a carefully planned, controlled, and conducted research design is the key to satisfying this assumption.

What if your independent variable does not allow for random assignment, such as an observed characteristic or attribute (e.g., sex) or a preexisting group (e.g., self-selection into levels)? This does not prohibit the use of these variables as an independent variable in ANOVA. Indeed, for many disciplines, random assignment is rarely if ever possible, and it is a preexisting condition or already defined group that is of interest to examine as an independent variable. In these cases, it is particularly essential that evidence be examined to determine the extent to which the assumption of independence is met.

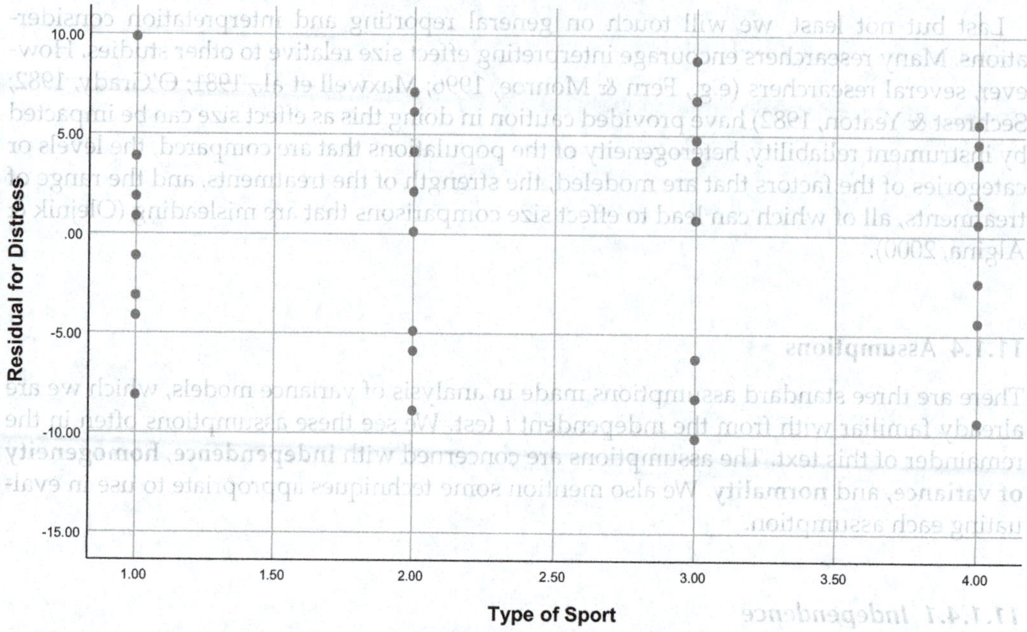

FIGURE 11.3
Residual plot by group for elite athlete example.

The simplest procedure for assessing independence is to examine residual plots by group. If the independence assumption is satisfied, then the residuals should fall into a random display of points for each group. If the assumption is violated, then the residuals will fall into some type of pattern. The Durbin-Watson statistic (Durbin & Watson, 1950, 1951, 1971) can be used to test for autocorrelation. Violations of the independence assumption generally occur in three situations: (1) when observations are collected over time; (2) when observations are made within blocks; or (3) when observation involves replication. For severe violations of the independence assumption, there is no simple "fix" (e.g., Scariano & Davenport, 1987). For the example data, a plot of the residuals by group is shown in Figure 11.3, and there does appear to be a random display of points for each group even though the units were not randomly assigned to group.

11.1.4.2 Homogeneity of Variance

The second assumption is that the variances of each population are equal. This is known as the assumption of **homogeneity of variance** or also sometimes referred to as **homoscedasticity**. In ANOVA models, the term *homogeneity of variance* is often used, while in regression, *homoscedasticity* is often used. Regardless, the terms *conceptually* relate to constant variance—i.e., the residuals are the same (i.e., *constant*) everywhere. A violation of the homogeneity of variance assumption can lead to bias in the SS_{with} term (recall that *within* measures variation of units within each group), as well as an increase in the Type I error rate (i.e., rejecting the null when it is really false) and possibly an increase in the Type II error rate.

Two sets of research studies have investigated violations of this assumption, classic work and more modern work. The classic work largely resulted from Box (1954) and Glass et al.

(1972). Their results indicated that the effect of the violation was small with equal or nearly equal n's across the groups. There is a more serious problem if the larger n's are associated with the smaller variances (actual observed $\alpha >$ nominal α, which is a liberal result; for example, if a researcher desires a nominal alpha of .05, the alpha actually observed will be greater than .05), or if the larger n's are associated with the larger variances (actual observed $\alpha <$ nominal α, which is a conservative result). [Note that Bradley's (1978) criterion is used in this text, where the actual α should not exceed 1.1 to 1.5 times the nominal alpha]. Thus, the suggestion from the classic work was that heterogeneity was a concern only when there were unequal n's. However, the classic work examined only minor violations of the assumption (the ratio of largest variance to smallest variance being relatively small), and unfortunately has been largely adapted in textbooks and by users.

There has been some research conducted since that time by researchers such as Brown and Forsythe (1974), and Wilcox (Wilcox, 1986, 1987, 1988, 1989), and nicely summarized by Coombs et al. (1996). In short, this work indicates that the effect of heterogeneity is more severe than previously thought (e.g., poor power; α can be greatly affected), even with equal n's (although having equal n's does reduce the magnitude of the problem). Thus F is not even robust to heterogeneity with equal n's (equal n's are sometimes referred to as a balanced design). However, heterogeneity is less problematic with a balanced design *and* when the assumption of normality holds (Wilcox, 2017).

Suggestions for dealing with such a violation include (a) using alternative procedures such as the Welch, Brown-Forsythe, and James procedures (Coombs et al., 1996; Glass & Hopkins, 1996; Keppel & Wickens, 2004; Myers et al., 2010; Wilcox, 1996, 2003), (b) reducing the alpha level and testing at a more stringent alpha level (e.g., alpha of .01 rather than the common .05) (e.g., Keppel & Wickens, 2004; Weinberg & Abramowitz, 2002), or (c) transforming Y (such as $\sqrt{Y}$, $1/Y$, or $\log Y$) (e.g., Keppel & Wickens, 2004; Weinberg & Abramowitz, 2002). The alternative procedures will be more fully described later in this chapter.

Examining the extent to which homogeneity has been met can be done visually. In a plot of residuals versus each value of X, the consistency of the variance of the conditional residual distributions may be examined simply by eyeballing the plot.

Another method for detecting violation of the homogeneity assumption is the use of formal statistical tests, as discussed also in Chapter 9. The traditional homogeneity tests (e.g., Levene's test) are commonly available in statistical software but are not robust to nonnormality, and this is the only test for homogeneity currently available in SPSS. For the example data, the residual plot of Figure 11.2 shows similar variances across the groups, and Levene's test suggests the variances are not different [F (3, 28) = .905, p = .451]. A recent simulation study by Wang et al. (2017) studied the performance of 14 homogeneity tests on controlling Type I error and power in one-way ANOVA. They found that the Ramsey conditional, O'Brien, Brown-Forsythe, bootstrap Brown-Forsythe, and Levene with squared deviation tests maintained adequate control of Type I errors and performed better than others reviewed, including maintaining acceptable power, across the simulated conditions. Recommendations for selecting a test for homogeneity of variance based on average cell size include the following: (a) when cell size is less than 10, O'Brien is the recommended test for homogeneity of variance as it maintains adequate Type I error control; (b) when cell size is greater than 10 but less than 20, the Ramsey conditional test is recommended as it also maintains adequate Type I error control; and (c) when the cell size is more than 20, the Brown-Forsythe, bootstrap Brown-Forsythe, and Ramsey conditional test are recommended as these tests provide adequate Type I error control and greater power (around .80).

11.1.4.3 Normality

The third assumption is that each of the populations follows the normal distribution (i.e., there is normality of the dependent variable for each category or group or level of the independent variable). The *F* test is relatively robust to moderate violations of this assumption (i.e., in terms of Type I and Type II error rates). Specifically, effects of the violation will be minimal except for small *n*'s, for unequal *n*'s, and/or for extreme nonnormality. As noted in our earlier discussion of homogeneity of variance, when there are equal sample sizes and the assumption of normality is violated, the results from a *F* test will not be robust unless the distributions of the group are equal (e.g., each group has the same degree of skew) (Wilcox, 2017). Wilcox (2017) suggests that *F* is robust to Type I errors when the group distributions are equal (e.g., the same skew across all groups).

Violation of the normality assumption may be a result of outliers. The simplest outlier detection procedure is to look for observations that are more than two or three standard deviations from their respective group mean. We recommend (and will illustrate later) inspection of residuals for examination of evidence of normality. Formal procedures for the detection of outliers are now available in many statistical packages.

The following graphical techniques can be used to examine residuals and detect violations of the normality assumption: (a) the frequency distributions of the residuals for each group (through stem-and-leaf plots, boxplots, histograms, residual plots), (b) the normal probability or quantile (Q-Q) plot, or (c) a plot of group means versus group variances (which should be independent of one another). There are also several statistical procedures available for the detection of nonnormality including skewness and kurtosis as well as formal tests for normality (e.g., the Shapiro-Wilk test, Shapiro & Wilk, 1965).

As we've learned previously, sample statistics such as **skewness** and **kurtosis** of the residuals can be reviewed. Values within an absolute value of 2.0 suggest evidence of normality. We can also divide the skew and kurtosis values by their standard errors to get *standardized skew and kurtosis* values. We can review those values to a critical value (e.g., ± 1.65 if alpha = .10; ± 1.96 if alpha = .05; ± 2.06 if alpha = .01) and determine if there is statistically significant skew and/or kurtosis. **D'Agostino's test** (D'Agostino, 1970) can be used to examine the null hypothesis that skewness equals zero, with a statistically significant D'Agostino's test indicating that there is statistically significant skewness. For kurtosis, we can use the **Bonett-Seier test for Geary's kurtosis** (Bonett & Seier, 2002). The null hypothesis states that data should have a Geary's kurtosis value equal to $\sqrt{2/\pi} = .7979$. Thus, a statistically significant Bonett-Seier test for Geary's kurtosis would indicate that there is statistically significant kurtosis. Thus, with these tests, as with Kolmogorov-Smirnov and Shapiro-Wilk, we do *not* want to find statistically significant results.

As is evident, many different tools can be used for testing the assumption of normality, and researchers should approach testing this assumption as collecting multiple forms of evidence to best understand the extent to which the assumption was met. A summary of several different types of evidence for examining normality is provided in Box 11.2.

Should you find yourself in a situation where there is a violation of normality, transformations can be used to normalize the data. For instance, a nonlinear relationship between *X* and *Y* may result in violations of the normality and/or homoscedasticity assumptions. Readers interested in learning more about potential data transformations are referred to sources such as Bradley (1982), Box and Cox (1964), or Mosteller and Tukey (1977).

In the example data, the residuals shown in Figure 11.3 appear to be somewhat normal in shape, especially considering the groups have fairly small *n*'s. This is suggested by the random display of points. In addition, as we will see later, for the residuals overall, skewness = −.2389 and kurtosis = −1.0191, indicating evidence of normality. Thus, it appears that all of

BOX 11.2 Evidence for Testing the Assumption of Normality

Evidence	Interpretation for Providing Evidence of Normality
Boxplot	Normality suggested when the quartiles are relatively evenly distributed with no outliers.
Histogram	Normality suggested with a relatively bell-shaped curve.
Skewness	Values within an absolute value of 2.0 suggest evidence of normality.
Kurtosis	Values within an absolute value of 2.0 suggest evidence of normality.
Standardized skew and standardized kurtosis	Divide the skew and kurtosis values by their standard errors to get *standardized skew and kurtosis* values. Review those values to a critical value (e.g., ±1.65 if alpha = .10; ±1.96 if alpha = .05; ±2.06 if alpha = .01). Standardized skew and kurtosis that are less than the critical value suggest evidence of normality.
D'Agostino's test	Tests the null hypothesis that skewness equals zero, with a statistically significant D'Agostino's test indicating that there is statistically significant skewness.
Bonett-Seier test for Geary's kurtosis	Tests the null hypothesis that data should have a Geary's kurtosis value equal to $\sqrt{2/\pi} = .7979$. A statistically significant test indicates that there is statistically significant kurtosis.
Quantile-quantile (Q-Q) plots	Plots that depict quantiles of the sample distribution to quantiles of the theoretical normal distribution. Points that fall on or closely to the diagonal line of the Q-Q plot suggest evidence of normality.
Detrended quantile-quantile plot	Evidence of normality is provided when the points exhibit little or no pattern around zero (the horizontal line).

TABLE 11.7

Assumptions, Evidence to Examine, and Effects of Violations: One-Factor ANOVA Design

Assumption	Evidence to Examine	Effect of Assumption Violation
Independence	• Scatterplot of residuals by group	Increased likelihood of a Type I and/or Type II error in the *F* statistic; influences standard errors of means and thus inferences about those means.
Homogeneity of variance	• Scatterplot of residuals by *X* • Formal test of equal variances (e.g., Levene's test)	Bias in SS_{with}; increased likelihood of a Type I and/or Type II error; less effect with equal or nearly equal *n*'s when normality can be assumed; effect decreases as *n* increases.
Normality	• Graphs of residuals (or scores) by group (e.g., boxplots, histograms, stem-and-leaf plots) • Skewness and kurtosis of residuals • Q-Q plots of residuals • Formal tests of normality of residuals • Plot of group means by group variances	Minimal effect with moderate violation; effect less severe with large *n*'s, with equal or nearly equal *n*'s, and/or with homogeneously shaped distributions (e.g., all groups have the same degree of skew).

our assumptions have been satisfied for the example data. We will delve further into examination of assumptions later as we illustrate how to use SPSS to conduct a one-way ANOVA.

A summary of the assumptions and the effects of their violation for the one-factor analysis of variance design are presented in Table 11.7.

11.2 Computing Parametric and Nonparametric Models Using SPSS

Next we consider the use of SPSS for the elite athlete example. Instructions for determining the one-way ANOVA using SPSS are presented first, followed by additional steps for examining the assumptions for the one-way ANOVA. Next, instructions for computing the Kruskal-Wallis and Brown and Forsyth are presented.

11.2.1 One-Way Analysis of Variance

Note that SPSS needs the data to be in a specific form for any of the analyses below to proceed, which is different from the layout of the data in Table 11.1. For a one-factor ANOVA, the dataset must consist of at least two variables or columns (if there are more than two variables, only two of which will be used in the one-factor ANOVA) (see Figure 11.4). *One column or variable indicates the levels or categories of the independent variable, and the second is for the dependent variable.* Each *row* then represents one unit (e.g., individual), indicating the level or group within which that unit is a member of (1, 2, 3, or 4 in our example), and their score on the dependent variable. Thus we wind up with two long columns of group values and scores as shown in the screenshot (Figure 11.4).

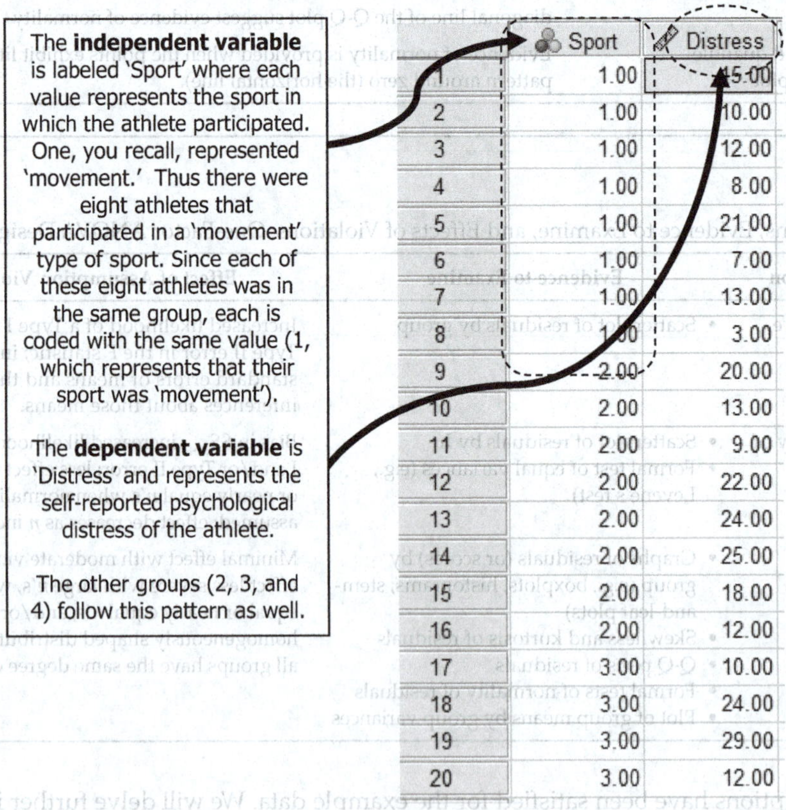
The **independent variable** is labeled 'Sport' where each value represents the sport in which the athlete participated. One, you recall, represented 'movement.' Thus there were eight athletes that participated in a 'movement' type of sport. Since each of these eight athletes was in the same group, each is coded with the same value (1, which represents that their sport was 'movement').
The **dependent variable** is 'Distress' and represents the self-reported psychological distress of the athlete.
The other groups (2, 3, and 4) follow this pattern as well.
Sport
Distress
1.00 15.00
2 1.00 10.00
3 1.00 12.00
4 1.00 8.00
5 1.00 21.00
6 1.00 7.00
7 1.00 13.00
8 1.00 3.00
9 2.00 20.00
10 2.00 13.00
11 2.00 9.00
12 2.00 22.00
13 2.00 24.00
14 2.00 25.00
15 2.00 18.00
16 2.00 12.00
17 3.00 10.00
18 3.00 24.00
19 3.00 29.00
20 3.00 12.00

FIGURE 11.4
First 20 cases of ANOVA data.

Step 1. To conduct a one-way ANOVA, go to "Analyze" in the top pulldown menu, then select "General Linear Model," and then select "Univariate." Following the screenshot for Step 1 (shown in Figure 11.5) produces the Univariate dialog box.

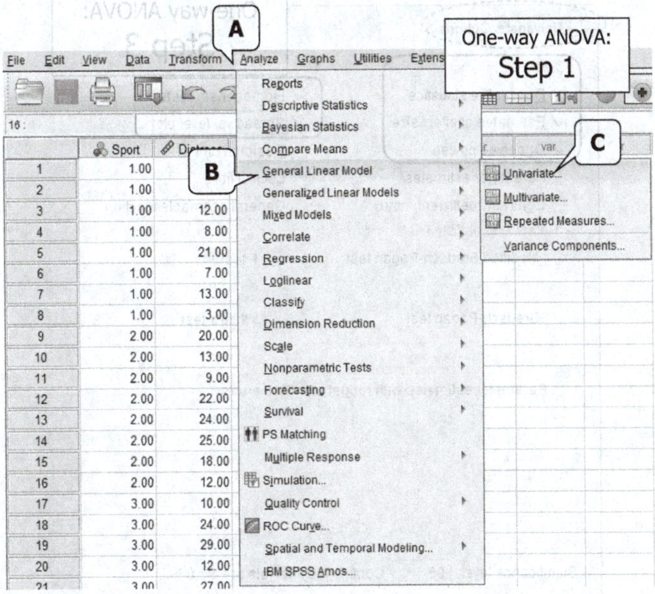

FIGURE 11.5
One-way ANOVA: Step 1.

Step 2. Click the dependent variable (e.g., psychological distress) and move it into the "Dependent Variable" box by clicking the arrow button. Click the independent variable (e.g., type of sport) and move it into the "Fixed Factors" box by clicking the arrow button. Next, click on "Options."

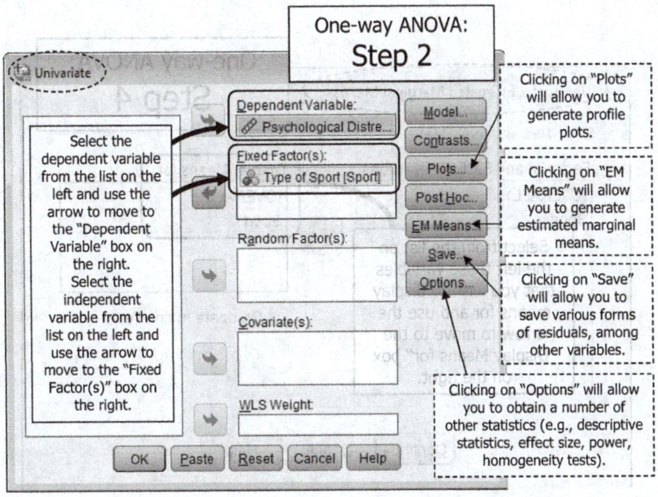

FIGURE 11.6
One-way ANOVA: Step 2.

Step 3. Clicking on "Options" will provide the option to select such information as "Descriptive statistics," "Estimates of effect size," "Observed power," and "Homogeneity tests." Click on "Continue" to return to the original dialog box.

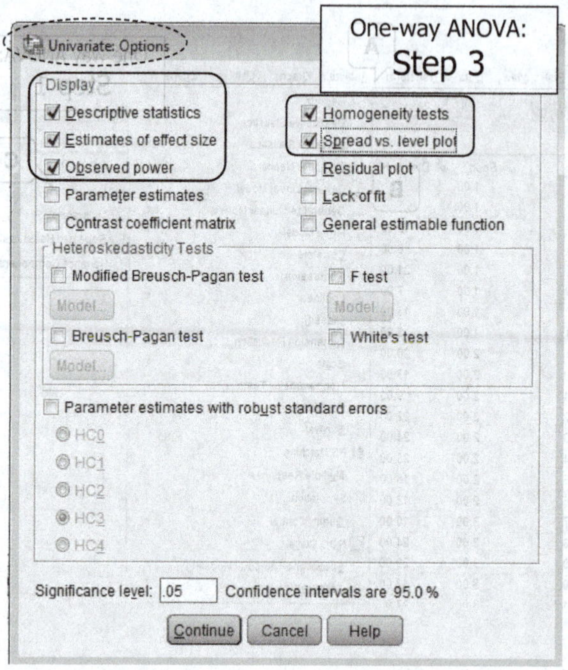

FIGURE 11.7
One-Way ANOVA: Step 3.

Step 4. Clicking on "EM Means" will provide the option to display the overall and factor means. Click on "Continue" to return to the original dialog box.

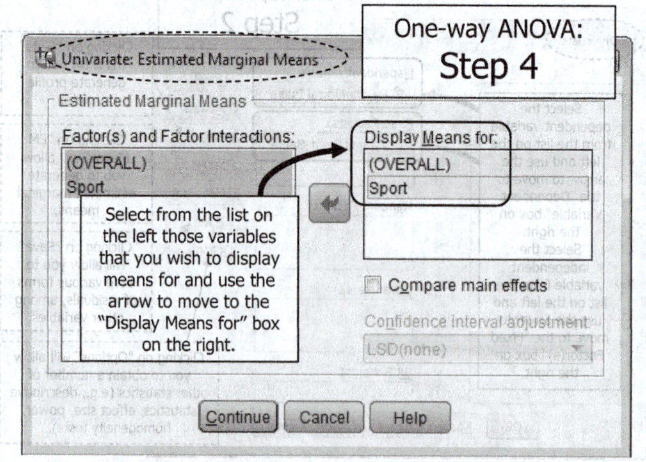

FIGURE 11.8
One-Way ANOVA: Step 4.

Step 5. From the Univariate dialog box, click on "Plots" to obtain a profile plot of means. Click the independent variable (e.g., type of sport, labeled as "Sport") and move it into the "Horizontal Axis" box by clicking the arrow button (see the screenshot for Step 5a in Figure 11.9). Then click on "Add" to move the variable into the "Plots" box at the bottom of the dialog box (see the screenshot for Step 5b in Figure 11.10). Click on "Continue" to return to the original dialog box.

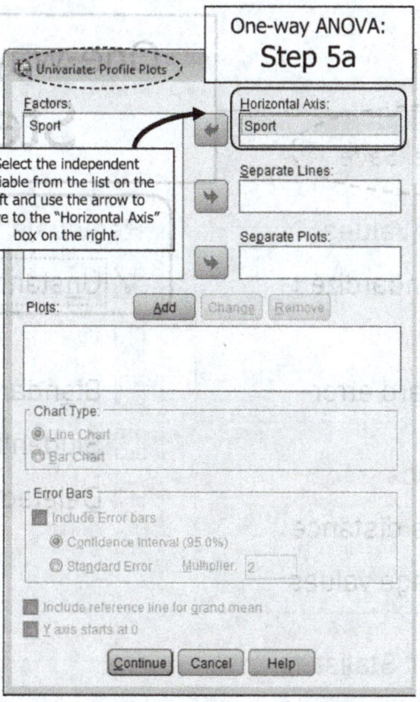

FIGURE 11.9
One-way ANOVA: Step 5a.

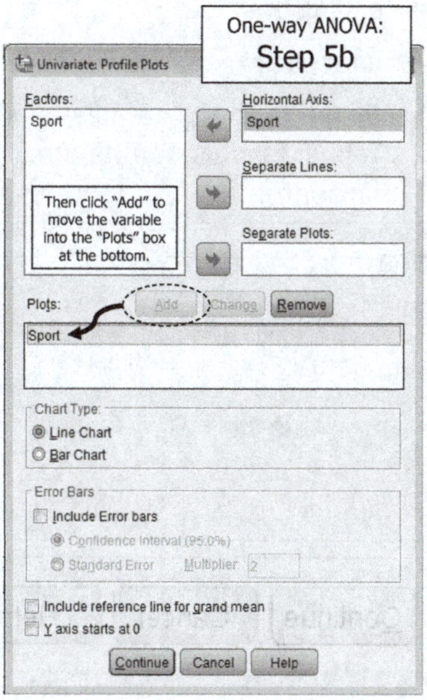

FIGURE 11.10
One-way ANOVA: Step 5b.

Step 6. From the Univariate dialog box, click on "Save" to select those elements that you want to save (in our case, we want to save the unstandardized residuals which will be used later to examine the extent to which normality and independence are met). From the Univariate dialog box, click on "OK" to return to generate the output.

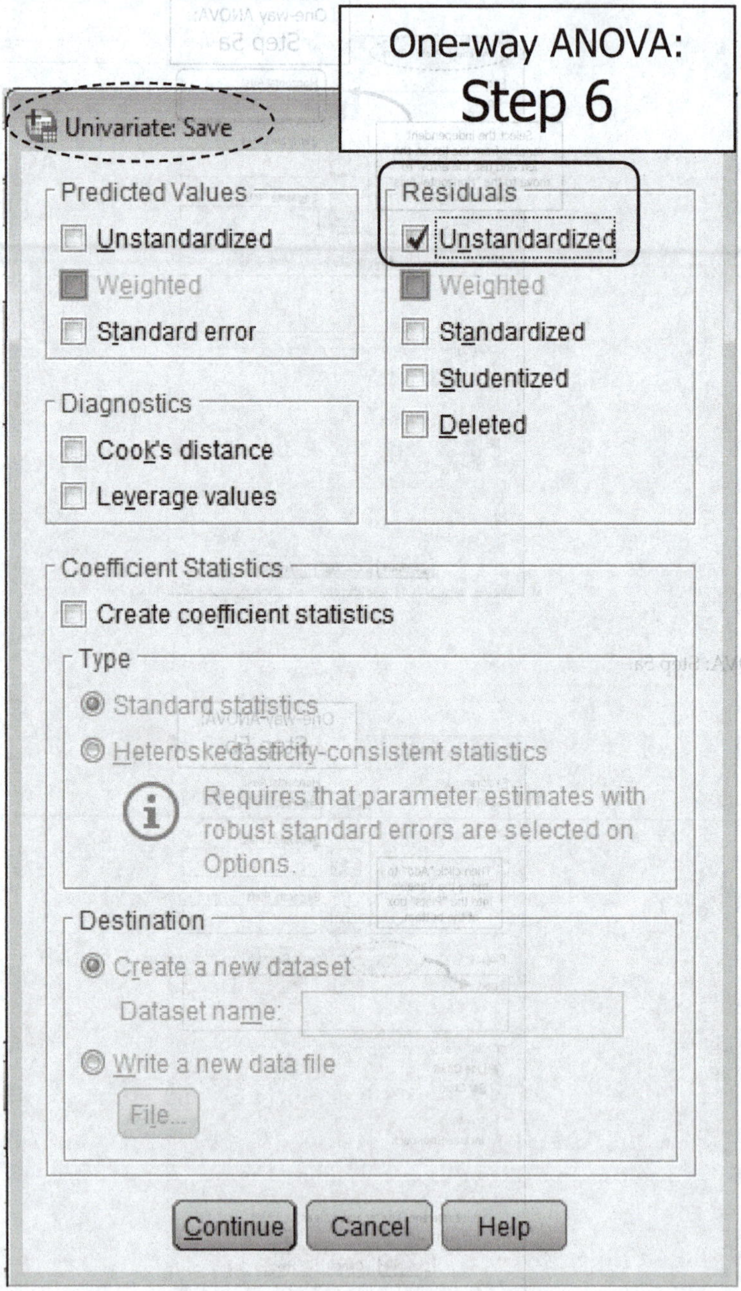

FIGURE 11.11
One-way ANOVA: Step 6.

11.2.1.1 Interpreting the Output for the One-Way Analysis of Variance

Annotated results are presented in Table 11.8 and the profile plot is shown in Figure 11.12.

TABLE 11.8

Selected SPSS Results for the Psychological Distress Example

Between-Subjects Factors

		Value Label	N
Type of Sport	1.00	Movement	8
	2.00	Target	8
	3.00	Fielding	8
	4.00	Territory	8

The table labeled "Between-Subjects Factors" provides sample sizes for each of the categories of the independent variable (recall that the independent variable is the 'between subjects factor').

Descriptive Statistics

Dependent Variable: Psychological Distress

Type of Sport	Mean	Std. Deviation	N
Movement	11.1250	5.48862	8
Target	17.8750	5.93867	8
Fielding	20.2500	7.28501	8
Territory	24.3750	5.09727	8
Total	18.4062	7.51283	32

The table labeled "Descriptive Statistics" provides basic descriptive statistics (means, standard deviations, and sample sizes) for each group of the independent variable.

Levene's Test of Equality of Error Variances[a,b]

		Levene Statistic	df1	df2	Sig.
Psychological Distress	Based on Mean	.905	3	28	.451
	Based on Median	.604	3	28	.618
	Based on Median and with adjusted df	.604	3	26.059	.618
	Based on trimmed mean	.883	3	28	.462

Tests the null hypothesis that the error variance of the dependent variable is equal across groups.

[a] Dependent variable: Psychological Distress

[b] Design: Intercept + Sport

The F test (and associated p value) for Levene's Test for Equality of Variances is reviewed to determine if equal variances can be assumed. In this case, we meet the assumption (as p is greater than α). Note that *df1* is degrees of freedom for the numerator (calculated as $J - 1$) and *df2* are the degrees of freedom for the denominator (calculated as $N - J$).

(continued)

TABLE 11.8 (continued)

Selected SPSS Results for the Psychological Distress Example

The row labeled **"SPORT"** is the independent variable or between groups variable. The *between groups mean square* (246.198) tells how much the group means vary. The degrees of freedom for between groups is $J - 1$ (3 in this example).

The omnibus *F* test is computed as:

$$F = \frac{MS_{betw}}{MS_{with}} = \frac{246.198}{36.112} = 6.818$$

The *p* value for the omnibus *F* test is .001. This indicates there is a statistically significant difference in the mean psychological distress based on the sport in which the athlete competes. The probability of observing these mean differences or more extreme mean differences by chance if the null hypothesis is really true (i.e., if the means really are equal) is substantially less than 1%. We reject the null hypothesis that all the population means are equal. For this example, this provides evidence to suggest that psychological distress differs based on the sport in which the athlete competes.

In one-way ANOVA, eta squared and partial eta squared are equal as there is just one independent variable. Thus, 'partial eta squared' on our one-way ANOVA output is really also eta squared, and is one measure of effect size computed as:

$$\eta_p^2 = \frac{SS_{betw}}{SS_{total}} = \frac{738.594}{1749.719} = .422$$

We can interpret this to mean that approximately 42% of the variation in the dependent variable (in this case, psychological distress) is accounted for by the sport in which the athlete competes.

Tests of Between-Subjects Effects

Dependent Variable: Psychological Distress

Source	Type III Sum of Squares	df	Mean Square	F	Sig.	Partial Eta Squared	Noncent. Parameter	Observed Power[b]
Corrected Model	738.594[a]	3	246.198	6.818	.001	.422	20.453	.956
Intercept	10841.281	1	10841.281	300.216	.000	.915	300.216	1.000
Sport	738.594	3	246.198	6.818	.001	.422	20.453	.956
Error	1011.125	28	36.112					
Total	12591.000	32						
Corrected Total	1749.719	31						

a. R Squared = .422 (Adjusted R Squared = .360)

b. Computed using alpha = .05

R squared is listed as a footnote underneath the table. *R* squared is the ratio of *sum of squares between* divided by *sum of squares total*:

$$R^2 = \frac{SS_{betw}}{SS_{total}} = \frac{738.594}{1749.719} = .422$$

and, in the case of one-way ANOVA, is also the simple bivariate Pearson correlation between the independent variable and dependent variable squared.

The row labeled **"Error"** is within groups. The *within groups mean square* tells us how much the observations within the groups vary (i.e., 36.112). The degrees of freedom for within groups is ($N-J$) or the total sample size minus the number of levels of the independent variable.

The row labeled "corrected total" is the *sum of squares total*. The degrees of freedom for the total is ($N-1$) or the total sample size minus 1.

Observed power tells whether our test is powerful enough to detect mean differences if they really exist. Power of .956 indicates that the probability of rejecting the null hypothesis if it is really false is about 96%; this represents strong power.

TABLE 11.8 (continued)

Selected SPSS Results for the Psychological Distress Example

Estimated Marginal Means

1. Grand Mean

Dependent Variable: Psychological Distress

Mean	Std. Error	95% Confidence Interval Lower Bound	Upper Bound
18.406	1.062	16.230	20.582

The 'Grand Mean' (in this case, 18.406) represents the overall mean, regardless of group membership, of the dependent variable. The 95% CI represents the CI of the grand mean.

2. Type of Sport

Dependent Variable: Psychological Distress

Type of Sport	Mean	Std. Error	95% Confidence Interval Lower Bound	Upper Bound
Movement	11.125	2.125	6.773	15.477
Target	17.875	2.125	13.523	22.227
Fielding	20.250	2.125	15.898	24.602
Territory	24.375	2.125	20.023	28.727

The table labeled **"Type of Sport"** provides descriptive statistics for each of the categories of the independent variable (notice that these are the same means reported previously). In addition to means, the *SE* and 95% CI of the means are reported.

Hold that thought! MCPs will be discussed in the next chapter.

Post Hoc Tests
Type of Sport

Multiple Comparisons

Dependent Variable: Psychological Distress
Tukey HSD

(I) Type of Sport	(J) Type of Sport	Mean Difference (I-J)	Std. Error	Sig.	95% Confidence Interval Lower Bound	Upper Bound
Movement	Target	-6.7500	3.00465	.135	-14.9536	1.4536
	Fielding	-9.1250*	3.00465	.025	-17.3286	-.9214
	Territory	-13.2500*	3.00465	.001	-21.4536	-5.0464
Target	Movement	6.7500	3.00465	.135	-1.4536	14.9536
	Fielding	-2.3750	3.00465	.858	-10.5786	5.8286
	Territory	-6.5000	3.00465	.158	-14.7036	1.7036
Fielding	Movement	9.1250*	3.00465	.025	.9214	17.3286
	Target	2.3750	3.00465	.858	-5.8286	10.5786
	Territory	-4.1250	3.00465	.526	-12.3286	4.0786
Territory	Movement	13.2500*	3.00465	.001	5.0464	21.4536
	Target	6.5000	3.00465	.158	-1.7036	14.7036
	Fielding	4.1250	3.00465	.526	-4.0786	12.3286

Based on observed means.

The error term is Mean Square(Error) = 36.112.

* The mean difference is significant at the 0.05 level.

(*continued*)

TABLE 11.8 (continued)

Selected SPSS Results for the Psychological Distress Example

Homogeneous Subsets

Psychological Distress

Tukey HSD[a,b]

		Subset	
Type of Sport	N	1	2
Movement	8	11.1250	
Target	8	17.8750	17.8750
Fielding	8		20.2500
Territory	8		24.3750
Sig.		.135	.158

Means for groups in homogeneous subsets are displayed.

Based on observed means.

The error term is Mean Square(Error) = 36.112.

[a] Uses Harmonic Mean Sample Size = 8.000.

[b] Alpha = 0.05.

Spread-versus-Level Plots

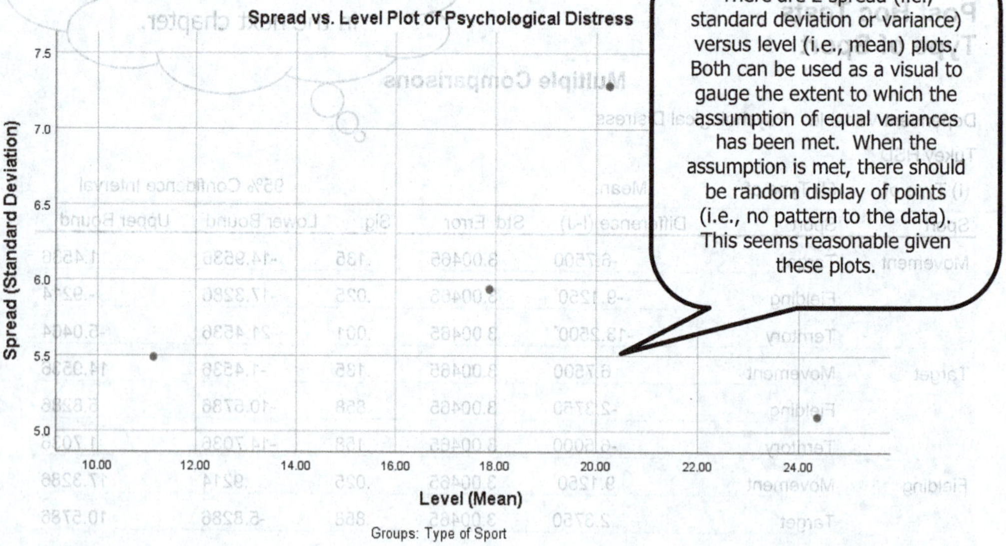
Spread vs. Level Plot of Psychological Distress
Spread (Standard Deviation)
7.5
7.0
6.5
6.0
5.5
5.0
10.00
12.00
14.00
16.00
18.00
20.00
22.00
24.00
Level (Mean)
Groups: Type of Sport
There are 2 spread (i.e., standard deviation or variance) versus level (i.e., mean) plots. Both can be used as a visual to gauge the extent to which the assumption of equal variances has been met. When the assumption is met, there should be random display of points (i.e., no pattern to the data). This seems reasonable given these plots.

TABLE 11.8 (continued)

Selected SPSS Results for the Psychological Distress Example

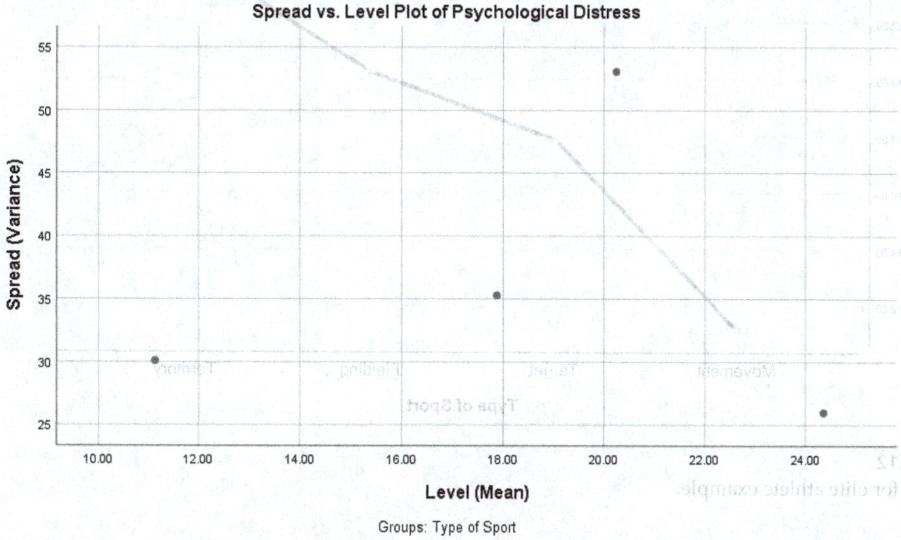

Profile Plots

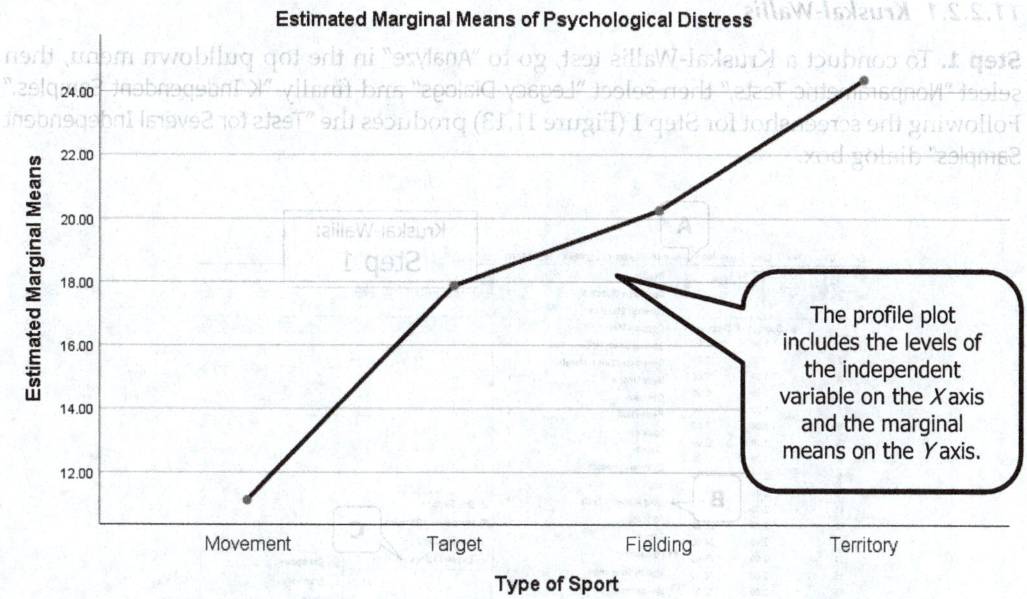

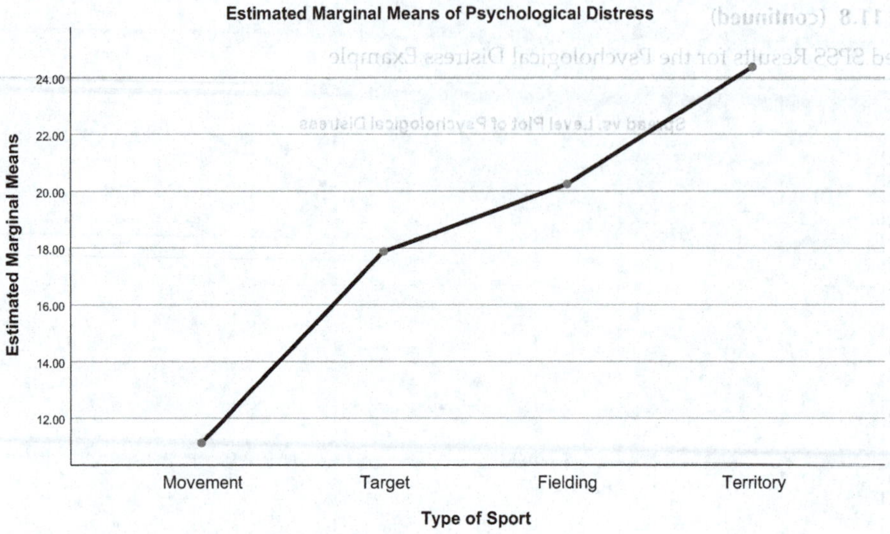

FIGURE 11.12
Profile plot for elite athlete example.

11.2.2 Nonparametric Procedures

Results from some of the recommended alternative procedures can be obtained from two other SPSS modules. Here we discuss the Kruskal-Wallis, Welch, and Brown-Forsythe procedures.

11.2.2.1 Kruskal-Wallis

Step 1. To conduct a Kruskal-Wallis test, go to "Analyze" in the top pulldown menu, then select "Nonparametric Tests," then select "Legacy Dialogs" and finally "K Independent Samples." Following the screenshot for Step 1 (Figure 11.13) produces the "Tests for Several Independent Samples" dialog box.

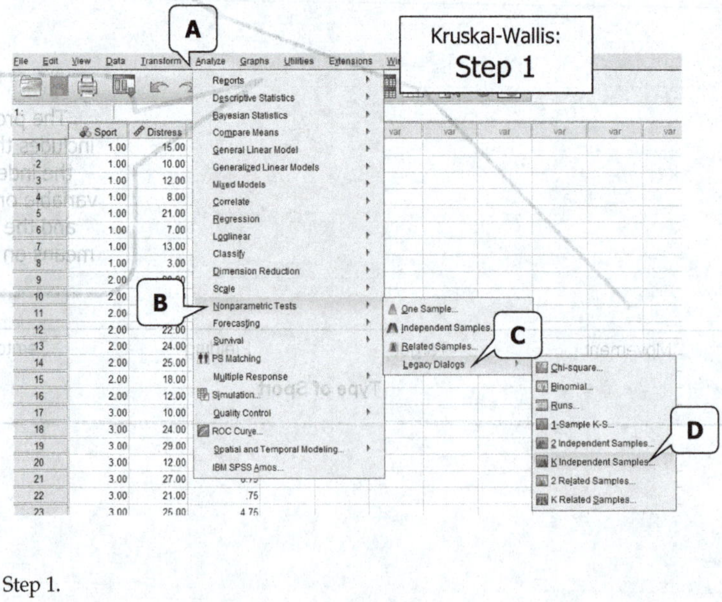

FIGURE 11.13
Kruskal-Wallis: Step 1.

Step 2. Next, from the main "Tests for Several Independent Samples" dialog box, click the dependent variable (e.g., psychological distress) and move it into the "Test Variable List" box by clicking on the arrow button. Next, click the grouping variable (e.g., type of sport) and move it into the "Grouping Variable" box by clicking on the arrow button. You will notice that there are two question marks next to the name of your grouping variable. This is SPSS letting you know that you need to define (numerically) which categories of the grouping variable you want to include in the analysis (this must be done by identifying a range of values for all groups of interest). To do that, click on "Define Range." We have four groups or levels of our independent variable (labeled 1, 2, 3, and 4 in our raw data); thus enter 1 as the minimum and 4 as the maximum. In the lower left portion of the screen under "Test Type," check "Kruskal-Wallis H" to generate this nonparametric test. Then click on "OK" to generate the results presented in Figure 11.14.

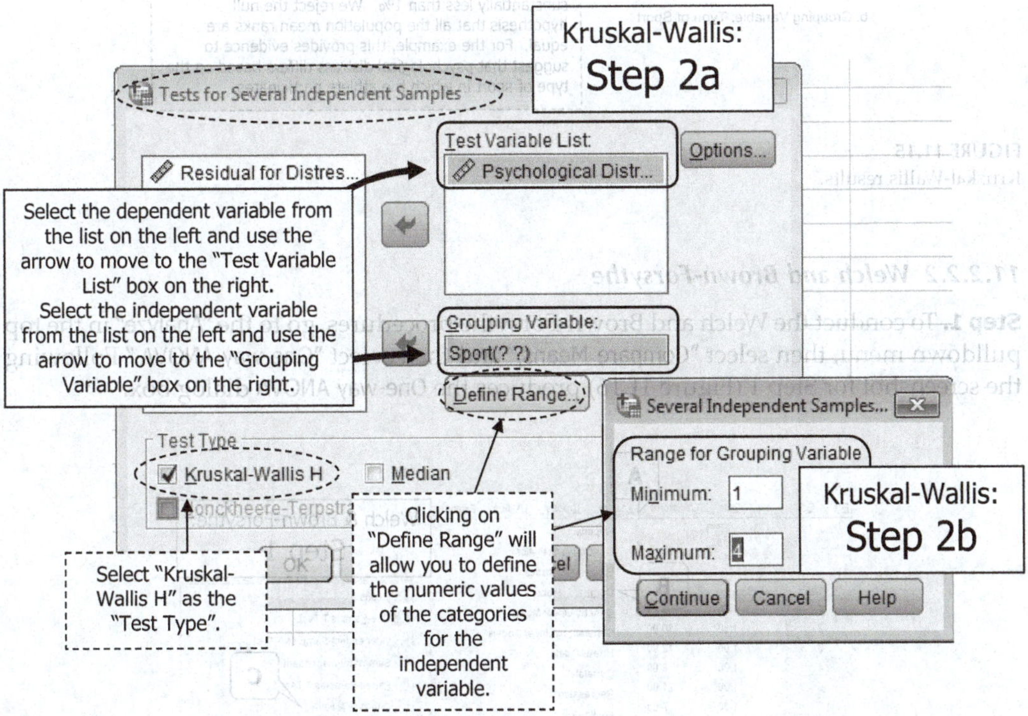

FIGURE 11.14
Kruskal-Wallis: Step 2a and 2b.

11.2.2.1.1 Interpreting the Output for Kruskal-Wallis

The Kruskal-Wallis is literally an analysis of variance of ranks. Thus the null hypothesis is that the mean ranks of the groups of the independent variable will not be significantly different. In this example, the results ($p = .005$) suggest statistically significant differences in the mean ranks of the dependent variable by group of the independent variable.

Kruskal-Wallis Test

Ranks

	Type of Sport	N	Mean Rank
Psychological Distress	Movement	8	7.75
	Target	8	15.25
	Fielding	8	18.75
	Territory	8	24.25
	Total	32	

The mean rank is the rank order, from smallest to largest, of the means of the dependent variable (psychological distress) by sport (i.e., type of sport).

Test Statistics[a,b]

	Psychological Distress
Kruskal-Wallis H	13.061
df	3
Asymp. Sig.	.005

a. Kruskal Wallis Test

b. Grouping Variable: Type of Sport

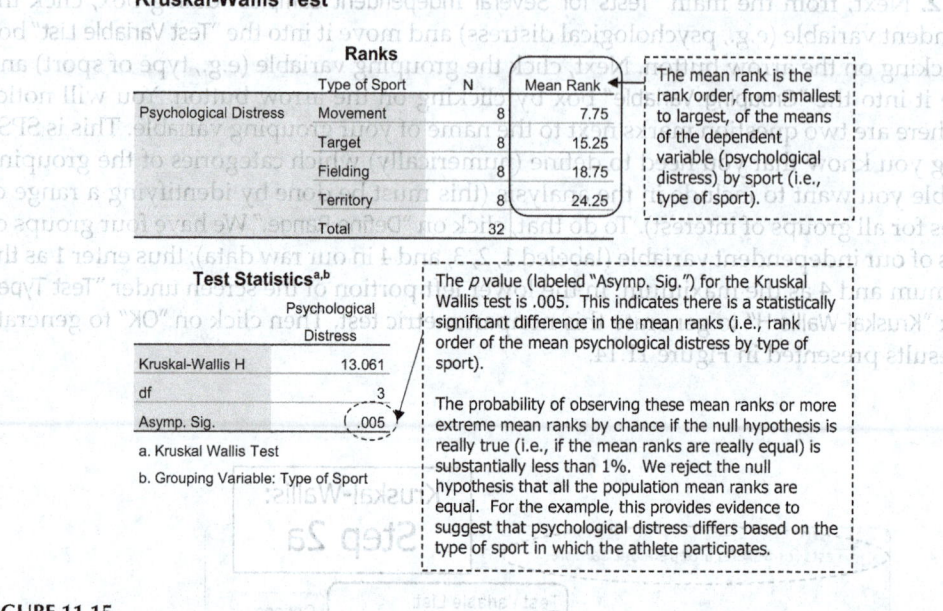

The *p* value (labeled "Asymp. Sig.") for the Kruskal Wallis test is .005. This indicates there is a statistically significant difference in the mean ranks (i.e., rank order of the mean psychological distress by type of sport).

The probability of observing these mean ranks or more extreme mean ranks by chance if the null hypothesis is really true (i.e., if the mean ranks are really equal) is substantially less than 1%. We reject the null hypothesis that all the population mean ranks are equal. For the example, this provides evidence to suggest that psychological distress differs based on the type of sport in which the athlete participates.

FIGURE 11.15
Kruskal-Wallis results.

11.2.2.2 Welch and Brown-Forsythe

Step 1. To conduct the Welch and Brown-Forsythe procedures, go to the "Analyze" in the top pulldown menu, then select "Compare Means," and then select "One-way ANOVA." Following the screenshot for Step 1 (Figure 11.16) produces the One-way ANOVA dialog box.

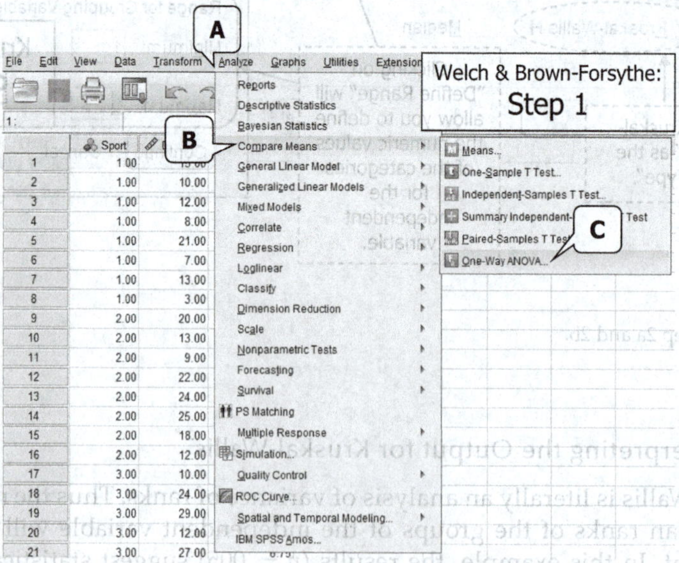

FIGURE 11.16
Welch and Brown-Forsythe: Step 1.

Step 2. Click the dependent variable (e.g., psychological distress) and move it into the "Dependent List" box by clicking the arrow button. Click the independent variable (e.g., type of sport) and move it into the "Factor" box by clicking the arrow button. Next, click on "Options."

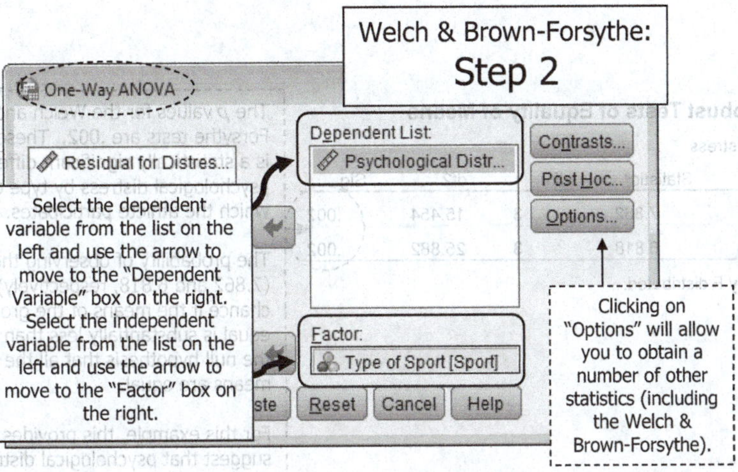

FIGURE 11.17
Welch and Brown-Forsythe: Step 2.

Step 3. Clicking on "Options" will provide the option to select such information as "Descriptive," "Homogeneity of variance test" (i.e., Levene's test for equal variances), "Brown-Forsythe," "Welch," and "Means plot." Click on "Continue" to return to the original dialog box. From the One-way ANOVA dialog box, click on "OK" to return and to generate the output.

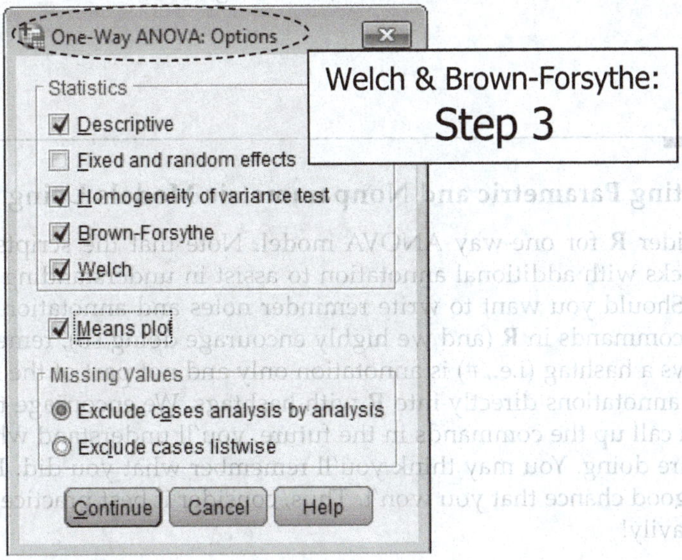

FIGURE 11.18
Welch and Brown-Forsythe: Step 3.

11.2.2.2.1 Interpreting the Output for the Welch and Brown-Forsythe

For illustrative purposes, and because the remainder of the one-way ANOVA results have been interpreted previously, only the results for the Welch and Brown-Forsythe procedures are displayed (Figure 11.19). Both tests suggest there are statistical differences between the groups in terms of the number of stats labs attended.

Robust Tests of Equality of Means

Psychological Distress

	Statistic[a]	df1	df2	Sig.
Welch	7.862	3	15.454	.002
Brown-Forsythe	6.818	3	25.882	.002

a. Asymptotically F distributed.

The p values for the Welch and Brown-Forsythe tests are .002. These indicate there is a statistically significant difference in mean psychological distress by type of sport in which the athlete participates.

The probability of observing the F statistics (7.862 and 6.818, respectively) or larger by chance if the means of the groups are really equal is substantially less than 1%. We reject the null hypothesis that all the population means are equal.

For this example, this provides evidence to suggest that psychological distress differs based on type of sport in which the athlete participates.

FIGURE 11.19
Welch and Brown-Forsythe results.

For further details on the use of SPSS for these procedures, be sure to examine books such as Page, Braver, and MacKinnon (2003), or Morgan, Leech, Gloeckner and Barrett (2012).

11.3 Computing Parametric and Nonparametric Models Using R

Next we consider **R** for one-way ANOVA model. Note that the scripts are provided within the blocks with additional annotation to assist in understanding how the command works. Should you want to write reminder notes and annotation to yourself as you write the commands in **R** (and we highly encourage doing so), remember that any text that follows a hashtag (i.e., #) is annotation only and not part of the **R** script. Thus, you can write annotations directly into **R** with hashtags. We encourage this practice so that when you call up the commands in the future, you'll understand what the various lines of code are doing. You may think you'll remember what you did. However, trust us. There is a good chance that you won't. Thus, consider it best practice when using **R** to annotate heavily!

11.3.1 Reading Data Into R

```
getwd()
```

R is always pointed to a directory on your computer. The *get working directory* function can be used to determine to which directory **R** is pointed. We will assume that we need to change the working directory, and will use the next line of code to set the working directory to the desired path.

```
setwd("E:/FolderName")
```

We use the *setwd* function to establish the working directory. To set the working directory, change what is in quotation marks to your file location. Also, if you are copying the directory name from your properties, you will need to change the backslash (i.e., \) to a forward slash (i.e., /).

```
Ch11_distress <- read.csv("Ch11_distress.csv")
```

The *read.csv* function reads our data into **R**. What's to the left of the '<-' will be what the data will be called in **R**. In this example, we're calling the R dataframe *Ch11_distress*. What's to the right of the '<-' tells **R** to find this particular csv file. In this example, our file is called *Ch11_distress.csv*. Make sure the extension (i.e., .csv) is included in your script. Also note that the name of your file should be in quotation marks within the parentheses.

```
names(Ch11_distress)
```

The *names* function will produce a list of variable names for each dataframe as follows. This is a good check to make sure your data have been read in correctly.

```
[1] "Sport"      "Distress"
```

```
View(Ch11_distress)
```

The *View* function will let you view the dataset in spreadsheet format in RStudio.

```
install.packages(car)
```

We will be using the *car* package for Levene's test. This function will install the package in **R**.

```
library(car)
```

The *library* function will load the *car* package in our library.

```
install.packages("compute.es")
```

We will use the *compute.es* package to compute effect sizes. The *install.packages* function will install the package in **R**.

```
library(compute.es)
```

The *library* function will load the *compute.es* package in our library.

```
Ch11_distress$SportF <- factor(Ch11_distress$Sport,
labels = c("movement", "target", "fielding", "territory"))
```

FIGURE 11.20
Reading data into **R**.

This command will create a new variable in our dataframe named *SportF*. We use the *factor* function to define the variable *Sport* as nominal with the four groups defined here (i.e., *movement, target, fielding, territory*). What is to the left of '<-' in the script creates the new *SportF*.

```
summary(Ch11_distress)
```

The *summary* function will produce basic descriptive statistics on all the variables in your dataframe. This is a great way to quickly check to see if the data have been read in correctly and get a feel for your data, if you haven't already. The output from the summary statement for this dataframe looks like this. Because we defined *SportF* as a factor, we are provided only the frequencies for each category in that variable.

```
     Sport          Distress          SportF
 Min.   :1.00   Min.   : 3.00   movement :8
 1st Qu.:1.75   1st Qu.:12.00   target   :8
 Median :2.50   Median :20.00   fielding  :8
 Mean   :2.50   Mean   :18.41   territory:8
 3rd Qu.:3.25   3rd Qu.:25.00
 Max.   :4.00   Max.   :30.00
```

```
Levels(Ch11_distress$SportF)
```

The *levels* function will output the categories of our factor variable, a good way to double check your coding of the categories.

```
[1] "movement"  "target"  "fielding"  "territory"
```

FIGURE 11.20 (continued)
Reading data into **R**.

11.3.2 Generating the One-Way ANOVA Model

```
Ch11_ANOVA <- aov(Distress ~ SportF, data=Ch11_distress)
```

The *aov* funtion will generate the one-way ANOVA model with *Distress* as the dependent variable and *SportF* as the independent variable. The dataframe from which we are pulling the data is defined by the *data* function. We are calling this object 'Ch11_ANOVA.'

```
summary(Ch11_ANOVA)
```

The *summary* function will provide the output from our ANOVA model:

```
            Df Sum Sq Mean Sq F value  Pr(>F)
SportF       3  738.6  246.20   6.818 0.00136 **
Residuals   28 1011.1   36.11
---
Signif. codes:  0 "***" 0.001 "**" 0.01 "*" 0.05 "." 0.1 " " 1
```

```
summary.lm(Ch11_ANOVA)
```

The *summary.lm* function will produce additional output, including R^2 which, in one-way ANOVA, is also the same value as partial eta squared (recall that in one-way ANOVA, eta squared is equal to partial eta squared).

```
Call:
aov(formula = Distress ~ SportF, data = Ch11_distress)
```

FIGURE 11.21
Generating the one-way ANOVA.

```
Residuals:
     Min       1Q   Median       3Q      Max
-10.2500  -4.5000   0.8125   4.2500   9.8750

Coefficients:
                Estimate Std. Error t value Pr(>|t|)
(Intercept)       11.125      2.125   5.236 1.45e-05 ***
SportFtarget       6.750      3.005   2.247 0.032741 *
SportFfielding     9.125      3.005   3.037 0.005125 **
SportFterritory   13.250      3.005   4.410 0.000139 ***
---
Signif. codes:  0 "***" 0.001 "**" 0.01 "*" 0.05 "." 0.1 " " 1

Residual standard error: 6.009 on 28 degrees of freedom
Multiple R-squared:  0.4221,  Adjusted R-squared:  0.3602
F-statistic: 6.818 on 3 and 28 DF,  p-value: 0.001361
```

Homogeneity Tests

```
leveneTest(Ch11_distress$Distress, Ch11_distress$SportF,
           center=mean)
```

The *leveneTest* function can be used to generate Levene's test for homogeneity of variance. There are multiple ways to center Levene's. For this illustration, we centered on the mean (i.e., *center=mean*).

```
Levene's Test for Homogeneity of Variance (center = mean)
      Df F value Pr(>F)
group  3  0.9047 0.4513
      28
```

We read this output as $F(3,28) = .9047$, $p = .4513$, indicating we have met the assumption of equal variances.

```
leveneTest(Ch11_ANOVA)
```

We can also run the *leveneTest* function on the object *(Ch11_ANOVA)* of our one-way ANOVA model results to generate Levene's test with the default centering of the median, which may provide more robust results. These results still provide evidence of meeting the assumption of equal variances, with $p = .618$.

```
Levene's Test for Homogeneity of Variance (center = median)
      Df F value Pr(>F)
group  3  0.6039 0.618
      28
```

```
install.packages("lawstat")
library(lawstat)
```

To install the *lawstat* package and load into the library.

```
levene.test(Ch11_distress$Distress,
            Ch11_distress$SportF,
            location = c("median"),
            bootstrap = TRUE,
            num.bootstrap = 1000,
            kruskal.test = FALSE,
            correction.method = c("zero.correction"))
```

FIGURE 11.21 (continued)
Generating the one-way ANOVA.

```
        bootstrap modified robust Brown-Forsythe Levene-type
        test based on the absolute deviations from the median
        with modified structural zero removal method and
        correction factor

data:  Ch11_distress$Distress
Test Statistic = 0.82624, p-value = 0.504
```

```
levene.test(Ch11_distress$Distress,
            Ch11_distress$SportF,
            location = c("median"),
            bootstrap = FALSE,
            kruskal.test = FALSE,
            correction.method = c("zero.correction"))
```

```
        modified robust Brown-Forsythe Levene-type test based
        on the absolute deviations from the median with
        modified structural zero removal method and correction
        factor

data:  Ch11_distress$Distress
Test Statistic = 0.82624, p-value = 0.4924
```

Effect Size

```
install.packages("sjstats")
library(sjstats)
```

The package *sjstats* can be used to generate multiple effect size indices in ANOVA. The *install.packages* and *library* functions will, respectively, install the package and then load it into our **R** library.

```
omega_sq(Ch11_ANOVA)
```

Using the object created from our ANOVA model, *Ch11_ANOVA*, we can generate omega squared with the *omega_sq* function.

```
    term omegasq
1 SportF   0.353
```

```
cohens_f(Ch11_ANOVA)
```

Using the object created from our ANOVA model, *Ch11_ANOVA*, we can generate Cohen's *f* with the *cohens_f* function.

```
    term cohens.f
1 SportF 0.8546738
```

```
eta_sq(Ch11_ANOVA)
```

Using the object created from our ANOVA model, *Ch11_ANOVA*, we can generate eta squared with the *eta_sq* function.

```
    term etasq
1 SportF 0.422
```

```
Ch11_distress$unstandardizedResiduals <- residuals(Ch11_ANOVA)
```

We also want to save our unstandardized residuals to the dataframe. We use the *residuals* function to compute unstandardized residuals from our *Ch11_ANOVA* model. To the left of '<-' will save the residuals as a variable named *unstandardizedResiduals* in our dataframe, *Ch11_distress*.

FIGURE 11.21 (continued)
Generating the one-way ANOVA.

11.3.3 Generating the Welch and Brown-Forsythe Tests

```
oneway.test(Distress ~ Sport, data = Ch11_distress)
```

The *oneway.test* function produces Welch's test results, which are as follows:

```
        One-way analysis of means (not assuming equal variances)

data:  Distress and Sport
F = 7.862, num df = 3.000, denom df = 15.454, p-value = 0.002055
```

```
install.packages("onewaytests")
library(onewaytests)
```

Install the *onewaytests* package and load into the **R** library.e

```
bf.test(Distress ~ SportF,
        Ch11_distress,
        alpha = .05,
        verbose = TRUE)
```

The *bf.test* function is used to generate the Brown-Forsythe test. Within parentheses, we define the dependent variable, *Distress,* independent variable, *SportF,* and dataframe, *Ch11_distress,* along with alpha, and the final command of *verbose=TRUE* which tells **R** to print the output to the console.

```
Brown-Forsythe Test
---------------------------------------------------------
 data : Distress and SportF

 statistic   : 6.817695
 num df      : 3
 denom df    : 25.88229
 p.value     : 0.001544356

 Result      : Difference is statistically significant.
---------------------------------------------------------
```

FIGURE 11.22
Generating the Welch and Brown-Forsythe Tests in **R**.

11.3.4 Generating the Kruskal-Wallis Test

```
kruskal.test(Distress ~ Sport, data = Ch11_distress)
```

The *kruskal.test* function produces results for the Kruskal-Wallis test. We define our model with the dependent variable, "Distress," and independent variable, "Sport." The dataframe we use is "Ch11_distress."

```
        Kruskal-Wallis rank sum test

data:  Distress by Sport
Kruskal-Wallis chi-squared = 13.061, df = 3, p-value =
0.004506
```

```
Ch11_distress$RankOrder <- rank(Ch11_distress$Distress)
```

This script produces a new variable in our dataframe called 'RankOrder', which is the rank for each value of the variable *Distress* in our *Ch11_distress* dataframe.

FIGURE 11.23
Generating the Kruskal-Wallis test.

```
by(Ch11_distress$RankOrder, Ch11_distress$Sport, mean)
```

The *by* function will produce the mean rank for each category of sport. The output looks like this:

```
Ch11_distress$Sport: movement
[1] 7.75
-------------------------------------------------------------
Ch11_distress$Sport: target
[1] 15.25
-------------------------------------------------------------
Ch11_distress$Sport: fielding
[1] 18.75
-------------------------------------------------------------
Ch11_distress$Sport: territory
[1] 24.25
```

FIGURE 11.23 (continued)
Generating the Kruskal-Wallis test.

11.4 Data Screening

As noted earlier, there are three standard assumptions made in analysis of variance models and will see these assumptions often in the remainder of this text. The assumptions are concerned with *normality*, *independence*, and *homogeneity of variance* (also called *homoscedasticity*).

11.4.1 Normality

As alluded to earlier in the chapter, understanding the distributional shape, specifically the extent to which normality is a reasonable assumption, is important. For the one-way ANOVA, the distributional shape for the residuals should be a normal distribution. Recall that when we ran our ANOVA model, we saved the unstandardized residuals to our datafile (we could have also reviewed the standardized or studentized residuals—and will illustrate the use of those in later chapters). We can again use "Explore" to examine the extent to which the assumption of normality is met. The general steps for accessing Explore have been presented in previous chapters, and will not be repeated here. Click the residual and move it into the "Dependent List" box by clicking on the arrow button. The procedures for selecting normality statistics were presented in Chapter 6 and remain the same here: click on "Plots" in the upper right corner. Place a checkmark in the boxes for "Normality plots with tests" and also for "Histogram." Then click "Continue" to return to the main Explore dialog box. Then click "OK" to generate the output. To identify normality by group, in the main dialog box, click the residual and move it into the Dependent List box, and click the independent variable and move to the "Factor List" box by clicking on the respective arrow buttons.

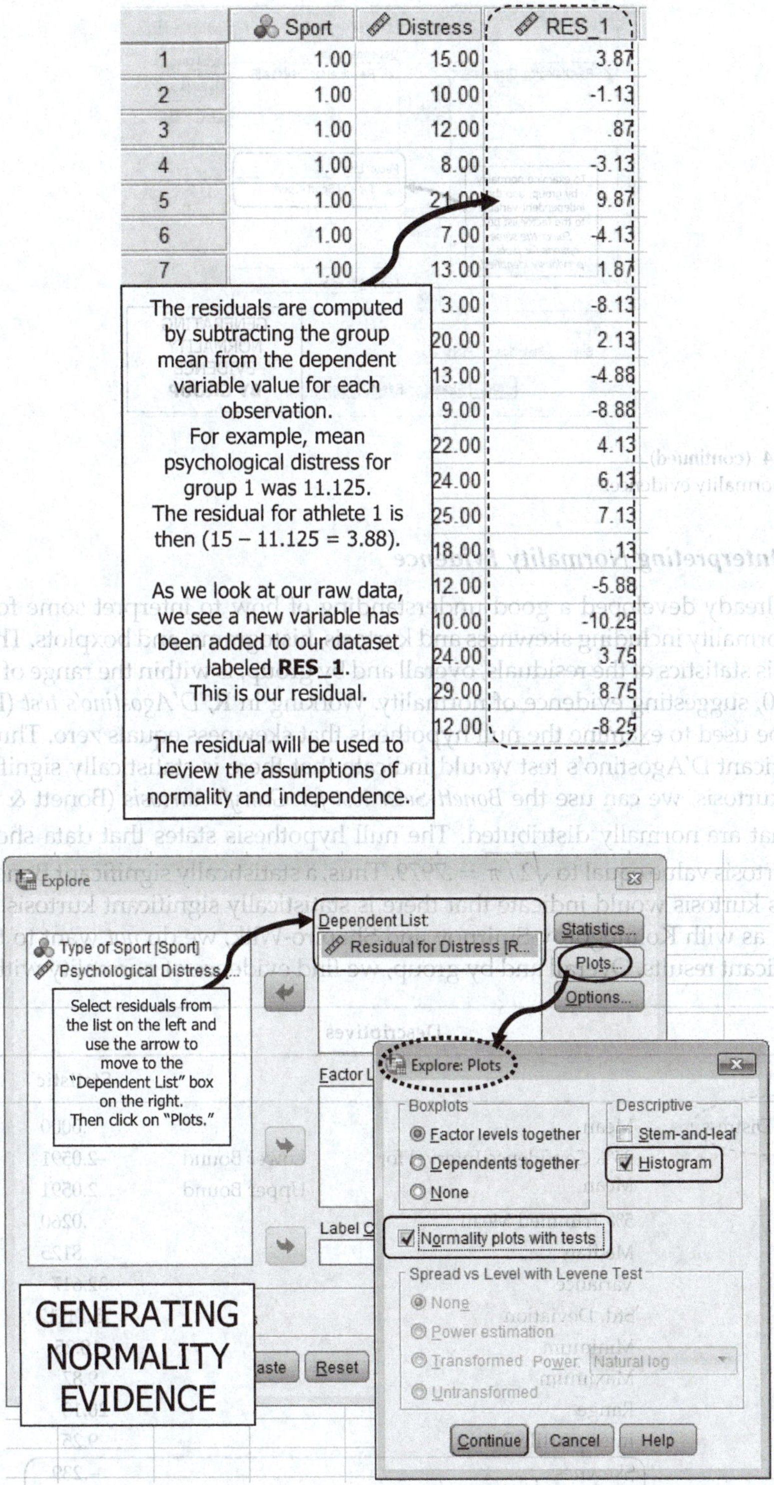

FIGURE 11.24
Generating normality evidence.

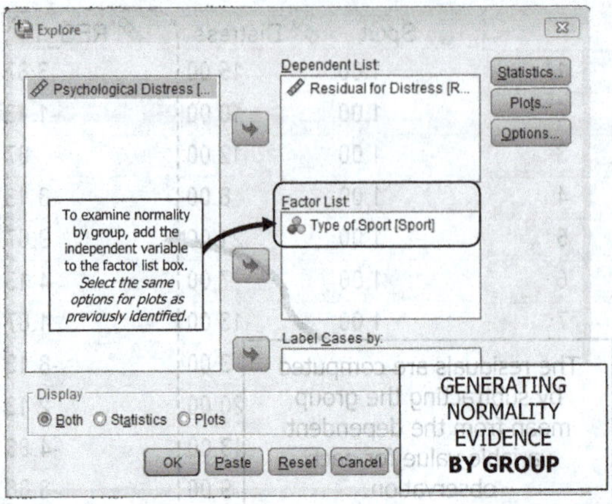

FIGURE 11.24 (continued)
Generating normality evidence.

11.4.1.1 Interpreting Normality Evidence

We have already developed a good understanding of how to interpret some forms of evidence of normality including skewness and kurtosis, histograms, and boxplots. The skewness and kurtosis statistics of the residuals, overall and by group, is within the range of an absolute value of 2.0, suggesting evidence of normality. Working in **R**, *D'Agostino's test* (D'Agostino, 1970) can be used to examine the null hypothesis that skewness equals zero. Thus, a statistically significant D'Agostino's test would indicate that there is statistically significant skewness. For kurtosis, we can use the *Bonett-Seier test for Geary's kurtosis* (Bonett & Seier, 2002) for data that are normally distributed. The null hypothesis states that data should have a Geary's kurtosis value equal to $\sqrt{2/\pi} = .7979$. Thus, a statistically significant Bonett-Seier test for Geary's kurtosis would indicate that there is statistically significant kurtosis. Thus, with these tests, as with Kolmogorov-Smirnov and Shapiro-Wilk, we do *not* want to find statistically significant results. Overall and by group, we find evidence of normality with p's > .05.

Descriptives

			Statistic	Std. Error
Residual for Distress	Mean		.0000	1.00959
	95% Confidence Interval for Mean	Lower Bound	−2.0591	
		Upper Bound	2.0591	
	5% Trimmed Mean		.0260	
	Median		.8125	
	Variance		32.617	
	Std. Deviation		5.71112	
	Minimum		−10.25	
	Maximum		9.87	
	Range		20.13	
	Interquartile Range		9.25	
	Skewness		−.239	.414
	Kurtosis		−1.019	.809

FIGURE 11.25
Normality evidence.

By group of the independent variable, we find the following, all indicating the normality assumption has been met.

	Type of Sport		Statistic	Std. Error
Residual for Distress	**Movement**	Skewness	.449	.752
		Kurtosis	.575	1.481
	Target	Skewness	−.315	.752
		Kurtosis	−1.522	1.481
	Fielding	Skewness	−.367	.752
		Kurtosis	−1.754	1.481
	Territory	Skewness	−.851	.752
		Kurtosis	.058	1.481

Working in **R**, we can generate various normality statistics as well.

```
install.packages("pastecs")
```

The *install.packages* function will install the *pastecs* package which we will use to generate various forms of normality evidence.

```
library(pastecs)
```

The *library* function will load the *pastecs* package.

```
stat.desc(Ch11_distress$unstandardizedResiduals,
    norm = TRUE)
```

The *stat.desc* function will generate normality indices on the variable "unstandardizedResiduals" in the dataframe "Ch11_distress" as follows. The *norm=TRUE* command will produce Shapiro-Wilk (*S-W*) results, which are displayed as *normtest.W* (which is the *S-W* statistic value) and *normtest.p* (which is the observed probability value).

Here, we see $SW = .958$ and the related $p = .240$. We see skew (.249) and kurtosis (−.976) for the "unstandardizedResidual" variable.

Skew, kurtosis, and *S-W* all indicate the assumption of normality has been met. As we know, we can divide the skew and kurtosis values by their standard errors to get a standardized value that can be used to determine if the skew and/or kurtosis is statistically different from zero. Since this output provides "2SE," we would simply divide this value by 2 to arrive at the standard error.

Note: You may have noticed that the skewness and kurtosis value that we've just generated differs from what we found in SPSS, which was skew = −.239 and kurtosis = −1.019. *This is because there are different ways to calculate skewness and kurtosis.* Let's use another package in **R** to calculate these statistics with different algorithms.

```
      nbr.val       nbr.null         nbr.na            min            max
 3.200000e+01   0.000000e+00   0.000000e+00  -1.025000e+01   9.875000e+00

        range            sum         median           mean        SE.mean
 2.012500e+01  -4.329870e-15   8.125000e-01  -1.353084e-16   1.009594e+00

 CI.mean.0.95            var        std.dev       coef.var       skewness
 2.059080e+00   3.261694e+01   5.711124e+00  -4.220819e+16  -2.169593e-01

    skew.2SE       kurtosis      kurt.2SE      normtest.W     normtest.p
-2.617390e-01  -1.168535e+00  -7.218785e-01   9.578412e-01   2.395168e-01
```

FIGURE 11.25 (continued)
Normality evidence.

```
install.packages("e1071")
```

The *install.packages* function will install the e1071 package which we will use to generate skewness and kurtosis.

```
library(e1071)
```

The *library* function will load the e1071 package.

```
skewness(Ch11_distress$unstandardizedResiduals, type=3)
skewness(Ch11_distress$unstandardizedResiduals, type=2)
skewness(Ch11_distress$unstandardizedResiduals, type=1)
```

The *skewness* function will generate skewness statistics on the variable(s) specified. The "type=" script defines how skewness is calculated. Specifying "type=2" will use the algorithm that is used by SPSS. Readers interested in learning more, including the algorithms for each of the three methods, are encouraged to review Joanes and Gill (1998). We see that using type=2, our skew is −.239, the same value as generated using SPSS.

```
# skewness(Ch11_distress$unstandardizedResiduals, type=3)
[1] -0.2169593

# skewness(Ch11_distress$unstandardizedResiduals, type=2)
[1] -0.2388885

# skewness(Ch11_distress$unstandardizedResiduals, type=1)
[1] -0.2275415
```

```
kurtosis(Ch11_distress$unstandardizedResiduals, type=3)
kurtosis(Ch11_distress$unstandardizedResiduals, type=2)
kurtosis(Ch11_distress$unstandardizedResiduals, type=1)
```

The *kurtosis* function will generate kurtosis statistics on the variable(s) we specify. The "type=" script defines how kurtosis is calculated. Specifying "type=2" will use the algorithm that is used by SPSS. Readers interested in learning more, including the algorithms for each of the three methods, are encouraged to review Joanes and Gill (1998). We see that using type=2, our kurtosis is −1.019, the same value as generated using SPSS.

```
# kurtosis(Ch11_distress$unstandardizedResiduals, type=3)
[1] -1.168535

# kurtosis(Ch11_distress$unstandardizedResiduals, type=2)
[1] -1.019064

# kurtosis(Ch11_distress$unstandardizedResiduals, type=1)
[1] -1.048471
```

Working in **R**, another way to test for normality is D'Agostino's test for skewness and the Bonett-Seier test for Geary's kurtosis.

```
install.packages("moments")
library(moments)
```

To conduct D'Agostino's test, we first have to install the *moments* package and then load it into our library. The null hypothesis for this test is that skewness equals zero. Thus, a statistically significant D'Agostino's test would indicate that there is statistically significant skewness.

```
agostino.test(Ch11_distress$unstandardizedResiduals)
```

The function *agostino.test* is generated using the variable "unstandardizedResiduals" from our "Ch11_distress" dataframe. The results suggest evidence of normality as $p = .544$, greater than alpha.

FIGURE 11.25 (continued)
Normality evidence.

```
        D'Agostino skewness test

data:  Ch11_distress$unstandardizedResiduals
skew = -0.22754, z = -0.60681, p-value = 0.544
alternative hypothesis: data have a skewness
```

```
agostino.test(Ch11_distress$unstandardizedResiduals[Ch11_distress$Sport==1])
agostino.test(Ch11_distress$unstandardizedResiduals[Ch11_distress$Sport==2])
agostino.test(Ch11_distress$unstandardizedResiduals[Ch11_distress$Sport==3])
agostino.test(Ch11_distress$unstandardizedResiduals[Ch11_distress$Sport==4])
```

By group, the results for the D'Agostino test provide evidence of normality by group with all p's > .05.

```
#agostino.test(Ch11_distress$unstandardizedResiduals[Ch11_distress$Sport==1])

        D'Agostino skewness test
data:  Ch11_distress$unstandardizedResiduals[Ch11_distress$Sport==1]
skew = 0.36014, z = 0.60580, p-value = 0.5446
alternative hypothesis: data have a skewness

#agostino.test(Ch11_distress$unstandardizedResiduals[Ch11_distress$Sport==2])

        D'Agostino skewness test
data:  Ch11_distress$unstandardizedResiduals[Ch11_distress$Sport==2]
skew = -0.25259, z = -0.42532, p-value = 0.6706
alternative hypothesis: data have a skewness

#agostino.test(Ch11_distress$unstandardizedResiduals[Ch11_distress$Sport==3])

        D'Agostino skewness test
data:  Ch11_distress$unstandardizedResiduals[Ch11_distress$Sport==3]
skew = -0.29418, z = -0.49518, p-value = 0.6205
alternative hypothesis: data have a skewness

#agostino.test(Ch11_distress$unstandardizedResiduals[Ch11_distress$Sport==4])
        D'Agostino skewness test
data: Ch11_distress$unstandardizedResiduals[Ch11_distress$Sport==4]
skew = -0.6827, z = -1.1426, p-value = 0.2532
alternative hypothesis: data have a skewness
```

```
bonett.test((Ch11_distress$unstandardizedResiduals))
```

The *bonett.test* function, generated using the variable "unstandardizedResiduals" from our Ch11_distress dataframe, performs the Bonett-Seier test for Geary's kurtosis for data that is normally distributed. The null hypothesis states that data should have a Geary's kurtosis value equal to $\sqrt{2/\pi} = .7979$. The results suggest evidence of normality as $p = .1232$, greater than alpha.

```
        Bonett-Seier test for Geary kurtosis

data:  (Ch11_distress$unstandardizedResiduals)
tau = 4.8125, z = -1.5413, p-value = 0.1232
alternative hypothesis: kurtosis is not equal to sqrt(2/pi)
```

```
bonett.test((Ch11_distress$unstandardizedResiduals[Ch11_distress$Sport==1]))
bonett.test((Ch11_distress$unstandardizedResiduals[Ch11_distress$Sport==2]))
bonett.test((Ch11_distress$unstandardizedResiduals[Ch11_distress$Sport==3]))
bonett.test((Ch11_distress$unstandardizedResiduals[Ch11_distress$Sport==4]))
```

By group, the results for the Bonett-Seier test for Geary's kurtosis for data that is normally distributed provide evidence of normality by group with all p's > .05.

FIGURE 11.25 (continued)
Normality evidence.

```
#bonett.test((Ch11_distress$unstandardizedResiduals[Ch11_distress$Sport==1]))

        Bonett-Seier test for Geary kurtosis
data:  (Ch11_distress$unstandardizedResiduals[Ch11_distress$Sport==1])
tau = 4.12500, z = -0.08177, p-value = 0.9348
alternative hypothesis: kurtosis is not equal to sqrt(2/pi)

#bonett.test((Ch11_distress$unstandardizedResiduals[Ch11_distress$Sport==2]))

        Bonett-Seier test for Geary kurtosis
data:  (Ch11_distress$unstandardizedResiduals[Ch11_distress$Sport==2])
tau = 4.9062, z = -1.2053, p-value = 0.2281
alternative hypothesis: kurtosis is not equal to sqrt(2/pi)

#bonett.test((Ch11_distress$unstandardizedResiduals[Ch11_distress$Sport==3]))

        Bonett-Seier test for Geary kurtosis
data: (Ch11_distress$unstandardizedResiduals[Ch11_distress$Sport==3])
tau = 6.1875, z = -1.5340, p-value = 0.125
alternative hypothesis: kurtosis is not equal to sqrt(2/pi)

#bonett.test((Ch11_distress$unstandardizedResiduals[Ch11_distress$Sport==4]))

        Bonett-Seier test for Geary kurtosis
data:  (Ch11_distress$unstandardizedResiduals[Ch11_distress$Sport==4])
tau = 4.03120, z = -0.68704, p-value = 0.4921
alternative hypothesis: kurtosis is not equal to sqrt(2/pi)
```

FIGURE 11.25 (continued)
Normality evidence.

The histogram of residuals, overall or by group, is not exactly what most researchers would consider a classic normally shaped distribution. Reviewing the residuals overall, it approaches a normal distribution and there is nothing to suggest normality may be an unreasonable assumption. By group, we will rely on other forms of normality evidence given the small group sizes make the histograms by group more difficult to visually evaluate.

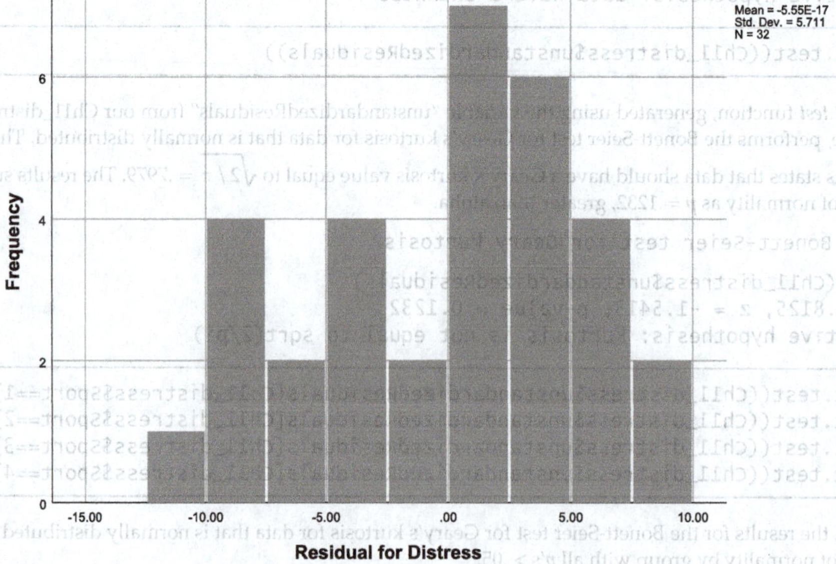

FIGURE 11.26
Histogram.

Two of the four histograms by group are presented. By group, the small group sizes are not conducive to suggesting normality. Thus, reviewing the normality evidence in aggregate will be helpful.

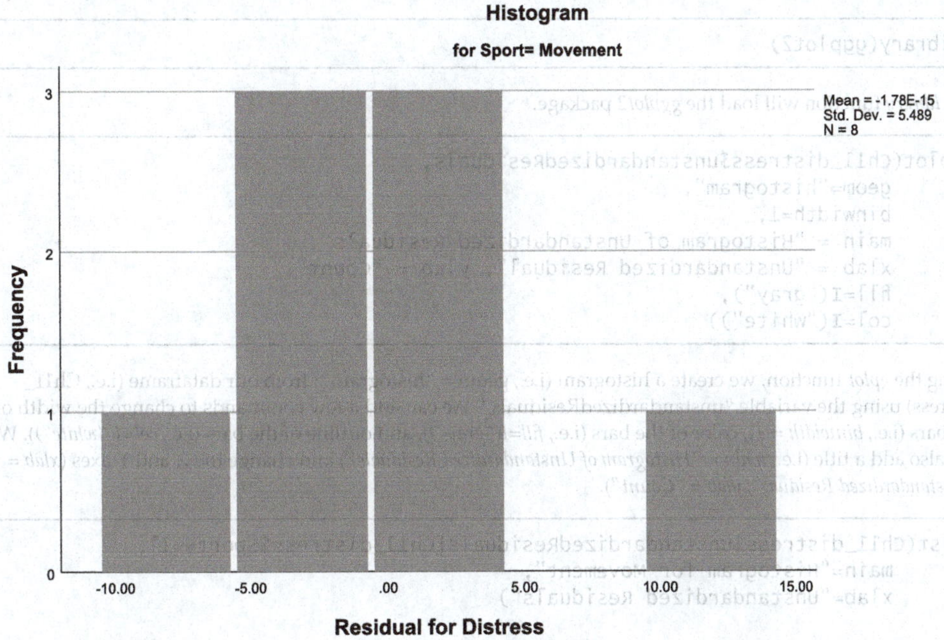

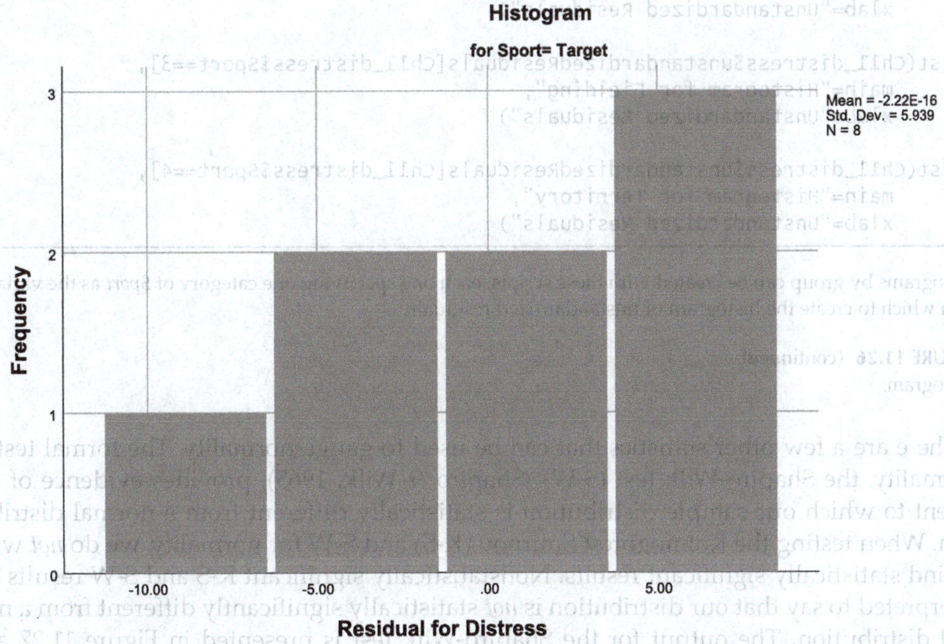

Working in **R**, we can generate a histogram using the *ggplot2* package.

FIGURE 11.26 (continued)
Histogram.

```
install.packages("ggplot2")
```

The *install.packages* function will install the *ggplot2* package which we can use to create various graphs and plots.

```
library(ggplot2)
```

The *library* function will load the *ggplot2* package.

```
qplot(Ch11_distress$unstandardizedResiduals,
      geom="histogram",
      binwidth=1,
      main = "Histogram of Unstandardized Residuals",
      xlab = "Unstandardized Residual", ylab = "Count",
      fill=I("gray"),
      col=I("white"))
```

Using the *gplot* function, we create a histogram (i.e., geom = "histogram") from our dataframe (i.e., Ch11_distress) using the variable "unstandardizedResiduals." We can add a few commands to change the width of the bars (i.e., *binwidth = 1*), color of the bars (i.e., *fill=I("gray")*), and outline of the bars (i.e., *col=I("white")*). We can also add a title (i.e., *main = "Histogram of Unstandardized Residuals"*) and change the *X* and *Y* axes (*xlab = "Unstandardized Residual", ylab = "Count"*).

```
hist(Ch11_distress$unstandardizedResiduals[Ch11_distress$Sport==1],
      main="Histogram for Movement",
      xlab="Unstandardized Residuals")

hist(Ch11_distress$unstandardizedResiduals[Ch11_distress$Sport==2],
      main="Histogram for Target",
      xlab="Unstandardized Residuals")

hist(Ch11_distress$unstandardizedResiduals[Ch11_distress$Sport==3],
      main="Histogram for Fielding",
      xlab="Unstandardized Residuals")

hist(Ch11_distress$unstandardizedResiduals[Ch11_distress$Sport==4],
      main="Histogram for Territory",
      xlab="Unstandardized Residuals")
```

Histograms by group can be created with these scripts, each one specifying one category of *Sport* as the variable with which to create the histogram of unstandardized residuals.

FIGURE 11.26 (continued)
Histogram.

There are a few other statistics that can be used to gauge normality. The formal test of normality, the Shapiro-Wilk test (S-W) (Shapiro & Wilk, 1965), provides evidence of the extent to which our sample distribution is statistically different from a normal distribution. When testing the Kolmogorov-Smirnov (K-S) and S-W for normality, we do *not* want to find statistically significant results. Nonstatistically significant K-S and S-W results are interpreted to say that our distribution is *not* statistically significantly different from a normal distribution. The output for the Shapiro-Wilk test is presented in Figure 11.27 and suggests that our sample distribution for residuals overall is not statistically significantly different than what would be expected from a normal distribution ($SW = .958$, $df = 32$,

$p = .240$), and the sample distribution for residuals by group is not statistically significantly different than what would be expected from a normal distribution (p's for all groups > .05).

Tests of Normality

	Kolmogorov-Smirnov[a]			Shapiro-Wilk		
	Statistic	df	Sig.	Statistic	df	Sig.
Residual for Distress	.112	32	.200*	.958	32	.240

* This is a lower bound of the true significance.

[a] Lilliefors Significance Correction

By group, we see evidence of normality as well.

Tests of Normality

		Kolmogorov-Smirnov[a]			Shapiro-Wilk		
	Type of Sport	Statistic	df	Sig.	Statistic	df	Sig.
Residual for Distress	**Movement**	.116	8	.200*	.985	8	.982
	Target	.169	8	.200*	.932	8	.531
	Fielding	.197	8	.200*	.905	8	.320
	Territory	.174	8	.200*	.933	8	.548

* This is a lower bound of the true significance.

[a] Lilliefors Significance Correction

Working in **R**, we saw earlier how the *stat.desc* function from the *pastecs* package could be used to generate the Shapiro-Wilk test, along with many other statistics. Should we want to generate *just* the Shapiro-Wilk test, we can run the following script.

```
shapiro.test(Ch11_distress$unstandardizedResiduals)
```

```
        Shapiro-Wilk normality test

data:  Ch11_distress$unstandardizedResiduals
W = 0.95784, p-value = 0.2395
```

```
tapply(Ch11_distress$unstandardizedResiduals,
       Ch11_distress$SportF, shapiro.test)
```

To generate the Shapiro-Wilk test by group, the *tapply* function can be used to apply the *shapiro.test* to the unstandardized residuals for all levels of the independent variable.

FIGURE 11.27
Shapiro-Wilk test.

Quantile-quantile (Q-Q) plots are also often examined to determine evidence of normality. Q-Q plots are graphs that plot quantiles of the theoretical normal distribution against quantiles of the sample distribution. Points that fall on or close to the diagonal line suggest evidence of normality. The Q-Q plot of residuals by group suggests relative normality.

Overall, the Q-Q plot suggests relative normality.

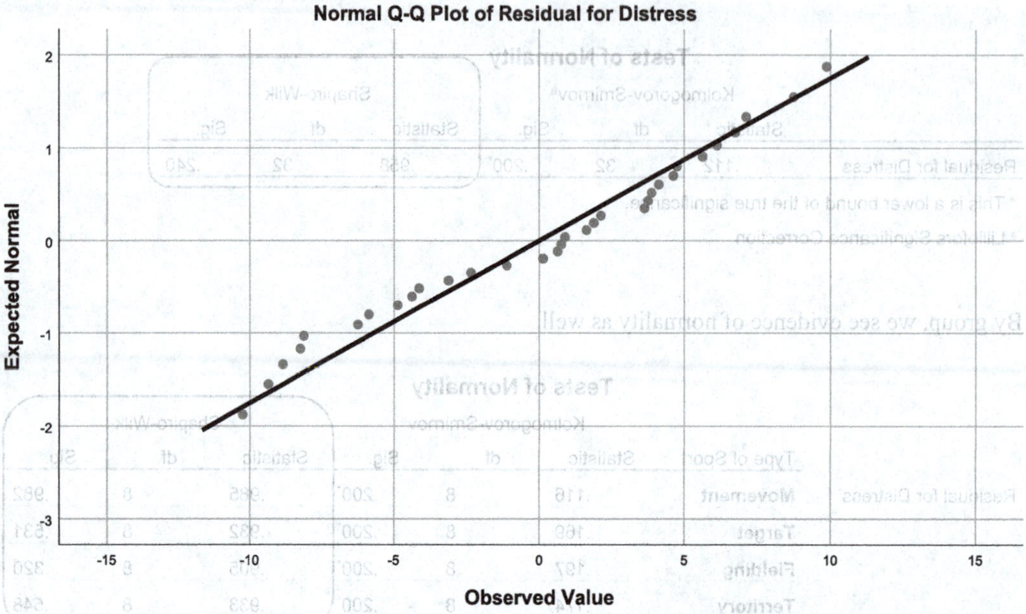

By group (for brevity, only two group graphs are presented), even with the small group sizes, there is general adherence to the diagonal line.

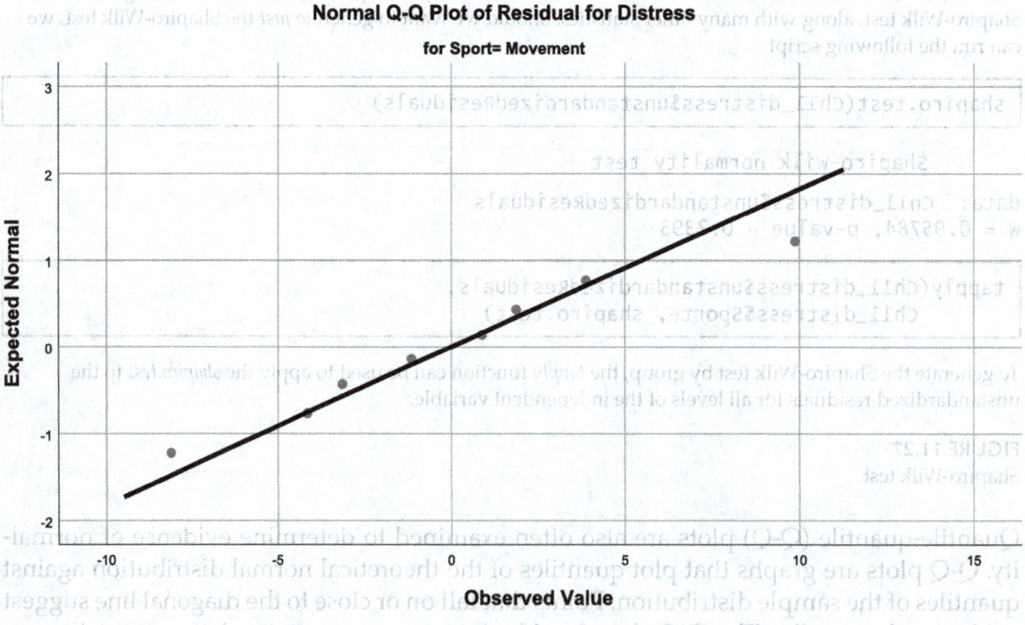

FIGURE 11.28
Q-Q plot.

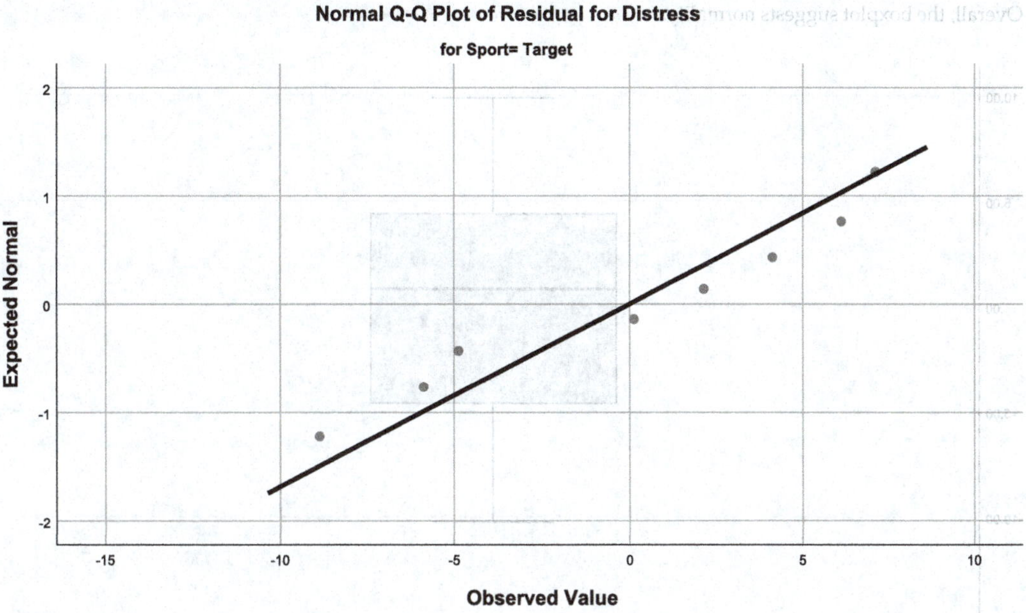

Working in **R**, we can use the *qplot* function to create a Q-Q plot of unstandardized residuals. The "data=" script defines the dataframe as "Ch11_distress."

```
qplot(sample=unstandardizedResiduals,
      data = Ch11_distress)
```

```
qqnorm(Ch11_distress$unstandardizedResiduals[Ch11_distress$Sport==1],
      main=‘movement’)
qqnorm(Ch11_distress$unstandardizedResiduals[Ch11_distress$Sport==2],
      main=‘target’)
qqnorm(Ch11_distress$unstandardizedResiduals[Ch11_distress$Sport==3],
      main=‘fielding’)
qqnorm(Ch11_distress$unstandardizedResiduals[Ch11_distress$Sport==4],
      main=‘territory’)
```

By group, Q-Q plots can be created with this script, with each command defining one category of the Sport variable.

FIGURE 11.28 (continued)
Q-Q plot.

Examination of the boxplot by group suggests a relatively normal distributional shape of residuals and no outliers.

Overall, the boxplot suggests normality.

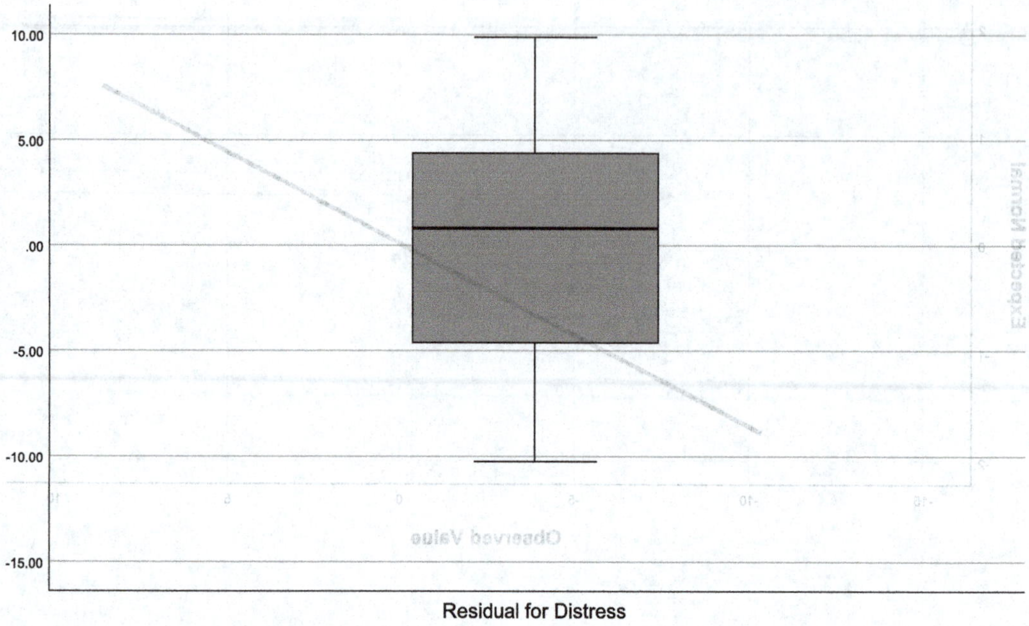

By group, even with the small group sizes, the distributions are generally acceptable in terms of normality (although fielding suggests more skew than the other groups) and do not suggest outliers.

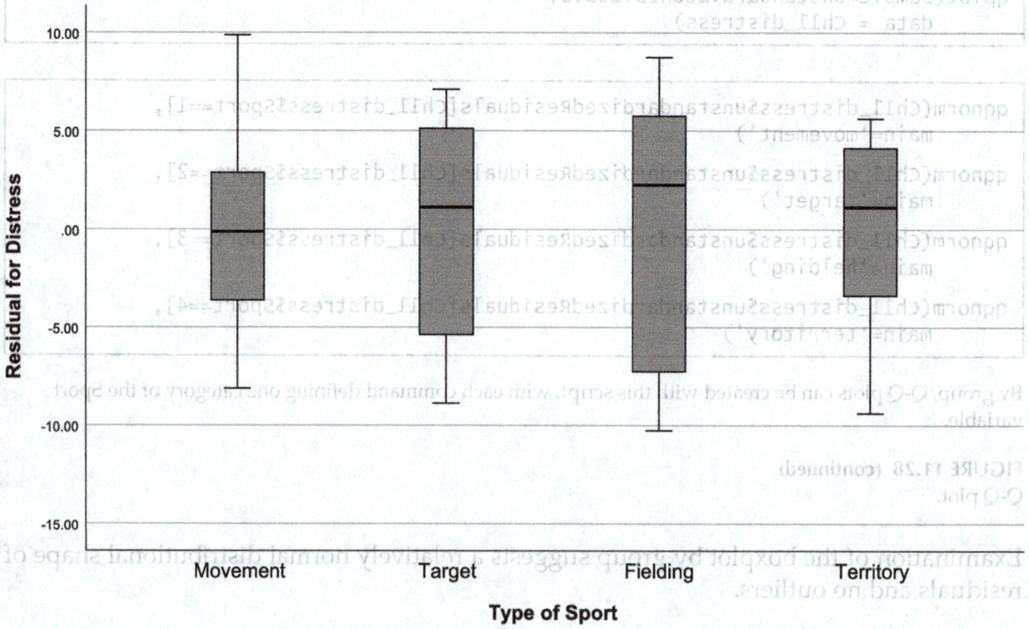

FIGURE 11.29
Boxplot

Working in **R**, we can generate a boxplot for unstandardized residuals using the *boxplot* function. To label the *Y* axis, we include the *ylab* command.

```
boxplot(Ch11_distress$unstandardizedResiduals,
        ylab="Unstandardized Residuals")
```

Adding the independent variable to the script produces a boxplot by group. The command *xlab* will print "Sport" to identify the *X* axis.

```
boxplot(Ch11_distress$unstandardizedResiduals~Ch11_distress$SportF,
        xlab="Sport", ylab="Unstandardized Residuals")
```

FIGURE 11.29 (continued)
Boxplot

Considering the forms of evidence we have examined, skewness and kurtosis statistics, the Shapiro-Wilk test, the Q-Q plot, and the boxplot, all suggest normality by group is a reasonable assumption. We can be reasonably assured we have met the assumption of normality of the dependent variable for each group of the independent variable.

11.4.2 Independence

The only assumption we have not tested for yet is independence. If subjects have been randomly assigned to conditions (in other words, the different levels of the independent variable), the assumption of independence has been met. In this illustration, we have an observational study—athletes were not randomly assigned to the type of sport in which they participated, and thus we cannot assume that the assumption of independence was met. Had we randomly assigned units to the levels of the independent variable, we would have confidence in having met this assumption. The example we've been following, with athletes in types of sports, is common in that we often use independent variables that do not allow random assignment, such as preexisting characteristics. We can plot residuals against levels of our independent variable using a scatterplot to get an idea of whether or not there are patterns in the data and thereby provide an indication of whether we have met this assumption. Remember that these variables were added to the dataset by saving the unstandardized residuals when we generated the ANOVA model.

Please note that some researchers do not believe that the assumption of independence can be tested. If there is not random assignment to groups, then these researchers believe this assumption has been violated—period. The plot that we generate will give us a general idea of patterns, however, in situations where random assignment was not performed.

The general steps for generating a simple scatterplot through "Scatter/dot" have been presented in Chapter 10, and they will not be reiterated here. From the "Simple Scatterplot" dialog screen, click the residual variable and move it into the "Y Axis" box by clicking on the arrow. Click the independent variable (e.g., type of sport) and move it into the "X Axis" box by clicking on the arrow. Then click "OK."

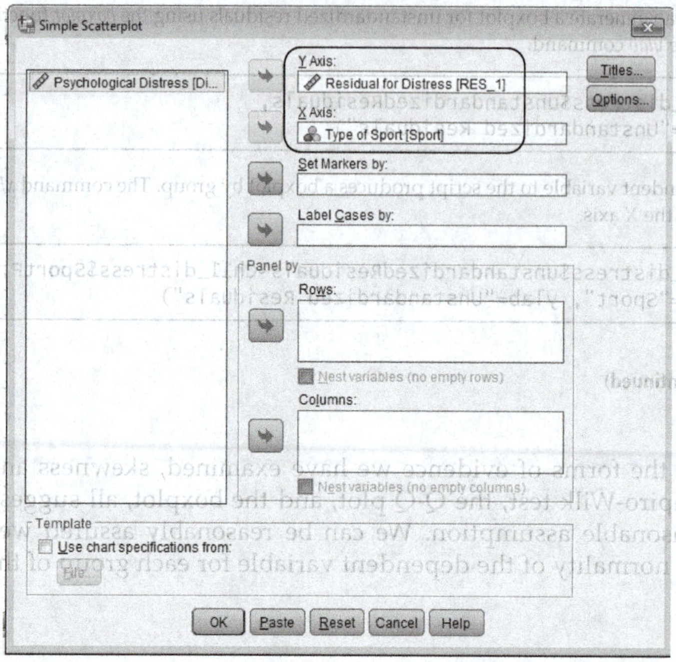

FIGURE 11.30
Generating a scatterplot.

Double click on the graph in the output to activate the chart editor. In the top toolbar within the chart editor, select "Options," then "Y Axis Reference Line."

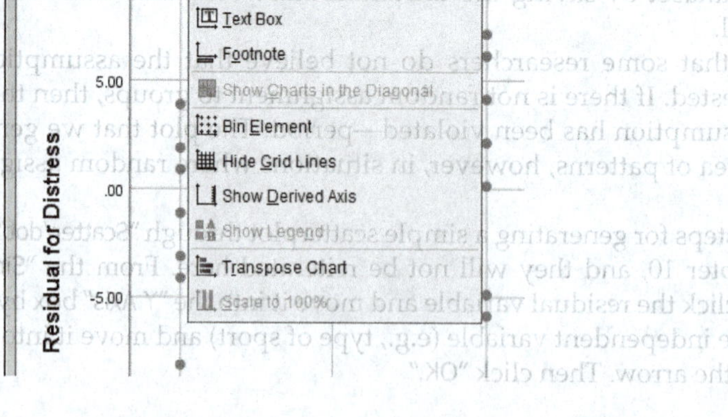

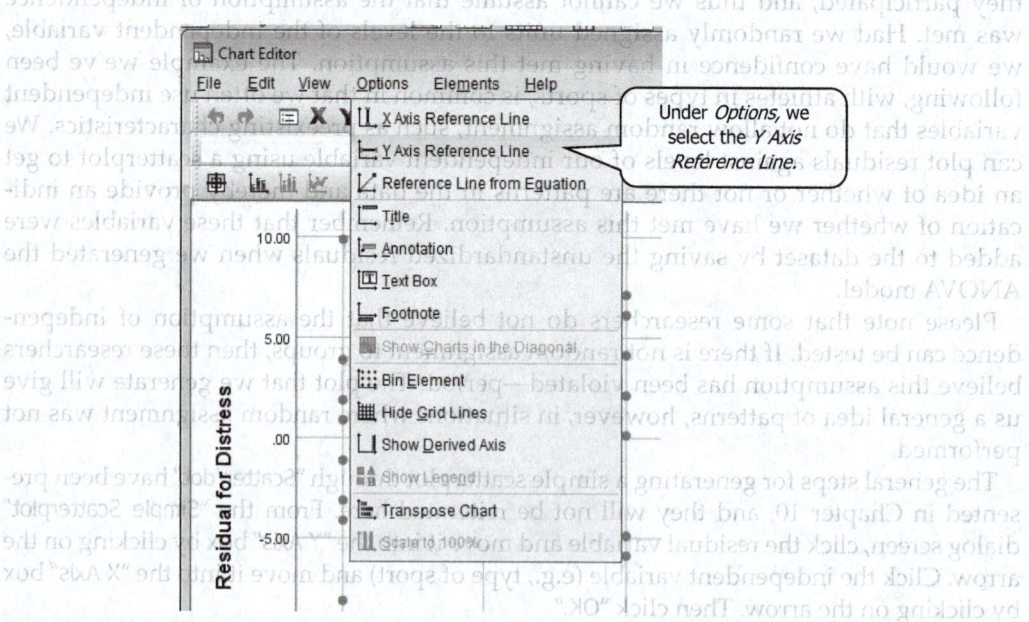

FIGURE 11.31
Chart editor.

Within the properties dialog box, we define the position for the *Y* axis reference line to be 0.

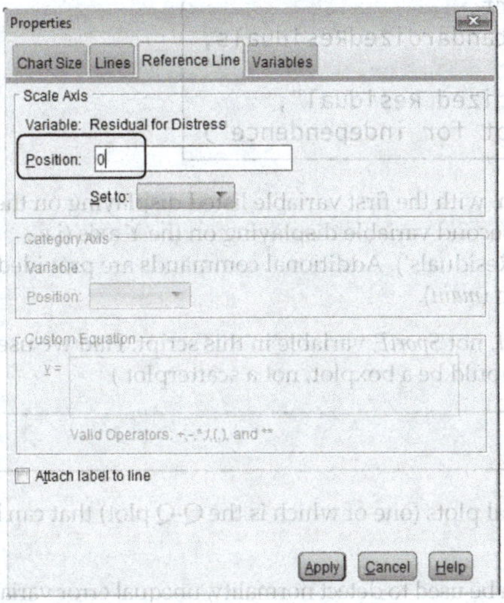

FIGURE 11.32
Adding a reference line.

11.4.2.1 Interpreting Independence Evidence

In examining the scatterplot for evidence of independence, the points should be falling relatively randomly above and below the reference line. In this example, our scatterplot suggests evidence of independence with a relatively random display of points above and below the horizontal line at zero. Thus, even though we had not met the assumption of independence through random assignment of cases to groups, this provides evidence that independence is a reasonable assumption.

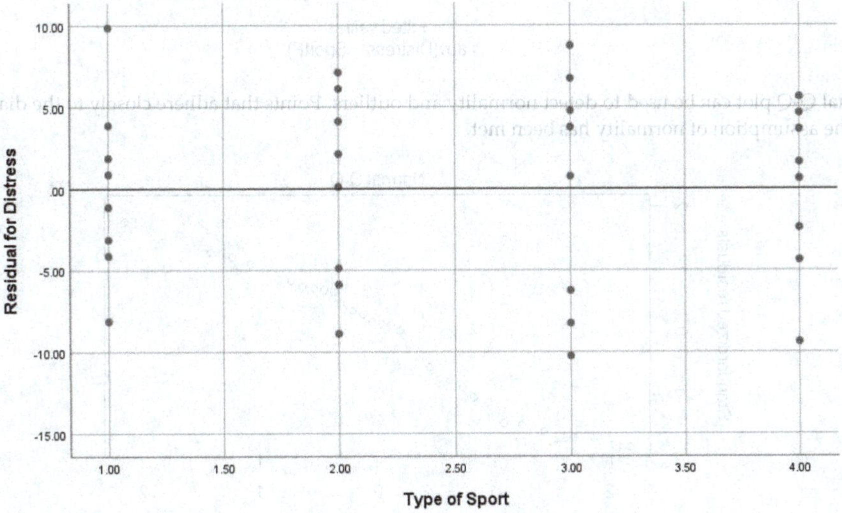

FIGURE 11.33
Scatterplot of residual by type of sport.

Working in R, we create a similar scatterplot.

```
plot(Ch11_distress$Sport,
     Ch11_distress$unstandardizedResiduals,
     xlab = "Sport",
     ylab = "Unstandardized Residual",
     main = "Scatterplot for independence")
```

Using the following *plot* function, with the first variable listed displaying on the *X* axis (e.g., 'Ch11_distress$Sport'), and the second variable displaying on the *Y* axis (i.e., 'Ch11_distress$unstandardizedResiduals'). Additional commands are provided to label the axes (*xlab* and *ylab*) and title the graph (*main*).

(Note that we are using our *Sport*, not *SportF*, variable in this script. Had we used *SportF*, the variable we defined as nominal, the plot generated would be a boxplot, not a scatterplot.)

```
plot(Ch11_ANOVA)
```

Using the *plot* function, additional plots (one of which is the Q-Q plot) that can be used for diagnostic purposes are created.

The residual versus fitted plot can be used to detect normality, unequal error variance and outliers. A random display of points, i.e., no patterns to the data, suggest assumptions of normality and equal variances have been met.

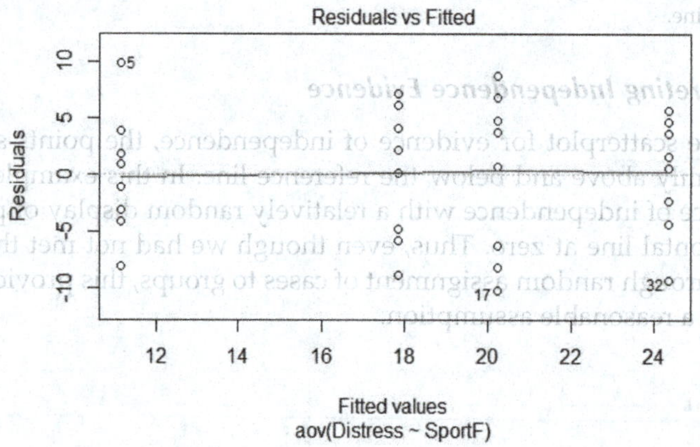

The normal Q-Q plot can be used to detect normality and outliers. Points that adhere closely to the diagonal line suggest the assumption of normality has been met.

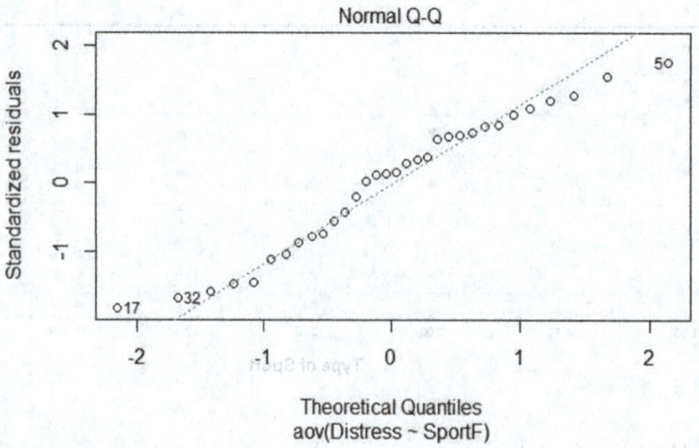

FIGURE 11.33 (continued)
Scatterplot of residual by type of sport.

The scale-location plot can be examined for evidence of equal variance. Relatively equally spaced points by group above and below a horizontal line (i.e., random and equal distribution of points and straight horizontal line) suggests evidence of meeting the assumption.

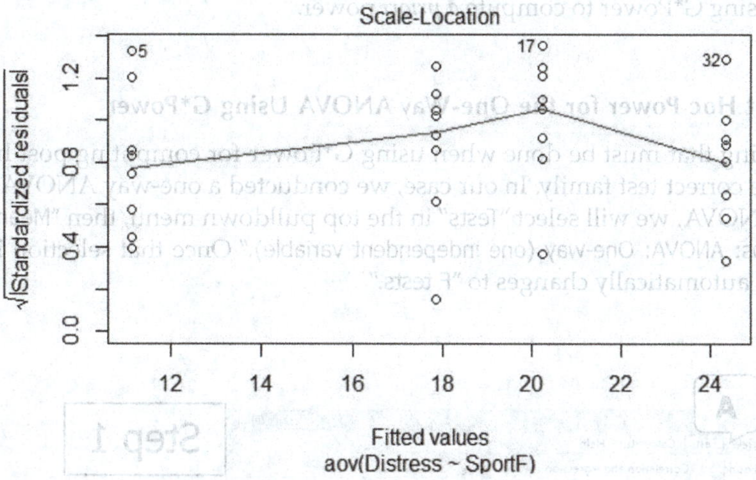

The constant leverage plot can be examined similarly as evidence of normality as well to determine points that may exert influence.

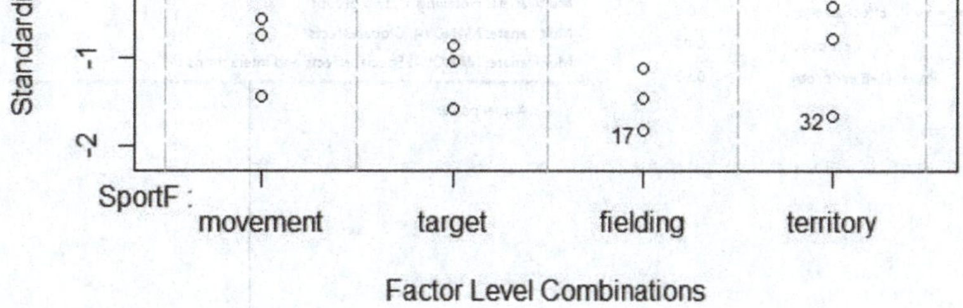

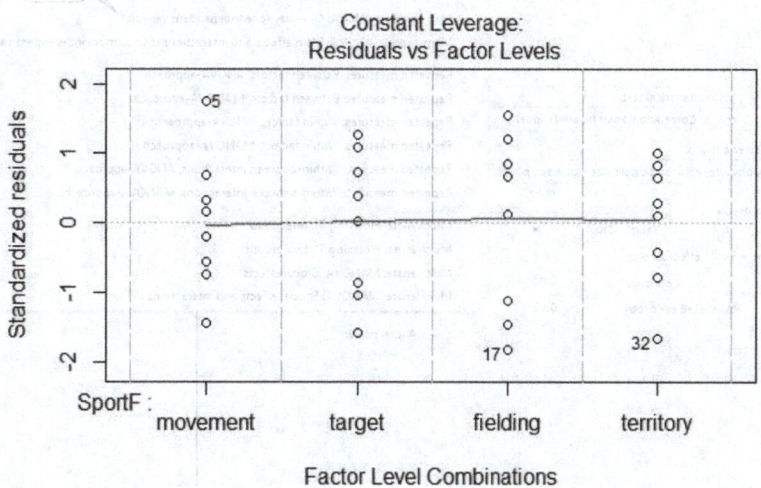

FIGURE 11.33 (continued)
Scatterplot of residual by type of sport.

11.4.3 Homogeneity of Variance

As we learned previously, another assumption to consider is that the variances of each population are equal. This is known as the assumption of *homogeneity of variance* or *homoscedasticity*. When generating ANOVA via SPSS, we requested Levene's test for examining homogeneity. Homogeneity tests using **R** were presented previously (see Figure 11.21).

11.5 Power Using G*Power

Using G*Power, post hoc power will be examined first. This will be following by an illustration of using G*Power to compute *a priori* power.

11.5.1 Post Hoc Power for the One-Way ANOVA Using G*Power

The first thing that must be done when using G*Power for computing post hoc power is to select the correct test family. In our case, we conducted a one-way ANOVA. To find the one-way ANOVA, we will select "Tests" in the top pulldown menu, then "Means," and then "Many groups: ANOVA: One-way (one independent variable)." Once that selection is made, the "Test family" automatically changes to "F tests."

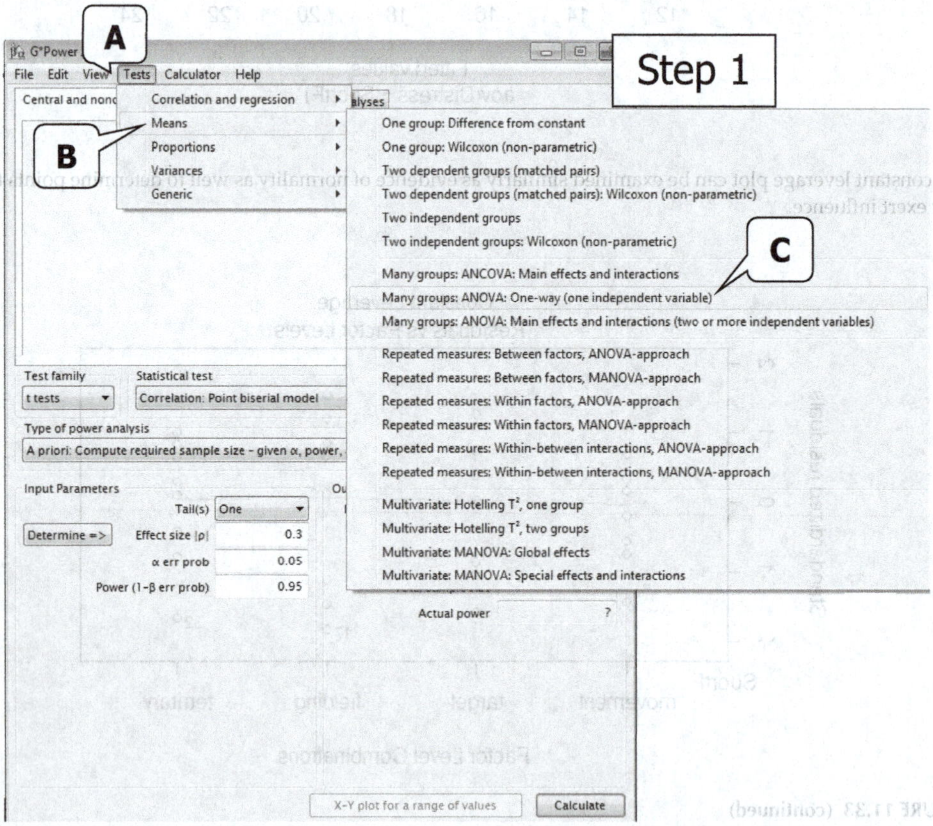

FIGURE 11.34
Power: Step 1.

The "Type of power analysis" desired then needs to be selected. To compute post hoc power, we need to select "Post hoc: Compute achieved power—given α, sample size, and effect size."

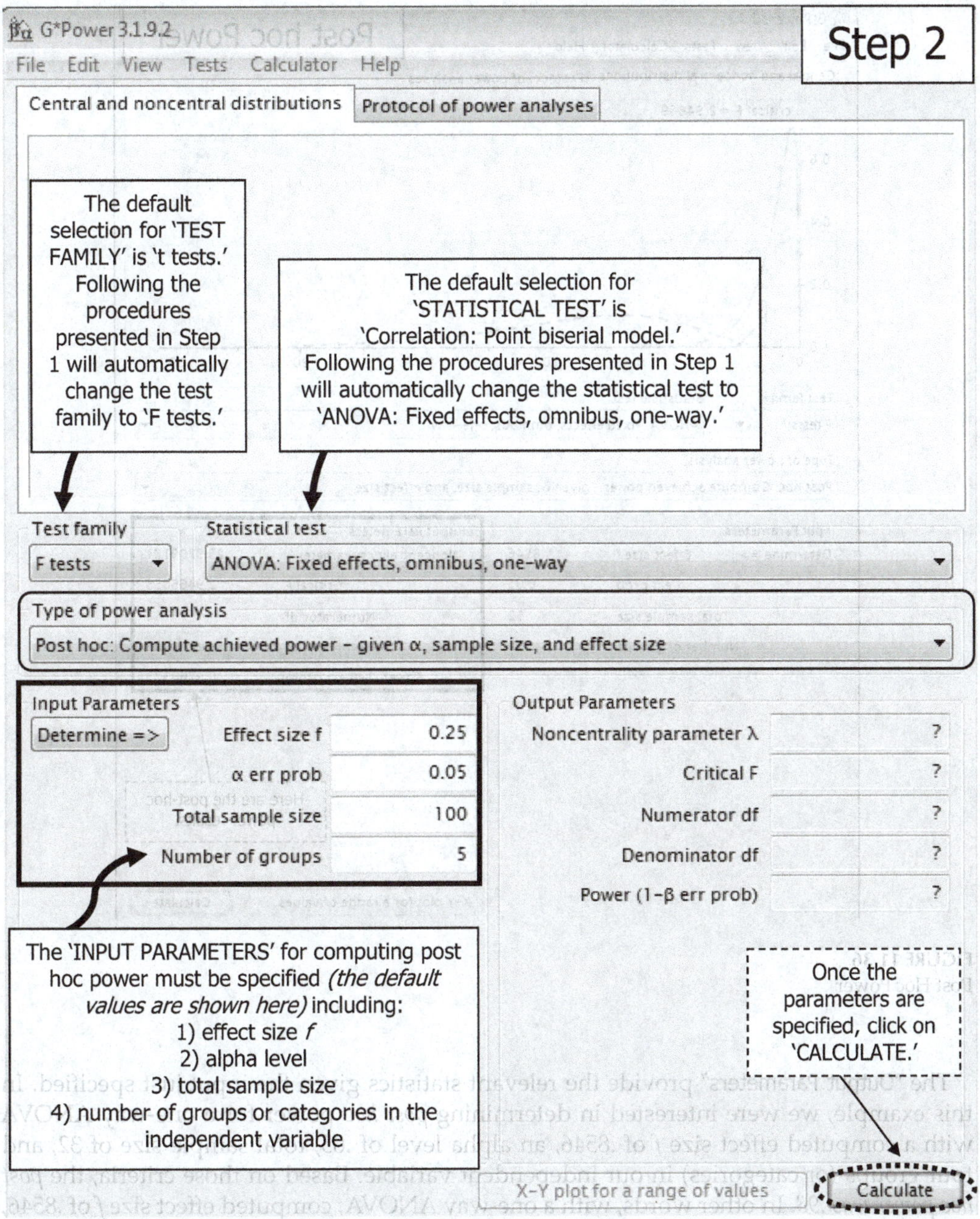

FIGURE 11.35
Power: Step 2.

The "Input Parameters" must then be specified. The first parameter is the effect size, *f*. In our example, the computed *f* effect size was .8546. The alpha level we used was .05, the total sample size was 32, and the number of groups (i.e., levels of the independent variable) was 4. Once the parameters are specified, click on "Calculate" to find the power statistics.

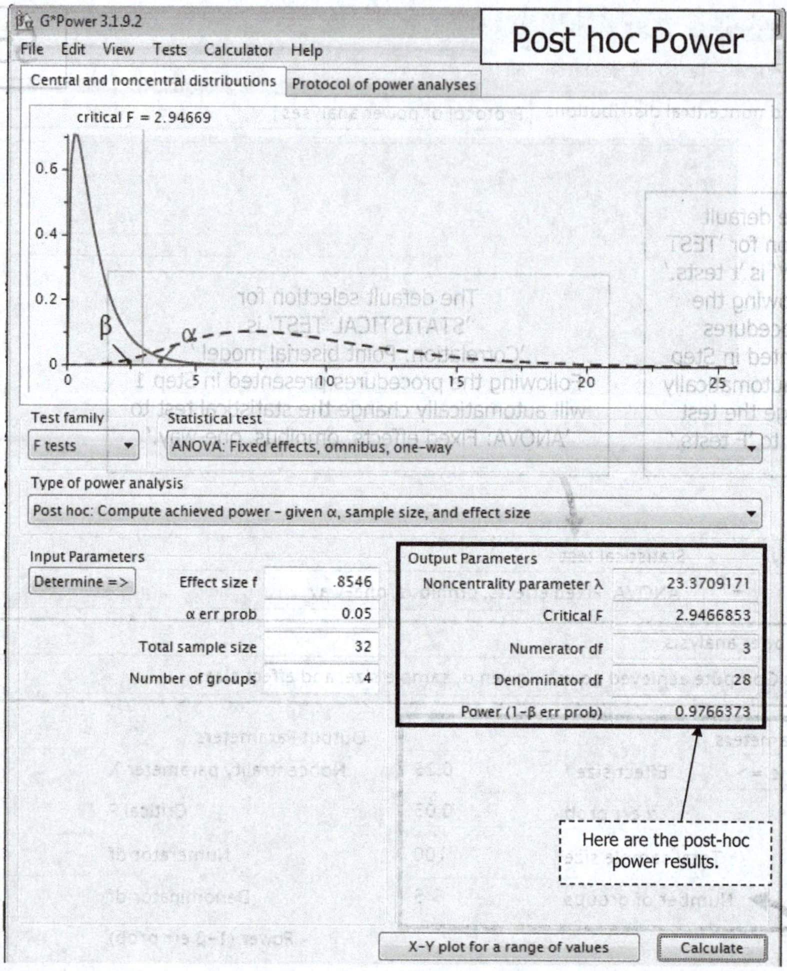

FIGURE 11.36
Post Hoc Power

The "**Output Parameters**" provide the relevant statistics given the input just specified. In this example, we were interested in determining *post hoc* power for a one-way ANOVA with a computed effect size f of .8546, an alpha level of .05, total sample size of 32, and four groups (or categories) in our independent variable. Based on those criteria, the *post hoc power was .98*. In other words, with a one-way ANOVA, computed effect size f of .8546, alpha level of .05, total sample size of 32, and four groups (or categories) in our independent variable, the post hoc power of our test was .98—*the probability of rejecting the null hypothesis when it is really false (in this case, the probability that the means of the dependent variable would be equal for each level of the independent variable) was 98%*, which would be considered more than sufficient power (sufficient power is often .80 or above). Note that this value is slightly different than the observed value reported in SPSS. Keep in mind that conducting power analysis *a priori* is recommended so that you avoid a situation where, post hoc, you find that the sample size was not sufficient to reach the desired level of power (given the observed parameters).

11.5.2 *A Priori* Power for the One-Way ANOVA Using G*Power

For *a priori* power, we can determine the total sample size needed given an estimated effect size *f*, alpha level, desired power, and number of groups of our independent variable. In this example, had we estimated a moderate effect *f* of .25 (this is the default in G*Power), alpha of .05, desired power of .80, and four groups in the independent variable, we would need a total sample size of 180 (or 45 per group in a balanced design).

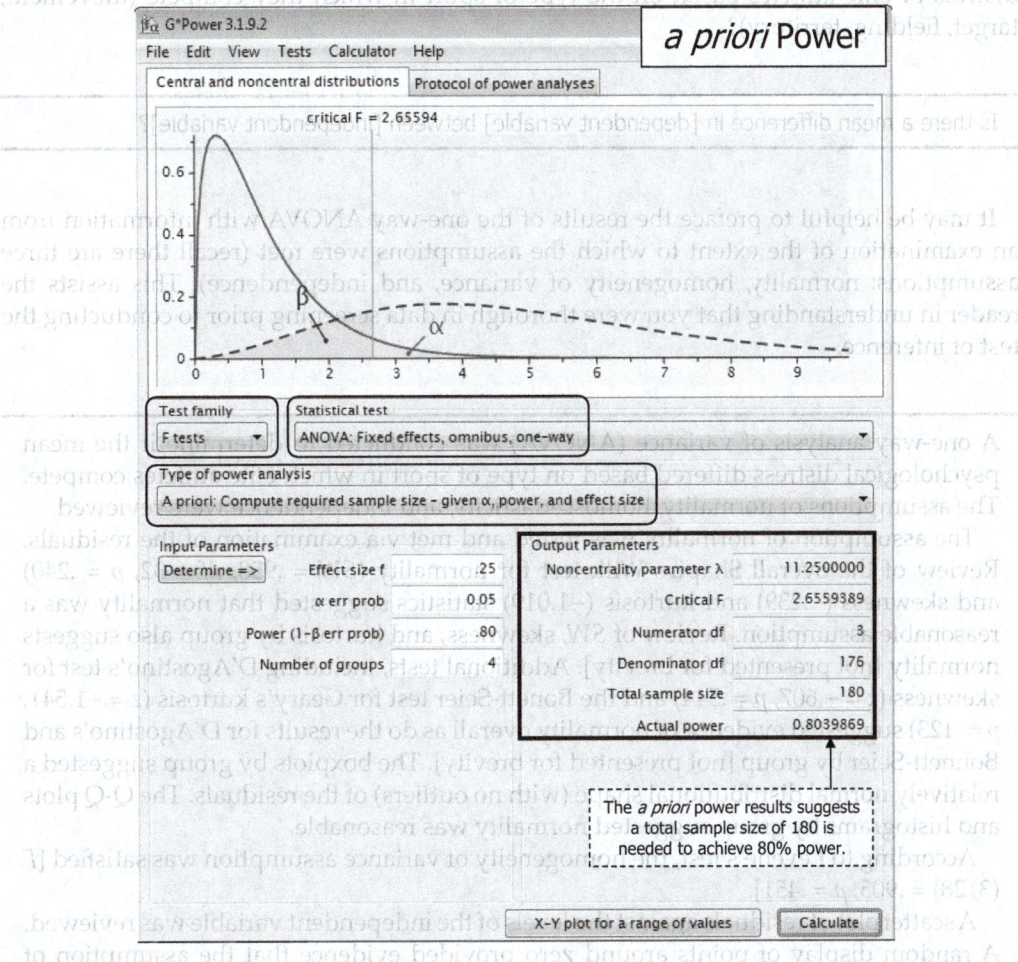

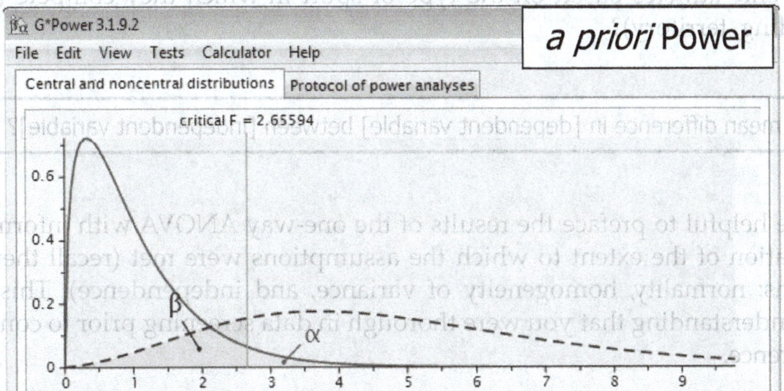

FIGURE 11.37
A priori power.

11.6 Research Question Template and Example Write-Up

Finally we come to an example paragraph of the results for the statistics lab example Recall that Ott Lier was working with Dr. Rhodes, one of the leading sports psychologists in the region. Dr. Rhodes is examining elite athletes and their vulnerability to psychological distress based on the sport in which they participate. Ott suggested that the following research question is: *Is there a mean difference in psychological distress of elite athletes based on the type of sport in which they participate?* Ott then generated a one-way ANOVA to test the inference.

A template for writing a research question for a one-way ANOVA is presented below. Please note that it is important to ensure the reader understands the levels or groups of the independent variable. This may be done parenthetically in the actual research question, as an operational definition, or specified within the methods section. In this example, parenthetically we could have stated the following: Is there a mean difference in psychological distress of elite athletes based on the type of sport in which they compete (movement, target, fielding, territory)?

Is there a mean difference in [dependent variable] between [independent variable]?

It may be helpful to preface the results of the one-way ANOVA with information from an examination of the extent to which the assumptions were met (recall there are three assumptions: normality, homogeneity of variance, and independence). This assists the reader in understanding that you were thorough in data screening prior to conducting the test of inference.

A one-way analysis of variance (ANOVA) was conducted to determine if the mean psychological distress differed based on type of sport in which elite athletes compete. The assumptions of normality, homoscedasticity, and independence were reviewed.

The assumption of normality was tested and met via examination of the residuals. Review of the overall Shapiro-Wilk test for normality ($SW = .958$, $df = 32$, $p = .240$) and skewness (–.239) and kurtosis (–1.019) statistics suggested that normality was a reasonable assumption. Review of *SW*, skewness, and kurtosis by group also suggests normality [not presented for brevity]. Additional tests, including D'Agostino's test for skewness ($z = -.607$, $p = .544$) and the Bonett-Seier test for Geary's kurtosis ($z = -1.541$, $p = .123$) suggested evidence of normality overall as do the results for D'Agostino's and Bonnett-Seier by group [not presented for brevity]. The boxplots by group suggested a relatively normal distributional shape (with no outliers) of the residuals. The Q-Q plots and histograms by group suggested normality was reasonable.

According to Levene's test, the homogeneity of variance assumption was satisfied [$F(3, 28) = .905$, $p = .451$].

A scatterplot of residuals against the levels of the independent variable was reviewed. A random display of points around zero provided evidence that the assumption of independence was met. (*Note:* Had there been random assignment to groups, we could have added an additional statement such as: "Random assignment of individuals to groups helped ensure that the assumption of independence was met. Additionally, a random display of points around zero provided evidence that the assumption of independence was met.")

Here is an APA-style example paragraph of results for the one-way ANOVA (remember that this will be prefaced by the previous paragraph reporting the extent to which the assumptions of the test were met).

The one-way ANOVA is statistically significant (F = 6.818, df = 3, 28, p = .001). This suggests that the mean psychological distress differs by type of sport in which the athlete participates. Based on Tukey's HSD post hoc multiple comparison results, mean psychological distress for athletes in movement sports was statistically significantly lower than for athletes in fielding (p = .025) and territory sports (p = .001) [we've kept this here as a placeholder and will revisit multiple comparison procedures in the next chapter]. The means and standard deviations of psychological distress for each type of sport were as follows: 11.125 (SD = 5.489) for athletes competing in movement sports, 17.875 (SD = 5.939) for athletes competing in target sports, 20.250 (SD = 7.285) for athletes competing in fielding sports, and 24.375 (SD = 5.097) for athletes competing in territory sports.

The effect size is rather large (ω^2=.35; suggesting about 35% of the variance of psychological distress is due to differences in the type of sport in which an elite athlete competes), and observed power is quite strong (.956).

For completeness, we also conducted several alternative procedures. The Kruskal-Wallis test (χ^2= 13.061, df = 3, p = .005), the Welch procedure (F_{Asymp} = 7.862, $df1$ = 3, $df2$ = 15.454, p = .002), and the Brown-Forsythe procedure (F_{Asymp} = 6.818, $df1$ = 3, $df2$ = 25.882, p = .002) also indicated a statistically significant effect of type of sport on psychological distress.

11.7 Additional Resources

This chapter has provided a preview into conducting one-way ANOVA. However, there are a number of areas that space limitations prevent us from delving into. For more in-depth coverage of ANOVA models, see Maxwell, Delaney, and Kelley (2018). For readers interested in one-way ANOVA when there is censored data (i.e., when some data cannot be observed due to resource limitations, such as cost or time), see Celik and Şenoglu (2018).

Problems

Conceptual Problems

1. Data for three independent random samples, each of size four, are analyzed by a one-factor analysis of variance fixed-effects model. If the values of the sample means are all equal, what is the value of MS_{betw}?
   a. 0
   b. 1
   c. 2
   d. 3

2. For a one-factor analysis of variance fixed-effects model, which of the following is always true?
   a. $df_{betw} + df_{with} = df_{total}$
   b. $SS_{betw} + SS_{with} = SS_{total}$
   c. $MS_{betw} + MS_{with} = MS_{total}$
   d. All of the above
   e. Both a and b
3. Suppose $n_1 = 19$, $n_2 = 21$, and $n_3 = 23$. For a one-factor ANOVA, the df_{with} would be
   a. 2
   b. 3
   c. 60
   d. 62
4. Suppose $n_1 = 19$, $n_2 = 21$, and $n_3 = 23$. For a one-factor ANOVA, the df_{betw} would be
   a. 2
   b. 3
   c. 60
   d. 62
5. Suppose $n_1 = 19$, $n_2 = 21$, and $n_3 = 23$. For a one-factor ANOVA, the df_{total} would be
   a. 2
   b. 3
   c. 60
   d. 62
6. Suppose $n_1 = 19$, $n_2 = 21$, and $n_3 = 23$. For a one-factor ANOVA, the df for the numerator of the F ratio would be which one of the following?
   a. 2
   b. 3
   c. 60
   d. 62
7. In a one-factor ANOVA, H_0 asserts that
   a. All of the population means are equal.
   b. The between-groups variance estimate and the within-groups variance estimate are both estimates of the same population residual variance.
   c. The within-groups sum of squares is equal to the between-groups sum of squares.
   d. Both a and b
8. For a one-factor ANOVA comparing three groups with $n = 10$ in each group, the F ratio has degrees of freedom equal to
   a. 2, 27
   b. 2, 29
   c. 3, 27
   d. 3, 29

9. For a one-factor ANOVA comparing five groups with $n = 50$ in each group, the F ratio has degrees of freedom equal to
   a. 4, 245
   b. 4, 249
   c. 5, 245
   d. 5, 249

10. Which of the following is not necessary in ANOVA?
   a. Observations are from random and independent samples.
   b. The dependent variable is measured on at least the interval scale.
   c. Populations have equal variances.
   d. Equal sample sizes are necessary.

11. If you find an F ratio of 1.0 in a one-factor ANOVA, it means that
   a. Between-groups variation exceeds within-groups variation
   b. Within-groups variation exceeds between-groups variation
   c. Between-groups variation is equal to within-groups variation
   d. Between-groups variation exceeds total variation

12. True or false? Suppose students in grades 7, 8, 9, 10, 11, and 12 were compared on absenteeism. If ANOVA were used rather than multiple t tests, then the probability of a Type I error will be less.

13. True or false? Mean square is another name for variance or variance estimate.

14. In ANOVA each independent variable is known as a level. True or false?

15. A negative F ratio is impossible. True or false?

16. Suppose that for a one-factor ANOVA with $J = 4$ and $n = 10$, the four sample means are all equal to 15. I assert that the value of MS_{with} is necessarily equal to zero. Am I correct?

17. With $J = 3$ groups, I assert that if you reject H_0 in the one-factor ANOVA you will necessarily conclude that all three group means are different. Am I correct?

18. True or false? The homoscedasticity assumption is that the populations from which each of the samples are drawn are normally distributed.

19. When analyzing mean differences among more than two samples, doing independent t tests on all possible pairs of means
   a. Decreases the probability of a Type I error
   b. Does not change the probability of a Type I error
   c. Increases the probability of a Type I error
   d. Cannot be determined from the information provided

20. Suppose for a one-factor fixed-effects ANOVA with $J = 5$ and $n = 15$, the five sample means are all equal to 50. I assert that the F test statistic cannot be significant. Am I correct?

21. True or false? The independence assumption in ANOVA is that the observations in the samples do not depend on one another.

22. True or false? For $J = 2$ and $\alpha = .05$, if the result of the independent t test is significant, then the result of the one-factor fixed-effects ANOVA is uncertain.

23. A statistician conducted a one-factor fixed-effects ANOVA and found the *F* ratio to be less than 0. I assert this means the between-groups variability is less than the within-groups variability. Am I correct?

24. Which of the following is *not* an alternative to the parametric one-factor fixed-effects ANOVA?
   a. Brown-Forsythe procedure
   b. Kruskal-Wallis test
   c. Levene's test
   d. Welch test

25. Which of the following is *not* a proportion of variance explained type of effect size measures that can be computed for one-way fixed-effects ANOVA?
   a. *d*
   b. ε^2
   c. η^2
   d. ω^2

26. A researcher computes a one-way fixed-effects ANOVA and finds ω^2=.07. Using Cohen's subjective standards, how would this effect size be interpreted?
   a. Small
   b. Moderate
   c. Large
   d. Very large

27. Which of the following do *not* provide evidence of the assumption of normality?
   a. Levene's test
   b. Q-Q plot
   c. Shapiro-Wilk test
   d. Skewness and kurtosis

28. The assumption of homoscedasticity deals with which one of the following?
   a. Equal population variances
   b. Independence
   c. Linearity
   d. Normality

Answers to Conceptual Problems

1. **a** (if the sample means are all equal, then MS_{betw} is 0.)
3. **c** (lose 1 *df* from each group; 63 − 3 = 60.)
5. **d** (equals the $df_{betw} + df_{with} = df_{total}$; 60 + 2 = 62.)
7. **d** (null hypothesis does not consider *SS* values.)
9. **a** (for between source = 5 − 1 = 4 and for within source = 250 − 5 = 245.)
11. **c** (an *F* ratio of 1.0 implies between- and within-groups variation are the same.)
13. **True** (mean square is a variance estimate.)

15. **True** (F ratio must be greater than or equal to 0.)
17. **No** (rejecting the null hypothesis in ANOVA only indicates that there is some difference among the means, not that all of the means are different.)
19. c (the more t tests conducted, the more likely a Type I error for the set of tests.)
21. **True** (basically the definition of independence.)
23. **No** (find a new statistician as a negative F value is not possible in this context.)
25. **a** (effect size d is interpreted as a standardized mean difference, not proportion of variance.)
27. **a** (Levene's test is used to examine the assumption of homogeneity of variances in ANOVA models, not normality.)

Computational Problems

1. Complete the following ANOVA summary table for a one-factor analysis of variance, where there are four groups receiving different headache medications, each with 16 observations, and $\alpha = .05$.

Source	SS	df	MS	F	Critical Value and Decision
Between	9.75	—	—	—	
Within	—	—	—		
Total	18.75	—			

2. A social psychologist wants to determine if type of music has any effect on the number of beers consumed by people in a tavern. Four taverns are selected that have different musical formats. Five people are randomly sampled in each tavern and their beer consumption monitored for three hours. Complete the following one-factor ANOVA summary table using $\alpha = .05$.

Source	SS	df	MS	F	Critical Value and Decision
Between	—	—	7.52	5.01	
Within	—	—	—		
Total	—	—			

3. A psychologist would like to know whether the season (fall, winter, spring, and summer) has any consistent effect on people's overall mood. In the middle of each season, the psychologist selects a random sample of $n = 25$ students. Each individual is given a questionnaire that assesses their overall mood (and results in a continuous composite score). A one-factor ANOVA was used to analyze these data. Complete the following ANOVA summary table (α =.05).

Source	SS	df	MS	F	Critical Value and Decision
Between	—	—	—	5.00	
Within	960	—	—		
Total	—	—			

4. The following five independent random samples are obtained from five normally distributed populations with equal variances. The dependent variable is the number of bank transactions in one month and the groups are five different banks.

Group 1	Group 2	Group 3	Group 4	Group 5
16	16	2	5	7
5	10	9	8	12
11	7	11	1	14
23	12	13	5	16
18	7	10	8	11
12	4	13	11	9
12	23	9	9	19
19	13	9	9	24

Use SPSS or **R** to conduct a one-factor analysis of variance to determine if the group means are equal using $\alpha = .05$.

5. The following three independent random samples are obtained from three normally distributed populations with equal variances. The dependent variable is starting hourly wage and the groups are the type of position (internship, co-op, work study).

Group 1: Internship	Group 2: Co-op	Group 3: Work Study
10	9	8
12	8	9
11	10	8
11	12	10
12	9	8
10	11	9
10	12	9
13	10	8

Conduct a one-factor analysis of variance to determine if the group means are equal using $\alpha = .05$. If needed, conduct Tukey's post hoc test. Report the extent to which the assumption of homogeneity of variances was met.

6. The following three independent random samples are obtained from three normally distributed populations with equal variances. The dependent variable is nurse's stress and the independent variable is hospital size.

Group 1	Group 2	Group 3
4	5	6
2	4	8
3	5	6
3	5	7
4	4	6
3	5	7
3	5	6
4	5	6

Conduct a one-factor analysis of variance to determine if the group means are equal using $\alpha = .05$. If needed, conduct Tukey's post hoc test. Report the extent to which the assumption of homogeneity of variances was met.

Answers to Computational Problems

1. $df_{betw} = 3$, $df_{with} = 60$, $df_{total} = 63$, $SS_{with} = 9$, $MS_{betw} = 3.25$, $MS_{with} = 0.15$, $F = 21.6666$, critical value = 2.76 (reject H_0).
3. $SS_{betw} = 150$, $SS_{total} = 1{,}110$, $df_{betw} = 3$, $df_{with} = 96$, $df_{total} = 99$, $MS_{with} = 50$, $MS_{with} = 10$, critical value approximately 2.7 (reject H_0).
5. The one-way ANOVA was statistically significant, $F = 9.629$, $df = 2, 21$, $p < .001$. Based on Tukey's HSD, there were statistically significantly different wages for work study students relative to either interns or co-op students. The assumption of homogeneity of variances was met, based on Levene's test [$F\ (2, 21) = 1.640$, $p = 2.18$].

Interpretive Problems

1. Using the survey1 dataset, which is accessible from the website, use SPSS or **R** to conduct a one-factor fixed-effects ANOVA, where political view is the grouping variable (i.e., independent variable) ($J = 5$) and the dependent variable is an interval or ratio variable of your choice. Also compute effect size and test for assumptions. Then write an APA-style paragraph describing the results.
2. Using the survey1 dataset, which is accessible from the website, use SPSS or **R** to conduct a one-factor fixed-effects ANOVA, where hair color is the grouping variable (i.e., independent variable) ($J = 5$) and the dependent variable is an interval or ratio variable of your choice. Also compute effect size and test for assumptions. Then write an APA-style paragraph describing the results.
3. Use the IPEDS2017 dataset, which is accessible from the website, use SPSS or **R** to conduct a one-factor fixed-effects ANOVA. Select an appropriate independent variable (e.g., *land grant institution*, LANDGRNT) and appropriate dependent variable (e.g., *total dormitory capacity*, ROOMCAP). Also compute effect size and test for assumptions. Then write an APA-style paragraph describing the results.

12

Multiple Comparison Procedures

Chapter Outline

Key Concepts

1. Contrast
2. Simple and complex contrasts
3. Planned and post hoc comparisons
4. Contrast- and family-based Type I error rates
5. Orthogonal contrasts

In this chapter our concern is with multiple comparison procedures that involve comparisons among the group means. Recall from Chapter 11 the one-factor analysis of variance where the means from two or more samples were compared. What do we do if the omnibus F test leads us to reject H_0? First, consider the situation where there are only two samples (e.g., assessing the effectiveness of two types of medication), and H_0 has already been rejected in the omnibus test. Why was H_0 rejected? The answer should be obvious. Those two sample means must be significantly different, as there is no other way that the omnibus H_0 could have been rejected (e.g., one type of medication is significantly more effective than the other based on an inspection of the means).

Second, consider the situation where there are more than two samples (e.g., three types of medication), and H_0 has already been rejected in the omnibus test. Why was H_0 rejected? The answer is not so obvious. This situation is one where a **multiple comparison procedure (MCP)** would be quite informative. Thus, for situations where there are at least three groups and the analysis of variance (ANOVA) H_0 has been rejected, some sort of MCP is necessary to determine which means, or combination of means, are different. Third, consider the situation where the researcher is not even interested in the ANOVA omnibus test, but is only interested in comparisons involving particular means (e.g., certain medications are more effective than a placebo). This is a situation where a MCP is useful for evaluating those specific comparisons.

If the ANOVA omnibus H_0 has been rejected, why not do all possible independent *t* tests? First let us return to a similar question from Chapter 11. There we asked about doing all possible pairwise independent *t* tests rather than an ANOVA. The answer there was to do an omnibus *F* test. The reasoning was related to the probability of making a Type I error (i.e., α), where the researcher incorrectly rejects a true null hypothesis. Although the alpha level for each *t* test can be controlled at a specified nominal level, say .05, what would happen to the overall alpha level for the set of *t* tests? The overall α level for the set of tests, often called the **family-wise Type I error rate**, would be larger than the α level for each of the individual *t* tests. The optimal solution, in terms of maintaining control over our overall α level as well as maximizing power, is to conduct **one overall omnibus test** that assesses the equality of all of the means simultaneously.

Let us apply the same concept to the situation involving multiple comparisons. Rather than doing all possible pairwise independent *t* tests, where the family-wise error rate could be quite large, *one should use a procedure that controls the family-wise error rate in some way. This can be done with multiple comparison procedures.* As pointed out later in the chapter, there are two main methods for taking the Type I error rate into account.

This chapter is concerned with several important new concepts, such as a contrast, planned versus post hoc comparisons, the Type I error rate, and orthogonal contrasts. The remainder of the chapter consists of selected multiple comparison procedures, including when and how to apply them. The terms *comparison* and *contrast* are used here synonymously. *Also, MCPs are applicable only for comparing levels of an independent variable that are fixed, in other words, for fixed-effects independent variables, and not for random-effects independent variables.* Our objectives are that by the end of this chapter, you will be able to (a) understand the concepts underlying the MCPs, (b) select the appropriate MCP for a given research situation, and (c) determine and interpret the results of MCPs.

12.1 What Multiple Comparison Procedures Are and How They Work

In the previous chapter, Ott Lier, one of four graduate students who assist in the statistics lab, was embarking on a very exciting research adventure. He continues to work towards completion of this project. As you may recall, Ott was assisting Dr. Rhodes, one of the region's leading sports psychologists, in examining elite athletes and vulnerability to psychological distress based on type of sport in which they participate. Our graduate student team successfully analyzed the data and used (as we saw in a previous chapter) one-way ANOVA to answer a research question. As we will see in this chapter, Ott will be expanding on the analysis as it relates to examining the group means.

The research lab has been contracted to work with one of the leading sports psychologists in the region, Dr. Rhodes. Dr. Rhodes is examining elite athletes and their vulnerability to psychological distress based on the type of sport in which they participate. Dr. Rhodes wants to determine if there is a difference in psychological stress based on type of sport (movement, target, fielding, or territory). Ott suggests the following research question is: *Is there a mean difference in psychological distress of elite athletes based on the type of sport in which they participate?* With one independent variable, Ott conducted a one-way ANOVA to answer Dr. Rhodes's question, where he rejected the null hypothesis. Now his task is to determine which type of sport (recall there were four) were statistically different on the outcome (i.e., psychological distress).

12.1.1 Characteristics

This section describes the most important characteristics of the multiple comparison procedures. We begin by defining a contrast, and then move into planned versus post hoc contrasts, the Type I error rates, and orthogonal contrasts.

12.1.1.1 Contrasts

A **contrast** is a weighted combination of the means. For example, a researcher may want to form contrasts that examine the following combinations of means: (a) Group 1 with Group 2, and (b) the combination (or average) of Groups 1 and 2 with Group 3. Statistically, a contrast is defined as follows:

$$\psi_i = c_1\mu_{.1} + c_2\mu_{.2} + \ldots + c_J\mu_{.J}$$

Where psi (ψ_i) is the particular contrast that is being investigated, the c_j are known as **contrast coefficients** (or **weights**), which are positive, zero, and negative values, and the μ_j are population group means. In other words, *a contrast is simply a particular combination of the group means, depending on which means the researcher is interested in comparing*. It should also be noted that to form a fair or legitimate contrast, $\sum c_j = 0$ for the equal n's or balanced case, and $\sum(n_j c_j) = 0$ for the unequal n's or unbalanced case.

For example, suppose we wish to compare the means of Groups 1 and 3 for $J = 4$ groups or levels, and we call this contrast 1. The contrast would be written as follows, where the means of Groups 2 and 4 are weighted as 0 since they are of no interest in this particular comparison:

$$\psi_1 = c_1\mu_{.1} + c_2\mu_{.2} + c_3\mu_{.3} + c_4\mu_{.4}$$
$$\psi_1 = (+1)\mu_{.1} + (0)\mu_{.2} + (-1)\mu_{.3} + (0)\mu_{.4}$$
$$\psi_1 = \mu_{.1} - \mu_{.3}$$

What hypotheses are we testing when we evaluate a contrast? The null and alternate hypotheses of any specific contrast can be written, respectively, simply as follows:

$$H_0 : \psi_i = 0$$

and

$$H_1 : \psi_i \neq 0$$

Thus we are testing whether a particular combination of means, as defined by the contrast coefficients, are different. How does this relate back to the omnibus *F* test? The null and alternate hypotheses for the omnibus *F* test can be written, respectively, in terms of contrasts as follows:

$$H_0\text{: } all\ \psi_i = 0$$

and

$$H_1\text{: } at\ least\ one\ \psi_i \neq 0$$

Here the omnibus test is used to determine whether any contrast that could be formulated for the set of *J* means is significant or not.

Contrasts can be divided into *simple or pairwise contrasts*, and *complex or nonpairwise contrasts*. A **simple or pairwise contrast** is a comparison involving only two means. Take as an example the situation where there are $J = 3$ groups. There are three possible distinct pairwise contrasts that could be formed: (a) $\mu_{.1} - \mu_{.2} = 0$ (comparing the mean of Group 1 to the mean of Group 2); (b) $\mu_{.1} - \mu_{.3} = 0$ (comparing the mean of Group 1 to the mean of Group 3); and (c) $\mu_{.2} - \mu_{.3} = 0$ (comparing the mean of Group 2 to the mean of Group 3). It should be obvious that a pairwise contrast involving Groups 1 and 2 is the same contrast whether it is written as $\mu_{.1} - \mu_{.2} = 0$, or as $\mu_{.2} - \mu_{.1} = 0$. In terms of *contrast coefficients*, these three contrasts for a simple or pairwise contrast could be written in the form of a table as in Table 2.1.

TABLE 2.1

Contract Coefficients for Simple or Pairwise Contrasts

	c_1	c_2	c_3
ψ_1: $\mu_{.1} - \mu_{.2} = 0$	+1	−1	0
ψ_2: $\mu_{.1} - \mu_{.3} = 0$	+1	0	−1
ψ_3: $\mu_{.2} - \mu_{.3} = 0$	0	+1	−1

where each contrast (i.e., ψ_1, ψ_2, ψ_3) is read across the table (left to right) to determine its contrast coefficients (i.e., c_1, c_2, c_3). For example, the first contrast, ψ_1, does not involve Group 3 because that contrast coefficient is zero (see c_3 for ψ_1), but does involve Groups 1 and 2 because those contrast coefficients are not zero (see c_1 and c_2 for ψ_1). The contrast coefficients are +1 for Group 1 (see c_1) and −1 for Group 2 (see c_2); consequently we are interested in examining the difference between the means of Groups 1 and 2.

Written in long form so that we can see where the contrast coefficients come from, the three contrasts are as follows:

$$\psi_1 = (+1)\mu_{.1} + (-1)\mu_{.2} + (0)\mu_{.3} = \mu_{.1} - \mu_{.2}$$

$$\psi_2 = (+1)\mu_{.1} + (0)\mu_{.2} + (-1)\mu_{.3} = \mu_{.1} - \mu_{.3}$$

$$\psi_3 = (0)\mu_{.1} + (+1)\mu_{.2} + (-1)\mu_{.3} = \mu_{.2} - \mu_{.3}$$

An easy way to remember the number of possible unique pairwise contrasts that could be written is ½[(J)(J – 1)] or $\left[(J)(J-1)\right]/2$. Thus for $J = 3$, the number of possible unique pairwise contrasts is 3, whereas for $J = 4$ the number of such contrasts is 6 (or ½[(4)(4 – 1)] = ½(4)(3) = ½(12) = 6).

A **complex contrast** is a comparison involving more than two means. Continuing with the example of $J = 3$ groups, we might be interested in testing the contrast of $\mu_{.1} - \left(\frac{1}{2}\right)(\mu_{.2} + \mu_{.3})$ [which could also be written as $\mu_{.1} - \left(\frac{\mu_{.2} + \mu_{.3}}{2}\right)$]. This contrast is a comparison of the mean for Group 1 (i.e., μ_1) with the average of the means for Groups 2 and 3 [i.e., $\left(\frac{\mu_{.2} + \mu_{.3}}{2}\right)$]. In terms of contrast coefficients, this contrast would be written as seen in Table 12.2.

TABLE 12.2

Complex Contract Coefficients

	c_1	c_2	c_3
$\psi_4 : \mu_{.1} - \frac{\mu_{.2}}{2} - \frac{\mu_{.3}}{2} = 0$	+1	–1/2	–1/2

Written in long form so that we can see where the contrast coefficients come from, this complex contrast is as follows:

$$\psi_4 = (+1)\mu_{.1} + \left(-\frac{1}{2}\right)\mu_{.2} + \left(-\frac{1}{2}\right)\mu_{.3}$$

$$\psi_4 = \mu_{.1} + \left(-\frac{1}{2}\right)\mu_{.2} + \left(-\frac{1}{2}\right)\mu_{.3}$$

$$\psi_4 = \mu_{.1} + \left(-\frac{\mu_{.2}}{2}\right) + \left(-\frac{\mu_{.3}}{2}\right) = 0$$

The number of unique complex contrasts is greater than ½[J (J – 1)], when J is at least 4. *In other words, the number of such contrasts that could be formed can be quite large when there are more than three groups.* It should be noted that the *total number of unique pairwise and complex contrasts is* $\left[1 + \left(\frac{1}{2}\right)(3^J - 1) - 2^J\right]$ (Keppel & Wickens, 2004). Thus for $J = 4$, one could form 25 total contrasts, $\left[1 + \left(\frac{1}{2}\right)(3^4 - 1) - 2^4\right] = 1 + \frac{(81-1)}{2} - 16 = 1 + 40 - 16 = 25$.

Many of the multiple comparison procedures are based on the same test statistic, which we introduce here as the **standard** ***t***. The **standard** ***t*** **ratio for a contrast** is given as follows:

$$t = \frac{\psi'}{s_{\psi'}}$$

Where $s_{\psi'}$ represents the standard error of the contrast as follows:

$$s_{\psi'} = \sqrt{MS_{error} \sum_{j=1}^{J} \left(\frac{c_j^2}{n_j}\right)}$$

where the prime (i.e.,′) indicates that this is a sample estimate of the population value of the contrast (i.e., based on sample data), and n_j refers to the number of observations in group j.

12.1.1.2 Planned Versus Post Hoc Comparisons

This section examines specific types of contrasts or comparisons. One way of classifying contrasts is whether the contrasts are formulated prior to the research or following a significant omnibus F test. **Planned contrasts** (also known as specific or *a priori* contrasts) involve particular comparisons that the researcher is interested in examining *prior* to data collection. These planned contrasts are generally based on theory, previous research, and/or specific hypotheses. Here the researcher is interested in certain specific contrasts *a priori*, where the number of such contrasts is usually small. *Planned contrasts are done without regard to the result of the omnibus F test (i.e., whether or not the overall F test is statistically significant).* In other words, the researcher is interested in certain specific contrasts, but not in the omnibus F test that examines all possible contrasts. In this situation the researcher could care less about the multitude of possible contrasts and need not even examine the overall F test; rather, the concern is only with a few contrasts of substantive interest. In addition, the researcher may not be as concerned with the family-wise error rate for planned comparisons because only a few of them will actually be carried out. Fewer planned comparisons are usually conducted (due to their specificity) than post hoc comparisons (due to their generality), so planned contrasts generally yield narrower confidence intervals, are more powerful, and have a higher likelihood of a Type I error than post hoc comparisons.

Post hoc contrasts are formulated such that the researcher provides no advance specification of the actual contrasts to be tested. This type of contrast is done *only* following a statistically significant omnibus F test. Post hoc is Latin for "after the fact," referring to contrasts tested after a statistically significant omnibus F in the ANOVA. Here the researcher may want to take the family-wise error rate into account somehow to achieve better overall Type I error protection. Post hoc contrasts are also known as *unplanned, a posteriori,* or *postmortem contrasts.* It should be noted that most MCPs (with the exception of post hoc contrasts) are not derived or based on finding a statistically significant F in the ANOVA.

12.1.1.3 The Type I Error Rate

The goal of multiple comparison procedures is to help ensure that some error rate is maintained and not exceeded so that we do not make a Type I error. **Type I error,** as you recall, is the probability of incorrectly rejecting a true null hypothesis. Type I error is sometimes referred to as **false positive**. Thus, when multiple comparisons are conducted, there is an increased chance of Type I error—or increased chance of false positives. The more multiple comparisons conducted, the higher the chance that there is a false positive—i.e., the higher the probability that a null comparison will be identified as statistically significant. The **false discovery rate** is the rate that comparisons identified as statistically significant are truly null (i.e., not statistically significant)—i.e., the ratio of the number of false positives to the number of total positives.

How does the researcher deal with the family-wise Type I error rate? Depending on the multiple comparison procedure selected, one may either *set alpha for each contrast* or *set alpha for a family of contrasts.* In the former category (i.e., alpha for each contrast), alpha is set for each individual contrast. The MCPs in this category are known as **contrast-based**. We designate the alpha level for contrast-based procedures as α_{pc}, as it represents the **per contrast** Type I error rate. Thus, alpha per contrast (i.e., α_{pc}) represents the *probability of making a Type I error (or false positive) for that particular contrast*.

In the latter category (i.e., alpha for a family of contrasts), alpha is set for a family or set of contrasts. The MCPs in this category are known as **family-wise**. Controlling for family-wise error controls for the probability of one or more false positives out of all comparison tests performed. We designate the alpha level for family-wise procedures as α_{fw}, as it represents the family-wise Type I error rate. Thus α_{fw} represents the *probability of making at least one Type I error in the family or set of contrasts*. When *all* the null hypotheses are true, the false discovery rate equals the family-wise error rate. When not all the null hypotheses are true, controlling for the family-wise error rate also controls the false discovery rate.

For **orthogonal (or independent or unrelated) contrasts**, the following property holds:

$$\alpha_{fw} = 1 - \left(1 - \alpha_{pc}\right)^{c}$$

where $c = J - 1$ orthogonal contrasts (as defined in the next section). For **nonorthogonal (or related or oblique) contrasts**, this property is more complicated, so we simply say the following:

$$\alpha_{fw} \leq c\alpha_{pc}$$

These properties should be familiar from the discussion in Chapter 11, where we were looking at the probability of a Type I error in the use of multiple independent *t* tests.

12.1.1.4 Orthogonal Contrasts

Let us begin this section by defining orthogonal contrasts. A set of contrasts is **orthogonal** if they represent nonredundant and independent (if the usual ANOVA assumptions are met) sources of variation. For *J* groups, you will only be able to construct $J - 1$ orthogonal contrasts in a set. However, more than one set of orthogonal contrasts may exist. Note that although the contrasts *within* each set are orthogonal, contrasts *across* such sets may not be orthogonal.

For purposes of simplicity, we first consider the **equal *n*'s or balanced case** (in other words, the sample sizes are the same for each group). *With equal observations per group, two contrasts are defined to be orthogonal if the products of their contrast coefficients sum to zero.* That is, two contrasts are orthogonal if the following holds:

$$\sum_{j=1}^{J}\left(c_j c_{j'}\right) = c_1 c_{1'} + c_2 c_{2'} + \ldots + c_J c_{J'} = 0$$

where *j* and *j*′ represent two distinct contrasts. Thus we see that orthogonality depends on the contrast coefficients, the c_j and *not* the group means, the $\mu_{.j}$.

For example, if $J = 3$, then we can form a set of two orthogonal contrasts. One such set is in Table 12.3. In this set of contrasts, the first contrast (ψ_1) compares the mean of Group 1 ($c_1 = +1$) to the mean of Group 2 ($c_2 = -1$). The second contrast (ψ_2) compares the average of the means of Group 1 $\left(c_1 = +\tfrac{1}{2}\right)$ and Group 2 $\left(c_2 = +\tfrac{1}{2}\right)$ to the mean of Group 3 $\left(c_3 = -1\right)$.

TABLE 12.3

Orthogonal Contrast

	c_1	c_2	c_3	
$\psi_1: \mu_{.1} - \mu_{.2} = 0$	+1	−1	0	
$\psi_2: \frac{1}{2}\mu_{.1} + \frac{1}{2}\mu_{.2} - \mu_{.3} = 0$	+½	+½	−1	
$\sum_{j=1}^{J}(c_j c_{j'}) =$	+½	−½	0	= 0

Thus, plugging these values into our equation produces the following:

$$\sum_{j=1}^{J}\left(c_j c_{j'}\right) = c_1 c_{1'} + c_2 c_{2'} + c_3 c_{3'}$$

$$\sum_{j=1}^{J}\left(c_j c_{j'}\right) = (+1)\left(+\frac{1}{2}\right) + (-1)\left(+\frac{1}{2}\right) + (0)(-1) = \left(+\frac{1}{2}\right) + \left(-\frac{1}{2}\right) + 0 = 0$$

If the sum of the contrast coefficient products for a set of contrasts is equal to zero, then we define this as an orthogonal set of contrasts.

A set of two contrasts that are *not* orthogonal is in Table 12.4, where we see that the set of contrasts does *not* sum to zero.

TABLE 12.4

Nonorthogonal Contrasts

	c_1	c_2	c_3	
$\psi_3: \mu_{.1} - \mu_{.2} = 0$	+1	−1	0	
$\psi_4: \mu_{.1} - \mu_{.3} = 0$	+1	0	−1	
$\sum_{j=1}^{J}(c_j c_{j'}) =$	+1	0	0	= +1

Thus, plugging these values into our equation produces the following, where we see that the product of the contrasts also does not sum to zero.

$$\sum_{j=1}^{J}\left(c_j c_{j'}\right) = c_1 c_{1'} + c_2 c_{2'} + c_3 c_{3'}$$

$$\sum_{j=1}^{J}\left(c_j c_{j'}\right) = (+1)(+1) + (-1)(0) + (0)(-1) = (+1) + 0 + 0 = +1$$

Consider a situation (Table 12.5) where there are three groups and we decide to form three pairwise contrasts, knowing full well that they cannot all be orthogonal to one another. For this set of contrasts, the first contrast (ψ_1) compares the mean of Group 1 ($c_1 = +1$) to the mean of Group 2 ($c_2 = -1$). The second contrast (ψ_2) compares the mean of Group 2 ($c_2 = +1$) to the mean of Group 3 ($c_3 = -1$), and the third contrast compares the mean of Group 1 ($c_1 = +1$) to the mean of Group 3 ($c_3 = -1$).

TABLE 12.5

Nonorthogonal Contrasts

	c_1	c_2	c_3
ψ_1: $\mu_{.1} - \mu_{.2} = 0$	+1	−1	0
ψ_2: $\mu_{.2} - \mu_{.3} = 0$	0	+1	−1
ψ_3: $\mu_{.1} - \mu_{.3} = 0$	+1	0	−1

Say that the group population means are $\mu_{.1} = 30$, $\mu_{.2} = 24$, and $\mu_{.3} = 20$. We find $\psi_1 = 6$ for the first contrast (i.e., ψ_1: $\mu_{.1} - \mu_{.2} = 30 - 24 = 6$), and $\psi_2 = 4$ for the second contrast (i.e., ψ_2: $\mu_{.2} - \mu_{.3} = 24 - 20 = 4$). Because these three contrasts are not orthogonal and contain totally redundant information about these means, $\psi_3 = 10$ for the third contrast by definition (i.e., ψ_3: $\mu_{.1} - \mu_{.3} = 30 - 20 = 10$). Thus, the third contrast contains no additional information beyond that contained in the first two contrasts.

Finally, for the unequal n's or unbalanced case, two contrasts are orthogonal if the following holds:

$$\sum_{j=1}^{J}\left(\frac{c_j c_{j'}}{n_j}\right)=0$$

The denominator n_j makes it more difficult to find an orthogonal set of contrasts that is of any interest to the applied researcher (see Pedhazur, 1997, for an example).

12.1.2 Selected Multiple Comparison Procedures

This section considers a selection of multiple comparison procedures (MCP). These represent the "best" procedures in some sense, in terms of ease of utility, popularity, and control of Type I and Type II error rates. Other procedures are briefly mentioned. In the interest of consistency, each procedure is discussed in the hypothesis testing situation based on a test statistic. Most, but not all, of these procedures can also be formulated as confidence intervals (sometimes called a **critical difference**), although these will not be discussed here. The first few procedures discussed are for planned comparisons, whereas the remainder of the section is devoted to post hoc comparisons. For each MCP, we describe its major characteristics, and then present the test statistic with an example using the data from Chapter 11.

Unless otherwise specified, each MCP makes the standard assumptions of normality, homogeneity of variance, and independence of observations. Some of the procedures do have additional restrictions, such as equal n's per group. Throughout this section we also presume that a two-tailed alternative hypothesis is of interest, although some of the MCPs can also be used with a one-tailed alternative hypothesis. In general, the MCPs are fairly robust to nonnormality (but not for extreme cases), but are not as robust to departures from homogeneity of variance or from independence (e.g., Pavur, 1988).

12.1.2.1 Planned Analysis of Trend

Trend analysis is a *planned MCP* useful when the groups represent different quantitative levels of a factor (i.e., an interval or ratio level independent variable). Examples of such a factor might be age, drug dosage, and different amounts of instruction, practice, or trials. Here, the researcher is interested in whether the sample means vary with a change in the amount of the independent variable. *We define trend analysis in the form of orthogonal polynomials, and assume that the levels of the independent variable are equally spaced (i.e., same distances between the levels of the independent variable, such as 100, 200, 300, and 400cc), and that the number of observations per group is the same.* This is the standard case; other cases are briefly discussed at the end of this section.

Orthogonal polynomial contrasts use the standard t test statistic, which is compared to the critical values of $\pm_{\alpha/2}t_{df(error)}$ obtained from the t table in Appendix Table A.2. The form of the contrasts is a bit different and requires a bit of discussion. *Orthogonal polynomial contrasts incorporate two concepts, orthogonal contrasts (recall these are unrelated or independent contrasts) and polynomial regression.* For J groups, there can be only $J - 1$ orthogonal contrasts in a set. In *polynomial regression*, we have terms in the model for a linear trend, a quadratic trend, a cubic trend, and so on. For example, linear trend is represented by a straight line (no bends), quadratic trend by a curve with one bend (e.g., U or upside-down U shapes), and cubic trend by a curve with two bends (e.g., S shape).

Now put those two ideas together. *A set of orthogonal contrasts can be formed where the first contrast evaluates a linear trend, the second a quadratic trend, the third a cubic trend, and so forth.* Thus for J groups, the highest order polynomial that can be formed is $J - 1$. With four groups, for example, one could form a set of three orthogonal contrasts to assess linear, quadratic, and cubic trend.

You may be wondering just how these contrasts are formed. For $J = 4$ groups, the contrast coefficients for the linear, quadratic, and cubic trends are found in Table 12.6.

TABLE 12.6

Orthogonal Polynomial Contrasts

	c_1	c_2	c_3	c_4
ψ_{linear}	−3	−1	+1	+3
$\psi_{quadratic}$	+1	−1	−1	+1
ψ_{cubic}	−1	+3	−3	+1

Where the contrasts can be written out as follows:

$$\psi_{linear} = (-3)\mu_{.1} + (-1)\mu_{.2} + (+1)\mu_{.3} + (+3)\mu_{.4}$$

$$\psi_{quadratic} = (+1)\mu_{.1} + (-1)\mu_{.2} + (-1)\mu_{.3} + (+1)\mu_{.4}$$

$$\psi_{cubic} = (-1)\mu_{.1} + (+3)\mu_{.2} + (-3)\mu_{.3} + (+1)\mu_{.4}$$

These contrast coefficients, for a number of different values of J, can be found in Appendix Table A.6. If you look in the table of contrast coefficients for values of J greater than 6, you see that the coefficients for the higher-order polynomials are not included. As an example, for $J = 7$, coefficients only up through a quintic trend are included. Although they could easily be derived and tested, these higher-order polynomials are usually not of interest to the researcher. In fact, it is rare to find anyone interested in polynomials beyond the cubic because they are difficult to understand and interpret (although statistically sophisticated, they say little to the applied researcher as the results must be interpreted in values that are highly complex). The contrasts are typically tested sequentially beginning with the linear trend and proceeding to higher-order trends (cubic then quadratic).

Using the example data on the elite athletes from Chapter 11, let us test for linear, quadratic, and cubic trends. While trend analysis may not be relevant for this data because the groups do not represent different quantitative levels of type of sport, we'll walk through the example for illustrative purposes and assume the levels are appropriate for trend analysis. Because $J = 4$, we can use the contrast coefficients given previously. The following are the computations, based on these mean values, to test the trend analysis. The critical values (where df_{error} is calculated as $N - J$ or $32 - 4 = 28$) are determined to be as follows: $\pm_{\alpha/2}t_{df(error)} = \pm_{.025}t_{28} = \pm 2.048$. The standard error for *linear trend* is computed as follows (where $n_j = 8$ for each of the $J = 4$ groups; MS_{error} was computed in the previous chapter and found to be 36.1116). Recall that the contrast equation for the linear trend is

$$\psi_{linear} = (-3)\mu_{.1} + (-1)\mu_{.2} + (+1)\mu_{.3} + (+3)\mu_{.4}$$

and thus these are the c_j values in the equation below (−3, −1, +1, and +3, respectively).

$$s_{\psi'} = \sqrt{MS_{error}\sum_{j=1}^{J}\left(\frac{c_j^2}{n_j}\right)}$$

$$s_{\psi'} = \sqrt{36.1116\left(\frac{(-3)^2}{8} + \frac{(-1)^2}{8} + \frac{(+1)^2}{8} + \frac{(+3)^2}{8}\right)} = \sqrt{36.1116\left(\frac{9}{8} + \frac{1}{8} + \frac{1}{8} + \frac{9}{8}\right)} = 9.5015$$

The standard error for *quadratic trend* is determined similarly. Recall that the contrast equation for the quadratic trend is

$$\psi_{quadratic} = (+1)\mu_{.1} + (-1)\mu_{.2} + (-1)\mu_{.3} + (+1)\mu_{.4}$$

and thus these are the c_j values in the equation below (+1, −1, −1, and +1, respectively).

$$s_{\psi'} = \sqrt{MS_{error}\sum_{j=1}^{J}\left(\frac{c_j^2}{n_j}\right)}$$

$$s_{\psi'} = \sqrt{36.1116\left(\frac{(+1)^2}{8} + \frac{(-1)^2}{8} + \frac{(-1)^2}{8} + \frac{(+1)^2}{8}\right)} = \sqrt{36.1116\left(\frac{1}{8} + \frac{1}{8} + \frac{1}{8} + \frac{1}{8}\right)} = 4.2492$$

The standard error for *cubic trend* is computed similarly. Recall that the contrast equation for the cubic trend is

$$\psi_{cubic} = (-1)\mu_{.1} + (+3)\mu_{.2} + (-3)\mu_{.3} + (+1)\mu_{.4}$$

and thus these are the c_j values in the equation below (−1, +3, −3, and +1, respectively).

$$s_{\psi'} = \sqrt{MS_{error} \sum_{j=1}^{J} \left(\frac{c_j^2}{n_j} \right)}$$

$$s_{\psi'} = \sqrt{36.1116 \left(\frac{(-1)^2}{8} + \frac{(+3)^2}{8} + \frac{(-3)^2}{8} + \frac{(+1)^2}{8} \right)} = \sqrt{36.1116 \left(\frac{1}{8} + \frac{9}{8} + \frac{9}{8} + \frac{1}{8} \right)} = 9.5015$$

Recall the following means for each group (as presented in the previous chapter; Table 12.7).

TABLE 12.7

Data and Summary Statistics for the Elite Athlete Example

	Psychological Distress by Type of Sport				
	Group 1: Movement (e.g., dance)	Group 2: Target (e.g., golf)	Group 3: Fielding (e.g., baseball)	Group 4: Territory (e.g., football)	Overall
	15	20	10	30	
	10	13	24	22	
	12	9	29	26	
	8	22	12	20	
	21	24	27	29	
	7	25	21	28	
	13	18	25	25	
	3	12	14	15	
Means	11.1250	17.8750	20.2500	24.3750	18.4063
Variances	30.1250	35.2679	53.0714	25.9821	56.4425

Thus, using the *contrast coefficients* (represented by the constant *c* values in the numerator of each term) and the values of the means for each of the four groups (represented by $\bar{Y}_{.1}$, $\bar{Y}_{.2}$, $\bar{Y}_{.3}$, $\bar{Y}_{.4}$), the test statistics are computed as follows:

$$t_{linear} = \frac{\psi_{linear}}{s_{\psi'}} = \frac{-3\bar{Y}_{.1} - 1\bar{Y}_{.2} + 1\bar{Y}_{.3} + 3\bar{Y}_{.4}}{s_{\psi'}}$$

$$t_{linear} = \frac{-3(11.1250) - 1(17.8750) + 1(20.2500) + 3(24.3750)}{9.5015} = 4.4335$$

$$t_{quadratic} = \frac{\psi_{quadratic}}{s_{\psi'}} = \frac{1\bar{Y}_{.1} - 1\bar{Y}_{.2} - 1\bar{Y}_{.3} + 1\bar{Y}_{.4}}{s_{\psi'}}$$

$$t_{quadratic} = \frac{1(11.1250) - 1(17.8750) - 1(20.2500) + 1(24.3750)}{4.2492} = -0.6178$$

$$t_{cubic} = \frac{\psi_{cubic}}{s_{\psi'}} = \frac{-1\bar{Y}_{.1} + 3\bar{Y}_{.2} - 3\bar{Y}_{.3} + 1\bar{Y}_{.4}}{s_{\psi'}}$$

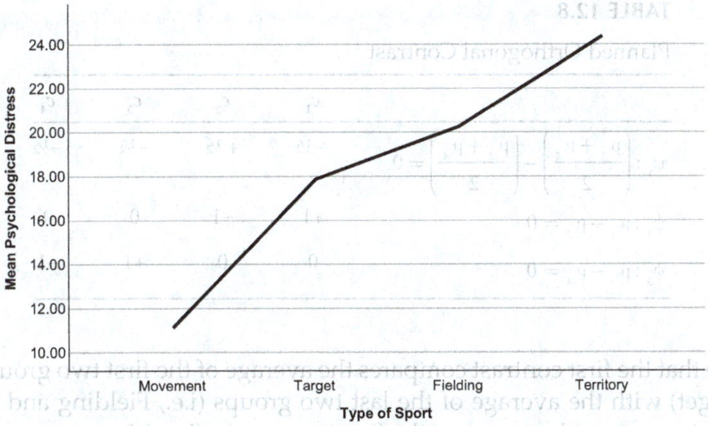

FIGURE 12.1
Profile plot for psychological distress example.

$$t_{cubic} = \frac{-1(11.1250)+3(17.8750)-3(20.2500)+1(24.3750)}{9.5015} = 0.6446$$

The *t* test statistic for the linear trend exceeds the *t* critical value. Thus, we see that there is a statistically significant *linear trend* in the means, but no significant *higher-order* trend (in other words, no significant quadratic or cubic trend). This should not be surprising as shown in the profile plot of the means of Figure 12.1, where there is a very strong linear trend, and that is about it. In other words, there is a steady increase in mean psychological distress as the type of sport increases from movement to target, fielding, and territory. Always plot the means so that you can interpret the results of the contrasts.

Let us make some final points about orthogonal polynomial contrasts. First, be particularly careful about extrapolating beyond the range of the levels investigated. The trend may or may not be the same outside of this range; that is, given only those sample means, we have no way of knowing what the trend is outside of the range of levels investigated. Second, in the unequal *n*'s or unbalanced case, it becomes difficult to formulate a set of orthogonal contrasts that make any sense to the researcher. See the discussion in the next section on planned orthogonal contrasts, as well as Kirk (2013). Third, when the levels are not equally spaced, this needs to be taken into account in the contrast coefficients (Kirk, 2013).

12.1.2.2 Planned Orthogonal Contrasts

Planned orthogonal contrasts (POC) are MCPs where the contrasts are defined ahead of time by the researcher (i.e., planned) and the set of contrasts are orthogonal (or unrelated). The POC method is a **contrast-based procedure** where the researcher is not concerned with control of the family-wise Type I error rate across the set of contrasts. The set of contrasts are *orthogonal*, so the number of contrasts should be small, and concern with the family-wise error rate is lessened.

Computationally, planned orthogonal contrasts use the standard *t* test statistic that is compared to the critical values of $\pm_{\alpha/2} t_{df(error)}$ obtained from the *t* table in Appendix Table A.2. Using the example dataset from Chapter 11, let us find a set of orthogonal contrasts and complete the computations. Since $J = 4$, we can find at most a set of three (or $J - 1$) orthogonal contrasts. One orthogonal set that seems reasonable for these data is in Table 2.8.

TABLE 12.8
Planned Orthogonal Contrast

	c_1	c_2	c_3	c_4
$\psi_1: \left(\frac{\mu_{.1}+\mu_{.2}}{2}\right)-\left(\frac{\mu_{.3}+\mu_{.4}}{2}\right)=0$	+ ½	+ ½	−½	−½
$\psi_2: \mu_{.1}-\mu_{.2}=0$	+1	−1	0	0
$\psi_3: \mu_{.3}-\mu_{.4}=0$	0	0	+1	−1

Here we see that the first contrast compares the average of the first two groups (i.e., Movement and Target) with the average of the last two groups (i.e., Fielding and Territory), the second contrast compares the means of the first two groups (i.e., Movement and Target), and the third contrast compares the means of the last two groups (Fielding and Territory). Note that the design is balanced (i.e., the equal n's case as all groups had a sample size of 8). What follows are the computations. The critical values are: $\pm_{\alpha/2}t_{df(error)} = \pm_{.025}t_{28} = \pm 2.048$.

The standard error for contrast 1 is computed as follows (where n_j = 8 for each of the J = 4 groups; MS_{error} was computed in the previous chapter and found to be 36.1116). The equation for contrast one is $\psi_1: \left(\frac{\mu_{.1}+\mu_{.2}}{2}\right)-\left(\frac{\mu_{.3}+\mu_{.4}}{2}\right)=0$ and thus the c_j values in the equation below (+1/2, +1/2, −1/2, −1/2, respectively, and these values are then squared which results in the value of .25).

$$s_{\psi'} = \sqrt{MS_{error}\sum_{j=1}^{J}\left(\frac{c_j^2}{n_j}\right)}$$

$$s_{\psi'} = \sqrt{36.1116\left(\frac{.25}{8}+\frac{.25}{8}+\frac{.25}{8}+\frac{.25}{8}\right)} = 2.1246$$

Similarly, the standard errors for contrasts 2 and 3 are computed below:

$$s_{\psi'} = \sqrt{MS_{error}\sum_{j=1}^{J}\left(\frac{c_j^2}{n_j}\right)} = \sqrt{36.1116\left(\frac{1}{8}+\frac{1}{8}\right)} = 3.0046$$

The **test statistics** are computed as follows:

$$t_1 = \frac{(1/2)\bar{Y}_{.1}+(1/2)\bar{Y}_{.2}-(1/2)\bar{Y}_{.3}-(1/2)\bar{Y}_{.4}}{s_{\psi'}}$$

$$t_1 = \frac{(1/2)(11.1250)+(1/2)(17.8750)-(1/2)(20.2500)-(1/2)(24.3750)}{2.1246} = -3.6772$$

$$t_2 = \frac{\bar{Y}_{.1}-\bar{Y}_{.2}}{s_{\psi'}} = \frac{11.1250-17.8750}{3.0046} = -2.2466$$

$$t_3 = \frac{\bar{Y}_3 - \bar{Y}_4}{s_{\psi'}} = \frac{20.2500 - 24.3750}{3.0046} = -1.3729$$

The result for contrast 1 is that the combined first two groups (Movement and Target) have statistically significantly lower psychological distress, on average, than the combined last two groups (Fielding and Territory). The result for contrast 2 is that Movement and Target groups are statistically significantly different from one another, on average. The result for contrast 3 is that the means of Fielding and Territory are not statistically significantly different from one another.

There is a practical problem with this procedure because (a) the contrasts that are of interest to the researcher may not necessarily be orthogonal, or (b) the researcher may not be interested in all of the contrasts of a particular orthogonal set. Another problem already mentioned occurs when the design is unbalanced, where an orthogonal set of contrasts may be constructed at the expense of meaningful contrasts. Our advice is simple.

1. If the contrasts you are interested in are not orthogonal, then use another MCP.
2. If you are not interested in all of the contrasts of an orthogonal set, then use another MCP.
3. If your design is not balanced and the orthogonal contrasts formed are not meaningful, then use another MCP.

In each case you need a different *planned* MCP. We recommend using one of the following procedures discussed later in this chapter: the Dunnett, Dunn (Bonferroni), or Dunn–Sidak procedure.

We defined the POC as a *contrast-based procedure*. One could also consider an alternative family-wise method where the α_{pc} level is divided among the contrasts in the set. This procedure is defined by $\alpha_{pc} = {}^{\alpha_{fw}}/_{c}$, where c is the number of orthogonal contrasts in the set (i.e., $c = J - 1$). As we show later, this borrows a concept from the Dunn (Bonferroni) procedure. If the variances are not equal across the groups, several approximate solutions have been proposed that take the individual group variances into account (Kirk, 2013).

12.1.2.3 Planned Contrasts With Reference Group: Dunnett Method

A third method of planned comparisons is attributed to Dunnett (1955) and thus referred to as the Dunnett method. It is designed to test pairwise contrasts where a reference group (e.g., a control or baseline group) is compared to each of the other $J - 1$ groups. Thus, a family of *prespecified* pairwise contrasts is to be evaluated. The Dunnett method is a *family-wise MCP* and is slightly more powerful than the Dunn procedure (another planned family-wise MCP). The test statistic is the standard t except that the standard error is simplified as follows:

$$s_{\psi'} = \sqrt{MS_{error}\left(\frac{1}{n_c} + \frac{1}{n_j}\right)}$$

where c is the reference group and j is the group to which it is being compared. The test statistic is compared to the critical values $\pm_{\alpha/2} t_{df(error),J-1}$, obtained from the Dunnett table located in Appendix Table A.7.

Using the example dataset, compare Group 1, the movement sport (used as a reference or baseline group), to each of the other three types of sports. The contrasts are found in Table 12.9.

TABLE 12.9
Planned Contrasts With Reference Group: Dunnett Method

	c_1	c_2	c_3	c_4
ψ_1: $\mu_{.1} - \mu_{.2} = 0$	+1	−1	0	0
ψ_2: $\mu_{.1} - \mu_{.3} = 0$	+1	0	−1	0
ψ_4: $\mu_{.1} - \mu_{.4} = 0$	+1	0	0	−1

The critical values are as follows: $\pm_{\alpha/2}t_{df(error),J-1} = \pm_{.025}t_{28,3} \approx \pm 2.48$

The standard error is computed as follows (where $n_c = 8$ for the reference group; $n_j = 8$ for each of the other groups; MS_{error} was computed in the previous chapter and found to be 36.1116).

$$s_{\psi'} = \sqrt{MS_{error}\left(\frac{1}{n_c} + \frac{1}{n_j}\right)} = \sqrt{36.1116\left(\frac{1}{8} + \frac{1}{8}\right)} = 3.00$$

The test statistics for the three contrasts (i.e., Group 1 to Group 2; Group 1 to Group 3; and Group 1 to Group 4) are computed as follows:

$$\textit{Movement to Target: } t_1 = \frac{\bar{Y}_{.1} - \bar{Y}_{.2}}{s_{\psi'}} = \frac{11.1250 - 17.8750}{3.0046} = -2.2466$$

$$\textit{Movement to Target: } t_2 = \frac{\bar{Y}_{.1} - \bar{Y}_{.3}}{s_{\psi'}} = \frac{11.1250 - 20.2500}{3.0046} = -3.0370$$

$$\textit{Movement to Fielding: } t_3 = \frac{\bar{Y}_{.1} - \bar{Y}_{.4}}{s_{\psi'}} = \frac{11.1250 - 24.3750}{3.0046} = -4.4099$$

Comparing the test statistics to the critical values, we see that the second group (i.e., Target) is not statistically significantly different from group one (i.e., Movement), but the third (Fielding) and fourth (Territory) groups are significantly different from group one (i.e., Movement).

If the variance of the reference group is different from the variances of the other $J - 1$ groups, then a modification of this method is described in Dunnett (1964). For related procedures that are less sensitive to unequal group variances, see Wilcox (1987) or Wilcox (1996) (e.g., variation of the Dunnett T3 procedure).

12.1.2.4 Other Planned Contrasts: Dunn (or Bonferroni) and Dunn–Sidak Methods

The Dunn (1961) procedure (commonly attributed to Dunn as the developer is unknown), also often called the **Bonferroni procedure** (because it is based on the Bonferroni inequality), is a planned family-wise MCP. *It is designed to test either pairwise or complex contrasts for balanced or unbalanced designs.* Thus this MCP is very flexible and may be used to test any planned contrast of interest. Dunn's method uses the standard t test statistic with one important exception. The alpha level is split up among the set of planned contrasts. Typically the per contrast alpha level (denoted as α_{pc}) is set at α/c, where c is the number of contrasts. That is, $\alpha_{pc} = \alpha_{fw}/c$. According to this rationale, the family-wise Type I error rate (denoted as α_{fw}) will be maintained at alpha. For example, if $\alpha_{fw} = .05$ is desired and there are five contrasts to be tested, then each contrast would be tested at the .01 level of significance (.05/5 = .01). We are reminded that alpha need not be distributed equally among the set of contrasts, as long as the sum of the individual α_{pc} terms is equal to α_{fw} (Keppel & Wickens, 2004; Rosenthal & Rosnow, 1985).

Computationally, the Dunn method uses the standard t test statistic, which is compared to the critical values of $\pm_{\alpha/c}t_{df(error)}$ for a two-tailed test obtained from the table in Appendix Table A.8. The table takes the number of contrasts into account without requiring you to physically split up the α. Using the example dataset from Chapter 11, for comparison purposes, let us test the same set of three orthogonal contrasts we evaluated with the POC method. These contrasts are in Table 12.10.

TABLE 12.10

Dunn Method

	c_1	c_2	c_3	c_4
$\psi_1: \left(\frac{\mu_{.1} + \mu_{.2}}{2}\right) - \left(\frac{\mu_{.3} + \mu_{.4}}{2}\right) = 0$	+ ½	+ ½	− ½	− ½
$\psi_2: \mu_{.1} - \mu_{.2} = 0$	+1	−1	0	0
$\psi_3: \mu_{.3} - \mu_{.4} = 0$	0	0	+1	−1

Below are the computations; the critical values include:

$$\pm_{\alpha/c}t_{df(error)} = \pm_{.05/3}t_{28} = \pm 2.539$$

The standard error for contrast 1 is computed as follows:

$$s_{\psi'} = \sqrt{MS_{error}\sum_{j=1}^{J}\left(\frac{c_j^2}{n_j}\right)} = \sqrt{36.1116\left(\frac{.25}{8} + \frac{.25}{8} + \frac{.25}{8} + \frac{.25}{8}\right)} = 2.1246$$

Similarly, the standard error for contrasts 2 and 3 is computed below:

$$s_{\psi'} = \sqrt{MS_{error}\sum_{j=1}^{J}\left(\frac{c_j^2}{n_j}\right)} = \sqrt{36.1116\left(\frac{1}{8} + \frac{1}{8}\right)} = 3.0046$$

The test statistics are computed as follows:

$$t_1 = \frac{(1/2)\bar{Y}_{.1} + (1/2)\bar{Y}_{.2} - (1/2)\bar{Y}_{.3} - (1/2)\bar{Y}_{.4}}{s_{\psi'}}$$

$$t_1 = \frac{(1/2)(11.1250) + (1/2)(17.8750) - (1/2)(20.2500) - (1/2)(24.3750)}{2.1246} = -3.6772$$

$$t_2 = \frac{\bar{Y}_{.1} + \bar{Y}_{.2}}{s_{\psi'}} = \frac{11.1250 - 17.8750}{3.0046} = -2.2466$$

$$t_3 = \frac{\bar{Y}_{.3} + \bar{Y}_{.4}}{s_{\psi'}} = \frac{20.2500 - 24.3750}{3.0046} = -1.3729$$

Notice that the test statistic values have not changed from the POC, but the critical value *has* changed. For this set of contrasts, then, we see the same results as were obtained via the POC procedure with the exception of contrast 2, which is now nonsignificant (i.e., only contrast 1 is significant). The reason for this difference lies in the critical values used, which were ±2.048 for the POC method and ±2.539 for the Dunn method. Here we see the conservative nature of the Dunn procedure because the critical value is larger than with the POC method, thus making it a bit more difficult to reject H_0.

The Dunn procedure is slightly conservative (i.e., not as powerful) in that the true α_{fw} may be less than the specified nominal α level. For example, if the nominal alpha (specified by the researcher) is .05, then the true alpha may be less than .05. *Thus when using the Dunn, you may be less likely to reject the null hypothesis (i.e., less likely to find a statistically significant contrast)*. A less conservative (i.e., more powerful) modification is known as the **Dunn-Sidak procedure** (Dunn, 1974; Sidak, 1967), and uses slightly different critical values. For more information see Kirk (2013), Keppel and Wickens (2004), and Wilcox (1987). The Bonferroni modification can also be applied to other MCPs.

12.1.2.5 Complex Post Hoc Contrasts: Scheffé and Kaiser-Bowden Methods

Another early MCP due to Scheffé (1953) is quite versatile. The Scheffé procedure can be used for any possible type of comparison, orthogonal or nonorthogonal, pairwise or complex, planned or post hoc, where the family-wise error rate is controlled. The Scheffé method is so general that the tests are quite conservative (i.e., less powerful), particularly for the pairwise contrasts. This is so because the family of contrasts for the Scheffé method consists of all possible linear comparisons. To control the Type I error rate for such a large family, the procedure has to be conservative (i.e., making it less likely to reject the null hypothesis if it is really true). *Thus we recommend the Scheffé method only for complex post hoc comparisons.*

The Scheffé procedure is the only MCP that is necessarily consistent with the results of the *F* ratio in the analysis of variance. If the *F* ratio is statistically significant, then this means that at least one contrast in the entire family of contrasts will be significant with the Scheffé method. Do not forget, however, that this family can be quite large and you may not even be interested in the contrast(s) that wind up being significant. If the *F* ratio is not statistically significant, then none of the contrasts in the family will be significant with the Scheffé method.

The test statistic for the Scheffé method is the standard t again. This is compared to the critical value $\sqrt{(J-1)\left({}_{\alpha}F_{J-1,df(error)}\right)}$ taken from the F table in Appendix Table A.4. In other words, the square root of the F critical value is adjusted by $J - 1$, which serves to increase the Scheffé critical value and make the procedure a more conservative one.

Consider a few example contrasts with the Scheffé method. Using the example data set from Chapter 11, for comparison purposes we test the same set of three orthogonal contrasts that were evaluated with the POC method. These contrasts are again as follows (Table 12.11).

TABLE 12.11
Scheffé Method

	c_1	c_2	c_3	c_4
$\psi_1: \left(\frac{\mu_{.1}+\mu_{.2}}{2}\right) - \left(\frac{\mu_{.3}+\mu_{.4}}{2}\right) = 0$	+ ½	+ ½	− ½	− ½
$\psi_2: \mu_{.1} - \mu_{.2} = 0$	+1	−1	0	0
$\psi_3: \mu_{.3} - \mu_{.4} = 0$	0	0	+1	−1

Below are the computations with the following critical value:

$$\sqrt{(J-1)\left({}_{\alpha}F_{J-1,df(error)}\right)} = \sqrt{(4-1)\left({}_{.05}F_{3,28}\right)} = \sqrt{(3)(2.95)} = 2.97$$

Standard error for contrast 1:

$$s_{\psi'} = \sqrt{MS_{error}\sum_{j=1}^{J}\left(\frac{c_j^2}{n_j}\right)} = \sqrt{36.1116\left(\frac{.25}{8}+\frac{.25}{8}+\frac{.25}{8}+\frac{.25}{8}\right)} = 2.1246$$

Standard error for contrasts 2 and 3:

$$s_{\psi'} = \sqrt{MS_{error}\left(\frac{1}{n_j}+\frac{1}{n_{j'}}\right)} = \sqrt{36.1116\left(\frac{1}{8}+\frac{1}{8}\right)} = 3.0046$$

The test statistics are computed as follows:

$$t_1 = \frac{(1/2)\bar{Y}_{.1} + (1/2)\bar{Y}_{.2} - (1/2)\bar{Y}_{.3} - (1/2)\bar{Y}_{.4}}{s_{\psi'}}$$

$$t_1 = \frac{(1/2)(11.1250) + (1/2)(17.8750) - (1/2)(20.2500) - (1/2)(24.3750)}{2.1246} = -3.6772$$

$$t_2 = \frac{\bar{Y}_{.1} + \bar{Y}_{.2}}{s_{\psi'}} = \frac{11.1250 - 17.8750}{3.0046} = -2.2466$$

$$t_3 = \frac{\bar{Y}_{.3} + \bar{Y}_{.4}}{s_{\psi'}} = \frac{20.2500 - 24.3750}{3.0046} = -1.3729$$

Using the Scheffé method, these results are precisely the same as those obtained via the Dunn procedure. There is somewhat of a difference in the critical values, which were 2.97 for the Scheffé method, 2.539 for the Dunn method, and 2.048 for the POC method. Here we see that the Scheffé procedure is even more conservative than the Dunn procedure, thus making it a bit more difficult to reject H_0.

For situations where the group variances are unequal, a modification of the Scheffé method less sensitive to unequal variances has been proposed by Brown and Forsythe (1974). Kaiser and Bowden (1983) found that the Brown-Forsythe procedure may cause the actual α level to exceed the nominal α level, and thus we recommend the Kaiser-Bowden modification. For more information see Kirk (2013), Wilcox (1987), and Wilcox (1996).

12.1.2.6 Simple Post Hoc Contrasts: Tukey HSD, Tukey-Kramer, Fisher LSD and Fisher-Hayter Tests

Tukey's (1953) honestly significant difference (HSD) test is one of the most popular post hoc MCPs. The HSD test is a family-wise procedure and is most appropriate for considering all pairwise contrasts with equal n's per group (i.e., a balanced design). The HSD test is sometimes referred to as the **studentized range test** because it is based on the sampling distribution of the studentized range statistic developed by William Sealy Gossett (forced to use the pseudonym "Student" by his employer, the Guinness brewery). For the traditional approach, the first step in the analysis is to rank order the means from largest ($\bar{Y}_{.1}$) to smallest ($\bar{Y}_{.J}$). The test statistic, or **studentized range statistic**, is computed as follows:

$$q_i = \frac{\bar{Y}_{.j} - \bar{Y}_{.j'}}{s_{\psi'}}$$

where

$$s_{\psi'} = \sqrt{\frac{MS_{error}}{n}}$$

and where i identifies the specific contrast, j and j = designate the two group means to be compared, and n represents the number of observations per group (equal n's per group is required). The test statistic is compared to the critical value $\pm\, {}_{\alpha}q_{df(error),\,J}$, where df_{error} is equal to $J\,(n - 1)$. The table for these critical values is given in Appendix Table A.9.

The first contrast involves a test of the largest pairwise difference in the set of J means (q_1) *(i.e., largest vs. smallest means)*. If these means are *not* statistically significantly different, then the analysis stops because no other pairwise difference could be significant. If these means *are* statistically significantly different, then we proceed to test the second pairwise difference involving the largest mean (i.e., q_2). Contrasts involving the largest mean are continued until a nonsignificant difference is found. Then the analysis picks up with the *second largest mean* and compares it with the smallest mean. Contrasts involving the second largest mean are continued until a nonsignificant difference is detected. The analysis continues with the *third largest mean* and the smallest mean, and so on, until it is obvious that no other pairwise contrast could be significant.

Finally, consider an example using the HSD procedure with the elite athlete data. Below are the computations, with the following critical value: $\pm {}_{\alpha}q_{df(error),J} = \pm {}_{.05}q_{28,4} \approx \pm 3.87$. The standard error is computed as follows where n represents the sample size per group:

$$s_{\psi'} = \sqrt{\frac{MS_{error}}{n}} = \sqrt{\frac{36.1116}{8}} = 2.1246$$

The test statistics are computed as follows:

Territory to Movement: $$q_1 = \frac{\bar{Y}_{.4} - \bar{Y}_{.1}}{s_{\psi'}} = \frac{24.3750 - 11.1250}{2.1246} = 6.2365$$

Territory to Target: $$q_2 = \frac{\bar{Y}_{.4} - \bar{Y}_{.2}}{s_{\psi'}} = \frac{24.3750 - 17.8750}{2.1246} = 3.0594$$

Fielding to Movement: $$q_3 = \frac{\bar{Y}_{.3} - \bar{Y}_{.1}}{s_{\psi'}} = \frac{20.2500 - 11.1250}{2.1246} = 4.2949$$

Fielding to Target: $$q_4 = \frac{\bar{Y}_{.3} - \bar{Y}_{.2}}{s_{\psi'}} = \frac{20.2500 - 17.8750}{2.1246} = 1.1179$$

Target to Movement: $$q_5 = \frac{\bar{Y}_{.2} - \bar{Y}_{.1}}{s_{\psi'}} = \frac{17.8750 - 11.1250}{2.1246} = 3.1771$$

Comparing the test statistic values to the critical value, these results indicate that the group means are significantly different for Groups 1 (Movement) and 4 (Territory) and for Groups 1 (Movement) and 3 (Fielding). Just for completeness, we examine the final possible pairwise contrast involving Groups 3 and 4. However, we already know from the results of previous contrasts that these means cannot possibly be significantly different. The test statistic result for this contrast is as follows:

Territory to Fielding: $$q_6 = \frac{\bar{Y}_{.4} - \bar{Y}_{.3}}{s_{\psi'}} = \frac{24.3750 - 20.2500}{2.1246} = 1.9415$$

Occasionally researchers need to summarize the results of their pairwise comparisons. Table 12.12 shows the results of Tukey's HSD contrasts for the example data. For ease of interpretation, the means are ordered from lowest to highest. The first row consists of the results for those contrasts that involve Group 1. Thus the mean for Group 1 (Movement) is statistically different from those of Groups 3 (Fielding) and 4 (Territory) only. None of the other pairwise contrasts were shown to be significant. Such a table could also be developed for other pairwise MCPs.

TABLE 12.12

Tukey HSD Contrast Test Statistics and Results

	Group 1: Movement	Group 2: Target	Group 3: Fielding	Group 4: Territory
Group 1 (mean = 11.1250)	–	3.1771	4.2949*	6.2365*
Group 2 (mean = 17.8750)		–	1.1179	3.0594
Group 3 (mean = 20.2500)			–	1.9415
Group 4 (mean = 24.3750)				–

$^{*} p < .05$; $_{.05}q_{28,4} = 3.87$

The HSD test has exact control of the family-wise error rate assuming normality, homogeneity, and equal n's (better than Dunn or Dunn-Sidak). The HSD procedure is more powerful than the Dunn (aka Bonferroni) or Scheffé procedures for testing all possible pairwise contrasts, although Dunn is more powerful for less than all possible pairwise contrasts. The HSD technique is the recommended MCP as a pairwise method in the equal n's situation and when there is homoscedasticity. The HSD test is reasonably robust to nonnormality, but not in extreme cases, and is not as robust as the Scheffé MCP.

There are several alternatives to the HSD for the unequal n's case. These include the Tukey-Kramer modification (Kramer, 1957; Tukey, 1953), which assumes normality and homogeneity. The Tukey-Kramer test statistic is the same as the Tukey HSD except that the standard error is computed as follows.

$$s_{\psi'} = \sqrt{MS_{error}\left[\frac{1}{2}\left(\frac{1}{n_1} + \frac{1}{n_2}\right)\right]}$$

The critical value is determined in the same way as with the Tukey HSD procedure.

If you are using SPSS to compute Tukey's MCP, you will find there are two options: Tukey and Tukey's b. Tukey's HSD is operationalized within SPSS as "Tukey," while "Tukey b" is a variation developed by Tukey that does not control the experiment-wise error rate (and thus is not recommended).

Fisher's (1942) **least significant difference (LSD) test**, also known as the protected t test, was the first MCP developed and is a pairwise post hoc procedure. It is a sequential procedure where a significant ANOVA F is followed by the LSD test in which all (or perhaps some) pairwise t tests are examined. The standard t test statistic is compared with the critical values of $\pm_{\alpha/2}t_{df(error)}$. The LSD test has precise control of the family-wise error rate for the three-group situation, assuming normality and homogeneity; but, as noted by Levin, Serlin, and Seaman (1994), for more than three groups, the protection deteriorates rather rapidly. In that case, a modification due to Hayter (1986) is suggested for more adequate protection.

The **Fisher-Hayter test** (also referred to as the Hayter-Fisher method) is a two-step procedure that was originally devised for equal sample sizes but also shown to work well with unbalanced designs when a modification is applied (Hayter, 1986). The Fisher-Hayter commences with a significant ANOVA F and then is followed by all pairwise comparisons using the studentized range distribution, with the comparisons treated as if there is one group less in the comparison, thereby being more powerful than the Tukey HSD.

In the case of unequal sample sizes, the Tukey-Kramer (relative to Fisher-Hayter) may have more power to detect the largest pairwise difference but is less powerful than the Fisher-Hayter in detecting all pairwise differences. The Fisher-Hayter can be applied in balanced and unbalanced designs and has excellent control of family-wise error (Keppel & Wickens, 2004).

12.1.2.7 Simple Post Hoc Contrasts for Unequal Variances: Games-Howell, Dunnett T3, and C Tests

When the group variances are unequal, several alternative procedures are available. These alternatives include the Games-Howell (Games & Howell, 1976), Dunnett T3, and Dunnett C (Dunnett, 1980) procedures. **Dunnett T3** is recommended for small sample sizes, $n < 50$ and **Games-Howell** for larger sample sizes, $n > 50$ (Maxwell, Delaney, & Kelley, 2018; Wilcox, 1995, 2003b). Games-Howell has been found to be slightly liberal, with an experiment-wise error rate above the nominal alpha, with smaller samples (Dunnett, 1980). **Dunnett C** performs about the same as Games-Howell (Wilcox, 1995, 2003b). For further details on these methods, please consult additional references (e.g., Benjamini & Hochberg, 1995; Hochberg, 1988; Kirk, 2013; Maxwell et al., 2018; Wilcox, 1987, 1995, 2003).

12.1.2.8 Follow-Up Tests to Kruskal-Wallis

Recall from Chapter 11 the nonparametric equivalent to the analysis of variance, the Kruskal–Wallis test. Several post hoc procedures are available to follow up a statistically significant overall Kruskal-Wallis test. The procedures discussed here are the nonparametric equivalents to the Scheffé and Tukey HSD methods. One may form pairwise or complex contrasts as in the parametric case. The test statistic is Z and computed as follows:

$$Z = \frac{\psi_i'}{s_{\psi'}}$$

where the standard error in the denominator is computed as:

$$s_{\psi'} = \sqrt{\left(\frac{N(N+1)}{12}\right)\sum_{j=1}^{J}\left(\frac{c_j^2}{n_j}\right)}$$

and where N is the total number of observations. For the Scheffé method, the test statistic Z is compared to the critical value $\sqrt{{}_{\alpha}\chi_{J-1}}$ obtained from the χ^2 table in Appendix Table A.3. For the Tukey HSD procedure, the test statistic Z is compared to the critical value $\left({}_{\alpha}q_{df(error),J}\right)/\sqrt{2}$ obtained from the table of critical values for the studentized range statistic in Appendix Table A.9.

Let us use the psychological distress data to illustrate. Do not forget that we use the ranked data as described in Chapter 11. The rank means for the groups are as follows: Group 1 (Movement) = 7.7500; Group 2 (Target) = 15.2500; Group 3 (Fielding) = 18.7500; and Group 4 (Territory) = 24.2500. Here we examine only two contrasts and then compare the results for both the Scheffé and Tukey HSD methods. The first contrast compares the first two types of sports to each other (i.e., Groups 1 and 2, Movement and Target), whereas the second contrast compares the first two types of sports (i.e., Movement and Target in aggregate) with the last two types of sports (i.e., Groups 3 and 4, Fielding and Territory in aggregate). In other words, we examine a pairwise contrast and a complex contrast, respectively. The results are given here. The critical values are as follows:

$$\textit{Scheffé}\ \sqrt{{}_{\alpha}\chi_{J-1}} = \sqrt{{}_{.05}\chi_{3}} = \sqrt{7.8147} = 2.7955$$

$$\textit{Tukey}\ \frac{{}_{\alpha}q_{df(error),J}}{\sqrt{2}} = \frac{{}_{.05}q_{28,4}}{\sqrt{2}} \approx \frac{3.87}{\sqrt{2}} = 2.7365$$

The standard error for contrast 1 is computed as:

$$s_{\psi'} = \sqrt{\left(\frac{N(N+1)}{12}\right)\sum_{j=1}^{J}\left(\frac{c_j^2}{n_j}\right)} = \sqrt{\left(\frac{32(32+1)}{12}\right)\left(\frac{1}{8}+\frac{1}{8}\right)} = 4.6904$$

The standard error for contrast 2 is calculated as follows:

$$s_{\psi'} = \sqrt{\left(\frac{N(N+1)}{12}\right)\sum_{j=1}^{J}\left(\frac{c_j^2}{n_j}\right)}$$

$$= \sqrt{\left(\frac{32(32+1)}{12}\right)\left(\frac{.25}{8}+\frac{.25}{8}+\frac{.25}{8}+\frac{.25}{8}\right)} = 3.3166$$

The test statistics are computed as follows:

$$Z_1 = \frac{\bar{Y}_{.1} - \bar{Y}_{.2}}{s_{\psi'}} = \frac{7.75 - 15.25}{4.6904} = -1.5990$$

$$Z_2 = \frac{(1/2)\bar{Y}_{.1} + (1/2)\bar{Y}_{.2} - (1/2)\bar{Y}_{.3} - (1/2)\bar{Y}_{.4}}{s_{\psi'}}$$

$$Z_2 = \frac{\left(\frac{1}{2}\right)(7.75) + \left(\frac{1}{2}\right)(15.25) - \left(\frac{1}{2}\right)(18.75) - \left(\frac{1}{2}\right)(24.25)}{3.3166} = -3.0151$$

For both procedures we find a statistically significant difference with the second contrast, but not with the first. These results agree with most of the other parametric procedures for these particular contrasts. That is, the first two groups are not statistically significantly different (only statistically significant with POC), whereas the first two groups in aggregate (Movement and Target) are statistically significantly different from the last two groups in aggregate (Fielding and Territory) (significant with all procedures). One could also devise nonparametric equivalent MCPs for methods other than the Scheffé and Tukey procedures.

12.1.3 Selecting the Proper Multiple Comparison Procedure

This chapter has attempted to summarize some of the most common MCPs. Box 12.1 is provided to assist in understanding typologies of MCPs, including simple versus complex contrasts and planned versus post hoc contrasts. Box 12.2 is provided to assist in summarizing some of the primary advantages and disadvantages of various multiple comparison procedures.

BOX 12.1 MCP Typologies

Typology	Definition
Simple versus complex comparison	
Simple or pairwise contrast	Comparison involving only two means
Complex or non-pairwise contrast	Comparison involving more than two means
Planned versus post hoc comparison	
Planned contrast (also known as specific or *a priori* contrast)	Comparisons that are determined without regard to the outcome of the omnibus *F* test
Post hoc comparison	Comparisons that are conducted only when the outcome of the omnibus *F* test is statistically significant

BOX 12.2 Advantages and Disadvantages of MCPs

	Advantage	Disadvantage
Planned Contrasts		
Trend analysis (planned polynomial MCP)	Can be used when groups represent different quantitative levels of a factor, allowing the examination of whether the sample means vary with a change in the amount of the independent variable	• Assumes equidistance between levels of the independent variable • Assumes equal *n*'s per group
Planned orthogonal contrast	• Contrasts are determined *a priori* • Unconcerned with control of family-wise Type I error rate across the set of contrasts	• The number of contrasts should be small • The contrasts that are of interest may not be orthogonal • Not all the contrasts of a particular orthogonal set may be of interest • Assumes equal *n*'s per group
Dunnett method (planned orthogonal contrast with reference group)	• Allows examination of pairwise contrasts where a reference group is compared to each of the other *J*-1 groups • More powerful than the Dunn MCP	• A modification of the procedure is needed in the presence of heteroscedasticity

(continued)

(continued)

Dunn method (also known as the Bonferonni method; planned orthogonal contrast)	• Can test pairwise or complex contrasts • Can deal with unbalanced groups	• Conservative (more difficult to reject the null hypothesis) relative to other MCPs • A modification (the Dunn-Sidak) is more powerful than the Dunn
Post hoc contrasts		
Scheffé (complex post hoc contrast)	• Can test orthogonal or nonorthogonal • Can test pairwise or complex contrasts • Can test planned or post hoc comparisions • Controls the family-wise error rate • The only MCP that is consistent with the results of the omnibus *F* test in ANOVA	• Even more conservative (more difficult to reject the null hypothesis) than the Dunn • The family of contrasts is potentially large and the contrast(s) that are statistically significant may not be of interest • Recommended only for complex post hoc comparisons • A modification of the procedure is needed in the presence of heteroscedasticity
Tukey's honestly significant difference (HSD) (simple post hoc comparison)	• Family-wise procedure with exact control of the family-wise error rate in the following conditions: normality (and is relatively robust to non-normality) and homogeneity are assumed and a balanced design • Most appropriate when considering all possible pairwise contrasts with equal *n*'s per group • More powerful than Dunn or Scheffé for testing all possible pairwise contrasts	• Not robust to extreme non-normality • Assumes a balanced design (Tukey-Kramer can be used for unbalanced designs) • Assumes homogeneity of variances
Fisher's least significance difference (LSD) test (pairwise post hoc comparison)	Precise control of the family-wise error rate for the three group situation	• Assumes normality and homogeneity of variances • Family-wise error rate deteriorates quickly with more than three groups
Fisher-Hayter test (pairwise post hoc comparison)	• More powerful than Tukey's HSD • Excellent control of family-wise error rate • Can be used with balanced or unbalanced designs	With unequal sample sizes, the Tukey-Kramer is more powerful in detecting the *largest* pairwise difference but is less powerful than the Fisher-Hayter in detecting *all* pairwise differences
Dunnett T3 (simple post hoc contrasts for unequal variances)	• Appropriate in the presence of heteroscedasticity • Recommended when $n < 50$	Not recommended for larger samples
Dunnett C tests (simple post hoc contrasts for unequal variances)	• Appropriate in the presence of heteroscedasticity • Recommended when $n > 50$	Not recommended for smaller samples
Games-Howell (simple post hoc contrasts for unequal variances)	• Appropriate in the presence of heteroscedasticity • Recommended when $n > 50$	Not recommended for smaller samples

Figure 12.2 is a flowchart to assist you in making decisions about which MCP to use. Not every statistician will agree with every decision on the flowchart as there is not total consensus about which MCP is appropriate in every single situation. Nonetheless, this is simply a guide. Whether you use it in its present form, or adapt it for your own needs, we hope you find the figure to be useful in your own research.

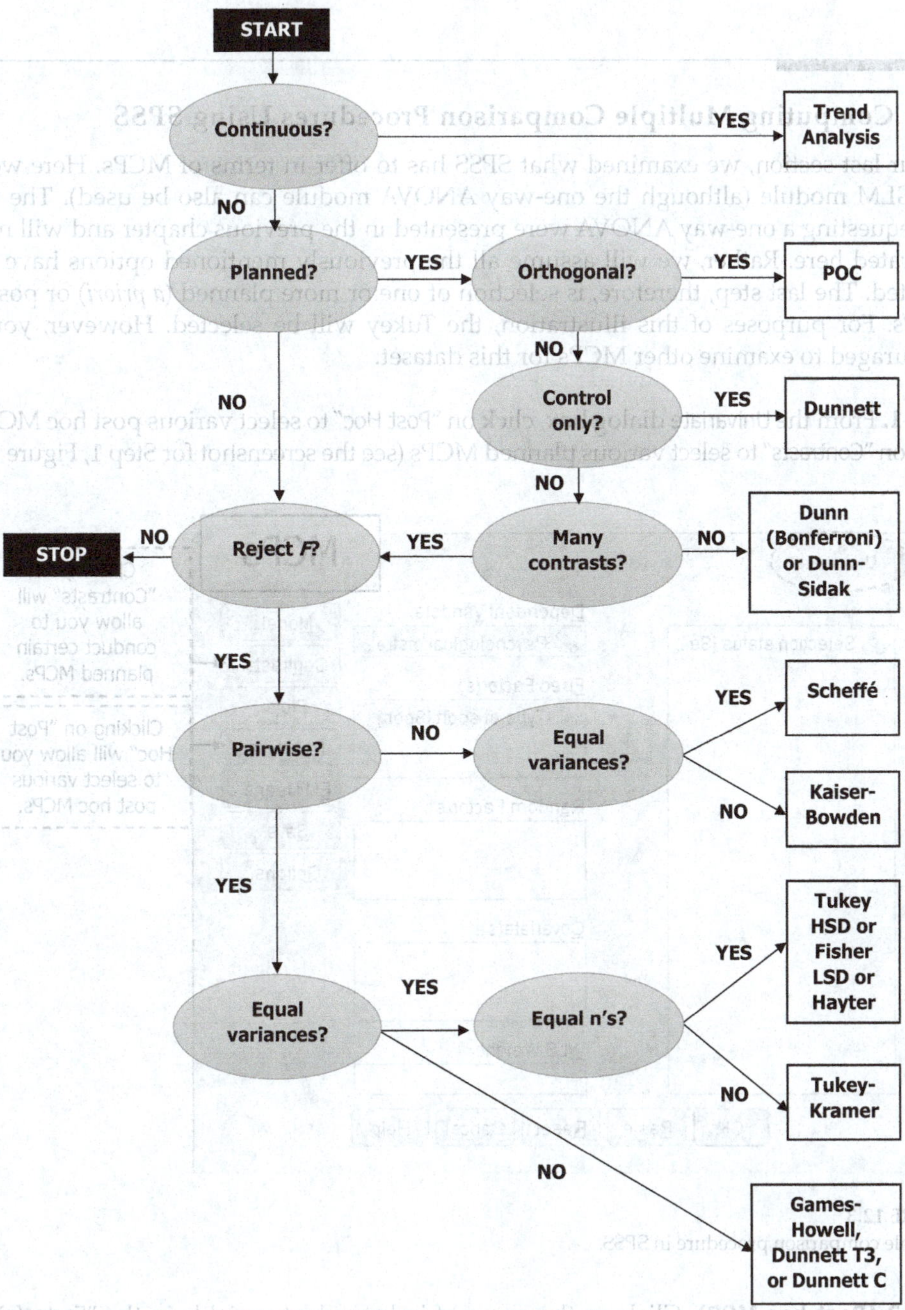

FIGURE 12.2
Flowchart of recommended MCPs.

At this point you should have met the following objectives: (a) be able to understand the concepts underlying the MCPs, (b) be able to select the appropriate MCP for a given research situation, and (c) be able to determine and interpret the results of MCPs. Chapter 13 returns to the analysis of variance again and discusses models for which there is more than one independent variable.

12.2 Computing Multiple Comparison Procedures Using SPSS

In our last section, we examined what SPSS has to offer in terms of MCPs. Here we use the GLM module (although the one-way ANOVA module can also be used). The steps for requesting a one-way ANOVA were presented in the previous chapter and will not be reiterated here. Rather, we will assume all the previously mentioned options have been selected. The last step, therefore, is selection of one or more planned (*a priori*) or post hoc MCPs. For purposes of this illustration, the Tukey will be selected. However, you are encouraged to examine other MCPs for this dataset.

Step 1. From the Univariate dialog box, click on "Post Hoc" to select various post hoc MCPs or click on "Contrasts" to select various planned MCPs (see the screenshot for Step 1, Figure 12.3).

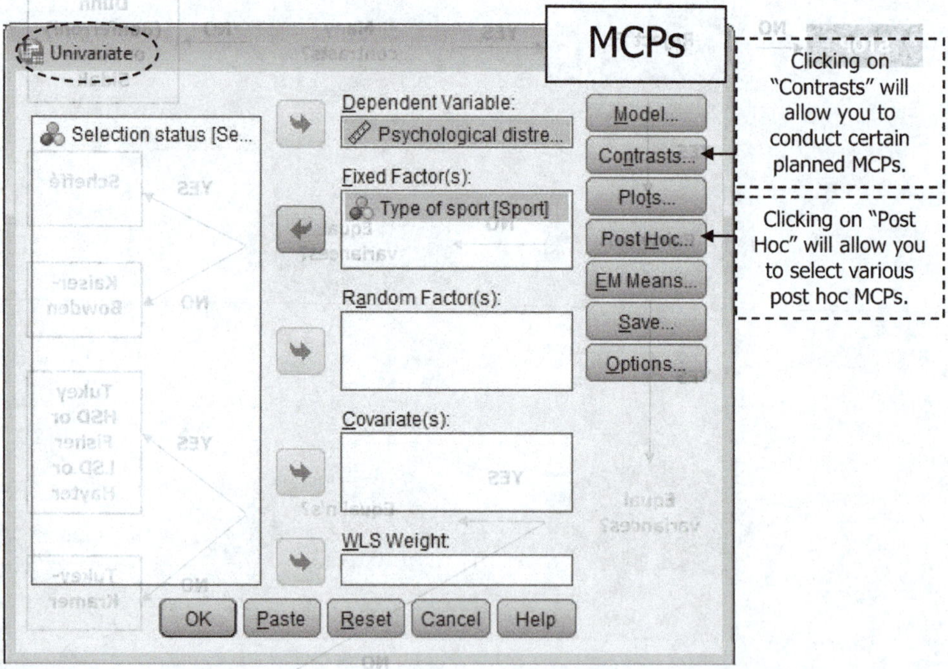

FIGURE 12.3
Multiple comparison procedure in SPSS.

Step 2 (Post hoc MCP). Click on the name of independent variable in the "Factor(s)" list box in the top left and move to the "Post Hoc Tests for" box in the top right by clicking on the arrow key. Check an appropriate MCP for your situation by placing a checkmark in the box next to the desired MCP. In this example, we will select "Tukey." Recall that SPSS operationalizes Tukey's HSD as *Tukey* within the ANOVA procedure. Click on "Continue" to return to the original dialog box. Click on "OK" to return to generate the output.

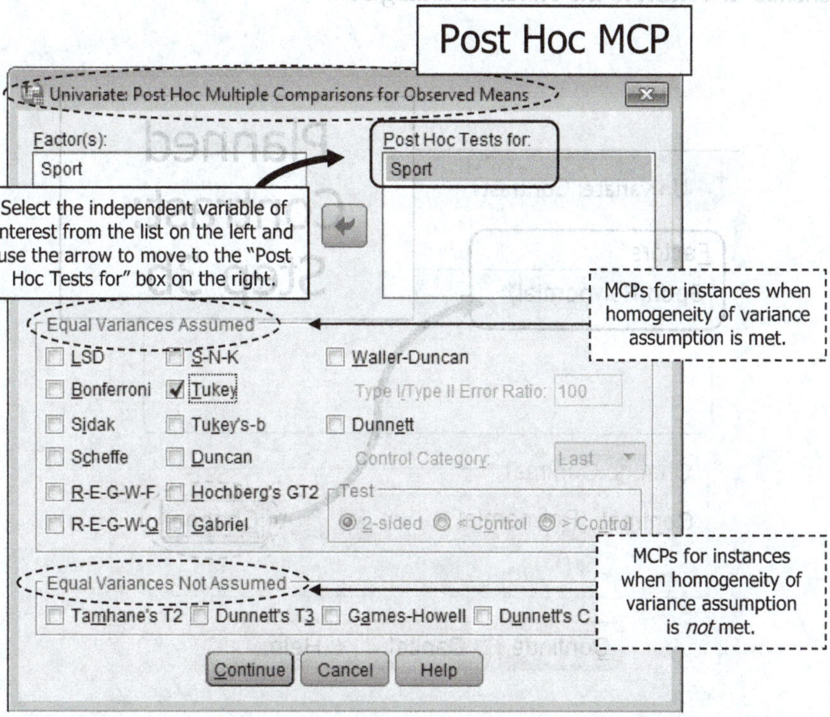

FIGURE 12.4
Post hoc MCP.

Step 3a (Planned MCP). To obtain trend analysis contrasts, click the "Contrasts" button from the "Univariate" dialog box (see the screenshot for Step 1, Figure 12.3). From the Contrasts dialog box, click the "Contrasts" pulldown and scroll down to "Polynomial."

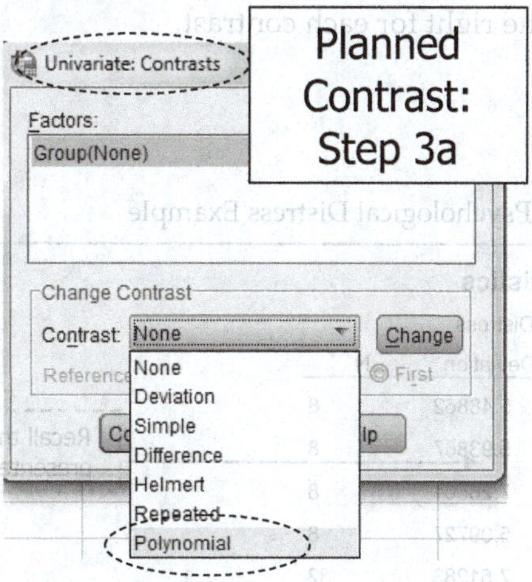

FIGURE 12.5
Planned contrast: Step 3a.

Step 3b. Click "Change" to select Polynomial and move it to be displayed in parentheses next to the independent variable. Recall that this type of contrast will allow testing of linear, quadratic, and cubic contrasts. Other specific planned contrasts are also available. Then click "Continue" to return to the Univariate dialog box.

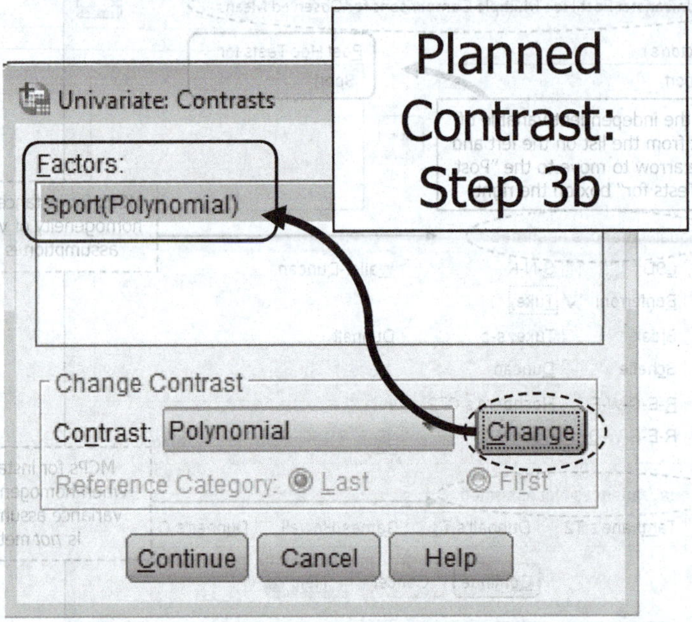

FIGURE 12.6
Planned contrast: Step 3b.

Interpreting the output. Annotated results from the Tukey HSD procedure, as one example of MCP, are shown in Table 12.13. Note that confidence intervals around a mean difference of zero are given to the right for each contrast.

TABLE 12.13
Tukey HSD SPSS Results for Psychological Distress Example

Descriptive Statistics

Dependent Variable: Psychological Distress

Type of Sport	Mean	Std. Deviation	N
Movement	11.1250	5.48862	8
Target	17.8750	5.93867	8
Fielding	20.2500	7.28501	8
Territory	24.3750	5.09727	8
Total	18.4062	7.51283	32

Recall the means of the groups as presented in the previous chapter.

TABLE 12.13 (continued)

Tukey HSD SPSS Results for Psychological Distress Example

Note that our selection of *Tukey* as the post hoc operationalizes to **Tukey's HSD**

'Mean difference' is simply the difference between the means of the two groups compared. For example, the mean difference of group 1 and group 2 is calculated as 11.1250 − 17.8750 = -6.7500

Multiple Comparisons

Dependent Variable: Psychological Distress

Tukey HSD

(I) Type of Sport	(J) Type of Sport	Mean Difference (I-J)	Std. Error	Sig.	95% Confidence Interval Lower Bound	Upper Bound
Movement	Target	-6.7500	3.00465	.135	-14.9536	1.4536
	Fielding	-9.1250*	3.00465	.025	-17.3286	-.9214
	Territory	-13.2500*	3.00465	.001	-21.4536	-5.0464
Target	Movement	6.7500	3.00465	.135	-1.4536	14.9536
	Fielding	-2.3750	3.00465	.858	-10.5786	5.8286
	Territory	-6.5000	3.00465	.158	-14.7036	1.7036
Fielding	Movement	9.1250*	3.00465	.025	.9214	17.3286
	Target	2.3750	3.00465	.858	-5.8286	10.5786
	Territory	-4.1250	3.00465	.526	-12.3286	4.0786
Territory	Movement	13.2500*	3.00465	.001	5.0464	21.4536
	Target	6.5000	3.00465	.158	-1.7036	14.7036
	Fielding	4.1250	3.00465	.526	-4.0786	12.3286

Based on observed means.

The error term is Mean Square(Error) = 36.112.

*. The mean difference is significant at the .05 level.

The standard error calculated in SPSS uses the harmonic mean (Tukey-Kramer modification) where n_j and n_k are the sample sizes for the two groups whose means are being compared (Toothaker, 1993):

$$s_{\psi'} = \sqrt{MS_{error}\left(\frac{1}{n_j}+\frac{1}{n_k}\right)}$$

$$s_{\psi'} = \sqrt{36.112\left(\frac{1}{8}+\frac{1}{8}\right)} = \sqrt{6.04275} = 3.00466$$

'Sig.' denotes the observed *p* value and provides the results of the contrasts. There are only two statistically significant contrasts. There is a statistically significant mean difference between: 1) group 1 (Movement) and group 3 (Fielding); and 2) between group 1 (Movement) and group 4 (Territory). Note that there are only 6 unique contrast results:

$$½[J(J-1)] = ½[4(4-1)] = ½(12) = 6.$$

However there are redundant results presented in the table. For example, the comparison of group 1 and 2 (presented in results row 1) is the same as the comparison of group 2 and 1 (presented in results row 2).

Toothaker, L. E. (1993). *Multiple comparison procedures*. Newbury Park, CA: Sage.

Homogeneous Subsets

Psychological Distress

Tukey HSD[a,b]

Type of Sport	N	Subset 1	Subset 2
Movement	8	11.1250	
Target	8	17.8750	17.8750
Fielding	8		20.2500
Territory	8		24.3750
Sig.		.135	.158

Means for groups in homogeneous subsets are displayed.

Based on observed means.

The error term is Mean Square(Error) = 36.112.

a. Uses Harmonic Mean Sample Size = 8.000.

b. Alpha = 0.05.

For each requested post hoc test that provides homogenous subset results, the groups are listed in order of *ascending* means. The means that are listed under each subset comprise a set of means that are ***not*** significantly different from each other. Movement isstatistically different from fielding and territory as they do not appear in the same subset together.

NOTE: Tests available in the MCP table generally has better properties than the homogenous subset tests and are the preferred focus for post hoc analysis.

12.3 Computing Multiple Comparison Procedures Using R

Next we consider **R** for multiple comparison procedures. Note that the scripts are provided within the blocks with additional annotation to assist in understanding how the command works. Should you want to write reminder notes and annotation to yourself as you write the commands in **R** (and we highly encourage doing so), remember that any text that follows a hashtag (i.e., #) is annotation only and not part of the **R** script. Thus, you can write annotations directly into **R** with hashtags. We encourage this practice so that when you call up the commands in the future, you'll understand what the various lines of code are doing. You may think you'll remember what you did. However, trust us. There is a good chance that you won't. Thus, consider it best practice when using **R** to annotate heavily!

12.3.1 Reading Data Into R

```
getwd()
```

R is always pointed to a directory on your computer. The *get working directory* function can be used to determine to which directory **R** is pointed. We will assume that we need to change the working directory, and will use the next line of code to set the working directory to the desired path.

```
setwd("E:/FolderName")
```

We use the *setwd* function to establish the working directory. To set the working directory, change what is in quotation marks to your file location. Also, if you are copying the directory name from your properties, you will need to change the forward slash (i.e., \) to a forward slash (i.e., /).

```
Ch11_distress <- read.csv("Ch11_distress.csv")
```

The *read.csv* function reads our data into **R**. What's to the left of the "<-" will be what the data will be called in **R**. In this example, we're calling the **R** dataframe "Ch11_distress." What's to the right of the "<-" tells **R** to find this particular csv file. In this example, our file is called "Ch11_distress.csv." Make sure the extension (i.e., .csv) is included in your script. Also note that the name of your file should be in quotation marks within the parentheses.

```
names(Ch11_distress)
```

The *names* function will produce a list of variable names for each dataframe as follows. This is a good check to make sure your data have been read in correctly.

```
[1] "Sport" "Distress"
```

```
View(Ch11_distress)
```

The *View* function will let you view the dataset in spreadsheet format in RStudio.

```
Ch11_distress$SportF <- factor(Ch11_distress$Sport,
labels = c("movement", "target", "fielding", "territory"))
```

FIGURE 12.7
Reading data into R.

This script will create a new variable in our dataframe named "SportF." We use the *factor* function to define the variable *Sport* as nominal with the four groups defined here (i.e., movement, target, fielding, territory). What is to the left of "<-" in the script creates the new *SportF* variable in our dataframe.

```
summary(Ch11_distress)
```

The *summary* function will produce basic descriptive statistics on all the variables in your dataframe. This is a great way to quickly check to see if the data have been read in correctly and to get a feel for your data, if you haven't already. The output from the summary statement for this dataframe looks like this. Because we defined SportF as a factor, we are provided only the frequencies for each category in that variable.

```
     Sport          Distress          SportF
Min.   :1.00   Min.   : 3.00   movement :8
1st Qu.:1.75   1st Qu.:12.00   target   :8
Median :2.50   Median :20.00   fielding  :8
Mean   :2.50   Mean   :18.41   territory:8
3rd Qu.:3.25   3rd Qu.:25.00
Max.   :4.00   Max.   :30.00
```

FIGURE 12.7 (continued)
Reading data into R.

12.3.2 Generating the One-Way ANOVA

```
Ch11_ANOVA <- aov(Distress ~ SportF, data=Ch11_distress)
```

The *aov* function will generate the one-way ANOVA model with "Distress" as the dependent variable and "SportF" as the independent variable. The dataframe from which we are pulling the data is defined by the *data* function. We are calling this object "Ch11_ANOVA."

FIGURE 12.8
Generating the one-way ANOVA.

12.3.3 Generating Tukey's Multiple Comparison Procedure

```
install.packages("multcomp")
```

The *install.packages* function will be used to install the *multcomp* package that is needed for the post hoc tests.

```
library(multcomp)
```

The *library* function will call up the package into our library.

```
PostHoc1<-glht(Ch11_ANOVA, linfct=mcp(SportF="Tukey"))
```

The *glht* function will generate Tukey's HSD post hoc analysis and name the object "PostHoc1." We could replace "Tukey" with "Dunnett" if we had wanted to run the Dunnett MCP rather than Tukey's.

```
summary(PostHoc1)
```

The *summary* function will output the results of the Tukey post hoc analysis from the previous command.

FIGURE 12.9
Generating Tukey's multiple comparison procedure.

```
    Simultaneous Tests for General Linear Hypotheses
Multiple Comparisons of Means: Tukey Contrasts

Fit: aov(formula = Distress ~ SportF, data = Ch11_distress)

Linear Hypotheses:
                            Estimate  Std. Error  t value  Pr(>|t|)
target - movement == 0       6.750     3.005      2.247     0.1356
fielding - movement == 0     9.125     3.005      3.037     0.0246
territory - movement == 0   13.250     3.005      4.410    <0.001
fielding - target == 0       2.375     3.005      0.790     0.8581
territory - target == 0      6.500     3.005      2.163     0.1585
territory - fielding == 0    4.125     3.005      1.373     0.5261

target - movement == 0
fielding - movement == 0 *
territory - movement == 0 ***
fielding - target == 0
territory - target == 0
territory - fielding == 0
---
Signif. codes: 0 '***' 0.001 '**' 0.01 '*' 0.05 '.' 0.1 ' ' 1
(Adjusted p values reported -- single-step method)
```

As we already know from the *F* test, there were differences between at least some of the types of sport. Tukey's post hoc tells us there are statistically significant differences between movement and fielding and between movement and territory.

```
confint(PostHoc1)
```

The *confint* function will output confidence intervals of the post hoc results. The lower confidence limit is labeled "lwr" and the upper confidence interval is "upr." The confidence intervals that do not contain zero suggest statistically significant differences in the outcome between those groups.

```
Simultaneous Confidence Intervals
Multiple Comparisons of Means: Tukey Contrasts

Fit: aov(formula = Distress ~ SportF, data = Ch11_distress)

Quantile = 2.7325
95% family-wise confidence level

Linear Hypotheses:
                            Estimate    lwr       upr
target - movement == 0       6.7500   -1.4601   14.9601
fielding - movement == 0     9.1250    0.9149   17.3351
territory - movement == 0   13.2500    5.0399   21.4601
fielding - target == 0       2.3750   -5.8351   10.5851
territory - target == 0      6.5000   -1.7101   14.7101
territory - fielding == 0    4.1250   -4.0851   12.3351
```

FIGURE 12.9 (continued)
Generating Tukey's multiple comparison procedure.

12.3.4 Generating Trend Analysis

```
contrasts(Ch11_distress$SportF)<-contr.poly(4)
```

To conduct a trend analysis, we use the *contr.poly* function. This defines "SportF" as the variable to conduct the contrast, using the Ch11_distress dataframe. This also defines four categories in that variable. Note that the categories need to be in ascending order in order to detect a meaningful trend. Our categories range from movement (1) to territory (4). Our categories are arguably not the best for trend analysis as they are not explicitly ordinal; however, for the sake of illustration, we will go with it!

```
Ch11trend <- aov(Distress ~ SportF, data=Ch11_distress)
```

We run our ANOVA model again.

```
summary.lm(Ch11trend)
```

Then we generate the output using the *summary.lm* function on the "Ch2trend" object. In the coefficient table, we see "Sport.L." The "L" refers to the linear trend. "Q" refers to the quadratic trend. "C" refers to the cubic trend. We see the only statistically significant trend is for the linear model.

```
Call:
aov(formula = Distress ~ Sport, data = Ch11_distress)

Residuals:
     Min        1Q    Median        3Q       Max
-10.2500   -4.5000    0.8125    4.2500    9.8750

Coefficients:
            Estimate Std. Error t value Pr(>|t|)
(Intercept)   18.406      1.062  17.327  < 2e-16 ***
Sport.L        9.419      2.125   4.433  0.00013 ***
Sport.Q       -1.313      2.125  -0.618  0.54172
Sport.C 1.370 2.125 0.645 0.52441
---
Signif. codes:
0 '***' 0.001 '**' 0.01 '*' 0.05 '.' 0.1 ' ' 1

Residual standard error: 6.009 on 28 degrees of freedom
Multiple R-squared: 0.4221, Adjusted R-squared: 0.3602
F-statistic: 6.818 on 3 and 28 DF, p-value: 0.001361
```

FIGURE 12.10
Generating trend analysis.

12.3.5 Generating Other MCPs

```
pairwise.t.test(Ch11_distress$Distress,
                Ch11_distress$Sport,
                paired = FALSE,
                p.adjust.method = "bonferroni")
```

FIGURE 12.11
Generating other MCPs.

Bonferroni and other methods can be computed using the pairwise *t* test function, *pairwise.t.test*, available in **R**. We first define the outcome (*Ch11_distress$Distress*) and independent variable (*Ch11_distress$Sport*). We indicate *paired = FALSE* as we do not actually have a matched sample—we want to conduct an independent *t* test. For the method, we will illustrate the Bonferroni; however, we could have used "BH" (Benjamin-Hochberg), "hochberg," "holm," "hommel," or "none" (the last of which is not recommended as it does not adjust the *p* value for multiple tests).

```
Pairwise comparisons using t tests with pooled SD

data: Ch11_distress$Distress and Ch11_distress$Sport

         movement target  fielding
target   0.19645  -       -
fielding 0.03075  1.00000 -
territory 0.00083 0.23522 1.00000

P value adjustment method: bonferroni
```

The results provide all possible pairwise comparisons. The values represent *p* values for the cells where the variables intersect. We see the same results with Bonferroni as we did with Tukey's post hoc results. More specifically, *movement* is statistically different from *fielding* ($p = .03075$) and *territory* ($p = .00083$).

FIGURE 12.11 (continued)
Generating other MCPs.

12.4 Research Question Template and Example Write-Up

In terms of an APA-style write-up, the MCP results for Tukey's HSD test for the statistics lab example are as follows.

Recall that our graduate research assistant, Ott, was working with one of the leading sports psychologists in the region, Dr. Rhodes. Dr. Rhodes is examining elite athletes and their vulnerability to psychological distress based on type of sport in which they participate. His research question was: *Is there a mean difference in psychological distress of elite athletes based on the type of sport in which they participate?* Ott then generated a one-way ANOVA as the test of inference. The APA-style example paragraph of results for the one-way ANOVA, prefaced by the extent to which the assumptions of the test were met, was presented in the previous chapter. Thus, only the results of the MCP (specifically the Tukey HSD) are presented here.

Post hoc analyses were conducted given the statistically significant omnibus ANOVA *F* test. Specifically, given the balanced design and equal variances, Tukey HSD multiple comparison tests were conducted on all possible pairwise contrasts. The following pairs of groups were found to be significantly different: Movement ($M = 11.125$, $SD = 5.4886$) and Fielding ($M = 20.2500$, $SD = 7.2850$) ($p = .025$); and Movement and Territory ($M = 24.3750$, $SD = 5.0973$) ($p = .001$). In other words, athletes who participate in sports related to Movement have statistically significantly lower psychological distress than athletes who participate in Fielding or Territory types of sports.

Problems

Conceptual Problems

1. True or false? The Tukey HSD procedure requires equal n's and equal means.
2. Applying the Dunn procedure, given a nominal family-wise error rate of .10 and two contrasts, what is the per contrast alpha?
   a. .01
   b. .05
   c. .10
   d. .20
3. Which of the following linear combinations of population means is not a legitimate contrast?
   a. $\frac{(\mu_{.1}+\mu_{.2}+\mu_{.3})}{3}-\mu_{.4}$
   b. $\mu_{.1}-\mu_{.4}$
   c. $\frac{(\mu_{.1}+\mu_{.2})}{2}-(\mu_{.3}+\mu_{.4})$
   d. $\mu_{.1}-\mu_{.2}+\mu_{.3}-\mu_{.4}$
4. When a one-factor fixed-effects ANOVA results in a significant F ratio for $J = 2$, one should follow the ANOVA with which one of the following procedures?
   a. Tukey HSD method
   b. Scheffé method
   c. Fisher-Hayter method
   d. None of the above
5. If a family-based error rate for alpha is desired, and hypotheses involving all pairs of means are to be tested, which method of multiple comparisons should be selected?
   a. Tukey HSD
   b. Scheffé
   c. Planned Orthogonal Contrasts
   d. Trend analysis
   e. None of the above
6. *A priori* comparisons are which one of the following?
   a. Planned in advance of the research
   b. Often arise out of theory and prior research
   c. May be done without examining the F ratio
   d. All of the above
7. True or false? For planned contrasts involving the control group, the Dunn procedure is most appropriate.
8. Which is not a property of planned orthogonal contrasts?
   a. The contrasts are independent.
   b. The contrasts are post hoc.

c. The sum of the cross-products of the contrast coefficients = 0.

d. If there are J groups, there are $J - 1$ orthogonal contrasts.

9. Which multiple comparison procedure is most flexible in the contrasts that can be tested?

a. Planned orthogonal contrasts

b. Newman-Keuls

c. Dunnett

d. Tukey HSD

e. Scheffé

10. Post hoc tests are necessary after an ANOVA given which one of the following?

a. H_0 is rejected with two groups.

b. Fail to reject the null hypothesis and there are more than two groups.

c. H_0 is rejected and there are more than two groups.

d. You should always do post hoc tests after an ANOVA.

11. True or false? Post hoc tests are done after ANOVA to determine why H_0 was *not* rejected.

12. True or false? Holding the α level and the number of groups constant, as the df_{error} increases, the critical value of the q decreases.

13. True or false? The Tukey HSD procedure maintains the family-wise Type I error rate at α.

14. True or false? The Dunnett procedure assumes equal numbers of observations per group.

15. For complex post hoc contrasts with unequal group variances, which of the following MCPs is most appropriate?

a. Kaiser-Bowden

b. Dunnett

c. Tukey HSD

d. Scheffé

16. The number of levels of the independent variable is six. How many orthogonal contrasts can be tested?

a. 1

b. 3

c. 5

d. 6

17. A researcher is interested in testing the following contrasts in a $J = 6$ study: Group 1 vs. 2; Group 3 vs. 4; and Group 5 vs. 6. I assert that these contrasts are orthogonal. Am I correct?

18. I assert that rejecting H_0 in a one-factor fixed-effects ANOVA with $J = 3$ indicates that all three pairs of group means are necessarily statistically significantly different using the Scheffé procedure. Am I correct?

19. For complex post hoc contrasts with equal group variances, which of the following MCPs is most appropriate?

a. Planned orthogonal contrasts

b. Dunnett

c. Tukey HSD

d. Scheffé

20. A researcher finds a statistically significant omnibus *F* test. For which one of the following will there be at least one statistically significant MCP?

a. Kaiser-Bowden

b. Dunnett

c. Tukey HSD

d. Scheffé

21. Suppose all $J = 4$ of the sample means are equal to 100. I assert that it is possible to find a significant contrast with some MCP. Am I correct?

22. True or false? In contrast-based multiple comparison procedures, alpha is set for each individual contrast.

23. When alpha is established for a family of contrasts, which of the following does it represent?

a. Contrast based alpha

b. Per contrast alpha

c. Probability of making a Type I error for a particular contrast

d. Probability of making at least one Type I error in a set of contrasts

24. Contrasts can be divided into which two of the following types?

a. Contrast and complex

b. Nonpairwise and complex

c. Pairwise and nonpairwise

d. Simple and pairwise

25. A trend analysis is evaluated in terms of which one of the following?

a. Oblique higher-order terms

b. Orthogonal polynomials

c. Pairwise contrast

d. Simple contrast

26. MCPs that apply trend analysis are usually conducted sequentially in which order?

a. Cubic, linear, quadratic

b. Linear, quadratic, cubic

c. Linear, cubic, quadratic

d. Quadratic, cubic, linear

27. A researcher has conducted a one-way ANOVA with an independent variable with 5 categories. How many orthogonal contrasts can be tested?

a. 2

b. 3

c. 4

d. 5

Answers to Conceptual Problems

1. **False** (requires equal n = s and equal variances; we hope the means are different.)
3. **c** (c is not legitimate as the contrast coefficients do not sum to 0.)
5. **a** (see flowchart of MCPs in Figure 12.2.)
7. **False** (use Dunnett procedure.)
9. **e** (Scheffé is most flexible of all MCPs; can test simple and complex contrasts.)
11. **False** (post hoc tests are conducted after ANOVA to determine why null *has* been rejected; post hoc tests are not needed when the null is not rejected.)
13. **True** (see characteristics of Tukey HSD.)
15. **a** (see Figure 12.2.)
17. **Yes** (each contrast is orthogonal to the others as they rely on independent information.)
19. **d** (see Figure 12.2.)
21. **No** (with equal sample means, the numerator of any t will be zero; thus nothing can possibly be significant.)
23. **d** (family-wise alpha represents the probability of making at least one Type I error in a set, or family, of contrasts.)
25. **b** (trend analysis is defined in the form of orthogonal polynomials.)
27. **c** (c (the number of orthogonal contrasts is one less than the number of levels or groups of the independent variable; in this case $J - 1 = 5 - 1 = 4$.)

Computational Problems

1. A one-factor fixed-effects analysis of variance is performed on data for 10 groups of unequal sizes and H_0 is rejected at the .01 level of significance. Using the Scheffé procedure, test the following contrast:

$$\bar{Y}_{.2} - \bar{Y}_{.5} = 0$$

at the .01 level of significance given the following information: $df_{with} = 40$, $\bar{Y}_{.2} = 10.8$, $n_2 = 8$, $\bar{Y}_{.5} = 15.8$, $n_2 = 8$, and $MS_{with} = 4$.

2. A one-factor fixed-effects ANOVA is performed on data from three groups of equal size ($n = 10$) and H_0 is rejected at the .01 level. The following values were computed: $MS_{with} = 40$ and the sample means are $\bar{Y}_{.1} = 4.5$, $\bar{Y}_{.2} = 12.5$, and $\bar{Y}_{.3} = 13.0$. Use the Tukey HSD method to test all possible pairwise contrasts.

3. A one-factor fixed-effects ANOVA is performed on data from three groups of equal size ($n = 20$) and H_0 is rejected at the .05 level. The following values were computed: $MS_{with} = 60$ and the sample means are $\bar{Y}_{.1} = 50$, $\bar{Y}_{.2} = 70$, and $\bar{Y}_{.3} = 85$. Use the Tukey HSD method to test all possible pairwise contrasts.

4. Consider the situation where there are $J = 4$ groups of subjects. Answer the following questions:
   a. Construct a set of orthogonal contrasts and show that they are orthogonal.
   b. Is the following contrast legitimate? Why or why not?

$$H_0: \mu_{.1} - (\mu_{.2} + \mu_{.3} + \mu_{.4})$$

   c. Using the same means, how might the contrast in part (b) be altered to yield a legitimate contrast?

5. Using the following data, conduct a one-factor fixed-effects ANOVA and perform Tukey's HSD using SPSS or **R**. Indicate which means are statistically significantly different based on Tukey's HSD.

Group	Outcome
1	10
1	13
1	12
1	11
1	10
2	15
2	16
2	14
2	17
2	16
3	17
3	18
3	16
3	17
3	16
4	21
4	22
4	20
4	21
4	22

6. Using the following data, conduct a one-factor fixed-effects ANOVA and perform Tukey's HSD using SPSS or **R**. Indicate which means are statistically significantly different based on Tukey's HSD.

Group	Outcome
1	36
1	45
1	32
1	57
1	46
1	60
1	23
1	32
1	60
1	45
2	57

2	47
2	32
2	42
2	42
2	53
2	60
2	33
2	64
2	37
3	23
3	61
3	58
3	52
3	28
3	52
3	43
3	64
3	47
3	62

Selected Answers to Computational Problems

1. Contrast = –5; standard error = 1; t = –5; critical values are 5.10 and –5.10; fail to reject.
3. Standard error = $\sqrt{60/20} = \sqrt{3} = 1.7321$
   - $q_1 = \frac{(85-50)}{1.7321} = 20.2073$
   - $q_2 = \frac{(85-70)}{1.7321} = 8.6603$
   - $q_3 = \frac{(70-50)}{1.7321} = 11.5470$
   - Critical values approximately 3.39 and –3.39; all contrasts are statistically significant.
5. Based on the one-factor fixed-effects ANOVA and Tukey's HSD (see the following table), there are statistically significant mean differences between the following groups:
   a. Group 1 and Group 2
   b. Group 1 and Group 3
   c. Group 1 and Group 4
   d. Group 2 and Group 4
   e. Group 3 and Group 4

Multiple Comparisons

Dependent Variable: outcome
Tukey HSD

(I) group	(J) group	Mean Difference (I-J)	Std. Error	Sig.	95% Confidence Interval Lower Bound	95% Confidence Interval Upper Bound
1.00	2.00	−4.4000*	.66332	.000	−6.2978	−2.5022
	3.00	−5.6000*	.66332	.000	−7.4978	−3.7022
	4.00	−10.0000*	.66332	.000	−11.8978	−8.1022
2.00	1.00	4.4000*	.66332	.000	2.5022	6.2978
	3.00	−1.2000	.66332	.305	−3.0978	.6978
	4.00	−5.6000*	.66332	.000	−7.4978	−3.7022
3.00	1.00	5.6000*	.66332	.000	3.7022	7.4978
	2.00	1.2000	.66332	.305	−.6978	3.0978
	4.00	−4.4000*	.66332	.000	−6.2978	−2.5022
4.00	1.00	10.0000*	.66332	.000	8.1022	11.8978
	2.00	5.6000*	.66332	.000	3.7022	7.4978
	3.00	4.4000*	.66332	.000	2.5022	6.2978

Based on observed means.
The error term is Mean Square(Error) = 1.100.
* The mean difference is significant at the 0.05 level.

6. Based on the one-factor fixed-effects ANOVA and Tukey's HSD (see the following table), there are statistically significant mean differences between *none* of the groups.

Multiple Comparisons

Dependent Variable: Outcome
Tukey HSD

(I) Group	(J) Group	Mean Difference (I-J)	Std. Error	Sig.	95% Confidence Interval Lower Bound	95% Confidence Interval Upper Bound
1.00	2.00	−3.1000	5.73262	.852	−17.3136	11.1136
	3.00	−5.4000	5.73262	.619	−19.6136	8.8136
2.00	1.00	3.1000	5.73262	.852	−11.1136	17.3136
	3.00	−2.3000	5.73262	.915	−16.5136	11.9136
3.00	1.00	5.4000	5.73262	.619	−8.8136	19.6136
	2.00	2.3000	5.73262	.915	−11.9136	16.5136

Based on observed means.
The error term is Mean Square(Error) = 164.315.

Interpretive Problems

1. For the interpretive problem you selected in Chapter 11 (using the survey1 dataset accessible from the website), select an *a priori* MCP, apply it using SPSS, and write an APA-style paragraph describing the results.
2. For the interpretive problem you selected in Chapter 11 (using the survey1 dataset accessible from the website), select a *post hoc* MCP, apply it using SPSS, and write an APA-style paragraph describing the results.
3. For the interpretive problem you selected in Chapter 11 (using the IPEDS2017 dataset accessible from the website), select a *post hoc* MCP, apply it using SPSS, and write an APA-style paragraph describing the results.

13

Factorial Analysis of Variance—Fixed-Effects Model

Chapter Outline

Key Concepts

1. Main effects
2. Interaction effects
3. Partitioning the sums of squares
4. The ANOVA model
5. Main effects contrasts, simple and complex interaction contrasts
6. Nonorthogonal designs

The last two chapters have dealt with the one-factor analysis of variance (ANOVA) model and various multiple comparison procedures (MCPs) for that model. In this chapter, we continue our discussion of analysis of variance models by extending the one-factor case to the two- and three-factor models. This chapter seeks an answer to the question: What should we do if there are multiple factors for which we want to make comparisons of the means? In other words, the researcher is interested in the effect of two or more independent variables or factors on the dependent (or criterion) variable. This chapter is most concerned with two- and three-factor models, but the extension to more than three factors, when warranted, is fairly simple.

For example, suppose that a researcher is interested in the effects of textbook choice and time of day on statistics achievement. Thus, one independent variable would be the textbook selected for the course, and the second independent variable would be the time of day the course was offered. The researcher hypothesizes that certain texts may be more effective in terms of achievement than others, and that student learning may be greater at certain times of the day. For the time-of-day variable, one might expect that students would not do as well in an early morning section or a late evening section than at other times of the day. In the example study, say that the researcher is interested in comparing three textbooks (A, B, and C) and three times of the day (early morning, mid-afternoon, and evening sections). Students would be randomly assigned to sections of statistics based on a combination of textbook and time of day. One group of students might be assigned to the section offered in the evening using textbook A. These results would be of interest to statistics instructors for selecting a textbook and optimal time of the day. This is just one example, but it should allow you to see how multiple independent variables can be applied within one model.

Most of the concepts used in this chapter are the same as those covered in Chapters 11 and 12. In addition, new concepts include main effects, interaction effects, multiple comparison procedures for main and interaction effects, and nonorthogonal designs. Our objectives are that by the end of this chapter, you will be able to (a) understand the characteristics and concepts underlying factorial ANOVA, (b) determine and interpret the results of factorial ANOVA, and (c) understand and evaluate the assumptions of factorial ANOVA.

13.1 What Two-Factor ANOVA Is and How It Works

Our very talented group of graduate students has been performing amazing statistical feats that have garnered rave reviews from those with which they have worked. We now find Ott Lier assisting one of the region's leading sports psychologists in examining elite athletes and vulnerability to psychological distress following selection procedures and player status (selection or deselection to remain on their team). Our graduate student team successfully analyzed the data (as we saw in a previous chapter) using one-way ANOVA to answer one research question using this data. As we will see in this chapter, Ott will be extending analysis to include an additional independent variable.

The research lab has been contracted to work with one of the leading sports psychologists in the region, Dr. Rhodes. Ott Lier, one of our very capable graduate students, has the pleasure of being selected to work with Dr. Rhodes. Dr. Rhodes is examining elite athletes and their vulnerability to psychological distress after selection procedures in which athletes are either selected or deselected for their team. Dr. Rhodes wants to determine if there is a difference in psychological stress based on type of sport (movement, target, fielding, or territory) and selection status (selected or deselected). Ott suggests the following research question is: *Is there a mean difference in psychological distress of elite athletes based on the type of sport and selection status?* With two independent variables, Ott determines that a factorial ANOVA is the best statistical procedure to use to answer Dr. Rhodes's question. His next task is to collect and analyze the data to address this research question.

This section describes the distinguishing characteristics of the two-factor ANOVA model, the layout of the data, the linear model, main effects and interactions, assumptions of the model and their violation, partitioning the sums of squares, the ANOVA summary table, multiple comparison procedures, effect size measures, confidence intervals, power, an example, and expected mean squares.

13.1.1 Characteristics

The first characteristic of the two-factor ANOVA model should be obvious by now; this model considers the effect of *two factors or independent variables* on one dependent variable. Each factor consists of two or more levels (or categories). This yields what we call a **factorial design** because more than a single factor is included. We see then that the two-factor ANOVA is an extension of the one-factor ANOVA. Why would a researcher want to complicate things by considering a second factor? Three reasons come to mind. First, the researcher may have a genuine interest in studying the second factor and, more specifically, how the second factor operates on the outcome in the presence of another factor. Rather than studying each factor separately in two analyses, the researcher includes both factors in the same analysis. This allows a test not only of the effect of each individual factor, known as **main effects**, but of the effect of both factors *collectively*. This latter effect is known as an **interaction effect** and provides information about whether the two factors are operating independent of one another (i.e., no interaction exists) or whether the two factors are operating *together* to produce some additional impact (i.e., an interaction exists). If two separate analyses were conducted, one for each independent variable, no information would be obtained about the interaction effect. As becomes evident, assuming a factorial ANOVA with two independent variables, the researcher will test three hypotheses: one for each factor or main effect individually and a third for the interaction between the factors. *Factorial ANOVA models with more than two independent variables will, accordingly, test for additional main effects and interactions.* This chapter spends considerable time discussing interactions.

A second reason for including an additional factor is an attempt to **reduce the error (or within-groups) variation**, which is variation that is unexplained by the first factor. The use of a second factor provides a more precise estimate of error variance. *For this reason, a two-factor design is generally more powerful than two one-factor designs, as the second factor and the interaction serve to control for additional extraneous variability.*

A third reason for considering two factors simultaneously is to provide *greater generalizability* of the results and to provide a more efficient and economical use of observations and resources. Thus the results can be generalized to more situations, and the study will be more cost efficient in terms of time and money.

For the two-factor ANOVA, every level of the first factor (hereafter known as factor A) is paired with every level of the second factor (hereafter known as factor B). In other words, *every combination of factors A and B is included in the design of the study*, yielding what is referred to as a **fully crossed design**. If some combinations are not included, then the design is not fully crossed and may form some sort of a nested design (see Chapter 16). Units (e.g., individuals or objects) are randomly assigned to one combination of the two factors. In other words, each individual responds to only one combination of the factors. If individuals respond to more than one combination of the factors, this would be some sort of repeated measures design, which we examine in Chapter 15. In this chapter we consider only models where all factors are fixed. Thus the overall design is known as a **fixed-effects model**. If one or both factors are random, then the design is not a fixed-effects model, which we discuss in Chapter 15. It is also a condition for factorial ANOVA that the dependent variable is measured at least at the interval level and the independent variables are categorical (either nominal or ordinal).

In this section of the chapter, for simplicity's sake, we impose the restriction that the number of observations is the same for each factor combination (i.e., equal or balanced *n*'s). This yields what is known as an **orthogonal design**, where the effects due to the factors (separately and collectively) are independent or unrelated. We leave the discussion of nonorthogonal (i.e., unequal *n*'s or unbalanced) factorial ANOVA until later in this chapter. In addition, there must be at least two observations per factor combination so as to have within-groups variation.

In summary, the characteristics of the two-factor analysis of variance fixed-effects model are as follows: (a) two independent variables (both of which are categorical) each with two or more levels, (b) the levels of both independent variables are fixed by the researcher, (c) subjects are randomly assigned to only one combination of these levels, (d) the two factors are fully crossed, and (e) the dependent variable is measured at least at the interval level. In the context of experimental design, the two-factor analysis of variance is often referred to as the **completely randomized factorial design**.

13.1.1.1 The Layout of the Data

Before we get into the theory and analysis of the data, let us examine one form in which the data can be placed, known as the layout of the data. We designate each observation as Y_{ijk}, where the j subscript tells us what level (or category) of factor A (i.e., independent variable 1) the observation belongs to, the k subscript tells us what level of factor B (i.e., independent variable 2) the observation belongs to, and the i subscript tells us the observation or identification number within that combination of factor A and factor B. For instance, Y_{321}

would mean that this is the third observation in the second level of factor A and the first level of factor B. The first subscript ranges over $i = 1, \ldots, n$, the second subscript ranges over $j = 1, \ldots, J$, and the third subscript ranges over $k = 1, \ldots, K$. Note also that the latter two subscripts denote the cell of an observation. Using the same example, we are referring to the third observation in the 21 cell. Thus, there are J levels of factor A, K levels of factor B, and n subjects in each cell, for a total of $JKn = N$ observations. For now, we consider the case where there are n subjects in each cell in order to simplify matters; this is referred to as the equal n's case. Later in this chapter we consider the unequal n's case.

The layout of the sample data is shown in Table 13.1. Here we see that each row represents the observations for a particular level of factor A (independent variable 1), and that each

TABLE 13.1

Layout for the Two-Factor ANOVA

	Level of Factor B				
Level of Factor A	**1**	**2**	**…**	***K***	**Row Mean**
1	Y_{111}	Y_{112}	…	Y_{11K}	$\bar{Y}_{.1.}$
	.	.	…	.	
	.	.	…	.	
	.	.	…	.	
	Y_{n11}	Y_{n12}	…	Y_{n1K}	
	$\bar{Y}_{.11}$	$\bar{Y}_{.12}$	…	$\bar{Y}_{.1K}$	
2	Y_{121}	Y_{122}	…	Y_{12K}	$\bar{Y}_{.2.}$
	.	.	…	.	
	.	.	…	.	
	.	.	…	.	
	Y_{n21}	Y_{n22}	…	Y_{n2K}	
	$\bar{Y}_{.21}$	$\bar{Y}_{.22}$	…	$\bar{Y}_{.2K}$	
.	.	.	…	.	.
	Y_{1J1}	Y_{1J2}	…	Y_{1JK}	
J	.	.	…	.	$\bar{Y}_{.J.}$
	.	.	…	.	
	Y_{nJ1}	Y_{nJ2}	…	Y_{nJK}	
	$\bar{Y}_{.J1}$	$\bar{Y}_{.J2}$	…	$\bar{Y}_{.JK}$	
Column Mean	$\bar{Y}_{..1}$	$\bar{Y}_{..2}$		$\bar{Y}_{..K}$	$\bar{Y}_{...}$

column represents the observations for a particular level of factor B (independent variable 2). At the bottom of each column are the column means $\left(\bar{Y}_{..k}\right)$, to the right of each row are the row means $\left(\bar{Y}_{.j.}\right)$, and in the lower right-hand corner is the overall mean $\left(\bar{Y}_{...}\right)$. We also need the cell means $\left(\bar{Y}_{.jk}\right)$, which are shown at the bottom of each cell. Thus, the layout is one form in which to think about the data.

13.1.1.2 The ANOVA Model

This section introduces the analysis of variance linear model, as well as estimation of the parameters of the model. The two-factor analysis of variance model is a form of the **general linear model,** like the one-factor ANOVA model of Chapter 11. The two-factor ANOVA fixed-effects model can be written in terms of **population parameters** as follows:

$$Y_{ijk} = \mu + \alpha_j + \beta_k + (\alpha\beta)_{jk} + \varepsilon_{ijk}$$

where Y_{ijk} is the observed score on the criterion (i.e., dependent variable) variable for individual i in level j of factor A (i.e., independent variable 1) and level k of factor B (i.e., independent variable 2) (or in the jk cell), μ is the overall or grand population mean (i.e., regardless of cell designation), α_j is the main effect for level j of factor A (row or effect of independent variable 1), β_k is the main effect for level k of factor B (column or effect of independent variable 2), $(\alpha\beta)_{jk}$ is the interaction effect for the combination of level j of factor A and level k of factor B, and ε_{ijk} is the random residual error for individual i in cell jk. The residual error can be due to individual differences, measurement error, and/or other factors not under investigation.

The population effects and residual error can be computed as follows:

$$\alpha_j = \mu_{.j.} - \mu$$

$$\beta_k = \mu_{..k} - \mu$$

$$(\alpha\beta)_{jk} = \mu_{.jk} - (\mu_{.j.} + \mu_{..k} - \mu)$$

$$\varepsilon_{ijk} = Y_{ijk} - \mu_{.jk}$$

That is, the **row effect,** α_j, is equal to the difference between the population mean of level j of factor A (i.e., one particular group or category of independent variable 1, $\mu_{.j.}$) and the overall population mean, μ. The **column effect,** β_k, is equal to the difference between the population mean of level k of factor B (i.e., one particular group or category of independent variable 2, $\mu_{..k}$) and the overall population mean, μ. The **interaction effect,** $(\alpha\beta)_{jk}$, is the difference between the population cell mean $\left(\mu_{.jk}\right)$ and the sum of the population mean of level j of factor A (i.e., one particular group or category of independent variable 1, $\mu_{.j.}$) and the population mean of level k of factor B (i.e., one particular group or category of independent variable 2, $\mu_{..k}$) subtracted from the overall population mean, μ. The **residual error,** ε_{ijk}, is equal to the difference between an individual's observed score, Y_{ijk}, and the population mean of cell jk, $\mu_{.jk}$.

The row, column, and interaction effects can also be thought of as the average effect of being a member of a particular row (i.e., a unit assigned to group or category A, B, or C of independent variable 1), *column* (i.e., a unit assigned to group or category X, Y, or Z of independent variable 2), *or cell* (e.g., a unit assigned to group A of independent variable 1 and group Y of independent variable 2), respectively. It should also be noted that the sum of the row effects is equal to zero, the sum of the column effects is equal to zero, and the sum of the interaction effects is equal to zero (both across rows and across columns). This implies, for example, that if there are any *nonzero* row effects, then the row effects will balance out around zero with some positive and some negative effects. Likewise for column and interaction effects.

You may be wondering why the interaction effect looks a little different from the main effects. We have given you the version that is solely a function of population means. A more intuitively convincing **conceptual version of the interaction effect** is as follows:

$$(\alpha\beta)_{jk} = \mu_{.jk} - \alpha_j - \beta_k - \mu$$

which is written in similar fashion to the row and column effects. Here we see that the interaction effect $\left[(\alpha\beta)_{jk}\right]$ is equal to the population cell mean $(\mu_{.jk})$ minus the following: (a) the row effect, (α_j); (b) the column effect, (β_k); and (c) the overall population mean, (μ). *In other words, the interaction is solely a function of cell means without regard to, or controlling for, its row effect, column effect, or the overall mean.*

To estimate the parameters of the model [μ, α_j, β_k, $(\alpha\beta)_{jk}$, and ε_{ijk}], the least squares method of estimation is used as the most appropriate for general linear models (e.g., regression, ANOVA). These sample estimates are represented by $\bar{Y}_{...}$, a_j, b_j, $(ab)_{jk}$, and e_{ijk}, respectively, where the latter four are computed as follows, respectively:

$$a_j = \bar{Y}_{.j.} - \bar{Y}_{...}$$

$$b_k = \bar{Y}_{..k} - \bar{Y}_{...}$$

$$(ab)_{jk} = \bar{Y}_{.jk} - \left(\bar{Y}_{.j.} + \bar{Y}_{..k} - \bar{Y}_{...}\right)$$

$$e_{ijk} = Y_{ijk} - \bar{Y}_{.jk}$$

Note that $\bar{Y}_{...}$ represents the overall sample mean, $\bar{Y}_{.j.}$ represents the sample mean for level *j* of factor A (independent variable 1), $\bar{Y}_{..k}$ represents the sample mean for level *k* of factor B (independent variable 2), and $\bar{Y}_{.jk}$ represents the sample mean for cell *jk* (the interaction of factor A and factor B).

For the two-factor ANOVA model, there are three sets of hypotheses, one for each of the main effects, and one for the interaction effect. The null and alternative hypotheses, respectively, for testing the main effect of factor A (independent variable 1) are as follows:

$$H_{01}: \mu_{.1.} = \mu_{.2.} = \ldots \mu_{.J.}$$

$$H_{11}: \text{not all the } \mu_{.j.} \text{ are equal}$$

The hypotheses for testing the main effect of factor B (independent variable 2) are noted as:

$$H_{02}: \mu_{..1} = \mu_{..2} = \ldots = \mu_{..K}$$

$$H_{12}: \text{not all the } \mu_{..k} \text{ are equal}$$

Finally, the hypotheses for testing the interaction effect (independent variable 1 with independent variable 2) are as follows:

$$H_{03}: \left(\mu_{.jk} - \mu_{.j.} - \mu_{..k} + \mu\right) = 0 \text{ for all } j \text{ and}$$

$$H_{13}: \text{not all the} \left(\mu_{.jk} - \mu_{.j.} - \mu_{..k} + \mu\right) \text{ are equal}$$

The null hypotheses can also be written in terms of row, column and interaction effects (which may make more intuitive sense to you) as follows:

$$H_{01}: \alpha_1 = \alpha_2 = \ldots = \alpha_J = 0$$
$$H_{02}: \beta_1 = \beta_2 = \ldots = \beta_K = 0$$
$$H_{03}: (\alpha\beta)_{jk} = 0 \text{ for all } j \text{ and } k$$

As in the one-factor model, all of the alternative hypotheses are written in a general form to cover the multitude of possible mean differences that could arise. These range from only two of the means being different to all of the means being different from one another. Also, because of the way the alternative hypotheses have been written, only a nondirectional alternative is appropriate. If one of the null hypotheses is rejected, then consider a multiple comparison procedure so as to determine which means, or combination of means, are significantly different (this is discussed later).

13.1.1.3 Main Effects and Interaction Effects

Finally, we come to a formal discussion of main effects and interaction effects. A **main effect** of factor A (independent variable 1) is defined as the effect of factor A, averaged across the levels of factor B (independent variable 2), on the dependent variable Y. More precisely, it represents the unique effect of factor A on the outcome Y, controlling statistically for factor B. A similar statement may be made for the main effect of factor B.

As far as the concept of interaction is concerned, things are a bit more complex. An **interaction** can be defined in any of the following ways: An interaction is said to exist if (a) certain combinations of the two factors produce effects *beyond* the effects of the two factors when those two factors are considered separately; (b) the mean differences among the levels of factor A are not constant across, and thus depend on, the levels of factor B; (c) there is *a joint effect* of factors A and B on Y; or (d) there is a *unique effect* that could not be predicted from knowledge of only the main effects.

Let us mention two fairly common examples of interaction effects. The first is known as an aptitude-treatment interaction (ATI). This means that the effectiveness of a particular treatment depends on the aptitude of the individual. In other words, some treatments are more effective for individuals with a high aptitude, and other treatments are more effective for those with a low aptitude. A second example is an interaction between treatment and sex. Here some treatments may be more effective for males and others may be more effective for females. This is often considered in gender studies research.

For some graphical examples of main and interaction effects, take a look at the various plots in Figure 13.1. Each plot represents the graph of a particular set of *cell means* (the mean of the dependent variable for a cell—the combination of a particular category of factor A and a particular category of factor B), sometimes referred to as a **profile plot**. On the ***X* axis** are the levels of factor A, the ***Y* axis** provides the cell means on the dependent variable Y, and the **separate lines** in the body of the plot represent the levels of factor B (although the specific placement of the two factors here is arbitrary; alternatively factor B could be plotted on the X axis and factor A as the separate lines). *Profile plots provide information about the possible existence of a main effect for A, a main effect for B, and/or an interaction effect.* A *main effect for factor A* can be examined by taking the means for each level of A and averaging them across the levels of B. If these marginal means for the levels of A are the same or nearly so, this would indicate no main effect for factor A. A *main effect for factor B* can be assessed by taking the means for each level of B and averaging them across the levels of A. If these marginal means for the levels of B are the same or nearly so, this would imply no main effect for factor B. An *interaction effect* is determined by whether the cell means for the levels of A are constant across the levels of B (or vice versa). This is easily viewed in a profile plot by checking to see whether or not the lines are parallel. *Parallel lines indicate no interaction, whereas nonparallel lines suggest that an interaction may exist.* Of course, the statistical significance of the main and interaction effects is a matter to be determined by the *F* test statistics (which we will soon learn). The profile plots give you only a rough idea as to the possible existence of the effects. For instance, lines that are nearly parallel will probably not show up as a significant interaction. It is suggested that the plot can be simplified if the factor with the most levels is shown on the *X* axis. This cuts down on the number of lines drawn.

The plots shown in Figure 13.1 represent the eight different sets of results possible for a two-factor design, that is, from no effects to all three effects being evident. To simplify matters, only two levels of each factor are used. Figure 13.1a indicates that there is no main effect for either factor A or B, and there is no interaction effect. The lines are horizontal (no A effect), lie nearly on top of one another (no B effect), and are parallel (no interaction effect). Figure 13.1b suggests the presence of an effect due to factor A only (the lines are not horizontal because the mean for A_1 is greater than the mean for A_2), but the lines are nearly on top of one another (no B effect) and are parallel (no interaction). In Figure 13.1c we see a separation between the lines for the levels of B (B_1 being greater than B_2); thus a main effect for B is likely, but the lines are horizontal (no A effect), and are parallel (no interaction).

For Figure 13.1d there are no main effects (the means for the levels of A are the same, and the means for the levels of B are the same), but an interaction is indicated by the lack of parallel lines. Figure 13.1e suggests a main effect for both factors, as shown by mean differences (A_1 less than A_2, and B_1 greater than B_2), but no interaction (the lines are parallel). In Figure 13.1f we see a main effect for A (A_1 less than A_2) and an interaction effect, but no main effect for B (little separation between the lines for factor B). For Figure 13.1g there appears to be a main effect for B (B_1 greater than B_2) and an interaction, but no main effect for A. Finally, in Figure 13.1h we see the likelihood of two main effects (A_1 less than A_2, and B_1 greater than B_2), and an interaction. Although these are clearly the only possible outcomes from a two-factor design, the precise pattern will differ depending on the obtained cell means. In other words, if your study yields a significant effect only for factor A, your profile plot need not look exactly like Figure 13.1b, but it will retain the same general pattern and interpretation.

In many statistics texts, a big deal is made about the type of interaction shown in the profile plot. They make a distinction between an ordinal interaction and a disordinal interaction. An **ordinal interaction** is said to exist when the lines are not parallel and they do not cross; ordinal here means the same relative order of the cell means is maintained across the levels of one of the factors. For example, the means for level 1 of factor B are always greater than the means for level 2 of B, regardless of the level of factor A. A **disordinal interaction** is said to exist when the lines are not parallel and they do cross. For example, the mean for B_1 is greater than the mean for B_2 at A_1, but the opposite is true at A_2. Dwelling on the distinction between the two types of interaction is not recommended as it can depend on how the plot is drawn (i.e., which factor is plotted on the *X* axis). That is, when factor A is plotted on the X axis a disordinal interaction may be shown, and when factor B is plotted on the *X* axis an ordinal interaction may be shown. The purpose of the profile plot is to simplify interpretation of the results; worrying about the type of interaction may merely serve to confuse that interpretation.

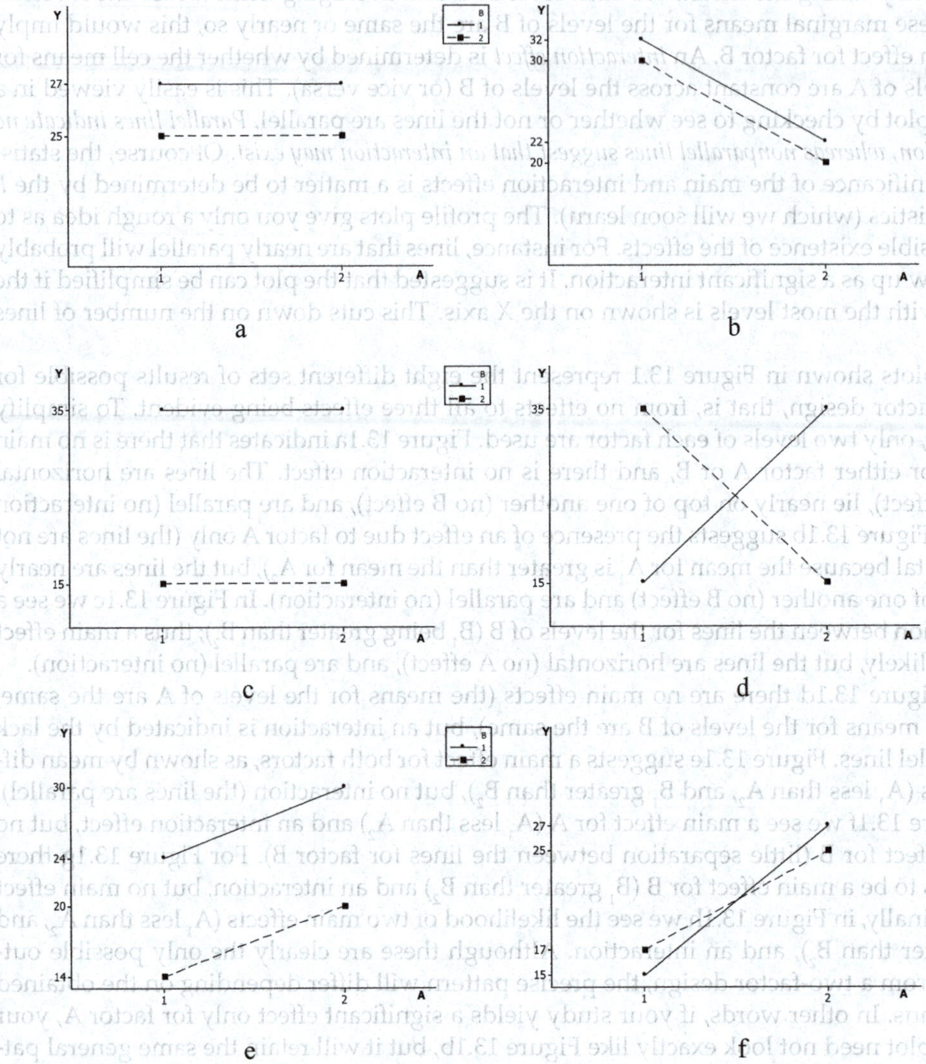

FIGURE 13.1
Display of possible two-factor ANOVA effects.

Let us take a moment to discuss how to deal with an interaction effect. Consider two possible situations, one where there is a significant interaction effect and one where there is no such effect. If there is *no* significant interaction effect, then the findings regarding the main effects can be generalized with greater confidence. In this situation, the main effects are known as **additive effects**, and an additive linear model with no interaction term could actually be used to describe the data. For example, the results might be that for factor A, the level 1 means always exceed those of level 2 by 10 points, across all levels of factor B. *Thus, we can make a blanket statement about the constant added benefits of* A_1 *over* A_2*, regardless of the level of factor B*. In addition, for the no-interaction situation, the main effects are statistically independent of one another; that is, *each of the main effects serves as an independent predictor* of *Y*.

If there *is* a significant interaction effect, then the findings regarding the main effects cannot be generalized with such confidence. In this situation, the main effects are not additive and the interaction term must be included in the linear model. For example, the results might be that (a) the mean for A_1 is greater than A_2 when considering B_1, but (b) the mean for A_1 is less than A_2 when considering B_2. *Thus, we cannot make a blanket statement about the constant added benefits of* A_1 *over* A_2*, because it depends on the level of factor B*. In addition, for the interaction situation, the main effects are not statistically independent of one another; that is, *each of the main effects does not serve as an independent predictor of Y*. In order to predict *Y* well, information is necessary about the levels of factors A and B. *Thus, in the presence of a significant interaction, generalizations about the main effects must be qualified*. A profile plot should be examined so that a proper graphical interpretation of the interaction and main effects can be made. A significant interaction serves as a warning that one cannot generalize statements about a main effect for A over all levels of B. If you obtain a significant interaction, this is an important result. Do not ignore it and go ahead to interpret the main effects.

13.1.1.4 Partitioning the Sums of Squares

As pointed out in Chapter 11, partitioning the sums of squares is an important concept in the analysis of variance. We will illustrate with a two factor model, but this can be extended to more than two factors. Let us begin with the **total sum of squares in** ***Y***, denoted here as SS_{total}. The term SS_{total} represents the amount of total variation among all of the observations without regard to row, column or cell membership. The next step is to partition the total variation into variation between the levels of factor A (denoted by SS_A), variation between the levels of factor B (denoted by SS_B), variation due to the interaction of the levels of factors A and B (denoted by SS_{AB}), and variation within the cells combined across cells (denoted by SS_{with}). In the two-factor analysis of variance, then, we can partition SS_{total} into the following:

$$SS_{total} = SS_A + SS_B + SS_{AB} + SS_{with}$$

Then computational formulas are used by statistical software to actually compute these sums of squares.

13.1.1.5 The ANOVA Summary Table

The next step is to assemble the ANOVA summary table. The purpose of the summary table is to simply summarize the analysis of variance. A general form of the summary table for the two-factor model is shown in Table 13.2. The first column lists the sources of variation

TABLE 13.2

Two-Factor Analysis of Variance Summary Table

Source	SS	df	MS	F
A	SS_A	$J-1$	MS_A	MS_A/MS_{with}
B	SS_B	$K-1$	MS_B	MS_B/MS_{with}
AB	SS_{AB}	$(J-1)(K-1)$	MS_{AB}	MS_{AB}/MS_{with}
Within	SS_{with}	$N-JK$	MS_{with}	
Total	SS_{total}	$N-1$		

in the model. We note that the total variation is divided into a within-groups source, and a general between-groups source, which is then subdivided into sources due to A, B, and the AB interaction. This is in keeping with the spirit of the one-factor model, where total variation was divided into a between-groups source (just one effect because there is only one factor and no interaction term) and a within-groups source. The second column provides the computed sums of squares.

The third column gives the degrees of freedom for each source. As always, degrees of freedom have to do with the number of observations that are free to vary in a particular context. Because there are J levels of factor A, then the number of degrees of freedom for the A source is equal to $J-1$. As there are J means and we know the overall mean, then only $J-1$ of the means are free to vary. This is the same rationale we have been using throughout this text. As there are K levels of factor B, there are $K-1$ degrees of freedom for the B source. For the AB interaction source, we take the product of the degrees of freedom for the main effects. Thus we have as degrees of freedom for AB the product $(J-1)(K-1)$. The degrees of freedom within groups is equal to the total number of observations minus the number of cells, $N-JK$. Finally, the degrees of freedom total can be written simply as $N-1$.

The fourth column provides the mean squares terms. In this column, the sum of squares terms are weighted by the appropriate degrees of freedom to generate the mean squares terms. Thus, for instance, $MS_S = SS_A/df_A$.

Finally, in the last column of the ANOVA summary table, we have the F values, which represent the summary statistics for the analysis of variance. There are three hypotheses that we are interested in testing, one for each of the two main effects and one for the interaction effect, so there will be three F test statistics. For the factorial fixed-effects model, each F value is computed by taking the MS for the source that you are interested in testing and dividing it by MS_{with}. Thus for each hypothesis, the same error term is used in forming the F ratio (i.e., MS_{with}). We return to the two-factor model for cases where the effects are not fixed in Chapter 15.

Each of the F test statistics is then compared with the appropriate F critical value so as to make a decision about the relevant null hypothesis. These critical values are found in the F table of Appendix Table A.4 as follows: for the test of factor A as ${}_{\alpha}F_{J-1,N-JK}$; for the test of factor B as ${}_{\alpha}F_{K-1,N-JK}$; and for the test of the interaction as ${}_{\alpha}F_{(J-1)(K-1),N-JK}$. Thus, with a two-factor model, testing two main effects and one interaction, there are three F tests and three decisions that must be made. Each significance test is one-tailed so as to be consistent with the alternative hypothesis. The null hypothesis is rejected if the F test statistic exceeds the F critical value.

Recall that these F tests are **omnibus tests** that tell only if there is an *overall* main effect or interaction effect. If the F test statistic does exceed the F critical value, and there is more than one degree of freedom for the source being tested, then it is not clear precisely why the null hypothesis was rejected. For example, if there are three levels of factor A and the null hypothesis for A is rejected, then we are not sure where the mean differences lie among the levels of A. In this case, some multiple comparison procedure should be used to determine where the mean differences are; this is the topic of the next section.

13.1.1.6 Multiple Comparison Procedures

In this section, we extend the concepts related to multiple comparison procedures (MCPs) covered in Chapter 12 to the two-factor ANOVA model. This model includes main and interaction effects; consequently you can examine contrasts of both main and interaction effects. In general, the procedures described in Chapter 12 can be applied to the two-factor situation. Things become more complicated as we have row and column means (i.e., marginal means), and cell means. Thus we have to be careful about which means are being considered.

Let us begin with contrasts of the *main effects*. If the effect for factor A is significant, and there are more than two levels of factor A, then we can form contrasts that compare the levels of factor A ignoring factor B. Here we would be comparing the means for the levels of factor A, which are marginal means as opposed to cell means. Considering each factor separately is strongly advised; considering the factors simultaneously is to be avoided. Some statistics texts suggest that you consider the design as a one-factor model with JK levels when using MCPs to examine main effects. This is inconsistent with the design and the intent of separating effects, and is not recommended.

For contrasts involving the *interaction*, our recommendation is to begin with a complex interaction contrast if there are more than four cells in the model. Thus, for example, in a 4 × 4 design that consists of four levels of factor A and four levels of factor B, one possibility is to test both 4 × 2 complex interaction contrasts. An example of one such contrast is as follows [where $\left(\bar{Y}_{.11}+\bar{Y}_{.21}+\bar{Y}_{.31}+\bar{Y}_{.41}\right)$, for example, is the sum of the cell means of each level of factor A for level 1 of factor B and $\left(\bar{Y}_{.12}+\bar{Y}_{.22}+\bar{Y}_{.32}+\bar{Y}_{.42}\right)$, is the sum of the cell means of each level of factor A for level 2 of factor B]:

$$\psi' = \frac{\left(\bar{Y}_{.11}+\bar{Y}_{.21}+\bar{Y}_{.31}+\bar{Y}_{.41}\right)}{4} - \frac{\left(\bar{Y}_{.12}+\bar{Y}_{.22}+\bar{Y}_{.32}+\bar{Y}_{.42}\right)}{4}$$

with a standard error of the following:

$$s_{\psi'} = \sqrt{MS_{with}\left(\sum_{j=1}^{J}\sum_{k=1}^{K}\frac{c_{jk}^2}{n_{jk}}\right)}$$

where n_{jk} is the number of observations in cell jk. This contrast would examine the interaction between the four groups in factor A and the first two groups in factor B. A second complex interaction contrast could consider the interaction between the four groups in factor A and the other two groups in factor B.

If the complex interaction contrast is significant, then follow this up with a simple interaction contrast that involves only four cell means. This is a single degree of freedom contrast because it involves only two levels of each factor (known as a **tetrad difference**). An example of such a contrast is the following:

$$\psi' = \left(\bar{Y}_{.11} - \bar{Y}_{.21}\right) - \left(\bar{Y}_{.12} - \bar{Y}_{.22}\right)$$

with a similar standard error term. Using the same example, this contrast would examine the interaction between the first two groups in factor A and the first two groups in factor B.

Most of the MCPs described in Chapter 12 can be used for testing main effects and interaction effects (although there is some debate about the appropriate use of interaction contrasts; see Boik, 1979; Marascuilo and Levin, 1970, 1976). Keppel and Wickens (2004) consider interaction contrasts in much detail. Finally, some statistics texts suggest the use of simple main effects in testing a significant interaction. These involve comparing, for example, the levels of factor A at a particular level of factor B, and are generally conducted by further partitioning the sums of squares. However, the simple main effects sums of squares represent a portion of a main effect plus the interaction effect. Thus, the simple main effect does not really help us to understand the interaction, and it is not recommended here.

13.1.1.7 Expected Mean Squares

As we asked in Chapter 11 for the one-factor fixed-effects model, for the two-factor fixed-effects model being considered here, we again ask the question, "How do we know which source of variation to use as the error term in the denominator?" That is, for the two-factor fixed-effects ANOVA model, how did we know to use MS_{with} as the error term in testing for the main effects and the interaction effect? As we learned in Chapter 11, an expected mean square for a particular source of variation represents the average mean square value for that source obtained if the same study were to be replicated an infinite number of times. For instance, the expected value of MS_A, denoted by $E(MS_A)$, is the average value of MS_A over repeated samplings.

Let us examine what the expected mean square terms actually look like for our two-factor fixed-effects model. Consider the two situations of (a) all of the H_0 actually being true and (b) all of the H_0 actually being false. If all of the H_0 are actually *true*, such that there really are no main effects or an interaction effect, then the expected mean squares are:

$$E(MS_A) = \sigma_\varepsilon^2$$

$$E(MS_B) = \sigma_\varepsilon^2$$

$$E(MS_{AB}) = \sigma_\varepsilon^2$$

$$E(MS_{with}) = \sigma_\varepsilon^2$$

and thus using MS_{with} as the error term will produce F values around 1.

If all of the H_0 are actually *false*, such that there really are main effects and an interaction effect, then the expected mean squares are as follows:

$$E(MS_A) = \sigma_\varepsilon^2 + \left(nK\sum_{j=1}^{J}\alpha_j^2\right) / (J-1)$$

$$E(MS_B) = \sigma_\varepsilon^2 + \left(nJ\sum_{k=1}^{K}\beta_k^2\right) / (K-1)$$

$$E(MS_{AB}) = \sigma_\varepsilon^2 + \left(n\sum_{j=1}^{J}\sum_{k=1}^{K}(\alpha\beta)_{jk}^2\right) / \left[(J-1)(K-1)\right]$$

$$E(MS_{with}) = \sigma_\varepsilon^2$$

and thus using MS_{with} as the error term will produce F values greater than 1.

There is a difference in the main and interaction effects between when H_0 is actually true as compared to when H_0 is actually false because in the latter situation there is a second term. The important parts of this second term are α, β, and $\alpha\beta$, which represent the effects for A, B and AB, respectively. The larger this part becomes, the larger the F ratio becomes. In comparing the two situations, we also see that $E(MS_{with})$ is the same whether H_0 is actually true or false, and thus it represents a reliable estimate of σ_ε^2. This term is *mean-free* because it does not depend on any mean differences.

Finally let us put all of this information together. In general, the **F ratio** represents

$$F = \frac{(systematic\ variability + error\ variability)}{error\ variability}$$

where, for the two-factor fixed-effects model, systematic variability is variability due to the main or interaction effects (i.e., between sources) and error variability is variability within. The F ratio is formed in a particular way because we want to isolate the systematic variability in the numerator. For this model, the only appropriate error term to use for each F ratio is MS_{with} because it does serve to isolate the systematic variability.

3.1.1.8 An Example

Consider the following illustration of the two-factor design. Here we expand on the example presented in Chapter 11 by adding a second factor to the model. Our dependent variable will again be psychological distress, factor A is type of sport in which the sampled athlete participates, and factor B is selection status (i.e., whether the athlete is deselected or selected to continue to compete on their team). Thus, the researcher is interested in whether the type of sport in which the athlete participates, the selection status (i.e., whether they are deselected or selected to continue to participate on their team), or the interaction of type of sport and selection status influences psychological distress. The categories of type of sport are defined again as (a) movement, (b) target, (c) fielding, and (d) territory. Selection status is defined as (a) deselected and (b) selected. This is not a manipulated design; i.e., this is truly an observational study where athletes were *not* randomly assigned to either type of sport or selection status. There were four athletes in each cell and eight cells (four levels of type of sport and two categories of selection status, thus 4 × 2 or 8 combinations of type of sport and selection status) for a total of 32 observations. Table 13.3 depicts the raw data and sample means for each cell (given beneath each cell), column, row, and overall.

The results are summarized in the ANOVA summary table as shown in Table 13.4. The F test statistics are compared to the following critical values obtained from Appendix Table A.4 (α = .05): ${}_{.05}F_{3,24} = 3.01$ for the A (i.e., type of sport) and AB (i.e., type of sport by selection status) effects; and ${}_{.05}F_{1,24} = 4.26$ for the B (i.e., selection status) effect. The test statistics exceed the critical values for the A and B effects only, so we can reject these H_0 and conclude that both the type of sport and selection status are related to mean differences in psychological distress. The interaction was shown not to be a significant effect. If you would like to see an example of a two-factor design where the interaction is significant, take a look at the end of chapter problems, computational problem 6.

TABLE 13.3

Data for the Elite Athlete Example: Psychological Distress by Type of Sport and Selection

	Selection (B)		
Sport (A)	**Deselected**	**Selected**	**Row Mean**
Movement (e.g., gymnastics, dance)	15	10	11.1250
	12	8	
	21	7	
	13	3	
	15.2500	7.0000	
Target (e.g., golf)	20	13	17.8750
	22	9	
	24	18	
	25	12	
	22.7500	13.0000	
Fielding (e.g., baseball)	24	10	20.2500
	29	12	
	27	21	
	25	14	
	26.2500	14.2500	
Territory (e.g., football)	30	22	24.3750
	26	20	
	29	25	
	28	15	
	28.2500	20.5000	
Column mean	23.1250	13.6875	18.4063 *(Overall mean)*

TABLE 13.4

Two-Factor Analysis of Variance Summary Table—Elite Athlete Example

Source	*SS*	*df*	*MS*	*F*
A	738.5938	3	246.1979	21.3504*
B	712.5313	1	712.5313	61.7911**
AB	21.8438	3	7.2813	0.6314*
Within	276.7500	24	11.5313	
Total	1749.7188	31		

$*\ {}_{.05}F_{3,24} = 3.01$

$**\ {}_{.05}F_{1,24} = 4.26$

Next we estimate the main and interaction effects. The *main effects for the levels of A* (i.e., type of sport) are estimated to be:

$Movement: a_1 = \bar{Y}_{.1.} - \bar{Y}_{...} = 11.1250 - 18.4063 = -7.2813$

$Target: a_2 = \bar{Y}_{.2.} - \bar{Y}_{...} = 17.8750 - 18.4063 = -0.5313$

$Fielding: a_3 = \bar{Y}_{.3.} - \bar{Y}_{...} = 20.2500 - 18.4063 = 1.8437$

$Territory: a_4 = \bar{Y}_{.4.} - \bar{Y}_{...} = 24.3750 - 18.4063 = 5.9687$

The *main effects for the levels of B* (selection status) are estimated to be:

$Deselected: b_1 = \bar{Y}_{..1} - \bar{Y}_{...} = 23.1250 - 18.4063 = 4.7187$

$Selected: b_2 = \bar{Y}_{..2} - \bar{Y}_{...} = 13.6875 - 18.4063 = -4.7187$

Finally, the *interaction effects for the combinations of the levels of factors A (type of sport) and B (selection status)* are:

$$(ab)_{11} = \bar{Y}_{.11} - \left(\bar{Y}_{.1.} + \bar{Y}_{..1} - \bar{Y}_{...}\right) = 15.2500 - \left(11.1250 + 23.1250 - 18.4063\right) = -0.5937$$

$$(ab)_{12} = \bar{Y}_{.12} - \left(\bar{Y}_{.1.} + \bar{Y}_{..2} - \bar{Y}_{...}\right) = 7.0000 - \left(11.1250 + 13.6875 - 18.4063\right) = 0.5938$$

$$(ab)_{21} = \bar{Y}_{.21} - \left(\bar{Y}_{.2.} + \bar{Y}_{..1} - \bar{Y}_{...}\right) = 22.7500 - \left(17.8750 + 23.1250 - 18.4063\right) = 0.1563$$

$$(ab)_{22} = \bar{Y}_{.22} - \left(\bar{Y}_{.2.} + \bar{Y}_{..2} - \bar{Y}_{...}\right) = 13.0000 - \left(17.8750 + 13.6875 - 18.4063\right) = -0.1562$$

$$(ab)_{31} = \bar{Y}_{.31} - \left(\bar{Y}_{.3.} + \bar{Y}_{..1} - \bar{Y}_{...}\right) = 26.2500 - \left(20.2500 + 23.1250 - 18.4063\right) = 1.2813$$

$$(ab)_{41} = \bar{Y}_{.41} - \left(\bar{Y}_{.4.} + \bar{Y}_{..1} - \bar{Y}_{...}\right) = 28.2500 - \left(24.3750 + 23.1250 - 18.4063\right) = -0.8437$$

$$(ab)_{42} = \bar{Y}_{.42} - \left(\bar{Y}_{.4.} + \bar{Y}_{..2} - \bar{Y}_{...}\right) = 20.5000 - \left(24.3750 + 13.6875 - 18.4063\right) = 0.8438$$

The profile plot shown in Figure 13.2 graphically depicts these effects. The main effect for type of sport (factor A) was statistically significant and has more than two levels, so let us consider one example of a multiple comparison procedure, Tukey's HSD test. Recall from Chapter 12 that the HSD test is a family-wise procedure most appropriate for considering all pairwise contrasts with a balanced design (which is the case for these data). The following are the computations:

The critical value (obtained from Appendix Table A.9):

$$_{\alpha}q_{df(with),\,J} = {}_{.05}q_{24,4} = 3.901$$

The standard error:

$$s_{\Psi'} = \sqrt{\frac{MS_{with}}{n}} = \sqrt{\frac{11.5313}{8}} = 1.2006$$

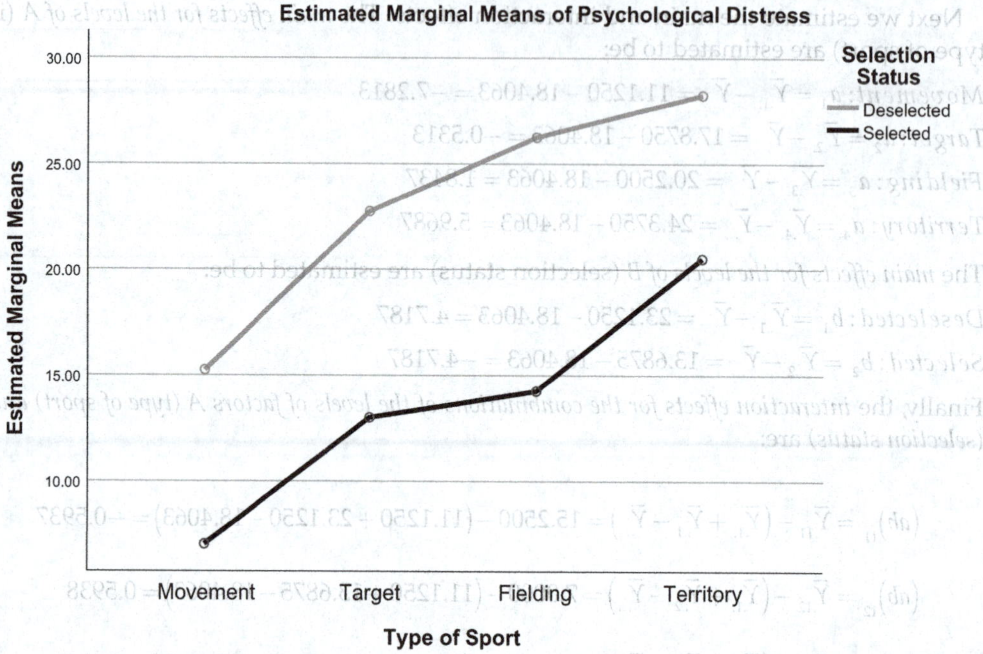

FIGURE 13.2
Profile plot for elite athlete example data.

The test statistics:

$$q_1 = \frac{\bar{Y}_{.4.} - \bar{Y}_{.1.}}{s_{\Psi'}} = \frac{24.3750 - 11.1250}{1.2006} = \mathbf{11.0361}^*$$

$$q_2 = \frac{\bar{Y}_{.4.} - \bar{Y}_{.2.}}{s_{\Psi'}} = \frac{24.3750 - 17.8750}{1.2006} = \mathbf{5.4140}^*$$

$$q_3 = \frac{\bar{Y}_{.4.} - \bar{Y}_{.3.}}{s_{\Psi'}} = \frac{24.3750 - 20.2500}{1.2006} = 3.4358$$

$$q_4 = \frac{\bar{Y}_{.3.} - \bar{Y}_{.1.}}{s_{\Psi'}} = \frac{20.2500 - 11.1250}{1.2006} = \mathbf{7.6004}^*$$

$$q_5 = \frac{\bar{Y}_{.3.} - \bar{Y}_{.2.}}{s_{\Psi'}} = \frac{20.2500 - 17.8750}{1.2006} = 1.9782$$

$$q_6 = \frac{\bar{Y}_{.2.} - \bar{Y}_{.1.}}{s_{\Psi'}} = \frac{17.8750 - 11.1250}{1.2006} = \mathbf{5.6222}^*$$

Recall that we compare the test statistic value to the critical value to make our hypothesis testing decision. If the test statistic value exceeds the critical value, we reject the null hypothesis and conclude that those means differ. For these tests, the results indicate that the means for the levels of factor *A* (type of sport) are statistically significantly different for levels 1 and 4 (i.e., the test statistic value is 11.0361 and the critical value is 3.901), 2 and 4, 1 and 3, and 1 and 2 (see equation results in bold). Thus, level 1 (movement) is significantly different from the other three types of sports, and levels 2 and 4 (target and fielding) are also significantly different. The only levels that are not statistically different are levels 2 and 3 $(q_5 = 1.9782)$ and levels 3 and 4 $(q_3 = 3.4358)$.

These results are somewhat different than those found with the one-factor model in Chapters 11 and 12 (where the significantly different levels were only 1 vs. 4 and 1 vs. 3). The MS_{with} has been reduced with the introduction of the second factor from 36.1116 to 11.5313 because SS_{with} has been reduced from 1,011.1250 to 276.7500. Although the *SS* and *MS* for the type of sport factor remain unchanged, this resulted in the *F* test statistic being considerably larger (increased from 6.8177 to 21.3504), although observed power was quite high in both models. Recall that this is one of the benefits we mentioned earlier about the use of additional factors in the model. Also, although the effect of factor B (selection status) was significant, there are only two levels, and thus we need not carry out any multiple comparisons (psychological distress is higher for deselected athletes). Finally, since the interaction was not significant, it is not necessary to consider any related contrasts.

13.1.2 Power

As mentioned in Chapter 11, power can be determined either in the planned (*a priori*) or observed (post hoc) power context. For planned power we typically use tables or power charts (e.g., Cohen, 1988; Murphy, Myors, & Wolach, 2009) or software (e.g., G*Power). These are particularly useful in terms of determining adequate sample sizes when designing a study. Observed power is reported by statistics software, such as SPSS, to indicate the actual power in a given study.

13.1.3 Effect Size

Various measures of effect size have been proposed. Let us examine some commonly used measures, which assume equal variances across the cells, and that are presented in Olejnik and Algina (2000). The formulas presented assume a two-factor design (factors A and B and the interaction of AB); however, these can easily be extended to additional factorial designs.

13.1.3.1 Proportion of Total Variance Effect Size

We begin with *proportion of total variance effect size* indices. *These effect size indices are interpreted as the proportion of total variability in the dependent variable that is accounted for by a factor (e.g., A, B, or the interaction AB).* One such effect size measure is the **omega squared statistic**, ω^2. We can determine ω^2 as follows and will offer two different ways to calculate the index, both of which should yield the same value:

$$\omega_A^2 = \frac{SS_A - (J-1)(MS_{with})}{SS_{total} + MS_{with}} = \frac{df_A(MS_A - MS_{with})}{SS_{total} + MS_{with}}$$

$$\omega_B^2 = \frac{SS_B - (K-1)(MS_{with})}{SS_{total} + MS_{with}} = \frac{df_B(MS_B - MS_{with})}{SS_{total} + MS_{with}}$$

$$\omega_{AB}^2 = \frac{SS_{AB} - (J-1)(K-1)(MS_{with})}{SS_{total} + MS_{with}} = \frac{df_{AB}(MS_{AB} - MS_{with})}{SS_{total} + MS_{with}}$$

Epsilon squared, ε^2, is another proportion of total variance effect size and can be computed as follows:

$$\varepsilon_A^2 = \frac{df_A(MS_A - MS_{with})}{SS_{total}}$$

$$\varepsilon_B^2 = \frac{df_B(MS_B - MS_{with})}{SS_{total}}$$

$$\varepsilon_{AB}^2 = \frac{df_{AB}(MS_{AB} - MS_{with})}{SS_{total}}$$

Eta squared, η^2, is the last proportion of total variance effect size that we'll discuss, and it can be computed as follows:

$$\eta_A^2 = \frac{SS_A}{SS_{total}}$$

$$\eta_B^2 = \frac{SS_B}{SS_{total}}$$

$$\eta_{AB}^2 = \frac{SS_{AB}}{SS_{total}}$$

3.1.3.2 Proportion of Partial Variance Effect Size

There are also **proportion of partial variance effect size** indices. These are referred to as *partial* because the effect size is computed by excluding other factors in the model when computing the effect size, and in this way controls other factors in the model. They are generally interpreted as the proportion of variation in the dependent variable, *Y*, explained by the effect of interest (i.e., by factor A, or factor B, or the AB interaction) that is *not* explained by other variables in the model. Generally, a proportion of partial variance effect size for a factor will be larger than a proportion of total variance for that same factor (Olejnik & Algina, 2000).

We can determine **partial omega squared** as follows:

$$\omega_{A,partial}^2 = \frac{df_A(MS_A - MS_{with})}{(df_A)(MS_A) + (N - df_A)(MS_{with})}$$

$$\omega_{B,partial}^2 = \frac{df_B(MS_B - MS_{with})}{(df_B)(MS_B) + (N - df_B)(MS_{with})}$$

$$\omega_{AB,partial}^2 = \frac{df_{AB}(MS_{AB} - MS_{with})}{(df_{AB})(MS_{AB}) + (N - df_{AB})(MS_{with})}$$

Partial epsilon squared is another proportion of partial variance effect size and can be computed as follows:

$$\varepsilon^2_{A,partial} = \frac{df_A(MS_A - MS_{with})}{SS_A + SS_{with}}$$

$$\varepsilon^2_{B,partial} = \frac{df_B(MS_B - MS_{with})}{SS_B + SS_{with}}$$

$$\varepsilon^2_{AB,partial} = \frac{df_{AB}(MS_{AB} - MS_{with})}{SS_{AB} + SS_{with}}$$

Partial eta squared is the estimate of effect size that can be requested when using SPSS for computing factorial ANOVA. We determine $\eta^2_{partial}$ as follows:

$$\eta^2_{A,partial} = \frac{SS_A}{SS_A + SS_{with}}$$

$$\eta^2_{B,partial} = \frac{SS_B}{SS_B + SS_{with}}$$

$$\eta^2_{AB,partial} = \frac{SS_{AB}}{SS_{AB} + SS_{with}}$$

13.1.3.3 Interpreting Effect Size

Using Cohen's (1988) subjective standards, these effect sizes, whether they are the proportion of total variance or proportion of partial variance, can be interpreted as follows: small effect, ω^2, ε^2, or $\eta^2 = .01$; medium effect, ω^2, ε^2, or $\eta^2 = .06$; large effect, ω^2, e^2, or $\eta^2 = .14$. See Table 13.5. Researchers interested in further discussion on effect size in

TABLE 13.5

Effect Sizes and Interpretations

Effect Size	Interpretation
Proportion of Total Variability Accounted For	
Omega squared (ω^2), epsilon squared (ε^2), and eta squared (η^2)	Proportion of total variability in the dependent variable that is accounted for by a factor (e.g., A, B, or AB) • Small effect = .01 • Medium effect = .06 • Large effect = .14
Proportion of Partial Variability Accounted For	
Partial omega squared ($\omega^2_{A,partial}$), partial epsilon squared ($\varepsilon^2_{A,partial}$), and partial eta squared ($\eta^2_{A,partial}$)	Proportion of total variability in the dependent variable that is accounted for by a factor (e.g., A, B, or AB) that is *not* explained by other variables in the model • Small effect = .01 • Medium effect = .06 • Large effect = .14

factorial designs are encouraged to review any number of resources (e.g., Cohen, 1988; Fidler & Thompson, 2001; Keppel & Wickens, 2004; Murphy et al., 2009; O'Grady, 1982; Wilcox, 1987).

13.1.3.4 Additional Effect Size Considerations

We will end our discussion on effect size with a few noteworthy items to consider as you compute and interpret effect sizes. Eta squared can be positively biased, overestimating the strength of the population relationship, and thus is best considered a descriptor of proportion of variance in the dependent variable explained for a particular sample (Maxwell, Arvey, & Camp, 1981). Thus, many researchers discourage reporting eta squared or partial eta squared, although you will still see it widely reported given that it is the only effect size value that is output from SPSS. Both epsilon squared and omega squared introduce a correction to this problem, and generally, both will be quite similar in value (Carroll & Nordholm, 1975). If you find yourself in a situation where epsilon squared or omega squared are negative, the standard is simply to set the effect size to zero (Olejnik & Algina, 2000).

One cautionary note in using omega squared, both the total and partial, is that the computation uses variance components from the expected mean squares for the source of variation, and the expected mean square assumes a balanced design (Olejnik & Algina, 2000). When sample sizes are not equal, researchers may wish to report a different measure of effect.

Also consider that proportion of total variance effect size indices are not comparable across studies that incorporate different factors (Olejnik & Algina, 2000). This is reasonable given that total variation is influenced by all the factors in the model. An even more stringent stumbling block pertains to proportion of partial variance effect size measures. Because the denominator for each factor and/or interaction differs when computing the proportion of partial variance effect size, these effects cannot be compared within the same study (Olejnik & Algina, 2000). Additionally, because the denominators differ in proportion of partial variance effect size, the sum of the partial measures of effect may total more than one, and this may occur even if the factors are orthogonal (i.e., balanced) (Olejnik & Algina, 2000).

Some researchers find interpreting proportion of variance effect sizes advantageous, as compared to standardized mean differences, given that the index ranges from 0 to 1 (Rosenthal, 1994). However, even large proportion of variance effect size values (e.g., .14+) suggest there is much variance that remains to be explained, and thus even large effects can be perceived as trivial (Rosenthal & Rubin, 1979).

Last but not least, we will touch on *general reporting and interpretation recommendations for effect size*. First, reporting effect size values for omnibus tests are rarely meaningful as the omnibus test is usually not the hypothesis test of interest (Rosnow & Rosenthal, 1988). Reporting effect size measures for factors and contrasts (e.g., A, B, and AB, as the computations provided here allow) are encouraged as those are likely where the real interest (and hypotheses of interest) lie (Olejnik & Algina, 2000). Second, many researchers encourage interpreting effect size relative to other studies. However, several researchers (e.g., Fern & Monroe, 1996; Maxwell et al., 1981; O'Grady, 1982; Sechrest & Yeaton, 1982) have provided caution in doing this as effect size can be impacted by instrument reliability, heterogeneity of the populations that are compared, the levels or categories of the factors that are modeled, the strength of the treatments, and the range of treatments, all of which can lead to effect size comparisons that are misleading (Olejnik & Algina, 2000). In our perspective, this doesn't mean that you should avoid interpreting effect size relative to other studies. Rather, recognizing these limitations and pointing out differences that are known when making those interpretations are important.

13.1.3.5 Effect Size Example

Let us estimate effect size given the elite athlete example and results that are presented in Table 13.9. The partial η^2 are determined to be the following:

$$\eta_A^2 = \frac{SS_A}{SS_A + SS_{with}} = \frac{738.5938}{738.5938 + 276.7500} = 0.7274$$

$$\eta_B^2 = \frac{SS_B}{SS_B + SS_{with}} = \frac{712.5313}{712.5313 + 276.7500} = 0.7203$$

$$\eta_{AB}^2 = \frac{SS_{AB}}{SS_{AB} + SS_{with}} = \frac{21.8438}{21.8438 + 276.7500} = 0.0732$$

We calculate ω^2 to be the following:

$$\omega_A^2 = \frac{SS_A - (J-1)(MS_{with})}{SS_{total} + MS_{with}} = \frac{738.5938 - (4-1)(11.5313)}{1749.7188 + 11.5313} = 0.3997$$

$$\omega_B^2 = \frac{SS_B - (K-1)(MS_{with})}{SS_{total} + MS_{with}} = \frac{712.5313 - (2-1)(11.5313)}{1749.7188 + 11.5313} = 0.3980$$

$$\omega_{AB}^2 = \frac{SS_{AB} - (J-1)(K-1)(MS_{with})}{SS_{total} + MS_{with}} = \frac{21.8438 - (4-1)(2-1)(11.5313)}{1749.7188 + 11.5313} = -0.007$$

Based on these effect size measures, using Cohen's subjective standards, one would conclude that there is a large effect for type of sport and for selection status, but very little effect for the type of interaction of sport and selection status. An example of interpretation is the following: Partial eta squared for the main effect for type of sport tells us that the proportion of variation in psychological distress explained by the type of sport in which the athlete participates that is *not* explained by selection status is about 73%. Omega squared for the main effect for type of sport tells us that proportion of total variability in the dependent variable that is accounted for by type of sport is about 40%. Interpretations for selection status and the interaction of sport by selection status can be made similarly.

13.1.3.6 Confidence Intervals for Effect Size

To refresh our memory, computing **confidence intervals** is valuable. As mentioned in Chapter 11, confidence intervals can be used for providing interval estimates of a population mean or mean difference; this gives us information about the accuracy of a sample estimate.

In the case of the two-factor model, we can form confidence intervals for row means, column means, cell means, the overall mean, as well as any possible contrast formed through a multiple comparison procedure. Note also that confidence intervals have been developed for effect sizes. The benefit in creating confidence intervals for effect size values is similar to that of creating confidence intervals for parameter estimates—*confidence intervals for the effect size provide an added measure of precision that is not obtained from knowledge of the effect size alone*. Computing confidence intervals for effect size indices, however, is not as straightforward as simply plugging in known values into a formula. Never fear; there are some nice online tools that can be used. For factorial ANOVA, Uanhoro's (2017) online calculator, available at https://effect-size-calculator.herokuapp.com/, uses the noncentral *F* method to compute confidence intervals for partial eta squared in fixed-effects ANOVA models that do not include covariates (i.e., ANCOVA, which we will study in a future chapter). As we see in Figure 13.3, and as we saw with one-way ANOVA, only four inputs are required: *F*, numerator and denominator degrees of freedom, and confidence interval. Note that because the *F* cannot be negative, the default setting for the 90% confidence interval is equivalent

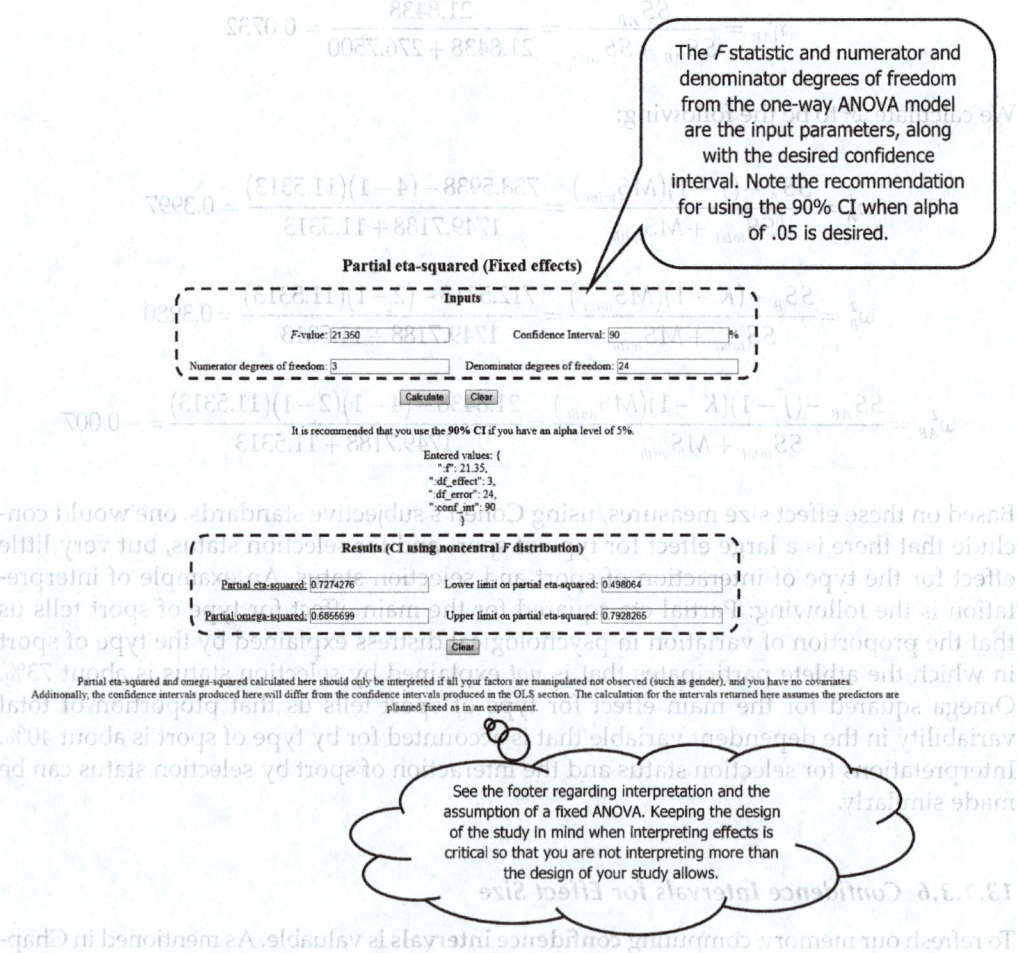

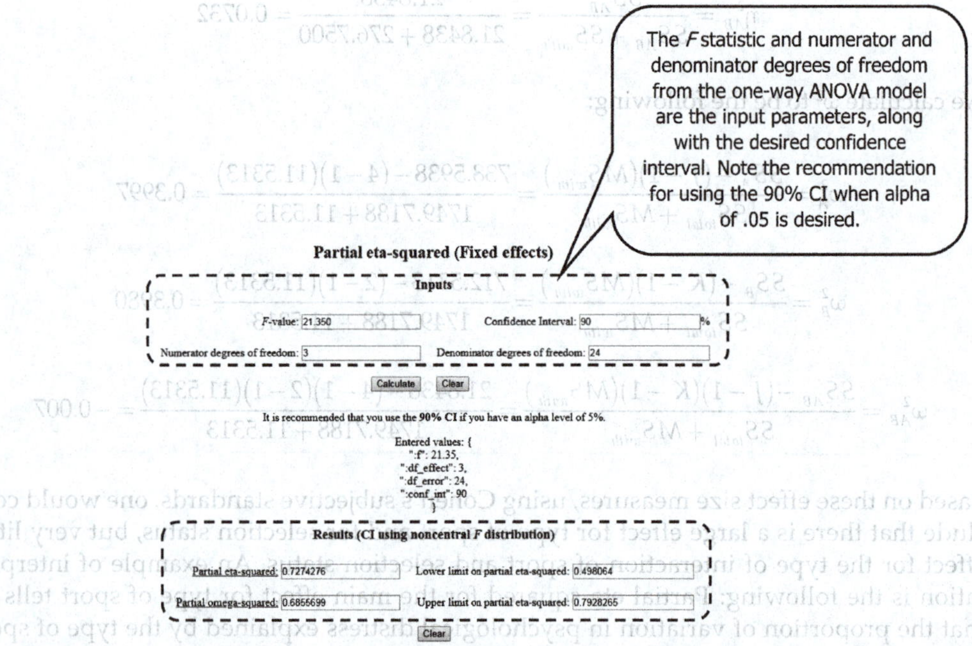

FIGURE 13.3
Confidence intervals for effect size.

to the 95% two-sided confidence interval (Smithson, 2003). Therefore, the site for the online calculator recommends that you "use the 90% CI if you have an alpha level of 5%."

We will use the results from our elite athlete data (see Table 13.9) and will illustrate with the main effect for type of sport; however, confidence intervals for results for all main effects and interactions can be computed similarly (see Figure 13.3). With an F of 21.350 and numerator and denominator degrees of freedom of 3 and 24, respectively, partial eta squared is .727 with lower and upper confidence limits of .498 and .793, respectively. Putting this in context of our example, if multiple random samples were drawn from the population, 95% of the samples could expect about 50%, at minimum, and 79%, at maximum, of the proportion of the outcome to be explained by the independent variable type of sport that is not explained by other variables in the model (specifically selection status).

13.1.4 Assumptions

In Chapter 11 we described in detail the assumptions for the one-factor analysis of variance. In the two-factor model, the assumptions are again concerned with **independence**, **homogeneity of variance**, and **normality**. A summary of the effects of their violation is provided in Table 13.6. The same methods for detecting violations described in Chapter 11 can be used for this model.

There are only two different wrinkles for the two-factor model as compared to the one-factor model. First, as the effect of heterogeneity is small with balanced designs (equal n's per cell) or nearly balanced designs, and/or with larger n's, this is a reason to strive for such a design. Unfortunately, there is very little research on this problem, except the classic (Box, 1954) article for a no-interaction model with one observation per cell. There are limited solutions for dealing with a violation of the homogeneity assumption, such as the Welch (1951) test, the Johansen (1980) procedure, and variations described by Wilcox (1996 or 2003). Transformations are not usually used, as they may destroy an additive linear model and create interactions that did not previously exist. Nonparametric techniques are not commonly used with the two-factor model, although see the description of the Brunner, Dette, and Munk (1997) procedure in Wilcox (2003). Second, the effect of nonnormality seems to be the same as heterogeneity (Miller, 1997).

TABLE 13.6

Assumptions and Effects of Violations for the Two-Factor ANOVA Design

Assumption	Effect of Assumption Violation
Independence	• Increased likelihood of a Type I and/or Type II error in the F statistic • Influences standard errors of means and thus inferences about those means
Homogeneity of variance	• Bias in SS_{with} • Increased likelihood of a Type I and/or Type II error • Less effect with balanced or nearly balanced design • Effect decreases as n increases
Normality	• Minimal effect with moderate violation • Minimal effect with balanced or nearly balanced design • Effect decreases as n increases

13.2 What Three-Factor and Higher-Order ANOVA Models Are and How They Work

13.2.1 Characteristics

All of the characteristics we discussed for the two-factor model apply to the three-factor model, with one obvious exception. There are three factors rather than two. This will result in three main effects (one for each factor, known as A, B, and C), three two-way interactions (known as AB, AC, and BC), and one three-way interaction (known as ABC). The only new concept is the three-way interaction, which may be stated as follows: "Is the AB interaction constant across all levels of factor C?" This may also be stated as "AC across the levels of B" or as "BC across the levels of A." These each have the same interpretation as there is only one way of testing the three-way interaction. In short, the three-way interaction can be thought of as the two-way interaction behaving differently across the levels of the third factor.

We do not explicitly consider models with more than three factors (compare Keppel & Wickens, 2004; Marascuilo & Serlin, 1988; Myers & Well, 1995). However, be warned that such models do exist, and that they will necessitate more main effects, more two-way interactions, more three-way interactions, as well as higher-order interactions—and thus more complex interpretations. Conceptually, the only change is to add these additional effects to the model.

13.2.2 The ANOVA Model

The model for the three-factor design is

$$Y_{ijkl} = \mu + \alpha_j + \beta_k + \gamma_l + (\alpha\beta)_{jk} + (\alpha\gamma)_{jl} + (\beta\gamma)_{kl} + (\alpha\beta\gamma)_{jkl} + \varepsilon_{ijkl}$$

where Y_{ijkl} is the observed score on the criterion (i.e., dependent) variable for individual i in level j of factor A, level k of factor B, and level l of factor C (or in the jkl cell), μ is the overall or grand population mean (i.e., regardless of cell designation), α_j is the effect for level j of factor A, β_k is the effect for level k of factor B, γ_l is the effect for level l of factor C, $\alpha\beta_{jk}$ is the interaction effect for the combination of level j of factor A and level k of factor B, $(\alpha\gamma)_{jl}$ is the interaction effect for the combination of level j of factor A and level l of factor C, $(\beta\gamma)_{kl}$ is the interaction effect for the combination of level k of factor B and level l of factor C, $(\alpha\beta\gamma)_{jkl}$ is the interaction effect for the combination of level j of factor A, level k of factor B, and level l of factor C, and ε_{ijkl} is the random residual error for individual i in cell jkl. Given that there are three main effects, three two-way interactions, and one three-way interaction, there will be an accompanying null and alternative hypothesis for each of these effects. At this point in your statistics career, the hypotheses should be obvious (simply expand on the hypotheses at the beginning of this chapter).

13.2.3 The ANOVA Summary Table

The ANOVA summary table for the three-factor model is shown in Table 13.7, with the usual columns for sources of variation, sums of squares, degrees of freedom, mean squares,

TABLE 13.7

Three-Factor Analysis of Variance Summary Table

Source	*SS*	*df*	*MS*	*F*
Between				
A	SS_A	$J-1$	MS_A	MS_A/MS_{with}
B	SS_B	$K-1$	MS_B	MS_B/MS_{with}
C	SS_C	$L-1$	MS_C	MS_C/MS_{with}
AB	SS_{AB}	$(J-1)(K-1)$	MS_{AB}	MS_{AB}/MS_{with}
AC	SS_{AC}	$(J-1)(L-1)$	MS_{AC}	MS_{AC}/MS_{with}
BC	SS_{BC}	$(K-1)(L-1)$	MS_{BC}	MS_{BC}/MS_{with}
ABC	SS_{ABC}	$(J-1)(K-1)(L-1)$	MS_{ABC}	MS_{ABC}/MS_{with}
Within	SS_{with}	$N-JKL$	MS_{with}	
Total	SS_{total}	$N-1$		

and *F*. A quick three-factor example dataset and the resulting ANOVA summary table from SPSS are shown in Table 13.8. Note that the only statistically significant effects are the main effect for B and the AC interaction ($p < .01$).

13.2.4 The Triple Interaction

Everything else about the three-factor design follows from the two-factor model. The assumptions are the same, MS_{with} is the error term used for testing each of the hypotheses in the fixed-effects model, and the multiple comparison procedures are easily utilized. The main new feature is the three-way interaction. If this interaction is significant, then this means that the two-way interaction is different across the levels of the third factor. This result will need to be taken into account prior to interpreting the two-way interactions and the main effects.

Although the inclusion of additional factors in the design should result in a reduction in MS_{with}, there is a price to pay for the study of additional factors. Although the analysis is simple for the computer, you must consider the possibility of significant higher-order interactions. If you find, for example, that the four-way interaction is significant, how do you deal with it? First you have to interpret this interaction, which could be difficult if it is unexpected. Then you may have difficulty in dealing with the interpretation of your other effects. Our advice is simple. *Do not include additional factors just because they sound interesting. Include only those factors that are theoretically or empirically important*. Then, if a significant higher-order interaction occurs, you will be in a better position to understand it because you will have already thought about its consequences. Reporting that an interaction is significant, but not interpretable, is not sound research. For additional discussion on this topic, see Keppel and Wickens (2004).

TABLE 13.8

Three-Factor Analysis of Variance Example—Raw Data and SPSS ANOVA Summary Table

Raw Data:

$A_1B_1C_1$: 8, 10, 12, 9

$A_1B_1C_1$: 23, 17, 21, 19

$A_1B_1C_1$: 22, 19, 16, 24

$A_1B_2C_2$: 33, 31, 27, 30

$A_2B_1C_1$: 16, 19, 21, 24

$A_2B_1C_2$: 6, 8, 11, 13

$A_2B_2C_1$: 27, 30, 31, 33

$A_2B_2C_2$: 16, 19, 21, 25

SPSS ANOVA Summary Table:

The row labeled **"A"** is the first independent variable or factor or between groups variable. The *between groups mean square* for factor A (.031) provides an indication of the variation in the dependent variable attributable to factor A.

The degrees of freedom for the sum of squares between groups for factor A is $J - 1$ ($df = 1$ in this example indicating 2 levels for factor A).

Similar interpretations are made for the other main effects and interactions.

The omnibus *F* test for the main effect for factor A (and computed similarly for the other main effects and interactions) is computed as follows, where MS_{with} is the mean square of the error term.

$$F = \frac{MS_A}{MS_{with}} = \frac{0.31}{8.698} = .004$$

The *p* value for the omnibus *F* test of the main effect for factor A is .953. This indicates there is not a statistically significant difference in the dependent variable based on factor A, averaged across the levels of Factors B and C. In other words, there is not a unique effect of factor A on the dependent variable, controlling for factors B and C. The probability of observing these mean differences or more extreme mean differences by chance if the null hypothesis is really true (i.e., if the population means really are equal) is about 95%.

We fail to reject the null hypothesis that the population means of factor A are equal. For this example, this provides evidence to suggest that the dependent variable does not differ, on average, across the levels of factor A, when controlling for factors B and C.

Tests of Between-Subjects Effects

Dependent Variable: OUTCOME

Source	Type III Sum of Squares	df	Mean Square	F	Sig.
Corrected Model	1702.219[a]	7	243.174	27.958	.000
Intercept	12840.031	1	12840.031	1476.219	.000
A	.031	1	.031	.004	.953
B	871.531	1	871.531	100.200	.000
C	.031	1	.031	.004	.953
A * B	.031	1	.031	.004	.953
A * C	830.281	1	830.281	95.457	.000
B * C	.031	1	.031	.004	.953
A * B * C	.281	1	.281	.032	.859
Error	208.750	24	8.698		
Total	14751.000	32			
Corrected Total	1910.969	31			

a. R Squared = .891 (Adjusted R Squared = .859)

The row labeled **"Error"** is within groups. The within groups sum of squares tells us how much variation there is within the cells combined across the cells (i.e., 208.750). The degrees of freedom for the sum of squares within groups is ($N - JKL$) or the sample size minus the number of levels of the independent variables [i.e., 32 – (2)(2)(2) = 24].

The row labeled **"corrected total"** is the sum of squares total. The degrees of freedom for the total is ($N - 1$) or the sample size minus one.

13.3 What the Factorial ANOVA With Unequal *n*'s Is and How It Works

Up until this point in the chapter, we have considered only the equal *n*'s or **balanced design**. *That is, the model used was where the number of observations in each cell was equal.* This served to make the formulas and equations easier to deal with. However, we do not need to assume that the *n*'s are equal. In this section we discuss ways to deal with the unequal *n*'s (or unbalanced) case for the two-factor model, although these notions can be transferred to higher-order models as well.

When *n*'s are unequal, things become a bit trickier as the main effects and the interaction effect are not orthogonal. In other words, the sums of squares cannot be partitioned into independent effects and thus the individual *SS* do not necessarily add up to the SS_{total}. As a result, several computational approaches have been developed. In the old days, prior to the availability of high-speed computers, the standard approach was to use unweighted means analysis. This is essentially an analysis of means, rather than raw scores, which are unweighted by cell size. This approach is only an approximate procedure. Due to the availability of quality statistical software, the unweighted means approach is no longer necessary. A rather silly approach, and one that we do not condone, is to delete enough data until you have an equal *n*'s model.

There are three more modern approaches to this case. Each of these approaches really test different hypotheses and thus may result in different results and conclusions: (a) the **sequential approach** (also known as the hierarchical sums of squares approach), (b) the **partially sequential approach** (also known as the partially hierarchical, or experimental design, or method of fitting constants approach), and (c) the **regression approach** (also known as the marginal means or unique approach). There has been considerable debate over the years about the relative merits of each approach (e.g., Applebaum & Cramer, 1974; Carlson & Timm, 1974; Cramer & Applebaum, 1980; Overall, Lee, & Hornick, 1981; Overall & Spiegel, 1969; Timm & Carlson, 1975). Below we describe what each approach is actually testing.

In the **sequential approach,** the effects being tested are:

$$\alpha \mid \mu$$
$$\beta \mid \mu, \alpha$$
$$\alpha\beta \mid \mu, \alpha, \beta$$

This indicates, for example, that the effect for factor B (β) is adjusted or controls for (as denoted by the vertical line) the overall mean (m) and the main effect due to factor A (a). Thus, each effect is adjusted for prior effects in the sequential order given (i.e., α, β αβ). Here the α effect is given theoretical or practical priority over the β effect. In SAS and SPSS, this is the **Type I sum of squares** method.

In the **partially sequential approach,** the effects being tested are:

$$\alpha \mid \mu, \beta$$
$$\beta \mid \mu, \alpha$$
$$\alpha\beta \mid \mu, \alpha, \beta$$

There is difference here because each main effect controls for the other main effect, but not for the interaction effect. In SAS and SPSS, this is the **Type II sum of squares** method. This is the only one of the three methods where the sums of squares will add up to the total sum of squares. Notice in the sequential and partially sequential approaches that the interaction is not taken into account in estimating the main effects, which is only fine if there is no interaction effect.

In the **regression approach**, the effects being tested are:

$$\alpha \mid \mu, \beta, \alpha\beta$$
$$\beta \mid \mu, \alpha, \alpha\beta$$
$$\alpha\beta \mid \mu, \alpha, \beta$$

In this approach, each effect controls for each of the other effects. In SAS and SPSS, this is the **Type III sum of squares** method (and is the default selection in SPSS). Many statisticians (Glass & Hopkins, 1996; Keppel & Wickens, 2004; Mickey, Dunn, & Clark, 2004), including the authors of this text, recommend exclusive use of the regression approach because each effect is estimated taking the other effects into account. The hypotheses tested in the sequential and partially sequential approaches are seldom of interest and are difficult to interpret (Carlson & Timm, 1974; Kirk, 2013; Overall, 1981; Timm & Carlson, 1975). The regression approach seems to be conceptually closest to the traditional analysis of variance in that each effect is estimated controlling for all other effects. When the *n*'s are equal, each of these three approaches tests the same hypotheses and yields the same results.

13.4 Computing Factorial ANOVA Using SPSS

In this section we take a look at SPSS for the elite athlete example. As already noted in Chapter 11, SPSS needs the data to be in a specific form for the analysis to proceed, which is different from the layout of the data in Table 13.1. For a two-factor ANOVA, the dataset must consist of three variables or columns, one for the level of factor A, one for the level of factor B, and the third for the dependent variable. Each row still represents one individual, indicating the levels of factors A and B within which the individual is a member, and their score on the dependent variable. As seen in the screenshot (Figure 13.4), for a two-factor ANOVA, the SPSS data are in the form of two columns that represent the group values (i.e., the two independent variables) and one column that represents the scores or values of the dependent variable.

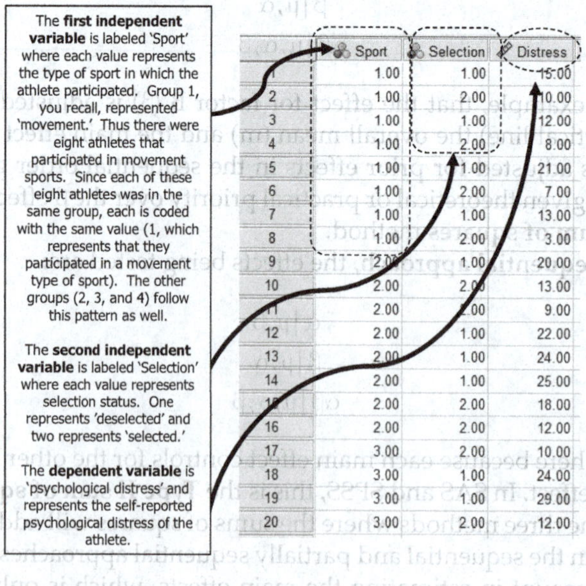
The **first independent variable** is labeled 'Sport' where each value represents the type of sport in which the athlete participated. Group 1, you recall, represented 'movement.' Thus there were eight athletes that participated in movement sports. Since each of these eight athletes was in the same group, each is coded with the same value (1, which represents that they participated in a movement type of sport). The other groups (2, 3, and 4) follow this pattern as well.
The **second independent variable** is labeled 'Selection' where each value represents selection status. One represents 'deselected' and two represents 'selected.'
The **dependent variable** is 'psychological distress' and represents the self-reported psychological distress of the athlete.

	Sport	Selection	Distress
1	1.00	1.00	15.00
2	1.00	2.00	10.00
3	1.00	1.00	12.00
4	1.00	2.00	8.00
5	1.00	1.00	21.00
6	1.00	2.00	7.00
7	1.00	1.00	13.00
8	1.00	2.00	3.00
9	2.00	1.00	20.00
10	2.00	2.00	13.00
11	2.00	2.00	9.00
12	2.00	1.00	22.00
13	2.00	1.00	24.00
14	2.00	1.00	25.00
15	2.00	2.00	18.00
16	2.00	2.00	12.00
17	3.00	2.00	10.00
18	3.00	1.00	24.00
19	3.00	1.00	29.00
20	3.00	2.00	12.00

FIGURE 13.4
First 20 cases of the factorial ANOVA data.

Step 1. To conduct a factorial ANOVA, go to "Analyze" in the top pulldown menu, then select "General Linear Model," and then select "Univariate." Following the screenshot for Step 1 (Figure 13.5) produces the Univariate dialog box.

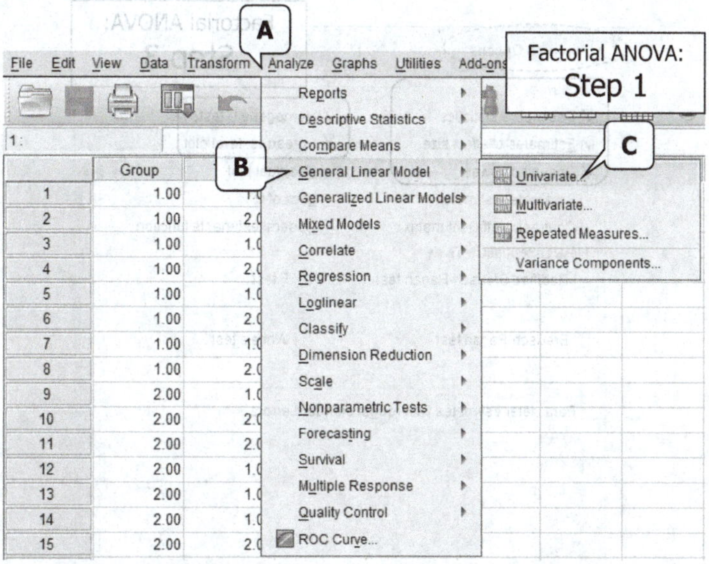

FIGURE 13.5
Factorial ANOVA: Step 1.

Step 2. Click the dependent variable (e.g., psychological distress) and move it into the "Dependent Variable" box by clicking the arrow button. Click the first independent variable (e.g., type of sport) and move it into the "Fixed Factors" box by clicking the arrow button. Follow this same step to move the second independent variable into the Fixed Factors box. Next, click on "Options."

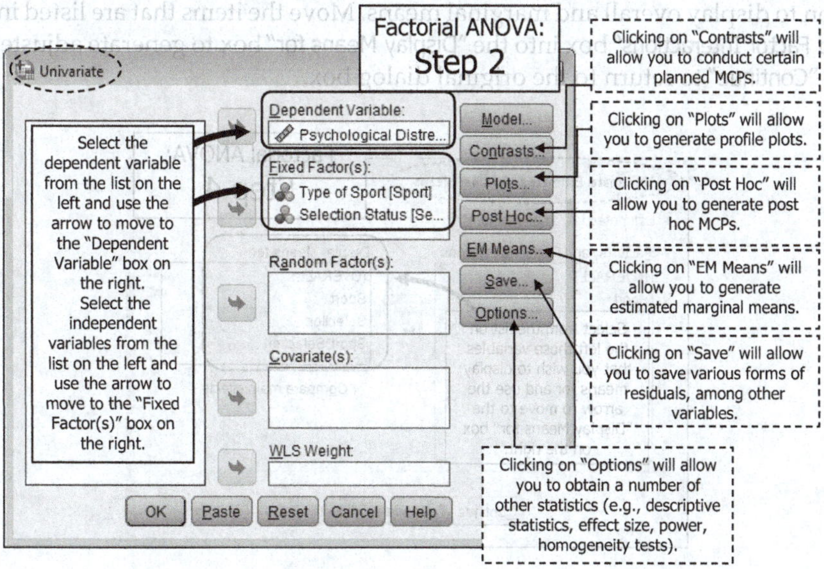

FIGURE 13.6
Factorial ANOVA: Step 2.

Step 3. Clicking on "Options" will provide the option to select such information as "Descriptive statistics," "Estimates of effect size," "Observed power," "Homogeneity tests" (i.e., Levene's test for equal variances), and "Spread vs. level plot." Click on "Continue" to return to the original dialog box.

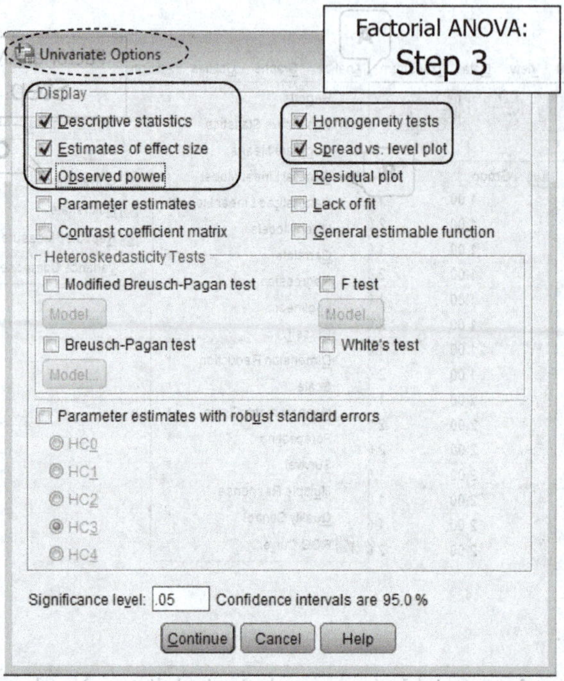

FIGURE 13.7
Factorial ANOVA: Step 3.

Step 4. Clicking on "EM Means" (see the main dialog box in Step 2, Figure 3.6) will provide the option to display overall and marginal means. Move the items that are listed in the "Factor(s) and Factor Interactions" box into the "Display Means for" box to generate adjusted means. Click on "Continue" to return to the original dialog box.

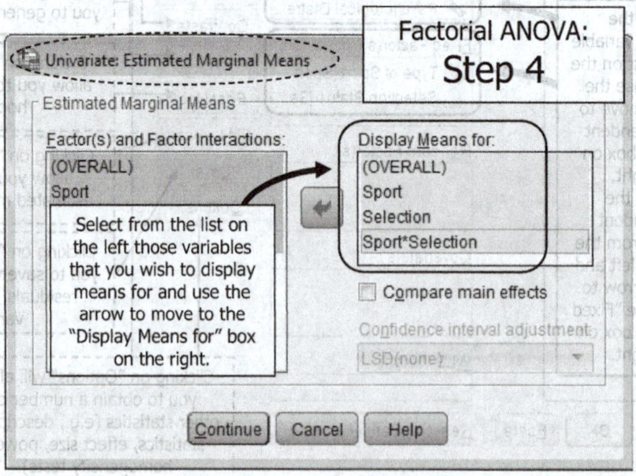

FIGURE 13.8
Factorial ANOVA: Step 4.

Step 5. From the Univariate dialog box, click on "Plots" to obtain a profile plot of means. Click the independent variable (e.g., type of sport labeled as "Sport") and move it into the "Horizontal Axis" box by clicking the arrow button (see screenshot for Step 5a, Figure 13.9). *(Tip: Placing the independent variable that has the most categories or levels on the horizontal axis of the profile plots will make for easier interpretation of the graph; however, this is really personal preference.)* Then click the second independent variable (e.g., "Selection") and move it into the "Separate Lines" box by clicking the arrow button (see Figure 13.9). Then click on "Add" to move the variable into the "Plots" box at the bottom of the dialog box (see the screenshot for Step 5b, Figure 13.10). Click on "Continue" to return to the original dialog box.

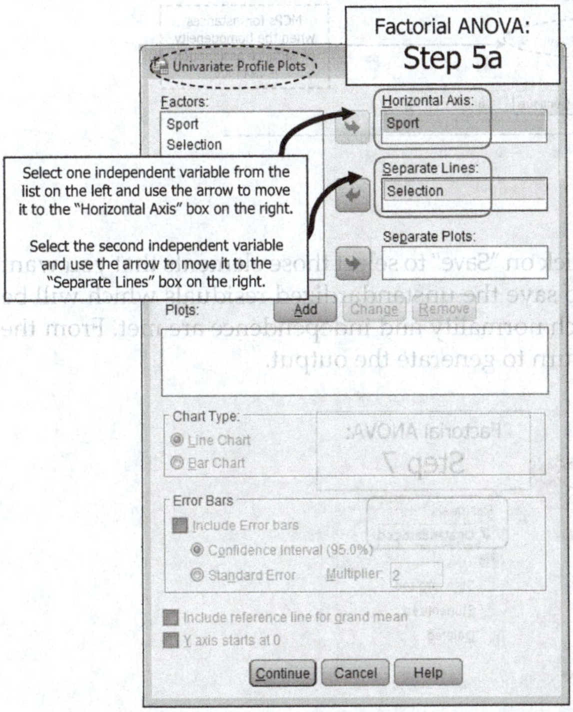

FIGURE 13.9
Factorial ANOVA: Step 5a.

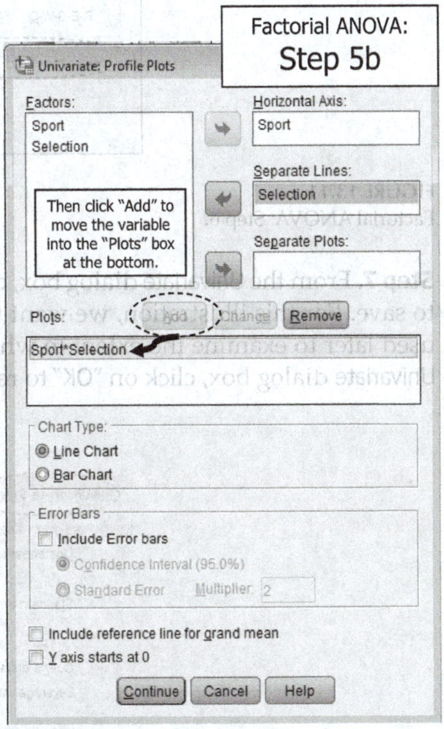

FIGURE 13.10
Factorial ANOVA: Step 5b.

Step 6. From the Univariate dialog box, click on "Post Hoc" to select various post hoc MCPs, or click on "Contrasts" to select various planned multiple comparison procedures (MCPs) (see main dialog box in screenshot for Step 2, Figure 13.6). From the "Post Hoc Multiple Comparisons for Observed Means" dialog box, click on the names of the independent variables in the "Factor(s)" list box in the top left (e.g., "Sport" and "Selection") and move them to the "Post Hoc Tests for" box in the top right by clicking on the arrow key. Check an appropriate MCP for your situation by placing a checkmark in the box next to the desired MCP. In this example, we will select Tukey, which is operationalized within SPSS as Tukey's HSD. Click on "Continue" to return to the original dialog box.

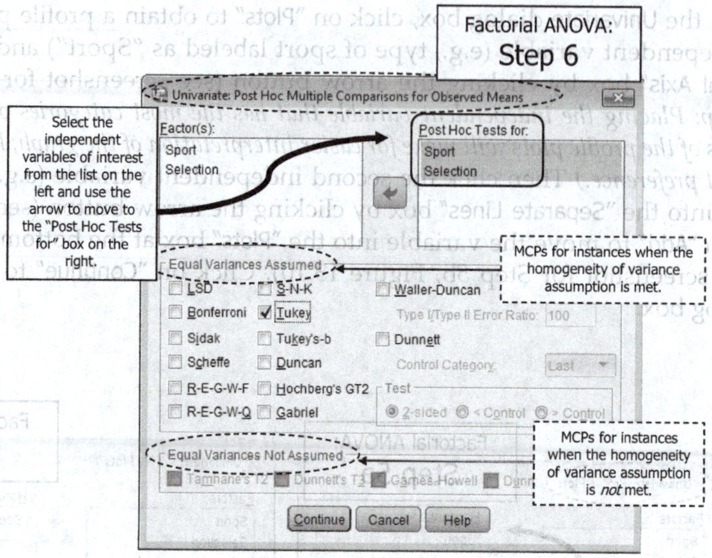

FIGURE 13.11
Factorial ANOVA: Step 6.

Step 7. From the Univariate dialog box, click on "Save" to select those elements that you want to save. For this illustration, we want to save the unstandardized residuals which will be used later to examine the extent to which normality and independence are met. From the Univariate dialog box, click on "OK" to return to generate the output.

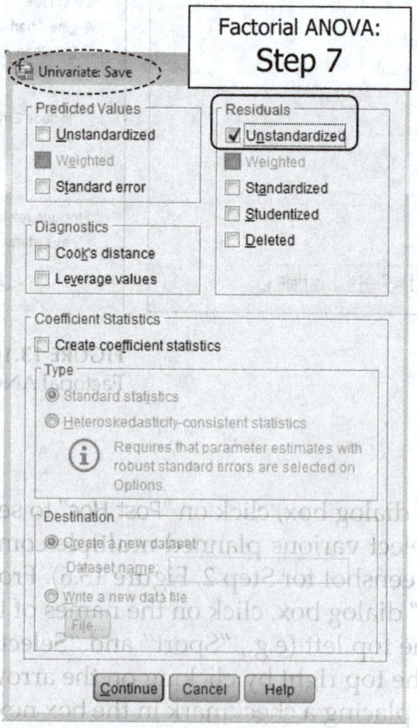

FIGURE 13.12
Factorial ANOVA: Step 7.

Interpreting the output. Annotated results are presented in Table 13.9 and the profile plot is shown in Figure 13.2. Note also that the SPSS ANOVA summary table will include additional sources of variation that we find not to be useful (i.e., corrected model, intercept, total); thus they are not annotated in Table 13.9.

TABLE 13.9

Selected SPSS Results for the Elite Athlete Psychological Distress Example

Between-Subjects Factors

		Value Label	N
Type of Sport	1.00	Movement	8
	2.00	Target	8
	3.00	Fielding	8
	4.00	Territory	8
Selection Status	1.00	Deselected	16
	2.00	Selected	16

The table labeled "Between-Subjects Factors" provides sample sizes for each of the categories of the independent variables (recall that the independent variables are the 'between subjects factors').

Descriptive Statistics

Dependent Variable: Psychological Distress

Type of Sport	Selection Status	Mean	Std. Deviation	N
Movement	Deselected	15.2500	4.03113	4
	Selected	7.0000	2.94392	4
	Total	11.1250	5.48862	8
Target	Deselected	22.7500	2.21736	4
	Selected	13.0000	3.74166	4
	Total	17.8750	5.93867	8
Fielding	Deselected	26.2500	2.21736	4
	Selected	14.2500	4.78714	4
	Total	20.2500	7.28501	8
Territory	Deselected	28.2500	1.70783	4
	Selected	20.5000	4.20317	4
	Total	24.3750	5.09727	8
Total	Deselected	23.1250	5.65538	16
	Selected	13.6875	6.09611	16
	Total	18.4062	7.51283	32

The table labeled "Descriptive Statistics" provides basic descriptive statistics (means, standard deviations, and sample sizes) for each cell of the design.

Levene's Test of Equality of Error Variances[a,b]

		Levene Statistic	df1	df2	Sig.
Psychological Distress	Based on Mean	.579	7	24	.766
	Based on Median	.417	7	24	.882
	Based on Median and with adjusted df	.417	7	15.398	.877
	Based on trimmed mean	.524	7	24	.807

Tests the null hypothesis that the error variance of the dependent variable is equal across groups.

a. Dependent variable: Psychological Distress

b. Design: Intercept + Sport + Selection + Sport * Selection

The *F* test (and associated *p* value) for Levene's Test for Equality of Error Variances is reviewed to determine if equal variances can be assumed. In this case, we meet the assumption (as *p* is greater than α). Note that *df1* is calculated as $(JK - 1)$ and *df2 is* calculated as $(N - JK)$.

(*continued*)

TABLE 13.9 (continued)

Selected SPSS Results for the Elite Athlete Psychological Distress Example

The omnibus *F* test for the main effect for 'Sport' (i.e., type of sport) (and computed similarly for the other main effects and interactions) is computed as $F = \frac{MS_A}{MS_{with}} = \frac{246.198}{11.531} = 21.350$

The *p* value for the omnibus *F* test for the main effect for 'sport' is .000. This indicates there is a statistically significant difference in the dependent variable based on type of sport, averaged across selection status (i.e., deselected or selected).

In other words, there is a unique effect of type of sport on psychological distress, controlling for selection status. The probability of observing these mean differences or more extreme mean differences by chance if the null hypothesis is really true (i.e., if the population means are really equal) is less than 1%. We reject the null hypothesis that the population means of type of sport are equal. For our example, this provides evidence to suggest that psychological distress differs, on average, across type of sport in which an athlete participates, when controlling for selection status.

Tests of Between-Subjects Effects

Dependent Variable: Psychological Distress

Source	Type III Sum of Squares	df	Mean Square	F	Sig.	Partial Eta Squared	Noncent. Parameter	Observed Power[b]
Corrected Model	1472.969[a]	7	210.424	18.248	.000	.842	127.737	1.000
Intercept	10841.281	1	10841.281	940.165	.000	.975	940.165	1.000
Sport	738.594	3	246.198	21.350	.000	.727	64.051	1.000
Selection	712.531	1	712.531	61.791	.000	.720	61.791	1.000
Sport * Selection	21.844	3	7.281	.631	.602	.073	1.894	.162
Error	276.750	24	11.531					
Total	12591.000	32						
Corrected Total	1749.719	31						

a. R Squared = .842 (Adjusted R Squared = .796)

b. Computed using alpha = .05

R^2 is listed as a footnote underneath the table. R^2 is the ratio of sum of squares between (i.e., combined *SS* for main effects and for the interaction) divided by sum of squares total:

$$R^2 = \frac{SS_{betw}}{SS_{total}}$$

$$R^2 = \frac{738.594 + 712.531 + 21.844}{1749.719} = .842$$

The row labeled **"Error"** is for within groups. The within groups sum of squares tells us how much variation there is within the cells combined across the cells (i.e., 276.750). The degrees of freedom for within groups is (N - JK) or the sample size minus the number of levels of the independent variables [i.e., 32 – (4)(2) = 24].

The row labeled **"Corrected Total"** is the sum of squares total. The degrees of freedom for the total is (N - 1) or the total sample size minus 1.

Observed power tells whether our test is powerful enough to detect mean differences if they really exist. Power of 1.000 indicates the maximum probability of rejecting the null hypothesis if it is really false (i.e., very strong power).

TABLE 13.9 (continued)

Selected SPSS Results for the Elite Athlete Psychological Distress Example

Estimated Marginal Means

1. Type of Sport

Dependent Variable: Psychological Distress

Type of Sport	Mean	Std. Error	95% Confidence Interval Lower Bound	Upper Bound
Movement	11.125	1.201	8.647	13.603
Target	17.875	1.201	15.397	20.353
Fielding	20.250	1.201	17.772	22.728
Territory	24.375	1.201	21.897	26.853

The table labeled **'Type of Sport'** provides descriptive statistics for each of the categories of the first independent variable. In addition to means, the *SE* and 95% CI of the means are reported.

2. Selection Status

Dependent Variable: Psychological Distress

Selection Status	Mean	Std. Error	95% Confidence Interval Lower Bound	Upper Bound
Deselected	23.125	.849	21.373	24.877
Selected	13.688	.849	11.935	15.440

The table labeled **'Selection Status'** provides descriptive statistics for each of the categories of the second independent variable. In addition to means, the *SE* and 95% CI of the means are reported.

3. Type of Sport * Selection Status

Dependent Variable: Psychological Distress

Type of Sport	Selection Status	Mean	Std. Error	95% Confidence Interval Lower Bound	Upper Bound
Movement	Deselected	15.250	1.698	11.746	18.754
	Selected	7.000	1.698	3.496	10.504
Target	Deselected	22.750	1.698	19.246	26.254
	Selected	13.000	1.698	9.496	16.504
Fielding	Deselected	26.250	1.698	22.746	29.754
	Selected	14.250	1.698	10.746	17.754
Territory	Deselected	28.250	1.698	24.746	31.754
	Selected	20.500	1.698	16.996	24.004

The table labeled **'Type of Sport * Selection Status'** provides descriptive statistics for each of the categories of the first independent variable by the second independent variable (i.e., cell means) (notice that these are the same means reported previously). In addition to means, the *SE* and 95% CI of the means are reported.

(continued)

TABLE 13.9 (continued)

Selected SPSS Results for the Elite Athlete Psychological Distress Example

Post Hoc Tests

When requested, post hoc tests are conducted for main effects that have more than two levels

Type of Sport

'Mean difference' is simply the difference between the means of the two levels of type of sport being compared. For example, the mean difference of Movement and Target is calculated as 11.1250 − 17.8750 = -6.7500.

Multiple Comparisons

Dependent Variable: Psychological Distress

Tukey HSD

(I) Type of Sport	(J) Type of Sport	Mean Difference (I-J)	Std. Error	Sig.	95% Confidence Interval Lower Bound	95% Confidence Interval Upper Bound
Movement	Target	-6.7500*	1.69788	.003	-11.4338	-2.0662
	Fielding	-9.1250*	1.69788	.000	-13.8088	-4.4412
	Territory	-13.2500*	1.69788	.000	-17.9338	-8.5662
Target	Movement	6.7500*	1.69788	.003	2.0662	11.4338
	Fielding	-2.3750	1.69788	.512	-7.0588	2.3088
	Territory	-6.5000*	1.69788	.004	-11.1838	-1.8162
Fielding	Movement	9.1250*	1.69788	.000	4.4412	13.8088
	Target	2.3750	1.69788	.512	-2.3088	7.0588
	Territory	-4.1250	1.69788	.098	-8.8088	.5588
Territory	Movement	13.2500*	1.69788	.000	8.5662	17.9338
	Target	6.5000*	1.69788	.004	1.8162	11.1838
	Fielding	4.1250	1.69788	.098	-.5588	8.8088

Based on observed means.

The error term is Mean Square(Error) = 11.531.

*. The mean difference is significant at the .05 level.

The standard error calculated in SPSS uses the harmonic mean (Tukey-Kramer modification) where n_j and n_k are the sample sizes for the two groups whose means are being compared (Toothaker, 1993):

$$s_{\psi'} = \sqrt{MS_{error}\left(\frac{1}{n_j} + \frac{1}{n_k}\right)}$$

$$s_{\psi'} = \sqrt{11.531\left(\frac{1}{8} + \frac{1}{8}\right)}$$

$$s_{\psi'} = \sqrt{2.88275} = 1.69766$$

'Sig.' denotes the observed p values and provides the results of the contrasts. There are four statistically significant mean differences between: 1) Movement and Target; 2) Movement and Fielding; 3) Movement and Territory; and 4) Target and Territory

Note that there are only ***6 unique contrast*** results:

$$\frac{1}{2}[J(J-1)] = \frac{1}{2}[4(4-1)] = \frac{1}{2}(12) = 6$$

Thus there are redundant results presented in the table. For example, the comparison of Movement and Target (presented in results row 1) is the same as the comparison of Target and Movement (presented in results row 2).

TABLE 13.9 (continued)

Selected SPSS Results for the Elite Athlete Psychological Distress Example

Homogeneous Subsets

Psychological Distress

Tukey HSD[a,b]

Type of Sport	N	Subset 1	Subset 2	Subset 3
Movement	8	11.1250		
Target	8		17.8750	
Fielding	8		20.2500	20.2500
Territory	8			24.3750
Sig.		1.000	.512	.098

Means for groups in homogeneous subsets are displayed.

Based on observed means.

The error term is Mean Square(Error) = 11.531.

a. Uses Harmonic Mean Sample Size = 8.000.

b. Alpha = .05.

This table displays the means for the types of sports that are *not* statistically significantly different. *We read the table by columns.* For example, in **subset 1,** the only mean displayed is Movement. *This indicates that Movement is statistically significantly different than all other sports.*

In **subset 2,** the means for Target and Fielding are displayed, indicating that those group means are 'homogeneous' or *not* significantly different. The means for Movement and Territory are not displayed in subset 2, which indicates those means *are* statistically different from each other.

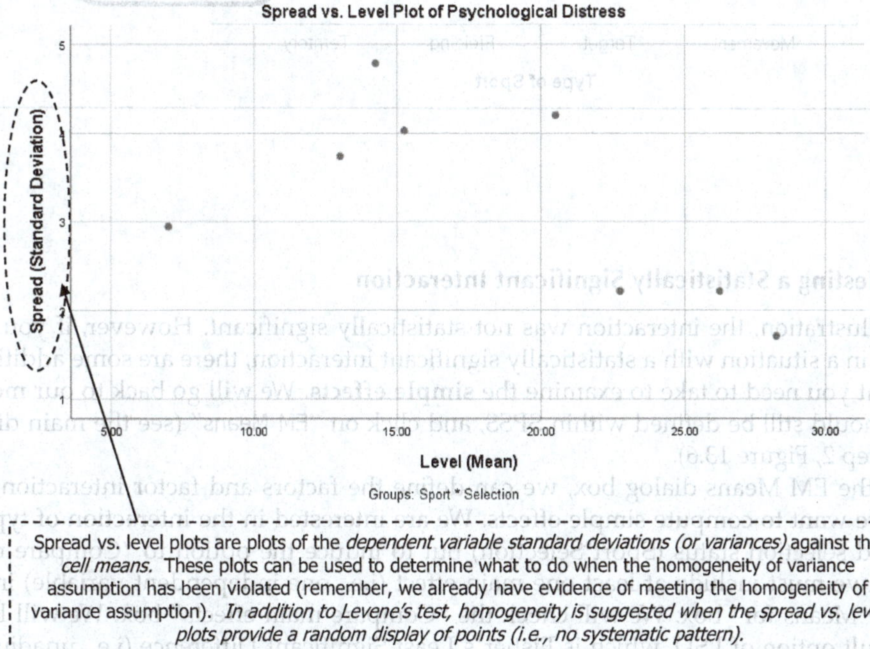

Spread vs. level plots are plots of the *dependent variable standard deviations (or variances)* against the *cell means.* These plots can be used to determine what to do when the homogeneity of variance assumption has been violated (remember, we already have evidence of meeting the homogeneity of variance assumption). *In addition to Levene's test, homogeneity is suggested when the spread vs. level plots provide a random display of points (i.e., no systematic pattern).*

If the plot suggests a linear relationship between the standard deviation and mean, transforming the data by taking the log of the dependent variable values may be a solution to the heterogeneity (since the calculation of logarithms requires positive values, this assumes all the data values are positive). If there is a linear relationship between the variance and mean, transforming the data by taking the square root of the dependent variable values may be a solution to the heterogeneity (since the calculation of square roots requires positive values, this assumes all the data values are positive).

Note: This plot displays the standard deviations. The plot for variances is not displayed for brevity, however you will find the variance plot looks nearly identical with the exception of the scale of the *Y* axis.

(*continued*)

TABLE 13.9 (continued)

Selected SPSS Results for the Elite Athlete Psychological Distress Example

Profile Plots

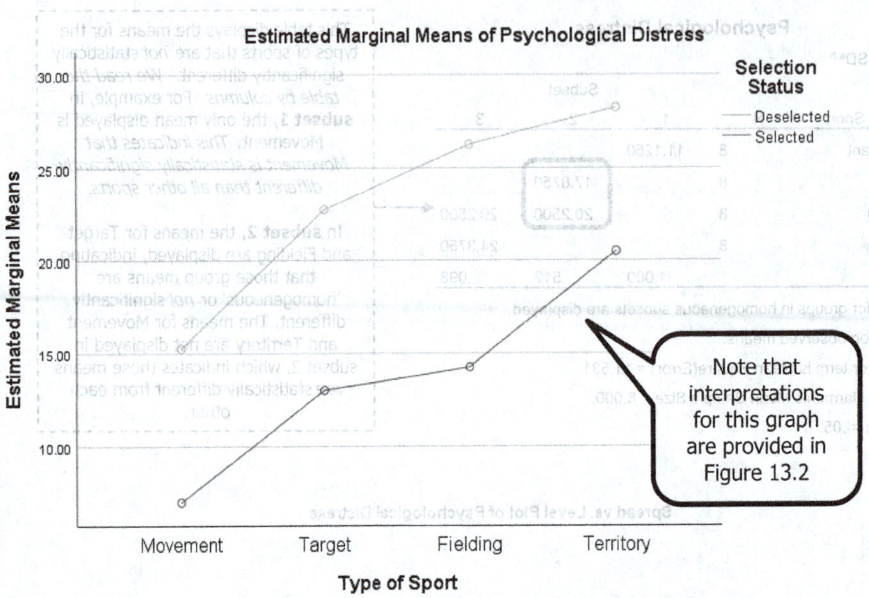

13.4.1 Testing a Statistically Significant Interaction

In this illustration, the interaction was not statistically significant. However, if you find yourself in a situation with a statistically significant interaction, there are some additional steps that you need to take to examine the **simple effects**. We will go back to our model, which should still be defined within SPSS, and click on "EM Means" (see the main dialog box in Step 2, Figure 13.6).

From the EM Means dialog box, we can define the factors and factor interactions for which we want to compute simple effects. We are interested in the interaction of type of sport and selection status (Sport*Selection) but to induce the option to "Compare main effects," we must include at least one main effect (i.e., one independent variable) in the "Display Means for" box. We will check the "Compare main effects" box. We will leave the default option of LSD, which is Fisher's Least Significant Difference (i.e., unadjusted probabilities). We could have selected Bonferroni; just remember that Bonferroni will be conservative if there are many comparisons that are made. Other options to which we are accustomed (e.g., Tukey's) are not available through the EM Means tool. Then click Continue to return to the main Univariate dialog box.

Interaction Step 2. Rather than clicking on "OK," we will click on "Paste" (see Figure 13.6). This will open a syntax box with the following script (for illustrative purposes, we have removed all other commands that are not necessary at this point):

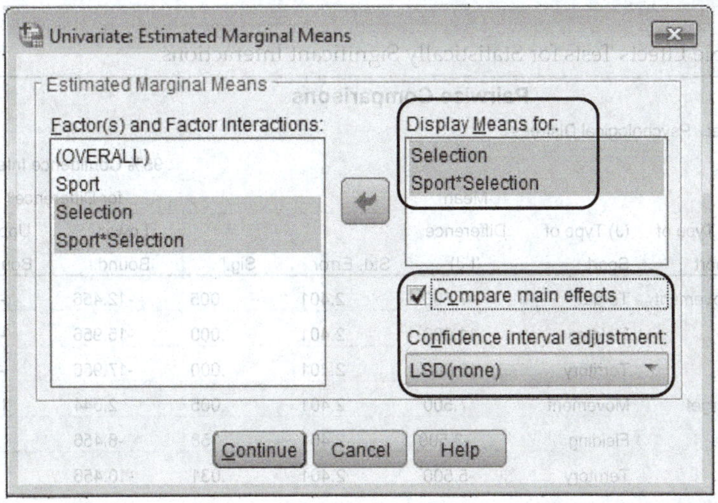

FIGURE 13.13
EM Means dialog box.

```
UNIANOVA Distress BY Sport Selection
/METHOD=SSTYPE(3)
/INTERCEPT=INCLUDE
/EMMEANS=TABLES(Selection) COMPARE ADJ(LSD)
/EMMEANS=TABLES(Sport*Selection)
/CRITERIA=ALPHA(0.05)
/DESIGN=Sport Selection Sport*Selection.
```

The line of code that reads /EMMEANS=TABLES(Sport*Selection) is the syntax that we will adjust by adding the syntax, COMPARE ADJ(LSD) and including the name of the factor of interest in parentheses in this syntax (i.e., **COMPARE (Sport) ADJ (LSD)** to our syntax). This line of syntax now reads:

```
/EMMEANS=TABLES(Sport*Selection) COMPARE (Sport) ADJ (LSD)
```

We will simply copy and paste this line of code back into the previous syntax, and remove the unnecessary line of code for comparing the main effect for selection (if we choose), and This will result in the following syntax (where ADJ specifies the adjustment to the p value for each pairwise comparison):

```
UNIANOVA Distress BY Sport Selection
/METHOD=SSTYPE (3)
/INTERCEPT=INCLUDE
/EMMEANS = TABLES (Sport * Selection) COMPARE (Sport) ADJ (LSD)
/CRITERIA=ALPHA (0.05)
/DESIGN=Sport Selection Sport*Selection.
```

We paste this into our syntax window, highlight these six lines of code, and then click the green triangle to run it (or click "Run," then "Selection" in the top toolbar of the syntax window) and generate our output, which now includes a test of simple effects.

Table 13.10 includes the new table of simple effects that is generated to test the interactions. Recall that an interaction means that the effect of one factor depends on the level

TABLE 13.10
Results of Simple Effects Tests for Statistically Significant Interactions

Pairwise Comparisons

Dependent Variable: Psychological Distress

Selection Status	(I) Type of Sport	(J) Type of Sport	Mean Difference (I-J)	Std. Error	Sig.[b]	95% Confidence Interval for Difference[b] Lower Bound	Upper Bound
Deselected	Movement	Target	-7.500*	2.401	.005	-12.456	-2.544
		Fielding	-11.000*	2.401	.000	-15.956	-6.044
		Territory	-13.000*	2.401	.000	-17.956	-8.044
	Target	Movement	7.500*	2.401	.005	2.544	12.456
		Fielding	-3.500	2.401	.158	-8.456	1.456
		Territory	-5.500*	2.401	.031	-10.456	-.544
	Fielding	Movement	11.000*	2.401	.000	6.044	15.956
		Target	3.500	2.401	.158	-1.456	8.456
		Territory	-2.000	2.401	.413	-6.956	2.956
	Territory	Movement	13.000*	2.401	.000	8.044	17.956
		Target	5.500*	2.401	.031	.544	10.456
		Fielding	2.000	2.401	.413	-2.956	6.956
Selected	Movement	Target	-6.000*	2.401	.020	-10.956	-1.044
		Fielding	-7.250*	2.401	.006	-12.206	-2.294
		Territory	-13.500*	2.401	.000	-18.456	-8.544
	Target	Movement	6.000*	2.401	.020	1.044	10.956
		Fielding	-1.250	2.401	.607	-6.206	3.706
		Territory	-7.500*	2.401	.005	-12.456	-2.544
	Fielding	Movement	7.250*	2.401	.006	2.294	12.206
		Target	1.250	2.401	.607	-3.706	6.206
		Territory	-6.250*	2.401	.016	-11.206	-1.294
	Territory	Movement	13.500*	2.401	00	8.544	18.456
		Target	7.500*	2.401	05	2.544	12.456
		Fielding	6.250*	2.	016	1.294	11.206

Based on estimated marginal means

*.Mean difference is significant at the 0.05 level.

b. Adjustment for multiple comparisons:

Least Significant Difference

(equivalent to no adjustments).

When players are *deselected,* there is no statistically significant difference in psychological distress between athletes in fielding as compared to territory sports. However, when players are *selected,* there is a statistically significant difference in psychological distress. More specifically, athletes in territory sports have statistically significantly more psychological distress when *selected* as compared to athletes in fielding sports (mean difference = -6.250, *p* = .016) but athletes in these sports are similar in psychological distress when *deselected.*

of another factor (and vice versa). In the elite athlete example, that would mean that the effect of selection status depends on the type of sport (and vice versa). In other words, the interaction means that psychological distress depends on the type of sport in which the athlete participates and selection status. Conversely, the effect of selection status on psychological distress depends on the type of sport in which the athlete participates. The simple effects, for which we just generated output, reveal the degree to which one independent variable is differentially effective at every level of the second independent variable.

Although we see lots of statistically significant results, we are specifically looking for comparisons where the results for a factor level are statistically significant in one level of a second factor but *not* statistically significant for the other level of that second factor. We see, for example, that *movement* is statistically significantly different than all other types of sports, regardless of whether the play is *deselected* or *selected*. In other words, we are not seeing an interaction between selection status and type of sport when considering the comparisons of *movement* to the other types of sport.

Our results for the simple effects of the interaction generate *one statistically significant simple effect*. Let's interpret the interaction of selection status (selected, deselected) with type of sport when the sports of *fielding* and *territory* are considered. When players are *deselected*, there is no statistically significant difference in psychological distress between athletes in fielding as compared to territory sports. However, when players are *selected*, there is a statistically significant difference in psychological distress. More specifically, athletes in territory sports have statistically significantly more psychological distress when *selected* as compared to athletes in fielding sports (mean difference = −6.250, $p = .016$) but athletes in these sports are similar in psychological distress when *deselected*. Because our omnibus F test for the interaction was not statistically significant, we will not interpret this comparison later in our write-up. However, it should provide an illustration that will assist you should you find a statistically significant interaction in your own research.

13.5 Computing Factorial ANOVA Using R

Next we consider **R** for factorial ANOVA. Note that the scripts are provided within the blocks with additional annotation to assist in understanding how the command works. Should you want to write reminder notes and annotation to yourself as you write the commands in **R** (and we highly encourage doing so), remember that any text that follows a hashtag (i.e., #) is annotation only and not part of the **R** script. Thus, you can write annotations directly into **R** with hashtags. We encourage this practice so that when you call up the commands in the future, you'll understand what the various lines of code are doing. You may think you'll remember what you did. However, trust us. There is a good chance that you won't. Thus, consider it best practice when using **R** to annotate heavily!

13.5.1 Reading Data Into R

```
getwd()
```

R is always pointed to a directory on your computer. The *get working directory* function can be used to determine to which directory **R** is pointed. We will assume that we need to change the working directory, and will use the next line of code to set the working directory to the desired path.

```
setwd("E:/FolderName")
```

We use the *setwd* function to establish the working directory. To set the working directory, change what is in quotation marks to your file location. Also, if you are copying the directory name from your properties, you will need to change the forward slash (i.e., \) to a forward slash (i.e., /).

```
Ch3_distress <- read.csv("Ch13_psychdistress.csv")
```

The *read.csv* function reads our data into **R**. What's to the left of the "<-" will be what the data will be called in **R**. In this example, we're calling the R dataframe "Ch13_distress." What's to the right of the "<-" tells **R** to find this particular csv file. In this example, our file is called "Ch13_psychdistress.csv." Make sure the extension (i.e., .csv) is included in your script. Also note that the name of your file should be in quotation marks within the parentheses.

```
names(Ch13_distress)
```

The *names* function will produce a list of variable names for each dataframe as follows. This is a good check to make sure your data have been read in correctly.

```
[1] "Sport" "Selection" "Distress"
```

```
View(Ch13_distress)
```

The *View* function will let you view the dataset in spreadsheet format in RStudio.

```
install.packages(car)
```

We will be using the *car* package for Levene's test. This function will install the package in **R**.

```
library(car)
```

The *library* function will load the *car* package in our library.

```
install.packages("compute.es")
```

We will use the *compute.es* package to compute effect sizes. The *install.packages* function will install the package in **R**.

```
library(compute.es)
```

The *library* function will load the *compute.es* package in our library.

```
Ch13_distress$SportF <- factor(Ch13_distress$Sport,
labels = c("movement", "target", "fielding", "territory"))
```

The *factor* function will create a new variable in our dataframe named "SportF." We use the *factor* function to define the variable *Sport* as nominal with the four groups defined here (i.e., movement, target, fielding, territory). What is to the left of "<-" in the script creates the new *SportF* variable in our dataframe.

FIGURE 13.14
Reading data into R.

```
Ch13_distress$SelectionF <- factor(Ch13_distress$Selection,
labels = c("deselected","selected"))
```

The *factor* function will create a new variable in our dataframe named "SelectionF." We use the *factor* function to define the variable *Selection* as nominal with the two groups defined here (i.e., deselected, selected). What is to the left of "<-" in the script creates the new *SelectionF* variable in our dataframe.

```
summary(Ch13_distress)
```

The *summary* function will produce basic descriptive statistics on all the variables in your dataframe. This is a great way to quickly check to see if the data have been read in correctly and to get a feel for your data, if you haven't already. The output from the summary statement for this dataframe looks like this. Because we defined *SportF* and *SelectionF* as factors, we are provided only the frequencies for each category in those variables.

```
     Sport          Selection        Distress          SportF       SelectionF
Min.   :1.00   Min.   :1.0   Min.   : 3.00   movement :8   deselected:16
1st Qu.:1.75   1st Qu.:1.0   1st Qu.:12.00   target   :8   selected  :16
Median :2.50   Median :1.5   Median :20.00   fielding :8
Mean   :2.50   Mean   :1.5   Mean   :18.41   territory:8
3rd Qu.:3.25   3rd Qu.:2.0   3rd Qu.:25.00
Max.   :4.00   Max.   :2.0   Max.   :30.00
```

FIGURE 13.14 (continued)
Reading data into R.

13.5.2 Generating the Factorial ANOVA

```
Ch13_2way <- aov(Distress ~ SportF*SelectionF, data=Ch13_distress)
```

The *aov* function will generate the factorial ANOVA model with "Distress" as the dependent variable and *SportF* and *SelectionF* as the independent variables. The main effects and the interaction of these variables will be generated with the command *Sport*Selection*. Had we included more independent variables, we would have simply continued adding them to this command line with asterisks such as A*B*C. We are using data from the Ch13_distress dataframe, and we are calling this object "Ch13_2way."

```
                  Df  Sum Sq  Mean Sq  F value   Pr(>F)
SportF             3   738.6    246.2   21.350 5.86e-07 ***
SelectionF         1   712.5    712.5   61.791 4.30e-08 ***
SportF:SelectionF  3    21.8      7.3    0.631    0.602
Residuals         24   276.7     11.5
---
Signif. codes: 0 '***' 0.001 '**' 0.01 '*' 0.05 '.' 0.1 ' ' 1
```

```
summary.lm(Ch13_2way)
```

The *summary.lm* function will produce additional output, including R^2.

```
Call:
aov(formula = Distress ~ SportF * SelectionF, data = Ch13_distress)
```

FIGURE 13.15
Generating factorial ANOVA.

```
Residuals:
   Min      1Q  Median      3Q     Max
-5.500  -2.250  -0.250   1.562   6.750

Coefficients:
                                   Estimate  Std. Error  t value   Pr(>|t|)
(Intercept)                          15.250       1.698    8.982   3.83e-09 ***
SportFtarget                          7.500       2.401    3.123    0.00462 **
SportFfielding                       11.000       2.401    4.581    0.00012 ***
SportFterritory                      13.000       2.401    5.414   1.46e-05 ***
SelectionFselected                   -8.250       2.401   -3.436    0.00216 **
SportFtarget:SelectionFselected      -1.500       3.396   -0.442    0.66264
SportFfielding:SelectionFselected    -3.750       3.396   -1.104    0.28041
SportFterritory:SelectionFselected    0.500       3.396    0.147    0.88417
---
Signif. codes: 0 '***' 0.001 '**' 0.01 '*' 0.05 '.' 0.1 ' ' 1

Residual standard error: 3.396 on 24 degrees of freedom
Multiple R-squared: 0.8418, Adjusted R-squared: 0.7957
F-statistic: 18.25 on 7 and 24 DF, p-value: 3.476e-08
```

```
Ch13_distress$unstandardizedResiduals <- residuals(Ch13_2way)
```

We also want to save our unstandardized residuals to the dataframe. We use the *residuals* function to compute unstandardized residuals from our Ch13_2way model. To the left of "<-" we will save the residuals as a variable named "unstandardizedResiduals" in our *Ch13_distress* dataframe.

```
install.packages("sjstats")
library(sjstats)
```

Installing and loading into the library the *sjstats* package will provide another great function for generating the ANOVA summary table, along with multiple effect size indices.

```
anova_stats(Ch13_2way)
```

	term	df	sumsq	meansq	statistic	p. value	etasq	partial.etasq
1	SportF	3	738.594	246.198	21.350	0.000	0.422	0.727
2	SelectionF	1	712.531	712.531	61.791	0.000	0.407	0.720
3	SportF:SelectionF	3	21.844	7.281	0.631	0.602	0.012	0.073
4	Residuals	24	276.750	11.531	NA	NA	NA	NA

	omegasq	partial.omegasq	cohens.f	power
1	0.400	0.656	1.634	1.000
2	0.398	0.655	1.605	1.000
3	-0.007	-0.036	0.281	0.183
4	NA	NA	NA	NA

FIGURE 13.15 (continued)
Generating factorial ANOVA.

13.5.3 Generating Tests for Homogeneity of Variance

```
install.packages("car")
library(car)
```

We use the *car* package to run Levene's Test so we will install using the *install.packages* function (if not already installed; if you have already installed this package, you can skip the install step) and then load into our library using the *car* package.

```
LeveneTest(Ch13_distress$Distress,
interaction(Ch13_distress$SportF,
Ch13_distress$SelectionF),
        center=mean)
```

```
Levene's Test for Homogeneity of Variance (center = mean)
      Df F value Pr(>F)
group  7 0.5785 0.7663
      24
```

We read this output as F(7,24) = .5785, p = .7663, indicating we have met the assumption of equal variances.

```
leveneTest(Ch13_2way)
```

We can also run the *leveneTest* function on the object (Ch13_2way) of our factorial ANOVA model results to generate Levene's test with the default centering of the median, which may provide more robust results. These results still provide evidence of meeting the assumption of equal variances, with $p = .882$.

```
Levene's Test for Homogeneity of Variance (center = median)
      Df F value Pr(>F)
group  7 0.4172 0.882
      24
```

FIGURE 13.16
Generating homoscedasticity tests.

13.5.4 Generating Post Hoc Tests

```
Ch13_tukey <- TukeyHSD(Ch13_2way)
```

The *TukeyHSD* function will generate Tukey's HSD post hoc analysis on our factorial ANOVA model, Ch13_2way, and will name the object "Ch13_tukey."

```
Ch13_tukey
```

This will output the results of the Tukey's HSD post hoc analysis from the previous command.

FIGURE 13.17
Generating post hoc comparisons.

```
Tukey multiple comparisons of means
  95% family-wise confidence level

Fit: aov(formula = Distress ~ SportF * SelectionF, data = Ch13_distress)
$SportF
                      diff        lwr       upr     p adj
target-movement      6.750  2.0662003  11.4338  0.0029427
fielding-movement    9.125  4.4412003  13.8088  0.0000901
territory-movement  13.250  8.5662003  17.9338  0.0000003
fielding-target      2.375 -2.3087997   7.0588  0.5122072
territory-target     6.500  1.8162003  11.1838  0.0042196
territory-fielding   4.125 -0.5587997   8.8088  0.0982713
```

As we already know from the *F* test, there were differences between at least some of the types of sport. Tukey's post hoc tells us there are statistically significant differences between *movement* and all other sports as well as differences between *territory* and *target*.

```
$SelectionF
                        diff        lwr       upr  p adj
selected-deselected -9.4375  -11.91539 -6.959613      0
```

As we already know from the *F* test, there is a statistically significant difference between the selection status groups. This confirms that finding again.

```
$'SportF:SelectionF'
                                              diff         lwr         upr
target:deselected-movement:deselected         7.50  -0.4524709  15.4524709
fielding:deselected-movement:deselected      11.00   3.0475291  18.9524709
territory:deselected-movement:deselected     13.00   5.0475291  20.9524709
```

For brevity, and because there was not a statistically significant omnibus interaction, the complete results for the post hoc comparisons of the "sport by selection" interaction are not presented here.

FIGURE 13.17 (continued)
Generating post hoc comparisons.

13.5.5 Computing Effect Size

```
install.packages("sjstats")
library(sjstats)
```

The package *sjstats* can be used to generate multiple effect size indices in ANOVA. The *install.packages* and *library* functions will, respectively, install the package and then load it into our **R** library.

```
omega_sq(Ch13_2way)
```

Using the object created from our ANOVA model, Ch13_2way, we can generate omega squared with the *omega_sq* function. We see that ω^2 for type of sport (i.e., A) is approximately .40, for selection status (i.e., B) is also about .40, and for the interaction of type of sport and selection status is about −.007.

```
               term  omegasq
1            SportF    0.400
2        SelectionF    0.398
3 SportF:SelectionF   -0.007
```

```
omega_sq(Ch13_2way, partial = TRUE)
```

Using the object created from our ANOVA model, Ch13_2way, we can generate partial omega squared with the *omega_sq* function, defining *partial = TRUE*. The partial variance effect size is interpreted as the proportion of variation in the dependent variable, *Y*, explained by the effect of interest (i.e., by factor A, or factor B, or the AB interaction) that is *not* explained by other variables in the model.

FIGURE 13.18
Generating effect size.

```
                 term  partial.omegasq
1              SportF            0.656
2          SelectionF            0.655
3   SportF:SelectionF           -0.036
```

```
cohens_f(Ch13_2way)
```

Using the object created from our ANOVA model, Ch13_2way, we can generate Cohen's *f* with the *cohens_f* function. The effect *f* can take on values from zero (when the means are equal) to an infinitely large positive value. This effect is interpreted as an approximate correlation index but can also be interpreted as the standard deviation of the standardized means (Cohen, 1988). Small effects for *f* = .1, moderate *f* = .25, and large effect *f* = .40.

```
                 term   cohens.f
1              SportF   1.633650
2          SelectionF   1.604568
3   SportF:SelectionF   0.280944
```

```
eta_sq(Ch13_2way)
```

Using the object created from our ANOVA model, Ch13_2way, we can generate eta squared with the *eta_sq* function.

```
                 term   etasq
1              SportF   0.422
2          SelectionF   0.407
3   SportF:SelectionF   0.012
```

```
eta_sq(Ch13_2way, partial = TRUE)
```

Using the object created from our ANOVA model, Ch13_2way, we can generate partial eta squared with the *eta_sq* function, defining *partial = TRUE*.

```
                 term  partial.etasq
1              SportF          0.727
2          SelectionF          0.720
3   SportF:SelectionF          0.073
```

```
anova_stats(Ch13_2way)
```

The *anova_stats* function can be used with our ANOVA model, Ch13_2way, to present a comprehensive summary, including effect size measures and power.

```
                 term  df    sumsq   meansq  statistic  p. value
1              SportF   3  738.594  246.198     21.350     0.000
2          SelectionF   1  712.531  712.531     61.791     0.000
3   SportF:SelectionF   3   21.844    7.281      0.631     0.602
4           Residuals  24  276.750   11.531         NA        NA

  etasq  partial.etasq  omegasq  partial.omegasq  cohens.f
1 0.422          0.727    0.400            0.656     1.634
2 0.407          0.720    0.398            0.655     1.605
3 0.012          0.073   -0.007           -0.036     0.281
4    NA             NA       NA               NA        NA

  power
1 1.000
2 1.000
3 0.183
4    NA
```

FIGURE 13.18 (continued)
Generating effect size.

13.6 Data Screening

13.6.1 Normality

We will use the residuals (which were requested and created through the "Save" option when generating our factorial ANOVA) to examine the extent to which normality was met.

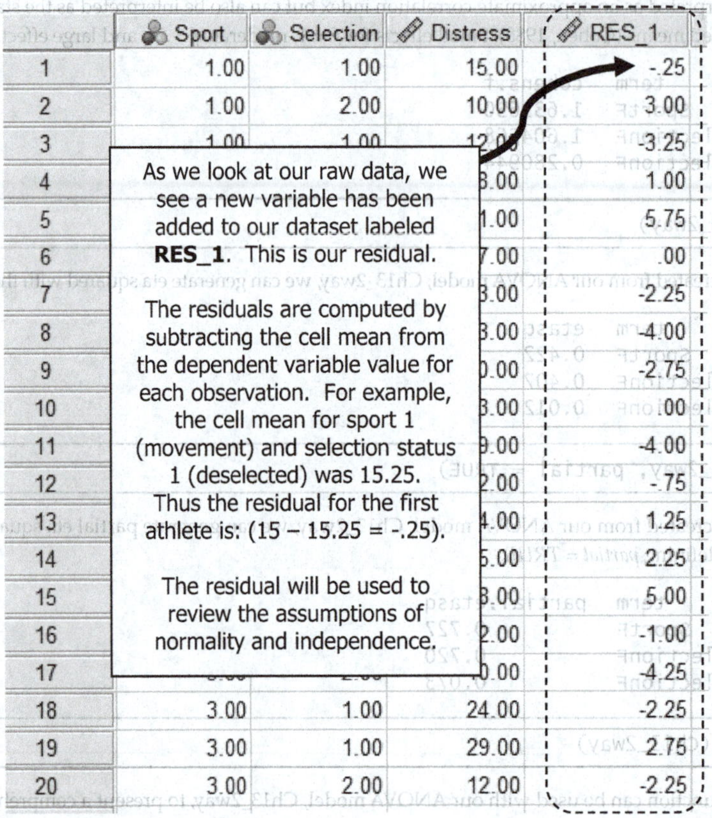

Sport
Selection
Distress
RES_1
As we look at our raw data, we see a new variable has been added to our dataset labeled **RES_1**. This is our residual.
The residuals are computed by subtracting the cell mean from the dependent variable value for each observation. For example, the cell mean for sport 1 (movement) and selection status 1 (deselected) was 15.25. Thus the residual for the first athlete is: (15 – 15.25 = -.25).
The residual will be used to review the assumptions of normality and independence.

FIGURE 13.19
First 20 cases of residual data.

As alluded to earlier in the chapter, understanding the distributional shape, specifically the extent to which normality is a reasonable assumption, is important. For factorial ANOVA, the distributional shape for the residuals should be a normal distribution. We can again use "Explore" to examine the extent to which the assumption of normality is met.

The general steps for accessing Explore have been presented in previous chapters, and will not be repeated here. Click the residual and move it into the "Dependent List" box by clicking on the arrow button. For dependent by group, click the factor variables (in this case, 'Sport' and 'Selection') and move to the "Factor List" box. The procedures for selecting normality statistics were presented in Chapter 6, and remain the same here: click on

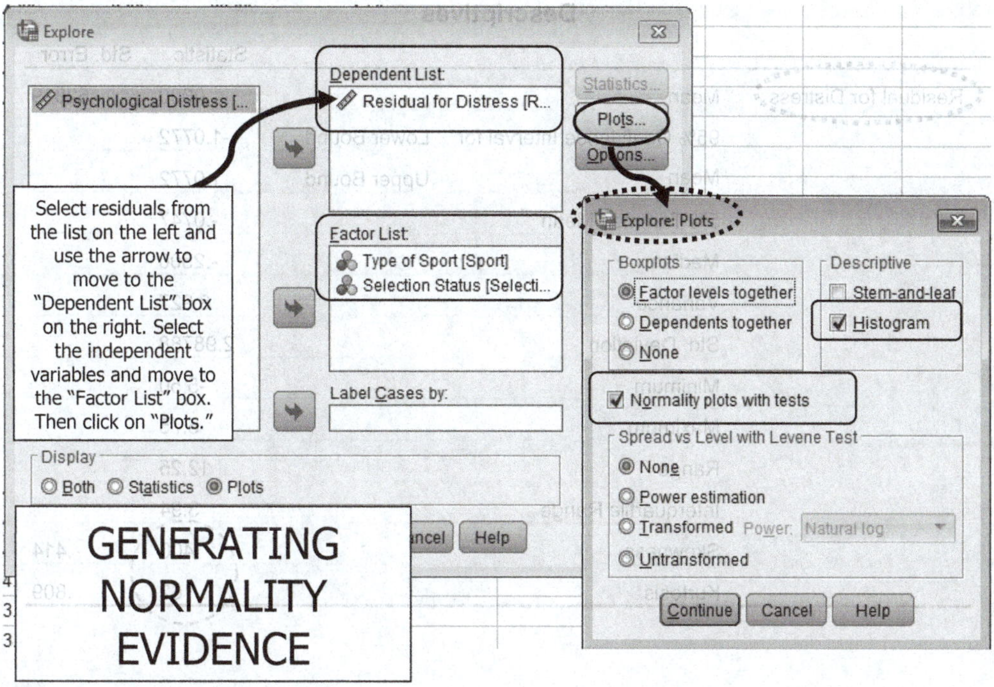

FIGURE 13.20
Generating normality evidence.

"Plots" in the upper right corner. Place a checkmark in the boxes for "Normality plots with tests" and also for "Histogram." Then click "Continue" to return to the main Explore dialog box. Then click "OK" to generate the output.

13.6.1.1 Interpreting Normality Evidence

We have already developed a good understanding of how to interpret some forms of evidence of normality including skewness and kurtosis, histograms, and boxplots. The skewness statistic of the residuals is .400 and kurtosis is −.162—both within the range of an absolute value of 2.0, suggesting some evidence of normality. By group, skewness and kurtosis are all within this range as well (for brevity, not presented here). Working in **R, D'Agostino's test** (D'Agostino, 1970) can be used to examine the null hypothesis that skewness equals zero. Thus, a statistically significant D'Agostino's test would indicate that there is statistically significant skewness. For kurtosis, we can use the **Bonett-Seier test for Geary's kurtosis** (Bonett & Seier, 2002) for data that is normally distributed. The null hypothesis states that data should have a Geary's kurtosis value equal to $\sqrt{2/\pi} = .7979$. Thus, a statistically significant Bonett-Seier test for Geary's kurtosis would indicate that there is statistically significant kurtosis. Thus, with these tests, as with Kolmogorov-Smirnov and Shapiro-Wilk, we do *not* want to find statistically significant results—and that's exactly what we found (i.e., $p >$ alpha).

Descriptives

			Statistic	Std. Error
Residual for Distress	Mean		.0000	.52819
	95% Confidence Interval for Mean	Lower Bound	-1.0772	
		Upper Bound	1.0772	
	5% Trimmed Mean		-.0747	
	Median		-.2500	
	Variance		8.927	
	Std. Deviation		2.98788	
	Minimum		-5.50	
	Maximum		6.75	
	Range		12.25	
	Interquartile Range		3.94	
	Skewness		.400	.414
	Kurtosis		-.162	.809

Working in **R**, we can generate various normality statistics as well.

```
install.packages("pastecs")
```

The *install.packages* function will install the *pastecs* package which we will use to generate various forms of normality evidence.

```
library(pastecs)
```

The *library* function will load the *pastecs* package.

```
stat.desc(Ch13_distress$unstandardizedResiduals,
        norm = TRUE)
```

The *stat.desc* function will generate normality indices on the variable "unstandardizedResiduals" in the dataframe Ch13_distress as follows. The *norm=TRUE* command will produce Shapiro-Wilk (S-W) results, which are displayed as *normtest.W* (which is the S-W statistic value) and *normtest.p* (which is the observed probability value).

Here, we see S-W = .977 and the related $p = .701$. We see skew (.363) and kurtosis (-.485) for the *unstandardizedResidual* variable.

Skew, kurtosis, and S-W all indicate the assumption of normality has been met. As we know, we can divide the skew and kurtosis values by their standard errors to get a standardized value that can be used to determine if the skew and/or kurtosis is statistically different from zero. Since this output provides "2SE," we would simply divide this value by 2 to arrive at the standard error.

FIGURE 13.21
Normality evidence.

Note: You may have noticed that the skewness and kurtosis value that we've just generated differs from what we found in SPSS, which was skew = .400 and kurtosis = −.162. This is because there are different ways to calculate skewness and kurtosis. Let's use another package in **R** to calculate these statistics with different algorithms.

```
         nbr.val       nbr.null         nbr.na            min
    3.200000e+01   0.000000e+00   0.000000e+00  -5.500000e+00

             max          range            sum         median
    6.750000e+00   1.225000e+01  -1.318390e-15  -2.500000e-01

            mean        SE.mean   CI.mean.0.95            var
   -4.119968e-17   5.281873e-01   1.077245e+00   8.927419e+00

         std.dev       coef.var       skewness       skew.2SE
    2.987879e+00  -7.252189e+16   3.633272e-01   4.383167e-01

        kurtosis      kurt.2SE     normtest.W     normtest.p
   -4.847138e-01-2.994385e-01   9.767450e-01   7.009705e-01
```

```
install.packages("e1071")
```

The *install.packages* function will install the e1071 package which we will use to generate skewness and kurtosis.

```
library(e1071)
```

The *library* function will load the e1071 package.

```
skewness(Ch13_distress$unstandardizedResiduals, type=3)
skewness(Ch13_distress$unstandardizedResiduals, type=2)
skewness(Ch13_distress$unstandardizedResiduals, type=1)
```

The *skewness* function will generate skewness statistics on the variable(s) specified. The "type=" script defines how skewness is calculated. Specifying "type=2" will use the algorithm that is used by SPSS. Readers interested in learning more, including the algorithms for each of the three methods, are encouraged to review Joanes and Gill (1998). We see that using type=2, our skew is .400, the same value as generated using SPSS.

```
# skewness(Ch13_distress$unstandardizedResiduals, type=3)
[1] 0.3633272

# skewness(Ch13_distress$unstandardizedResiduals, type=2)
[1] 0.4000506

# skewness(Ch13_distress$unstandardizedResiduals, type=1)
[1] 0.3810486
```

```
kurtosis(Ch13_distress$unstandardizedResiduals, type=3)
kurtosis(Ch13_distress$unstandardizedResiduals, type=2)
kurtosis(Ch13_distress$unstandardizedResiduals, type=1)
```

The *kurtosis* function will generate kurtosis statistics on the variable(s) we specify. The "type=" script defines how kurtosis is calculated. Specifying "type=2" will use the algorithm that is used by SPSS. Readers interested

FIGURE 13.21 (continued)
Normality evidence.

in learning more, including the algorithms for each of the three methods, are encouraged to review Joanes and Gill (1998). We see that using type=2, our kurtosis is −.162, the same value as generated using SPSS.

```
# kurtosis(Ch13_distress$unstandardizedResiduals, type=3)
[1] -0.4847138

# kurtosis(Ch13_distress$unstandardizedResiduals, type=2)
[1] -0.162271

# kurtosis(Ch13_distress$unstandardizedResiduals, type=1)
[1] -0.3198199
```

Working in **R**, another way to test for normality is D'Agostino's test for skewness and the Bonett-Seier test for Geary's kurtosis.

```
install.packages("moments")
library(moments)
```

To conduct D'Agostino's test, we first have to install the *moments* package and then load it into our library. The null hypothesis for this test is that skewness equals zero. Thus, a statistically significant D'Agostino's test would indicate that there is statistically significant skewness.

```
agostino.test(Ch13_distress$unstandardizedResiduals)
```

The function *agostino.test* is generated using the variable "unstandardizedResiduals" from our Ch13_distress dataframe. The results suggest evidence of normality as $p = .3154$, greater than alpha.

```
        D'Agostino skewness test

data: Ch13_distress$unstandardizedResiduals
skew = 0.38105, z = 1.00390, p-value = 0.3154
alternative hypothesis: data have a skewness
```

```
bonett.test((Ch13_distress$unstandardizedResiduals))
```

The *bonett.test* function, generated using the variable "unstandardizedResiduals" from our Ch13_distress dataframe, performs the Bonett-Seier test for Geary's kurtosis for data that is normally distributed. The null hypothesis states that data should have a Geary's kurtosis value equal to $\sqrt{2/\pi} = .7979$. The results suggest evidence of normality as $p = .7488$, greater than alpha.

```
        Bonett-Seier test for Geary kurtosis

data: (Ch13_distress$unstandardizedResiduals)
tau = 2.31250, z = 0.32019, p-value = 0.7488
alternative hypothesis: kurtosis is not equal to sqrt(2/pi)
```

```
agostino.test(Ch3_distress$unstandardizedResiduals[Ch3_distress$Sport==1])
agostino.test(Ch3_distress$unstandardizedResiduals[Ch3_distress$Sport==2])
agostino.test(Ch3_distress$unstandardizedResiduals[Ch3_distress$Sport==3])
agostino.test(Ch3_distress$unstandardizedResiduals[Ch3_distress$Sport==4])
agostino.test(Ch3_distress$unstandardizedResiduals[Ch3_distress$Selection==1])
agostino.test(Ch3_distress$unstandardizedResiduals[Ch3_distress$Selection==2])
```

FIGURE 13.21 (continued)
Normality evidence.

By group, the results for the D'Agostino test provide evidence of normality by group with all p's > .05. For brevity, only the results from 'Selection' are presented.

```
# agostino.test(Ch3_distress$unstandardizedResiduals[Ch3_distress$Selection==1])

        D'Agostino skewness test

data: Ch3_distress$unstandardizedResiduals[Ch3_distress$Selection == 1]
skew = 0.68393, z = 1.37170, p-value = 0.1702
alternative hypothesis: data have a skewness

# agostino.test(Ch3_distress$unstandardizedResiduals[Ch3_distress$Selection==2])

D'Agostino skewness test

data: Ch3_distress$unstandardizedResiduals[Ch3_distress$Selection == 2]
skew = 0.26226, z = 0.54189, p-value = 0.5879
alternative hypothesis: data have a skewness
```

```
bonett.test((Ch3_distress$unstandardizedResiduals))
```

The *bonett.test* function, generated using the variable *unstandardizedResiduals* from our *Ch3_distress* dataframe, performs the Bonett-Seier test for Geary's kurtosis for data that is normally distributed. The null hypothesis states that data should have a Geary's kurtosis value equal to $\sqrt{2/\rho} = .7979$. The results suggest evidence of normality as $p = .7488$, greater than alpha.

```
Bonett-Seier test for Geary kurtosis

data: (Ch3_distress$unstandardizedResiduals)
tau = 2.31250, z = 0.32019, p-value = 0.7488
alternative hypothesis: kurtosis is not equal to sqrt(2/pi)
```

```
bonett.test((Ch3_distress$unstandardizedResiduals[Ch3_distress$Sport==1]))
bonett.test((Ch3_distress$unstandardizedResiduals[Ch3_distress$Sport==2]))
bonett.test((Ch3_distress$unstandardizedResiduals[Ch3_distress$Sport==3]))
bonett.test((Ch3_distress$unstandardizedResiduals[Ch3_distress$Sport==4]))
bonett.test((Ch3_distress$unstandardizedResiduals[Ch3_distress$Selection==1]))
bonett.test((Ch3_distress$unstandardizedResiduals[Ch3_distress$Selection==2]))
```

By group, the results for the Bonett-Seier test for Geary's kurtosis for data that is normally distributed provide evidence of normality by group with all p's > .05. For brevity, only the results from 'Selection' are presented.

```
# bonett.test((Ch13_distress$unstandardizedResiduals[Ch13_distress$Selection==1]))

Bonett-Seier test for Geary kurtosis

data: (Ch3_distress$unstandardizedResiduals[Ch3_distress$Selection == 1])
tau = 1.90630, z = -0.38564, p-value = 0.6998
alternative hypothesis: kurtosis is not equal to sqrt(2/pi)

# bonett.test((Ch3_distress$unstandardizedResiduals[Ch3_distress$Selection==2]))

Bonett-Seier test for Geary kurtosis
data: (Ch3_distress$unstandardizedResiduals[Ch3_distress$Selection == 2])
tau = 2.71880, z = 0.16969, p-value = 0.8653
alternative hypothesis: kurtosis is not equal to sqrt(2/pi)
```

FIGURE 13.21 (continued)
Normality evidence.

As suggested by the skewness statistic, the histograms of residuals, overall, are slightly positively skewed, but it approaches a normal distribution and there is nothing to suggest that normality may be an unreasonable assumption. Similarly, the histograms by group suggest some skew (not presented for brevity). Additional normality indices will be reviewed to better understand the extent that normality may be reasonable.

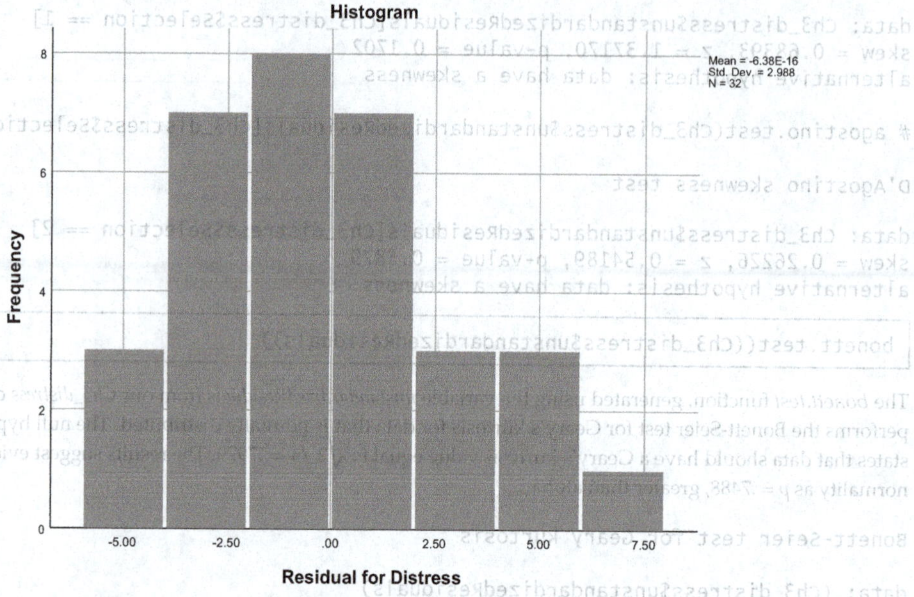

Working in **R**, we can generate a histogram using the *ggplot2* package.

```
install.packages("ggplot2")
```

The *install.packages* function will install the *ggplot2* package which we can use to create various graphs and plots.

```
library(ggplot2)
```

The *library* function will load the *ggplot2* package.

```
qplot(Ch13_distress$unstandardizedResiduals,
      geom="histogram",
      binwidth=1,
      main = "Histogram of Unstandardized Residuals",
      xlab = "Unstandardized Residual", ylab = "Count",
      fill=I("gray"),
      col=I("white"))
```

Using the *gplot* function, we create a histogram (i.e., geom = "histogram") from our dataframe (i.e., Ch13_distress) using the variable "unstandardizedResiduals." We can add a few commands to change the width of the bars (i.e., *binwidth = 1*), color of the bars (i.e., *fill=I("gray")*), and outline of the bars (i.e., *col=I("white")*). We can also add a title (i.e., *main = "Histogram of Unstandardized Residuals"*) and change the *X* and *Y* axes (*xlab = "Unstandardized Residual", ylab = "Count"*).

FIGURE 13.22
Histogram.

```
hist(Ch3_distress$unstandardizedResiduals[Ch3_distress$Sport==1],
      main="Histogram for Movement",
      xlab="Unstandardized Residuals")

hist(Ch3_distress$unstandardizedResiduals[Ch3_distress$Sport==2],
      main="Histogram for Target",
      xlab="Unstandardized Residuals")

hist(Ch3_distress$unstandardizedResiduals[Ch3_distress$Sport==3],
      main="Histogram for Fielding",
      xlab="Unstandardized Residuals")

hist(Ch3_distress$unstandardizedResiduals[Ch3_distress$Sport==4],
      main="Histogram for Territory",
      xlab="Unstandardized Residuals")

hist(Ch3_distress$unstandardizedResiduals[Ch3_distress$Selection==1],
      main="Histogram for Deselected",
      xlab="Unstandardized Residuals")

hist(Ch3_distress$unstandardizedResiduals[Ch3_distress$Selection==2],
      main="Histogram for Selected",
      xlab="Unstandardized Residuals")
```

Histograms by group can be created with these scripts, each one specifying one category of *Sport* or *Selection* as the variable with which to create the histogram of unstandardized residuals.

FIGURE 13.22 (continued)
Histogram.

There are a few other statistics that can be used to gauge normality. The formal test of normality, the Shapiro-Wilk test (*SW*) (Shapiro & Wilk, 1965), provides evidence of the extent to which our sample distribution is statistically different from a normal distribution. The output for the Shapiro-Wilk test is presented in Figure 13.23 and suggests that our sample distribution for residuals is not statistically significantly different than what would be expected from a normal distribution ($SW = .977$, $df = 32$, $p = .701$), nor are the residuals by group statistically significantly different than what would be expected from a normal distribution.

Tests of Normality

	Kolmogorov-Smirnov[a]			Shapiro-Wilk		
	Statistic	df	Sig.	Statistic	df	Sig.
Residual for Distress	.094	32	.200*	.977	32	.701

*. This is a lower bound of the true significance.

a. Lilliefors Significance Correction

Working in **R,** the *stat.desc* function from the *pastecs* package can be used to generate the Shapiro-Wilk test, along with many other statistics. Should we want to generate *just* the *S-W* test, we can run the following script.

FIGURE 13.23
Shapiro-Wilk test of normality.

```
shapiro.test(Ch1_distress$unstandardizedResiduals)
```

```
        Shapiro-Wilk normality test
data: Ch13_distress$unstandardizedResiduals
W = 0.97674, p-value = 0.701
```

```
tapply(Ch13_distress$unstandardizedResiduals,
       Ch13_distress$SportF, shapiro.test)

tapply(Ch13_distress$unstandardizedResiduals,
 Ch13_distress$SelectionF, shapiro.test)
```

To generate the Shapiro-Wilk test by group, the *tapply* function can be used to apply the *shapiro.test* to the unstandardized residuals for all levels of the independent variable.

FIGURE 13.23 (continued)
Shapiro-Wilk test of normality.

Quantile-quantile (Q-Q) plots are also often examined to determine evidence of normality. Q-Q plots are graphs that plot quantiles of the theoretical normal distribution against quantiles of the sample distribution. Points that fall on or close to the diagonal line suggest evidence of normality. The Q-Q plot of residuals, overall and by group, suggest relative normality.

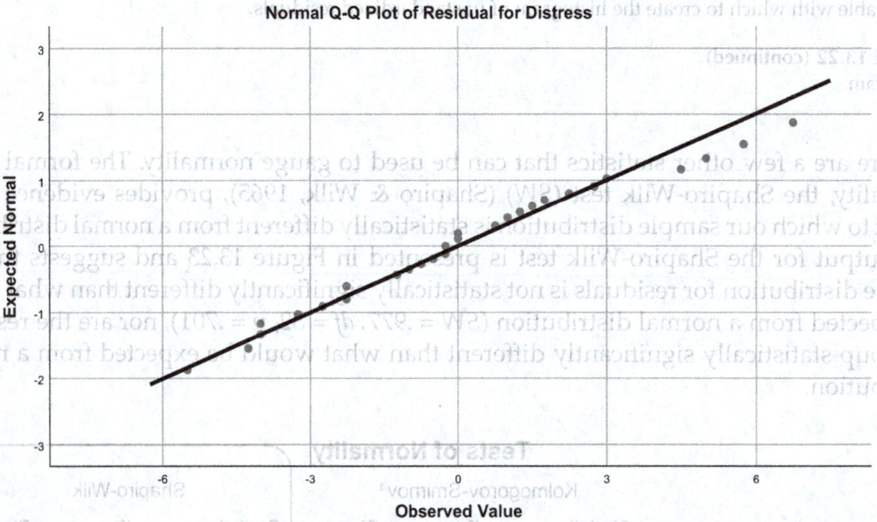

Working in **R**, we can use the *qplot* function to create a Q-Q plot of unstandardized residuals. The "data=" script defines the dataframe as Ch13_distress.

```
qplot(sample=unstandardizedResiduals,
    data = Ch13_distress)
```

FIGURE 13.24
Normal Q-Q Plot

```
qqnorm(Ch13_distress$unstandardizedResiduals[Ch3_distress$Sport==1],
        main='movement')

qqnorm(Ch13_distress$unstandardizedResiduals[Ch3_distress$Sport==2],
        main='target')

qqnorm(Ch13_distress$unstandardizedResiduals[Ch3_distress$Sport==3],
        main='fielding')

qqnorm(Ch13_distress$unstandardizedResiduals[Ch3_distress$Sport==4],
        main='territory')

qqnorm(Ch13_distress$unstandardizedResiduals[Ch3_distress$Selection==1],
        main='deselected')

qqnorm(Ch13_distress$unstandardizedResiduals[Ch3_distress$Selection==2],
        main='selected')
```

By group, QQ plots can be created with this script, with each command defining one category of the *Sport* and *Selection* variables.

FIGURE 13.24 (continued)
Normal Q-Q Plot

Examination of the boxplot suggests a relatively normal distributional shape of residuals and no outliers, overall and by group.

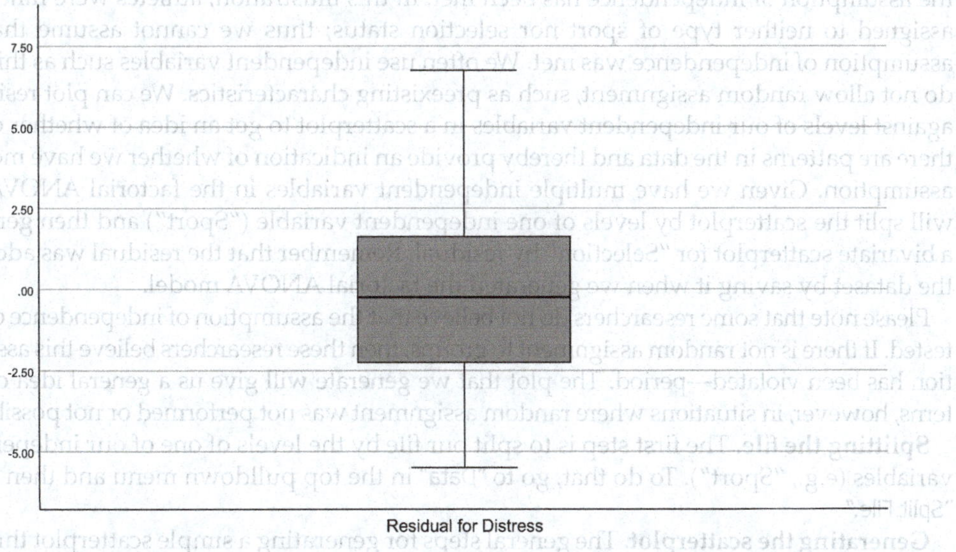

Working in R, we can generate a boxplot for unstandardized residuals using the *boxplot* function. To label the *Y* axis, we include the *ylab* command.

FIGURE 13.25
Boxplot.

```
boxplot(Ch13_distress$unstandardizedResiduals,
        ylab="Unstandardized Residuals")
```

Adding the independent variable to the script produces a boxplot by group. The command *xlab* will print *Sport* to identify the *X* axis.

```
boxplot(Ch13_distress$unstandardizedResiduals~Ch13_distress$SportF,
        xlab="Sport", ylab="Unstandardized Residuals")

boxplot(Ch13_distress$unstandardizedResiduals~Ch13_distress$SelectionF,
        xlab="Selection", ylab="Unstandardized Residuals")
```

FIGURE 13.25 (continued)
Boxplot.

Considering the forms of evidence we have examined, skewness and kurtosis statistics, the Shapiro-Wilk test, the Q-Q plot, and the boxplot, all suggest normality is a reasonable assumption. We can be reasonably assured that we have met the assumption of normality of the dependent variable for each group of the independent variable.

13.6.2 Independence

The only assumption we have not tested for yet is independence. As we discussed in reference to the one-way ANOVA, if subjects have been randomly assigned to conditions (or to the different combinations of the levels of the independent variables in a factorial ANOVA), the assumption of independence has been met. In this illustration, athletes were randomly assigned to neither type of sport nor selection status; thus we cannot assume that the assumption of independence was met. We often use independent variables such as this that do not allow random assignment, such as preexisting characteristics. We can plot residuals against levels of our independent variables in a scatterplot to get an idea of whether or not there are patterns in the data and thereby provide an indication of whether we have met this assumption. Given we have multiple independent variables in the factorial ANOVA, we will split the scatterplot by levels of one independent variable ("Sport") and then generate a bivariate scatterplot for "Selection" by residual. Remember that the residual was added to the dataset by saving it when we generated the factorial ANOVA model.

Please note that some researchers do not believe that the assumption of independence can be tested. If there is not random assignment to groups, then these researchers believe this assumption has been violated—period. The plot that we generate will give us a general idea of patterns, however, in situations where random assignment was not performed or not possible.

Splitting the file. The first step is to split our file by the levels of one of our independent variables (e.g., "Sport"). To do that, go to "Data" in the top pulldown menu and then select "Split File."

Generating the scatterplot. The general steps for generating a simple scatterplot through "Scatter/dot" are likely not new to you (from the top toolbar in SPSS, go to Graphs -> Legacy Dialogs -> Scatter/Dot). From the "Simple Scatterplot" dialog screen, click the residual variable and move it into the "Y Axis" box by clicking on the arrow. Click the independent variable that was not used to split the file (e.g., 'Selection Status') and move it into the "X Axis" box by clicking on the arrow. Then click "OK."

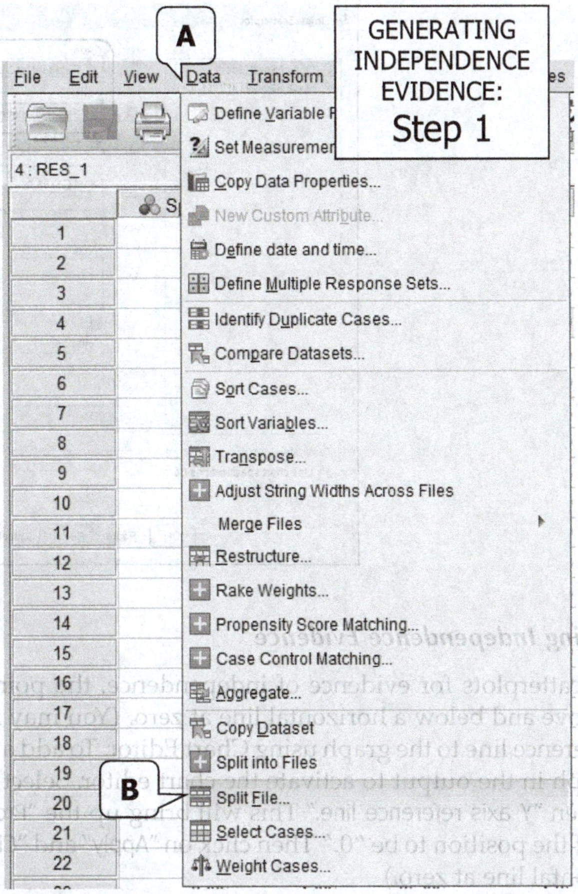

FIGURE 13.26
Generating independence evidence: Step 1.

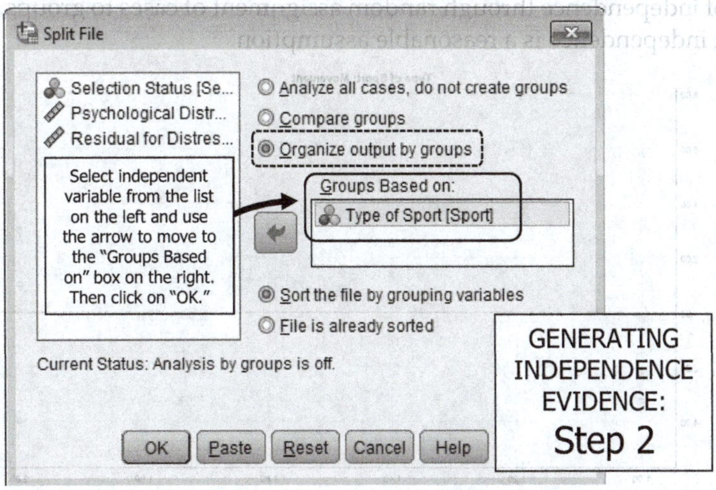

FIGURE 13.27
Generating independence evidence: Step 2.

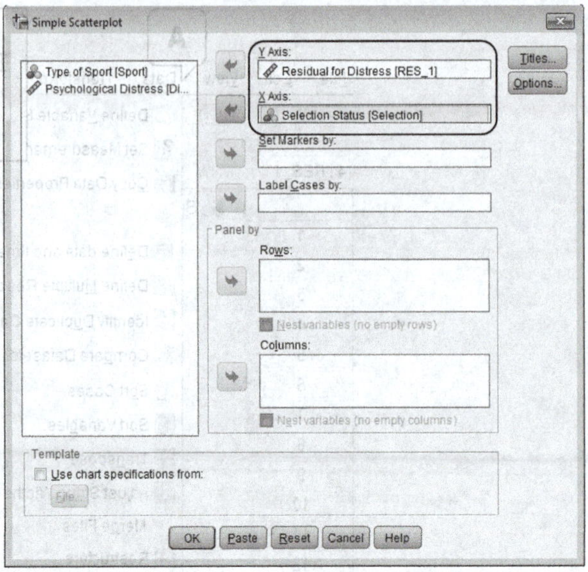

FIGURE 13.28
Generating a scatterplot.

13.6.2.1 Interpreting Independence Evidence

In examining the scatterplots for evidence of independence, the points should fall relatively randomly above and below a horizontal line at zero. (You may recall in Chapter 11 that we added a reference line to the graph using Chart Editor. To add a reference line, double click on the graph in the output to activate the chart editor. Select "Options" in the top pulldown menu, then "Y axis reference line." This will bring up the "Properties" dialog box. Change the value of the position to be "0." Then click on "Apply" and "Close" to generate the graph with a horizontal line at zero.)

In this example, our scatterplot for each type of sport generally suggests evidence of independence with a relatively random display of residuals above and below the horizontal line at zero for each category of time. Thus, even though we have not met the assumption of independence through random assignment of cases to groups, this provides evidence that independence is a reasonable assumption.

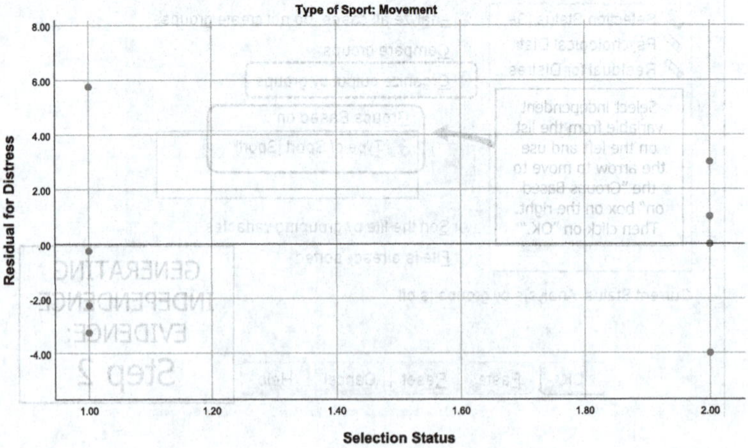

FIGURE 13.29
Residual plots.

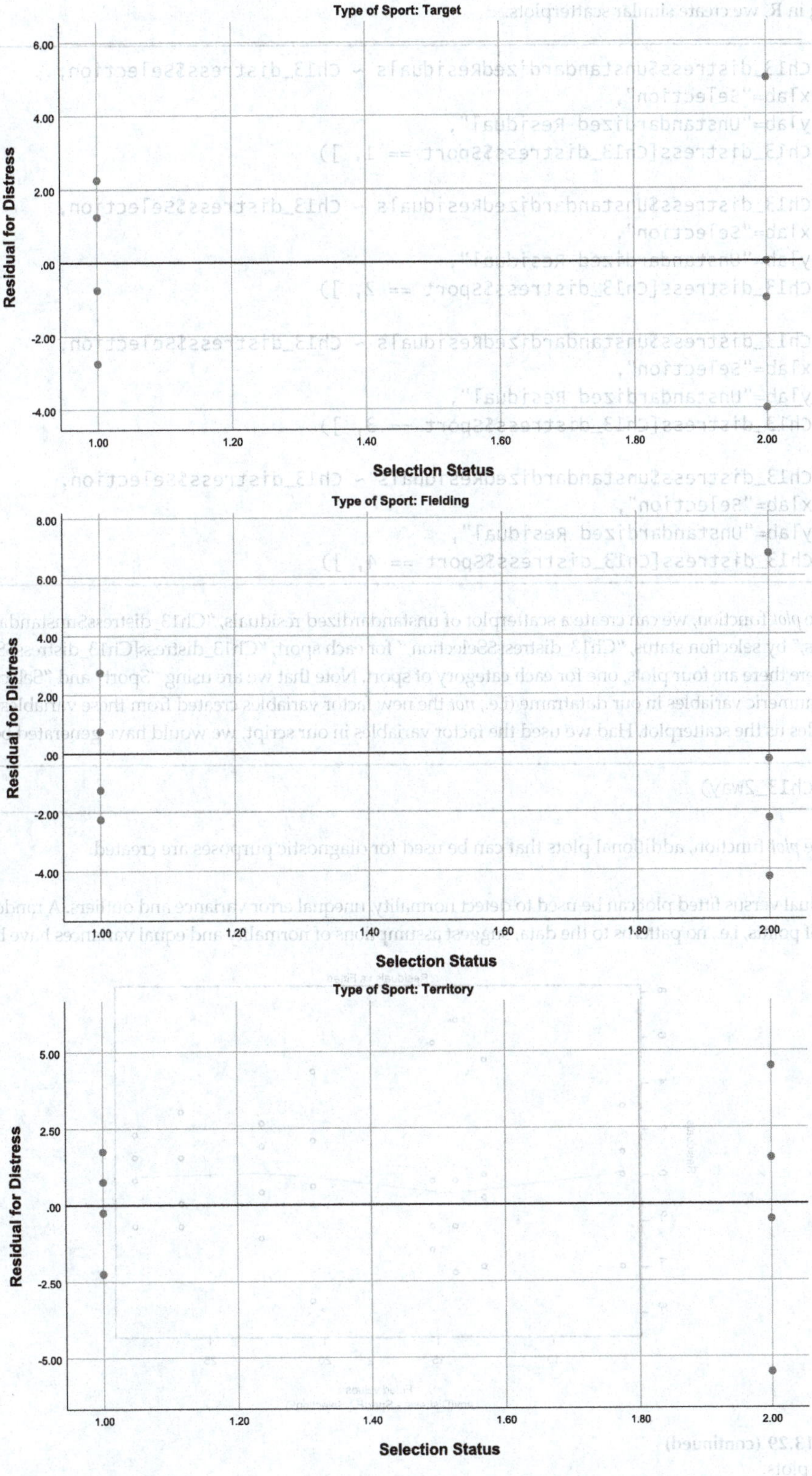

FIGURE 13.29 (continued)
Residual plots.

Working in **R**, we create similar scatterplots.

```
plot(Ch13_distress$unstandardizedResiduals ~ Ch13_distress$Selection,
     xlab="Selection",
     ylab="Unstandardized Residual",
     Ch13_distress[Ch13_distress$Sport == 1, ])

plot(Ch13_distress$unstandardizedResiduals ~ Ch13_distress$Selection,
     xlab="Selection",
     ylab="Unstandardized Residual",
     Ch13_distress[Ch13_distress$Sport == 2, ])

plot(Ch13_distress$unstandardizedResiduals ~ Ch13_distress$Selection,
     xlab="Selection",
     ylab="Unstandardized Residual",
     Ch13_distress[Ch13_distress$Sport == 3, ])

plot(Ch13_distress$unstandardizedResiduals ~ Ch13_distress$Selection,
     xlab="Selection",
     ylab="Unstandardized Residual",
     Ch13_distress[Ch13_distress$Sport == 4, ])
```

Using the *plot* function, we can create a scatterplot of unstandardized residuals, "Ch13_distress$unstandardized Residuals," by selection status, "Ch13_distress$Selection," for each sport, "Ch13_distress[Ch13_distress$Sport == 1,]," where there are four plots, one for each category of sport. Note that we are using "Sport" and "Selection," the original numeric variables in our dataframe (i.e., *not* the new factor variables created from these variables). Doing so provides us the scatterplot. Had we used the factor variables in our script, we would have generated boxplots.

```
plot(Ch13_2way)
```

Using the *plot* function, additional plots that can be used for diagnostic purposes are created.

The residual versus fitted plot can be used to detect normality, unequal error variance and outliers. A random display of points, i.e., no patterns to the data, suggest assumptions of normality and equal variances have been met.

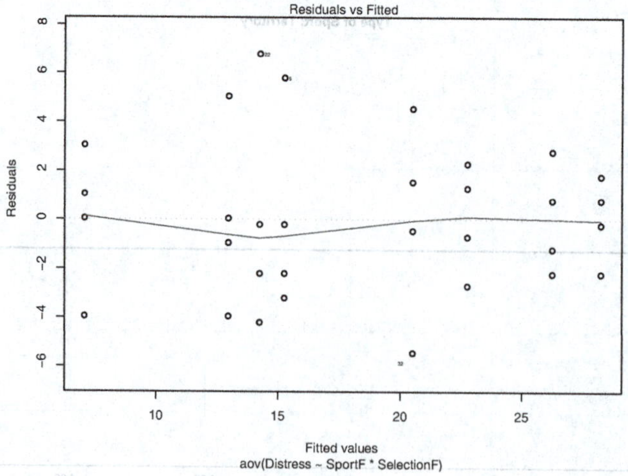

FIGURE 13.29 (continued)
Residual plots.

The normal Q-Q plot can be used to detect normality and outliers. Points that adhere closely to the diagonal line suggest the assumption of normality has been met.

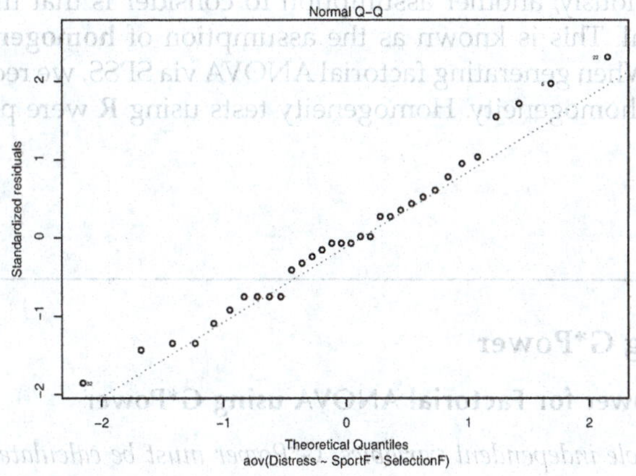

The scale-location plot can be examined for evidence of equal variance. Relatively equally spaced points by group above and below a horizontal line (i.e., random and equal distribution of points and straight horizontal line) suggests evidence of meeting the assumption.

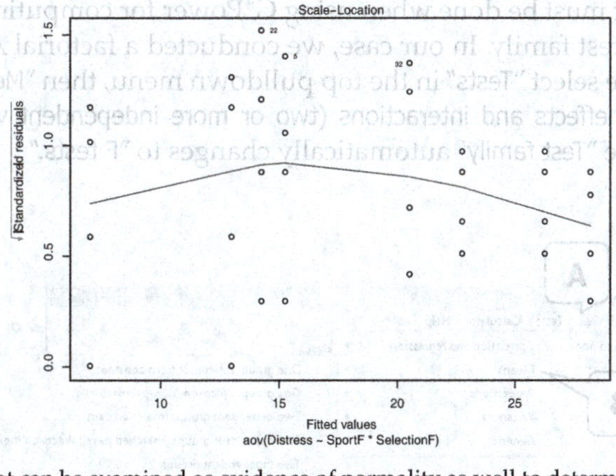

The constant leverage plot can be examined as evidence of normality as well to determine points that may exert influence.

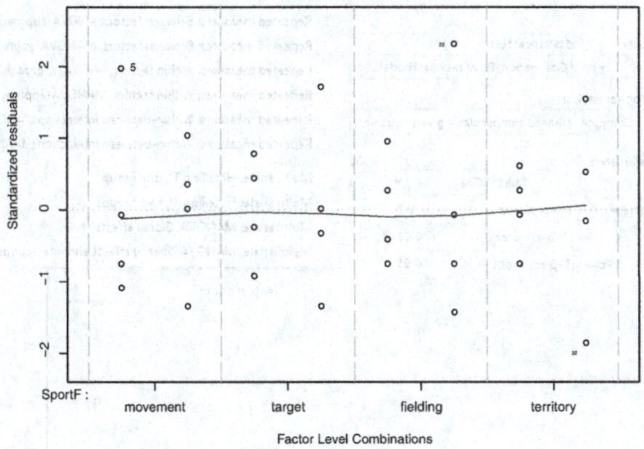

FIGURE 13.29 (continued)
Residual plots.

13.6.3 Homogeneity of Variance

As we learned previously, another assumption to consider is that the variances of each population are equal. This is known as the assumption of **homogeneity of variance** or **homoscedasticity**. When generating factorial ANOVA via SPSS, we requested a number of tests for examining homogeneity. Homogeneity tests using **R** were presented previously (see Figure 13.16).

13.7 Power Using G*Power

13.7.1 Post Hoc Power for Factorial ANOVA using G*Power

*When there are multiple independent variables, G*Power must be calculated for each main effect and for each interaction.* We will illustrate computing post hoc power for the **main effect** for type of sport, but note that computing power for the other main effect(s) and interaction(s) are similarly obtained.

The first thing that must be done when using G*Power for computing post hoc power is to select the correct test family. In our case, we conducted a factorial ANOVA. To find the factorial ANOVA, we select "Tests" in the top pulldown menu, then "Means" and then "Many groups: ANOVA: Main effects and interactions (two or more independent variables)." Once that selection is made, the "Test family" automatically changes to "F tests."

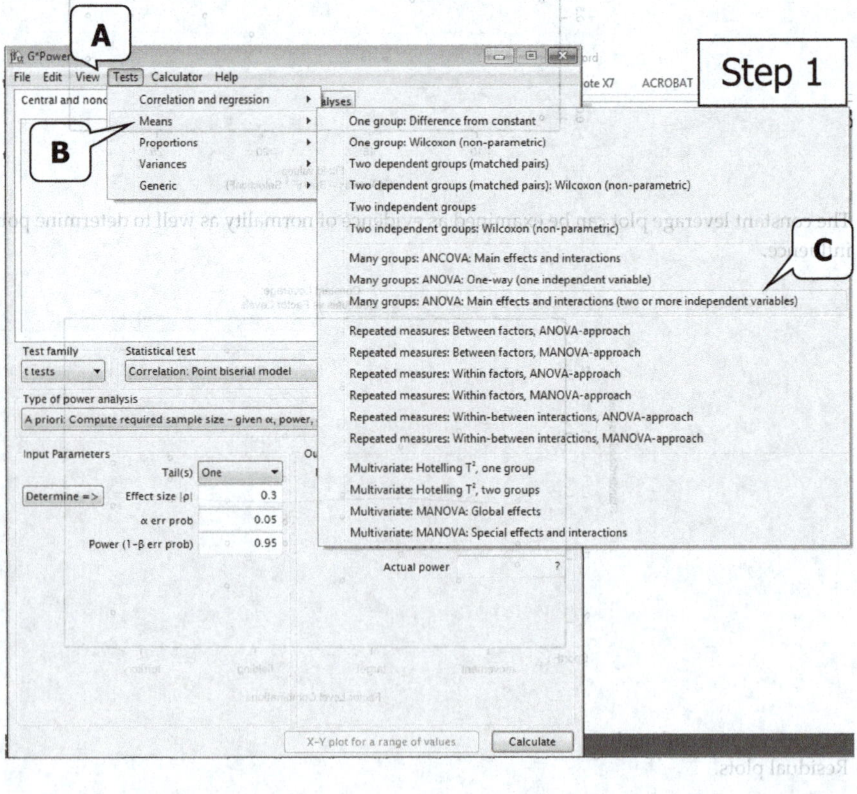

FIGURE 13.30
Power: Step 1.

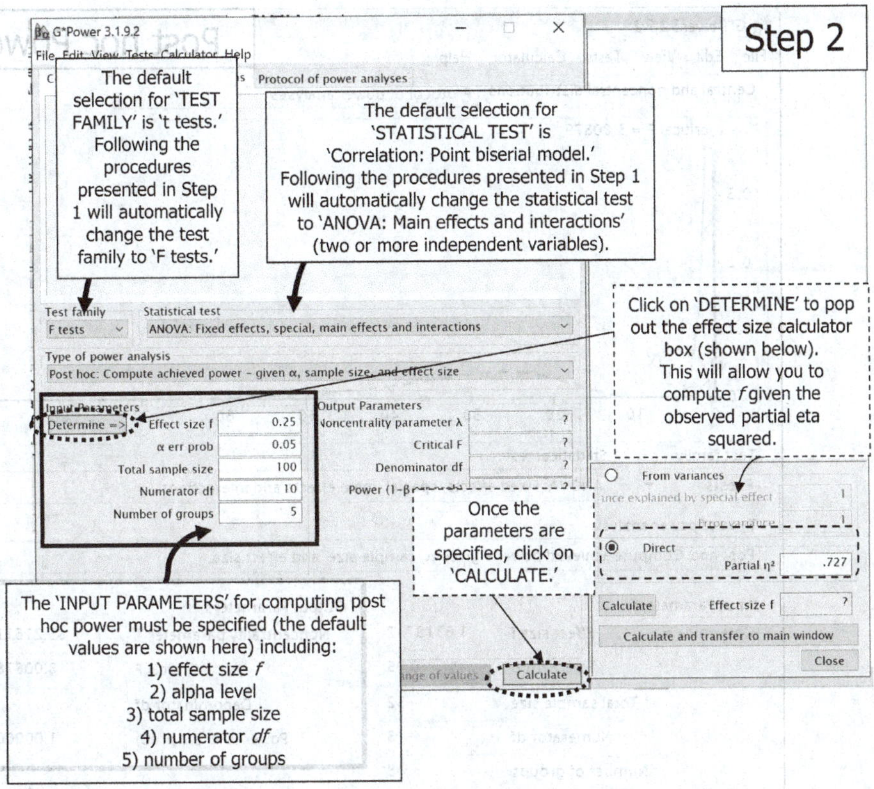

FIGURE 13.31
Power: Step 2.

The "Type of power analysis" desired then needs to be selected. To compute post hoc power, we need to select "Post hoc: Compute achieved power—given α, sample size, and effect size."

The "Input Parameters" must then be specified. We compute the effect size *f* last, so skip that for the moment. In our example, the alpha level we used was .05 and the total sample size was 32. The numerator *df* for type of sport (recall that we are computing post hoc power for the main effect for type of sport here) is equal to the number of categories of this variable (i.e., 4) minus 1; thus there are three degrees of freedom for type of sport. The *number of groups* is equal to the product of the number of levels or categories of the independent variables, or $(J)(K)$. In this example, the number of groups or cells then equals $(J)(K) = (4)(2) = 8$.

We skipped filling in the first parameter, the effect size *f*, for a reason. SPSS provided only a partial eta squared effect size. Thus, we will use the pop out effect size calculator in G*Power to compute the effect size *f* (we saved this parameter for last as the calculation is based on the previous values just entered). To pop out the effect size calculator, click on "Determine" which is displayed under "Input Parameters." In the pop out effect size calculator, click on the radio button for "Direct" and then enter the partial eta squared value for type of sport that was calculated in SPSS (i.e., .727). Clicking on "Calculate" in the pop out effect size calculator will calculate the effect size *f*. Then click on "Calculate and transfer to main window" to transfer the calculated effect size (i.e., 1.6318712) to the "Input Parameters." Once the parameters are specified, click on "Calculate" to find the power statistics.

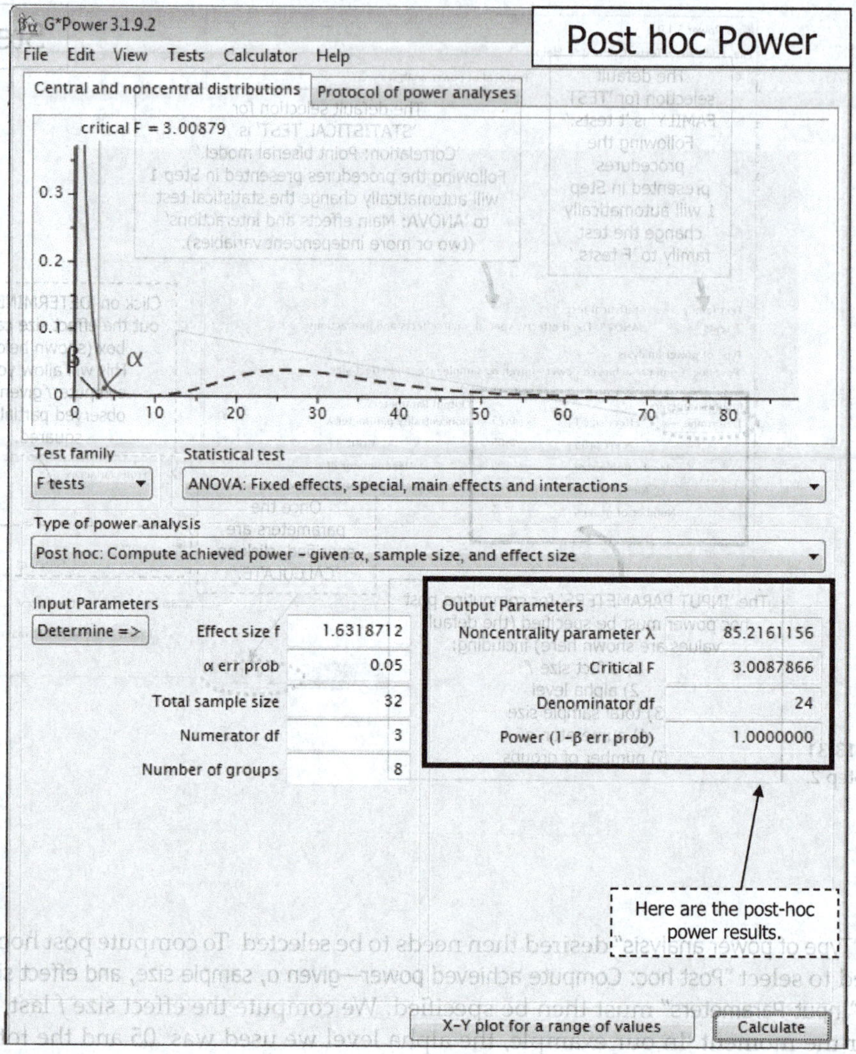

FIGURE 13.32
Post hoc power results.

The "Output Parameters" provide the relevant statistics given the input just specified. In this example, we were interested in determining post hoc power for a two-factor ANOVA with a computed effect size *f* of 1.632, an alpha level of .05, total sample size of 32, numerator degrees of freedom of three and eight groups or cells. Based on those criteria, the post hoc power for the main effect of type of sport was 1.00. In other words, with the input parameters we defined, the *post hoc* power of our main effect was 1.00—the probability of rejecting the null hypothesis when it is really false (in this case, the probability that the means of the dependent variable would be equal for each level of the independent variable) was 1.00, which would be considered maximum power (sufficient power is often .80 or above). Note that this value is the same as that reported in SPSS. Keep in mind that conducting power analysis *a priori* is recommended so that you avoid a situation where, post hoc, you find that the sample size was not sufficient to reach the desired level of power (given the observed parameters).

13.7.1.1 Power for Interactions

Calculation of power for interactions is conducted similarly. Calculating *f* from the input of .727 for partial eta squared results in the following output for interaction power. The *post hoc* power of the interaction effect for this test was .204—the probability of rejecting the null hypothesis when it is really false (in this case, the probability that the means of the dependent variable would be equal for each cell) was about 20%, which would be considered very low power (sufficient power is often .80 or above). Note that this value is not the same as that reported in SPSS.

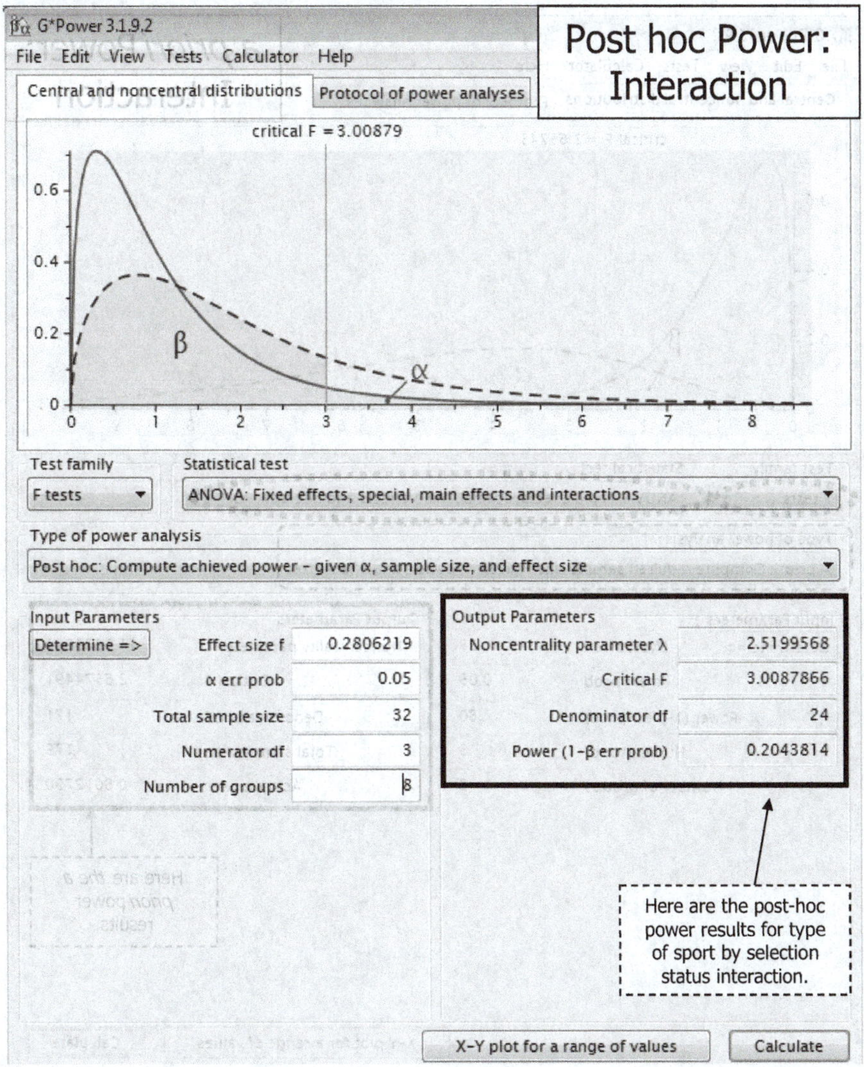

FIGURE 13.33
Post hoc power interaction results.

13.7.2 *A Priori* Power for Factorial ANOVA Using G*Power

For *a priori* power, we can determine the total sample size needed for the main effects and/or interactions given an estimated effect size *f*, alpha level, desired power, numerator degrees of freedom (i.e., number of categories of our independent variable or interaction, depending on which *a priori* power is of interest), and number of groups or cells (i.e., the product of the number of levels of the independent variables). We follow Cohen's (1988) conventions for effect size (i.e., small $f = .10$; moderate $f = .25$; large $f = .40$). In this example, had we estimated a moderate effect f of .25, alpha of .05, desired power of .80, numerator degrees of freedom of three [four types of sports, two categories in selection status, thus $(4 - 1)(2 - 1) = 3$], and number of groups of eight (i.e., four types of sports, two categories in selection status, thus $4 \times 2 = 8$), we would need a total sample size of 179 (or about 22 or 23 individuals per cell).

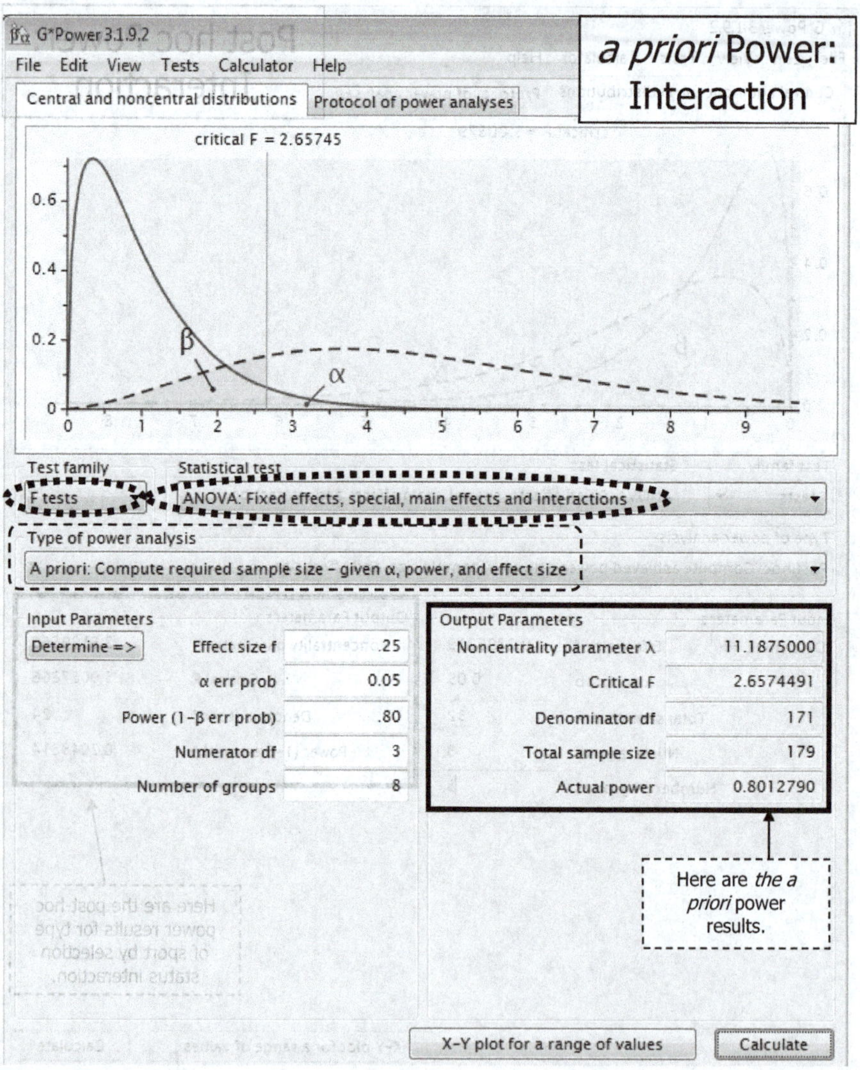

FIGURE 13.34
A priori power interaction results.

13.8 Research Question Template and Example Write-Up

Finally we come to an example paragraph of the results for the two-factor elite athlete example. Recall that our graduate research assistant, Ott, was working with Dr. Rhodes, one of the leading sports psychologists in the region. Dr. Rhodes was interested in examining elite athletes and their vulnerability to psychological distress after selection procedures in which athletes are either selected or deselected for their team and/or to continue in their athletic field. Ott then generated a factorial ANOVA as the test of inference. A template for writing a research question for a factorial ANOVA is presented in this section. This is illustrated assuming a two-factor model, but it can easily be extended to more than two factors. As we noted in Chapter 11, it is important to ensure the reader understands the levels or groups of the independent variables. This may be done parenthetically in the actual research question, as an operational definition, or specified within the methods section. In this example, parenthetically we could have stated the following: *Is there a mean difference in psychological distress of elite athletes based on the type of sport in which they participate (movement, target, fielding, or territory) and selection status (deselected or selected)?*

Is there a mean difference in [dependent variable] based on [independent variable 1] and [independent variable 2]?

It may be helpful to preface the results of the factorial ANOVA with information on an examination of the extent to which the assumptions were met (recall there are three assumptions: normality, homogeneity of variance, and independence). This assists the reader in understanding that you were thorough in data screening prior to conducting the test of inference.

A factorial analysis of variance (ANOVA) was conducted to determine if the mean psychological distress of elite athletes differed based on type of sport in which they participated (i.e., movement, target, fielding, or territory) and selection status (deselected or selected). The assumptions of normality, homoscedasticity, and independence were reviewed.

The assumption of normality was tested and met via examination of the residuals. Review of the overall Shapiro-Wilk test for normality (SW = .977, df = 32, p = .701), and skewness (.400) and kurtosis (−.162) statistics, suggested that normality was a reasonable assumption. Normality of residuals by group was also reasonable, as results for the Shapiro-Wilk test for normality by group were all non-statistically significant. Skewness and kurtosis of residuals by group were all within the range of an absolute value of 2.0, suggesting normality by group was reasonable. Additional tests, including the overall D'Agostino's test for skewness (z = 1.00, p = .315) and the Bonett-Seier test for Geary's kurtosis (z = .320, p = .749) suggested evidence of normality. The results for D'Agostino's test for skewness and the Bonett-Seier test for Geary's kurtosis by group were all non-statistically significant, suggesting normality is reasonable. The boxplots of residuals, overall and by group, suggested a relatively normal distributional shape (with no outliers). The Q-Q plots and histograms suggested normality was reasonable, although the plots by group reflected some non-normality. In aggregate, the results suggest normality by group is reasonable.

According to Levene's test, the homogeneity of variance assumption was satisfied [F (7, 24) = .579, p = .766].

Scatterplots of residuals against the levels of the independent variables were reviewed. A random display of points around zero provided evidence that the assumption of independence was met in the absence of random assignment to groups. [*Note:* Had there been random assignment to groups, we could have also stated, "Random assignment of individuals to groups helped ensure that the assumption of independence was met."]

Here is an APA-style example paragraph of results for the factorial ANOVA (remember that this will be prefaced by the previous paragraph reporting the extent to which the assumptions of the test were met).

The interaction of type of sport by selection status is not statistically significant ($F_{sport*selection}$ = 21.844, df = 3,24, p = .602), but there are statistically significant main effects for both type of sport (F_{sport} = 21.350, df = 3,24, p = .001) and selection status ($F_{selection}$ = 61.791, df = 1,24, p = .001).

Effect sizes are large for both type of sport status (partial $\eta^2_{sport} = .727$, $\omega^2_{sport} = .400$) and selection status (partial $\eta^2_{selection} = .720$; $\omega^2_{selection} = .398$) but very small for the interaction of sport by selection status (partial $\eta^2_{sport*selection} = -.007$; $\omega^2_{sport*selection} = .007$.). Partial eta squared for the main effect for type of sport tells us that the proportion of variation in psychological distress explained by the type of sport in which the athlete participates that is *not* explained by selection status is about 73%. Partial eta squared for the main effect for selection status tells us that the proportion of variation in psychological distress explained by whether the athlete is selected or deselected that is *not* explained by the type of sport in which they participate is about 72%. Omega squared for the main effect for type of sport tells us that proportion of total variability in the dependent variable that is accounted for by type of sport is about 40%. Omega squared for the main effect for selection status tells us that proportion of total variability in the dependent variable that is accounted for by selection status is about 40%.

Observed power for type of sport and selection status is maximal (i.e., 1.000). However, the test of the interaction of sport by selection status was underpowered, with observed power of only .162.

Post hoc analyses were conducted given the statistically significant omnibus ANOVA F tests for the main effects. The profile plot (Figure 13.2) summarizes these differences. Tukey's HSD tests were conducted on all possible pairwise contrasts. For the main effect of type of sport, Tukey's HSD post hoc comparisons revealed that athletes in "movement" sports had statistically significantly lower psychological distress than all the other types of sports, and that athletes in "target" sports had statistically significantly lower psychological distress than the athletes in "territory" types of sports. More specifically, the following pairs of types of sports were found to be significantly different ($p < .05$):

- Movement (M = 11.125, SD = 5.4886) and Target (M = 17.875, SD = 1.201);
- Movement and Fielding (M = 20.2500, SD = 7.2850);

- Movement and Territory (M = 24.3750, SD = 5.0973); and
- Target and Territory.

In other words, athletes enrolled in "movement" types of sports had statistically significantly less psychological distress than athletes who participated in any of the three other types of sports (i.e., target, fielding, and territory).

For the main effect of selection status, a comparison of means revealed that athletes who were deselected for their sport (M = 23.125, SD = .849) had statistically significantly higher psychological distress than athletes who were selected (M = 13.688, SD = .849).

13.9 Additional Resources

This chapter has provided a preview into conducting factorial ANOVA. However, there are a number of areas that space limitations prevent us from delving into. For more in-depth coverage of ANOVA models, see Maxwell, Delaney, and Kelley (2018) and Keppel and Wickens (2004), among others.

Problems

Conceptual Problems

1. You are given a two-factor design with the following cell means (cell 11 = 25; cell 12 = 75; cell 21 = 50; cell 22 = 50; cell 31 = 75; cell 32 = 25). Assume that the within-cell variation is small. Which one of the following conclusions seems most probable?
   a. The row means are significantly different.
   b. The column means are significantly different.
   c. The interaction is significant.
   d. All of the above.
2. In a two-factor ANOVA, one independent variable has five levels and the second has four levels. If each cell has seven observations, what is df_{with}?
   a. 20
   b. 120
   c. 139
   d. 140
3. In a two-factor ANOVA, df_{with} one independent variable has three levels or categories and the second has three levels or categories. What is df_{AB}, the interaction degrees of freedom?
   a. 3
   b. 4

c. 6
d. 9

4. Which of the following conclusions would result in the greatest generalizability of the main effect for factor *A* across the levels of factor B? The interaction between the independent variables *A* and *B* was

a. Not significant at the .25 level.
b. Significant at the .05 level.
c. Significant at the .01 level.
d. Significant at the .001 level.

5. In a two-factor fixed-effects ANOVA tested at an alpha of .05, the following *p* values were found: main effect for factor *A*, $p = .06$; main effect for factor B, $p = .09$; interaction *AB*, $p = .02$. What can be interpreted from these results?

a. There is a statistically significant main effect for factor *A*.
b. There is a statistically significant main effect for factor B.
c. There is a statistically significant main effect for factors *A* and *B*.
d. There is a statistically significant interaction effect.

6. In a two-factor fixed-effects ANOVA, $F_A = 2$, $df_A = 3$, $df_B = 6$, $df_{AB} = 18$, and $df_{with} = 56$. The null hypothesis for factor A can be rejected

a. At the .01 level.
b. At the .05 level, but not at the .01 level.
c. At the .10 level, but not at the .05 level.
d. None of the above

7. In ANOVA the interaction of two factors is certainly present when

a. The two factors are positively correlated.
b. The two factors are negatively correlated.
c. Row effects are not consistent across columns.
d. Main effects do not account for all of the variation in *Y*.
e. Main effects do account for all of the variation in *Y*.

8. For a design with four factors, how many *total* interactions will there be?

a. 4
b. 8
c. 11
d. 12
e. 16

9. Degrees of freedom for the *AB* interaction are equal to which one of the following?

a. $df_A - df_B$
b. $(df_A)(df_B)$
c. $df_{with} - (df_A + df_B)$
d. $df_{total} - df_{with}$

10. A two-factor experiment means that the design necessarily includes which one of the following?

a. Two independent variables
b. Two dependent variables
c. An interaction between the independent and dependent variables
d. Exactly two separate groups of subjects

11. Two independent variables are said to interact when which one of the following occurs?

a. Both variables are equally influenced by a third variable.
b. These variables are differentially affected by a third variable.
c. Each factor produces a change in the subjects' scores.
d. The effect of one variable depends on the second variable.

12. True or false? If there is an interaction between the independent variables textbook and time of day, this means that the textbook used has the same effect at different times of the day.

13. True or false? If the *AB* interaction is significant, then at least one of the two main effects must be significant.

14. For a two-factor fixed-effects model, if the degrees of freedom for testing factor A = 2,24, then I assert that the degrees of freedom for testing factor B will necessarily be = 2,24. Am I correct?

Questions 15 through 17 are based on the following ANOVA summary table (fixed-effects):

Source	*df*	*MS*	*F*
A	2	45	4.5
B	1	70	7.0
AB	2	170	17.0
Within	60	10	

15. For which source of variation is the null hypothesis rejected at the .01 level of significance?

a. A
b. B
c. AB
d. All of the above

16. How many cells are there in the design?

a. 1
b. 2
c. 3
d. 5
e. None of the above

17. The total sample size for the design is which one of the following?
   a. 66
   b. 68
   c. 70
   d. None of the above

Questions 18 through 20 are based on the following ANOVA summary table (fixed-effects):

Source	*df*	*MS*	*F*
A	2	164	5.8
B	1	80	2.8
AB	2	68	2.4
Within	9	28	

18. For which source of variation is the null hypothesis rejected at the .01 level of significance?
   a. *A*
   b. *B*
   c. *AB*
   d. All of the above
19. How many cells are there in the design?
   a. 1
   b. 2
   c. 3
   d. 6
   e. None of the above
20. The total sample size for the design is which one of the following?
   a. 10
   b. 15
   c. 20
   d. 25
21. Which of the following assumptions is applicable in ANOVA but not in factorial ANOVA? Select all that apply?
   a. Equal variances
   b. Independent
   c. Normality
   d. All of the above
   e. None of the above
22. In the absence of random assignment to groups, which one of the following can be used to examine the extent to which the assumption of independence has been met?

a. Boxplot of residuals by levels of factor *A*
b. Scatterplot of residuals to categories of the independent variables
c. Shapiro-Wilk test
d. Spread versus level plots

23. The following table is provided in your output. Which groups have statistically significantly different means on the outcome based on Tukey's MCP?

DEPENDENT VARIABLE

Tukey HSD[a,b,c]

Group	N	Subset 1	Subset 2
A	1000	1.6524	
B	1000		1.8304
C	1000		1.8490
D	1000		1.9691

Means for groups in homogeneous subsets are displayed.

Based on observed means.

a. Group A is statistically different from Groups B, C, and D.
b. Groups B, C, and D are statistically different from each other.
c. Groups A and B differ, but Groups C and D are not statistically different.
d. Groups C and D differ, but Groups A and B are not statistically different.

24. A researcher finds a p value of .04 for Levene's test. Which of the following can be concluded if the alpha level is .05?

a. The assumption of equal variances has been violated.
b. The assumption of normality has been met.
c. There is a statistically significant main effect for this factor.
d. There is a statistically significant omnibus test.

25. An inappropriate way to deal with factorial ANOVA with unequal n's includes which one of the following?

a. Deleting data until n's are equal
b. Partially sequential approach
c. Regression approach
d. Sequential approach

Answers to Conceptual Problems

1. **c** (a plot of the cell means reveals an interaction.)

3. **b** (product of the number of degrees of freedom for each main effect; $(J - 1)(K - 1) = (2)(2) = 4$.)

5. **d** (p less than alpha only for the interaction term.)
7. **c** (c is one definition of an interaction.)
9. **b** (interaction df = product of main effects df.)
11. **d** (the effect of one factor depends on the second factor; see definition of interaction.)
13. **False** (when the interaction is significant, this implies nothing about the main effects.)
15. **c** (check F table for critical values; only reject for interaction.)
17. **a** (as $df_{total} = 65$, then total sample size = 66.)
19. **d** (3 levels of A, 2 levels of B, thus 6 cells.)
21. **e** (all assumptions of ANOVA are also applicable to factorial ANOVA; these include independence, homogeneity of variance, and normality.)
23. **a** (interpreting the subset columns, Group A is statistically different from Groups B, C, and D; however, Groups B, C, and D are not statistically different from each other.)
25. **a** (with factorial ANOVA with unequal n's, the inappropriate way to deal with the unbalance is to delete data until the sample sizes of the groups are the same.)

Computational Problems

1. Complete the following ANOVA summary table for a two-factor fixed-effects analysis of variance, where there are two levels of factor A (drug) and three levels of factor B (dosage). Each cell includes 26 patients and $\alpha = .05$.

Source	*SS*	*df*	*MS*	*F*	Critical Value	Decision
A	6.15	–	–	–	–	–
B	10.60	–	–	–	–	–
AB	9.10	–	–	–	–	–
Within	–	–	–			
Total	250.85	–				

2. Complete the following ANOVA summary table for a two-factor fixed-effects analysis of variance, where there are three levels of factor A (program) and two levels of factor B (gender). Each cell includes four individuals and $\alpha = .01$.

Source	*SS*	*df*	*MS*	*F*	Critical Value	Decision
A	3.64	–	–	–	–	–
B	.57	–	–	–	–	–
AB	2.07	–	–	–	–	–
Within	–	–	–			
Total	8.18	–				

3. Complete the following ANOVA summary table for a two-factor fixed-effects analysis of variance, where there are two levels of factor A (undergraduate versus

graduate) and two levels of factor *B* (treatment). Each cell includes four students and $\alpha = .05$.

Source	*SS*	*df*	*MS*	*F*	Critical Value	Decision
A	14.06	–	–	–	–	–
B	39.06	–	–	–	–	–
AB	1.56	–	–	–	–	–
Within	–	–	–			
Total	723.43	–				

4. Conduct a two-factor fixed-effects ANOVA to determine if there are any effects due to *A* (task type), *B* (task difficulty), or the *AB* interaction ($\alpha = .01$). Conduct Tukey's HSD post hoc comparisons, if necessary. The following are the scores from the individual cells of the model:

   A_1B_1: 41, 39, 25, 25, 37, 51, 39, 101
   A_1B_2: 46, 54, 97, 93, 51, 36, 29, 69
   A_1B_3: 113, 135, 109, 96, 47, 49, 68, 38
   A_2B_1: 86, 38, 45, 45, 60, 106, 106, 31
   A_2B_2: 74, 96, 101, 124, 48, 113, 139, 131
   A_2B_3: 152, 79, 135, 144, 52, 102, 166, 155

5. An experimenter is interested in the effects of strength of reinforcement (factor *A*), type of reinforcement (factor B), and sex of the adult administering the reinforcement (factor C) on children's behavior. Each factor consists of two levels. Thirty-two children are randomly assigned to 8 cells (i.e., 4 per cell), one for each of the factor combinations. Using the scores from the individual cells of the model that follow, conduct a three-factor fixed-effects analysis of variance ($\alpha = .05$). If there are any significant interactions, graph and interpret the interactions.

   $A_1B_1C_1$: 3, 6, 3, 3
   $A_1B_1C_2$: 4, 5, 4, 3
   $A_1B_2C_1$: 7, 8, 7, 6
   $A_1B_2C_2$: 7, 8, 9, 8
   $A_2B_1C_1$: 1, 2, 2, 2
   $A_2B_1C_2$: 2, 3, 4, 3
   $A_2B_2C_1$: 5, 6, 5, 6
   $A_2B_2C_2$: 10, 10, 9, 11

6. A replication study dataset of the example from this chapter is given below (A = type of sport, *B* = selection status; same levels). Using the scores from the individual cells of the model that follow, conduct a two-factor fixed-effects analysis of variance ($\alpha = .05$). Are the results different as compared to the original dataset?

A_1B_1: 10, 8, 7, 3
A_1B_2: 15, 12, 21, 13
A_2B_1: 13, 9, 18, 12
A_2B_2: 20, 22, 24, 25
A_3B_1: 24, 29, 27, 25
A_3B_2: 10, 12, 21, 14
A_4B_1: 30, 26, 29, 28
A_4B_2: 22, 20, 25, 15

7. Using the following data, conduct a two-factor fixed-effects ANOVA to determine if there are any effects due to A (intervention), B (group), or the AB interaction (a = .05). Conduct Tukey HSD post hoc comparisons, if necessary.

Intervention	Group	Outcome
1	1	69
1	1	67
1	1	55
1	1	72
1	1	70
1	1	59
1	1	63
1	1	64
1	2	69
1	2	74
1	2	71
1	2	67
2	2	69
2	2	64
2	2	54
2	2	58
2	3	58
2	3	62
2	3	56
2	3	60
1	3	64
1	3	56
1	3	55
1	3	64

8. Using the following data, conduct a two-factor fixed-effects ANOVA to determine if there are any effects due to A (intervention), B (group), or the AB interaction (a = .05). Conduct Tukey HSD post hoc comparisons, if necessary.

Intervention	Group	Outcome
1	1	69
1	1	72
1	1	63
1	1	74
1	2	67
1	2	70
1	2	64
1	2	71
1	3	55
1	3	59
1	3	69
1	3	67
2	1	69
2	1	58
2	1	56
2	1	56
2	2	64
2	2	58
2	2	60
2	2	55
2	3	54
2	3	62
2	3	64
2	3	64

Answers to Computational Problems

1. $SS_{with} = 225$; $df_A = 1$; $df_B = 2$; $df_{AB} = 2$; $df_{with} = 150$; $df_{total} = 155$; $MS_A = 6.15$; $MS_B = 5.30$; $MS_{AB} = 4.55$; $MS_{with} = 1.50$; $F_A = 4.10$; $F_B = 3.5333$; $F_{AB} = 3.0333$; critical value for A is approximately 3.91, thus reject H_0 for A; critical value for B and AB approximately 3.06, thus reject H_0 for B and fail to reject H_0 for AB.
3. See completed table below:

Source	*SS*	*df*	*MS*	*F*	Critical Value	Decision
A	14.06	1	14.06	.25	4.75	Fail to reject H_0
B	39.06	1	39.06	.70	4.75	Fail to reject H_0
AB	1.56	1	1.56	.03	4.75	Fail to reject H_0
Within	668.75	12	55.73			
Total	723.43	15				

5. $F_A = 4.0541$; $F_B = 210.1622$; $F_C = 31.7838$; $F_{AB} = 7.9459$; $F_{AC} = 13.1351$; $F_{BC} = 10.3784$; $F_{ABC} = 4.0541$; all but ABC and A are significant.
7. $F_{intervention} = 3.723$, $p = .069$; $F_{group} = 3.185$, $p = .064$; $F_{intervention*group} = 2.666$, $p = .119$; fail to reject H_0 for intervention, group, and the intervention by group interaction. No post hoc comparisons are needed given there were no hypotheses rejected.

Interpretive Problems

1. Building on the interpretive problem from Chapter 11, utilize the survey1 dataset, which is accessible from the website. Use SPSS or **R** to conduct a two-factor fixed-effects ANOVA, including effect size, where political view is factor A ($J = 5$), gender is factor B ($K = 2$), and the dependent variable is the same one that you used for interpretative problem #1 in Chapter 11. Then write an APA-style paragraph summarizing the results.
2. Building on the interpretive problem from Chapter 11, use the survey1 dataset, which is accessible from the website. Use SPSS or **R** to conduct a two-factor fixed-effects ANOVA, including effect size, where hair color is factor A (i.e., one independent variable) ($J = 5$), gender is factor B (a new factor, $K = 2$), and the dependent variable is an interval or ratio variable of your choice. Then write an APA-style paragraph describing the results.
3. Building on the interpretive problem from Chapter 11, use the IPEDS2017 dataset, which is accessible from the website. Use SPSS or **R** to conduct a factorial ANOVA. To the model that you created in Chapter 11, add a second independent variable. Compute the results of the factorial ANOVA. Also compute effect size and test for assumptions. Then write an APA-style paragraph describing the results.

14

Introduction to Analysis of Covariance: The One-Factor Fixed-Effects Model with a Single Covariate

Chapter Outline

Key Concepts

1. Statistical adjustment
2. Covariate
3. Adjusted means

4. Homogeneity of regression slopes
5. Independence of the covariate and the independent variable

We have now considered several different analysis of variance (ANOVA) models. As we moved through Chapter 13, we saw that the inclusion of additional factors helped to reduce the residual or uncontrolled variation. These additional factors served as experimental design controls, in that their inclusion in the design helped to reduce the uncontrolled variation. In fact, this could be the reason an additional factor is included in a factorial design.

In this chapter a new type of variable, known as a **covariate**, is incorporated into the analysis. Rather than serving as an "experimental design control," the covariate serves as a "statistical control" where uncontrolled variation is reduced statistically in the analysis. Thus a model where a covariate is used is known as **analysis of covariance** (ANCOVA). We are most concerned with the one-factor fixed-effects model here, although this model can be generalized to any of the other ANOVA designs considered in this text. That is, any of the ANOVA models discussed in the text can also include a covariate, and thus become an ANCOVA model. Additionally, multiple covariates can be included in a model, although our discussion will focus on the inclusion of just one covariate.

Most of the concepts used in this chapter have already been covered in the text. In addition, new concepts include statistical adjustment, covariate, adjusted means, and two important assumptions, homogeneity of regression slopes and independence of the covariate and the independent variable. Our objectives are that by the end of this chapter, you will be able to (a) understand the characteristics and concepts underlying ANCOVA; (b) determine and interpret the results of ANCOVA, including adjusted means and multiple comparison procedures; and (c) understand and evaluate the assumptions of ANCOVA.

14.1 What ANCOVA Is and How It Works

We have been following a superbly talented group of graduate students. We now find Addie Venture assisting with experimental data from her institution's Exercise Physiology and Wellness Institute. As we will see in this chapter, Addie will be examining data generated from an experiment of athletes.

Addie Venture and her group of graduate researchers have been extremely successful in providing support to researchers in a number of areas. We now find Addie assisting Dr. Waung, the university's director of the Exercise Physiology and Wellness Institute, with an experimental study to determine if there was a mean difference in self-rated physical performance based on the use of caffeine in an attempt to facilitate improved athletic performance. Twelve athletes were randomly assigned to ingest either a caffeinated (treatment) or decaffeinated (control) beverage prior to physical activity. Prior to random assignment to sections, participants were also measured on mental fatigue. After random assignment, participants completed a 2000-meter self-paced jog and were then asked to self-rate their physical performance. Addie is now ready to examine this data. Addie's research question that she recommends to Dr. Waung is: *Is there a mean difference in self-rated physical performance based on caffeine ingestion, controlling for mental fatigue?* With one independent variable and one covariate for which to control, Addie determines that an analysis of covariance (ANCOVA) is the best statistical procedure to use to answer the question. Her next task is to analyze the data to address the research question.

In this section, we describe the distinguishing characteristics of the one-factor fixed-effects ANCOVA model. However, before we begin an extended discussion of these characteristics, consider the following example (a situation similar to which we find Addie Venture with her project with Dr. Waung).

14.1.1 Characteristics

Imagine a situation where a statistics professor is scheduled to teach two sections of introductory statistics. The professor, being a cunning researcher, decides to perform a little experiment where Section 1 is taught using the traditional lecture method and Section 2 is taught with more innovative methods using extensive graphics, computer simulations, and computer-assisted and calculator-based instruction, as well as using mostly small-group and self-directed instruction. The professor is interested in which section performs better in the course.

Before the study/course begins, the professor thinks about whether there are other variables related to statistics performance that should somehow be taken into account in the design. An obvious one is ability in quantitative methods. From previous research and experience, the professor knows that ability in quantitative methods is highly correlated with performance in statistics and decides to give a measure of quantitative ability in the first class and use that as a covariate in the analysis. A *covariate* (e.g., quantitative ability) is defined as a source of variation not controlled for in the design of the experiment, but that the researcher believes to affect the dependent variable (e.g., course performance). The covariate is used to *statistically adjust* the dependent variable. For instance, if Section 1 has higher quantitative ability than Section 2 going into the study, then it would be wise to take this into account in the analysis. Otherwise Section 1 might outperform Section 2 due to their higher quantitative ability rather than due to the method of instruction. This is precisely the point of the analysis of covariance. Some of the more typical examples of covariates in education and the behavioral sciences, depending on the study of course, are pretest (where the dependent variable is the posttest), prior achievement, weight, IQ, aptitude, age, experience, previous training, motivation, and grade point average.

Let us now begin with the characteristics of the ANCOVA model. The first set of characteristics is obvious because they carry over from the one-factor fixed-effects ANOVA model. *There is a single independent variable or factor with two or more levels or categories (thus the independent variable continues to be either nominal or ordinal in measurement scale)*. The *levels of the independent variable are fixed* by the researcher rather than randomly sampled from a population of levels. Once the levels of the independent variable are selected, *subjects or individuals are somehow assigned to these levels or groups*. Each subject is then exposed to only one level of the independent variable (although ANCOVA with repeated measures is also possible, but is not discussed here). In our example, method of statistics instruction is the independent variable with two levels or groups, the traditional lecture method and the cutting-edge method.

Situations where the researcher is able to randomly assign subjects to groups are known as **true experimental designs**. Situations where the researcher does not have control over which level a subject is assigned to are known as **quasi-experimental designs**. This lack of control may occur for one of two reasons. First, the groups may be already in place when the researcher arrives on the scene; these groups are referred to as **intact groups** (e.g., based on class assignments made by students at the time of registration). Second, it may be theoretically impossible for the researcher to assign subjects to groups (e.g., income level). Thus a distinction is typically made about whether or not the researcher can control the assignment of subjects to groups. The distinction between the use of ANCOVA in true and quasi-experimental situations has been quite controversial over the past few decades; we look at it in more detail later in this chapter. For further information on true experimental designs and quasi-experimental designs, we suggest you consider Campbell and Stanley (1966), Cook and Campbell (1979), and Shadish, Cook, and Campbell (2002). In our example again, if assignment to groups is random, then we have a true experimental design. If assignment to groups is not random, perhaps already assigned at registration, then we have a quasi-experimental design.

One final item in the first set of characteristics has to do with the measurement scales of the variables. In the analysis of covariance, it is assumed the *dependent variable is measured at the interval level or better*. If the dependent variable is measured at the ordinal level, then nonparametric procedures described toward the end of this chapter should be considered. It is also assumed that the *covariate is measured at the interval level or better*. Lastly, as indicated previously, the *independent variable must be a grouping or categorical variable*.

The remaining characteristics have to do with the uniqueness of the analysis of covariance. As already mentioned, the analysis of covariance is a form of statistical control developed specifically to reduce unexplained error variation. The covariate (sometimes known as a *concomitant variable*, as it accompanies or is associated with the dependent variable), is a source of variation not controlled for in the design of the experiment, but believed to affect the dependent variable. In a factorial design, for example, a factor could be included to reduce error variation. However, this represents an experimental design form of control as it is included as a factor in the model.

In ANCOVA, the dependent variable is adjusted statistically to remove the effects of the portion of uncontrolled variation represented by the covariate. The group means on the dependent variable are adjusted so that they now represent groups with the same means on the covariate. The analysis of covariance is essentially an analysis of variance on these "adjusted means." This needs further explanation. Consider first the situation of the randomized true experiment where there are two groups. Here it is unlikely that the two groups will be statistically different on any variable related to the dependent measure. The two groups should have roughly equivalent means on the covariate, although 5% of the time we would expect a significant difference due to chance at $\alpha = .05$. Thus, we typically do not see preexisting differences between the two groups on the covariate in a true experiment—that is the value and beauty of random assignment, especially as it relates to ANCOVA. The advantage of ANCOVA in randomized studies, as compared to other types of statistical designs, is *increased precision* and *unbiased estimates* of treatment effects. However, the relationship between the covariate and the dependent variable is important. If these variables are linearly related (discussed later), then the use of the covariate in the analysis will serve to reduce the unexplained variation in the model. The greater the magnitude of the correlation, the more uncontrolled variation can be removed, as shown by a reduction in mean square error.

Let us divert for a moment to ensure we understand statistical precision and bias. **Precision** refers to the size of deviations from an estimate (e.g., mean) that occurs when the same sampling procedures using the same sampling frame and sample size are repeated. Estimates that are more precise, for example, have more narrow confidence intervals. **Bias** refers to the difference between an estimate's expected value and the true value of the parameter. Thus, bias basically means that an estimate is systematically "off," either overestimating or underestimating the true population parameter.

BOX 14.1 Precision and Bias and the Relationship to ANCOVA

Term	Definition
Precision	The size of deviations from an estimate (e.g., mean) that occurs when the same sampling procedures using the same sampling frame and sample size are repeated.
Bias	The difference between an estimate's expected value and the true value of the parameter and basically means that an estimate is systematically "off," either overestimating or underestimating the true population parameter.
How these concepts relate to ANCOVA	The advantage of ANCOVA in randomized studies, as compared to other types of statistical designs, is *increased precision* and *unbiased estimates* of treatment effects through the inclusion of the covariate.

Consider next the situation of the **quasi-experiment**, that is, *without randomization to groups or levels of the independent variable.* Here it is more likely that the two groups will be statistically different on the covariate as well as other variables related to the dependent variable. Thus, there may indeed be a preexisting difference between the two groups on the covariate. If the groups do differ on the covariate and we ignore it by conducting an ANOVA, our ability to get a precise estimate of the group effects will be reduced as the group effect will be confounded with the effect of the covariate. For instance, if a significant group difference is revealed by the ANOVA, we would not be certain if there was truly a group effect or whether the effect was due to preexisting group differences on the covariate, or some combination of group and covariate effects. The analysis of covariance takes the covariate mean difference into account as well as the linear relationship between the covariate and the dependent variable.

Thus, the covariate is used to (a) reduce error variation, (b) take any preexisting group mean difference on the covariate into account, (c) take into account the relationship between the covariate and the dependent variable, and (d) yield a more precise and less biased estimate of the group effects. If error variation is reduced, the analysis of covariance will be more powerful and require smaller sample sizes than the analysis of variance Keppel & Wickens, 2004; Mickey, Dunn, & Clark, 2004; Myers, Lorch, & Well, 2010). If error variation is not reduced, the analysis of variance is more powerful. A more extensive comparison of ANOVA versus ANCOVA is given in Chapter 16. In addition, as shown later, one degree of freedom is lost from the error term for each covariate used. This results in a larger critical value for the F test and makes it a bit more difficult to find a statistically significant F test statistic. This is the major cost of using a covariate. If the covariate is not effective in reducing error variance, then we are worse off than if we had ignored the covariate. Importance references on ANCOVA include Elashoff (1969) and Huitema (2011).

14.1.1.1 The Layout of the Data

Before we get into the theory and subsequent analysis of the data, let us examine the layout of the data. We designate each observation on the dependent or criterion variable as Y_{ij}, where the j subscript tells us what group or level the observation belongs to and the i subscript tells us the observation or identification number within that group. The first subscript ranges over $i = 1, \ldots, n_j$ and the second subscript ranges over $j = 1, \ldots, J$. Thus,

TABLE 14.1

Layout for the One-Factor ANCOVA

Level of the Independent Variable							
1		2		…		J	
Y_{11}	X_{11}	Y_{12}	X_{12}	…	Y_{1J}	X_{1J}	
Y_{21}	X_{21}	Y_{22}	X_{22}	…	Y_{2J}	X_{1J}	
…	…	…	…	…	…	…	
Y_{n1}	X_{n1}	Y_{n2}	X_{n2}	…	Y_{nJ}	Y_{nJ}	
$\bar{Y}_{.1}$	$\bar{X}_{.1}$	$\bar{Y}_{.2}$	$\bar{X}_{.2}$	…	$\bar{Y}_{.J}$	$\bar{X}_{.J}$	

there are J levels of the independent variable and n_j subjects in group j. We designate each observation on the covariate as X_{ij}, where the subscripts have the same meaning.

The layout of the data is shown in Table 14.1. Here we see that each pair of columns represents the observations for a particular group or level of the independent variable on the dependent variable (i.e., Y) and the covariate (i.e., X). At the bottom of the pair of columns for each group j are group means $(\bar{Y}_{.j}, \bar{X}_{.j})$. Although the table shows there are n observations for each group, we need not make such a restriction, as this was done only for purposes of simplifying the table.

14.1.1.2 The ANCOVA Model

The analysis of covariance model is a form of the general linear model much like the models shown in the last few chapters of this text. The **one-factor ANCOVA fixed-effects model** can be written in terms of population parameters as follows:

$$Y_{ij} = \mu_Y + \alpha_j + \beta_w\left(X_{ij} - \mu_X\right) + \varepsilon_{ij}$$

where Y_{ij} is the observed score on the dependent variable for individual i in group j, μ_Y is the overall or grand population mean (i.e., regardless of group designation) for the dependent variable Y, α_j is the group effect for group j, β_w is the within-groups regression slope from the regression of Y on X (i.e., the covariate), X_{ij} is the observed score on the covariate for individual i in group j, μ_X is the overall or grand population mean (i.e., regardless of group designation) for the covariate X, and ε_{ij} is the random residual error for individual i in group j. The residual error can be due to individual differences, measurement error, and/or other factors not under investigation. As you would expect, the least squares sample estimators for each of these parameters are as follows: $\bar{Y}$ for μ_Y, $\bar{X}$ for μ_X, a_j for α_j, b_w for β_w, and e_{ij} for ε_{ij}. Just like in the analysis of variance, the sum of the group effects is equal to zero. This implies that if there are any nonzero group effects, then the group effects will balance out around zero with some positive and some negative effects.

The hypotheses consist of testing the equality of the adjusted means (defined by $\mu'_{.j}$ and discussed later) as follows:

$$H_0: \mu'_{.1} = \mu'_{.2} = \ldots = \mu'_{.J}$$

$$H_1: \textit{not all the } \mu'_{.j} \textit{ are equal}$$

14.1.1.3 The ANCOVA Summary Table

We turn our attention to the familiar summary table, this time for the one-factor ANCOVA model. A general form of the summary table is shown in Table 14.2. Under the first column you see the following sources: adjusted between-groups variation, adjusted within-groups variation, variation due to the covariate, and total variation. The second column notes the sums of squares terms for each source (i.e., $SS_{betw(adj)}$, $SS_{with(adj)}$, SS_{cov}, SS_{total}). Recall that the *between* source represents the independent variable being systematically studied and the *within* source represents the error or residual.

The third column gives the degrees of freedom for each source. For the adjusted between-groups source (i.e., the independent variable controlling for the covariate), because there are J group means, the $df_{betw(adj)}$ is $J - 1$, the same as in the one-factor ANOVA model. For the adjusted within-groups source, because there are N total observations and J groups, we would expect the degrees of freedom within to be $N - J$, because that was the case in the one-factor ANOVA model. However, as we pointed out earlier in the characteristics of the ANCOVA model, a price is paid for the use of a covariate. The price here is that we lose one degree of freedom from the within term for single covariate, so that $df_{with(adj)}$ is $N - J - 1$. For multiple covariates, we lose one degree of freedom for each covariate used (see later discussion). This degree of freedom has gone to the covariate source such that df_{cov} is equal to 1. Finally, for the total source, as there are N total observations, the df_{total} is the usual $N - 1$.

The fourth column gives the mean squares for each source of variation. As always, the mean squares represent the sum of squares weighted by their respective degrees of freedom. Thus $\left[MS_{betw(adj)} = SS_{betw(adj)} /(J-1)\right]$, $\left[MS_{with(adj)} = SS_{with(adj)} /(N-J-1)\right]$, and $\left[MS_{cov} = SS_{cov} /1\right]$. The last column in the ANCOVA summary table is for the F values. Thus for the one-factor fixed-effects ANCOVA model, the F value tests for differences between the adjusted means (i.e., to test for differences in the mean of the dependent variable based on the levels of the independent variable when controlling for the covariate) and is computed as $F = MS_{betw(adj)} / MS_{with(adj)}$. A second F value, which is obviously not included in the ANOVA model, is the test of the covariate. To be specific, this F statistic is actually testing the hypothesis of H_0: $\beta_w = 0$. If the slope is equal to zero, then the covariate and the dependent variable are unrelated. This F value is equal to $F = MS_{cov} / MS_{with(adj)}$. If the F test for the covariate is *not* statistically significant (and has a negligible effect size), the researcher may want to consider removing that covariate from the model.

The critical value for the test of difference between the adjusted means is ${}_{\alpha}F_{J-1,N-J-1}$. The critical value for the test of the covariate is ${}_{\alpha}F_{1,N-J-1}$. The null hypotheses in each case are

TABLE 14.2

One-Factor Analysis of Covariance Summary Table

Source	SS	*df*	MS	F
Covariate	SS_{cov}	1	MS_{cov}	$MS_{cov}/MS_{with(adj)}$
Between adjusted (i.e., independent variable)	$SS_{betw(adj)}$	$J-1$	$MS_{betw(adj)}$	$MS_{betw(adj)}/MS_{with(adj)}$
Within adjusted (i.e., Error)	$SS_{with(adj)}$	$N-J-1$	$MS_{with(adj)}$	
Total	SS_{total}	$N-1$		

rejected if the F test statistic exceeds the F critical value. The critical values are found in the F table of Appendix Table A.4.

If the F test statistic for the adjusted means exceeds the F critical value, and there are more than two groups, then it is not clear exactly how the means are different. In this case, some multiple comparison procedure may be used to determine which means are different (see later discussion). For the test of the covariate (i.e., the within-groups regression slope), we hope that the F test statistic *does* exceed the F critical value. Otherwise, the power and precision of the test of the adjusted means in ANCOVA will be lower than the test of the unadjusted means in ANOVA because the covariate is not significantly related to the dependent variable. (As stated previously, if the F test for the covariate is *not* statistically significant and has a negligible effect size, the researcher may want to consider removing that covariate from the model).

14.1.1.4 Partitioning the Sum of Squares

As seen already, the partitioning of the sums of squares is the backbone of all general linear models, whether we are dealing with an ANOVA model, an ANCOVA model, or a linear regression model. As always, the first step is to partition the total variation into its relevant parts or sources of variation. As we have learned from the previous section, the sources of variation for the one-factor ANCOVA model are adjusted between groups (i.e., the independent variable), adjusted within groups (i.e., error), and the covariate. This is written as follows:

$$SS_{total} = SS_{betw(adj)} + SS_{with(adj)} + SS_{cov}$$

From this point the statistical software is used to handle the remaining computations.

14.1.1.5 Adjusted Means and Related Procedures

In this section we formally define the adjusted mean and briefly examine several multiple comparison procedures. We have spent considerable time already discussing the analysis of the adjusted means. Now it is time to define them. The **adjusted mean** is denoted by $\bar{Y}'_{.j}$ and estimated by

$$\bar{Y}'_{.j} = \bar{Y}_{.j} - b_w\left(\bar{X}_{.j} - \bar{X}_{..}\right)$$

Here it should be noted that the adjusted mean is simply equal to the unadjusted mean (i.e., $\bar{Y}_{.j}$) minus the adjustment [i.e., $b_w\left(\bar{X}_{.j} - \bar{X}_{..}\right)$]. The adjustment is a function of the within-groups regression slope (i.e., b_w) and the difference between the group mean and the overall mean for the covariate (i.e., the difference being the group effect, $\bar{X}_{.j} - \bar{X}_{..}$). No adjustment will be made if (a) $b_w = 0$ (i.e., X and Y are unrelated), or (b) the group means on the covariate are all the same. Thus, in both cases $\bar{Y}_{.j} = \bar{Y}'_{.j}$. In all other cases, at least some adjustment will be made for some of the group means (although not necessarily for all of the group means).

You may be wondering how this adjustment actually works. Let us assume the covariate and the dependent variable are positively correlated such that b_w is also positive, and there are two treatment groups with equal n's that differ on the covariate. If Group 1 has a higher mean on *both* the covariate and the dependent variable than Group 2, then the adjusted means will be closer together than the unadjusted means. For our first example, we have the following conditions:

$$b_w = 1, \bar{Y}_{.1} = 50, \bar{Y}_{.2} = 30, \bar{X}_{.1} = 20, \bar{X}_{.2} = 10, \bar{X}_{..} = 15$$

The adjusted means are determined as follows:

$$\bar{Y}'_{.1} = \bar{Y}_{.1} - b_w(\bar{X}_{.1} - \bar{X}_{..}) = 50 - 1(20 - 15) = 45$$

$$\bar{Y}'_{.2} = \bar{Y}_{.2} - b_w(\bar{X}_{.2} - \bar{X}_{..}) = 30 - 1(10 - 15) = 35$$

This is shown graphically in Figure 14.1a. In looking at the covariate X, we see that Group 1 has a higher mean $(\bar{X}_{.1} = 20)$ than Group 2 $(\bar{X}_{.2} = 10)$ by 10 points. The vertical line represents the overall mean on the covariate $(\bar{X}_{..} = 15)$. In looking at the dependent variable Y, we see that Group 1 has a higher mean $(\bar{Y}_{.1} = 50)$ than Group 2 $(\bar{Y}_{.2} = 30)$ by 20 points. The diagonal lines represent the regression lines for each group, with $b_w = 1.0$. The points at which the regression lines intersect (or cross) the vertical line $(\bar{X}_{..} = 15)$ represent on the Y scale the values of the adjusted means. Here we see that the adjusted mean for Group 1 $(\bar{Y}'_{.1} = 45)$ is larger than the adjusted mean for Group 2 $(\bar{Y}'_{.2} = 35)$ by 10 points. Thus, because of the preexisting difference on the covariate, the adjusted means here are somewhat closer together than the unadjusted means (10 points vs. 20 points, respectively).

If Group 1 has a higher mean on the covariate and a lower mean on the dependent variable than Group 2, then the adjusted means will be further apart than the unadjusted means. As a second example, we have the following slightly different conditions:

$$b_w = 1, \bar{Y}_1 = 30, \bar{Y}_2 = 50, \bar{X}_1 = 20, \bar{X}_2 = 10, \bar{X}_{..} = 15$$

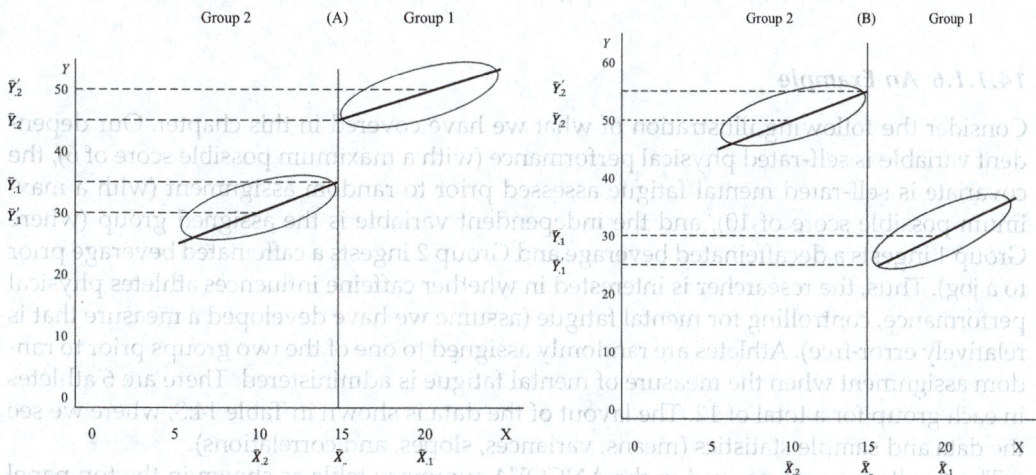

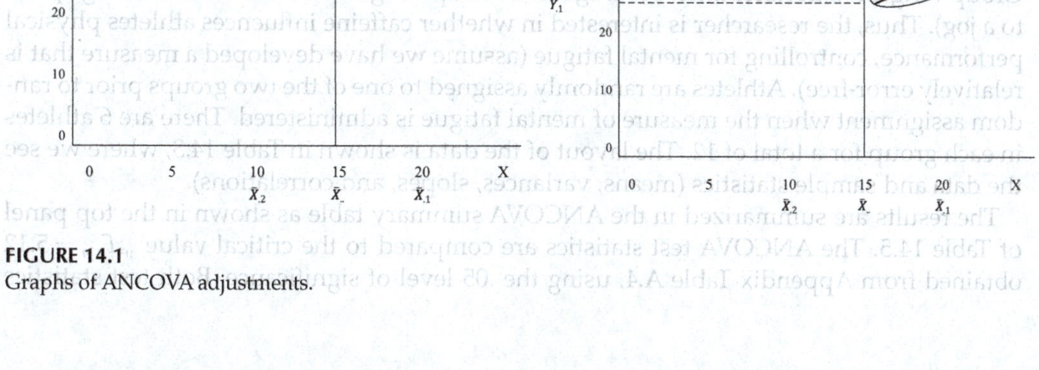

FIGURE 14.1
Graphs of ANCOVA adjustments.

Then the adjusted means become as follows:

$$\bar{Y}'_{.1} = \bar{Y}_{.1} - b_w\left(\bar{X}_{.1} - \bar{X}_{..}\right) = 30 - 1(20 - 15) = 25$$

$$\bar{Y}'_{.2} = \bar{Y}_{.2} - b_w\left(\bar{X}_{.2} - \bar{X}_{..}\right) = 50 - 1(10 - 15) = 55$$

This is shown graphically in Figure 14.1b where the unadjusted means differ by 20 points and the adjusted means differ by 30 points. There are obviously other possible situations.

Let us briefly examine multiple comparison procedures (MCPs) for use in the analysis of covariance situation. Most of the procedures described in Chapter 12 can be adapted for use with a covariate, although a few procedures are not mentioned here as critical values do not currently exist. The adapted procedures involve a different form of the standard error of a contrast. The contrasts are formed based on adjusted means, of course. Let us briefly outline just a few procedures. Each of the test statistics has as its numerator the contrast ψ', such as $\psi' = \bar{Y}'_{.1} - \bar{Y}'_{.2}$. The standard errors do differ somewhat depending on the specific MCP, just as they do in ANOVA.

The example procedures briefly described here are easily translated from the ANOVA context into the ANCOVA context. Dunn's (or the Bonferroni) method is appropriate to use for a small number of planned contrasts (still utilizing the critical values from Appendix Table A.8). Scheffé's procedure can be used for unplanned complex contrasts with equal group variances (again based on the *F* table in Appendix Table A.4). Tukey's HSD test is most desirous for unplanned pairwise contrasts with equal *n*'s per group. There has been some discussion in the literature about the appropriateness of this test in ANCOVA. Most statisticians currently argue that the procedure is only appropriate when the covariate is fixed, when in fact it is almost always random. As a result the Bryant-Paulson (Bryant & Paulson, 1976) generalization of the Tukey procedure has been developed for the random covariate case. The test statistic is compared to the critical value ${}_{\alpha}q_{X,df(error),J}$ taken from Appendix Table A.10, where *X* is the number of covariates. If the group sizes are unequal, the harmonic mean can be used in ANCOVA (Huitema, 2011). A generalization of the Tukey-Bryant procedure for unequal *n*'s ANCOVA was developed by Hochberg and Varon-Salomon (1984) (see also Hochberg & Tamhane, 1987; Miller, 1997).

14.1.1.6 An Example

Consider the following illustration of what we have covered in this chapter. Our dependent variable is self-rated physical performance (with a maximum possible score of 6), the covariate is self-rated mental fatigue assessed prior to random assignment (with a maximum possible score of 10), and the independent variable is the assigned group (where Group 1 ingests a decaffeinated beverage and Group 2 ingests a caffeinated beverage prior to a jog). Thus, the researcher is interested in whether caffeine influences athletes physical performance, controlling for mental fatigue (assume we have developed a measure that is relatively error-free). Athletes are randomly assigned to one of the two groups prior to random assignment when the measure of mental fatigue is administered. There are 6 athletes in each group for a total of 12. The layout of the data is shown in Table 14.3, where we see the data and sample statistics (means, variances, slopes, and correlations).

The results are summarized in the ANCOVA summary table as shown in the top panel of Table 14.5. The ANCOVA test statistics are compared to the critical value ${}_{.05}F_{1,9} = 5.12$ obtained from Appendix Table A.4, using the .05 level of significance. Both test statistics exceed the critical value, so we reject H_0 in each case. We conclude that (a) physical performance means do differ for the two groups when adjusted (or controlling) for mental fatigue (i.e., the between adjusted test of the independent variable controlling for the covariate), and (b) the slope of the regression of Y (i.e., dependent variable) on X (i.e., covariate) is statistically significantly different from zero (i.e., the test of the covariate). Just to be complete, the results for the analysis of variance (ANOVA) on Y are shown in the bottom panel of Table 14.4. We see that in the analysis of the unadjusted means (i.e., the ANOVA), there is

TABLE 14.3

Data and Summary Statistics for the Physical Performance Example

	Group 1 (Decaffeinated)		Group 2 (Caffeinated)		Overall	
Statistic	Physical Performance (Y)	Mental Fatigue (X)	Physical Performance (Y)	Mental Fatigue (X)	Physical Performance (Y)	Mental Fatigue (X)
	1	4	1	1		
	2	3	2	3		
	3	5	4	2		
	4	6	5	4		
	5	7	6	5		
	6	9	6	7		
Means	3.5000	5.6667	4.0000	3.6667	3.7500	4.6667
Variances	3.5000	4.6667	4.4000	4.6667	3.6591	5.3333
b_{YX}	0.8143		0.8143		0.5966	
r_{YX}	0.9403		0.8386		0.7203	
Adjusted means	2.6857		4.8143			

TABLE 14.4

One-Factor ANCOVA and ANOVA Summary Tables

Source	SS	df	MS	F
ANCOVA				
Covariate	20.8813	1	20.8813	21.9641*
Adjusted between (i.e., independent variable)	10.8127	1	10.8127	11.3734*
Adjusted within (i.e., error)	8.5560	9	0.9507	
Total	40.2500	11		
ANOVA				
Between	0.7500	1	0.7500	0.1899**
Within	39.5000	10	3.9500	
Total	40.2500	11		

* $_{.05}F_{1,9} = 5.12$
** $_{.05}F_{1,10} = 4.96$

no significant group difference. Thus the adjustment (i.e., ANCOVA which controlled for the covariate, mental fatigue) yielded a different statistical result. The covariate also "did its thing" in that a reduction in MS_{with} resulted due to the strong relationship between the covariate and the dependent variable (i.e., $r_{XY} = 0.7203$ overall).

Let us next examine the group physical performance means, as shown previously in Table 14.3. Here we see that with the *unadjusted* physical performance means (i.e., prior to controlling for the covariate), there is a 0.5000-point difference in favor of Group 2 (the group that ingested caffeine prior to a self-paced jog), whereas for the *adjusted* physical performance means (i.e., the ANCOVA results which controlled for mental fatigue), there is a 2.1286-point difference in favor of Group 2. In other words, the adjustment (i.e., controlling for mental fatigue) in this case resulted in a greater difference between the adjusted physical performance means than between the unadjusted physical performance means. Since there are only two groups, a multiple comparison procedure is unnecessary (although we illustrate this in the SPSS section).

14.1.1.7 ANCOVA Without Randomization

As referenced previously in the discussion of assumptions, there has been a great deal of discussion and controversy over the years, particularly in education and the behavioral sciences, about the use of the analysis of covariance in situations where randomization is not conducted. **Randomization** is defined as an experiment where individuals are randomly assigned to groups (or cells in a factorial design). In the Campbell and Stanley (1966) system of experimental design, these designs are known as **true experiments**. (Do not confuse random assignment with random selection, the latter of which deals with how the cases are sampled from the population.)

In certain situations, randomization either has not occurred or is not possible due to circumstances in the study. The best example is the situation where there are **intact groups**, which are groups that have been formed prior to the researcher arriving on the scene. Either the researcher chooses not to randomly assign these individuals to groups through a reassignment (e.g., it is just easier to keep the groups in their current form), or the researcher cannot randomly assign them (legally, ethically, or otherwise). When randomization does not occur, the resulting designs are known as **quasi-experimental**. For instance, in classroom research, the researcher is almost never able to come into a school and randomly assign students to classrooms. Once students are given their class assignments at the beginning of the year, this cannot be altered. On occasion, the researcher might be able to pull a few students out of several classrooms, randomly assign them to small groups, and conduct a true experiment. In general, this is possible only on a very small scale and for short periods of time.

Let us briefly consider the issues as it relates to ANCOVA, as not all statisticians agree. In *true experiments* (i.e., with randomization), there is no cause for concern (except for dealing with the statistical assumptions). The analysis of covariance is more powerful and has greater precision for true experiments than for quasi-experiments. So if you have a choice, go with a true experimental situation (which is a big *if*). In a true experiment, the probability that the groups differ on the covariate or any other concomitant variable is equal to α. That is, the likelihood that the group means will be different on the covariate is small, and thus the adjustment in the group means may be small. The payoff is in the possibility that the error term will be greatly reduced.

In *quasi-experiments*, as it relates to ANCOVA, there are several possible causes for concern. Although this is the situation where the researcher needs the most help, this is also the situation where less help is available. Here it is more likely that there will be statistically significant differences among the group means on the covariate. Thus the adjustment in the group means can be substantial (assuming that b_w is different from zero). Because there are significant mean differences on the covariate, any of the following may occur: (a) it is likely that the groups may be different on other important characteristics as well, which have not been controlled for either statistically or experimentally; (b) the homogeneity of regression slopes assumption is less likely to be met; (c) adjusting for the covariate may remove part of the treatment effect; (d) equating groups on the covariate may be an extrapolation beyond the range of possible values that occur for a particular group (e.g., the examples on trying to equate men and women (Lord, 1960, 1967) or trying to equate mice and elephants (Ferguson & Takane, 1989); these groups should not be equated on the covariate because their distributions on the covariate do not overlap); (e) although the slopes may be equal for the range of X's obtained, when extrapolating beyond the range of scores, the slopes may not be equal; (f) the standard errors of the adjusted means may increase, making tests of the adjusted means not significant; and (g) there may be differential growth in the groups confounding the results (e.g., adult vs. child groups).

Although one should be cautious about the use of ANCOVA in quasi-experiments, this is not to suggest that ANCOVA should never be used in such situations. Schneider, Avivi-Reich, and Mozuraitis (2015) provide recommendations for conducting ANCOVA in various situations, including experimental designs where there is both random selection and random assignments, as well as quasi-experimental designs where it cannot be assumed that the covariate is equal across the population. Just be extra careful and do not go too far in terms of interpreting your results. If at all possible, replicate your study. For further discussion, see Huitema (2011), Porter and Raudenbush (1987), or Schneider et al. (2015).

14.1.1.8 More Complex ANCOVA Models

The one-factor ANCOVA model can be extended to more complex models in the same way as we expanded the one-factor ANOVA model. Thus, we can consider ANCOVA designs that involve any of the following characteristics: (a) factorial designs (i.e., having more than one factor or independent variable); (b) fixed-, random-, and mixed-effects designs; (c) repeated measures and split-plot (mixed) designs; (d) hierarchical designs; and (e) randomized block designs. Conceptually, there is nothing new for these types of ANCOVA designs, and you should have no trouble getting a statistical package to do such analyses. For further information on these designs, or for information on how one can also utilize multiple covariates in an analysis of covariance design, see any number of excellent references (Huitema, 2011; Keppel & Wickens, 2004; Kirk, 2014; Myers et al., 2010; Page, Braver, & MacKinnon, 2003).

14.1.1.9 Nonparametric ANCOVA Procedures

In situations where the assumptions of normality, homogeneity of variance, and/or linearity have been seriously violated, one alternative is to consider nonparametric ANCOVA procedures. Some rank ANCOVA procedures have been proposed by Quade (1967), Puri and Sen (1969), Conover and Iman (1982), Rutherford (1992), Mansouri and Zhang (2018). For a description of such procedures, see these references as well as Huitema (2011), Harwell (1992), Harwell (2003), or Wilcox (2003a).

14.1.2 Sample Size

As you have likely gauged in the discussion of sample size in other chapters, there are not suggested sample size guidelines that we will offer in consideration of computing ANCOVA. We know there are many elements that work together to impact sample size. These include the alpha level (where smaller alphas require larger sample size), power (where increased power requires larger sample size), effect size (where larger effect size estimates decrease sample size), and variation in the data (where increased variance increases required sample size). Rather than attempt to suggest criteria for the number of cases required in ANCOVA, we encourage researchers to compute required sample size based on power analysis, as we will illustrate later. We also encourage researchers to consider work that has been done in this area. For example, a two-step method for computing sample size with ANCOVA using one covariate was proposed by Borm, Fransen, and Lemmens (2007). Shan and Ma (2014) proposed an exact approach that produces power closer to the pre-specified power when the correlation between the dependent variable and covariate is large. Researchers interested in sample size determination with more complex ANCOVA models that include multiple covariates are encouraged to review Shieh (2017).

14.1.3 Power

Given a fixed sample size, ANCOVA is more powerful than ANOVA, and this has been demonstrated (e.g., Egbewale, Lewis, & Sim, 2014; Van Breukelen, 2006). Approaching power from a slightly different angle, a smaller sample size is needed in ANCOVA to obtain the same power in ANOVA (Maxwell, Delaney, & Kelley, 2018). How large the sample size needs to be in ANCOVA to achieve a desired power is best gauged by conducting a power analysis using power tables (e.g., Cohen, 1988) or appropriate software (e.g., G*Power).

14.1.4 Effect Size

For the one-factor ANCOVA model, effect size works exactly the same as in the factor-ANOVA model, except that they are based on adjusted means (Cohen, 1988), and as we will see in SPSS, partial eta squared is still the effect size reported in SPSS. The effect size representing the *standardized difference between adjusted means for a two-group design* (i.e., two groups or categories in the independent variable) can be computed as follows (Maxwell et al., 2018):

$$d = \frac{\bar{Y}_1' - \bar{Y}_2'}{\sqrt{MS_{with(adj)}}}$$

Where $\bar{Y}_1'$ and $\bar{Y}_2$ represent the adjusted means of the two groups in the study.

Effect size values for the proportion of total variance (specifically for eta squared, epsilon squared, and omega squared) for the omnibus test can be computed as follows. In effect size indices that represent the proportion of total variance, the variance due to the independent variable (i.e., the "effect of interest") is expressed as a proportion of the sum of the error variance and the total variance (i.e., the variance due to all factors) (Olejnik & Algina, 2000, p. 268). Because effect size values that represent the proportion of total variance are influenced by all the factors in the model, these effect size indices cannot be compared across models that incorporate different factors or different research designs (Olejnik & Algina, 2000).

Eta squared for group effects in ANCOVA, representing the proportion of total variance, can be computed as follows (Olejnik & Algina, 2000), where SS_{effect} corresponds to our notation of $SS_{betw(adj)}$:

$$\eta^2 = \frac{SS_{effect}}{SS_{total}} = \frac{SS_{betw(adj)}}{SS_{total}}$$

Epsilon squared for group effects in ANCOVA, representing the proportion of total variance in the dependent variable that is explained by the independent variable after the effects of the covariate have been removed, can be computed as follows (Olejnik & Algina, 2000):

$$\varepsilon^2 = \frac{df_{effect}\left(MS_{effect} - MS_{error}\right)}{SS_{total}} = \frac{df_{betw(adj)}\left(MS_{betw(adj)} - MS_{with(adj)}\right)}{SS_{total}}$$

Omega squared for group effects in ANCOVA, representing the proportion of total variance in the dependent variable that is explained by the independent variable after the effects of the covariate have been removed, can be computed as follows (Olejnik & Algina, 2000):

$$\omega^2 = \frac{df_{effect}\left(MS_{effect} - MS_{error}\right)}{SS_{total} + MS_{error}} = \frac{df_{betw(adj)}\left(MS_{betw(adj)} - MS_{with(adj)}\right)}{SS_{total} + MS_{with(adj)}}$$

Where df_{effect} corresponds to our notation of $df_{betw(adj)}$ and MS_{effect} corresponds to our notation of $MS_{betw(adj)}$. MS_{error} corresponds to our notation of $MS_{with(adj)}$. Using the example data and results (presented in Table 14.7), we find omega squared to be as follows:

$$\omega^2 = \frac{df_{betw(adj)}\left(MS_{betw(adj)} - MS_{with(adj)}\right)}{SS_{total} + MS_{with(adj)}} = \frac{1(10.812 - .951)}{40.250 + .951} = \frac{9.861}{21.201} = .465$$

Epsilon squared and omega squared will yield similar values (Carroll & Nordholm, 1975). Both epsilon squared and omega squared can result in negative values when *F* is less than one. In the event this occurs, setting the effect size value to zero is typical practice (Olejnik & Algina, 2000).

We will leave our discussion of effect size measures with a few cautionary notes discussed in Olejnik and Algina (2000). Omega squared effect size indices are derived from expected mean squares variance components. Expected means squares assume a balanced design, and in the absence of balance, omega squared is not recommended (Vaughan & Corballis, 1969). Small sample sizes (e.g., N = 15 and N = 30) can detrimentally impact epsilon squared and omega squared by producing large standard errors for these effects (Carroll & Nordholm, 1975).

TABLE 14.5
Effect Sizes and Interpretations

Effect Size	Interpretation
Standardized difference between adjusted means for a two-group design (*d*)	Standardized mean difference controlling for the covariate • Small effect, $d = .20$ • Medium effect, $d = .50$ • Large effect, $d = .80$
Eta squared (η^2)	Proportion of total variability in the dependent variable that is accounted for by the independent variable after controlling for the covariate • Small effect, $\eta^2 = .01$ • Medium effect, $\eta^2 = .06$ • Large effect, $\eta^2 = .14$
Epsilon squared (ε^2)	Proportion of total variability in the dependent variable that is accounted for by the independent variable after controlling for the covariate • Small effect, $\varepsilon^2 = .01$ • Medium effect, $\varepsilon^2 = .06$ • Large effect, $\varepsilon^2 = .14$
Omega squared (ω^2)	Proportion of total variability in the dependent variable that is accounted for by the independent variable after controlling for the covariate • Small effect, $\omega^2 = .01$ • Medium effect, $\omega^2 = .06$ • Large effect, $\omega^2 = .14$

14.1.5 Assumptions

The introduction of a covariate requires several assumptions beyond the traditional ANOVA assumptions. For the familiar assumptions (e.g., independence of observations, homogeneity, and normality), the discussion is kept to a minimum as these have already been described in Chapters 11 and 13. The new assumptions are as follows: (a) linearity, (b) independence of the covariate and the independent variable, (c) the covariate is measured without error, and (d) homogeneity of the regression slopes. In this section, we describe each assumption, how each assumption can be evaluated, the effects that a violation of the assumption might have, and how one might deal with a serious violation. Later in the chapter, when we illustrate how to use SPSS and **R** to generate ANCOVA, we will specifically test for the assumptions of independence of observations, homogeneity of variance, normality, linearity, independence of the covariate and the independent variable, and homogeneity of regression slopes.

14.1.5.1 Independence

As we learned previously, the assumption of independence of observations can be met by (a) keeping the assignment of individuals to groups (i.e., to the levels or categories of the independent variable) separate through the design of the experiment (specifically random assignment—not to be confused with random selection), and (b) keeping the individuals separate from one another through experimental control so that the scores on the dependent variable *Y* are independent across subjects (both within and across groups).

As in previous ANOVA models, the use of independent random samples is also crucial in the analysis of covariance. The *F* ratio is very sensitive to violation of the independence assumption in terms of increased likelihood of a Type I and/or Type II error. A violation of the independence assumption may affect the standard errors of the sample adjusted means and thus influence any inferences made about those means. One purpose of random assignment of individuals to groups is to achieve independence. If each individual is observed only once and individuals are randomly assigned to groups, then the independence assumption is usually met. Random assignment is important for valid interpretation of both the *F* test and multiple comparison procedures. Otherwise, the *F* test and adjusted means may be biased.

The simplest procedure for assessing independence is to examine residual plots by group. If the independence assumption is satisfied, then the residuals should fall into a random display of points. If the assumption is violated, then the residuals will fall into some type of cyclical pattern. As discussed in Chapter 11, the Durbin-Watson statistic (Durbin & Watson, 1950, 1951, 1971) can be used to test for autocorrelation. Violations of the independence assumption generally occur in the three situations we mentioned in Chapter 11: time series data, observations within blocks, or replication. For severe violations of the independence assumption, there is no simple "fix," such as the use of transformations or nonparametric tests (Scariano & Davenport, 1987).

14.1.5.2 Homogeneity of Variance

The second assumption is that the variances of each population are the same, known as the homogeneity of variance or homoscedasticity assumption. A violation of this assumption may lead to bias in the SS_{with} term, as well as an increase in the Type I error rate, and possibly an increase in the Type II error rate. A summary of Monte Carlo research on ANCOVA assumption violations by Harwell (2003) indicates that the effect of the violation is negligible with equal or nearly equal *n*'s across the groups. There is a more serious problem if the larger *n*'s are associated with the smaller variances (actual or observed $\alpha >$ nominal or stated α selected by the researcher, which is a liberal result), or if the larger *n*'s are associated with the larger variances (actual $\alpha <$ nominal α, which is a conservative result).

In a plot of *Y* versus the covariate *X* for each group, the variability of the distributions may be examined for evidence of the extent to which this assumption is met. Another method for detecting violation of the homogeneity assumption is the use of formal statistical tests for homoscedasticity (e.g., Levene's), as discussed in Chapter 11 and as we illustrate using SPSS and **R** later in this chapter. Several solutions are available for dealing with a violation of the homogeneity assumption. These include the use of variance stabilizing transformations or other ANCOVA models that are less sensitive to unequal variances, such as nonparametric ANCOVA procedures (described at the end of this chapter).

14.1.5.3 Normality

The third assumption is that each of the populations follows the normal distribution. Based on the classic work by Box and Anderson (1962) and Atiqullah (1964), as well as the summarization of modern Monte Carlo work by Harwell (2003), the *F* test is relatively robust to nonnormal *Y* distributions, "minimizing the role of a normally distributed *X*" (Harwell, 2003, p. 62). Thus we need only really be concerned with serious nonnormality (although "serious nonnormality" is a subjective call made by the researcher).

We will examine residuals for this assumption, and the following graphical techniques can be used to detect violation of the normality assumption: (a) frequency distributions (such as stem-and-leaf plots, boxplots, or histograms), or (b) normal probability plots. There are also several statistical procedures available for the detection of nonnormality [e.g., the Shapiro-Wilk test (Shapiro & Wilk, 1965)]. If the assumption of normality is violated, transformations can also be to normalize the data, as previously discussed in Chapter 11. In addition, nonparametric ANCOVA has been shown to be robust to nonnormality, have reasonable power, and preserve the nominal alpha level (Wu & Lai, 2015), and one can use one of the rank ANCOVA procedures previously mentioned.

14.1.5.4 Linearity

The next assumption is that the regression of Y (i.e., the dependent variable) on X (i.e., the covariate) is linear. If the relationship between Y and X is not linear, then use of the usual ANCOVA procedure is not appropriate, just as linear regression (see Chapter 17) would not be appropriate in cases of nonlinearity. In ANCOVA (as well as in correlation and linear regression), we fit a straight line to the data points in a scatterplot. When the relationship is nonlinear, a straight line will not fit the data particularly well. In addition, the magnitude of the linear correlation will be smaller. If the relationship is not linear, the estimate of the group effects will be biased, and the adjustments made in SS_{with} and SS_{betw} will be smaller.

Violations of the linearity assumption can generally be detected by looking at scatterplots of Y versus X, overall and for each group or category of the independent variable. Once a serious violation of the linearity assumption has been detected, two alternatives can be used: transformations and nonlinear ANCOVA. Transformations on one or both variables can be used to achieve linearity (Keppel & Wickens, 2004). The second option is to use nonlinear ANCOVA methods as described by Huitema (2011) and Keppel and Wickens (2004).

14.1.5.5 Fixed Independent Variable

The fifth assumption states that the levels of the independent variable are fixed by the researcher. This results in a fixed-effects model rather than a random-effects model. As in the one-factor ANOVA model, the one-factor ANCOVA model is the same computationally in the fixed- and random-effects cases. The summary of Monte Carlo research by Harwell (2003) indicates that the impact of a random effect on the F test is minimal.

14.1.5.6 Independence of the Covariate and the Independent Variable

A condition of the ANCOVA model (although not an assumption) requires that the covariate and the independent variable be independent. That is, the covariate is not influenced by the independent or treatment variable. If the covariate is affected by the treatment itself, then the use of the covariate in the analysis either (a) may remove part of the treatment effect or produce a spurious (inflated) treatment effect, or (b) may alter the covariate scores as a result of the treatment being administered prior to obtaining the covariate data. The obvious solution to this potential problem is to obtain the covariate scores prior to the administration of the treatment. In other words, be alert prior to the study for possible covariate candidates. Thus, in a true experiment, the treatment (i.e., independent variable) and covariate are not related by default of random assignment and thereby the assumption of independence of the covariate and independent variable are met. If randomization is not possible, closely matching participants on the covariate may also help to ensure the assumption is not violated.

Let us consider an example where this condition is obviously violated. A psychologist is interested in which of several hypnosis treatments is most successful in reducing or eliminating cigarette smoking. A group of heavy smokers is randomly assigned to the hypnosis treatments. After the treatments have been completed, the researcher suspects that some patients are more susceptible to hypnosis (i.e., are more suggestible) than others. By using suggestibility as a covariate after the study is completed, the researcher would not be able to determine whether group differences were a result of hypnosis treatment, suggestibility, or some combination. Thus, the measurement of suggestibility after the hypnosis treatments have been administered would be ill-advised. An extended discussion of this condition is given in Maxwell et al. (2018).

Evidence of the extent to which this assumption is met can be done by examining mean differences on the covariate across the levels of the independent variable. If the independent variable has only two levels, an independent t test would be appropriate. If the independent variable has more than two categories, a one-way ANOVA would suffice. If the groups are not statistically different on the covariate, then that lends evidence that the assumption of independence of the covariate and the independent variable has been met. If the groups are statistically different on the covariate, then the groups are not likely to be equivalent.

14.1.5.7 Covariate Measured Without Error

An assumption that we have not yet discussed in this text is that the covariate is measured without error. This is of special concern in education and the behavioral sciences, where variables are often measured with considerable measurement error. In the presence of measurement error, in randomized experiments, b_w (i.e., the within-groups regression slope from the regression of the dependent variable, Y, on the covariate, X) will be underestimated so that less of the covariate effect is removed from the dependent variable (i.e., the adjustments will be smaller). In addition, the reduction in the unexplained variation will not be as great and the F test will not be as powerful when there is measurement error. The F test is generally conservative in terms of Type I error (the actual observed alpha will be less than the nominal alpha which was selected by the researcher—the nominal alpha is often .05). However, the treatment effects will not be biased. In quasi-experimental designs, b_w will also be underestimated with similar effects. However, the treatment effects may be seriously biased. A method by Porter (1967) is suggested for this situation.

There is considerable discussion about the effects of measurement error (Cohen, Cohen, West, & Aiken, 2003; Keppel & Wickens, 2004; Lord, 1960, 1967, 1969; Mickey et al., 2004; Pedhazur, 1997; Porter, 1967; Reichardt, 1979; Weisberg, 1985). Obvious violations of this assumption can be detected by computing the reliability of the covariate prior to the study or from previous research. This is the minimum that should be done. One may also want to consider the *validity* of the covariate as well, where validity may be defined as the extent to which an instrument measures what it was intended to measure. While this is the first mention in the text of measurement error, it is certainly important that all measures included in a model—regardless of which statistical procedure is being conducted—are measured such that the scores provide high reliability and validity.

14.1.5.8 Homogeneity of Regression Slopes

The final assumption puts forth that the slope of the regression line between the dependent variable and covariate is the same for each category of the independent variable. Here we assume that $\beta_1 = \beta_2 = \ldots = \beta_J$. This is an important assumption because it allows us to use b_w, the sample estimator of β_w, as the within-groups regression slope, and some researchers have noted that this is *the most important assumption* (Shieh, 2017). Assuming that the group slopes are parallel allows us to test for group intercept differences, *which is all we are really doing when we test for differences among the adjusted means.* Without this assumption of homogeneity of regression slopes, groups can differ on *both* the regression slope and intercept, and β_w cannot legitimately be used. If the slopes differ, then the regression lines interact in some way. As a result, the size of the group differences in Y (i.e., the dependent variable) will depend on the value of X (i.e., the covariate). For example, Treatment 1 may be most effective on the dependent variable for low values of the covariate, Treatment 2 may be most effective on the dependent variable for middle values of the covariate, and Treatment 3 may be most effective on the dependent variable for high values of the covariate. Thus, we do not have constant differences on the dependent variable between the groups of the independent variable across the values of the covariate. A straightforward interpretation is not possible, which is the same situation in factorial ANOVA when the interaction between factor A and factor B is found to be significant. *Thus, unequal slopes in ANCOVA represent a type of interaction.*

There are other potential outcomes if this assumption is violated. Without homogeneous regression slopes, the use of β_w can yield biased adjusted means and can affect the F test. Earlier simulation studies by Peckham (1968) and Glass, Peckham, and Sanders (1972) suggest that for the one-factor fixed-effects model, the effects will be minimal. Later analytical research by Rogosa (1980) suggests that there is little effect on the F test for balanced designs with equal variances, but the F is less robust for mild heterogeneity. However, a summary of modern Monte Carlo work by Harwell (2003) indicates that the effect of slope heterogeneity on the F test is (a) negligible with equal n's and equal covariate means (randomized studies), (b) modest with equal n's and unequal covariate means (nonrandomized studies), and (c) modest with unequal n's.

A formal statistical procedure is often conducted to test for homogeneity of slopes using statistical software (we will illustrate this later in this chapter), although the eyeball method (i.e., see if the slopes look about the same by reviewing scatterplots of the dependent variable and covariate for each category of the independent variable) can be a good starting point. Some alternative tests for equality of slopes when the variances are unequal are provided by Tabatabai and Tan (1985).

Several alternatives are available if the homogeneity of slopes assumption is violated. The first is to use the concomitant variable not as a covariate but as a blocking variable. This will work because this assumption is not made for the randomized block design (see Chapter 16). A second option, and not a very desirable one, is to analyze each group separately with its own slope or subsets of the groups having equal slopes. A third possibility is to utilize interaction terms between the covariate and the independent variable and conduct a regression analysis (see Agresti, 2018). A fourth option is to use the Johnson-Neyman (Johnson & Neyman, 1936) technique, whose purpose is to determine the values of X (i.e., the covariate) that are related to significant group differences on Y (i.e., the dependent variable). Interested readers are referred to Huitema (2011) or Wilcox (1987). A fifth option is use more modern robust methods (e.g., Maxwell et al., 2018; Wilcox, 2003b).

A summary of the ANCOVA assumptions is presented in Table 14.6.

TABLE 14.6
Assumptions and Effects of Violations—One-Factor ANCOVA

Assumption	Effect of Assumption Violation
Independence	• Increased likelihood of a Type I and/or Type II error in *F* • Affects standard errors of means and inferences about those means
Homogeneity of variance	• Bias in SS_{with}; increased likelihood of a Type I and/or Type II error • Negligible effect with equal or nearly equal *n*'s • Otherwise more serious problem if the larger *n*'s are associated with the smaller variances (increased α) or larger variances (decreased α)
Normality	• *F* test relatively robust to nonnormal *Y*, minimizing the role of nonnormal X
Linearity	• Reduced magnitude of r_{XY} • Straight line will not fit data well • Estimate of group effects biased • Adjustments made in *SS* smaller
Fixed-effect	• Minimal impact
Covariate & factor are independent	• May reduce/increase group effects; may alter covariate scores

Covariate measured without error	• True experiment:
	  • b_W underestimated
	  • adjustments smaller
	  • reduction in unexplained variation smaller
	  • *F* less powerful
	  • reduced likelihood of Type I error
	• Quasi-experiment:
	  • b_W underestimated
	  • adjustments smaller
	  • group effects seriously biased

Homogeneity of slopes	• Negligible effect with equal *n*'s in true experiment • Modest effect with equal *n*'s in quasi-experiment • Modest effect with unequal *n*'s

14.2 Computing ANCOVA Using SPSS

Next we consider SPSS for the *physical performance* (i.e., dependent variable) example that includes *treatment group* as the independent variable and *mental fatigue* as the covariate (Ch14_fatigue.sav). As noted in previous chapters, SPSS needs the data to be in a specific form for the analysis to proceed, which is different from the layout of the data in Table 14.1. For a one-factor ANCOVA with a single covariate, the dataset must contain three variables or columns: one for the level of the factor or independent variable, one for the covariate, and a third for the dependent variable. The screenshot in Figure 14.2 presents an example of the dataset for the physical performance example. Each row still represents one individual, displaying the level of the factor (or independent variable) for which they are a member, as well as their scores on the covariate and the scores for the dependent variable.

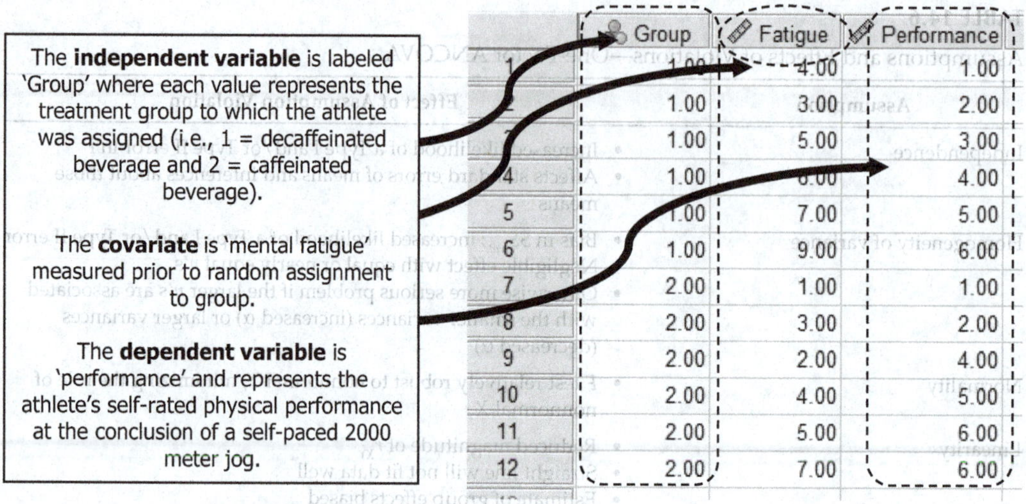

The **independent variable** is labeled 'Group' where each value represents the treatment group to which the athlete was assigned (i.e., 1 = decaffeinated beverage and 2 = caffeinated beverage).
The **covariate** is 'mental fatigue' measured prior to random assignment to group.
The **dependent variable** is 'performance' and represents the athlete's self-rated physical performance at the conclusion of a self-paced 2000 meter jog.
Group
Fatigue
Performance

FIGURE 14.2
Data.

Step 1. To conduct an ANCOVA, go to "Analyze" in the top pulldown menu, then select "General Linear Model," and then select "Univariate." Following the screenshot for Step 1 (Figure 14.3) produces the Univariate dialog box.

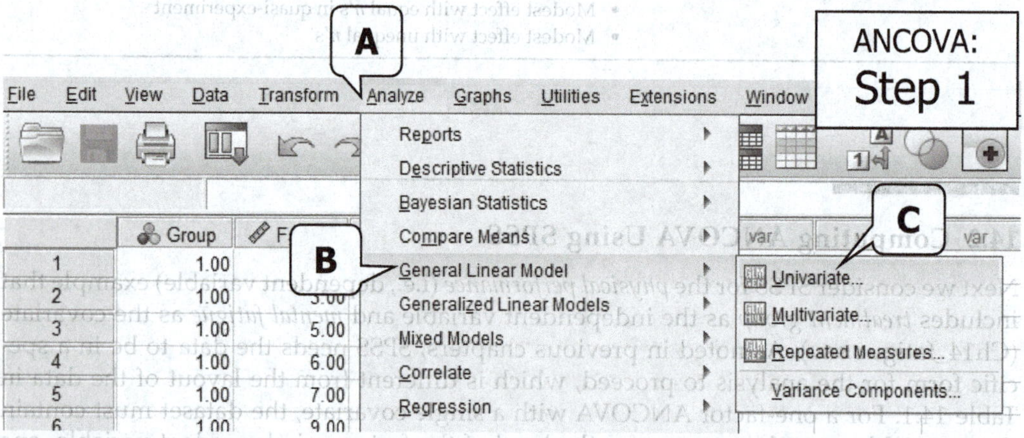

FIGURE 14.3
ANCOVA: Step 1.

Step 2. From the Univariate dialog box (see Step 2, shown in Figure 14.4), click the dependent variable (e.g., self-rated physical performance) and move it into the "Dependent Variable" box by clicking the arrow button. Click the independent variable (e.g., group) and move it into the "Fixed Factor(s)" box by clicking the arrow button. Click the covariate (e.g., fatigue) and move it into the "Covariate(s)" box by clicking the arrow button. Next, click on "Options."

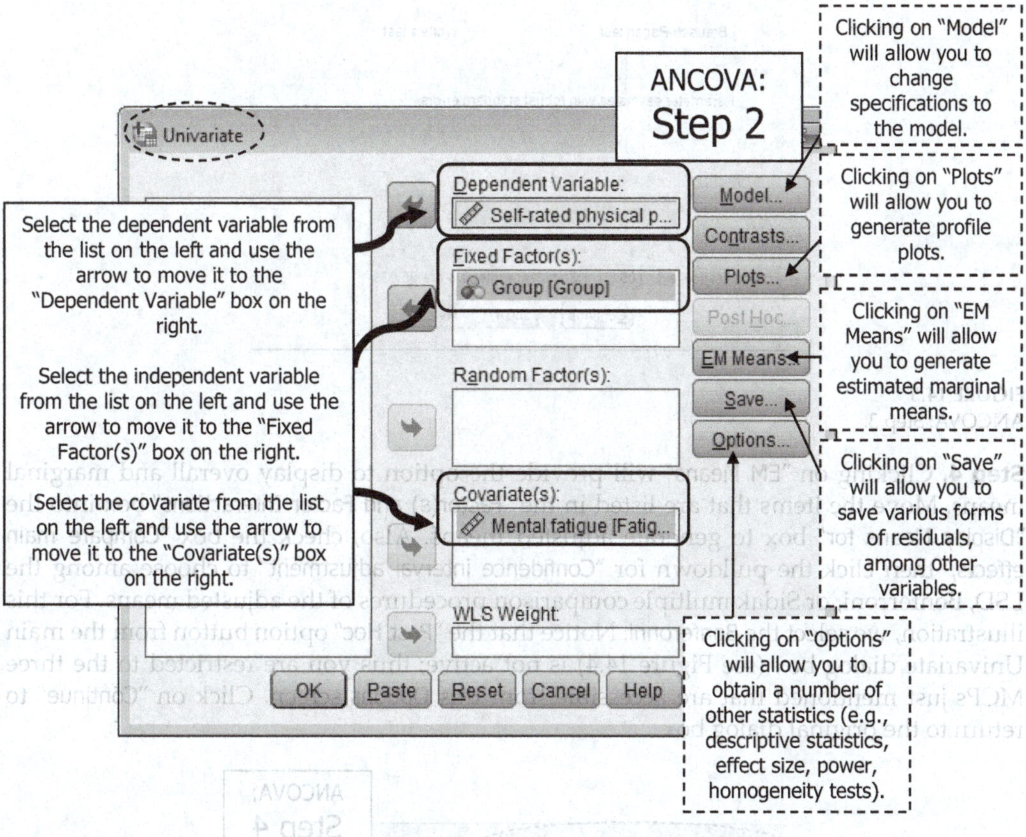

FIGURE 14.4
ANCOVA: Step 2.

Step 3. Clicking on "Options" will provide the option to select such information as "Descriptive Statistics," "Estimates of effect size," "Observed power," and "Homogeneity tests." Click on "Continue" to return to the original dialog box.

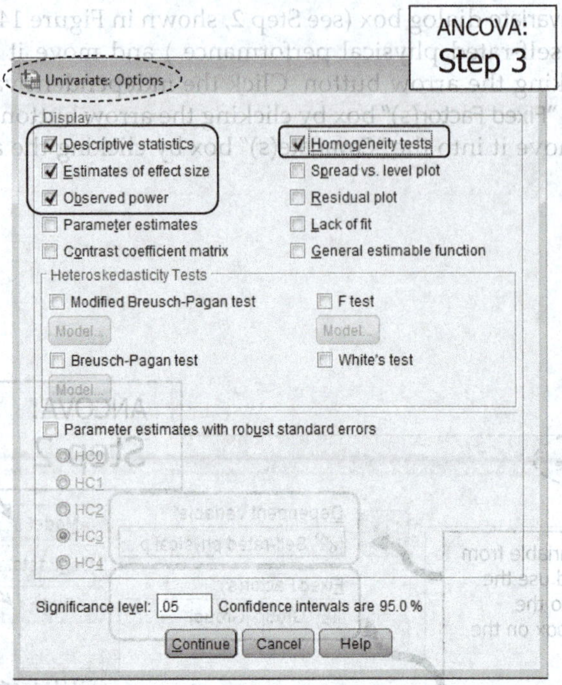

FIGURE 14.5
ANCOVA: Step 3.

Step 4. Clicking on "EM Means" will provide the option to display overall and marginal means. Move the items that are listed in the "Factor(s) and Factor Interactions" box into the "Display Means for" box to generate adjusted means. Also, check the box "Compare main effects," then click the pulldown for "Confidence interval adjustment" to choose among the LSD, Bonferroni, or Sidak multiple comparison procedures of the adjusted means. For this illustration, we select the Bonferonni. Notice that the "Post Hoc" option button from the main Univariate dialog box (see Figure 14.4) is not active; thus you are restricted to the three MCPs just mentioned that are accessible from this Options screen. Click on "Continue" to return to the original dialog box.

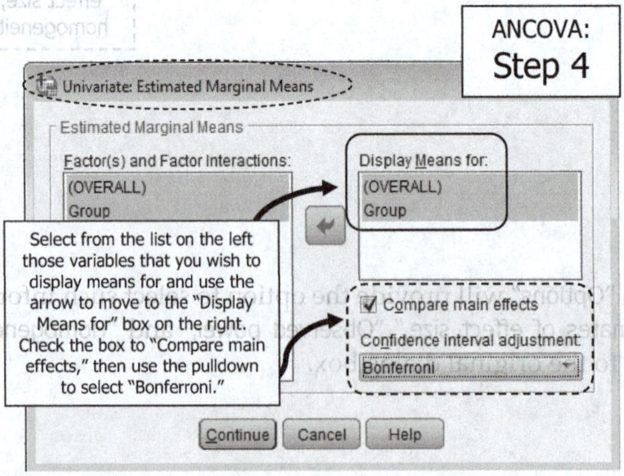

FIGURE 14.6
ANCOVA: Step 4.

Step 5. From the "Univariate" dialog box (see Figure 14.4), click on "Plots" to obtain a profile plot of means. Click the independent variable (e.g., statistics course section, "Group") and move it into the "Horizontal Axis" box by clicking the arrow button (see screenshot Step 5a, shown in Figure 14.7). Then click on "Add" to move the variable into the "Plots" box at the bottom of the dialog box (see screenshot for Step 5b, shown in Figure 14.8). Click on "Continue" to return to the original dialog box.

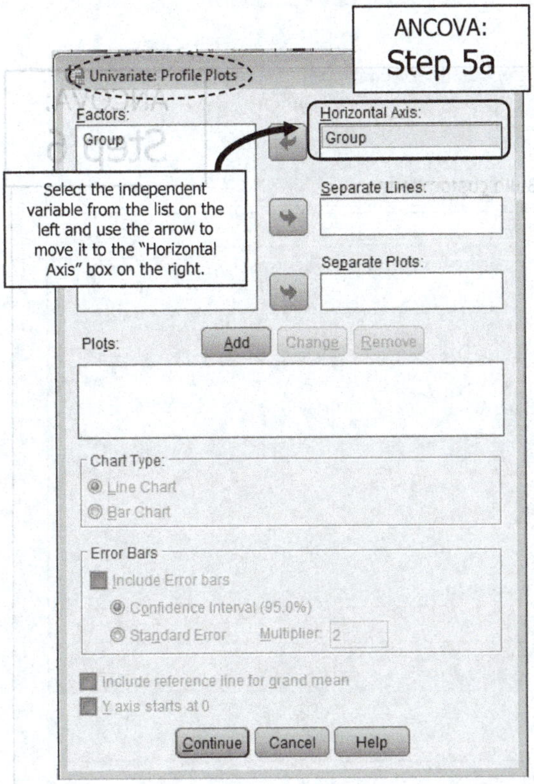

FIGURE 14.7
ANCOVA: Step 5a.

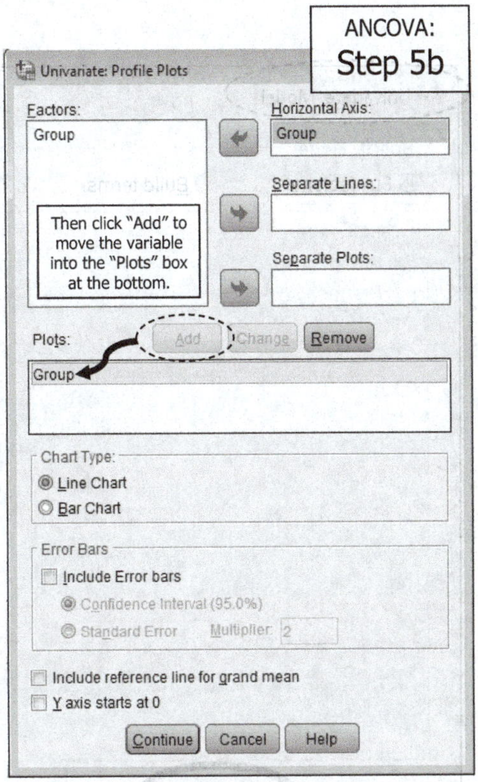

FIGURE 14.8
ANCOVA: Step 5b.

Step 6. Finally, in order to generate the appropriate sources of variation and results as recommended in this chapter, from the main Univariate dialog box (see Step 2, Figure 14.4), you need to click on the "Model" button. Then select "Type I" from the "Sum of squares" pull-down menu. Click on "Continue" to return to the original dialog box.

You may be asking yourself why we need to utilize the Type I sum of squares, as up until this point in the text we have always recommended the Type III (which is the default in SPSS). In a study conducted by Li and Lomax (2011), the following were confirmed with SPSS (as well as with SAS). First, when generating the Type I sum of squares, the covariate is extracted first, then the treatment is estimated controlling for the covariate. The Type I sum of squares will also correctly add up to the total sum of squares. Second, when generating the Type III sum of squares, each effect is estimated controlling for each of the other effects. In other words, the covariate is computed controlling for the treatment, and the treatment is determined controlling for the covariate. The former is not of interest as the treatment is administered after the covariate has been measured; thus no such control is necessary. Also, the Type III sum of squares will not add up to the total sum of squares, as the covariate sum of squares will be different than when using Type I. Thus, you do not want to estimate the covariate controlling for the treatment, and thus you want to use the Type I, not Type III, in the ANCOVA context. In other words, Type I sum of squares is sequential, with each term adjusted for the term that precedes it in the model.

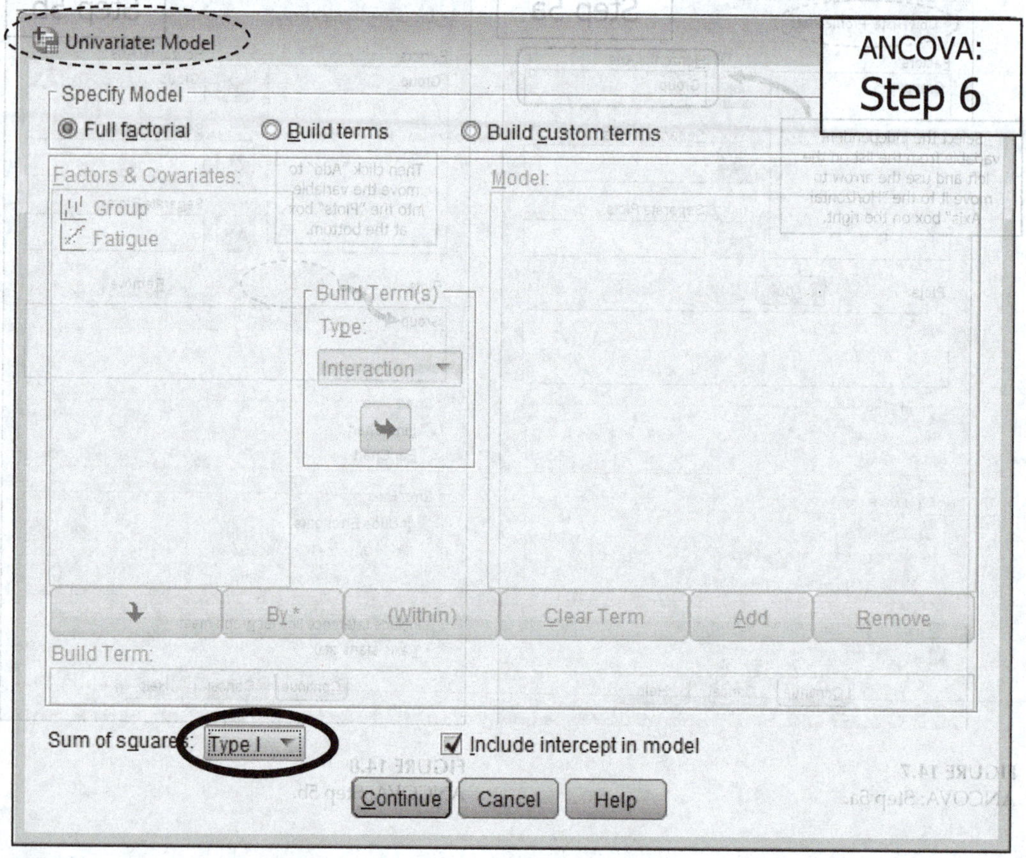

FIGURE 14.9
ANCOVA: Step 6.

Step 7. From the "Univariate" dialog box (see Step 2, Figure 14.4), click on "Save" to select those elements that you want to save (here we want to save the unstandardized residuals for later use in order to examine the extent to which normality and independence are met). Click on "Continue" to return to the original dialog box. From the Univariate dialog box, click on "OK" to return to generate the output.

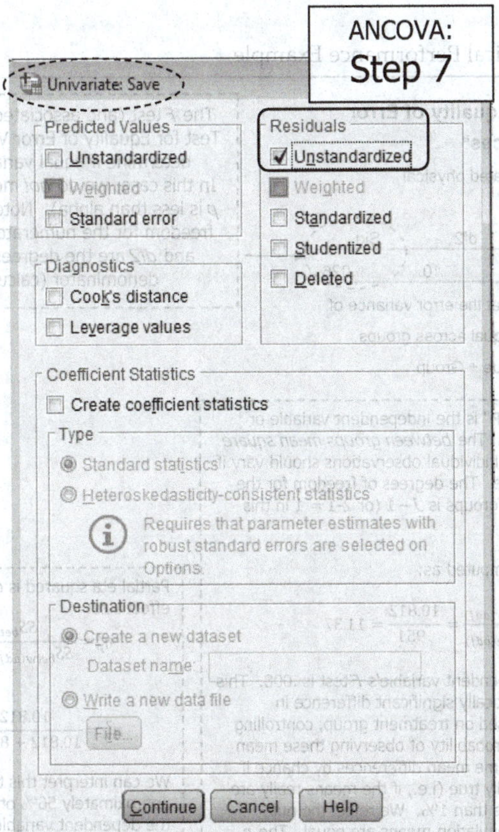

FIGURE 14.10
ANCOVA: Step 7.

Interpreting the output. Annotated results are presented in Table 14.7.

TABLE 14.7
SPSS Results for the Physical Performance Example

Between-Subjects Factors

		Value Label	N
Group	1.00	Control (decaffeinated beverage)	6
	2.00	Treatment (caffeinated beverage)	6

The table labeled "Between-Subjects Factors" provides sample sizes for each of the categories of the independent variable (recall that the independent variable is the 'between subjects factor').

Descriptive Statistics

Dependent Variable: Self-rated physical performance

Group	Mean	Std. Deviation	N
Control (decaffeinated beverage)	3.5000	1.87083	6
Treatment (caffeinated beverage)	4.0000	2.09762	6
Total	3.7500	1.91288	12

The table labeled "Descriptive Statistics" provides basic descriptive statistics (means, standard deviations, and sample sizes) for each group of the independent variable.

(continued)

TABLE 14.7 (continued)

SPSS Results for the Physical Performance Example

Levene's Test of Equality of Error Variances[a]

Dependent Variable: Self-rated physical performance

F	df1	df2	Sig.
6.768	1	10	.026

Tests the null hypothesis that the error variance of the dependent variable is equal across groups.

a. Design: Intercept + Fatigue + Group

The *F* test (and associated *p* value) for Levene's Test for Equality of Error Variances is reviewed to determine if equal variances are assumed. In this case, we do *not* meet the assumption (as *p* is less than alpha). Note that *df1* is degrees of freedom for the numerator (calculated as $J - 1$) and *df2* are the degrees of freedom for the denominator (calculated as $N - J$).

The row labeled **"GROUP"** is the independent variable or between groups variable. The *between groups mean square* (10.812) tells how much individual observations should vary if the null hypothesis is true. The degrees of freedom for the sum of squares between groups is $J - 1$ (or 2-1 = 1 in this example).

The omnibus *F* test is computed as:

$$F = \frac{MS_{betw(adj)}}{MS_{with(adj)}} = \frac{10.812}{.951} = 11.37$$

The *p* value for the independent variable's *F* test is .008. This indicates there is a statistically significant difference in physical performance based on treatment group, controlling for mental fatigue. The probability of observing these mean differences or more extreme mean differences by chance if the null hypothesis is really true (i.e., if the means really are equal) is substantially less than 1%. We reject the null hypothesis that all the population means are equal. The *p* value for the covariate's *F* test is .001. This indicates there is a statistically significant relationship between the covariate (mental fatigue) and physical performance.

Partial eta squared is one measure of effect size:

$$\eta_p^2 = \frac{SS_{betw(adj)}}{SS_{betw(adj)} + SS_{error}}$$

$$\eta_p^2 = \frac{10.812}{10.812 + 8.557} = .558$$

We can interpret this to say that approximately 56% of the variation in the dependent variable (in this case, statistics quiz score) is accounted for by the instructional method when controlling for aptitude.

Tests of Between-Subjects Effects

Dependent Variable: Self-rated physical performance

Source	Type I Sum of Squares	df	Mean Square	F	Sig.	Partial Eta Squared	Noncent. Parameter	Observed Power[b]
Corrected Model	31.693[a]	2	15.846	16.667	.001	.787	33.333	.993
Intercept	168.750	1	168.750	177.483	.000	.952	177.483	1.000
Fatigue *(covariate)*	20.881	1	20.881	21.961	.001	.709	21.961	.986
Group *(ind. variable)*	10.812	1	10.812	11.372	.008	.558	11.372	.850
Error	8.557	9	.951					
Total	209.000	12						
Corrected Total	40.250	11						

a. R Squared = .787 (Adjusted R Squared = .740)

b. Computed using alpha = .05

R^2 is listed as a footnote underneath the table. R^2 is the ratio of $SS_{betw(adj)}$ and SS_{cov} divided by SS_{total}:

$$R^2 = \frac{SS_{betw(adj)} + SS_{cov}}{SS_{total}}$$

$$R^2 = \frac{10.812 + 20.881}{40.250} = .787$$

The row labeled **"Error"** is within groups. The within groups mean square tells us how much the observations within the groups really vary (i.e., .951). The degrees of freedom for the sum of squares within groups is (N-J-1) or the sample size minus the number of levels of the independent variable minus one.

The row labeled "corrected total" is the sum of squares total. The degrees of freedom for the total is (N-1) or the sample size minus one.

Observed power tells whether our test is powerful enough to detect mean differences if they really exist. Power of .850 indicates that the probability of rejecting the null hypothesis if it is really false is about 85%, strong power.

TABLE 14.7 (continued)

SPSS Results for the Physical Performance Example

Estimated Marginal Means

1. Grand Mean

Dependent Variable: Self-rated physical performance

Mean	Std. Error	95% Confidence Interval Lower Bound	Upper Bound
3.750[a]	.281	3.113	4.387

a. Covariates appearing in the model are evaluated at the following values: Mental fatigue = 4.6667.

The 'Grand Mean' (in this case, 3.750) represents the overall mean, regardless of group membership in the independent variable. The 95% CI represents the CI of the grand mean. Here, 95% of the time, the true grand mean will be between 3.113 and 4.387.

2. Group

Estimates

Dependent Variable: Self-rated physical performance

Group	Mean	Std. Error	95% Confidence Interval Lower Bound	Upper Bound
Control (decaffeinated beverage)	2.686[a]	.423	1.729	3.642
Treatment (caffeinated beverage)	4.814[a]	.423	3.858	5.771

a. Covariates appearing in the model are evaluated at the following values: Mental fatigue = 4.6667.

The table labeled **"Group"** provides descriptive statistics for each of the categories of the independent variable, controlling for the covariate (notice that these are NOT the same means reported previously; also note the table footnote). In addition to means, the *SE* and 95% CI of the means are reported.

'Mean difference' is simply the difference between the adjusted group means of the two groups compared. For example, the mean difference of group 1 and group 2, controlling for the covariate, is calculated as 2.686 – 4.814 = -2.12. Because there are only two groups to our independent variable, the values in the table are the same (in absolute value) for row 1 as compared to row 2 (the exception is that the CI for the difference is switched).

Pairwise Comparisons

Dependent Variable: Self-rated physical performance

(I) Group	(J) Group	Mean Difference (I-J)	Std. Error	Sig.[b]	95% Confidence Interval for Difference[b] Lower Bound	Upper Bound
Control (decaffeinated beverage)	Treatment (caffeinated beverage)	-2.129*	.631	.008	-3.556	-.701
Treatment (caffeinated beverage)	Control (decaffeinated beverage)	2.129*	.631	.008	.701	3.556

Based on estimated marginal means

*. The mean difference is significant at the .05 level.

b. Adjustment for multiple comparisons: Bonferroni.

'Sig.' denotes the observed *p* value and provides the results of the Bonferroni post hoc procedure. There is a statistically significant adjusted mean difference in the outcome between groups of the independent variable (controlling for the covariate).

Because we had only two groups, requesting post hoc results really was not necessary. We could have reviewed the *F* test and then the adjusted means to determine which group had the higher adjusted mean. The pairwise comparison results will become more valuable when the ANCOVA includes independent variables with more than two categories.

Note there are redundant results presented in the table. The comparison of group 1 and 2 (presented in results row 1) is the same as the comparison of group 2 and 1 (presented in results row 2).

(continued)

TABLE 14.7 (continued)

SPSS Results for the Physical Performance Example

The table labeled **"Univariate Tests"** is simply an omnibus *F* test. In the case of one independent variable, the row labeled "Contrast" provides the same results for the independent variable as that presented in the summary table previously. The results from this table suggest there is a statistically significant difference in adjusted mean physical performance based on treatment group when controlling for mental fatigue.

Univariate Tests

Dependent Variable: Self-rated physical performance

	Sum of Squares	df	Mean Square	F	Sig.	Partial Eta Squared	Noncent. Parameter	Observed Power[a]
Contrast	10.812	1	10.812	11.372	.008	.558	11.372	.850
Error	8.557	9	.951					

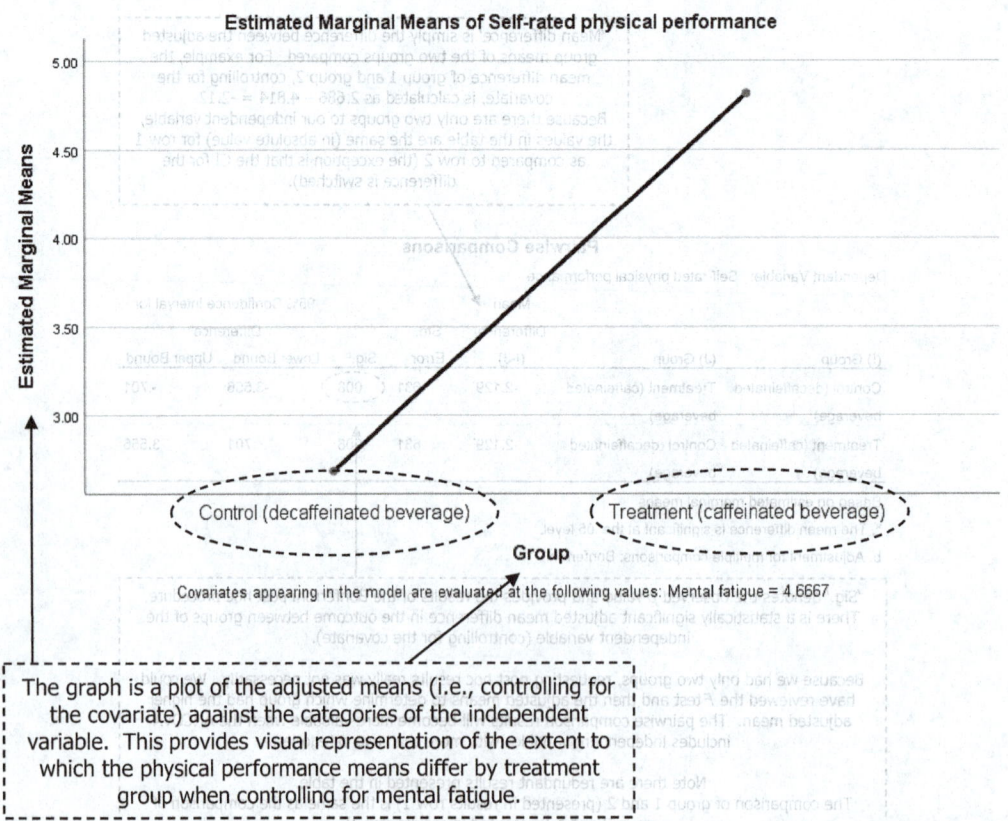

The F tests the effect of Group. This test is based on the linearly independent pairwise comparisons among the estimated marginal means.

a. Computed using alpha = .05

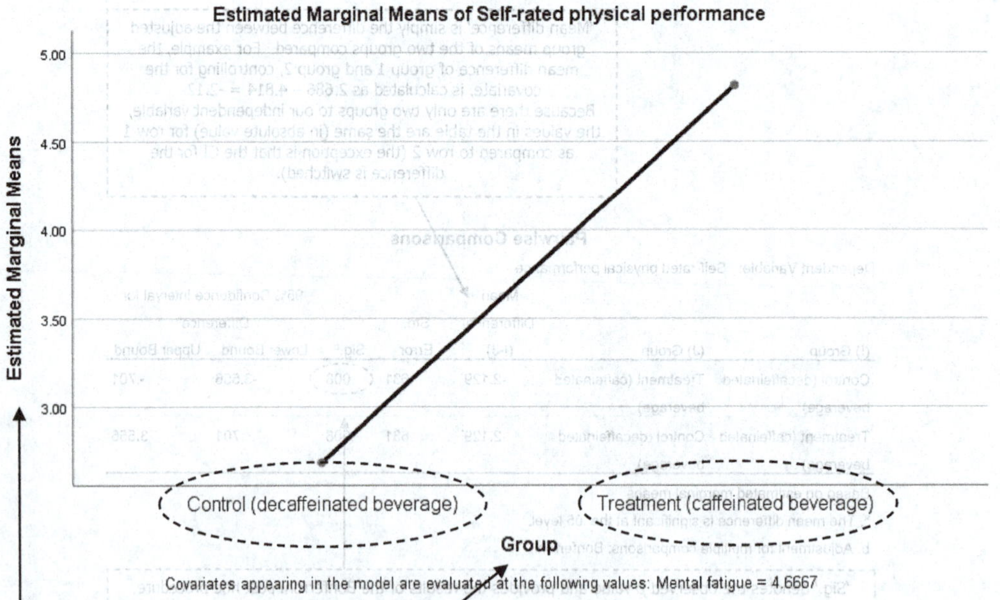

The graph is a plot of the adjusted means (i.e., controlling for the covariate) against the categories of the independent variable. This provides visual representation of the extent to which the physical performance means differ by treatment group when controlling for mental fatigue.

14.3 Computing ANCOVA Using R

Next we consider **R** for the ANCOVA model. Note that the scripts are provided within the blocks with additional annotation to assist in understanding how the command works. Should you want to write reminder notes and annotation to yourself as you write the commands in **R** (and we highly encourage doing so), remember that any text that follows a hashtag (i.e., #) is annotation only and not part of the **R** script. Thus, you can write annotations directly into **R** with hashtags. We encourage this practice so that when you call up the commands in the future, you'll understand what the various lines of code are doing. You may think you'll remember what you did. However, trust us. There is a good chance that you won't. Thus, consider it best practice when using **R** to annotate heavily!

14.3.1 Reading Data Into R

```
getwd()
```

R is always pointed to a directory on your computer. The *get working directory* function can be used to determine to which directory **R** is pointed. We will assume that we need to change the working directory, and will use the next line of code to set the working directory to the desired path.

```
setwd("E:/FolderName")
```

We use the *setwd* function to establish the working directory. To set the working directory, change what is in quotation marks to your file location. Also, if you are copying the directory name from your properties, you will need to change the forward slash (i.e., \) to a forward slash (i.e., /).

```
Ch14_fatigue <- read.csv("Ch14_fatigue.csv")
```

The *read.csv* function reads our data into **R**. What's to the left of the "<-" will be what the data will be called in **R**. In this example, we're calling the **R** dataframe "Ch14_fatigue." What's to the right of the "<-" tells **R** to find this particular csv file. In this example, our file is called "Ch14_fatigue.csv." Make sure the extension (i.e., .csv) is included in your script. Also note that the name of your file should be in quotation marks within the parentheses.

```
names(Ch14_fatigue)
```

The *names* function will produce a list of variable names for each dataframe as follows. This is a good check to make sure your data have been read in correctly.

```
[1] "Group"    "Fatigue"    "Performance"
```

```
View(Ch14_fatigue)
```

The *View* function will let you view the dataset in spreadsheet format in RStudio.

```
Ch14_fatigue$GroupF <- factor(Ch14_fatigue$Group,
                       labels = c("control",
                       "treatment"))
```

FIGURE 14.11
Reading data into **R**.

This command will create a new variable in our dataframe named "GroupF." We use the *factor* function to define the variable "Group" as nominal with the two groups defined here (i.e., control, treatment). What is to the left of "<-" in the script creates the new GroupF variable in our dataframe.

```
summary(Ch14_fatigue)
```

The *summary* function will produce basic descriptive statistics on all the variables in your dataframe. This is a great way to quickly check to see if the data have been read in correctly and to get a feel for your data, if you haven't already. The output from the summary statement for this dataframe looks like this. Because we defined GroupF as a factor, we are provided only the frequencies for each category in that variable.

```
    Group         Fatigue        Performance        GroupF
Min.   :1.0   Min.   :1.000   Min.   :1.00   control  :6
1st Qu.:1.0   1st Qu.:3.000   1st Qu.:2.00   treatment:6
Median :1.5   Median :4.500   Median :4.00
Mean   :1.5   Mean   :4.667   Mean   :3.75
3rd Qu.:2.0   3rd Qu.:6.250   3rd Qu.:5.25
Max.   :2.0   Max.   :9.000   Max.   :6.00
```

FIGURE 14.11 (continued)
Reading data into **R**.

14.3.2 Generating the ANCOVA Model

```
ANCOVA_fatigue <- lm(Performance ~ Fatigue+GroupF, data=Ch14_fatigue)
```

The *lm* function will generate the ANCOVA model with "Performance" as the dependent variable and "Group" as the independent variable, with "Fatigue" as the covariate. The dataframe from which we are pulling the data is defined by the *data* function. We are calling this object "ANCOVA_fatigue."

```
anova(ANCOVA_fatigue)
```

This command will output the results, which we see here:

```
Analysis of Variance Table

Response: Performance
          Df  Sum Sq Mean Sq F value   Pr(>F)
Fatigue    1 20.8807 20.8807  21.961 0.001142 **
GroupF     1 10.8122 10.8122  11.372 0.008228 **
Residuals  9  8.5571  0.9508
---
Signif. codes:
0 '***' 0.001 '**' 0.01 '*' 0.05 '.' 0.1 ' ' 1
```

```
summary(ANCOVA_fatigue)
```

The *summary* function will provide additional output from our ANCOVA model:

```
Call:
lm(formula = Performance ~ Fatigue + GroupF, data = Ch14_fatigue)

Residuals:
    Min      1Q  Median     3Q    Max
-1.4571 -0.7429  0.1357 0.6857 1.3571
```

FIGURE 14.12
Generating ANCOVA in **R**.

```
Coefficients:
                 Estimate Std. Error t value  Pr(>|t|)
(Intercept)       -1.1143     0.9015  -1.236  0.247732
Fatigue            0.8143     0.1427   5.705  0.000293 ***
GroupFtreatment    2.1286     0.6312   3.372  0.008228 **
---
Signif. codes: 0 '***' 0.001 '**' 0.01 '*' 0.05 '.' 0.1 ' ' 1

Residual standard error: 0.9751 on 9 degrees of freedom
Multiple R-squared: 0.7874, Adjusted R-squared: 0.7402
F-statistic: 16.67 on 2 and 9 DF, p-value: 0.000942
```

```
install.packages("sjstats")
```

The *install.packages* function will install *sjstats*.

```
library(sjstats)
```

The *library* function will call the *sjstats* package into the library.

```
anova_stats(ANCOVA_fatigue)
```

The *anova_stats* function, applied to our ANCOVA model (i.e., ANCOVA_fatigue) will produce the ANOVA summary table, along with multiple effect size indices.

```
term              df sumsq meansq statistic p. value etasq
1 Fatigue        1 20.881 20.881 21.961 0.001   0.519
2 GroupF         1 10.812 10.812 11.372 0.008   0.269
3 Residuals 9  8.557  0.951        NA      NA      NA

  partial.etasq  omegasq partial.omegasq cohens.f power
1      0.709     0.484           0.636 1.562    0.996
2      0.558     0.239           0.464 1.124    0.911
3         NA        NA              NA    NA       NA
```

```
omega_sq(ANCOVA_fatigue)
omega_sq(ANCOVA_fatigue, partial = TRUE)
cohens_f(ANCOVA_fatigue)
eta_sq(ANCOVA_fatigue)
eta_sq(ANCOVA_fatigue, partial = TRUE)
```

Had we wanted a specific effect size value, we could have generated the above code.

```
# omega_sq(ANCOVA_fatigue)
     term omegasq
1 Fatigue  0.484
2 GroupF   0.239

# omega_sq(ANCOVA_fatigue, partial = TRUE)
     term partial.omegasq
1 Fatigue           0.636
2 GroupF            0.464
```

FIGURE 14.12 (continued)
Generating ANCOVA in R.

```
# cohens_f(ANCOVA_fatigue)
     term cohens.f
1 Fatigue 1.562097
2 GroupF  1.124067

# eta_sq(ANCOVA_fatigue)
     term etasq
1 Fatigue 0.519
2 GroupF  0.269

# eta_sq(ANCOVA_fatigue, partial = TRUE)
     term partial.etasq
1 Fatigue 0.709
2 GroupF  0.558
```

```
Ch14_fatigue$unstandardizedResiduals <- residuals(ANCOVA_fatigue)
```

We also want to save our unstandardized residuals to the dataframe. We use the *residuals* function to compute unstandardized residuals from our *ANCOVA_fatigue* model. To the left of "<-" we will save the residuals as a variable named "unstandardizedResiduals" in our dataframe, *Ch14_fatigue*.

FIGURE 14.12 (continued)
Generating ANCOVA in R.

14.4 Data Screening

The assumptions that we will test for in our ANCOVA model include: (a) independence of observations; (b) homogeneity of variance (this was previously generated; thus you can examine Table 14.6 for this assumption as it will not be reiterated here); (c) normality; (d) linearity; (e) independence of the covariate and the independent variable; and (f) homogeneity of regression slopes. We will examine the assumptions after generating the ANCOVA results. This is because many of the tests for assumptions are based on examination of the residuals, which were requested when generating the ANCOVA.

14.4.1 Independence

If subjects have been randomly assigned to conditions (in other words, the different levels of the independent variable), the assumption of independence has been met. In this illustration, students were randomly assigned to group (i.e., ingest caffeinated versus decaffeinated beverage), and thus the assumption of independence was met. As we have learned in previous chapters, however, we often use independent variables that do not allow random assignment (e.g., intact groups). We can plot residuals against levels of the independent variable in a scatterplot to get an idea of whether or not there are patterns in the data and thereby provide an indication of the extent to which we have met this assumption. Remember that these variables were added to the dataset by saving the unstandardized residuals when we generated the ANCOVA model.

Note that some researchers do not believe that the assumption of independence can be tested. If there is not random assignment to groups, then these researchers believe this assumption has been violated—period. The plot that we generate will give us a general idea of patterns, however, in situations where random assignment was not performed.

The general steps for generating a simple scatterplot through "Scatter/dot" have been presented in Chapter 10, and they will not be reiterated here. From the "Simple Scatterplot" dialog screen, click the residual variable and move it into the "Y Axis" box by clicking on the arrow. Click the independent variable (e.g., group) and move it into the "X Axis" box by clicking on the arrow. Then click "OK."

14.4.1.1 Interpreting Independence Evidence

In examining the scatterplot for evidence of independence, the points should fall relatively randomly above and below the horizontal reference line at zero. In this example, the scatterplot does suggest evidence of independence with relative randomness of points above and below the horizontal line at zero.

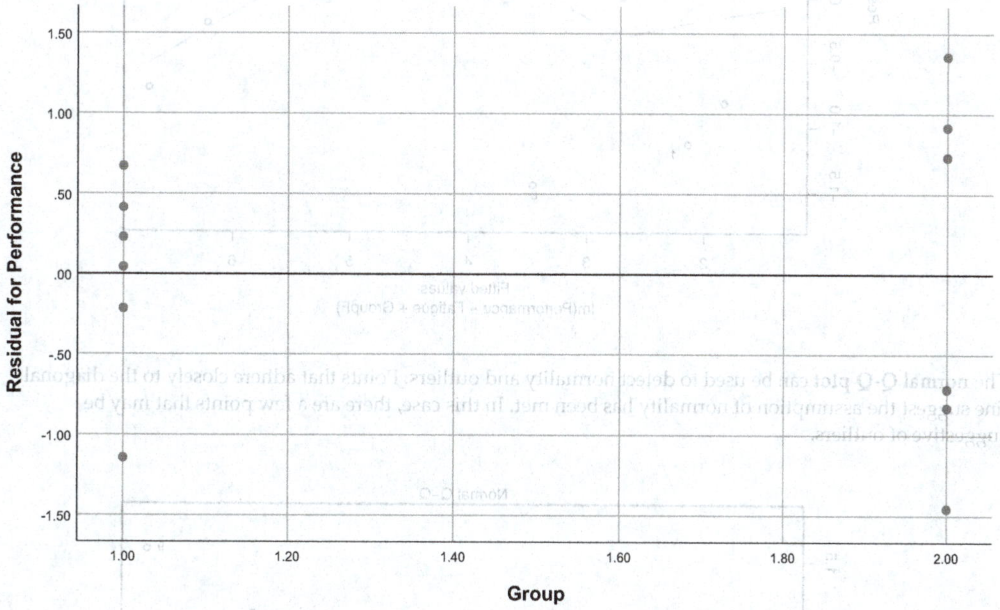

Working in **R**, we create a similar scatterplot.

```
plot(Ch14_fatigue$Group,
     Ch14_fatigue$unstandardizedResiduals,
     xlab = "Group",
     ylab = "Unstandardized Residual",
     main = "Scatterplot for Independence")
```

Using the following *plot* function, with the first variable listed displaying on the X axis (e.g., "Ch14_fatigue$Group"), and the second variable displaying on the *Y* axis (i.e., "Ch14_fatigue$unstandardized Residuals"). Additional commands are provided to label the axes (*xlab* and *ylab*) and title the graph (*main*).

(Note that we are using our "Group" variable, not *GroupF*, in this script. Had we used *GroupF*, the variable we defined as nominal, the plot generated would be a boxplot, not a scatterplot.)

FIGURE 14.13
Independence evidence.

```
plot(ANCOVA_fatigue)
```

Using the *plot* function, additional plots that can be used for diagnostic purposes are created.

The **residual versus fitted plot** can be used to detect normality, unequal error variance, and outliers. A random display of points, i.e., no patterns to the data, suggest assumptions of normality and equal variances have been met.

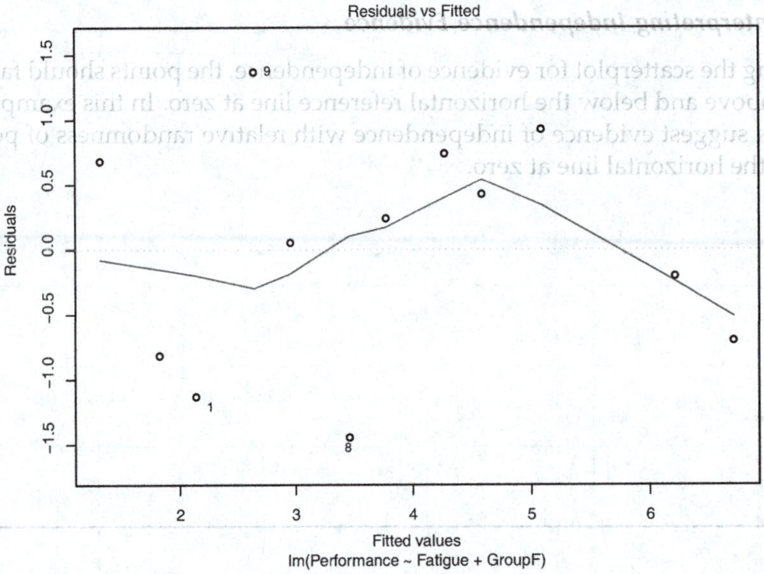

The **normal Q-Q plot** can be used to detect normality and outliers. Points that adhere closely to the diagonal line suggest the assumption of normality has been met. In this case, there are a few points that may be suggestive of outliers.

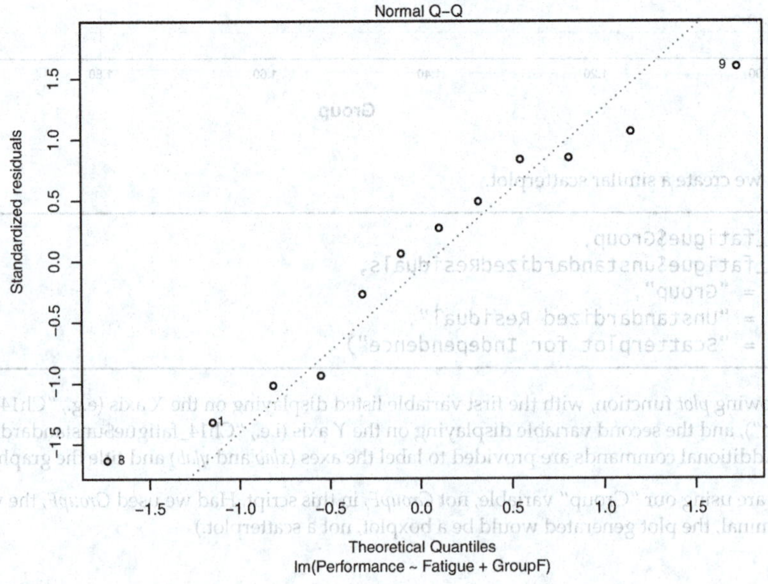

FIGURE 14.13 (continued)
Independence evidence.

The **scale-location plot** can be examined for evidence of equal variance. Relatively equally spaced points by group above and below a horizontal line (i.e., random and equal distribution of points and straight horizontal line) suggests evidence of meeting the assumption. There is some evidence in this graph to suggest heteroscedasticity.

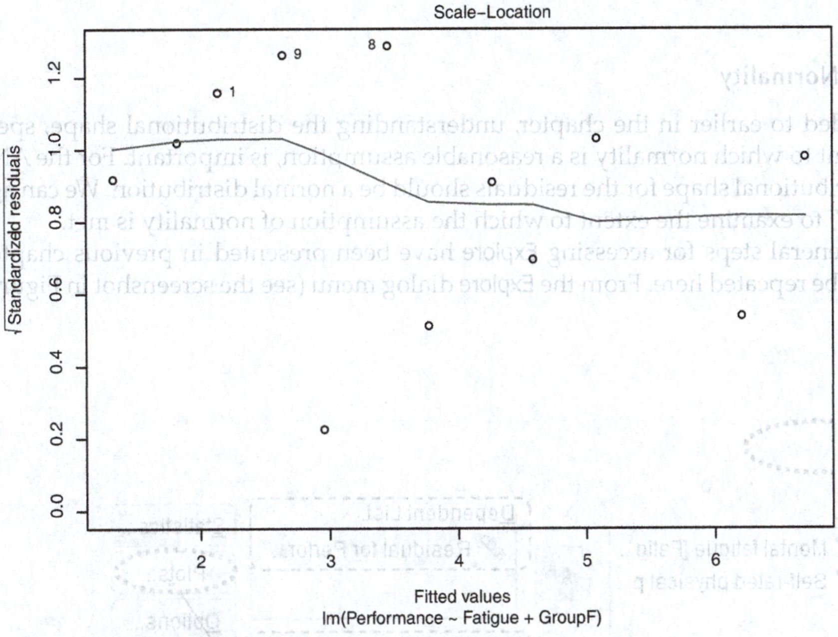

The **constant leverage plot** can be examined as evidence of normality as well to determine points that may exert influence.

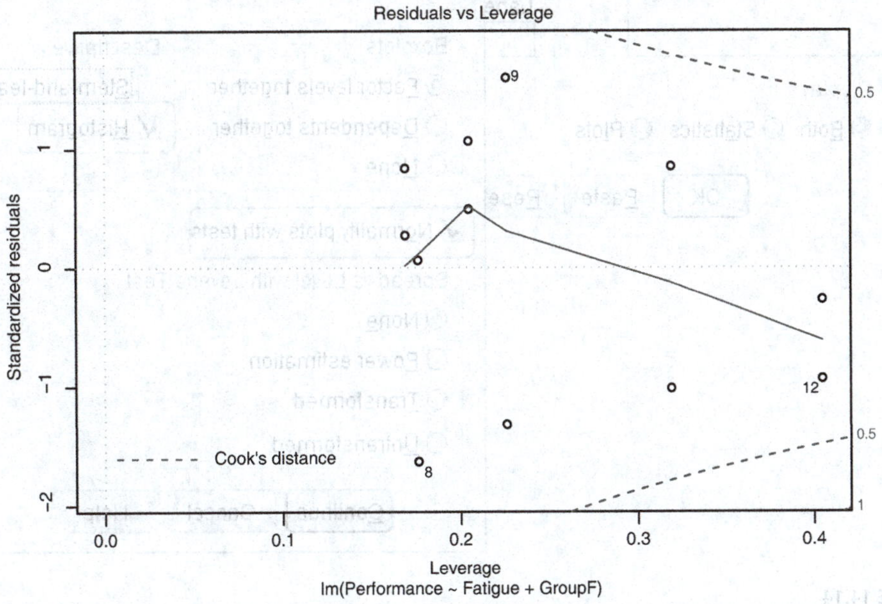

FIGURE 14.13 (continued)
Independence evidence.

14.4.2 Homogeneity of Variance

As we learned previously, another assumption to consider is that the variances of each population are equal. This is known as the assumption of **homogeneity of variance**. When generating factorial ANOVA via SPSS, we requested Levene's test (see Figure 14.5).

14.4.3 Normality

As alluded to earlier in the chapter, understanding the distributional shape, specifically the extent to which normality is a reasonable assumption, is important. For the ANCOVA, the distributional shape for the residuals should be a normal distribution. We can again use "Explore" to examine the extent to which the assumption of normality is met.

The general steps for accessing Explore have been presented in previous chapters, and will not be repeated here. From the Explore dialog menu (see the screenshot in Figure 14.14),

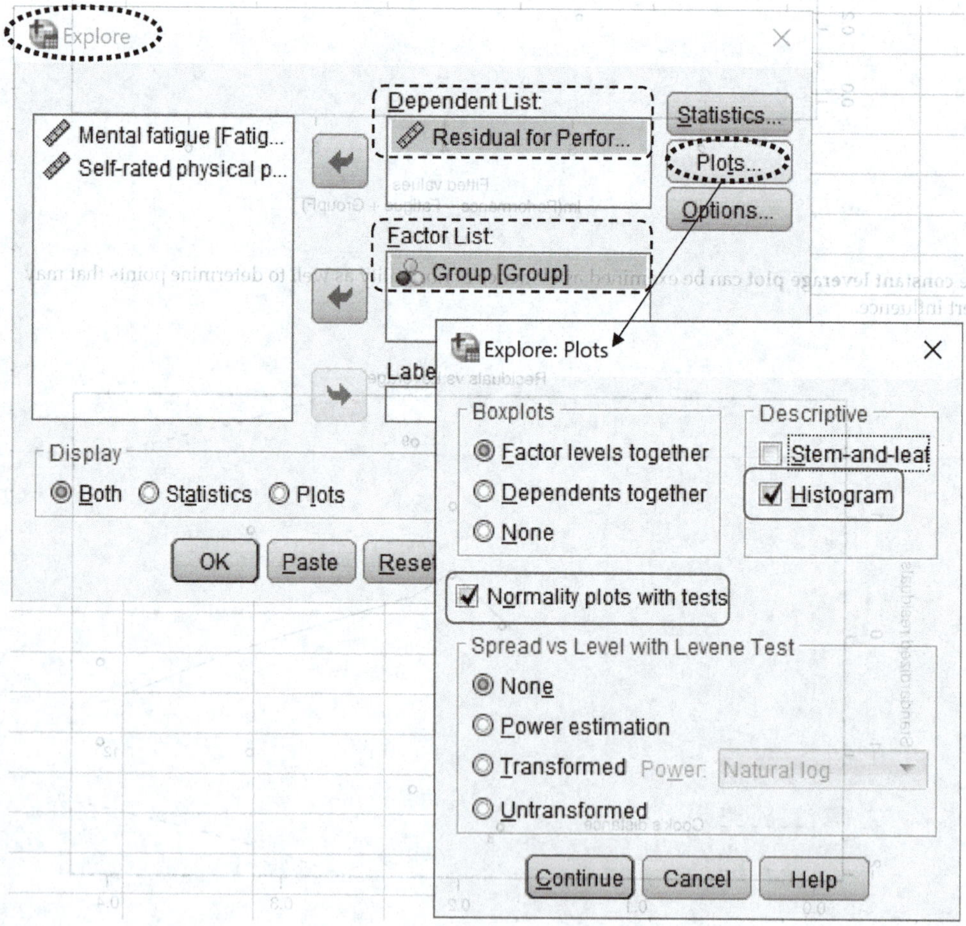

FIGURE 14.14
Generating normality evidence.

click the residual and move it into the "Dependent List" box by clicking on the arrow button. Moving the independent variable ("Group") to the "Factor List" box will generate normality by group. The procedures for selecting normality statistics include the following: click on "Plots" in the upper right corner. Place a checkmark in the boxes for "Normality plots with tests" and also for "Histogram." Then click "Continue" to return to the main Explore dialog box. Then click "OK" to generate the output.

14.4.3.1 Interpreting Normality Evidence

We have already developed a good understanding of how to interpret some forms of evidence of normality including skewness and kurtosis, histograms, and boxplots. Here we examine the output for these statistics again. The overall skewness statistic of the residuals is −.237 and kurtosis is −1.024—both are within the range of an absolute value of 2.0 and 7.0, respectively, suggesting some evidence of normality (see the "Descriptives" output in Figure 14.15). By group, skew suggests normality but there is slight non-normality based on kurtosis (treatment skew = −.076, kurtosis = −2.303; control skew = −1.296, kurtosis = 2.015).

Descriptives

			Statistic	Std. Error
Residual for Performance	Mean		.0000	.25461
	95% Confidence Interval for Mean	Lower Bound	-.5604	
		Upper Bound	.5604	
	5% Trimmed Mean		.0056	
	Median		.1357	
	Variance		.778	
	Std. Deviation		.88200	
	Minimum		-1.46	
	Maximum		1.36	
	Range		2.81	
	Interquartile Range		1.51	
	Skewness		-.237	.637
	Kurtosis		-1.024	1.232

Working in **R**, we can generate various normality statistics as well.

```
install.packages("pastecs")
```

The *install.packages* function will install the *pastecs* package which we will use to generate various forms of normality evidence.

```
library(pastecs)
```

FIGURE 14.15
Normality evidence.

The *library* function will load the *pastecs* package.

```
stat.desc(Ch14_fatigue$unstandardizedResiduals,
        norm = TRUE)
```

The *stat.desc* function will generate normality indices on the variable "unstandardizedResiduals" in the dataframe Ch14_fatigue as follows. The *norm=TRUE* command will produce Shapiro-Wilk results (*SW*), which are displayed as *normtest.W* (which is the *SW* statistic value) and *normtest.p* (which is the observed probability value).

Here, we see overall $SW = .965$ and the related $p = .854$. (by group, control $SW = .911$, $p = .4426$; treatment $SW = .902$, $p = .3832$). We see skew (−.181) and kurtosis (−.141) for the "unstandardizedResidual" variable.

Skew, kurtosis, and *SW* all indicate the assumption of normality has been met. As we know, we can divide the skew and kurtosis values by their standard errors to get a standardized value that can be used to determine if the skew and/or kurtosis is statistically different from zero. Since this output provides "2SE," we would simply divide this value by 2 to arrive at the standard error.

Note: You may have noticed that the overall skewness and kurtosis value that we've just generated differs from what we found in SPSS, which was skew = −.237 and kurtosis = −1.024. This is because there are different ways to calculate skewness and kurtosis. Let's use another package in **R** to calculate these statistics with different algorithms.

```
     nbr.val        nbr.null         nbr.na           min            max
1.200000e+01   0.000000e+00   0.000000e+00  -1.457143e+00   1.357143e+00

       range             sum         median          mean        SE.mean
2.814286e+00  -1.276756e-15   1.357143e-01  -1.064009e-16   2.546112e-01

CI.mean.0.95             var        std.dev      coef.var       skewness
5.603954e-01   7.779221e-01   8.819989e-01  -8.289394e+15  -1.813642e-01

    skew.2SE        kurtosis       kurt.2SE    normtest.W     normtest.p
-1.422906e-01  -1.408656e+00  -5.715804e-01   9.651737e-01   8.543019e-01
```

```
install.packages("e1071")
```

The *install.packages* function will install the **e1071** package which we will use to generate skewness and kurtosis.

```
library(e1071)
```

The *library* function will load the **e1071** package.

```
skewness(Ch14_fatigue$unstandardizedResiduals, type=3)
skewness(Ch14_fatigue$unstandardizedResiduals, type=2)
skewness(Ch14_fatigue$unstandardizedResiduals, type=1)
```

The *skewness* function will generate skewness statistics on the variable(s) specified. The "type=" script defines how skewness is calculated. Specifying "type=2" will use the algorithm that is used by SPSS. Readers interested in learning more, including the algorithms for each of the three methods, are encouraged to review Joanes and Gill (1998). We see that using type=2, our skew is −.237, the same value as generated using SPSS.

```
# skewness(Ch14_fatigue$unstandardizedResiduals, type=3)
[1] -0.1813642
```

FIGURE 14.15 (continued)
Normality evidence.

```
#skewness(Ch14_fatigue$unstandardizedResiduals, type=2)
[1]   -0.2374222
```

```
# skewness(Ch14_fatigue$unstandardizedResiduals, type=1)
[1] -0.2066495
```

```
kurtosis(Ch14_fatigue$unstandardizedResiduals, type=3)
kurtosis(Ch14_fatigue$unstandardizedResiduals, type=2)
kurtosis(Ch14_fatigue$unstandardizedResiduals, type=1)
```

The *kurtosis* function will generate kurtosis statistics on the variable(s) we specify. The "type=" script defines how kurtosis is calculated. Specifying "type=2" will use the algorithm that is used by SPSS. Readers interested in learning more, including the algorithms for each of the three methods, are encouraged to review Joanes and Gill (1998). We see that using type=2 our kurtosis is −1.024, the same value as generated using SPSS.

```
# kurtosis(Ch14_fatigue$unstandardizedResiduals, type=3)
[1] -1.408656
```

```
# kurtosis(Ch14_fatigue$unstandardizedResiduals, type=2)
1]   -1.024246
```

```
# kurtosis(Ch14_fatigue$unstandardizedResiduals, type=1)
[1] -1.106169
```

```
shapiro.test(Ch14_fatigue$unstandardizedResiduals)
```

Had we wanted to generate only the Shapiro-Wilk test, the shapiro.test function could be used.

```
        Shapiro-Wilk normality test

data:  Ch14_fatigue$unstandardizedResiduals
W = 0.96517, p-value = 0.8543
```

Working in **R**, another way to test for normality is D'Agostino's test for skewness and the Bonett-Seier test for Geary's kurtosis.

```
install.packages("moments")
library(moments)
```

To conduct D'Agostino's test, we first have to install the *moments* package and then load it into our library. The null hypothesis for this test is that skewness equals zero. Thus, a statistically significant D'Agostino's test would indicate that there is statistically significant skewness.

```
agostino.test(Ch14_fatigue$unstandardizedResiduals)
```

The function *agostino.test* is generated using the variable "unstandardizedResiduals" from our Ch14_fatigue dataframe. The results suggest evidence of normality as $p = .6967$, greater than alpha.

```
        D'Agostino skewness test

data: Ch14_fatigue$unstandardizedResiduals
skew = -0.20665, z = -0.38974, p-value = 0.6967
alternative hypothesis: data have a skewness
```

FIGURE 14.15 (continued)
Normality evidence.

```
agostino.test(Ch14_fatigue$unstandardizedResiduals[Ch14_fatigue$Group==1])
agostino.test(Ch14_fatigue$unstandardizedResiduals[Ch14_fatigue$Group==2])
```

This test can also be generated by group of the independent variable. Given the small sample size by group in this illustration, however, results are not available.

```
bonett.test((Ch14_fatigue$unstandardizedResiduals))
```

The *bonett.test* function, generated using the variable "unstandardizedResiduals" from our Ch14_fatigue dataframe, performs the Bonett-Seier test for Geary's kurtosis for data that are normally distributed. The null hypothesis states that data should have a Geary's kurtosis value equal to $\sqrt{2/\pi} = .7979$. The results suggest evidence of normality as $p = .293$, greater than alpha.

```
        Bonett-Seier test for Geary kurtosis

data: (Ch14_fatigue$unstandardizedResiduals)
tau = 0.72619, z = -1.05160, p-value = 0.293
alternative hypothesis: kurtosis is not equal to sqrt(2/pi)
```

```
bonett.test((Ch14_fatigue$unstandardizedResiduals[Ch14_fatigue$Group==1]))
bonett.test((Ch14_fatigue$unstandardizedResiduals[Ch14_fatigue$Group==2]))
```

This test can also be generated by group of the independent variable. By group, the results for the Bonett-Seier test for Geary's kurtosis for data that is normally distributed provide evidence of normality by group with both p's > .05.

```
# bonett.test((Ch14_fatigue$unstandardizedResiduals[Ch14_fatigue$Group==1]))

        Bonett-Seier test for Geary kurtosis

data: (Ch14_fatigue$unstandardizedResiduals[Ch14_fatigue$Group == 1])
tau = 0.45238, z = 0.26847, p-value = 0.7883
alternative hypothesis: kurtosis is not equal to sqrt(2/pi)

# bonett.test((Ch14_fatigue$unstandardizedResiduals[Ch14_fatigue$Group==2]))

        Bonett-Seier test for Geary kurtosis

data: (Ch14_fatigue$unstandardizedResiduals[Ch14_fatigue$Group == 2])
tau = 1.0000, z = -1.9487, p-value = 0.05133
alternative hypothesis: kurtosis is not equal to sqrt(2/pi)
```

FIGURE 14.15 (continued)
Normality evidence.

The histogram of residuals, overall and by group (not presented here), is not what most would consider normal in shape, and this is largely an artifact of the small sample size. Because of this, we will rely more heavily on the other forms of normality evidence.

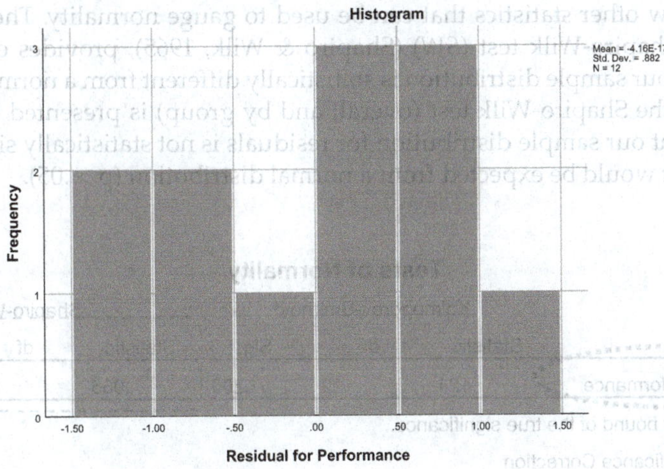

Working in **R**, we can generate a histogram using the *ggplot2* package.

```
install.packages("ggplot2")
```

The *install.packages* function will install the *ggplot2* package which we can use to create various graphs and plots. If you have already installed *ggplot2* previously, there is no need to run this script again.

```
library(ggplot2)
```

The library function will load the ggplot2 package.

```
qplot(Ch14_fatigue$unstandardizedResiduals,
      geom="histogram",
      binwidth=.5,
      main = "Histogram of Unstandardized Residuals",
      xlab = "Unstandardized Residual", ylab = "Count",
      fill=I("gray"),
      col=I("white"))
```

Using the *qplot* function, we create a histogram (i.e., geom = "histogram") from our dataframe (i.e., Ch14_fatigue) using the variable "unstandardizedResiduals." We can add a few commands to change the width of the bars (i.e., *binwidth* = .5), color of the bars (i.e., *fill=I("gray")*), and outline of the bars (i.e., *col=I("white")*). We can also add a title (i.e., *main = "Histogram of Unstandardized Residuals"*) and change the *X* and *Y* axes (*xlab = "Unstandardized Residual", ylab = "Count"*).

```
hist(Ch14_fatigue$unstandardizedResiduals[Ch14_fatigue$Group==1],
     main="Histogram for Control",
     xlab="Unstandardized Residuals")
```

```
hist(Ch14_fatigue$unstandardizedResiduals[Ch14_fatigue$Group==2],
     main="Histogram for Control",
     xlab="Unstandardized Residuals")
```

Histograms by group can be created with these scripts, each one specifying one category of Group as the variable with which to create the histogram of unstandardized residuals.

FIGURE 14.16
Histogram.

There are a few other statistics that can be used to gauge normality. The formal test of normality, the Shapiro-Wilk test (*SW*) (Shapiro & Wilk, 1965), provides evidence of the extent to which our sample distribution is statistically different from a normal distribution. The output for the Shapiro-Wilk test (overall and by group) is presented in Figure 14.17 and suggests that our sample distribution for residuals is not statistically significantly different than what would be expected from a normal distribution ($p > .05$).

Tests of Normality

	Kolmogorov-Smirnov[a]			Shapiro-Wilk		
	Statistic	df	Sig.	Statistic	df	Sig.
Residual for Performance	.124	12	.200*	.965	12	.854

*. This is a lower bound of the true significance.

a. Lilliefors Significance Correction

```
shapiro.test(Ch14_fatigue$unstandardizedResiduals)
```

Working in **R**, had we wanted to generate only the Shapiro-Wilk test, the *shapiro.test* function could be used.

```
        Shapiro-Wilk normality test

data:  Ch14_fatigue$unstandardizedResiduals
W = 0.96517, p-value = 0.8543
```

```
tapply(Ch14_fatigue$unstandardizedResiduals,
       Ch14_fatigue$GroupF, shapiro.test)
```

To generate the Shapiro-Wilk test by group, the *tapply* function can be used to apply the *shapiro.test* to the unstandardized residuals for all levels of the independent variable.

```
$control

        Shapiro-Wilk normality test
data:  X[[i]]
W = 0.91093, p-value = 0.4426

$treatment

        Shapiro-Wilk normality test
data:  X[[i]]
W = 0.90156, p-value = 0.3832
```

FIGURE 14.17
Shapiro-Wilk test of normality.

Quantile-quantile (Q-Q) plots are also often examined to determine evidence of normality. Q-Q plots are graphs that plot quantiles of the theoretical normal distribution against quantiles of the sample distribution. Points that fall on or close to the diagonal line suggest evidence of normality. The Q-Q plot of residuals shown below suggests relative normality.

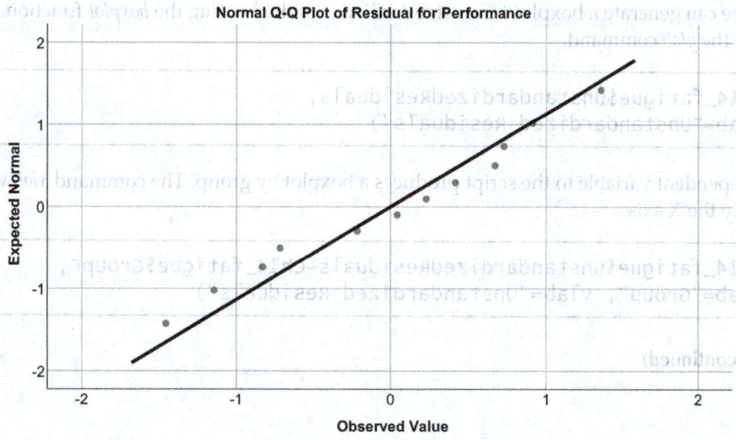

Working in **R**, we can use the *qplot* function to create a Q-Q plot of unstandardized residuals. The "data=" script defines the dataframe as "Ch14_fatigue."

```
qplot(sample=unstandardizedResiduals,
      data = Ch14_fatigue)
```

```
qqnorm(Ch14_fatigue$unstandardizedResiduals[Ch14_fatigue$Group==1],
       main='control')

qqnorm(Ch14_fatigue$unstandardizedResiduals[Ch14_fatigue$Group==2],
       main='treatment')
```

By group, QQ plots can be created with this script, with each command defining one category of the *Group* variable.

FIGURE 14.18
Normal Q-Q plot

Examination of the boxplot by group in Figure 14.19 suggests a relatively normal distributional shape of residuals and no outliers for both groups.

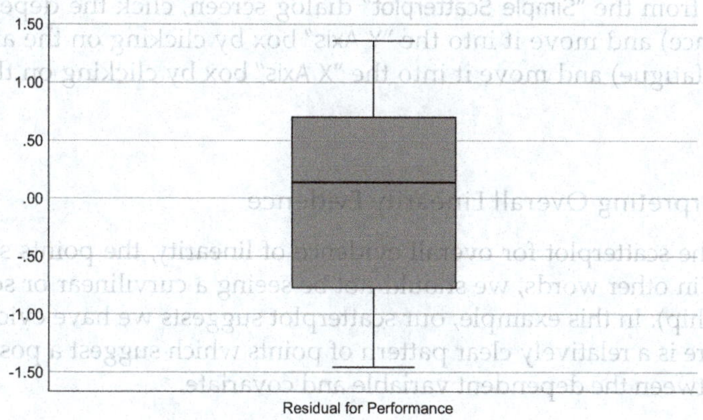

FIGURE 14.19
Boxplot.

Working in **R**, we can generate a boxplot for unstandardized residuals using the *boxplot* function. To label the *Y* axis, we include the *ylab* command.

```
boxplot(Ch14_fatigue$unstandardizedResiduals,
        ylab="Unstandardized Residuals")
```

Adding the independent variable to the script produces a boxplot by group. The command *xlab* will print Group to identify the *X* axis.

```
boxplot(Ch14_fatigue$unstandardizedResiduals~Ch14_fatigue$GroupF,
        xlab="Group", ylab="Unstandardized Residuals")
```

FIGURE 14.19 (continued)
Boxplot.

Considering the forms of evidence we have examined, skewness and kurtosis statistics, histogram, the Shapiro-Wilk test, the Q-Q plot, and the boxplot, all suggest normality is a reasonable assumption. We can be reasonably assured we have met the assumption of normality of the dependent variable for each group of the independent variable.

14.4.4 Linearity

Recall that the assumption of linearity means that the regression of the dependent variable (i.e., "physical performance" in this illustration) on the covariate (i.e., "mental fatigue") is linear. Evidence of the extent to which this assumption is met can be done by examining scatterplots of the dependent variable versus the covariate—both overall and also for each category or group of the independent variable.

14.4.4.1 Overall Linearity Evidence

The general steps for generating a simple scatterplot through "Scatter/dot" have been presented in Chapter 10, and they will not be reiterated here. To generate the overall scatterplot, from the "Simple Scatterplot" dialog screen, click the dependent variable (i.e., performance) and move it into the "Y Axis" box by clicking on the arrow. Click the covariate (i.e., fatigue) and move it into the "X Axis" box by clicking on the arrow. Then click "OK."

14.4.4.1.1 Interpreting Overall Linearity Evidence

In examining the scatterplot for overall evidence of linearity, the points should fall relatively linearly (in other words, we should not be seeing a curvilinear or some other nonlinear relationship). In this example, our scatterplot suggests we have evidence of overall linearity as there is a relatively clear pattern of points which suggest a positive and linear relationship between the dependent variable and covariate.

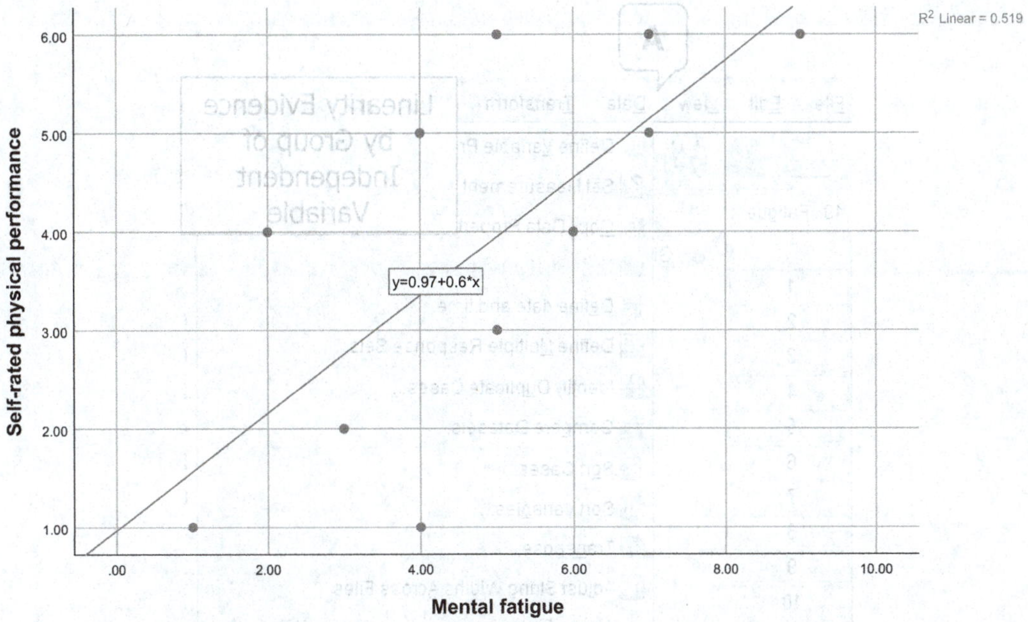

Working in **R**, we can generate a similar scatterplot.

```
plot(Ch14_fatigue$Fatigue,
     Ch14_fatigue$Performance,
     xlab = "Fatigue",
     ylab = "Performance",
     main = "Scatterplot for Independence")
```

Using the *plot* function, with the first variable listed displaying on the *X* axis (e.g., "Ch14_fatigue$Fatigue"), and the second variable displaying on the *Y* axis (i.e., "Ch14_fatigue$Performance"). Additional commands are provided to label the axes (*xlab* and *ylab*) and title the graph (*main*).

FIGURE 14.20
Scatterplot.

14.4.4.2 Linearity Evidence by Group

To generate the scatterplot of the dependent variable and covariate for each group of the independent variable, we must first split the data file. To do this, go to "Data" in the top pulldown menu. Then select "Split File."

From the Split File dialog screen, select the radio button for "Organize output by groups," and then click the independent variable and move it into the "Groups Based on" box by clicking on the arrow. Then click "OK."

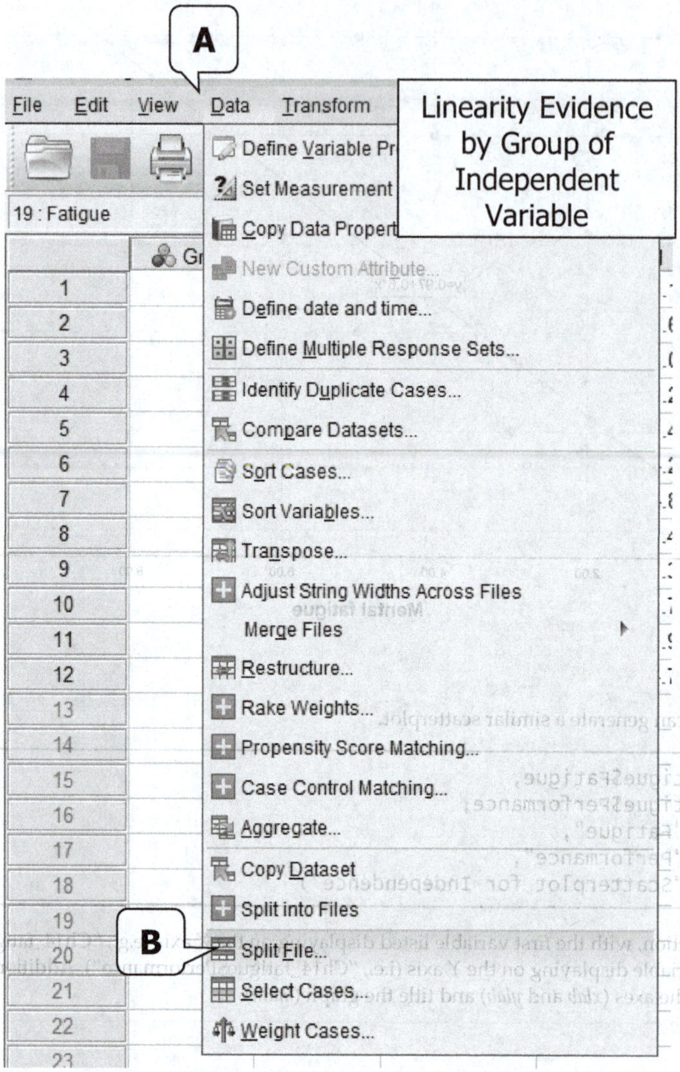

FIGURE 14.21
Linearity by group of independent variable.

After splitting the file, the next step is to generate the scatterplot of the dependent variable by covariate. Because we have split the file, there will be two scatterplots generated: one for the treatment (i.e., ingestion of caffeinated beverage) and one for the control (i.e., ingestion of decaffeinated beverage). Because we have just generated the overall scatterplot, the selections made previously will remain, and thus from the "Simple Scatterplot" dialog screen, simply click "OK" to generate the output.

14.4.4.2.1 Interpreting Evidence of Linearity Evidence by Group

In examining the scatterplot for evidence of linearity by group of the independent variable, our interpretation should remain the same: the points should fall relatively linearly

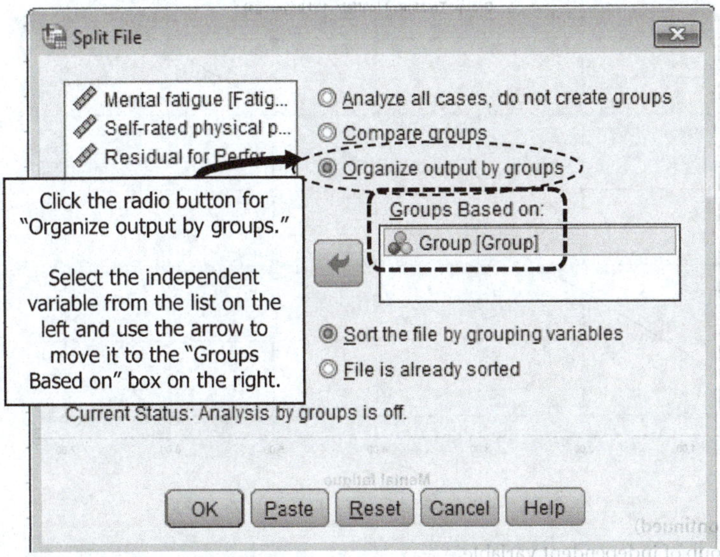

FIGURE 14.22
Split file.

(in other words, we should not see a curvilinear or some other nonlinear relationship). In this example, our scatterplots suggest we have evidence of linearity by group of the independent variable as there is a relatively clear pattern of points which suggest a positive and linear relationship between the dependent variable and covariate for each group of the independent variable.

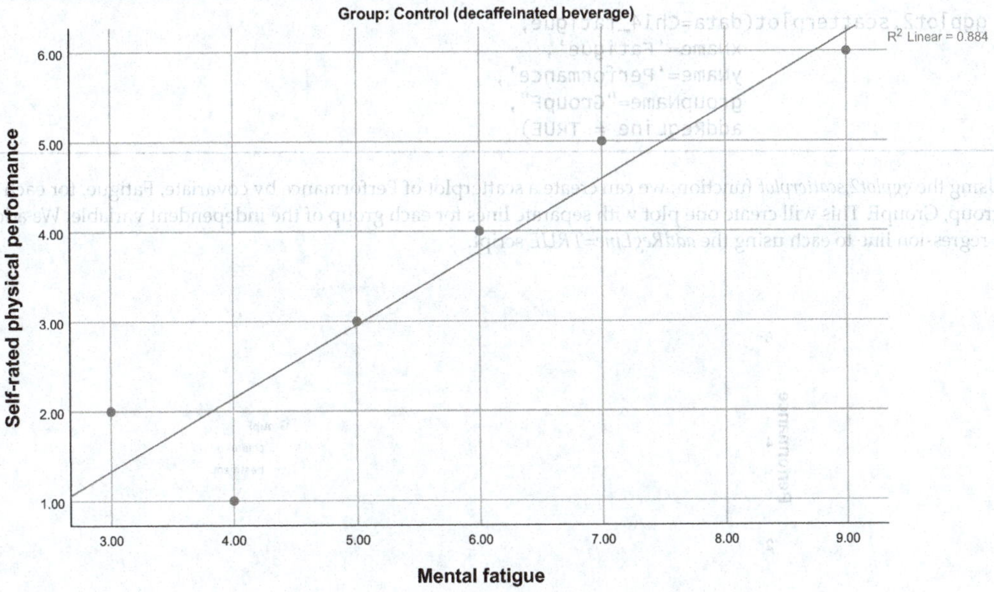

FIGURE 14.23
Scatterplot by group of independent variable.

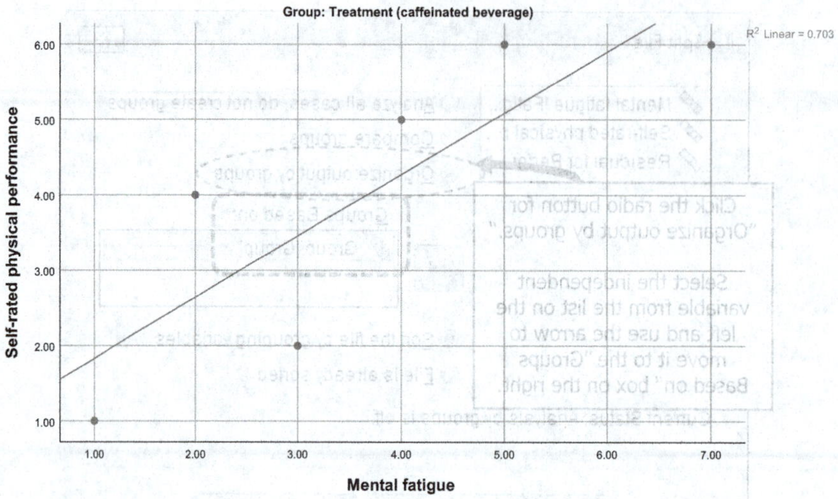

FIGURE 14.23 (continued)
Scatterplot by group of independent variable.

Working in **R**, we create a similar plot.

```
Install.package("devtools")
library(devtools)
install_github("easyGgplot2", "kassambara")
library(easyGgplot2)
```

For this plot, we will use the *easyGgplot2* package. To use this package, we need devtools installed and loaded in our library and will use the *install_github* function to install *easyGgplot2* and kassambara directly from GitHub. We then load *easyGgplot2* in our library.

```
ggplot2.scatterplot(data=Ch14_fatigue,
                    xName='Fatigue',
                    yName='Performance',
                    groupName="GroupF",
                    addRegLine = TRUE)
```

Using the *ggplot2.scatterplot* function, we can create a scatterplot of Performance by covariate, Fatigue, for each group, GroupF. This will create one plot with separate lines for each group of the independent variable. We add a regression line to each using the *addRegLine=TRUE* script.

FIGURE 14.24
Scatterplot by group of independent variable.

14.4.5 Independence of Covariate and Independent Variable

Recall the assumption of independence of the covariate and independent variable. In other words, the levels of the independent variable should not differ on the covariate. If subjects have been randomly assigned to conditions (in other words, the different levels of the independent variable), the assumption of independence of the covariate and independent variable has likely been met. In this illustration, athletes were randomly assigned to treatment group (i.e., ingestion of caffeinated or decaffeinated beverage), and thus the assumption of independence of the covariate and independent variable was likely met. As we have learned in previous chapters, however, we often use independent variables that do not allow random assignment. Evidence of the extent to which this assumption is met can be done by examining mean differences on the covariate based on the independent variable. If the independent variable has only two levels, an independent *t* test would be appropriate. If the independent variable has more than two categories, a one-way ANOVA would suffice. If the groups are not statistically different on the covariate, then that lends evidence that the assumption of independence of the covariate and the independent variable has been met.

We have two levels of our independent variable, thus we will generate an independent *t* test. The general steps for generating an independent *t* test have been presented in Chapter 8, and they will not be reiterated here. From the "Independent Samples *T* Test" dialog screen, click the covariate (e.g., mental fatigue) and move it into the "Test Variable(s)" box by clicking on the arrow. Click the independent variable (e.g., treatment group) and move it into the "Grouping Variable" box by clicking on the arrow. Click the "Define Groups" box and enter "1" for "Group 1" and '2' for "Group 2." Then click "Continue" to return to the main the "Independent Samples *T* Test" dialog screen and click on "OK" to generate the output.

14.4.5.1 Interpreting Evidence of Independence of Covariate and Independent Variable

In examining the independent *t* test results, evidence of independence of the covariate and independent variable is provided when the test results are *not* statistically significant. In this example, our results suggest we have evidence of independence of the covariate and independent variable as the results are *not* statistically significant, $t(10)$, = 1.604, p = .140. Thus, we have likely met this assumption through random assignment of cases to groups, and this provides further confirmation that we have not violated the assumption of independence of the covariate and independent variable.

Independent Samples Test

		Levene's Test for Equality of Variances		t-test for Equality of Means						
									95% Confidence Interval of the Difference	
		F	Sig.	t	df	Sig. (2-tailed)	Mean Difference	Std. Error Difference	Lower	Upper
Mental fatigue	Equal variances assumed	.000	1.000	1.604	10	.140	2.00000	1.24722	-.77898	4.77898
	Equal variances not assumed			1.604	10.000	.140	2.00000	1.24722	-.77898	4.77898

FIGURE 14.25
Independent *t* test results.

Working in **R**, we can compute a *t* test when we have two groups or an ANOVA if there are more than two groups. For illustrative purposes, we'll run an ANOVA.

```
Ch14_independence <- aov(Ch14_fatigue$Fatigue ~ Ch14_fatigue$GroupF)
```

The *aov* function will generate the ANOVA model with *Fatigue* as the dependent variable and *GroupF* as the independent variable. We are using data from the *Ch14_fatigue* dataframe, and we are calling this object "Ch14_independence." Recall that in a two-group situation, $F = t^2$ or $\sqrt{F} = t$. Thus, $\sqrt{F} = \sqrt{2.571} = t$, we find $t = 1.603$, which is roughly equivalent (likely due to rounding) that we found using SPSS.

```
                    Df Sum Sq Mean Sq F value Pr(>F)
Ch14_fatigue$GroupF  1  12.00  12.000   2.571   0.14
Residuals           10  46.67   4.667
```

FIGURE 14.25 (continued)
Independent *t* test results.

14.4.6 Homogeneity of Regression Slopes

Step 1. In order the test the homogeneity of slopes assumption, you will need to rerun the ANCOVA analysis. Keep every screen the same as before, *with one exception*. Return to the main Univariate dialog box (see Step 2) and click on "Model." From the Model dialog box, click on the "Build terms" radio button to build a custom model to include the interaction between the independent and covariate variables. To do this, under the "Build Term(s)" pulldown in the middle of the dialog box, select "Main effects."

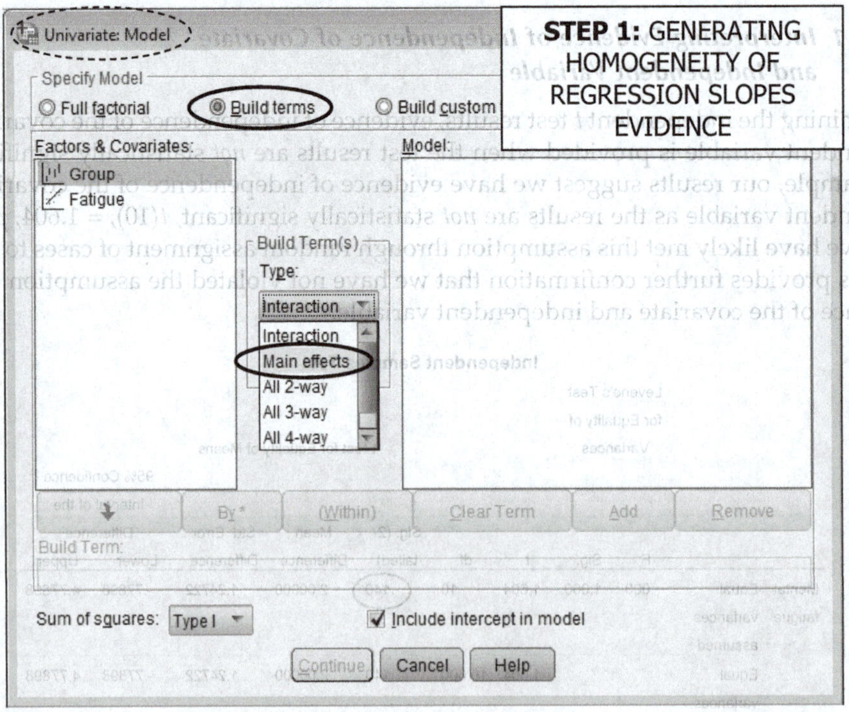

FIGURE 14.26
Homogeneity of regression slopes: Step 1.

Step 2. Click the independent variable and move it into the Model box by clicking on the arrow button. Next, click the covariate and move it into the Model box by clicking on the arrow button. This will place "Group" and "Fatigue" in the Model box on the right of the screen.

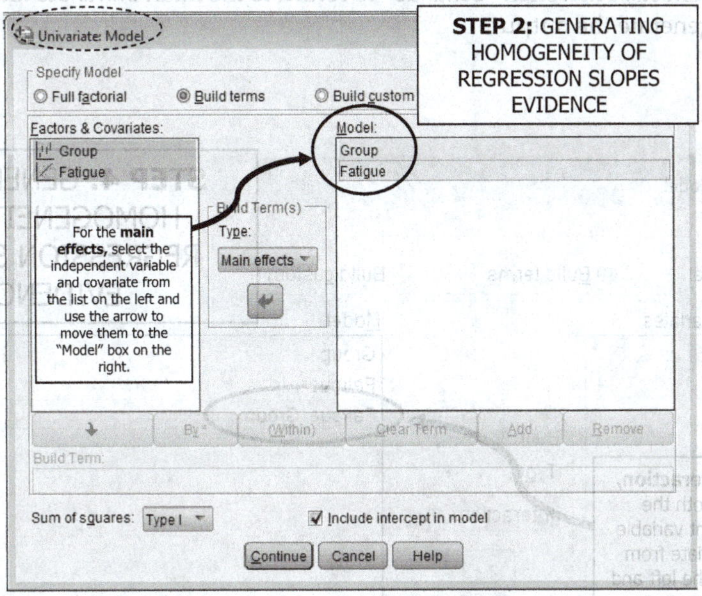

FIGURE 14.27
Homogeneity of regression slopes: Step 2.

Step 3. Then, from the Build Term(s) pulldown menu, select "Interaction."

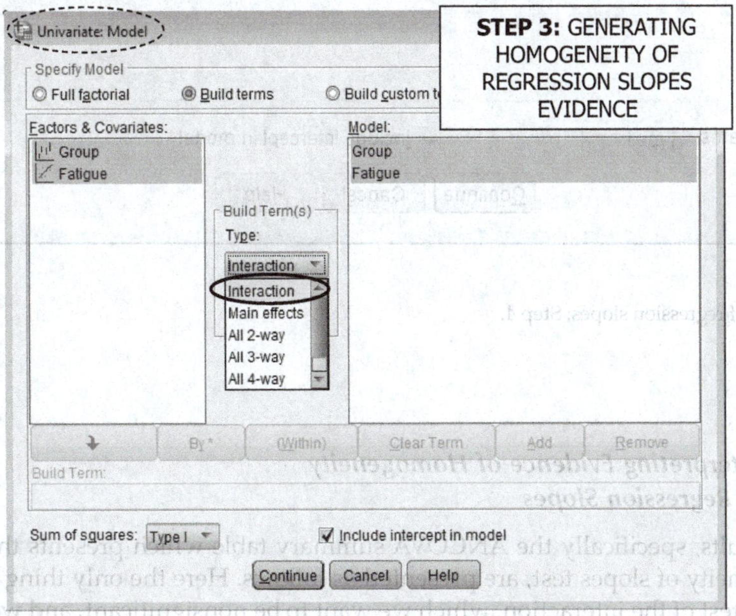

FIGURE 14.28
Homogeneity of regression slopes: Step 3.

Step 4. From the left "Factors & Covariates" box, click both variables at the same time (e.g., using the shift key) and use the arrow key to move the interaction of Fatigue*Group into the Model box on the right. There should now be *three terms* in the Model box: the interaction and two main effects. Then click "Continue" to return to the main Univariate dialog box. Then click "OK" to generate the output.

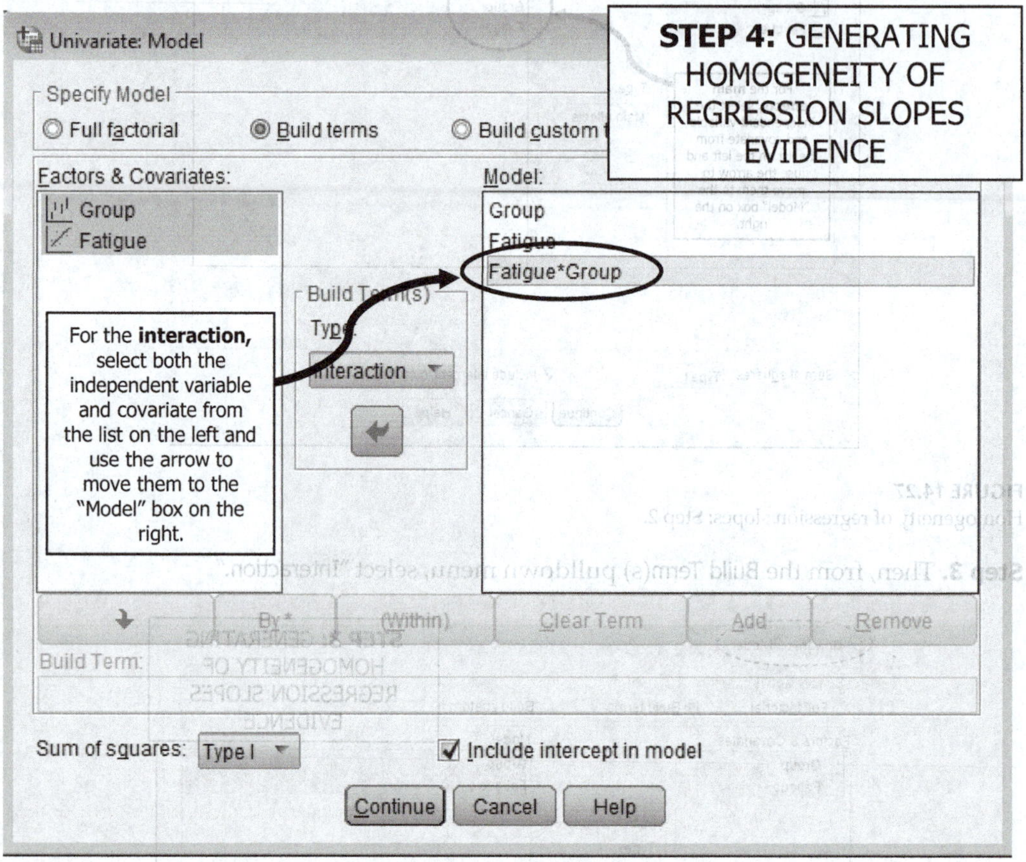

FIGURE 14.29
Homogeneity of regression slopes: Step 4.

14.4.6.1 *Interpreting Evidence of Homogeneity of Regression Slopes*

Selected results, specifically the ANCOVA summary table which presents the results for the homogeneity of slopes test, are presented as follows. Here the only thing that we care about is the test of the interaction, which we want to be nonsignificant, and we find this to be the case: F (1, 8) = .000, p = 1.000. This indicates that we have met the homogeneity of regression slopes assumption.

Tests of Between-Subjects Effects

Dependent Variable: Self-rated physical performance

Source	Type I Sum of Squares	df	Mean Square	F	Sig.	Partial Eta Squared	Noncent. Parameter	Observed Power[b]
Corrected Model	31.693[a]	3	10.564	9.876	.005	.787	29.629	.955
Intercept	168.750	1	168.750	157.763	.000	.952	157.763	1.000
Group	.750	1	.750	.701	.427	.081	.701	.115
Fatigue	30.943	1	30.943	28.928	.001	.783	28.928	.997
Group * Fatigue	.000	1	.000	.000	1.000	.000	.000	.050
Error	8.557	8	1.070					
Total	209.000	12						
Corrected Total	40.250	11						

a. R Squared = .787 (Adjusted R Squared = .708)

b. Computed using alpha = .05

Working in **R**, we can examine homogeneity of regression slopes by building in an interaction term in the model.

```
HRS <- aov(Performance ~ Fatigue + GroupF + Fatigue:GroupF,
        data=Ch14_fatigue)
```

We use the *aov* function to generate our model, which takes the form of *dependent variable ~ covariate + independent variable + covariate:independent variable interaction*. We name this function *HRS* (i.e., homogeneity of regression slopes).

```
Anova(HRS, type="II")
```

We use the *Anova* function on our object, defining Type II sum of squares as *type = "II"*.

```
Anova Table (Type II tests)

Response: Performance
               Sum Sq  Df F  value    Pr(>F)
Fatigue        30.9429  1   28.928  0.0006628 ***
GroupF         10.8122  1   10.108  0.0130104 *
Fatigue:GroupF  0.0000  1    0.000  1.0000000
Residuals       8.5571  8
---
Signif. codes: 0 '***' 0.001 '**' 0.01 '*' 0.05 '.' 0.1 ' ' 1
```

FIGURE 14.30
Homogeneity of regression slopes evidence.

14.5 Power Using G*Power

Generating power analysis for ANCOVA models follows similarly to that for ANOVA and factorial ANOVA. In particular, if there is more than one independent variable, we must test for main effects and interactions separately. Because we have only one independent variable for our ANCOVA model, our illustration assumes only one main effect. If there were additional independent variables and/or interactions, we would have followed these steps for those as well.

14.5.1 Post Hoc Power for ANCOVA Using G*Power

The first thing that must be done when using G*Power for computing post hoc power is to select the correct test family. In our case, we conducted an ANCOVA. To find ANCOVA, we will select "Tests" in the top pulldown menu, then "Means," and then "Many groups: ANCOVA: Main effects and interactions." Once that selection is made, the "Test family" automatically changes to "F tests."

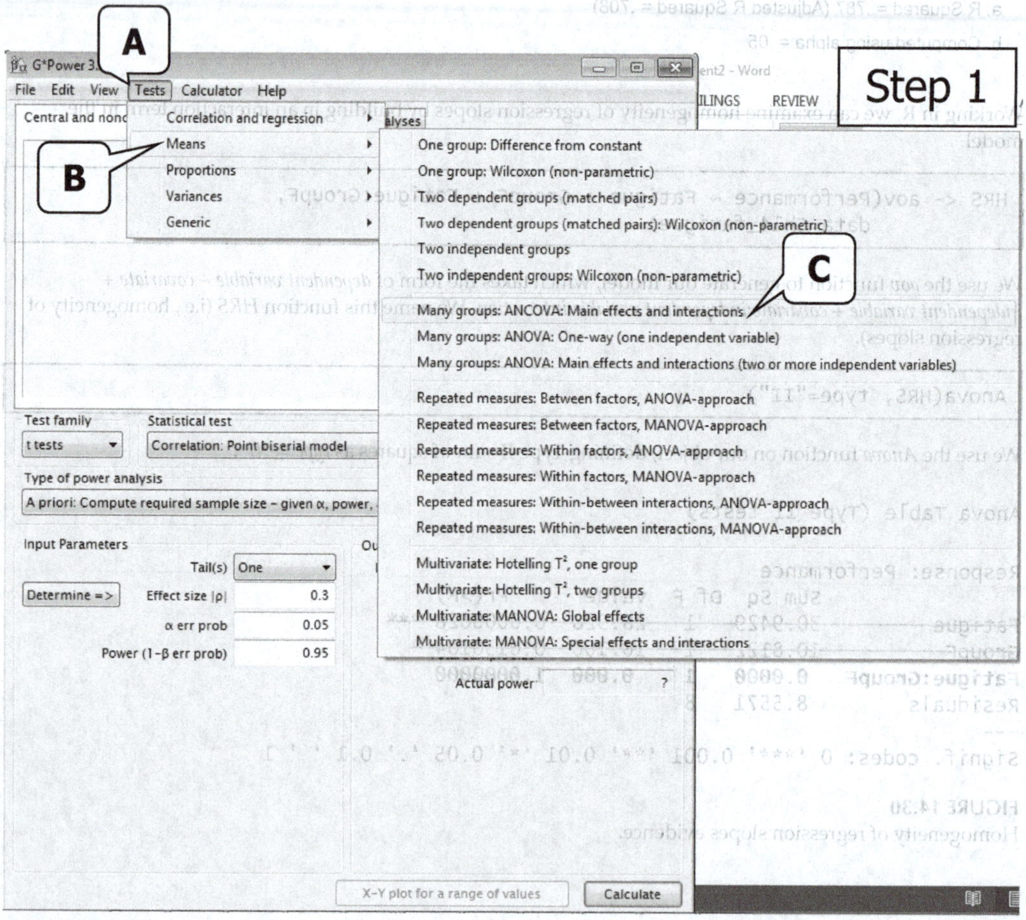

FIGURE 14.31
Power: Step 1.

The "Type of power analysis" desired then needs to be selected. To compute post hoc power, we need to select "Post hoc: Compute achieved power—given α, sample size, and effect size."

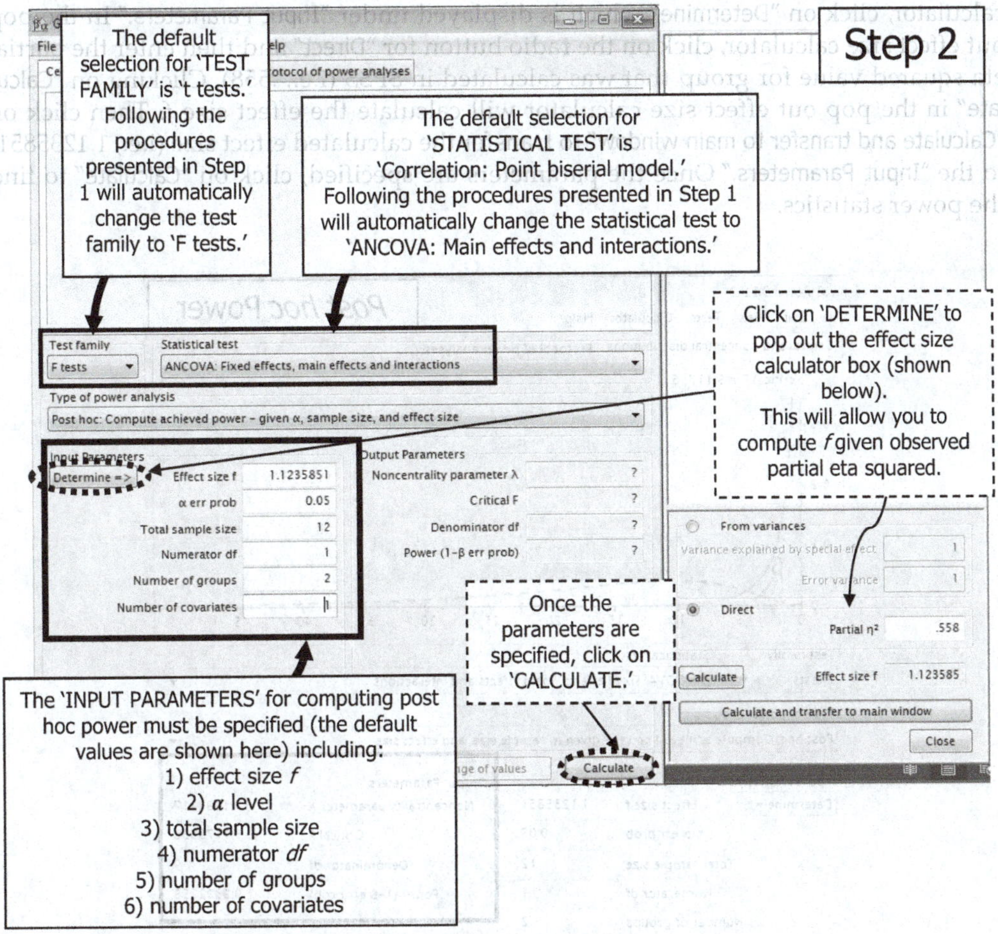

FIGURE 14.32
Power: Step 2.

The "Input Parameters" must then be specified. We will compute the effect size *f* last so we skip that for the moment. In our example, the alpha level we used was .05 and the total sample size was 12. The *numerator degrees of freedom* for group (our independent variable) is equal to the number of categories of this variable (i.e., 2) minus 1; thus there is one degree of freedom for the numerator. The *number of groups* equals, in the case of an ANCOVA with multiple independent variables, the product of the number of levels or categories of the independent variables or $(J)(K)$. In this example, we have only one independent variable. Thus the number of groups when there is only one independent variable is equal to the number of categories of this independent variable (i.e., 2). The last parameter that must be inputted is the number of covariates. In this example, we have only one covariate; thus we enter 1 in this box.

We skipped filling in the first parameter, the effect size *f*, for a reason. SPSS provides only a partial eta squared measure of effect size. Thus we will use the pop out effect size calculator in G*Power to compute the effect size *f* (we saved this parameter for last as the calculation is based on the previous values just entered). To pop out the effect size calculator, click on "Determine" which is displayed under "Input Parameters." In the pop out effect size calculator, click on the radio button for "Direct" and then enter the partial eta squared value for group that was calculated in SPSS (i.e., .558). Clicking on "Calculate" in the pop out effect size calculator will calculate the effect size *f*. Then click on "Calculate and transfer to main window" to transfer the calculated effect size (i.e., 1.1235851) to the "Input Parameters." Once the parameters are specified, click on "Calculate" to find the power statistics.

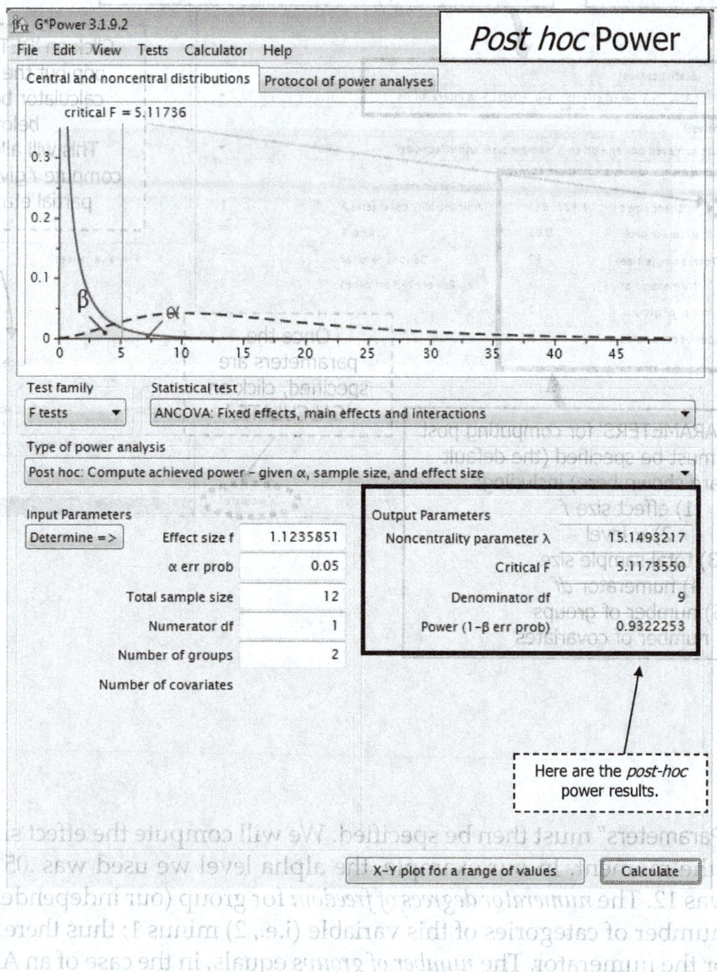

FIGURE 14.33
Post hoc power.

The "Output Parameters" provide the relevant statistics given the input just specified. In this example, we were interested in determining post hoc power for an ANCOVA with a computed effect size *f* of 1.1235851, an alpha level of .05, total sample size of 12, numerator degrees of freedom of one, two groups, and one covariate.

Based on those criteria, the post hoc power for the main effect of treatment group (i.e., our only independent variable) was .93. In other words, with an ANCOVA, computed effect size *f* of 1.124, alpha level of .05, total sample size of 12, numerator degrees of freedom of one, two groups, and one covariate, the post hoc power of our main effect for this test was .93—the probability of rejecting the null hypothesis when it is really false (in this case, the probability that the adjusted means of the dependent variable would be equal for each level of the independent variable, controlling for the covariate) was about 93%, which would be considered more than sufficient power (sufficient power is often .80 or above). Note that this value differs slightly than that reported in SPSS. Keep in mind that conducting power analysis *a priori* is recommended so that you avoid a situation where, post hoc, you find that the sample size was not sufficient to reach the desired level of power (given the observed parameters).

14.5.2 *A Priori* Power for ANCOVA Using G*Power

For *a priori* power, we can determine the total sample size needed for the main effects and/or interactions given an estimated effect size *f*, alpha level, desired power, numerator degrees of freedom (i.e., number of categories of our independent variable and/or interaction, depending on which *a priori* power we are interested in and depending on the number of independent variables), number of groups (i.e., the number of categories of the independent variable *in the case of only one independent variable* OR the product of the number of levels of the independent variables *in the case of multiple independent variables*), and the number of covariates. We follow Cohen's (1988) conventions for effect size (i.e.,

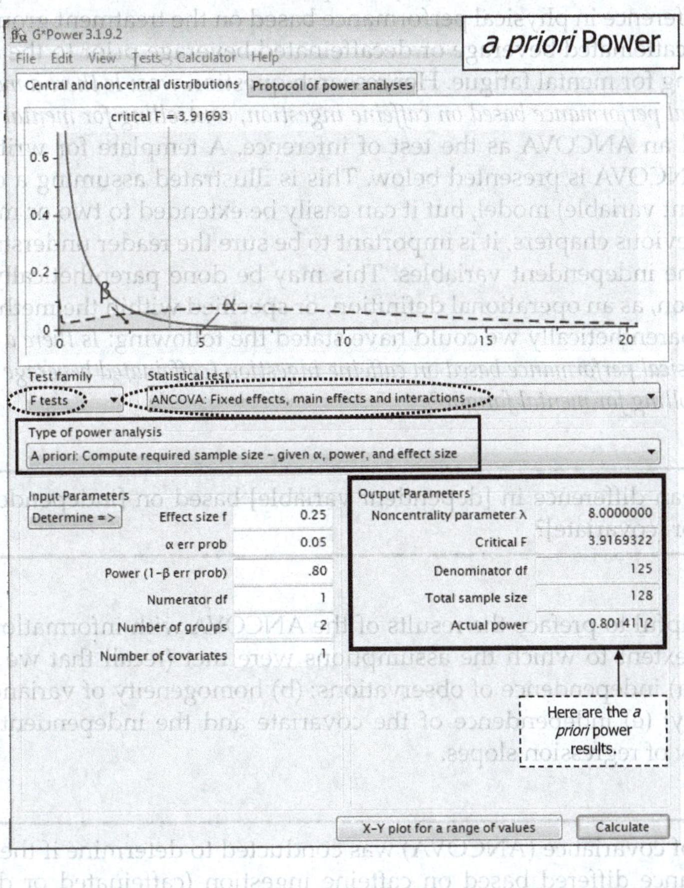

FIGURE 14.34
A priori power

small $f = .10$; moderate $f = .25$; large $f = .40$). In this example, had we estimated a moderate effect f of .25, alpha of .05, desired power of .80, numerator degrees of freedom of one (two categories in our independent variable, thus $2 - 1 = 1$), number of groups of two (i.e., there is only one independent variable and there were two categories), and one covariate, we would need a total sample size of 128.

14.6 Research Question Template and Example Write-Up

Finally we come to an example paragraph of the results for the physical performance example. Recall that our graduate research assistant, Addie, was assisting Dr. Waung, the university's director of the Exercise Physiology and Wellness Institute, with an experimental study to determine if there was a mean difference in self-rated physical performance based on caffeine use in an attempt to facilitate improved athletic performance. Twelve athletes ingested either caffeinated (treatment) or decaffeinated (control) beverage prior to physical activity. Prior to random assignment to sections, participants were also measured on mental fatigue. After random assignment, participants completed a 2000-meter self-paced jog and were then asked to self-rate their physical performance. She was looking to see if there was a mean difference in physical performance based on the treatment group (two categories: ingesting caffeinated beverage or decaffeinated beverage prior to the self-paced jog) while controlling for mental fatigue. Her research question was: *Is there a mean difference in self-rated physical performance based on caffeine ingestion, controlling for mental fatigue?* Addie then generated an ANCOVA as the test of inference. A template for writing a research question for ANCOVA is presented below. This is illustrated assuming a one-factor (i.e., one independent variable) model, but it can easily be extended to two or more factors. As we noted in previous chapters, it is important to be sure the reader understands the levels or groups of the independent variables. This may be done parenthetically in the actual research question, as an operational definition, or specified within the methods section. In this example, parenthetically we could have stated the following: *Is there a mean difference in self-rated physical performance based on caffeine ingestion (caffeinated beverage or decaffeinated beverage), controlling for mental fatigue?*

Is there a mean difference in [dependent variable] based on [independent variable], controlling for [covariate]?

It may be helpful to preface the results of the ANCOVA with information on an examination of the extent to which the assumptions were met (recall that we tested several assumptions: (a) independence of observations; (b) homogeneity of variance; (c) normality; (d) linearity; (e) independence of the covariate and the independent variable; and (f) homogeneity of regression slopes.

An analysis of covariance (ANCOVA) was conducted to determine if the mean physical performance differed based on caffeine ingestion (caffeinated or decaffeinated beverage), while controlling for mental fatigue. The assumptions of ANCOVA, including independence, homogeneity of variance, normality, linearity, independence of the covariate and independent variable, and homogeneity of regression slopes were examined.

Independence of observations was met by random assignment of athletes to group. This assumption was also confirmed by review of a scatterplot of residuals against the levels of the independent variable. A random display of points around zero provided further evidence that the assumption of independence was met.

According to Levene's test, the **homogeneity of variance** assumption was not satisfied [F (1, 10) = 6.768, p = .026]. However, heterogeneity is less problematic with a balanced design *and* when the assumption of normality holds, as is the case with this study.

The assumption of **normality** was tested and met via examination of the residuals. Review of the Shapiro-Wilk test for normality (overall SW = .965, df = 12, p = .854; treatment SW = .902, df = 6, p = .383; control SW = .911, df = 6, p = .443) and skewness (overall, −.237; treatment = −.076; control = −1.296) and kurtosis (overall, −1.024; treatment = −2.303; control = 2.015) statistics generally suggested that normality was reasonable (though kurtosis was a bit high). Additional tests, including D'Agostino's test for skewness (z = −.390, p = .697) and the Bonett-Seier test for Geary's kurtosis (overall, z = −1.051, p = .293; treatment, z = −1.949, p = .0513; control, z = .268, p = .788) suggested evidence of normality. The boxplots by group suggested a relatively normal distributional shape (with no outliers) of the residuals. The Q-Q plots suggested normality was reasonable. The histograms by group suggested some non-normality, but that was expected given the small sample size. In general, there is evidence that normality has been met.

Linearity of the dependent variable with the covariate was examined with scatterplots, both overall and by group of the independent variable. Overall, the scatterplot of the dependent variable with the covariate suggested a positive linear relationship. This same pattern was present for the scatterplot of the dependent variable with the covariate when disaggregated by the categories of the independent variables.

Independence of the covariate and independent variable was met by random assignment of athletes to treatment group. This assumption was also confirmed by an independent t test which examined the mean difference on the covariate (i.e., mental fatigue) by independent variable (i.e., caffeinated or decaffeinated beverage ingestion). The results were not statistically significant, $t(10)$, = 1.604, p = .140, which further confirms evidence of independence of the covariate and independent variable. There was not a mean difference in physical performance based on whether or not the athlete ingested caffeine prior to the self-paced jog.

Homogeneity of regression slopes was suggested by similar regression lines evidenced in the scatterplots of the dependent variable and covariates by group (reported earlier as evidence for linearity). This assumption was confirmed by a nonstatistically significant interaction of aptitude by group, F (1, 8) = .000, p = 1.000.

Here is an APA-style example paragraph of results for the ANCOVA (remember that this will be prefaced by the previous paragraph reporting the extent to which the ANCOVA assumptions were met).

The results of the ANCOVA suggest a statistically significant effect of the covariate, mental fatigue, on the dependent variable, physical performance ($F_{fatigue}$ = 21.961; *df* = 1,9; *p* = .001). More importantly, there is a statistically significant effect for treatment group (F_{group} = 11.372; *df* = 1,9; *p* = .008), with a large effect size and strong power (ω^2 = .465, observed power = .850). The effect size suggests that about 47% of the variance in physical performance can be accounted for by treatment group when controlling for mental fatigue. Follow-up tests were conducted to evaluate the pairwise differences among the adjusted means of physical performance by treatment group. [Had there been more than two groups, including a statement similar to this would be needed: Follow-up tests were conducted to evaluate the pairwise differences among the adjusted means of physical performance by treatment group.]

The *unadjusted* group physical performance mean (i.e., prior to controlling for mental fatigue) was larger for the caffeinated group (*M* = 4.00, *SD* = 2.10) as compared to the decaffeinated group (*M* = 3.50, *SD* = 1.87) by only .50. However, the *adjusted mean* for the caffeinated group (*M* = 4.814, *SE* = .423) as compared to the decaffeinated group (*M* = 2.686, *SE* = .423) was larger by 2.128. Thus, the use of the covariate resulted in a large significant difference between the treatment groups. In summary, athletes assigned to the caffeinated group outperformed athletes in the decaffeinated group on physical performance when controlling for mental fatigue.

If our independent variable had more than two groups, we would have needed to evaluate and report the results of a post hoc multiple comparison procedure when generating SPSS (recall that we asked for Bonferroni post hoc results). The following provides a template for how these results may have been written, had our analyses required them.

Follow-up tests were conducted to evaluate the pairwise differences among the adjusted means of [dependent variable] based on [independent variable]. The [post hoc procedure selected, e.g., Bonferroni] was applied to control for the risk of increased Type I error across all pairwise comparisons. Pairwise comparisons revealed [report specific results, including means and standard deviations here].

14.7 Additional Resources

This chapter has provided a preview into conducting ANCOVA. However, there are a number of areas that space limitations prevent us from delving into. For those of you who are interested in learning more about ANCOVA, or if you find yourself in a sticky situation in your analyses, you may wish to look into the following, among many other excellent resources.

- For more in-depth coverage of ANCOVA models, see Huitema (2011), Maxwell et al. (2018), and Rutherford (2011).

- The use of ANCOVA when the design contains comparisons of participants sampled from different populations (i.e., classification designs where participants are classified into two or more mutually exclusive groups according to criteria (e.g., age, gender) and this classification is then used as a between-subjects factor in subsequent analysis) (Schneider et al., 2015).
- Alternative models that can be considered for ANCOVA when interested in examining pretest-posttest effects, such as using a change, gain, or difference score and using residual scores (Kisbu-Sakarya, MacKinnon, & Aiken, 2013; Maxwell et al., 2018).

Problems

Conceptual Problems

1. Oscar wants to determine whether adults who can elect to work at home differ in their work engagement as compared to adults who are required to work in an office setting. Oscar randomly assigns 10 employees to be assigned to work in an office setting or be provided the option to work at home. After six months, Oscar measures adults on their work engagement. Is ANCOVA appropriate given this scenario?

2. Joe wants to determine whether the time to run the Magic Mountain Marathon (ratio level variable) differs, on average, for nonprofessional athletes who complete a 12-week endurance training program as compared to those who complete a 4-week endurance training program. Joe randomly assigns nonprofessional athletes to one of the two training programs. In conducting this experiment, Joe also wants to control for the number of prior marathons in which the participant has run. Is ANCOVA appropriate given this scenario?

3. Tami has generated an ANCOVA. In testing the assumptions, she reviews a scatterplot of the residuals for each category of the independent variable. For which assumption is Tami likely reviewing evidence?

a. Homogeneity of regression slopes

b. Homogeneity of variance

c. Independence of observations

d. Independence of the covariate and the independent variable

e. Linearity

4. Wesley has generated an ANCOVA. In his model, there is one independent variable which has three categories (type of phone: Blackberry, iPhone, and Droid) and one covariate (amount of time spent on desktop or laptop computer). In testing the assumptions, he reviews a one-way ANOVA, the dependent variable being amount of time spent on desktop or laptop computer and the independent variable being type of phone. For which assumption is Wesley likely reviewing evidence?

a. Homogeneity of regression slopes

b. Homogeneity of variance

c. Independence of observations

d. Independence of the covariate and the independent variable
e. Linearity

5. If the correlation between the covariate X and the dependent variable Y differs markedly in the two treatment groups, it seems likely that
   a. The assumption of normality is suspect.
   b. The assumption of homogeneity of slopes is suspect.
   c. A nonlinear relation exists between X and Y.
   d. The adjusted means for Y differ significantly.
6. If for both the treatment and control groups the correlation between the covariate X and the dependent variable Y is substantial but negative, the error variation for ANCOVA as compared to that for ANOVA is
   a. Less.
   b. About the same.
   c. Greater.
   d. Unpredictably different.
7. An experiment was conducted to compare three different instructional strategies. Fifteen subjects were included in each group. The same test was administered prior to and after the treatments. If both pretest and IQ are used as covariates, what are the degrees of freedom for the error term?
   a. 2
   b. 40
   c. 41
   d. 42
8. The effect of a training program concerned with educating heart attack patients to the benefits of moderate exercise was examined. A group of recent heart attack patients was randomly divided into two groups; one group received the training program and the other did not. The dependent variable was the amount of time taken to jog three laps, with the weight of the patient after the program used as a covariate. Examination of the data after the study revealed that the covariate means of the two groups differed. Which of the following assumptions is most clearly violated?
   a. Linearity
   b. Homogeneity of slopes
   c. Independence of the treatment and the covariate
   d. Normality
9. In ANCOVA, the covariate is a variable which should have a
   a. Low positive correlation with the dependent variable
   b. High positive correlation with the independent variable
   c. High positive correlation with the dependent variable
   d. Zero correlation with the dependent variable

10. In ANCOVA how will the correlation of zero between the covariate and the dependent variable appear?

a. Unequal group means on the dependent variable

b. Unequal group means on the covariate

c. Regression of the dependent variable on the covariate with $b_w = 0$.

d. Regression of the dependent variable on the covariate with $b_w = 1$

11. Which of the following is not a necessary requirement for using ANCOVA?

a. Covariate scores are not affected by the treatment.

b. There is a linear relationship between the covariate and the dependent variable.

c. The covariate variable is the same measure as the dependent variable.

d. Regression slopes for the groups are similar.

12. Which of the following is the most desirable situation to use ANCOVA?

a. The slope of the regression line equals zero.

b. The variance of the dependent variable for a specific covariate score is relatively large.

c. The correlation between the covariate and the dependent variable is –.95.

d. The correlation between the covariate and the dependent variable is .60.

13. A group of students was randomly assigned to one of three instructional strategies. Data from the study indicated an interaction between slope and treatment group. It seems likely that

a. The assumption of normality is suspect.

b. The assumption of homogeneity of slopes is suspect.

c. A nonlinear relation exists between X and Y.

d. The covariate is not independent of the treatment.

14. If the mean on the dependent variable GPA (*Y*) for persons of middle social class (*X*) is higher than for persons of lower and higher social classes, one would expect that

a. The relationship between *X* and *Y* is curvilinear.

b. The covariate *X* contains substantial measurement error.

c. GPA is not normally distributed.

d. Social class is not related to GPA.

15. If both the covariate and the dependent variable are assessed after the treatment has been concluded, and if both are affected by the treatment, the use of ANCOVA for these data would likely result in

a. An inflated *F* ratio for the treatment effect.

b. An exaggerated difference in the adjusted means.

c. An underestimate of the treatment effect.

d. An inflated value of the slope b_w.

16. When the covariate correlates +.5 with the dependent variable, I assert that the adjusted MS_{with} from the ANCOVA will be less than the MS_{with} from the ANOVA. Am I correct?

17. For each of two groups, the correlation between the covariate and the dependent variable is substantial, but negative in direction. I assert that the error variance for ANCOVA, as compared to that for ANOVA, is greater. Am I correct?
18. True or false? In ANCOVA, X is known as a factor.
19. A study was conducted to compare six types of diets. Twelve subjects were included in each group. Their weights were taken prior to and after treatment. If pre-weight is used as a covariate, what are the degrees of freedom for the error term?
    a. 5
    b. 65
    c. 66
    d. 71
20. A researcher conducts both a one-factor ANOVA and a one-factor ANCOVA on the same data. In comparing the adjusted group means to the unadjusted group means, they find that for each group, the adjusted mean is equal to the unadjusted mean. I assert that the researcher must have made a computational error. Am I correct?
21. The correlation between the covariate and the dependent variable is zero. I assert that ANCOVA is still preferred over ANOVA. Am I correct?
22. If there is a nonlinear relationship between the covariate X and the dependent variable Y, then it is very likely that
    a. There will be less reduction in SS_{with}.
    b. The group effects will be biased.
    c. The correlation between X and Y will be smaller in magnitude.
    d. All of the above
23. Which of the following assumptions is not shared between ANCOVA and ANOVA?
    a. Homogeneity of variance
    b. Independence
    c. Linearity
    d. Normality
24. The assumption of normality in ANCOVA is concerned with the distributional shape of which one of the following?
    a. Covariate
    b. Dependent variable
    c. Independent variable
    d. Residuals
25. The regression of the dependent variable on the covariate is assumed to be which one of the following?
    a. Independent
    b. Homogenous
    c. Linear
    d. Multicollinear

26. If units have been randomly assigned to conditions within the independent variable, which one of the following assumptions have likely been met?
    a. Homogeneity of variance
    b. Independence of the covariate and independent variable
    c. Linearity
    d. Normality
27. True or false? In ANCOVA, the independent variable is statistically adjusted to remove the effects of that part of uncontrolled variation in the covariate.

Answers to Conceptual Problems

1. **No** (there is no covariate mentioned for which to control.)
3. **c** (evidence of meeting the assumption of independence can be examined by a scatterplot of residuals by group or category of the independent variable; a random display of points suggests the assumption is met.)
5. **b** (see discussion on homogeneity of regression slopes.)
7. **b** (14 *df* per group, 3 groups, 42 *df* – 2 *df* for covariates = 40.)
9. **c** (want covariate having a high correlation with the dependent variable.)
11. **c** (the covariate and dependent variable need not be the same measure; could be pretest and posttest, but it does not have to be.)
13. **b** (an interaction indicates that the regression lines are not parallel across the groups.)
15. **c** (a post hoc covariate typically results in an underestimate of the treatment effect, due to confounding or interference of the covariate.)
17. **No** (if the correlation is substantial, then error variance will be reduced in ANCOVA regardless of its sign.)
19. **b** (11 *df* per group, 6 groups, 66 *df* – 1 *df* for covariate = 65.)
21. **No** (there will be no adjustment due to the covariate and one *df* will be lost from the error term.)
23. **c** (linearity is an assumption applicable to ANCOVA but not ANOVA.)
25. **c** (regression of the dependent variable on the covariate is assumed to be linear in ANCOVA.)
27. **False** (in ANCOVA, the *dependent variable*, not the independent variable, is statistically adjusted to remove the effects of that part of uncontrolled variation in the covariate.)

Computational Problems

1. Consider the analysis of covariance situation where the dependent variable Y is the posttest of an achievement test and the covariate X is the pretest of the same test. Given the data that follow, where there are three groups, (a) calculate the adjusted Y values assuming that $b_w = 1.00$, and (b) determine what effects the adjustment had on the posttest results.

Group	X	$\bar{X}$	Y	$\bar{Y}$
	40		120	
1	50	50	125	125
	60		130	
	70		140	
2	75	75	150	150
	80		160	
	90		160	
3	100	100	175	175
	110		190	

2. Malani wants to determine whether children whose preschool classroom has a window differ in their receptive vocabulary as compared to children whose classroom does not have a window. At the beginning of the school year, Malani randomly assigns 10 children at Rainbow Butterfly Preschool to one of two different classrooms: one classroom which has a window that looks out onto a grassy area or another classroom that has no windows. At the end of the school year, Malani measures children on their receptive vocabulary. Below are two independent random samples (classroom with and without window) of paired values on the covariate (*X*; receptive vocabulary measured at beginning of school year) and the dependent variable essay score (*Y*; receptive vocabulary measured at the end of the school year). Conduct an analysis of variance on *Y*, an analysis of covariance on *Y* using *X* as a covariate, and compare the results ($\alpha = .05$). Determine the unadjusted and adjusted means.

Classroom With Window		Classroom Without Window	
X	Y	X	Y
80	105	80	95
75	100	85	100
85	105	90	105
70	100	85	100
90	110	95	105

3. Below are four independent random samples (different methods of instruction) of paired values on the covariate IQ (*X*) and the dependent variable essay score (*Y*). Conduct an analysis of variance on *Y*, an analysis of covariance on *Y* using *X* as a covariate, and compare the results ($\alpha = .05$). Determine the unadjusted and adjusted means.

Group 1		Group 2		Group 3		Group 4	
X	Y	X	Y	X	Y	X	Y
94	14	80	38	92	55	94	24
96	19	84	34	96	53	94	37
98	17	90	43	99	55	98	22
100	38	97	43	101	52	100	43

Group 1		Group 2		Group 3		Group 4	
X	*Y*	*X*	*Y*	*X*	*Y*	*X*	*Y*
102	40	97	61	102	35	103	49
105	26	112	63	104	46	104	24
109	41	115	93	107	57	104	41
110	28	118	74	110	55	108	26
111	36	120	76	111	42	113	70
130	66	120	79	118	81	115	63

4. A communications researcher wants to know which of five versions of commercials for a new television show is most effective in terms of viewing likelihood. Each commercial is viewed by six students. A one-factor ANCOVA was used to analyze these data where the covariate was amount of television previously viewed per week. Complete the ANCOVA summary table below ($\alpha = .05$).

Source	*SS*	*df*	*MS*	*F*	Critical Value	Decision
Between adjusted	96	–	–	–	–	–
Within adjusted	192	–	–			
Covariate	–	–	–	–	–	–
Total	328	–				

5. Dr. Lee wants to determine whether prescribed workouts improve quality of movement for pre-professional athletes. College athletes were randomly assigned to either a specific prescribed movement plan (treatment) or instructed to choose their own workout (comparison group). Quality of movement was measured prior to random assignment and after 6 weeks of participation in the study. The data appear below, with athletes randomly assigned to treatment group and measured on the covariate (*X*; baseline quality of movement) and the dependent variable (*Y*; quality of movement at 6 weeks post treatment). Compute ANCOVA on *Y* using *X* as a covariate, and determine the results to the null hypothesis that the adjusted means are all equal ($\alpha = .05$). Should there be a statistically significant group effect, indicate which group had the higher mean quality of movement.

Group	Baseline (X)	Post (Y)
Prescribed movement plan	30	61
Prescribed movement plan	35	57
Prescribed movement plan	40	58
Prescribed movement plan	36	53
Prescribed movement plan	38	56
Comparison	42	49
Comparison	34	46
Comparison	39	45
Comparison	43	48
Comparison	41	47

Answers to Computational Problems

1. The adjusted group means are all equal to 150; this resulted because the adjustment moved the mean for Group 1 up to 150 and the mean for Group 3 down to 150.
3. ANOVA results: $SS_{betw} = 4{,}763.275$, $SS_{with} = 9{,}636.7$, $df_{betw} = 3$, $df_{with} = 36$, $MS_{betw} = 1{,}587.758$, $MS_{with} = 267.686$, $F = 5.931$, critical value approximately 2.88 (reject H_0).

   Unadjusted means in order: 32.5, 60.4, 53.1, 39.9.

   ANCOVA results: $SS_{betw} = 5{,}402.046$, $SS_{with} = 3{,}880.115$, $df_{betw} = 3$, $df_{with} = 35$, $MS_{betw} = 1{,}800.682$, $MS_{with} = 110.8604$, $F = 16.24$, critical value approximately 2.88 (reject H_0), $SS_{cov} = 5{,}117.815$, $F_{cov} = 46.164$, critical value approximately 4.12 (reject H_0).

   Adjusted means in order: 30.7617, 61.2544, 53.1295, 40.7544.
5. The results of the ANCOVA suggest a statistically significant effect of the covariate, baseline quality of movement, on the dependent variable post-treatment quality of movement ($F_{baseline} = 12.469$, $p = .010$). Additionally, there is a statistically significant effect for workout plan ($F_{workoutplan} = 27.792$, $p = .001$) with prescribed workouts producing greater average quality of movement ($M_{prescribed} = 56.870$, $SE_{prescribed} = 1.215$; $M_{comparison} = 47.130$, $SE_{comparison} = 1.215$).

Interpretive Problems

1. Using the same data you selected for the first interpretative problem for Chapter 11, select an appropriate covariate and then generate a one-factor ANCOVA (including testing the assumptions of both the ANOVA and ANCOVA). Compare and contrast the results of the ANOVA and ANCOVA. Which method would you select and why?
2. Using the same data you selected for the second interpretative problem for Chapter 11, select an appropriate covariate and then generate a one-factor ANCOVA (including testing the assumptions of both the ANOVA and ANCOVA). Compare and contrast the results of the ANOVA and ANCOVA. Which method would you select and why?
3. Using the same data you selected for the third interpretative problem for Chapter 11, select an appropriate covariate and then generate a one-factor ANCOVA (including testing the assumptions of both the ANOVA and ANCOVA). Compare and contrast the results of the ANOVA and ANCOVA. Which method would you select and why?

15

Random- and Mixed-Effects Analysis of Variance Models

Chapter Outline

Key Concepts

1. Fixed-, random-, and mixed-effects models
2. Repeated measures models
3. Compound symmetry/sphericity assumption
4. Friedman repeated measures test based on ranks
5. Split-plot or mixed designs (i.e., both between- and within-subjects factors)

In this chapter we continue our discussion of the analysis of variance (ANOVA) by considering models in which there is a random-effects factor, previously introduced in Chapter 11. These models include the one-factor and factorial designs, as well as repeated measures designs. As becomes evident, repeated measures designs are used when there is at least one factor where each individual is exposed to all levels of that factor. This factor is referred to as a **repeated factor**, for obvious reasons. This chapter is mostly concerned with one- and two-factor random-effects models, the two-factor mixed-effects model, and one- and two-factor repeated measures designs.

It should be noted that effect size measures, power, and confidence intervals can be determined in the same fashion for the models in this chapter as for previously described ANOVA models. The standard effect size measures already described are applicable (i.e., ω^2 and η^2), although the intraclass correlation coefficient, ρ_I, can be utilized for random effects (similarly interpreted). For additional discussion of these issues in the context of this chapter, see Cohen (1988), Fidler and Thompson (2001), Keppel and Wickens (2004), Murphy, Myors, and Wolach (2009), Wilcox (2003), and Wilcox (1996).

Many of the concepts used in this chapter are the same as those covered in Chapters 11 through 14. In addition, the following new concepts are addressed: random- and mixed-effects factors, repeated measures factors, the compound symmetry/sphericity assumption, and mixed designs. Our objectives are that by the end of this chapter, you will be able to (a) understand the characteristics and concepts underlying random- and mixed-effects ANOVA models, (b) determine and interpret the results of random- and mixed-effects ANOVA models, and (c) understand and evaluate the assumptions of random- and mixed-effects ANOVA models.

15.1 The One-Factor Random-Effects Model

This section describes the distinguishing characteristics of the one-factor random-effects ANOVA model, the linear model, the ANOVA summary table and expected mean squares, assumptions and their violation, and multiple comparison procedures.

15.1.1 Characteristics of the Model

The characteristics of the one-factor *fixed-effects* ANOVA model have already been covered in Chapter 11. These characteristics include (a) one factor (or independent variable) with two or more levels, (b) all levels of the factor of interest are included in the design (i.e., a fixed-effects factor), (c) subjects are randomly assigned to one level of the factor, and (d) the dependent variable is measured at least at the interval level. Thus, the overall design is a fixed-effects model, where there is one factor and the individuals respond to only one level of the factor. If individuals respond to more than one level of the factor, then this is a repeated measures design, as shown later in this chapter.

The characteristics of the one-factor *random-effects* ANOVA model are the same with one obvious exception. This has to do with the selection of the levels of the factor. In the fixed-effects case, researchers select all of the levels of interest, because they are interested only in making generalizations (or inferences) about those particular levels. Thus, in replications of this design, each replicate would use precisely the same levels. Considering analyses that are conducted on individuals, examples of factors that are typically fixed include socioeconomic status, sex, specific types of drug treatment, age group, weight, or marital status.

In the random-effects case, researchers randomly select levels from the population of levels because they are interested in making generalizations (or inferences) about the entire population of levels, not merely those that have been sampled. Thus in replications of this design, each replicate need not have the same levels included. The concept of random selection of factor levels from the population of levels is the same as the random selection of subjects from the population. Here the researcher is making an inference from the sampled levels to the population of levels, instead of making an inference from the sample of individuals to the population of individuals. In a random-effects design, then, a random sample of factor levels is selected in the same way as a random sample of individuals is selected.

For instance, a researcher interested in instructor effectiveness may have randomly sampled instructors from one discipline (i.e., the independent variable) from the population of instructors in a university system. Generalizations can then be made about all instructors in that university system that could have been sampled. Other examples of factors that are typically random include *randomly selected* preexisting groups such as classrooms, organizations, buildings, observers or raters, or time (seconds, minutes, hours, days, weeks, etc.). It should be noted that in many settings, the random selection of groups or units such as organizations, schools, or classrooms is not often possible as those decisions are not under the researcher's control. Here we would need to consider such factors as fixed rather than random effects.

15.1.2 The ANOVA Model

The one-factor ANOVA random-effects model is written in terms of population parameters as

$$Y_{ij} = \mu + a_j + \varepsilon_{ij}$$

where Y_{ij} is the observed score on the dependent variable for individual i in level j of factor A, μ is the overall or grand population mean, a_j is the random effect for level j of factor A, and ε_{ij} is the random residual error for individual i in level j. The residual error can be due to individual differences, measurement error, and/or other factors not under investigation. Note that we use a_j to designate the random effects to differentiate them from a_j in the fixed-effects model.

Because the random-effects model consists of only a sample of the effects from the population, the sum of the sampled effects is not necessarily zero. For instance, we may select a sample having only positive effects (e.g., all very effective instructors). If the entire population of effects were examined, then the sum of those effects would indeed be zero.

For the one-factor random-effects ANOVA model, the hypotheses for testing the effect of factor A are written in terms of equality of the variances among the means of the random levels, as follows (i.e., the means for each level are about the same and thus the variability among those means is about zero). It should be noted that the sign for the alternative hypothesis is "greater than" reflecting the fact that the variance cannot be negative.

$$H_0: \sigma_a^2 = 0$$

$$H_1: \sigma_a^2 > 0$$

Recall for the one-factor fixed-effects ANOVA model that the hypotheses for testing the effect of factor A are written in terms of equality of the means of the groups (as presented here):

$$H_0: \mu_{.1} = \mu_{.2} = \ldots = \mu_{.J}$$

$$H_1: not\,all\,the\,\mu_{.j}\,are\,equal$$

This reflects the difference in the inferences made in the random- and fixed-effects models. In the fixed-effects case, the null hypothesis is about specific population means; in the random-effects case, the null hypothesis is about variation among the entire population of means. As becomes evident, the difference in the models is reflected in the multiple comparison procedures.

15.1.3 ANOVA Summary Table and Expected Mean Squares

Here there are very few differences between the one-factor random-effects and one-factor fixed-effects models. The sources of variation are still A (or between), within, and total. The sums of squares, degrees of freedom, mean squares, *F* test statistic, and critical value are determined in the same way as in the fixed-effects case. Obviously then, the ANOVA summary table looks the same as well. Using the example from Chapter 11, assuming the model is now a random-effects model, we obtain a test statistic $F = 6.8177$, which is again significant at the .05 level.

As in Chapters 11 and 13, the formation of a proper *F* ratio is related to the expected mean squares. If H_0 is actually *true*, then the *expected mean squares* are as follows:

$$E(MS_A) = \sigma_\varepsilon^2$$

$$E(MS_{with}) = \sigma_\varepsilon^2$$

and thus the ratio of expected mean squares is:

$$\frac{E(MS_A)}{E(MS_{with})} = 1$$

where the expected value of *F* is $E(F) = df_{with} / (df_{with} - 2)$, and σ_ε^2 is the population variance of the residual errors.

If H_0 is actually *false*, then the expected mean squares are as follows:

$$E(MS_A) = \sigma_\varepsilon^2 + n\sigma_a^2$$

$$E(MS_{with}) = \sigma_\varepsilon^2$$

and thus the ratio of the expected mean squares is as follows:

$$\frac{E(MS_A)}{E(MS_{with})} > 1$$

Where $E(F) > df_{with} / (df_{with} - 2)$ and σ_a^2 is the population variance of the levels of factor A.

Thus the important part of $E(MS_A)$ is the magnitude of the second term $n\sigma_a^2$.

As in previous ANOVA models, the proper *F* ratio should be formed as follows:

$$F = \frac{(systematic\,variability + error\,variability)}{error\,variability}$$

For the one-factor random-effects model, the only appropriate *F* ratio is MS_A / MS_{with} because it does serve to isolate the systematic variability (i.e., the variability between the levels or groups in factor A, the independent variable). That is, the within term must be utilized as the error term in the F ratio.

15.1.4 Assumptions and Violation of Assumptions

In Chapter 11 we described the assumptions for the one-factor fixed-effects model. The assumptions are nearly the same for the one-factor random-effects model, and we need not devote much attention to them here. In short, the assumptions are again concerned with the distribution of the dependent variable scores, specifically that scores are random and independent, coming from normally distributed populations with equal population variances. The effect of assumption violations and how to deal with them have been thoroughly discussed in Chapter 11 (although see, for example, Wilcox, 2003, for alternative procedures when variances are unequal).

Additional assumptions must be made for the random-effects model. These assumptions deal with the effects for the levels of the independent variable, the a_j. First, here are a few words about the a_j. The random group effects a_j are computed, in the population, by the following:

$$a_j = \mu_{.j} - \mu_{..}$$

For example, a_3 represents the effect for being a member of Group 3. If the overall mean $\mu_{..}$ is 60 and the mean of Group 3 (i.e., μ_3) is 100, then the group effect would be

$$a_3 = \mu_{.3} - \mu_{..} = 100 - 60 = 40$$

In other words, the effect for being a member of Group 3 is an increase of 40 points over the overall mean.

The assumptions are that the a_j group effects are randomly and independently sampled from the normally distributed population of group effects, with a population mean of zero and a population variance of σ_a^2. Stated another way, there is a population of group effects out there from which we are taking a random sample. For example, with teacher as the factor of interest, we are interested in examining the effectiveness of teachers as measured by academic performance of students in their class. We take a random sample of teachers from the population of second-grade teachers. For these teachers we measure their effectiveness in the classroom via student performance and generate an effect for each teacher (i.e., the a_j). These effects indicate the extent to which a particular teacher is more or less effective than the population average of teachers. Their effects are known as random effects as the teachers are randomly selected. In selecting teachers, each teacher is selected independently of all other teachers to prevent a biased sample.

The effects of the violation of the assumptions about the a_j are the same as with the dependent variable scores. The F test is quite robust to nonnormality of the a_j terms, and unequal variances of the a_j terms. However, the F test is quite sensitive to nonindependence among the a_j terms, with no known solutions. A summary of the assumptions and the effects of their violation for the one-factor random-effects model is presented in Table 15.1.

TABLE 15.1

Assumptions and Effects of Violations: One-Factor Random-Effects Model

Assumption	Effect of Assumption Violation
Independence	• Increased likelihood of a Type I and/or Type II error in *F* • Affects standard errors of means and inferences about those means
Homogeneity of variance	• Bias in SS_{with}; increased likelihood of a Type I and/or Type II error • Small effect with equal or nearly equal *n*'s; otherwise effect decreases as *n* increases
Normality	• Minimal effect with equal or nearly equal *n*'s

15.1.5 Multiple Comparison Procedures

Let us think for a moment about the use of multiple comparison procedures for the random-effects model. In general, the researcher is not usually interested in making inferences about just the levels of A that were sampled. Thus, estimation of the a_j terms does not provide us with any information about the a_j terms that were not sampled. Also, the a_j terms cannot be summarized by their mean, as they do not necessarily sum to zero for the levels sampled, only for the population of levels.

15.2 The Two-Factor Random-Effects Model

In this section, we describe the distinguishing characteristics of the two-factor random-effects ANOVA model, the linear model, the ANOVA summary table and expected mean squares, assumptions of the model and their violation, and multiple comparison procedures.

15.2.1 Characteristics of the Model

The characteristics of the one-factor random-effects ANOVA model have already been covered in this chapter, and those of the two-factor fixed-effects model in Chapter 13. Here we extend and combine these characteristics to form the two-factor random-effects model. These characteristics include (a) two factors (or independent variables) each with two or more levels, (b) the levels of each of the factors are randomly sampled from the population of levels (i.e., two random-effects factors), (c) subjects are randomly assigned to one combination of the levels of the two factors, and (d) the dependent variable is measured at least at the interval level. Thus the overall design is a random-effects model, with two factors, and the individuals respond to only one combination of the levels of the two factors (note that this is not a popular model in education and the behavioral sciences; in factorial designs we typically see a random-effects factor with a fixed-effects factor). If individuals respond to more than one combination of the levels of the two factors, then this is a repeated measures design (discussed later in this chapter).

15.2.2 The ANOVA Model

The two-factor ANOVA random-effects model is written in terms of population parameters as

$$Y_{ijk} = \mu + a_j + b_k + (ab)_{jk} + \varepsilon_{ijk}$$

where Y_{ijk} is the observed score on the dependent variable for individual i in level j of factor A and level k of factor B (or in the jk cell), μ is the overall or grand population mean (i.e., regardless of cell designation), a_j is the random effect for level j of factor A (row effect), b_k is the random effect for level k of factor B (column effect), $(ab)_{jk}$ is the interaction random effect for the combination of level j of factor A and level k of factor B, and ε_{ijk} is the random residual error for individual i in cell jk. The residual error can be due to individual differences, measurement error, and/or other factors not under investigation. Note that we use a_j, b_k, and $(ab)_{jk}$ to designate the random effects to differentiate them from the α_j, β_k, and $(\alpha\beta)_{jk}$ in the fixed-effects model. Finally, there is no requirement that the sum of the main or interaction effects is equal to zero as only a sample of these effects are taken from the population of effects.

There are three sets of hypotheses, one for each of the two main effects and one for the interaction effect. The null and alternative hypotheses, respectively, for testing the main effect of factor A (i.e., independent variable A) follows. The null hypothesis tests whether the variance among the means for the random effect of independent variable A is equal to zero (i.e., the means for each level of factor A are about the same; thus, the variability among those means is about zero). It should be noted that the sign for the alternative hypothesis is "greater than," reflecting the fact that the variance cannot be negative.

$$H_{01}: \sigma_a^2 = 0$$
$$H_{11}: \sigma_a^2 > 0$$

The hypotheses for testing the main effect of factor B (i.e., independent variable B) similarly test whether the variance among the means for the random effect of independent variable B is equal to zero (i.e., the means for each level of factor B are about the same and thus the variability among those means is about zero). It should be noted that the sign for the alternative hypothesis is "greater than," reflecting the fact that the variance cannot be negative.

$$H_{02}: \sigma_b^2 = 0$$
$$H_{12}: \sigma_b^2 > 0$$

Finally, the hypotheses for testing the interaction effect are presented next. In this case, the null hypothesis tests whether the variance among the means for the interaction of the random effects of factors A and B is equal to zero (i.e., the means for each AB cell are about the same and thus the variability among those means is about zero). It should be noted that the sign for the alternative hypothesis is "greater than," reflecting the fact that the variance cannot be negative.

$$H_{03}: \sigma_{ab}^2 = 0$$
$$H_{13}: \sigma_{ab}^2 > 0$$

These hypotheses again reflect the difference in the inferences made in the random- and fixed-effects models. In the fixed-effects case, the null hypotheses are about means, whereas in the random-effects case the null hypotheses are about *variation* among the means.

15.2.3 ANOVA Summary Table and Expected Mean Squares

Here there are very few differences between the two-factor fixed-effects and random-effects models. The sources of variation are still A, B, AB, within, and total. The sums of squares, degrees of freedom, and mean squares are determined the same as in the fixed-effects case. However, the F test statistics are different due to the expected mean squares, as are the critical values used. The F test statistics are formed for the test of factor A (i.e., the main effect for independent variable A) as follows:

$$F = \frac{MS_A}{MS_{AB}}.$$

for the test of factor B (i.e., the main effect for independent variable B) as presented here:

$$F = \frac{MS_B}{MS_{AB}}$$

and for the test of the AB interaction as indicated:

$$F = \frac{MS_{AB}}{MS_{with}}$$

Recall that in the fixed-effects model, the MS_{with} was used as the error term for all three hypotheses. However, in the random-effects model, the MS_{with} is used as the error term *only* for the test of the interaction. The MS_{AB} is used as the error term for the tests of both main effects. The critical values used are those based on the degrees of freedom for the numerator and denominator of each hypothesis tested. Thus, using the example from Chapter 13, assuming that the model is now a random-effects model, we obtain the following as our test statistic for the test of factor A (i.e., the main effect for independent variable A):

$$F_A = \frac{MS_A}{MS_{AB}} = \frac{246.1979}{7.2813} = 33.8124$$

for the test of factor B, the test statistic is computed as follows:

$$F_B = \frac{MS_B}{MS_{AB}} = \frac{712.5313}{7.2813} = 97.8577$$

and for the test of the AB interaction, we find the following:

$$F_{AB} = \frac{MS_{AB}}{MS_{with}} = \frac{7.2813}{11.5313} = 0.6314$$

The critical value for the test of factor A is found in the F table of Appendix Table 4 as $_{\alpha}F_{J-1,(J-1)(K-1)}$, which for the example is $_{.05}F_{3,3} = 9.28$, and is significant at the .05 level. The critical value for the test of factor B is found in the F table as $_{\alpha}F_{J-1,(J-1)(K-1)}$, which for the example is $_{.05}F_{1,3} = 10.13$, and is significant at the .05 level. The critical value for the test of the interaction is found in the F table as $_{\alpha}F_{J-1,(J-1)(K-1),N-JK}$, which for the example is $_{.05}F_{3,24} = 3.01$, and is not significant at the .05 level. It just so happens for the example data that the results for the random- and fixed-effects models are the same. This will not always be the case.

The formation of the proper F ratios is again related to the expected mean squares. Recall that our hypotheses for the two-factor random-effects model are based on variation among the means of the random effects (rather than the means as seen in the fixed-effects case). If H_0 is actually *true* (i.e., there is no variation among the means of the random effects), then the *expected mean squares* are all equals, as noted as follows:

$$E(MS_A) = \sigma_\varepsilon^2$$
$$E(MS_B) = \sigma_\varepsilon^2$$
$$E(MS_{AB}) = \sigma_\varepsilon^2$$
$$E(MS_{with}) = \sigma_\varepsilon^2$$

where σ_ε^2 is the population variance of the residual errors.

If H_0 is actually *false* (i.e., there *is* variation among the means of the random effects), then the expected mean squares are as follows:

$$E(MS_A) = \sigma_\varepsilon^2 + n\sigma_{ab}^2 + Kn\sigma_a^2$$
$$E(MS_B) = \sigma_\varepsilon^2 + n\sigma_{ab}^2 + Jn\sigma_a^2$$
$$E(MS_{AB}) = \sigma_\varepsilon^2 + n\sigma_{ab}^2$$
$$E(MS_{with}) = \sigma_\varepsilon^2$$

where σ_a^2, σ_b^2, and σ_{ab}^2 are the population variances of A, B and AB, respectively.

As in previous ANOVA models, the proper F ratio should be formed as follows:

$$F = \frac{(\textit{systematic variability} + \textit{error variability})}{\textit{error variability}}$$

For the two-factor random-effects model, the appropriate error term for the main effects is MS_{AB} and the appropriate error term for the interaction effect is MS_{with}.

15.2.4 Assumptions and Violation of Assumptions

Previously we described the assumptions for the one-factor random-effects model. The assumptions are nearly the same for the two-factor random-effects model and we need not devote much attention to them here. As before, the assumptions are concerned with the distribution of the dependent variable scores, and of the random-effects [sampled levels of the independent variables, the a_j, b_k, and their interaction $(ab)_{jk}$]. However, there are a few new wrinkles. Little is known about the effect of unequal variances (i.e., heterogeneity)

TABLE 15.2
Assumptions and Effects of Violations: Two-Factor Random-Effects Model

Assumption	Effect of Assumption Violation
Independence	Little is known about the effects of dependence; however, based on the fixed-effects model, we might expect the following: • Increased likelihood of a Type I and/or Type II error in F • Affects standard errors of means and inferences about those means
Homogeneity of variance	Little is known about the effects of heteroscedasticity; however, based on the fixed-effects model, we might expect the following: • Bias in SS_{with} • Increased likelihood of a Type I and/or Type II error • Small effect with equal or nearly equal n's • Otherwise effect decreases as n increases
Normality	• Minimal effect with equal or nearly equal n's • Otherwise substantial effects

or dependence (i.e., violation of the assumption of independence) for this random-effects model, although we expect the effects to be the same as for the fixed-effects model. For violation of the normality assumption, effects are known to be substantial. A summary of the assumptions and the effects of their violation for the two-factor random-effects model is presented in Table 15.2.

15.2.5 Multiple Comparison Procedures

The story of multiple comparisons for the two-factor random-effects model is the same as that for the one-factor random-effects model. In general, the researcher is not usually interested in making inferences about just the levels of A, B, or AB that were sampled, and thus performing multiple comparison procedures in a two-factor random-effects model is a moot point. Thus, estimation of the a_j, b_k, or $(ab)_{jk}$ terms do not provide us with any information about the a_j, b_k, or $(ab)_{jk}$ terms that were not sampled. Also, the a_j, b_k, or $(ab)_{jk}$ terms cannot be summarized by their means, as they will not necessarily sum to zero for the levels sampled, only for the population of levels.

15.3 The Two-Factor Mixed-Effects Model

This section describes the distinguishing characteristics of the two-factor *mixed-effects* ANOVA model, the linear model, the ANOVA summary table and expected mean squares, assumptions of the model and their violation, and multiple comparison procedures.

15.3.1 Characteristics of the Model

The characteristics of the two-factor random-effects ANOVA model have already been covered in the preceding section, and those of the two-factor fixed-effects model in Chapter 13. Here we combine these characteristics to form the two-factor mixed-effects model. These characteristics include (a) two factors (or independent variables) each with two or more levels, (b) the levels for one of the factors are randomly sampled from the population of levels (i.e., the random-effects factor) and all of the levels of interest for the second factor are included in the design (i.e., the fixed-effects factor), (c) subjects are randomly selected and assigned to one combination of the levels of the two factors, and (d) the dependent variable is measured at least at the interval level. Thus, the overall design is a mixed-effects model, with one fixed-effects factor and one random-effects factor, and individuals respond to only one combination of the levels of the two factors. If individuals respond to more than one combination, then this is a repeated measures design.

15.3.2 The ANOVA Model

There are actually two variations of the two-factor mixed-effects model, one where factor A is fixed and factor B is random, and the other where factor A is random and factor B is fixed. The labeling of a factor as A or B is arbitrary, so we consider only the former variation where A is fixed and B is random. For the latter variation merely switch the labels of the factors. The two-factor ANOVA mixed-effects model is written in terms of population parameters as

$$Y_{ijk} = \mu + \alpha_j + b_k + (ab)_{jk} + \varepsilon_{ijk}$$

where Y_{ijk} is the observed score on the dependent variable for individual *i* in level *j* of factor A and level *k* of factor B (or in the *jk* cell), μ is the overall or grand population mean (i.e., regardless of cell designation), α_j is the fixed effect for level *j* of factor A (row effect), b_k is the random effect for level *k* of factor B (column effect), $(ab)_{jk}$ is the interaction mixed effect for the combination of level *j* of factor A and level *k* of factor B, and ε_{ijk} is the random residual error for individual *i* in cell *jk*. The residual error can be due to individual differences, measurement error, and/or other factors not under investigation. Note that we use b_k and $(\alpha b)_{jk}$ to designate the random and mixed effects respectively to differentiate them from β_k and $(\alpha\beta)_{jk}$ in the fixed-effects model.

As shown in Figure 15.1, due to the nature of the mixed-effects model, only some of the columns are randomly selected for inclusion in the design. Each cell of the design will include row (α), column (*b*), and interaction (α*b*) effects. With an equal *n*'s model, if we sum these effects for a given column, then the effects will sum to zero. However, if we sum these effects for a given row, then the effects will not sum to zero, as some columns were not sampled.

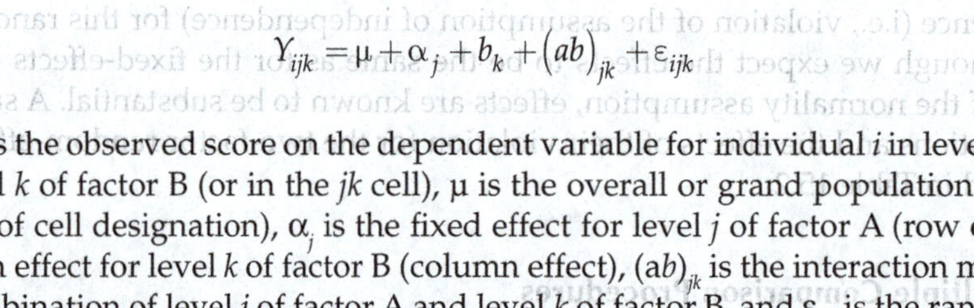

FIGURE. 15.1
Conditions for the two-factor mixed-effects model: although all four levels of factor A are selected by the researcher (A is fixed), only three of the six levels of factor B are selected (B is random). If the levels of B selected are 1, 3, and 6, then the design will only consist of the shaded cells. In each cell of the design are row, column, and cell effects. If we sum these effects for a given column, then the effects will sum to zero. If we sum these effects for a given row, then the effects will not sum to zero (due to missing cells).

The null and alternative hypotheses, respectively, for testing the effect of factor A are presented below. These hypotheses reflect testing the equality of means of the levels of independent variable A (the fixed-effect).

$$H_{01}: \mu_{.1.} = \mu_{.2.} = \ldots \mu_{.J.}$$
$$H_{11}: \textit{not all the } \mu_{.j.} \textit{ are equal}$$

The hypotheses for testing the effect of factor B, the random effect, follow. The null hypothesis tests whether the variance among the means for the random effect of independent variable B is equal to zero (i.e., the means for each level of factor B are about the same and thus the variability among those means is about zero). It should be noted that the sign for the alternative hypothesis is "greater than," reflecting the fact that the variance cannot be negative.

$$H_{02}: \sigma_b^2 = 0$$
$$H_{12}: \sigma_b^2 > 0$$

Finally, the hypotheses for testing the interaction effect are presented next. In this case, the null hypothesis tests whether the variance among the means for the interaction of the random effects of factors A and B is equal to zero (i.e., the means for each AB cell are about the same and thus the variability among those means is about zero). It should be noted that the sign for the alternative hypothesis is "greater than," reflecting the fact that the variance cannot be negative.

$$H_{03}: \sigma_{ab}^2 = 0$$
$$H_{13}: \sigma_{ab}^2 > 0$$

These hypotheses reflect the difference in the inferences made in the mixed-effects model. Here we see that the hypotheses about the fixed-effect A (i.e., the main effect for independent variable A) are about *means*, whereas the hypotheses involving the random-effect B (i.e., the main effect of B and the interaction effect AB) are about *variation among the means* as these involve a random effect.

15.3.3 ANOVA Summary Table and Expected Mean Squares

There are very few differences between the two-factor fixed-effects, random-effects, and mixed-effects models. The sources of variation for the mixed-effects model are again A (the fixed effect), B (the random effect), AB (the interaction effect), within, and total. The sums of squares, degrees of freedom, and mean squares are determined the same as in the fixed-effects case. However, the *F* test statistics are different in each of these models, as well as the critical values used. The *F* test statistics are formed for the test of factor A, the fixed effect, as seen here:

$$F_A = \frac{MS_A}{MS_{AB}}$$

for the test of factor B, the random effect, is computed as follows:

$$F_B = \frac{MS_B}{MS_{with}}$$

and for the test of the AB interaction, the mixed effect, as indicated here:

$$F_{AB} = \frac{MS_{AB}}{MS_{with}}$$

Recall that in the fixed-effects model, the MS_{with} is used as the error term for all three hypotheses. However, in the random-effects model, the MS_{with} is used as the error term only for the test of the interaction, and the MS_{AB} is used as the error term for the tests of both main effects. Finally, in the mixed-effects model, the MS_{with} is used as the error term for the test of factor B (the random effect) and the interaction (i.e., AB), whereas the MS_{AB} is used as the error term for the test of factor A (the fixed effect). The critical values used are those based on the degrees of freedom for the numerator and denominator of each hypothesis tested.

Thus, using the example from Chapter 13, let us assume the model is now a mixed-effects model where factor A, the fixed effect, is the type of sport in which the athlete participates (four categories). Factor B, the random effect, is selection status (two randomly chosen categories from levels such as selected as starter, selected as second string, etc.). We obtain as our test statistic for the test of factor A, the fixed effect of type of sport, as follows:

$$F_A = \frac{MS_A}{MS_{AB}} = \frac{246.1979}{7.2813} = 33.8124$$

for the test of factor B, the random effect of selection status, the test statistic is computed as:

$$F_B = \frac{MS_B}{MS_{with}} = \frac{712.5313}{11.5313} = 61.7911$$

and for the test of the AB (fixed by random effect, type of sport by selection status) interaction, we find a test statistic as follows:

$$F_{AB} = \frac{MS_{AB}}{MS_{with}} = \frac{7.2813}{11.5313} = 0.6314$$

The critical value for the test of factor A (the fixed effect, type of sport) is found in the F table as ${}_{\alpha}F_{J-1,(J-1)(K-1)}$, which for the example is ${}_{.05}F_{3,3} = 9.28$, and is statistically significant at the .05 level. The critical value for the test of factor B (the random-effect, selection status) is found in the F table as ${}_{\alpha}F_{K-1,N-JK}$, which for the example is ${}_{.05}F_{1,24} = 4.26$, and is significant at the .05 level. The critical value for the test of the interaction between type of sport and selection status is found in the F table as ${}_{\alpha}F_{J-1,(J-1)(K-1),N-JK}$, which for the example is ${}_{.05}F_{3,24} = 3.01$, and is not significant at the .05 level. It just so happens for the example data that the results for the mixed-, random-, and fixed-effects models are the same. This is not always the case.

The formation of the proper *F* ratio is again related to the expected mean squares. If H_0 is actually *true* (i.e., the variance among the means is zero), then the *expected mean squares* are as follows:

$$E(MS_A) = \sigma_\varepsilon^2$$
$$E(MS_B) = \sigma_\varepsilon^2$$
$$E(MS_{AB}) = \sigma_\varepsilon^2$$
$$E(MS_{with}) = \sigma_\varepsilon^2$$

where σ_ε^2 is the population variance of the residual errors.

If H_0 is actually *false* (the variance among the means is *not* equal to zero), then the expected mean squares are as follows:

$$E(MS_A) = \sigma_\varepsilon^2 + n\sigma_{\alpha b}^2 + Kn\left[\sum_{j=1}^{J} \alpha_j^2 / (J-1)\right]$$
$$E(MS_B) = \sigma_\varepsilon^2 + Jn\sigma_b^2$$
$$E(MS_{AB}) = \sigma_\varepsilon^2 + n\sigma_{\alpha b}^2$$
$$E(MS_{with}) = \sigma_\varepsilon^2$$

where all terms have been previously defined.

As in previous ANOVA models, the proper *F* ratio should be formed as follows:

$$F = \frac{(systematic\ variability + error\ variability)}{error\ variability}$$

For the two-factor mixed-effects model, MS_{AB} must be used as the error term for the test of A, and MS_{with} must be used as the error term for the test of B and for the interaction test.

15.3.4 Assumptions and Violation of Assumptions

Previously we described the assumptions for the two-factor random-effects model. The assumptions are nearly the same for the two-factor mixed-effects model, and we need not devote much attention to them here. As before, the assumptions are concerned with the distribution of the dependent variable scores and of the random effects. However, note that not much is known about the effects of dependence or heteroscedasticity for random effects, although we expect the effects are the same as for the fixed-effects case. A summary of the assumptions and the effects of their violation for the two-factor mixed-effects model are presented in Table 15.3.

15.3.5 Multiple Comparison Procedures

For multiple comparisons in the two-factor mixed-effects model, the researcher is not usually interested in making inferences about just the levels of the random-effect factor (i.e., B) or the interaction (i.e., AB) that were randomly sampled. Thus, estimation of the b_k or $(ab)_{jk}$

TABLE 15.3
Assumptions and Effects of Violations: Two-Factor Mixed-Effects Model

Assumption	Effect of Assumption Violation
Independence	Little is known about the effects of dependence; however, based on the fixed-effects model, we might expect the following: • Increased likelihood of a Type I and/or Type II error in F • Affects standard errors of means and inferences about those means
Homogeneity of variance	Little is known about the effects of heteroscedasticity; however, based on the fixed-effects model, we might expect the following: • Bias in SS_{with} • Increased likelihood of a Type I and/or Type II error • Small effect with equal or nearly equal n's • Otherwise effect decreases as n increases
Normality	• Minimal effect with equal or nearly equal n's • Otherwise substantial effects

terms does not provide us with any information about the b_k or $(ab)_{jk}$ terms not sampled. Also, the b_k or $(ab)_{jk}$ terms cannot be summarized by their means as they will not necessarily sum to zero for the levels sampled, only for the population of levels. However, inferences about the fixed-factor A can be made in the same way they were made for the two-factor fixed-effects model. We have already used the example data to look at some multiple comparison procedures in Chapter 13.

This concludes our discussion of random- and mixed-effects models for the one- and two-factor designs. For three-factor designs, see Keppel and Wickens (2004). In the major statistical software, the analysis of random effects can be treated as follows: in SAS PROC GLM, use the RANDOM statement to designate random effects; in SPSS GLM, random effects can also be designated, either in the point-and-click mode (by using the "Random Factor(s)" box) or in the syntax mode to designate random effects.

15.4 The One-Factor Repeated Measures Design

In this section, we describe the distinguishing characteristics of the one-factor repeated measures ANOVA model, the layout of the data, the linear model, assumptions of the model and their violation, the ANOVA summary table and expected mean squares, multiple comparison procedures, alternative ANOVA procedures, and an example.

15.4.1 Characteristics of the Model

The one-factor repeated measures model is the logical extension to the dependent t test. Although in the dependent t test there are only two measurements for each subject (e.g., the same individuals measured prior to an intervention and then again after an intervention), in the one-factor repeated measures model two *or more* measurements can be examined. The characteristics of the one-factor repeated measures ANOVA model are somewhat similar to the one-factor fixed-effects model, yet there are a number of obvious exceptions. The first unique characteristic has to do with the fact that each subject responds to each level of factor A. This is in contrast to the nonrepeated case where each subject is exposed to only one level of factor A. This design is often referred to as a **within-subjects design**, as each subject responds to each level of factor A. Thus, subjects serve as their own controls such that individual differences are taken into account. This was not the case in any of the previously discussed ANOVA models. As a result, subjects' scores are not independent across the levels of factor A. Compare this design to the one-factor fixed-effects model where total variation was decomposed into variation due to A (or between) and due to the residual (or within). In the one-factor repeated measures design, residual variation is further decomposed into variation due to subjects and variation due to the interaction between A and subjects. The reduction in the residual sum of squares yields a more powerful design as well as more precision in estimating the effects of A, and thus is more economical in that fewer subjects are necessary than in previously discussed models (Murphy et al., 2009).

The one-factor repeated measures design is also a mixed model. The subjects factor is a random effect, whereas the A factor is almost always a fixed effect. For example, if time is the fixed effect, then the researcher can examine phenomena over time. Finally, the one-factor repeated measures design is similar in some ways to the two-factor mixed-effects design except with one subject per cell. In other words, the one-factor repeated measures design is really a special case of the two-factor mixed-effects design with $n = 1$ per cell. Unequal n's can happen only when subjects miss the administration of one or more levels of factor A.

On the down side, the repeated measures design includes some risk of carry-over effects from one level of A to another because each subject responds to all levels of A. Remember that the repeated factor must be the same measure (or equated) at each measurement occasion. As examples of the carry-over effect, subjects' performance may be altered due to fatigue (decreased performance), practice (increased performance), or sensitization (increased performance) effects. These effects may be minimized by (a) counterbalancing the order of administration of the levels of A so that each subject does not receive the same order of the levels of A (this can also minimize problems with the compound symmetry assumption; see subsequent discussion), (b) allowing some time to pass between the administration of the levels of A, or (c) matching or blocking similar subjects with the assumption of subjects within a block being randomly assigned to a level of A. This last method is a type of randomized block design (see Chapter 16).

15.4.2 The Layout of the Data

The layout of the data for the one-factor repeated measures model is shown in Table 15.4. Here we see the columns designated as the levels of factor A and the rows as the subject. Thus, the columns or "levels" of factor A represent the different measurements. An example is measuring children on reading performance before, immediately after, and six months after they participate in a reading intervention. Row, column and overall means are also shown in Table 15.4, although the subject means are seldom of any utility (and thus are not reported in research studies). Here you see that the layout of the data looks the same as the two-factor model, although there is only one observation per cell.

TABLE 15.4

Layout for the One-Factor Repeated Measures ANOVA

	Level of Factor A (Repeated Factor)				
Level of Factor S	**1**	**2**	**. . .**	**J**	**Row Mean**
1	Y_{11}	Y_{12}	. . .	Y_{1J}	$\bar{Y}_{1.}$
2	Y_{21}	Y_{22}	. . .	Y_{2J}	$\bar{Y}_{2.}$
. . .					
n	Y_{n1}	Y_{n2}		Y_{nJ}	$\bar{Y}_{n.}$
Column Mean	$\bar{Y}_{.1}$	$\bar{Y}_{.2}$	. . .	$\bar{Y}_{.J}$	$\bar{Y}_{..}$

15.4.3 The ANOVA Model

The one-factor repeated measures ANOVA model is written in terms of population parameters as

$$Y_{ij} = \mu + \alpha_j + s_i + (s\alpha)_{ij} + \varepsilon_{ij}$$

where Y_{ij} is the observed score on the dependent variable for individual i responding to level j of factor A, μ is the overall or grand population mean, α_j is the fixed effect for level j of factor A, s_i is the random effect for subject i of the subject factor, $(s\alpha)_{ij}$ is the interaction between subject i and level j, and ε_{ij} is the random residual error for individual i in level j. The residual error can be due to measurement error, and/or other factors not under investigation. From the model you can see this is similar to the two-factor model only with one observation per cell. Also, the fixed effect is denoted by α and the random effect by s; thus we have a mixed-effects model. Lastly, for the equal n's model the effects for α and $s\alpha$ sum to zero for each subject (or row).

The hypotheses for testing the effect of factor A are as follows. The null hypothesis indicates that the means for each measurement are the same.

$$H_{01}: \mu_{.1} = \mu_{.2} = \ldots \mu_{.J}$$

$$H_{11}: \textit{not all the } \mu_{.j} \textit{ are equal}$$

The hypotheses are written in terms of means because factor A is a fixed effect (i.e., all sampled cases have been measured).

15.4.4 Assumptions and Violation of Assumptions

Previously we described the assumptions for the two-factor mixed-effects model. The assumptions are nearly the same for the one-factor repeated measures model (since it is similar to the two-factor mixed-effects model) and are again mainly concerned with the distribution of the dependent variable scores and of the random effects.

A new assumption is known as **compound symmetry** and states that the covariances between the scores of the subjects across the levels of the repeated factor A are constant. In other words, the covariances for all pairs of levels of the fixed factor are the same across the population of random effects (i.e., the subjects). The analysis of variance is not particularly robust to a violation of this assumption. In particular, the assumption is often violated when factor A is time, as the relationship between adjacent levels of A is stronger than when the levels are farther apart. For example, consider the previous illustration of children measured in reading performance before, after, and six months after intervention. The means of the pre- and immediate post-reading performance will likely be more similar than the means of the pre- and six months post-reading performance. If the assumption is violated, three alternative procedures are available. The first is to limit the levels of factor A (i.e., the repeated measures factor) either to those that meet the assumption, or to limit the number of repeated measures to two (in which case there would be only one covariance and thus nothing to assume). The second and more plausible alternative is to use adjusted *F* tests. These are reported shortly. The third is to use multivariate analysis of variance (MANOVA), which makes no compound symmetry assumption, but is slightly less powerful. For readers interested in MANOVA, a number of excellent multivariate textbooks can be referred to (e.g., Hahs-Vaughn, 2016).

Huynh and Feldt (1970) showed that the compound symmetry assumption is a sufficient but not necessary condition for the validity of the *F* test. Thus, the *F* test may also be valid under less stringent conditions. The necessary and sufficient condition for the validity of the *F* test is known as **sphericity**. This assumes that the variance of the difference scores for each pair of factor levels is the same (e.g., with $J = 3$ levels, the variance of the difference score between levels 1 and 2 is the same as the variance of the difference score between levels 1 and 3, which is the same as the variance of the difference score between levels 2 and 3; thus another type of homogeneity of variance assumption). Further discussion of sphericity is beyond the scope of this text (see, for example, Keppel & Wickens, 2004; Kirk, 2014; Myers, Lorch, & Well, 2010). A summary of the assumptions and the effects of their violation for the one-factor repeated measures design is presented in Table 15.5.

TABLE 15.5

Assumptions and Effects of Violations: One-Factor Repeated Measures Model

Assumption	Effect of Assumption Violation
Independence	Little is known about the effects of dependence; however, based on the fixed-effects model, we might expect the following: • Increased likelihood of a Type I and/or Type II error in *F* • Affects standard errors of means and inferences about those means
Homogeneity of variance	Little is known about the effects of heteroscedasticity; however, based on the fixed-effects model, we might expect the following: • Bias in SS_{SA} • Increased likelihood of a Type I and/or Type II error • Small effect with equal or nearly equal *n*'s • Otherwise effect decreases as *n* increases
Normality	• Minimal effect with equal or nearly equal *n*'s • Otherwise substantial effects
Sphericity	• *F* not particularly robust • Consider usual *F* test, Geisser-Greenhouse conservative *F* test, and adjusted (Huynh-Feldt) *F* test, if necessary

15.4.5 ANOVA Summary Table and Expected Mean Squares

The sources of variation for this model are similar to those for the two-factor model, except that there is no within-cell variation. The ANOVA summary table is shown in Table 15.6, where we see the following sources of variation: A (i.e., the repeated measure), subjects (denoted by S), the SA interaction, and total. The test of subject differences is of no real interest. Quite naturally, we expect there to be variation among the subjects. From the table, we see that although three mean square terms can be computed, only one F ratio results for the test of factor A; thus, the subjects effect cannot be tested anyway as there is no appropriate error term. This is subsequently shown through the expected mean squares.

Next we need to consider the sums of squares for the one-factor repeated measures model. If we take the total sum of squares and decompose it, we have the following:

$$SS_{total} = SS_A + SS_B + SS_{SA}$$

These three terms can then be computed by statistical software. The degrees of freedom, mean squares, and F ratio are determined as shown in Table 15.6.

The formation of the proper F ratio is again related to the expected mean squares. If H_0 is actually *true* (in other words, the means are the same for each of the measures), then the *expected mean squares* are as follows:

$$E(MS_A) = \sigma_\varepsilon^2$$
$$E(MS_S) = \sigma_\varepsilon^2$$
$$E(MS_{SA}) = \sigma_\varepsilon^2$$

where σ_ε^2 is the population variance of the residual errors.

If H_0 is actually *false* (i.e., the means are not the same for each of the measures), then the expected mean squares are as follows:

$$E(MS_A) = \sigma_\varepsilon^2 + \sigma_{s\alpha}^2 + n\left[\sum_{j=1}^{J} \alpha_j^2 / (J-1)\right]$$
$$E(MS_S) = \sigma_\varepsilon^2 + J\sigma_s^2$$
$$E(MS_{SA}) = \sigma_\varepsilon^2 + \sigma_{s\alpha}^2$$

TABLE 15.6

One-Factor Repeated Measures ANOVA Summary Table

Source	SS	df	MS	F
A	SS_A	$J-1$	MS_A	MS_A/MS_{SA}
S	SS_S	$n-1$	MS_S	
SA	SS_{SA}	$(J-1)(n-1)$	MS_{SA}	
Total	SS_{total}	$N-1$		

where σ_s^2 and $\sigma_{s\alpha}^2$ represent variability due to subjects and to the interaction of factor A and subjects, respectively, and other terms are as before.

As in previous ANOVA models, the proper *F* ratio should be formed as follows:

$$F = \frac{(\textit{systematic variability} + \textit{error variability})}{\textit{error variability}}$$

For the one-factor repeated measures model, MS_{SA} must be used as the error term for the test of A and there is no appropriate error term for the test of S or the test of SA (although that is fine as we are not really interested in those tests anyway since they refer to the individual cases).

As noted earlier in the discussion of assumptions for this model, the *F* test is not very robust to violation of the compound symmetry assumption. This assumption is often violated in education and the behavioral sciences; consequently, statisticians have spent considerable time studying this problem. Research suggests that the following sequential procedure be used in the test of factor A. First, do the usual *F* test that is quite liberal in terms of rejecting H_0 too often. If H_0 is not rejected, then stop. If H_0 is rejected, then continue with step 2, which is to use the Geisser and Greenhouse (1958) conservative *F* test. For the model being considered here, the degrees of freedom for the *F* critical value are adjusted to be 1 and $n - 1$. If H_0 is rejected, then stop. This would indicate that both the liberal and conservative tests reached the same conclusion to reject H_0. If H_0 is not rejected, then the two tests did not reach the same conclusion, and a further test (a tie-breaker) should be undertaken. Thus in step 3 an adjusted *F* test is conducted. The adjustment is known as Box's (Box, 1954) correction (usually referred to as the Huynh and Feldt (1970) procedure. Here the numerator degrees of freedom are $(J-1)\varepsilon$, and the denominator degrees of freedom are $(J-1)(n-1)\varepsilon$, where ε is a correction factor (not to be confused with the residual term ε). The correction factor is quite complex and is not shown here (see, for example, Keppel & Wickens, 2004; Myers et al., 2010). Most major statistical software conducts the Geisser-Greenhouse and Huynh-Feldt tests. The Huynh-Feldt test is recommended due to greater power (Keppel & Wickens, 2004; Myers et al., 2010); thus when available, you can simply use the Huynh and Feldt procedure rather than the previously recommended sequence.

15.4.6 Multiple Comparison Procedures

If the null hypothesis for repeated factor (i.e., factor A) is rejected and there are more than two levels of the factor, then the researcher may be interested in which means or combinations of means are different (in other words, which measurement means differ from one another). This could be assessed, as we have seen in previous chapters, by the use of some multiple comparison procedure (MCP). In general, most of the MCPs outlined in Chapter 12 can be used in the one-factor repeated measures model (see additional discussion in Keppel & Wickens, 2004; Mickey, Dunn, & Clark, 2004).

It has been shown that these MCPs are seriously affected by a violation of the compound symmetry assumption. In this situation two alternatives are recommended. The first alternative is, rather than using the same error term for each contrast (i.e., MS_{SA}), to use a separate error term for each contrast tested. Then many of the MCPs previously covered in Chapter 12 can be used. This complicates matters considerably (Keppel & Wickens, 2004; Kirk, 2013). A second alternative, recommended by Maxwell (1980) and Wilcox (1987), involves the use of multiple dependent t tests where the α level is adjusted much like the Bonferroni procedure. Maxwell concluded that this procedure is better than many of the other MCPs. For other similar procedures, see Hochberg and Tamhane (1987).

15.4.7 Alternative ANOVA Procedures

There are several alternative procedures to the one-factor repeated measures ANOVA model. These include the Friedman (1937) test, as well as others, such as the Agresti and Pendergast (1986) test. The Friedman test, like the Kruskal-Wallis test, is a nonparametric procedure based on ranks. However, the Kruskal-Wallis test cannot be used in a repeated measures model as it assumes that the individual scores are independent. This is obviously not the case in the one-factor repeated measures model where each individual is exposed to all levels of factor A.

Let us outline how the Friedman test is conducted. First, scores are ranked within subject. For instance, if there are $J = 4$ levels of factor A, then the scores for each subject would be ranked from 1 to 4. From this, one can compute a mean ranking for each level of factor A. The null hypothesis essentially becomes a test of whether the mean rankings for the levels of A are equal. The test statistic is a χ^2 statistic. In the case of tied ranks, either the available ranks can be averaged, or a correction factor can be used as done with the Kruskal-Wallis test (see Chapter 11). The test statistic is compared to the critical value of ${}_{\alpha}\chi^2_{J-1}$ (see Appendix Table A.3). The null hypothesis that the mean rankings are the same for the levels of factor A will be rejected if the test statistic exceeds the critical value.

You may also recall from the Kruskal-Wallis test the problem with small n's in terms of the test statistic not being precisely distributed as χ^2. The same problem exists with the Friedman test when $J < 6$ and $n < 6$, so we suggest you consult the table of critical values in (Marascuilo & McSweeney, 1977, Table A22). The Friedman test, like the Kruskal-Wallis test, assumes that the population distributions have the same shape (although not necessarily normal) and variability, and that the dependent measure is continuous. For a discussion of other alternative nonparametric procedures, see Agresti and Pendergast (1986), Myers and Well (1995), and Wilcox (1987, 1996, 2003). For information on more advanced within-subjects ANOVA models, see Cotton (1998), Keppel and Wickens (2004), and Myers et al. (2010).

Various multiple comparison procedures (MCPs) can be used for the Friedman test. For the most part, these MCPs are analogs to their parametric equivalents. In the case of planned (or a priori) pairwise comparisons, one may use multiple matched-pair Wilcoxon tests (i.e., a form of the Kruskal-Wallis test for two groups) in a Bonferroni form (i.e., taking the number of contrasts into account through an adjustment of the α level; for example, if there are six contrasts with an alpha of .05, the adjusted alpha would be .05/6 or .008). For post hoc comparisons, numerous parametric analogs are available. For additional discussion on MCPs for this model, see Marascuilo and McSweeney (1977).

15.4.8 An Example

Let us consider an example to illustrate the procedures used for this model. The data are shown in Table 15.7 where there are eight dancers, each of whom has been evaluated by four ballet instructors (who will be referred to as "raters") on ballet technique. First, let us take a look at the results for the parametric ANOVA model, as shown in Table 15.8. The F test statistic is compared to the usual F test critical value of ${}_{.05}F_{3,21} = 3.07$, which is

TABLE 15.7

Data for the Ballet Technique Example One-Factor Design: Raw Scores and Rank Scores on the Ballet Technique Task by Subject and Instructor

	Rater 1		Rater 2		Rater 3		Rater 4	
Subject	**Raw**	**Rank**	**Raw**	**Rank**	**Raw**	**Rank**	**Raw**	**Rank**
1	3	1	4	2	7	3	8	4
2	6	2	5	1	8	3	9	4
3	3	1	4	2	7	3	9	4
4	3	1	4	2	6	3	8	4
5	1	1	2	2	5	3	10	4
6	2	1	3	2	6	3	10	4
7	2	1	4	2	5	3	9	4
8	2	1	3	2	6	3	10	4

TABLE 15.8

One-Factor Repeated Measures ANOVA Summary Table for the Ballet Technique Example

Source	*SS*	*df*	*MS*	*F*
Within subjects:				
Rater (A)	198.125	3	66.042	73.477*
Error (SA)	18.875	21	.899	
Between subjects:				
Error (S)	14.875	7	2.125	
Total	231.875	31		

$^*\,_{.05}F_{3,21} = 3.07$

significant. For the Geisser-Greenhouse conservative procedure, the test statistic is compared to the critical value of $_{.05}F_{1,7} = 5.59$, which is also significant. The two procedures both yield a statistically significant result; thus we need not be concerned with a violation of the compound symmetry assumption. As an example MCP, the Bonferroni procedure determined that all pairs of raters are significantly different from one another, except for Rater 1 versus Rater 2.

Finally, let us take a look at the Friedman test. The test statistic is $\chi^2 = 22.9500$. This test statistic is compared to the critical value $_{.05}\chi^2_3 = 7.8147$, which is significant. Thus the conclusions for the parametric ANOVA and nonparametric Friedman tests are the same here. This will not always be the case, particularly when ANOVA assumptions are violated.

15.5 The Two-Factor Split-Plot or Mixed Design

Through the previous chapters, we have learned about many statistical procedures as our talented set of graduate students have assisted others and conducted studies of their own. What is in store for the group now?

For the past few chapters, we have followed Addie, Challie, Oso, and Ott, an extraordinarily talented group of graduate students working in a research lab, as they have successfully examined various questions. Knowing the success this group of students have achieved thus far, their faculty advisor feels confident that Oso can assist another faculty member at the university. Oso is working with Dr. Kilauea, the coordinator of the dance program. Dr. Kilauea has conducted an experiment in which eight ballet dancers were randomly assigned to one of two dance instructors. Each dancer was then assessed on ballet technique (e.g., body alignment, hip placement, feet placement) by four raters. Dr. Kilauea wants to know the following: if there is a mean difference in ballet technique based on instructor; if there is a mean difference in ballet technique based on rater; and if there is a mean difference in ballet technique based on the rater by instructor interaction. The research questions presented to Dr. Kilauea from Oso includes the following:

- *Is there a mean difference in ballet technique based on instructor?*
- *Is there a mean difference in ballet technique based on rater?*
- *Is there a mean difference in ballet technique based on rater by instructor?*

With one between-subjects independent variable (i.e., instructor) and one within-subjects factor (i.e., rating on ballet technique), Oso determines that a two-factor split-plot ANOVA is the best statistical procedure to use to answer Dr. Kilauea's question. His next task is to assist Dr. Kilauea in analyzing the data.

In this section, we describe the distinguishing characteristics of the two-factor split-plot or mixed ANOVA design, the layout of the data, the linear model, assumptions and their violation, the ANOVA summary table and expected mean squares, multiple comparison procedures, and an example.

15.5.1 Characteristics of the Model

The characteristics of the two-factor split-plot or mixed ANOVA design are a combination of the characteristics of the one-factor repeated measures and the two-factor fixed-effects models. It is unique because there are two factors, only one of which is repeated. For this reason the design is often called a **mixed design**. Thus, one of the factors is a *between-subjects* factor, the other is a *within-subjects* factor, and the result is known as a **split-plot design** (from agricultural research). Each subject then responds to every level of the repeated factor, but to only one level of the nonrepeated factor. Subjects then serve as their own controls for the repeated factor, but not for the nonrepeated factor. The other characteristics carry over from the one-factor repeated measures model and the two-factor model.

15.5.2 The Layout of the Data

The layout of the data for the two-factor split-plot or mixed design is shown in Table 15.9. Here we see the rows designated as the levels of factor A, the between-subjects or nonrepeated factor, and the columns as the levels of factor B, the within-subjects or repeated factor. Within each factor level combination or cell are the subjects. Notice that the same subjects appear at all levels of factor B (the within-subjects factor, the repeated measure), but only at one level of factor A (the between-subjects factor). Row, column, cell, and overall means are also shown. Here you see that the layout of the data looks much the same as the two-factor model.

TABLE 15.9

Layout for the Two-Factor Split-Plot or Mixed ANOVA

Level of Factor A (Nonrepeated Factor)	Level of Factor B (Repeated Factor) 1	2	...	K	Row Mean
1	Y_{111}	Y_{112}	...	Y_{11K}	
	.	.	...	.	
	.	.	...	.	$\bar{Y}_{.1.}$
	.	.	...	.	
	Y_{n11}	Y_{n12}	...	Y_{n1K}	
	$\bar{Y}_{.11}$	$\bar{Y}_{.12}$	...	$\bar{Y}_{.1K}$	
2	Y_{121}	Y_{122}	...	Y_{12K}	
	.	.	...	.	$\bar{Y}_{.2.}$
	.	.	...	.	
	Y_{n21}	Y_{n22}	...	Y_{n2K}	
	$\bar{Y}_{.21}$	$\bar{Y}_{.22}$	...	$\bar{Y}_{.2K}$	
.	.	.	...	.	.
.	.	.	...	.	.
.	.	.	...	.	.
J	Y_{1J1}	Y_{1J2}	...	Y_{1JK}	
	.	.	...	.	
	.	.	...	.	$\bar{Y}_{.J.}$
	.	.	...	.	
	Y_{nJ1}	Y_{nJ2}	...	Y_{nJK}	
	$\bar{Y}_{.J1}$	$\bar{Y}_{.J2}$	...	$\bar{Y}_{.JK}$	
Column Mean	$\bar{Y}_{..1}$	$\bar{Y}_{..2}$		$\bar{Y}_{..K}$	$\bar{Y}_{...}$

Note: Each subject is measured at all levels of factor B, but at only one level of factor A.

15.5.3 The ANOVA Model

The two-factor split-plot model can be written in terms of population parameters as follows:

$$Y_{ijk} = \mu + \alpha_j + s_{i(j)} + \beta_k + (\alpha\beta)_{jk} + (\beta s)_{ki(j)} + \varepsilon_{ijk}$$

where Y_{ijk} is the observed score on the dependent variable for individual i in level j of factor A (the between-subjects factor) and level k of factor B (i.e., the jk cell, the within-subjects factor or repeated measure), μ is the overall or grand population mean (i.e., regardless of cell designation), α_j is the effect for level j of factor A (row effect for the nonrepeated factor), $s_{i(j)}$ is the effect of subject i that is nested within level j of factor A (i.e., $i(j)$ denotes that i is nested within j), β_k is the effect for level k of factor B (column effect for the repeated factor), $(\alpha b)_{jk}$ is the interaction effect for the combination of level j of factor A and level k of factor B, $(\beta s)_{ki(j)}$ is the interaction effect for the combination of level k of factor B (the within-subjects factor, the repeated measure) and subject i that is nested within level j of factor A (the between-subjects factor), and ε_{ijk} is the random residual error for individual i in cell jk.

We use the terminology "subjects are nested within factor A" to indicate that a particular subject S_i is exposed to only one level of factor A (the between-subjects factor), level j. This observation is then denoted in the subjects effect by $S_{i(j)}$ and in the interaction effect by $(\beta s)_{ki(j)}$. This is due to the fact that not all possible combinations of subject with the levels of factor A are included in the model. A more extended discussion of designs with nested factors is given in Chapter 16. The residual error can be due to individual differences, measurement error, and/or other factors not under investigation. We assume for now that A and B are fixed-effects factors and that S is a random-effects factor.

It should be mentioned that for the equal n's model, the sum of the row effects, the sum of the column effects, and the sum of the interaction effects are all equal to zero, both across rows and across columns. This implies, for example, that if there are any nonzero row effects, then the row effects will balance out around zero with some positive and some negative effects.

The hypotheses to be tested here are exactly the same as in the nonrepeated two-factor ANOVA model (see Chapter 13). For the two-factor ANOVA model, there are three sets of hypotheses, one for each of the main effects, and one for the interaction effect. The null and alternative hypotheses, respectively, for testing the main effect of factor A (between-subjects factor) are as follows:

$$H_{01}: \mu_{.1.} = \mu_{.2.} = \ldots \mu_{.J.}$$

$$H_{11}: \textit{not all the } \mu_{.j.} \textit{ are equal}$$

The hypotheses for testing the main effect of factor B (within-subjects factor, i.e., the repeated measure) are noted as:

$$H_{02}: \mu_{..1} = \mu_{..2} = \ldots \mu_{..K}$$

$$H_{12}: \textit{not all the } \mu_{..k} \textit{ are equal}$$

Finally, the hypotheses for testing the interaction effect (i.e., the between- by within-factors effect) are as follows:

$$H_{03}: (\mu_{.jk} - \mu_{.j.} - \mu_{..k} + \mu) = 0 \textit{ for all } j \textit{ and } k$$

$$H_{13}: \textit{not all the } (\mu_{.jk} - \mu_{.j.} - \mu_{..k} + \mu) = 0$$

If one of the null hypotheses is rejected, then the researcher may want to consider a multiple comparison procedure so as to determine which means or combination of means are significantly different (discussed later in this chapter).

15.5.4 Assumptions and Violation of Assumptions

Previously we described the assumptions for the different two-factor models and the one-factor repeated measures model. The assumptions for the two-factor split-plot or mixed design are actually a combination of these two sets of assumptions.

The assumptions can be divided into two sets of assumptions, one for the between-subjects factor and one for the within-subjects (or repeated measures) factor. For the between-subjects factor, we have the usual assumptions of population scores being random, independent, and normally distributed with equal variances. For the within-subjects factor (i.e., the repeated measure), the assumption is the already familiar compound symmetry assumption. For this design, the assumption involves the population covariances for all pairs of the levels of the within-subjects factor (i.e., k and k') being equal, at each level of the between-subjects factor (for all levels j). To deal with this assumption, we look at alternative F tests in the next section. A summary of the assumptions and the effects of their violation for the two-factor split-plot or mixed design are presented in Table 15.10.

15.5.5 ANOVA Summary Table and Expected Mean Squares

The ANOVA summary table is shown in Table 15.11, where we see the following sources of variation: A, S, B, AB, BS, and total. The table is divided into within-subjects sources and between-subjects sources. The between-subjects sources are A and S, where S will be used as the error term for the test of factor A. The within-subjects sources are B, AB, and BS, where BS will be used as the error term for the test of factor B and of the AB interaction. This will become clear when we examine the expected mean squares shortly.

TABLE 15.10
Assumptions and Effects of Violations: Two-Factor Split-Plot or Mixed Model

Assumption	Effect of Assumption Violation
Independence	• Increased likelihood of a Type I and/or Type II error in F • Affects standard errors of means and inferences about those means
Homogeneity of variance	• Bias in error terms • Increased likelihood of a Type I and/or Type II error • Small effect with equal or nearly equal n's • Otherwise effect decreases as n increases
Normality	• Minimal effect with equal or nearly equal n's • Otherwise substantial effects
Sphericity	• F not particularly robust • Consider usual F test, Geisser-Greenhouse conservative F test, and adjusted (Huynh-Feldt) F test, if necessary

TABLE 15.11

Two-Factor Split-Plot or Mixed Model ANOVA Summary Table

Source	*SS*	*df*	*MS*	*F*
Between subjects:				
A	SS_A	$J-1$	MS_A	MS_A/MS_A
S	SS_S	$J(n-1)$	MS_S	
Within subjects:				
B	SS_B	$K-1$	MS_B	MS_B/MS_{BS}
AB	SS_{AB}	$(J-1)(K-1)$	MS_{AB}	MS_{AB}/MS_{BS}
BS	SS_{BS}	$(K-1)J(n-1)$	MS_{BS}	
Total	SS_{total}	$N-1$		

Next we need to consider the sums of squares for the two-factor mixed design. Taking the total sum of squares and decomposing it yields the following:

$$SS_{total} = SS_A + SS_S + SS_B + SS_{AB} + SS_{BS}$$

We leave the computation of these five terms for statistical software. The degrees of freedom, mean squares, and F ratios are computed as shown in Table 15.11.

The formation of the proper F ratio is again related to the expected mean squares. If H_0 is actually *true* (i.e., the means are really equal), then the *expected mean squares* are as follows:

$$E(MS_A) = \sigma_\varepsilon^2$$

$$E(MS_S) = \sigma_\varepsilon^2$$

$$E(MS_B) = \sigma_\varepsilon^2$$

$$E(MS_{AB}) = \sigma_\varepsilon^2$$

$$E(MS_{BS}) = \sigma_\varepsilon^2$$

where σ_ε^2 is the population variance of the residual errors.

If H_0 is actually *false* (i.e., the means are really not equal), then the expected mean squares are as follows:

$$E(MS_A) = \sigma_\varepsilon^2 + K\sigma_s^2 + nK\left[\sum_{j=1}^{J}\alpha_j^2/(J-1)\right]$$

$$E(MS_S) = \sigma_\varepsilon^2 + K\sigma_s^2$$

$$E(MS_B) = \sigma_\varepsilon^2 + \sigma_{\beta s}^2 + nJ\left[\sum_{k=1}^{K}\beta_k^2/(K-1)\right]$$

$$E(MS_{AB}) = \sigma_\varepsilon^2 + \sigma_{\beta s}^2 + n\left[\sum_{j=1}^{J}\sum_{k=1}^{K}(\alpha\beta)_{jk}^2/(J-1)(K-1)\right]$$

$$E(MS_{BS}) = \sigma_\varepsilon^2 + \sigma_{\beta s}^2$$

where $\sigma^2_{\beta s}$ represents variability due to the interaction of factor B (the within-subjects or repeated measures factor) and subjects, and the other terms are as before.

As in previous ANOVA models, the proper F ratio should be formed as follows:

$$F = \frac{(\textit{systematic variability} + \textit{error variability})}{\textit{error variability}}$$

For the two-factor split-plot design, the error term for the proper test of factor A (the between-subjects factor) is the S term, whereas the error term for the proper tests of factor B (the within-subjects or repeated measures factor) and the AB interaction is the BS interaction. For models where factors A and B are not both fixed-effects factors, see Keppel and Wickens (2004).

As the compound symmetry assumption is often violated, we again suggest the following sequential procedure to test for B (the repeated measure) and for AB (the within-by between-subjects factor interaction). First, do the usual F test, which is quite liberal in terms of rejecting H_0 too often. If H_0 is not rejected, then stop. If H_0 is rejected, then continue with Step 2, which is to use the Geisser-Greenhouse (1958) conservative F test. For the model under consideration here, the degrees of freedom for the F critical values are adjusted to be 1 and $J(n - 1)$ for the test of B, and $J - 1$ and $J(n - 1)$ for the test of the AB interaction. There is no conservative test necessary for factor A, the between-subjects nonrepeated factor, as the assumption does not apply; thus, the usual test is all that is necessary for the test of A. If H_0 for B and/or AB is rejected, then stop. This would indicate that both the liberal and conservative tests reached the same conclusion to reject H_0. If H_0 is not rejected, then the two tests did not yield the same conclusion, and an adjusted F test is conducted. The adjustment is known as Box's (1954) correction [or the Huynh and Feldt (1970) procedure]. Most major statistical software conducts the Geisser-Greenhouse and Huynh-Feldt tests.

15.5.6 Multiple Comparison Procedures

Consider the situation where the null hypothesis for any of the three hypotheses is rejected (i.e., for A, B, and/or AB). If there is more than one degree of freedom in the numerator for any of these hypotheses, then the researcher may be interested in which means or combinations of means are different. This could be assessed again by the use of some multiple comparison procedure (MCP). Thus, the procedures outlined in Chapter 13 (i.e., for main effects, and for simple and complex interaction contrasts) for the regular two-factor ANOVA model can be adapted to this model.

However, it has been shown that the MCPs involving the repeated factor are seriously affected by a violation of the compound symmetry assumption. In this situation, two alternatives are recommended. The first alternative is, rather than using the same error term for each contrast involving the repeated factor (i.e., MS_B or MS_{AB}), to use a separate error term for each contrast tested. Then many of the MCPs previously covered in Chapter 12 can be used. This complicates matters considerably (Keppel & Wickens, 2004; Kirk, 2014). The second and simpler alternative is suggested by Shavelson (1996). He recommended that the appropriate error terms be used in MCPs involving the main effects, but for interaction contrasts both error terms be pooled (or added) together (this procedure is conservative, yet simpler than the first alternative).

15.5.7 An Example

Consider now an example problem to illustrate the two-factor mixed design. Here we expand on the example presented earlier in this chapter by adding a second factor to the model. The data are shown in Table 15.12 where there are eight dancers, each of whom has been evaluated by four raters on ballet technique (rater is the *within-subjects factor* as each individual has been evaluated by four raters). Ratings on ballet technique can range from 1 (lowest rating) to 10 (highest rating). Each dancer was also randomly assigned to one of two ballet instructors. Thus, factor A is the between-subjects factor. In this illustration, factor A represents the dance instructors, where we see that four subjects are randomly assigned to level 1 of factor A (i.e., ballet instructor 1) and the remaining four to level 2 of factor A (i.e., ballet instructor 2). Thus, factor B (i.e., rater) is repeated (the within-subjects factor) and factor A (i.e., ballet instructor) is not repeated (the between-subjects factor). The ANOVA summary table is shown in Table 15.13.

The test statistics are compared to the following usual F test critical values: for factor A (the between-subjects factor that tests mean differences based on instructor), ${}_{.05}F_{1,6} = 5.99$, which is not statistically significant; for factor B (the within-subjects factor that tests mean differences based on repeated ratings), ${}_{.05}F_{3,18} = 3.16$, which is significant; and for AB, ${}_{.05}F_{3,18} = 3.16$, which is also statistically significant. For the Geisser-Greenhouse conservative procedure, the test statistics are compared to the following critical values: for factor A (i.e., between-subjects factor, ballet instructor) no conservative procedure is necessary; for factor B (i.e., within-subjects factor or the repeated measure), ${}_{.05}F_{1,6} = 5.99$, which is also significant; and for the interaction AB (ballet instructor by rater), ${}_{.05}F_{1,6} = 5.99$, which is also significant. The usual and Geisser-Greenhouse procedures both yield a statistically significant result for factor B (rater) and for the interaction AB (ballet instructor by rater); thus we need not be concerned with a violation of the sphericity assumption. A profile plot of the interaction is shown in Figure 15.2.

TABLE 15.12

Data for the Ballet Technique Example Two-Factor Design: Raw Scores on the Ballet Technique Task by Instructor and Rater

Factor A (Nonrepeated Factor)		Factor B (Repeated Factor)			
Ballet Instructor	**Subject**	**Rater 1**	**Rater 2**	**Rater 3**	**Rater 4**
1	1	3	4	7	8
	2	6	5	8	9
	3	3	4	7	9
	4	3	4	6	8
2	5	1	2	5	10
	6	2	3	6	10
	7	2	4	5	9
	8	2	3	6	10

TABLE 15.13

Two-Factor Split-Plot ANOVA Summary Table for the Ballet Technique Example

Source	SS	df	MS	F
Between subjects:				
Instructor (A)	6.125	1	6.125	4.200**
Error (S)	8.750	6	1.458	
Within subjects:				
Rater (B)	198.125	3	66.042	190.200*
Instructor x Rater	12.625	3	4.208	12.120*
Error (BS)	6.250	18	0.347	
Total	231.875	31		

$^{*}{}_{.05}F_{3,18} = 3.16$

$^{**}{}_{.05}F_{1,6} = 5.99$

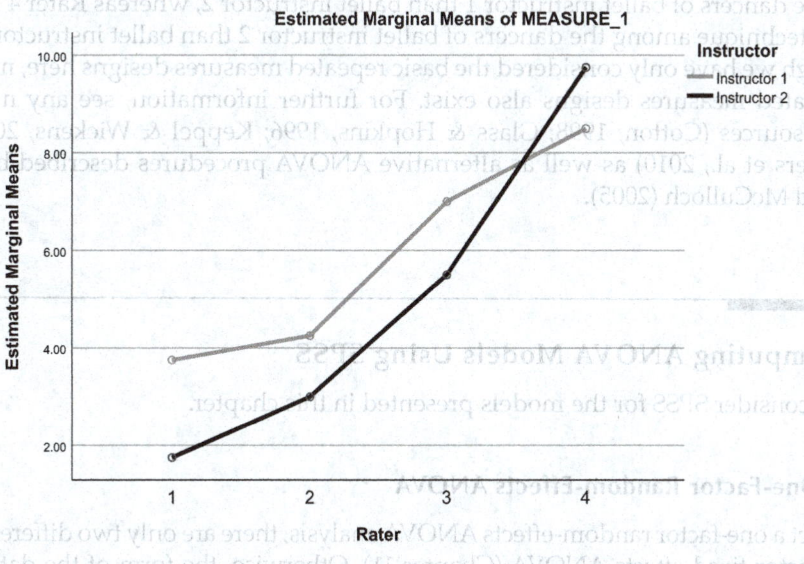

FIGURE 15.2
Profile plot for example data.

There is a significant AB (i.e., instructor by rater) interaction, so we should follow this up with simple interaction contrasts, each involving only four cell means. As an example of a MCP, consider the following contrast:

$$\psi' = \frac{(\bar{Y}_{.11} - \bar{Y}_{.21}) - (\bar{Y}_{.14} - \bar{Y}_{.24})}{4} = \frac{(3.75 - 1.75) - (8.50 - 9.75)}{4} = 0.8125$$

with a standard error computed as follows:

$$se_{\psi'} = \sqrt{MS_{BS}\left(\frac{\sum_{j=1}^{J}\sum_{k=1}^{K} c_{jk}^2}{n_{jk}}\right)} = \sqrt{0.3472\left(\frac{1/16+1/16+1/16+1/16}{4}\right)} = 0.1473$$

Using the Scheffé procedure, we formulate the following as the test statistic:

$$t = \frac{\psi'}{se_{\psi'}} = \frac{0.8125}{0.1473} = 5.5160$$

This is compared with the critical value presented here:

$$\sqrt{(J-1)(K-1)\,{}_{\alpha}F_{(J-1)(K-1),(K-1)J(n-1)}} = \sqrt{3\left({}_{.05}F_{3,18}\right)} = \sqrt{3(3.16)} = 3.0790$$

Thus, we may conclude that the tetrad interaction difference between the first and second levels of factor A (ballet instructor) and the first and fourth levels of factor B (rater, the repeated measure) is significant. In other words, Rater 1 finds better ballet technique among the dancers of ballet instructor 1 than ballet instructor 2, whereas Rater 4 finds better ballet technique among the dancers of ballet instructor 2 than ballet instructor 1.

Although we have only considered the basic repeated measures designs here, more complex repeated measures designs also exist. For further information, see any number of excellent sources (Cotton, 1998; Glass & Hopkins, 1996; Keppel & Wickens, 2004; Kirk, 2014; Myers et al., 2010) as well as alternative ANOVA procedures described by Wilcox (2003) and McCulloch (2005).

15.6 Computing ANOVA Models Using SPSS

Next we consider SPSS for the models presented in this chapter.

15.6.1 One-Factor Random-Effects ANOVA

To conduct a one-factor random-effects ANOVA analysis, there are only two differences from the one-factor fixed-effects ANOVA (Chapter 11). Otherwise, the form of the data and the conduct of the analyses are exactly the same. In terms of the form of the data, one column or variable indicates the levels or categories of the independent variable (i.e., the random factor), and the second is for the dependent variable. Each row then represents one individual, indicating the level or group that individual is a member of (1, 2, 3, or 4 in our example; recall that for the one-factor random-effects ANOVA, these categories are randomly selected from the population of categories), and their score on the dependent variable. Thus, we wind up with two long columns of group values and scores as shown in the screenshot in Figure 15.3. The data used to illustrate has measured customer satisfaction based on the location visited by the customer. The independent variable, location, is a random factor rather than fixed as the locations were randomly selected from the population of all locations. The dependent variable is a measure of customer satisfaction with their experience.

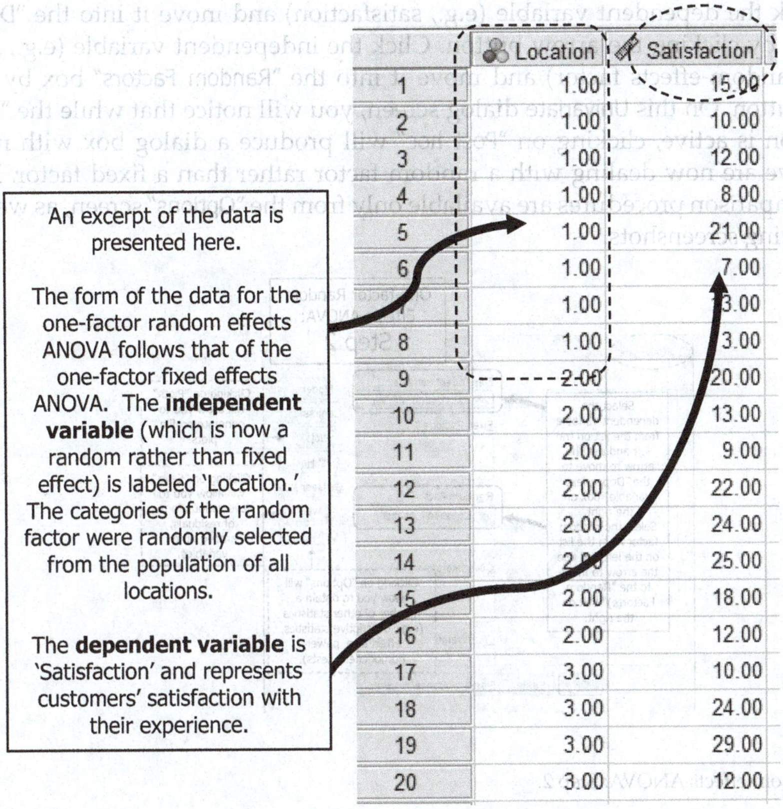

An excerpt of the data is presented here.

The form of the data for the one-factor random effects ANOVA follows that of the one-factor fixed effects ANOVA. The **independent variable** (which is now a random rather than fixed effect) is labeled 'Location.' The categories of the random factor were randomly selected from the population of all locations.

The **dependent variable** is 'Satisfaction' and represents customers' satisfaction with their experience.

	Location	Satisfaction
1	1.00	15.00
2	1.00	10.00
3	1.00	12.00
4	1.00	8.00
5	1.00	21.00
6	1.00	7.00
7	1.00	3.00
8	1.00	3.00
9	2.00	20.00
10	2.00	13.00
11	2.00	9.00
12	2.00	22.00
13	2.00	24.00
14	2.00	25.00
15	2.00	18.00
16	2.00	12.00
17	3.00	10.00
18	3.00	24.00
19	3.00	29.00
20	3.00	12.00

FIGURE 15.3
One-factor random-effects ANOVA data.

Step 1. To conduct a one-factor random-effects ANOVA, go to "Analyze" in the top pull-down menu, then select "General Linear Model," and then select "Univariate." Following the screenshot for Step 1 (shown in Figure 15.4) produces the Univariate dialog box.

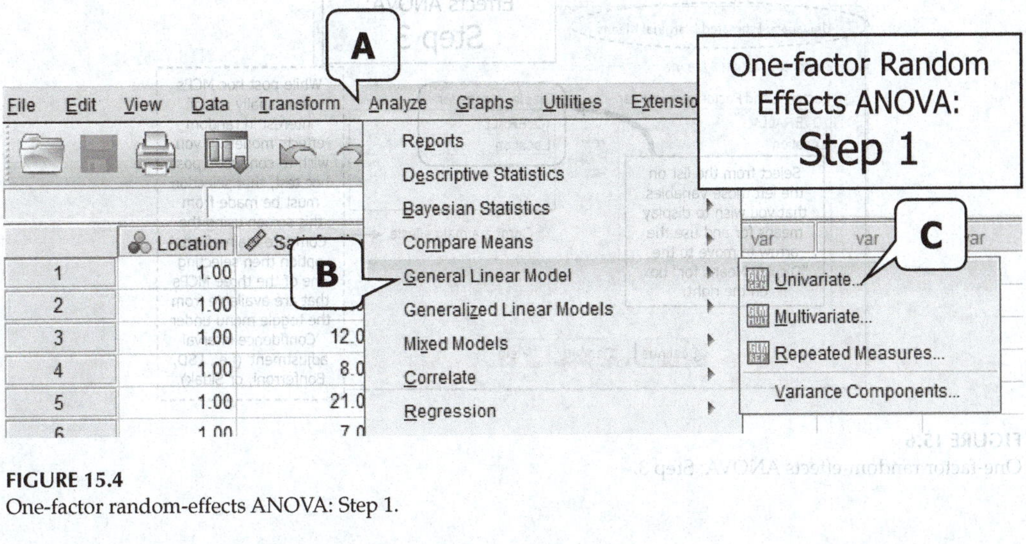

FIGURE 15.4
One-factor random-effects ANOVA: Step 1.

Step 2. Click the dependent variable (e.g., satisfaction) and move it into the "Dependent Variable" box by clicking the arrow button. Click the independent variable (e.g., location; this is the random-effects factor) and move it into the "Random Factors" box by clicking the arrow button. On this Univariate dialog screen, you will notice that while the "Post hoc" option button is active, clicking on "Post hoc" will produce a dialog box with no active options as we are now dealing with a random factor rather than a fixed factor. Post hoc multiple comparison procedures are available only from the "Options" screen, as we will see in the following screenshots.

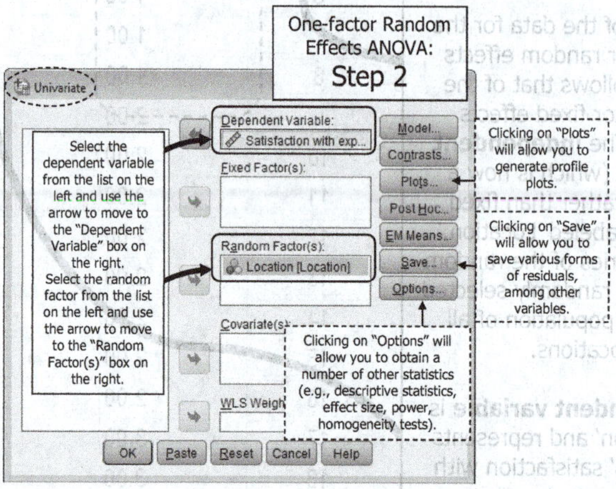

FIGURE 15.5
One-factor random-effects ANOVA: Step 2.

Step 3. Clicking on "EM Means" provides the option to display marginal and overall means. Click on "Continue" to return to the original dialog box. *Note that if you are interested in a multiple comparison procedure for testing mean differences of the random effect, post hoc MCPs are available only from this screen.* To select a post hoc procedure, click on "Compare main effects" and use the toggle menu to reveal the Tukey LSD, Bonferroni, and Sidak procedures. However, we have already mentioned that MCPs are not generally of interest for this model.

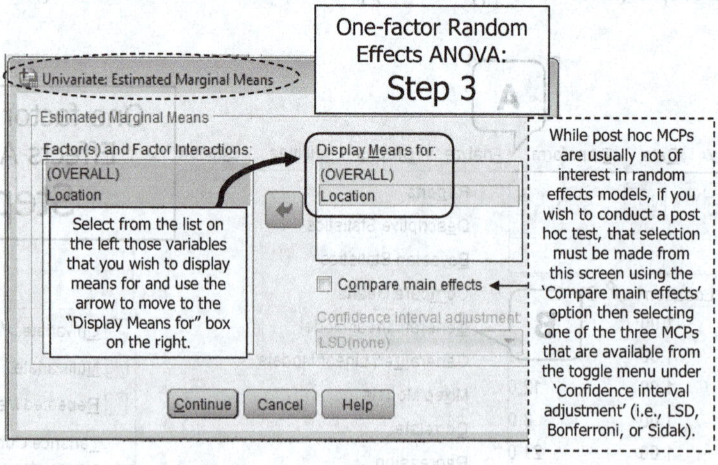

FIGURE 15.6
One-factor random-effects ANOVA: Step 3.

Step 4. Clicking on "Options" provides the option to select such information as "Descriptive statistics," "Estimates of effect size," "Observed power," and "Homogeneity tests" (i.e., Levene's test for equal variances). Click on "Continue" to return to the original dialog box.

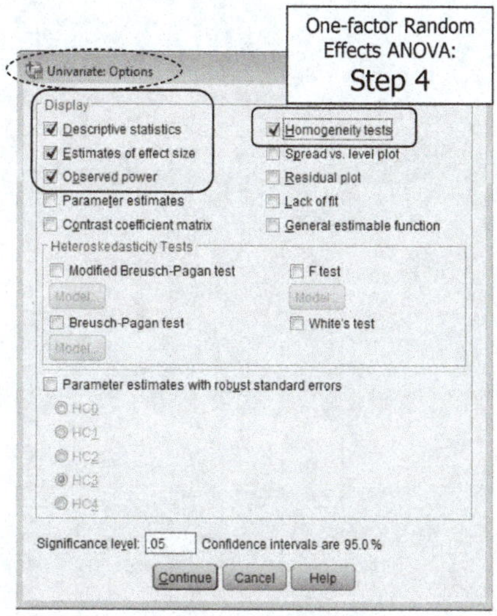

FIGURE 15.7
One-factor random-effects ANOVA: Step 4.

Step 5. From the Univariate dialog box, click on "Plots" to obtain a profile plot of means. Click the random factor (e.g., "Location") and move it into the "Horizontal Axis" box by clicking the arrow button (see screenshot for Step 5a, Figure 15.8). Then click on "Add" to move the variable into the "Plots" box at the bottom of the dialog box (see screenshot for Step 5b, Figure 15.9). Click on "Continue" to return to the original dialog box.

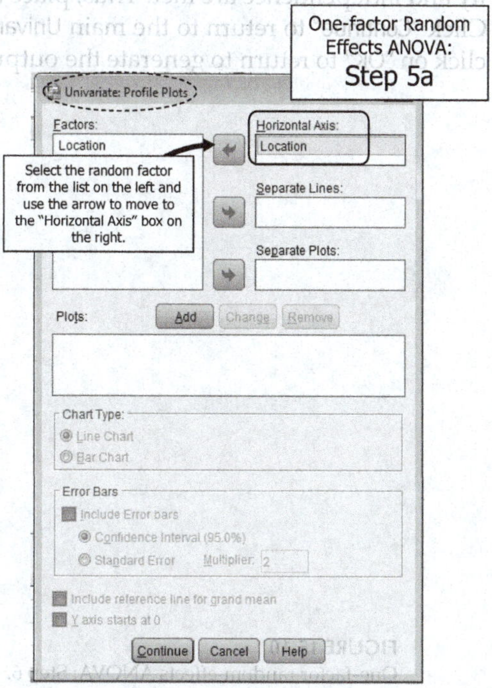

FIGURE 15.8
One-factor random-effects ANOVA: Step 5a.

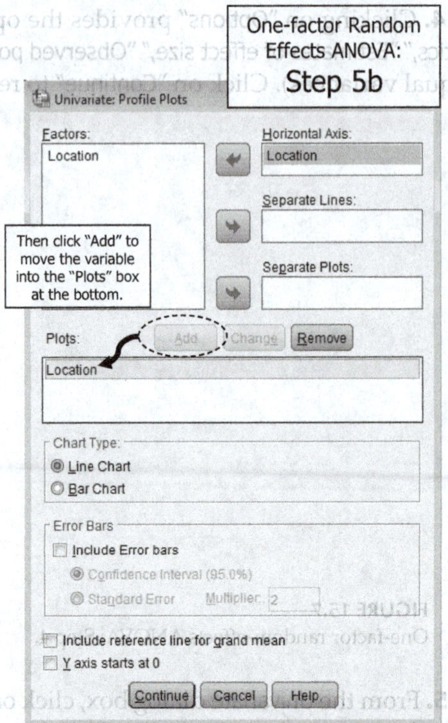

FIGURE 15.9
One-factor random-effects ANOVA: Step 5b.

Step 6. From the Univariate dialog box (see the screenshot for Step 2, Figure 15.5), click on "Save" to select those elements that you want to save. In our case, we want to save the unstandardized residuals which will be used later to examine the extent to which normality and independence are met. Thus, place a checkmark in the box next to "Unstandardized." Click "Continue" to return to the main Univariate dialog box. From the Univariate dialog box, click on "OK" to return to generate the output.

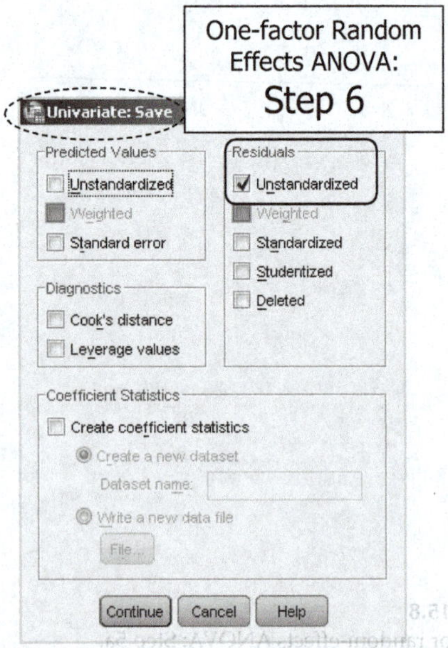

FIGURE 15.10
One-factor random-effects ANOVA: Step 6.

15.6.2 Two-Factor Random-Effects ANOVA

To run a two-factor random-effects ANOVA model, there are the same two differences from the two-factor fixed-effects ANOVA (covered in Chapter 13). First, on the GLM screen (shown in the screenshot in Figure 15.11), click both factor names into the "Random Factor(s)" box rather than the "Fixed Factor(s)" box. Second, the same situation exists with MCPs: if you are interested in a multiple comparison procedure for the random factors, post hoc MCPs are available only from the "EM Means" screen. However, we have already mentioned that MCPs are not generally of interest for this model. For brevity, the subsequent screenshots are not presented.

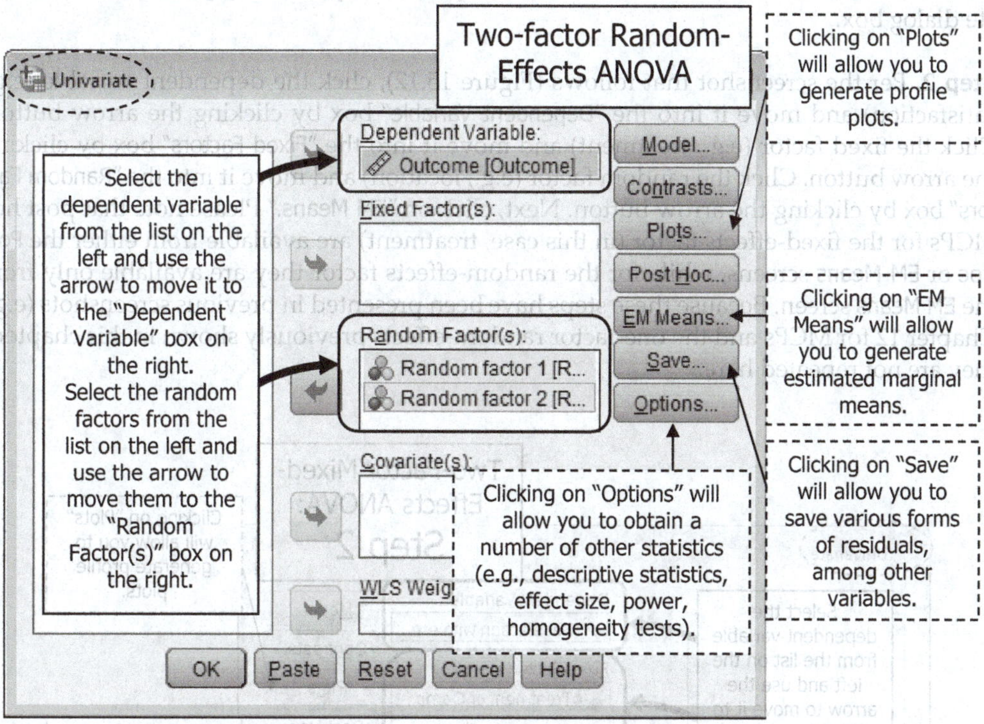

FIGURE 15.11
Two-factor random-effects ANOVA.

15.6.3 Two-Factor Mixed-Effects ANOVA

To conduct a two-factor mixed-effects ANOVA, there are three differences from the two-factor fixed-effects ANOVA when using SPSS to analyze the model. The first is that both a random and a fixed effect factor must be defined (see the screenshot for Step 2, Figure 15.12). The second difference is that post hoc MCPs for the fixed-effects factor are available from either the "Post Hoc" or "EM Means" screens, while for the random-effects factor they are available only from the "EM Means" screen. The third difference is related to the output provided by SPSS. Unfortunately, the *F* statistic for any main effect that is random in a mixed-effects model is computed incorrectly in SPSS because the wrong error term is used when implementing the SPSS point-and-click mode. As described in Lomax and Surman (2007) and extended by Li and Lomax (2011), you need to either (a) compute the *F* statistics by hand from the *MS* values (which are correct), (b) use SPSS syntax where the user indicates the proper error terms, or (c) use a different software package (e.g., SAS, where the user also provides the proper error terms). These options are not presented here. Rather, readers are referred to the appropriate references. For the purpose of this illustration, we will use the satisfaction data. The dependent variable is satisfaction with the customer experience. Assignment to an intervention or comparison group will be a fixed factor, and the location will be a random factor.

Step 1. To conduct a one-factor fixed-effects ANOVA, go to "Analyze" in the top pulldown menu, then select "General Linear Model," and then select "Univariate." Following screenshot one for the one-factor random-effects ANOVA presented previously produces the Univariate dialog box.

Step 2. Per the screenshot that follows (Figure 15.12), click the dependent variable (e.g., satisfaction) and move it into the "Dependent Variable" box by clicking the arrow button. Click the fixed factor (e.g., treatment) and move it into the "Fixed Factors" box by clicking the arrow button. Click the random factor (e.g., location) and move it into the "Random Factors" box by clicking the arrow button. Next, click on "EM Means." Please note that post hoc MCPs for the fixed-effects factor (in this case, treatment) are available from either the Post Hoc or EM Means screens, while for the random-effects factor they are available only from the EM Means screen. Because these steps have been presented in previous screenshots (e.g., Chapter 12 for MCPs and the one-factor random-effects previously shown in this chapter), they are not repeated here.

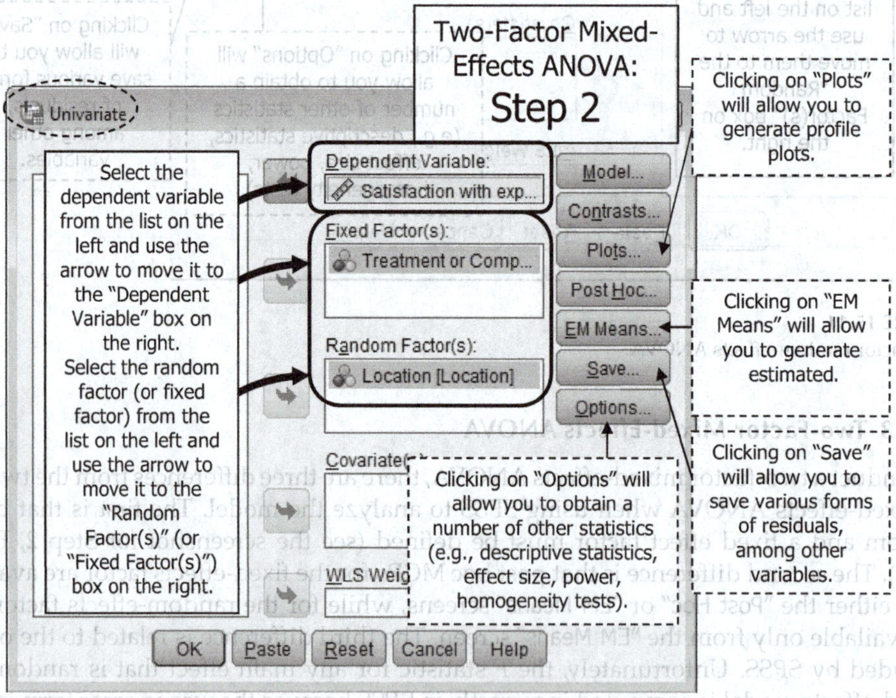

FIGURE 15.12
Two-factor mixed-effects ANOVA: Step 2.

15.6.4 One-Factor Repeated Measures ANOVA

In order to run a one-factor repeated measures ANOVA model, the data have to be in the form suggested by the following screenshot. Each row represents one dancer in our sample. All of the scores for each subject must be in one row of the dataset and each level of the repeated factor is a separate variable (represented by the columns). For example, if there are four raters who assess each dancer's ballet technique, there will be variables for each rater (e.g., Rater1 through Rater4; example dataset on the website). In this illustration, we have both raw scores and ranked data for each of the four raters. When using ANOVA for repeated measures, we will apply the raw scores. The ranked scores will be of value only when computing the nonparametric version of ANOVA (i.e., the Friedman test) which will be covered later in this chapter.

	Rater1_raw	Rater2_raw	Rater3_raw	Rater4_raw	Rater1_rank	Rater2_rank	Rater3_rank	Rater4_rank
1	3.00	4.00	7.00	8.00	1.00	2.00	3.00	4.00
2	6.00	5.00	8.00	9.00	2.00	1.00	3.00	4.00
3	3.00	4.00	7.00	9.00	1.00	2.00	3.00	4.00
4	3.00	4.00	6.00	8.00	1.00	2.00	3.00	4.00
5	1.00	2.00	5.00	10.00	1.00	2.00	3.00	4.00
6	2.00	3.00	6.00	10.00	1.00	2.00	3.00	4.00
7	2.00	4.00	5.00	9.00	1.00	2.00	3.00	4.00
8	2.00	3.00	6.00	10.00	1.00	2.00	3.00	4.00

> For the repeated measures ANOVA, each row represents one dancer in our sample. Each column represents one level of the repeated measures factor. For this illustration, four raters assessed the ballet technique of each dancer in the sample, thus there are four columns that represent the raw scores of each of the raters (Rater1_raw, Rater2_raw, etc.) and four scores that represent the ranked scores of each of the raters (Rater1_rank, Rater2_rank, etc.).

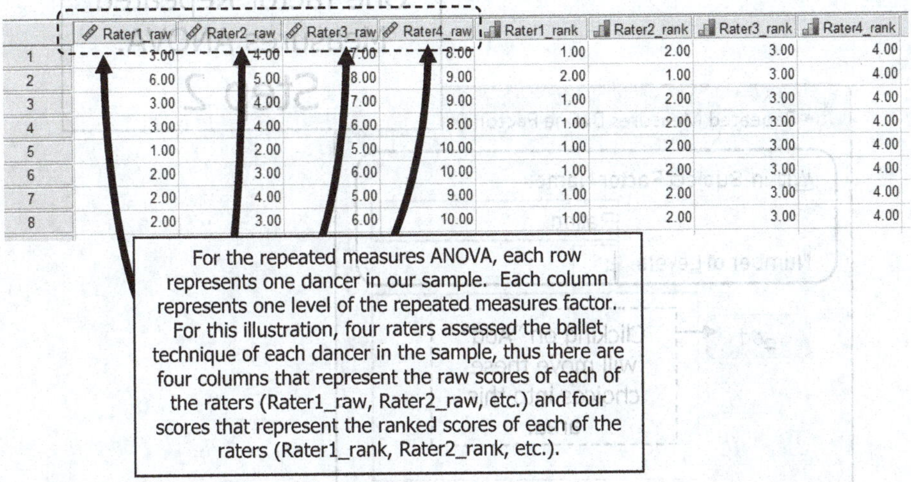

FIGURE 15.13
Repeated measures ANOVA data.

Step 1. To conduct a one-factor repeated measures ANOVA, go to "Analyze" in the top pull-down menu, then select "General Linear Model," and then select "Repeated Measures." Following the screenshot for Step 1 (Figure 15.14) produces the Repeated Measures dialog box.

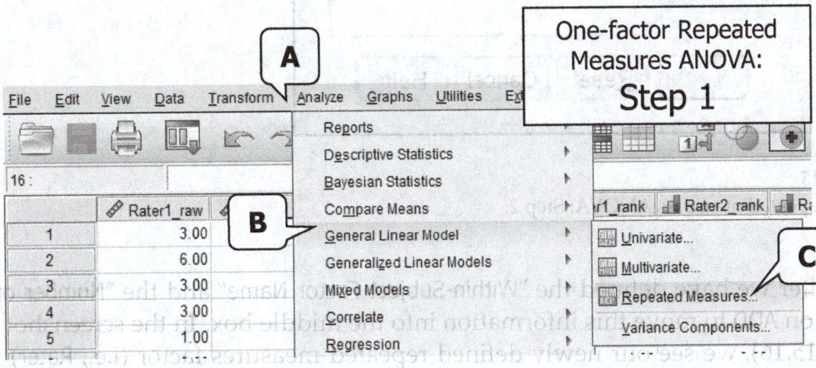

FIGURE 15.14
One-factor repeated measures ANOVA: Step 1.

Step 2. The "Repeated Measures Define Factor(s)" dialog box will appear (see Figure 15.15). In the box under "Within-Subject Factor Name," enter the name you wish to call the repeated factor. For this illustration, we will label the repeated measure "Rating." It is necessary to define a name for the repeated factor as there is no single variable representing this factor (recall that the columns in the dataset represent the repeated measures); in the dataset there is one variable for each level of the factor (in other words, one variable for each different rater or measurement). Again, in our example, there are four levels of rater (i.e., four raters) and thus four variables. Thus we name the within-subjects factor "Rating." The "Number of Levels" indicates the number of measurements of the repeated measure. In this example, there were four raters, and thus the "number of levels" of the factor is 4.

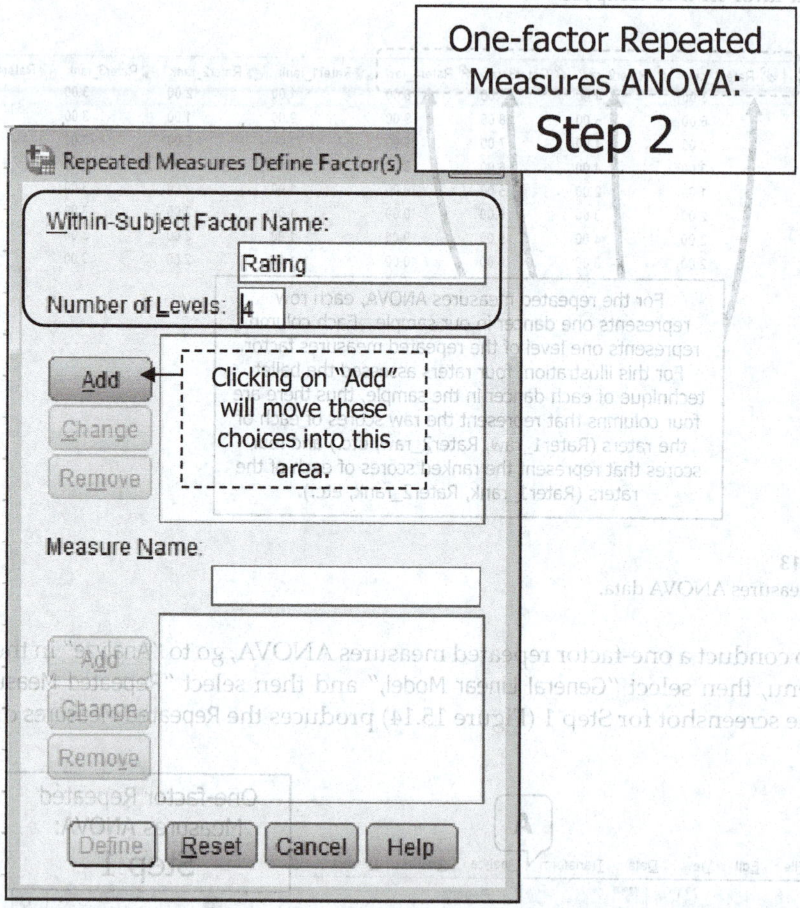

FIGURE 15.15
One-factor repeated measures ANOVA: Step 2.

Step 3. After we have defined the "Within-Subject Factor Name" and the "Number of Levels," then click on ADD to move this information into the middle box. In the screenshot for Step 3 (Figure 15.16), we see our newly defined repeated measures factor (i.e., Rater) with "4" indicating that there are four levels: Rater(4). Finally, click on "Define" to open the main Repeated Measures dialog box.

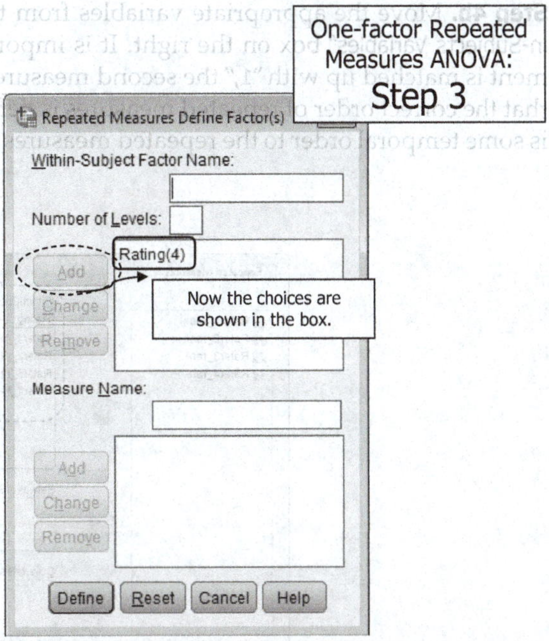

FIGURE 15.16
One-factor repeated measures ANOVA: Step 3.

Step 4a. From the Repeated Measures dialog box (see the screenshot for Step 4a, Figure 15.17), we see a heading called "Within-Subjects Variables" with the newly defined factor rater in parentheses. In this illustration, the values of 1 through 4 represent each one of the four raters that we just defined through the screenshot in Figure 15.16. Preceding each of the levels of the repeated factor are lines with question marks. This is the software's way of asking us to define which variable from the list on the left represents the first measurement (or the first rater in our illustration).

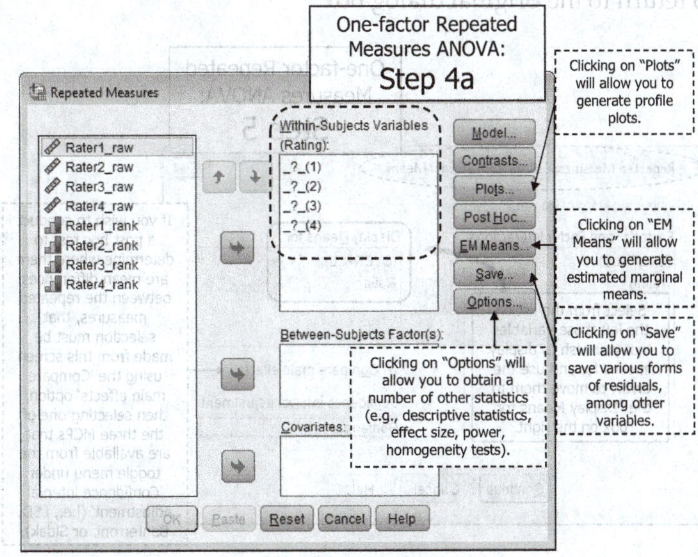

FIGURE 15.17
One-factor repeated measures ANOVA: Step 4a.

Step 4b. Move the appropriate variables from the variable list on the left into the "Within-Subjects Variables" box on the right. It is important to make sure that the first measurement is matched up with "1," the second measurement is matched with "2," and so forth so that the correct order of repeated measures is defined. This is especially critical when there is some temporal order to the repeated measures (e.g., pre-, post-, 3 months after post, etc.).

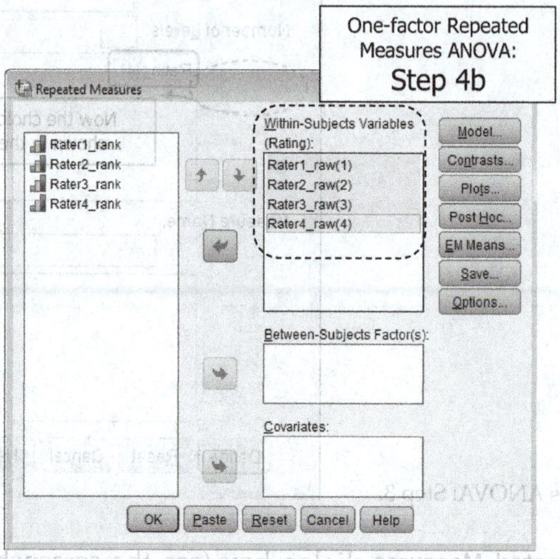

FIGURE 15.18
One-factor repeated measures ANOVA: Step 4b.

Step 5. From the Univariate dialog box (see the screenshot in Figure 15.17), clicking on "EM Means" will provide the option to compute marginal and overall means. For the one-factor repeated measures ANOVA, this dialog box is the proper place to obtain *post hoc* multiple comparison procedures including Tukey's LSD, Bonferroni, and Sidak procedures. Click on "Continue" to return to the original dialog box.

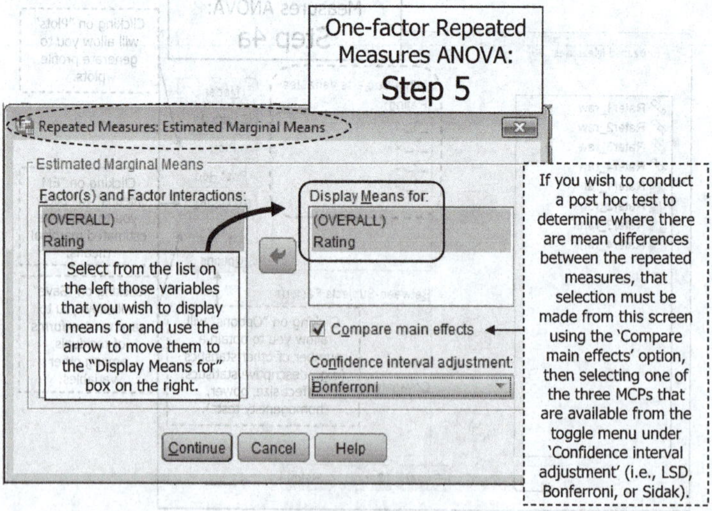

FIGURE 15.19
One-factor repeated measures ANOVA: Step 5.

Step 6. From the Univariate dialog box (see the screenshot in Figure 15.17), clicking on "Options" will provide the option to select such information as "Descriptive statistics," "Estimates of effect size," "Observed power," and "Homogeneity tests." Click on "Continue" to return to the original dialog box.

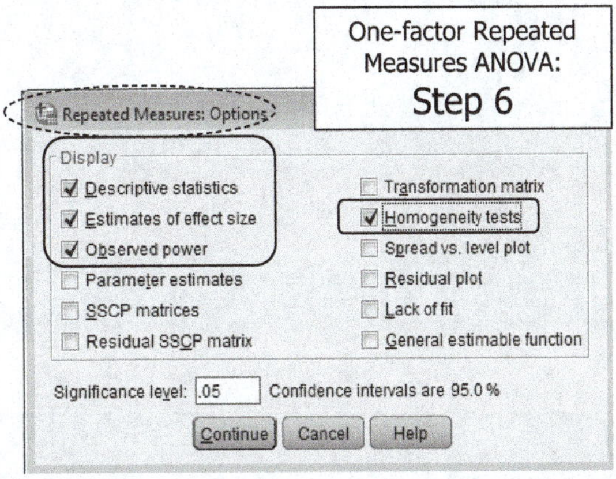

FIGURE 15.20
One-factor repeated measures ANOVA: Step 6.

Step 7. From the Univariate dialog box (see the screenshot in Figure 15.17), click on "Plots" to obtain a profile plot of means. Click the repeated measure factor (e.g., "Rater") and move it into the "Horizontal Axis" box by clicking the arrow button (see the screenshot for Step 7a in Figure 15.21). Then click on "Add" to move the variable into the "Plots" box at the bottom of the dialog box (see the screenshot for Step 7b in Figure 15.22). Click on "Continue" to return to the original dialog box.

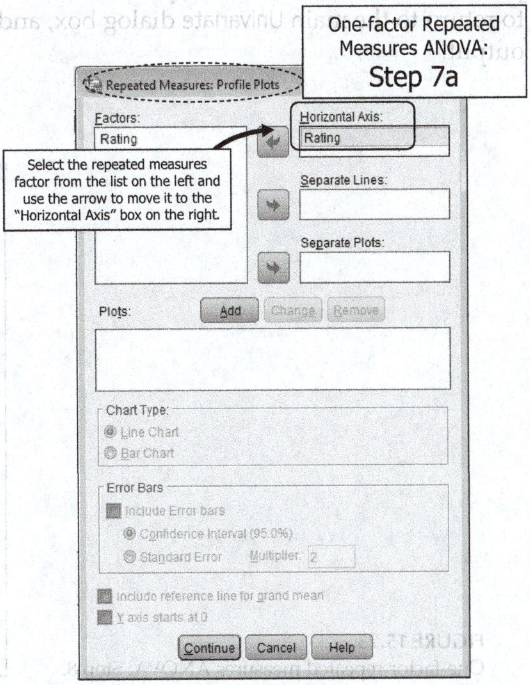

FIGURE 15.21
One-factor repeated measures ANOVA: Step 7a.

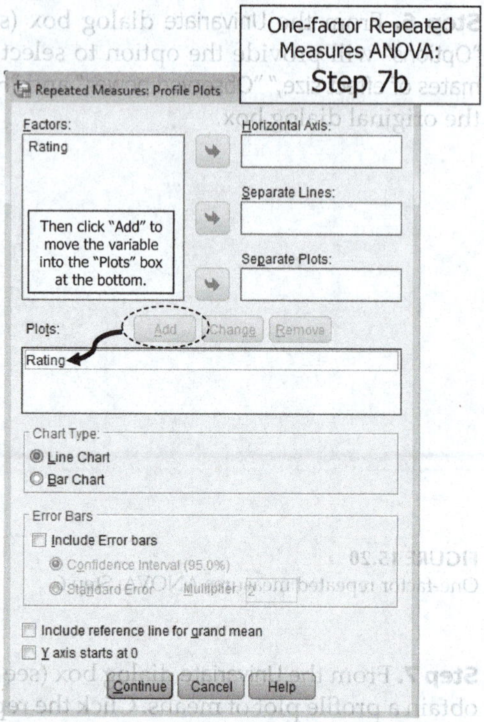

FIGURE 15.22
One-factor repeated measures ANOVA: Step 7b.

Step 8. From the Univariate dialog box (see the screenshot in Figure 15.17), click on "Save" to select those elements that you want to save (in our case, we want to save the unstandardized residuals which will be used later to examine the extent to which normality and independence are met). To do this, place a checkmark next to "Unstandardized." Click "Continue" to return to the main Univariate dialog box, and then click on "OK" to return to generate the output.

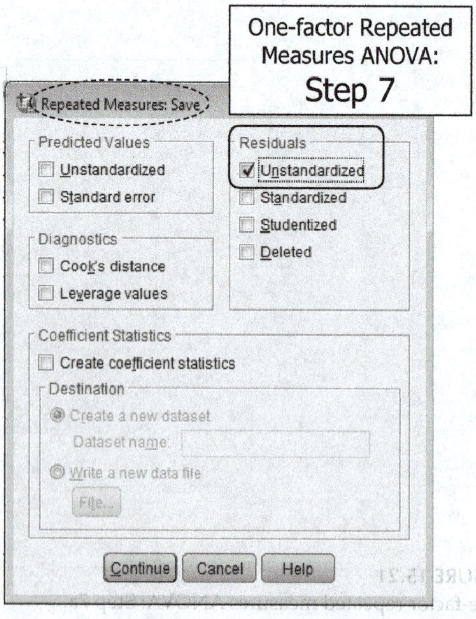

FIGURE 15.23
One-factor repeated measures ANOVA: Step 8.

Interpreting the output. Annotated results are presented in Table 15.14.

TABLE 15.14

One-Factor Repeated Measures ANOVA SPSS Results for the Ballet Technique Example

Within-Subjects Factors

Measure: MEASURE_1

Rating	Dependent Variable
1	Rater1_raw
2	Rater2_raw
3	Rater3_raw
4	Rater4_raw

Descriptive Statistics

	Mean	Std. Deviation	N
Rater1_raw	2.7500	1.48805	8
Rater2_raw	3.6250	.91613	8
Rater3_raw	6.2500	1.03510	8
Rater4_raw	9.1250	.83452	8

The table labeled "Descriptive Statistics" provides basic descriptive statistics (means, standard deviations, and sample sizes) for each rater of the repeated measure.

Multivariate Tests[a]

Effect		Value	F	Hypothesis df	Error df	Sig.	Partial Eta Squared	Noncent. Parameter	Observed Power[c]
Rating	Pillai's Trace	.967	48.650[b]	3.000	5.000	.000	.967	145.949	1.000
	Wilks' Lambda	.033	48.650[b]	3.000	5.000	.000	.967	145.949	1.000
	Hotelling's Trace	29.190	48.650[b]	3.000	5.000	.000	.967	145.949	1.000
	Roy's Largest Root	29.190	48.650[b]	3.000	5.000	.000	.967	145.949	1.000

a. Design: Intercept

Within Subjects Design: Rating

b. Exact statistic

c. Computed using alpha = .05

The table labeled "Multivariate Tests" provides results for the multivariate test of mean differences between the repeated measures. Multivariate tests are provided when there are three or more levels of the within-subjects factor. These results are generally more conservative than the univariate results (in other words, you may be less likely to find statistically significant multivariate results as compared to univariate results.) *Note that the multivariate tests do not require meeting the assumption of sphericity.* Thus if the assumption of sphericity is met, reporting univariate results is recommended.

If results for the multivariate tests are reported, of the four test results, Wilks' Lambda is recommended. In this example, all four multivariate criteria produce the same results—specifically that there is a statistically significant multivariate mean difference (as noted by p less than α.)

(continued)

TABLE 15.14 (continued)

One-Factor Repeated Measures ANOVA SPSS Results for the Ballet Technique Example

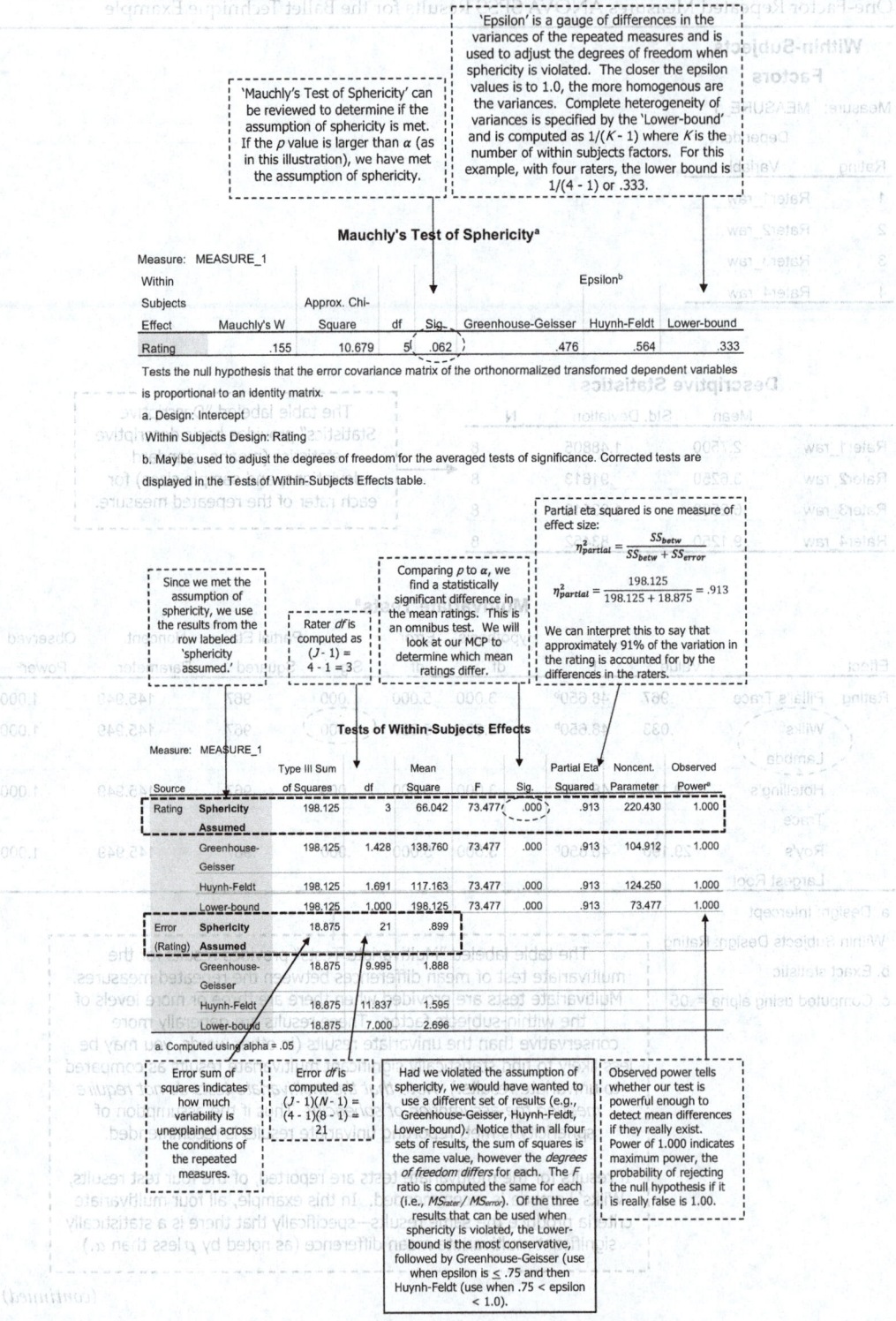

'Mauchly's Test of Sphericity' can be reviewed to determine if the assumption of sphericity is met. If the p value is larger than α (as in this illustration), we have met the assumption of sphericity.

'Epsilon' is a gauge of differences in the variances of the repeated measures and is used to adjust the degrees of freedom when sphericity is violated. The closer the epsilon values is to 1.0, the more homogenous are the variances. Complete heterogeneity of variances is specified by the 'Lower-bound' and is computed as $1/(K - 1)$ where K is the number of within subjects factors. For this example, with four raters, the lower bound is $1/(4 - 1)$ or .333.

Mauchly's Test of Sphericity[a]

Measure: MEASURE_1

Within Subjects Effect	Mauchly's W	Approx. Chi-Square	df	Sig.	Epsilon[b] Greenhouse-Geisser	Huynh-Feldt	Lower-bound
Rating	.155	10.679	5	.062	.476	.564	.333

Tests the null hypothesis that the error covariance matrix of the orthonormalized transformed dependent variables is proportional to an identity matrix.

a. Design: Intercept
Within Subjects Design: Rating

b. May be used to adjust the degrees of freedom for the averaged tests of significance. Corrected tests are displayed in the Tests of Within-Subjects Effects table.

Partial eta squared is one measure of effect size:

$$\eta^2_{partial} = \frac{SS_{betw}}{SS_{betw} + SS_{error}}$$

$$\eta^2_{partial} = \frac{198.125}{198.125 + 18.875} = .913$$

We can interpret this to say that approximately 91% of the variation in the rating is accounted for by the differences in the raters.

Since we met the assumption of sphericity, we use the results from the row labeled 'sphericity assumed.'

Rater df is computed as $(J - 1) = 4 - 1 = 3$

Comparing p to α, we find a statistically significant difference in the mean ratings. This is an omnibus test. We will look at our MCP to determine which mean ratings differ.

Tests of Within-Subjects Effects

Measure: MEASURE_1

Source		Type III Sum of Squares	df	Mean Square	F	Sig.	Partial Eta Squared	Noncent. Parameter	Observed Power[a]
Rating	Sphericity Assumed	198.125	3	66.042	73.477	.000	.913	220.430	1.000
	Greenhouse-Geisser	198.125	1.428	138.760	73.477	.000	.913	104.912	1.000
	Huynh-Feldt	198.125	1.691	117.163	73.477	.000	.913	124.250	1.000
	Lower-bound	198.125	1.000	198.125	73.477	.000	.913	73.477	1.000
Error (Rating)	Sphericity Assumed	18.875	21	.899					
	Greenhouse-Geisser	18.875	9.995	1.888					
	Huynh-Feldt	18.875	11.837	1.595					
	Lower-bound	18.875	7.000	2.696					

a. Computed using alpha = .05

Error sum of squares indicates how much variability is unexplained across the conditions of the repeated measures.

Error df is computed as $(J - 1)(N - 1) = (4 - 1)(8 - 1) = 21$

Had we violated the assumption of sphericity, we would have wanted to use a different set of results (e.g., Greenhouse-Geisser, Huynh-Feldt, Lower-bound). Notice that in all four sets of results, the sum of squares is the same value, however the *degrees of freedom differs* for each. The F ratio is computed the same for each (i.e., MS_{rater} / MS_{error}). Of the three results that can be used when sphericity is violated, the Lower-bound is the most conservative, followed by Greenhouse-Geisser (use when epsilon is $\leq .75$ and then Huynh-Feldt (use when $.75 <$ epsilon < 1.0).

Observed power tells whether our test is powerful enough to detect mean differences if they really exist. Power of 1.000 indicates maximum power, the probability of rejecting the null hypothesis if it is really false is 1.00.

TABLE 15.14 (continued)

One-Factor Repeated Measures ANOVA SPSS Results for the Ballet Technique Example

The output from the 'Tests of Within-subjects Contrasts' will not be used. Polynomial contrasts do not make sense for the rater factor.

Tests of Within-Subjects Contrasts

Measure: MEASURE_1

Source	Rating	Type III Sum of Squares	df	Mean Square	F	Sig.	Partial Eta Squared	Noncent. Parameter	Observed Power[a]
Rating	Linear	189.225	1	189.225	103.685	.000	.937	103.685	1.000
	Quadratic	8.000	1	8.000	18.667	.003	.727	18.667	.957
	Cubic	.900	1	.900	2.032	.197	.225	2.032	.235
Error (Rating)	Linear	12.775	7	1.825					
	Quadratic	3.000	7	.429					
	Cubic	3.100	7	.443					

a. Computed using alpha = .05

The output from the 'Tests of Between-Subjects Effects' will not be used as there is no between subjects factor.

Tests of Between-Subjects Effects

Measure: MEASURE_1

Transformed Variable: Average

Source	Type III Sum of Squares	df	Mean Square	F	Sig.	Partial Eta Squared	Noncent. Parameter	Observed Power[a]
Intercept	946.125	1	946.125	445.235	.000	.985	445.235	1.000
Error	14.875	7	2.125					

a. Computed using alpha = .05

Estimated Marginal Means

1. Grand Mean

Measure: MEASURE_1

Mean	Std. Error	95% Confidence Interval Lower Bound	Upper Bound
5.438	.258	4.828	6.047

The 'Grand Mean' (in this case, 5.438) represents the overall mean, regardless of the rater. The 95% CI represents the CI of the grand mean.

(continued)

TABLE 15.14 (continued)

One-Factor Repeated Measures ANOVA SPSS Results for the Ballet Technique Example

2. Rating

Estimates

Measure: MEASURE_1

Rating	Mean	Std. Error	95% Confidence Interval Lower Bound	95% Confidence Interval Upper Bound
1	2.750	.526	1.506	3.994
2	3.625	.324	2.859	4.391
3	6.250	.366	5.385	7.115
4	9.125	.295	8.427	9.823

The table labeled **"Rating"** provides descriptive statistics for each of the four raters. In addition to means, the *SE* and 95% CI of the means are reported.

'Mean difference' is simply the difference between the means of the two raters being compared. For example, the mean difference of rater 1 and rater 2 is calculated as 2.750 − 3.625 = −.875.

Pairwise Comparisons

Measure: MEASURE_1

(I) Rating	(J) Rating	Mean Difference (I-J)	Std. Error	Sig.[b]	95% Confidence Interval for Difference[b] Lower Bound	95% Confidence Interval for Difference[b] Upper Bound
1	2	-.875	.295	.126	-1.948	.198
	3	-3.500*	.267	.000	-4.472	-2.528
	4	-6.375*	.706	.000	-8.940	-3.810
2	1	.875	.295	.126	-.198	1.948
	3	-2.625*	.263	.000	-3.581	-1.669
	4	-5.500*	.567	.000	-7.561	-3.439
3	1	3.500*	.267	.000	2.528	4.472
	2	2.625*	.263	.000	1.669	3.581
	4	-2.875*	.549	.007	-4.871	-.879
4	1	6.375*	.706	.000	3.810	8.940
	2	5.500*	.567	.000	3.439	7.561
	3	2.875*	.549	.007	.879	4.871

Based on estimated marginal means

*. The mean difference is significant at the .05 level.

b. Adjustment for multiple comparisons: Bonferroni.

'Sig.' denotes the observed *p* value and provides the results of the Bonferroni post-hoc procedure. There is a statistically significant mean difference between:

1. rater 1 and rater 3
2. rater 1 and rater 4
3. rater 2 and rater 3
4. rater 2 and rater 4
5. rater 3 and rater 4

The only groups for which there is not a statistically significant mean difference is between raters 1 and 2.

Note there are redundant results presented in the table. The comparison of rater 1 and 2 (presented in results for rater 1) is the same as the comparison of rater 2 and 1 (presented in results for rater 2) and so forth.

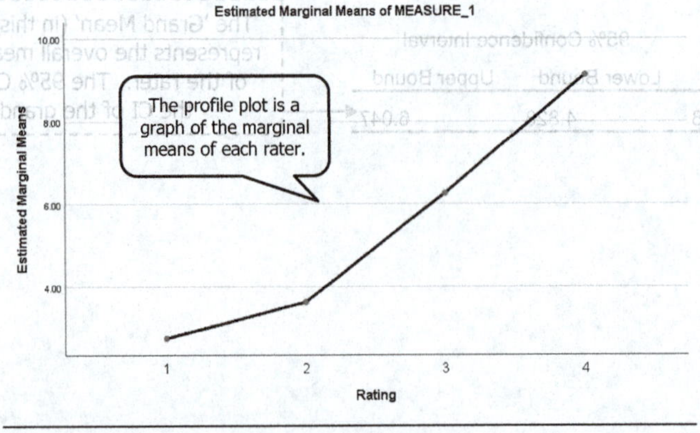

15.6.5 Friedman's Test: Nonparametric One-Factor Repeated Measures ANOVA

Step 1. The nonparametric version of the repeated measures ANOVA is Friedman's test. To compute Friedman's test, go to "Analyze" in the top pulldown menu, then select "Nonparametric Tests," then "Legacy Dialogs," and then finally "K Related Samples." Following the screenshot for Step 1 (shown in Figure 15.24) produces the "Tests for Several Related Samples" dialog box.

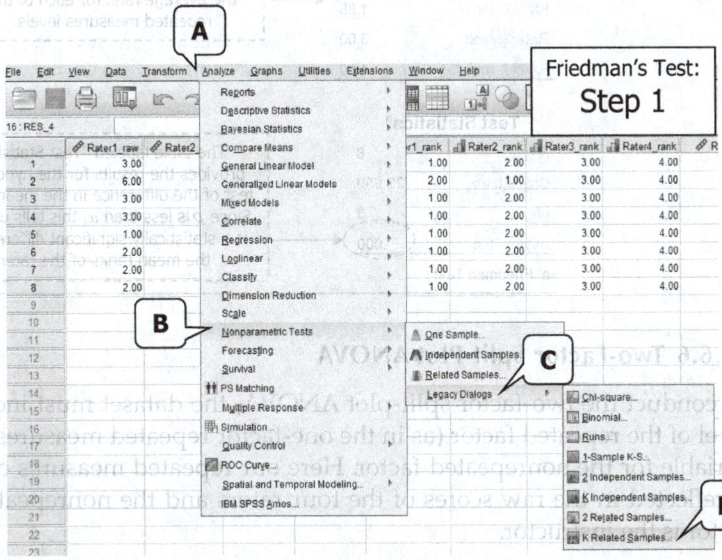

FIGURE 15.24
Friedman's test: Step 1.

Step 2. Recall that the Friedman test operates using ranked data, not continuous raw scores as with the repeated measures ANOVA; thus we will work with the ranked variables in our dataset for this test. From the Tests for Several Related Samples dialog box, click the variables representing the *ranked levels* of the repeated factor into the "Test Variables" box by using the arrow key in the middle of the dialog box. Under Test Type at the bottom left, check Friedman. Then click on "OK" to return to generate the output.

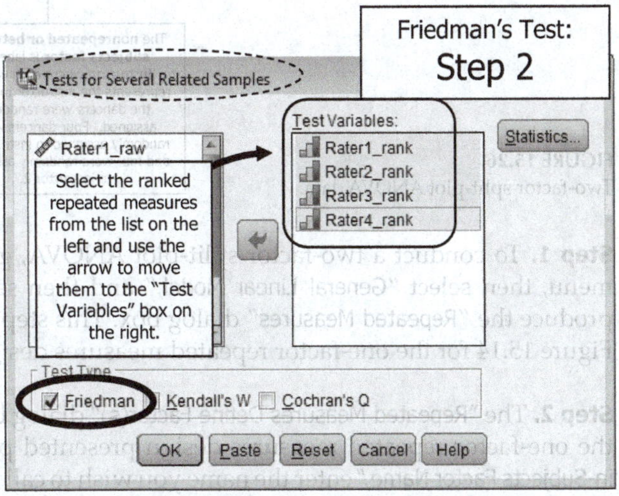

FIGURE 15.25
Friedman's test: Step 2

Interpreting the output. Annotated results are presented in Table 15.15.

TABLE 15.15
Friedman's test SPSS results for the ballet technique example.

Ranks

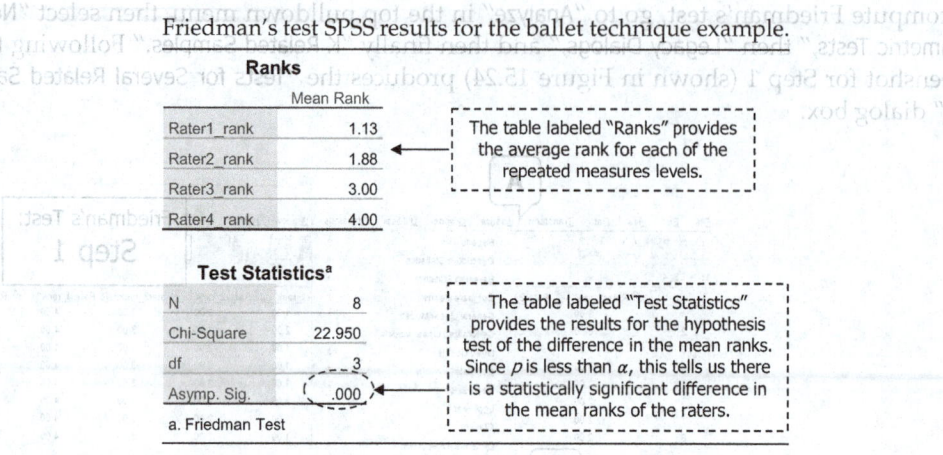

	Mean Rank
Rater1_rank	1.13
Rater2_rank	1.88
Rater3_rank	3.00
Rater4_rank	4.00

The table labeled "Ranks" provides the average rank for each of the repeated measures levels.

Test Statistics[a]

N	8
Chi-Square	22.950
df	3
Asymp. Sig.	.000

a. Friedman Test

The table labeled "Test Statistics" provides the results for the hypothesis test of the difference in the mean ranks. Since p is less than α, this tells us there is a statistically significant difference in the mean ranks of the raters.

15.6.6 Two-Factor Split-Plot ANOVA

To conduct the two-factor split-plot ANOVA, the dataset must include variables for each level of the repeated factor (as in the one-factor repeated measures ANOVA), and another variable for the nonrepeated factor. Here our repeated measures or within-subjects factor is reflected in the raw scores of the four raters and the nonrepeated or between-subjects factor is the instructor.

	Instructor	Rater1_raw	Rater2_raw	Rater3_raw	Rater4_raw
1	1.00	3.00	4.00	7.00	8.00
2	1.00	6.00	5.00	8.00	9.00
3	1.00	3.00	4.00	7.00	9.00
4	1.00	3.00	4.00	6.00	8.00
5	2.00	1.00	2.00	5.00	10.00
6	2.00	2.00	3.00	6.00	10.00
7	2.00	2.00	4.00	5.00	9.00
8	2.00	2.00	3.00	6.00	10.00

The **nonrepeated or between subjects factor** is labeled 'Instructor' where each value represents the instructor to which the dancers were randomly assigned. Four dancers were randomly assigned to instructor 1 and four were randomly assigned to instructor 2.

The **repeated measures** or **within subjects factor** is labeled 'Rater' where there are four different raters, each reflected in the score they assigned to each of the eight dancers. (We will use the raw scores of the raters for the two-factor split-plot ANOVA.)

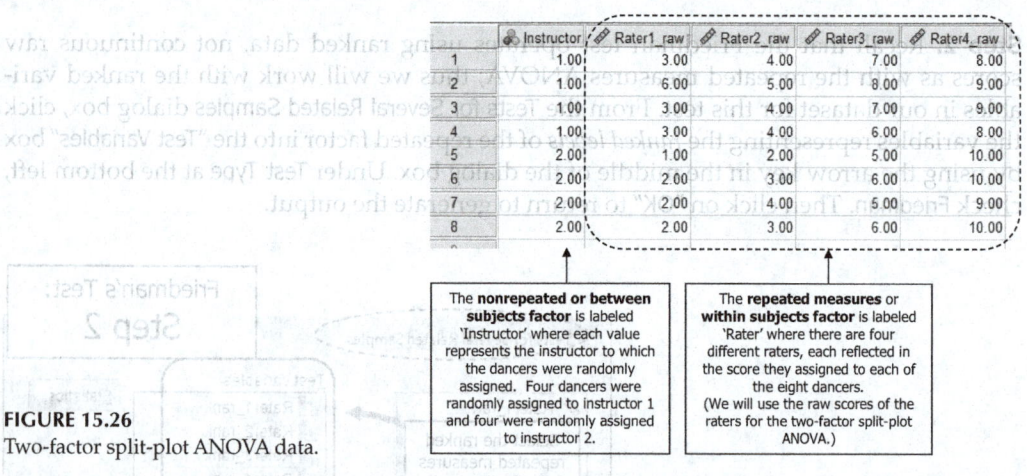

FIGURE 15.26
Two-factor split-plot ANOVA data.

Step 1. To conduct a two-factor split-plot ANOVA, go to "Analyze" in the top pulldown menu, then select "General Linear Model," and then select "Repeated Measures." This will produce the "Repeated Measures" dialog box. This step has been presented previously (see Figure 15.14 for the one-factor repeated measures design) and will not be reiterated here.

Step 2. The "Repeated Measures Define Factor(s)" dialog box will appear (see Figure 15.15 for the one-factor repeated measures design presented previously). In the box under "Within-Subjects Factor Name," enter the name you wish to call the repeated factor. For this example we label the repeated factor "Rating." It is necessary to define a name for the repeated factor as there is no single variable representing this factor (recall that the columns in the dataset represent the repeated measures); in the dataset there is one variable for each level of the factor (in other words, one variable for each different rater or measurement). Again, in our example, there are four levels of rater (i.e., four raters) and thus four variables. The "number of levels" indicates the number of measurements of the repeated factor. Here there were four raters, and thus the "number of levels" of the factor is 4.

Step 3. After defining the "Within-Subjects Factor Name" and the "number of levels," then click on ADD to move this information into the middle box. In Figure 15.16 for the one-factor repeated measures design presented previously, we see our newly defined repeated factor (i.e., Rating) with "4" indicating it was measured by four raters: Rating(4). Finally, click on "Define" to open the main Repeated Measures dialog box.

Step 4a. From the Repeated Measures dialog box (see Figures 15.17 and 15.18 for the one-factor repeated measures design presented previously), we see a heading called "Within-Subjects Variables" with the newly defined factor rater in parentheses. Here the values of 1 through 4 represent each one of the four raters. Preceding each of the levels of the repeated factor are lines with question marks. This is the software's way of asking us to define which variable represents the first measurement (or the first rater in our illustration).

Step 4b. Move the appropriate variables from the variable list on the left into the "Within-Subjects Variables" box on the right. It is important to make sure that the first measurement is matched up with "1," the second measurement is matched with "2," and so forth so that the correct order of repeated measures is defined.

Step 5. Once the "Within-Subjects Variables" are defined, the next step is to define the between-subjects or nonrepeated factor, as we see in the screenshot that follows (Figure 15.27). Move the appropriate variable from the variable list on the left into the "Between-Subjects Factor(s)" box on the right. From this, point, the options and selections work as we have seen when conducting other ANOVA models.

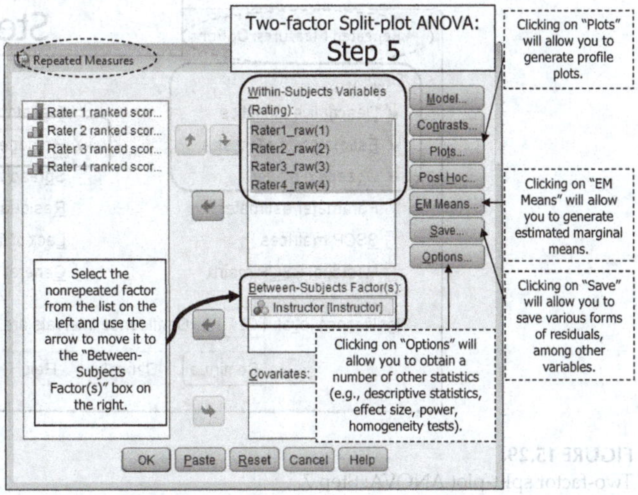

FIGURE 15.27
Two-factor split-plot ANOVA: Step 5.

Step 6. From the Repeated Measures dialog box, clicking on "EM Means" will provide the option to display overall and marginal means (see the screenshot in Figure 15.28). For the two-factor split-plot ANOVA, this dialog box is the proper place to obtain post hoc multiple comparison procedures for the *repeated measure*. Post hoc procedures include Tukey's LSD, Bonferroni, and Sidak procedures. Click on "Continue" to return to the original dialog box.

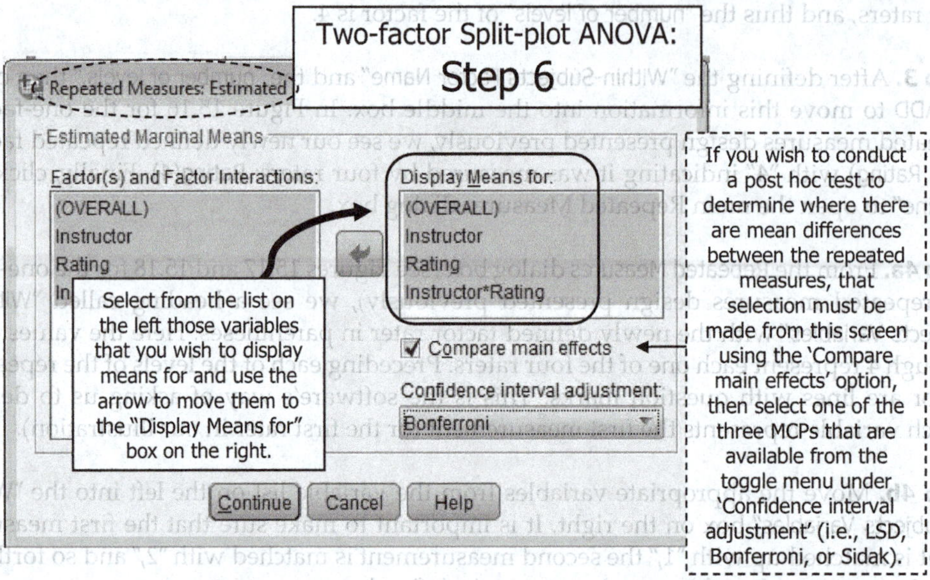

FIGURE 15.28
Two-factor split-plot ANOVA: Step 6

Step 7. From the Repeated Measures dialog box, clicking on "Options" will provide the option to select such information as "Descriptive statistics," "Estimates of effect size," "Observed power," and "Homogeneity tests." Click on "Continue" to return to the original dialog box.

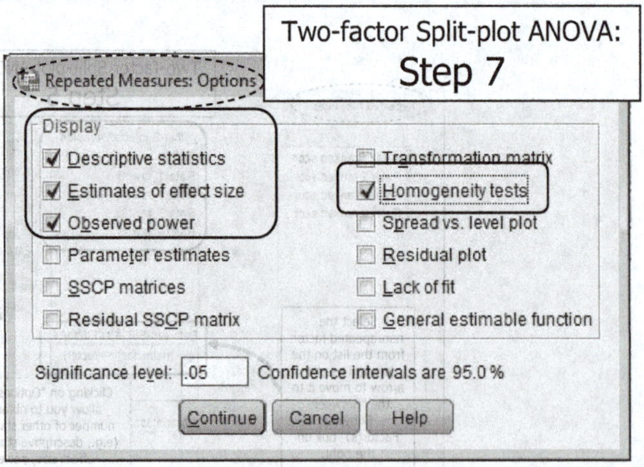

FIGURE 15.29
Two-factor split-plot ANOVA: Step 7.

Step 8. Click on the name of the nonrepeated or between-subjects factor in the "Factor(s)" list box in the top left and move it to the "Post Hoc Tests for" box in the top right by clicking on the arrow key. Check an appropriate MCP for your situation by placing a checkmark in the box next to the desired MCP. In this example, we select Tukey (see the screenshot for Step 8 shown in Figure 15.30). Click on "Continue" to return to the original dialog box.

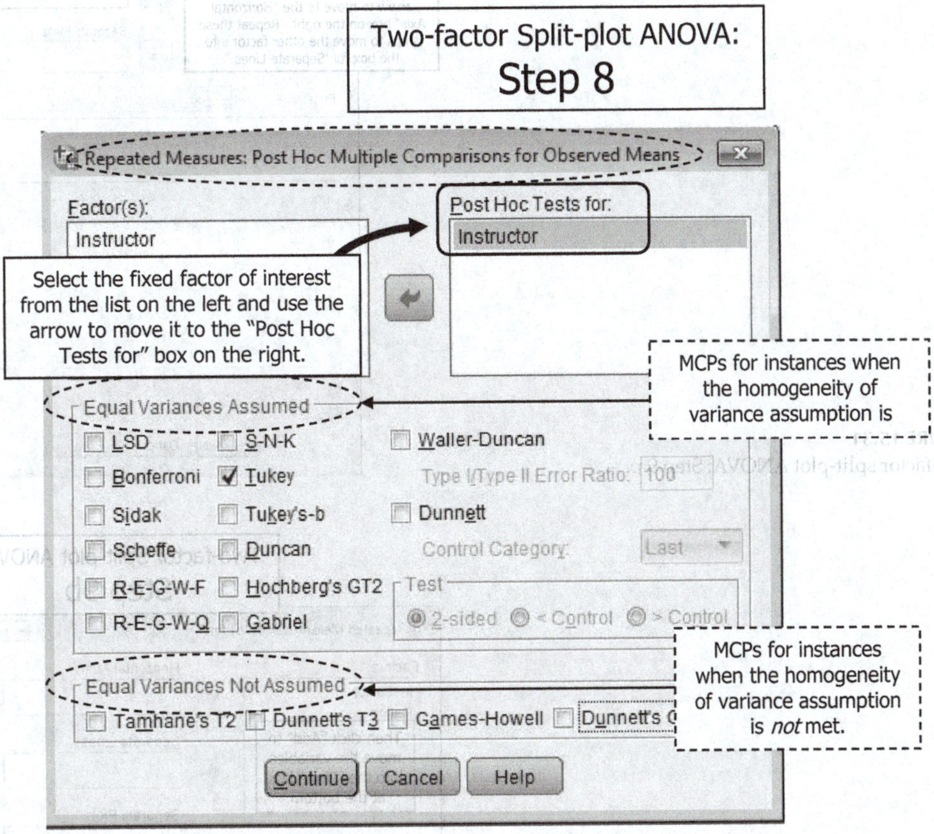

FIGURE 15.30
Two-factor split-plot ANOVA: Step 8.

Step 9. From the Repeated Measures dialog box, click on "Plots" to obtain a profile plot of means. Click the repeated measures factor (e.g., rating) and move it into the "Horizontal Axis" box by clicking the arrow button. Then click the nonrepeated factor (e.g., instructor) and move it into the "Separate Lines" box by clicking the arrow button. Then click on "Add" to move this into the "Plots" box at the bottom of the dialog box (see the screenshots for Steps 9a and 9b, Figures 15.31 and 15.32). Click on "Continue" to return to the original dialog box. (*Tip:* Placing the factor that has the most categories or levels on the horizontal axis of the profile plot will make for easier interpretation of the graph. In this case, there were four raters and two instructors, thus we placed "rater" on the horizontal axis. You can graph multiple plots, so trying different placement of factors on the axis or lines may produce a more desirable plot given your situation.)

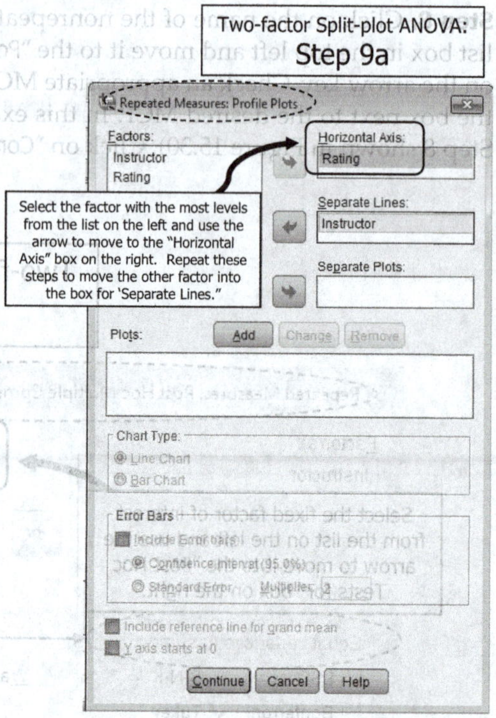

FIGURE 15.31
Two-factor split-plot ANOVA: Step 9a.

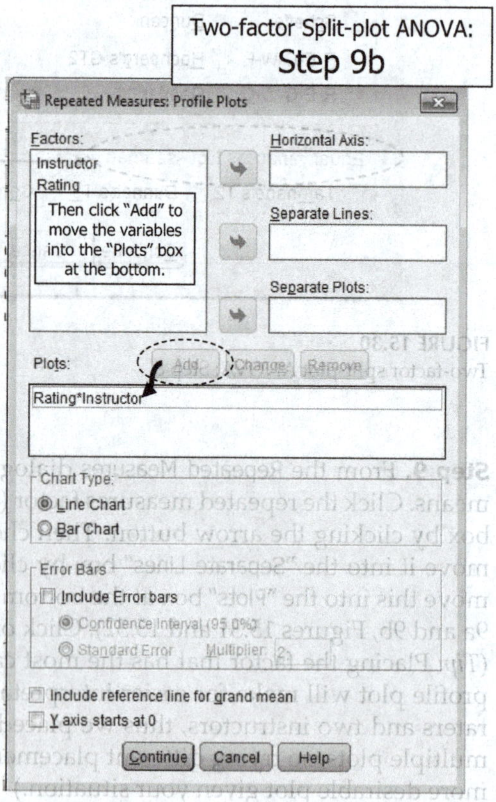

FIGURE 15.32
Two-factor split-plot ANOVA: Step 9b.

Step 10. From the Repeated Measures dialog box, click on "Save" to select those elements that you want to save (here we want to save the unstandardized residuals which will be used later to examine the extent to which normality and independence are met). To do this, place a checkmark next to "Unstandardized." Click "Continue" to return to the main Repeated Measures dialog box. From there, click on "OK" to generate the output.

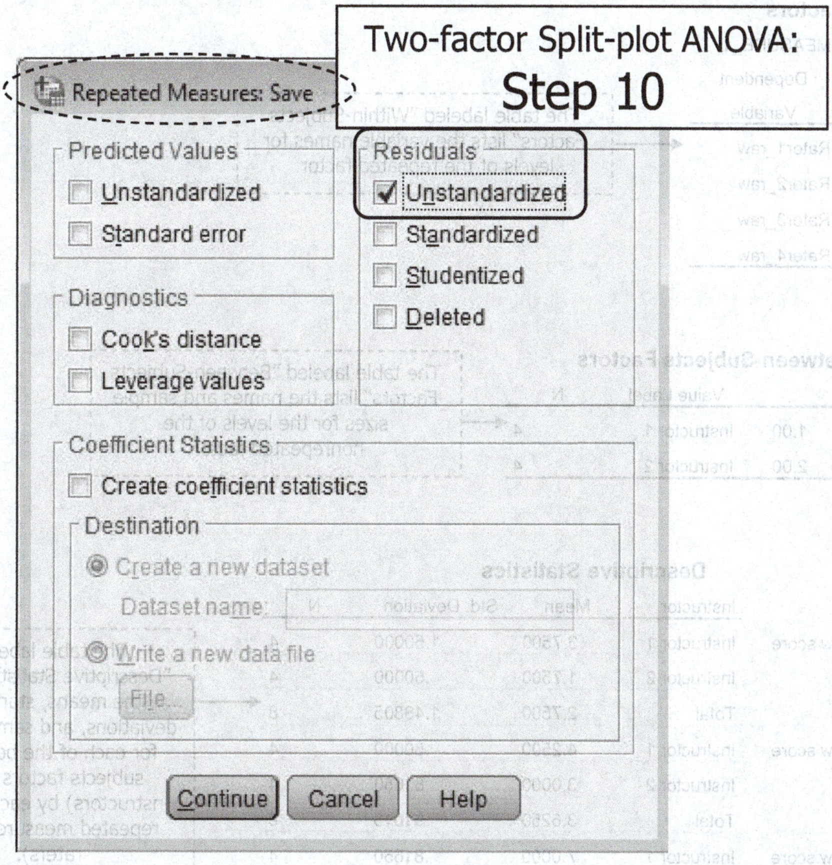

FIGURE 15.33
Two-factor split-plot ANOVA: Step 10.

Interpreting the output. Annotated results are presented in Table 15.16. Note that statistically significant interactions can be examined with simple effects, following the same steps as detailed in factorial ANOVA.

TABLE 15.16

Two-Factor Split-plot ANOVA SPSS Results for the Ballet Technique Example

Within-Subjects Factors

Measure: MEASURE_1

Rating	Dependent Variable
1	Rater1_raw
2	Rater2_raw
3	Rater3_raw
4	Rater4_raw

The table labeled "Within-Subjects Factors" lists the variable names for levels of the repeated factor.

Between-Subjects Factors

		Value Label	N
Instructor	1.00	Instructor 1	4
	2.00	Instructor 2	4

The table labeled "Between-Subjects Factors" lists the names and sample sizes for the levels of the nonrepeated factor.

Descriptive Statistics

	Instructor	Mean	Std. Deviation	N
Rater 1 raw score	Instructor 1	3.7500	1.50000	4
	Instructor 2	1.7500	.50000	4
	Total	2.7500	1.48805	8
Rater 2 raw score	Instructor 1	4.2500	.50000	4
	Instructor 2	3.0000	.81650	4
	Total	3.6250	.91613	8
Rater 3 raw score	Instructor 1	7.0000	.81650	4
	Instructor 2	5.5000	.57735	4
	Total	6.2500	1.03510	8
Rater 4 raw score	Instructor 1	8.5000	.57735	4
	Instructor 2	9.7500	.50000	4
	Total	9.1250	.83452	8

The table labeled "Descriptive Statistics" lists the means, standard deviations, and sample sizes for each of the between subjects factors (i.e., instructors) by each of the repeated measures (i.e., raters).

TABLE 15.16 (continued)

Two-Factor Split-plot ANOVA SPSS Results for the Ballet Technique Example

Multivariate Tests[a]

Effect		Value	F	Hypothesis df	Error df	Sig.	Partial Eta Squared	Noncent. Parameter	Observed Power[c]
Rating	Pillai's Trace	.983	74.892[b]	3.000	4.000	.001	.983	224.677	1.000
	Wilks' Lambda	.017	74.892[b]	3.000	4.000	.001	.983	224.677	1.000
	Hotelling's Trace	56.169	74.892[b]	3.000	4.000	.001	.983	224.677	1.000
	Roy's Largest Root	56.169	74.892[b]	3.000	4.000	.001	.983	224.677	1.000
Rating * Instructor	Pillai's Trace	.899	11.925[b]	3.000	4.000	.018	.899	35.774	.860
	Wilks' Lambda	.101	11.925[b]	3.000	4.000	.018	.899	35.774	.860
	Hotelling's Trace	8.944	11.925[b]	3.000	4.000	.018	.899	35.774	.860
	Roy's Largest Root	8.944	11.925[b]	3.000	4.000	.018	.899	35.774	.860

a. Design: Intercept + Instructor
Within Subjects Design: Rating

b. Exact statistic

c. Computed using alpha = .05

The table labeled "Multivariate Tests" provides results for the multivariate test of mean differences for the repeated measures factor (i.e., 'Rating'), and for the between- by within-subjects interaction (i.e., 'Rating*Instructor'). Multivariate tests are provided when there are three or more levels of the within-subjects factor. These results are generally more conservative than the univariate results (in other words, you may be less likely to find statistically significant multivariate results as compared to univariate results.). *Note that the multivariate tests do not require meeting the assumption of sphericity.* Thus if the assumption of sphericity is met, reporting univariate results is recommended.

If results for the multivariate tests are reported, of the four test criteria, Wilks' Lambda is recommended. In this example, all four multivariate criteria produce the same results—specifically that there is a statistically significant multivariate mean difference for the repeated measures factor and a statistically significant between- by within-subjects interaction (as noted by p less than α).

'Epsilon' is a gauge of differences in the variances of the repeated measures. The closer the epsilon value is to 1.0, the more homogenous are the variances. Complete heterogeneity of variances is specified by the 'Lower-bound' and is computed as $1/(K - 1)$ where K is the number of within subjects levels. For this example, with four raters, the lower bound is 1/(4-1) or .333.

'Mauchly's Test of Sphericity' can be reviewed to determine if the assumption of sphericity is met. If the p value is larger than α (as in this illustration), we have met the assumption of sphericity.

Mauchly's Test of Sphericity[a]

Measure: MEASURE_1

Within Subjects Effect	Mauchly's W	Approx. Chi-Square	df	Sig.	Epsilon[b] Greenhouse-Geisser	Huynh-Feldt	Lower-bound
Rating	.429	4.001	5	.557	.706	1.000	.333

Tests the null hypothesis that the error covariance matrix of the orthonormalized transformed dependent variables is proportional to an identity matrix.

a. Design: Intercept + Instructor
Within Subjects Design: Rating

b. May be used to adjust the degrees of freedom for the averaged tests of significance. Corrected tests are displayed in the Tests of Within-Subjects Effects table.

(continued)

TABLE 15.16 (continued)

Two-Factor Split-plot ANOVA SPSS Results for the Ballet Technique Example

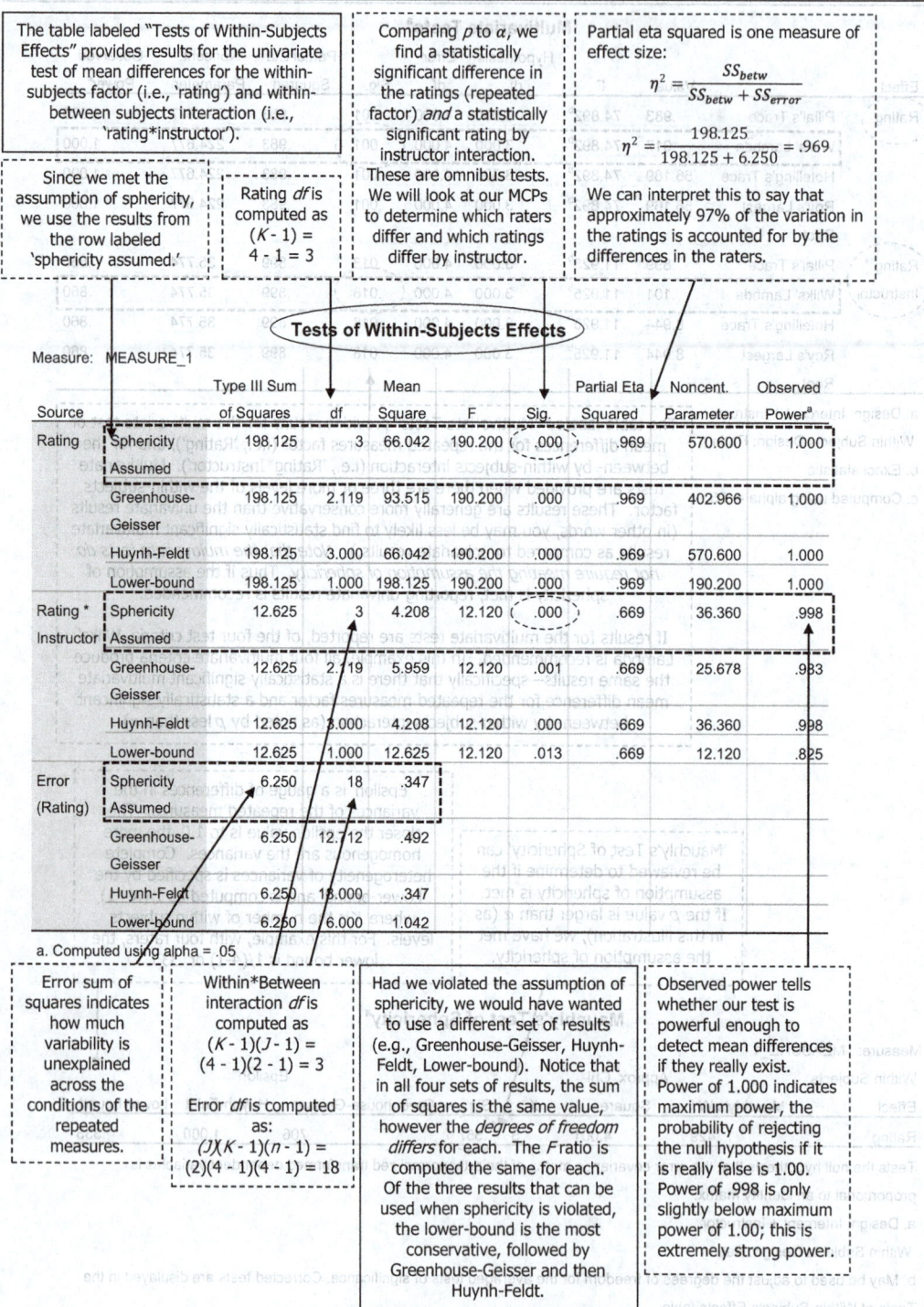

The table labeled "Tests of Within-Subjects Effects" provides results for the univariate test of mean differences for the within-subjects factor (i.e., 'rating') and within-between subjects interaction (i.e., 'rating*instructor').

Since we met the assumption of sphericity, we use the results from the row labeled 'sphericity assumed.'

Rating *df* is computed as $(K - 1) = 4 - 1 = 3$

Comparing p to α, we find a statistically significant difference in the ratings (repeated factor) *and* a statistically significant rating by instructor interaction. These are omnibus tests. We will look at our MCPs to determine which raters differ and which ratings differ by instructor.

Partial eta squared is one measure of effect size:

$$\eta^2 = \frac{SS_{betw}}{SS_{betw} + SS_{error}}$$

$$\eta^2 = \frac{198.125}{198.125 + 6.250} = .969$$

We can interpret this to say that approximately 97% of the variation in the ratings is accounted for by the differences in the raters.

Tests of Within-Subjects Effects

Measure: MEASURE_1

Source		Type III Sum of Squares	df	Mean Square	F	Sig.	Partial Eta Squared	Noncent. Parameter	Observed Power[a]
Rating	Sphericity Assumed	198.125	3	66.042	190.200	.000	.969	570.600	1.000
	Greenhouse-Geisser	198.125	2.119	93.515	190.200	.000	.969	402.966	1.000
	Huynh-Feldt	198.125	3.000	66.042	190.200	.000	.969	570.600	1.000
	Lower-bound	198.125	1.000	198.125	190.200	.000	.969	190.200	1.000
Rating * Instructor	Sphericity Assumed	12.625	3	4.208	12.120	.000	.669	36.360	.998
	Greenhouse-Geisser	12.625	2.119	5.959	12.120	.001	.669	25.678	.983
	Huynh-Feldt	12.625	3.000	4.208	12.120	.000	.669	36.360	.998
	Lower-bound	12.625	1.000	12.625	12.120	.013	.669	12.120	.825
Error (Rating)	Sphericity Assumed	6.250	18	.347					
	Greenhouse-Geisser	6.250	12.712	.492					
	Huynh-Feldt	6.250	18.000	.347					
	Lower-bound	6.250	6.000	1.042					

a. Computed using alpha = .05

Error sum of squares indicates how much variability is unexplained across the conditions of the repeated measures.

Within*Between interaction *df* is computed as $(K - 1)(J - 1) = (4 - 1)(2 - 1) = 3$

Error *df* is computed as: $(J)(K - 1)(n - 1) = (2)(4 - 1)(4 - 1) = 18$

Had we violated the assumption of sphericity, we would have wanted to use a different set of results (e.g., Greenhouse-Geisser, Huynh-Feldt, Lower-bound). Notice that in all four sets of results, the sum of squares is the same value, however the *degrees of freedom differs* for each. The *F* ratio is computed the same for each. Of the three results that can be used when sphericity is violated, the lower-bound is the most conservative, followed by Greenhouse-Geisser and then Huynh-Feldt.

Observed power tells whether our test is powerful enough to detect mean differences if they really exist. Power of 1.000 indicates maximum power, the probability of rejecting the null hypothesis if it is really false is 1.00. Power of .998 is only slightly below maximum power of 1.00; this is extremely strong power.

TABLE 15.16 (continued)

Two-Factor Split-plot ANOVA SPSS Results for the Ballet Technique Example

Tests of within subjects contrasts can be especially helpful in the case of repeated measures over time.
Linear effect of repeated measures tests whether the means of the outcome increase or decrease over time.
Quadratic effect of repeated measure tests whether the means have a single curve or bend over time.
Cubic effect of repeated measures tests for two curves or bends in the plot of means over time.

Tests of Within-Subjects Contrasts

Measure: MEASURE_1

Source	Rating	Type III Sum of Squares	df	Mean Square	F	Sig.	Partial Eta Squared	Noncent. Parameter	Observed Power[a]
Rating	Linear	189.225	1	189.225	302.760	.000	.981	302.760	1.000
	Quadratic	8.000	1	8.000	48.000	.000	.889	48.000	1.000
	Cubic	.900	1	.900	3.600	.107	.375	3.600	.359
Rating * Instructor	Linear	9.025	1	9.025	14.440	.009	.706	14.440	.883
	Quadratic	2.000	1	2.000	12.000	.013	.667	12.000	.821
	Cubic	1.600	1	1.600	6.400	.045	.516	6.400	.563
Error (Rating)	Linear	3.750	6	.625					
	Quadratic	1.000	6	.167					
	Cubic	1.500	6	.250					

a. Computed using alpha = .05

Levene's Test of Equality of Error Variances[a]

		Levene Statistic	df1	df2	Sig.
Rater 1 raw score	Based on Mean	3.600	1	6	.107
	Based on Median	.400	1	6	.550
	Based on Median and with adjusted df	.400	1	3.659	.564
	Based on trimmed mean	2.704	1	6	.151
Rater 2 raw score	Based on Mean	.158	1	6	.705
	Based on Median	.429	1	6	.537
	Based on Median and with adjusted df	.429	1	5.880	.537
	Based on trimmed mean	.188	1	6	.680
Rater 3 raw score	Based on Mean	.000	1	6	1.000
	Based on Median	.000	1	6	1.000
	Based on Median and with adjusted df	.000	1	3.000	1.000
	Based on trimmed mean	.000	1	6	1.000
Rater 4 raw score	Based on Mean	1.000	1	6	.356
	Based on Median	1.000	1	6	.356
	Based on Median and with adjusted df	1.000	1	3.000	.391
	Based on trimmed mean	1.000	1	6	.356

Tests the null hypothesis that the error variance of the dependent variable is equal across groups.

a. Design: Intercept + Instructor
Within Subjects Design: Rating

The F test (and associated p values) for Levene's Test for Equality of Error Variances is reviewed to determine if equal variances can be assumed. In this case, we meet the assumption (as p is greater than α).

Note that *df1* is degrees of freedom for the numerator (calculated as $J - 1$) and *df2* are the degrees of freedom for the denominator (calculated as $N - J$).

SPSS computes Levene's test four different ways and reports the associated statistic and significance for each. All test the same null hypothesis (which is noted in the footnote of the table) and are thus interpreted the same way (i.e., as a test of equal population error variances across all cells). For this illustration, we will interpret the results 'based on mean' and will use the corresponding p value to interpret the extent of meeting the assumption of homogeneity.

(continued)

TABLE 15.16 (continued)

Two-Factor Split-plot ANOVA SPSS Results for the Ballet Technique Example

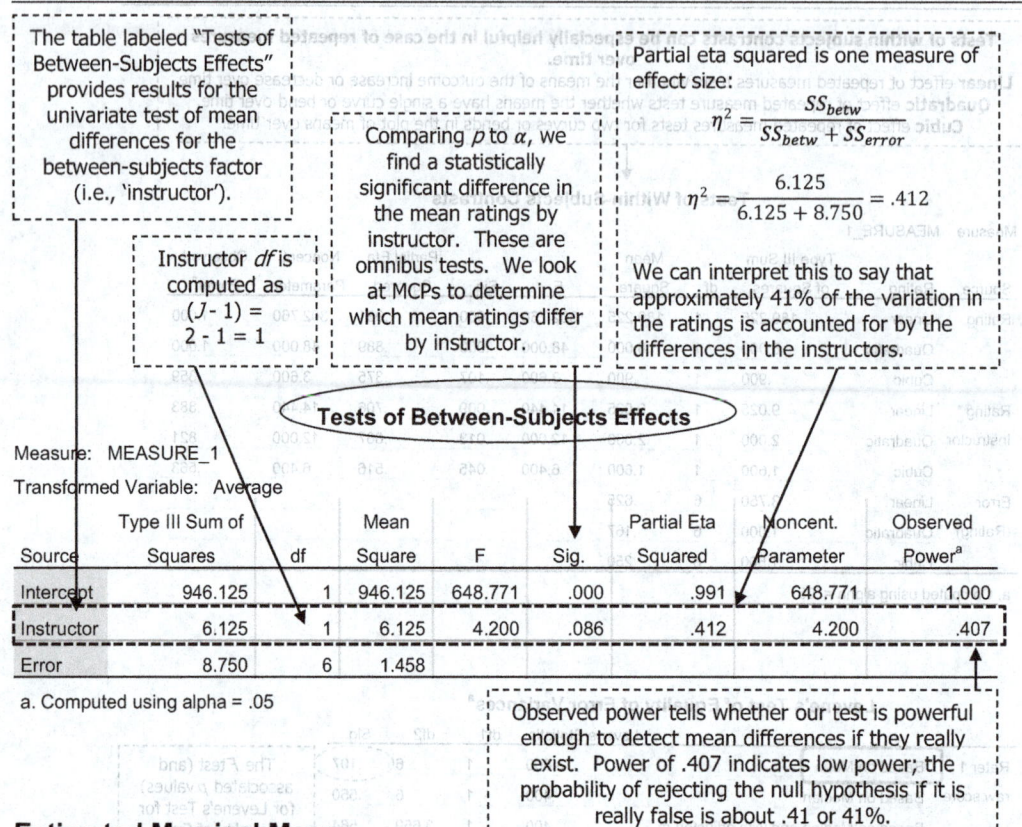

The table labeled "Tests of Between-Subjects Effects" provides results for the univariate test of mean differences for the between-subjects factor (i.e., 'instructor').

Instructor *df* is computed as $(J - 1) = 2 - 1 = 1$

Comparing p to α, we find a statistically significant difference in the mean ratings by instructor. These are omnibus tests. We look at MCPs to determine which mean ratings differ by instructor.

Partial eta squared is one measure of effect size:

$$\eta^2 = \frac{SS_{betw}}{SS_{betw} + SS_{error}}$$

$$\eta^2 = \frac{6.125}{6.125 + 8.750} = .412$$

We can interpret this to say that approximately 41% of the variation in the ratings is accounted for by the differences in the instructors.

Tests of Between-Subjects Effects

Measure: MEASURE_1
Transformed Variable: Average

Source	Type III Sum of Squares	df	Mean Square	F	Sig.	Partial Eta Squared	Noncent. Parameter	Observed Power[a]
Intercept	946.125	1	946.125	648.771	.000	.991	648.771	1.000
Instructor	6.125	1	6.125	4.200	.086	.412	4.200	.407
Error	8.750	6	1.458					

a. Computed using alpha = .05

Observed power tells whether our test is powerful enough to detect mean differences if they really exist. Power of .407 indicates low power; the probability of rejecting the null hypothesis if it is really false is about .41 or 41%.

Estimated Marginal Means

1. Grand Mean

Measure: MEASURE_1

Mean	Std. Error	95% Confidence Interval Lower Bound	Upper Bound
5.438	.213	4.915	5.960

The 'Grand Mean' (in this case, 5.438) represents the overall mean, regardless of the rater or instructor. The 95% CI represents the CI of the grand mean.

2. Instructor

Estimates

Measure: MEASURE_1

Instructor	Mean	Std. Error	95% Confidence Interval Lower Bound	Upper Bound
Instructor 1	5.875	.302	5.136	6.614
Instructor 2	5.000	.302	4.261	5.739

The table for **"Instructor"** provides descriptive statistics for each of the levels of our between-subjects factor. In addition to means, the *SE* and 95% CI of the means are reported.

TABLE 15.16 (continued)

Two-Factor Split-plot ANOVA SPSS Results for the Ballet Technique Example

'Mean difference' is simply the difference between the means of the two categories of our between-subjects factor. For example, the mean difference of instructor 1 and instructor 2 is calculated as 5.875 – 5.000 = .875

Pairwise Comparisons

Measure: MEASURE_1

(I) Instructor	(J) Instructor	Mean Difference (I-J)	Std. Error	Sig.[a]	95% Confidence Interval for Difference[a] Lower Bound	Upper Bound
Instructor 1	Instructor 2	.875	.427	.086	-.170	1.920
Instructor 2	Instructor 1	-.875	.427	.086	-1.920	.170

Based on estimated marginal means

a. Adjustment for multiple comparisons: Bonferroni.

'Sig.' denotes the observed *p* value and provides the results of the Bonferroni *post hoc* procedure. There is not a statistically significant mean difference in ratings between instructor 1 and 2.

Note there are redundant results presented in the table. The comparison of instructor 1 and 2 (presented in the first row) is the same as the comparison of instructor 2 and 1 (presented in the second row).

The contrast output from the 'Univariate Tests' will not be used here.

Univariate Tests

Measure: MEASURE_1

	Sum of Squares	df	Mean Square	F	Sig.	Partial Eta Squared	Noncent. Parameter	Observed Power[a]
Contrast	1.531	1	1.531	4.200	.086	.412	4.200	.407
Error	2.188	6	.365					

The F tests the effect of Instructor. This test is based on the linearly independent pairwise comparisons among the estimated marginal means.

a. Computed using alpha = .05

3. Rating

Estimates

Measure: MEASURE_1

Rating	Mean	Std. Error	95% Confidence Interval Lower Bound	Upper Bound
1	2.750	.395	1.783	3.717
2	3.625	.239	3.039	4.211
3	6.250	.250	5.638	6.862
4	9.125	.191	8.658	9.592

The table labeled **"Rating"** provides descriptive statistics for the rating of each of the four raters. In addition to means, the *SE* and 95% CI of the means are reported.

(continued)

TABLE 15.16 (continued)

Two-Factor Split-plot ANOVA SPSS Results for the Ballet Technique Example

'Mean difference' is simply the difference between the means of the two raters being compared. For example, the mean difference of rater 1 and rater 2 is calculated as 2.750 − 3.625 = -.875.

Pairwise Comparisons

Measure: MEASURE_1

(I) Rating	(J) Rating	Mean Difference (I-J)	Std. Error	Sig.[b]	95% Confidence Interval for Difference[b] Lower Bound	Upper Bound
1	2	-.875	.280	.122	-1.955	.205
	3	-3.500*	.270	.000	-4.543	-2.457
	4	-6.375*	.375	.000	-7.824	-4.926
2	1	.875	.280	.122	-.205	1.955
	3	-2.625*	.280	.000	-3.705	-1.545
	4	-5.500*	.339	.000	-6.808	-4.192
3	1	3.500*	.270	.000	2.457	4.543
	2	2.625*	.280	.000	1.545	3.705
	4	-2.875*	.191	.000	-3.613	-2.137
4	1	6.375*	.375	.000	4.926	7.824
	2	5.500*	.339	.000	4.192	6.808
	3	2.875*	.191	.000	2.137	3.613

Based on estimated marginal means

*. The mean difference is significant at the .05 level.

b. Adjustment for multiple comparisons: Bonferroni.

'Sig.' denotes the observed *p* value and provides the results of the Bonferroni *post hoc* procedure. There is a statistically significant mean difference in ratings of writing between:

1. rater 1 and rater 3
2. rater 1 and rater 4
3. rater 2 and rater 3
4. rater 2 and rater 4
5. rater 3 and rater 4

The only groups for which there is not a statistically significant mean difference is raters 1 and 2.

Note there are redundant results presented in the table. The comparison of rater 1 and 2 (presented in results for rater 1) is the same as the comparison of group 2 and 1 (presented in results for rater 2) and so forth.

Multivariate test results for 'rating', which were presented earlier in the output (note that earlier output included results for rating and rating*instructor), are provided again. See earlier output for interpretations.

Multivariate Tests

	Value	F	Hypothesis df	Error df	Sig.	Partial Eta Squared	Noncent. Parameter	Observed Power[b]
Pillai's trace	.983	74.892[a]	3.000	4.000	.001	.983	224.677	1.000
Wilks' lambda	.017	74.892[a]	3.000	4.000	.001	.983	224.677	1.000
Hotelling's trace	56.169	74.892[a]	3.000	4.000	.001	.983	224.677	1.000
Roy's largest root	56.169	74.892[a]	3.000	4.000	.001	.983	224.677	1.000

Each F tests the multivariate effect of Rating. These tests are based on the linearly independent pairwise comparisons among the estimated marginal means.

a. Exact statistic

b. Computed using alpha = .05

TABLE 15.16 (continued)

Two-Factor Split-plot ANOVA SPSS Results for the Ballet Technique Example

4. Instructor * Rating

Measure: MEASURE_1

				95% Confidence Interval	
Instructor	Rating	Mean	Std. Error	Lower Bound	Upper Bound
Instructor 1	1	3.750	.559	2.382	5.118
	2	4.250	.339	3.422	5.078
	3	7.000	.354	6.135	7.865
	4	8.500	.270	7.839	9.161
Instructor 2	1	1.750	.559	.382	3.118
	2	3.000	.339	2.172	3.828
	3	5.500	.354	4.635	6.365
	4	9.750	.270	9.089	10.411

The table for **"Instructor*Rating"** provides descriptive statistics for each of the combinations of instructor by rater (or cell). In addition to means, the *SE* and 95% CI of the means are reported.

Profile Plots

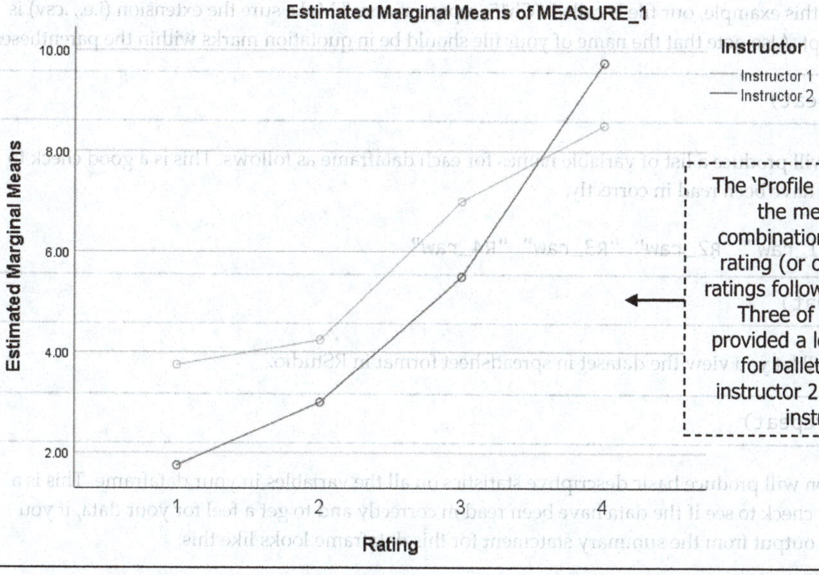

The 'Profile plot' is a graph of the means for each combination of instructor by rating (or cell). We see the ratings follow a similar pattern. Three of the four raters provided a lower mean rating for ballet technique for instructor 2 (as compared to instructor 1).

15.7 Computing ANOVA Models Using R

15.7.1. The One-Factor Repeated Measures Design

Next we consider **R** for the one-factor repeated measures ANOVA model. Note that the scripts are provided within the blocks with additional annotation to assist in understanding how the command works. Should you want to write reminder notes and annotation to yourself as you write the commands in **R** (and we highly encourage doing so), remember that any text that follows a hashtag (i.e., #) is annotation only and not part of the **R** script. Thus, you can write annotations directly into **R** with hashtags. We encourage this practice so that when you call up the commands in the future, you'll understand what the various lines of code are doing. You may think you'll remember what you did. However, trust us. There is a good chance that you won't. Thus, consider it best practice when using **R** to annotate heavily!

```
getwd()
```

R is always pointed to a directory on your computer. The *get working directory* function can be used to determine to which directory **R** is pointed. We will assume that we need to change the working directory, and will use the next line of code to set the working directory to the desired path.

```
setwd("E:/FolderName")
```

We use the *setwd* function to establish the working directory. To set the working directory, change what is in quotation marks to your file location. Also, if you are copying the directory name from your properties, you will need to change the backslash (i.e., \) to a forward slash (i.e., /).

```
Ch15_repeat <- read.csv("Ch15_repeatraw.csv")
```

The *read.csv* function reads our data into **R**. What's to the left of the "<-" will be what the data will be called in **R**. In this example, we're calling the **R** dataframe "Ch15_repeat." What's to the right of the "<-" tells **R** to find this particular csv file. In this example, our file is called "Ch15_repeatraw.csv." Make sure the extension (i.e., .csv) is included in your script. Also note that the name of your file should be in quotation marks within the parentheses.

```
names(Ch15_repeat)
```

The *names* function will produce a list of variable names for each dataframe as follows. This is a good check to make sure your data have been read in correctly.

```
[1] "ID"    "R1_raw" "R2_raw" "R3_raw" "R4_raw"
```

```
View(Ch15_repeat)
```

The *View* function will let you view the dataset in spreadsheet format in RStudio.

```
summary(Ch15_repeat)
```

The *summary* function will produce basic descriptive statistics on all the variables in your dataframe. This is a great way to quickly check to see if the data have been read in correctly and to get a feel for your data, if you haven't already. The output from the summary statement for this dataframe looks like this:

```
       ID            R1_raw          R2_raw           R3_raw
 Min.   :1.00   Min.   :1.00   Min.   :2.000   Min.   :5.00
 1st Qu.:2.75   1st Qu.:2.00   1st Qu.:3.000   1st Qu.:5.75
 Median :4.50   Median :2.50   Median :4.000   Median :6.00
 Mean   :4.50   Mean   :2.75   Mean   :3.625   Mean   :6.25
 3rd Qu.:6.25   3rd Qu.:3.00   3rd Qu.:4.000   3rd Qu.:7.00
 Max.   :8.00   Max.   :6.00   Max.   :5.000   Max.   :8.00
     R4_raw
 Min.   : 8.000
 1st Qu.: 8.750
 Median : 9.000
 Mean   : 9.125
 3rd Qu.:10.000
 Max.   :10.000
```

FIGURE 15.34
Reading data into **R**.

15.7.2 Restructuring Data for the One-Factor Repeated Measures ANOVA Model

```
install.packages(reshape)
library(reshape2)
```

We will install the *reshape* package and load *reshape2* to convert our wide format data to long format.

```
Ch15long <-melt(Ch15_repeat, id.vars = c("ID"),
          measure.vars = ,
          variable.name = "rater",
          value.name = "ranking")
```

We are creating a new dataset named "Ch15long." The *melt* function will transform our "wide" format data to "long" format. In other words, there will be multiple rows of data for each measurement occasion but just one column for the repeated measure. Within parentheses, we see we are using the Ch15_repeat dataframe to do this. The ID variable we want to keep but not split apart so we include the *id.vars=c("ID")* command. If there were other nonrepeated measures, we would have listed those here as well. The last two lines tell us that variable.name defines the column heading for the Rater and *value.name* defines the column heading for the rank score.

```
names(Ch15long)
```

The *names* function will produce a list of variable names for our new dataframe as follows. This is a good check to make sure we have restructured the data correctly and retained the ID variable.

```
[1] "ID"       "rater" "ranking"
```

```
View(Ch15long)
```

The *View* function will let you view the dataset in spreadsheet format in RStudio.

```
Ch15long$rater<-as.numeric(Ch15long$rater)
```

The *as.numeric* function will change the string to numeric values for the variable *rater* that is located in our Ch15long dataframe.

```
Ch15long<-within(Ch15long,
          {rater <- factor(rater)
          ID <- factor(ID)})
```

The *within* function will define rater and ID as factors within the Ch15long dataframe.

```
View(Ch15long)
```

The *View* function will let you view the dataset in spreadsheet format in RStudio.

FIGURE 15.35
Restructuring data for the one-factor repeated measures ANOVA model.

15.7.3 Generating the One-Factor Repeated Measures ANOVA Model

```
repeatedANOVA <- aov(ranking~rater+Error(ID), data=Ch15long)
```

The *aov* function will model the one-factor repeated measures ANOVA with "ranking" as the repeated measure, "rater" as the variable that defines who completed the ranking, and "ID" as the ID variable. The data comes from the *Ch15long* dataframe, and we are creating an object called "repeatedANOVA" from the model.

```
summary(repeatedANOVA)
```

The *summary* function will provide output from our repeated measures ANOVA model.

```
Error: ID
          Df Sum Sq Mean Sq F value Pr(>F)
Residuals  7  14.88   2.125

Error: Within
          Df Sum Sq Mean Sq F value   Pr(>F)
rater      3 198.13   66.04   73.48 2.66e-11 ***
Residuals 21  18.87    0.90
---
Signif. codes:  0 "***" 0.001 "**" 0.01 "*" 0.05 "." 0.1 " " 1
```

```
resid <- proj(repeatedANOVA)
Ch15long$unstandardizedResiduals <- resid[[3]][, "Residuals"]
```

After running the repeated measures ANOVA, save the residuals using this script.

FIGURE 15.36
Generating the one-factor repeated measures ANOVA model.

15.7.4 Computing Friedman's Test in R: Nonparametric One-Factor Repeated Measures ANOVA

Next we consider **R** for Friedman's test, the nonparametric version of the one-factor repeated measures ANOVA model.

```
if (!require("devtools")) {
  install.packages("devtools")
}
devtools::install_github("b0rxa/scmamp")
library("scmamp")
```

The **R** package *devtools* will be used when generating our model. If this package is not installed, this command will install the pack and load what is required.

```
reprank <- read.csv (file="E:/FolderName/Ch15_repeatrank.csv", head=T, sep=",")
```

The *read.csv* function will read in our csv file, recognize the column headers as names (i.e., *head=T*) and recognize that it is a comma delimited file (i.e., *sep= ","*).

FIGURE 15.37
Computing Friedman's test in R.

```
reprank
```

To see the data in our console, we type in its name and see the data displayed as follows.

```
  R1_rank R2_rank R3_rank R4_rank
1       1       2       3       4
2       2       1       3       4
3       1       2       3       4
4       1       2       3       4
5       1       2       3       4
6       1       2       3       4
7       1       2       3       4
8       1       2       3       4
```

```
reprank.matrix <- data.matrix(reprank)
```

Next, using the *data.matrix* function, we take the dataframe "reprank" and convert it to a matrix labeled *reprank.matrix*.

```
reprank.matrix
```

To see the data in our console, we type in its name and see the data displayed as follows.

```
     R1_rank R2_rank R3_rank R4_rank
[1,]       1       2       3       4
[2,]       2       1       3       4
[3,]       1       2       3       4
[4,]       1       2       3       4
[5,]       1       2       3       4
[6,]       1       2       3       4
[7,]       1       2       3       4
[8,]       1       2       3       4
```

```
friedmanTest(reprank.matrix)
```

The *friedmanTest* function can be used to run Friedman's test on the matrix we just created, *reprank.matrix*. The results provided are as follows:

```
       Friedman's rank sum test
data: reprank.matrix
Friedman's chi-squared = 22.95, df = 3, p-value = 4.136e-05
```

FIGURE 15.37 (continued)
Computing Friedman's test in **R**.

15.7.5 Computing the Two-Factor Split-Plot or Mixed Design in R

Next we consider **R** for the two-factor split-plot or mixed ANOVA model.

15.7.5.1 Reading Data Into R

```
getwd()
```

R is always pointed to a directory on your computer. The *get working directory* function can be used to determine to which directory **R** is pointed. We will assume that we need to change the working directory, and will use the next line of code to set the working directory to the desired path.

FIGURE 15.38
Reading data into **R**.

```
setwd("E:/FolderName")
```

We use the *setwd* function to establish the working directory. To set the working directory, change what is in quotation marks to your file location. Also, if you are copying the directory name from your properties, you will need to change the backslash (i.e., \) to a forward slash (i.e., /).

```
Ch15split <- read.csv("Ch15_splitplot.csv", header = TRUE)
```

The *read.csv* function reads our data into **R**. What's to the left of the "<-" will be what the data will be called in **R**. In this example, we're calling the **R** dataframe "Ch15_split." What's to the right of the "<-" tells **R** to find this particular csv file. In this example, our file is called "Ch15_splitplot.csv." Make sure the extension (i.e., .csv) is included in your script. Also note that the name of your file should be in quotation marks within the parentheses. We are reading in the first row of data as headers with "header = TRUE." Note that this data include the instructor variable and the raw rankings.

```
names(Ch15split)
```

The *names* function will produce a list of variable names for each dataframe as follows. This is a good check to make sure your data have been read in correctly.

```
[1] "ID"          "Instructor" "R1_raw"     "R2_raw"     "R3_raw"     "R4_raw"
```

```
View(Ch15split)
```

The *View* function will let you view the dataset in spreadsheet format in RStudio.

```
summary(Ch15split)
```

The *summary* function will produce basic descriptive statistics on all the variables in your dataframe. This is a great way to quickly check to see if the data have been read in correctly and to get a feel for your data, if you haven't already. The output from the summary statement for this dataframe looks like this:

```
       ID           Instructor        R1_raw          R2_raw          R3_raw
 Min.   :1.00   Min.   :1.0   Min.   :1.00   Min.   :2.000   Min.   :5.00
 1st Qu.:2.75   1st Qu.:1.0   1st Qu.:2.00   1st Qu.:3.000   1st Qu.:5.75
 Median :4.50   Median :1.5   Median :2.50   Median :4.000   Median :6.00
 Mean   :4.50   Mean   :1.5   Mean   :2.75   Mean   :3.625   Mean   :6.25
 3rd Qu.:6.25   3rd Qu.:2.0   3rd Qu.:3.00   3rd Qu.:4.000   3rd Qu.:7.00
 Max.   :8.00   Max.   :2.0   Max.   :6.00   Max.   :5.000   Max.   :8.00
     R4_raw
 Min.   : 8.000
 1st Qu.: 8.750
 Median : 9.000
 Mean   : 9.125
 3rd Qu.:10.000
 Max.   :10.000
```

```
install.packages(reshape)
library(reshape2)
```

We will install the *reshape* package and load *reshape2* to convert our wide format data to long format.

FIGURE 15.38 (continued)
Reading data into **R**.

```
Ch15splitlong<-melt(Ch15split, id.vars = c("ID", "Instructor"),
          measure.vars = ,
          variable.name = "rater",
          value.name = "rating")
```

We are creating a new dataset named "Ch15splitlong." The *melt* function will transform our "wide" format data to "long" format. In other words, there will be multiple rows of data for each measurement occasion but just one column for the repeated measure. Within parentheses, we see we are using the Ch15_split dataframe to do this. The ID and instructor variables we want to keep but not split apart so we include the *id.vars=c("ID", "Instructor")* command. If there were other nonrepeated measures, we would have listed those here as well. The last two lines tell us that *variable.name* defines the column heading for the rater and *value.name* defines the column heading for the rating.

```
names(Ch15splitlong)
```

The *names* function will produce a list of variable names for each variable in our dataframe as follows.

```
[1] "ID"            "Instructor" "rater"        "rating"
```

```
View(Ch15splitlong)
```

The *View* function will let you view the dataset in spreadsheet format in RStudio.

```
Ch15splitlong$rater<-as.numeric(Ch15splitlong$rater)
```

The *as.numeric* function will change the string to numeric values for the variable "rater" that is located in our "Ch15splitlong" dataframe.

```
Ch15splitlong$Instructor=factor(Ch15splitlong$Instructor)
Ch15splitlong$rater=factor(Ch15splitlong$rater)
Ch15splitlong$ID=factor(Ch15splitlong$ID)
```

The *factor* function will be used to define variables *Instructor, rater,* and *ID* as nominal within the dataframe Ch15splitlong.

FIGURE 15.38 (continued)
Reading data into **R**.

15.7.5.2 Generating the Two-Factor Split-Plot ANOVA

```
install.packages(reshape)
library(reshape2)
```

We will install the *reshape* package and load *reshape2* to convert our wide format data to long format.

```
Ch15splitlong<-melt(Ch15split, id.vars = c("ID", "Instructor"),
          measure.vars = ,
          variable.name = "rater",
          value.name = "rating")
```

FIGURE 15.39
Two-Factor Split Plot ANOVA in **R**.

We are creating a new dataset named "Ch15splitlong." The *melt* function will transform our "wide" format data to "long" format. In other words, there will be multiple rows of data for each measurement occasion but just one column for the repeated measure. Within parentheses, we see we are using the Ch15_split dataframe to do this. The *ID* and *Instructor* variables we want to keep but not split apart so we include the *id.vars=c("ID", "Instructor")* command. If there were other nonrepeated measures, we would have listed those here as well. The last two lines tell us that *variable.name* defines the column heading for the Rater and *value.name* defines the column heading for the rank score.

```
names(Ch15splitlong)
```

The *names* function will produce a list of variable names for our new dataframe as follows. This is a good check to make sure we have restructured the data correctly and retained the ID variable.

```
[1] "ID"          "Instructor" "rater"       "rating"
```

```
View(Ch15splitlong)
```

The *View* function will let you view the dataset in spreadsheet format in RStudio.

```
Ch15splitlong$raterF<-as.numeric(Ch15splitlong$rater)
```

The variable "rater" is currently in our dataframe as a string variable. The *as.numeric* function will change rater to numeric (i.e., define a numeric value for each string category). To the left of "<-" tells **R** to create a new variable in our dataframe called "raterF."

```
Ch15splitlong$InstructorF=factor(Ch15splitlong$Instructor)
Ch15splitlong$rater=factor(Ch15splitlong$rater)
Ch15splitlong$ID=factor(Ch15splitlong$ID)
```

The *factor* function defines "InstructorF," "rater," and "ID" as factors in our dataframe.

```
modelsplit <- aov(rating ~ Instructor*rater + Error(ID),
                  data = Ch15splitlong)
```

The *aov* function is used to generate the two-factor split-plot ANOVA model using the dataframe Ch15splitlong. The dependent variable is "rating," and the within-subjects factor is "rater." The repeated measures are nested within rater. We model error based on the ID.

```
summary(modelsplit)
```

The *summary* function will provide output from our split-plot ANOVA model.

```
Error: ID
           Df Sum Sq Mean Sq F value Pr(>F)
Instructor  1  6.125   6.125     4.2 0.0863 .
Residuals   6  8.750   1.458
---
Signif. codes:  0 "***" 0.001 "**" 0.01 "*" 0.05 "." 0.1 " " 1

Error: Within
                 Df Sum Sq Mean Sq F value   Pr(>F)
rater             3 198.13   66.04  190.20 8.13e-14 ***
```

FIGURE 15.39 (continued)
Two-Factor Split Plot ANOVA in **R**.

```
Instructor:rater  3  12.62    4.21   12.12 0.000141 ***
Residuals        18   6.25    0.35
---
Signif. codes:  0 "***" 0.001 "**" 0.01 "*" 0.05 "." 0.1 " " 1
```

Our output corresponds to the tests of within-subjects effects (i.e., rater, instructor*rater, and error) and between-subjects effects (i.e., instructor) that we found using SPSS.

```
Ch15splitlong$unstandardizedResiduals <- residuals(modelsplit)
```

We also want to save our unstandardized residuals to the dataframe. We use the *residuals* function to compute unstandardized residuals from our *modelsplit* model. To the left of "<-" will save the residuals as a variable named "unstandardizedResiduals" in our dataframe, "Ch15splitlong$unstandardizedResiduals."

```
install.packages("ggplot2")
```

We can graph the data using the *ggplot2* package. If this is not already installed, the *install.packages* function is used to install the package in **R**.

```
library(ggplot2)
```

The *library* function is used to call up the *ggplot2* package.

```
ggplot(Ch15splitlong, aes(y=rating, x=rater,
shape=Instructor, color=rating)) + geom_point()
```

The *ggplot* function can be used to create a plot from our dataframe, Ch15splitlong, with "rating" on the *Y* axis and "rater" on the *X* axis. We allow shapes to define the different instructors using the *shaper=Instructor* command.

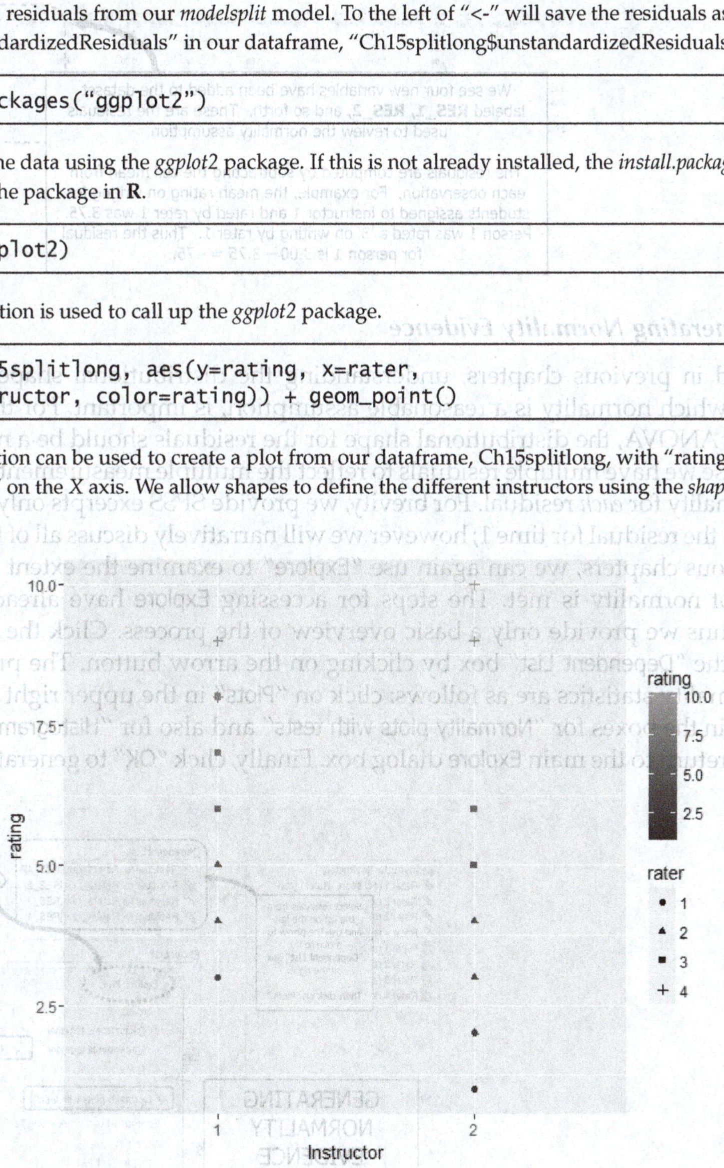

FIGURE 15.39 (continued)
Two-Factor Split Plot ANOVA in **R**.

15.8 Data Screening for the Two-Factor Split-Plot ANOVA

Now let's examine our data for the assumptions of the two-factor split-plot ANOVA.

15.8.1 Normality

We use the residuals (which we requested and created through the "Save" option when generating our two-factor split-plot ANOVA) to examine the extent to which normality was met.

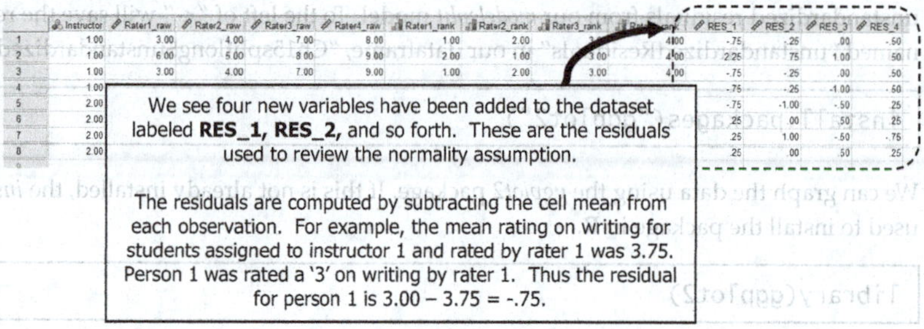

We see four new variables have been added to the dataset labeled **RES_1, RES_2,** and so forth. These are the residuals used to review the normality assumption.
The residuals are computed by subtracting the cell mean from each observation. For example, the mean rating on writing for students assigned to instructor 1 and rated by rater 1 was 3.75. Person 1 was rated a '3' on writing by rater 1. Thus the residual for person 1 is 3.00 – 3.75 = -.75.

FIGURE 15.40
Normality data.

15.8.1.1 *Generating Normality Evidence*

As mentioned in previous chapters, understanding the distributional shape, specifically the extent to which normality is a reasonable assumption, is important. For the two-factor mixed design ANOVA, the distributional shape for the residuals should be a normal distribution. Because we have multiple residuals to reflect the multiple measurements, we need to examine normality for *each* residual. For brevity, we provide SPSS excerpts only for "RES_1" which reflects the residual for time 1; however we will narratively discuss all of the residuals.

As in previous chapters, we can again use "Explore" to examine the extent to which the assumption of normality is met. The steps for accessing Explore have already been presented, and thus we provide only a basic overview of the process. Click the residual and move it into the "Dependent List" box by clicking on the arrow button. The procedures for selecting normality statistics are as follows: click on "Plots" in the upper right corner. Place a checkmark in the boxes for "Normality plots with tests" and also for "Histogram." Then click "Continue" to return to the main Explore dialog box. Finally, click "OK" to generate the output.

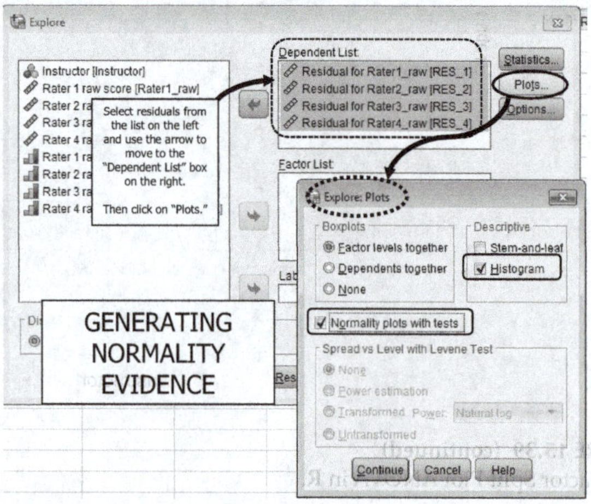

FIGURE 15.41
Generating normality evidence.

15.8.1.2 Interpreting Normality Evidence

We have already developed a good understanding of how to interpret some forms of evidence of normality including skewness and kurtosis, histograms, and boxplots. Next we see the output for this evidence. The skewness statistic of the residuals for rater 1 is 1.675 and kurtosis is 3.136—skewness being within the range of an absolute value of 2.0 suggesting evidence of normality but some non-normality based on kurtosis. For the other three residuals, all skewness and kurtosis statistics (not shown here) are within an absolute value of 2.0, respectively, suggesting evidence of normality.

Descriptives

			Statistic	Std. Error
Residual for Rater1_raw	Mean		.0000	.36596
	95% Confidence Interval for Mean	Lower Bound	-.8654	
		Upper Bound	.8654	
	5% Trimmed Mean		-.0833	
	Median		-.2500	
	Variance		1.071	
	Std. Deviation		1.03510	
	Minimum		-.75	
	Maximum		2.25	
	Range		3.00	
	Interquartile Range		1.00	
	Skewness		1.675	.752
	Kurtosis		3.136	1.481

FIGURE 5.42
Normality evidence.

As suggested by the skewness statistic, the histogram of residuals is positively skewed, and the histogram also provides a visual display of the leptokurtic distribution.

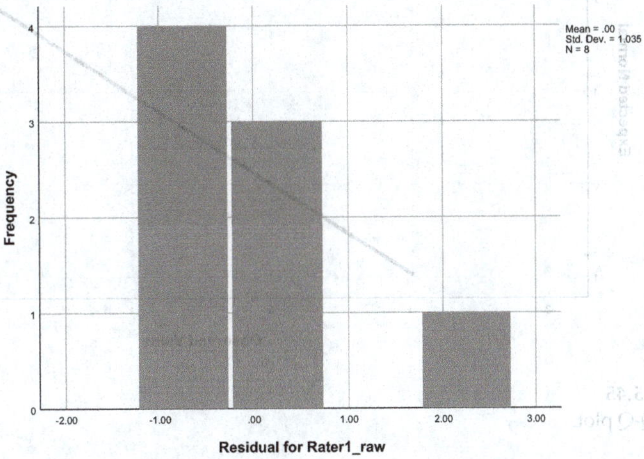

FIGURE 15.43
Histogram.

There are a few other statistics that can be used to gauge normality. The formal test of normality, the Shapiro-Wilk test (*SW*) (Shapiro & Wilk, 1965), provides evidence of the extent to which the sample distribution is statistically different from a normal distribution. The output for the Shapiro-Wilk test is presented in Figure 15.44 and suggests that our sample distributions for three of the four residuals (specifically residuals for raters 2, 3, and 4) are not statistically significantly different than what would be expected from a normal distribution, as those *p* values are greater than alpha. However, the distribution for the residual for rater 1 *is* statistically significantly different than a normal distribution ($SW = .745$, $df = 8$, $p = .007$).

Tests of Normality

	Kolmogorov-Smirnov[a]			Shapiro-Wilk		
	Statistic	df	Sig.	Statistic	df	Sig.
Residual for Rater1_raw	.280	8	.065	.745	8	.007
Residual for Rater2_raw	.250	8	.150	.913	8	.374
Residual for Rater3_raw	.152	8	.200*	.965	8	.857
Residual for Rater4_raw	.316	8	.018	.828	8	.057

*. This is a lower bound of the true significance.

a. Lilliefors Significance Correction

FIGURE 15.44
Shapiro-Wilk test of normality.

Quantile-quantile (Q-Q) plots are also often examined to determine evidence of normality. These graphs plot quantiles of the theoretical normal distribution against quantiles of the sample distribution. Points that fall on or close to the diagonal line suggest evidence of normality. The Q-Q plot of residuals for rater 1 shown below suggests some nonnormality (for brevity, the plots for the other raters are not shown).

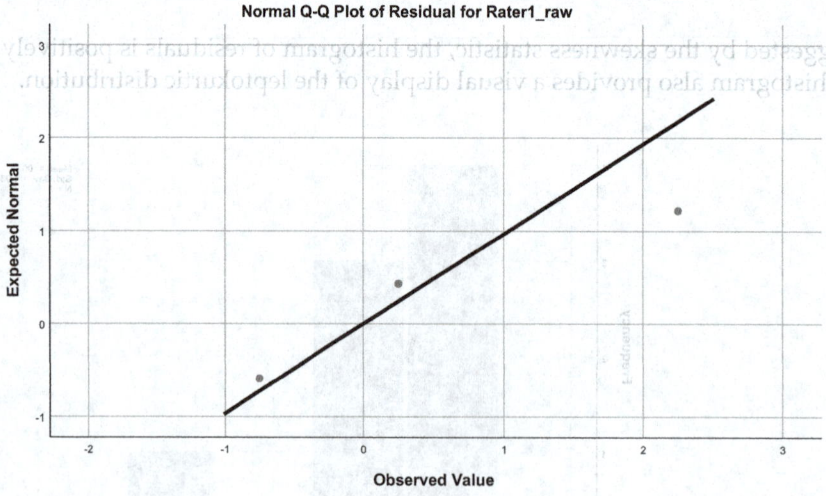

FIGURE 15.45
Normal Q-Q plot.

Examination of the boxplot for rater 1 (Figure 15.46) also suggests a nonnormal distributional shape of residuals with one outlier. For brevity, the boxplots for the remaining residuals are not presented but suggest normality.

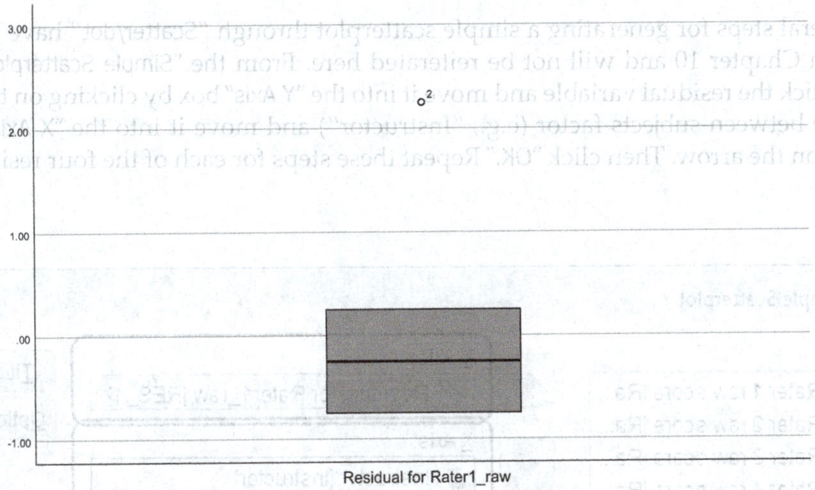

FIGURE 15.46
Boxplot.

For three of the four residuals (residuals for raters 2, 3, and 4), the forms of evidence we have examined—skewness and kurtosis statistics, the Shapiro-Wilk test, the Q-Q plot, and the boxplot—all suggest normality is a reasonable assumption. We can be reasonably assured we have met the assumption of normality for residuals for raters 2, 3, and 4. However, all forms of evidence suggest nonnormality for the residual for rater 1.

15.8.2 Independence

The only assumption we have not tested for yet is independence. As we discussed in reference to the one-way ANOVA, if subjects have been randomly assigned to conditions (in other words, the different levels of the between-subjects factor), the assumption of independence has been met. In this illustration, students were randomly assigned to instructor and thus the assumption of independence was met. However, we often use between-subjects factors that do not allow random assignment, such as preexisting characteristics (e.g., sex or education level). We can plot residuals against levels of our between-subjects factor using a scatterplot to get an idea of whether or not there are patterns in the data and thereby provide an indication of whether we have met this assumption. In this illustration, we only have one between-subjects factor. If there were multiple between-subjects factors, we would split the scatterplot by levels of one between-subjects factor and then generate a bivariate scatterplot for the other between-subjects factor by residual (as we did with factorial ANOVA). Remember that the residual was added to the dataset by saving it when we generated the two-factor split-plot ANOVA model.

Please note that some researchers do not believe that the assumption of independence can be tested. If there is not random assignment to groups, then these researchers believe this assumption has been violated—period. The plot that we generate will give us a general idea of patterns, however, in situations where random assignment was not performed.

15.8.2.1 Generating the Scatterplot

The general steps for generating a simple scatterplot through "Scatter/dot" have been presented in Chapter 10 and will not be reiterated here. From the "Simple Scatterplot" dialog screen, click the residual variable and move it into the "Y Axis" box by clicking on the arrow. Click the between-subjects factor (e.g., "Instructor") and move it into the "X Axis" box by clicking on the arrow. Then click "OK." Repeat these steps for each of the four residuals.

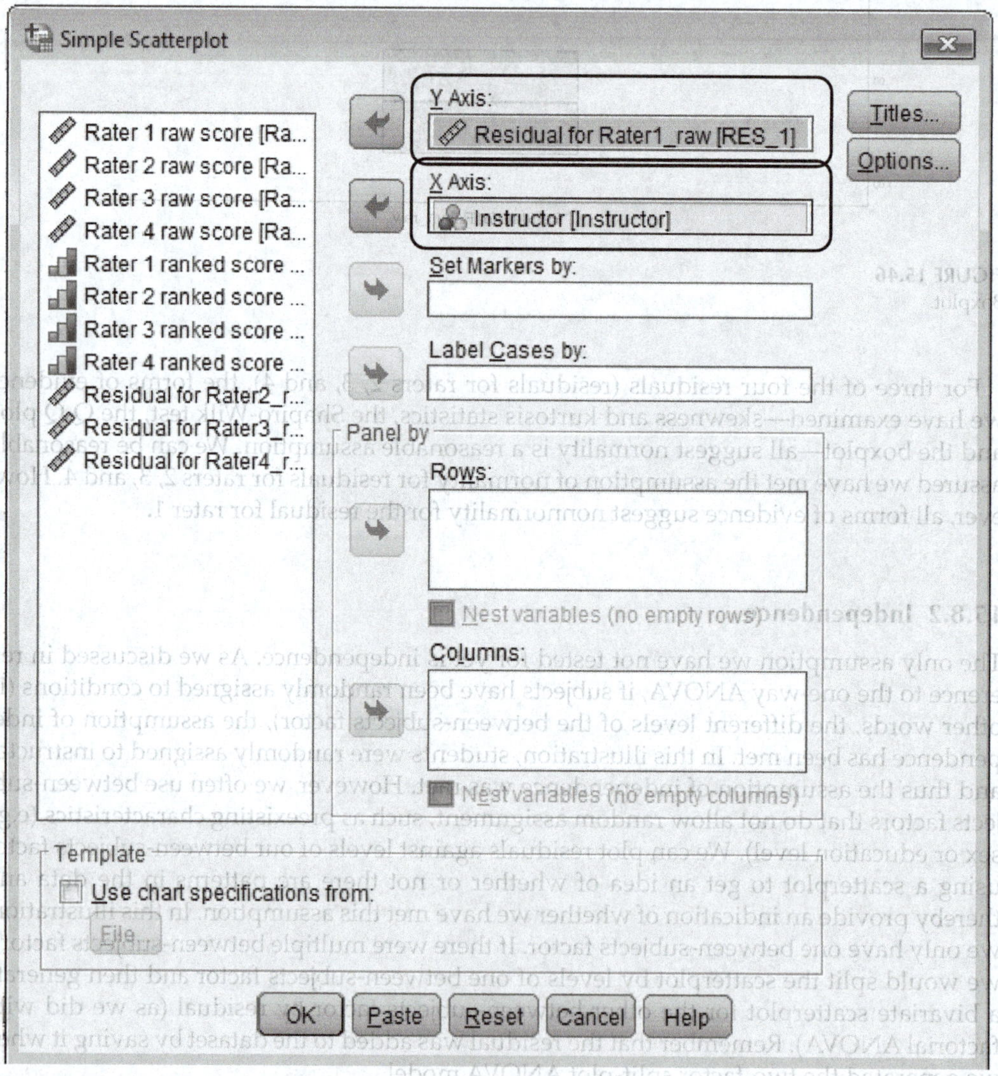

FIGURE 15.47
Generating scatterplot.

15.8.2.2 Interpreting Independence Evidence

In examining the scatterplots for evidence of independence, the points should fall relatively randomly above and below a horizontal line at zero. (You may recall in Chapter 11 that we added a reference line to the graph using Chart Editor. To add a reference line, double click on the graph in the output to activate the chart editor. Select "Options" in the top pulldown menu, then "Y axis reference line." This will bring up the "Properties" dialog box. Change the value of the position to be "0." Then click on "Apply" and "Close" to generate the graph with a horizontal line at zero.)

Here our scatterplot for each residual generally suggests evidence of independence with a relatively random display of residuals above and below the horizontal line at zero for each category of time (note that only the scatterplot of the residual for rater 3 by instructor is presented). If we had not met the assumption of independence through random assignment of cases to groups, this provides evidence that independence was a reasonable assumption.

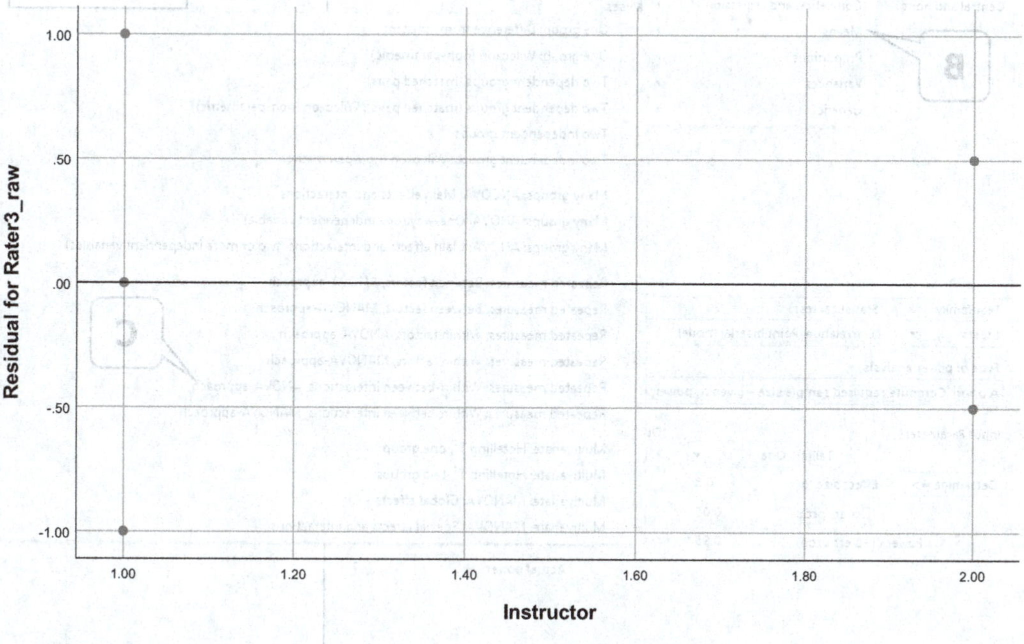

FIGURE 15.48
Scatterplot.

15.9 Power Using G*Power

15.9.1 Post Hoc Power for Two-factor Split-plot ANOVA

Generating power analyses for a two-factor split-plot ANOVA models follow similarly to that for ANOVA, factorial ANOVA, and ANCOVA. In particular, if there is more than one independent variable, we must test for main effects and interactions separately. The first thing that must be done when using G*Power for computing post hoc power is to select the correct test family. In our case, we conducted a two-factor split-plot ANOVA. Because we have both between, within, and interaction terms, the type of statistical test selected depends on which part of the model power is to be estimated. In this illustration, let us first determine power for the within-between subjects interaction. To find this design, we select "Tests" in the top pulldown menu, then "Means," and then "ANOVA: Repeated measures, within-between interactions." Once that selection is made, the "Test family" automatically changes to "F tests." (Note that had we wanted to determine power for the between-subjects main effect, we would have selected "ANOVA: Repeated measures, between factors." For the within-subjects main effect, we would have selected "ANOVA: Repeated measures, within factors.")

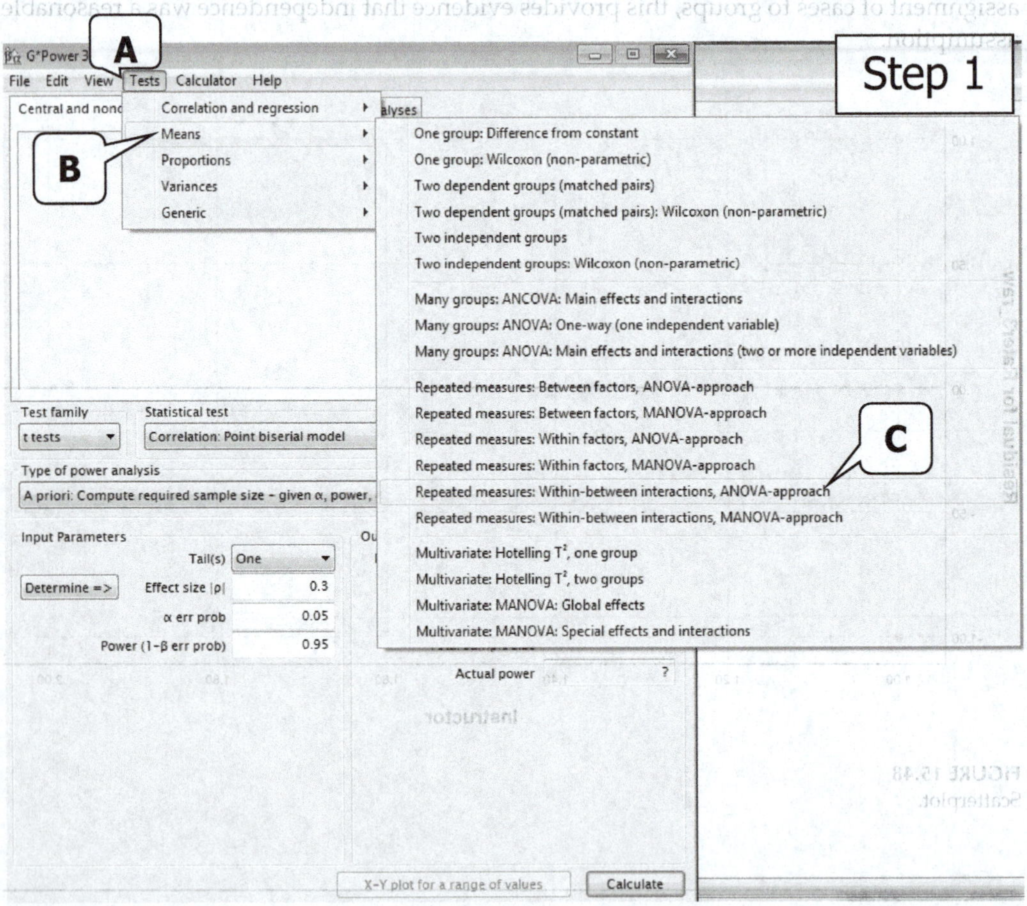

FIGURE 15.49
Post hoc power for two-factor split-plot ANOVA using G*Power.

The "Type of power analysis" desired needs to be selected. To compute *post hoc* power, select "Post hoc: Compute achieved power—given α, sample size, and effect size."

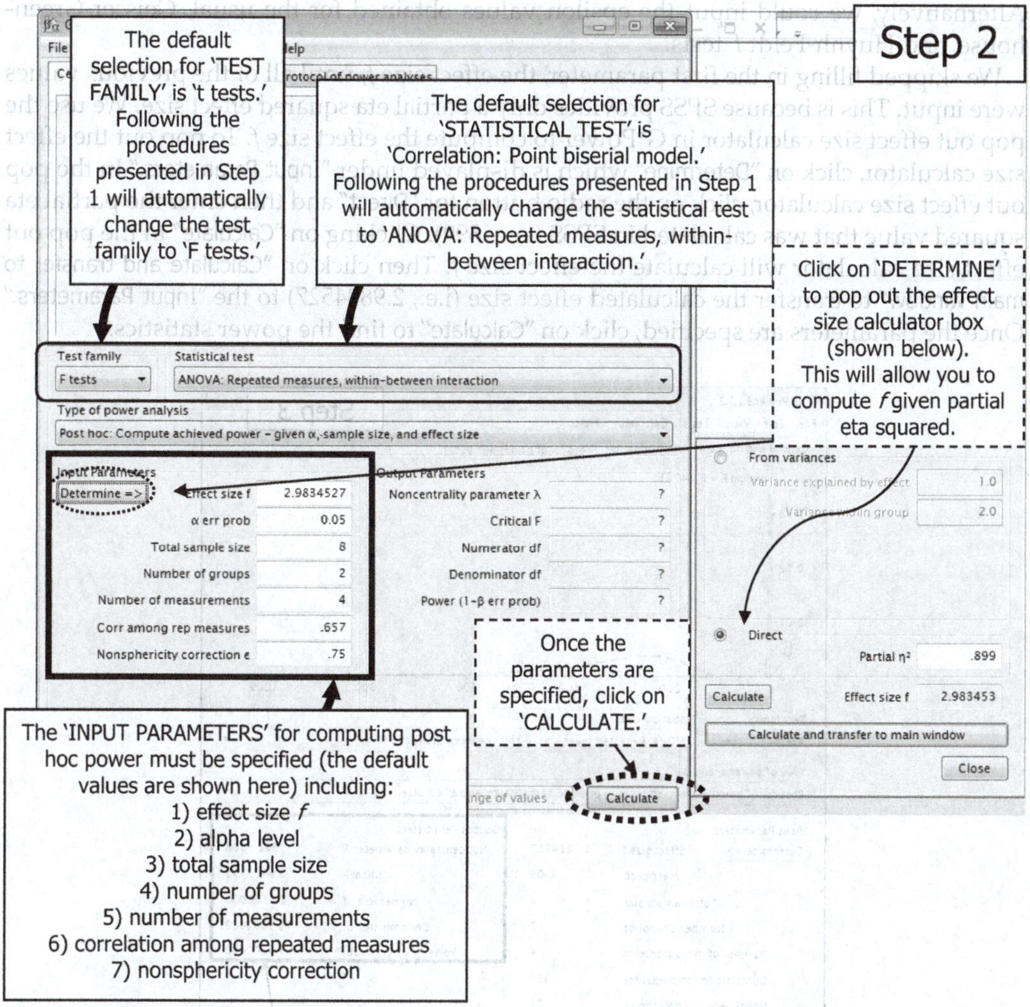

FIGURE 15.50
Post hoc power for two-factor split-plot ANOVA: Step 2.

The "Input Parameters" must then be specified. We will compute the effect size *f* last so we skip that for the moment. In our example, the alpha level we used was .05 and the total sample size was 8. The *number of groups*, in the case of a two-factor split-plot ANOVA with one nonrepeated factor having two categories, equals two. The next parameter is the number of measurements. This refers to the number of levels of the repeated factor, which in this illustration is four. Next, we have to input the correlation among repeated measures. We will estimate this parameter as the average correlation among all bivariate correlations of the repeated measures. For our raters, the Pearson correlation coefficients were: r_{12} = .865, r_{13} = .881, r_{14} = −.431, r_{23} = .716, r_{24} = −.677, and r_{34} = −.372 and thus the average correlation was .657 (in absolute value terms). The last parameter to define is the nonsphericity correction epsilon, ε. Epsilon ranges from 0 to 1, with 0 indicating the assumption is violated completely and 1 being perfect sphericity. Acceptable sphericity is approximately .75 or higher. One option is to input an acceptable level of sphericity; thus we input .75 here.

Alternatively, we could input the epsilon values obtained for the usual, Geisser-Greenhouse, and Huynh-Feldt *F* tests.

We skipped filling in the first parameter, the effect size *f*, until all of the previous values were input. This is because SPSS provides only a partial eta squared effect size. We use the pop out effect size calculator in G*Power to compute the effect size *f*. To pop out the effect size calculator, click on "Determine" which is displayed under "Input Parameters." In the pop out effect size calculator, click on the radio button for "Direct" and then enter the partial eta squared value that was calculated in SPSS (i.e., .899). Clicking on "Calculate" in the pop out effect size calculator will calculate the effect size *f*. Then click on "Calculate and transfer to main window" to transfer the calculated effect size (i.e., 2.9834527) to the "Input Parameters." Once the parameters are specified, click on "Calculate" to find the power statistics.

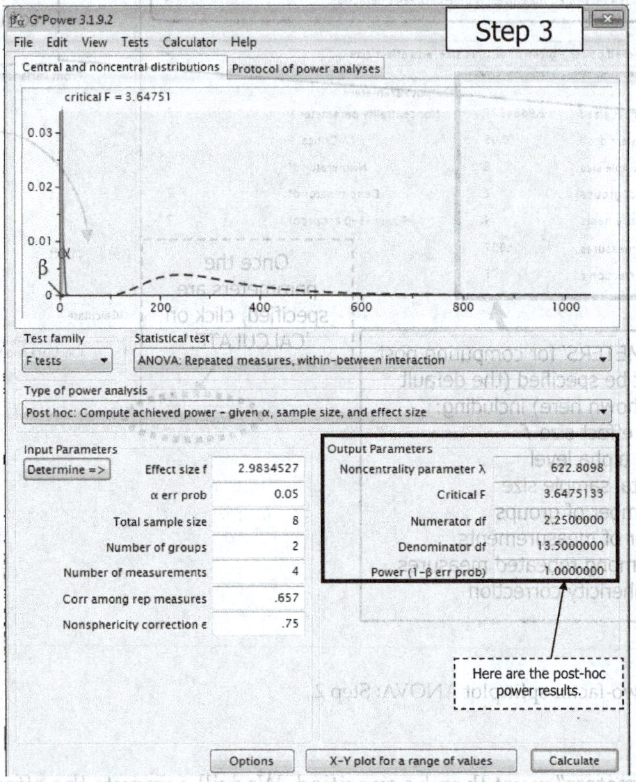

FIGURE 15.51
Post hoc power for two-factor split-plot ANOVA: Step 3.

The "Output Parameters" provide the relevant statistics given the input just specified. In this example, we were interested in determining post hoc power for the within-between interaction in a two-factor split-plot ANOVA with a computed effect size *f* of 2.9834527, an alpha level of .05, total sample size of 8, two groups, four measurements, an average correlation among repeated measures of .657, and epsilon sphericity correction of .75. Based on those criteria, the post hoc power of our within-between interaction effect for this test was 1.000—the probability of rejecting the null hypothesis when it is really false (in this case, the probability that the means of the dependent variable would be equal for each level of the independent variable) was at the maximum (i.e., 100%) (sufficient power is often .80 or above). Note that this is the same value as that reported in SPSS. Keep in mind that conducting power analysis *a priori* is recommended so that you avoid a situation where, post hoc, you find that the sample size was not sufficient to reach the desired level of power (given the observed parameters).

15.9.2 *A Priori* Power for Two-Factor Split-Plot ANOVA

For *a priori* power, we can determine the total sample size needed for the main effects and/or interactions given an estimated effect size f, alpha level, desired power, number of groups (i.e., the number of categories of the independent *variable in the case of only one independent variable* OR the product of the number of levels of the independent variables *in the case of multiple independent variables*), number of measurements, correlation among repeated measures, and nonsphericity correction epsilon. We follow Cohen's (1988) convention for effect size (i.e., small $f = .10$; moderate $f = .25$; large $f = .40$). In this example, had we wanted to determine *a priori* power for a within-between interaction and had estimated a moderate effect f of .25, alpha of .05, desired power of .80, number of groups was two (i.e., we have only one independent variable and there were two categories), four measurements, a moderate correlation among repeated measures of .50, and a nonsphericity correction epsilon of .75, we would need a total sample size of 30 (i.e., 15 cases per group given two levels to our independent variable).

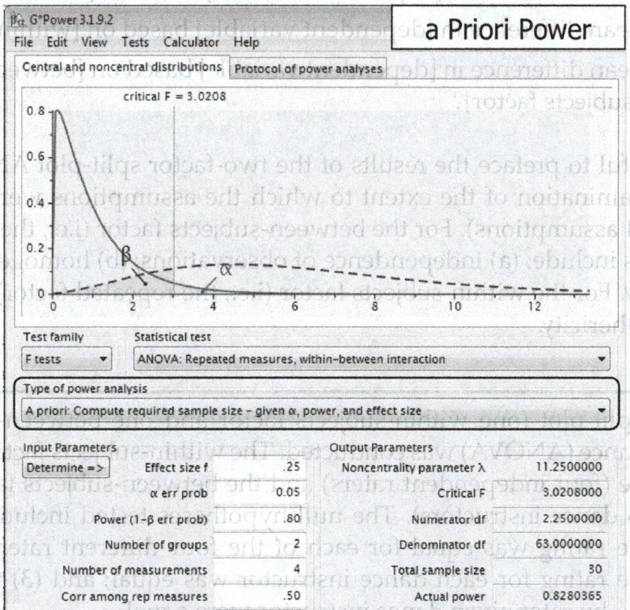

FIGURE 15.52
A priori power for two-factor split-plot ANOVA.

15.10 Research Question Template and Example Write-Up

Finally, here is an example paragraph just for the results of the two-factor split-plot design (feel free to write similar paragraphs for the other models in this chapter). Recall that our graduate research assistant, Oso Wyse, was assisting the coordinator of the dance program, Dr. Kilauea. Dr. Kilauea wanted to know if there is a mean difference in ballet technique based on instructor; if there is a mean difference in ballet technique based on rater; and if there is a mean difference in ballet technique based on rater by instructor. The research questions presented to Dr. Kilauea from Oso's work include the following:

- *Is there a mean difference in ballet technique based on instructor?*
- *Is there a mean difference in ballet technique based on rater?*
- *Is there a mean difference in ballet technique based on rater by instructor?*

Oso then assisted Dr. Kilauea in generating a two-factor split-plot ANOVA as the test of inference, and a template for writing the research questions for this design is presented in this section. As we noted in previous chapters, it is important to ensure the reader understands the levels or groups of the factor(s). This may be done parenthetically in the actual research question, as an operational definition, or specified within the methods section.

- Is there a mean difference in [dependent variable] based on [between-subjects factor]?
- Is there a mean difference in [dependent variable] based on [within-subjects factor]?
- Is there a mean difference in [dependent variable] based on [between-subjects factor] by [within-subjects factor]?

It may be helpful to preface the results of the two-factor split-plot ANOVA with information on an examination of the extent to which the assumptions were met (recall that we tested several assumptions). For the between-subjects factor (i.e., the nonrepeated factor), assumptions include: (a) independence of observations; (b) homogeneity of variance; and (c) normality. For the within-subjects factor (i.e., the repeated factor), we examine the assumption of sphericity.

A two-factor split-plot (one within-subjects factor and one between-subjects factor) analysis of variance (ANOVA) was conducted. The within-subjects factor was rating on ballet technique (four independent raters) and the between-subjects factor was dance instructor (two dance instructors). The null hypotheses tested include: (1) the mean ballet technique rating was equal for each of the four different raters; (2) the mean ballet technique rating for each dance instructor was equal; and (3) the mean ballet technique rating by rater given dance instructor were equal.

There were no missing data and no univariate outliers. The assumption of *sphericity* was met ($\chi^2 = 4.001$, Mauchly's $W = .429$, $df = 5$, $p = .557$); therefore, the results reported reflect univariate results. The sphericity assumption was further upheld in that the same results were obtained for the usual, Geisser-Greenhouse, and Huynh-Feldt F tests. The assumption of *homogeneity of variance* was met for the ballet technique rating of all raters [rater 1, $F(1, 6) = 3.600$, $p = .107$; rater 2, $F(1, 6) = .158$, $p = .705$; rater 3, $F(1, 6) = 0.000$, $p = 1.000$; and rater 4, $F(1, 6) = 1.000$, $p = .356$].

The assumption of *normality* was tested via examination of the residuals. Review of the Shapiro-Wilk test for normality (SW_{rater1} = .745, *df* = 8, *p* = .007; SW_{rater2} = .913, *df* = 8, *p* = .374; SW_{rater3} = .965, *df* = 8, *p* = .857; SW_{rater4} = .828, *df* = 8, *p* = .057), and skewness (rater 1 = 1.675; rater 2 = .290; rater 3 = .000; rater 4 = −.571) and kurtosis (rater 1 = 3.136; rater 2 = .272; rater 3 = −.700; rater 4 = −1.729) statistics suggest that normality was a reasonable assumption for raters 2, 3, and 4, but nonnormality was suggested for rater 1. The boxplot suggested a relatively normal distributional shape (with no outliers) of the residuals for raters 2 through 4. The boxplot of the residuals for rater 1 suggested nonnormality with one outlier. The Q-Q plots suggested normality was reasonable for the residuals of raters 2, 3, and 4, but suggested nonnormality for rater 1. Thus, while there was nonnormality suggested by the residuals for rater 1, the two-factor split-plot ANOVA is robust to violations of normality with equal sample sizes of groups as is evident in this design.

Random assignment of individuals to dance instructor helped ensure that the assumption of *independence* was met. Additionally, a scatterplot of residuals against the levels of the between-subjects factor was reviewed. A relatively random display of points around zero provided further evidence that the assumption of independence was met.

Here is an APA-style example paragraph of results for the two-factor split-plot ANOVA (remember that this will be prefaced by the previous paragraph reporting the extent to which the assumptions of the test were met).

The results for the univariate ANOVA indicate:

1. A statistically significant within-subjects main effect for rater (F_{rater} = 198.125, *df* = 3,18, *p* = .001) (rater 1, *M* = 2.750, *SE* = .395; rater 2, *M* = 3.625, *SE* = .239; rater 3, *M* = 6.250, *SE* = .250; rater 4, *M* = 9.125, *SE* = .191).
2. A statistically significant within-between subjects interaction effect between rater and dance instructor ($F_{\text{rater x instructor}}$ = 12.625, *df* = 3,18, *p* = .001) (for brevity, we have not included the means and standard errors here, however you may want to include those in the narrative or in tabular form).
3. A nonstatistically significant between-subjects main effect for dance instructor ($F_{instructor}$ = 4.200, *df* = 1,6, *p* = .086) (dance instructor 1, *M* = 5.875, *SE* = .302; dance instructor 2, *M* = 5.000, *SE* = .302).

Effect sizes were rather large for the significant effects (partial η^2_{rater} = .969, power = 1.000; partial $\eta^2_{rater\ x\ instructor}$ = .669, power = .998) with more than sufficient observed power, but less so for the nonsignificant effect (partial $\eta^2_{instructor}$ = .412, power = .407) which had less than desired power.

The statistically significant *main effect for the within-subjects factor* suggests that there are mean differences in ballet technique rating by rater. The raters were quite inconsistent in that Bonferroni multiple comparison procedures revealed statistically significant differences among all pairs of raters except for rater 1 versus rater 2. The nonstatistically significant *main effect for the between-subjects factor* suggests that there are not differences, on average, in ballet technique rating per dance instructor. Most valuable in our findings is the interaction for the between-within factor (i.e., dance instructor by rater). In examining confidence intervals of the *interaction for the between-within factor*, nonoverlapping confidence intervals suggest statistically significant differences. We see that the patterns evident for the within-subjects factors echo here as well. For both dance instructor 1 and dance instructor 2, there are statistically significant differences among all pairs of raters except for rater 1 versus rater 2. Examining the statistically significant interaction using simple effects, we find for all raters, there is a statistically significant difference between instructor 1 and instructor 2 (rater 1, $p = .045$; rater 2, $p = .040$; . . .). For instructor 1, there is a statistically significant difference between rater 1 and 4 ($p = .001$) and rater 1 and 4 ($p = .001$) . . . [report results of simple effects; for brevity only a few are included here!]. From the profile plot in Figure 15.2, we see that while rater 4 found the dancers of instructor 2 to have better ballet technique, the other raters liked the ballet technique by the dancers of instructor 1.

15.11 Additional Resources

This chapter has provided a preview into conducting a number of ANOVA models. However, there are a number of areas that space limitations prevent us from delving into. For those of you who are interested in learning more about ANOVA models, or if you find yourself in a sticky situation in your analyses, you may wish to look into the following, among many other excellent resources.

- For more in-depth coverage of ANOVA models, see Maxwell, Delaney, and Kelley (2018), Kirk (2014) and Keppel and Wickens (2004), among others

Problems

Conceptual Problems

1. When an ANOVA design includes a random factor that is crossed with a fixed factor, the design illustrates which type of model?
   a. Fixed
   b. Mixed
   c. Random
   d. Crossed
2. The denominator of the F ratio used to test the interaction in a two-factor ANOVA is MS_{with} in which one of the following?
   a. Fixed-effects model
   b. Random-effects model
   c. Mixed-effects model
   d. All of the above

3. A course consists of five units, the order of presentation of which is varied (counterbalanced). A researcher used a 5 × 2 ANOVA design with order (five different randomly selected orders) and gender serving as factors. Which ANOVA model is illustrated by this design?

a. Fixed-effects model

b. Random-effects model

c. Mixed-effects model

d. Nested model

4. A researcher conducts a study where children are measured on frequency of sharing at three different times over the course of the academic year. Which ANOVA model is most appropriate for analysis of this data?

a. One-factor random-effects model

b. Two-factor random-effect model

c. Two-factor mixed-effects model

d. One-factor repeated measures design

e. Two-factor split-plot design

5. A health care researcher wants to make generalizations about the number of patients served by after hour clinics in her region. She randomly samples clinics and collects data on the number of patients served. Which ANOVA model is most appropriate for analysis of this data?

a. One-factor random-effects model

b. Two-factor random-effect model

c. Two-factor mixed-effects model

d. One-factor repeated measures design

e. Two-factor split-plot design

6. A preschool teacher randomly assigns children to classrooms—some with windows and some without windows. She wants to know if there is a mean difference in receptive vocabulary based on type of classroom (with and without windows) and whether this varies by classroom teacher. Which ANOVA model is most appropriate for analysis of this data?

a. One-factor random-effects model

b. Two-factor random-effect model

c. Two-factor mixed-effects model

d. One-factor repeated measures design

e. Two-factor split-plot design

7. True or false? If a given set of data was analyzed with both a one-factor fixed-effects model and a one-factor random-effects model, the *F* ratio for the random-effects model will be greater than the *F* ratio for the fixed-effects model.

8. True or false? A repeated measures design is necessarily an example of the random-effects model.

9. Suppose researchers A and B perform a two-factor ANOVA on the same data, but that A assumes a fixed-effects model and B assumes a random-effects model. I assert that if A finds the interaction significant at the .05 level, B will also find the interaction significant at the .05 level. Am I correct?

10. I assert that MS_{with} should always be used as the denominator for all F ratios in any two-factor analysis of variance. Am I correct?

11. I assert that in a one-factor repeated measures ANOVA and a two-factor split-plot ANOVA, the SS_{total} will be exactly the same when using the same data. Am I correct?

12. Football players are each exposed to all three different counterbalanced coaching strategies, one per month. This is an example of which type of model?

a. One-factor fixed-effects ANOVA model

b. One-factor repeated-measures ANOVA model

c. One-factor random-effects ANOVA model

d. One-factor fixed-effects ANCOVA model

13. A two-factor split-plot design involves which of the following?

a. Two repeated factors

b. Two nonrepeated factors

c. One repeated factor and one nonrepeated factor

d. Farmers splitting up their land into plots

14. The interaction between factors L and M can be assessed only if which one of the following occurs?

a. Both factors are crossed.

b. Both factors are random.

c. Both factors are fixed.

d. Factor L is a repeated factor.

15. True or false? A student factor is almost always random.

16. In a two-factor split-plot design, there are two interaction terms. Hypotheses can actually be tested for how many of those interactions?

a. 0

b. 1

c. 2

d. Cannot be determined

17. True or false? In a one-factor repeated measures ANOVA design, the F test is quite robust to violation of the sphericity assumption, and thus we never need to worry about it.

18. True or false? Assumptions for the two-factor split-plot ANOVA include consideration only for the between-subjects factors.

19. The assumption of sphericity is applicable to which ANOVA models? Select all that apply.

a. One-factor random effects

b. Two-factor random effects

c. Two-factor mixed effects

d. One-factor repeated measures
e. Two-factor split-plot

20. Which one of the following is a type of equal variance assumption?
a. Independence
b. Multicollinearity
c. Normality
d. Sphericity

Answers to Conceptual Problems

1. **b** (When there are both random and fixed factors, then the design is mixed.)
3. **c** (Gender is fixed, and order is random; thus it is a mixed-effects model.)
5. **a** (Clinics were randomly selected from the population; thus the one-factor random-effects model is appropriate.)
7. **False** (The *F* ratio will be the same for both the one-factor random- and fixed-effects models.)
9. **Yes** (The test of the interaction is exactly the same for both models yielding the same *F* ratio.)
11. **Yes** (SS_{total} is the same for both models; the total amount of variation is the same, it is just divided up in different ways; review the example dataset in this chapter.)
13. **c** (See definition of design.)
15. **True** (Rarely is one interested in particular students, thus students are usually random.)
17. **False** (The *F* test is not very robust in this situation and we should be concerned about it.)
19. **d and e** (The assumption of sphericity is applicable to the within-subjects factor—i.e., repeated factor—so it is applicable to both the one-factor repeated measures and two-factor split-plot ANOVA designs.)

Computational Problems

1. Complete the following ANOVA summary table for a two-factor model, where there are three levels of factor A (fixed method effect) and two levels of factor B (random teacher effect). Each cell of the design includes 4 students ($\alpha = .01$).

Source	*SS*	*df*	*MS*	*F*	Critical Value	Decision
A	3.64	–	–	–	–	–
B	0.57	–	–	–	–	–
AB	2.07	–	–	–	–	–
Within	–	–	–			
Total	8.18	–				

2. A researcher tested whether aerobics increased the fitness level of eight undergraduate students participating over a four-month period. Students were measured at the end of each month using a 10-point fitness measure (10 being most fit). The data are shown here. Conduct an ANOVA to determine the effectiveness of the program, using a = .05. Use the Bonferroni method to detect exactly where the differences are among the time points (if they are different).

Subject	Time 1	Time 2	Time 3	Time 4
1	3	4	6	9
2	4	7	5	10
3	5	7	7	8
4	1	3	5	7
5	3	4	7	9
6	2	5	6	7
7	1	4	6	9
8	2	4	5	6

3. Using the same data as in Computational Problem #2, conduct a two-factor split-plot ANOVA, where the first four subjects participate in a step aerobics problem and the last four subjects participate in a spinning program ($\alpha = .05$).
4. To examine changes in teaching self-efficacy, 10 teachers were measured on their self-efficacy towards teaching at the beginning of their teaching career and at the end of their first and third years of teaching. The teaching self-efficacy scale ranged from 0 to 100, with higher scores reflecting greater teaching self-efficacy. The data are shown here. Conduct a one-factor repeated measures ANOVA to determine mean differences across time, using $\alpha = .05$. Use the Bonferroni method to detect if and/or where the differences are among the time points.

Subject	Beginning Year 1	End Year 1	End Year 3
1	35	50	45
2	50	75	82
3	42	51	56
4	70	72	71
5	65	50	81
6	92	42	69
7	80	82	88
8	78	76	79
9	85	60	83
10	64	71	89

5. Using the same data as in Computational Problem #4, conduct a two-factor split-plot ANOVA, where the first five subjects participate in a mentoring program and the last five subjects do not participate in a mentoring program ($\alpha = .05$).

6. You are a statistical consultant, and a researcher comes to you with the following partial SPSS output (sphericity assumed). In a two-factor split-plot ANOVA design, rater is the repeated (or within-subjects) factor, gender of the rater is the nonrepeated (or between-subjects) factor, and the dependent variable is history exam scores. (a) Are the effects significant (which you must determine, as significance is missing, using $\alpha = .05$)? (b) What are the implications of these results in terms of rating the history exam?

Tests of Within-Subjects Effects

Source	Type III *SS*	*df*	*MS*	*F*
RATER	298.38	3	99.46	30.47
RATER*GENDER	184.38	3	61.46	18.83
ERROR(RATER)	58.75	18	3.26	

Tests of Between-Subjects Effects

Source	Type III *SS*	*df*	*MS*	*F*
GENDER	153.13	1	153.13	20.76
ERROR	44.25	6	7.38	

7. To examine changes in stress, 10 patients with generalized anxiety disorder were measured on their subjective stress at baseline, after 6 weeks of participating in mindfulness meditation training, and after 12 weeks of participation. Self-reported stress ranged from 0 to 50, with higher scores reflecting greater stress. The data are shown here. Conduct a one-factor repeated measures ANOVA to determine mean differences across time, using $\alpha = .05$. Use the Bonferroni method to detect if and/or where the differences are among the time points.

Subject	Baseline	After 6 Weeks	After 12 Weeks
1	48	43	40
2	40	38	35
3	43	40	34
4	48	44	41
5	46	42	36
6	41	38	35
7	49	45	39
8	44	40	37
9	43	40	34
10	42	37	33

8. To examine changes in stress, 20 patients with generalized anxiety disorder were measured on their subjective stress at baseline and then randomly assigned to receive either mindfulness meditation intervention (1) or stress management education (0).

The patients were measured again on subjective stress after 6 weeks and after 12 weeks of participation in the study. Self-reported stress ranged from 0 to 50, with higher scores reflecting greater stress. The data are shown here. Conduct a two-factor split-plot ANOVA to determine mean differences across time and group, using $\alpha = .05$.

Subject	Intervention	Baseline	After 6 Weeks	After 12 Weeks
1	1	48	43	40
2	1	40	38	35
3	1	43	40	34
4	1	48	44	41
5	1	46	42	36
6	1	41	38	35
7	1	49	45	39
8	1	44	40	37
9	1	43	40	34
10	1	42	37	33
11	0	47	46	43
12	0	46	46	44
13	0	49	47	45
14	0	48	45	43
15	0	40	39	39
16	0	43	41	40
17	0	42	40	39
18	0	44	42	41
19	0	45	44	43
20	0	47	45	44

Answers to Computational Problems

1. $SS_{with} = 1.9$, $df_A = 2$, $df_B = 1$, $df_{AB} = 2$, $df_{with} = 18$, $df_{total} = 23$, $MS_A = 1.82$, $MS_B = .57$, $MS_{AB} = 1.035$, $MS_{with} = .1056$, $F_A = 1.7585$, $F_B = 5.3977$, $F_{AB} = 9.8011$, critical value for AB = 6.01 (reject H_0 for AB), critical value for B = 8.29 (fail to reject H_0 for B), critical value for A = 99 (fail to reject H_0 for A).

3. $SS_{time} = 126.094$, $SS_{time\ x\ program} = 2.594$, $SS_{program} = 3.781$, $MS_{time} = 42.031$, $MS_{time\ x\ program} = 0.865$, $MS_{program} = 3.781$, $F_{time} = 43.078$ ($p < .001$), $F_{time\ x\ program} = 0.886$ ($p > .05$), $F_{program} = 0.978$ ($p > .05$).

5. $SS_{time} = 691.467$, $SS_{time\ x\ mentor} = 550.400$, $SS_{mentor} = 1968.300$, $MS_{time} = 345.733$, $MS_{time\ x\ mentor} = 275.200$, $MS_{mentor} = 1968.300$, $F_{time} = 2.719$ ($p = .096$), $F_{time\ x\ mentor} = 2.164$ ($p = .147$), $F_{mentor} = 7.073$ ($p < .001$).

7. $SS_{subjects} = 206.833$, $SS_{time} = 320.600$, $SS_{subjects\ x\ time} = 18.067$, $MS_{subjects} = 22.981$, $MS_{time} = 160.300$, $MS_{subjects\ x\ time} = 1.004$, $F = 159.708$, $p < .000$ (reject H_0); with Bonferroni, all contrasts are statistically significant at alpha = .05.

Interpretive Problem

1. In Chapter 13, you built on the interpretive problem from Chapter 11 utilizing the survey1 dataset from the website. SPSS or **R** was used to conduct a two-factor fixed-effects ANOVA, including effect size, where political view is factor A ($J = 5$), gender is factor B ($K = 2$), and the dependent variable is the same one that you used for Interpretative problem #1 in Chapter 11. Now, in addition to the two-factor fixed-effects ANOVA, conduct both a random-effects and a mixed-effects design. Determine whether the nature of the factors makes any difference in the results.
2. In Chapter 13, you built on the interpretive problem from Chapter 11 utilizing the survey1 dataset from the website. SPSS or **R** was used to conduct a two-factor fixed-effects ANOVA, including effect size, where hair color is factor A (i.e., one independent variable) ($J = 5$), gender is factor B (a new factor, $K = 2$), and the dependent variable is an interval or ratio variable of your choice. Now, in addition to the two-factor fixed-effects ANOVA, conduct both a random-effects and a mixed-effects design. Determine whether the nature of the factors makes any difference in the results.

16

Hierarchical and Randomized Block Analysis of Variance Models

Chapter Outline

Key Concepts

1. Crossed designs and nested designs
2. Confounding
3. Randomized block designs
4. Methods of blocking

In the last several chapters our discussion has dealt with different analysis of variance (ANOVA) models. In this chapter we complete our discussion of the analysis of variance by considering models in which there are multiple factors, but where at least one of the factors is either a hierarchical (or nested) factor or a blocking factor. As we define these models, summarized in Box 16.1, we shall see that this results in a hierarchical (or nested) design and a blocking design, respectively.

BOX 16.1 Summary of Hierarchical and Randomized Block ANOVA Models

Model	Summary
Two-factor hierarchical ANOVA model	One factor is nested within another factor. • A two-factor nested design (or incomplete factorial design) of factor *B* being nested within factor *A* is one where the levels of factor *B* occur for only one level of factor *A*. **Nesting** is a particular type of confounding among the factors being investigated, where the *AB* interaction is part of the *B* effect (or is **confounded** with B) and therefore cannot be investigated. • Also known as a nested design, hierarchical design or multilevel model
Two-factor randomized block design for $n = 1$	Two factors, each with at least two levels. One factor is known as the **treatment factor** (although this factor could also be an observable factor). The second factor is known as the **blocking factor**, which is a nuisance factor for which control is desired. • Each block represents the formation of a matched set of individuals, that is, matched on the blocking variable, but not necessarily matched on any other nuisance variable. The purpose of the blocking factor is to reduce residual variation. • Each subject falls into only one block in the design and is subsequently randomly assigned to one level of the treatment factor within that block. There is only one subject for each treatment-block level combination. As a result, the model does not include an interaction term, and this is a distinguishing feature of this model. • Designs that include one or more blocking factors are known as **randomized block designs,** *matching designs*, or *treatment by block designs*.
Two-factor randomized block design for $n > 1$	For two-factor randomized block designs with more than one observation per cell, the characteristics are exactly the same as with the $n = 1$ model, with the obvious exception that when $n > 1$, an interaction term exists.
Friedman test	This is the nonparametric equivalent to the two-factor randomized block ANOVA model, and it is based on mean ranks.

In this chapter we are mostly concerned with the two-factor hierarchical (or nested) model and the two-factor randomized block model, although these models can be generalized to designs with more than two factors. Most of the concepts used in this chapter are the same as those covered in previous chapters. In addition, new concepts include crossed and nested factors, confounding, blocking factors, and methods of blocking. Our objectives are that by the end of this chapter, you will be able to (a) understand the characteristics and concepts underlying hierarchical and randomized block ANOVA models, (b) determine and interpret the results of hierarchical and randomized block ANOVA models, (c) understand and evaluate the assumptions of hierarchical and randomized block ANOVA models, and (d) compare different ANOVA models and select an appropriate model.

16.1 What Hierarchical and Randomized Block ANOVA Models Are and How They Work

Throughout the text, we have followed a savvy group of graduate students on statistical analysis adventures. In this chapter, we see one of those students, Challie Lenge, embarking on a new journey.

The quad of graduate students have enjoyed the complex statistical analyses that they have been tasked with and are looking forward to another challenging task. This time, Challie Lenge will be working with a psychology faculty member involved in a clinical trial through their institution's medical center. Dr. Mayfield has conducted an experiment in which hospice patients were randomly assigned to one of two interventions (massage therapy or music therapy) and one of four different interventionists. There were 24 hospice patients who participated; thus there were six patients in each intervention-interventionist combination. Each patient was assessed on quality of life at the conclusion of the study. Dr. Mayfield wants to know the following: if there is a mean difference in quality of life based on intervention (music therapy or massage therapy) and if there is a mean difference in quality of life between interventionist. Challie suggests the following research questions to Dr. Mayfield:

- *Is there a mean difference in quality of life based on intervention?*
- *Is there a mean difference in quality of life based on interventionist?*

With one between-subjects independent variable (i.e., intervention, either music therapy or massage therapy) and one hierarchical or nested factor (i.e., interventionist/clinician), Challie determines that a two-factor hierarchical ANOVA is the best statistical procedure to use to answer Dr. Mayfield's question. Her next task is to assist Dr. Mayfield in analyzing the data.

16.1.1 Characteristics of the Two-Factor Hierarchical Model

In this section, we describe the distinguishing characteristics of the two-factor hierarchical ANOVA model, the layout of the data, the linear model, the ANOVA summary table and expected mean squares, and multiple comparison procedures.

The characteristics of the two-factor fixed-, random-, and mixed-effects models have already been covered in earlier chapters. Here we consider a special form of the two-factor model where *one factor is nested within another factor*. The best introduction to this model is via an example. Suppose you are interested in which of several different interventions (e.g., music therapy, massage therapy, art therapy) results in the highest level of quality of life among hospice patients. Thus, quality of life is the dependent variable and type of intervention is one factor. A second factor is the interventionist or therapist (i.e., the person who performs the intervention, such as the massage therapist or music therapist). That is, you may also believe that some therapists are more effective than others, which results in different levels of quality of life. However, each therapist has only one caseload of patients and only one type of intervention in which they are trained. In other words, all combinations of the intervention and interventionist (aka therapist) factors are not possible. This design is known as a **nested design**, **hierarchical design**, or **multilevel model** because the interventionist factor is nested within the intervention factor. This is in contrast to a two-factor **crossed design**, where all possible combinations of the two factors are included. The two-factor designs described in Chapters 13 and 15 were all crossed designs.

Let us give a more precise definition of crossed and nested designs. A two-factor completely crossed design (or **complete factorial design**) is one where every level of factor A occurs in combination with every level of factor B. A two-factor nested design (or **incomplete factorial design**) of factor B being nested within factor A is one where the levels of factor B occur for only one level of factor A. We denote this particular nested design as **B(A)**, which is read as *factor B being nested within factor A* (in other references, you may see this written as B:A or as B|A). To return to our example, the therapist factor (factor B) is nested within the intervention factor (factor A), as each therapist utilizes only one type of intervention (e.g., music therapy or massage therapy). The outcome measured is quality of life. Thus, a researcher may select a nested design to examine the extent to which patient quality of life differs given that therapists are nested within intervention. The researcher is likely most interested in the treatment (e.g., type of intervention) but recognizes that the context (i.e., the person providing the intervention, i.e., the interventionist, therapist, or clinician) may contribute to differences in the outcome, and can model this statistically through a hierarchical ANOVA.

These models are shown graphically in Figure 16.1. In Figure 16.1a, a **completely crossed or complete factorial design** is shown where there are two levels of factor A and six levels of factor B. Thus, there are 12 possible factor combinations that would all be included in a completely crossed design. The shaded region indicates the combinations that might be included in a nested or incomplete factorial design where factor B (e.g., interventionist) is nested within factor A (e.g., intervention). Although the number of levels of each factor remains the same, factor B now has only three levels within each level of factor A. For A_1 we see only B_1, B_2, and B_3, whereas for A_2 we see only B_4, B_5, and B_6. Thus, only 6 of the possible 12 factor combinations are included in the nested design. For example, level 1 of factor B occurs only in combination with level 1 of factor A. In summary, Figure 16.1a shows that the nested or incomplete factorial design consists of only a portion of the completely crossed design (the shaded regions).

In Figure 16.1b, we see the **nested design** depicted in its more traditional form. Here you see that the six factor combinations not included are not even shown (e.g., A_1 with B_4). Other examples of the two-factor nested design are as follows: (a) student is nested within teacher (or classroom), (b) faculty member is nested within department, (c) individual is nested within neighborhood, (d) county is nested within state, (e) employee is nested within employer, (f) patient is nested within doctor, (g) chapter is nested within book.

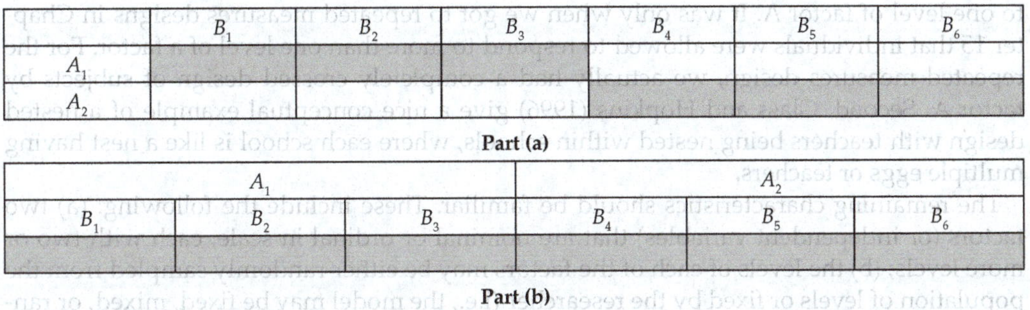

(a) The *completely crossed design*. The shaded region indicates the cells that would be included in a nested design where factor *B* is nested within factor A. In the nested design, factor *A* has two levels and factor *B* has three levels within each level of factor A. You see that only 6 of the 12 possible cells are filled in the nested design.

(b) The same nested design in *traditional form*. The shaded region indicates the cells included in the nested design (i.e., the same six as shown in the first part).

FIGURE 16.1
Two-factor completely crossed versus nested designs.

Thus, with this design, one factor is nested within another factor, rather than the two factors being crossed. As is shown in more detail later in this chapter, the nesting characteristic has some interesting and distinct outcomes. For now, some brief mention should be made of these outcomes. **Nesting** is a particular type of confounding among the factors being investigated, where the *AB* interaction is part of the *B* effect (or is **confounded** with B) and therefore cannot be investigated. (Going back to the previous example, this means that the therapist by intervention interaction effect is confounded with the therapist main effect, and thus teasing apart those effects is not possible.) In the ANOVA model and the ANOVA summary table, there will not be an interaction term or source of variation. This is due to the fact that each level of factor *B* (the nested factor, such as the therapist) occurs in combination with only one level of factor *A* (the nonnested factor, such as the treatment). We cannot compare for a particular level of *B* (e.g., the interventionist) all levels of factor *A* (e.g., intervention), as a certain level of *B* only occurs with one level of A.

Confounding may occur for two reasons. First, the confounding may be intentional due to practical reasons, such as a reduction in the number of individuals to be observed. Fewer individuals would be necessary in a nested design, as compared to a crossed design, due to the fact that there are fewer cells in the model. Second, the confounding may be absolutely necessary because crossing may not be possible. For example, school is nested within school district because a particular school can be a member of only one school district. The nested factor (here factor B) may be a nuisance variable that the researcher wants to take into account in terms of explaining or predicting the dependent variable *Y*. An error commonly made is to ignore the nuisance variable *B* and go ahead with a one-factor design using only factor A. This design may result in a biased test of factor *A* such that the *F* ratio is inflated. Thus H_0 would be rejected more often that it should be, serving to increase the actual α level over that specified by the researcher and thereby increase the likelihood of a Type I error. The *F* test is then too liberal.

Let us make two further points about this first characteristic. First, in the one-factor ANOVA design discussed in Chapter 11, we have already seen nesting going on in a different way. Here subjects were nested within factor *A* because each subject only responded to one level of factor A. It was only when we got to repeated measures designs in Chapter 15 that individuals were allowed to respond to more than one level of a factor. For the repeated measures design, we actually had a completely crossed design of subjects by factor A. Second, Glass and Hopkins (1996) give a nice conceptual example of a nested design with teachers being nested within schools, where each school is like a nest having multiple eggs or teachers.

The remaining characteristics should be familiar. These include the following: (a) two factors (or independent variables) that are nominal or ordinal in scale, each with two or more levels; (b) the levels of each of the factors may be either randomly sampled from the population of levels or fixed by the researcher (i.e., the model may be fixed, mixed, or random); (c) subjects are randomly assigned to only one combination of the levels of the two factors; and (d) the dependent variable is measured at least at the interval level. If individuals respond to more than one combination of the levels of the two factors, then this is a repeated measures design (see Chapter 15).

For simplicity, we again assume the design is balanced. For the two-factor nested design, a design is balanced if (a) the number of observations within each factor combination (or cell) is the same (in other words, the sample size for each cell of the design is the same), and (b) the number of levels of the nested factor within each level of the other factor is the same. The first portion of this statement should be quite familiar from factorial designs, so no further explanation is necessary. The second portion of this statement is unique to this design and requires a brief explanation. As an example, say factor *B* is nested within factor *A* (i.e., the nonnested factor) and factor *A* has two levels. On the one hand, factor *B* may have the same number of levels for each level of factor A. This occurs if there are three levels of factor *B* under level 1 of factor *A* (i.e., A_1) and also three levels of factor *B* under level 2 of factor *A* (i.e., A_2). On the other hand, factor *B* may not have the same number of levels for each level of factor A. This occurs if there are three levels of factor *B* under A_1 and only two levels of factor *B* under A_2. If the design is unbalanced, you are encouraged to use a more modern hierarchical analytic approach that goes beyond least squares estimation and uses, for example, maximum likelihood estimation (Maxwell, Delaney, & Kelley, 2018). See the discussion, for example, in Kirk (2013) and Dunn and Clark (1987).

16.1.1.1 The Layout of the Data for the Two-Factor Hierarchical Model

The layout of the data for the two-factor nested design is shown in Table 16.1. To simplify matters, we have limited the number of levels of the factors to two levels of factor *A* (e.g., intervention or treatment group) and three levels of factor *B* (e.g., interventionist or therapist). This serves only as an example layout because many other possibilities obviously exist. Here we see the major set of columns designated as the levels of factor A, the nonnested factor (e.g., intervention), and for each level of A, the minor set of columns are the levels of factor B, the nested factor (e.g., interventionist). Within each factor level combination or cell are the subjects. Means are shown for each cell, for the levels of factor A, and overall. Note that the means for the levels of factor *B* need not be shown, as they are the same as the cell means. For instance, $\bar{Y}_{.11}$ is the same as $\bar{Y}_{..1}$ (not shown) as B_1 only occurs once. This is another result of the nesting.

16.1.1.2 The Two-Factor Hierarchical ANOVA Model

The nested factor is almost always random (Glass & Hopkins, 1996; Keppel, 1991; Mickey, Dunn, & Clark, 2004; Page, Braver & MacKinnon, 2003). In other words, the levels of the

TABLE 16.1
Layout for the Two-Factor Nested Design

	A_1			A_2		
	B_1	B_2	B_3	B_4	B_5	B_6
	Y_{111}	Y_{112}	Y_{113}	Y_{124}	Y_{125}	Y_{126}
	.	.	.	.	.	.
	Y_{n11}			Y_{n24}	Y_{n25}	Y_{n26}
Cell means	$\bar{Y}_{.11}$	$\bar{Y}_{.12}$	$\bar{Y}_{.13}$	$\bar{Y}_{.24}$	$\bar{Y}_{.25}$	$\bar{Y}_{.26}$
A means	$\bar{Y}_{.1.}$				$\bar{Y}_{.2.}$	
Overall mean			$\bar{Y}_{...}$			

nested factor are a random sample of the population of levels. For example, in the case of teachers (or classrooms) nested within teaching pedagogy, it is often the case that a random sample of the teachers (or classrooms) is selected rather than specific teachers (which would be a fixed-effects factor). This can be extended to any number of examples where groups or clusters are nested within the factor of interest (e.g., intervention). Thus, the nested factor (i.e., the teacher factor) is a random factor. As a result, the two-factor nested ANOVA is often a mixed-effects model where the nonnested factor is fixed (i.e., all the levels of interest for the nonnested factor are included in the model) and the nested factor is random. The two-factor mixed-effects nested ANOVA model is written in terms of **population parameters** as follows:

$$Y_{ijk} = \mu + \alpha_j + b_{k(j)} + \varepsilon_{ijk}$$

where Y_{ijk} is the observed score on the dependent variable for individual i in level j of factor A (where A is the nonnested factor) and level k of factor B (or in the jk cell) (where B is the nested factor), μ is the overall or grand population mean (i.e., regardless of cell designation), α_j is the fixed effect for level j of factor A, $b_{k(j)}$ is the random effect for level k of factor B, and e_{ijk} is the random residual error for individual i in cell jk. Notice that there is no interaction term in the model, and also that the effect for factor B is denoted by $b_{k(j)}$. *This tells us that the levels of factor B are nested within factor A*. The residual error can be due to individual differences, measurement error, and/or other factors not under investigation. We consider the fixed-, mixed-, and random-effects cases later in this chapter.

For the two-factor mixed-effects nested ANOVA model, there are only two sets of hypotheses, one for each of the main effects, because there is no interaction effect. The null and alternative hypotheses, respectively, for testing the effect of factor A (nonnested factor) are as follows. The null hypothesis for testing the effect of factor A is similar to what we have seen in previous chapters for fixed-effects factors and written as the means of the levels of factor A are the same.

$$H_{01}: \mu_{.1.} = \mu_{.2.} = \cdots = \mu_{.j.}$$

$$H_{11}: \text{not all the } \mu_{.j.} \text{ are equal}$$

The hypotheses for testing the effect of factor B, because this is a random-effects factor, are written as the *variation among the means*, and are presented as below.

$$H_{02}: \sigma_b^2 = 0$$
$$H_{12}: \sigma_b^2 > 0$$

These hypotheses reflect the inferences made in the fixed-, mixed-, and random-effects models (as fully described in Chapter 15). For *fixed main effects*, the null hypotheses are about *means*, whereas for *random main effects*, the null hypotheses are about *variation among the means*. As we already know, the difference in the models is also reflected in the multiple comparison procedures. As before, we do need to pay particular attention to whether the model is fixed, mixed, or random. The assumptions about the two-factor nested model are exactly the same as with the two-factor crossed model (discussed in Chapters 13 and 15), and thus we need not provide any additional discussion other than to remind you of the assumptions regarding normality, homogeneity of variance, and independence (of observations within cells). In addition, procedures for determining power and confidence intervals are the same as with the two-factor crossed model.

16.1.1.3 ANOVA Summary Table and Expected Mean Squares for the Two-Factor Hierarchical Model

The computations of the two-factor mixed-effects nested model are somewhat similar to those of the two-factor mixed-effects crossed model. The main difference lies in the fact that there is no interaction term. The ANOVA summary table is shown in Table 16.2, where we see the following sources of variation: A, B(A), within cells, and total. There we see that only two *F* ratios can be formed, one for each of the two main effects, because no interaction term is estimated (recall that this is because not all possible combinations of *A* and *B* occur).

If we take the **total sum of squares** and decompose it, we have the following:

$$SS_{total} = SS_A + SS_{B(A)} + SS_{with}$$

We leave the computations involving these terms to the statistical software. The degrees of freedom, mean squares, and *F* ratios are determined as shown in Table 16.2, assuming a mixed-effects model. The critical value for the test of factor A is ${}_{\alpha}F_{J-1,J(K_{(j)}-1)}$ and for the

TABLE 6.2

Two-Factor Nested Design ANOVA Summary Table: Mixed Effects Model

Source	SS	Df	MS	F
A	SS_A	$J-1$	MS_A	$MS_A/MS_{B(A)}$
B(A)	$SS_{B(A)}$	$J(K_{(j)}-1)$	$MS_{B(A)}$	$MS_{B(A)}/MS_{with}$
Within	SS_{with}	$JK_{(j)}(n-1)$	MS_{with}	
Total	SS_{total}	$N-1$		

test of factor B is $_{\alpha}F_{J(K_{(j)}-1),JK_{(j)}(n-1)}$. Let us explain something about the degrees of freedom. The degrees of freedom for B(A) are equal to $J(K_{(j)} - 1)$. This means that for a design with two levels of factor A (e.g., intervention, the nonnested factor) and three levels of factor B (e.g., interventionist, the nested factor) within each level of A (for a total of six levels of B), the degrees of freedom are equal to 2(3 – 1) = 4. This is not the same as the degrees of freedom for a completely crossed design where df_B would be 5 (i.e., 6 – 1 = 5). The degrees of freedom for within are equal to $JK_{(j)}(n - 1)$. For this same design with $n = 10$, then the degrees of freedom within are equal to (2)(3)(10 – 1) = 54 (i.e., 6 cells with 9 degrees of freedom per cell).

The appropriate **error terms** for each of the fixed-, random-, and mixed-effects models are described in the following two paragraphs. For the *fixed-effects model*, both F ratios use the within source as the error term. For the *random-effects model*, the appropriate error term for the test of A is $MS_{B(A)}$ and for the test of B is MS_{with}. For the *mixed-effects model where A is fixed and B is random*, the appropriate error term for the test of A is $MS_{B(A)}$ and for the test of B is MS_{with}. As already mentioned, this is the predominant model in the social sciences. Finally, for the *mixed-effects model where A is random and B is fixed*, both F ratios use the within source as the error term. These are now described by the expected mean squares.

The formation of the proper F ratios is again related to the **expected mean squares.** If H_0 is actually *true*, then the expected mean squares are as follows:

$$E(MS_A) = \sigma_\varepsilon^2$$

$$E\left(MS_{B(A)}\right) = \sigma_\varepsilon^2$$

$$E(MS_{with}) = \sigma_\varepsilon^2$$

If H_0 is actually *false*, then the expected mean squares for the *fixed-effects case* are as follows:

$$E(MS_A) = \sigma_\varepsilon^2 + nK_{(j)}\left[\frac{\sum_{j=1}^{J}\alpha_j^2}{J-1}\right]$$

$$E\left(MS_{B(A)}\right) = \sigma_\varepsilon^2 + n\left[\frac{\sum_{j=1}^{J}\sum_{k=1}^{K}\beta_{k(j)}^2}{J\left(K_{(j)}-1\right)}\right]$$

$$E(MS_{with}) = \sigma_\varepsilon^2$$

Thus, the appropriate F ratios both involve using the *within source* as the error term.

If H_0 is actually *false*, then the expected mean squares for the *random-effects case* are as follows:

$$E(MS_A) = \sigma_\varepsilon^2 + n\sigma_{b(a)}^2 + nK_{(j)}\sigma_a^2$$

$$E\left(MS_{B(A)}\right) = \sigma_\varepsilon^2 + n\sigma_{b(a)}^2$$

$$E(MS_{with}) = \sigma_\varepsilon^2$$

Thus, the appropriate error term for the test of A (i.e., the nonnested factor) is $MS_{B(A)}$ and the appropriate error term for the test of B (i.e., the nested factor) is MS_{with}.

If H_0 is actually *false*, then the expected mean squares for the *mixed-effects case where A is fixed and B is random* are as follows:

$$E(MS_A) = \sigma_\varepsilon^2 + n\sigma_{b(a)}^2 + nK_{(j)}\left[\frac{\sum_{j=1}^{J}\alpha_j^2}{J-1}\right]$$

$$E(MS_{B(A)}) = \sigma_\varepsilon^2 + n\sigma_{b(a)}^2$$

$$E(MS_{with}) = \sigma_\varepsilon^2$$

Thus, the appropriate error term for the test of *A* (nonnested) is $MS_{B(A)}$ and the appropriate error term for the test of *B* (nested) is MS_{with}.

Finally, if H_0 is actually *false*, then the expected mean squares for the *mixed-effects case where A is random and B is fixed* are as follows:

$$E(MS_A) = \sigma_\varepsilon^2 + nK_{(j)}\sigma_a^2$$

$$E(MS_{B(A)}) = \sigma_\varepsilon^2 + n\left[\frac{\sum_{j=1}^{J}\sum_{k=1}^{K}\beta_{k(j)}^2}{J(K_{(j)}-1)}\right]$$

$$E(MS_{with}) = \sigma_\varepsilon^2$$

Thus, the appropriate *F* ratios both involve using the *within source* as the error term.

16.1.1.4 Multiple Comparison Procedures for the Two-Factor Hierarchical Model

This section considers multiple comparison procedures (MCPs) for the two-factor nested design. First of all, the researcher is usually not interested in making inferences about random effects. Second, for MCPs based on the levels of factor *A* (the nonnested factor), there is nothing new to report. Third, for MCPs based on the levels of factor *B* (the nested factor), this is a different situation. The researcher is not usually as interested in MCPs about the nested factor as compared to the nonnested factor because inferences about the levels of factor *B* are not even generalizable across the levels of factor A, due to the nesting. If you are nonetheless interested in MCPs for factor B, by necessity you have to look within a level of *A* to formulate a contrast. Otherwise MCPs are conducted as before. For more complex nested designs, see Myers (1979), Keppel and Wickens (2004), Kirk (2013), Mickey et al. (2004), or Myers, Lorch, and Well (2010).

16.1.1.5 An Example of the Two-Factor Hierarchical Model

Let us consider an example to illustrate the procedures in this section. The data are shown in Table 16.3. Factor *A* is approach to the teaching of reading (basal vs. whole language approaches), and factor *B* is teacher. Thus, there are two teachers using the basal approach and two different teachers using the whole language approach. The researcher is interested in the effects these factors have on student's reading comprehension in the first grade. Thus the dependent variable is a measure of reading comprehension. Six students are randomly assigned to each approach-teacher combination for small-group instruction. This particular example is a *mixed model*, where factor A (instructional method) is a fixed effect and factor B (teacher) is a random effect. This could easily translate to other examples. For example, factor A is a healthcare treatment and factor B is provider, with some doctors using one type of healthcare approach and the remaining doctors using a different approach. The outcome could be improvement in health (e.g., lower blood pressure). The results are shown in the ANOVA summary table of Table 16.4.

TABLE 16.3

Data for the Teaching Reading Example: Two-Factor Nested Design

	Reading Approaches			
	A_1 (Basal)		A_2 (Whole Language)	
	Teacher B_1	Teacher B_2	Teacher B_3	Teacher B_4
	1	1	7	8
	1	3	8	9
	2	3	8	11
	4	4	10	13
	4	6	12	14
	5	6	15	15
Cell means	2.8333	3.8333	10.0000	11.6667
A means	3.3333		10.8333	
Overall mean		7.0833		

TABLE 16.4

Two-Factor Nested Design ANOVA Summary Table: Teaching Reading Example

Source	*SS*	*df*	*MS*	*F*
A	337.5000	1	337.5000	59.5585*
B(A)	11.3333	2	5.6667	0.9524**
Within	119.0000	20	5.9500	
Total	467.8333	23		

* $_{.05}F_{1,2} = 18.51$
** $_{.05}F_{2,20} = 3.49$

From Appendix Table A.4, the critical value for the test of factor A is $_{\alpha}F_{J-1,J(K_{(j)}-1)} = {}_{.05}F_{1,2} = 18.51$, and the critical value for the test of factor B is $_{\alpha}F_{J(K_{(j)}-1),JK_{(j)}(n-1)} = {}_{.05}F_{2,20} = 3.49$. Thus there is a statistically significant difference between the two approaches to reading instruction at the .05 level of significance, and there is no significant difference between the teachers. When we look at the means for the levels of factor A, we see that the mean comprehension score for the whole language approach ($\bar{Y}_{.2.} = 10.8333$) is greater than the mean for the basal approach ($\bar{Y}_{.1.} = 3.3333$). Because there were only two levels of the reading approach tested (whole language and basal), no post hoc multiple comparisons are really necessary. Rather, the mean reading comprehension scores for each approach can be merely examined to determine which mean was statistically significantly larger.

16.1.2 Characteristics of the Two-Factor Randomized Block Model for $n = 1$

In this section, we describe the distinguishing characteristics of the two-factor randomized block ANOVA model for one observation per cell, the layout of the data, the linear model, assumptions and their violation, the ANOVA summary table and expected mean squares, multiple comparison procedures, and methods of block formation.

The characteristics of the two-factor randomized block ANOVA model are quite similar to those of the regular two-factor ANOVA model, as well as sharing a few characteristics with the one-factor repeated measures ANOVA design. There is one obvious exception, which has to do with the nature of the factors being used. Here there will be two factors, each with at least two levels. One factor is known as the **treatment factor** and is referred to here as factor A (a treatment factor is technically what we have been considering in Chapters 11 through 15; although as we'll soon discuss, this factor does not have to truly be a "treatment" but can be an observable attribute). The second factor is known as the **blocking factor** and is referred to here as factor B. A blocking factor is a new concept and requires some discussion.

Take an ordinary one-factor ANOVA design, where the single factor is a treatment factor (e.g., method of exercising) and the researcher is interested in its effect on some dependent variable (e.g., percentage of body fat). Despite individuals being randomly assigned to a treatment group, the groups may be different due to a nuisance variable operating in a nonrandom way. For instance, Group 1 may consist of mostly older adults and Group 2 may consist of mostly younger adults. Thus, it is likely that Group 2 will be favored over Group 1 because age, the nuisance variable, has not been properly balanced out across the groups by the randomization process.

One way to deal with this problem is to control the effect of the nuisance variable by incorporating it into the design of the study. Including the blocking or nuisance variable as a factor in the design should result in a reduction in residual variation (due to some additional portion of individual differences being explained) and an increase in power (Glass & Hopkins, 1996; Keppel & Wickens, 2004). The blocking factor is selected based on the strength of its relationship to the dependent variable, where an unrelated blocking variable would not reduce residual variation. It would be reasonable to expect, then, that variability among individuals within a block (e.g., within younger adults) should be less than variability among individuals between blocks (e.g., between younger and older adults). *Thus, each block represents the formation of a matched set of individuals, that is, matched on the blocking variable, but not necessarily matched on any other nuisance variable.* Using our example, we expect that in general, adults within a particular age block (i.e., the older or younger blocks) will be more similar in terms of variables related to body fat than adults across blocks.

Let us consider several examples of blocking factors. Some blocking factors are naturally occurring blocks such as siblings, friends, neighbors, plots of land, and time. Other blocking factors are not naturally occurring, but can be formulated by the researcher. Examples of this type include grade point average, age, weight, aptitude test scores, intelligence test scores, socioeconomic status, and school or district size. Note that the examples of blocking factors here represent a variety of measurement scales (categorical as well as continuous). Later we will discuss how to deal with the blocking factor based on its measurement scale in the discussion of method of block formation.

Let us make some summary statements about characteristics of blocking designs. First, designs that include one or more blocking factors are known as **randomized block designs**, also known as *matching designs* or *treatment by block designs. The researcher's main interest is in the treatment factor*. The purpose of the blocking factor is to reduce residual variation. Thus, the researcher is not as much interested in the test of the blocking factor (possibly not at all) as compared to the treatment factor. Thus, there is at least one blocking factor and one treatment factor, each with two or more levels. Second, each subject falls into only one block in the design and is subsequently randomly assigned to one level of the treatment factor within that block. Thus subjects within a block serve as their own controls such that some portion of their individual differences is taken into account. As a result, the scores of subjects are not independent within a particular block. Third, for purposes of this section, we assume there is only one subject for each treatment-block level combination. *As a result, the model does not include an interaction term*, and this is a distinguishing feature of this model. Later in this chapter, we consider the multiple observations case, where there is an interaction term in the model. Finally, the dependent variable is measured at least at the interval level.

16.1.2.1 The Layout of the Data for the Two-Factor Randomized Block Design for n = 1

The layout of the data for the two-factor randomized block model is shown in Table 16.5. Here we see the columns designated as the levels of the blocking factor *B* and the rows as the levels of the treatment factor A. Row, block, and overall means are also shown. Here you see that the layout of the data looks the same as the two-factor model, but with a single observation per cell.

TABLE 16.5
Layout for the Two-Factor Randomized Block Design

	Level of Factor B				
Level of Factor A	**1**	**2**	**...**	**K**	**Row Mean**
1	Y_{11}	Y_{12}	...	Y_{1K}	$\bar{Y}_{1.}$
2	Y_{21}	Y_{22}	...	Y_{2K}	$\bar{Y}_{2.}$
.	.	.	...	.	.
.	.	.	...	.	.
.	.	.	...	.	.
J	Y_{J1}	Y_{J2}	...	Y_{JK}	$\bar{Y}_{J.}$
Block mean	$\bar{Y}_{.1}$	$\bar{Y}_{.2}$	...	$\bar{Y}_{.K}$	$\bar{Y}_{..}$ *(overall mean)*

16.1.2.2 The Two-Factor Randomized Block Design for n = 1 ANOVA Model

The two-factor fixed-effects randomized block ANOVA model is written in terms of *population parameters* as follows:

$$Y_{jk} = \mu + \alpha_j + \beta_k + \varepsilon_{jk}$$

where Y_{jk} is the observed score on the dependent variable for the individual responding to level j of factor A and level k of block B, μ is the overall or grand population mean, α_j is the fixed effect for level j of factor A, β_k is the fixed effect for level k of the block B, and ε_{jk} is the random residual error for the individual in cell jk. The residual error can be due to measurement error, individual differences, and/or other factors not under investigation. You can see this is similar to the two-factor fully crossed model with one observation per cell (i.e., $i = 1$ making the i subscript unnecessary), and with no interaction term included. Also, the effects are denoted by α and β given we have a fixed-effects model. Note that the row and column effects both sum to zero in the fixed-effects model.

The hypotheses for testing the effect of factor A are as follows, where the null indicates that the means of the levels of factor A are equal:

$$H_{01}: \mu_{1.} = \mu_{2.} = \ldots = \mu_{J.}$$

$$H_{11}: \text{not all the } \mu_{j.} \text{ are equal}$$

For testing the effect of factor B (the blocking factor), the hypotheses are presented here, where the null hypothesis is that the means of the levels of the blocking factor are equal.

$$H_{02}: \mu_{.1} = \mu_{.2} = \ldots = \mu_{.K}$$

$$H_{12}: \text{not all the } \mu_{.k} \text{ are equal}$$

The factors are both fixed, so the hypotheses are written in terms of means.

16.1.2.3 ANOVA Summary Table and Expected Mean Squares

The sources of variation for this model are similar to those of the regular two-factor model, except that there is no interaction term. The ANOVA summary table is shown in Table 16.6, where we see the following sources of variation: A (treatments), B (blocks), residual, and total. The test of block differences is usually of no real interest. In general, we expect there to be differences between the blocks. From the table, we see that two F ratios can be formed.

TABLE 16.6

Two-Factor Randomized Block Design ANOVA Summary Table

Source	SS	Df	MS	F
A	SS_A	$J-1$	MS_A	MS_A/MS_{res}
B	SS_B	$K-1$	MS_B	MS_B/MS_{res}
Residual	SS_{res}	$(J-1)(K-1)$	MS_{res}	
Total	SS_{total}	$N-1$		

If we take the total sum of squares and decompose it, we have the following equation:

$$SS_{total} = SS_A + SS_B + SS_{res}$$

The remaining computations are determined by the statistical software. The degrees of freedom, mean squares, and F ratios are also shown in Table 16.6.

Earlier in our discussion of the two-factor randomized block design, we mentioned that the F test is not very robust to violation of the sphericity assumption. We again recommend the following sequential procedure be used in the test of factor A. First, perform the usual F test, which is quite liberal in terms of rejecting H_0 too often, where the degrees of freedom are $J - 1$ and $(J - 1)(K - 1)$. If H_0 is not rejected, then stop. If H_0 is rejected, then continue with step 2, which is to use the Geisser and Greenhouse (1958) conservative F test. For the model we are considering here, the degrees of freedom for the F critical value are adjusted to be 1 and $K - 1$. If H_0 is rejected, then stop. This would indicate that both the liberal and conservative tests reached the same conclusion, that is, to reject H_0. If H_0 is not rejected, then the two tests did not reach the same conclusion, and a further test should be undertaken. Thus, in step 3, an adjusted F test is conducted. The adjustment is known as Box's (1954) correction (the Huynh and Feldt (1970) procedure). Here the degrees of freedom are equal to $(J - 1)(\varepsilon)$ and $(J - 1)(K - 1)(\varepsilon)$, where ε is the correction factor (e.g., Kirk, 2013). It is now fairly standard for the major statistical software to conduct the Geisser-Greenhouse and Huynh-Feldt tests.

Based on the expected mean squares (not shown here for simplicity), the residual is the proper error term for the fixed-, random-, and mixed-effects models. *Thus, MS_{res} is the proper error term for every version of this model.* One may also be interested in an assessment of the effect size for the treatment factor A; note that the effect size of the blocking factor B is usually not of interest, and further discussion on effect size is provided later in the chapter. Finally, the procedures for determining confidence intervals and power are the same as in previous models.

16.1.2.4 Multiple Comparison Procedures

If the null hypothesis for either the A (treatment) or B (blocking) factor is rejected and there are more than two levels of the factor for which statistical significance was found, then the researcher may be interested in which means or combinations of means are different. This could be assessed, as put forth in previous chapters, by the use of some multiple comparison procedure (MCP). In general, the use of MCPs outlined in Chapter 12 is unchanged as long as the sphericity assumption is met. If the assumption is not met, then MS_{res} is not the appropriate error term, and the alternatives recommended in Chapter 15 should be considered (e.g., Boik, 1981; Kirk, 2013; Maxwell, 1980).

16.1.2.5 Methods of Block Formation

There are different methods available for the formation of blocks depending on the nature of the blocking variable. As we see, the methods have to do with whether the blocking factor is an ordinal or an interval/ratio variable, and whether the blocking factor is a fixed or a random effect. This discussion borrows heavily from the work of Pingel (1969) in defining five such methods. The first method is the **predefined value blocking method**, *where the blocking factor is an ordinal variable.* Here the researcher specifies K different population values of the blocking variable. For each of these values (i.e., a fixed effect), individuals are randomly assigned to the levels of the treatment factor. Thus, individuals within a block have the same value on the blocking variable. For example, if class rank is the blocking variable, the levels might be the top third, middle third, and bottom third of the class.

The second method is the **predefined range blocking method**, *where the blocking factor is an interval or ratio variable*. Here the researcher specifies K mutually exclusive ranges in the population distribution of the blocking variable, where the probability of obtaining a value of the blocking variable in each range may be specified as $1/K$. For each of these ranges (i.e., a fixed effect), individuals are randomly assigned to the levels of the treatment factor. Thus, individuals within a block are in the same range on the blocking variable. For example, if a score that ranges from 0 to 100 is the blocking variable, the levels might be 0–32, 33–66, and 67–100.

The third method is the **sampled value blocking method**, *where the blocking variable is an ordinal variable*. Here the researcher randomly samples K population values of the blocking variable (i.e., a random effect). For each of these values, individuals are randomly assigned to the levels of the treatment factor. Thus individuals within a block have the same value on the blocking variable. For example, if class rank is again the blocking variable, only this time measured in tenths, the researcher might randomly select 3 levels from the population of 10 levels.

The fourth method is the **sampled range blocking method**, *where the blocking variable is an interval or ratio variable*. Here the researcher randomly samples N individuals from the population, such that $N = JK$, where K is the number of blocks desired (i.e., a fixed effect) and J is the number of treatment groups. These individuals are ranked according to their values on the blocking variable from 1 to N. The first block consists of those individuals ranked from 1 to J, the second block of those ranked from $J + 1$ to $2J$, and so on. Finally, individuals within a block are randomly assigned to the J treatment groups. For example, consider a placement exam score as the blocking variable, where there are $J = 4$ treatment groups, $K = 10$ blocks, and thus $N = JK = 40$ individuals. The top four ranked individuals on the placement exam would constitute the first block, and they would be randomly assigned to the four groups. The next four ranked individuals would constitute the second block, and so on.

The fifth method is the **post hoc blocking method**. Here the researcher has already designed the study and collected the data, without the benefit of a blocking variable. After the fact, a blocking variable is identified and incorporated into the analysis. It is possible to implement any of the four preceding procedures on a post hoc basis.

Based on the research of Pingel (1969), some statements can be made about the precision of these blocking methods in terms of a reduction in residual variability as well as better estimation of the treatment effect. In general, for an ordinal blocking variable, the predefined value blocking method is more precise than the sampled value blocking method. Likewise, for an interval or ratio blocking variable, the predefined range blocking method is more precise than the sampled range blocking method. Finally, the post hoc blocking method is the least precise of the methods discussed. For discussion of selecting an optimal number of blocks, we suggest you consider Feldt (1958; highly recommended), as well as Keppel and Wickens (2004) and Myers et al. (2010). These researchers make the following recommendations about the optimal number of blocks (where r_{XY} is the correlation between the blocking factor X, in a randomized block design, and the dependent variable Y):

- if $r_{XY} = .2$, then use five blocks;
- if $r_{XY} = .4$, then use four blocks,

- if $r_{XY} = .6$, then use three blocks, and
- if $r_{XY} = .8$, then use two blocks.

16.1.2.6 An Example

Let us consider an example to illustrate the procedures in this section. The data are shown in Table 16.7. The blocking factor is age (i.e., 20, 30, 40, and 50 years of age), the treatment factor is number of workouts per week (i.e., 1, 2, 3, and 4), and the dependent variable is amount of weight lost during the first month. Presume we have a fixed-effects model. Table 16.8 contains the resultant ANOVA summary table.

The test statistics are both compared to the usual F test critical value of $_{.05}F_{3,9} = 3.86$ (from Appendix Table A.4), so that both main effects tests are statistically significant. The Geisser-Greenhouse conservative procedure is necessary for the test of factor A; here the test statistic is compared to the critical value of $_{.05}F_{1,3} = 10.13$, which is also significant. The two procedures both yield a statistically significant result, so we need not be concerned with a violation of the sphericity assumption for the test of A. In summary, the effects of amount of exercise undertaken and age on amount of weight lost are both statistically significant at the .05 level of significance.

Next we need to test the *additivity assumption* using Tukey's (1949) test of additivity. The F test statistic is equal to 0.1010, which is compared to the critical value of $_{.05}F_{1,8} = 5.32$ from Appendix Table A.4. The test is nonsignificant, so the model is additive and the assumption has been met.

TABLE 16.7

Data for the Exercise Example: Two-Factor Randomized Block Design

	Age				
Exercise Program	**20**	**30**	**40**	**50**	**Row Means**
1/week	3	2	1	0	1.5000
2/week	6	5	4	2	4.2500
3/week	10	8	7	6	7.7500
4/week	9	7	8	7	7.7500
Block means	7.0000	5.5000	5.0000	3.7500	5.3125 *(overall mean)*

TABLE 16.8

Two-Factor Randomized Block Design ANOVA Summary Table: Exercise Example

Source	*SS*	*df*	*MS*	*F*
A	21.6875	3	7.2292	18.2648*
B	110.1875	3	36.7292	92.7974*
Residual	3.5625	9	0.3958	
Total	135.4375	15		

$^*\, _{.05}F_{3,9} = 3.86$

As an example of a MCP, the Tukey HSD procedure is used to test for the equivalence of exercising once a week (j = 1) and four times a week (j = 4), where the contrast is written as $\bar{Y}_{4.} - \bar{Y}_{1.}$. The mean amount of weight lost for these groups are 1.5000 for the once a week program and 7.7500 for the four times a week program. The standard error is computed as:

$$s_{\psi'} = \sqrt{\frac{MS_{res}}{J}} = \sqrt{\frac{0.3958}{4}} = 0.3146$$

and the studentized range statistic is as follows:

$$q = \frac{\bar{Y}_{4.} - \bar{Y}_{1.}}{s_{\psi'}} = \frac{7.75 - 1.50}{0.3146} = 19.8665$$

The critical value is ${}_{\alpha}q_{9,4} = 4.415$ (from Appendix Table A.9). The test statistic exceeds the critical value; thus we conclude that the mean amount of weight lost for groups 1 (exercise once per week) and 4 (exercise four times per week) are statistically significantly different at the .05 level (i.e., more frequent exercise helps one to lose more weight).

16.1.3 Characteristics of the Two-Factor Randomized Block Design for $n > 1$

For two-factor randomized block designs with more than one observation per cell, there is little that we have not already covered. First, the characteristics are exactly the same as with the n = 1 model, with the obvious exception that when $n > 1$, an interaction term exists. Second, the layout of the data, the model, the ANOVA summary table, and the multiple comparison procedures are the same as in the regular two-factor model. Third, the assumptions are the same as with the n = 1 model, except the assumption of additivity is not necessary because an interaction term exists. The sphericity assumption is required for those tests using MS_{AB} as the error term. We do not mean to minimize the importance of this popular model; however, there really is no additional information to provide beyond what we have already presented. For a discussion of other randomized block designs, see Kirk (2014).

16.1.4 Characteristics of the Friedman Test

There is a nonparametric equivalent to the two-factor randomized block ANOVA model. The test was developed by Friedman (1937) and is based on mean ranks. For the case of n = 1, the procedure is precisely the same as the Friedman test for the one-factor repeated measures model (see Chapter 15). For the case of $n > 1$, the procedure is slightly different. First, all of the scores within each block are ranked for that block. For instance, if there are J = 4 levels of factor A and n = 10 individuals per cell, then each block's scores would be ranked from 1 to 40 (i.e., nJ). From this, a mean ranking can be determined for each level of factor A. The null hypothesis tests whether the mean rankings for each of the levels of A are equal. The test statistic is a χ^2, which is compared to the critical value of ${}_{\alpha}\chi^2_{J-1}$ (see Appendix Table A.3), where the null hypothesis is rejected if the test statistic exceeds the critical value.

In the case of tied ranks, either the available ranks can be averaged, or a correction factor can be used (see Chapter 15). You may also recall the problem with small n's in terms of the test statistic not being precisely distributed as a χ^2. For situations where $J < 6$ and $n < 6$, consult the table of critical values in Marascuilo and McSweeney (1977, Table A-22, p. 521). The Friedman test assumes that the population distributions have the same shape (although not necessarily normal) and the same variability, and that the dependent measure is continuous. For alternative nonparametric procedures, see the discussion in Chapter 15.

Various multiple comparison procedures (MCPs) can be used for the nonparametric two-factor randomized block model. For the most part, these MCPs are analogs to their parametric equivalents. In the case of planned pairwise comparisons, one may use multiple matched-pair Wilcoxon tests in a Bonferroni form (i.e., taking the number of contrasts into account by splitting up the α level). Due to the nature of planned comparisons, these are more powerful than the Friedman test. For post hoc comparisons, two example MCPs are the Tukey HSD analog for pairwise contrasts, and the Scheffé analog for complex contrasts. For additional discussion about the use of MCPs for this model, see Marascuilo and McSweeney (1977). For an example of the Friedman test, return to Chapter 15. Finally, note that MCPs are not usually conducted on the blocking factor as they are rarely of interest to the applied researcher.

16.1.5 Comparison of Various ANOVA Models

How do some of the ANOVA models we have considered compare in terms of power and precision? Recall again that **power** is defined as the probability of rejecting H_0 when H_0 is false, and **precision** is defined as a measure of our ability to obtain good estimates of the treatment effects. The classic literature on this topic revolves around the correlation between the dependent variable Y and the concomitant variable X (i.e., r_{XY}), where the concomitant variable can be either a covariate or a blocking factor. First, let us compare the one-factor ANOVA and one-factor ANCOVA models. If r_{XY}, the correlation between the covariate X and the dependent variable Y, is not statistically significantly different from zero, then the amount of unexplained variation will be the same in the two models. Thus, no statistical adjustment will be made on the group means. In this situation, the ANOVA model is more powerful, as we lose one degree of freedom for each covariate used in the ANCOVA model. If r_{XY} *is* significantly different from zero, then the amount of unexplained variation will be smaller in the ANCOVA model as compared to the ANOVA model. Here the ANCOVA model is more powerful and is more precise as compared to the ANOVA model. Second, compare the one-factor ANOVA and two-factor randomized block designs. If r_{XY}, the correlation between the blocking factor X and the dependent variable Y, is not statistically significantly different from zero, then the blocking factor will not account for much variability in the dependent variable. One recommendation is that if $r_{XY} < 2$, then ignore the concomitant variable (whether it is a covariate or a blocking factor), and use the one-factor analysis of variance. Otherwise, take the concomitant variable into account somehow, either as a covariate or blocking factor.

How should we take the concomitant variable into account if it correlates with the dependent variable at *greater* than .20 (i.e., $r_{XY} > 20$)? The two best possibilities are the analysis of covariance design (ANCOVA, Chapter 14) and the randomized block ANOVA design (discussed in this chapter). That is, the concomitant variable can be used either as a covariate through a statistical form of control (i.e., ANCOVA), or as a blocking factor through an experimental design form of control (i.e., randomized block ANOVA). As suggested by the classic work of Feldt (1958), if $.20 < r_{XY} < .40$, then use the concomitant variable as a blocking factor in a randomized block design as it is the most powerful and precise design. If $r_{XY} >$ .60, then use the concomitant variable as a covariate in an ANCOVA design as it is the most powerful and precise design. If $.40 < r_{XY} < .60$, then the randomized block and ANCOVA designs are about equal in terms of power and precision.

However, Maxwell, Delaney, and Dill (1984) showed that the correlation between the covariate and dependent variable should not be the ultimate criterion in deciding whether to use an ANCOVA or a randomized block design. These designs differ in the following two ways: (a) whether the concomitant variable is treated as continuous (ANCOVA) or categorical (randomized block), and (b) whether individuals are assigned to groups based on the concomitant variable (randomized blocks) or without regard to the concomitant variable (ANCOVA). Thus the Feldt (1958) comparison of these particular models is not a fair one in that the models differ in these two ways. The ANCOVA model makes full use of the information contained in the concomitant variable, whereas in the randomized block model, some information is lost due to the categorization. In examining nine different models, Maxwell and colleagues suggest that r_{XY} should not be the sole factor in the choice of a design (given that r_{XY} is at least .3), but that two other factors be considered. The first factor is whether scores on the concomitant variable are available prior to the assignment of individuals to groups. If so, power will be increased by assigning individuals to groups based on the concomitant variable (i.e., blocking). The second factor is whether X (the concomitant variable) and Y (the dependent variable) are linearly related. If so, the use of ANCOVA with a continuous concomitant variable is more powerful because linearity is an assumption of the model (Keppel & Wickens, 2004; Myers et al., 2010). If not, either the concomitant variable should be used as a blocking variable, or some sort of nonlinear ANCOVA model should be used.

There are a few other decision criteria you may want to consider in choosing between the randomized block and ANCOVA designs. First, in some situations, blocking may be difficult to carry out. For instance, we may not be able to find enough homogeneous individuals to constitute a block. If the blocks formed are not very homogeneous, this defeats the whole purpose of blocking. Second, the interaction of the independent variable and the concomitant variable may be an important effect to study. In this case, use the randomized block design with multiple individuals per cell. If the interaction is significant, this violates the assumption of homogeneity of regression slopes in the analysis of covariance design, but does not violate any assumption in the randomized block design with $n > 1$. Third, it should be obvious by now that the assumptions of the ANCOVA design are much more restrictive than in the randomized block design. Thus when important assumptions are likely to be seriously violated, the randomized block design is preferable.

There are other alternative designs for incorporating the concomitant variable as a pretest, such as an analysis of variance on gain (the difference between posttest and pretest), or a mixed (split-plot) design where the pretest and posttest measures are treated as the levels of a repeated factor. Based on the research of Huck and McLean (1975) and Jennings (1988), the ANCOVA model is generally preferred over these other two models. For further discussion see Reichardt (1979), Huitema (2011), or Kirk (2013).

16.1.6 Sample Size

16.1.6.1 Hierarchical ANOVA Model Sample Size

Sample size is often a difficult question to answer with single-level analyses, and the question of sufficient sample size becomes even more complex to answer with multilevel models. In general, in multilevel models (i.e., hierarchical models), *the sample size at the highest level is primarily of most concern because the sample size at that level is always smaller than at the lowest level* (Maas & Hox, 2005). In a two-level model, such as a two-factor hierarchical ANOVA, the "highest-level" sample size would be the sample size at the group or cluster level (i.e., nested factor). The following discussion of sample size is in the context of multilevel modeling in general and goes a bit beyond what has been covered in this chapter as most current research on hierarchical models has been in the context of estimation methods such as full maximum likelihood or restricted maximum likelihood. We'll proceed regardless, as this may help framing how to think about sample size in a hierarchical design. Additionally, you may be using hierarchical ANOVA with a maximum likelihood estimation, and in those cases, this is completely applicable. A few guidelines exist for minimum group sample size, including more than 10 groups (Snijders & Bosker, 1999), assuming restricted maximum likelihood is the estimation method, and a minimum of 30 groups (Kreft & de Leeuw, 1998). Sample size of the number of cases within groups (i.e., at the lowest level in a multilevel model) is less of a concern, and groups with even just one observation in them should be retained. While those groups will not contribute to the within-group variances, they will contribute to the between-group variance and overall average.

In addition to considering the sample sizes at each level, the proportion of variation in the outcome between groups, i.e., **intraclass correlation coefficient (ICC)**, as well as the estimation method, i.e., **full maximum likelihood (FML)** or **restricted maximum likelihood (RML)**, are also considerations. Simulation research has been conducted that has conditioned on estimation methods (FML, RML), number of groups (30, 50, 100), size of groups (5, 30, 50), and ICC (.1, .2, .3) (Maas & Hox, 2005). In all conditions, regression coefficients and variance components are unbiased. However, the standard errors of the variances at level 2 are underestimated when the number of groups is fewer than 100; however, the bias is, "in practice, probably acceptable" (Maas & Hox, 2005, p. 91). Conditions were also tested with only 10 groups based on work by Snijders and Bosker (1999). While the regression coefficients and level 1 variance components were unbiased, the level 2 variance components were overestimated, and the standard errors were unacceptably underestimated, suggesting that 10 groups at level 2 is insufficient for estimating MLM (Maas & Hox, 2005). Optimal Design (Spybrook, Raudenbush, Liu, Congdon, & Martinez, 2006) is a freely accessible online program designed to estimate power and sample size in group randomized designs and can be used *a priori* or post hoc. Even if you are not in a situation where randomization of groups will be or has been done, Optimal Design may provide the best available information for estimating sample size in a hierarchical design.

16.1.6.2 Randomized Block ANOVA Sample Size

In general, randomized block designs have more power that completely randomized designs of equal size (Festing, 2014). In terms of sample size, there are no magic numbers that can be suggested. Rather, we encourage you to determine sample size based on power tables or software (e.g., G*Power).

16.1.7 Power

A discussion of power has been intertwined throughout this chapter. As noted previously, recall that procedures for determining power in the hierarchical ANOVA model are the same as with the two-factor crossed model. Depending on your situation, the use of software such as Optimal Design may be appropriate.

16.1.8 Effect Size

Traditional effect sizes considered in ANOVA include omega squared (ω^2), eta squared (η^2), and partial eta squared $\left(\eta_p^2\right)$. *Omega squared* is interpreted as the proportion of the variation of the dependent variable that is attributed to variation in the independent variable. *Eta squared* is interpreted as the proportion of total variability in the dependent variable that is accounted for by variation in each main effect, interaction, and error in the model. *Partial eta squared* is interpreted as the proportion of total variability in the dependent variable attributed to a factor and that is not explained by other factors in the model. However, as pointed out by Olejnik and Algina (2003), Cohen's effect sizes are based on "unrestricted populations" (p. 446); in other words, designs that do *not* include controls or blocking variables. Thus, effect sizes that work well in simpler ANOVA models (e.g., omega squared and eta squared) do not work well with more complex ANOVA models such as nested and randomized block designs. *Failing to consider the design (e.g., nested random effects) when calculating the effect size can result in biased estimates.* Wampold and Serlin (2000) found that ignoring the nested model can lead not only to inflated Type I error rates but grossly overstated effects. For example, when 30% of the variance in the outcome was due to the cluster, a moderate effect was produced when the actual treatment effect was zero (Wampold & Serlin, 2000).

To address this and other shortcomings of effect size in more complicated ANOVA models, researchers are encouraged to consider other, more appropriate, effect size indices. For example, Olejnik and Algina (2003) proposed generalized eta squared and generalized omega squared effect size statistics that take into account research design features.

16.1.8.1 Hierarchical ANOVA Effect Size

For the **hierarchical ANOVA model with a random nested factor**, the **overall omega squared** ($\hat{\omega}^2$) is the appropriate effect size measure (Olejnik & Algina, 2000). This effect size represents the proportion of total variance of the dependent variable accounted for by the respective factor. In this case, both factors may be random, or one factor is fixed while the other is random. Applying Cohen's (1988) conventions for interpretation, a small overall omega squared hat is .01, medium is .06, and large is .14. Maxwell et al. (2018) provide the following formula:

$$\hat{\omega}_A^2 = \frac{\sum \hat{\alpha}_j^2 / a}{\left(\sum \hat{\alpha}_j^2 / a\right) + \hat{\alpha}_\beta^2 + \hat{\alpha}_\varepsilon^2}$$

Where

$$\frac{\sum \hat{\alpha}_j^2}{a} = \left(\frac{(a-1)}{a}\right)\left(\frac{\left(MS_A - MS_{B(A)}\right)}{bn}\right)$$

$$\hat{\alpha}_\beta^2 = \frac{MS_{B(A)} - MS_{with}}{n}$$

$$\hat{\alpha}_\varepsilon^2 = MS_{with}$$

a = number of levels of factor A
b = number of levels per nest (not the total number of levels of factor B)

Partial omega squared, $\hat{\omega}^2_{partial}$, is for assessing partial variance; e.g., other factors in the design are controlled by excluding them from the computation (proportion of total variability in the dependent variable attributed to a factor and that is not explained by other factors in the model). Generally, for the same effect, *a proportion of partial variance effect size will be larger than the proportion of total variance effect size* (Olejnik & Algina, 2000). Applying Cohen's (1988) conventions for interpretation, a small partial omega squared hat is .01, medium is .06, and large is .14.

$$\hat{\omega}^2_{A.partial} = \frac{MS_A - MS_{AB}}{MS_A + (n)(K)(MS_{error}) - MS_{AB}}$$

$$\hat{\omega}^2_{B.partial} = \frac{MS_B - MS_{AB}}{MS_B + (n)(J)(MS_{error}) - MS_{AB}}$$

where

J = number of levels in factor A
K = number of levels in factor B

Maxwell et al. (2018) provide the following formula for the effect of the nonnested factor, where $\sum \hat{\alpha}_j^2 / a$ and $\hat{\sigma}^2_\varepsilon$ were defined previously.

$$\hat{\omega}^2_{A,partial} = \frac{\sum \hat{\alpha}_j^2 / a}{\left(\sum \hat{\alpha}_j^2 / a\right) + \hat{\sigma}^2_\varepsilon}$$

Partial intraclass correlation coefficient, $\hat{\rho}^2_{I:B(A),\,partial}$, for assessing the effect of the nested factor, can be computed as follows (Maxwell et al., 2018):

$$\hat{\rho}^2_{I:B(A),partial} = \frac{\hat{\sigma}^2_\beta}{\hat{\sigma}^2_\beta + \hat{\sigma}^2_\varepsilon}$$

where

$$\hat{\sigma}^2_\beta = \frac{MS_{B(A)} - MS_{with}}{n}$$

$$\hat{\sigma}^2_\varepsilon = MS_{with}$$

If we follow conventions for ICC in general that are presented by Hox, Moerbeek, and van de Schoot (2017) and apply these to partial ICC, a small effect is .05, moderate is .10, and large is .15. In cases where higher ICCs are reasonable based on a prior information, small is .10, medium is .20, and large is .30. *We caution readers on applying conventions for interpreting the size of the effect, regardless of which effect size is interpreted.* As noted by Hox et al. (2017), what is small versus moderate versus large very much depends on the context.

Thus, we encourage readers to review related literature to compare and make interpretations of the size of the effect rather than apply effect size conventions.

For the two-factor nested ANOVA example presented in the illustration throughout the test, we find the following overall $\hat{\omega}_A^2$ of .70:

$$\hat{\omega}_A^2 = \frac{\sum \hat{\alpha}_j^2 / a}{\left(\sum \hat{\alpha}_j^2 / a\right) + \hat{\sigma}_\beta^2 + \hat{\sigma}_\varepsilon^2} = \frac{13.83}{13.83 + (-.012) + 5.95} = \frac{13.83}{19.77} = .70$$

where

$$\frac{\sum \hat{\alpha}_j^2}{a} = \left(\frac{(a-1)}{a}\right)\left(\frac{MS_A - MS_{B(A)}}{bn}\right) = \left(\frac{2-1}{2}\right)\left(\frac{337.50 - 5.667}{(2)(24)}\right) = .5\left(\frac{331.833}{48}\right) = 13.83$$

$$\hat{\sigma}_\beta^2 = \frac{MS_{B(A)} - MS_{with}}{n} = \frac{5.667 - 5.95}{24} = \frac{-.283}{24} = -.012$$

$$\hat{\sigma}_\varepsilon^2 = MS_{with} = 5.95$$

a = number of levels of factor A = 2
b = number of levels per nest (not the total number of levels of factor B) = 2

And, for the effect of level *A* (i.e., nonnested factor, in this case the intervention) can be computed as follows:

$$\hat{\omega}_{A,partial}^2 = \frac{\sum \hat{\alpha}_j^2 / a}{\left(\sum \hat{\alpha}_j^2 / a\right) + \hat{\sigma}_\varepsilon^2} = \frac{13.83}{13.83 + 5.95} = \frac{13.83}{19.78} = .70$$

16.1.8.2 Two-factor Randomized Block Effect Size

For the **two-factor randomized block**, the **overall omega squared** ($\hat{\omega}^2$) is the appropriate effect size measure and can be calculated as follows (Olejnik & Algina, 2000):

$$\hat{\omega}_A^2 = \frac{J(MS_A - MS_{AB})}{SS_{total} + MS_A + MS_B - MS_{AB}}$$

$$\hat{\omega}_B^2 = \frac{K(MS_B - MS_{AB})}{SS_{total} + MS_A + MS_B - MS_{AB}}$$

$$\hat{\omega}_{AB}^2 = \frac{JK(MS_{AB} - MS_{error})}{SS_{total} + MS_A + MS_B - MS_{AB}}$$

where

J = number of levels in factor A
K = number of levels in factor B

TABLE 16.9

Effect Sizes and Interpretations

Effect Size	Interpretation
Overall omega squared ($\hat{\omega}^2$)	Proportion of the variation of the dependent variable that is attributed to variation in the factor (i.e., independent variable) • Small effect, $\omega_A^2 = .01$ • Medium effect, $\omega_A^2 = .06$ • Large effect, $\omega_A^2 = .14$
Partial omega squared for level A (nonnested factor) $\left(\hat{\omega}_{partial}^2\right)$	Proportion of total variability in the dependent variable attributed to the nonnested factor that is not explained by other variables in the model • Small effect, $\omega_{A,partial}^2 = .01$ • Medium effect, $\omega_{A,partial}^2 = .06$ • Large effect, $\omega_{A,partial}^2 = .14$
Partial intraclass correlation coefficient for the effect of level B (nested factor) $\left(\hat{\rho}_{I:B(A),\,partial}^2\right)$	Proportion of variation in the dependent variable due to the random factor of B nested within A; conventions based on Hox et al. (2017) with values in parentheses denoting cases where higher ICCs are reasonable based on *a priori* information • Small effect $\hat{\rho}_{I:B(A),partial}^2 = .05$ (.10) • Medium effect $\hat{\rho}_{I:B(A),partial}^2 = .10$ (.20) • Large effect $\hat{\rho}_{I:B(A),partial}^2 = .15$ (.30)

Hox, J. J., Moerbeek, M., & van de Schoot, R. (2017). *Multilevel analysis: Techniques and applications* (3rd ed.). New York, NY: Routledge.

Partial omega squared is for assessing partial variance, e.g., other factors in the design are controlled by excluding them from the computation. Generally, for the same effect, *a proportion of partial variance effect size will be larger than the proportion of total variance effect size* (Olejnik & Algina, 2000). Applying Cohen's (1988) conventions for interpretation, a small partial omega squared hat is .01, medium is .06, and large is .14. Partial omega squared can be computed as follows:

$$\hat{\omega}_{A.partial}^2 = \frac{MS_A - MS_{AB}}{MS_A + (n)(K)(MS_{error}) - MS_{AB}}$$

$$\hat{\omega}_{B.partial}^2 = \frac{MS_B - MS_{AB}}{MS_B + (n)(J)(MS_{error}) - MS_{AB}}$$

where

J = number of levels in factor A
K = number of levels in factor B

16.1.9 Assumptions

16.1.9.1 Assumptions of Hierarchical Models

As noted previously, the assumptions of the two-factor hierarchical model are the same as with the two-factor crossed model (Chapters 13 and 15). These include normality, homogeneity of variance, and independence of observations within cells.

16.1.9.2 Assumptions of the Two-Factor Randomized Block ANOVA

In Chapter 15 we described the assumptions for the one-factor repeated measures ANOVA model. The assumptions are nearly the same for the two-factor randomized block model, and we need not devote much attention to them here. As before, the assumptions are mainly concerned with independence, normality, and homogeneity of variance. As these have been presented previously, we will not devote additional time on them here.

Another assumption is **compound symmetry** and is necessary because the observations within a block are not independent. *The assumption states that the population covariances for all pairs of the levels of the treatment factor A (i.e., j and j′) are equal.* The analysis of variance is not particularly robust to a violation of this assumption. If the assumption is violated, three alternative procedures are available. The first is to limit the levels of factor A, either to those that meet the assumption, or to two levels (in which case there is only one covariance). The second, and more plausible, alternative is to use adjusted *F* tests. These are reported shortly. The third is to use multivariate analysis of variance, which has no compound symmetry assumption but is slightly less powerful. This method is beyond the scope of this text, but you may refer to Hahs-Vaughn (2016).

Huynh and Feldt (1970) showed that the compound symmetry assumption is a sufficient but unnecessary condition for the test of treatment factor *A* to be *F* distributed. Thus the *F* test may also be valid under less stringent conditions. The necessary and sufficient condition for the validity of the F test of *A* is known as *sphericity*. *The assumption of sphericity is met when the variance of the difference scores for each pair of factor levels is the same.* Further discussion of sphericity is beyond the scope of this text (e.g., Keppel & Wickens, 2004; Kirk, 2013), although we have previously discussed sphericity for repeated measures designs in Chapter 15.

A final assumption purports that there is no interaction between the treatment and blocking factors. This is obviously an assumption of the model because no interaction term is included. Such a model is often referred to as an *additive model*, and thus this assumption is referred to as the **assumption of additivity**. As was mentioned previously, in this model the interaction is confounded with the error term. Violation of the additivity assumption results in the test of factor *A* to be negatively biased; thus there is an increased probability of committing a Type II error. As a result, if H_0 is rejected, then we are confident that H_0 is really false. If H_0 is not rejected, then our interpretation is ambiguous as H_0 may or may not be really true (due to an increased probability of a Type II error). Here you would not know whether H_0 was true or not, as there might really be a difference, but the test may not be powerful enough to detect it. Also, the power of the test of factor *A* is reduced by a violation of the additivity assumption. The assumption may be tested by Tukey's (1949) test of additivity (see Kirk, 2013; Timm, 2002), which generates an *F* test statistic that is compared to the critical value of ${}_{\alpha}F_{1,[(J-1)(K-1)-1]}$. If the test is not statistically significant, then the model is additive and the assumption has been met. If the test *is* significant, then the model is *not* additive and the assumption has *not* been met. A summary of the assumptions and the effects of their violation for this model are presented in Table 16.10.

TABLE 16.10

Assumptions and Effects of Violations: Two-Factor Randomized Block ANOVA

Assumption	Effect of Assumption Violation
Independence	• Increased likelihood of a Type I and/or Type II error in F • Affects standard errors of means and inferences about those means
Homogeneity of variance	• Small effect with equal or nearly equal n's • Otherwise effect decreases as n increases
Normality	• Minimal effect with equal or nearly equal n's
Sphericity	• Fairly serious effect
No interaction between treatment and blocks	• Increased likelihood of a Type II error for the test of factor A and thus reduced power

16.2 Mathematical Introduction Snapshot

Let's summarize some of the mathematics that underlie the models we've covered. The *two-factor mixed-effects nested ANOVA* model is written in terms of population parameters as follows:

$$Y_{ijk} = \mu + \alpha_j + b_{k(j)} + \varepsilon_{ijk}$$

where Y_{ijk} is the observed score on the dependent variable for individual i in level j of factor A and level k of factor B (or in the jk cell), μ is the overall or grand population mean (i.e., regardless of cell designation), α_j is the fixed effect for level j of factor A, $b_{k(j)}$ is the random effect for level k of factor B, and ε_{ijk} is the random residual error for individual i in cell jk. The distinguishing feature of this model is the lack of an interaction term.

The *two-factor fixed-effects randomized block ANOVA* model is written in terms of population parameters as follows:

$$Y_{jk} = \mu + \alpha_j + \beta_k + \varepsilon_{jk}$$

where Y_{jk} is the observed score on the dependent variable for the individual responding to level j of factor A and level k of block B, μ is the overall or grand population mean, α_j is the fixed effect for level j of factor A, β_k is the fixed effect for level k of the block B, and ε_{jk} is the random residual error for the individual in cell jk. This is similar to the two-factor fully crossed model with one observation per cell (i.e., $i = 1$ making the i subscript unnecessary), and with no interaction term included. Also, the effects are denoted by α and β given we have a fixed-effects model.

16.3 Computing Hierarchical and Randomized Block ANOVA Models Using SPSS

In this section we examine SPSS for the models presented in this chapter. We begin with the two-factor hierarchical ANOVA and then follow with the two-factor randomized block ANOVA.

16.3.1 Computing the Two-Factor Hierarchical ANOVA Using SPSS

To conduct a two-factor hierarchical (or nested) ANOVA, there are a few differences from other ANOVA models we have considered in this text. We will illustrate computation of the model that follows the point-and-click method, as we have done in previous chapters, and will be using the "twofactor_nested.sav" data. It is important to note that the most recent versions of SPSS offer increasing ability to generate multilevel models using more modern analytic procedures (i.e., going beyond least squares estimation), and readers interested in more complex regression models using SPSS are referred to Heck, Tabata, and Thomas (2014). For this illustration, we will walk through the GLM steps as we have with previous ANOVA models.

In terms of the form of the data, one column or variable indicates the levels or categories of the independent variable (i.e., the fixed factor), one column indicates the levels of the nested factor, and the one variable represents the outcome or the dependent variable. Each row represents one individual, indicating the level or group of the nonnested factor (massage therapy or music therapy, in our example), the level or group of the nested factor (interventionist, therapist, or clinician 1, 2, 3, or 4), and their score on the dependent variable. Thus we have three columns which represent the nonnested factor (factor A), the nested factor (factor B), and the outcome value or dependent variable, as shown in Figure 6.2.

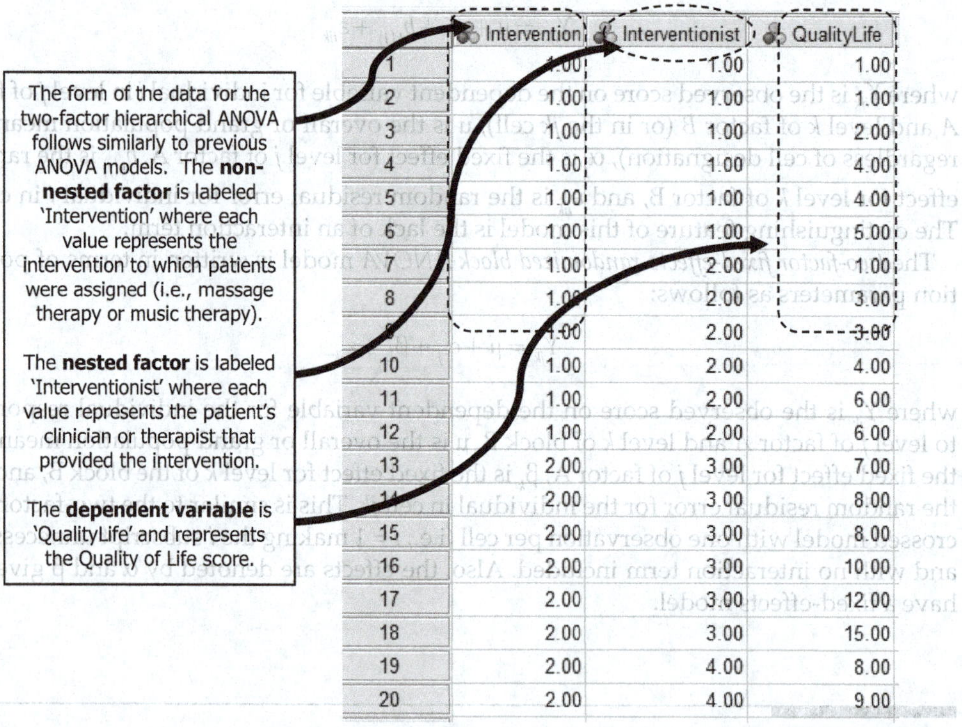
The form of the data for the two-factor hierarchical ANOVA follows similarly to previous ANOVA models. The **non-nested factor** is labeled 'Intervention' where each value represents the intervention to which patients were assigned (i.e., massage therapy or music therapy).
The **nested factor** is labeled 'Interventionist' where each value represents the patient's clinician or therapist that provided the intervention.
The **dependent variable** is 'QualityLife' and represents the Quality of Life score.

	Intervention	Interventionist	QualityLife
1	1.00	1.00	1.00
2	1.00	1.00	1.00
3	1.00	1.00	2.00
4	1.00	1.00	4.00
5	1.00	1.00	4.00
6	1.00	1.00	5.00
7	1.00	2.00	1.00
8	1.00	2.00	3.00
9	1.00	2.00	3.00
10	1.00	2.00	4.00
11	1.00	2.00	6.00
12	1.00	2.00	6.00
13	2.00	3.00	7.00
14	2.00	3.00	8.00
15	2.00	3.00	8.00
16	2.00	3.00	10.00
17	2.00	3.00	12.00
18	2.00	3.00	15.00
19	2.00	4.00	8.00
20	2.00	4.00	9.00

FIGURE 16.2
Data for the two-factor hierarchical ANOVA.

Step 1. To conduct a two-factor hierarchical ANOVA, go to "Analyze" in the top pulldown menu, then select "General Linear Model," and then select "Univariate." Following the screenshot for Step 1 (shown in Figure 16.3) produces the Univariate dialog box.

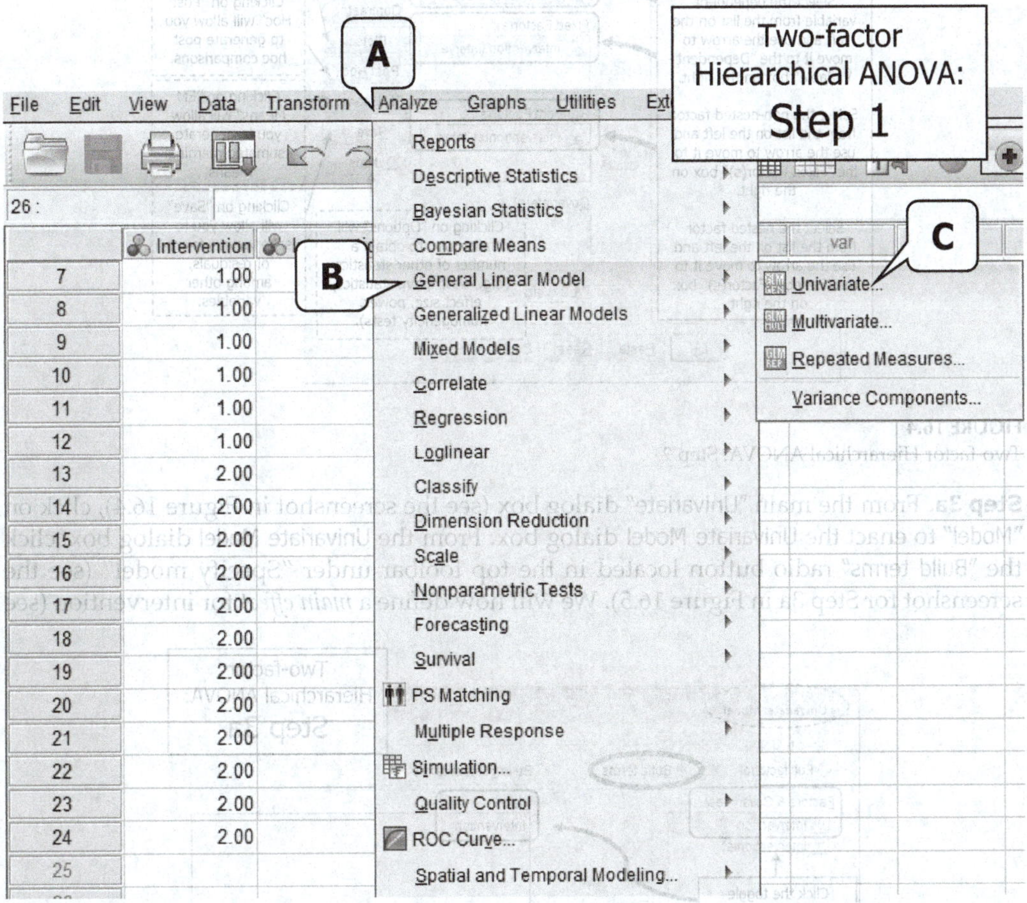

FIGURE 16.3
Two-factor Hierarchical ANOVA: Step 1.

Step 2. Click the dependent variable (e.g., Quality of Life score) and move it into the "Dependent Variable" box by clicking the arrow button. Click the nonnested factor (e.g., intervention; this is a fixed-effects factor) and move it into the "Fixed Factor(s)" box by clicking the arrow button. Click the nested variable (e.g., interventionist; this is a random-effects factor) and move it into the "Random Factor(s)" box by clicking the arrow button.

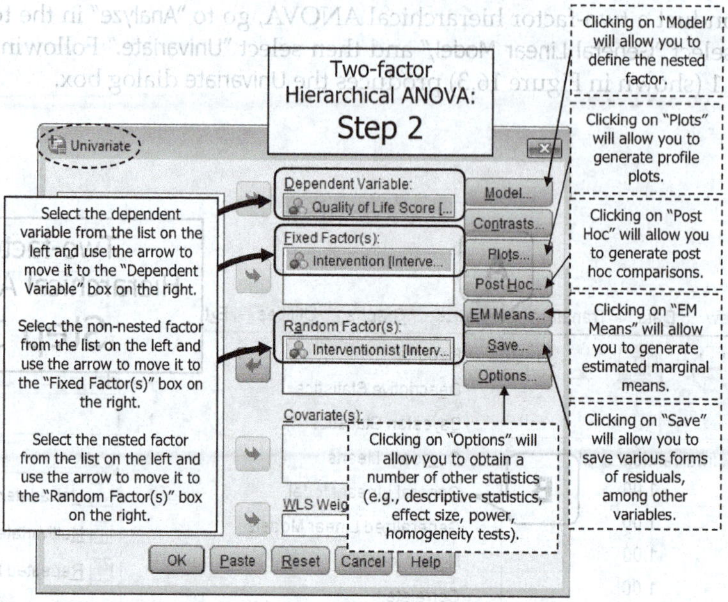

FIGURE 16.4
Two-factor Hierarchical ANOVA: Step 2.

Step 3a. From the main "Univariate" dialog box (see the screenshot in Figure 16.4), click on "Model" to enact the Univariate Model dialog box. From the Univariate Model dialog box, click the "Build terms" radio button located in the top toolbar under "Specify model" (see the screenshot for Step 3a in Figure 16.5). We will now define a *main effect* for intervention (see

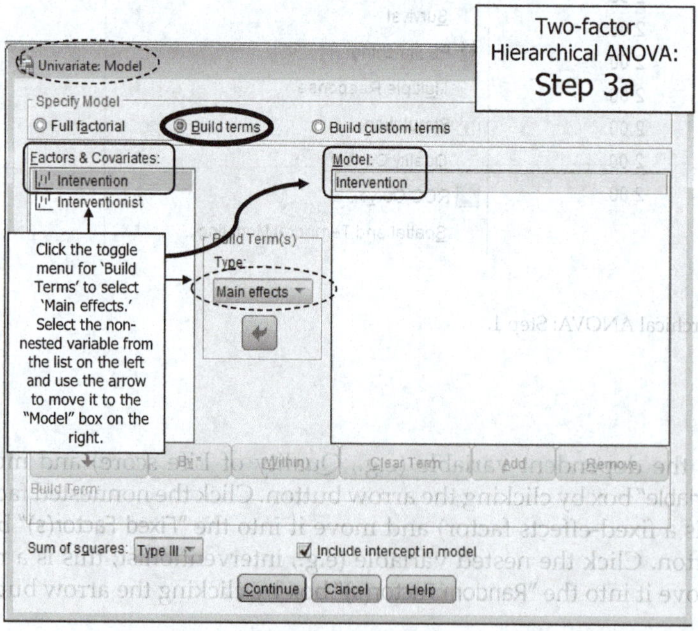

FIGURE 16.5
Two-factor hierarchical ANOVA: Step 3a.

Figure 16.5). To do this, click the "Build terms" toggle menu in the center of the page and select "Main effects." Click the nonnested factor (in this illustration, "Intervention") from the Factors & Covariates list on the left and move to the "Model" box on the right by clicking the arrow.

Step 3b. We will now define an *interaction effect* for intervention by interventionist (see the screenshot for Step 3b in Figure 16.6). To do this, click the "Build terms" toggle menu in the center of the page and select "Interaction." Click both the nonnested factor (e.g., "Intervention") and nested factor (e.g., "Interventionist") from the Factors & Covariates list on the left and move them to the "Model" box on the right by clicking the arrow. The interaction term is necessary to trick SPSS into computing the main effect of B(A) for the nested factor (which SPSS calls "intervention*interventionist," but is actually "interventionist"), and thus generate the proper ANOVA summary table. Thus the model should *not* include a main effect term for "Interventionist."

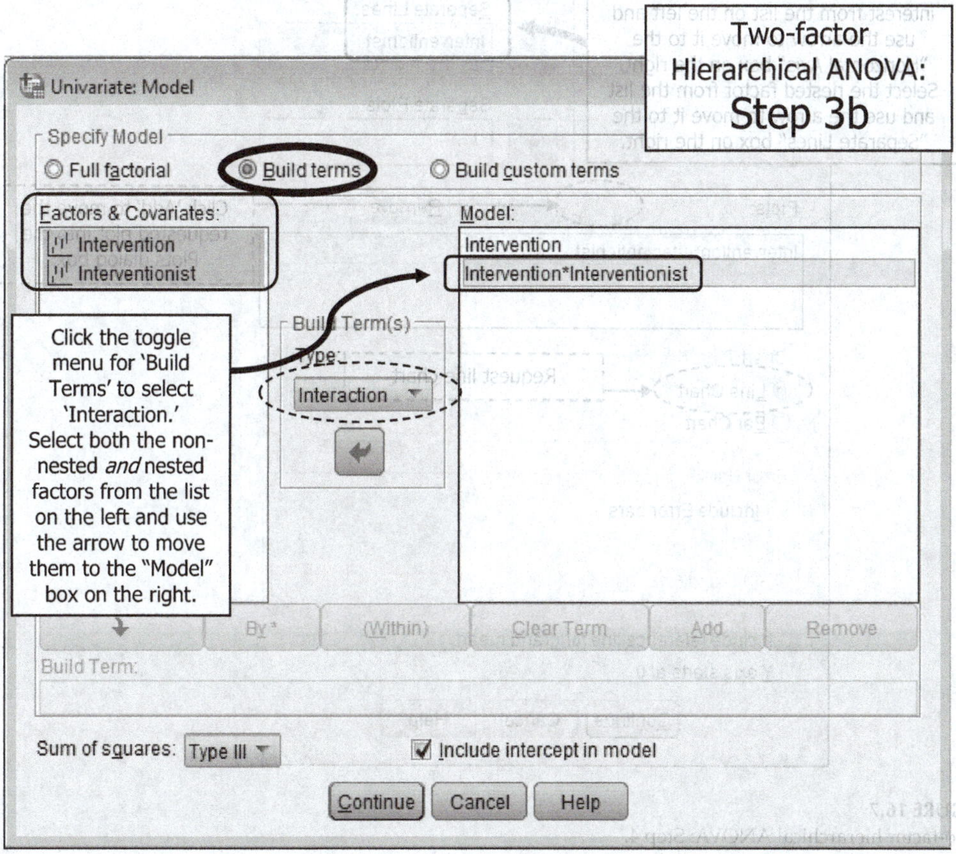

FIGURE 16.6
Two-factor Hierarchical ANOVA: Step 3b.

Step 4. From the Univariate dialog box (see Figure 16.4), clicking on "Plots" will provide the option to graph various profile plots. From the Univariate Profile Plots dialog box, click on the name of the nonnested factor in the "Factor(s)" list box in the top left and move it to the "Horizontal Axis" box in the top right by clicking on the arrow key. Then click on the name of the nested factor in the Factor(s) list box in the top left and move it to the "Separate Lines" box in the right by clicking on the arrow key. Next, click on "Add" to create the command to generate the plot in the dialog box in the middle. Select the radio button for "Line Chart" under Chart Type. Click on "Continue" to return to the original dialog box.

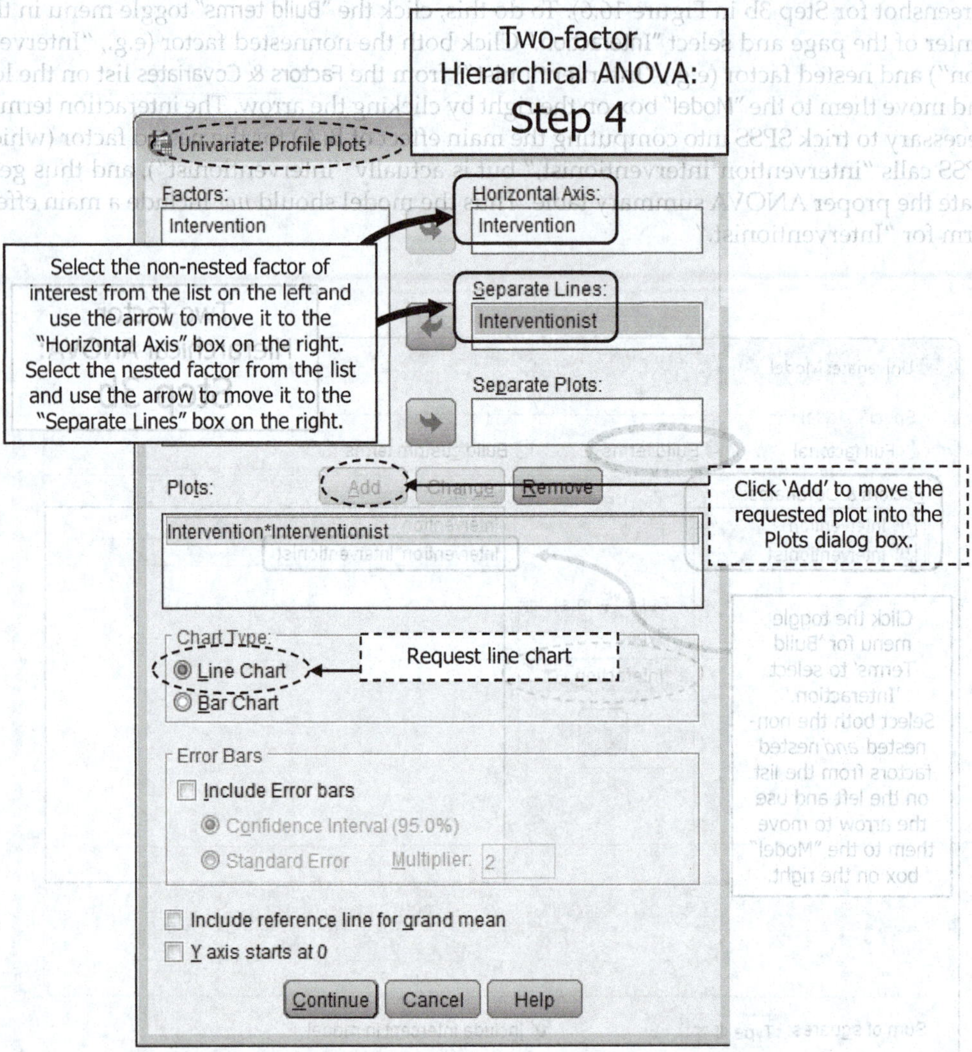

FIGURE 16.7
Two-factor hierarchical ANOVA: Step 4.

Step 5. From the Univariate dialog box (see Figure 16.4), clicking on "Post hoc" will provide the option to select *post hoc* multiple comparison procedures for the nonnested factor. From the Univariate Post Hoc Multiple Comparisons for Observed Means dialog box, click on the name of the nonnested factor in the "Factor(s)" list box in the top left and move it to the "Post Hoc Tests for" box in the top right by clicking on the arrow key. Check an appropriate MCP for your situation by placing a checkmark in the box next to the desired MCP. In this example, we select Tukey. Click on "Continue" to return to the original dialog box. (*Note:* Because we only have two treatments, this step is unnecessary as we can simply compare the means of the groups. The steps have been provided so that you can see the process in the event you have three or more groups in your own research.)

It is important to note that Li and Lomax (2011) found that the standard errors of the MCPs for the nonnested factor in SPSS point-and-click mode are not correct. More specifically, SPSS point-and-click uses MS_{with} as the error term in computing the MCP standard error rather than $MS_{B(A)}$ as the error term. There is no way to generate the correct results solely with SPSS point-and-click, unless hand computations using the correct error term are utilized or other software programs (e.g., SPSS syntax) are also involved.

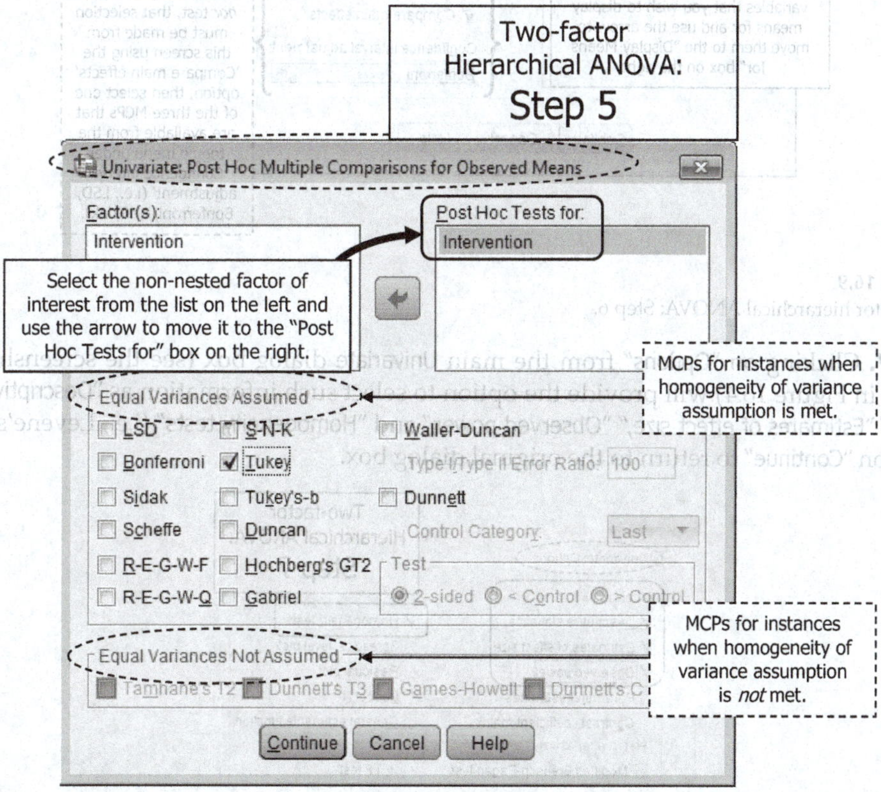

FIGURE 16.8
Two-factor hierarchical ANOVA: Step 5.

Step 6. From the Univariate dialog box (see Figure 16.4), clicking on "EM Means" will provide the option to select estimated marginal means. From the Univariate Estimated Marginal Means dialog box, click on "(OVERALL)" and the names of the non-nested and nested factors in the "Factor(s) and Factor Interactions" list box in the top left and move it to the "Display Means for" box in the top right by clicking on the arrow key. *Note that if you are interested in a multiple comparison procedure for the nested factor (although generally not of interest for this model), post hoc MCPs are available only from this screen.* To select a post hoc procedure, click on "Compare main effects" and use the toggle menu to reveal the Tukey LSD, Bonferroni, and Sidak procedures. For illustration purposes, we'll select Bonferroni. However, we have already mentioned that MCPs are not generally of interest for the nested factor. Click on "Continue" to return to the original dialog box.

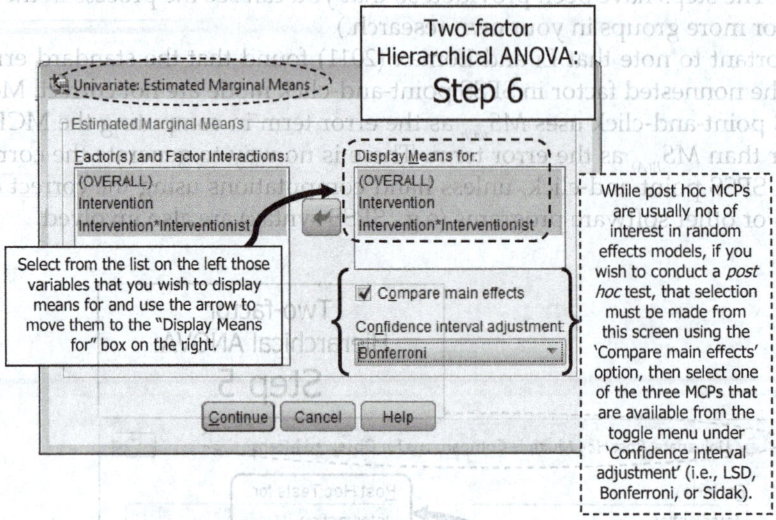

FIGURE 16.9
Two-factor hierarchical ANOVA: Step 6.

Step 7. Clicking on "Options" from the main Univariate dialog box (see the screenshot for Step 2 in Figure 16.4) will provide the option to select such information as "Descriptive statistics," "Estimates of effect size," "Observed power," and "Homogeneity tests" (i.e., Levene's test). Click on "Continue" to return to the original dialog box.

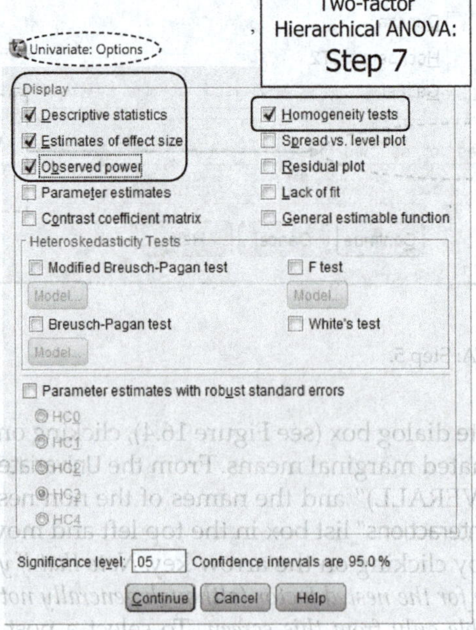

FIGURE 16.10
Two-factor Hierarchical ANOVA: Step 7.

Step 8. From the "Univariate" dialog box (see the screenshot for Step 2 in Figure 16.4), click on "Save" to select those elements you want to save. Here we want to save the unstandardized residuals to be used to examine the extent to which normality and independence are met. Thus, place a checkmark in the box next to "Unstandardized." Click "Continue" to return to the main "Univariate" dialog box. From the Univariate dialog box, click on "OK" to generate the output.

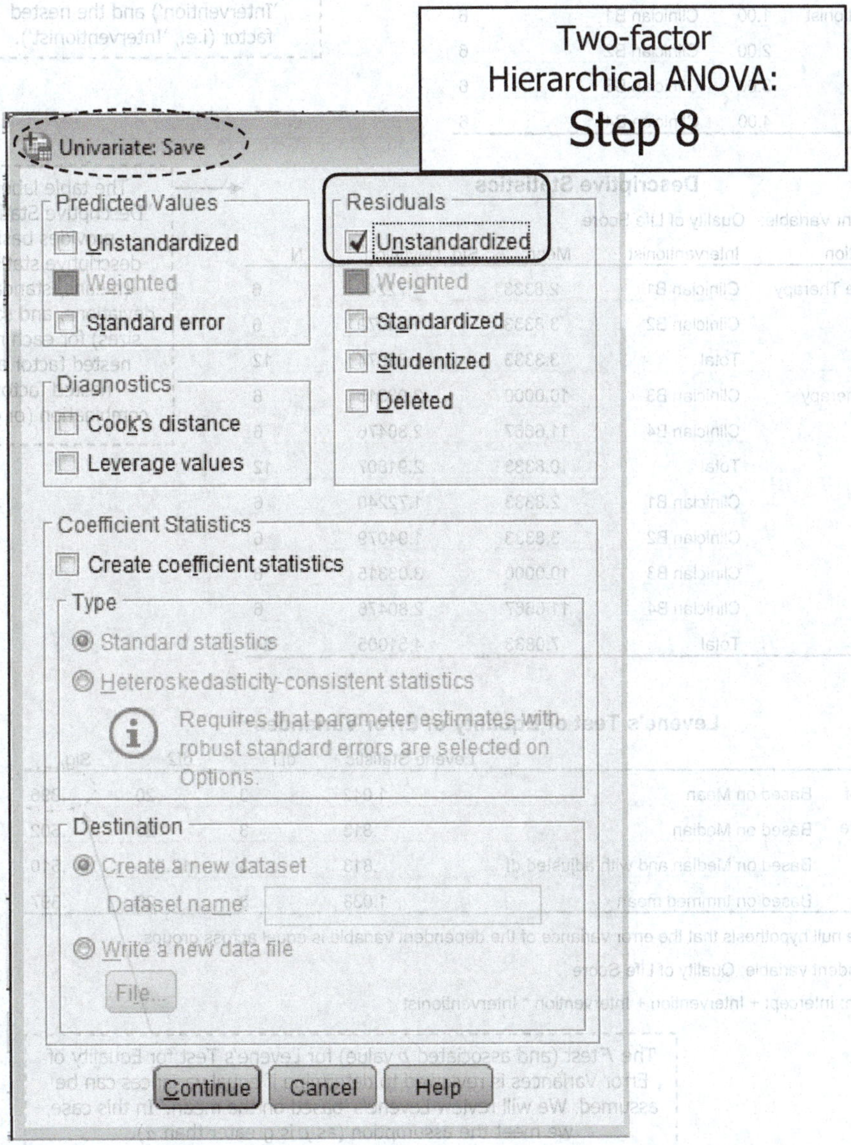

FIGURE 16.11
Two-factor hierarchical ANOVA: Step 8.

Interpreting the Output. Annotated results are presented in Table 16.11.

TABLE 16.11

Two-Factor Hierarchical ANOVA SPSS Results for the Quality of Life Intervention Example

Between-Subjects Factors

		Value Label	N
Intervention	1.00	Massage Therapy	12
	2.00	Music Therapy	12
Interventionist	1.00	Clinician B1	6
	2.00	Clinician B2	6
	3.00	Clinician B3	6
	4.00	Clinician B4	6

The table labeled "Between-Subjects Factors" lists the variable names and sample sizes for the non-nested factor (i.e., 'Intervention') and the nested factor (i.e., 'Interventionist').

Descriptive Statistics

Dependent Variable: Quality of Life Score

Intervention	Interventionist	Mean	Std. Deviation	N
Massage Therapy	Clinician B1	2.8333	1.72240	6
	Clinician B2	3.8333	1.94079	6
	Total	3.3333	1.82574	12
Music Therapy	Clinician B3	10.0000	3.03315	6
	Clinician B4	11.6667	2.80476	6
	Total	10.8333	2.91807	12
Total	Clinician B1	2.8333	1.72240	6
	Clinician B2	3.8333	1.94079	6
	Clinician B3	10.0000	3.03315	6
	Clinician B4	11.6667	2.80476	6
	Total	7.0833	4.51005	24

The table labeled "Descriptive Statistics" provides basic descriptive statistics (means, standard deviations, and sample sizes) for each non-nested factor and nested factor combination (or cell).

Levene's Test of Equality of Error Variances[a,b]

		Levene Statistic	df1	df2	Sig.
Quality of Life Score	Based on Mean	1.042	3	20	.396
	Based on Median	.813	3	20	.502
	Based on Median and with adjusted df	.813	3	12.531	.510
	Based on trimmed mean	1.038	3	20	.397

Tests the null hypothesis that the error variance of the dependent variable is equal across groups.

a. Dependent variable: Quality of Life Score

b. Design: Intercept + Intervention + Intervention * Interventionist

The *F* test (and associated *p* value) for Levene's Test for Equality of Error Variances is reviewed to determine if equal variances can be assumed. We will review Levene's 'based on the mean.' In this case, we meet the assumption (as *p* is greater than α).

TABLE 16.11 (continued)

Two-Factor Hierarchical ANOVA SPSS Results for the Quality of Life Intervention Example

Comparing p to α, we find a statistically significant difference in intervention. This is an omnibus test. We will look at our MCPs to determine which mean ratings differ.

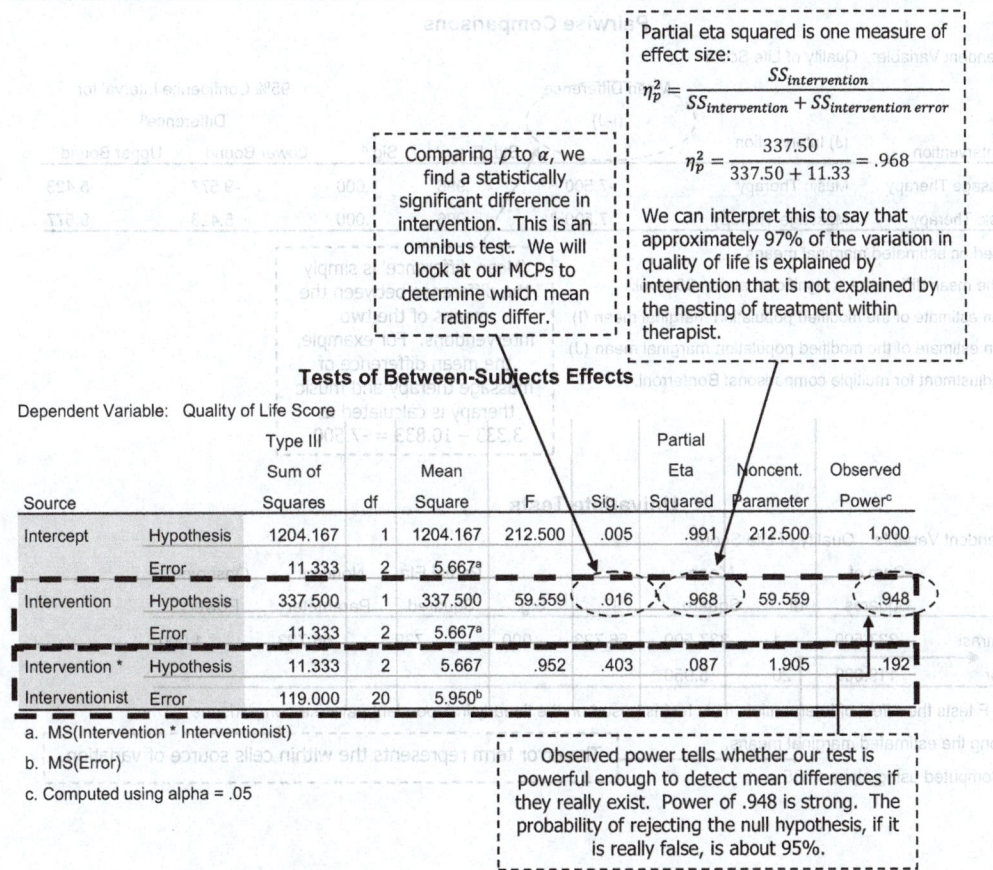

Partial eta squared is one measure of effect size:

$$\eta_p^2 = \frac{SS_{intervention}}{SS_{intervention} + SS_{intervention\ error}}$$

$$\eta_p^2 = \frac{337.50}{337.50 + 11.33} = .968$$

We can interpret this to say that approximately 97% of the variation in quality of life is explained by intervention that is not explained by the nesting of treatment within therapist.

Tests of Between-Subjects Effects

Dependent Variable: Quality of Life Score

Source		Type III Sum of Squares	df	Mean Square	F	Sig.	Partial Eta Squared	Noncent. Parameter	Observed Power[c]
Intercept	Hypothesis	1204.167	1	1204.167	212.500	.005	.991	212.500	1.000
	Error	11.333	2	5.667[a]					
Intervention	Hypothesis	337.500	1	337.500	59.559	.016	.968	59.559	.948
	Error	11.333	2	5.667[a]					
Intervention * Interventionist	Hypothesis	11.333	2	5.667	.952	.403	.087	1.905	.192
	Error	119.000	20	5.950[b]					

a. MS(Intervention * Interventionist)

b. MS(Error)

c. Computed using alpha = .05

Observed power tells whether our test is powerful enough to detect mean differences if they really exist. Power of .948 is strong. The probability of rejecting the null hypothesis, if it is really false, is about 95%.

Estimated Marginal Means

1. Grand Mean

Dependent Variable: Quality of Life Score

Mean	Std. Error	95% Confidence Interval Lower Bound	95% Confidence Interval Upper Bound
7.083[a]	.498	6.045	8.122

a. Based on modified population marginal mean.

The **'Grand Mean'** (in this case, 7.083) represents the overall Quality of Life score, regardless of the intervention or interventionistThe 95% CI represents the CI of the grand mean.

2. Intervention

Estimates

Dependent Variable: Quality of Life Score

Intervention	Mean	Std. Error	95% Confidence Interval Lower Bound	95% Confidence Interval Upper Bound
Massage Therapy	3.333[a]	.704	1.864	4.802
Music Therapy	10.833[a]	.704	9.364	12.302

a. Based on modified population marginal mean.

The table for **"Intervention"** provides descriptive statistics for each of the interventions. In addition to means, the *SE* and 95% CI of the means are reported.

(*continued*)

TABLE 16.11 (continued)

Two-Factor Hierarchical ANOVA SPSS Results for the Quality of Life Intervention Example

Pairwise Comparisons

Dependent Variable: Quality of Life Score

(I) Intervention	(J) Intervention	Mean Difference (I-J)	Std. Error	Sig.[d]	95% Confidence Interval for Difference[d] Lower Bound	Upper Bound
Massage Therapy	Music Therapy	-7.500*,b,c	.996	.000	-9.577	-5.423
Music Therapy	Massage Therapy	7.500*,b,c	.996	.000	5.423	9.577

Based on estimated marginal means

*. The mean difference is significant at the .05 level.

b. An estimate of the modified population marginal mean (I).

c. An estimate of the modified population marginal mean (J).

d. Adjustment for multiple comparisons: Bonferroni.

'Mean difference' is simply the difference between the means of the two interventions. For example, the mean difference of massage therapy and music therapy is calculated as 3.333 − 10.833 = -7.500.

Univariate Tests

Dependent Variable: Quality of Life Score

	Sum of Squares	df	Mean Square	F	Sig.	Partial Eta Squared	Noncent. Parameter	Observed Power[a]
Contrast	337.500	1	337.500	56.723	.000	.739	56.723	1.000
Error	119.000	20	5.950					

The F tests the effect of Intervention. This test is based on the linearly independent pairwise comparisons among the estimated marginal means.

a. Computed using alpha = .05

The error term represents the within cells source of variation.

3. Intervention * Interventionist

Dependent Variable: Quality of Life Score

Intervention	Interventionist	Mean	Std. Error	95% Confidence Interval Lower Bound	Upper Bound
Massage Therapy	Clinician B1	2.833	.996	.756	4.911
	Clinician B2	3.833	.996	1.756	5.911
	Clinician B3	.[a]	.	.	.
	Clinician B4	.[a]	.	.	.
Music Therapy	Clinician B1	.[a]	.	.	.
	Clinician B2	.[a]	.	.	.
	Clinician B3	10.000	.996	7.923	12.077
	Clinician B4	11.667	.996	9.589	13.744

a. This level combination of factors is not observed, thus the corresponding population marginal mean is not estimable.

The table for **"Intervention* Interventionist"** provides descriptive statistics for each of the intervention-interventionist combinations. In addition to means, the *SE* and 95% CI of the means are reported. Note the footnote in reference to the missing mean values. This is because this is not a completely crossed design (i.e., the clinicians provided only one intervention).

TABLE 16.11 (continued)

Two-Factor Hierarchical ANOVA SPSS Results for the Quality of Life Intervention Example

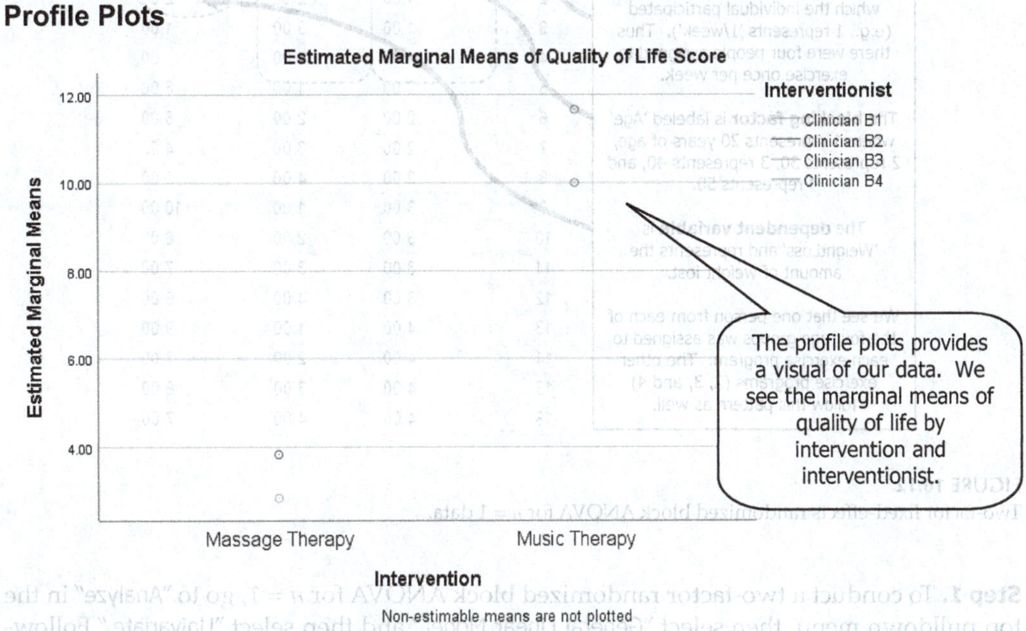

Please see eResource for figure in full color

16.3.2 Computing the Two-Factor Fixed-Effects Randomized Block ANOVA for $n = 1$ Using SPSS

To run a two-factor fixed-effects randomized block ANOVA for $n = 1$, there a few differences from the regular two-factor fixed-effects ANOVA that we see later as we build the model in SPSS. Additionally, the test of additivity is not available in SPSS, nor are the adjusted F tests (i.e., the Geisser-Greenhouse and Huynh-Feldt procedures). All other ANOVA procedures that you are familiar with will operate as before.

In terms of the form of the data, it looks just as we saw with the two-factor fixed-effects ANOVA, with the exception that now we have one treatment factor and one blocking variable. The dataset must therefore consist of three variables or columns, one for the level of the treatment factor, one for the level of the blocking factor, and the third for the dependent variable. Each row still represents one individual, indicating the levels of the treatment and blocking factors to which the individual is a member, and their score on the dependent variable. As seen in the screenshot (Figure 16.12), for a two-factor fixed-effects randomized block ANOVA, the SPSS data take the form of two columns that represent the group values (i.e., the treatment and blocking factors) and one column that represents the scores on the dependent variable.

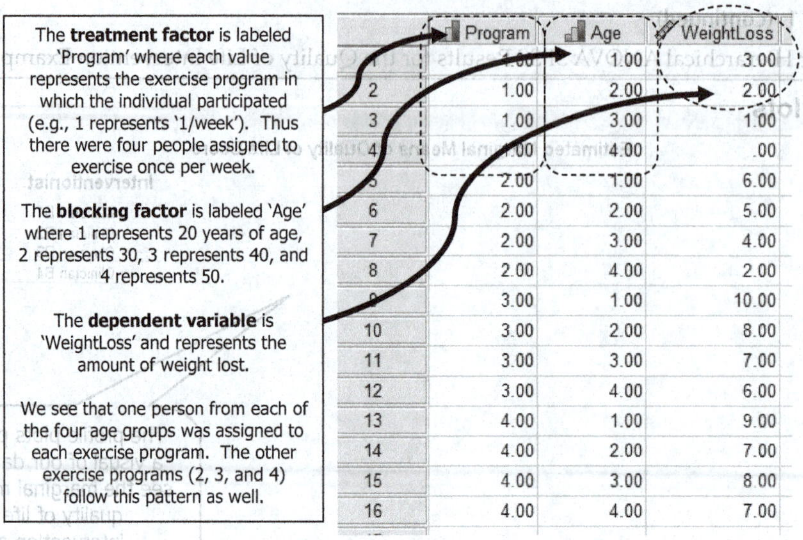
The **treatment factor** is labeled 'Program' where each value represents the exercise program in which the individual participated (e.g., 1 represents '1/week'). Thus there were four people assigned to exercise once per week.
The **blocking factor** is labeled 'Age' where 1 represents 20 years of age, 2 represents 30, 3 represents 40, and 4 represents 50.
The **dependent variable** is 'WeightLoss' and represents the amount of weight lost.
We see that one person from each of the four age groups was assigned to each exercise program. The other exercise programs (2, 3, and 4) follow this pattern as well.
Program
Age
WeightLoss

	Program	Age	WeightLoss
1	1.00	1.00	3.00
2	1.00	2.00	2.00
3	1.00	3.00	1.00
4	1.00	4.00	.00
5	2.00	1.00	6.00
6	2.00	2.00	5.00
7	2.00	3.00	4.00
8	2.00	4.00	2.00
9	3.00	1.00	10.00
10	3.00	2.00	8.00
11	3.00	3.00	7.00
12	3.00	4.00	6.00
13	4.00	1.00	9.00
14	4.00	2.00	7.00
15	4.00	3.00	8.00
16	4.00	4.00	7.00

FIGURE 16.12
Two-factor fixed-effects randomized block ANOVA for $n = 1$ data.

Step 1. To conduct a two-factor randomized block ANOVA for $n = 1$, go to "Analyze" in the top pulldown menu, then select "General Linear Model," and then select "Univariate." Following the screenshot for Step 1 (Figure 16.13) produces the Univariate dialog box.

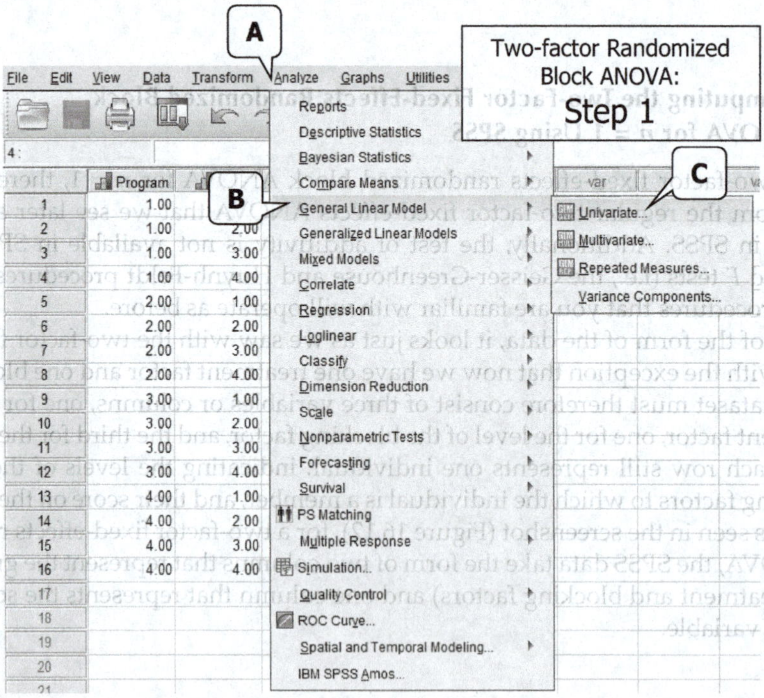

FIGURE 16.13
Two-factor fixed-effects randomized block ANOVA for $n = 1$: Step 1.

Step 2. Click the dependent variable (e.g., weight loss) and move it into the "Dependent Variable" box by clicking the arrow button. Click the treatment factor and the blocking factor and move them into the "Fixed Factors" box by clicking the arrow button.

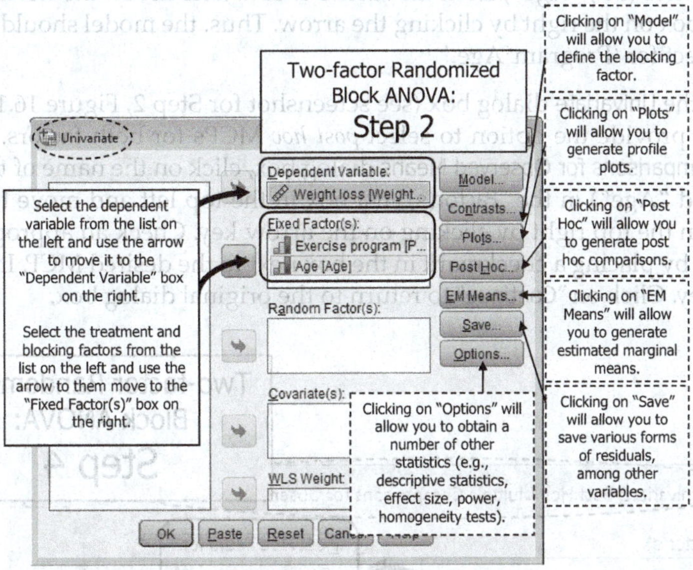

FIGURE 16.14
Two-factor fixed-effects randomized block ANOVA for $n = 1$: Step 2.

Step 3. From the main Univariate dialog box (see the screenshot for Step 2 (Figure 16.14), click on "Model" to enact the Univariate Model dialog box. From the Univariate Model dialog box, click the "Custom" radio button (see the screenshot for Step 3 in Figure 16.15). We will now

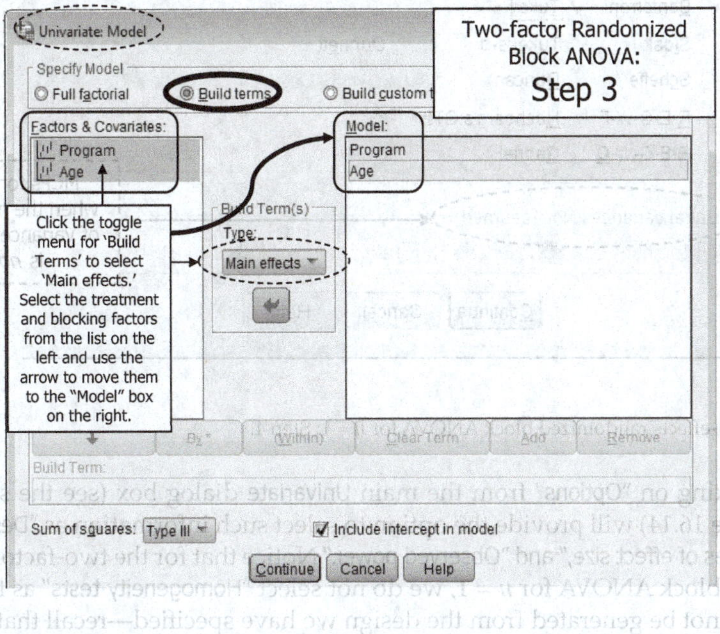

FIGURE 16.15
Two-factor fixed-effects randomized block ANOVA for $n = 1$: Step 3.

define the effects necessary for this model, a main effect for both exercise program and for age. We will *not* define an interaction. To do this, click the "Build terms" toggle menu in the center of the page and select "Main effect." Click the treatment factor (i.e., "Program") and the blocking factor (i.e., "Age") from the Factors & Covariates list on the left and move them to the "Model" box on the right by clicking the arrow. Thus. the model should *not* include an interaction effect for 'Program*Age.'

Step 4. From the Univariate dialog box (see screenshot for Step 2, Figure 16.14), clicking on "Post hoc" will provide the option to select *post hoc* MCPs for both factors. From the Post Hoc Multiple Comparisons for Observed Means dialog box, click on the name of the factors (i.e., "Program" and "Age") in the "Factor(s)" list box in the top left and move to the "Post Hoc Tests for" box in the top right by clicking on the arrow key. Check an appropriate MCP for your situation by placing a checkmark in the box next to the desired MCP. In this example, we select Tukey. Click on "Continue" to return to the original dialog box.

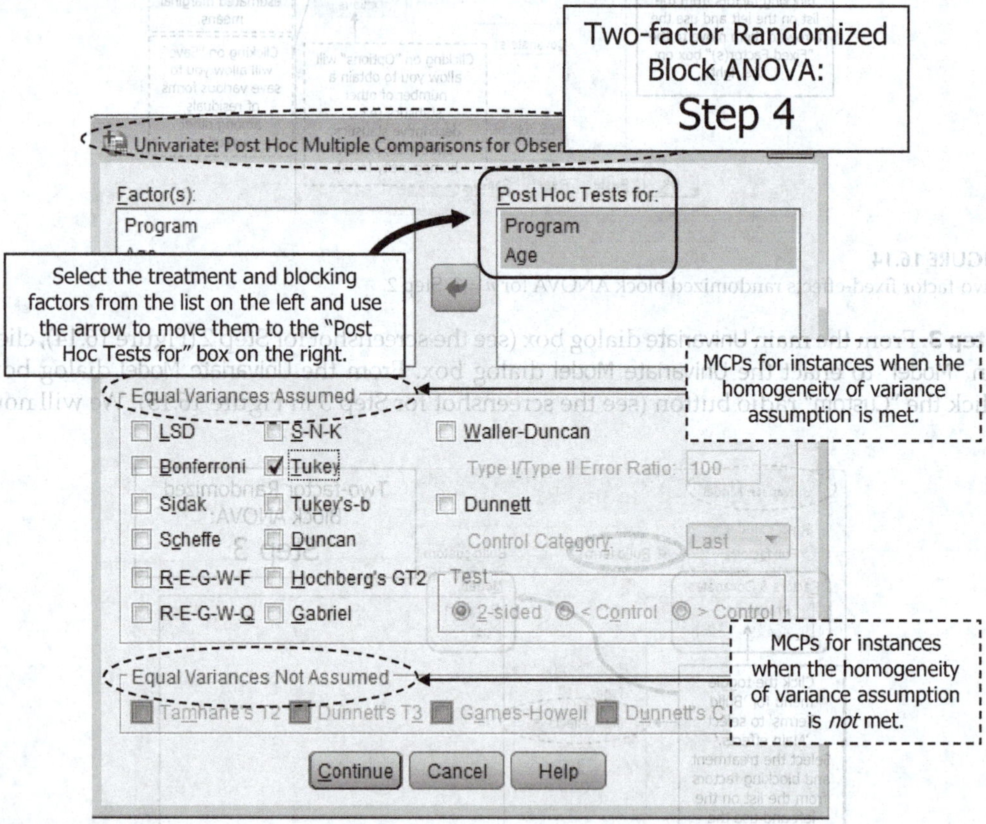

FIGURE 16.16
Two-factor fixed-effects randomized block ANOVA for $n = 1$: Step 4.

Step 5. Clicking on "Options" from the main Univariate dialog box (see the screenshot for Step 2, Figure 16.14) will provide the option to select such information as "Descriptive statistics," "Estimates of effect size," and "Observed power." Notice that for the two-factor fixed-effects randomized block ANOVA for $n = 1$, we do not select "Homogeneity tests" as the results for Levene's cannot be generated from the design we have specified—recall that there is only one individual per age group in each exercise program. Thus, there is no within-cell variation to calculate. This is not an issue with randomized block designs with $n > 1$. Click on "Continue" to return to the original dialog box.

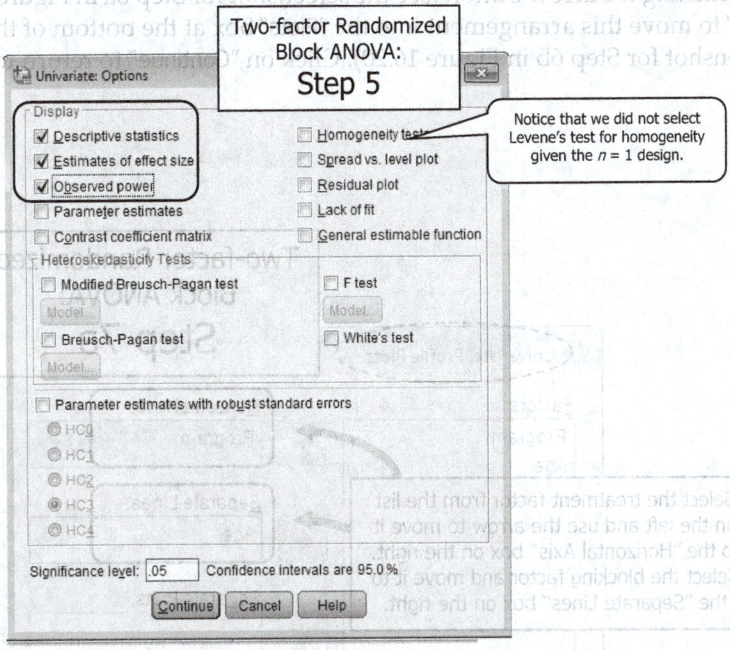

FIGURE 16.17
Two-factor fixed-effects randomized block ANOVA for $n = 1$: Step 5.

Step 6. From the Univariate dialog box (see the screenshot for Step 2, Figure 16.14), clicking on "EM Means" will provide the option to select estimated marginal means. From the Univariate Estimated Marginal Means dialog box, click on "(OVERALL)" and the names of the nonnested and nested factors in the "Factor(s) and Factor Interactions" list box in the top left and move it to the "Display Means for" box in the top right by clicking on the arrow key. Click on "Continue" to return to the original dialog box.

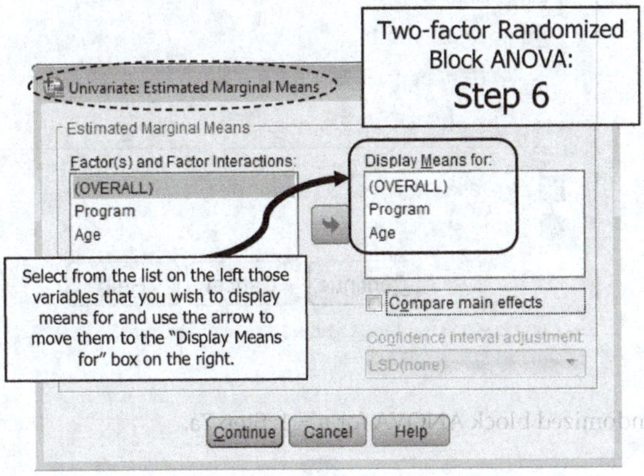

FIGURE 16.18
Two-factor fixed-effects randomized block ANOVA for $n = 1$: Step 6.

Step 7. From the Univariate dialog box, click on "Plots" to obtain a profile plot of means. Click the treatment factor (e.g., "Program") and move it into the "Horizontal Axis" box by clicking the arrow button. Click the blocking factor (e.g., "Age") and move it into the "Separate Lines" box by clicking the arrow button (see the screenshot for Step 6a in Figure 16.19). Then click on "Add" to move this arrangement into the "Plots" box at the bottom of the dialog box (see the screenshot for Step 6b in Figure 16.20). Click on "Continue" to return to the original dialog box.

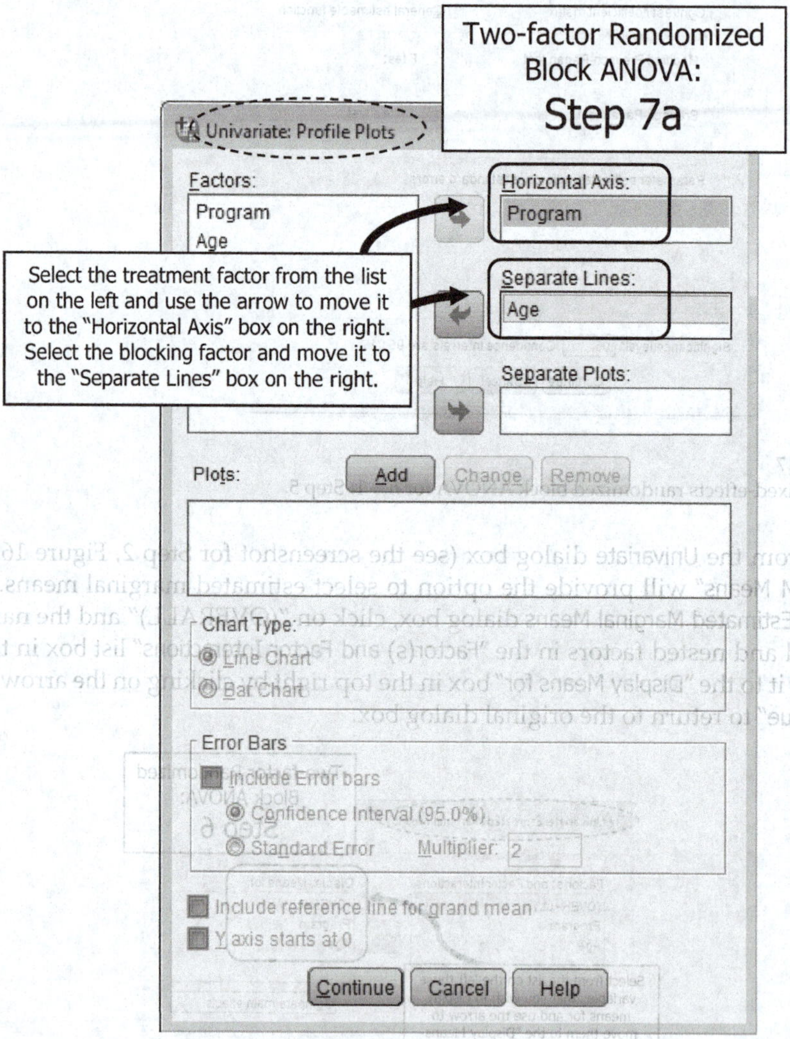

FIGURE 16.19
Two-factor fixed-effects randomized block ANOVA for $n = 1$: Step 7a.

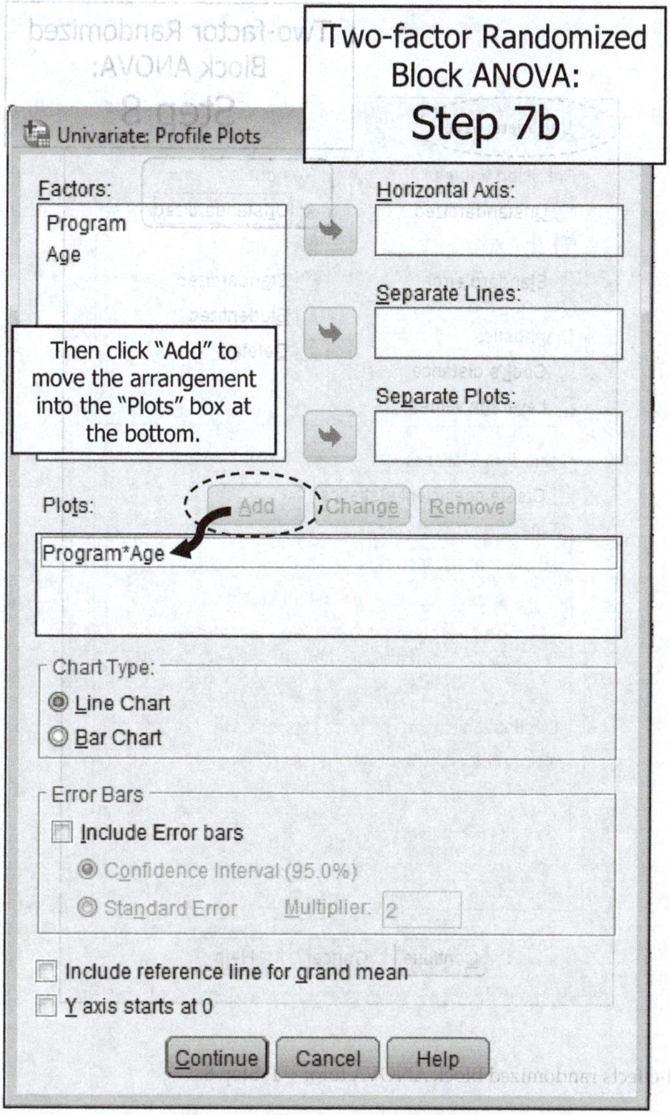

FIGURE 16.20 Two-factor fixed-effects randomized block ANOVA for $n = 1$: Step 7b.

Step 8. From the Univariate dialog box (see the screenshot for Step 2, Figure 16.14), click on "Save" to select those elements you want to save. Here we save the unstandardized residuals to use later to examine the extent to which normality and independence are met. Thus, place a checkmark in the box next to "Unstandardized." Click "Continue" to return to the main Univariate dialog box. From there, click on "OK" to return and generate the output.

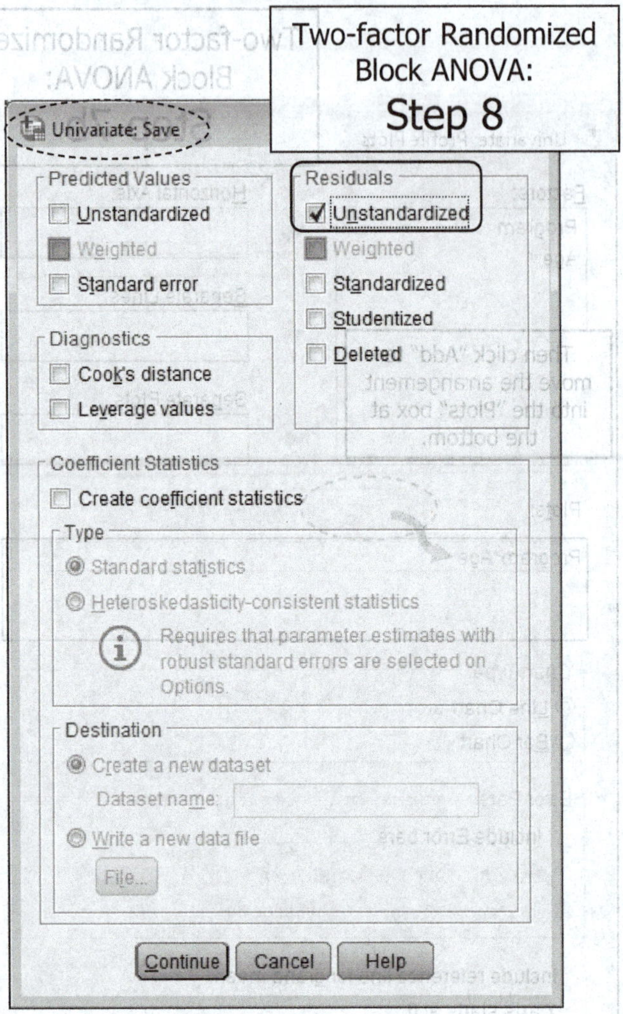

FIGURE 16.21
Two-factor fixed-effects randomized block ANOVA for $n = 1$: Step 8.

16.3.2.1 Interpreting the Output

Annotated results are presented in Table 16.12.

16.3.3 Computing the Two-Factor Fixed-Effects Randomized Block ANOVA for $n > 1$ Using SPSS

To run a two-factor randomized block ANOVA for $n > 1$, the procedures are exactly the same as with the regular two-factor ANOVA. However, the adjusted F tests are not available.

TABLE 16.12

Two-Factor Randomized Block ANOVA for $n = 1$ SPSS Results for the Exercise Program Example

Between-Subjects Factors

		Value Label	N
Exercise program	1.00	1/week	4
	2.00	2/week	4
	3.00	3/week	4
	4.00	4/week	4
Age	1.00	20 years old	4
	2.00	30 years old	4
	3.00	40 years old	4
	4.00	50 years old	4

The table labeled "Between-Subjects Factors" lists the variable names and sample sizes for the levels of treatment factor (i.e., 'exercise program') and the blocking factor (i.e., 'age').

Descriptive Statistics

Dependent Variable: Weight loss

Exercise program	Age	Mean	Std. Deviation	N
1/week	20 years old	3.0000	.	1
	30 years old	2.0000	.	1
	40 years old	1.0000	.	1
	50 years old	.0000	.	1
	Total	1.5000	1.29099	4
2/week	20 years old	6.0000	.	1
	30 years old	5.0000	.	1
	40 years old	4.0000	.	1
	50 years old	2.0000	.	1
	Total	4.2500	1.70783	4
3/week	20 years old	10.0000	.	1
	30 years old	8.0000	.	1
	40 years old	7.0000	.	1
	50 years old	6.0000	.	1
	Total	7.7500	1.70783	4
4/week	20 years old	9.0000	.	1
	30 years old	7.0000	.	1
	40 years old	8.0000	.	1
	50 years old	7.0000	.	1
	Total	7.7500	.95743	4
Total	20 years old	7.0000	3.16228	4
	30 years old	5.5000	2.64575	4
	40 years old	5.0000	3.16228	4
	50 years old	3.7500	3.30404	4
	Total	5.3125	3.00486	16

The table labeled "Descriptive Statistics" provides basic descriptive statistics (means, standard deviations, and sample sizes) for each treatment factor-blocking factor combination.

Because there was only one individual per age group in each exercise program, there is no within cell variation to calculate (and thus missing values for the standard deviation).

(continued)

TABLE 16.12 (continued)

Two-Factor Randomized Block ANOVA for $n = 1$ SPSS Results for the Exercise Program Example

Comparing p to α, we find a statistically significant difference in weight loss based for both exercise program and age group. These are omnibus tests. We will look at *post hoc* tests to determine which exercise programs and age groups statistically differ on weight loss.

Partial eta squared is one measure of effect size calculated as:

$$\eta^2 = \frac{SS_{program}}{SS_{program} + SS_{error}}$$

$$\eta^2 = \frac{110.187}{110.187 + 3.563} = .969$$

Tests of Between-Subjects Effects

Dependent Variable: Weight loss

Source	Type III Sum of Squares	df	Mean Square	F	Sig.	Partial Eta Squared	Noncent. Parameter	Observed Power[b]
Corrected Model	131.875[a]	6	21.979	55.526	.000	.974	333.158	1.000
Intercept	451.563	1	451.563	1140.789	.000	.992	1140.789	1.000
Program	110.187	3	36.729	92.789	.000	.969	278.368	1.000
Age	21.688	3	7.229	18.263	.000	.859	54.789	.999
Error	3.563	9	.396					
Total	587.000	16						
Corrected Total	135.438	15						

a. R Squared = .974 (Adjusted R Squared = .956)

b. Computed using alpha = .05

Observed power tells whether our test is powerful enough to detect mean differences if they really exist. Power of 1.00 indicates maximum power, the probability of rejecting the null hypothesis if it is really false is about 100%.

Estimated Marginal Means

1. Grand Mean

Dependent Variable: Weight loss

Mean	Std. Error	95% Confidence Interval Lower Bound	Upper Bound
5.313	.157	4.957	5.668

The 'Grand Mean' (in this case, 5.313) represents the overall mean, regardless of the exercise program or age. The 95% CI represents the CI of the grand mean.

2. Exercise program

Dependent Variable: Weight loss

Exercise program	Mean	Std. Error	95% Confidence Interval Lower Bound	Upper Bound
1/week	1.500	.315	.788	2.212
2/week	4.250	.315	3.538	4.962
3/week	7.750	.315	7.038	8.462
4/week	7.750	.315	7.038	8.462

The table for **"Exercise program"** provides descriptive statistics for each of the programs. In addition to means, the *SE* and 95% CI of the means are reported.

TABLE 16.12 (continued)

Two-Factor Randomized Block ANOVA for $n = 1$ SPSS Results for the Exercise Program Example

3. Age

Dependent Variable: Weight loss

Age	Mean	Std. Error	95% Confidence Interval Lower Bound	Upper Bound
20 years old	7.000	.315	6.288	7.712
30 years old	5.500	.315	4.788	6.212
40 years old	5.000	.315	4.288	5.712
50 years old	3.750	.315	3.038	4.462

The table for **"Age"** provides descriptive statistics for each of the age groups. In addition to means, the *SE* and 95% CI of the means are reported.

Post Hoc Tests

Exercise program

'Mean difference' is simply the difference between the means of the categories of our program factor. For example, the mean difference of exercising once per week and exercising twice per week is calculated as 1.500 – 4.250 = -2.750.

Multiple Comparisons

Dependent Variable: Weight loss

Tukey HSD

(I) Exercise program	(J) Exercise program	Mean Difference (I-J)	Std. Error	Sig.	95% Confidence Interval Lower Bound	Upper Bound
1/week	2/week	-2.7500*	.44488	.001	-4.1388	-1.3612
	3/week	-6.2500*	.44488	.000	-7.6388	-4.8612
	4/week	-6.2500*	.44488	.000	-7.6388	-4.8612
2/week	1/week	2.7500*	.44488	.001	1.3612	4.1388
	3/week	-3.5000*	.44488	.000	-4.8888	-2.1112
	4/week	-3.5000*	.44488	.000	-4.8888	-2.1112
3/week	1/week	6.2500*	.44488	.000	4.8612	7.6388
	2/week	3.5000*	.44488	.000	2.1112	4.8888
	4/week	.0000	.44488	1.000	-1.3888	1.3888
4/week	1/week	6.2500*	.44488	.000	4.8612	7.6388
	2/week	3.5000*	.44488	.000	2.1112	4.8888
	3/week	.0000	.44488	1.000	-1.3888	1.3888

Based on observed means.

The error term is Mean Square(Error) = .396.

*. The mean difference is significant at the .05 level.

'Sig.' denotes the observed *p* value and provides the results of the Tukey *post hoc* procedure. There is a statistically significant mean difference in weight loss for all exercise programs except for exercising 3 vs. 4 times per week ($p = 1.000$). Note there are redundant results presented in the table. The comparison of exercising 1/week vs. 2/week (row 1) is the same as the comparison of 2/week vs. 1/week (row 4).

(*continued*)

TABLE 16.12 (continued)

Two-Factor Randomized Block ANOVA for $n = 1$ SPSS Results for the Exercise Program Example

Homogeneous Subsets

Weight loss

Tukey HSD[a,b]

Exercise program	N	Subset 1	Subset 2	Subset 3
1/week	4	1.5000		
2/week	4		4.2500	
3/week	4			7.7500
4/week	4			7.7500
Sig.		1.000	1.000	1.000

Means for groups in homogeneous subsets are displayed.

Based on observed means.

The error term is Mean Square(Error) = .396.

a. Uses Harmonic Mean Sample Size = 4.000.

b. Alpha = .05.

"Homogenous Subsets" provides a visual representation of the MCP. For each subset, the means that are printed are homogeneous, or not significantly different. For example, in subset 1 the mean weight loss for exercising once per week (regardless of age group) is 1.50. This is statistically significantly different than the mean weight loss for exercising 2, 3, or 4 times per week (as reflected by empty cells in row 1). Similar interpretations are made for contrasts involving exercising 2, 3, and 4 times per week.

Age

'Mean difference' is simply the difference between the means of the age groups (i.e., the blocking factor). For example, the mean weight loss difference of 20 year olds to 30 year olds is calculated as 7.000 − 5.500 = 1.5000.

Dependent Variable: Weight loss

Tukey HSD

(I) Age	(J) Age	Mean Difference (I-J)	Std. Error	Sig.	95% Confidence Interval Lower Bound	95% Confidence Interval Upper Bound
20 years old	30 years old	1.5000*	.44488	.034	.1112	2.8888
	40 years old	2.0000*	.44488	.007	.6112	3.3888
	50 years old	3.2500*	.44488	.000	1.8612	4.6388
30 years old	20 years old	-1.5000*	.44488	.034	-2.8888	-.1112
	40 years old	.5000	.44488	.685	-.8888	1.8888
	50 years old	1.7500*	.44488	.015	.3612	3.1388
40 years old	20 years old	-2.0000*	.44488	.007	-3.3888	-.6112
	30 years old	-.5000	.44488	.685	-1.8888	.8888
	50 years old	1.2500	.44488	.080	-.1388	2.6388
50 years old	20 years old	-3.2500*	.44488	.000	-4.6388	-1.8612
	30 years old	-1.7500*	.44488	.015	-3.1388	-.3612
	40 years old	-1.2500	.44488	.080	-2.6388	.1388

Based on observed means.

The error term is Mean Square(Error) = .396.

*. The mean difference is significant at the .05 level.

'Sig.' denotes the observed p value and provides the results of the Tukey *post hoc* procedure. There is a statistically significant mean difference in weight loss for:

- 20 and 30 year olds ($p = .034$)
- 20 and 40 year olds ($p = .007$)
- 20 and 50 year olds ($p < .001$)
- 30 and 50 year olds ($p = .015$)

Note there are redundant results presented in the table. The comparison of 20 year olds to 30 year olds is the same as the comparison of 30 year olds to 20 year olds, and so forth.

TABLE 16.12 (continued)

Two-Factor Randomized Block ANOVA for $n = 1$ SPSS Results for the Exercise Program Example

Homogeneous Subsets

Weight loss

Tukey HSD[a,b]

Age	N	Subset 1	Subset 2	Subset 3
50 years old	4	3.7500		
40 years old	4	5.0000	5.0000	
30 years old	4		5.5000	
20 years old	4			7.0000
Sig.		.080	.685	1.000

Means for groups in homogeneous subsets are displayed.

Based on observed means.

The error term is Mean Square(Error) = .396.

a. Uses Harmonic Mean Sample Size = 4.000.

b. Alpha = .05.

> **"Homogenous Subsets"** provides a visual representation of the MCP. For each subset, the means that are printed are homogeneous, or not significantly different. For example, in subset 1 the mean weight loss for 50 year olds (regardless of exercise program) is 3.750. This is statistically significantly different than the mean weight loss for individuals in the 30 and 20 year old age groups (as they are not printed in subset 1).

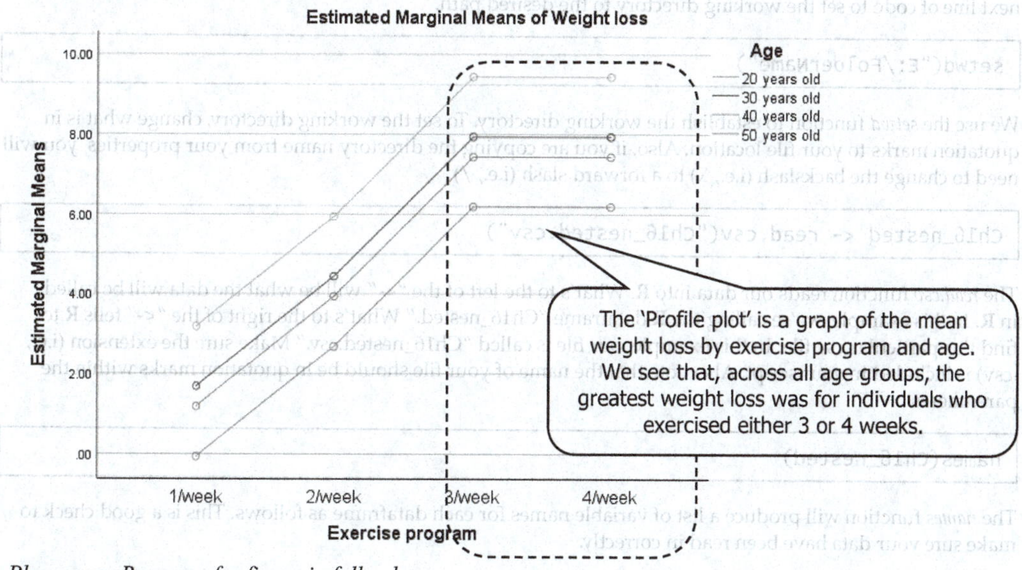

Please see eResource for figure in full color

16.3.4 Computing the Friedman Test Using SPSS

Lastly, the Friedman test can be run as previously described in Chapter 15.

16.4 Computing Hierarchical and Randomized Block Analysis of Variance Models Using R

16.4.1 Two-Factor Hierarchical ANOVA in R

Next we consider **R** for the two-factor hierarchical ANOVA model. The commands are provided within the blocks with additional annotation to assist in understanding how the command works. Should you want to write reminder notes and annotation to yourself as you write the commands in **R** (and we highly encourage doing so), remember that any text that follows a hashtag (i.e., #) is annotation only and not part of the **R** code. Thus, you can write annotations directly into **R** with hashtags. We encourage this practice so that when you call up the commands in the future, you'll understand what the various lines of code are doing. You may think you'll remember what you did. However, trust us. There is a good chance that you won't. Thus, consider it best practice when using **R** to annotate heavily!

16.4.1.1 Reading Data Into R

```
getwd()
```

R is always pointed to a directory on your computer. The *get working directory* function can be used to determine to which directory **R** is pointed. We will assume that we need to change the working directory, and will use the next line of code to set the working directory to the desired path.

```
setwd("E:/FolderName")
```

We use the *setwd* function to establish the working directory. To set the working directory, change what is in quotation marks to your file location. Also, if you are copying the directory name from your properties, you will need to change the backslash (i.e., \) to a forward slash (i.e., /).

```
Ch16_nested <- read.csv("Ch16_nested.csv")
```

The *read.csv* function reads our data into **R**. What's to the left of the "<-" will be what the data will be called in **R**. In this example, we're calling the **R** dataframe "Ch16_nested." What's to the right of the "<-" tells **R** to find this particular csv file. In this example, our file is called "Ch16_nested.csv." Make sure the extension (i.e., .csv) is included in your script. Also note that the name of your file should be in quotation marks within the parentheses.

```
names(Ch16_nested)
```

The *names* function will produce a list of variable names for each dataframe as follows. This is a good check to make sure your data have been read in correctly.

```
[1] "Tx"   "Intvnst"   "Quality"
```

```
View(Ch16_nested)
```

FIGURE 16.22
Reading data into R.

The **View** function will let you view the dataset in spreadsheet format in RStudio.

```
Ch16_nested$TxF <- factor(Ch16_nested$Tx,
                          labels = c("massage therapy", "music therapy"))
Ch16_nested$IntvnstF <- factor(Ch16_nested$Intvnst,
                          labels = c(1,2,3,4))
```

This script will create a new variable in our dataframe named "TxF." We use the *factor* function to define the variable "Tx" as categorical with the two groups defined here (i.e., *massage therapy, music therapy*). We do this similarly for the "Intvnst" variable. What is to the left of "<-" in the script creates two new variables in our dataframe named "TxF" and "IntvnstF." We could have also done this by just renaming the variables rather than creating new ones.

```
summary(Ch16_nested)
```

The *summary* function will produce basic descriptive statistics on all the variables in your dataframe. This is a great way to quickly check to see if the data have been read in correctly and to get a feel for your data, if you haven't already. The output from the summary statement for this dataframe looks like this. Because we defined IntvnstF and TxF as factors, we are provided only the frequencies for each category in those variables.

```
      Tx           Intvnst          Quality       IntvnstF              TxF
Min.   :1.0   Min.   :1.00   Min.   : 1.000   1:6       massage therapy:12
1st Qu.:1.0   1st Qu.:1.75   1st Qu.: 3.750   2:6       music therapy  :12
Median :1.5   Median :2.50   Median : 6.500   3:6
Mean   :1.5   Mean   :2.50   Mean   : 7.083   4:6
3rd Qu.:2.0   3rd Qu.:3.25   3rd Qu.:10.250
Max.   :2.0   Max.   :4.00   Max.   :15.000
```

FIGURE 16.22 (continued)
Reading data into **R**.

16.4.1.2 Generating the Two-Factor Nested ANOVA Model

```
install.packages("nlme")
library(nlme)
```

The *install.packages* and *library* functions will be used to, respectively, install the *nlme* package and load it into our library. This packages is used for linear and nonlinear mixed effects modeling.

```
Ch16nest = aov(Quality ~ TxF +Error(IntvnstF), Ch16_nested)
```

The *aov* function will be used to define our model. We will create an object from the results called "Ch16nest." The dependent variable is "Quality" and we include one nonnested factor, *TxF*, and one random effect for the interventionist, defined as *Error(IntvnstF)*. The dataframe is Ch16_nested.

```
summary(Ch16nest)
```

The *summary* function will output the results of our model, *Ch16nest*.

FIGURE 16.23
Generating the two-factor nested ANOVA.

```
Error: IntvnstF
          Df Sum Sq Mean Sq F value Pr(>F)
TxF        1  337.5  337.5    59.56 0.0164 *
Residuals  2   11.3    5.7
---
Signif. codes: 0 '***' 0.001 '**' 0.01 '*' 0.05 '.' 0.1 ' ' 1

Error: Within
          Df Sum Sq Mean Sq F value Pr(>F)
Residuals 20    119    5.95
```

FIGURE 16.23 (continued)
Generating the two-factor nested ANOVA.

16.4.1.3 Generating a Post Hoc Test

```
install.packages("TukeyC")
library(TukeyC)
```

The *install.packages* and *library* functions will be used to, respectively, install the *TukeyC* package and load it into our library. This package is used for post hoc analyses.

```
tuk = TukeyC(Ch16_nested,
             model = 'Quality ~ TxF + Error(IntvnstF)',
             error = 'IntvnstF',
             which = 'TxF',
             fl1=1,
             sig.level = 0.05)
```

The *TukeyC* function will be used to generate the post hoc test. The dataframe is Ch16_nested. We define our model, error, and predictor for which we are examining the post hoc results (in this example, *TxF*).

```
summary(tuk)
```

The *summary* function will output the results.

```
Groups of means at sig.level = 0.05
                Means G1 G2
music therapy   10.83 a
massage therapy  3.33    b

Matrix of the difference of means above diagonal and
respective p-values of the Tukey test below diagonal values
                music therapy massage therapy
music therapy           0.000             7.5
massage therapy         0.016             0.0
```

FIGURE 16.24
Generating a post hoc test.

16.4.2 Two-Factor Fixed-Effects Randomized Block ANOVA in R

Next we consider **R** for the two-factor fixed-effects randomized block ANOVA model. The commands are provided within the blocks with additional annotation to assist in understanding how the command works. As noted previously, should you want to write reminder notes and annotation to yourself as you write the commands in **R**, any text that follows a hashtag (i.e., #) is annotation only and not part of the **R** code.

16.4.2.1 Reading Data Into R

```
getwd()
```

R is always pointed to a directory on your computer. The *get working directory* function can be used to determine to which directory **R** is pointed. We will assume that we need to change the working directory, and will use the next line of code to set the working directory to the desired path.

```
setwd("E:/FolderName")
```

We use the *setwd* function to establish the working directory. To set the working directory, change what is in quotation marks to your file location. Also, if you are copying the directory name from your properties, you will need to change the backslash (i.e., \) to a forward slash (i.e., /).

```
Ch16_block <- read.csv("Ch16_block.csv")
```

The *read.csv* function reads our data into **R**. What's to the left of the "<-" will be what the data will be called in **R**. In this example, we're calling the **R** dataframe "Ch16_block." What's to the right of the "<-" tells **R** to find this particular csv file. In this example, our file is called "Ch16_block.csv." Make sure the extension (i.e., .csv) is included in your script. Also note that the name of your file should be in quotation marks within the parentheses.

```
names(Ch16_block)
```

The *names* function will produce a list of variable names for each dataframe as follows. This is a good check to make sure your data have been read in correctly.

```
[1] "Program" "Age" "WtLoss"
```

```
View(Ch16_block)
```

The *View* function will let you view the dataset in spreadsheet format in RStudio.

```
Ch16_block$ProgramF <- factor(Ch16_block$Program,
                       labels=c("1/week", "2/week","3/week","4/week"))
```

The *factor* command is used to define the categorical variables. What is to the left of "<-" is creating a new variable in our dataframe (i.e., Ch16_block), named "ProgramF." To the right of "<-" is defining the variable Program in the dataframe as a categorical variable with four categories with the labels defined here.

```
Ch16_block$Age <-ordered(Ch16_block$Age,
                 labels=c("20", "30", "40", "50"))
```

The command to the left of "<-" is writing over the variable in our dataframe (i.e., Ch16_block), named Age and defining it as an ordinal variable. To the right of "<-" is defining the variable Age in the dataframe with four categories which have labels of 20, 30, 40, and 50.

FIGURE 16.25
Reading data into **R**.

```
summary(Ch16_block)
```

The *summary* command will produce basic descriptive statistics on all the variables in your dataframe. This is a great way to quickly check to see if the data have been read in correctly and get a feel for your data, if you haven't already. The output from the summary statement for this dataframe looks like this.

```
    Program       Age      WtLoss             ProgramF
Min.    :1.00   20:4  Min.    : 0.000    1/week:4
1st Qu.:1.75   30:4  1st Qu.: 2.750    2/week:4
Median :2.50   40:4  Median : 6.000    3/week:4
Mean   :2.50   50:4  Mean   : 5.312    4/week:4
3rd Qu.:3.25         3rd Qu.: 7.250
Max.   :4.00         Max.   : 10.000
```

FIGURE 16.25 (continued)
Reading data into R.

16.4.2.2 Generating the Two-Factor Fixed-Effects Randomized Block ANOVA

```
BlockModel <- aov(WtLoss ~ ProgramF + Age, Ch16_block)
```

The *aov* function is used to generate our model randomized block ANOVA model. We create an object from those results called "BlockModel." "WtLoss" is our dependent variable. "ProgramF" is the treatment (i.e., independent variable), and "Age" is the blocking factor. We are using data from the dataframe Ch16_block.

```
summary(BlockModel)
```

Because we created an object from our model, we run the *summary* function to output the results.

```
           Df Sum Sq Mean Sq F value    Pr(>F)
ProgramF    3 110.19   36.73   92.79 4.35e-07 ***
Age         3  21.69    7.23   18.26 0.000362 ***
Residuals   9   3.56    0.40
---
Signif. codes: 0 '***' 0.001 '**' 0.01 '*' 0.05 '.' 0.1 ' ' 1
```

FIGURE 16.26
Generating the two-factor fixed-effects randomized block ANOVA.

16.5 Data Screening

16.5.1 Examining Assumptions for the Two-Factor Hierarchical ANOVA

The assumptions for the two-factor hierarchical ANOVA that we will examine include normality homogeneity of variance, and independence of observations within cells.

16.5.1.1 Normality

We will use the residuals (which were requested and created through the "Save" option) to examine the extent to which normality was met.

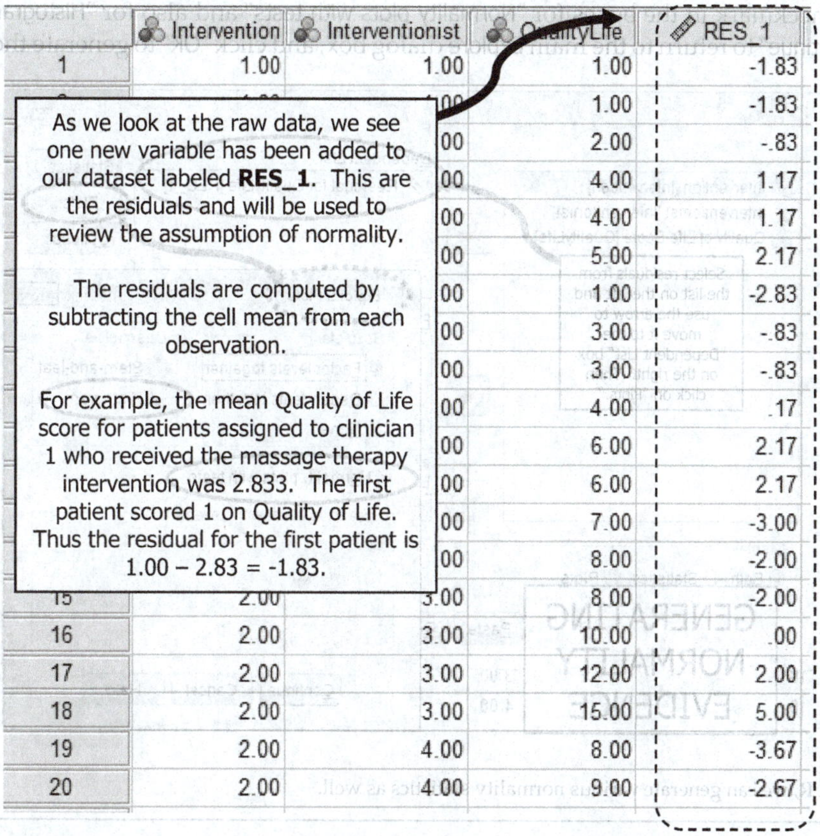

Intervention
Interventionist
QualityLife
RES_1
As we look at the raw data, we see one new variable has been added to our dataset labeled **RES_1**. This are the residuals and will be used to review the assumption of normality.
The residuals are computed by subtracting the cell mean from each observation.
For example, the mean Quality of Life score for patients assigned to clinician 1 who received the massage therapy intervention was 2.833. The first patient scored 1 on Quality of Life. Thus the residual for the first patient is 1.00 – 2.83 = -1.83.

Working in **R**, we can save the unstandardized residuals using the following command. The *proj* function will create a matrix giving projections of the data given the terms of the model. That matrix will be used to compute residuals. We created a new variable in our dataframe called "unstandardizedResiduals" (i.e., "Ch16_nested$unstandardizedResiduals").

```
Ch16nest.pr <- proj(Ch16nest)
Ch16_nested$unstandardizedResiduals <- Ch16nest.pr[['Within']][,'Residuals']
```

FIGURE 16.27
Two-factor hierarchical ANOVA residuals.

As described in earlier ANOVA chapters, understanding the distributional shape, specifically whether normality is a reasonable assumption, is important. For the two-factor hierarchical ANOVA, the residuals should be normally distributed.

As in previous chapters, we use "Explore" to examine whether the assumption of normality is met. The general steps for accessing Explore have been presented in previous chapters and will not be repeated here. Click the residual and move it into the "Dependent List" box by clicking on the arrow button. The procedures for selecting normality statistics were presented in Chapter 6 and remain the same here: click on "Plots" in the upper right corner.

Place a checkmark in the boxes for "Normality plots with tests" and also for "Histogram." Then click "Continue" to return to the main Explore dialog box, and click "OK" to generate the output.

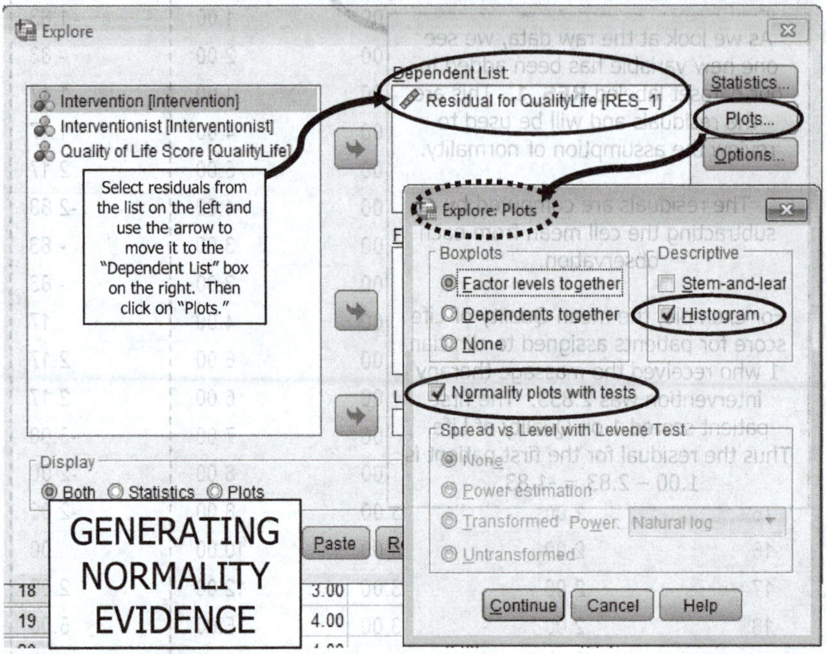

Working in **R**, we can generate various normality statistics as well.

```
install.packages("pastecs")
```

The *install.packages* command will install the *pastecs* package which we will use to generate various forms of normality evidence.

```
library(pastecs)
```

The *library* function will load the *pastecs* package.

```
stat.desc(Ch16_nested$unstandardizedResiduals,
          norm = TRUE)
```

The *stat.desc* will generate normality indices on the variable "unstandardizedResiduals" in the dataframe Ch16_nested as follows. The *norm=TRUE* command will produce Shapiro-Wilk results (*SW*), which are displayed as *normtest.W* (which is the *S-W* statistic value) and *normtest.p* (which is the observed probability value). Here, we see *S-W* = .960 and the related $p = .44$.

We see skew (.249) and kurtosis (−.976), along with $SW = .960$, $p = .442$ for the "unstandardizedResidual" variable. All indicate the assumption of normality has been met. As we know, we can divide the skew and kurtosis values by their standard errors to get a standardized value that can be used to determine if the skew and/or kurtosis is statistically different from zero. Since this output provides "2SE," we would simply divide this value by 2 to arrive at the standard error.

FIGURE 16.28
Generating normality evidence.

Note: You may have noticed that the skewness and kurtosis value that we've just generated differs from what we found in SPSS, which was skew = .284 and kurtosis = −.693 This is because there are different ways to calculate skewness and kurtosis. Let's use another package in **R** to calculate these statistics with different algorithms.

```
     nbr.val        nbr.null          nbr.na            min
2.400000e+01   0.000000e+00   0.000000e+00  -3.666667e+00

         max           range             sum         median
5.000000e+00   8.666667e+00   7.216450e-16  -3.333333e-01

        mean         SE.mean    CI.mean.0.95            var
3.008661e-17   4.643056e-01   9.604894e-01   5.173913e+00

     std.dev        coef.var        skewness       skew.2SE
2.274624e+00   7.560253e+16   2.494060e-01   2.640553e-01

    kurtosis        kurt.2SE     normtest.W    normtest.p
-9.764138e-01-5.319450e-01   9.601899e-01   4.422514e-01
```

```
install.packages("e1071")
```

The *install.packages* function will install the **e1071** package which we will use to generate skewness and kurtosis.

```
library(e1071)
```

The *library* function will load the **e1071** package.

```
skewness(Ch16_block$unstandardizedResiduals, type=3)
skewness(Ch16_block$unstandardizedResiduals, type=2)
skewness(Ch16_block$unstandardizedResiduals, type=1)
```

The *skewness* function will generate skewness statistics on the variable(s) we specify. The "type=" script defines how skewness is calculated. Specifying "type=2" will use the algorithm that is used by SPSS. Readers interested in learning more, including the algorithms for each of the three methods, are encouraged to review Joanes and Gill (1998). We see that using "type=2," our skew is .284, the same value as generated using SPSS.

```
# skewness(Ch16_nested$unstandardizedResiduals, type=3)
[1] 0.249406

# skewness(Ch16_nested$unstandardizedResiduals, type=2)
[1] 0.2839088

# skewness(Ch16_nested$unstandardizedResiduals, type=1)
[1] 0.2658471
```

```
kurtosis(Ch16_block$unstandardizedResiduals, type=3)
kurtosis(Ch16_block$unstandardizedResiduals, type=2)
kurtosis(Ch16_block$unstandardizedResiduals, type=1)
```

The *kurtosis* function will generate kurtosis statistics on the variable(s) we specify. The "type=" script defines how kurtosis is calculated. Specifying "type=2" will use the algorithm that is used by SPSS. Readers interested in learning more, including the algorithms for each of the three methods, are encouraged to review Joanes and Gill (1998). We see that using "type=2," our kurtosis is −.693, the same value as generated using SPSS.

FIGURE 16.28 (continued)
Generating normality evidence.

```
# kurtosis(Ch16_nested$unstandardizedResiduals, type=3)
[1] -0.9764138

# kurtosis(Ch16_nested$unstandardizedResiduals, type=2)
[1] -0.6927686

# kurtosis(Ch16_nested$unstandardizedResiduals, type=1)
[1] -0.7966245
```

```
shapiro.test(Ch16_nested$unstandardizedResiduals)
```

Had we wanted to generate only the Shapiro-Wilk test, the *shapiro.test* function could be used.

```
        Shapiro-Wilk normality test

data: Ch16_nested$unstandardizedResiduals
W = 0.96019, p-value = 0.4423
```

Working in **R**, another way to test for normality is **D'Agostino's test** for skewness and the **Bonett-Seier test** for **Geary's kurtosis**.

```
install.packages("moments")
library(moments)
```

To conduct D'Agostino's test, we first have to install the *moments* package and then load it into our library. The null hypothesis for this test is that skewness equals zero. Thus, a statistically significant D'Agostino's test would indicate that there is statistically significant skewness.

```
agostino.test(Ch16_nested$unstandardizedResiduals)
```

The function *agostino.test* is generated using the variable "unstandardizedResiduals" from our Ch16_nested dataframe. The results suggest evidence of normality as $p = .526$, greater than alpha.

```
        D'Agostino skewness test

data:  Ch16_nested$unstandardizedResiduals
skew = 0.26585, z = 0.63406, p-value = 0.526
alternative hypothesis: data have a skewness
```

```
bonett.test((Ch16_nested$unstandardizedResiduals))
```

The *bonett.test* function, generated using the variable "unstandardizedResiduals" from our Ch16_nested dataframe, performs the Bonett-Seier test for Geary's kurtosis for data that are normally distributed. The null hypothesis states that data should have a Geary's kurtosis value equal to $\sqrt{2/\pi} = .7979$. The results suggest evidence of normality as $p = .147$, greater than alpha.

```
        Bonett-Seier test for Geary kurtosis

data: (Ch16_nested$unstandardizedResiduals)
tau = 1.9167, z = -1.4508, p-value = 0.1468
alternative hypothesis: kurtosis is not equal to sqrt(2/pi)
```

FIGURE 16.28 (continued)
Generating normality evidence.

16.5.1.1.1 Interpreting Normality Evidence

By this point, we have had a substantial amount of practice in interpreting quite a range of normality statistics and interpret them again in reference to the hierarchical ANOVA model assumption of normality. The skewness statistic of the residuals is .284 and kurtosis is −.693—both being within the range of what would be considered normal (i.e., an absolute value of 2.0), suggesting some evidence of normality. Working in **R** (see Figure 16.28), D'Agostino's test (D'Agostino, 1970) can be used to examine the null hypothesis that skewness equals zero. Thus, a statistically significant D'Agostino's test would indicate that there is statistically significant skewness. For kurtosis, we can use the Bonett-Seier test for Geary's kurtosis (Bonett & Seier, 2002) for data that are normally distributed. The null hypothesis states that data should have a Geary's kurtosis value equal to $\sqrt{2/\pi} = .7979$. Thus, a statistically significant Bonett-Seier test for Geary's kurtosis would indicate that there is statistically significant kurtosis. Thus, with these tests, as with Kolmogorov-Smirnov and Shapiro-Wilk, we do *not* want to find statistically significant results—which is exactly what was found in this illustration.

As suggested by the skewness statistic, the histogram of residuals is slightly positively skewed, and the histogram also provides a visual display of the slightly platykurtic distribution.

Descriptives

			Statistic	Std. Error
Residual for QualityLife	Mean		.0000	.46431
	95% Confidence Interval for Mean	Lower Bound	-.9605	
		Upper Bound	.9605	
	5% Trimmed Mean		-.0648	
	Median		-.3333	
	Variance		5.174	
	Std. Deviation		2.27462	
	Minimum		-3.67	
	Maximum		5.00	
	Range		8.67	
	Interquartile Range		4.08	
	Skewness		.284	.472
	Kurtosis		-.693	.918

FIGURE 16.29
Normality evidence.

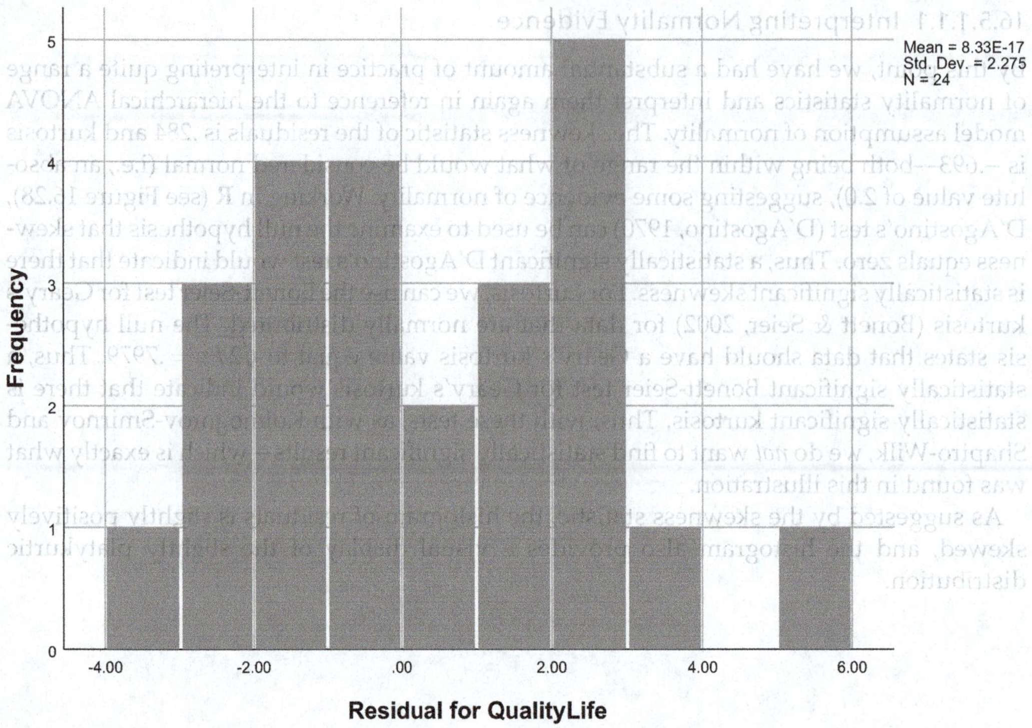

Working in **R**, we can generate a histogram using the *ggplot2* package.

```
install.packages("ggplot2")
```

The *install.packages* function will install the *ggplot2* package which we can use to create various graphs and plots. Remember, if this package has previously been installed, there is no need to install again.

```
library(ggplot2)
```

The *library* function will load the *ggplot2* package.

```
qplot(Ch16_nested$unstandardizedResiduals,
      geom="histogram",
      binwidth=0.5,
      main = "Histogram of Unstandardized Residuals",
      xlab = "Unstandardized Residual", ylab = "Count",
      fill=I("gray"),
      col=I("white"))
```

Using the *qplot* command, we create a histogram (i.e., geom = "histogram") from our dataframe (i.e., Ch16_nested) using the variable "unstandardizedResiduals." We can add a few commands to change the width of the bars (i.e., *binwidth=0.5*), color of the bars (i.e., *fill=I("gray")*), and outline of the bars (i.e., *col=I("white")*). We can also add a title (i.e., *main = "Histogram of Unstandardized Residuals"*) and change the X and Y axes (*xlab = "Unstandardized Residual", ylab = "Count"*).

FIGURE 16.30
Histogram.

There are a few other statistics that can be used to gauge normality. The formal test of normality, the Shapiro-Wilk test (*SW*) (Shapiro & Wilk, 1965), provides evidence of the extent to which our sample distribution is statistically different from a normal distribution. The output for the Shapiro-Wilk test is presented in Figure 16.31 and suggests that our sample distribution for the residual is not statistically significantly different than what would be expected from a normal distribution as the *p* value is greater than α.

Tests of Normality

	Kolmogorov-Smirnov[a]			Shapiro-Wilk		
	Statistic	df	Sig.	Statistic	df	Sig.
Residual for QualityLife	.123	24	.200*	.960	24	**.442**

*. This is a lower bound of the true significance.

a. Lilliefors Significance Correction

Working in **R**, we used the *stat.desc* function from the *pastecs* package to generate *SW* earlier, along with many other statistics.

```
shapiro.test(Ch16_nested$unstandardizedResiduals)
```

Had we wanted to generate only the Shapiro-Wilk test, the *shapiro.test* function could be used.

```
        Shapiro-Wilk normality test

data: Ch16_nested$unstandardizedResiduals
W = 0.96019, p-value = 0.4423
```

FIGURE 16.31
Shapiro-Wilk test of normality.

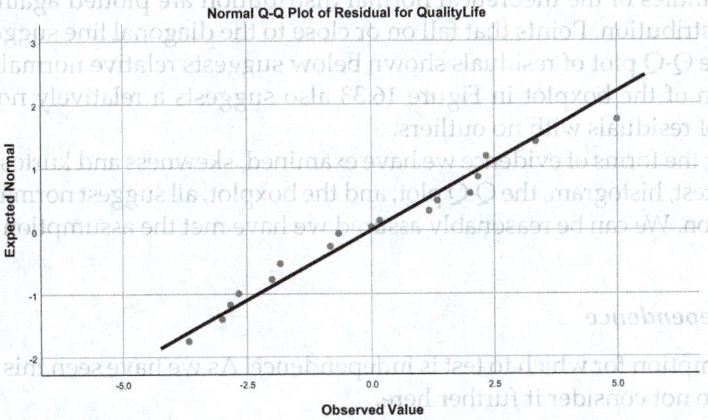

Working in **R,** we can use the *qplot* command to create a Q-Q plot of unstandardized residuals.

```
qplot(sample=unstandardizedResiduals,
    data = Ch16_nested)
```

FIGURE 16.32
Normal Q-Q plot.

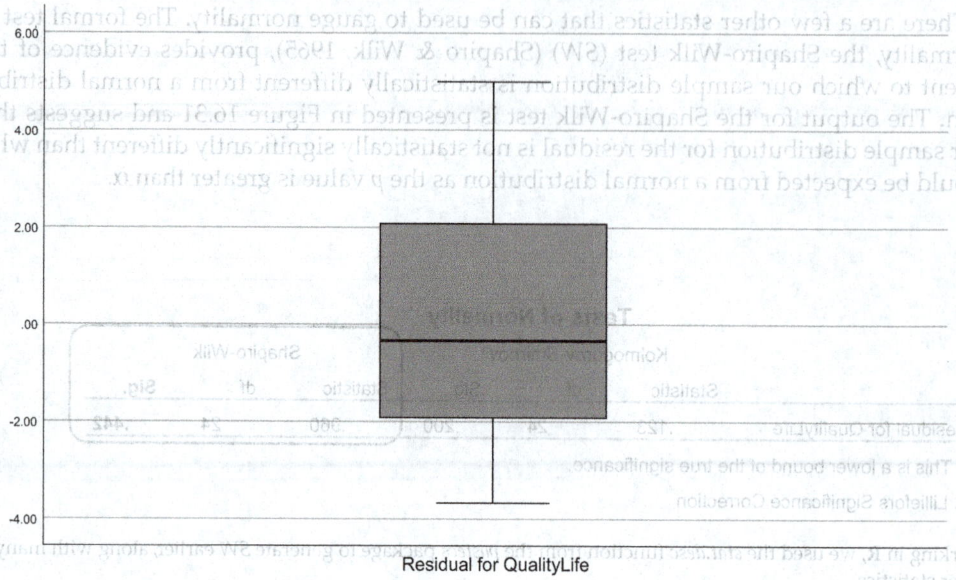

Working in **R,** we can generate a boxplot for unstandardized residuals using the *boxplot* function. To label the *Y* axis, we include the *ylab* command.

```
boxplot(Ch16_nested$unstandardizedResiduals,
        ylab="unstandardized residual")
```

FIGURE 16.33
Residual Boxplot.

Quantile-quantile (Q-Q) plots are also often examined to determine evidence of normality, where quantiles of the theoretical normal distribution are plotted against quantiles of the sample distribution. Points that fall on or close to the diagonal line suggest evidence of normality. The Q-Q plot of residuals shown below suggests relative normality.

Examination of the boxplot in Figure 16.33 also suggests a relatively normal distributional shape of residuals with no outliers.

Considering the forms of evidence we have examined, skewness and kurtosis statistics, the Shapiro-Wilk test, histogram, the Q-Q plot, and the boxplot, all suggest normality is a reasonable assumption. We can be reasonably assured we have met the assumption of normality.

16.5.1.2 Independence

Another assumption for which to test is independence. As we have seen this tested in other designs, we do not consider it further here.

16.5.1.3 Homogeneity of Variance

Homogeneity is the assumption of equal variances. In SPSS, Levene's test is used to examine this assumption. The results are provided in Table 16.11 and suggest that the variance of the error term is constant across groups in our model. In other words, we have met the homogeneity of variance assumption.

16.5.2 Examining Assumptions for the Two-Factor Fixed-Effects Randomized Block ANOVA for $n = 1$

The assumptions for the two-factor randomized block ANOVA that we will examine include normality, independence, and homoscedasticity (or homogeneity of variance).

16.5.2.1 Normality

We use the residuals (which were requested and created through the "Save" option when generating our model) to examine the extent to which normality was met. As shown in previous ANOVA chapters, understanding the distributional shape, specifically the extent to which normality is a reasonable assumption, is important. For the two-factor randomized block ANOVA, the residuals should be a normal distribution. Because the steps for generating normality evidence were presented previously in the chapter for the two-factor hierarchical ANOVA model, they will not be reiterated here.

16.5.2.1.1 Interpreting Normality Evidence

By this point, we have had a substantial amount of practice in interpreting quite a range of normality statistics. Here we interpret them again, only now in reference to the two-factor randomized block ANOVA model. The skewness statistic of the residuals is −.154 and kurtosis is −.496—both being within the range of what would be considered normal (i.e., an absolute value of 2.0), suggesting some evidence of normality.

Descriptives

			Statistic	Std. Error
Residual for WeightLoss	Mean		.0000	.12183
	95% Confidence Interval for Mean	Lower Bound	-.2597	
		Upper Bound	.2597	
	5% Trimmed Mean		.0069	
	Median		.0625	
	Variance		.238	
	Std. Deviation		.48734	
	Minimum		-.94	
	Maximum		.81	
	Range		1.75	
	Interquartile Range		.87	
	Skewness		-.154	.564
	Kurtosis		-.496	1.091

FIGURE 16.34
Two-factor randomized block ANOVA normality evidence.

Working in **R**, we can generate various normality statistics as well.

```
install.packages("pastecs")
```

The *install.packages* function will install the *pastecs* package which we will use to generate various forms of normality evidence.

```
library(pastecs)
```

The *library* function will load the *pastecs* package.

```
stat.desc(Ch16_block$unstandardizedResiduals,
norm = TRUE
```

The *stat.desc* will generate normality indices on the variable "unstandardizedResiduals" in the dataframe Ch16_block as follows. The *norm=TRUE* command will produce Shapiro-Wilk results (*SW*). We see skew (−.127) and kurtosis (−.985) along with *SW* = .965, *p* = .757 for the "unstandardizedResidual" variable. All indicate the assumption of normality has been met. As we know, we can divide the skew and kurtosis values by their standard errors to get a standardized value that can be used to determine if the skew and/or kurtosis is statistically different from zero. Since this output provides "2SE," we would simply divide this value by 2 to arrive at the standard error.

Note: You may have noticed that the skewness and kurtosis value that we've just generated differs from what we found in SPSS, which was skew = .284 and kurtosis = −.693 This is because there are different ways to calculate skewness and kurtosis. Let's use another package in **R** to calculate these statistics with different algorithms.

```
      nbr.val        nbr.null          nbr.na             min
 1.600000e+01    0.000000e+00    0.000000e+00   -9.375000e-01

          max           range             sum          median
 8.125000e-01    1.750000e+00   -5.551115e-17    6.250000e-02

         mean         SE.mean    CI.mean.0.95             var
-3.469447e-18    1.218349e-01    2.596850e-01    2.375000e-01

      std.dev        coef.var        skewness        skew.2SE
 4.873397e-01   -1.404661e+17   -1.265598e-01   -1.121373e-01

     kurtosis        kurt.2SE      normtest.W      normtest.p
-9.849269e-01   -4.514808e-01    9.652256e-01    7.566056e-01
```

```
install.packages("e1071")
```

The *install.packages* function will install the **e1071** package which we will use to generate skewness and kurtosis.

```
library(e1071)
```

The *library* function will load the **e1071** package.

```
skewness(Ch16_block$unstandardizedResiduals, type=3)
skewness(Ch16_block$unstandardizedResiduals, type=2)
skewness(Ch16_block$unstandardizedResiduals, type=1)
```

FIGURE 16.34 (continued)
Two-factor randomized block ANOVA normality evidence.

The *skewness* function will generate skewness statistics on the variable(s) we specify. The "type=" script defines how skewness is calculated. Specifying "type=2" will use the algorithm that is used by SPSS. Readers interested in learning more, including the algorithms for each of the three methods, are encouraged to review Joanes and Gill (1998). We see that using "type=2," our skew is −.154, the same value as generated using SPSS.

```
# skewness(Ch16_block$unstandardizedResiduals, type=3)
[1] -0.1265598

# skewness(Ch16_block$unstandardizedResiduals, type=2)
[1] -0.1542825

# skewness(Ch16_block$unstandardizedResiduals, type=1)
[1] -0.1394245
```

```
kurtosis(Ch16_block$unstandardizedResiduals, type=3)
kurtosis(Ch16_block$unstandardizedResiduals, type=2)
kurtosis(Ch16_block$unstandardizedResiduals, type=1)
```

The *kurtosis* function will generate kurtosis statistics on the variable(s) we specify. The "type=" script defines how kurtosis is calculated. Specifying "type=2" will use the algorithm that is used by SPSS. Readers interested in learning more, including the algorithms for each of the three methods, are encouraged to review Joanes and Gill (1998). We see that using "type=2," our kurtosis is −.496, the same value as generated using SPSS.

```
# kurtosis(Ch16_block$unstandardizedResiduals, type=3)
[1] -0.9849269

# kurtosis(Ch16_block$unstandardizedResiduals, type=2)
[1] -0.4964841

# kurtosis(Ch16_block$unstandardizedResiduals, type=1)
[1] -0.7072946
```

FIGURE 16.34 (continued)
Two-factor randomized block ANOVA normality evidence.

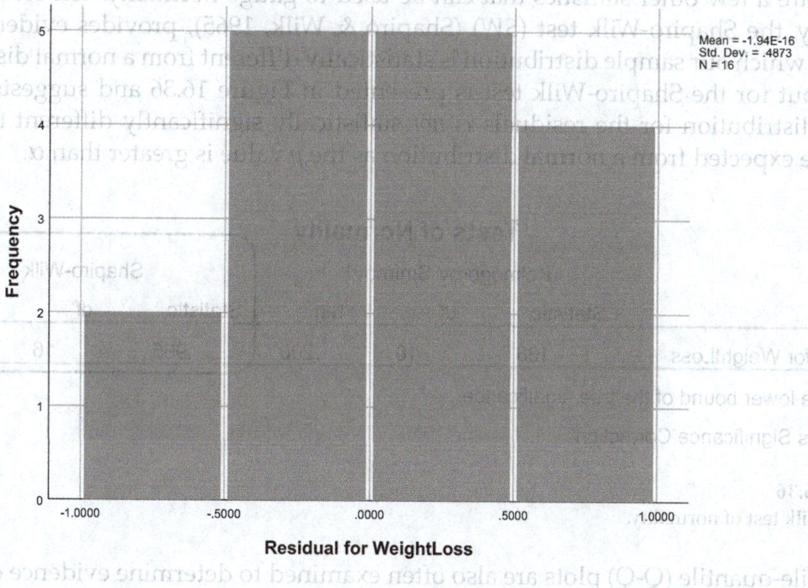

FIGURE 16.35
Histogram.

Working in R, we can generate a histogram using the *ggplot2* package.

```
install.packages("ggplot2")
```

The *install.packages* function will install the *ggplot2* package which we can use to create various graphs and plots. Remember, if this package has previously been installed, there is no need to install again.

```
library(ggplot2)
```

The *library* function will load the *ggplot2* package.

```
qplot(Ch16_block$unstandardizedResiduals,
      geom="histogram",
      binwidth=0.5,
      main = "Histogram of Unstandardized Residuals",
      xlab = "Unstandardized Residual", ylab = "Count",
      fill=I("gray"),
      col=I("white"))
```

Using the *qplot* function, we create a histogram (i.e., geom = "histogram") from our dataframe (i.e., Ch16_block) using the variable "unstandardizedResiduals." We can add a few commands to change the width of the bars (i.e., *binwidth=0.5*), color of the bars (i.e., *fill=I("gray")*), and outline of the bars (i.e., *col=I("white")*). We can also add a title (i.e., *main = "Histogram of Unstandardized Residuals"*) and change the X and Y axes (*xlab = "Unstandardized Residual", ylab = "Count"*).

FIGURE 16.35 (continued)
Histogram.

As suggested by the skewness statistic, the histogram of residuals is slightly negatively skewed, and the histogram also provides a visual display of the slightly platykurtic distribution.

There are a few other statistics that can be used to gauge normality. The formal test of normality, the Shapiro-Wilk test (*SW*) (Shapiro & Wilk, 1965), provides evidence of the extent to which our sample distribution is statistically different from a normal distribution. The output for the Shapiro-Wilk test is presented in Figure 16.36 and suggests that our sample distribution for the residuals is *not* statistically significantly different than what would be expected from a normal distribution as the p value is greater than α.

Tests of Normality

	Kolmogorov-Smirnov[a]			Shapiro-Wilk		
	Statistic	df	Sig.	Statistic	df	Sig.
Residual for WeightLoss	.136	16	.200*	.965	16	.757

*. This is a lower bound of the true significance.

a. Lilliefors Significance Correction

FIGURE 16.36
Shapiro-Wilk test of normality.

Quantile-quantile (Q-Q) plots are also often examined to determine evidence of normality where quantiles of the theoretical normal distribution are plotted against quantiles of the sample distribution. Points that fall on or close to the diagonal line suggest evidence of normality. The Q-Q plot of residuals shown below suggests relative normality.

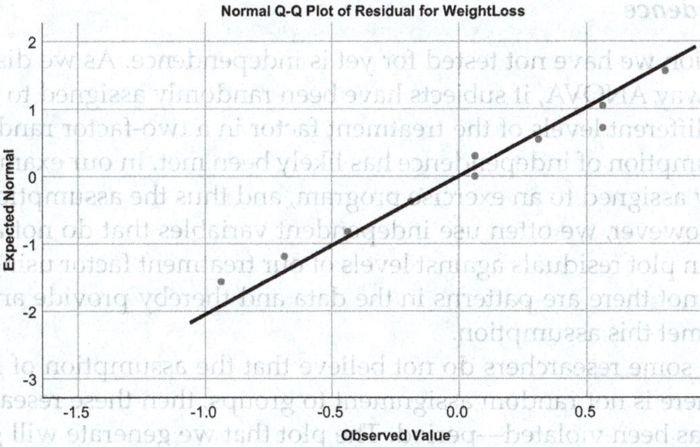

Working in **R,** we can use the *qplot* function to create a Q-Q plot of unstandardized residuals.

```
qplot(sample=unstandardizedResiduals,
     data = Ch6_block)
```

FIGURE 16.37
Q-Q plot.

Examination of the boxplot in Figure 16.38 also suggests a relatively normal distributional shape of residuals with no outliers.

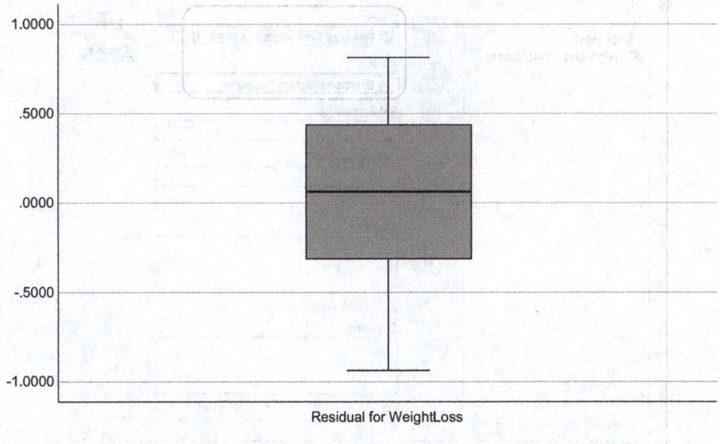

Working in **R,** we can generate a boxplot for unstandardized residuals using the *boxplot* function. To label the *Y* axis, we include the *ylab* command.

```
boxplot(Ch16_block$unstandardizedResiduals,
        ylab="unstandardized residual")
```

FIGURE 16.38
Residual boxplot.

Considering the forms of evidence we have examined, skewness and kurtosis statistics, the Shapiro-Wilk test, histogram, the Q-Q plot, and the boxplot, all suggest normality is a reasonable assumption. We can be reasonably assured we have met the assumption of normality.

16.5.2.2 Independence

The only assumption we have not tested for yet is independence. As we discussed in reference to the one-way ANOVA, if subjects have been randomly assigned to conditions (in other words, the different levels of the treatment factor in a two-factor randomized block ANOVA), the assumption of independence has likely been met. In our example, individuals were randomly assigned to an exercise program, and thus the assumption of independence was met. However, we often use independent variables that do not allow random assignment. We can plot residuals against levels of our treatment factor using a scatterplot to see whether or not there are patterns in the data and thereby provide an indication of whether we have met this assumption.

Please note that some researchers do not believe that the assumption of independence can be tested. If there is not random assignment to groups, then these researchers believe this assumption has been violated—period. The plot that we generate will give us a general idea of patterns, however, in situations where random assignment was not performed.

16.4.2.2.1 Generating the Scatterplot

The general steps for generating a simple scatterplot through "Scatter/dot" have been presented in Chapter 10, and they will not be reiterated here. From the "Simple Scatterplot" dialog screen, click the residual variable and move it into the "Y Axis" box by clicking on the arrow. Click the independent variable that we wish to display (e.g., "Exercise Program") and move it into the "X Axis" box by clicking on the arrow. Then click "OK."

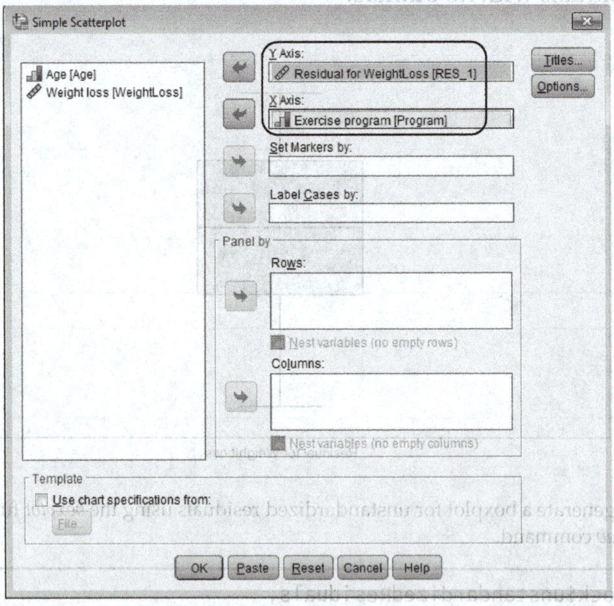

Working in **R**, we create a similar scatterplot using the following *plot* command, with the first variable listed displaying on the *X* axis (e.g., "Ch16_block$Program"), and the second variable displaying on the *Y* axis (i.e., "Ch16_block$unstandardized.residuals"). Additional commands are provided to label the axes (*xlab* and *ylab*) and title the graph (*main*). *Note:* We use the "Program" (not the "ProgramF") variable on the *X* axis. Had we generated the plot with "ProgramF," a scatterplot would have automatically been generated.

FIGURE 16.39
Generating a scatterplot.

```
plot(Ch16_block$Program,
    Ch16_block$unstandardizedResiduals,
    xlab = "program",
    ylab = "unstandardized residuals",
    main = "Scatterplot for independence")
```

Using the *plot* function, additional plots (one of which is the Q-Q plot) that can be used for diagnostic purposes are created.

```
plot(BlockModel)
```

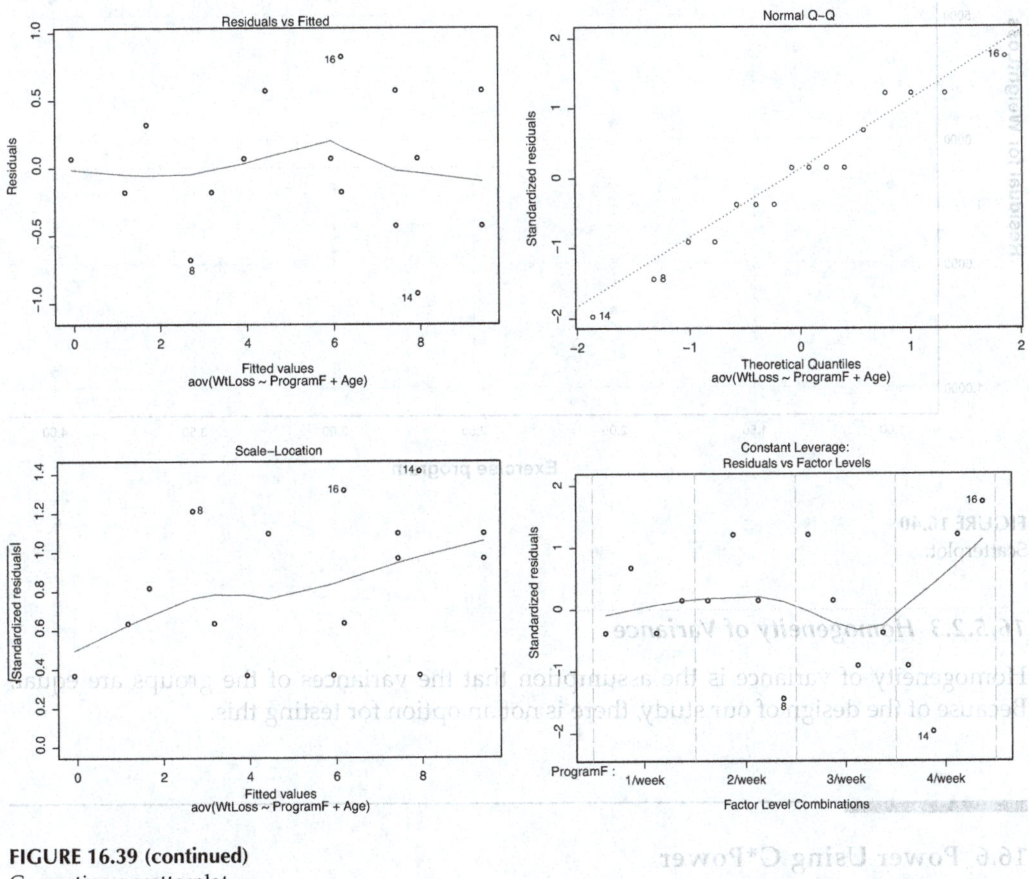

FIGURE 16.39 (continued)
Generating a scatterplot.

16.4.2.2.2 Interpreting Independence Evidence

In examining the scatterplot for evidence of independence, the points should be fall relatively randomly above and below a horizontal line at zero. (You may recall in Chapter 11 that we added a reference line to the graph using Chart Editor. To add a reference line, double click on the graph in the output to activate the chart editor. Select "Options" in the top pulldown menu, then "Y axis reference line." This will bring up the "Properties" dialog box. Change the value of the position to be "0." Then click on "Apply" and "Close" to generate the graph with a horizontal line at zero.)

In this example, our scatterplot for exercise program by residual generally suggests evidence of independence with a relatively random display of residuals above and below the horizontal line at zero. Thus, had we not met the assumption of independence through random assignment of cases to groups, this would have provided evidence that independence was a reasonable assumption.

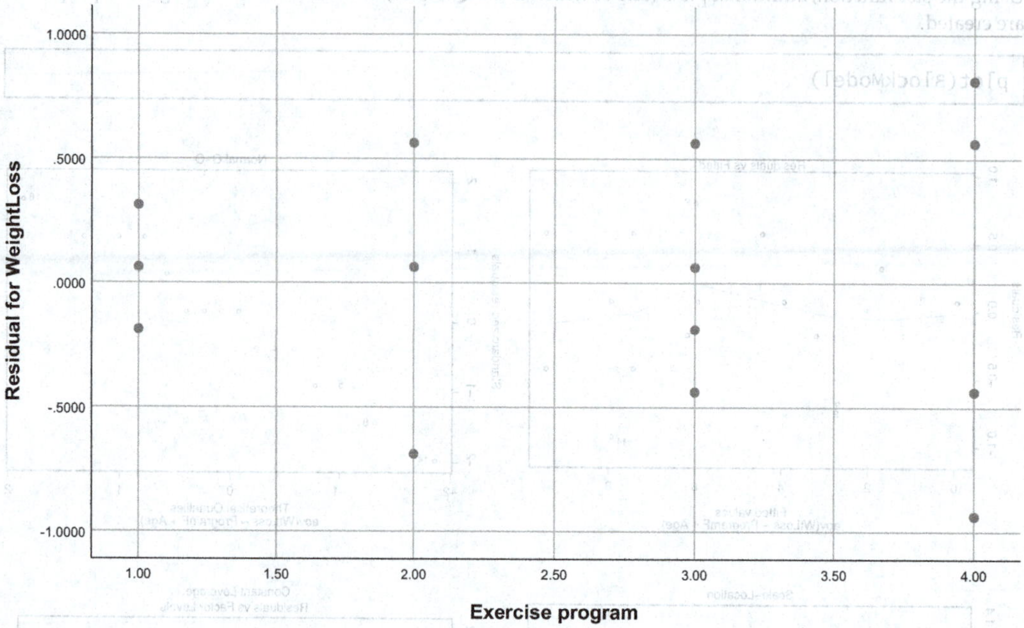

FIGURE 16.40
Scatterplot.

16.5.2.3 Homogeneity of Variance

Homogeneity of variance is the assumption that the variances of the groups are equal. Because of the design of our study, there is not an option for testing this.

16.6 Power Using G*Power

G*Power provides power calculations for the two-factor randomized block ANOVA model. In G*Power, just treat this design as if it were a regular two-factor ANOVA model.

16.7 Research Question Template and Example Write-up

Finally, here is an example paragraph just for the results of the *two-factor hierarchical ANOVA* design (feel free to write a similar paragraph for the two-factor randomized block ANOVA example). Recall that our graduate research assistant, Challie Lenge, was assisting a psychology faculty member, Dr. Mayfield, in a clinical trial conducted through the institution's medical center. Dr. Mayfield wanted to know the following: if there is a mean difference in quality of life for hospice patients based on type of intervention (massage therapy or music therapy), and if there is a mean difference in quality of life based on interventionist or clinician assigned to provide the intervention. The research questions presented to Dr. Mayfield from Challie include the following:

- *Is there a mean difference in quality of life based on intervention?*
- *Is there a mean difference in quality of life based on the interventionist?*

Challie then assisted Dr. Mayfield in generating a two-factor hierarchical ANOVA as the test of inference, and a template for writing the research questions for this design is presented here. As we noted in previous chapters, it is important to ensure the reader understands the levels of the factor(s). This may be done parenthetically in the actual research question, as an operational definition, or specified within the methods section.

- Is there a mean difference in [dependent variable] based on [nonnested factor]?
- Is there a mean difference in [dependent variable] based on [nested factor]?

It may be helpful to preface the results of the two-factor hierarchical ANOVA with information on an examination of the extent to which the assumptions were met. The assumptions include: (a) homogeneity of variance, and (b) normality.

A two-factor hierarchical analysis of variance (ANOVA) was conducted. The dependent variable was quality of life. The nonnested factor was intervention (massage therapy or music therapy) and the nested factor was interventionist or clinician (four interventionists or clinicians). The null hypotheses tested included: (1) the mean quality of life was equal for each of the interventions, and (2) the mean quality of life for each interventionist was equal.

The data were screened for missingness and violation of assumptions prior to analysis. There were no missing data. The assumption of *homogeneity of variance* was met via Levene's test (F (3, 20) = 1.042, p = .396). The assumption of *normality* was tested via examination of the residuals. Review of the Shapiro-Wilk test (SW = .960, df = 24, p = .442) and skewness (.284) and kurtosis (−.693) statistics suggested that normality was a reasonable assumption. Additional tests, including D'Agostino's test for skewness (z = .634, p = .526) and the Bonett-Seier test for Geary's kurtosis (z = −1.451, p = .147) suggested evidence of normality. The boxplot displayed a relatively normal distributional shape (with no outliers) of the residuals. The Q-Q plot and histogram suggested normality was tenable.

Here is an APA-style example paragraph of results for the two-factor hierarchical ANOVA (remember that this will be prefaced by the previous paragraph reporting the extent to which the assumptions of the test were met).

The results for the two-factor hierarchical ANOVA indicate:

1. A statistically significant main effect for intervention ($F_{intervention} = 59.559$, $df = 1,2$, $p = .016$).
2. A nonstatistically significant nested effect for interventionist (i.e., clinician) ($F_{interventionist} = .952$, $df = 2, 20$, $p = .403$).

Overall effect size as measured by $\hat{\omega}_A^2$ was .70 with high observed power (.948). The partial effect for the effect of intervention was also large (partial $\hat{\omega}_{A,partial}^2 = .70$) but with lower power (.192). The results of this study provide evidence to suggest that quality of life is significantly higher for hospice patients who received music therapy as the intervention ($M = 10.833$, $SE = .704$) as compared to massage therapy ($M = 3.333$, $SE = .704$). The results also suggest that mean scores for quality of life are comparable for hospice patients regardless of the clinician who provided the intervention.

16.8 Additional Resources

This chapter has provided a preview into conducting hierarchical (nested) and randomized block ANOVA. However, there are a number of areas that space limitations prevent us from delving into. For those that are interested in learning more about ANOVA models, or find yourself in a sticky situation in your analyses, you may wish to look into the following, among many other excellent resources.

- For more in-depth coverage of ANOVA models, see Maxwell et al. (2018), Kirk (2014) and Keppel and Wickens (2004), among others.
- To learn more about multilevel models, in general, see Raudenbush and Bryk (2002), Hox et al. (2017), Snijders and Bosker (2012), among many other excellent sources.

Problems

Conceptual Problems

1. A researcher wants to know if the number of professional development courses that a teacher completes differs based on the format that the professional development is offered (online, mixed mode, face-to-face). The researcher randomly samples 100 teachers employed in the district. Believing that years of teaching experience may be a concomitant variable, the researcher ranks the teachers on years of experience and places them in categories that represent five-year intervals. The researcher then randomly selects four years of experience blocks. The teachers within those blocks are then randomly assigned to professional development format. Which of the following methods of blocking is employed here?

a. Predefined value blocking
b. Predefined range blocking
c. Sampled value blocking
d. Sampled range blocking

2. To study the effectiveness of three spelling methods, 45 subjects are randomly selected from the fourth graders in a particular elementary school. Based on the order of their IQ scores, subjects are grouped into IQ groups (low = 75–99, average = 100–115, high = 116–130), 15 in each group. Subjects in each group are randomly assigned to one of the three methods of spelling, five each. Which of the following methods of blocking is employed here?
   a. Predefined value blocking
   b. Predefined range blocking
   c. Sampled value blocking
   d. Sampled range blocking

3. A researcher is examining preschoolers' knowledge of number identification. Fifty preschoolers are grouped based on socioeconomic status (low, moderate, high). Within each SES group, students are randomly assigned to one of two treatment groups: one which incorporates numbers through individual, small group, and whole group work with manipulatives, music, and art; and a second which incorporates numbers through whole group study only. Which of the following methods of blocking is employed here?
   a. Predefined value blocking
   b. Predefined range blocking
   c. Sampled value blocking
   d. Sampled range blocking

4. If three teachers employ method *A* and three other teachers employ method B, then which one of the following is suggested?
   a. Teachers are nested within method.
   b. Teachers are crossed with methods.
   c. Methods are nested within teacher.
   d. Cannot be determined.

5. The interaction of factors *A* and *B* can be assessed only if which one of the following occurs?
   a. Both factors are fixed.
   b. Both factors are random.
   c. Factor *A* is nested within factor B.
   d. Factors *A* and *B* are crossed.

6. In a two-factor design, factor *A* is nested within factor *B* for which one of the following?
   a. At each level of *A* each level of *B* appears.
   b. At each level of *A* unique levels of *B* appear.
   c. At each level of *B* unique levels of *A* appear.
   d. Cannot be determined.

7. Five teachers use an experimental method of teaching statistics, and five other teachers use the traditional method. If factor M is method of teaching, and factor T is teacher, this design can be denoted by which one of the following?
   a. T(M)
   b. T x M
   c. M x T
   d. M(T)
8. True or false? If factor *C* is nested within factors *A* and B, this is denoted as *AB*(*C*).
9. True or false? A design in which all levels of each factor are found in combination with each level of every other factor is necessarily a nested design.
10. True or false? To determine if counseling method E is uniformly superior to method C for the population of counselors, from which random samples are taken to conduct a study, one needs a nested design with a mixed model.
11. I assert that the predefined value method of block formation is more effective than the sampled value method in reducing unexplained variability. Am I correct?
12. For the interaction to be tested in a two-factor randomized block design, it is required that which one of the following occurs?
    a. Both factors be fixed
    b. Both factors be random
    c. $n = 1$
    d. $n > 1$
13. Five medical professors use a computer-based method of teaching, and five other medical professors use a lecture-based method of teaching. A researcher is interested in student outcomes for those enrolled in classes taught by these instructional methods. This is an example of which type of design?
    a. Completely crossed design
    b. Repeated measures design
    c. Hierarchical design
    d. Randomized block design
14. In a randomized block study, the correlation between the blocking factor and the dependent variable is .35. I assert that the residual variation will be smaller when using the blocking variable than without. Am I correct?
15. A researcher is interested in examining the number of suspensions of high school students based on random assignment participation in a series of self-awareness workshops. The researcher believes that age may be a concomitant variable. Applying a two-factor randomized block ANOVA design to the data, is age an appropriate blocking factor?
16. In a two-factor hierarchical design with two levels of factor *A* and three levels of factor *B* nested within each level of A, how many *F* ratios can be tested?
    a. 1
    b. 2
    c. 3
    d. Cannot be determined

17. If the correlation between the concomitant variable and dependent variable is −.80, which of the following designs is recommended?

a. ANCOVA

b. One-factor ANOVA

c. Randomized block ANOVA

d. All of the above

18. True or false? IQ must be used as a treatment factor.

19. Which of the following blocking methods best estimates the treatment effects?

a. Predefined value blocking

b. Post hoc predefined value blocking

c. Sampled value blocking

d. Sampled range blocking

20. The assumption of normality for the two-factor hierarchical ANOVA is concerned with which of the following?

a. Dependent variable

b. Independent variable

c. Nested factor

d. Residual

21. True or false? The assumption of normality for the two-factor hierarchical ANOVA differs from the two-factor crossed model.

22. The assumptions for the two-factor randomized block ANOVA model are nearly identical to which one of the following?

a. Dependent *t* test

b. Factorial ANOVA

c. One-factor repeated measures ANOVA

d. Two-factor hierarchical ANOVA

23. Why is the assumption of compound symmetry with two-factor randomized block ANOVA necessary?

a. Observations within a block are not independent.

b. The distribution of residuals cannot be assumed normal.

c. The means of the levels of the blocking factor are equal.

d. The population covariances for all pairs of the dependent variable are equal.

24. An interaction between the treatment and blocking factors in a two-factor randomized block ANOVA results in which one of the following?

a. Compound symmetry

b. Multicollinearity

c. Rejection of the null hypothesis

d. Violation of the additivity assumption

25. In a two-factor randomized block ANOVA, a multiple comparison procedure is needed in which of the following situations?

a. When the null hypothesis for the treatment is rejected and it has more than two levels.

b. When the null hypothesis for the blocking factor is rejected and it has more than two levels.

c. Both a and b only.

d. Either a or b.

Answers to Conceptual Problems

1. **d** (teachers are ranked according to a ratio blocking variable; a random sample of blocks are drawn; then teachers within the blocks are assigned to treatment.)
3. **a** (children are randomly assigned to treatment based on ordinal SES value.)
5. **d** (interactions occur only among factors that are crossed.)
7. **a** (this is the notation for teachers nested within methods; see also problem 2.)
9. **False** (cannot be a nested design; must be a crossed design.)
11. **Yes** (see the discussion on the types of blocking.)
13. **c** (physician is nested within method.)
15. **Yes** (age is an appropriate blocking factor here.)
17. **a** (use of a covariate is best for large correlations.)
19. **a** (see the summary of the blocking methods.)
21. **False** (assumptions for the two-factor nested model and assumptions for the two-factor crossed model are the same.)
23. **a** (the assumption of compound symmetry with two-factor randomized block ANOVA is needed because the observations within a block are not independent.)
25. **d** (a multiple comparison procedure is needed for two-factor randomized block ANOVA when either or both of the following occur: the null hypothesis for the treatment is rejected and it has more than two levels; *or* when the null hypothesis for the blocking factor is rejected and it has more than two levels.)

Computational Problems

1. An experiment was conducted to compare three types of behavior modification (1, 2, and 3) using age as a blocking variable (4-, 6-, and 8-year-old children). The mean scores on the dependent variable, number of instances of disruptive behavior, are listed here for each cell. The intention of the treatments is to minimize the number of disruptions.

Type of Behavior Modification	Age: 4 years	6 years	8 years
1	20	40	40
2	50	30	20
3	50	40	30

Use these cell means to graph the interaction between type of behavior modification and age.

a. Is there an interaction between type of behavior modification and age?

b. What kind of recommendation would you make to teachers?

2. An experiment was conducted to compare four different preschool curricula that were adopted in four different classrooms. Reading readiness proficiency was used as a blocking variable (below proficient, at proficient, above proficient). The mean scores on the dependent variable, letter recognition, are listed here for each cell. The intention of the treatment (i.e., the curriculum) is to increase letter recognition.

	Reading Readiness Proficiency		
Curriculum	**Below**	**At**	**Above**
1	12	20	22
2	20	24	18
3	16	16	20
4	15	18	25

Use these cell means to graph the interaction between curriculum and reading readiness proficiency.

a. Is there an interaction between type of curriculum and reading readiness proficiency?

b. What kind of recommendation would you make to teachers?

3. An experimenter tested three sales pitches (subtle, moderate, pushy) on morning versus afternoon shoppers. Thus, shopping time of day (morning or afternoon) is a blocking variable. The dependent measure was the number of sales during a 2-week period. There were five subjects in each cell. Complete the ANOVA summary table below, assuming a fixed-effects model, where $\alpha = .50$.

Source	*SS*	*df*	*MS*	*F*	Critical Value	Decision
Sales pitch (A)	200	–	–	–	–	–
Time of day (B)	100	–	–	–	–	–
Interaction (AB)	20	–	–	–	–	–
Within	240	–	–			
Total	–	–				

4. An experiment was conducted to determine if there was a mean difference in weight for women based on type of aerobics exercise program participated (low impact vs. high impact). Body mass index (BMI) was used as a blocking variable to represent below, at, or above recommended BMI. The data are shown below. Conduct a two-factor randomized block ANOVA ($\alpha = .05$) and Bonferroni MCPs using SPSS to determine the results of the study.

Subject	Exercise Program	BMI	Weight
1	1	1	100
2	1	2	135
3	1	3	200
4	1	1	95
5	1	2	140
6	1	3	180
7	2	1	120
8	2	2	152
9	2	3	176
10	2	1	128
11	2	2	142
12	2	3	220

5. A mathematics professor wants to know which of three approaches to teaching calculus resulted in the best test performance (section 1, 2, or 3). Scores on a placement exam were used as a blocking variable (block 1: 200–400; block 2: 401–600; block 3: 601–800). The data are shown below. Conduct a two-factor randomized block ANOVA (α = .05) and Bonferroni MCPs using SPSS to determine the results of the study.

Subject	Section	Placement Exam	Test Score
1	1	1	90
2	1	2	93
3	1	3	100
4	2	1	88
5	2	2	90
6	2	3	97
7	3	1	79
8	3	2	85
9	3	3	92

6. A restaurant owner (who owns multiple franchise locations) wants to know which of three recipes for a signature dish (mild, medium, spicy) resulted in the best sales, blocking on section of town in which the restaurant is located (section 1, 2, or 3). The data are shown below. Conduct a two-factor randomized block ANOVA (a = .05) and Bonferroni MCPs using SPSS to determine the results of the study.

Subject	Section of Town	Recipe	Sales
1	1	1	90
2	1	2	93
3	1	3	100

4	2	1	88
5	2	2	90
6	2	3	97
7	3	1	79
8	3	2	85
9	3	3	92

7. A restaurant owner wants to know which of three recipes for a signature dish (mild =1, medium = 2, spicy = 3) resulted in the best sales, with recipe nested within chef (chef 1, 2, or 3). The data are shown below. Conduct a two-factor hierarchical ANOVA ($\alpha = .50$) and Bonferroni MCPs using SPSS to determine the results of the study.

Chef	Recipe	Sales
1.00	1.00	45.00
1.00	2.00	52.00
1.00	3.00	59.00
2.00	1.00	38.00
2.00	2.00	41.00
2.00	3.00	52.00
3.00	1.00	40.00
3.00	2.00	50.00
3.00	3.00	62.00
1.00	1.00	45.00
1.00	2.00	48.00
1.00	3.00	60.00
2.00	1.00	38.00
2.00	2.00	41.00
2.00	3.00	50.00
3.00	1.00	43.00
3.00	2.00	55.00
3.00	3.00	65.00

Answers to Computational Problems

1. a. Yes
   b. At age 4, type 1 is most effective; at age 6, type 2 is most effective; and at age 8, type 2 is most effective.

3. $SS_{total} = 560$, $df_A = 2$, $df_B = 1$, $df_{AB} = 2$, $df_{\text{with}} = 24$, $df_{\text{total}} = 29$, $MS_A = 100$, $MS_B = 100$, $MS_{AB} = 10$, $MS_{\text{with}} = 10$, $F_A = 10$, $F_B = 10$, $F_{AB} = 1$, critical value for $B = 4.26$ (reject H_0 for B), critical value for A and $AB = 3.40$ (reject H_0 for A and fail to reject H_0 for AB).

5. $F_{\text{section}} = 44.385$, $p = .002$; $F_{\text{placement}} = 61.000$, $p = .001$; thus reject H_0 for both effects. Bonferroni results: all but sections 1 and 2 are different, and all blocks are statistically different.

7. $F_{\text{recipe}} = 6.961$, $p < .001$; thus reject H_0 for the main effect of recipe. Bonferroni results: all flavors (i.e., mild, medium, and spicy) of recipes are statistically different.

Interpretive Problems

1. The following is the first one-factor ANOVA interpretive problem you developed in Chapter 11: *Using the survey1 dataset, which is accessible from the website, use SPSS or **R** to conduct a one-factor fixed-effects ANOVA, where political view is the grouping variable (i.e., independent variable) (J = 5) and the dependent variable is an interval or ratio variable of your choice. Also compute effect size and test for assumptions. Then write an APA-style paragraph describing the results.*

   Take the one-factor ANOVA interpretive problem you developed in Chapter 11. What are some reasonable blocking variables to consider? Which type of blocking would be best in your situation? Select this blocking variable from the same dataset and conduct a two-factor randomized block ANOVA. Compare these results with the one-factor ANOVA results (without the blocking factor) to determine how useful the blocking variable was in terms of reducing residual variability.

2. The following is the second one-factor ANOVA interpretive problem you developed in Chapter 11: *Using the survey1 dataset, which is accessible from the website, use SPSS or **R** to conduct a one-factor fixed-effects ANOVA, where hair color is the grouping variable (i.e., independent variable) (J = 5) and the dependent variable is an interval or ratio variable of your choice. Also compute effect size and test for assumptions. Then write an APA-style paragraph describing the results.*

   Take this one-factor ANOVA interpretive problem you developed in Chapter 11. What are some reasonable blocking variables to consider? Which type of blocking would be best in your situation? Select this blocking variable from the same dataset and conduct a two-factor randomized ANOVA. Compare these results with the one-factor ANOVA results (without the blocking factor) to determine how useful the blocking variable was in terms of reducing residual variability.

3. The following is the third one-factor ANOVA interpretive problem you developed in Chapter 11: *Using the IPEDS2017 dataset, which is accessible from the website, use SPSS or **R** to conduct a one-factor fixed-effects ANOVA. Select an appropriate independent variable (e.g., land grant institution, LANDGRNT) and appropriate dependent variable (e.g., total dormitory capacity, ROOMCAP). Also compute effect size and test for assumptions. Then write an APA-style paragraph describing the results.*

   Take this one-factor ANOVA interpretive problem you developed in Chapter 11. What are some reasonable blocking variables to consider? Which type of blocking would be best in your situation? Select this blocking variable from the same dataset and conduct a two-factor randomized ANOVA. Compare these results with the one-factor ANOVA results (without the blocking factor) to determine how useful the blocking variable was in terms of reducing residual variability.

17

Simple Linear Regression

Chapter Outline

Key Concepts

1. Slope and intercept of a straight line
2. Regression model
3. Prediction errors/residuals
4. Standardized and unstandardized regression coefficients
5. Proportion of variation accounted for; coefficient of determination

In Chapter 10 we considered various bivariate measures of association. Specifically, the chapter dealt with the topics of scatterplot, covariance, types of correlation coefficients, and their resulting inferential tests. Thus the chapter was concerned with addressing the question of the extent to which two variables are associated or related. In this chapter we extend our discussion of two variables to address the question of the extent to which one variable can be used to predict or explain another variable.

Beginning in Chapter 11 we examined various analysis of variance (ANOVA) models. It should be mentioned again that ANOVA and regression are both forms of the same general linear model (GLM), where the relationship between one or more independent variables and one dependent variable is evaluated. The major difference between the two procedures is that in ANOVA, the independent variables are discrete variables (i.e., nominal or ordinal), while in regression, the independent variables are continuous variables (i.e., interval or ratio; however, we will see later how we can apply dichotomous variables in regression models). Otherwise there is considerable overlap of these two procedures in terms of concepts and their implementation. Note that a continuous variable can be transformed into a discrete variable. For example, the GRE-Quantitative exam is a continuous variable scaled from 130 to 170. It could be made into a discrete variable, such as low (130–139), average (140–159), and high (160–170).

When considering the relationship between two variables (say X and Y), the researcher usually determines some measure of relationship between those variables, such as a correlation coefficient (e.g., r_{XY}, the Pearson product-moment correlation coefficient), as we did in chapter 10. Another way of looking at how two variables may be related is through regression analysis, in terms of prediction or explanation. That is, we evaluate the ability of one variable to predict or explain a second variable. Here we adopt the usual notation where X is defined as the **independent** or **predictor variable**, and Y as the **dependent** or **criterion variable**.

For example, an admissions officer might want to use a placement exam score to predict graduate-level grade point averages (GPA) to make admissions decisions for a sample of applicants to a university or college. The research question of interest is how well does the placement exam (the independent or predictor variable) predict or explain performance in graduate school (the dependent or criterion variable)? This is an example of simple linear regression where only a single predictor variable is included in the analysis. The utility of the placement exam in predicting GPA requires that these variables have a correlation different from zero. Otherwise the placement exam will not be very useful in predicting GPA. For education and the behavioral sciences, the use of a single predictor does not usually result in reasonable prediction or explanation. Thus, Chapter 18 considers the case of multiple predictor variables through multiple linear regression analysis.

In this chapter, we consider the concepts of slope, intercept, regression model, unstandardized and standardized regression coefficients, residuals, proportion of variation accounted for, tests of significance, and statistical assumptions. Our objectives are that by the end of this chapter, you will be able to (a) understand the concepts underlying simple linear regression, (b) determine and interpret the results of simple linear regression, and (c) understand and evaluate the assumptions of simple linear regression.

17.1 What Simple Linear Regression Is and How It Works

In this chapter, we find Ott Lier stretching his statistical skills.

Ott Lier, along with the additional graduate research assistants working in the statistics and research lab, has continued to expand his palette of statistical skills and has been brought into a project with the Human Resources Department of a large employer in their area. Ott will be working with Dr. Randall, the director of Human Resources. Dr. Randall wants to know if work optimism can be used to predict employment success. If this is possible, Dr. Randall anticipates changes to their onboarding and training of employees to hopefully increase employment success. Ott suggests the following research question to Dr. Randall: *Can employment success be predicted from work optimism?* Ott determines that a simple linear regression is the best statistical procedure to use to answer Dr. Randall's question. His next task is to assist Dr. Randall in analyzing the data.

Let us consider the basic concepts involved in simple linear regression. Many years ago when you had algebra, you learned about an equation used to describe a straight line:

$$Y = bX + a$$

Here the predictor variable X is used to predict the criterion variable Y. The **slope** of the line is denoted by b and indicates the number of Y units the line changes for a one-unit change in X. You may find it easier to think about the slope as measuring tilt or steepness. The Y-intercept is denoted by a and is the point at which the line intersects or crosses the Y axis. To be more specific, a is the value of Y when X is equal to zero. Hereafter we use the term **intercept** rather than Y-intercept to keep it simple.

Consider the plot of the straight line $Y = 0.5X + 1.0$ as shown in Figure 17.1. Here we see that the line clearly intersects the Y axis at $Y = 1.0$; thus the intercept is equal to one. The

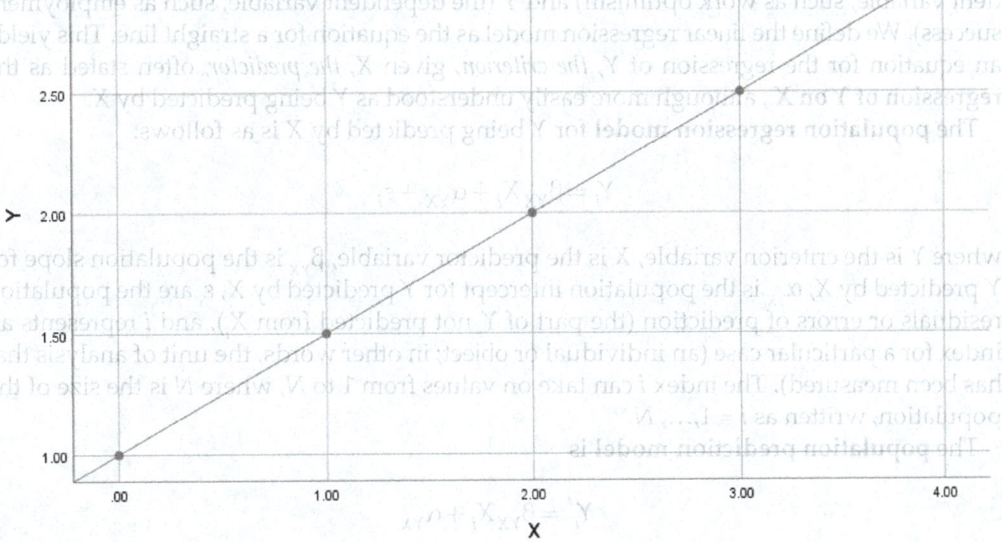

FIGURE 17.1
Plot of line: $Y = 0.5\,X + 1.0$.

slope of a line is defined, more specifically, as the change in Y (numerator) divided by the change in X (denominator).

$$b = \frac{\Delta Y}{\Delta X} = \frac{Y_2 - Y_1}{X_2 - X_1}$$

For instance, take two points shown in Figure 17.1, (X_1, Y_1) and (X_2, Y_2), that fall on the straight line with coordinates (0, 1) and (4, 3), respectively. We compute the slope for those two points to be (3 − 1)/(4 − 0) = 0.5. If we were to select any other two points that fall on the straight line, then the slope for those two points would also be equal to 0.5. That is, regardless of the two points on the line that we select, the slope will always be the same, constant value of 0.5. This is true because we only need two points to define a particular straight line. That is, with the points (0, 1) and (4, 3) we can draw only one straight line that passes through both of those points, and that line has a slope of 0.5 and an intercept of 1.0.

Let us take the concepts of slope, intercept, and straight line and apply them in the context of correlation so that we can study the relationship between the variables X and Y. If the slope of the line is a positive value (e.g., Figure 17.1), as X increases, Y also increases, then the correlation will be positive. If the slope of the line is zero, such that the line is parallel or horizontal to the X axis, as X increases Y remains constant, then the correlation will be zero. If the slope of the line is a negative value, as X increases Y decreases (i.e., the line decreases from left to right), then the correlation will be negative. Thus the sign of the slope corresponds to the sign of the correlation.

17.1.1 Characteristics

17.1.1.1 The Population Simple Linear Regression Model

Let us take these concepts and apply them to simple linear regression. Consider the situation where we have the entire population of individual's scores on both variables X (the independent variable, such as work optimism) and Y (the dependent variable, such as employment success). We define the linear regression model as the equation for a straight line. This yields an equation for the regression of Y, *the criterion,* given X, *the predictor,* often stated as the **regression of Y on X**, although more easily understood as Y being predicted by X.

The **population regression model** for Y being predicted by X is as follows:

$$Y_i = \beta_{YX} X_i + \alpha_{YX} + \varepsilon_i$$

where Y is the criterion variable, X is the predictor variable, β_{YX} is the population slope for Y predicted by X, α_{YX} is the population intercept for Y predicted by X, ε_i are the population residuals or errors of prediction (the part of Y_i not predicted from X_i), and i represents an index for a particular case (an individual or object; in other words, the unit of analysis that has been measured). The index i can take on values from 1 to N, where N is the size of the population, written as $i = 1, \ldots, N$.

The **population prediction model** is

$$Y_i' = \beta_{YX} X_i + \alpha_{YX}$$

where Y_i' is the predicted value of Y for a specific value of X. That is, Y_i is the *actual or observed score* obtained by individual i, while Y_i' is the *predicted score* based on their X score for that same individual (in other words, you are using the value of X to predict what Y will be). Thus, we see that the population prediction error is defined as follows:

$$\varepsilon_i = Y_i - Y_i'$$

There is only one difference between the regression and prediction models. The regression model explicitly includes prediction error as ε_i, whereas the prediction model includes prediction error implicitly as part of the predicted score Y_i' (i.e., there is some error in the predicted values).

Consider for a moment a practical application of the difference between the regression and prediction models. Frequently a researcher will develop a regression model for a population where X and Y are both known, and then use the prediction model to actually predict Y when only X is known (i.e., Y will not be known until later). Using the employment example, the human resources officer first develops a regression model for a population of employees currently employed at the organization so as to have a current measure of work optimism. This yields the slope and intercept. Then the prediction model is used to predict future employment success and to help make training and onboarding decisions for future populations of incoming employees based on their work optimism.

A simple method for determining the population slope (β_{YX}) and intercept (α_{YX}) is computed as follows:

$$\beta_{YX} = \rho_{XY}\left(\frac{\sigma_Y}{\sigma_X}\right)$$

and

$$\alpha_{YX} = \mu_Y - \beta_{YX}\mu_X$$

where σ_Y and σ_X are the population standard deviations for Y and X respectively, ρ_{XY} is the population correlation between X and Y (simply the Pearson correlation coefficient, rho), and μ_Y and μ_X are the population means for Y and X respectively. Note that the previously used mathematical method for determining the slope and intercept of a straight line is not appropriate in regression analysis with real data.

17.1.1.2 The Sample Simple Linear Regression Model

Our discussion of the sample simple linear regression model begins with coverage of the unstandardized and standardized models. This is followed by prediction errors, least squares criterion, coefficient tests, significance tests, and confidence intervals.

17.1.1.2.1 Unstandardized Regression Model

Let us return to the real world of sample statistics and consider the sample simple linear regression model. As usual, Greek letters refer to population parameters and English letters refer to sample statistics. The **sample regression model** for predicting Y from X is computed as:

$$Y_i = b_{YX}X_i + a_{YX} + e_i$$

where Y and X are as before (i.e., the dependent and independent variables respectively), b_{YX} is the sample slope for Y predicted by X, a_{YX} is the sample intercept for Y predicted by X, e_i are sample residuals or errors of prediction (the part of Y_i not predictable from X_i), and i represents an index for a case (an individual or object). The index i can take on values from 1 to n, where n is the size of the sample, and is written as $i = 1,\ldots, n$.

The **sample prediction model** is computed as follows:

$$Y_i' = b_{YX}X_i + a_{YX}$$

where Y_i' is the predicted value of Y for a specific value of X. We define the sample prediction error as the difference between the *actual score* obtained by individual i (i.e., Y_i) and the *predicted score* based on the X score for that individual (i.e., Y_i'). In other words, the residual is that part of Y that is *not* predicted by X. The goal of the prediction model is to include an independent variable X that minimizes the residual; this means that the independent variable does a nice job of predicting the outcome. Computationally, the residual (or error) is computed as:

$$e_i = Y_i - Y_i'$$

The difference between the regression and prediction models is the same as previously discussed, except now we are dealing with a sample rather than a population.

The sample slope (b_{YX}) and intercept (a_{YX}) can be determined by

$$b_{YX} = r_{YX}\left(\frac{s_Y}{s_X}\right)$$

and

$$a_{YX} = \bar{Y} - b_{YX}\bar{X}$$

where s_Y and s_X are the sample standard deviations for Y and X respectively, r_{YX} is the sample correlation between X and Y (again the Pearson correlation coefficient, rho), and $\bar{Y}$ and $\bar{X}$ are the sample means for Y and X, respectively. The **sample slope (b_{YX})** is referred to alternately as (a) the expected or predicted change in Y for a one-unit change in X, and (b) the unstandardized or raw regression coefficient. The **sample intercept (a_{YX})** is referred to alternately as (a) the point at which the regression line intersects (or crosses) the Y axis, and (b) the value of Y when X is zero.

Consider now the analysis of a realistic example to be followed throughout this chapter. Let us use work optimism (a continuous score) to predict employment success (also a continuous score). The work optimism scale has a possible range of 20 to 80 points, and the employment success scale has a possible range of 0 to 50 points. Given the sample of 10 employees shown in Table 17.1, let us work through a simple linear regression analysis. The observation numbers ($i = 1, \ldots, 10$), and values for the work optimism score (the independent variable, X) and employment success core (the dependent variable, Y) variables are given in the first three columns of the table, respectively. The other columns are discussed as we go along.

The sample statistics for the work optimism score (the independent variable) are $\bar{X} = 55.5$ and $s_X = 13.1339$, for the employment success core (the dependent variable) are $\bar{Y} = 38$ and $s_Y = 7.5130$, and the correlation r_{YX} is 0.9177. The sample slope (b_{YX}) and intercept (a_{YX}) are computed as follows:

TABLE 17.1

Employment Example Regression Data

Employee	Work Optimism (X)	Employment Success (Y)	Residual (*e*)	Predicted Employment Success (Y′)
1	37	32	3.7125	28.2875
2	45	36	3.5125	32.4875
3	43	27	−4.4375	31.4375
4	50	34	−1.1125	35.1125
5	65	45	2.0125	42.9875
6	72	49	2.3375	46.6625
7	61	42	1.1125	40.8875
8	57	38	−0.7875	38.7875
9	48	30	−4.0625	34.0625
10	77	47	−2.2875	49.2875

$$b_{YX} = r_{YX}\left(\frac{s_Y}{s_X}\right) = 0.9177\left(\frac{7.5130}{13.1339}\right) = 0.5250$$

and

$$a_{YX} = \bar{Y} - b_{YX}\bar{X} = 38 - 0.5250(55.5) = 8.8625$$

Let us interpret the slope and intercept values. A **slope** of 0.5250 means that if your score on work optimism is increased by one point, then your predicted score on employment success (i.e., the dependent variable) will be increased by 0.5250 points or about one-half of one point. An **intercept** of 8.8625 means that if your score on work optimism is zero, then your score on employment success is 8.8625. The sample simple linear regression model, given these values, becomes

$$Y_i = b_{YX}X_i + a_{YX} + e_i = 0.5250X_i + 8.8625 + e_i$$

If your score on work optimism is 63, then your **predicted score** on employment success is the following:

$$Y_i' = 0.5250(63) + 8.8625 = 41.9375$$

Thus, based on the prediction model developed, your predicted score on employment success is approximately 42; however, as becomes evident, predictions are generally not perfect.

17.1.1.2.2 Standardized Regression Model

Up until now, the computations in simple linear regression have involved the use of raw scores. For this reason, we call this the *unstandardized regression model.* The slope estimate is an unstandardized or raw regression slope because it is the predicted change in *Y* raw score units for a one raw score unit change in X. We can also express regression in **standard z score units** for both X and Y as follows:

$$z(X_i) = \frac{X_i - \bar{X}}{s_X}$$

and

$$z(Y_i) = \frac{Y_i - \bar{Y}}{s_Y}$$

In both cases, the numerator is the difference between the observed score and the mean, and the denominator is the standard deviation (and dividing by the standard deviation standardizes the value). The means and variances of both standardized variables (i.e., z_X and z_Y) are 0 and 1, respectively.

The **sample standardized linear prediction model** becomes the following where $z(Y_i')$ is the standardized predicted value of Y:

$$z(Y_i') = (b_{YX}^*)(z(X_i)) = (r_{YX})(z(X_i))$$

Thus the **standardized regression slope, b_{YX}^***, sometimes referred to as a **beta weight**, is equal to r_{YX}, i.e., the simple bivariate correlation between X and Y. No intercept term is necessary in the prediction model as the mean of the z scores for both X and Y is zero (i.e., $a_{YX}^* = \bar{Z}_Y - b_{YX}^* \bar{Z}_X = 0$). In summary, *the standardized slope is equal to the correlation coefficient* and *the standardized intercept is equal to zero*.

For our employment example, the sample standardized linear prediction model is

$$z(Y_i') = (.9177)(z(X_i))$$

The slope of .9177 would be interpreted as the expected increase in employment success in z score (i.e., standardized score) units for a one z score (i.e., standardized score) unit increase in the work optimism score. A one z score unit increase is also the same as a one standard deviation increase because the standard deviation of z is equal to one (recall from Chapter 4 that the mean of a standardized z score is 0 with a standard deviation of 1).

When should you consider use of the standardized versus unstandardized regression analyses? According to Pedhazur (1997), the standardized regression slope b^* is not very stable from sample to sample. For example, at Organization Q, the standardized regression slope b^* would vary across different employee types (or samples), whereas the unstandardized regression slope b would be much more consistent across employee types. Thus, in simple regression most researchers prefer the use of b. We see later that the standardized regression slope b^* has some utility in multiple regression analysis.

17.1.1.2.3 Prediction Errors

Previously we mentioned that perfect prediction of Y from X is extremely unlikely, only occurring with a perfect correlation between X and Y (i.e., r_{YX}, also noted as r_{XY}, = ±1.0). When developing the regression model, the values of the outcome, Y, are known. Once the slope and intercept have been estimated, we can then use the prediction model to predict the outcome (*Y*) from the independent variable (*X*) when the values of *Y* are *unknown*. We have already defined the predicted values of *Y* as *Y*′. In other words, *a predicted value Y′ can be computed by plugging the obtained value for X into the prediction model*. It can be shown that $Y_i = Y_i'$ for all *i* only when there is perfect prediction. However, this is extremely unlikely in reality, particularly in simple linear regression using a single predictor.

We can determine a value of *Y*′ for each of the *i* cases (individuals or objects) from the prediction model. In comparing the actual *Y* values to the predicted *Y* values, we obtain the **residuals** *as the difference between the observed* (Y_i) *and predicted values* (Y_i'), computed as follows:

$$e_i = Y_i - Y_i'$$

for all $i = 1, \ldots, n$ individuals or objects in the sample. The residuals, e_i, are also known as **errors of estimate**, or **prediction errors**, and are that portion of Y_i that is not predictable from X_i. The residual terms are random values that are unique to each individual or object.

The residuals and predicted values for the employment example are shown in the last two columns of Table 17.1, respectively. Consider observation 2, where the observed work optimism score is 45 and the observed employment success core is 36. The predicted employment success score is 32.4875 and the residual is +3.5125. This indicates that person 2 had a higher observed employment success score than was predicted using the work optimism score as a predictor. We see that a **positive residual** indicates the observed criterion score is larger than the predicted criterion score, whereas a **negative residual** (such as in observation 3) indicates the observed criterion score is smaller than the predicted criterion score. For observation 3, the observed work optimism score is 43, the observed employment success score is 27, the predicted employment success score is 31.4375, and thus the residual is -4.4375. Person 2 scored higher on employment success than we predicted, and person 3 scored lower on employment success than we predicted.

The regression example is shown graphically in the **scatterplot** of Figure 17.2, where the straight diagonal line represents the regression line. *Individuals falling above the regression line have positive residuals* (e.g., observation 1) (in other words, the difference between the observed score, represented as a dot on the graph, is greater in value than the predicted value, which is represented by the regression line) *and individuals falling below the regression line have negative residuals* (e.g., observation 3) (in other words, the difference between the observed score is less in value than the predicted value, which is represented by the regression line). The residual is, very simply, *the vertical distance between the observed score (represented by the 'dots' in the scatterplot (Figure 17.2) and the regression line.* In the residual column of Table 17.1 we see that one-half of the residuals are positive and one-half are negative, and in Figure 17.2 that one-half of the points fall above the regression line and one-half below the regression line. It can be shown that the mean of the residuals is always zero (i.e., $\bar{e} = 0$), as the sum of the residuals is always zero. This results from the fact that the mean of the observed criterion scores is equal to the mean of the predicted criterion scores (i.e., $\bar{Y} = \bar{Y}'$; 38 for the example data).

17.1.1.2.4 Least Squares Criterion

How was one particular method selected for determining of the slope and intercept? Obviously, some standard procedure has to be used. Thus, there are statistical criteria that help us decide which method to use in determining the slope and intercept. The criterion

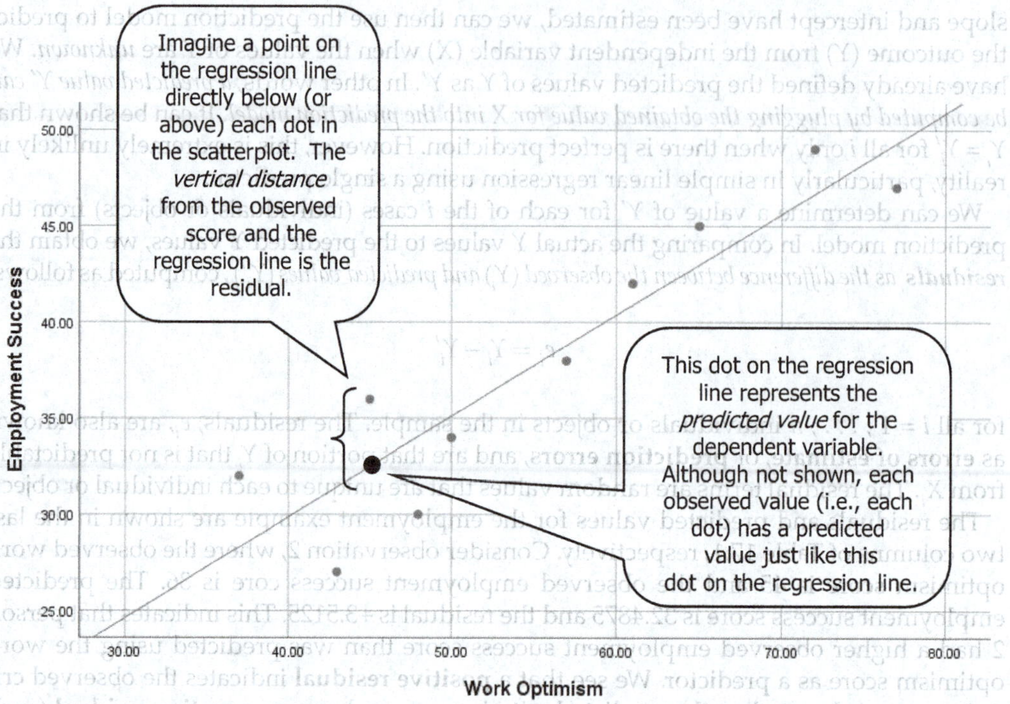

FIGURE 17.2
Scatterplot for employment example.

usually used in linear regression analysis (and in all general linear models, for that matter) is the **least squares criterion.** According to the least squares criterion, *the sum of the squared prediction errors or residuals is smallest.* That is, we want to find that regression line, defined by a particular slope and intercept, which results in the smallest sum of the squared residuals (recall that the residual is the difference between the observed and predicted values for the outcome). Since the residual is the vertical difference between the observed and predicted value, the regression line is simply the line that minimizes that vertical distance. Given the value that we place on the accuracy of prediction, this is the most logical choice of a method for estimating the slope and intercept.

In summary then, the least squares criterion gives us a particular slope and intercept, and thus a particular regression line, such that the sum of the squared residuals is smallest. We often refer to this particular method for determining the slope and intercept as **least squares estimation** or ordinary least squares (OLS), because *b* and *a* represent sample estimates of the population parameters b and α obtained using the least squares criterion.

17.1.1.2.5 Proportion of Predictable Variation (Coefficient of Determination)

How well is the criterion variable *Y* predicted by the predictor variable *X*? For our example, we want to know how well employment success scores are predicted by work optimism scores. Let us consider two possible situations with respect to this example. First, if the work optimism score is found to be a really good predictor of employment success scores, then instructors could use the work optimism score to individualize onboarding and training based on work optimism of the employee. They could, for example, provide enhanced onboarding to employees with low work optimism scores, or in general, adjust the level of training to fit the optimism of their employees. Second, if work optimism is not found to be a very good predictor of employment success scores, then human resources representatives would not find very much use for the work optimism score in terms of their preparation for employment. They could search for some other more useful predictor, such as employee engagement or career readiness. In other words, if a predictor is not found to be particularly useful in predicting the criterion variable, then other relevant predictors should be considered.

How do we determine the utility of a predictor variable? The simplest method involves partitioning the total sum of squares in Y, which we denote as SS_{total} (sometimes written as SS_Y). This process is much like partitioning the sum of squares in the analysis of variance.

In simple linear regression, we can partition SS_{total} as follows:

$$SS_{total} = SS_{reg} + SS_{res}$$

$$\sum_{i=1}^{n}\left(Y-\bar{Y}\right)^2 = \sum_{i=1}^{n}\left(Y'-\bar{Y}\right)^2 + \sum_{i=1}^{n}\left(Y-Y'\right)^2$$

where SS_{total} is the total sum of squares in Y, SS_{reg} is the sum of squares of the regression of Y predicted by X (sometimes written as $SS_{Y'}$) (and represented in the equation as $\sum_{i=1}^{n}\left(Y'-\bar{Y}\right)^2$), SS_{res} is the sum of squares of the residuals (and represented in the equation as $\sum_{i=1}^{n}\left(Y-Y'\right)^2$), and the sums are taken over all observations from $i = 1, \ldots, n$. Thus, SS_{total} represents the total variation in the observed Y scores, SS_{reg} the variation in Y predicted by X, and SS_{res} the variation in Y not predicted by X.

The equation for SS_{reg} uses information about the difference between the predicted value of Y and the mean of Y: $\sum_{i=1}^{n}\left(Y'-\bar{Y}\right)^2$. Thus the SS_{reg} is essentially examining how much better the line of best fit (i.e., the predicted value of Y) is as compared to the mean of Y (recall that a slope of zero is a horizontal line, which is the mean of Y). The equation for SS_{res} uses information about the difference between the observed value of Y and the predicted value of Y: $\sum_{i=1}^{n}\left(Y-Y'\right)^2$. Thus the SS_{res} *is providing an indication of how "off" or inaccurate the model is*. The closer SS_{res} is to zero, the better the model fit (as more variability of the dependent variable is being explained by the model; in other words, the independent variables are doing a good job of prediction when the SS_{res} is smaller). Since $r_{XY}^2 = \frac{SS_{reg}}{SS_{total}}$, we can write SS_{total}, SS_{reg}, and SS_{res} as follows:

$$SS_{total} = \frac{n\sum_{i=1}^{n} Y^2 - \left(\sum_{i=1}^{n} Y\right)^2}{n}$$

$$SS_{reg} = \left(r_{XY}^2\right)\left(SS_{total}\right)$$

$$SS_{res} = \left(1-r_{XY}^2\right)\left(SS_{total}\right)$$

where r_{XY}^2 is the squared sample correlation between X and Y **(which, as we know, is the same as the squared sample correlation between Y and X, r_{XY}^2)**, commonly referred to as the **coefficient of determination**. The coefficient of determination in simple linear regression is not only the squared simple bivariate Pearson correlation between X and Y, but also $r_{XY}^2 = \frac{SS_{reg}}{SS_{total}}$ which tells us that it is the proportion of the total variation of the dependent variable (i.e., the denominator) that has been explained by the regression model (i.e., the numerator). Thus, the coefficient of determination can be used both as a measure of **effect size** (described in a later section) and as a **test of significance** (described in the next section). With the sample data of predicting employment success scores from work optimism, let us determine the sums of squares. We can write SS_{total} as follows:

$$SS_{total} = \frac{n\sum_{i=1}^{n} Y^2 - \left(\sum_{i=1}^{n} Y\right)^2}{n} = \frac{10(14,948) - (380^2)}{10} = 508.00$$

We already know that $r_{XY} = .9177$, so by squaring it, we obtain $r_{XY}^2 = .8422$. Next we can determine SS_{reg} and SS_{res} as follows:

$$SS_{reg} = (r_{XY}^2)(SS_{total}) = (.8422)(508.00) = 427.8376$$

$$SS_{res} = (1 - r_{XY}^2)(SS_{total}) = (1 - .8422)(508.00) = 80.1624$$

Given the squared correlation between X and Y ($r_{XY}^2 = .8422$), work optimism predicts approximately 84% of the variation in employment success, which is clearly a large effect size. Significance tests are discussed in the next section.

17.1.1.2.6 Significance Tests and Confidence Intervals

This section describes four procedures used in the simple linear regression context. The first two are tests of statistical significance that generally involve testing whether or not X is a significant predictor of Y. Then we consider two confidence interval techniques.

Test of Significance of r_{XY}^2. The first test is the test of the significance of r_{XY}^2 *(alternatively known as the test of the proportion of variation in Y predicted or explained by X)*. It is important that r_{XY}^2 be different from zero in order to have reasonable prediction. The null and alternative hypotheses, respectively, are as follows where the null indicates that the correlation between X and Y will be zero:

$$H_0 : \rho_{XY}^2 = 0$$

$$H_1 : \rho_{XY}^2 > 0$$

This test is based on the following test statistic:

$$F = \frac{r^2/m}{(1-r^2)/(n-m-1)}$$

where F indicates that this is an F statistic, r^2 is the coefficient of determination, $1 - r^2$ is the proportion of variation in Y that is not predicted by X, m is the number of predictors (which in the case of simple linear regression is always 1), and n is the sample size. The F test statistic is compared to the F critical value, always a one-tailed test (given that a squared value cannot be negative) and at the designated level of significance α, with degrees of freedom equal to m (i.e., the number of independent variables) and $(n - m - 1)$, as taken from the F table in Appendix Table A.4. That is, the tabled critical value is ${}_{\alpha}F_{m,(n-m-1)}$.

For the employment example, we determine the test statistic to be the following:

$$F = \frac{r^2/m}{(1-r^2)/(n-m-1)}$$

$$F = \frac{.8422/1}{(1-.8422)/(10-1-1)} = 42.6971$$

From Appendix Table A.4, the critical value, at the .05 level of significance, with degrees of freedom of 1 (i.e., one predictor) and 8 (i.e., $n - m - 1 = 10 - 1 - 1 = 8$) is ${}_{.05}F_{1,8} = 5.32$. The test statistic exceeds the critical value; thus we reject H_0 and conclude that ρ^2_{XY} is not equal to zero at the .05 level of significance (i.e., work optimism does predict a significant proportion of the variation on employment success).

***Test of Significance of b_{YX}*.** The second test is the test of the significance of the slope or regression coefficient, b_{YX}. In other words, *is the unstandardized regression coefficient statistically significantly different from zero?* This is actually the same as the test of b^*, the standardized regression coefficient, so we need not develop a separate test for the standardized regression coefficient. The null and alternative hypotheses, respectively, are as follows, where the null hypothesis states that the regression coefficient is equal to zero and the alternative states that it is not equal to zero.

$$H_0: \beta_{YX} = 0$$

$$H_1: \beta_{YX} \neq 0$$

To test whether the regression coefficient is equal to zero, we need a standard error for the slope b. However, first we need to develop some new concepts. The first new concept is the **variance error of estimate**. Although this is the correct term, it is easier to consider this as the **variance of the residuals**. The variance error of estimate, or variance of the residuals, is defined as follows:

$$s^2_{res} = \frac{\sum e_i^2}{df_{res}} = \frac{SS_{res}}{df_{res}} = MS_{res}$$

where the summation is taken from $i = 1, \ldots, n$ and $df_{res} = (n - m - 1)$ (or $n - 2$ if there is only a single predictor). Two degrees of freedom are lost because we have to estimate the population slope and intercept, β and α, from the sample data. The variance error of estimate indicates the amount of variation among the residuals. *If there are some extremely large residuals, this will result in a relatively large value of s^2_{res}, indicating poor prediction overall. If the residuals are generally small, this will result in a comparatively small value of s^2_{res}, indicating good prediction overall.*

The next new concept is the **standard error of estimate** (sometimes known as the **root mean square error**). *The standard error of estimate is simply the positive square root of the variance error of estimate, and thus is the standard deviation of the residuals or errors of estimate.* We denote the standard error of estimate as s_{res}.

The final new concept is the **standard error of b**. We denote the standard error of b as s_b and define it as

$$s_b = \frac{s_{res}}{\sqrt{\frac{n\sum X^2 - \left(\sum X\right)^2}{n}}} = \frac{s_{res}}{\sqrt{SS_X}}$$

where the summation is taken over $i = 1, \ldots, n$. We want s_b to be small to reject H_0, so we need s_{res} to be small and SS_X to be large. In other words, we want there to be a large spread of scores in X. *If the variability in X is small, it is difficult for X to be a significant predictor of Y.*

Now we can put these concepts together into a **test statistic** to test the significance of the slope b. As in many significance tests, the test statistic is formed by the ratio of a parameter estimate divided by its respective standard error. A ratio of the parameter estimate of the slope b to its standard error s_b is formed as follows:

$$t = \frac{b}{s_b}$$

The test statistic t is compared to the critical values of t (in Appendix Table A.2), a two-tailed test for a nondirectional H_1, at the designated level of significance a, and with degrees of freedom of $(n - m - 1)$. That is, the tabled critical values are $\pm_{(\alpha/2)} t_{(n-m-1)}$ for a two-tailed test.

In addition, all other things being equal (i.e., same data, same degrees of freedom, same level of significance), both of these significance tests (i.e., the test of significance of the squared bivariate correlation between X and Y and the test of significance of the slope) will yield the exact same result. That is, if X is a significant predictor of Y, then H_0 will be rejected in both tests. If X *is not* a significant predictor of Y, then H_0 will not be rejected for either test. *In simple linear regression, each of these tests is a method for testing the same general hypothesis and logically should lead the researcher to the exact same conclusion.* Thus, there is no need to implement both tests.

We can also form a **confidence interval around the slope b**. As in most confidence interval procedures, it follows the form of the sample estimate plus or minus the tabled critical value multiplied by the standard error. The confidence interval (CI) around b is formed as follows:

$$CI(b) = b \pm_{(\alpha/2)} t_{(n-m-1)} (s_b)$$

Recall that the null hypothesis was written as $H_0: \beta_{YX} = 0$. Therefore, *if the confidence interval contains zero, then β is not significantly different from zero at the specified α level.* This is interpreted to mean that in $(1 - \alpha)$% of the sample confidence intervals that would be formed from multiple samples, β will be included. This procedure assumes homogeneity of variance (discussed later in this chapter); for alternative procedures see Wilcox (1996, 2003).

Now we can determine the second test statistic for the employment example. We specify $H_0: \beta_{YX} = 0$ (i.e., the null hypothesis is that the slope is equal to zero; visually a slope of zero is a horizontal line) and conduct a two-tailed test. First the variance error of estimate is as follows:

$$s^2_{res} = \frac{\sum e_i^2}{df_{res}} = \frac{SS_{res}}{df_{res}} = MS_{res}$$

$$s^2_{res} = \frac{80.1578}{8} = 10.0197$$

The standard error of estimate, s_{res}, is $\sqrt{10.0197} = 3.1654$. Next, the standard error of b is computed as:

$$s_b = \frac{s_{res}}{\sqrt{\dfrac{n\sum X^2 - \left(\sum X\right)^2}{n}}} = \frac{s_{res}}{\sqrt{SS_X}} = \frac{3.1654}{\sqrt{1552.50}} = .0803.$$

Finally, we determine the test statistic to be as follows:

$$t = \frac{b}{s_b} = \frac{.5250}{.0803} = 6.5380$$

To evaluate the null hypothesis, we compare this test statistic to its critical values $\pm_{(.025)}t_{(8)} = \pm 2.306$. The test statistic exceeds the critical value, so H_0 is rejected in favor of H_1 (recall that we're not "accepting" the alternative hypothesis, simply finding evidence to support the alternative hypothesis). We conclude that the slope is indeed significantly different from zero, at the .05 level of significance.

Finally let us determine the confidence interval for the slope b as follows:

$$CI(b) = b \pm_{(\alpha/2)} t_{(n-m-1)}(s_b) = b \pm_{.025} t_8(s_b)$$

$$CI(b) = 0.5250 \pm (2.306)(0.0803) = (0.3398, 0.7102)$$

The interval does not contain zero, the value specified in H_0; thus we conclude that the slope β is significantly different from zero, at the .05 level of significance.

Confidence Interval for the Predicted Mean Value of Y. The third procedure is to develop a confidence interval for the predicted mean value of Y, denoted by $\bar{Y}_0'$, for a specific value of X_0. Alternatively, $\bar{Y}_0'$ is referred to as the **conditional mean of *Y* given X_0** (more about conditional distributions in the next section). In other words, for a particular predictor score X_0, how confident can we be in the predicted mean for Y?

The standard error of $\bar{Y}_0'$ is as follows:

$$s\left(\bar{Y}_0'\right) = s_{res}\sqrt{\left(\frac{1}{n}\right) + \left[\frac{\left(X_0 - \bar{X}\right)^2}{SS_X}\right]}$$

In looking at this equation, the further X_0 is from $\bar{X}$, the larger the standard error. Thus, the standard error depends on the particular value of X_0 selected. In other words, we expect to make our best predictions at the center of the distribution of X scores, and to make our poorest predictions for extreme values of X. Thus, the closer the value of the predictor is to the center of the distribution of the X scores, the better the prediction will be.

A confidence interval around $\bar{Y}_0'$ is formed as follows:

$$CI\left(\bar{Y}_0'\right) = \bar{Y}_0' \pm_{(\alpha/2)} t_{(n-2)}\left[s\left(\bar{Y}_0'\right)\right]$$

Our interpretation is that in $(1-\alpha)\%$ of the sample confidence intervals that would be formed from multiple samples, the population mean value of Y for a given value of X will be included.

Let us consider an example of this confidence interval procedure with the employment data. If we take a work optimism score of 50, the predicted score on employment success is 35.1125. A confidence interval for the predicted mean value of 35.1125 is as follows:

$$s\left(\bar{Y}_0'\right) = s_{res}\sqrt{\left(\frac{1}{n}\right) + \left[\frac{\left(X_0 - \bar{X}\right)^2}{SS_X}\right]}$$

$$s\left(\bar{Y}_0'\right) = 3.1654\sqrt{\left(\frac{1}{10}\right) + \left[\frac{(50-55)^2}{1552.50}\right]} = 1.0786$$

$$CI\left(\bar{Y}_0'\right) = \bar{Y}_0' \pm {}_{(\alpha/2)}t_{(n-2)}\left[s\left(\bar{Y}_0'\right)\right] = \bar{Y}_0' \pm {}_{.025}t_8\left[s\left(\bar{Y}_0'\right)\right]$$

$$CI\left(\bar{Y}_0'\right) = 35.1125 \pm (2.306)(1.0786) = (32.6252, 37.5998)$$

In Figure 17.3 the confidence interval around $\bar{Y}_0'$ given X_0 is plotted as the pair of curved lines closest to the regression line. Here we see graphically that the width of the confidence interval increases the further we move from X (where X = 55.5000).

Prediction Interval for Individual Values of Y. The fourth and final procedure is to develop a prediction interval for an individual predicted value of Y_0' at a specific individual value of X_0. That is, the predictor score for a particular individual is known, but the criterion score for that individual has not yet been observed. This is in contrast to the confidence interval just discussed where the individual Y scores have already been observed. Thus, the *confidence interval deals with the mean of the predicted values, while the prediction interval deals with an individual predicted value not yet observed.*

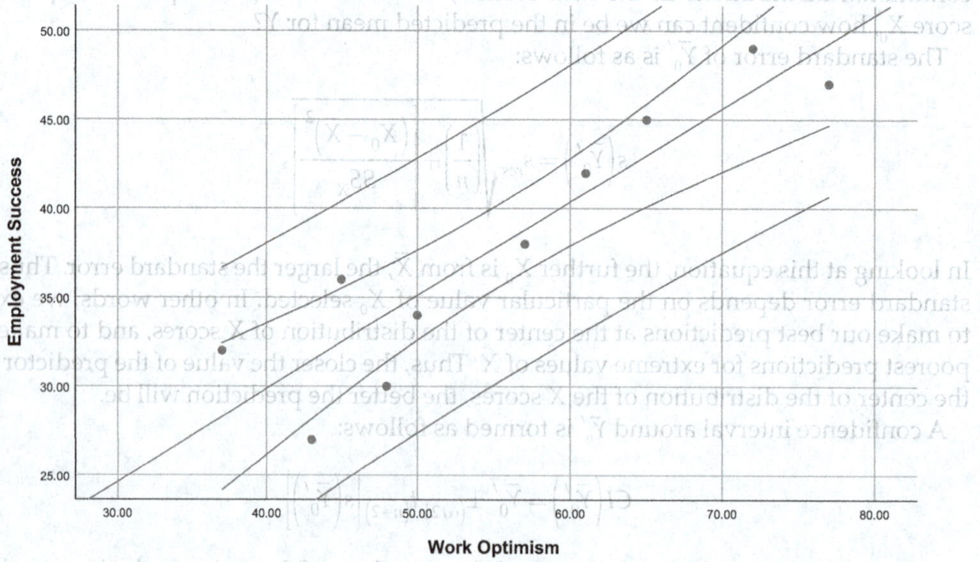

FIGURE 17.3
Confidence intervals for the employment example. Curved lines closest to the regression line represent the 95% CI; lines furthest from the regression line represent the 95% predicted interval (PI)

The standard error of Y_0' is as follows:

$$s(Y_0') = s_{res}\sqrt{1 + \left(\frac{1}{n}\right) + \left[\frac{(X_0 - \bar{X})^2}{SS_X}\right]}$$

The standard error of Y_0' is similar to the standard error of $\bar{Y}_0'$ with the addition of 1 to the equation. Thus the standard error of Y_0' will always be greater than the standard error of $\bar{Y}_0'$ as there is greater uncertainty about individual values than about the mean. The further X_0 is from $\bar{X}$, the larger the standard error. Thus the standard error again depends on the particular value of X, where we have more confidence in predictions for values of X close to $\bar{X}$.

The **prediction interval (PI)** around Y_0' is formed as follows:

$$PI(Y_0') = Y_0' \pm_{(\alpha/2)} t_{(n-2)}\left[s(Y_0')\right]$$

Our interpretation of the prediction interval is that in $(1-\alpha)\%$ of the sample prediction intervals that would be formed from multiple samples, the new observation Y_0 for a given value of X will be included.

Consider an example of this prediction interval procedure with the employment data. If we take a work optimism score of 50, the predicted score on employment success is 35.1125. A prediction interval for the predicted individual value of 35.1125 is as follows:

$$s(Y_0') = s_{res}\sqrt{1 + \left(\frac{1}{n}\right) + \left[\frac{(X_0 - \bar{X})^2}{SS_X}\right]} = 3.1654\sqrt{1 + \left(\frac{1}{10}\right) + \left[\frac{(50-55)^2}{1552.50}\right]} = 3.3441$$

$$PI(Y_0') = Y_0' \pm_{(\alpha/2)} t_{(n-2)}\left[s(Y_0')\right] = Y_0' \pm_{.025} t_8\left[s(Y_0')\right]$$

$$PI(Y_0') = 35.1125 \pm (2.306)(3.3441) = (27.4010, 42.8240)$$

In Figure 17.3, the prediction interval around Y_0' given X_0 is plotted as the pair of curved lines furthest from the regression line. Here we see graphically that the *prediction interval is always wider than its corresponding confidence interval.*

17.1.2 Sample Size

A widely heard convention for sample size in regression is that a researcher needs at least 10 cases for every independent variable in the model. In the case of simple linear regression, that would suggest a sample size of 10 provides sufficient power. In some cases, this may be sufficient, but in other cases, this may be quite insufficient. Rather than suggest there are general guidelines that work for "guesstimating" sample size, we recommend performing power analyses to estimate sample size given known or anticipated parameters. Should you choose to throw caution to the wind and decide not to systematically explore sample size as a function of power, we will reiterate Darlington and Hayes (2017, p. 521) in that "larger is generally better."

17.1.3 Power

With simple linear regression, we have only one predictor and one dependent variable. As we will later see in the illustration using G*Power, power in simple linear regression is a function of directionality of the test (i.e., one- or two-tailed), size of the population effect (i.e., effect size), level of significance, slope specified in the null hypothesis (usually 0), and the standard deviation of both the predictor and outcome. To determine sample size for a desired level of power, we suggest that you consult power tables (e.g., Cohen, 1988) or power software such as G*Power (note that Liu includes syntax for using **R**, SAS, and SPSS) (Erdfelder, Faul, & Buchner, 1996; Faul, Erdfelder, Buchner, & Lang, 2009; Faul, Erdfelder, Lang, & Buchner, 2007; Liu, 2014). If you're interested in learning more about power, we encourage you to consult any of a number of excellent resources (e.g., Aberson, 2010; Cohen, 1988; Liu, 2014; Murphy, Myors, & Wolach, 2014).

17.1.4 Effect Size

There are multiple effect size indices that can be considered in simple linear regression. We will discuss the coefficient of determination and f^2.

17.1.4.1 Coefficient of Determination

Recall that r_{XY}^2 is the squared sample correlation between X and Y, i.e., the *coefficient of determination*, introduced earlier. The coefficient of determination in simple linear regression is not only the squared simple bivariate Pearson correlation between X and Y, but also $r_{XY}^2 = \frac{SS_{reg}}{SS_{total}}$ which tells us that it is the proportion of the total variation of the dependent variable (i.e., the denominator) that has been explained by the regression model (i.e., the numerator). In other words, r_{XY}^2 indicates the proportion of total variation in the dependent variable Y that is predicted from the set of predictor variables. There is no objective gold standard as to how large the coefficient of determination needs to be in order to say a meaningful proportion of variation has been predicted. The coefficient is determined not just by the quality of the predictor variable included in the model, but also by the quality of relevant predictor variables not included in the model, as well as by the amount of total variation in the dependent variable Y. According to the subjective standards of Cohen (1988), a small effect size for the coefficient of determination is defined as $r_{XY}^2 = .01$ a medium effect size as $r_{XY}^2 = .09$ and a large effect size as $r_{XY}^2 = .025$ Interpretation of effect size can be made based on a comparison to similar studies; what is considered a "small" effect using Cohen's conventions may actually be quite large in comparison to other related studies that have been conducted. In lieu of a comparison to other studies, such as in those cases where there are no or minimal related studies, then Cohen's subjective standards may be appropriate. For additional information on effect size measures in regression, we suggest you consider Steiger and Fouladi (1992), Mendoza and Stafford (2001), and Smithson (2001) (which also includes some discussion of power).

17.1.4.2 f²

The coefficient of determination (i.e., the squared multiple correlation coefficient), r_{XY}^2, can also be used to compute a globalized f^2, sometimes referred to as **Cohen's** f^2 (Cohen, 1988), which is $f^2 = \left(r_{XY}^2\right) / \left(1 - r_{XY}^2\right)$. *Note that Cohen's f^2 is a ratio of two proportions.* More specifically, it is the ratio of (1) the proportion of variation in the dependent variables uniquely explained by the independent variable to (2) the proportion of variation in the dependent variable unexplained by *any* variable in the model (Darlington & Hayes, 2017). In simple linear regression, with only one predictor, this ratio of proportions is expressed very simply as the globalized f^2. Note that Cohen's f^2 is *not* a proportion itself, because while it cannot be smaller than zero, it has no upper bound (Darlington & Hayes, 2017). Thus, *f^2 can be greater than one, and thus interpretations of f^2 cannot follow similarly as correlation coefficients.*

In many instances, *a localized effect* is of interest. In other words, the proportion of variation in the outcome is uniquely explained by one variable in the model. As we'll see in the multiple regression chapter, the computation for the localized effect differs given multiple predictors. With a single predictor in simple linear regression, we are concerned only with the globalized f^2.

17.1.4.3 Confidence Intervals for Effect Size

Confidence intervals (CI) can be computed for correlations, and thus in the case of simple linear regression, these CI are also the CI for the regression model and the CI for the effect size. *Larger CI suggest lower precision, and smaller CI reflect higher precision.* An excellent online calculator for computing all types of effect sizes and their confidence intervals is provided by Dr. David B. Wilson and is available through the Campbell Collaboration (see https://campbellcollaboration.org/research-resources/effect-size-calculator.html). Although designed for use when conducting meta-analyses, the online calculator comes in handy whenever an effect size and its CI are desired.

Let's take an example with our employment data that will be used later. Correlating work optimism and employment success, we find a Pearson correlation of .918 (which will also be the model R in our simple linear regression). Using Campbell's effect size calculator for a correlation, along with the sample size, we find the 95% CI of (.6833, .9808) (see Figure 17.4). Because the confidence interval does not contain 0, our null value (i.e.,

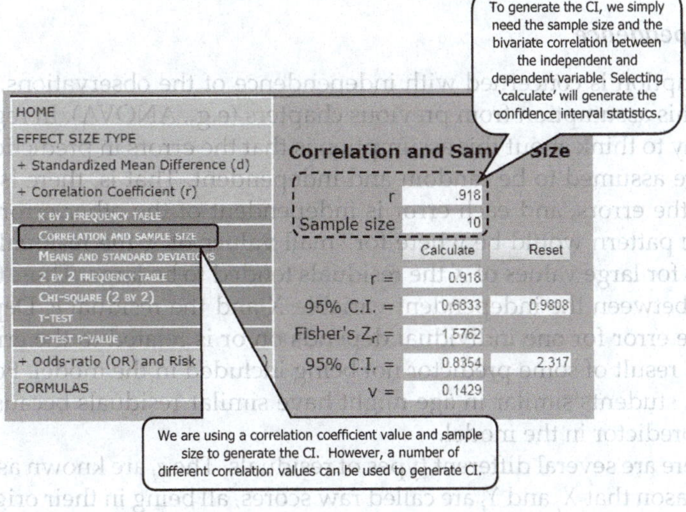

FIGURE 17.4
Computing correlation CI using the Campbell Collaboration Online Calculator.

TABLE 17.2
Effect Sizes and Interpretations

Effect Size	Interpretation
r_{XY}^2	• Squared simple bivariate Pearson correlation between X and Y • Proportion of the total variation of the dependent variable (i.e., the denominator) that has been explained by the regression model (i.e., the numerator) • Cohen's standards: o $r_{XY}^2 = .01$, small o $r_{XY}^2 = .09$, medium o $r_{XY}^2 = .25$, large
Cohen's f^2	• Ratio of (1) the proportion of variation in the dependent variables uniquely explained by the independent variable to (2) the proportion of variation in the dependent variable unexplained by *ANY* variable in the model • Cohen's standards: o $f^2 = .02$, small o $f^2 = .15$, medium o $f^2 = .35$, large

reflecting no relationship), this may provide evidence to suggest a statistically significant relationship between the independent variable and the outcome.

For additional information on effect size measures in regression, we suggest you consider Darlington and Hayes (2017), Steiger and Fouladi (1992), Mendoza and Stafford (2001), and Smithson (2001, which also includes some discussion of power).

17.1.5 Assumptions

In this section, we consider the following assumptions involved in simple linear regression: (a) independence; (b) homogeneity; (c) normality; (d) linearity; and (e) fixed X. Some discussion is also devoted to the effects of assumption violations and how to detect them.

17.1.5.1 Independence

The first assumption is concerned with independence of the observations. We should be familiar with this assumption from previous chapters (e.g., ANOVA). In regression analysis, another way to think about this assumption is that the errors in prediction or the residuals (i.e., e_i) are assumed to be random and independent. That is, there is no systematic pattern about the errors, and each error is independent of the other errors. An example of a systematic pattern would be where for small values of X the residuals tended to be small, whereas for large values of X the residuals tended to be large. Thus, there would be a relationship between the independent variable X and the residual e. Dependent errors occur when the error for one individual depends on or is related to the error for another individual as a result of some predictor not being included in the model. For our employment example, students similar in age might have similar residuals because age was not included as a predictor in the model.

Note that there are several different types of residuals. The e_i are known as **raw residuals** for the same reason that X_i and Y_i are called raw scores, all being in their original scale. The raw residuals are on the same raw score scale as Y, but with a mean of zero and a variance of S^2_{res}. Some researchers dislike raw residuals as their scale depends on the scale of Y, and therefore they must temper their interpretation of the residual values. Several different types of **standardized residuals** have been developed, including the original form of standardized residual e_i/S_{res}. These values are measured along the z score scale with a mean of 0 and a variance of 1, and approximately 95% of the values are within ±2 units of zero. Later in our illustration of SPSS, we will use **studentized residuals** for diagnostic checks. Studentized residuals, a type of standardized residual, are more sensitive to detecting outliers. Some researchers prefer these or other variants of standardized residuals over raw residuals because they find it easier to detect large residuals. However, if you really think about it, one can easily look at the middle 95% of the raw residuals by just considering the range of ±2 standard errors (i.e., ±2 S_{res}) around zero. Readers interested in learning more about other types of standardized residuals are referred to a number of excellent resources (e.g., Atkinson, 1987; Cook & Weisberg, 1982; Dunn & Clark, 1987; Kleinbaum, Kupper, Muller, & Nizam, 1998; Weisberg, 2014).

The simplest procedure for assessing the assumption of independence is to examine a scatterplot (Y versus X) or a residual plot (e.g., e versus X). *If the independence assumption is satisfied, there should be a random display of points. If the assumption is violated, the plot will display some type of pattern.* For example, the negative residuals tend to cluster together and positive residuals tend to cluster together. As we know from ANOVA, violation of the independence assumption generally occurs in the following three situations: (a) when the observations are collected over time [the independent variable is a measure of time; consider using the Durban-Watson test (Durbin & Watson, 1950, 1951, 1971)]; (b) observations are made within blocks, such that the observations within a particular block are more similar than observations in different blocks; or (c) when observation involves replication. Lack of independence affects the estimated standard errors, being under- or overestimated. For serious violations one could consider using generalized or weighted least squares as the method of estimation.

17.1.5.2 Homoscedasticity

The second assumption is **homogeneity of variance** or **homoscedasticity**, which should also be a familiar assumption (e.g., ANOVA). When discussed in the context of ANOVA, this assumption is usually referred to as homogeneity of variance; in the context of regression, it is usually referred to as homoscedasticity. This assumption must be reframed a bit in the regression context by examining the concept of a **conditional distribution**. In regression analysis, a conditional distribution is defined as the distribution of Y for a particular value of X. For instance, in the employment example, we could consider the conditional distribution of employment success scores when work optimism = 50; in other words, what the distribution of Y looks like for $X = 50$. *We call this a conditional distribution because it represents the distribution of Y conditional on a particular value of X (sometimes denoted as $Y \mid X$, read as Y given X).* Alternatively we could examine the conditional distribution of the prediction errors, that is, the distribution of the prediction errors conditional on a particular value of X (i.e., $e \mid X$, read as e given X). Thus, the homogeneity or homoscedasticity assumption is that the conditional distributions have a constant variance for all values of X.

In a plot of the Y scores or the residuals versus X, the consistency of the variance of the conditional distributions can be examined. A common violation of this assumption occurs when the conditional residual variance increases as X increases. Here the residual plot is cone- or fan-shaped where the cone opens toward the right. An example of this violation would be where weight is predicted by age, as weight is more easily predicted for young children than it is for adults. Thus, residuals would tend to be larger for adults than for children.

If the homogeneity assumption is violated, estimates of the standard errors are larger, and although the regression coefficients remain unbiased, the validity of the significance tests is affected. In fact, with larger standard errors, it is more difficult to reject H_0, therefore resulting in a larger number of Type II errors. Minor violations of this assumption will have a small net effect; more serious violations occur when the variances are greatly different. In addition, nonconstant variances may also result in the conditional distributions being nonnormal in shape.

If the homogeneity assumption is seriously violated, the simplest solution is to use some sort of transformation, known as **variance stabilizing transformations** (e.g., Weisberg, 2014). Commonly used transformations are the log or square root of Y (e.g., Kleinbaum et al., 1998). These transformations can also often improve on the nonnormality of the conditional distributions. However, this complicates things in terms of dealing with transformed variables rather than the original variables. A better solution is to use generalized or weighted least squares (Weisberg, 2014). A third solution is to use a form of robust estimation (e.g., Carroll & Ruppert, 1982; Kleinbaum et al., 1998; Wilcox, 2003).

17.1.5.3 Normality

The third assumption of **normality** should also be a familiar one. In regression, the normality assumption is that the conditional distributions of either Y or the prediction errors (i.e., residuals) are normal in shape. That is, *for all values of X, the scores on Y or the prediction errors are normally distributed.* Oftentimes nonnormal distributions are largely a function of one or a few extreme observations, known as **outliers**, and thus we will begin our discussion here. Extreme values (i.e., outliers) may cause nonnormality and seriously affect the regression results. The regression estimates are quite sensitive to outlying observations such that the precision of the estimates is affected, particularly the slope. Also, the coefficient of determination can be affected. In general, the regression line will be pulled toward the outlier, because the least squares principle always attempts to find the line that best fits all of the points.

There are a number of different recommendations for crudely detecting outliers from a residual plot or scatterplot. A commonly used convention is to define an outlier as an observation that is more than two or three standard errors from the mean (i.e., a large distance from the mean). The outlier observation may be a result of (a) a simple recording or data entry error, (b) an error in observation, (c) an improperly functioning instrument, (d) inappropriate use of administration instructions, or (e) a true outlier. If the outlier is the result of an error, correct the error if possible and redo the regression analysis. If the error cannot be corrected, then the observation could be deleted. If the outlier represents an accurate observation, then this observation may contain important theoretical information, and one would be more hesitant to delete it (or perhaps seek out similar observations).

A simple procedure to use for single case outliers (i.e., in situations where there is just one outlier) is to perform *two* regression analyses, both with and without the outlier being included. A comparison of the regression results will provide some indication of the effects of the outlier. Other methods for detecting and dealing with outliers are available, but are not described here (e.g., Barnett & Lewis, 1994; Beckman & Cook, 1983; Dennis Cook, 1977, 2000; David & Daryl, 1978; Hawkins, 1980; Kleinbaum et al., 1998; Mickey, Dunn, & Clark, 2004; Pedhazur, 1997; Rousseeuw & Leroy, 1987; Wilcox, 2003).

Beyond examination and treatment for outliers, how does one go about detecting violation of the normality assumption? There are two commonly used procedures. *The simplest procedure involves checking for symmetry in a histogram, frequency distribution, boxplot, or skewness and kurtosis statistics.* Although **nonzero kurtosis** (i.e., a distribution that is either flat, platykurtic, or has a sharp peak, leptokurtic) will have minimal effect on the regression estimates, **nonzero skewness** (i.e., a distribution that is not symmetric with either a positive or negative skew) will have much greater impact on these estimates. Thus, finding asymmetrical distributions is a must. There are different conventions for determining how extreme skewness can be and still retain a relatively normal distribution. One simple guideline is that skewness values within ±2.0 are considered relatively normal, with more liberal researchers applying a ±3.0 guideline, and more conservative researchers using ±1.0. Another recommendation for determining how extreme a skewness value must be for the distribution to be considered nonnormal is as follows: Skewness values outside the range of plus or minus two standard errors of skewness suggest a distribution that is nonnormal. Applying this suggestion to a hypothetical example, if the standard error of skewness is .85, then any value of skewness outside of −2(.85) to +2(.85), or −1.7 to +1.7, would be considered nonnormal. It is important to note that this second recommendation is sensitive to small sample sizes and should only be considered as a general guide. For the employment example the skewness value for the raw residuals is −0.2692. Based on the simple guideline, and the most stringent convention that skewness values within ±1.0 are considered relatively normal, there is evidence of normality in this illustration.

Another useful graphical technique is the normal probability plot (or Q-Q plot). With normally distributed data or residuals, the points on the normal probability plot will fall along a straight diagonal line, whereas nonnormal data will not. There is a difficulty with this plot because there is no criterion with which to judge deviation from linearity. A normal probability plot of the raw residuals for the employment example is shown in Figure 17.5. Together, the skewness and normal probability plot results indicate that the

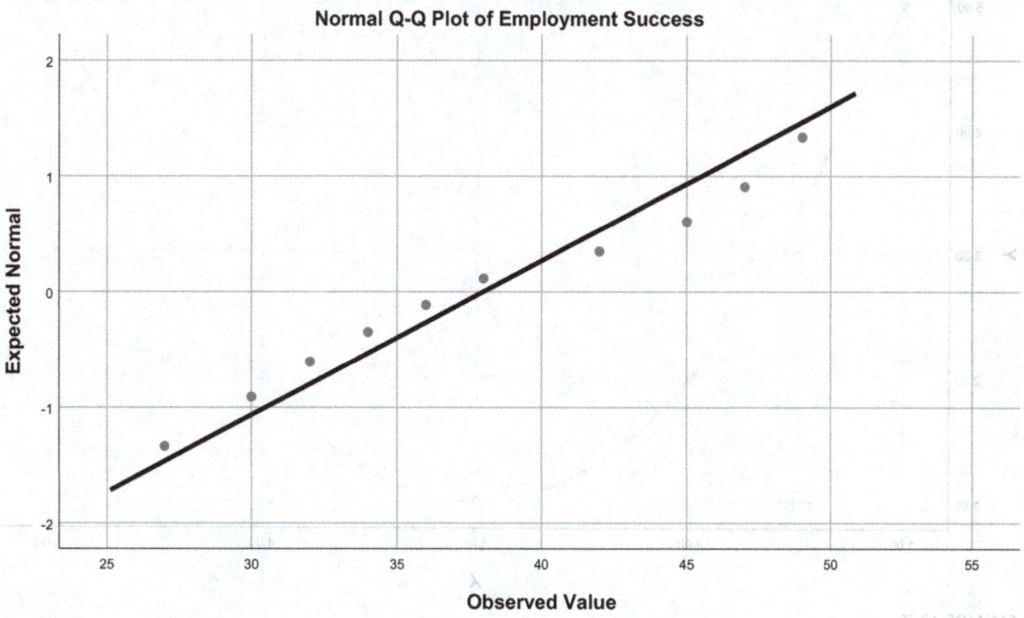

FIGURE 17.5
Normal probability plot for employment example.

normality assumption is satisfied. It is recommended that skewness and/or the normal probability plot be considered at a minimum.

Several statistical procedures are available for the detection of nonnormality (e.g., Andrews, 1971; Belsley, Kuh, & Welsch, 1980; Ruppert & Carroll, 1980; Wu, 1985). As we learned in previous chapters, the Kolmogorov-Smirnov (K-S) (Chakravart, Laha, & Roy, 1967) with Lilliefor's significance (Lilliefors, 1967), and the Shapiro-Wilk (*SW*) (Shapiro & Wilk, 1965) are tests that provide evidence of the extent to which our sample distribution is statistically different from a normal distribution.

In cases of nonnormality, various transformations are available to transform a nonnormal distribution into a normal distribution. The most commonly used transformations to correct for nonnormality in regression analysis are to transform the dependent variable using the log (to correct for positive skew) or the square root (to correct for positive or negative skew). However, again there is the problem of dealing with transformed variables measured along some other scale than that of the original variables.

17.1.5.4 Linearity

The fourth assumption is **linearity**. This assumption simply indicates that there is a linear relationship between X and Y, which is also assumed for most types of correlations. Consider the scatterplot and regression line in Figure 17.6 where X and Y are not linearly related. Here X and Y form a perfect curvilinear relationship as all of the points fall precisely on a curve. However, fitting a straight line to these points will result in a slope of zero as indicated by the solid horizontal line, not useful at all for predicting Y from X (as the predicted score for all cases will be the mean of Y). For example, age and performance are not linearly related.

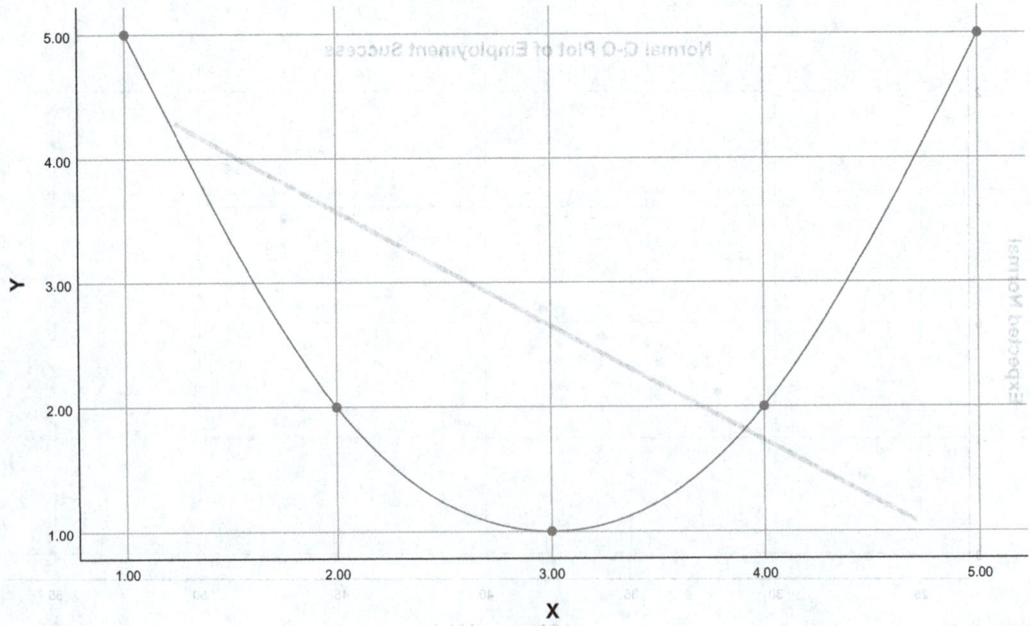

FIGURE 17.7

If the relationship between X and Y is linear, then the sample slope and intercept will be unbiased estimators of the population slope and intercept, respectively. The linearity assumption is important because, regardless of the value of X_i, we always expect Y_i to increase by b_{XY} units for a one-unit increase in X_i. If a nonlinear relationship exists, this means that the expected increase in Y_i depends on the value of X_i. Strictly speaking, linearity in a model refers to there being linearity in the parameters of the model (i.e., slope β and intercept a).

Detecting violation of the linearity assumption can often be done by looking at the scatterplot of *Y* versus *X*. If the linearity assumption is met, we expect to see no systematic pattern of points. While this plot is often satisfactory in simple linear regression, less obvious violations are more easily detected in a residual plot. If the linearity assumption is met, we expect to see a horizontal band of residuals mainly contained within $\pm 2s_{res}$ or $\pm 3s_{res}$ (or standard errors) across the values of *X*. If the assumption is violated, we expect to see a systematic pattern between *e* and *X*. Therefore, we recommend you examine both the scatterplot and the residual plot. A residual plot for the employment example is shown in Figure 17.7. Even with a very small sample, we see a fairly random display of residuals, and therefore feel fairly confident that the linearity assumption has been satisfied.

A hypothesis test for linearity can also be conducted in which a linear relationship is compared to a quadratic or cubic relationship. We will illustrate this later using SPSS.

If a serious violation of the linearity assumption has been detected, how should we deal with it? There are two alternative procedures that the researcher can utilize, **transformations** or **nonlinear models**. The first option is to transform either one or both of

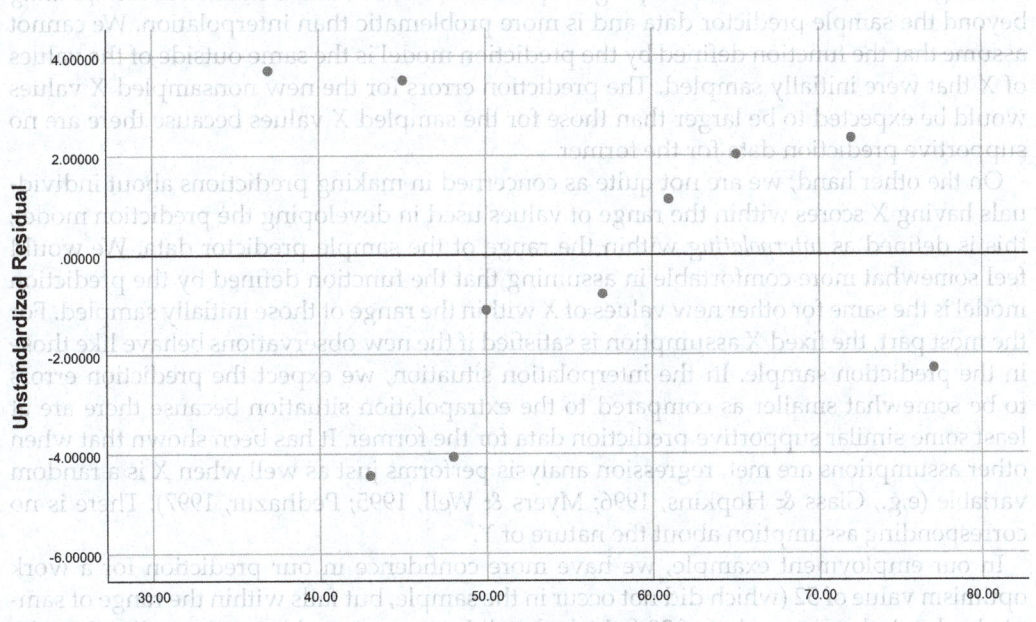

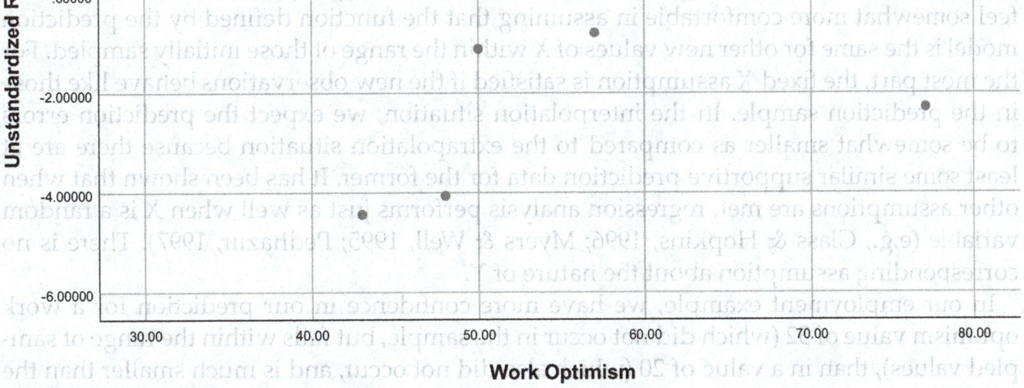

FIGURE 17.7
Residual plot for employment example.

the variables to achieve linearity. That is, the researcher selects a transformation that subsequently results in a linear relationship between the transformed variables. Then the method of least squares can be used to perform a linear regression analysis on the transformed variables. However, when dealing with transformed variables measured along a different scale, results need to be described in terms of the transformed rather than the original variables. A better option is to use a nonlinear model to examine the relationship between the variables in their original scale (see Wilcox, 1996, 2003; also discussed in Chapter 18).

17.1.5.5 Fixed X

The fifth and final assumption is that the values of X are **fixed**. That is, X is a fixed variable rather than a random variable. This results in the regression model being valid only for those particular values of X that were actually observed and used in the analysis. Thus, the same values of X would be used in replications or repeated samples. You may recall a similar concept in the fixed-effects analysis of variance models previously considered.

Strictly speaking, the regression model and its parameter estimates are valid only for those values of X actually sampled. The use of a prediction model, based on one sample of individuals, to predict Y for another sample of individuals may also be suspect. Depending on the circumstances, the new sample of individuals may actually call for a different set of parameter estimates. Two obvious situations that come to mind are the **extrapolation** and **interpolation** of values of X. In general we may not want to make predictions about individuals having X scores (i.e., scores on the independent variable) that are outside of the range of values used in developing the prediction model; this is defined as *extrapolating* beyond the sample predictor data and is more problematic than interpolation. We cannot assume that the function defined by the prediction model is the same outside of the values of X that were initially sampled. The prediction errors for the new nonsampled X values would be expected to be larger than those for the sampled X values because there are no supportive prediction data for the former.

On the other hand, we are not quite as concerned in making predictions about individuals having X scores within the range of values used in developing the prediction model; this is defined as *interpolating* within the range of the sample predictor data. We would feel somewhat more comfortable in assuming that the function defined by the prediction model is the same for other new values of X within the range of those initially sampled. For the most part, the fixed X assumption is satisfied if the new observations behave like those in the prediction sample. In the interpolation situation, we expect the prediction errors to be somewhat smaller as compared to the extrapolation situation because there are at least some similar supportive prediction data for the former. It has been shown that when other assumptions are met, regression analysis performs just as well when X is a random variable (e.g., Glass & Hopkins, 1996; Myers & Well, 1995; Pedhazur, 1997). There is no corresponding assumption about the nature of Y.

In our employment example, we have more confidence in our prediction for a work optimism value of 52 (which did not occur in the sample, but falls within the range of sampled values), than in a value of 20 (which also did not occur, and is much smaller than the smallest value sampled, 37). In fact, this is precisely the rationale underlying the prediction interval previously developed, where the width of the interval increased as an individual's score on the predictor (X_i) moved away from the predictor mean ($\bar{X}$).

TABLE 17.3

Assumptions and Violation of Assumptions: Simple Linear Regression

Assumption	Effect of Assumption Violation
Independence	• Influences standard errors of the model
Homogeneity	• Bias in S^2_{res} • May inflate standard errors and thus increase likelihood of a Type II error • May result in nonnormal conditional distributions
Normality	• Less precise slope, intercept, and R^2
Linearity	• Bias in slope and intercept • Expected change in *Y* is not a constant and depends on value of *X* • Reduced magnitude of coefficient of determination
Values of X fixed	• Extrapolating beyond the range of *X*: prediction errors larger, may also bias slope and intercept • Interpolating within the range of *X*: smaller effects than in extrapolation; if other assumptions met, negligible effect

A summary of the assumptions and the effects of their violation for simple linear regression is presented in Table 17.3.

17.1.5.6 Summary

The simplest procedure for assessing assumptions, and thus perhaps where you want to begin (but not end!) your examination of assumptions, is via plots of residuals. Take the employment problem as an example. Although sample size is quite small in terms of looking at conditional distributions, it would appear that all of our assumptions have been satisfied. All of the residuals are within two standard errors of zero, and there does not seem to be any systematic pattern in the residuals. The distribution of the residuals is nearly symmetrical, and the normal probability plot looks good. The scatterplot also strongly suggests a linear relationship.

17.2 Mathematical Introduction Snapshot

To summarize the mathematics that underlie simple linear regression, we first examined the *population regression model* for *Y* being predicted by *X*, which was as follows:

$$Y_i = \beta_{YX} X_i + \alpha_{YX} + \varepsilon_i$$

where *Y* is the criterion variable, *X* is the predictor variable, β_{YX} is the population slope for *Y* predicted by *X*, α_{YX} is the population intercept for *Y* predicted by *X*, ε_i are the population residuals or errors of prediction (the part of Y_i not predicted from X_i), and *i* represents an index for a particular case (an individual or object; in other words, the unit of analysis that has been measured). The index *i* can take on values from 1 to *N*, where *N* is the size of the population, written as $i = 1,\ldots,N$.

The *population prediction model* is as follows:

$$Y_i' = \beta_{YX} X_i + \alpha_{YX}$$

where Y_i' is the predicted value of Y for a specific value of X. That is, Y_i is the *actual or observed score* obtained by individual i, while Y_i' is the *predicted score* based on their X score for that same individual (in other words, you are using the value of X to predict what Y will be).

The *sample regression model* for predicting Y from X is computed as:

$$Y_i = b_{YX} X_i + a_{YX} + e_i$$

where Y and X are as before (i.e., the dependent and independent variables respectively), b_{YX} is the sample slope for Y predicted by X, a_{YX} is the sample intercept for Y predicted by X, e_i are sample residuals or errors of prediction (the part of Y_i not predictable from X_i), and i represents an index for a case (an individual or object). The index i can take on values from 1 to n, where n is the size of the sample, and is written as $i = 1,\ldots,n$.

The *sample prediction model* is computed as follows:

$$Y_i' = b_{YX} X_i + a_{YX}$$

where Y_i' is the predicted value of Y for a specific value of X. We define the sample prediction error as the difference between the *actual score* obtained by individual i (i.e., Y_i) and the *predicted score* based on the X score for that individual (i.e., Y_i'). The sample slope $\left(b_{XY}\right)$ and intercept $\left(a_{YX}\right)$. can be determined by

$$b_{YX} = r_{YX}\left(\frac{s_Y}{s_X}\right)$$

and

$$a_{YX} = \bar{Y} - b_{YX}\bar{X}$$

where s_Y and s_X are the sample standard deviations for Y and X respectively, r_{YX} is the sample correlation between X and Y (again the Pearson correlation coefficient, rho), and $\bar{Y}$ and $\bar{X}$ are the sample means for Y and X, respectively.

One method for determining the utility of a predictor variable is by partitioning the total sum of squares in Y, which we denote as SS_{total} (also SS_Y):

$$SS_{total} = SS_{reg} + SS_{res} = \sum_{i=1}^{n}\left(Y - \bar{Y}\right)^2 = \sum_{i=1}^{n}\left(Y' - \bar{Y}\right)^2 + \sum_{i=1}^{n}\left(Y - Y'\right)^2$$

where SS_{total} is the total variation in the observed Y scores Y, SS_{reg} is the sum of squares of the regression of Y predicted by X (i.e., variation in Y predicted by X, also $SS_{Y'}$) (and represented in the equation as $\sum_{i=1}^{n}\left(Y' - \bar{Y}\right)^2$), SS_{res} is the sum of squares of the residuals (i.e., the variation in Y not predicted by X; and represented in the equation as $\sum_{i=1}^{n}\left(Y' - \bar{Y}\right)^2$), and the sums are taken over all observations from $i = 1,\ldots,n$. Since $r_{XY}^2 = \frac{SS_{reg}}{SS_{total}}$, we can write SS_{total}, SS_{reg}, and SS_{res} as follows:

$$SS_{toatl} = \frac{n\sum_{i=1}^{n} Y^2 - \left(\sum_{i=1}^{n} Y\right)^2}{n}$$

$$SS_{reg} = \left(r_{XY}^2\right)\left(SS_{total}\right)$$

$$SS_{res} = \left(1 - r_{XY}^2\right)\left(SS_{total}\right)$$

where r_{XY}^2 is the squared sample correlation between X and Y, i.e., the *coefficient of determination.* The coefficient of determination in simple linear regression is not only the squared simple bivariate Pearson correlation between X and Y, but also $r_{XY}^2 = \frac{SS_{reg}}{SS_{total}}$ which tells us that it is the proportion of the total variation of the dependent variable (i.e., the denominator) that has been explained by the regression model (i.e., the numerator) and thus is a valuable effect size index.

17.3 Computing Simple Linear Regression Using SPSS

Next we consider SPSS for the simple linear regression model. Before we conduct the analysis, let us review the data. With one independent variable and one dependent variable, the dataset must consist of two variables or columns, *one for the independent variable* and *one for the dependent variable.* Each row still represents one individual or unit that has been measured, with the value of the independent variable for that particular case and their score on the dependent variable. In the screenshot in Figure 17.8, we see the SPSS dataset is in the form of two columns representing one independent variable (work optimism) and one dependent variable (employment success).

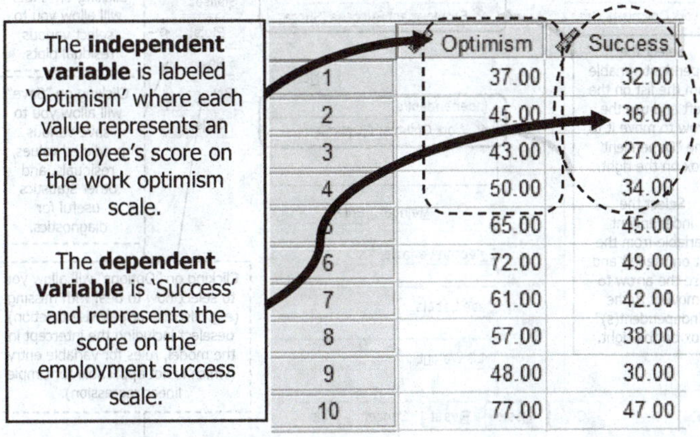
The **independent variable** is labeled 'Optimism' where each value represents an employee's score on the work optimism scale.
The **dependent variable** is 'Success' and represents the score on the employment success scale.
Optimism
Success
1 37.00 32.00
2 45.00 36.00
3 43.00 27.00
4 50.00 34.00
5 65.00 45.00
6 72.00 49.00
7 61.00 42.00
8 57.00 38.00
9 48.00 30.00
10 77.00 47.00

FIGURE 17.8
Data for the simple linear regression model.

Step 1. To conduct a simple linear regression, go to "Analyze" in the top pulldown menu, then select "Regression," and then select "Linear." Following the screenshot for Step 1 (Figure 17.9) produces the "Linear Regression" dialog box.

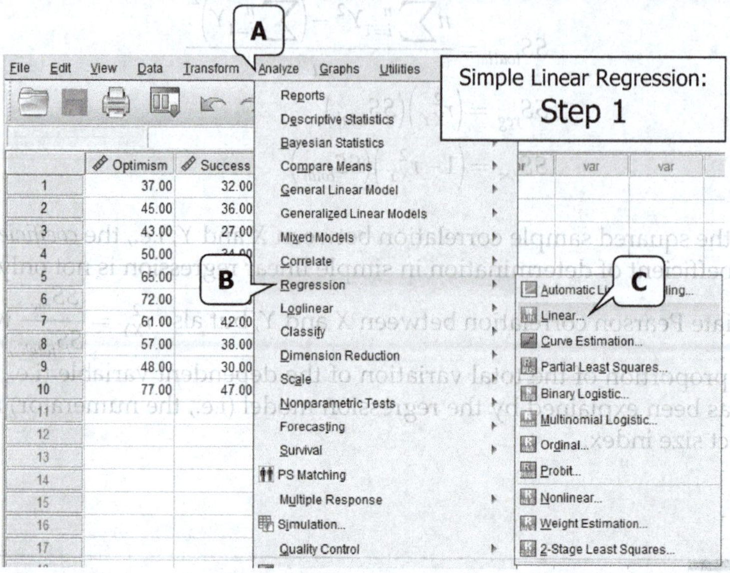

FIGURE 17.9
Conducting simple linear regression: Step 1.

Step 2. Click the dependent variable (e.g., "Success") and move it into the "Dependent" box by clicking the arrow button. Click the independent variable and move it into the "Independent(s)" box by clicking the arrow button (see the screenshot for Step 2, Figure 17.10).

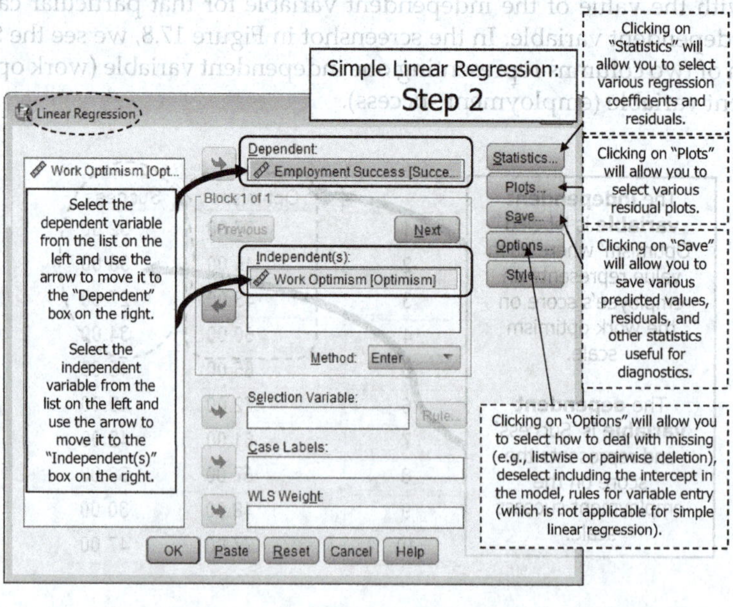

FIGURE 17.10
Conducting simple linear regression: Step 2.

Step 3. From the Linear Regression dialog box (see Figure 17.10), clicking on "Statistics" will provide the option to select various regression coefficients and residuals. From the Statistics dialog box (see the screenshot for Step 3, Figure 17.11), place a checkmark in the box next to the following: (1) estimates; (2) confidence intervals; (3) model fit; (4) descriptives; (5) Durbin-Watson; and (6) casewise diagnostics. Click on "Continue" to return to the original dialog box.

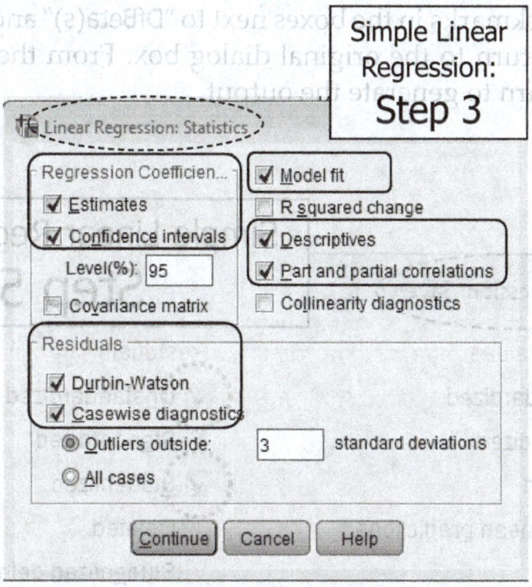

FIGURE 17.11
Conducting simple linear regression: Step 3.

Step 4. From the Linear Regression dialog box (see Figure 1.10), clicking on "Plots" will provide the option to select various residual plots. From the Plots dialog box, place a checkmark in the box next to the following: (1) histogram; (2) normal probability plot. Click on "Continue" to return to the original dialog box.

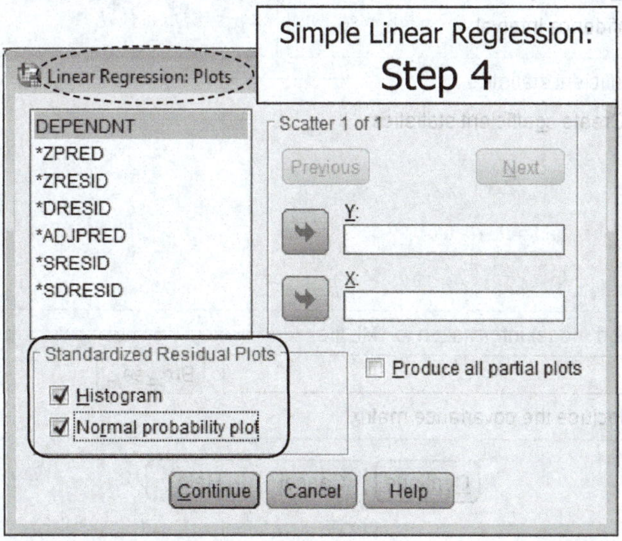

FIGURE 17.12
Conducting simple linear regression: Step 4.

Step 5. From the Linear Regression dialog box (see Figure 17.10), clicking on "Save" will provide the option to save various predicted values, residuals, and statistics that can be used for diagnostic examination. From the Save dialog box under "Predicted Values," place a checkmark in the box next to "Unstandardized." Under the heading "Residuals," place checkmarks in the boxes next to "Unstandardized" and "Studentized." Under the heading "Distances," place checkmarks in the boxes next to "Mahalanobis" and "Cook's.: Under the heading "Influence Statistics," place checkmarks in the boxes next to "DfBeta(s)" and "Standardized DfBeta(s)." Click on "Continue" to return to the original dialog box. From the Linear Regression dialog box, click on "OK" to return to generate the output.

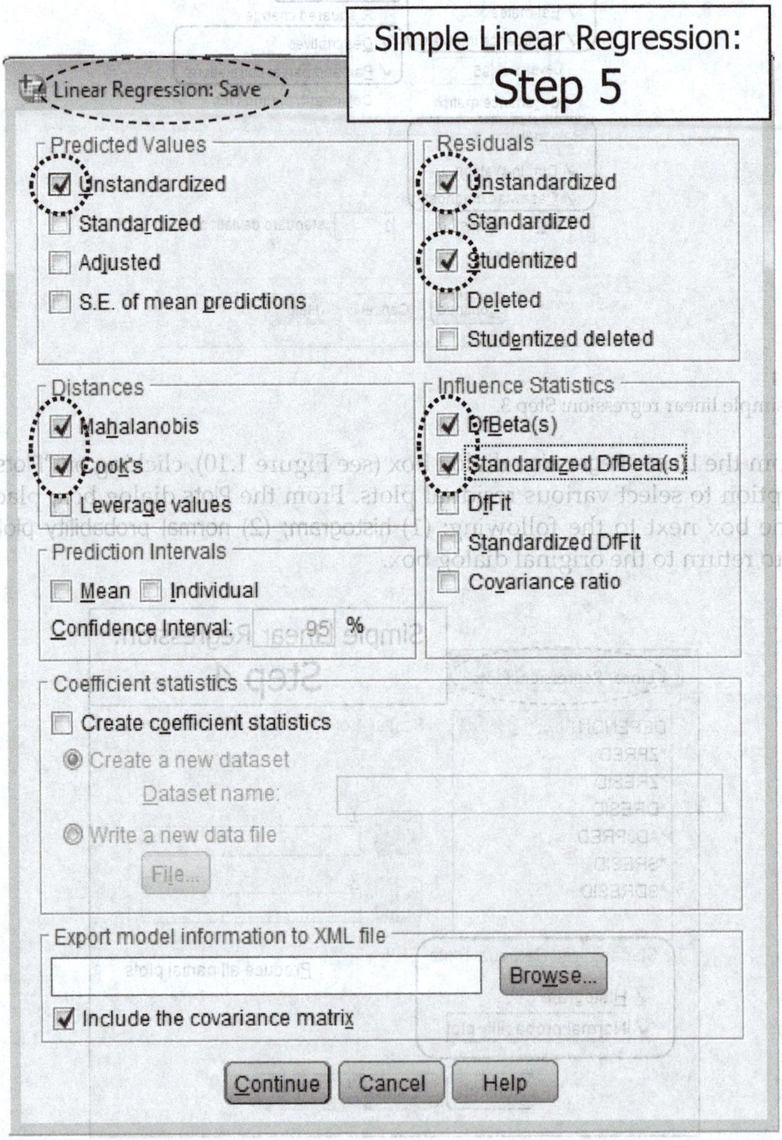

FIGURE 17.13
Conducting simple linear regression: Step 5.

Interpreting the output. Annotated results are presented in Table 17.4. In Chapters 18 and 19 we see other regression modules in SPSS which allow you to consider, for example, generalized or weighted least squares regression, nonlinear regression, and logistic regression. Additional information on regression analysis in SPSS is provided in texts such as Darlington and Hayes (2017).

TABLE 17.4

Selected SPSS Results for the Employment Example

Descriptive Statistics

	Mean	Std. Deviation	N
Employment Success	38.0000	7.51295	10
Work Optimism	55.5000	13.13393	10

The table labeled "Descriptive Statistics" provides basic descriptive statistics (means, standard deviations, and sample sizes) for the independent and dependent variables.

Correlations

		Employment Success	Work Optimism
Pearson Correlation	Employment Success	1.000	.918
	Work Optimism	.918	1.000
Sig. (1-tailed)	Employment Success	.	.000
	Work Optimism	.000	.
N	Employment Success	10	10
	Work Optimism	10	10

The table labeled "Correlations" provides the correlation coefficient value ($r = .918$), p value ($<.001$), and sample size ($N = 10$) for the simple bivariate Pearson correlation between the independent and dependent variables. There is a statistically significant bivariate correlation between GRE-Q and midterm exam score.

Variables Entered/Removed[a]

Model	Variables Entered	Variables Removed	Method
1	Work Optimism[b]		Enter

a. Dependent Variable: Employment Success

b. All requested variables entered.

"Variables Entered/Removed" lists the independent variables included in the model and the method by which they were entered (i.e., 'Enter'). With a single predictor, there is only one way for variables to enter the model. However, we will talk further about this in multiple linear regression.

(continued)

TABLE 17.4 (continued)

Selected SPSS Results for the Employment Example

'Adjusted *R* square' is an estimate of how well the model would fit other data from the same population and is calculated as:

$$R^2_{adj} = 1 - (1 - R^2)\left(\frac{n-1}{n-m-1}\right)$$

If an additional independent variable were entered in the model, an increase in R^2_{adj} indicates the new variable is adding value to the model. Negative R^2_{adj} values can occur and indicate the model fits the data VERY poorly.

Model Summary[b]

					Change Statistics					
Model	R	R Square	Adjusted R Square	Std. Error of the Estimate	R Square Change	F Change	df1	df2	Sig. F Change	Durbin-Watson
1	.918[a]	.842	.822	3.16540	.842	42.700	1	8	.000	1.287

a. Predictors: (Constant), Work Optimism

b. Dependent Variable: Employment Success

R in simple linear regression is the simple bivariate Pearson correlation between *X* and *Y*.

R^2 in simple linear regression is the squared simple bivariate Pearson correlation between *X* and *Y*. It represents the proportion of variance in the dependent variable that is explained by the independent variable.

Durbin-Watson is a test of independence of the residuals. Ranging from 0 to 4, values of 2 indicate uncorrelated errors. Values less than 1 or greater than 3 indicate a likely assumption violation.

Total sum of squares is partitioned into *SS* regression and *SS* residual. When the regression *SS* equals zero, this indicates that the independent variable has provided no information in terms of explaining the dependent variable.

The *F* statistic is computed as

$$F = \frac{MS_{regression}}{MS_{residual}} = \frac{427.842}{10.020}$$

The *p* value (.000) indicates we reject the null hypothesis. The prediction equation provides a better fit to the data than estimating the predicted value of *Y* to be equal to the mean of *Y*.

ANOVA[a]

Model		Sum of Squares	df	Mean Square	F	Sig.
1	Regression	427.842	1	427.842	42.700	.000[b]
	Residual	80.158	8	10.020		
	Total	508.000	9			

a. Dependent Variable: Employment Success

b. Predictors: (Constant), Work Optimism

TABLE 17.4 (continued)

Selected SPSS Results for the Employment Example

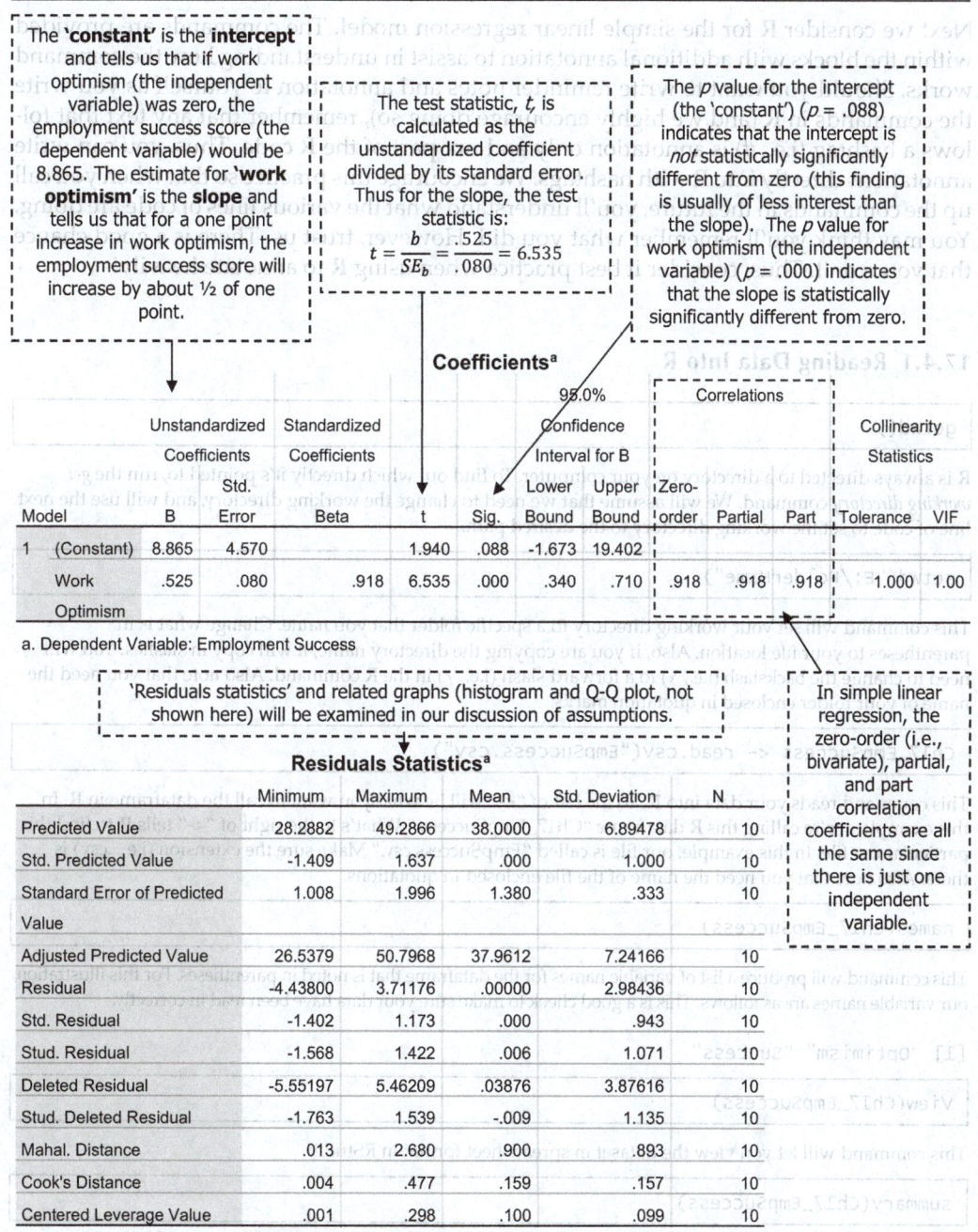

The **'constant'** is the **intercept** and tells us that if work optimism (the independent variable) was zero, the employment success score (the dependent variable) would be 8.865. The estimate for **'work optimism'** is the **slope** and tells us that for a one point increase in work optimism, the employment success score will increase by about ½ of one point.

The test statistic, *t*, is calculated as the unstandardized coefficient divided by its standard error. Thus for the slope, the test statistic is:

$$t = \frac{b}{SE_b} = \frac{.525}{.080} = 6.535$$

The *p* value for the intercept (the 'constant') (*p* = .088) indicates that the intercept is *not* statistically significantly different from zero (this finding is usually of less interest than the slope). The *p* value for work optimism (the independent variable) (*p* = .000) indicates that the slope is statistically significantly different from zero.

Coefficients[a]

Model		Unstandardized Coefficients B	Unstandardized Coefficients Std. Error	Standardized Coefficients Beta	t	Sig.	95.0% Confidence Interval for B Lower Bound	95.0% Confidence Interval for B Upper Bound	Correlations Zero-order	Correlations Partial	Correlations Part	Collinearity Statistics Tolerance	Collinearity Statistics VIF
1	(Constant)	8.865	4.570		1.940	.088	-1.673	19.402					
	Work Optimism	.525	.080	.918	6.535	.000	.340	.710	.918	.918	.918	1.000	1.00

a. Dependent Variable: Employment Success

In simple linear regression, the zero-order (i.e., bivariate), partial, and part correlation coefficients are all the same since there is just one independent variable.

'Residuals statistics' and related graphs (histogram and Q-Q plot, not shown here) will be examined in our discussion of assumptions.

Residuals Statistics[a]

	Minimum	Maximum	Mean	Std. Deviation	N
Predicted Value	28.2882	49.2866	38.0000	6.89478	10
Std. Predicted Value	-1.409	1.637	.000	1.000	10
Standard Error of Predicted Value	1.008	1.996	1.380	.333	10
Adjusted Predicted Value	26.5379	50.7968	37.9612	7.24166	10
Residual	-4.43800	3.71176	.00000	2.98436	10
Std. Residual	-1.402	1.173	.000	.943	10
Stud. Residual	-1.568	1.422	.006	1.071	10
Deleted Residual	-5.55197	5.46209	.03876	3.87616	10
Stud. Deleted Residual	-1.763	1.539	-.009	1.135	10
Mahal. Distance	.013	2.680	.900	.893	10
Cook's Distance	.004	.477	.159	.157	10
Centered Leverage Value	.001	.298	.100	.099	10

a. Dependent Variable: Employment Success

17.4 Computing Simple Linear Regression Using R

Next we consider **R** for the simple linear regression model. The commands are provided within the blocks with additional annotation to assist in understanding how the command works. Should you want to write reminder notes and annotation to yourself as you write the commands in **R** (and we highly encourage doing so), remember that any text that follows a hashtag (i.e., #) is annotation only and not part of the **R** code. Thus, you can write annotations directly into **R** with hashtags. We encourage this practice so that when you call up the commands in the future, you'll understand what the various lines of code are doing. You may think you'll remember what you did. However, trust us. There is a good chance that you won't. Thus, consider it best practice when using **R** to annotate heavily!

17.4.1 Reading Data Into R

```
getwd()
```

R is always directed to a directory on your computer. To find out which directly it's pointed to, run the *get working directory* command. We will assume that we need to change the working directory, and will use the next line of code to set the working directory to the desired path.

```
setwd("E:/FolderName")
```

This command will set your working directory to a specific folder that you name. Change what is in parentheses to your file location. Also, if you are copying the directory name, it will copy in slashes. You will need to change the backslash (i.e., \) to a forward slash (i.e., /) in the **R** command. Also note that you need the name of your folder enclosed in quotation marks.

```
Ch17_EmpSuccess <- read.csv("EmpSuccess.csv")
```

This command reads your data into **R**. To the left of "<-" will be what you want to call the dataframe in **R**. In this example, we're calling this **R** dataframe "Ch17_EmpSuccess." What's to the right of "<-" tells **R** to find this particular csv file. In this example, our file is called "EmpSuccess.csv." Make sure the extension (i.e., .csv) is there. Also note that you need the name of the file enclosed in quotations.

```
names(Ch17_EmpSuccess)
```

This command will produce a list of variable names for the dataframe that is noted in parentheses. For this illustration, our variable names are as follows. This is a good check to make sure your data have been read in correctly.

```
[1] "Optimism" "Success"
```

```
View(Ch17_EmpSuccess)
```

This command will let you view the dataset in spreadsheet format in RStudio.

```
summary(Ch17_EmpSuccess)
```

The *summary* command will produce basic descriptive statistics on all the variables in your dataframe. This is a great way to quickly check to see if the data have been read in correctly and get a feel for your data, if you haven't already. The output from the summary statement for this dataframe looks like this.

FIGURE 17.14
Reading data into **R**.

```
  Optimism       Success
Min.   :37.00   Min.   :27.00
1st Qu.:45.75   1st Qu.:32.50
Median :53.50   Median :37.00
Mean   :55.50   Mean   :38.00
3rd Qu.:64.00   3rd Qu.:44.25
Max.   :77.00   Max.   :49.00
```

FIGURE 17.14 (continued)
Reading data into **R**.

17.4.2 Generating the Simple Linear Regression Model

```
EmpSuccess <- lm(formula = Success ~ Optimism,
data = Ch17_EmpSuccess)
```

The *lm* command is the code to run the multiple linear regression model. In this example, we're creating an object named "EmpSuccess." The formula defines our dependent variable as "Success," and it is predicted by "Optimism." The data comes from "Ch17_EmpSuccess."

```
summary(EmpSuccess)
```

Run the *summary* command to see the results from the multiple linear regression model displayed in the RStudio console. If you don't run the summary line of code, since we created an object from our model, there won't be any results output!

```
Residuals:
    Min      1Q  Median      3Q     Max
-4.4380 -1.9932  0.1626  2.2568  3.7118

Coefficients:
            Estimate Std. Error t value Pr(>|t|)
(Intercept)  8.86473    4.56965   1.940 0.088358 .
Optimism     0.52496    0.08034   6.535 0.000181 ***
---
Signif. codes:  0 "***" 0.001 "**" 0.01 "*" 0.05 "." 0.1 " " 1

Residual standard error: 3.165 on 8 degrees of freedom
Multiple R-squared:  0.8422,	Adjusted R-squared:  0.8225
F-statistic:  42.7 on 1 and 8 DF,  p-value: 0.0001814
```

```
anova(EmpSuccess)
```

This command generates the ANOVA summary table from the multiple regression model, i.e., the object we created called "EmpSuccess."

```
Analysis of Variance Table

Response: Success
          Df Sum Sq Mean Sq F value    Pr(>F)
Optimism   1 427.84  427.84    42.7 0.0001814 ***
Residuals  8  80.16   10.02
---
Signif. codes:  0 "***" 0.001 "**" 0.01 "*" 0.05 "." 0.1 " " 1
```

FIGURE 17.15
Generating the simple linear regression model and ANOVA summary table.

Comparing our output from R to SPSS, we see that, with the exception of small rounding error, the results for the coefficients are the same. There is additional output from R that we don't receive from SPSS.

17.4.3 Generating Correlation Coefficients

```
install.packages("Hmisc")
```

This command will install a package, *Hmisc,* that will allow us to generate the correlation matrix and related *p* values.

```
library("Hmisc")
```

We need to install the package only once in **R.** However, we need to load the package to our library each time we use it. Thus, after installing the package, we load the package with the *library* command.

```
cor(Ch17_EmpSuccess)
```

This command will generate a correlation table using all the variables in our datafram. The default matrix is Pearson.

```
           Optimism   Success
Optimism 1.0000000 0.9177195
Success  0.9177195 1.0000000
```

FIGURE 17.16
Generating correlation coefficients.

17.4.4 Generating Confidence Intervals of Coefficient Estimates

```
confint(EmpSuccess, level =.95)
```

Because we created an object from our model (i.e., EmpSuccess), we can easily request additional stats. With the *confint* command, we can obtain confidence intervals for the coefficient estimates. With the *level* command, we set the confidence interval to 95% (i.e., the complement of our alpha level). The lower confidence interval is displayed as 2.5%, and the upper confidence interval is displayed as 97.5%.

```
                  2.5 %     97.5 %
(Intercept) -1.6728948 19.4023634
Optimism     0.3397038  0.7102157
```

FIGURE 17.17
Generating confidence intervals of coefficient estimates

17.5 Data Screening

As you may recall, there were a number of assumptions associated with simple linear regression. These included the following: (a) independence; (b) homogeneity of variance; (c) linearity; and (d) normality. Although fixed values of X are assumed, this is not an assumption that can be tested, but is instead related to the use of the results (i.e., extrapolation and interpolation).

Before we begin to examine assumptions, let us review the values that we requested to be saved to our datafile (see the dataset screenshot in Figure 17.18).

1. **PRE_1** values are the **unstandardized predicted values** (i.e., Y_i').
2. **RES_1** values are the **unstandardized residuals,** simply the difference between the observed and predicted values. For person 1, for example, the observed value for employment success (i.e., the dependent variable) was 32 and the predicted value was 28.28824. Thus the unstandardized residual is simply 32–28.28824 or 3.71176.
3. **SRE_1** values are the **studentized residuals,** a type of standardized residual that is more sensitive to outliers as compared to standardized residuals. Studentized residuals are computed as the unstandardized residual divided by an estimate of the standard deviation with that case removed. As a guideline, studentized residuals with an absolute value greater than 3 are considered outliers (Stevens, 1984). Studentized residuals, as compared to standardized residuals, are more sensitive for detecting outlying cases.
4. **MAH_1** values are **Mahalanobis distance values,** which can be helpful in detecting outliers. These values can be reviewed to determine cases that are exerting leverage. Barnett and Lewis (1994) produced a table of critical values for evaluating Mahalanobis distance. Squared Mahalanobis distances divided by the number of variables (D^2 / df) which are greater than 2.5 (for small samples) or 3 to 4 (for large samples) are suggestive of outliers (Hair et al, 2006). Later, we will follow another convention for examining these values using the chi-square distribution.
5. **COO_1** values are **Cook's distance values** and provide an indication of influence of individual cases. As a guideline, Cook's values greater than 1.0 suggest that case is potentially problematic.
6. **DFB0_1** and **DFB1_1** values are **unstandardized DfBeta values** for the intercept and slope, respectively. These values provide estimates of the intercept and slope when the case is removed.
7. **SDB0_1** and **SDB1_1** values are **standardized DfBeta values** for the intercept and slope, respectively, and are easier to interpret as compared to their unstandardized counterparts. Standardized DfBeta values greater than an absolute value of two suggest that the case may be exerting undue influence on the parameters of the model (i.e., the slope and intercept).

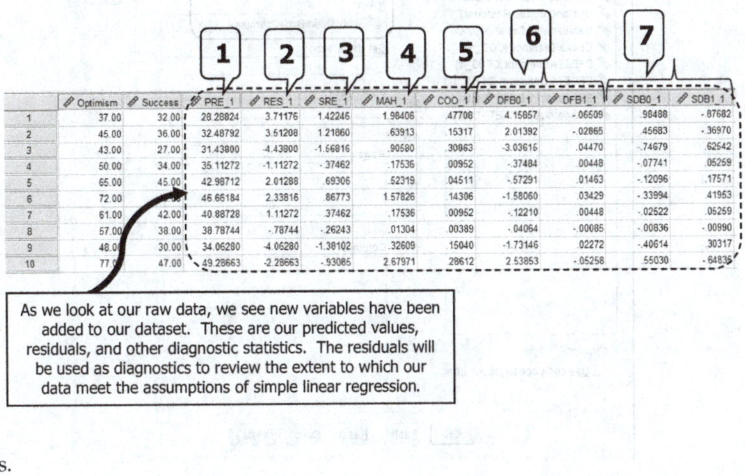

	Optimism	Success	PRE_1	RES_1	SRE_1	MAH_1	COO_1	DFB0_1	DFB1_1	SDB0_1	SDB1_1
1	37.00	32.00	28.28824	3.71176	1.42246	1.98406	.47708	4.15857	-.06509	.98488	-.87682
2	45.00	36.00	32.48792	3.51208	1.21860	.63913	.15317	2.01392	-.02865	.45683	-.36970
3	43.00	27.00	31.43800	-4.43800	-1.66816	.90580	.30863	-3.03616	.04470	-.74679	.62542
4	50.00	34.00	35.11272	-1.11272	-.37462	.17536	.00952	-.37484	.00448	-.07741	.05269
5	65.00	45.00	42.98712	2.01288	.69306	.52319	.04511	-.57291	.01463	-.12096	.17571
6	72.00	[illegible]	46.66184	2.33816	.86773	1.57826	.14306	-1.58060	.03429	-.33994	.41953
7	61.00	42.00	40.88728	1.11272	.37462	.17536	.00952	-.12210	.00448	-.02522	.05269
8	57.00	38.00	38.78744	-.78744	-.26243	.01304	.00389	-.04064	-.00085	-.00836	-.00990
9	48.0	30.00	34.06280	-4.06280	-1.38102	.32609	.15040	-1.73146	.02272	-.40614	.30317
10	77.0	47.00	49.28663	-2.28663	-.93085	2.67971	.28612	2.53853	-.05258	.55030	-.64835

1
2
3
4
5
6
7
As we look at our raw data, we see new variables have been added to our dataset. These are our predicted values, residuals, and other diagnostic statistics. The residuals will be used as diagnostics to review the extent to which our data meet the assumptions of simple linear regression.

FIGURE 17.18
Saved variables.

Working in **R**, we can include the following commands to produce similar additional variables in our dataframe.

```
Ch17_EmpSuccess$unstandardizedPredicted <- predict(EmpSuccess)
```

What is to the left of "<-" tells **R** to save a new variable in our dataframe (i.e., Ch17_EmpSuccess) that is called "unstandardizedPredicted." What is to the right of "<-" tells **R** to created unstandardized predicted values using the simple linear regression results from the object EmpSuccess.

```
Ch17_EmpSuccess$unstandardizedResiduals <- resid(EmpSuccess)
```

Similarly, this command saves unstandardized residuals, using the simple linear regression results from the object EmpSuccess, into our dataframe.

```
Ch17_EmpSuccess$studentized.residuals <- rstudent(EmpSuccess)
```

Similarly, this command saves studentized residuals, using the simple linear regression results from the object EmpSuccess, into our dataframe.

```
Ch17_EmpSuccess$cook <- cooks.distance(EmpSuccess)
```

Similarly, this command saved Cook's distance, an influence statistic, using the simple linear regression results from the object EmpSuccess.

```
Ch17_EmpSuccess$dfbeta <- dfbeta(EmpSuccess)
```

Similarly, this command saves dfbeta values, using the simple linear regression results from the object EmpSuccess.

FIGURE 17.18 (continued)
Saved variables.

17.5.1 Independence

We now plot the studentized residuals (which were requested and created through the "Save" option) against the values of X to examine the extent to which independence was met. The general steps for generating a simple scatterplot through "Scatter/dot" have been presented in Chapter 10, and they will not be reiterated here. From the "Simple Scatterplot" dialog screen, click the studentized residual variable and move it into the "Y Axis" box by clicking on the arrow. Click the independent variable X and move it into the "X Axis" box by clicking on the arrow. Then click "OK."

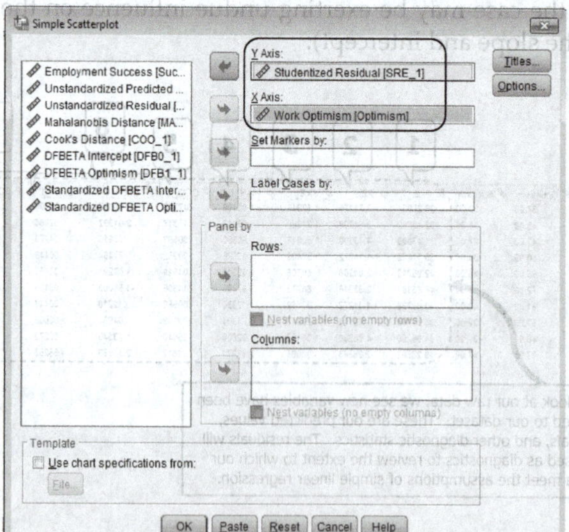

FIGURE 17.19
Plotting to examine independence.

Working in **R**, we create a similar scatterplot using the following *plot* command, with the first variable listed displaying on the *X* axis (e.g., "Ch17_Empsuccess$Optimism"), and the second variable displaying on the *Y* axis (i.e., "Ch17_Empsuccess$studentized.residuals"). Additional commands are provided to label the axes (*xlab* and *ylab*) and title the graph (*main*).

```
plot(Ch17_EmpSuccess$Optimism,
    Ch17_EmpSuccess$studentized.residuals,
    xlab = "work optimism",
    ylab = "studentized residuals",
    main = "Scatterplot for independence")
```

FIGURE 17.19 (continued)
Plotting to examine independence.

Interpreting independence evidence. If the assumption of independence is met, the points should fall randomly within a band of −2.0 to +2.0. Here we have evidence of independence, especially given the small sample size, as all points are within an absolute value of 2.0 and fall relatively randomly.

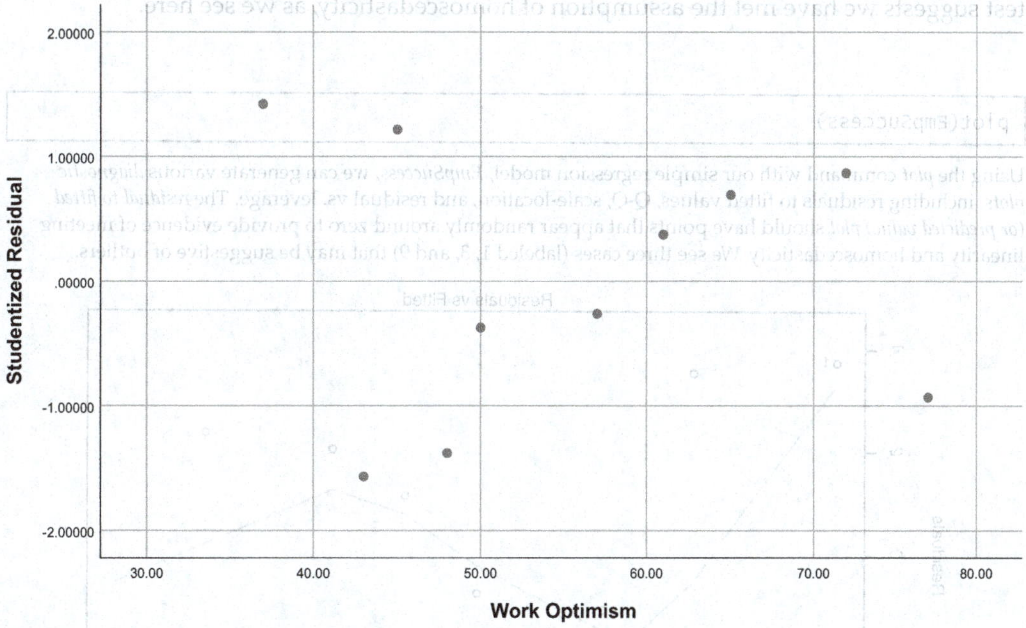

FIGURE 17.20
Scatterplot for examining the assumption of independence.

17.5.2 Homoscedasticity

We can use the same plot of studentized residuals against *X* values (used earlier for independence) to examine the extent to which homogeneity was met. Recall that homogeneity is when the dependent variable has the same variance for all values of the independent variable. Evidence of meeting the assumption of homogeneity is a plot where the spread of residuals appears fairly constant over the range of *X* values (i.e., a random display of points). If the spread of the residuals increases or decreases across the plot from left to right, this may indicate that the assumption of homogeneity has been violated. Here we have evidence of homogeneity.

There are a number of additional plots that are helpful diagnostics. We can also examine homogeneity of variance, or homoscedasticity, by looking at the spread of residuals over the range of predicted values, referred to as the *residual to fitted (or predicted value) plot*—again, looking for there to be a fairly constant spread. In other words, we're looking for a relatively random display of points. If the display of residuals increases or decreases across the plot, then there may be an indication that the assumption of homoscedasticity has been violated.

The *scale-location plot* provides evidence of the extent to which the residuals are spread equally across all values of the predictor. A random display of points suggests evidence of homoscedasticity.

The *residual vs. leverage plot* can be reviewed for influential cases, which would be evident by outlying values at the upper or lower right corners. Cases outside the dashed lines are suggestive of influential cases.

Working in **R**, we can also generate the *nonconstant error variance test* to determine if there is homogeneity of variance. The null hypothesis of this test is constant error variance, and the alternative hypothesis is that the error variance changes with the level of the fitted values, or with the linear combination of independent variables. A nonstatistically significant test suggests we have met the assumption of homoscedasticity, as we see here.

```
plot(EmpSuccess)
```

Using the *plot* command with our simple regression model, *EmpSuccess,* we can generate various *diagnostic plots,* including residuals to fitted values, Q-Q, scale-location, and residual vs. leverage. The *residual to fitted (or predicted value) plot* should have points that appear randomly around zero to provide evidence of meeting linearity and homoscedasticity. We see three cases (labeled 1, 3, and 9) that may be suggestive of outliers.

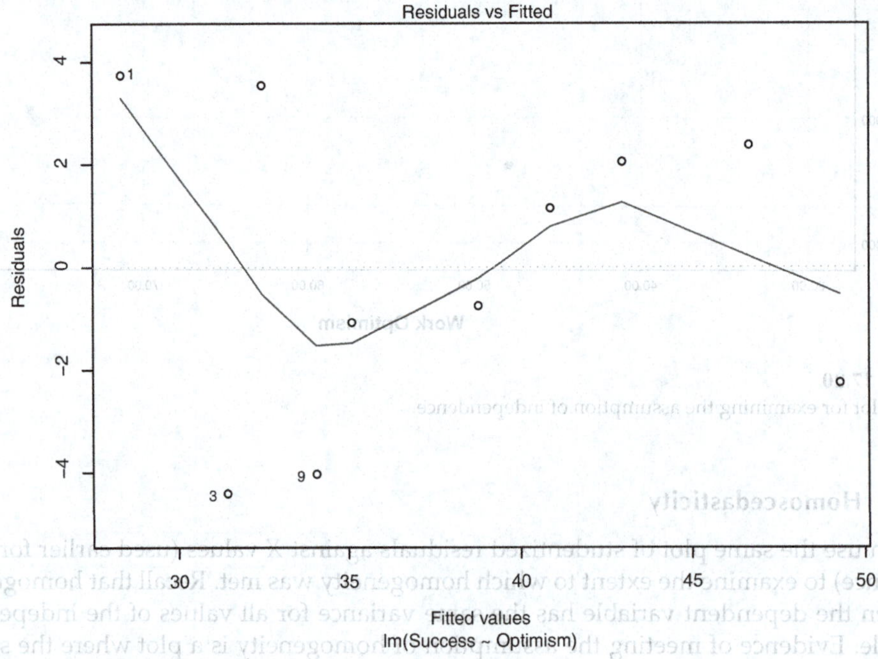

FIGURE 17.21
Residual plots and nonconstant error variance test in **R**.

The *scale-location plot* provides evidence of the extent to which the residuals are spread equally across all values of the predictor. A random display of points suggests evidence of homoscedasticity.

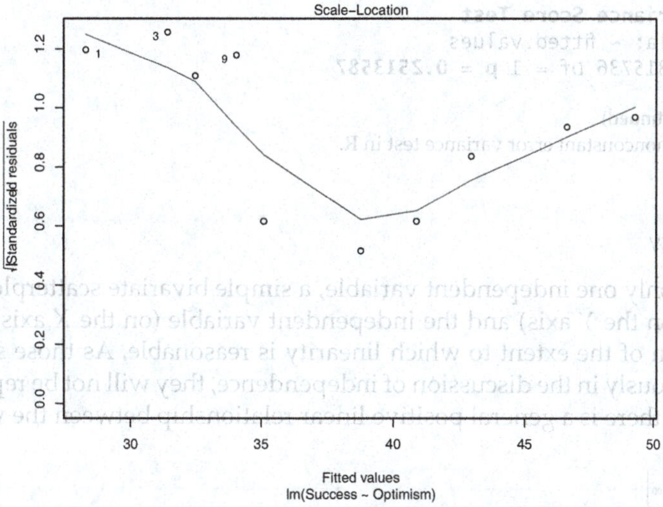

The *residual vs. leverage plot* can be reviewed for influential cases, which would be evident by outlying values at the upper or lower right corners. Cases outside the dashed lines are suggestive of influential cases. In this example, there are cases that are close, but are not beyond the dashed lines, which suggests evidence that there are no outlying cases.

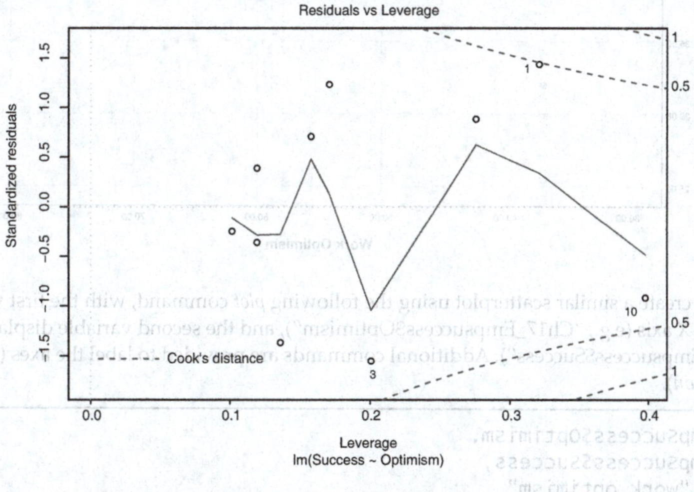

The nonconstant error variance test, the *ncvTest* function, is part of the *car* package, so we first install *car* using the *install.packages* function and then load it into our library using the *library* function.

We use our multiple linear regression object (i.e., 'EmpSuccess') with the *ncvTest* function to conduct the nonconstant error variance test.

```
install.packages("car")
library(car)
ncvTest(GGPA_MultReg)
```

FIGURE 17.21 (continued)
Residual plots and nonconstant error variance test in **R**.

The results produce a chi-squared test. Based on the *p* value (.251), our test is not statistically significant which indicates we have met the assumption of homoscedasticity.

```
Non-constant Variance Score Test
Variance formula: ~ fitted.values
Chisquare = 1.315736 Df = 1 p = 0.2513587
```

FIGURE 17.21 (continued)
Residual plots and nonconstant error variance test in **R**.

17.5.3 Linearity

Since we have only one independent variable, a simple bivariate scatterplot of the dependent variable (on the *Y* axis) and the independent variable (on the *X* axis) will provide a visual indication of the extent to which linearity is reasonable. As those steps have been presented previously in the discussion of independence, they will not be repeated here. For this scatterplot, there is a general positive linear relationship between the variables.

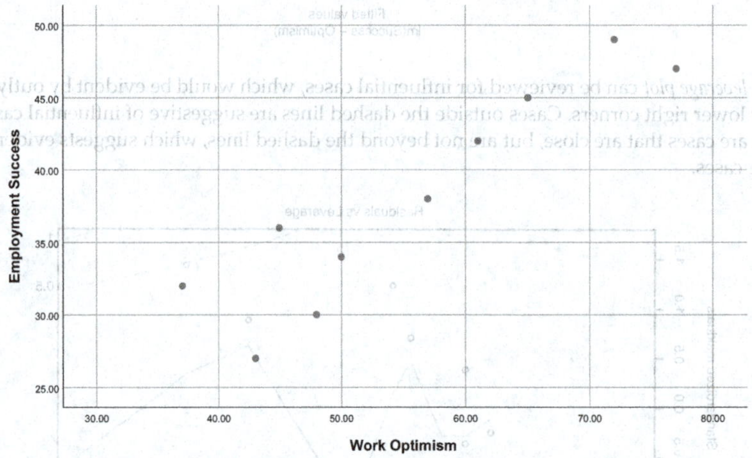

Working in **R**, we create a similar scatterplot using the following *plot* command, with the first variable listed displaying on the *X* axis (e.g., "Ch17_Empsuccess$Optimism"), and the second variable displaying on the *Y* axis (i.e., "Ch17_Empsuccess$Success"). Additional commands are provided to label the axes (*xlab* and *ylab*) and title the graph (*main*).

```
plot(Ch17_EmpSuccess$Optimism,
     Ch17_EmpSuccess$Success,
     xlab = "work optimism",
     ylab = "employment success",
     main = "Scatterplot for Linearity")
```

FIGURE 17.22
Scatterplot to Examine Linearity

Additionally, the plot of studentized residuals against X values (used earlier for independence) can be used to examine the extent to which linearity was met. We highly recommend examining this residual plot as it is more sensitive to detecting independence violations. Here a random display of points within an absolute value of 2 or 3 suggests further evident of linearity.

17.5.3.1 Hypothesis Tests to Examine Linearity Using SPSS

Another way to test for linearity is to conduct a hypothesis test using curve estimation to determine if there is a statistically significant linear (versus quadratic or cubic) relationship.

Step 1. To conduct curve estimation, go to "Analyze" in the top pulldown, then select "Regression," and then select the "Curve estimation" procedure.

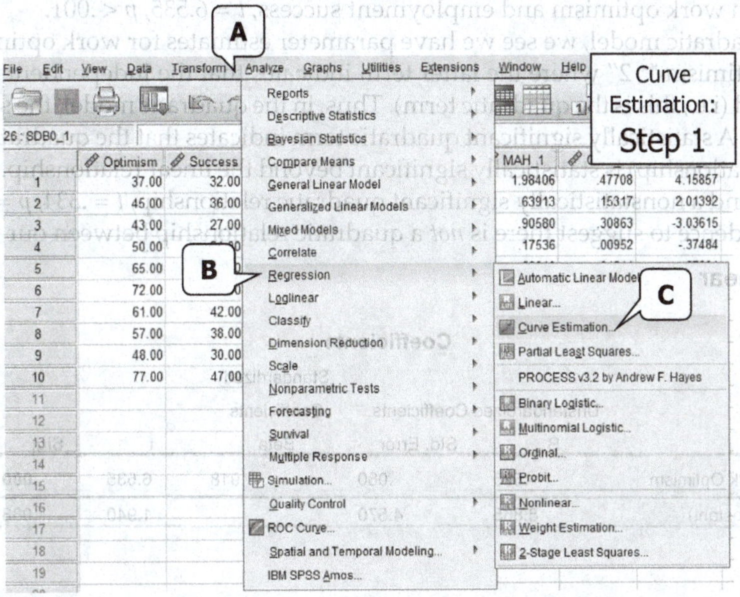

FIGURE 17.23
Hypothesis test for linearity: Step 1.

Step 2. Move the dependent variable to the "Dependent(s)" box, and the independent variable to the "Independent Variable" box. Under "Models," select "Linear," "Quadratic," and "Cubic."

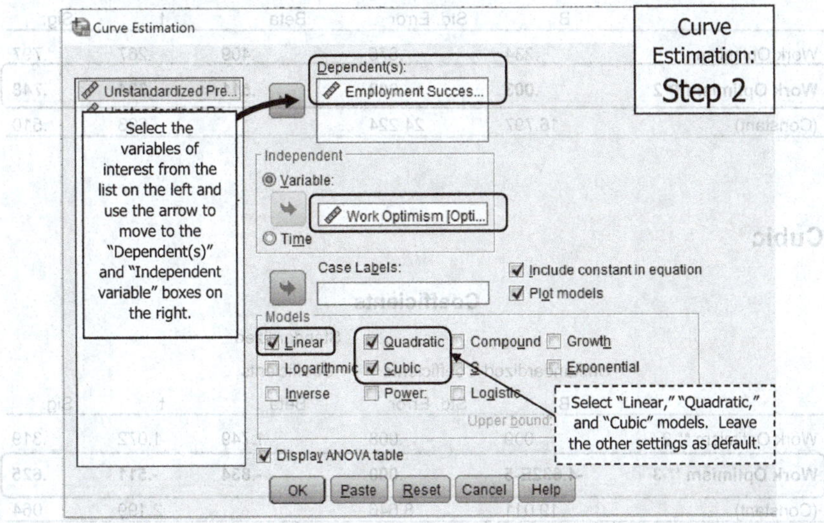

FIGURE 17.24
Hypothesis test for linearity: Step 2.

17.5.3.1.1 Interpreting Hypothesis Tests to Examine Linearity

For purposes of examining linearity, we are only concerned with the output for the "coefficients" (see Figure 17.25). Each coefficient hypothesis test is estimating whether the standardized coefficient is statistically different from zero. Finding statistical significance for the coefficient in the *linear model* provides evidence to suggest a linear relationship between the variables. For this illustration, we find a statistically significant linear relationship between work optimism and employment success, $t = 6.535$, $p < .001$.

For the quadratic model, we see we have parameter estimates for work optimism as well as "work optimism ** 2" where the latter term indicates that the independent variable has been squared (i.e., this is the quadratic term). Thus, in the quadratic model, the squared term is of interest. A statistically significant quadratic term indicates that the quadratic trend (i.e., quadratic relationship) is statistically significant beyond the linear relationship. In this illustration, we find a nonstatistically significant quadratic relationship, $t = .334$, $p = .748$, which provides evidence to suggest there is *not* a quadratic relationship between our variables.

Linear

Coefficients

	Unstandardized Coefficients		Standardized Coefficients		
	B	Std. Error	Beta	t	Sig.
Work Optimism	.525	.080	.918	6.535	**.000**
(Constant)	8.865	4.570		1.940	.088

Quadratic

Coefficients

	Unstandardized Coefficients		Standardized Coefficients		
	B	Std. Error	Beta	t	Sig.
Work Optimism	.234	.875	.409	.267	.797
Work Optimism ** 2	**.003**	**.008**	**.511**	**.334**	**.748**
(Constant)	16.797	24.224		.693	.510

Cubic

Coefficients

	Unstandardized Coefficients		Standardized Coefficients		
	B	Std. Error	Beta	t	Sig.
Work Optimism ** 2	.009	.008	1.749	1.072	.319
Work Optimism ** 3	**-4.632E-5**	**.000**	**-.834**	**-.511**	**.625**
(Constant)	19.011	8.646		2.199	.064

FIGURE 17.25
Hypothesis test for linearity: results.

Next, we examine the results of the cubic model. We find that a new term called "work optimism ** 3" has been estimated in this model. This term represented the cubic term. This model is estimating the extent to which there is a cubic trend, above and beyond the linear and quadratic relationships. A statistically significant cubic term suggests evidence that there is a cubic relationship between the variables. In this illustration, we find a non-statistically significant relationship, $t = -.511$, $p = .625$. Thus, we have evidence to suggest that there is not a cubic relationship between our variables.

Looking at all three models, linear, quadratic, and cubic, we have evidence to suggest linearity between our variables given the nonstatistically significant nonlinear quadratic and cubic trends.

17.5.4 Normality

17.5.4.1 Generating Normality Evidence

Understanding the distributional shape, specifically the extent to which normality is a reasonable assumption, is important in simple linear regression just as it was in ANOVA models. We again examine residuals for normality, following the same steps as with the previous ANOVA designs. We also use various diagnostics to examine our data for influential cases. Let us begin by examining the unstandardized residuals for normality. For simple linear regression, the distributional shape of the unstandardized residuals should be a normal distribution. Because the steps for generating normality evidence were presented previously in the chapters for ANOVA models, they will not be provided here.

17.5.4.2 Interpreting Normality Evidence

By now we have had a substantial amount of practice in interpreting quite a range of normality statistics. We interpret them again in reference to the assumption of normality for the unstandardized residuals in simple linear regression. The skewness statistic of the residuals is –.269 and kurtosis is –1.369—both being within the range of what would be expected from a normal distribution (an absolute value of 2.), suggesting some evidence of normality.

Descriptives

			Statistic	Std. Error
Unstandardized Residual	Mean		.0000000	.94373849
	95% Confidence Interval for Mean	Lower Bound	-2.1348848	
		Upper Bound	2.1348848	
	5% Trimmed Mean		.0403471	
	Median		.1626409	
	Variance		8.906	
	Std. Deviation		2.98436314	
	Minimum		-4.43800	
	Maximum		3.71176	
	Range		8.14976	
	Interquartile Range		5.36232	
	Skewness		-.269	.687
	Kurtosis		-1.369	1.334

FIGURE 17.26
Normality evidence.

Working in **R**, we can generate various normality statistics as well.

```
install.packages("pastecs")
```

This command will install the *pastecs* package which we will use to generate various forms of normality evidence.

```
library(pastecs)
```

This command will load the *pastecs* package.

```
stat.desc(Ch17_EmpSuccess$unstandardizedResiduals,
        norm = TRUE)
```

This command will generate normality indices on the variable "unstandardizedResiduals" in the dataframe Ch17_EmpSuccess as follows. Should you want to generate normality indices on different residuals (e.g., studentized), just switch out the residual variable name in the *stat.desc* function. The *norm=TRUE* command will produce Shapiro-Wilk results (*SW*).

Looking at the results, we see skew (–.194) and kurtosis (–1.64) along with $SW = .927$, $p = .416$ for the "time" variable. All indicate the assumption of normality has been met. As we know, we can divide the skew and kurtosis values by their standard errors to get a standardized value that can be used to determine if the skew and/or kurtosis is statistically different from zero. Since this output provides "2SE," we would simply divide this value by 2 to arrive at the standard error.

Note: You may have noticed that the skewness and kurtosis value that we've just generated differs from what we found in SPSS, which was skew = –.269 and kurtosis = –.1.369. This is because there are different ways to calculate skewness and kurtosis. Let's use another package in **R** to calculate these statistics with different algorithms.

```
     nbr.val       nbr.null        nbr.na           min
1.000000e+01  0.000000e+00  0.000000e+00 -4.438003e+00

         max          range           sum        median
3.711755e+00  8.149758e+00  1.332268e-15  1.626409e-01

        mean        SE.mean  CI.mean.0.95           var
1.333135e-16  9.437385e-01  2.134885e+00  8.906423e+00

     std.dev       coef.var      skewness      skew.2SE
2.984363e+00  2.238605e+16 -1.938327e-01-1.410630e-01

    kurtosis       kurt.2SE    normtest.W    normtest.p
-1.639214e+00-6.142834e-01  9.267260e-01  4.164719e-01
```

```
install.packages("e1071")
```

This command will install the e1071 package which we will use to generate skewness and kurtosis.

```
library(e1071)
```

This command will load the e1071 package.

```
skewness(Ch17_EmpSuccess$unstandardizedResiduals, type=3)
skewness(Ch17_EmpSuccess$unstandardizedResiduals, type=2)
skewness(Ch17_EmpSuccess$unstandardizedResiduals, type=1)
```

FIGURE 17.26 (continued)
Normality evidence.

The *skewness* function will generate skewness statistics on the variable(s) we specify. The "type=" script defines how skewness is calculated. Specifying "type=2" will use the algorithm that is used by SPSS. Readers interested in learning more, including the algorithms for each of the three methods, are encouraged to review Joanes and Gill (1998). We see that using "type=2," our skew is –.269, the same value as generated using SPSS.

```
# skewness(Ch17_EmpSuccess$unstandardizedResiduals, type=3)
[1] -0.1938327
# skewness(Ch17_EmpSuccess$unstandardizedResiduals, type=2)
[1] -0.2692121
# skewness(Ch17_EmpSuccess$unstandardizedResiduals, type=1)
[1] -0.2270196
```

```
kurtosis(Ch17_EmpSuccess$unstandardizedResiduals, type=3)
kurtosis(Ch17_EmpSuccess$unstandardizedResiduals, type=2)
kurtosis(Ch17_EmpSuccess$unstandardizedResiduals, type=1)
```

The *kurtosis* function will generate kurtosis statistics on the variable(s) we specify. The "type=" script defines how kurtosis is calculated. Specifying "type=2" will use the algorithm that is used by SPSS. Readers interested in learning more, including the algorithms for each of the three methods, are encouraged to review Joanes and Gill (1998). We see that using "type=2," our kurtosis is –1.369, the same value as generated using SPSS.

```
# kurtosis(Ch17_EmpSuccess$unstandardizedResiduals, type=3)
[1] -1.639214
# kurtosis(Ch17_EmpSuccess$unstandardizedResiduals, type=2)
[1] -1.369316
# kurtosis(Ch17_EmpSuccess$unstandardizedResiduals, type=1)
[1] -1.320017
```

FIGURE 17.26 (continud)
Normality evidence.

While we have a very small sample size, the histogram reflects the skewness and kurtosis statistics.

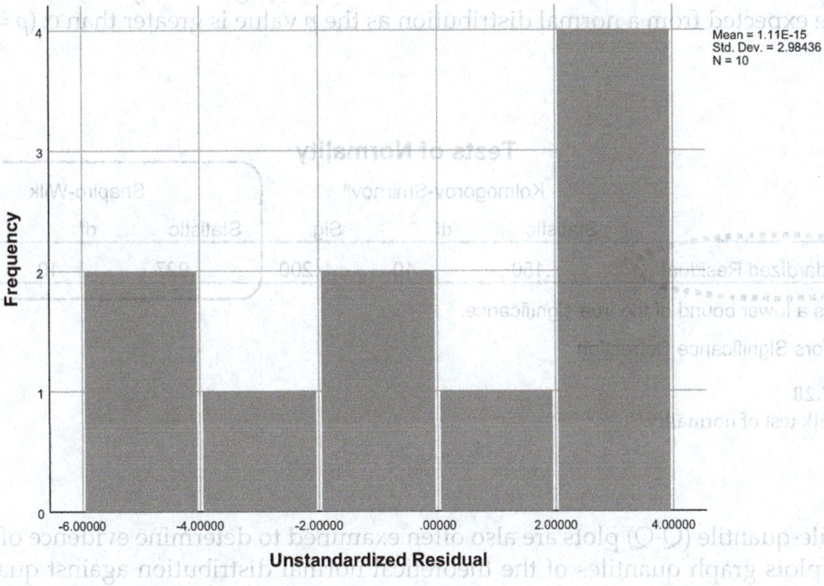

FIGURE 17.27
Histogram of unstandardized residuals.

Working in **R**, we can generate a histogram using the *ggplot2* package.

```
install.packages("ggplot2")
```

The *install.packages* function will install the *ggplot2* package which we can use to create various graphs and plots.

```
library(ggplot2)
```

The *library* function will load the *ggplot2* package.

```
qplot(Ch17_EmpSuccess$unstandardizedResiduals,
      geom="histogram",
      binwidth=0.5,
      main = "Histogram of Unstandardized Residuals",
      xlab = "Unstandardized Residual", ylab = "Count",
      fill=I("gray"),
      col=I("white"))
```

Using the *gplot* function, we create a histogram (i.e., geom = "histogram") from our dataframe (i.e., Ch17_EmpSuccess) using the variable "unstandardizedResiduals." We can add a few commands to change the width of the bars (i.e., *binwidth = 0.5*), color of the bars (i.e., *fill=I("gray")*), and outline of the bars (i.e., *col=I("white")*). We can also add a title (i.e., *main = "Histogram of Unstandardized Residuals"*) and change the *X* and *Y* axes (*xlab = "Unstandardized Residual", ylab = "Count"*).

FIGURE 17.27 (continued)
Histogram of unstandardized residuals.

There are a few other statistics that can be used to gauge normality. The formal test of normality, the Shapiro-Wilk test (*SW*) (Shapiro & Wilk, 1965), provides evidence of the extent to which our sample distribution is statistically different from a normal distribution. The output for the Shapiro-Wilk test is presented in Figure 17.28 and suggests that our sample distribution for the residual is *not* statistically significantly different than what would be expected from a normal distribution as the p value is greater than α ($p = .416$).

Tests of Normality

	Kolmogorov-Smirnov[a]			Shapiro-Wilk		
	Statistic	df	Sig.	Statistic	df	Sig.
Unstandardized Residual	.150	10	.200*	.927	10	.416

*. This is a lower bound of the true significance.

a. Lilliefors Significance Correction

FIGURE 17.28
Shapiro-Wilk test of normality.

Quantile-quantile (Q-Q) plots are also often examined to determine evidence of normality. Q-Q plots graph quantiles of the theoretical normal distribution against quantiles of the sample distribution. Points that fall on or close to the diagonal line suggest evidence of normality. The Q-Q plot of residuals shown below suggests relative normality.

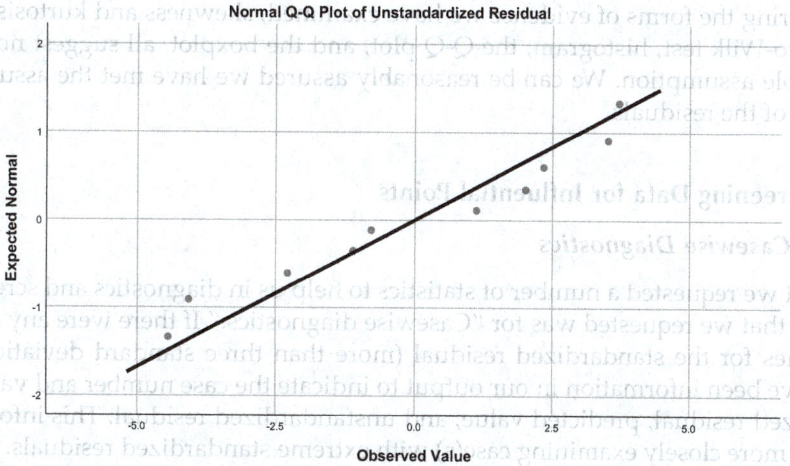

Working in **R**, we can use the *gplot* command to create a Q-Q plot of unstandardized residuals.

```
qplot(sample=unstandardizedResiduals,
    data = Ch17_EmpSuccess)
```

FIGURE 17.29
Normal Q-Q plot.

Examination of the boxplot shown in Figure 17.30 also suggests a relatively normal distributional shape of residuals with no outliers.

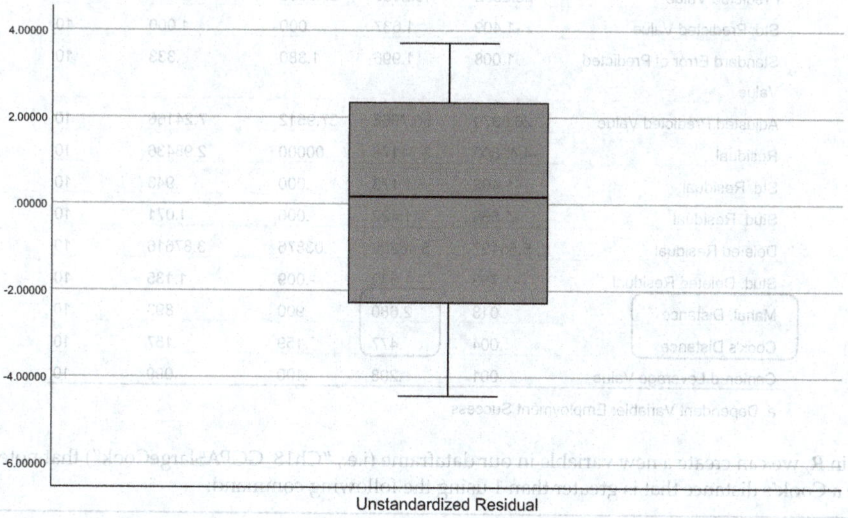

Working in **R**, we can generate a boxplot for unstandardized residuals using the *boxplot* function. To label the *Y* axis, we include the *ylab* command.

```
boxplot(Ch17_EmpSuccess$unstandardizedResiduals,
      ylab="unstandardized residual")
```

FIGURE 17.30
Boxplot of unstandardized residual.

Considering the forms of evidence we have examined, skewness and kurtosis statistics, the Shapiro-Wilk test, histogram, the Q-Q plot, and the boxplot, all suggest normality is a reasonable assumption. We can be reasonably assured we have met the assumption of normality of the residuals.

17.5.5 Screening Data for Influential Points

17.5.5.1 Casewise Diagnostics

Recall that we requested a number of statistics to help us in diagnostics and screening our data. One that we requested was for "Casewise diagnostics." If there were any cases with large values for the standardized residual (more than three standard deviations), there would have been information in our output to indicate the case number and values of the standardized residual, predicted value, and unstandardized residual. This information is useful for more closely examining case(s) with extreme standardized residuals.

17.5.5.2 Cook's Distance

Cook's distance provides an overall measure for the influence of individual cases. Values greater than one suggest that the case may be problematic in terms of undue influence on the model. In examining the residual statistics provided in the following table, we see that the maximum value for Cook's distance is .477, well under the point at which we should be concerned.

Residuals Statistics[a]

	Minimum	Maximum	Mean	Std. Deviation	N
Predicted Value	28.2882	49.2866	38.0000	6.89478	10
Std. Predicted Value	-1.409	1.637	.000	1.000	10
Standard Error of Predicted Value	1.008	1.996	1.380	.333	10
Adjusted Predicted Value	26.5379	50.7968	37.9612	7.24166	10
Residual	-4.43800	3.71176	.00000	2.98436	10
Std. Residual	-1.402	1.173	.000	.943	10
Stud. Residual	-1.568	1.422	.006	1.071	10
Deleted Residual	-5.55197	5.46209	.03876	3.87616	10
Stud. Deleted Residual	-1.763	1.539	-.009	1.135	10
Mahal. Distance	.013	2.680	.900	.893	10
Cook's Distance	.004	.477	.159	.157	10
Centered Leverage Value	.001	.298	.100	.099	10

a. Dependent Variable: Employment Success

Working in **R**, we can create a new variable in our dataframe (i.e., "Ch18_GGPA$largeCook") that notes cases that have a Cook's distance that is greater than 1 using the following command:

```
Ch17_EmpSuccess$largeCook <- Ch17_EmpSuccess$cook > 1
```

We can then run the *sum* function to find out how many large Cook's values there are, and there are none.

```
sum(Ch17_EmpSuccess$largeCook)
```

```
[1] 0
```

FIGURE 17.31
Residual statistics.

17.5.5.3 Mahalanobis Distances

Mahalanobis distances are measures of the distance from each case to the mean of the independent variable for the remaining cases. We can use the value of Mahalanobis distance as a test statistic value using the chi-square distribution. With only one independent variable and one dependent variable, we have two degrees of freedom. Given an alpha level of .05, the chi-square critical value is 5.99. Thus any Mahalanobis distance greater than 5.99 suggests that case is an outlier. With a maximum distance of 2.680 (see the previous table), there is no evidence to suggest there are outliers in our data.

17.5.5.4 DfBeta

We also asked to save DfBeta values. These values provide another indication of the influence of cases. The DfBeta provides information on the change in the predicted value when the case is deleted from the model. For standardized DfBeta values, values greater than an absolute value of 2.0 should be examined more closely. Looking at the minimum (–.87682) and maximum (.62542) DfBeta values for the slope (i.e., Optimism), we do not have any cases that suggest undue influence.

Descriptive Statistics

	N	Minimum	Maximum	Mean	Std. Deviation
DFBETA Optimism	10	-.06509	.04470	-.0021866	.03608593
Standardized DFBETA Optimism	10	-.87682	.62542	-.0275752	.47302980
Valid N (listwise)	10				

Working in **R**, we can request DfBetas from our simple regression model, i.e., *EmpSuccess*, using the following command, and we will name this object "Ch17dfbeta":

```
Ch17dfbeta <- dfbetas(EmpSuccess)
```

Next, we want to define the range within which there may be influence. Values outside the range of an absolute value of 2 may be influential points. We define the range of our object (i.e., "Ch17dfbeta") to be < –2 and > 2. We will create an objects from this called "Ch17dfbetasummary."

```
Ch17dfbetasummary <- Ch17dfbeta < -2 | Ch17dfbeta > 2
```

Now, all we need to do is run the *sum* function to see how many DfBeta values are outside this range, and we see there are none.

```
sum(Ch17dfbetasummary)
```

```
[1] 0
```

FIGURE 17.32
Interpreting DfBeta values for influential points

17.6 Power Using G*Power

A priori and post hoc power could again be determined using the specialized software described previously in this text (e.g., G*Power); alternatively, you can consult *a priori* power tables (e.g., Cohen, 1988). As an illustration, we use G*Power to compute the *post hoc* power of our test.

17.6.1 Post Hoc Power

The first thing that must be done when using G*Power to compute *post hoc* power is to select the correct test family. Here we conducted simple linear regression. To find regression select "Tests" in the top pulldown menu then "Correlation and regression" and then "Linear bivariate regression: One group, size of slope." Once that selection is made, the "Test family" automatically changes to "t tests."

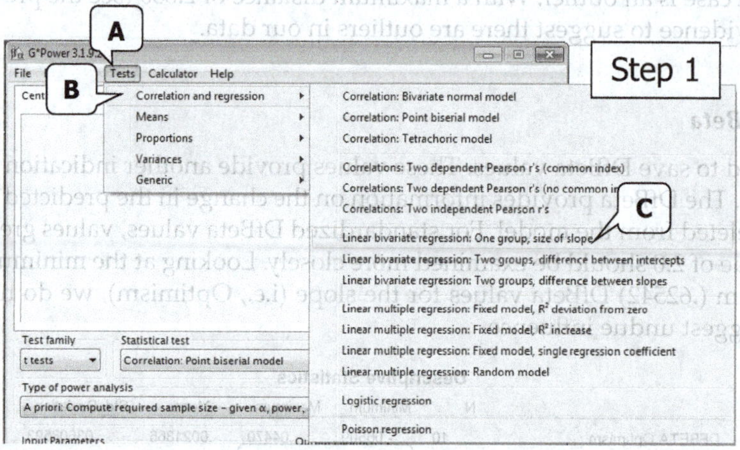

FIGURE 17.33
Post hoc power for simple linear regression: Step 1.

The "Type of power analysis" desired then needs to be selected. To compute post hoc power, select "Post hoc: Compute achieved power—given α, sample size, and effect size."

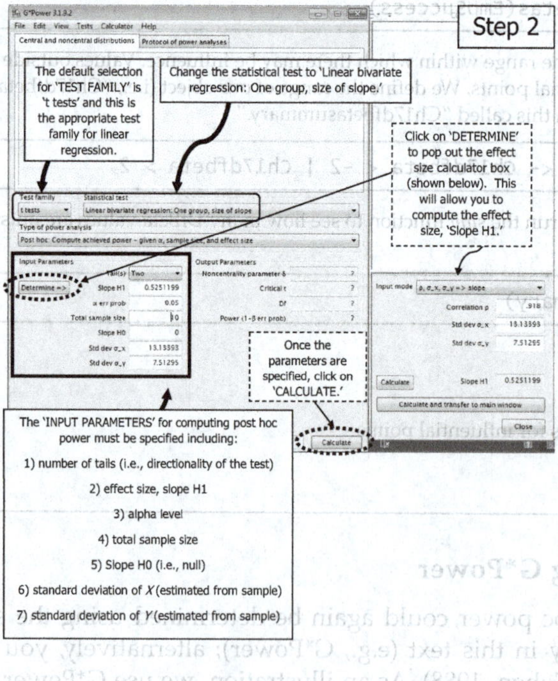

FIGURE 17.34
Computing Post Hoc Power: Step 2

The "Input Parameters" must then be specified. In our example, we conducted a two-tailed test. We will compute the effect size, *Slope H1*, last so we skip that for the moment. The alpha level we used was .05 and the total sample size was 10. The *Slope H0* is the slope specified in the null hypothesis—thus a value of zero. The last two parameters to be specified are for the standard deviation of *X*, the independent variable, and the standard deviation of *Y*, the dependent variable.

We skipped filling in the second parameter, the effect size, *Slope H1*, for a reason. We will use the pop out effect size calculator in G*Power to compute the effect size *Slope H1*. To pop out the effect size calculator, click on "Determine" displayed under "Input Parameters." In the pop out effect size calculator, click the toggle menu to select ρ, σ*x*, σ*y* => *slope*. Input the values for the correlation coefficient of *X* and *Y*, the standard deviation of *X*, and the standard deviation of *Y*. Click on "Calculate" in the pop out effect size calculator to compute the effect size *Slope H1*. Then click on "Calculate and transfer to main window" to transfer the calculated effect size (i.e., 0.5251199) to the "Input Parameters." Once the parameters are specified, click on "Calculate" to find the power statistics.

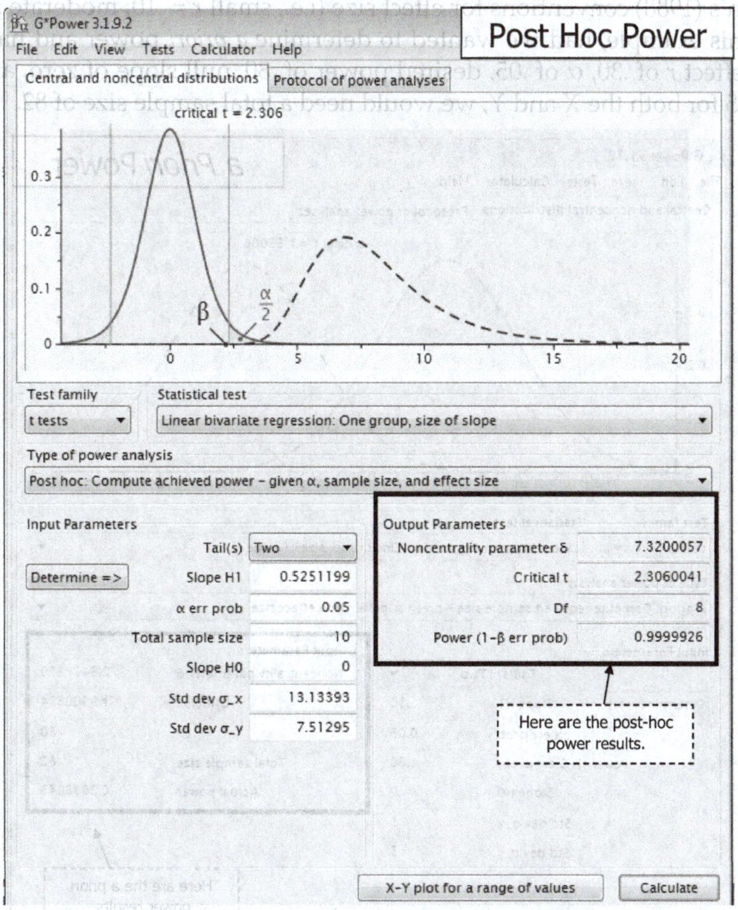

FIGURE 17.35
Post hoc power results.

The "Output Parameters" provide the relevant statistics given the input just specified. Here we were interested in determining post hoc power for simple linear regression with a two-tailed test, a computed effect size *Slope H1* of 0.5251199, an alpha level of .05, total sample size of 10, a hypothesized null slope of zero, a standard deviation of X (i.e., work optimism) of 13.13393, and a standard deviation of Y (i.e., employment success) of 7.51295. Based on those criteria, the post hoc power for the simple linear regression was .9999926. In other words, for these conditions the post hoc power of our simple linear regression was nearly 1.00—the probability of rejecting the null hypothesis when it is really false (in this case, the probability that the slope is zero) was around the maximum (i.e., 1.00; sufficient power is often .80 or above). Keep in mind that conducting power analysis *a priori* is recommended so that you avoid a situation where, post hoc, you find that the sample size was not sufficient to reach the desired level of power (given the observed parameters).

17.6.2 *A Priori* Power

For *a priori* power, we can determine the total sample size needed for simple linear regression given the directionality of the test, an estimated effect size *Slope H1*, α level, desired power, slope for the null hypothesis (i.e., zero), and the standard deviations of X and Y. We follow Cohen's (1988) conventions for effect size (i.e., small $r = .10$; moderate $r = .30$; large $r = .50$). In this example, had we wanted to determine *a priori* power and had estimated a moderate effect r of .30, α of .05, desired power of .80, null slope of zero, and standard deviation of 5 for both the X and Y, we would need a total sample size of 82.

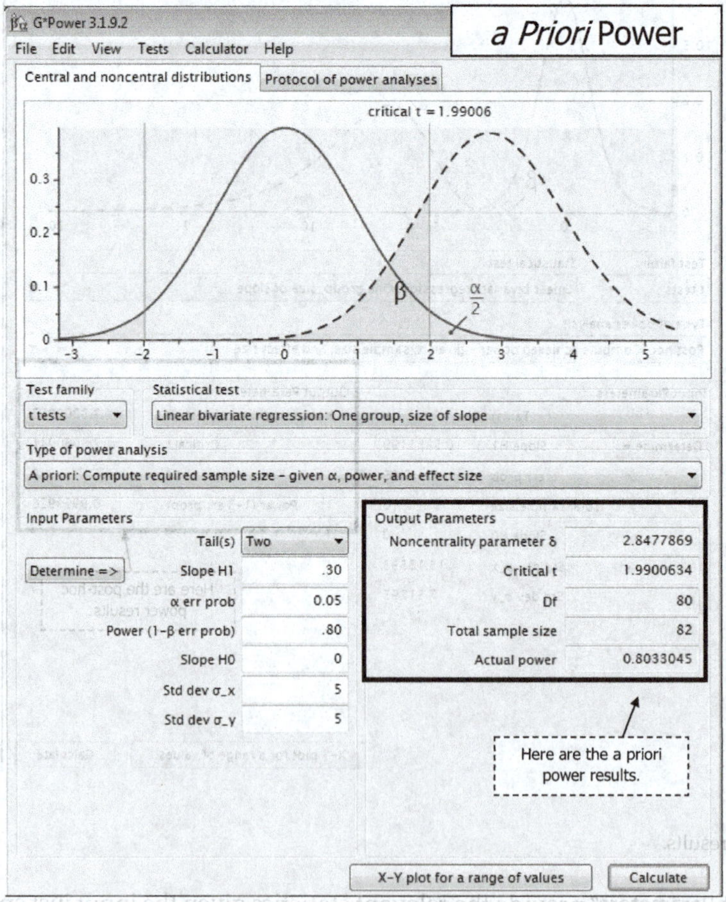

FIGURE 17.36
A priori power results.

17.7 Research Question Template and Example Write-Up

Finally, here is an example paragraph for the results of the simple linear regression analysis. Recall that our graduate research assistant, Ott Lier, was assisting the Human Resources director, Dr. Randall. Dr. Randall wanted to know if employment success could be predicted by work optimism. The research question presented to Dr. Randall from Ott included the following: *To what extent can employment success be predicted from work optimism?*

Ott then assisted Dr. Randall in generating a simple linear regression model as the test of inference. A template for writing the research question for this design is presented below.

To what extent can [dependent variable] be predicted from [independent variable]?

It may be helpful to preface the results of the simple linear regression with information on an examination of the extent to which the assumptions were met. The assumptions include: (a) independence; (b) homogeneity of variance; (c) normality; (d) linearity; and (e) fixed values of X.

A simple linear regression analysis was conducted to determine if employment success (dependent variable) could be predicted from work optimism (independent variable). The null hypothesis tested was that the regression coefficient (i.e., the slope) was equal to zero. The data were screened for missingness and violation of assumptions prior to analysis. There was no missing data.

Linearity. The scatterplot of the independent variable (work optimism) and the dependent variable (employment success) indicates that the assumption of linearity is reasonable—as work optimism increases, employment success scores generally increase as well. With a random display of points falling within an absolute value of 2, a scatterplot of unstandardized residuals against values of the independent variable provided further evidence of linearity.

Normality. The assumption of normality was tested via examination of the unstandardized residuals. Review of the Shapiro-Wilk test for normality ($SW = .927$, $df = 10$, $p = .416$) and skewness (−.269) and kurtosis (−1.369) statistics suggested that normality was a reasonable assumption. The boxplot suggested a relatively normal distributional shape (with no outliers) of the residuals. The Q-Q plot and histogram suggested normality was reasonable.

Independence. A relatively random display of points in the scatterplot of studentized residuals against values of the independent variable provided evidence of independence. The Durbin-Watson statistic was computed to evaluate independence of errors and was 1.287, which is considered acceptable. This suggests that the assumption of independent errors has been met.

Homoscedasticity. A relatively random display of points, where the spread of residuals appears fairly constant over the range of values of the independent variable (in the scatterplot of studentized residuals against values of the independent variable) provided evidence of homogeneity of variance. The results of the nonconstant error variance test also provide evidence of homoscedasticity, $\chi^2 = 1.32$, $df = 1$, $p = .25$.

Here is an APA-style example paragraph of results for the simple linear regression analysis (remember that this will be prefaced by the previous paragraph reporting the extent to which the assumptions of the test were met).

The results of the simple linear regression suggest that a significant proportion of the total variation in employment success was predicted by work optimism. In other words, an employee's work optimism is a good predictor of their employment success, $F(1, 8) = 42.700$, $p < .001$. Additionally, we find: (a) the unstandardized slope (.525) and standardized slope (.918) are statistically significantly different from zero ($t = 6.535$, $df = 8$, $p < .001$); with every one point increase in work optimism, employment success will increase by approximately ½ of one point; (b) the confidence interval around the unstandardized slope does not include zero (.340, .710) further confirming that work optimism is a statistically significant predictor of employment success; and (c) the intercept (or average employment success score when work optimism is zero) was 8.865. Multiple R^2 indicates that approximately 84% of the variation in employment success was predicted by work optimism scores. According to Cohen (1988), this suggests a large effect.

17.8 Additional Resources

This chapter has provided a preview into conducting simple linear regression analysis. However, there are a number of areas that space limitations prevent us from delving into. For those of you who are interested in learning more about simple linear regression, or if you find yourself in a sticky situation in your analyses, you may wish to look into the following, among many other excellent resources.

- A comprehensive overview of regression, including managing irregularities, among other topics (Darlington & Hayes, 2017)
- A comprehensive treatment of the mathematics of regression (Olive, 2017)
- Comprehensive coverage of regression, including extensions of the linear model (e.g., boosting linear regression, Bayesian linear models), among other topics (Fahrmeir, Kneib, Lang, & Marx, 2013)

Problems

Conceptual Problems

1. A regression intercept represents which one of the following?
   a. The slope of the line
   b. The amount of change in Y given a one-unit change in X
   c. The value of Y when X is equal to zero
   d. The strength of the relationship between X and Y

2. The regression line for predicting final exam grades in history from midterm scores in the same course is found to be $Y' = .61X + 3.12$. If the value of X increases from 74 to 75, the value of Y will do which one of the following?
   a. Increase by .61 points
   b. Increase by 1.00 points

c. Increase by 3.12 points
d. Decrease by .61 points

3. The regression line for predicting salary of principals from cumulative GPA in graduate school is found to be $Y' = 35000X + 37000$. What does the value of 37000 represent?
a. Average cumulative GPA
b. The criterion value
c. The mean salary of principals when cumulative GPA is zero
d. The standardized regression coefficient given an intercept of zero.

4. The regression line for predicting salary of principals from cumulative GPA in graduate school is found to be $Y' = 35000X + 37000$. What does the value of 35000 represent?
a. The amount of change in Y given a one-unit change in X
b. The correlation between X and Y
c. The intercept value
d. The value of Y when X is equal to zero

5. You are given that $\mu_X = 14$, $\sigma_X^2 = 36$, $\mu_Y = 14$, $\sigma_Y^2 = 49$, and $Y = 14$ is the prediction equation for predicting Y from X. Which of the following is the variance of the predicted values of Y'?
a. 0
b. 14
c. 36
d. 49

6. In regression analysis, the prediction of Y is *most* accurate for which of the following correlations between X and Y?
a. –.90
b. –.30
c. +.20
d. +.80

7. If the relationship between two variables is linear, then which one of the following is correct?
a. All of the points must fall on a curved line.
b. The relationship is best represented by a curved line.
c. All of the points must fall on a straight line.
d. The relationship is best represented by a straight line.

8. If both X and Y are measured on a z score scale, the regression line will have a slope of which one of the following?
a. 0.00
b. +1 or –1
c. r_{XY}
d. s_Y/s_X

9. If the simple linear regression equation for predicting Y from X is $Y' = 25$, then the correlation between X and Y is which one of the following?
a. 0.00
b. 0.25

c. 0.50
d. 1.00

10. Which one of the following is correct for the unstandardized regression slope?
a. It may never be negative.
b. It may never be greater than +1.00.
c. It may never be greater than the correlation coefficient r_{XY}.
d. None of the above

11. If two individuals have the same score on the predictor, their residual scores will be which one of the following?
a. Be necessarily equal
b. Depend *only* on their observed scores on *Y*
c. Depend *only* on their predicted scores on *Y*
d. Depend *only* on the number of individuals that have the same predicted score

12. If $r_{XY} = .6$, the proportion of variation in *Y* that is *not* predictable from *X* is which one of the following?
a. .36
b. .40
c. .60
d. .64

13. Homogeneity assumes which one of the following?
a. The range of *Y* is the same as the range of *X*.
b. The *X* and *Y* distributions have the same mean values.
c. The variability of the *X* and the *Y* distributions is the same.
d. The conditional variability of *Y* is the same for all values of *X*.

14. Which one of the following is suggested to examine the extent to which homogeneity of variance has been met?
a. Scatterplot of Mahalanobis distances against standardized residuals
b. Scatterplot of studentized residuals against unstandardized predicted values
c. Simple bivariate correlation between *X* and *Y*
d. Shapiro-Wilk test results for the unstandardized residuals

15. Which one of the following is suggested to examine the extent to which normality has been met?
a. Scatterplot of Mahalanobis distances against standardized residuals
b. Scatterplot of studentized residuals against unstandardized predicted values
c. Simple bivariate correlation between *X* and *Y*
d. Shapiro-Wilk test results for the unstandardized residuals

16. The linear regression slope b_{YX} represents which one of the following?
a. Amount of change in *X* expected from a one unit change in *Y*
b. Amount of change in *Y* expected from a one unit change in *X*
c. Correlation between *X* and *Y*
d. Error of estimate of *Y* from *X*

17. True or false? If the correlation between *X* and *Y* is zero, then the best prediction of *Y* that can be made is the mean of *Y*.

18. True or false? If *X* and *Y* are highly nonlinear, linear regression is more useful than the situation where *X* and *Y* are highly linear.

19. True or false? If the pretest (*X*) and the posttest (*Y*) are positively correlated, and your friend receives a pretest score below the mean, then the regression equation would predict that your friend would have a posttest score that is above the mean.

20. Two variables are linearly related so that given *X*, *Y* can be predicted without error. I assert that r_{XY} must be equal to either +1.0 or −1.0. Am I correct?

21. I assert that the simple regression model is structured so that at least two of the actual data points will necessarily fall on the regression line. Am I correct?

22. Which one of the following is *not* a metric that can be used as a measure of effect in simple linear regression?

a. Coefficient of determination

b. Mahalanobis distance

c. r_{XY}^2

d. Squared sample correlation between *X* and *Y*

23. What prevents Cohen's f^2 from being interpreted with the same conventions as correlation coefficients?

a. It can be smaller than zero.

b. It cannot be greater than one.

c. It has no upper bound.

d. It is a proportion.

24. The assumption of independence in simple linear regression deals with which one of the following?

a. Bivariate correlation coefficient

b. Independent variable

c. Dependent variable

d. Residuals

Answers to Conceptual Problems

1. c (see definition of intercept; a and b refer to the slope and d to the correlation.)

3. c (the intercept is 37000 which represents average salary when cumulative GPA is zero.)

5. a (the predicted value is a constant mean value of 14 regardless of *X*, thus the variance of the predicted values is 0.)

7. d (linear relationships are best represented by a straight line, although all of the points need not fall on the line.)

9. a (if the slope = 0, then the correlation = 0.)

11. b (with the same predictor score, they will have the same residual score; whether the residuals are the same will depend only on the observed *Y*.)

13. d (see definition of homogeneity.)

15. **d** (various pieces of evidence for normality can be assessed, including formal tests such as the Shapiro-Wilk test.)
17. **True** (the value of Y is irrelevant when the correlation = 0, so the mean of Y is the best prediction.)
19. **False** (if the variables are positively correlated, then the slope would be positive and a low score on the pretest would predict a low score on the posttest.)
21. **No** (the regression equation may generate any number of points on the regression line.)
23. **c** (Cohen's f^2 is a ratio of two proportions but itself is *not* a proportion, thus it has no upper bound and cannot be interpreted with the same conventions as correlation coefficients.)

Computational Problems

1. You are given the following pairs of scores on X (number of hours studied) and Y (quiz score).

X	Y
4	5
4	6
3	4
7	8
2	4

   a. Find the linear regression model for predicting Y from X.
   b. Use the prediction model obtained to predict the value of Y for a new person who has a value of 6 for X.

2. You are given the following pairs of scores on X (preschool social skills) and Y (receptive vocabulary at the end of kindergarten).

X	Y
25	60
30	45
42	56
45	58
36	42
50	38
38	35
47	45
32	47
28	57
31	56

   a. Find the linear regression model for predicting Y from X.
   b. Use the prediction model obtained to predict the value of Y for a new child who has a value of 48 for X.

3. The prediction equation for predicting Y (pain indicator) from X (drug dosage) is $Y = 2.5X + 18$. What is the observed mean for Y if $\mu_X = 40$ and $\sigma_X^2 = 81$?

4. You are given the following pairs of scores on X (# of years working) and Y (# of raises).

X	Y
2	2
2	1
1	1
1	1
3	5
4	4
5	7
5	6
7	7
6	8
4	3
3	3
6	6
6	6
8	10
9	9
10	6
9	6
4	9
4	10

Perform the following computations using $\alpha = .05$.

a. The regression equation of Y predicted by X
b. Test of the significance of X as a predictor
c. Plot Y versus X
d. Compute the residuals
e. Plot residuals versus X

5. The prediction equation for predicting Y (customer satisfaction) from X (customer experience) is $Y = 5X + 8$. What is the observed mean for Y if $\mu_X = 25$ and $\sigma_X^2 = 16$?

Answers to Computational Problems

1. a. b (slope) = .8571, a (intercept) = 1.9716; b. Y = (outcome) = 7.1142

3. Given $Y = 2.5X + 18$ and knowing that $\mu_X = 40$ and $\sigma_X^2 = 81$. Then plug in the values to the equation for the intercept: $\alpha_{YX} = \mu_Y - \beta_{YX}\mu_X$. This leads to: $18 = \mu_Y - (25)(40)$ Thus, $\mu_Y = 18 + 100 = 118$.

5. The prediction equation for predicting Y (customer satisfaction) from X (customer experience) is $Y = 5X + 8$. We know that $\mu_X = 25$ and $\sigma_X^2 = 16$. Then plug in the values to the equation for the intercept: $\alpha_{YX} = \mu_Y - \beta_{YX}\mu_X$. This leads to: $8 = \mu_Y - (5)(25)$. Thus, $\mu_Y = 8 + 125 = 133$.

Interpretive Problems

1. With the survey1 data accessible from the website, your task is to use SPSS or **R** to find a suitable single predictor of current GPA. In other words, select several potential predictors that seem reasonable, and conduct a simple linear regression analysis for each of those predictors individually. Which of those is the best predictor of current GPA? What is the interpretation of the effect size? Write up the results following APA style.
2. With the survey1 data accessible from the website, your task is to use SPSS or **R** to find a suitable single predictor of the number of hours exercised per week. In other words, select several potential predictors that seem reasonable, and conduct a simple linear regression analysis for each of those predictors individually. Which of those is the best predictor of the number of hours of exercise? What is the interpretation of the effect size? Write up the results following APA style.
3. Using the volcano data (Ch17_volcano) accessible from the website, compute a simple linear regression using SPSS or **R** with number of injuries as the dependent variable and volcano elevation as the independent variable. Interpret the findings, including a measure of effect size. Write up the results following APA style.

18

Multiple Linear Regression

Chapter Outline

Key Concepts

1. Partial and semipartial (part) correlations
2. Standardized and unstandardized regression coefficients
3. Coefficient of multiple determination and multiple correlation

Modeling prediction is one of the most common methods of quantitative analysis. This leads us to multiple regression analysis, where we are able to model two or more predictors to predict or explain the criterion variable. Here we adopt the usual notation where the X's are defined as the *independent* or *predictor variables*, and Y as the *dependent* or *criterion variable*.

For example, an admissions officer might use Graduate Record Exam (GRE) scores to predict graduate-level grade point averages (GPA) to make admissions decisions for a sample of applicants to your favorite local university or college. The admissions office may decide that including only one variable omits a number of other factors that relate to GPA. Other potentially useful predictors might be undergraduate GPA, ratings of recommendation letters, scored writing samples, and/or an evaluation from a personal interview. The research question of interest would now be, *how well do the GRE, undergraduate GPA, recommendation ratings, writing sample scores, and/or interview scores (the independent or predictor variables) predict performance in graduate school (the dependent or criterion variable)*? This is an example of a situation where multiple regression analysis using multiple predictor variables might be the method of choice.

This chapter considers the concepts of partial, semipartial, and multiple correlations, standardized and unstandardized regression coefficients, and the coefficient of multiple determination, as well as introduces a number of other types of regression models. Our objectives are that by the end of this chapter, you will be able to (a) determine and interpret the results of partial and semipartial correlations, (b) understand the concepts underlying multiple linear regression, (c) determine and interpret the results of multiple linear regression, (d) understand and evaluate the assumptions of multiple linear regression, and (e) have a basic understanding of other types of regression models.

18.1 What Multiple Linear Regression Is and How It Works

The group of graduate students in the statistics lab have developed into quite a group of statistics gurus, their skills being sought from across the university campus and beyond. Today, we find Addie Venture taking the lead on an existing on-campus project.

Dr. Golly, the assistant dean in the Graduate Student Services office, seeks advice from Addie Venture on a special project. Dr. Golly is interested in estimating the extent to which graduate grade point average can be predicted by scores on the overall Graduate Record Exam (GRE-total) and undergraduate grade point average. From her recent statistical trek in regression, Addie knows that questions delving into relationships and prediction with continuous outcomes and multiple predictors can be examined using multiple regression. Addie suggests the following research question to Dr. Golly: *Can graduate grade point average be predicted by scores on the overall Graduate Record Exam (GRE-total) and undergraduate grade point average?* Addie determines that a multiple linear regression is the appropriate statistical procedure to use to answer Dr. Golly's question. Excited for the first project of the semester, Addie then proceeds to assist Dr. Golly in analyzing the data and interpreting the results.

18.1.1 Characteristics

Prior to a discussion of regression analysis, we need to consider two related concepts in correlational analysis, partial and semipartial correlations. Multiple regression analysis involves the use of two or more predictor variables, which can be either or both continuous or categorical, and one criterion variable that is continuous in scale (we will work with binary outcomes in the proceeding chapter); thus there are at a minimum three variables involved in the analysis. If we think about these variables in the context of the Pearson correlation, we have a problem, because this correlation can be used to relate only two variables at a time. How do we incorporate additional variables into a correlational analysis? The answer is through partial and semipartial correlations, and later in this chapter, multiple correlations.

18.1.1.1 Partial Correlation

First we discuss the concept of **partial correlation**. The simplest situation consists of three variables, which we label X_1, X_2, and X_3. Here an example of a partial correlation would be the correlation between X_1 and X_2 where X_3 is *held constant* (i.e., controlled or partialed out). That is, *the influence of X_3 is removed from both X_1 and X_2 (both have been adjusted for X_3)*. Thus, the partial correlation here represents the linear relationship between X_1 and X_2 independent of the linear influence of X_3. This particular partial correlation is denoted by $r_{12.3}$, where the *X*'s are not shown for simplicity and the dot indicates that the variables preceding it are to be correlated and the variable(s) following it are to be partialed out. We compute $r_{12.3}$ as follows:

$$r_{12.3} = \frac{r_{12} - r_{13}r_{23}}{\sqrt{(1-r_{13}^2)(1-r_{23}^2)}}$$

Let us take an example of a situation where a partial correlation might be computed. Say a researcher is interested in the relationship between height (X_1) and weight (X_2). The sample consists of individuals ranging in age (X_3) from 6 months to 65 years. The sample correlations are for: height (X_1) and weight (X_2), $r_{12} = .7$; height (X_1) and age (X_3), $r_{13} = .1$; and weight (X_2) and age (X_3), $r_{23} = .6$. We compute the correlation between height and weight, controlling for age, $r_{12.3}$, as follows:

$$r_{12.3} = \frac{r_{12} - r_{13}r_{23}}{\sqrt{(1-r_{13}^2)(1-r_{23}^2)}} = \frac{.7-(.1)(.6)}{\sqrt{(1-.01)(1-.36)}} = .8040.$$

We see here that the bivariate correlation between height and weight, ignoring age ($r_{12} = .7$), is smaller than the partial correlation between height and weight controlling for age ($r_{12.3} = .8040$). *That is, the relationship between height and weight is stronger when age is held constant (i.e., for a particular age) than it is across all ages.* Although we often talk about holding a particular variable constant, in reality variables such as age cannot be held constant artificially.

Holding age constant would be an **experimental control**—controlling for the effects of age by collecting height and weight data from everyone who has the same age. It is important to note that this is not the same as achieving **statistical control**—controlling for the effects of age by correlating the residuals of a regression to predict height from age with the residuals from a regression to predict weight from age.

Some rather interesting partial correlation results can occur in particular situations. At one extreme, if both the correlation between height (X_1) and age (X_3), r_{13}, and weight (X_2) and age (X_3), r_{23}, equal zero, then the correlation between height (X_1) and weight (X_2) will equal the partial correlation between height and weight controlling for age, $r_{12} = r_{12.3}$. That is, *if the variable being partialed out is uncorrelated with each of the other two variables, then the partialing process will logically not have any effect*.

At the other extreme, *if either r_{13} or r_{23} equals 1, then $r_{12.3}$ cannot be calculated as the denominator is equal to zero* (in other words, at least one of the terms in the denominator is equal to zero which results in the product of the two terms in the denominator equaling zero and thus a denominator of zero—and you cannot divide by zero). Thus in this situation (where either r_{13} or r_{23} is perfectly correlated at 1.0), the partial correlation (i.e., $r_{12.3}$, partial correlation between height and weight controlling for age) is not defined. Later in this chapter we refer to this as *perfect collinearity*, which is a serious problem.

In between these extremes, it is possible for the partial correlation to be greater than or less than its corresponding bivariate correlation (including a change in sign), and even for the partial correlation to be equal to zero when its bivariate correlation is not. For significance tests of partial and semipartial correlations, we refer you to your favorite statistical software.

18.1.1.2 Semipartial (Part) Correlation

Next, the concept of **semipartial correlation** (also called a **part correlation**) is discussed. The simplest situation consists again of three variables, which we label X_1, X_2, and X_3. Here an example of a semipartial correlation would be the correlation between X_1 and X_2 where X_3 is removed from X_2 only. That is, the influence of X_3 is removed from X_2 only. Thus the semipartial correlation here represents the linear relationship between X_1 and X_2 after that portion of X_2 that can be linearly predicted from X_3 has been removed from X_2. This particular semipartial correlation is denoted by $r_{1(2.3)}$, where the X's are not shown for simplicity and within the parentheses the dot indicates that the variable(s) following it are to be removed from the variable preceding it. Another use of the semipartial correlation is when we want to examine the predictive power in the prediction of Y from X_1 after removing X_2 from the prediction. A method for computing $r_{1(2.3)}$ is as follows:

$$r_{1(2.3)} = \frac{r_{12} - r_{13}r_{23}}{\sqrt{\left(1 - r_{23}^2\right)}}$$

Let us take an example of a situation where a semipartial correlation might be computed. Say a researcher is interested in the relationship between GPA (X_1) and GRE scores (X_2). The researcher would like to remove the influence of intelligence (IQ: X_3) from GRE scores, but not from GPA. The simple bivariate correlation between GPA and GRE is $r_{12} = .5$; between GPA and IQ is $r_{13} = .3$; and between GRE and IQ is $r_{23} = .7$. We compute the semipartial correlation that removes the influence of intelligence (IQ: X_3) from GRE scores (X_2), but not from GPA (X_1) (i.e., $r_{1(2.3)}$) as follows:

$$r_{1(2.3)} = \frac{r_{12} - r_{13}r_{23}}{\sqrt{\left(1 - r_{23}^2\right)}} = \frac{.5 - (.3)(.7)}{\sqrt{(1 - .49)}} = .4061$$

Thus, the bivariate correlation between GPA (X_1) and GRE scores (X_2) ignoring IQ (X_3) ($r_{12} = .50$) is larger than the semipartial correlation between GPA and GRE controlling for IQ in GRE ($r_{1(2.3)} = .4061$). As was the case with partial correlations, various values of a semipartial correlation can be obtained depending on the combination of the bivariate correlations. For more information on partial and semipartial correlations, see Glass and Hopkins (1996), Hays (1988), and Pedhazur (1997).

Now that we have considered the correlational relationships among two or more variables (i.e., partial and semipartial correlations), let us move on to an examination of the multiple regression model where there are two or more predictor variables.

Let us take the concepts we have learned in this and the previous chapter and place them into the context of multiple linear regression. For purposes of brevity, we do not consider the population situation because the sample situation is invoked 99.44% of the time. In this section we discuss the unstandardized and standardized multiple regression models, the coefficient of multiple determination, multiple correlation, tests of significance, and statistical assumptions.

18.1.1.3 Unstandardized Regression Model

The sample multiple linear regression model for predicting Y from m predictors $X_{1,2,...,m}$ is

$$Y_i = b_1 X_{1i} + b_2 X_{2i} + \ldots + b_m X_{mi} + a + e_i$$

where Y is the **criterion variable** (also known as the dependent variable); the X_k's are the **predictor (or independent) variables** where $k = 1, \ldots, m$; b_k is the **sample partial slope** of the regression line for Y as predicted by X_k, a is the **sample intercept** of the regression line for Y as predicted by the set of X_k's; e_i are the **residuals or errors of prediction** (the part of Y not predictable from the X_k's); and i represents an index for an individual or object. The index i can take on values from 1 to n where n is the size of the sample (i.e., $i = 1, \ldots, n$). The term **partial slope** is used because it represents the slope of Y for a particular X_k in which we have partialled out the influence of the other X_k's, much as we did with the partial correlation.

The **sample prediction model** is

$$Y_i' = b_1 X_{1i} + b_2 X_{2i} + \ldots + b_m X_{mi} + a$$

Where Y_i' is the predicted value of Y for specific values of the X_k's, and the other terms are as before. There is only one difference between the regression and prediction models. The regression model explicitly includes prediction error as e_i, whereas the prediction model includes prediction error implicitly as part of the predicted score Y_i' (i.e., there is some error in the predicted values). The goal of the prediction model is to include an independent variable X that minimizes the residual; this means that the independent variable does a nice job of predicting the outcome. We can compute residuals, the e_i, for each of the i individuals or objects by comparing the actual Y values with the predicted Y values as

$$e_i = Y_i - Y_i'$$

for all $i = 1, \ldots, n$ individuals or objects in the sample.

Determining the sample partial slopes and the intercept in the multiple predictor case is rather complicated. To keep it simple, we use a two-predictor model for illustrative purposes. Generally we rely on statistical software for implementing multiple regression analysis. For the two-predictor case, the sample partial slopes (b_1 and b_2) and the intercept (a) can be determined as follows:

$$b_1 = \frac{(r_{Y1} - r_{Y2}r_{12})s_Y}{(1 - r_{12}^2)s_1}$$

$$b_2 = \frac{(r_{Y2} - r_{Y1}r_{12})s_Y}{(1 - r_{12}^2)s_2}$$

$$a = \bar{Y} - b_1\bar{X}_1 - b_2\bar{X}_2$$

The sample partial slope b_1 is referred to alternately as (a) the expected or predicted change in Y for a one-unit change in X_1 with X_2 held constant (or for individuals with the same score on X_2), and (b) the unstandardized or raw regression coefficient for X_1. Similar statements may be made for b_2. Note the similarity of the partial slope equation to the semipartial correlation. The sample intercept is referred to as the value of the dependent variable Y when the values of the independent variables X_1 and X_2 are both zero.

An alternative method for computing the sample partial slopes that involves the use of a partial correlation is as follows:

$$b_1 = r_{Y1.2}\left(\frac{s_Y\sqrt{1 - r_{Y2}^2}}{s_1\sqrt{1 - r_{12}^2}}\right)$$

$$b_2 = r_{Y2.1}\left(\frac{s_Y\sqrt{1 - r_{Y1}^2}}{s_2\sqrt{1 - r_{12}^2}}\right)$$

What statistical criterion is used to arrive at the particular values for the partial slopes and intercept? The criterion usually used in multiple linear regression analysis [and in all general linear models (GLM) for that matter] is the **least squares criterion**. *The least squares criterion arrives at those values for the partial slopes and intercept such that the sum of the squared prediction errors or residuals is smallest*. That is, we want to find that regression model, defined by a particular set of partial slopes and an intercept, which has the smallest sum of the squared residuals. We often refer to this particular method for calculating the slope and intercept as **least squares estimation,** because a and the b_k's represent sample estimates of the population parameters α and the β_k's, which are obtained using the least squares criterion. Recall from simple linear regression that the residual is simply the vertical distance from the observed value of Y to the predicted value of Y, and the line of best fit minimizes this distance. This concept still applies to multiple linear regression with the exception that we are now in a three-dimensional (or more) plane given there are multiple independent variables.

18.1.1.4 Standardized Regression Model

Up until this point in the chapter, everything in multiple linear regression analysis has involved the use of raw scores. For this reason we referred to the model as the

unstandardized regression model. Often we may want to express the regression in terms of standard z score units rather than in raw score units. The means and variances of the standardized variables (e.g., z_1, z_2, z_Y) are 0 and 1, respectively. The **sample standardized linear prediction model** becomes the following:

$$z(Y_i') = b_1^* z_{1i} + b_2^* z_{2i} + \ldots + b_m^* z_{mi}$$

where b_k^* represents a **sample standardized partial slope** (sometimes called **beta weights**) and the other terms are as before. As was the case in simple linear regression, no intercept term is necessary in the standardized prediction model as the mean of the z scores for all variables is 0. (Recall that the intercept is the value of the dependent variable when the scores on the independent variables are all zero. *Thus in a standardized prediction model, the dependent variable will equal zero when the values of the independent variables are equal to their means—i.e., zero*). The **sample standardized partial slopes** are, in general, computed by the following equation:

$$b_k^* = b_k \left(\frac{s_k}{s_Y} \right)$$

For the two-predictor case, the standardized partial slopes can be calculated by

$$b_1^* = b_1 \left(\frac{s_1}{s_Y} \right)$$

or

$$b_1^* = \frac{r_{Y1} - (r_{Y2} r_{12})}{(1 - r_{12}^2)}$$

and

$$b_2^* = b_2 \left(\frac{s_2}{s_Y} \right)$$

or

$$b_2^* = \frac{r_{Y2} - (r_{Y1} r_{12})}{(1 - r_{12}^2)}$$

If the two predictors are *uncorrelated* (i.e., $r_{12} = 0$), then the standardized partial slopes are equal to the simple bivariate correlations between the dependent variable and the independent variables (i.e., $b_1^* = r_{Y1}$ and $b_2^* = r_{Y2}$) because the rest of the equation goes away, as we see here. In the latter "mathematical introduction snapshot," we provide an illustration of this using the example data in the chapter.

$$b_1^* = \frac{r_{Y1} - (r_{Y2} r_{12})}{(1 - r_{12}^2)} = \frac{r_{Y1} - r_{Y2}(0)}{(1 - 0)} = r_{Y1}$$

When would you want to use the standardized versus unstandardized regression analyses? According to Pedhazur (1997), b_k^* is sample specific and is not very stable across different samples due to the variance of X_k changing (as the variance of X_k increases, the value of b_k^* also increases, all else being equal). For example, the example we will review later with data from Ivy-Covered University, b_k^* would vary across different graduating classes (or samples) while b_k would be much more consistent across classes. Thus most researchers prefer the use of b_k to compare the influence of a particular predictor variable across different samples and/or populations. Pedhazur also states that the b_k^* is of "limited value" (p. 321), but could be reported along with the b_k. As Pedhazur and others have reported, the b_k^* can be deceptive in determining the relative importance of the predictors as they are affected by the variances and covariances of both the included predictors and the predictors not included in the model. Thus we recommend the b_k for general purpose use.

18.1.1.5 Coefficient of Multiple Determination and Multiple Correlation

An obvious question now is, how well is the criterion variable predicted or explained by the set of predictor variables? For our example, we are interested in how well graduate grade point averages (the dependent variable) are predicted by GRE total scores and undergraduate grade point averages. In other words, *what is the utility of the set of predictor variables?*

The simplest method involves the partitioning of the familiar total sum of squares in Y, which we denote as SS_{total}. In multiple linear regression analysis, we can write SS_{total} as follows:

$$SS_{total} = \frac{\left[n\sum Y_i^2 - \left(\sum Y_i\right)^2\right]}{n}$$

$$\text{or } SS_{total} = (n-1)s_Y^2$$

where we sum over Y from $i = 1, \ldots, n$. Next we can conceptually partition SS_{total} as

$$SS_{total} = SS_{reg} + SS_{res}$$

$$\sum\left(Y_i - \bar{Y}\right)^2 = \sum\left(Y_i' - \bar{Y}\right)^2 + \sum\left(Y_i - Y_i'\right)^2$$

where SS_{reg} is the regression sum of squares due to the prediction of Y from the X_k's (often written as $SS_{Y'}$), and SS_{res} is the sum of squares due to the residuals.

Before we consider computation of SS_{reg} and SS_{res}, let us look at the **coefficient of multiple determination**. Recall the coefficient of determination that is applicable to simple linear regression, r_{XY}^2. We now consider the *multiple predictor version* of r_{XY}^2, here denoted as $R_{Y.1,\ldots,m}^2$, which we will shorthand as R^2. The subscript tells us that Y is the criterion (or dependent) variable and that $X_{1,\ldots,m}$ are the predictor (or independent) variables (with m representing the total number of independent variables). The simplest procedure for computing R^2 is as follows:

$$R_{Y.1,\ldots,m}^2 = b_1^* r_{Y1} + b_2^* r_{Y2} + \ldots + b_m^* r_{Ym}$$

The coefficient of multiple determination tells us *the proportion of total variation in the dependent variable Y that is predicted from the set of predictor variables* (i.e., $X_{1,\ldots,m}$'s). Often we see the coefficient in terms of *SS* as follows:

$$R^2_{Y.1,\ldots,m} = \frac{SS_{reg}}{SS_{total}}$$

Thus, one method for computing the sums of squares regression and residual, SS_{reg} and SS_{res}, is from the coefficient of multiple determination, R^2 (an index that can also be used a measure of effect size) as follows:

$$SS_{reg} = R^2\left(SS_{total}\right)$$
$$SS_{res} = \left(1-R^2\right)\left(SS_{total}\right) = SS_{total} - SS_{reg}$$

Note also that $R_{Y.1,\ldots,m}$ is referred to as the ***multiple correlation coefficient*** so as not to confuse it with a simple bivariate correlation coefficient. In the latter 'mathematical introduction snapshot,' we provide an illustration using the example data in the chapter.

It should be noted that R^2 is sensitive to sample size and to the number of predictor variables. As sample size and/or the number of predictor variables increase, R^2 will increase as well. *R* is a biased estimate of the population multiple correlation due to sampling error in the bivariate correlations and in the standard deviations of *X* and *Y*. Because *R* systematically overestimates the population multiple correlation, an adjusted coefficient of multiple determination has been devised. The adjusted R^2 (denoted as R^2_{adj}) is calculated as follows:

$$R^2_{adj} = 1 - \left(1 - R^2\right)\left(\frac{n-1}{n-m-1}\right)$$

Thus, R^2_{adj} adjusts for sample size and for the number of predictors in the model; this allows us to compare models fitted to the same set of data with different numbers of predictors or with different samples of data. The difference between the squared multiple correlation (aka coefficient of multiple determination), R^2, and the adjusted squared multiple correlation (aka adjusted coefficient of multiple determination), R^2_{adj}, is called **shrinkage**.

When *n* is small relative to *m*, the amount of bias can be large as R^2 can be expected to be large by chance alone. In this case the adjustment will be quite large, as it should be. In addition, with small samples, the regression coefficients (i.e., the b_k's) may not be very good estimates of the population values. When *n* is large relative to *m*, bias will be minimized and generalizations are likely to be better about the population values.

For the example data, we determine the adjusted multiple coefficient of determination R^2_{adj} to be as follows:

$$R^2_{adj} = 1 - \left(1 - R^2\right)\left(\frac{n-1}{n-m-1}\right) = 1 - \left(1 - .9089\right)\left(\frac{11-1}{11-2-1}\right) = .8861$$

In this case, the adjusted multiple coefficient of determination indicates a very small adjustment in comparison to R^2.

18.1.1.6 Significance Tests

Here we describe two procedures used in multiple linear regression analysis. These involve testing the significance of the overall regression model and of each individual partial slope (or regression coefficient).

18.1.1.6.1 Test of Significance of the Overall Regression Model

The first test is the test of significance of the overall regression model, or alternatively the *test of significance of the coefficient of multiple determination*. This is a test of all of the b_k's simultaneously, an examination of overall model fit of the independent variables in aggregate. The null and alternative hypotheses, respectively, are as follows:

$$H_0: \beta_1 = \beta_2 = \ldots = \beta_k = 0$$
$$H_1: \text{not all the } \beta_k = 0$$

If H_0 is rejected, then one or more of the individual regression coefficients (i.e., the b_k) is statistically significantly different from zero (if the assumptions are satisfied, as discussed later). If H_0 is not rejected, then none of the individual regression coefficients will be significantly different from zero.

The test is based on the following test statistic:

$$F = \frac{R^2/m}{(1-R^2)(n-m-1)}$$

where F indicates that this is an F statistic, m is the number of predictors or independent variables, and n is the sample size. The F test statistic is compared to the F critical value, always a one-tailed test (by default, this value can never be negative given the terms in the equation, so this will always be a *directional test*) and at the designated level of significance, with *degrees of freedom* being m and $(n - m - 1)$, as taken from the F table (see Appendix). That is, the tabled critical value is ${}_{\alpha}F_{m,(n-m-1)}$. The test statistic can also be written in equivalent form as

$$F = \frac{SS_{reg}/df_{reg}}{SS_{res}/df_{res}} = \frac{MS_{reg}}{MS_{res}}$$

Where the degrees of freedom regression equals the number of independent variables, $df_{reg} = m$, and degrees of freedom residual equals the difference between the sample size, number of independent variables, and one, $df_{res} = (n - m - 1)$.

18.1.1.6.2 Test of Significance of b_k

The second test is the test of the statistical significance of each individual partial slope or regression coefficient, b_k. *That is, are the individual unstandardized regression coefficients statistically significantly different from zero?* This is actually the same as the test of b^*_k, so we need not develop a separate test for b^*_k. The null and alternative hypotheses, respectively, are as follows:

$$H_0: \beta_k = 0$$
$$H_1: \beta_k \neq 0$$

where β_k is the population partial slope for X_k.

In multiple regression it is necessary to compute a standard error for each regression coefficient b_k. The **variance error of estimate, s^2_{res}**, is similarly defined for multiple linear regression and computed as:

$$s^2_{res} = \frac{SS_{res}}{df_{res}} = MS_{res}$$

where $df_{res} = (n - m - 1)$. Degrees of freedom are lost as we have to estimate the population partial slopes and intercept, the β_k's and α, respectively, from the sample data. *The variance error of estimate indicates the amount of variation among the residuals.* The standard error of estimate is simply the positive square root of the variance error of estimate and is the standard deviation of the residuals or errors of estimate. We call it the **standard error of estimate**, denoted as s_{res}.

Finally, we need to compute a **standard error** for each b_k. Denote the standard error of b_k as $s(b_k)$ and define it as follows:

$$s(b_k) = \frac{s_{res}}{\sqrt{(n-1)(s_k^2)(1-R_k^2)}}$$

where s_k^2 is the **sample variance** for predictor X_k, and R_k^2 is the **squared multiple correlation** between X_k and the remaining X_k's. R_k^2 represents the overlap between that predictor (X_k) and the remaining predictors. In the case of two predictors, the squared multiple correlation R_k^2 is equal to the simple bivariate correlation between the two independent variables r_{12}^2.

The test statistic, t, for testing the significance of the regression coefficients, b_k's, is as follows:

$$t = \frac{b_k}{s(b_k)}$$

The test statistic t is compared to the critical values of t, a two-tailed test for a nondirectional H_1, at the designated level of significance, and with degrees of freedom $(n - m - 1)$, as taken from the t table in Appendix Table A.2. Thus, the tabled critical values are $\pm_{(\alpha/2)}t_{(n-m-1)}$ for a two-tailed test.

We can also form a *confidence interval around b_k* as follows:

$$CI(b_k) = b_k \pm_{(\alpha/2)} t_{(n-m-1)} s(b_k)$$

Recall that the null hypothesis tested is $H_0 = \beta_k = 0$. Therefore, if the confidence interval contains zero, then the regression coefficient b_k is not statistically significantly different from zero at the specified α level. This is interpreted to mean that in $(1 - \alpha)\%$ of the sample confidence intervals that would be formed from multiple samples, β_k will be included. In the latter "mathematical introduction snapshot," we provide an illustration using the example data in the chapter.

18.1.1.6.3 Other Tests

One can also form confidence intervals for the predicted mean of Y and the prediction intervals for individual values of Y.

18.1.1.7 Methods of Entering Predictors

There are many different ways in which predictor variables can be entered in a regression model, none of which are necessarily right or wrong—although we highly discourage the use of a few. We will begin with what is likely the most common method of entering independent variables, and that is simultaneous regression. There are other methods of entering the independent variables where the predictor variables are entered (or selected) systematically; here the set of predictors has not been selected *a priori*. This class of models is referred to as **sequential regression** (also known as **variable selection procedures**). This section introduces a brief description of the following sequential regression procedures: backward elimination, forward selection, stepwise selection, all possible subsets regression, and hierarchical regression.

18.1.1.7.1 Simultaneous Regression

The multiple predictor model which we have considered thus far can be viewed as **simultaneous regression**. That is, *all of the predictors to be used are entered (or selected) simultaneously*, such that all of the regression parameters are estimated simultaneously; here the set of predictors has been selected *a priori*. In computing these regression models, we have used the default setting in SPSS of the method of entry as "Enter," which enters the set of independent variables in aggregate.

18.1.1.7.2 Backward Elimination

First consider the backward elimination procedure. Here variables are eliminated from the model based on their **minimal contribution** to the prediction of the criterion variable. In the first stage of the analysis, all potential predictors are included in the model. In the second stage, that predictor is deleted from the model that makes the smallest contribution to the prediction of the dependent variable. This can be done by eliminating that variable having the smallest t or F statistic such that it is making the smallest contribution to R^2_{adj}. In subsequent stages, that predictor is deleted that makes the next smallest contribution to the prediction of the outcome Y. The analysis continues until each of the remaining predictors in the model is a significant predictor of Y. This could be determined by comparing the t or F statistics for each predictor to the critical value, at a preselected level of significance. Some computer programs use as a stopping rule the maximum F-to-remove criterion, where the procedure is stopped when all of the selected predictors' F values are greater than the specified F criterion. Another stopping rule is where the researcher stops at a predetermined number of predictors (see Hocking, 1976; Thompson, 1978). In SPSS, this is the **backward** method of entering predictors.

18.1.1.7.3 Forward Selection

In the forward selection procedure, variables are added or selected into the model based on their **maximal contribution** to the prediction of the criterion variable. Initially, none of the potential predictors are included in the model. In the first stage, the predictor is added to the model that makes the largest contribution to the prediction of the dependent variable. This can be done by selecting that variable having the largest t or F statistic such that it is making the largest contribution to R^2_{adj}. In subsequent stages, the predictor is selected that makes the next largest contribution to the prediction of Y. The analysis continues until each of the selected predictors in the model is a significant predictor of the outcome Y, whereas none of the unselected predictors is a significant predictor. This could be determined by comparing the t or F statistics for each predictor to the critical value, at a preselected level of significance. Some computer programs use as a stopping rule the minimum F-to-enter criterion, where the procedure is stopped when all of the unselected predictors' F values are less than the specified F criterion. For the same set of data and at the same level of significance, the backward elimination and forward selection procedures may not necessarily result in the exact same final model due to the differences in how variables are selected. In SPSS, this is the **forward** method of entering predictors.

18.1.1.7.4 Stepwise Selection

The stepwise selection procedure is a modification of the forward selection procedure with one important difference. *Predictors that have been selected into the model can at a later step be deleted from the model*; thus, the modification conceptually involves a backward elimination mechanism. This situation can occur for a predictor when a significant contribution at an earlier step later becomes a nonsignificant contribution given the set of other predictors in the model. Thus a predictor loses its significance due to new predictors being added to the model.

The stepwise selection procedure is as follows. Initially, none of the potential predictors are included in the model. In the first step, that predictor is added to the model that makes the largest contribution to the explanation of the dependent variable. This can be done by selecting that variable having the largest t or F statistic such that it is making the largest contribution to R^2_{adj}. In subsequent stages, the predictor is selected that makes the next largest contribution to the prediction of Y. Those predictors that have entered at earlier stages are also checked to see if their contribution remains significant. If not, then that predictor is eliminated from the model. The analysis continues until each of the predictors remaining in the model is a significant predictor of Y, while none of the other predictors is a significant predictor. This could be determined by comparing the t or F statistics for each predictor to the critical value, at a specified level of significance. Some computer programs use as stopping rules the minimum F-to-enter and maximum F-to-remove criteria, where the F-to-enter value selected is usually equal to or slightly greater than the F-to-remove value selected (to prevent a predictor from continuously being entered and removed). For the same set of data and at the same level of significance, the backward elimination, forward selection, and stepwise selection procedures may not necessarily result in the exact same final model, due to differences in how variables are selected. In SPSS, this is the **stepwise** method of entering predictors.

18.1.1.7.5 All Possible Subsets Regression

Another sequential regression procedure is known as all possible subsets regression. Let us say, for example, that there are five potential predictors. In this procedure, all possible one-, two-, three-, and four-variable models are analyzed (with five predictors, there is only a single five-predictor model). Thus there will be 5 one-predictor models, 10 two-predictor models, 10 three-predictor models, and 5 four-predictor models. The best k predictor model can be selected as the model that yields the largest R^2_{adj}. For example, the best three-predictor model would be that model of the 10 estimated that yields the largest R^2_{adj}. With today's powerful computers, this procedure is easier and more cost efficient than in the past. However, the researcher is not advised to consider this procedure, or for that matter, any of the other sequential regression procedures, when the number of potential predictors is large. Here the researcher is allowing number crunching to take precedence over thoughtful analysis. Also, the number of models will be equal to 2^m, so that for 10 predictors there are 1,024 possible subsets. Obviously examining that number of models is not a thoughtful analysis.

18.1.1.7.6 Hierarchical Regression

In hierarchical regression, *the researcher specifies a priori a sequence for the individual predictor variables* (not to be confused with hierarchical linear models, which is a regression approach for analyzing nested data collected at multiple levels, such as child, classroom, and school). The analysis proceeds in a forward selection, backward elimination, or stepwise selection mode according to a researcher-specified, *theoretically based sequence*, rather than an unspecified statistically based sequence. This variable selection method is different from those previously discussed in that the *researcher determines the order of entry from a careful consideration of the available theory research*, instead of the software dictating the sequence.

A type of hierarchical regression is known as **setwise regression** (also called **blockwise, chunkwise**, or **forced stepwise regression**). Here the researcher specifies *a priori* a sequence for sets of predictor variables. This procedure is similar to hierarchical regression in that the researcher determines the order of entry of the predictors. The difference is that the setwise method uses sets of predictor variables at each stage rather than one individual predictor variable at a time. The sets of variables are determined by the researcher so that variables within a set share some common theoretical ground (e.g., home background variables in one set and aptitude variables in another set). Variables within a set are selected according to one of the sequential regression procedures. The variables selected for a particular set are then entered in the specified theoretically based sequence. In SPSS, this is conducted by entering predictors in **blocks** and selecting their desired method of entering variables in each block (e.g., simultaneously, forward, backward, stepwise).

18.1.1.7.7 Commentary on Sequential Regression Procedures

Let us make some comments and recommendations about the sequential regression procedures, which are summarized in Box 18.1. First, numerous statisticians have noted problems with stepwise methods (i.e., backward elimination, forward selection, and stepwise selection) (e.g., Derksen & Keselman, 1992; Huberty, 1989; Mickey, Dunn, & Clark, 2004; Miller, 1984, 1990; Wilcox, 2003). These problems include the following: (a) selecting noise rather than important predictors; (b) highly inflated R^2 and R^2_{adj} values; (c) confidence intervals for partial slopes that are too narrow; (d) p values that are not trustworthy; (e) important predictors being barely edged out of the model, making it possible to miss the true model; and (f) potentially heavy capitalization on chance given the number of models analyzed.

Second, theoretically based regression models have become the norm in many disciples (and the stepwise methods of entry are driven by mathematics of the models rather than theory). Thus hierarchical regression either has or will dominate the landscape of the sequential regression procedures. Thus, we strongly encourage you to consider more extended discussions of hierarchical regression (Cohen, Cohen, West, & Aiken, 2003; Pedhazur, 1997; Tabachnick & Fidell, 2013, 2019).

If you are working in an area of inquiry where research evidence is scarce or nonexistent, then you are conducting exploratory research. Thus, you are probably trying to simply identify the key variables. Here hierarchical regression is not appropriate, as a theoretically driven sequence cannot be developed as there is no theory to guide its development. Here we recommend the use of all possible subsets regression (Kleinbaum, Kupper, Muller, & Nizam, 1998). For additional information on the sequential regression procedures, see Cohen and Cohen (1983), Weisberg (1985), Miller (1990), Pedhazur (1997), and Kleinbaum et al. (1998).

18.1.1.8 Nonlinear Relationships

Here we discuss how to deal with nonlinearity. We formally introduce several multiple regression models for when the criterion variable does not have a linear relationship with the predictor variables.

First consider polynomial regression models. In polynomial models, powers of the predictor variables (e.g., squared, cubed) are used. In general, a sample polynomial regression model that includes one quadratic term is as follows:

$$Y = b_1X_1 + b_2X^2 + \ldots + b_mX^m + a + e$$

where the independent variable X is taken from the first power through the mth power, and the i subscript for observations has been deleted to simplify matters. If the model consists only of X taken to the first power, then this is a **simple linear regression model** (or **first-degree polynomial;** this is a straight line and what we have studied to this point). A **second-degree polynomial** includes X taken to the second power (or **quadratic model**; this is a curve with one bend in it rather than a straight line). A **third-degree polynomial** includes X taken to the third power (or **cubic model;** this is a curve with two bends in it).

A polynomial model with multiple predictors can also be utilized. An example of a second-degree polynomial model with two predictors (X_1 and X_2) is illustrated in the following equation:

$$Y_i = b_1X_1 + b_2X_1^2 + \ldots + b_3X_2 + b_4X_2^2 + a + e$$

It is important to note that when whenever a higher-order polynomial is included in a model (e.g., quadratic, cubic, and more), the first-order polynomial must also be included in the model. In other words, it is not appropriate to include a quadratic term X^2 without also including the first-order polynomial X. For more information on polynomial regression models, see Weisberg (1985), Bates and Watts (1988), Seber and Wild (1989), Pedhazur (1997), and Kleinbaum et al. (1998). Alternatively, one might transform the criterion variable and/or the predictor variables to obtain a more linear form, as previously discussed.

18.1.1.9 Interactions

Another type of model involves the use of an interaction term, a term with which you may be familiar from factorial ANOVA. These can be implemented in any type of regression model. We can write a simple two-predictor interaction-type model as follows:

$$Y = b_1X_1 + b_2X_1 + b_3X_1X_2 + a + e$$

where $X_1 X_2$ represents the interaction of predictor variables 1 and 2. An interaction can be defined as occurring when the relationship between Y and X_1 depends on the level of X_2. In other words, X_2 is a **moderator variable**. For example, suppose one were to use years of education and age to predict political attitude. The relationship between education and attitude might be moderated by age. In other words, the relationship between education and attitude may be different for older versus younger individuals. If age were a moderator, we would expect there to be an interaction between age and education in a regression model. Note that if the predictors are very highly correlated, collinearity is likely. Moderation is covered in more detail in the final chapter. For more information on interaction models, see Cohen and Cohen (1983), Berry and Feldman (1985), Kleinbaum et al. (1998), Weinberg and Abramowitz (2002), and Meyers, Gamst, and Guarino (2006).

18.1.1.10 Categorical Predictors

So far we have only considered continuous predictors—independent variables that are interval or ratio in scale. There may be times, however, that you wish to use a categorical predictor—an independent variable that is nominal or ordinal in scale. For example, gender, grade level (e.g., freshman, sophomore, junior, senior), highest education earned (less than high school, high school graduate, etc.) are all categorical variables that may be very interesting and theoretically appropriate to include in either a simple or multiple regression model. Given their scale (i.e., nominal or ordinal), however, we must recode the values prior to analysis so that they are on a scale of zero and one. This is called "dummy coding" as this type of recoding makes the model work. For example, males might be coded as zero and females coded as one. When there are more than two categories to the categorical predictor, multiple dummy coded variables must be created—*specifically one minus the number of levels or categories of the categorical variable.* Thus, in the case of grade level where there are four categories (freshman, sophomore, junior, senior), three of the four categories would be dummy coded and included in the regression model as predictors. The category that is "left out" is the reference category, or that category to which all other levels are compared. The easiest way to understand this is perhaps to examine the data. In the screenshot in Figure 18.1, the first column represents grade level where

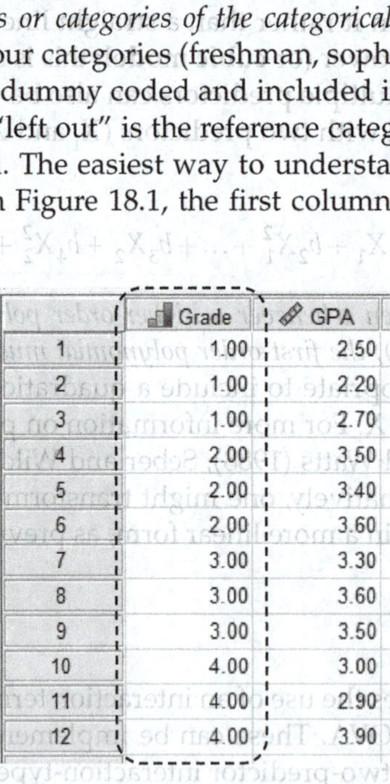

	Grade	GPA
1	1.00	2.50
2	1.00	2.20
3	1.00	2.70
4	2.00	3.50
5	2.00	3.40
6	2.00	3.60
7	3.00	3.30
8	3.00	3.60
9	3.00	3.50
10	4.00	3.00
11	4.00	2.90
12	4.00	3.90

FIGURE 18.1
Grade level (categorical variable).

1 = freshman, 2 = sophomore, 3 = junior, and 4 = senior. Dummy coding the grade levels will result in additional columns being created.

Dummy coding the grade levels will result in additional columns being created. To easily do this in SPSS, go to "Transform," then "Create Dummy Variables" (see Figure 18.2).

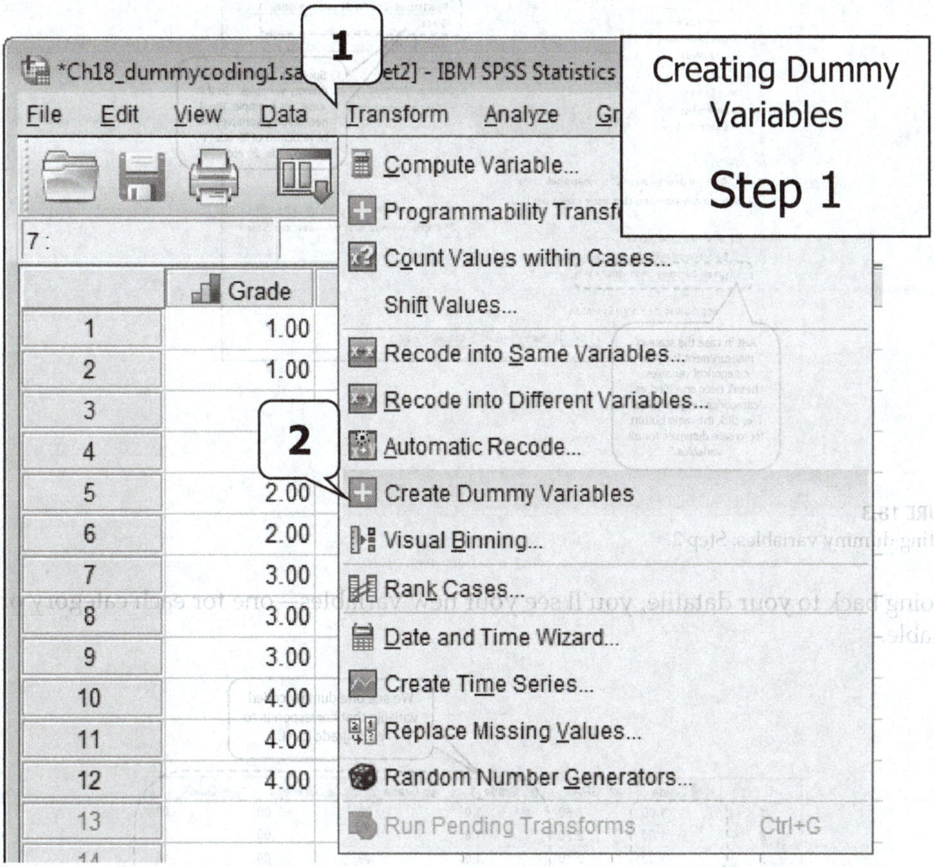

FIGURE 18.2
Creating dummy variables: Step 1.

From the Create Dummy Variables dialog box (see Figure 18.3), click on the categorical variable for which you want to create dummy values and click the arrow to move into the "Create Dummy Variables for:" box. Place a check in the box to "Create main-effect dummies" and assign a "Root Name." The root name is essentially a prefix to the new dummy variables that will be created. If you have correctly specified the measurement scale of your variables as either nominal or ordinal in SPSS, then nothing else is needed. However, if your variables are not correctly specified, or if you have a scale (i.e., interval or ratio) variable that you want to create dummy variables for, then you'll need to select the radio button for "Create dummies for all variables." After your selections are made, click "OK." (Note that you are **highly encouraged** to make sure the measurement scales of your variables in your datafile are correctly defined! This is just good data cleaning practice!)

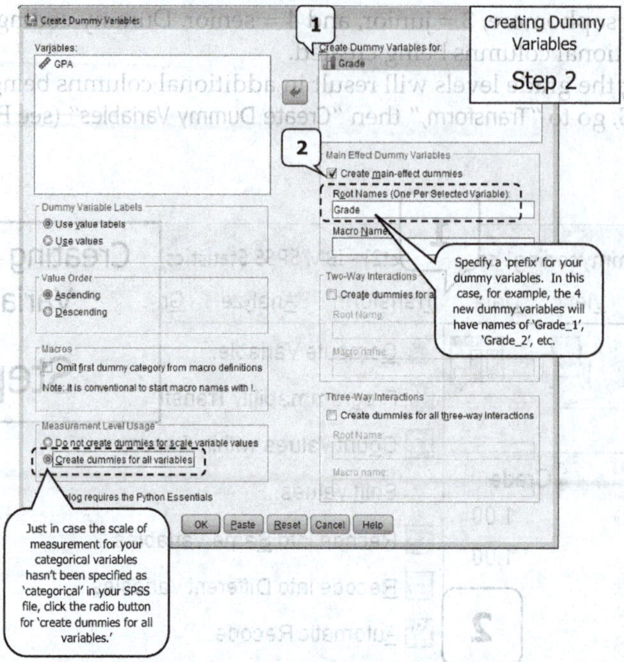

FIGURE 18.3
Creating dummy variables: Step 2.

Going back to your datafile, you'll see your new variables—one for each category of the variable.

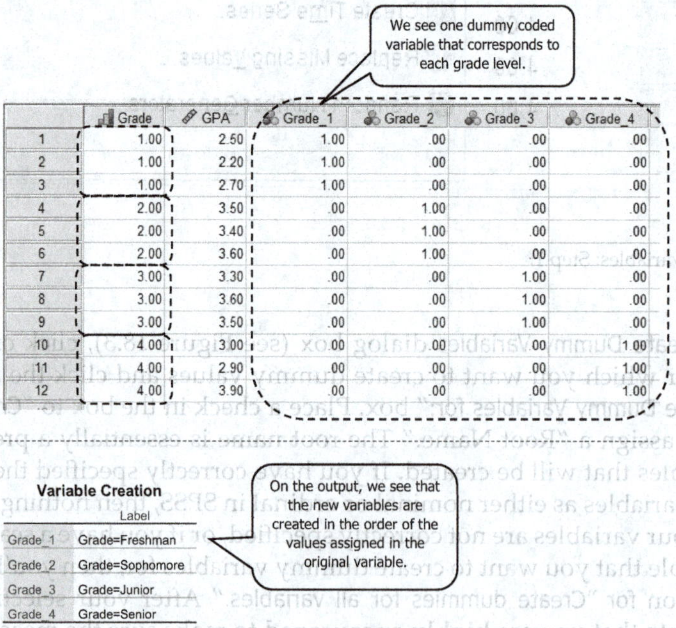

	Grade	GPA	Grade_1	Grade_2	Grade_3	Grade_4
1	1.00	2.50	1.00	.00	.00	.00
2	1.00	2.20	1.00	.00	.00	.00
3	1.00	2.70	1.00	.00	.00	.00
4	2.00	3.50	.00	1.00	.00	.00
5	2.00	3.40	.00	1.00	.00	.00
6	2.00	3.60	.00	1.00	.00	.00
7	3.00	3.30	.00	.00	1.00	.00
8	3.00	3.60	.00	.00	1.00	.00
9	3.00	3.50	.00	.00	1.00	.00
10	4.00	3.00	.00	.00	.00	1.00
11	4.00	2.90	.00	.00	.00	1.00
12	4.00	3.90	.00	.00	.00	1.00

Variable Creation

	Label
Grade_1	Grade=Freshman
Grade_2	Grade=Sophomore
Grade_3	Grade=Junior
Grade_4	Grade=Senior

FIGURE 18.4
Newly created dummy variables.

In terms of generating the analysis and the point-and-click use of SPSS to compute the regression model, nothing changes. The steps are the same regardless of whether the predictors are continuous or categorical. Now let us discuss *why* dummy coding works in this situation. The point biserial correlation is appropriate when one variable is dichotomous and the other variable is interval or ratio. The point biserial correlation is a variant of the Pearson product-moment correlation, and we can use the Pearson as a variant of the point biserial. Thus while we will not have a linear relationship between a continuous outcome and a binary variable, the mathematics that underlie the model will hold.

Consider the example output for predicting grade point average (GPA) based on grade level, where "senior" is the reference category. We see that the intercept (i.e., "constant") is statistically significant as is "freshman." The interpretation of the intercept remains the same regardless of the scale of the predictors. The intercept represents grade point average (the dependent variable) when all the predictors are zero. In this case, this means that grade point average is 3.267 for *seniors* (the reference category). The only statistically significant predictor is "freshman." This is interpreted to say that mean GPA decreases by .800 points for freshmen *as compared to seniors*. The nonstatistically significant regression coefficients for "sophomore" and "junior" indicate that mean GPA is similar for these grade levels as compared to seniors. The interpretation for dummy variable predictors is always in reference to the category that was "left out." In this case, that was "seniors."

Coefficients[a]

Model		Unstandardized Coefficients B	Unstandardized Coefficients Std. Error	Standardized Coefficients Beta	t	Sig.
1	(Constant)	3.267	.183		17.892	.000
	Grade=Freshman	-.800	.258	-.704	-3.098	.015
	Grade=Sophomore	.233	.258	.205	.904	.393
	Grade=Junior	.200	.258	.176	.775	.461

a. Dependent Variable: GPA

FIGURE 18.5
Regression model with dummy variables.

It is important to note that even though "sophomore" and "junior" were not statistically significant, they should be retained in the model as they represent (along with "freshman") a group. Dropping one or more dummy coded indicator variables that represent a group will change the reference category. For example, if "sophomore" and "junior" were dropped from the model, the interpretation would then become the mean GPA for freshmen *as compared to all other grade levels*. Thus, careful thought needs to be put into dropping one or more indicators that are part of a set.

18.1.2 Sample Size

We will start and end with the same recommendation: Estimate sample size using power software or tables and consult current advances related to estimating sample size based on simulation research. With that said, you don't have to look far to find sample size guidelines and recommendations. For example, you have likely read in other textbooks or had a colleague recommend that there be at least 10 cases for every independent variable in the multiple regression model. This is an inappropriate way to estimate sample size. A fair body of research has examined minimum sample size in the context of multiple linear regression, and some consensus that sample size considerations differ depending on the goal of your research—either testing a hypothesis test estimating a parameter (Algina & Olejnik, 2000; Maxwell, 2000)—with larger sample sizes needed for estimation of a prediction equation (e.g., Pedhazur, 1997), as compared to sample sizes needed for testing a hypothesis related to the multiple correlation coefficient (Maxwell, 2000). Using simulation research, recent research suggests that the squared multiple correlation coefficient does have a relationship with overall sample size and the ratio of the sample size to predictors. Simulation research to examine the sample size needed to ensure the sample regression equation performed similarly to the population regression equation, Knofszynski (2008) examined more than 23 million simulated samples and found that the need for a large sample size increases as the squared multiple correlation coefficient diminishes (Knofszynski, 2008). More specifically, as the squared multiple correlation coefficient nears zero, there is a quicker increase in the need for a larger sample size, and this pattern is constant across varying numbers of predictors, however the sample size does not dramatically increase as the number of predictors increases. For example, with a squared multiple correlation coefficient of .10 and three predictors, a sample size of 1800 is needed to achieve "excellent prediction level" (Knofszynski, 2008, p. 438). In comparison, with a square multiple correlation coefficient of .50, again with three predictors, a sample size of 220 is needed to achieve "excellent" (Knofszynski, 2008). When R^2 is .90, a sample size of only 15 or 7 is needed to achieve "excellent" or "good" prediction, respectively (Knofszynski, 2008). As we know, sample size and power are inextricably intertwined, and attempting to separate the two is futile. The best recommendation is to estimate sample size using power software and to consult current advances based on simulation research such as Knofszynski (2008).

18.1.3 Power

With a large number of predictors, power is reduced, and there is an increased likelihood of a Type I error across the total number of significance tests (i.e., one for each predictor and overall). In multiple regression, power is a function of sample size, the number of predictors, the level of significance, and the size of the population effect (i.e., for a given predictor, or overall). With multiple regression, there are several estimates of power that may be of interest to researchers including power for the *group of all predictors* (**R^2 model**), power for *one group of predictors as compared to another group of predictors* (**R^2 change**), and power for a *single predictor within the model* (i.e., **regression coefficient**) (Aberson, 2010). Because adding predictors increases the value of R^2, it is easy to fall into the trap of mindlessly including additional predictors (Murphy, Myors, & Wolach, 2014). However, powering for the group of all predictors (R^2 model) is affected by both the number of predictors and the amount of variance explained. *Increasing the number of predictors can decrease power as they use degrees of freedom for testing the null hypothesis, or may increase power by increasing the model* R^2 (Aberson, 2010). The ideal situation occurs when there is a parsimonious number of predictors that explain a large proportion of the variance (i.e., fewer predictors that explain a lot of variance is more powerful than a lot of predictors that explain the same amount of variance) (Aberson, 2010). As we will learn later in the "Assumptions" section, the more that predictors correlate with each other (i.e., multicollinearity), the less unique variance is explained (i.e., the value of R^2 change is determined by unique variation explained of the predictors; it is desirable to have predictors that explain substantial variance in the outcome over and above the other predictors), and thus power is reduced in the presence of multicollinearity (Aberson, 2010).

To determine how large a sample you need relative to the estimate of power in which you're interested, we suggest that you consult power tables (e.g., Cohen, 1988) or power software (were Liu includes syntax for using **R**, SAS, and SPSS) (Erdfelder, Faul, & Buchner, 1996; Faul, Erdfelder, Buchner, & Lang, 2009; Faul, Erdfelder, Lang, & Buchner, 2007; Liu, 2014). We will later illustrate how to use G*Power for estimating power. If you're interested in learning more about power, we encourage you to consult any of a number of excellent resources (e.g., Aberson, 2010; Cohen, 1988; Liu, 2014; Murphy et al., 2014).

18.1.4 Effect Size

There are multiple effect size indices that can be considered in the context of multiple linear regression. We will discuss effect size in the form of R^2 (i.e., multiple R squared or the coefficient of determination), partial R^2, f^2, and partial f^2.

18.1.4.1 Coefficient of Multiple Determination, R^2

One effect size in multiple linear regression is the *coefficient of multiple determination* or *multiple correlation coefficient*, introduced previously. The coefficient of multiple determination indicates the proportion of total variation in the dependent variable Y that is predicted from the set of predictor variables. There is no objective gold standard as to how large the coefficient of determination needs to be in order to say a meaningful proportion of variation has been predicted. The coefficient is determined not just by the quality of the predictor variables included in the model, but also by the quality of relevant predictor variables not included in the model, as well as by the amount of total variation in the dependent variable Y. According to the subjective standard of Cohen (1988), a small effect size is defined as $R^2 = .02$, a medium effect size as $R^2 = .13$, and a large effect size as $R^2 = .26$.

18.1.4.2 Multiple Partial R^2

The **multiple partial R^2**, symbolized by Cohen (1988) as $R^2_{YB.A}$, is computed as:

$$R^2_{YB.A} = \frac{R^2_{Y.A,B} - R^2_{Y.A}}{1 - R^2_{Y.A}} = \frac{R^2_{Y.(B.A)}}{1 - R^2_{Y.A}}$$

$R^2_{YB.A}$ is the proportion of that part of the total variation in the dependent variable, Y, uniquely explained by predictor, B, removing the influence of the set of predictors. A. In other words, A is partialed from both Y and B; A is held constant or statistically controlled. $R^2_{Y.A,B}$ represents the proportion of variance in Y accounted for by predictors A and B, and $R^2_{Y.A}$ represents the proportion of variance in Y accounted for by predictor A (Cohen, 1988). The numerator, therefore, represents the proportion of variation in Y that is uniquely accounted for by predictor, B, and can be conceived as a squared multiple semipartial (i.e., part) correlation. In the case of only two predictors, the multiple partial R^2 equates to the squared term of our earlier discussion of partial correlations. According to the subjective standard of Cohen (1988), a small effect size is defined as $R^2 = .02$, a medium effect size as $R^2 = .13$, and a large effect size as $R^2 = .26$.

18.1.4.3 f^2

The squared multiple correlation coefficient can also be used to compute f^2, which is computed as:

$$f^2 = \frac{R^2}{(1 - R^2)}$$

Interpreting f^2, it is the ratio of (1) the proportion of variation in the dependent variable uniquely explained by the independent variables to (2) the proportion of variation in the dependent variable unexplained by *any* variable in the model. The numerator, therefore, reflects the unique proportion of variance in Y for which the predictors account. The denominator reflects the proportion of variance in Y unaccounted for by the model. According to Cohen's (1988) conventions, a small effect size is defined as $f^2 = .02$, a medium effect size as $f^2 = .15$, and a large effect size as $f^2 = .35$.

18.1.4.4 Partial f^2

Similar to the computation of f^2, we can use the squared multiple partial correlations to compute $f^2_{partial}$ (Cohen, 1988). It is computed as:

$$f^2_{partial} = \frac{R^2_{YB.A}}{(1 - R^2_{YB.A})}.$$

Interpreting $f^2_{partial}$, $R^2_{YB.A}$ is the proportion of the total variation in the dependent variable, Y, uniquely explained by predictor(s), B, removing the influence of the set of predictors, A (i.e., the contribution of B over and above what is accounted for by A). In other words, A is partialed from both Y and B; A is held constant or statistically controlled. Thus, we can interpret $f^2_{partial}$ as the proportion of Y accounted for by predictor(s) B when the set of predictors, A, are held constant. According to the subjective standard of Cohen (1988), a small effect size is defined as $f^2_{partial} = .02$, a medium effect size as $f^2_{partial} = .13$, and a large effect size as $f^2_{partial} = .26$.

18.1.4.5 Additional Effect Size Considerations

For partial effects, standardized slopes or beta weights have been commonly reported as measures of effect size as they represent the number of standard deviation units the outcome variable will change for a one-unit standard deviation increase in the respective predictor variable. However, we discourage this practice. In simple linear regression, we saw that the standardized slope equals the Pearson correlation coefficient. With multiple linear regression, this is not the case as there are multiple independent variables. In multiple linear regression, the beta weight is influenced by the extent of overlap between the respective independent variable and the remaining independent variables (i.e., collinearity). The larger the overlap, the larger the beta weight. Thus, using the beta weight as a measure of effect size can be problematic, particularly if there is quite a bit of overlap between the independent variables.

TABLE 18.1

Effect Sizes and Interpretations

Effect Size	Interpretation
R^2	• Coefficient of multiple determination or squared multiple correlation coefficient • Proportion of total variation in the dependent variable Y that is predicted from the set of predictor variables • Cohen's conventions: ∘ $R^2 = .02$, small ∘ $R^2 = .13$, medium ∘ $R^2 = .26$, large
$f^2 = \frac{R^2}{1-R^2}$	• Ratio of: (1) the proportion of variation in the dependent variable uniquely explained by the independent variables to (2) the proportion of variation in the dependent variable unexplained by *any* variable in the model • Cohen's standards: ∘ $f^2 = .02$, small ∘ $f^2 = .15$, medium ∘ $f^2 = .35$, large
$R^2_{YB.A} = \frac{R^2_{Y.A,B} - R^2_{Y.A}}{1-R^2_{Y.A}}$	• Multiple partial R^2 • Proportion of variation in Y that is accounted for by predictor(s), B, when holding the set of independent variables A constant; i.e., A is partialed out from both Y and B • Cohen's conventions: ∘ $R^2 = .02$, small ∘ $R^2 = .13$, medium ∘ $R^2 = .26$, large
$f^2_{partial} = \frac{R^2_{YB.A}}{1-R^2_{YB.A}}$	• Multiple partial f^2 • Proportion of variation in Y that is accounted for by predictor(s), B, when holding the set of independent variables A constant; i.e., A is partialed out from both Y and B • Cohen's conventions: ∘ $R^2 = .02$, small ∘ $R^2 = .13$, medium ∘ $R^2 = .26$, large

Table 18.1 provides a summary of multiple linear regression effect size indices and guidelines for interpretation. For additional information on effect size measures in regression, we suggest you consider Steiger and Fouladi (1992), Mendoza and Stafford (2001) (2001), and Smithson (2001; which also includes some discussion of power).

Confidence intervals (CI) can be computed for R^2, and these CI reflect precision of the estimated R^2. *Larger CI suggest lower precision, and smaller CI reflect higher precision.* A R^2 CI that includes the null value (i.e., $R^2 = 0$) may provide evidence to suggest a nonstatistically significant relationship between the set of independent variables and the outcome. We can also use the online effect size calculator by Uanhoro (2017) to compute confidence intervals. There are four values that must be input: R^2, the confidence interval (i.e., complement of alpha), and the numerator (i.e., effect) and denominator (i.e., error) degrees of freedom. Inputting these values, we are provided the confidence interval of .5927733, .9690771.

18.1.5 Assumptions

For the most part, the assumptions of multiple linear regression analysis are the same as that with simple linear regression. The assumptions are concerned with: (a) independence,

(b) homoscedasticity, (c) normality, (d) linearity, (e) fixed X, and (f) noncollinearity. When the first four assumptions are met, the coefficients produced by the ordinary least squares regression will be the best linear unbiased estimators (BLUE) (according to the Gauss-Markov theorem, ordinary least squares estimators will be BLUE in that they are unbiased, linear, and have the smallest variation of all estimators that are linear and unbiased). In other words, the smallest mean square error for the estimators will be produced (Meuleman, Loosveldt, & Emonds, 2013). This section also mentions those techniques appropriate for evaluating each assumption. Readers who are interested in expanded coverage of diagnostics related to assumptions are encouraged to review the chapter by Meuleman et al. (2013).

18.1.5.1 Independence

The first assumption is concerned with **independence** of the observations. The simplest procedure for assessing independence is to examine residual plots of e versus the predicted values of the dependent variable Y' and of e versus each independent variable X_k (alternatively, one can look at plots of observed values of the dependent variable Y versus predicted values of the dependent variable Y' and of observed values of the dependent variable Y versus each independent variable X_k). If the independence assumption is satisfied, the residuals should fall into a random display of points. If the assumption is violated, the residuals will fall into some sort of pattern. Lack of independence affects the estimated standard errors of the model. For serious violations, one could consider generalized or weighted least squares as the method of estimation (e.g., Myers, 1986; Weisberg, 1985), or some type of transformation. The residual plots shown in Figure 18.6 do not suggest any independence problems for the graduate grade point average (GGPA) example, where Figure 18.6a represents the residual e versus the predicted value of the dependent variable Y', Figure 18.6b represents e versus GRETOT, and Figure 18.6c represents e versus undergraduate grade point average (UGPA).

18.1.5.2 Homoscedasticity

The second assumption is **homoscedasticity**, where the conditional distributions have the same constant variance for all values of X. In the residual plots, the consistency of the variance of the conditional distributions may be examined.

The **nonconstant error variance test** can also be used to examine this assumption. The null hypothesis for this test is that there is constant error variance; the alternative hypothesis is that the error variance changes at levels of the fitted values (i.e., with the linear combination of the independent variables). A nonstatistically significant nonconstant error variance test suggests the assumption of homoscedasticity has been met.

If the homoscedasticity assumption is violated, estimates of the standard errors are larger, and the conditional distributions may also be nonnormal. Solutions to violation of this assumption include variance stabilizing transformations (such as the square root or log of Y), generalized or weighted least squares (Myers, 1986; Weisberg, 1985), or robust regression (Kleinbaum et al., 1998; Myers, 1986; Wilcox, 1996, 2003; Wu, 1985). Due to the small sample size, homoscedasticity cannot really be assessed for the example data.

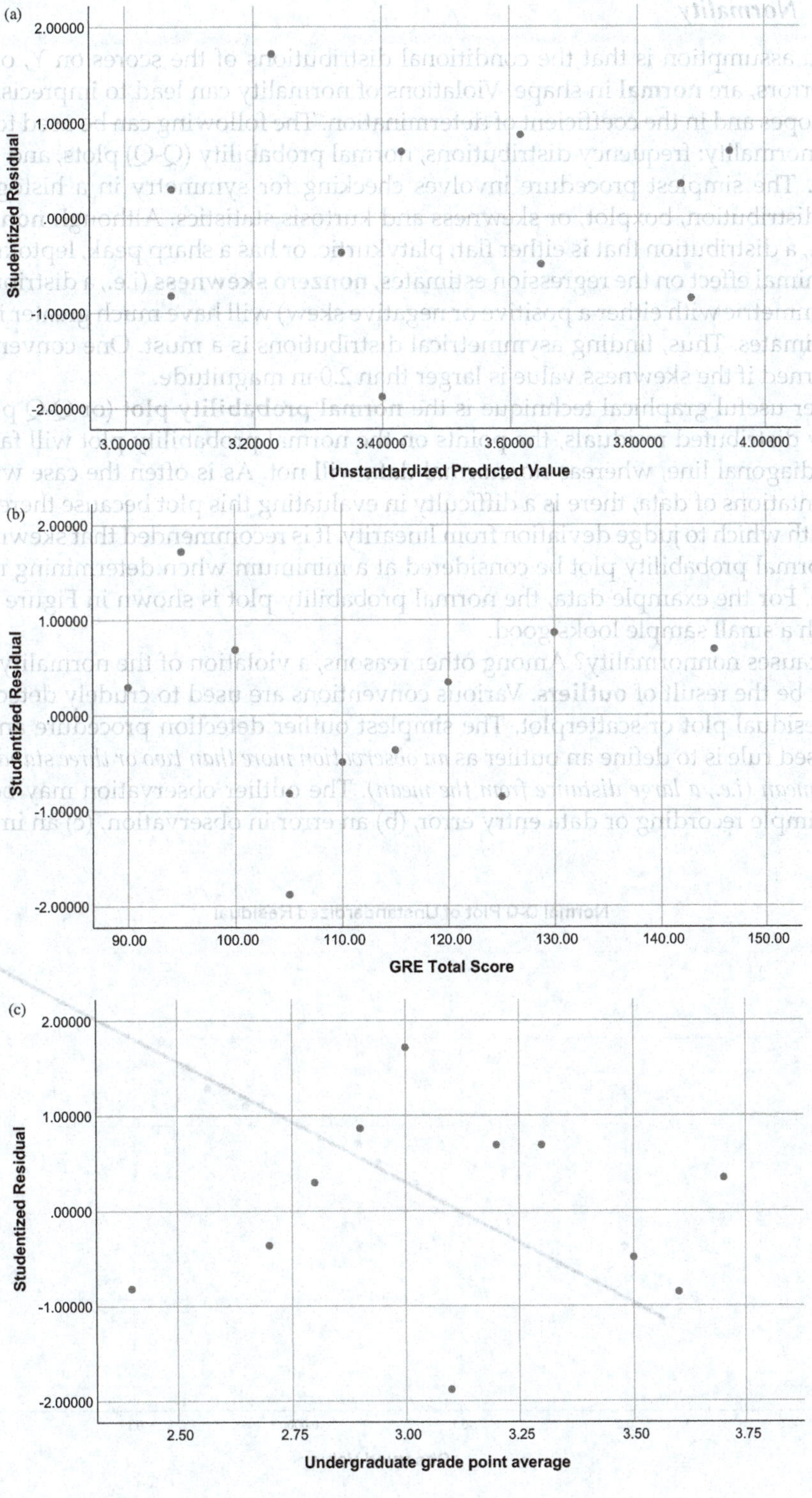

FIGURE 18.6
Residual plots for GRE-GPA example: (a), (b), (c).

18.1.5.3 Normality

The third assumption is that the conditional distributions of the scores on *Y*, or the prediction errors, are **normal** in shape. Violations of normality can lead to imprecision in the partial slopes and in the coefficient of determination. The following can be used to examine data for normality: frequency distributions, normal probability (Q-Q) plots, and skewness statistics. The simplest procedure involves checking for symmetry in a histogram, frequency distribution, boxplot, or skewness and kurtosis statistics. Although **nonzero kurtosis** (i.e., a distribution that is either flat, platykurtic, or has a sharp peak, leptokurtic) will have minimal effect on the regression estimates, **nonzero skewness** (i.e., a distribution that is not symmetric with either a positive or negative skew) will have much greater impact on these estimates. Thus, finding asymmetrical distributions is a must. One convention is to be concerned if the skewness value is larger than 2.0 in magnitude.

Another useful graphical technique is the **normal probability plot** (or Q-Q plot). With normally distributed residuals, the points on the normal probability plot will fall along a straight diagonal line, whereas nonnormal data will not. As is often the case with visual reprensentations of data, there is a difficulty in evaluating this plot because there is no criterion with which to judge deviation from linearity. It is recommended that skewness and/or the normal probability plot be considered at a minimum when determining normality evidence. For the example data, the normal probability plot is shown in Figure 18.7, and even with a small sample looks good.

What causes nonnormality? Among other reasons, a violation of the normality assumption may be the result of **outliers**. Various conventions are used to crudely detect outliers from a residual plot or scatterplot. The simplest outlier detection procedure and a commonly used rule is to define an outlier as *an observation more than two or three standard errors from the mean (i.e., a large distance from the mean)*. The outlier observation may be a result of (a) a simple recording or data entry error, (b) an error in observation, (c) an improperly

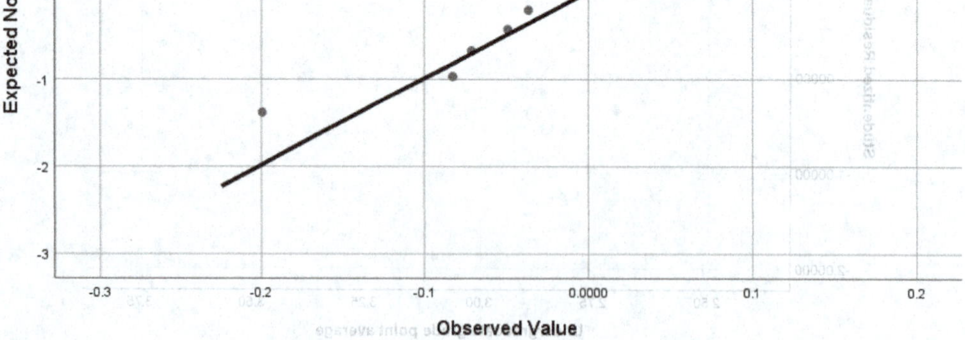

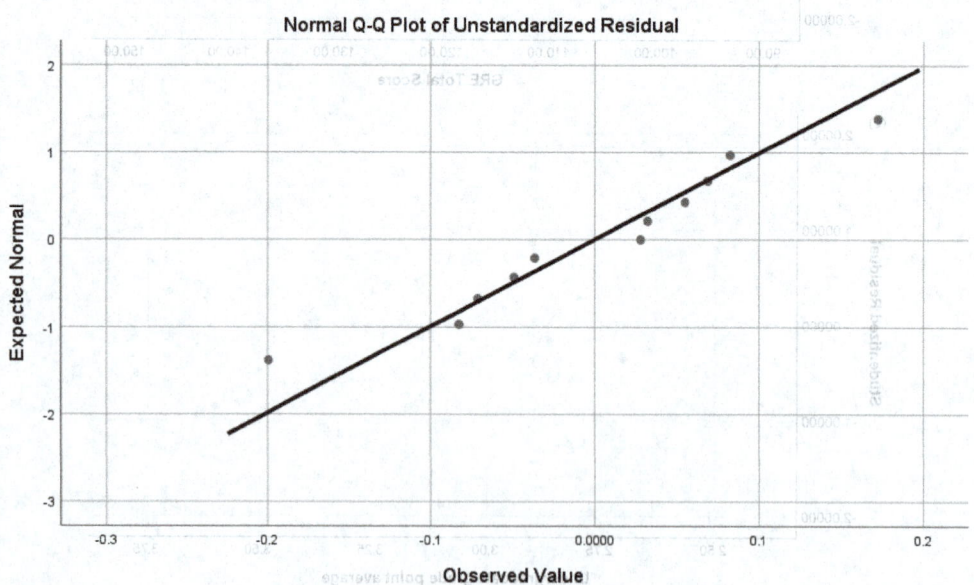

FIGURE 18.7
Q-Q plot.

functioning instrument, (d) inappropriate use of administration instructions, or (e) a true outlier. If the outlier results from an error, try to correct the error, and then redo the regression analysis. If the error cannot be corrected, then deleting the observation is possible. If the outlier represents an accurate observation, however, then this observation may contain important theoretical information, and one would be more hesitant to delete it (or perhaps seek out similar observations). Thus, implementing a different approach for dealing with the outlier is needed. A simple procedure to use for single case outliers (i.e., just one outlier) is to perform two regression analyses, one with the outlier being included and one without. Comparing the results of these analyses will provide some indication of the effects of the outlier. Other methods include robust regression (Kleinbaum et al., 1998; Wilcox, 1996, 2003), and nonparametric regression (Miller, 1997; Rousseeuw & Leroy, 1987; Wu, 1985).

What happens if you find other types of nonnormality (i.e., beyond outliers)? Transformations can be used to normalize the data. The most commonly used transformations to correct for nonnormality in regression analysis are to transform the dependent variable using the log (to correct for positive skew) or the square root (to correct for positive or negative skew). However, again there is the challenge of interpreting transformed variables measured along a scale other than that of the original variables.

18.1.5.4 Linearity

The fourth assumption is **linearity**, that there is a linear relationship between the observed scores on the dependent variable Y and the values of the independent variables, X_k's. If satisfied, then the sample partial slopes and intercept are unbiased estimators of the population partial slopes and intercept, respectively. The linearity assumption is important because regardless of the value of X_k, we always expect Y to increase by b_k units for a one-unit increase in X_k, controlling for the other X_k's. If a nonlinear relationship exists, this means that the expected increase in Y depends on the value of X_k; that is, the expected increase is not a constant value. Strictly speaking, *linearity in a model refers to there being linearity in the parameters of the model* (i.e., α and the β_k's).

Violation of the linearity assumption can be detected through residual plots. The residuals should be located within a band of $\pm 2\, s_{res}$ (or standard errors), indicating no systematic pattern of points. Residual plots for the GGPA example were shown previously in Figure 18.1. Even with a very small sample, we see a fairly random pattern of residuals, and therefore feel fairly confident that the linearity assumption has been satisfied. Note also that there are other types of residual plots developed especially for multiple regression analysis, such as the added variable and partial residual plots (Larsen & McCleary, 1972; Mansfield & Conerly, 1987; Weisberg, 1985). Procedures to deal with nonlinearity include transformations (of one or more of the X_k's and/or of Y) and other regression models (discussed later in this chapter).

18.1.5.5 Fixed X

The fifth assumption is that the values of X_k are **fixed**, where the independent variables X_k are fixed variables rather than random variables. This results in the regression model being valid only for those particular values of X_k that were actually observed and used in the analysis. Thus, the same values of X_k would be used in replications or repeated samples.

Strictly speaking, the regression model and its parameter estimates are valid only for those values of X_k actually sampled. The use of a prediction model developed to predict the dependent variable Y, based on one sample of individuals, may be suspect for another sample of individuals. Depending on the circumstances, the new sample of individuals may actually call for a different set of parameter estimates. Generally we may not want to make predictions about individuals having combinations of X_k scores outside of the range of values used in developing the prediction model; this is defined as *extrapolating* beyond the sample predictor data. On the other hand, we may not be quite as concerned in making predictions about individuals having combinations of X_k scores within the range of values used in developing the prediction model; this is defined as *interpolating* within the range of the sample predictor data.

It has been shown that when other assumptions are met, regression analysis performs just as well when X is a random variable (e.g., Glass & Hopkins, 1996; Myers & Well, 1995; Pedhazur, 1997; Wonnacott & Wonnacott, 1981). There is no such assumption about Y.

18.1.5.6 Noncollinearity

Considering simple and multiple linear regression, the final assumption is unique to multiple linear regression analysis (as compared to simple linear regression), but will be quite common throughout multivariate procedures that we cover. A violation of this assumption is known as collinearity, where there is a very strong linear relationship between two or more of the predictors.

Although multicollinearity does not impact overall model fit or model predictions (Kutner, Nachtscheim, & Neter, 2005), the presence of severe collinearity is problematic in several respects. First, it will lead to instability of the regression coefficients across samples, where the estimates will bounce around quite a bit in terms of magnitude and even occasionally result in changes in sign (perhaps opposite of expectation). This occurs because the standard errors of the regression coefficients become larger, thus making it more difficult to achieve statistical significance. Another result that may occur involves an overall regression that is significant, but none of the individual predictors are significant. Collinearity will also restrict the utility and generalizability of the estimated regression model. While the potential impact of multicollinearity can be severe, it is not uncommon for authors to fail to report diagnostics for identifying multicollinearity (e.g., nearly 99.9% of clinical and epidemiological studies from 2004 to 2013 did *not* explicitly address examination of this assumption) (Vatcheva, Lee, McCormick, & Rahbar, 2016). *Don't be one of those authors!*

Recall from earlier in the chapter the notion of partial regression coefficients, where the other predictors were held constant. In the presence of severe collinearity, the other predictors cannot really be held constant because they are so highly intercorrelated. Collinearity may be indicated when there are large changes in estimated coefficients due to (a) a variable being added or deleted, and/or (b) an observation being added or deleted (Chatterjee & Price, 1977). **Singularity** is a special case of multicollinearity; it is perfect multicollinearity and occurs when two or more items/variables perfectly predict and are therefore perfectly redundant. This can occur, for example, when a composite variable as well as its component variables are used as predictors in the same model (e.g., including GRETOT, GRE-Quantitative, and GRE-Verbal as predictors).

How do we detect violations of this assumption? The simplest procedure is to conduct a series of special regression analyses, one for each X, where that predictor is predicted by all of the remaining X's (i.e., the criterion variable is not involved). If any of the resultant R_k^2 values are close to one (greater than .9 is a good guideline), then there may be a collinearity problem. However, the large R^2 value may also be due to small sample size; thus more data would be useful in this type of situation. For the example data, R_{12}^2 = .091 and therefore collinearity is not a concern.

Also, if the number of predictors is greater than or equal to n, then perfect collinearity is a possibility. Another statistical method for detecting collinearity is to compute a variance inflation factor (VIF) for each predictor, which is equal to $1 / (1 - R_k^2)$. The VIF is defined as the inflation that occurs for each regression coefficient above the ideal situation of uncorrelated predictors. Many suggest that the largest VIF should be less than 10 in order to satisfy this assumption (Myers, 1990; Stevens, 2009; Wetherill, 1986).

There are several possible methods for dealing with a collinearity problem. First, one can remove one or more of the correlated predictors. Second, ridge regression techniques, and ridge-related techniques (e.g., partial ridge regression, which have been shown to be superior to other existing methods), can be used (Chandrasekhar, Bagyalakshmi, Srinivasan, & Gallo, 2016; Hoerl & Kennard, 1970a, 1970b; Marquardt & Snee, 1975; Singh, 2010; Wetherill, 1986). Third, principal component scores resulting from principal component analysis can be utilized rather than raw scores on each variable (Kleinbaum et al., 1998; Myers, 1986; Weisberg, 1985; Wetherill, 1986). Fourth, transformations of the variables can be used to remove or reduce the extent of the problem. The final solution, and probably our last choice, is to use simple linear regression, as collinearity cannot exist with a single predictor.

18.1.5.7 Summary of Assumptions

For the GGPA example, although sample size is quite small in terms of looking at conditional distributions, it would appear that all of our assumptions have been satisfied. All of the residuals are within two standard errors of zero, and there does not seem to be any systematic pattern in the residuals. The distribution of the residuals is nearly symmetric and the normal probability plot looks good. A summary of the assumptions and the effects of their violation for multiple linear regression analysis is presented in Table 18.2.

TABLE 18.2

Assumptions and Violation of Assumptions: Multiple Linear Regression Analysis

Assumption	Effect of Assumption Violation
Independence	• Influences standard errors of the model
Homogeneity	• Bias in s_{res}^2 • May inflate standard errors and thus increase likelihood of a Type II error • May result in nonnormal conditional distributions
Normality	• Less precise slopes, intercept, and R^2
Linearity	• Bias in slope and intercept • Expected change in Y is not a constant and depends on value of X
Fixed X values	• Extrapolating beyond the range of X combinations: prediction errors larger, may also bias slopes and intercept • Interpolating within the range of X combinations: smaller effects than above; if other assumptions met, negligible effect
Noncollinearity of X's	• Regression coefficients can be quite unstable across samples (as standard errors are larger) • R^2 may be significant, yet none of the predictors are significant • Restricted generalizability of the model

18.2 Mathematical Introduction Snapshot

Throughout the chapter we have woven some of the mathematics of multiple linear regression. Now, let's consider the analysis illustrated using the data with which Addie, our graduate researcher, is working. We use the GRE Quantitative + Verbal Total (GRETOT) and undergraduate grade point average (UGPA) to predict graduate grade point average (GGPA). GRETOT has a possible range of 40 to 160 points, sand GPA is defined as having a possible range of 0.00 to 4.00 points. Given the sample of 11 statistics students as shown in Table 18.3, let us work through a multiple linear regression analysis.

As sample statistics, we compute for GRETOT (X_1 or subscript 1) that the mean is $\bar{X}_1$ = 112.7273 and the variance is s_1^2= 266.8182, for UGPA (X_2 or subscript 2) that the mean is $\bar{X}_2$ = 3.1091 and the variance is $s_2^2 = 0.1609$, and for GGPA (Y), a mean of $\bar{Y} = 3.5000$ and variance of $s_Y^2 = 0.1100$. In addition, we compute the bivariate correlation between the dependent variable (graduate GPA) and GRE total, $r_{Y1} = .7845$; between the dependent variable (graduate GPA) and undergraduate GPA, $r_{Y2} = .7516$; and between GRE total and undergraduate GPA, $r_{12} = .3011$. The sample partial slopes (b_1 and b_2) and intercept (a) are determined as follows:

$$b_1 = \frac{(r_{Y1} - r_{Y2}r_{12})s_Y}{(1-r_{12}^2)s_1} = \frac{[.7845-(.7516)(.3011)](.3317)}{(1-.3011^2)(16.3346)} = .0125$$

$$b_2 = \frac{(r_{Y2} - r_{Y1}r_{12})s_Y}{(1-r_{12}^2)s_2} = \frac{[.7516-(.7845)(.3011)](.3317)}{(1-.3011^2)(.4011)} = .4687$$

$$a = \bar{Y} - b_1\bar{X}_1 - b_2\bar{X}_2$$

$$a = 3.500 - (.0125)(112.7273) - (.4687)(3.1091) = .6337$$

Let us interpret the partial slope and intercept values. A partial slope of .0125 for GRETOT would mean that if your score on the GRETOT was increased by 1 point, then your graduate grade point average would be increased by .0125 points, controlling for undergraduate

TABLE 18.3

GRE-GPA example data

Student	GRE-Total (X_1)	Undergraduate GPA (X_2)	Graduate GPA (Y)
1	145	3.2	4.0
2	120	3.7	3.9
3	125	3.6	3.8
4	130	2.9	3.7
5	110	3.5	3.6
6	100	3.3	3.5
7	95	3.0	3.4
8	115	2.7	3.3
9	105	3.1	3.2
10	90	2.8	3.1
11	105	2.4	3.0

grade point average. Likewise, a partial slope of .4687 for UGPA would mean that if your undergraduate grade point average was increased by 1 point, then your graduate grade point average would be increased by .4687 points, controlling for GRETOT. An intercept of .6337 would mean that if your scores on the GRETOT and UGPA were both 0, then your graduate grade point average would be .6337. However, it is impossible to obtain a GRETOT score of 0 because 40 points is the minimum score possible. In a similar way, an undergraduate student could not obtain a UGPA of 0 and be admitted to graduate school. This is not to say that the regression equation is incorrect, but just to point out how the interpretation of "GRETOT and UGPA were both 0" is a bit meaningless in context.

To put all of this together then, the sample multiple linear regression model is

$$Y_1 = b_1 X_{1i} + b_2 X_{2i} + a + e_i$$

$$Y_1 = .0125(X_{1i}) + .4687(X_{2i}) + .6337 + e_i$$

In other words, if your score on the GRETOT was 130 and your UGPA was 3.5, then your predicted score on the GGPA would be computed as:

$$Y_i' = .0125(130) + .4687(3.50) + .6337 = 3.8992$$

Based on the prediction equation, we predict your GGPA to be around 3.9; however, predictions are usually somewhat less than perfect, even with two predictors.

For the GGPA example, we compute the overall F test statistic as the following:

$$F = \frac{R^2 / m}{(1 - R^2)(n - m - 1)}$$

$$F = \frac{.9089 / 2}{(1 - .9089)(11 - 2 - 1)} = 39.9078$$

or as

$$F = \frac{SS_{reg} / df_{reg}}{SS_{res} / df_{res}} = \frac{MS_{reg}}{MS_{res}} = \frac{.9998 / 2}{.1002 / 8} = 39.9122$$

The critical value, at the .05 level of significance, is ${}_{.05}F_{2,8} = 4.46$. The test statistic exceeds the critical value, so we reject H_0 and conclude that all of the partial slopes are not equal to zero at the .05 level of significance (the two F test statistics differ slightly due to rounding error).

For our graduate grade point average example, the standardized partial slopes are equal to

$$b_1^* = b_1\left(\frac{s_1}{s_Y}\right) = (.0125)\left(\frac{16.3346}{.3317}\right) = .6156$$

and

$$b_2^* = b_2\left(\frac{s_2}{s_Y}\right) = (.4687)\left(\frac{.4011}{.3317}\right) = .5668$$

The prediction model is then as follows:

$$z(Y_i') = .6156 z_{1i} + .5668 z_{2i}$$

The standardized partial slope of .6156 for GRETOT would be interpreted as the expected increase in GGPA in z score units for a one z score unit increase in the GRETOT, controlling for UGPA. A similar statement may be made for the standardized partial slope of UGPA. The b_k^2 can also be interpreted as the expected standard deviation change in the dependent variable Y associated with a one standard deviation change in the independent variable X_k when the other X_k's are held constant.

With the example of predicting GGPA from GRETOT and UGPA, let us examine the partitioning of the total sum of squares SS_{total} as follows:

$$SS_{total} = (n-1)(s_Y^2) = (10)(.1100) = 1.100$$

Next, we can determine the multiple correlation coefficient R^2 as

$$R^2_{Y.1,\ldots,m} = b_1^*(r_{Y1}) + b_2^*(r_{Y2}) + \ldots + b_m^*(r_{Ym})$$

$$R^2_{Y.1,\ldots,m} = (.6156)(.7845) + (.5668)(.7516) = .9089$$

We can also partition SS_{total} into SS_{reg} and SS_{res}, where

$$SS_{reg} = (R^2)(SS_{total}) = (.9089)(1.1000) = .9998$$

$$SS_{res} = (1 - R^2)(SS_{total}) = (1 - .9089)(1.1000) = .1002$$

Finally, let us summarize these results for the example data. We found that the coefficient of multiple determination (R^2) was equal to .9089. Thus, the GRE total score and the undergraduate grade point average predicts around 91% of the variation in the graduate grade point average. This would be quite satisfactory for the college admissions officer in that there is little variation left to be explained, although this result is quite unlikely in actual research in education and the behavioral sciences. Obviously there is a large effect size here.

Let us compute the second test statistic for the GGPA example. We specify the null hypothesis to be $\beta_k = 0$ (i.e., the slope is zero) and conduct two-tailed tests. First the variance error of estimate is

$$s_{res}^2 = \frac{SS_{res}}{df_{res}} = \frac{.1022}{8} = .0125$$

The standard error of estimate, s_{res}, is .1118. Next, the standard errors of the b_k are found to be

$$s(b_1) = \frac{s_{res}}{\sqrt{(n-1)(s_1^2)(1-r_{12}^2)}} = \frac{.1118}{\sqrt{(10)(266.8182)(1-.3011^2)}} = .0023$$

$$s(b_2) = \frac{s_{res}}{\sqrt{(n-1)(s_2^2)(1-r_{12}^2)}} = \frac{.1118}{\sqrt{(10)(.1609)(1-.3011^2)}} = .0924$$

Finally, we find the t test statistics to be computed as follows:

$$t_1 = \frac{b_1}{s(b_1)} = \frac{.0125}{.0023} = 5.4348$$

$$t_2 = \frac{b_2}{s(b_2)} = \frac{.4687}{.0924} = 5.0725$$

To evaluate the null hypotheses, we compare these test statistics to the critical values of $\pm_{.025}t_8 = \pm 2.306$. Both test statistics exceed the critical value; consequently H_0 is rejected in favor of H_1 for both predictors. We conclude that both partial slopes are indeed statistically significantly different from zero at the .05 level of significance.

Finally, let us compute the confidence intervals for the b_k's as follows:

$$CI(b_1) = b_1 \pm_{(\alpha/2)} t_{(n-m-1)} \left[s(b_1)\right]$$

$$CI(b_1) = b_1 \pm_{.025} t_8 \left[s(b_1)\right] = .0125 \pm (2.306)(.0023) = (.0072, .0178)$$

$$CI(b_2) = b_2 \pm_{(\alpha/2)} t_{(n-m-1)} \left[s(b_2)\right]$$

$$CI(b_2) = b_2 \pm_{.025} t_8 \left[s(b_2)\right] = .4687 \pm (2.306)(.0924) = (.2556, .6818)$$

The intervals do not contain zero, the value specified in H_0; thus we again conclude that both b_k's are significantly different from zero at the .05 level of significance.

18.3 Computing Multiple Linear Regression Using SPSS

Next we consider SPSS for the multiple linear regression model using the Ch18.GGPA data. Before we conduct the analysis, let us review the data. With one dependent variable and two independent variables, the dataset must consist of three variables or columns, one for each independent variable and one for the dependent variable. Each row still represents one individual, indicating the value of the independent variables for that particular case and their score on the dependent variable. As seen in the screenshot in Figure 18.8, for a multiple linear regression analysis therefore, the SPSS data are in the form of three columns that represent the two independent variables (GRE total score and undergraduate GPA) and one dependent variable (graduate grade point average).

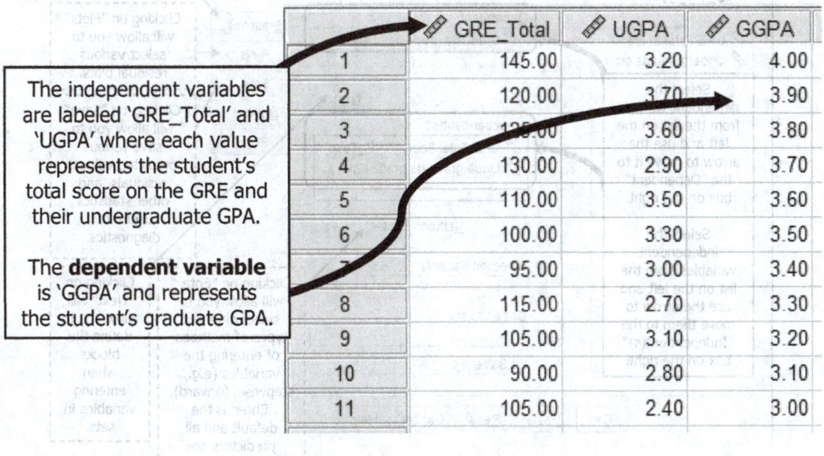
The independent variables are labeled 'GRE_Total' and 'UGPA' where each value represents the student's total score on the GRE and their undergraduate GPA.
The **dependent variable** is 'GGPA' and represents the student's graduate GPA.

	GRE_Total	UGPA	GGPA
1	145.00	3.20	4.00
2	120.00	3.70	3.90
3	[illegible]	3.60	3.80
4	130.00	2.90	3.70
5	110.00	3.50	3.60
6	100.00	3.30	3.50
7	95.00	3.00	3.40
8	115.00	2.70	3.30
9	105.00	3.10	3.20
10	90.00	2.80	3.10
11	105.00	2.40	3.00

FIGURE 18.8
SPSS data.

Step 1. To conduct a simple linear regression, go to "Analyze" in the top pulldown menu, then select "Regression," and then select "Linear." Following the screenshot for Step 1 (Figure 18.9) produces the "Linear Regression" dialog box.

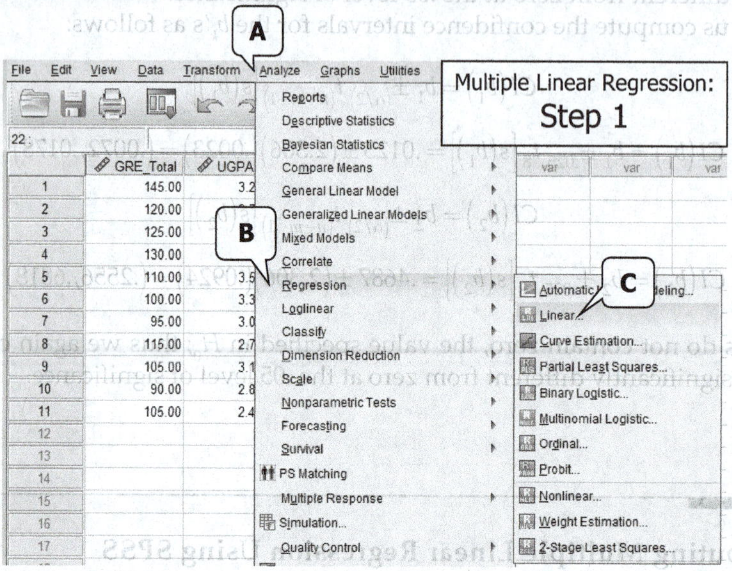

FIGURE 18.9
Multiple linear regression: Step 1.

Step 2. Click the dependent variable (e.g., "GGPA") and move it into the "Dependent" box by clicking the arrow button. Click the independent variables and move them into the "Independent(s)" box by clicking the arrow button (see the screenshot in Figure 18.10).

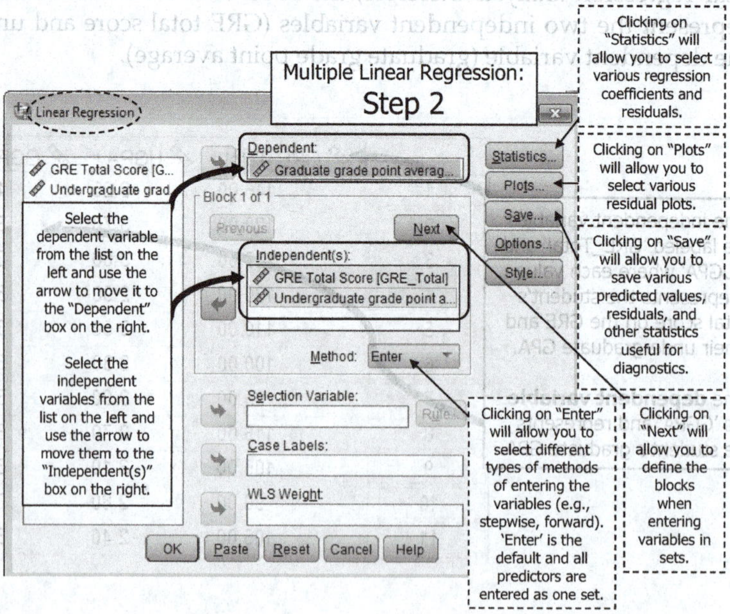

FIGURE 18.10
Multiple linear regression: Step 2.

Step 3. From the Linear Regression dialog box (see Figure 18.10), clicking on "Statistics" will provide the option to select various regression coefficients and residuals. From the Statistics dialog box (see the screenshot in Figure 18.11), place checkmarks in the box next to the following: (1) "Estimates"; (2) "Confidence intervals"; (3) "Model fit"; (4) "R squared change"; (5) "Descriptives"; (6) "Part and partial correlations"; (7) "Collinearity diagnostics"; (8) "Durbin-Watson"; and (9) "Casewise diagnostics." For this example we apply an alpha level of .05; thus, we will leave the default confidence interval percentage at 95. If we were using a different alpha, the confidence interval would be the complement of alpha (e.g., $\alpha = .01$ then $CI = 1 - .01 = .99$). We will also leave the default of "3 standard deviations" for defining outliers for the casewise diagnostics. Click on "Continue" to return to the original dialog box.

Let's quickly address the **Durbin-Watson test**. The Durbin-Watson test is a test of autocorrelation, and specifically whether adjacent residuals are correlated. It is a test that is usually conducted with time series data. The underlying principle is that correlated residuals should be more similar to their neighbors than other, random pairs of residuals. The Durbin-Watson test then examines the sum of squared differences between neighboring residuals to the sums of squared residuals. Because the examination is on adjacency, how the cases are ordered makes a difference.

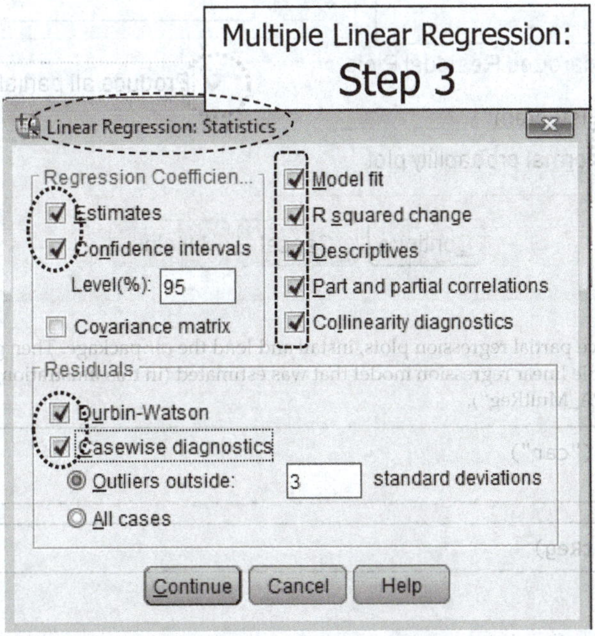

Working in **R,** we can generate the Durbin-Watson test using the following command, where 'GGPA_MultReg' is the object created when we generated our multiple linear regression model. In other words, you will need to compute the multiple linear regression model before you can produce the Durbin Watson test.

```
durbinWatsonTest(GGPA_MultReg)
```

FIGURE 18.11
Multiple linear regression: Step 3.

Step 4. From the Linear Regression dialog box (see Figure 18.10), clicking on "Plots" will provide the option to select various residual plots. From the Plots dialog box, place checkmarks in the boxes next to the following: (1) "Histogram"; (2) "Normal probability plot"; and

(3) "Produce all partial plots." Click on "Continue" to return to the original dialog box. We can use this dialog box to generate various residual plots, which can be used to check assumptions. For this illustration, we'll save the residuals and plot them later as that provides greater flexibility in how we can work with them.

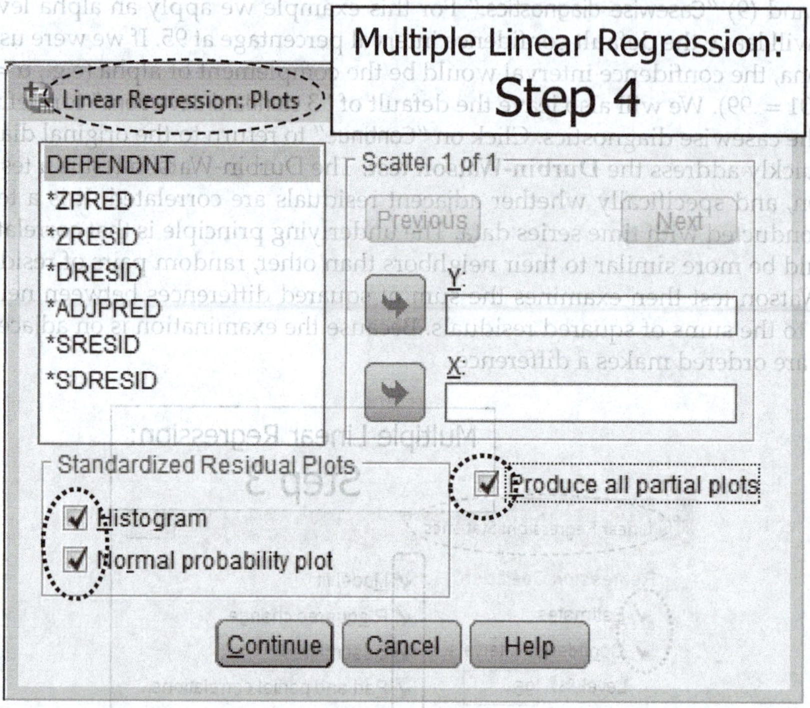

Working in **R**, to produce partial regression plots, install and load the *car* package. Then generate the *avPlots* command on the multiple linear regression model that was estimated (in this illustration, we called the regression model "GGPA_MultReg").

```
install.packages("car")
library(car)
```

```
avPlots(GGPA_MultReg)
```

FIGURE 18.12
Multiple linear regression: Step 4.

Step 5. From the Linear Regression dialog box (see Figure 18.10), clicking on "Save" will provide the option to save various predicted values, residuals, and statistics that can be used for diagnostic examination. From the Save dialog box under the heading of "Predicted Values," place a checkmark in the box next to "Unstandardized." Under the heading "Residuals," place a checkmarks in the boxes next to "Unstandardized" and "Studentized." Under the heading "Distances," place checkmarks in the boxes next to "Mahalanobis," "Cook's," and "Leverage values." Under the heading "Influence Statistics," place a checkmark in the box next to "Standardized DfBeta(s)." Click on "Continue" to return to the original dialog box. From the Linear Regression dialog box, click on "OK" to return and generate the output.

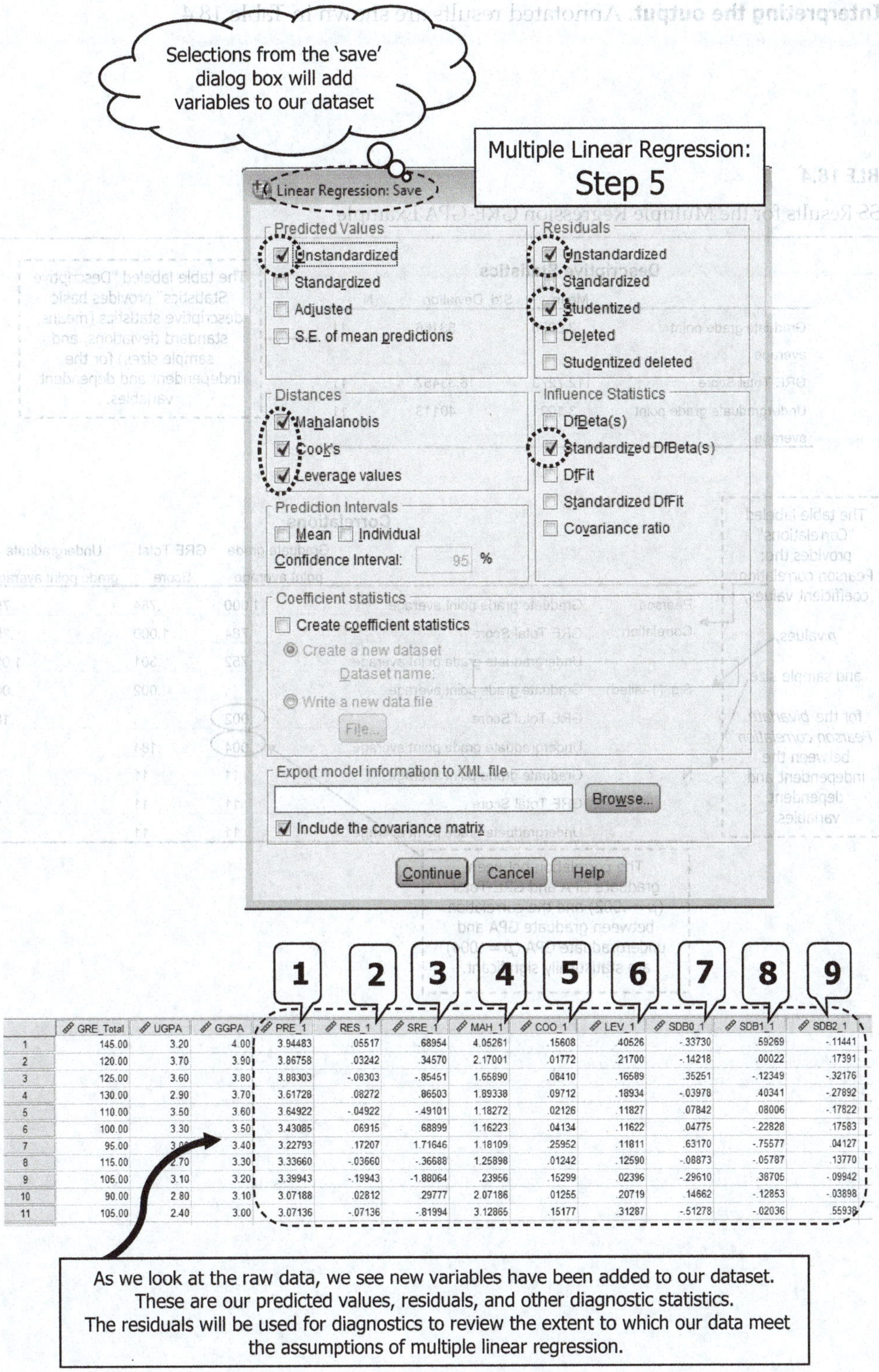

	GRE_Total	UGPA	GGPA	PRE_1	RES_1	SRE_1	MAH_1	COO_1	LEV_1	SDB0_1	SDB1_1	SDB2_1
1	145.00	3.20	4.00	3.94483	.05517	.68954	4.05261	.15608	.40526	-.33730	.59269	-.11441
2	120.00	3.70	3.90	3.86758	.03242	.34570	2.17001	.01772	.21700	-.14218	.00022	.17391
3	125.00	3.60	3.80	3.88303	-.08303	-.85451	1.65890	.08410	.16589	.35251	-.12349	-.32176
4	130.00	2.90	3.70	3.61728	.08272	.86503	1.89338	.09712	.18934	-.03978	.40341	-.27892
5	110.00	3.50	3.60	3.64922	-.04922	-.49101	1.18272	.02126	.11827	.07842	.08006	-.17822
6	100.00	3.30	3.50	3.43085	.06915	.68899	1.16223	.04134	.11622	.04775	-.22828	.17583
7	95.00	3.0[illegible]	3.40	3.22793	.17207	1.71646	1.18109	.25952	.11811	.63170	-.75577	.04127
8	115.00	2.70	3.30	3.33660	-.03660	-.36688	1.25898	.01242	.12590	-.08873	-.05787	.13770
9	105.00	3.10	3.20	3.39943	-.19943	-1.88064	.23956	.15299	.02396	-.29610	.38705	-.09942
10	90.00	2.80	3.10	3.07188	.02812	.29777	2.07186	.01255	.20719	.14662	-.12853	-.03898
11	105.00	2.40	3.00	3.07136	-.07136	-.81994	3.12865	.15177	.31287	-.51278	-.02036	.55938

FIGURE 18.13
Multiple linear regression: Step 5.

Interpreting the output. Annotated results are shown in Table 18.4.

TABLE 18.4

SPSS Results for the Multiple Regression GRE-GPA Example

Descriptive Statistics

	Mean	Std. Deviation	N
Graduate grade point average	3.5000	.33166	11
GRE Total Score	112.7273	16.33457	11
Undergraduate grade point average	3.1091	.40113	11

The table labeled "Descriptive Statistics" provides basic descriptive statistics (means, standard deviations, and sample sizes) for the independent and dependent variables.

The table labeled "Correlations" provides the: Pearson correlation coefficient values, *p* values, and sample size for the *bivariate Pearson correlation* between the independent and dependent variables.

Correlations

		Graduate grade point average	GRE Total Score	Undergraduate grade point average
Pearson Correlation	Graduate grade point average	1.000	.784	.752
	GRE Total Score	.784	1.000	.301
	Undergraduate grade point average	.752	.301	1.000
Sig. (1-tailed)	Graduate grade point average	.	.002	.004
	GRE Total Score	.002	.	.184
	Undergraduate grade point average	.004	.184	.
N	Graduate grade point average	11	11	11
	GRE Total Score	11	11	11
	Undergraduate grade point average	11	11	11

The correlation between graduate GPA and GRE-Total ($p = .002$) and the correlation between graduate GPA and undergraduate GPA ($p = .004$) are statistically significant.

TABLE 18.4 (continued)

SPSS Results for the Multiple Regression GRE-GPA Example

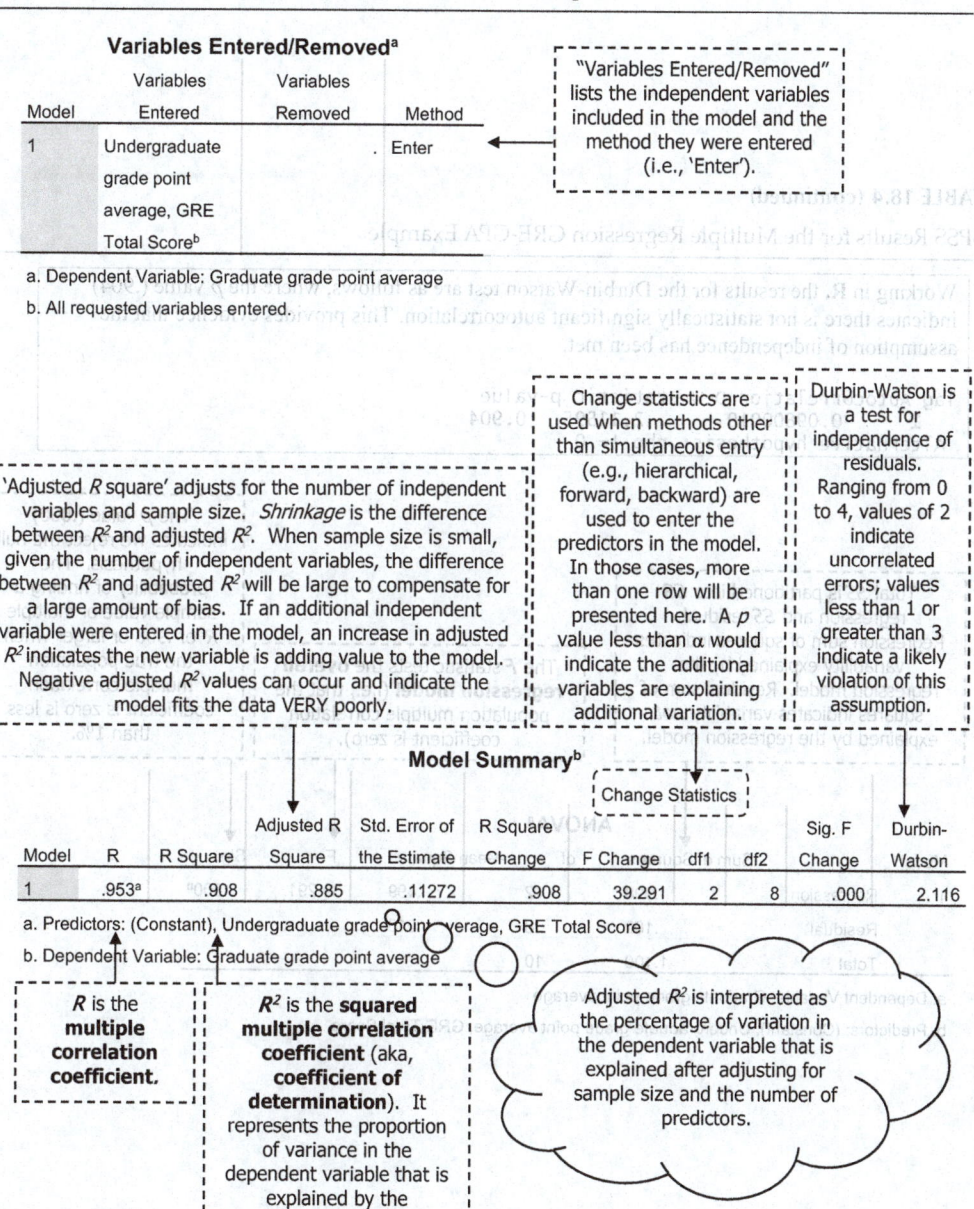

Variables Entered/Removed[a]

Model	Variables Entered	Variables Removed	Method
1	Undergraduate grade point average, GRE Total Score[b]	.	Enter

a. Dependent Variable: Graduate grade point average

b. All requested variables entered.

"Variables Entered/Removed" lists the independent variables included in the model and the method they were entered (i.e., 'Enter').

'Adjusted R square' adjusts for the number of independent variables and sample size. *Shrinkage* is the difference between R^2 and adjusted R^2. When sample size is small, given the number of independent variables, the difference between R^2 and adjusted R^2 will be large to compensate for a large amount of bias. If an additional independent variable were entered in the model, an increase in adjusted R^2 indicates the new variable is adding value to the model. Negative adjusted R^2 values can occur and indicate the model fits the data VERY poorly.

Change statistics are used when methods other than simultaneous entry (e.g., hierarchical, forward, backward) are used to enter the predictors in the model. In those cases, more than one row will be presented here. A p value less than α would indicate the additional variables are explaining additional variation.

Durbin-Watson is a test for independence of residuals. Ranging from 0 to 4, values of 2 indicate uncorrelated errors; values less than 1 or greater than 3 indicate a likely violation of this assumption.

Model Summary[b]

Model	R	R Square	Adjusted R Square	Std. Error of the Estimate	Change Statistics: R Square Change	F Change	df1	df2	Sig. F Change	Durbin-Watson
1	.953[a]	.908	.885	.11272	.908	39.291	2	8	.000	2.116

a. Predictors: (Constant), Undergraduate grade point average, GRE Total Score

b. Dependent Variable: Graduate grade point average

R is the **multiple correlation coefficient.**

R^2 is the **squared multiple correlation coefficient** (aka, **coefficient of determination**). It represents the proportion of variance in the dependent variable that is explained by the independent variables.

Adjusted R^2 is interpreted as the percentage of variation in the dependent variable that is explained after adjusting for sample size and the number of predictors.

(*continued*)

TABLE 18.4 (continued)

SPSS Results for the Multiple Regression GRE-GPA Example

Working in **R,** the results for the Durbin-Watson test are as follows, where the *p* value (.904) indicates there is not statistically significant autocorrelation. This provides evidence that the assumption of independence has been met.

```
lag Autocorrelation D-W Statistic p-value
   1     -0.09800019      2.11595   0.904
 Alternative hypothesis: rho != 0
```

Total *SS* is partitioned into *SS* regression and *SS* residual. Regression sum of squares indicates variability explained by the regression model. Residual sum of squares indicates variability *not* explained by the regression model.

The *F* statistic tests the **overall regression model** (i.e., that the population multiple correlation coefficient is zero).

The *p* value (.000) indicates we reject the null hypothesis. The probability of finding a sample value of multiple R^2 of .908 or larger when the true population multiple correlation coefficient is zero is less than 1%.

ANOVA[a]

Model		Sum of Squares	df	Mean Square	F	Sig.
1	Regression	.998	2	.499	39.291	.000[b]
	Residual	.102	8	.013		
	Total	1.100	10			

a. Dependent Variable: Graduate grade point average

b. Predictors: (Constant), Undergraduate grade point average, GRE Total Score

TABLE 18.4 (continued)

SPSS Results for the Multiple Regression GRE-GPA Example

The **'constant'** is the **intercept** and the unstandardized coefficient tells us that when all the predictors were zero, graduate GPA (the dependent variable) would be .638. The 'GRE-Total' and 'UGPA' are the slopes. For every one point increase in GRE-Total, graduate GPA will increase by about 1/10 of one point (holding constant undergraduate GPA). For every one point increase in undergraduate GPA, graduate GPA will increase by about ½ of one point (holding constant GRE-Total).

The test statistic, *t*, is calculated as the *unstandardized coefficient divided by its standard error.* Thus the slope for *undergraduate GPA* is calculated as (difference due to rounding):

$$t = \frac{.469}{.093} = 5.043$$

The *p* value for the intercept (the 'constant') (*p* = .087) indicates that the intercept is *not* statistically significantly different from zero (this finding is usually of less interest than the slopes). The *p* values for GRE-Total and undergraduate GPA (the independent variables) (*p* = .001) indicate that the slopes are statistically significantly different from zero.

Coefficients[a]

Model	Unstandardized Coefficients B	Unstandardized Coefficients Std. Error	Standardized Coefficients Beta	t	Sig.	95.0% Confidence Interval for B Lower Bound	95.0% Confidence Interval for B Upper Bound	Correlations Zero-order	Correlations Partial	Correlations Part	Collinearity Statistics Tolerance	Collinearity Statistics VIF
1 (Constant)	.638	.327		1.954	.087	-.115	1.391					
GRE Total Score	.012	.002	.614	5.447	.001	.007	.018	.784	.887	.585	.909	1.100
Undergrad GPA	.469	.093	.567	5.030	.001	.254	.684	.752	.872	.541	.909	1.100

a. Dependent Variable: Graduate grade point average

Zero-order correlations are the simple bivariate Pearson correlations between the dependent variable and the independent variables.

Collinearity statistics are reviewed under assumptions.

The **partial correlation** of .887 is the correlation between GRE-Total and graduate GPA (dependent variable) when the linear effect of undergraduate GPA has been removed from both GRE-Total and graduate GPA (i.e., 'controlling' for or holding constant undergraduate GPA). Squaring this indicates that 78.7% of the variation in graduate GPA that is not explained by undergraduate GPA *is* explained by GRE-Total.

The **part correlation** of .585, when squared (i.e., .342) indicates that GRE-Total explains an additional 34% of the variance in graduate GPA over and above the variance in graduate GPA which is explained by undergraduate GPA.

(*continued*)

TABLE 18.4 (continued)

SPSS Results for the Multiple Regression GRE-GPA Example

'Collinearity diagnostics' will be examined in our discussion of assumptions.

Collinearity Diagnostics[a]

Model	Dimension	Eigenvalue	Condition Index	Variance Proportions (Constant)	Variance Proportions GRE Total Score	Variance Proportions Undergraduate grade point average
1	1	2.981	1.000	.00	.00	.00
	2	.012	15.727	.03	.86	.40
	3	.007	20.537	.97	.13	.60

a. Dependent Variable: Graduate grade point average

'Residual statistics' and related graphs (histogram and Q-Q plot of standardized residuals, not presented here) will be examined in our discussion of assumptions.

Residuals Statistics[a]

	Minimum	Maximum	Mean	Std. Deviation	N
Predicted Value	3.0714	3.9448	3.5000	.31597	11
Std. Predicted Value	-1.357	1.408	.000	1.000	11
Standard Error of Predicted Value	.038	.079	.058	.011	11
Adjusted Predicted Value	3.0599	3.9117	3.4954	.30917	11
Residual	-.19943	.17207	.00000	.10082	11
Std. Residual	-1.769	1.527	.000	.894	11
Stud. Residual	-1.881	1.716	.017	1.008	11
Deleted Residual	-.22531	.21754	.00458	.12935	11
Stud. Deleted Residual	-2.355	2.020	.000	1.145	11
Mahal. Distance	.240	4.053	1.818	1.048	11
Cook's Distance	.012	.260	.092	.081	11
Centered Leverage Value	.024	.405	.182	.105	11

a. Dependent Variable: Graduate grade point average

TABLE 18.4 (continued)

SPSS Results for the Multiple Regression GRE-GPA Example

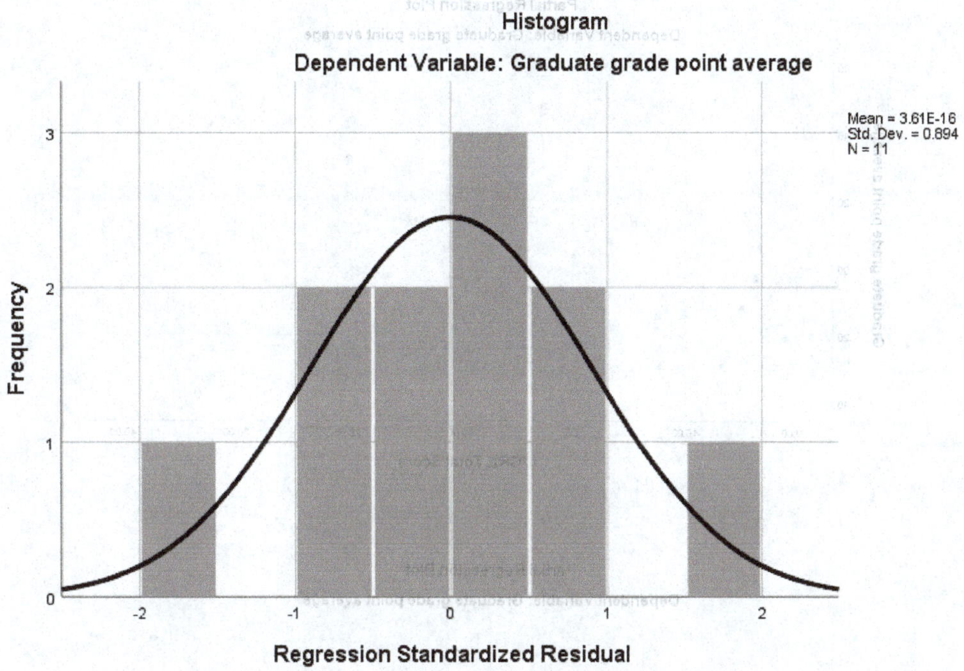

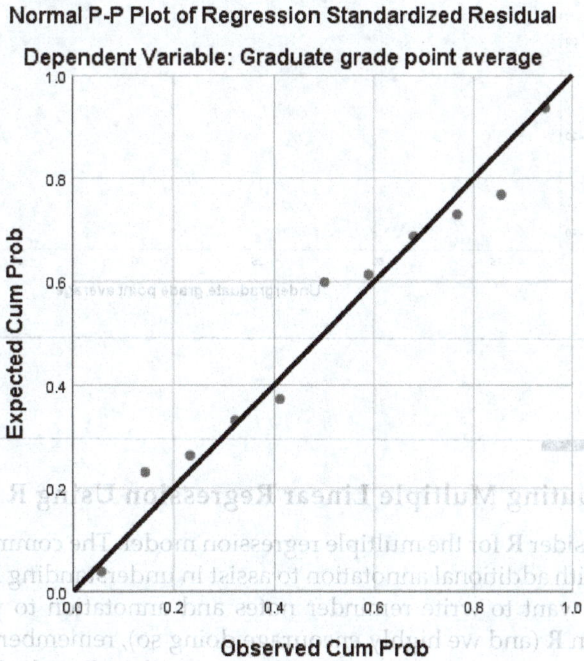

(continued)

TABLE 18.4 (continued)

SPSS Results for the Multiple Regression GRE-GPA Example

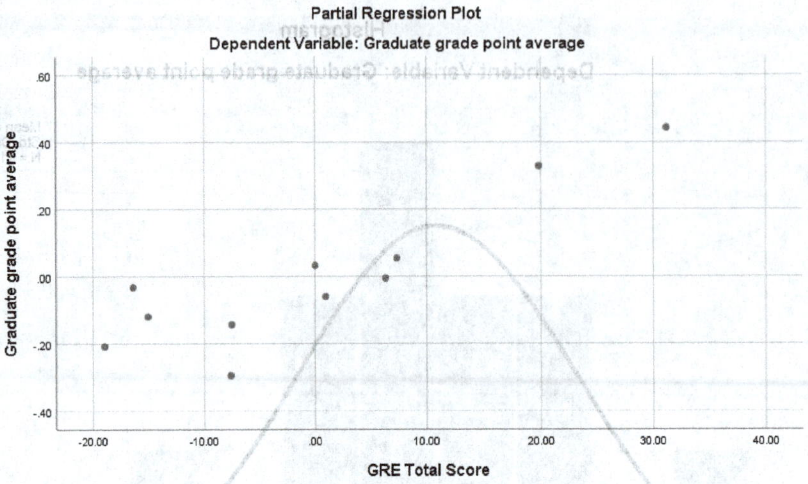

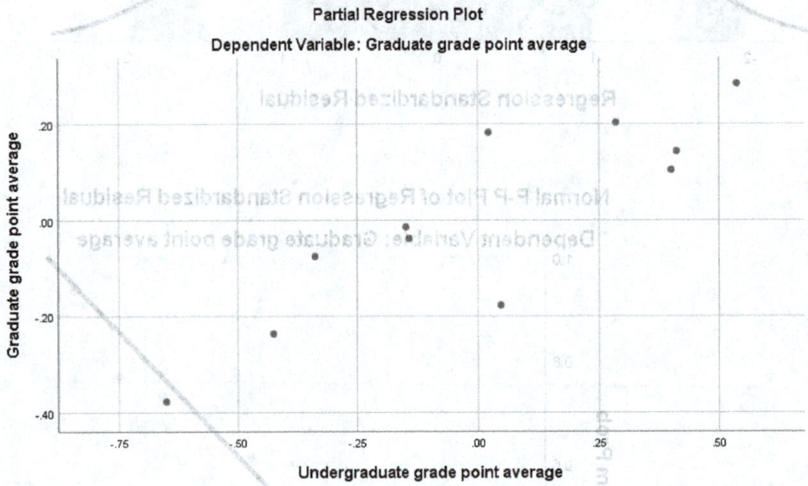

18.4 Computing Multiple Linear Regression Using R

Next we consider **R** for the multiple regression model. The commands are provided within the blocks with additional annotation to assist in understanding how the command works. Should you want to write reminder notes and annotation to yourself as you write the commands in **R** (and we highly encourage doing so), remember that any text that follows a hashtag (i.e., #) is annotation only and not part of the **R** code. Thus, you can write annotations directly into **R** with hashtags. We encourage this practice so that when you call up the commands in the future, you'll understand what the various lines of code are doing. You may think you'll remember what you did. However, trust us. There is a good chance that you won't. Thus, consider it best practice when using **R** to annotate heavily!

18.4.1 Reading Data Into R

In this illustration, we are pulling in data that is currently in a .csv file.

```
getwd()
```

R is always directed to a directory on your computer. To find out which directly it's pointed to, run the *get working directory* command. We will assume that we need to change the working directory, and will use the next line of code to set the working directory to the desired path.

```
setwd("E:/FolderName")
```

This command will set your working directory to a specific folder that you name. Change what is in parentheses to your file location. Also, if you are copying the directory name, it will copy in slashes. You will need to change the backslash (i.e., \) to a forward slash (i.e., /) in the **R** command. Also note that you need the name of your folder enclosed in quotation marks.

```
Ch18_GGPA <- read.csv("Ch18_GGPA.csv")
```

This command reads your data into **R**. To the left of "<-" will be what you want to call the dataframe in **R**. In this example, we're calling this **R** dataframe "Ch18_GGPA." What's to the right of "<-" tells **R** to find this particular csv file. In this example, our file is called "Ch18_GGPA.csv." Make sure the extension (i.e., .csv) is there. Also note that you need the name of the file enclosed in quotations.

```
names(Ch18_GGPA)
```

This command will produce a list of variable names for the dataframe that is noted in parentheses. For this illustration, our variable names are as follows. This is a good check to make sure your data have been read in correctly.

```
[1] "GRE_Total" "UGPA"      "GGPA"
```

```
View(Ch18_GGPA)
```

This command will let you view the dataset in spreadsheet format in RStudio.

```
summary(Ch18_GGPA)
```

The *summary* command will produce basic descriptive statistics on all the variables in your dataframe. This is a great way to quickly check to see if the data have been read in correctly and get a feel for your data, if you haven't already. The output from the summary statement for this dataframe looks like this.

```
   GRE_Total          UGPA            GGPA
 Min.   : 90.0   Min.   :2.400   Min.   :3.00
 1st Qu.:102.5   1st Qu.:2.850   1st Qu.:3.25
 Median :110.0   Median :3.100   Median :3.50
 Mean   :112.7   Mean   :3.109   Mean   :3.50
 3rd Qu.:122.5   3rd Qu.:3.400   3rd Qu.:3.75
 Max.   :145.0   Max.   :3.700   Max.   :4.00
```

FIGURE 18.14
Reading data into R.

18.4.2 Generating the Multiple Regression Model and Saving Values

With these commands, we will generate the multiple regression model and save variables that can be used for data screening.

```
GGPA_MultReg <- lm(formula = GGPA ~ UGPA + GRE_Total,
                   data = Ch18_GGPA)
```

The *lm* command is the code to run the multiple linear regression model. In this example, we're naming our model (i.e., our object) "GGPA_MultReg." The formula defines our dependent variable as "GGPA" and it is predicted by "UGPA" and "GRE_Total." The data come from the Ch18_GGPA dataframe.

```
summary(GGPA_MultReg)
```

Run the *summary* command to see the results from the multiple regression model. The output includes a few residual statistics, coefficient estimates and related statistics, R^2, R^2_{adj}, and the overall F test. Note that if you don't run the summary line of code, since we created an object with our model, there won't be any results output from the *lm* command!

```
Residuals:
     Min       1Q   Median       3Q      Max
-0.19943 -0.06029  0.02812  0.06216  0.17207

Coefficients:
            Estimate Std. Error t value Pr(>|t|)
(Intercept) 0.637906    0.326537   1.954 0.086517 .
UGPA        0.468670    0.093181   5.030 0.001015 **
GRE_Total   0.012463    0.002288   5.447 0.000611 ***
---
Signif. codes:  0 "***" 0.001 "**" 0.01 "*" 0.05 "." 0.1 " " 1

Residual standard error: 0.1127 on 8 degrees of freedom
Multiple R-squared: 0.9076, Adjusted R-squared: 0.8845
F-statistic: 39.29 on 2 and 8 DF, p-value: 7.289e-05
```

```
anova(GGPA_MultReg)
```

The *anova* command will generate the ANOVA summary table for the multiple regression model.

```
Analysis of Variance Table

Response: GGPA
          Df  Sum Sq Mean Sq F value    Pr(>F)
UGPA       1 0.62147 0.62147  48.916 0.0001133 ***
GRE_Total  1 0.37689 0.37689  29.665 0.0006112 ***
Residuals  8 0.10164 0.01270
---
Signif. codes:  0 "***" 0.001 "**" 0.01 "*" 0.05 "." 0.1 " " 1
```

```
vcov(GGPA_MultReg)
```

The *vcov* command will generate the covariance matrix for the model parameters.

```
              (Intercept)          UGPA     GRE_Total
(Intercept)  0.1066264269 -1.975867e-02 -3.906768e-04
UGPA        -0.0197586732  8.682693e-03 -6.419572e-05
GRE_Total   -0.0003906768 -6.419572e-05  5.236241e-06
```

FIGURE 18.15
Generating multiple linear regression in **R** and saving variables.

Working in **R**, we can generate the Durbin-Watson test using the following command, where 'GGPA_MultReg' is the object created when we generated our multiple linear regression model. In other words, you will need to compute the multiple linear regression model before you can produce the Durbin Watson test.

```
durbinWatsonTest(GGPA_MultReg)
```

For diagnostic purposes, we can save additional variables to the dataframe which will be used later for checking assumptions.

```
Ch18_GGPA$unstandardizedPredicted <- predict(GGPA_MultReg)
```

This command saves unstandardized predicted values.

```
Ch18_GGPA$unstandardizedResiduals <- resid(GGPA_MultReg)
```

This command saves unstandardized residuals.

```
Ch18_GGPA$standardized.residuals <- rstandard(GGPA_MultReg)
```

This command saves standardized residuals. We expect standardized residuals to be within a range of −2.0 to +2.0.

```
Ch18_GGPA$studentized.residuals <- rstudent(GGPA_MultReg)
```

This command saves studentized residuals.

```
Ch18_GGPA$cook <- cooks.distance(GGPA_MultReg)
```

This command saves Cook's distance, an influence statistic.

```
Ch18_GGPA $leverage <- hatvalues(GGPA_MultReg)
```

This command saves the leverage values.

FIGURE 18.15 (continued)
Generating multiple linear regression in **R** and saving variables.

18.4.3 Generating Correlation Coefficients

```
install.packages("Hmisc")
```

There are many ways to generate correlations in **R**. For this illustration, we will use the *Hmisc* package. This command will install the *Hmisc* package that will allow us to generate the correlation matrix and related *p* values.

```
library("Hmisc")
```

This will load the package so we can use it.

```
cor(Ch18_GGPA)
```

This command will generate a simple correlation table. The default matrix is Pearson.

```
          GRE_Total      UGPA      GGPA
GRE_Total 1.0000000 0.3010711 0.7844854
UGPA      0.3010711 1.0000000 0.7516460
GGPA      0.7844854 0.7516460 1.0000000
```

FIGURE 18.16
Generating correlation coefficients in **R**.

```
res2 <- rcorr(as.matrix(Ch18_GGPA))
res2
```

This command will generate a matrix correlation table with all variables in our Ch18_GGPA dataframe and will also generate *p* values for the coefficients and sample size. We see the strongest correlation between GGPA and GRE_Total at $r = .78$.

```
          GRE_Total UGPA GGPA
GRE_Total      1.00 0.30 0.78
UGPA           0.30 1.00 0.75
GGPA           0.78 0.75 1.00

n= 11

P
          GRE_Total UGPA   GGPA
GRE_Total           0.3683 0.0042
UGPA      0.3683           0.0076
GGPA      0.0042    0.0076
```

FIGURE 18.16 (continued)
Generating correlation coefficients in **R**.

18.4.4 Generating Confidence Intervals of Coefficient Estimates

```
confint(GGPA_MultReg, level =.95)
```

Because we named our model as an object, we can easily request additional statistics on it. With the *confint* command, we can obtain confidence intervals for the coefficient estimates. With the *level* command, we set the confidence interval to 95% and thus are provided the lower confidence interval as 2.5% and upper confidence interval as 97.5%.

```
                   2.5 %     97.5 %
(Intercept) -0.115089982 1.39090147
UGPA         0.253794259 0.68354566
GRE_Total    0.007186535 0.01774012
```

FIGURE 18.17
Generating confidence intervals of coefficient estimates in R.

18.5 Data Screening

As you may recall, there were a number of assumptions associated with multiple linear regression. These included: (a) independence; (b) homoscedasticity; (c) linearity; (d) normality; and (e) noncollinearity. Although fixed values of X were discussed in assumptions, this is not an assumption that will be tested, but is instead related to the use of the results (i.e., extrapolation and interpolation). Before we begin to examine assumptions, let us review the values that we requested to be saved to our dataset (see Figure 18.13).

1. PRE_1 values are the unstandardized predicted values (i.e., Y_i').
2. RES_1 values are the unstandardized residuals, simply the difference between the observed and predicted values. For student 1, for example, the observed value for the graduate GPA (i.e., the dependent variable) was 4 and the predicted value was 3.94483. Thus the unstandardized residual is simply 4 − 3.94483 or .05517.
3. SRE_1 values are the studentized residuals, a type of standardized residual that is more sensitive to outliers as compared to standardized residuals. Studentized residuals are computed as the unstandardized residual divided by an estimate of the standard deviation with that case removed. As a rule of thumb, studentized residuals with an absolute value greater than 3 are considered outliers (Stevens, 1984).
4. MAH_1 values are Mahalanobis distance values which measure how far that particular case is from the average of the independent variable and thus can be helpful in detecting outliers. These values can be reviewed to determine cases that are exerting leverage. Barnett and Lewis (1994) produced a table of critical values for evaluating Mahalanobis distance. Squared Mahalanobis distances divided by the number of variables $\left(D^2/df\right)$ which are greater than 2.5 (for small samples) or 3 to 4 (for large samples) are suggestive of outliers (Hair, Black, Babin, Anderson, & Tatham, 2006). Later, we follow another convention for examining these values using the chi-square distribution.
5. COO_1 values are Cook's distance values and provide an indication of influence of individual cases. As a rule of thumb, Cook's values greater than one suggest that case is potentially problematic.
6. LEV_1 values are leverage values, a measure of distance from a respective case to the average of the predictor.
7. SDB0_1, SDB1_1 and SDB2_1 values are standardized DfBeta values for the intercept and slopes, respectively, and are easier to interpret as compared to their unstandardized counterparts. Standardized DfBeta values greater than an absolute value of two suggest that the case may be exerting undue influence on the calculation of the parameters in the model (i.e., the slopes and intercept).

18.5.1 Independence

Here we will plot: (1) studentized residuals (which were requested and created through the "Save" option when generating our model) against unstandardized predicted values; and (2) studentized residuals against each independent variable to examine the extent to which independence was met. The general steps for generating a simple scatterplot through "Scatter/dot" in SPSS have been presented in Chapter 10, and they will not be reiterated here. From the "Simple scatterplots" dialog screen, click the studentized residual and move it to the *Y* axis box by clicking the arrow. Similarly, move the unstandardized predicted value variable into the *X* axis box. Then click "OK" to generate the plot. Repeat these steps to plot the studentized residual to each independent variable. If the assumption of independence is met, the points should fall randomly within a band of −2.0 to +2.0, which is what we see in the graphs presented previously (see Figure 18.1).

Working in **R**, we create similar scatterplots using the following *plot* commands, with the first variable listed displaying on the *X* axis (e.g., "Ch18_GGPA$unstandardizedPredicted"), and the second variable displaying on the *Y* axis (i.e., "Ch18_GGPA$studentized.residuals"). Additional commands are provided to label the axes (*xlab* and *ylab*) and title the graph (*main*).

```
plot(Ch18_GGPA$unstandardizedPredicted,
     Ch18_GGPA$studentized.residuals,
     xlab = "unstandardized predicted values",
     ylab = "studentized residuals",
     main = "Scatterplot for independence")

plot(Ch18_GGPA$UGPA,
     Ch18_GGPA$studentized.residuals,
     xlab = "undergraduate GPA",
     ylab = "studentized residuals",
     main = "Scatterplot for independence")

plot(Ch18_GGPA$GRE_Total,
     Ch18_GGPA$studentized.residuals,
     xlab = "GRE Total",
     ylab = "studentized residuals",
     main = "Scatterplot for independence")
```

FIGURE 18.18 (continued)
Generating plots in R for independence evidence.

18.5.2 Homoscedasticity

Recall that homogeneity of variance, or homoscedasticity, is evident when the spread of residuals is fairly constant over the range of unstandardized predicted values and observed values of the independent variables. In other words, we're looking for a relatively random display of points. If the display of residuals increases or decreases across the plot, then there may be an indication that the assumption of homoscedasticity has been violated. The plots used to examine independence (see Figure 18.1) can also be used for homoscedasticity: (1) studentized residuals against unstandardized predicted values and (2) studentized residuals against each independent variable to examine the extent to which independence was met.

Working in **R**, we can generate the *nonconstant error variance test* to determine if there is homogeneity of variance. The null hypothesis of this test is constant error variance, and the alternative hypothesis is that the error variance changes with the level of the fitted values, or with the linear combination of independent variables. A nonstatistically significant test suggests we have met the assumption, as we see here.

We use our multiple linear regression object (i.e., "GGPA_MultReg") with the *ncvTest* command to conduct the nonconstant error variance test. Note that this function runs from the package *car*; thus, make sure that *car* is installed and loaded in your library prior to running.

```
ncvTest(GGPA_MultReg)
```

The results produce a chi-squared test. Based on the *p* value (.463), our test is not statistically significant which indicates we have met the assumption of homoscedasticity.

```
Non-constant Variance Score Test
Variance formula: ~ fitted.values
Chisquare = 1.315736    Df = 1    p = 0.463052
```

FIGURE 18.19
Non-Constant Error Variance Test in R

18.5.3 Linearity

Since we have more than one independent variable, we have to take a different approach to examining linearity than what was done with simple linear regression. However, we can use the same information gleaned from our examination of independence and homoscedasticity for reviewing the assumption of linearity. As noted previously, the residuals should be located within a band of $\pm 2s_{res}$ (or standard errors), indicating no systematic pattern of points. Residual plots for the GGPA example are shown in Figure 18.1. Even with a very small sample, we see a fairly random pattern of residuals, and therefore feel fairly confident that the linearity assumption has been satisfied.

We can also review the partial regression plots that we asked for when generating the regression model (see Figure 18.12 for generating partial regression plots in **R**). A separate partial regression plot is provided for each independent variable, where we are looking for linearity (rather than some type of polynomial). Even with a small sample size, the partial regression plots suggest evidence of linearity.

18.5.4 Normality

Understanding the distributional shape, specifically the extent to which normality is a reasonable assumption, is important in multiple linear regression just as it was in simple linear regression. Normality can be understood by examining residuals as well as various diagnostics to examine our data for influential cases. Let us begin by examining the unstandardized residuals for normality. Because the steps for generating normality evidence were presented in previous chapters (see, for example, Chapter 16), they will not be repeated here.

18.5.4.1 Interpreting Normality Evidence

By this point, we are well versed in interpreting quite a range of normality statistics and will do the same for multiple linear regression. The skewness statistic of the residuals is −.336 and kurtosis is .484—both being within the range of what would be considered normal (approximately an absolute value of 2.0), suggesting some evidence of normality.

Descriptives

			Statistic	Std. Error
Unstandardized Residual	Mean		.0000000	.03039717
	95% Confidence Interval for Mean	Lower Bound	-.0677291	
		Upper Bound	.0677291	
	5% Trimmed Mean		.0015202	
	Median		.0281190	
	Variance		.010	
	Std. Deviation		.10081601	
	Minimum		-.19943	
	Maximum		.17207	
	Range		.37150	
	Interquartile Range		.14051	
	Skewness		-.336	.661
	Kurtosis		.484	1.279

FIGURE 18.20
Normality evidence.

Given the very small sample size, the histogram reflects as normal a distribution as might be expected.

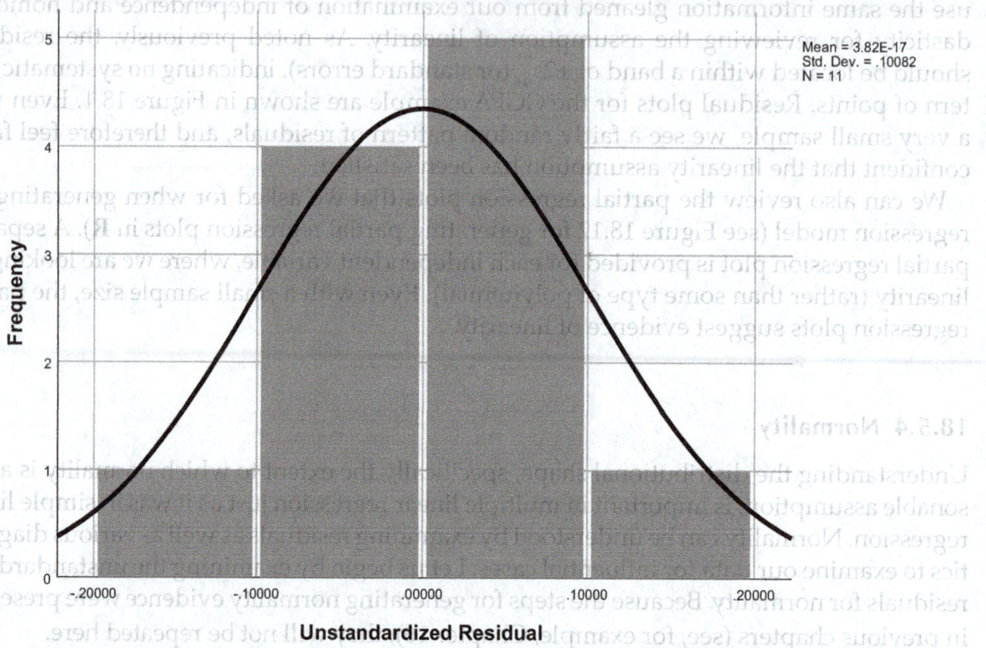

Working in **R**, we can generate a histogram using the *ggplot2* package.

```
install.packages("ggplot2")
```

This command will install the *ggplot2* package which we can use to create various graphs and plots.

```
library(ggplot2)
```

This command will load the *ggplot2* package.

```
qplot(Ch18_GGPA$unstandardizedResiduals,
      geom="histogram",
      main = "Histogram of Unstandardized Residuals",
      xlab = "Unstandardized Residual", ylab = "Count",
      fill=I("gray"),
      col=I("white"))
```

Using the *gplot* command, we create a histogram (i.e., geom = "histogram") from our dataframe (i.e., Ch18_GGPA) using the variable *unstandardizedResiduals.* We can add a few commands to change the color of the bars (i.e., *fill=I("gray")*), and outline of the bars (i.e., *col=I("white")*). We can also add a title (i.e., *main = "Histogram of Unstandardized Residuals"*) and change the *X* and *Y* axes (*xlab = "Unstandardized Residual", ylab = "Count"*).

FIGURE 18.21
Histogram.

There are a few other statistics that can be used to gauge normality. The results for the formal test of normality, the Shapiro-Wilk test (*SW*) (Shapiro & Wilk, 1965), is presented below and suggests that our sample distribution for the residual is *not* statistically significantly different than what would be expected from a normal distribution as the p value is greater than α (p = .918).

Tests of Normality

	Kolmogorov-Smirnov[a]			Shapiro-Wilk		
	Statistic	df	Sig.	Statistic	df	Sig.
Unstandardized Residual	.155	11	.200*	.973	11	.918

*. This is a lower bound of the true significance.

a. Lilliefors Significance Correction

Working in **R**, we can generate various normality statistics as well.

```
install.packages("pastecs")
```

This command will install the *pastecs* package which we will use to generate various forms of normality evidence.

```
library(pastecs)
```

This command will load the *pastecs* package.

```
stat.desc(Ch18_GGPA$unstandardizedResiduals,
          norm = TRUE)
```

This command will generate normality indices on the variable "unstandardizedResiduals" in the dataframe Ch18_GGPA as follows. The *norm=TRUE* command will produce Shapiro- Wilk results (*SW*). We see skew (−.250) and kurtosis (−.694), along with *SW* = .973, p = .918 for the "unstandardized residual" variable. All indicate the assumption of normality has been met. As we know, we can divide the skew and kurtosis values by their standard errors to get a standardized value that can be used to determine if the skew and/or kurtosis is statistically different from zero. Since this output provides "2SE," we would simply divide this value by 2 to arrive at the standard error.

Note: You may have noticed that the skewness and kurtosis value that we've just generated differs from what we found in SPSS, which was skew = −.336 and kurtosis = .484. This is because there are different ways to calculate skewness and kurtosis. Let's use another package in **R** to calculate these statistics with different algorithms.

```
      nbr.val       nbr.null         nbr.na            min
 1.100000e+01   0.000000e+00   0.000000e+00  -1.994318e-01
          max          range            sum         median
 1.720684e-01   3.715003e-01  -1.387779e-17   2.811903e-02
         mean        SE.mean   CI.mean.0.95            var
-1.261617e-18   3.039717e-02   6.772912e-02   1.016387e-02
      std.dev       coef.var       skewness       skew.2SE
 1.008160e-01  -7.991015e+16  -2.502561e-01  -1.893907e-01
     kurtosis      kurt.2SE      normtest.W     normtest.p
-6.940916e-01  -2.712533e-01   9.733156e-01   9.178945e-01
```

```
install.packages("e1071")
```

This command will install the e1071 package which we will use to generate skewness and kurtosis.

FIGURE 18.22
Normality evidence: Shapiro-Wilk test.

```
library(e1071)
```

This command will load the e1071 package.

```
skewness(Ch18_GGPA$unstandardizedResiduals, type=3)
skewness(Ch18_GGPA$unstandardizedResiduals, type=2)
skewness(Ch18_GGPA$unstandardizedResiduals, type=1)
```

This command will generate skewness statistics on the variable(s) we specify. The "type=" script defines how skewness is calculated. Specifying "type=2" will use the algorithm that is used by SPSS. Readers interested in learning more, including the algorithms for each of the three methods, are encouraged to review Joanes and Gill (1998). We see that using "type=2," our skew is −.336, the same value as generated using SPSS.

```
# skewness(Ch18_GGPA$unstandardizedResiduals, type=3)
[1] -0.2502561

# skewness(Ch18_GGPA$unstandardizedResiduals, type=2)
[1] -0.3364554

# skewness(Ch18_GGPA$unstandardizedResiduals, type=1)
[1] -0.2887179
```

```
kurtosis(Ch18_GGPA$unstandardizedResiduals, type=3)
kurtosis(Ch18_GGPA$unstandardizedResiduals, type=2)
kurtosis(Ch18_GGPA$unstandardizedResiduals, type=1)
```

This command will generate kurtosis statistics on the variable(s) we specify. The "type=" script defines how kurtosis is calculated. Specifying "type=2" will use the algorithm that is used by SPSS. Readers interested in learning more, including the algorithms for each of the three methods, are encouraged to review Joanes and Gill (1998). We see that using "type=2," our kurtosis is .484, the same value as generated using SPSS.

```
# kurtosis(Ch18_GGPA$unstandardizedResiduals, type=3)
[1] -0.6940916

# kurtosis(Ch18_GGPA$unstandardizedResiduals, type=2)
[1] 0.483582

# kurtosis(Ch18_GGPA$unstandardizedResiduals, type=1)
[1] -0.2098508
```

FIGURE 18.22 (continued)
Normality evidence: Shapiro-Wilk test.

Quantile-quantile (Q-Q) plots are also often examined to determine evidence of normality. The Q-Q plot of residuals suggests relative normality with points that fall on or close to the diagonal line suggesting evidence of normality.

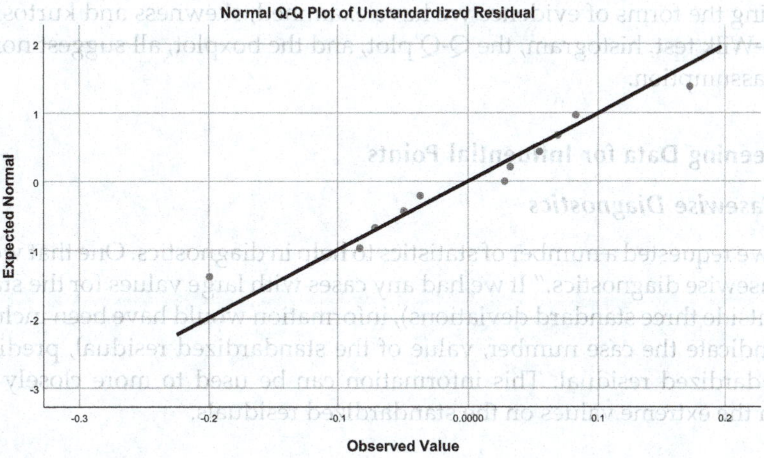

Working in **R**, we can use the *gplot* command to create a Q-Q plot of the variable *unstandardizedResiduals* from the dataframe Ch18_GGPA.

```
qplot(sample=unstandardizedResiduals,
      data = Ch18_GGPA)
```

FIGURE 18.23
Q-Q plot.

The boxplot in Figure 18.24 also suggests a relatively normal distribution of residuals with no outliers.

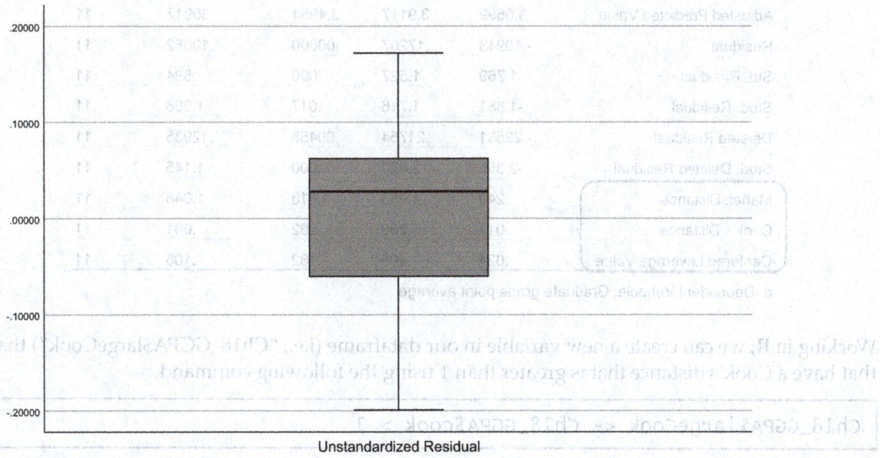

Working in **R**, we can generate a boxplot for unstandardized residuals using the *boxplot* function. To label the *Y* axis, we include the *ylab* command.

```
boxplot(Ch18_GGPA$unstandardizedResiduals,
        ylab="unstandardized residual")
```

FIGURE 18.24
Boxplot.

Considering the forms of evidence we have examined, skewness and kurtosis statistics, the Shapiro-Wilk test, histogram, the Q-Q plot, and the boxplot, all suggest normality is a reasonable assumption.

18.5.5 Screening Data for Influential Points

18.5.5.1 Casewise Diagnostics

Recall that we requested a number of statistics to help in diagnostics. One that we requested was for "Casewise diagnostics." If we had any cases with large values for the standardized residual (outside three standard deviations), information would have been included in our output to indicate the case number, value of the standardized residual, predicted value, and unstandardized residual. This information can be used to more closely examining case(s) with the extreme values on the standardized residuals.

18.5.5.2 Cook's Distance

Cook's distance provides an overall measure for the influence of individual cases. Values greater than one suggest that the case may be problematic in terms of undue influence on the model. Examining the residual statistics in our output (see following table), we see that the maximum value for Cook's distance is .260, well under the point at which we should be concerned.

Residuals Statistics[a]

	Minimum	Maximum	Mean	Std. Deviation	N
Predicted Value	3.0714	3.9448	3.5000	.31597	11
Std. Predicted Value	-1.357	1.408	.000	1.000	11
Standard Error of Predicted Value	.038	.079	.058	.011	11
Adjusted Predicted Value	3.0599	3.9117	3.4954	.30917	11
Residual	-.19943	.17207	.00000	.10082	11
Std. Residual	-1.769	1.527	.000	.894	11
Stud. Residual	-1.881	1.716	.017	1.008	11
Deleted Residual	-.22531	.21754	.00458	.12935	11
Stud. Deleted Residual	-2.355	2.020	.000	1.145	11
Mahal. Distance	.240	4.053	1.818	1.048	11
Cook's Distance	.012	.260	.092	.081	11
Centered Leverage Value	.024	.405	.182	.105	11

a. Dependent Variable: Graduate grade point average

Working in **R**, we can create a new variable in our dataframe (i.e., "Ch18_GGPA$largeCook") that notes cases that have a Cook's distance that is greater than 1 using the following command:

```
Ch18_GGPA$largeCook <- Ch18_GGPA$cook > 1
```

We can then run the *sum* command to find out how many large Cook's values there are.

```
sum(Ch18_GGPA$largeCook)
```

We can write similar commands for the centered leverage values.

FIGURE 18.25
Screening data for influential points

18.5.5.3 Mahalanobis Distances

Mahalanobis distances are measures of the distance from each case to the mean of the independent variable for the remaining cases. We can use the value of Mahalanobis distance as a test statistic value with the chi-square distribution. With two independent variables and one dependent variable, we have three degrees of freedom. Given an alpha level of .05 (alpha of .001 if you want to be a bit more liberal), the chi-square critical value is 7.82. Thus any Mahalanobis distance greater than 7.82 suggests that case is an outlier. With a maximum of 4.053 (see Figure 18.25), there is no evidence to suggest there are outliers in our data.

18.5.5.4 Centered Leverage Values

Centered leverage values less than .20 suggest there are no problems with cases that are exerting undue influence (see Figure 18.25). Values greater than .5 indicate problems.

18.5.5.5 DfBeta

We also asked to save DfBeta values. These values provide another indication of the influence of cases. DfBeta provides information on the change in the predicted value when the case is deleted from the model. For standardized DfBeta values, values greater than an absolute value of 2.0 should be examined more closely. Looking at the minimum and maximum DfBeta values, there are no cases suggestive of undue influence.

Statistics

		Standardized DFBETA Intercept	Standardized DFBETA GRE_Total	Standardized DFBETA UGPA
N	Valid	11	11	11
	Missing	0	0	0
Minimum		-.51278	-.75577	-.32176
Maximum		.63170	.59269	.55938

Working in **R,** we can request DfBetas from our multiple regression model using the following command, and we will name this object "Ch18_dfbeta":

```
Ch18_dfbeta <- dfbetas(GGPA_MultReg)
```

Next, we want to define the range within which there may be influence. Values outside the range of an absolute value of 2 may be influential points. We define the range of our object (i.e., "Ch18_dfbeta") to be < −2 and > 2. We will create an object from this called "Ch18_dfbetasummary."

```
Ch18_dfbetasummary <- Ch18_dfbeta < -2 | Ch18_dfbeta > 2
```

Now, all we need to do is run the *sum* function to see how many DfBeta values are outside this range, and we see there are none.

```
sum(Ch18_dfbetasummary)
```

[1] 0

FIGURE 18.26
Screening for influential points: DfBeta.

18.5.5.6 Diagnostic Plots

A number of diagnostic plots can be generated from the values we saved. For example, a plot of Cook's distance against centered leverage values provides a way to identify influential cases (i.e., cases with leverage of .50 or above and Cook's distance of 1.0 or greater). Here there are no cases that suggest undue influence.

```
plot(GGPA_MultReg)
```

The *plot* command will graph a plot of residuals to fitted values. Note that you have to hit the return key in the RStudio console to generate the plot.

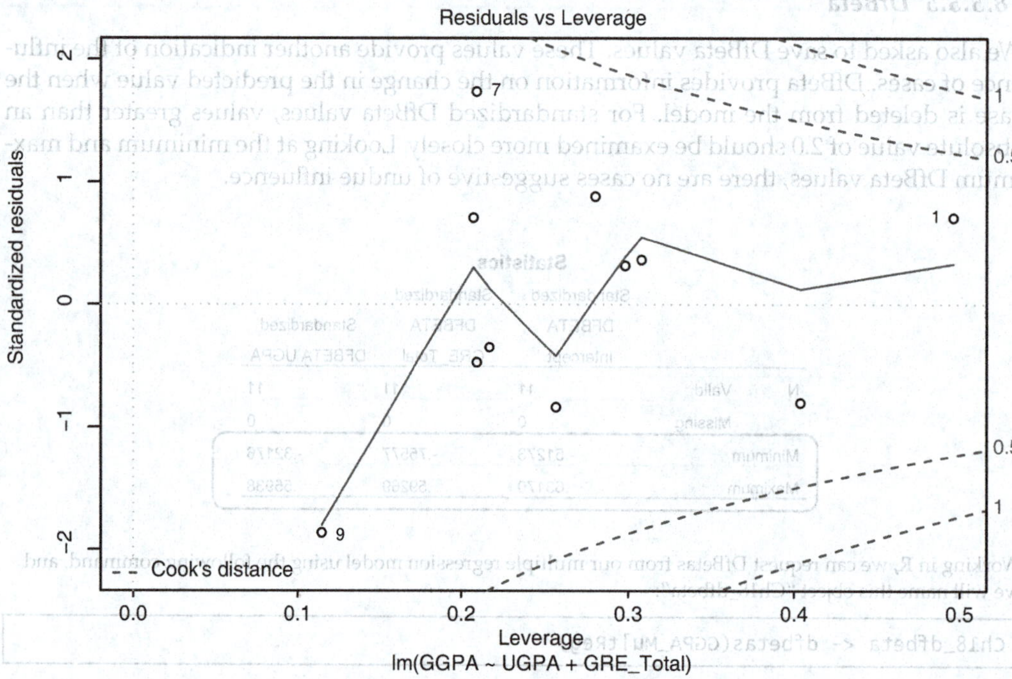


```
layout(matrix(c(1,2,3,4),2,2))
plot(GGPA_MultReg)
```

The *plot* function generates diagnostic plots, and we can use the *layout* command to plot four graphs per page.

FIGURE 18.27
Screening for influential points: diagnostic plots.

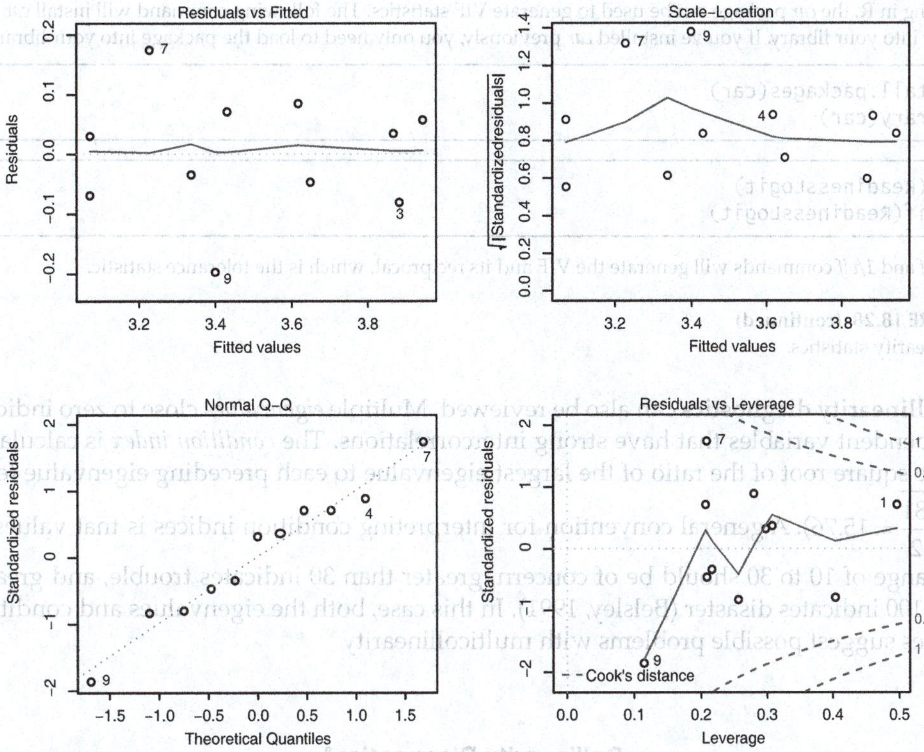

FIGURE 18.27 (continued)
Screening for influential points: diagnostic plots.

18.5.6 Noncollinearity

Detecting multicollinearity can be done by reviewing the **VIF** and **tolerance statistics.** From the table in Figure 18.28, we see tolerance and VIF values. *Tolerance* is calculated as $(1 - R^2)$ and values close to zero (a recommendation is .10 or less) suggest potential multicollinearity problems. Why? A tolerance of .10 suggests that 90% (or more) of the variance in one of the independent variables can be explained by another independent variable. *VIF* is the "variance inflation factor" and is the reciprocal of tolerance where $VIF = \frac{1}{tolerance}$. VIF values greater than 10 (which correspond to a tolerance of .10) suggest potential multicollinearity.

Collinearity Statistics	
Tolerance	VIF
.909	1.100
.909	1.100

FIGURE 18.28
Collinearity statistics.

Working in **R**, the *car* package can be used to generate VIF statistics. The following command will install *car* and load it into your library. If you've installed *car* previously, you only need to load the package into your library.

```
install.packages(car)
library(car)
```

```
vif(ReadinessLogit)
1/vif(ReadinessLogit)
```

The *vif* and *1/vif* commands will generate the VIF and its reciprocal, which is the tolerance statistic.

FIGURE 18.28 (continued)
Collinearity statistics.

Collinearity diagnostics can also be reviewed. Multiple *eigenvalues* close to zero indicate independent variables that have strong intercorrelations. The *condition index* is calculated as the square root of the ratio of the largest eigenvalue to each preceding eigenvalue (e.g., $\sqrt{\frac{2.981}{.012}} = 15.76$). A general convention for interpreting condition indices is that values in the range of 10 to 30 should be of concern, greater than 30 indicates trouble, and greater than 100 indicates disaster (Belsley, 1991). In this case, both the eigenvalues and condition indices suggest possible problems with multicollinearity.

Collinearity Diagnostics[a]

Model	Dimension	Eigenvalue	Condition Index	Variance Proportions (Constant)	GRE Total Score	Undergraduate grade point average
1	1	2.981	1.000	.00	.00	.00
	2	.012	15.727	.03	.86	.40
	3	.007	20.537	.97	.13	.60

a. Dependent Variable: Graduate grade point average

FIGURE 18.29
Collinearity diagnostics.

Noncollinearity can also be examined by computing regression models where each independent variable is considered the outcome and is predicted by the remaining independent variables (the dependent variable is not included in these models). If any of the resultant R_k^2 values are close to one (greater than .9 is a good guideline to follow), then there may be a collinearity problem. For the example data, $R_{12}^2 = .091$, and therefore collinearity is not a concern. Note that in multiple regression situations where there are two independent variables (as in this example with GRE-Total and undergraduate GPA), only one regression needs to be conducted to check for multicollinearity as the results for regressing undergraduate GPA on GRE-Total are the same as regressing GRE-Total on undergraduate GPA.

18.6 Power Using G*Power

A priori and post hoc power can be determined using the specialized software described previously in this text (e.g., G*Power), or you can consult *a priori* power tables (e.g., Cohen, 1988). As an illustration, we use G*Power to first compute the post hoc power of our test. This is followed by an illustration of how to compute *a priori* power.

18.6.1 Post Hoc Power

The first thing that must be done when using G*Power for computing post hoc power is to select the correct test family. In our case, we conducted multiple linear regression. To find regression, we select "Tests" in the top pulldown menu, then "Correlation and regression," and then "Linear multiple regression: Fixed model, R^2 deviation from zero." This will allow us to determine power for the hypothesis that the overall multiple R^2 is equal to zero (i.e., power for the overall regression model). Once that selection is made, the "Test family" automatically changes to "F test."

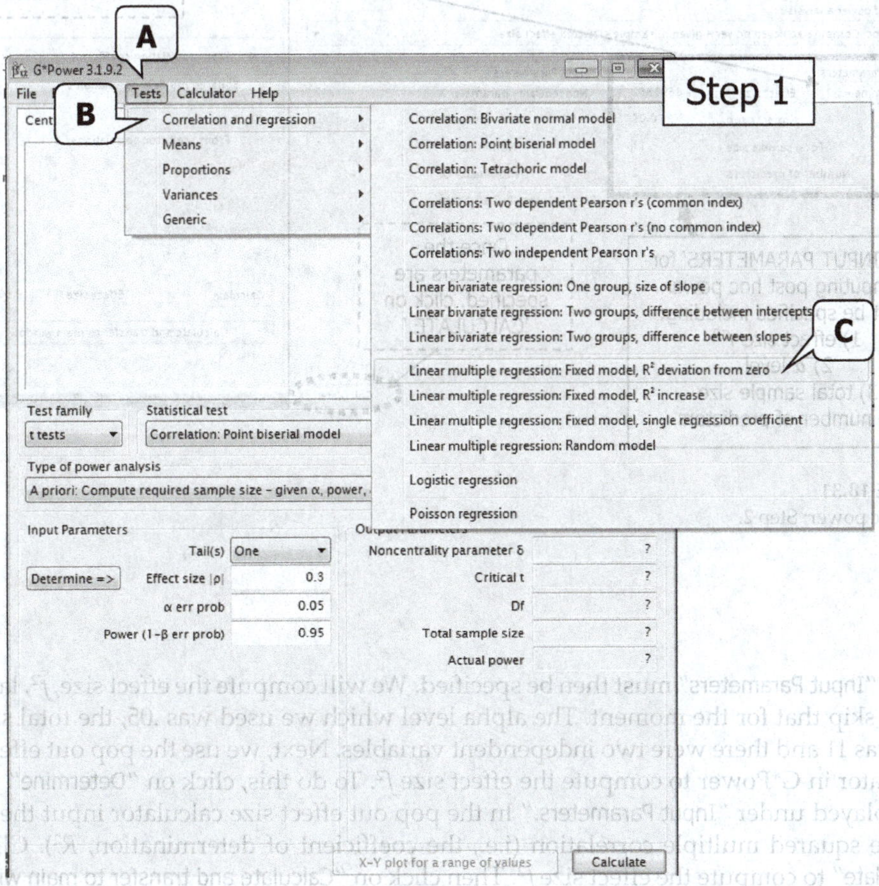

FIGURE 18.30
Post hoc power: Step 1.

The "Type of power analysis' desired needs to be selected. To compute post hoc power, select "Post hoc: Compute achieved power—given α, sample size, and effect size."

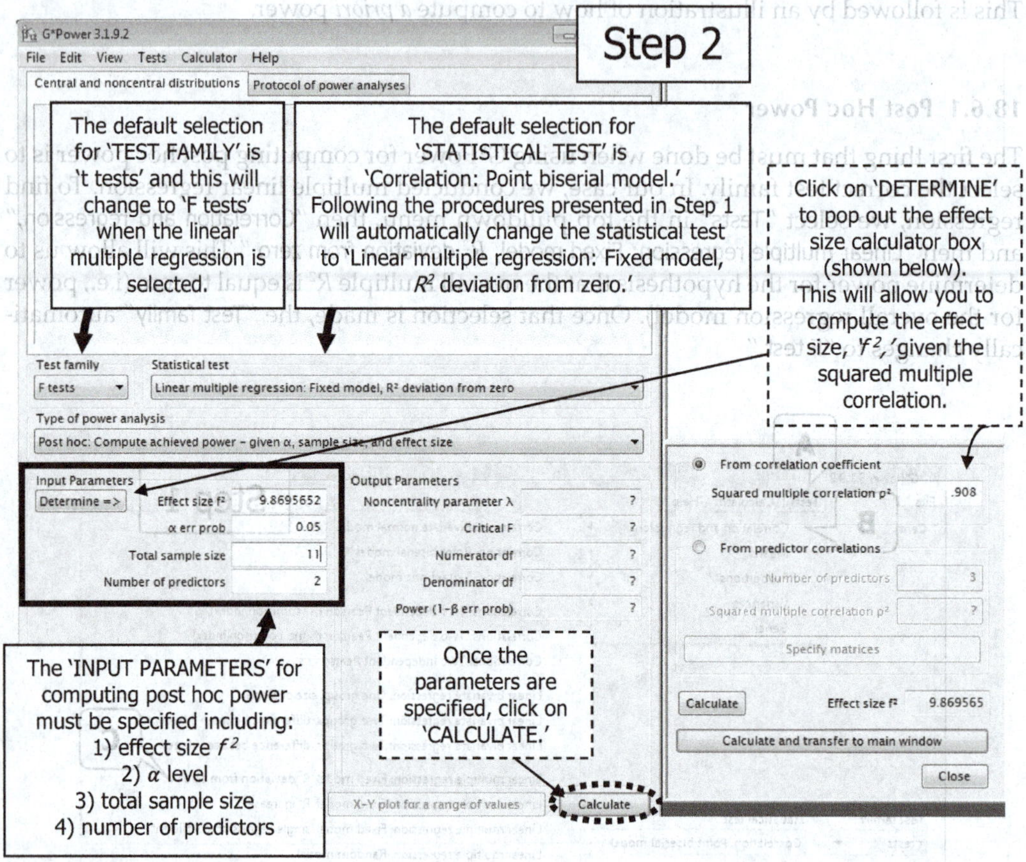

FIGURE 18.31
Post hoc power: Step 2.

The "Input Parameters" must then be specified. We will compute the effect size, f^2, last and so we skip that for the moment. The alpha level which we used was .05, the total sample size was 11 and there were two independent variables. Next, we use the pop out effect size calculator in G*Power to compute the effect size f^2. To do this, click on "Determine" which is displayed under "Input Parameters." In the pop out effect size calculator input the value for the squared multiple correlation (i.e., the coefficient of determination, R^2). Click on "Calculate" to compute the effect size f^2. Then click on "Calculate and transfer to main window" to transfer the calculated effect size (i.e., 9.8695652) to the "Input Parameters." Once the parameters are specified, click on "Calculate" to find the power statistics.

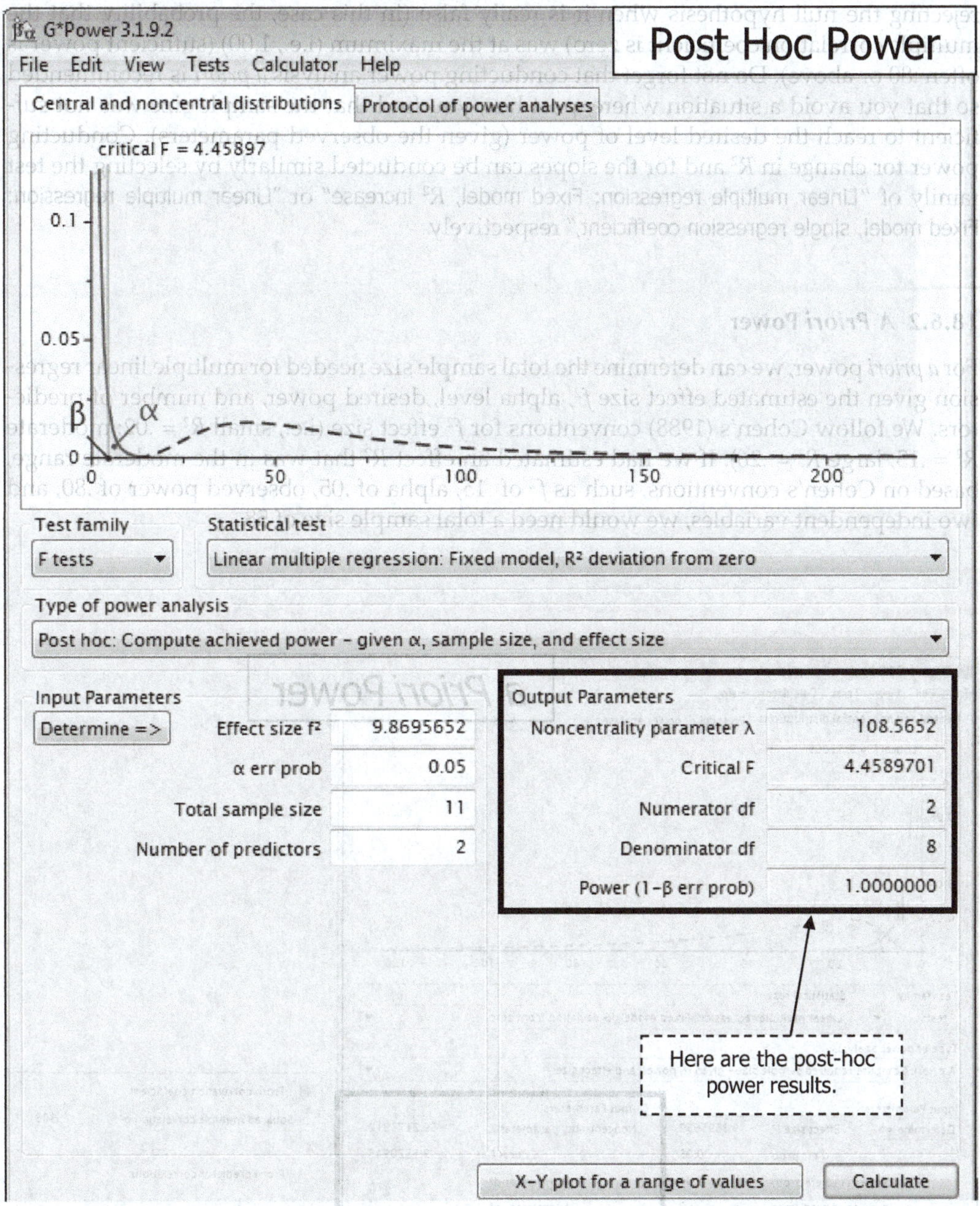

FIGURE 18.32
Post hoc power results.

The "Output Parameters" provide the relevant statistics given the input just specified. Here we were interested in determining *post hoc* power for a multiple linear regression with a computed effect size f^2 of 9.8695652, an alpha level of .05, total sample size of 11, and two predictors. Based on those criteria, the post hoc power for the overall multiple linear regression model is 1.0000. In other words, given the input parameters, the probability of rejecting the null hypothesis when it is really false (in this case, the probability that the multiple correlation coefficient is zero) was at the maximum (i.e., 1.00) (sufficient power is often .80 or above). Do not forget that conducting power analysis *a priori* is recommended so that you avoid a situation where, post hoc, you find that the sample size was not sufficient to reach the desired level of power (given the observed parameters). Conducting power for change in R^2 and for the slopes can be conducted similarly by selecting the test family of "Linear multiple regression: Fixed model, R^2 increase" or "Linear multiple regression: Fixed model, single regression coefficient," respectively.

18.6.2 *A Priori* Power

For *a priori* power, we can determine the total sample size needed for multiple linear regression given the estimated effect size f^2, alpha level, desired power, and number of predictors. We follow Cohen's (1988) conventions for f^2 effect size (i.e., small $R^2 = .02$; moderate $R^2 = .13$; large $R^2 = .26$). If we had estimated an effect R^2 that was in the moderate range, based on Cohen's conventions, such as f^2 of .15, alpha of .05, observed power of .80, and two independent variables, we would need a total sample size of 58.

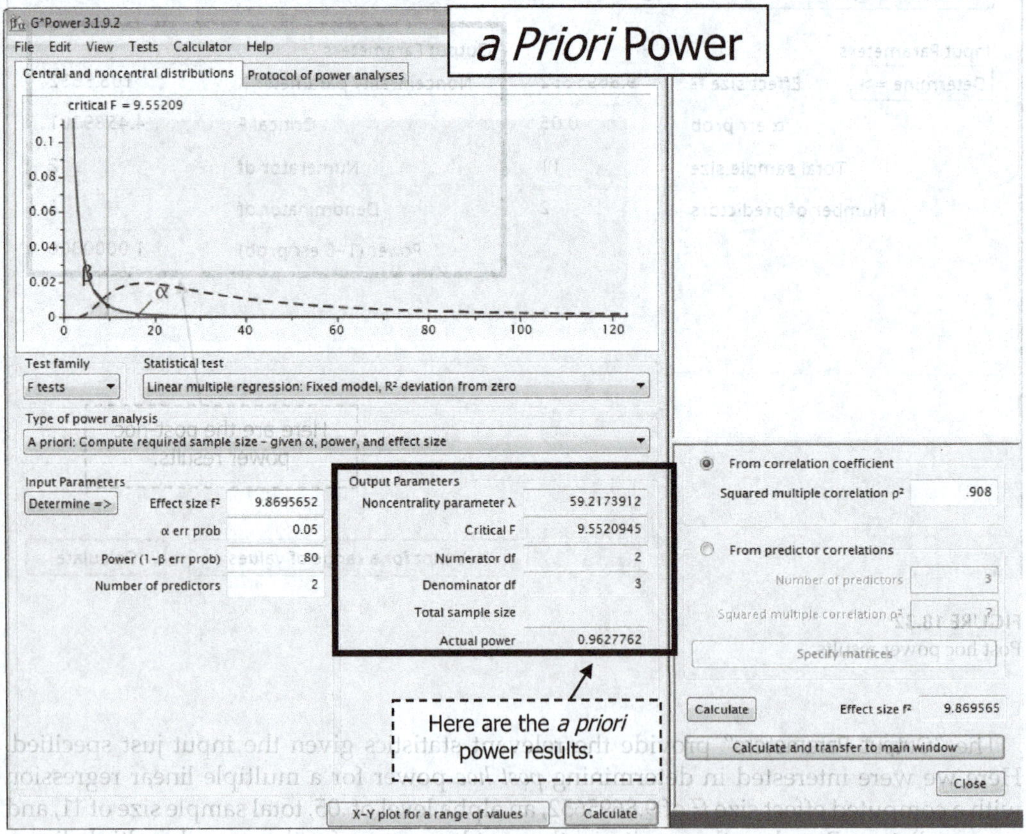

FIGURE 18.33
A priori power results

18.7 Research Question Template and Example Write-Up

Finally, here is an example write-up for the results of the multiple linear regression analysis. Recall that our graduate research assistant, Addie Venture, was assisting the assistant dean in Graduate Student Services, Dr. Golly. Dr. Golly wanted to know if graduate GPA could be predicted by the total score on the required graduate entrance exam (GRE-Total) and by undergraduate GPA. The research question presented to Dr. Golly by Addie included the following: *Can graduate GPA be predicted from the GRE-Total and undergraduate GPA?*

Addie then assisted Dr. Golly in generating a multiple linear regression as the test of inference, and a template for writing the research question for this design is presented here.

Can [dependent variable] be predicted from [list the set of independent variables]?

It may be helpful to preface the results of the multiple linear regression with information on an examination of the extent to which the assumptions were met. The assumptions include: (a) independence; (b) homoscedasticity; (c) normality; (d) linearity; (e) noncollinearity; and (f) values of *X* are fixed. Because the last assumption (fixed *X*) is based on interpretation, it will not be discussed here.

A multiple linear regression model was conducted to determine if graduate GPA (dependent variable) could be predicted from GRE-Total scores and undergraduate GPA (independent variables). The null hypotheses tested were that the multiple R^2 was equal to zero and that the regression coefficients (i.e., the slopes) were equal to zero. The data were screened for missingness and violation of assumptions prior to analysis. There were no missing data.

Linearity. Review of the partial scatterplot of the independent variables (GRE-Total and undergraduate GPA) and the dependent variable (graduate GPA) indicate linearity is a reasonable assumption. Additionally, with a random display of points falling within an absolute value of two, a scatterplot of unstandardized residuals to predicted values provided further evidence of linearity.

Normality. The assumption of normality was tested via examination of the unstandardized residuals. Review of the Shapiro-Wilk test for normality ($SW = .973$, $df = 11$, $p = .918$) and skewness (−.336) and kurtosis (.484) statistics suggested that normality was a reasonable assumption. The boxplot suggested a relatively normal distributional shape (with no outliers) of the residuals. The Q-Q plot and histogram suggested normality was reasonable. Examination of casewise diagnostics, including Mahalanobis distance, Cook's distance, DfBeta values, and centered leverage values, suggested there were no cases exerting undue influence on the model.

Independence. A relatively random display of points in the scatterplots of studentized residuals against values of the independent variables and studentized residuals against predicted values provided evidence of independence. The Durbin-Watson statistic was computed to evaluate independence of errors and was 2.116, which is considered acceptable. This suggests that the assumption of independent errors has been met.

Homoscedasticity. A relatively random display of points, where the spread of residuals appears fairly constant over the range of values of the independent variables (in the scatterplots of studentized residuals against predicted values and studentized residuals against values of the independent variables) provided evidence of homoscedasticity. The nonconstant error test was not statistically significant, $\chi^2 = .539$, $df = 1$, $p = .463$, providing further evidence that there is homogeneity of variance.

Noncollinearity. Tolerance was greater than .10 (.909) and the variance inflation factor was less than 10 (1.100), suggesting that multicollinearity was not an issue. However, the eigenvalues for the predictors were close to zero (.012 and .007) and the respective condition indices were in the range of concern (between 10 and 30, 15.727 and 20.537 respectively). A review of GRE-Total regressed on undergraduate GPA, however, produced R^2 of .091 which suggests noncollinearity. Thus, though there is some isolated cause for concern, the evidence in aggregate suggests that multicollinearity is not an issue.

Here is an example write-up of the results for the multiple linear regression (remember that this will be prefaced by the previous paragraph reporting the extent to which the assumptions of the test were met).

The results of the multiple linear regression suggest that a significant proportion of the total variation in graduate GPA was predicted by GRE-Total and undergraduate GPA, $F(2, 8) = 39.291$, $p < .001$. Additionally, we find:

a. For GRE-Total, the unstandardized partial slope (.012) and standardized partial slope (.614) are statistically significantly different from zero ($t = 5.447$, $df = 8$, $p < .001$). This indicates that with every one-point increase in the GRE-Total score, graduate GPA will increase by approximately 1/100 of one point when controlling for undergraduate GPA.

b. For undergraduate GPA, the unstandardized partial slope (.469) and standardized partial slope (.567) are statistically significantly different from zero ($t = 5.030$, $df = 8$, $p < .001$). This indicates that with every one-point increase in undergraduate GPA, graduate GPA will increase by approximately ½ of one point when controlling for GRE-Total.

c. The confidence intervals around the unstandardized partial slopes do not include zero (GRE-Total, .007, .018; undergraduate GPA, .254, .684) further confirming that these variables are statistically significant predictors of graduate GPA. Thus GRETOT and UGPA were shown to be statistically significant predictors of GGPA, both individually and collectively.

d. The intercept (or average graduate GPA when GRE-Total and undergraduate GPA is zero) was .638, not statistically significantly different from zero ($t = 1.954$, $df = 8$, $p = .087$).

e. R^2 indicates that approximately 91% of the variation in graduate GPA was predicted by the model (i.e., GRE-Total scores and undergraduate GPA). Interpreted according to Cohen (1988), this suggests a large effect. Cohen's f^2, computed as $f^2 = \frac{R^2}{1-R^2}$, was 9.87, a large effect, and represents the proportion of variation in graduate GPA uniquely explained by the model (i.e., GRE-Total scores and undergraduate GPA) to the proportion of variation in graduate GPA unexplained by the model.

f. Estimated post hoc power to predict multiple R^2 was at the maximum, 1.00.

18.8 Additional Resources

This chapter has provided a preview into conducting multiple linear regression analysis. However, there are a number of areas related to regression and various regression models that space limitations prevent us from delving into. For those of you who are interested in learning more, or if you find yourself in a sticky situation in your analyses, you may wish to look into the following, among many other excellent resources:

- General references related to regression (Olive, 2017; Welc, Esquerdo, & Springer-Link, 2018).
- Bayesian regression (Wang, Faraway, & Yue Ryan, 2018).
- Classification and regression trees (CART), random forests, bagging, boosting, and more (Berk, 2016).
- Nonlinearity in one or more independent variables (Knafl & Ding, 2016)
- Obtaining robust multicollinearity diagnostics when outliers are present (Sinan & Alkan, 2015)
- Quantile regression (Koenker, Chernozhukov, He, & Peng, 2017)
- Regression discontinuity (Hausman & Rapson, 2017; Lee, 2016) and extension of RDD to regression kink design (Card, Lee, Pei, & Weber, 2016)
- Transformations and weighting with heteroscedastic data (Ruppert, 2014)

Problems

Conceptual Problems

1. The correlation of salary and cumulative grade point average controlling for socioeconomic status is an example of which one of the following?
   a. Bivariate correlation
   b. Partial correlation
   c. Regression correlation
   d. Semipartial correlation
2. The most accurate predictions are made when the standard error of estimate equals which one of the following?
   a. $\bar{Y}$
   b. s_Y
   c. 0
   d. 1
3. True or false? The intercept can take on a positive value only.
4. True or false? Adding an additional predictor to a regression equation will necessarily result in an increase in R^2.
5. True or false? The best prediction in multiple regression analysis will result when each predictor has a high correlation with the other predictor variables and a high correlation with the dependent variable.

6. Consider the following two situations:

   Situation 1: $r_{Y1} = .6 \quad r_{Y2} = .5 \quad r_{12} = .0$

   Situation 2: $r_{Y1} = .6 \quad r_{Y2} = .5 \quad r_{12} = .2$

   I assert that the value of R^2 will be greater in Situation 2. Am I correct?
7. Values of variables X_1, X_2, and X_3 are available for a sample of 50 students. The value of $r_{12} = .6$. I assert that if the partial correlation $r_{12.3}$ were calculated it would be larger than .6. Am I correct?
8. A researcher is building a regression model. There is theory to suggest that science ability can be predicted by literacy skills when controlling for child characteristics (e.g., age and socioeconomic status). Which one of the following variable selection procedures is suggested?
   a. Backward elimination
   b. Forward selection
   c. Hierarchical regression
   d. Stepwise selection
9. I assert that the forward selection, backward elimination, and stepwise regression methods will always arrive at the same final model, given the same dataset and level of significance? Am I correct?
10. I assert the R^2_{adj} will always be larger for the model with the most predictors. Am I correct?
11. True or false? In a two-predictor regression model, if the correlation among the predictors is .95 and VIF is 20, then we should be concerned about collinearity.
12. A researcher is examining how weight is related to age and number of hours exercised per week. The researcher wishes to remove the influence of age from the number of hours exercised per week but not from weight. Which coefficient should the researcher compute?
   a. Bivariate correlation
   b. Partial correlation
   c. Regression correlation
   d. Semipartial correlation
13. Which of the following types of evidence are appropriate for examining the extent to which the assumption of normality has been met?
   a. Maximum value of Cook's distance
   b. Scatterplot of studentized residuals and unstandardized predicted values
   c. Shapiro-Wilk test
   d. Variance inflation factor value
14. A researcher is computing a multiple linear regression model and is interested in including a nominal variable that has four categories. How do you suggest the researcher pursue this?
   a. Create dummy variables and include all four of the dummy variables.
   b. Create dummy variables and include three of the four dummy variables.
   c. Include the nominal variable in the model as is.
   d. Exclude the nominal variable as multiple linear regression cannot deal with variables of this measurement scale.

Answers to Conceptual Problems

1. b (partial correlations correlate two variables while holding constant a third.)
3. **False** (the intercept can be any value.)
5. **False** (best prediction is when there is a high correlation of the predictors with the dependent variable and low correlations among the predictors.)
7. **No** (the partial correlation may be larger than, the same as, or smaller than .6.)
9. **No** (as discussed, these methods may yield different final models.)
11. **True** (that is precisely the situation when we should be very concerned about collinearity.)
13. c (the Shapiro-Wilk test of normality is one of several types of normality evidence that can be used to examine residuals for meeting the assumption of normality.)

Computational Problems

1. You are given the following data, where X_1 (hours of professional development) and X_2 (aptitude test scores) are used to predict Y (annual salary in thousands):

Y	X_1	X_2
40	100	10
50	200	20
50	300	10
70	400	30
65	500	20
65	600	20
80	700	30

Determine the following values: intercept; b_1, b_2, SS_{res}; SS_{reg}; F; s^2_{res}; $s(b_1)$; $s(b_2)$; t_1; t_2.

2. You are given the following data, where X_1 (final percentage in science class) and X_2 (number of absences) are used to predict Y (standardized science test score in third grade):

Y	X_1	X_2
300	65	7
480	98	0
350	70	3
420	80	2
400	82	0
335	70	3
370	75	4
390	80	1
485	99	0
415	95	2
375	88	3

Determine the following values: intercept; b_1, b_2, SS_{res}; SS_{reg}; F; s^2_{res}; $s(b_1)$; $s(b_2)$; t_1; t_2.

3. Complete the missing information for this regression model ($df = 23$).

Y'	=	25.1	+	$1.2\,X_1$	+	$1.0\,X_2$	−	$.50\,X_3$	
		(2.1)		(1.5)		(1.3)		(.06)	standard errors
		(11.9)		( )		( )		( )	*t* ratios
				( )		( )		( )	Significant at .05?

4. Consider a sample of elementary school children. Given that r(strength, weight) = .6, r(strength, age) = .7, and r(weight, age) = .8, what is the first-order partial correlation coefficient between strength and weight holding age constant?

5. For a sample of 100 adults, you are given that $r_{12} = .55$, $r_{13} = .80$, and $r_{23} = .70$. What is the value of $r_{1(2.3)}$?

6. A researcher would like to predict salary from a set of four predictor variables for a sample of 45 subjects. Multiple linear regression analysis was utilized. Complete the following summary table ($\alpha = .05$) for the test of significance of the overall regression model:

Source	SS	df	MS	F	Critical Value and Decision
Regression	–	–	20	–	
Residual	400	–	–		
Total	–	–			

7. Calculate the partial correlation $r_{12.3}$ and the part correlation $r_{1(2.3)}$ from the following bivariate correlations: $r_{12} = .5$, $r_{13} = .8$, $r_{23} = .9$.

8. Calculate the partial correlation $r_{13.2}$ and the part correlation $r_{1(3.2)}$ from the following bivariate correlations: $r_{12} = .21$, $r_{13} = .40$, $r_{23} = -.38$.

9. You are given the following data, where X_1 (verbal aptitude) and X_2 (prior reading achievement) are to be used to predict Y (reading achievement):

Y	X_1	X_2
2	2	5
1	2	4
1	1	5
1	1	3
5	3	6
4	4	4
7	5	6
6	5	4
7	7	3
8	6	3
3	4	3
3	3	6
6	6	9
6	6	8
10	8	9

Y	X_1	X_2
9	9	6
6	10	4
6	9	5
9	4	8
10	4	9

Determine the following values: intercept; b_1, b_2, SS_{res}; SS_{reg}; F; s^2_{res}; $s(b_1)$; $s(b_2)$; t_1; t_2.

10. You are given the following data, where X_1 (years of teaching experience) and X_2 (salary in thousands) are to be used to predict Y (morale):

Y	X_1	X_2
125	1	24
130	2	30
145	3	32
115	2	28
170	6	40
180	7	38
165	5	48
150	4	42
195	9	56
180	10	52
120	2	33
190	8	50
170	7	49
175	9	53
160	6	49

Determine the following values: intercept; b_1, b_2, SS_{res}; SS_{reg}; F; s^2_{res}, $s(b_1)$; $s(b_2)$; t_1; t_2.

11. A researcher has conducted a multiple linear regression. The maximum value for Mahalanobis distance in their model is 8.26. They have tested at alpha of .05 and have three independent variables and one dependent variable. Given this scenario, do the researchers have cause for concern for possible outliers?

Answers to Computational Problems

1. intercept = 28.0952, b_1 = .0381, b_2 = .8333, SS_{res} = 21.4294, SS_{reg} = 1,128.5706, F = 105.3292 (reject at .01), s^2_{res} = 5.3574, $s(b_1)$ = .0058, $s(b_2)$ = .1545, t_1 = 6.5343 (reject at .01), t_2 = 5.3923 (reject at .01).

3. in order, the t values are 0.8 (not significant), 0.77 (not significant), −8.33 (significant).

5. $r_{1(2.3)}$ = −.0140.

7. $r_{12.3}$ = −.8412, $r_{1(2.3)}$ = −.5047.

9. intercept = −1.2360, b_1 = .6737, b_2 = .6184, SS_{res} = 58.3275, SS_{reg} = 106.6725, F = 15.5453 (reject at .05), s^2_{res} = 3.4310, $s(b_1)$ = .1611, $s(b_2)$ = .2030, t_1 = 4.1819 (reject at .05), t_2 = 3.0463 (reject at .05).

11. Given alpha of .05, three independent variables and one dependent variable, there are four degrees of freedom. This results in a chi-square critical value of 9.49. Any Mahalanobis distance value would need to be *greater* than 9.49 to raise concern. Thus, with the maximum value of Mahalanobis distance in their model being 8.26, the researchers do *not* have cause for concern for possible outliers.

Interpretive Problems

1. Using SPSS or **R**, develop a multiple regression model with data supplied for other chapters in this textbook. Write up your results, including interpretation of effect size and testing of assumptions.
2. Use SPSS or **R** to develop a multiple regression model with data available on the textbook's website from the 2017 IPEDS (https://nces.ed.gov/ipeds/). Select one continuous variable as the dependent variable [e.g., 12-month instructional activity credit hours: undergraduates (CDACTUA)] and find at least two strong predictors from among the remaining variables in the dataset. Write up the results in APA style, including testing for the assumptions. Determine and interpret a measure of effect size.
3. Use SPSS or **R** to develop a logistic regression model with data available on the textbook's website from the 2017 NHIS* family file (https://www.cdc.gov/nchs/nhis/). Select one binary variable as the dependent variable [e.g., "# family members receiving Women, Infants, Children (WIC) benefits" (FWICCT)] and find at least two strong predictors from among the remaining variables in the dataset. Write up the results in APA style, including testing for the assumptions. Determine and interpret a measure of effect size.

* It is important to note that we are using only one data file from the NHIS *and* the NHIS is a *complex sample* (i.e., not a simple random sample). Per NHIS (see https://www.cdc.gov/nchs/nhis/about_nhis.htm#sample_design), "The sampling plan follows a multistage area probability design that permits the representative sampling of households and non-institutional group quarters (e.g., college dormitories)… The current sampling plan was implemented in 2016… [It] is a sample of clusters of addresses that are located in primary sampling units (PSU's). A PSU consists of a county, a small group of contiguous counties, or a metropolitan statistical area." In the NHIS dataset, you will find, for example, a "weight" variable, which is used to adjust for the complex survey design. We won't get into the technical aspects of this, but when the data are analyzed to adjust for the sampling design (including nonsimple random sampling procedure and disproportionate sampling) the end results are then representative of the intended population. The purpose of the text is not to serve as a primer for understanding complex samples, and thus readers interested in learning more about complex survey designs are referred to any number of excellent resources (Hahs-Vaughn, 2005; Hahs-Vaughn, McWayne, Bulotskey-Shearer, Wen, & Faria, 2011a, 2011b; Lee, Forthofer, & Lorimor, 1989; Skinner, Holt, & Smith, 1989). Additionally, so as to not complicate matters any more than necessary, the applications in the textbook do not illustrate how to adjust for the complex sample design. *As such, if you do not adjust for the complex sampling design, the results that you see should not be interpreted to represent any larger population but only that select sample of individuals who actually completed the survey.* I want to stress that the reason why the sampling design has not been illustrated in the

textbook applications is because the point of this section of the textbook is to illustrate how to use statistical software to generate various procedures and how to interpret the output, and not to ensure the results are representative of the intended population. *Please do not let this discount or diminish the need to apply this critical step in your own analyses when using complex survey data as quite a large body of research exists that describes the importance of effectively analyzing complex samples as well as provides evidence of biased results when the complex sample design is not addressed in the analyses* (Hahs-Vaughn, 2005, 2006a, 2006b; Hahs-Vaughn et al., 2011a, 2011b; Kish & Frankel, 1973, 1974; Korn & Graubard, 1995; Lee et al., 1989; Lumley, 2004; Pfeffermann, 1993; Skinner et al., 1989).

19

Logistic Regression

Chapter Outline

Key Concepts

1. Logit
2. Odds
3. Odds ratio

In the previous chapter we examined ordinary least squares (OLS) regression—multiple regression models—that allow us to examine the relationship between one or more predictors when the outcome is continuous. In this chapter, we are introduced to logistic regression, which can also be used when the outcome is categorical and that allows model prediction. Logistic regression and discriminant analysis (which is discussed in an upcoming chapter) share similarities, and there can be confusion on when one is more appropriate than the other. Understanding that you may not be fully familiar with discriminant analysis, we'll offer the condensed version of how the two procedures contrast. The assumptions of multivariate normality and equal variance-covariance matrices, which are required in discriminant analysis, do not hold for logistic regression. Thus, logistic regression is more robust than discriminant analysis when these assumptions are not met. Additionally, logistic regression is oftentimes less interpretatively challenging than discriminant analysis given that it falls within the regression family, more common to many researchers as compared to discriminant analysis.

For the purposes of this chapter, we will concentrate on binary logistic regression which is used when the outcome has only two categories (i.e., dichotomous, binary, or sometimes referred to as a Bernoulli outcome). The logistic regression procedure appropriate for more than two categories is called multinomial (or polytomous) logistic regression. Readers interested in learning more about multinomial logistic regression will be provided some additional references later in this chapter. Also in this chapter we discuss methods that can be used to enter predictors in logistic regression models. Our objectives are by the end of this chapter you will be able to: (a) understand the concepts underlying logistic regression, (b) determine and interpret the results of logistic regression, (c) understand and evaluate the assumptions of logistic regression, and (d) have a basic understanding of methods of entering the covariates.

19.1 What Logistic Regression Is and How It Works

Oso Wyse, one of the four amazingly talented statistical gurus in the statistics and research lab, has just had a conversation with his faculty advisor. He finds himself embarking on a challenging statistical project.

Oso Wyse finds himself on his final statistical expedition as a graduate research assistant in the stats and research lab. After introduction from his faculty advisor, Oso meets with Dr. Malani, a faculty member in the early childhood department. Dr. Malani has collected data on children who will be entering kindergarten in the fall. Interested in kindergarten readiness issues, Dr. Malani wants to know if scores from a teacher observation scale for social development and family structure (single family versus two-family home) can predict whether children are prepared or unprepared to enter kindergarten. Oso suggests the following research question to Dr. Malani: *Can kindergarten readiness (prepared vs. unprepared) be predicted by social development and family structure (single family vs. two-family home)?* Given that the outcome is dichotomous, Oso determines that binary logistic regression is the appropriate statistical procedure to use to answer Dr. Malani's question. Oso then proceeds with assisting Dr. Malani in analyzing the data.

If the dependent variable is binary (i.e., dichotomous or having only two categories), then ordinary least squares (OLS) regression, described earlier in this text, is inappropriate. Although OLS regression can easily accommodate dichotomous independent variables through dummy coding (i.e., assignment of 1 and 0 to the categories where "1" is traditionally coded as the category of interest, i.e., case outcome; "0" is traditionally coded as the non-case outcome or reference category), it is an entirely different case when the *outcome* is dichotomous. Applying OLS regression to a binary outcome creates problems. For example, a dichotomous outcome violates normality and homogeneity assumptions in OLS regression. In addition, OLS estimates are based on linear relationships between the independent and dependent variables, and forcing a linear relationship (as seen in Figure 19.1) in the case of a binary outcome is erroneous [although we found at least one author (Hellevik, 2009) who argues that OLS regression can be used with dichotomous outcomes]. As seen in this figure, there is obviously not a linear relationship between age at kindergarten entry and reading proficiency (i.e., proficient or not proficient).

As part of the regression family, logistic regression still allows a prediction to be made; however, now the prediction is whether or not the unit under investigation falls into one of the two categories of the dependent variable. Initially used mostly in the hard sciences, this method has become more broadly popular as there are many situations where researchers want to examine outcomes that are discrete, rather than continuous, in nature. Some examples of dichotomous dependent variables are pass/fail, surviving surgery/not, admit/reject, vote for/against, employ/not, win/lose, or purchase/not. Logistic regression has been applied in a wide variety of situations. As just a few examples, Mehta and colleagues examined public housing and rental assistance and its relationship to asthma (Mehta, Dooley, Kane, Reid, & Shah, 2018). Berg and Brännström (2018) used logistic regression

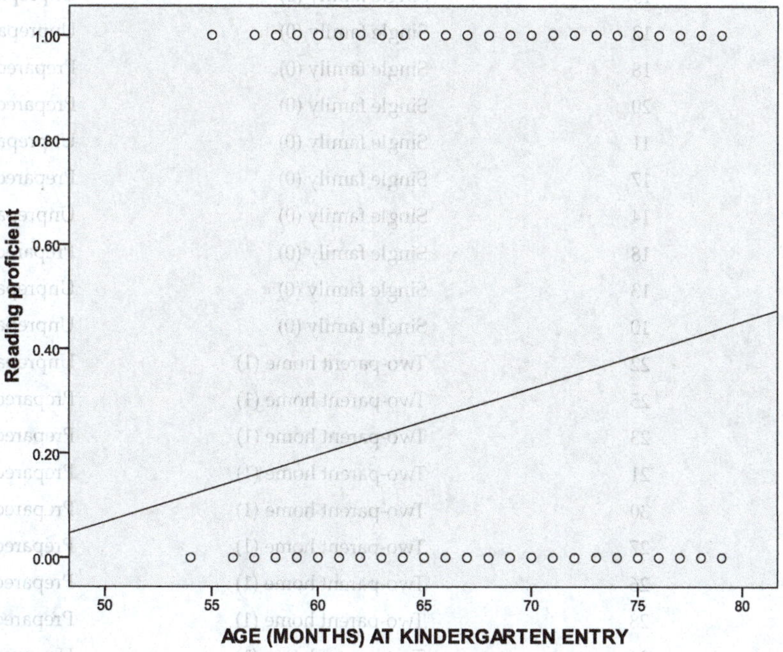

FIGURE 19.1
Nonlinearity of binary outcome.

to model the extent to which children who were evicted were then placed in out-of-home care. McGrath and colleagues (McGrath, Hall, Peterson, Kraemer, & Vincent, 2017) used logistic regression to determine whether muscle strength can protect against development of osteoporosis. Cox et al (2016) predicted the likelihood of college graduation based on factors outside of academics using logistic regression.

The idea of using a dichotomous variable was introduced in Chapter 18 on multiple regression as the concept of a *dummy variable*, where the first condition is indicated by a value of 1 (e.g., prepared for kindergarten), whereas a value of 0 indicates the opposite condition (e.g., unprepared for kindergarten). Understanding the coding of 0 and 1 is very important for interpretation purposes. Again, "1" is traditionally the case outcome (with results interpreted in terms of cases) and "0" the non-case or reference category. For the purposes of this text, our discussion will concentrate on dichotomous outcomes where logistic regression is appropriate (i.e., binary logistic regression, referred to throughout this chapter simply as logistic regression). Conditions for which there are more than two possible categories for the dependent variable (e.g., three categories, such as "above satisfactory performance," "satisfactory performance," and "below satisfactory performance"), multinomial logistic regression may be appropriate. An example of the data structure for a logistic regression model with a binary outcome (prepared vs. unprepared for kindergarten), one continuous predictor (social development) and one dichotomous dummy coded predictor (family structure: single parent vs. two-parent home) is presented in Table 19.1.

TABLE 19.1
Kindergarten Readiness Example Data

Child	Social Development (X_1)	Family Structure (X_2)	Kindergarten Readiness (Y)
1	15	Single family (0)	Unprepared (0)
2	12	Single family (0)	Unprepared (0)
3	18	Single family (0)	Prepared (1)
4	20	Single family (0)	Prepared (1)
5	11	Single family (0)	Unprepared (0)
6	17	Single family (0)	Prepared (1)
7	14	Single family (0)	Unprepared (0)
8	18	Single family (0)	Prepared (1)
9	13	Single family (0)	Unprepared (0)
10	10	Single family (0)	Unprepared (0)
11	22	Two-parent home (1)	Unprepared (0)
12	25	Two-parent home (1)	Prepared (1)
13	23	Two-parent home (1)	Prepared (1)
14	21	Two-parent home (1)	Prepared (1)
15	30	Two-parent home (1)	Prepared (1)
16	27	Two-parent home (1)	Prepared (1)
17	26	Two-parent home (1)	Prepared (1)
18	28	Two-parent home (1)	Prepared (1)
19	24	Two-parent home (1)	Unprepared (0)
20	30	Two-parent home (1)	Prepared (1)

19.1.1 Characteristics

19.1.1.1 Logistic Regression Equation

As we learned previously with ordinary least squares regression, knowledge of the independent variable(s) provides the information necessary to be able to estimate a precise numerical value of the dependent variable, a predicted value. The following formula recaps the sample multiple regression equation where Y is the predicted outcome for individual i based on: (a) the Y intercept, a, the value of Y when all predictor values are zero; (b) the product of the value of the independent variables, X's, and the regression coefficients, b_k; and (c) the residual, ε_i:

$$Y_i = a + b_1 X_1 + \ldots + b_m X_m + \varepsilon_i$$

As we see, the logistic regression equation is similar in concept to simple and multiple linear regression, but operates much differently. In logistic regression, the binary dependent variable is transformed into a logit variable (which is the natural log of the odds of the dependent variable occurring or not occurring) and the parameters are then estimated using maximum likelihood. The end result is that the odds of an event occurring are estimated through the logistic regression model (whereas OLS estimates a precise numerical value of the dependent variable).

To understand how the logistic regression equation operates, there are three primary computational concepts that must be understood: probability, odds, and the logit. These express the same thing, only in different ways (Menard, 2000). Let us first consider probability.

19.1.1.2 Probability

The overarching difference between OLS regression (i.e., simple and multiple linear regression that we've been learning about) and logistic regression is the measurement scale of the outcome. With OLS regression, our outcome is continuous in scale (i.e., interval or ratio measurement scale). In binary logistic regression, our outcome is dichotomous—one of two categories. Let us use kindergarten readiness ("prepared for kindergarten" coded as "1" vs. "unprepared" coded as "0") as an example of our logistic regression outcome. Therefore, what the regression equation allows us to predict is substantially different for OLS as compared to logistic regression. In comparison to OLS, which allows us to compute a precise numerical value (e.g., a specific predicted score for the dependent variable), the logistic regression equation allows us to compute a *probability*—more specifically, the *probability* that the dependent variable will occur. The logistic regression equation, therefore, generates predicted probabilities that fall between values of 0 and 1. The probability of a case or unit being classified into the lowest numerical category [i.e., $P(Y = 0)$ or, in the case of our example, the probability that a child will be "unprepared"' for kindergarten] is equal to 1 minus the probability that it falls within the highest numerical category [i.e., $P(Y = 1)$ or the probability that a child will be 'prepared' for kindergarten]. This equates to $P(Y = 0) = 1 - P(Y = 1)$. Applied to our example, the probability that a child will be unprepared for kindergarten is equal to one minus the probability that a child will be prepared for kindergarten. In other words, the knowledge of the probability of one category occurring (e.g., unprepared for kindergarten) allows us to easily determine the probability that the other category will occur (e.g., prepared) as the total probability must equal 1.0. Remember, however, that probabilities have to fall within the range of 0 to 1. As we know, it is not possible to have a negative probability, nor is it possible to have a probability greater than 1 (i.e., greater than 100%). If we try to model the probability as the dependent variable in our OLS equation, it is mathematically possible that the predicted values would be negative or greater than 1—values that are outside the range of what is feasible when considering probabilities. Therefore, this is where our logistic regression equation takes a turn from what we learned with linear regression.

19.1.1.3 Odds and Logit (or Log Odds)

So far, we have talked about the outcome of our logistic regression equation as being a probability, and we also know that predicted probabilities must be between 0 and 1. As we think about how to estimate probabilities, we will see that this takes a few steps to achieve. Rather than the dependent variable being a probability, if it were an *odds value*, then values greater than 1 would be possible and appropriate. **Odds** are simply the ratio of the probability of the dependent variable's two outcomes. The odds that the outcome of a binary variable is 1 (i.e., public school attendance) rather than 0 (or private school attendance), is simply the ratio of the odds that Y equals 1 to the odds that Y does not equal 1. In mathematical terms, this can be written as follows:

$$Odds\,(Y=1)=\frac{P(Y=1)}{1-P(Y=1)}$$

As we see in Table 19.2, when the probability that $Y = 1$ (e.g., prepared for kindergarten) equals .50 (column 1 in Table 19.2), then $1 - P(Y = 1)$ (or unprepared for kindergarten) is .50 (column 2) and the odds are equal to 1.00 (column 3). When the probability of $Y = 1$ (e.g., prepared) is very small (say, .100 or less), then the odds for being prepared for kindergarten are also very small and approach zero (i.e., the smaller the probability that a child is prepared for kindergarten). However, as the probability of $Y = 1$ (e.g., being prepared for kindergarten) increases, the odds (column 3) increase tremendously. Thus, the

TABLE 19.2
Illustration of Logged Odds

$P(Y = 1)$	$1 - P(Y = 1)$	$Odds(Y=1)=\frac{P(Y=1)}{1-P(Y=1)}$	$\ln[Odds(Y=1)]=\ln\left[\frac{P(Y=1)}{1-P(Y=1)}\right]=Logit(Y)$
.001	.999	.001/.999 = .001	*ln*(.001) = −6.908
.100	.900	.100/.900 = .111	*ln*(.111) = −2.198
.300	.700	.300/.700 = .429	*ln*(.429) = −.846
.500	.500	.500/.500 = 1.000	*ln*(1.000) = 0.000
.700	.300	.700/.300 = 2.333	*ln*(2.333) = .847
.900	.100	.900/.100 = 9.000	*ln*(9.000) = 2.197
.999	.001	.999/.001 = 999.000	*ln*(999) = 6.907

issue that we are faced with when using odds is that while odds can be infinitely large, we are still limited in that the minimum value is zero and we still do not have data that can be modeled linearly. When $P(Y = 1) < .5$, the slope below an odds of 1.0 is very steep; yet when $P(Y = 1) > .5$, the slope above odds of 1.0 is much more gradual. It might also be worth noting at this point that the reciprocal odds have the same magnitude of effect but are asymmetrical, and the natural log functions to create a symmetrical outcome variable.

Changing the scale of the odds by taking the natural logarithm of the odds (also called *logit Y* or *log odds*) provides us with a value of the dependent variable that can theoretically range from negative infinity to positive infinity. Thus, taking the log odds of *Y* creates a linear relationship between *X* and the probability of *Y* (Pampel, 2000). The natural log of the odds is calculated as follows, with the residual being the difference between the predicted probability and the actual value of the dependent variable (0 or 1):

$$ln\left[\frac{P(Y=1)}{1-P(Y=1)}\right] = Logit(Y)$$

In column 4 of Table 19.2, we see what happens when the logit transformation is made. As the odds increase from 1 to positive infinity, the logit (or log odds) of *Y* becomes larger and larger (and remains positive). As the odds decrease from 1 to 0, the logit (or log odds) of *Y* is negative and grows larger and larger (in absolute value).

The logit of *Y* equation is interpreted very similarly to that of OLS. For each one-unit change in the independent variable, the logistic regression coefficients represent the change in the predicted log odds of being in a category. In comparison to OLS regression, the regression coefficients have the exact same interpretation. The difference in interpretation with logistic regression is that the outcome now represents a *log odds* rather than a precise numerical value as we saw with OLS regression. Linking the logit back to probabilities, a one-unit change in the logit equals a bigger change in probabilities that are near the center as compared to the extreme values. This happens because of the linearization once we take the natural log. Taking the natural log stretches the *S*-shaped curve into a linear form; thus, the values at the extreme are stretched less, so to speak, as compared to the values in the middle (Pampel, 2000). By working with log odds, our familiar additive regression equation is applicable:

$$ln\left[\frac{P(Y=1)}{1-P(Y=1)}\right] = Logit(Y) = a + \beta_1 X_1 + \beta_2 X_2 + \ldots + \beta_m X_m$$

It is important to note that although we were accustomed to examining standardized regression coefficients in OLS regression, it is not the norm that standardized coefficients are computed for logistic regression models by statistical software. Standardization is ordinarily accomplished by taking the product of the unstandardized regression coefficient and the ratio of the standard deviation of *X* to the standard deviation of *Y*. The interpretation of a standard deviation change in a continuous variable thus makes sense; however, this is not the case for a dichotomous variable, nor is it the case for the log odds (which is the predicted outcome and which does not have a standard deviation).

While interpretation of the logistic equation is relatively straightforward as it holds many similarities to OLS regression, log odds are not a metric that we use often. Therefore, understanding what it means when a predictor, *X*, has some effect on the log odds, *Y*, can be difficult. This is where odds come back into the picture.

If we exponentiate the logit (*Y*) (i.e., the outcome of our logistic regression equation), then it converts back to the odds (see the following equation). Now we can interpret the independent variables as affecting the odds (rather than log odds) of the outcome:

$$Odds(Y=1) = e^{logit(Y)} = e^{ln[Odds(Y=1)]} = e^{\alpha+\beta_1 X_1+\beta_2 X_2+\ldots+\beta_m X_m} = \left(e^{\alpha}\right)\left(e^{\beta_1 X_1}\right)\left(e^{\beta_2 X_2}\right)\ldots\left(e^{\beta_m X_m}\right)$$

As can be seen here, the exponentiation creates an equation that is multiplicative rather than additive, and this then changes the interpretation of the exponentiated coefficients. In previous regression equations we have studied, when the product of the regression coefficient and its predictor is zero, that variable adds nothing to the prediction of the dependent variable. In a multiplicative environment, a value of zero corresponds to a coefficient of 1. In other words, a coefficient of 1 will not change the value of the odds (i.e., the outcome). Coefficients greater than 1 increase the odds, and coefficients less than 1 decrease the odds. In addition, the odds will change more the greater the distance the value is from 1.

Converting the odds back to a probability can be done through the following formula:

$$P(Y=1) \frac{Odds(Y=1)}{1+Odds(Y=1)} = \frac{e^{\alpha+\beta_1 X_1+\beta_2 X_2+\ldots+\beta_m X_m}}{1+e^{\alpha+\beta_1 X_1+\beta_2 X_2+\ldots+\beta_m X_m}}$$

Probability values close to one indicate increased likelihood of occurrence. In our example, since "1" indicates kindergarten preparedness, a probability close to one would indicate a child was more likely to be prepared for kindergarten. Children with probabilities close to zero suggest a decreased probability of being prepared for kindergarten (and increased probability of not being prepared for kindergarten).

19.1.1.4 Estimation and Model Fit

Now that we understand the logistic regression process and resulting equations a bit better, it is time to turn our attention to how the equation is estimated and how we can determine how well the model fits. We previously learned with multiple regression that the data from the observed values of the independent variables in the sample were used to estimate or predict the values of the dependent variable. In logistic regression, we are also using the knowledge of the values of our predictor(s) to estimate the outcome (i.e., log odds). Now we are using a method called *maximum likelihood estimation* to estimate the values of the parameters (i.e., the logistic coefficients). As we just learned, the dependent variable in a logistic regression model is transformed into a logit value, which is the natural log of the odds of the dependent variable occurring or not occurring. Maximum likelihood estimation is then applied to the model and estimates the odds of occurrence after transformation into the logit. The "likelihood" in maximum likelihood refers to the likelihood of the data occurring given a specific value for population parameters that have been assumed. It is the probability of the data contingent upon a parameter-estimate that is being maximized. Whereas in OLS the sum of squared distance of the observed data to the regression line was minimized, in maximum likelihood the log likelihood is maximized.

The log of the likelihood function (sometimes abbreviated as *LL*) that results from ML estimation then reflects the likelihood of observing the sample statistics given the population parameters. The log likelihood provides an index of how much has not been explained in the model after the parameters have been estimated, and as such, the *LL* can be used as an indicator of model fit. The values of the log likelihood function vary from zero to negative infinity, with values closer to zero suggesting better model fit and larger values (in absolute value terms) indicating poorer fit. The log likelihood value will approach zero the closer the likelihood value is to one. When this happens, this suggests the observed data could be generated from these population parameters. In other words, the smaller the log likelihood, the better the model fit. It follows therefore, that the log likelihood value will grow more negative the closer the likelihood function is to zero. This suggests that the observed data are *less* likely to be generated from these population parameters.

Maximum likelihood estimation performed by statistical software usually begins the estimation process with all regression coefficients equal to the most conservative estimate (i.e., the least squares estimates). Better model fit is accomplished through the use of an algorithm which generates new sets of regression coefficients that produce larger log likelihoods. This is an iterative process that stops when the selection of new parameters creates very little change in the regression coefficients and very small increases in the log likelihood—so small that there is little value in any further estimation.

19.1.1.5 Significance Tests

As with multiple regression, there are two tests of significance in logistic regression. Specifically, these involve testing the significance of the overall logistic regression model and testing the significance of each of the logistic regression coefficients.

19.1.1.5.1 Test of Significance of the Overall Regression Model

The first test is the test of statistical significance to determine overall model fit and provides evidence of the extent to which the predicted values accurately represent the observed values (Xie, Pendergast, & Clarke, 2008). We consider several overall model tests including: (a) change in log likelihood; (b) Hosmer and Lemeshow's goodness of fit test; (c) pseudo-variance explained; and (d) predicted group membership. Additional work (e.g., Xie et al., 2008) has recently been conducted on new methods to assess model fit, but these are not currently available in statistical software, nor easily computed. Also in this section, we briefly address sensitivity, specificity, false positive, false negative and cross-validation.

19.1.1.5.1.1 Change in Log Likelihood

One way to test overall model fit is the likelihood ratio test. This test is based on the change in the log likelihood function from a smaller model (often the baseline or intercept only model) to a larger model that includes one or more predictors (sometimes referred to as the fitted model). Although we indicate that the smaller model is often the intercept only model, this test can also be used to examine changes in model fit from one fitted model to another fitted model, and we will discuss this in a bit. This likelihood ratio test is similar to the overall F test in OLS regression and tests the null hypothesis that all the regression coefficients are equal to zero. Using statistical notation, we can denote the null and alternative hypotheses for the regression coefficients as follows:

$$H_0\colon \beta_1 = \beta_2 = \cdots = \beta_m = 0$$

$$H_1\colon \textit{Not all the}\, \beta_m = 0$$

For explanation purposes, we assume the smaller model is the baseline or intercept only model. The baseline log likelihood is estimated from a logistic regression model that includes only the constant (i.e., intercept) term. The model log likelihood is estimated from the logistic regression model that includes the constant and the relevant predictor(s). By multiplying the difference in these log likelihood functions by −2, a chi-square test is produced with degrees of freedom equal to the difference in the degrees of freedom of the models ($df = df_{model} - df_{baseline}$) (where "model" refers to the fitted model that includes one or more predictors). In the case of the constant only model, there is only one parameter estimated (i.e., the intercept), so there is only one degree of freedom. In models that include independent variables, the degrees of freedom are equal to the number of independent variables in the model plus one for the constant. The larger the difference between the baseline and model LL values, the better the model fit. It is important to note that the log likelihood difference test assumes nested models. In other words, all elements that are included in the baseline or smallest model must also be included in the fitted model. As alluded to previously, the change in log likelihood test can be used for more than just comparing the intercept only model to a fitted model. Researchers often use this test in the model building process to determine if adding predictors (or sets of predictors) aids in model fit by comparing one fitted model to another fitted model. In general, the change in log likelihood is computed as follows:

$$\chi^2 = 2(LL_{model} - LL_{baseline})$$

19.1.1.5.1.2 Hosmer-Lemeshow Goodness of Fit Test

The Hosmer-Lemeshow goodness of fit test is another tool that can be used to examine overall model fit. The Hosmer-Lemeshow statistic is computed by dividing cases into deciles (i.e., 10 groups) based on their predicted probabilities. Then a chi-square value is computed based on the observed and expected frequencies. This is a chi-square test for which the researcher does *not* want to find statistical significance. Nonstatistically significant results for the Hosmer-Lemeshow test indicate the model has acceptable fit. In other words, the predicted or estimated model is not statistically significantly different from the observed values. Although the Hosmer-Lemeshow test can easily be requested in SPSS, it has been criticized for being conservative (i.e., lacking sufficient power to detect lack of fit in instances such as nonlinearity of an independent variable), too likely to indicate model fit when five or fewer groups (based on the decile groups created in computing the statistic) are used to calculate the statistic, and offers little diagnostics to assist the researcher when the test indicates poor model fit (Hosmer, Hosmer, LeCessie, & Lemeshow, 1997). Additionally, this test can be overly conservative unless one has very large sample sizes.

19.1.1.5.1.3 Pseudo-Variance Explained

Another overall model fit index for logistic regression is pseudo-variance explained. This index is akin to multiple R^2 (or the coefficient of determination) in OLS regression and can also be considered an effect size measure for the model. The reason these values are considered pseudo-variance explained in logistic regression is that the variance in a dichotomous outcome, as evident in logistic regression, differs as compared to the variance of a continuous outcome, as present in OLS regression.

There are a number of multiple R^2 pseudo-variance explained values that can be computed in logistic regression. Pseudo R^2 measures can be used to interpret one model and as a goodness of fit when comparing multiple models. However, these uses assume there are benchmark values for interpretation and the only influence on the value is the explanatory power provided by the independent variable(s) (Hemmert, Schons, Wieseke, & Schimmelpfennig, 2018). Of these, SPSS automatically computes the Cox and Snell and Nagelkerke indices. There is, however, no consensus on which (if any) of the pseudo-variance explained indices are best and many researchers choose not to report any of them in their published results. In fact, a meta-analysis of studies (1997 to 2011) that had conducted logistic regression and pseudo R^2, Hemmert and colleagues found, among other findings, that the distribution of observations in the outcome and the number of independent variable substantially impact pseudo R^2 (e.g., asymmetrical distributions decreases pseudo R^2, and increasing the number of independent variables increases pseudo R^2) (Hemmert et al., 2018). If you do choose to use and/or report one or more of these values, they should be used only as a guide "without attributing great importance to a precise figure" (Pampel, 2000, p. 50). Additionally, should you use pseudo R^2, review Hemmert et al.'s (2018) study as they identify additional pseudo R^2 values you may wish to consider as well as considerations for interpreting and reporting.

We discuss the following: (a) Cox and Snell (1989); (b) Nagelkerke (1991); (c) Hosmer and Lemeshow (1989); (d) Aldrich and Nelson (1984); (e) Harrell (1986); and (f) traditional R^2.

The Cox and Snell R^2 (1989) is computed as the ratio of the likelihood values raised to the power of $2/n$ (where n is sample size). A problematic is that the computation is such that the theoretical maximum of one cannot be obtained, even when there is perfect prediction:

$$R_{CS}^2 = 1 - \left(\frac{LL_{baseline}}{LL_{model}}\right)^{2/n}$$

Nagelkerke (1991) adjusts the Cox and Snell value so that the maximum value of one can be achieved, and it is computed as follows:

$$R_N^2 = \frac{R_{CS}^2}{1 - \left(LL_{baseline}\right)^{2/n}}$$

Hosmer and Lemeshow's (1989) R^2 is the proportional reduction in the log likelihood (in absolute value terms). Although not provided by SPSS, it can easily be computed by the ratio of the model to baseline $-2LL$. Ranging from zero to one, this value provides an indication of how much the badness of fit of the baseline model is improved by the inclusion of the predictors in the fitted model. Hosmer and Lemeshow's (1989) R^2 is computed as:

$$R_L^2 = \frac{-2LL_{model}}{-2LL_{baseline}}$$

Harrell (1986) proposed that Hosmer and Lemeshow's R^2 be adjusted for the number of parameters (i.e., independent variables) in the model. This adjustment (where m equals the number of independent variables in the model) to the computation makes this R^2 value akin to the adjusted R^2 in OLS regression. It is computed as:

$$R_{LA}^2 = \frac{(-2LL_{model}) - 2m}{-2LL_{baseline}}$$

Aldrich and Nelson (1984) provided an alternative to the R_L^2 that is equivalent to the squared contingency coefficient. This measure has the same problem as the Cox and Snell R^2; the theoretical maximum of one cannot be obtained even when the independent variable(s) perfectly predict the outcome. It is computed as:

$$pseudo\,R^2 = \frac{-2LL_{model}}{-2LL_{model} + n}$$

The traditional R^2, the coefficient of determination as used in simple and multiple regression, can also be used in logistic regression (only with binary logistic regression, as the mean and variance of a dichotomous variable make sense; however, the mean, for example, in a dummy coded variable situation, is equal to the proportion of cases in the category labeled as 1). R^2 can be computed by correlating the observed values of the binary dependent variable with the predicted values (i.e., predicted probabilities) obtained from the logistic regression model and then squaring the correlated value. Predicted probability values can easily be saved when generating logistic regression models in SPSS.

19.1.1.5.1.4 Predicted Group Membership

Another test of model fit for logistic regression can be accomplished by evaluating predicted to observed group membership. Assuming a cut value of .50, cases with predicted probabilities at .5 or above are predicted as 1 and predicted probabilities below .5 are predicted as 0. A crosstab table of predicted to observed predicted probabilities provides the frequency and percentage of cases correctly classified. Correct classification would be seen in cases that have the same value for both the predicted and observed values. A perfect model produces 100% correctly classified cases. A model that classifies no better than chance would provide 50% correctly classified cases. Press's Q is a chi-square statistic with one degree of freedom that can be used as a formal test of classification accuracy. It is computed as:

$$Q = \frac{\left[N - (nK)\right]^2}{N(K-1)}$$

where N is the total sample size, n represents the number of cases that were correctly classified, and K equals the number of groups. As with other chi-square statistics we have examined, this test is sensitive to sample size. Also, it is important to note that focusing solely on the correct classification overall (as is done with Press's Q) may result in overlooking one or more groups that have unacceptable classification. The researcher should evaluate the classification of each group in addition to the overall classification.

Sensitivity is the probability that a case coded as 1 for the dependent variable (aka "positive") is classified correctly. In other words, sensitivity is the percentage of correct predictions of the cases that are coded as 1 for the dependent variable. In the kindergarten readiness example that we will review later, of those 12 children who were prepared for kindergarten (i.e., coded as 1 for the dependent variable), 11 were correctly classified. Thus the sensitivity is 11/12 or about 92%.

Specificity is the probability that a case coded as 0 for the dependent variable (aka "negative") is classified correctly. In other words, specificity is the percentage of correct predictions of the cases that are coded as 0 for the dependent variable. In the kindergarten readiness example that we will review later, of those 8 children who were unprepared for kindergarten (i.e., coded as 0 for the dependent variable), 7 were correctly classified. Thus the specificity is 7/8 or 87.5%.

False positive rate is the probability that a case coded as 0 for the dependent variable (aka "negative") is classified *incorrectly*. In other words, this is the percentage of cases in error where the dependent variable is predicted to be 1 (i.e., prepared), but in fact the observed value is 0 (i.e., unprepared). In the kindergarten readiness example that we will review later, of those 8 children who were unprepared for kindergarten (i.e., coded as 0 for the dependent variable), 1 was incorrectly classified. Thus the false positive rate is 1/8 or 12.5%. The false positive rate is also computed as one minus specificity.

False negative rate is the probability that a case coded as 1 for the dependent variable (aka "positive") is classified *incorrectly*. In other words, this is the percentage of cases in error where the dependent variable is predicted to be 0 (i.e., unprepared), but in fact the observed value is 1 (i.e., prepared). In the kindergarten readiness example that we will review later, of those 12 children who were prepared for kindergarten (i.e., coded as 1 for the dependent variable), 1 was incorrectly classified. Thus the false negative rate is 1/12 or about 8%. The false negative rate is also computed as one minus sensitivity.

19.1.1.5.1.5 Cross-Validation

A recommended best practice in logistic regression is to cross-validate the results. If the sample size is sufficient, this can be accomplished by using 75%–80% of the sample to derive the model and then use the remaining cases (the holdout sample) to determine its accuracy. With cross-validation, you are in essence testing the model on two samples—a primary sample (which represents the largest percentage of the sample size) and a holdout sample (that which remains). If classification accuracy of the holdout sample is within 10% of the primary sample, this provides evidence of the utility of the logistic regression model.

19.1.1.6 Test of Significance of the Logistic Regression Coefficients

The second test in logistic regression is the test of the statistical significance of each regression coefficient, b_k. This test allows us to determine if the individual coefficients are statistically significantly different from zero. The null and alternative hypothesis can be illustrated in the same mathematical notation as we used with OLS regression:

$$H_0: \beta_k = 0$$

$$H_0: \beta_k \neq 0$$

Interpreting the test provides evidence of the probability of obtaining the observed sample coefficient by chance if the null hypothesis was true (i.e., if the population regression coefficient value was zero). The Wald statistic, which follows a chi-square distribution, is used as the test statistic for regression coefficients in SPSS. This is calculated by squaring the ratio of the regression coefficient divided by its standard error:

$$W = \frac{\beta_k^2}{SE_{\beta_k^2}}$$

When the logistic regression coefficients are large (in absolute value), rounding error can create imprecision in estimation of the standard errors. This can result in inaccuracies in testing the null hypothesis, and more specifically, increased Type II errors (i.e., failing to reject the null hypothesis when the null hypothesis is false). An alternative to the Wald test, in situations such as this, is the difference in log likelihood test previously described to compare models with and without the variable of interest (Pampel, 2000).

Raftery (1995) proposed a Bayesian information criterion (BIC), computed as the difference between the chi-square value and the natural log of the sample size, that could also be applied to testing logistic regression coefficients:

$$BIC = \chi^2 - \ln n$$

To reject the null hypothesis, the BIC should be positive (i.e., greater than zero). That is, the chi-square value must be greater than the natural log of the sample size. BIC values below zero suggest that the variable contributes little to the model. BIC values between 0 and +2 are considered weak; between 2 and 6, positive; between 6 and 10, strong; and more than 10, very strong.

Beyond determining statistical significance of the individual predictors, you may also want to assess which predictors are adding the most to the model. In OLS regression, we examined the standardized regression coefficients. There are no traditional standardized regression coefficients provided in SPSS for logistic regression, but they are easy to calculate. Simply standardize the predictors before generating the logistic regression model, and then run the model as desired. You can then interpret the logistic regression coefficients as standardized regression coefficients (if necessary, review the multiple regression chapter).

We can also form a confidence interval around the logistic regression coefficient, b_k. The confidence interval formula is the same as in OLS regression: the logistic regression coefficient plus or minus the product of the tabled critical value and the standard error:

$$CI(b_k) = b_k \pm_{(a/2)} t_{(n-m-1)} s_b$$

The null hypothesis that we tested was H_0: $\beta_k = 0$. It follows that if our confidence interval contains zero, then the logistic regression coefficient (b_k) is not statistically significantly different from zero at the specified significance level. We can interpret this to say that β_k will be included in $(1 - \alpha)\%$ of the sample confidence intervals formed from multiple samples.

19.1.1.7 Methods of Predictor Entry

The three categories of model building that will be discussed include: (a) simultaneous logistic regression; (b) stepwise logistic regression; and (c) hierarchical regression.

19.1.1.7.1 Simultaneous Logistic Regression

With simultaneous logistic regression, all the independent variables of interest are included in the model in one set. This method of model building is usually used when the researcher does not hypothesize that some predictors are more important than others. This method of entry allows you to evaluate the contribution of an independent variable over and above that of all other predictors in the model (i.e., each independent variable is evaluated as if it was the last one to enter the equation). One problem that may be encountered with this method of entry is related to strong correlations between the predictor and the outcome. An independent variable that has a strong bivariate correlation with the dependent variable may indicate a weak correlation when entered simultaneously with other predictors. In SPSS, this method of entry is referred to as "Enter."

19.1.1.7.2 Stepwise Logistic Regression

Stepwise logistic regression is a data-driven model building technique where the computer algorithms drive variable entry rather than theory. Issues with this type of technique have previously been outlined in the discussion associated with this method in multiple regression and thus are not rehashed here. If stepwise logistic regression is determined to be the most appropriate strategy to build your model, Hosmer, Lemeshow, and Sturdivant (2000) suggest setting a more liberal criteria for variable inclusion (e.g., α = .15 to .20). They also provide specific recommendations on dealing with interaction terms and scales of variables. Because it is only in unusual instances that this method of model building is appropriate (e.g., exploratory research), additional coverage of the suggestions by Hosmer and Lemeshow is not presented.

SPSS offers forward and backward stepwise methods. For both forward and backward methods, options include conditional, LR, and Wald. The differences between these options are mathematically driven. The LR method of entry uses the $-2LL$ for estimating entry of independent variables. The conditional method also uses the likelihood ratio test, but one that is considered to be computationally quicker. The Wald method applies the Wald test to determining entry of the independent variables. With forward stepwise methods, the model begins with a constant only and, based on some criterion, independent variables are added one at a time until a specified cutoff is achieved (e.g., all independent variables included in the model are statistically significant and any additional variables not included in the model are not statistically significant). Backward stepwise methods work in the reverse fashion where initially all independent variables (and the constant) are included. Independent variables are then removed until only those that are statistically significant remain in the model, and including an omitted independent variable would not improve the model.

19.1.1.7.3 Hierarchical Regression

In hierarchical regression, the researcher specifies *a priori* a sequence for the individual predictor variables (not to be confused with hierarchical linear models, which is a regression approach for analyzing nested data collected at multiple levels, such as child, classroom, and school). The analysis proceeds in a forward selection, backward elimination, or stepwise selection mode according to a researcher specified, theoretically based sequence, rather than an unspecified statistically based sequence. In SPSS, this is conducting by entering predictors in **blocks** and selecting their desired method of entering variables in each block (e.g., simultaneously, forward, backward, stepwise). Because this method was explained in detail in reference to multiple regression and operation of this method of variable selection is the same in logistic regression, additional information will not be presented.

19.1.2 Sample Size

Simulation research suggests that logistic regression is best used with large samples. Samples of size 100 or greater are needed to accurately conduct tests of significance for logistic regression coefficients (Long, 1997). Note that for illustrative purposes, the example in this chapter uses a sample size of 20. We recognize this is insufficient in practice, but have used it for greater ease in presenting the data.

19.1.3 Power

Power in logistic regression can be computed *a priori* (which is ideal) using software such as G*Power to determine requisite sample size as well as post hoc. It is important to note the relationship between goodness of fit and power in the context of logistic regression. For example, the power of the Hosmer-Lemeshow goodness of fit statistic in detecting ill fit (e.g., nonlinearity in predictor variables) (Xie et al., 2008).

19.1.4 Effect Size

There are a number of effect size indices that may be considered in logistic regression, and a concise summary is presented in Table 19.4. We have already talked about multiple R^2 pseudo-variance explained values which can be used not only to gauge model fit, but also as measures of effect size. Another important statistic in logistic regression is the **odds ratio** (*OR*), also an effect size index that is similar to R^2. The odds ratio is computed by exponentiating the logistic regression coefficient e^{b_k}. Conceptually this is the odds for one category (e.g., prepared for kindergarten) divided by the odds for the other category (e.g., unprepared for kindergarten). The null hypothesis to be tested is that $OR = 1$, which indicates that there is no relationship between a predictor variable and the dependent variable. If an odds ratio of 1 indicates no effect, then an odds ratio *greater than one* indicates higher odds of the outcome occurring. An odds ratio of *less than one* indicates lower odds of the outcome occurring. Thus, assuming we are interesting in finding a relationship between the outcome and some event, we want to find *OR* to be significantly different from 1.

When the independent variable is **continuous,** the odds ratio represents the amount by which the odds change for a one-unit increase in the independent variable. When the odds ratio is greater than one, the independent variable increases the odds of occurrence. When the odds ratio is less than one, the independent variable decreases the odds of occurrence. The odds ratio is provided in SPSS output as "Exp(B)" in the table labeled "Variables in the Equation." In predicting kindergarten readiness, social development is a continuous covariate with a resulting odds ratio of 2.631. We can interpret this odds ratio to be that for every one-unit increase in social development, the odds of being ready for kindergarten (i.e., prepared) increase by 263%, controlling for the other variables in the model.

In the case of **categorical** variables, including dichotomous, multinomial, and ordinal variables, odds ratios are often interpreted in terms of their relative size or the change in odds ratios in comparing models. Consider first the case of a **dichotomous** variable. In the model predicting kindergarten readiness, type of household is one independent variable included in the model where a two-parent home is coded as "1" and a single-parent home as "0." An odds ratio of .002 indicates that the odds of being prepared for kindergarten (compared to unprepared for kindergarten) are decreased by a factor of .002 by being in a single parent home (as opposed to living in a two-family home). We could also state that the odds that a child from a single parent home will be prepared for kindergarten are .998 (i.e., 1 – .002).

In the case of a categorical variable with more than two categories, the odds ratio is interpreted relative to the reference (or left out) category. For example, say we have a predictor in our model that is mother's education level with categories that include: (1) less than high school diploma; (2) high school diploma or GED; and (3) at least some college. Say we set the last category ("at least some college") as the reference category. An odds ratio of .86 for the category of "high school diploma or GED" for mother's education level suggests that the odds of being prepared for kindergarten (as compared to unprepared) decrease by a factor of .86 when the child's mother has a high school diploma or GED, relative to when the child's mother has at least some college, when the other variables in the model are controlled.

Confidence intervals (CI) can be computed for odds ratios, and these CI reflect precision of the estimated OR. *Larger CI suggest lower precision, and smaller CI reflect higher precision.* An odds ratio with a CI that includes the null value (i.e., $OR = 1$) may provide evidence to suggest a nonstatistically significant relationship between the independent variable and the outcome. There are a number of resources that make for easy computing of effect sizes as well as their confidence intervals. We will illustrate two online calculators for computing odds ratio in the case of two groups (e.g., treatment and control) and their confidence intervals. One is provided by Dr. David B. Wilson and is available through the Campbell Collaboration (seehttps://campbellcollaboration.org/research-resources/effect-size-calculator.html). Although designed for use when conducting meta-analyses, the online calculator comes in handy whenever an effect size and its CI are desired. Let's take an example using our kindergarten readiness data that will be used later. We see in Table 19.3 a crosstabulation of type of household (which will serve as a proxy for treatment/control) by kindergarten readiness. This is a 2 × 2 frequency table.

Using Campbell's effect size calculator for a 2 × 2 table and treating "two-parent household" as the treatment and "prepared" as the desired (i.e., "yes") outcome, we find an odds ratio of 6, *OR CI* of (.8117, 44.3512). Because the confidence interval contains 1, our null value (i.e., $OR = 1$), this may provide evidence to suggest a nonstatistically significant relationship between the independent variable and the outcome.

TABLE 19.3

Type of Household by Kindergarten Readiness Crosstabulation

		Kindergarten Readiness	
		Unprepared	**Prepared**
Type of Household	Single-parent household	6	4
	Two-parent household	2	8

We can also use the online effect size calculator by Uanhoro (2017) to compute confidence intervals. This calculator uses the **R** package *epitools* for computing the *OR* and their confidence intervals. Selecting "unconditional maximum likelihood estimation (Wald)" as the method for the *OR* (which uses the normal approximation; see Figure 19.2) will produce identical results as Campbell's effect size calculator (*OR* = 6; .*CI*, 8117, 44.3512). An added benefit of Uanhoro (2017) is that, in addition to the Wald method for estimation, there are three additional methods provided for calculating the *OR* (https://effect-size-calculator.herokuapp.com/#oddsriskabsolute-ratios--number-needed-to-treat). These include: (1) median-unbiased estimation (mid-*p*); (2) conditional maximum likelihood estimation (Fisher); and (3) small sample adjustment (small). Confidence intervals for mid-*p* and Fisher are computed using exact methods, which is useful in cases where the sample size is small or there is sparse data structure (e.g., rare events) (Hirji, Tsiatis, & Mehta, 1989). Confidence intervals for the "small" method are computed using the normal approximation with small sample adjustment. When using Uanhoro's calculator to calculate relative risk, there are three methods for estimating: (1) unconditional maximum likelihood estimation (Wald); (2) small sample adjustment (small); and (3) bootstrap estimation (boot).

From either of these calculators, we're also provided the **risk ratio**. The risk ratio is computed as the risk of incident in one group divided by the risk of incidence in the other group. In our example of kindergarten preparedness, the "risk" of being "prepared" in the two-parent household was 8/10 or 80%, and the risk of being "prepared" in the single-parent household was 4/10 or 40%. Thus, the risk ratio is simply the incidence of exposure in the "treatment" (i.e., two-parent) group divided by the incidence of exposure in the "control" (i.e., single-parent) group or .80/.40 = 2. A *risk ratio of less than 1* indicates that "exposure" is associated with a reduction in risk; i.e., a decreased risk of the outcome in the exposed group. A *risk ratio greater than 1*, as we see in this example, indicates an increased risk of the outcome in the exposed group. In our illustration, with a RR of 2, there is an increased "risk" of being prepared (which is a good thing!) in children from

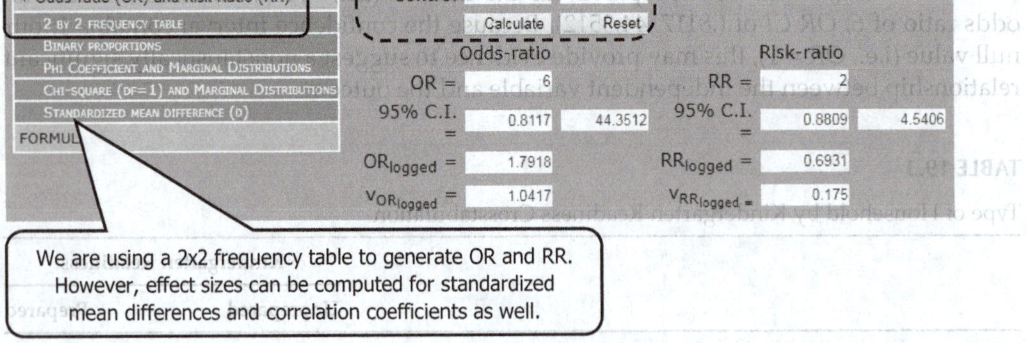

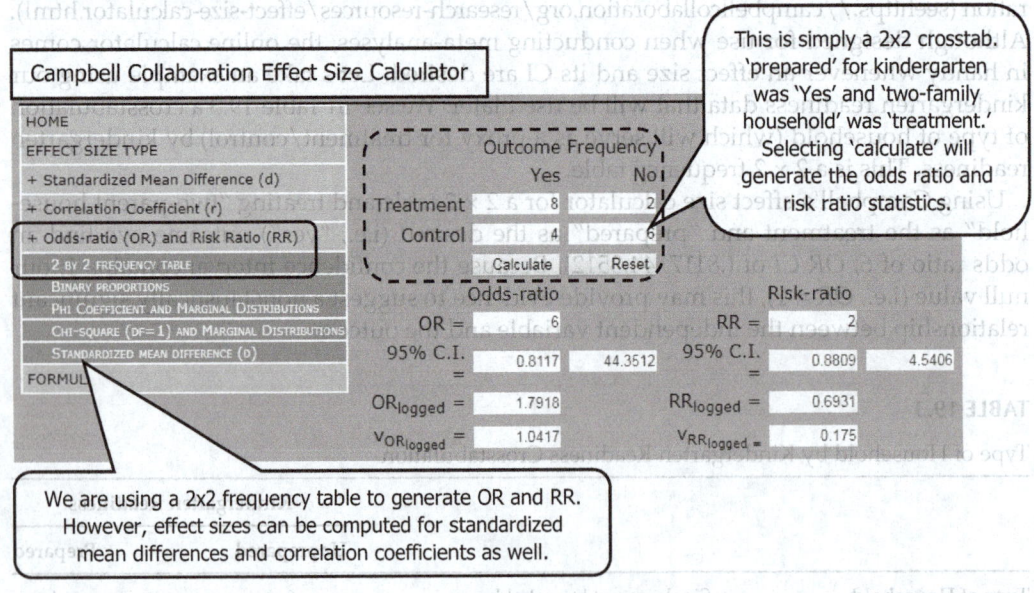

FIGURE 19.2
Computing *OR* CI using the Campbell Collaboration Online Calculator or Uanhoro's Effect Size Calculator.

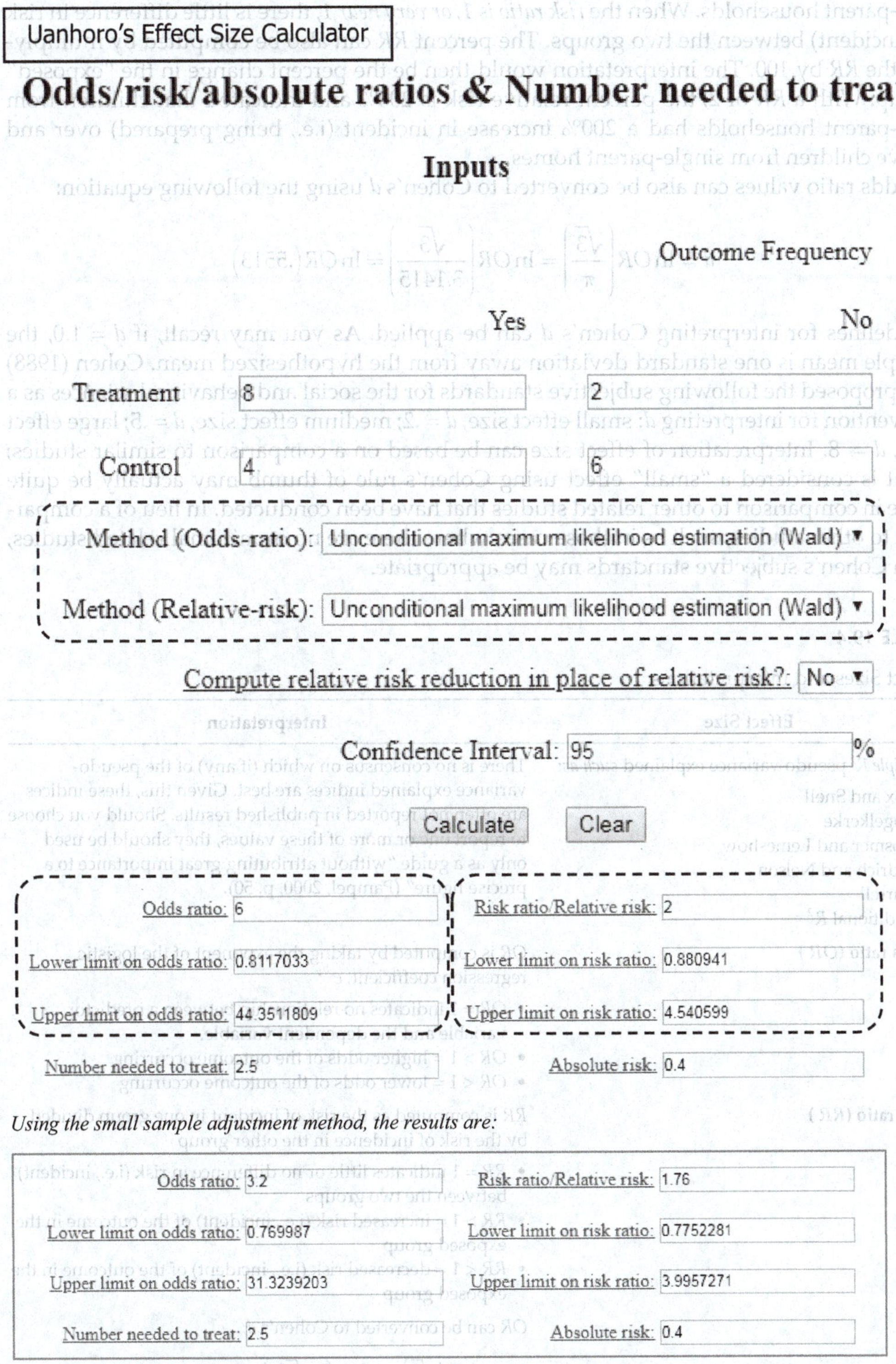

FIGURE 19.2 (continued)
Computing *OR* CI using the Campbell Collaboration Online Calculator or Uanhoro's Effect Size Calculator.

two-parent households. When the *risk ratio is 1, or very near 1,* there is little difference in risk (or incident) between the two groups. The percent *RR* can also be computed by multiplying the *RR* by 100. The interpretation would then be the percent change in the "exposed" group. With a *RR* of 2, the percent relative risk is 200% and indicated that children from two-parent households had a 200% increase in incident (i.e., being prepared) over and above children from single-parent homes.

Odds ratio values can also be converted to Cohen's *d* using the following equation:

$$d = \ln OR\left(\frac{\sqrt{3}}{\pi}\right) = \ln OR\left(\frac{\sqrt{3}}{3.1415}\right) = \ln OR(.5513)$$

Guidelines for interpreting Cohen's *d* can be applied. As you may recall, if $d = 1.0$, the sample mean is one standard deviation away from the hypothesized mean. Cohen (1988) has proposed the following subjective standards for the social and behavioral sciences as a convention for interpreting *d*: small effect size, $d = .2$; medium effect size, $d = .5$; large effect size, $d = .8$. Interpretation of effect size can be based on a comparison to similar studies; what is considered a "small" effect using Cohen's rule of thumb may actually be quite large in comparison to other related studies that have been conducted. In lieu of a comparison to other studies, such as in those cases where there are no or minimal related studies, then Cohen's subjective standards may be appropriate.

TABLE 19.4

Effect Sizes and Interpretations

Effect Size	Interpretation
Multiple R^2 pseudo-variance explained *such as:* • Cox and Snell • Nagelkerke • Hosmer and Lemeshow • Aldrich and Nelson • Harrell • traditional R^2	There is no consensus on which (if any) of the pseudo-variance explained indices are best. Given this, these indices are often not reported in published results. Should you choose to report one or more of these values, they should be used only as a guide "without attributing great importance to a precise figure" (Pampel, 2000, p. 50).
Odds ratio (*OR*)	*OR* is computed by taking the exponent of the logistic regression coefficient, e^{b_k} • $OR = 1$ indicates no relationship between a predictor variable and the dependent variable. • $OR > 1$ = higher odds of the outcome occurring • $OR < 1$ = lower odds of the outcome occurring
Risk ratio (*RR*)	*RR* is computed as the risk of incident in one group divided by the risk of incidence in the other group • $RR = 1$ indicates little or no difference in risk (i.e., incident) between the two groups • $RR > 1$ = increased risk (i.e., incident) of the outcome in the exposed group • $RR < 1$ = decreased risk (i.e., incident) of the outcome in the exposed group
d	*OR* can be converted to Cohen's *d*: $d = \ln OR\left(\frac{\sqrt{3}}{\pi}\right) = \ln OR\left(\frac{\sqrt{3}}{3.1415}\right) = \ln OR(.5513)$

19.1.5 Assumptions

Compared to OLS regression, the assumptions of logistic regression are somewhat relaxed; however four primary assumptions must still be considered: (a) noncollinearity; (b) linearity; (c) independence of errors; and (d) values of *X* are fixed. In this section, we also discuss conditions that are needed in logistic regression as well as diagnostics that can be performed to more closely examine the data.

19.1.5.1 Noncollinearity

Noncollinearity is applicable to logistic regression models with multiple predictors just as it was in multiple regression (but is not applicable when there is only one predictor in any regression model). This assumption has already been explained in detail in Chapter 18 on multiple regression and thus will not be reiterated other than to explain tools that can be used to detect multicollinearity. Although most standard statistical software does not provide an option to easily generate collinearity statistics in logistic regression, you can generate an OLS regression model (i.e., a traditional multiple linear regression) with the same variables used in the logistic regression model and request collinearity statistics there. Because it is only the collinearity statistics that are of interest, do not be concerned in generating an OLS regression model that violates some of the OLS basic assumptions (e.g., normality). We have previously discussed tolerance and the variance inflation factor as two collinearity diagnostics (where tolerance is computed as $1-R_k^2$ where R_k^2 is the variance in each independent variable, *X*, explained by the other independent variables and VIF is $\frac{1}{1-R_k^2}$. In reviewing these statistics, tolerance values of less than .20 suggest multicollinearity exists, and values of less than .10 suggest serious multicollinearity. VIF values greater than 10 indicate a violation of noncollinearity.

The effects of a violation of noncollinearity in logistic regression are the same as that in multiple regression. First, it will lead to instability of the regression coefficients across samples, where the estimates will bounce around quite a bit in terms of magnitude, and even occasionally result in changes in sign (perhaps opposite of expectation). This occurs because the standard errors of the regression coefficients become larger, thus making it more difficult to achieve statistical significance. Another result that may occur involves an overall regression that is significant, but none of the individual predictors are significant. Violation will also restrict the utility and generalizability of the estimated regression model.

19.1.5.2 Linearity

In OLS regression, the dependent variable is assumed to have a linear relationship with the continuous independent variable(s), but this does not hold in logistic regression. Because the outcome in logistic regression is a logit, the assumption of linearity in logistic regression refers to linearity between *logit of the dependent variable* and the continuous independent variable(s). Hosmer and Lemeshow (1989) suggest several strategies for detecting nonlinearity, the easiest of which to apply is likely the Box-Tidwell transformation. This strategy is also valuable as it is not overly sensitive to minor violations of linearity. This involves generating a logistic regression model that includes all independent variables of interest along with an interaction term for each—the interaction term being the product of the continuous independent variable and its natural log [i.e., X * ln (X)]. Statistically significant interaction terms suggest nonlinearity. It is important to note that the assumption of linearity is applicable only for continuous predictors. A violation of linearity can result in biased parameters estimates, as well as the expected change in the logit of Y not being constant across the values of X. The Hosmer-Lemeshow test has decreased power in detecting lack of fit in situations where linearity is violated (Xie et al., 2008).

19.1.5.3 Independence of Errors

Independence of errors is applicable to logistic regression models just as it is with OLS regression, and a violation of this assumption can result in underestimated standard errors (and thus overestimated test statistic values and perhaps finding statistical significance more often than is really viable, as well as affecting confidence intervals). This assumption has already been explained in detail during the discussion of multiple regression assumptions and thus additional information will not be provided here.

19.1.5.4 Fixed X

The last assumption is that the values of X_k are **fixed**, where the independent variables X_k are fixed variables rather than random variables. Because this assumption was discussed in detail in relation to multiple regression, we only summarize the main points. When X is fixed, the regression model is valid only for those particular values of X_k that were actually observed and used in the analysis. Thus, the same values of X_k would be used in replications or repeated samples. As discussed in the previous regression chapter (Chapter 18), generally we may not want to make predictions about individuals having combinations of X_k scores outside of the range of values used in developing the prediction model; this is defined as *extrapolating* beyond the sample predictor data. On the other hand, we may not be quite as concerned in making predictions about individuals having combinations of X_k scores within the range of values used in developing the prediction model; this is defined as *interpolating* within the range of the sample predictor data. Table 19.5 summarizes the assumptions of logistic regression and the impact of their violation.

TABLE 19.5

Assumptions and Violation of Assumptions: Logistic Regression Analysis

Assumption	Effect of Assumption Violation
Noncollinearity of *X*'s	• Regression coefficients can be quite unstable across samples (as standard errors are larger) • Restricted generalizability of the model
Linearity	• Bias in slopes and intercept • Expected change in logit of Y is not a constant and depends on value of X
Independence	• Influences standard errors of the model and thus hypothesis tests and confidence intervals
Values of *X*'s are fixed	• Extrapolating beyond the range of X combinations: prediction errors larger, may also bias slopes and intercept • Interpolating within the range of X combinations: smaller effects than when extrapolating; if other assumptions met, negligible effect

19.1.5.5 Conditions

Although not assumptions, the following conditions should be met with logistic regression: nonzero cell counts; nonseparation of data; lack of influential points; and sufficient sample size.

19.1.5.5.1 Nonzero Cell Counts

The first condition is related to nonzero cell counts in the case of nominal independent variables. A zero cell count occurs when the outcome is constant for one or more categories of a nominal independent variable (e.g., all females pass the course). This results in high standard errors because entire groups of individuals have odds of 0 or 1. Strategies to remove zero cell counts include recoding the categories (e.g., collapsing categories) or adding a constant to each cell of the crosstab table. If the overall model fit is what is of primary interest, then you may choose not to do anything about zero cell counts. The overall relationship between the set of predictors and the dependent variable is not generally impacted by zero cell counts. However, if zero cell counts are retained and the results of the individual predictors are what is of interest, it would be wise to provide a limitation to your results recognizing higher standard errors that are produced due to zero cell counts as well as caution that the values of the individual regression coefficients may be affected. Careful review of the data prior to computing the logistic regression model can help thwart potential problems with zero cell counts.

19.1.5.5.2 Nonseparation of Data

Another condition that should be examined is that of complete or quasi-complete separation. Complete separation arises when the dependent variable is perfectly predicted and results in an inability to estimate the model. Quasi-complete separation occurs when there is less than complete separation and results in extremely large coefficients and standard errors. These conditions may occur when the number of variables equals (or nearly equals) the number of cases in the dataset, such that large coefficients and standard errors result.

19.1.5.5.3 Lack of Influential Points

Outliers and influential cases are problematic in logistic regression analysis just as with OLS regression. Severe outliers can cause the maximum likelihood estimator to reduce to zero (Croux, Flandre, & Haesbroeck, 2002). Residual analysis and other diagnostic tests are equally beneficial for detecting miscoded data and unusual (and potentially influential) cases in logistic regression as it is in OLS regression. SPSS and other statistical software, including **R**, provides the option for saving a number of values including predicted values, residuals, and influence statistics. Both probabilities and group membership predicted values can be saved. Residuals that can be saved include: (a) unstandardized; (b) logit; (c) studentized; (d) standardized; and (e) deviance. The three types of influence values that can be saved include Cook's, leverage values, and DfBetas.

The wide variety of values that can be saved suggests that there are many types of diagnostics that can be performed. Review should be conducted when standardized or studentized residuals are greater than an absolute value of 3.0 and DfBeta values are greater than one. Leverage values greater than $(m+1)/N$ (where m equals the number of independent variables) indicate an influential case (values closer to 1 suggest problems, while those closer to 0 suggest little influence). If outliers or influential cases are found, it is up to you to decide if removal of the case is warranted. It may be that they, while uncommon, are completely plausible so that they are retained in the model. If they are removed from the model, it is important to report the number of cases that were removed prior to analysis (and evidence to suggest what caused you to remove them). A review of Chapter 18 on multiple regression provides further details on diagnostic analysis of outliers and influential cases.

19.2 Mathematical Introduction Snapshot

To summarize the mathematics that underlie logistic regression, odds are simply the ratio of the probability of the dependent variable's two outcomes and computed as:

$$Odds(Y=1) = \frac{P(Y=1)}{1-P(Y=1)}$$

Changing the scale of the odds by taking the natural logarithm of the odds (aka *logit Y* or *log odds*) provides us with a value of the dependent variable that can theoretically range from negative infinity to positive infinity and thus creates a linear relationship between *X* and the probability of *Y* (Pampel, 2000). The natural log of the odds is calculated as follows:

$$\ln\frac{P(Y=1)}{1-P(Y=1)} = Logit(Y)$$

and working with log odds, our familiar additive regression equation is applicable:

$$ln\left[\frac{P(Y=1)}{1-P(Y=1)}\right] = Logit(Y) = a + \beta_1 X_1 + \beta_2 X_2 + \ldots + \beta_m X_m$$

If we exponentiate the logit (*Y*) (i.e., the outcome of our logistic regression equation), then it converts back to the odds (as noted by the calculation here) which allows us to interpret the independent variables as affecting the odds (rather than log odds) of the outcome:

$$Odds(Y=1) = e^{logit(Y)} = e^{ln[Odds(Y=1)]} = e^{\alpha+\beta_1 X_1+\beta_2 X_2+\ldots+\beta_m X_m} = \left(e^{\alpha}\right)\left(e^{\beta_1 X_1}\right)\left(e^{\beta_2 X_2}\right)\ldots\left(e^{\beta_m X_m}\right)$$

Converting the odds back to a probability can be done through the following formula:

$$P(Y=1) = \frac{Odds(Y=1)}{1+Odds(Y=1)} = \frac{e^{\alpha+\beta_1 X_1+\beta_2 X_2+\ldots+\beta_m X_m}}{1+e^{\alpha+\beta_1 X_1+\beta_2 X_2+\ldots+\beta_m X_m}}$$

Probability values close to one indicate increased likelihood of occurrence.

19.3 Computing Logistic Regression Using SPSS

Next we consider SPSS for the logistic regression model. Before we conduct the analysis, let us review the data (Ch19.readiness.sav) (note that we recognize the sample size of 20 does not meet minimum sample size criteria previously specified; however for illustrative purposes we felt it important to be able to show the entire dataset, and this would have been more difficult with the recommended sample size for logistic regression). With one dependent variable and two independent variables, the dataset must consist of three variables or columns, one for each independent variable and one for the dependent variable. Each row still represents one individual. As seen in the screenshot in Figure 19.3, the SPSS data are in the form of three columns that represent the two independent variables (a continuous teacher administered social development scale and household—a dichotomous variable, single vs. two-adult household) and one binary dependent variable (kindergarten readiness screening test—prepared vs. not prepared). As our dependent variable is dichotomous, we will conduct binary logistic regression. When the dependent variable consists of more than two categories, multinomial logistic regression is appropriate (although not illustrated here).

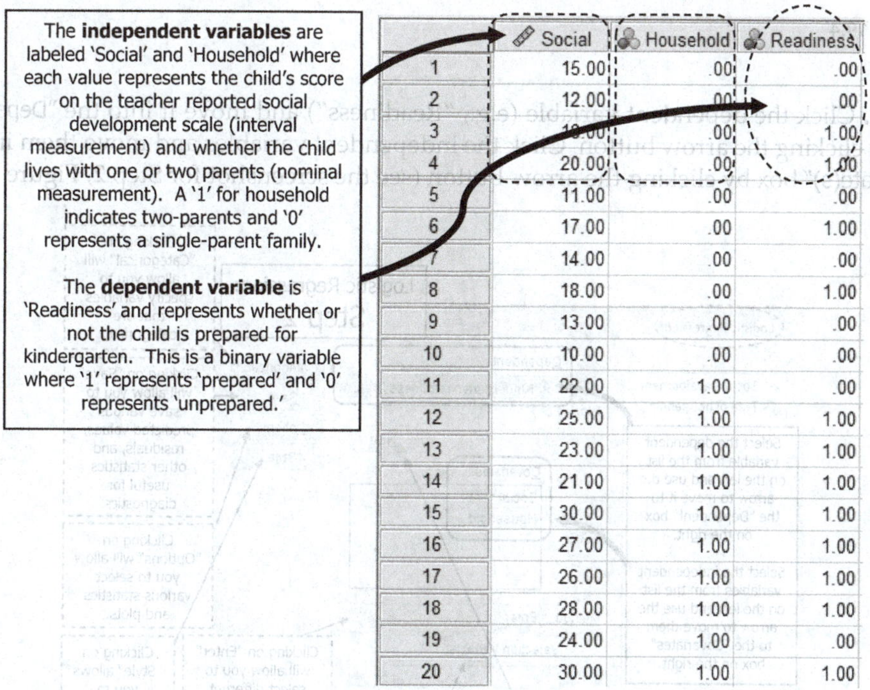

FIGURE 19.3
SPSS data.

Step 1. To conduct a binary logistic regression, go to "Analyze" in the top pulldown menu, then select "Regression," and then select "Binary Logistic." Following the screenshot below (see screenshot for Step 1, Figure 19.4) produces the "Logistic Regression" dialog box.

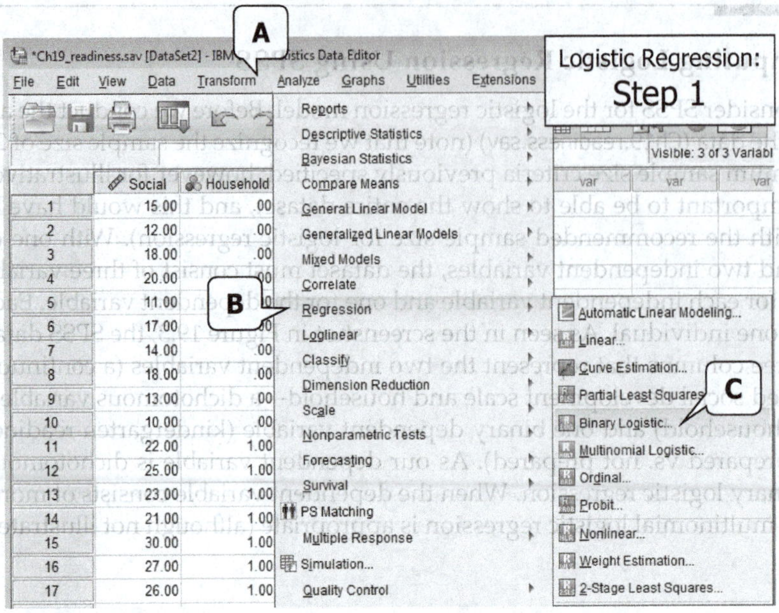

FIGURE 19.4
Step 1.

Step 2. Click the dependent variable (e.g., "Readiness") and move it into the "Dependent" box by clicking the arrow button. Click the independent variables and move them into the "Covariate(s)" box by clicking the arrow button (see the screenshot for Step 2, Figure 19.5).

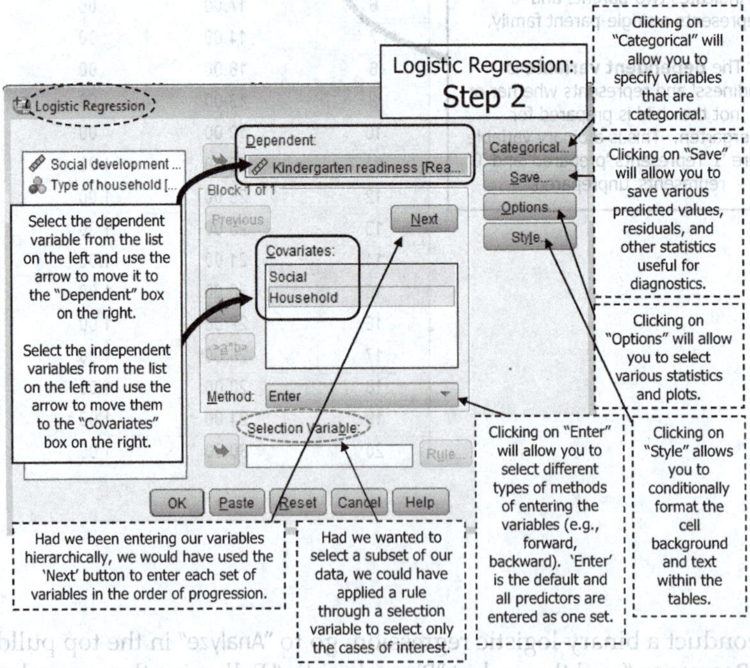

FIGURE 19.5
Step 2.

Step 3. From the Logistics Regression dialog box (see Figure 19.5), clicking on "Categorical" will provide the option to define as categorical those variables that are nominal or ordinal in scale as well as to select which category of the variable is the reference category through the Define Categorical Variables dialog box (see the screenshot for Figure 19.6). From the list of covariates on the left, click the categorical covariate(s) (e.g., "Household") and move it into the "Categorical Covariates" box by clicking the arrow button. By default, "(Indicator)" will appear next to the variable name. Indicator refers to traditional dummy coding and you have the option of selecting which value is the reference category. For binary variables (only two categories), using the "Last" value as the reference category means that the category coded with the largest value will be the category "left out" of the model (or referent), and using the "First" value as the reference category means that the category coded with the smallest value will be the category "left out" of the model. Here two-parent households were coded as 1 and single-parent households as 0. We use single-parent households (coded as 0) as the reference category. Thus we select the radio button for "First" (see Figure 9.6) to define single-parent households as the reference category.

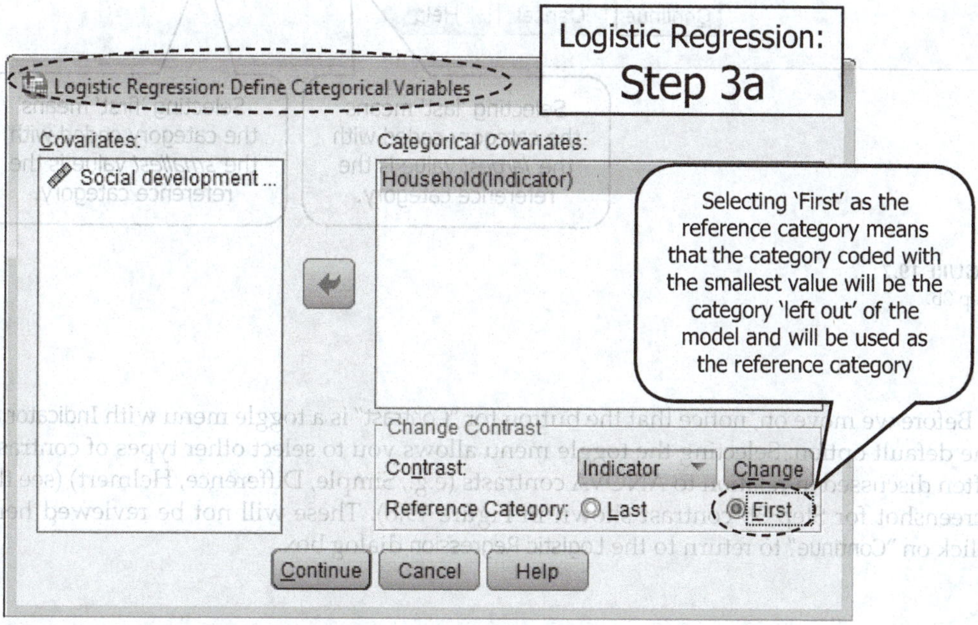

FIGURE 19.6
Step 3a.

Next, we need to click the button labeled "Change" (see the screenshot in Figure 19.7) to define the first value (i.e., zero or single parent household) as the reference (or "left out") category. By doing that, the name of our categorical covariate will now read Household(Indicator(first)). Had we had a categorical variable with more than two categories, we could just define the variable as categorical within logistic regression and select either the first or last value as the reference category. If neither the first or last were what you wanted as the reference category, then some recoding of the data is necessary.

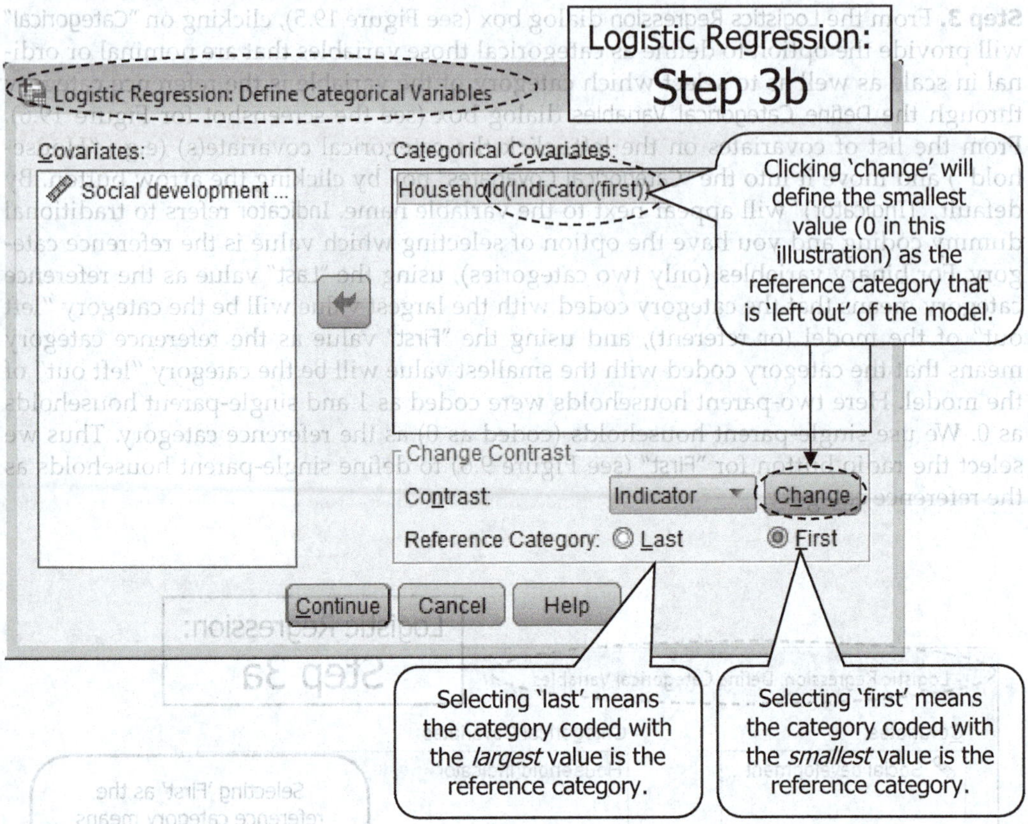
Logistic Regression:
Step 3b
Logistic Regression: Define Categorical Variables
Covariates:
Social development ...
Categorical Covariates:
Household(Indicator(first))
Clicking 'change' will define the smallest value (0 in this illustration) as the reference category that is 'left out' of the model.
Change Contrast
Contrast:
Indicator
Change
Reference Category:
Last
First
Continue
Cancel
Help
Selecting 'last' means the category coded with the *largest* value is the reference category.
Selecting 'first' means the category coded with the *smallest* value is the reference category.

FIGURE 19.7
Step 3b.

Before we move on, notice that the button for "Contrast" is a toggle menu with Indicator as the default option. Selecting the toggle menu allows you to select other types of contrasts often discussed in relation to ANOVA contrasts (e.g., Simple, Difference, Helmert) (see the screenshot for Step 3b contrast shown in Figure 19.8). These will not be reviewed here. Click on "Continue" to return to the Logistic Regression dialog box.

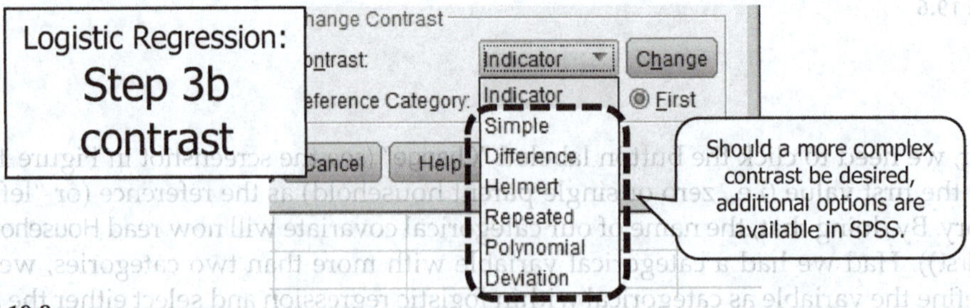
Logistic Regression:
Step 3b
contrast
Indicator
Change
Indicator
First
Simple
Difference
Helmert
Repeated
Polynomial
Deviation
Should a more complex contrast be desired, additional options are available in SPSS.

FIGURE 19.8
Step 3b contrast.

Step 4. From the Logistic Regression dialog box (see Figure 19.6), clicking on "Save" will provide the option to save various predicted values, residuals, and statistics that can be used for diagnostic examination (see the screenshot in Figure 19.9). From the Save dialog box under the heading "Predicted Values," place checkmarks in the boxes next to "Probabilities" and "Group membership." Under the heading "Residuals," place a checkmark in the box next to "Standardized." Under the heading "Influences," place checkmarks in the boxes next to "Cook's," "Leverage values," and "DfBeta(s)." Click on "Continue" to return to the original dialog box.

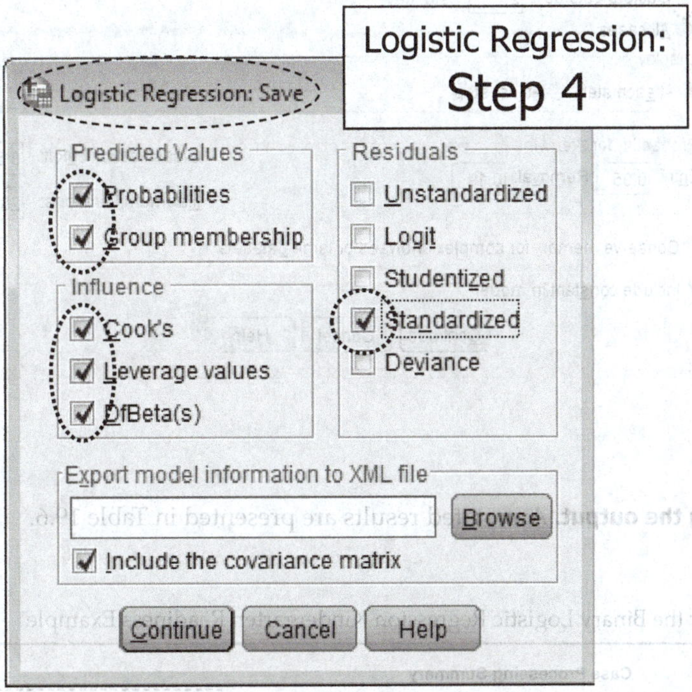

FIGURE 19.9
Step 4.

Step 5. From the Logistic Regression dialog box (see screenshot Step 2 Figure 19.6), clicking on "Options" will allow you to generate various statistics and plots. From the Options dialog box (see the screenshot for Step 5 in Figure 19.10) under the heading "Statistics and Plots," place checkmarks in the boxes next to "Classification plots," "Hosmer-Lemeshow goodness-of-fit," "Casewise listing of residuals," "Outliers outside," and "CI for exp(B)." For Outliers outside, you must specify a numeric value of standard deviations to define what you consider to be an outlier. Common values may be 2 (in a normal distribution, 95% of cases will be within +2 standard deviations), 3 (in a normal distribution, about 99% of cases will be within +3 standard deviations), or 3.29 (in a normal distribution, about 99.9% of cases will be within +3.29 standard deviations). For this illustration, we will use a value of 2. For CI for exp(*B*), you must specify a confidence interval. This should be the complement of the alpha being tested. If you are using an alpha of .05, then the CI will be 1 – .05 or 95. All the remaining options in the Options dialog box will be left as the default settings. Click on "Continue" to return to the original dialog box. From the Logistic Regression dialog box, click on "OK" to generate the output.

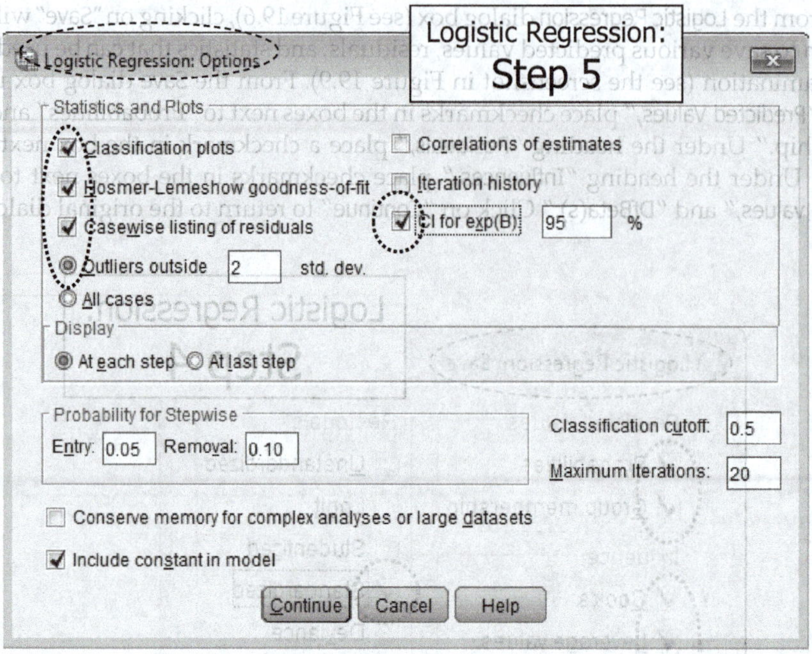

FIGURE 19.10
Step 5.

Interpreting the output. Annotated results are presented in Table 19.6.

TABLE 19.6
SPSS Results for the Binary Logistic Regression Kindergarten Readiness Example

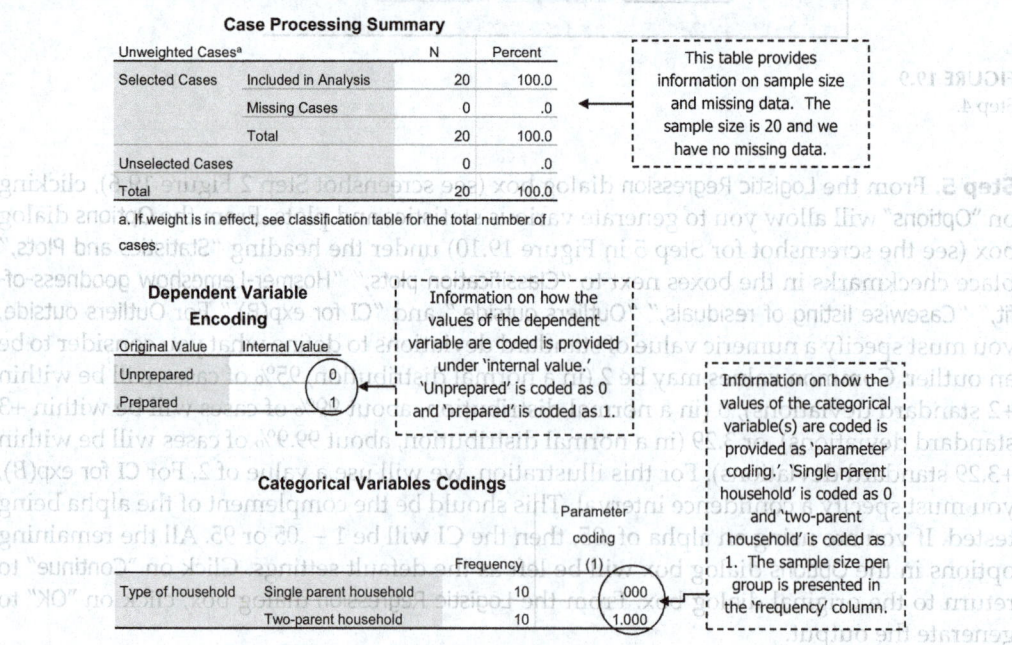

Case Processing Summary

Unweighted Cases[a]		N	Percent
Selected Cases	Included in Analysis	20	100.0
	Missing Cases	0	.0
	Total	20	100.0
Unselected Cases		0	.0
Total		20	100.0

a. If weight is in effect, see classification table for the total number of cases.

This table provides information on sample size and missing data. The sample size is 20 and we have no missing data.

Dependent Variable Encoding

Original Value	Internal Value
Unprepared	0
Prepared	1

Information on how the values of the dependent variable are coded is provided under 'internal value.' 'Unprepared' is coded as 0 and 'prepared' is coded as 1.

Categorical Variables Codings

		Frequency	Parameter coding (1)
Type of household	Single parent household	10	.000
	Two-parent household	10	1.000

Information on how the values of the categorical variable(s) are coded is provided as 'parameter coding.' 'Single parent household' is coded as 0 and 'two-parent household' is coded as 1. The sample size per group is presented in the 'frequency' column.

TABLE 19.6 (continued)

SPSS Results for the Binary Logistic Regression Kindergarten Readiness Example

Block 0 is a summary of the model with the *constant only* (i.e., none of the predictors are included). The **classification table** provides the percentage of cases correctly predicted given the constant only. *Without including covariates,* we can correctly predict children who are prepared for kindergarten 100% of the time but fail to predict any children (0%) who are unprepared. Here all children are predicted to be prepared.

Block 0: Beginning Block

Classification Table[a,b]

	Observed		Predicted		
			Kindergarten readiness		Percentage
			Unprepared	Prepared	Correct
Step 0	Kindergarten readiness	Unprepared	0	8	.0
		Prepared	0	12	100.0
	Overall Percentage				60.0

a. Constant is included in the model.
b. The cut value is .500

Variables in the Equation

		B	S.E.	Wald	df	Sig.	Exp(B)
Step 0	Constant	.405	.456	.789	1	.374	1.500

Variables not in the Equation

			Score	df	Sig.
Step 0	Variables	Social development	8.860	1	.003
		Type of household(1)	3.333	1	.068
	Overall Statistics		11.168	2	.004

Variables not in the equation provides an indication of whether each covariate will statistically significantly contribute to predicting the outcome. Only social development ($p = .003$) is of value in the logistic model. The value of 11.168 for **overall statistics** is a residual chi-square statistic. Since the p value for the residual chi-square statistic indicates statistical significance ($p = .004$), this indicates that including the two covariates improves the model as compared to the constant only model.

(*continued*)

TABLE 19.6 (continued)

SPSS Results for the Binary Logistic Regression Kindergarten Readiness Example

Block 1: Method = Enter

Method = Enter indicates that the method of entering the predictors was simultaneous entry (recall this is the default method in SPSS and is called "Enter").

Omnibus Tests of Model Coefficients

		Chi-square	df	Sig.
Step 1	Step	15.793	2	.000
	Block	15.793	2	.000
	Model	15.793	2	.000

The -2LL for the constant only model is computed as the sum of chi-square for the constant only model and -2LL for the full model:

$$\chi^2_{Model} + (-2LL) = 15.793 + 11.128 = 26.921$$

Model Summary

Step	-2 Log likelihood	Cox & Snell R Square	Nagelkerke R Square
1	11.128[a]	.546	.738

a. Estimation terminated at iteration number 7 because parameter estimates changed by less than .001.

Model summary statistics provide overall model fit. For good model fit, the value of *-2LL* for the full model (11.128) should be less than *-2LL* for the constant only model (26.921). This is a chi-square value with degrees of freedom equal to the number of parameters in the full model (i.e., 2 predictors plus one constant) minus the number of parameters in the baseline model (i.e., 1). Thus there are 2 *df.* Using the chi-square table, with an alpha of .05 and 2 *df,* the critical value is 5.99. Since 11.128 is larger than the critical value, we reject the null hypothesis that the best prediction model is the constant only model. *In other words, the full model (with predictors) is better at predicting kindergarten readiness than the constant only model.*

The two R^2 values are pseudo R^2 and are interpreted similarly to multiple R^2. These can be used as effect size indices for logistic regression and Cohen's interpretations for correlation can be used to interpret. Both values indicate a large effect.

Hosmer and Lemeshow Test

Step	Chi-square	df	Sig.
1	4.691	7	.698

As a measure of classification accuracy, *non-statistical significance (p = .698) indicates good model fit for the Hosmer and Lemeshow test.* This test is affected by small sample size, however; caution should be used when interpreting the results of this test when sample size is less than 50.

TABLE 19.6 (continued)

SPSS Results for the Binary Logistic Regression Kindergarten Readiness Example

Contingency Table for Hosmer and Lemeshow Test

		Kindergarten readiness = Unprepared		Kindergarten readiness = Prepared		
		Observed	Expected	Observed	Expected	Total
Step 1	1	2	1.988	0	.012	2
	2	2	1.922	0	.078	2
	3	1	1.651	1	.349	2
	4	2	1.292	0	.708	2
	5	0	.607	2	1.393	2
	6	1	.404	2	2.596	3
	7	0	.100	2	1.900	2
	8	0	.030	2	1.970	2
	9	0	.005	3	2.995	3

The **classification table** provides information on how well group membership was predicted. Cells on the *diagonal* indicate *correct* classification. For example, children who were prepared for kindergarten were accurately classified 91.7% of the time as compared to unprepared children (87.5%). Overall, 90% of children were correctly classified. This is computed as the number of correctly classified cases divided by total sample size:

$$\frac{7+11}{20} = .90$$

Classification Table[a]

	Observed		Predicted: Kindergarten readiness Unprepared	Predicted: Kindergarten readiness Prepared	Percentage Correct
Step 1	Kindergarten readiness	Unprepared	7	1	87.5
		Prepared	1	11	91.7
	Overall Percentage				90.0

a. The cut value is .500

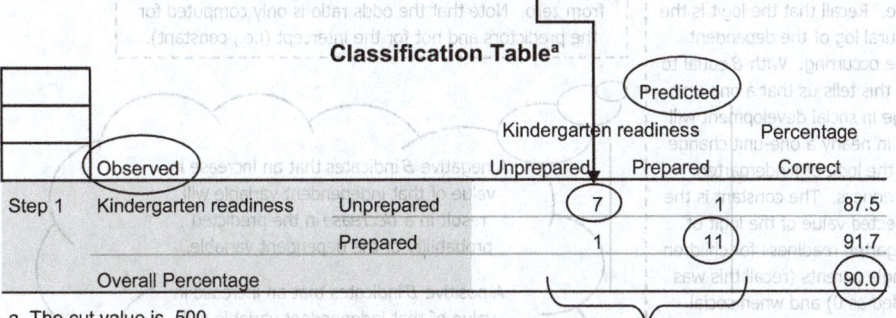

Using Press's *Q* and given the chi-square critical value of 3.841 ($df = 1$), we find:

$$Q = \frac{[N-(nK)]^2}{N(K-1)} = \frac{[20-(18)(2)]^2}{20(2-1)} = 12.8$$

We reject the null hypothesis. There is evidence to suggest that the predictions are statistically significantly better than chance.

(continued)

TABLE 19.6 (continued)

SPSS Results for the Binary Logistic Regression Kindergarten Readiness Example

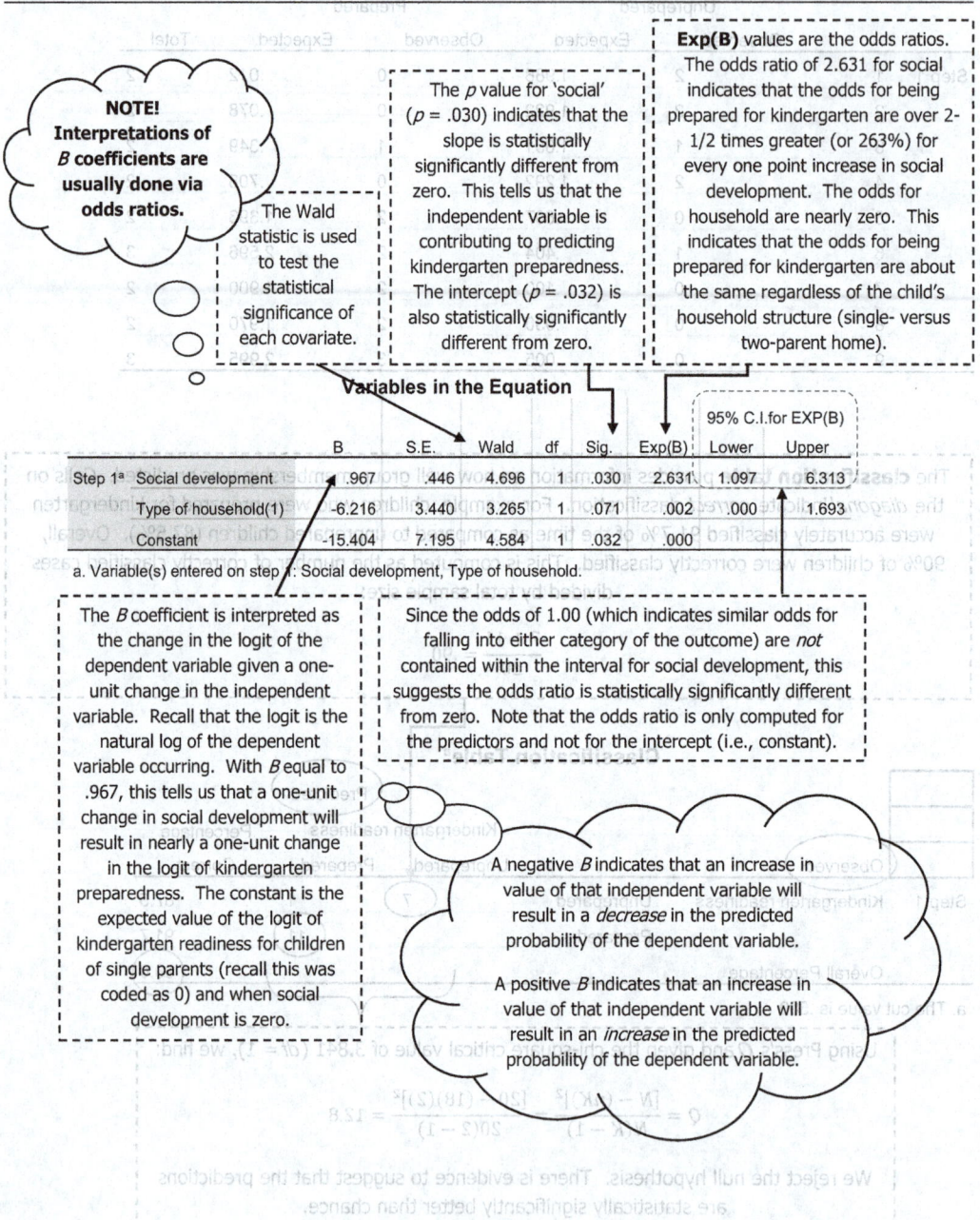

NOTE! Interpretations of *B* coefficients are usually done via odds ratios.

The Wald statistic is used to test the statistical significance of each covariate.

The *p* value for 'social' (*p* = .030) indicates that the slope is statistically significantly different from zero. This tells us that the independent variable is contributing to predicting kindergarten preparedness. The intercept (*p* = .032) is also statistically significantly different from zero.

Exp(B) values are the odds ratios. The odds ratio of 2.631 for social indicates that the odds for being prepared for kindergarten are over 2-1/2 times greater (or 263%) for every one point increase in social development. The odds for household are nearly zero. This indicates that the odds for being prepared for kindergarten are about the same regardless of the child's household structure (single- versus two-parent home).

Variables in the Equation

		B	S.E.	Wald	df	Sig.	Exp(B)	95% C.I.for EXP(B) Lower	Upper
Step 1ᵃ	Social development	.967	.446	4.696	1	.030	2.631	1.097	6.313
	Type of household(1)	-6.216	3.440	3.265	1	.071	.002	.000	1.693
	Constant	-15.404	7.195	4.584	1	.032	.000		

a. Variable(s) entered on step 1: Social development, Type of household.

The *B* coefficient is interpreted as the change in the logit of the dependent variable given a one-unit change in the independent variable. Recall that the logit is the natural log of the dependent variable occurring. With *B* equal to .967, this tells us that a one-unit change in social development will result in nearly a one-unit change in the logit of kindergarten preparedness. The constant is the expected value of the logit of kindergarten readiness for children of single parents (recall this was coded as 0) and when social development is zero.

Since the odds of 1.00 (which indicates similar odds for falling into either category of the outcome) are *not* contained within the interval for social development, this suggests the odds ratio is statistically significantly different from zero. Note that the odds ratio is only computed for the predictors and not for the intercept (i.e., constant).

A negative *B* indicates that an increase in value of that independent variable will result in a *decrease* in the predicted probability of the dependent variable.

A positive *B* indicates that an increase in value of that independent variable will result in an *increase* in the predicted probability of the dependent variable.

TABLE 19.6 (continued)

SPSS Results for the Binary Logistic Regression Kindergarten Readiness Example

```
            Step number: 1

            Observed Groups and Predicted Probabilities

         4 +                                                                                                    +
           I                                                                                                    I
           I                                                                                                    I
    F      I                                                                                                    I
    R    3 +                                                                                                   P+
    E      I                                                                                                   PI
    Q      I                                                                                                   PI
    U      I                                                                                                   PI
    E    2 +U                                                                                        P        PP+
    N      IU                                                                                        P        PPI
    C      IU                                                                                        P        PPI
    Y      IU                                                                                        P        PPI
         1 +U U  U       U        P       U           U                       P       P         U    P   P   PPP+
           IU U  U       U        P       U           U                       P       P         U    P   P   PPPI
           IU U  U       U        P       U           U                       P       P         U    P   P   PPPI
           IU U  U       U        P       U           U                       P       P         U    P   P   PPPI
Predicted   ----------+---------+---------+---------+---------+---------+---------+---------+---------+----------
  Prob:     0        .1        .2        .3        .4        .5        .6        .7        .8        .9         1
  Group:    UUUUUUUUUUUUUUUUUUUUUUUUUUUUUUUUUUUUUUUUUUUUUUUUUUPPPPPPPPPPPPPPPPPPPPPPPPPPPPPPPPPPPPPPPPPPPPPPPPP

            Predicted Probability is of Membership for Prepared
            The Cut Value is .50
            Symbols: U - Unprepared
                     P - Prepared
            Each Symbol Represents .25 Cases.
```

"P" indicates "prepared for kindergarten" and "U" indicates "unprepared for kindergarten." P's to the left of .50 indicate misclassified cases. U's to the right of .50 indicate misclassified cases.

Although there are 4 U's, this represents a frequency of one.

Casewise List[b]

Case	Selected Status[a]	Observed Kindergarten readiness	Predicted	Predicted Group	Temporary Variable Resid	ZResid	SResid
14	S	P**	.214	U	.786	1.918	2.102
19	S	U**	.832	P	-.832	-2.226	-2.106

a. S = Selected, U = Unselected cases, and ** = Misclassified cases.

b. Cases with studentized residuals greater than 2.000 are listed.

Recall we told SPSS to identify residuals that were outside 2 standard deviations. Based on that decision, cases 14 and 19 were identified as potential outliers. We review this output in the discussion on outliers.

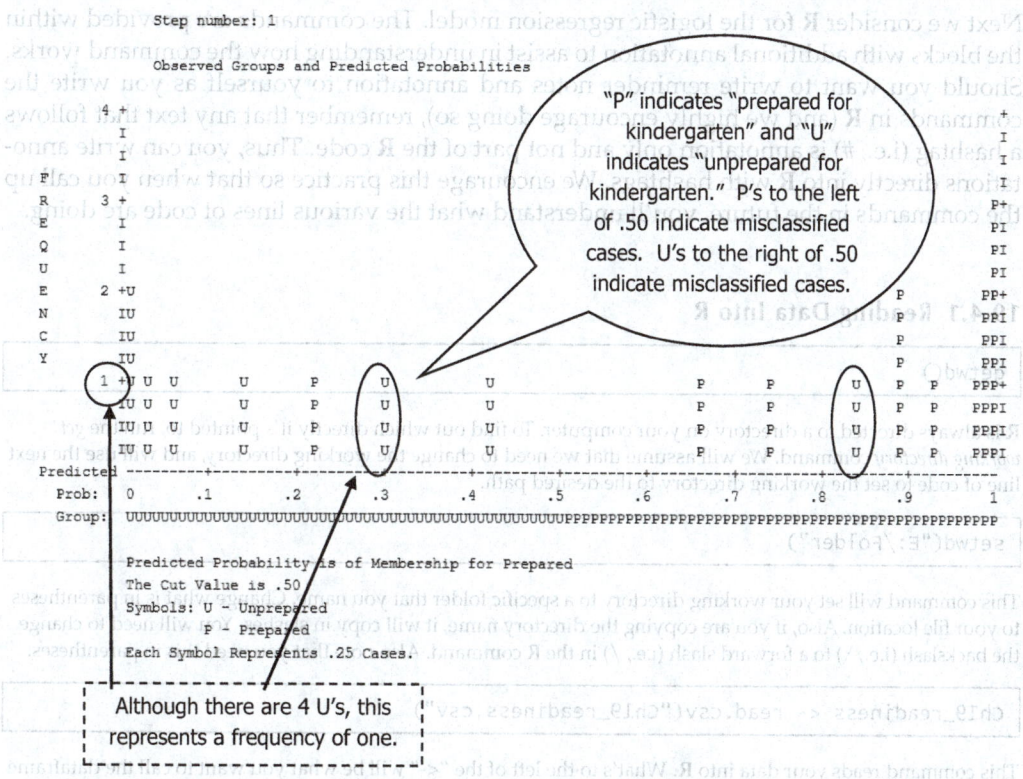

19.4 Computing Logistic Regression Using R

Next we consider **R** for the logistic regression model. The commands are provided within the blocks with additional annotation to assist in understanding how the command works. Should you want to write reminder notes and annotation to yourself as you write the commands in **R** (and we highly encourage doing so), remember that any text that follows a hashtag (i.e., #) is annotation only and not part of the **R** code. Thus, you can write annotations directly into **R** with hashtags. We encourage this practice so that when you call up the commands in the future, you'll understand what the various lines of code are doing.

19.4.1 Reading Data Into R

```
getwd()
```

R is always directed to a directory on your computer. To find out which directly it's pointed to, run the *get working directory* command. We will assume that we need to change the working directory, and will use the next line of code to set the working directory to the desired path.

```
setwd("E:/Folder")
```

This command will set your working directory to a specific folder that you name. Change what is in parentheses to your file location. Also, if you are copying the directory name, it will copy in slashes. You will need to change the backslash (i.e., \) to a forward slash (i.e., /) in the **R** command. Also note that you need this in parentheses.

```
Ch19_readiness <- read.csv("Ch19_readiness.csv")
```

This command reads your data into **R**. What's to the left of the "<-" will be what you want to call the dataframe in **R**. In this example, we're calling this **R** dataframe "Ch19_readiness." What's to the right of the "<-" tells **R** to find this particular csv file. In this example, our file is called "Ch19_readiness.csv." Make sure the extension (i.e., .csv) is there. Also note that you need this in quotations.

```
names(Ch19_readiness)
```

This command will produce a list of variable names for the dataframe as follows:

[1] "Social" "Household" "Readiness"

This is a good check to make sure your data have been read in correctly.

```
View(Ch19_readiness)
```

This command will let you view the dataset in spreadsheet format in RStudio.

```
Ch19_readiness$Household <- factor(Ch19_readiness$Household)
```

This tells **R** to treat the variable "Household" as categorical.

```
Ch19_readiness$Readiness <- factor(Ch19_readiness$Readiness)
```

This tells R to treat the variable "Readiness"' as categorical.

FIGURE 19.11
Reading data into **R**.

```
summary(Ch19_readiness)
```

The *summary* command will produce basic descriptive statistics on all the variables in your dataframe. This is a great way to quickly check to see if the data have been read in correctly and get a feel for your data, if you haven't already. The output from the summary statement for this dataframe looks like this. Because we defined Household and Readiness as categorical, we get only a few summary stats.

```
        Social     Household   Readiness
Min.    :10.00     0:10        0: 8
1st Qu. :14.75     1:10        1:12
Median  :20.50
Mean    :20.20
3rd Qu. :25.25
Max.    :30.00
```

FIGURE 19.11 (continued)
Reading data into **R**.

19.4.2 Generating the Logistic Regression Model and Saving Values

With these commands, we will generate the logistic regression model and save variables that can be used for data screening.

```
ReadinessLogit <- glm(formula = Readiness ~ Social + Household,
                      family="binomial",
                      data =Ch19_readiness)
```

The *glm* function will run the logistic regression model. In this example, we're naming our model *ReadinessLogit*. The formula defines our dependent variable as "Readiness," and it is predicted by "Social" and "Household." The command *family = "binomial"* tells **R** to compute a logistic regression model using a binomial distribution.

```
summary(ReadinessLogit)
```

The *summary* function will generate the results from the logistic regression model. If you don't run the summary line of code, since we named our model, there won't be any results output!

```
Deviance Residuals:
     Min        1Q     Median       3Q       Max
-1.88892  -0.24308    0.06327  0.41366   1.75662

Coefficients:
              Estimate  Std. Error  z value  Pr(>|z|)
(Intercept)   -15.4035      7.1941   -2.141    0.0323 *
Social          0.9675      0.4465    2.167    0.0302 *
Household1     -6.2162      3.4402   -1.807    0.0708 .
---
Signif. codes:
0 '***' 0.001 '**' 0.01 '*' 0.05 '.' 0.1 ' ' 1

(Dispersion parameter for binomial family taken to be 1)

    Null deviance: 26.920 on 19 degrees of freedom
Residual deviance: 11.128 on 17 degrees of freedom
AIC: 17.128
Number of Fisher Scoring iterations: 6
```

FIGURE 19.12
Generating the logistic regression model and saving variables.

```
ReadinessLogit2 <- glm(formula = Readiness ~ Social,
                       family="binomial",
                       data =Ch19_readiness)

anova(ReadinessLogit, ReadinessLogit2,
    test = "Chisq") #to compare 2 models
```

There are a number of model fit tests that can be conducted. As an example, if we want to compare one model with fewer predictors (for illustrative purposes, the model has been re-ran as *ReadinessLogit2* with only "Social" as the predictor) to another model, we can do so. The *anova* function with *test = "Chisq"* will generate the likelihood ratio test to compare the two models, *ReadinessLogit* and *ReadinessLogit2*. This test generates the likelihood ratio test to compare the likelihood of the data under the full model (i.e., *ReadinessLogit*) against the likelihood of the data in the reduced model (i.e., *ReadinessLogit2*). A statistically significant likelihood ratio test means we reject the null hypothesis that the reduced model is better than the full model. In other words, a statistically significant likelihood ratio test provides evidence against the reduced model and in favor of the full model. We see $p = .02319$, suggesting the full model, with both predictors, is better model fit than the reduced model with only one predictor.

```
Analysis of Deviance Table

Model 1: Readiness ~ Social + HouseholdF
Model 2: Readiness ~ Social
  Resid. Df Resid. Dev Df Deviance Pr(>Chi)
1 17 11.128
2 18 16.282-1 -5.1541 0.02319 *
---
Signif. codes: 0 '***' 0.001 '**' 0.01 '*' 0.05 '.' 0.1 ' ' 1
```

```
install.packages("zoo")
library(lmtest)
lrtest(ReadinessLogit, ReadinessLogit2)
```

The likelihood ratio test can also be conducted using the *lrtest* function from the *zoo* package. In parentheses, we input the two models to compare.

```
Likelihood ratio test

Model 1: Readiness ~ Social + HouseholdF
Model 2: Readiness ~ Social
#Df LogLik Df Chisq Pr(>Chisq)
1 3-5.5638
2 2-8.1409-1 5.1541 0.02319 *
---
Signif. codes: 0 '***' 0.001 '**' 0.01 '*' 0.05 '.' 0.1 ' ' 1
```

```
install.packages("survey")
library(survey)
regTermTest(ReadinessLogit, "Social")
regTermTest(ReadinessLogit, "HouseholdF")
```

The Wald test can be generated using the *regTermTest* function from the *survey* package. Within parentheses, we define our logistic regression model (i.e., *ReadinessLogit*) and one of the predictors. Thus, the number of tests generated will equal the number of predictors for which you want to generate the Wald test. The Wald test tests the alternative hypothesis that the coefficient of an independent variable in the model is not equal to zero. Failing to reject the hypothesis provides evidence that removing the variable from the model will not

FIGURE 19.12 (continued)
Generating the logistic regression model and saving variables.

substantially impact the model fit. Not surprising, we see that we could remove the "Household" predictor and our model fit would not be detrimentally impacted.

```
# regTermTest(ReadinessLogit, "Social")
Wald test for Social
  in glm(formula = Readiness ~ Social + Household, family = "binomial",
    data = Ch19_readiness)
F = 4.696185  on 1 and 17 df: p= 0.044723
```

```
# regTermTest(ReadinessLogit, "Household")
Wald test for Household
 in glm(formula = Readiness ~ Social + Household, family = "binomial",
    data = Ch19_readiness)
F = 3.264941  on 1  and 17 df:  p= 0.088507
```

```
install.packages("caret")
library(caret)
varImp(ReadinessLogit)
```

Using the *varImp* function from the *caret* package our our logistic model, *ReadinessLogit*, we can examine variable importance by reviewing the absolute value of the *t* test statistic for each predictor. The measure has a maximum value of 100, with values closer to 100 suggesting greater variable importance.

```
             Overall
Social      2.167068
HouseholdF1 1.806915
```

```
Ch19_readiness$predicted.probabilities <- fitted(ReadinessLogit)
```

The *fitted* function saves the predicted probabilities generated from the "ReadinessLogit" object. Within the parentheses is the name of our logistic regression model (i.e., *ReadinessLogit*). To the left of "<-" is the command that will save the predicted probabilities with the name of *predicted.probabilities* to our dataframe (i.e., *Ch19_readiness*). The remaining variables that we are generating are created and saved to our dataframe similarly.

```
Ch19_readiness$cook <- cooks.distance(ReadinessLogit)
```

The *cooks.distance* function will save Cook's distance, an influence statistic, generated from the "ReadinessLogit" object to our dataframe *Ch19_readiness* and will label the variable "cook."

```
Ch19_readiness$leverage <- hatvalues(ReadinessLogit)
```

The *hatvalues* function saves the leverage values generated from the *ReadinessLogit* object to our dataframe *Ch19_readiness* and will label the variable "leverage."

```
Ch19_readiness$standardized.residuals <- rstandard(ReadinessLogit)
```

The *rstandard* function saves standardized residuals generated from the *ReadinessLogit* object.

```
Ch19_readiness$studentized.residuals <- rstudent(ReadinessLogit)
```

The *rstudent* function saves studentized residuals generated from the *ReadinessLogit* object.

FIGURE 19.12 (continued)
Generating the logistic regression model and saving variables.

```
Ch19_readiness$dfbeta <- dfbeta(ReadinessLogit)
```

The *dfbeta* function saves DfBeta values generated from the *ReadinessLogit* object.

```
write.csv(Ch19_readiness,"Ch19diag.csv")
```

If you want to save the data that you just created and export to Excel, you can use this command to write a csv file.

FIGURE 19.12 (continued)
Generating the logistic regression model and saving variables

Comparing our output from **R** to SPSS, we see that, with the exception of small rounding error, the results for the coefficients are the same. There is additional output from **R** that we don't receive from SPSS. For example, the deviance residuals (which are −2*log likelihood) are a model fit measure and can be used to compare the null model (i.e., intercept only model) with the model which includes predictors.

19.4.3 Generating Confidence Intervals of Coefficient Estimates

```
confint(ReadinessLogit)
```

Because we named our model, we can easily request additional stats. With the *confint* command, we can obtain confidence intervals for the coefficient estimates. These CI are based on the profiled log-likelihood function.

```
                   2.5 %       97.5 %
(Intercept)  -35.3699318  -5.1530264
Social         0.3232473   2.1935459
Household1   -15.3437530  -0.7315369
```

```
confint.default(ReadinessLogit)
```

With the *confint.default* statement, we can get *CI* based on just the standard errors.

```
                    2.5 %      97.5 %
(Intercept) -29.50365894  -1.3034231
Social        0.09246227   1.8425236
Household1  -12.95885210   0.5265212
```

FIGURE 19.13
Generating confidence intervals of coefficient estimates

19.4.4 Exponentiating Coefficients

```
exp(coef(ReadinessLogit))
```

Use the *exp* command to exponentiate the coefficients and interpret them as odds-ratios. For the intercept and Household variables, we see "−07" and "−03," respectively. This indicates we need to move the decimals that number of places to the left.

```
(Intercept)        Social   Household1
2.043276e-07 2.631339e+00 1.996888e-03
```

FIGURE 19.14
Exponentiating coefficients.

19.4.5 Producing Odds Ratios and Their Confidence Intervals

Earlier, we illustrated two online calculators that can be used for computing *OR* and confidence intervals. However, it's also very easy to compute *OR* and confidence intervals using the logistic regression model generated in **R**.

```
exp(cbind(OR=coef(ReadinessLogit),
confint.default(ReadinessLogit)))
```

This statement will produce odds ratios and their confidence intervals based on standard errors. Had we just used the *confint* command, the *CI* produced would be based on the profiled log-likelihood function. Use the *cbind* command to place the coefficients and *CI* in columns.

	OR	2.5 %	97.5 %
(Intercept)	2.043276e-07	1.537176e-13	0.2716005
Social	2.631339e+00	1.096872e+00	6.3124485
Household1	1.996888e-03	2.355277e-06	1.6930324

FIGURE 19.15
Producing odds ratios and their confidence intervals

19.5 Data Screening

Previously we described a number of assumptions used in logistic regression. These included: (a) noncollinearity; (b) linearity between the predictors and logit of the dependent variable; and (c) independence of errors. We also reviewed the data to ensure there are no outliers.

Before we begin to examine assumptions, let us review the values that we requested to be saved to our datafile (see the SPSS dataset screenshot in Figure 19.16 , as well as Figure 19.12 for producing the variables earlier in **R**).

1. PRE_1 values are the predicted probabilities.
2. PGR_1 is the predicted group membership (here group membership is either prepared or unprepared for kindergarten).
3. COO_1 values are Cook's influence statistics. As a general suggestion, Cook's values greater than one suggest that case is potentially problematic.
4. LEV_1 values are leverage values. As a general guide, leverage values less than .20 suggest there are no problems with cases exerting undue influence. Values greater than .5 indicate problems.
5. ZRE_1 values are standardized residuals computed as the residual divided by an estimate of the standard deviation of the residual. Standardized residuals have a mean of zero and standard deviation of one.

6, 7, 8. DFB0_1, DFB1_1 and DFB2_1 values are DfBeta values and indicate the difference in a beta coefficient if that particular case were excluded from the model.

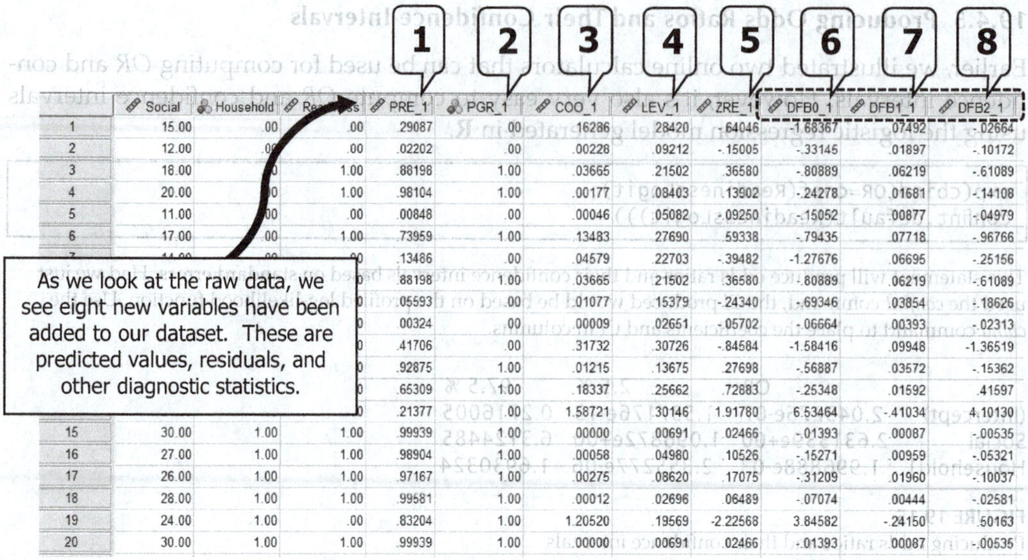
1
2
3
4
5
6
7
8
As we look at the raw data, we see eight new variables have been added to our dataset. These are predicted values, residuals, and other diagnostic statistics.

	Social	Household	Readiness	PRE_1	PGR_1	COO_1	LEV_1	ZRE_1	DFB0_1	DFB1_1	DFB2_1
1	15.00	.00	.00	29087	.00	16286	28420	-.64046	-1.68367	07492	-.02664
2	12.00	.00	.00	.02202	.00	.00228	.09212	-.15005	-.33145	.01897	-.10172
3	18.00	[illegible]	1.00	.88198	1.00	.03665	.21502	.36580	-.80889	.06219	-.61089
4	20.00	[illegible]	1.00	.98104	1.00	.00177	.08403	.13902	-.24278	.01681	-.14108
5	11.00	[illegible]	.00	.00848	.00	.00046	.05082	-.09250	-.15052	.00877	-.04979
6	17.00	.00	1.00	.73959	1.00	13483	27690	.59338	-.79435	.07718	-.96766
7	[illegible]	[illegible]	[illegible]	.13486	.00	.04579	.22703	-.39482	-1.27676	.06695	-.25156
[illegible]	[illegible]	[illegible]	[illegible]	.88198	1.00	.03665	.21502	.36580	-.80889	.06219	-.61089
[illegible]	[illegible]	[illegible]	[illegible]	.05593	.00	.01077	.15379	-.24340	-.69346	.03854	-.18626
[illegible]	[illegible]	[illegible]	[illegible]	00324	.00	.00009	.02651	-.05702	-.06664	.00393	-.02313
[illegible]	[illegible]	[illegible]	[illegible]	.41706	.00	.31732	.30726	-.84584	-1.58416	.09948	-1.36519
[illegible]	[illegible]	[illegible]	[illegible]	.92875	1.00	.01215	.13675	.27698	-.56887	.03572	-.15362
[illegible]	[illegible]	[illegible]	[illegible]	.65309	1.00	.18337	.25662	.72883	-.25348	.01592	.41597
[illegible]	[illegible]	[illegible]	[illegible]	.21377	.00	1.58721	.30146	1.91780	6.53464	-.41034	4.10130
15	30.00	1.00	1.00	.99939	1.00	.00000	.00691	.02466	-.01393	.00087	-.00535
16	27.00	1.00	1.00	.98904	1.00	.00058	.04980	.10526	-.15271	.00959	-.05321
17	26.00	1.00	1.00	.97167	1.00	.00275	.08620	.17075	-.31209	.01960	-.10037
18	28.00	1.00	1.00	.99581	1.00	.00012	.02696	.06489	-.07074	.00444	-.02581
19	24.00	1.00	.00	.83204	1.00	1.20520	.19569	-2.22568	3.84582	-.24150	.50163
20	30.00	1.00	1.00	.99939	1.00	.00000	.00691	.02466	-.01393	.00087	-.00535

FIGURE 19.16
Saved data.

19.5.1 Noncollinearity

It is not possible to request multicollinearity statistics, such as tolerance and VIF, using logistic regression in SPSS or **R**. We can, however, estimate those values by running the same variables in a multiple regression model and requesting only the collinearity statistics. We are not interested in the parameter estimates of the model—only the collinearity statistics. Tolerance values of less than .10 and VIF values of greater than 10 indicate multicollinearity (Menard, 1995). Because the steps for generating multiple regression were presented previously in the text, we will not reiterate them here. Rather, we will merely present the applicable portion of the output of this model. From the output that follows with a tolerance of .248 and VIF of 4.037, we have evidence that we do not have multicollinearity. In examining collinearity diagnostics, a general guideline for interpreting condition indices is that values in the range of 10 to 30 should be of concern, greater than 30 indicates trouble, and greater than 100 indicates disaster (Belsley, 1991). Here the condition index of dimension three (14.259) is within the range of cause for concern. The last three columns refer to variance proportions. Multiplying these values by 100 provides a percentage of the variance of the regression coefficient that is related to a particular eigenvalue. Multicollinearity is suggested when covariates have high percentages associated with a small eigenvalue (and large condition index). Thus, for purposes of reviewing for multicollinearity, concentrate only on the rows with small eigenvalues. In this example 100% of the variance of the regression coefficient for social development and 73% for type of household are related to eigenvalue 3 (the dimension with the smallest eigenvalue and largest condition index). This suggests some concern for multicollinearity. In summary, we have met the assumption of noncollinearity with the tolerance and VIF values, but there is some concern for multicollinearity with the condition index and variance proportion values.

Coefficients[a]

Model		Collinearity Statistics	
		Tolerance	VIF
1	Social development	.248	4.037
	Type of household	.248	4.037

a. Dependent Variable: Kindergarten readiness

Collinearity Diagnostics[a]

Model	Dimension	Eigenvalue	Condition Index	Variance Proportions		
				(Constant)	Social development	Type of household
1	1	2.683	1.000	.00	.00	.01
	2	.303	2.974	.05	.00	.25
	3	.013	**14.259**	.95	**1.00**	**.73**

a. Dependent Variable: Kindergarten readiness

Working in **R**, the *car* package can be used to generate VIF statistics. The following command will install *car* and load it into your library. If you've installed the package previously, you only need to load the package into your library.

```
install.packages(car)
library(car)
```

```
vif(ReadinessLogit)
1/vif(ReadinessLogit)
```

The *vif* command will generate the VIF and its reciprocal (using the *1/vif* command), which is the tolerance statistic.

FIGURE 19.17
Collinearity output and **R** code.

19.5.2 Linearity

Recall that the linearity assumption is applicable only to continuous variables. Thus, we will test this assumption only for social development. The Tidwell transformation test can be used to test that the assumption of linearity has been met. To generate this test, for each *continuous* independent variable we must first create an interaction term that is the product of the independent variable and its natural log (*ln*). Here we have only one continuous independent variable—social development. Thus, only one interaction term will be created.

Step 1. To create an interaction term of our continuous variable and the natural log of this variable, go to "Transform" in the top pulldown menu, then select "Compute Variable." Following the screenshot for Step 1 (Figure 19.18) produces the "Compute Variable" dialog box.

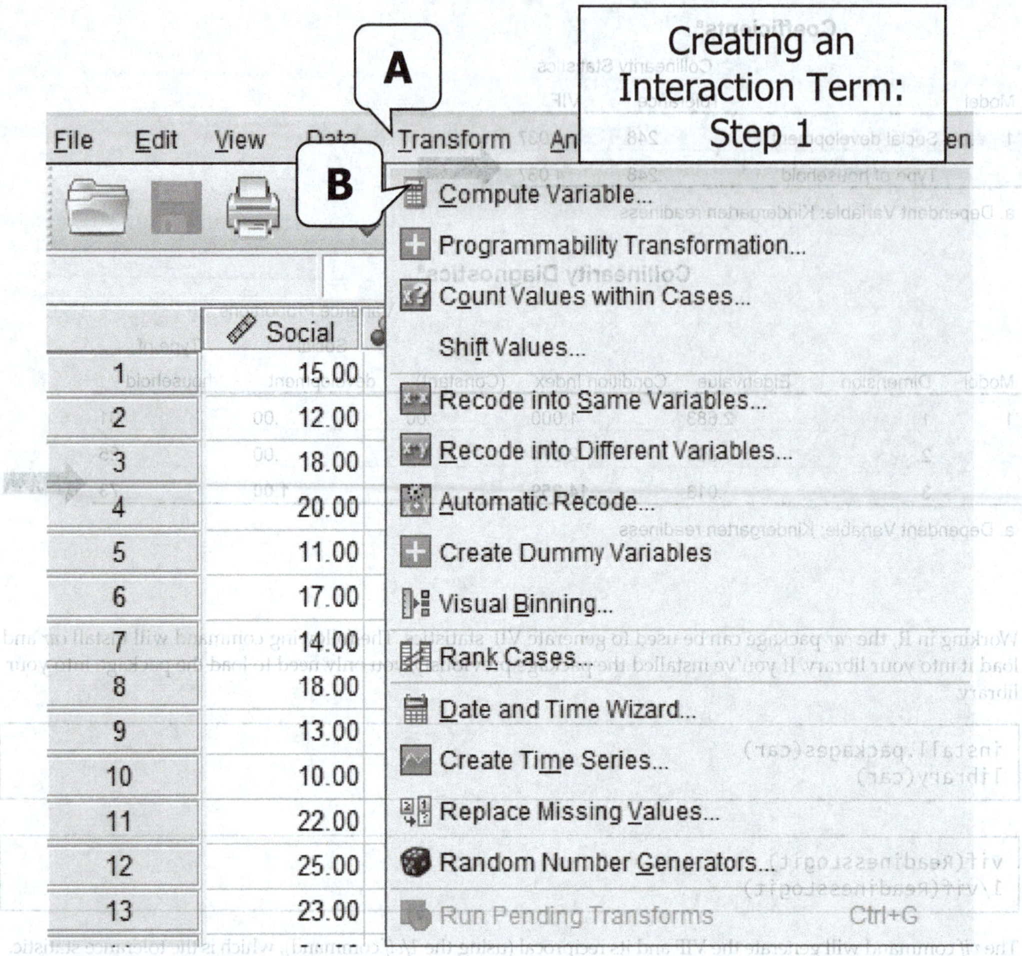

FIGURE 19.18
Creating an interaction term: Step 1.

Step 2. In the Target Variable box in the upper left corner, enter the variable name that you want to appear as the column header (see the screenshot for Step 2, Figure 19.19). Since this is the column header name, this name cannot begin with special characters or numbers and cannot have any spaces. If you wish to define the label for this variable (i.e., what will appear on the output; this *can* include special characters, spaces, and numbers), then click on the "Type & Label" box directly underneath "Target Variable," where additional text to define the name of the variable can be included. Next, click on the continuous covariate (i.e., social development) and move it into the Numeric Expression box by clicking on the arrow in the middle of the screen. Using either the keyboard on screen or your keyboard, click on the asterisks key (i.e.,*). This will be used as the multiplication sign. Next, under Function group, click on "Arithmetic" to display all of the basic mathematical functions. From this alphabetized list click on Ln (natural log). To move this function into the Numeric Expression box, click on the arrow key in the right central part of the dialog box.

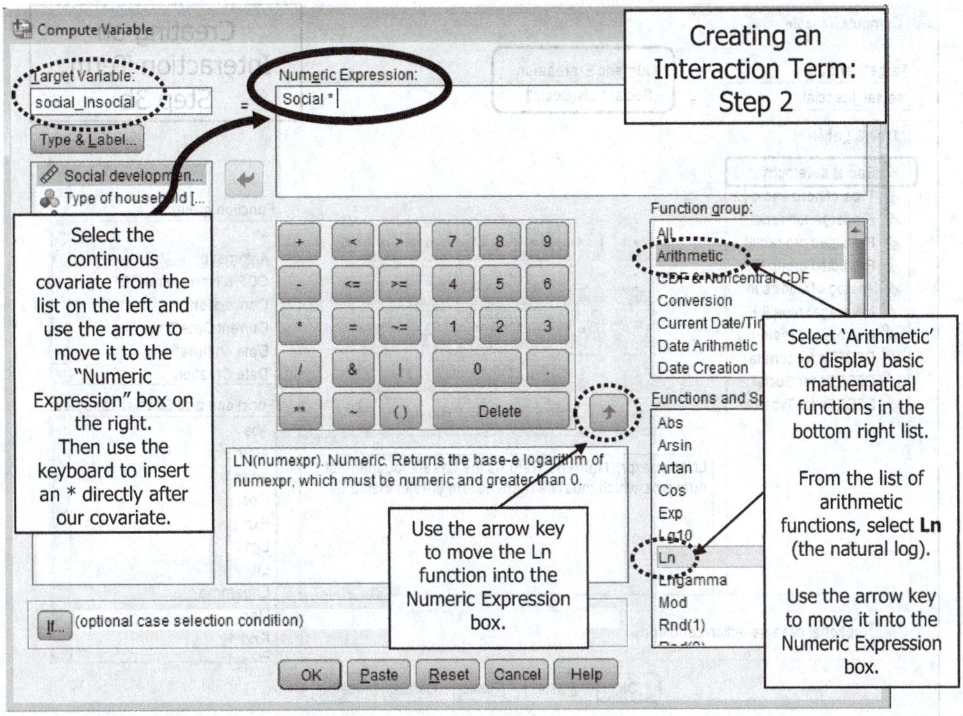

FIGURE 19.19
Creating an interaction term: Step 2.

Step 3. Once the natural log function is displayed in the Numeric Expression box, a question mark enclosed inside parentheses will appear (see screenshot for Step 3a, Figure 19.20). This is SPSS's way of asking for which variable you want the natural log computed. Here it is the continuous covariate, social development.

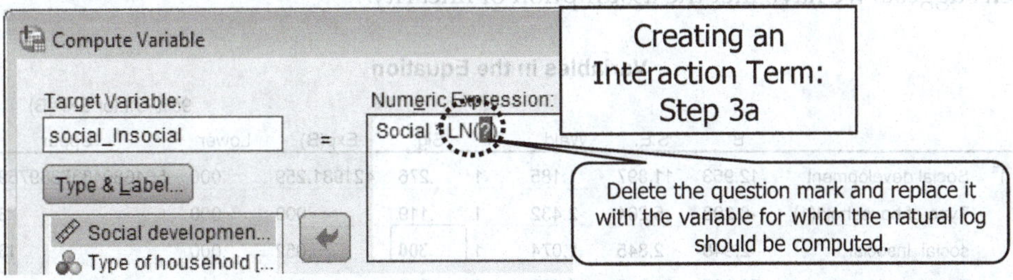

FIGURE 19.20
Creating an interaction term: Step 3a.

Here we want to compute the natural log for the continuous covariate, social development. To move this variable into the parentheses, use the backspace or delete key to remove the question mark. Then, click on the continuous covariate, social development, and move it into the parentheses next to LN in the Numeric Expression box by clicking on the arrow in the middle of the screen (see the screenshot for Step 3b, Figure 19.21). The numeric expression should then read: Social*LN(Social). Click "OK" to compute and create the new variable in the dataset.

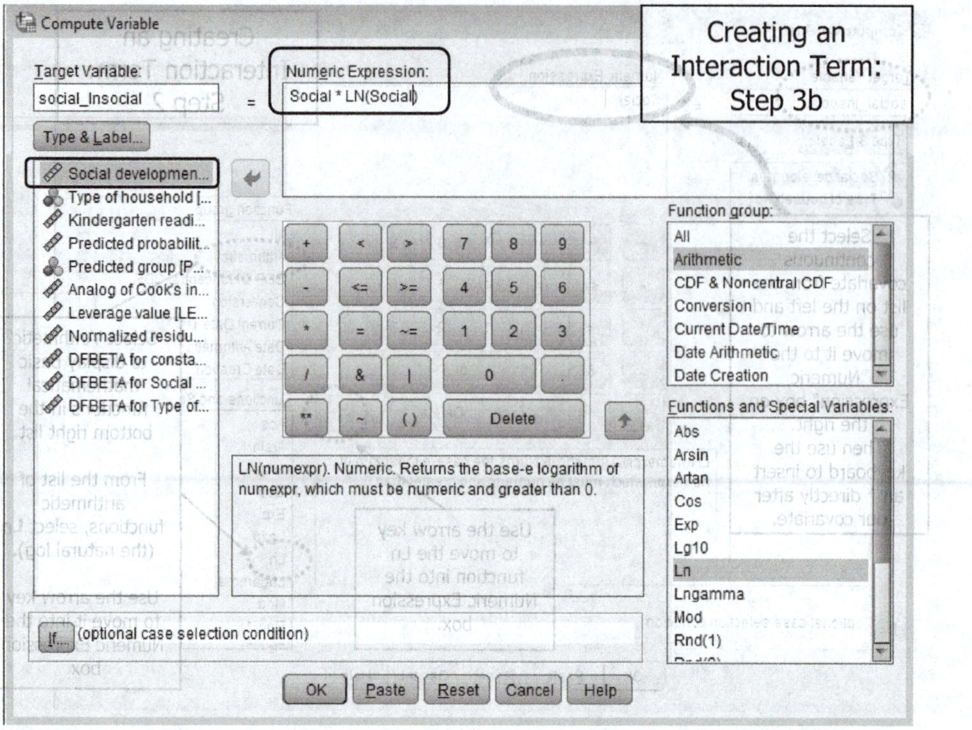

FIGURE 19.21
Creating an interaction term: Step 3b.

Step 4. The next step is to include the newly created variable (i.e., the interaction of the continuous variable with its natural log) into the logistic regression model, along with the other predictors. As those steps have been presented previously, they will not be reiterated here. The output indicates that the interaction term is not statistically significant ($p = .300$), which suggests we have met the assumption of linearity.

Variables in the Equation

		B	S.E.	Wald	df	Sig.	Exp(B)	95% C.I.for EXP(B) Lower	Upper
Step 1[a]	Social development	12.953	11.897	1.185	1	.276	421981.259	.000	5646804337369759.000
	Type of household(1)	-8.208	5.264	2.432	1	.119	.000	.000	8.236
	social_lnsocial	-2.948	2.845	1.074	1	**.300**	.052	.000	13.845
	Constant	-76.228	64.345	1.403	1	.236	.000		

a. Variable(s) entered on step 1: Social development, Type of household, social_lnsocial.

Working in **R**, we create the natural log of the variable "social development" with the following script and save it to our dataframe, naming the new variable "logsocial."

```
Ch19_readiness$logsocial
<- log(Ch19_readiness$Social)*Ch19_readiness$Social
```

FIGURE 19.22
Interaction Output

Next, we include the new variable, "logsocial,' into the logistic equation with this command. We name the new object "ReadinessLogit2."

```
ReadinessLogit2 <- glm(formula = Readiness ~ Social + Household +logsocial,
                       family="binomial",
                       data =Ch19_readiness)
```

Finally, we review the output of the new model with the *summary* function.

```
summary(ReadinessLogit2)
```

FIGURE 19.22 (continued)
Interaction Output

19.5.3 Independence

We plot the standardized residuals (which were requested and created through the "Save" option) against the values of X to examine the extent to which independence was met. The general steps for generating a simple scatterplot through "Scatter/dot" have been presented in a previous chapter (see Chapter 10), and they will not be repeated here. We will create one graph for each independent variable in our model. For the first graph in this example, place the standardized residual (called "normalized residual" in SPSS) on the Y axis and the independent variable (in this case, "social development") on the X axis. For the second graph, repeat these steps, keeping the standardized residual (called "normalized residual") on the Y axis, and move the second independent variable ("household") on the X axis.

Interpreting independence evidence. If the assumption of independence is met, the points should fall randomly within a band of −2.0 to +2.0. Here we have pretty good evidence of independence, especially given the small sample size relative to logistic regression, as all but one point (case 19) is within an absolute value of 2.0.

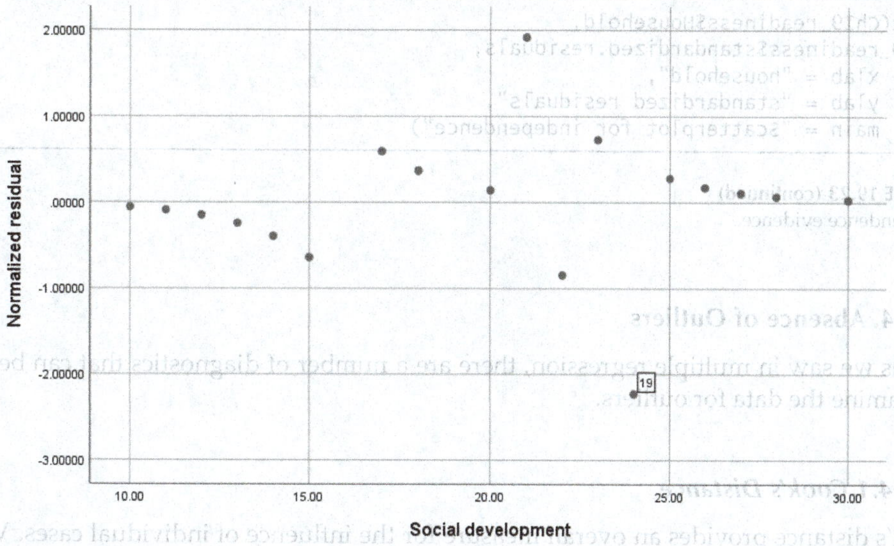

FIGURE 19.23
Independence evidence.

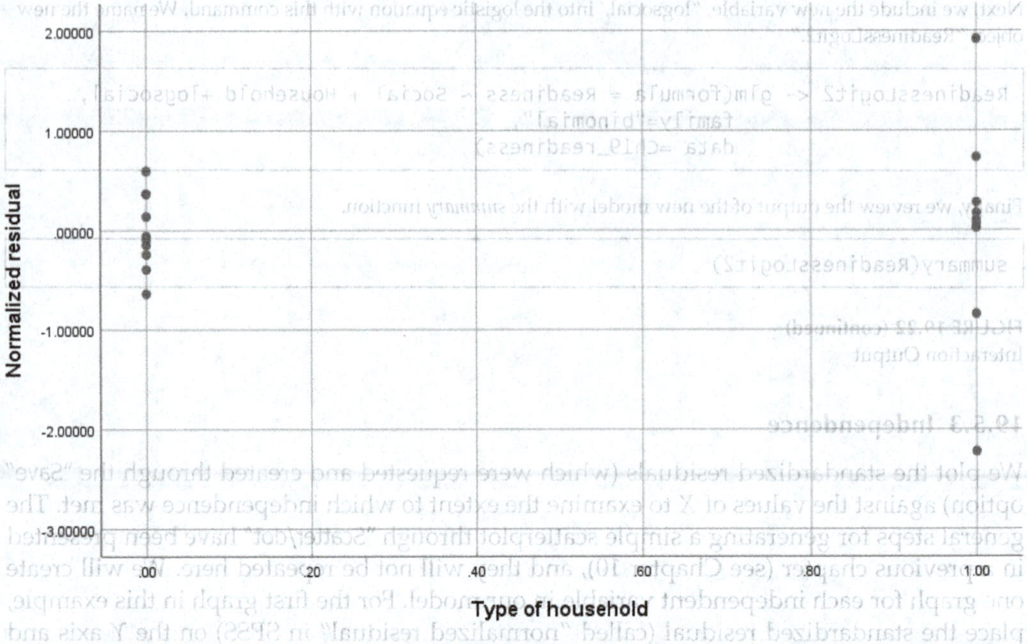

Working in **R**, we create plots using the *plot* function, with the first variable listed displaying on the *X* axis (i.e., "Ch19_readiness$Social"), and the second variable displaying on the *Y* axis (i.e., "Ch19_readiness$standardized.residuals"). **R** will automatically produce a boxplot for the "household" variable given that it is categorical in scale.

```
plot(Ch19_readiness$Social,
Ch19_readiness$standardized.residuals,
      xlab = "social",
      ylab = "standardized residuals",
      main = "Scatterplot for independence")
```

```
plot(Ch19_readiness$Household,
Ch19_readiness$standardized.residuals,
      xlab = "household",
      ylab = "standardized residuals",
      main = "Scatterplot for independence")
```

FIGURE 19.23 (continued)
Independence evidence.

19.5.4. Absence of Outliers

Just as we saw in multiple regression, there are a number of diagnostics that can be used to examine the data for outliers.

19.5.4.1 Cook's Distance

Cook's distance provides an overall measure for the influence of individual cases. Values greater than one suggest that a case may be problematic in terms of undue influence on the model. Examining the residual statistics provided in the binary logistic regression output (see the table in Figure 19.24, we see that the maximum value for Cook's distance is 1.58, which indicates at least one influential point.

19.5.4.2 Leverage Values

These values range from 0 to 1, with values close to 1 indicating greater leverage. As a general rule, leverage values greater than $(m + 1)/n$ (where m equals the number of independent variables; here $(2+1)/20 = .15$ indicates an influential case. With a maximum of .307, there is evidence to suggest one or more cases are exerting leverage.

19.5.4.3 DfBeta

We saved the DfBeta values as another indication of the influence of a case. The DfBeta provides information on the change in the predicted value when the case is deleted from the model. For logistic regression, the DfBeta values should be smaller than one. Looking at the minimum and maximum DfBeta values for the intercept (labeled "constant") and for household, we have at least one case that is suggestive of undue influence.

Descriptive Statistics

	N	Minimum	Maximum
Analog of Cook's influence statistics	20	.00000	1.58721
Leverage value	20	.00691	.30726
Normalized residual	20	-2.22568	1.91780
DFBETA for constant	20	-1.68367	6.53464
DFBETA for Social development	20	-.41034	.09948
DFBETA for Type of household(1)	20	-1.36519	4.10130
Valid N (listwise)	20		

Working in **R**, we can display the minimum and maximum values (along with other statistics) of all the variables in the dataframe with the *summary* function defined four our dataframe, Ch19_readiness. If you have a large dataset and want to review only the variables of interest, they can be listed in parentheses, separated by commas, such as ("Ch19_readiness$cook, Ch19_readiness$leverage")

```
summary(Ch19_readiness)
```

FIGURE 19.24
DfBeta output.

From our logistic regression output, we can review the Casewise List to determine cases with studentized residuals larger than two standard deviations (recall from the Options dialog box that we told SPSS to identify residuals outside two standard deviations). Here there were two cases (cases 14 and 19) that were identified as outliers and the relevant statistics (e.g., observed group, predicted value, predicted group, residual, and standardized residual) are provided. We examine these cases to make sure there was not a data entry error. If the data are correct, then we determine whether to keep or filter out the case(s).

Casewise List[b]

		Observed			Temporary Variable		
Case	Selected Status[a]	Kindergarten readiness	Predicted	Predicted Group	Resid	ZResid	SResid
14	S	P**	.214	U	.786	1.918	2.102
19	S	U**	.832	P	-.832	-2.226	-2.106

a. S = Selected, U = Unselected cases, and ** = Misclassified cases.
b. Cases with studentized residuals greater than 2.000 are listed.

FIGURE 19.25
Casewise output.

Since we have a small dataset, we can easily review the values of our diagnostics and see which cases are problematic in terms of exerting undue influence and/or outliers. Those that are circled are values that fall outside of the recommended guidelines and thus are suggestive of outlying or influential cases. Due to the already small sample size, we will not filter out any of these potentially problematic cases. However, in this situation (i.e., with diagnostics that suggest one or more influential cases), you may want to consider filtering out those cases or, at a minimum, reviewing the data to be sure that there was not a data entry error for that case.

PRE_1	PGR_1	COO_1	LEV_1	ZRE_1	DFB0_1	DFB1_1	DFB2_1
.999392	1.00	.000004	.006911	.024661	-.013932	.000875	-.005351
.999392	1.00	.000004	.006911	.024661	-.013932	.000875	-.005351
.995807	1.00	.000117	.026963	.064891	-.070741	.004442	-.025813
.989041	1.00	.000581	.049804	.105262	-.152712	.009590	-.053211
.971670	1.00	.002750	.086198	.170750	-.312087	.019597	-.100367
.928748	1.00	.012153	.136749	.276980	-.568875	.035722	-.153621
.832036	1.00	1.205197	.195686	-2.225679	3.845816	-.241498	.501633
.653086	1.00	.183375	.256624	.728829	-.253484	.015918	.415970
.417058	.00	.317320	.307255	-.845835	-1.584165	.099477	-1.365193
.213769	.00	1.587210	.301455	1.917797	6.534642	-.410342	4.101298
.981041	1.00	.001773	.084029	.139017	-.242779	.016815	-.141077
.881982	1.00	.036653	.215020	.365801	-.808894	.062192	-.610891
.881982	1.00	.036653	.215020	.365801	-.808894	.062192	-.610891
.739590	1.00	.134832	.276901	.593380	-.794347	.077183	-.967663
.290873	.00	.162857	.284197	-.640457	-1.683669	.074919	-.026642
.134862	.00	.045786	.227035	-.394822	-1.276762	.066947	-.251561
.055928	.00	.010766	.153789	-.243396	-.693464	.038535	-.186256
.022018	.00	.002284	.092122	-.150046	-.331452	.018975	-.101723
.008483	.00	.000458	.050824	-.092499	-.150523	.008774	-.049789
.003241	.00	.000089	.026507	-.057023	-.066639	.003932	-.023128

FIGURE 19.26
Reviewing diagnostic values

19.5.5 Assessing Classification Accuracy

In addition to examining Press's *Q* for classification accuracy, we can generate a kappa statistic. Kappa is the proportion of agreement above that expected by chance. A kappa statistic of 1.0 indicates perfect agreement whereas a kappa of 0 indicates chance agreement. Negative values can occur and indicate weaker than chance agreement. General rules of interpretation for kappa are: small, < .30; moderate, .30 to .50; large, > .50.

Step 1. Kappa statistics are generated through the "Crosstab" procedure (go to "Analyze" in the top pulldown menu, then "Descriptive statistics," and then "Crosstabs"). Once the Crosstabs dialog box is open, select the dependent variable from the list on the left and use the arrow key to move it to "Row(s)." Select the predicted group (PGR_1) from the list on the left and use the arrow key to move it to Column(s) (see the screenshot for Step 1, Figure 19.27).

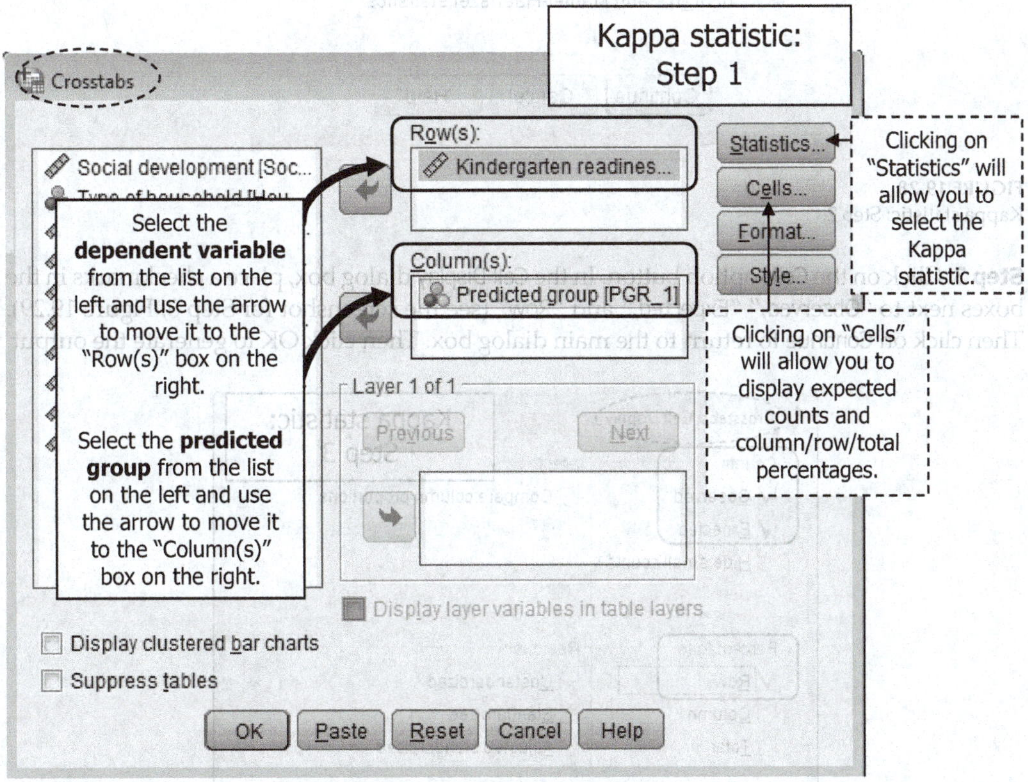

FIGURE 19.27
Kappa statistic: Step 1.

Step 2. Click on the Statistics option button. Place a checkmark in the box next to "Kappa" (see the screenshot for Step 2, Figure 19.28). Then click on Continue to return to the main dialog box.

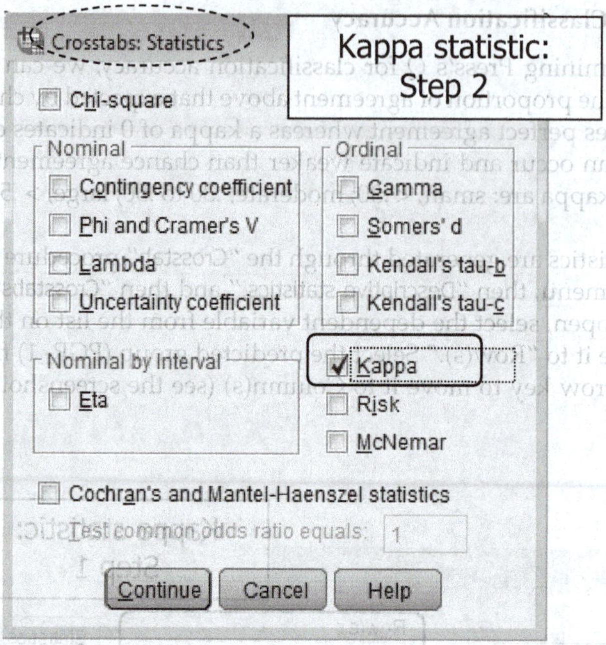

FIGURE 19.28
Kappa statistic: Step 2.

Step 3. Click on the Cells option button. In the Cell Display dialog box, place a checkmarks in the boxes next to "Observed," "Expected," and "Row" (see the screenshot for Step 3, Figure 19.29). Then click on Continue to return to the main dialog box. Then click OK to generate the output.

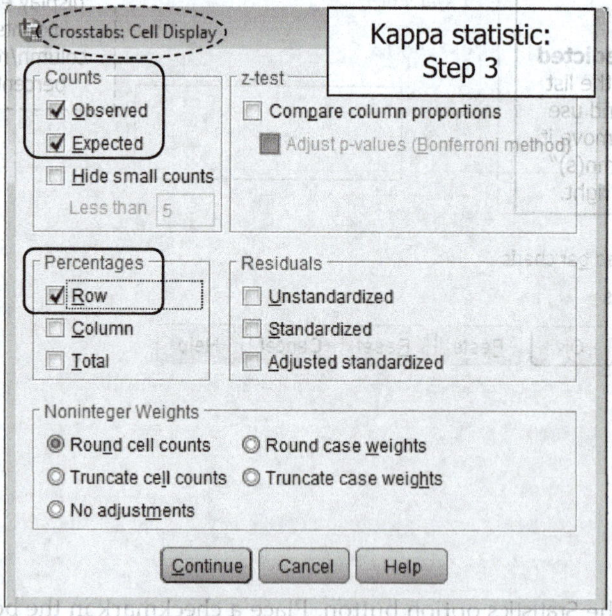

FIGURE 19.29
Kappa statistic: Step 3.

The crosstab table is interpreted as we have seen in the past. The columns represent the predicted group membership and the rows represent the observed group membership. This table should look familiar to the one that was provided to us with the logistic regression results. What is of most interest is the table labeled "Symmetric Measures," as this table contains the Kappa statistic. With a Kappa statistic of .792, and using our conventions for interpretation, this is considered to be a large value, which suggests strong agreement.

Kindergarten readiness * Predicted group Crosstabulation

			Predicted group		
			Unprepared	Prepared	Total
Kindergarten readiness	Unprepared	Count	7	1	8
		Expected Count	3.2	4.8	8.0
		% within Kindergarten readiness	87.5%	12.5%	100.0%
	Prepared	Count	1	11	12
		Expected Count	4.8	7.2	12.0
		% within Kindergarten readiness	8.3%	91.7%	100.0%
Total		Count	8	12	20
		Expected Count	8.0	12.0	20.0
		% within Kindergarten readiness	40.0%	60.0%	100.0%

Symmetric Measures

		Value	Asymptotic Standard Error[a]	Approximate T[b]	Approximate Significance
Measure of Agreement	**Kappa**	.792	.140	3.540	.000
N of Valid Cases		20			

a. Not assuming the null hypothesis.

b. Using the asymptotic standard error assuming the null hypothesis.

Working in **R**, we can use the *caret* package to generate a number of accuracy statistics, including Kappa.

```
install.packages("caret")
library(caret)
```

First, we need to install *caret* and load it into our library.

```
threshold <- 0.5
```

FIGURE 19.30
Kappa output and ROC curve.

Next, we set our *threshold* level. For this illustration, we will use a threshold of .50.

```
confusionMatrix(factor(Ch19_readiness$predicted.probabilities>threshold),
                factor(Ch19_readiness$Readiness==1),
                positive="TRUE")
```

The *confusionMatrix* function will generate the predicted group classification table (called a "confusion matrix") as well as a number of statistics.

```
Confusion Matrix and Statistics

          Reference
Prediction FALSE TRUE
     FALSE     7    1
     TRUE      1   11

               Accuracy : 0.9
                 95% CI : (0.683, 0.9877)
    No Information Rate : 0.6
    P-Value [Acc > NIR] : 0.003611

                  Kappa : 0.7917
 Mcnemar's Test P-Value : 1.000000

            Sensitivity : 0.9167
            Specificity : 0.8750
         Pos Pred Value : 0.9167
         Neg Pred Value : 0.8750
             Prevalence : 0.6000
         Detection Rate : 0.5500
   Detection Prevalence : 0.6000
      Balanced Accuracy : 0.8958

       'Positive' Class : TRUE
```

The model has accuracy of predicting of about 90% ("accuracy: 0.9"). Using the four quadrants of our classification table and labeling the cells as A (upper left), B (upper right), C (bottom left), and D (bottom right) (you may remember this from working with contingency tables in an earlier chapter), specificity and sensitivity can be calculated.

The true negative rate is **specificity** and is calculated as $A/(A+B)$. Noted on the R output as .8750.
The true positive rate is **sensitivity** and is calculated as $D/(C+D)$. Noted on the R output as .9167.

```
install.packages("ROCR")
library(ROCR)
```

To generate the ROC curve, we will install and use the *ROCR* package. The *install.packages* and *library* commands will install and call *ROCR* into our library, respectively.

```
predReadiness <- prediction(predict(ReadinessLogit),
                Ch19_readiness$Readiness)
perfReadiness <- performance(predReadiness,"tpr","fpr")
```

FIGURE 19.30 (continued)
Kappa output and ROC curve.

We will create an object called "predReadiness" using our logistic model (i.e., *ReadinessLogit*). The performance measures that we request include the true positive rate (*tpr*) and false positive rate (*fpr*).

```
plot(perfReadiness)
```

Our ROC curve is displayed using the *plot* function.

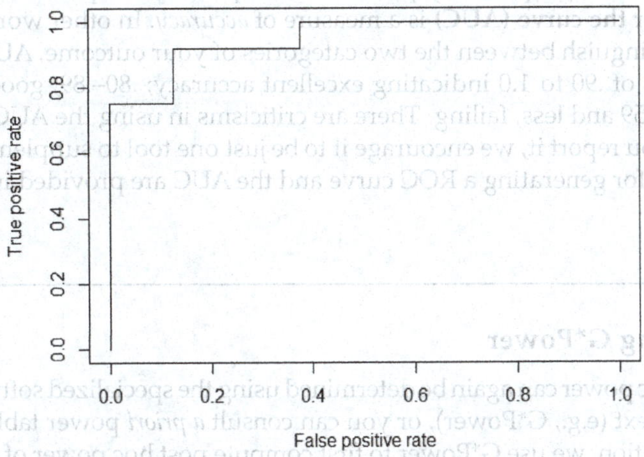


```
performance(predReadiness, 'auc')
```

To find the area under the curve (AUC), we use the *performance* function, inserting our predicted object (predReadiness) and requesting the AUC (*auc*). The output is a scalar, .9479167. AUC ranges from 0 to 1, with 1 indicating 100% specificity and 100% sensitivity. In this example, the AUC is about .95, indicating very good specificity and sensitivity.

```
An object of class "performance"
Slot "x.name":
[1] "None"

Slot "y.name":
[1] "Area under the ROC curve"

Slot "alpha.name":
[1] "none"

Slot "x.values":
list()

Slot "y.values":
[[1]]
[1] 0.9479167

Slot "alpha.values":
list()
```

FIGURE 19.30 (continued)
Kappa output and ROC curve.

19.5.5.1 ROC Curves and AUC

Another way to determine classification accuracy is using the **Receiver Operator Characteristic (ROC) curve,** developed during World War II for analyzing radar images and discovered as a useful tool for evaluating medical results in the 1970s. ROC curves plot the true positive rate (sensitivity) to the false positive rate (1-specificity). Each point on the ROC curve is a sensitivity/specificity pair that corresponds to a specific decision threshold. The **area under the curve (AUC)** is a measure of *accuracy*. In other words, how well a parameter can distinguish between the two categories of your outcome. AUC ranges from 0 to 1, with values of .90 to 1.0 indicating excellent accuracy; .80–.89, good; .70–.79, fair; .60–.69, poor; and .59 and less, failing. There are criticisms in using the AUC (Hand, 2009), and thus should you report it, we encourage it to be just one tool to supplement your analysis. **R** commands for generating a ROC curve and the AUC are provided in Figure 19.30.

19.6 Power Using G*Power

A priori and post hoc power can again be determined using the specialized software described previously in this text (e.g., G*Power), or you can consult *a priori* power tables (e.g.,Cohen, 1988). As an illustration, we use G*Power to first compute post hoc power of our example.

19.6.1 Post Hoc Power

The first thing that must be done when using G*Power for computing *post hoc* power is to select the correct test family. For logistic regression we select "Tests" in the top pulldown menu, then "Correlation and regression," and finally "Logistic regression." Once that selection is made, the "Test family" automatically changes to "z tests."

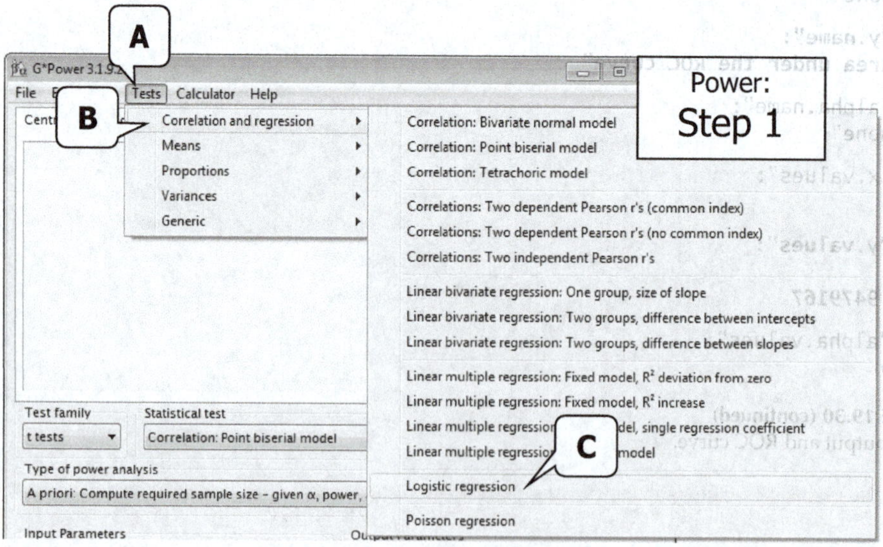

FIGURE 19.31
Post hoc power.

The "Type of power analysis" desired then needs to be selected. To compute post hoc power, select "Post hoc: Compute achieved power—given α, sample size, and effect size." For this illustration, we will compute power for the continuous covariate.

The "Input Parameters" must then be specified. In our example we conducted a two-tailed test. The odds ratio for our continuous variable social development was 2.631. The probability that $Y = 1$ given that $X = 1$ under the null hypothesis is set to .50. The alpha level we used was .05 and the total sample size was 20. "R^2 other X" refers to the squared correlation between social development and our other covariate. In this case, the simple bivariate correlation between these variables is .867 and the squared correlation is .752. Social development is a continuous variable, thus it follows a normal distribution. The last two parameters to be specified are for the mean and standard deviation of our covariate. In this case, the mean of social development was 20.20 and the standard deviation was 6.39. Once the parameters are specified, click on "Calculate" to find the power statistics.

The "Output Parameters" provide the relevant statistics for the input just specified. In this example, we were interested in determining post hoc power for a logistic regression model. Based on the criteria specified, the post hoc power was substantially less than 1. In other words, the probability of rejecting the null hypothesis when it is really false was significantly less than 1% (sufficient power is often .80 or above). This finding is not surprising given the very small sample size. Keep in mind that conducting power analysis *a priori* is recommended so that you avoid a situation where, post hoc, you find that the sample size was not sufficient to reach the desired level of power (given the observed parameters).

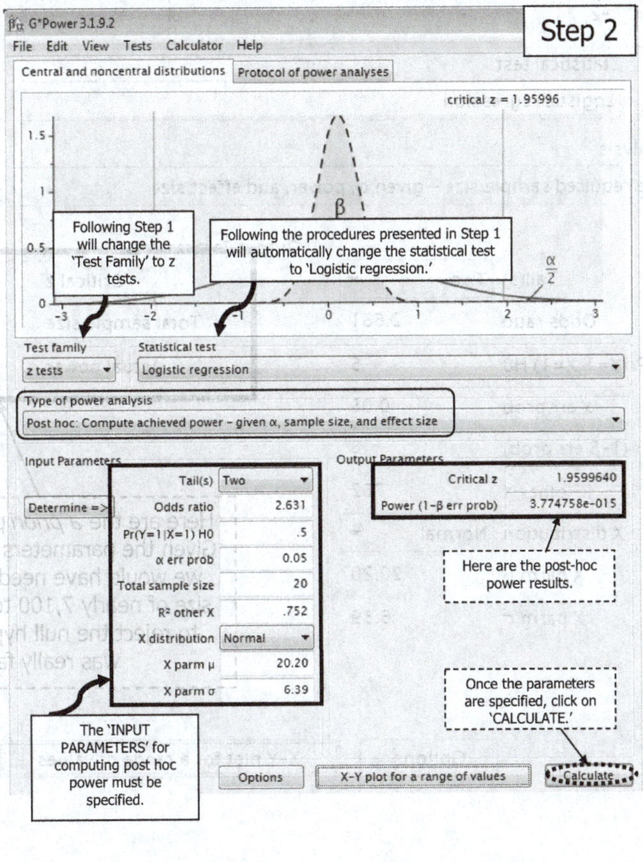

FIGURE 19.32
Post hoc power: Step 2.

19.6.2 *A Priori* Power

For *a priori* power, we can determine the total sample size needed for logistic regression given the same parameters just discussed. In this example, had we wanted an *a priori* power of .80 given the same parameters just defined, we would need a total sample size of 7094.

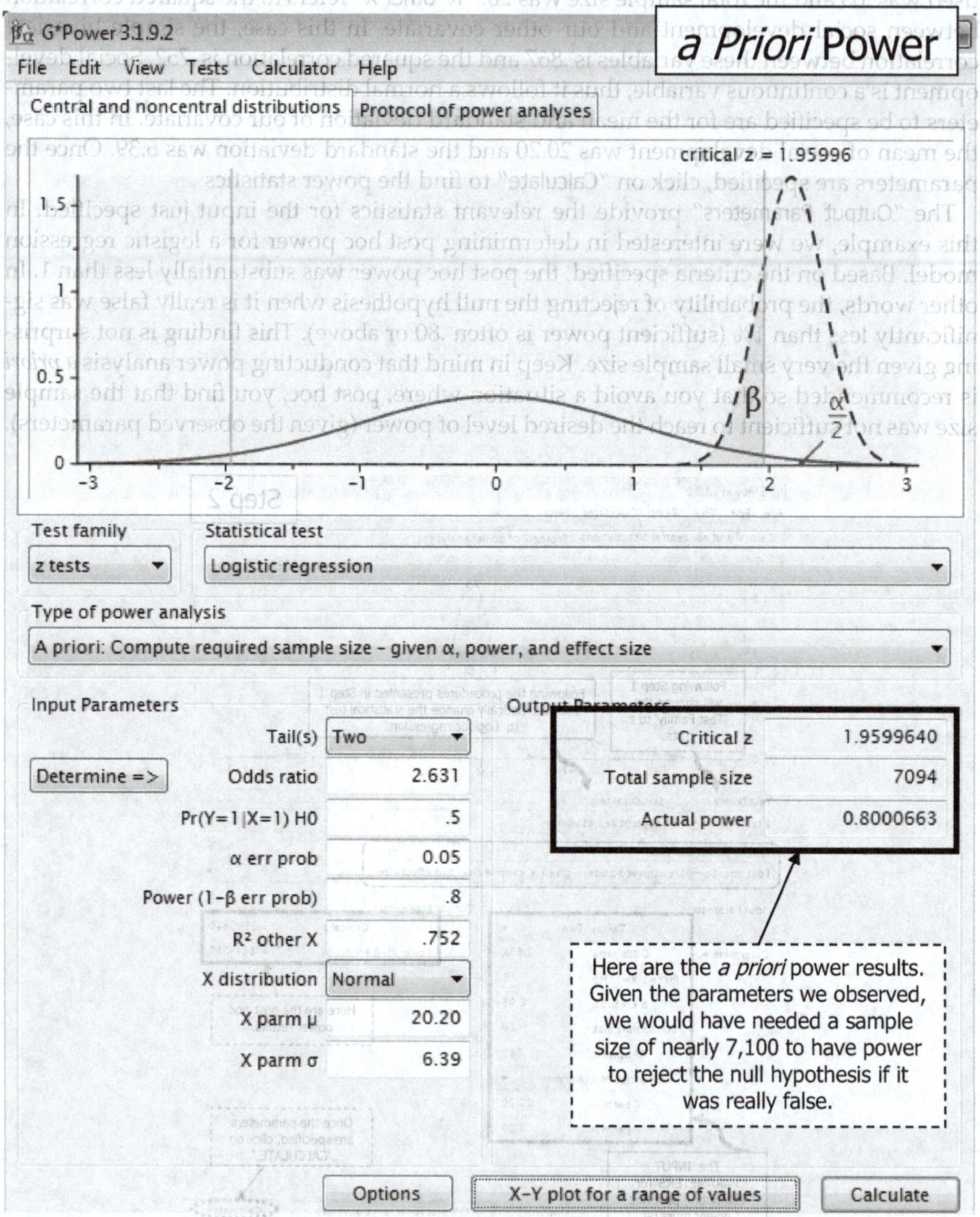

FIGURE 19.33
A priori power.

19.7 Research Question Template and Example Write-Up

Finally, here is an example paragraph for the results of the logistic regression analysis. Recall that our graduate research assistant, Oso Wyse, was assisting Dr. Malani, a faculty member in the early childhood department. Dr. Malani wanted to know if kindergarten readiness (prepared vs. unprepared) could be predicted by social development (a continuous variable) and type of household (single- vs. two-parent home). The research question presented to Dr. Malani from Oso included the following: *Can kindergarten readiness be predicted from social development and type of household?*

Oso then assisted Dr. Malani in generating a logistic regression as the test of inference, and a template for writing the research question for this design is presented as follows:

Can [dependent variable] be predicted from [list independent variables]?

It may be helpful to preface the results of the logistic regression with information on an examination of the extent to which the assumptions were met. The assumptions include: (a) independence; (b) linearity; and (c) noncollinearity. We will also examine the data for outliers and influential points.

Logistic regression was conducted to determine whether social development and type of household (single parent vs. two-parent home) could predict kindergarten readiness.

The assumptions of logistic regression were tested. Specifically, these include: (a) noncollinearity; (b) linearity; and (c) independence of errors.

In terms of **noncollinearity**, a VIF value of 4.037 (below the value of 10.0 which indicates the point of concern) and tolerance of .248 (above the value of .10 which suggests multicollinearity) provided evidence of noncollinearity. However, there was some concern for multicollinearity. In examining the collinearity diagnostics, a condition index value of 14.259 was observed, which falls within the range of concern (specifically 10–30). Review of the variance proportions suggested that 100% of the variance of the regression coefficient for social development and 73% for type of household were related to the smallest eigenvalue. This also suggests concern for multicollinearity. Thu while we met the assumption of noncollinearity with the tolerance and VIF values, but there is some concern for multicollinearity with the condition index and variance proportion values.

Linearity was assessed by re-estimating the model and including, along with the original predictors, an interaction term which was the product of the continuous independent variable (i.e., social development) and its natural logarithm. The interaction term was not statistically significant, thus providing evidence of linearity (social*ln(social), B = -2.948, SE = 2.845, Wald = 1.074, df = 1, p = .300).

Independence was assessed by examining a plot of the standardized residuals against values of each independent variable. With the exception of one case which was slightly outside the band, all cases were within an absolute value of 2.0 thus indicating the assumption of independence has been met.

In reviewing for **outliers and influential points**, Cook's distance values were generally within the recommended range of less than 1.0, although the maximum value was 1.587. Leverage values ranged from .007 to .307, well under the recommended .50, suggesting outliers were not problematic. DfBeta values beyond one also suggested cases that may be exerting influence on the model. Based on the evidence reviewed, there are some cases that are suggestive of outlying and influential points. Due to the small sample size however, these cases were retained. Readers are urged to interpret the results with caution given the possible influence of outliers.

Here is an example paragraph of results for the logistic regression (remember that this will be prefaced by the previous paragraph reporting the extent to which the assumptions of the test were met).

Logistic regression analysis was then conducted to determine whether kindergarten readiness (prepared vs. unprepared) could be predicted from social development and type of household (single versus two-parent home). Good model fit was evidenced by nonstatistically significant results on the Hosmer and Lemeshow test, χ^2 (n = 20) = 4.691, df = 7, p =.698, and large effect size indices when interpreted using Cohen (1988) (Cox and Snell R^2 = .546; Nagelkerke R^2 = .738). These results suggest that the predictors, as a set, reliably distinguished between children who are ready for kindergarten (i.e., prepared) versus unprepared. Of the two predictors in the model, only social development was a statistically significant predictor of kindergarten readiness (Wald = 4.696, df = 1, p = .030). The odds ratio for social development suggests that for every one-point increase in social development, the odds are about 2 and 2/3 greater for being prepared for kindergarten as compared to unprepared. Type of household was not statistically significant, which suggests that the odds for being prepared for kindergarten (relative to unprepared) are similar regardless of being raised in a single parent versus a two-parent household. The table below presents the results for the model including the regression coefficients, Wald statistics, odds ratios, and 95% confidence intervals for the odds ratios. This is followed by a table which presents the group means and standard deviations of each predictor for both children who are prepared and unprepared for kindergarten.

Logistic Regression Results

						95% CI for Exp(*B*)	
	B	***SE***	**Wald**	***p***	**Exp(*B*)**	**Lower**	**Upper**
Intercept (constant)	−15.404	7.195	4.584	.032	NA		
Social development	.967	.446	4.696	.030	2.631	1.097	6.313
Type of household (two-parent home)	−6.216	3.440	3.265	.071	.002	.000	1.693

Group Means (and Standard Deviations) of Predictors

Predictor	**Prepared for Kindergarten**	**Unprepared for Kindergarten**
Social development	23.58 (4.74)	15.13 (5.14)
Type of household (two-parent home)	.67 (.49)	.25 (.46)

Overall, the logistic regression model accurately predicted 90% of the children in our sample, with children who are prepared for kindergarten slightly more likely to be classified correctly (91.7% of children prepared for kindergarten and 87.5% of children unprepared correctly classified). To account for chance agreement in classification, the Kappa coefficient was computed and found to be .792, a large value. Additionally, Press's Q was calculated to be 12.8, providing evidence that the predictions based on the logistic regression model are statistically significantly better than chance. The area under the ROC curve was approximately .95, indicating very good specificity and sensitivity. Post hoc power, calculated using G*Power, was less than .01 indicating very weak power.

19.8 Additional Resources

This chapter has provided a preview into conducting logistic regression analysis. However, there are a number of areas that space limitations prevent us from delving into. For those of you who are interested in learning more, or if you find yourself in a sticky situation in your analyses, you may wish to look into the following, among many other excellent resources:

- In-depth coverage of logistic regression (Hilbe, 2016; Osborne, 2015).
- Comprehensive overview of ROC curves, including going beyond the basics with a discussion on Bayesian methods (Krzanowski & Hand, 2009).
- Application of logistic regression with randomized trials and covariate adjustment (Jiang et al., 2017).
- Rare events and imbalanced data (Maalouf, Homouz, & Trafalis, 2018).

Problems

Conceptual Problems

1. Which one of the following represents the primary difference between OLS regression and logistic regression?
   a. Computer processing time to estimate the model
   b. The measurement scales of the independent variables that can be included in the model
   c. The measurement scale of the dependent variable
   d. The statistical software that must be used to estimate the model
2. Which one of the following is NOT an assumption of logistic regression?
   a. Independence
   b. Homogeneity of variance
   c. Linearity
   d. Noncollinearity

3. Which one of the following is NOT an appropriate dependent variable for binary logistic regression?
   a. Bernoulli
   b. Dichotomous
   c. Multinomial
   d. One variable with two categories
4. Which of the following would NOT be appropriate outcomes to examine with binary logistic regression?
   a. Employment status (employed; unemployed not looking for work; unemployed looking for work)
   b. Enlisted member of the military (member vs. non-member)
   c. Marital status (married vs. not married)
   d. Recreational athlete (athlete vs. nonathlete)
5. Which of the following represents what is being predicted in binary logistic regression?
   a. Mean difference between two groups
   b. Odds that the unit of analysis belongs to one of two groups
   c. Precise numerical value
   d. Relationship between one group compared to the other group
6. True or false? While probability, odds, and log odds may be computationally different, they all relay the same basic information.
7. A researcher is studying diet soda drinking habits and has coded "diet soda drinker" as "1" and "non diet soda drinker" as "0." Which of the following is a correct interpretation given a probability value of .52?
   a. The odds of being a diet soda drinker are about equal to those of not being a diet soda drinker.
   b. The odds of being a diet soda drinker are substantially greater than not being a diet soda drinker.
   c. The odds of being a diet soda drinker are substantially less than not being a diet soda drinker.
   d. Cannot be determined from the information provided.
8. A researcher has computed the odds ratio to study the relative odds of participating in family counseling, and has coded "participation" as "1" and "nonparticipation" as "0," based on family stability (a continuous variable). Which of the following is a correct interpretation given an odds ratio of .25?
   a. Families that are more stable participate in family counseling.
   b. The odds of being a stable family are about the same as compared to families that are not stable.
   c. For every one-unit increase in family stability, the odds of participating in family counseling decrease by 75%.
   d. For families that participate in counseling, the odds of family stability are 25% more likely.

9. Which of the following is a correct interpretation of the logit?
   a. The log odds become larger as the odds increase from 1 to 100.
   b. The log odds become smaller as the odds increase from 1 to 100.
   c. The log odds stay relatively stable as the odds decrease from 1 to 0.
   d. The change in log odds becomes larger when the independent variables are categorical rather than continuous.
10. Which of the following correctly contrasts the estimation of OLS regression as compared to logistic regression?
    a. The sum of the squared distance of the observed data to the regression line is minimized in logistic regression. The log likelihood function is maximized in OLS regression.
    b. The sum of the squared distance of the observed data to the regression line is maximized in logistic regression. The log likelihood function is minimized in OLS regression.
    c. The sum of the squared distance of the observed data to the regression line is maximized in OLS regression. The log likelihood function is minimized in logistic regression.
    d. The sum of the squared distance of the observed data to the regression line is minimized in OLS regression. The log likelihood function is maximized in logistic regression.
11. Which of the following is NOT a test that can be used to evaluate overall model fit for logistic regression models?
    a. Change in log likelihood
    b. Hosmer-Lemeshow goodness of fit
    c. Cox and Snell R squared
    d. Wald test
12. A researcher is studying diet soda drinking habits and has coded "diet soda drinker" as "1" and "non diet soda drinker" as "0." She has predicted drinking habits based on the individual's weight (measured in pounds). Given this scenario, which of the following is a correct interpretation of an odds ratio of 1.75?
    a. For every one-unit increase in being a diet soda drinker, the odds of putting on an additional pound increase by 75%.
    b. For every one-unit increase in being a diet soda drinker, the odds of putting on an additional pound decrease by 75%.
    c. For every one-pound increase in weight, the odds of attending being a diet soda drinker decrease by 75%.
    d. For every one-pound increase in weight, the odds of attending being a diet soda drinker increase by 75%.
13. A researcher is studying pet ownership and has coded "pet owner" as "1" and "non pet owner" as "0." He has predicted owning a pet based on the individual's household income. Given this scenario, which of the following is a correct interpretation of an odds ratio of 1.90?
    a. For pet owners, the odds of having higher household income increase by 90%.
    b. The odds of being a pet owner, as compared to not being a pet owner, are about the same.

c. For every one-unit increase in household income, the odds of being a pet owner decrease by 90%.
d. For every one-unit increase in household income, the odds of being a pet owner increase by 90%.

Answers to Conceptual Problems

1. c (The measurement scale of the dependent variable is the main difference between multiple regression and logistic regression.)
3. c (Multinomial.)
5. b (Odds that the unit of analysis belongs to one of two groups.)
7. a (The odds of being a diet soda drinker are about equal to those of not being a diet soda drinker, with .50 being exactly equal.)
9. a (The log odds become larger as the odds increase from 1 to 100.)
11. d (Wald test (assesses significance of individual predictors).)
13. d (For every one-unit increase in household income, the odds of pet owner increase by 90%.)

Computational Problems

1. You are given the following data, where X_1 (high school cumulative grade point average) and X_2 (participation in school-sponsored athletics; 0 = nonathlete and 1 = athlete; use 0 as the reference category) are used to predict Y (college enrollment immediately after high school, "1," versus delayed college enrollment or no enrollment, "0").

X_1	X_2	Y
4.15	1	1
2.72	0	1
3.16	0	0
3.89	1	1
4.02	1	1
1.89	0	0
2.10	0	1
2.36	1	1
3.55	0	0
1.70	0	0

Determine the following values based on simultaneous entry of independent variables: intercept; $-2LL$; constant; b_1; b_2; $se(b_1)$; $se(b_2)$; odds ratios; $Wald_1$; $Wald_2$.

2. You are given the following data, where X_1 (participation in high school honors classes; yes = 1, no = 0; use 0 as the reference category) and X_2. (participation in co-op program in college; yes = 1; no = 0; use 0 as the reference category) are used to predict Y (baccalaureate graduation with honors = 1 versus graduation without honors = 0).

X_1	X_2	Y
0	1	1
0	0	1
1	0	0
1	1	1
1	1	1
0	0	0
1	0	1
0	1	1
1	0	0
0	0	0

Determine the following values based on simultaneous entry of independent variables: intercept; −2*LL*; constant; b_1; b_2; $se(b_1)$; $se(b_2)$; odds ratios; $Wald_1$; $Wald_2$.

3. You are given the following data, where X_1 (high frequency social media user; yes = 1, no = 0; use 0 as the reference category) and X_2 (regularly consume coffee; yes = 1; no = 0; use 0 as the reference category) are used to predict Y (regularly exercise = 1 versus do not regularly exercise = 0).

X_1	X_2	Y
0	1	1
0	1	1
0	1	1
0	0	1
0	0	1
0	1	0
0	1	0
0	1	1
0	1	0
0	0	0
1	0	0
1	0	0
1	1	0
1	1	1
1	1	1
1	1	0
1	1	0
1	1	0

Determine the following values based on simultaneous entry of independent variables: intercept; −2*LL*; constant; b_1; b_2; $se(b_1)$. ; $se(b_2)$; odds ratios; $Wald_1$; $Wald_2$; *p*

Answers to Computational Problems

1. $-2LL = 7.558$; $b_{HSGPA} = -.366$; $b_{athlete} = 22.327$; $b_{constant} = .219$; $se\left(b_{HSGPA}\right) = 1.309$; $se\left(b_{athlete}\right) = 20006.861$; odds $\text{ratio}_{\text{HSGPA}} = .693$; odds $\text{ratio}_{\text{athlete}} < .001$; $Wald_{HSGPA} = .078$; $Wald_{athlete} = .000$
3. $-2LL = 22.342$; $b_{SocMed} = -1.533$; $b_{coffee} = .387$; $b_{constant} = .138$; $se\left(b_{SocMed}\right) = 1.050$; $se\left(b_{coffee}\right) = 1.145$; odds $\text{ratio}_{\text{SocMed}} = .216$; odds $\text{ratio}_{\text{coffee}} = 1.472$; $Wald_{SocMed} = 2.132$; $Wald_{coffee} = .114$; $p_{SocMed} = .216$; $p_{coffee} = .736$; $p_{constant} = .893$

Interpretive Problems

1. Use SPSS or **R** to develop a logistic regression model with data available on the website from the Division I-A Football Bowl Subdivision (FBS) obtained from ESPN during January 2016 (n = 128; FBS_2015.sav or FBS_2015.csv) (http://espn.go.com/college-football/statistics/team/_/stat/total/sort/totalYards). Utilize "top quartile in overall efficiency" as the dependent (binary) variable to find at least two strong predictors from among the continuous variables in the dataset. Write up the results in APA style, including testing for the assumptions. Determine and interpret a measure of effect size.
2. Use SPSS or **R** to develop a logistic regression model with data available on the textbook's website from the 2017 IPEDS (https://nces.ed.gov/ipeds/). Select one binary variable as the dependent variable [e.g., "institution provides on-campus housing" (ROOM)] and find at least two strong predictors from among the remaining variables in the dataset. Write up the results in APA style, including testing for the assumptions. Determine and interpret a measure of effect size.
3. Use SPSS or **R** to develop a logistic regression model with data available on the textbook's website from the 2017 NHIS* family file (https://www.cdc.gov/nchs/nhis/). Select one binary variable as the dependent variable [e.g., "any family member need help with an activity of daily living (ADL)" (FLAADLYN')] and find at least two strong predictors from among the remaining variables in the dataset. Write up the results in APA style, including testing for the assumptions. Determine and interpret a measure of effect size.

* It is important to note that the NHIS is a *complex sample* (i.e., not a simple random sample). Per NHIS (see https://www.cdc.gov/nchs/nhis/about_nhis.htm#sample_design), "The sampling plan follows a multistage area probability design that permits the representative sampling of households and noninstitutional group quarters (e.g., college dormitories) … The current sampling plan was implemented in 2016 … [It] is a sample of clusters of addresses that are located in primary sampling units (PSU's). A PSU consists of a county, a small group of contiguous counties, or a metropolitan statistical area." In the NHIS dataset, you will find, for example, a "weight" variable, which is used to adjust for the complex survey design. We won't get into the technical aspects of this, but when the data are analyzed to adjust for the sampling design (including non-simple random sampling procedure and disproportionate sampling) the end results are then representative of the intended population. The purpose of the text is not to serve as a primer for understanding complex samples, and thus readers interested in learning more about complex survey designs are referred to any number of excellent resources (Hahs-Vaughn, 2005; Hahs-Vaughn, McWayne, Bulotskey-Shearer, Wen, & Faria, 2011a, 2011b; Lee, Forthofer, & Lorimor, 1989; Skinner, Holt, & Smith, 1989). Additionally, so as to not complicate matters

any more than necessary, the applications in the textbook do not illustrate how to adjust for the complex sample design. *As such, if you do not adjust for the complex sampling design, the results that you see should not be interpreted to represent any larger population but only that select sample of individuals who actually completed the survey.* I want to stress that the reason why the sampling design has not been illustrated in the textbook applications is because the point of this section of the textbook is to illustrate how to use statistical software to generate various procedures and how to interpret the output and not to ensure the results are representative of the intended population. *Please do not let this discount or diminish the need to apply this critical step in your own analyses when using complex survey data as quite a large body of research exists that describes the importance of effectively analyzing complex samples as well as provides evidence of biased results when the complex sample design is not addressed in the analyses* (Hahs-Vaughn, 2005, 2006a, 2006b; Hahs-Vaughn et al., 2011a, 2011b; Kish & Frankel, 1973, 1974; Korn & Graubard, 1995; Lee et al., 1989; Lumley, 2004; Pfeffermann, 1993; Skinner et al., 1989).

20

Mediation and Moderation

Chapter Outline

Key Concepts

1. Mediation
2. Moderation
3. Direct effect
4. Indirect effect

In the previous three chapters, we have considered various regression models, specifically looking at using one or more independent variables to predict an outcome. In this chapter we build on our knowledge of regression to examine other ways in which variables can relate in a regression model.

When considering the relationship between two variables (say X and Y), the researcher usually determines some measure of relationship between those variables, such as a correlation coefficient (e.g., r_{XY}, the Pearson product-moment correlation coefficient), as we did in Chapter 10. Another way of looking at how two variables may be related is through regression analysis, in terms of prediction or explanation. That is, we evaluate the ability of one variable to predict or explain a second variable. With Chapters 18 and 19, we considered the case of multiple predictor variables through multiple linear regression analysis and logistic regression.

In this chapter we consider *differential effects* of predictors. In other words, a predictor may be more or less effective on the outcome in a given situation, where that "given situation" is that the predictor is being mediated or moderated in its relationship to the dependent variable. Our objectives are that by the end of this chapter, you will be able to (a) understand the concepts underlying mediation and moderation, (b) determine and interpret the results of a mediated and moderated model, and (c) understand and evaluate the assumptions of and conditions under which mediation and moderation can be examined.

20.1 What Mediation Is and How It Works

Let us consider the basic concepts involved in a simple mediation model. The underlying framework for mediation is to examine the *way* in which the independent variable relates to the dependent variable. For example, there may be a direct effect of the independent variable on the dependent variable, but there may also be an indirect effect where the independent variable passes influence through another variable, the mediator, and the mediator then to the dependent variable. We will focus on a simple mediation model, but this can be extended to complex models with multiple mediators.

20.1.1 Characteristics

Before we begin our discussion of mediation, we will have a quick and concise refresher on the simple and multiple regression models. As we learned in simple linear regression, the **population regression model** for the regression of *Y, the criterion*, given X, *the predictor,* often stated as the **regression of *Y* on *X***, although more easily understood as ***Y* being predicted by *X*** is:

$$Y_i = \beta_{YX} X_i + \alpha_{XY} + \varepsilon_i$$

where Y_i is the criterion variable, X_i is the predictor variable, β_{YX} is the population slope for Y_i predicted by X_i, α_{YX} is the population intercept for Y_i predicted by X_i, ε_i are the population residuals or errors of prediction (the part of Y_i not predicted from X_i), and *i* represents an index for a particular case (an individual or object; in other words, the unit of analysis that has been measured). The index *i* can take on values from 1 to *N*, where *N* is the size of the population, written as $i = 1, \ldots, N$.

The **population prediction model** is

$$Y_i' = \beta_{YX} X_i + \alpha_{YX}$$

where Y_i' is the predicted value of Y for a specific value of X. That is, Y_i is the *actual or observed score* obtained by individual i, while Y_i' is the *predicted score* based on their X score for that same individual (in other words, you are using the value of X to predict what Y will be). Thus, we see that the population prediction error is defined as follows:

$$\varepsilon_i = Y_i - Y_i'$$

There is only one difference between the regression and prediction models. The regression model explicitly includes prediction error as ε_i, whereas the prediction model includes prediction error *implicitly* as part of the predicted score Y_i' (i.e., there is some error in the predicted values).

The **sample multiple linear regression model** for predicting Y_i from m predictors $X_{1,2,\ldots,m}$ is

$$Y_i = b_1 X_{1i} + b_2 X_{2i} + \ldots + b_m X_{mi} + a + e_i$$

where Y_i is the **criterion variable** (i.e., the dependent variable); the X_k's are the **predictor (or independent) variables** where $k = 1, \ldots, m$; b_k is the **sample partial slope** of the regression line for Y as predicted by X_k, a is the **sample intercept** of the regression line for Y_i as predicted by the set of X_k's; e_i are the **residuals or errors of prediction** (the part of Y_i not predictable from the X_k's); and i represents an index for an individual or object. The index i can take on values from 1 to n where n is the size of the sample (i.e., $i = 1, \ldots, n$). The term **partial slope** is used because it represents the slope of Y for a particular X_k in which we have partialed out the influence of the other X_k's, much as we did with the partial correlation.

The **sample prediction model** is

$$Y_i' = b_1 X_{1i} + b_2 X_{2i} + \ldots + b_m X_{mi} + a$$

Where Y_i' is the predicted value of the outcome for specific values of the X_k's, and the other terms are as before. There is only one difference between the regression and prediction models. The regression model explicitly includes prediction error as e_i whereas the prediction model includes prediction error implicitly as part of the predicted score Y_i' (i.e., there is some error in the predicted values). The goal of the prediction model is to include an independent variable X that minimizes the residual; this means that the independent variable does a nice job of predicting the outcome. We can compute residuals, the e_i, for each of the i individuals or objects by comparing the actual Y values (i.e., Y_i) with the predicted Y values (i.e., Y_i') as

$$e_i = Y_i - Y_i'$$

for all $i = 1, \ldots, n$ individuals or objects in the sample.

Now let's consider the case of multiple predictors, but in the context of **mediation**. Let us first visualize what is happening in mediation. For ease we will drop the subscripts and superscripts with the exception of the direct effect, c'. In Figure 20.1, we have one independent variable, X, one mediator variable, M, and one dependent variable, Y. The arrows show us that the independent variable can be related to the dependent variable by two different paths. One path of influence from X to Y is *direct;* i.e., the arrow which goes directly from X to Y. In this path, X is the antecedent which influences Y, the consequent. The **direct effect** is notated as c' and can be interpreted as follows: two cases that differ by one unit on the independent variable, X, but are equal on the mediator, M, will differ by c' units on the dependent variable, Y. We see this in the following equation:

$$c' = \left[Y' \mid (X = x, M = m)\right] - \left[Y' \mid (X = x - 1, M = m)\right]$$

Where Y' is the estimated outcome which is conditioned on (i.e., |) the remaining values in parentheses where x is any value of the independent variable, X, and m is any value of the mediator, M. A **positive sign for** c' (i.e., positive direct effect) indicates that the case that is one unit higher on X is estimated to be higher on Y. A **negative sign for** c' (i.e., negative direct effect) indicates that the case that is one unit higher on X is estimated to be lower on Y. Y is the group mean in the case of a binary X, and therefore in situations where the independent variable is dichotomous, c' is estimating the difference between the two group means holding the mediator constant (i.e., the adjusted mean difference in ANCOVA).

The **indirect effect** is the second path of influence from the independent variable, X, to the independent variable, Y. It is is *indirect* as we see an arrow leads from X to the mediator, M, then from M to Y. In this indirect path, X is the antecedent which influences M, the consequent, then antecedent M influences Y, the consequent. In other words, the independent variable influences the mediating variable which in turn then influences the dependent variable. In the indirect effect path, path a represents how much two cases which differ by one unit on the independent variable, X, differ on the mediator, M. A positive sign for a indicates that a case higher on the independent variable is higher on the mediator. A negative sign for a indicates that the case higher on the independent variable is lower on the mediator. The b coefficient is interpreted as c' except with the mediator, M, rather than the independent variable, X, as the antecedent. In path b, we find that two cases that differ by one unit on the mediator, M, but are equal on X will differ by b units on the dependent variable, Y. The product, ab, is the *indirect effect* of the independent variable, X, on the dependent variable, Y, through the mediator, M. We can interpret the indirect effect as follows: two cases that differ by one unit on the mediator, M, but are equal on the independent variable, X, will differ by b units on the dependent variable, Y. A positive sign for ab (i.e., both a and b are positive *or* both are negative) indicates that the case higher on the independent variable is higher on the dependent variable. A negative sign for ab (i.e., either a and b, but *not both*, are negative) indicates that the case higher on the independent variable is lower on the dependent variable.

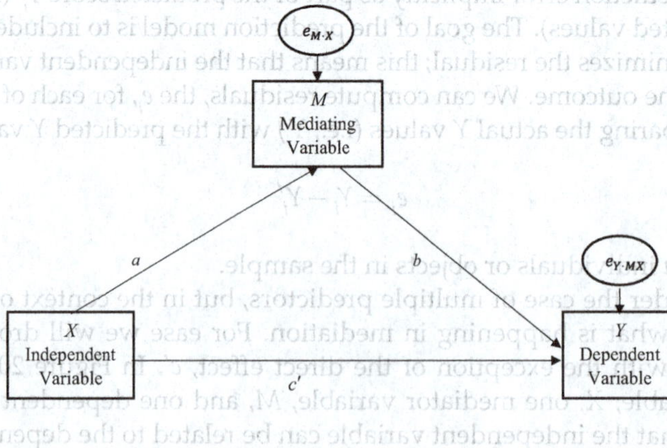

FIGURE 20.1
Simple mediation model.

The **total effect** of the independent variable on the dependent variable is c and indicates how much two cases that differ by one unit on the independent variable will differ on the dependent variable:

$$c = \left[Y' \mid (X = x)\right] - \left[Y' \mid (X = x - 1)\right] = c' + ab$$

A summary of the effects is presented in Box 20.1.

BOX 20.1 Summary of Mediating Effects

Path	Effects	Interpretation
a	Indirect effect of the independent variable on the mediator	How much two cases that differ by one unit on the independent variable, X, will differ on the mediator, M
b	Indirect effect of the mediator on the dependent variable	Two cases that differ by one unit on the mediator but are equal on the independent variable will differ by b units on the dependent variable
ab	Indirect effect of the independent variable on the dependent variable through the mediator	Two cases that differ by one unit on the mediator but are equal on the independent variable will differ by b units on the dependent variable
c'	Direct effect of the independent variable on the dependent variable	Two cases that differ by one unit on the independent variable, X, but are equal on M will differ by c' units on the dependent variable
c	Total effect of the independent variable on the dependent variable	How much two cases that differ by one unit on the independent variable will differ on the dependent variable

20.1.1.1 Additional Mediation Models

The mediation model in Figure 20.1 is the simplest mediation model that can be conceived. There are many more configurations that may exist, with more X's and more M's as well as mediated moderated models, multilevel mediation, and more. This chapter is designed to provide an overview into mediation and to whet your appetite to learn as you consider more advanced models in your own research.

20.1.2 Sample Size

Estimating sample size for mediation models is more complicated than with multiple linear regression. Although some guidelines for estimating sample size with mediated models have been provided (e.g., Fritz & MacKinnon, 2007), using Monte Carlo simulation to estimate sample size is recommended (Schoemann, Boulton, & Short, 2017). This is detailed further in the discussion of power.

20.1.3 Power

As with sample size, power in mediation models is also more complicated than with multiple linear regression. This is due to the formation of indirect effect as a product of two

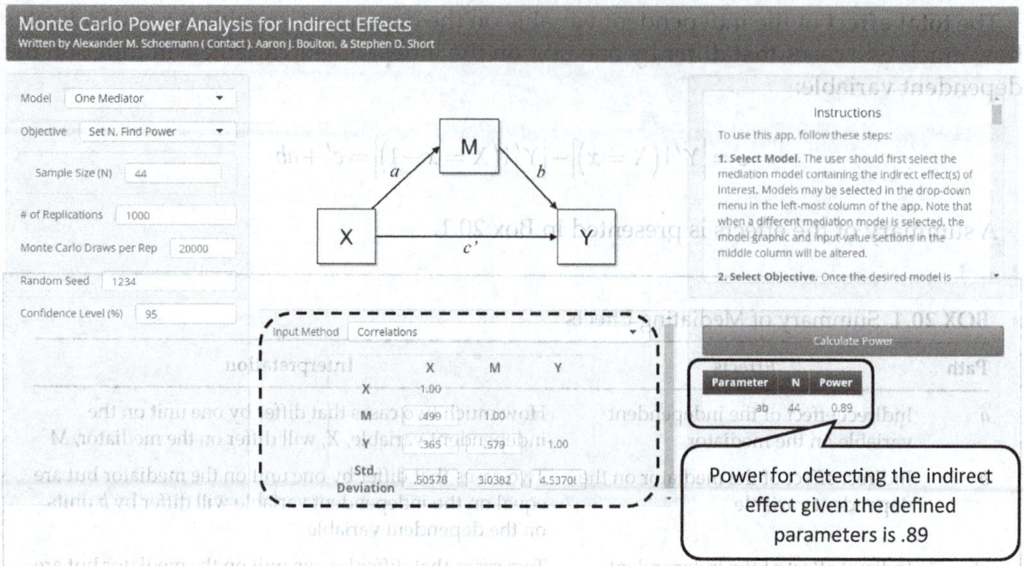

FIGURE 20.2
Power analysis for indirect effects.

effects, and as noted by Hayes (2013, p. 141), "with no agreed upon way of quantifying the magnitude of those effects or their product (something you need to do to assess the power to detect an effect of a given size)." The literature on power within mediation is not voluminous; however, there are tables for determining sample sizes needed for detecting indirect effects of a given size (Fritz & MacKinnon, 2007). Additional literature from Zhang (2014) illustrates estimating power in mediation using bootstrap methods through Monte Carlo simulation. Packages in **R**, such as *powerMediation* (Qiu, 2018), can be used to determine power and/or sample size in mediation analysis. *MedPower* is an online tool for computing power and sample size for mediation models (Kenny, n.d.). Schoemann et al. (2017) provide an app that uses Monte Carlo simulation for computing power for indirect effects. Using Schoemann et al. (2017), for example, we see in Figure 20.2, given the correlations and standard deviations from the variables in the model that will be estimated later using SPSS and **R**, along with the default settings for the simulation (i.e., 1000 replications, 20,000 Monte Carlo draws per rep, and 95% confidence level), the power for detecting the indirect effect given a sample size of 44 is *.89*—which is strong power.

20.1.4 Effect Size

As with other elements related to mediation, effect size in mediation analysis is a growing area of research and discussion (e.g., Lachowicz, Preacher, & Kelley, 2018; Preacher & Kelley, 2011) and there are multiple effect size indices that can be considered. We will focus on partially and completely standardized effects using notation from Hayes (2013), summarized in Box 20.2, but will touch on a few other indices that may be encountered in the literature but that are not recommended for use.

BOX 20.2 Effect Sizes in Mediation Models

Effect Size	Formula	Interpretation
Partially standardized direct effect	$c'_{ps} = \frac{c'}{SD_Y}$	Independent of the indirect effect (i.e., mediating effect), a unit that is one unit higher on the independent variable will be c'_{ps} standard deviations different on the dependent variable
Partially standardized indirect effect	$ab_{ps} = \frac{ab}{SD_Y}$	Two cases that differ by one unit on the independent variable will differ by ab_{ps} standard deviations in the dependent variable as a result of the effect of the independent variable on the mediator
Partially standardized total effect	$c_{ps} = \frac{c}{SD_Y} = c'_{ps} + ab_{ps}$	Two cases that differ by one unit on the independent variable will differ by c_{ps} standard deviations on the outcome as a result of the *combined direct and indirect effects* by which the independent variable affects the dependent variable
Completely standardized direct effect	$c'_{cs} = \frac{(SD_X)(c')}{SD_Y} = (SD_X)(c'_{ps})$	Independent of the indirect effect (i.e., mediating effect), a unit that is one standard deviation unit higher on the independent variable will be c'_{cs} standard deviations different on the dependent variable
Completely standardized indirect effect (i.e., index of mediation)	$ab_{cs} = \frac{(SD_X)(ab)}{SD_Y} = (SD_X)(ab_{ps})$	Two cases that differ by one standard deviation unit on the independent variable will differ by ab_{cs} standard deviations in the dependent variable as a result of the effect of the independent variable on the mediator; in other words, the expected standard deviation change in *the dependent variable* for a one standard deviation increase in the independent variable through the mediating variable
Completely standardized total effect	$c_{cs} = \frac{(SD_X)(c)}{SD_Y} = (c'_{cs})(ab_{cs})$	Two cases that differ by one standard deviation unit on the independent variable will differ by c_{cs} standard deviations on the outcome as a result of the *combined direct and indirect effects* by which the independent variable affects the dependent variable

20.1.4.1 Partially Standardized Effect

The **partially standardized effect** is an effect that is relative to the standard deviation (not the original metric) of the outcome, *Y*. In other words, the independent variable, *X*, remains in its original metric, but the partially standardized effects are rescaled to the standard deviation of the dependent variable, *Y*. This means that the size of the partially standardized effect depends on the scale of the independent variable, *X*.

The **partially standardized direct effect** can be computed as:

$$c'_{ps} = \frac{c'}{SD_Y}$$

The interpretation of the partially standardized *direct effect* is that, independent of the indirect effect (i.e., mediating effect), a unit that is one unit higher on the independent variable will be c'_{ps} standard deviations different on the dependent variable.

The **partially standardized indirect effect** can be computed as:

$$ab_{ps} = \frac{ab}{SD_Y}$$

The interpretation of the partially standardized *indirect effect* is that two cases that differ by one unit on the independent variable will differ by ab_{ps} standard deviations in the dependent variable as a result of the effect of the independent variable on the mediator.

As the total effect of the independent variable, X, is the sum of the direct and indirect effects, the **partially standardized total effect** is the sum of the partially standardized direct and indirect effects, computed as:

$$c_{ps} = \frac{c}{SD_Y} = c'_{ps} + ab_{ps}$$

The interpretation of the partially standardized *total effect* is that two cases that differ by one unit on the independent variable will differ by c_{ps} standard deviations on the outcome as a result of the *combined direct and indirect effects* by which the independent variable affects the dependent variable.

In the case that the independent variable, X, is *dichotomous*, then the partially standardized direct effect and the partially standardized indirect effect are interpreted as the number of standard deviations in the dependent variable, Y, that the groups differ, on average, due to the direct and indirect effects. The direct and indirect effects in the case of binary X sum to the total estimated mean difference in the outcome between the two categories.

20.1.4.2 Completely Standardized Effect

When the scaling of the independent variable, X, is removed from the partially standardized effects, the direct and indirect effects are then expressed in the form of a difference in standard deviations in the dependent variable, Y, between units that differ by one standard deviation on the independent variable, X. The **completely standardized direct effect** then is computed as follows:

$$c'_{cs} = \frac{(SD_X)(c')}{SD_Y} = (SD_X)(c'_{ps})$$

The completely standardized direct effect is interpreted as: independent of the indirect effect (i.e., mediating effect), a unit that is one standard deviation unit higher on the independent variable will be c'_{ps} standard deviations different on the dependent variable.

The **completely standardized indirect effect** is computed as:

$$ab_{cs} = \frac{(SD_X)(ab)}{SD_Y} = (SD_X)(ab_{ps})$$

The completely standardized indirect effect is interpreted as follows: Two cases that differ by one standard deviation unit on the independent variable will differ by ab_{cs} standard deviations in the dependent variable as a result of the effect of the independent variable on the mediator. In other words, the expected standard deviation change in *the dependent variable* for a one standard deviation increase in the independent variable through the mediating variable

Note that when the direct and indirect effects are computed using standardized regression coefficients, *or* when all variables in the model are standardized, they will equate to the completely standardized direct and indirect effects (Preacher & Hayes, 2008b).

The **completely standardized total effect** is computed as:

$$c_{cs} = \frac{(SD_X)(c)}{SD_Y} = (c'_{cs})(ab_{cs})$$

The completely standardized total effect is interpreted as follows: Two cases that differ by one standard deviation unit on the independent variable will differ by c_{cs} standard deviations on the outcome as a result of the *combined direct and indirect effects* by which the independent variable affects the dependent variable.

Note that in a simple regression model that estimates the dependent variable from a single independent variable, the completely standardized total effect is equal to the standardized regression coefficient for X. Additionally, when the independent variable is binary, the completely standardized effect is usually not meaningful and is thus not recommended (Hayes, 2013).

20.1.4.3 Other Effect Size Indices for Mediation Models

As is sometimes the case, statistics may be reported even if they are not best practice, and this includes effect sizes in the context of mediation. Thus, we summarize these effects simply because you may find them in the literature; however, we do not encourage their use, as has been recommended by other researchers (e.g., Hayes, 2013).

The **ratio of the indirect effect to total effect** is an effect size for mediation models that is sometimes reported. Problematic with this effect size index is that this proportion may compute to be less than zero (when either but not both *ab* or *c* is less than zero) or greater than one (when *c* is closer in value to zero than *ab*) (Hayes, 2013). Research also suggests that it is unstable from sample to sample (MacKinnon, Warsi, & Dwyer, 1995). Simulation research suggests that a sample of at least 500 is needed for this effect size to produce a trustworthy effect size estimate (MacKinnon et al., 1995).

The **ratio of the indirect effect to the direct effect** is the ratio of the indirect effect, *ab*, to the direct effect, *c′*. Problematic with this effect size index is that as the direct effect, *c′*, nears zero, the ratio will dramatically increase in size. Thus, from sample to sample, small changes in the indirect effect dramatically alter the value of ratio. Simulation research suggests that a sample of at least 2000 is needed for this effect size index to produce a trustworthy effect size estimate (MacKinnon et al., 1995).

The **proportion of variance** in the dependent variable, *Y*, that is explained by the indirect effect, *ab*, is another effect size index that is sometimes reported. This effect size becomes problematic when the indirect effect, *ab*, exists in the absence of a relationship between the independent variable, *X*, and the dependent variable, *Y*. In other words, the indirect effect, *ab*, is larger, in absolute value terms, than the direct effect, *c*. When this occurs, this proportion of variance effect size can be negative and thus interpretable.

Kappa squared, κ^2, is the ratio of the indirect effect, *ab*, to the maximum possible value of *ab* given the data. While this is a promising effect size index, recent simulation research illustrated that the original derivation of the maximum possible value was computationally in error (Wen & Fan, 2015). Thus software that implemented kappa squared was also in error. Should this be corrected, this effect size may be considered as another appropriate effect size in the future (Hayes, 2013).

20.1.5 Assumptions

By default, moderation and mediation require at least two independent variables, thus the assumptions that must be met are those of multiple regression, including: (a) independence, (b) homoscedasticity, (c) normality, (d) linearity, (e) fixed X, and (f) noncollinearity. Beyond these, there are no further assumptions that must be considered for mediation or moderation. In terms of homoscedasticity, the PROCESS macro that will be illustrated has an option for regression that does not assume homoscedasticity, such as heteroscedasticity-consistent covariance estimators.

20.2 What Moderation Is and How It Works

Moderation is said to occur when the effect of the independent variable, *X*, in terms of size (small or large effect), sign (positive or negative), or strength (weak or strong), on some dependent variable, *Y*, depends on or can be predicted by moderating variable, *W*. In other words, *W* moderates the effect of *X* on *Y*; there is an interaction of *W* and *X* in their influence on *Y*. This is conceptually depicted in Figure 20.3.

While the term *moderation* may be new to you, the concept is likely not as interactions in factorial ANOVA represent moderation. Moderation is simply examining whether the effect of one variable on the dependent variable differs across levels of another variable. While

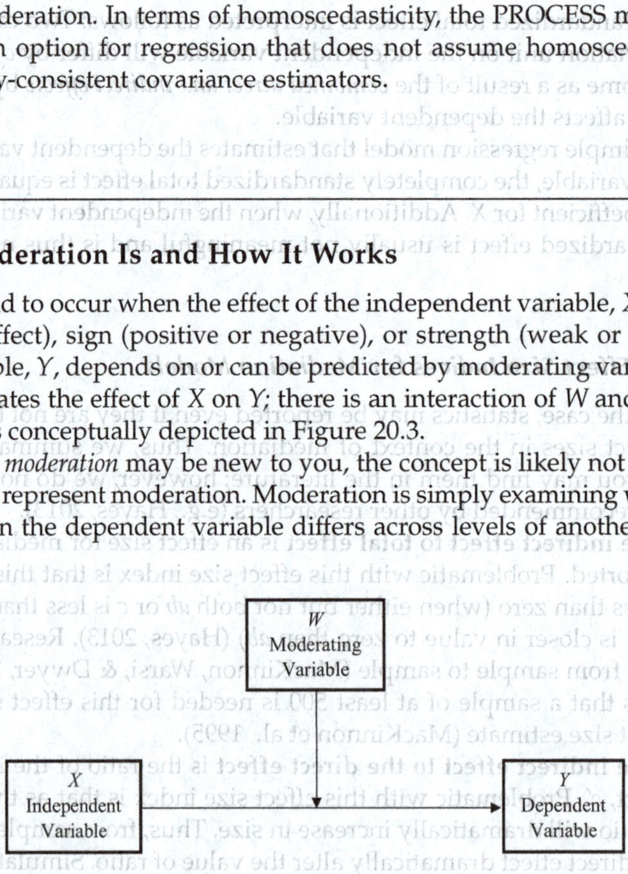

FIGURE 20.3
Conceptual simple moderation model.

factorial ANOVA assumes categorical variables for both X and W, we will illustrate moderation via regression, which is not conditioned on the variables being categorical. Additionally, we will work within the framework of ordinary least squares regression using **moderated multiple regression** (MMR). MMR is an inferential approach to examining moderation that consists of comparing two least-squares regression equations (Aiken & West, 1991).

20.2.1 Characteristics

We noted previously the sample multiple linear regression model. Let's consider this model for predicting Y from 2 predictors:

$$Y_i = b_1X + b_2W + a + e_i$$

where Y_i is the criterion variable (also known as the dependent variable); X is one predictor (or independent) variable and W is a second antecedent variable; b_k is the sample partial slope of the regression line for Y_i as predicted by X or W; a is the sample intercept of the regression line for Y_i as predicted by the set of predictors; e_i are the residuals or errors of prediction (the part of Y_i not predictable from the predictors); and i represents an index for an individual or object. The index i can take on values from 1 to n where n is the size of the sample (i.e., $i = 1, \ldots, n$).

The sample prediction model, therefore, is

$$Y_i' = b_1X + b_2W + a$$

Where Y_i' is the predicted value of the dependent variable for specific values of the predictors, and the other terms are as before. We interpret X, for example, as a one-unit change in X results in a b_1 change in Y_i', and this is *unconditional* on W. In other words, the effect of X on Y_i' does not depend on the moderating variable, W. The value of X does not change, i.e., it is *invariant*, across all values of the moderating variable. Similar interpretations can be made for W and b_2—the effect of W on Y_i' does not depend on the independent variable, X; W on Y_i' is unconditional on X. The value of W does not change, i.e., it is *invariant*, across all X values.

A **simple linear moderation model** has the following form:

$$Y_i = b_1X + b_2W + b_3XW + a + e_i$$

With the **sample prediction moderation model** being:

$$Y_i' = b_1X + b_2W + b_3XW + a$$

where XW is simply the product of X and W (i.e., there is not mathematical magic needed to construct XW; XW results from simply multiplying X by W).

In the simple moderated model, b_1 is interpreted as the *conditional effect of* X on the dependent variable when the moderating variable is zero. In other words, it is the difference in Y_i' for two cases that differ by *one* on X but differ by *zero* on W. It is important to note that b_1 is *not* interpreted as a main effect or as the effect of X on the dependent variable when controlling for W.

A similar interpretation can be made for b_2: It is the *conditional effect of* W on the dependent variable when X is zero. In other words, it is the difference in Y_i' for two cases that

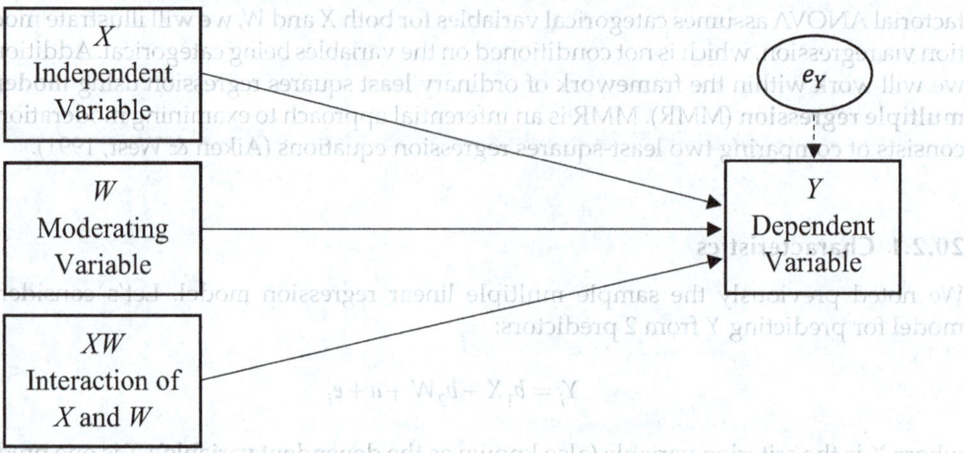

FIGURE 20.4
Simple moderation model.

differ by *one* on *W* but differ by *zero* on *X*. It is important to note that b_2 is *not* interpreted as a main effect or as the effect of *W* on the dependent variable when controlling for *X*.

Statistically, this model is depicted in Figure 20.4. It is important to note that *X* and *W* should always be included in the model when there is a moderating effect included, even if *X* and/or *W* are not statistically significant (Hayes, 2013).

By including the interaction term, *XW*, we are testing that the effect of *X* on the outcome is **conditional** on *W*. In other words, the effect of *X* on Y_i' is dependent (aka "conditioned") on *W*. In contrast, in an *unconditional* model, the effect of *X* on *Y* is invariant across all values of *W*. The coefficients for *X* and *W*, in a model that includes the moderating term *XW*, are *conditional effects*, with the condition being that the other variable is zero (note that when the moderating term is not included in the model, partial effects (not conditional effects) are estimated).

For two cases that differ on *X* by a unit, the difference in the dependent variable for a one-unit increase (or decrease) in *W* is a change of b_3 units. In other words, as *W* increases by one unit, for two cases that differ on *X* by a unit, the dependent variable will change by b_3 units. These interpretations are predicated on *W* being the moderating variable. If, however, *X* is the moderating variable, then b_3 represents the difference in the dependent variable for a one unit increase (or decrease) in *X* for two cases that differ by a unit on *W*. The degree to which the slopes are not parallel in a moderation model is dependent on b_3. As the absolute value of b_3 increases, the slopes will become increasingly nonparallel.

20.2.1.1 Probing an Interaction

Graphs are an excellent way to visualize an interaction, as we have already seen with factorial ANOVA. However to really understand what's happening when an interaction occurs, the interaction needs to be *probed* more deeply. In other words, does a statistically significant interaction mean that *X* effects *Y* for cases that are low on the moderator? High on the moderator? Somewhere in between? The *test of the interaction* (i.e., the inferential test of the coefficient) establishes that an interaction is or is not statistically significant—i.e., whether the relationship between the independent and dependent variables systematically varies as a function of the moderator. If there is a statistically significant interaction, this justifies the next step—*probing*. The *test of the interaction* is *not* the same thing as *probing for an interaction.* Probing for the interaction is necessary to better understand what is happening within the interaction and to understand where the differential variation on the moderator occurs. As researchers, we want to say more than just the effect of *X* on *Y* depends on *W*, and we usually want to say at what point(s) the effect of *X* on *Y* depends on *W*.

A common technique for probing an interaction is the **pick-a-point approach** (Rogosa, 1980). In this approach, the conditional effect of *X* on *Y* is computed using one or more values of *W*, and this is followed by a test of inference. Modern statistical software eliminates the need for computing this by hand, which can be prone to error. If you are so inclined, however, Cohen, Cohen, West, and Aiken (2003) provide an example of hand calculation for the pick-a-point approach. Using the PROCESS macro, as illustrated later, the pick-a-point approach is implemented and output provided automatically. We will illustrate the approach applying the 16th, 50th, and 84th percentiles, as recommended by Hayes (2013) as they correspond to relatively low, moderate, and high values of the moderating variable. In the case that *W* is *normally distributed*, these values also correspond, respectively, to one standard deviation below the mean (16th percentile), the mean (i.e., 50th percentile in a normal distribution), and one standard deviation above the mean (i.e., 84th percentile) on the moderating variable. And regardless of the distributional shape of *W*, the 16th, 50th, and 84th percentiles will always be within the range of the observed data.

The challenge with the pick-a-point approach is the selection of often arbitrary values of the moderating variable and the fact that the values selected are sample specific (Hayes, 2013). The **Johnson-Neyman** (JN) technique (Johnson & Neyman, 1936) eliminates these issues, The JN technique was originally proposed as a way to handle violations of homogeneity of regression in ANCOVA mean difference tests for two groups. Bauer and Curran (2005) extended the work to more general regression models. The JN technique can be applied only with continuous moderating variables. The JN technique can be considered as the reverse of the pick-a-point approach in that values of *W* are derived at the point where the interaction is statistically significant (Hayes, 2013). In other words, the values of *W* where the conditional effect of *X* on *Y* changes from nonstatistically significant to statistically significant.

Hayes (2013, p. 255) refers to the JN technique as identifying "regions of significance" for the effect of *X* on *Y*. If the JN technique results in *two solutions*, this suggests that the conditional effect of *X* on *Y* is statistically significant in one of the two fashions: $JN_{W1} \le W \le JN_{W2}$ *or* $JN_{W1} \ge W$ *and* $W \ge JN_{W2}$. In other words, the region of significance is either contained within two points (i.e., $JN_{W1} \le W \le JN_{W2}$) on *W* or it is outside two points of *W* (*i.e.,* $JN_{W1} \ge W$ *and* $W \ge JN_{W2}$).

If JN results in only *one solution*, this suggests that the conditional effect of X on *Y* is statistically significant when one of the following but not both occur: $W \ge JN_{W1}$ *or* when $W \le JN_{W1}$. In other words, the region of significance is either above (i.e., $W \ge JN_{W1}$) or below (i.e., $W \le JN_{W1}$) some value of *W*, but not between them, and not in both directions.

It may also be the case that the JN technique results in *no solution.* This can happen when the conditional effect of *X* on *Y* is statistically significant across *all* values of *W* (i.e., the entire range of values of *W*) *or* when the conditional effect of X on *Y* is statistically significant across *no* values of *W*.

20.2.1.2 Centering

Researchers working with moderated models may want to consider centering the X and W variables. This can assist in avoiding multicollinearity (Aiken & West, 1991) and may also increase the interpretability of the regression intercept. As noted by Hayes (2013), however, centering to avoid multicollinearity is largely a myth. In terms of interpretation, on the other hand, centering *is* something that many researchers may want to consider.

When centering is not applied, the intercept is interpreted as the value of the dependent variable when all the predictors are *zero*. If either X or W are not zero, then the intercept has no meaning. In comparison, if the predictors are centered at the average, for example, the intercept becomes the value of the dependent variable when the predictors are at their *average*. In the case of mean centering X and W, b_1 is interpreted as the difference in Y between two cases that differ by one unit on X among cases that are *at the mean* of W. For b_2, we find it is interpreted as the difference in Y between two cases that differ by one unit on W among cases that are *at the mean* of X.

A model estimated without mean centering is mathematically equivalent (e.g., R^2 and $MS_{residual}$) to a model estimated with mean centering. The coefficients and related estimates (*t*, *p*, *SE*) for X and W will differ as they are estimating effects for cases at the average (rather than zero). However, the regression coefficient for the interaction, XW, will be the same regardless of centering. Thus, the test of the moderation will result in the same conclusion regardless of mean centering or not mean centering.

20.2.2 Sample Size

As with multiple regression, there exists conventions for sample size needed for detecting a moderating effect. Stone-Romero and Anderson (1994) found that samples of at least 120 were needed to detect moderate and large moderating effects. Aguinis (2004) recommends a sample size of at least 100 for detecting a moderating effect. Throughout the text, however, we have discouraged the application of conventions for determining sample size, as there are so many factors that need to be considered and applying a one-size-fits-all determination for sample size is thus not best practice. Rather, we suggest estimating sample size with, for example, power software. Shieh (2009), for example, provides SAS IML and **R** code for calculating power and sample size.

20.2.3 Power

Powering a study for a main effect is different from powering a study for an interaction. Aguinis (2004) grouped factors that impact power in moderated multiple regression into five categories: variable distributions; variable operationalization; sample size; predictor variable correlations; and interactive effects of these factors impacting power. We will start our discussion of power within the context of these categories.

The first category relates to the **distribution of the variables**. Aguinis and Stone-Romero (1997) found that power in MMR is dramatically decreased when the variance of the predictor, X, is smaller in the sample than in the population. Range restriction of the independent variable, X, in turn restricts the range of the interaction, XW, and this detrimentally impacts the ability to find a population moderating effect. Another aspect related to variable distribution concerns transformations of outcome variables. Transforming Y, specifically log transformations to correct for nonnormally skewed distributions, has been found to underestimate the moderating effect and decrease power (i.e., which indicates an increased change of a Type II error) (Russell & Dean, 2000).

The second factor impacting power relates to **variable operationalization**, which includes measurement error, operationalization of the dependent variable, and categorizing continuous variables (Aguinis, 2004). The probability of Type II errors increases in the presence of inadequate reliability when testing moderation (Aguinis, 2004). Low reliability of modeled variables is so problematic that measurement error is considered by some researchers to be the most impactful factor on power in MMR (Kromrey & Foster-Johnson, 1999). The measurement scale of the variables included in MMR also impacts power. In particular, the use of Likert items for either or both the independent and/or dependent variable have been shown to decrease power to detect a moderating effect (e.g., Russell & Bobko, 1992). Artificially categorizing (e.g., creating dichotomy or multicategory) a continuous variable has also been found to decrease power in detecting moderating effects.(e.g., Mason & Tu, 1996).

Sample size, both overall and subgroup, can impact power in MMR. Generally in testing hypotheses, regardless of statistical approach, larger sample sizes result in increased power. For MMR, overall sample size is particularly critical. For example, Stone-Romero and Anderson (1994) found that samples of at least 120 were needed to detect moderate and large moderating effects. As noted previously, estimating overall sample size via a power analysis program may mitigate problems with decreased power in MMR. In addition to overall sample size, however, the group sizes within the moderating variable (i.e., subgroups) also impact power. Unequal sizes of the subgroups impact power above and beyond the total sample size (Aguinis, 2004). There is decreased power when one group is substantially smaller than the other group, regardless of the total sample size (Stone-Romero, Alliger, & Aguinis, 1994).

The fourth factor identified by Aguinis (2004) that impacts power in MMR relates to **predictor variable correlations**. Researchers have found that multicollinearity does not detrimentally impact MMR (Cronbach, 1987). However, a weak relationship between the independent and dependent variable (i.e., first-order effect) may limit detection of a moderating effect (Rogers, 2002). In other words, the strength of the relationship between the independent and dependent variable places a cap on the size of the moderating effect.

The last factor relates to **interaction effects between these aspects that impact power**. For example, as noted by Aguinis (2004, p. 78), "the combined effects on power of the simultaneous presence of small total sample size, large measurement error, and unequal sample sizes across the moderator-based subgroups are greater than the sum of the individual effects of these factors." Additionally, the presence of just one factor that detrimentally impacts power can dramatically decrease power even if the other factors are powered sufficiently (Aguinis, 2004).

Researchers interested in assessing power for moderation have a number of resources to consult. For example, Shieh (2009) illustrates power and sample size calculations for detecting moderating effects. Calculating power for moderating effects in cluster randomized designs has also been illustrated (e.g., Dong, Kelcey, & Spybrook, 2018; Dong & Society for Research on Educational, 2014; Spybrook & Kelcey, 2014).

20.2.4 Effect Size

A common effect size for moderated multiple regression is f^2 (Aiken & West, 1991), computed as follows:

$$f^2 = \frac{R_2^2 - R_1^2}{1 - R_2^2}$$

Where R_1^2 is the proportion of variance in the dependent variable that is accounted for by the effects of the independent variable (X) and moderating variable (W), and R_2^2 is the proportion of variance in the dependent variable that is accounted for by the effects of the independent variable, moderating variable, and interaction term (XW). Conventions for interpreting f^2 are offered by Cohen (1988), with small effects of $f^2 = .02$, moderate effects of $f^2 = .15$, and large effects of $f^2 = .35$. Aguinis, Beaty, Boik, and Pierce (2005) proposed a modified f^2 that is appropriate to use when there are categorical moderators when homogeneity of error is violated. An online calculator (see http://www.hermanaguinis.com/mmr/index.html) is available for computed modified f^2.

When the independent, moderating, and dependent variables have metrics that are interpretable (e.g., number of XYZ, dummy coding), the direction and strength of the conditional effects represent an unstandardized effect size (Bodner, 2017). Standardized regression coefficients can be interpreted as effect size, although this practice is debatable (Smithson & Shou, 2017). With continuous moderators, Bodner (2017) presents an approach for conditional effects expressed in standardized mean differences and semi-partial correlations.

20.2.5 Assumptions

The usual assumptions of multiple linear regression are applicable for moderated multiple regression and include: linearity; residuals that are homoscedastic, normally distributed, and independent; and lack of multicollinearity. When there is a categorical moderator, homogeneity of (within-group) error variance assumption—i.e., homoscedasticity—is particularly important to preventing increased probability of Type I and Type II errors.

20.3 Computing Mediation and Moderation Using SPSS

We will first consider SPSS for mediation using the PROCESS macro. This will be followed by illustration for moderation.

20.3.1 Installing the PROCESS Macro

An excellent computational tool for observed variable path analysis-based moderation and mediation is PROCESS (Hayes, n.d.). In addition to estimating coefficients, standard errors (including heteroscedasticity-constant standard errors), and similar statistics, PROCESS provides direct and indirect effects for mediation models (including percent bootstrap and Monte Carlo confidence intervals for indirect effects), conditional effects in moderation models, and conditional indirect effects in conditional process models with a single mediator or with multiple mediators. Additionally, it provides options for probing interactions as well as generates effect size indices for direct, indirect, and total effects. There are a number of templates for estimating models, and models can be custom built as well. These are just a few of the rich tools that PROCESS provides.

PROCESS can be used by writing syntax within SPSS or by installing a custom dialog menu that can be used in the navigational menu within SPSS. We will illustrate using the latter. To install PROCESS as a custom menu tool, visit http://processmacro.org and click "Download" from the top navigational menu. From this page, you will have access to download the latest version of PROCESS (version 3.2.01 at the time of writing) (note, however, that you will need administrator privilege to install). Once installed, PROCESS is provided as an option from the regression menu.

20.3.2 Computing Mediation Analysis Using SPSS

Next we consider SPSS for computing mediation. Before we conduct the analysis, let us review the data. We are using the "Ch20_medmod.sav" data. For this illustration, the dependent variable is "DV," the independent variable is "TRTMT," and the mediating variable is "M1" (see Figure 20.5).

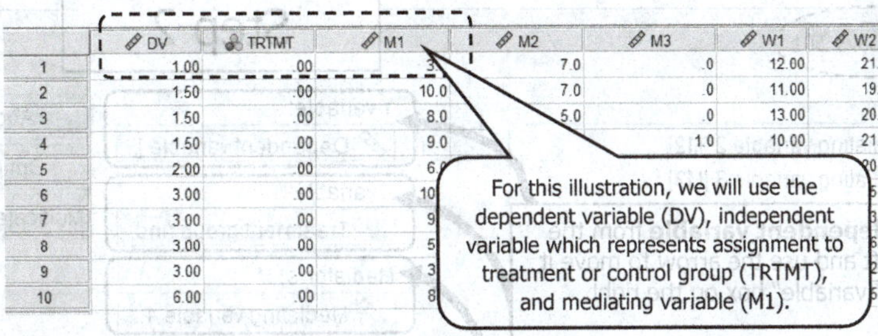

FIGURE 20.5
Mediation data (first 10 cases).

Step 1. To conduct a mediated regression model, go to "Analyze" in the top pulldown menu, then select "Regression," and then select "PROCESS." Following the screenshot for Step 1 (Figure 20.6) produces the "PROCESS" dialog box.

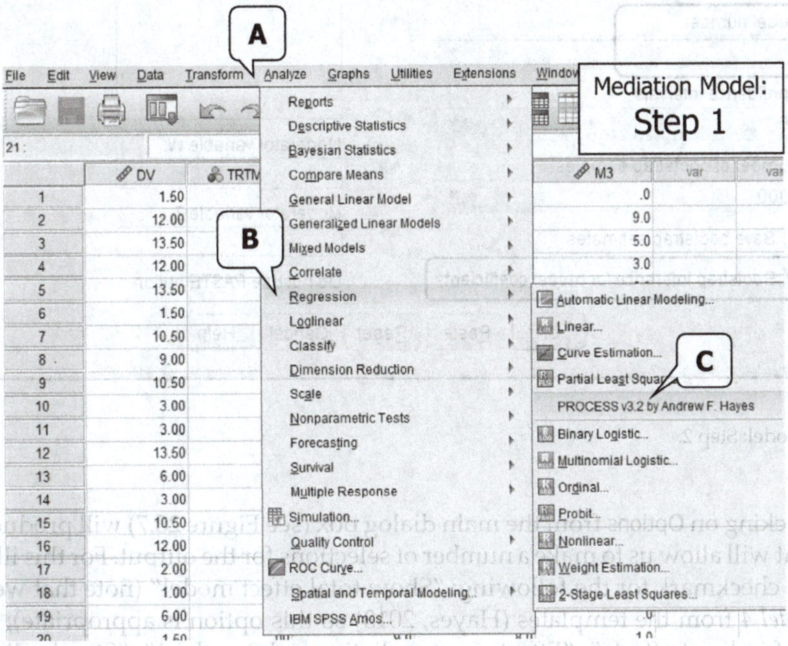

FIGURE 20.6
Mediation model: Step 1.

Step 2. Click the dependent variable (e.g., "DV") and move it into the "Y variable" box by clicking the arrow button. Click the independent variable (e.g., "TRTMT") and move into the "X Variable" box by clicking the arrow button. Click the mediating variable (e.g., "M1") and move to the "Mediator(s) M" box by clicking the arrow button (see the screenshot for Step 2, Figure 20.7). We are using model 4 from the templates, so use the toggle menu to select "4" for "Model number." We will leave the default settings for confidence intervals (i.e., 95) and number of bootstrap samples (e.g., 5000). To obtain the bootstrap inference for model coefficients, place a check in the respective box.

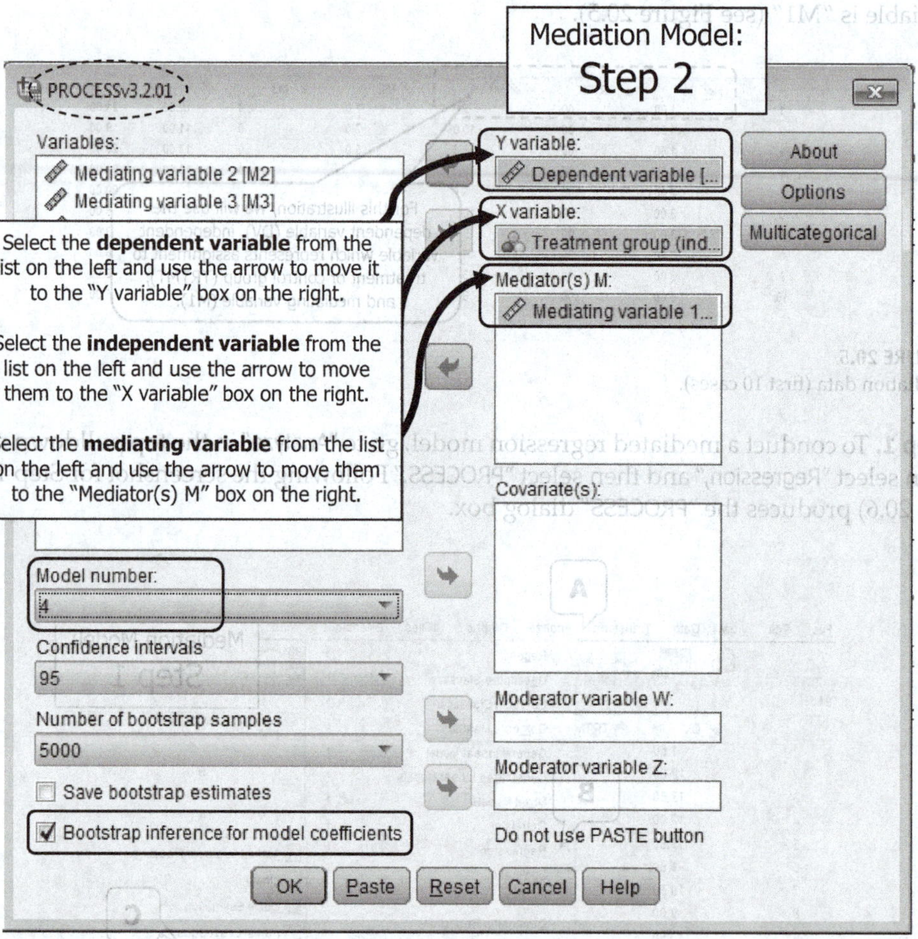

FIGURE 20.7
Mediation Model: Step 2.

Step 3. Clicking on Options from the main dialog box (see Figure 20.7) will produce the dialog box that will allow us to make a number of selections for the output. For this illustration, we place a checkmark for the following: "Show total effect model" (note that we are computing *model 4* from the templates (Hayes, 2013) so this option is appropriate); "Pairwise contrasts of indirect effects"; "Effect size (mediation-only models)"; "Standardized coefficients (mediation-only models)." Using the toggle menu, we select "HC4" (Cribari-Neto,

2004) for the heteroscedasticity-consistent inference. HC4 takes large leverage values into account when constructing the standard errors, and has been shown to outperform HC3 in the presence of high leverage points and error distributions that are nonnormal (Hayes & Cai, 2007). Using HC3 or HC4 is recommended (Hayes & Cai, 2007). Then click "Continue" to return to the main dialog box.

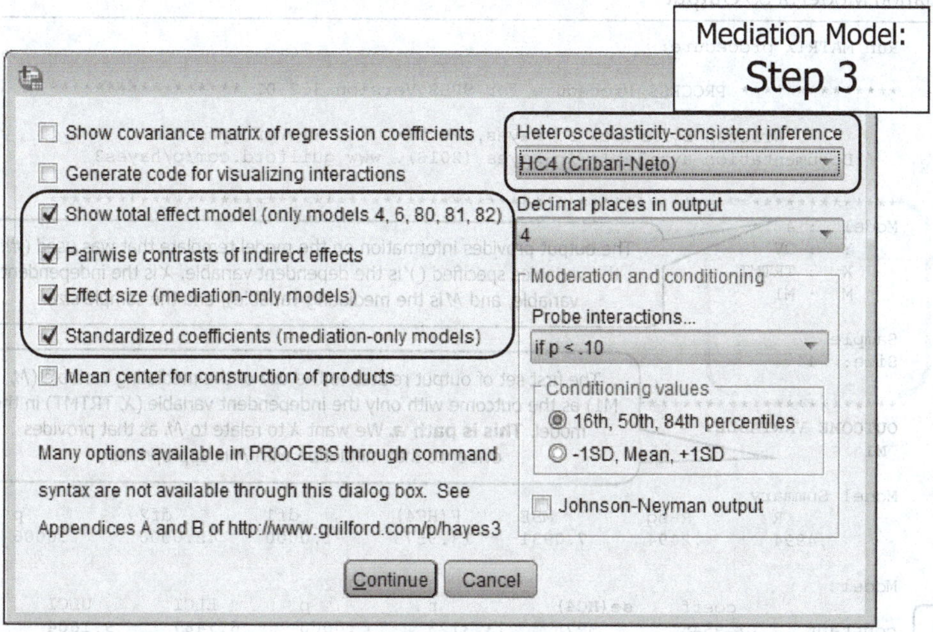

FIGURE 20.8
Mediation model: Step 3.

20.3.2.1 Interpreting Mediation Output

From the output in Table 20.1, we see the mediation analyses is actually a series of models. Among other findings, the mediating variable fully (or completely) mediates the relationship between the independent variable and the outcome.

Note that for the bootstrapped confidence intervals, assumptions about the shape of the sampling distribution are not made. As a result, bootstrapped confidence intervals handle irregularities of the *ab* sampling distribution and yield more accurate inferences than the normal theory approach, which results in increased power (relative to the normal theory approach) (Hayes, 2013). As bootstrapped confidence intervals are derived void of any assumptions of the size of the parameter, it is incorrect to state that intervals that do not include zero are statistically significant. Thus, a bootstrapped confidence interval that is entirely above zero will support a conclusion of a positive indirect effect, but it would technically be incorrect to conclude to reject the null hypothesis that the estimate = 0 with an observed probability of no more than .05 (Hayes, 2013). In practice, however, the interpretation of a bootstrapped confidence interval leads to a similar substantive interpretation—i.e., intervals that do not contain zero provide "evidence that the effect is positive to a 'statistically significant' degree" (Hayes, 2013, p. 101).

TABLE 20.1

Mediation Model SPSS Output

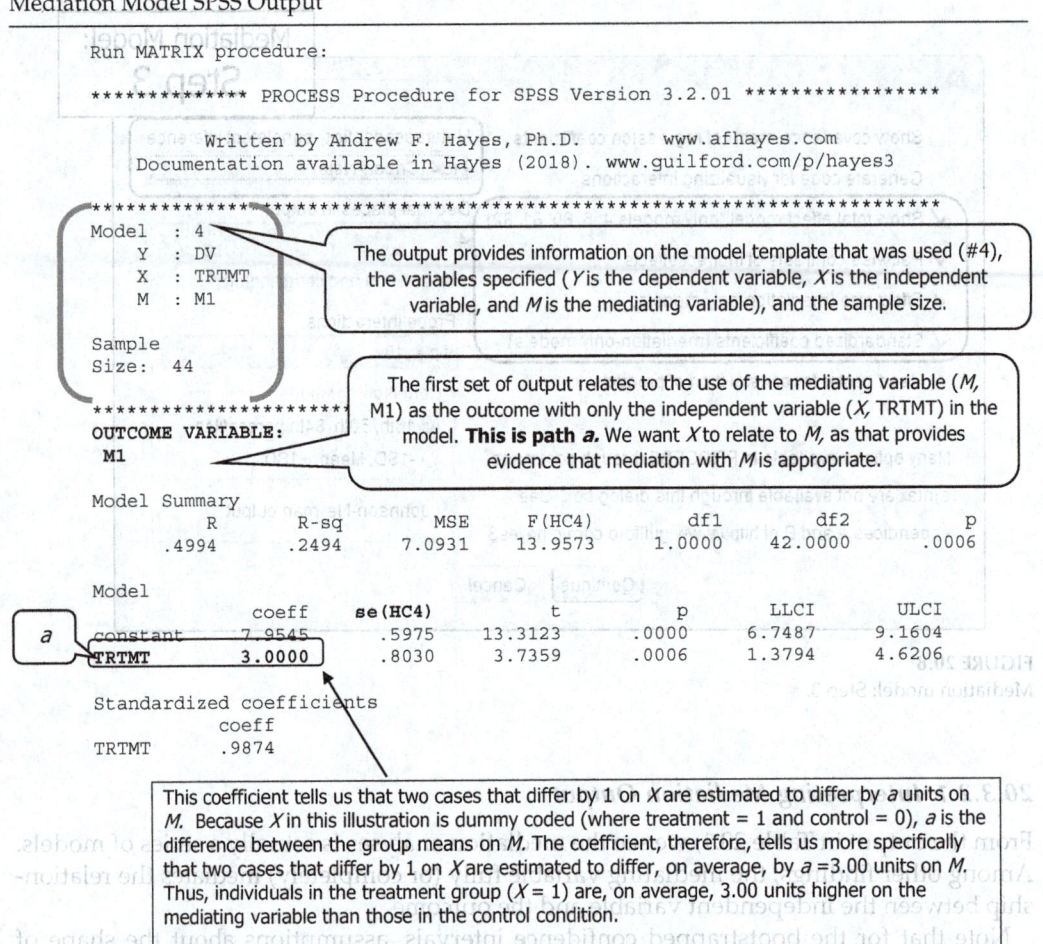

```
Run MATRIX procedure:

************** PROCESS Procedure for SPSS Version 3.2.01 *****************

          Written by Andrew F. Hayes, Ph.D.       www.afhayes.com
    Documentation available in Hayes (2018).  www.guilford.com/p/hayes3

**************************************************************************
Model   : 4
    Y   : DV
    X   : TRTMT
    M   : M1

Sample
Size:   44

**************************************************************************
OUTCOME VARIABLE:
 M1

Model Summary
          R       R-sq        MSE      F(HC4)        df1        df2          p
      .4994      .2494     7.0931     13.9573     1.0000    42.0000      .0006

Model
              coeff     se(HC4)          t          p       LLCI       ULCI
constant     7.9545       .5975    13.3123      .0000     6.7487     9.1604
TRTMT        3.0000       .8030     3.7359      .0006     1.3794     4.6206

Standardized coefficients
             coeff
TRTMT        .9874
```

The output provides information on the model template that was used (#4), the variables specified (*Y* is the dependent variable, *X* is the independent variable, and *M* is the mediating variable), and the sample size.

The first set of output relates to the use of the mediating variable (*M*, M1) as the outcome with only the independent variable (*X*, TRTMT) in the model. **This is path *a*.** We want *X* to relate to *M*, as that provides evidence that mediation with *M* is appropriate.

a

This coefficient tells us that two cases that differ by 1 on *X* are estimated to differ by *a* units on *M*. Because *X* in this illustration is dummy coded (where treatment = 1 and control = 0), *a* is the difference between the group means on *M*. The coefficient, therefore, tells us more specifically that two cases that differ by 1 on *X* are estimated to differ, on average, by *a* =3.00 units on *M*. Thus, individuals in the treatment group (*X* = 1) are, on average, 3.00 units higher on the mediating variable than those in the control condition.

The standard errors are constructed using heteroscedasticity consistent methods. For this illustration, we requested HC4. HC4 takes large leverage values into consideration. HC4 has been shown to outperform HC3 in the presence of high leverage points and error distributions that are nonnormal (Cribari-Neto, 2004). Using HC3 or HC4 has been recommended (Hayes & Cai, 2007).

TABLE 20.1 (continued)

Mediation Model SPSS Output

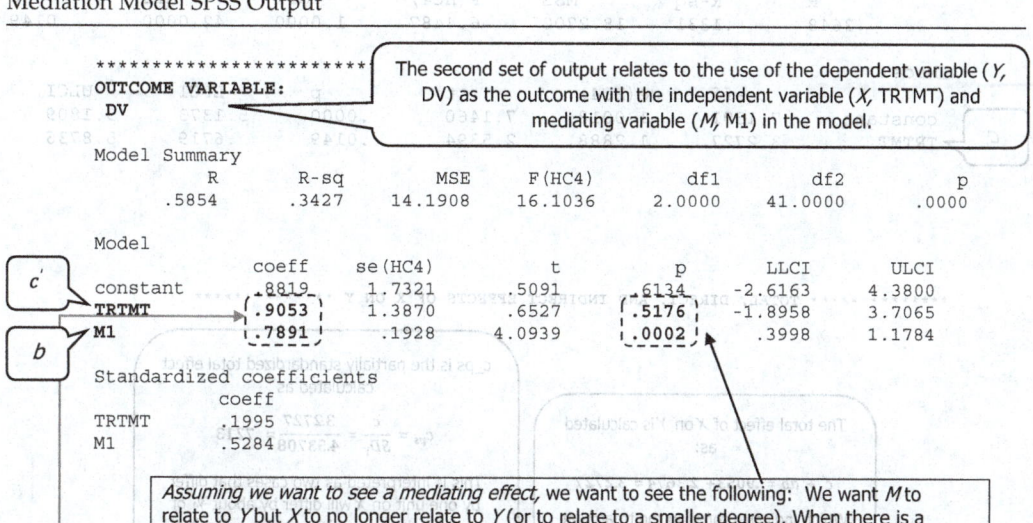

```
**************************
OUTCOME VARIABLE:
 DV

Model Summary
          R       R-sq        MSE     F(HC4)        df1        df2          p
      .5854      .3427    14.1908    16.1036     2.0000    41.0000      .0000

Model
              coeff    se(HC4)          t          p       LLCI       ULCI
constant      .8819     1.7321      .5091      .6134    -2.6163     4.3800
TRTMT         .9053     1.3870      .6527      .5176    -1.8958     3.7065
M1            .7891      .1928     4.0939      .0002      .3998     1.1784

Standardized coefficients
          coeff
TRTMT     .1995
M1        .5284
```

The second set of output relates to the use of the dependent variable (*Y*, DV) as the outcome with the independent variable (*X*, TRTMT) and mediating variable (*M*, M1) in the model.

c′

b

Assuming we want to see a mediating effect, we want to see the following: We want *M* to relate to *Y* but *X* to no longer relate to *Y* (or to relate to a smaller degree). When there is a mediating effect, the relation between *X* and *Y* will decrease or disappear altogether. If the relationship between *X* and *Y* completely disappears, this indicates that there is **full mediation.** In other words, *M* fully mediates the relationship between *X* and *Y*. If some relationship between *X* and *Y* remains after the mediator is included in the model, but that relationship is smaller in magnitude, this indicates that there is **partial mediation.** In other words, *M* partially mediates the relationship between *X* and *Y*. In this illustration, we see that *X* is not statistically significant (p = .5026) but *M* is statistically significant (p = .0001). Thus, there is full mediation as the relationship between the treatment and the outcome has completely disappeared with the inclusion of the mediator. *This suggests that the mediator fully mediates the relationship between the treatment and the outcome.*

The **coefficient for *X*** tells us that two people that differ by one unit on *X* but are equal on *M* are estimated to differ by .9053 units on the outcome. Since *X* is a binary variable (treatment = 1, control = 0), this coefficient suggests that independent of the effect of *M* on *Y*, individuals assigned to the treatment condition are estimated to be nearly 1 point higher (specifically .9053 higher), on average, on the outcome than those assigned to the control condition.

The **coefficient for *M*** tells us that two people who are equal on *X* (i.e., assigned to the same condition) but that differ by one unit on *M* are estimated to differ by .7891 units on the dependent variable. The sign for *b* (i.e., the mediating variable) is positive, which indicates that individuals who are higher on the mediating variable, *M*, are also estimated to be higher on the dependent variable.

(continued)

TABLE 20.1 (continued)

Mediation Model SPSS Output

```
************************** TOTAL EFFECT MODEL ****************************
OUTCOME VARIABLE:
 DV

Model Summary
          R       R-sq        MSE      F(HC4)        df1        df2          p
      .3648      .1331    18.2700      6.4487     1.0000    42.0000      .0149

Model
              coeff     se(HC4)        t          p       LLCI       ULCI
constant     7.1591      1.0018     7.1460     .0000     5.1373     9.1809
TRTMT        3.2727      1.2888     2.5394     .0149      .6719     5.8736
```

c

```
************** TOTAL, DIRECT, AND INDIRECT EFFECTS OF X ON Y **************
```

The total effect of *X* on *Y* is calculated as:

$c' + ab = .9053 + 2.3674 = 3.2727$

Which indicates those in the treatment group were, on average, about 3-1/4 units higher on the outcome than those in the control group.

c_ps is the partially standardized total effect calculated as

$$c_{ps} = \frac{c}{SD_Y} = \frac{3.2727}{4.53708} = .7213$$

This is interpreted as two cases that differ by one unit on *X* will differ by about ¾ of one standard deviation on *Y* as a result of the *combined direct and indirect effects* by which *X* affects *Y*.

```
Total effect of X on Y
     Effect     se(HC4)          t          p       LLCI       ULCI       c_ps
     3.2727      1.2888     2.5394      .0149      .6719     5.8736      .7213
```

This provides information on the direct effect of *X* on *Y* (i.e., path *c*′)

```
Direct effect of X on Y
     Effect     se(HC4)          t          p       LLCI       ULCI      c'_ps
      .9053      1.3870      .6527      .5176    -1.8958     3.7065      .1995
```

This provides information on the mediating effect; the *ab* effect—the indirect effect of treatment assignment *(X)* on the dependent variable *(Y)* through the mediator. This is calculated simply as the product of the coefficients (with the difference here due to rounding):

$ab = 3.00 \; .7891 = 2.3673$

c′_ps is the partially standardized direct effect calculated as

$$c_{ps} = \frac{c'}{SD_Y} = \frac{9053}{4.53708} = .1995$$

This is interpreted as, independent of the indirect effect, an individual in the treatment group is estimated to be about .20 standard deviations higher on *Y*.

```
Indirect effect(s) of X on Y:
        Effect    BootSE   BootLLCI   BootULCI
M1      2.3674     .7573      .9776     3.9406
```

ab

The indirect effect of *X* on *Y* is the product of the effect of the independent variable, *X*, on the mediating variable, *M*, (i.e., path *a*) and the effect of *M* on the outcome, *Y*, when *X* is held constant (i.e., path *b*). The 95% bootstrap confidence intervals are provided.

TABLE 20.1 (continued)

Mediation Model SPSS Output

The partially standardized indirect effect of X on Y is a measure of effect size calculated as:

$$ab_{ps} = \frac{ab}{SD_Y} = \frac{2.3674}{4.5371} = .5218$$

```
Partially standardized indirect effect(s) of X on Y:
      Effect     BootSE    BootLLCI    BootULCI
M1     .5218      .1652      .2261       .8722
```

The partially standardized indirect effect rescales *ab* to the standard deviation of *Y* but maintains the original metric of *X*. Thus, the size of the partially standardized indirect effect depends on the scale of *X*.

The **partially standardized indirect** effect of *X* on *Y* tells us that two individuals who differ by one unit on *X* differ by about # standard deviation units on *Y* as a result of the effect of *M*, which in turn affects *Y*. In this illustration, since *X* is binary, the partially standardized indirect effect of *X* on *Y* tells us that two individuals who differ by one unit on *X* differ by about ½ of one standard deviation unit on *Y*, on average, as a result of the effect of *M*, which in turn affects *Y*. More specifically, those in the treatment group were, on average, about ½ of one standard deviation higher on the outcome as a result of the indirect effect through the mediating variable, *M*, than those in the control condition.

The bootstrapped confidence interval tells us that the this difference could be as low as about ¼ of one standard deviation and as high as nearly 9/10 of one standard deviation.

```
*********** BOOTSTRAP RESULTS FOR REGRESSION MODEL PARAMETERS ************

OUTCOME VARIABLE:
 M1

             Coeff    BootMean     BootSE    BootLLCI    BootULCI
constant    7.9545      7.9586      .5889      6.8000      9.1111
TRTMT       3.0000      2.9919      .7981      1.4060      4.5513

----------

OUTCOME VARIABLE:
 DV

             Coeff    BootMean     BootSE    BootLLCI    BootULCI
constant     .8819       .9200     1.6775     -2.3398      4.2559
TRTMT        .9053       .9525     1.3869     -1.7333      3.7262
M1           .7891       .7833      .1888       .3864      1.1410

*********************** ANALYSIS NOTES AND ERRORS ************************

Level of confidence for all confidence intervals in output:
  95.0000

Number of bootstrap samples for percentile bootstrap confidence intervals:
  5000

NOTE: Standardized coefficients for dichotomous or multicategorical X are in
      partially standardized form.

NOTE: A heteroscedasticity consistent standard error and covariance matrix
estimator was used.

------ END MATRIX -----
```

(Callouts: *a* → TRTMT coefficient for M1; *c′* → TRTMT coefficient for DV; *b* → M1 coefficient for DV.)

The bootstrapped confidence interval results lend evidence to support the conclusions from the hypothesis tests presented earlier. Among others, that *M* fully mediates the relationship between *X* and *Y* given that 0 is within the interval for *X* and is not within the interval for *M*.

Cribari-Neto, F. (2004). Asymptotic inference under heteroskedasticity of unknown form. *Computational Statistics and Data Analysis, 45*, 215-233. doi:10.1016/S0167-9473(02)00366-3

Hayes, A. F., & Cai, L. (2007). Using heteroskedasticity-consistent standard error estimators in OLS regression: An introduction and software implementation. *Behavior Research Methods, 39*(4), 709-722.

20.3.3 Computing Moderation Analysis Using SPSS

Next we consider SPSS for computing moderation. Before we conduct the analysis, let us review the data. We are using the "Ch20_medmod.sav" data. For this illustration, the dependent variable is "DV," the independent variable is "TRTMT," and the moderating variable is "W1." Note in Figure 20.2 that there is no interaction term, *XW*, that represents the interaction between the moderating variable and independent variable. Using the PROCESS macro, there is no need to compute the interaction.

Step 1. To conduct a simple moderation model, the first step is the same as followed for conducting mediation. Go to "Analyze" in the top pulldown menu, then select "Regression," and then select "PROCESS." Following the screenshot presented earlier in Figure 20.6 (Step 1) produces the "PROCESS" dialog box.

Step 2. Click the dependent variable (e.g., "DV") and move it into the "Y variable" box by clicking the arrow button. Click the independent variable (e.g., TRTMT) and move into the "X Variable" box by clicking the arrow button. Click the moderating variable (e.g., W) and move to the "Moderator (W)" box by clicking the arrow button (see the screenshot for Step 2, Figure 20.9). We are using model 1 from the templates (Hayes, 2013), so use the toggle menu to select "1" for "Model number." We will leave the default settings for confidence intervals (i.e., 95) and number of bootstrap samples (e.g., 5000). To obtain the bootstrap inference for model coefficients, place a check in the respective box.

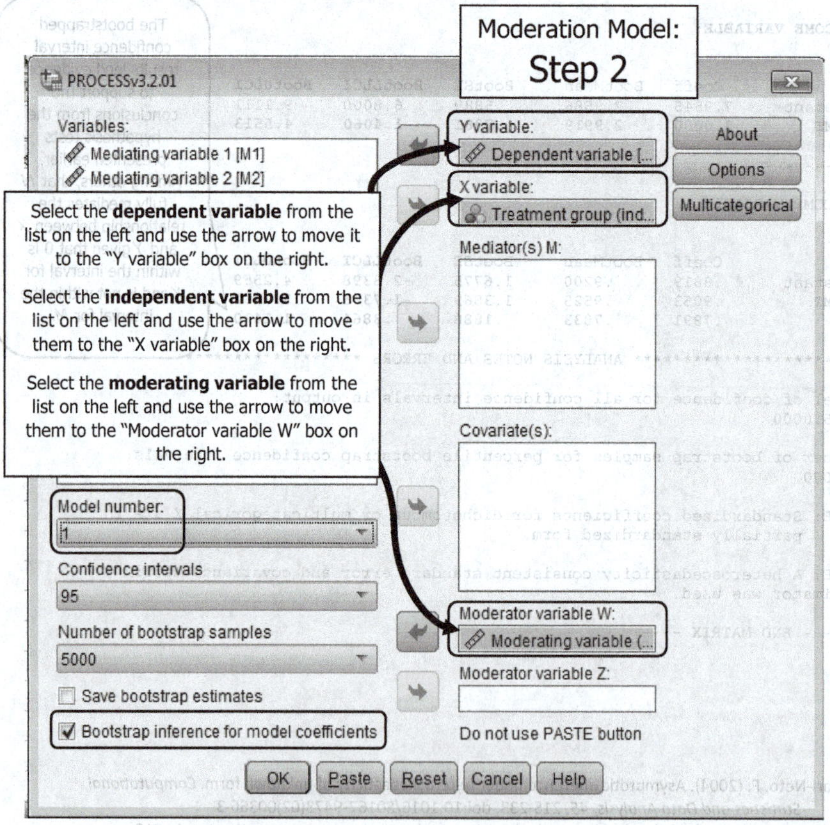

FIGURE 20.9
Simple moderation: Step 2.

Step 3. Clicking on Options from the main dialog box (see Figure 20.9) will produce the dialog box that will allow us to make a number of selections for the output. For this illustration, we place a checkmark in the respective box to generate code for visualizing interactions. Using the toggle menu, we select "HC4" (Cribari-Neto, 2004) for the heteroscedasticity-consistent inference. HC4 takes large leverage values into account when constructing the standard errors, and has been shown to outperform HC3 in the presence of high leverage points and error distributions that are nonnormal (Hayes & Cai, 2007). Using HC3 or HC4 is recommended (Hayes & Cai, 2007). In the "Moderation and conditioning" box, we leave the default settings for "Probe interactions," and place a checkmark for Johnson-Neyman output. Then click "Continue" to return to the main dialog box. Note that the default conditioning values for probing interactions is the 16th, 50th, and 84th percentiles. When *W* is normally distributed, this corresponds, respectively, to one standard deviation below the mean, the mean, and one standard deviation above the mean.

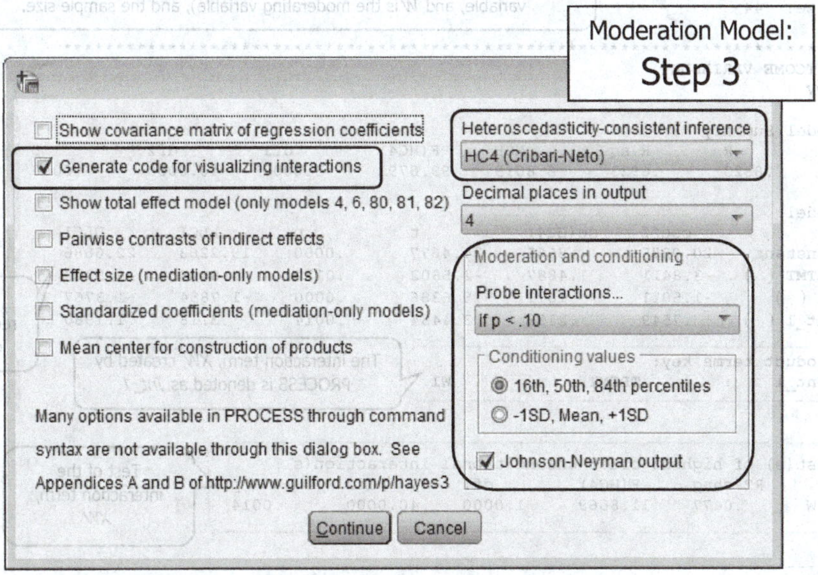

FIGURE 20.10
Moderation model: Step 3.

20.3.3.1 Interpreting Moderation Output

Annotated results are presented in Table 20.2. The OLS regression coefficient for b_1 (i.e., *X*) is −3.8411. This is interpreted as the difference in the outcome (noted as *DV* on the output) between the treatment and control group among those with a value of 0 on the moderating variable, *W* (noted as *W1* in the output). Of cases with *W* = 0, those in the treatment group (*X* =1) had lower values on the dependent variable as noted by the negative sign of the coefficient. Mathematically this is a correct interpretation; however, 0 does not occur in our range of *W* in this particular example. Thus, in this example, this interpretation interpolates beyond the range of the available data and provides an example where centering makes sense.

The OLS regression coefficient for b_2 (i.e., *W*) is −1.5811. This coefficient is interpreted as the difference in the dependent variable between two cases that differ by one unit on *W* when *X* is 0. In this illustration, *X* of zero refers to the control group so this *is* an interpretable coefficient. This is the conditional effect of the moderating variable, *W*, on the outcome,

TABLE 20.2

Moderation Model SPSS Output

Matrix

```
Run MATRIX procedure:

************** PROCESS Procedure for SPSS Version 3.2.01 ****************

          Written by Andrew F. Hayes, Ph.D.       www.afhayes.com
    Documentation available in Hayes (2018). www.guilford.com/p/hayes3

**************************************************************************
Model  : 1
    Y  : DV
    X  : TRTMT
    W  : W1

Sample
Size:  44
```

The output provides information on the model template that was used (#1), the variables specified (*Y* is the dependent variable, *X* is the independent variable, and *W* is the moderating variable), and the sample size.

```
**************************************************************************
OUTCOME VARIABLE:
 DV

Model Summary
          R       R-sq        MSE     F(HC4)        df1        df2          p
      .8320      .6923     6.8099    99.0793     3.0000    40.0000      .0000

Model
              coeff    se(HC4)          t          p       LLCI       ULCI
constant    20.9575      .8565    24.4677      .0000    19.2263    22.6886
TRTMT ( )   -3.8411     1.4887    -2.5802      .0137    -6.8499     -.8323
W1 ( )      -1.5811      .1011   -15.6386      .0000    -1.7854    -1.3767
Int_1 ( )     .7549      .2192     3.4434      .0014      .3118     1.1980

Product terms key:
 Int_1    :        TRTMT    x        W1
```

b_1 (constant), b_2 (W1), b_3 (Int_1)

OLS regression output

The interaction term, *XW*, created by PROCESS is denoted as *Int_1*

```
Test(s) of highest order unconditional interaction(s):
       R2-chng     F(HC4)        df1        df2          p
X*W      .0477    11.8569     1.0000    40.0000      .0014
```

Test of the interaction term, *XW*

```
----------
    Focal predict: TRTMT    (X)
          Mod var: W1       (W)
```

The **first row** represents the effect of *X* on *Y* conditioned on *W* being low (i.e., 16th percentile or one standard deviation below the mean)—an effect of -.0667. The second row represents the effect of *X* on *Y* conditioned on *W* being moderate (i.e., 50th percentile)—an effect of 2.9528. The third row represents the effect of *X* on *Y* conditioned on *W* being high (i.e., 84th percentile or one standard deviation above the mean)—an effect of 4.4626.

```
Conditional effects of the focal predictor at values of the moderator(s):

         W1     Effect    se(HC4)          t          p       LLCI       ULCI
     5.0000     -.0667      .6851     -.0973      .9230    -1.4513     1.3180
     9.0000     2.9528      .8956     3.2972      .0021     1.1428     4.7629
    11.0000     4.4626     1.2430     3.5902      .0009     1.9504     6.9748
```

These 'conditional effects' values are based on the equation: $\theta_{X\to Y} = b_1 + b_3W$ and the effect (i.e., regression coefficient) represents the effect of *X* on *Y* among those relatively low (i.e., 16th percentile), moderate (i.e., 50th percentile), and high (i.e., 84th percentile) on *W*, the moderating variable.

(continued)

TABLE 20.2 (continued)

Moderation Model SPSS Output

Moderator value(s) defining Johnson-Neyman significance region(s):

Value	% below	% above
6.8479	27.2727	72.7273

Johnson-Neyman results for probing an interaction. The region of significance for the effect of *X* on *Y*. The Johnson-Neyman technique shows that the relationship between *X* and *Y* is significant when *W* is **greater than 6.8479** but not significant with lower values.

Conditional effect of focal predictor at values of the moderator:

W1	Effect	se(HC4)	t	p	LLCI	ULCI
3.0000	-1.5764	.9379	-1.6807	.1006	-3.4721	.3193
3.5000	-1.1990	.8609	-1.3928	.1714	-2.9389	.5409
4.0000	-.8215	.7915	-1.0379	.3055	-2.4213	.7782
4.5000	-.4441	.7321	-.6067	.5475	-1.9237	1.0354
5.0000	-.0667	.6851	-.0973	.9230	-1.4513	1.3180
5.5000	.3108	.6533	.4757	.6369	-1.0097	1.6312
6.0000	.6882	.6390	1.0770	.2879	-.6033	1.9797
6.5000	1.0657	.6433	1.6565	.1055	-.2346	2.3659
6.8479	1.3283	.6572	2.0211	.0500	.0000	2.6565
7.0000	1.4431	.6659	2.1671	.0362	.0972	2.7890
7.5000	1.8205	.7050	2.5823	.0136	.3956	3.2454
8.0000	2.1980	.7581	2.8994	.0060	.6658	3.7301
8.5000	2.5754	.8224	3.1316	.0032	.9133	4.2375
9.0000	2.9528	.8956	3.2972	.0021	1.1428	4.7629
9.5000	3.3303	.9756	3.4137	.0015	1.3586	5.3020
10.0000	3.7077	1.0609	3.4949	.0012	1.5636	5.8519
10.5000	4.0852	1.1503	3.5513	.0010	1.7602	6.4101
11.0000	4.4626	1.2430	3.5902	.0009	1.9504	6.9748
11.5000	4.8400	1.3382	3.6167	.0008	2.1353	7.5448
12.0000	5.2175	1.4355	3.6345	.0008	2.3161	8.1189
12.5000	5.5949	1.5345	3.6461	.0008	2.4936	8.6963
13.0000	5.9724	1.6348	3.6532	.0007	2.6682	9.2765

Data for visualizing the conditional effect of the focal predictor:
Paste text below into a SPSS syntax window and execute to produce plot.

```
DATA LIST FREE/
   TRTMT       W1          DV          .
BEGIN DATA.
      .0000     5.0000    13.0522
    1.0000     5.0000    12.9855
      .0000     9.0000     6.7279
    1.0000     9.0000     9.6807
      .0000    11.0000     3.5658
    1.0000    11.0000     8.0284
END DATA.
GRAPH/SCATTERPLOT=
 W1       WITH      DV       BY       TRTMT      .
```

To visualize the graph, copy and paste into SPSS syntax as noted. The graph, based on this syntax, is pasted here.

TABLE 20.2 (continued)

Moderation Model SPSS Output

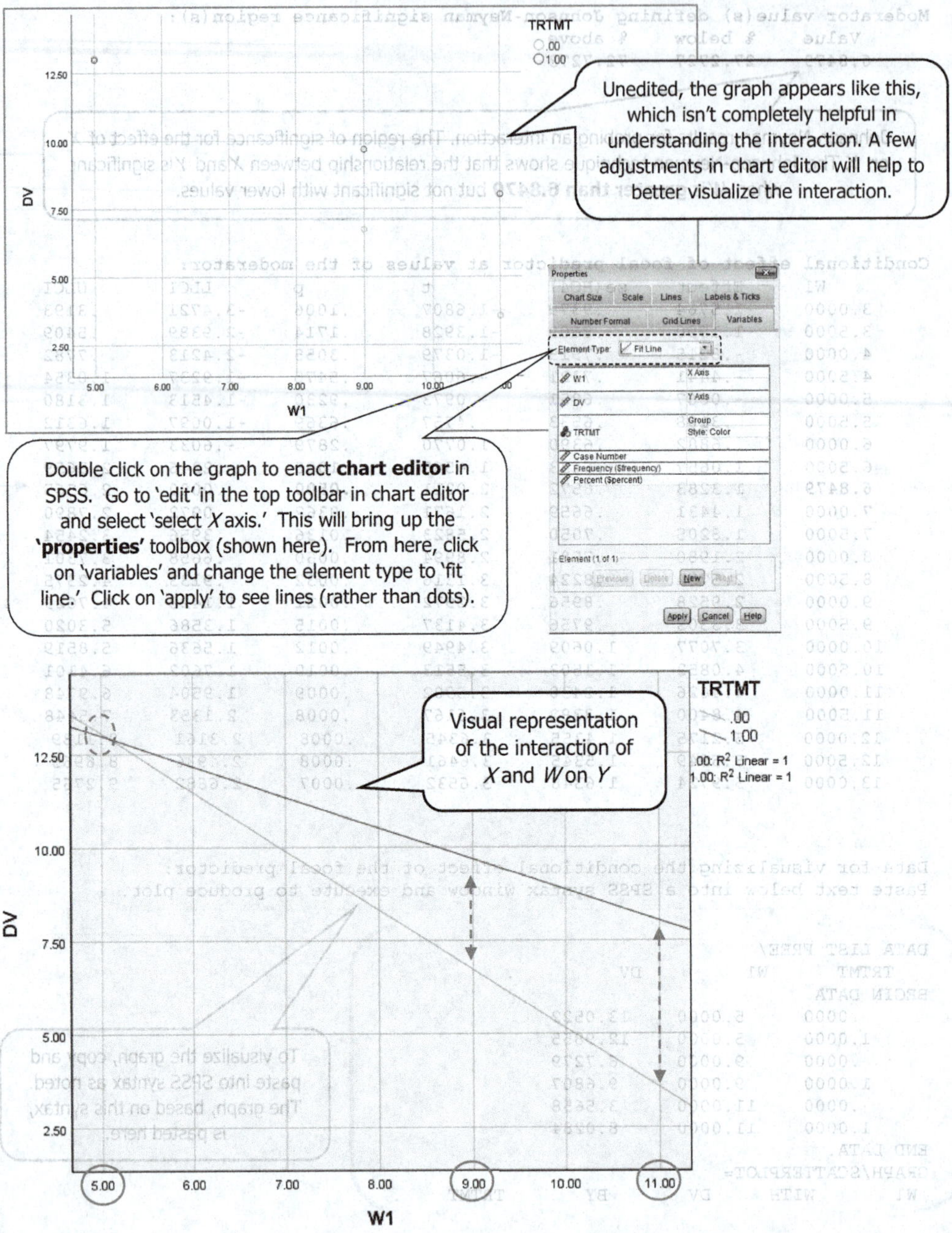
TRTMT
.00
1.00
12.50
10.00
7.50
5.00
2.50
DV
5.00 6.00 7.00 8.00 9.00 10.00
W1
Unedited, the graph appears like this, which isn't completely helpful in understanding the interaction. A few adjustments in chart editor will help to better visualize the interaction.
Properties
Chart Size Scale Lines Labels & Ticks
Number Format Grid Lines Variables
Element Type: Fit Line
W1 X Axis
DV Y Axis
TRTMT Group Style: Color
Case Number
Frequency ($frequency)
Percent ($percent)
Element (1 of 1)
Previous Delete New Redo
Apply Cancel Help
Double click on the graph to enact **chart editor** in SPSS. Go to 'edit' in the top toolbar in chart editor and select 'select *X* axis.' This will bring up the **'properties'** toolbox (shown here). From here, click on 'variables' and change the element type to 'fit line.' Click on 'apply' to see lines (rather than dots).
Visual representation of the interaction of *X* and *W* on *Y*
TRTMT
.00
1.00
.00: R² Linear = 1
1.00: R² Linear = 1
12.50
10.00
7.50
5.00
2.50
DV
5.00 6.00 7.00 8.00 9.00 10.00 11.00
W1

(*continued*)

TABLE 20.2 (continued)

Moderation Model SPSS Output

> The **first row** represents the effect of *X* on *Y* conditioned on *W* being low (i.e., 16th percentile or one standard deviation below the mean)—an effect of -.0667. The second row represents the effect of *X* on *Y* conditioned on *W* being moderate (i.e., 50th percentile)—2.9528. The third row represents the effect of *X* on *Y* conditioned on *W* being high (i.e., 84th percentile or one standard deviation above the mean)—4.4626

```
Conditional effects of the focal predictor at values of the moderator(s):

         W1      Effect     se(HC4)          t          p       LLCI       ULCI
     5.0000     -.0667       .6851      -.0973      .9230    -1.4513     1.3180
     9.0000     2.9528       .8956      3.2972      .0021     1.1428     4.7629
    11.0000     4.4626      1.2430      3.5902      .0009     1.9504     6.9748
```

For example, given the conditional effects presented earlier (copied and pasted here in the box above just to make it easier), when ***W*** **= 5.00**, i.e., *relatively low—one standard deviation below the mean—* **the conditional effect of *X* on *Y* is -.667,** computed as follows. We see at this point, one standard deviation below the mean, there is not a statistically significant conditional effect (*p* = .9230), and that is visualized on the graph by the lines for the two groups in *X* overlaying each other.

$$\theta_{X \to Y} = b_1 + b_3 W = -3.8411 + (.7549)(5.00) = -3.8411 + 3.7745 = -.066$$

```
*********** BOOTSTRAP RESULTS FOR REGRESSION MODEL PARAMETERS ****
OUTCOME VARIABLE:
 DV

              Coeff    BootMean      BootSE    BootLLCI    BootULCI
constant    20.9575     21.0859       .8917     19.7238     23.1469
TRTMT       -3.8411     -3.8229      1.5965     -6.7705      -.3999
W1          -1.5811     -1.5949       .1051     -1.8312     -1.4212
Int_1         .7549       .7500       .2276       .2648      1.1572
```

> The bootstrapped confidence interval results lend evidence to support the conclusions from the hypothesis tests presented earlier. Among others, that *W* moderates the relationship between *X* and *Y* given that 0 is not within the interval for *Int_1*, the interaction term.

```
********************** ANALYSIS NOTES AND ERRORS ************************

Level of confidence for all confidence intervals in output:
  95.0000

Number of bootstrap samples for percentile bootstrap confidence intervals:
  5000

W values in conditional tables are the 16th, 50th, and 84th percentiles.

NOTE: A heteroscedasticity consistent standard error and covariance matrix
estimator was used.

------ END MATRIX -----
```

Y, among those in the control group (i.e., $X = 0$). The sign for the coefficient is negative, which indicates that those higher on *W* had lower scores on the outcome variable.

The regression coefficient for the interaction, *Int_1*, is .7549 and indicates how the effect of X on the dependent variable changes as *W* changes by one unit. In this illustration, the interaction is statistically significant, which suggests the effect of *X* (independent variable) on *Y* (dependent variable) depends on *W* (moderating variable). As *W* increases by one unit, the difference in the dependent variable between those in the treatment and control group increases by .7549 units (i.e., a positive effect, so the effect moves toward larger values on the number as *W* increases).

As noted previously, we requested probing interactions with the default conditioning values of the 16th, 50th, and 84th percentiles, and when *W* is normally distributed, this corresponds, respectively, to one standard deviation below the mean, the mean, and one standard deviation above the mean. We see in the graph that the moderating effect of *W* on X occurs at higher values of the moderator.

20.4 Computing Mediation and Moderation Using R

Next we consider **R** for computing mediation and moderation. The commands are provided within the blocks with additional annotation to assist in understanding how the command works. Should you want to write reminder notes and annotation to yourself as you write the commands in **R** (and we highly encourage doing so), remember that any text that follows a hashtag (i.e., #) is annotation only and not part of the **R** code. Thus, you can write annotations directly into **R** with hashtags. We encourage this practice so that when you call up the commands in the future, you'll understand what the various lines of code are doing. You may think you'll remember what you did. However, trust us. There is a good chance that you won't. Thus, consider it best practice when using **R** to annotate heavily!

20.4.1 Reading Data Into R

```
getwd()
```

R is always pointed to a directory on your computer. The *get working directory* function can be used to determine to which directory **R** is pointed. We will assume that we need to change the working directory, and will use the next line of code to set the working directory to the desired path.

```
setwd("E:/FolderName")
```

We use the *setwd* function to establish the working directory. To set the working directory, change what is in quotation marks to your file location. Also, if you are copying the directory name from your properties, you will need to change the backslash (i.e., \) to a forward slash (i.e., /).

```
Ch20_med <- read.csv("Ch20_medmod.csv")
```

The *read.csv* function reads our data into **R**. What's to the left of the "<-" will be what the data will be called in **R**. In this example, we're calling the R dataframe "Ch20_med." What's to the right of the "<-" tells **R** to find this particular csv file. In this example, our file is called "Ch20_medmod.csv." Make sure the extension (i.e.,

FIGURE 20.11
Reading data into R.

.csv) is included in your script. Also note that the name of your file should be in quotation marks within the parentheses.

```
names(Ch20_med)
```

The *names* function will produce a list of variable names for each dataframe as follows. This is a good check to make sure your data have been read in correctly.

```
[1] "DV"      "TRTMT" "M1"      "M2"      "M3"      "W1"      "W2"
"
```

```
View(Ch20_med)
```

The *View* function will let you view the dataset in spreadsheet format in RStudio.

```
Ch20_med$TRTMTf <- factor(Ch20_med$TRTMT,
labels = c("treatment", "control"))
```

This command will create a new variable in our dataframe named "TRTMTf." We use the *factor* function to define the variable TRTMT as nominal with the two groups defined here (i.e., *treatment, control*). What is to the left of "<-" in the script creates the new TRTMTf variable in our dataframe.

```
summary(Ch20_med)
```

The *summary* function will produce basic descriptive statistics on all the variables in your dataframe. This is a great way to quickly check to see if the data have been read in correctly and to get a feel for your data, if you haven't already. The output from the summary statement for this dataframe looks like this. Because we defined TRTMTf as a factor, we are provided only the frequencies for each category in that variable.

```
       DV              TRTMT            M1               M2
Min.    : 1.000   Min.    :0.0   Min.    : 3.000   Min.    : 4.000
1st Qu.: 5.250   1st Qu.:0.0   1st Qu.: 7.750   1st Qu.: 7.000
Median :10.500   Median :0.5   Median :10.000   Median : 7.000
Mean    : 8.795   Mean    :0.5   Mean    : 9.455   Mean    : 8.136
3rd Qu.:13.500   3rd Qu.:1.0   3rd Qu.:12.000   3rd Qu.: 9.250
Max.    :13.500   Max.    :1.0   Max.    :16.000   Max.    :14.000

       M3               W1               W2             TRTMTf
Min.    : 0.000   Min.    : 3.000   Min.    : 5.00   control   :22
1st Qu.: 0.750   1st Qu.: 6.000   1st Qu.:10.00   treatment:22
Median : 3.000   Median : 9.000   Median :15.00
Mean    : 4.455   Mean    : 8.409   Mean    :14.45
3rd Qu.: 6.250   3rd Qu.:10.000   3rd Qu.:19.00
Max.    :16.000   Max.    :13.000   Max.    :25.00
```

FIGURE 20.11 (continued)
Reading data into **R**.

20.4.2 Generating a Mediation Model Using R

```
model_a <- lm(M1 ~ TRTMTf,
              Ch20_med)
```

The *lm* function is used to generate a linear regression model with the mediating variable, "M1," as the outcome and the treatment variable, TRTMTf, as the independent variable. The data come from "Ch20_med" and the object is named "model_a." This will produce the coefficient for *a*.

FIGURE 20.12
Generating a mediating model in **R**.

```
summary(model_a)
```

The *summary* function is used to produce the output for model_a.

```
Call:
lm(formula = M1 ~ TRTMTf, data = Ch20_med)

Residuals:
    Min      1Q  Median      3Q     Max 
-4.9545 -1.9545  0.0455  2.0455  5.0455 

Coefficients:
                Estimate Std. Error t value Pr(>|t|)    
(Intercept)       7.9545     0.5678  14.009  < 2e-16 ***
TRTMTftreatment   3.0000     0.8030   3.736 0.000558 ***
---
Signif. codes:  0 "***" 0.001 "**" 0.01 "*" 0.05 "." 0.1 " " 1
Residual standard error: 2.663 on 42 degrees of freedom
Multiple R-squared: 0.2494, Adjusted R-squared: 0.2316
F-statistic: 13.96 on 1 and 42 DF, p-value: 0.0005579
```

```
model_bc <- lm(DV ~ TRTMTf + M1,
             Ch20_med)
```

The *lm* function is used to generate a linear regression model with the dependent variable, DV, as the outcome and the treatment variable, TRTMTf, and mediating variable, M1, as the independent variables. The data come from "Ch20_med" and the object is named "model_bc." This will produce coefficients for *c′* and *b*.

```
summary(model_bc)
```

The *summary* function is used to produce the output for model_bc.

```
Call:
lm(formula = DV ~ TRTMTf + M1, data = Ch20_med)

Residuals:
    Min      1Q  Median      3Q     Max 
-7.3894 -2.4932  0.5241  3.0323  6.3050 

Coefficients:
                Estimate Std. Error t value Pr(>|t|)    
(Intercept)       0.8819     1.9129   0.461 0.647223    
TRTMTftreatment   0.9053     1.3110   0.691 0.493744    
M1                0.7891     0.2183   3.616 0.000812 ***
---
Signif. codes:  0 "***" 0.001 "**" 0.01 "*" 0.05 "." 0.1 " " 1

Residual standard error: 3.767 on 41 degrees of freedom
Multiple R-squared: 0.3427, Adjusted R-squared: 0.3106
F-statistic: 10.69 on 2 and 41 DF, p-value: 0.0001838
```

```
model_c <- lm(DV ~ TRTMTf,
             Ch20_med)
```

The *lm* function is used to generate a linear regression model with the dependent variable, *DV*, as the outcome and the treatment variable, TRTMTf, as the independent variable. The data come from Ch20_med and the object is named "model_c." This will produce the coefficient for path *c*.

FIGURE 20.12 (continued)
Generating a mediating model in **R**.

```
summary(model_c)
```

The *summary* function is used to produce the output for *model_c*.

```
Call:
lm(formula = DV ~ TRTMTf, data = Ch20_med)

Residuals:
    Min      1Q  Median      3Q     Max
-8.9318 -4.1591  0.9545  3.0682  6.3409

Coefficients:
                Estimate Std. Error t value Pr(>|t|)
(Intercept)       7.1591     0.9113   7.856  8.9e-10 ***
TRTMTftreatment   3.2727     1.2888   2.539   0.0149 *
---
Signif. codes:  0 "***" 0.001 "**" 0.01 "*" 0.05 "." 0.1 " " 1

Residual standard error: 4.274 on 42 degrees of freedom
Multiple R-squared: 0.1331, Adjusted R-squared: 0.1125
F-statistic: 6.449 on 1 and 42 DF, p-value: 0.01489
```

```
install.packages("mediation")
library(mediation)
```

The *install.packages* function is used to install the package, *mediation*. The *library* function is used to load the package into our library.

```
med1 <- mediate(model_a, model_bc,
                treat ='TRTMTf', mediator = 'M1',
                boot = TRUE, sims = 5000)
```

The *mediate* function is used to compute bootstrapped confidence intervals from our models which estimated the coefficients for *a*, *b*, and *c*′, which were models *model_a* and *model_bc*. The script, "sims = 5000," will generate 5,000 bootstrapped samples.

```
summary(med1)
```

The *summary* function is used to produce the output for the bootstrapped results from *med1*. **ACME** is the **average causal mediation effect**, or *ab*, and is 2.367 in this model. The ACME is the mediation effect and is the indirect effect of *X* on *Y* (i.e., the effect of *X* on *Y* through the mediator). An ACME confidence interval that is statistically significant indicates a statistically significant mediating effect. **ADE** is the **average direct effect**, or *c*′, and is .905 in this model. This is the direct effect of *X* on *Y* after taking into account the mediating (or indirect) effect of *M*. From the results, we also see the *total effect* is 3.273. This is the coefficient for *c* and is the total effect of *X* on *Y* without the mediator. It is calculated as the sum of the indirect (i.e., mediation) effect (i.e., 2.367 in this model) and direct effect (i.e., .905 in this model).

```
Causal Mediation Analysis
Nonparametric Bootstrap Confidence Intervals with the Percentile Method
                 Estimate 95% CI Lower 95% CI Upper p-value
ACME                2.367        0.992        3.935    0.00
ADE                 0.905       -1.676        3.741    0.49
Total Effect        3.273        0.750        5.654    0.01
Prop. Mediated      0.723        0.244        2.481    0.01
Sample Size Used: 44
```

```
plot(med1)
```

FIGURE 20.12 (continued)
Generating a mediating model in **R**.

The *plot* function can be used to generate a plot of the confidence intervals. We see that the average direct effect confidence interval crosses zero, indicating that the direct effect of *X* on *Y* after taking the mediator into account is not statistically significant. In comparison, the mediation effect (ACME) and the total effect do not cross zero, indicating those effects are statistically significant.

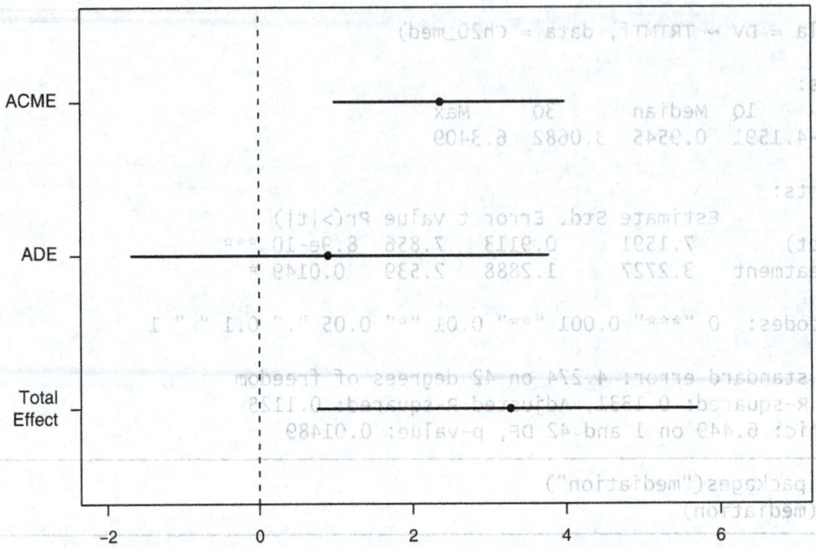

Mediation models, as with most procedures, can be computed with different packages, and different packages provide different tools and output. Let's look at an example using the *MBESS* package, which provides a number of effect size estimates.

```
install.packages("MBESS")
library(MBESS)
```

The *MBESS* package is first installed then loaded into our library using the *install.packages* and *library* functions.

```
mediation(x=Ch20_med$TRTMT,
          mediator=Ch20_med$M1,
          dv=Ch20_med$DV)
```

Next, we define our mediation model with *X, mediator,* and *dv* from the dataframe Ch20_med.

The estimates for path *c* are provided first.

```
$Y.on.X
$Y.on.X$Regression.Table

                 Estimate  Std. Error t value  p(>>|t|) Low Conf Limit
Intercept.Y_X 7.159091  0.9112933 7.855968 8.900653e-10     5.3200265
c (Regressor) 3.272727  1.2887634 2.539432 1.489384e-02     0.6718975
              Up Conf Limit
Intercept.Y_X      8.998155
c (Regressor)      5.873557
$Y.on.X$Model.Fit
       Residual standard error (RMSE) numerator df denominator df
Values                       4.274345            1             42
       F-Statistic p-value (F)       R^2    Adj R^2 Low Conf Limit
```

FIGURE 20.12 (continued)
Generating a mediating model in **R**.

```
Values     6.448716  0.01489384 0.133104 0.1124636      0.004776991
        Up Conf Limit
Values      0.3505862
```

The estimates for path *a* are provided next.

```
$M.on.X
$M.on.X$Regression.Table

                 Estimate Std. Error   t value      p(>|t|) Low Conf Limit
Intercept.M_X    7.954545  0.5678137 14.009075 1.986718e-17       6.808651
a (Regressor)    3.000000  0.8030099  3.735944 5.579076e-04       1.379460
                 Up Conf Limit
Intercept.M_X          9.10044
a (Regressor)          4.62054

$M.on.X$Model.Fit
        Residual standard error (RMSE) numerator df denominator df
Values                        2.663282            1             42
        F-Statistic  p-value (F)       R^2   Adj R^2 Low Conf Limit
Values     13.95728 0.0005579076 0.2494274 0.2315566      0.05511564
        Up Conf Limit
Values     0.4743653
```

The estimates for paths *c*′ and *b* are provided next.

```
$Y.on.X.and.M
$Y.on.X.and.M$Regression.Table

                        Estimate Std. Error   t value      p(>|t|)
Intercept.Y_XM         0.8818695  1.9128789 0.4610169 0.6472228096
c.prime (Regressor)    0.9053181  1.3110235 0.6905430 0.4937437886
b (Mediator)           0.7891364  0.2182535 3.6156865 0.0008122274
                      Low Conf Limit Up Conf Limit
Intercept.Y_XM            -2.9812678      4.745007
c.prime (Regressor)       -1.7423477      3.552984
b (Mediator)               0.3483644      1.229908

$Y.on.X.and.M$Model.Fit
        Residual standard error (RMSE) numerator df denominator df
Values                        3.767066            2             41
        F-Statistic  p-value (F)      R^2   Adj R^2 Low Conf Limit
Values     10.68782 0.0001837648 0.342692 0.3106282      0.1012886
        Up Conf Limit
Values       0.547119
Many effect size values are estimated.
```

Many effect size values are estimated.

```
$Effect.Sizes
                                                      Estimate
Indirect.Effect                                     2.36740922
Indirect.Effect.Partially.Standardized              0.52179137
Index.of.Mediation                                  0.26391192
R2_4.5                                              0.12545916
R2_4.6                                              0.06030367
R2_4.7                                              0.17597043
Maximum.Possible.Mediation.Effect                   9.35535239
ab.to.Maximum.Possible.Mediation.Effect_kappa.squared 0.25305399
Ratio.of.Indirect.to.Total.Effect                   0.72337504
```

FIGURE 20.12 (continued)
Generating a mediating model in R.

```
Ratio.of.Indirect.to.Direct.Effect              2.61500276
Success.of.Surrogate.Endpoint                   1.09090909
Residual.Based_Gamma                            0.10865859
Residual.Based.Standardized_gamma               0.11610848
ES.for.two.groups                               0.78337195
SOS                                             0.94256516
```

The *MBESS* package documentation provides a summary of the effect size measures provided in the output (Kelley, 2018, pp. 66–67):

- Indirect.Effect = *ab*
- Indirect.Effect.Partially. Standaedized = $ab_{ps} = \frac{ab}{SD_Y}$ (MacKinnon, 2008)
- Index.of. Mediation = $ab = \left(\frac{SD_x}{SD_Y}\right)$ (Preacher & Hayes, 2008a)
- R2_4.5 = index of explained variance (equation 4.5 in MacKinnon, 2008)
- R2_4.6 = index of explained variance (equation 4.6 in MacKinnon, 2008)
- R2_4.7 = index of explained variance (equation 4.7 in MacKinnon, 2008)
- Maximum.Possible.Mediation.Effect = "the maximum attainable value of the mediation effect (i.e., the indirect effect), in the direction of the observed indirect effect, that could have been observed, conditional on the sample variances and on the magnitudes of relationships among some of the variables" (Kelley, 2018, p. 66).
- ab.to.Maximum.Possible.Mediation.Effect_kappa.squared = the proportion of the maximum possible indirect effect; the indirect effect is the numerator and the maximum possible mediation effect is the denominator (Preacher & Kelley, 2011)
- Ratio.of.Indirect.to.Total.Effect = ratio of the indirect effect to the total effect (Freedman, 2002); this effect size is also referred to as *mediation ratio* (Ditlevsen, Christensen, Lynch, Damsgaard, & Keiding, 2005) and as the *relative indirect effect* (Huang, Sivaganesan, Succop, & Goodman, 2004); "often loosely interpreted as the *relative indirect effect*" (Kelley, 2018, p. 66).
- Ratio.of.Indirect.to.Direct. Effect = ratio of the indirect effect to the direct effect (Sobel, 1982)
- Success.of.Surrogate.Endpoint = success of a surrogate endpoint (Buyse & Molenberghs, 1998)
- Residual.Based_Gamma = residual based index (Preacher & Kelley, 2011)
- Residual.Based.Standardized_gamma = standardized residual based index, where the scales of *M* and *Y* are removed by using standardized values of *M* and *Y* (Preacher & Kelley, 2011)
- ES.for.two.groups = Hansen and McNeal (1996) effect size for two groups, applicable when *X* is binary and coded with values of 0 and 1
- SOS = shared over simple effects (SOS) index; computed as the ratio of the variation in the outcome, *Y*, explained by both the independent variable, *X*, and mediating variable, *M*, divided by the variation in *Y* explained by *X* (Lindenberger & Pötter, 1998)

```
upsilon(Ch20_med$TRTMT, Ch20_med$M1, Ch20_med$DV,
        conf.level = 0.95,
        bootstrap = TRUE,
        bootstrap.package = "lavaan",
        bootstrap.type="ordinary", B = 1000,
        boot.data.out=FALSE)
```

To generate the upsilon effect size (Lachowicz et al., 2018), the *upsilon* function is used (note that at the time of writing, this function can be used with simple mediation models only). The first line defines *X, M,* and *Y*. Bootstrapped confidence intervals are generate with the "bootstrap = TRUE" script. The default bootstrap package is *lavaan,* and the other option is *boot.* The type of bootstrap confidence interval is *ordinary*, which is the default. When using *lavaan,* the other option is *bollen.stine.* We generate 1000 bootstrap replications with *B = 1000.* Bootstrapped data will be generated only if *boot.data.out = TRUE.* In this case, we have not requested the data by indicating *FALSE.* (Be patient—the bootstrapping may take several minutes to run!)

```
                 Estimate 95% ordinary LCL 95% ordinary UCL
Upsilon        0.06964950       0.01251146        0.1860631
Adj Upsilon 0.06026125       0.00619668        0.1714112
```

FIGURE 20.12 (continued)
Generating a mediating model in **R**.

20.4.3 Generating a Moderation Model Using R

So as not to be confusing with the mediation example, we will read our data in again, but this time call our dataframe a name unique to the moderation illustration, specifically "Ch20_mod."

```
getwd()
setwd("E:\filename")
Ch20_mod <- read.csv("Ch20_medmod.csv")
```

```
install.packages("devtools")
devtools::install_github("markhwhiteii/processr")
library(processr)
```

The *processr* package in **R** allows users to specify models 1, 4, 7, and 14. To access *processr*, we will first install *devtools* (if not already installed), and then run the "install_github" script to download *processr.* The *processr* package runs through *lavaan,* and *lavaan* requires continuous inputs. As such, when using *processr*, any dichotomous variables must be numeric and coded as 0 and 1 (i.e., we will not use the recoded factor variable for the treatment variable).

```
mod1result <- model1(iv="TRTMT", dv="DV",
                     mod="W1", data=Ch20_mod)

mod1result
```

We use the *model1* function to denote Model 1 from Hayes and define the independent variable, "iv," dependent variable, "dv," and moderating variable, "mod." The data come from Ch20_mod. We name the object "mod1result," and use the mod1result script to output our results. The results provide the coefficients along with estimates for three values of the moderating variable allowing us to see the effect of *X* on *Y* conditioned on *W* being low (one standard deviation below the mean)—an effect of 5.756, moderate (the mean)—an effect of 8.409, and high (one standard deviation above the mean)—an effect of 11.062.

```
# A tibble: 7 x 5
  term            estimate std.error statistic  p.value
  <chr>              <dbl>     <dbl>     <dbl>    <dbl>
1 intercept         21.0       1.88      11.1   8.01e-14
2 TRTMT             -3.84      2.66      -1.44  1.57e- 1
3 W1                -1.58      0.206     -7.67  2.21e- 9
4 interaction        0.755     0.303      2.49  1.70e- 2
5 when W1 = 5.756     0.504     1.12      0.449 6.56e- 1
6 when W1 = 8.409     2.51      0.793     3.16  2.98e- 3
7 when W1 = 11.062    4.51      1.13      3.98  2.86e- 4
```

```
mod2result <- model1(iv="W1", dv="DV",
mod="TRTMT", data=Ch20_mod)
mod2result
```

If we swap the roles of the independent and moderating variables, we can see the effect of the moderating variable at levels of the independent variable.

```
# A tibble: 6 x 5
  term         estimate std.error statistic  p.value
  <chr>           <dbl>     <dbl>     <dbl>    <dbl>
1 intercept      21.0       1.88      11.1   8.01e-14
2 W1             -1.58      0.206     -7.67 2.21e- 9
3 TRTMT          -3.84      2.66      -1.44 1.57e- 1
4 interaction     0.755     0.303      2.49 1.70e- 2
```

FIGURE 20.13
Generating a moderating model in **R**.

```
5 when TRTMT = 0    -1.58      0.206    -7.67 2.21e- 9
6 when TRTMT = 1    -0.826     0.222    -3.72 6.17e- 4
```

Now let's look at another way to examine moderation using **R**. We will generate two models: one without the interaction term and one with the term, and will then compare the models.

```
Mod1 <- lm(DV ~ TRTMTf + W1,
data = Ch20_mod)
```

The *lm* function is used to generate a linear regression model with the outcome, DV, and the treatment variable, TRTMTf, as the independent variable, and the moderating variable, W1. No interaction term is included in this model. The data come from Ch20_mod and the object is named "Mod1."

```
summary(fitMod)
```

The *summary* function is used to produce the output.

```
Residuals:
    Min      1Q  Median      3Q     Max
-6.5795 -1.9992  0.4091  2.1770  4.8848

Coefficients:
                 Estimate Std. Error t value Pr(>|t|)
(Intercept)       17.9125     1.5195  11.788 9.49e-15 ***
TRTMTftreatment    2.4886     0.8415   2.958  0.00513 **
W1                -1.2322     0.1604  -7.681 1.83e-09 ***
---
Signif. codes:  0 "***" 0.001 "**" 0.01 "*" 0.05 "." 0.1 " " 1

Residual standard error: 2.77 on 41 degrees of freedom
Multiple R-squared:  0.6445,  Adjusted R-squared:  0.6272
F-statistic: 37.17 on 2 and 41 DF,  p-value: 6.181e-10
```

Next, we generate the same model but include the interaction term.

```
Mod2 <- lm(DV ~ TRTMTf + W1 + TRTMTf*W1,
data = Ch20_mod)
```

The *lm* function is used to generate a linear regression model with the moderating variable, *W1*, the outcome, *DV*, and the treatment variable, *TRTMTf*, as the independent variable, along with an interaction term *XW*, specifically *TRTMTf*W1* in this dataframe. The data come from *Ch20_mod* and the object is named "Mod2."

```
summary(Mod2)
```

The *summary* function is used to produce the output.

```
Residuals:
    Min      1Q  Median      3Q     Max
-7.3546 -1.1344  0.5217  1.7758  3.8193

Coefficients:
                    Estimate Std. Error t value Pr(>|t|)
(Intercept)          20.9575     1.8825  11.133 8.01e-14 ***
TRTMTftreatment      -3.8411     2.6624  -1.443    0.157
```

FIGURE 20.13 (continued)
Generating a moderating model in **R**.

```
W1                     -1.5811     0.2061  -7.672 2.21e-09 ***
TRTMTftreatment:W1   0.7549     0.3031   2.490    0.017 *
---
Signif. codes:  0 "***" 0.001 "**" 0.01 "*" 0.05 "." 0.1 " " 1

Residual standard error: 2.61 on 40 degrees of freedom
Multiple R-squared: 0.6923, Adjusted R-squared: 0.6692
F-statistic: 29.99 on 3 and 40 DF, p-value: 2.507e-10
```

```
anova(Mod1, Mod2)
```

Then we compare the models using the *ANOVA* function. We see there is a statistically significant difference ($p = .01701$).

```
Analysis of Variance Table

Model 1: DV ~ TRTMTf + W1
Model 2: DV ~ TRTMTf + W1 + TRTMTf * W1
  Res.Df    RSS Df Sum of Sq      F  Pr(>F)
1     41 314.63
2     40 272.40  1    42.236 6.2022 0.01701 *
---
Signif. codes:  0 "***" 0.001 "**" 0.01 "*" 0.05 "." 0.1 " " 1
```

What about centering?

```
Xc <- c(scale(Ch20_mod$TRTMT, center=TRUE, scale=FALSE))
```

Should we want to run the model with variables that are centered, this script will create a new variable, *Xc*, that is a *centered predictor*.

```
Wc<- c(scale(Ch20_mod$W1, center=TRUE, scale=FALSE))
```

Should we want to run the model with variables that are centered, this script will create a new variable, "Wc," that is a *centered moderator*.

```
fitMod2 <- lm(DV ~ TRTMTf + Wc + TRTMTf*Wc,
              data = Ch20_mod)
```

Let's first generate a model that centers *W* but not *X*, given that 0 for *X* is an interpretable value (i.e., the control group). The *lm* function is used to generate a linear regression model with the dependent variable, "DV," the centered moderating variable, "Wc," and the uncentered treatment variable, *TRTMTf*, as the independent variable. The data come from *Ch20_mod* and the object is named "fitMod2."

```
summary(fitMod2)
```

The *summary* function is used to produce the output. We see that the intercept is now 7.66 and is interpreted as the value of *Y* for those in the control group ($X = 0$) when *W* is at the average.

```
Residuals:
    Min      1Q  Median      3Q     Max
-7.3546 -1.1344  0.5217  1.7758  3.8193
```

FIGURE 20.13 (continued)
Generating a moderating model in R.

```
Coefficients:
                      Estimate Std. Error t value Pr(>|t|)
(Intercept)             7.6622     0.5602  13.677  < 2e-16 ***
TRTMTftreatment         2.5068     0.7927   3.162 0.00298 **
Wc                     -1.5811     0.2061  -7.672 2.21e-09 ***
TRTMTftreatment:Wc      0.7549     0.3031   2.490 0.01701 *
---
Signif. codes:  0 "***" 0.001 "**" 0.01 "*" 0.05 "." 0.1 " " 1

Residual standard error: 2.61 on 40 degrees of freedom
Multiple R-squared: 0.6923, Adjusted R-squared: 0.6692
F-statistic: 29.99 on 3 and 40 DF, p-value: 2.507e-10
```

If *both* X and W are centered, our script and output appears as such:

```
Xc <- c(scale(Ch20_mod$TRTMT, center=TRUE, scale=FALSE))
Wc<- c(scale(Ch20_mod$W1, center=TRUE, scale=FALSE))
fitMod3 <- lm(DV ~ Xc + Wc + Xc*Wc, data = Ch20_mod)
summary(fitMod3)
```

```
Residuals:
    Min      1Q  Median      3Q     Max
-7.3546 -1.1344  0.5217  1.7758  3.8193
Coefficients:
             Estimate Std. Error t value Pr(>|t|)
(Intercept)    8.9155     0.3964  22.494  < 2e-16 ***
Xc             2.5068     0.7927   3.162 0.00298 **
Wc            -1.2036     0.1516  -7.942 9.48e-10 ***
Xc:Wc          0.7549     0.3031   2.490 0.01701 *
---
Signif. codes:  0 "***" 0.001 "**" 0.01 "*" 0.05 "." 0.1 " " 1
Residual standard error: 2.61 on 40 degrees of freedom
Multiple R-squared: 0.6923, Adjusted R-squared: 0.6692
F-statistic: 29.99 on 3 and 40 DF, p-value: 2.507e-10
```

FIGURE 20.13 (continued)
Generating a moderating model in **R**.

20.5 Additional Resources

This chapter has provided a preview of conducting moderated and mediated regression. However, once again, space limitations prevent us from delving too deeply into these advanced topics. For those who are interested in a deeper dive, there are quite a number of excellent resources to turn, including the following, among many others:

- A comprehensive overview of moderation and mediation, including details on using the PROCESS macro in SPSS (Hayes, 2013)
- Dr. David A. Kenny's mediation website, http://davidakenny.net/cm/mediate.htm, and moderation website, http://davidakenny.net/cm/moderation.htm
- Dr. Andrew F. Hayes's webpage with links for SPSS, SAS, and Mplus macros and code, among other useful resources, http://www.afhayes.com/index.html

Problems

Conceptual Problems

1. A researcher is examining team performance and wants to look at the relationship between communication and collaboration. The researcher believes that communication may interact with timing. Which of the following types of models would you recommend the researcher examine?
   a. Mediation
   b. Moderation
   c. Neither
   d. Both
2. A researcher wants to examine the relationship between intelligence in early adulthood and physical performance in late adulthood. However, they believe there may be an indirect effect of intelligence on physical performance through education. Which of the following types of models would you recommend the researcher examine?
   a. Mediation
   b. Moderation
   c. Neither
   d. Both
3. A researcher wants to examine the relationship between stress and high-risk behavior and believes there may be an indirect effect of stress on high-risk behavior through depression. Which of the following types of models would you recommend the researcher examine?
   a. Mediation
   b. Moderation
   c. Neither
   d. Both
4. A researcher wants to examine the relationship between job demands and health and believes that job demands may interact with cultural values. Which of the following types of models would you recommend the researcher examine?
   a. Mediation
   b. Moderation
   c. Neither
   d. Both
5. True or false? Power for moderated multiple regression can be determined in the same way that power for multiple linear regression is determined.
6. A researcher has conducted a moderated multiple regression analysis and finds f^2 of .40. Using Cohen's (1988) conventions, this can be interpreted in which one of the following ways?
   a. Small effect
   b. Moderate effect
   c. Large effect
   d. Cannot be determined without additional information

7. A particularly important assumption to consider with moderated multiple regression is which one of the following?
   a. Homoscedasticity
   b. Lack of multicollinearity
   c. Linearity
   d. Normality of residuals
8. Which one of the following effect sizes are recommended for mediation analyses?
   a. Kappa squared
   b. Partially standardized indirect effect
   c. Proportion of variance in the independent variable that is explained by the indirect effect
   d. Ratio of the indirect to direct effect
9. For which of the following effects is the size of the effect dependent on the scale of the independent variable?
   a. Completely standardized indirect effect
   b. Completely standardized total effect
   c. Partially standardized direct effect
   d. None of the above
10. The pick-a-point approach is used for which of the following?
   a. To test a direct effect
   b. To test an indirect effect
   c. To probe an interaction
   d. To test an interaction

Answers to Conceptual Problems

1. **b** (an interaction of communication and timing on collaboration suggests a moderating relationship.)
3. **a** (an indirect effect of depression suggests that the researcher examine the relationship between stress and high-risk behavior as mediated by depression.)
5. **False** (power in multiple moderated regression is more complicated than in multiple linear regression and thus additional factors need to be considered.)
7. **a** (homoscedasticity is an especially important assumption in moderated analyses.)
9. **c** (in partially standardized effects, the independent variable remains in its original metric; thus the size of the partially standardized effect depends on the scale of X.)

Computational Problems

1. Using the Ch20_medmod data, conduct a simple mediation model (Figure 20.1) to test the mediating effect of M2 on the relationship between DV and TRTMT. Report the path coefficients and related parameter estimates for *a*, *b*, *ab*, *c*, and *c′*. Indicate if there is full, partial, or no mediation.
2. Using the Ch20_medmod data, conduct a simple moderation model (Figure 20.3) to test the moderating effect of W2 on the relationship between DV and TRTMT. Probe

interactions using the 16th, 50th, and 84th percentiles and the Johnson-Neyman technique. Report the path coefficients and related parameter estimates for b_1, b_2, and b_3, along with results for probing the interactions.

Answers to Computational Problems

1. The path coefficients and related parameter estimates include:

a. $a = 1.544$, $SE = .6292$, $t = 2.4562$, $p = .0183$

b. $b = .3338$, $SE = .2481$, $t = 2.7677$, $p = .0084$

c. $ab = 1.0612$

d. $c = 3.2727$, $SE = 1.2888$, $t = 2.5394$, $p = .0149$

e. $c' = 2.2116$, $SE = 1.3205$, $t = 1.6748$, $p = .1016$

f. There is full mediation as the effect of TRTMT on the DV is no longer statistically significant when the mediating variable, M1, is included in the model (see paths b and c').

Please see eResource for figure in full color

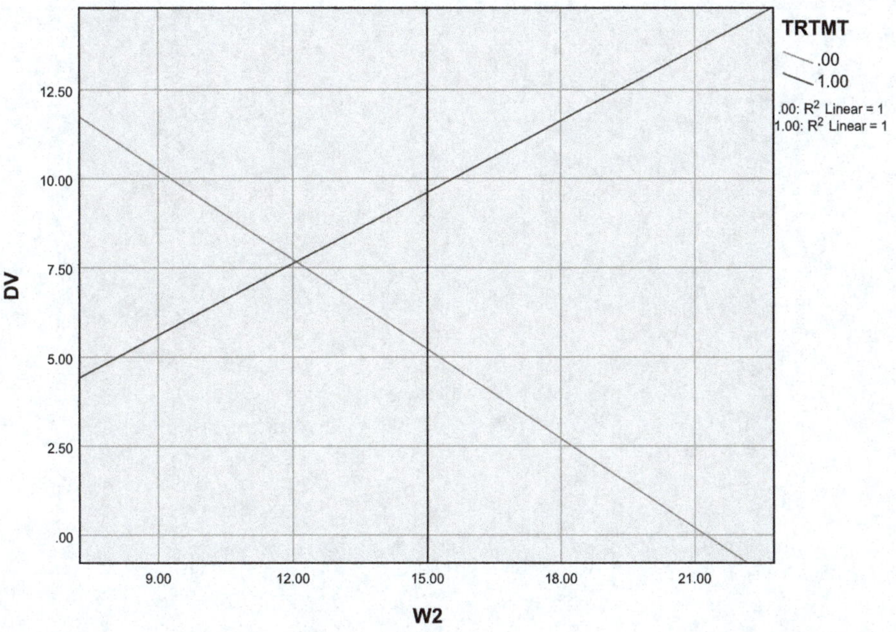

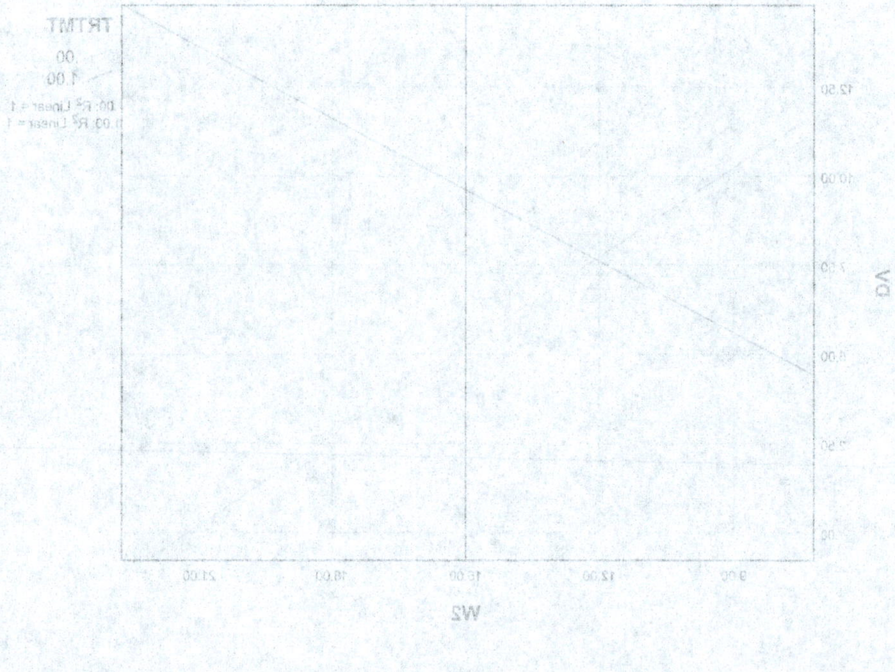

Appendix: Tables

TABLE A.1

Standard Unit Normal Distribution.

z	*P(z)*	*z*	*P(z)*	*z*	*P(z)*	*z*	*P(z)*
0.00	0.5000000	0.32	0.6255158	0.64	0.7389137	0.96	0.8314724
0.01	0.5039894	0.33	0.6293	0.65	0.7421539	0.97	0.8339768
0.02	0.5079783	0.34	0.6330717	0.66	0.7453731	0.98	0.8364569
0.03	0.5119665	0.35	0.6368307	0.67	0.7485711	0.99	0.8389129
0.04	0.5159534	0.36	0.6405764	0.68	0.7517478	1.00	0.8413447
0.05	0.5199388	0.37	0.6443088	0.69	0.7549029	1.01	0.8437524
0.06	0.5239222	0.38	0.6480273	0.70	0.7580363	1.02	0.8461358
0.07	0.5279032	0.39	0.6517317	0.71	0.7611479	1.03	0.848495
0.08	0.5318814	0.40	0.6554217	0.72	0.7642375	1.04	0.85083
0.09	0.5358564	0.41	0.659097	0.73	0.7673049	1.05	0.8531409
0.10	0.5398278	0.42	0.6627573	0.74	0.77035	1.06	0.8554277
0.11	0.5437953	0.43	0.6664022	0.75	0.7733726	1.07	0.8576903
0.12	0.5477584	0.44	0.6700314	0.76	0.7763727	1.08	0.8599289
0.13	0.5517168	0.45	0.6736448	0.77	0.7793501	1.09	0.8621434
0.14	0.55567	0.46	0.6772419	0.78	0.7823046	1.10	0.8643339
0.15	0.5596177	0.47	0.6808225	0.79	0.7852361	1.11	0.8665005
0.16	0.5635595	0.48	0.6843863	0.80	0.7881446	1.12	0.8686431
0.17	0.5674949	0.49	0.6879331	0.81	0.7910299	1.13	0.8707619
0.18	0.5714237	0.50	0.6914625	0.82	0.7938919	1.14	0.8728568
0.19	0.5753454	0.51	0.6949743	0.83	0.7967306	1.15	0.8749281
0.20	0.5792597	0.52	0.6984682	0.84	0.7995458	1.16	0.8769756
0.21	0.5831662	0.53	0.701944	0.85	0.8023375	1.17	0.8789995
0.22	0.5870644	0.54	0.7054015	0.86	0.8051055	1.18	0.8809999
0.23	0.5909541	0.55	0.7088403	0.87	0.8078498	1.19	0.8829768
0.24	0.5948349	0.56	0.7122603	0.88	0.8105703	1.20	0.8849303
0.25	0.5987063	0.57	0.7156612	0.89	0.8132671	1.21	0.8868606
0.26	0.6025681	0.58	0.7190427	0.90	0.8159399	1.22	0.8887676
0.27	0.6064199	0.59	0.7224047	0.91	0.8185887	1.23	0.8906514
0.28	0.6102612	0.60	0.7257469	0.92	0.8212136	1.24	0.8925123
0.29	0.6140919	0.61	0.7290691	0.93	0.8238145	1.25	0.8943502
0.30	0.6179114	0.62	0.7323711	0.94	0.8263912	1.26	0.8961653
0.31	0.6217195	0.63	0.7356527	0.95	0.8289439	1.27	0.8979577

(continued)

TABLE A.1 (continued)

The Standard Unit Normal Distribution

z	P(z)	z	P(z)	z	P(z)	z	P(z)
1.28	0.8997274	1.68	0.9535213	2.08	0.9812372	2.48	0.9934309
1.29	0.9014747	1.69	0.954486	2.09	0.9816911	2.49	0.9936128
1.30	0.9031995	1.70	0.9554345	2.10	0.9821356	2.50	0.9937903
1.31	0.9049021	1.71	0.9563671	2.11	0.9825708	2.51	0.9939634
1.32	0.9065825	1.72	0.9572838	2.12	0.982997	2.52	0.9941323
1.33	0.9082409	1.73	0.9581849	2.13	0.9834142	2.53	0.9942969
1.34	0.9098773	1.74	0.9590705	2.14	0.9838226	2.54	0.9944574
1.35	0.911492	1.75	0.9599408	2.15	0.9842224	2.55	0.9946139
1.36	0.913085	1.76	0.9607961	2.16	0.9846137	2.56	0.9947664
1.37	0.9146565	1.77	0.9616364	2.17	0.9849966	2.57	0.9949151
1.38	0.9162067	1.78	0.962462	2.18	0.9853713	2.58	0.99506
1.39	0.9177356	1.79	0.963273	2.19	0.9857379	2.59	0.9952012
1.40	0.9192433	1.80	0.9640697	2.20	0.9860966	2.60	0.9953388
1.41	0.9207302	1.81	0.9648521	2.21	0.9864474	2.61	0.9954729
1.42	0.9221962	1.82	0.9656205	2.22	0.9867906	2.62	0.9956035
1.43	0.9236415	1.83	0.966375	2.23	0.9871263	2.63	0.9957308
1.44	0.9250663	1.84	0.9671159	2.24	0.9874545	2.64	0.9958547
1.45	0.9264707	1.85	0.9678432	2.25	0.9877755	2.65	0.9959754
1.46	0.927855	1.86	0.9685572	2.26	0.9880894	2.66	0.996093
1.47	0.9292191	1.87	0.9692581	2.27	0.9883962	2.67	0.9962074
1.48	0.9305634	1.88	0.969946	2.28	0.9886962	2.68	0.9963189
1.49	0.9318879	1.89	0.970621	2.29	0.9889893	2.69	0.9964274
1.50	0.9331928	1.90	0.9712834	2.30	0.9892759	2.70	0.996533
1.51	0.9344783	1.91	0.9719334	2.31	0.9895559	2.71	0.9966358
1.52	0.9357445	1.92	0.9725711	2.32	0.9898296	2.72	0.9967359
1.53	0.9369916	1.93	0.9731966	2.33	0.9900969	2.73	0.9968333
1.54	0.9382198	1.94	0.9738102	2.34	0.9903581	2.74	0.996928
1.55	0.9394292	1.95	0.9744119	2.35	0.9906133	2.75	0.9970202
1.56	0.9406201	1.96	0.9750021	2.36	0.9908625	2.76	0.9971099
1.57	0.9417924	1.97	0.9755808	2.37	0.991106	2.77	0.9971972
1.58	0.9429466	1.98	0.9761482	2.38	0.9913437	2.78	0.9972821
1.59	0.9440826	1.99	0.9767045	2.39	0.9915758	2.79	0.9973646
1.60	0.9452007	2.00	0.9772499	2.40	0.9918025	2.80	0.9974449
1.61	0.9463011	2.01	0.9777844	2.41	0.9920237	2.81	0.9975229
1.62	0.9473839	2.02	0.9783083	2.42	0.9922397	2.82	0.9975988
1.63	0.9484493	2.03	0.9788217	2.43	0.9924506	2.83	0.9976726
1.64	0.9494974	2.04	0.9793248	2.44	0.9926564	2.84	0.9977443
1.65	0.9505285	2.05	0.9798178	2.45	0.9928572	2.85	0.997814
1.66	0.9515428	2.06	0.9803007	2.46	0.9930531	2.86	0.9978818
1.67	0.9525403	2.07	0.9807738	2.47	0.9932443	2.87	0.9979476

z	P(z)	z	P(z)	z	P(z)	z	P(z)
2.88	0.9980116	3.17	0.9992378	3.46	0.9997299	3.75	0.9999116
2.89	0.9980738	3.18	0.9992636	3.47	0.9997398	3.76	0.999915
2.90	0.9981342	3.19	0.9992886	3.48	0.9997493	3.77	0.9999184
2.91	0.9981929	3.20	0.9993129	3.49	0.9997585	3.78	0.9999216
2.92	0.9982498	3.21	0.9993363	3.50	0.9997674	3.79	0.9999247
2.93	0.9983052	3.22	0.999359	3.51	0.9997759	3.80	0.9999277
2.94	0.9983589	3.23	0.999381	3.52	0.9997842	3.81	0.9999305
2.95	0.9984111	3.24	0.9994024	3.53	0.9997922	3.82	0.9999333
2.96	0.9984618	3.25	0.999423	3.54	0.9997999	3.83	0.9999359
2.97	0.998511	3.26	0.9994429	3.55	0.9998074	3.84	0.9999385
2.98	0.9985588	3.27	0.9994623	3.56	0.9998146	3.85	0.9999409
2.99	0.9986051	3.28	0.999481	3.57	0.9998215	3.86	0.9999433
3.00	0.9986501	3.29	0.9994991	3.58	0.9998282	3.87	0.9999456
3.01	0.9986938	3.30	0.9995166	3.59	0.9998347	3.88	0.9999478
3.02	0.9987361	3.31	0.9995335	3.60	0.9998409	3.89	0.9999499
3.03	0.9987772	3.32	0.9995499	3.61	0.9998469	3.90	0.9999519
3.04	0.9988171	3.33	0.9995658	3.62	0.9998527	3.91	0.9999539
3.05	0.9988558	3.34	0.9995811	3.63	0.9998583	3.92	0.9999557
3.06	0.9988933	3.35	0.9995959	3.64	0.9998637	3.93	0.9999575
3.07	0.9989297	3.36	0.9996103	3.65	0.9998689	3.94	0.9999593
3.08	0.998965	3.37	0.9996242	3.66	0.9998739	3.95	0.9999609
3.09	0.9989992	3.38	0.9996376	3.67	0.9998787	3.96	0.9999625
3.10	0.9990324	3.39	0.9996505	3.68	0.9998834	3.97	0.9999641
3.11	0.9990646	3.40	0.9996631	3.69	0.9998879	3,98	0.9999655
3.12	0.9990957	3.41	0.9996752	3.70	0.9998922	3.99	0.999967
3.13	0.999126	3.42	0.9996869	3.71	0.9998964	4.00	0.9999683
3.14	0.9991553	3.43	0.9996982	3.72	0.9999004		
3.15	0.9991836	3.44	0.9997091	3.73	0.9999043		
3.16	0.9992112	3.45	0.9997197	3.74	0.999908		

Values computed by the authors using R.

TABLE A.2

Percentage Points of the *t* Distribution

	$\alpha_1 = .10$	.05	.025	.01	.005	.0025	.001	.0005
v	$\alpha_2 = .20$	.10	.050	.02	.010	.0050	.002	.0010
1	3.077684	6.313752	12.7062	31.82052	63.65674	127.3213	318.3088	636.6192
2	1.885618	2.919986	4.302653	6.964557	9.924843	14.08905	22.32712	31.59905
3	1.637744	2.353363	3.182446	4.540703	5.840909	7.453319	10.21453	12.92398
4	1.533206	2.131847	2.776445	3.746947	4.604095	5.597568	7.173182	8.610302
5	1.475884	2.015048	2.570582	3.36493	4.032143	4.773341	5.89343	6.868827
6	1.439756	1.94318	2.446912	3.142668	3.707428	4.316827	5.207626	5.958816
7	1.414924	1.894579	2.364624	2.997952	3.499483	4.029337	4.78529	5.407883
8	1.396815	1.859548	2.306004	2.896459	3.355387	3.832519	4.500791	5.041305
9	1.383029	1.833113	2.26215	2.821438	3.249836	3.689662	4.296806	4.780913
10	1.372184	1.812461	2.228139	2.763769	3.169273	3.581406	4.1437	4.586894
11	1.36343	1.795885	2.200985	2.718079	3.105807	3.496614	4.024701	4.436979
12	1.356217	1.782288	2.178813	2.680998	3.05454	3.428444	3.929633	4.317791
13	1.350171	1.770933	2.160369	2.650309	3.012276	3.372468	3.851982	4.220832
14	1.34503	1.76131	2.144787	2.624494	2.976843	3.325696	3.78739	4.140454
15	1.340606	1.75305	2.13145	2.60248	2.946713	3.286039	3.732834	4.072765
16	1.336757	1.745884	2.119905	2.583487	2.920782	3.251993	3.686155	4.014996
17	1.333379	1.739607	2.109816	2.566934	2.898231	3.22245	3.645767	3.965126
18	1.330391	1.734064	2.100922	2.55238	2.87844	3.196574	3.610485	3.921646
19	1.327728	1.729133	2.093024	2.539483	2.860935	3.173725	3.5794	3.883406
20	1.325341	1.724718	2.085963	2.527977	2.84534	3.153401	3.551808	3.849516
21	1.323188	1.720743	2.079614	2.517648	2.83136	3.135206	3.527154	3.819277
22	1.321237	1.717144	2.073873	2.508325	2.818756	3.118824	3.504992	3.792131
23	1.31946	1.713872	2.068658	2.499867	2.807336	3.103997	3.484964	3.767627
24	1.317836	1.710882	2.063899	2.492159	2.79694	3.090514	3.466777	3.745399
25	1.316345	1.708141	2.059539	2.485107	2.787436	3.078199	3.450189	3.725144
26	1.314972	1.705618	2.055529	2.47863	2.778715	3.066909	3.434997	3.706612
27	1.313703	1.703288	2.051831	2.47266	2.770683	3.05652	3.421034	3.689592
28	1.312527	1.701131	2.048407	2.46714	2.763262	3.046929	3.408155	3.673906
29	1.311434	1.699127	2.04523	2.462021	2.756386	3.038047	3.39624	3.659405
30	1.310415	1.697261	2.042272	2.457262	2.749996	3.029798	3.385185	3.645959
40	1.303077	1.683851	2.021075	2.423257	2.704459	2.971171	3.306878	3.550966
60	1.295821	1.670649	2.000298	2.390119	2.660283	2.914553	3.231709	3.4602
120	1.288646	1.657651	1.97993	2.357825	2.617421	2.859865	3.159539	3.373454
∞	1.281552	1.644854	1.959964	2.326348	2.575829	2.807034	3.090232	3.290527

Values computed by the authors using **R**.

TABLE A.3

Percentage Points of the χ^2 Distribution

	Alpha							
υ	**0.990**	**0.975**	**0.950**	**0.900**	**0.100**	**0.050**	**0.025**	**0.010**
1	0.000157088	0.000982069	0.00393214	0.01579077	2.705543	3.841459	5.023886	6.634897
2	0.02010067	0.05063562	0.1025866	0.210721	4.60517	5.991465	7.377759	9.21034
3	0.1148318	0.2157953	0.3518463	0.5843744	6.251389	7.814728	9.348404	11.34487
4	0.2971095	0.4844186	0.710723	1.063623	7.77944	9.487729	11.14329	13.2767
5	0.5542981	0.8312116	1.145476	1.610308	9.236357	11.0705	12.8325	15.08627
6	0.8720903	1.237344	1.635383	2.204131	10.64464	12.59159	14.44938	16.81189
7	1.239042	1.689869	2.16735	2.833107	12.01704	14.06714	16.01276	18.47531
8	1.646497	2.179731	2.732637	3.489539	13.36157	15.50731	17.53455	20.09024
9	2.087901	2.700389	3.325113	4.168159	14.68366	16.91898	19.02277	21.66599
10	2.558212	3.246973	3.940299	4.865182	15.98718	18.30704	20.48318	23.20925
11	3.053484	3.815748	4.574813	5.577785	17.27501	19.67514	21.92005	24.72497
12	3.570569	4.403789	5.226029	6.303796	18.54935	21.02607	23.33666	26.21697
13	4.106915	5.008751	5.891864	7.041505	19.81193	22.36203	24.7356	27.68825
14	4.660425	5.628726	6.570631	7.789534	21.06414	23.68479	26.11895	29.14124
15	5.229349	6.262138	7.260944	8.546756	22.30713	24.99579	27.48839	30.57791
16	5.812212	6.907664	7.961646	9.312236	23.54183	26.29623	28.84535	31.99993
17	6.40776	7.564186	8.67176	10.08519	24.76904	27.58711	30.19101	33.40866
18	7.014911	8.230746	9.390455	10.86494	25.98942	28.8693	31.52638	34.80531
19	7.63273	8.906516	10.11701	11.65091	27.20357	30.14353	32.85233	36.19087
20	8.260398	9.590777	10.85081	12.44261	28.41198	31.41043	34.16961	37.56623
21	8.897198	10.2829	11.59131	13.2396	29.61509	32.67057	35.47888	38.93217
22	9.542492	10.98232	12.33801	14.04149	30.81328	33.92444	36.78071	40.28936
23	10.19572	11.68855	13.09051	14.84796	32.0069	35.17246	38.07563	41.6384
24	10.85636	12.40115	13.84843	15.65868	33.19624	36.41503	39.36408	42.97982
25	11.52398	13.11972	14.61141	16.47341	34.38159	37.65248	40.64647	44.3141
26	12.19815	13.8439	15.37916	17.29188	35.56317	38.88514	41.92317	45.64168
27	12.8785	14.57338	16.1514	18.1139	36.74122	40.11327	43.19451	46.96294
28	13.56471	15.30786	16.92788	18.93924	37.91592	41.33714	44.46079	48.27824
29	14.25645	16.04707	17.70837	19.76774	39.08747	42.55697	45.72229	49.58788
30	14.95346	16.79077	18.49266	20.59923	40.25602	43.77297	46.97924	50.89218
40	22.16426	24.43304	26.5093	29.05052	51.80506	55.75848	59.34171	63.69074
50	29.70668	32.35736	34.76425	37.68865	63.16712	67.50481	71.4202	76.15389
60	37.48485	40.48175	43.18796	46.45889	74.39701	79.08194	83.29767	88.37942
70	45.44172	48.75756	51.73928	55.32894	85.52704	90.53123	95.02318	100.4252
80	53.54008	57.15317	60.39148	64.27784	96.5782	101.8795	106.6286	112.3288
90	61.75408	65.64662	69.12603	73.29109	107.565	113.1453	118.1359	124.1163
100	70.06489	74.22193	77.92947	82.35814	118.498	124.3421	129.5612	135.8067

Values computed by the authors using **R**.

TABLE A.4

Percentage Points of the F Distribution

v_2 \ v_1	1	2	3	4	5	6	7	8	9	10	12	15	20	24	30	40	60	120	Infinity
alpha = .10																			
1	39.86346	49.5	53.59324	55.83296	57.24008	58.20442	58.90595	59.43898	59.85759	60.19498	60.70521	61.22034	61.74029	62.00205	62.26497	62.52905	62.79428	63.06064	63.32812
2	8.526316	9	9.16179	9.243416	9.292626	9.32553	9.349081	9.36677	9.380544	9.391573	9.408132	9.424711	9.441309	9.449616	9.457927	9.466244	9.474565	9.482891	9.491222
3	5.538319	5.462383	5.390773	5.342644	5.309157	5.284732	5.266195	5.251671	5.239996	5.230411	5.215618	5.200313	5.184482	5.176365	5.168111	5.159719	5.151187	5.142513	5.133695
4	8.526316	4.324555	4.19086	4.10725	4.050579	4.009749	3.978966	3.95494	3.935671	3.919876	3.895527	3.87036	3.844338	3.830994	3.817422	3.803615	3.789568	3.775275	3.76073
5	4.544771	3.779716	3.619477	3.520196	3.452982	3.404507	3.367899	3.339276	3.316281	3.297402	3.268239	3.238011	3.20665	3.190523	3.174084	3.157324	3.14023	3.122792	3.104996
6	3.77595	3.463304	3.288762	3.180763	3.107512	3.054551	3.014457	2.983036	2.957741	2.936935	2.904721	2.871222	2.83634	2.818345	2.79996	2.781169	2.761952	2.74229	2.722162
7	3.589428	3.257442	3.074072	2.960534	2.883344	2.827392	2.78493	2.75158	2.724678	2.70251	2.668111	2.63223	2.594732	2.575327	2.555457	2.535096	2.514218	2.492792	2.470786
8	3.457919	3.113118	2.923796	2.806426	2.726447	2.668335	2.624135	2.589349	2.561238	2.538037	2.501958	2.464216	2.424637	2.404097	2.383016	2.361362	2.339097	2.316181	2.292566
9	3.360303	3.006452	2.812863	2.69268	2.610613	2.550855	2.505313	2.469406	2.44034	2.416316	2.378885	2.339624	2.298322	2.276827	2.25472	2.231958	2.208493	2.18427	2.159227
10	3.285015	2.924466	2.727673	2.605336	2.521641	2.460582	2.413965	2.37715	2.347306	2.322604	2.284051	2.243515	2.200744	2.178426	2.155426	2.131691	2.107161	2.081765	2.055422
11	3.225202	2.859511	2.660229	2.536188	2.451184	2.389067	2.341566	2.303997	2.273502	2.24823	2.208725	2.167094	2.123046	2.100005	2.076214	2.05161	2.026118	1.999652	1.972109
12	3.176549	2.806796	2.605525	2.480102	2.394022	2.331024	2.28278	2.244575	2.213525	2.187764	2.147437	2.104851	2.059677	2.035993	2.011492	1.986102	1.959732	1.932278	1.903615
13	3.136205	2.763167	2.560273	2.433705	2.346724	2.282979	2.234103	2.19535	2.16382	2.137635	2.096588	2.05316	2.006982	1.982718	1.957575	1.931466	1.904287	1.875915	1.846196
14	3.102213	2.726468	2.522224	2.394692	2.306943	2.242559	2.193134	2.153904	2.121955	2.095396	2.053714	2.009535	1.962453	1.937663	1.911933	1.885163	1.857234	1.828001	1.797283
15	3.073186	2.695173	2.489788	2.361433	2.273022	2.208082	2.158178	2.11853	2.086209	2.059319	2.01707	1.972216	1.924314	1.899044	1.872774	1.845393	1.816764	1.78672	1.755052
16	3.04811	2.668171	2.461811	2.332745	2.243758	2.178329	2.128003	2.087982	2.055331	2.028145	1.985386	1.939921	1.891272	1.865561	1.838792	1.810841	1.781557	1.750747	1.718169
17	3.026232	2.644638	2.437434	2.307747	2.218253	2.152392	2.101689	2.061336	2.028388	2.000936	1.957716	1.911695	1.862361	1.836242	1.80901	1.780528	1.750627	1.71909	1.685641
18	3.006977	2.623947	2.416005	2.285772	2.195827	2.129581	2.078541	2.037889	2.004674	1.97698	1.93334	1.886811	1.836845	1.810348	1.782685	1.753706	1.723222	1.690993	1.656706
19	2.9899	2.605612	2.397022	2.266303	2.175956	2.109364	2.05802	2.017098	1.983639	1.955725	1.911702	1.864705	1.814155	1.787307	1.759241	1.729793	1.698758	1.665869	1.630774
20	2.974653	2.589254	2.380087	2.248934	2.158227	2.091322	2.039703	1.998534	1.964853	1.936738	1.892363	1.844935	1.793843	1.766667	1.738223	1.708334	1.676776	1.643256	1.60738
21	2.960956	2.574569	2.364888	2.233345	2.142311	2.075123	2.023252	1.981858	1.947974	1.919674	1.874975	1.827148	1.775551	1.748068	1.719268	1.688962	1.656907	1.622782	1.586151
22	2.948585	2.561314	2.35117	2.219274	2.127944	2.060497	2.008397	1.966796	1.932725	1.904255	1.859255	1.811057	1.758989	1.731217	1.702083	1.671382	1.638853	1.604147	1.566785
23	2.937356	2.54929	2.338727	2.206512	2.114911	2.047227	1.994915	1.953124	1.91888	1.890252	1.844974	1.796431	1.743921	1.715878	1.686428	1.655352	1.622371	1.587107	1.549035
24	2.927117	2.538332	2.32739	2.194882	2.103033	2.035132	1.982625	1.940658	1.906255	1.87748	1.831942	1.783076	1.730152	1.701854	1.672104	1.640673	1.60726	1.571459	1.532696
25	2.917745	2.528305	2.317017	2.184242	2.092165	2.024062	1.971376	1.929246	1.894693	1.865782	1.820003	1.770834	1.71752	1.688981	1.658947	1.627177	1.59335	1.557031	1.517597
26	2.909132	2.519096	2.307491	2.174469	2.082182	2.013893	1.961039	1.918758	1.884067	1.855028	1.809023	1.759571	1.70589	1.677122	1.646819	1.614725	1.580502	1.543683	1.503595
27	2.901192	2.510609	2.298712	2.165463	2.072981	2.004519	1.95151	1.909087	1.874267	1.845109	1.798891	1.749173	1.695144	1.66616	1.635601	1.603198	1.568595	1.531293	1.490568
28	2.893846	2.502761	2.290595	2.157136	2.064473	1.995851	1.942696	1.900141	1.865199	1.83593	1.789513	1.739543	1.685187	1.655997	1.625193	1.592496	1.557527	1.519759	1.478412
29	2.887033	2.495483	2.283069	2.149415	2.056583	1.987811	1.934521	1.891842	1.856786	1.827412	1.780807	1.7306	1.675932	1.646547	1.615511	1.582531	1.54721	1.50899	1.467036
30	2.880695	2.488716	2.276071	2.142235	2.049246	1.980333	1.926916	1.884121	1.848958	1.819485	1.772704	1.722272	1.667309	1.637737	1.606479	1.573228	1.537569	1.498912	1.456365
40	2.835354	2.440369	2.226092	2.09095	1.99682	1.926879	1.872522	1.828863	1.792902	1.762686	1.714563	1.662411	1.605151	1.574111	1.541076	1.505625	1.467157	1.424757	1.376912
60	2.791068	2.393255	2.177411	2.040986	1.94571	1.87472	1.819393	1.774829	1.73802	1.707009	1.657429	1.603368	1.543486	1.510718	1.475539	1.437342	1.395201	1.347568	1.291464
120	2.747807	2.347338	2.129991	1.992302	1.895875	1.823812	1.767476	1.721959	1.684248	1.652379	1.601204	1.545002	1.482072	1.447226	1.409379	1.367602	1.32034	1.264573	1.192563
Infinity	2.705543	2.302585	2.083796	1.94486	1.847271	1.774107	1.71672	1.670196	1.631517	1.598718	1.545779	1.487142	1.420599	1.383177	1.341867	1.295126	1.23995	1.168605	1.000018

υ_2	υ_1: 1	2	3	4	5	6	7	8	9	10	12	15	20	24	30	40	60	120	Infinity
alpha = .05																			
1	161.4476	199.5	215.7073	224.5832	230.1619	233.986	236.7684	238.8827	240.5433	241.8817	243.906	245.9499	248.0131	249.0518	250.0951	251.1432	252.1957	253.2529	254.3144
2	18.51282	19	19.16429	19.24679	19.29641	19.32953	19.35322	19.37099	19.38483	19.3959	19.41251	19.42914	19.44577	19.45409	19.46241	19.47074	19.47906	19.48739	19.49573
3	10.12796	9.552094	9.276628	9.117182	9.013455	8.940645	8.886743	8.845238	8.8123	8.785525	8.744641	8.70287	8.66019	8.638501	8.616576	8.594411	8.572004	8.549351	8.52645
4	7.708647	6.944272	6.591382	6.388233	6.256057	6.163132	6.094211	6.041044	5.998779	5.964371	5.911729	5.857805	5.802542	5.774389	5.745877	5.716998	5.687744	5.658105	5.628072
5	6.607891	5.786135	5.409451	5.192168	5.050329	4.950288	4.875872	4.81832	4.772466	4.735063	4.677704	4.618759	4.558131	4.527153	4.495712	4.463793	4.43138	4.398454	4.364997
6	5.987378	5.143253	4.757063	4.533677	4.387374	4.283866	4.206658	4.146804	4.099016	4.059963	3.999935	3.938058	3.874189	3.841457	3.808164	3.774286	3.739797	3.704667	3.668866
7	5.591448	4.737414	4.346831	4.120312	3.971523	3.865969	3.787044	3.725725	3.676675	3.636523	3.574676	3.51074	3.444525	3.410494	3.375808	3.34043	3.304323	3.267445	3.229751
8	5.317655	4.45897	4.066181	3.837853	3.687499	3.58058	3.500464	3.438101	3.38813	3.347163	3.283939	3.218406	3.150324	3.11524	3.079406	3.042778	3.005303	2.966923	3.229751
9	5.117355	4.256495	3.862548	3.633089	3.481659	3.373754	3.292746	3.229583	3.178893	3.13728	3.072947	3.006102	2.936455	2.900474	2.863652	2.825933	2.787249	2.747525	2.927575
10	4.964603	4.102821	3.708265	3.47805	3.325835	3.217175	3.135465	3.071658	3.020383	2.978237	2.912977	2.845017	2.774016	2.737248	2.699551	2.660855	2.621077	2.580122	2.537878
11	4.844336	3.982298	3.587434	3.35669	3.203874	3.094613	3.01233	2.94799	2.896223	2.853625	2.787569	2.71864	2.646445	2.608974	2.570489	2.530905	2.490123	2.448024	2.40447
12	4.747225	3.885294	3.490295	3.259167	3.105875	2.99612	2.913358	2.848565	2.796375	2.753387	2.686637	2.616851	2.543588	2.505482	2.466279	2.42588	2.384166	2.340995	2.296198
13	4.667193	3.805565	3.410534	3.179117	3.025438	2.915269	2.832098	2.766913	2.714356	2.671024	2.603661	2.53311	2.458882	2.420196	2.380334	2.33918	2.296596	2.252414	2.206432
14	4.60011	3.738892	3.343889	3.11225	2.958249	2.847726	2.764199	2.698672	2.645791	2.602155	2.534243	2.463003	2.387896	2.348678	2.308207	2.26635	2.22295	2.177811	2.130693
15	4.543077	3.68232	3.287382	3.055568	2.901295	2.790465	2.706627	2.640797	2.587626	2.543719	2.475313	2.403447	2.327535	2.287826	2.246789	2.204276	2.160105	2.114056	2.065847
16	4.493998	3.633723	3.238872	3.006917	2.852409	2.741311	2.657197	2.591096	2.537667	2.493513	2.42466	2.352223	2.27557	2.235405	2.193841	2.150711	2.105813	2.058895	2.009635
17	4.451322	3.591531	3.196777	2.964708	2.809996	2.69866	2.614299	2.547955	2.494291	2.449916	2.380654	2.307693	2.230354	2.189766	2.147708	2.103998	2.058411	2.010663	1.960386
18	4.413873	3.554557	3.159908	2.927744	2.772853	2.661305	2.576722	2.510158	2.456281	2.411702	2.342067	2.268622	2.190648	2.149665	2.107143	2.062885	2.016643	1.9681	1.91684
19	4.38075	3.521893	3.12735	2.895107	2.740058	2.628318	2.543534	2.47677	2.422699	2.377934	2.307954	2.234063	2.155497	2.114143	2.071186	2.02641	1.979544	1.930237	1.878025
20	4.351244	3.492828	3.098391	2.866081	2.71089	2.598978	2.514011	2.447064	2.392814	2.347878	2.277581	2.203274	2.124155	2.082454	2.039086	1.993819	1.946358	1.896318	1.84318
21	4.324794	3.4668	3.072467	2.8401	2.684781	2.572712	2.487578	2.420462	2.366048	2.320953	2.250362	2.17567	2.096033	2.054004	2.010248	1.964515	1.916486	1.865739	1.811703
22	4.30095	3.443357	3.049125	2.816708	2.661274	2.549061	2.463774	2.396503	2.341937	2.296696	2.225831	2.150778	2.070656	2.028319	1.984195	1.938018	1.889445	1.838018	1.783107
23	4.279344	3.422132	3.027998	2.795539	2.639999	2.527655	2.442226	2.374812	2.320105	2.274728	2.203607	2.128217	2.047638	2.005009	1.960537	1.913938	1.864844	1.81276	1.756997
24	4.259677	3.402826	3.008787	2.776289	2.620654	2.508189	2.422629	2.355081	2.300244	2.254739	2.18338	2.107673	2.026664	1.98376	1.938957	1.891955	1.84236	1.789642	1.733049
25	4.241699	3.38519	2.991241	2.75871	2.602987	2.49041	2.404728	2.337057	2.282097	2.236474	2.164891	2.088887	2.007471	1.964306	1.919188	1.871801	1.821727	1.768395	1.710992
26	4.225201	3.369016	2.975154	2.742594	2.58679	2.474109	2.388314	2.320527	2.265453	2.219718	2.147926	2.071642	1.989842	1.946428	1.90101	1.853255	1.802719	1.748795	1.6906
27	4.210008	3.354131	2.960351	2.727765	2.571886	2.459108	2.373208	2.305313	2.250131	2.204292	2.132303	2.055755	1.97359	1.92994	1.884236	1.836129	1.785149	1.73065	1.671682
28	4.195972	3.340386	2.946685	2.714076	2.558128	2.445259	2.35926	2.291264	2.235982	2.190044	2.117869	2.041071	1.958561	1.914686	1.868709	1.820263	1.768857	1.7138	1.654076
29	4.182964	3.327654	2.93403	2.701399	2.545386	2.432434	2.346342	2.278251	2.222874	2.176844	2.104493	2.027458	1.94462	1.900531	1.854293	1.805523	1.753704	1.698107	1.637644
30	4.170877	3.31583	2.922277	2.689628	2.533555	2.420523	2.334344	2.266163	2.210697	2.16458	2.092063	2.014804	1.931653	1.88736	1.840872	1.79179	1.739574	1.683452	1.622265
40	4.084746	3.231727	2.838745	2.605975	2.449466	2.335852	2.249024	2.18017	2.124029	2.077248	2.003459	1.924463	1.838859	1.792937	1.744432	1.692797	1.637252	1.57661	1.508904
60	4.001191	3.150411	2.758078	2.525215	2.36827	2.254053	2.166541	2.096968	2.040098	1.992592	1.917396	1.836437	1.747984	1.700117	1.649141	1.594273	1.534314	1.467267	1.389276
120	3.920124	3.071779	2.680168	2.447237	2.289851	2.175006	2.08677	2.016426	1.958763	1.910461	1.833695	1.750497	1.65868	1.608437	1.554343	1.495202	1.429013	1.351886	1.253858
Infinity	3.841459	2.995732	2.604909	2.371932	2.2141	2.098598	2.009591	1.938414	1.879886	1.830704	1.752172	1.666386	1.570522	1.517293	1.459099	1.393962	1.318032	1.221395	1.000023

(continued)

υ_2	υ_1: 1	2	3	4	5	6	7	8	9	10	12	15	20	24	30	40	60	120	Infinity
alpha = .01																			
1	4052.181	4999.5	5403.352	5624.583	5763.65	5858.986	5928.356	5981.07	6022.473	6055.847	6106.321	6157.285	6208.73	6234.631	6260.649	6286.782	6313.03	6339.391	6365.864
2	98.50251	99	99.1662	99.24937	99.2993	99.33259	99.35637	99.37421	99.38809	99.3992	99.41585	99.43251	99.44917	99.4575	99.46583	99.47416	99.4825	99.49083	99.49916
3	34.11622	30.81652	29.4567	28.7099	28.23708	27.91066	27.6717	27.48918	27.34521	27.22873	27.05182	26.87219	26.68979	26.59752	26.50453	26.41081	26.31635	26.22114	26.12517
4	21.19769	18	16.69437	15.97702	15.52186	15.20686	14.97576	14.79889	14.65913	14.5459	14.37359	14.1982	14.01961	13.92906	13.83766	13.74538	13.6522	13.5581	13.46305
5	16.25818	13.27393	12.05995	11.39193	10.96702	10.67225	10.45551	10.28931	10.15776	10.05102	9.888275	9.722219	9.552646	9.466471	9.379329	9.291189	9.202015	9.111771	9.020417
6	13.74502	10.92477	9.779538	9.148301	8.745895	8.466125	8.259995	8.101651	7.976121	7.874119	7.718333	7.558994	7.395832	7.312721	7.228533	7.143222	7.056737	6.969023	6.880021
7	12.24638	9.546578	8.451285	7.846645	7.460435	7.191405	6.992833	6.840049	6.718752	6.620063	6.469091	6.314331	6.155438	6.074319	5.99201	5.908449	5.823566	5.737286	5.649525
8	11.25862	8.649111	7.590992	7.006077	6.631825	6.370681	6.177624	6.02887	5.910619	5.814294	5.666719	5.515125	5.359095	5.279264	5.19813	5.11561	5.031618	4.946052	4.858799
9	10.56143	8.021517	6.991917	6.422085	6.056941	5.80177	5.612865	5.467123	5.351129	5.256542	5.111431	4.962078	4.807995	4.728998	4.648582	4.566649	4.483087	4.397769	4.31055
10	10.04429	7.559432	6.552313	5.994339	5.636326	5.385811	5.200121	5.056693	4.942421	4.849147	4.70587	4.55814	4.405395	4.326929	4.246933	4.165287	4.081855	3.996481	3.90898
11	9.646034	7.205713	6.21673	5.6683	5.316009	5.06921	4.886072	4.744468	4.63154	4.539282	4.397401	4.250867	4.099046	4.02091	3.941132	3.859573	3.776071	3.690436	3.602442
12	9.330212	6.926608	5.952545	5.411951	5.064343	4.820574	4.639502	4.499365	4.38751	4.296054	4.155258	4.009619	3.858433	3.780485	3.700789	3.619181	3.535473	3.44944	3.360809
13	9.073806	6.700965	5.73938	5.20533	4.861621	4.620363	4.440997	4.302062	4.191078	4.100267	3.960326	3.815365	3.664609	3.586753	3.507042	3.425293	3.341287	3.25476	3.165393
14	8.861593	6.514884	5.563886	5.035378	4.694964	4.45582	4.277882	4.139946	4.02968	3.939396	3.800141	3.655697	3.505222	3.427387	3.347596	3.265641	3.181274	3.094191	3.004018
15	8.683117	6.358873	5.416965	4.89321	4.555614	4.318273	4.141546	4.004453	3.894788	3.80494	3.66624	3.522194	3.371892	3.294029	3.21411	3.131906	3.047135	2.959453	2.868426
16	8.530965	6.226235	5.292214	4.772578	4.43742	4.201634	4.025947	3.889572	3.780415	3.690931	3.552687	3.408947	3.258737	3.180811	3.100733	3.018248	2.933046	2.844737	2.752824
17	8.39974	6.112114	5.185	4.668968	4.335939	4.101505	3.926719	3.790964	3.682242	3.593066	3.455198	3.311694	3.161518	3.083502	3.003241	2.920458	2.834806	2.745852	2.653033
18	8.28542	6.012905	5.09189	4.579036	4.247882	4.014637	3.840639	3.705422	3.597074	3.508162	3.370608	3.227286	3.077097	2.998974	2.918516	2.83542	2.749309	2.659701	2.565963
19	8.184947	5.925879	5.010287	4.500258	4.170767	3.938573	3.765269	3.630525	3.522503	3.433817	3.296527	3.153343	3.003109	2.924866	2.844201	2.760786	2.674211	2.583944	2.48928
20	8.095958	5.848932	4.938193	4.43069	4.102685	3.871427	3.69874	3.564412	3.456676	3.368186	3.23112	3.088041	2.937735	2.859363	2.778485	2.694749	2.607708	2.516783	2.421191
21	8.016597	5.780416	4.874046	4.368815	4.042144	3.811725	3.63959	3.505632	3.398147	3.30983	3.172953	3.029951	2.879556	2.80105	2.719955	2.635896	2.548393	2.456813	2.360294
22	7.945386	5.719022	4.816606	4.313429	3.987963	3.758301	3.58666	3.453034	3.345773	3.257606	3.120891	2.977946	2.827447	2.748802	2.66749	2.583111	2.495149	2.402919	2.305477
23	7.881134	5.663699	4.764877	4.263567	3.939195	3.710218	3.539024	3.405695	3.298634	3.210599	3.074025	2.931118	2.780504	2.70172	2.620191	2.535496	2.447081	2.354209	2.25585
24	7.822871	5.613591	4.718051	4.218445	3.89507	3.666717	3.495928	3.362867	3.255985	3.168069	3.031615	2.888732	2.737997	2.659072	2.577329	2.492321	2.403461	2.309955	2.210685
25	7.769798	5.567997	4.675465	4.17742	3.854957	3.627174	3.456754	3.323937	3.217217	3.129406	2.993056	2.850186	2.699325	2.62026	2.538305	2.45299	2.363691	2.269562	2.16939
26	7.721254	5.526335	4.63657	4.13996	3.818336	3.591075	3.420993	3.288399	3.181824	3.094108	2.957848	2.814982	2.663991	2.584787	2.502624	2.417007	2.327279	2.232536	2.131471
27	7.676684	5.488118	4.600907	4.105622	3.78477	3.557991	3.388219	3.255827	3.149385	3.061754	2.925573	2.782703	2.63158	2.552239	2.469872	2.38396	2.293812	2.198465	2.096517
28	7.635619	5.452937	4.568091	4.074032	3.753895	3.527559	3.358073	3.225868	3.119547	3.031992	2.895881	2.753	2.601744	2.522268	2.439701	2.353501	2.262941	2.167001	2.06418
29	7.597663	5.420445	4.537795	4.044873	3.725399	3.499475	3.330252	3.198219	3.092009	3.004524	2.868472	2.725577	2.574188	2.494579	2.411817	2.325335	2.234372	2.137851	2.034166
30	7.562476	5.390346	4.50974	4.017877	3.699019	3.473477	3.304499	3.172624	3.066516	2.979094	2.843095	2.70018	2.548659	2.468921	2.385967	2.299211	2.207854	2.110762	2.006225
40	7.3141	5.178508	4.312569	3.828294	3.51384	3.291012	3.123757	2.992981	2.88756	2.800545	2.664827	2.521616	2.368876	2.287998	2.203382	2.114232	2.019411	1.917191	1.804707
60	7.077106	4.977432	4.125892	3.649047	3.338884	3.118674	2.953049	2.82328	2.718454	2.631751	2.496116	2.352297	2.197806	2.115364	2.028479	1.936018	1.836259	1.72632	1.600647
120	6.850893	4.78651	3.9491	3.479531	3.173545	2.955854	2.791764	2.662906	2.558574	2.472077	2.3363	2.191504	2.034588	1.950018	1.860005	1.762849	1.655693	1.532992	1.380528
Infinity	6.634897	4.60517	3.781622	3.319176	3.017254	2.801982	2.63933	2.511279	2.407333	2.320925	2.184747	2.038528	1.878312	1.790826	1.696406	1.592268	1.47299	1.324585	1.000033

Values computed by the authors using **R**.

TABLE A.5

Fisher's Z Transformed Values

r	Z	r	Z	r	Z	r	Z
0.00	0.000000	0.25	0.2554128	0.50	0.5493061	0.75	0.9729551
0.01	0.01000033	0.26	0.2661084	0.51	0.5627298	0.76	0.9962151
0.02	0.02000267	0.27	0.2768638	0.52	0.5763398	0.77	1.020328
0.03	0.030009	0.28	0.2876821	0.53	0.5901452	0.78	1.045371
0.04	0.04002135	0.29	0.2985663	0.54	0.6041556	0.79	1.071432
0.05	0.05004173	0.30	0.3095196	0.55	0.6183813	0.80	1.098612
0.06	0.06007216	0.31	0.3205454	0.56	0.6328332	0.81	1.127029
0.07	0.07011467	0.32	0.3316471	0.57	0.6475228	0.82	1.156817
0.08	0.08017133	0.33	0.3428283	0.58	0.6624627	0.83	1.188136
0.09	0.09024419	0.34	0.3540925	0.59	0.6776661	0.84	1.221174
0.10	0.1003353	0.35	0.3654438	0.60	0.6931472	0.85	1.256153
0.11	0.1104469	0.36	0.3768859	0.61	0.7089214	0.86	1.293345
0.12	0.120581	0.37	0.3884231	0.62	0.7250051	0.87	1.33308
0.13	0.1307399	0.38	0.4000597	0.63	0.7414161	0.88	1.375768
0.14	0.1409256	0.39	0.4118	0.64	0.7581737	0.89	1.421926
0.15	0.1511404	0.40	0.4236489	0.65	0.7752987	0.90	1.472219
0.16	0.1613867	0.41	0.4356112	0.66	0.7928136	0.91	1.527524
0.17	0.1716667	0.42	0.447692	0.67	0.8107431	0.92	1.589027
0.18	0.1819827	0.43	0.4598967	0.68	0.829114	0.93	1.65839
0.19	0.1923372	0.44	0.4722308	0.69	0.8479558	0.94	1.738049
0.20	0.2027326	0.45	0.4847003	0.70	0.8673005	0.95	1.831781
0.21	0.2131713	0.46	0.4973113	0.71	0.8871839	0.96	1.94591
0.22	0.2236561	0.47	0.5100703	0.72	0.907645	0.97	2.092296
0.23	0.2341895	0.48	0.5229843	0.73	0.9287274	0.98	2.29756
0.24	0.2447741	0.49	0.5360603	0.74	0.9504794	0.99	2.646652

TABLE A.6

Orthogonal Polynomials

J	Trend	j = 1	2	3	4	5	6	7	8	9	10	Σc_j^2
J = 3	Linear	−1	0	1								2
	Quadratic	1	−2	1								6
J = 4	Linear	−3	−1	1	3							20
	Quadratic	1	−1	−1	1							4
	Cubic	−1	3	−3	1							20
J = 5	Linear	−2	−1	0	1	2						10
	Quadratic	2	−1	−2	−1	2						14
	Cubic	−1	2	0	−2	1						10
	Quartic	1	−4	6	−4	1						70
J = 6	Linear	−5	−3	−1	1	3	5					70
	Quadratic	5	−1	−4	−4	−1	5					84
	Cubic	−5	7	4	−4	−7	5					180
	Quartic	1	−3	2	2	−3	1					28
	Quintic	−1	5	−10	10	−5	1					252
J = 7	Linear	−3	−2	−1	0	1	2	3				28
	Quadratic	5	0	−3	−4	−3	0	5				84
	Cubic	−1	1	1	0	−1	−1	1				6
	Quartic	3	−7	1	6	1	−7	3				154
	Quintic	−1	4	−5	0	5	−4	1				84
J = 8	Linear	−7	−5	−3	−1	1	3	5	7			168
	Quadratic	7	1	−3	−5	−5	−3	1	7			168
	Cubic	−7	5	7	3	−3	−7	−5	7			264
	Quartic	7	−13	−3	9	9	−3	−13	7			616
	Quintic	−7	23	−17	−15	15	17	−23	7			2184
J = 9	Linear	−4	−3	−2	−1	0	1	2	3	4		60
	Quadratic	28	7	−8	−17	−20	−17	−8	7	28		2772
	Cubic	−14	7	13	9	0	−9	−13	−7	14		990
	Quartic	14	−21	−11	9	18	9	−11	−21	14		2002
	Quintic	−4	11	−4	−9	0	9	4	−11	4		468
J = 10	Linear	−9	−7	−5	−3	−1	1	3	5	7	9	330
	Quadratic	6	2	−1	−3	−4	−4	−3	−1	2	6	132
	Cubic	−42	14	35	31	12	−12	−31	−35	−14	42	8580
	Quartic	18	−22	−17	3	18	18	3	−17	−22	18	2860
	Quintic	−6	14	−1	−11	−6	6	11	1	−14	6	780

Source: Reprinted from Pearson, E. S., and Hartley, H. O., *Biometrika Tables for Statisticians*, Cambridge University Press, Cambridge, UK, 1966, Table 47. With permission of Biometrika Trustees.

TABLE A.7

Critical Values for Dunnett's Procedure

df	1	2	3	4	5	6	7	8	9
One tailed, α = .05									
5	2.02	2.44	2.68	2.85	2.98	3.08	3.16	3.24	3.30
6	1.94	2.34	2.56	2.71	2.83	2.92	3.00	3.07	3.12
7	1.89	2.27	2.48	2.62	2.73	2.82	2.89	2.95	3.01
8	1.86	2.22	2.42	2.55	2.66	2.74	2.81	2.87	2.92
9	1.83	2.18	2.37	2.50	2.60	2.68	2.75	2.81	2.86
10	1.81	2.15	2.34	2.47	2.56	2.64	2.70	2.76	2.81
11	1.80	2.13	2.31	2.44	2.53	2.60	2.67	2.72	2.77
12	1.78	2.11	2.29	2.41	2.50	2.58	2.64	2.69	2.74
13	1.77	2.09	2.27	2.39	2.48	2.55	2.61	2.66	2.71
14	1.76	2.08	2.25	2.37	2.46	2.53	2.59	2.64	2.69
15	1.75	2.07	2.24	2.36	2.44	2.51	2.57	2.62	2.67
16	1.75	2.06	2.23	2.34	2.43	2.50	2.56	2.61	2.65
17	1.74	2.05	2.22	2.33	2.42	2.49	2.54	2.59	2.64
18	1.73	2.04	2.21	2.32	2.41	2.48	2.53	2.58	2.62
19	1.73	2.03	2.20	2.31	2.40	2.47	2.52	2.57	2.61
20	1.72	2.03	2.19	2.30	2.39	2.46	2.51	2.56	2.60
24	1.71	2.01	2.17	2.28	2.36	2.43	2.48	2.53	2.57
30	1.70	1.99	2.15	2.25	2.33	2.40	2.45	2.50	2.54
40	1.68	1.97	2.13	2.23	2.31	2.37	2.42	2.47	2.51
60	1.67	1.95	2.10	2.21	2.28	2.35	2.39	2.44	2.48
120	1.66	1.93	2.08	2.18	2.26	2.32	2.37	2.41	2.45
∞	1.64	1.92	2.06	2.16	2.23	2.29	2.34	2.38	2.42
One tailed, α = .01									
5	3.37	3.90	4.21	4.43	4.60	4.73	4.85	4.94	5.03
6	3.14	3.61	3.88	4.07	4.21	4.33	4.43	4.51	4.59
7	3.00	3.42	3.66	3.83	3.96	4.07	4.15	4.23	4.30
8	2.90	3.29	3.51	3.67	3.79	3.88	3.96	4.03	4.09
9	2.82	3.19	3.40	3.55	3.66	3.75	3.82	3.89	3.94
10	2.76	3.11	3.31	3.45	3.56	3.64	3.71	3.78	3.83
11	2.72	3.06	3.25	3.38	3.48	3.56	3.63	3.69	3.74
12	2.68	3.01	3.19	3.32	3.42	3.50	3.56	3.62	3.67
13	2.65	2.97	3.15	3.27	3.37	3.44	3.51	3.56	3.61
14	2.62	2.94	3.11	3.23	3.32	3.40	3.46	3.51	3.56
15	2.60	2.91	3.08	3.20	3.29	3.36	3.42	3.47	3.52
16	2.58	2.88	3.05	3.17	3.26	3.33	3.39	3.44	3.48
17	2.57	2.86	3.03	3.14	3.23	3.30	3.36	3.41	3.45
18	2.55	2.84	3.01	3.12	3.21	3.27	3.33	3.38	3.42
19	2.54	2.83	2.99	3.10	3.18	3.25	3.31	3.36	3.40
20	2.53	2.81	2.97	3.08	3.17	3.23	3.29	3.34	3.38
24	2.49	2.77	2.92	3.03	3.11	3.17	3.22	3.27	3.31

(*continued*)

TABLE A.7 (continued)

Critical Values for Dunnett's Procedure

df	1	2	3	4	5	6	7	8	9
One tailed, α = .01									
30	2.46	2.72	2.87	2.97	3.05	3.11	3.16	3.21	3.24
40	2.42	2.68	2.82	2.92	2.99	3.05	3.10	3.14	3.18
60	2.39	2.64	2.78	2.87	2.94	3.00	3.04	3.08	3.12
120	2.36	2.60	2.73	2.82	2.89	2.94	2.99	3.03	3.06
∞	2.33	2.56	2.68	2.77	2.84	2.89	2.93	2.97	3.00
Two tailed, α = .05									
5	2.57	3.03	3.29	3.48	3.62	3.73	3.82	3.90	3.97
6	2.45	2.86	3.10	3.26	3.39	3.49	3.57	3.64	3.71
7	2.36	2.75	2.97	3.12	3.24	3.33	3.41	3.47	3.53
8	2.31	2.67	2.88	3.02	3.13	3.22	3.29	3.35	3.41
9	2.26	2.61	2.81	2.95	3.05	3.14	3.20	3.26	3.32
10	2.23	2.57	2.76	2.89	2.99	3.07	3.14	3.19	3.24
11	2.20	2.53	2.72	2.84	2.94	3.02	3.08	3.14	3.19
12	2.18	2.50	2.68	2.81	2.90	2.98	3.04	3.09	3.14
13	2.16	2.48	2.65	2.78	2.87	2.94	3.00	3.06	3.10
14	2.14	2.46	2.63	2.75	2.84	2.91	2.97	3.02	3.07
15	2.13	2.44	2.61	2.73	2.82	2.89	2.95	3.00	3.04
16	2.12	2.42	2.59	2.71	2.80	2.87	2.92	2.97	3.02
17	2.11	2.41	2.58	2.69	2.78	2.85	2.90	2.95	3.00
18	2.10	2.40	2.56	2.68	2.76	2.83	2.89	2.94	2.98
19	2.09	2.39	2.55	2.66	2.75	2.81	2.87	2.92	2.96
20	2.09	2.38	2.54	2.65	2.73	2.80	2.86	2.90	2.95
24	2.06	2.35	2.51	2.61	2.70	2.76	2.81	2.86	2.90
30	2.04	2.32	2.47	2.58	2.66	2.72	2.77	2.82	2.86
40	2.02	2.29	2.44	2.54	2.62	2.68	2.73	2.77	2.81
60	2.00	2.27	2.41	2.51	2.58	2.64	2.69	2.73	2.77
120	1.98	2.24	2.38	2.47	2.55	2.60	2.65	2.69	2.73
∞	1.96	2.21	2.35	2.44	2.51	2.57	2.61	2.65	2.69
Two tailed, α = .01									
5	4.03	4.63	4.98	5.22	5.41	5.56	5.69	5.80	5.89
6	3.71	4.21	4.51	4.71	4.87	5.00	5.10	5.20	5.28
7	3.50	3.95	4.21	4.39	4.53	4.64	4.74	4.82	4.89
8	3.36	3.77	4.00	4.17	4.29	4.40	4.48	4.56	4.62
9	3.25	3.63	3.85	4.01	4.12	4.22	4.30	4.37	4.43
10	3.17	3.53	3.74	3.88	3.99	4.08	4.16	4.22	4.28
11	3.11	3.45	3.65	3.79	3.89	3.98	4.05	4.11	4.16
12	3.05	3.39	3.58	3.71	3.81	3.89	3.96	4.02	4.07
13	3.01	3.33	3.52	3.65	3.74	3.82	3.89	3.94	3.99
14	2.98	3.29	3.47	3.59	3.69	3.76	3.83	3.88	3.93
15	2.95	3.25	3.43	3.55	3.64	3.71	3.78	3.83	3.88
16	2.92	3.22	3.39	3.51	3.60	3.67	3.73	3.78	3.83

df	1	2	3	4	5	6	7	8	9
Two tailed, α = .01									
17	2.90	3.19	3.36	3.47	3.56	3.63	3.69	3.74	3.79
18	2.88	3.17	3.33	3.44	3.53	3.60	3.66	3.71	3.75
19	2.86	3.15	3.31	3.42	3.50	3.57	3.63	3.68	3.72
20	2.85	3.13	3.29	3.40	3.48	3.55	3.60	3.65	3.69
24	2.80	3.07	3.22	3.32	3.40	3.47	3.52	3.57	3.61
30	2.75	3.01	3.15	3.25	3.33	3.39	3.44	3.49	3.52
40	2.70	2.95	3.09	3.19	3.26	3.32	3.37	3.41	3.44
60	2.66	2.90	3.03	3.12	3.19	3.25	3.29	3.33	3.37
120	2.62	2.85	2.97	3.06	3.12	3.18	3.22	3.26	3.29
∞	2.58	2.79	2.92	3.00	3.06	3.11	3.15	3.19	3.22

Source: Reprinted from Dunnett, C.W., *J.Am. Stat. Assoc.*, 50, 1096, 1955 Table 1a and Table 1b With permission of the American Statistical Association; Dunnett, C. W., *Biometrics, 20*, 482, 1964, Table II and Table III. With permission of the Biometric Society.

The columns represent *J* = number of treatment means (excluding the control).

TABLE A.8
Critical Values for Dunn's (Bonferroni's) Procedure

		Number of Contrasts										
ν	α	2	3	4	5	6	7	8	9	10	15	20
2	0.01	14.071	17.248	19.925	22.282	24.413	26.372	28.196	29.908	31.528	38.620	44.598
	0.05	6.164	7.582	8.774	9.823	10.769	11.639	12.449	13.208	13.927	17.072	19.721
	0.10	4.243	5.243	6.081	6.816	7.480	8.090	8.656	9.188	9.691	11.890	13.741
	0.20	2.828	3.531	4.116	4.628	5.089	5.512	5.904	6.272	6.620	8.138	9.414
3	0.01	7.447	8.565	9.453	10.201	10.853	11.436	11.966	12.453	12.904	14.796	16.300
	0.05	4.156	4.826	5.355	5.799	6.185	6.529	6.842	7.128	7.394	8.505	9.387
	0.10	3.149	3.690	4.115	4.471	4.780	5.055	5.304	5.532	5.744	6.627	7.326
	0.20	2.294	2.734	3.077	3.363	3.610	3.829	4.028	4.209	4.377	5.076	5.626
4	0.01	5.594	6.248	6.751	7.166	7.520	7.832	8.112	8.367	8.600	9.556	10.294
	0.05	3.481	3.941	4.290	4.577	4.822	5.036	5.228	5.402	5.562	6.214	6.714
	0.10	2.751	3.150	3.452	3.699	3.909	4.093	4.257	4.406	4.542	5.097	5.521
	0.20	2.084	2.434	2.697	2.911	3.092	3.250	3.391	3.518	3.635	4.107	4.468
5	0.01	4.771	5.243	5.599	5.888	6.133	6.346	6.535	6.706	6.862	7.491	7.968
	0.05	3.152	3.518	3.791	4.012	4.197	4.358	4.501	4.630	4.747	5.219	5.573
	0.10	2.549	2.882	3.129	3.327	3.493	3.638	3.765	3.880	3.985	4.403	4.718
	0.20	1.973	2.278	2.503	2.683	2.834	2.964	3.079	3.182	3.275	3.649	3.928
6	0.01	4.315	4.695	4.977	5.203	5.394	5.559	5.704	5.835	5.954	6.428	6.782
	0.05	2.959	3.274	3.505	3.690	3.845	3.978	4.095	4.200	4.296	4.675	4.956
	0.10	2.428	2.723	2.939	3.110	3.253	3.376	3.484	3.580	3.668	4.015	4.272
	0.20	1.904	2.184	2.387	2.547	2.681	2.795	2.895	2.985	3.066	3.385	3.620
7	0.01	4.027	4.353	4.591	4.782	4.941	5.078	5.198	5.306	5.404	5.791	6.077
	0.05	2.832	3.115	3.321	3.484	3.620	3.736	3.838	3.929	4.011	4.336	4.574
	0.10	2.347	2.618	2.814	2.969	3.097	3.206	3.302	3.388	3.465	3.768	3.990
	0.20	1.858	2.120	2.309	2.457	2.579	2.684	2.775	2.856	2.929	3.214	3.423
8	0.01	3.831	4.120	4.331	4.498	4.637	4.756	4.860	4.953	5.038	5.370	5.613
	0.05	2.743	3.005	3.193	3.342	3.464	3.589	3.661	3.743	3.816	4.105	4.316
	0.10	2.289	2.544	2.726	2.869	2.967	3.088	3.176	3.254	3.324	3.598	3.798
	0.20	1.824	2.075	2.254	2.393	2.508	2.605	2.690	2.765	2.832	3.095	3.286
9	0.01	3.688	3.952	4.143	4.294	4.419	4.526	4.619	4.703	4.778	5.072	5.287
	0.05	2.677	2.923	3.099	3.237	3.351	3.448	3.532	3.607	3.675	3.938	4.129
	0.10	2.246	2.488	2.661	2.796	2.907	3.001	3.083	3.155	3.221	3.474	3.658
	0.20	1.799	2.041	2.212	2.345	2.454	2.546	2.627	2.696	2.761	3.008	3.185
10	0.01	3.580	3.825	4.002	4.141	4.256	4.354	4.439	4.515	4.584	4.852	5.046
	0.05	2.626	2.860	3.027	3.157	3.264	3.355	3.434	3.505	3.568	3.813	3.989
	0.10	2.213	2.446	2.611	2.739	2.845	2.934	3.012	3.080	3.142	3.380	3.552
	0.20	1.779	2.014	2.180	2.308	2.413	2.501	2.578	2.646	2.706	2.941	3.106
11	0.01	3.495	3.726	3.892	4.022	4.129	4.221	4.300	4.371	4.434	4.682	4.860
	0.05	2.586	2.811	2.970	3.094	3.196	3.283	3.358	3.424	3.484	3.715	3.880
	0.10	2.166	2.412	2.571	2.695	2.796	2.881	2.955	3.021	3.079	3.306	3.468
	0.20	1.763	1.993	2.154	2.279	2.380	2.465	2.539	2.605	2.663	2.888	3.048
12	0.01	3.427	3.647	3.804	3.927	4.029	4.114	4.189	4.256	4.315	4.547	4.714
	0.05	2.553	2.770	2.924	3.044	3.141	3.224	3.296	3.359	3.416	3.636	3.793
	0.10	2.164	2.384	2.539	2.658	2.756	2.838	2.910	2.973	3.029	3.247	3.402
	0.20	1.750	1.975	2.133	2.254	2.353	2.436	2.508	2.571	2.628	2.845	2.999

ν	α	Number of Contrasts 2	3	4	5	6	7	8	9	10	15	20
13	0.01	3.371	3.582	3.733	3.850	3.946	4.028	4.099	4.162	4.218	4.438	4.595
	0.05	2.526	2.737	2.886	3.002	3.096	3.176	3.245	3.306	3.361	3.571	3.722
	0.10	2.146	2.361	2.512	2.628	2.723	2.803	2.872	2.933	2.988	3.198	3.347
	0.20	1.739	1.961	2.116	2.234	2.331	2.412	2.482	2.544	2.599	2.809	2.958
14	0.01	3.324	3.528	3.673	3.785	3.878	3.956	4.024	4.084	4.138	4.347	4.497
	0.05	2.503	2.709	2.854	2.967	3.058	3.135	3.202	3.261	3.314	3.518	3.662
	0.10	2.131	2.342	2.489	2.603	2.696	2.774	2.841	2.900	2.953	3.157	3.301
	0.20	1.730	1.949	2.101	2.217	2.312	2.392	2.460	2.520	2.574	2.779	2.924
15	0.01	3.285	3.482	3.622	3.731	3.820	3.895	3.961	4.019	4.071	4.271	4.414
	0.05	2.483	2.685	2.827	2.937	3.026	3.101	3.166	3.224	3.275	3.472	3.612
	0.10	2.118	2.325	2.470	2.582	2.672	2.748	2.814	2.872	2.924	3.122	3.262
	0.20	1.722	1.938	2.088	2.203	2.296	2.374	2.441	2.500	2.553	2.754	2.896
16	0.01	3.251	3.443	3.579	3.684	3.771	3.844	3.907	3.963	4.013	4.206	4.344
	0.05	2.467	2.665	2.804	2.911	2.998	3.072	3.135	3.191	3.241	3.433	3.569
	0.10	2.106	2.311	2.453	2.563	2.652	2.726	2.791	2.848	2.898	3.092	3.228
	0.20	1.715	1.929	2.077	2.190	2.282	2.359	2.425	2.483	2.535	2.732	2.871
17	0.01	3.221	3.409	3.541	3.644	3.728	3.799	3.860	3.914	3.963	4.150	4.284
	0.05	2.452	2.647	2.783	2.889	2.974	3.046	3.108	3.163	3.212	3.399	3.532
	0.10	2.096	2.296	2.439	2.547	2.634	2.706	2.771	2.826	2.876	3.066	3.199
	0.20	1.709	1.921	2.068	2.179	2.270	2.346	2.411	2.488	2.519	2.713	2.849
18	0.01	3.195	3.379	3.508	3.609	3.691	3.760	3.820	3.872	3.920	4.102	4.231
	0.05	2.439	2.631	2.766	2.869	2.953	3.024	3.085	3.138	3.186	3.370	3.499
	0.10	2.088	2.287	2.426	2.532	2.619	2.691	2.753	2.806	2.857	3.043	3.174
	0.20	1.704	1.914	2.059	2.170	2.259	2.334	2.399	2.455	2.505	2.696	2.830
19	0.01	3.173	3.353	3.479	3.578	3.658	3.725	3.784	3.835	3.881	4.059	4.185
	0.05	2.427	2.617	2.750	2.852	2.934	3.004	3.064	3.116	3.163	3.343	3.470
	0.10	2.080	2.277	2.415	2.520	2.605	2.676	2.738	2.791	2.839	3.023	3.152
	0.20	1.699	1.908	2.052	2.161	2.250	2.324	2.388	2.443	2.493	2.682	2.813
20	0.01	3.152	3.329	3.454	3.550	3.629	3.695	3.752	3.802	3.848	4.021	4.144
	0.05	2.417	2.605	2.736	2.836	2.918	2.986	3.045	3.097	3.143	3.320	3.445
	0.10	2.073	2.269	2.405	2.508	2.593	2.663	2.724	2.777	2.824	3.005	3.132
	0.20	1.695	1.902	2.045	2.154	2.241	2.315	2.378	2.433	2.482	2.668	2.798
21	0.01	3.134	3.308	3.431	3.525	3.602	3.667	3.724	3.773	3.817	3.987	4.108
	0.05	2.408	2.594	2.723	2.822	2.903	2.970	3.028	3.080	3.125	3.300	3.422
	0.10	2.067	2.261	2.396	2.498	2.581	2.651	2.711	2.764	2.810	2.989	3.114
	0.20	1.691	1.897	2.039	2.147	2.234	2.306	2.369	2.424	2.472	2.656	2.785
22	0.01	3.118	3.289	3.410	3.503	3.579	3.643	3.698	3.747	3.790	3.957	4.075
	0.05	2.400	2.584	2.712	2.810	2.889	2.956	3.014	3.064	3.109	3.281	3.402
	0.10	2.061	2.254	2.387	2.489	2.572	2.641	2.700	2.752	2.798	2.974	3.096
	0.20	1.688	1.892	2.033	2.141	2.227	2.299	2.361	2.415	2.463	2.646	2.773

(*continued*)

TABLE A.8 (continued)

Critical Values for Dunn's (Bonferroni's) Procedure

		Number of Contrasts										
ν	α	2	3	4	5	6	7	8	9	10	15	20
23	0.01	3.103	3.272	3.392	3.483	3.558	3.621	3.675	3.723	3.766	3.930	4.046
	0.05	2.392	2.574	2.701	2.798	2.877	2.943	3.000	3.050	3.094	3.264	3.383
	0.10	2.056	2.247	2.380	2.481	2.563	2.631	2.690	2.741	2.787	2.961	3.083
	0.20	1.685	1.888	2.028	2.135	2.221	2.292	2.354	2.407	2.455	2.636	2.762
24	0.01	3.089	3.257	3.375	3.465	3.539	3.601	3.654	3.702	3.744	3.905	4.019
	0.05	2.385	2.566	2.692	2.788	2.866	2.931	2.988	3.037	3.081	3.249	3.366
	0.10	2.051	2.241	2.373	2.473	2.554	2.622	2.680	2.731	2.777	2.949	3.070
	0.20	1.682	1.884	2.024	2.130	2.215	2.286	2.347	2.400	2.448	2.627	2.752
25	0.01	3.077	3.243	3.359	3.449	3.521	3.583	3.635	3.682	3.723	3.882	3.995
	0.05	2.379	2.558	2.683	2.779	2.856	2.921	2.976	3.025	3.069	3.235	3.351
	0.10	2.047	2.236	2.367	2.466	2.547	2.614	2.672	2.722	2.767	2.938	3.058
	0.20	1.679	1.881	2.020	2.125	2.210	2.280	2.341	2.394	2.441	2.619	2.743
26	0.01	3.066	3.230	3.345	3.433	3.505	3.566	3.618	3.664	3.705	3.862	3.972
	0.05	2.373	2.551	2.675	2.770	2.847	2.911	2.966	3.014	3.058	3.222	3.337
	0.10	2.043	2.231	2.361	2.460	2.540	2.607	2.664	2.714	2.759	2.928	3.047
	0.20	1.677	1.878	2.016	2.121	2.205	2.275	2.335	2.388	2.435	2.612	2.735
27	0.01	3.056	3.218	3.332	3.419	3.491	3.550	3.602	3.647	3.688	3.843	3.952
	0.05	2.368	2.545	2.668	2.762	2.838	2.902	2.956	3.004	3.047	3.210	3.324
	0.10	2.039	2.227	2.356	2.454	2.534	2.600	2.657	2.707	2.751	2.919	3.036
	0.20	1.675	1.875	2.012	2.117	2.201	2.270	2.330	2.383	2.429	2.605	2.727
28	0.01	3.046	3.207	3.320	3.407	3.477	3.536	3.587	3.632	3.672	3.825	3.933
	0.05	2.383	2.539	2.661	2.755	2.830	2.893	2.948	2.995	3.038	3.199	3.312
	0.10	2.036	2.222	2.351	2.449	2.528	2.594	2.650	2.700	2.744	2.911	3.027
	0.20	1.672	1.872	2.009	2.113	2.196	2.266	2.326	2.378	2.424	2.599	2.720
29	0.01	3.037	3.197	3.309	3.395	3.464	3.523	3.574	3.618	3.658	3.809	3.916
	0.05	2.358	2.534	2.655	2.748	2.823	2.886	2.940	2.967	3.029	3.189	3.301
	0.10	2.033	2.218	2.346	2.444	2.522	2.588	2.644	2.693	2.737	2.903	3.018
	0.20	1.671	1.869	2.006	2.110	2.193	2.262	2.321	2.373	2.419	2.593	2.713
30	0.01	3.029	3.188	3.298	3.384	3.453	3.511	3.561	3.605	3.644	3.794	3.900
	0.05	2.354	2.528	2.649	2.742	2.816	2.878	2.932	2.979	3.021	3.180	3.291
	0.10	2.030	2.215	2.342	2.439	2.517	2.582	2.638	2.687	2.731	2.895	3.010
	0.20	1.669	1.867	2.003	2.106	2.189	2.258	2.317	2.369	2.414	2.587	2.707
40	0.01	2.970	3.121	3.225	3.305	3.370	3.425	3.472	3.513	3.549	3.689	3.787
	0.05	2.323	2.492	2.606	2.696	2.768	2.827	2.878	2.923	2.963	3.113	3.218
	0.10	2.009	2.189	2.312	2.406	2.481	2.544	2.597	2.644	2.686	2.843	2.952
	0.20	1.656	1.850	1.983	2.083	2.164	2.231	2.288	2.338	2.382	2.548	2.663
60	0.01	2.914	3.056	3.155	3.230	3.291	3.342	3.386	3.425	3.459	3.589	3.679
	0.05	2.294	2.456	2.568	2.653	2.721	2.777	2.826	2.869	2.906	3.049	3.146
	0.10	1.989	2.163	2.283	2.373	2.446	2.506	2.558	2.603	2.643	2.793	2.897
	0.20	1.643	1.834	1.963	2.061	2.139	2.204	2.259	2.308	2.350	2.511	2.621

		Number of Contrasts										
ν	α	2	3	4	5	6	7	8	9	10	15	20
120	0.01	2.859	2.994	3.067	3.158	3.215	3.263	3.304	3.340	3.372	3.493	3.577
	0.05	2.265	2.422	2.529	2.610	2.675	2.729	2.776	2.816	2.852	2.967	3.081
	0.10	1.968	2.138	2.254	2.342	2.411	2.469	2.519	2.562	2.600	2.744	2.843
	0.20	1.631	1.817	1.944	2.039	2.115	2.178	2.231	2.278	2.319	2.474	2.580
∞	0.01	2.806	2.934	3.022	3.089	3.143	3.188	3.226	3.260	3.289	3.402	3.480
	0.05	2.237	2.388	2.491	2.569	2.631	2.683	2.727	2.766	2.800	2.928	3.016
	0.10	1.949	2.114	2.226	2.311	2.378	2.434	2.482	2.523	2.560	2.697	2.791
	0.20	1.618	1.801	1.925	2.018	2.091	2.152	2.204	2.249	2.289	2.438	2.540

Source: Table 1 reprinted from Games, P. A. (1977), An improved *t* table for simultaneous control of *g* contrasts. *Journal of the American Statistical Association*, *72*, 531–534. Reprinted with permission of the American Statistical Association, www.amstat.org and by permission of the publisher (Taylor & Francis Ltd., www.tandfonline.com.

TABLE A.9

Critical Values for the Studentized Range Statistic

v	J or r: 2	3	4	5	6	7	8	9	10
$\alpha = .10$									
1	8.929	13.44	16.36	18.49	20.15	21.51	22.64	23.62	24.48
2	4.130	5.733	6.773	7.538	8.139	8.633	9.049	9.409	9.725
3	3.328	4.467	5.199	5.738	6.162	6.511	6.806	7.062	7.287
4	3.015	3.976	4.586	5.035	5.388	5.679	5.926	6.139	6.327
5	2.850	3.717	4.264	4.664	4.979	5.238	5.458	5.648	5.816
6	2.748	3.559	4.065	4.435	4.726	4.966	5.168	5.344	5.499
7	2.680	3.451	3.931	4.280	4.555	4.780	4.972	5.137	5.283
8	2.630	3.374	3.834	4.169	4.431	4.646	4.829	4.987	5.126
9	2.592	3.316	3.761	4.084	4.337	4.545	4.721	4.873	5.007
10	2.563	3.270	3.704	4.018	4.264	4.465	4.636	4.783	4.913
11	2.540	3.234	3.658	3.965	4.205	4.401	4.568	4.711	4.838
12	2.521	3.204	3.621	3.922	4.156	4.349	4.511	4.652	4.776
13	2.505	3.179	3.589	3.885	4.116	4.305	4.464	4.602	4.724
14	2.491	3.158	3.563	3.854	4.081	4.267	4.424	4.560	4.680
15	2.479	3.140	3.540	3.828	4.052	4.235	4.390	4.524	4.641
16	2.469	3.124	3.520	3.804	4.026	4.207	4.360	4.492	4.608
17	2.460	3.110	3.503	3.784	4.004	4.183	4.334	4.464	4.579
18	2.452	3.098	3.488	3.767	3.984	4.161	4.311	4.440	4.554
19	2.445	3.087	3.474	3.751	3.966	4.142	4.290	4.418	4.531
20	2.439	3.078	3.462	3.736	3.950	4.124	4.271	4.398	4.510
24	2.420	3.047	3.423	3.692	3.900	4.070	4.213	4.336	4.445
30	2.400	3.017	3.386	3.648	3.851	4.016	4.155	4.275	4.381
40	2.381	2.988	3.349	3.605	3.803	3.963	4.099	4.215	4.317
60	2.363	2.959	3.312	3.562	3.755	3.911	4.042	4.155	4.254
120	2.344	2.930	3.276	3.520	3.707	3.859	3.987	4.096	4.191
∞	2.326	2.902	3.240	3.478	3.661	3.808	3.931	4.037	4.129

v	J or r: 11	12	13	14	15	16	17	18	19
$\alpha = .10$									
1	25.24	25.92	26.54	27.10	27.62	28.10	28.54	28.96	29.35
2	10.01	10.26	10.49	10.70	10.89	11.07	11.24	11.39	11.54
3	7.487	7.667	7.832	7.982	8.120	8.249	8.368	8.479	8.584
4	6.495	6.645	6.783	6.909	7.025	7.133	7.233	7.327	7.414
5	5.966	6.101	6.223	6.336	6.440	6.536	6.626	6.710	6.789
6	5.637	5.762	5.875	5.979	6.075	6.164	6.247	6.325	6.398
7	5.413	5.530	5.637	5.735	5.826	5.910	5.838	6.061	6.130
8	5.250	5.362	5.464	5.558	5.644	5.724	5.799	5.869	5.935
9	5.127	5.234	5.333	5.423	5.506	5.583	5.655	5.723	5.786
10	5.029	5.134	5.229	5.317	5.397	5.472	5.542	5.607	5.668
11	4.951	5.053	5.146	5.231	5.309	5.382	5.450	5.514	5.573
12	4.886	4.986	5.077	5.160	5.236	5.308	5.374	5.436	5.495
13	4.832	4.930	5.019	5.100	5.176	5.245	5.311	5.372	5.429

	J or r								
v	11	12	13	14	15	16	17	18	19
α = .10									
14	4.786	4.882	4.970	5.050	5.124	5.192	5.256	5.316	5.373
15	4.746	4.841	4.927	5.006	5.079	5.147	5.209	5.269	5.324
16	4.712	4.805	4.890	4.968	5.040	5.107	5.169	5.227	5.282
17	4.682	4.774	4.858	4.935	5.005	5.071	5.133	5.190	5.244
18	4.655	4.746	4.829	4.905	4.975	5.040	5.101	5.158	5.211
19	4.631	4.721	4.803	4.879	4.948	5.012	5.073	5.129	5.182
20	4.609	4.699	4.780	4.855	4.924	4.987	5.047	5.103	5.155
24	4.541	4.628	4.708	4.780	4.847	4.909	4.966	5.021	5.071
30	4.474	4.559	4.635	4.706	4.770	4.830	4.886	4.939	4.988
40	4.408	4.490	4.564	4.632	4.695	4.752	4.807	4.857	4.905
60	4.342	4.421	4.493	4.558	4.619	4.675	4.727	4.775	4.821
120	4.276	4.353	4.422	4.485	4.543	4.597	4.647	4.694	4.738
∞	4.211	4.285	4.351	4.412	4.468	4.519	4.568	4.612	4.654

	J or r								
v	2	3	4	5	6	7	8	9	10
α = .05									
1	17.97	26.98	32.82	37.08	40.41	43.12	45.40	47.36	49.07
2	6.085	8.331	9.798	10.88	11.74	12.44	13.03	13.54	13.99
3	4.501	5.910	6.825	7.502	8.037	8.478	8.853	9.177	9.462
4	3.927	5.040	5.757	6.287	6.707	7.053	7.347	7.602	7.826
5	3.635	4.602	5.218	5.673	6.033	6.330	6.582	6.802	6.995
6	3.461	4.339	4.896	5.305	5.628	5.895	6.122	6.319	6.493
7	3.344	4.165	4.681	5.060	5.359	5.606	5.815	5.998	6.158
8	3.261	4.041	4.529	4.886	5.167	5.399	5.597	5.767	5.918
9	3.199	3.949	4.415	4.756	5.024	5.244	5.432	5.595	5.739
10	3.151	3.877	4.327	4.654	4.912	5.124	5.305	5.461	5.599
11	3.113	3.820	4.256	4.574	4.823	5.028	5.202	5.353	5.487
12	3.082	3.773	4.199	4.508	4.751	4.950	5.119	5.265	5.395
13	3.055	3.735	4.151	4.453	4.690	4.885	5.049	5.192	5.318
14	3.033	3.702	4.111	4.407	4.639	4.829	4.990	5.131	5.254
15	3.014	3.674	4.076	4.367	4.595	4.782	4.940	5.077	5.198
16	2.998	3.649	4.046	4.333	4.557	4.741	4.897	5.031	5.150
17	2.984	3.628	4.020	4.303	4.524	4.705	4.858	4.991	5.108
18	2.971	3.609	3.997	4.277	4.495	4.673	4.824	4.956	5.071
19	2.960	3.593	3.977	4.253	4.469	4.645	4.794	4.924	5.038
20	2.950	3.578	3.958	4.232	4.445	4.620	4.768	4.896	5.008
24	2.919	3.532	3.901	4.166	4.373	4.541	4.684	4.807	4.915
30	2.888	3.486	3.845	4.102	4.302	4.464	4.602	4.720	4.824
40	2.858	3.442	3.791	4.039	4.232	4.389	4.521	4.635	4.735
60	2.829	3.399	3.737	3.977	4.163	4.314	4.441	4.550	4.646
120	2.800	3.356	3.685	3.917	4.096	4.241	4.363	4.468	4.560
∞	2.772	3.314	3.633	3.858	4.030	4.170	4.286	4.387	4.474

(continued)

TABLE A.9 (continued)

Critical Values for the Studentized Range Statistic

v	11	12	13	14	15	16	17	18	19
	J or *r*								
$\alpha = .05$									
1	50.59	51.96	53.20	54.33	55.36	56.32	57.22	58.04	58.83
2	14.39	14.75	15.08	15.38	15.65	15.91	16.14	16.37	16.57
3	9.717	9.946	10.15	10.35	10.53	10.69	10.84	10.98	11.11
4	8.027	8.208	8.373	8.525	8.664	8.794	8.914	9.028	9.134
5	7.168	7.324	7.466	7.596	7.717	7.828	7.932	8.030	8.122
6	6.649	6.789	6.917	7.034	7.143	7.244	7.338	7.426	7.508
7	6.302	6.431	6.550	6.658	6.759	6.852	6.939	7.020	7.097
8	6.054	6.175	6.287	6.389	6.483	6.571	6.653	6.729	6.802
9	5.867	5.983	6.089	6.186	6.276	6.359	6.437	6.510	6.579
10	5.722	5.833	5.935	6.028	6.114	6.194	6.269	6.339	6.405
11	5.605	5.713	5.811	5.901	5.984	6.062	6.134	6.202	6.265
12	5.511	5.615	5.710	5.798	5.878	5.953	6.023	6.089	6.151
13	5.431	5.533	5.625	5.711	5.789	5.862	5.931	5.995	6.055
14	5.364	5.463	5.554	5.637	5.714	5.786	5.852	5.915	5.974
15	5.306	5.404	5.493	5.574	5.649	5.720	5.785	5.846	5.904
16	5.256	5.352	5.439	5.520	5.593	5.662	5.720	5.786	5.843
17	5.212	5.307	5.392	5.471	5.544	5.612	5.675	5.734	5.790
18	5.174	5.267	5.352	5.429	5.501	5.568	5.630	5.688	5.743
19	5.140	5.231	5.315	5.391	5.462	5.528	5.589	5.647	5.701
20	5.108	5.199	5.282	5.357	5.427	5.493	5.553	5.610	5.663
24	5.012	5.099	5.179	5.251	5.319	5.381	5.439	5.494	5.545
30	4.917	5.001	5.077	5.147	5.211	5.271	5.327	5.379	5.429
40	4.824	4.904	4.977	5.044	5.106	5.163	5.216	5.266	5.313
60	4.732	4.808	4.878	4.942	5.001	5.056	5.107	5.154	5.199
120	4.641	4.714	4.781	4.842	4.898	4.950	4.998	5.044	5.086
∞	4.552	4.622	4.685	4.743	4.796	4.845	4.891	4.934	4.974

v	2	3	4	5	6	7	8	9	10
	J or *r*								
$\alpha = .01$									
1	90.03	135.0	164.3	185.6	202.2	215.8	227.2	237.0	245.6
2	14.04	19.02	22.29	24.72	26.63	28.20	29.53	30.68	31.69
3	8.261	10.62	12.17	13.33	14.24	15.00	15.64	16.20	16.69
4	6.512	8.120	9.173	9.958	10.58	11.10	11.55	11.93	12.27
5	5.702	6.976	7.804	8.421	8.913	9.321	9.669	9.972	10.24
6	5.243	6.331	7.033	7.556	7.973	8.318	8.613	8.869	9.097
7	4.949	5.919	6.543	7.005	7.373	7.679	7.939	8.166	8.368
8	4.746	5.635	6.204	6.625	6.960	7.237	7.474	7.681	7.863
9	4.596	5.428	5.957	6.348	6.658	6.915	7.134	7.325	7.495
10	4.482	5.270	5.769	6.136	6.428	6.669	6.875	7.055	7.213
11	4.392	5.146	5.621	5.970	6.247	6.476	6.672	6.842	6.992
12	4.320	5.046	5.502	5.836	6.101	6.321	6.507	6.670	6.814
13	4.260	4.964	5.404	5.727	5.981	6.192	6.372	6.528	6.667

	J or *r*								
v	2	3	4	5	6	7	8	9	10
$\alpha = .01$									
14	4.210	4.895	5.322	5.634	5.881	6.085	6.258	6.409	6.543
15	4.168	4.836	5.252	5.556	5.796	5.994	6.162	6.309	6.439
16	4.131	4.786	5.192	5.489	5.722	5.915	6.079	6.222	6.349
17	4.099	4.742	5.140	5.430	5.659	5.847	6.007	6.147	6.270
18	4.071	4.703	5.094	5.379	5.603	5.788	5.944	6.081	6.201
19	4.046	4.670	5.054	5.334	5.554	5.735	5.889	6.022	6.141
20	4.024	4.639	5.018	5.294	5.510	5.688	5.839	5.970	6.087
24	3.956	4.546	4.907	5.168	5.374	5.542	5.685	5.809	5.919
30	3.889	4.455	4.799	5.048	5.242	5.401	5.536	5.653	5.756
40	3.825	4.367	4.696	4.931	5.114	5.265	5.392	5.502	5.599
60	3.762	4.282	4.595	4.818	4.991	5.133	5.253	5.356	5.447
120	3.702	4.200	4.497	4.709	4.872	5.005	5.118	5.214	5.299
∞	3.643	4.120	4.403	4.603	4.757	4.882	4.987	5.078	5.157

	J or *r*								
v	11	12	13	14	15	16	17	18	19
$\alpha = .01$									
1	253.2	260.0	266.2	271.8	277.0	281.8	286.3	290.4	294.3
2	32.59	33.40	34.13	34.81	35.43	36.00	36.53	37.03	37.50
3	17.13	17.53	17.89	18.22	18.52	18.81	19.07	19.32	19.55
4	12.57	12.84	13.09	13.32	13.53	13.73	13.91	14.08	14.24
5	10.48	10.70	10.89	11.08	11.24	11.40	11.55	11.68	11.81
6	9.301	9.485	9.653	9.808	9.951	10.08	10.21	10.32	10.43
7	8.548	8.711	8.860	8.997	9.124	9.242	9.353	9.456	9.554
6	8.027	8.176	8.312	8.436	8.552	8.659	8.760	8.854	8.943
9	7.647	7.784	7.910	8.025	8.132	8.232	8.325	3.412	8.495
10	7.356	7.485	7.603	7.712	7.812	7.906	7.993	8.076	8.153
11	7.128	7.250	7.362	7.465	7.560	7.649	7.732	7.809	7.883
12	6.943	7.060	7.167	7.265	7.356	7.441	7.520	7.594	7.665
13	6.791	6.903	7.006	7.101	7.188	7.269	7.345	7.417	7.485
14	6.664	6.772	6.871	6.962	7.047	7.126	7.199	7.268	7.333
15	6.555	6.660	6.757	6.845	6.927	7.003	7.074	7.142	7.204
16	6.462	6.564	6.658	6.744	6.823	6.898	6.967	7.032	7.093
17	6.381	6.480	6.572	6.656	6.734	6.806	6.873	6.937	6.997
18	6.310	6.407	6.497	6.579	6.655	6.725	6.792	6.854	6.912
19	6.247	6.342	6.430	6.510	6.585	6.654	6.719	6.780	6.837
20	6.191	6.285	6.371	6.450	6.523	6.591	6.654	6.714	6.771
24	6.017	6.106	6.186	6.261	6.330	6.394	6.453	6.510	6.563
30	5.849	5.932	6.008	6.078	6.143	6.203	6.259	6.311	6.361
40	5.686	5.764	5.835	5.900	5.961	6.017	6.069	6.119	6.165
60	5.528	5.601	5.667	5.728	5.785	5.837	5.886	5.931	5.974
120	5.375	5.443	5.505	5.562	5.614	5.662	5.708	5.750	5.790
∞	5.227	5.290	5.348	5.400	5.448	5.493	5.535	5.574	5.611

Source: Table 3 from Harter, H. L. (1960). Tables of range and studentized range. *Annals of Mathematical Statistics, 31*, 1122–1147. By permission of the Institute of Mathematical Statistics.

TABLE A.10

Critical Values for the Bryant–Paulson Procedure

$\alpha = .05$

v	$J = 2$	$J = 3$	$J = 4$	$J = 5$	$J = 6$	$J = 7$	$J = 8$	$J = 10$	$J = 12$	$J = 16$	$J = 20$
X = 1											
2	7.96	11.00	12.99	14.46	15.61	16.56	17.36	18.65	19.68	21.23	22.40
3	5.42	7.18	8.32	9.17	9.84	10.39	10.86	11.62	12.22	13.14	13.83
4	4.51	5.84	6.69	7.32	7.82	8.23	8.58	9.15	9.61	10.30	10.82
5	4.06	5.17	5.88	6.40	6.82	7.16	7.45	7.93	8.30	8.88	9.32
6	3.79	4.78	5.40	5.86	6.23	6.53	6.78	7.20	7.53	8.04	8.43
7	3.62	4.52	5.09	5.51	5.84	6.11	6.34	6.72	7.03	7.49	7.84
8	3.49	4.34	4.87	5.26	5.57	5.82	6.03	6.39	6.67	7.10	7.43
10	3.32	4.10	4.58	4.93	5.21	5.43	5.63	5.94	6.19	6.58	6.87
12	3.22	3.95	4.40	4.73	4.98	5.19	5.37	5.67	5.90	6.26	6.53
14	3.15	3.85	4.28	4.59	4.83	5.03	5.20	5.48	5.70	6.03	6.29
16	3.10	3.77	4.19	4.49	4.72	4.91	5.07	5.34	5.55	5.87	6.12
18	3.06	3.72	4.12	4.41	4.63	4.82	4.98	5.23	5.44	5.75	5.98
20	3.03	3.67	4.07	4.35	4.57	4.75	4.90	5.15	5.35	5.65	5.88
24	2.98	3.61	3.99	4.26	4.47	4.65	4.79	5.03	5.22	5.51	5.73
30	2.94	3.55	3.91	4.18	4.38	4.54	4.69	4.91	5.09	5.37	5.58
40	2.89	3.49	3.84	4.09	4.29	4.45	4.58	4.80	4.97	5.23	5.43
60	2.85	3.43	3.77	4.01	4.20	4.35	4.48	4.69	4.85	5.10	5.29
120	2.81	3.37	3.70	3.93	4.11	4.26	4.38	4.58	4.73	4.97	5.15
X = 2											
2	9.50	13.18	15.59	17.36	18.75	19.89	20.86	22.42	23.66	25.54	26.94
3	6.21	8.27	9.60	10.59	11.37	12.01	12.56	13.44	14.15	15.22	16.02
4	5.04	6.54	7.51	8.23	8.80	9.26	9.66	10.31	10.83	11.61	12.21
5	4.45	5.68	6.48	7.06	7.52	7.90	8.23	8.76	9.18	9.83	10.31
6	4.10	5.18	5.87	6.37	6.77	7.10	7.38	7.84	8.21	8.77	9.20
7	3.87	4.85	5.47	5.92	6.28	6.58	6.83	7.24	7.57	8.08	8.46
8	3.70	4.61	5.19	5.61	5.94	6.21	6.44	6.82	7.12	7.59	7.94
10	3.49	4.31	4.82	5.19	5.49	5.73	5.93	6.27	6.54	6.95	7.26
12	3.35	4.12	4.59	4.93	5.20	5.43	5.62	5.92	6.17	6.55	6.83
14	3.26	3.99	4.44	4.76	5.01	5.22	5.40	5.69	5.92	6.27	6.54
16	3.19	3.90	4.32	4.63	4.88	5.07	5.24	5.52	5.74	6.07	6.33
18	3.14	3.82	4.24	4.54	4.77	4.96	5.13	5.39	5.60	5.92	6.17
20	3.10	3.77	4.17	4.46	4.69	4.88	5.03	5.29	5.49	5.81	6.04
24	3.04	3.69	4.08	4.35	4.57	4.75	4.90	5.14	5.34	5.63	5.86
30	2.99	3.61	3.98	4.25	4.46	4.62	4.77	5.00	5.18	5.46	5.68
40	2.93	3.53	3.89	4.15	4.34	4.50	4.64	4.86	5.04	5.30	5.50
60	2.88	3.46	3.80	4.05	4.24	4.39	4.52	4.73	4.89	5.14	5.33
120	2.82	3.38	3.72	3.95	4.13	4.28	4.40	4.60	4.75	4.99	5.17

α = .05

v	$J = 2$	$J = 3$	$J = 4$	$J = 5$	$J = 6$	$J = 7$	$J = 8$	$J = 10$	$J = 12$	$J = 16$	$J = 20$
X = 3											
2	10.83	15.06	17.82	19.85	21.45	22.76	23.86	25.66	27.08	29.23	30.83
3	6.92	9.23	10.73	11.84	12.72	13.44	14.06	15.05	15.84	17.05	17.95
4	5.51	7.18	8.25	9.05	9.67	10.19	10.63	11.35	11.92	12.79	13.45
5	4.81	6.16	7.02	7.66	8.17	8.58	8.94	9.52	9.98	10.69	11.22
6	4.38	5.55	6.30	6.84	7.28	7.64	7.94	8.44	8.83	9.44	9.90
7	4.11	5.16	5.82	6.31	6.70	7.01	7.29	7.73	8.08	8.63	9.03
8	3.91	4.88	5.49	5.93	6.29	6.58	6.83	7.23	7.55	8.05	8.42
10	3.65	4.51	5.05	5.44	5.75	6.01	6.22	6.58	6.86	7.29	7.62
12	3.48	4.28	4.78	5.14	5.42	5.65	5.85	6.17	6.43	6.82	7.12
14	3.37	4.13	4.59	4.93	5.19	5.41	5.59	5.89	6.13	6.50	6.78
16	3.29	4.01	4.46	4.78	5.03	5.23	5.41	5.69	5.92	6.27	6.53
18	3.23	3.93	4.35	4.66	4.90	5.10	5.27	5.54	5.76	6.09	6.34
20	3.18	3.86	4.28	4.57	4.81	5.00	5.16	5.42	5.63	5.96	6.20
24	3.11	3.76	4.16	4.44	4.67	4.85	5.00	5.25	5.45	5.75	5.98
30	3.04	3.67	4.05	4.32	4.53	4.70	4.85	5.08	5.27	5.56	5.78
40	2.97	3.57	3.94	4.20	4.40	4.56	4.70	4.92	5.10	5.37	5.57
60	2.90	3.49	3.83	4.08	4.27	4.43	4.56	4.77	4.93	5.19	5.38
120	2.84	3.40	3.73	3.97	4.15	4.30	4.42	4.62	4.77	5.01	5.19

α = .01

v	$J = 2$	$J = 3$	$J = 4$	$J = 5$	$J = 6$	$J = 7$	$J = 8$	$J = 10$	$J = 12$	$J = 16$	$J = 20$
X = 1											
2	19.09	26.02	30.57	33.93	36.58	38.76	40.60	43.59	45.95	49.55	52.24
3	10.28	13.32	15.32	16.80	17.98	18.95	19.77	21.12	22.19	23.82	25.05
4	7.68	9.64	10.93	11.89	12.65	13.28	13.82	14.70	15.40	16.48	17.29
5	6.49	7.99	8.97	9.70	10.28	10.76	11.17	11.84	12.38	13.20	13.83
6	5.83	7.08	7.88	8.48	8.96	9.36	9.70	10.25	10.70	11.38	11.90
7	5.41	6.50	7.20	7.72	8.14	8.48	8.77	9.26	9.64	10.24	10.69
8	5.12	6.11	6.74	7.20	7.58	7.88	8.15	8.58	8.92	9.46	9.87
10	4.76	5.61	6.15	6.55	6.86	7.13	7.35	7.72	8.01	8.47	8.82
12	4.54	5.31	5.79	6.15	6.48	6.67	6.87	7.20	7.46	7.87	8.18
14	4.39	5.11	5.56	5.89	6.15	6.36	6.55	6.85	7.09	7.47	7.75
16	4.28	4.96	5.39	5.70	5.95	6.15	6.32	6.60	6.83	7.18	7.45
18	4.20	4.86	5.26	5.56	5.79	5.99	6.15	6.42	6.63	6.96	7.22
20	4.14	4.77	5.17	5.45	5.68	5.86	6.02	6.27	6.48	6.80	7.04
24	4.05	4.65	5.02	5.29	5.50	5.68	5.83	6.07	6.26	6.56	6.78
30	3.96	4.54	4.89	5.14	5.34	5.50	5.64	5.87	6.05	6.32	6.53
40	3.88	4.43	4.76	5.00	5.19	5.34	5.47	5.68	5.85	6.10	6.30
60	3.79	4.32	4.64	4.86	5.04	5.18	5.30	5.50	5.65	5.89	6.07
120	3.72	4.22	4.52	4.73	4.89	5.03	5.14	5.32	5.47	5.69	5.85

(continued)

TABLE A.10 (continued)

Critical Values for the Bryant–Paulson Procedure

α = .01

v	$J = 2$	$J = 3$	$J = 4$	$J = 5$	$J = 6$	$J = 7$	$J = 8$	$J = 10$	$J = 12$	$J = 16$	$J = 20$
X = 2											
2	23.11	31.55	37.09	41.19	44.41	47.06	49.31	52.94	55.82	60.20	63.47
3	11.97	15.56	17.91	19.66	21.05	22.19	23.16	24.75	26.01	27.93	29.38
4	8.69	10.95	12.43	13.54	14.41	15.14	15.76	16.77	17.58	18.81	19.74
5	7.20	8.89	9.99	10.81	11.47	12.01	12.47	13.23	13.84	14.77	15.47
6	6.36	7.75	8.64	9.31	9.85	10.29	10.66	11.28	11.77	12.54	13.11
7	5.84	7.03	7.80	8.37	8.83	9.21	9.53	10.06	10.49	11.14	11.64
8	5.48	6.54	7.23	7.74	8.14	8.48	8.76	9.23	9.61	10.19	10.63
10	5.02	5.93	6.51	6.93	7.27	7.55	7.79	8.19	8.50	8.99	9.36
12	4.74	5.56	6.07	6.45	6.75	7.00	7.21	7.56	7.84	8.27	8.60
14	4.56	5.31	5.78	6.13	6.40	6.63	6.82	7.14	7.40	7.79	8.09
16	4.42	5.14	5.58	5.90	6.16	6.37	6.55	6.85	7.08	7.45	7.73
18	4.32	5.00	5.43	5.73	5.98	6.18	6.35	6.63	6.85	7.19	7.46
20	4.25	4.90	5.31	5.60	5.84	6.03	6.19	6.46	6.67	7.00	7.25
24	4.14	4.76	5.14	5.42	5.63	5.81	5.96	6.21	6.41	6.71	6.95
30	4.03	4.62	4.98	5.24	5.44	5.61	5.75	5.98	6.16	6.44	6.66
40	3.93	4.48	4.82	5.07	5.26	5.41	5.54	5.76	5.93	6.19	6.38
60	3.83	4.36	4.68	4.90	5.08	5.22	5.35	5.54	5.70	5.94	6.12
120	3.73	4.24	4.54	4.75	4.91	5.05	5.16	5.35	5.49	5.71	5.88
X = 3											
2	26.54	36.26	42.64	47.36	51.07	54.13	56.71	60.90	64.21	69.25	73.01
3	13.45	17.51	20.17	22.15	23.72	25.01	26.11	27.90	29.32	31.50	33.13
4	9.59	12.11	13.77	15.00	15.98	16.79	17.47	18.60	19.50	20.87	21.91
5	7.83	9.70	10.92	11.82	12.54	13.14	13.65	14.48	15.15	10.17	16.95
6	6.85	8.36	9.34	10.07	10.65	11.13	11.54	12.22	12.75	13.59	14.21
7	6.23	7.52	8.36	8.98	9.47	9.88	10.23	10.80	11.26	11.97	12.51
8	5.81	6.95	7.69	8.23	8.67	9.03	9.33	9.84	10.24	10.87	11.34
10	5.27	6.23	6.84	7.30	7.66	7.96	8.21	8.63	8.96	9.48	9.88
12	4.94	5.80	6.34	6.74	7.05	7.31	7.54	7.90	8.20	8.65	9.00
14	4.72	5.51	6.00	6.36	6.65	6.89	7.09	7.42	7.69	8.10	8.41
16	4.56	5.30	5.76	6.10	6.37	6.59	6.77	7.08	7.33	7.71	8.00
18	4.44	5.15	5.59	5.90	6.16	6.36	6.54	6.83	7.06	7.42	7.69
20	4.35	5.03	5.45	5.75	5.99	6.19	6.36	6.63	6.85	7.19	7.45
24	4.22	4.86	5.25	5.54	5.76	5.94	6.10	6.35	6.55	6.87	7.11
30	4.10	4.70	5.06	5.33	5.54	5.71	5.85	6.08	6.27	6.56	6.78
40	3.98	4.54	4.88	5.13	5.32	5.48	5.61	5.83	6.00	6.27	6.47
60	3.86	4.39	4.72	4.95	5.12	5.27	5.39	5.59	5.75	6.00	6.18
120	3.75	4.25	4.55	4.77	4.94	5.07	5.18	5.37	5.51	5.74	5.90

Source: Tables 1A and 1B from Bryant, J. L. & Paulson, A. S. (1976). An extension of Tukey's method of multiple comparisons to experimental designs with random concomitant variables, *Biometrika*, *63*, 631–638. By permission of Oxford University Press.

References

Aberson, C. L. (2010). *Applied power analysis for the behavioral sciences.* New York, NY: Routledge.

Agresti, A. (2013). *Categorical data analysis.* Hoboken, NJ: Wiley-Interscience.

Agresti, A. (2018). *Statistical methods for the social sciences* (5th ed.). Upper Saddle River, NJ: Pearson.

Agresti, A., & Pendergast, J. (1986). Comparing mean ranks for repeated measures data. *Communications in Statistics: Theory and Method, 15,* 1417–1433.

Aguinis, H. (2004). *Regression analysis for categorical moderators.* New York, NY: Guilford.

Aguinis, H., & Stone-Romero, E. F. (1997). Methodological artifacts in moderated multiple regression and their effects on statistical power. *Journal of Applied Psychology, 82*(1), 192–206. doi: 10.1037/0021-9010.82.1.192.

Aguinis, H., Beaty, J. C., Boik, R. J., & Pierce, C. A. (2005). Effect size and power in assessing moderating effects of categorical variables using multiple regression: A 30-year review. *Journal of Applied Psychology, 90*(1), 94–107.

Aiken, L. S., & West, S. G. (1991). *Multiple regression: Testing and interpreting interactions.* Newbury Park, CA: Sage Publications.

Aldrich, J. H., & Nelson, F. D. (1984). *Linear probability, logit, and probit models.* Beverly Hills, CA: Sage.

Algina, J., & Keselman, H. J. (2003). Approximate confidence intervals for effect sizes. *Educational and Psychological Measurement, 63*(4), 537–553.

Algina, J., & Olejnik, S. (2000). Determining sample size for accurate estimation of the squared multiple correlation coefficient. *Multivariate Behavioral Research, 35,* 119–136.

Algina, J., Blair, R. C., & Coombs, W. T. (1995). A maximum test for scale: Type I error rates and power. *Journal of Educational and Behavioral Statistics, 20*(1), 27–39.

Algina, J., Keselman, H. J., & Penfield, R. D. (2005). Effect sizes and their intervals: The two-level repeated measures case. *Educational and Psychological Measurement, 65*(2), 241–258.

American Psychological Association. (2010). *Publication manual of the American Psychological Association.* Washington, DC: American Psychological Association.

Amrhein, V., & Greenland, S. (2018). Remove, rather than redefine, statistical significance. *Nature Human Behaviour, 2*(1), 4.

Andrews, D. F. (1971). Significance tests based on residuals. *Biometrika, 58,* 139–148.

Applebaum, M. I., & Cramer, E. M. (1974). Some problems in the nonorthogonal analysis of variance. *Psychological Bulletin, 81,* 335–343.

Atiqullah, M. (1964). The robustness of the covariance analysis of a one-way classification. *Biometrika, 51*(3/4), 365–373.

Atkinson, A. C. (1987). *Plots, transformations, and regression.* Oxford, UK: Oxford University Press.

Barnett, V., & Lewis, T. (1994). *Outliers in statistical data* (3rd ed.). Chichester, UK: Wiley.

Basu, S., & DasGupta, A. (1995). Robustness of standard confidence intervals for location parameters under departure from normality. *The Annals of Statistics, 23*(4), 1433–1442.

Batanero, C., & Chernoff, E. J. (2018). *Teaching and learning stochastics: Advances in probability education research.* Cham, Switzerland: Springer.

Bates, D. M., & Watts, D. G. (1988). *Nonlinear regression analysis and its applications.* New York, NY: Wiley.

Bauer, D. J., & Curran, P. J. (2005). Probing interactions in fixed and multilevel regression: Inferential and graphical techniques. *Multivariate Behavioral Research, 40*(3), 373–400.

Beal, S. L. (1987). Asymptotic confidence intervals for the difference between two binomial parameters for use with small samples. *Biometrics,* (4), 941–950. doi:10.2307/2531547

Beckman, R. J., & Cook, R. D. (1983). Outliers [in statistical data]. *Technometrics, 25,* 119–149.

Belsley, D. A. (1991). *Conditioning diagnostics: Collinearity and weak data in regression.* New York, NY: Wiley.

Belsley, D. A., Kuh, E., & Welsch, R. E. (1980). *Regression diagnostics.* New York, NY: Wiley.

Benjamin, D. J., Berger, J. O., Johannesson, M., Nosek, B. A., Wagenmakers, E. J., Berk, R., . . . Fehr, E. (2018). Redefine statistical significance. *Nature Human Behaviour*, *2*(1), 6–10.

Benjamini, Y., & Hochberg, Y. (1995). Controlling the false discovery rate: A practical and powerful approach to multiple testing. *Journal of the Royal Statistical Society. Series B*, *57*(1), 289–300.

Berg, L., & Brännström, L. (2018). Evicted children and subsequent placement in out-of-home care: A cohort study. *PLoS ONE, 13*(4), 1–13. doi: 10.1371/journal.pone.0195295.

Berk, R. A. (2016). *Statistical learning from a regression perspective* (2nd ed.). Cham, Switzerland: Springer.

Berry, W. D., & Feldman, S. (1985). *Multiple regression in practice*. Beverly Hills, CA: Sage.

Bodner, T. E. (2017). Standardized effect sizes for moderated conditional fixed effects with continuous moderator variables. *Frontiers in Psychology, 8*. doi: 10.3389/fpsyg.2017.00562.

Boik, R. (1981). A priori tests in repeated measures designs: Effects of nonsphericity. *Psychometrika, 46*(3), 241–255.

Boik, R. J. (1979). Interactions, partial interactions, and interaction contrasts in the analysis of variance. *Psychological Bulletin, 86*(5), 1084–1089. doi: 10.1037/0033–2909.86.5.1084.

Bonett, D. G., & Seier, E. (2002). A test of normality with high uniform power. *Computational Statistics and Data Analysis, 40*, 435–445. doi:10.1016/S0167-9473(02)00074-9

Bonett, D. G., & Wright, T. A. (2000). Sample size requirements for estimating Pearson, Kendall and Spearman correlations. *Psychometrika, 65*(1), 23–28. doi:10.1007/BF02294183

Borm, G. F., Fransen, J., & Lemmens, W. A. J. G. (2007). A simple sample size formula for analysis of covariance in randomized clinical trials. *Journal of Clinical Epidemiology, 60*, 1234–1238. doi: 10.1016/j.jclinepi.2007.02.006.

Box, G. E. P. (1954). Some theorems on quadratic forms applied in the study of analysis of variance problems, II: Effects of Inequality of variance and of correlation between errors in the two-way classification. *The Annals of Mathematical Statistics, 25*(3), 484–498.

Box, G. E. P., & Anderson, S. L. (1962). *Robust tests for variances and effect of non-normality and variance heterogeneity on standard tests* (Technical Report Number 7, Ordinance Project Number TB 2–0001 (832)). Retrieved from Bryant, J. L., & Paulson, A. S. (1976). An extension of Tukey's method of multiple comparisons to experimental designs with random concomitant variables. *Biometrika, 63*(3), 631–638.

Box, G. E. P., & Cox, D. R. (1964). An analysis of transformations. *Journal of the Royal Statistical Society, 26*(Series B), 211–243.

Bradley, J. V. (1978). Robustness? *The British Journal of Mathematical and Statistical Psychology, 31*(2), 144–152.

Bradley, J. V. (1982). The insidious L-shaped distribution. *Bulletin of the Psychonomic Society, 20*(2), 85–88.

Brown, M. B., & Forsythe, A. B. (1974). The ANOVA and multiple comparisons for data with heterogeneous variances. *Biometrics,* (4), 719–724. doi: 10.2307/2529238.

Brunner, E., Dette, H., & Munk, A. (1997). Box-type approximations in nonparametric factorial sesigns. *Journal of the American Statistical Association, 92*(440), 1494–1502. doi: 10.2307/2965420.

Bryant, J. L., & Paulson, A. S. (1976). An extension of Tukey's method of multiple comparisons to experimental designs with random concomitant variables. *Biometrika, 63*(3), 631–638.

Buyse, M., & Molenberghs, G. (1998). Criteria for the validation of surrogate endpoints in randomized experiments. *Biometrics, 54*(3), 1014–1029.

Campbell, D. T., & Stanley, J. C. (1966). *Experimental and non-experimental designs*. Chicago: Rand McNally.

Card, D., Lee, D. S., Pei, Z., & Weber, A. (2016). *Regression kink design: Theory and practice* . Retrieved from Cambridge, MA: https://www.nber.org/papers/w22781.pdf.

Carlson, J. E., & Timm, N. H. (1974). Analysis of nonorthogonal fixed-effects designs. *Psychological Bulletin, 81*(9), 563–570. doi: 10.1037/h0036936.

Carroll, R. J., & Ruppert, D. (1982). Robust estimation in heteroscedastic linear models. *Annals of Statistics, 10*, 429–441.

Carroll, R. J., & Schneider, H. (1985). A note on levene's tests for equality of variances. *Statistics and Probability Letters, 3*, 191–194. doi:10.1016/0167-7152(85)90016-1

Carroll, R., & Nordholm, L. A. (1975). Sampling characteristics of Kelley's epsilon2 and Hays' omega2. *Educational & Psychological Measurement, 35*, 541–554.

Celik, N., & Senoglu, B. (2018). Robust estimation and testing in one-way ANOVA for Type II censored samples: skew normal error terms. *Journal of Statistical Computation and Simulation, 88*(7), 1382–1393. doi: 10.1080/00949655.2018.1433670.

Chakravart, I. M., Laha, R. G., & Roy, J. (1967). *Handbook of methods of applied statistics* (Vol. 1). New York, NY: Wiley.

Chambers, J. M. (1983). *Graphical methods for data analysis*. Belmont, CA: Wadsworth.

Chandrasekhar, C. K., Bagyalakshmi, H., Srinivasan, M. R., & Gallo, M. (2016). Partial ridge regression under multicollinearity. *Journal of Applied Statistics, 43*(13), 2462–2473. doi: 10.1080/02664763.2016.1181726.

Chatterjee, S., & Price, B. (1977). *Regression analysis by example*. New York, NY: Wiley.

Cleveland, W. S. (1994). *The elements of graphing data* (Rev. ed.). Murray Hill, NJ: AT&T Bell Laboratories.

Clinch, J. J., & Keselman, H. J. (1982). Parametric alternatives to the analysis of variance. *Journal of Educational Statistics, 7*.

Coe, P. R., & Tamhane, A. C. (1993). Small sample confidence intervals for the difference, ratio, and odds ratio of two success probabilities. *Communications in Statistics-Simulation and Computation, 22*, 925–938.

Cohen, J. (1968). Multiple regression as a general data-analytic system. *Psychological Bulletin, 70*(6), 426–443. doi: 10.1037/h0026714.

Cohen, J. (1988). *Statistical power analysis for the behavioral sciences* (2nd ed.). Hillsdale, NJ: Lawrence Erlbaum.

Cohen, J., & Cohen, P. (1983). *Applied multiple regression/correlation analysis for the behavioral sciences* (2nd ed.). Hillsdale, NJ: Erlbaum.

Cohen, J., Cohen, P., West, S. G., & Aiken, L. S. (2003). *Applied multiple regression/correlation analysis for the behavioral sciences* (3rd ed.). Mahwah, NJ: Lawrence Erlbaum Associates.

Conover, W. J., & Iman, R. L. (1981). Rank transformations as a bridge between parametric and nonparametric statistics. *The American Statistician*, (3), 124–129. doi:10.2307/2683975

Conover, W. J., & Iman, R. L. (1982). Analysis of covariance using the rank transformation. *Biometrics*, (3), 715–724. doi: 10.2307/2530051.

Cook, R. D. (1977). Detection of influential observation in linear regression. *Technometrics, 19*(1), 15.

Cook, R. D. (2000). Detection of influential observation in linear regression. *Technometrics, 42*(1), 65–68. doi: 10.2307/1271434.

Cook, R. D., & Campbell, D. T. (1979). *Quasi-experimentation: Design and analysis issues for field settings*. Chicago, IL: Rand McNally.

Cook, R. D., & Weisberg, S. (1982). *Residuals and influence in regression*. London, England: Chapman & Hall.

Coombs, W. T., Algina, J., & Oltman, D. O. (1996). Univariate and multivariate omnibus hypothesis tests selected to control Type I error rates when population variances are not necessarily equal. *Review of Educational Research, 66*(2), 137–179.

Cotton, J. W. (1998). *Analyzing within-subjects experiments*. Mahwah, NJ: Lawrence Erlbaum.

Cowles, M., & Davis, C. (1982). On the origins of the .05 level of statistical significance. *American Psychologist, 37*(5), 553–558. doi:10.1037/0003-066X.37.5.553

Cowles, M., & Davis, C. (1982). On the origins of the .05 level of statistical significance. *American Psychologist, 37*(5), 553–558. doi: 10.1037/0003-066X.37.5.553.

Cox, B., Reason, R., Nix, S., & Gillman, M. (2016). Life happens (outside of college): Non-college life-events and students' likelihood of graduation. *Research in Higher Education, 57*(7), 823–844. doi: 10.1007/s11162-016-9409-z.

Cox, D. R., & Snell, E. J. (1989). *Analysis of binary data* (2nd ed.). London: Chapman and Hall.

Cramer, E. M., & Applebaum, M. I. (1908). Nonorthogonal analysis of variance--Once again. *Pyschological Bulletin, 87*(51–57).

Crane, H. (2018). The impact of *p*-hacking on "redefine statistical significance". *Basic & Applied Social Psychology, 40*(4), 219–235. doi:10.1080/01973533.2018.1474111

Crane, H. (2018). The impact of *p*-hacking on "redefine statistical significance". *Basic & Applied Social Psychology, 40*(4), 219–235. doi: 10.1080/01973533.2018.1474111.
Crawley, M. J. (2013). *The R book* (2nd ed.). Hoboken, NJ: John Wiley & Sons.
Cribari-Neto, F. (2004). Asymptotic inference under heteroskedasticity of unknown form. *Computational Statistics and Data Analysis, 45*, 215–233. doi: 10.1016/S0167–9473(02)00366–3.
Cristea, I. A., & Ioannidis, J. P. A. (2018). P values in display items are ubiquitous and almost invariably significant: A survey of top science journals. *PLoS One, 13*(5), 1–15. doi:10.1371/journal.pone.0197440
Cristea, I. A., & Ioannidis, J. P. A. (2018). P values in display items are ubiquitous and almost invariably significant: A survey of top science journals. *PLoS ONE, 13*(5), 1–15. doi: 10.1371/journal.pone.0197440.
Cronbach, L. J. (1987). Statistical tests for moderator variables: Flaws in analyses recently proposed. *Psychological Bulletin*, (3), 414–417.
Croux, C., Flandre, C., & Haesbroeck, G. (2002). The breakdown behavior of the maximum likelihood estimator in the logistic regression model. *Statistics and probability letters, 60*, 377–386.
Cumming, G., & Calin-Jageman, R. (2017). *Introduction to the new statistics: Estimation, open science, and beyond*. New York, NY: Routledge.
Cumming, G., & Finch, S. (2001). A primer on the understanding, use, and calculation of confidence intervals that are based on central and noncentral distributions. *Educational and Psychological Measurement, 61*(4), 532–574.
D'Agostino, R. B. (1970). Transformation to normality of the null distribution of g1. *Biometrika, 57*(3), 679–681.
D'Agostino, R. B., Belanger, A., & D'Agostino, R. B. J. (1990). A suggestion for using powerful and informative tests of normality. *The American Statistician*, (4), 316–321. doi:10.2307/2684359
Darlington, R. B., & Hayes, A. F. (2017). *Regression analysis and linear models*. New York, NY: Guilford.
David, F. A., & Daryl, P. (1978). Finding the outliers that matter. *Journal of the Royal Statistical Society. Series B (Methodological), 40*(1), 85.
Derksen, S., & Keselman, H. J. (1992). Backward, forward and stepwise automated subset selection algorithms: Frequency of obtaining authentic and noise variables. *British Journal of Mathematical and Statistical Psychology, 45*, 265–282.
Ditlevsen, S., Christensen, U., Lynch, J., Damsgaard, M. T., & Keiding, N. (2005). The mediation proportion: A structural equation approach for estimating the proportion of exposure effect on outcome explained by an intermediate variable. *Epidemiology, 15*(1), 114–120. doi: 10.1097/01.ede.0000147107.76079.07.
Dong, N., & Society for Research on Educational, E. (2014). *Power analysis to detect the effects of a continuous moderator in 2-level simple cluster random assignment experiments*. Retrieved from Evanston, IL: https://login.ezproxy.net.ucf.edu/login?auth=shibb&url=https://search.ebscohost.com/login.aspx?direct=true&db=eric&AN=ED562787&site=eds-live&scope=site
Dong, N., Kelcey, B., & Spybrook, J. (2018). Power analyses for moderator effects in three-level cluster randomized trials. *Journal of Experimental Education, 86*(3), 489–514.
Duncan, G. T., & Layard, M. W. J. (1973). A Monte-Carlo study of asymptotically robust tests for correlation coefficients. *Biometrika, 60*(3), 551–558.
Dunn, O. J. (1961). Multiple comparisons among means. *Journal of the American Statistical Association*, (293), 52–64. doi: 10.2307/2282330.
Dunn, O. J. (1974). On multiple tests and confidence intervals. *Communications in Statistics, 3*(1), 101–103.
Dunn, O. J., & Clark, V. (1987). *Applied statistics: Analysis of variance and regression* (2nd ed.). New York, NY: Wiley, c1987.
Dunn, O. J., & Clark, V. A. (1987). *Applied statistics: Analysis of variance and regression*. New York, NY: Wiley.
Dunnett, C. W. (1955). A multiple comparison procedure for comparing several treatments with a control. *Journal of the American Statistical Association*, (272), 1096–1121. doi: 10.2307/2281208.
Dunnett, C. W. (1964). New tables for multiple comparisons with a control. *Biometrics*, (3), 482–491. doi: 10.2307/2528490.

Dunnett, C. W. (1980). Pairwise multiple comparisons in the unequal variance case. *Journal of the American Statistical Association, 75*(372), 796–800. doi: 10.2307/2287161.

Durbin, J., & Watson, G. S. (1950). Testing for serial correlation in least squares regression: I. *Biometrika, 37*(3/4), 409–428.

Durbin, J., & Watson, G. S. (1950). Testing for serial correlation in least squares regression. *Biometrika, 37*, 409–428.

Durbin, J., & Watson, G. S. (1951). Testing for serial correlation in least squares regression: II. *Biometrika, 38*(1/2), 159–178.

Durbin, J., & Watson, G. S. (1951). Testing for serial correlation in least squares regression, II. *Biometrika, 38*, 159–178.

Durbin, J., & Watson, G. S. (1971). Testing for serial correlation in least squares regression: III. *Biometrika, 58*(1), 1–19.

Durbin, J., & Watson, G. S. (1971). Testing for serial correlation in least squares regression, III. *Biometrika, 58*, 1–19.

Egbewale, B. E., Lewis, M., & Sim, J. (2014). Bias, precision and statistical power of analysis of covariance in the analysis of randomized trials with baseline imbalance: A simulation study. *BMC Medical Research Methodology*, 14–49.

Elashoff, J. D. (1969). Analysis of covariance: A delicate instrument. *American Educational Research Journal, 6*(3), 383–401.

Erdfelder, E., Faul, F., & Buchner, A. (1996). GPOWER: A general power analysis program. *Behavior Research Methods, Instruments & Computers, 28*(1), 1–11.

Fahrmeir, L., Kneib, T., Lang, S., & Marx, B. (2013). *Regression: Models, methods, and applications*. Berlin, Heidelberg: Springer.

Faul, F., Erdfelder, E., Buchner, A., & Lang, A.-G. (2009). Statistical power analysis using G*Power 3.1: Tests for correlation and regression analyses. *Behavior Research Methods, 41*(4), 1149–1160.

Faul, F., Erdfelder, E., Lang, A.-G., & Buchner, A. (2007). G*Power 3: A flexible statistical power analysis program for the social, behavioral, and biomedical sciences. *Behavior Research Methods, 39*(2), 175–191.

Feldt, L. (1958). A comparison of the precision of three experimental designs employing a concomitant variable. *Psychometrika, 23*(4), 335–354.

Ferguson, G. A., & Takane, Y. (1989). *Statistical analysis in psychology and education* (6th ed.). New York, NY: McGraw Hill.

Fern, E. F., & Monroe, K. B. (1996). Effect-size estimates: Issues and problems in interpretation. *Journal of Consumer Research, 23*(2), 89–105.

Festing, M. F. W. (2014). Randomized block experimental designs can increase the power and reproducibility of laboratory animal experiments. *ILAR Journal, 55*(3), 472–476.

Fidler, F., & Thompson, B. (2001). Computing correct confidence intervals for ANOVA fixed-and random-effects effect sizes. *Educational and Psychological Measurement, 61*(4), 575–604.

Finch, S., & Cumming, G. (2009). Putting research in context: Understanding confidence intervals from one or more studies. *Journal of Pediatric Psychology, 34*(9), 903–916.

Fink, A. (2002). *How to sample in surveys* (2nd ed.). Thousand Oaks, CA: Sage.

Fisher, R. A. (1925). *Statistical methods for research workers* (2d ed., rev. and enl. ed.). Edinburgh, London: Oliver and Boyd.

Fisher, R. A. (1926). The arrangement of field experiments. *Journal of the Ministry of Agriculture, 33*, 503–513.

Fisher, R. A. (1935). Statistical tests. *Nature, 136*(3438), 474.

Fisher, R. A. (1942). *The design of experiments* (3d ed.). Edinburgh, UK: Oliver and Boyd.

Freedman, L. S. (2002). Confidence intervals and statistical power of the 'validation' ratio for surrogate or intermediate endpoints. *Journal of Statistical Planning and Inference, 96*, 143–153.

Friedman, M. (1937). The use of ranks to avoid the assumption of normality implicit in the analysis of variance. *Journal of the American Statistical Association*, (200), 675–701. doi: 10.2307/2279372.

Friedman, M. (1937). The use of ranks to avoid the assumption of normality implicit in the analysis of variance. *Journal of the American Statistical Association, 32*(200), 675–701. doi: 10.2307/2279372.

Fritz, M. S., & MacKinnon, D. P. (2007). Required sample size to detect the mediated effect. *Psychological Science, 18*(3), 233–239. doi: 10.1111/j.1467-9280.2007.01882.x.

Gabor, A. (1990). *The man who discovered quality: How W. Edwards Deming brought the quality revolution to America: The stories of Ford, Xerox, and GM* (1st ed.). New York, NY: Times Books.

Games, P. A., & Howell, J. F. (1976). Pairwise multiple comparison procedures with unequal N's and/or variances: A Monte Carlo study. *Journal of Educational Statistics, 1*(2), 113–125. doi: 10.2307/1164979.

Geisser, S., & Greenhouse, S. W. (1958). An extension of Box's results on the use of the F distribution in multivariate analysis. *The Annals of Mathematical Statistics*, (3), 885.

Geisser, S., & Greenhouse, S. W. (1958). An extension of Box's results on the use of the F distribution in multivariate analysis. *The Annals of Mathematical Statistics, 29*(3), 885.

Ghosh, B. K. (1979). A comparison of some approximate confidence intervals for the binomial parameter. *Journal of the American Statistical Association, 74*, 894–900.

Glass, G. V., & Hopkins, K. D. (1996). *Statistical methods in education and psychology* (3rd ed.). Boston, MA: Allyn and Bacon.

Glass, G. V., Peckham, P. D., & Sanders, J. R. (1972). Consequences of failure to meet assumptions underlying the fixed effects analyses of variance and covariance. *Review of Educational Research*, (3), 237–288.

Greenwood, P. E., & Nikulin, M. S. (1996). *A guide to chi-squared testing*. New York, NY: John Wiley & Sons.

Grissom, R. J., & Kim, J. J. (2005). *Effect sizes for research: A broad practical approach*. Mahway, NJ: Lawrence Erlbaum Associates.

Grissom, R. J., & Kim, J. J. (2012). *Effect sizes for research: Univariate and multivariate applications* (2nd ed.). New York NY: Routledge.

Hahs-Vaughn, D. L. (2005). A primer for using and understanding weights with national datasets. *Journal of Experimental Education, 73*(3), 221–248.

Hahs-Vaughn, D. L. (2006a). Analysis of data from complex samples. *International Journal of Research & Method in Education, 29*(2), 163–181.

Hahs-Vaughn, D. L. (2006b). Weighting omissions and best practices when using large-scale data in educational research. *Association for Institutional Research Professional File*, (101), 1–9.

Hahs-Vaughn, D. L. (2016). *Applied multivariate statistical concepts*. New York, NY: Routledge/Taylor & Francis.

Hahs-Vaughn, D. L., McWayne, C. M., Bulotskey-Shearer, R. J., Wen, X., & Faria, A. (2011a). Complex sample data recommendations and troubleshooting. *Evaluation Review, 35*(3), 304–313. doi:10.1177/0193841X11412070

Hahs-Vaughn, D. L., McWayne, C. M., Bulotskey-Shearer, R. J., Wen, X., & Faria, A. (2011b). Methodological considerations in using complex survey data: An applied example with the Head Start Family and Child Experiences Survey. *Evaluation Review, 35*(3), 269–303.

Hair, J. F., Black, W. C., Babin, B. J., Anderson, R. E., & Tatham, R. L. (2006). *Multivariate data analysis* (6th ed.). Upper Saddle River, NJ: Pearson Prentice Hall.

Hancock, G. R., & Mueller, R. O. (2010). *The reviewer's guide to quantitative methods in the social sciences*. New York, NY: Routledge.

Hand, D. J. (2009). Measuring classifier performance: a coherent alternative to the area under the ROC curve. *Machine Learning, 77*(1), 103.

Hansen, W. B., & McNeal, R. B., Jr. (1996). The law of maximum expected potential effect: Constraints placed on program effectiveness by mediator relationships. *Health Education Research, 11*(4), 501–507. doi: 10.1093/her/11.4.501.

Harlow, L. L., Mulaik, S. A., & Steiger, J. H. (Eds.). (1997). *What if there were no significance tests?* Mahwah, NJ: Lawrence Erlbaum Associates.

Harrell, F. E. J. (1986). The LOGIST procedure. In I. SAS Institute (Ed.), *SUGI supplemental library user's guide* (5 ed., pp. 269–293). Cary, NC: SAS Institute, Inc.

Hartley, J. (1992). A postscript to Wainer's "Understanding graphs and tables". *Educational Researcher, 21*, 25–26. doi:10.2307/1176844

Harwell, M. R. (1992). Summarizing Monte Carlo results in methodological research. *Journal of Educational Statistics*, (4), 297–313. doi: 10.2307/1165126.

Harwell, M. R. (2003). Summarizing Monte Carlo results in methodological research: The single--factor, fixed-effects ANCOVA case. *Journal of Educational and Behavioral Statistics, 28*, 45–70.

Hausman, C., & Rapson, D. S. (2017). *Regression discontinuity in time: Considerations for empirical applications*. Cambridge, MA: National Bureau of Economic Research.

Hawkins, D. M. (1980). *Identification of outliers*. London; New York, NY: Chapman and Hall.

Hayes, A. F. (2013). *Introduction to mediation, moderation, and conditional process analysis: A regression-based approach*. New York, NY: Guilford.

Hayes, A. F. (n.d.). The PROCESS macro for SPSS and SAS (Version 3.2). Retrieved from http://processmacro.org/index.html

Hayes, A. F., & Cai, L. (2007). Using heteroskedasticity-consistent standard error estimators in OLS regression: An introduction and software implementation. *Behavior Research Methods, 39*(4), 709–722.

Hays, W. L. (1988). *Statistics* (4th ed.). New York, NY: Holt, Rinehart and Winston.

Hayter, A., J. (1986). The maximum familywise error rate of Fisher's least significant difference test. *Journal of the American Statistical Association, 81*(396), 1000–1004. doi: 10.2307/2289074.

Heck, R. H., Tabata, L. N., & Thomas, S. L. (2014). *Multilevel and longitudinal modeling with IBM SPSS* (2nd ed.). New York, NY: Routledge.

Hellevik, O. (2009). Linear versus logistic regression when the dependent variable is a dichotomy. *Quality and Quantity, 43*(1), 59–74.

Hemmert, G. A. J., Schons, L. M., Wieseke, J., & Schimmelpfennig, H. (2018). Log-likelihood-based pseudo-R2 in logistic regression. *Sociological Methods & Research, 47*(3), 507–531. doi: 10.1177/0049124116638107.

Heyde, C. C., Seneta, E., Crepel, P., Feinberg, S. E., & Gain, J. (Eds.). (2001). *Statisticians of the centuries*. New York, NY: Springer.

Hilbe, J. M. (2016). *Practical guide to logistic regression*. Boca Raton: CRC Press/Taylor & Francis.

Hirji, K. F., Tsiatis, A. A., & Mehta, C. R. (1989). Median unbiased estimation for binary data. *The American Statistician, 43*(1), 7. doi: 10.2307/2685158.

Hochberg, Y. (1988). A sharper Bonferroni procedure for multiple tests of significance. *Biometrika, 75*(4), 800–802.

Hochberg, Y., & Tamhane, A. C. (1987). *Multiple comparison procedures*. New York, NY: Wiley.

Hochberg, Y., & Varon-Salomon, Y. (1984). On Simultaneous Pairwise Comparisons in Analysis of Covariance. *Journal of the American Statistical Association*, (388), 863–866. doi: 10.2307/2288716.

Hocking, R. R. (1976). The analysis and selection of variables in linear regression. *Biometrics, 32*(1), 1–49.

Hoenig, J. M., & Heisey, D. M. (2001). The abuse of power: The pervasive fallacy of power calculations for data analysis. *The American Statistician, 55*(1), 19–24.

Hoerl, A. E., & Kennard, R. W. (1970a). Ridge regression: Application to non-orthogonal models. *Technometrics, 12*, 591–612.

Hoerl, A. E., & Kennard, R. W. (1970b). Ridge regression: Biased estimation for non-orthogonal models. *Technometrics, 12*, 55–67.

Hogg, R. V., & Craig, A. T. (1995). *Introduction to mathematical statistics* (5th ed.). Englewood Cliffs, NJ: Prentice Hall.

Hosmer, D. W., & Lemeshow, S. (1989). *Applied logistic regression*. New York, NY: Wiley.

Hosmer, D. W., Hosmer, T., LeCessie, S., & Lemeshow, S. (1997). A comparison of goodness-of-fit tests for the logistic regression model. *Statistics in Medicine, 16*, 965–980.

Hosmer, D. W., Lemeshow, S., & Sturdivant, R. X. (2000). *Applied logistic regression* (2nd ed.). Hoboken, NJ: John Wiley & Sons, Inc.

Howard, W. (1984). How to display data badly. *The American Statistician, 38*(2), 137–147. doi:10.2307/2683253

Howell, D. C. (2010). *Statistical methods for psychology* (7th ed.). Belmont, CA: Thomson Wadsworth.

Hox, J. J., Moerbeek, M., & van de Schoot, R. (2017). *Multilevel analysis: Techniques and applications* (3rd ed.). New York, NY: Routledge.

Huang, B., Sivaganesan, S., Succop, P., & Goodman, E. (2004). Statistical assessment of mediational effects for logistic mediational models. *Statistics in Medicine, 23*(17), 2713–2728.

Huberty, C. J. (1989). Problems with stepwise methods--Better alternatives. In B. Thompson (Ed.), *Advances in social science methodology* (Vol. 1, pp. 43–70). Greenwich, CT: JAI Press.

Huck, S. W. (2000). *Reading statistics and research* (3rd ed.). New York, NY: Longman.

Huck, S. W. (2012). *Reading statistics and research* (6th ed.). Boston, MA: Pearson.

Huck, S. W. (2016). *Statistical misconceptions.* New York, NY: Routledge.

Huck, S. W., & McLean, R. A. (1975). Using a repeated measures ANOVA to analyze the data from a pretest-posttest design: A potentially confusing task. *Psychological Bulletin, 82*(4), 511–518. doi: 10.1037/h0076767.

Huitema, B. E. (2011). *Analysis of covariance and alternatives statistical methods for experiments, quasi-experiments, and single-case studies* (2nd ed.). Hoboken, NJ: Wiley.

Huynh, H., & Feldt, L. S. (1970). Conditions under which mean square ratios in repeated measurements designs have exact F-distributions. *Journal of the American Statistical Association, 65*(332), 1582. doi: 10.2307/2284340.

Huynh, H., & Feldt, L., S. . (1970). Conditions under which mean square ratios in repeated measurements designs have exact F-distributions. *Journal of the American Statistical Association,* (332), 1582. doi: 10.2307/2284340.

Jaeger, R. M. (1984). *Sampling in education and the social sciences.* New York, NY: Longman.

James, G. S. (1951). The comparison of several groups of observations when the ratios of the population variances are unknown *Biometrika, 38*(3/4), 324–329.

Jennings, E. (1988). Models for pretest-posttest data: Repeated measures ANOVA revisited. *Journal of Educational Statistics, 13*(3), 273. doi: 10.2307/1164655.

Jiang, H., Kulkarni, P. M., Mallinckrodt, C. H., Shurzinske, L., Molenberghs, G., & Lipkovich, I. (2017). Covariate adjustment for logistic regression analysis of binary clinical trial data. *Statistics in Biopharmaceutical Research, 9*(1), 126–134.

Joanes, D. N., & Gill, C. A. (1998). Comparing measures of sample skewness and kurtosis. *Journal of the Royal Statistical Society. Series D (The Statistician)*(1), 183–189.

Johansen, S. (1980). The Welch-James approximation to the distribution of the residual sum of squares in a weighted linear regression. *Biometrika, 67*(1), 85–93.

Johnson, P. O., & Neyman, J. (1936). Tests of certain linear hypotheses and their application to some educational problems. *Statistical Research Memoirs, 1*, 57–93.

Kaiser, L. D., & Bowden, D. C. (1983). Simultaneous confidence intervals for all linear contrasts of means with heterogenous variances. *Communications in Statistics: Theory and Methods, 12*(1), 73–88.

Kalton, G. (1983). *Introduction to survey sampling.* Thousand Oaks, CA: Sage.

Keller, D. K. (2006). *The tao of statistics: A path to understanding (with no math).* Thousand Oaks, CA: Sage.

Kelley, K. (2018). Package MBESS (Version 4.4.3). Retrieved from https://cran.r-project.org/web/packages/MBESS/MBESS.pdf

Kenny, D. A. (n.d.). Power and N computations for mediation. Retrieved from https://davidakenny.shinyapps.io/MedPower/

Keppel, G. (1991). *Design and analysis: A researcher's handbook* (3rd ed.). Englewood Cliffs, NJ: Prentice-Hall, Inc.

Keppel, G., & Wickens, T. D. (2004). *Design and analysis: A researcher's handbook* (4th ed.). Upper Saddle River, NJ: Pearson Prentice Hall.

Kim, Y. J., & Cribbie, R. A. (2018). ANOVA and the variance homogeneity assumption: Exploring a better gatekeeper. *British Journal of Mathematical and Statistical Psychology, 71*(1), 1–12. doi:10.1111/bmsp.12103

Kinney, J. J. (2015). *Probability an introduction with statistical applications* (2nd ed.). Hoboken, NJ: John Wiley & Sons, Inc.

Kirk, R. E. (2013). *Experimental design: Procedures for the behavioral sciences* (4th ed.). Thousand Oaks, CA: Sage Publications, Inc.

Kirk, R. E. (2014). *Experimental design: Procedures for the behavioral sciences*. Thousand Oaks, CA: Sage.

Kisbu-Sakarya, Y., MacKinnon, D. P., & Aiken, L. S. (2013). A Monte Carlo comparison study of the power of the analysis of covariance, simple difference, and residual change scores in testing two-wave data. *Educational & Psychological Measurement, 73*(1), 47–62. doi: 10.1177/0013164412450574.

Kish, L., & Frankel, M. R. (1973, October 17). *Inference from complex samples*. Paper presented at the annual meeting of the Royal Statistical Society.

Kish, L., & Frankel, M. R. (1974). Inference from complex samples. *Journal of the Royal Statistical Society, Series B, 36*, 1–37.

Kleinbaum, D. G., Kupper, L. L., Muller, K. E., & Nizam, A. (1998). *Applied regression analysis and other multivariable models* (3rd ed.). Pacific Grove, CA: Duxbury.

Knafl, G. J., & Ding, K. (2016). *Adaptive regression for modeling nonlinear relationships*. Cham, Switzerland: Springer.

Knofszynski, G. T. (2008). Sample sizes when using multiple linear regression for prediction. *Educational and Psychological Measurement, 68*(3), 431–442.

Koenker, R., Chernozhukov, V., He, X., & Peng, L. (2017). *Handbook of quantile regression* (1st ed.). Boca Raton, FL: CRC Press.

Koren, J. (Ed.). (1970). *The history of statistics, their development and progress in many countries, in memoirs to commemorate the seventy fifth anniversary of The American Statistical Association*. New York, NY: Macmillan.

Korn, E. L., & Graubard, B. I. (1995). Examples of differing weighted and unweighted estimates from a sample survey. *American Statistician, 49*, 291–305.

Kramer, C. Y. (1957). Extension of multiple range tests to group correlated adjusted means. *Biometrics*, (1), 13–18. doi: 10.2307/3001898.

Kreft, I., & de Leeuw, J. (1998). *Introducing multilevel modeling*. Thousand Oaks, CA: Sage.

Kromrey, J. D., & Foster-Johnson, L. (1999). Statistically differentiating between interaction and nonlinearity in multiple regression analysis: A Monte Carlo investigation of a recommended strategy. *Educational & Psychological Measurement, 59*(3), 392–413. doi: 10.1177/00131649921969947.

Kruskal, W. H., & Wallis, W. A. (1952). Use of ranks in one-criterion variance analysis. *Journal of the American Statistical Association, 47*(260), 583–621. doi: 10.2307/2280779.

Kruskal, W. H., & Wallis, W. A. (1953). Errata: Use of ranks in one-criterion variance analysis. *Journal of the American Statistical Association, 48*(264), 907–911. doi: 10.2307/2281082.

Krzanowski, W. J., & Hand, D. J. (2009). *ROC curves for continuous data*. Boca Raton, FL: CRC Press.

Kutner, M., Nachtscheim, C., & Neter, J. (2005). *Applied linear statistical models* (5th ed.). New York, NY: McGraw Hill.

Lachowicz, M. J., Preacher, K. J., & Kelley, K. (2018). A novel measure of effect size for mediation analysis. *Psychological Methods, 23*(2), 244–261. doi: 10.1037/met0000165.

Lamb, G. S. (1984). What you always wanted to know about six but were afraid to ask. *Journal of Irreproducible Results, 29*, 18–20.

Lance, C. E., & Vandenberg, R. J. (2009). *Statistical and methodological myths and urban legends: Doctrine, verity and fable in the organizational and social sciences*. New York, NY: Routledge.

Larsen, W. A., & McCleary, S. J. (1972). The use of partial residual plots in regression anlaysis. *Technometrics, 14*, 781–790.

Lee, E. S., Forthofer, R. N., & Lorimor, R. J. (1989). *Analyzing complex survey data*. Newbury Park, CA: Sage.

Lee, M.-J. (2016). *Matching, regression discontinuity, difference in differences, and beyond*. New York, NY: Oxford University Press.

Levene, H. (1960). Robust tests for equality of variances. In I. Olkin (Ed.), *Contributions to probability and statistics: Essays in honor of Harold Hotelling* (pp. 278–292). Palo Alto, CA: Stanford University Press.

Levin, J. R., Serlin, R. C., & Seaman, M. A. (1994). A controlled, powerful multiple-comparison strategy for several situations. *Psychological Bulletin, 115*(1), 153–159.

Levy, P. S., & Lemeshow, S. (2011). *Sampling of populations: Methods and applications* (4th ed.). Hoboken, NJ: John Wiley & Sons.

Li, J., & Lomax, R. G. (2011). Analysis of variance: what is your statistical software actually doing? *Journal of Experimental Education, 79*, 279–294.

Li, J., & Lomax, R. G. (2011). Analysis of variance: what is your statistical software actually doing? *The Journal of Experimental Education, 79*, 279–294.

Lilliefors, H. (1967). On the Kolmogorov-Smirnov test for normality with mean and variance unknown. *Journal of the American Statistical Association, 62*, 399–402.

Lindenberger, U., & Pötter, U. (1998). The complex nature of unique and shared effects in hierarchical linear regression: Implications for developmental psychology. *Psychological Methods, 3*(2), 218–230. doi: 10.1037/1082–989X.3.2.218.

Liu, X. S. (2014). *Statistical power analysis for the social and behavioral sciences: Basic and advanced techniques*. New York, NY: Routledge.

Lomax, R. G., & Surman, S. H. (2007). Factorial ANOVA in SPSS: Fixed-, random-, and mixed-effects models. In S. S. Sawilowsky (Ed.), *Real data analysis*. Greenwich, CT: Information Age.

Long, J. S. (1997). *Regression models for categorical and limited dependent variables*. Thousand Oaks, CA: SAGE.

Lord, F. M. (1960). Large-sample covariance analysis when the control variable is fallible. *Journal of the American Statistical Association*, (290), 307–321. doi: 10.2307/2281743.

Lord, F. M. (1967). A paradox in the interpretation of group comparisons. *Psychological Bulletin, 68*(5), 304–305. doi: 10.1037/h0025105.

Lord, F. M. (1969). Statistical adjustments when comparing preexisting groups. *Psychological Bulletin, 72*(5), 336–337. doi: 10.1037/h0028108.

Lumley, T. (2004). Analysis of complex survey samples. *Journal of Statistical Software, 9*(8), 1–19.

Maalouf, M. m. m. k. a. a., Homouz, D., & Trafalis, T. B. (2018). Logistic regression in large rare events and imbalanced data: A performance comparison of prior correction and weighting methods. *Computational Intelligence, 34*(1), 161–174. doi: 10.1111/coin.12123.

Maas, C. J. M., & Hox, J. J. (2005). Sufficient sample size for multilevel modeling. *Methodology: European Journal of Research Methods for the Behavioral and Social Sciences, 1*(3), 86–92.

MacKinnon, D. P. (2008). *Introduction to statistical mediation analysis*. New York, NY: Lawrence Erlbaum Associates.

MacKinnon, D. P., Warsi, G., & Dwyer, J. H. (1995). A simulation study of mediated effect measures. *Multivariate Behavioral Research, 30*(1), 41–62. doi: 10.1207/s15327906mbr3001_3.

Mansfield, E. R., & Conerly, M. D. (1987). Diagnostic value of residual and partial residual plots. *The American Statistician, 41*, 107–116.

Mansouri, H., & Zhang, F. (2018). Simultaneous rank tests in analysis of covariance based on pairwise ranking. Retrieved from https://arxiv.org/pdf/1802.03884.pdf

Marascuilo, L. A., & Levin, J. R. (1970). Appropriate post hoc comparisons for interaction and nested hypotheses in analysis of variance designs: The elimination of Type IV errors. *American Educational Research Journal, 7*(3), 397–421.

Marascuilo, L. A., & Levin, J. R. (1976). The simultaneous investigation of interaction and nested hypotheses in two-factor analysis of variance designs. *American Educational Research Journal, 13*(1), 61–65.

Marascuilo, L. A., & McSweeney, M. (1977). *Nonparametric and distribution-free methods for the social sciences*. Monterey, CA: Brooks/Cole.

Marascuilo, L. A., & Serlin, R. C. (1988). *Statistical methods for the social and behavioral sciences*. New York, NY: Freeman.

Marquardt, D. W., & Snee, R. D. (1975). Ridge regression in practice. *The American Statistician, 29*, 3–19.

Mason, C. A., & Tu, S. (1996). Assessing moderator variables: Two computer simulation studies. *Educational & Psychological Measurement, 56*(1), 45–62. doi: 10.1177/0013164496056001003.

Maxwell, S. E. (1980). Pairwise multiple comparisons in repeated measures designs. *Journal of Educational & Behavioral Statistics, 5*(3), 269.

Maxwell, S. E. (2000). Sample size and multiple regression analysis. *Psychological Methods, 5*, 434–458.

Maxwell, S. E., Arvey, R. D., & Camp, C. J. (1981). Measures of strength of association: A comparative examination. *Journal of Applied Psychology, 66*(5), 525–534.

Maxwell, S. E., Delaney, H. D., & Dill, C. A. (1984). Another look at ANCOVA versus blocking. *Psychological Bulletin, 95*, 136–147. doi: 10.1037/0033–2909.95.1.136.

Maxwell, S. E., Delaney, H. D., & Kelley, K. (2018). *Designing experiments and analyzing data*. New York, NY: Routledge.

McCulloch, C. E. (2005). Repeated measures ANOVA, RIP? *CHANCE, 19*, 29–33.

McGrath, R. P., Hall, O. T., Peterson, M. D., Kraemer, W. J., & Vincent, B. M. (2017). Muscle strength is protective against osteoporosis in an ethnically diverse sample of adults *Journal of Strength & Conditioning Research, 31*(9), 2586–2589.

Mehta, A. J. a. b. o., Dooley, D. P., Kane, J., Reid, M., & Shah, S. N. (2018). Subsidized housing and adult asthma in Boston, 2010–2015. *American Journal of Public Health, 108*(8), 1059–1065. doi: 10.2105/AJPH.2018.304468.

Menard, S. (1995). *Applied logistic regression analysis*. Thousand Oaks, CA: Sage.

Menard, S. (2000). *Applied logistic regression analysis* (2nd ed.). Thousand Oaks, CA: Sage.

Mendoza, J. L., & Stafford, K. L. (2001). Confidence intervals, power calculation, and sample size estimation for the squared multiple correlation coefficient under the fixed and random regression models: A computer program and useful standard tables. *Educational and Psychological Measurement, 61*, 650–667.

Mendoza, J. L., & Stafford, K. L. (2001). Confidence intervals, power calculatino, and sample size estimation for the squared multiple correlation coefficient under the fixed and random regression models: A computer program and useful standard tables. *Educational and Psychological Measurement, 61*, 650–667.

Meuleman, B., Loosveldt, G., & Emonds, V. (2013). Regression analysis: Assumptions and diagnostics. In H. Best & C. Wolf (Eds.), *Handbook of regression analysis and causal inference* (pp. 83–110). London, England: SAGE.

Meyers, L. S., Gamst, G., & Guarino, A. J. (2006). *Applied multivariate research: Design and interpretation*. Thousand Oaks, CA: Sage.

Mickey, R. M., Dunn, O. J., & Clark, V. A. (2004). *Applied statistics: Analysis of variance and regression* (3rd ed.). Hoboken, NJ: Wiley.

Miller, A. J. (1984). Selection of subsets of regression variables (with discussion). *Journal of the Royal Statistical Society, A*, (147), 389–425.

Miller, A. J. (1990). *Subset selection in regression*. New York, NY: Chapman & Hall.

Miller, R. G. (1997). *Beyond ANOVA: Basics of applied statistics*. Boca Raton, FL: CRC Press.

Morgan, G. A., Leech, N. L., Gloeckner, G. W., & Barrett, K. C. (2012). *IBM SPSS for introductory statistics: Use and interpretation* (5th ed.). Boca Raton, FL: CRC Press/Taylor & Francis Group.

Mosteller, F., & Tukey, J. W. (1977). *Data analysis and regression*. Reading, MA: Addison-Wesley.

Murphy, K. R., Myors, B., & Wolach, A. (2009). *Statistical power analysis: A simple and general model for traditional and modern hypothesis tests* (3rd ed.). New York, NY: Routledge/Taylor & Francis Group.

Murphy, K. R., Myors, B., & Wolach, A. (2014). *Statistical power analysis: A simple and general model for traditional and modern hypothesis tests* (4th ed.). New York, New York: Routledge/Taylor & Francis Group.

Myers, J. L., & Well, A. D. (1995). *Research design and statistical analysis*. Mahwah, NJ: Lawrence Erlbaum Associates.

Myers, J. L., Lorch, R. F., & Well, A. (2010). *Research design and statistical analysis* (3rd ed.). New York, NY: Routledge.

Myers, R. H. (1979). *Fundamentals of experimental design* (4th ed.). Boston, MA: Allyn and Bacon.

Myers, R. H. (1986). *Classical and modern regression with applications*. Boston, MA: Duxbury.

Myers, R. H. (1990). *Classical and modern regression with applications* (2nd ed.). Boston, MA: Duxbury.

Nagelkerke, N. J. D. (1991). A note on a general devision of the coefficient of determination. *Biometrika, 78*, 691–692.

Neyman, J. (1950). *First course in probability and statistics*. New York, NY: Holt.

Neyman, J., & Pearson, E. S. (1933). The testing of statistical hypotheses in relation to probabilities a priori. *Proceedings of the Cambridge Philosophical Society: Mathematical & Physical Sciences, 29*(4), 492–510.

Noreen, E. W. (1989). *Computer-intensive methods for testing hypotheses: An introduction*. New York, NY: Wiley.

O'Grady, K. E. (1982). Measures of explained variance: Cautions and limitations. *Psychological Bulletin, 92*(3), 766–777. doi: 10.1037/0033–2909.92.3.766.

Olejnik, S. F., & Algina, J. (1987). Type I error rates and power estimates of selected parametric and nonparametric tests of scale. *Journal of Educational Statistics*, (1), 45–61. doi:10.2307/1164627

Olejnik, S., & Algina, J. (2000). Measures of effect size for comparative studies: Applications, interpretations, and limitations. *Contemporary Educational Psychology, 25*(3), 241–286.

Olejnik, S., & Algina, J. (2000). Measures of effect size for comparative studies: Applications, interpretations, and limitations. *Contemporary Educational Psychology, 25*(3), 241–286.

Overall, J. E., Lee, D. M., & Hornick, C. W. (1981). Comparison of two strategies for analysis of variance in nonorthogonal designs. *Psychological Bulletin, 90*, 367–375. doi:10.1037/0033-2909.90.2.367

Olejnik, S., & Algina, J. (2003). Generalized eta and omega squared statistics: Measures of effect size for some common research designs. *Psychological Methods, 8*(4), 434–447.

Olive, D. J. (2017). *Linear regression*. Cham, Switzerland: Springer International Publishing.

Olive, D. J. (2017). *Linear regression*. Switzerland: Springer.

Olofsson, P. (2007). *Probabilities: The little numbers that rule our lives*. Hoboken, NJ: Wiley-Interscience.

Osborne, J. W. (2015). *Best practices in logistic regression*. Los Angeles, CA: Sage.

Overall, J. E. (1981). Comparison of two strategies for analysis of variance in nonorthogonal designs. *Psychological Bulletin, 90*, 367–375. doi: 10.1037/0033–2909.90.2.367.

Overall, J. E., & Spiegel, D. K. (1969). Concerning least squares analysis of experimental data. *Pyschological Bulletin, 72*, 311–322.

Page, M. C., Braver, S. L., & MacKinnon, D. P. (2003). *Levine's guide to SPSS for analysis of variance* (2nd ed.). Mahwah, NJ: Lawrence Erlbaum Associates Publishers.

Pampel, F. C. (2000). *Logistic regression: A primer*. Thousand Oaks, CA: SAGE.

Pavur, R. (1988). Type I error rates for multiple comparison procedures with dependent data. *The American Statistician*, (3), 171–173. doi: 10.2307/2684994.

Pearson, E. S. (1978). *The history of statistics in the 17th and 18th centuries*. New York, NY: Macmillan.

Peckham, P. D. (1968). *An investigation of the effects of non-homogeneity of regression slopes upon the F-test of analysis of covariance*. Unpublished doctoral dissertation. University of Colorado, Boulder, CO.

Pedhazur, E. J. (1997). *Multiple regression in behavioral research* (3rd ed.). Fort Worth, TX: Harcourt Brace.

Pfeffermann, D. (1993). The role of sampling weights when modeling survey data. *International Statistical Review, 61*(2), 317–337.

Pingel, L. A. (1969). *A comparison of the effects of two methods of block formation on design precision*. Paper presented at the American Educational Research Association, Los Angeles, CA.

Porter, A. C. (1967). *The effects of using fallible variables in the analysis of covariance*. Unpublished doctoral dissertation. University of Wisconsin. Madison, WI.

Porter, A. C., & Raudenbush, S. W. (1987). Analysis of covariance: Its model and use in psychological research. *Journal of Counseling Psychology, 34*, 383–392. doi: 10.1037/0022–0167.34.4.383.

Preacher, K. J., & Hayes, A. F. (2008a). Contemporary approaches to assessing mediation in communication research. In A. F. Hayes, M. D. Slater, & L. B. Snyder (Eds.), *The Sage sourcebook of advanced data analysis methods for communication research*. (pp. 13–54). Thousand Oaks, CA: Sage Publications, Inc.

Preacher, K. J., & Hayes, A. F. (2008b). Asymptotic and resampling strategies for assessing and comparing indirect effects in multiple mediator models. *Behavior Research Methods, 40*(3), 879–891.

Preacher, K. J., & Kelley, K. (2011). Effect size measures for mediation models: Quantitative strategies for communicating indirect effects. *Psychological Methods, 16*(2), 93–115.

Puri, M. L., & Sen, P. K. (1969). Analysis of covariance based on general rank scores. *The Annals of Mathematical Statistics*, (2), 610–618.

Qiu, W. (2018). *Powermediation:* Power/sample size calculation for mediation analysis (Version R package version 3.1.0). Retrieved from https://cran.r-project.org/web/packages/powerMediation/powerMediation.pdf

Quade, D. (1967). Rank analysis of covariance. *Journal of the American Statistical Association*, (320), 1187–1200. doi: 10.2307/2283769.
Raftery, A. E. (1995). Bayesian model selection in social research. *Sociological Methodology, 25*, 111–163.
Rahlf, T. (2017). *Data visualisation with R: 100 examples*. Cham, Switzerland: Springer International Publishing.
Ramsey, P. H. (1989). Critical values of Spearman's rank order correlation. *Journal of Educational Statistics, 14*, 245–253.
Ramsey, P. H. (1994). Testing variances in psychological and educational research. *Journal of Educational Statistics*, (1), 23–42. doi:10.2307/1165175
Raudenbush, S. W., & Bryk, A. S. (2002). *Hierarchical linear models: Applications and data analysis methods* (2nd ed.). Thousand Oaks, CA: Sage.
Reichardt, C. S. (1979). The statistical analysis of data from nonequivalent control group designs. In T. D. Cook & D. T. Campbell (Eds.), *Quasi-experimentation: Design and analysis issues for field settings*. Chicago, IL: Rand McNally.
Robbins, N. B. (2005). *Creating more effective graphs*. Hoboken, NJ: Wiley-Interscience.
Rogers, W. M. (2002). Theoretical and mathematical constraints of interactive regression models. *Organizational Research Methods, 5*(3), 212–230. doi: 10.1177/10928102005003002.
Rogosa, D. R. (1980). Comparing non-parallel regression lines. *Psychological Bulletin, 88*, 307–321.
Rosenthal, R. (1994). Parametric measures of effect size. In H. Cooper & L. V. Hedges (Eds.), *The handbook of research synthesis* (pp. 231–244). New York, NY: Russell Sage Foundation.
Rosenthal, R., & Rosnow, R. L. (1985). *Contrast analysis: Focused comparisons in the analysis of variance*. Cambridge, NY: Cambridge University Press.
Rosenthal, R., & Rubin, D. B. (1979). A note on percent variance explained as a measure of the importance of effects. *Journal of Applied Social Psychology, 9*(5), 395–396. doi: 10.1111/j.1559-1816.1979.tb02713.x.
Rosnow, R. L., & Rosenthal, R. (1988). Focused tests of significance and effect size estimation in counseling psychology. *Journal of Counseling Psychology, 35*(2), 203–208.
Rousseeuw, P. J., & Leroy, A. M. (1987). *Robust regression and outlier detection*. New York, NY: Wiley.
Rudas, T. (2004). *Probability theory a primer*. Thousand Oaks, CA: Sage.
Ruppert, D. (2014). Transformation and weighting. In M. Davidian, X. Lin, J. S. Morris, & L. A. Stefanski (Eds.), *The work of Raymond J. Carroll: The impact and influence of a statistician* (pp. 155–161). Switzerland: Springer.
Ruppert, D., & Carroll, R. J. (1980). Trimmed least squares estimation in the linear model. *Journal of the American Statistical Association, 75*, 828–838.
Russell, C. J., & Bobko, P. (1992). Moderated regression analysis and Likert scales: Too coarse for comfort. *Journal of Applied Psychology, 77*(3), 336–342.
Russell, C. J., & Dean, M. A. (2000). To log or not to log: Bootstrap as an alternative to the parametric estimation of moderation effects in the presence of skewed dependent variables. *Organizational Research Methods, 3*(2), 166–185. doi: 10.1177/109442810032002.
Rutherford, A. (1992). Alternatives to traditional analysis of covariance. *British Journal of Mathematical and Statistical Psychology, 45*(2), 197–223. doi: 10.1111/j.2044-8317.1992.tb00988.x.
Rutherford, A. (2011). *ANOVA and ANCOVA a GLM approach* (2nd ed.). Hoboken, NJ: Wiley.
Sahay, A. (2016). *Applied regression and modeling: A computer integrated approach* (1st ed.). New York, NY: Business Expert Press.
Scariano, S. M., & Davenport, J. M. (1987). The effects of violation of independence assumptions in the one-way ANOVA. *The American Statistician, 41*(2), 123–129.
Scheffé, H. (1953). A Method for judging all contrasts in the analysis of variance. *Biometrika, 40*(1/2), 87–104.
Schmid, C. F. (1983). *Statistical graphics: Design principles and practices*. New York, NY: Wiley.
Schneider, B. A., Avivi-Reich, M., & Mozuraitis, M. (2015). A cautionary note on the use of the Analysis of Covariance (ANCOVA) in classification designs with and without within-subject factors. *Frontiers in Psychology, 6*, 1–12. doi: 10.3389/fpsyg.2015.00474/full; 10.3389/fpsyg.2015.00474

Schoemann, A. M., Boulton, A. J., & Short, S. D. (2017). Determining power and sample size for simple and complex mediation models. *Social Psychological and Personality Science, 8*(4), 379–386. doi: 10.1177/1948550617715068.

Seber, G. A. F., & Wild, C. J. (1989). *Nonlinear regression*. New York, NY: Wiley.

Sechrest, L., & Yeaton, W. H. (1982). Magnitudes of experimental effects in social science research. *Evaluation Review, 6*(5), 579–600.

Shadish, W. R., Cook, T. D., & Campbell, D. T. (2002). *Experimental and quasi-experimental designs for generalized causal inference*. Boston: Houston Mifflin.

Shan, G., & Ma, C. (2014). A comment on sample size calculation for analysis of covariance in parallel arm studies. *Journal of Biometrics and Biostatistics, 5*(1). doi: 10.4172/2155–6180.1000184.

Shapiro, S. S., & Wilk, M. B. (1965). An analysis of variance test for normality (complete samples). *Biometrika, 52*(3–4), 591–611.

Shapiro, S. S., & Wilk, M. B. (1965). An analysis of variance test for normality (complete samples). *Biometrika, 52*(3 and 4), 591–611.

Shavelson, R. J. (1996). *Statistical reasoning for the behavioral sciences* (3rd ed.). Boston: Allyn and Bacon.

Shear, B. R. B. S. C. E., Nordstokke, D. W., & Zumbo, B. D. (2018). A note on using the nonparametric Levene test when population means Are unequal. *Practical Assessment, Research & Evaluation, 23*(13), 1–11.

Shieh, G. (2009). Detecting interaction effects in moderated multiple regression with continuous variables power and sample size considerations. *Organizational Research Methods, 12*(3), 510–528. doi: 10.1177/1094428108320370.

Shieh, G. (2017). Power and sample size calculations for contrast analysis in ANCOVA. *Multivariate Behavioral Research, 52*(1), 1–11. doi: 10.1080/00273171.2016.1219841

Sidak, Z. (1967). Rectangular confidence regions for the means of multivariate normal distributions. *Journal of the American Statistical Association, 62*(318), 626–633. doi: 10.2307/2283989.

Sinan, A., & Alkan, B. B. (2015). A useful approach to identify the multicollinearity in the presence of outliers. *Journal of Applied Statistics, 42*(5), 986-993.

Singh, R. m. r. y. c. (2010). A survey of ridge regression for liprovement over ordinary least squares. *IUP Journal of Computational Mathematics*, 3(4), 54–74.

Skinner, C. J., Holt, D., & Smith, T. M. F. (Eds.). (1989). *Analysis of complex samples*. New York: Wiley.

Skinner, C. J., Holt, D., & Smith, T. M. F. (Eds.). (1989). *Analysis of complex samples*. New York, NY: Wiley.

Smithson, M. (2001). Correct confidence intervals for various regression effect sizes and parameters: The importance of noncentral distributions in computing intervals. *Educational and Psychological Measurement, 61*(4), 605–632.

Smithson, M. (2003). Noncentral confidence intervals for standardized effect sizes. In *Confidence intervals* (pp. 33–41). Thousand Oaks, CA: Sage.

Smithson, M., & Shou, Y. (2017). Moderator effects differ on alternative effect-size measures. *Behavior Research Methods, 49*(2), 747–757. doi: 10.3758/s13428-016-0735-z.

Snijders, T. A. B., & Bosker, R. J. (1999). *Multilevel analysis: An introduction to basic and advanced multilevel modeling*. Thousand Oaks, CA: Sage.

Snijders, T. A. B., & Bosker, R. J. (2012). *Multilevel analysis: An introduction to basic and advanced multilevel modeling* (2nd ed.). Thousand Oaks, CA: SAGE.

Sobel, M. E. (1982). Asymptotic confidence intervals for indirect effects in structural equation models. In S. Leinhardt (Ed.), *Sociological Methodology* (pp. 290–312). Washington, DC: American Sociological Association.

Spybrook, J., & Kelcey, B. (2014). *Power calculations for binary moderator in cluster randomized trials*. Retrieved from https://login.ezproxy.net.ucf.edu/login?auth=shibb&url=https://search.ebscohost.com/login.aspx?direct=true&db=eric&AN=ED562789&site=eds-live&scope=site

Spybrook, J., Raudenbush, S., Liu, X., Congdon, R., & Martinez, A. (2006). Optimal design (Version 1.76): University of Michigan. Retrieved from http://sitemaker.umich.edu/group-based/optimal_design_software

Steiger, J. H., & Fouladi, R. T. (1992). R2: A computer program in interval estimation power calculation, and hypothesis testing for the squared multiple correlation. *Behavior Research Methods, Instruments & Computers, 4*, 581–582.

Stevens, J. P. (1984). Outliers and influential data points in regression analysis. *Psychological Bulletin, 95*(2), 334–344.

Stevens, J. P. (2009). *Applied multivariate statistics for the social sciences* (5th ed.). New York, NY: Psychology Press.

Stigler, S. M. (1986). *The history of statistics: The measurement of uncertainty before 1900*. Cambridge, MA: Belknap Press of Harvard University Press.

Stone-Romero, E. F., & Anderson, L. E. (1994). Relative power of moderated multiple regression and the comparison of subgroup correlation coefficients for detecting moderating effects. *Journal of Applied Psychology, 79*(3), 354–359.

Stone-Romero, E. F., Alliger, G. M., & Aguinis, H. (1994). Type II error problems in the use of moderated multiple regression for the detection of moderating effects of dichotomous variables. *Journal of Management, 20*(1), 167–178. doi: 10.1177/014920639402000109.

Storer, B. E., & Kim, C. (1990). Exact properties of some exact test statistics for comparing two binomial proportions. *Journal of the American Statistical Association*, (409), 146–155. doi:10.2307/2289537

Sudman, S. (1976). *Applied sampling*. New York, NY: Academic Press.

Tabachnick, B. G., & Fidell, L. S. (2013). *Using multivariate statistics* (6th ed.). Boston, MA: Pearson.

Tabachnick, B. G., & Fidell, L. S. (2019). *Using multivariate statistics* (7th ed.). Boston, MA: Pearson.

Tabatabai, M. A., & Tan, W. Y. (1985). Some comparative studies on testing parallelism of several straight lines under heteroscedastic variances. *Communications in Statistics: Simulation and Computation, 14*(4), 837–844.

Thompson, B. (2016). The case for using the general linear model as a unifying conceptual framework for teaching statistics and psychometric theory. *Journal of Methods and Measurement in the Social Sciences, 6*(2), 30–41. doi: 10.2458/azu_jmmss.v6i2.18801.

Thompson, M. L. (1978). Selection of variables in multiple regression. Part I: A review and evaluation. Part II: Chosen procedures, computations and examples. *International Statistical Review, 46*, 1–19 and 129–146.

Tijms, H. (2004). *Understanding probability: Chance rules in everyday life*. New York, NY: Cambridge University Press.

Timm, N. H. (2002). *Applied multivariate analysis*. New York, NY: Springer.

Timm, N. H., & Carlson, J. E. (1975). Analysis of variance through full rank models . *Multivariate Behavioral Research Monographs, 75* (1), 120–143.

Tomarken, A., & Serlin, R. C. (1986). Comparison of ANOVA alternatives under variance heterogeneity and specific noncentrality structures. *Psychological Bulletin, 99*, 90–99.

Trafimow, D., Amrhein, V., Areshenkoff, C. N., Barrera-Causil, C. J., Beh, E. J., Bilgic, Y. K., . . . Marmolejo-Ramos, F. (2018). Manipulating the alpha level cannot cure significance testing. *Frontiers in Psychology, 9*, 1–7. doi:10.3389/fpsyg.2018.00699

Trafimow, D., Amrhein, V., Areshenkoff, C. N., Barrera-Causil, C. J., Beh, E. J., Bilgic, Y. K., . . . Marmolejo-Ramos, F. (2018). Manipulating the alpha level cannot cure significance testing. *Frontiers in Psychology, 9*, 1–7. doi: 10.3389/fpsyg.2018.00699.

Tufte, E. R. (2001). *The visual display of quantitative information* (2nd ed.). Cheshire, CT: Graphics Press.

Tukey, J. W. (1949). One degree of freedom for non-additivity. *Biometrics*, (3), 232. doi: 10.2307/3001938.

Tukey, J. W. (1953). *The problem of multiple comparisons*. Princeton, NJ: Princeton University.

Tukey, J. W. (1977). *Exploratory data analysis*. Reading, MA: Addison-Wesley.

Uanhoro, J. O. (2017). *Effect size calculators*. Retrieved from https://effect-size-calculator.herokuapp.com/

Van Belle, G. (2002). *Statistical rules of thumb*. New York, NY: Wiley-Interscience.

Van Breukelen, G. J. P. (2006). ANCOVA versus change from baseline had more power in randomized studies and more bias in nonrandomized studies. *Journal of Clinical Epidemiology, 59*, 920–925. doi: 10.1016/j.jclinepi.2006.02.007.

Vatcheva, K. P., Lee, M., McCormick, J. B., & Rahbar, M. H. (2016). Multicollinearity in regression analyses conducted in epidemiologic studies. *Epidemiology, 6*(2).

Vaughan, G. M., & Corballis, M. C. (1969). Beyond tests of significance: Estimating strength of effects in selected ANOVA designs. *Psychological Bulletin, 72*(3), 204–213. doi: 10.1037/h0027878.

Vogt, W. P. (2005). *Dictionary of statistics and methodology: A nontechnical guide for the social sciences* (3rd ed.). Los Angeles, CA: Sage.

Voinov, V., Balakrishnan, N., & Nikulin, M. S. (2013). *Chi-squared goodness of fit tests with applications* (1st ed.). Waltham, MA: Academic Press.

Wainer, H. (1992). Understanding graphs and tables. *Educational Researcher, 21*(1), 14–23.

Wainer, H. (2000). *Visual revelations: Graphical tales of fate and deception from Napoleon Bonaparte to Ross Perot*. Mahwah, NJ: Lawrence Erlbaum Associates.

Wallgren, A., Wallgren, B., Persson, R. S., Jorner, U., & Haaland, J-A. (1996). *Graphing statistics and data: Creating better charts*. Thousand Oaks, CA: Sage.

Wampold, B. E., & Serlin, R. C. (2000). The consequence of ignoring a nested factor on measures of effect size in analysis of variance. *Psychological Methods, 5*(4), 425–433.

Wang, X., Faraway, J. J., & Yue Ryan, Y. (2018). *Bayesian regression modeling with INLA* (1st ed.). Boca Raton, FL: CRC Press.

Wang, Y., Rodríguez de Gil, P., Chen, Y.-H., Kromrey, J. D., Kim, E. S., Pham, T., . . . Romano, J. L. (2017). Comparing the performance of approaches for testing the homogeneity of variance assumption in one-factor ANOVA models. *Educational and Psychological Measurement, 77*(2), 305–329. doi: 10.1177/0013164416645162.

Wang, Y., Rodríguez de Gil, P., Chen, Y-H., Kromrey, J. D., Kim, E. S., Pham, T., . . . Romano, J. L. (2017). Comparing the performance of approaches for testing the homogeneity of variance assumption in one-factor ANOVA models. *Educational and Psychological Measurement, 77*(2), 305–329. doi:10.1177/0013164416645162

Weinberg, S. L., & Abramowitz, S. K. (2002). *Data analysis for the behavioral sciences using SPSS*. Cambridge, UK.: Cambridge University Press.

Weisberg, S. (1985). *Applied linear regression* (2nd ed.). New York, NY: Wiley.

Weisberg, S. (2014). *Applied linear regression* (4th ed.). Hoboken, NJ: Wiley.

Welc, J., Esquerdo, P. J. R., & SpringerLink. (2018). *Applied regression analysis for business: Tools, traps and applications*. Cham, Switzerland: Springer International Publishing.

Welch, B. L. (1951). On the comparison of several mean values: An alternative approach. *Biometrika, 38*(3/4), 330–336.

Wen, Z., & Fan, X. (2015). Monotonicity of effect sizes: Questioning kappa-squared as mediation effect size measure. *Psychological Methods, 20*(2), 193–203. doi: 10.1037/met0000029.

Wetherill, G. B. (1986). *Regression analysis with applications*. London, England: Chapman & Hall.

Wickham, H., & Grolemund, G. (2017). *R for data science*. Sebastopol, CA: O'Reilly Media.

Wilcox, R. R. (1986). Controlling power in a heteroscedastic ANOVA procedure. *British Journal of Mathematical and Statistical Psychology, 39*(1), 65–68. doi: 10.1111/j.2044–8317.1986.tb00845.x.

Wilcox, R. R. (1987). *New statistical procedures for the social sciences: Modern solutions to basic problems*. Hillsdale, NJ: Lawrence Erlbaum Associates.

Wilcox, R. R. (1988). A new alternative to the ANOVA F and new results on James's second-order method. *British Journal of Mathematical and Statistical Psychology, 41*(1), 109–117. doi: 10.1111/j.2044–8317.1988.tb00890.x.

Wilcox, R. R. (1989). Adjusting for unequal variances when comparing means in one-way and two-way fixed effects ANOVA models. *Journal of Educational Statistics, 14*(3), 269–278. doi: 10.2307/1165019.

Wilcox, R. R. (1993). Comparing one-step M-estimators of location when there are more than two groups. *Psychometrika, 58*(1), 71–78. doi:10.1007/BF02294471

Wilcox, R. R. (1993). Comparing one-step M-estimators of location when there are more than two groups. *Psychometrika, 58*(1), 71–78. doi: 10.1007/BF02294471.

Wilcox, R. R. (1995). *Statistics for the social sciences*. San Diego, CA: Academic Press.

Wilcox, R. R. (1996). *Statistics for the social sciences*. San Diego, CA: Academic.

Wilcox, R. R. (2003). *Applying contemporary statistical procedures*. San Diego, CA: Academic Press.

Wilcox, R. R. (2012). *Introduction to robust estimation and hypothesis testing* (3rd ed.). Boston, MA: Academic Press.

Wilcox, R. R. (2017). *Introduction to robust estimation and hypothesis testing* (4th ed.). Burlington, MA: Elsevier.

Wilkinson, L. (2005). *The grammar of graphics* (2nd ed.). New York, NY: Springer.

Wonnacott, T. H., & Wonnacott, R. J. (1981). *Regression: A second course in statistics*. New York, NY: Wiley.

Wu, L. L. (1985). Robust M-estimation of location and regression. In N. B. Tuma (Ed.), *Sociological Methodology* (pp. 316–388). San Francisco, CA: Jossey-Bass.

Wu, L. L. (1985). Robust M-estimation of location and regression. In N. B. Tuma (Ed.), *Sociological Methodology* (pp. 316–388). San Francisco, CA: Jossey-Bass.

Wu, X. W., & Lai, D. (2015). Comparison of statistical methods for pretest–posttest designs in terms of type I error probability and statistical power. *Communications in Statistics: Simulation & Computation, 44*(2), 284–294. doi: 10.1080/03610918.2013.775295.

Xie, X.-J., Pendergast, J., & Clarke, W. (2008). Increasing the power: A practical approach to goodness-of-fit test for logistic regression models with continuous predictors. *Computational Statistics and Data Analysis, 52*, 2703–2713. doi: 10.1016/j.csda.2007.09.027.

Yu, M. C., & Dunn, O. J. (1982). Robust tests for the equality of two correlation coefficients: A Monte Carlo study. *Educational & Psychological Measurement, 42*, 987–1004.

Yuan, K.-H., & Maxwell, S. (2005). On the post hoc power in testing mean differences. *Journal of Educational and Behavioral Statistics, 30*(2), 141–167. doi:10.3102/10769986030002141.

Zhang, Z. (2014). Monte Carlo based statistical power analysis for mediation models: Methods and software. *Behavior Research Methods, 46*(4), 1184–1198.

Zimmerman, D. W. (1997). A note on interpretation of the paired-samples t test. *Journal of Educational and Behavioral Statistics, 22*(3), 349–360. doi:10.2307/1165289

Zimmerman, D. W. (1997). A note on interpretation of the paired-samples t test. *Journal of Educational and Behavioral Statistics, 22*(3), 349–360. doi: 10.2307/1165289.

Zumbo, B. D., & Nordstokke, D. W. (2010). A new nonparametric Levene test for equal variances. *Psicológica, 32*(2), 401–430.

Name Index

Subject Index

Note: Numbers in *italic* indicate figures and numbers in **bold** indicate tables on the corresponding page.

THE ENCYCLOPEDIA OF

SCHIZOPHRENIA AND OTHER PSYCHOTIC DISORDERS

THIRD EDITION

Richard Noll, Ph.D.

Foreword by
Leonard George, Ph.D.

Facts On File
An imprint of Infobase Publishing

For Wolfgang Noll,
My beautiful boy of seven summers,
Sol invictus

The Encyclopedia of Schizophrenia and Other Psychotic Disorders, Third Edition

Facts On File, Inc.
An imprint of Infobase Publishing
132 West 31st Street
New York NY 10001

Library of Congress Cataloging-in-Publication Data

Noll, Richard, 1959–
The Encyclopedia of schizophrenia and other psychotic disorders / Richard Noll; foreword by Leonard George. — 3rd ed.
p. cm.
Includes index.
ISBN 0-8160-6405-9 (alk. paper)
1. Schizophrenia—Encyclopedias. 2. Schizophrenia—Information services—Directories. I. Title.
RC514.N63 2006
616.89′003—dc22 2005056749

Facts On File books are available at special discounts when purchased in bulk quantities for businesses, associations, institutions, or sales promotions. Please call our Special Sales Department in New York at (212) 967-8800 or (800) 322-8755.

You can find Facts On File on the World Wide Web at http://www.factsonfile.com

Text and cover design by Cathy Rincon

Printed in the United States of America

VB Hermitage 10 9 8 7 6 5 4 3 2 1

This book is printed on acid-free paper.

CONTENTS

FOREWORD: THE HAUNTED ANIMAL

Our species is haunted by madness. One in every 100 of us will fall prey to it at some time in our lives, and of those, one in 10 will be driven by misery or confusion to take their own lives. Not only the afflicted suffer, of course. As Aristotle famously noted, we are social animals, profoundly linked with each other, and derangements of the psyche (the technical term is *psychoses*) strain the social web, burdening family, friends, communities, and economies. Directly or indirectly, madness touches us all.

Has it always been so? Experts disagree as to whether some forms of psychosis, such as schizophrenia, may have arisen over the last few centuries. But people showing the common mark of the psychotic disorders—disturbed contact with physical and social reality, leading to mental anguish and inability to live well—can be found in every culture on earth today and were likely among our ancestors at prehistory's dawn.

Throughout history, madness has been a terrible scourge and, also, a mirror. Beliefs about psychosis reflect the framework with which societies define reality. Traditional cultures going back to the Old Stone Age did not draw a line between animate and nonliving as we do today. Rather, the cosmos and everything in it was ensouled. In dreams and visions, a person's soul could wander in the invisible lands of the spirits. A soul's distress implied trouble in the spirit realm. Perhaps the soul had been kidnapped by a sorcerer or lost its way in the otherworld. Maybe the body had been invaded by some dark ghost. Or the person might have skewed the balance of the world by breaking a taboo laid down by spirits. A shaman may have been called in to divine the problem and heal the deranged person, by finding the wayward soul or extracting the invader—often literally by sucking it out of the body through a tube of bone or bark—or cutting a deal with the peeved sprite whose taboo had been slighted. Shamans lived on the cusp between seen and unseen worlds and partook of the weirdness of that liminal space, so their actions were often inscrutable. Ironically, many modern scholars who studied preliterate healing practices confused the patient's state with that of the doctor, seeing symptoms of psychosis in the odd behavior of shamans. The present work's author, Dr. Richard Noll, exposed the fallacy of the "schizophrenia metaphor" of shamanism in one of his earliest research papers.

The notion that madness can be caused by spiritual forces endured into the worldviews of the early civilizations—indeed, it has survived to the present. With the Vatican's blessing, a Roman college still offers courses in the study of demonic possession and exorcism, training priests to discern the signs of the devil's hand in severely disturbed behavior and the right techniques of "sucking out" the pest—no longer with a shaman's bone, but with sprays of holy water and chants of scripture. Dr. Noll's published collection of psychiatric case reports of the "possession syndrome" is the most important study of this topic in many decades.

In ancient Greece, all sorts of mental and physical maladies were taken to be the mischief of the *kakodaimones,* personifications of malign forces in one's character or environment, or else the result

of the gods' displeasure. Sufferers might make a pilgrimage to a temple-complex of the healing deity Asklepios. There, they would ease their souls by strolling through gardens and groves and attending the theater. At the climax of the therapy, they spent the night in the temple, where they prayed for a visit from the divine healer. Asklepios's favorite animal was the snake (which still curls around Asklepios's wand in the symbol of the medical profession)—feeling it slither over one's body in the darkened temple was a sure sign of good prognosis.

Hippocrates founded a medical tradition that sought natural causes for ailments. The cosmos was an interplay of four elements (air, fire, earth, and water), and the human being, as a *mikrokosmos* (small replica of the cosmos), featured the circulation of airy blood, fiery yellow bile, earthy black bile, and watery phlegm. If the balanced flow of these four humors was upset, illness of body or mind could ensue. Too much yellow bile could trigger bouts of mania, while an excess of black bile (*melan choler* in Greek) could lead to a deep melancholy. Either extreme could fray the sufferer's contact with reality for a while. The Hippocratic doctor would advise a moderate lifestyle—neither too much nor too little sleep, food, exercise, socializing. He might also try to bleed the excess humor from the body. Hippocratic medicine, as reformulated by Galen in the second century A.D., remained vital for classifying and treating madness well into the Enlightenment.

Christian authorities through the ages viewed madness in many ways. Christ's call to compassion for the sick drew Christian doctors to treat psychotic sufferers as patients who needed medical help, often of the Hippocratic/Galenic variety. Christianity cast the world as a battle between the Lord and Lucifer over the fate of souls, so it is no surprise that hurt psyches would be seen as casualties of that spiritual war. Folk healers peddled charms to keep Satan's spawn at bay or drive them out or offered to cut open the scalp of the mad person and remove the "folly stone" that had sprouted in the brain. With a little sleight of hand, they could give the plucked stone to the patient's grateful family as a keepsake—and then leave town as fast as possible.

By the later Middle Ages, the Catholic project of a universal church was in dire straits. The grip of Islam on Africa and the Middle East was not seriously loosened by the Crusades. Within western Europe itself, heresies like Catharism and Waldensianism threatened the Catholic monopoly of faith. The Black Death's ravages were strangely unresponsive to prayer, raising further doubts. Clearly, Christendom was under sustained attack by a potent foe. It could only be the devil, aided by a "fifth column" of perverse humans. This conclusion was drawn not by the ignorant masses but by the leading intellectual lights of the church, setting the foundation for the Great Witch Hunt. Deviant behaviors that were taken as signs of humoral imbalance in the past now marked a person as either a demonic victim or collaborator. The prescription for psychosis was often exorcism. As well as the pronouncement of holy mutterings, torturing the bewitched person was encouraged to discomfit the resident demon. The "witches" accused of sending the demons got even worse treatment. Tens of thousands confessed under torture. But some eagerly shared their tales of flying through the air at night on a goat or broom to the witches' sabbaths, where in Satan's honor they would kiss a giant cat beneath the tail, feast on babies' flesh, and plot spells to blight crops and abort good Christian fetuses. These delusional souls were freed from their psychoses by the stake or the noose.

There never were any witches. But the witch-hunters' fantasies surfaced again in the late 20th century as a wave of "ritual Satanic abuse" reports spread around the world. Investigators found no credible evidence for the alleged global conspiracy of devil-worshippers. Dr. Noll's timely writings on this topic helped eventually to stem the irrational tide.

In the 1400s, as the Witch Hunt was unleashed, the Renaissance bloomed in Italy. A brighter conception of humanity and nature gradually spread. No longer was the world the chessboard of God and devil, but a wondrous creation to be explored by the miracle that is humanity, "noble in reason, infinite in faculty," as Shakespeare put it. This rebirth of a proud and ingenious curiosity led to the rise of modern science. Mad people were no longer thought soiled by Satan's touch but somehow diseased. In the absence of useful treatments,

they were locked in "insane asylums" or "madhouses" in the care of a new breed of medical specialist, the "mad-doctor." Patients' disruptive acts had to be managed in these settings, leading to an era of inventive restraints. And the mad-doctors devised many clever means to try to shock or stress patients out of their psychoses. These methods were often not so different from those of the witch interrogators, but with much kinder motive.

The humanistic wisdom of the Renaissance bore fruit in the rise of democratic governments and legally enshrined human rights in Europe and the Americas. Seen with humanists' eyes, the denizens of the madhouses looked to be unfortunate kin, not only saddled with mental illness, but stripped of dignity and jailed in dungeons. Such was the view of the great reformers like Pinel, Rush, and Tuke, who began the process (which is not yet complete in some parts of the world) of unchaining the mad and treating them decently. But there were still no viable theories to explain the cause of psychosis or guide its treatment. Other areas of medicine were starting to see breakthroughs—scientists found the cause of many diseases to be microorganisms, and soon were creating vaccines. Medicine's trend was to focus on biology and neglect psychological and social factors in illness and health.

The imprint of this split between body and psyche has been clear in the disciplines of psychiatry and psychology since their inception in the 19th century. Camps of specialists framed the puzzle of psychosis as either biological or psychosocial. Their research produced a series of dead ends instead of insights. Each view had its turn dominating academic and popular culture. More harm than good came of these fractured perspectives. The reign of psychoanalysis for several decades was notably unhelpful. Dr. Noll's archival research, published in several articles and books, has shed much-needed light on this complex era.

The madness that haunts us still evades our grasp. Millions around the world succumb, and few recover fully. But there is good news. A revolution is taking place in our conceptions of health, illness, and recovery. Researchers have found that the most useful approach to health problems is to weigh the full range of biological and psychosocial influences. We suffer not just as ill bodies or as ill minds but as ill persons. In broad strokes, this "biopsychosocial" model is like the holistic vision of the ancients, but now confirmed, revised, and empowered by the tools of modern science. And it seems that psychosis is finally yielding some of its secrets to this approach. Let us hope that more and more effective therapies will be the result.

The study of psychosis is one of the fastest changing areas in health science. And its long history holds deep lessons that must never be lost. How are we to embrace this vast topic? We can have no better guide in the world than Dr. Richard Noll. The first two editions of the present book established it as the best single-volume resource for anyone wishing to learn about the history and current science of psychotic disorders. This, the third edition, is a masterpiece of erudition and clarity. Experts will find nuggets of knowledge that they missed in decades of study; nonspecialists will be introduced to the landscape of psychosis in straightforward language that is grounded in rock-solid scholarship. The best way to use this book—indeed, the best way for us to advance in our struggle with psychosis—may be to follow the advice of the alchemists of old: *"Ora, lege, lege, lege, relege, labora, et invenies"*—"Pray, read, read, read, reread, work, and you will find!" If we do so diligently, one day humankind may no longer be the haunted animal.

—Leonard George, Ph.D., R.Psych.
Department of Psychology, Capilano College
North Vancouver, British Columbia

PREFACE TO THE THIRD EDITION

This third edition of *The Encyclopedia of Schizophrenia and Other Psychotic Disorders* is a completely revised and updated reference to all the medical, scientific, and historical aspects of these ancient afflictions. The entries in this book have been carefully selected for their usefulness in the years to come.

This volume points both forward and backward in time. In addition to providing entries that summarize all the current theories, findings, and treatments for schizophrenia since the second edition was completed in the summer of 1999, this book has been thoroughly revised to place the science of schizophrenia into its historical context. Thus, this book combines the latest scholarly research in the history of medicine and psychiatry with the vast scientific research literature on the diagnosis, etiology, pathophysiology, course, outcome, and treatment of schizophrenia. There is no other reference work that combines these two perspectives in such depth.

For this edition, many entries have been combined into larger, more comprehensive essays. This change is most evident in the entries for two of the most rapidly changing areas of research in schizophrenia: antipsychotic drugs and genetics studies. The latest scientific information for all entries is distilled and explained in plain language, thoroughly embedded in the new historical scholarship on those topics. Extensive reviews of the latest findings on endocrine and immune system alterations, brain abnormalities, and blood vessel alterations in schizophrenia likewise combine historical and scientific perspectives. New research findings regarding the course and outcome of schizophrenia and possible new environmental risk factors are discussed in entries for those topics.

Since the last edition, an explosion of new scholarship on the history of psychiatry has broadened our understanding of the historical trajectory of the evolution of dementia praecox (1893) into schizophrenia (1908). Extensive, entirely new entries for these disorders appear in this edition, as well as for related psychotic disorders such as manic-depressive illness (1899) and bipolar disorder (1980). Disorders that may be biologically related to schizophrenia, such as schizotypal personality disorder, also received thorough updating. So have entries for psychotic disorders that appear to be distinct from schizophrenia and manic-depressive illness, such as paranoia, chronic delusional states in French psychiatry, and the atypical psychotic disorders. The history of treatments for schizophrenia and other psychotic disorders is covered in depth in new or significantly revised entries on psychosurgery, insulin coma therapy, metrazol shock therapy, and electroconvulsive therapy.

Throughout this book, there will be many references to the *Diagnostic and Statistical Manual of Mental Disorders, 4th ed., text revision,* or *DSM-IV-TR* (2000), produced by the American Psychiatric Association, and *The International Classification of Diseases, 10th ed.,* or *ICD-10* (1992), created by the World Health Organization. They are the two most often used diagnostic manuals for mental disorders throughout the world. The diagnostic criteria for schizophrenia

from these two volumes are included in appendixes in this volume.

Rather than including a huge bibliography at the end of the book and in order to prevent all the flipping of pages back and forth as the reader attempts to locate a particular reference, full citations of references are included after each entry. Publications in English, German, and French—the three primary languages in the history of psychiatry—are provided for scholars and for European readers of this volume. Those reference sources have been chosen carefully according to three criteria: (1) the source is recommended as the best review of the relevant research in a particular area, (2) the source represents the first mention of an important theory or research finding in print, and (3) the source refers directly to a passage quoted in the entry or cites a major representative work of the person listed in a biographical entry. The users of this book are encouraged to read further, and it is hoped that the extensive references provided with the entries will encourage further exploration in the spirit of the proverb that was a favorite among the ancient alchemists, *liber librum aperit* ("one book opens another").

There are many long citations from rare psychiatric texts and especially from autobiographical accounts. Our best feeling for what life must have been like for patients, their family members, and physicians alike over the past two centuries comes from such vivid reports. Many of these quotations are from volumes that are so obscure that they can only be found in the rare book collections of *some* specialized libraries, and care has been taken to select those passages that particularly make the history of psychiatry "come alive" for the reader.

No other book like this presently exists for understanding schizophrenia and the other psychotic disorders. It is hoped that the reader will find it of value when trying to come to grips with a subject that has mystified humankind for centuries.

—Richard Noll, Ph.D.
Allentown, Pennsylvania

MADNESS, PSYCHOSIS, SCHIZOPHRENIA: A BRIEF HISTORY

The history of schizophrenia is the history of psychiatry. The earliest clear description of this disease dates to only 1809—at about the time that the very first psychiatric textbooks were being written by dedicated physicians who worked in "madhouses" and "asylums" with the "insane." They collected their observations of lunatics, devised classifications for them, speculated as to the causes of their afflictions, and even performed crude autopsies on their bodies to see if they could discover the secret of madness. The profession of psychiatry grew out of the efforts of these physicians to understand and cure diseases of the mind, particularly those tragic, chronic mental illnesses that condemned thousands to debilitated lives in institutions. Therefore, the psychotic disorders, and schizophrenia in particular, have always been at the very heart of the concerns of the psychiatric profession and are in fact responsible for its existence.

As we enter the 21st century hardly a month goes by in which some new discovery in genetics is not announced, and the mission to explore the genetics of schizophrenia will no doubt occupy a prominent position in the research of the next decade. But our late 20th-century cultural persona of schizophrenia as primarily a "genetically transmitted disease" forces us to reexamine certain historical problems related to schizophrenia. Specifically, what is its ever-changing story over the centuries? What other masks has it worn on the various stages of human history? What guesses have been made as to its possible etiology? What have been the fads and fashions in its research?

The many individual entries in this encyclopedia provide detailed synopses of these topics, but below is a brief summary of the highlights of the history of this disease.

Did Schizophrenia Exist in Antiquity?

If schizophrenia is truly a brain disease that has a strong basis in genetics, then there should be evidence that this severe mental disorder has afflicted people for hundreds, if not thousands, of years. "Madness" has been reported in every society on record, no matter how ancient or how primitive, and descriptions of hallucinations, delusions, and bizarre behavior are often reported in association with "madness." For example, in an attempt to trace schizophrenia back to ancient Babylonian accounts (3000 B.C.) or to early Sanskrit texts from India, translation of descriptions of mental illness from these cultures have been collected in articles published in 1985 by D. V. Jeste and his colleagues and in 1984 by C. V. Haldipur. But it is still not clear from this historical evidence that schizophrenia—as we know it, as a disease with a particular course that begins in adolescence or early adulthood, with characteristic signs and symptoms, and a chronic deteriorating course (at least in the type of schizophrenia that seems to be the most "genetic")—existed in the ancient eras. This point (and the larger ramifications of this entire issue) has been eloquently argued and documented by psychiatrist E. Fuller Torrey in his book *Schizophrenia and Civilization* (1980).

There are many reasons for this doubt. First, ancient descriptions of madness that involved delusional, hallucinating, or confused individuals could be accounts of any number of physical or mental disorders. The same argument holds true for 19th- and 20th-century anthropological descriptions of "schizophrenia" or "psychosis" in preliterate (formerly called "primitive") societies. For example, these same symptoms could be

produced by head trauma, brain infections, injury due to birth complications, strokes, or by any number of other known organic mental disorders. Or they could be descriptions of the other psychotic disorders, such as bipolar disorder (manic-depressive psychosis) or any of the atypical psychotic disorders. What is missing in these accounts are descriptions of the full course of the disease process over time.

Another issue regarding "schizophrenia" in so-called primitive societies should also be addressed. In the 20th century there has been a long tradition among some anthropologists (usually psychoanalytically oriented) and certain psychiatrists and psychologists who are "armchair anthropologists" that the magico-religious healers and diviners known as shamans have perhaps been persons who would otherwise be labeled schizophrenic or certainly psychotic in our culture. The theory goes: since their bizarre behavior is accepted (visions, ecstatic trances, etc.) and since prominent social roles have been created for them, they seem to adapt just fine without any further deterioration. This absurd ethnocentric notion has unfortunately persisted with some very prominent proponents, often with those who have little or no true expertise in the study of shamanism, schizophrenia, or both. The "schizophrenia metaphor" of shamanism is unfounded.

Psychosis in Europe up to 1600

Since antiquity, persons with psychotic disorders and other forms of mental illness have been left to themselves, sent off in "ships of fools," locked in cages, "flogged into reason," chained, or simply killed, in some instances. Until the 1500s, the care of the insane in Europe—what little was offered—had been the responsibility of monks and nuns. For example, the oldest institution for the insane in England, the Bethlem Royal Hospital ("Bedlam"), was first established in 1247 as a priory, and by 1329 it functioned as a hospital. The patients were serviced by a 13th-century religious order known as the Bethlehemites, and on their habits they wore the special insignia of a red star with a dark blue center. The city of London took control of the place in 1346, and in 1547 it was made into a royal institution, headed by physicians, and the name was changed to St. Mary of Bethlehem. This was later changed to its present name, the Bethlehem Royal Hospital.

The reigning theory of madness was based on the antiphlogistic or humoral theory of disease. This theory had been in vogue since the time of Hippocrates (460–377 B.C.) and was elaborated upon by Galen (A.D. 129–199). Both mental and physical disorders were considered by Galen to be caused by an excess (*plethora*) of one of the four humors: black bile, yellow bile, blood, and phlegm. The cure was to remove the excess by bleeding the patient or by using purgatives or laxatives. Remnants of the humoral theory formed the basis of asylum treatment for persons with schizophrenia and the other psychotic disorders until well into the 19th century and are graphically described by the fathers of psychiatry in the earliest psychiatric textbooks.

The "New Philosophy" and Madness—the 1600s

Many social and historical changes converged in the 17th century (especially in England) to change this dark state of affairs for people with mental disorders. First, societies began to incarcerate mentally ill people in central institutions (jails, hospitals) where many of them could be observed together for long periods of time. Second, physicians (crude as their art may have been at the time, an era that medical historian Guy Williams has dubbed the Age of Agony) began to be put in charge of the care of the mentally ill in these institutions. The institution of private madhouses for the care of the insane (at a profit) also began in this era and also involved physicians. And third, with the influence of Francis Bacon's "new philosophy," which sparked science as we know it, the concept of "disease" began to take on new meaning. This was largely due to the influence of the English physician Thomas Sydenham (1624–89), often referred to as the "English Hippocrates," who emphasized the direct observation of illnesses and suggested their classification according to syndromes, or groups of symptoms. This differed from the centuries-old identification of diseases usually

by a single symptom, such as was the case with the ancient mental disorder known as "fury."

The 1700s: Madness Is Classified

Throughout the 1700s, physicians who doctored to the mentally ill in madhouses (both public and private) began to be recognized for their medical specialty and were called mad-doctors or lunatic-doctors in England and its colonies. The more scientifically minded mad-doctors began to study the symptoms of mental illness for the first time in terms of syndromes, and many of them contributed treatises and classifications of their insane patients. In this endeavor, the British led the way, and such figures as William Battle of St. Luke's Hospital in London, John Haslam of "Bedlam" in London, and William Cullen of Edinburgh became world-famous authorities through their written observations on madness. Daringly, Haslam even reported on his autopsies of corpses of Bedlam patients, in an age where such practices were discouraged by British laws, and "bodysnatchers" supplied medical students and professors with such commodities. Each author devised his own unique classification system for mental disorders, often borrowing concepts used for centuries, as well as coining new terms and phrases. It is certain that many cases of what we would now call schizophrenia were probably classified under one or more of these early attempts to devise a more scientific method of understanding mental illness.

The 1800s: Psychiatry (and Schizophrenia) Begins

Following the early lead of the British, after 1801 it was the French who dominated the medical study of the mentally ill until mid-century, when the Germans began their domination of this field. Indeed, the devotion of the early French *aliénistes* (Pinel, Esquirol, and the members of the "Esquirol Circle") to the study and classification of mental disorders directly led to the development of a distinct medical specialty for mental illness, which is now universally known as "psychiatry." The French were the first to include lectures on mental illness in their medical schools, and the British followed suit by the 1820s.

In 1801 French physician Philippe Pinel published his famous treatise on insanity (*l'aliénation mentale*, or "mental alienation," which led physicians who specialized in the care of the mentally ill to be called "alienists" in England). The first edition of Pinel's *Traité médico-philosophique sur l'aliénation mentale, ou la manie* established him as the world's leading authority on mental illness and helped to persuade the world that the mentally ill could be treated in a more humane manner through his philosophy of "moral treatment." When Pinel was put in charge of the large institution for insane men in Paris following the French Revolution, he became famous for freeing 53 patients from their chains—without any disastrous consequences. Indeed, one of them, a former French soldier named Chevigné, became his bodyguard. The legend of Pinel unshackling the insane fit well with the revolutionary and democratic spirit of the times, and it helped to free the psychological chains in the minds of caretakers of the mentally ill, that their charges were nothing more than beasts and should be treated as such. Variations of the "moral treatment" were already being developed in England by William Tuke at the York Retreat and by Vincenzo Chiarugi, often referred to as "the Pinel of Italy." This more humane treatment philosophy was not widely adopted in Europe until the mid-1800s, and even in England, it took the reformist physician John Conolly's "nonrestraint movement" in the 1840s to bring lasting changes finally in the asylums in that country.

In the young United States, Philadelphia physician Benjamin Rush of the Pennsylvania Hospital began to study the insane patients within his institution and published a book on the subject, his *Medical Inquiries and Observations upon the Diseases of the Mind* of 1812, the only major American textbook of psychiatry to appear until the 1880s. Thus, American physicians played almost no role in the scientific description and classification of mental disorders until the 20th century.

Schizophrenia now enters the picture. In 1809 the very first clinical descriptions of schizophrenia as we know it appeared in print in two separate works. Working independently in their respective

countries, John Haslam of the Bethlem Royal Hospital in London and Philippe Pinel of the Salpêtrière asylum in Paris both produced expanded second editions of books on mental illness that had been published previously; they contain the first complete reports of what we now know as schizophrenia in its "chronic" (or "Type II") form. The expanded second edition of 1809 of Pinel's original 1801 treatise has never been translated into English (a translation of the first edition appeared as early as 1806). Pinel's description of *démence* in the first edition strongly resembles the thought disorder of schizophrenia, and this concept was apparently illustrated with case material in the second edition that seemed to confirm this connection. However, the following case history reproduced here from Haslam's 1809 *Observations on Madness and Melancholy* may be the first valid historical evidence in the English language for schizophrenia:

> There is a form of insanity which occurs in young persons; and, as far as these cases have been the subject of my observation, they have been more frequently noticed in females. Those whom I have seen, have been distinguished by prompt capacity and lively disposition; and in general have become the favorites of parents and tutors, by their faculty in acquiring knowledge, and by a prematurity of attainment. This disorder commences, about or shortly after, the period of menstruation, and in many instances has been unconnected with hereditary taint; as far as could be ascertained by minute enquiry. The attack is almost imperceptible; some months usually elapse before it becomes the subject of particular notice; and fond relatives are frequently deceived by the hope that it is only an abatement of excessive vivacity, conducing to a prudent reserve, and steadiness of character. A degree of apparent thoughtfulness and inactivity precede, together with the diminution of the ordinary curiosity, concerning that which is passing before them; and they therefore neglect those objects and pursuits which formerly proved sources of delight and instruction. The sensibility appears to be considerably blunted; they do not bear the same affection towards their parents and relations; they become unfeeling to kindness, and careless of reproof. To their companions they show a cold civility, but take no interest whatever in their concerns. If they read a book they are unable to give any account of its contents; sometimes, with steadfast eyes, they will dwell for an hour on one page, and then turn over a number in a few minutes. It is very difficult to persuade them to write, which most readily develops their state of mind; much time is consumed and little is produced. The subject is reportedly begun, but they seldom advance beyond a sentence or two; the orthography becomes puzzling, and by endeavoring to adjust the spelling the subject vanishes. As their apathy increases they are negligent of their dress, and inattentive to personal cleanliness. Frequently they seem to experience transient impulses of passion, but these have no source in sentiment; the tears, which trickle down at one time, are as unmeaning as the loud laugh which succeeds them; and it often happens that a momentary gust of anger, with its attendant invectives, ceases before the threat can be concluded. As the disorder increases, the urine and feces are passed without restraint, and from the indolence which accompanies it, they generally become corpulent. Thus in the interval between puberty and manhood, I have painfully witnessed this hopeless and degrading change, which in a short time has transformed the most promising and vigorous intellect into a slavering and bloated idiot.

Haslam is describing what 20th-century British psychiatrist Timothy J. Crow has named "Type II schizophrenia" or the "Pinel-Haslam syndrome"; insidious onset, negative symptoms (attention deficits, problems in information processing, apathy, poverty of speech, loss of curiosity in people and activities), and gradual cognitive deterioration.

The cognitive deterioration described by Haslam, or *démence,* as Pinel termed it, was later elaborated upon by French *aliéniste* Benedict Augustin Morel in his descriptions of mental "degeneration," for which he coined the term *démence précoce* in 1853. Whereas the concept of degeneration probably referred to cases that we would label schizophrenia today, it also referred to cases of one of the most frequently encountered psychotic disorders of the 19th and early 20th century, the "general paralysis

of the insane," which was later found to be caused by tertiary syphilis.

After Morel's introduction of degeneration theory in the 1850s, and Jules Baillarger's very first description of the "double-formed insanity" (what we now call bipolar disorder) in 1854, the French alienists subsided in importance, and it was the Germans, led by Wilhelm Griesinger, who began to dominate psychiatry until well into the 20th century (except, perhaps, for Charcot's contributions in Paris in the 1880s to the understanding of hysteria and the use of hypnosis). Griesinger's 1861 textbook, *Die Pathologie und Therapie der Psychische Krankheiten (The Pathology and Therapy of Mental Disorders)*, provided a detailed classification of mental disorders that was based on the notion that they were organically based, indeed, that they were all largely diseases of the brain. Although not a new notion, the work of Griesinger and later German psychiatrists and neurologists helped to establish the biological approach in psychiatry. Because of the contributions of the Germans, the biological approach is the central research strategy in the study of schizophrenia and the psychotic disorders today.

The 1840s was the pivotal decade in the history of the profession of psychiatry. By this time the actual word *psychiatry* was in use in both Germany and England, and the very first professional associations of such physicians were formed in Germany, England, France, and in the United States. In 1844, 13 superintendents of state asylums from across America met together in Philadelphia and formed the organization that is now known as the American Psychiatric Association. In the 1870s, following the study of wounded veterans of the American Civil War, the first professional society for the medical specialty of neurology was founded. Thus the study of mental disorders now had two branches of medicine with two very different philosophies, which remained at odds with one another until well into the 20th century.

With the Germans taking the lead, psychiatry began to resemble its present form. Indeed, by the end of the 19th century our present notion of psychosis as a disorder involving a gross impairment in reality testing (a "break with reality") and the creation of a new reality had taken shape. Even today psychosis encompasses phenomena that were labeled "insanity," "alienation," and "dementia" or degeneration in the 19th century.

The "Clinical Method" of Psychopathology

In 1863 Karl Kahlbaum of Prussia published his Habilitation (the equivalent of a second doctoral dissertation in Germany, necessary for becoming a university professor), *Die Gruppirung der psychischen Krankheiten (The Classification of Psychiatric Diseases)*. In this book, Kahlbaum described a class of progressively degenerating psychotic disorders that he grouped under the term "Vesania typical" (typical insanity). In 1866 Kahlbaum became the director of a private psychiatric clinic in Görlitz, Prussia, a small town near Dresden. He was accompanied by his younger assistant, Ewald Hecker, and together they conducted a series of research studies on young psychotic patients that would eventuate in a major influence on the development of modern psychiatry. Together Kahlbaum and Hecker were the first to describe and name such syndromes as dysthymia, cyclothymia, paranoia, catatonia, and hebephrenia. These are just the diagnostic labels that survived into history. In an attempt to overthrow the confusion of the past, including the inclination of physicians since pagan antiquity to group all mental disorders as forms of either "mania" or "melancholia" (terms that were not distilled down to their present meaning until the period between 1850 and 1900), Kahlbaum made the mistake of coining new names for just about every syndrome. Though acknowledged as a major psychiatric thinker in the 19th century, perhaps second only to Emil Kraepelin, his classification system was too novel and idiosyncratic to be widely adopted, and thus Kahlbaum receded into the shadows of history.

Perhaps their most lasting contribution to psychiatry was the introduction of the "clinical method" from medicine to the study of mental diseases, a method which is now known as psychopathology. Other than Morel's claims about his degeneration theory, the element of time had largely been missing from definitions of mental disorders. Psychiatrists made pronouncements about prognosis that

were *not* based on careful observations of the changing symptoms of patients over time. Mad-doctors, alienists, and other physicians who wrote about the insane arbitrarily invented names for insanities and described their characteristic signs and symptoms based on a short-term, cross-sectional observation period of their lunatic patients. When the element of time was added to the concept of diagnosis, a diagnosis became more than just a description of a collection of symptoms: diagnosis now also defined prognosis (course and outcome). An additional feature of the clinical method was that the characteristic symptoms that define syndromes should be described without any prior assumption of brain pathology (although such links could be made later as scientific knowledge progressed). Karl Kahlbaum first made his appeal for the adoption of the clinical method in psychiatry in his 1874 book on catatonia. Without Kahlbaum and Hecker there would be no dementia praecox.

Dementia Praecox (1893)

In 1891 Emil Kraepelin left his position at the university in Dorpat (now Tartu, Estonia) to become a professor and director of the psychiatric clinic at the university in Heidelberg, Germany. Convinced of the value of Kahlbaum's suggestions for a more exact qualitative clinical method in psychiatry, Kraeplin realized that by adding a quantitative component to such a research program (which Kahlbaum never did), he could place psychiatry on a more scientific foundation. Quantification helped to eliminate any subjective biases on the part of the researcher. He began the first such research program of this nature in the history of psychiatry at Heidelberg in 1891, collecting data about every new patient that was admitted to the clinic (and not just "interesting cases," as had been the case in the past) and summarizing them on specially prepared index cards, his famous *Zahlkarten*. He had been keeping data on such cards since at least 1887. In his posthumously published *Memoirs* (which was first published in German 61 years after his death), Kraepelin described his method:

> . . . after the first thorough examination of a new patient, each of us had to throw in a note [in a "diagnosis box"] with his diagnosis written on it. After a while, the notes were taken out of the box, the diagnoses were listed, and the case was closed, the final interpretation of the disease was added to the original diagnosis. In this way, we were able to see what kind of mistakes had been made and were able to follow-up the reasons for the wrong original diagnosis (p. 61).

Kraepelin was obsessed with finding patterns in the data on these cards, taking them home with him or on vacation at times. In 1893, two years after starting his more rigorous research program in Heidelberg, the fourth edition of Kraepelin's textbook, *Psychiatrie,* reflected some preliminary impressions derived from the analysis of his cards. Diagnosis of clinical syndromes according to signs and symptoms, the traditional approach, was now augmented by indications of course and outcome (prognosis). In that edition he introduced a class of psychotic disorders he called "psychic degenerative processes." Three of these came directly from the work of Kahlbaum and Hecker: dementia paranoides (a sudden-onset, degenerative form of Kahlbaum's paranoia); catatonia (directly from Kahlbaum's 1874 monograph on the subject); and dementia praecox, which was essentially Hecker's hebephrenia (as described in 1871). Dementia praecox was hebephrenia and would remain so in Kraepelin's thinking for six more years.

In March 1896 the fifth edition of Kraepelin's textbook appeared. In it Kraepelin stated that he was confident of the value of his clinical method of using qualitative and quantitative data collected over a long period of observation of patients as a way of developing a diagnosis that included prognosis (course and outcome):

> What convinced me of the superiority of the clinical method of diagnosis (followed here) over the traditional one, was the *certainty with which we could predict (in conjunction with our new concept of disease) the future course of events.* Thanks to it the student can now find his way more easily in the difficult subject of psychiatry.

In the 1896 fifth edition, dementia praecox (still essentially hebephrenia), dementia paranoides, and

catatonia are separate psychotic disorders included among "metabolic disorders leading to dementia." In the sixth edition of *Psychiatrie* of 1899, Kraepelin reordered the psychiatric cosmos for the next century by grouping most of the insanities into two large categories, dementia praecox and manic-depressive illness. They were distinguished by the following characteristics: (1) dementia praecox was primarily a disorder of intellectual functioning, whereas manic-depressive illness was primarily a disorder of affects or mood, (2) dementia praecox had a uniformly deteriorating course and a poor prognosis, whereas manic-depressive insanity had a course of acute exacerbations followed by complete remissions with no lasting deterioration of intellectual functioning, and (3) there were no recoveries from dementia praecox, whereas in manic-depressive illness there were many complete recoveries. In 1899 dementia praecox took its now familiar form as a heterogenous class of psychotic disorders comprised of hebephrenic, catatonic, and paranoid forms. These forms have persisted until today, through Eugen Bleuler's 1908 description of schizophrenia (to which he added a fourth form, dementia simplex, or simple schizophrenia) to the main types of schizophrenia in *DSM-IV-TR* (the paranoid, catatonic, and disorganized types, with the latter retaining its historical designation as the hebephrenic type in *ICD-10* [1992]).

But what caused this terrible disease of rapid intellectual (cognitive) deterioration (dementia), mainly in the young (between 15 and 25 years old), and mainly in males? Kraepelin believed that heredity predisposed persons with dementia praecox to develop abnormalities in the metabolic functioning of the sex glands (gonads) after puberty, leading to an autointoxication (self-poisoning) process that eventually affected the brain. Autointoxication theories of various diseases, physical and mental, were highly influential from the 1890s to the 1920s in psychiatry.

Schizophrenia (1908)

Not everyone agreed with Kraepelin's emphasis on classification by prognosis. Indeed one Swiss psychiatrist, Eugen Bleuler, began to question the notion, observing that there were many different courses to the disorder, and that some persons with dementia praecox would plateau at a particular level of deficit and stay at that level for the rest of their lives, without degenerating any further. In 1908 Bleuler published a paper challenging Kraepelin's views, and suggested that the disorder be renamed *schizophrenia* (from two Greek words meaning "to split" and "mind") to remove the emphasis on prognosis suggested by the term *dementia praecox.* Bleuler had been using the term schizophrenia in lectures to his medical staff at the Burghölzli Hospital in Zurich, Switzerland, prior to this time. In 1911 Bleuler published his classic monograph, *Dementia Praecox oder die Gruppe der Schizophrenien.* His description of schizophrenia (to which he added a fourth subtype, Otto Diem's "simple schizophrenia") was hailed as a major contribution, and the ideas in Bleuler's 1911 book are still largely reflected in the classification systems in use today. No one has ever matched Bleuler's insightful description of this disease.

Bleuler had believed he was further developing Kraepelin's concepts of dementia praecox rather than inventing an entirely new disorder. Bleuler's objections to Kraepelin's dementia praecox were many, however. He objected (as many others did, particularly British psychiatrists) that there was no "dementia" in the classical, organic sense of the term (for example, as in today's Alzheimer's disease), but instead an intellectual deterioration that may or may not end up looking like dementia. He noted the deterioration was not progressive, with episodes of partial remission or complete recovery occurring in some cases. The term *praecox* was also objectionable to Bleuler, since he had encountered cases of schizophrenia that occurred during midlife (currently named late-onset schizophrenia). There were also cases of "latent schizophrenia," according to Bleuler, in which the psychotic disorder was not triggered by an endogenous disease process but by personal experiences, such as trauma. Bleuler went so far as to believe that cases of latent schizophrenia were more common than cases of manifest schizophrenia. Bleuer also noted the existence of people with paranoid personality disorders who resembled cases of dementia praecox. Bleuler widened Kraepelin's concept of dementia praecox by arguing that these cases, too, should be considered

part of the disease (an idea that has taken hold in our current notions of schizophrenia spectrum disorders, especially schizotypal personality disorder). Influenced by his associate Carl Gustav Jung and by Sigmund Freud and the psychoanalytic movement, Bleuler believed in the possibility of psychogenic or reactive triggers for schizophrenia, which Kraepelin did not allow.

In sum, Bleuler greatly widened the circumference of persons whom he considered should be diagnosed with dementia praecox. He also left open the possibilities for various courses and outcomes, and better prognoses, than Kraepelin did. He emphasized the heterogeneous nature of schizophrenia, with the possibility that multiple disease processes may underlie it, whereas Kraepelin held to the conviction that dementia praecox was one disease with at least three forms. It was therefore Bleuler's wider concept of schizophrenia that took hold, especially in America, and dominated psychiatry until 1980. In that year, the narrower diagnostic criteria and pessimistic prognosis for schizophrenia became the official diagnosis of this disorder in *DSM-III*. This narrower, "neo-Kraepelinian" definition of schizophrenia persists today.

The "Mind Twist Men" versus the "Brain Spot Men"

In the late 1800s and early 1900s a great battle erupted in American medicine that was to have a profound influence on the practice of psychiatry and on attitudes toward dementia praecox and schizophrenia.

The conflict raged between those traditional physicians who preferred the knowledge derived from the practice of medicine as an art and those who argued for the greater role of knowledge gained from laboratory studies to make the practice of medicine a science. Until the late 19th century, medical training had followed the master-apprentice model. One learned medical practice by observing one's mentor, and then by doing it oneself. Clinical lore and personal anecdotes were the only "evidence" to be trusted—especially in such a backward discipline of medicine as psychiatry, which was held in very low esteem by the rest of the medical profession. Such had been the basis of medical training for thousands of years, dating back to the Hippocratic literature of the ancient Greeks.

By the late 1860s, claims for the clinical relevance of basic science conducted in laboratories were being vigorously voiced by physicians in the United States. These physicians argued that personal anecdotes and clinical folklore were a bad way to conduct medical practice. Instead, new studies in anatomy, chemistry, and other scientific disciplines should be relied upon to make medical practice more scientific. Of course, as we enter the 21st century, we now know that these medical discontents prevailed. However, circa 1900, this victory was not apparent, and the psychiatry of the 20th century remained the only major subdiscipline of American medicine to reject laboratory science and its evidence that mental diseases may have biological causes.

Why did psychiatry remain in such a primitive state throughout most of the 20th century? The responsibility for this tragedy lies in the influence of two prominent American schools of psychiatry that were suspicious of laboratory science and rejected the claims of Kraepelin and his followers that dementia praecox or schizophrenia was caused by heredity (genetics) or other biological causes. The first of these schools, Adolf Meyer's "biosocial reaction" school, had an early influence from circa 1910 to the 1950s. The second of these schools, Sigmund Freud's psychoanalysis, had a profound and devastating influence on American psychiatry and retarded its development as a scientific branch of medicine from the 1920s to the 1970s.

The Meyerians. While acknowledging the potential value of laboratory research in psychiatry, prominent psychiatrists in America such as the Swiss émigrés Adolf Meyer and August Hoch preferred to rely upon the ability of the trained clinician to analyze the biosocial factors in the life of the "whole person" that contributed to the psychological and behavioral "reactions" that constituted all known mental disorders, including dementia praecox. The literature of Meyer and his supporters is laced throughout with polemics against the "failed" or "outdated" practice of psychiatrists who modeled their thinking and their fatalistic diagnostic and prognostic pronouncements on the medical pathologists. Most mental disorders, they

argued, were viewed by these older psychiatrists to be as irreversible as nervous tissue damage, or as irrefutable as the fateful hand dealt by heredity. Furthermore, the Meyerians pointed out—and with some truth—that the neuropathological, biochemical, and serological laboratory studies and the statistical studies of heredity had not proven themselves to be of any real relevance to the diagnosis and treatment of patients. Because the "can do" philosophy of the Meyerians blended so well with similar American cultural values of pragmatism and functionalism, personified in the figure of William James (1842–1910), in the first two decades of this century, they paved the way for the resounding acceptance of psychoanalytic theory by the 1920s in American psychiatry.

The Psychoanalysts. Psychoanalysis, like the Meyerian philosophy, rejected "pessimistic" hereditarian views and argued that patients could actually be understood and changed through the application of this new method. By World War I, even neurologically trained physicians such as James Jackson Putnam, Smith Ely Jelliffe, and William Alanson White had converted to the more optimistic worldview of Freudian psychoanalysis.

The Kraepelinians. The "old"—or perhaps more aptly put "Old World"—psychiatric perspective castigated by Adolf Meyer was primarily the 19th-century French (B. A. Morel, Valentin Magnan) and particularly German emphasis on hereditary degeneration theory, and in particular its avocation by the German psychiatrist Emil Kraepelin. One disorder in particular, dementia praecox, was often the focus of the heated charges and countercharges hurled between the Kraepelinians, the Meyerians, and the psychoanalysts. The biological and hereditarian etiology of dementia praecox (the disorder described and named by Kraepelin in the sixth edition of his *Psychiatrie* in 1899 as composed of the psychotic disorders paranoia, catatonia, and hebephrenia) indicated in his opinion an extremely poor prognosis for any patient that manifested the symptoms. Manic-depressive insanity, the nondeteriorating and sometimes remitting form of serious psychotic disturbance, was described by Kraepelin in the sixth edition of his *Psychiatrie* in 1899 and met with far greater acceptance among the Meyerians and psychoanalysts. Yet, Kraepelin insisted that it, too, had a firm etiologic basis in biological processes and that therefore both dementia praecox and manic-depressive insanity could be investigated through laboratory methods. The growth in laboratory studies of these illnesses are reflected in the bulkiness of volume III of the eighth edition of *Psychiatrie,* published in 1913, which is primarily concerned with dementia praecox and manic-depressive insanity.

While Kraepelin's diagnostic terms *dementia praecox* and *manic-depressive insanity* were adopted by American psychiatrists in the first quarter of this century, the etiologic and prognostic ideas of Kraepelin underwent considerable revisioning. This new—or perhaps more aptly put "New World"—dynamic or functional interpretation of dementia praecox was forged by the hands of Adolf Meyer, Smith Ely Jelliffe, and August Hoch, who coauthored a seminal monograph in 1911 containing their revisionist perspectives.

There was a small group of American physicians who believed that Kraepelin's theories about dementia praecox and schizophrenia were correct. They, too, viewed this devastating disorder as first and foremost a brain disease. They, too, knew that heredity (genetics) played a strong role in the cause and development of this disease. This group was led by Bayard Taylor Holmes (1852–1924) of Chicago and Elmer Ernest Southard (1876–1920) of Harvard Medical School in Boston.

Bayard Taylor Holmes was the editor of *Dementia Praecox Studies,* the first scientific or medical journal in any language to be named after a psychiatric disorder. During its short life (1918–22), *Dementia Praecox Studies* not only provided extensive bibliographic essays and reviews of published laboratory reports from several nations but also provided translations of selected experimental studies of unpublished doctoral theses from the original German or French. Perhaps most important, *Dementia Praecox Studies* served as the primary place of publication for the experimental reports of the Research Laboratory of the Psychopathic Hospital of Cook County (Illinois) and for the editorials of its director, Holmes. Bayard Taylor Holmes was also a noted Chicago surgeon and, in 1895, the unsuccessful Socialist candidate for mayor of Chicago.

Dementia Praecox Studies was the only journal ever produced by the handful of Kraepelinian physicians in the United States. Like Emil Kraepelin, they believed that mental disorders were first and foremost brain diseases with neuropathological, biochemical, infectious, and genetic causes. But from the 1910s until the late 1960s American psychiatry was dominated by the followers of Adolf Meyer's "psychosocial reaction" theory and Sigmund Freud's pseudoscience of psychoanalysis. These traditions of "mind twist men" (see below) were suspicious of laboratory science and rejected biological and genetic causes for mental disorders. The premature death from pneumonia of pathologist Elmer Ernest Southard left the "brain spot men" without a prominent spokesman. The death of Bayard Holmes in 1924 essentially ended the Kraepelinian movement in America for decades.

The opening pages of the January 1918 edition of *Dementia Praecox Studies* contain the following invitation from Herman Campbell Stevens for the submission of laboratory research reports: "The purpose of this publication is to arouse interest in the subject of dementia praecox. . . . How little is known about the disease is apparent from a reading of the standard treatises on psychiatry and from the current literature. It is the purpose of this journal to serve as a clearinghouse for scientifically established facts with regard to dementia praecox. Any competent and contentious study of a morphological, biochemical, or psychiatric nature will be accepted. It is the aim of the editors to encourage research in the hope that a rational therapy and prophylaxis will result." Bayard Holmes unabashedly expressed his "faith" in the hypothesis that "disease of the mind is the result of organic disease of the body," and as "in spite of the magnitude of this problem there is a great scarcity of books and monographs dealing with the physical, chemical and biologic conditions of the unfortunate victims of this disease," he urges "the publication of a journal devoted exclusively to the study from the organic point of view, of one part of the field of mental disease, viz., dementia praecox."

The most prominent bearer of the torch for Kraepelin in America was the neuropathologist—and arch-critic of Adolf Meyer—E. E. Southard. Southard was the first to describe (in 1915) cortical atrophy as a clear pathology in the brains of persons with dementia praecox. But when Southard died prematurely, so, too, did the only promise of a serious American program of neuropathological research on dementia praecox and manic-depressive insanity. Southard, with his characteristic humor, referred to the Meyerians and the psychoanalysts as "mind twist men" and Kraepelinians (such as himself) as "brain spot men," monikers as apt as any others applied since.

American Psychiatry and the Tragic Years of Psychoanalysis

Although laboratory research on the neurological, biochemical, and genetic causes and associated pathologies of schizophrenia continued in Munich at Kraepelin's Deutsche Forschungsanstalt fuer Psychiatrie (German Research Institute for Psychiatry) from 1917 until World War II, in America such research was the exception and not the rule. After the deaths of Southard and Holmes, Henry Cotton, N. D. C. Lewis, George Kirby, Seymour Kety (after the war), and a handful of others continued to look for biological evidence of the cause and characteristic disease processes in schizophrenia but failed miserably. This failure emboldened American, French, and British psychiatrists who had come under the influence of the ideas of psychoanalysts such as Sigmund Freud, Carl Gustav Jung, and Alfred Adler. Unfortunately, psychoanalytically oriented psychiatrists drew the wrong conclusion from the failure of laboratory science, and thousands of persons with schizophrenia and their family members suffered for it.

From the 1920s until the 1970s, psychoanalysis dominated American psychiatry, diverting the search for new drug treatments and basic biological research into a blind alley. Psychoanalysis was a covert ideology with absolutely no scientific evidence to support it. Psychoanalytic organizations maintained a cultlike, secret society social structure, which only added to its apparent mystery and allure to the "uninitiated" lay public. However, because so many prominent physicians converted to it, psychoanalysis and figures such as Sigmund Freud and Carl Jung enjoyed a legitimacy that was not deserved. Throughout the 20th century psy-

choanalysts blamed the victim—or the victim's mother—as the "cause" of schizophrenia (or other psychiatric illnesses). Just imagine the pain caused by such a theory! And yet, the "refrigerator mothers" and "schizophrenogenic mothers" seemed like real villains to psychiatrists. Medical students were trained to view the mothers of schizophrenics as "pathogens," as if they were viruses. This same tragedy of blaming the afflicted person or a family member for the "cause" of schizophrenia was additionally promoted in the various "family interaction theories" of the 1950s to 1970s that became so beloved of psychiatric social workers in particular. Family interaction theorists blamed unhealthy communication patterns within the entire family—thus making everyone share the blame for causing schizophrenia.

It took major advances in medical technology, specifically the computer revolution and the rise of new techniques in neuroimaging, genetics research, and psychopharmacology to swing the pendulum back to Kraepelin's search for the biological causes of the psychotic disorders.

Historians of science now regard psychoanalysis as a pseudoscience that inexplicably dominated a subdiscipline of medicine—psychiatry—and unnecessarily maintained a 19th-century attitude toward the causes and treatment of mental disorders. Psychoanalysis was the dominant medical pseudoscience of the 20th century, as phrenology was in the 19th century and animal magnetism was in the 18th century.

The 1970s: Schizophrenia Becomes a Physical Disease Once Again

Advances in the technology to study biochemistry, brain function and structure, genetics, and the development of brain imaging techniques (e.g., the CT scan) all converged to stimulate a biological renaissance in the study of schizophrenia and the psychotic disorders in the 1970s. Suddenly it was appropriate to speak of schizophrenia as a "brain disease," and psychoanalytic and family interaction models largely began to be ignored as legitimate causes of this disease (although it was found that psychosocial factors can have an effect on relapse rates in persons with schizophrenia). Genetic transmission was now estimated to be responsible for about 80 percent of the cause of schizophrenia, with other unknown environmental factors comprising the other 20 percent. Viral theories of the cause of schizophrenia were also resurrected after first being mentioned by Kraepelin and Bleuler almost a century before. Perinatal factors in the development of schizophrenia again began to be studied in earnest. Cross-cultural studies of the prevalence rates of schizophrenia were initiated by the World Health Organization. Twins studies and adoption studies conducted in the 1960s helped to form new and complex theories of the genetic transmission of schizophrenia in the 1970s and 1980s. After decades of disappointment and neglect, the search for the causes of schizophrenia once again was viewed as a promising endeavor.

The 1980s, 1990s, and Beyond

The last two decades of the 20th century brought more scientific progress than the last 100 years combined in the understanding and treatment of schizophrenia and other psychotic disorders.

We now know for a fact that genetics plays a key role in the cause and development of schizophrenia and bipolar disorder. Several candidates for the locus of the genes that cause schizophrenia are the subject of intense scrutiny. The mode of genetic transmission remains a mystery; however, the National Institute of Mental Health Schizophrenia Genetics Initiative that began in 1989 is collecting and analyzing the DNA of persons with schizophrenia and their entire families in order to find a solution. Environmental factors still play an important role, too, in the development of the psychotic disorders, but no one knows what they are or how they interact with genes.

Unfortunately, at the dawn of the 21st century most of the evidence concerning the "causes" of schizophrenia comes from epidemiological studies and not from the identification of a characteristic process of cellular pathology (as is the case in other diseases, including Alzheimer's disease). As two editorials that appeared in 1999 in *The New England Journal of Medicine* and *Nature Neuroscience* remind us, no one knows what causes schizophrenia.

Advances in brain imaging technology, neurochemistry, and neuropathology have produced sophisticated new models of schizophrenia based on the notion of disconnection between certain neural circuits or pathways in the brain. The prefrontal region of the frontal lobe and the temporal lobe are the two cortical regions most affected in schizophrenia. Subcortical structures such as the thalamus, a major relay center for messages traveling throughout the brain, and the hippocampus and cerebellum also have been implicated in schizophrenia.

With the push to make psychiatry a true medical science, the traditional schizophrenia subtypes of Kraepelin and Bleuler have been called into question by quantitative studies of the symptoms of schizophrenia. Although Timothy Crow offered the first major reconceptualization of schizophrenia with his Type I/Type II concept of syndromes characterized by positive and negative symptoms, respectively, others have used the statistical technique of factor analysis to come up with new "dimensions" of schizophrenia. Prominent schizophrenia researchers such as Peter F. Liddle and Nancy Andreasen have posited three syndromes for schizophrenia, and Mark Lenzenweger has argued for four. All of these dimensional models of schizophrenia claim that neuroimaging, neuropathological, and neuropsychological data provide a better "fit" with these new dimensions than the old, traditional clinical subtypes of Kraepelin and Bleuler.

The introduction of clozapine as the first of the new class of antipsychotic medications was the first major innovation in the treatment of psychosis to appear in 30 years. Pharmaceutical companies have a variety of new antipsychotics in the pipeline, and as more is understood about the interaction of the more than 100 different neurotransmitters in the brain, more effective drugs will continue to be designed and brought to market.

As we enter the 21st century the dominant explanatory paradigm in schizophrenia research is the neurodevelopmental model. First proposed by R. H. Murray in 1985 and D. R. Weinberger in 1986, the neurodevelopmental model claims that the causes of schizophrenia originate in subtle abnormalities that occur sometime during the early development of the nervous system of the fetus. This approach has sparked new research into a wide variety of old topics of schizophrenia research, such as childhood-onset schizophrenia. Whether neurodevelopmental schizophrenia turns out to be the main illness or is found to be only one of several subtypes of schizophrenia remains to be seen. Still, no one can dispute the fact that schizophrenia research will be one of the most fascinating areas of science as the new century unfolds.

Andreasen, N. C. "Editorial: Understanding the Causes of Schizophrenia," *New England Journal of Medicine* 340 (February 25, 1999).

Andreasen, N. C., and M. Flaum. "Schizophrenia: The Characteristic Symptoms," *Schizophrenia Bulletin* 17 (1991): 27–49.

"Editorial: What Causes Schizophrenia?" *Nature Neuroscience* 2 (April 1999).

Haldipur, C. V. "Madness in Ancient India: Concepts of Madness in Charaka Samhita (1st century A.D.)," *Comprehensive Psychiatry* 25 (1984): 335–344.

Haslam, J. *Observations on Madness and Melancholy.* London: J. Callon, 1809.

Jeste, D. V. "Did Schizophrenia Exist before the Eighteenth Century?" *Comprehensive Psychiatry* 26 (1985): 493–503.

Noll, R. "The American Reaction to Dementia Praecox, 1900," *History of Psychiatry* 15 (2004): 127–128.

Pinel, P. *Traité médico-philosophique sur l'aliénation mentale.* 2nd ed. Paris: J. A. Brosson, 1809.

Torrey, E. F. *Schizophrenia and Civilization.* New York: Jason Aronson, 1980.

Warner, J. H. "Ideals of Science and Their Discontent in Late Nineteenth-Century American Medicine," *Isis* 82 (1991): 454–478.

Williams, G. *The Age of Agony: The Art of Healing, ca. 1700–1800.* Chicago: Academy Chicago Publishers, 1986.

ENTRIES A–Z

A

abaissement du niveau mental Literally, a "lowering of the level (or threshold) of consciousness." Today, this idea is usually expressed by the term ALTERED STATE OF CONSCIOUSNESS.

French psychiatrist Pierre JANET (1859–1947) coined this term to refer to the apparent weakening of volitional control of consciousness and the subsequent DISSOCIATION (or "splitting") of consciousness into autonomous parts that may not even be aware of one another. Although Janet noted that this *abaissement* was common in forms of psychological automatisms such as found in multiple personalities, hysterics, the trance behavior of mediums, and in automatic writing, the term was adopted and used extensively by Swiss psychiatrist C. G. JUNG (1875–1961) in his famous 1907 monograph, *Über die Psychologie der Dementia Praecox: Ein Versuch* (The psychology of dementia praecox) to describe DEMENTIA PRAECOX (later "SCHIZOPHRENIA"). Jung felt that the *abaissement* was the "primary condition" and "the root of the schizophrenic disorder." He thought it resulted from both psychological and physiological causes. In dementia praecox, Jung argued that the *abaissement* caused the following effects commonly observed in schizophrenics: (1) the loss of whole regions of normally controlled contents of consciousness, (2) split-off fragments of the personality, (3) the prevention of normal trains of thought from being consistently carried through and completed, (4) a decrease in the responsibility and proper reaction of the ego, (5) constriction and distortion of thoughts and feelings, and (6) a lowering of the threshold of consciousness (as in an altered state), thereby allowing normally inhibited content of the unconscious to enter consciousness in the form of autonomous invasions.

Jung was briefly (in 1902) a student of Janet's in Paris and was greatly influenced by him. *Abaissement du niveau mental* was a term used frequently by C. G. Jung in his later writings.

Janet, P. *L'Automatisme Psychologique*. Paris: Alcon, 1890.

Jung, C. G. *Über die Psychologie der Dementia praecox: Ein Versuch*. Halle a.S., 1907.

abilify See ANTIPSYCHOTIC DRUGS.

ablation studies In the late 19th and early 20th centuries, the modern neurosciences (then called the "brain sciences") were coming into being, just as the clinical syndromes of DEMENTIA PRAECOX and manic-depressive PSYCHOSIS were simultaneously being identified and described by Emil KRAEPELIN (1856–1926). It was natural that the investigative techniques of gross anatomy and neuropathology of the new "brain sciences" would be applied to the study of the brains of deceased patients that had suffered from these MENTAL DISORDERS. The many ablation studies of the brains of schizophrenics and manic-depressives involved the removal and systematic destruction of the brain tissue in order to look for structural abnormalities. Brain tissue was commonly ablated slice by slice, with careful records kept to document unusual formations. Not surprisingly, most of these studies were inconclusive due to the imprecision of this gross procedure. Modern brain imaging techniques and biochemical and genetic strategies of investigation have been more successful in detecting the subtle physiological abnormalities in the brains of people suffering from SCHIZOPHRENIA or manic-depressive psychosis.

See also BRAIN ABNORMALITIES IN SCHIZOPHRENIA; BRAIN IMAGING STUDIES IN SCHIZOPHRENIA.

aboulia In 19th-century psychiatry, aboulia was a "disorder of the will" or "a form of insanity characterized by an inability to exert the will." Before the rise of PSYCHOANALYSIS and behaviorism in the 20th century, many psychiatrists considered aboulia as the central characteristic of most MENTAL DISORDERS. Hence, much of what we would now call psychotherapy was actually "will-training," that is, training people to concentrate better, to focus their attention on tasks better, and to control their impulses.

DEMENTIA PRAECOX and SCHIZOPHRENIA were considered primarily disorders of the will by many psychiatrists. According to Emil KRAEPELIN, the essence of dementia praecox/schizophrenia was "that destruction of conscious volition . . . which is manifest in the loss of energy and drive, in disjointed volitional behavior. This rudderless state leads to impulsive instinctual activity: there is no planned reflection which suppresses impulses as they arise or directs them into proper channels."

Aboulia is again being considered in contemporary schizophrenia research because so many researchers have implicated the abnormal functioning of the frontal lobe—the seat of inhibition and "executive functioning" or "supervisory mental processes." Frontal lobe dysfunctions result in a disorder of volition or will, a symptom sometimes also called "AVOLITION."

See also BRAIN ABNORMALITIES IN SCHIZOPHRENIA.

Berrios, G. E., and M. Gili. "Will and Its Disorders: A Conceptual History," *History of Psychiatry* 6 (1995): 87–104.

Kraepelin, E. "Patterns of Mental Disorder (1920)," trans. H. Marshall. In *Themes and Variations in European Psychiatry,* edited by S. R. Hirsch and M. Shepherd. Bristol, England: Wright, 1974.

Morice, R., and A. Delahunty. "Frontal/Executive Impairments in Schizophrenia," *Schizophrenia Bulletin* 22 (1996): 125–137.

abuse of psychiatric patients The mentally ill have been ridiculed and scorned throughout human history. Although the efforts to humanize the treatment of the mentally ill through the "moral medicine" movement of the early 19th century resulted in many reforms in some asylums for the insane, reports have continued until present times of periodic abuses—both psychological and physiological—in psychiatric facilities throughout the world. It is often thought that the tremendous power that the staff of such institutions wields over the (usually) involuntarily committed, mentally ill patient can sometimes corrupt even the most empathetic and well-intentioned caregiver at stressful times.

Through the centuries, a massive and disturbing literature of first-person accounts has been created that documents such abuses. A small book published anonymously in London in 1752, entitled *Low-Life, Or One Half of the World Knows Not How the Other Half Lives,* describes the torturous conditions of the chained patients at the BETHLEM ROYAL HOSPITAL ("BEDLAM"), in which the author reports observing the nurses stealing for themselves the best portions of food that were originally intended for the patients. Sadly, even today such abuses by staff are frequently reported in large psychiatric institutions, and not only food but also property and even money often mysteriously disappear from patients who, when they complain, are told they are either confused, delusional, or lying. In *The New York World* newspaper in 1887, a serialized story entitled "Ten Days in a Mad House" described similar abuses. It was written by journalist-celebrity Elizabeth Seaman (née Cochrane), who, under the pseudonym Nellie BLY, faked mental illness and gained admission to the New York City Lunatic Asylum on Blackwell's Island (briefly named "Welfare Island" in the 1940s but now changed to "Roosevelt Island"). This account was published in book form in 1888.

Perhaps the most famous—and influential—autobiographical account was Clifford BEERS's *A Mind That Found Itself* (1908). Beers, a businessman who underwent a brief psychotic episode, was first put in a private sanitarium and then a state hospital. He described the repeated abuses of patients by attendants and how kindly new staff members were soon transformed into sadists through peer pressure. Beers writes:

> I soon observed that the only patients who were not likely to be subjected to abuse were the very

> ones least in need of care and treatment . . . The patient too weak, physically or mentally, to attend to his own wants was frequently abused because of that very helplessness which made it necessary for attendants to wait upon him.

He also relates the following anecdote, still familiar to those who work in today's psychiatric institutions:

> One attendant, on the very day he had been discharged for choking a patient into an insensibility so profound that it had been necessary to call a physician to restore him, said to me, "They are getting pretty damned strict these days, discharging a man for simply *choking* a patient." This illustrates the attitude of many attendants.

Beers eventually improved, wrote his autobiography, and founded the MENTAL HYGIENE MOVEMENT in the United States. His early efforts are still bearing fruit with the many mental patients' advocacy groups, especially the National Alliance for the Mentally Ill.

As much as we may prefer not to believe it, abuses are still a part of the world of almost any institution that serves an inpatient population of people who have chronic mental illnesses. A short autobiographical account by Leopold Bellak, a prominent psychiatrist, SCHIZOPHRENIA researcher, and professor at the Albert Einstein College of Medicine in New York City, includes a story that almost anyone today who has ever worked in such facilities will find familiar. These are the sort of events that go on *sub rosa* in the culture of the psychiatric hospital but that no one will openly admit to, especially administrators, who often do not want either to hear of such cases or believe them when reported. This leaves the honest witness to suffer the brunt of the negative consequences for his or her accusations, with the actual abuser often remaining unaffected. Bellak describes his first clinical experiences as a psychiatric aide on a chronic psychotic ward in 1938 and 1939:

> The utter sense of hopelessness fostered in institutions run in very poor and dictatorial fashion by an ill-trained staff was often hardly better than that described in *One Flew Over the Cuckoo's Nest*. Acts of sadism were tolerated, if not encouraged. On my first day as a psychiatric aide in a high-class sanitarium, I was put under the tutelage of an experienced psychiatric aide. Among his first words of wisdom to me were that if I should find it necessary to hit a patient, I should hit him in the abdomen in order to leave no telltale marks. Seeing a patient put into wet packs was the closest thing I could imagine to a rape.

In many countries today, political prisoners are sometimes incarcerated and abused in psychiatric institutions, a practice that led to the withdrawal of the Soviet Union from the WORLD PSYCHIATRIC ASSOCIATION in 1983, when it became clear that the USSR was likely to be expelled. As a result of the glasnost of the Gorbachev era, an official delegation of 26 Americans (including 14 psychiatrists and 2 lawyers) selected by the NATIONAL INSTITUTE OF MENTAL HEALTH (NIMH) visited four Soviet psychiatric hospitals in February and March 1989 to investigate such reports. In July 1989 the investigative team released its report, claiming that many of the patients they examined had no discernible MENTAL DISORDERS and that the maximum security prisons in the Soviet Union still had the characteristics of "psychiatric prisons." They found that many patients had been incarcerated for "anti-Soviet thoughts" or undesirable political behavior. Drugs were used for "punitive rather than therapeutic purposes," and patients were denied most rights, especially the right to have a say in their treatment. Based on these grim findings, the delegation recommended that the Soviet Union not be readmitted to the World Psychiatric Association. However, due to the political climate of openness and optimism toward the changes in Soviet society, on October 18, 1989, the World Psychiatric Association voted to readmit the Soviet All-Union Society of Psychiatrists and Narcologists, but with the stipulation that it would be subject to suspension if the Soviets did not end their misuse of psychiatry against political dissidents. Despite the negative report and recommendations of the NIMH, the AMERICAN PSYCHIATRIC ASSOCIATION voted in favor of readmission.

The abuse of persons suffering from mental disorders, particularly those inpatients residing

in institutions, has also occurred for centuries in the form of involuntary participation in medical experiments aimed at preventing, treating, or curing mental disorders. In the given historical context of their respective eras, radical procedures were introduced as "rational treatments" that followed logically from a (then) current medical theory of the cause (etiology) or the disease process (pathophysiology) of mental disorders. Because of the severity of deterioration in functioning that occurs over time, persons with schizophrenia have been disproportionately abused in such experiments. Perhaps the best documented example of such abuse is that perpetuated by psychiatrist Henry A. COTTON and his associates at the New Jersey State Hospital at Trenton between 1918 and 1932. Like many prominent physicians in his day, Cotton believed that infections in various parts of the body (the teeth, gums, colon, stomach, cervix, testicles, and so on) could be transmitted to the brain via the blood and cause severe mental disorders such as DEMENTIA PRAECOX (schizophrenia) and manic-depressive insanity (BIPOLAR DISORDER). Unlike the majority of those physicians, Cotton chose to use his authority as superintendent and medical director of his state hospital to immediately remove most or all the teeth of recent admissions and to perform radical surgeries to eliminate the sources of focal infection. Hundreds of thousands of teeth were removed and more than 2,000 major surgical procedures were performed, resulting in the deaths of hundred of people. His own early statistics indicated a mortality rate of about 30 percent, and he was well aware of this fact, as historian Andrew Scull has documented. Although Cotton was recognized for his humane innovations at Trenton after taking control in 1907, eliminating many forms of physical restraint and replacing abusive hospital staff, and although his surgical treatments were indeed congruent with current medical theory, his continued use of such procedures even when an outside evaluator was able to show they did not eliminate mental illness, is horrifying. A similar story of abuse, PSYCHOSURGERY, also began with a seemingly rational treatment for mental illness but led to the disabling or death of an estimated 40,000 to 50,000 persons from the 1930s to the 1960s.

See also BEERS, CLIFFORD W.; CHEMICAL RESTRAINT; MECHANICAL RESTRAINT.

Beers, Clifford. *A Mind That Found Itself: An Autobiography.* New York: Longmans, Green, 1908.

Bellak, L. "An Idiosyncratic Overview." In *Disorders of the Schizophrenic Syndrome*, edited by L. Bellak. New York: Basic Books, 1979.

Peterson, D., ed. *A Mad People's History of Madness.* Pittsburgh, Pa.: University of Pittsburgh Press, 1982.

Pressman, Jack. *Last Resort: Psychosurgery and the Limits of Medicine.* Cambridge: Cambridge University Press, 1998.

Scull, Andrew. *Madhouse: A Tragic Tale of Megalomania and Modern Medicine.* New Haven, Conn.: Yale University Press, 2005.

accessory symptoms The name given by Eugen BLEULER in his 1911 classic, *Dementia Praecox, Or the Group of Schizophrenias,* to the symptoms of SCHIZOPHRENIA that may also appear in other types of mental illness. This is in contrast to the "fundamental symptoms" that uniquely characterize schizophrenia. Among the most easily recognizable of the accessory symptoms are HALLUCINATIONS and DELUSIONS. Bleuler emphasizes what an important role these accessory symptoms play in the life of the afflicted individual when he writes:

> It is not often that the fundamental symptoms are so markedly exhibited as to cause the patient to be hospitalized in a mental institution. It is primarily the accessory phenomena which makes his retention at home impossible, or it is they which make the psychosis manifest and give occasion to require psychiatric help. These accessory symptoms may be present throughout the whole course of this disease, or only in entirely arbitrary periods of illness.

Bleuler, E. *Dementia Praecox, Or the Group of Schizophrenia.* Translated by Joseph Zinkin. 1911. Reprint, New York: International Universities Press, 1950.

acedia Also spelled "accidia," it is a word that originated in the Middle Ages to refer to the apa-

thetic self-neglect or uncaring behavior of those who are melancholic (depressed) or otherwise mentally ill. In medieval Europe, the church designated Accidia (or sloth) as the fourth of the Seven Cardinal (Deadly) Sins. Acedia also described an impoverishment of mental energy, which, it was felt, could be reversed in an individual through an experience of "conversion," in which lost faith is recovered and psychological revitalization occurs. Thus, acedia was related to "MELANCHOLIA" or "DEPRESSION." This term was used in the 19th century but is now considered obsolete.

Jackson, S. W. *Melancholia and Depression: From Hippocratic Times to Modern Times.* New Haven, Conn.: Yale University Press, 1986.

acromania A diagnostic term used in the 18th and 19th centuries to label a "confirmed" or "incurable madness."

acting-out A common bit of jargon in the day-to-day conversation of mental health professionals today; it refers to the expression of socially inappropriate sexual and aggressive behaviors. It has its origins in psychoanalytic theory, in that sexual and aggressive instinctual impulses, which we normally repress, inhibit, or sublimate, are not held back (either unconsciously or in fantasy) and are instead "acted-out" in behavior. More often than not it refers to violent behavior, and if a psychiatric patient is engaged in acting-out behavior it is said that he or she is "going-off" (i.e., like the firing of a rocket or an explosion).

active phase of schizophrenia The period of time that the characteristic symptoms of SCHIZOPHRENIA are present. According to *DSM-IV-TR* (2000), two or more of the five characteristic symptoms must be "present for a significant portion of time during a one-month period (or less if successfully treated)." These five characteristic symptoms are:

(1) DELUSIONS
(2) HALLUCINATIONS
(3) disorganized speech (e.g., frequent derailment or incoherence)
(4) grossly disorganized or catatonic behavior
(5) negative symptoms, i.e., affective flattening, ALOGIA, or AVOLITION.

Returning to a method of diagnosing schizophrenia based on only one symptom that had been proposed in the past (see FIRST-RANK SYMPTOMS), *DSM-IV-TR* states that the identification of the active phase of schizophrenia may be identified by only one characteristic symptom if "delusions are bizarre" or "hallucinations consist of a voice keeping up a running commentary on the person's behavior or thoughts, or two or more voices conversing with each other."

Although to receive a *DSM-IV-TR* diagnosis of schizophrenia, these symptoms of the active phase must be in evidence for at least one month (or less if successfully treated); attenuated forms of two or more of these active phase symptoms (such as odd beliefs or unusual experiences) or the presence of NEGATIVE SYMPTOMS must also be in evidence for a period of six months as either part of a PRODROMAL PHASE or a RESIDUAL PHASE. To receive a diagnosis of schizophrenia in *ICD-10* (1992), the characteristic symptoms of the active phase must be in evidence for more than one month, and although a prodromal phase is acknowledged, since such a syndrome cannot be identified reliably as belonging specifically to schizophrenia and not to any other MENTAL DISORDER, it is not included in this one-month duration.

The European definition of the active phase in *ICD-10* has a strict one-month minimum to be met before "an acute schizophrenia-like psychotic disorder" can be diagnosed as schizophrenia. However, the range of characteristic symptoms is wider in Europe than in North America.

The North American psychiatric definition of what constitutes an active phase of schizophrenia changed between 1987 and 1994. *DSM-IV's* inclusion of negative symptoms as part of the active phase of schizophrenia and the lengthening of the time frame for the active phase are the two most significant departures from *DSM-III-R* of 1987.

acute In reference to diseases, *acute* refers to those that are sudden in onset and generally rather short-lived. However, acute phases of a disease are those periods when symptoms that are generally dormant can flare up.

acute and transient psychotic disorders One of the five types of ATYPICAL PSYCHOTIC DISORDERS found in *ICD-10* (1992) that cannot be readily classified as SCHIZOPHRENIA or as a mood disorder with psychotic features. The others in this category are persistent delusional disorders, induced DELUSIONAL DISORDER, SCHIZOAFFECTIVE DISORDER, and schizotypal disorder. Acute and transient psychotic disorders fall into two categories determined by the amount of time it took for the disorder to change from a nonpsychotic to a clearly psychotic state: abrupt onset (onset within 48 hours) or acute onset (onset in more than 48 hours but less than two weeks). If the onset is acute, *ICD-10* indicates it must be specified if it is associated with acute stress two weeks or less before the start of psychotic symptoms. These disorders are also subdivided according to whether POLYMORPHIC PSYCHOTIC SYMPTOMS are present or whether those typical of schizophrenia are present. If the symptoms are similar to those of schizophrenia, and if they last at least one month, the diagnosis is changed to schizophrenia. If the symptoms are polymorphic and nonschizophrenic, the diagnosis need not be changed after one month. However, after three months it may be changed to that of a persistent delusional disorder. DELUSIONS, HALLUCINATIONS, and incomprehensible or incoherent speech, or any combination of these, are the psychotic symptoms that are most often present in these disorders.

acute-chronic distinction The criterion in SCHIZOPHRENIA research that traditionally explores cognitive, perceptual, and behavioral differences in schizophrenics based on the amount of time they have been diagnosed with the disorder and have been hospitalized. Generally, ACUTE schizophrenics are those who have not been institutionalized for more than 3.5 years, and chronic schizophrenics are those whose total time spent in institutions has been six years or more. Acute schizophrenics have been found to differ from chronic schizophrenics across many neurophysiological and neuropsychological variables.

Studying schizophrenia by dividing persons into acute and chronic subgroups has virtually disappeared since the 1990s. Instead, a great deal of attention has been paid to trying to identify and understand the PRODROMAL PHASE of schizophrenia, which predates the "first episode" or first acute or active phase of characteristic psychotic symptoms. Additionally, the many cognitive and physical changes that occur as the illness persists over the years (in decades past simply lumped together as aspects of "chronic schizophrenia") are being identified and studied in detail.

See also ACUTE SCHIZOPHRENIA; CHRONIC SCHIZOPHRENIA; PRODROMAL PHASE.

acute delirius mania A late 19th-century term for the acute forms of CATATONIC EXCITEMENT. The syndrome was often described as an acute MENTAL DISORDER with a rapid onset and course, resembling DELIRIUM caused by fever, during which the patient would experience a rise in temperature, rapidly reach exhaustion, and then possibly death. Other names for this syndrome were Bell's syndrome or disease, typhomania, *Délire aigu*, delirius mania, acute delirium, delirium grave, mania gravis, and delirium acutum.

Fürstner, C. "Über delirium acutum," *Archiv für Psychiatrie* 11 (1881): 517–538.

acute recoverable psychosis Limited psychotic episode for which complete remission can occur. Acute recoverable psychoses (ARPs) is a generic term proposed for the psychotic disorders that generally last only from two weeks up to six months. These disorders may be predominantly affective, confusional (resembling organic mental disorders), or SCHIZOPHRENIA-like (usually distinguished by paranoid and nonparanoid varieties). It has been suggested that the shared core symptoms and characteristic natural history of the schizophrenia-like

ARPs indicate they are variants of the same underlying disorder, despite the many diagnostic labels.

See also ATYPICAL PSYCHOTIC DISORDERS.

Munro, A. "Schizophrenia-like Illnesses." In *New Perspectives in Schizophrenia,* edited by M. N. Menuck and M. V. Seeman. New York: Macmillan, 1985.

acute schizophrenia The ACUTE phase of SCHIZOPHRENIA is when the symptoms first flare up into a full PSYCHOSIS. However, "acute" can also refer to the length of time that active schizophrenic symptoms are evident or refer to a hypothesized variant of schizophrenia that has a better prognosis than CHRONIC SCHIZOPHRENIA. The ACUTE-CHRONIC DISTINCTION in studies of schizophrenia refers to the amount of time that has elapsed since the clear diagnosis of schizophrenia has been made. Many studies have shown psychological and behavioral differences between those patients in the early or acute stages of the illness versus those in the later or chronic stages of schizophrenia. For research purposes, acute schizophrenics are those who have had less than a total of 3.5 years' hospitalization. Studies have shown that chronic schizophrenics have more severe thought disorder and other cognitive deficits than acute schizophrenics, but many have argued that this deterioration may be due to the debilitating effects of institutionalization rather than being a result of the illness itself. Acute schizophrenia is often conceptually confused with REACTIVE SCHIZOPHRENIA, the type of schizophrenia in which patients are found to have a better pre-breakdown history and eventually improve, versus those who follow a lifelong chronic course.

Schizophrenia researchers no longer design studies along the lines of the acute-chronic distinction. The arbitrary criterion that a certain number of years or less of hospitalization defines acute schizophrenia is no longer used in contemporary schizophrenia research. Nor is the criterion provided in *DSM-III* (1980) and *DSM-III-R* (1987) that "chronic schizophrenia" is defined by an illness that has been in evidence for at least two years. Instead, research is focused more narrowly on groups identified as manifesting "first-episode schizophrenia" or "recent-onset schizophrenia" in which the active symptoms have been apparent for only days, weeks, or months. These terms have almost entirely replaced the old notion of acute schizophrenia.

ADD psychosis The acronym for "attention deficit disorder," a clinical diagnostic entity proposed by Leopold Bellak in 1985. Bellak claims that many cases of SCHIZOPHRENIA (perhaps as many as 10 percent) are misdiagnosed and are instead examples of "ADD PSYCHOSIS." ADD psychosis is organic in origin, and it is thought to constitute the end result of a particular neurological deficit (attention deficit disorder) on personality organization. Attention deficit disorder (a common childhood diagnosis given to children who are hyperactive and dyslexic, among other attributes) was formerly called "minimal brain dysfunction," and the concept of ADD psychosis is the lifelong extension of these neurological deficits into adulthood. Many of Bellak's proposed symptoms (primarily NEGATIVE SYMPTOMS) and associated neurological findings for ADD psychosis seem to be similar to Crow's Type II schizophrenia and Carpenter's "deficit syndrome."

See also CROW'S HYPOTHESIS; DEFICIT SYMPTOMS/SYNDROME.

Bellak, L. "ADD Psychosis as a Separate Entity," *Schizophrenia Bulletin* 11 (1985): 523–527.

adolescent insanity A term coined in 1873 by Thomas Clouston, a Scottish psychiatrist and lecturer in psychiatry at the University of Edinburgh. He sometimes also called this syndrome "developmental insanity." Clouston identified adolescent insanity as a psychotic syndrome with an AGE AT ONSET between 18 and 24 years. Clouston said males were predominantly affected and that 30 percent of the cases developed into a more serious "secondary DEMENTIA." A family history of such psychosis was noticed in 65 percent of his cases when compared with 25 percent of cases of insanity with other diagnoses. Clouston's concept of adolescent insanity never became popular and was forgotten after Emil KRAEPELIN elaborated his concept of DEMENTIA PRAECOX in 1896. Clous-

ton was not at all pleased by being ignored for his contribution, and in a 1904 textbook on psychiatry he wrote: "Since I first used the term in 1873 and described its general characteristics it has become generally accepted by writers in psychiatry. Lately, however, Kraepelin has taken the term Dementia Praecox and applied it to practically my whole group of adolescent cases, making it cover the curable and incurable. I strongly object. . . ." Clouston's syndrome is now regarded as one of the precursors to the NEURODEVELOPMENTAL MODEL OF SCHIZOPHRENIA that has become the overarching paradigm at the end of the 20th century.

Clouston, T. S. *Clinical Lectures on Mental Diseases, Sixth Edition.* London: Churchill, 1904.

O'Connell, P., et al. "Developmental Insanity or Dementia Praecox: Was the Wrong Concept Adopted?" *Schizophrenia Research* 23 (1997): 97–106.

adoption method and studies One of the research strategies to resolve the "nature versus nurture" controversy in the investigation of the causes of MENTAL DISORDERS. Adoption studies have tended to strongly support the argument for the genetic basis for many psychiatric disorders, including SCHIZOPHRENIA, BIPOLAR DISORDER (manic-depressive disorder), and even alcoholism.

Adoption studies have been carried out in two ways: in the first method, children separated at birth from parents with a psychiatric disorder, and then raised by adoptive parents, are located. If these offspring show a prevalence for, say, schizophrenia that is the same as might be expected if they had been raised at home by their schizophrenic parent(s), then the argument is supported that genetics rather than environment is the primary cause of schizophrenia. A second method used in adoption studies is to look at all children who have been adopted, matching those in a group who develop schizophrenia (or another mental disorder), and then matching other adoptees in a control group who have not developed schizophrenia. Research is then conducted on both the biological and adoptive relatives of these individuals in these two groups. If the schizophrenia adoptees show a higher prevalence of schizophrenia in their biological relatives but not their adoptive ones, then the genetic explanation for schizophrenia is supported.

The very first published study using these adoptive methods in schizophrenia research was reported by L. L. Heston in the *British Journal of Psychiatry* in 1966. In the late 1960s, a famous series of adoption studies using these two methods was conducted in Denmark by David Rosenthal and Seymour Kety. All of these studies have consistently shown that adopted children who develop schizophrenia are many times more likely to have biological relatives who have developed schizophrenia rather than adoptive relatives who have done so. In the 1980s Rosenthal and Kety and their associates published reviews of clinical studies using the adoptive methods that support this genetic hypothesis in AFFECTIVE DISORDERS (such as bipolar disorder) as well.

In the 1990s the Danish data underwent further analyses and was supplemented by an ongoing Finnish Adoptive Family Study of Schizophrenia. The Danish study found that biological relatives of schizophrenic adoptees are more likely to have typical "narrowly defined" schizophrenia but also have more "latent" nonpsychotic forms of the illness. In the initial 1971 published report of the Danish study, Rosenthal and his colleagues termed these latent, nonpsychotic forms of the disorder "SCHIZOPHRENIA SPECTRUM DISORDERS (SSD)" to indicate a potential underlying biological commonality between schizophrenia and other mental disorders. The results of the Finnish study, first published in 1991, are consistent with previous studies of adoptees, finding a lifetime prevalence rate of 9.4 percent in the adopted-away children of schizophrenic parents and a lifetime prevalence in a control group of adoptees of 1.2 percent. Therefore, adopted-away children of mothers suffering from schizophrenia bear a four-times greater risk of developing schizophrenia later in life than those adopted-away children whose mothers did not have schizophrenia. The Finnish study of Tienari and colleagues provided support for both strong genetic and strong environmental main effects as well as gene-environment interaction effects. People who develop schizophrenia are "genetically sensitive" to their environments.

See also GENETICS STUDIES.

Heston, L. L. "Psychiatric Disorders in Foster Home Reared Children of Schizophrenic Mothers," *British Journal of Psychiatry* 112 (1966): 819–825.

Tienari, P. J., and L. C. Wynne. "Adoption Studies of Schizophrenia," *Annals of Medicine* 26 (1994): 233–237.

Wahlberg, K. E., L. C. Wynne, et al. "Gene-Environment Interaction in Vulnerability to Schizophrenia: Findings from the Finnish Adoptive Family Study of Schizophrenia," *American Journal of Psychiatry* 154 (1997): 355–362.

Wender, P. H., S. S. Kety, D. Rosenthal, et al. "Psychiatric Disorders in the Biological and Adoptive Families of Adopted Individuals with Affective Disorders," *Archives of General Psychiatry* 43 (1986): 923–929.

affect The behavioral expression of what is interpreted by others as an inner, subjective emotion or mood. For centuries, the term *affect* has often been used interchangeably with *mood.* Affect, emotion, and mood are now three distinct concepts in psychiatry, with emotion referring to an immediate inner state of feeling that is fluid and changeable, and mood referring to a general emotional state that grips a person for a long period of time (such as DEPRESSION or MANIA). Facial expressions, tone of voice, body language, content of speech, and observable actions can all be interpreted as affects corresponding to privately experienced emotions or moods. However, outwardly expressed affect can be incongruent or totally contradictory with what a person is truly feeling inside. Additionally, the affect expressed by a person can conflict with social norms in social interactions. The clinical term *inappropriate affect* is often used to refer to these examples. Persons with SCHIZOPHRENIA have long been observed to display inappropriate affect, and these behaviors are social cues to others of psychological disturbance.

See also AFFECTIVE DISORDERS.

Owens, H., and J. S. Maxmen. "Mood and Affect: A Semantic Confusion," *American Journal of Psychiatry* 136 (1979): 97–99.

affective disorders Throughout history, the word *affective* has been related to terms such as mood, emotion, passion, feeling, sentiment, euphoria, dysphoria, euthymia, dysthymia, cyclothymia, and so on. All these terms have been used to describe inner, subjective states of experience that are difficult to put into words. Since the time of the ancient Greeks, the two main broad categories for dozens of mental illnesses caused by a disorder of affect have been MELANCHOLIA and MANIA. By the latter half of the 19th century, concepts of melancholia and mania that had taken on a variety of meanings since antiquity were redefined in modern clinical forms as DEPRESSION and mania.

The affective disorders were renamed MOOD DISORDERS in 1987 with the publication of *DSM-III-R,* and remain so in *DSM-IV-TR* (2000). These are a group of MENTAL DISORDERS in which there is a disturbance of mood, accompanied by a full or partial manic or depressive syndrome, which is not due to any other physical or mental disorder. The Mood Disorders (Depressive Disorders, BIPOLAR DISORDERS, Mood Disorder Due to a General Medical Condition, Substance-Induced Mood Disorder) are characterized by "mood episodes" (Major Depressive Episode, Manic Episode, Mixed Episode, and Hypomanis Episode). Like SCHIZOPHRENIA, there is evidence that the development of the various mood disorders is influenced, in part, by genetics.

For centuries it had been noticed that alterations of mania and melancholia could afflict the same person at various times, but it was only in 1850 that a French ALIENIST, Jean-Pierre FALRET, proposed at a lecture to the Paris Psychiatric Society that this might be evidence of a single underlying disorder, a CIRCULAR INSANITY (*la folie circulaire*). In 1854 he and another French alienist, Jules-Gabriel-Francois BAILLARGER, published papers at almost the same time making this assertion (Baillarger called it the "double-formed insanity"). After 1899, when Emil KRAEPELIN essentially grouped all the AFFECTIVE DISORDERS under the broad diagnostic category of "manic-depressive illness" (*das manisch-depressive Irrsein*) and distinguished it from DEMENTIA PRAECOX (schizophrenia), all persons manifesting an affective or mood disorder were regarded as manic-depressive or potentially manic-depressive. In 1957, based on longitudinal studies of families with members who suffered from affective disorders, German psychiatrist Karl Leonhard

(1904–88) presented evidence that "monopolar" depression or mania were distinct illnesses from "bipolar" illness. However, the official separation of MANIC-DEPRESSIVE ILLNESS from major depression as distinct disorders did not occur until 1980, when *DSM-III* introduced the term *bipolar disorder* to replace Kraepelin's term. German psychiatrist Karl Kleist (1879–1960) had originally coined the term *bipolar* in 1953.

The relationship between schizophrenia and mood disorders, particularly the bipolar disorders, is the subject of much ongoing debate and research. Although Kraepelin distinctly separated dementia praecox from manic-depressive illness as the two main forms of insanity, it is still not clear among prominent psychiatrists and researchers if they are separate diseases or two ends of the spectrum of the same underlying disease. For example, in clinical situations, a person suffering from bipolar disorder with psychotic features (DELUSIONS and HALLUCINATIONS), particularly the sort of PARANOIA that accompanies manic episodes, can be indistinguishable from someone suffering from PARANOID SCHIZOPHRENIA.

Causes of Affective Disorders

Like schizophrenia, affective disorders are thought to be characterized by ETIOLOGIC HETEROGENEITY. Multiple causes—experiential (e.g., psychological trauma), social, genetic, biochemical (neurotransmitter dysfunction), endocrine dysfunction (particularly the thyroid gland and the hypothalamic-pituitary-adrenal glands axis), immune system dysfunction, biorhythm dysfunction, brain structure abnormalities, viral infection—have been proposed. A clear summary of the evidence and issues in the causes of affective disorders can be found in the chapter on "Causes" in E. Fuller Torry and Michael Knable's 2002 book, *Surviving Manic Depression: A Manual on Bipolar Disorder for Patients, Families and Providers.*

See also ANTIDEPRESSANT DRUGS; MANIC-DEPRESSIVE ILLNESS; SCHIZOAFFECTIVE DISORDER.

Berrios, G. E. "Mood Disorders: Clinical Section." In *A History of Clinical Psychiatry*, edited by G. E. Berrios and R. Porter. London: Athlone Press, 1995.

Taylor, A. M. "Are Schizophrenia and Affective Disorder Related? A Selected Literature Review," *American Journal of Psychiatry* 149 (1992): 22–32.

Torrey, E. F., and M. B. Knable. "Are Schizophrenia and Bipolar Disorder One Disease or Two? Introduction to the Symposium," *Schizophrenia Research* 39 (1999): 93–94.

Torrey, E. F., and M. B. Knable. *Surviving Manic Depression: A Manual on Bipolar Disorder for Patients, Families and Providers.* New York: Basic Books, 2002.

affective disturbances One of the "Four A's" (AUTISM, AFFECTIVE DISTURBANCES, ASSOCIATION DISTURBANCES, AMBIVALENCE) that Eugen BLEULER proposed as the fundamental symptoms of SCHIZOPHRENIA. Since then, this disturbance in the ability of schizophrenics to feel and/or express the full range of human emotions has been included in most definitions of schizophrenia. In *Dementia Praecox, Or the Group of Schizophrenias* (1911), Bleuler writes:

> Patients with schizophrenia react differently to their affective disturbances. The majority are not aware of them and consider their reaction as normal. The more intelligent, however, may reason about it quite acutely. At the beginning they sense the emotional emptiness as rather painful, so that they may be easily mistaken for melancholics. One of our catatonics considered himself as "insensitized"; one of Jung's patients could not pray any more because of "hardening of her feelings." Later, they tend to displace the changes in themselves to the outer world which itself becomes hollow, empty, strange, because of these affective changes. Often the element of strangeness has a touch of the uncanny and the hostile.

Bleuler, E. *Dementia Praecox, Or the Group of Schizophrenias*, trans. Joseph Zinkin. 1911. Reprint, New York: International Universities Press, 1950.

Africa Many studies have been done in Africa since the 1930s to determine how prevalent SCHIZOPHRENIA is on this continent. The majority of impressions from around Africa is that the prevalence of schizophrenia is quite low. Most of the disorders described in these reports resemble an ACUTE RECOVERABLE PSYCHOSIS rather than schizo-

phrenia. Unfortunately, there is as yet no conclusive study that can give a reasonable estimate of the prevalence of schizophrenia in Africa.

after-care movement The original name for the organized efforts of mental health professionals in Europe (and later the United States) to provide support services for deinstitutionalized mental patients so that they will not relapse and require readmission. A physician by the name of Lindpainter initiated this movement in Nassau, Germany, in 1829. It became so popular that it was advocated by psychiatrist Jean FALRET in France in 1841 and instituted in England in 1871, by an organization called the Guild of Friends of the Infirm in Mind.

The first outpatient clinic devoted to the prevention of mental disorders was founded at the Pennsylvania Hospital in Philadelphia in 1885, and other organized efforts to provide financial and social assistance to discharged mental patients were started in America at around this time. Forms of HYDROTHERAPY, various emetics, and some pharmacological substances were administered. Due to the excessive amount of psychiatric patients "deinstitutionalized" in the United States in the 1950s (estimated to be about 200,000 between 1955 and 1967), the United States government began to provide federal funds for Community Mental Health Centers (CMHCs) in 1963 to provide after-care for these people. However, studies have shown that only a small percentage of discharged psychiatric patients have received consistent care from the CMHCs. The lack of a major effort to provide housing for these individuals led to the phenomenon in the United States of the tens (and perhaps hundreds) of thousands of "mentally ill homeless" on American streets by the late 1980s.

age at onset The general age range at which a particular disorder is thought to begin. Some disorders can begin to afflict a person at any age, but most have particular critical periods in the life cycle during which they are more likely to appear. However, the insidious nature of many psychiatric symptoms often makes it difficult to pinpoint exactly when a particular mental disorder is thought to begin.

In SCHIZOPHRENIA, it has been commonly observed that the first major signs of this psychotic disorder occur during adolescence or early adulthood, usually between age 15 and 25. However, cases of LATE-ONSET SCHIZOPHRENIA occurring after the age of 45 have been reported in the literature. Early-onset schizophrenia is more characteristic of males than females, with 1980s studies of late-onset schizophrenia indicating a high female-to-male ratio and a predominance of paranoid symptoms. The average age of onset for BIPOLAR DISORDERS has been found to be about 30 (average range, ages 20 to 40), with occurrences of brief manic or HYPOMANIC EPISODES in early adulthood leading up to the development of a psychotic disorder at about this time.

It has long been known that many physical illnesses (such as multiple sclerosis or Alzheimer's disease) have typical age ranges of onset, and the establishment of similar patterns in many MENTAL DISORDERS supports the belief that they are essentially biological in nature and not caused by supernatural forces or psychoanalytic demons such as "unresolved conflicts" or "SCHIZOPHRENOGENIC MOTHERS." Schizophrenia and bipolar disorder are thought to be disorders characterized by incomplete age-dependent penetrance, which is a term in genetics research that refers to the likelihood that someone with a particular genetic predisposition will develop a corresponding disorder at a particular time in the life cycle.

See also INCOMPLETE PENETRANCE.

Hafner, H., et al. "Causes and Consequences of the Gender Difference in Age at Onset of Schizophrenia," *Schizophrenia Bulletin* 24 (1998): 87–98.

Keith, S. J., and S. M. Matthews. "The Diagnosis of Schizophrenia: A Review of Onset and Duration Issues," *Schizophrenia Bulletin* 17 (1991): 51–67.

AIDS and psychiatric patients Although no studies of the incidence and prevalence of Acquired Immune Deficiency Syndrome (AIDS) in psychiatric patients have been conducted (as of early

1989), the institutionalized populations and deinstitutionalized "street people" are at high risk for contracting this disorder. This will no doubt be an important issue in the future. As many institutionalized patients contract and develop AIDS, the need will arise for special psychiatric inpatient units designed for those that need to be placed on body fluid precautions. State hospitals in particular are believed to be fertile breeding ground for the spread of this disorder; several high-risk populations (IV drug abusers, prisoners, promiscuous patients with impulse control disorders) are combined in the wards of these institutions and freely engage in high-risk sexual behaviors. Male wards in psychiatric hospitals—as in prisons—are known for their promotion of homosexual practices, and sometimes these same patients engage in sexual activities with members of the opposite sex when given free hours on the grounds during the day.

Recognizing this danger, and the ethical problems AIDS poses for psychiatrists, the AMERICAN PSYCHIATRIC ASSOCIATION's Ad Hoc Committee on AIDS Policy issued AIDS policy guidelines, which were published in full in the *American Journal of Psychiatry* in April 1988. The APA's "Guidelines for Inpatient Psychiatric Units" recommends to psychiatrists that, "Regardless of HIV serologic status, all inpatients should be considered potentially at risk for transmitting or receiving HIV infection."

During the early years of the AIDS epidemic, there was some concern that the confusion and other signs of mental deterioration documented in AIDS patients might be misdiagnosed as signs of SCHIZOPHRENIA or other MENTAL DISORDERS. But a major study released by the WORLD HEALTH ORGANIZATION in 1988 indicates that mental deterioration is evident only in the later, more serious stages of the illness, when the diagnosis of AIDS has already become evident through the detectable presence of human immunodeficiency virus (HIV) antibodies in the blood.

American Psychiatric Association. "AIDS Policy: Guidelines for Inpatient Psychiatric Units," *American Journal of Psychiatry* 145 (1988): 4.

Woody, G. E., et al. "Psychiatric Symptoms, Risky Behavior, and HIV Infection," *NIDA Research Monographs* 172 (1997): 156–170.

AIDS and schizophrenia See HIV AND SCHIZOPHRENIA.

AIDS dementia complex Since 1981, when AIDS was first observed to occur in the United States in homosexual males, there has been an intense effort to identify the signs and symptoms of the disorder. One of the features that has been observed in many persons who have developed AIDS is a marked mental deterioration. It is now known that HIV-positive persons also develop symptoms of an ORGANIC MENTAL DISORDER—namely, DEMENTIA—which is due to the direct infection of the brain by HIV (human immunodeficiency virus). In fact, the syndrome that was first described in a 1986 publication by researcher B. A. Navia and colleagues as the "AIDS dementia complex" has been found to be the initial clinical presentation of AIDS in as many as one-fourth of all patients. Based on this work, the diagnostic criteria for AIDS formed by the Centers for Disease Control in the United States has modified the criteria to allow the diagnosis of AIDS solely on the basis of dementia in a seropositive (that is, tested positive for HIV in the blood) individual without any other evidence of an opportunistic infection or Karposi's sarcoma. Besides the usual signs of dementia—forgetfulness, poor concentration, confusion, slowed thinking—there are movement problems (loss of balance, leg weakness) and more serious psychiatric symptoms, such as DEPRESSION, apathy, and even the thought disorder or mania of PSYCHOSIS. The later stages of the disorder are marked by the most severe forms of these symptoms.

There has been some concern that the early stages of AIDS dementia complex may be misdiagnosed as SCHIZOPHRENIA, although a routine HIV test should help to clear up the issue. Research on the retroviruses stimulated by AIDS may lead to a better understanding of the causes of the psychotic disorders. VIRAL THEORIES OF SCHIZOPHRENIA have long been suggested.

Jones, G. H. "HIV and the Onset of Schizophrenia," *The Lancet* 1 (1987): 982.

Navia, B. A., et al. "The AIDS Dementia Complex. I. Clinical Features," *Annals of Neurology* 19 (1986): 517–524.

———. "AIDS Dementia Complex as the Presenting Sole Manifestation of HIV Infection," *Annals of Neurology* 44 (1987): 65–69.

akathisia A symptom found in many psychiatric patients treated with ANTIPSYCHOTIC DRUGS. The term was coined in a 1901 article in the French journal *Review neurologique* by a neurologist from Prague, Ladislav Haskovec (1866–1944), and is derived from Greek word for "the inability to sit down." It is usually defined as the compulsion to be in motion. Patients with akathisia report feeling restless, uncomfortable with remaining still, and needing to pace or fidget continually. The neurological mechanism for this behavior is not well understood. Akathisia seems to be a symptom that appears in patients who are treated with high-potency conventional antipsychotic drugs. Sometimes this symptom can be alleviated by lowering the dosage, switching to a lower-potency drug, or by administering a contra-active drug such as the ones used to treat acute dystonic reactions (namely, anticholinergic and antiparkinsonian agents, antihistamines, and benzodiazepines). When the side effects are refractory, psychiatric experts often suggest adding propranolol as an adjunct treatment.

Akathisia is a classic early sign of Parkinson's disease. The fact that antipsychotic drugs may produce serious Parkinsonian side effects has been known since the first clinical trials of CHLORPROMAZINE (THORAZINE), a PHENOTHIAZINE, in France in 1952. Akathisia and other Parkinsonian side effects may have been known to have been associated with the use of phenothiazine-type drugs as early as 1947. Akathisia is a side effect that occurs in up to 20 to 25 percent of persons taking antipsychotic medication. It is also a lesser side effect of selective-serotonin reuptake inhibitor (SSRI) drugs such as Prozac used in the treatment of depression and anxiety. *DSM-IV* (1994) suggested that a new syndrome called "neuroleptic-induced acute akathisia" may possibly be added as a diagnostic category in future editions.

akinesia See BRADYKINESIA.

Akineton See ANTIPARKINSONIAN DRUGS.

alcohol amnestic disorder See KORSAKOV'S PSYCHOSIS.

alienation mentale See MENTAL ALIENATION.

alienism An obsolete 19th-century term for the study and treatment of mental diseases. In France this medical discipline was referred to as *MÉDICINE MENTALE*. It predates "PSYCHIATRY" as a conventional label for this profession. The word *psychiatry* was first used in English to describe this profession in 1846, following the reintroduction of the word *psychiatrics* by FEUCHTERSLEBEN in 1845. From about the mid-1800s this profession was also called "medical psychology" or "mental science."

alienist An archaic, obsolete term for a psychiatrist that was commonly used in the 1800s. The French term for this professional was *aliéniste*. Other commonly used terms for psychiatrists, especially in England, were "mental pathologist" and "psychiater" (from the German word of the same spelling). "Lunatic doctor" and "MAD-DOCTOR" were terms more commonly employed in the 17th and 18th centuries. These men frequently worked in "mad-houses" and later "lunatic asylums." MENTAL ALIENATION—first used in the 15th century as a term for mental illness—became the standard term for mental illness in the late 18th and early 19th centuries, hence the derivation of the label for this type of professional. "Alienists" also referred to those psychiatric experts who were requested to make legal competency determinations in court, especially at LUNACY TRIALS.

allele One of several alternative forms of a GENE. Alleles always occupy the same place ("locus") on a CHROMOSOME.

almshouses Houses founded by private charities for the reception and support of the (usually) poor. These are the famous "poor houses" that provided "indoor relief." Mentally ill individuals were frequently guests at almshouses. The word dates back

to medieval times, when it referred to the house where the alms of the monastery were dispensed to the needy. Many such institutions were built in the United States during the Age of Reform from the 1820s to the 1840s, as were many penitentiaries and asylums for the mentally ill. In Pennsylvania, the famous Philadelphia Poorhouse was utilized by the many medical schools for the training of new physicians. Today's rough equivalent of almshouses are rescue missions and halfway houses. Perhaps the best historical description of these institutions can be found in the chapter entitled "The Almshouse Experience," in David J. Rothman's book on the rise of institutions in America.

Rothman, D. J. *The Discovery of the Asylum: Social Order and Disorder in the New Republic.* Boston: Little, Brown, 1971.

alogia One of the NEGATIVE SYMPTOMS of SCHIZOPHRENIA. Alogia is the term now used in place of "poverty of speech" to refer to the underproduction of speech, the abbreviation of speech, or the relative lack of any attempt to speak (mutism) that is often manifest in persons with schizophrenia.

altered state of consciousness Psychologist Charles Tart, who is commonly regarded as a leading authority on altered states of consciousness (ASCs), often defines an ASC as a "qualitative alteration in the overall patterning of mental functioning, such that the experiencer feels his consciousness is radically different from the way it functions ordinarily."

In an effort to understand the phenomenology of SCHIZOPHRENIA, the subjective reports of schizophrenic experience began to be collected in the 1960s and compared with other unusual ASCs—such as those reported in "mystical" experience or in the psychedelic experiences of those who have ingested hallucinogenic substances. A famous paper was published in 1966 by Malcom Bowers and D. X. Freedman, which suggested that some schizophrenics have "psychedelic experiences" during the onset of their psychosis. However, further phenomenological studies of the ASCs of schizophrenics in the 1970s and 1980s have not supported the contention that they are similar to mystical or drug-induced ASCs. In the early 1960s hallucinogens were called psychotomimetic or "psychosis-mimicking" drugs, but this term has fallen out of conventional usage.

In 1961 psychiatrists Humphrey Osmond (who coined the word *psychedelic*) and Abram Hoffer designed a diagnostic test for schizophrenia, the Hoffer-Osmond Diagnostic Test, the first to be based on the subjective reports of schizophrenic experiences of perceptual distortions. It was believed that this test distinguished schizophrenia from other psychiatric disorders based on the uniqueness of the phenomenology of the ASCs experienced by schizophrenics. A later scale whose items were also derived from autobiographical accounts of schizophrenics was devised in 1970 by Osmond and psychologist A. Moneim El-Meligi—the Experiential World Inventory. This self-report inventory of 400 items purported to measure subjective changes with scales for five major phenomenological categories: sensory perception, time perception, body perception, self perception, and perception of others. Neither of these phenomenologically based measures ever became popular, and they have not been used in research since the early 1970s.

Bowers, M., and D. X. Freedman. "Psychedelic Experiences in Acute Psychosis," *Archives of General Psychiatry* 15 (1966): 240–248.

El-Meligi, A. M., and H. Osmond. *EWI: Manual for the Clinical Use of the Experiential World Inventory.* New York: Mens Sana Press, 1970.

Alzheimer, Alois (1864–1915) German neurologist who is best remembered for identifying Alzheimer's disease (a form of presenile dementia) in 1906, but who also published research on SCHIZOPHRENIA and MANIC-DEPRESSIVE ILLNESS. Starting in 1903 he worked under Emil KRAEPELIN in the research laboratory at the University of Munich. Along with German neurologist Franz Nissl (1860–1919), these three men conducted research on the underlying disease processes in the nervous system that caused MENTAL DISORDERS

such as DEMENTIA PRAECOX; they made major contributions to the field of neuropathology. Earlier Nissl had invented new staining techniques that allowed for the study of nerve cells, and Alzheimer discovered the organic disease process in the ailment that is still known by his name. Alzheimer considered dementia praecox an essentially organic disease of the brain.

Alzheimer is credited for conducting the very first neurohistological study of schizophrenia (dementia praecox). In 1897 Alzheimer published a paper in which he described abnormal nerve cells in the cortex of young patients with psychotic disorders who did not have a known organic brain disease. Alzheimer believed that dementia praecox (schizophrenia), presenile dementia (later called Alzheimer's disease) and epilepsy were all organic brain diseases. However, he did not believe that hysteria or manic-depressive illness were organic brain diseases. Thus, in the early 20th century there were numerous published reports of neuropathological studies on dementia praecox (schizophrenia) and epilepsy, but none on the mood disorders. He held a professorship at Breslau University and taught there from 1912 until his death in 1915.

Alzheimer, A. "Beitrage zur pathologischen Anatomie der Hirnrinde und zur anatomischen Grundlagen der Psychosen," *Monatsschrift Psychiatrie und Neurologie* 2 (1897): 82–120.

amantadine See ANTIPARKINSONIAN DRUGS.

ambivalence The presence of two contradictory drives, tendencies, emotions, or thoughts that are aimed at the same person, object, or goal. These contradictory urges may be unconscious, conscious, or only partly conscious, but in SCHIZOPHRENIA they are a very common phenomenon that tends to paralyze the willful, volitional actions of the afflicted. For example, a commonly reported experience of people with schizophrenia is that, when they try to express a thought or feeling or attempt an action, their minds suddenly become flooded with many different and often contradictory choices, and they are unable to focus on only one. One of Eugen BLEULER's higher-functioning patients once told him that, "When one expresses a thought, one always sees the counter thought. This intensifies itself and becomes so rapid that one doesn't really know which was the first." Another of his patients expressed the ambivalence so characteristic of schizophrenia by telling Bleuler, "I am a human being like yourself, even though I am not a human being." Bleuler reports that example in his classic 1911 book, *Dementia Praecox, Or the Group of Schizophrenias*, in which "ambivalence" is described as one of the "fundamental symptoms" of schizophrenia. AMBIVALENCE is one of Bleuler's famous "Four A's" (AUTISM, ASSOCIATIONS DISTURBANCES, AFFECTIVE DISTURBANCES, ambivalence), which he felt were the central identifying symptoms of schizophrenia that differentiated it from other mental disorders. Bleuler identified three types of ambivalence in schizophrenia: affective ambivalence, ambivalence of will, and intellectual ambivalence. Modern theorists think that schizophrenic ambivalence may be due to disorders in attention that disable the individual's ability to focus attention on one goal or thought and screen out all other contradictory "noise" that might otherwise flood the mind.

See also ATTENTION, DISORDERS IN.

Bleuler, E. *Dementia Praecox, Or the Group of Schizophrenias*, trans. Joseph Zinkin. 1911. Reprint, New York: International Universities Press, 1950.

ambulatory schizophrenic This is a term for a person with SCHIZOPHRENIA whose level of functioning is high enough that inpatient care is not generally required. It is also applied to schizophrenic patients within psychiatric institutions who can be trusted to reside on open wards or be allowed frequent brief visits into the surrounding community. The term seems to be slowly falling out of conventional usage, with the synonym "high-functioning" replacing "ambulatory" as a label for these schizophrenics.

See also BORDERLINE SCHIZOPHRENIA.

amenomania In his 1812 psychiatric manual, *Medical Inquiries and Observations upon the Diseases*

of the Mind, American alienist Benjamin RUSH claimed that, "Amenomania is a common form of partial insanity." By the examples he gives, it seems that Rush used this term to describe what we might now call a DELUSIONAL DISORDER in people who may not be paralyzed by mental illness but who have fixed delusions or eccentric beliefs on certain topics that may be quite bizarre.

In particular, Rush believed this disorder was found "most frequently in the enthusiasts in religion," which explains his derivation of the word. The grandiose religious delusions that characterize amenomania, Rush claims, may also be indicative of what we now call BIPOLAR DISORDER or PARANOID SCHIZOPHRENIA, for people with amenomania believe they are "the peculiar favourites of heaven." They converse with angels and with spirits of the dead, they see visions, and they believe they are "exalted into beings of the highest order." Rush describes a familiar psychotic DELUSION still encountered in a few patients today when he reports, "I have seen two instances of persons, who believed themselves to be the Messiah."

Psychologist Milton Rokeach experimentally grouped three such schizophrenic patients together in the same environment and described the results in 1964 in his unique book, *The Three Christs of Ypsilanti.*

Rokeach, M. *The Three Christs of Ypsilanti.* New York: Alfred A. Knopf, 1964.

Rush, B. *Medical Inquiries and Observations on the Diseases of the Mind.* Philadelphia: Kimber & Richardson, 1812.

American Psychiatric Association The professional organization of physicians who specialize in the practice of PSYCHIATRY. The precursor to the APA was founded at a meeting in Philadelphia on October 16, 1844, by "the original thirteen" physicians: Francis T. Stribling, Samuel B. Woodward, Samuel White, Isaac RAY, Pliny EARLE, Thomas KIRKBRIDE, Aramiah BRIGHAM, Luther Bell, William AWL, John Galt, Nehemia Cuter, John Butler, and Charles H. Steadman. The original name decided upon by these men was the Association of Medical Superintendents of American Institutions for the Insane. Benjamin RUSH—the "father of American psychiatry"—was a physician at the Pennsylvania Hospital in Philadelphia in the early 1800s and his image appears on the modern logo for this organization. In that founding year the association also published the first English-language psychiatric journal, the *American Journal of Insanity,* which in 1921, under the urging of then-APA president William Alanson White, changed its name to the *American Journal of Psychiatry.* The association changed its name to the American Medico-Psychological Association in 1893 and then to its present title, the American Psychiatric Association, in 1921.

The American Psychiatric Association is responsible for the continually revised editions of the *Diagnostic and Statistical Manual of Mental Disorders,* which is the most widely accepted diagnostic manual used in North America. The most recent edition was *DSM-IV-TR,* published in 2000.

McGovern, C. M. *Masters of Madness: Social Origins of the American Psychiatric Profession.* Hanover and London: University Press of New England, 1985.

American Psychological Association The professional society of American psychologists. It was founded in July 1892 by G. Stanley Hall (1844–1924), a professor of psychology at Clark University in Worcester, Massachusetts.

amine The name for a type of organic compound that contains nitrogen. Amines function as NEUROTRANSMITTERS in the brain. CATECHOLAMINES are a type of amine.

See also DOPAMINE HYPOTHESIS.

amisulpride See ANTIPSYCHOTIC DRUGS.

amphetamine psychosis An obsolete diagnostic term for the psychotic episodes brought on in some people by the ingestion of amphetamine (usually in the form of the "street drug" methamphetamine, or "speed") or similarly acting substances. Irritability, paranoid delusions, and even violent behavior may be exhibited during these acute psychotic episodes.

The main pharmacological effect of amphetamine is believed to be the release of CATECHOLAMINES, one of which, dopamine, is hypothesized to cause schizophrenic symptoms when there is an excess of it. Amphetamine activates or worsens preexisting psychotic symptoms, and ANTIPSYCHOTIC DRUGS work as a potent antidote to the psychosis produced by extreme amphetamine intoxication. Thus, the biochemical properties and effects of amphetamine have been studied as a model for understanding the underlying biochemical processes in schizophrenia.

See also BIOCHEMICAL THEORIES OF SCHIZOPHRENIA; DOPAMINE HYPOTHESIS.

anhedonia The chronic inability to experience pleasure. It is often a sign of a MOOD DISORDER, such as a depressive episode, but can also be found in schizophrenics as a form of their AFFECTIVE DISTURBANCES.

animal models of schizophrenia Animals have long been used in a variety of experimental research studies in many areas of medicine. Animals are routinely used in neurobiological, neurochemical, neuroendocrine, genetics, and pharmacological research, for example, to test hypotheses that would be injurious, lethal, and therefore ethically forbidden if performed on human beings. Attempts to induce behaviors or physiological changes in animals that are similar to those found in persons with SCHIZOPHRENIA have a long history in psychiatric research. However, the development of reliable "models" of the etiology (cause) and pathophysiology of schizophrenia date to only the early 1970s. These animal models focused on pharmacologically manipulating the NEUROTRANSMITTER DOPAMINE and studying the resulting changes in pathophysiology and behavior. Such animal research led, in part, to the DOPAMINE HYPOTHESIS of schizophrenia, first posited by Solomon Snyder and his colleagues in 1976 in the *American Journal of Psychiatry*. The dopamine hypothesis of the cause of schizophrenia was subsequently rejected in its strict monocausal form, as other neurotransmitters were linked to the disorder. Animal models of schizophrenia based on direct manipulations of the dopaminergic system have outlived their usefulness and are no longer conducted in their classical form. However, dopamine is still implicated in the pathophysiology of schizophrenia, and dopamine receptors in the brain remain a target of ANTIPSYCHOTIC DRUGS.

The problem with animal models of schizophrenia is that they are most reliable when focusing on a single issue (e.g., the effects of manipulating the levels of dopamine in the nervous system) but not multiple factors. Since schizophrenia is characterized by a multiplicity of factors leading to its (unknown) cause and resulting in its (still largely unknown) pathophysiology, the development of a single animal model of schizophrenia is doubtful. However, two schizophrenia researchers at the NATIONAL INSTITUTE OF MENTAL HEALTH, the National Institutes of Health, in Bethesda, Maryland, Daniel Weinberger (chief of the Clinical Brain Disorders branch), and B. K. Lipska (chief of the Unit on Animal Models, Clinical Brain Disorders branch), propose that future animal models should focus on three emerging areas of schizophrenia research: (1) testing the NEURODEVELOPMENTAL MODEL OF SCHIZOPHRENIA by experimentally inducing disruption in the development of animal brain development at various stages of embryonic or fetal development through maternal malnutrition, the introduction of possible teratogens (such as viruses) that may disrupt the creation or maturation of nerve cells *in utero*, the creation of lesions in the brains of newly born animals, inducing "stress" in neonates, and so on, (2) the use of drugs to study the possible role that the neurotransmitter glutamate, particularly the "hypofunctioning" of the glutamatergic system of the brain, plays in the underlying pathophysiology of schizophrenia, and (3) genetics, particularly by inserting transgenic mutations in developing embryos or knocking out certain genes that are candidates for the development of schizophrenia in human beings.

The functioning of the immune system in schizophrenia is an additional area of research that lends itself to animal models. In a study published in *Neuroscience Biobehavior Review* in June 2005, a team of researchers in Zurich, Switzerland, investigated the long-known epidemiological

link between bacterial or viral infections in pregnant mothers and the later higher risk of the post-puberty development of schizophrenia in their children. Using pregnant mice in a series of different conditions, they argue this epidemiological link in schizophrenia is mediated by the prenatal activation of the fetal immune system in response to the elevation of the maternal cytokine level due to infection. This study combined assumptions from the neurodevelopmental model and theories of IMMUNE SYSTEM ALTERATIONS IN SCHIZOPHRENIA.

The National Institutes of Health provides the latest information of animal models used in genetics research on its Web site: www.nih.gov/science/models.

Lipska, B. K., and D. R. Weinberger. "Animal Models of Schizophrenia." In *Schizophrenia.* 2nd ed., edited by S. R. Hirsch and D. R. Weinberger. Oxford: Blackwell, 2003.

Meyer, U., et al. "Towards an Immuno-Precipitated Neurodevelopmental Animal of Schizophrenia," *Neuroscience Biobehavior Review* 15 (June 2005): 913–947.

animal spirits A prescientific concept used to explain the cause of MENTAL DISORDERS, particularly mania. A 17th-century treatise by Thomas Willis, *De anima brutorum* (1672), claims that "animal spirits" were distillations from the blood contained in the brain. Their production in the brain was thought to irritate the nervous system and stimulate intellectual functioning so severely that mania would be the result.

anticholinergic effects The effect of some drugs that act as antagonists to the actions of cholinergic nerve fibers, usually of the parasympathetic nervous system. Such cholinergic nerve cells or fibers are those that use acetylcholine as their NEUROTRANSMITTERS. Drugs that have anticholinergic effects block the transmission of this neurotransmitter, thus preventing the communication between nerve cells and thereby altering behavior.

Most psychoactive drugs have anticholinergic effects in both the central and the peripheral nervous systems. The types of drugs that have anticholinergic effects are heterocyclic antidepressants, antipsychotics, antihistamines, ANTIPARKINSONIAN DRUGS, and some hypnotics. If a patient is taking a combination of these drugs (such as an antipsychotic drug with an antidepressant—a common combination) or if an overdose of these drugs is taken, the additive anticholinergic effects can cause a crisis. The combination of signs and symptoms that indicate there is too much of an effect is called the "anticholinergic syndrome." At its worst, a patient suffering from an anticholinergic syndrome will have confusion, DELIRIUM with disorientation, agitation, visual and AUDITORY HALLUCINATIONS, anxiety, restlessness, pseudoseizures, and perhaps even thought disorder (e.g., delusions). Dry mouth, constipation, urinary retention, decreased sweating, increased body temperature, flushing, discoordination, and tachycardia are common but far less serious side effects due to anticholinergic syndrome. The treatment for the anticholinergic syndrome is anticholinesterase drug therapy.

anticipation (genetic) A phenomenon observed over time in some genetic diseases in which each successive generation develops the disease at a progressively earlier age and with a course that is more severe. This phenomenon was noted in the 19th century and was cited as evidence for the medical theory of hereditary DEGENERATION. A useful historical survey of the survival of this idea was provided by German psychiatric researcher Manfred Spitzer in the journal *Nervenarzt* in 1995.

The term *anticipation* was first used in the context of degeneration theory (and with reference to DEMENTIA PRAECOX) in the published text of an invited Huxley Lecture by F. W. Mott, delivered at the Charing Cross Hospital Medical School in London in 1910. Mott was a physician at Charing Cross Hospital as well as a pathologist for the London County Asylums and Fullerian Professor of Physiology at the Royal Institution. Presenting charts of various pedigrees as evidence for the heredity basis of nervous and mental diseases, Mott noted that, "almost invariably in the case of insane parents and offspring, the offspring is affected earlier than the parent." He proposed a name for this phenomenon: "the law of anticipation." Mott did

place limits on this process of intergenerational degeneration, stating that "the general tendency is for insanity not to proceed beyond three generations. . . . Not infrequently the stock dies out by the inborn tendency to insanity manifesting itself in the form of congenital imbecility or insanity of adolescence—dementia praecox." This is a good thing, according to Mott: "thus rotten twigs are continually breaking off the tree of life."

In an important paper published in 1992, R. I. Richards and G. R. Sutherland were the first to propose the possible underlying molecular mechanism for the phenomenon of anticipation: the repeating of a three nucleotide sequence (e.g., CAG or CTG). These three-letter repeats (triplet repeats) enlarge further in the genomes of each successive generation, and longer repeats are correlated with more severe disease. Because of this proliferation of the three-letter repeats in succeeding generations, they also are called trinucleotide expansions. Triplet repeats are known to cause at least 13 different neurodegenerative disorders, making them an attractive focus of research on SCHIZOPHRENIA. However, there is a fundamental difference between schizophrenia and these other disorders. These neurodegenerative disorders are caused by single genes and follow classic patterns of Mendelian inheritance, whereas schizophrenia is thought to be a disorder caused, in part, by many genes and follows confusing NON-MENDELIAN PATTERNS OF TRANSMISSION. The possibility that genetic anticipation caused by triplet repeats is part of the schizophrenia disease process was first proposed by Anne Bassett and W. G. Honer in an article published in the *American Journal of Human Genetics* in 1994.

Anticipation is currently of great interest in GENETICS STUDIES of schizophrenia, particularly those involving genetic association studies. Anticipation is also of great interest to researchers studying CHILDHOOD-ONSET SCHIZOPHRENIA. No candidate trinucleotide repeat has yet been conclusively linked to schizophrenia. Promising trinucleotide expansions in schizophrenia such as CAG and CTG have not been reliably confirmed in replication studies—a familiar and frustrating pattern in almost all areas of biological research on schizophrenia.

Since so many genetic diseases manifest anticipation, a central public-access online database of known trinucleotide sequences called Satellog was established in June 2005 to assist geneticists in their research. The name of this database refers to the fact that trinucleotide repeats are also known as satellite repeats. However, methodological problems with identifying anticipation in diseases and psychiatric disorders such as schizophrenia were identified as early as 1945 by Lionel S. Penrose (1898–1972), then the Galton Professor of Eugenics at University College London in England: "This finding, which in one form or another, is characteristic of mental hospital data, has in the past been attributed to a tendency for progressive degeneration or anticipation of diseases in succeeding generations. Such an explanation, which is not in accordance with the concepts of modern genetics, is unnecessary, because the more likely explanations are close at hand." He further developed his warning about possible "ascertainment bias" in documenting anticipation in a 1948 article published in the *Annals of Eugenics.*

Whether the proposed mechanism of trinucleotide repeats can fully explain the phenomenon of anticipation is doubtful, and even if a definitive genetic pattern of nucleotide repeats is found in some forms of schizophrenia, the phenomenon of anticipation in this disease—for which there is some suggestive evidence—may have to be accounted for by factors as yet unknown.

Bassett, A. S., and W. G. Honer. "Evidence for Anticipation in Schizophrenia," *American Journal of Human Genetics* 54 (1994): 864–870.

McInnis, M. G., et al. "Anticipation in Schizophrenia: A Review and Reconsideration," *American Journal of Medical Genetics* 88 (1999): 686–693.

Missirlis, P., et al. "Sattelog: A Database for the Identification and Prioritization of Satellite Repeats in Disease Association Studies," *BMC Bioinformatics* 6 (June 2005): 145–150.

Mott, F. W. "The Huxley Lecture on Hereditary Aspects of Nervous and Mental Diseases," *British Medical Journal* 2 (October 8, 1910): 1,013–1,020.

Penrose, L. S. "The Problem of Anticipation in Pedigrees of Dystrophia Myotonics," *Annals of Eugenics* 14 (1948): 125–132.

———. "Survey of Cases of Familial Mental Illness (1945)," *European Archives of Clinical Neuroscience* 240 (1991): 314–324.

Richards, R. I., and G. R. Sutherland. "Dynamic Mutations: A New Class of Mutations Causing Human Disease," *Cell* 70 (1992): 709–712.

Spitzer, M., and L. Hermle. "Von der Degeneration zur Antizipation," *Nervenarzt* 66 (1995): 187–196.

Vaswan, M., and S. Kapur. "Genetic Basis of Schizophrenia. Trinucleotide Repeats: An Update," *Progress in Neuropsychopharmacology and Biological Psychiatry* 25 (August 2001): 1,187–1,201.

antidepressant drugs The class of psychoactive drugs that alleviate the symptoms of depression. The term *antidepressant* was coined by Max Lurie in 1952 but did not come into common usage until the 1960s. The first drugs used specifically for depression were amphetamines. The first designer drug marketed as a treatment for "mild depression" (in 1942) was Benzedrine (racemic amphetamine sulfate), the first of the amphetamine drugs developed and introduced by the pharmaceutical company Smith Kline and French in 1936. Two years later, it was being recommended as a treatment for obesity, and for at least the next 30 years amphetamines were prescribed as "diet pills" by physicians. Dexadrine (dextroamphetamine sulfate) appeared in 1946, followed by a drug that combined Dexadrine with a barbiturate, amobarbital (Amytal).

The second generation of antidepressants involved two separate categories of drugs. Monoamine oxidase inhibitors (MAO inhibitors) included drugs such as iproniazid (Marsilid), developed in 1952 for tuberculosis but first used in PSYCHIATRY in 1957. It was discovered by Nathan Kline. Tricyclic antidepressants were first introduced in 1957 with imipramine (Tofranil) after its discovery by Roland Kuhn. In the decades after they were developed, researchers found that drugs of both these classes increased levels of serotonin and norepinephrine in the brain, giving rise to the idea—still unproven—that depression was caused by deficiencies of these NEUROTRANSMITTERS in the brain. It should be repeated in this age of Prozac that there is no evidence that depression is caused by a lack of serotonin or any other chemical in the brain.

The first two generations of antidepressants were designed in an era in which little was known about neurotransmitters (called neurohumors or neurohormones prior to the 1960s) in the brain, and indeed many neurotransmitters had still not been discovered yet. The third generation of designer drugs for the treatment of depression (and now anxiety as well) were created from theories of "reuptake inhibition" based on this new knowledge. These drugs inhibited the reuptake of monoamine neurotransmitters such as DOPAMINE, norepinepherine, and serotonin. In 1979 the drug mianserin appeared under the trade name Athymil in France and in the United Kingdom as Norval. Others were trazodone (Desyrel), released in the United States in 1982, and maprotiline (Ludiomil), first used in France in 1975 and in America in 1981. Other drugs of this generation, which are sometimes called "atypical antidepressants," are amoxapine (Ascendin), bupropion (Wellbutrin, Zyban), clomipramine (Anafranil), and venlafaxine (Effexor).

The fourth generation of antidepressant drugs are the SSRIs, or selective serotonin reuptake inhibitors. Since these drugs work selectively on serotonin in the brain, there are fewer anticholinergic or antihistaminic side effects, allowing for little or no sedation and little impairment of learning, memory, and cognition. The SSRIs are also used in the treatment of anxiety disorders and obsessive compulsive disorder. Prozac, introduced in the United States in 1988 (but approved by the FDA in December 1987), is arguably the most famous drug in the history of medicine. Other SSRIs that followed Prozac were sertraline, introduced as Zoloft in the United States in 1992; paroxetine, marketed as Paxil in 1992; fluvoxamine, trade name Luvox, 1995; citalopram, trade name Celexa, 1998; and escitalopram (Lexapro), introduced in the United States in 2002.

How they are thought to work (pharmacodynamics) The first promising modern biological (neurotransmitter) theory for the pathophysiology (and perhaps the cause) of a MENTAL DISORDER was the "catecholamine theory of depression," first proposed in a highly influential article by Harvard psychiatrist Joseph Schildkraut (1934–) published in 1965 in the *American Journal of Psychiatry.* It had long been suspected that the monoamines (CATECHOLAMINES and INDOLAMINES) were involved in

depression. Dopamine and norepinepherine are catecholamines, whereas serotonin is an indolamine. The role of catecholamines in the "causation" of depression was noted as early as 1959 by Canadian psychiatrist Abram Hoffer at a conference on depression at McGill University in Montreal, but his speculation had no effect on psychiatrists or psychopharmacologists. The catecholamine theory of depression resulted from investigations into how antidepressant drugs such as MAO inhibitors and the tricyclic antidepressants affected brain chemistry. Both types of antidepressants were found to act on the neurotransmitter norepinepherine. Schildkraut's theory that abnormally low levels of the catecholamine neurotransmitter norepinepherine was associated with depression dominated psychiatric thinking in the 1970s and early 1980s. In the 1980s, the role of norepinepherine as the sole factor in depression was discredited when another similar "neurotransmitter deficit" theory involving serotonin emerged, leading to the production of designer SSRIs such as Prozac. SSRIs work by keeping more serotonin at receptor sites. The 1968 discovery that the tricyclic antidepressant imipramine blocked the reuptake of serotonin led to the speculation by Swedish pharmacologist Arvid Carlsson (1923–) that this specific action might be a contributing source of its antidepressant effect. Carlsson and his colleagues Kjell Fuxe and Urban Ungerstedt published their discovery that year in the *Journal of Pharmacy and Pharmacology.* Research on the connection between blockade of serotonin reuptake and the alleviation of depression soon followed, resulting in the first SSRI to be marketed as an antidepressant, zimeldine (Zelmid), in Europe in 1982. It was withdrawn from the market in 1983 because it caused Guillan-Barré syndrome in some persons who took it.

Since the late 1980s, the dominant biological theory of DEPRESSION is the monocausal neurotransmitter theory that deficient levels of serotonin at receptor cites in the brain produce depression (expanded in the 21st century to anxiety, obsessional thoughts, and social phobias). Depression, however, is a highly complex syndrome involving not only neurotransmitters (of which there are more than 100, only a few of which have been studied in detail), but cognitive, emotional, social, experiential, and genetic factors as well in its production. The humoral metaphor of a dyscrasia, an imbalance in bodily fluids, as a cause of disease is still quite strong with regard to the presumed low levels of serotonin and depression.

The use of antidepressant drugs in schizophrenia Persons with schizophrenia do indeed experience depression. In a review of studies by S. G. Siris published in 1991, it was concluded that about 25 percent of persons with schizophrenia also suffer from depression. This is not surprising considering the countless disappointments and losses persons with schizophrenia experience in interpersonal relationships and occupational goals/achievements. Depression occurs throughout the course of schizophrenia, both prior to and after the onset of the active phase of symptoms. Depression is a common part of the RESIDUAL PHASE of schizophrenia following the storm of active psychotic symptoms. *ICD-10* includes a formal diagnostic category of postpsychotic depression for this, whereas *DSM-IV-TR* mentions postpsychotic depression in an appendix. Antidepressant medication is often prescribed along with antipsychotic medication, although treatment of depression in schizophrenia with antidepressant drugs but without also administering antipsychotic drugs is not recommended. In a major review of the double-blind, placebo-controlled studies of the use of antidepressant drugs along with first-generation ANTIPSYCHOTIC DRUGS in schizophrenia by S. G. Siris and C. Bench in 2003, the results were said to be mixed but generally favorable. There was some weak evidence that SSRIs and some tricyclics might alleviate some NEGATIVE SYMPTOMS in some persons with schizophrenia. The symptoms of severe depression (ANHEDONIA, AVOLITION, ALOGIA, AKATHISIA, AKINESIA, and so on) can often mimic negative symptoms, so the negative symptoms of schizophrenia may actually not have been alleviated. However, some antidepressants—particularly SSRIs such as Prozac and Paxil—have been linked to the onset of manic episodes and psychotic episodes. Several of the ATYPICAL ANTIPSYCHOTICS, such as olanzapine (Zyprexa), have been found to lessen depressive symptoms and are often used to treat bipolar disorder.

Side effects However, although the SSRIs are in widespread use, there are severe side effects. If too

much serotonin accumulates in the central nervous system through the use of SSRIs, the "serotonin syndrome" may occur. The serotonin syndrome is characterized by disorientation, confusion, hypomania, agitation, restlessness, fever, chills, sweating, diarrhea, hypertension, tachycardia, ataxia, increased reflexes, and myoclonus. Visual hallucinations have also been reported. The symptoms vanish 24 to 48 hours after drug use is discontinued. When use of SSRIs is halted, the "serotonin withdrawal syndrome" manifests in about 60 percent of people who have taken these drugs. Withdrawal symptoms include anxiety, agitation, crying spells, irritability, dizziness, vertigo, nausea, vomiting, diarrhea, fatigue, chills, sensations of electric shocks, insomnia, and vivid dreams.

Akathisia as a side effect of SSRI use has been increasingly linked to suicidal behavior, violence, and homicidal behavior.

Sexual dysfunction occurs in up to 80 percent of persons treated with SSRIs, although some more conservative estimates place it within the 30 to 40 percent range, reflecting a more restrictive definition of the range of what constitutes a sexual dysfunction. This fact was kept hidden by pharmaceutical companies for many years prior to the introduction of SSRIs to the market in the 1980s. Since the first SSRIs were marketed as antidepressants, and since the alleviation of depression was touted as its main effect, the fact that more sexual dysfunction occurs in persons taking these drugs than the alleviation of depressive symptoms has led critics of the pharmaceutical industry to question the very meaning of what a drug's main effect may be. From an iconoclastic point of view, if we are to categorize drugs by their main effect, then there may be better evidence that the SSRIs are "sexual-dysfunction-inducing drugs" rather than antidepressants.

See also DEPRESSION.

Healy, D. *The Antidepressant Era.* Cambridge, Mass.: Harvard University Press, 1997.

———. *The Creation of Psychopharmacology.* Cambridge, Mass.: Harvard University Press, 2002.

Julien, R. M. *A Primer of Drug Action,* 10th ed. New York: Worth, 2005.

Schildkraut, J. "The Catecholamine Hypothesis of Depression: A Review of Supporting Evidence," *American Journal of Psychiatry* 122 (1965): 509–522.

Siris, S. G., and C. Bench. "Depression and Schizophrenia." In *Schizophrenia.* 2nd ed., edited by S. R. Hirsch and D. Weinberger. Oxford: Blackwell, 2003.

antiparkinsonian drugs These are drugs that are administered to relieve PARKINSONISM, the side effects of antipsychotic drugs that will usually appear within weeks or a few months after beginning antipsychotic drug therapy. Patients who suffer from this side effect exhibit a triad of signs: tremors (usually in the hands but also in the wrists and elbows), rigidity (extreme tension in muscles that make the body actually feel rigid), and AKINESIA or BRADYKINESIA (an absence or a slowness of body or facial muscle motion). Common ANTIPARKINSONIAN DRUGS are amantadine (trade name Symmetrel), BENZTROPINE (Cogentin), biperiden (Akineton), and DIPHENHYDRAMINE (Benadryl). Parkinson's syndrome, which is induced by ANTIPSYCHOTIC DRUGS, should not be confused with Parkinson's disease, which is a progressive neurological disorder that is not reversible.

antipsychiatry See LAING, RONALD DAVID.

anti-psychosis A curative substance that the prescient Daniel H. Tuke hypothesized, in 1881, would one day be created to reverse the symptoms of mental disorders. His prophetic remarks were delivered on August 2 in London in his presidential address to the Medico-Psychological Association in which he lamented the special problems of "psychological" medicine as opposed to the more forthright "organic" medicine:

> It must be frankly granted that Psychological Medicine can boast, as yet, of no specifics, nor is it likely, perhaps, that such a boast will ever be made. It may be difficult to suppress the hope, but we cannot entertain the expectation that some future Sydenham will discover an *anti-psychosis* which will as safely and speedily cut short an attack of mania or melancholia as bark an attack of ague.

Today's ANTIPSYCHOTIC DRUGS are named, in part, as a memorial to Tuke's farsightedness.

Tuke, D. H. *Chapters in the History of the Insane in the British Isles.* London: Keegan, Paul, Trench & Co., 1882.

antipsychotic drugs The class of drugs that suppress or alleviate psychotic symptoms (primarily POSITIVE SYMPTOMS such as hallucinations and delusions). The term *antipsychotic drugs* was used for the first time to refer to these pharmacological agents by a German-Canadian psychiatrist, Heinz Lehmann of Montreal, in an article published in the *Canadian Medical Association Journal* in 1961. They are also commonly referred to as neuroleptics (coined by Jean Delay of France in 1955), antischizophrenic agents, and major tranquilizers (which is a misnomer). From 1955 to the 1990s, antipsychotic drugs were most often referred to as neuroleptics in Europe and major tranquilizers in the United States. Smith Kline and French introduced CHLORPROMAZINE (THORAZINE) in 1955 just months before another new drug that revolutionized outpatient psychiatry, the famous "minor" tranquilizer mebrobamate (Miltown), so in a marketing contrast to Miltown, Thorazine was soon sold to physicians by pharmaceutical companies as a "major tranquilizer." Antipsychotic drugs are the treatment of choice for SCHIZOPHRENIA and other psychotic disorders, but some—particularly those introduced since 1990—have been used effectively in the treatment of MANIC EPISODES (particularly "mixed" or dysphoric mania) and have an antidepressant effect as well.

Historical Background

Prior to 1952 there were only weakly effective drugs for treating persons suffering from schizophrenia or other psychotic disorders. Most of the drugs used by MAD-DOCTORS and ALIENISTS in asylums were used to sedate patients in order to reduce suffering, promote prolonged sleep, and thereby improve patient management by asylum staff. These drugs were widely in use from at least 1840 until the mid-20th century, and they include opiates, hyocine, digitalis, chloral (after 1869), bromides, barbiturates (after 1903), anticholinergic agents, and paraldehyde (a distinctly foul-smelling drug when exhaled by asylum patients that led to its characteristic odor permeating mental institutions prior to the introduction of chlorpromazine). These are the drugs that enjoyed a long life in the asylum, but in reality almost anything and everything was tried on asylum patients in a desperate effort to find effective treatment.

In 1931 two physicians from India, Ganneth Sen and Katrick Bose, published a report of their research using an extract from the roots of the Rauwolfia plant. Rauwolfia had been used for centuries in traditional Indian medicine for the treatment of mental illness because of its ability to calm excited persons. Sen and Bose recommended its use for high blood pressure as well as the treatment of psychiatric disorders. Three chemists working for the Ciba pharmaceutical company in Basel, Switzerland, isolated the sedative agent from the plant, the alkaloid reserpine. In April 1954 Nathan Kline published a report in the *Annals of the New York Academy of Sciences* on the effectiveness of reserpine and a preparation of its whole root (marketed as Raudixin for hypertension) on the inpatients at Rockland State Hospital in Orangeburg, New York. The following year, the effectiveness of RESERPINE for the treatment of anxiety and depression was confirmed in a randomized and controlled experiment conducted by David Lewis Davies and Michael Shepard of the Maudsley Hospital in England. They published their report in the British medical journal *Lancet,* but their results were largely overlooked due to the explosion of interest in chlorpromazine (Thorazine) at that time. Reserpine was used in psychiatric practice until 1961, when it was taken off the market due to adversive side effects.

In 1955 approximately 559,000 persons were residing in American psychiatric hospitals. In 1956, two years after the first antipsychotic drug chlorpromazine (Thorazine in the United States; Largactil in Europe) was approved for use in America (as an anti-emetic, not an antipsychotic), the number of inpatients began to drop steadily on a year-by-year basis. Patients who responded well to these drugs (not all, by any means, but a significant number) soon became well enough to be released back into the community. A similar pattern followed in the United Kingdom in the 1960s. If only the numbers are considered, from the perspective of local and national governments that funded psychiatric inpatient care, "deinstitutionalization" was a success. By 1983 fewer than

220,000 persons resided in psychiatric hospitals in the United States. By the 1990s most persons with schizophrenia were quickly stabilized on antipsycotic drugs and discharged somewhat rapidly. There is no question that antipsychotic drugs have had a profound effect on the practice of psychiatry and in the treatment of schizophrenia. However, the introduction of chlorpromazine and the PHENOTHIAZINES into psychiatric practice was perhaps only partly responsible for this emptying of the wards of psychiatric hospitals. Other factors are social and financial. In America, changing the care of persons with mental disorders from inpatient institutions to the community shifted the financial responsibility from the states to the federal government. In Japan, the introduction of phenothiazines was actually followed by an increase, not a decrease, in the population of psychiatric institutions.

The first of the phenothiazine antihistamine drugs, promethazine (synthesized in 1947), had been used by French naval surgeon Henri Laborit (1914–95) as an agent to deepen anesthesia and to relax patients prior to surgery. Working with the phenothiazine nucleus, in December 1950, French biochemist Paul Charpentier synthesized more potential pharmacological agents and developed the second phenothiazine, chlorpromazine. It was found to produce a calmness, disinterest, and detachment from external stimuli, and conscious sedation in patients who took it—a condition Laborit called an "artificial hibernation." Laborit believed there might be a therapeutic effect on psychosis. As he put it in his early 1952 article in *Presse Medicale:* "These findings allow one to anticipate certain indications for the use of this compound in psychiatry. . . ." At his suggestion, in 1952 chlorpromazine was tested in clinical trials on patients at the Val-de Grace military hospital in Paris by Pierre Hamon, Jean Paraire, and Jean Velluz. Shortly following this first psychiatric trial, at the Ste.-Anne Mental Hospital in Paris, Jean Delay and Pierre Deniker conducted a clinical trial on psychotic patients and found an alleviation of HALLUCINATIONS and DELUSIONS occurred without the patients being unduly sedated by the drug. After only three months of their chlorpromazine clinical trial, Delay and Deniker became the first to publish scientific claims of success in articles that appeared in the *Presse Medicale* and *Annales-Medico-Psychologiques* in 1952. Although none of these men—Laborit, Hamon, Paraire, Velluz, Delay, or Deniker—was ever awarded the Nobel Prize for the discovery of the antipsychotic properties of chlorpromazine, they fought bitterly with one another over who should be credited with priority in the discovery. This very public controversy probably led the Nobel committees to pass over them continually for the Nobel Prize in medicine.

Clinical trials followed in Lyons, France, and in 1953 in Basel, Switzerland, the United States, and Canada. A common—almost miraculous—observation in these trials was that some chronic patients who were noncommunicative for years suddenly "woke up" and became responsive to their environment. Many reported that the voices they heard were gone, and some were surprised at what year it was and how high prices had become. By the late 1950s many people believed that chlorpromazine had become a wonder drug along the lines of penicillin, a marvel of modern medical science.

The phenothiazines dominated the treatment of schizophrenia and other psychotic disorders for decades, and many are still in use. Following the approval of chlorpromazine (Thorazine) for use in the United States in March 1954, and the pharmaceutical company Smith Kline and French immediately experienced enormous profits, other phenothiazine "major tranquilizers" followed: prochlorperazine, 1957 (marketed as Compazine in 1956); perphenazine, patented in 1956, marketed as Trilafon in 1957; thioridazine, 1958 (Mellaril, 1959); trifluoperazine, 1959 (Stelazine, 1958); fluphenazine, 1960 (Prolixin, 1960). The next class of antipsychotic drugs, the butyrophenomes, was used in Europe from 1959 onward. However, the first of these drugs, haloperidol (Haldol), was not introduced in the United States until 1967. By the 1980s it became the most widely prescribed antipsychotic drug in the United States.

Antipsychotic drugs are now classified into three broad groups or "generations," the preferred terminology of the WORLD PSYCHIATRIC ASSOCIATION: conventional, typical, or first-generation antipsychotics (1954–75), which are grouped into three chemical classes: the phenothiazines, begin-

ning with chlorpromazine (Thorazine) in 1954; the butyrophenomes, beginning in 1959 with haloperidol (marketed as Haldol in America in 1967); the THIOXANTHENES, beginning with thiothixene (Navane); and miscellaneous or alternative agents to the phenothiazines, introduced first in the early 1970s, such as LOXAPINE (Loxitane), molindone (Moban), and pimozide (Orap); atypical or second-generation antipsychotics, beginning in 1990 (no new antipsychotic drugs were marketed in the United States between 1975 and 1990) with the introduction of clozapine (Clozaril), and followed by RISPERIDONE (RISPERDAL) in 1993, OLANZAPINE (Zyprexa) in 1996, sertinole (Serlect) in 1997, quetiapine (Seroquel) in 1999, ziprasidone (GEODON) in 2000, aripiprazole (Abilify) in 2003, and zotepine (not approved for use in North America but available in Europe and in many countries worldwide); and third-generation antipsychotics, beginning with amisulpride (Solian) in 2005. Amulsipride is considered to be the start of a new generation of drugs because, although it is often referred to as an atypical antipsychotic, it has a different effect on the NEUROTRANSMITTERS of the brain than the other atypical agents and, in low doses, is effective in the treatment of dysthymia and depression.

How they are thought to work (pharmacodynamics) First-generation antipsychotics work, in part, by blocking certain receptor sites for the neurotransmitter DOPAMINE, particularly the D_2 receptors. Until the 1990s, the blocking of D_2 receptors was thought to be the sole mechanism for reducing psychotic symptoms. Second-generation or atypical antipsychotic drugs also block, or are antagonists, at the same dopamine receptor sites, but they all have a second action, usually the antagonism of the serotonin $5HT_2$ receptors. In general, to be considered an "atypical" antipsychotic, the blocking of serotonin $5HT_2$ receptor must be greater, and occur at lower doses, than the D_2 receptor blockade. The serotonin psychedelic drug LSD (banned from production and distribution in the United States since 1966) is thought to produce its characteristic hallucinations and "psychosis-mimicking" state by being an agonist of $5HT_2$. Aripiprazole (Abilify) works differently by being a partial agonist at D_2 receptors and at serotonin $5HT_{1a}$ receptors, and an antagonist at serotonin $5HT_2$ receptors. The first third-generation drug, amisulpride (Solian), is the first atypical that does not block serotonin receptors, but instead blocks two different dopamine receptors, D_2 and D_3, in the limbic system of the brain but not the basal ganglia (the part of the brain that is primarily linked to producing the Parkinsonian side effects of antipsychotic medication).

Since there are more than 100 identifiable neurotransmitters and only a select few have been studied in depth, future generations of antipsychotic drugs will no doubt target other neurotransmitter systems. In particular, the neurotransmitter glutamate, which has been linked to schizophrenia since 1980, will be of particular interest to psychopharmacologists in the decades to come.

Pharmacogenetics It has long been observed by physicians and researchers that not everyone responds to a given medication in the same way. Some respond only to lower doses, some to higher, and some not at all. Ethnic differences, in particular, have been noted, and the underlying reasons for these differences in response to medication have been sought by identifying the genes that code for drug metabolizing enzymes (DMEs), which are known to be different between Caucasians, Asians, black Africans, and African Americans. With the rise of medical genomics—an entirely new approach to disease and health based on knowledge of genetic differences—pharmaceutical companies have been keen to apply this new knowledge to the development of new drugs. This field is known as pharmacogenetics, a term first used as early as 1959 by F. Vogel in an article in a German pediatric journal in reference to the speculation that adverse drug reactions might be due to genetic differences between people. Designer drugs which are based on slight differences in genes between people (single nucleotide polymorphisms, SNPs or "snips") and can target treatment-resistant patients with a variety of diseases are a long-term development goal of pharmaceutical companies. Such designer drugs might be developed for the treatment of schizophrenia, although currently no such pharmacogenomic drugs for schizophrenia yet exist.

Side effects It was noticed at least as early as 1953 that chlorpromazine (Thorazine) produced serious side effects (dyskinesias and AKATHISIA) in some patients. As early as 1956 there was a published

report that such side effects continued for months in some patients after being completely taken off phenothiazines. As the new era of phenothiazine use continued, severe and bizarre movement disorders (tremors, rigidity, eye-rolls, grimaces, excessive drooling) became increasingly apparent. By 1957 the syndrome later renamed (in 1964) TARDIVE DYSKINESIA (TD) had been described in an article by a German physician, Matthais Schoenecker, in *Der Nervenarzt.* The emergence of such severe side effects was an unwelcome surprise to those few psychiatrists in the 1950s and 1960s who connected them with the use of phenothiazines. This was especially true in America, a country where mental hospital staff and physicians were amazed as they saw patients "wake up" and regain their humanity on an almost daily basis. But considering the massive doses of these drugs patients were initially administered in the early days (particularly in the United States, where daily doses of 3,000 mg a day were routine as compared with the 150 mg a day given in Europe to patients), it is a wonder that more physicians, patients, and families did not sound the alarm earlier. Most preferred to attribute the side effects to "psychodynamic" (unconscious impulses) or other "spontaneous" biological causes and not to the new drugs. The turning point was the publication of a book in 1965, *The Action of Neuroleptic Drugs,* by Hans-Joachim Haase and Paul Janssen, which detailed the serious side effects of large doses and long-term use. Still, despite the fact that the authors were a prominent psychiatrist and a world-renowned psychopharmacologist, the idea that such serious side effects were caused by these psychiatric "wonder drugs" was met with strong initial resistance by American psychiatrists until a joint task force formed by the Food and Drug Administration and the American College of Neuropsychopharmacology published a convincing report documenting such side effects in 1973. As law professor and historian Sheldon Gelman put it in his 1999 book, *Medicating Schizophrenia: A History,* "Except to a few researchers, tardive dyskinesia remained invisible until the early 1970s. It was as if the disorder simply did not exist" (p. 88).

The adverse effects of antipsychotic drug use fall into several categories:

Central nervous system effects: we now know that these drugs cause acute EXTRAPYRAMIDAL SYNDROMES (EPS) as a serious side effect early in the course of treatment. EPS is characterized by a triad of symptoms: (a) dystonias (involuntary muscle spasms, sustained abnormal posturing of the face, tongue, limbs, trunk); (b) akathisia; and (c) PARKINSONISM (not to be confused with Parkinson's disease). Long-term use of the first-generation antipsychotics leads to brain damage and a chronic syndrome of the above triad of symptoms, TD. Unlike TD, the acute EPS side effects are usually completely reversible through lowering the dosage of ANTIPSYCHOTIC DRUGS or withdrawing them completely for a time (a "drug holiday"). Anticholinergic side effects are also quite common with the first-generation antipsychotics in particular: dry mouth, dilated pupils and blurred vision, increased heart rate, constipation, urinary retention, dizziness, and drying of lung secretions. Side effects can be reversed by giving the patient ANTIPARKINSONIAN DRUGS, anticholinergic drugs, or antiadrenergic drugs. Tardive dyskinesia is managed by these same drugs but is not reversible. Clozapine is the only effective drug for persons with TD. Atypical antipsychotics cause far fewer side effects and because of this are often preferred in the early years of treatment of schizophrenia. However, there are concerns specific to the long-term use of clozapine. Persons taking clozapine must have their blood cell counts monitored weekly to prevent agranulocytosis, a dangerous lowering of the white blood cell counts. Alterations in normal EEG patterns and, at times, seizures may occur. All antipsychotic drugs lower the seizure threshold, making them more likely.

Thermoregulatory adverse effects: The most severe is NEUROLEPTIC MALIGNANT SYNDROME (NMS), which can be fatal in 5 to 20 percent of cases if unnoticed and untreated. The syndrome resembles an older one known as lethal catatonia in the pre–antipsychotics era. *DSM-IV* criteria for NMS indicate that muscle rigidity and hyperthermia (a body temperature of 101–104 degrees Fahrenheit) must be present. The clinical picture of NMS is similar to CATATONIA. Both typical and atypical antipsychotic drugs can cause NMS, and it can happen at any point during treatment. Hyperthermia and hypothermia (a core body temperature below 95 degrees Fahrenheit) may also occur,

with hypothermia associated with sudden unexplained deaths that coincide with the administration of antipsychotic drugs.

Other miscellaneous adverse effects: Sedation is a problem in about 40 percent of persons taking clozapine, as is extreme weight gain. Weight gain is also a serious side effect of olanzapine, but the other atypical antipsychotics also cause weight gain to a greater or lesser degree. Several atypical agents also affect heart rhythms and blood pressure. Changes in the relative numbers of blood corpusules (blood dyscrasias) may also occur with the use of first-generation antipsychotics and with clozapine. Leukopenia (abnormally low white blood cell counts) is the most common, and agranulocytosis (granulocyte count below 500/mm) may be life threatening. There is also an increased risk of developing diabetes and hyperglycemia with these drugs. Excessive salivation (sialorrhea) happens to almost all patients who take clozapine. Dry mouth (xerostomia) is also common. Constipation can be a problem with first-generation antipsychotics and clozapine. Transient elevation of liver enzymes occurs with the use of all antipsychotics. Extended use of the phenothiazines (such as chlorpromazine) can lead to changes in the cornea, lens, and retinas of the eyes. Sexual dysfunctions are common. Treatment with phenothiazines can cause photosensitivity and lead to sunburns or rashes.

DSM-IV-TR (2000) includes a new category for "medication induced movement disorders." Specific diagnostic criteria are offered for the following syndromes: Neuroleptic-induced Parkinsonism; Neuroleptic Malignant Syndrome, Neuroleptic-induced Acute Dystonia, Neuroleptic-induced Acute Akathisia, Neuroleptic-induced Tardive Dyskinesia, Medication-induced Postural Tremor, and Medication-induced Movement Disorder Not Otherwise Specified. Thus, the treatment of standard mental disorders has led to side effects that have now created a whole new category of mental disorders to accompany, not replace, the earlier diagnoses.

Administration of drugs and compliance In 2004 the American Psychiatric Association (APA) issued a revision of its practice guidelines for the psychopharmacological treatment of persons with schizophrenia. The guidelines offer treatment algorithms, or decision paths, for physicians to follow when treating newly psychotic individuals, when practicing maintence therapy as a follow-up, and for patients who are "treatment resistant" and for whom antipsychotic drugs do not seem to work. Atypical antipsychotics such as risperidol, which produce fewer acute EPS side effects and which, if used long-term, may prevent the development of tardive dyskinesia, are the first-line treatments for schizophrenia. The guidelines offer suggested combinations of drugs in such refractory cases and, if all else fails, ECT (electroconvulsive therapy) as a last resort. Suggestions are also given for how to manage acute side effects such as EPS and tardive dyskinesia in chronic patients.

It has long been known that persons with schizophrenia have a difficult time complying with medication treatment after they are released from inpatient settings. Forgetting to take medication, or consciously choosing not to, has been associated with higher rates of relapse and hospitalizations. It is estimated that noncompliance rates in persons with schizophrenia who are living in the community range between 24 percent and 63 percent. The avoidance of side effects is often cited as a reason persons with schizophrenia do not take their medications, but due to the problems many persons have in focusing their attention, many simply forget or are easily distracted by other events in their daily lives. Injectable forms of medications such as Prolixin have been developed to solve this problem. Depending on the medication or the dose, the effect of injectable forms of antipsychotic drugs can last weeks.

However, medication compliance is not just a problem with persons with schizophrenia who are patients. Psychiatrists who treat persons with schizophrenia have been studied in the United States by the Schizophrenia Patient Outcomes Research Team (PORT) and have been found to be lacking in adherence to evidenced-based treatment guidelines set by the American Psychiatric Association. Physician-conformance to APA guidelines was found to be "modest at best." A common problem was the tendency of psychiatrists to engage in "polypharmacy"—the administration of more than one antipsychotic drug, or combinations of antipsychotic drugs and other types of drugs—when there was no scientific evidence to recommend such combinations.

Subtype differences in treatment responsiveness Recent GENETICS STUDIES of schizophrenia have not, as yet, identified characteristic schizophrenia subtype profiles for each of the classic forms of schizophrenia (paranoid, hebephrenic [disorganized], catatonic types). The lack of firm underlying biological knowledge of possible differences in the causes (etiologies) and pathophysiologies of the different schizophrenia subtypes, researchers and pharmaceutical companies who manufacture antipsychotic drugs have increasingly tended to regard schizophrenia as a single heterogeneous disorder rather than several different disorders (the classic subtypes). Fewer studies examine subtype differences than a quarter century ago, and antipsychotic drugs are marketed for "schizophrenia"—not for "paranoid schizophrenia," "disorganized schizophrenia" (hebephrenia prior to 1994), or "catatonic schizophrenia." An additional subtype of schizophrenia, the "undifferentiated type," was added to *DSM-III* in 1980 to refer to patients who do not manifest dominant symptoms of the three classic subtypes and which may include a mixture of symptoms from each. The undifferentiated type category is among the most widely used today in psychiatric institutions and also adds to the perception that schizophrenia may be one disease because there are no treatment differences between the classic subtypes. The presence of positive and negative symptoms, not classic subtypes, guide treatment. However, some differences in the responsiveness of the classic schizophrenia subtypes to treatment have been documented in the literature of the past 40 years. Since antipsychotic drugs have always worked best to alleviate positive symptoms, persons with paranoid schizophrenia (a subtype characterized entirely by positive symptoms such as paranoid delusions and auditory hallucinations of voices) have generally responded quite well to these drugs. Persons with the disorganized type of schizophrenia (hebephrenia) and the catatonic type (catatonia) have traditionally been treatment-resistant. Although catatonia (a syndrome that is essential to the diagnosis of the catatonic subtype of schizophrenia but which may be a separate syndrome of its own) has long been thought to have virtually vanished since the introduction of antipsychotic drugs in 1952, since 1983 there have been reports that it has been mislabeled, or relabeled, as neuroleptic malignant syndrome. In the pre–antipsychotic era literature, catatonia was treated effectively with barbiturates and electroshock therapy. The potency of barbiturates in essentially curing catatonia through the induction of prolonged sleep was documented as early as 1930 by W. J. Bleckwenn in the *Archives of Neurology and Psychiatry.* In 1983 physicians Gregory Fricchione and Ned Cassem of the Massachusetts General Hospital in Boston reported in an article in the *Journal of Clinical Psychopharmacology* that lorazepam (Ativan), a benzodiazepine "minor tranquilizer," reversed neuroleptic malignant syndrome. Later at Stony Brook Hospital in New York, Fricchione and Max Fink found that barbiturates, lorazepam, and ECT all were 100 percent effective in curing NMS, thus adding weight to the evidence that NMS and "lethal catatonia" were perhaps one and the same syndrome (with NMS being an iatrogenic form of lethal catatonia caused by the use of antipsychotic drugs). Although electroconvulsive therapy (ECT) is effective in the treatment of core catatonic symptoms (mutism, stupor, akathisia, clouded consciousness), the evidence is less clear that ECT works to alleviate core psychotic symptoms such as delusions and hallucinations. Treatment of catatonia or suspected NMS with benzodiazepines or barbiturates is therefore recommended first before using ECT. Although the combination of ECT with antipsychotic drugs has been explored in some studies, indicating that ECT may work best in patients with acute exacerbations and short episode duration, there is not enough evidence upon which to base treatment recommendations for psychiatrists as to when ECT can be used in conjunction with antipsychotic drugs. HEBEPHRENIA, or the disorganized type of schizophrenia, continues to be the most treatment-resistant form of schizophrenia due to the presence of negative symptoms, which still do not respond well to any present antipsychotic drug. Still, the notion that "one treatment fits all" remains dominant in the current pharmacological response to schizophrenia.

Relapse, treatment-resistant schizophrenia, and the natural course of the disease Several studies have shown that, on average, if a group of persons with schizophrenia that is in remission (the residual type) is switched from treatment with an antipsy-

cotic drug to a placebo, approximately 65 to 85 percent of them will relapse within one year. A variety of studies estimate that 20 to 33 percent of persons with schizophrenia exhibit treatment refractoriness to antipsychotic drugs and that an additional number, about 15 percent, experience an alleviation of symptoms with placebo treatment alone in double-blind studies. Clozapine is recommended as the treatment of choice in chronic treatment-resistant schizophrenia, demonstrating a therapeutic effect in about 30 percent of such persons.

Antipsychotic drugs do not "cure" schizophrenia: their main function is to significantly lower the probability of total relapse into psychosis by reducing the positive symptoms (hallucinations and delusions). Based on interpretations of the various long-term follow-up studies of schizophrenia, antipsychotic drugs do not seem to slow or stop whatever natural disease process is at work in schizophrenia. Antipsychotic drugs do not have any demonstrable effect on the various patterns of the COURSE AND OUTCOME OF SCHIZOPHRENIA. One controversial literature review by the noted schizophrenia researcher Richard Jed Wyatt (1939–2002) disputed this conclusion. In his reanalysis of 22 studies, Wyatt argued that early intervention with antipsychotic drugs in persons undergoing their first episode of active symptoms increased the likelihood of lessening the severity the long-term course of the disease. He additionally suggested that perhaps even going so far as to identifying young persons at-risk for schizophrenia and giving them antipsychotic medication as a preventive measure before they suffer hallucinations and delusions may delay or prevent the first-episode onset of schizophrenia. In an even more controversial claim, Wyatt suggested such actions might prevent the "brain damage" the schizophrenia disease process produces. However, although the evidence is abundant that long-term treatment with antipsychotic drugs produces irreversible brain damage that results in the syndrome known as tardive dyskinesia, there is still no clear evidence that a psychotic episode leads directly to irreversible structural brain damage. Although the evidence for brain changes in schizophrenia is clear, it is not clear that active phases of the illness in which delusions and hallucinations are floridly present causes them or follows such changes as part of the progressing underlying disease process. Wyatt's argument that withholding the use of antipsychotic drugs leads to brain damage currently has no evidence to support it.

Summary

In essence, the effect of the usage of antipsychotic drugs in schizophrenia can be summed up in the following way: (a) antipsychotic drugs alleviate positive symptoms in most, but certainly not all, persons with schizophrenia, especially in the early years of the disease, with 20 to 33 percent of all persons with schizophrenia demonstrating little or no response to antipsychotic drugs, (2) the use of these drugs is correlated with, but is perhaps not the sole cause of, less overall hospitalization time and shorter stays in inpatient settings, (3) although the use of antipsychotic drugs, is beneficial in reversing acute exacerbations of psychosis, and help persons function better in daily life in the short term by eliminating hallucinations and delusions, there is as yet no evidence that the use of these drugs dramatically improves negative symptoms, or overall interpersonal functioning over the life span, (4) there is no evidence that antipsychotic drugs affect the natural disease course of schizophrenia, and (5) the history of psychiatry repeatedly has documented that, for at least 15 to 20 years after the introduction of new psychopharmacologic agents (such as antipsychotics or antidepressants), pharmaceutical companies and hopeful physicians tend to deny (consciously or unconsciously) the harmful side effects of these drugs and have highly biased positive views of their therapeutic power and potential.

American Psychiatric Association. "Practice Guideline for the Treatment of Patients with Schizophrenia, Second Edition," *American Journal of Psychiatry* 161 (2004), February Supplement.

Ban, T., D. Healy, and E. Shorter, eds. *Reflections on Twentieth-Century Psychopharmacology.* Budapest: Animula, 2004.

Barnes, T. R. E., P. Buckley, and S. S. Schultz. "Treatment-resistant Schizophrenia." In *Schizophrenia.* 2nd ed., edited by S. R. Hirsch and D. Weinberger. Oxford: Blackwell, 2003.

Delay, J., P. Deniker, and J.-M. Harl. "Utilisation en therapeutique psychiatrique d'une phenothiazine d'action centrale elective (4560 RP)," *Annales Medico-Psychologique* 110 (1952): 112–117.

Fenton, W. S. "Determinants of Medication Compliance in Schizophrenia: Empirical and Clinical Findings," *Schizophrenia Bulletin* 23 (1997): 635–651.

Gelman, S. *Medicating Schizophrenia: A History.* New Brunswick, N.J.: Rutgers University Press, 1999.

Healy, D. *The Creation of Psychopharmacology.* Cambridge, Mass., and London: Harvard University Press, 2002.

Julien, R. M. *A Primer of Drug Action.* 10th ed. New York: Worth, 2005.

Kline N. S., and A. M. Stanley. "Use of Reserpine in a Neuropsychiatric Hospital," *Annals of the New York Academy of Medicine* 61 (1955): 85–91.

Laborit, H., P. Hugenard, and R. Alluaume. "Un nouveau stabilisateur vegetatif (le 4560 RP)," *Presse Medicale* 60 (1952): 206–208.

Lehman, A. F., and D. M. Steinwachs. "Patterns of Usual Care for Schizophrenia: Initial Results from the Schizophrenia Patient Outcomes Research Team (PORT) Client Survey," *Schizophrenia Bulletin* 24 (1998): 11–20.

Lieberman, J. A., and R. M. Murray, eds. *Comprehensive Care of Schizophrenia: A Textbook of Clinical Management.* London: Martin Dunitz, 2001.

McGlashan, T. H. "Early Detection and Intervention in Schizophrenia Research," *Schizophrenia Bulletin* 22 (1996): 327–345.

Sen, G., and K. Bose. "*Rauwolfia Serpentina,* a New Indian Drug for Insanity and High Blood Pressure," *Indian Medical World* 61 (1931): 194–201.

Vogel, F. "Moderne Probleme der Humangenetik," *Ergebnisse innere Medizin und Kinderheilkunde* 12 (1959): 52–125.

antisocial behavior Behavior that is disrupting or harmful to society as a whole. Persons who are experiencing a psychotic disorder may, due to their lack of full contact with reality, commit antisocial acts against others or against property. Sometimes extreme violence—such as assaults or even homicides—have been known to result. If such persons are legally judged insane, then they are generally not considered responsible for the antisocial behavior committed while under the influence of the psychotic disorder. Particularly dangerous diagnostic categories include those afflicted with the psychotic hostility and delusional beliefs characteristic of some people with PARANOID SCHIZOPHRENIA or the manic episodes of BIPOLAR DISORDER.

anxiety A symptom of most MENTAL DISORDERS that is usually described as a feeling of uneasiness, apprehension, or dread. Anxiety can be a pervasive feeling that is not associated with any one person or thing in particular, which is generally how most definitions distinguish it from fear, which usually does have an object. Anxiety can be overwhelming in the ACUTE RECOVERABLE PSYCHOSES and in active phases of BIPOLAR DISORDER. Schizophrenics commonly report anxiety, especially during the PRODROMAL PHASE, when the awareness of frighteningly new psychotic symptoms causes anxiety, and during periods in chronic schizophrenia, when exacerbations of psychotic symptoms occur. From a psychoanalytic point of view, anxiety is a sign that the ego has not successfully been able to keep unpleasant or threatening thoughts or feelings entirely out of awareness, so that, even though the actual content of the threatening thought or feeling may be unconscious, the unpleasant effects are still experienced as anxiety.

APA nomenclature The terminology and diagnostic schemata devised and continually revised by the American Psychiatric Association in its continuing editions of the *Diagnostic and Statistical Manual of Mental Disorders.* This term is often used in contradistinction to ICD nomenclature, the diagnostic schemata for mental disorders found in the WORLD HEALTH ORGANIZATION's continuing revisions of the *International Classification of Diseases.*

apathy A symptom present in many mental disorders but especially in DEPRESSION, ORGANIC MENTAL DISORDERS (due to brain damage), and in SCHIZOPHRENIA. This symptom of "uncaring" or of "lack of interest in the self or in the world" is pervasive, like a MOOD DISORDER, and is indicative of the AFFECTIVE DISTURBANCES of schizophrenia.

Argentina The only prevalence study of SCHIZOPHRENIA conducted in Argentina found a low rate of 1.1 per 1,000.

Torrey, E. F. *Schizophrenia and Civilization.* New York: Jason Aronson, 1980.

Arieti, Silvano (1914–1981) An American psychiatrist and psychoanalyst long recognized as a leading authority on SCHIZOPHRENIA. He was a professor of clinical psychiatry at the New York Medical College and was a training analyst and supervisor at the William Alanson White Institute for Psychoanalysis. For many years he was editor in chief of *The American Handbook of Psychiatry.* His most significant contribution to the study of schizophrenia was his comprehensive volume, *Interpretation of Schizophrenia,* which was hailed soon after the appearance of the first edition in 1955 as the most complete presentation on the disorder since Eugen BLEULER's in 1911. A significantly revised and expanded second edition appeared in 1974. His psychoanalytic orientation is evident throughout the volume, particularly in the sections concerning psychotherapy and schizophrenics.

Arieti, S. *Interpretation of Schizophrenia.* Rev. 2nd ed. New York: Basic Books, 1974.

aripiprazole See ANTIPSYCHOTIC DRUGS.

Aristotelian thinking A concept used by Silvano ARIETI to denote the usual rational, logical processes employed by "normal" human beings. In his book *Interpretation of Schizophrenia,* Arieti contrasts Aristotelian thinking in normals with the more "primitive" and irrational logic that he calls PALEOLOGIC THOUGHT and that, he argues, characterizes schizophrenics. This idea fit in well with psychoanalytic notions of SCHIZOPHRENIA being an expression of REGRESSION to a more primitive and infantile mode of reasoning and experiencing the world. Arieti writes in the 1974 revised edition of his classic volume: "The paleologic type of organization is archaic or incomplete in comparison to the Aristotelian. The schizophrenic patient, when he thinks in a typically schizophrenic way, uses non-Aristotelian cognitive organizations."

Arnold, Thomas (1742–1816) The author of *Observations on the Nature, Kinds, Causes, and Prevention of Insanity, Lunacy or Madness* (1782), an important achievement in the development of modern psychiatry. Arnold was an Edinburgh-trained English physician who had studied under William Cullen. After completing his medical training, he opened a private mad-house in Leicester, which provided him with the important observations on mental disorders that he then used to create the classification system outlined in his 1782 book. He classified MENTAL DISORDERS according to their symptom clusters, as it is still done today, and he divided them into two main classes: "ideal insanity," which referred to disorders of perception such as HALLUCINATIONS and illusions; and "notional insanity," those disorders characterized by DELUSIONS. This system influenced later authors of psychiatric works. Two other influential books by Arnold are *A Case of Hydrophobia Successfully Treated* (1793) and *Observations on the Management of the Insane* (1809).

art, schizophrenic The relationship between "madness" and "creativity" has been the subject of speculation for at least 2,000 years. Master artists such as Vincent Van Gogh (1853–90), who clearly suffered from a mental illness that led to his incarceration in an asylum and eventual suicide, or abstract expressionist Jackson Pollock (1912–1956), who was hospitalized for severe alcoholism in 1938 and whose psychotic-like drawings were later published by his analyst, have stimulated the argument over whether madmen and artists draw from the same unconscious well for their inspiration.

Psychiatrists and psychologists have studied the artwork of schizophrenics in particular for more than a century. The very first psychiatrist to study the artwork of mental patients was Max Simon, whose groundbreaking paper, *"L'Imagination dans la folie: Étude sur les dessins, plans, descriptions, et costumes des aliénés,"* was published in the French psychiatric journal *Annales Médico-Psychologiques* in 1876. Simon correlated five major classifications of artistic style with five different classes of MENTAL DISORDERS. As have most subsequent psychiatric commentators, Simon noted the similarities in style of psychotic art with the creations of small children and of people in primitive societies. In 1880 the famous Italian criminologist and psychopathologist Cesare

Lombroso (1836–1909) wrote a paper, "On the Art of the Insane," which was published as a chapter in his book *The Man of Genius* in 1888. In addition to reaffirming Simon's observations, Lombroso remarked on the prevalence of sexual symbolism in the artwork of psychotics. German psychiatrist Fritz Mohr constructed the first diagnostic test based on the drawings of mental patients in 1906.

Perhaps the most famous book on schizophrenic art was published in German in 1922 (and translated into English and published in 1972)—the classic work *Bildnerei der Geisteskranken (Artistry of the Mentally Ill)* by Hans Prinzhorn (1886–1933). Prinzhorn was a psychiatrist at the Heidelberg Psychiatric Clinic and amassed a unique collection of 5,000 pieces of artwork produced by psychiatric patients from institutions in Germany, Austria, Switzerland, Italy, and the Netherlands between 1890 and 1920. Prinzhorn detailed the case histories of "ten schizophrenic artists" along with reproductions of their artwork. His approach to schizophrenic art was essentially aesthetic, and he concluded that the content of the artwork had no value as a diagnostic tool. Prinzhorn made the interesting observation that HALLUCINATIONS were rarely depicted in the art of schizophrenics. He identified the "components" of the "schizophrenic configuration" that distinguish schizophrenic art from other styles (such as similar productions by children and "primitives") and argues that the "schizophrenic outlook" is most closely mirrored by the abstract art of the 20th century. Prinzhorn concludes: "Existing artistic abilities are therefore not necessarily destroyed by the schizophrenic process but can in fact maintain themselves unchanged over long periods. . . . We have also demonstrated that during the progress of schizophrenia, while the patient declines into a highly confused, unapproachable final state with all the typical symptoms in their greatest extremes, his superficial, craftsmanlike dexterity develops great configurative power which allows him to produce pictures of undoubted artistic quality."

Many psychoanalytic papers have been published on schizophrenic art since 1918, perhaps the most notable being Ernst Kris's paper, "Comments on Spontaneous Artistic Creations by Psychotics," which was included in his chapter on "The Art of the Insane" in his famous book, *Psychoanalytic Explorations in Art* (1952). Sexual and aggressive expressions of the id that characterize primitive and infantile PRIMARY PROCESS thinking are examined in the art of schizophrenics in these writings. The practical use of artistic creations as a tool in the psychotherapy of schizophrenics was described by Margaret Naumberg in 1950 in her book, *Schizophrenic Art: Its Meaning in Psychotherapy.* In the second edition (1974) of Silvano ARIETI's *Interpretation of Schizophrenia,* more examples of this form of art therapy with psychotics are provided, with a psychoanalytic interpretation of these productions.

The use of creative techniques in psychotherapy (such as drawing, painting, sculpture, dance) was pioneered by Swiss psychiatrist C. G. JUNG (1875–1961), who interpreted such material as if it gave a snapshot or X-ray of the patient's internal world. Although not technically schizophrenic, but apparently often on the brink of psychosis, artist Jackson Pollock spent several years in analysis with Jungian analyst Dr. Joseph Henderson, who eventually allowed the publication of many of the drawings that Pollock did during therapy in *Jackson Pollock: Psychoanalytic Drawings (1970).* In excerpts from a previously unpublished lecture on his former patient (but reproduced in the Pollock biography by B. H. Friedman, *Jackson Pollock: Energy Made Visible* [1972]), Henderson makes the following observations that are typical of many Jungian psychoanalytic interpretations: "Following a prolonged period of representing human figures and animals in an anguished, dismembered or lamed condition, there came a new development in the drawings Pollock made during therapy. This was not merely the dissociation of schizophrenia, though he was frequently close to it. It has seemed to me a parallel with similar states of mind ritually induced among tribal societies or in shamanistic trance states. In this light the patient appears to have been in a state similar to the novice in a tribal initiation rite during which he is ritually dismembered at the onset of an ordeal whose goal is to change him from a boy into a man." Similar Jungian interpretations of schizophrenic experience and art are found in the writings of the Jungian analyst John Weir Perry.

Honoring the long tradition of schizophrenic art, the quarterly research review publication of the NATIONAL INSTITUTE OF MENTAL HEALTH,

Schizophrenia Bulletin, continues to feature on its cover the artwork created by current and former mental patients, with a description of the piece by its author included in the "About the Cover" section following the table of contents.

Friedman, B. H. *Jackson Pollock: Energy Made Visible.* New York: McGraw-Hill, 1972.

Kris, E. *Psychoanalytic Explorations in Art.* New York: International Universities Press, 1952.

Lombroso, C. *The Man of Genius.* 1880. Reprint, London: Scott, 1895.

Naumberg, M. *Schizophrenic Art: Its Meaning in Psychotherapy.* New York: Grune & Stratton, 1950.

Prinzhorn, H. *Artistry of the Mentally Ill: A Contribution to the Psychology and Psychopathology of Configuration.* Translated by E. v. Brockdorff from the 2nd German edition. (1922). New York: Springer-Verlag, 1972.

Simon, M. "L'Imagination dans le folie: Étude sur les dessins, plans, descriptions, et costumes des aliénés," *Annales Médico-Psychologiques* 16 (1876): 358–390.

Wysuph, C. I. *Jackson Pollock: Psychoanalytic Drawings.* New York: Horizon Press, 1970.

"as-if" personality See BORDERLINE CASES; BORDERLINE SCHIZOPHRENIA.

Asperger's disorder See AUTISM, INFANTILE.

association disturbances One of THE "FOUR A'S" (association disturbances, AFFECTIVE DISTURBANCES, AMBIVALENCE, AUTISM) that Eugen BLEULER identified as the "fundamental symptoms" that uniquely characterize SCHIZOPHRENIA. Bleuler devoted a large section of his 1911 classic, *Dementia Praecox, Or the Group of Schizophrenias,* to the description of these association disturbances in schizophrenia. In one paragraph he summarizes his basic observations on association disturbances in schizophrenia:

> In the normal thinking process, the numerous actual and latent images combine to determine each association. In schizophrenia, however, single images or whole combinations may be rendered ineffective, in an apparently haphazard fashion. Instead, thinking operates with ideas and concepts which have no, or a completely insufficient, connection with the main idea and should therefore be excluded from the thought-process. The result is that thinking becomes confused, bizarre, incorrect, abrupt. Sometimes, all the associative threads fail and the thought chain is totally interrupted; after such "blocking," ideas may emerge which have no recognizable connection with preceding ones.

Today this association disturbance in schizophrenia is referred to as a form of FORMAL THOUGHT DISORDER.

See also LOOSENING OF ASSOCIATIONS.

Bleuler, E. *Dementia Praecox, Or the Group of Schizophrenias,* trans. Joseph Zinkin. 1911. Reprint, New York: International Universities Press, 1950.

Association of Medical Officers of Asylums and Hospitals for the Insane The first and oldest professional psychiatric association in the world, it was founded in Great Britain in 1841. In 1865 its name was changed to the Medico-Psychological Association of Great Britain and Ireland. It became the Royal Medico-Psychological Association in 1926 and eventually changed to its present title, the Royal College of Psychiatrists, in 1971. The association began publication of a professional journal, *The Asylum Journal,* in 1842 but later changed its name to the *Journal of Mental Science.* It is now published by the Royal College of Psychiatrists as the *British Journal of Psychiatry.*

Association of Medical Superintendents of American Institutions for the Insane The initial name for the professional society of American psychiatrists, founded in 1844, that is known today as the AMERICAN PSYCHIATRIC ASSOCIATION.

Association Studies See GENETICS STUDIES.

asthenic type One of the types of physique that psychiatrist and neurologist Ernst Kretschmer

claimed to be representative of schizophrenics (*schizophrenes*) in his 1921 book, *Körperbau und Charakter* (Physique and character). Asthenic types were excessively thin and looked taller than they truly were. Other physical types, such as the ATHLETIC TYPE and the dysplastic type, were also thought by Kretschmer to be prevalent among schizophrenics. Kretschmer concludes: "There is a clear biological affinity between the psychic disposition of the schizophrenes and the bodily disposition characteristic of the asthenics, athletics, and certain dysplastics." Although Kretschmer's theory of how certain temperaments were related to specific types of physique has not been taken seriously for many decades, he nonetheless deserves credit as one of the pioneers in the search for the BIOLOGICAL MARKERS OF SCHIZOPHRENIA.

Kretschmer, E. *Physique and Character: An Investigation of the Nature of Constitution and of the Theory of Temperament.* 1921. Reprint, New York: The Humanities Press, 1951.

asylums A word that originally meant a place of sanctuary—such as a church or monastery—*asylum* later became the word of choice to designate institutions for the insane, particularly in the very late 18th and throughout the 19th centuries. Using the word *hospital* as the official name for institutions for the mentally disordered did not come into vogue in the United States until the State Care Act was passed into law in 1890, officially replacing the term *asylum* with *hospital* in the system of state mental hospitals that this legislation mandated. A similar official shift in terminology followed suit in Great Britain shortly thereafter.

For centuries the mentally ill were treated in general hospitals, but more often than not they were relegated to the streets, poor-houses, and prisons. Sometimes small houses or "one-man asylums" were built to contain particularly troublesome psychotics. In the 17th and 18th centuries, especially in England, hospitals and private "madhouses" were created to incarcerate the mentally ill, although the royal hospitals also treated the general medical problems of the community. With the humanistic movement toward the adoption of moral medicine in the early 1800s, much legislation in England (and subsequently the United States) was passed regulating the care of the mentally ill by setting up national programs of institutions and licensing the operators of private madhouses. Private psychiatric facilities presently refer to themselves as clinics or institutes. Now there is a trend, particularly in the United States, to change the names of public institutions for the mentally ill from hospitals to psychiatric centers.

The first institution in the United States built solely for the care of the insane was opened in Williamsburg, Virginia, in 1769. By 1830 only 13 hospitals and asylums existed in the United States, mostly in the Atlantic states but also as far west as Ohio and Kentucky. Generally their patient population was relatively small, no more than 50 or so for most of them, but a few had a capacity of 200 or more. However, in the 1830s and 1840s a definite shift in public opinion toward the "deviant and dependant" led to the notion that institutions should be built and utilized as places of first resort for intervention. Not only were asylums constructed in record numbers for the insane, but also penitentiaries for the criminal, orphan asylums for homeless children, ALMSHOUSES for the poor, and reformatories for delinquents. It was not that overwhelming new numbers of these people were suddenly appearing but simply that the general public and government's philosophy of dealing with these social problems changed. By 1860, of the 33 states then in existence, 28 had asylums for the insane. Incredibly, between 1840 and 1870 the number of people involuntarily committed to state-run institutions in the United States increased from 2,500 to more than 74,000—far higher than the rate of growth for the population of the United States in that period (only three and one half times). By 1955, just prior to the largest waves in the deinstitutionalization of psychiatric patients, that number had swollen to 559,000 patients in psychiatric hospitals.

See also COMMITMENT.

Deutsch, A. *The Mentally Ill in America: A History of Their Care and Treatment from Colonial Times.* 2nd ed. New York: Columbia University Press, 1949.

Rothman, D. J. *The Discovery of the Asylum: Social Order and Disorder in the New Republic.* Boston: Little, Brown, 1971.

asyndetic thinking A term coined by psychiatrist Norman Cameron to describe the apparent lack of causal linkage or connectedness between elements in the language of schizophrenics. Cameron contributed to the study of the unique structure of schizophrenic language in two noted papers written in the 1930s and listed below.

See also COGNITIVE STUDIES OF SCHIZOPHRENIA.

Cameron, N. "Deterioration and Regression in Schizophrenic Thinking," *Journal of Abnormal and Social Psychology* 34 (1939): 265.

———. "Reasoning, Regression and Communication in Schizophrenics," *Psychological Monographs* 50, no. 1 (1938).

athletic type One of the three main "types of physique" that Ernst Kretschmer proposed were characteristic of "schizophrenes" in his 1921 book *Körperbau und Charakter (Physique and Character)*. The ASTHENIC TYPE was the most clearly associated with schizophrenics; also the dysplastic type was common. The athletic type, according to Kretschmer, "is recognized by the strong development of the skeleton, the musculature and also the skin." Kretschmer attempted to devise a taxonomic system of body types that correlated with particular psychological types, in particular those with the psychotic disorders of SCHIZOPHRENIA (whom he referred to as "schizophrenes") and manic-depressive psychosis (whom, following FALRET, he referred to as "circulars").

atropine intoxication therapy A little-used form of treatment for SCHIZOPHRENIA introduced by G. R. Forrer in the late 1940s in which a coma would be induced in patients through the toxic state produced by injections of atropine. Never very popular, this procedure was discontinued in light of the ostensible effectiveness of INSULIN COMA THERAPY.

See also COMA THERAPY; NITROGEN INHALATION THERAPY.

Forrer, G. R. "Atropine Toxicity in the Treatment of Schizophrenia," *Journal of the Michigan Medical Society* 49 (1950): 184–185.

attention, disorders in An almost universal characteristic of SCHIZOPHRENIA that has been observed since earliest times is the inability of an individual with the disorder to willfully focus his or her attention on a thought, feeling, object, or activity for any great length of time before it is disrupted. Since the late 1950s, this problem in functioning has been referred to as attentional deficits or disorders of attention.

Schizophrenics have been observed to have extreme difficulty in sustaining and selectively focusing their attention. This has been true not only in the earliest clinical descriptions of the disorder, but also in many experimental studies of schizophrenic cognition conducted since 1961. In the 1913 English translation of his papers on *Dementia Praecox and Paraphrenia,* Emil KRAEPELIN observed in his schizophrenic patients that "it is quite common for them to lose both inclination and ability on their own initiative to keep their attention fixed for any length of time." Oftentimes unsophisticated family members or other caretakers of schizophrenics tragically mistake these "gaps" in attention that disrupt activity as signs that the afflicted person is "lazy" or "being difficult." These short circuits in the willful activities of schizophrenics are instead almost universal characteristics of the disease, particularly in the nonparanoid subtypes of schizophrenia.

In 1961 Andrew McGhie and James Chapman published a classic paper on this topic that influenced the next several decades of the experimental study of schizophrenia. In their published report, the authors collected representative statements from schizophrenics about their own inner experiences and concluded that in schizophrenia "a primary disorder is that of a decrease in the selective and inhibitory functions of attention." In other words, McGhie and Chapman were arguing that the selective "filtering" mechanism that we all use to screen out unwanted ideas and feelings, when we are focusing our attention on something else, is not functioning properly in schizophrenics. They find it difficult to screen out all these unwanted stimuli from inside themselves and from the outside world, and this disrupts not only their ability to think and communicate, but it also distorts their perceptions and sensations.

Reports by McGhie and Chapman's patients illustrate the disorders in attention characteristic of schizophrenia:

> "It's as if I am too wide awake—very, very alert. I can't relax at all. Everything seems to go through me. I just can't shut things out."
>
> "My concentration is very poor. I jump from one thing to another. If I am talking to someone they only need to cross their legs or scratch their heads and I am distracted and I forget what I am saying."
>
> "I can't concentrate on television because I can't watch the screen and listen to what is being said at the same time. I can't seem to take in two things like this at the same time, especially when one of them means watching and the other means listening. On the other hand I always seem to be taking in too much at the one time and then I can't handle it and can't make sense of it."
>
> "Sometimes when people speak to me my head is overloaded. It's too much to hold at once. It goes out as quickly as it goes in. It makes you forget what you just heard because you can't get hearing it long enough. It's just words in the air unless you can figure it out from their faces."

Since McGhie and Chapman's paper was published, many experimental studies have been conducted to understand the disorders of attention in schizophrenia. This research has been a trend in COGNITIVE STUDIES OF SCHIZOPHRENIA, which use metaphors of the mind derived from the computer sciences to examine INFORMATION PROCESSING IN SCHIZOPHRENIA. Some of this research has attempted to correlate certain attention deficits with deficits in the specific information processing abilities of the two cerebral hemispheres of the brain.

In the search for childhood predictors of later adult schizophrenia, research has focused on disturbances in attention in children as one possible way to predict the later development of schizophrenia. In an ongoing LONGITUDINAL STUDY, psychologists Barbara A. Cornblatt and L. Erlenmeyer-Kimling of the New York State Psychiatric Institute are following a group of children evaluated for "global attention deficits" that may prove to be a "marker of risk" for schizophrenia. (See also HIGH-RISK STUDIES; NONPARANOID SCHIZOPHRENIA.)

In the late 1990s, the ability of persons with schizophrenia to screen out relevant from irrelevant sensations was studied under the new term SENSORIMOTOR GATING. Attempts to improve the ability of schizophrenics to focus their attention through "attention training" have produced only mild and temporary improvements.

Cornblatt, B. A., and J. G. Keilp. "Impaired Attention, Genetics, and Pathophysiology of Schizophrenia," *Schizophrenia Bulletin* 20 (1994): 31–46.

Cornblatt, B. A., and L. Erlenmeyer-Kimling. "Global Attentional Deviance as a Marker of Risk for Schizophrenia: Specificity and Predictive Validity," *Journal of Abnormal Psychology* (1985): 470–486.

McGhie, A., and J. Chapman. "Disorders of Attention and Perception in Early Schizophrenia," *British Journal of Medical Psychology* 34 (1961): 103–117.

Medalia, A., et al. "Effectiveness of Attention Training in Schizophrenia," *Schizophrenia Bulletin* 24 (1998): 147–152.

Swerdlow, N. R., et al. "Using an Animal Model of Deficient Sensorimotor Gating to Study the Pathophysiology and New Treatments of Schizophrenia," *Schizophrenia Bulletin* 24 (1998): 303–316.

attention-deficit hyperactivity disorder (ADHD) See HYPERKINESIA.

atypical antipsychotics See ANTIPSYCHOTIC DRUGS.

atypical psychotic disorders The generic term for psychotic disorders with a sudden onset, short duration, and complete or almost complete remission and return to normal functioning. More than 200 synonyms or partial synonyms for these disorders have been documented. These BRIEF PSYCHOTIC DISORDERS, as they are called in *DSM-IV-TR* (2000), or ACUTE AND TRANSIENT PSYCHOTIC DISORDERS, as they are grouped in *ICD-10* (1992), have historically been those that do not fall within the two great psychotic disorders described in 1899 by Emil KRAEPELIN, DEMENTIA PRAECOX (later,

SCHIZOPHRENIA) and MANIC-DEPRESSIVE ILLNESS. Since these disorders are periodic, cyclic, and have a good prognosis, Kraepelin tended to subsume them under his concept of manic-depressive illness as forms of MANIA. Today they are regarded as a large and little-understood group of psychotic disorders that do not easily fit the diagnostic categories of schizophrenia or of the AFFECTIVE DISORDERS and which are therefore regarded separately. The incidence of these disorders is believed to be greater in developing, or Third World, countries than in First World countries (such as the western European countries, the United Kingdom, the United States, and Japan). In First World (developed) countries they are generally split into two main types, depending on the length of time they are in evidence: (1) a group of chronic persistent delusional disorders, and (2) a group of acute and transient disorders with POLYMORPHIC PSYCHOTIC SYMPTOMS.

Cultural differences in diagnosis In North America, where *DSM-IV-TR* is most widely used, these disorders are now referred to as "brief psychotic disorders." Formerly they were referred to as "brief psychotic reactions" in *DSM-III* (1980) and *DSM-III-R* (1987), but the word *reaction* was dropped because it implied a particular cause of the psychotic disorder—a reaction to a stressful event or events—and this was not found in all cases. Although *ICD-10* (1992) is used worldwide and is promoted by the WORLD HEALTH ORGANIZATION as the standard diagnostic reference book, individual countries refuse to give up traditional terms that have a long history. For example, in France the term BOUFFÉE DELIRANTE has been used quite popularly since the 1890s for these disorders. In Germany, where Karl Kahlbaum first proposed the term DYSPHRENIA for these disorders in 1863, the term CYCLOID PSYCHOSES is still quite popular. In Scandinavian countries, the terms REACTIVE PSYCHOSES, psychogenic psychoses, and schizophreniform psychoses are still popular following a long history dating back to a 1916 book by Danish psychiatrist August Wimmer (1872–1937) on psychogenic forms of mental disease. In Japan, the term *atypical psychoses* has been the most popular term for these disorders since a 1941 publication by Japanese psychiatrist Hisatoshi Mitsuda that first described these disorders. In Japan the prognosis is usually presumed to be favorable, but in the 1980s and 1990s a residual "defect syndrome" has been found in a small proportion of these patients, launching a debate over the differential diagnosis between certain atypical psychoses and schizophrenia. In Japan these disorders are seen to have etiological (causal) links to genetics; epilepsy, with an increased risk of epilepsy found in relatives of patients with atypical psychoses; and endocrinological disorders such as luteal insufficiency and latent hypothyroidism.

Culture-bound syndromes There are some disorders that do not fit easily into Western diagnostic categories in psychiatry that are specific to particular populations or cultural areas of the world. These "culture-bound syndromes" (for example, *amok* among the Malay, or various forms of spirit possession) are considered separately from psychotic disorders in *ICD-10* because many of them more closely fit other diagnostic categories (such as personality disorders or dissociative disorders) rather than Western concepts of psychosis. *ICD-10* provides a list of these culture-specific syndromes and offers suggested Western psychiatric diagnoses that may be analogous to them.

The issue of misdiagnosis There are numerous medical conditions and medications that may cause symptoms of psychosis. Invariably these may present as atypical psychoses. A useful text that describes these conditions and offers suggestions for making the differential diagnosis between a medical disorder and a mental disorder is *Distinguishing Psychological from Organic Disorders* by Robert L. Taylor.

Marneros, A., and F. Pillman. *Brief Psychoses—The Acute and Transient Psychotic Disorders.* Cambridge: Cambridge University Press, 2003.

Pillman, F., and A. Marneros. "Brief and Acute Psychoses: The Development of Concepts," *History of Psychiatry* 14 (2003): 161–177.

Pull, C. B., J. M. Cloos, and N. V. Murthy. "Atypical Psychotic Disorders." In *Schizophrenia.* 2nd ed., edited by S. R. Hirsch and D. Weinberger. Cambridge: Blackwell, 2003.

Taylor, R. L. *Distinguishing Psychological from Organic Disorders: Screening for Psychological Masquerade.* London: Free Association Books, 2000.

auditory hallucinations Perhaps the most common type of HALLUCINATION found in the psychotic disorders. These are hallucinations of sound, and they are found across many diagnostic categories and are even experienced in rare instances by "normals" who do not exhibit signs of a MENTAL DISORDER. Strictly speaking, auditory hallucinations may indicate a psychotic disorder only when they are accompanied by gross impairment in REALITY TESTING.

Auditory verbal hallucinations (AVHs)—specifically the hearing of voices—is the most common type of hallucination experienced by person with SCHIZOPHRENIA. It is estimated that approximately 50 percent of all schizophrenics have experienced AVHs. The voices are usually identified as being male or female and do not usually belong to anyone known to the person experiencing them. The voices quiet if the experiencer is engaged in meaningful conversation, but they intensify if there is no background noise in the immediate environment or if the background noise has no meaning. *DSM-IV-TR* (2000) states that schizophrenia can be diagnosed if only one of the following characteristic symptoms has been in evidence for a significant portion of a one-month period (or less if successfully treated): AVHs of a voice keeping up a running commentary on the person's behavior or thoughts, or AVHs of two or more voices conversing with one another. AVHs are one of the most common POSITIVE SYMPTOMS of schizophrenia.

The hearing of "voices" is the most common type of auditory hallucination reported, but individuals have also reported hallucinations of "clicks," "rushing noises," and "music." A common misconception, which is no longer supported by recent research on the psychotic disorders, is that the hearing of "voices" is a definite sign of schizophrenia. Indeed, even in conventional clinical practice today one of the most common (and usually one of the first) questions asked of a patient upon admission to a psychiatric crisis center or a psychiatric hospital is, "Have you been hearing voices?" If the answer is "yes," then the patient is usually diagnosed as schizophrenic. To illustrate how clinicians place too much emphasis on "hearing voices" as a symptom of schizophrenia, Stanford University psychologist David L. Rosenham had normal volunteers go to psychiatric hospitals and report that they had been hearing voices for about three weeks. This was their only reported symptom. Not only were most of them admitted, but they were also given schizophrenic diagnoses. Rosenham's remarkable report of this experiment, "On Being Sane in Insane Places," was published in *Science* in 1973 and received much publicity.

In the 1919 English translation of the eighth edition of his famous textbook of psychiatry, *Dementia Praecox and Paraphrenia,* Emil KRAEPELIN observes that "the hearing of voices" was "the symptom peculiarly characteristic of dementia praecox." He noted that, as a rule, what the voices say is "unpleasant and disturbing." These voices tease, mock, threaten, and abuse the suffering patient. However, Kraepelin also reports that some of his patients heard "good voices" at times. A common characteristic of these auditory hallucinations is that, "Many of the voices make remarks about the thoughts and doings of the patient." Another quality that Kraepelin thought was specific to the auditory hallucinations of schizophrenics was that "the patient's own thoughts appear to them to be spoken aloud." One of Kraepelin's patients told him, "I have the feeling as if someone beside me said out loud what I think."

In *Dementia Praecox, Or the Group of Schizophrenias* (1911), Eugen BLEULER argued that hallucinations were one of the accessory symptoms of schizophrenia that could be found in other disorders (such as manic-depressive psychosis) as well. However, Bleuler thought that auditory hallucinations were more common in schizophrenia than in other disorders. "Almost every schizophrenic who is hospitalized hears 'voices,' occasionally or continually." Bleuler adds that,

> The most common auditory hallucination is that of speech. The "voices" of our patients embody all their strivings and fears, and their entire transformed relationship to the external world. . . . For the patient, as for his attendant, the "voices" become, above all, the representatives of the pathological or hostile powers. The voices not only speak to the patient, but they pass electricity through his body, beat him, paralyze him, take his thoughts away.

Different types of auditory hallucinations were among the 11 FIRST-RANK SYMPTOMS of schizophrenia proposed by the German psychiatrist Kurt Schneider in his phenomenologically based textbook, *Clinical Psychopathology* (1959). The presence of any one of these 11 symptoms was proposed as sufficient to make the diagnosis of schizophrenia. In this sense, it is said that each of these symptoms—including the auditory hallucinations of voices—is PATHOGNOMONIC of schizophrenia, at least according to Schneider.

The psychoanalytic interpretation of auditory hallucinations was only briefly discussed by Sigmund FREUD (1857–1939). In his essay "Metapsychological Supplement to the Theory of Dreams" (1916), Freud made reference to the "dream hallucination" and compared it to schizophrenic auditory hallucinations. Although he noted that both of these were examples of REGRESSION, he suggested that an additional factor in schizophrenia was a disturbance in "that institution of the ego" concerned with the "testing of reality." In his famous 1914 paper "On Narcissism," Freud makes it clear that the "voices" heard in schizophrenic auditory hallucinations do not represent the *superego* itself, as might be thought, given the critical, moralistic judgments and threats made by the voices, but instead Freud thought that these voices represent the regressive undoing or deterioration of the superego. Freud writes: "The voices as well as the indefinite number of speakers, are brought into the foreground again by the disease, and so the evolution of conscience is regressively reproduced."

Later psychoanalytic writers mostly agree with psychoanalyst Otto Fenichel, who, in his textbook *The Psychoanalytic Theory of the Neuroses* (1945), believes that schizophrenic auditory hallucinations serve as a defense: they are "substitutes for perception" after a break with reality. "Inner conflicts are projected and experienced as if they were external perceptions," Fenichel explains.

PSYCHOANALYSIS is now only a historical curiosity of the 20th century, like animal magnetism and phrenology in the 18th and 19th centuries. Although such speculations by Freud and his followers were highly influential on psychiatric thinking from the 1920s until the 1970s, advances in the brain sciences have refuted all the major claims of psychoanalysis. Psychoanalysis is now regarded as a pseudoscience and has no place in ethical psychiatric practice.

The invention of brain imaging technologies in the 1970s has allowed researchers to observe an active, living human brain hallucinating in real time. Increasingly more sophisticated techniques for observing or "capturing" the metabolic activity of the brain during auditory hallucinations have used such measures as regional cerebral blood flow (rCBF), positron emission tomography (PET scans), single photon emission computed tomography (SPECT), and functional magnetic resonance imaging (fMRI). Computer generated images of regional neuronal activity have given us pictures of the various parts of the brain that "light up" when someone is experiencing an auditory hallucination.

The first published study that showed the auditory hallucinations were not "imaginary" (or products of some vague Freudian "superego" or "defense mechanism") but due to the activity of a specific region of the brain was conducted by P. K. McGuire and colleagues. It appeared in the British medical journal *Lancet* in 1993. Using SPECT technology to study regional cerebral blood flow (blood rushes to a part of the brain when that part is being used), they found that auditory hallucinations were associated with increased rCBF in Broca's area of the brain (an area associated with language expression) and, to a lesser extent, in the medial frontal cortex and left medial temporal cortex.

Since 1993 numerous brain imaging studies have confirmed that auditory hallucinations are associated with activity in the parts of the brain that govern the hearing and speaking of words. These functional imaging studies have also confirmed that there is an abnormal interaction between areas of the brain known as the prefrontal area (where so-called executive control of the brain, mind, and body take place) and the auditory association areas in the temporal lobe of the brain (particularly Heschl's gyrus). When these areas are activated during auditory hallucinations, such hallucinations are "heard" as "real" by the person with schizophrenia.

Both conventional and atypical antipsychotics have been the treatment of choice for auditory hallucinations. However, in 25 to 30 percent of cases,

drugs do not stop the "voices." Numerous psychological techniques have been developed to help persons with schizophrenia cope with their hallucinations. Almost all these techniques produced some limited benefit to such persons by reducing their feeling of distress caused by the hallucinations, but none of the techniques effectively eliminated the frequency of the hallucinations. The strategies that have been tried are (1) distracting activities, such as listening to music, (2) behavioral activities, such as exercise, and (3) cognitive training to teach patients to ignore the voices in their heads.

The very few other clinical studies of auditory hallucinations have generally been in phenomenological research on the relationship of certain types of hallucinations with certain diagnostic categories. Auditory hallucinations have been found to occur across diagnostic categories, including in psychotic depressions and BIPOLAR DISORDER, but the auditory hallucination of "voices" may be most common in the paranoid subtype of schizophrenia.

Asaad, G., and B. Shapiro. "Hallucinations: Theoretical and Clinical Overview," *American Journal of Psychiatry* 143 (1986): 1,088–1,097.

David, A. S. "Auditory Hallucinations: Phenomenology, Neuropsychology, and Neuroimaging Update," *Acta Psychiatrica Scandinavica* 395 (1999): 95–104.

Dierks, T., et al. "Activation of Heschl's Gyrus during Auditory Hallucinations," *Neuron* 22 (1999): 615–621.

Frith, C. "The Role of the Prefrontal Cortex in Self-Consciousness: The Case of Auditory Hallucinations," *Philosophical Transactions of the Royal Society of London. B. Biological Sciences* 1346 (1996): 1,505–1,512.

Leudar, I., and P. Thomas. *Voices of Reason, Voices of Insanity: Studies of Verbal Hallucinations.* London: Routledge, 2000.

McGuire, P. K., G. M. S. Shah, and R. M. Murray. "Increased Blood Flow in Broca's Area during Auditory Hallucinations in Schizophrenia," *Lancet* 342 (1993): 70–796.

Shergill, S., R. M. Murray, and P. K. McGuire. "Auditory Hallucinations: A Review of Psychological Treatments," *Schizophrenia Research* 32 (1998): 137–150.

Australia Several studies have been done on the Australian aborigines to determine their prevalence rates for schizophrenia; two of the better ones both came up with a rate of 4.4 per 1,000. Schizophrenia prevalence rates for the rest of the continent as a whole still need to be determined.

Autenreith, Ferdinand (1772–1835) A German physician who believed in the curability of acute psychotic disorders. He is remembered as the inventor of the "padded room." A more sinister invention of Autenreith's was a metal mask that would fit over the faces of mental patients, preventing them from making too much noise by limiting the amount of movement of their jaws. He also devised bulblike gags to perform the same function.

See also MECHANICAL RESTRAINT.

autism Eugen BLEULER coined this term in 1910 as one of the "FOUR A'S" (ASSOCIATION DISTURBANCES, AFFECTIVE DISTURBANCES, AMBIVALENCE, AUTISM) that Eugen Bleuler proposed as the FUNDAMENTAL SYMPTOMS that uniquely distinguish SCHIZOPHRENIA from other MENTAL DISORDERS. It refers to the unresponsiveness of many schizophrenics to their environment, thus seeming like they are in a "world of their own." In *Dementia Praecox, Or the Group of Schizophrenias* (1911), Bleuler makes the following observations on autism:

> The most severe schizophrenics, who have no more contact with the outside world, live in a world of their own. They have encased themselves with their desires and wishes (which they consider fulfilled) or occupy themselves with the trials and tribulations of their precursory ideas; they have cut themselves off as much as possible from any contact with the external world.

Bleuler then concludes, "This detachment from reality, together with the relative and absolute predominance of the inner life, we term autism." This symptom in children has led to the identification of infantile autism.

Bleuler, E. *Dementia Praecox, Or the Group of Schizophrenias.* Translated by Joseph Zinkin. 1911. Reprint, New York: International Universities Press, 1950.

autism, infantile A brain disease of infancy and childhood first described by psychiatrist Leo Kanner (1894–1981) in 1943. It was formerly called Kanner's syndrome but is now known as autistic disorder, the most severe and prototypical form of the general diagnostic category known as pervasive developmental disorders in *DSM-III-R*. Through the years, many other diagnostic terms have been used for this class of disorders, including atypical development, symbiotic psychosis, childhood psychosis, and childhood schizophrenia, but all these terms are now obsolete.

Autistic disorder is usually apparent in a child's behavior within the first two to three years of life. The child generally does not respond well to touching or other forms of social interaction, is slow to develop language, develops many unusual stereotyped and repetitive behaviors, and can become fascinated with certain inanimate objects (such as a spinning fan or faucets). Although some children can experience improvements in language, social, and other skills around the ages of five or six, this is not true in every case. Puberty can bring about marked changes either for the better or worse. The disease has a lifelong manifestation, although a small minority of these children go on to live relatively independent lives. The majority remain handicapped, with about 25 percent experiencing epileptic seizures before adulthood. About 50 percent remain within the mentally retarded range of intellectual functioning.

Studies in England and the United States have found that the prevalence of autistic disorder in the population is about four to five children out of every 10,000. Males are three to four times more likely to be afflicted with this disorder than females.

It is now known that autistic disorder is a brain disease that has nothing to do with child-rearing practices—especially the supposedly monstrous REFRIGERATOR MOTHER of autistic children, who Kanner believed was the cause of the disorder. Autistic disorder has been associated with maternal rubella, anoxia during birth, encephalitis, infantile spasms, tuberous sclerosis, untreated phenylketonuria, and the fragile X syndrome. A genetic basis is indicated by studies that show that autistic disorder is more common in siblings than in the general population. Candidate genes for autism have been found.

It was formerly thought that autism was a form of a childhood psychosis that would eventually develop into SCHIZOPHRENIA, but most recent research seems to indicate that they are two different disorders. Sancte de Santis described a childhood psychotic disorder in 1906, *dementia praecoxissima,* which he thought was related to DEMENTIA PRAECOX in adults. There was much confusion over whether infantile autism was a form of CHILDHOOD SCHIZOPHRENIA, until Kanner separated the two in 1943. Autism was officially removed from the diagnostic class of schizophrenic disorders in the 1970s, primarily as a result of the six published studies on the childhood psychoses published by Kolvin and his colleagues in 1971.

Autism, like schizophrenia, is viewed by many researchers as being a "spectrum disorder": that is, the disease manifests in several forms to a greater or lesser degree and may have underlying genetic relationships to other mental disorders. *DSM-IV-TR* (2000) includes Autistic Disorder in the category of Pervasive Developmental Disorders, many of which, in decades past, were diagnosed as infantile autism or childhood schizophrenia. These include Rett's Disorder, Childhood Disintegrative Disorder, and Asperger's Disorder. Autistic Disorder is characterized by a triad of impairments: qualitative impairment in social interaction (inability to look others in the eye, lack of curiosity in the world around them except for certain objects or movements of objects that fascinate them), qualitative impairments in communication (particularly delay in, or total lack of, development of spoken language), and restricted repetitive and stereotyped patterns of behavior, interest, and activities. Many children diagnosed with autism also have a secondary diagnosis of mental retardation due to an IQ below 70 and severe deficits in their ability to perform typical activities of daily living. In the first four years of life, autism is often easily distinguished from mental retardation as a primary diagnosis because mentally retarded children tend to seek out social interaction and are more interpersonally "present" than children who are developing autism. Asperger's disorder is a separate diagnosis in *DSM-IV-TR,* but many researchers and clinicians still argue that

it may be a form of "higher-functioning" autism. Although impairments in social interactions and repetitive and stereotyped patterns of behavior are part of the picture, unlike Autistic Disorder, there is no clinically significant general delay in language (for example, single words are used by age two, communicative phrases by age three). Also unlike Autistic Disorder, there is no clinically significant delay in cognitive development or in the development of age-appropriate self-help skills, adaptive behavior (other than social interaction), and curiosity about the world around them. In Asperger's disorder, IQ levels are generally higher and the possibility of holding jobs and engaging in other "normal" activities is greater as they become adults. The disorder is named after Viennese pediatrician Hans Asperger (1906–80), who published a paper in 1944 in the medical journal *Archiv fuer Psychiatrie und Nervenkrankheiten* on a condition he called "autistic psychopathy." This paper went largely unnoticed until 1981, when Lorna Gladys Wing, a child psychiatrist working at the Maudsley Hospital in London, published a paper in *Psychological Medicine* proposing that a new diagnostic term, Asperger's syndrome, be given to those autistic children who do not display developmental delays in language and communication. She distinguished Asperger's syndrome from the typical definition of autism of Leo Kanner. An earlier clinical description of a child with Asperger's syndrome actually appeared in an article by G. E. Ssucharewa in 1926 in the *Monatsschrift fuer Psychiatrie und Neurologie.*

DeMyer, M. K., J. N. Hingtgen, and R. K. Jackson. "Infantile Autism Reviewed: A Decade of Research," *Schizophrenia Bulletin* 7 (1981): 388–451.

Kolvin, J., et al. "Studies in the Childhood Psychoses. II. The Phenomenology of Childhood Psychosis," *British Journal of Psychiatry* 118 (1971): 385–395.

autistic savants Formerly called idiot savants, a term coined in 1887 by the pioneer in the study of mental retardation, J. Langdon Down, for "children who, while feebleminded, exhibit special faculties which are capable of being cultivated to a very great extent." Autistic savants, though often mentally retarded, almost invariably develop from an early history of autistic disorder. Psychiatrist Darold Treffert proposes that this phenomenon be renamed the "savant syndrome" in his book, *Extraordinary People: Understanding "Idiot Savants"* (1989). He identifies two subtypes: "talented savants" or "Savant I," who have "skills that are remarkable simply in contrast to the handicap"; and "prodigious savants" or "Savant II," which is a much rarer form of the condition in which "the ability or brilliance is not only spectacular in contrast to the handicap, but would be spectacular even if viewed in a normal person."

The savant syndrome is six times more likely to occur in males than females. Although the condition is rare, some estimates indicate that as many as 9.8 percent of those children diagnosed with autistic disorder may exhibit this syndrome. And even more rare are the cases of the "prodigious savants," or "Savant II," with less than 100 cases on record in the past 150 years.

The common talent of all children and adults with the savant syndrome is phenomenal memory ability. This enables the sometimes spectacular performance of skills in the following areas: calendar calculating, music (usually the piano), rapid numbers calculating and mathematics, art (painting, drawing, and sculpting), and sometimes mechanical ability. The memorization of enormous amounts of information has been documented in some prodigious savants.

Treffert has found that one of the more common patterns is a "triad" of blindness, mental retardation, and musical ability.

In 1988 a movie, *Rain Man,* won the Academy Award for best picture for its depiction of a prodigious savant, or "Savant II." The many remarkable feats of memory ability and calculating ability dramatized in the film were all based on actual anecdotes reported in the clinical literature and are generally accurate re-creations.

Treffert, D. "The Idiot Savant: A Review of the Syndrome," *American Journal of Psychiatry* 145 (1988): 563–572.

autoimmune hypothesis See IMMUNE SYSTEM ALTERATIONS IN SCHIZOPHRENIA.

autointoxication as the cause of dementia praecox (schizophrenia) There were two primary biological theories about the cause of DEMENTIA PRAECOX and SCHIZOPHRENIA from 1896 until the 1930s: heredity (genetics) and autointoxication. Whereas histories of biological psychiatry have focused almost exclusively on HEREDITY—since it has turned out that genetics does indeed play an influential role in the cause (ETIOLOGY) of the disease—they have tended to ignore the autointoxication or focal infection (focal sepsis) theories that were so promising a century ago. This is due to the fact that such theories of the cause of schizophrenia lost prominence by the 1930s. Breakthroughs in bacteriology and endocrinology had a profound influence on not only Emil KRAEPELIN (1856–1926) but many others as well, all of whom were convinced of the rationality of the notion that perhaps all diseases, both physical and mental, were caused by self-poisoning processes in the body. Kraepelin was not alone in the belief that dementia praecox was due to an endogenous process of autointoxication or focal infection which led to a poisoning of the brain and the production of the characteristic signs and symptoms of this chronic, devastating form of insanity. Then as now, the etiologic heterogeneity of dementia praecox and its successor, schizophrenia, cannot be explained by heredity or genetics alone. To understand fully Kraepelin's view of dementia praecox and its implications for subsequent research on the causes of schizophrenia, we must first understand the cognitive categories of the medical world in which he lived and worked, an era dominated by the new bacteriological and endocrinological paradigms emerging from the laboratory revolution in medicine that began in the late 1800s.

Autointoxication theory in medicine and psychiatry With the general acceptance of the germ theory of disease by 1880 due to the efforts of Louis Pasteur in France and Robert Koch in Germany, the new medical science of bacteriology offered a novel and potentially fruitful paradigm for comprehending illness. Following the replicable laboratory demonstration that bacteria or microbes were involved in processes such a putrefaction, fermentation, and infection, it was a natural cognitive leap to hypothesize that they were involved in the etiology and pathophysiology of many—if not most—diseases. Initially it was argued that diseases were not caused by the bacterial organisms acting directly but instead by the toxins they produced. Poisonous ptomaines (the products of proteins formed in putrefaction) or "toxalbumins" were formed that could be circulated through the body's bloodstream and produce a wide variety of diseases affecting almost every organ. In the original, classical form of autointoxication theory, the intestines were most often cited as the locus of this systemic self-poisoning process, with the kidneys and liver assuming lesser importance in theoretical speculation.

The disease theory of autointoxication first appears in the German medical literature. Hermann Senator (1834–1911), a clinical professor at Berlin University, had speculated as early as 1868 that "self-infection" arising in the intestines could be a source of disease elsewhere in the body. Later, in 1884, he argued that mental disturbances could be caused by this process, claiming that the acute delirium of diabetic coma may have its origin in *Selbstinfektion*.

However, it was the work of French physicians that fueled the rapid expansion of this theory to all categories of disease, including mental disorders. Autointoxication theory rose to international prominence in medicine after the 1887 publication of *Lecons sur les auto-intoxications dans les maladies* by Charles-Jacques Bouchard (1837–1915), an eminent professor of pathology at the University of Paris. For both Senator and Bouchard—the founders of autointoxication theory—the disease-causing poisons were the products of putrefactive processes in the intestines. Although a normal part of the digestive process, under certain conditions (such as fecal stasis) the overproduction of these toxins could not be filtered by the liver or kidneys and, as they entered other organs, disease would result. Bouchard's vision of the inner life of the human body is dramatic: "I have said that the organism, in its normal, as in its pathological state, is a receptacle and a laboratory of poisons. . . . Man is in this way constantly living under the chance of being poisoned; he is always working toward his own destruction; he makes continual attempts at suicide by intoxication."

It was not until 1893, however, that we find the first indications that autointoxication theory is being seriously discussed as a possible etiology for mental disorders. On August 1 of that year, at the Fourth Session of the French Congress of Psychological Medicine held in La Rochelle, "Rapporteurs" François-André Chevalier-Lavaure, a physician from Aix-en-Provence, and Emmanuel Regis, a physician from Bordeaux, drew attention to the value of autointoxication as a possible organic cause of madness by organizing and leading a panel on "Auto-intoxication in Mental Disease." This topic had been the subject of Chevalier-Lavaure's doctoral dissertation in 1890, the first substantive treatment of this issue in the history of psychiatry. In their presentation, they argued that it was difficult to distinguish between cases of autointoxication and those of infection from sources outside the body, but that a clear diagnostic distinction should be made between "infectious" insanity (mental disturbances following acute infectious diseases, such as meningio-encephalitis) and "visceral insanity," which is "associated with disease of the internal organs" and is "also very probably due to autointoxication." As Kraepelin would be three years later, in 1896, when he speculated that dementia praecox was caused by autointoxication, Regis and Chevalier-Lavaure were cautious about the extant scientific basis of their claims: "Indeed, we are inclined it [visceral insanity] as the most typical illustration of the influence of auto-intoxication on the mental faculties. There is not as yet sufficient experimental evidence, however, in favor of this assumption to enable us to assert that such is actually the case; for in respect especially of the mental disturbances that are dependent on digestive troubles we know next to nothing about the concomitant changes in the chemistry of the gastric digestion and toxicity of the intestinal contents."

Hermann Senator had already proposed in 1884 that such self-infection would have profound effects on the nervous system and the brain. When Bouchard's book first appeared in English in January 1894, Thomas Oliver noted in his translator's preface that, "The part played by auto-intoxication in mental diseases is attracting attention." In 1895 systematic extensions of autointoxication theory to psychiatry were offered in the German medical literature by D. E. Jacobson of Copenhagen and in the American medical literature by Albert E. Sterne of Indianapolis. Even Julius von Wagner-Jauregg (1857–1940), who would later win a Nobel Prize for his therapy for neurosyphilis, speculated that disturbed mental states may be caused by the influence of intestinal toxins on brain cells (Wagner-Jauregg 1896). According to Veronika Jahn in a 1975 monograph on this subject, the gastrointestinal tract continued to be the most often cited etiologic locus of "autointoxication psychoses" in psychiatric circles.

Although the rise of the bacteriological paradigm after 1880 initiated and fueled autointoxication theory, advances in the understanding of metabolic processes and the endocrine system between 1890 and 1905—the year Ernest Starling first proposed the modern concept of the "hormone"—added a new endogenous etiological hypothesis: metabolic or "interstitial autointoxication" due to the over- or underproduction of internal secretions in the glands with ducts (liver, pancreas, and kidney), those without ducts (thyroid, adrenals, pituitary), and especially the sex glands (gonads). The medical and psychiatric literatures on autointoxication prior to World War I reflect the confusion in the emerging discipline of endocrinology regarding the nature of hormones and their similarities to enzymes, general metabolites, drugs, toxins, antitoxins, and vitamins. The noted Russian psychiatric researcher Aleksandr Ivanovich Iushchenko (1869–1936) of St. Petersburg extensively reviewed this confusing literature in a series of lectures in 1911, which were later published and translated into German in 1914. He argued that dementia praecox was not due to an autointoxication arising in the intestines but rather was caused by glandular dysfunctions, especially disease processes in the parathyroid. Dementia praecox as a disease arising secondarily from metabolic disorders causing autointoxication would remain a central (if unsupported) etiologic hypothesis for its first 40 years, beginning with the speculative medical cognition of Emil Kraepelin himself.

Emil Kraepelin: Metabolic autointoxication as the cause of dementia praecox Impressed with recent advances in the understanding of metabolic

disorders (*Stoffwechselerkrankungen*) and with the plausibility of autointoxication theory, Kraepelin positioned his new diagnostic entity of dementia praecox squarely within the context of these new medical paradigms. In the general discussion of the causes of the insanities that opens the 1896 fifth edition of his *Psychiatrie,* Kraepelin notes that many of the characteristic signs of glandular or metabolic disorders appear during the development of mental deterioration, especially in dementia praecox (pages 36–37). Later in this book (p. 439), in his very first detailed description of dementia praecox in a chapter on *"Die Stoffwechselerkrankungen,"* Kraepelin states that he has "serious objections" to the point of view that dementia praecox is caused by "inadequate constitutional faculties" or "hereditary degeneration (*erblischen Entartung*)." Instead, he offers an alternate hypothesis: "I consider it more likely that what we have here is a tangible morbid process in the brain (*einen greifbaren Krankheitsvorgang im Gehirne*). Only in this way does the quick descent into severe dementia become at all comprehensible." He admits the failure of neuropathological studies to find any characteristic cellular pathology in dementia praecox but attributes this to an inadequate effort to search for such morbid changes. What then causes this "tangible morbid process in the brain" if it is not heredity? Kraepelin is clear on this point: "In light of our current experience, I would assume that we are dealing here with an autointoxication (*Selbstvergiftung*), whose immediate causes lie somewhere in the body."

Kraepelin, however, makes a major departure from classic autointoxication theory by rejecting the intestines as the source of toxins. Instead, Kraepelin posits the *locus morbi* in the gonads: "If we consider the tendency for the illness to strike at the age when sexual development is still taking place, then it is not out of the question for there to be a connection between the illness and some processes taking place in the sexual organs. These are, of course, only provisional and very indefinite hypotheses."

Kraepelin's metabolic autointoxication theory of dementia praecox was not uniformly welcomed by psychiatrists. Perhaps the most direct attack on this thesis came from Adolf MEYER (1866–1950), later to become one of the most prominent psychiatrists in the United States, in his review of the 1896 fifth edition of Kraepelin's textbook. "As long as chemistry can not furnish more accurate data and methods, the theory of intoxication and auto-intoxication so often resorted to by Kraepelin will be a *terminus technicus* for our ignorance." But such critics did not deter Kraepelin. In the 1899 sixth edition of his textbook, Kraepelin continues to make the argument that the sex glands are the source of the toxins that poison the brain and produce dementia praecox, but his claims are now more nuanced: "In view of the close connection for the disease with the developmental age, with menstrual disorders and reproduction, and in view of the absence of any recognizable external cause, the most obvious thing to think of is probably an *autointoxication* which could possibly be in some close or distant connection with processes in the genital organs." However, Kraepelin now tempers his earlier dismissal of the role of heredity in the cause of dementia praecox, adopting a view that presages modern vulnerability models of the etiology of schizophrenia: "The frequency of hereditary disposition to mental disturbances and their physical and mental symptoms would only signify a lowered resistance to the actual cause of the disease."

Although many followed Kraepelin and accepted autointoxication as the probable cause of the dementia praecox/schizophrenia, most diverged from Kraepelin by insisting that the intestines were the true locus of the "self-infection" and not the sex glands. Still, metabolic autointoxication as a possible cause of dementia praecox was an hypothesis that intrigued Kraepelin for at least two decades. In the third volume of the final, 1913 eighth edition of his *Psychiatrie,* Kraepelin (p. 931) cautiously asserts that it is still too early to make etiological conclusions about dementia praecox, but that it generally might be said that "a number of facts" (*eine Reihe von Tatsachen*) about dementia praecox suggest "an autointoxication as a result of a metabolic disturbance might be probable to some extent" (*einer Selbstvergiftung infolge einer Stoffwechselstorung bis zu einem gewissen Grade wahrscheinlich*).

Dementia praecox soon became an accepted diagnostic entity in Britain, and slightly later in America, where the first serious publications on

dementia praecox began to appear in 1900. In these first American notices, the importance of Kraepelin's new scientific nomenclature is uniformly lauded, with heredity mentioned as the most probable cause of the disorder. Autointoxication is not mentioned. Perhaps this is due to the fact that the autointoxication theory of the etiology of mental disorders did not meet with the immediate interest that it did in Britain, where the theory mutated into a new variant that originated in dentistry: focal infection theory.

Focal infection as the cause of dementia praecox In 1900 the British physician William Hunter suggested that "oral sepsis" was the root source of bacterial infections that would spread to other parts of the body such as the heart, lungs, stomach, intestines, and—a speculation conducive to the application of this theory to Kraepelin's autointoxication theory of dementia praecox—even the sex glands. Secondary localized diseases would then develop from the pathogenic effect of these bacteria, producing toxins as by-products that would cause further systemic sequalae. With autointoxication theory gaining wider acceptance in medicine after 1900, especially through its promotion by the British surgeon Sir William Arbuthnot Lane and John Harvey Kellog of Battle Creek, Michigan, focal infection theory in British dentistry seemed to be the next logical step in its evolution, although it, too, eventually proved to be an unfounded theory that had no scientific evidence to back it up. Focal infection as a cause of insanity was proposed by the British psychiatrist Lewis Bruce of Scotland in 1906 and neurologist Henry Upson of Cleveland, Ohio, in 1907. In outlining his theory that dementia praecox was caused by dental impaction, Upson claimed in 1909, "In several cases I have watched the development of an alveolar abcess and the simultaneous development of an acute psychosis, which was finally relieved by the extraction of the offending teeth." After the prominent Chicago physician Frank Billings, a former president of the American Medical Association, publicized his conversion to focal infection theory in 1916, physicians and psychiatrists concerned with finding the cause and cure of dementia praecox were emboldened to consider radical new theories of etiology and the rational treatments that would follow from them.

Rational therapeutics and surgical solutions The theories of autointoxication and focal infection were attractive to Kraepelin and others not only because of their central assumptions about the etiology of dementia praecox but also because they held out the very real promise of viable treatments or even a cure. As Kraepelin well knew, without knowledge of the cause of dementia praecox, there could be no effective rational therapy. Yet, despite his belief in autointoxication, Kraepelin did not direct his energies, or those of his talented research associates such as Franz Nissl and Alois ALZHEIMER, to finding internal sites of autointoxication or focal infection. Rather, he focused his research group on neuropathololological studies, studies of hereditary patterns of transmission, and the development of psychopharmacological agents designed specifically for use in psychiatry.

Sources of autointoxication or infection in the body, if located properly, could be treated with Listerizing sprays or ointments, colonic irrigations, or, as Sir William Arbuthnot Lane demonstrated with his colectomies as a cure for chronic constipation, surgery. For the cure of mental illness, several physicians in America and Britain decided that surgery would be the most rational treatment. The first to do so was Newdigate M. Owensby (1882–1952), chief physician at the Bay View Asylum in Baltimore, Maryland. His experimental procedure was reported in *The New York Times* on December 20, 1907. Hypothesizing that the symptoms of dementia praecox were caused by an oversecretion of the thyroid gland (due to diseased blood vessels in the gland), which poisoned the brain, in July 1907 Owensby chose "the worst patient in the asylum" and cut away the diseased portion of the thyroid. In October 1907 the man was discharged, symptom-free. By December 1907 Owensby had operated on at least four other patients, reporting therapeutic success in all of them. The second to do so was Bayard Taylor HOLMES (1852–1924), a professor of medicine and a specialist in abdominal surgery in Chicago. Holmes was an avid proponent of biological psychiatry and founded and edited the journal *DEMENTIA PRAECOX STUDIES* between 1918 and 1922, a periodical devoted to disseminating scientific information about the possible organic causes of dementia praecox. It is believed to be the first med-

ical journal named after a mental disorder. After conducting less than a year of his own laboratory research, in 1915 Holmes hit upon a focal infection theory of the etiology of dementia praecox—an ergotism-like toxemia caused by fecal stasis in the cecum. The following year Holmes began performing cecostomies and appendicostomies, constructing a stoma in the side of his subjects to allow daily irrigations of the colon with water and magnesium sulfate to eliminate psychotic symptoms. Between 1916 and 1918, in private hospitals and in his short-lived (1917–18) Psychiatric Research Laboratory of the Psychopathic Hospital at Cook County Hospital in Chicago, Holmes and his associates performed major surgery on at least 22 persons suffering from dementia praecox. The first one was his own son, Ralph Loring Holmes, who had developed dementia praecox at age 17 while in his first year of medical school. Ralph never recovered from his May 1916 cecostomy and died four days after the experimental surgical procedure.

The third physician to advocate surgery as a treatment of dementia praecox was Henry A. COTTON (1876–1933), the superintendent of the New Jersey State Hospital at Trenton from 1907 to 1930 and an innovative psychiatrist who had studied with Kraepelin and Alzheimer in Munich for two years. Heavily influenced by Kraepelin's own belief in autointoxication as a cause of dementia praecox, and impressed by the dental theory of focal infection, starting in 1918 Cotton routinely had all the teeth removed from the psychiatric patients to stem the production of psychotic symptoms. By the following year he began even more radical procedures, removing part or all of the colon, cervix, ovaries, testes, or appendix of dementia praecox patients and claimed enormous success. More than 2,000 persons received experimental surgery as psychiatric treatment at the state hospital in Trenton and in Cotton's private clinic, although the pace of this endeavor slowed considerably after a political investigation into Cotton's excesses led to a public scandal and his own mental breakdown. Hundreds of his patients died following surgery. Historian Andrew Scull relates the details of this horrific gothic tale in his 2005 book, *Madhouse: A Tragic Tale of Megalomania and Modern Medicine.* The fourth physician to treat dementia praecox through dental and abdominal surgery was Thomas C. Graves, the medical superintendent of the Rubery Hill and Hollymoore Mental Hospital in Birmingham, England.

Autointoxication or focal infection as explanations for the cause of a wide variety of diseases, both acute and chronic, continued to be promoted as a general theory in medicine and biological psychiatry until the early 1930s. By that time, numerous clinical studies spurred by advances in medical technology had found little scientific evidence for endogenous autointoxication as the presumed cause of dozens of diseases, as the theory's proponents had claimed. The autointoxication and focal infection theories of dementia praecox likewise vanished from serious consideration, never to return in their original form, as "schizophrenia" supplanted the Kraepelin's old nosological category and etiological speculation. However, viral infections, endocrine disturbances, and even theories of too much of the neurotransmitter dopamine "poisoning" the brain and causing schizophrenia are all analogues to the autointoxication theory of the cause of dementia praecox/schizophrenia proposed by Kraepelin and other physicians more than a century ago.

See also DEMENTIA PRAECOX; ENDOCRINE DISORDER HYPOTHESIS; VIRAL THEORIES OF SCHIZOPHRENIA.

Holmes, B. T. "A Guide to the Documents in Evidence of the Toxaemia of Dementia Praecox," *Dementia Praecox Studies* 3 (1920): 23–107.

Jahn, V. *Die gastrointestinalen Autointoxikationspsychosen des spaeten 19. Jahrhunderts.* Zurich: Juris Druck, 1975.

Kraepelin, E. *Psychiatrie. Ein Lehrbuch für Studirende und Aerzte. Achte, vollstandig umgearbeitete Auflage.* 3 vols. Leipzig: Verlag von Johann Ambrosius Barth, 1908–1913.

———. *Psychiatrie. Ein Lehrbuch für Studirende und Aerzte. Funfte, vollstandig umgearbeitete Auflage.* Leipzig: Verlag von Johann Ambrosius Barth, 1896.

———. *Psychiatrie. Ein Lehrbuch für Studirende und Aerzte. Sechste, vollstandig umgearbeitete Auflage.* Leipzig: Verlag von Johann Ambrosius Barth, 1899.

———. *Psychiatry: A Textbook for Students and Physicians.* Vol. 2. Canton, Mass.: Science History Publications, 1990 [A translation fo Kraepelin's 6th edition of 1899].

Meyer, A. "Book Review," *American Journal of Insanity* 53 (1896): 298–302.

Noll, R. "Historical Review: Autointoxication and Focal Infection Theories of Dementia Praecox," *World Journal of Biological Psychiatry* 5 (2004): 66–72.

———. "Infections Insanities, Surgical Solutions: Bayard Taylor Holmes, Dementia Praecox, and Laboratory Science in Early Twentieth-Century America," *History of Psychiatry* 17 (2006): 183–204.

Regis, E., and F. A. Chevalier-Lavaure. "Auto-intoxication in Mental Diseases," *The Medical Week* 11 (1893): 373.

Scull, A. *Madhouse: A Tragic Tale of Megalomania and Modern Medicine.* New Haven, Conn.: Yale University Press, 2005.

Senator, H. "Ueber ein Fall von Hydrothionamie und uber Selbstinfektion durch abnorme Verdauungsvorgange," *Berliner klinische Wochenschrift* 5 (1868): 254.

———. "Ueber Selbstinfektion durch abnorme Zersetzungsvorgange und ein dadurch bedingtes (dyskrasisches) Coma (Kussmaulscher Symptomenkomplex des "diabetischen Coma)," *Zeitschrift für klinische Medizin* 7 (1884): 7–8.

avolition See ABOULIA.

Awl, William See "CURE-AWL, DR."

axonal pruning See CORTICAL PRUNING AS A CAUSE OF SCHIZOPHRENIA.

B

bad news technique Perhaps one of the earliest "cognitive" psychotherapeutic techniques on record is the practice of inventing false "bad news" to tell patients in order to quell their manic mood states. There is evidence that this rather sadistic "counter-cognitions" technique was used in the BETHLEM ROYAL HOSPITAL in England as early as the 1500s to change the behavior of unmanageable patients.

Baillarger, Jules-Gabriel-François (1809–1890) One of the most eminent of the French psychopathologists of the 19th century. Baillarger was a student of ESQUIROL and founded the famous *Annales Médico-Psychologiques* in 1843, the very first French professional publication devoted to the study of psychological medicine. His research contributions include one of the first descriptions (in 1854) of MANIC-DEPRESSIVE PSYCHOSIS, which he called *folie à double forme.* Baillarger's revolutionary connection between alternating melancholic and manic phases, which he hypothesized to be of a single disorder and independent of MENTAL DISORDERS characterized solely by DEPRESSION or solely by MANIA, is a concept later used by KRAEPELIN in his definition of manic-depressive psychosis and is still employed today in modern diagnostic systems. A mere two weeks after Baillarger presented his new diagnostic entity, another student of Esquirol's, Pierre FALRET, claimed instead that it was he who had first described such a condition in a paper published in 1851—but only in 1854 did he call it *la folie circulaire,* the term historically associated with Falret. Both Baillarger and Falret are thus given the distinction of being the first clinicians to describe manic-depressive psychosis or BIPOLAR DISORDER.

See also BIPOLAR DISORDER; CIRCULAR INSANITY; MANIC-DEPRESSIVE ILLNESS.

balderdash syndrome Another name for GANSER'S SYNDROME.

balmy Slang for "eccentric" or "mad." Some scholars have suggested that the term is derived from a 17th-century private madhouse in London known as Balmes House. It was later known as the Whitmore House or Warburton's madhouse.

Barison, Ferdinando An influential theorist—particularly in Italy—of schizophrenic thinking styles. Differing from those theorists who held that schizophrenics tended to be more concrete in their thinking than normals, Barison argued that schizophrenics become overly abstract in their ideas and speech. Barison thought that schizophrenics employed abstractions in order to cover up the gaps in their thought processes caused by the disease process, thus repairing the "dissociative" breaks in the organization of the typical schizophrenic mind. This viewpoint was largely adopted by psychiatrist Silvano ARIETI in his discussion of the "pseudoabstract form and content" of schizophrenic thought and language in his *Interpretation of Schizophrenia* (1974).

Barison, F. "L'Astrazione formale de pensiero quale sintomo di schizofrenia," *Schizophrenie* 3 (1934).

basket men The colloquial term used to refer to the male attendants of the BETHLEM ROYAL HOSPITAL in

London as late as the 17th century. It was a holdover from medieval times when the hospital was a monastery. "Basket men" was a term for the hospitallers (usually monks or nuns) who would go out into the community—baskets in hand—begging for alms and food, which would then be carried back to the hospital for the care of the hospitallers, their patients, and prisoners in the public jails. Such "alms-baskets" held a highly symbolic significance, for the phrase "to go to the basket" meant to go to prison—a common place to find the mentally ill prior to the reforms of the 19th century. Along with other unfortunate individuals, the mentally ill person might also be termed a "basket-scrambler," meaning one who scrambles for the dole from a basket (i.e., who lives on charity).

Bateson, Gregory (1904–1985) An anthropologist by training, Bateson (and his associates) in 1956 formulated the famous DOUBLE-BIND THEORY of communication patterns in the families of schizophrenics. Bateson was the son of the famous British biologist William Bateson, who coined the word *genetics;* his father named him after Gregor Mendel. After completing his M.A. in anthropology at Cambridge, Bateson conducted fieldwork in New Guinea. He met and married Margaret Mead, a pioneer in cultural anthropology, with whom he conducted important fieldwork in Bali. Their marriage lasted 14 years. Bateson is noted for his broad theoretical concerns in cybernetics, communications theory (which has influenced family-therapy theorists), the family dynamics of SCHIZOPHRENIA, and his work with John Lilly on man-dolphin communication at the Oceanographic Institute in Hawaii. Until his death in 1985, Bateson was a frequent lecturer and scholar-in-residence at the Esalen Institute in Big Sur, California.

Lipset, D. *Gregory Bateson: The Legacy of a Scientist.* Englewood Cliffs, N.J.: Prentice Hall, 1980.

bath of surprise A type of immersion therapy, used until the 19th century, in which the mentally ill person was plunged without warning into cold water. ESQUIROL, in his *Mental Maladies: A Treatise on Insanity* (first English translation, 1845), lists several forms of cold water treatment for patients, but the bath of surprise "consists of plunging the patient into water when he least expects it." Esquirol goes on to say that, "We administer it, by precipitating him into a reservoir, a river, or the sea. It is the fright which renders this means efficacious in overcoming sensibility. We can conceive the vivid impression that a patient experiences, who falls unexpectedly into the water, with the fear of being drowned." However, Esquirol admits that he has no data supporting the usefulness of this form of therapy and confesses, "I have never made use of it, but I am certain it has been fatal." Incredibly, instead of the bath of surprise, Esquirol recommends throwing the patient out of a third-story window in order to effect a cure: "When I hear of it (the bath of surprise) being prescribed, I should prefer rather, that they advised to precipitate the patient from the third story, because we have known some insane persons cured by falling upon the head."

Esquirol, J. E. D. *Mental Maladies: A Treatise on Insanity.* Translated by E. K. Hunt. 1838. Reprint, Philadelphia: Lea and Blanchard, 1845.

baths One of the most ancient forms of treatment for mental illness. It is included by Philippe PINEL as one of the three forms of the "usual treatment" ("bleeding, bathing, and pumping") for the mentally ill in asylums circa 1801. Various pseudoscientific theories were put forth at the time to account for the calming or shocking effect of baths that seemed temporarily to reduce active psychotic symptoms. In Daniel Hack Tuke's *A Dictionary of Psychological Medicine* of 1892, a full 10 pages is devoted to the variations on this basic form of treatment for the mentally ill. Indeed, 15 different categories of "bath" are listed in that reference work, as follows:

1. Prolonged warm or hot baths
2. Prolonged warm baths with the addition of cold to the head
3. Prolonged warm sitz baths
4. Prolonged warm baths medicated with mustard
5. Prolonged cold baths

6. Dip baths
7. Baths of surprise
8. Suffusion of tepid and cold water from pails
9. Douches
10. Showers
11. Packing in the wet sheets
12. Packing in the dry sheets
13. Packing in mustard and water sheets
14. Hot air (Turkish) baths
15. Vapour (Russian) baths

Many of these types of bath treatments survived until well into the 20th century.

See also HYDROTHERAPY.

Williams, D. "Baths." In *A Dictionary of Psychological Medicine,* Vol. 1, edited by D. H. Tuke. London: J. & A. Churchill, 1892.

Battie, William (1703–1776) An English physician and anatomist who was the first (and only) psychiatrist ever to be elected president of the Royal College of Physicians, a distinction he earned in 1764. Beginning in 1742 he served on the board of governors of the BETHLEM ROYAL HOSPITAL. However, due to the abusive conditions for patients at "Bedlam," in 1751 Battie founded Saint Luke's Hospital for Lunatics and later acquired two private madhouses. Battie instituted important reforms for the treatment of the mentally ill, many of which were outlined in his classic *Treatise on Madness* (1758), which is a milestone in the history of psychiatry. He advocated the training of the caretakers of the insane and called for research into the causes of insanity for the purposes of prevention. Battie is also remembered for his vicious battles fought with John Munro, who ran "Bedlam," over administrative and treatment philosophies for the care of the insane. The slang expression that a mentally ill person is "batty" or has "gone batty" may have originated in England with the expression that a person has "gone to Battie's," i.e., to Battie's private madhouse.

Beck, Samuel Jacob (1896–?) Romanian-born psychologist, later educated at Harvard and Columbia, who eventually headed the psychology laboratory at the Michael Reese Hospital in Chicago, Illinois. After psychologist David Levy imported the RORSCHACH TEST from Switzerland around 1925, Beck was the first American psychologist to publish research using the test; he also published the first Rorschach manual in English in 1937. Beck pioneered the use of the Rorschach as a diagnostic test for SCHIZOPHRENIA.

bedlam A well-known euphemism, even today, for pandemonium or chaos—like that found in "mad-houses." There was never a place officially named Bedlam. Instead, the word was a colloquial corruption of Bethlem, from the BETHLEM ROYAL HOSPITAL in London. An arresting portrayal of what the real "Bedlam" may have been like is to be found in certain scenes in the motion picture *Bedlam* (RKO, 1946), produced by Val Lewton, in which the chilling chiaroscuro suggests horrors of the asylum that the camera itself does not fully depict for the audience. However, the asylum images of life in "Bedlam" that are explicitly revealed bear a striking resemblance to those in the famous painting *Courtyard with Lunatics,* completed by Spanish artist Francisco Goya in 1793, which gives a graphic portrayal of asylum life in the 18th century. Since Lewton was known for the many literary and artistic allusions in his films (including many to Goya), he probably drew upon this painting (as well as Goya's etchings) for his motion picture conception of "Bedlam."

bed saddle A severe form of MECHANICAL RESTRAINT for patients that survived into the 20th century. For example, the bed saddle was reported in use at St. Elizabeth's Hospital in Washington, D.C., until removed from use by William Alanson White after he became superintendent of that institution in October 1903. In his memoirs, White describes the bed saddle:

> One day in my first month at the hospital. In going through the wards of the institution I found a colored patient strapped to the bed by means of what was known as a "bed saddle." This bed saddle was

> made of thin strips of metal in the form of a cross strapped to the bed, and the patient was strapped to it with his arms extended in the position of crucifixion. I had never seen such an apparatus before and immediately issued an order discontinuing its use. I had been trained in the belief that physical restraint was unnecessary, yet in the very hospital where this was a fundamental principle a certain amount of physical restraint had actually been used. I had never seen such a cruel apparatus as this, so I felt justified in ordering its discontinuance.

A standing form of this device was known as the CRUCIFORM STANCE or harness.

White, W. A. *William Alanson White: An Autobiography of a Purpose.* Garden City, N.Y.: Doubleday, Doran, 1938.

Beers, Clifford W. (1876–1943) Beers, an American businessman, underwent a mental breakdown and attempted to commit suicide by jumping out of a window in June 1900, at the age of 24. PARANOIA, AUDITORY HALLUCINATIONS, and continual thoughts of suicide had plagued him for several years. After regaining his sanity and his eventual release, Beers wrote an autobiography, *A Mind That Found Itself* (1908), which detailed his treatment—and abuse—in mental institutions. The horrors of these institutions as depicted by Beers shocked the public of his day and helped to win him supporters for his National Committee for Mental Health (later called the National Association for Mental Health), the first major psychiatric patient-advocacy organization in the United States. Beers relates in his book how he would deliberately get himself transferred to the worst wards of the hospital—the "violent wards"—so that he could thoroughly investigate the institution for his later reform efforts. The sad fact is that the reader of Beers's book today who has worked any significant amount of time in psychiatric hospitals will find many of Beers's experiences familiar—suggesting that almost a century after the publication of this book many ugly conditions have still not changed in public institutions for the care of the mentally ill.

See also ABUSE OF PSYCHIATRIC PATIENTS.

Beers, C. *A Mind That Found Itself.* Garden City, N.Y.: Doubleday, 1908.

behavior therapy The behavioral model of MENTAL DISORDERS holds that SCHIZOPHRENIA should not be considered the expression of an underlying mental "disease" but instead reflects the learning of a repertoire of "maladaptive behaviors" that can be corrected through using the operant conditioning techniques of behavior therapy. However, behaviorists have never constructed a complete theory about the recalcitrant maladaptive behaviors of schizophrenics, and long-term success, with behavioral techniques, of patients with schizophrenia has not been demonstrated. Behavior therapists focus on changing selected target behaviors of a patient (e.g., bizarre dressing, excessive smoking or coffee drinking, AUDITORY HALLUCINATIONS) and try to eliminate them systematically through the manipulation of "reinforcement contingencies" based on the general principles of learning that have been found to be effective in changing the behavior of animals and "normals."

The studies of psychologist T. Aylion and his colleagues in the 1960s were some of the first applying behavior therapy to institutionalized schizophrenics. A much-publicized behavioral technique that was designed to shape the behavior of entire wards of patients was the "token economy programs" that were popular in the late 1960s and early 1970s. Tokens were introduced on wards as a money substitute that could reward adaptive behaviors and help extinguish or reduce maladaptive ones. The problem with such programs was that they could only work in small environments where there was a highly motivated and highly trained staff on all three shifts of a 24-hour day—committed to following the rules of the behavioral program to the letter without "giving in" to the immediate maladaptive demands of the patients. Currently, social skills training programs based on learning theory and behavior therapy paradigms are gaining attention. Modeling, problem solving, and reinforcement techniques are used to improve the ability of schizophrenics to hold a conversation, be assertive, etc.

Whether any of the above forms of behavior therapy techniques for individuals or groups has long-

lasting effects is questionable. Schizophrenics who do well in such programs in the highly structured environment of an institution lose such skills as soon as they are back in the community and without constant support and reminders as environmental cues. The evidence suggests that the newly learned behaviors instituted by these programs are thus not generalizable. Furthermore, the disease process itself—as schizophrenia is more and more viewed as a brain disease of as yet unknown etiology—seems to sabotage the ability of the nervous system to allow psychosocially induced changes in thinking and behavior to remain permanently and lead to long-term improvements in the level of social and occupational functioning. Behavior therapy—and social skills training programs based on these principles—is thus of limited value in the treatment of schizophrenia.

Ayllon, T. "Some Behavioral Problems Associated with Eating in Chronic Schizophrenic Patients." In *Case Studies in Behavior Modification,* edited by L. Ullman and L. Krasner. New York: Holt, Rinehart & Winston, 1965.

Kazdin, A. E. "The Failure of Some Patients to Respond to Token Programs," *Journal of Behavior Therapy and Experimental Psychiatry* 4 (1973): 7–14.

Lieberman, R. P., W. D. Spaulding, and P. W. Corrigan. "Cognitive-Behavioural Therapies in Psychiatric Rehabilitation." In *Schizophrenia,* edited by S. R. Hirsch and D. R. Weinberger. London: Blackwell Science, 1995, pp. 605–625.

Penn, D. L., and K. T. Mueser. "Research Update on the Psychosocial Treatment of Schizophrenia," *American Journal of Psychiatry* 153 (1996): 607–617.

Belgian cage A wooden cage for the restraint of individuals with severe MENTAL DISORDERS. It stood on short posts. Such a cage was on display at a national exhibition in Brussels in 1880. Older names for such forms of MECHANICAL RESTRAINT, were the "idiot's cage" or "lunatic's cage."

Bellevue Hospital A hospital in New York City whose psychiatric ward achieved the notoriety in the United States that "Bedlam" had earned in England. Special wards reserved specifically for the mentally ill, called "insane pavilions," were first instituted at Bellevue Hospital in 1826. In 1839 a city "mad-house" was constructed and opened on Blackwell's Island (now Roosevelt Island) on the East River of New York City to handle the overwhelming population of the mentally ill that Bellevue was unable to confine. In the mid-20th century, saying that someone "belongs in Bellevue" was equivalent to saying that they were insane. By 2005 such references to Bellevue in popular culture and in everyday conversation had virtually disappeared on a national level, although it maintains a diminishing reputation as a "madhouse" to locals.

Bell's mania or disease A late-19th-century term for CATATONIC EXCITEMENT.

Benadryl The trade name for DIPHENHYDRAMINE, an antihistamine and anticholinergic drug that is used to treat the sometimes severe side effects that patients can experience after the initiation of antipsychotic drug therapy or after a significant increase in dosage. These side effects (stiffness; tremors; lockjaw; involuntary motions of the mouth, tongue, and hands; involuntary eye rolls), which usually occur within hours or days of administering ANTIPSYCHOTIC DRUGS, are acute dystonic reactions that can be reversed with antiparkinsonian agents such as Benadryl, Cogentin, or Akineton. These side effects are acute and are not to be confused with chronic reactions (to years of treatment with antipsychotic drugs) that are known as TARDIVE DYSKINESIA, which is treated with drugs other than Benadryl.

See also ANTIPARKINSONIAN DRUGS.

benign stupors Swiss psychiatrist August HOCH (1868–1919) proposed this term to refer to a certain "reactive type" of manic-depressive insanity that mimicked the symptoms of the catatonic type of DEMENTIA PRAECOX but which did not have the poor prognosis suggested by KRAEPELIN. Stanley McCormick (1874–1947), an insane heir to the

fortune of the famous McCormick family of Chicago, was treated by Hoch in the final years of his life and may have been the model for this proposed psychiatric disorder. Hoch's concept of benign stupors, influenced by the "reactive psychiatry" of Adolf MEYER, never became popular and is no longer in use.

Hoch, A. *Benign Stupors: A Study of a New Manic-Depressive Reaction Type*. New York: Macmillan, 1921.

Noll, R. "Styles of Psychiatric Practice, 1906–1925: Clinical Evaluations of the Same Patient by James Jackson Putnam, Adolf Meyer, August Hoch, Emil Kraepelin, and Smith Ely Jelliffe," *History of Psychiatry* 10 (1999): 145–189.

benztropine See ANTIPARKINSONIAN DRUGS.

Bethlem Royal Hospital ("Bedlam") The oldest mental hospital in England, which stood at the present site of the Liverpool Street Railway Station in London. Originally established as a priory in 1247, by 1329 records show that it was functioning as a hospital. The patients were serviced by a religious order of Hospitallers founded in the 13th century and called the "Bethlehemites." The insignia on their habits was a red star with a dark blue center. In 1346 the City of London took control of the priory and hospital from the bishop of Bethlehem, and by 1403 it is recorded that six mentally ill patients resided there.

The person who was brought to the Bethlem Hospital for incarceration when it was relocated in Moorfields entered gates that were topped, on either side, with sculptures of reclining but manacled male nudes, created by Caius Gabriel Cibber in 1677. Such a person may very well have felt that he or she were crossing through the gates of Hell and into the netherworld. These depicted "Raving Madness" (a heavily chained, taut-muscled and -fisted madman whose mouth is opened in an anguishing grimace) and "Melancholy Madness" (a more passive figure, lying on his stomach, a stuporous expression on his face). Noted English poet Alexander Pope referred to them as the "brazen brainless brothers" in his work *The Dunciad*.

Financial scandals and stories of abuse and torture in the public media marked the next several centuries of the institution's existence—until the 1870s, when official investigations finally reported nothing out of the ordinary at the hospital. Probably not without coincidence, this change followed a period of over a century (from 1728 to 1852) in which the Bethlem Royal Hospital was directed by physician members of the Monro family for four generations (James, John, Thomas, Edward Thomas). In an investigative report of the Committee on Madhouses presented to the House of Commons in 1815 it was noted that many patients were chained and manacled with heavy irons. An American Marine named James Norris had been chained continually for 12 years (since 1804), and a female patient was found to have been restrained in such a manner for eight years. Due to these abuses, particularly of Norris, superintendent Thomas Monro and apothecary John HASLAM were fired from the Bethlem Royal Hospital (Monro through forced retirement). Surgeon Bryan CROWTHER, who was responsible for routinely bleeding all the patients at Bethlem every spring regardless of the type or severity of illness, escaped a similar fate when he died shortly before the committee began its hearings. Monro's only defense against the charges of abusive treatment of patients made by the investigative commission was a weak one: "It was handed down to me by my father, and I do not know any better practice."

An autobiographical account of confinement in "Bedlam" was circulated in 1818 by a former patient, Urbane Metcalf. He describes the hospital as having four main "galleries" (more like cellblocks than wards), with the worst, the "basement gallery," described as follows:

> It is to be observed that the basement is appropriated for those patients who are not cleanly in their persons, and who, on that account have no beds, but lay on straw with blankets and a rug; but I am sorry to say, it is too often made a place of punishment, to gratify the unbounded cruelties of the keepers.

The hospital was first made into a royal institution in 1547, and the official name became the

Hospital of St. Mary of Bethlehem. Later this was shortened to Bethlehem Hospital and then to the Bethlem Royal Hospital. The institution moved several times over the years, with the final move occurring in 1920, to its present location in Monks Orchard, Eden Park, Beckenham, Kent. In 1948 it formed an association with Maudsley Hospital and now serves as a postgraduate teaching hospital for psychiatry.

Recent scholarship by the archivist at the Bethlehem Royal Hospital, Patricia Allderidge, questions the "house of horrors" image of "Bedlam" that has been perpetuated for the past 200 years. While noting in a paper published in 1985 that some patients were chained at the hospital, this was standard practice in asylums at the time (see BICÊTRE). After examining the original hospital records in the famous case of Norris (whose real first name is James and not William, as is often reported), she notes that he was quite possibly the most dangerous patient that the hospital staff had ever encountered. A large, strong seaman, Norris was continually making murderous assaults on staff until finally, in 1804, he was cuffed in an iron harness and chained to a post for good (as he is often pictured in drawings). The media attention to the Committee on Madhouses enquiry into this case truly helped to develop the stereotype of the hellish Bedlam, although Allderidge claims that the primary source materials (which have only been open since 1967) do not reveal much else that was extraordinary about the treatment at Bedlam vis-à-vis other asylums at that time.

See also BEDLAM.

Allderidge, P. "Bedlam: Fact or Fantasy?" In *The Anatomy of Madness: Essays in the History of Psychiatry,* Vol. 1, edited by W. Byrnum, R. Porter & M. Shephard. London: Tavistock, 1985.

———. *Cibber's Figures from the Gates of Bedlam.* London: Victoria and Albert Museum Masterpieces, No. 14, 1977.

Metcalf, U. *The Interior of Bethlehem Hospital.* London: 1818.

———. *Report of the Committee for Better Regulation of Madhouses.* London: Baldwin, Craddock, & Joy, 1815.

Tuke, D. H. *Chapters in the History of the Insane in the British Isles.* London: Kegan Paul, Trench, 1882.

bibliotherapy The reading of books as a therapeutic activity for the mentally ill. Such an activity can help focus the mind of some afflicted persons and give them a sense of structure and organization to help combat chaotic thought processes. For psychotic patients the value is extremely limited, but some patients—particularly those who have PARANOID SCHIZOPHRENIA or BIPOLAR DISORDER—seem to get satisfaction from the activity. Due to the religious preoccupations of many psychotic patients, the Bible remains one of the most common books read and reread by patients in today's psychiatric hospitals, as has been the case for almost two centuries.

In his *Medical Inquiries and Observations on the Diseases of the Mind* (1812), American psychiatrist Benjamin RUSH recommended that the person responsible for the care of the mentally ill should engage them in bibliotherapy: "His business should be, to divert them from conversing upon all the subjects upon which they had been deranged, to tell them pleasant stories, to read to them select passages from entertaining books, and to oblige them to read to him." A pioneer in the psychotherapy of schizophrenia, Swiss psychiatrist and psychoanalyst C. G. JUNG reports in his autobiography the case of a "schizophrenic old woman" whose auditory hallucinations of "voices" told her to let Jung test her knowledge of the Bible. As Jung (1961) tells it,

> She brought along an old, tattered, much-read Bible, and at each visit I had to assign her a chapter to read. The next time I had to test her on it. I did this for about seven years, once every two weeks. At first I felt very odd in this role, but after a while I realized what the lessons signified. In this way her attention was kept alert, so that she did not sink deeper into the disintegrating dream.

Jung reports a partial cure with this bibliotherapy method, admitting that "I would not have imagined that these memory exercises could have a therapeutic effect."

Jung, C. G. *Memories, Dreams, Reflections.* New York: Pantheon, 1961.

Rush, Benjamin. *Medical Inquiries and Observations Upon the Diseases of the Mind.* Philadelphia: Kimber & Richardson, 1812.

Bicêtre In 1793, following the French Revolution, Philippe PINEL was appointed as physician in charge of this mental institution in Paris, renowned as one of the worst in the world. The Bicêtre became a hospital in 1656 but was essentially a holding tank for all of the undesirables of society. By the time Pinel took charge of the institution, it contained only insane males, whereas the females were kept at the SALPÊTRIÈRE, also in Paris. Scores of patients, regardless of their illness, were heavily chained and often beaten by sadistic attendants. Records show that riots by the patients were not infrequent and led to the injuries and deaths of many of the attendants—often convicted criminals themselves. Pinel is frequently depicted as stunning the world by unchaining scores of these patients and by instituting policies for the minimum mechanical restraint necessary for maintaining order. Etchings and an 1876 painting by Tony Robert-Fleury depicting Pinel singlehandedly unchaining the mentally ill helped perpetuate this myth, although in the 1809 second edition of his famous textbook Pinel gives credit to the chief male nurse of the Bicêtre, Jean-Baptiste Pussin (1746–1809), for freeing the first 40 patients on May 23, 1789.

In his 1801 classic, *A Treatise on Insanity* (tr., 1806), Pinel argues that "coercion must always appear to be the result of necessity," and that with the changes he brought about at the Asylum de Bicêtre with his philosophy of "moral treatment:"

> I can assert, from accurate personal knowledge, that the maxims of enlightened humanity prevail throughout every department of its management; that the domestics and keepers are not allowed, on any pretext whatever, to strike a madman; and that straight waistcoats, superior force, and seclusion for a limited time, are the only punishments inflicted.

Pinel, P. *A Treatise on Insanity* (1801). Translated from the French by D. D. Davis and M. D. Sheffield. England: W. Todd, 1806.

biochemical theories of schizophrenia Biochemical theories of the causes of SCHIZOPHRENIA are among the oldest in history. Almost all the biochemical theories assume that schizophrenia is caused by abnormal metabolic or enzymatic processes in the chemistry of the brain. Thus, when present-day mental health professionals explain to the family member of a schizophrenic that the brain disease is caused by a "chemical imbalance," it is because of the suggestive evidence for certain aberrant "autointoxicating" chemical processes in the brain. However, there are many different theories involving many different chemicals and biochemical processes in the nervous system, and no one biochemical theory can as yet be targeted as the best explanation for the sole cause of schizophrenia (or of all its subtypes).

Autointoxication The idea that schizophrenia was perhaps caused by such an "autointoxicating" process in the brain was proposed from the very first by Emil KRAEPELIN in his initial description of dementia praecox in 1896. He wrote:

> For these reasons I consider it more likely that what we have here is a tangible morbid process occurring in the brain. Only in this way does the quick descent into severe dementia become at all comprehensible. It is true that morbid anatomy has so far been quite unable to help us here, but we should not forget that reliable methods have not yet been employed in a serious search for morbid changes. In the light of our current experience, I would assume that we are dealing with an autointoxication, whose immediate causes lie somewhere in the body.

Another early theorist to propose a metabolic disturbance as the cause of schizophrenia was the Swiss psychiatrist C. G. JUNG. In his 1907 classic, *The Psychology of Dementia Praecox,* Jung proposes that purely psychological causes (COMPLEXES) may be primary but are not enough to explain the devastating effects of schizophrenia. He proposed in addition the presence of a mysterious "hypothetical X, or metabolic toxin (?)" as perhaps the organic cause of this mental disorder. "Dementia praecox favors the appearance of anomalies in the metabolism—toxins, perhaps, which injure the brain in a more or less irreparable manner, so that the highest psychic functions become paralyzed,"

Jung wrote early in his monograph. Furthermore, he expressed the hope in 1907 that "a more perfect chemistry or anatomy of the future will perhaps demonstrate the objective metabolic anomalies or toxic effects associated (with dementia praecox)."

Endocrine theories By the mid-1930s most of the prominent proponents of AUTOINTOXICATION AS A CAUSE OF DEMENTIA PRAECOX (SCHIZOPHRENIA) had vanished from the scenes. Sources of internal foci of infection were no longer thought to be the cause of poisons sent to the brain that caused psychotic symptoms. However, with the rise of endocrinology as a medical science, ENDOCRINE ALTERATIONS IN SCHIZOPHRENIA became a major focus of biochemical research in schizophrenia beginning in the 1920s. A significant proponent of such research was Nolan D. C. Lewis (1889–1979), a noted child psychiatrist who for a time served as the head of the New York State Psychiatric Institute. "Internal secretions" (hormones), enzymes, and a wide variety of other biochemical substances were examined in persons with schizophrenia. Then as now, findings were inconsistent and difficult to understand. The various CONVULSIVE THERAPIES that became popular in the 1930s (such as electroshock therapy or insulin coma therapy) were thought to work by producing biochemical changes in the brain, but there was never any conclusive evidence to support this.

Transmethylation hypotheses Based on studies of how hallucinogenic drugs, particularly LSD-25, worked on the brain to produce "psychotogenic" (psychosis-causing) effects, from at least 1957 to the mid-1970s the dominant theories of schizophrenia were based on various "inappropriate methylation" or TRANSMETHYLATION HYPOTHESES. The term *transmethylation* was coined by the organic chemist John Harley-Mason of Cambridge University in England. The first publication advocating this hypothesis was published in 1952 in the *Journal of Mental Science* and coauthored by Humphrey Osmond (1917–2004) and John Smythies. The assumption was that if the body of a person with schizophrenia was producing LSD-like or mescaline-like substances, then metabolites of these chemicals should be detectable in the blood or urine. For two decades schizophrenia researchers searched for enzymes that converted one biochemical molecule into another less-active substance or its detectable metabolite after breakdown. A prominent proponent of this line of research during this era was Seymour Kety (1915–2000), the head of the neuroscience laboratories at the NATIONAL INSTITUTE OF MENTAL HEALTH.

No endogenous psychotogen, no psychosis-causing metabolite, was ever found in persons with schizophrenia. However, the basic research conducted within the framework of the transmethylation hypotheses led to many useful discoveries, including the metabolites of DOPAMINE and serotonin, which had applications to other fields of research, such as psychopharmacology. By the late 1960s the focus of research had shifted from the search for toxic metabolites to instabilities of the methylation process itself. By the late 1970s the transmethylation hypothesis had been replaced by a new one: the DOPAMINE HYPOTHESIS. Research into the various transmethylation hypotheses slowed to a trickle and had virtually disappeared by the 21st century. The last such publication in this tradition appeared in 1999, reporting the "experimental psychosis" induced by the ingestion of Ayahoasca, a South American hallucinogenic beverage prepared by boiling two plants found in the Amazon region.

Neurotransmitters Following the discovery of receptors for acetylcholine, dopamine, serotonin, and other NEUROTRANSMITTERS starting in 1970, biochemical research in schizophrenia has been dominated by the study of neurotransmitter systems in the central nervous system. The hypothesis that an excessive production of dopamine flooded its receptor sites and caused the POSITIVE SYMPTOMS of schizophrenia led to a "single-system" theory of the cause of schizophrenia. With increased knowledge about the involvement of some of the other 100 or more neurotransmitter systems in schizophrenia (GABA, serotonin, glutamate, and so on), such single-system theories are no longer held to be valid. Changes in the biochemistry of specific parts of the brain, such as the hypothalamus and portions of the frontal lobe, have emerged from this research. A comprehensive review of research on the neurotransmitters implicated in the pathophysiology of schizophrenia can be found in the chapter on the neurochemistry of schizophrenia by Moghaddam and Krystal published in Steven Hirsch and Daniel Weinberger's 2003 volume, *Schizophrenia* (2nd ed).

By 2005 research on the biochemical/neurochemical theories of schizophrenia focused on three major areas of abnormal processes in the brain involving (1) monoamine mechanisms (dopamine, serotonin, and noradrenaline, and their common degraditive enzyme, MAO); (2) amino acid neurotransmitters (the inhibitory amino acid neurotransmitter pathways of gamma-aminobutryic acid [GABA] and glutamate, an excitatory neurotransmitter); and (3) neuropeptides (opioids and cholecystokinin [CCK]).

Given the fact that there are more than 100 neurotransmitters in the brain, and many of them interact with each other and with neuropeptides, researchers in this field are increasingly reluctant to believe in "single-system" theories of the neurochemistry of schizophrenia. Neurochemical studies are now regularly combined with postmortem work, functional brain imaging data, and other sources of information about what really happens in the brain of a person with schizophrenia. New theories of schizophrenia no longer propose simple "chemical imbalances" but instead are highly complex, interactive models that combine multiple neurotransmitter systems with neural circuitry. Most of these theories focus on pathways between the cortex and the subcortical regions of the limbic system of the brain. An entire issue of *Schizophrenia Bulletin* published in 1998 (vol. 24, no. 2) was devoted to these "New Models of the Pathophysiology of Schizophrenia."

With the promising findings in genetics regarding schizophrenia, biochemical theories have been linked to genetic theories of the causes of schizophrenia. The assumption is that a particular genetic abnormality predisposes an individual to developing a metabolic disorder in the brain. However, while this linkage is suggestive based on our knowledge of the genetic causes of other types of diseases, concrete evidence linking the two in the causes of schizophrenia is still lacking. Furthermore, it must be remembered that, other than through genetic causes, biochemical imbalances may derive from such things as environmental stress, infectious diseases, and trauma—all of which have historically been implicated in various theories of the cause of schizophrenia.

Jung, C. G. *The Psychology of Dementia Praecox,* in *The Collected Works of C. G. Jung.* Vol. 3. Princeton, N.J.: Princeton University Press, 1960; first published, 1907.

Kraepelin, E. "Dementia praecox," from *Psychiatrie.* In *The Clinical Roots of the Schizophrenia Concept: Translations of Seminal European Contributions on Schizophrenia,* edited by J. Cutting and M. Shepherd. 1896. Reprint, Cambridge: Cambridge University Press, 1987.

Moghaddam, B., and J. H. Krystal. "The Neurochemistry of Schizophrenia." In *Schizophrenia.* 2nd ed., edited by S. R. Hirsch and D. Weinberger. Cambridge: Blackwell, 2003.

Osmond, H., and J. R. Smythies. "Schizophrenia: A New Approach," *Journal of Mental Science* 98 (1952): 309–315.

Pomilio, A. B., et al. "Ayahoasca: An Experimental Psychosis that Mirrors the Transmethylation Hypothesis of Schizophrenia," *Journal of Ethnopharmacology* 65 (April 1999): 29–51.

biogenic amine hypothesis The hypothesis that abnormalities in the structure, production, and transmission of the biogenic amines are the cause of many mental disorders, especially psychotic disorders. The three primary groups of biogenic amines that are suspected to play this role are the CATECHOLAMINES (such as the NEUROTRANSMITTER DOPAMINE), the INDOLAMINES (such as the neurotransmitter serotonin), and the HISTAMINES.

biological markers of schizophrenia The search for certain biological "signs" or "markers" in the biochemistry and neurophysiology of SCHIZOPHRENIA is one of the most important searches presently underway in schizophrenia research laboratories. If it can be shown that certain biochemical or neurophysiological processes are different in schizophrenics than in normals, then further tests can be devised to determine why this is so, perhaps giving scientific clues to the causes of schizophrenia. Furthermore, certain measurable differences found in schizophrenics may then be developed into a useful physiological method for making the diagnosis of schizophrenia (much as we now have tests for many other physical diseases). Ideally, such tests could then be used in GENETIC COUNSEL-

ING (if genetics tests are developed) or in prenatal screening by determining the liability to schizophrenia. At present, although it is almost certain that schizophrenia is a brain disease with a physiological cause, there are no certain biological markers that can be looked for through medical tests in the same way that, for example, diabetes can be diagnosed.

Biological markers for schizophrenia are sought in research on the following areas: neuroanatomy, both gross and histologic (neuropathology, computed tomography, magnetic resonance imaging); dynamic brain functioning (positron emission tomography, mapping of the brain's electrical activity); neuroendocrine measures; neurophysiological measures (tracking of eye movements, electroencephalogram); molecular genetics; biochemical measures; and the biochemical response to the administration of various psychoactive drugs.

See also BRAIN ABNORMALITIES IN SCHIZOPHRENIA; BRAIN IMAGING TECHNIQUES; BIOCHEMICAL THEORIES OF SCHIZOPHRENIA; CARDIOVASCULAR HYPOPLASIA; ENDOCRINE DISORDER HYPOTHESIS; EYE-MOVEMENT ABNORMALITIES IN SCHIZOPRENIA; PLATELET MONOAMINE OXIDASE ACTIVITY HYPOTHESIS.

biperiden See ANTIPARKINSONIAN DRUGS.

bipolar disorder Until the publication of *DSM-III* in 1980 and *ICD-10* in 1992, a person suffering from a major depressive episode was diagnosed with MANIC-DEPRESSIVE ILLNESS even though they may have never experienced a manic episode. This was due to the conceptualization of manic-depression proposed by Emil KRAEPELIN in 1899 as a single disease resulting in the manifestation of almost all the known severe and/or chronic AFFECTIVE DISORDERS (now termed "mood disorders"). Evidence that there may actually be "monopolar" syndromes of DEPRESSION and MANIA in addition to the "bipolar" manic-depressive illness was first presented in 1957 in a book by a German psychiatrist, Karl Leonhard (1904–88), *Die Aufteilung der endogenen Psychosen* (The Classification of Endogenous Psychoses). Leonard borrowed the term *bipolar* to refer to manic-depressive illness from another German psychiatrist, Karl Kleist (1879–1960), who first used the term (and *unipolar* as well) in 1953. His conclusions were based on years of longitudinal research on the course and outcome of manic-depressive disorder. Leonhard's work inspired numerous studies of this issue by other researchers throughout the 1960s, and by the 1970s it was believed that unipolar depression and bipolar manic-depression were in fact separate syndromes.

In 1980 *DSM-III* introduced the new terms *major depression* and *bipolar disorder* to replace manic-depression as it had been defined since 1899. As forms of Affective Disorders (a new umbrella category), the diagnosis of a manic episode was now the key to receiving a bipolar diagnosis. This still implied that persons who are "bipolar" would one day experience at least one bout of major depression, but we now know that this is not the case. In *DSM-IV* (2000), the category of Mood Disorders includes separate categories for (plural) Depressive Disorders and Bipolar Disorders. Bipolar Disorders are divided into Bipolar I Disorder (where a full manic episode has been diagnosed) and Bipolar II disorder (where hypomanic episodes are present with recurrent episodes of major depression). Each of the forms of Bipolar I disorder is defined according to whether the most recent episode was major depression, mania, or a mixed episode. Specifiers for each of the bipolar disorders are added if psychotic features present, if there is a seasonal pattern, if there is or is not interepisode recovery, if there are catatonic features, if the onset was postpartum, and if the course of a person's illness indicated rapid cycling (four or more manic, major depressive, or mixed episodes in a 12-month period).

Most of the research conducted since the adoption of the RESEARCH DIAGNOSTIC CRITERIA (1978) and *DSM-III* (1980) supports the notion that unipolar depression and bipolar disorder are in fact two separate syndromes. However, the focus has primarily been on major depression, which has a lifetime risk of approximately 5 percent in the United States, and not on bipolar disorder, which has a risk of approximately 1 percent (almost identical to schizophrenia). Studies conducted in Europe indicate the

prevalence rate for bipolar disorder may be as high as 5 percent. Prior to 1980, manic-depressive illness also tended to be neglected by researchers, with most of the attention going to dementia praecox and schizophrenia.

Symptoms and Diagnostic Path

Despite the prominence of this disorder in psychiatry since 1899, very little is still known about the various courses of bipolar disorder, its various outcomes, its ETIOLOGY (causes), and its pathophysiology (underlying biological abnormalities associated with the disease process that causes it). What is known can be summarized below:

Age of onset The rule of thumb since Kraepelin was that most persons with manic-depression or bipolar disorder experienced their first manic episode prior to age 25. This assumption has been disputed in a major study conducted by the Institute of Psychiatry in London by Noel Kennedy and colleagues that was published in the *American Journal of Psychiatry* in 2005. In this study, all cases of first-episode PSYCHOSIS, mania, or hypomania in adults treated at a psychiatric facility in London between 1965 and 1999 were analyzed. They found that the average age of onset of a manic episode was 32.9 years. A major gender difference was found, with an average age of onset for men at 30 years and one for women at 35 years. Half of all the men experienced a manic episode before age 25, and by age 35 almost 80 percent of men had done so. In women, only one-third had experienced mania before the age of 25, and just 64 percent by the age of 35.

A family history of affective disorders is associated with an earlier age of onset. Onset before the age of 17 is associated with a more severe course of the illness.

Comorbidity Persons with bipolar disorder are extremely likely to develop another mental disorder at some point in their lives. The two most common comorbid conditions are anxiety disorders (primarily panic disorder and social phobia) and substance abuse (primarily alcohol and marijuana).

Season of birth effect As with schizophrenia, studies have found season of birth effects for bipolar disorder and unipolar depression. Persons with bipolar disorder are more likely than the general population to be born in December through March. Persons with unipolar depression are more likely to be born in the period from March through May.

Frequency of episodes Studies have indicated that, for most persons with bipolar disorder, the disease starts slowly and picks up severity over the years. The durations between the first, second, and third episodes are much longer than the time between bouts of mania, depression, or mixed states as the years go by. Earlier age of onset is associated with an increased frequency of episodes and a continuity of symptoms between full episodes. Later episodes are less likely to include euphoric mania and more likely to become increasingly dysphoric and/or psychotic.

Cycle patterns The classic CIRCULAR INSANITY pattern identified by Falret in 1854 of mania alternating with depression is actually quite rare. Most persons with bipolar disorder have a variety of alterations (mania-mania-mania-depression-mania, for just one example). Untreated, depressive episodes last longer than manic episodes. Seasonal patterns have been noted, with depression more likely in the winter and mania or hypomania more likely in the spring and summer. Anniversary reactions to past traumatic events seem to trigger annual manic or depressive episodes in some persons.

Rapid cycling Rapid cycling is defined in *DSM-IV-TR* as four distinct episodes in a calendar year, each separated by two months of normal functioning or by a switch in polarity (mania to depression, or vice versa). One consistent finding is that rapid cycling is far more common in women than in men. Continuous or ultradian (ultrafast) cycling is associated with a severe course of the illness.

Mixed episodes Since the early 1990s, a great deal of research has been devoted to those episodes that seem to be a mixture of mania and depression. Such MIXED STATES are now generally termed *dysphoric mania.* They are associated with later stages of the illness, with more suicidal thoughts and suicide attempts, and with poorer outcomes than patients who experience pure or euphoric mania. Mixed states occur in about 40 percent of persons with bipolar disorder during the course of a lifetime.

Psychotic features Pronounced and persistent delusions or hallucinations are a bad prognostic

sign in bipolar disorder. Psychotic features are associated with greater disability and a more severe and chronic course of the illness.

Sleep For a person with bipolar disorder, the duration and quality of sleep is the key to preventing relapse. Lack of sleep has been known to ignite a manic episode.

Treatment Options and Outlook

LITHIUM has been the standard treatment for manic episodes since the 1950s. However, it was only approved for use in the United States in 1970. Lithium also works to alleviate the depressive episodes in bipolar disorder. However, lithium does not work for everyone. Recent recommended treatment algorithms (decision trees) for psychiatrists to follow suggest that the type of manic episode is the most important determinant of what medication to use. For euphoric mania (the classic type), lithium is the first choice. Lithium works less well for dysphoric mania and psychotic mania. Antipsychotic drugs such as olanzapine (Zyprexa) or mood-stabilizers such as divalproex sodium or valproate (Depakote or Depakene), carbamazepine (Tegretol), lamotrigine (Lamictal), topiramate (Topamax), or gabapentin (Neurontin) are found to work better for these two types of mania. Some antidepressant drugs (such as some of the SSRIs) have actually been known to ignite a manic episode and therefore are not usually prescribed.

Genetics Like schizophrenia, bipolar disorder runs in families. Twins studies and adoption studies have indicated patterns that support the suspicion that genetics plays a role in family transmission. Although far fewer studies of bipolar disorder have been conducted than those on schizophrenia, concordance rates for identical twins have averaged around 44 percent. No strong candidate genes for bipolar disorder have been identified.

Bipolar disorder and schizophrenia Near the end of his career, Emil Kraepelin admitted that, in practice, it was sometimes quite difficult to diagnose cases differentially of manic-depression from cases of schizophrenia. When pronounced psychotic features are present in a mood disorder, especially during a manic episode, this is indeed the case. In reviewing the evidence for a connection between manic-depression and bipolar disorder in their excellent book *Surviving Manic-Depression* (2002), E. Fuller Torrey and Michael Knable of the Stanley Research Foundation of Bethesda, Maryland, concluded, "In fact, the findings for manic-depressive illness more closely approximate those for schizophrenia than for unipolar depression."

The issue of whether schizophrenia and bipolar disorder were one disease or two separate diseases was the subject of a one-day symposium on April 17, 1999, associated with the International Congress on Schizophrenia Research. The results of this symposium were published in a special issue of *Schizophrenia Research* in 1999. The basic conclusion that many of the RISK FACTORS for the two disorders were similar (family history, roughly the same season of birth effect, similar 1 percent lifetime risk for the disorder in the general population), but that the clinical pictures of the two disorders were quite different (course and outcome, neuropsychological findings, neuroimaging findings, gender differences). Whether schizophrenia and manic-depression are two separate disorders or different expression of an underlying "unitary psychosis" is still an open question.

Akiskal, H. S., et al. "Re-evaluating the Prevalence of and Diagnostic Composition within the Broad Clinical Spectrum of Bipolar Disorders," *Journal of Affective Disorders* 59 (2000): S5–S30.

Kennedy, N. et al. "Gender Difficiences in Incidence and Age at Onset of Mania and Bipolar Disorder over a 35-year Period in Cambridge, England." *American Journal of Psychiatry* 162 (2005) 257–262.

Goldberg, J. F., and M. Harrow, eds. *Bipolar Disorders: Clinical Course and Outcomes.* Washington, D.C., and London: American Psychiatric Press, 1999.

Sato, T., et al. "The Boundary between Mixed and Manic Episodes in the *ICD-10* Classification," *Acta Psychiactrica Scandinavica* 106 (2002): 109–116.

Suppes, T., E. B. Dennehy, and E. Wells Gibbons. "The Longitudinal Course of Bipolar Disorder," *Journal of Clinical Psychiatry* 61 (2000): 23–30 (supplement 9).

Suppes, T., et al. "Report of the Texas Consensus Conference Panel on Medication Treatment of Bipolar Disorder 2000," *Journal of Clinical Psychiatry* 63 (April 2002): 288–299.

Torrey, E. F., and M. B. Knable. *Surviving Manic Depression: A Manual on Bipolar Disorder for Patients, Families and Providers.* New York: Basic Books, 2002.

Birch, John (1745–1815) Birch was a British surgeon and is perhaps the first to use ELECTROSHOCK THERAPY for mental illness. In the late 1700s Birch founded an "electric department" at London's St. Thomas Hospital and used electricity to treat his patients stricken with MELANCHOLIA and other assumed MENTAL DISORDERS. He "passed shocks through the brain," as is reported in a book by George Adams (the man who made Birch's special electrical instrument), *An Essay on Electricity, Explaining the Principles of That Useful Science, and Describing the Instruments* (London, 1799).

birth order and schizophrenia In the late 1950s and early 1960s many studies were conducted to determine whether a person's rank in birth order among his or her siblings was correlated to the later development of SCHIZOPHRENIA. This research was partially conducted to test hypotheses generated by psychoanalytic theory, which predicted that the extraordinary oedipal demands made upon the first-born male child might (in combination with a "SCHIZOPHRENOGENIC MOTHER") produce adult schizophrenia. The make-up or "constellation" of schizophrenic families, determined by such things as the sex and birth order rank of children, was also of interest to "family systems" theorists who practice family therapy. However, major reviews of these studies have almost uniformly concluded that there is no association between birth order and the development of schizophrenia.

Erlenmeyer-Kimling, L., E. Van Den Bosch, and B. Denham. "The Problem of Birth Order and Schizophrenia: A Negative Conclusion," *British Journal of Psychiatry* 115 (1969): 659–678.

bizarre ideation A common descriptive term found in the diagnostic assessments of clinicians examining psychotic patients. It refers to the grossly aberrant expressed thoughts of someone with a psychotic mental disorder. It is often used as a more colorful euphemism for the more clinical term DELUSION.

blacks, incidence of schizophrenia in In the United States, blacks are given the diagnosis of SCHIZOPHRENIA at a greater rate than whites. The most conservative studies indicate that the rate for blacks is at least one and a half times that for whites. There are several reasons suggested for this discrepancy. One is that most clinicians in the United States are white, and that the labeling of blacks with such a serious diagnosis is an expression, consciously or unconsciously, of racism. Others have suggested reasons based on epidemiological grounds, namely that there is a strong association between schizophrenia and lower socioeconomic status—regardless of race—in large cities. This association does not seem to be as strong for smaller cities or rural areas. Demographic studies show that blacks tend to be clustered in major metropolitan areas and less so in smaller cities or rural areas. Studies of schizophrenia rates in rural American areas show no difference between whites and blacks. Thus, those who cite such epidemiological data suggest that the higher schizophrenia rates among black Americans are due to environmental factors—the harsh life of poverty in large urban areas—rather than racial factors.

Kramer, M. "Population Changes and Schizophrenia, 1970–1985." In *The Nature of Schizophrenia,* edited by L. Wynne et al. New York: Wiley, 1978.

bleeding The deliberate opening of a blood vessel (venesection) or the more localized use of cupping glasses and leeches to draw blood was one of the most common forms of medical treatment for both physical and MENTAL DISORDERS for thousands of years. It gained in popularity as a psychiatric treatment after William Harvey's discovery of the circulation of blood in 1628 and was extensively employed for many physical and mental diseases until the 19th century. Galen, in the second century A.D., recommends it as a treatment for fevers. Due to the HUMORAL THEORY OF MENTAL ILLNESS of Hippocrates (fifth century B.C.) it was thought that insanity was caused by an excess of "hot blood"

or of particular humors, which thus needed to be drawn off from the body. The word for this condition of excess—the Greek *plethora*—is still used today, although not in its original, humoral sense.

Bloodletting was a common medical practice for centuries, although in the 12th century priests and monks (who were long involved in the medical treatment of the sick and poor) were forbidden to use it or other physical treatments by Pope Innocent II and instead were ordered to concentrate on religious matters of the soul. To compensate for this loss of medical specialists, a group of lay specialists known as barbers or barber-surgeons arose to meet the demand for bloodletting services. In England, a subspecialty group known as Lay-Barbers or Surgeons of the Short Robe was one of the groups represented in the Guild of the Barber-Surgeons, which was formed in 1210. Later legislation restricted the Lay-Barbers to bloodletting, wound surgery, cupping, leeching, the extraction of teeth, the giving of enemas, and—the only service that the barbers of today still perform—shaving. To distinguish themselves from the Surgeons of the Long Robe, who performed amputations and other services that the surgeons of today still provide, the Lay-Barbers placed a striped pole or sign outside their doors, under which was attached a "bleeding bowl" to advertise the nature of their services. The barber-pole represented the stick held and squeezed in the patient's hand to help increase the flow of blood from a wound produced on a vein in the arm (the same place where blood is most commonly drawn today), with the white stripe on the pole symbolizing the tourniquet tied around the arm above the opened vein and the red stripe, of course, symbolizing the blood. This is the way barber poles still appear today. Sometimes on the older poles a blue line might appear, which symbolized the appearance of the veins in the body.

There were three main bloodletting techniques. In venesection, sometimes called "breathing a vein," a vein (usually on the arm or foot) was opened with a sharp-pointed, double-edged, and straight-bladed cutting instrument known in ancient Greece and Rome as a phlebotome (from the Greek words for "a vein" and "to cut") or later as a lancet. The noted British medical journal *The Lancet* is named after this bloodletting instrument. A practitioner would be advised to carry a variety of lancets of various sizes for different-size veins. They could be either the manually applied type or, later, a "spring-lancet," in which a spring-propelled device could be released to mechanically push into and puncture a vein. Special "bleeding bowls" with internal gradations marked to measure the amount of blood collected were used, with some of the finer ones made of pewter. It was considered an art not to spill a drop of blood anywhere but in these bowls.

A second method, "wet cupping," involved the application to the surface of the skin of a glass (usually) cup that had first been exhausted of air inside (usually through holding it over a flame until the flame expired), causing the skin to puff up (tumefy). After the skin responded in this manner, the cup was lifted and several incisions were made (sometimes with special devices, with multiple, razor-sharp blades, known as "scarificators"), and the cup reapplied to collect the blood.

The third method, "leeching," involved applying the freshwater parasitic invertebrate still known as *Hirudo medicinalis* to various parts of the body. The animal would then attach itself to the skin through its three-pronged bite and would engorge itself until full (in the largest leeches, about an ounce of blood). Cupping the wound after the leech was removed would then obtain much more blood, since leeches inject an anticoagulant substance into the blood and such wounds would not readily clot or heal. The word *leech* is actually an old Anglo-Saxon word for a "healer" or "to heal," and for many centuries the animal was more commonly known by its ancient Latin name, *hirudo*. With the popularity of the medical practice of bloodletting, the word *leech* only later began to refer to the animal itself.

That the anemia caused by an excessive loss of blood could weaken anyone—and thus diminish their symptoms of mental illness—is no surprise. Many individuals lost their lives through this misguided form of treatment based on an incorrect theory. The history of psychiatry seems to be particularly prone to such tragic treatments, usually based upon some new scientific discovery (as the treatment of bleeding followed the discovery of the circulation of the blood), particularly since there are also modern examples of dangerous treatments based on little or no scientific theory—20th-century

equivalents of "bleeding," such as PSYCHOSURGERY, the COMA THERAPIES, and the CONVULSIVE THERAPIES for schizophrenics.

Up until the 19th century, all the patients in the BETHLEM ROYAL HOSPITAL in London were bled several times every summer, regardless of the severity or type of disorder, and as a commonly reported form of punishment. In 18th-century France, prior to their transfer to the care of Philippe PINEL at the BICÊTRE Asylum in the 1790s, the mentally ill patients of Paris's oldest hospital were bled so often that the general public referred to bleeding as the *"traitement de l'Hôtel-Dieu."* French mental patients were usually bled once or twice in the spring and autumn and then bathed (or simply cast) into cold water. Pinel did not advocate bleeding, nor did J. E. D. ESQUIROL, who bluntly stated in his 1838 psychiatric manual that "I do not believe it necessary to prescribe bloodletting in the treatment of insanity."

Perhaps the greatest advocate of bleeding among the fathers of modern psychiatry was the American Benjamin RUSH of Philadelphia. In his 1812 textbook, *Medical Inquiries and Observations on the Diseases of the Mind,* he gives modern readers a glimpse into this long-rejected practice as a treatment for "mania":

> Blood-letting is indicated by the extraordinary success which has attended its artificial use in the United States, and particularly in the Pennsylvania Hospital. In the use of bleeding in this state of madness, the following rules should be observed:
>
> It should be copious on the first attack of the disease. From 20 to 30 ounces of blood may be taken at once, unless fainting be induced before that quantity be drawn. It will do most service if the patient be bled in a standing posture. The effects of this early and copious bleeding are wonderful in calming mad people. It often prevents the necessity of using any other remedy, and sometimes it cures in a few hours.

Rush's treatment of choice (which he picked up during his training in Edinburgh and London, where he witnessed the regime at Bedlam and St. Luke's) did not meet with widespread approval in the United States, and by 1832 was no longer in use in American asylums. By the mid-1800s, the use of bleeding as a treatment for mental illness had almost entirely disappeared in Europe as well, leading the noted German psychiatrist Wilhelm GRIESINGER to write in 1845 that, "The use of bleeding . . . has in recent times been considerably restricted, and all are agreed that the necessity for venesection is not to be inferred from delirium, or any of its forms, even the most active, excited, and furious."

The best source of information on the medical practice of bleeding for modern readers is the essay and illustrations in a catalog of "bloodletting instruments" in the collection of the Smithsonian Institution in Washington, D.C., published in 1979 by Audrey Davis and Toby Appel.

Brain, P. *Galen on Bloodletting: A Study of the Origins, Development and Validity of His Opinions, with a Translation of the Three Works.* Cambridge: Cambridge University Press, 1986.

Davis, A., and T. Appel. *Bloodletting Instruments in the National Museum of History and Technology,* Smithsonian Studies in History and Technology, Number 41. Washington, D.C.: Smithsonian Institution Press, 1979.

Earle, P. "Bloodletting in Mental Disorder," *American Journal of Insanity* 10 (1854): 387–405.

Esquirol, J. E. D. *Mental Maladies, A Treatise on Insanity,* trans. E. K. Hunt. Philadelphia: Lea & Blanchard, 1845; first published, 1838.

Griesinger, W. *Mental Pathology and Therapeutics.* 2nd ed., trans. C. L. Robertson. 1845. Reprint, New York: William Wood & Co., 1882.

Rush, B. *Medical Inquiries and Observations Upon the Diseases of the Mind.* Philadelphia: Kimber & Richardson, 1812.

Bleuler, Eugen (1857–1939) An empathetic healer and prominent Swiss psychiatrist who coined the term *SCHIZOPHRENIA* in a 1908 paper and who gave its clearest and unsurpassed description in his classic book, *Dementia Praecox, Or the Group of Schizophrenias,* in 1911. Bleuler was born in Zollikon, near Zurich, where his ancestors were largely farmers. After earning his diploma, he served his medical residency at the Waldau mental hospital near Bern. He then left to study in Paris with such noted French psychiatrists as Jean Martin Charcot

and Victor Magnon. In 1885 he returned to Zurich to serve as assistant to August Forel, the chief of the BURGHÖLZI HOSPITAL. The following year, Bleuler at the age of 29 became the director of a mental hospital, the Reinau, located in a former monastery on an island in the Rhine River.

Bleuler's next 12 years were spent at Reinau and provided him the intimate experience of the everyday life of schizophrenics that he based his later theoretical work on. Bleuler lived in the same building with 800-plus patients (considered some of the worst and most chronic in this "backwater" institution) and devoted himself selflessly to every aspect of their care. Still a bachelor, Bleuler spent almost all his waking hours with his patients and succeeded in his goal of attaining a close emotional rapport (*affektiver Rapport*) with each of them. Despite his relative youthfulness, the patients and the attendants addressed him as "Father" out of reverence.

This devotion to understanding the inner world of the schizophrenic patient he carried with him to the Burghölzi mental hospital when he succeeded his mentor Forel as the director in 1896. His lectures to his new staff, based on his observations made during his 12 years at Reinau, were the basis of his later book on schizophrenia. He organized work therapy programs (*Arbeitstherapie*) for the patients and would visit the wards several times at any hour during the day. He was also insistent that his staff demonstrate the same devotion as Bleuler himself to understanding the patients—a revolutionary approach in the days when physicians were rarely seen by the patients at all, let alone involved in discussions with them. Over the years, his staff contained individuals who would later become famous for their own contributions to psychiatry and psychoanalysis: C. G. JUNG, Karl Abraham, A. A. Brill, Ernest Jones, and Ludwig Binswanger. Alphonse Maeder (cited in Ellenberger's book, *The Discovery of the Unconscious*), who also became well known, described what life was like with Eugen Bleuler in those legendary days at the Burghölzi:

> The patient was the focus of interest. The student learned how to talk with him. Burghölzi was in that time a kind of factory where you worked very much and were poorly paid. Everyone from the professor to the young resident was totally absorbed by his work. Abstinence from alcoholic drinks was imposed on everyone. Bleuler was kind to all and never played the role of the chief.

Bleuler was briefly associated with Sigmund FREUD's psychoanalytic movement but broke with Freud in 1910. He is credited with coining the word *depth psychology*, which refers to the psychology of the unconscious mind made famous by Freud and Jung.

Bleuler, E. *Dementia Praecox, Or the Group of Schizophrenias.* Translated by Joseph Zinkin. 1911. Reprint, New York: International Universities Press, 1950.

Ellenberger, H. *The Discovery of the Unconscious.* New York: Basic Books, 1970.

Bleuler, Manfred (1903–1990) Son of Eugen BLEULER and a major contributor to the study of schizophrenia in his own right. Manfred assumed his father's former position as the director of the Zürich Psychiatric University Clinic at the Burghölzi in 1942. He remained in this position for 27 years and was known for his long-term studies of schizophrenic patients and their families. Like his father, Manfred also placed a great importance on understanding the inner world of those afflicted with schizophrenia. In 1979 he wrote:

> A healthy life exists buried beneath this confusion. Somewhere deep within himself the schizophrenic is in touch with reality despite his hallucinations. He has common sense in spite of his delusions and confused thinking. He hides a warm and human heart behind his sometimes shocking affective behavior. We must know how to approach the schizophrenic. We must enter and feel with him his vision of reality. We must never relinquish this endeavor.

Bleuler, M. "My Sixty Years with Schizophrenics." In *Disorders of the Schizophrenic Syndrome,* edited by L. Bellak. New York: Basic Books, 1979.

———. *The Schizophrenic Disorders: Long-Term Patient and Family Studies,* trans. S. M. Clemens. 1972. Reprint, New Haven, Conn.: Yale University Press, 1978.

Bleuler's syndrome The eponymous label given by British psychiatric researcher T. J. Crow to his proposed "Type I" SCHIZOPHRENIA, which is the variety characterized by positive symptoms, good response to psychotropic medication, and a relative lack of intellectual impairment. This last characteristic is why Crow named Type I schizophrenia after Eugen BLEULER, whose contribution to the study of schizophrenia was his recognition that there were forms of schizophrenia that did not necessarily follow the strict degenerative course that Emil KRAEPELIN thought characterized all dementia praecox. Kraepelin's concept of dementia praecox more closely fits Crow's Type II schizophrenia, which he named the PINEL-HASLAM SYNDROME after the two famous alienists who each, apparently, provided the first clinical descriptions of this disorder in books that they published in 1809.

See also CROW'S HYPOTHESIS.

Crow, T. J. "The Two-syndrome Concept: Origins and Current Status," *Schizophrenia Bulletin* 11 (1985): 471–485.

blocking A very common symptom of SCHIZOPHRENIA wherein a person has an abrupt loss of their train of thought, feeling as though he or she is suddenly "blanking out" in mid-sentence. Many schizophrenics describe this experience as a sudden loss of all thoughts and feelings, leaving awareness "empty" or filled with "nothingness." Often they cannot remember what they were previously saying or thinking when asked after such an experience. One paranoid schizophrenic patient that the author knew would scream out, "They just killed me right now!" to describe his anxiety over the frequent, sudden loss of his inner world. The term was used by Eugen BLEULER as early as 1911.

bloodletting See BLEEDING.

blood of the insane, studies of Blood has always been regarded as a carrier of information about the essence—physical, mental, spiritual—of the individual person. Humoral medicine, of course, posited blood as one of the primary causative factors in disease and offered rational treatments—such as BLEEDING—for the cure of physical and mental maladies. For asylum physicians and researchers intrigued by the stories that blood may reveal, there were at least four questions that needed to be addressed:

(1) Is the blood of diseased persons different from the blood of healthy ones?
(2) Can specific diseases be diagnosed by specific changes in the blood?
(3) Is the cause of madness in the blood itself? In other words, is "mad" blood "bad" blood? (the question of etiology)
(4) Are differences in the blood of the insane merely clues to the hidden causes of madness that are to be found elsewhere in the body? (the question of pathophysiology)

Unclear about the exact parameters of the clinical syndromes confronting asylum physicians, and not knowing how to define operationally mental illnesses such as DEMENTIA PRAECOX or manic-depressive insanity except as vaguely "organic" or "biological," most laboratory researchers simply applied methods inspired by the latest conceptual or technological innovations in the various medical sciences and hoped there would be a serendipitous payoff in the search for the ETIOLOGY, pathophysiology, and treatment of psychiatric disorders.

In the past 150 years, four general approaches to the examination of the blood of the insane have framed experimental research:

(1) the corpuscular richness paradigm (1854)
(2) the metabolic paradigm (circa 1895)
(3) the immunoserodiagnostic paradigm (1906)
(4) the medical genomics paradigm (2005)

The corpuscular richness paradigm The first quantitative laboratory investigation of the blood of asylum patients was conducted in 1854 by W. Lauder Lindsay, then an assistant physician at the Crichton Royal Institution at Dumfries, and published in January 1855 just as he assumed a new position as superintendent and chief medical officer of James Murray's Royal Asylum for Lunatics in Perthshire, Scotland. Lauder Lindsay created the

initial paradigm for this type of laboratory research in PSYCHIATRY by focusing on the relative numbers or proportions of the structural elements of blood as counted through microscopic observation. In doing so, Lauder Lindsay was applying laboratory logic—but not the time-consuming procedures—inspired by Karl Vierordt's pioneering 1852 publication in which the first blood cell counts were reported. The studies of Vierordt and Lauder Lindsay were conducted within the context of the first phase in the history of modern hematology in which the focus was on the quantification of various cell types within the blood. Staining techniques that could more accurately reveal the structural characteristics of the blood only came into general use after 1877, when Paul Ehrlich (1854–1915), while still a medical student, developed a triacid stain that enabled the clear microscopic definition of the nucleus, cytoplasm, and other details of cells in thin films of dried blood on glass slides.

In his unprecedented experiment, Lauder Lindsay used a needle to prick the fingers of 236 insane patients and 36 officers and attendants of the Crichton Royal Institution and Southern Counties Asylum at Dumfries. A simple blood smear on glass slides was examined using a microscope from Nachet in Paris, with a magnifying power of "180 to 380 diameters." His procedural remarks are colorful:

> As a general rule, the insane are extremely bad subjects for such experiments. . . . They are extremely sensitive, restless and suspicious of operative interference, even of a slight nature. Many obstinately refused to allow their fingers to be pricked. Some did so from a firm conviction that a deep-laid conspiracy against their lives or welfare lurked under the cloak of apparently simple experiment; others simply objected to become tools of experiment or amusement; some declined on the plea that in their greatly debilitated condition they could ill afford to spare even a single drop of blood; others lacked courage to submit to the operation; some demanded full explanations of the motives which led to my making the singular request of allowing their finger to be pricked by a needle; in others this formed the keynote of their delusions, delirium or vituperation, for days or weeks after the experiment was attempted in them. On the other hand, many, who could not appreciate the objects of experiment, submitted cheerfully . . . some presented their fingers under the impression that, from the single drop of blood, the state of their constitution, the chances of cure, and the period of their removal, could infallibly be predicted; others from curiosity to see the appearance from which their own blood, or that of their companions, presented under a microscope . . . some carried this laudable curiosity to a great extent, begging most earnestly not only to see their own blood at different periods of the day, but that of fellow-patients and attendants, evidently strongly impressed with the belief that between their own blood and that of companions who exhibited most different traits of character or conduct, or between that of insane patients and sane attendants, there should exist a perceptible difference. On various occasions, I was obliged to demonstrate the condition of my own blood under the microscope, to satisfy the curiosity thus awakened (1855: 82).

Documenting the relative proportion of serum, fibrin, and globules in the blood of the insane and noninsane, as well as a comparison of the form and structures of the red and white corpuscles, he attributed differences in the blood of the insane to the presence of other physical diseases that were equally present in noninsane persons. Diagnostic differences among the insane did not yield corresponding differences in the blood. His negative findings are summarized more succinctly in his later June 1857 annual report as superintendent and chief medical officer of Murray's Royal Asylum for Lunatics: "insanity and the different types and phases thereof are not characterized by a particular morbid state of the blood, and tend to show that insanity must be placed in the category of ordinary physical diseases" (1857: 15).

Lauder Lindsay was a Scottish precursor to what historian Edward Shorter referred to as "the first biological psychiatry" launched in the 1860s by Germans such as Wilhelm GRIESINGER (1817–68). Additionally, Lauder Lindsay expressed his faith in laboratory medicine as a means not only to discover the causes of mental disorders but also as a medium for dispelling discrimination against the mentally ill:

> Researches of this nature will tend greatly to break down the unfounded prejudices still existing in the public mind regarding the special nature of insanity, and to propagate, among the profession as well as the public, more correct opinions of the mutual relations of the healthy and morbid states of mind and body, and more particularly the reaction of physical disease on mental phenomena. It will hereby be found that insanity is much more a corporeal disease than is at present believed, or, at least, is more intimately connected with, or inseparable from, various of the ordinary physical diseases to which human flesh is heir (1855: 78).

Reflecting the assumptions and practices of the "morphologic era" in the early history of hematology, subsequent innovators in biological psychiatry also focused on the "corpuscular richness" of the blood. Blood was taken from insane persons, diluted, and then the corpuscles in a certain volume of that dilution were counted using such instruments as Gower's Haemacytometer. The relative proportion of red and white blood cells (blood dyskrasias) was of particular interest, as was the amount of hemoglobin, and many who followed this research paradigm claimed these amounts differed before, during, and after an individual's bout with madness. By 1892 S. Rutherford Macphail could review the extant literature up to that time and conclude that there was an overall "deficiency of the corpuscular richness of the blood met with in the first stages of insanity," and that a "close connection" exists "between improvement in the quality of the blood, and mental recovery, the converse which exists in cases of persistent and incurable dementia." The corpuscular richness paradigm continued to be followed not only by American and British researchers but also by those in Germany and France.

Following the division of dementia praecox from manic-depressive insanity by Emil KRAEPELIN in the 6th edition of his *Psychiatrie* (1899), serological studies focused on distinguishing these two diseases from each other and from persons without MENTAL DISORDERS. Experiments designed to test the corpuscular richness hypothesis were, not surprisingly, often contradictory. This was especially true with regard to MANIC-DEPRESSIVE ILLNESS. However, a 1920 review by Bayard Taylor HOLMES (1852–1924)—an ardent American proponent of biological psychiatry and the founder (in 1918) of *DEMENTIA PRAECOX STUDIES*, the first medical journal named after a mental disorder—concluded that the blood in dementia praecox "is at times highly concentrated, exhibiting polycythemia [an excess of red blood cells] with leucopenia [a decrease in white blood cells]," and that "the morphological changes in the blood are excessively rapid, almost instantaneous, and when the ratio of corpuscles approaches the normal, there is often a betterment in the mental condition of the patient." This latter statement by Holmes referred to a phenomenon known as the "blood crisis," in which the exacerbation of psychotic symptoms was correlated with a rapid diminishing of white blood cells and an overproduction of red blood cells, the reversal of which accompanied a return to relative normalcy. A rational treatment for dementia praecox derived from this experimental observation involved the injection of patients with sodium nucleate (salts of yeast acids used in the treatments of anemia, rheumatism, and gout) to increase the white blood cell count.

By the 1920s serological studies in psychiatry were no longer conducted within the corporeal richness paradigm. Two more promising serological paradigms—the metabolic paradigm and the immunoserodiagnostic paradigm—captured the imagination of researchers after 1900 following advances in endocrinology and immunology.

The metabolic paradigm Throughout the latter half of the 19th century, physiologists sought to understand the mechanisms of metabolism. For most of that time, physiological changes in the body were explained by theories of nervous regulation. Between 1890 and 1905—the year Ernest Starling first proposed the modern concept of "hormone"—metabolism was increasingly explained by theories of chemical regulation through secreting organs such as glands. Endocrinology emerged from physiology in a recognizable form in the years following British physiologist Edward Schaefer's address "On Internal Secretions" to the British Medical Association in Physiology in London on August 2, 1895. *Internal secretions* was a term introduced by physiologist Claude Bernard in 1855, but reframed by

Schaefer in terms of clinical medicine. Metabolic diseases as a separate category of illness were caused by the overproduction or underproduction of internal secretions in the glands with ducts (liver, pancreas, and kidneys), those without ducts (thyroid, adrenals, pituitary), and the sex glands (gonads). As Schaefer proposed in his famous lecture, secreting organs, both with and without ducts, return secreted materials to the blood. The ductless glands, however, produce only internal secretions. Blood thus became the medium through which to detect and measure internal secretions, or, later in the 20th century, hormones and NEUROTRANSMITTERS.

This emerging new endocrinological paradigm was immediately seized upon by the first biological psychiatrists. If an overproduction or underproduction of internal secretions could produce physical diseases such as diabetes, why not also insanity? Since it was clear that the brain was the organ underlying mental diseases, perhaps the true etiology of the insanities originated elsewhere in the body, places where substances toxic to the brain (internal secretions, ptomaines, bacteria, and so on) were produced and then transmitted to the central nervous system via the blood. This autointoxication theory of mental disorders first became prominent in France in 1893 and influenced a generation of ALIENISTS, neurologists, and psychiatric researchers. And indeed the most prominent among them was Emil Kraepelin. From the fifth edition of *Psychiatrie* in 1896 until the eighth edition in 1913, autointoxication (*Selbstvergiftung*) arising from a metabolic disturbance, probably in the sex glands—and not heredity—was Kraepelin's prime candidate for the cause of dementia praecox.

The early experimental literature on the search for traces of internal secretions in the blood of the insane reflects the confusion in the emerging field of endocrinology regarding the nature of hormones and their similarities to enzymes, general metabolites, drugs, toxins, antitoxins, and vitamins. These studies are too numerous, perplexing, and contradictory to summarize here. Perhaps the most extensive early review of this literature was conducted by the Russian psychiatric researcher Aleksandr Ivanovich Iushchenko (1869–1936) in a series of lectures delivered in 1911 and then translated into German and published in 1914. He hypothesized that dementia praecox was caused by glandular dysfunctions, especially disease processes in the parathyroid. Modern endocrinological research into the biological substrates of dementia praecox/SCHIZOPHRENIA began in the 1920s, increased in number from the late 1950s to the 1980s due to researchers looking for metabolites as part of the TRANSMETHYLATION HYPOTHESIS and has declined somewhat in the past 20 years. The early literature was reviewed in the work of one of its major proponents, Nolan D. C. Lewis (1889–1959), who believed the thyroid, adrenal, and gonads were implicated in dementia praecox.

Most of the research into the metabolic disorder hypothesis of schizophrenia has yielded little of value. The past half-century of research is confounded by the fact that endocrine abnormalities in schizophrenia may be due to stress caused by the illness itself or the effects of antipsychotic medications. The best evidence for an endocrine link to schizophrenia involves the anterior pituitary gland. The anterior pituitary contains gland cells that respond to releasing or inhibiting factors from the hypothalamus, which eventually may be found to be the source of the myriad confusing findings of endocrine dysfunction in schizophrenia.

Endocrinological research provided a direct and important analogical bridge that led to the discovery of neurotransmitters in the brain. Following the 1921 discovery by Otto Loewi (1873–1961) of a substance in the brain later identified as acetylcholine, neurotransmitters were referred to as neurohormones or neurohumors. Indeed, the term *neurotransmitter* did not come into use until the 1960s. Neurotransmitter theories of the pathophysiology of schizophrenia (not the etiology—an important distinction to remember) involving the measurement of serotonin (1954), DOPAMINE (1966), glutamate (1980), and so on, in the blood or cerebral spinal fluid (CSF), evolved directly from the metabolic paradigm in studies of the blood of the insane.

The immunoserodiagnostic paradigm By 1890 the discovery of "reactions" in the blood to foreign organisms or substances, as evidenced by the production of detectable "antitoxins," "antigens," "defensive ferments," or "antibodies," led to the

rise of immunology in medicine. Following the general acceptance of the germ theory of disease by 1880 and advances in bacteriology that demonstrated microorganisms could directly or indirectly cause diseases, between 1890 and 1910 the development of serologic tests such as agglutination, the precipitin reaction, and complement fixation revolutionized the diagnosis of infectious diseases. The development of the Wasserman reaction test for neurosyphilis in 1906 was a turning point for biological psychiatry. It had long been suspected that the many asylum patients with GENERAL PARALYSIS OF THE INSANE were suffering from the long-term effects of the syphilis bacterium in their nervous systems. For the first time, there was a blood test for madness—at least for one variety of madness, anyway. Could such immunoserodiagnostic tests for the other insanities be developed? Could one serologic test be developed that could differentially diagnose the major forms of insanity, dementia praecox, and manic-depressive illness?

In 1909 two German researchers from Eppendorf created a minor sensation when they injected patients with cobra venom and found that all the dementia praecox patients, and a portion of the manic-depressive subjects, invariably reacted to the toxin, while other psychiatric patients and normals did not. The excitement over the "Much-Holzmann psycho-reaction" was over within two years. Although the "Much-Holzmann psycho-reaction" was quickly discredited by other researchers, it was the first promising differential diagnostic immunoserologic finding for dementia praecox and manic-depressive insanity. Another more promising BLOOD TEST FOR SCHIZOPHRENIA, the Abderhalden defensive ferments reaction test, would cause an international sensation in 1913.

In an era in which autointoxication theory influenced medical and psychiatric cognition, researchers posited that bacteria in the intestines spread throughout the body and caused damage to internal organs. These damaged organs would release debris such as "toxic albumins" into the bloodstream, which would then be carried to the brain and cause the symptoms of insanity. Such theories were many and varied, as were the hypothetical substances that could be detected in the blood of the insane. In only one example, Bayard Taylor Holmes of Chicago believed he had produced experimental support for the theory that fecal stasis in the cecum led to the bacterial production of the same toxic amines that were implicated in ergotism, resulting in the poisoning of the brain and eventual psychosis. An excess of histamine in the blood was claimed as evidence for this mechanism.

The immunoserodiagnostic paradigm continues to this day in schizophrenia research, with not only the blood but also the cerebral spinal fluid examined for antibodies to possible pathogens. Evidence for allergic reactions to foods, viruses transmitted from cats to humans, and a lengthy list of other possible pathogens is weak. Viruses in particular are suspected to be involved in the etiology of some forms of schizophrenia and bipolar disorder, although no confirmatory antibodies have yet been detected.

In the late 1990s there was renewed interest in searching for IMMUNE SYSTEM ALTERATIONS IN SCHIZOPHRENIA and other mental disorders. A 2004 review of this literature by researchers from the Netherlands led to the hypothesis that lymphocytes—which make up about 20 percent of all white blood cells—might carry information that reflects the metabolism of brain cells and might be utilized as an indirect probe of a limited number of cellular functions, including gene expression. They proposed focusing on the T (thymus-derived) cell, B (bone-marrow-derived) cell, and NK cell subpopulations of lymphocytes. Other increases or decreases in specific lymphocytes have been found in schizophrenia. The return of interest to numerical or morphological changes in the white blood cells harkens back to the early 20th century research by Lundvall, Holmes, and others intrigued by correlating changes in the blood with changes in symptoms in dementia praecox.

Medical genomics In January 2005 an international team of researchers reported the results of a pilot study in which they claimed to have developed a blood test that could differentially diagnose schizophrenia from bipolar disorder and from normal controls. Collecting RNA from blood samples, the researchers found that schizophrenia and BIPOLAR DISORDER exhibited unique expressed genome signatures. If the follow-up studies confirm the

preliminary report published in the *American Journal of Medical Genetics Part B: Neuropsychiatric Genetics* by Ming T. Tsuang, C. C. Liew, and colleagues, this development signals not only a new paradigm in serological studies of mental disorders—that of medical genomics—but also promises the attainment of the holy grail of biological psychiatry: a blood test for madness.

Is this the dawning of a "third biological psychiatry"? The trajectory of history from a solitary Scottish asylum physician counting the blood cells of his lunatic patients under a weak microscope in 1854 to this recent report by a team of geneticists in three different countries is nothing less than breathtaking.

See also ENDOCRINE ALTERATIONS IN SCHIZOPHRENIA; GENETICS STUDIES.

Holmes, B. T. "A Guide to the Documents in Evidence of the Toxaemia of Dementia Praecox." *Dementia Praecox Studies* 3 (1920): 23–107.

Justschenko, A. I. *Das Wesen der Geisteskrankheiten und deren biologische-chemische Untersuchungen.* Dresden and Leipzig, Verlag von Theodor Steinkopf, 1914.

Kraepelin, E. *Psychiatrie. Ein Lehrbuch für Studierende und Aerzte. Fuenfte, vollstaendig umgearbeitete Auflage.* Leipzig: Verlag von Johann Ambrosius Barth, 1896.

Lauder Lindsay, W. "The Histology of the Blood in the Insane," *Journal of Psychological Medicine and Mental Pathology* 1 (1855): 78–93.

———. *Thirtieth Annual Report of the Directors of James Murray's Royal Asylum for Lunatics.* Perthshire, Scotland: Printed by order of the Directors by James Dewar Jr., 1857.

Macphail, S. R. "Blood of the Insane." In D. H. Tuke (ed.), *A Dictionary of Psychological Medicine,* Vol. I. Philadelphia: P. Blakiston and Son, 1892.

Noll, R. "The Blood of the Insane," *History of Psychiatry,* in press.

Tsuang, M. T., N. Nossova, T. Yager, et al. "Assessing the Validity of Blood-based Gene Expression Profiles for the Classification of Schizophrenia and Bipolar Disorder: A Preliminary Report," *American Journal of Medical Genetics Part B: Neuropsychiatric Genetics,* 133B (2005): 1–5.

blood test for schizophrenia There is no diagnostic blood test for schizophrenia or any other MENTAL DISORDER. The cause of SCHIZOPHRENIA is unknown, the nature of the biological disease process is unclear, and even today it is not known if it is one disease with many forms or many diseases with similar symptoms, courses, and outcomes. Given this situation, it is next to impossible to develop a blood test that could differentially diagnose schizophrenia from other mental disorders and from persons with no mental disorders. However, twice in history—once in 1913 and again in January 2005—the world's attention was caught by the announcement of the development of just such a blood test for schizophrenia.

The story of the first blood test for dementia praecox (1912) In May 1913 at the annual meeting of the German Psychiatrists Association in Breslau, a presentation of experimental research findings by August Fauser (1856–1938), a psychiatrist from Stuttgart, created an international sensation that would capture the imagination of medical researchers for the next several years. At that conference, Fauser reported that he had used a recently invented immunodiagnostic test in an examination of the blood of 250 psychiatric patients and found it could differentially diagnose DEMENTIA PRAECOX from other psychiatric disorders. Furthermore, Fauser claimed that this blood test could also differentiate normal controls from persons suffering from severe mental disorders. Fauser's stunning announcement of the discovery of a blood test for madness held out the promise that PSYCHIATRY would now share in the success of other medical sciences that had been revolutionized by laboratory studies in bacteriology, endocrinology, and serology. This remarkable new immunoserodiagnostic tool was known as the Abderhalden defensive ferments reaction test, originally developed in 1909 by the Swiss biochemist Emil Abderhalden (1877–1950) as a purported method of diagnosing pregnancy. Abderhalden continually refined his procedure and central concept—that of the "defensive ferments," the *Schutzfermente* or *Abwehrfermente*—and a 1912 book on his discovery went through two more editions by 1914. The third edition of 1913 included a bibliography of more than 400 published studies using his serodiagnostic technique.

In a lecture on October 27, 1912, in Halle at a congress of German Psychiatrists and Neurologists,

Abderhalden himself had suggested that his new blood test might be applied to the study of nervous and mental disorders. Fauser, under the direct guidance of Abderhalden, carried out this research plan and published a short research report on his findings on December 26, 1912. But it was Fauser's presentation at the May 1913 meeting of the German Psychiatrists Association that caught the world's attention. For a very brief—but exciting—period in the history of psychiatry, many researchers in Europe and North America believed that psychiatry now had the equivalent of the Wasserman reaction test for dementia praecox.

Fauser's claim to have found a blood test that could differentially diagnose dementia praecox from other psychiatric illness and from healthy persons was, for a time, internationally accepted as valid because of the congruence of his specific findings with the etiological speculations of Emil Kraepelin. Kraepelin believed the disease was caused by "a tangible morbid process in the brain (*einen greifbaren Krankheitsvorgang im Gehirn*)." Furthermore, Kraepelin speculated that the brain is affected by "an autointoxication (*Selbstvergiftung*)" that originated elsewhere in the body. Rejecting notions prevalent in medicine at the time that bodily autointoxications primarily arose from the intestines, KRAEPELIN held to the notion that dementia praecox was caused by a metabolic disturbance originating in the sex glands.

One of the major claims of Abderhalden's defensive ferments reaction test was that it could identify diseased internal organs in the body through a reaction of hypothesized "defensive ferments (*die Abwehrfermente*)" in the blood of a patient when it came into contact with tissue from corresponding human organs taken from a cadaver. The assumption by Abderhalden was that debris from a diseased organ, toxalbumins, would end up in the bloodstream. Since such material was poisonous to the blood and not excreted through the kidneys, the blood produced "defensive ferments" or enzymes which dissolved this debris, catabolizing it and making it into a peptone and amino acid. Specific defensive ferments would be produced in the blood only when coming into contact with tissue from specific organs, and this process could be experimentally replicated in a test tube outside of a living body. An experimental reaction indicating the creation of defensive ferments in the blood in response to contact with corresponding tissue would result in a bright violet color. Such a color would confirm which organ in a patient's body was diseased.

Thus, Fauser found that defensive ferments in the blood of all persons with severe mental disorders caused a reaction against tissue from the cerebral cortex, thereby supporting Kraepelin's contention that dementia praecox is caused by a tangible morbid process in the brain. Fauser further corroborated Kraepelin when he reported that he found defensive ferments reacted against sex gland tissue only in the blood of persons with dementia praecox and not in those diagnosed as manic-depressive, hysteric, or with purely degenerative insanity. The serum of male patients reacted only with testicular tissue, and the serum of female patients only with ovarian tissue.

Fauser's report, and subsequent research publications from his clinic, immediately inspired replication efforts around the world. The most notable of these was a study conducted with the blood of 106 psychiatric patients at the Sheppard and Enoch Pratt Hospital in Baltimore by the noted virologist Charles E. Simon. In an article published in the May 30, 1914, issue of *The Journal of the American Medical Association,* Simon provided a critical review of the work of Fauser and subsequent researchers who did not confirm Fauser's findings, pointing out possible flaws in their use of Abderhalden's complex methodology as a reason for conflicting results. In Simon's own study, the sex-gland reaction was found in nearly all dementia praecox patients, but he directly rejects Fauser's claim that such a reaction is exclusive to dementia praecox. Simon also directly accused Fauser of manipulating his data to achieve the expected outcome. According to Simon,

> In surveying the literature just outlined, one cannot help being impressed . . . by the wonderful apparent uniformity of the results reported by Fauser, and on the other by the total lack of uniformity of those obtained by others. . . . The thought naturally suggests itself that two factors may have been operative to this end, namely that

> Fauser was carried away by his enthusiasm and allowed himself to be influenced unduly in the direction of his own wishes, and that [others] lacked complete control of the technic. As a matter of fact, there is good ground for the belief that both factors were operative (p. 1,703).

Despite an acute awareness of the chaos in the medical literature on what Simon renamed the "Abderhalden-Fauser Reaction," he insisted on the reality of Abderhalden's proposed "defensive ferments" and on the method for detecting them: "It is my firm conviction that . . . Abderhalden's basic work in this field should be viewed as one of the most important contributions to modern experimental science" (Simon, 1914: 1702).

Charles E. Simon never again mentioned the "Abderhalden-Fauser Reaction" in any subsequent publications—and for a very good reason. In the four months before Simon's paper appeared in print, a series of devastating critiques of Abderhalden's defensive ferments reaction test began to appear in German medical journals. Serious criticisms of Abderhalden's methods and even the veracity of the defensive ferments continued in English language journals.

With the wisdom of hindsight, it is known why the Abderhalden defensive ferments reaction test did not revolutionize biological psychiatry: Abderhalden's defensive ferments simply do not exist. They never did. All the reports of positive results with the Abderhalden reaction test were based on error—if not worse. Indeed, in an article published in the May 14, 1998, issue of *Nature,* two German scholars accuse Emil Abderhalden of outright fraud rather than incompetence. The issue of error versus fraud was explored in depth in a 2000 article by Kaasch.

But surely the hundreds of published experimental reports of positive findings using Abderhalden's test were not fraudulent? There is, of course, another explanation: human fallibility. Since the reaction depended on the ability to perceive a particular color, the method was not quantitative. Instead, it was highly subjective. Some researchers saw the color all the time, some saw the color some of the time, and some never saw it no matter how carefully they followed Abderhalden's procedures. The story of the rise and fall of Abderhalden's blood test is more akin to a social psychology experiment on perceptual bias and the consensual nature of reality rather than fraud perpetuated on a massive international scale. August Fauser and his colleagues in Stuttgart clearly saw the color every time it fit their preconceptions about the locus of the diseased organs in dementia praecox. Because of this highly subjective element, the hundreds of experimental reports often wildly conflicted in their results. Charles Simon was therefore correct in his suspicion of experimental bias on the part of Fauser but failed to discern the essential weakness in Abderhalden's method. By 1917 it was clear to most of the world that Abderhalden's defensive ferments did not exist and that the method purported to detect them was flawed. In 1920 Jacques Loeb could write to a biochemist colleague, "Nobody speaks of the Abderhalden reaction any more in the United States and I am very much surprised to see that in his journal Abderhalden still continues that myth." However, scientific articles reporting the use of Abderhalden's test continued to appear in German publications for several more decades.

Despite the general rejection of Abderhalden's defensive ferments and the test purporting to detect them, a minority of physicians in the United States continued to believe in them and in their promise to revolutionize biological psychiatry. These physicians were Albert Sterne of Indianapolis, Bayard Taylor HOLMES of Chicago, and Henry A. COTTON of Trenton. What united these men in their continued belief in Abderhalden and his test was their strong belief in autointoxication and focal infection theories of the cause of dementia praecox and other mental disorders.

The second blood test for schizophrenia (2005) It has been known for some time that both schizophrenia and MANIC-DEPRESSIVE ILLNESS (BIPOLAR DISORDER) have a significant genetic component. Blood relations of persons with schizophrenia or bipolar disorder are more likely also to have the same disorder than persons with whom there is no genetic relatedness. Although the specific genes underlying these disorders are still largely unknown, some candidate genes have been tentatively identified on chromosomes that are implicated in both disorders (specifically, chromosomes 10, 13, 18, and

22). The promise of medical genomics for finding the causes and potential treatments for schizophrenia and bipolar disorder has long been promoted by pharmaceutical and genomics companies. But the genetic heterogeneity of both disorders, and the complex environmental factors that surely must also be involved in the ETIOLOGY of these disorders, has seemed to push the pay-off of basic genetics research further and further into the future. This is why the January 2005 report of a pilot study of a gene-based diagnostic blood test for schizophrenia and bipolar disorder is so stunning.

Ming T. Tsuang, director of the Institute of Behavioral Genomics at the University of California, San Diego, and his international team of colleagues from the United States, Canada, and Taiwan employed a procedure for using RNA derived from white blood cells. This procedure—known as "the Sentinel Principle"—was invented and patented by C. C. Liew, chief scientist of ChondroGene, a private genomics firm in Toronto, Canada. They took blood from 30 subjects with schizophrenia, 16 with bipolar disorder, and 28 normal controls. Using a microarray analysis, they found that each disease state exhibited a unique expressed genome signature, allowing for the objective biological differential diagnosis of mental disorders for perhaps the first time in history. They examined eight candidate biomarker genes and with 95 to 97 percent accuracy were able to use them as blood biomarkers to discriminate between schizophrenia, bipolar disorder, and normal controls. As they conclude in their abstract: "We therefore propose that blood cell–derived RNA may have significant value for performing diagnostic functions and identifying disease biomarkers in schizophrenia and BPD."

Abderhalden, E. "Ausblicke ueber die Verwertbarkeit der Ergebnisse neuerer Forschungen auf dem Gebiete des Zellstoffwechsels zur Loesung von Fragestellungen auf dem Gebiete der Pathologie des Nervensystems," *Deutsche medizinische Wochenschrift* 48 (November 28, 1912): 2,252–2,255.

———. *Defensive Ferments of the Animal Organism.* 3rd ed. William Wood and Company, New York, 1914.

———. *Die Abwehrfermente des Tierischen Organismus.* Berlin: Springer, 1913.

Deichmann, U., and B. Müller-Hill. "The Fraud of Abderhalow's Enzymes." *Nature* 393 (1998): 309–311.

Fauser, A. "Die Serologie in der Psychiatrie: Rueckblicke und Ausblicke," *Muenchener medizinische Wochenschrift* 60 (September 9, 1913): 1,984–1,989.

———. "Einige Untersuchungsergebnisse und klinische Ausblicke auf Grund der Abderhaldenschen Anschauungen und Methodik," *Deutsche medizinische Wochenschrift* 52 (December 26, 1912): 2,446–2,451.

———. "Pathologische-serologische Befunde bei Geisteskrankheiten auf Grund der Abderhaldenschen Anschauung und Methodik," *Allgemeine Zeitschrift für Psychiatrie und psychisch-gerichtliche Medizin* 70 (May 31, 1913): 841–849.

———. "Zur Frage des Vorhandenseins spezifischer Schutzfermente im Serum vom Geisteskranken," *Muchener medizinische Wochenschrift* 11 (March 18, 1913): 584–586.

Kaasch, M. "Sensation, Irrtum, Betrug?—Emil Abderhalden und die Geschichte der Abwehrfermente," *Acta Historica Leopoldina* 36 (2000): 145–210.

Simon, C. E. "The Abderhalden-Fauser Reaction in Mental Diseases with Special Reference to Dementia Praecox," *Journal of the American Medical Association* 62 (May 30, 1914): 1,701–1,706.

Tsuang, M. T., N. Nossova, T. Yager, et al. "Assessing the Validity of Blood-based Gene Expression Profiles for the Classification of Schizophrenia and Bipolar Disorder: A Preliminary Report," *American Journal of Medical Genetics Part B: Neuropsychiatric Genetics* 133B (January 2005): 1–5.

blood transfusion Down through the centuries the idea has persisted that mental illness might be caused by abnormalities in the blood. The practice of BLEEDING attempted to cure the mentally ill by drawing significant quantities of blood from the afflicted until a change in symptoms could be noted. Similarly, the idea of blood transfusions as a possible treatment of mental illness developed in Europe in the late 1550s. A French physician, Jean-Baptiste Denis, performed the first recorded transfusion of blood from dog to dog. At a meeting of the Royal Society on November 23, 1667, Richard Lower demonstrated the transfusion of sheep's blood into a divinity student, Arthur Coga. This event was recorded by Samuel Pepys in his famous diary. Besides France and England, these transfu-

sion treatments were recommended in Germany by physicians Klein and Ettmüller, the latter of which suggested this form of treatment in his 1682 *Chirurgia Transfusoria.*

A 20th-century resurrection of this "bad blood" theory of the cause of mental illness was made in 1977 by psychiatrists J. Wagemaker and R. Cade, who noticed a significant improvement in a paranoid schizophrenic patient following hemodialysis for kidney disease. They hypothesized that an unknown "toxin," which caused schizophrenic symptoms, may have been removed through hemodialysis. Although a further study using hemodialysis on schizophrenics with no kidney disease proved promising and attracted media attention, replications of this study by others have not found the same results.

See also HEMODIALYSIS TREATMENT OF SCHIZOPHRENIA.

blood vessel alterations in schizophrenia Beginning with the ancient Greek and Roman humoral theory of medicine, blood has been associated in various ways with the cause of insanity. By the 19th century, the focus shifted to the vessels that transported blood throughout the body. The possibility that psychotic disorders might be caused by pathological changes in the circulatory system was proposed by the great neuroanatomist Theodor Meynert (1833–92). In 1884 Meynert proposed that the insanities were caused by pathological changes in the circulatory system. Since the brain was fed oxygen and nutrients through the blood-brain barrier (as we now call it), any damage to the blood vessels feeding the brain would cause neuropathology. Meynert, who is best remembered for his contributions to our understanding of the structure and functioning of the central nervous system (as well as for being Sigmund FREUD's professor in Vienna), was a major influence on the first biological psychiatrists of the late 19th century by convincing them that the foundation of mental illnesses illness could be found in studies of neuroanatomy and neuropathology.

After the introduction of DEMENTIA PRAECOX (1893) and SCHIZOPHRENIA (1908) as identifiable psychotic syndromes, attention again turned to the structure and function of the blood vessels in persons with this disease. In his classic 1911 volume *Dementia Praecox, or the Group of Schizophrenias,* Eugen BLEULER discusses abnormalities of the "vasomotor system" in schizophrenia, stating, "We do not yet know anything fundamental about the tensions within the vascular system in psychoses (p. 166)." A page later he then adds the observation, "The fragility of the blood vessels which appears in many schizophrenics, both acute and chronic, seems to indicate a real vascular pathology."

Between 1923 and 1925, while working as a staff psychiatrist under superintendent William Alanson White (1870–1937) of St. Elizabeth's Hospital in Washington, D.C., Noland D. C. Lewis (1889–1979) and his colleagues performed or reviewed the records of autopsies on 4,800 mental patients, of which 601 were diagnosed with dementia praecox (schizophrenia). Lewis concluded that a biological marker of schizophrenia was a primary hypoplasia (underdevelopment or atrophy of tissue or an organ) of the cardiovascular system. Dementia praecox patients, it was found, were characterized by small hearts and a hypoplasia through the vascular system. This, it was hypothesized, led to a general reduction of oxygen to the brain (cerebral hypoxemia), thereby contributing to the development of dementia praecox. According to Lewis, another contributing factor to the development of dementia praecox was the dysfunction of the thyroid and adrenal glands and the gonads. Several confirmatory replications of Lewis's study were performed by others and reported until about 1940. After that time, there was little interest in the role of the vascular system in the etiology or pathophysiology of schizophrenia until 2005.

The inflammatory-vascular theory of schizophrenia (2005) In 2005 D. R. Hanson and Irving L. Gottesman, two prominent researchers in the genetics of schizophrenia, proposed a "genetic-vascular-inflammatory" theory of schizophrenia in the online electronic journal *BMC Medical Genetics.* The theory proposes that the physiological abnormalities leading to illness involve the disruption of the "exquisitely precise regulation of the delivery

of energy and oxygen required for normal brain function." They propose that abnormalities in the metabolism of the central nervous system (as evidenced by abnormal cerebral regional blood flow) arise because genetically modulated inflammatory reactions damage the microvascular system of the brain in reaction to environmental agents. These would include infections, hypoxia, and physical trauma. Damage would accumulate with repeated exposure to triggering agents resulting in exacerbation and deterioration, or healing with their removal. Hansen and Gottesman are proposing "a chronic, smoldering, inflammation of the blood vessels alone" as the source of the many BRAIN ABNORMALITIES IN SCHIZOPHRENIA. And since blood must feed the cells in all areas of the brain, it is no surprise that a century of brain studies in schizophrenia have implicated almost every area of the brain to the disease at one time or another. This theory also brings IMMUNE SYSTEM ABNORMALITIES back into consideration with the hypothesis of the inflammation of the blood vessels leading directly to damage of the blood-brain barrier.

Hansen, D. R., and L. L. Gottesman. "Schizophrenia: A Genetic-Inflammatory-Vascular Synthesis," *BMC Medical Genetics* 6 (2005): 1,471–1,492.

Lewis, N. D. C. "Pathology of Dementia Praecox," *Journal of Nervous and Mental Disease* 62 (1925): 25–260.

Meynert, T. *Klinische Vorlesungen uber Psychiatrie.* Vienna: Braumuller, 1890.

blunted affect A commonly used descriptive term for a significant reduction in the (normal) intensity of the expressed emotions of a person. This is one of the major symptomatic expressions of SCHIZOPHRENIA but can also be witnessed in those persons who are depressed. A related term, FLAT AFFECT, refers to the nearly complete absence of any emotions whatsoever, with the voice sounding monotonous and the face rigid.

Bly, Nellie (1867–1922) The pseudonym of an American journalist for the *New York World,* Elizabeth Seaman (née Cochrane), who faked insanity and gained admittance to the New York City Lunatic Asylum (formerly "mad-house") on Blackwell's Island (now Roosevelt Island). Her serialized exposé was entitled "Ten Days in a Mad House," with the engaging subtitle "Feigning insanity in order to reveal asylum horrors. The trying ordeal of the *New York World*'s girl correspondent." Her articles were published in book form the following year.

Bly detailed abuses involving the unnecessary use of restraints, cruelty to patients by attendants, and unsanitary conditions. These were the same kinds of maltreatment documented by Charles Dickens when he went to the asylum on Blackwell's Island during his trip to America in 1842.

Bly, N. *Ten Days in a Mad House.* New York: 1888.

boarding homes The mentally ill have long resided in boarding homes in the United States, but this type of residence has proliferated since the DEINSTITUTIONALIZATION of psychiatric patients from state hospitals, which began in the 1950s. The idea was that it would be more "normal" for patients to live in the community in such homes. However, in the United States such homes are often found to be undersupervised, with their high turnover rates not infringing upon their profitability to the private owners, who generally have no professional training for supervising such patients. Many psychiatric patients actually prefer the relatively close supervision of the psychiatric hospital, where there are always other people around in case of danger. A cogent critique of the problem of the "homeless mentally ill" in the 1980s is provided in a book by psychiatrist E. Fuller Torrey.

Torrey, E. F. *Nowhere to Go: The Tragic Odyssey of the Homeless Mentally Ill.* New York: HarperPerennial, 1988.

body image in schizophrenia A commonly reported phenomenon in SCHIZOPHRENIA is the experience of distortions in body image. The afflicted person feels, fears, or believes that the physical body itself is changing and will look different to others. Such body distortions can take bizarre

forms in people with schizophrenia and are fully experienced as "real" by them. A former patient of the author's was fully experiencing the feeling that his face had turned into that of a dog's, and that this was how people were actually perceiving him. Others may believe that they have huge, gaping holes in the middle of their torsos through which they experience the wind passing, or feel much thinner or fatter than they really are. The issue of a person's body image has been much discussed in recent years, with the phenomenon of females with anorexia nervosa having the delusional belief that they are being perceived as fat when, in fact, they are emaciated.

Boerhaave, Hermann (1668–1738) A Dutch physician, known for his psychiatric interests. He is acknowledged as the inventor of the "spinning chair," a device of mechanical restraint that was designed to render patients unconscious.

See also CIRCULATING SWING.

borderline cases No diagnostic system is perfect, especially when it comes to identifying mental disorders, and so over the years they must constantly be revised. New categories must be added and others discarded. In the 20th century, the concept that there could be cases that fall between "NEUROSIS" and "PSYCHOSIS" because they have the features of each began to take hold when it was discovered that more and more patients could not be evenly classified by this simple dichotomy. These have been called "borderline cases." However, following the dichotomy of psychotic disorders identified by KRAEPELIN in 1899s, it has generally been found that these so-called borderline cases seemed to be related either to SCHIZOPHRENIA (DEMENTIA PRAECOX) or to BIPOLAR DISORDER (manic-depressive psychosis). Those borderline cases that seemed more closely to resemble schizophrenia are now labeled SCHIZOTYPAL PERSONALITY DISORDER (see BORDERLINE SCHIZOPHRENIA), and those that are allied with manic-depressive psychosis are now called BORDERLINE PERSONALITY DISORDER. However, this distinction was also reflected in the clustering of other types of similar personality disorders in the *Diagnostic and Statistical Manual of Mental Disorders, Third Edition, Revised* (1987), with "Cluster A" consisting of schizotypal, paranoid, and schizoid personality disorders. These people are said to appear "odd or eccentric." "Cluster B" is grouped into borderline, antisocial, histrionic, and narcissistic personality disorders, in all of which an individual's behavior appears "dramatic, emotional or erratic."

Spitzer, R. L., J. Endicott, and M. Gibbon. "Crossing the Border into Borderline Personality and Borderline Schizophrenia," *Archives of General Psychiatry* 36 (1979): 17–24.

borderline neuroses See BORDERLINE SCHIZOPHRENIA.

borderline personality disorder Although the descriptions of this disorder differ, the most widely accepted diagnostic description is an erratic pattern of interpersonal relationships characterized by extremes of overidealization and devaluation, problems with self-identity, emotional instability (usually depicted as vaccillating between intense feelings and displays of anger and an "emptiness" depression), and, in the most severe forms of the disorder, self-mutilation and suicide threats and attempts. During stressful periods, psychotic symptoms (such as BIZARRE DELUSIONS or HALLUCINATIONS) can appear. For example, a woman whose daily occupation requires a significant amount of reasoning ability and responsibility (e.g., as a social worker) may nonetheless suddenly be afraid to open the door of her apartment to pay for the pizza she ordered over the telephone, for fear that the delivery boy had poisoned it.

Borderline personality disorder is apparently becoming more common than in the past and is generally diagnosed more in females than in males. Males with similar symptoms tend to be involved in antisocial activities (e.g., stealing, violence, substance abuse) acted-out against others and thus are usually given the diagnosis of antisocial personality disorder. Since this disorder is often difficult for most people to identify, fictional examples from motion

pictures or television are sometimes referred to in the training of mental health professionals. Some fictionalized examples of extreme forms of the disorder are the roles of actresses Glenn Close in the movie *Fatal Attraction* (1987) and Meryl Streep in the movie *Plenty* (1985).

Borderline personality disorder is the best example of the types of BORDERLINE CASES that resemble affective disorders, such as BIPOLAR DISORDER, rather than those that resemble schizophrenia.

See also ANTISOCIAL BEHAVIOR.

borderline schizophrenia A term that became popular in the 1920s but is no longer in use for the type of disorder in which a person has what resembles SCHIZOPHRENIA across many traits but is not fully psychotic and does not have all the symptoms of schizophrenia. Such individuals might now be commonly diagnosed as having a SCHIZOTYPAL PERSONALITY DISORDER. The concept that some patients fall between "NEUROSIS" and "psychosis" with their mental illness is expressed in the use of the word *borderline*. In psychoanalytic publications, this concept formerly meant patients who were intermediate between the groups that were clearly "analyzable" (such as those with neurotic disorders) and "non-analyzable" (those who are psychotic).

Other clinical terms used over the years that overlap with borderline schizophrenia (with the person who coined them and in what year) are as follows: borderline neurosis (L. P. Clark, 1919); impulsive character (W. Reich, 1925); INCIPIENT SCHIZOPHRENIA (Glover, 1932); SCHIZOAFFECTIVE DISORDER (Kasanin, 1933); AMBULATORY SCHIZOPHRENIA (Zilboorg, 1941); "as-if" personality (H. Deutsch, 1942); LATENT PSYCHOSIS (Federn, 1947); pseudoneurotic schizophrenia (Hoch & Polatin, 1949); and LATENT SCHIZOPHRENIA (Bychowski, 1953). It is also thought that Eugen BLEULER attempted to identify this type of "borderline" person with the term *compensated schizophrenic* in 1911.

Stone, M. H. "The Borderline Syndrome: Evolution of the Term, Genetic Aspects, and Prognosis." In *Essential Papers on Borderline Disorders: One Hundred Years at the Border*, edited by M. H. Stone. New York: New York University Press, 1986.

bouffée délirante Throughout the history of PSYCHIATRY, there has been a distinction been psychotic disorders that are chronic (such as SCHIZOPHRENIA) and those that have a sudden onset, a brief duration, and then just as suddenly disappear. *Bouffée délirante* is a brief psychotic disorder characterized by a sudden onset ("like a bolt from the blue") of DELUSIONS and HALLUCINATIONS of any kind (auditory, visual, tactile, olfactory, gustatory) with a rapid acceleration of often changing delusional features (for example, persecution, megalomania, or hypochondriasis). The disorder disappears completely after a period of weeks or months. Persons who suffer such disorders return to their previous level of functioning and usually remain in full remission. In French psychiatry, the brief or acute psychotic disorder known as the *bouffée délirante* has been an important diagnostic category for more than a century. In the past, this diagnosis was three times more likely to be used by French psychiatrists than that of ACUTE SCHIZOPHRENIA. As recently as 1999, it was reported that the diagnosis of *bouffée délirante polymorphe* was given to as many as one-third of persons admitted with acute psychotic symptoms.

Bouffée délirante was first described in separate books published in 1886 by Honore Saury (1854–?) and Paul-Maurice Legrain (1860–1939), students of the French *alieniste* Valentin Magnan (1835–1916) of the Ste.-Anne Mental Hospital in Paris. In 1893 Magnan proposed this diagnostic category in the context of DEGENERATION THEORY, of which he was a major proponent. The connection of this disorder with degeneration began to disappear in French psychiatry around 1910. The prominent French psychiatrist Henry Ey (1900–77) emphasized the distinction in course and prognosis between *bouffée délirante* and schizophrenia rather than the symptoms, a characteristic feature of French psychiatry as a whole.

See also ACUTE AND TRANSIENT PSYCHOTIC DISORDERS; BRIEF PSYCHOTIC DISORDER; POLYMORPHIC PSYCHOTIC SYMPTOMS.

Ferrey, G. "Evolution et prognostic des troubles psychotiques aigus (bouffée délirante polymorphe)," *Encéphale* 25 (1999): 26–32.

Legrain, P.-M. *Du Délire Chez Dégénérés.* Paris: Deshaye et Lecrosoier, 1886.

Magnan, V. *Lecons cliniques sur les maladies mentales.* 2nd ed. Paris: Battaille, 1893.

Pichot, P. "The Concept of 'Bouffée Délirante' with Special Reference to the Scandinavian Concept of Reactive Psychosis," *Psychopathology* 19 (1986): 35–43.

boundary disturbances in schizophrenia This is a type of perceptual distortion that many schizophrenics report in which they feel they are merging or blending into or are part of another person. Such persons may describe the anxiety felt when in the presence of others as being due to the frightening feeling that they are "sliding into" another person and thus losing the sense of individual identity. Such experiences—although terrifying for most psychotics—have been reported by "normals" who have ingested certain hallucinogens, thus giving rise to the research in the experiential similarities between SCHIZOPHRENIA and hallucinogenic states.

bradykinesia One of the triad of signs of PARKINSONISM that is an adverse effect of the administration of ANTIPSYCHOTIC DRUGS. Along with tremor and rigidity, bradykinesia (or AKINESIA) can occur in patients within weeks to months after the beginning of antipsychotic drug therapy. Bradykinesia is a slowness of motion, whereas akinesia (less common and more severe) is an absence of motion that is not caused by a general paralysis. The person with bradykinesia will frequently seem to have a masklike face, with little expressiveness and infrequent and slow eye blinking. The motions of such a patient can seem "zombielike." The bradykinetic patient is said to turn his or her body "en bloc," as if rigidly frozen into a body without joints. Drooling is a common associated phenomenon with the triad of Parkinsonian symptoms.

Brady- is a prefix that means "slow" and is used in many other clinical behavioral terms.

See also ANTIPARKINSONIAN DRUGS.

brain abnormalities in schizophrenia The search for abnormal structures in the brains of schizophrenics has a long history, beginning with the 19th-century ABLATION STUDIES and continuing with the sophisticated technology of BRAIN IMAGING TECHNIQUES today. It is known that autopsies were performed on the deceased patients at the BETHLEM ROYAL HOSPITAL in London, England, in the early 1800s, as well as in Paris, France, by PINEL and ESQUIROL at about the same time. Between 1802 and 1804, Pinel conducted more than 250 autopsies or "openings" (*ouvertures*) of corpses of deceased mental patients. Only about one-fourth of these patients showed cerebral lesions, thus confirming the belief of Pinel and his student Esquirol after their *recherches cadavériques* that insanity was more likely to be caused by visceral lesions than by brain abnormalities.

The brains of persons with SCHIZOPHRENIA have been studied using two basic approaches, one for dead brains and one for living brains.

The first—and oldest—of these is called *neuropathology.* Neuropathology is the science that correlates autopsy findings in dead brains with the symptoms and behaviors of the person with schizophrenia when they were alive. There are two general types of evidence in neuropathology: macroscopic findings, which involve the observation and measurement of larger structures in the brain (such as the early ablation studies that found lesions with the naked eye); and histological findings, which involve the microscopic examination of the structure and neurochemistry of the various types of cells in the brain (neurons, glial cells). The earliest neuropathological study of the brains of persons with DEMENTIA PRAECOX (schizophrenia) and other psychotic disorders was conducted in Germany by Alois ALZHEIMER (1864–1915) and published in 1897. Alzheimer and Franz Nissl (inventor of a famous staining technique that allows for the study of nerve cells) continued their neuropathological investigation of dementia praecox under Emil KRAEPELIN (1856–1926) in Germany in the very first multidisciplinary research program devoted to discovering the biological causes of MENTAL DISORDERS. The findings of this remarkable research group were summarized in the thick third volume (1913) of four in the eighth edition of Kraepelin's textbook *Psychiatrie.* In the United States, this neuropathological approach was continued in a 1915 study of the brains of

persons with dementia praecox by the prominent Harvard Medical School neuropathologist E. E. Southard (1876–1920). Southard counted himself with Kraepelin and Alzheimer as one of the "brain spot men" in psychiatry who believed schizophrenia was a brain disease. He and the other Kraepelinians were opposed to "mind twist men" such as Adolf MEYER (1866–1950) and Sigmund FREUD, who denied the importance of heredity and brain disease and instead claimed that mental disorders were caused by reactions to environmental stresses (Meyer) or early childhood experiences (Freud).

Due to the lack of technological breakthroughs in the methods of neuropathological research, and the rise of the influence of Freud and psychoanalysis in psychiatry in the United States and Great Britain after the First World War, virtually no neuropathological studies of schizophrenia were conducted from the mid-1920s to the early 1950s. During that time, there were no neuropathological investigations of AFFECTIVE DISORDERS such as manic-depressive illness, a state of affairs that persisted into the late 1990s, when the Stanley Foundation of Bethesda, Maryland, began collecting and comparing the brains of persons with schizophrenia, BIPOLAR DISORDER, and major DEPRESSION. At the 1st International Congress of Neuropathology, which was held in Rome, Italy, in 1953, the general consensus among the world's leading experts was that there were no pathological changes in the nervous system of schizophrenics—a conclusion that greatly strengthened the prominence of theories like Freudian psychoanalysis, which denied the role of biological disease processes in favor of the "schizophrenogenic mother" and other experiential/environmental causes of mental disorders. It would not be until 33 years later, at the 4th World Congress of Biological Psychiatry held in Philadelphia in 1985, that a symposium specifically on the "Neuropathology of Schizophrenia"—the first in history—would be held. By 1990 professional neuropathologists could no longer ignore the growing evidence of brain abnormalities in schizophrenia, and a workshop on "The Neuropathology of Schizophrenia" was held at the XIth International Congress of Neuropathology in Kyoto, Japan. The renewal of interest in the neuropathology of schizophrenia sprang almost directly from the innovative research of German neuropathologist Bernhard Bogerts. Bogerts and his research group published their first of many postmortem studies of schizophrenia in 1983.

The second major approach in neuropathology is the use of BRAIN IMAGING TECHNIQUES (or "neuroimaging" as it is now commonly called) to study the brains of living persons. Neuroimaging studies have examined both the structure and the functioning of living brains of persons with schizophrenia. The very first neuroimaging study of structural abnormalities in schizophrenia was conducted by E. D. Johnstone and colleagues using a CT SCAN. It was published in 1976. Since then, many other studies of structure have used not only CT but also MRI to measure size and volume of certain brain structures. Many other studies have used techniques that look at the functioning of living brains, such as positron emission tomography (PET) and single photo emission computed tomography (SPECT) and functional magnetic resonance imaging (fMRI), which combines both structure and function in its computer generated images.

The scientific literature on the neuropathology of schizophrenia is gigantic and growing weekly. Prominent experts in the field of schizophrenia disagree about the interpretation of almost every neuropathological finding. Neuropathological theories of schizophrenia come and go on a regular basis, with few of them ever completely ruled out. It is distressing to realize how little we know about the brains of persons with schizophrenia. However, a major critical review of the literature on the neuropathology of schizophrenia by Paul J. Harrison was published in the scientific journal *Brain* in 1999. Harrison weighed the strength of the evidence for various claims, and the strongest findings are as follows:

Macroscopic findings (in descending order of certainty):

1. Enlarged lateral and third ventricles of the brain. *Background:* Ventricles are the "spaces" between the lobes of the brain through which the cerebrospinal fluid passes. The first researcher to describe enlarged cerebral ventricles in the postmortem examination of brains from deceased psychotic patients was Ewald Hecker (1843–1909) in 1871.

Hecker described the psychotic disorder HEBEPHRENIA, which Kraepelin later incorporated as one of the three subtypes of dementia praecox. Enlarged ventricles were also described in Johnstone's 1976 CT study and have been described many times since, thus justifying Harrison's certainty about the strength of this finding.

2. Decreased cortical volume. *Background:* There have been many descriptions of the smaller, lighter brains of persons with schizophrenia.

3. Enlarged ventricles and decreased cortical volume are found in persons who have just suffered through their first experience of schizophrenia. *Background:* This strong finding means that brain abnormalities are not due to the progression of the disease, nor are they due to the effects of antipsychotic medications on the brain. The brains of persons who develop schizophrenia are structurally abnormal before they get ill for the very first time.

4. The temporal lobe (including the hippocampus) loses disproportionately more volume than the other areas of the brain.

5. Decreased thalamic volume. *Background:* The thalamus, a major relay center for circuits that send messages traveling throughout the brain, is smaller and lighter than normal in persons with schizophrenia.

6. Cortical volume loss affects gray matter rather than white matter. *Background:* The two large hemispheres of the cortex are made up of different types of cells. The shrinkage of the brains of people with schizophrenia seems to occur in the gray matter, largely made of neurons, rather than the white matter, largely made of glial cells.

7. Enlarged basal ganglia is secondary to antipsychotic medication. *Background:* The basal ganglia, an important structure in the extrapyramidal motor system of the brain, is rich in the NEUROTRANSMITTER DOPAMINE. Because so many antipsychotic drugs work by affecting dopamine pathways in the brain, long-term use of such drugs seems to affect the structure of the brain in areas such as the basal ganglia that are part of the dopamine system.

Histological findings (in decreasing order of certainty):

1. Absence of gliosis as an intrinsic feature
2. Smaller cortical and hippocampal neurons
3. Fewer neurons in dorsal thalamus
4. Reduced synaptic and dendritic markers in hippocampus
5. Maldistribution of white matter neurons
6. Entorhirnal cortex dysplasia
7. Cortical or hippocampal neuron loss
8. Disarray of hippocampal neurons

Harrison also added two additional neuropathological findings: (1) Contrary to speculation since the 1930s, evidence of Alzheimer's disease is not more common in the brains of persons with schizophrenia than in the general population and (2) pathology (brain abnormality) is connected to asymmetries in the cerebral hemispheres in the brain.

As so many others have concluded since Southard did in 1915, Harrison also suggests that the brain abnormalities in schizophrenia most likely originate in the developing embryo and fetus and continue on through childhood and adolescence, culminating in the first episode of schizophrenia in young adulthood in most cases. Such theories of FETAL NEURAL DEVELOPMENT AND SCHIZOPHRENIA, or "neurodevelopmental schizophrenia," as it is sometimes called, have dominated the field since 1986. Michael Knable and Daniel Weinberger of the NATIONAL INSTITUTE OF MENTAL HEALTH (NIMH) argue that "schizophrenia is a developmental abnormality affecting the connectivity of the prefrontal and medial temporal cortices." This so-called disconnection hypothesis of schizophrenia has been defined in many different ways with reference to many different brain regions and neural pathways. Neuropathological studies of the brains of human fetuses at high-risk for developing schizophrenia later in life are lacking, which make it difficult to test hypotheses about the neurodevelopmental causes of schizophrenia.

Two of the major reviewers of the evidence for brain abnormalities in schizophrenia—P. J. Harrison of Oxford University in England and Bernhard Bogerts of the University of Magdeburg, Germany, agree that the best interpretation of all these findings is that much of the evidence clearly points away from the notion that schizophrenia is a progressively neurodegenerative disease, like Alzheimer's disease, and therefore, by default, the findings generally fit the NEURODEVELOPMENTAL

MODEL OF SCHIZOPHRENIA but do not prove it. They agree on consistent evidence for:

(1) cellular changes in the hippocampal formation, a finding first reported in 1984
(2) cellular changes in the dorsal prefrontal cortex (DPFC), first noticed in postmortem studies in the 1990s
(3) decreased volume in the mediodorsal thalamic nucleus

A problem with most neuropathological studies of schizophrenia until the year 2000 was that most changes in the brains of schizophrenics were compared to normal controls and not to the brains of persons who had suffered from other psychiatric disorders (such as bipolar disorder). It is not known if brain abnormalities are similar or distinctively different from persons suffering other psychotic disorders, affective disorders, or personality disorders (for which there are no postmortem brain studies).

Abnormalities in other areas of the brains of persons with schizophrenia have been proposed. Schizophrenia researcher Nancy Andreasen (1938–) of the University of Iowa, noted for leading the research group that published the first MRI study of schizophrenia in 1986, has proposed that abnormalities in the cerebellum, particularly shrinkage in size over time, is correlated with the persistence of negative symptoms, psychosis, and psychosocial impairment. These assumptions form the basis of her COGNITIVE DYSMETRIA theory.

Bogerts, B. "The Neuropathology of Schizophrenia Diseases: Historical Aspects and Present Knowledge," *European Archives of Psychiatry and Clinical Neuroscience* 249 (1999): Supplement 4, IV2–IV13.

Harrison, P. J. "The Neuropathology of Schizophrenia: A Critical Review of the Data and Their Interpretation," *Brain* 122 (1999): 593–624.

Knable, M. B., and D. R. Weinberger. "Are Mental Diseases Brain Diseases? The Contributions of Neuropathology to Understanding of Schizophrenic Psychoses," *European Archives of Psychiatry and Clinical Neuroscience* 245 (1995): 224–230.

Southard, E. E. "The Mind Twist and the Brain Spot Hypotheses in Psychopathology and Neuropathology," *Psychological Bulletin* 11 (1914): 117–130.

———. "On the Topographical Distribution of Cortex Lesions and Abnormalities in Dementia Praecox, with Some Account of Their Functional Significance," *American Journal of Insanity* 71 (1915): 603–671.

———. "Psychopathology and Neuropathology: The Problems of Teaching and Research Contrasted," *Journal of the American Medical Association* 18 (1912): 914.

Wassink, T. H., N. C. Andreasen, P. Nopoulos, and M. Flaum. "Cerebellar Morphology as a Predictor of Symptom and Psychosocial Outcome in Schizophrenia," *Biological Psychiatry* 45 (1999): 41–48.

brain imaging studies of schizophrenia Also called neuroimaging techniques, these are technologically sophisticated methods for studying the structure and functioning of the brains of living human beings by generating "pictures" or "images" that can then be studied and compared with images from the brains of others. These techniques have revolutionized the neurosciences.

Techniques for "seeing" into a living body and examining its internal structure has a long history in medicine. After the invention of the X-ray technique in 1895 by the German physicist W. C. Roentgen (1845–1923), it was applied the following year by Harvey Cushing (1896–1939) of Johns Hopkins University in Baltimore to a patient who had suffered spinal cord damage due to a bullet injury to the neck. The extensive diagnostic use of X-rays to investigate the living brain and nervous system was pioneered by Arthur Schuller (1874–1957) of Vienna, who published a book on this application in 1918. Beginning in 1918 another technique with a long history in 20th century medicine, the air encephalography, ventriculography, or pneumoencephalography, was introduced at Johns Hopkins. This technique involved injecting air into the space around the spinal cord, which allowed for a clearer contrast image in X-ray studies. The first application of pneumoencephalography to the study of SCHIZOPHRENIA in 1927 found an anomaly that has been a consistent finding in some (but not most) persons with schizophrenia: enlarged cerebral ventricles. This first study was conducted in a mental hospital near Jena, Germany, by Walter Jacobi and H. Winkler under the supervision

of Hans Berger (1873–1941), who had invented the EEG and was experimenting with it at this time. Other techniques that were introduced to image the living brain were carotid arteriography (1947), radionucleotide brain scanning (1948), and the measurement of cerebral blood flow (1948). The measurement of regional cerebral blood flow, or RCBF, played an important role in understanding schizophrenia in the years prior to the introduction of modern neuroimaging technologies. The first modern technique was the CT SCAN, pioneered for use by G. N. Hounsfield in 1973. The first report of the use of brain imaging techniques to study schizophrenic brains was the classic report by E. D. Johnstone and his colleagues published in the British medical journal *Lancet* in 1976. Many other types of brain imaging techniques have been developed and used in schizophrenia research since then.

CT (computerized tomography) scans and nuclear magnetic resonance (NMR), also called MAGNETIC RESONANCE IMAGING (MRI), generate images of the structure of the brain. MRI images are considered to be clearer and of more value. The dynamics of brain functioning, however, are studied with brain imaging techniques such as brain electrical activity mapping (BEAM), cerebral blood flow imaging (also known as regional cerebral blood flow, or rCBF), positron emission tomography (PET SCANS), single photon emission computed tomography (SPECT), and magnetoencephalography (MEG).

Brain imaging studies of schizophrenia have become an important area of research. The neuroimaging studies of the 1970s and 1980s focused on brain structure in schizophrenia, with the first CT study appearing in 1976 and the first MRI study appearing in 1984. However, since the first PET study of schizophrenia appeared in 1980, the vast majority of studies since then has examined the functioning brains of persons with schizophrenia, usually as they performed certain psychological tasks (memory tasks and so on). Most of these recent studies have used (1) a variety of different types of PET techniques using different radioactive materials to trace the many different ways in which brain metabolism works, (2) functional magnetic resonance imaging (fMRI), which came into use in the mid-1990s, and (3) three-dimensional magnetic resonance imaging (3D MRI), first used in schizophrenia research by DeQuardo in 1996.

After 24 years of the widespread use of neuroimaging techniques in schizophrenia research, one fact clearly stands out: almost every region of the brain has been implicated in schizophrenia by at least one or more of these hundreds of studies.

Since these technologies are new, and innovations seem to appear at a rapid rate, it is difficult to arrive at conclusions about schizophrenia with absolute certainty. It is hard to generalize findings from one study to another. Technologies differ; different regions of the brain are examined from one study to another, the tasks they are asked to perform while being scanned differ, and there are serious statistical issues regarding the ways in which this computerized technology measures the brain and then constructs a computer generated image from many thousands of tiny "approximate" measurements. Because these technologies are so new and relatively rare (because they are so expensive to obtain and maintain), researchers know that just about any brain imaging study of schizophrenia is a novel contribution to the field. Some, unfortunately, are not careful about the logic of their experimental design. Many principal investigators who manage neuroimaging research teams are medically trained psychiatrists with little or no background in experimental psychology, a problem that may lead to design flaws and to the wrong interpretation of neuroimaging results. A common bit of gossip among researchers in this field concerns some researchers with deep pockets whose goal is simply to produce impressive color photos of a schizophrenia brain "lighting up" when performing just about any task. Such images can be impressive to administrators with little expertise in neuroimaging when requesting grants or increases in funding. Fortunately, these researchers are in the minority. It is therefore not surprising to find that so many brain imaging studies seem to contradict one another, as has been the case with the issue of HYPOFRONTALITY as a "finding" about the brains of schizophrenics.

University of Pennsylvania schizophrenia researchers Ruben Gur and Raquel Gur remind researchers to keep four basic principles in mind before making claims of new scientific findings

about schizophrenia based on brain imaging studies:

1. First, carry out extensive studies on healthy subjects before leaping to patient studies.
2. Remember to incorporate standard resting measures of brain activity as well as activation measures (as when the subject is asked to perform a psychological task, such as a memory or spatial problem).
3. Suspend judgment until data are available on large, well-characterized, samples of persons with schizophrenia.
4. Integrate functional neuroimaging data with clinical variables and other measures of brain structure and function.

What have brain imaging studies of schizophrenia taught us about the disease? In general, there are two categories of findings which result from the brain imaging techniques used:

(1) Structural imaging studies (CT, MRI) have consistently provided support for evidence first noticed in autopsies that the brains of some schizophrenics have less tissue and less volume than normal brains. The problem seems to be worse for the tissue of the temporal lobes of the brain, particularly the left, and is also true for regions of the frontal lobe and other areas (the hippocampus, the cerebellum, and so on). The reduction in the volume of brain tissue results in the enlargement of the "spaces" or ventricles between the various lobes of the brain, a fact that has also been repeatedly confirmed in these imaging studies. Furthermore, brain imaging studies have confirmed that these structural abnormalities are present even in the earliest phases of the illness and therefore were most likely in existence before the first psychotic symptoms appeared.

(2) Functional imaging studies (PET, SPECT, fMRI) of schizophrenia have documented a widespread disturbance of brain functioning. This seems to be especially true for the connections between two areas: the frontal and temporal lobes. However, many other areas of the brain seem to function abnormally in schizophrenia as well when compared to the functioning of normal brains.

These functional imaging studies are the primary basis of the so-called DISCONNECTION THEORIES OF SCHIZOPHRENIA. These theories claim that there is a dynamic imbalance between different regions of the brain, and as such they do not cooperate with one another in a normal fashion. Various versions of this disconnection theory have been proposed that implicate different regions of the brain. The most prominent disconnection theory involves the "fronto-temporal network." As one of the most prominent researchers in functional imaging studies of schizophrenia, Peter F. Liddle, describes the general "disconnection" hypothesis, "the essential functional abnormality in schizophrenia is a disturbance of functional connectivity in the neural networks serving the supervisory mental functions responsible for the initiation, selection and monitoring of self-generated mental activity."

Some support for neurodevelopmental and disconnection theories of schizophrenia have come from MAGNETIC RESONANCE SPECTROSCOPY IMAGING (MRSI) studies of both adults and children with schizophrenia and their biological relatives. These studies show that people with schizophrenia, both children and adults, and their biological relatives have a smaller than normal regional NAA (N-acetylaspartate) chemical signal, indicating neuron damage or abnormalities in functioning of certain neural circuits or pathways.

The results of neuroimaging studies of schizophrenia have been combined with postmortem studies of BRAIN ABNORMALITIES IN SCHIZOPHRENIA and with studies of cognitive functioning (memory, spatial ability, and so on) to give us a fuller picture of what is happening inside the brain of a person with schizophrenia.

Buchsbaum, M. S., et al. "Positron Emission Tomography Studies of Abnormal Glucose Metabolism in Schizophrenia," *Schizophrenia Bulletin* 24 (1998): 343–364.

Buckley, P. F. "Structural Brain Imaging in Schizophrenia." In *Schizophrenia. Psychiatric Clinics of North America*, edited by P. F. Buckley. Philadelphia: W. B. Saunders, 1998, pp. 77–92.

DeQuardo, J. R., et al. "Landmark-based Morphometric Analysis in First-break Schizophrenia," *Biological Psychiatry* 45 (1999): 1,321–1,328.

Frith, C. D. "Functional Brain Imaging and the Neuropathology of Schizophrenia," *Schizophrenia Bulletin* 23 (1997): 525–527.
Gur, R. C., and R. E. Gur. "Hypofrontality in Schizophrenia: RIP," *Lancet* 3 (June 1995): 1,383–1,384.
Hounsfield, G. N. "Computerized Transverse Axial Scanning (Tomography)," *British Journal of Radiology* 46 (1973): 1,016–1,022.
Johnstone, E. D., et al. "Cerebral Ventricular Size and Cognitive Impairment in Chronic Schizophrenia," *Lancet* 2 (1976): 924–926.
Liddle, P. F. "Brain Imaging." In *Schizophrenia*, edited by Hirsch, S. R., and D. R. Weinberger. London: Blackwell Science, 1995, pp. 425–439.
McCarley, R. W., et al. "Neuroimaging and the Cognitive Neuroscience of Schizophrenia," *Schizophrenia Bulletin* 22 (1996): 703–725.

brain injury and psychosis See MEDICAL DISORDERS THAT MIMIC PSYCHOTIC DISORDERS.

brain tumors and psychosis See MEDICAL DISORDERS THAT MIMIC PSYCHIATRIC DISORDERS.

brief psychotic disorder In *DSM-IV-TR* (2000), a psychotic disorder lasting at least one day but less than one month that results in a full return to premorbid levels of functioning. The presence of one or more of the following symptoms must be in evidence: DELUSIONS, HALLUCINATIONS, disorganized speech, or grossly disorganized or catatonic behavior. There are three types:

(1) with a marked stressor preceding the onset of symptoms (*brief reactive psychosis*)
(2) without a marked stressor, indicating the psychosis is not a reaction to stress or trauma
(3) with postpartum onset (onset within four weeks of giving birth (postpartum psychosis) In *ICD-10* (1992) these are known as ACUTE AND TRANSIENT PSYCHOTIC DISORDERS. After one month, if the symptoms persist, in *DSM-IV-TR* the diagnosis is changed to SCHIZOPHRENIFORM DISORDER. If symptoms of schizophreniform disorder persist more than six months, the diagnosis may then be changed to schizophrenia, schizoaffective disorder, an atypical affective disorder, or a psychotic disorder not otherwise specified.

See also ATYPICAL PSYCHOTIC DISORDERS.

Brierre de Boismont, Alexandre (1798–1881) A noted French *aliéniste* who is most remembered for his comprehensive study of HALLUCINATIONS published in 1853. This study examined the phenomenon of hallucinations not only in the mentally ill, but also in hypnosis ("magnetic visions"), religious experience, and in other ALTERED STATES OF CONSCIOUSNESS. Brierre de Boismont was a disciple of ESQUIROL and was a member of the famous "Esquirol Circle."

Brierre de Boismont, A. *Hallucinations: Or, the Rational History of Apparitions, Visions, Dreams, Ecstasy, Magnetism and Somnambulism.* Philadelphia: Lindsay & Blakiston, 1853.

Brigham, Amariah (1798–1848) One of the original 13 founders of the American Psychiatric Association in 1844 (then called the Association of Medical Superintendents of American Institutions for the Insane). In 1843 he became the superintendent of the newly opened Utica State Hospital in New York. The following year, in 1844, he started the *American Journal of Insanity*, which later became the *American Journal of Psychiatry*, as it is known today. He printed it in the hospital with the assistance of patients in work programs.

Broadmoor Hospital Broadmoor has achieved notoriety in the British Isles as the place where the most homicidal of "homicidal maniacs" are kept. Since it opened its doors in 1863, Broadmoor has been where the most dangerous or violent mentally ill criminals have been placed. Prior to its construction in Crowthorne, Berkshire, such dangerous patients were kept in a special "gallery" at the BETHLEM ROYAL HOSPITAL in London.

Brosius, C. M. (1825–1910) A German psychiatrist who, along with Wilhelm GRIESINGER, is noted for quickly and successfully instituting policies of nonrestraint for the patients in German asylums and hospitals in the mid-1800s. German institutions took the lead in this more humane treatment of the mentally ill, whereas hospitals in the rest of Europe, notably England and France, only significantly improved near the end of the 1800s.

Broussais, Francois Joseph Victor (1772–1838) A French physician, army surgeon, and professor of general pathology of the University of Paris who was a bitter enemy of Philippe PINEL. Broussais entertained the theory that mental illness was caused by gastrointestinal "irritation." BLEEDING, PURGING, and diets were suggested as treatments for this irritation.

Broussais, F. J. V. *De l'irritation et de la folie.* Paris: 1828.

Bucknill, Sir John Charles (1817–1897) A major figure in 19th-century British PSYCHIATRY, Bucknill was an important advocate of nonrestraint policies and the boarding-out of mental patients from the hospitals to community placements. Superintendent of the Devon Asylum from 1844 to 1862, he also became the first president of the Association of Medical Officers of Asylums and Hospitals for the Insane (now the Royal College of Psychiatrists), and in 1862 he rose to the prominent position of Lord Chancellor's Visitor in Lunacy. Bucknill was also the first honorary member of the American Psychiatric Association; together with D. H. Tuke he wrote a standard textbook, *A Manual of Psychological Medicine,* in 1858 (2nd ed., 1882) that was widely used for many years.

Burghölzi Hospital The famous psychiatric hospital and clinic that is associated with the University of Zürich in Switzerland. After accepting a position as professor of medicine at the University in 1860, Wilhelm GRIESINGER assisted in planning and overseeing the construction of the new hospital. Griesinger also became its first director upon opening. Other famous directors of the Burghölzi over the years have been August Forel, Eugen BLEULER, and Manfred BLEULER. Burghölzi holds a special significance for the history of the scientific study of SCHIZOPHRENIA and the psychotic disorders because it was while they worked together there that Eugen Bleuler and C. G. JUNG wrote their famous monographs on "DEMENTIA PRAECOX," and it is the place where the term *schizophrenia* was first coined and used. Jung also carried out his famous diagnostic "word-association" experiments at Burghölzi in the early 20th century. The Burghölzi was the site of a noted longitudinal study of schizophrenia, carried out by Manfred Bleuler.

See also COURSE OF SCHIZOPHRENIA.

butyrophenones See ANTIPSYCHOTIC DRUGS.

C

cacodemonomania This is one of the two types of DEMONOMANIA identified by ESQUIROL in his chapter on the topic in his 1838 textbook, *Des Maladies mentales*. The word is used to refer to those mentally ill persons who believe they are possessed by, or in contact with, evil spirits or Satan himself. It is derived from two Greek words, *kakos* and *daimon*, for "bad" and "demon." The word *daimon* in the classical world did not have a bad connotation, as Esquirol notes, but had more of the meaning of a "guardian spirit" or "spiritual guide," which a person could consult. Esquirol asserts the diagnosis of cacodemonomania should be applied to "all those unfortunate beings who fancied that they were possessed by the devil, and in his power; who were convinced that they have been present at the imaginary assemblies of evil spirits, or who feared damnation, and the misery of eternal fire."

Possession by "evil spirits" has been attributed as a cause of mental illness for thousands of years. Cacodemonomania can still be witnessed from time to time in certain individuals even today, and a modern case of this disorder, reported in the psychiatric literature as recently as 1987, can be found reprinted in the volume by Richard Noll listed below.

Esquirol, J. E. D. *Mental Maladies, A Treatise on Insanity*, trans. E. K. Hunt. 1838. Reprint, Philadelphia: Lea & Blanchard, 1845.

Kemp, S., and K. Williams. "Demonic Possession and Mental Disorder in Medieval and Early Modern Europe," *Psychological Medicine* 17 (1987): 21–29.

Noll, R. *Vampires, Werewolves and Demons: Twentieth Century Reports in the Psychiatric Literature*. New York: Brunner/Mazel, 1991.

Salmons, P. H., and D. J. Clarke. "Cacodemonomania," *Psychiatry* 50 (1987): 50–54.

Cameron, Donald (1901–1967) A British psychiatrist who became the first president of the World Psychiatric Association. While a professor of psychiatry at McGill University in Montreal, Canada, in the 1940s, Cameron helped popularize the form of treatment of SCHIZOPHRENIA known as INSULIN COMA THERAPY in North America.

camisole A heavy-canvas coat, reaching from neck to waist, with long, closed sleeves that are designed to wrap the wearer's arms across the chest and are tied with cords behind the wearer's back. Apparently, the 19th-century term *camisole* was merely a euphemism for a type of STRAITJACKET, a term that had taken on a negative connotation by the end of the 1800s. In *A Mind That Found Itself*, Clifford BEERS graphically describes his torturous experience of being placed in a camisole in 1902, and describes this type of mechanical restraint as follows: "A camisole is a type of straight-jacket; and a very convenient type it is for those who resort to such methods of restraint, for it enables them to deny the use of a straight-jacket all. A straight-jacket, indeed, is not a camisole, just as electrocution is not hanging."

Beers, C. *A Mind That Found Itself*. New York: Doubleday, 1908.

Canada The only major study of prevalence rates for SCHIZOPHRENIA in Canada was carried out by research psychiatrist H. M. B. Murphy and his colleagues in the 1960s. In a survey of 14 Canadian villages with different ethnic compositions, he found an overall age-corrected prevalence rate of 4.6 per 1,000 in Canada. However, considering that he used a much narrower (at the time)

definition of schizophrenia than was accepted in the United States, the Canadian rate would have been much higher if the broader, American criteria had been used. Murphy found that traditional, "Old French" villages had a much higher rate of schizophrenia than other types, measuring twice as high as Anglo-Protestant villages. Furthermore, Canadian Catholics as a whole had a much higher rate of schizophrenia than Canadian Protestants.

Many studies have also been conducted in Canada on the native Canadian Inuit populations. Hudson Bay Inuit groups were found to have higher prevalence rates for schizophrenia, with studies ranging from 12.7 to 30.4 per 1,000.

Schizophrenia may also be especially prevalent among Canadian Indians, particularly the Cree and Salteaux Indians of northern Saskatchewan, where the age-corrected prevalence rate was 11.0 in one study. The same study looked at the non-Indian population in the area and found that the age-corrected prevalence rate for schizophrenia was only 2.4 per 1,000.

Murphy, H. B. M., and M. Lemieux. "The Problem of High Schizophrenic Prevalence in One Type of French-Canadian Rural Community," *Canadian Psychiatric Association Journal* 12 (1967): 72–81.

Sampath, H. "Prevalence of Psychiatric Disorders in a Southern Baffin Island Eskimo Settlement," *Canadian Psychiatric Association Journal* 19 (1974): 363–367.

Roy, C., et al. "The Prevalence of Mental Disorders among Saskatchewan Indians," *Journal of Cross-Cultural Psychiatry* 1 (1970): 383–392.

candidate genes Genes that are believed to be implicated in the cause of a particular disease (pathogenesis).

See also BIOLOGICAL MARKERS OF SCHIZOPHRENIA; GENETICS STUDIES; GENOME.

Capgras syndrome A delusional condition that some psychotic individuals develop in which they believe that a person, usually closely related in some way, has been replaced by an impostor or a "double." The DELUSION is often quite fixed and can be very distressing for the concerned family member, friend, or caretaker whose identity is constantly denied even when confronted with the absurdity of the notion. Usually the person accused of being an "impostor" or a "replacement" is also thought to bear bad intentions toward the delusional person.

The very first case was described by Jean Marie Capgras (1873–1950) and J. Reboul-Lachaux in 1923: a woman with a chronic paranoid psychosis who insisted that various individuals involved in her life had been replaced by "doubles." Their name for the condition was *l'illusion des sosies,* or "the illusion of doubles," but it is now almost universally known as the Capgras syndrome.

Capgras syndrome is one of the MISIDENTIFICATION SYNDROMES that are sometimes witnessed in psychotic individuals. As is the case with many fictional works of horror or science fiction that exploit common human fears, the 1956 motion picture *Invasion of the Body Snatchers* is based on a premise very similar to the fearful experience of persons suffering from Capgras syndrome.

Recent neuroimaging and neuropsychological studies of Capgras syndrome suggest that this delusional disorder is associated with right hemisphere abnormalities in the brain.

Capgras, J. M., and J. Reboul-Lachaux. "L'illusion des 'soises' dans um delire systematize chronique," *Annales Medico-Psychologiques* 81 (1923): 186–193.

Edelstyn, N. M., and F. Oyebode. "A Review of the Phenomenology and the Cognitive Neuropsychological Origins of the Capgras Syndrome," *International Journal of Geriatric Psychiatry* 14 (1999): 48–59.

carbamazepine A drug generally known by its trade name, Tegretol, used to treat seizure disorders. However, it has come into use in psychiatric centers as a treatment for certain psychotic patients who tend toward violence. It is structurally related to the heterocyclic antidepressants (such as imipramine and others) and to another anticonvulsant, phenytoin (trade name, Dilantin). It is also used in the treatment of some forms of BIPOLAR DISORDER.

carbon dioxide therapy One of the somatic or physical therapies for SCHIZOPHRENIA that was used

by American psychiatrists from 1929 until the late 1940s. In 1929 Arthur Solomon Loevenhart of the University of Wisconsin published a report that indicated that the inhalation of carbon dioxide produced a "cerebral stimulation" that alleviated catatonic symptoms in schizophrenia, MANIC-DEPRESSIVE ILLNESS, and involutional MELANCHOLIA (DEPRESSION in late life). Patients breathed in a gas mixture of 30 percent carbon dioxide, far greater than the average atmospheric amount of .03 percent. Patients were given as many as 150 inhalation sessions. This form of therapy has not been used since the 1940s.

Loevenhart, A. S., W. F. Lorenz, and R. M. Waters. "Cerebral Stimulation," *Journal of the American Medical Association* 92 (1929): 880–883.

cardiazol therapy See METRAZOL SHOCK THERAPY.

cardiovascular hypoplasia See BLOOD VESSEL ALTERATIONS IN SCHIZOPHRENIA.

catalepsy Another name for CATATONIC WAXY FLEXIBILITY, or *flexibilitas cera*.

catathymic crisis The crisis state induced in a person who is aware that he or she is developing a psychosis, or for whom an existing psychotic state is worsening. The terrible fear and anxiety caused by this awareness of a loss of control and a degeneration into mental chaos somehow leads the person to commit a violent or other antisocial act. As first described by Wertham in 1937, the crisis-provoked act is intended as a cry for help by the afflicted person. Wertham writes: "One gains the impression that the violent act in these cases prevents the developments that would be far more serious for the patient's health. The overt act seems to be a rallying point for the constructive forces of the personality."

Wertham, F. "The Catathymic Crisis," *Archives of Neurology and Psychiatry* 37 (1937): 974.

catatonia, or catatonic type Catatonia is a syndrome of abnormal movement. It can be associated with mood disorders (such as major DEPRESSION) or with disorders of cognitive deterioration or deficit (SCHIZOPHRENIA). Catatonic behavior can take many forms (see the entries below), from stupor (the classic picture of catatonia that we all have), to excitement, catalepsy (catatonic waxy flexibility), negativism, mutism, apparently voluntary assumption of inappropriate or bizarre posturing, stereotyped movements, off mannerisms, prominent grimacing, echolalia, or echopraxia. All these characteristics are part of the clinical picture of the "catatonic type" of schizophrenia in *DSM-IV-TR* (2000), any two of which are necessary for a diagnosis of this type.

Catatonia was considered an independent psychotic disorder in its own right until 1899. In that year Emil KRAEPELIN reframed catatonia as a "form" of DEMENTIA PRAECOX along with hebephrenic and paranoid forms. In 1911 Eugen BLEULER likewise considered catatonia as a subtype of schizophrenia and not as an independent disorder.

Catatonia (*Katatonia*) was a term coined by Karl Ludwig KAHLBAUM as early as 1868, but he first used it in print in his 1874 monograph, *Die Katatonie, oder das Spannungsirresein*. In Kahlbaum's view, catatonia was essentially a motility psychosis, a disorder of movement, which manifested in overactive and underactive forms. In the decades after 1899, as first Kraepelin's dementia praecox, then Bleuler's schizophrenia, were accepted by psychiatrists in primarily German and English-speaking countries (but not so in France or French-speaking countries until, arguably, sometime after *DSM-III* appeared in 1980), catatonia lost its independence. After the introduction of CHLORPROMAZINE and the PHENOTHIAZINES in MENTAL HOSPITALS after 1954, it was claimed that catatonia had virtually disappeared because of the effects of ANTIPSYCHOTIC DRUGS. However, such symptoms do indeed still appear in patients treated with these drugs but are now often interpreted as aspects of their side effects, particularly a form known as the NEUROLEPTIC MALIGNANT SYNDROME (or NMS), which can be lethal. Indeed, "lethal catatonia" had long been described in the old psychiatric literature and the symptoms and lethal course are similar to that of

NMS. Catatonia has long been known to respond to treatment with barbiturates, benzodiazepines, and electroconvulsive therapy. There is no firm scientific evidence from biological, genetic, or longitudinal studies of schizophrenia that catatonia is a distinct subtype of schizophrenia, but for historical and clinical reasons it is kept within schizophrenia as a variant of this disorder.

Kahlbaum, K. *Die Katatonie, oder das Spannungsirresein.* Berlin: Hirschwald, 1874.

catatonic excitement A behavior that occurs intermittently in catatonic persons in which they move about in a very active fashion without any apparent purpose and seemingly unguided by environmental cues. This excited motor behavior can occur between periods of other types of less mobile catatonic behavior. In the late 19th century, catatonic excitement was sometimes thought to result in death from exhaustion, and other names for it included "acute delirius mania," "BELL'S MANIA," and "BELL'S DISEASE."

See also AKATHISIA; NEUROLEPTIC MALIGNANT SYNDROME.

catatonic negativism A seemingly purposeless resistance to all attempts, whether physical or verbal, to being moved. If the person is passive, he or she may simply be unresponsive. When in a more active state, the person may be oppositional and do the opposite of what is asked.

catatonic posturing The bizarre or unusual postures that catatonic persons can maintain for a long period of time.

catatonic rigidity The maintenance of a muscularly tense, rigid position by a catatonic person, despite the forceful efforts of others to move him or her.

catatonic stupor The common image of a catatonic person's behavior. The person behaves as if in a stupor, hardly moving and relatively unresponsive to his or her environment.

catatonic waxy flexibility This is a behavior found in persons with the rare catatonic subtype of SCHIZOPHRENIA in which a person's body or limbs can be molded into a particular position and will remain passively in place, as if the person were a doll or made of wax. An older medical term for waxy flexibility is *cera flexibilitas.*

catecholamines A class of biogenic amines that includes the NEUROTRANSMITTERS dopamine, epinephrine, and norepinephrine.

See also BIOGENIC AMINE HYPOTHESIS; DOPAMINE HYPOTHESIS; INDOLAMINES; HISTAMINES.

cats and schizophrenia The current widespread practice of humans keeping cats as house pets did not begin until the middle of the 1700s and became very popular by the end of the 1800s. The rise in rates of insanity from 1750 until the present parallels this phenomenon. The question is: Do cats cause insanity? At least two controlled studies have found that persons with SCHIZOPHRENIA and BIPOLAR DISORDER have had a greater exposure to cats in childhood compared with persons who do not have those MENTAL DISORDERS. This issue has been explored in the context of VIRAL THEORIES by E. Fuller Torrey of the Stanley Research Foundation in Bethesda, Maryland. In the past decade several studies have found evidence that *Toxoplasmosis,* an infectious disease caused by a virus in cat feces or in undercooked meat, may be implicated in schizophrenia. Several studies have found antibodies to this virus in persons with schizophrenia as well as in the mothers of persons with schizophrenia.

CAT scan See CT SCAN.

causality, teleologic An aspect of the thinking of schizophrenics, as identified by Silvano ARIETI, in

which events in the world are interpreted as purposeful and due to somebody's will. Arieti compares this aspect of schizophrenic cognition to the thought patterns of children and people in primitive societies. Teleologic causality is contrasted with "deterministic causality," the more rational and scientific way in which most "civilized" normal adults attribute causes to events they experience.

cautery treatment A rather primitive form of "shock treatment" used on the mentally ill in the 18th and early 19th centuries in which they would be touched on the head or neck with a hot iron poker. Alternatively, the ancient technique of igniting moxa (small combustible cones from a plant that was introduced into Europe from Asia) on the skin to cauterize it. A treatment manual advocating the use of this method was written by French psychiatrist L. Valentin and published in 1815. ESQUIROL was greatly influenced by this book and successfully applied the treatment himself. This is how he described its use:

> I cannot omit making some remarks respecting the use of fire and moxa, applied to the top of the head, and over the occiput or neck in mania. Doctor L. Valentin has published some valuable observations concerning the cure of mania by the application of fire. I have many times applied the iron at a red heat to the neck, in mania complicated with fury, and sometimes with success.

Esquirol, J. E. D. *Mental Maladies, A Treatise on Insanity* (1838), trans. E. K. Hunt. Philadelphia: Lea & Blanchard, 1845; first published, 1838.

Valentin, L. *An Essay and Observations Concerning the Good Effects of the Actual Cautery, Applied to the Head in Various Disorders.* 8 vols. Nancy: 1815.

cera flexibilitas See CATATONIC WAVY FLEXIBILITY.

Cerletti, Ugo (1877–1963) Italian psychiatrist and inventor of ELECTROSHOCK (or "electroconvulsive") THERAPY. Cerletti was inspired to invent this treatment in a rather macabre way—by observing the reactions of pigs who were given electrical shocks just before slaughter. Together with his colleague, Lucio Bini, Cerletti perfected his new treatment, and the very first schizophrenic to receive this treatment did so on April 15, 1938. Electroconvulsive therapy, or ECT as it is commonly referred to, was considered a safer and more humane type of CONVULSIVE THERAPY than the one invented by Hungarian psychiatrist VON MEDUNA, in which convulsions were induced by pharmacological means.

Cerletti had a varied medical career, undergoing training in Turin, Rome, Paris, and Heidelberg, where he was exposed to Emil KRAEPELIN and his associates. Cerletti seems to have always been attracted to unconventional ideas about medical treatments for MENTAL DISORDERS. Near the end of his life, he attempted to find a chemical alternative to his own electroshock therapy, which would have none of the harsh side effects of the convulsive therapies. He concocted a serum, from the brains of animals that had been subjected to repeated electroshock sessions, that he thought would have the same therapeutic effect as electroshock therapy. This serum was alleged to contain a special chemical created in these animal brains from the treatments—vitalizing substances that Cerletti called *aeroagomines*—which he believed he could inject into schizophrenics and obtain similar results. However, Cerletti's work in this area has been discounted.

Cerletti, U. "Old and New Information about Electroshock," *American Journal of Psychiatry* 107 (1950): 87–94.

Cerletti, U., and L. Bini. "L'Electroshock," *Arch. Gen. Neurol. Psichiatr. Psicoanal.* 19 (1938): 266.

ceruloplasmin hypothesis In 1957 Swiss biochemist S. Akerfeldt announced research findings that suggested that an increased level of the copper-containing substance ceruloplasmin might be related to the development of SCHIZOPHRENIA. He developed a relatively simple test, which he thought could discriminate between the BIOLOGICAL MARKERS OF SCHIZOPHRENIA and other mental diseases.

Despite media attention, his theory was soon disproved when it was found that the level of ceruloplasmin depended on the amount of ascorbic acid (vitamin C) in the blood, and institutionalized psychiatric patients have been known to have low serum ascorbic acid levels.

See also TRANSMETHYLATION HYPOTHESIS OF SCHIZOPHRENIA.

Akerfeldt, S. "Oxidation of N_1N-Dimenthyl-p-phenylenediamine by Serum from Patients with Mental Disease," *Science* 125 (1957): 117–123.

Ceylon (Sri Lanka) A 1974 study of the prevalence rate for SCHIZOPHRENIA in Ceylon (now Sri Lanka) found a rate of 3.7 per 1,000.

Wijesinghe, C. P., et al. "Survey of Psychiatric Morbidity in a Semi-urban Population in Sri Lanka," *Acta Psychiatrica Scandinavica* 58 (1978): 413–441.

chemical restraint The use of drugs, as opposed to MECHANICAL RESTRAINTS (such as straps, STRAITJACKETS, MUFFS) to subdue psychiatric patients. Although ANTIPSYCHOTIC DRUGS were only brought into use in 1952 to treat psychotic disorders by reducing their symptoms, many different types of drugs have been used for centuries to restrain patients engaged in undesirable behaviors. Often such pharmacological agents were used as punishment. In the 18th and 19th centuries, such drugs may have been administered as a daily "physic" said to improve the health of a patient. Camphor and opiates in particular are mentioned in these early accounts. By the end of the 19th century many sedatives had been created that were then widely used (often to the point of excess) in mental hospitals. In his autobiography of his life as a mental patient, Clifford BEERS makes the following remarks about chemical restraint:

> Chemical restraint (sometimes called medical restraint) consists in the use of temporarily paralyzing drugs—hyoscine being the popular "dose." By the use of such drugs a troublesome patient may be rendered unconscious and kept so for hours at a time. Indeed, very troublesome patients (especially when attendants are scarce) are not infrequently kept in a stupefied condition for days, or even for weeks—but only in institutions where the welfare of the patients is lightly regarded.

Chemical restraint is one of the main instruments of psychiatric abuse in many countries.

See also ABUSE OF PSYCHIATRIC PATIENTS.

Beers, C. *A Mind That Found Itself.* New York: Doubleday, 1908.

chemistry of the brain See BIOCHEMICAL THEORIES OF SCHIZOPHRENIA.

cheromania A term used in the Middle Ages to describe the unnatural euphoric reaction to epidemics (such as the plague) and other disasters. It is equivalent to the elation reported in "maniacs" in archaic psychiatric textbooks and to the same behavior in persons undergoing a "manic episode" in today's nomenclature.

Chiarugi, Vincenzo (1759–1820) Sometimes referred to as the "Pinel of Italy." Chiarugi was an Italian physician appointed in 1789 by the Grand Duke Pietro Leopoldo of Tuscany to head the Hospital of Bonifacio in Florence. His work with the mentally ill at that hospital led to his publishing several works regarding mental illness, including a volume of 100 observations on mental illness. He believed that psychoses were the result of a deterioration of the brain, thus linking him with modern theories of the organic etiology of mental illness. He was also an early reformer and an opponent of cruel or unnecessary forms of restraint, and he shares an historic distinction as one of the earliest proponents of nonrestraint policies, with PINEL in France and William Tuke of the YORK RETREAT in England. A translation of an indicative passage from one of Chiarugi's works is provided by historian of psychiatry George Mora:

> It is a supreme moral duty and medical obligation to respect the insane individual as a person. It is especially necessary for the person who treats the mental patient to gain his confidence and trust. It is best, therefore, to be tactful and understanding and try to lead the patient to the truth and to instill reason in him little by little in a kind way. . . . The attitude of doctors and nurses must be authoritative and impressive, but at the same time pleasant and adapted to the impaired mind of the patient. . . . Generally it is better to follow the patient's inclinations and give him as many comforts as is advisable from a medical and practical standpoint.

Chiarugi, V. *Della pazzia in genere e in specie trattato medico analitico con una centuria di observazioni.* Florence: 1973–1974.

———. *On Insanity and Its Classification,* ed. and trans. G. Mora. Canton, Mass.: Science History Publications, 1987.

Mora, G. Vincenzo. "Chiarugi (1759–1820) and His Psychiatric Reform in Florence in the Late 18th Century," *Journal of the History of Medicine* 14 (1959): 431.

childhood-onset schizophrenia Childhood-onset schizophrenia is a very rare form of SCHIZOPHRENIA. It is defined by the onset of the typical psychotic symptoms of schizophrenia before the 18th birthday. This disorder is now sometimes called "neurodevelopmental schizophrenia." Although it had practically disappeared from the scientific literature, in 1994 several studies were published that resurrected interest in this disorder. Since then, there has been an explosion of research on the very small population of children who could be located that have childhood-onset schizophrenia. Although childhood-onset schizophrenia is rare, it resembles the "adolescent-onset" and "adult-onset" versions of schizophrenia. There are similarities between childhood, adolescent, and adult-onset schizophrenias in terms of their poor premorbid histories, their performance on psychological tests, and certain neuroanatomical and neuroimaging findings. Thus, it is thought that childhood-onset schizophrenia is continuous with at least some of the later-onset versions of schizophrenia and not a separate disease process. For example, abnormalities in the cerebral ventricles of children with schizophrenia tend to worsen in adolescence. Also, in MAGNETIC RESONANCE SPECTROSCOPY IMAGING studies, smaller than normal regional chemical signals for N-acetylaspartate (NAA) are found in childhood-onset schizophrenics, adult-onset schizophrenics, and biological relatives of schizophrenics. In general, the course of childhood-onset schizophrenia is more severe than the later-onset varieties of this disease.

No one knows why there is an earlier age of onset in this disorder. Several possible factors behind early onset are: (1) increased genetic load, especially if both parents are schizophrenic or have a high-risk for schizophrenia themselves, (2) increased exposure to harmful environmental forces, either during fetal development, infancy, or early childhood, that affect the brain and nervous system, (3) precocious brain maturation (the brain develops abnormally fast in some respects and not in others, causing a disconnection between different areas of brain functioning), and (4) perhaps a premature exposure of the nervous system to hormones that are only usually released during puberty.

Other names for this disorder that can still be found in the literature are childhood schizophrenia, developmental psychosis, childhood psychosis, symbiotic psychosis, and atypical development. *DSM-IV* (1994) allows the diagnosis of schizophrenia in children only if prominent DELUSIONS and HALLUCINATIONS are present for at least a month in a child who has already been known to have a history of autistic disorder or a pervasive developmental disorder.

Since the neurodevelopmental model of schizophrenia has emerged as a dominant scientific paradigm, the study of childhood-onset schizophrenia is combined with the data from studies of FETAL NEURAL DEVELOPMENT, adolescent-onset, adult-onset, and LATE-ONSET schizophrenia to construct a picture of the natural course of this terrible disease over the human life span.

Alaghband-Rad, J., S. D. Hamburger, J. N. Giedd, J. A. Frazier, and J. L. Rapoport. "Childhood-onset Schizophrenia:

Biological Markers in Relation to Clinical Characteristics," *American Journal of Psychiatry* 154 (1997): 64–68.

Howells, J. G., and W. R. Guirguis. "Childhood Schizophrenia 20 Years Later," *American Journal of Psychiatry* 41 (1984): 123–128.

McKenna, K., C. T. Gordon, and J. L. Rapoport. "Childhood Onset Schizophrenia: Timely Neurobiological Research," *Journal of the American Academy of Child and Adolescent Psychiatry* 33 (1994): 771–781.

Murray, R. M. "Toward an Aetiological Classification of Schizophrenia," *Lancet* 1 (1985): 1,023–1,026.

Rapoport, J. L., J. Giedd, S. Kumra, et al. "Childhood-onset Schizophrenia: Progressive Ventricular Change during Adolescence," *Archives of General Psychiatry* 54 (1997): 897–903.

childhood psychosis See CHILDHOOD SCHIZOPHRENIA.

children at risk for schizophrenia See HIGH-RISK STUDIES.

chiromania An archaic term for madness caused by MASTURBATION, a common belief of psychiatrists throughout the 19th century and earlier. It is derived from the Greek words for "hand" and "insanity."

chlorpromazine The first true ANTIPSYCHOTIC DRUG, approved for use in the United States in March 1954. The drug is a PHENOTHIAZINE and is more commonly known by its trade name, THORAZINE; it was named by the manufacturer, Smith, Kline, and French, after the Norse god of thunder, Thor.

choromania An archaic term for the uncontrollable impulse to dance or sway. The famous "dancing manias" that were epidemic in the Middle Ages are another example of this. Perhaps the classic reference to "dancing manias" or "frenzies" is the work of the 19th-century German scholar J. F. C. Hecker, and translations of representative excerpts of his writings can be found in the appendix to a book by psychiatrist Harold Mersky of the London Psychiatric Hospital, London, Ontario, Canada.

Hecker, J. F. C. *Die grossen Volkskrankheiten des Mittelalters, Historisch-pathologische Untersuchungen . . .*, ed. August Hirsch. Berlin: Th.Chr.Fr.Enslin, 1865.

Mersky, H. *The Analysis of Hysteria.* London: Baillière Tindall, 1979.

chromosome Within the nucleus of each cell in the human body there are rodlike organic bodies (normally 46 in humans) called chromosomes, which are the bearers of GENES. Each chromosome is made up of an extended double helix of DNA and associated proteins. Chromosomes are arranged in 23 different pairs. One pair, made up of the X and Y chromosomes, is called the sex chromosomes and is responsible for the transmission of genetic information regarding sex differentiation. The other 22 pairs (numbered from 1 to 22) are called autosomes. The 46 chromosomes in humans were first observed directly by scientists when new techniques were developed by Tijo and Levan in 1956. Since that time, a series of studies have been conducted on large samples of psychiatric patients of varying diagnoses—especially schizophrenics—with little success in detecting specific abnormalities. This has changed with the development of clearer research diagnostic criteria for schizophrenia and the more advanced research technologies of molecular genetics.

A series of techniques known as chromosome mapping attempt to determine the position of specific genes on specific chromosomes and then construct a diagram of each chromosome showing the relative position of genes. There are estimated to be between 25,000 to 30,000 human genes, most of which are yet to be identified.

See also GENETICS STUDIES.

Tijo, H., and A. Levan. "The Chromosome Number of Man," *Hereditas* 42 (1956): 1–6.

chronic delusional states in French psychiatry National differences have always played a role in the history of science and medicine. In PSYCHIATRY, where most MENTAL DISORDERS are syndromes (clusters of symptoms) that do not meet the criteria for disease in the sense of having an identifiable

underlying cellular pathology, national traditions and culture-specific folklore shape (socially construct) clusters of symptoms into diagnostic syndromes that may differ from standard classification of mental disorders that are found in *ICD-10* and *DSM-IV-TR*. Historically, this has been especially true in France, where diagnostic systems arising in Germany (such as that of Emil KRAEPELIN) and "Anglo-Saxon" countries such as England and the United States have met with resistance. The French antipathy toward German psychiatric classification began in the early 1900s as a reflection of the political and cultural nationalism that played a role in bringing about the First World War (1914–18). Even today, definitions of what constitutes SCHIZOPHRENIA, the delusional disorders, and the brief psychotic disorders are viewed differently in French psychiatry.

Since approximately 1909, French psychiatry has placed delusions at the center of its definition of psychotic disorders. This trend began with the work of Valentin Magnan (1835–1916) and his colleagues in the 1880s on "chronic delusional insanity." However, although Magnan linked his "systematic delusions" to processes of DEGENERATION or nondegeneration, by the First World War, degeneration theory began to decline in importance in French psychiatry. Again, anti-German sentiment may have played a role, because German psychiatry emphasized hereditary causes and disorders with chronic, progressively deteriorating course like DEMENTIA PRAECOX. Since then, French psychiatry has adopted an elaborate classification system for chronic delusional states that, under current diagnostic systems, might be regarded as forms of PARANOID SCHIZOPHRENIA, PERSISTENT DELUSIONAL DISORDERS, DELUSIONAL DISORDER, and PARANOID PERSONALITY DISORDER. To this day French psychiatrists are more likely to emphasize nonschizophrenia delusional syndromes and more narrowly diagnose schizophrenia in everyday practice.

Currently, chronic delusional states are divided into three main categories:

(1) chronic interpretative psychosis (also known as systematized or paranoic psychoses)
(2) chronic hallucinatory psychosis
(3) chronic imaginative (or paraphrenic or fantastic) psychosis

Chronic interpretive psychosis There are two types of chronic interpretive psychosis, intellectual delusional states and emotional delusional states. Both were described in 1909 by Paul Serieux (1864–1947) and J. M. Capgras in their seminal book, *Les Folies Raisonnantes: le Delire d'Interpretation (Intelligent Insanity: Delusional Interpretation)*. In intellectual delusional states, facts that were perceived correctly at first are misinterpreted due to false reasoning. Eventually the delusions arising from this misinterpretation progressively conquer all other aspects of mental activity. The delusions are systematized and complex, there are no prominent hallucinations, intellectual functioning is unimpaired, and the course is chronic. In emotional delusional states, the delusional premise does not spread beyond the theme of the delusion and the persons or persons involved in the delusion. The two most common variants of emotional delusional states are (a) vindictive delusional states (e.g., the "litigious paranoia" of persons who are constantly involved in legal suits against others whom they perceive as having "wronged" them) and (b) sentimental delusional states (delusional jealousy and erotomania).

Chronic hallucinatory psychosis This disorder was first described in 1911 by Gilbert-Louis-Simeon Ballet (1853–1916), a Parisian psychiatrist working at the famous mental hospital the Hotel-Dieu. The symptoms of this disorder, which Ballet believed was rooted in HEREDITY, were:

(a) persistent hallucinatory activity
(b) delusions, most frequently of persecution
(c) clear sensorium, unimpaired speech, relatively normal behavior, and unimpaired intellectual functioning.

In more recent French psychiatric descriptions of this disorder, additional features are:

(a) onset in middle or late adult life
(b) absence of schizophrenic thought disorder
(c) relatively good functioning prior to the onset of the disorder

Chronic imaginative psychosis This delusional disorder is characterized by magical thinking, fantastic and grandiose delusions, and confabulation. All this is in stark contrast to the otherwise good contact with reality the person exhibits. This disorder was first described by Ferdinand-Pierre-Louis-Ernest Dupré (1862–1921) in 1910 in an article in the journal *L'Encephale (The Brain).* This diagnosis is rarely made by French psychiatrists today.

The continuing influence of the chronic delusional states of French psychiatry is reflected in the diagnostic criteria for DELUSIONAL DISORDER in *DSM-IV-TR* (2000) and PERSISTENT DELUSIONAL DISORDERS in *ICD-10* (1992).

See also PARANOIA; PARAPHRENIA.

Magnan, V. "Chronic Delusional Insanity of Systematic Evolution," trans. A. Marie and J. MacPherson, *American Journal of Insanity* 51 (1895): 37–57; 175–198; 524–538; 52 (1896): 397–415.

Pichot, P. "The Diagnosis and Classification of Mental Disorders in the French-speaking Countries: Background, Current Values and Comparison with other Classifications." In *Sources and Traditions of Classification in Psychiatry,* edited by N. Sartorius, et al. Toronto: Hofgrete and Huber, 1990.

chronic schizophrenia The idea that some forms of SCHIZOPHRENIA seem to follow a chronic lifetime course without improvement is as old as the concept of schizophrenia itself. It has always been observed throughout the history of PSYCHIATRY that there were some psychotic disorders that improved and some that ended in permanent deterioration or "dementia." Indeed, KRAEPELIN's concept of "DEMENTIA PRAECOX," which he formed in 1893, was based entirely on the idea that it was a progressively degenerative disorder with a poor prognosis. He called this mental deterioration the *Verblodungs-process.* However, his 1899 definition of the MANIC-DEPRESSIVE PSYCHOSES (see also BIPOLAR DISORDER) was of a group of psychotic disorders with a relatively good prognosis for improvement. Eugen BLEULER produced the still prevalent picture of schizophrenia as having acute and chronic forms in his 1911 *Dementia Praecox, Or the Group of Schizophrenias.*

Schizophrenia has long been conceptualized as pairs of opposites across many different dimensions. The acute/chronic distinction and the reactive/process distinction are essentially equivalent, expressing the idea that there is a form of schizophrenia with a sudden onset and a better prognosis (acute or reactive) and a form that has an insidious onset that gradually develops from early in life and does not seem to get any better (chronic or process). In recent years the term *chronic schizophrenia* has been falling out of use in the clinical research literature (although it is still part of the everyday jargon of mental health professionals) due to the appearance of more descriptive terms for this apparent strain of schizophrenia.

The traditional notion of "chronic schizophrenia" is now being redefined. In the psychiatric research literature chronic schizophrenia is characterized by its NEGATIVE SYMPTOMS, such as restricted emotional range, poverty of speech, reduction of curiosity in the immediate environment around a person, an apathetic or diminished sense of "purpose" in the afflicted person, and a reduced need to engage in social interactions. Negative symptoms are based on the idea that something is "taken away" from a person. When they endure, they have been called "deficit symptoms." There is a vast amount of research that also shows that chronic schizophrenics also show certain "soft neurological signs" and sometimes structural and functional abnormalities in the brain.

See also ACUTE-CHRONIC DISTINCTION; COURSE AND OUTCOME OF SCHIZOPHRENIA; CROW'S HYPOTHESIS; DEFICIT SYMPTOMS; DEGENERATION; PINEL-HASLAM SYNDROME; POSITIVE SYMPTOMS.

circular insanity The name given in 1854 by FALRET to what we now call BIPOLAR DISORDER. The term was widely used in English-language literature until KRAEPELIN's new definition of the disorder and invention of the term MANIC-DEPRESSIVE ILLNESS. People stricken with this mental disorder were often referred to as "circulars," much in the same way that we presently refer to them as "manic-depressives."

See also MANIC-DEPRESSIVE ILLNESS.

Ritti, A. "Circular Insanity." In *A Dictionary of Psychological Medicine*, 2 vols., edited by D. H. Tuke. Philadelphia: P. Blakiston & Son, 1892.

circulating swing A form of treatment for the mentally ill that was popular throughout the 18th and into the early 19th centuries in which patients would be rapidly spun around in a circular motion. Although Dutch physician Herman Boerhaave (1668–1738) may have been the first to use such a device, the first working model of a circulating swing is credited to English physician John Mason Cox, who describes the device in his 1806 book, *Practical Observations on Insanity:*

> His *swing* formed by suspending a Windsor chair to a hook in the ceiling, by two ropes to hind legs and two to fore, joined by a sliding knot to regulate elevation: patient in a straight waistcoat, and a leathern strap around his waist, buckled to the bars behind; legs fastened by straps to the front ones of the chair; then turned around.

Reflecting the many mechanical variations of this basic concept by innovative physicians in other asylums, it was also called the "GYRATOR" or "gyrating chair," "rotary machine," "spinning chair," "rotating swing" or "chair" and also "Darwin's chair" or "machine," since it was suggested by Erasmus Darwin (1731–1802), the physician grandfather of Charles Darwin, as a form of treatment for patients with many different types of ailment. The device attributed to Darwin consisted of a boxlike chair (or bed, apparently), which was suspended by an iron rod from the ceiling. The patient would be tightly strapped into this seat. A small wooden platform was built next to the chair on which another person could push another rod back and forth, which generated the rotation of the rod on which the chair was suspended. Psychiatrists Alexander and Selesnick reproduce an 18th-century illustration of this machine in their book on the history of psychiatry.

It is said that the circulating swing could be driven up to 100 rotations per minute, causing considerable disorientation, vomiting, purging, bleeding from the eyes, and eventual unconsciousness in patients. Needless to say, treatment sessions lasted only a matter of minutes. ESQUIROL, who called it "the machine of Darwin" in 1838, was apparently the first to introduce this rotary machine to France, but he discourages its use along with the following report:

> Doctor Martin, physician of the hospital at Antiquaille, where to this day the insane of Lyons are treated, has informed me that he has been frightened at the accidents which the insane had met with, who had been submitted to the influence of this machine. They fall into a state of syncope, and had also copious evacuations both by vomiting and purging, which prostrated them extremely.

Esquirol notes at the bottom of the page of his *Mental Maladies* in 1838 that, "Since the first edition of this article was published, the rotary machine has been every where abandoned."

American psychiatrist Benjamin RUSH was an enthusiastic advocate of his "gyrater," as well as a stationary "coercion chair," which he referred to as his "TRANQUILLIZER." However, he utilized a form of the circulating swing and had suggestions for technical improvements on the machine. The circulating swing was also part of the regimen recommended by 18th-century Englishman John HASLAM (of "Bedlam").

See also HAYNER'S WHEEL; MECHANICAL RESTRAINT.

Alexander, F. G., and S. T. Selesnick. *The History of Psychiatry.* New York: Harper & Row, 1966.

Esquirol, J. E. D. *Mental Maladies, A Treatise on Insanity,* trans. E. K. Hunt. Philadelphia: Lea and Blanchard, 1845; first published, 1838.

Scull, A. "The Domestication of Madness," *Medical History* 27 (1983): 233–248.

clanging A frequently observed speech anomaly, in persons with psychotic disorders, in which words are spoken for the way they sound, rather than for what they mean. This can sometimes appear like bizarre punning or attempts at rhyming. "I am the needle-nose who knows. Like the rose in his hair, OK?" is an example of the clanging found in psychotic speech patterns. BLEULER

(in 1911) referred to these language anomalies as "clang associations."

See also LANGUAGE ABNORMALITIES IN SCHIZOPHRENIA.

Clérambault-Kandinsky syndrome A syndrome characterized by delusions of being controlled. It was identified by Gaétan Gatian de Clérambault (1872–1934), a French psychiatrist who was prominent in identifying several CHRONIC DELUSIONAL STATES IN FRENCH PSYCHIATRY.

Clérambault's syndrome (or de Clérambault's syndrome) See EROTOMANIA.

climate as a cause of insanity Many early authorities on mental illness claimed that the nature of a particular climate could cause such disorders. Both Benjamin RUSH and J. E. D. ESQUIROL agreed that temperate climates, which had frequent alterations of hot and cold, were the most likely to cause insanity. These ideas exist in a modern form in studies of the EPIDEMIOLOGY of mental disorders, which show that incidence and prevalence rates are different in different parts of the world—particularly for SCHIZOPHRENIA.

See also VIRAL THEORIES OF SCHIZOPHRENIA.

clown syndrome See *FAXENSYNDROM*.

clozapine See ANTIPSYCHOTIC DRUGS.

CNS The acronym for "central nervous system," essentially designating the brain, the spinal cord, and their associated processes. The "peripheral nervous system" refers to the sensory (afferent) and motor (efferent) nerve cells that connect the remainder of the body with the central nervous system.

Cogentin See ANTIPARKINSONIAN DRUGS.

cognitive-behavior therapy See BEHAVIOR THERAPY.

cognitive dysmetria theory of schizophrenia A DISCONNECTION THEORY OF SCHIZOPHRENIA proposed by Nancy Andreasen of the University of Iowa College of Medicine. Relying primarily on functional brain imaging data, Andreasen and her associates have developed a model that implicates the "connectivity" of NEURAL CIRCUITS between the prefrontal region of the frontal lobe of the brain, the subcortical nuclei of the thalamus, and the cerebellum. A disruption in this circuitry produces what Andreasen has called "cognitive dysmetria." Cognitive dysmetria means the person with schizophrenia has difficulties in prioritizing, processing, coordinating, and responding to information. This "poor mental coordination" is a fundamental cognitive deficit in SCHIZOPHRENIA and may account for the broad diversity of its symptoms.

See also ABOULIA.

Andreasen, N. A., et al. "'Cognitive Dysmetria' as an Integrative Theory of Schizophrenia: A Dysfunction in Cortical-Subcortical-Cerebellar Circuitry?" *Schizophrenia Bulletin* 24 (1998): 203–218.

cognitive studies of schizophrenia In the late 1950s a revolution began in the way experimental studies in psychology were conducted. Advances in cybernetics, linguistics (particularly the work of Noam Chomsky), and the computer sciences gave rise to a new type of psychology. Called "cognitive psychology," it borrowed the metaphors of information processing from the computer sciences to approach the study of human thought and experience in a new way—by examining the human mind's processes of encoding, transforming, storing, and using information for regulating behavior. Thought and language abnormalities had long been noted by SCHIZOPHRENIA researchers, but cognitive psychology extended the study of schizophrenia to find patterns of information processing in sensation, perception, memory, motor (movement) processes, and, in particular, the ability to focus one's attention. Studies comparing schizophrenic and normal information processing almost always find significant differences between these two groups. One line of evidence tends to indicate that some schizophrenics

have information processing problems associated with the left hemisphere of the brain when compared to normals. Furthermore, cognitive studies have helped document evidence for distinct subdivisions within schizophrenics, thus giving more suggestive evidence for subtype differences than had hitherto been possible with strictly behavioral or biological approaches. An example of this is the highly successful demonstration across numerous studies that there are distinct differences between the paranoid subtype of schizophrenia and the nonparanoid subtypes. Indeed, a special issue of *Schizophrenia Bulletin,* edited by experimental psychologist Peter Magaro, was devoted to this evidence in 1981. An excellent review of the experimental studies of "schizophrenic cognition" was published by Canadian psychologist Leonard George in 1985.

In the 1990s the rise of the neurodevelopmental model inspired researchers to investigate new aspects of the cognitive deficits that people with schizophrenia exhibit. The cognitive studies of disorders of ATTENTION are now grounded in neurophysiology in studies of SENSORIMOTOR GATING, the idea that the thalamus acts as a "gate" that separates relevant from irrelevant stimuli and then relays this information to the appropriate circuits of neural networks in the brain. In the case of schizophrenia, "gating" breaks down and irrelevant stimuli competes with relevant stimuli in the brain, causing the experiences and behaviors we observe as the symptoms of schizophrenia. Many studies have found deficits in the working memory of schizophrenics, which is the type of short-term memory needed for tasks such as memorizing an unfamiliar telephone number just long enough to be able to dial it before forgetting it. Working memory is often compared to the RAM facility of a computer.

See also NEUROPSYCHOLOGICAL STUDIES OF SCHIZOPHRENIA.

George, L., and R. Neufeld. "Cognition and Symptomatology in Schizophrenia," *Schizophrenia Bulletin* 11 (1985): 264–285.

Knight, R. A., and S. M. Silverstein. "The Role of Cognitive Psychology in Guiding Research on Cognitive Deficits in Schizophrenia." In *Origins and Development of Schizophrenia: Advances in Experimental Psychopathology,* edited by M. F. Lenzenweger and R. H. Dwarkin. Washington, D.C.: American Psychological Association, 1998.

Magaro, P. A., ed. "Special Issue: Paranoia," *Schizophrenia Bulletin* 7 (1981): 4.

collective insanity See FOLIE À DEUX.

Columbia-Greystone Project A PSYCHOSURGERY research project initiated in 1947 combining the psychiatric research scientists of Columbia University Medical Center in New York City and the psychiatric patients of the New Jersey State Hospital at Greystone Park. The goal was to refine the methods of psychosurgery as a treatment for mental disorders, specifically to find the critical locations in the frontal lobes where more limited incisions could maximize the benefits and minimize the sometimes terrible after-effects. A review of this research was published in 1949. The group called itself the "Columbia-Greystone Associates" and was co-led by Fred Mettler, a professor of anatomy at Columbia University, and Marcus Currey, the medical superintendent and CEO of the Greystone Park State Hospital. Mettler was also a board member of the NATIONAL INSTITUTE OF MENTAL HEALTH (NIMH) at the time, and his influence led to the large supporting grant from the NIMH, totaling hundreds of thousands of dollars, that funded the project.

The project had two phases: a 1947–48 study and a 1951–52 study. In the first study, the more important of the two, a series of 19 patients underwent a psychosurgical procedure known as a TOPECTOMY, a more localized and focal procedure than the traditional "ice pick" lobotomies performed by Walter FREEMAN, the world's leading authority on psychosurgery. They also explored other "open" methods (i.e., procedures that required the surgical opening of the skull), but their results were all rather inconclusive. Realizing the less than spectacular results they were getting with their methods, the associates then invited Freeman to perform a series of his famous TRANSORBITAL LOBOTOMIES on a series of patients at Greystone Park in October 1948. Of this tragic failure, which

led him to abandon the hope of an assembly-line approach to treating chronic psychiatric patients (largely schizophrenics) with transorbital lobotomies, Freeman later wrote:

> Of the 18 patients operated upon . . . there was not a single one that I would have chosen from my own practice. The results were as bad as I anticipated. Furthermore, in one patient the icepick broke, leaving a small bit embedded in the base of the brain. Fortunately, there was no unfavorable effects, but the embarrassment was mine [cited in Shutts, 1982].

Mettler, F. A., ed. *Selective Partial Ablation of the Frontal Cortex.* New York: Hoeber, 1949.

coma therapy In the 20th century, several biological treatments were developed for SCHIZOPHRENIA that were based on the deliberate induction of a comatose state in the patient, with the assumption that the patient would reawaken in a much improved state. The most famous variety of coma therapy was INSULIN COMA THERAPY, developed by psychiatrist Manfred SAKEL and his associates in Austria in 1936, in which a deep hypoglycemic coma was induced in schizophrenics as a sort of "shock" to their system. While coma therapy was widely used (along with PSYCHOSURGERY and ELECTROSHOCK THERAPY) throughout the 1940s and 1950s, it disappeared after the introduction of ANTIPSYCHOTIC DRUGS for the treatment of schizophrenia. Other forms of coma therapy for schizophrenia involved inducing a comatose state through inhaling pure nitrogen or by injections of atropine, but neither of these forms were widely utilized. No rational theory explaining why coma therapy worked for some patients was ever formulated.

See also NITROGEN INHALATION THERAPY.

command hallucination Despite media depictions of "psychotic killers" who carry out murderous crimes "because God told me to," the phenomenon of command hallucinations is relatively uncommon in psychotics. When such hallucinations are present, they tend to be in the form of a "voice" telling the person to do various acts, some of which may be harmful to self or others. Many patients resist the commands and experience great fear and anxiety because of them. For example, a patient once cried out to the author in the middle of a conversation, "They're trying to get me to kill myself, but I won't do it!" He apparently had just then experienced a command-type AUDITORY HALLUCINATION urging him to commit suicide. Sometimes, however, psychotic individuals *do* give in to the commands, and suicide and/or acts of violence can be carried out against others.

Commissioners in Lunacy Commissioned by the British government in 1845, this committee of 15 individuals was endowed with the power to inspect existing madhouses and asylums and refuse or approve the licensure of new ones. The commissioners' jurisdiction extended over England and Wales, unlike previous regulatory boards, which had jurisdiction just over London and a seven mile radius around it. The direct precursors to the Commissioners in Lunacy were the committee of five medical commissioners from the College of Physicians empowered in 1774, and its successor, the Metropolitan Commissioners in Lunacy, established in 1828.

commitment One of the most frightening experiences anyone can imagine is being involuntarily committed to a MENTAL HOSPITAL. The many autobiographical accounts of such traumatic events by ex-mental patients have served only to stimulate the public's imagination, and they have been depicted frequently in fictional accounts in literature, motion pictures and on television. There have been many critics of the role of psychiatrists, which gives them extraordinary power over others usually granted only to judges or the police, and many of these critics have been psychiatrists themselves, notably Thomas Szaz and R. D. LAING (1927–89). Szaz caused a stir in 1963 with his book *Law, Liberty and Psychiatry* because he called for eliminating all forms of involuntary commitment. In his 1985

autobiography, Laing bluntly expresses his view of the powers of psychiatry when he writes:

> Thus, society expects psychiatry to perform two very special functions. To lock certain people up, and to stop and, if possible, change certain states of mind and types of conduct in the name of curing mental illnesses . . . These two tasks are placed on psychiatry. It is ensured that psychiatrists carry out these tasks by giving them the *power* to do so, a power *they* can't refuse, if they want to practice psychiatry.

In the United States, each state is responsible for making its own commitment laws. In most cases, they are understandably vague (given the great variety of symptoms and behaviors exhibited in persons with severe mental disorders), but since the 1970s states have generally focused narrowly on the issue of dangerousness, specifically whether the person is a danger to himself or others. Generally it takes the written approval of only one or two psychiatrists to commit someone involuntarily to a mental hospital. That such a process is needed in the treatment of severe mental illness is largely unquestioned, since in floridly psychotic states of mind people can—and do—engage in harmful acts against themselves or others. Judgment is impaired during such episodes, and a person who is indeed suffering from a severe mental illness may not know that he or she requires help. This is known as lack of INSIGHT.

Most of the laws governing commitment have been transformed over the years to become more humane, largely due to the lobbying efforts of patient advocacy groups since the end of the 1800s. It has become progressively more difficult to commit someone to a psychiatric hospital, and laws have been changed to require frequent psychiatric and judicial review to expedite the earliest possible release.

One of the abuses of the power of commitment held by psychiatrists was the commitment of married women to "insane asylums" at their husband's request even though they were not truly insane. Such power was granted to the superintendents of asylums by some state legislatures, notably in Illinois, whose 1851 commitment law declared: "married women . . . may be entered or detained in the hospital (the state asylum at Jacksonville, Illinois) at the request of the husband of the woman . . . without evidence of insanity required in other cases." These laws were eventually changed after the intense lobbying efforts of one such woman, Elizabeth Parsons Ware Packard, who in 1860 was committed by her husband (the Reverend Theophilus Packard) to the Illinois State Asylum at Jacksonville and was incarcerated there for three years. She apparently drew her husband's ire for expressing philosophical differences on religious matters. The commitment was carried out by two doctors who were members of her husband's church and judged her insane by merely feeling her pulse. She kept a diary while in the asylum and produced many publications based on it over the years. An 1867 investigation of the Jacksonville asylum found 148 such women committed there. Packard persuaded the Illinois state legislature to change the commitment law that year, and she persuaded Iowa to do the same in 1872. Efforts by groups in the MENTAL HYGIENE MOVEMENT working with the AMERICAN PSYCHIATRIC ASSOCIATION helped to abolish such inhumane laws in the United States by the 1930s.

See also LUNACY TRIALS.

Laing, R. D. *Wisdom, Madness, and Folly: The Making of a Psychiatrist.* New York: McGraw-Hill, 1985.

Packard, E. P. W. *Marital Power Exemplified in Mrs. Packard's Trial, and Self-Defense from the Charge of Insanity; or, Three Year's Imprisonment for Religious Belief, by the Arbitrary Will of a Husband, with an Appeal to the Government to so Change the Laws so as to Afford Legal Protection to Married Women.* Hartford: Case, Lockwood, 1866.

Szaz, T. *Law, Liberty and Psychiatry.* New York: Macmillan, 1963.

communicated insanity See FOLIE À DEUX.

community mental health centers Following the pattern of the DEINSTITUTIONALIZATION of the mentally ill from psychiatric institutions in the United States in the 1950s, it soon became clear that these discharged patients were not receiving the proper

care in the community. In a 1961 report entitled *Action for Mental Health,* the Joint Commission on Mental Illness and Health recommended the establishment of federally funded community-based mental health centers so that seriously ill patients could be treated closer to home and be kept out of psychiatric hospitals. In a special message to Congress in February 1963, President John F. Kennedy proposed a system of "Community Mental Health Centers" to be set up around the United States. President Kennedy optimistically argued that, "when carried out, reliance on the cold mercy of custodial isolation will be supplanted by the open warmth of community concern and capability." Community care was designed to be a replacement for confinement in state hospitals.

Unfortunately, as many studies have shown, right from the start CMHCs have treated only a small percentage of discharged psychiatric patients—at most, only 10 to 15 percent of the new cases admitted to the CMHCs were for people with serious psychiatric diagnoses such as SCHIZOPHRENIA. Instead of providing services to the seriously mentally ill—as was the idea behind the plan—CMHCs have overwhelmingly provided counseling and psychotherapy for people with marital problems, family problems, relationship problems, and other interpersonal problems. In many settings valuable treatment resources are being drained by court-mandated "therapy" for individuals as a form of "pretrial intervention" so that they do not have to schedule full trials and be sent to already overcrowded jails. Such individuals often include sociopaths (especially juveniles) who are poorly motivated to change their behavior and see their weekly appointments with a therapist at the local CMHC as merely a way of staying out of jail.

It was estimated that, by 1987, more than 800 CMHCs were granted more than $3 billion in federal funds to maintain this system but without any appreciable improvement in the care of the seriously mentally ill. An illuminating critique of the CMHC system in the United States and its almost exclusive treatment of the "worried well" is provided by psychiatrist E. Fuller Torrey in his section on "The Failure of the Community Health Centers" in his book, *Surviving Schizophrenia.*

Goldman, H. H., et al. "Community Mental Health Centers and the Treatment of Severe Mental Disorder," *American Journal of Psychiatry* 137 (1980): 83–86.

Torrey, E. F. *Surviving Schizophrenia: A Family Manual.* 2nd ed. New York: Harper & Row, 1988.

comorbidity Comorbidity refers to the simultaneous presence in an individual of two or more distinctly different diseases or mental disorders. Their simultaneous presence may be due entirely to coincidence. In epidemiology, comorbidity is studied to see if there is a correlation between the two or more diseases or disorders arising in the same persons at the same time, implying perhaps a deeper, causal relationship. Correlations can be positive, meaning that when one disease is present there is a higher than expected rate of another specific disease also being present. In situations of negative comorbidity, there is a lower than expected rate of the occurrence of another specific disease.

It has long been noted that persons with SCHIZOPHRENIA suffer from a variety of physical diseases that are due to poor self-care or neglect within the medical system. It has been estimated that between 46 percent and 80 percent of inpatients and between 20 percent and 40 percent of outpatients with schizophrenia have been found to have ongoing physical diseases. In about half these cases the medical condition was thought to make schizophrenic symptoms worse. The true rates of comorbidity of schizophrenia with other diseases or disorders is unknown because such persons are deliberately left out of research studies on schizophrenia in order to eliminate possible confounding variables in the interpretation of results.

Comorbidity with other diseases and disorders Persons with schizophrenia have higher-than-expected rates of infection (particularly pulmonary tuberculosis), diabetes, arteriosclerotic disease and myocardial infarction, middle ear disease, irritable bowel syndrome, and HIV infection. In the United States, it is estimated that approximately 5 percent to 7 percent of persons with schizophrenia are infected with HIV.

On the other hand, schizophrenia is negatively comorbid with rheumatoid arthritis and cancer,

particularly lung cancer in men with schizophrenia. This finding is in stark contrast to everyday clinical experience with schizophrenia as it is apparent many persons with schizophrenia are heavy smokers. Indeed, the best estimates based on research are that 73 percent of males and 53 percent of females who are schizophrenic smoke cigarettes. No one knows the reasons behind this negative comorbidity of schizophrenia and lung cancer, but some have suggested that ANTIPSYCHOTIC DRUGS may provide some sort of long-term anticancer protection.

Substance abuse is the most common comorbid disorder associated with schizophrenia. Use of alcohol, cannabis (marijuana), cocaine, methamphetamine and a whole host of other substances, legal and illegal, are known to be contributing factors in relapse and may be involved in triggering the first psychotic episode. In a 10-country study conducted by the WORLD HEALTH ORGANIZATION (WHO) it was found that 57 percent of males with schizophrenia abused alcohol, and another 24 to 41 percent of all persons with schizophrenia abused street drugs, primarily cannabis and cocaine. The WHO singled out cannabis use (smoking marijuana) as a significant predictor of poor outcome, indicating that it is associated with relapse.

Jablensky, A. "The Epidemiological Horizon." In *Schizophrenia.* 2nd ed., edited by S. R. Hirsch and D. Weinberger. Cambridge: Blackwell, 2003.

Compazine See ANTIPSYCHOTIC DRUGS.

complex A term used by C. G. JUNG to describe organized clusters of feelings that take on a life of their own and that exist in all of us. The term was first used by the German philosopher and psychiatrist Theodor Ziehen (1862–1950) as "emotionally charged complex of representations" (*gefühlsbetonter Vorstellungskomplex*) to explain the underlying cluster of feelings that caused delayed reactions in the course of his experiments with the word association test, later made famous by Jung. Jung thought that the mind's basic structure is made up of autonomous "feeling-toned complexes" (*gefühlsbetonter Komplex*), nodal points, or clusters of affect whose dynamics are observed in the phenomenon we call "personality." Jung felt that the "ego" was essentially a complex, and although it was the most important one, it was only one among many. The ego could be influenced and even paralyzed by other such clusters of feelings, which we experience when we suddenly feel we are losing control when mad, joyful, etc., in everyday life. Everyone has complexes, but in normals they work together within a functional system that is adaptive for the survival of the individual. In mental disorders, particularly severe ones such as schizophrenia or multiple personality disorder, their strength is greater and their autonomy from the ego more extreme due to DISSOCIATION, thus disabling the personality, as Jung observes, with "a multiplication of its centers of gravity."

In schizophrenia, Jung thought that the disturbances in the will of the individual, and his or her hallucinations and delusions, represented the pathological work of complexes. In his famous monograph *The Psychology of Dementia Praecox* (1907), he demonstrated how the nature of complexes in schizophrenia fits in with descriptions of similar phenomena in the psychoanalytic theories of Sigmund FREUD. Although Jung recognized that dementia praecox was caused by a "toxin" that led to an irreversible disease process in the brain, he was largely under the influence of the psychological approach of Freud at this time and felt that it was possible for the "feeling-toned complex" to make the changes in the chemistry of the brain to produce the toxin. In this respect he differed significantly from his supervisor, Eugen BLEULER, who felt that the organic disease process in the brain came first and that the complexes only gave the psychotic symptoms their form but did not cause them. In 1908 Bleuler and Jung published a paper together that contrasted their views on this issue. After his break with Freud, Jung returned much later to a more organic view of the causes of schizophrenia.

Jung thought that ancient reports of demoniacal possession (see DEMONOMANIA) were simply due to the work of complexes that had become too strong and had begun to form alternate egos in the personality of the afflicted. Jung's "complex

theory" is at the center of his entire psychology, which was briefly referred to as "complex psychology" but is now more widely known as "analytical psychology."

See also ABAISSEMENT DU NIVEAU MENTAL; MULTIPLE PERSONALITY AND SCHIZOPHRENIA.

Bleuler, E., and C. G. Jung. "Komplexe und Krankheitsursachen bei Dementia Praecox," *Zentralblatt für Nervenheilkunde und Psychiatrie* 31:19 (1908): 220–227.

Jung, C. G. "The Psychogenesis of Schizophrenia," *Journal of Mental Science* 85 (1939): 999–1,011.

———. "The Psychology of Dementia Praecox," in *The Collected Works of C. G. Jung*, Vol. 3. 1907. Reprint, Princeton, N.J.: Princeton University Press, 1960.

compos mentis A Latin term for "sanity" that has found its way into jurisprudence over the centuries. *Non compos mentis* is its opposite, meaning "not in full possession of mental faculties." The expression apparently is derived from the Roman author Tacitus, who uses it in his *Annals*.

See also INSANITY.

concordance rate The rate of agreement, association, or correlation between two individuals (or types of individuals) and a given trait. Concordance rates are most often encountered in discussions of twins studies of SCHIZOPHRENIA and BIPOLAR DISORDER that have sought evidence for the genetic transmission of these diseases. For example, since we known that MONOZYGOTIC TWINS (also known as identical twins) share all the same genes, we known that they must be highly concordant for traits like eye and hair color, blood type, and most physical characteristics. DIZYGOTIC TWINS, on the other hand, who have on the average only half their genes in common, will resemble each other no more than other siblings, making them discordant across many traits. Concordance rates are often presented as decimaled numbers that represent a correlation coefficient, and the closer the number is to 1.0 the more concordant two individuals or groups are for a given trait. If schizophrenia (or bipolar disorder) is the result of genetic inheritance, then the assumption in research studies is that monozygotic twins should *both* develop the disease at higher rates (that is, with concordance rates closer to 1.0) than dizygotic twins, where perhaps only one member is likely to develop the disorder.

Almost all research studies have shown that monozygotic twins do indeed have a higher concordance for schizophrenia and for bipolar disorder than dizygotic twins. On the average, most studies show that the concordance rate for schizophrenia is three times higher in monozygotic twins than in dizygotic twins. Furthermore, the risk for schizophrenia is 40 to 60 times higher in monozygotic twins than in the general population. In patients with bipolar disorder, the concordance rate is approximately .43 for monozygotic twins.

Also supporting the hypothesis of the genetic transmission of schizophrenia are recent re-analyses of these twin studies data, in which it is found not only that monozygotic twins are more concordant for schizophrenia than dizygotic twins, but also that within these pairs of monozygotic twins, those that have a greater presence of NEGATIVE SYMPTOMS (which have been associated with a more degenerative, more "genetic" variety of schizophrenia) have a higher concordance rate (.52) than those monozygotic twins who have a lesser presence of such symptoms (.36).

After decades of research on monozygotic (identical) twins, it has been found that the concordance rate for schizophrenia among identical twins is close to 50 percent, which means that a large portion of whatever it is that causes schizophrenia is not due to genetic factors.

See also CHRONIC SCHIZOPHRENIA; CONSANGUINITY METHOD; CROW'S HYPOTHESIS; DEFICIT SYMPTOMS; GENETICS STUDIES; TWINS METHOD AND STUDIES.

Moldin, S. O., and I. I. Gottesman. "Genes, Experience and Chance in Schizophrenia: Positioning for the 21st Century," *Schizophrenia Bulletin* 23 (1997): 547–561.

concretization An aspect of schizophrenic thought patterns in which abstract thoughts or feelings are "concretized," usually in bizarre ways. For example, during an exacerbation of the psychosis a schizophrenic may feel a loss of control, which causes considerable anxiety. If paranoid, the individual may

attribute this distress to the effect of a particular facial expression someone in his immediate environment may just have manifested—perhaps without any awareness of or conscious interaction with the paranoid patient. The notion that humans tend to think in two broad modes—the concrete and the abstract—was first proposed by the psychologist Kurt GOLDSTEIN in 1939. Goldstein noticed that concrete thinking was particularly found in brain-damaged patients and, to a lesser degree, in schizophrenics. Psychologist and psychoanalyst Silvano ARIETI picked up on this idea and asserted that the "process of active concretization" formed the essential basis of the way in which the thinking of people is changed by SCHIZOPHRENIA when compared to normal thinking processes.

Arieti, S. *Interpretation of Schizophrenia.* 2nd ed. New York: Basic Books, 1974.

Goldstein, K. *The Organism.* New York: American Books, 1939.

confabulation This is the unconcious fabrication of facts or events that is often noted in brain-damaged individuals and in those persons with amnestic disorders. They confabulate due to gaps in memory, and the fabricated response to questions are facile attempts to fill in these gaps, but without any awareness of the person that he or she is confabulating. This is different than lying or DELUSIONS, which are found in the psychotic disorders and are not the response to memory impairment.

confidentiality Individuals have the right to privacy. Special relationships between a person and certain specific medical, mental health, or legal representatives are protected by this right of privacy, and many statutes have established the privileged nature of communications made during the course of professional relationships. A breach of confidentiality by a practitioner is a basis of malpractice actions against that person. Patients of mental health professionals should expect that what is discussed or included as part of treatment is private information, to be released to others only by the patient's (ideally, written) consent.

See also LEGAL ISSUES IN SCHIZOPHRENIA.

confusion A psychological state of disorientation that is found across many different types of MENTAL DISORDERS (including ORGANIC MENTAL DISORDERS) but in particular is evident in the psychotic disorders. It is usually evident during exacerbations of a PSYCHOSIS.

conjugal insanity See FOLIE À DEUX.

Conolly, John (1794–1866) An English psychiatrist and reformer. After graduating from Edinburgh University, Conolly studied in France, where he was influenced by the "moral treatment" of Philippe PINEL. Returning to England, in 1839 he became the chief physician to the Hanwell Asylum in Middlesex and there began to practice his own moral treatment of the mentally ill, including the abolition of MECHANICAL RESTRAINTS. He remained there for four years. He wrote many books on his philosophy of treatment; although they were controversial for their time, they were also highly influential. As the guiding leader of the NONRESTRAINT MOVEMENT, Conolly's ideas spread throughout Europe and America. Indeed, his ideas were held in very high regard in the United States and were partially the inspiration that brought together the 13 founders of the AMERICAN PSYCHIATRIC ASSOCIATION in 1844.

Conolly, J. *An Inquiry Concerning the Indications of Insanity with Suggestions for the Better Protection and Cure of the Insane.* London: 1830.

———. *The Treatment of the Insane without the Use of Mechanical Restraints.* London: Smith, Elder, 1856.

consanguinity method One of the methods of conducting GENETICS STUDIES of SCHIZOPHRENIA and other MENTAL DISORDERS (such as BIPOLAR DISORDER), which are assumed to have a genetic basis. The consanguinity method is based on a simple idea: If a particular disease is assumed to be genetic in origin, then the disease will be more prevalent in relatives of an afflicted person than in the general population as a whole. The afflicted person is known in these studies as the INDEX CASE. The

assumption in consanguinity studies is that the closer a relative is biologically to the index case, the more likely he or she is to develop the disorder. Twins studies are based on this principle but for many reasons are considered more scientifically powerful evidence than traditional consanguinity studies.

The very first published study on the genetics of schizophrenia was the consanguinity study conducted by Ernst Rüdin in 1916. He apparently carried out this study at the urging of Emil KRAEPELIN. Rüdin, as expected, found a significant increase in the prevalence rate of schizophrenia in the biological relatives of his index cases. He also recognized that the gene seemed to be passed on in NON-MENDELIAN PATTERNS OF TRANSMISSION. Further studies were conducted in Europe by Schultz in 1932 and in the United States by KALLMANN in 1938.

Rüdin, E. *Zur Vererburg und Neuentstehung der Dementia Praecox.* Berlin: Springer-Verlag, 1916.

Slater, E. "A Review of Earlier Evidence on Genetic Factors in Schizophrenia." In *The Transmission of Schizophrenia,* edited by D. Rosenthal and S. Kety. Oxford: Pergamon Press, 1968.

Zerbin-Rüdin, E., and K. S. Kendler. "Ernst Rüdin and His Geneologic-Demographic Department in Munich: An Introduction to Their Family Studies of Schizophrenia," *American Journal of Medical Genetics* 67 (1996): 332–337.

contagious insanity See FOLIE À DEUX.

continuous sleep therapy Swiss psychiatrist Jakob Kläsi developed this form of therapy for schizophrenics in the early 1920s. Kläsi induced a prolonged sleep in his patients with the use of barbiturates. These periods of sleep lasted a week or more, and the patient was only allowed to eat or perform bodily functions upon wakings, after which more barbiturates would be administered and the patient would be put back to sleep. His only theory to rationalize this treatment was that SCHIZOPHRENIA was the result of a pathological excitement that resulted from an inflammatory process in the brain that could be alleviated through rest, as other inflammatory conditions could be. However, the complications of the procedure (toxicity, the development of respiratory problems and pneumonia) outweighed the apparent therapeutic benefits, and thus the treatment was not widely used.

See also SLEEP TREATMENT.

Diethelm, O. "An Historical View of Somatic Treatment in Psychiatry," *American Journal of Psychiatry* 95 (1938): 1,165–1,179.

Kläsi, J. "Über die therapeutische Anwendung der 'Dauernarkose' mittels sominifens bei Schizophrenen," *Z. Neurol. Psychiatr.* 74 (1922): 557–592.

continuum of psychosis See *EINHEITSPSYCHOSE*.

convulsive therapies Although no sound scientific theories have ever supported their use, the convulsive therapies were among the most widely used somatic treatments for SCHIZOPHRENIA in the 20th century. The basic idea is that deliberately inducing a convulsion or seizure—either by drugs or electricity—somehow has a therapeutic effect in schizophrenia.

The first report of a convulsive therapy was by the Hungarian psychiatrist L. von MEDUNA in 1935. von Meduna apparently believed (without any supporting scientific evidence) that epilepsy and schizophrenia were biologically incompatible and that, therefore, inducing a convulsive seizure in schizophrenics would be therapeutic. He used camphor and metrazol to induce these convulsions and reported successful results. However, his relapse rate was high, and his "convulsive therapy" was found to be more effective with patients with AFFECTIVE DISORDERS (such as DEPRESSION) than with schizophrenics. This similar beneficial result with people with severe affective disorders has also been found to be true for ELECTROSHOCK THERAPY (now commonly referred to as ECT, or "electroconvulsive therapy"), which was first used by CERLETTI and Bini in 1938. Since the 1970s ECT has been infrequently used for schizophrenia in the United States.

See also METRAZOL SHOCK THERAPY.

Fink, M. "Convulsive Therapy: A Review of the First 55 Years," *Journal of Affective Disorders* 63 (2001): 1–15.

copro-psychiatrie A 19th-century "school" of PSYCHIATRY that claimed that mental illnesses, and particularly the psychotic disorders, were caused by diseases of the digestive tract, particularly the intestines and bowels. These physicians primarily studied the feces, urine, and other bodily "secretions of the insane." In the second (1861) edition of his famous textbook, *Die Pathologie und Therapie der Psychische Krankheit* (the first was in 1845), German psychiatrist Wilhelm GRIESINGER notes that this "peculiar bud from the stem of the 'Somatic School' has . . . gone out of fashion."

See also AUTOINTOXICATION AS A CAUSE OF DEMENTIA PRAECOX.

cortical pruning as a cause of schizophrenia This is a theory that proposes a developmental process ("cortical" or "axonal pruning") that is extended past its normal point of termination (at about age 16) and goes on to cause SCHIZOPHRENIA. In the brain, neurons ("brain cells") pass messages back and forth to one another through a vast web of interconnections. From the nucleus of the neuron, a "message" travels down a branchlike structure called the "axon." The point at which information from one cell passes to another is a gap separating the axons called a "synapse." Biochemical NEUROTRANSMITTERS such as DOPAMINE, serotonin, and norepinepherine all cross this gap to affect the adjoining neuron.

Starting with the postmortem studies of P. R. Huttenlocher, published in 1979, it was discovered that there are major changes in the number of synapses (especially in the prefrontal cortex) throughout childhood and adolescence. "Synaptic density" (think of this as the thick branches of a tree or bush—the axons—intercrossing one another) increases in this cortical area until about ages five to seven, and then it begins a gradual decline until about age 16, when the density of synapses seems to level off to average adult levels. It is estimated that as much as 30 percent to 40 percent of these interconnections between brain cells disappear or "fall off" or are "pruned" (as one would a tree or shrub), and as a result the brain is measured to be less "active" or have less "energy" ("reduced cerebral metabolism"), particularly in the prefrontal cortical regions. This process is called axonal pruning.

A theory for a possible contributing cause of schizophrenia based on this normal process of "cortical" or "axonal pruning" was first put forth by Irving Feinberg in 1982, and developed by researchers Ralph Hoffman and Steven Dobscha in a paper published in 1989. In that paper, they hypothesized that the normal developmental process of cortical pruning that happens to us all in childhood and adolescence, and especially its measured reduction of cerebral metabolism in the prefrontal cortex, may actually cause schizophrenia if the process continues into late adolescence and early adulthood.

A computer model simulation of what the effect of cortical pruning would be in normals was conducted by Hoffman and Dobscha, and it was found that such experiences as DELUSIONS and HALLUCINATIONS and other psychotic symptoms might be experienced by humans. Another prominent schizophrenia researcher, Letten Saugstad of Norway, proposed that the cortical pruning process is implicated in the development of manic-depressive psychosis as well, with the hypothesis being that very early puberty is the necessary factor in the development of manic-depressive psychosis, and extremely late puberty the necessary factor in the development of schizophrenia. If the onset of puberty is viewed as coinciding with the last major step in brain development (the end of the cortical pruning process), then manic-depressiveness may result from the earlier than normal termination of the cortical pruning process.

Cortical pruning theories of mental illness have not been supported. As of 2005, such a theory of schizophrenia has been rejected.

Feinberg, I. "Schizophrenia and Late Maturational Brain Changes in Man," *Psychopharmacology Bulletin,* 18 (1982): 29–31.

———. "Schizophrenia: Caused by a Fault in Programmed Synaptic Elimination during Adolescence?" *Journal of Psychiatric Research* 4 (1982/1983): 319–334.

Hoffman, R. E., and S. K. Dobscha. "Cortical Pruning and the Development of Schizophrenia: A Computer Model," *Schizophrenia Bulletin* 15 (1989): 477–490.

Huttenlocher, P. R. "Synaptic Density in Human Frontal Cortex—Evidence for Synaptic Elimination during

Normal Development," *Neuro-science Letters* 33 (1979), 247–252.

Saugstad, L. F. "Social Class, Marriage, and Fertility in Schizophrenia," *Schizophrenia Bulletin* 15 (1989): 9–43.

Cotard's syndrome A relatively uncommon delusional syndrome, usually found in people with a psychotic disorder (usually, PARANOID SCHIZOPHRENIA) or with an ORGANIC MENTAL DISORDER, in which he or she denies his or her own existence or the existence of the external world. For this reason, French psychiatrist Jules Cotard (1840–89) introduced this idea in 1880 at a meeting in Paris of the Societé Médico-Psychologique by calling it *le délire de négation* (delusions of negation). Cotard first published his ideas on this newly identified syndrome in 1882. Another French psychiatrist, Séglas, named this condition the Cotard Syndrome in 1897. Schizophrenics who exhibit Cotard's syndrome may make statements such as "I'm dead" or "I'm not here or anywhere. I'm a ghost." Nonpsychotic conditions that are probably related to Cotard's syndrome are feelings of DEREALIZATION or DEPERSONALIZATION.

Cotard, J. "Du délire des négations," *Archives de Neurologie* 11 (1882): 152–170: and 12: 282–296.

Séglas, J. *La Délire de Négation.* Vol. 1. Paris: Masson, 1897.

cottage system Another name for the centuries-old system of caring for the mentally ill in which they are maintained in the community rather than in institutions. Belgium's GHEEL COLONY, which is almost 1,000 years old, is an example of how long this system has been maintained.

Cotton, Henry A. See FOCAL INFECTION AS CAUSE OF PSYCHOTIC DISORDERS.

course and outcome of schizophrenia From antiquity until the second half of the 1800s, all insanities were thought to fall within two broad categories, MANIA and MELANCHOLIA. These two terms did not have the meaning they have today until the end of the 1800s. Speculation as to the course and outcome of the multitude of mental disorders forced to fit into these two ancient categories was varied and not based on any scientific study. For example, Benedict Morel in France speculated in 1857 that both mania and melancholia were the result of hereditary DEGENERATION and, over successive generations, ended in idiocy and death. Therefore, all mental disturbances were ultimately signs of degeneration and doomed an individual or his or her children to dementia and death.

With the efforts of German psychiatrists such as Karl Ludwig KAHLBAUM (beginning in 1863) and Emil KRAEPELIN (beginning in 1883) to identify and classify syndromes of MENTAL DISORDERS, it soon became apparent that one way of distinguishing seemingly similar mental disorders from one another was by course and outcome. Some mental disorders could be temporary and result in full recovery; others seemed to flare up occasionally and leave lasting deficits that became worse over the course of a person's life.

The importance of course and outcome proved to be crucial in the history of PSYCHIATRY beginning with the publication of the sixth edition of Kraepelin's textbook, *Psychiatrie.* In the 1899 edition, Kraepelin divided and reclassified all the known "insanities" (psychotic disorders) into two main categories: DEMENTIA PRAECOX and MANIC-DEPRESSIVE ILLNESS. His main criterion for dividing the insanities this way was prognosis. Manic-depressive illness was characterized by exacerbating and remitting episodes, many full recoveries, no cognitive deterioration (dementia), and an excellent prognosis. Persons with manic-depressive illness could often return to full intellectual, social, and occupational functioning between episodes. On the other hand, dementia praecox in its three main forms (paranoid, hebephrenic, and catatonic) was a degenerative disease characterized by a progressive deteriorating course and outcome. From the time he introduced the concept of dementia praecox in 1893, he had largely viewed dementia praecox in this unforgiving way, but by 1920 he had admitted the existence of cases of partial or full recovery (the existence of which Eugen BLEULER had insisted upon from the first description of SCHIZOPHRENIA in 1908).

Kraepelin identified two main patterns across the life spans of people with dementia praecox: "simple" (insidious, slow, and chronic) and "undulating" (episodic, with psychotic symptoms flaring up and subsiding at times, yet leaving a core deficit in cognitive functioning that worsens until death). Since Kraepelin's time there has been much interest in the "natural history of schizophrenia," that is, the typical pattern or patterns the disorder demonstrates over long periods of time. Wilhelm Meyer-Gross of Heidelburg University in Germany was the first to conduct a long-term follow-up study of 294 patients diagnosed with schizophrenia. In his 1932 publication of his results, Mayer-Gross reported that 17 years after first being diagnosed with schizophrenia, approximately 30 percent were found to be "practically cured, living at home, socially adjusted," 19 percent were in institutions, 5 percent were "living at home, employed, but poorly socially adjusted," and 3.5 percent were "living at home, but manifestly ill." Strikingly, 42.5 percent were dead, most having died in MENTAL HOSPITALS. In 1941 Manfred BLEULER, son of Eugen Bleuler, published early data on the possible course types of schizophrenia and devoted most of his career to long-term follow-up studies of persons with chronic mental disorders.

Longitudinal or long-term follow-up studies have examined the types of onset (sudden or insidious), patterns of exacerbations and remissions of psychotic symptoms, changes in cognitive functioning (attention, working memory, episodic or autobiographical memory, executive functions) over time, and the end state (full recovery to mild, moderate, or severe deterioration by the end of the time period of study).

There have been five major longitudinal studies of the course and outcome in schizophrenia since 1972, and all five have rejected Kraepelin's fatalistic definition of dementia praecox as always ending in a state of chronic dementia. All of them also reject Kraepelin's early division of the course of dementia praecox into two patterns, simple and undulating, with one outcome, dementia. In fact, the number of different courses of schizophrenia is not known for certain. Estimates based on research have varied widely from four to 79 different possible patterns that combine course and outcome.

Results from the five major longitudinal studies have been appearing in print since 1972. Two were conducted in Switzerland: The BURGHÖLZLI HOSPITAL Study (1972) conducted by Manfred Bleuler and his colleagues (designated in the chart below by "B"), and the Lausanne Investigations (1976) conducted by Luc Ciompi and colleagues (L). Two additional studies were conducted in the United States: the Vermont Longitudinal Research Project (1987) conducted by Courtenay Harding and colleagues at Vermont's only state hospital (V), and the Chicago study (1991) conducted by J. T. Marengo and colleagues (C). A worldwide study of 14 different geographical locations in developing and developed countries was conducted by the WORLD HEALTH ORGANIZATION in its collaborative International Study of Schizophrenia (ISoS) project (2001). Since Switzerland and the United States are developed or First World countries, the ISoS results are particularly interesting because of the addition of data from developing countries and reflect the much better outcome for persons with schizophrenia in those parts of the world.

The common patterns found in the five major longitudinal studies are generally divided into eight course types for schizophrenia. In the chart below, adapted from a chart prepared by H. Haefner and W. An der Heiden and published in 2003, the numbers represent the percentage of persons with schizophrenia that fit each of the eight course and outcome combinations:

Based on these five major longitudinal studies, 10 North American long-term follow-up studies that lasted a minimum of 10 years, and the genetic, biochemical, psychopharmacological, neuropathological, neuroimaging, and neuropsychological picture of schizophrenia as it now stands, the following conclusions about the course and outcome of schizophrenia may be drawn from our present state of scientific knowledge:

1. In developed countries, schizophrenia is a chronic disease, causing impairment (neurocognitive, social, and occupational) that lasts a lifetime. In developing countries, schizophrenia follows a less severe course and has a better outcome. No one knows why this is so.

	Onset	Course type	End state	L	B	V	C	ISoS
1	Acute	Undulating	Recovery/Mild	25.4	30–40/25–35	7	10.8	29.4
2	Chronic	Simple	Moderate/Severe	24.1	10–20	4	36.5	14.4
3	Acute	Undulating	Moderate/Severe	11.9	5	4	9.5	4.9
4	Chronic	Simple	Recovery/Mild	10.1	5–10	12	4.1	10.4
5	Chronic	Undulating	Recovery/Mild	9.6	–	38	6.8	22.6
6	Acute	Simple	Moderate/Severe	8.3	5–15	3	13.5	9.1
7	Chronic	Undulating	Moderate/Severe	5.3	–	27	12.2	4
8	Acute	Simple	Recovery/Mild	5.3	5	5	6.8	5.3

2. When compared to other mental disorders, such as BIPOLAR DISORDER, the outcome for schizophrenia is worse.
3. Schizophrenia is not a neurodegenerative disease that begins after puberty, as Kraepelin believed. Negative symptoms and cognitive impairment are present in the prodromal phase, years before the first episode of schizophrenia. Cognitive impairment does not ever improve over the course of schizophrenia, but it also does not significantly worsen either. Measurable brain abnormalities, such as enlarged ventricles (when present, which is in a minority of persons with schizophrenia), do not worsen over time. Most of the destructive impact of schizophrenia occurs early in the process, during the years-long prodromal phase or around the time of the first psychotic episode. Antipsychotic drugs do not improve most negative symptoms and they do not improve cognitive functioning (attention, working memory, autobiographical memory, executive functioning). "Full recovery" unfortunately implies some residual cognitive impairment will remain.
4. The underlying disease processes in schizophrenia, while mostly disabling and chronic, do not get progressively worse over the life span. In fact, people with schizophrenia suffer most of their loss of functioning early in the disease process. After five to 10 years their symptoms reach a "plateau" and either do not get worse or go into partial remission. This again argues against a view of schizophrenia as a neurodegenerative disease.
5. There is no firm scientific evidence, from these longitudinal studies, biological research, or GENETICS STUDIES, to support the clinical subtypes of schizophrenia found in *DSM-IV-TR* (paranoid, disorganized, catatonic, undifferentiated, residual) or *ICD-10* (paranoid, hebephrenic, catatonic, undifferentiated, residual, or simple). Therefore, although in practice clinicians believe that the paranoid subtypes have a better prognosis than the nonparanoid subtypes, this is not supported by longitudinal studies. Clinicians have no scientific basis for making a prognosis based on the presenting clinical subtype. The only firm scientific evidence for possible subtypes of schizophrenia is for forms of the disorder with an acute onset or an insidious onset, and these are associated with good prognosis and poor prognosis, respectively.
6. Primary negative symptoms are stable over time and are not affected by environmental factors. Positive symptoms (HALLUCINATIONS and DELUSIONS) are unstable over time and are influenced by environmental factors. The stability of negative symptoms contradicts the hypothesis that schizophrenia is a progressive neurodegenerative disease, as Kraepelin believed.
7. Schizophrenia is associated with an increased risk of suicide, physical illness, and an average life span that is 10 to 15 years less than the general population.
8. ANTIPSYCHOTIC DRUGS do not work in as many as one-third of all persons with schizophrenia. Antipsychotic drugs do not prevent brain damage in schizophrenia. Antipsychotic drugs do not directly work on the underlying causes of schizophrenia and therefore do not alter the natural course of the disease process.
9. The causes of schizophrenia are unknown.
10. In individual cases, it is impossible to predict the course or outcome of schizophrenia.

Bleuler, M. *Krankheitsverlauf, Persoenlichkeit, und Verwandtschaft der Schizophrener und Ihrer Gegenseitigen Beziehungen.* Leipzig: George Thieme, 1941.

Haefner, H., and W. An der Heiden. "Course and Outcome of Schizophrenia." In *Schizophrenia. 2nd ed.*, edited by S. R. Hirsch and D. Weinberger. Cambridge: Blackwell, 2003.

Mayer-Gross, W. "Die Klinik (der Schizophrenie)." In *Handbuch der Geisteskrankheiten. Band IX. Spezieller Teil V: Die Schizophrenie*, edited by O. Bumke. Berlin: Springer, 1932.

McGlashan, T. H. "A Selective Review of Recent North American Studies of Schizophrenia," *Schizophrenia Bulletin* 14 (1988): 515-542.

creativity and psychosis Is there a relationship between "madness" and creativity? Thousands of years of popular speculation have thought so. The first of the now familiar "pathographies" of famous creative individuals began to appear in the mid-1800s, led by the works of French alienist J. J. Moreau de Tours (1804–84) and German psychiatrist P. J. Möbius (1853–1907), who wrote psychiatric interpretations of the creative lives of Rousseau, Goethe, Schopenhauer, and Nietzsche. In the 20th century, psychologists have tried to answer this question experimentally by comparing the thought processes of schizophrenics with those of highly creative nonschizophrenic individuals. It has long been reported that when highly creative nonschizophrenics are given traditional diagnostic tests, they tend to score higher on psychopathology than "normals." However, there is no evidence that these people or other highly creative individuals are more susceptible to SCHIZOPHRENIA than the general population.

A review of these studies on creativity and schizophrenia was published by J. A. Keefe and P. A. Magaro in 1980. Although there was no direct evidence of a link between the two, schizophrenics and creative nonschizophrenics did share several qualities in the styles of their thinking: both used language in very unusual ways, both had deviant, idiosyncratic views of reality when compared to other people, and both tended to be perceived as "eccentric" by others. An important distinction to be made is that one of the hallmarks of a schizophrenic is the inability to focus attention in a normal, sustained manner, and such attention is necessary for planning and carrying out all activities of life—including creative ones. Thus, being "schizophrenic" does not make one creative, nor vice versa.

However, there has been much speculation that many highly creative people throughout history may have been afflicted (or blessed, as the case may be) with BIPOLAR DISORDER. The thought disorder of schizophrenia is generally absent in manic-depressives, but there is an incredible rush of energy due to the manic phase of the illness that can keep creative people working on projects literally for days with little or no sleep. Such persons may have been Vincent Van Gogh, Edgar Allan Poe, Handel, Berlioz, F. Scott Fitzgerald, Eugene O'Neill, and Virginia Woolf. The anecdotal evidence for a connection between MANIC-DEPRESSIVE ILLNESS and creativity is quite strong.

Alcoholism, either in connection with bipolar illness or alone, is prominently represented in creative individuals. Writers in particular seem to be prone to alcoholism, and the first five American Nobel laureates for literature (Lewis, O'Neill, Faulkner, Hemingway, and Steinbeck) were all alcoholics.

There has also been some speculation, based on anecdotal evidence, that relatives of highly creative people are often schizophrenic or manic-depressives. For example, Albert Einstein's son Edward (born in 1910) was afflicted with schizophrenia. James Joyce's daughter Lucia was a diagnosed schizophrenic who spent most of her life in mental institutions. British horror writer Ramsey Campbell's mother was schizophrenic, and Jane Fonda's mother (Frances Seymour Brokow) committed suicide in a mental hospital in 1950 by slitting her own throat. The exact nature of her severe illness is not known. Even famous psychiatrists have not been exempt, for the mothers of both Harry Stack Sullivan and C. G. JUNG are known to have had serious MENTAL DISORDERS that may have resulted in psychiatric hospitalization. Indeed, both Stack and Jung themselves are known to have had periods in their lives when psychotic-like symptoms and a general functional breakdown were known to occur. Thus, the question of madness and creativity

is an intriguing one that will continue to generate endless speculation.

See also ART, SCHIZOPHRENIC.

Dykes, M., and A. McGhie. "A Comparative Study of Attentional Strategies of Schizophrenic and Highly Creative Normal Subjects," *British Journal of Psychiatry* 128 (1976): 50–56.

Jamison, K. R. *Touched with Fire: Manic-Depressive Illness and Temperament.* New York: Free Press, 1993.

Keefe, J. A., and P. A. Magaro. "Creativity and Schizophrenia: An Equivalence of Cognitive Processing," *Journal of Abnormal Psychology* 89 (1980): 390–398.

Croatia Some parts of Croatia have some of the highest prevalence rates for SCHIZOPHRENIA in the world; the northwestern coastal area has a prevalence rate twice as high as that of other areas. Rates for manic depression are also high in Croatia. The Istrian Peninsula in Croatia has a particularly high rate (about 7.4 per 1,000) when compared to other areas of Croatia (from 2.9 to 4.2 per 1,000).

Lemkau, P. V. "Selected Aspects of the Epidemiology of Psychoses in Croatia," *American Journal of Epidemiology* 94 (1971): 112–117.

cross-cultural studies It has long been reported that severe MENTAL DISORDERS such as SCHIZOPHRENIA and MANIC-DEPRESSIVE ILLNESS seem to be more prevalent in technologically developed Western countries than in developing countries in the Third World. This is a very old observation. As early as 1835 British psychiatrist J. C. Prichard (1786–1848) noted in his text *A Treatise on Insanity* that "insanity belongs almost exclusively to civilized races of man: it scarcely exists among savages, and is rare in barbarous countries." Other prominent figures in psychiatry in the 19th century who expressed these views were Isaac RAY, Dorothea DIX, Edward Jarvis, and Pliny EARLE.

In the 19th and early 20th centuries, many anecdotal reports by psychiatrists and anthropologists about mental disorders in "primitive" societies supported the view that schizophrenia in particular seemed to be uncommon. The more scientific epidemiological studies of the prevalence of schizophrenia show that it is found in different amounts in different parts of the world. In reviewing all this data, psychiatrist E. Fuller Torrey published a fascinating book in 1980 on *Schizophrenia and Civilization* in which he argued that "schizophrenia appears to be a disease of civilization, with a close correlation between its prevalence and the degree of civilization."

However, diagnostic criteria can be very different from culture to culture, and many diseases that look like schizophrenia (such as manic-depressive psychosis in its earliest stage, certain metabolic disorders, or ORGANIC MENTAL DISORDERS caused by strokes, tumors, or lesions induced by head trauma) may not in fact be so. To correct these problems and to construct a true picture of schizophrenia worldwide, many rigorous, scientific, long-term follow-up studies have been conducted in many areas of the world. The three most important studies have been major projects of the WORLD HEALTH ORGANIZATION: the International Pilot Study of Schizophrenia (IPSS), which was carried out in nine countries (Denmark, India, Colombia, Nigeria, United Kingdom, Soviet Union, Czechoslovakia, Taiwan, and the United States) between 1968 and the early 1970s; the Determinants of Outcome Study, conducted between 1983 and 1985 in 10 countries, using methods that were improvements over the IPSS study of a decade earlier; and the International Study of Schizophrenia (ISoS) and its follow-up studies, completed in 1997. The ISoS looked at 14 different geographical locations in both developed and developing countries. All these studies have shown that schizophrenic patients in less-industrialized societies (as in the Third World) have a significantly better outcome than do those schizophrenics in industrialized nations. However, these studies also show a core of "worst outcome" schizophrenics, and these groups seem to match the familiar descriptions of CHRONIC SCHIZOPHRENIA known in Western societies, where it is thought to be more genetically based and more "organic" and degenerative in nature than the "acute-onset" types. "Acute onset psychoses" were found, instead, to predominate in the non-Western world.

Whether these cross-cultural differences are due to sociocultural differences (Third World countries being more "sociocentric," Western societies more "egocentric") or to the prevalence of different, less chronic strains of schizophrenia in Third World countries is presently unknown.

Jablensky, A., et al. "Schizophrenia: Manifestations, Incidence and Course in Different Cultures. A World Health Organization Ten-Country Study," *Psychological Medicine Monographs Supplement* 20 (1992): 1–97.

Lin, K. M., and A. M. Kleinman. "Psychopathology and Clinical Course of Schizophrenia: A Cross-Cultural Perspective," *Schizophrenia Bulletin* 14 (1988): 555–567.

Torrey, E. F. *Schizophrenia and Civilization.* New York: Jason Aronson, 1980.

Crow's hypothesis For many years, researchers sought to combine all the highly diversified studies of SCHIZOPHRENIA into a single theory that could account for all the new findings that advances in technology had brought. In essence, the desire was for a theory that could account for the symptoms of schizophrenia and relate them to specific biological processes. Furthermore, such a theory would have to be testable. In 1980 psychiatrist T. J. Crow did just that. He published his concept of schizophrenia as essentially a "two-syndrome" disease and connected findings on the symptomatology of schizophrenia with the biochemical and neurophysiological qualities of the disease. He named these two subtypes of schizophrenia Type I and Type II; because it has been so popular with those who carry out schizophrenia research, the theory is commonly referred to as Crow's hypothesis or two-syndrome paradigm.

Type I schizophrenia is thought by Crow to be characterized by an acute onset, generally normal intellectual functioning, no discernible abnormalities in the structure of the brain, and a good response to ANTIPSYCHOTIC DRUGS. It is thought to be caused by an excess of dopamine production in the brain and is generally associated with POSITIVE SYMPTOMS (symptoms that seem to be additions to the personality, such as hallucinations and delusions). Most important, it is associated with the absence of NEGATIVE SYMPTOMS (those symptoms that represent something taken away from the personality, such as poverty of speech, poverty of content of speech, restricted affect, psychomotor retardation, reduced desire for social interaction, and constricted thought process).

In Type II schizophrenia, characteristics include insidious onset (i.e., it develops slowly, like a chronic illness), intellectual deterioration, enlarged ventricles in the brain, poor response to antipsychotic drugs, and prominent negative symptoms. Thus, the difference in Type I versus Type II schizophrenia is based not only on the predominance of unrelated symptoms (positive versus negative) but also the fact that Type II schizophrenia is clearly characterized by structural BRAIN ABNORMALITIES. Type II, therefore, is the subtype of schizophrenia that most resembles traditional brain diseases.

Although Crow's hypothesis generated considerable research, it did not stand the test of time. By the 1990s his "two-syndrome" concept had been replaced by new research schemes derived from statistical studies of the symptoms of schizophrenia. These factor-analytic studies rejected the notion of "syndromes" and "diagnostic subtypes" and instead replaced them with various "dimensions" of psychopathology. Instead of Crow's two syndromes, proposals for three and four dimensional alternatives have been offered by Nancy Andreasen (3), Peter Liddle (3), and Mark Lenzenweger and Robert Dworkin (4).

Crow, T. J. "Molecular Pathology of Schizophrenia: More Than One Disease Process?" *British Medical Journal* 280 (1980): 66–86.

———. "The Two-syndrome Concept: Origins and Current Status," *Schizophrenia Bulletin* 11 (1985): 471–486.

Lenzenweger, M. F., and R. H. Dworkin. "The Dimensions of Schizophrenia Phenomenology? Not One or Not Two, At Least Three, Perhaps Four," *British Journal of Psychiatry* 168 (1996): 432–440.

Crowther, Bryan (1765–1814) A surgeon of the BETHLEM ROYAL HOSPITAL who wrote a book in 1811 of his observations made during the dissections of the brains of deceased "Bedlam" patients. He

was assisted by apothecary John HASLAM in these autopsies, who also incorporated his observations in a book. He is thus one of the early investigators to use neuropathological methods to look for BRAIN ABNORMALITIES in the severely mentally ill. In his book, Crowther also mentioned that, as surgeon to the Bethlem Royal Hospital, he routinely practiced the BLEEDING of patients every spring regardless of the type or severity of their illness.

When John Haslam was interrogated in 1815 by a committee of the House of Commons about alleged abuses at "Bedlam," it came up in his testimony that Crowther was a raging alcoholic who needed to be put in MECHANICAL RESTRAINT at times. Haslam told the committee: "Mr. Crowther was generally insane, and mostly drunk. He was so insane as to have a straight-waistcoat." Haslam and the superintendent of Bethlem, Thomas Monro, were dismissed as a result of the committee's findings, but Crowther died shortly before the committee opened its hearings—escaping, no doubt, a similar fate.

Crowther, B. *Practical Remarks on Insanity, to Which Is Added a Commentary on the Dissection of the Brains of Maniacs, with Some Account of Diseases Incident to the Insane.* London: 1811.

Report of the Committee for Better Regulation of Madhouses. London: Baldwin, Craddock, & Joy, 1815.

cruciform stance A form of MECHANICAL RESTRAINT in which a disobedient patient was harnessed and tied in a standing position to a cross-shaped metal structure. Patients were then left on this structure for many hours or days at a time. An eminent 19th-century German psychiatrist, Heinrich Wilhelm Neumann (1814–84), recommended the cruciform stance or harness as "the best possible punishment for the worst transgressions of the insane." The horizontal form of this mode of mechanical restraint was known as the BED SADDLE and survived into the 20th century.

Kreapelin, E. *One Hundred Years of Psychiatry,* trans. W. Baskin. 1917. Reprint, New York: Philosophical Library, 1962.

CT scan Abbreviation for "computed tomography," in BRAIN IMAGING STUDIES used to image the structure of the brain. It is the same as the more commonly known term CAT scan or computerized axial tomography. Information is gathered from the body in cross-sectional planes, as if examining the body with X-rays slice by slice. An image is created by a computer synthesis of X-ray transmission data obtained from many different directions through each plane. Image by image (or "slice" by "slice") the body is studied, and abnormalities are searched for in the computer-generated images. CT scans and other brain-imaging techniques are now commonly being used to study brain abnormalities in schizophrenia and have led to discoveries about how the brains of people with SCHIZOPHRENIA are different from the brains of normals. It is the first of the many new brain-imaging techniques developed since the first published report of the use of a CT scan in 1973; its first use in schizophrenia research was reported in 1976.

See also BRAIN IMAGING STUDIES OF SCHIZOPHRENIA.

Cullen, William (1710–1790) A noted British physician and one of the influential instructors of Benjamin RUSH. He is remembered for founding the Glasgow Medical School in Scotland and for a system of classifying mental disorders that influenced later psychiatrists, notably Philippe PINEL and RUSH. Cullen is also remembered for coining the term *NEUROSIS,* a class of diseases with a physiological basis in the nervous system. One of these, Vesania, was an ancient Latin term for "insanity," used until the end of the 18th century. His treatment recommendations for mental illness were largely those also used for other physical disorders: BLEEDING, PURGING, bathing, and changes in diet.

Cullen, William. *First Lines of the Practice of Physic, with Practical and Explanatory Notes by John Rotheram.* Edinburgh: Bell, Bradfute, etc., 1796.

"Cure-Awl, Dr." This was the derisive nickname of physician William AWL, the first superintendent

(in 1838) of the Ohio State Asylum for the Insane and one of the 13 founders of the AMERICAN PSYCHIATRIC ASSOCIATION. The nickname derives from his incredible claim in 1842 that under his direction the Ohio Asylum had achieved a 100 percent cure rate for insanity.

Exaggerated claims of the curability of severe mental illness were not uncommon in the mid-19th century in the young United States, and such claims were considered a source of national pride. In fact, the preponderance of such claims in the 1830s and 1840s led to a "cult of the asylum" in the United States, led by Dorothea DIX, who cited this evidence in her lobbying efforts to state legislators to build more asylums. Without evidence to the contrary, state after state mandated the construction of state asylums for the insane, and Dix was credited for being personally responsible for 32 of them. It wasn't until 1877 that these fabricated statistics were finally shown to be false in an influential book by Pliny EARLE, another of the 13 founders of the American Psychiatric Association.

Earle, P. *The Curability of the Insane.* Philadelphia: Blakiston, 1877.

Rothman. D. J. *The Discovery of the Asylum: Social Order and Disorder in the New Republic.* Boston: Little, Brown, 1971.

cycloid psychoses A variety of BRIEF PSYCHOTIC DISORDERS that have played an influential role in German and Scandinavian psychiatry. The term first appears in the work of German psychiatrist Karl Kleist (1879–1960) in 1926 in the *Archiv fuer Psychiatrie und Nervenkrankheiten (Archives for Psychiatry and Nervous Disease)* as "cycloid degeneration psychoses" to refer to two types of transient psychotic disorders: the confusional psychoses that alternated between agitated confusion and stupor, and the motility psychoses that alternated between hyperkinesis and akinesis. The term "cycloid psychoses" replaced a term used by Kleist for the same disorders in a 1921 publication, "sudden, fully-formed, constitutional psychoses (*autochthone konstitutionelle Psychosen*)." The cycloid psychoses have a sudden onset and a brief duration with full recovery, though in some instances they may reoccur. Kleist was a major critic of Emil KRAEPELIN's 1899 division of the psychotic disorders into two main categories, DEMENTIA PRAECOX and MANIC-DEPRESSIVE ILLNESS, and believed there were many psychotic disorders that fell between these two but that could not be reduced to either. Kleist, following his teacher Carl Wernicke (1848–1905), believed in the possibility of localizing these MENTAL DISORDERS in functionally unstable areas of the brain and classifying them according to their underlying neurological impairment. This was in opposition to SCHIZOPHRENIA, which Kleist believed was caused by the degenerative progressive atrophying of nerve cells in the brain.

Kleist and Karl Leonhard (1904–88), his colleague in Frankfurt, Germany, in the mid-1930s, eventually identified at least 26 cycloid psychoses that were schizophrenia-like and cyclical (like manic depression). In 1953 Kleist introduced the terms *unipolar* and *bipolar* to differentiate the cycloid psychoses in an article published in the *Monatsschrift fuer Psychiatrie und Neurologie.* In 1957, in *Die Aufteilung der endogenen Psychosen (The Classification of Endogenous Psychoses),* Leonhard grouped psychotic disorders into three large categories of "endogenous psychoses": one, the affective, or phasic psychoses (with "bipolar" distinguished from "monopolar" types); two, the cycloid psychoses; and three the schizophrenia psychoses, which he broke down into "systematic" (stable symptoms picture, systematized delusions) and "nonsystematic" psychoses (fluctuating or polymorphic symptom picture, fluctuating severity). In his book, Leonhard insisted that "Cycloid psychoses are completely cured in every phase. Should it be otherwise in a particular case, we deal with misdiagnosis." The concept of cycloid psychoses is still popular in German psychiatry.

See also DYSPHRENIA.

Beckmann, H., and E. Franzek. "Cycloid Psychoses and Their Differentiations from Affective and Schizophrenia Psychoses." In *Contemporary Psychiatry,* edited by F. Henn, N. Sartorius, H. Helmchen, and H. Lauter. Heidelberg: Springer, 2001.

Beckmann, H., and K.-J. Neumarker, eds. *Endogenous Psychoses: Leonhard's Impact on Psychiatry.* Berlin: Ullstein Mosby, 1995.

Kleist, K. "Autochthone Degenerationspsychosen," *Zeitschrift fuer gesamte Neurologieund Psychiatrie* 69 (1921): 1–11.

cytogenetics This is the area of specialization within genetics that is concerned with the study of the structure and function of the cell, and especially the study of the CHROMOSOMES.

D

Darwin's chair (or machine) See CIRCULATING SWING.

Daseinanalyse Literally, the "analysis of existence," a method and mode of treatment formulated by Ludwig Binswanger (1881–1966) in the 1950s that was based on understanding the experiential structures of the inner worlds of mentally ill persons. Binswanger had worked at the BURGHÖLZI HOSPITAL under Eugen BLEULER and C. G. JUNG in the first years of the 20th century. He constructed this revision of FREUD's psychoanalysis with the ideas of phenomenological philosophers Heidegger and Husserl. His emphasis on carefully describing the inner experiences of schizophrenics (the phenomenology of schizophrenic experience) had great influence on subsequent studies of the afflicted individual's experience of his or her own disease process. It influenced British PSYCHIATRY, in particular in the 1950s and 1960s, and especially the work of R. D. LAING.

Binswanger thought that the experiential world of schizophrenics was characterized by four qualities:

1. A breakdown in the consistency of natural experience. To get out of this situation, they construct DELUSIONS to minimize the anxiety felt about the inner chaos and to reestablish order in the world.
2. A splitting-off of experiential consistency into rigid pairs of alternatives. The world is seen as good/bad, pure/evil, yes/no. These alternatives are often grandiose, inflated, "exaggerated ideals." When choices in the world are limited in this dualistic way, the schizophrenic cannot help but sometimes to fall into the darkness of making the negative choice, therefore viewing him- or herself only in terms of deficiency, imperfection, or "sin."
3. A process of "covering." The schizophrenic tries to "cover-up" through thoughts, words, and behaviors the awful negative aspect of existence (the *Dasein,* in Binswanger's terminology) that is unbearable to the schizophrenic. This naturally leads to an inflated notion of the preferred alternative for viewing existence.
4. An experience of existence as being "worn away," as though by friction. No longer can the person find a way in or out of his way of being, and this eventually fatigues him and leads to a renunciation or resignation of the world, what Binswanger calls an "existential retreat."

In 1957 Binswanger published a series of five case histories of schizophrenics that he treated using his *daseinanalyse.* Despite a significant amount of interest in its philosophy and its phenomenological approach to clinical situations, daseinanalysis never was a widely accepted treatment for schizophrenics and is today an uncommon treatment mode in general.

Binswanger, L. *Being-in the-World: Selected Papers of Ludwig Binswanger.* Translated and edited by J. Neddleman. New York: Basic Books, 1963.

———. *Schizophrenie.* Pfullingen: Gunther Neske Verlag, 1957.

day hospitals An alternative to commitment to psychiatric institutions, day hospitals provide care for severely mentally ill people during the day, after which they are allowed to go home at night. This is generally viewed as a cheaper and more humane alternative to full-time care in institutions, which

are usually the sponsors of such programs. A rarer version of this idea involves "night hospitals," where patients return at night after spending the day in a community setting. Both are forms of what is commonly referred to as "partial hospitalization." The earliest recorded operating day hospital was opened in the Soviet Union in the 1930s. It was not until 1946 that the movement began in Britain with the opening of a day hospital in London by a British psychiatrist by the name of Bierer. Day hospitals were introduced in North America in 1947 by Donald Cameron, a psychiatrist from McGill University in Montreal, Canada.

See also COMMUNITY MENTAL HEALTH CENTERS.

Vaughan, P. J. "Developments in Psychiatric Day Care," *British Journal of Psychiatry* 147 (1985): 1–4.

deficit symptoms/syndrome These are the primary, enduring NEGATIVE SYMPTOMS of SCHIZOPHRENIA that are not considered secondary to other factors (e.g., DEPRESSION or ANXIETY, the effects of ANTIPSYCHOTIC DRUGS, or the environmental deprivation found in institutions). These terms were first proposed in a 1985 paper by W. T. Carpenter and his colleagues on deficit and nondeficit forms of schizophrenia. They are intended as a clarification and an alternative to CROW'S HYPOTHESIS of "Type I" and "Type II" schizophrenia. In Crow's two subtypes, POSITIVE SYMPTOMS (such as delusions and hallucinations) predominate in Type I but can also appear on a transient basis in Type II schizophrenia. The negative symptoms in Type II schizophrenia (restricted affect, diminished social drive, anhedonia, diminished intellectual ability) can also be transient in some cases, due to the secondary factors listed above. Carpenter and his coworkers wish to restrict more closely the two proposed subtypes of schizophrenia to one displaying a "primary enduring core of deficit symptoms" and one that does not. This proposed diagnostic category of "schizophrenia with deficit syndrome" would then most clearly be related to the variety of the disease most associated with neurological deterioration and a chronic course.

See also CHRONIC SCHIZOPHRENIA; COURSE AND OUTCOME OF SCHIZOPHRENIA.

Carpenter, W. T., D. W. Heinrichs, and A. M. Wagman. "Deficit and Nondeficit Forms of Schizophrenia: The Concept," *American Journal of Psychiatry* 145 (1988): 578–583.

Defoe, Daniel (1661–1736) Best remembered as the author of *Robinson Crusoe* (1719), Defoe was prolific writer and social critic who took a particularly keen interest in the humane treatment of the mentally ill. He wrote many articles on the abusive conditions in private madhouses, arguing that they should be inspected and licensed, which they eventually were. He published his own journal, known as the *Review,* and from time to time included articles of his own with themes like the 1706 "Scheme for the Management of Mad-houses."

degeneration theory In his *Traité des dégénérescences physiques, intellectuelles et morales de l'espece humaine* (Treatise on the Physical, Intellectual and Moral Degeneration of the Human Species) of 1857, the French alienist Benedict-Augustin Morel proposed the theory that physical and mental diseases were caused by immorality, substance abuse, masturbation, and living in unsanitary urban centers. These experiences in the life of an individual led to the hereditary transmission of a these physical, mental, and moral weaknesses to one's children. Each generation would thus pass along this hereditary taint, making each less and less fit to survive. It was believed (without statistical evidence until the end of the 1800s) that this process of DEGENERATION from an original healthy "type" would end family lines when the last generations were populated with persons who were too physically ill, insane, demented, or mentally retarded ("idiocy," "cretinism," or "feeble-mindedness") to survive and reproduce. This notion of "hereditary taint" or "bad blood" was akin to the notion of "original sin in the germ plasm"—that is, one was born burdened by the sins of the fathers (previous generations). Degeneration theory was an important influence in PSYCHIATRY in the latter half of the 19th century, particularly in France with the work of Valentin Magnan, in England with the work of Henry Mausdley, and in Germany in the work of Emil KRAEPELIN.

After its introduction by Emil Kraepelin in 1893, DEMENTIA PRAECOX (or *demence precoce*, a term first used by Morel in 1860) was viewed within this context as evidence of a "blood line" nearing the end of its degeneration process because it was a form of dementia arising in young people that is usually only seen in old age. Forms of insanity such as dementia praecox (SCHIZOPHRENIA) were thought to have an earlier AGE OF ONSET and a more severe course in each new generation. Today this phenomenon is known as genetic ANTICIPATION. It has been observed to occur in some neurodegenerative diseases and is being studied for its possible connection to schizophrenia. Degeneration theory became a dominant medical theory and a major source of PARANOIA among the public by the end of the 19th century, fueled in no small part by the popular hysteria provoked by the 1892 book *Entartung* (published in English as *Degeneration* in 1895). As an accepted theory in medicine, degeneration theory finally subsided in importance in the 1920s.

Backed by the authority of Francis Galton (1822–1911) in England, in the first half of the 20th century programs of EUGENICS (a term Galton coined) led to the promotion of selective breeding among humans to produce stronger blood lines of healthy human beings, forced sterilization of the insane, the immoral, and the criminal, and, in Nazi Germany, the murder of individuals (such as persons with dementia praecox/schizophrenia) who were deemed too biologically "unfit" to live and reproduce. The geneticist Eolf Axl Carlson traced the tragic history of eugenics in his 2001 volume, *The Unfit: A History of a Bad Idea.*

Emil Kraepelin, dementia praecox and degeneration It has long been asserted that Emil Kraepelin considered dementia praecox as evidence of the correctness of degeneration theory. We know from his autobiographical "self-assessment" that he wrote in 1920, and which remained unpublished until almost 80 years after his death, that he personally believed in degeneration theory and advocated eugenic programs to stop the "deterioration of the race" of the German people (*Volk*). But "degeneration" was more often used in his psychiatric publications to refer to the processes of progressive intellectual (dementia), physical, and social deterioration that occurred in an individual as part of a disease process that, in most persons, began only after puberty. For example, he originally introduced dementia praecox in 1893 as one of the insanities in the category of "psychic degenerative processes." In 1896 Emil Kraepelin estimated that in approximately 70 percent of the cases of dementia praecox he had observed, "hereditary predisposition" was present and "the so-called signs of degeneration were frequently observed" (*Psychiatrie,* 6th ed., p. 97) However, this hereditary predisposition did not lead directly to dementia praecox but instead to a metabolic self-poisoning of the body, or AUTOINTOXICATION (*Selbstvergiftung*), probably arising from the sex glands, which eventually affected the brain and produced psychotic symptoms (HALLUCINATIONS and DELUSIONS) and dementia. This belief was shared by another prominent German psychiatrist, Wilhelm Weygandt (1870–1939), who speculated in 1907 that "I should like to put forward a tentative explanation of dementia precox of my own. . . . I would suggest that so far as the organic side is concerned the most plausible concept is one of autotoxic damage affecting genetically predisposed brains." Kraepelin's use of the concept of degeneration should thus be viewed from these two perspectives: first, and most important, as a description of the course and outcome of a disease process, and only secondarily as evidence supporting the grander medical, social, cultural, and political claims of degeneration theory.

See also CHRONIC DELUSIONAL STATES IN FRENCH PSYCHIATRY; GENETICS STUDIES.

Carlson, E. A. *The Unfit: A History of a Bad Idea.* Cold Spring Harbor, N.Y.: Cold Spring Harbor Laboratory Press, 2001.

Engstrom, E., W. Burgmair, and M. M. Weber. "Emil Kraepelin's 'Self-Assessment': Clinical Autobiography in Historical Context," *History of Psychiatry* 13 (2002): 89–119.

Genil-Perrin, G. *Historie des origines et de l'évolution de l'idée de dégénérescence en médecine mentale.* Paris: 1913.

Morel, B. A. *Traité des dégénérescences physiques, intellectuelles et morales de l'espèce humaine.* Paris: 1857.

Weygandt, W. "Kritische Bemerkungen zur Psychologie der Dementia Praecox," *Monatsschrift für Psychiatrie und Neurologie* 22 (1907): 289–301.

deinstitutionalization With the advent of ANTIPSYCHOTIC DRUGS in the mid-1950s, and with the growing concern over the costs of institutionalizing large numbers of people and the harmful effects such living conditions might have, starting in 1955 literally hundreds of thousands of psychiatric patients were released—all too often to the streets—with little or no support services available to them. In 1955 there were approximately 559,000 patients in public psychiatric facilities in the United States, but by the mid-1980s that number had dwindled to about 110,000. The greatest number were released between 1965 and 1980, when an estimated 358,000 patients were sent back into the community to live. This process, although initially well-intentioned, led to the alarming problem of the homeless mentally ill, the "street people," that characterizes the last quarter of the 20th century.

Talbott, J. A. "Deinstitutionalization: Avoiding the Disasters of the Past," *Hospital and Community Psychiatry* 30 (1979): 621–624.

Torrey, E. F. *Nowhere to Go: The Tragic Odyssey of the Homeless Mentally Ill.* New York: Harper/Perennial, 1989.

délire de négation See COTARD'S SYNDROME.

délire d' énormité Literally the "delusion of enormity," a psychotic delusion that a person has undergone a massive increase in size. Such a person may insist that he or she fills up the entire room or is as large as the earth or perhaps even the entire universe. In some cases, it has been known to alternate with COTARD'S SYNDROME (the "delusion of negation"), and in fact it has been referred to as a "manic" form of Cotard's syndrome.

Enoch, M. D., and W. H. Trethowan. "Cotard's Syndrome." In *Uncommon Psychiatric Syndromes,* 2nd ed., edited by Enoch and Trethowan. Bristol: John Wright & Sons, 1979.

delirium An acute, reversible mental state characterized by clouded consciousness, confusion, extreme mental and motor excitement, defective perception, impaired memory, and a rapid flow of disconnected ideas. DELUSIONS and HALLUCINATIONS can accompany delirious states. Delirium is a symptom of an organic brain disorder, for it has a physiological basis (fevers, toxic effects from drugs or alcohol, exhaustion, etc.). Delirium is reversible, which distinguishes it from dementia, which is not.

From the time of ancient Greece and Rome, "delirium" has referred to a disturbance in the train of thinking, associated with physical disease. In 19th-century France, the term began to be used in reference to such a disturbance in thinking but without any connection to physical disease. For example Philippe PINEL uses the term *délire* to refer both to disturbances in logical reasoning and judgment (delusions) as well as to organic brain disease. In Great Britain and Germany, the distinction between "delusion" and "delirium" was largely maintained throughout the 19th century and is the basis of our modern definitions of these terms.

Berrios, G. E. "Delirium and Confusion in the 19th Century: A Conceptual History," *British Journal of Psychiatry* 139 (1981): 439–449.

delusion Historically, one of the primary symptoms of a psychotic disorder. The German psychiatrist Karl Jaspers once wrote that "Since time immemorial Delusion has been taken as the basic characteristic of madness." Although there is disagreement in the many different theories and definitions of what exactly a delusion is, a delusion is defined "a false personal belief based on incorrect inference about external reality" and is firmly maintained despite the consensually accepted beliefs of most others. Individuals with delusions will generally hold on to their beliefs even when confronted with strong evidence that contradicts their beliefs. In this sense, delusions are said to be "fixed," as if unchangeably cemented into the mind. Delusions are sometimes referred to as "ideational symptoms," because they involve a disturbance in ideas or cognition, whereas HALLUCINATIONS are sometimes called "perceptual" or "sensational symptoms," since they represent a disturbance in the processes of sensation and perception.

The first use of the word *delusion* in the English language in reference to mental disorder was in 1552, and the word's derivation can be traced back to a form of the Latin verb meaning "to play false." In Great Britain in the first half of the 19th century, the word *delusion* was used in a medical sense to refer to perceptual disorders (similar to our present use of the word *illusion*), but after 1850 it appears to have taken on its present meaning of "wrong belief."

See also CHRONIC DELUSIONAL STATES IN FRENCH PSYCHIATRY.

Arthur, A. Z. "Theories and Explanations of Delusions: A Review," *American Journal of Psychiatry* 121 (1964): 105–115.

Garety, P. "Delusions: Problems in Definition and Measurement," *British Journal of Medical Psychology* 58 (1985): 25–34.

Schmidt, G. "A Review of the German Literature on Delusion Between 1914 and 1939." In *The Clinical Roots of the Schizophrenia Concept,* edited by J. Cutting and M. Shepherd. Cambridge: Cambridge University Press, 1987.

delusional disorder A classification of psychotic disorders that first appeared in the 1987 *DSM-III-R.* The essential characteristic of delusional disorder is the persistent presence of a DELUSION that is not "bizarre" and is not due to any other psychotic disorder (such as SCHIZOPHRENIA, SCHIZOPHRENIFORM DISORDER, or a mood disorder such as bipolar illness). Persons with this disorder do not have obviously odd or peculiar behavior. As *DSM-III-R* stated, "A common characteristic of people with Delusional Disorder is the apparent normality of their behavior and appearance when their delusional ideas are not being discussed or acted upon." Yet they secretly (or in some cases, not so secretly) harbor a delusion that profoundly disagrees with reality. Formerly, this type of disorder was called paranoid disorder, but there are many different types of delusions that have nothing to do with "PARANOIA" (which is commonly interpreted as unfounded suspiciousness). The disorder rarely causes interruptions in intellectual or occupational functioning, and in most studies the average age of onset seems to be between 40 and 55.

There are seven different subtypes of delusional disorder: *erotomanic* (more traditionally known as Clérambault's syndrome), in which the delusion is that another person, usually of a higher social status, is in love with the subject; the *grandiose,* in which a person is convinced that he or she is "special" due to an inflated sense of power, identity, wealth, or special relationship to a deity or a special person (such as a celebrity); the *jealous,* in which the delusion is that one's sexual partner is unfaithful; the *persecutory,* in which the delusion involves a convincing belief that one is being purposely maligned or singled out for harassment in some way; the *somatic,* in which the person is convinced that he or she has some disease, mental disorder, or physical defect; the mixed type, in which delusions characteristic of one or more of the above types are present, but no one these predominates; and finally, a category of unspecified type for delusions that do not fit in the above categories.

In *ICD-10* (1992), this category of psychotic disorders is divided into *delusional disorder, other persistent delusional disorder,* and *unspecified persistent delusional disorder.* Delusions that are not related to schizophrenic delusions (that is, those that are "other than completely impossible or culturally inappropriate") must be present for at least three months. No hallucinations in any modality can be in evidence. The subtypes of persistent delusions are as follows: persecutory, litiginous, self-referential, grandiose, hypochondriacal (somatic), jealous, and erotomanic.

Delusional disorder has its roots in a long tradition in French psychiatry that identified a class of psychotic disorders that do not fall within the categories of schizophrenia (DEMENTIA PRAECOX) or a mood disorder (MANIC-DEPRESSIVE ILLNESS).

See also CHRONIC DELUSIONAL STATES IN FRENCH PSYCHIATRY; PARANOIA; PARAPHRENIA.

Dowbiggin, I. "Delusional Disorder." In *A History of Clinical Psychiatry: The Origin and History of Psychiatric Disorders,* edited by G. E. Berrios and R. Porter. London and New Brunswick, N.J.: Athlone Press, 1995.

delusional jealousy The false belief that one's sexual partner is engaging in sexual activities with others. This DELUSION of infidelity is also known

as the OTHELLO SYNDROME. Delusional jealousy is considered a psychotic disorder, whereas "obsessional jealousy" is the term used for persons with neurotic disorders. "Pathological jealousy" was first described by Karl Jaspers in 1910.

delusional perception A term for a phenomenon noticed in certain psychotic disorders in which the distinction between a DELUSION and an HALLUCINATION is not clear. It almost appears as if those individuals who are delusional are also caught in a process that changes their perceptual processes. Thus, when asked about their experiences, it is often difficult to distinguish whether the events described are simply delusions (bizarre ideas) or actual hallucinatory experiences that were "perceived" with the senses. This term (also called "perceptual delusions") is more often described in the German and French psychiatric literature than in the English-language literature.

Matussek, P. "Studies in Delusional Perception." In *The Clinical Roots of the Schizophrenia Concept: Translations of Seminal European Contributions on Schizophrenia,* edited by J. Cutting and M. Shepherd. Cambridge: Cambridge University Press, 1987.

delusions, bizarre A totally implausible idea or belief that is idiosyncratic and would not be believed as true by anyone. For example, a psychotic individual may believe that singer Diana Ross is the "Antichrist" or that singer Madonna is the biblical "Whore of Babylon."

delusions, grandiose A common psychotic delusion found particularly in PARANOID SCHIZOPHRENIA and in manic-depressive psychosis, in which a person has a highly exaggerated sense of his or her importance, identity, knowledge, or influence. For example, a psychotic individual may claim to own IBM and generously offer to write a hospital staff member a check for $5 million if they would only help that person escape or be discharged from the hospital. Many religious delusions are grandiose (e.g., "I'm Jesus Christ").

delusions, mood-congruent A delusion whose content matches the particular manic or depressed mood state that a person is in. For example, the delusion that one has AIDS or cancer when, in fact, one does not is consistent with a depressed mood in an individual. If in a manic mood state, grandiose delusions in particular may be mood-congruent (e.g., claims of owning millions of dollars or of being the most brilliant writer in the world).

delusions, mood-incongruent A delusion whose content does not match the particular mood state that a person is experiencing. These are the opposite of MOOD-CONGRUENT DELUSIONS.

delusions, nihilistic Commonly found in schizophrenia, these delusions involve the conviction that one does not exist, or that external reality does not exist. This is also referred to as COTARD'S SYNDROME.

delusions, persecutory One of the most common types of DELUSION found in PARANOID SCHIZOPHRENIA, and occasionally in other psychotic disorders as well. It is the delusion that the psychotic individual is being singled out, and even pursued for special abuse, by persons or "forces," and that this places the mentally disordered person in a constant state of danger. Delusions of being poisoned are common. Although known since antiquity, and included in ESQUIROL's descriptions of "monomania," the earliest comprehensive treatment of persecutory delusions was perhaps given by German psychiatrist Carl Wilhelm Ideler (1795–1860) in 1948. These delusions were also referred to as "persecutory delirium" by French psychiatrist Ernest Charles Lasègue in 1852.

Ideler, C. W. *Der Wahnsinn.* Bremen: 1848.

delusions, somatic A delusional belief about the structure of functioning of one's body. For example, a male schizophrenic patient may fully believe that he is pregnant, or a psychotic woman may believe

that a team of doctors kidnapped her during the night and removed her uterus and genitalia.

delusions, systematized An organized system of delusions that all refer to a similar theme and that form the basis for a psychotic individual's incorrect interpretation of new experiences. For example, a psychotic person who has failed a psychology licensing examination may believe that the members of the licensing board in that state are involved in a conspiracy against the afflicted person and, furthermore, that these board members are responsible for the person's inability to find a parking space. The term *systematic* or *systematized delusions* originated in the work of French psychiatrist Valentin Magnan of Paris. The idea was first put forth in a series of articles published in 1888 in *Le Progrès médical,* then in a monograph published in 1892 with his colleague Paul Sérieu (1864–1947), entitled *Le délire chronique à évolution systématique.* Such systematized delusions were not only organized but persistent, unlike the disorganized and transient delusions found in other psychotic disorders.

See also BOUFFÉE DÉLIRANTE; CHRONIC DELUSIONAL STATES IN FRENCH PSYCHIATRY.

delusions of being controlled One of the most common types of delusion found in SCHIZOPHRENIA, it involves the idea that a person's thought, feeling, and behavior are controlled by some external force (e.g., "Kate is controlling my thoughts"). This is also known as the Clérambault-Kandinsky syndrome.

delusions of passion See EROTOMANIA.

delusions of poverty The delusion that a person is totally devoid of any material possessions, or that such possessions will soon be taken away from the person, rendering him or her poverty-stricken.

delusions of reference The delusions that people, objects, or events in an individual's immediate environment have an unusual or "special" significance. This significance is usually of a negative or threatening quality, but not always. For example, a psychotic individual may believe that the expression on television newsman Dan Rather's face is a secret message that is intended just for that person.

demence A term used by both Philippe PINEL in 1801 and Benjamin RUSH in 1812 to describe what we would now call THOUGHT DISORDER—disconnected and disorganized thoughts that are strung together without any logical order. Pinel describes the "special character of dementia" that is still observed in schizophrenics today:

> Rapid succession or uninterrupted alternation of undulated ideas, and evanescent and unconnected emotions. Continually repeated acts of extravagance; complete forgetfulness of every previous state; diminished sensibility to external impressions; abolition of the faculty of judgment; perceptual activity.

Benjamin Rush preferred to rename this condition "dissociation," as he believed that this constituted its primary symptom. However, Rush's use of this term is different than the more commonly accepted definition of DISSOCIATION by Pierre JANET (1859–1947). Dissociation was "an association of unrelated perceptions, or ideas, from the inability of the mind to perform the operations of judgement and reason." Furthermore, "ideas, collected together without order, frequently constitute a paroxysm of the disease." Rush's emphasis on ASSOCIATION DISTURBANCES was later also emphasized by Eugen BLEULER in 1911 as one of the four PRIMARY SYMPTOMS OF SCHIZOPHRENIA.

Pinel, P. *A Treatise on Insanity* 1801. Reprint, Sheffield: W. Todd, 1806.

Rush, B. *Medical Inquiries and Observations upon Diseases of the Mind.* Philadelphia: Kimber & Richardson, 1812.

dementia Dementia is an ORGANIC MENTAL SYNDROME that is characterized by impairment in short- and long-term memory, disturbances in the ability to think abstractly, impaired judgment,

and personality changes; there is also evidence of other abnormal brain functioning. In personality changes, a person may not seem himself or herself, may become withdrawn, and a once lively personality may become flat. A once neat person may start to appear sloppy and apathetic. When social judgment is impaired by the organic brain disease process that produced the dementia, some people may become irritable, impulsive, or paranoid. They may wander about and become lost. Alzheimer's disease (primary degenerative dementia of the Alzheimer's type) is the picture of extreme dementia that most of us are familiar with.

According to modern definition, dementia may not necessarily be progressively degenerative, and actually may go into remission in some circumstances. However, in the 19th century the older idea of dementia was that it referred to chronic insanity or that it was a progressively degenerative brain disease that led to death (see DEGENERATION). With advances in the science of neurology in the second half of the 19th century, specific chronic brain disorders were identified that involved dementia, although conditions that could not be conclusively identified as "organic" were also recognized as "vesanic dementias." The idea of vesanic dementias contributed to the formation of the idea of PSYCHOSIS in the latter half of the 19th century.

Berrios, G. E. "Dementia during the 17th and 18th Centuries," *Psychological Medicine* (1987).

dementia infantalis A term first used in 1930 by Austrian psychiatrist Theodore Heller to describe CHILDHOOD ONSET SCHIZOPHRENIA. He thought that dementia infantalis was present in children before the age of four. It is sometimes referred to as "Heller's disease."

See also AUTISM, INFANTILE.

dementia paralytica See GENERAL PARALYSIS OF THE INSANE.

dementia paranoides A term coined by Emil KRAEPELIN in the fourth edition of his textbook, *Psychiatrie,* to characterize a psychotic disorder with a sudden onset and disorganized delusions, which progresses rapidly into DEMENTIA. Dementia paranoides was one of the "psychic processes of degeneration" in this 1893 textbook, along with DEMENTIA PRAECOX and CATATONIA. However, in the fifth edition of 1896, Kraepelin placed these three disorders under the category of "metabolic disorders leading to dementia." In 1899 dementia praecox ballooned into one of the two great insanities (along with MANIC-DEPRESSIVE ILLNESS), and dementia paranoides, catatonia, and HEBEPHRENIA were now merely forms of dementia praecox. Sigmund FREUD's famous interpretation of the autobiography of the psychotic Daniel Paul Schreber, formerly a presiding judge on Saxony's highest court, is where this term figures most prominently in his writings. Since Schreber was a homosexual, this helped support Freud's theory that homosexual panic was at the root of paranoia.

See also PARANOID SCHIZOPHRENIA.

Freud, S. "Psycho-analytic Notes on an Autobiographical Account of a Case of Paranoia (Dementia Paranoides)." In *The Standard Edition of the Complete Psychological Works of Sigmund Freud,* edited by J. Strachey. 1911. Reprint, New York: Macmillan, 1964.

dementia praecocissima This term was first used in 1905 by Italian psychiatrist Sante De Sanctis (1862–1935) to describe a form of dementia praecox that had its onset before puberty. De Sanctis is generally credited for being the first to describe what later become known as CHILDHOOD SCHIZOPHRENIA.

De Sanctis, S. *Neuropsichiatria infantile. Patalogia e diagnostica.* Turin: Lattes, 1925.

———. "On Some Varieties of Dementia Praecox," tr. M. Osborn. In *Modern Perspectives in International Child Psychiatry,* edited by J. G. Howells. 1906. Reprint, Edinburgh: Oliver & Boyd, 1969.

dementia praecox A term that referred to a psychotic disorder marked by rapid cognitive disintegration beginning soon after the clear onset of

the disease, usually in the years following puberty. Cognitive disintegration did not mean an impairment of intelligence but instead referred to a disruption in the various mental functions that we now commonly refer to as attention, memory, and goal-directed thinking (executive functions). DEMENTIA in this older sense meant "incoherence." The primary disturbance in dementia praecox was not one of mood (as was the case in MANIC-DEPRESSIVE ILLNESS), but of cognition. From the outset, dementia praecox was viewed as a progressively degenerating disease from which no one recovered.

Démence précoce (1853, 1860) This psychotic disorder was first mentioned by the French alienist Benedict-Augustin Morel in 1853, but later described in his 1860 textbook, *Traité des maladies mentales.* Morel introduced this term to define a disorder striking primarily men in their teenage or young adult years. Following the first clear disruption in their lives, their intellectual functioning rapidly declined. Morel placed this insanity within the larger context of his DEGENERATION THEORY. These young men were beginning a rapid intellectual deterioration that would result in total disability and possible death. Morel, however, did not conduct any long-term or quantitative research on the course and outcome of *démence précoce* (KRAEPELIN would be the first in history to do that), so this prognosis was based on speculation.

The contributions of Karl Kahlbaum and Ewald Hecker (1863–1874) In 1863 Karl KAHLBAUM (1828–99) of Prussia published his Habilitation (the equivalent of a second doctoral dissertation in Germany, necessary for becoming a university professor), *Die Gruppirung der psychischen Krankheiten* (The Classification of Psychiatric Diseases). In this book, Kahlbaum described a class of progressively degenerating psychotic disorders that he grouped under the term *Vesania typical* (typical insanity). In 1866 Kahlbaum became the director of a private psychiatric clinic in Görlitz, Prussia, a small town near Dresden. He was accompanied by his younger assistant, Ewald Hecker (1843–1909), and together they conducted a series of research studies on young psychotic patients that would eventuate in a major influence on the development of modern PSYCHIATRY. Together Kahlbaum and Hecker were the first to describe and name such syndromes as dysthymia, cyclothymia, PARANOIA, CATATONIA, and HEBEPHRENIA.

Perhaps their most lasting contribution to psychiatry was the introduction of the "clinical method" from medicine to the study of mental diseases, a method which is now known as psychopathology. Other than Morel's claims about his degeneration theory, the element of time had largely been missing from definitions of mental disorders. Psychiatrists made pronouncements about prognosis that were not based on careful observations of the changing symptoms of patients over time. MAD-DOCTORS, ALIENISTS, and other physicians who wrote about the insane arbitrarily invented names for insanities and described their characteristic signs and symptoms based on a short-term, cross-sectional observation period of their lunatic patients. When the element of time was added to the concept of diagnosis, a diagnosis became more than just a description of a collection of symptoms: diagnosis now also defined prognosis (course and outcome). An additional feature of the clinical method was that the characteristic symptoms that define syndromes should be described without any prior assumption of brain pathology (although such links could be made later as scientific knowledge progressed). Karl Kahlbaum first made his appeal for the adoption of the clinical method in psychiatry in his 1874 book on catatonia. Without Kahlbaum and Hecker there would be no dementia praecox.

Emil Kraepelin and dementia praecox (1893) In 1891 Emil Kraepelin left his position at the university in Dorpat (now Tartu, Estonia) to become a professor and director of the psychiatric clinic at the university in Heidelberg, Germany. Convinced of the value of Kahlbaum's suggestions for a more exact qualitative clinical method in psychiatry (which Kahlbaum never applied himself), Kraeplin realized that by adding a quantitative component to such a research program he could place psychiatry on a more scientific foundation. Quantification helped to eliminate any subjective biases on the part of the researcher. He began the first such research program of this nature in the history of psychiatry at Heidelberg in 1891, collecting data about every new patient that was admitted to the clinic (and not just "interesting cases," as had been

the case in the past) and summarizing them on specially prepared index cards, his famous *Zählkarten*. He had been keeping data on such cards since 1887. In his posthumously published *Memoirs* (which was first published in German 61 years after his death), Kraepelin described his method:

> . . . after the first thorough examination of a new patient, each of us had to throw in a note [in a "diagnosis box"] with his diagnosis written on it. After a while, the notes were taken out of the box, the diagnoses were listed, and the case was closed, the final interpretation of the disease was added to the original diagnosis. In this way, we were able to see what kind of mistakes had been made and were able to follow-up the reasons for the wrong original diagnosis (p. 61).

Kraepelin was obsessed with finding patterns in the data on these cards, taking them home with him or on vacation at times. In 1893, two years after starting his more rigorous research program in Heidelberg, the fourth edition of Kraepelin's textbook, *Psychiatrie*, reflected some preliminary impressions derived from the analysis of his cards. Clinical syndromes involved not only a diagnosis according to signs and symptoms, but one which also included course and outcome. In that edition, he introduced a class of psychotic disorders he called psychic degenerative processes. Three of these came directly from the work of Kahlbaum and Hecker: DEMENTIA PARANOIDES (a sudden-onset, degenerative form of Kahlbaum's paranoia; catatonia (directly from Kahlbaum's 1874 monograph on the subject; and dementia praecox, which was essentially Hecker's hebephrenia (as described in 1871). Dementia praecox was hebephrenia and would remain so in Kraepelin's thinking for six more years.

In March 1896 the fifth edition of Kraepelin's textbook appeared. In it, Kraepelin stated that he was confident of the value of his clinical method of using qualitative and quantitative data collected over a long period of observation of patients as a way of developing a diagnosis that included prognosis (course and outcome):

> What convinced me of the superiority of the clinical method of diagnosis (followed here) over the traditional one, was the *certainty with which we could predict (in conjunction with our new concept of disease) the future course of events*. Thanks to it the student can now find his way more easily in the difficult subject of psychiatry.

In the 1896 fifth edition, dementia praecox (still essentially hebephrenia), dementia paranoides, and catatonia are separate psychotic disorders included among "metabolic disorders leading to dementia."

In the sixth edition of *Psychiatrie* of 1899, Kraepelin reordered the psychiatric cosmos for the next century by grouping most of the insanities into two large categories, dementia praecox and manic-depressive illness. They were distinguished by the following characteristics: dementia praecox was primarily a disorder of intellectual functioning, whereas manic-depressive illness was primarily a disorder of affects or mood, dementia praecox had a uniformly deteriorating course and a poor prognosis, whereas manic-depressive insanity had a course of acute exacerbations followed by complete remissions with no lasting deterioration of intellectual functioning, and there were no recoveries from dementia praecox, whereas in manic-depressive illness there were many complete recoveries. In 1899 dementia praecox took its now-familiar form as a heterogenous class of psychotic disorders comprised of hebephrenic, catatonic, and paranoid forms. These forms have persisted until today through Eugen BLEULER'S SCHIZOPHRENIA of 1908 (to which he added a fourth form, dementia simplex, or simple schizophrenia), and the main types of schizophrenia in *DSM-IV-TR* (the paranoid, catatonic, and disorganized types, with the latter retaining its historical designation as the hebephrenic type in *ICD-10* [1992]).

In the seventh edition of 1904, there was little change in the description of dementia praecox, but Kraepelin does admit for the first time that in a small number of cases recovery from dementia praecox might occur.

The eighth edition of Kraepelin's *Psychiatrie* was a four-volume opus, each of which appeared in different years between 1909 and 1915. In this edition, dementia praecox became one of the "endogenous dementias." It is in the 1913 third

volume (second part) of this edition that Kraepelin adjusts his concept of prognosis to admit that a partial remisison of symptoms occurred in approximately 26 percent of his patients. This brought dementia praecox in line with Eugen Bleuler's claims about schizophrenia, which he had insisted from the start (in 1908) that (a) in many cases there was no fateful progressive deterioration, (b) in some cases the symptoms did indeed remit for periods of time, and (c) there were cases of complete recovery.

The eighth edition of 1913 is also notable for the fact that Kraepelin increased the number of forms of dementia to 11. However, the three classical original subtypes would remain as the most influential description of this disorder for the century that followed.

The eighth edition of *Psychiatrie* was the last Kraepelin would produce in his lifetime. He was working on a ninth edition with Johannes Lange (1891–1938) but died in 1926 before it could be completed. Lange finished the bulk of it and published it in 1927.

Etiology Kraepelin realized that the state of scientific knowledge was such that definitive claims about the cause of dementia praecox could not be made. Heredity clearly played a role, as Kraepelin and his research associates had demonstrated this in quantitative research. As a result of following the clinical method suggested by Kahlbaum, Kraepelin set aside claims about underlying brain disease or specific neuropathology in the diagnostic descriptions of his mental disorders. However, from the fifth edition of 1896 to the third volume of the eighth edition of 1913, it was clear that Kraepelin believed that dementia praecox was caused by a poisoning of the brain and "autointoxication," probably arising from the sex glands after puberty. Kraepelin's ideas about AUTOINTOXICATION AS A CAUSE OF DEMENTIA PRAECOX is covered in depth in a separate entry in this volume.

Dementia praecox is a universal human disease Kraepelin believed that dementia praecox was not a culture-bound syndrome and that it represented a disease process that could be found all over the world. Kraepelin himself loved to travel, and in Asia he observed that dementia praecox was similar to the European form of the illness in Chinese, Japanese, Tamil, and Malay patients, leading him to suggest in the eighth edition of *Psychiatrie* that "we must therefore seek the real cause of dementia praecox in conditions which are spread all over the world, which thus do not lie in race or in climate, in food or in any other general circumstance of life. . . ."

Treatment Without knowing the cause of dementia praecox or manic-depressive illness, Kraepelin repeatedly stated that there could be no treatments specific to these conditions. Treatment for these insanities was the same for any institutionalized patient with any diagnosis: the occasional use of drugs (opiates, barbiturates, and so on) to alleviate acute episodes of distress, prolonged baths (greatly admired by Kraepelin as a humane method of calming patients), and occupational activities (if possible). Kraepelin himself had experimented with hypnosis early in his career and found it lacking. Psychotherapy as such was not part of the medical cognition of Kraepelin. In fact, Kraepelin detested both FREUD and JUNG for introducing diagnostic terms and forms of treatment that had no empirical basis.

The reception of dementia praecox By 1899 Kraepelin himself had counted almost 20 German-language publications that made reference to his new diagnostic term, dementia praecox. In the decade after 1899, the number of German-language publications using Kraepelin's categories of dementia praecox and manic-depressive illness as a basis for clinical speculation and experimental research exploded. German-language psychiatric concepts were always introduced much faster in America (than, say, Britain) where émigré German, Swiss, and Austrian physicians essentially created American psychiatry. Swiss-emigree Adolf MEYER, arguably the most influential psychiatrist in America for the first half of the 20th century, published the first critique of dementia praecox in an 1896 book review of the fifth edition of Kraepelin's textbook. But it was not until 1900 that the first three American publications regarding dementia praecox appeared, one of which was a translation of a few sections of Kraepelin's sixth edition of 1899 on dementia praecox. Because so many influential American physicians began to take psychoanalysis seriously after Freud and Jung attended a conference at Clark University in 1909, dementia

praecox and, after 1911, Bleuler's schizophrenia were openly accepted. Until 1910 Bleuler had been peripherally connected through Jung to Freud's psychoanalytic movement, and this eased the adoption of his broader version of dementia praecox (schizophrenia) in America over Kraepelin's more narrow and prognostically more negative one. Until the late 1950s the terms dementia praecox and schizophrenia were used interchangeably in American psychiatry. The reception of dementia praecox as an accepted diagnosis in British psychiatry came much slower, perhaps taking hold only around the time of the First World War. In France an older psychiatric tradition regarding the psychotic disorders (see the entry for CHRONIC DELUSIONAL DISORDERS IN FRENCH PSYCHIATRY) predated Kraepelin, and the French never fully adopted Kraepelin's classification system. Instead the French maintained an independent classification system throughout the 20th century. After 1980, when *DSM-III* totally reshaped psychiatric diagnosis, French psychiatry began finally to alter its views of diagnosis to converge with the North American system. Kraepelin thus finally conquered France via America.

The "neo-Kraepelinians" and DSM-III (1980) Editions of the *Diagnostic and Statistic Manual of Mental Disorders* since the first one in 1952 had reflected views of schizophrenia as "reactions" or "psychogenic" (*DSM-I*), or as manifesting Freudian notions of "defense mechanisms" (as in *DSM-II* of 1968, in which the symptoms of schizophrenia were interpreted as "psychologically self-protected). The diagnostic criteria were wide, including either concepts that no longer exist or that are now labeled as personality disorders (for example, SCHIZOTYPAL PERSONALITY DISORDER). There was also no mention of the dire prognosis Kraepelin had made. Schizophrenia seemed to be more prevalent and more treatable than either Kraepelin or Bleuler would have allowed.

As a direct result of the effort to construct RESEARCH DIAGNOSTIC CRITERIA in the 1970s that were independent of any clinical diagnostic manual, Kraepelin's ideas began to return in prominence. For research purposes, the definition of schizophrenia returned to the narrow range allowed by Kraepelin's dementia praecox. Furthermore, the disorder was a progressively deteriorating one once again, with the notion that recovery, if it happened at all, was rare. This revision of schizophrenia became the basis of the diagnostic criteria in *DSM-III*. Some of the psychiatrists who worked to bring about this revision referred to themselves as the neo-Kraepelinians.

Berrios, G. E., and R. Hauser. "The Early Development of Kraepelin's Ideas on Classification," *Psychological Medicine* 18 (1988): 813–822.

Diem, O. "Die einfach demente Form der Dementia praecox," *Archiv für Psychiatrie und Nervenkrankheiten* 37 (1903): 111–187.

Hecker, E. "Die Hebephrenie," *Virchows Archiv für pathologische Anatomie* 52 (1871): 392–449.

Jablensky, A., et al. "Kraepelin Revisited: A Reassessment and Statistical Analysis of Dementia Praecox and Manic-Depressive Insanity in 1980," *Psychological Medicine* 23 (1993): 843–858.

Kahlbaum, K. *Die Gruppierung der psychischen Krankheiten und die Eintheilung der Seelenstorungen*. Danzig, 1863.

———, K. *Die Katatonie oder das Spannungsirresein*. Berlin: Hirschwald, 1874.

Kraepelin, E. "Dementia praecox." In *The Clinical Roots of the Schizophrenia Concept: Translations of Seminal European Contributions On Schizophrenia*, edited by J. Cutting and M. Shepherd. 1896. Reprint (5th ed.), Cambridge: Cambridge University Press, 1987.

Kraepelin, E. *Memoirs*, Berlin: Springer-Verlag, 1987.

Dementia Praecox Studies The first scientific or medical journal in any language to be named after a psychiatric disorder. During its short life (1918 to 1922), *Dementia Praecox Studies* not only provided extensive bibliographic essays and reviews of published laboratory reports from several nations but also provided translations of selected experimental studies of unpublished doctoral theses from the original German or French. Perhaps most important, *Dementia Praecox Studies* served as the primary place of publication for the experimental reports of the Research Laboratory of the Psychopathic Hospital of Cook County (Illinois) and the editorials of its director, the noted Chicago surgeon and, in 1895, the unsuccessful Socialist candidate for mayor of Chicago, Bayard Taylor HOLMES, M.D. (1852–1924).

Dementia Praecox Studies was the only journal ever produced by the handful of Kraepelinian physicians in the United States. Like Emil KRAEPELIN, they believed that MENTAL DISORDERS were first and foremost brain diseases with neuropathological, biochemical, infectious, and genetic causes. But from the 1890s until the late 1960s, American psychiatry was dominated by the followers of Adolf MEYER's "psychosocial reaction" theory and Sigmund FREUD's pseudoscience of PSYCHOANALYSIS. These traditions of "mind twist men" were suspicious of laboratory science and rejected biological and genetic causes for mental disorders. The premature death from pneumonia of Harvard Medical School pathologist Elmer Ernest Southard (1876–1920) left the "brain spot men" without a prominent spokesman. The death of Bayard Holmes in 1924 essentially ended the Kraepelinian movement in America for decades.

The opening pages of the January 1918 edition contain the following invitation from Herman Campbell Stevens for the submission of laboratory research reports: "The purpose of this publication is to arouse interest in the subject of dementia praecox. . . . How little is known about the disease is apparent from a reading of the standard treaties on psychiatry and from the current literature. It is the purpose of this journal to serve as a clearing-house for scientifically established facts with regard to dementia praecox. Any competent and contentious study of a morphological, biochemical or psychiatric nature will be accepted. It is the aim of the editors to encourage research in the hope that a rational therapy and prophylaxis will result." Bayard Holmes unabashedly expressed his "faith" in the hypothesis that "disease of the mind is the result of organic disease of the body," and as "in spite of the magnitude of this problem there is a great scarcity of books and monographs dealing with the physical, chemical and biologic conditions of the unfortunate victims of this disease," he urges "the publication of a journal devoted exclusively to the study from the organic point of view, of one part of the field of mental disease, viz., dementia praecox."

Holmes, B. "Prospectus of *Dementia Praecox Studies*," *Dementia Praecox Studies* 1 (January 1918), unnumbered appendix to the first issue.

Stevens, H. C. "Our Point of View," *Dementia Praecox Studies* 1 (January 1918): 1–2.

demoniac A person who is "possessed" by demons or evil spirits. In all cultures, whether simple or complex and technological, there is usually a belief that mental illness was caused by such discarnate entities.

See also CACODEMONOMANIA; POSSESSION SYNDROME.

demonomania A 19th-century term for a type of mental disorder in which a person believes his or her thoughts, feelings, or behaviors are due to the direct influence of, or communication with, "spiritual" entities. ESQUIROL devoted an entire chapter in this disorder in his 1838 *Mental Maladies*, which he said is composed of "all those forms of delirium which have reference to religious beliefs." He identifies two distinct subtypes of demonomania, depending on whether the person believes he or she is influenced by "good" or "bad" spirits. The first of these, *theomania*, "would have designated that class of the insane, who believe that they are God, who imagine that they have conversations and intimate communications with the Holy Spirit, angels and saints, and who pretend to be inspired, and to have received a commission from heaven to convert men." The second type of demonomania, CACODEMONOMANIA, involves such imagined contact with evil spirits or the Devil. Esquirol uses the word *demonomania* to refer to both "good" and "evil" spiritual influences rather than just evil ones since, as he correctly points out, "The word demon among the ancients was not understood in a bad sense. It signified the Divinity, a tutelary Genius, a guardian Spirit. . . ." Esquirol suggests he is thus "preserving the primitive significance of this word."

See also POSSESSION SYNDROME.

Esquirol, J. E. D. *Mental Maladies, A Treatise on Insanity*, trans. E. K. Hunt. Philadelphia: Lea & Blanchard, 1845; first published, 1838.

Noll, R. *Vampires, Werewolves, and Demons: Twentieth Century Reports in the Psychiatric Literature*. New York: Brunner/Mazel, 1991.

denial A type of defense mechanism in which a person does not seem to be aware of some aspect of external reality or of himself that is obvious to others. This type of behavior is commonly observed in people with psychotic disorders, and in its extreme forms denial can give an individual's statements an almost delusional quality.

See also DELUSION.

Denmark See SCANDINAVIA.

depersonalization An aberration of the sense or experience of oneself in which the feeling of the "reality" of one's experience is missing. People experiencing depersonalization claim that they feel distant from their own experience, that it is "dreamlike," or that reality has an uncanny "strangeness" to it. They may feel that they are automatons, or that their experience is "automatic" and not "spontaneous" in any way. Feelings that one's extremities have changed in size sometimes accompany this syndrome. Depersonalization can occur in normals for temporary periods of time (particularly in adolescents, with estimates that as many as 70 percent of them experience it at one time or another), but it is also experienced by those individuals who are diagnosed with SCHIZOTYPAL PERSONALITY DISORDER, SCHIZOPHRENIA, or, when not psychotic, depersonalization disorder, which is one of the DISSOCIATIVE DISORDERS.

depression When depression is present in an individual afflicted with one of the psychotic disorders it is considered a dangerous sign. Suicide is far more likely to result from depression in psychotic individuals. Studies have shown that for SCHIZOPHRENIA, an individual is most likely to commit suicide within the first 10 years of the onset of the disease.

Depression has always been a type of AFFECTIVE DISORDER, but there has been more recognition that many people who are diagnosed with schizophrenia suffer from depression. This depression may be caused by the underlying schizophrenic disease process, the realization by the person that his or her mental capacities are deteriorating, or as a side effect of antipsychotic medication. Many schizophrenics are thus also given ANTIDEPRESSANT DRUGS along with their antipsychotic medication. Sometimes people who are suffering from a severe depression can hear AUDITORY HALLUCINATIONS and, in many ways, appear to be schizophrenic. However, clinicians must make the sometimes difficult differential diagnosis between this depression with psychotic features and true schizophrenia.

See also ANTIPSYCHOTIC DRUGS.

DeLisi, L. E. *Depression in Schizophrenia.* Washington, D.C.: American Psychiatric Press, 1990.

Sands, J. R., and M. Harrow. "Depression during the Longitudinal Course of Schizophrenia," Schizophrenia Bulletin 25 (1999): 157–171.

derealization This is the component of DEPERSONALIZATION in which one's sense of the reality of one's world is disturbed. Depersonalization includes alterations in the sense of identity (e.g., the feeling of being an automaton), in addition to derealization.

dereistic thinking A word coined by Eugen BLEULER in 1912 to describe a type of intense fantasy activity that totally ignores any contradictions with reality and that may seem quite realistic. Bleuler constructed the term "dereistic" from two Latin words meaning "away from reality." Dereistic thinking sometimes occurs in the daydreams of normal people, but it is found in its clearest (and most reality-free) forms in dreams, the hallucinations and delusions of schizophrenics, and in mythology. Bleuler's concept of dereistic thinking resembles a similar process later referred to by his colleague at the BURGHÖLZI HOSPITAL in Zurich, C. G. JUNG, as "active imagination." Dereistic thinking also resembles the descriptions of REGRESSION or of "regression in the service of the ego" by Sigmund FREUD and his followers.

Bleuler, E. *Textbook of Psychiatry.* 4th ed. Translated by A. A. Brill. 1916. Reprint, New York: Macmillan, 1924.

De Sanctis, Sante (1862–1935) An Italian physician and a professor of psychiatry at the University of Rome who is perhaps best remembered for his 1905 description of DEMENTIA PRAECOCISSIMA, a childhood form of DEMENTIA PRAECOX. He wrote on a wide variety of topics, including dreams, experimental psychiatry, and forensic psychiatry. In 1932 he published an autobiography of his life and career in PSYCHIATRY.

deteriorating psychoses A 19th-century term for psychotic disorders marked by their DEGENERATION, such as DEMENTIA PRAECOX.

developmental insanity See ADOLESCENT INSANITY

diagnosis, differential One of the most important determinants of treatment is the diagnosis of the disorder. This is extremely important when it comes to severe MENTAL DISORDERS such as SCHIZOPHRENIA or BIPOLAR DISORDER, which often require different classes of drugs and which have different courses. Often one of the first diagnostic decisions that a clinician must make is whether the patient is psychotic (out of touch with reality) or not. If so, then: Are the symptoms due to one of the psychotic disorders, or are they due to an organic mental disorder (such as an underlying neurological disease or intoxication)? If a known organic brain disease, or intoxication, can be ruled out, then the clinician must decide which among the various psychotic disorders best fits the history of the person's illness and the type of symptoms that person is displaying. Often a difficult differential diagnosis must be made between schizophrenia (particularly the paranoid subtype) and a manic episode with psychotic features.

The two most commonly used diagnostic system are the AMERICAN PSYCHIATRIC ASSOCIATION'S *DSM-IV-TR* (2000) and the WORLD HEALTH ORGANIZATION'S *ICD-10* (1992).

American Psychiatric Association, *Diagnostic and Statistical Manual of Mental Disorders.* 4th ed, text revision. Washington, D.C.: American Psychiatric Association, 2000.

World Health Organization, *Mental Disorders: Glossary and Guide to Their Classification in Accordance with the Tenth Revision of the International Classification of Diseases.* Geneva, Switzerland: World Health Organization, 1992.

diathesis-stress theories One of the main categories of genetic theories of SCHIZOPHRENIA. Diathesis-stress theories all posit that it is the interaction between genetic heritage (the "diathesis" or "inherited predisposition," which places the person at "high-risk" for the development of the disease) and stressors in the environment that causes the disease. Diathesis-stress theories are polygenetic ones. The diathesis is often assumed to involve the additive effect of the operation of a large number of genes, sometimes called schizophrenic polygenes. These theories hold that the more schizophrenic polygenes an individual inherits, the more vulnerable that person is to stressors in the environment that can induce the onset of schizophrenia.

A famous theory of the diathesis-stress causes of schizophrenia was put forth by clinical psychologist Paul Meehl in 1962. Meehl proposed that a genetic predisposition for particular kinds of neurological defects, which he called SCHIZOTAXIA, must interact with the experiences of environmental social learning to produce a type of person that may be called a schizotype. If the schizotype is subjected to certain stressors that are severe enough, that person will develop schizophrenia. Meehl's theory fits in with the other polygenetic diathesis-stress theories because it accounts for the interaction of heredity and the environment in the production of schizophrenia, and it allows for a wide range of schizophrenia-like disorders that the schizotype can exhibit without experiencing the extreme stressors that could cause schizophrenia. Furthermore, it assumes that the environment may be the source of the development of one over the other type of schizophrenic subtype.

Diathesis-stress theories based on polygenetic assumptions are still among the most widely accepted theories with researchers who are trying to learn the causes of severe MENTAL DISORDERS such as schizophrenia and BIPOLAR DISORDER. These theories are the latest battleground in the long-standing "nature v. nurture" debate in science.

Yet, with increases in our knowledge of the causes of diseases, it is becoming clearer and clearer that the nature-nurture distinction is becoming more and more blurred. Epidemiologist Brian McMahon succinctly lists the problems in understanding the complexity of gene-environment interactions:

1. It has become clear that there is no disease that is determined entirely by genetic or environmental factors.
2. There is, evidently, more overlap in the time of operation of genetic and environmental factors than was previously suspected.
3. Just as the environment may exert its effect through the genetic mechanism of mutation, so may genetic factors operate by changing the environment.
4. The roles of genes and environment, and the nature of the specific factors involved, may be quite different in individuals with identical manifestations.

See also GENETIC TRANSMISSION; HIGH-RISK STUDIES.

MacMahon, B. "Gene-environment Interaction in Human Disease." In *The Transmission of Schizophrenia*, edited by D. Rosenthal and S. Kety. Oxford: Pergamon Press, 1968.

Meehl, P. "Schizotaxia, Schizotypy, Schizophrenia," *American Psychologist* 17 (1962): 827–828.

dibenzodiazepine See ANTIPSYCHOTIC DRUGS.

dibenzoxazepine See ANTIPSYCHOTIC DRUGS.

dihydroindolone See ANTIPSYCHOTIC DRUGS.

dimensions of schizophrenia SCHIZOPHRENIA has always been characterized as a "heterogeneous" disorder made up of several different clinical "subtypes" or, perhaps, several different diseases. Emil KRAEPELIN posited three forms for his DEMENTIA PRAECOX (1899): PARANOIA, HEBEPHRENIA, and CATATONIA. Eugen BLEULER added a fourth to his schizophrenia concept (1908), a subtype called "simple schizophrenia." Both of the current major diagnostic manuals of mental disorders, *DSM-IV* (1994) and *ICD-10* (1992), base their diagnostic criteria for schizophrenia on Kraepelin's and Bleuler's clinical subtypes.

"Subtype" models of schizophrenia were based on clinical observation of symptoms and the grouping and classification of those symptoms by individual researchers. By the 1970s a movement arose to reexamine these traditional subtypes using the new findings in neuropathology, genetics neuroimaging, and neuropsychology as a basis for a new model of schizophrenia. In 1980 T. J. Crow proposed the first of these new models, his "two-syndrome concept" of schizophrenia involving Type I (positive symptoms, later onset, better prognosis) and Type II (negative symptoms, earlier onset, and poorer prognosis). CROW'S HYPOTHESIS generated a great deal of additional research and, by 1987, its claims were being challenged by new statistical studies of the symptoms of schizophrenia using factor analysis that led to new "dimensional models" of schizophrenia.

Factor analysis is a statistical technique that, when used in studies of schizophrenic symptoms quantified with the use of structured interviews, identified groups of related symptoms that tend to coexist in an individual. Closely related symptoms "load" onto a single "factor" or "dimension." Factor analysis does not identify discrete clusters of patients (which is what subtype models like those of Kraepelin, Bleuler, or *DSM-IV-TR* claim to do). However, it does identify clusters of symptoms that may be related to ongoing findings on the biological processes in schizophrenia. Proponents of dimensional models claim that this is indeed the case, and that statistically created, quantitative dimensional models are better indicators of possible underlying neuropathology in schizophrenia.

The first dimensional model of schizophrenia using factor analysis was proposed by Peter F. Liddle in 1987. Liddle's factor analytic studies came up with four dimensions for three newly proposed syndromes for schizophrenia: (1) a psychomotor poverty syndrome, (2) a disorganization syndrome, and (3) a reality distortion syndrome.

According to Liddle, there is a disconnection of the neuronal networks in the brain that serve supervisory mental functions (the executive mental functions, usually associated with the frontal lobe).

Most factor analytic studies of schizophrenic symptoms come up with three or four dimensions. Most recently, Mark Lenzenweger has proposed a four-dimension model of schizophrenia: (1) reality distortion (HALLUCINATIONS, DELUSIONS), (2) disorganization (positive formal thought disorder, bizarre behavior), (3) negative symptoms (flattened affect, AVOLITION, ALOGIA, asociality), and (4) premorbid social functioning.

Whether the traditional clinical subtypes of schizophrenia or the new dimensional models will prevail in the future is presently unknown.

Liddle, P. F. "Inner Connections within the Domain of Dementia Praecox: Role of Supervisory Processes in Schizophrenia," *European Archives of Psychiatry and Clinical Neuroscience* 245 (1995): 210–215.

———. "The Symptoms of Chronic Schizophrenia: A Re-Examination of the Positive-Negative Dichotomy," *British Journal of Psychiatry* 151 (1987): 145–151.

Lenzenweger, M. F. "Schizophrenia: Refining the Phenotype, Resolving Endophenotypes," *Behaviour Research and Therapy* 37 (1999): 281–295.

diminished responsibility A legal term in England that has been used since the 13th century as an argument to plea the innocence of mentally ill offenders. Prior to this time insanity was viewed as an affliction from God to punish sinfulness, and therefore criminal activities by such individuals were not viewed with compassion. The concept of "guilty, but insane" was introduced only in 1843.

See also INSANITY DEFENSE; M'NAUGHTEN RULES.

diphenhydramine See ANTIPARKINSONIAN DRUGS.

disconnection theories of schizophrenia It has long been known that specialized NEURAL CIRCUITS in the human brain connect disparate regions of the cortex and subcortical structures to perform specific types of tasks. There are many such neural networks in the brain, and much research has been done to learn how these functionally specialized "systems" or "populations of neurons" work in normal human brains as they perform very simple tasks (for example, a simple memory or spatial task). There is much about the functioning of the normal human brain that we still do not understand.

The problem is therefore compounded when we try to understand the "connectivity" of different regions of the human brain when these same simple tasks are performed by persons with SCHIZOPHRENIA. A growing class of theories of schizophrenia claim there is an abnormal connection in the circuitry between different regions of the brain and that these regions do not cooperate on specific tasks the way they would in a brain belonging to a person who does not have schizophrenia. These disconnection theories, as they are called, are now a major focus of investigation in schizophrenia research. A primary source of data supporting these various complementary theories comes from functional BRAIN IMAGING studies. Although some theories compete with one another, most complement one another and overlap to a greater or lesser degree.

The major disconnection theories are as follows: (1) Schizophrenia is a deficit of neuronal connectivity between the frontal lobe and the temporal lobe of the brain. This theory is associated with the studies of Daniel Weinberger, K. J. Friston, C. D. Frith, and Peter Liddle. (2) The positive symptoms of schizophrenia are due to a dysfunction of the temporolimbic cortex. This is a theory associated with the work of the German neuropathologist B. Bogerts. (3) Schizophrenia is due to a deficit in the connectivity between the thalamus (a major relay center for messages throughout the brain). This is a theory proposed by E. G. Jones. (4) Schizophrenia is due to a dysfunction in cortical-subcortical-cerebellar circuitry. This theory, known as the "cognitive dysmetria" theory, is proposed by Nancy Andreasen.

Friston, K. J. "Schizophrenia and the Disconnection Hypothesis," *Acta Scandinavica Psychiatrica* 99 (1999): 68–79.

Friston, K. J., and C. D. Frith. "Schizophrenia: A Disconnection Syndrome?" *Clinical Neurosciences* 3 (1995), 89–97.

disorganized type One of the classic subtypes of SCHIZOPHRENIA in *DSM-IV-TR* (2000), better known throughout the history of psychiatry as HEBEPHRENIA (first described by Ewald Hecker in 1871). In *ICD-10* (1992), this form of schizophrenia is still known as the "hebephrenic type." This syndrome is marked by incoherence (disorganized speech), disorganized behavior, an obvious LOOSENING OF ASSSOCIATIONS, and FLAT AFFECT. Affect is also often inappropriate. Sometimes there can be a "silliness" to it, including giggling, strange mannerisms, frequent somatic (hypochondriacal) complaints, and unusual facial grimaces or other odd behavior. There may be AUDITORY HALLUCINATIONS of voices or DELUSIONS, but the delusions are unsystematic and grossly illogical.

Hebephrenia was Emil KRAEPELIN'S model for DEMENTIA PRAECOX in the 1893 and 1896 editions of his textbook, *Psychiatrie.* In those editions, dementia praecox (hebephrenia), DEMENTIA PARANOIDES, and CATATONIA were grouped together as three separate but related psychotic disorders. It was only in the 1899 edition that hebephrenia becomes only one of three forms of dementia praecox, along with catatonia and the paranoid form. The hebephrenic (disorganized), catatonic, and paranoid forms of schizophrenia are still recognized in current diagnostic manuals. The disorganized type (hebephrenia) is still regarded as the most chronic. NEGATIVE SYMPTOMS (constricted emotional range and intellectual abilities, ALOGIA, AVOLITION, and so on) seem to predominate over POSITIVE SYMPTOMS (HALLUCINATIONS and delusions). In clinical lore it is also associated with earlier age of onset and afflicts males far more than females. However, the scientific basis of dividing schizophrenia into these subtypes is currently questionable. Clinical experience and research studies indicate that most persons with schizophrenia have symptoms of one or more of the subtypes during their lives (hence the category UNDIFFERENTIATED TYPE for these persons), and there is no current biological or genetic basis for discriminating schizophrenia into various types. The disorganized type, however, is "classical" schizophrenia.

disorientation This is the clinical term most often used for people who have an obvious organic mental syndrome (such as DELIRIUM or DEMENTIA) and who are confused about who they are, where they are, or what day of the week, month, or even year it is. A common shorthand notation for this, often seen in clinical progress notes, is "disoriented X 3" (i.e., disoriented in three spheres of normal experience).

dissociation This is literally a splitting of the normally coherent and integrated functions of consciousness, particularly identity and memory. It is the defining characteristic of the DISSOCIATIVE DISORDERS, which include dissociative identity disorder, psychogenic fugue, psychogenic amnesia, and depersonalization disorder.

The concept of dissociation was apparently introduced by French ALIENIST J. J. Moreau de Tours in 1845. Pierre JANET (1859–1947) provided the first extensive psychological elaboration of this concept in his classic work, *L'Automatisme Psychologique,* in 1889 to describe systems of associated ideas that have been split off from consciousness and exist in a parallel life along with the dominant stream of consciousness. Janet referred to dissociation as *"dèsagrègation."* As this "disaggregation" or "dissociation" (as became the customary translation and use of this word in English) strengthens around its thematic core, referred to by Janet as "subconscious fixed ideas," the gap between these parallel streams of consciousness are widened, and *existences secondes,* or "secondary existences," are then created. Janet felt that this was a pathological—not a normal—psychological process and was to be found in hysteria, hypnosis, and in instances of "dual consciousness" or multiple personality.

Joseph Breuer (1842–1925) and Sigmund FREUD (1856–1939) also contributed to the study of dissociative phenomena with their interpretation of the famous case of "Anna O." reported in 1895 in their book, *Studies On Hysteria,* Anna O. was treated by Breuer from 1880 to 1882 for a series of psychosomatic problems and peculiar dissociative absences. However, Breuer and Freud disagreed as to the fundamental nature of these absences, with Breuer interpreting these phenomena as a form of "autohypnosis" and Freud insisting that their basic reason for existing was to serve as a DEFENSE

MECHANISM. It is Freud's basic claim that has been accepted by generations of clinicians, although Breuer's autohypnotic hypothesis has been resurrected recently as a major factor in the early childhood creation of multiple personalities. Only Swiss psychoanalyst and psychiatrist C. G. JUNG (1875–1961) seems to have included a nonpathological interpretation of dissociation as a major part of his psychological theories.

See also COMPLEX; MULTIPLE PERSONALITY.

Bliss, E. L. "A Reexamination of Freud's Basic Concepts from Studies of Multiple Personality Disorder," *Dissociation* 1 (1988): 36–40.

Moreau de Tours, J. J. *Du hachisch et de l'aliénation mentale: Etudes psychologiques.* Paris: Fortin, Masson, & Cie, 1845.

Noll, R. "Multiple Personality, Dissociation, and C. G. Jung's Complex Theory," *Journal of Analytical Psychology* 34 (1989), 353–370.

van der Hart, O., and B. Friedman. "A Reader's Guide to Pierre Janet on Dissociation: A Neglected Intellectual Heritage," *Dissociation,* 2 (1989): 3–16.

dissociative disorders A category of mental disorders first created in 1980 in *DSM-III* whose primary symptom is DISSOCIATION. Disturbances in identity and memory characterize these disorders. The dissociative disorders can often be mistaken for more serious psychotic disorders such as SCHIZOPHRENIA. Since there is no significant break with reality, persons suffering from dissociative disorders are not considered psychotic. This concept is recognized even by the legal system in the United States, where there have been instances of individuals with multiple personality disorder who have committed serious crimes but who have not been judged "insane" because they were not technically psychotic. An example of this is the sensational case of convicted rapist Billy Milligan in Ohio in the 1970s; he suffered from multiple personality disorder but was not judged legally insane.

A more traditional clinical term for the dissociative disorders is "hysterical neuroses, dissociative type." In *ICD-9* (1978), these disorders were included among those subtypes listed for "Hysteria."

Keyes, D. *The Minds of Billy Milligan.* New York: Random House, 1981.

Putnam, F. W. "Dissociation as a Response to Extreme Trauma." In *Childhood Antecedents of Multiple Personality,* edited by R. Kluft. Washington, D.C.: American Psychiatric Press, 1985.

distractibility A descriptive clinical term for when a person's attention seems to be easily diverted to unimportant or irrelevant events in the person's immediate environment. This is a characteristic found in many people who do not have diagnosable MENTAL DISORDERS, and such people are often referred to as "dreamy," "spacey," or "spaced-out." However, in certain psychotic disorders such as SCHIZOPHRENIA this distractibility can be extreme, and such disturbances in the processes of attention are often said to be one of the primary characteristics of schizophrenia.

See also ATTENTION, DISORDERS IN; COGNITIVE STUDIES OF SCHIZOPHRENIA.

Dix, Dorothea Lynde (1802–1887) It is said by historian of psychiatry Gregory Zilboorg in his 1941 classic, *A History of Medical Psychology,* that "The history of medical psychology in America during the nineteenth century is the history of the AMERICAN PSYCHIATRIC ASSOCIATION and the life of Dorothea Dix." Dix was a retired schoolteacher who, starting in 1841, became one of the most noted reformers of the care of the mentally ill in the 19th century. Her investigations of the terrible conditions suffered by the mentally ill and the poor in ALMSHOUSES, prisons, and the few institutions that existed fueled her energetic campaign of petitions to state legislatures and the Congress of the United States, and to the Parliament in England, to allocate funds to build more humane institutions for the care of the mentally ill. It is estimated that between the 1840s and 1880s she was directly responsible for the building of 32 new state asylums for the insane in the United States.

In an 1848 "Memorial" address to Congress in Washington, D.C., Dix reported that during her investigations she had seen "more than 9000 idiots, epileptics and insane in the United States, destitute

of appropriate care and protection . . . bound with galling chains, bowed beneath fetters and heavy iron balls attached to drag-chains, lacerated with ropes, scourged with rods and terrified beneath storms of execration and cruel blows; now subject to jibes and scorn and torturing tricks; now abandoned to the most outrageous violations."

Dix remained a reformer until late in her life. As repayment for her achievements in the care-taking of others, she was given a permanent apartment on the grounds of the New Jersey State Hospital at Trenton, where she lived out most of her remaining years.

See also ABUSE OF PSYCHIATRIC PATIENTS; ASYLUMS; BEERS, CLIFFORD W.

Deutsch, A. *The Mentally Ill in America.* Garden City, N.Y.: Doubleday, 1937, chapter 9.

Tiffany, F. *The Life of Dorothea Lynde Dix.* Boston: 1891.

Zilboorg, G. *A History of Medical Psychology.* New York: W. W. Norton, 1941.

dizygotic twins "Fraternal" or "nonidentical" twins. Dizygotic twins are thought to share about 50 percent of their genes in common, compared to the nearly 100 percent shared by MONOZYGOTIC TWINS. This makes for an interesting comparison between these two types of twin-pairs in GENETICS STUDIES of SCHIZOPHRENIA and BIPOLAR DISORDER, and some of the most suggestive evidence that these MENTAL DISORDERS have a genetic basis is the fact that a particular disease is much more likely to appear in both monozygotic twins than in both dizygotic twins.

See also CONCORDANCE RATE; CONSANGUINITY METHOD; TWINS METHOD AND STUDIES.

DMPEA The acronym for dimethoxphenethylamine, once thought to be one of the BIOLOGICAL MARKERS OF SCHIZOPHRENIA. DMPEA is a product of a chemical process known as transmethylation (in biochemistry, the transference of a methyl group from one compound to another). In 1963 scientists Friedhoff and Van Winkle found increased concentrations (when compared to normal controls) of DMPEA in the urine of 60 percent of acute schizophrenics who were not treated with ANTIPSYCHOTIC DRUGS. Furthermore, they found the even more suggestive evidence of higher than normal concentrations of DMPEA in the urine of 71 percent of male paranoid schizophrenics and in 75 percent of female paranoid schizophrenics. However, further research on the role of this and other compounds produced by the biochemical process of transmethylation found in the body fluids of schizophrenics, has not indicated a specific relationship to this or any other mental disorder.

See also BIOCHEMICAL THEORIES; TRANSMETHYLATION HYPOTHESIS.

Friedhoff, J. J., and E. Van Winkle. "Conversion of Dopamine to 3,4-dimethoxyphenylacetic Acid in Schizophrenia Patients," *Nature* 199 (1963): 1,271–1,272.

Luchins, D., T. A. Ban, and H. E. Lehmann. "A Review of Nicotinic Acid, N-methylated Indolamines and Schizophrenia," *International Journal of Pharmacopsychiatry* 13 (1978): 16–33.

DNA marker See MOLECULAR MARKER.

Dollhaus An old German term for "madhouse."

dominant In genetics, a trait observable in an individual (called the PHENOTYPE) and caused by one ALLELE (the term for an alternative form of a gene) is said to be dominant with respect to another trait known to be caused by a second allele, if the individual carrying both alleles shows signs only of the first trait and not the second.

dopamine A chemical substance in the brain that functions as a NEUROTRANSMITTER, that is, it is involved in the communication between neurons in the brain. Dopamine is one of the CATECHOLAMINES. For the most part, dopamine is thought to play the role of an inhibitor of functions. It has been found to be implicated in the motor (movement) control systems of the brain, and especially in SCHIZOPHRENIA.

See also DOPAMINE HYPOTHESIS.

dopamine hypothesis A NEUROTRANSMITTER theory of the cause (ETIOLOGY) of SCHIZOPHRENIA that was popular in the 1970s and 1980s but which is now regarded as too simplistic. Interestingly, this theory of the cause of schizophrenia arose from studying how its main form of treatment, ANTIPSYCHOTIC DRUGS, worked in the cortex of the brain to eliminate HALLUCINATIONS and DELUSIONS (POSITIVE SYMPTOMS). Antipsychotic drugs were found to do so by blocking dopamine at its receptor sites. This led to the hypothesis that the brain was producing dopamine in excess of normal levels—although then, as today, there is no way to know exactly what "normal" levels of dopamine in the brain may be. This hypothesized overproduction of dopamine was evidence of a neurological dysfunction, so therefore there must be a dysfunction of the dopaminergic system, and that dysfunction causes schizophrenia. The dopamine hypothesis replaced another of the BIOCHEMICAL THEORIES OF SCHIZOPHRENIA, the various forms of the TRANSMETHYLATION HYPOTHESIS, which, other than genetics, had been the dominant biological theory of the cause of schizophrenia since the 1950s. The dopamine hypothesis of schizophrenia in its fully articulated form was first proposed by Solomon Snyder and his colleagues in an article published in the *American Journal of Psychiatry* in 1976. However, the evolution of the dopamine hypothesis has a much longer history.

In 1957 the Swedish neuroscientist Arvid Carlsson (1923–) discovered that dopamine acted as a neurotransmitter in the brain. His research report was published the following year in the journal *Science.* His work on DOPAMINE and the role of the CATECHOLAMINES as neurotransmitters eventually led to Carlsson sharing the Nobel Prize in medicine in 2000.

Although antipsychotic drugs had been used since 1952, no one was sure exactly how they worked on the brain to reduce psychotic symptoms. The first suggestion that a neurotransmitter may be implicated not only in the pharmacodynamics of antipsychotic drugs, but that there may be a link to the cause of MENTAL DISORDERS such as schizophrenia, was put forth in 1954 in a paper by David Wolley and Edward Shaw. They suggested a role for the newly discovered (1953) neurotransmitter serotonin (5HT), but their paper had virtually no impact on fellow researchers.

In 1963 Arvid Carlsson and his colleague Margit Lindqvist published a famous paper reporting that they had demonstrated that CHLORPROMAZINE and haloperidol worked on the catecholamine systems in the brain, reducing activity by acting on the postsynaptic neurons. Although this 1963 paper is cited in many publications by schizophrenia researchers as the first place the dopamine hypothesis of schizophrenia is mentioned, in fact, dopamine is not specifically mentioned at all in the paper. Three years later, pharmacologist Jacques van Rossum, a professor of pharmacology at the medical faculty of the University of Nijmegen in the Netherlands, published a paper that specified dopamine as the catecholamine system that was blocked at the postsynaptic neuron by antipsychotic drugs. This 1966 paper contained the first mention of the term *dopamine hypothesis* and the first formal description of its connection to schizophrenia:

> When the hypothesis of dopamine blockade by neuroleptic agents can be further substantiated it may have fargoing consequences for the pathophysiology of schizophrenia. Overstimulation of dopamine receptors could then be part of the etiology. Obviously, such an overstimulation may be caused by overproduction of dopamine, production of substances with dopamine actions (methoxy derivatives), abnormal susceptibility of the receptors, etc.

Van Rossum's paper is also sometimes cited as the first description of how dopamine is blocked at its "receptor sites" by antipsychotic drugs, but the idea of "receptors" had not been defined in the mid-1960s. In fact, the first neurotransmitter receptor (for acetylcholine) was not discovered until 1970. The development of radio-labeling techniques for research on neurotransmitter systems in the nervous system led to an explosion of interest in research on receptors by 1972.

In 1974 Solomon Snyder of Johns Hopkins University reported the discovery of dopamine receptors. He and his colleagues discovered two types: D_{-1} and D_{-2} receptors. Furthermore, they discovered that antipsychotic drugs worked by binding

selectively to D_{-2} receptors and not D_{-1} receptors. Since all antipsychotic drugs worked by binding to the D_{-2} receptor, it was thought that there must be a dysfunction or abnormality in the D_{-2} receptor that caused PSYCHOSIS. This was the basis of the DOPAMINE HYPOTHESIS of schizophrenia put forth by Solomon Snyder in 1976. Since van Rossum's 1966 article had not made much of an impact on his contemporaries, Snyder's did, and it is Snyder who gets the credit for initiating a new phase of research in schizophrenia. However, by the 1980s Snyder backed off from this single-system theory of a neurotransmitter dysfunction cause of schizophrenia and criticized this logic. In the 1980s Arvid Carlsson also became a critic of this single-system dopamine hypothesis of schizophrenia.

The dopamine hypothesis of schizophrenia, although discarded in its original form as a causal theory, still exerts its influence on the pharmaceutical industry. The idea that selected neurotransmitter receptors can be targeted (for blockade or activation) by specific drugs, and that psychiatric symptoms would lessen from this action, has until recently pushed psychopharmacological research and marketing to cling to single-transmitter theories of the causes of mental illnesses (e.g., dopamine for schizophrenia, serotonin for depression, and so on). Such specificity is attractive not only to researchers, but also to those marketing new drugs: single-transmitter drugs are easier to comprehend by a largely science-blind public. Pharmaceutical companies make use of ancient metaphors from the humoral theory of medicine to explain how these drugs work: DEPRESSION or schizophrenia is caused by an "imbalance" of a specific "chemical." Therefore, the way to restore health is by restoring the balance of the chemical (humor) in the brain by the use of a drug.

There are known to be more than 100 neurotransmitter systems in the brain, and if one system is altered by drugs, it is still not understood how this affects other neurotransmitter systems. Newer generations of psychoactive drugs work on multiple receptors of two or more neurotransmitters, and the effect on the rest of the brain may be correspondingly more complicated to discern. However, although a dysfunction in the dopaminergic system is no longer posited as the single cause of schizophrenia, there is no doubt that dopamine plays a role in the pathophysiology of positive symptoms such as delusions and hallucinations.

The "revised" dopamine hypothesis of schizophrenia As a part of the new NEURODEVELOPMENTAL THEORY OF SCHIZOPHRENIA proposed by Daniel Weinberger of The NATIONAL INSTITUTE OF MENTAL HEALTH in Bethesda, Maryland, a "revised" version of the dopamine hypothesis has been proposed. The "revised" dopamine hypothesis is an attempt to account for NEGATIVE SYMPTOMS and cognitive impairment, serious features of schizophrenia that cannot be explained by the original dopamine theory that only accounts for positive symptoms. In the revised view, schizophrenia is associated with (but not necessarily caused by) a dopamine imbalance involving an excess of dopamine production in the subcortical structures of the brain (the mesolimbic system) and an underproduction of dopamine production in the prefrontal cortex. Subcortical dopamine projections might be hyperactive, hyperstimulating D_{-2} receptors and producing hallucinations and delusions. Dopamine projections to the prefrontal cortex might be hypoactive, resulting in the hyperstimulation of D_{-1} receptors, negative symptoms, and cognitive impairment.

Both dopamine hypotheses have little experimental support. To date, there is still no compelling evidence that documents abnormalities of dopamine functioning in schizophrenia. Postmortem neuropathological studies of the brains of persons with schizophrenia have been inconclusive. Brain imaging studies using PET (positron emission tomography) or SPECT (single photon emission computerized tomography) have been used for receptor imaging in living subjects, particularly the D_{-2} receptor. While the hyperactivity of subcortical transmission at D_{-2} receptors has been supported, other aspects of the revised dopamine hypothesis have not. Speculations about dopamine dysfunction and the production of negative symptoms and cognitive impairment, and the claim that positive symptoms become independent of the dopamine system and "take on a life of their own" in chronic, treatment-resistant schizophrenia, are unsupported with hard evidence. The revised dopamine hypothesis, like its predecessor, will probably have a short shelf life in science.

In fact, as any practicing clinician can tell the researchers, there is strong evidence against both dopamine hypotheses: antipsychotic drugs do not always alleviate hallucinations and delusions, and in fact may not do so in up to a third of all persons experiencing these psychotic symptoms. Corroboration of this clinical observation can be found in studies that, in some persons, hallucinations and delusions are present when, in fact, there seems to be measurably normal levels of synaptic dopamine. Blocking the D_{-2} receptors of these persons with antipsychotic drugs has little or no effect on their psychotic symptoms. This may mean that other neurotransmitter systems acting independently of the dopaminergic system may also produce positive symptoms.

Baumeister, A. A., and J. L. Francis. "Historical Development of the Dopamine Hypothesis of Schizophrenia," *Journal of the History of the Neurosciences* 11 (2002): 265–277.

Carlsson, A. "The Current Status of the Dopamine Hypothesis," *Neuropsychopharmacology* 1 (1988): 179–186.

Carlsson, A., and M. Lindqvist. "The Effect of Chlorpromazine on the Formation of 3-Methoxytyramine and Normetanephrine in Mouse Brain," *Acta Pharmacologica* 20 (1963): 140–144.

Healy, D. *The Creation of Psychopharmacology.* Cambridge, Mass.: Harvard University Press, 2002.

Laruelle, M. "Dopamine Transmission in the Schizophrenic Brain." In *Schizophrenia.* 2nd ed., edited by S. R. Hirsch and D. Weinberger. Cambridge: Blackwell, 2003.

Snyder, S. "The Dopamine Hypothesis of Schizophrenia: Focus on the Dopamine Receptor," *American Journal of Psychiatry* 133 (1976): 197–202.

Van Rossum, J. M. "The Significance of Dopamine Receptor Blockade in the Mechanism of Action of Neuroleptic Drugs," *Archives of International Pharmacodynamics and Therapeutics* 60 (1966): 492–494.

Wolley, D. W., and E. Shaw. "A Biochemical and Pharmacological Suggestion about Certain Mental Disorders," *Proceedings of the National Academy of Sciences of the United States of America* 40 (1954): 228–231.

double-bind theory One of the most widely discussed theories of the cause of SCHIZOPHRENIA, from the 1950s to the 1970s, although it is now generally regarded as of little scientific significance. This theory was derived from communications and cybernetics research and was first put forth by Gregory BATESON and his colleagues in 1956. Essentially, it places the cause of schizophrenia in the interaction patterns of the family, and this theory was the basis of much later family interaction research.

Essentially, the double-bind theory centers on the incongruence between the basic content of primary communications and the underlying meaning (expressed by tone of voice, gestures or context of the communication), which incongruence is called metacommunications. Bateson and his colleagues purported to find that, in the families of schizophrenics, the schizophrenic member is caught in a double-bind when incongruent messages are communicated and the recipient must respond to the incongruent message without being given the opportunity to clarify the incongruence in the message. For example, the parent of a schizophrenic may say, "Of course I love you," while wearing a facial expression of disgust or while doing something intrusive or harmful to the afflicted person. A lifetime of such aberrant communications since early childhood is thus thought to produce schizophrenia. The double-bind theory has remained just that, with no carefully controlled scientific study to validate its claims.

See also FAMILY INTERACTION THEORIES.

Bateson, G., et al. "Towards a Theory of Schizophrenia," *Behavioral Science* 1 (1956): 251–264.

double conscience or consciousness These are 19th-century terms that refer to multiple personality disorder, in which one or more alternate personalities would coexist with the ego of the "birth personality." The very first complete medical case history of a person with multiple personalities was that of the young American woman Mary Reynolds, first reported in 1817.

Mitchell, S. L. "A Double Consciousness or a Duality of Person, in the Same Individual," *Medical Repository* 3 (1817): 185–186.

Mitchell, S. W. "Mary Reynolds: A Case of Double Consciousness," *Transactions of the College of Physicians of Philadelphia* 10 (1888): 366–389.

double insanity See FOLIE À DEUX.

douche One of the primary modes of alleviating the active symptoms of mental illness since antiquity; in particular, in mental institutions in the 18th and 19th centuries the patient would be forced under a shower of (usually) ice-cold water. This was done in many fashions, including: by physically restraining the patient and pouring buckets of cold water over his or her head (as in the SPREAD-EAGLE CURE), or by using a "douching machine" in which a patient would be strapped in a chair beneath an apparatus that forced strong jets of cold water down onto his or her head. The reproduction of a design drawing of such an apparatus from the 1820s is provided in the first volume of Howells and Osborn's *A Reference Companion to the History of Abnormal Psychology.*

ESQUIROL describes the use of the douche on the mentally ill in his 1838 textbook, *Mental Maladies:*

> The douche consists in pouring water upon the head from a greater or less height. It was known to the ancients; and is administered in different ways. . . . The patient received the douche, seated in an arm chair; or better, plunged into a bath of tepid or cold water.
>
> The douche produces its effects, both by the action of the cold, and the percussion. It exercises a sympathetic influence upon the epigastrium. It causes cardialgia, and desires to vomit. After its action ceases, the patients are pale, and sometimes sallow. It also acts morally, as a means of repression; a douche often sufficing to calm a raging excitement, to break up dangerous resolutions, or force a patient to obedience. . . . The douche ought to be applied with discretion, and never immediately after a repast. . . . Its employment ought to be continued but a few minutes at a time, and its administration never left to servants. They may abuse it, and we ought not to be ignorant that the douche is not exempt from grave accidents.

In describing the douche method of BATHS for the mentally ill included in Tuke's *A Dictionary of Psychological Medicine,* 14 other means of administering baths are discussed in detail. One of them sounds like the "Chinese water-torture" of motion picture fame:

> Schneider and Morel shaved their patients' heads, and placed them under an intermittent stream of water, which fell drop by drop on the back of the scalp . . .

See also HYDROTHERAPY.

Esquirol, J. E. D. *Mental Maladies, A Treatise on Insanity,* trans. E. K. Hunt. Philadelphia: Lea & Blanchard, 1845; first published, 1838.

Howells, J. G., and M. L. Osborn. *A Reference Companion to the History of Abnormal Psychology.* 2 vols. Westport, Conn.: Greenwood Press, 1984.

Williams, D. "Baths." In *A Dictionary of Psychological Medicine.* Vol. 1, edited by D. H. Tuke. London: J. & A. Churchill, 1892.

dreams in schizophrenia There is no scientific evidence to suggest that the dream content of persons with SCHIZOPHRENIA (or any other mental disorder) are markedly different from "normals." Throughout the 20th century, psychoanalysts, including FREUD and JUNG, made such erroneous claims, and the misconception that schizophrenic dreams are somehow different from those of nonschizophrenics is widespread in the public. All these claims were based on clinical anecdotes and not from more rigorously designed quantitative studies of dream content. It is now the conventional wisdom in cognitive neuroscience that psychoanalysis was merely a pseudoscience (like phrenology or astrology) with no scientific support for any of its claims. The speculations of Freud and Jung and their devotees about dreams and the "unconscious mind" have only historical, not scientific, significance. The only consistent finding in quantitative dream research studies is that "patient populations" (not just persons suffering from schizophrenia, but people suffering from depression and a whole host of other disorders)

have fewer "friends" appearing in their dreams. Instead, when contrasted with the dream content of "normals," the characters in their dreams tend to be family members or strangers. There are also fewer "friendly interactions" with people in their dreams. None of this points to some special status for the dreams of schizophrenics, but instead points to the generally accepted theory that there is more in common between our waking and dreaming lives than there is discontinuity (as Freud and Jung would have us believe).

An ongoing quantitative study of dreams is being conducted by G. William Domhoff of the University of California, Santa Cruz.

Domhoff, G. W. "New Rationales and Methods for Quantitative Dream Research Outside the Laboratory," *Sleep* 21 (1998): 398–404.

Maharaj, N. *An Investigation into the Structure of Schizophrenic Dreams,* Doctoral Dissertation, Leiden University, The Netherlands, 1997.

drug holiday A "vacation" from taking ANTIPSYCHOTIC DRUGS that is necessary from time to time so that the psychiatrist can assess the further need of medication for a patient.

drug psychoses A category of organic psychotic conditions, listed in *ICD-10* (1992), for those psychoses induced by the ingestion of various drugs (e.g., amphetamines, barbiturates, opiates, and hallucinogens). There is a break with reality, and HALLUCINATIONS and DELUSIONS may be present. They can be due to the active intoxicating effects of the substances, or to the effects of withdrawal.

See also AMPHETAMINE PSYCHOSIS; SUBSTANCE-INDUCED PSYCHOTIC DISORDER.

DSM-IV *The Diagnostic and Statistical Manual of Mental Disorders, Fourth Edition,* appeared in 1994 as the latest in a series of major revisions of the "Bible" of psychiatrists. The earlier editions were *DSM-I* (1952), *DSM-II* (1968), *DSM-III* (1980), and *DSM-III-R* (1987). The AMERICAN PSYCHIATRIC ASSOCIATION has periodically updated its diagnostic manuals to be consistent with advances in research on mental disorders. The later editions have attempted to be phenomenologically based (i.e., focused on descriptions of behaviors in various MENTAL DISORDERS) and have attempted to be free of pejorative theoretical assumptions. For example, the word *NEUROSIS* was no longer included when *DSM-III* came out in 1980, since it referred to a concept from psychoanalytic theory that did not always match current research on the various disorders. Teams of psychiatrists are continually working in committees to collect research information and to revise, eliminate, or create new diagnostic categories for each revision of the manual. *DSM-IV-TR* (2000) is just such a revision.

Originally designed for use in the United States, it is now one of the most widely used diagnostic manuals for mental disorders in the world.

The diagnostic criteria have changed considerably over the many editions of the *DSM*s. This is especially true for SCHIZOPHRENIA. Although Emil KRAEPELIN's narrowly defined view of schizophrenia dominated the early part of the century, by the 1950s BLEULER's more inclusive concept of schizophrenia and the influence of psychoanalytic pseudoscience on American mental health professionals led to a broadening of the definition of what it meant to be a schizophrenic—and often with disastrous consequences for those persons stigmatized with that inappropriate label. The broad definition of schizophrenia and the influence of psychoanalytic language finally disappeared in 1980 with the publication of *DSM-III.* Currently, the narrow "Neo-Kraepelinian" definition of schizophrenia is the accepted standard and continues to find scientific evidence in support of it.

dual diagnosis The presence of two existing mental disorders in a person that requires the granting of two different diagnostic labels. This term is most often used to describe those "dually diagnosed" patients who are mentally retarded as well as schizophrenic (or carry some other psychotic diagnosis). One of the growing problems in the post-psychedelic era of the 1960s is the large number of YOUNG ADULT CHRONIC PATIENTS who are abusers of drugs and alcohol and who also seem to

have a serious (often psychotic) MENTAL DISORDER. These patients are also dually diagnosed and in the United States are sometimes referred to as "double trouble" patients.

ducking See BATH OF SURPRISE; BATHS; HYDROTHERAPY.

duplex personality See DOUBLE CONSCIENCE OR CONSCIOUSNESS.

dysphrenia A BRIEF PSYCHOTIC DISORDER or ACUTE AND TRANSIENT PSYCHOTIC DISORDER described by the German psychiatrist Karl Ludwig KAHLBAUM (1829–99) in his Habilitation thesis, *Die Gruppirung psychicher Krankheiten* (*The Classification of Mental Diseases*) in 1863. Dysphrenia was a severe psychotic disorder of sudden onset and short duration. Symptoms were mixed or "impure" and varied widely from case to case (in modern terms, a syndrome characterized by POLYMORPHIC PSYCHOTIC SYMPTOMS). Kahlbaum assumed that the underlying cause (etiology) of the psychosis involved an underlying disease process of an epileptic, sexual, or rheumatic nature. Persons suffering from dysphrenia recovered in full without any long lasting effect. In his highly influential book, Kahlbaum distinguished dysphrenia from the spectrum of typical psychotic disorders, or *vesania typica*, which were all stages of a single underlying disease process that was progressive in nature. He believed that a different disease process (epileptic, sexual, or rheumatic) provoked an exacerbation of the same underlying disease process found in progressive and chronic psychotic disorders but "without leaving a lasting alteration in the elements that serve its expression" (p. 67).

Kahlbaum's group of chronic and progressively deteriorating psychotic disorders, which he grouped under the *vesania typica* concept, was a major source of inspiration for Emil KRAEPELIN when he proposed his heterogeneous disease concept of DEMENTIA PRAECOX in 1896. Kraepelin was aware of the existence of brief psychotic disorders, but these disorders were difficult to reconcile with his view of dementia praecox as a progressively chronic disease. Starting in 1893, in successive editions of his famous textbook, *Psychiatrie*, Kraepelin placed brief psychotic disorders under the category of "periodic" insanities. In 1899, when he introduced MANIC-DEPRESSIVE ILLNESS as a psychotic disorder that was periodic but continually remitting and manifesting a better prognosis than dementia praecox, Kraepelin considered brief psychotic disorders as subtypes of MANIA.

Kahlbaum, K. L. *Die Gruppirung psychicher Krankheiten*. Danzig, 1863.

E

Earle, Pliny (1809–1892) Earle was a psychiatrist and one of the 13 founders of the AMERICAN PSYCHOLOGICAL ASSOCIATION in 1844. He had traveled widely in Europe and was knowledgeable about European treatments for mental illness. He held several important positions in his lifetime, including that of medical superintendent of the Bloomingdale Asylum in New York in 1844 and the State Lunatic Hospital at Northampton, Massachusetts in 1864, where he remained for the next 21 years. He is perhaps best remembered for pioneering the teaching of PSYCHIATRY in American medical schools, and for his 1887 book, *The Curability of the Insane,* which sharply contradicted the wildly inflated claims of "curability" of the insane that had been made by various superintendents of ASYLUMS in the United States during the previous 40 years.

écho de la pensée Literally, "echo of the thought." This is a characteristic of schizophrenic thought disorder that is commonly called "thought broadcasting." A psychotic individual exhibiting *écho de la pensée* believes that his private thoughts are being sent out into the minds of other people, who may then speak them for him. In more-deteriorated psychotic states, the person may not even recognize these thoughts as his or her own and attribute them entirely to other people.

echolalia The spontaneous (yet persistent) repetition of the words and phrases of others. It is as if the listening person is an "echo" of the speaker's speech. For example, the speaker may ask, "Does that belong to you?" only to be met with the response (usually in a mumbling, mocking, or staccato tone) "Belong to you. Belong to you." Informally, it is sometime called "parroting" after the behavior of parrots. This symptom is found in SCHIZOPHRENIA (particularly the DISORGANIZED TYPE) and especially in autistic children or individuals with certain brain disorders.

See also AUTISM, INFANTILE; LANGUAGE ABNORMALITIES IN SCHIZOPHRENIA.

ECT The acronym for "electroconvulsive therapy" is the most recent attempt to neutralize the negative connotations most people associate with the method's original name, ELECTROSHOCK THERAPY.

EEG studies of schizophrenia German psychiatrist Hans Berger (1873–1941) invented the electroencephalogram in 1924 and first published the results of his studies of the electrical activity of the human brain in 1929. The EEG (as it is still known today) employed electrodes, which were attached to the scalp in strategic locations around the head, to map the electrical activity of the different regions of the brain. In the decade that followed this discovery there was great hope that the EEG could be used in psychiatry as a diagnostic tool, the assumption being that the brain wave patterns of people with particular mental disorders would differ from one another and from the patterns of people without diagnosable disorders. Although applications were found in neurology, PSYCHIATRY eventually found the EEG was of little diagnostic value.

EEG studies of schizophrenics generally showed more abnormalities than those of nonschizophrenic persons, but no specific brain wave abnormality could be linked to SCHIZOPHRENIA. However,

an improvement on the classical EEG methodology has been the use of event-related potentials, also known as ERPs, which have been a much more promising BIOLOGICAL MARKER OF SCHIZOPHRENIA. Whereas most EEG studies are conducted while the subject is at rest, ERPs involve the presentation of a flash of light, a tone or a very mild electrical stimulus to a subject so that the responding electrical activity in the brain can be recorded. ERPs are very useful because they are a nonintrusive way (unlike the surgical implantation of electrodes in the brain) of measuring the neural activity in relation to sensory, motor, and cognitive processes.

A large literature exists of ERP research that has been conducted with people diagnosed with schizophrenia. Three lines of evidence have been considered to be most promising in the search for biological markers: (1) Certain brain wave abnormalities in schizophrenics (technically, amplitude reductions in middle and late positive components) are thought to be related to dysfunctions in attention, which are found in some schizophrenics and in some individuals at high-risk for schizophrenia (2) ERP patterns have been found to differ from those of people diagnosed with other mental disorders and (3) certain aspects of the electrical activity of the brain measured by ERPs seem to be genetically determined (i.e., the brain may be predisposed to react to certain types of stimuli in specific ways).

In the 1990s, the EEG technique was combined with new BRAIN IMAGING technology in studies of the functioning and structure of the brains of persons with schizophrenia. Studies combining EEG activity with PET SCAN measurements have found abnormal functioning in the connections between the left frontal lobe and the temporal lobe. One study combining MAGNETIC RESONANCE IMAGING (MRI) with EEG found that the reduction of volume in the left superior temporal gyrus was strongly correlated with a decrease in the amplitude of the P3 (or P300) peak, which has been a commonly reported phenomenon reported in EEG studies of the brains of schizophrenics. This "latency of the P300 cortical ERP," as this abnormality is called, may be additional evidence that at least one form of schizophrenia resembles diseases like dementia, Alzheimer's disease, multiple sclerosis, Huntington's chorea, and Parkinson's disease. The same P300 latency is found in all these diseases and is also found during normal aging.

See also ATTENTION, DISORDERS IN; HIGH-RISK STUDIES.

Berger, H. "Über das Elektrenkephalogramm des Menschen," *Archiv für Psychiatrie und Nervenkrankheiten* 98 (1933): 231–255.

Erlenmeyer-Kimling, L. "Biological Markers for the Liability to Schizophrenia." In *Biological Perspectives of Schizophrenia,* edited by H. Helmchen and F. A. Henn. New York: Wiley, 1987.

Holzman, P. S. "Recent Studies of Psychophysiology in Schizophrenia," *Schizophrenia Bulletin* 13 (1987): 49–76.

McCarley, R. W., et al. "Auditory P300 Abnormalities and Left Superior Temporal Gyrus Volume Reduction in Schizophrenia," *Archives of General Psychiatry* 50 (1993): 190–197.

Morrison-Stewart, S. L., et al. "Coherence on Electroencephalography and Aberrant Functional Organization of the Brain in Schizophrenic Patients during Activation Tasks," *British Journal of Psychiatry* 159 (1991): 636–644.

O'Donnell, B. F. "Increased Rate of P300 Latency Prolongation with Age in Schizophrenia," *Archives of General Psychiatry* 52 (1995): 544–549.

Egas Moniz, António Caetano de Abreu Freire (1874–1955) A Portuguese neurologist who performed the first PSYCHOSURGERY (a term he coined) on a human being (a LEUCOTOMY) on November 15, 1935. For the invention of this procedure he won a Nobel Prize in physiology and medicine in 1949. Egas Moniz spells out his rationale for the leucotomy in the first book on psychosurgery, *Tentatives Opératoires dans le Traitement de Certaines Psychoses (Experimental Surgery in the Treatment of Certain Psychoses),* which was published in France in the spring of 1936: "To cure these patients it is necessary to destroy the arrangements of cellular connections, more or less fixed, that must exist in the brain and particularly those that are linked with the frontal lobes." Egas Moniz's work inspired Walter FREEMAN to perform the first leucotomy in the United States and to popularize the practice of psychosurgery.

Egas Moniz, A. *Tentatives Opératoires dans le Traitement de Certaines Psychoses.* Paris: Masson, 1936.

egocentricity Individuals with psychotic disorders are sometimes described as being egocentric in the same way that, for example, an infant is egocentric: impulses are expressed without regard to the context of social situation. Thus, psychotic individuals may engage in activities that are socially repugnant, bizarre, or simply inconsiderate. According to psychoanalytic theory, energy ("libido") is withdrawn from the external world and drawn back into the internal world in psychotic individuals. Thus, the person becomes more interested in his or her internal world and its needs rather than the demands of external reality. In this way, the concept of egocentricity is related to descriptions of the autism of some psychotic individuals, particularly schizophrenics.

Einheitspsychose In German, a "unitary psychosis," the idea that all mental illnesses (certainly all of the psychotic disorders) are simply variations of the same underlying disease process (the EINHEITSPSYCHOSE) and are not separate mental disorders with no apparent relationship to one another. This idea was first applied to mental illness by the Belgian ALIENIST Joseph Guislain (1797–1860) in 1833.

The eminent German psychiatrist Wilhelm GRIESINGER describes this idea in the "Form of Mental Disease" chapter in his 1861 classic, *Mental Pathology and Therapeutics.* He proposes that there are "two grand groups" or "fundamental states of mental anomalies": (1) those characterized by disturbances in emotional states (what we would call MOOD DISORDERS), and (2) those characterized by "disorders of the intellect and will" (the "thought disorder" characteristic of SCHIZOPHRENIA and related "spectrum" disorders). Griesinger believed that these types of disorder fit a degenerative pattern, with the mood disorders ("states of depression" then "states of exaltation" or manic states) developing eventually into more serious disorders in which thinking functions deteriorate ("states of mental weakness"), leading to the total degeneration of the mind. Griesinger writes:

> Observation shows, further, that in the great majority of cases, those conditions which form the first leading group *precede* those of the second group; that the latter generally appear only as consequences and *terminations* of the first, when the cerebral affection has not been cured. There is, moreover, again presented within the first group, in a great proportion of cases, a certain definite *succession* of the various forms of emotional states, whence there results a method of viewing insanity which recognizes in the different *forms,* different *stages* of one morbid process; which may, indeed, be modified, interrupted, or transformed by the most varied intercurrent pathological circumstances, but which, on the whole, pursues a constantly progressive course, which may proceed even to complete destruction of the mental life.

The idea of the *Einheitspsychose* returned in a theory by the noted British schizophrenia researcher Timothy J. Crow. He postulated in a 1986 article that all the psychotic disorders are distributed along a continuum that extends from unipolar depression through bipolar (manic-depressive) and schizoaffective psychosis to schizophrenia—a progressive degeneration from bad to worse. This matched Griesinger's observations exactly: that the psychotic disorders characterized by disturbances in emotion degenerate into psychoses characterized by disturbances of will and thought. Crow added a 20th-century twist to this idea by proposing that this spectrum of disorders is caused by a single gene; in other words, there is a single genetic locus where significant variation occurs in defect that predisposes to all these psychotic disorders. In a 1989 article he reviewed the evidence that the defective gene has a locus on the sex chromosomes, particularly the X chromosome. Crow guessed the "psychosis gene" was located somewhere on the X chromosome. He was wrong.

Crow, T. J. "The Continuum of Psychosis and Its Implications for the Structure of the Gene," *British Journal of Psychiatry* 149 (1986): 419–429.

DeLisi, L. E., and T. J. Crow. "Evidence for a Sex Chromosome Locus for Schizophrenia," *Schizophrenia Bulletin* 15 (1989): 431–440.

Griesinger, W. *Mental Pathology and Therapeutics*. Translated by C. L. Robertson and J. Rutherford. 1845. Reprint, New York: William Wood & Co., 1882.

Vleigen, J. *Die Einheitpsychose*. Stuttgart: F. Enke, 1980.

elective mutism A symptom found in some people who are diagnosed with a psychotic disorder who, for whatever reason, simply refuse to talk. This has been described particularly in connection with CATATONIA.

electronarcosis therapy Since at least the 1870s, asylum physicians who were at a loss as to how to treat persons in acute episodes of psychotic disorders experimented with sedative drugs (usually opium derivatives or barbiturates) to induce long periods of sleep. This SLEEP TREATMENT procedure was targeted specifically for SCHIZOPHRENIA by Jakob Kläsi in the 1922 and was used in the United States and Europe from the 1920s to the 1940s. In the Soviet Union a technique was developed for electrically stimulating the brain stem of persons with schizophrenia to induce prolonged sleep without drugs. This electronarcosis therapy was introduced as early as 1936 in the Soviet Union and was used well into the 1960s. Electronarcosis was also used by psychiatrists in the early 1960s in the former German Democratic Republic (communist East Germany). Electronarcosis therapy is no longer used for the treatment of schizophrenia today.

Wortis, J. *Soviet Psychiatry*. Baltimore: Williams and Wilkins, 1950.

electroshock therapy Now more commonly known as electroconvulsive therapy, or "ECT," it is a form of treatment designed by Italian psychiatrist Ugo CERLETTI and his colleagues in Rome to treat severe mental illness by electrically inducing seizures. An alleviation of symptoms followed the deliberate induction of such seizures. It was considered an improvement on other types of CONVULSIVE THERAPIES, which had many toxic side effects associated with the use of drugs to induce such powerful seizures. The very first patient to receive this treatment (a schizophrenic) did so on April 15, 1938. Electroshock therapy then became one of the most widely used forms of treatment for schizophrenia until the 1970s, when it became clear that ANTIPSYCHOTIC DRUGS were a more effective means of controlling psychotic symptoms and that ECT was much more effective with severe depression than with schizophrenia.

Cerletti experimented with pigs before attempting the procedure on humans. Most other psychiatrists were afraid to try this new procedure, but not Cerletti. In a rather macabre account of the very first electroshock treatment ever administered, D. J. Impastato relates the details of this historic (and horrific) event:

> Now came the search for Rome's first patient. For obvious reasons this was not a simple matter. Then, luckily, a patient from North Italy was admitted to the clinic who was a catatonic schizophrenic and who spoke an incomprehensible gibberish. He was unable to give his name or state anything about himself. No one could identify him. Dr. Cerletti decided he should be the historic patient. Following adequate preparations the first treatment was given in 1938. Present were Cerletti, Bini, Longhi, Accornero, Kalinowsky and Fleischer. The patient was brought in, and the machine was set at 1/10 of a second and 70 volts and the shock given. Naturally, the low dosage resulted in a petit mal reaction. After the electric spasm, which lasted a fraction of a second, the patient burst out into song. The Professor suggested that another treatment with a higher voltage be given. The staff objected. They stated that if another treatment were given the patient would probably die and wanted further treatment postponed until the morrow. The Professor knew what that meant. He decided to go ahead right then and there, but before he could say so the patient suddenly sat up and pontifically proclaimed, no longer in a jargon, but in clear Italian: "Non una seconda! Mortifera!" (Not again, it will kill me). This made the Professor think and swallow, but his courage was not lost. He gave the order to proceed at a higher voltage and a longer time: and the first electroconvulsion in man ensued. Thus was

born EST out of one man and over the objection of his assistants.

No scientifically satisfying theory has ever been put forth to justify or explain the use of electroshock therapy for SCHIZOPHRENIA. Like most treatments for mental illness over the last several centuries, as soon as a new scientific discovery is made it is quickly adapted for use on the mentally ill in the hope that a new treatment or cure can finally be found. When it was discovered that blood circulated in the body, BLEEDING and BLOOD TRANSFUSIONS (often using animal blood) were quickly tried on the insane. When Hungarian psychiatrist von MEDUNA put forth the scientifically unsound theory that, since epilepsy and schizophrenia were biologically incompatible, deliberately inducing seizures (by chemical means) in schizophrenics would cure it, such methods were widely tried and efforts were made to improve upon them. Electroshock therapy was such an improvement, despite the fact that the initial theory to explain its beneficial effects was unsound.

Electric shocks that were too weak to produce convulsions were used almost 200 years before Cerletti to treat illness, but it was only around 1804 that a use for psychosis is recorded. A machine that produced electric shocks from weak electric currents was set up in the Middlesex Hospital in England in 1767 to treat various ailments, and shocks were applied to various parts of the body. At about this time American inventor and statesman Benjamin Franklin suffered unconsciousness and retrograde amnesia after a severe electric shock during one of his electricity experiments, and he apparently suggested its use for the treatment of the insane. In the 1790s British surgeon John BIRCH used his machine to "pass shocks through the brain" of depressed patients at London's Saint Thomas Hospital; this may be the first recorded use of electric shocks applied directly to the brain to treat a mental disorder. In 1838 ESQUIROL reviewed the reports of the use of electricity in the treatment of mental illness, including his own experiments with its use:

> Gmelin and Perfect affirm, that they have effected cures by electricity. At the Salpêtrière, during two summers, those of 1823 and 1824, I submitted to the influence of electricity a large number of our insane women. One only was cured, in the course of my experiments. This was a young and very strong girl, who had become a maniac in consequence of a fright, which suppressed her menses. She had been insane for a month, and was electrized for fifteen days. At the menstrual period, the discharge appeared, and she was immediately restored.

Although electroshock therapy is still sometimes used for schizophrenia, this is quickly becoming an outmoded form of treatment for the disease, at least in the United States. Symptomatic relief is often only temporary, and a major review of the bulk of the research published prior to 1980 has concluded that electroshock therapy has not been shown to improve the quality of life of schizophrenic patients.

In June 1985 the NATIONAL INSTITUTE OF MENTAL HEALTH in the United States convened a Consensus Development Conference on Electroconvulsive Therapy and issued a summary statement on the body of scientific evidence about ECT. The panel of experts concluded that "The evidence for the efficacy of ECT in schizophrenia is not compelling but is strongest for those schizophrenic patients with a shorter duration of illness, a more acute onset, and more intense affective symptoms. ECT has not been useful in chronically ill schizophrenic patients." When is ECT indicated? The expert panel found that "The efficacy of ECT has been established most convincingly in the treatment of delusional and severe endogenous depressions, which make up a clinically important minority of depressive disorders." However, the panel warns that there are "significant side effects, especially acute confusional states and persistent memory deficits for events during the months surrounding ECT treatment."

Due in no small part to the supportive studies of Max Fink (1923–) and others, in the early 21st century some researchers and clinicians are advocating a role for ECT in treatment-resistant schizophrenia.

Arndt, R. "Electricity." In *A Dictionary of Psychological Medicine*. Vol. 1, edited by D. H. Tuke. London: J. & A. Churchill, 1892.

Esquirol, J. E. D. *Mental Maladies, A Treatise on Insanity,* trans. E. K. Hunt. 1838. Reprint, Philadelphia: Lea and Blanchard, 1845.

Harms, E. "Origins and Early History of Electrotherapy and Electroshock," *American Journal of Psychiatry* 12 (1955): 933.

Impastato, D. J. "The Story of the First Electroshock Treatment," *American Journal of Psychiatry* 116 (1960): 1,113–1,114.

National Institutes of Health, *Electroconvulsive Therapy,* Consensus Development Conference Statement, 1985, vol. 5, no. 11. Bethesda, Md.: U.S. Dept. of Health and Human Services, National Institutes of Health, Office of Medical Applications of Research.

Salzman, C. "The Use of ECT in the Treatment of Schizophrenia," *American Journal of Psychiatry* 137 (1980): 1,032–1,041.

EMD An acronym for "eye movement dysfunction," perhaps one of the most promising candidates for a BIOLOGICAL MARKER for schizophrenia.

See also EYE MOVEMENT ABNORMALITIES IN SCHIZOPHRENIA.

endocrine alterations in schizophrenia The human body is viewed in Western medicine as being composed of several major "systems." In the 20th century, these systems, which were conceptualized and studied as if they operated in isolation from one another, became increasingly integrated. Recent medical research has focused on how the nervous system, the immune system, and the endocrine system communicate with one another in both disease and health. The endocrine system is composed of the subcortical structure known as the hypothalamus, its connection to the pituitary gland (the "master gland" in the brain that "controls" the activity of the system of other glands throughout the body), and the various hormones produced by the glands, which have a stimulating effect on both the nervous system and the immune system as well as other aspects of growth and metabolism. The scientific discipline devoted to the study of metabolic processes is called endocrinology. A related field, neuroendocrinology, focuses specifically on the interdependence of the endocrine and nervous systems.

History of the rise of endocrinology Throughout the latter half of the 19th century, physiologists sought to understand the mechanisms of metabolism. For most of that time, physiological changes in the body were explained by theories of nervous regulation. Between 1890 and 1905—the year Ernest Starling first proposed the modern concept of "hormone"—metabolism was increasingly explained by theories of chemical regulation through secreting organs such as glands. Endocrinology emerged from physiology in a recognizable form in the years following British physiologist Edward Schaefer's address "On Internal Secretions" to the British Medical Association in Physiology in London on August 2, 1895. *Internal secretions* was a term introduced by physiologist Claude Bernard in 1855 but reframed by Schaefer in terms of clinical medicine. Metabolic diseases as a separate category of illness were caused by the overproduction or underproduction of internal secretions in the glands with ducts (liver, pancreas, and kidneys), those without ducts (thyroid, adrenals, pituitary), and the sex glands (gonads). As Schaefer proposed in his famous lecture, secreting organs, both with and without ducts, return secreted materials to the blood. The ductless glands, however, produce only internal secretions. Blood (and later the cerebral spinal fluid) thus became the medium through which to detect and measure internal secretions, or later in the 20th century, hormones and NEUROTRANSMITTERS (originally called neurohormones).

Dementia praecox as an endocrine disorder (1896) This emerging new endocrinological paradigm was immediately seized upon by the first biological psychiatrists. If an overproduction or underproduction of internal secretions could produce physical diseases such as diabetes, why not also insanity? Since it was clear that the brain was the organ underlying mental diseases, perhaps the true ETIOLOGY of the insanities originated elsewhere in the body, places where substances toxic to the brain (internal secretions, ptomaines, bacteria, and so on) were produced and then transmitted to the central nervous system via the blood. This AUTOINTOXICATION theory of mental disorders first became prominent in France in 1893 and influenced a generation of alienists, neurologists, and psychiatric researchers. And indeed the most prominent among them was Emil KRAEPELIN.

Edward Shorter, in his 1997 volume, *A History of Psychiatry: From the Era of the Asylum to the Age of Prozac,* emphasized the irony that Kraepelin, the icon of the first biological psychiatry, was instrumental in putting an end to it because he was "agnostic about cause" and had "declared [brain] anatomy to be unimportant." This is only partially correct. Although Shorter correctly reports that Kraepelin introduced DEMENTIA PRAECOX in 1896 as a "metabolic disorder," the close connection between metabolic disorders and autointoxication theory in Kraepelin's medical cognition was not explored by Shorter. Kraepelin is perhaps better characterized as having been "tentative about cause" rather than agnostic. From the fifth edition of *Psychiatrie* in 1896 until the eighth edition in 1913, autointoxication (*Selbstvergiftung*) arising from a metabolic disturbance, probably in the sex glands—and not heredity—was Kraepelin's prime candidate for the cause of dementia praecox.

The search for "internal secretions" in dementia praecox (schizophrenia) The early experimental literature on the search for traces of internal secretions in the BLOOD OF THE INSANE reflects the confusion in the emerging field of endocrinology regarding the nature of hormones and their similarities to enzymes, general metabolites, drugs, toxins, antitoxins, and vitamins. These studies are too numerous, perplexing, and contradictory to summarize here. Perhaps the most extensive early review of this literature was conducted by the Russian psychiatric researcher Aleksandr Ivanovich Iushchenko (1869–1936) in a series of lectures delivered in 1911 and then translated into German and published in 1914. He hypothesized that dementia praecox was caused by glandular dysfunctions, especially disease processes in the parathyroid. In 1920 Bayard Taylor HOLMES, a major proponent of the autointoxication theory of dementia praecox, published a massive bibliography of works relating to the "toxaemia of dementia praecox" that remains the best source of information on early 20th century endocrine studies in dementia praecox (SCHIZOPHRENIA).

From hormones to neurohormones Endocrinological research provided a direct and important analogical bridge that led to the discovery of neurotransmitters in the brain. Following the 1921 discovery by Otto Loewi (1873–1961) of a substance in the brain later identified as acetylcholine, neurotransmitters were referred to as neurohormones or neurohumors. Indeed, the term *neurotransmitter* did not come into use until the 1960s. Neurotransmitter theories of the pathophysiology of schizophrenia (not the etiology—an important distinction to remember) involving the measurement of serotonin, DOPAMINE, glutamate, and so on, in the blood or cerebral spinal fluid (CSF) evolved directly from the metabolic paradigm in studies of the blood of the insane.

The "modern" era of endocrinology Modern endocrinological research into the biological substrates of dementia praecox/schizophrenia began in the 1920s, increased in number from the 1960s to the 1980s, and has declined markedly in the past 20 years. The early literature was reviewed in the works of one of its major proponents, Nolan D. C. Lewis (1889–1959), who believed the thyroid, adrenals, and gonads were implicated in dementia praecox. In the 21st century, publications of basic research on the endocrinology of schizophrenia have slowed to a trickle. Most of the research into the endocrine disorder hypothesis of schizophrenia has yielded little of value. There is no consistent or conclusive evidence for the role of the endocrine system in the cause (etiology) or pathophysiology (disease process) of schizophrenia.

The introduction of ANTIPSYCHOTIC DRUGS in 1952 has made endocrine research in schizophrenia more difficult. Endocrine abnormalities found in schizophrenia research may be due to the effects of antipsychotic medications. Recently, however, a few studies have once again examined the role of the sex glands and sex hormones in schizophrenia—a return to the initial 1896 hypothesis of the cause of dementia praecox put forth by Emil KRAEPELIN. The best evidence for an endocrine link to schizophrenia involves the anterior pituitary gland. The anterior pituitary contains gland cells that respond to releasing or inhibiting factors from the hypothalamus, which eventually may be found to be the source of the myriad confusing findings of endocrine dysfunction in schizophrenia.

See also DOPAMINE HYPOTHESIS; IMMUNE SYSTEM ALTERATIONS IN SCHIZOPHRENIA; METABOLIC DISORDER HYPOTHESIS.

Holmes, B. T. "A Guide to the Documents in Evidence of the Toxaemia of Dementia Praecox," *Dementia Praecox Studies* 3 (1920): 23–107.

Justschenko, A. I. *Das Wesen der Geisteskrankheiten und deren biologische-chemische Untersuchungen.* Dresden and Leipzig, Verlag von Theodor Steinkopf, 1914.

Kraepelin, E. *Psychiatrie. Ein Lehrbuch für Studierende und Aerzte.Fuenfte, vollstaendig umgearbeitete Auflage.* Leipzig: Verlag von Johann Ambrosius Barth, 1896.

Lewis, N. D. C. *Constitutional Factors in Dementia Praecox, with Particular Attention to Circulatory System and Some of the Endocrine Glands.* New York: Nervous and Mental Disease Publishing Co., 1923.

———. *Research in Dementia Praecox.* New York: National Committee For Mental Health, 1936.

Lieberman, J. A., and A. R. Koreen. "Neurochemistry and Neuroendocrinology of Schizophrenia: A Selective Review," *Schizophrenia Bulletin* 19 (1993): 371–429.

Schaefer, E. "Address in Physiology: On Internal Secretions," *Lancet* 2 (1895): 321–324.

Shorter, E. *A History of Psychiatry, From the Era of the Asylum to the Age of Prozac.* New York: John Wiley and Sons, 1997.

Stevens, J. R. "Schizophrenia: Reproductive Hormones and the Brain," *American Journal of Psychiatry* 159 (2002): 713–719.

Welbourn, R. B. "Endocrine Diseases." In *Companion Encyclopedia of the History of Medicine, Volume I,* edited by Bynum, W. F. and R. Porter. London and New York: Routledge, 1993.

endogenous psychosis See PSYCHOSIS.

endophenotype In genetics research, an endophenotype is perhaps best thought of as a BIOLOGICAL MARKER of a particular MENTAL DISORDER. It is a biological abnormality that is a much more direct result of the hypothesized genetic defect than the actual symptoms and behaviors of the disorder itself. For example, such an abnormality could be sought as a marker that indicates a person is genetically vulnerable to developing the disorder. It would then be said that the endophenotype demonstrates greater penetrance (i.e., it occurs with greater frequency) than the mental illness itself. The endophenotype may be found in the close relatives of the person with the disorder (known as the INDEX CASE or the PROBAND), but the symptoms of the mental illness itself may be fully evident only in the person in question.

See also CANDIDATE GENES; CONCORDANCE RATE; GENETICS STUDIES; INCOMPLETE PENETRANCE.

England Studies of the prevalence rates for schizophrenia in England have found substantial differences in different parts of the country, thus producing a mixed picture. Some researchers have suggested that if the diagnostic criteria differences between England and the United States were resolved, England would have a higher prevalence rate than the United States. A 1965 study of a working-class area by South London's Maudsley Institute found a prevalence rate of 3.4 per 1,000. One clear fact is that in England, schizophrenia occurs much more often in the lower socioeconomic groups. Scotland has a higher rate of schizophrenia than England.

Studies done on immigrants to the United Kingdom who suffer from their first episode of schizophrenia show that Asian immigrants tend to have a considerably lower relapse and readmission rate than white British-born citizens, whereas Afro-Caribbean immigrants have higher rates. The differences are thought to be due to the degree to which the immigrant group retains its traditional cultural values and group cohesion after moving to a new country. In Asians these qualities were maintained, whereas in Afro-Caribbeans in Britain these qualities were not maintained.

Birchwood, M., et al. "The Influence of Ethnicity and Family Structure on Relapse in First-Episode Schizophrenia. A Comparison of Asian, Afro-Caribbean and White Patients," *British Journal of Psychiatry* 161 (1992): 783–790.

Torrey, E. F. *Schizophrenia and Civilization.* New York: Jason Aronson, 1980.

environmental causes of schizophrenia The environmental causes of schizophrenia are unknown. Over the years, epidemiological studies have pointed to numerous possibilities: infections (such

as viruses), the weather, the seasons, pregnancy complications, emotional traumas such as early parental loss, unhealthy expressed emotion styles in families, toxins, and a whole host of others. After a century of research, no one is certain of an environmental cause for schizophrenia. What is sure is that there is a genetic component to the origins and development of psychotic disorders such as schizophrenia, and that genetics do interact with (unknown) environmental factors.

See also RISK FACTORS; SEASONALITY OF BIRTH.

enzyme In biochemistry, an enzyme is a protein, secreted by cells, that acts as a catalyst to induce chemical changes in other substances, itself remaining largely unchanged by the process. For this reason enzymes arc also called "biocatalysts," "biocatalyzers," and "organic catalysts." Most modern enzymes, as they are discovered, are named by adding the suffix "-ase" to the name of the substance on which the enzyme acts or activates, and/or the type of reaction it causes.

enzyme disorder hypothesis One of the BIOCHEMICAL THEORIES OF SCHIZOPHRENIA is that the disease is caused by abnormal enzyme activity. In fact, between 1957 and 1979 one of the most active areas in schizophrenia research was the search for metabolic (i.e., biochemical, neurochemical, neuroendocrinologic) changes in certain substances (neuroenzymes, neurohormones, neuropeptides and their metabolites) in the neurophysiology of people diagnosed with schizophrenia.

Several diverse areas of research have yielded biological markers of uncertain significance. First, there was suggestive evidence for elevations in the activity of the enzyme creatine kinase (CK) during acute psychotic phases of schizophrenia and affective disorders. This was first reported by H. Y. Meltzer in 1968, and later work by him indicated that serum CK activity was genetically regulated.

Second, many studies since 1941 (by Birkhauser) have indicated decreased levels of the enzyme monoamine oxidase, or "MAO," in the blood platelets of psychiatric patients, particularly schizophrenics. Much of the interest in this work was stimulated by a series of studies conducted by researchers Murphy and Wyatt and published in 1972. It was thought that this decrease in MAO activity may be a genetic marker of vulnerability to a range of mental disorders, not just schizophrenia.

Third, some reports indicated a decrease in the activity of the enzyme dopamine-beta-hydroxylase ("DBH") in the blood and the cerebrospinal fluid ("CSF") of schizophrenics. The first published finding of this DBH abnormality was by scientists Wise and Stein in 1973.

Fourth, many other enzymes (such as choline acetyltransferase and glutamic acid decarboxylase), other NEUROTRANSMITTERS than DOPAMINE (such as GABA, norepinepherine and serotonin), and peptides (such as the endorphins) have also been investigated as possible causal factors in the development of SCHIZOPHRENIA.

The research in this area is often incomprehensible to those not educated in the language of biochemistry, but a 1987 review by Meltzer published in *Schizophrenia Bulletin* provided one of the more accessible sources of information in this important area of schizophrenia research.

See also METABOLIC DISORDER HYPOTHESIS; TRANSMETHYLATION HYPOTHESIS.

Berger, P. A. "Biochemistry and the Schizophrenias: Old Concepts and New Hypotheses," *Journal of Nervous and Mental Disease* 169 (1981): 90–99.

Birkhauser, V. H. "Cholinesterase und monoaminoxydase in zentralen nervensystem," *Schweitzer. Med. Woch.* 71 (1941): 750–752.

Meltzer, H. Y. "Creatin Kinase and Aldolase in Serum: Abnormality Common to Acute Psychoses," *Science* 159 (1968): 1370.

———. "Biological Studies in Schizophrenia," *Schizophrenia Bulletin* 13 (1987): 77–114.

Wise, C. D., and L. Stein. "Dopamine-beta-hydroxylase Deficits in the Brains of Schizophrenic Patients," *Science* 181 (1973): 344–347.

epidemiology Epidemiology is an area of study that combines the methods of many different disciplines (demographic, sociological, psychological,

and medical) to study diseases. Of particular interest is the incidence and prevalence of a disease in a population, the demographic factors involved (e.g., race, sex, area inhabited), the natural history of the disease (e.g., age of onset, subtypes), and how the disease affects the environment. Most medical phenomena have been studied in this way, including the epidemiology of mental disorders.

Incidence and prevalence rates for a disease are the two most commonly encountered epidemiological statistics in research reports. Incidence refers to how frequently a particular disease occurs in a given population, whereas prevalence refers to the total number of cases of a particular disorder in a population in a given time period. Both incidence and prevalence rates can vary from study to study, depending upon the demographic characteristics of the area. Studies of the prevalence of SCHIZOPHRENIA have reported lifetime prevalence rates averaging 1 percent in the general population. For bipolar disorder (manic-depressive psychosis), prevalence rates have ranged from .4 percent to 1.2 percent of the adult population of the United States. Some research (summarized by L. F. Saugstad in 1989) indicates a marked increase of manic-depressive psychosis over the previous 30 years in several countries (mainly Scandinavia).

Perhaps the most readable source of information on the epidemiology of schizophrenia is psychiatrist E. Fuller Torrey's book, *Schizophrenia and Civilization* (1980). Chapter by chapter he reviews the epidemiological evidence collected on schizophrenia. Torrey reaches the following conclusions:

1. Schizophrenia appears to be a disease of civilization, since it appears to be found in more urban and technologically advanced areas of the world than in so-called "Third World" countries.
2. In the United States, prevalence rates for schizophrenia have ranged from 1.1 to 4.7 persons per 1,000.
3. Chinese-Americans and Mexican-Americans appear to have low schizophrenia rates. Schizophrenia is more common among the lower socioeconomic groups, among blacks, and among urban dwellers.
4. Scandinavian prevalence rates for schizophrenia are two to three times that of the United States. Rates also appear to be higher in the Soviet Union and Eastern European countries, but may be very low in Southern European countries, especially in Italy.
5. The two areas of the world with perhaps the highest prevalence rates for schizophrenia (and for manic-depressive psychosis) are Croatia, in Yugoslavia and—in particular—Western Ireland. In fact, the likelihood that a person will be hospitalized for schizophrenia in certain counties in Ireland is higher than 1 in 25 (4 percent), the highest of any area in the world. The counties most affected are Mayo, Sligo, Roscommon, Galway, Clare, Kerry, Cork, and Waterford. Irish immigrants to the United States and Canada have also traditionally had high rates of psychiatric hospitalization.
6. The prevalence rate for schizophrenia in Japan is about 2.3 per 1,000.
7. Schizophrenics may have a typical "season of birth," since, according to Torrey, studies indicate that—for unknown reasons—schizophrenics are disproportionately born in the late winter and early spring months in the Northern Hemisphere.
8. There is evidence that there are cultural differences in the response to antipsychotic medication. Europeans have been found to require lower doses of certain drugs than American patients.

Since viruses follow seasonal patterns and have been studied with epidemiological approaches, it has been suggested that some of this data point to the role of viruses in the case of schizophrenia. However, a 1985 comprehensive review of the epidemiological evidence on schizophrenia by William W. Eaton of the Center for Epidemiological Studies at the NATIONAL INSTITUTE OF MENTAL HEALTH concluded that genetics is the most important factor worldwide in the development of this disorder. Current interpretations of the vast literature on the epidemiology of schizophrenia by Assen Jablensky (1997 and 2003) confirm Torrey's summary and support Eaton's conclusion about the importance of genetics.

See also CROSS-CULTURAL STUDIES; GENETICS STUDIES; RISK FACTORS; VIRAL THEORIES OF SCHIZOPHRENIA.

Eaton, W. W. "Epidemiology of Schizophrenia," *Epidemiological Review* 7 (1985): 105–126.

Jablensky, A. "The Epidemiological Horizon." In *Schizophrenia*, edited by S. R. Hirsch and D. R. Weinberger. London: Blackwell Science, 2003.

———. "The 100-Year Epidemiology of Schizophrenia," *Schizophrenia Research* 28 (1997): 111–125.

Rawnsley, K. *Epidemiology of Affective Psychoses*. London: Cambridge University Press, 1982.

Saugstad, L. F. "Social Class, Marriage, and Fertility in Schizophrenia," *Schizophrenia Bulletin* 15 (1989): 11–43.

Torrey, E. F. "Geographical Distribution of Insanity in America: Evidence for an Urban Factor," *Schizophrenia Bulletin* 16 (1990): 591–604.

———. *Schizophrenia and Civilization*. New York: Jason Aronson, 1980.

epilepsy and schizophrenia There has been a long controversy as to whether epilepsy and schizophrenia are related in any way. For example, the CONVULSIVE THERAPIES were invented by von MEDUNA in the 1930s and were based on a scientifically unsupported theory that epilepsy and schizophrenia are biologically incompatible; it was thought that inducing a seizure in schizophrenics might "cure" them. Many studies both pro and con have explored this relationship. One finding that seems to be reliable is that the symptoms of one type of seizure disorder, temporal lobe epilepsy, very often resemble schizophrenia in presentation. In fact, evidence presented by K. Davison in 1983 suggests that as much as 17 percent of people suffering from temporal lobe epilepsy display some symptoms of schizophrenia. In particular, temporal lobe epileptics have been known to have symptoms that resemble PARANOID SCHIZOPHRENIA, including grandiose, mystical, and religious DELUSIONS and HALLUCINATIONS.

Davison, K. "Schizophrenia-like Psychoses Associated with Organic Cerebral Disorders: A Review," *Psychiatric Developments* 1 (1983): 1–34.

epistaxis From the Greek, meaning a "nosebleed." Profuse bleeding from the nose was one of the variations of BLEEDING as a treatment for mental illness in the 18th and early 19th centuries. ESQUIROL in 1838 mentions its successful use in the treatment of a young man.

equinoxes Certain times of the year were thought to cause madness or exacerbate its symptoms more than at other times. For example, the mentally ill were called "lunatics" because of the mistaken belief that the phases of the moon, particularly the full moon, had a role in causing madness. The vernal and autumnal equinoxes, were singled out by many authorities in centuries past as critical periods for the development of "madness." ESQUIROL notes in 1838 that "a house for the insane is most disturbed, and requires more careful supervision, at the period of the equinoxes." Philippe PINEL, however, differed, writing in 1801 that the critical period of "maniacal paroxysms" "generally being immediately after the summer solstice, are continued with more or less violence during the heat of summer, and commonly terminate towards the decline of autumn."

Esquirol, J. E. D. *Mental Maladies, A Treatise on Insanity*. Translated by E. K. Hunt. 1838. Reprint, Philadelphia: Lea and Blanchard, 1845.

Pinel, P. *A Treatise on Insanity*. 1801. Reprint, Sheffield: W. Todd, 1806.

erotic jealousy syndrome See OTHELLO SYNDROME.

erotomania "Love is a madness" (*furor amoris*) the Roman orator and statesman Cicero once wrote, and indeed there are very few human experiences that can generate more DELUSIONS than our erotic passions can. Forms of "love-madness" have been called *erotomania* at least since the 17th century. The word first appears in English in 1640 in a book by Jacques Ferrand, which was originally published in French in 1623, entitled *Erotomania or a Cure of Love or Erotique Melancholy*. For the next several centuries different authors defined erotomania in different ways, often confusing what we now know as nymphomania for this essentially delusional phenomenon.

Erotomania is often referred to as CLÉRAMBAULT'S SYNDROME after French psychiatrist Gaétan Gatian de Clérambault (1872–1934). In an article published in December 1920, Clérambault described erotomania as a type of "passional psychosis" (*les delires passionels*), his term for a category of delusional states in which a paranoid delusion is accompanied with passionate feeling. Clérambault, as head of the psychiatric emergency service of the Paris Prefectures of Police, was interested in how such delusional states led persons to commit crimes. Clérambault identified very specific characteristics of this delusional syndrome: "A conviction of being in amorous communication with a person of much higher rank, who has been the first to fall in love and the first to make advances." Clérambault thought that women in particular were susceptible to this delusion, and he published supporting case histories of women who had developed delusional beliefs that particularly desirable men (who, in reality, may never have met the women or had any contact with them) had fallen in love with them. This picture of erotomania was termed *pure erotomania* by Clérambault to distinguish it from the descriptions of other psychiatric authorities, who tended to define it as a form of PARANOIA.

As a type of delusional syndrome, erotomania generally does not appear alone and is usually an aspect of a serious psychotic disorder, such as SCHIZOPHRENIA or BIPOLAR DISORDER. A tragic modern example of this is would be presidential assassin John Hinckley Jr.'s erotomanic fascination with the actress Jodie Foster, which led him to attempt to assassinate President Ronald Reagan in 1981, in order to forever link their names together in history.

In French psychiatry (which has always resisted outside diagnostic systems), erotomania holds a special place as a separate delusional disorder. In *DSM-IV-TR* (2000) it is a subtype of DELUSIONAL DISORDER. In *ICD-10* (1992) it is similarly considered a subtype of PERSISTENT DELUSIONAL DISORDERS. Erotomanic delusions have been known to be present in persons suffering from schizophrenia, bipolar disorder, and major DEPRESSION, but these other disorders are the primary diagnosis, and the erotomanic delusions are secondary.

Enoch, M. D., and W. H. Trethowan. "De Clérambault's Syndrome." In *Uncommon Psychiatric Syndromes*. 2nd ed., edited by Enoch and Trethowan. Bristol, England: John Wright & Sons, 1979.

Segal, J. H. "Erotomania Revisited! From Kraepelin to *DSM-III-R*," *American Journal of Psychiatry* 146 (1989): 1,261–1,266.

erotomania, paranoid type See PARANOIA EROTICA.

erotomania proper The name given in 1882 by J. C. Bucknill and D. H. Tuke to what was later called pure erotomania. Following a distinction made in 1838 by ESQUIROL, Bucknill and Tuke distinguished the delusional syndrome of erotomania from those syndromes in which the sexual passions were actually acted out, such as nymphomania. They write:

> Erotomania, in its extended signification, not infrequently follows upon religious melancholy. . . . It is not uncommon in the old, and . . . in persons who have been patterns of chastity during life. . . . It is more frequent among women than in men, and . . . among the unmarried and widows than the married. . . . It may attack any age; but the sentimental form—erotomania proper—more especially affects the young, and those of an ardent, susceptible temperament. . . . Erotomania is often complicated with hysteria, and sometimes with hypochondriasis.

Bucknill, J. C., and D. H. Tuke. *A Manual of Psychological Medicine*. 2nd ed. London: J. & A. Churchill, 1882.

erotomanic type One of the variants of DELUSIONAL DISORDER as defined in *DSM-IV-TR* (2000). It corresponds to EROTOMANIA as defined by de Clérambault.

ERP The acronym for "event-related potentials." See also EEG STUDIES OF SCHIZOPHRENIA.

Esquirol, Jean-Étienne-Dominique (1772–1840) A student of Philippe PINEL's at the SALPÊTRIÈRE in

Paris and the author of the 1838 book *Des Maladies Mentales,* a classic textbook in the field of PSYCHIATRY, or *médecine mentale* as it was then called. A recent study of the 19th-century French psychiatric profession by Goldstein concludes that until well past the middle of the century, approximately 95 percent of all French *aliénistes* had studied in Paris with either Pinel or Esquirol. Esquirol received his doctorate in 1805 with the completion of his thesis, entitled "Passions Considered as Causes, Symptoms, and Therapeutic Means of Mental Diseases." He won the position of an attending physician at the Salpêtrière in 1811, and in that year instituted the very first official training courses on mental diseases for medical students and other physicians. A select group of young physicians who had trained under Esquirol and had become his disciples formed the "Esquirol Circle," an informal intellectual society that met for Sunday luncheons, which were presided over by Esquirol himself. Many of these "Circle" members became famous in their own right as their careers developed during the 19th century, notably, J.-P. FALRET, A. J. F. BRIERRE DE BOISMONT, J.-J. Moreau de Tours, and Jules BAILLARGER.

The search for BIOLOGICAL MARKERS of mental disorders has always existed in one form or another, and in Esquirol's day PHYSIOGNOMY was considered an important diagnostic tool. According to an entry for March 22, 1818, in the diary of Sir Alexander Morison, which described his visit to the Salpêtrière, Esquirol showed Morison his large personal collection of plaster casts of the faces of insane persons. The search for physiological markers of insanity also led Esquirol to become involved in the autopsies of deceased patients, referred to at that time as "openings (*ouvertures*) of corpses." Following the lead of his mentor Philippe PINEL, who also conducted *recherches cadavériques* between 1802 and 1804, Esquirol believed that visceral lessions were more likely to cause insanity than brain abnormalities, particularly in melancholics in which, he purported, the transverse colon was displaced.

Esquirol traveled widely in his life and inspected many institutions for the insane throughout Europe. His review of the inhumane conditions in French institutions moved him enough to write a strong report of his experiences to the French minister of the interior in 1818. In 1823 he was named inspector general of the faculty of medicine at the Salpêtrière; he left in 1825 to become the superintendent of the Maison de Charenton, one of France's oldest mental hospitals. The Maison de Charenton was the place where the Marquis de Sade was held for many years until his death. Esquirol spent 15 years working on his famous textbook, which was instantly recognized as a classic and translated into Italian, English, and German soon after publication. Esquirol is particularly remembered for providing the first clear description of HALLUCINATIONS and, especially, how they differ from illusions.

Esquirol, J. E. D. *Des Maladies Mentales.* 2 vols. Paris: J. B. Baillière, 1838.

Goldstein, J. *Console and Classify: The French Psychiatric Profession in the Nineteenth Century.* Cambridge: Cambridge University Press, 1987.

Mora, G. "On the Bicentenary of the Birth of Esquirol (1772–1840), the First Complete Psychiatrist," *American Journal of Psychiatry* 129 (1972): 562–566.

etherization After the anesthetic properties of ether were discovered in 1846, it was highly recommended for use in American asylums, from about 1849 to 1860, for acute excitements and for agitated depression. In France it was especially given to those patients suffering from mental DEGENERATION, most likely those suffering from the general paralysis of the insane and dementia praecox. However, this form of somatic treatment for mental illness fell into decline in the remaining decades of the 19th century.

The discovery of ether's effects also eclipsed the use of hypnosis as anesthesia during surgery. British "civil-surgeon" James Esdaille had perfected the use of hypnosis anesthesia to perform thousands of minor operations and about 300 major ones (including 19 amputations) between 1846 and 1848, in the experimental "Mesmeric Hospital" that he had been granted permission to establish in Calcutta, India, by the governor of Bengal. Although the medical discipline of anesthesiology evolved from the early surgical use of ether, the use of hypnosis anesthesia during surgery did not come into any significant use again until the 20th century.

Bramwell, J. M. *Hypnotism: Its History, Practice and Theory.* London: Alexander Morning, 1906.
Diethelm, O. "Somatic Treatment in Psychiatry," *American Journal of Psychiatry* 95 (1938): 1,165–1,179.

ethnicity and schizophrenia See BLACKS, INCIDENCE OF SCHIZOPHRENIA IN; CROSS-CULTURAL STUDIES; EPIDEMIOLOGY; RISK FACTORS.

etiologic heterogeneity This is essentially a term for expressing the idea that a single disease may have many different causes (etiologies). This idea, which is prominent in GENETICS STUDIES, is derived from the growing body of evidence that several MENTAL DISORDERS—especially SCHIZOPHRENIA and BIPOLAR DISORDER—are in reality a *spectrum* of disorders, not just a single, homogeneous disease entity. The subtypes of schizophrenia and bipolar disorder, while somehow related, may develop from different causes. Etiologic heterogeneity may result from NONALLELIC GENETIC HETEROGENEITY, PHENOCOPIES, or both.

See also GENETIC TRANSMISSION.

Tsuang, M. T., and Farone, S. V. "The Case for Heterogenity in the Etiology of Schizophrenia," *Schizophrenia Research* 17 (1995): 161–175.

etiology The cause or causes of a disease.

evacuants Now called "laxatives," these were substances that induced defecation in order to "purge" (and therefore "purify") the body. Evacuants and purgatives, especially emetics that caused vomiting, were a popular form of treatment for the mentally ill. The use of these substances continued in one form or another until the late 19th and early 20th centuries. Wilhelm GRIESINGER, the noted German psychiatric authority, writes of the significance of evacuants for the treatment of mental illness in the 1861 second edition of his famous textbook:

> Those medicines which act upon the digestive canal are the oldest, and still those that are most frequently used. Besides their evident indication in constipation—which is common in these diseases–, and very often better obviated by dietetic means and mild clysters than by medicines—they are also given with advantage in all recent cases associated with cerebral congestion, and are the chief remedy in acute inflammatory states of the brain.

Evacuants are no longer used as a treatment for mental illness, although laxatives may be prescribed for a limited time to counteract the constipation that may be one of the side effects of some types of ANTIPSYCHOTIC DRUGS.

Griesinger, W. *Mental Pathology and Therapeutics.* 1861. Reprint, New York: William Wood & Company, 1882.

exacerbations Those periods when the symptoms of a disease flare up and become worse. They then may go into remission. Many of the psychotic disorders are characterized by exacerbations and remissions. Such is also the case with most other mental and physical diseases (such as multiple sclerosis). These ACUTE episodes may accompany a more chronic course of an illness, such as the POSITIVE SYMPTOMS (delusions and hallucinations) of schizophrenia, which may wax and wane over the lifetime course of a disease.

See also COURSE OF SCHIZOPHRENIA.

existential analysis See DASEINANALYSE.

exogenous psychosis See PSYCHOSIS.

exorcism Throughout history, many diseases—and mental illnesses in particular—were thought to be the result of "possession" by malevolent spirits or "demons." Therefore, the remedy for this, exorcism, entailed the forceful removal of these entities by magical means. This spirit possession theory of disease and exorcism has been recorded in "primitive" societies worldwide and is mentioned in historical works dating back as far as ancient Egypt.

In the New Testament, particularly the Gospel according to Mark (A.D. 64), one of the defining attributes of Jesus is his magical ability to cast out "devils" from "demoniacs" and thereby cure them. As a treatment, formal exorcisms by practitioners of all sorts, clerical or otherwise, were carried out with regularity in Europe until the 17th century.

See also CACODEMONOMANIA; POSSESSION SYNDROME.

Kemp, S., and K. Williams. "Demonic Possession and Mental Disorder in Medieval and Early Modern Europe," *Psychological Medicine* 17 (1987): 21–29.

Noll, R. *Vampires, Werewolves and Demons: Twentieth Century Reports in the Psychiatric Literature*. New York: Brunner/Malec, 1991.

Smith, M. *Jesus the Magician*. San Francisco: Harper & Row, 1978.

expressed emotion It has long been suspected that the behavior of the family has an influence on the development of mental illness in afflicted family members. Proponents of most FAMILY INTERACTION THEORIES propose that abnormal communication patterns actually cause mental illness, and many theories have been put forth to describe the role of the family in the cause of schizophrenia. However, the research in this area has been difficult and so far inconclusive, and many of the older research tends to disregard entirely the role of biological factors in the causation of SCHIZOPHRENIA. Instead, many researchers have turned their attention to the effect of the family on the course of an illness. These studies try to identify family behavior patterns that influence—either positively or negatively—the mental illness of a particular family member. The strength of this approach is that it is not incompatible with the impressive body of research that points to significant biological factors in the causation of mental illness (particularly schizophrenia).

One of the most significant findings is that the "expressed emotion" or "EE" within a particular family environment is a suggestive predictor of relapse in patients after their discharge from hospital care. EE was measured in families indirectly by analyzing interviews with family members (without the patient being present). The first published report on EE appeared in 1962 and was the result of the work in England of Brown and colleagues; replications of this work that consistently support the role of EE in relapse continued into the 1980s. The consistent finding is that patients returning to families with low levels of EE have consistently lower relapse rates and had less of a need for antipsychotic medication. The conclusion is that in people with schizophrenia (at least in its earliest years of manifestation), there is a lower tolerance for intense environmental stimuli, particularly critical or intensely emotional comments or interactions involving family members. Thus, a family environment that is relatively supportive and emotionally undemanding may help a person with schizophrenia to reduce dependence on medication and help prevent relapse. Given this finding, other research has been conducted that has had trained families of schizophrenics with high levels of EE (high emotional overinvolvement of family members and high numbers of critical comments) monitor their interactions and actually lower their levels of EE. Controlled studies have shown that relapse rates can be significantly reduced for patients whose families can learn to lower their usually high levels of EE.

Some research has examined other variables than EE as the source of important influences on the course of a family member's mental illness. For example, an important study by the UCLA Family Project (reported by Goldstein in 1985) found that instead of EE, which is measured indirectly, other factors, such as a directly measured index of a family's "affective style" or "AS" and a family's "communication deviance" or "CD," had more of an effect either independently or together in the development of schizophrenia.

More research clearly needs to be done in this area. But what is important about these studies is the knowledge that, to some extent, schizophrenia can be managed by reducing or changing emotional interactions within the family.

Brown, G. W., J. T. L. Birley, and J. K. Wing. "Influence of Family Life on the Course of Schizophrenic Disorders: A Replication," *British Journal of Psychiatry* 121 (1972): 241–258.

Goldstein, M. J. "Family Factors That Antedate the Onset of Schizophrenia and Related Disorders: The Results

of a Fifteen Year Prospective Longitudinal Study," *Acta Psychiatrica Scandinavica* 71, Suppl. 319 (1985): 7–18.

Hooley, J. M., and J. Hiller. "Expressed Emotion and Pathogenesis of Relapse in Schizophrenia." In *Origins and Development of Schizophrenia: Advances in Experimental Psychopathology,* edited by M. F. Lenzenweger and R. H. Dworkin, 447–468. Washington, D.C.: American Psychological Association, 1998.

expressivity In genetics, expressivity is the extent to which a given phenotype, or observable trait, is manifest in an individual. It is the extent to which a trait (an observable behavior or a physical characteristic), known to be caused by the influence of a particular gene or genes that predisposes an individual to that trait, can be observed in the individual.

extrapyramidal symptoms/syndromes In the human body, the extrapyramidal system encompasses those parts of the central nervous system that are responsible for the coordination and integration of body movements. Perhaps the most serious drawback to the use of ANTIPSYCHOTIC DRUGS in the treatment of the psychotic disorders is their very serious adverse effects on the extrapyramidal system. The symptoms that these side effects produce can include tremors, muscular rigidity, drooling, eyes rolling upward toward the forehead, odd or jerky movements, blurred vision, dry mouth, odd motions of the tongue and hands, and a shuffling gait. There are four extrapyramidal syndromes: acute dystonic reactions, AKATHISIA, PARKINSONISM, and TARDIVE DYSKINESIA. Of these, the first three syndromes can be alleviated with drugs such as BENADRYL or COGENTIN, or through the reduction or cessation of antipsychotic medication. However, the fourth of these syndromes, tardive dyskinesia, is a chronic condition that develops from the prolonged use of antipsychotic medication (usually many years, although sensitivity levels differ from person to person).

eye movement abnormalities in schizophrenia One of the clearest candidates for being a BIOLOGICAL MARKER OF SCHIZOPHRENIA is certain eye movement dysfunctions. These abnormalities were first detected in schizophrenics in 1908 by researchers Diefendorf and Dodge, and have been studied for their possible link to schizophrenia ever since. The majority of these studies have involved "smooth pursuit eye movements" (SPEM), that is, those eye movements made when following a moving object. With recent advances in technology, scientists have also found that eye movement dysfunctions are detectable even while the eyes are focused on a stationary target.

Overall, smooth pursuit eye movements have been found to be abnormal in about 50 percent to 85 percent of schizophrenics in most studies, with the same dysfunctions found in about 8 percent of the general population. Furthermore, 40 percent to 50 percent of first-degree relatives of schizophrenics also have smooth pursuit eye movement abnormalities. The rate of abnormalities in persons with bipolar disorder (30 percent to 50 percent) is thought to be inflated due to LITHIUM treatment, and the number of first-degree relatives of manic-depressives that have these abnormalities is just 10 percent to 13 percent—only slightly above the rate for the general population. Thus, smooth pursuit eye movement abnormalities seem to be a genetically transmitted dysfunction and are thus becoming more and more accepted as a solid biological marker for schizophrenia. There is great hope that SPEM dysfunction is, indeed, such a marker, since it could then be used as a predictor for identifying which high-risk individuals are at true genetic risk for one day developing schizophrenia.

Diefendorf, A. R., and R. Dodge. "An Experimental Study of the Ocular Reactions of the Insane from Photographic Records," *Brain* 31 (1908): 451–489.

Erlenmeyer-Kimling, L. "Biological Markers for the Liability to Schizophrenia." In *Biological Perspectives of Schizophrenia,* edited by H. Helmchen and F. Hein. New York: Wiley, 1987.

Levy, D. L., P. S. Holzman, S. Matthysse, and N. R. Mendell. "Eye Tracking Dysfunction and Schizophrenia: A Critical Perspective," *Schizophrenia Bulletin* 19 (1994): 461–536.

eyes, subduing patients with See FIXING.

F

factor analytic models of schizophrenic symptoms See DIMENSIONS OF SCHIZOPHRENIA.

"Factors of Insanities, The" In 1894 John Hughlings Jackson (1835–1911), a British neurologist who is still considered one of the most important in his field, published a paper on "The Factors of Insanities" in which he proposed some very important ideas that are still used today. In particular, Jackson defined the difference between POSITIVE SYMPTOMS and NEGATIVE SYMPTOMS and their relationship to the nervous system. In the 1980s, these concepts became especially important in SCHIZOPHRENIA research with the work of research psychiatrist Nancy Andreason (1938–). Jackson divided the presenting symptoms found in the psychotic disorders according to whether they are the result of the "dissolution" of certain centers in the brain (the negative symptoms), or whether they are caused by the remaining "healthy nervous arrangements" left intact but nonetheless affected in their functioning by the destruction of neural tissue in other parts of the brain (the positive symptoms). The positive symptoms, then, should disrupt the normally complex integrative functions of the higher cortical functions (for example, thoughts and perceptions) and make them caricatures—less differentiated, less complex, and more automatic or involuntary variations (such as delusions and hallucinations). Jackson wrote:

> We must not speak crudely of disease causing the symptoms of insanity. Popularly the expression may pass, but properly speaking disease of the highest centres no more causes positive mental states, however abnormal they may seem, than opening flood gates causes water to flow or cutting the vagi causes the heart to beat more frequently. Disease only causes the negative element of the mental condition: the positive mental element, say a delusion, obviously an elaborate delusion however absurd it may be signifies activities of the healthy nervous arrangements, signifies evolution going on in what remains of the highest cerebral centres.

Jackson's observation that the "disease" or "dissolution" of brain tissue is related to negative symptoms influenced Crow's "type II schizophrenia," in which negative symptoms, such as flat affect, poverty of speech, blocking, are correlated with structural abnormalities in the brain.

See also BRAIN ABNORMALITIES IN SCHIZOPHRENIA.

Jackson, J. H. "The Factors of Insanities." In *Selected Writings*. Vol. 2. 1894. Reprint, New York: Basic Books, 1958.

Falret, Jean-Pierre (1794–1870) A noted French *aliéniste* who was a member of the "Esquirol Circle," the group of influential physicians to the insane females at the SALPÊTRIÈRE in Paris (males were kept at another hospital, the BICÊTRE), who met regularly for case seminars with their mentor, J. E. D. ESQUIROL. Falret joined the medical staff at this hospital in 1815. After assuming charge of the section for lunatics at the Salpêtrière in 1841, Falret began a program of treatment based on the belief that religion should play a role in psychiatric treatment, a belief that sharply contrasted with his mentors Pinel and Esquirol. He induced a cleric—a certain Abbé Christophe—to come to the hospital and lead group religious activities that included

hours of praying, singing, and biblical recitations. He believed that religious practice helped to bring about the cure of mental illness and to avoid relapses. In addition, as he told a journalist in the 1840s, religion played another role in the lives of his female patients at the Salpêtrière because, "Not being able to give them a lover to comfort the solitude of their hearts, I seek to give them God."

Falret is best remembered for his 1854 description of *la folie circulaire,* or the CIRCULAR INSANITY, as it became known in English and which is now known as BIPOLAR DISORDER. However, his linkage of phases of MELANCHOLIA and MANIA together into a separate disorder from either of these mental disorders alone had been preceded only two weeks earlier by fellow "Esquirol Circle" member Jules BAILLARGER's published description of *la folie à double forme.* Thus, it is Baillarger who was given credit for what was later named by KRAEPELIN as MANIC-DEPRESSIVE insanity. Falret, however, claimed he had published a description of this disorder in 1851 but did not use the term *la folie circulaire* in that earlier paper. Falret stressed the role of heredity in the transmission of this disorder, and he argued that the disorder was more commonly found in women.

Falret's other contributions include: in 1853, authoritative diagnostic indicators for the GENERAL PARALYSIS OF THE INSANE; and in 1822 *the* first published study of suicide that used statistical data. He believed that suicide was the result of a combination of predisposing and environmental causal factors.

Falret, J.-P. *De l'hypochondrie et du suicide.* Paris: 1822.

———. "Marche de la folie," *Gazette des Hôpitaux,* January 14, 1851.

———. "Mémoire sur la folie circulaire, forme de maladie mentale caractérisée par la reproduction successive et régulière de l'état manaiaque, de l'état mélancolique, et d'un intervalle lucide plus ou moins prolongé," *Bulletin de l'Académie Impériale de Médecine* 19 (February 14, 1854): 382–400.

———. *Recherches sur la folie paralytique et les diverses paralysies générales.* Paris: 1853.

Goldstein, J. *Console and Classify: The French Psychiatric Profession in the Nineteenth Century.* Cambridge: Cambridge University Press, 1987.

Falret, Jules-Philippe-Joseph (1824–1902) A French *aliéniste* and the son of Jean-Pierre FALRET. He continued his father's work in the understanding of the "circular insanity" and of the general paralysis of the insane. However, he is perhaps best remembered for his identification (along with Ernest Charles Lasègue) in 1877 of a form of "communicated" or "shared" delusional disorder, which is still known as FOLIE À DEUX.

Lasègue, E., and J.-Ph.-J. Falret. "La folie à deux (ou folie communiquée)," *Annales médico-psychologique* 18 (1877): 321.

family care The placement of mentally ill people in households under the care of unrelated families. In Europe this tradition has persisted since at least the 1300s in Gheel, Belgium, where a shrine to the patron saint of the mentally ill, Saint Dymphna, attracted far too many of the afflicted seeking miracle cures for the local hospital to handle. Thus, a tradition of boarding the mentally ill in private households began and is continued to this day on a reduced scale under the sponsorship of the Belgian government. Foster home care of the mentally ill became more prevalent in Europe only in the 19th century. British psychiatrist Henry MAUDSLEY, who dominated the field in his country in the latter third of the 1800s, strongly advocated the return of the most chronic patients to the care of their own families. In the United States, the very first such formal foster home program was apparently instituted in Massachusetts in 1885.

family interaction theories Popular from the 1950s to the 1970s, this group of theories asserts that severe mental illness (and in particular schizophrenia) is caused by abnormal family communication patterns. The assumption is that the underlying pathological communication patterns of the family create the mental illness in a selected person who is the "scapegoat" or the bearer of the "sick role" for the other members of the family, which acts together in an organized whole usually called a "system." Treating the mentally ill person ("the identified patient") is often depicted by pro-

ponents of family interaction as a group "family therapy" during which pathological communication patterns can be pointed out and changed, thus, theoretically, healing or curing the "identified patient." When applied to SCHIZOPHRENIA, most of these theories usually completely ignore biological evidence for the cause of the psychosis.

The family interaction theories were derived from the interest of PSYCHOANALYSIS in family dynamics as the cause of schizophrenia. For example, psychoanalyst Frieda FROMM-REICHMANN first used the term *schizophrenogenic mother* in 1948 to single out the mother as the primary cause of schizophrenia in her children. This concept was later "verified" in a study of 25 mothers of schizophrenics by Trude Tietze in 1949. Also in the 1940s, Leo Kanner wrote about the role of the "refrigerator mother" as the cause of AUTISM in infancy and childhood.

By the 1950s, more sophisticated family interaction theories were proposed that shifted from the focus on the single mother-child relationship to the study of the family as an interactive system that works together as a whole. As early as 1949 Theodore Lidz and his colleagues at Yale University began to publish work on the study of communication patterns in families with schizophrenic members. The family triad of father, mother, and schizophrenic child was of particular interest, and two typical patterns of families were discerned, schizmatic, and skewed. In the "skewed family," an unempathetic and intrusive mother is the guilty party, and she paired with an ineffectual male who is passive and perhaps mentally ill or alcoholic himself. The lack of a strong male role model and the over-intrusiveness of the mother tends to produce schizophrenic sons in these families, according to Lidz. In families characterized by a "marital schism," the entire family (rather than just the mother) seems to be at war with one another, with the parents continually threatening separation and undercutting one another. Lidz believed this sort of pattern was more characteristic of the lives of female schizophrenic patients that he and his colleagues studied.

In 1956 Gregory BATESON and his colleagues at Stanford University (the "Palo Alto Group") proposed the theory of the double bind (see DOUBLE-BIND THEORY). The theory is that schizophrenia develops in people from families that engage in "double-bind" communications, i.e., communications in which the content of the verbally expressed message does not match, or is "incongruent," with the underlying message expressed in the tone of voice, gesture, facial expression, or context of the message. For example, "I love you" may be said while the parent may have a facial expression of total apathy, or perhaps during a situation in which the parent is being particularly cruel to the child. The double-bind theory was the basis of further elaborations of "family systems theory" by Jay Haley, one of Bateson's original colleagues, and a major influence in the development of "family therapy" as a treatment modality. The essence of the rationale for using family therapy as the treatment for schizophrenia was expressed by Haley in a 1962 article when he notes, "It became apparent that it was not entirely reasonable to have a child driven mad by his family, then hospitalize him and get him on his feet and send him right back into his family to be driven mad again."

Other family interaction theorists have invented other terms for the types of family communications that seem to cause a schizophrenic break in one of the children. For example, in research spanning more than a decade Wynne and various colleagues have identified deviant styles of parental communication that may lead to the development of thought disorder in genetically susceptible children. Communication deviance (CD) is thought to comprise such characteristics as the lack of firm commitment to ideas, unusual language patterns, and problems in bringing closure to ideas or in interactions with others. However, it cannot be as yet determined whether the CD of the parents is the expression of a latent genetic trait, such as deficits in attention that have not fully developed into schizophrenia (but which their child *is* experiencing as schizophrenia), or whether it is the parents' response to daily communication with a psychotic child. Several prospective studies of children at high risk for schizophrenia are currently underway to determine whether family factors such as CD are present prior to the development of schizophrenia.

In the 1988 edition of *Surviving Schizophrenia,* E. Fuller Torrey asserts that, "Family interaction

theories, like psychoanalytic theories, have by now been discarded and for many of the same reasons." He argues that research has been of poor quality or has not held up to replication by others, and that it fails to distinguish between family communication patterns that cause schizophrenia versus those that are caused by it. However, research in this area continues, since at present only a portion of the "cause" of schizophrenia can be attributed to genetics, suggesting that the environment—specifically, family interaction patterns—may still play a significant role in the development, or at least the severity of the course, of schizophrenia.

See also EXPRESSED EMOTION.

Bateson, G., et al. "Towards a Theory of Schizophrenia," *Behavioral Science* 1 (1956): 251–264.

Lidz, R., and T. Lidz. "The Family Environment of Schizophrenic Patients," *American Journal of Psychiatry* 106 (1949): 332–345.

Lidz, T. *The Origin and Treatment of Schizophrenic Disorders.* New York: Basic Books, 1973.

Tietze, T. "A Study of Mothers of Schizophrenic Patients," *Psychiatry* 12 (1949): 55–65.

Wynne, L. C., et al. "Schizophrenics and Their Families: Research on Parental Communication." In *Developments in Psychiatric Research,* edited by J. M. Tanner. London: Hodder & Stoughton, 1977.

family studies (genetics) See CONSANGUINITY METHOD.

family therapy See FAMILY INTERACTION THEORIES.

farming (as treatment) The physical exercise of work has long been employed in the treatment of some mentally ill persons, and well into this century many institutions continued the practice of using patients to help farm or take care of the institutional grounds. However, due to the decline of a farming-based society, most institutions now have pragmatic "occupational therapy" training programs that are designed to help patients gain and maintain skills they will need upon discharge back to an urban community. ESQUIROL in particular recommended farming as the best form of therapeutic physical exercise for the mentally ill, particularly depressed people. In 1838 he writes:

> Corporeal exercises, riding on horseback, the game of tennis, fencing, swimming and traveling, especially in melancholy, should be employed, in aid of other means of treatment. The culture of the earth, with a certain class of the insane, may be advantageously substituted for all other exercises. We know the result to which a Scottish farmer arrived, by the use of labor. He rendered himself celebrated by the cure of certain insane persons, whom he obliged to labor in his fields.

Esquirol, J. E. D. *Mental Maladies. A Treatise on Insanity,* trans. E. K. Hunt. Philadelphia: Lea and Blanchard, 1845; first published, 1838.

Faxensyndrom Also known as the clown syndrome, it is a form of reactive MENTAL DISORDER, found in prisoners, that simulates a true psychosis. "Childish" or "silly" behavior predominates in this syndrome as a dissociated reaction to the confines of prison. It was first identified by Eugen BLEULER, and it is related to the more commonly described GANSER'S SYNDROME, also known as "prison psychosis."

Bleuler, E. "Das Faxensyndrom," *Psychiatr.-Neurol. Wochenschrift* 12 (1910–11): S. 375.

Feighner research criteria In the 1970s, researchers in the field of SCHIZOPHRENIA began to develop specific criteria for defining schizophrenia that would be universally acceptable and used in all future studies. For many decades, scientists had been conducting research studies on "schizophrenics" without any commonly accepted definition of what a "schizophrenic" was. Furthermore, many studies did not list their criteria for defining schizophrenia, and many studies reported using "schizophrenics" as a single generic group without regard to important differences in the subtypes of schizophrenia. Hence, most of the research prior to 1980 is not cited in scientific journals today, because the

patients that were used then might not match the generally accepted definition of the schizophrenic subjects used in research today. The assumption is that the knowledge gained in those earlier studies may not be generalizable to the results of today.

The Feighner research criteria were developed at the Washington University School of Medicine in St. Louis and first proposed in a 1972 publication. They were referred to as the Feighner criteria because of the name of the senior author of the publication. The Feighner criteria consists of suggested diagnostic criteria for 14 mental disorders (including schizophrenia), criteria that would ensure that all future research used subjects with the same characteristics. The Feighner criteria was used extensively in schizophrenia research throughout the 1970s. Other research criteria that were also proposed in the early 1970s were the New Haven Schizophrenia Index and the WORLD HEALTH ORGANIZATION International Pilot Study of Schizophrenia Criteria, revised by Carpenter, Strauss and Bartko and called the "CSB system" or the "WHO Flexible System." However, in 1975 the RESEARCH DIAGNOSTIC CRITERIA (or RDC) was developed by Robert Spitzer (1932–) of the New York State Psychiatric Research Institute and Eli Robins (1921–95) of the Washington University School of Medicine in St. Louis, and it is the RDC that has been the most widely accepted research criteria in the study of schizophrenia.

Endicott, J., et al. "Diagnostic Criteria for Schizophrenia: Reliabilities and Agreement between Systems," *Archives of General Psychiatry* 39 (1982): 864–889.

Feighner, J. P., et al. "Diagnostic Criteria for Use in Psychiatric Research," *Archives of General Psychiatry* 20 (1972): 57–63.

feigned insanity Ever since laws began to accept that some severely mentally ill people could commit criminal acts for which they were not responsible due to their loss of reason, there have been otherwise-normal criminals and selected others who have "feigned" or "simulated" insanity to escape imprisonment or other punishment for criminal acts. In his 1801 classic, *A Treatise on Insanity*, Philippe PINEL devotes an entire section to "Feigned Mania: The Method of Ascertaining It." In this section he provides two illustrative case histories, one being a case of "feigned mania" in a political prisoner (whom Pinel humanely does not reveal to the authorities and thus spares the dissident a return to prison) and another exemplifying genuine mental illness. Pinel makes the observation, still all too true today (as anyone who has worked in a state psychiatric facility will admit), that "A guilty prisoner sometimes counterfeits insanity in order to escape the vengeance of the law, preferring confinement in a lunatic hospital to the punishment due to his crime." However, Pinel is honest about the difficulty of identifying simulated insanity.

> It may be thought astonishing, that in an object of so much importance as that of ascertaining the actual existence of mental derangement, there is yet no definite rule to guide us in so delicate an examination. In fact, there appears no other method than what is adopted in other departments of natural history: that of ascertaining whether the facts which are observed belong to any one of the established varieties of mental derangement, or to any of its complications with other disorders.

American physician Isaac RAY, whose 1838 book, *A Treatise On the Medical Jurisprudence of Insanity*, was perhaps the greatest contribution made by American psychiatry in the 19th century, devotes several chapters to such topics as "Simulated Insanity," "Concealed Insanity," and "Simulated Somnambulism." He criticizes the practice of using the courtroom testimony of physicians who have no experience working with the mentally ill in distinguishing cases of simulated insanity from genuine ones:

> Those who have been longest acquainted with the manners of the insane, and whose practical acquaintance with the disease furnishes the most satisfactory guaranty of the correctness of their opinions, assure us that insanity is not feigned easily, and consequently that no attempt at imposition can long escape the efforts of one properly qualified to expose it.

Ray states that all cases of simulated insanity betray a common characteristic: "The grand fault committed by impostors is, that in their anxiety to produce an imitation that shall deceive, they overdo the character they assume, and present nothing but a clumsy caricature." He then describes specific symptoms of "mania" that are often clumsily mimicked, and he gives physicians guidelines on how to trick the suspected simulator, urging them to "contrive some plan for outwitting the pretender, and entrapping him in his own toils."

Many techniques have been employed through the centuries to detect feigned insanity. Ray relates a tale reported by Benjamin RUSH of Philadelphia in which Rush was called in by the courts to determine whether a man who had just been condemned to execution was "feigning madness" or not. Incredibly, Rush based his decision on the man's PULSE, which he found "twenty beats more frequent than in the natural state," and therefore, "he decided, chiefly on the strength of this fact, that the prisoner was really mad." With the rise of experimental research on psychology and psychophysiology at the end of the 19th century, objective techniques were eventually sought for use in forensic psychiatric situations. Swiss psychiatrist C. G. JUNG was a pioneer in the creation of a diagnostic device with the famous "word association" test, which had already been used in psychiatric research by others. Jung reports the application of his word association tests to forensic issues, including determining cases of "simulated insanity" in a series of papers he published between 1903 and 1908.

Today our knowledge of the psychotic disorders (particularly schizophrenia and bipolar disorder) is so widely distributed that, in most legal situations, it would be highly unlikely for someone to simulate them successfully for any great length of time. However, in nonforensic situations in which it is rarely expected that the presenting patient is lying about his or her symptoms, an impostor can gain admittance to psychiatric facilities by perhaps just claiming to "hear voices." Such was the ruse reported in a famous 1973 article by psychologist David Rosenhan and his associates at Stanford University, who sent normal impostors to a psychiatric facility and who instructed them to report only such auditory hallucinations. Most of them were admitted to the facility with a diagnosis of schizophrenia. Rosenhan's criticisms of psychiatric diagnostic practices have, in turn, been criticized by many others (see Spitzer's 1976 article) who defend the actions of the admitting psychiatrists in the Rosenhan study as rational decisions based on the context in which the claims of psychotic symptoms were made.

Jung, C. G. "On Simulated Insanity." In *The Collected Works of C. G. Jung, Volume 1: Psychiatric Studies,* edited by H. Read, M. Fordham and G. Adler. 1903. Reprint, Princeton, N.J.: Princeton University Press, 1970.

Pinel, P. *A Treatise on Insanity.* Translated by D. D. Davis. 1801. Reprint, Sheffield, England: W. Todd, 1806. .

Ray, I. *A Treatise On the Medical Jurisprudence of Insanity.* Boston: Charles C. Little and James Brown, 1838.

Rosenhan, D. L. "On Being Sane in Insane Places," *Science* 179 (1973): 250–258.

Spitzer, R. L. "More on Pseudoscience in Science and the Case for Psychiatric Diagnosis," *Archives of General Psychiatry* 33 (1976): 459–470.

Ferriar, John (1761–1815) Scottish physician who served at the Manchester Lunatic Asylum in England. He is remembered for his careful empirical observations and case histories of mental illness, provided in his 1792 book, *Medical Histories and Reflections.* He criticized BLEEDING and PURGING as treatments for mental illness and was one of the first to recommend isolation rather than mechanical restraints for violent patients. He is credited for introducing the term "hysterical conversion" into the psychiatric vocabulary.

Ferriar, J. *Medical Histories and Reflections.* London: 1792.

fertility The ability to reproduce children. Fertility rates for people diagnosed with the psychotic disorders have been determined on various populations in many countries over many decades. The low marriage rates for schizophrenic patients (particularly males) also contribute to low rates of marital fertility (the rate of children per marriage). When census data are

used, marital fertility rates for SCHIZOPHRENIA and for manic-depressive psychosis (BIPOLAR DISORDER) are lower than the norm for the population as a whole. On the whole, no studies have found evidence of any physiological dysfunction that might impair fertility in those people diagnosed with schizophrenia. Therefore the lower rates of fertility are probably due to the severe disruption in the ability to form and maintain social relationships with others.

Saugstad, L. F. "Social Class, Marriage, and Fertility in Schizophrenia," *Schizophrenia Bulletin* 15 (1989): 9–43.

fetal neural development and schizophrenia Brain abnormalities may develop early in the lives of people later diagnosed with SCHIZOPHRENIA and may already be in existence before the full onset of the disease occurs. In many areas of the brain that demonstrate structural abnormalities, particularly those involving the subcortical structures of the LIMBIC SYSTEM (e.g., the hippocampus and parahippocampal areas, amygdala, dorsolateral frontal cortex, and the globus pallidus), the damage is thought to arise during the development of the nervous system in the fetus during gestation. During fetal neural development, certain nerve cells (neurons) actually travel to specific spots (a process called neuronal migration) and form very specific connections with one another to create distinct structures in the brain (a process called the specification of cerebral cortical areas). In fact, some researchers have argued that there is a strong possibility that the development of schizophrenia later in life is related to a defect in genes controlling the migration and interconnection of these young neurons during fetal neural development.

A conference on fetal neural development and schizophrenia was held in Washington, D.C., from May 31 to June 1, 1988, and included many of the major researchers in schizophrenia and experts in brain imaging and neuropathology. A summary of the conference proceedings published in *Schizophrenia Bulletin* in 1989 listed the following findings as possible evidence that disturbances in the development of the nervous system of the fetus may be the source of the brain anomalies found in schizophrenia:

1. Recent neuropathological studies have found structural deviance that has been interpreted as evidence of fetal neural development, most likely in the second trimester.
2. Helsinki residents whose *second trimester* of gestation overlapped a particularly severe viral epidemic evidenced an increased rate of hospital diagnoses of schizophrenia. First or third trimester exposure was not associated with an elevation of rates of schizophrenia.
3. Two clinical studies have found that disturbances of gestation during the second trimester are linked to childhood and adult psychoses.
4. The extensive literature on the prenatal and perinatal experiences of schizophrenic patients contains evidence that schizophrenic patients have suffered considerably more prenatal and perinatal complications than controls. Indeed, some perinatal complications may actually be the result of a prenatal insult.
5. Minor physical anomalies are benign congenital abnormalities associated with the disruptions of fetal development. These external signs have been used as indices of otherwise cryptic fetal neural maldevelopment. Several investigators have reported that schizophrenic patients have a significantly elevated incidence of these anomalies.
6. Several investigators have found that the brains of schizophrenic patients are significantly reduced in volume. Such findings could reflect a failure in fetal neural development.

It is hoped that by studying the role of fetal neural development in schizophrenia the interaction of both genetic (neuronal migration and specification of areas) and environmental (viruses, birth complications) factors can be better understood.

At the dawn of the 21st century, the reigning scientific paradigm in schizophrenia research is the neurodevelopmental model. This theory was first articulated in 1986 by Daniel Weinberger of the NATIONAL INSTITUTE OF MENTAL HEALTH. Weinberger argued that the causes of schizophrenia begin in the womb, long before birth, and are not found in adolescence or adulthood, as many had previously thought.

The normal development of the human nervous system through early life, from embryo to fetus to infancy, childhood, adolescence, and adulthood, is still not well understood, however. Current textbooks in human embryology are filled mainly with references to embryological research on mice, chicks, zebrafish, and fruit flies—not human beings. Not only human embryology, but also developmental biology and developmental genetics are still very much in their infancy as scientific disciplines. There is so much that we do not know about normal processes that it is difficult to pinpoint the abnormalities in human fetal neural development that may be evidence of the disease process of schizophrenia. Hence, a severe limitation of Weinberger's neurodevelopmental model is that it still must refer to evidence from animal studies of fetal neural development to look for analogues to presumed causes of schizophrenia in human fetuses. Actual neuropathological evidence of schizophrenia from human fetal tissue does not yet exist.

See also NEURODEVELOPMENTAL MODEL OF SCHIZOPRENIA; PERINATAL FACTORS HYPOTHESIS.

Gilbert, S. F. *Developmental Biology*. 4th ed. Sunderland, Mass.: Sinauer Associates, 1994.

Langman, J. *Medical Embryology*. 4th ed. Baltimore: Williams & Wilking, 1989.

Larsen, W. J. *Human Embryology*. 2nd ed. New York: Churchill Livingstone, 1997.

Lyon, M., et al. "Fetal Neural Development and Schizophrenia," *Schizophrenia Bulletin* 15 (1989): 149–161.

Rakic, P. "Specification of Cerebral Cortical Areas," *Science* 241 (1988): 170–176.

Weinberger, D. R. "The Pathogenesis of Schizophrenia: A Neurodevelopmental Theory." In *The Neurology of Schizophrenia*, edited by H. A. Nasrallah and D. R. Weinberger. Amsterdam: Elsevier, 1986, pp. 397–406.

Feuchtersleben, Ernst von (1806–1849) Feuchtersleben was an influential Austrian physician whose primary contribution was the invention of many clinical terms still used today. For example, in 1845 Feuchtersleben coined the word *PSYCHOSIS* to refer to mental illness that was not due to identifiable diseases in the tissue of the nervous system. He proposed this term as a counterpart to *NEUROSIS*, already long in use to refer to a mental disorder that is due to the pathology of nervous tissue (unlike today's colloquial usage, which does not carry that emphasis on physiological causes of the disorder). Feuchtersleben also coined or popularized many other terms still in use today, most importantly *psychopathology, psychopathy*, and *psychiatrics*.

Feuchtersleben, E. v. *Lehrbuch der ärztlichen Seelenkunde*. Vienna: 1845.

fever therapy Throughout the centuries there have been many anecdotal reports of improvements in the mentally ill following physical illnesses that were accompanied by fever. For example, in the mid-1700s Malcolm Flemyng (?–1764), an English physician, made the observation that "intermittent fevers strengthen the nerves." In a chapter on "The Causes of the Disease" in his 1911 text *Dementia Praecox, Of the Group Of Schizophrenias*, Eugen BLEULER also notes, "yet we often see that mentally ill patients improve extensively after having had fever."

In 1887 Austrian neurologist and psychiatrist Julius Wagner von Jaureg (1857–1940) first proposed the idea that the introduction of fevers might be therapeutic for patients with certain mental illnesses, specifically those with the disorder known as the GENERAL PARALYSIS OF THE INSANE, which was later found conclusively to be the result of syphilis. His first experiments, in which he inoculated these "paretics" with malarial organisms, were conducted in 1917. He achieved significantly beneficial results with this malarial fever treatment, and in 1927 he won a Nobel Prize for this work.

"Malaria treatment" was first used in the United States on the patients at St. Elizabeth's Hospital in Washington, D.C., in 1922, at the initiative of its superintendent, William Alanson White, who ordered from Puerto Rico a supply of 12 mosquitoes contaminated with benign tertian malaria. Eleven of the mosquitoes died in transit, but the sole surviving insect was placed in a small cage and then strapped to the arm of a schizophrenic. After being bitten through the wire mesh of the cage, blood continued to be drawn from this

schizophrenic so as to infect 12 other syphilitics and induce the curative fevers in them. The first published report of this syphilotherapy appeared in 1924. Also in 1924, the then-29-year-old Walter FREEMAN, of later "PSYCHOSURGERY" fame, was made director of the research laboratories (bacteriology, psychology, pathology, and roentgenology) at St. Elizabeth's and subsequently continued this research. Prior to "malaria therapy," fevers were induced in patients with substances such as sterile milk and other proteins, with the intention of alleviating symptoms or producing a cure. The artificial production of fevers as a treatment for several mental illnesses was used in American institutions such as the New Jersey State Hospital at Trenton throughout the 1930s.

Lewis, N. D. C., et al. "Malaria Treatment of Paretic Neuro-syphilis," *American Journal of Psychiatry* 4 (1924): 175–188.

Finland See SCANDINAVIA.

fire and moxa treatment See CAUTERY TREATMENT.

first break The first clear onset of the schizophrenic illness in a person's life. It is an old term in the SCHIZOPHRENIA literature that is derived from the notion of a "first (nervous) breakdown." The term "first-break schizophrenics" is still used to designate those people who come to the attention of mental health professionals for the very first time with the clear psychotic symptoms of schizophrenia. "First-episode schizophrenics" is a current term for this.

first-degree relatives In the search for the genetic basis of MENTAL DISORDERS, it is assumed that the closer the relationship between an afflicted person and his blood relatives, the more likely these blood relatives will also manifest signs of the disorder. The parents, siblings (brothers and sisters), and children of an afflicted person are known as "first-degree relatives," whereas grandparents, cousins, aunts and uncles, and nieces and nephews are known as "second-degree relatives." In studies of the transmission of SCHIZOPHRENIA using the CONSANGUINITY METHOD, it has generally been concluded, since the first studies were completed in 1916, that the first-degree relatives of an afflicted person (the "index case") are nine times more likely than people in the general population to develop this disorder.

See also GENETICS STUDIES.

first-rank symptoms Due to the extremely complex nature of SCHIZOPHRENIA, many different systems using different criteria have been proposed for its diagnosis. Some systems are based on theory, whereas others are based primarily on phenomenology, i.e., the presence (or absence) of certain carefully described symptoms that are commonly observed in schizophrenic patients in clinical practice. This pragmatic approach to psychiatric diagnosis was characteristic of the "phenomenological school" of German psychiatry, which included such representatives as Jaspers, Mayer-Gross, Kleist, Leonhard, and, especially, Kurt Schneider. A phenomenological approach developed by Schneider in the 1939 book *Psychischer Befund und Psychiatrische Diagnose* (published in subsequent editions as *Klinische Psychopathologie*) purported to identify only those symptoms that he thought would discriminate schizophrenia from other forms of mental illness. The identified symptoms would be considered "pathognomonic" of schizophrenia.

Schneider identified 11 characteristic symptoms of schizophrenia, which he called "first-rank symptoms," the presence of any one of which would be sufficient for diagnosing a person with schizophrenia. The first three of Schneider's first-rank symptoms are forms of auditory hallucinations: (1) the patient hears voices speaking his or her thought out loud, (2) the patient experiences himself or herself as the subject about which the voices are discussing or arguing, and (3) the patient hears voices commenting on his or her actions as they are performed. The fourth symptom is a delusional percept, a two-stage process in which a patient's normal perception is followed by a highly personalized delusional interpretation of the perception.

The fifth through eleventh symptoms on Schneider's list are best characterized as serious defects in the experience of the normal boundaries that separate the self from the environment: (5) in somatic passivity, the patient experiences him- or herself as the passive and reluctant recipient of body sensations that are imposed from the outside (6) in thought withdrawal, the patient believes his thoughts are being taken out of his mind by some external force (7) in thought broadcast, the private thoughts in the mind of the patient are experienced as being magically transferred into the minds of others and (8) in thought insertion, the patients experience certain thoughts as being inserted into their head by others. First-rank symptoms, 9 through 11 consist of affect, impulses, and motor activity that are experienced as imposed and controlled from outside the patient's body.

Schneider's first-rank symptoms were adopted in Europe and in many other parts of the world as a primary method of diagnosing schizophrenia. The first-rank symptoms became familiar to American psychiatrists only in the 1970s, and although many of the individual symptoms are mentioned in *DSM-IV-TR* (2000), they have not achieved the prominence attributed to them in other parts of the world. Many research studies have been conducted that show that the first-rank symptoms are not pathognomonic of schizophrenia, that the mere presence of any one of the 11 is not sufficient for giving someone a diagnosis of schizophrenia. For example, AUDITORY HALLUCINATIONS can occur in other mental disorders, such as bipolar disorder or in depression with psychotic features. Furthermore, Schneider's first-rank symptoms seem to represent only the POSITIVE SYMPTOMS of schizophrenia (DELUSIONS and HALLUCINATIONS) and do not take into account the presence of NEGATIVE SYMPTOMS (FLAT AFFECT, poverty of speech, etc.) in some forms of schizophrenia.

See also AUDITORY HALLUCINATIONS; SUBJECTIVE EXPERIENCE IN SCHIZOPHRENIA.

Carpenter, W. T., J. S. Strauss, and S. Muleh. "Are There Pathognomonic Symptoms of Schizophrenia?," *Archives of General Psychiatry* 28 (1973): 847B–852.

Schneider, K. *Clinical Psychopathology.* Translated by M. W. Hamilton. New York: Grune & Stratton, 1959.

five-point restraints The label given to a technique of restraining violent patients in a psychiatric setting. It refers to the practice of tying a violent patient to a bed, usually with thick cotton cords. Each ankle is tied to a leg of the bed as the patient either lies or is restrained physically on the bed, and the wrists are tied to portions of the bed frame on either side of the patient's body. This technique is called FOUR-POINT RESTRAINTS. For particularly violent patients, a bed sheet or another restraint cord is wrapped across the chest and under the arms and tied under the bed to keep the patient restrained flat on his or her back.

See also MECHANICAL RESTRAINT.

fixing A technique recommended by some 18th- and early 19th-century physicians who worked with "lunatics" or "madmen" to subdue unmanageable patients by "fixing," "setting," or "catching the patients by the eye." Although it is unclear whether this practice was derived from the hypnotic induction techniques of practitioners of the "animal magnetism" of Franz Anton Mesmer (1734–1815), which was popular at the time, this willful gazing or staring into the eyes of patients in order to quiet them was recommended by English physician William Pargeter (1760–1810) in his 1792 book, *Observations on Maniacal Disorders.* However, this practice was ridiculed by John HASLAM in his 1798 manual, *Observations on Insanity.* Nonetheless, American physician Benjamin RUSH of Philadelphia's Pennsylvania Hospital recommended this practice as an effective "Remedie for Mania" in his 1812 textbook, *Medical Inquiries and Observations Upon the Diseases of the Mind.* After isolating the violent patient from his family and placing him in a private chamber in either "a public or private madhouse," Rush then gives physicians the following advice:

> This preliminary measure being taken, the first object of the physician, when he enters the cell, or chamber, of his deranged patient, should be to catch his EYE, and look him out of countenance. The dread of the eye was early imposed upon every beast of the field. The tyger, the mad bull, and the enraged dog, all fly from it: now a man deprived of

his reason partakes so much of the nature of those animals, that he is for the most part easily terrified, or composed, by the eye of a man who possesses his reason. I know this dominion of the eye over mad people is denied by Mr. Haslam, from his supposing that it consists simply in imparting to the eye a stern or ferocious look. This may sometimes be necessary; but a much greater effect is produced, by looking the patient out of countenance with a mild and steady eye, and varying its aspect from the highest degree of sternness, down to the mildest degree of benignity; for there are keys in the eye, if I may be allowed the expression, which should be suited to the state of the patient's mind, with the same exactness that musical tones should be suited to the depression of spirits in hypochondriasis. Mr. Haslam again asks, "Where is the man that would trust himself alone with a madman, with no other means of subduing him than by his eye?" This may be, and yet the efficacy of the eye as a calming remedy may not be called in question. It is but one of several other remedies that are proper to tranquilize him, and, when used alone, may not be sufficient to that purpose. Who will deny the efficacy of bleeding for the cure of madness? and yet who would rely upon it exclusively, without the aid of other remedies? In favour of the power of the eye, in conjunction with other means, in composing mad people, I can speak from the experience of many years. It has been witnessed by several hundred students of medicine in our hospital, and once by several of the managers of the hospital, in the case of a man recently brought into their room, and whose conduct for a considerable time resisted its efficacy.

The most famous case of a "cure" using the technique of "fixing" by a physician was the successful treatment of King George III of England for an attack of "MANIA" in 1788 by MAD-DOCTOR Francis Willis, who demonstrated his use of "the EYE" to a parliamentary committee inquiring into the physician's activities.

Rush, B. *Medical Inquiries and Observations upon the Diseases of the Mind.* Philadelphia: Kimber & Richardson, 1812.
Scull, A. "The Domestication of Madness," *Medical History* 27 (1983): 233–248.

flat affect One of the NEGATIVE SYMPTOMS of SCHIZOPHRENIA. In flat affect there is virtually no expression of affect, and in behavior this may mean that the person speaks in a monotone and that the face is relatively immobile and without expression. Although some contemporary critics of the use of ANTIPSYCHOTIC DRUGS point to such behavior as evidence that these substances reduce people suffering with schizophrenia to "zombies," in fact, such behavioral qualities have been described for more than a century, long before the widespread use of antipsychotic drugs in the 1950s.

flexibilitas cerea See CATATONIC WAXY FLEXIBILITY.

flight of ideas This term refers to the rapid, continuous flow of a person's speech in which there are quick jumps form topic to topic. These rapid shifts are usually based on common associations, plays on words, or are in response to events happening in the immediate environment. "Ideas" literally "fly" rapidly from the mouth of the person speaking, and this is a very characteristic symptom of someone experiencing a MANIC EPISODE. This can be a sign of BIPOLAR DISORDER, as well as a sign of ORGANIC MENTAL DISORDERS, SCHIZOPHRENIA, or acute reactive psychoses. Flight of ideas may also appear in nonpsychotic conditions, such as an acute reaction to stress.

See also LANGUAGE ABNORMALITIES IN SCHIZOPHRENIA.

flogging In the Middle Ages, a common practice in Europe (especially in German-speaking areas) was the ritual beating or "flogging" of wandering, mentally ill people before escorting them back to the towns from which they originated. At other times, public flogging (sometimes at a whipping post) was the prescribed treatment for the inappropriate behavior of the mentally ill. In his *Dialogue of Cumfort* of 1533, Sir Thomas More of England relates the story of an instance when he ordered the public flogging of "a lunatic" for disruptive behavior in church during the Mass. Apparently the mentally ill person in question would lift the skirts of praying

women just as the Host was elevated by the priest during the ceremony. More ordered his seizure and he was flogged until the lesson "was beaten home. For he could then very well rehearse his faults himself, and speak and treat very well, and promise to do afterward as well" (cited in Tuke).

Formally prescribed beatings were common even in institutions for the insane until the early 1800s. Although the practice had disappeared in English and French institutions by the 1820s, it was still a part of the treatment regime in German asylums. Reviewing primarily rare German-language texts from the 18th and early 19th centuries, Emil KRAEPELIN documents this form of "treatment" in his 1917 historical sketch, *Hundert Jahre Psychiatre (One Hundred Years of Psychiatry)*:

> Rivaling chains in popularity was the lash. Müller (in 1700) related that in the Juliusspital attendants were generously provided with many restraining and punitive devices—chains, manacles, shackles, and efficient, leather-encased bullwhips. They made ample use of these instruments whenever a patient complained, littered his quarters, or became recalcitrant or abusive. "Thrashing was almost part of the daily routine," he concluded. Lichtenberg explained that thrashings were often better for lunatics than anything else, and that they helped them to adjust to the harsh realities of daily life. Even Reil, the enthusiastic champion of mental care for the insane, noted that the straight jacket, confinement, hunger, and a few lashes with the bullwhip would readily bring patients into line. Frank was also of the opinion that a "light blow" was "effective in dealing with malicious or unreasonable patients." Autenreith found that women who persisted in going around naked quickly dressed in response to a few applications of the lash. . . .

See also ABUSE OF PSYCHIATRIC PATIENTS.

Kraepelin, E. *One Hundred Years of Psychiatry.* Translated by W. Baskin. 1917. Reprint, New York: Philosophical Library, 1962.

Marx, O. "Descriptions of Psychiatric Care in Some Hospitals during the First Half of the 19th Century," *Bulletin of the History of Medicine* (1967): 208–214.

Tuke, D. H. *Chapters in the History of the Insane in the British Isles.* London: Kegan, Paul, Trench, 1882.

fluphenazine See ANTIPSYCHOTIC DRUGS.

focal infection as cause of psychotic disorders A disputed autointoxication theory of the cause of mental illness that has not been seriously considered since the 1930s. The short-lived "focal infection" theory of American psychiatrist Henry A. COTTON (1876–1933), which he first formulated and investigated in 1916, held that the "functional psychoses" were due to chronic infections in specific areas of the body that nonetheless had an effect on the entire physiological system. It was proposed by Cotton that the weakest infections would result only in "psychoneuroses" in people, but the stronger the infection the more severe the disorder it produced, with DEMENTIA PRAECOX (SCHIZOPHRENIA) apparently the result of the most severe systemic focal infections. These infected areas may not appear to be infected nor give the patient any unusual distress, but they were verified as being infected through laboratory tests. The primary areas of focal infection were thought to be the teeth and tonsils. From these areas infections then spread (by constantly swallowing the bacteria originating in the mouth) to the stomach and lower intestinal tract (including the duodenum, small intestine, gall bladder, appendix, and colon) and the genitourinary tract. In mentally ill women, Cotton claimed in 1922, the cervix was infected in about 80 percent of the cases—even in virgins.

From 1916 to 1918 Cotton investigated the suspected foci of infection on the patients of the New Jersey State Hospital at Trenton, where he was the superintendent. By July 1918 Cotton decided to take his bizarre theory one step further and actually devised a surgical procedure of treatment based on the theory that this would cure PSYCHOSIS. In an October 1922 article that summarizes his work, Cotton explained his rationale with the following claim: "For the general practitioner can, not only arrest many cases after a psychosis has developed, but, better still, by eliminating the foci of infection can

easily prevent the occurrence of a psychosis." Thus, between 1918 and 1922, Cotton and medical and surgical colleagues from other disciplines performed "detoxication" surgery on some 1,400 patients, removing teeth, tonsils, colons, parts of the stomach and intestines, and glandular tissue form the cervix. In 38 women, full hysterectomies were performed, and some patients—both male and female—also lost their thyroid glands. Cotton claimed that, because of this "detoxication" surgery, the recovery rate from psychosis from 1918 to 1922 jumped to 80 percent of all cases, up from an average of 37 percent for the 10-year period prior to 1918.

Even in Cotton's time, this theory and his surgical techniques for "arresting" psychosis were considered bizarre by many of his contemporaries. In a publication of the remarks of other prominent psychiatrists following Cotton's research summary article in the *American Journal of Psychiatry* in 1922, one critic made the following remarks to Cotton:

> Now, to my mind a colostomy or a colectomy is a somewhat serious operation. Mr. Cotton speaks of them in a way that would almost lead one to think the operation as simple and as devoid of danger as the extraction of a tooth . . . we find ourselves told by the friends of patients, people who have heard of these activities and this theory, not through medical publications, seldom through their family physicians, but through lay journals and the daily press, that something is being done at Trenton by Dr. Cotton and his associates which the rest of us are not doing, and they are demanding that we shall adopt these theories and follow the methods pursued at Trenton.
>
> We should study this matter so carefully and so thoroughly, not being carried away by the enthusiasm of Dr. Cotton. . . . Shall we have our daughter's uterine cervix enucleated, or the tonsils cut out, or the colon removed in whole or part, or my son's teeth extracted with a hope of recovery from dementia praecox or some other bad mental state(?) . . .

The support of the popular media, however, was not enough to keep Cotton in good scientific standing. A carefully designed study to test Cotton's theory was conducted in 120 patients at the New York State Psychiatric Institute on Ward's Island in New York City by the medical director (George Kirby) and a bacteriologist (Nicholas Kopeloff). They found that the removal of focal infections in 58 of the cases did not result in a higher improvement rate than that of the other 62. Surgical work was done on infected teeth, tonsils, sinuses, and genitals, but not on the intestinal tract. Furthermore, the study strongly criticized as "unsatisfactory" from a scientific point of view Cotton's methods for establishing focal infection. Thus, the study conclusively rejected Cotton's claim that focal infection is the cause of functional psychoses.

Until his death in 1933, hundreds of patients died from such operations performed by Cotton and his staff at Trenton.

Cotton, H. A. "The Etiology and Treatment of the So-called Functional Psychoses. Summary of Results Based on the Experience of Four Years," *American Journal of Psychiatry* 2 (1922): 157–210.

Kopeloff, N., and G. H. Kirby. "Focal Infection and Mental Disease," *American Journal of Psychiatry,* 3 (1923): 149–199.

Scull, A. *Madhouse: A Tragic Tale of Megalomania and Modern Medicine.* New Haven, Conn.: Yale University Press, 2005.

folie à deux Literally a "psychosis of two." Folie à deux is a MENTAL DISORDER afflicting at least two closely related persons in which identical delusions and sometimes psychotic behavior are shared and, indeed, strongly supported by each of the partners. Although this disorder is most commonly found in relationships between two people, case histories have been published that show that it can afflict as many as 12 persons in a family (*folie à famille*). In DSM-IV-TR (2000), the diagnosis of shared psychotic disorder was given to those people who were initially not psychotic, but in whom a delusion or delusions develop as the result of a close relationship with another person who already had the delusion prior to the relationship. The many case histories that have been recorded indicate that the "primary case" individual may have a higher IQ or some other elevated social status when compared to the person or persons in whom the psychosis is induced.

Because this disorder occurs in the context of close and longlasting relationships, folie à deux seems to follow a chronic course that can be eliminated only partially by treatment.

French alienists Ernest-Charles Lasègue (1816–83) and Jules-Philippe-Joseph FALRET (1824–1902) first described and named this disorder in a famous paper published in 1877 (translated into English and published in 1964) in which they provide seven case history examples of folie à deux. Prior to this time and as early as 1838, similar disorders had been called "infectiousness of insanity" (Ideler) or "psychic infection" (Hoffbauer), but the conditions under which they occurred were not described. Lasègue and Falret describe these conditions that lead to the "contagion on insanity" in the following way:

> In "folie à deux," one individual is the active element; being more intelligent than the other he creates the delusion and gradually imposes it upon the second or passive one; little by little the latter resists the pressure of his associate, continuously reacting to correct, modify, and coordinate the delusional material. The delusion soon becomes their common cause to be repeated to all in almost identical fashion.

Other names given to folie à deux after the time of Lasègue and Falret have been as follows: "contagious insanity" (Seguin); "reciprocal insanity" (Parsons); "psychosis of association" (Gralnick); "induced insanity" (Lehman, 1883); "insanity by contagion" (Carrier); "double insanity" (Tuke); "collective insanity" (Ireland); "conjugal insanity" (Rhein); "influenced psychosis" (Gordon); "mystic paranoia" (Pike). *DSM-III* (1980) referred to this syndrome as shared paranoid disorder. *DSM-IV-TR* (2000) refers to it as "shared psychotic disorder," and (*ICD-10* (1992) refers to it as "induced delusional disorder."

At least four different subtypes of folie à deux have been suggested over the years:

1. *Folie imposée,* in which the psychotic delusions of the psychotic "primary case" are induced in a mentally healthy person and disappear in the healthy person after the individuals are separated.
2. *Folie simultanée,* in which two related persons who are morbidly predisposed in some way simultaneously develop a paranoid and depressive psychosis.
3. *Folie communiquée,* in which the delusional ideas are induced in a second person, after that person had initially resisted them for a long period of time, and are maintained in the second person even when the related persons are separated.
4. *Folie induite,* in which a relationship between two psychotic persons results in the weaker person's adoption of new delusions that initially belonged only to the stronger one—a commonly observed phenomenon in many psychiatric hospitals even today.

When a group of people (such as a family) succumbs to the delusional beliefs of a stronger personality within the group, this has been termed *folie à plusieurs* or *folie partagée* ("shared madness"). The famous "Manson family" case of the late 1960s would be a good example of this phenomenon.

Dewhurst, K., and J. Todd. "The Psychosis of Association—Folie à Deux," *Journal of Nervous and Mental Disease* 124 (1956): 451.

Enoch, M. D., and W. H. Trethowan. *Uncommon Psychiatric Disorders.* 2nd ed. Bristol, U.K.: John Wright & Sons, 1979.

Lasègue, C., and J. Falret. "La folie à deux (ou folie communiquée)," *Annales Medico-psychologique* 18 (1877): 321. English translation by R. Michaud in *American Journal of Psychiatry* 121, Suppl. (1964).

folie à double forme This is the very first name given by BAILLARGER in 1854 to the MENTAL DISORDER we know as manic-depressive PSYCHOSIS.

See also BIPOLAR DISORDER.

folie à famille See FOLIE À DEUX.

folie circulaire The name given to manic-depressive psychosis by FALRET in 1854—but two weeks after BAILLARGER's publication of a description of this syndrome. Although the two

famous French ALIENISTS argued over who was first in describing this disorder, Falret's term was more widely used in the English psychiatric literature of the late 1800s, and as a result, people whom we would now call "manic-depressives" were referred to as "circulars" until the early 1900s.

See also BIPOLAR DISORDER.

food allergies as a cause of psychosis With the rise in interest in the effects of nutrition on the mind and the emotions in the 1960s, many have suggested that even such serious mental disorders as SCHIZOPHRENIA and BIPOLAR DISORDER may be due to imbalances in nutrition. In particular, a commonly discussed theory is that these psychotic disorders may be due to the effects of allergic reactions to certain substances in various foods. Since the list of possible allergens in food is gigantic, it has been difficult to support this hypothesis in controlled research studies, although many researchers who hold to the principles of "orthomolecular psychiatry" have continued the search. Most adequately controlled studies have not been able to find evidence of antibodies in the bodies of schizophrenics that would support the notion that the physical system was fighting a substance that it was allergic to. However, it is probable that nutrition does, in some way, contribute either to the development of some psychotic disorders or at least affects the course of the disease.

See also MEGAVITAMIN THERAPY; TRANSMETHYLATION HYPOTHESIS.

Kinnell, H. G., et al. "Food Antibodies in Schizophrenia," *Psychological Medicine* 12 (1982): 85–89.

formal thought disorder A central characteristic of many psychotic disorders, and SCHIZOPHRENIA in particular, in which the form of thought processes is disturbed. This is distinguished from disturbances in the content of thought (such as BIZARRE IDEATION). Formal thought disorder may include such commonly observed phenomena in the psychotic disorders as LOOSENING OF ASSOCIATION, INCOHERENCE, BLOCKING, CLANGING, ECHOLALIA, NEOLOGISMS, PERSEVERATION, and POVERTY OF CONTENT OF SPEECH.

formication This is the term for a tactile HALLUCINATION (a hallucination of touch) in which a person believes insects or other living creatures are crawling around under the person's skin. Although it is rare among the psychotic disorders, it can be more commonly found in people who may exhibit signs of an ORGANIC PSYCHOSIS induced by substance abuse, particularly cocaine intoxication, or may be a part of delirium tremens in alcoholism. In Europe, formication may be one of the defining symptoms of a delusional syndrome known as the MONOSYMPTOMATIC HYPOCHONDRIACAL PSYCHOSIS.

Four A's, the A useful mnemonic term invented by later generations of scholars to refer to the four FUNDAMENTAL SYMPTOMS OF SCHIZOPHRENIA proposed by Eugen BLEULER in 1911. The "Four A's" are AUTISM, AFFECTIVE DISTURBANCES, ASSOCIATION DISTURBANCES, and AMBIVALENCE.

four-point restraints See FIVE-POINT RESTRAINTS.

Franklin, Benjamin (1706–1790) Early American statesman and scientist. He founded the Pennsylvania Hospital in Philadelphia in 1752, the first hospital in the United States and the place where Benjamin RUSH served (starting in 1785) and made his observations of the mentally ill (who had been allowed admission since the hospital first opened its doors). The original buildings are still used today, at their location on Pine Street in Philadelphia. Franklin and Rush were political as well as scientific contemporaries, and Franklin's signature can be seen just below Rush's on the Declaration of Independence. Franklin's experiments in electricity led to the development of treatments by physicians that consisted of passing weak electrical currents into patients to cure a variety of ills—including mental illness. Franklin was chosen by King Louis XVI of France to chair the famous royal commission to investigate "animal magnetism" in March 1784. The eight other members included the distinguished scientist Lavoisier and Guillotin, the inventor of the famous device of execution used extensively during the Reign of Terror following

the French Revolution. The committee essentially debunked Franz Anton Mesmer's claims about the special "fluids" that were supposedly transferred from the operator to the patient and that supposedly caused the sometimes wondrous manifestations. In its report, the committee did not deny that healing and curing was effected by the use of animal magnetism, but asserted that the mechanism at work was simply "imagination."

See also ELECTROSHOCK THERAPY.

Laurence, J.-R., and C. Perry. *Hypnosis, Will and Memory: A Psycho-Legal History.* New York: Guilford, 1988.

McConnkey, K. M., and C. Perry. "Benjamin Franklin and Mesmerism," *International Journal of Clinical and Experimental Hypnosis* 33 (1985): 122–130.

Freeman, Walter (1895–1972) The "father of lobotomy." Freeman was born into a prominent Philadelphia medical family and studied neurology in Philadelphia and in Europe. Upon the recommendation of former mentors, in 1924, at the age of 29, Freeman was hired by William Alanson White to direct the research laboratories of St. Elizabeth's Hospital in Washington, D.C. His influential contact in Europe with Wagner-Jauregg, who invented the "malaria treatment" for syphilis, led to Freeman's continuation of this FEVER THERAPY work at St. Elizabeth's in the 1920s. He remained at St. Elizabeth's until 1933, when he required recuperation for a "nervous breakdown" caused by overwork and the ingestion of the barbiturate Nembutal, which he had taken every night for many years. At a neurological conference in London in August 1935, Freeman met António EGAS MONIZ, a Portuguese neurosurgeon who had been conducting PSYCHOSURGERY experiments with animals. Egas Moniz excited Freeman with his theories about behavior change through psychosurgery; after returning to Portugal, Egas Moniz performed the first psychosurgery on a human subject (a chronic, severely depressed female patient from a local mental hospital) on November 15, 1935. Egas Moniz published his classic book on the subject in the spring of 1936 and sent a copy to Freeman.

Freeman and his colleague James Watts studied Egas Moniz's book; after procuring the "Moniz leucotome"—the surgical instrument designed by Egas Moniz for psychosurgery—they practiced these techniques on the brains of cadavers. Finally, on September 14, 1936, Freeman and Watts performed the first American leucotomy (psychosurgery on the white fibers that connect the frontal lobe to the rest of the brain) on a 63-year-old woman who had been admitted to George Washington University Hospital in Washington, D.C., with "agitated depression." In November 1936, Freeman used the term *lobotomy* for the first time to describe these operations instead of Egas Moniz's term, *leucotomy.* Lobotomy simply referred to the severing of the nerve fibers of a lobe of the brain. However, Freeman streamlined psychosurgery with the invention of the technique of transorbital lobotomies, in which a gold-plated icepick was inserted directly into the frontal lobes of the brain through the corner of each eye socket (the orbit of the eye) rather than drilling through the skull, as was Egas Moniz's technique. This allowed for the "assembly-line" approach to psychosurgery that enabled the procedure to be performed quickly and with a minimum of preparation on large numbers of patients. In January 1946, Freeman performed the first transorbital lobotomies, assembly-line-style "icepick surgery," on 10 patients in his consulting office. Since the "leucotome" was too fragile for such a procedure, on this historic occasion Freeman used an ordinary icepick found in his kitchen drawer at home.

Based on their lobotomies of 80 patients, Freeman and Watts published their famous textbook, *Psychosurgery,* in 1942, and became world-renowned. Although later discontinued as a dangerous and inhumane technique, it is estimated that, due to the influence of Freeman and Watts, as many as 30,000 lobotomies were performed in the United States in the 1940s and the 1950s. Freeman had high hopes for psychosurgery as a treatment for the psychotic disorders, in particular, schizophrenia. In the preface to the 1950 second edition of *Psychosurgery,* Freeman and Watts argue, "Even more important from the strictly psychiatric point of view is the recognition that some chronically disturbed schizophrenic patients may become completely restored to effective citizenship." On a personal mission to make state hospitals obso-

lete with psychosurgery, Freeman made dozens of road trips to a dozen or more states in the early 1950s and performed rapid transorbital lobotomies on thousands of mental patients in V.A. and state hospitals. Freeman informally dubbed his missionary travels "Operation Icepick." Many patients still exist in psychiatric hospitals today who were subjected to surgery, their condition either unchanged or worse.

When the U.S. Food and Drug Administration approved the use of CHLORPROMAZINE in March 1954, PSYCHOSURGERY and the chemical CONVULSIVE THERAPIES gradually fell into disuse. Treatment with antipsychotic drugs began to be viewed as the most humane treatment for the psychotic disorders, and there was a public and scientific backlash directed at Freeman and his psychosurgery work. Freeman moved from Washington to California in 1954 and never again performed lobotomies on such a grand scale. He performed his last lobotomy on a previously lobotomized woman at Herrick Memorial Hospital in Berkley, California, in February 1967, when he was 72. Freeman died of cancer in May 1972.

See also COLUMBIA-GREYSTONE PROJECT.

Egas Moniz, A. *Tentatives Opératoires dans le Traitement de Certaines Psychoses*. Paris: Masson, 1936.

Freeman, W., and J. Watts. *Psychosurgery*. 1942. Reprint, Springfield, Ill.: Charles C. Thomas, 1950.

Shutts, D. *Lobotomy: Resort to the Knife*. New York: Van Nostrand Reinhold, 1982.

Fregoli's syndrome One of the delusional MISIDENTIFICATION SYNDROMES of the psychotic disorders (along with the CAPGRAS SYNDROME and the INTERMETAMORPHOSIS SYNDROME. In this delusion, a familiar person, who is seen as a persecutor, exists in the bodies of various others in the immediate environment, who are unknown to the delusional person. The afflicted person recognizes that physical differences exist between the body of the persecutor and the bodies of the people in which the persecutor is thought to exist. This distinguishes Fregoli's syndrome from Capgras syndrome, in which the physical body of the "impostor" is transformed to match the delusion as well. This syndrome was first reported by French psychiatrists Courbon and Fail in 1927, in the case of a woman who felt that a famous actor of that time, Fregoli, was making himself known to her by occupying the bodies of various persons in her environment. The actor Fregoli was known for his effectiveness at changing facial expression on stage and was in this regard similar to the famous American silent screen actor Lon Chaney—"The Man of a Thousand Faces." Cases of Fregoli's syndrome are extremely rare and may involve an organic component.

Courbon, P., and G. Fail. "Syndrome d'illusion de Fregoli et schizophrénie," *Bull. Soc. Clin. Med. Ment.* 15 (1927): 121.

Christodoulou, G. N. "Delusional Hyper-identification of the Fregoli-type: Organic Pathogenic Contributors," *Acta Psychiatrica Scandanavica* 54 (1977): 305.

Freud, Sigmund (1856–1939) An Austrian-Jewish neurologist and the creator of PSYCHOANALYSIS, the famous "talking cure," which had a profound influence on the treatment of mental illness in the 20th century. Today's various psychotherapies all owe a major debt to Freud and psychoanalysis for demonstrating that certain MENTAL DISORDERS can be treated or even cured through the use of psychotherapeutic techniques that were not physical (such as drugs or baths). Although the bulk of Freud's clinical experience was not with patients suffering from severe psychotic disorders (unlike that of his one-time disciple, C. G. JUNG), Freud proposed and revised several theories about psychosis during the course of his lifetime.

Due largely to the influence of the German psychiatric literature in the latter half of the 19th century, by Freud's time the terms *neurosis* and *psychosis* had become mutually exclusive categories, and Freud's earliest writings reflect this distinction. As early as 1894, in a letter to his mentor Wilhelm Fliess ("Draft H," dated January 24), Freud speaks of the psychoses as being composed of "hallucinatory confusion," "paranoia," and "hysterical psychosis." From the earliest, Freud considered the psychoses as disruptions in the way in which a person relates to the outside world. Since Freud determined that many of the psychological and psychosomatic symptoms found in his neurotic

consulting-room patients were due to an inner "defensive" conflict between the drive to express sexuality and the efforts to "repress" these feelings and ideas, in his earliest work he mentions "defense psychoses" that are likewise the result of a defensive conflict against sexuality. In other words, people with psychotic disorders defended against their sexual drives by "projecting" the source of their problems on the outside world (e.g., "hallucinations" are internal images or thoughts experienced as "external"; paranoid delusions are the projection of internal strife on the outside world). In fact, their problems are internal in origin. Psychotic people thus withdraw from the external social world because it is mistakenly perceived as a threat.

Between 1911 and 1914, Freud developed his first detailed model of the mind ("the psychical apparatus"). His interpretation of the case history of the paranoid psychosis of Schreber, and his famous 1914 essay "On Narcissism," both led to an interpretation of psychosis as a withdrawal of libido (the energy of the sexual instinct) from its normal attachment to objects and people of the external world (object-love) and a return to an infantile attachment on the self ("infantile auto-eroticism"). This withdrawal of energy to an infantile state was a process of "regression" to a state of "primary narcissism." In practical terms, this means that Freud thought that psychotics "regressed" to an egocentric mental state akin to that experienced by preverbal infants, as evidenced by the loss of connection to the "real world" ("abandonment of object-love") that is observed in people with psychotic disorders. After this withdrawal of libido, there is an ineffective attempt to reestablish a connection with the "object world" of external reality, but this is instead done with the projection of delusions and hallucinations, which take the place of reality. Psychotic symptoms were thus seen by Freud as a defense, a way of shutting out the demands of the external world.

In the early 1920s, Freud developed his second theory of the psychical apparatus—the famous structural theory of the interplay of the ego, id, and superego in psychic life. While convalescing from the first of many major surgical operations for cancer during the last 16 years of his life, Freud wrote a short paper in 1923 on "Neurosis and Psychosis," which described how these two clinical classes of disorders could be caused by specific disturbed relationships among the three parts of the human mind. In this paper, Freud distinguishes among "transference neuroses" (the type of distorted relationship that arises in a patient in psychoanalysis in which the patient transfers to the analyst infantile thoughts and feelings that were originally "projected" onto the parents), "narcissistic neuroses" and the "psychoses" based on the following formulas: "Transference neuroses correspond to a conflict between the ego and the id; narcissistic neuroses, to a conflict between the ego and the superego; and psychoses, to one between the ego and the external world." Furthermore, in psychosis, the ego was thought to be in the service of the id, and the main defense mechanism it employed was denial or disavowal.

Even after Freud was forced by the Nazis into exile in England from his native Vienna in June 1938, he continued to write about the psychoanalytic theory of psychosis. In his very last major piece of writing, the unfinished book, *An Outline of Psycho-Analysis* (1940), Freud explained that "the precipitating cause of the outbreak of a psychosis is either that reality has become intolerably painful or that the instincts have become extraordinarily intensified." Yet, as is commonly observed in people afflicted with the psychotic disorders, no one is ever completely out of touch with reality when in a psychotic state, and there are "healthy" parts of the mind that are always intact. Freud graphically describes this phenomenon in the following passage from the same paragraph of the *Outline:*

> The problem of psychoses would be simple and perspicuous if the ego's detachment from reality could be carried through completely. But that seems to happen only rarely or perhaps never. Even in a state so far removed from the reality of the external world as one of hallucinatory confusion, one learns from patients after their recovery that at the time in some corner of their mind (as they put it) there was a normal person hidden, who, like a detached spectator, watched the hubbub of illness go past him.

Although true psychotics were generally considered "unanalyzable," Freud's psychoanalysis was used by some of his later followers to treat dementia praecox (schizophrenia). Notable analysts include Abraham, Federn, Sullivan, FROMM-REICHMANN, Searles, and John Rosen, who developed a hybrid treatment ("direct analysis") that he used with institutionalized patients. Although claims of success abound in this literature, with our present knowledge of the course of SCHIZOPHRENIA and the strong biological basis for the disease process, there is much skepticism of claims of lasting therapeutic success using this modality of treatment. Indeed, by 1980 the use of psychoanalysis for the treatment of the psychotic disorders had virtually disappeared in practice.

Freud, S. "The Loss of Reality in Neurosis and Psychosis," *Standard Edition,* 19 (1924): 183–190.

———. "Neurosis and Psychosis," *Standard Edition,* 19 (1924): pp. 149–154.

———. "On Narcissism: An Introduction," *Standard Edition,* 14 (1914): 67–104.

———. "An Outline of Psycho-Analysis," *Standard Edition,* Vol. 23. 1940. pp. 139–208.

———. "Psychoanalytic Notes on an Autobiographical Account of a Case Paranoia (Dementia Paranoides)," *Standard Edition,* 12 (1911): pp. 3–82.

———. *Standard Edition of the Complete Works of Sigmund Freud.* Edited by James Strachey and Anna Freud. 24 vols. London: The Hogarth Press and the Institute of Psychoanalysis, 1953–1974.

Fromm-Reichmann, Frieda (1890–1957) A German psychoanalyst and a student of Harry Stack Sullivan at the Chestnut Lodge sanitarium in Rockville, Maryland. Sullivan was another psychoanalyst known for his psychotherapeutic efforts with schizophrenics, and he worked with Fromm-Reichmann after her exile from Nazi Germany in 1934. Fromm-Reichmann developed her own style of treatment, which she called "psychoanalytically-oriented psychotherapy," which indicated that she was departing from the classical Freudian psychoanalytic procedure in her treatment of schizophrenia. Many of her essays on her treatment of SCHIZOPHRENIA (written from 1939 onward) are attempts to describe the inner experiences of the patient and the therapist working with such traditionally "difficult" patients. She described the "loneliness" of the schizophrenic patient and contradicted traditional psychoanalytic notions that the person suffering from schizophrenia gladly seeks out his or her withdrawal from interpersonal relationships. Fromm-Reichmann instead argued that the schizophrenic is eager to reestablish relationships with others but is prevented by a profound sense of mistrust that originates from the earliest relationships with the mother. Fromm-Reichmann was the first to use the term *SCHIZOPHRENOGENIC MOTHER* to identify the mother's role in causing the disorder, but it was only popularized through its later use by psychoanalyst Trude Tietze, in 1949.

It is believed that Fromm-Reichmann unintentionally caused pain in thousands of patients and their families in the 1950s and 1960s by using her considerable authority in psychoanalytic circles to legitimize the idea that the mother of someone with schizophrenia was to blame for the illness. Like FREUD and almost every other psychoanalyst, she sincerely believed that the cause of schizophrenia was to be found in a disturbed early childhood relationship with one's mother. Psychoanalysts like Fromm-Reichmann vigorously denied that schizophrenia could have a physical cause, and they denied the role of HEREDITY or genetics even though the scientific evidence had been accumulating for that fact since at least 1916. Psychoanalysts held experimental, quantitative, medical, and biological research in contempt, believing blindly in a dubious pseudoscience (psychoanalysis) created by a neurologist (Freud) who ignored the work of KRAEPELIN and others on the physical causes of mental disorders. For many mothers in the 1950s and 1960s, this unscientific "medical finding" by a highly psychoanalytic psychiatric establishment proved to be a disaster, as Edward Dolnick illustrates in his book on this black chapter in medical history, *Madness on the Couch.*

Dolnick, Edward. *Madness on the Couch: Blaming the Victim in the Heyday of Psychoanalysis.* New York: Simon & Schuster, 1998.

Fromm-Reichmann, F. *Psychoanalysis and Psychotherapy: Selected Papers.* Edited by D. M. Bullard. Chicago: University of Chicago Press, 1959.

functional psychoses This is a term popular since about 1915 to denote the group of psychotic disorders that do not have a known organic cause (ETIOLOGY). Four primary groups of psychotic disorders have been considered "functional." DEMENTIA PRAECOX and manic-depressive psychosis have long been described as the two main functional psychoses, although the acute recoverable psychoses and chronic paranoid psychoses have also been traditionally regarded as functional psychoses. The term *functional* is also used to point out the importance of psychological or environmental factors in the development of these psychoses. Functional psychoses are distinguished from the "organic psychoses," which are psychotic disorders caused by known organic disease processes in the brain (e.g., the dementias).

Perhaps the earliest use of the term *functional psychosis* is found in a psychiatric textbook by German psychiatrist Emanuel Ernst Mendel (1839–1907) in 1907:

> . . . there is a great difference of opinion amongst authors as to how to divide those mental diseases in which no anatomical findings have hitherto been met and which do not belong under any of the forms named. They are designated as functional psychoses, by which it is not said that anatomical changes do not exist, but only that we have so far been unable to verify them.

The term has not been used as frequently in the past decade or so, since the prevailing viewpoint is that both schizophrenia and BIPOLAR DISORDER are essentially organic (e.g., genetic, biochemical) in origin. Thus, the dichotomy between "functional" and "organic" psychotic disorders is beginning to disappear.

Mendel, E. *Textbook of Psychiatry.* Translated by W. C. Krauss. Philadelphia: F. A. Davis, 1907.

fundamental states of manic-depressive insanity When elaborating his description of manic-depressive insanity (a term he originated), Emil KRAEPELIN noted that "manic-depressives" suffered only from a "periodical insanity" and thus were not psychotic all the time. This was a major difference that separated manic-depressive insanity from DEMENTIA PRAECOX, the other "functional psychosis" identified and named by him. However, Kraepelin noticed that manic-depressives seemed to fall into four main categories of personality types, or temperament, when they were in the "free intervals between the attacks" or if the full development of the disease had not yet occurred. These four manic-depressive "fundamental states" are as follows: (1) the "depressive temperament," which is characterized by a "permanent gloomy emotional stress in all the experiences of life", (2) "manic temperament," the opposite of the depressive temperament, which Kraepelin also refers to as "constitutional excitement", (3) the "irritable temperament," which is a mixture of the manic and depressed fundamental states in which these people exhibit a chronic hypersensitivity and irritability, and (4) the "cyclothymic temperament," which is characterized by the "frequent, more or less regular fluctuations of the psychic state to the manic or to the depressive side."

By identifying these fundamental temperaments, Kraepelin was supporting the contemporary idea that mental disorders may be grouped into categories that are actually spectrum disorders, i.e., that similarities can be found in the symptoms between certain psychotic disorders and less serious personality disorders, which may suggest that they are points on a spectrum of psychopathology. Bipolar disorder, for example, may share the same underlying disease process as BORDERLINE PERSONALITY DISORDER, and schizophrenia may likewise be a variant of SCHIZOTYPAL PERSONALITY DISORDER and SCHIZOPHRENIFORM DISORDER.

See also MANIC-DEPRESSIVE ILLNESS.

Kraepelin, E. *Manic-Depressive Insanity and Paranoia.* Translated by R. M. Barclay and edited by G. M. Robertson. Edinburgh: E. & S. Livingstone, 1921.

fundamental symptoms of schizophrenia When Eugen BLEULER coined the term *SCHIZOPHRENIA* and described this group of disorders in his famous 1911 textbook, he described them as being com-

prised of a group of "fundamental symptoms" that were "permanent," "specific," and "characteristic" of schizophrenia and not of any other mental disorder. Therefore, the fundamental symptoms are said to be pathognomonic of schizophrenia, according to Bleuler. These are in contrast to the ACCESSORY SYMPTOMS of schizophrenia (e.g., hallucinations and delusions), which may be found in other mental disorders as well. A shorthand label for these fundamental symptoms is THE FOUR A'S, namely, AUTISM, AMBIVALENCE, AFFECTIVE DISTURBANCES, and ASSOCIATION DISTURBANCES.

Bleuler, E. *Dementia Praecox, Or the Group of Schizophrenias*, trans. J. Zinkin. 1911. Reprint, New York: International Universities Press, 1950.

fury (or furor) An excited state of uncontrollable violence and anger that has, since ancient times, been associated with the mental disorder of MANIA. Under Roman law, the Latin word *furor* referred to the mental disorder in which people (the *furiosi*) became manic and violent but were not legally responsible for their actions. The second major category of insanity in ancient Rome comprised those people who were mentally handicapped in a cognitive sense, such as the mentally retarded or, it is assumed, those others who experienced psychotic disorders that led to intellectual degeneration (the *mente capti*). They, too, were not responsible for their criminal acts. For almost 2,000 years "furor" or "fury" has been mentioned by authorities on mental illness as either a separate syndrome of its own or as a synonym for mania. In his 1801 textbook *A Treatise on Insanity*, Philippe PINEL confesses that patients of this type are extremely difficult to treat. He writes:

> I have found maniacal fury without delirium, which in France is called folie raisonnante, whether continued, periodical, or subject to irregular returns and independent of the influence of the seasons, the variety of the disorder most unyielding to the action of remedies. A madman of this description condemned himself to the most absolute confinement for eight years. During the whole of that time he was extremely agitated. He cried, threatened, and, whenever his arms were at liberty, broke to pieces whatever came in his way, without manifesting any error of the imagination, or any lesion of the faculties of perception, judgment and reasoning. Other madmen, subject to periodical accessions of extreme violence, are frequently sensible of the impending paroxysm, give warning of the necessity of their immediate confinement, announce the decline and termination of their effervescent fury, and retain during their lucid intervals the recollection of their extravagances.

As for the treatment of fury, Pinel recommends the following: "Opium, camphire (camphor) in large doses, sudden emersion in cold water, blisters, the moxa, and copious bleedings." However, almost four decades later (in 1838), Pinel's famous pupil, the French alienist J. E. D. ESQUIROL, devotes an entire chapter to "Fury" in his book *Mental Maladies*, primarily to put forth the idea that fury is a symptom, not a separate disorder, and that it may be found in many mental illnesses besides mania. "Fury . . . does not require special treatment," Esquirol writes, further arguing:

> It is because fury has been taken for insanity itself . . . that so many grave errors have been committed in the treatment of the furiously insane. They were bled to excess, with the intention of abating their vital force, and it was not perceived that the loss of blood augmented the evil, and that it composed the sick only by depriving them of the power of reaction, necessary for the solution of the disorder.
>
> This symptom has been the cause of the most general, as well as fatal errors in the treatment of the insane. Seeing among them only the furious, all the insane have been treated like dangerous and mischievous animals, ready to destroy and exterminate every thing; against whom it was necessary to protect society. Hence dungeons, cells, grates, chains and blows; means which, by exasperating the delirium, were a principal obstacle to its cure. Ever since these unfortunate people have been treated with kindness, the number of the furious has diminished to such a degree that, in hospitals well kept, and properly arranged, among many

> hundred insane people, not one can be found in a state of fury.

For the second half of the 19th century, "fury" as a separate form of insanity fell into disuse as a concept. However, it has long been noted (and is true today) that in certain manic states people can become irritable, hostile and, at times, violent. This can be true during certain manic phases of BIPOLAR DISORDER, a fact recognized by German psychiatrist Emil KRAEPELIN in the eighth edition of his famous *Textbook* on psychiatry (which appeared in four volumes between 1909 and 1915), in which he mentions the violent variety called the "raving mania" or "acute delirious mania."

See also MANIA.

Esquirol, J. E. D. *Mental Maladies, A Treatise on Insanity.* Translated by E. K. Hunt. 1838. Reprint, Philadelphia: Lea & Blanchard, 1845.

Kraepelin, E. *Manic-Depressive Insanity and Paranoia.* Translated by R. M. Barclay and edited by G. M. Robinson. Edinburgh: E. & S. Livingstone, 1921.

Pinel, P. *A Treatise on Insanity.* Translated by D. D. Davis. 1801. Reprint, Sheffield, England: W. Todd, 1806.

G

Ganser's syndrome A rare psychotic syndrome (a cluster of symptoms) that likely occurs as a response to overwhelming stress. It has often been referred to as "PRISON PSYCHOSIS," since, from the time it was first described by German psychiatrist Sigbert J. M. Ganser (1853–1931) in 1897, it has often (but not always) been found in people in confinement, primarily prisoners. Most of the case histories of the past several decades, however, have concerned people who are not confined and who are not prisoners.

The distinguishing hallmark of Ganser's Syndrome is the symptom of "approximate answers," i.e., blatantly incorrect, absurd, and sometimes silly responses to direct questions that required a simple factual answer. In his 1897 lecture titled "A Peculiar Hysterical State," Ganser emphasized the "inability" of his patients (all prisoners) to "answer correctly the simplest questions which were asked of them, even though by many of their answers they have grasped, in a large part, the sense of the question, and in their answers they betray at once a baffling ignorance and a surprising lack of knowledge which they most assuredly once possessed or still possess." Ganser would ask his patients simple questions, and they would give the following responses to him: "Have you eyes? I have no eyes. How many fingers do you have? Eleven. How many legs does a horse have? Three." Ganser remarked on how these people would deliberately pass over the correct answer and select an obviously false one. He concluded, however, that they were not malingering, but that this was a genuine symptom of a mental disorder.

The symptom of approximate answers is sometimes referred to by the German word *Vorbeireden,* meaning "to talk past the point." However, Ganser never used this term himself. Further case studies of Ganser's syndrome have found that there is usually a clouding of consciousness, as well as reports of hallucinations, delusions and later periods of amnesia for the intervals when the symptoms of Ganser's syndrome were present. Although Ganser thought it was a form of hysteria, it is most often considered either a true psychotic disorder or simple malingering, an instance of FEIGNED INSANITY. However, due to reports of clouded consciousness, amnestic episodes, and its possible origin as a reaction to extreme stress, it is classified among the nonspecific dissociative disorders under that category in *DSM-IV* (1994).

See also *FAXENSYNDROM.*

Auerbach, D. B. "The Ganser Syndrome." In *Extraordinary Disorders of Human Behavior,* edited by C. H. Friedman & R. A. Faguet. New York: Plenum, 1982.

Ganser, S. J. "Über einen eigenartigen hysterischen dämmerzustand," *Arch. Psychiatr. Nervenkr.* 30 (1898): 633. An English translation by C. F. Shorer appears in the *British Journal of Criminology* 5 (1965): 120.

gating See ATTENTION, DISORDERS IN; SENSORIMOTOR GATING.

Genain quadruplets The Genain quadruplets are a rare set of monozygotic ("identical") sisters who all developed SCHIZOPHRENIA in the mid-1950s when they were in their twenties. They have been studied by David Rosenthal and his colleagues at the NATIONAL INSTITUTE OF MENTAL HEALTH (NIMH) in Bethesda, Maryland, at periodic intervals ever since. At the time of their initial hospitalization at NIMH in the 1950s, they were extensively studied in the hope that they

could provide clues to the genetic transmission of schizophrenia. Being monozygotic quadruplets, they were genetically identical. However, the four sisters all differed in the severity of their disorder, and this has remained true throughout their lives. They were last under extensive study at NIMH in 1981, but an update on their progress was published in *Schizophrenia Bulletin* in 1988 by NIMH scientists Allan Mirsky and Olive Quinn; it revealed that the then-57-year-old sisters "are faring about as well now as they ever have in their adult lives."

The name Genain is a pseudonym chosen by Rosenthal and is derived from the Greek for "dreadful gene." Likewise, the names for the sisters, given in birth order, were Nora, Iris, Myra, and Hester and were chosen from the acronym NIMH. Rosenthal summarized the initial psychological and physiological studies conducted in the 1950s in his book, *The Genain Quadruplets* (1963). Rosenthal felt that the Genain quadruplets were evidence of the genetic determination of schizophrenic subtypes, since they all developed nonparanoid types of schizophrenia, thus fitting the pattern of monozygotic twins. The 1981 follow-up study at NIMH utilized all the neurological and biochemical techniques of investigation that had been developed since the 1950s. He and his researchers found that there were similar biological and biochemical abnormalities in the quadruplets when compared to normals, but that their CT SCANS were all normal, showing no evidence of ventricular enlargement and little atrophy of brain tissue.

See also BRAIN ABNORMALITIES IN SCHIZOPHRENIA; BRAIN IMAGING TECHNIQUES; TWINS METHOD AND STUDIES.

Mirsky, A. F., and O. W. Quinn. "The Genain Quadruplets," *Schizophrenia Bulletin* 14 (1988): 595–612.

Rosenthal, D. *The Genain Quadruplets.* New York: Basic Books, 1963.

gender differences in schizophrenia It has long been observed that there are many differences between men and women who are afflicted with SCHIZOPHRENIA. This observation is almost a century old. In Emil KRAEPELIN's original description of DEMENTIA PRAECOX in the 1896 fifth edition of his famous textbook, *Psychiatrie,* he makes the observation that: "Men appear to be three times more likely than women to suffer from the forms of illness described here." In the 1980s, as researchers collected evidence on the heterogeneity of schizophrenia, gender differences became an increasingly important area of research. Some of the major findings can be summarized here:

(1) Men have an earlier age of onset for schizophrenia than women.
(2) Men with schizophrenia have a poorer premorbid history than women with schizophrenia.
(3) Males have more NEGATIVE SYMPTOMS than females.
(4) Neurocognitive functioning is different across many parameters between males and females with schizophrenia.
(5) Males have a poorer course of schizophrenia than females.
(6) Males have a poorer response to antipsychotic drugs than females.
(7) Males have more structural and functional brain abnormalities than women. Thus, by almost any measure, women with schizophrenia as a whole tend to do better than men with the disorder.

A special issue of *Schizophrenia Bulletin* published in 1990 was devoted to the theme of "Gender and Schizophrenia."

As of this writing there is still no plausible scientific explanation for the gender differences we know to exist in schizophrenia.

Bryant, N. L., et al. "Gender Differences in Temporal Lobe Structures of Patients with Schizophrenia: A Volumetric MRI Study," *American Journal of Psychiatry* 156 (1999): 603–609.

Goldstein, J. M., and M. T. Tsuang. "Gender and Schizophrenia: An Introduction and Synthesis of Findings," *Schizophrenia Bulletin* 16:2 (1990): 179–184.

gender-identity confusion A commonly reported experience, usually during the onset of SCHIZOPHRENIA or during periods of exacerbations, in which a person becomes confused about which

gender he or she is. They tend to feel themselves transforming into the opposite sex. If it occurs in a man, he may feel he is becoming a woman, and in extreme cases may report the feeling of being "pregnant." This symptom is not to be confused with the "switching" into an alternate personality of the opposite sex that sometimes occurs in multiple personality disorder, as this phenomenon is situation-specific and is not related to the pervasive sense of one's entire being undergoing the sexual transformation that is found in psychotic states.

gene The word *gene* is derived from an ancient Greek word meaning "birth." It is often defined as the functional unit of heredity, or sometimes as an inherited "Mendelian factor" transmitted from parent to offspring. Each gene occupies a specific place on a CHROMOSOME, and this place is called the locus (plural: loci). Each gene is able to reproduce itself exactly at each cell division and is capable of directing the formation of an enzyme or other protein. Genes normally occur in pairs in all cells as a consequence of the fact that all chromosomes are paired (except the sex chromosomes X and Y of the male). If any one of a series of two or more different genes must occupy the same locus on a chromosome, it is referred to as an allele.

general paralysis of the insane This was the name given to a mental and physical disorder suffered by large numbers of people admitted to asylums in the 19th century; early in this century the disorder was conclusively found to be the effects of the tertiary stage of syphilis (neurosyphilis). People suffering from general paralysis of the insane (often referred to as "paretics" due to the paresis, or muscular weakening, that characterized the disorder) would first experience difficulties in speaking, then movement problems, epileptic-like convulsions, then a more paralytic stage, which would develop to the point where these people would need constant help in feeding, dressing, hygiene, and simply moving their bodies in any desired manner. Psychological symptoms would almost invariably begin with DEPRESSION, then DELUSIONS (sometimes grandiose ones), then a degeneration of memory and other cognitive functions that rendered the sufferer psychologically—as well as physically—paralyzed.

It has been suggested by medical historian George Rosen that the condition may have been observed in the mentally ill as early as 1672 by English physician Thomas Willis (1621–75), and a mental disorder with similar symptoms was also described by John HASLAM in 1798. The label "general paralysis of the insane" was given to the disorder in 1826 by French ALIENIST Louis Calmeil (1798–1895). However, the progression of stages in the disorder were accurately described first by another French alienist, Antoine-Leurente Bayle (1799–1858), in 1822. As a result, this disorder was commonly known in France throughout the 19th century as *"la maladie de Bayle."* In reviewing the psychiatric literature of his day, German psychiatrist Wilhelm GRIESINGER (1817–68) found that estimates from asylums in many European countries put the number of admissions of patients with this disorder at anywhere from 6 percent to 25 percent of total admissions by 1861, with France reporting the highest rates.

With the growing interest in the study of the brain and the nervous system in the latter half of the 1800s some researchers began to suspect that syphilis might be related to the cause of general paralysis of the insane. In 1905 two German researchers identified the spiral-shaped bacterium that caused syphilis, *SPIROCHAETA PALLIDA* (later renamed) *TREPONEMA PALLIDUM*). In 1906 German bacteriologist August von Wassermann and his colleagues devised the diagnostic blood test for syphilis that still bears his name, and in 1913 the issue was finally laid to rest when the syphilitic organism was found in the brains of paretics by Noguchi and Moore.

See also DEGENERATION.

Bayle, A. L. *Traité des maladies du cerveau et de ses membranes.* Paris: 1826.

Noguchi, H., and J. W. Moore. "A Demonstration of Treponema Pallidum in the Brain in Cases of General Paralysis," *Journal of Experimental Medicine* 17 (1913): 232–238.

Rosen, G. *Madness in Society: Chapters in the Historical Sociology of Mental Illness.* Chicago: University of Chicago Press, 1968.

genetic counseling for schizophrenia With the advances made in linking certain medical disorders to specific genes (e.g., Huntington's chorea with chromosome 4, in 1983), more and more prospective parents have sought genetic counseling to discover the risks involved when there is a family history of a particular disease. This presents difficulties for those who seek genetic counseling for schizophrenia, since the patterns of transmission are still unknown. The only solid information that can presently be offered are risk factors calculated by certain computer programs that are based on a polygenetic or multifactorial model for the transmission of SCHIZOPHRENIA. These computer programs can calculate the risks for each combination of affected or unaffected family members, ranging from a risk of 1 percent (the base rate found in the general population) to over 50 percent (when both biological parents and other relatives have the illness). Given this lack of knowledge, should a genetic counselor ever advise schizophrenics or their mates not to have children? In this situation, a well-known textbook on genetic counseling by Fuhrmann and Vogel argues that the risks are high enough even with present knowledge always to discourage having children. Others, however, may argue only that this advice should "usually" be given in this situation. For example, in a 1976 article a major figure in schizophrenia research, L. Erlenmeyer-Kimling, observes that, "Parenthood and schizophrenia tend to mix poorly." She adds the following explanation:

> In addition to the genetic risks to the children of schizophrenic parents, there is considerable likelihood that any children of such parents will be exposed to a disrupted home environment, and frequently to a grossly unsuitable one. The birth of a child often exacerbates the patient's illness, and the responsibilities of bringing up the children tend to trigger further difficulties.

An experimental program for genetic counseling for schizophrenia was set up in London's Maudsley Hospital Genetic Clinic in 1983–84, with the results reported by Adrianne Reveley in 1985. Most of the cases inquired about the risk of potential offspring developing schizophrenia in situations where (a) one of the prospective parents was schizophrenic or (b) when a relative of one of the two prospective parents had schizophrenia. Contrary to the strong opinions of some scholars in the field, in practice, genetic counselors cannot scientifically make these decisions for people, and the staff at the Maudsley Clinic did not do so. Their philosophy should be remembered by those who either seek or give genetic counseling for schizophrenia: "It is not the role of a genetic counsellor to advise individuals, but rather to present the evidence of risk, and provide enough information for those seeking counsel to make their own decisions."

A similar situation presently exists for the genetic counseling of bipolar disorder. A review of this issue by Cadoret in 1976 (still valid today) concludes that such counseling might be so tentative at present as to be virtually useless.

See also GENETIC TRANSMISSION.

Cadoret, R. J. "The Genetics of Affective Disorder and Genetic Counseling," *Social Biology* 23 (1976): 116–122.

Erlenmeyer-Kimling, L. "Schizophrenia: A Bag of Dilemmas," *Social Biology* 23 (1976): 123–134.

Gottesman, I. I., and S. O. Moldin. *Schizophrenia and Genetic Risks: A Guide to Genetic Counseling.* Arlington, Va.: NAMI, 1992.

Reveley, A. "Genetic Counselling for Schizophrenia," *British Journal of Psychiatry* 147 (1985): 107–112.

genetic heterogeneity This is one of the possible modes of the GENETIC TRANSMISSION of SCHIZOPHRENIA. It is also sometimes referred to as ETIOLOGIC HETEROGENEITY. The idea is that schizophrenia (or other psychotic disorders such as BIPOLAR DISORDER) may be caused by any one of a number of single genes, located, perhaps, even on different chromosomes, each one of which is entirely capable of predisposing to the disease without the additional effect of other genes.

genetic markers of vulnerability In the search for BIOLOGICAL MARKERS OF SCHIZOPHRENIA and bipolar disorder, the assumption is that certain mea-

surable physiological processes accompany specific diseases and, it is hoped, may be related to the cause of the disease. Furthermore, it is hoped that these characteristic biological markers are indeed true genetic markers for the disorder, that is, that the biological characteristic and the disease are genetically linked and follow related patterns of genetic transmission. Identifying such a biological characteristic (such as "smooth pursuit eye movement abnormalities" in SCHIZOPHRENIA) may then be considered a sign or a marker of the genetic vulnerability of the person with the marker for the disease to which it is linked.

According to a report on *Behavioral Genetics* by the NATIONAL INSTITUTE OF MENTAL HEALTH (NIMH), a genetic marker must meet the following criteria:

1. The characteristic must be associated with an increased likelihood of the illness (although all people with the illness need not show the characteristic nor vice versa). It is then a marker for the illness, though not necessarily a genetic one.
2. It must be heritable and not be a secondary effect of the illness. That is, it must be genetic and not a result of having had the illness.
3. It must be observable (or evocable) in the well state in addition to the ill state. Since the marker is a predisposition to the illness, not a marker of the illness itself, we should expect it in at least some well relatives and the recovered ill.
4. Transmission of both the characteristic and the illness must be related within pedigrees. This demonstration shows the characteristic is a necessary or contributing genetic factor in an illness.

Therefore, the search for genetic markers is a quest for the underlying biological predisposition or vulnerability to a particular disease that is detectable in the afflicted person during periods of remission as well as when actively symptomatic. This shifts the attention of research away from studying just those periods when the disease is most visible.

There are several strategies for searching for genetic markers of vulnerability. In well-state studies, patients, either in remission or actively psychotic, along with their relatives who do not have psychotic disorders can be matched according to a marker they all share, and which distinguishes them from "normals" who do not have the marker nor the disorder. For example, EYE-MOVEMENT ABNORMALITIES may be such a marker for schizophrenia, since it has been found in many schizophrenics and their nonschizophrenic relatives and is thought to have a genetic basis. Or, such genetically vulnerable people and normals may be distinguished from one another if they have different reactions to a specific drug that is experimentally administered for a short period, a technique known as a PHARMACOLOGIC CHALLENGE.

Once a suspected biological marker of vulnerability is identified, it can be analyzed according to how highly correlated the transmission of the marker and the disorder is in families. One of the most powerful statistical procedures for this is SEGREGATION ANALYSIS. In segregation analysis, the observed frequency of illness in a SIBSHIP (the group of all siblings of the afflicted person, and their parents) or in a pedigree (the multigenerational extended family group) is compared with a hypothetical pattern of inheritance that is based on a particular model of a mode of genetic transmission (for example, possible patterns based on the theory that only one gene is the cause of the disorder or the theory that more than one gene is, in combination, responsible for the disease).

If a biological marker is identified that seems to be transmitted throughout a family in a highly similar manner to the way the disease is inherited, then the next strategy would be to link the marker to a single CHROMOSOME or to a location on a specific chromosome. The marker is then called a LINKED MARKER. This search for disease-related genes is done through a statistical procedure known as LINKAGE ANALYSIS. Linkage analysis is considered more sensitive than segregation analysis for detecting a single "locus" or place that is responsible for predisposition to the illness (monogenetic transmission), and it is less suited to a model of genetic transmission that hypnothesizes that many genetic places or loci, and perhaps the environment, may be responsible together for predisposition to the illness (polygenetic transmission). Therefore, the linkage of a particular disorder to a specific chromosome (such as the linkage

of schizophrenia to abnormalities on chromosome 6) only lets us know where on the chromosome the genetic predisposition may originate and does not necessarily tell us anything about the actual cause of the disorder, which may involve many factors, both genetic and environmental.

With remarkable improvements in PCR (polymerase chain reaction) techniques and computerized DNA sequencing technology during the l990s, vast screenings of large areas of the human genome are now possible. Current approaches to finding the genes that make people susceptible to schizophrenia still include linkage analysis, association studies, searches for chromosome abnormalities, the DNA analysis of other physical or mental disorders or syndromes that may resemble schizophrenia in some of their characteristics, studies of ANTICIPATION, and (genetic) efforts to facilitate genetic analysis by reducing the phenotypic complexity of the disease (primarily FACTOR ANALYTIC STUDIES OF THE SYMPTOMS OF SCHIZOPHRENIA). Large-scale ongoing studies of hundreds of families that have schizophrenic members are conducted by the NIMH Genetics Initiative for Schizophrenia, which uses all these new genomic technologies. NIMH and other laboratories in the United States and Europe have found many weak CHROMOSOME LINKAGES TO SCHIZOPHRENIA. However, it must be emphasized that these linkages are not strong ones and that there are no certain genetic markers for schizophrenia.

See also CANDIDATE GENES; CHROMOSOME ABNORMALITIES; GENETIC TRANSMISSION.

Karayiorgou, M., and J. A. Gorgos. "Dissecting the Genetic Complexity of Schizophrenia," *Molecular Psychiatry* 2 (1997): 211–223.

National Institute of Mental Health. *Behavioral Genetics, Science Monographs No. 2,* DHEW Publication No. (ADM) 80–876. Washington, D.C.: U.S. Gov't. Printing Office, 1980.

genetics studies The idea that "madness" or "insanity" is inherited in some way from generation to generation has been hypothesized for thousands of years. Although family patterns of disease were observed, the causes people attributed them to were not scientific. The "sins of the father" (or perhaps some other family member), which may have brought a Divine curse upon the family, were considered to be manifested in the mental illness of certain family members. Or people simply attributed the mental illness in an afflicted family to "bad blood."

Many of the earliest psychiatric manuals from the early 1800s all comment on the fact that some mental disorders are associated with certain families and not others. By mid-century, so many informal studies had been compiled by alienists at various asylums that Wilhelm GRIESINGER could write in 1860:

> Statistical investigations strengthen very remarkably the opinion generally held by physicians and the laity, that in the greater number of cases of insanity a hereditary predisposition lies at the bottom of the malady; and I believe that we might, without hesitation, affirm that there is really no circumstance more powerful than this (page 106).

Heredity and variation in the 19th century The science of genetics is an early 20th-century creation. Throughout the late 18th and the entire 19th centuries, discussions instead revolved around the issues of heredity and variation. HEREDITY is the transmission of "characters" (physical and behavioral traits) from past generations to new ones. Variability referred to the changes in inherited characters or traits from one generation to the next. Variability also referred to the differences among individuals of the same generation. Animal breeders and horticulturalists (plant breeders) had evolved techniques over the centuries to blend "bloodlines" to create new ones that possessed characters or traits that were desirable in their livestock, crops, or flowers. These techniques of "hybridization"—the art of the creation of hybrids—were documented since the late 1700s in a sizeable literature that influenced Charles Darwin (1809–82). It also influenced the generation of biologists after Darwin's death who eventually developed new ideas and statistical methods that evolved into the science of genetics. Because animal and plant breeders deliberately created hybrids to combine desirable char-

acters or traits in new generations that had been stable in old generations, they viewed unstable characters or traits (variation) as undesirable. Their assumption was that heredity and variation were two violently opposing forces, and that variation could be mastered through the carefully controlled art of breeding hybrid animals or plants over many generations.

It was inevitable that the theories and techniques of animal and plant breeders would be applied to human beings. Of particular interest was the persistence of undesirable characters or traits in human beings, or the creation of new ones in new generations (variability)—such as immorality, addictions, or mental illnesses—and how to prevent them from being passed on to future generations.

Throughout history it had been recognized that some mental disorders are associated with certain families and not others. The inheritance of insanity became a particular concern in the 1800s, when there was a sharp rise in the numbers of person developing psychotic disorders in Europe and America. For example, the question "whether heredity?" was one of the routine inquiries that MAD-DOCTORS made at the BETHLEM ROYAL HOSPITAL ("Bedlam") and is reflected in patient records as early as the 1820s. In his *Traite des degenerescences physiques, intellectuelles et morales de l'espece humaine* (Treatise on the Physical, Intellectual and Moral Degeneration of the Human Species) of 1857, the French ALIENIST Benedict-Augustin MOREL proposed the theory that physical and mental diseases, immorality, substance abuse, and living in unsanitary urban centers, led to the hereditary transmission of a physical, mental, and moral weakness of one's children. Each generation would thus pass this along, making each less and less fit to survive. This process of DEGENERATION would end family lines when the last generations were populated with persons who were too physically ill, mentally retarded, or insane to survive and reproduce. This notion of "hereditary taint" or "bad blood" was akin to the notion of "original sin in the germ plasm"—that is, one was born burdened by the sins of the fathers (previous generations). Dementia praecox—a term first used by Morel—was seen as evidence of a "bloodline" nearing the end of its degeneration process because it was a form of dementia arising in young people that is usually only seen in old age. Forms of insanity such as DEMENTIA PRAECOX (SCHIZOPHRENIA) were thought to have an earlier AGE OF ONSET and a more severe course in each new generation. Today this phenomenon is known as genetic ANTICIPATION. It has been observed to occur in some neurodegenerative diseases and is being studied for its possible connection to schizophrenia. DEGENERATION THEORY became a dominant medical theory and a major source of paranoia among the public by the end of the 19th century but subsided in importance by the end of the First World War.

Backed by the authority of Francis Galton (1822–1911) in England, in the first half of the 20th century programs of EUGENICS (a term Galton coined) led to the promotion of selective breeding among humans to produce stronger bloodlines of healthy human beings; forced sterilization of the insane, the immoral, and the criminal; and, in Nazi Germany, the murder of individuals (such as persons with dementia praecox/schizophrenia) who were deemed too biologically "unfit" to live and reproduce. The geneticist Eolf Axl Carlson traced the tragic history of eugenics in his 2001 volume, *The Unfit: A History of a Bad Idea.*

Dementia praecox and degeneration In his first detailed clinical description of dementia praecox in 1896, Emil KRAEPELIN estimated that in approximately 70 percent of the cases he had observed, "hereditary predisposition" was present and "the so-called signs of degeneration were frequently observed" (*Psychiatrie,* 6th edition, p. 97). However, this hereditary predisposition did not lead directly to dementia praecox but instead to a metabolic self-poisoning of the body, or AUTOINTOXICATION (*Selbstvergiftung*), probably arising from the sex glands, which eventually affected the brain and produced psychotic symptoms (hallucinations and delusions) and dementia. This belief was shared by another prominent German psychiatrist, Wilhelm Weygandt (1870–1939), who speculated in 1907 that, "I should like to put forward a tentative explanation of dementia precox of my own. . . . I would suggest that so far as the organic side is concerned the most plausible concept is one of autotoxic damage affecting genetically predisposed brains."

Genetics in the 20th century Although heredity and variation were known facts, no one knew

their underlying biological mechanisms. Heredity and variation were major components of Darwinian evolutionary theory (although the Darwinians put a positive spin on variation as a desirable strength in populations, enhancing the ability of populations to survive and reproduce). However, Charles Darwin died in 1882 without knowing anything about genes. The usual turning point cited by historians is the reputed "rediscovery" of an 1866 article in which a way to study hereditary units was proposed. In the year 1900, at least three different biologists published papers in which they cited a forgotten and/or ignored research report by the monk Gregor Mendel (1822–84). Mendel had analyzed eight years of garden experiments that traced the hereditary transmission of characteristics (traits) in hybrids he created from different lineages of peas. Proposing formulas for the prediction of the appearance of characteristics in future species, and reporting that his actual findings matched his predictions (much too well, others said later, indicating unconscious bias on the part of Mendel—or worse, deliberate falsification), Mendel was turned into a hero and an icon for the transformation for the study of heredity into a science. Although he has used the term in a private letter in 1905, British biologist William Bateson proposed that this new science be called "genetics" in a lecture in 1906. In 1909 the Danish biologist Wilhelm Johannsen (1857–1927) proposed that a hypothetical basic biological unit of heredity be called the "gene." In the same book, *Elemente der Exacten Erblichkeiten* (Elements of Exact Heredity), Johannsen introduced the terms PHENOTYPE and GENOTYPE. A lecture tour of the United States in 1911 helped promote these ideas there, influencing the prominent geneticist T. H. Morgan (1866–1945) of Columbia University. Johannsen insisted that this orienting concept of the gene be free of any speculation about its material nature, and this open-ended view of the gene led to a multitude of debates about the nature of the gene throughout the 20th century: Was the gene a corpuscule or a chemical? Was it found in the nucleus of cells or in the cytoplasm of cells? Were the chromosomes themselves genes or were the genes segments of the chromosomes? Was the gene stable and unchanging, or instable and mutating? Was it a protein (a theory popular in the 1930s and 1940s) or was it composed of nucleic acids (as was suspected by 1950, and reflected in the 1953 discovery by James Watson and Francis Crick that the DNA molecule had a double helix structure of two chains of nucleic acids twisted around each other)? Did the gene have a definite structure, or should it be defined solely in terms of functions (for example, as the physiological unit that guides development and growth)? How do environmental forces affect genes—or do they? Many of these questions have been answered to the satisfaction of biologists. And yet, how, precisely, a gene should be defined is still a matter of debate among many biologists and philosophers of science. As one such philosopher of science, Philip Kitcher, put it in 1992, "A gene is anything a competent biologist chooses to call a gene."

Psychiatric genetics It was inevitable that the statistical study of the inheritance of traits or characteristics would be applied to persons with mental disorders and their families. Influenced by Galton's pioneering of statistical techniques of correlation in his studies of the transmission of genius and other traits, 19th-century proponents of degeneration theory in medicine used simple statistical procedures to trace hereditary taint in families. Galton's basic statistical tools were refined and exceeded by new statistical techniques and research methods invented by R. A. Fisher (1918) and Sewall Wright (1912). Fisher and Wright extended Mendel's single-gene model of the transmission of characters or traits to a new model in which predictions can be made about the probabilities of multiple genes combining to have effects that result in measurable traits. This introduction of quantitative genetics continues to have a profound effect on genetics research.

The first true attempt to discern the role of genetics in the development of mental disorders was a study conducted in Germany and published in 1916 (see below), and from this eventually developed a specialty known as psychiatric genetics. There were two influential centers of psychiatric genetics prior to the 1970s: the German psychiatric research group centered around Emil Kraepelin in Munich in the first third of the 20th century, and the British research group led by Eliot Slater (who had first trained in Munich) beginning in 1935 at the

Maudsley Hospital in London. Slater set up the first psychiatric research unit at that hospital in 1959, and in 1971 he published the first true textbook in the field of psychiatric genetics, *The Genetics of Mental Disorders.* Starting in the late 1960s, a third group of influential researchers into the genetics of mental disorders was led by Semour Kety and David Rosenthal at the NATIONAL INSTITUTE OF MENTAL HEALTH (NIMH), the Institutes of Health, in Bethesda, Maryland. In addition to the ongoing schizophrenia research at NIMH, significant medical genomic research continues at deCODE genetics in Reykjavik, Iceland, led by Dr. Kari Stefansson.

Following the influence of Harvard biologist E. O. Wilson, whose theory of sociobiology (1975) proposed that complex social behaviors in all species, including humans, had a strong genetic influence, the 1980s witnessed the rise of behavioral genetics as a scientific discipline. Behavioral genetics research involves sorting out how much of schizophrenia (and other disorders) is due to the influence of genes and how much is due to environmental factors. Behavioral genetics is an influential area of research in the early 21st century, providing an important data base for an equally influential subdiscipline of psychology known as evolutionary psychology. Evolutionary psychology examines present-day behaviors (mating, parenting, cooperation, competition, and so on) as reflecting adaptations formed in the prehistoric human past. Genes are assumed to play a key role in shaping the structure and functions of the human brain, which is itself a product of Darwinian natural selection.

Genetic theories of the causes of mental disorders were highly unpopular in mainstream psychiatry from the 1920s to the 1970s, when the profession was dominated by Freudian psychoanalysts who placed the root cause of adult mental life, normal and abnormal, in early childhood experiences before the age of five. The adoption of the pseudoscience of eugenics as a state policy by the National Socialist government in Germany (1933–45), and the subsequent exposure of the Holocaust, also fueled extreme environmentalism as a backlash to hereditary theories of mental illness. By the late 1960s, the results of the family, twins, and adoption studies reviewed below eventually provided strong evidence for the biological roots of schizophrenia and manic-depressive illness and directly refuted the claims of psychoanalysts, paving the way for the return of biological psychiatry in the 1980s.

Today research methodologies for studying the role of the genetics in schizophrenia fall into two broad categories: behavioral genetics, which consists of the inferences we can indirectly draw about the influence of genes on complex human behaviors and diseases (such as schizophrenia), and is characterized by the methods found in family, twin, and adoption studies; and molecular genetics, which is devoted to discovering the actual sequences of DNA (genes) linked or associated with the expression of schizophrenia as a disease process. Although the causal links connecting molecular genetics and behavioral genetics are currently unknown, the great assumption is that this tremendous gap in understanding will vanish through future research.

Behavioral Genetics

Family studies Perhaps the historical starting point for psychiatric genetics is the 1916 study by Ernst Rüdin (1874–1952) of Munich, Germany. In *Zur Vererbung und Neuentstheung der Dementia Praecox* (*On the Inheritability and Cause of Dementia Praecox*), he studied patients with dementia praecox (schizophrenia) using the CONSANGUITY METHOD. The consanguity method involves constructing family trees of genetic relatedness, or "pedigrees," centered on one person as a starting point who is the "proband" or "index case." It is essentially a demographic method that involves interviews or correspondence with as many members of an afflicted person's family or friends of the family (such as parish priests, in Rüdin's case) as is possible in order to document the presence or absence of schizophrenia throughout the family.

Rüdin, who worked under Kraepelin in Munich, compiled data on 701 families with 4,823 children living in Bavaria who had a family member who had been diagnosed with dementia praecox. He found higher rates of schizophrenia in children for which one parent was schizophrenic (6.2 percent of children) than in children who had two healthy, unaffected parents (4.5 percent of the children).

Although this indicated a hereditary component to dementia praecox, the production of schizophrenic children by two healthy parents pointed to the complexities of the pattern of genetic transmission, as too did the relatively small number of schizophrenic children produced when there was one schizophrenic parent. From this point onward, researchers began to suspect that schizophrenia followed a pattern of NON-MENDELIAN PATTERNS OF TRANSMISSION. Further family studies of schizophrenia continued throughout the 20th century, many finding similar perplexing patterns of genetic transmission of schizophrenia in families. The most notable of these was perhaps the research of Franz J. Kallman (1897–1965), a German immigrant to the United States who worked at the New York State Psychiatric Institute. His 1938 volume, *The Genetics of Schizophrenia,* is regarded by many behavioral geneticists as the true starting point for the study of the genetics of schizophrenia.

Since 1916, more than 40 family studies of schizophrenia have been published. They consistently show that schizophrenia runs in families. All studies show that the lifetime risk of developing schizophrenia increased with the degree of genetic relatedness to the schizophrenic index case (or proband) that is the starting point of the pedigree in such studies. Those closer "in blood" to the person with schizophrenia consistently are shown to bear a higher risk of also developing the disease. The average risk for first-degree relatives of a person with schizophrenia (parents, siblings, children) is 9 percent, and for second-degree relatives (grandparents, grandchildren, and so on) is 4 percent. The average lifetime risk of the general population is approximately 1 percent. When the various amounts of risk averaged for first-degree relatives are broken down according to relationship, new patterns emerge: the median risk for each parent was 6 percent, for each sibling 9 percent, and for each child 13 percent. Since the vast majority of persons with schizophrenia are born to two biological parents who do not have the disease, the lower risk of 6 percent reflects this fact. One parent with schizophrenia (and rates for mothers and fathers are the same) conveys a 13 percent risk to each child, whereas two persons with schizophrenia who produce a child gives it a 46 percent risk of developing schizophrenia later in life.

The "family design" or consanguity method also forms the basis of HIGH-RISK STUDIES of schizophrenia. In these studies, children with mothers who suffer from schizophrenia are studied from birth into adulthood. Since such children are at genetic "high-risk" for developing schizophrenia by early adulthood, their cognitive, emotional, and behavioral development is thoroughly studied over time. Currently, there are 15 long-term follow-up studies being conducted that have been coordinated through the Risk Research Consortium since 1984, consisting of the continuous study of at least 1,200 children with a schizophrenic mother and 1,400 children born to parents without schizophrenia. As these children age, new studies will be published using this data.

The problem with traditional family studies is that they do not provide a method of figuring out how much of schizophrenia might be due to genetic inheritance, and how much might be due to "nurture" or environmental causes. Two other methods have been developed to address the issue of "genetics v. environment" or "nature v. nurture": the twins studies and adoption studies.

Twins studies: logic of the design Studies of twin pairs in which one member is affected with schizophrenia provide strong evidence for both the influence of genetics and the role of environmental factors in the development of the disease process in schizophrenia. Twins studies compare the CONCORDANCE RATE for schizophrenia in MONOZYGOTIC TWINS ("identical twins," who are assumed to share 100 percent of their genes and thus are natural "clones" of one another) with that for the disease in DIZYGOTIC TWINS (who are assumed to have 50 percent of their genes in common). If schizophrenia is a genetically transmitted disease, then the likelihood that both MZ twins would develop the disease, if one of them has it, should be much higher than the likelihood of the same thing happening in pairs of DZ twins. In fact, based on the relative percentages of shared genes (100 percent v. 50 percent), the assumed prediction is that MZ twins will both be affected with schizophrenia at twice the rate of DZ twins. Additionally, the concordance rates for DZ twins, one of which has schizophrenia, should be

higher than randomly selected twin pairs from the general population in which schizophrenia may or may not be present. Such a pattern would indicate the clear influence of genetics in schizophrenia. In all twins studies of persons with schizophrenia since the very first one in 1928, the general pattern has always been along these lines (MZ more than DZ more than nonaffected twin pairs in the general population), although the actual concordance rates have been far less than the predicted concordance rates of 100 percent for MZ twin pairs and 50 percent for DZ twin pairs—indicating once again that genetics is not the whole story behind the development of schizophrenia.

Twins studies are used to calculate an estimate known as heritability. Using a formula based on the MZ/DZ ratio, the heritability statistic (h) can be estimated. Heritability is defined as that proportion of phenotypic variance that is due to genetic variance in a population. The portion of variance found in a population that is not due to genotypic variance is therefore assumed to be due to unknown environmental influences or error. There is both narrow heritability (that corresponding to the assumptions of the animal breeders) and broad heritability (that corresponding to most known genetic phenomena, which involve multiple genes and complex traits). There are drawbacks to the usefulness of the heritability statistic, however. Heritability changes in populations over time and place and is therefore highly sensitive to environmental changes. Citing the heritability of a disease is often used incorrectly to imply cause, but a high heritability statistic (such as found in twins studies of schizophrenia) merely means that genes play a significant role in a given population at a given time in a given environment but that this may not have been true in the past or will be true in the future.

Twins studies: "premodern" studies using varying diagnostic definitions of "schizophrenia" The first application of the twins design to study the genetics of psychiatric disorders was conducted by Hans Luxenburger (1894–1976) in Munich. While employed at the German Psychiatric Research Institute founded by Emil Kraepelin and his associates, Luxenberger located 211 twin pairs in which one twin had been diagnosed with dementia praecox (schizophrenia) in a Bavarian asylum. Publishing his results in 1928 in the *Zeitschrift fuer die gesamte Neurologie und Psychiatrie* (Journal of Combined Neurology and Psychiatry), Luxenburger reported concordance rates of 64 percent for MZ twins and 0 percent for DZ twins—a very strong indication of the genetic basis of schizophrenia. How to explain the fact that there were pairs of identical (MZ) twins in which one twin had schizophrenia and the other didn't? Could the discordant MZ pairs be evidence for a "nongenetic schizophrenia" caused by something other than heredity? Looking specifically at the 36 percent of MZ pairs that were discordant for schizophrenia Luxenburger found that first-degree relatives had the same risk for developing schizophrenia as the concordant MZ pairs. This finding gave support to the notion that genes that predispose a person to schizophrenia are indeed spread throughout the family of biological relatives of a person with schizophrenia and that nongenetic forms of schizophrenia are probably uncommon. Otherwise, families of the discordant MZ pairs, assuming that the one MZ twin with schizophrenia has a nongenetic form of the disorder, would have little or no affected members. This was not found to be the case. Virtually every schizophrenia study using the twins method has replicated Luxenburger's finding. Even though one twin in a discordant MZ pair has not been afflicted with the disease, that twin still has the same high genetic risk for developing the disease as the other twin who has schizophrenia. What, then, threw the genetic switch that started the schizophrenia disease process in one identical twin and not in another? Environmental factors must be the missing clue to this puzzle, but they remain a mystery.

With respect to fraternal or DZ twins who are not genetically identical, the general finding in twins studies is that the children of the DZ twin with schizophrenia are at a much greater risk for developing the disease than the children of the DZ twin who is not afflicted. This, too, lends support to the theory that schizophrenia is a brain disease with a strong genetic component.

Three other early genetics studies of schizophrenia in twins added weight to the arguments against the extreme environmentalism of Freudian psychoanalysis among the American and British psychiatric elite of the mid-20th century. In a

study published in the journal *California and Western Medicine* in 1932, a Los Angeles private practice psychiatrist, Aaron J. Rosanoff (1878–1943), found a concordance rate of 85 percent for schizophrenia in 48 MZ twin pairs and a rate of 38 percent in 79 DZ twin pairs. In 1946 Franz J. Kallman published a study in the *American Journal of Psychiatry* that found concordance rates of 89 percent for MZ twin pairs and 15 percent for DZ twin pairs. British psychiatric researcher Eliot SLATER (1904–83) reported concordance rates of 75 percent for MZ and 11 percent for DZ in his 1953 book, *Psychotic and Neurotic Illnesses in Twins*. Thus, consistently strong evidence suggesting a hereditary or genetic component to the cause of schizophrenia has accumulated since the early 20th century.

Twins studies: "modern" studies using equivalent diagnostic definitions of schizophrenia Until the development in 1978 of the FEIGHNER CRITERIA for diagnosing schizophrenia and other mental disorders, diagnostic definitions of schizophrenia widened and narrowed throughout the 20th century. Such a diversity of opinions about how to define and identify persons with schizophrenia makes the pre–1980 scientific literature on schizophrenia difficult to generalize to the more "modern," narrowly defined view that has been in existence since *DSM-III* of 1980 adopted the Feighner diagnostic criteria for schizophrenia. *DSM-III* narrowed the definition of schizophrenia in a manner that brought it closer to Emil Kraepelin's early views of dementia praecox and separated schizophrenia from other mental disorders (such as schizoaffective disorder, schizotypal disorder, and schizoid personality disorder), which were previously diagnosed as forms of schizophrenia since the time of Eugen BLEULER's 1911 volume, *Dementia Praecox, or the Group of Schizophrenias*. A further tightening of the diagnostic criteria was reflected in *DSM-III-R* (1987) and *ICD-10* (1992). This tightening of the diagnostic criteria for schizophrenia since 1980 has produced stronger data for the role of genetics in this disease.

The first twin study to use "modern" diagnostic criteria was conducted by S. Onstead and colleagues in Norway and published in 1991.Using the *DSM-III-R* definition of schizophrenia, they found concordance rates of 48 percent for the MZ twin pairs and 4 percent for the DZ twin pairs. The results of five recent studies in Europe and Japan published between 1996 and 1999 that used both *ICD-10* and *DSM-III-R* definitions of schizophrenia were combined and analyzed by researchers Cardno and Gottesman in an article that appeared in the *American Journal of Medical Genetics* in 2000. When using the *DSM-III-R* definition of schizophrenia, concordance rates were 50 percent for MZ twin pairs and 4.1 percent for DZ twin pairs, indicating a liability-heritability estimate of 88 percent. Using *ICD-10* criteria, the concordance rates were 42.4 (MZ), 3.9 (DZ), and a heritability estimate of 83 percent. Cardno and Gottesman stress that two important conclusions can be drawn from these data: first, that schizophrenia is a strongly genetic disorder and nongenetic forms of schizophrenia (phenocopies), if they exist, are relatively uncommon. Second, people who are at genetic risk for developing schizophrenia but do not have it possess genotypes that are not expressed. (That is, despite having the genes that may cause schizophrenia, these genes do not "switch on" and begin the disease process.)

Still, although there is evidence that schizophrenia is a "strongly" genetic disorder, the recent (post 1996) MZ concordance rates for schizophrenia of 42 to 50 percent still do not match the MZ concordance rate of 100 percent for Huntington's disease, a monogenetic neurological disease. Perhaps the characterization of schizophrenia as "strongly" genetic is best retermed "suggestively" genetic.

Adoption studies Despite the strongly suggestive evidence from twins studies that genetics plays a role in the development of schizophrenia, many critics flipped the data upside down and emphasized the opposite conclusion: that nongenetic factors are equally important. In particular, critics focused on the fact that the twins in these studies were raised in the same homes. The idea that there may have been something about the "shared environment" of these twins—sharing the same mother, father, experiences, and so on—that could be the true cause of schizophrenia. To investigate this issue, Leonard Heston (1930–), a psychiatry resident at the University of Oregon Medical School, conducted a study of children of mothers suffering from schizophrenia who had been given up for adoption. Adopted children were raised by

persons with whom they shared no genes. Also, the "shared environment" of schizophrenic parents and children in previously studies was eliminated. Heston found that children of schizophrenic mothers who had been given up for adoption had an 11 percent risk for developing the disease (5 of 47 children of schizophrenia mothers), which corresponds closely to the 9 or 10 percent risk of a child of a schizophrenic parent. In other words, the genetic risk was the same, regardless of what environment the child was raised in. Heston published his results in 1966 in the *British Journal of Psychiatry.*

Two major adoption studies conducted in Denmark by three schizophrenia researchers at the National Institute of Mental Health in Bethesda, Maryland—Seymour Kety (1915–2000), David Rosenthal (1919–96), and Paul Wender (1934–)—in collaboration with Danish psychiatrist Fini Schulsinger (1923–)—confirmed Heston's conclusions. Using Danish adoption registers, the researchers examined the records of approximately 5,500 children adopted between 1924 and 1947, and 10,000 of their 11,000 biological parents. Of these, they found 44 biological mothers (two-thirds of the parents) or fathers (one-third of the parents) who had been diagnosed with schizophrenia and whose children had been adopted away. The 44 adopted-away children of a schizophrenic parent were matched against 67 control children who had been adopted away and whose biological parents had no psychiatric history. A 7 percent risk for developing schizophrenia (3 of 44 children of schizophrenics) was found, with no risk found among the control adoptees whose biological parents had no psychiatric history. This famous study using the adoptees' study method was published in the *Journal of Psychiatric Research* in 1968.

A second study based on the same data used a different method combining the methods of adoption studies with that of family studies. In examining the medical histories of the extended family members of the 47 of the approximately 5,500 adopted children who had developed schizophrenia, and matching them against 47 children who had not developed schizophrenia, they found that first-degree biological relatives of schizophrenic adoptees had a 5 percent risk for developing schizophrenia, and a 0 percent risk for first-degree relatives of adoptees who had no mental illness. When the researchers broadened their definition of schizophrenia to include "schizophrenia spectrum disorders" (nonpsychotic disorders thought to be related to schizophrenia but that are not as severe, such as schizoid personality disorder), they found much higher rates of risk among the biological parents of adopted-away children with schizophrenia 20.3 percent, than among biological parents of nonaffected adopted-away children, 5.8 percent. These famous Danish studies further confirmed the role of heredity in the development of not only schizophrenia but also "schizophrenia spectrum" disorders. The results of this first adoptees family design was published in the journal *Behavior Genetics* in 1976.

The most recent adoption study of schizophrenia was carried out by P. Tienari and colleagues in Finland and published in *Acta Psychiatrica Scandinavica* in 1991. They found lifetime prevalence risk for developing schizophrenia that was consistent with earlier adoption studies, a 9.4 percent risk for adopted-away children of schizophrenic parents, and an analogous risk of only 1.2 percent in adopted-away children of nonaffected parents. However, an interesting finding of the Finnish adoption study pointed to an association between the genetic predisposition to schizophrenia and psychological abnormalities in the adopting parents. Whether this evidence for a specific "shared environment" effect is supported in future studies remains to be seen.

Critics of some of the adoption studies, such as E. Fuller Torrey and R. H. Yolken, argue that "shared environment" effects cannot be ruled out. In an article they published in *Brain Research Reviews* in 2000, Torrey and Yolken note that the adopted-away children in these studies shared a uterine environment with their mothers. Factors such as oxygenation, possible exposure to drugs, chemical agents, or infectious agents (such as viruses) may be part of the common shared environment of mother and child that has had a more important influence on the development of schizophrenia than genes. Also, many of the adopted-away children in adoption studies lived with their biological mother for weeks or months before being adopted, thereby sharing a postnatal environment.

Subtype differences One of the enduring dilemmas in schizophrenia research is whether or not scientists are studying one disease or several related diseases. The noted schizophrenia researcher Irving Gottesman and others take the position that the various classical subtypes of schizophrenia (paranoid schizophrenia, hebephrenia or the disorganized subtype, catatonic schizophrenia, and so on) are perhaps best viewed as expressions of a single disease process on a continuum from less to more severe forms of the disorder and are not genetically distinct disorders. In fact, genetics studies of schizophrenia do not provide support for these classic subtype differences, indicating that future diagnostic manuals that may be based on as-yet undiscovered facts about the biological nature of schizophrenia may no longer include such subtypes. The only evidence suggestive of a genetic basis for a subtype of schizophrenia involves (a) the classic hebephrenic or disorganized subtype, considered to be a much more chronic and disabling form of the disorder, and (b) T. J. Crow's Type II schizophrenia, which is characterized by early onset, poorer prognosis, and predominance of negative symptoms. However, even this genetic evidence is weak and may not be supported in future studies.

Molecular Genetics

Molecular biology The computer revolution that began in the 1970s and has changed our world forever has been the driving force behind an analogous revolution in biology. Increasingly new and more powerful computing technologies have enabled us to study life at the level of molecules, resulting in the current international effort to understand the location and functioning of the genes in the human genome. This effort will be followed by the rise of proteomics, the study of the formation and dynamics of proteins. All that genes do, after all, is code for specific proteins. The causal link between genes, proteins, and the development of complex bodily structures and behaviors (including diseases such as schizophrenia) is a task that may very well take us into the 22nd century. Still, the current revolution in molecular genetics will go hand in hand with future studies of behavioral genetics in an effort to close the yawning chasm of our gap in knowledge of how segments of certain DNA molecules and a person suffering from schizophrenia are somehow causally related. At present, the two primary methods for identifying the genes involved in schizophrenia are linkage analysis and association studies.

Linkage analysis Linkage analysis is a useful method for locating single genes that have a powerful effect. These genes are located through tracing DNA markers that are linked, or are in close proximity to them, on a particular chromosome. Until the development in 1980 by D. Botstein and colleagues of the technique of using restriction fragment length polymorphisms (RFLP) as a mapping tool, it was not possible to search reliably for specific candidate genes for schizophrenia. In the late 1980s, RFLP research was supplanted by the development of new methods for detecting variations within genomic DNA. These also led to the identification of segments of DNA on chromosomes that could be used as "DNA markers" that could be traced through the pedigrees of families afflicted with schizophrenia and other diseases. There are several different classes of DNA markers that are used in this research, such as restriction endonucleases (REs), variable number of tandem repeats (VNTRs), simple sequence repeat (SSR) polymorphisms, and single nucleotide polymorphisms (SNPs or "snips"). In linkage analysis, DNA must be taken from many members of different generations in multiple families in which schizophrenia is present (multiply affected pedigrees). Linkage analysis is a powerful technique for tracing monogenetic traits (such as the single genes leading to monogenetic diseases like Huntington's disease) but is a much less powerful technique for identifying the genes underlying complex traits—like most human behaviors or diseases such as schizophrenia.

The completion of the first draft of the Human Genome Sequence in 1999, and the availability of this map for researchers, has accelerated research in the search for the candidate genes that are implicated in the cause and/or pathophysiology of schizophrenia. Specific regions of almost every chromosome have been suspected of containing schizophrenia genes, but many of the studies have not found confirmation in replication attempts by other researchers,

The first linkage analyses in schizophrenia research both implicated segments of chromosome

5. In an article published in the British journal *Lancet* in 1988, Anne Bassett and her colleagues published a study of an Asian-Canadian family in Vancouver in which they identified a locus on chromosome 5q found in a young man with schizophrenia and his schizophrenic uncle but which did not appear in the rest of the family. That same year, in an article published in *Nature*, Robin Sherrington and colleagues reported the results of the first true linkage analysis of schizophrenia, using data from 7 British and Icelandic families. They, too, found a link between schizophrenia and chromosome 5q (specifically, 5q11-13). Replication studies by others found that the results of these two studies were due to false positives and therefore were incorrect. Other linkage studies over the past 18 years have implicated the following regions: chromosome 22q, chromosome 8p, chromosome 6p, chromosome 10p, chromosome 6q, chromosome 13q, chromosome 15q13-q14, chromosome 18, chromosome 1q, and the X chromosome. Overall, at the present time there is no reliable agreement about the involvement of any of these regions in schizophrenia, although chromosomes 6, 8, 13, and 22 hold the most promise at present for the location of schizophrenia susceptibility genes.

One recent finding of great interest has been the location of a candidate gene for schizophrenia, *neuregulin 1*, that was found on region 8p in an Icelandic study conducted by Hreinn Stefansson and colleagues. The results were published in the *American Journal of Human Genetics* in 2002. This particular gene plays a role in the expression and activation of neurotransmitter receptors in the central nervous system, especially receptors for glutamate, a neurotransmitter that has been linked to the pathophysiology of schizophrenia since 1980.

Candidate genes for schizophrenia found on chromosomes 1, 1, 20, and 22 were found in a unique study by Ming T. Tsuang, C. C. Liew, and their colleagues in which they claim to have developed an RNA-based blood test for differentially diagnosing schizophrenia from bipolar disorder and from other psychiatric disorders and normal controls. These candidate genes have been previously linked to inflammatory/immunological processes in the body and to human brain development (this latter finding perhaps lending support to the NEURODEVELOPMENTAL MODEL OF SCHIZOPHRENIA). This study, published in January 2005 in the *American Journal of Medical Genetics Part B (Neuropsychiatric Genetics)* may be the first step toward developing a reliable diagnostic BLOOD TEST FOR SCHIZOPHRENIA.

Association studies Due to the confusing results of linkage studies, it is thought that perhaps schizophrenia is not caused by the expression of one or more powerful genes, but instead by multiple genes of small effect, none of which alone is necessary or sufficient to cause the disorder. Linkage analysis cannot detect small-effect genes contributing in an additive way with other such genes, nor can it detect small-effect genes interacting with other genes, nor small-effect genes interacting with the environment. The methods of association studies are more sensitive to detecting genes with small effects.

Association studies compare the frequencies of genetic marker alleles in a group of persons with schizophrenia and to those found in a sample of control subjects who do not have schizophrenia. A statistically significant difference suggests (a) a tight linkage to a marker allele and a disease mutation (linkage disequillibrium), or (b) the marker allele itself contributes to the cause of schizophrenia. The assumption is that the two loci are so close together that they have not been separated by recombination over several generations. Alleles at the two loci are therefore assumed to be "associated," even in individuals with schizophrenia from different families.

Candidate genes Candidate genes that have been examined to see if there is an association to schizophrenia have primarily been those that code for proteins that are involved in the neurochemistry of the disorder—specifically, dopamine, serotonin, and glutamate receptors. The inspiration for these genetic studies derived from the DOPAMINE HYPOTHESIS of schizophrenia. It had been suggested in 1966 by Jac van Rossum that antipsychotic drugs worked by blocking dopamine at the post-synaptic receptor cite, so the next logical step was to infer that schizophrenia might be caused by a dysfunction of the dopamine neurotransmitter system in the brain. By 1972 the technology of radio-labeling allowed, for the first time, the positive identification of neurotransmitter receptors in the brain. Five dopamine

receptors have been identified since then, two D1 receptors and three D2 receptors. ANTIPSYCHOTIC DRUGS work on the D2 receptors and not the D1 receptors. The regions of the chromosomes that code for these D2 receptors are now known, and are located on chromosomes 3 and 11. Seven serotonin receptors have been identified (5HT-1 to 5HT-7) and the corresponding genes have been located. Three genes linked to dopamine and serotonin are among the top 12 candidate genes for schizophrenia thus far (see below). However, none of these genes for dopamine or serotonin receptors have been conclusively linked to the cause of schizophrenia—meaning that schizophrenia is not caused by a neurotransmitter dysfunction—but they certainly must play a role in the pathophysiology of the disorder.

As of July 2005, the strongest evidence for candidate genes for schizophrenia centers on four genes: *DISC1* (*Disturbed in schizophrenia 1*), located on chromosome 1 (1q42.2); *DTNBP1* (*Dystrobrevin binding protein 1*), located on chromosome 6 (6p22.3); *NRG1* (*Neuregulin1*), located on chromosome 8 (8p12); and *RGS4* (*Regulator of G-protein signaling 4*), located on chromosome 1 (1q23.3). Eight other candidate genes have less support but are still considered possibilities: *AKT1* (14q32.33); *COMT* (22q11.21); *DRD3* (3q13.31), the dopamine receptor D3 gene; *G30/G72* (13q33.2); HTR2A (13q14.2), the serotonin receptor 2A gene; *PRODH* (22q11.21); *SLC6A4* (17q11.2), the serotonin transporter gene; and *ZDHHC8* (22q11.21).

Treatment implications of genetics studies of schizophrenia The most likely innovation in the treatment of schizophrenia that may follow from basic genetic research is the development of designer drugs tailored to treatment-resistant patients. Medical geonmics companies are focusing their research on single nucleotide polymorphisms (SNPs or "snips"), very small differences in the same gene in a population, which may be responsible for the commonly observed fact in medicine that some persons respond to a new drug but others do not. The term for this area of research—*pharmacogenetics*—was first used in an article by F. Vogel in a German pediatrics journal in 1959 in reference to the speculation that adverse effects of medication in some persons and not in others may be due to genetic differences. As of September 2005, no such pharmacogenetic drugs for schizophrenia have been developed. Gene therapy for the treatment of disease has turned out to be an exceedingly problematic (and sometimes dangerous) experimental therapy and is unlikely to be an option for persons with schizophrenia at anytime in the near future.

Useful Web Sites

Trying to keep up with the almost daily reports of new research on the genetics of schizophrenia is difficult. The Web sites of the following associations continually post new scientific information relating to the genetics of schizophrenia and other mental disorders and genetic counseling: the International Society of Psychiatric Genetics (www.ispg.net), the Behavior Genetics Association (www.bga.org), the International Society for Twin Studies (www.ists.qimr.edu.au), and the National Society of Genetic Counselors (www.nsgc.org). For more information on the terminology and history of genetics, see the Web site of the Cold Spring Harbor Laboratory (http:vector/cshl/org).

Summary

The following conclusions can be drawn from the present state of research into the genetics of schizophrenia:

(1) Schizophrenia is a familial disease, passed from one generation to another within a family in unpredictable ways, and genes are involved in transmitting a vulnerability to the disease.
(2) Almost all 23 chromosomes have been implicated as continuing regions where possible genes linked to schizophrenia may reside, but the evidence for specific candidate genes is generally weak and contradictory. There is no evidence of "schizogenes" that directly lead to the development of schizophrenia that are analogous to the gene that causes Huntington's disease, to name one example.
(3) Behavioral genetics studies of schizophrenia indicate that nongenetic factors play a sizeable role in the cause and pathophysiology of schizophrenia, and some RISK FACTORS are well known from epidemiological studies.
(4) Schizophrenia is not caused by a chemical imbalance in the brain (i.e., dopamine system dysfunctioning) as so many family members of people with schizophrenia are told every

day, but such neurotransmitter irregularities are instead representative of the disease process (pathophysiology).

(5) Estimates of the high heritability of schizophrenia derived from twins studies must be interpreted with caution. High heritability does not imply causation.

(6) Schizophrenia is most probably related to the activity of multiple genes with small effects.

(7) The cause of schizophrenia is unknown. What is known is that genes alone do not cause schizophrenia.

Botstein, D., R. L. White, M. H. Skolnik, and R. W. Davis. "Construction of a Genetic Linkage Map in Man Using Restriction Fragment Length Polymorphisms (RFLPs)," *American Journal of Human Genetics* 32 (1980): 314–331.

Carlson, E. A. *The Unfit: A History of a Bad Idea.* Cold Spring Harbor, N.Y.: Cold Spring Harbor Laboratory Press, 2001.

Gottesman, I. I. *Schizophrenia Genesis: The Origin of Madness.* New York: W. H. Freman, 1991.

Griesinger, W. *Mental Pathology and Therapeutics,* trans. C. L. Robinson and J. Rutherford. 1860 (German). Reprint, New York: William Wood and Co., 1882.

Johannsen, W. *Elemente der Exacten Erblichkeitslehre.* Jena: Gustav Fischer, 1909.

Kitcher, P. "Gene: Current Usages." In *Keywords in Evolutionary Biology,* edited by Evelyn Fox Keller and Elisabeth A. Lloyd. Cambridge, Mass.: Harvard University Press, 1992.

Kraepelin, E. *Psychiatrie. Ein Lehrbuch für Studirende und Aerzte. Funfte, vollstandig umgearbeitete Auflage.* Leipzig, Verlag von Johann Ambrosius Barth, 1896.

Prasad, S., et al. "Molecular Genetics of Schizophrenia: Past, Present, Future," *Journal of Bioscience* 27 (February 2002): 35–52.

Riley, B., P. J. Asherton, and P. McGuffin. "Genetics and Schizophrenia." In *Schizophrenia.* 2nd ed., edited by S. R. Hirsch and D. Weinberger. Oxford: Blackwell, 2003.

Slater, E., and V. Cowie. *The Genetics of Mental Disorders.* Oxford: Oxford University Press, 1971.

Stefansson, H., et al. "*Neuregulin 1* and Susceptibility to Schizophrenia," *American Journal of Human Genetics* 71 (2002): 877–892.

Sullivan, P. F. "The Genetics of Schizophrenia," *PLoS Medicine* 2 (July 2005): e212 (www.plosmedicine.org).

Torrey, E. F., and R. H. Yolken. "Familial and Genetic Mechanisms in Schizophrenia," *Brain Research Reviews* 31 (2000): 113–117.

Tsuang, M. T., et al. "Assessing the Validity of Blood-based Gene Expression Profiles for the Classification of Schizophrenia and Bipolar Disorder: A Preliminary Report," *American Journal of Medical Genetics Part B—Neuropsychiatric Genetics* 133B (January 2005): 1–5.

Vogel, F. "Moderne Probleme der Humangenetik," *Erbgebnisse innere Medizin und Kinderheilkunde* 12 (1959): 52–125.

Weygandt, W. "Kritische Bemerkungen zur Psychologie de Dementia praecox," *Monatsschrift für Psychiatrie und Neurologie* 22 (1907): 289–301.

genetic transmission Despite almost 90 years of the study of the genetics of SCHIZOPHRENIA, the pattern of the transmission of the disease from family member to family member is unknown. Several possible models of the mode of genetic transmission of schizophrenia have been proposed.

There are, however, essentially two major varieties. One type of model proposes that a single major gene has defects that predispose an individual to a particular disease. This is known as a monogenetic transmission model. It is also sometimes called the "generalized single locus (GSL) model" or, by others, a "Mendelian pattern," since the defective gene in classical MENDELIAN TRANSMISSION patterns (the first genetic transmission patterns ever identified) is either a dominant gene, a recessive gene, or a sex-linked gene (a single gene located on a sex chromosome). This is the oldest model for the genetic transmission of schizophrenia and was first proposed by Rosanoff and Orr in 1911. This monogenetic model of genetic transmission is the type more likely to be detected through LINKAGE ANALYSIS statistical procedures, which are considered more powerful than SEGREGATION ANALYSIS in the detecting of a single gene that may be responsible for the predisposition to schizophrenia.

More than 3,000 physical diseases (albeit somewhat rare ones) have been found to be monogenetic and are transmitted according to Mendelian patterns. Much research continues to be conducted in the hope that mental illnesses may also be transmitted in this "single gene" fashion.

The second type is polygenetic models of transmission, sometimes called "non-Mendelian models of transmission." The assumption here is that the genetic predisposition to a particular disease is the result of an additive effect. That is, the predisposition exists only through the combined effects of several genes. There are many physical characteristics that are polygenetically determined in all of us, such as height and intelligence. Furthermore, many physical illnesses such as diabetes are polygenetically determined. MENTAL DISORDERS, especially schizophrenia and BIPOLAR DISORDER, are likewise thought to be more likely to follow a polygenetic pattern of transmission. Computer models of transmission that also account for environmental factors in the development of the disease are called MULTIFACTORIAL THRESHOLD MODELS OF GENETIC TRANSMISSION, first proposed by Falconer in 1965 and adapted to schizophrenia by Gottesman and Shields in 1967. This is a form of a DIATHESIS-STRESS THEORY of schizophrenia.

Another idea that combines concepts from the monogenetic and polygenetic models is the GENETIC HETEROGENEITY of a particular disorder. The hypothesis here is that the same disease (schizophrenia) may be caused by any one of a number of genes located in different places (multiple loci). Any one of these genes alone would be sufficient to cause the disorder. Thus, while conflicting results of research may place the "schizophrenia-gene" at first on chromosome 5, then chromosome X, this may just be confirming evidence for the genetic heterogeneity of schizophrenia.

There continues to be much debate among researchers as to whether schizophrenia and the psychotic disorders follow a monogenetic or a polygenetic mode of transmission, or a "mixed model" of the two. As of 2006 the mode of genetic transmission of schizophrenia is unknown.

Falconer, D. S. "The Inheritance of Liability to Certain Diseases Estimated from the Incidence among Relatives," *Annals of Human Genetics* 29 (1965): 51–76.

Garver, D. L., et al. "Schizophrenia and the Question of the Genetic Heterogeneity," *Schizophrenia Bulletin* 15 (1989): 421–430.

Gottesman, I. I., and J. Shields. "A Polygenetic Theory of Schizophrenia," *Proceedings of the National Academy of Sciences of the United States of America* 58 (1967): 199–205.

Rosanoff, A. J., and F. L. Orr. "A Study in Insanity in the Light of Mendelian Theory," *American Journal of Insanity* 68 (1911): 221–261.

Rosenthal, D., and S. Kety. *The Transmission of Schizophrenia.* Oxford: Pergamon Press, 1968.

genome A combination of the words *gene* and *chromosome,* the word genome is the complete set of chromosomes derived from one parent; or it can refer to the total gene complement of a set of chromosomes found in higher life forms. On April 27, 1989, an announcement was made at Cold Spring Harbor Laboratory in New York State, a major genetics research center, that an international organization of geneticists was being formed to initiate an immense project to identify and define all human genes and genetic material. In 1999 an announcement was made of the completion of the first draft of the human genome. By 2005 it was estimated that there are 25,000 genes in the human genome.

genotype The genetic composition of an individual. It may also refer to a gene combination at any one locus or with respect to any specified combination of loci.

Geodon See ANTIPSYCHOTIC DRUGS.

Germany Prevalence studies for SCHIZOPHRENIA conducted in the 1930s found prevalence rates ranging from 1.9 to 2.6 per 1,000. Current evidence suggests that the prevalence rates have not changed in Germany since the 1930s.

Torrey, E. F. *Schizophrenia and Civilization.* New York: Jason Aronson, 1980.

Ghana The West African country of Ghana (formerly the Gold Coast) has been the subject of several SCHIZOPHRENIA prevalence studies since the

1940s. The most striking finding is that in one area of northern Ghana the prevalence of schizophrenia increased sharply between 1937 and 1963. Since this coincided with the pervasive introduction of Western cultural influences, the Ghana studies are often cited by E. Fuller Torrey as possible indications that schizophrenia is a "disease of civilization."

Torrey, E. F. *Schizophrenia and Civilization.* New York: Jason Aronson, 1980.

Gheel Colony Gheel, Belgium, has been the home of a shrine to Saint Dymphna, the patron saint of the mentally ill, since the 11th century. Many miraculous cures are said to have taken place there. However, by the 14th century the large number of mentally ill pilgrims was becoming unmanageable, and a hospital and humane system of family care were established. Mentally ill pilgrims would be placed in local households and be under the foster care of family members. Although as recently as the late 1930s it was reported that as many as 4,000 mentally ill persons were under foster care in the community, by the 1960s this number had been significantly reduced, with about 1,700 being served in 1970. However, the Belgian Ministry of Public Health still provides psychiatric services for these people in the Gheel Colony. The hospital that works with the families of the area is called the Rijkspsychiatrisch Ziekenhuis-Centrum voor Gezinsverpleging (the "State Psychiatric Hospital Center for Family Care.").

The Gheel Colony is a remarkable example of how the severely mentally ill can be integrated into society as an alternative to institutionalization. Attempts to copy the "Gheel model" of care in Great Britain and the United States in the 19th century were known as the "cottage system" or as "boarding-out," but no successful long-term program based on the Gheel Colony has ever been devised.

American psychiatrist William Alanson While made a series of trips, beginning in 1906, to visit European hospitals for mental disease. In his memoirs, he gives a colorful description of the unique system of community care for the mentally ill at Gheel:

> One of the most interesting of my visits was to Gheel, in Belgium, where the patients for the most part live with the families that make up this settlement. The hospital itself, the so-called *asile fermé,* occupies the central position. The little town of Gheel consists for the most part of a few stores on one side of a single street, and the country for twenty miles about is occupied by peasants who live upon and cultivate the land. This condition has been maintained over many centuries. The patients who are sent there are studied in the central asylum and if found to be sufficiently reliable are sent out to the little farm cottages, where they live with the peasant's families. The doctor makes his rounds once a month on his bicycle, sees the patient, chats with him and weighs him, the weight being considered one of the outstanding evidences that the patient is being properly cared for. I visited a number of these homes and found that the patient's room was a plain affair furnished only with a bed and a chair and perhaps a table and a rug, with a crucifix at the head of the bed. The patient himself, treated as a member of the family, could usually be found downstairs or nearby, engaged in the household work or the work of the farm.

Parry-Jones, W. L. "The Model of the Gheel Lunatic Colony and Its Influence on the Nineteenth-Century Asylum System in Britain." In *Madhouses, Mad-Doctors, and Madmen: The Social History of Psychiatry in the Victorian Era,* edited by A. Scull. London: Athlone Press, 1981.
White, W. A. *William Alanson White: The Autobiography of a Purpose.* Garden City, N.Y.: Doubleday, Doran, 1938.

glossolalia This is the technical term for the phenomenon of "speaking in tongues," the bizarre babbling and emission of sounds that is often part of an ecstatic religious ritual involving an altered state of consciousness. Although the phenomenon is ancient in origin, it is commonly observed in certain fundamentalist Christian or "charismatic" Roman Catholic gatherings, especially in the United States and Canada. The speech in glossolalia may seem like the NEOLOGISMS or WORD SALAD of a psychotic disorder, but it is in fact an innocuous situation-specific behavior that does not necessarily indicate a mental disorder.

Goodman, F. *Speaking in Tongues: A Cross-Cultural Study of Glossolalia.* Chicago: University of Chicago Press, 1972.

glutamate hypothesis Glutamate is the main neurotransmitter in both the sensory and motor neural circuits of the cerebral cortex of the brain. In 1980 J. Kim and three other colleagues published a study in which it was hypothesized that a "hypoactivity" of the glutamanergic system may be linked to the pathophysiology of schizophrenia. This glutamate hypothesis of schizophrenia in its pure form has already been rejected, just as the simple "single-system" forms of the DOPAMINE HYPOTHESIS (1966) and the SEROTONIN HYPOTHESIS (1954) have been. Since 1980 numerous studies of the activity of glutamate in schizophrenia have been conducted. Glutamate receptor genes, glutamate receptor binding, and glutamate receptor expression in the cortical, striatal, and temporal lobe structures in the brain have been examined in the past decade. The exact role of glutamate in schizophrenia is presently unknown.

Kim, J., et al. "Low Cerebralspinal Fluid Glutamate in Schizophrenic Patients and a New Hypothesis on Schizophrenia," *Neuroscience Letters* 20 (1980): 379–382.

Goffman, Erving (1922–1988) Goffman was a noted Canadian sociologist who is best remembered for his book *Asylums* (1961), which contained a series of essays on his research on the interactive effects of institutions and the persons who are confined and work in them. Goffman conducted his research between 1954 and 1957 as a visiting member of the Laboratory of Socio-environmental Studies of the NATIONAL INSTITUTE OF MENTAL HEALTH in Bethesda, Maryland. For a period of one year (1955–56) he worked "undercover" in St. Elizabeth's Hospital in Washington, D.C., one of the country's largest mental hospitals with a census of over 7,000 patients. His depictions of the social world of the "hospital inmate," especially how this world is subjectively experienced by this person, offer a picture of how such institutions systematically dehumanize not only their "inmates," but the staff as well. He especially emphasized the ways in which inmates survive in the closed worlds of "total institutions" by "making-do" in a bad situation. The thesis of Goffman's book is that perhaps the most important influence on the behavior of a mental hospital patient is the institutional environment and not the illness, and that the reactions and adjustments of a patient in a mental hospital are similar to those of inmates in other types of institutions (e.g., prisons).

Goffman, E. *Asylums: Essays on the Social Situation of Mental Patients and Other Inmates.* New York: Doubleday, 1961.

Goldstein, Kurt (1878–1965) A German psychiatrist perhaps most remembered for his studies of brain-damaged patients and schizophrenics. He proposed the idea that there were two essential types of thought, "concrete" and "abstract," and that brain-damaged people and schizophrenics had lost their capacity for abstract thought and instead exhibited concrete thought patterns. Goldstein felt that brain damaged people adopted the "concrete attitude" to avoid ANXIETY and "catastrophic reactions"—an agitated state of panic and rage that is a reaction to the frustrations brought on by the limitations imposed in thought and action by brain damage. His contribution to the study of SCHIZOPHRENIA was the further recognition of the fact that, at least in some forms of the disorder, it resembles an organic brain disease.

Goldstein, K. *The Organism.* New York: American Books, 1939.

———. "The Significance of Psychological Research in Schizophrenia," *Journal of Nervous and Mental Disease* 97 (1943): 261–279.

governess psychosis In the 19th century, when much less was known about the causes of the psychotic disorders, it was thought that certain occupations might predispose one to madness. Sometimes the exposure to certain chemicals or materials was the reputed cause, such as the

chemical used by hatters or shoemakers, or the vapors inhaled from the mining of lead (causing a form of insanity known in 19th-century Scotland as "mill-reeck"). However, most of the time no such material causes could be found. Artists, poets, and other creative people are perhaps the best known example, but (at least in Europe) the profession of being a "governess" to the children of wealthy parents was also commonly regarded as possibly contributing to the development of a serious mental illness—especially DEMENTIA PRAECOX (SCHIZOPHRENIA). In the conventional folk wisdom of the time, and even in psychiatric journals, it was commonly speculated that there was a mental disorder known as a "governess-psychosis." This topic was taken so seriously in the latter half of the 19th century that Eugen BLEULER felt the need to consider the issue in his chapter on "The Causes of the Disease" in his 1911 book, *Dementia Praecox, Or the Group of Schizophrenias:*

> For decades the idea has been preserved that governesses were especially prone to develop schizophrenia. Some authors even spoke of a "governess-psychosis"; and it has been maintained that governesses suffer a particularly severe (and unpleasant) form of the disease. There may be something in this, inasmuch as young women become governesses who have ambitions of raising their social standing beyond their capacities and among whom there must be many with schizophrenic predisposition. The treatment they often receive at the hands of their employers gives occasion for determining a schizophrenia. However, it must certainly be first established whether or not governesses really do suffer in greater numbers than members of other vocations.

See also MAD HATTER, MAD AS A HATTER.

Bleuler, E. *Dementia Praecox, Or the Group of Schizophrenias,* trans. J. Zinkin. 1911. Reprint, New York: International Universities Press, 1950.

grandiose type One of the common types of delusional (paranoid) disorder. GRANDIOSE DELUSIONS are often those in which a person is convinced that he or she has some special ability or status that elevates him or her above all others. These may be delusions of unlimited riches, of the possession of special powers or abilities, or that the person has been given a divine calling of some sort. People may even believe that they are a famous person. However, in delusional disorder, these usually fixed delusions do not impair intellectual, social, and occupational functioning as similar grandiose delusions do in the paranoid subtype of schizophrenia. The early 19th-century French descriptions of the mental disorder that Esquirol named MONOMANIA are perhaps most clearly found today in this grandiose type of delusional disorder.

See also PARANOID SCHIZOPHRENIA.

grandiosity An inflated belief about one's importance, worth, knowledge, or identity. In the psychotic disorders, GRANDIOSE DELUSIONS are common, particularly in the paranoid subtype of schizophrenia and in the manic phase of BIPOLAR DISORDER. A manic individual with grandiose delusions may believe that he or she has a "special message" or "talent" that no one in the world has, or may grossly overestimate their assets and create huge debts while on a shopping spree or in business transactions. People with the paranoid subtype of schizophrenia may believe that they are a famous rock music star (Mick Jagger and Madonna seem to be the favorites in American psychiatric hospitals) or are married to one.

See also PARANOID SCHIZOPHRENIA.

Griesinger, Wilhelm (1817–1868) German psychiatrist who is regarded as the "father of biological psychiatry." The 1861 second edition of Griesinger's famous textbook, *Mental Pathology and Therapeutics,* was a turning point in the history of psychiatry as it shifted the center of major scientific contributions in the field from France, whose *aliénistes* had dominated psychiatry in the first half of the 19th century, to Germany. German psychiatrists dominated the field well into the early 20th century.

Born in Stuttgart, Griesinger was educated in Germany, Switzerland, and France. After finishing his medical studies, he took a position at the

Winnenthal asylum in Württemberg. His two years there seem to have been the only period in which he was involved in full-time clinical work with patients, as he held mainly administrative and teaching positions throughout the remainder of his life. His experience at Württemberg formed the basis of the ideas and observations of his 1845 first edition. After accepting a position as professor of medicine in Zurich in 1860, Griesinger was in charge of planning and supervising the construction of a large new hospital for the treatment of the mentally ill—the famous BURGHÖLZI HOSPITAL, which Eugen BLEULER later managed in the early 20th century. He also founded a major psychiatric journal, which continues to be published today—the *Archiv für Psychiatrie und Nervenkrankheit.*

Griesinger made a major contribution to psychiatry with his strong emphasis on the brain and nervous system as the source of all mental disorders. His classifications of mental disorders and their clinical descriptions were widely adopted in Germany and elsewhere. His scientific philosophy still reigns today in our current research efforts to unlock the secrets of the psychotic disorders:

> Insanity being a disease, and that disease being an affection of the brain, it can therefore only be studied in a proper manner from the medical point of view. The anatomy, physiology, and pathology of the nervous system, and the whole range of special pathology and therapeutics, constitute preliminary knowledge most essential to the medical psychologist.

Griesinger, W. "The Care and Treatment of the Insane in Germany," *Journal of Mental Science* 14 (1868–69): 1–34.

———. *Mental Pathology and Therapeutics.* 2nd ed., trans. C. L. Robertson and J. Rutherford. 1861. Reprint, New York: William Wood, 1882.

Marx, O. M. "Wilhelm Griesinger and the History of Psychiatry: A Reassessment," *Bulletin of the History of Medicine* 46 (1972): 522–544.

group psychotherapy Group therapy came into vogue in the latter half of the 20th century, and from an administrative and therapeutic point of view it seemed the perfect treatment for institutionalized patients. Group meetings of a wide variety have been almost universally adopted by those who perform psychiatric services in institutional or quasi–institutional settings (e.g., aftercare programs), particularly since the resources do no exist to provide every patient with consistent individualized treatment.

Insight-oriented group therapy, which is designed to explore deeply personal emotional issues, has until recently been the primary mode of group-oriented treatment for institutionalized schizophrenics. Although patients with less serious psychiatric diagnoses (that is, nonpsychotic disorders) may benefit from such emotionally intense group experiences, research shows that insight-oriented group psychotherapy may actually worsen psychotic symptoms. At best, as J. M. Kane concludes in 1989 in a major review of the research on the effectiveness of different treatments in schizophrenia,

> Many clinicians have suggested the value of group therapy during the inpatient phase of the treatment of schizophrenia. Several review articles have appeared on this topic. . . . By and large, the results from studies designed to assess the impact of group therapy when used with or without medication have not been positive, though there are some exceptions.

Instead, much of the research indicates that the focus should be shifted from the idea that the disease process in schizophrenia is somehow being alleviated through insight-oriented group (or individual) therapy, as it most probably is not, to the idea that the focus of groups should be a structured program that teaches adaptive social and vocational skills. Likewise, the research indicates that insight-oriented family therapy (see FAMILY INTERACTION THEORIES), which views the cause of the illness in family interaction patterns, should instead be replaced by structured psychoeducational programs for family members that can teach them how their behavior affects the course of the schizophrenic relative's illness and how to accentuate the positive aspects of that influence. Such

"family management strategies" can reduce the rate of relapse for schizophrenia (see EXPRESSED EMOTION).

Given the evidence that traditional insight-oriented "group therapy" is essentially useless in arresting the schizophrenic disease process, this knowledge should have profound effects on the treatment of schizophrenics in public institutions. For example, psychiatrists and psychologists would no longer be necessary for conducting "group therapy," since individuals with only a high school or college degree could be given specialized training in the methods of structured psychoeducational or supportive programming for schizophrenics. Such policies could have profound economic benefits since these people could be hired at far lower wages than clinical personnel and yet with the same therapeutic effect for the patients.

Conceptions of "group therapy" for the treatment of schizophrenics therefore have changed radically in the 1980s. When the patient is hospitalized during the acute stages of the psychosis, structured interaction with the patient, either individually or in a group situation, should be supportive and psychoeducational. However, research shows that inpatient "social skills" or "reality-adaptive-supportive therapy" or post-discharge "family management strategies" in combination with antipsychotic drugs are more effective than just the drugs alone; the research also indicates that the positive effects of these psychosocial strategies are only good for a year or so after discharge. Schizophrenia is, after all, in most of its manifestations a chronic brain disease of an unknown origin, and it appears that the organic disease process eventually counteracts the therapeutic gains of psychosocial treatment, no matter how intense or consistent the program may be. The true therapy of the future for schizophrenia will almost certainly be biologically based. And although "group therapy" is almost universally mandated by the administrators of state hospitals as part of the "usual treatment" of institutionalized patients, it may one day be regarded as quaint and as ultimately useless as the "usual treatments" of the 19th century—bleeding, bathing, and purging—seem to us today.

Penn, D. L., and K. T. Mueser. "Research Update on the Psychosocial Treatment of Schizophrenia," *American Journal of Psychiatry* 153 (1996): 607–617.

gustatory hallucination This is a hallucination of taste. People who report gustatory hallucinations often report an unpleasant taste in their mouth. This type of HALLUCINATION is less common than other types, particularly AUDITORY HALLUCINATIONS.

gyrator (or "gyrater") A mechanical device invented by Benjamin RUSH and used at the Pennsylvania Hospital in Philadelphia in the early 1800s. Based on the CIRCULATING SWING used by English physician Joseph Mason Cox (1762–1822) at the Fishponds Private Lunatic Asylum in Stapleton, England, the gyrator was a machine on which a patient would apparently sit and be rapidly spun around by its gyrations to bring the blood to the brain. In his 1812 textbook, *Medical Inquiries and Observations Upon the Diseases of the Mind,* Rush describes his "gyrater" under the heading of "Exercise" as a recommended treatment:

> EXERCISE. This should consist of swinging, seesaw, and an exercise discovered by Dr. Cox, which promises more than either of them, and that is, subjecting the patient to a rotary motion, so as to give a centrifugal direction of the blood towards the brain. He tells us he has cured eight persons of torpid madness by this mode of exercise. I have contrived a machine for this purpose in the hospital, which produces the same effects upon the body which are mentioned by Dr. Cox. These are vertigo and nausea, and a general perspiration. I have called it a Gyrater. It would be more perfect, did it permit the head to be placed at a greater distance from its center of motion. It produces great changes in the pulse.

Not satisfied with the "gyrater" he invented for use at the Pennsylvania Hospital, Rush provides the following suggestions for a more effective machine:

> A cheap contrivance, to answer all its purposes, might easily be made, by placing a patient upon

a board moved at its centre upon a pivot, with his head toward one of its extremities, and then giving it a rotary motion. The centrifugal force of the blood would exceed, in this way, that which it receives from the chair employed by Dr. Cox or from the gyrater in the Pennsylvania Hospital.

Many descriptions of Rush's "gyrater" incorrectly describe it as this latter machine suggested by Rush as an improvement on the gyrater.

Rush B. *Medical Inquiries and Observations upon the Diseases of the Mind.* Philadelphia: Kimber & Richardson, 1812.

H

hair pulling See TRICHTILLOMANIA.

Haiti See BOUFFÉE DÉLIRANTE.

Haldol See ANTIPSYCHOTIC DRUGS.

hallucination A hallucination is an event that is experienced as a sensory perception (e.g., the sound of a voice, the sight of someone or something) but, in fact, is not real. The relevant sensory organs, such as the ears or eyes, are not physically stimulated, yet the person reports a sensory experience. A hallucination is experienced as real, and it may be perceived as originating from outside a person's body (as with the usual sensory experiences of sight and sound), or it may be felt to come from within a person's own body. For example, a person may report "hearing voices," but the voices may be experienced as coming from within the head rather than from outside it. A delusional interpretation (if present) of a hallucination, may be consistent with a person's belief system or, if the person is psychotic, with his delusional system. Hallucinations are distinguished from delusions in that a hallucination is a disturbance of perception whereas a delusion represents a pathological distortion of normal ideation.

Hallucinations occur in the form of one or more of the five senses: sight (VISUAL HALLUCINATIONS), sound (AUDITORY HALLUCINATIONS), taste (GUSTATORY HALLUCINATIONS), touch (TACTILE HALLUCINATIONS), and smell (OLFACTORY HALLUCINATIONS). Hallucinations can be mood congruent or mood incongruent in content, with either a manic or depressed mood. For example, a depressed individual who is also experiencing auditory hallucinations may hear voices telling him that he is worthless, useless or perhaps may urge self-mutilation or suicide.

Hallucinations are only to be considered a symptom of a psychotic disorder if there is also a clearly demonstrated break with reality in the mental state of the individual. Hallucinations are often thought of as immediately signifying that a person is psychotic, but this is not the case. People who have many other types of MENTAL DISORDERS, such as effective disorder and even personality disorder, can experience transient hallucinations. Even normal individuals can experience transient hallucinations from time to time. The most commonly reported hallucinatory experience reported in people without mental disorders is hearing a voice calling one's own name. Hallucinations that occur within the context of intense religious experiences are not necessarily to be considered a sign of mental illness.

The word *hallucination* first appeared in the English language in 1572 in a work by Johann Kaspar Lavater, referring to "ghostes and spirites walking by nyght" (in other words, "apparitions"). However, its original derivation is from a Greek word meaning "to wander in mind." J. E. D. ESQUIROL was the first to recognize the importance of hallucinations as a symptom of mental disorder in his 1838 textbook, *Des Maladies Mentales.* In the chapter "Hallucinations," Esquirol constructs a definition of hallucinations that is still the basis of the one employed in the most current diagnostic manual of mental disorder—*DSM-IV* (1994). Esquirol defines a hallucination as "a thorough conviction of the perception of a sensation, when no external object, suited to excite the sensation, has impressed the senses." Esquirol was also the first

to emphasize the distinction between a hallucination and an ILLUSION, in which an actual external stimulus is misperceived or misinterpreted. A pupil of Esquirol's and a member of the "Esquirol Circle," A. J. F. BRIERRE DE BOISMONT, wrote the first comprehensive textbook on the clinical and cultural manifestations of hallucinations, and this book was translated into English and published in 1853.

Hallucinations (as well as delusions) were regarded as an important symptom of schizophrenia by many of the early authorities on schizophrenia, but they differed in regard to how necessary the presence of hallucinations in a person was to making the diagnosis of schizophrenia. For example, although many authorities have considered hallucinations, particularly auditory hallucinations, as a defining sign of schizophrenia as Kurt Schneider did with his FIRST-RANK SYMPTOMS, others have proposed that different symptoms might be better criteria for defining schizophrenia. Eugen BLEULER, for example, argued in 1911 that hallucinations and delusions are not among the four PRIMARY SYMPTOMS OF SCHIZOPHRENIA but instead are merely the ACCESSORY SYMPTOMS of the disorder. However, Bleuler realized how serious these accessory symptoms could be for the afflicted person. For as he remarks in his 1911 classic, *Dementia Praecox, Or the Group of Schizophrenias:*

> It is not often that the fundamental symptoms are so markedly exhibited as to cause the patient to be hospitalized in a mental institution. It is primarily the accessory phenomena which make his retention at home impossible, or it is they which make the psychosis manifest and give occasion to require psychiatric help.

Hallucinations, along with delusions, are considered to be the POSITIVE SYMPTOMS of schizophrenia. The most recent comprehensive review article on the theories and research findings on hallucinations was published in 1986 and was authored by G. Asaad and B. Shapiro.

With the introduction of BRAIN IMAGING techniques into the research on schizophrenia, particularly those that allow for "images" of a functioning brain (positron emission tomography and functional magnetic resonance imaging), in the 1990s many researchers succeeded in "capturing" auditory hallucinations while a person with schizophrenia was actually experiencing them. New "dysconnection," or "disconnection," theories of schizophrenia point to imbalances in the neural connection networks between the left frontal and left temporal lobes of the brain in their explanations of auditory hallucinations in schizophrenia.

Asaad, I., and B. Shapiro. "Hallucinations: Theoretical and Clinical Overview," *American Journal of Psychiatry,* 143 (1986): 1,088–1,097.

Brierre de Boismont, A. *Hallucinations, or, The Rational History of Apparitions, Visions, Dreams, Ecstasy, Magnetism and Somnambulism.* Philadelphia: Lindsay & Blakiston, 1853.

Esquirol, J. E. D. *Mental Maladies, A Treatise on Insanity,* trans. E. K. Hunt. 1838. Reprint, Philadelphia: Lea & Blanchard, 1845.

Sarbin, T. R., and J. B. Juhasz. "The Historical Background of the Concept of Hallucination, *Journal of the History of the Behavioral Sciences* 3 (1967): 339–358.

Stern, E., and D. A. Silbersweig. "Neural Mechanisms Underlying Hallucinations in Schizophrenia: The Role of Abnormal Fronto-Temporal Interactions." In *Origins and Development of Schizophrenia: Advances in Experimental Psychopathology,* edited by M. F. Lenzenweger and R. H. Dworkin. Washington, D.C.: American Psychological Association, 1998.

hallucinatory verbigeration This is the term given by Emil KRAEPELIN in the eighth edition (1909–15) of his famous textbook, *Psychiatrie,* for the type of AUDITORY HALLUCINATION in which a patient hears essentially the same meaningless sentences over and over again. One of Kraepelin's patients wrote down the following nonsense sentences that he heard over and over again as an auditory hallucination: "For we ourselves can always hope that we should let ourselves pray other thoughts. For we ourselves wish to know who would let the swine's head be tormented to death with us foolishly."

Kraepelin, E. *Dementia Praecox and Paraphrenia.* Translated by R. M. Barclay and edited by G. M. Robertson. Edinburgh: E. & S. Livingstone, 1919.

haloperidol See ANTIPSYCHOTIC DRUGS.

handcuffs Until the mid-1800s, many extreme methods of MECHANICAL RESTRAINT were still in use in European asylums. Handcuffs were included among these instruments, which were more often used for punitive measures than therapeutic ones. One variant on the form of handcuffs that we think of today was a type that would hook onto iron rings on a heavy iron belt that circled the waist. Handcuffs were routinely employed at the asylum in Middlesex, England, until English physician John CONOLLY, a leading figure of the NONRESTRAINT MOVEMENT, became superintendent there in 1839.

harness, cruciform See BED SADDLE; CRUCIFORM STANCE.

Hartford Retreat An American private institution for the humane treatment of mental illness that was founded in Hartford, Connecticut, in 1824. It was based on the famous YORK RETREAT in England. For most of its first several decades, the Hartford Retreat admitted all patients who could pay and only a small portion of those who could not. However, these patients had to meet certain criteria and could not have a history of chronic mental illness. What's more, they would be discharged within six months regardless of their progress. Since "discharge rates" were often touted as "curability rates," the Hartford Retreat was praised by many, including Dorothea DIX and British author Charles Dickens, who visited it on his trip to America in 1842 and found it to be one of the few institutions in America that was worthy of merit.

However, when the retreat requested and received state funds in 1843, for the next two decades it shifted its role from one of a curative institution to a custodial one. More poor and chronic cases were admitted, and superintendents of the institution complained of the growing numbers of "filthy, noisy, or dangerous pauper lunatics" that filled its wards. In 1866 the state of Connecticut appropriated funds for a state asylum, allowing the Hartford Retreat to revert to a private institution for the wealthy. It later changed its name to the Institute for Living.

Goodheart, L. B. *Mad Yankees: The Hartford Retreat for the Insane in Nineteenth-Century Psychiatry.* Amherst: University of Massachusetts Press, 2004.

Haslam, John (1764–1844) An apothecary and researcher at the BETHLEM ROYAL HOSPITAL ("Bedlam"), Haslam produced some of the finest of the early psychiatric manuals; the 1798 *Observations On Insanity* and its expanded second edition of 1809, retitled *Observations on Madness and Melancholy.* He performed autopsies on the patients at Bedlam and described his observations in his written works. He also provided clinical descriptions of what were later known as general paralysis of the insane and the chronic, more degenerative form of schizophrenia now described by British psychiatrist T. J. Crow as Type II schizophrenia. Because Haslam and Philippe PINEL both seemed to provide the first descriptions of cases of this type of schizophrenia in 1809, Crow has given the name PINEL-HASLAM SYNDROME to Type II schizophrenia (see CROW'S HYPOTHESIS).

Haslam's descriptions of case histories seem to give a complete description of the disease process in CHRONIC SCHIZOPHRENIA, as we have come to know it, with an insidious onset in adolescence or early adulthood, classical signs and symptoms and a chronic deteriorating course. Prior to this time, many mental disorders had been described throughout the centuries, and although hallucinations and delusions had been commonly reported they had never been accompanied by descriptions of the developmental course of the disease. Therefore, Haslam and Pinel's simultaneous (but independent) publications of these case histories give us the first definite HISTORICAL EVIDENCE FOR SCHIZOPHRENIA as a distinct disease.

Haslam's descriptions in his 1798 book of what we now know as BIPOLAR DISORDER predate the French psychiatrist BAILLARGER's first thorough description in 1854 of a single disorder that combines both depressed and manic mood swings. When discussing "mania" and "melancholia" he insightfully asserts: "I would strongly oppose their being considered as opposite diseases." In a later passage in the same book, Haslam gives a

description of patients with bipolar disorder that is still accurate today:

> . . . for we see every day the most furious maniacs suddenly sink into a profound melancholy; and the most depressed and miserable objects, become violent and raving. We have patients in the Bethlehem Hospital, whose lives are divided between furious and melancholic paroxisms, and who, under both states, retain the same set of ideas.

In his writings, Haslam recommended the "gentleness of manner and kindness of treatment" of the insane popularized by Pinel with his *traitement moral* ("moral treatment"). However, some of his activities at "Bedlam" were deemed abusive by a House of Commons investigation in 1815, and he was fired from the staff of that institution without a pension after more than 20 years' service. At the time of his dismissal he was 56 years old and is credited by historians with knowing more about mental illness than any of his contemporaries in Britain. His works on the clinical and legal aspects of mental illness remain classics in the field and were influential in the early days of psychiatry.

See also BETHLEM ROYAL HOSPITAL.

Haslam, J. *Considerations on the Moral Management of Insane Persons.* London: Hunter, 1817.

———. *Medical Jurisprudence, as It Relates to Insanity, according to the Law of England.* London: 1809.

———. *Observations on Insanity, with Practical Remarks on the Disease, and an Account of the Morbid Appearances On Dissection.* London: F. & C. Rivington, 1798.

———. *Observations on Madness and Melancholy.* London: J. Callon, 1809.

Leigh, D. "John Haslam, M.D.—1764–1844, Apothecary to Bethlem," *Journal of the History of Medicine* 10 (1955): 17–44.

Hayner's wheel A device that was originally designed as a form of treatment for mental illness but was more often used as a form of MECHANICAL RESTRAINT for agitated patients. The "hollow wheel," as it was also called, was a huge, padded circular treadmill on which a patient was forced to walk for hours or days at a time. The device was not unlike those we know today, which are commonly placed in the cages of pet mice or hamsters. With prodding from the "keepers" (as the psychiatric aides or attendants were called in those days), the patient would be "encouraged" to run the treadmill until exhausted. It was used in several German asylums in the 19th century, after its construction by a German psychiatrist named Hayner, who later renounced its use. Apparently, the idea for this machine was first proposed by one of the first German psychiatrists, Johann Christian Reil (1759–1813) of the University of Halle, who recommended many varieties of what he referred to as "non-injurious torture" as effective treatments for mental illness. In the 1890s, while at the Heidelberg Clinic, Emil KRAEPELIN acquired one of Hayner's wheels for the small museum of mechanical restraint that he set up for the medical students under his tutelage.

hebephrenia One of the three distinct psychotic disorders, recognized in the last half of the 19th century, that Emil KRAEPELIN grouped together under his unifying concept of DEMENTIA PRAECOX in 1899. Hebephrenia was the name given to a psychotic disorder identified by German psychiatrist Ewald Hecker (1843–1909) in 1871, which would begin in adolescence or adulthood and result in a rapid disorganization or DEGENERATION. Hecker believed that in this disorder a person's psychological state was arrested at the developmental stage of puberty, thus resulting in severe problems in late adolescence and early adulthood, when more mature psychological integration was required. Hecker derived the name of this disorder from "Hebe," the name of the ancient Greek goddess of youth.

Hecker is given credit by Kraepelin for being the first to point out the characteristic AGE AT ONSET in dementia praecox (schizophrenia). However, in his description of dementia praecox in 1896, Kraepelin does not completely accept Hecker's description of hebephrenia as a disorder in which a depressed state is followed by a manic state, after which mental degeneration quickly follows. Instead, Kraepelin accepts the expanded definition of hebephrenia proposed in a doctoral dissertation by Daraszkiewicz in 1892, which allows for the most severe

cases—including the "depressed forms"—that end in profound mental deterioration.

Kraepelin later referred to hebephrenia as "silly dementia," since often a nonsensical, illogical "silliness" marks the dementia praecox patients with this subtype of the disorder. In the eighth edition (1909–15) of his textbook, *Psychiatrie,* Kraepelin describes this variant of dementia praecox in the following manner:

> That form of dementia praecox which we have called above "silly dementia" is in many respects nearly related to simple insidious dementia. In its clinical picture there appears beside the progressive devastation of the psychic life *incoherence* in thinking, feeling, and action. . . .
>
> The development of the disease is accomplished in almost four-fifths of the cases quite gradually; often an insidious change of the psychic personality precedes the appearance of more distinct morbid phenomena by many years. In the remaining patients the disorder begins in a subacute form; in a few cases it breaks out suddenly. In the preliminary stage there are sometimes nervous troubles, complaints of lassitude, headaches, feeling of giddiness, fainting-fits, irritability, disorders of sleep. The patients become absent-minded, forgetful, negligent; they tire easily, they cannot collect their thoughts any more; they appear lacking in ideas and understanding, they are silly and lazy; they fail in daily tasks, change their occupation, because it is too difficult for them, set aside their work, or give it up entirely.

Kraepelin's description of hebephrenia matches the current diagnostic subtype of schizophrenia known as the DISORGANIZED TYPE that can be found *DSM-IV* (1994). The descriptions of hebephrenia as comprising an insidious onset with the full outbreak of psychotic symptoms in adolescence or early adulthood (usually between ages 15 and 25), and the resulting cognitive disintegration, are all incorporated in modern descriptions of SCHIZOPHRENIA.

Daraskiewicz, L. *Über Hebephrenie, insbesondere deren schwere Form.* Doctoral dissertation, Laakmans, Dorpat, 1892.

Hecker, E. "Die Hebephrenie," *Virchows Archiv für pathologische Anatomie* 52 (1871): 392–449.

Kraepelin, E. *Dementia Praecox and Paraphrenia.* Translated by R. M. Barclay and edited by G. M. Robertons. Edinburgh: E. & S. Livingstone, 1919.

hebephrenic type In the World Health Organization's 10th revision of the *International Classification of Diseases,* or *ICD-10,* this is one of the mental disorders classified under the category of schizophrenic psychoses. It is equivalent to the classical descriptions of HEBEPHRENIA and to current descriptions of the subtype of SCHIZOPHRENIA known as the DISORGANIZED TYPE, which is described in *DSM-IV* (1994).

hemispheric asymmetries in schizophrenia See LATERALITY IN SCHIZOPHRENIA.

hemodialysis treatment of schizophrenia Between the 1930s, when techniques for the CONVULSIVE THERAPIES, COMA THERAPY, and PSYCHOSURGERY were being introduced, and the early 1970s, no new somatic treatment for SCHIZOPHRENIA was introduced. In the 1970s physician R. Cade noticed that the psychotic symptoms of a patient diagnosed with the paranoid subtype of schizophrenia had improved greatly after treatment with hemodialysis for a kidney disease. Cade and colleague J. Wagemaker Jr. theorized that the dialysis might have removed some sort of toxic substance from the blood of the patient that had been responsible for causing the psychotic symptoms. They followed up this observation by submitting to hemodialysis a group of patients who were diagnosed with schizophrenia but who did not have any kidney disease. They were encouraged by seemingly positive results and published them in 1977. However, several attempts at replication by other researchers have failed (most recently in 1983), suggesting that hemodialysis as a treatment for schizophrenia is not very effective and therefore is not recommended.

See also TRANSMETHYLATION HYPOTHESIS.

Carpenter, W. T., et al. "The Therapeutic Efficacy of Hemodialysis in Schizophrenia," *New England Journal of Medicine* 308 (1983): 669–675.

Wagemaker, J., and R. Cade. "The Use of Hemodialysis in Chronic Schizophrenia," *American Journal of Psychiatry* 134 (1977): 684–685.

hemorrhoids, production of as treatment In his 1838 book on *Mental Maladies*, J. E. D. ESQUIROL recommends BLEEDING as a treatment for severe mental illness only if it is performed locally through cupping with leeches. For both the severe forms of depression ("lypemania or melancholy") and of mania, Esquirol recommends the application of leeches to the anus to produce hemorrhoids (varicose veins of the anus). He writes:

> Pursuing the atrabile into the circulation, the humorists deduce from blood-letting a general precept against melancholy ... Nevertheless, we may have recourse to local sanguine evacuations; now at the epigastrium, when the stomach is the seat of an active irritation; now, to the vulva, when we wish to reestablish the menstrual flux; or to the anus, when we desire to renew a hemorrhoidal discharge; and finally to the head, when there are signs of cerebral congestion. I have sometimes applied leeches with success to the side of the head, when lypemaniacs complained of a fixed pain in the part.

This form of treatment is a vestige of the type of thinking that resulted from the influence of the HUMORAL THEORY of disease and mental illness, in which an excess of humors in the blood (a condition called *plethora*) needed to be drained off to restore a healthful balance in the patient.

Esquirol, J. E. D. *Mental Maladies. A Treatise on Insanity.* Translated by E. K. Hunt. 1838. Reprint, Philadelphia: Lea & Blanchard, 1845.

heredity See GENETICS STUDIES.

heritability of psychotic disorders Heritability is a quantitative concept from population genetics and is used widely in studies of behavioral genetics. In a given population, heritability is that portion of the variation in a measurable trait (such as IQ, or extraversion-introversion) or a disease (such as SCHIZOPHRENIA) that is due solely to genetic factors. It is expressed as the ratio of the total genetic variance in a population to the phenotypic variance in a population. In the broad sense, then, heritability is a statistic that indicates the degree to which a trait is genetically determined. In the narrow sense, it is the degree to which a trait is transmitted from parent to offspring. If a trait (or a disease) has a heritability estimate of 1.00, that means that 100 percent of the trait or disease is assumed to be caused by the action of genes.

TWINS METHOD AND STUDIES have provided most of the estimates of the heritability of the various psychotic disorders, including estimates for schizophrenia. The most recent estimates are derived from the Maudsley Twin Psychosis Series at Maudsley Hospital in London, England, and were reported in a publication in February 1999. Heritability estimates for schizophrenia, SCHIZOAFFECTIVE DISORDER, and MANIA (BIPOLAR DISORDER) were determined using various diagnostic criteria for each disorder (Research Diagnostic Criteria, *DSM-II-R*, and *ICD-10*). Despite slight differences in the diagnostic criteria for these three disorders, the heritability estimates were all within the same range and were quite high. All were between 82 percent and 85 percent. Thus, it was once again confirmed that genes play a significant role in the origins and development of the psychotic disorders.

Cardno, A. G., et al. "Heritability Estimates for Psychotic Disorders: The Maudsley Twin Psychosis Series," *Archives of General Psychiatry* 56 (1999): 162–168.

high-functioning schizophrenic See AMBULATORY SCHIZOPHRENIC.

high-risk studies Also called the "risk-for-schizophrenia" research, high-risk studies evaluate children who are considered to be at a higher than average statistical risk for developing SCHIZOPHRENIA later in life. These studies hope to clarify several questions that researchers have about the disease process in schizophrenia. For example,

one hope is that by studying children before the onset of the disorder it will be possible to identify the initial, core "warning signs" of the full onset of the disorder and separate them from the later symptoms of the disorder. Furthermore, if specific environmental influences that precede the onset of schizophrenia can be identified, perhaps further research can then tell us whether schizophrenia can be prevented in vulnerable individuals by changing or altering these environmental influences in some way.

Most of the high-risk research has tended to use children with at least one biological parent who has schizophrenia. As the family studies research using the CONSANGUINITY METHOD to find evidence of the genetic transmission of schizophrenia have indicated, children with one schizophrenic parent have a lifetime risk of approximately 12 percent, whereas individuals who have two biological parents diagnosed with schizophrenia have a much higher risk, of 35 percent to 46 percent. Individuals with a schizophrenic biological parent also have a greater risk for developing one of the schizophrenia "spectrum" disorders (e.g., schizotypal personality disorder, schizophreniform disorder, and schizoaffective disorder).

However, it is estimated that 85 percent to 90 percent of all persons diagnosed with schizophrenia do not have a schizophrenic parent. Therefore, high-risk studies that use just the children of schizophrenic parents may not apply to the much larger number of individuals who will develop schizophrenia but who do not have schizophrenic parents. To take this possibility into account, a complementary research strategy using "behavioral markers of risk" has been developed, which defines an individual's risk status based on his or her own specific behavioral disturbances. The ongoing New York High-Risk Project, which is being conducted by researcher L. Erlenmeyer-Kimling of the New York State Psychiatric Institute, has been studying two selected samples since the 1970s consisting of children of schizophrenics. This group periodically undergoes a battery of neuropsychological and psychophysiological tests that measure three primary "biobehavioral domains" of possible predictors of liability to psychopathology: attentional and information-processing capacities, neuromotor functioning, and psychophysiological processes. They theorize that these primary areas of disturbance create problems in social functioning as the child grows older. Their results have indicated greater problems in fine motor coordinations, attentions, and information processing (AIP) in the children of schizophrenics.

Besides the presumed genetic risk factor in schizophrenia, risk factors related to the physical environment have long been explored in the high-risk studies as contributors to the development of schizophrenia. Some of the most suggestive childhood history factors that may increase the risk for developing schizophrenia are: (1) obstetrical complications, (2) the season of birth (a higher percentage of schizophrenics are born in the winter and spring months), (3) prenatal stress of the mother, and (4) early exposure to certain viral infections.

In a major review of the evidence from 24 high-risk studies conducted since 1952, which was published in *Schizophrenia Bulletin* in 1988, researcher Joan Asarnow of the UCLA Neuropsychiatric Institute reaches the following conclusions about the state of our knowledge concerning children at-risk for schizophrenia:

- Some high-risk children can be distinguished from their peers by signs of neurointegrative problems, social impairments, and early symptomatology. Although some abnormalities can be identified as early as infancy, impairments are more pronounced in middle childhood and adolescence.
- Particular deficits in attention-information processing, neuromotor functions, and social behavior may be associated with specific risk for schizophrenia. The form of these deficits may vary with the age of the individual, and future work is needed to clarify developmental patterns within the same individuals. Other deficiencies are shown by children whose parents have other psychiatric disorders, as well as in samples of clinically disturbed children.
- Strong evidence currently exists from the risk-for-schizophrenia and general psychopathology literature that some attributes of the family environment are associated with increased risk for the onset of the disorder. These attributes include: family communication deviance, negative affective

> style, high expressed emotion, and general disturbance in the family environment. It is still unclear whether these family attributes hold specific risk for schizophrenia or are associated with increased risk for a variety of disorders and dysfunctions. However, the current evidence . . . points to the highest rates of schizophrenia spectrum disorders in individuals exposed to both disturbed rearing environments and genetic risk (inferred from the presence of schizophrenia in at least one biological parent). Future studies need to explicate the mechanisms by which environmental attributes, individual attributes and genetic predisposition may interact to influence risk for schizophrenia.

In the 1990s, innovation in the methods of data collection in high-risk studies included advanced techniques for genetic screening and new brain imaging technologies. These neuroimaging studies allow for the long-term assessment of changes in both the structure and the function of children at high-risk for developing schizophrenia as these children age.

Asarnow, J. R. "Children at Risk for Schizophrenia: Converging Lines for Evidence," *Schizophrenia Bulletin* 14 (1988): 613–631.

Cornblatt, B. A., et al. "High-Risk Research in Schizophrenia: New Strategies, New Designs." In *Origins and Development of Schizophrenia: Advances in Experimental Psychopathology*, edited by M. F. Lenzenweger and R. H. Dworkin. Washington, D.C.: American Psychological Association, 1998.

Erlenmeyer-Kimling, L., et al. "Prediction from Longitudinal Assessments of High-Risk Children." In *Origins and Development of Schizophrenia: Advances in Experimental Psychopathology*, edited by M. F. Lenzenweger and R. H. Dworkin. Washington, D.C.: American Psychological Association, 1998.

Hill, Robert Gardiner (1811–1878) English physician who served as the resident surgeon at the Lincoln Asylum in England. Known as a persuasive advocate of nonrestraint policies in the treatment of institutionalized patients, he put such policies into effect at Lincoln in 1838 and is given credit by Wilhelm GRIESINGER for being the first to do so. In an 1838 book he argues that, "in a properly constructed building, with sufficient number of suitable attendants, restraint is never necessary, never justifiable, and always injurious."

See also ABUSE OF PSYCHIATRIC PATIENTS; CHEMICAL RESTRAINT; MECHANICAL RESTRAINT; NONRESTRAINT MOVEMENT.

Hill, R. G. *Lunacy: Its Past and Present.* London: Longman, Green, Reader & Dyer, 1870.

———. *Total Abolition of Personal Restraint in the Treatment of the Insane.* London: Simpkin, Marshall, 1838.

histamines Histamine (HA), a biogenetic amine, is a NEUROTRANSMITTER that has been linked to the regulation of several important functions of the central nervous system. These include arousal, cognition, neuroendocrine regulation, and circadian rhythyms. Animal model research on neurodegeneration conducted by L. Fernandez-Novona and R. Cacabelos of Spain has shown that histamine may have a cytotoxic (cell-poisoning) effect. Histamine has been examined in studies of Alzheimer's disease and SCHIZOPHRENIA. The BIOGENIC AMINE HYPOTHESIS of the cause of schizophrenia has tended to focus on the CATECHOLAMINES (such as DOPAMINE) and the INDOLAMINES (such as serotonin) and not the histamines. An "autointoxication" theory of the cause of dementia praecox first put forth in 1916 by Chicago surgeon and bacteriologist Bayard Taylor HOLMES implicated an overproduction of histamine—or "hyperhistaminia"—in the intestines as a source of poisons carried to the brain, which caused psychotic symptoms.

See also AUTOINTOXICATION AS A CAUSE OF DEMENTIA PRAECOX (SCHIZOPHRENIA).

Fernandez-Novona, L., and R. Cacabelos. "Histamine Function in Brain Disorders," *Behavioral Brain Research* 124 (October 2001): 213–233.

Holmes, B. T., and J. Retinger. "The Relation of Cecal Stasis to Dementia Praecox," *Lancet-Clinic* 116 (1916): 145–150.

historical evidence of schizophrenia If SCHIZOPHRENIA is truly a brain disease that has a strong

basis in genetics, then there should be evidence that this severe mental disorder has afflicted people for hundreds, if not thousands, of years. "Madness" has been reported in every society on record to a greater or lesser degree, and descriptions of HALLUCINATIONS, DELUSIONS, and bizarre behavior are often reported in association with ancient mental disorders. In an attempt to trace schizophrenia back to ancient Babylonian accounts (3000 B.C.) or to early Sanskrit texts from India, translations of descriptions of mental illness were collected in articles published in 1985 by D. V. Jeste and his colleagues and in 1984 by C. V. Haldipur. But it is still unclear from this historical evidence that schizophrenia—as we know it, a disease with a particular course that begins in adolescence or early adulthood, with characteristic signs and symptoms and a chronic deteriorating course (at least in the type of schizophrenia that seems to be the most "genetic")—existed in ancient times. This point (and the larger ramifications of this entire issue) has been eloquently argued and documented by psychiatrist E. Fuller Torrey in his book *Schizophrenia and Civilization* (1980).

There are many reasons for this uncertainty. First, ancient descriptions of "madness," which involved delusional, hallucinating, or confused individuals, could be accounts of any number of physical or mental disorders. For example, these symptoms could be produced by head trauma, brain infections, injury due to birth complications, strokes or any number of other known, organic mental disorders. Or, they could be descriptions of the other psychotic disorders, such as bipolar disorder or any of the acute reactive psychoses. What is missing in these ancient accounts are descriptions of the full course of the disease process over time.

Several changes in traditional thought developed in the 1600s (especially in England), which converged to change this state of affairs. First, societies began to incarcerate mentally ill people in central institutions (jails, hospitals), where many of them could be observed together for long periods of time. Secondly, physicians began to be put in charge of the care of the mentally ill in these institutions, as, for example, happened at the BETHLEM ROYAL HOSPITAL in England during the 17th century. And third, the concept of *disease* began to take on a new meaning, largely due to the influence of English physician Thomas Sydenham (1624–89), often referred to as the "English Hippocrates," who emphasized the direct observation of illnesses and suggested their classification according to syndromes or groups of symptoms. This differed from centuries of the identification of diseases usually by a single symptom, as was the case with the mental disorder known as FURY. Throughout the 1700s physicians who doctored to the mentally ill ("mad-doctors," or "lunatic doctors," as their specialty of medical practice came to be known) contributed treatises and textbooks based on their idiosyncratic observations and classifications of the mentally ill.

Eventually, in 1809, the very first clinical descriptions of schizophrenia as we know it appeared in print. Working independently in their respective countries, John HASLAM of the Bethlem Royal Hospital in London and Philippe PINEL of the Salpêtrière asylum in Paris produced expanded second editions of books on mental illness, which had been published previously, that contain the first complete reports of what we now know as schizophrenia in its "chronic" form. The expanded second edition of Pinel's work, *Traité médico-philosophique sur l'aliénation mentale, ou la manie* (first edition, 1801), has never been translated into English. Pinel's description of DÉMENCE in the first edition, which strongly resembles the thought disorder of schizophrenia, was apparently illustrated with case material in the second edition that seemed to confirm this connection. However, the following case history, which is reproduced from Haslam's 1809 *Observations on Madness and Melancholy,* may be the first valid historical evidence in the English language that we have for schizophrenia:

> there is a form of insanity which occurs in young persons; and, as far as these cases have been the subject of my observation, they have been more frequently noticed in females. Those whom I have seen, have been distinguished by prompt capacity and lively disposition; and in general have become the favorites of parents and tutors, by their faculty in acquiring knowledge, and by a prematurity of attainment. This disorder commences, about or shortly after, the period of menstruation, and in

> many instances has been unconnected with hereditary taint; as far as could be ascertained by minute enquiry. The attack is almost imperceptible; some months usually elapse before it becomes the subject of particular notice; and fond relatives are frequently deceived by the hope that it is only an abatement of excessive vivacity, conducing to a prudent reserve, and steadiness of character. A degree of apparent thoughtfulness and inactivity precede, together with a diminution of the ordinary curiosity, concerning that which is passing before them; and they therefore neglect those objects and pursuits which formerly proved sources of delight and instruction. The sensibility appears to be considerably blunted; they do not bear the same affection towards their parents and relations; they become unfeeling to kindness, and careless of reproof. To their companions they show a cold civility, but take no interest whatever in their concerns. If they read a book they are unable to give any account of its contents; sometimes, with steadfast eyes, they will dwell for an hour on one page, and then turn over a number in a few minutes. It is very difficult to persuade them to write, which most readily develops their state of mind; much time is consumed and little produced. The subject is reportedly begun, but they seldom advance beyond a sentence or two: the orthography becomes puzzling, and by endeavoring to adjust the spelling the subject vanishes. As their apathy increases they are negligent of their dress and inattentive to personal cleanliness. Frequently they seem to experience transient impulses of passion, but these have no source in sentiment; the tears, which trickle down at one time, are as unmeaning as the loud laugh which succeeds them; and it often happens that a momentary gust of anger, with its attendant invectives, ceases before the threat can be concluded. As the disorder increases, the urine and feces are passed without restraint, and from the indolence which accompanies it, they generally become corpulent. Thus in the interval between puberty and manhood, I have painfully witnessed this hopeless and degrading change, which in a short time has transformed the most promising and vigorous intellect into a slavering and bloated idiot.

Haslam is describing what British psychiatrist T. J. Crow has named Type II schizophrenia or the PINEL-HASLAM SYNDROME: insidious onset, NEGATIVE SYMPTOMS (attention deficits, problems in information processing, apathy, poverty of speech, loss of curiosity in people and activities), and gradual cognitive deterioration. This *démence*, as Pinel called it, was later elaborated upon by French alienist B. A. Morel in his descriptions of mental DEGENERATION, and was used by Morel to coin the term *démence précoce* in 1852. Emil KRAEPELIN borrowed this term to describe our modern clinical picture of DEMENTIA PRAECOX in 1893.

Haldipur, C. V. "Madness in Ancient India: Concepts of Madness in Charaka Samhita (1st century A.D.)," *Comprehensive Psychiatry* 25 (1984): 335–344.

Haslam, J. *Observations on Madness and Melancholy*. London: J. Callon, 1809.

Jeste, D. V. "Did Schizophrenia Exist before the Eighteenth Century?" *Comprehensive Psychiatry* 26 (1985), 493–503.

Pinel, P. *Traité médico-philosophique sur l'aliénation mentale*. 2nd ed. Paris: J. A. Brosson, 1809.

Torrey, E. F. *Schizophrenia and Civilization*. New York: Jason Aronson, 1980.

HIV and schizophrenia Persons with SCHIZOPHRENIA and other psychotic disorders are more susceptible to high-risk behaviors that may lead to HIV infection than persons without any diagnosable mental disorder. Studies have shown that persons with severe psychiatric disorders such as schizophrenia have less knowledge about the dangers of HIV infection and are less concerned about such infection than "healthy" control group members. According to a study conducted in Italy and published in 1997, HIV infection in schizophrenic patients may increase the severity of depression and may reduce tolerability to antipsychotic medication.

See also AIDS AND PSYCHIATRIC PATIENTS.

Gottesman, I. I., and C. S. Groome. "HIV/AIDS Risks as a Consequence of Schizophrenia," *Schizophrenia Bulletin* 23 (1997): 675–684.

Grassi, L., et al. "HIV-Risk Behavior and Knowledge about HIV/AIDS among Patients with Schizophrenia," *Psychological Medicine* 29 (1999): 171–179.

Mauri, M. C., et al. "Schizophrenia Patients before and after HIV Infection: A Case-Control Study," *Encephale* 23 (1997): 437–441.

HIV CNS disease A disease of the central nervous system (the brain and spinal cord) that is due to infection with the human immunodeficiency virus (HIV), implicated in acquired immunodeficiency syndrome (AIDS). The symptoms of such a disease process may resemble many MENTAL DISORDERS, including such psychotic disorders as SCHIZOPHRENIA and BIPOLAR DISORDER. However, the most common symptom is DEMENTIA. The clinical signs and symptoms of the AIDS DEMENTIA COMPLEX were first clearly identified by B. A. Navia and his colleagues in 1986.

Bridge, T. P., A. F. Mirsky, and F. K. Goodwin. *Psychological Neuropsychiatric, and Substance Abuse Aspects of AIDS*, Vol. 44. New York: Raven Press, 1988.

Hoch, August (1868–1919) A Swiss psychiatrist who emigrated to America in 1887 and is best remembered for his posthumously published book *Benign Stupors: A Study of a New Manic-Depressive Reaction Type* (New York: Macmillan, 1921). Hoch had returned to Europe in 1893–94 to train under Emil KRAEPELIN in Heidelberg, Germany. Together they conducted a series of psychological experiments (primarily word-association tests) concerning mental performance under a variety of conditions (fatigue, etc.). Upon arrival in America Hoch first worked at Johns Hopkins Hospital in Baltimore. After returning from Germany, he was a staff psychiatrist at McLean Hospital in Belmont, Massachusetts, from 1895 until 1908. With the help of his friend and fellow Swiss émigré Adolf MEYER, Hoch became a professor of psychiatry at Cornell University Medical College in 1909. In 1910 he replaced Meyer as the chief of the New York Psychiatric Institute at the Manhattan State Hospital on Ward's Island in New York City.

Hoch became a convert to Meyer's view that all mental disorders, including DEMENTIA PRAECOX or SCHIZOPHRENIA, were "reactions" to psychosocial stressors and not caused by heredity (genetics) as Kraepelin and his followers argued. In his last years, poor health forced Hoch to retire to California, where he was the live-in psychiatrist for Stanley McCormick of the wealthy and influential McCormick family of Chicago.

Meyer, A. "August Hoch, MD" (obituary), *Archives of Neurology and Psychiatry* 2 (1919): 576.

Meyer, A., S. E. Jelliffe, and A. Hoch. *Dementia Praecox: A Monograph*. Boston: R. G. Badger, 1911.

Noll, R. "Styles of Psychiatric Practice, 1906–1925: Clinical Evaluations of the Same Patient by James Jackson Putnam, Adolf Meyer, August Hoch, Emil Kraepelin, and Smith Ely Jelliffe," *History of Psychiatry* 10 (1999): 145–189.

holergasia A complete disorganization of mental activity. This was one of the many terms of psychological processes proposed by Swiss psychiatrist Adolf MEYER in the early 20th century that never became really popular and have since disappeared. Holergasia is probably equivalent to the FORMAL THOUGHT DISORDER of the DISORGANIZED TYPE of SCHIZOPHRENIA. Meyer, who came to the United States in 1892, was perhaps the most important figure in American psychiatry from about 1910 to 1940. His new name for schizophrenia, *parergasia*, was never adopted by anyone outside his close circle of followers.

Meyer, A., S. E. Jelliffe, and A. Hoch. *Dementia Praecox, A Monograph*. Boston: R. G. Badger, 1911.

Hollingshead & Redlich See SOCIAL DRIFT THEORY.

hollow wheel See HAYNER'S WHEEL.

Holmes, Bayard Taylor (1852–1924) It is through the psychotic illness in 1905 of Ralph Loring Holmes, his 17-year-old son, that Bayard Taylor Holmes enters the history of psychiatry. Holmes was personally devastated by his son's illness. His anguish was exacerbated by feelings of impotence,

for although his professional life was devoted to improving medical education in Chicago, he had a complete lack of expertise in psychiatry. Holmes, however, had a combative nature and decided to tackle his ignorance and his son's illness head on. Weary of relying on the advice of colleagues and some of the most respected psychiatrists in America while watching his son deteriorate further, Holmes semi-retired from his surgical practice and his position as professor of surgical pathology and bacteriology at College of Physicians and Surgeons in Chicago to care for his son himself. He also vowed to use his scientific expertise to find both a cause and a cure for dementia praecox. He soon became a prominent advocate for reforms in the institutional care of the mentally ill, compiled a bibliographic collection of more than 8,000 international scientific articles, dissertations, and books concerning laboratory studies of dementia praecox, and from 1918 to 1922 was the editor of what is believed to be the first medical journal named after a psychiatric disorder: *DEMENTIA PRAECOX STUDIES*.

Using equipment and lab space loaned by medical colleagues, in January 1915 Holmes began his own laboratory studies of dementia praecox. Within a few months, to his satisfaction, he hit upon a viable organic theory of the cause of dementia praecox: an ergotism-like toxemia caused by fecal stasis in the cecum led to an autointoxication process that poisoned the brain. In May 1916, he developed and experimented with a rational treatment based on this theory: abdominal surgery and daily irrigations of the colon as a way to reduce psychotic symptoms. Between May 1916 and January 1918 Holmes and his associates performed cecostomies on at least 22 dementia praecox patients. Holmes tested his surgical procedures, as well as other forms of treatment, on additional patients with DEMENTIA PRAECOX between April 1917 and February 1918 at an experimental inpatient unit he founded: the Psychiatric Research Laboratory of the Psychopathic Hospital, Cook County Hospital, in Chicago, Illinois.

Until recently, Bayard Holmes did not appear in any histories of psychiatry. During his lifetime he was a major critic of just about every prominent figure in American psychiatry. He believed Adolf MEYER was deliberately deceptive in his use of jargon. Freud's psychoanalysis was "a distinctly mystical theory, insusceptible of either proof or refutation," he wrote in 1914. Eugenics was a "pseudoscience," he claimed in 1916. Holmes was especially appalled at the lack of laboratories in mental hospitals. He made it clear in many opinion pieces in medical journals that he detested the psychiatric profession for its lack of interest in laboratory science and for making false claims to the unsuspecting public about scientific knowledge of causes and effective cures. Holmes firmly believed in AUTOINTOXICATION AS A CAUSE OF DEMENTIA PRAECOX (SCHIZOPHRENIA) and could not imagine how the followers of Meyer and Freud could ignore the fact that dementia praecox was an organic disease. Holmes died at his vacation home in Fairhope, Alabama, on April 1, 1924, discouraged that he could not convince the medical and psychiatric communities to take up the challenge to find the biological cause and cure of the illness that had so disabled his son.

In May 1916, Ralph Loring Holmes was the very first person in the history of medicine to undergo abdominal surgery as a treatment for dementia praecox. His father, Bayard Taylor Holmes, performed the procedure himself at Lakeside Hospital in Chicago. Ralph died from the procedure four days later.

See also PSYCHOSURGERY.

Beatty, W. K. "Bayard Taylor Holmes—A Forgotten Man," *Proceedings of the Institute of Medicine of Chicago* 34 (1981): 120–123.

Noll, R. "Infectious Insanities, Surgical Solutions: Bayard Taylor Holmes, Dementia Praecox, and Laboratory Science in Early Twentieth-century America," *History of Psychiatry*, 17 (2006): 183–204.

Horn's sack An early German psychiatrist who worked in the Berlin asylum, Ernst Horn (1774–1848) is largely remembered as the inventor of a sack that was put over unmanageable patients in order to calm them down and place them under control. A patient died from suffocation in one of Horn's sacks, and the resulting court case earned Horn considerable notoriety. Horn's sack was a long, wide bag that was reinforced with oilcloth.

Emil KRAEPELIN describes its use in his short historical book, *One Hundred Years of Psychiatry* (1917):

> The bag was pulled over the patient's head and tied beneath his feet. "It restraints the patient," explained Horn. "It shocks him by making him aware of his confinement and causes him to suspect or realize the fruitlessness of any attempt to stir up troubles." He also claimed that many restless, troublesome lunatics—even after other measures had failed to make them obedient, orderly and calm—responded to it by developing a more serene state of mind, by becoming more tractable, and by becoming more responsive to other, indirect, psychic treatments. Many patients who refused to eat were so impressed by the threat of the bag "that they took a new lease on life and began once more to enjoy the food which they had stubbornly refused."

Apparently, Horn was also an advocate of the CRUCIFORM STANCE, a standing form of the BED SADDLE.

Kraepelin, E. *One Hundred Years of Psychiatry.* Translated by W. Baskin. 1917. Reprint, New York: Philosophical Library, 1962.

hospitalism A term for the apathy and loss of ambition or creativity that was first noticed by Emelyn Lincoln Coolidge in 1909 in children who were hospitalized for a long time. Today we would refer to this as the effects of INSTITUTIONALIZATION. It is a type of "learned helplessness" that develops from being too dependent upon a caregiving staff in an institutional setting for too long a time.

In the 1940s the psychoanalyst René Spitz used this term to denote whatever physical or psychological disturbances occur in infants up to 18 months old who undergo a prolonged stay in a hospital or other similar institution where they are completely separated from their mother. Spitz did research in orphanages, nurseries, and other institutions in which infants and young children were separated from their mothers. Spitz thought that when a baby is cared for in an institutional setting in which the caregivers are anonymous and for which no emotional link is established, the child will develop a series of disorders, which are collectively called "hospitalism." These disorders are: (1) retardation of bodily development, (2) retardation of body mastery, (3) retardation of adaptation to the world, (4) retardation of language ability, (5) a reduced resistance to disease, and (6) in the most extreme cases, emaciation and eventual death. Spitz thought the damage caused by this rupture in the earliest mother-child relationship was long-lasting and led to chronic problems, potentially including schizophrenia.

In studies of schizophrenia, the effects of institutionalization must be taken into account and separated from the observable behaviors of the schizophrenic subjects that are caused first and foremost by the disease process. This is the basis of the ACUTE-CHRONIC DISTINCTION in schizophrenia research.

Coolidge, E. L. *Care of Infants Who Must Be Separated from Their Mothers Because of Some Especial Need on the Part of the Child,* Papers of the American Academy of Medicine. Conference on Prevention of Infant Mortality. Washington, D.C.: 1909.

Spitz, R. A. "Hospitalism—An Enquiry into the Genesis of Psychiatric Conditions in Early Childhood," *Psychoanalytic Study of the Child* 1 (1945): 53–74.

Hôtel-Dieu, l' Founded in 1656, l'Hôtel Dieu is the oldest hospital in Paris. In 1660 the French Parliament declared that it should provide special accommodations for "mad men and women." In the early 1790s, during the French Revolution, many of the mentally ill patients were removed from the hospital and transferred to the care of Philippe PINEL at the BICÊTRE Asylum. Prior to this time the patients there were subjected to BLEEDING so often that the technique was commonly referred to by the public as the *traitement de l'Hôtel-Dieu.*

Hoxton madhouses These were private "madhouses" in the Hoxton section of London, England. In the early 1700s practically all mentally ill in London were in one of the Hoxton madhouses. Like "Bellevue" in the United States, the word

"Hoxton" took on the ominous meaning of a place of banishment for the mentally ill, and sometimes was used as a synonym for "madness" or "lunacy" itself.

See also PRIVATE MADHOUSES.

Morris, A. D. *The Hoxton Madhouses.* London: 1958.

humoral theory of mental illness This theory of health and disease is thought to have been formulated by Hippocrates (460–377 B.C.) and expanded upon by Galen (A.D. 129–199). The ancient Greek notion that the universe was comprised entirely of four elements (earth, air, fire, water), which were each associated with a particular quality (dry, cold, hot, moist), formed the basis of Hippocrates' empirical medicine. Hippocrates associated four essential characteristics—the humors (from the Latin word for moisture)—of the human body with combinations of the elemental qualities. These four humors were blood, yellow bile, black bile, and phlegm; their relative quantities in relation to one another led to good health or to disease. Each of these humors was then associated with its ascendancy during a particular season: spring (blood); summer (yellow bile); autumn (black bile); winter (phlegm). Galen later paired combinations of qualities to each of the humors and their seasons of ascendancy: blood was warm and moist, yellow bile warm and dry, black bile cold and dry, and phlegm cold and moist.

Both physical and mental illnesses were considered by Galen to be caused by an excess of humors. What we would call acute diseases tended to be the result of an excess of blood or yellow bile, whereas an excess of black bile or phlegm was associated with more chronic ailments. Black bile in particular caused mental distress, and an excess of it produced MELANCHOLIA or "DEPRESSION," as we know it. Black bile could build up in the blood, the stomach or elsewhere. Therefore Galen recommended what would later become the standard regimen for the institutionalized mentally ill, what PINEL referred to as the "usual treatment" of bleeding, bathing, and purging. These treatments were recommended to either draw off the unwanted excess humor in certain disorders (by BLEEDING or PURGING) or to counteract the effects of the abnormal balance of humors (through temperature-specific baths or douches). Reestablishing the flow of blood in menstruation or from hemorrhoids with the use of leeches was thought by Galen to assist especially in the elimination of the disease-causing humor. Vestiges of the old Galenic humor theory of mental illness can especially be seen in the psychiatric texts of the first half of the 1800s, particularly in J. E. D. ESQUIROL's writings.

See also HEMORRHOIDS, PRODUCTION OF AS A TREATMENT.

Jackson, S. W. "Galen—On Mental Disorders," *Journal of the History of the Behavioral Sciences* 5 (1969): 365–384.

hurry of the spirits A term used popularly in 18th century England for "madness" or "lunacy." William BATTIE uses it in his famous 1758 book, *A Treatise On Madness.*

hydropathic institutions In Europe (especially Germany) in the mid-1800s, special clinics were set up to provide HYDROTHERAPY to mentally ill people as an alternative to commitment to the traditional asylums. These "hydropathic" clinics or institutions could provide outpatient treatment. Thus, people who did not suffer from severe mental disorders did not have to be institutionalized to receive treatment—a very modern concept. However, the established psychiatric authorities of the time—notably Wilhelm GRIESINGER in Germany—strongly criticized these practices as potentially dangerous since they could be performed outside the supervision of the medical profession. In the 1861 second edition of his *Mental Pathology and Therapeutics* (originally published in 1845), Griesinger expresses the following opinions about hydropathic institutions:

> In the first edition of this work, I have already expressed my opinion of the treatment in hydropathic institutions. Since then facts from all quarters have been elicited proving the injury which it generally inflicts on the mentally diseased. Most asylum physicians are in a position to contribute examples of this: Flemming, Erlenmeyer, Dam-

erow, Sponholz, etc., have expressed themselves decidedly upon this point. This violent procedure seems much to favor the transition to general paralysis. The absurdity of sending patients to cold-water establishments, instead of into lunatic asylums, would be incredible were it not of daily occurrences, still, it is evident that, in certain cases, the occasional use of wet compresses, cold sitzbaths, and, above all, cold washing followed by dry friction, can, under special indications, be beneficially employed.

Despite these criticisms, hydropathic institutions did not disappear, but instead flourished in the 1880s and 1890s as places of treatment for those from the upper classes suffering from the Victorian Age malady of "nervousness" or NEURASTHENIA, the term for this condition coined by physician George Miller Beard (1839–83) of New York in the 1870s. They specialized in a variety of hydrotherapeutic techniques involving both hot and cold bathing, including being wrapped alternately in hot and cold wet sheets, spraying from showering devices, and other such activities. The ancient spas at such places as Baden-Baden, Carlsbad, and Marienbad, which offered natural thermal spring waters, were also popular as forms of hydrotherapy.

Drinka, G. F. *The Birth of Neurosis: Myth, Malady, and the Victorians.* New York: Simon & Schuster, 1984.

Griesinger, W. *Mental Pathology and Therapeutics,* trans. C. L. Robertson and J. Rutherford. New York: William Wood & Co., 1882.

hydrotherapy Literally "water therapy," since the late 19th century the term for the various types of baths or DOUCHES that were one of the primary modes of treatment of the institutionalized mentally ill. It was particularly used for those patients who had become agitated or unmanageable in some way. In the latter half of the 1800s "hydrotherapy" took on the meaning of a particular procedure for a tub bath, which became popular in German psychiatric institutions and then was copied in other places, including the United States. Special treatment rooms were set up that contained large tubs, which would be filled with water and usually heated to between 98 and 102 degrees Fahrenheit. However, cold water baths were sometimes prescribed as well. A thick canvas cover was stretched over the top of the tub and tethered along the rim of the tub, with a hole cut at one end to allow the patient's head to be exposed. A "bathmaster" or "bathmistress" would oversee the treatment sessions, during which a patient would be left immersed in the tub for hours or, in some cases of extreme agitation, days at a time. Not surprisingly, a state of relaxation resulted and behavioral compliance was restored.

While working at the psychiatric clinic at Heidelberg University between 1891 and 1903, Emil KRAEPELIN relied primarily on hydrotherapy for agitated patients, with great success. As he reports in his *Memoirs:*

> By procuring English fireclay tubs and by employing more staff and using the baths during the night, our equipment became more and more complete. The baths were especially successful when they were applied for weeks and months. Slowly, but surely, they became the most important method for dealing with states of agitation, and isolation became completely superfluous.

In the 1890s the primary authority on hydrotherapy in the United States was Dr. Simon Baruch of Bellevue Hospital in New York City. Hydrotherapy equipment was later instituted at St. Elizabeth's Hospital in Washington, D.C., after a visiting physician from there reviewed the hydrotherapy procedures at Bellevue in 1897. When William Alanson White became superintendent of St. Elizabeth's in 1904, he implemented a policy of eliminating the more inhumane forms of physical restraint (straitjackets, bed saddles, etc.) and promoted instead the use of hydrotherapy. By the 1920s, hydrotherapy was the primary mode of treatment for institutionalized patients at St. Elizabeth's, and statistics show that between the summers of 1923 and 1924 a total of 106,816 warm-tub hydrotherapy sessions were prescribed for over 4,000 patients. Hydrotherapy declined in use in the 1930s when the COMA, CONVULSIVE, and ELECTROSHOCK THERAPIES all came into vogue in institutions.

Kraepelin, E. *Memoirs.* Translated by C. Wooding-Deane. Berlin: Springer-Verlag, 1987.

hyperkinesia Excessive movement and restlessness. When accompanied by impulsivity and poor attention span, it is a behavioral sign of a childhood disorder, attention-deficit hyperactivity disorder (ADHD). It is estimated that one-third of children who manifest ADHD (usually before age 4) continue to show signs of the disorder in adulthood. Hyperkinesis is also one of the traditional symptoms of CATATONIC EXCITEMENT.

hypnosis and psychosis In the 19th century a small number of physicians attempted to use hypnotism ("mesmerism") to treat "insanity" in institutionalized patients. For example, in the 1840s in India, British surgeon James Esdaile attempted to cure the mental illnesses of patients of the Calcutta Asylum during a six-month period but was generally disappointed with the results. However, in a few cases, people with less debilitating disorders responded to Esdaile's hypnotic inductions. In one case, a man who had cut his throat during a MANIC EPISODE had emergency surgery performed on him by Esdaile while the patient was under "mesmeric anesthesia." British physician John Elliotson, who largely initiated the explosion of interest in mesmerism in England in 1837 and founded the *Zoist,* a mesmeric medical journal in 1843, recommended the use of hypnotism for HYSTERIA. In Paris, the famous hypnotic experiments (beginning in 1878) of neurologist Jean-Martin Charcot (1825–93) with the institutionalized female patients of the Salpêtrière asylum led to the acceptance of hypnotism by the medical establishment.

In the 20th century there have been many research studies to determine: (1) if people with psychotic disorders can be hypnotized (questionable, due to problems in focusing attention noted particularly in schizophrenia), and (2) whether this may be a beneficial form of treatment. The leading authority on this issue is psychologist Elgin Baker of the Indiana University School of Medicine, who published a review of this issue in 1983. In reviewing the research, Baker found that "psychotics" and "borderlines" were comparable to normal subjects and neurotic subjects in their ability to be hypnotized (hypnotic susceptibility). However, Baker recommends that hypnotism be used as one of many other possible treatment techniques in psychotherapy—and in accordance with an overall treatment plan that may even include ANTIPSYCHOTIC DRUGS, which apparently do not reduce the hypnotic susceptibility of psychotic patients.

Baker, E. L. "The Use of Hypnotic Techniques with Psychotics," *American Journal of Clinical Hypnosis* 25 (1983): 283–288.

Bramwell, J. M. *Hypnotism: Its History, Practice and Theory.* London: Alexander Moring, 1906.

Owen, A. R. G. *Hysteria, Hypnosis and Healing in the Work of J.-M. Charcot.* New York: Garrett, 1971.

hypochondriasis Sometimes called "hypochondria." The contemporary meaning of this disorder is of a preoccupation with the belief and accompanying fear that one has a serious disease; based on a misinterpretation of bodily sensations, when in fact physical examination and medical reassurances to the contrary present proof that one does not have the imagined disease. This belief is not of delusional intensity, so there is no break with reality. It is not known how many people develop this disorder, but the numbers of men and women afflicted seem to be equal, and it seems to follow a chronic course throughout a person's lifetime. Apparent predisposing factors seem to be a past history of an actual serious disease (e.g., a heart attack) in the person's life or in the life of a family member. In *DSM-III-R* this was listed as one of the somatoform disorders, a group of mental disorders that have physical symptoms, which at first seem to have a physical cause.

In the psychotic disorders, particularly schizophrenia, people may report odd physical symptoms in various parts of their bodies (e.g., the head, the genitals), which seems to be more common in the initial stages of the first definite onset of the disorder, or in periodic exacerbations in the first years of the disorder. This is especially true for those diagnosed with one of the three nonparanoid subtypes

of schizophrenia, particularly the DISORGANIZED TYPE OF HEBEPHRENIC TYPE that Emil Kraepelin called the "silly dementia." Although others often interpret these reports by schizophrenics as efforts at malingering or as hypochondriasis, this is generally not the case. Such reports seem to be the experience of genuine effects of the disease process on the nervous system.

"Hypochondria" has been used to describe mental disorders at least since the time of Galen, who may have been the first to use it. *Hypochondrium* is the Greek word for an area just below the lower ribs, and Galen believed this was the place of origin of one of the three forms of *melancholia.* Over the centuries the words *hypochondriasis* and *hypochondria* were used as synonyms for hypochondriacal melancholy, a type of depression accompanied by flatulence and gastrointestinal problems. In the late 1600s, these terms were separated from melancholia (depression) by medical scholars, although hypochondriasis and melancholy were closely related well into the 1800s. However, the connection between an "imaginary illness" and hypochondria was apparent by the early 1600s to some medical scholars. By the 1800s, hypochondriasis differed from other, true forms of mental disorder, such as "hypochondriacal insanity," which were considered a more severe pathological development of "noninsane" hypochondriasis.

Jackson, S. W. *Melancholia and Depression: From Hippocratic Times to Modern Times.* New Haven, Conn.: Yale University Press, 1986.

Kenyon, F. E. "Hypochondriasis: A Survey of Some Historical, Clinical and Social Aspects," *International Journal of Psychiatry* 2 (1966): 308–326.

Savage, G. H. "Hypochondriasis and Insanity." In *A Dictionary of Psychological Medicine,* edited by D. H. Tuke. Philadelphia: P. Blakiston & Son, 1892.

hypofrontality Also referred to as "cerebral metabolic hypofrontality," or "metabolic hypofrontality," it refers to the results of some studies of the patterns of blood flow in the brain, showing that some schizophrenics have a much lower than normal blood flow in the frontal lobe (specifically, the prefrontal regions) of the brain. The original study that discovered this abnormality was conducted by researchers Ingvar and Franzen and published in 1974. They determined this "hypofrontality" by using a then-new BRAIN IMAGING TECHNIQUE known as regional cerebral blood flow (rCBF). In people diagnosed with schizophrenia, the more "hypofrontal" they appeared, the more they were observed to manifest the NEGATIVE SYMPTOMS of schizophrenia (e.g., they were more withdrawn, there was greater "ALOGIA" or poverty of speech, more disturbances in attention). The implication of this research is that this metabolic hypofrontality may be convincing evidence of a primary brain process (a lowered metabolism in the front part of the brain) that produces the observable symptoms of schizophrenia. However, the "hypofrontality" research has been somewhat inconsistent in that all the studies using the rCBF brain imaging technique seem to replicate Ingvar and Franzen's original finding, but studies that use PET SCANS (positron emission tomography) to measure cerebral metabolism have been much less consistent.

Despite the inconsistencies across studies, by 1995 the finding of hypofrontality in schizophrenia had reached the status of a "paradigm." Most researchers accepted it as a major truth about the abnormal brains of persons with schizophrenia. This success was due, primarily, to the vigorous promotion of this hypothesis by two National Institute of Mental Health researchers, Daniel Weinberger and Karen Faith Berman, in the late 1980s. However, the claim that hypofrontality was a "trait-like" pathophysiologic characteristic of schizophrenia has been weakened considerably by other studies. These additional studies suggest that the images of lower metabolic activity in the prefrontal cortex of the brain (hypofrontality) may depend on the specific cognitive demands of the experimental task employed in the study (in other words, they are task-dependent or state-specific), and may therefore not be due to any continuous abnormality in the around-the-clock operation of a brain addled by schizophrenia. By 2005 references to a static "hypofrontality" have virtually disappeared in the literature on schizophrenia.

The hypofrontality controversy in schizophrenia is a useful case study in the history of science, for in it we see how quickly a scientific "finding" that

seems so certain and true can be just as quickly overturned by more carefully designed and controlled research.

Curtis, V. A., et al. "Attenuated Frontal Activation in Schizophrenia May Be Task Dependent," *Schizophrenia Research* 37 (1999): 35–44.

Gur, R. C., and R. E. Gur. "Hypofrontality in Schizophrenia: RIP," *Lancet* 3 (June 1995): 1,383–1,384.

Weinberger, D. R., and K. F. Berman. "Prefrontal Function in Schizophrenia: Confounds and Controversies," *Philosophical Transactions of the Royal Society of London. B. Biological Sciences* 351 (1996): 1,495–1,503.

hypomanic episode This is a less serious version of a fully developed MANIC EPISODE that is indicative of a MOOD DISORDER, particularly BIPOLAR DISORDER. The predominant mood in a hypomanic episode is usually described as expansive, elevated, or irritable. A hypomanic episode is not serious enough to cause impairment in social and occupational functioning, and it does not develop into the sometimes psychotic features (delusions, hallucinations) that may accompany a manic episode. "Hypomania" was first described by Berlin psychiatrist Emanuel Ernst Mendel (1839–1907) in 1881.

hysteria *Hysteria* is the Greek word for uterus. From ancient times, a significant number of mental and physical disorders in women were believed to be caused by the wandering of a restless womb in the female body. Thus, there has always been a connection between hysterical symptoms and sexuality in women. Hysteria was initially identified by the Hippocratic school in the fifth century B.C. A large number of symptoms have been attributed to hysteria, many of which have survived into today's diagnostic manuals. Among the most ancient and most often reported symptoms have been spasms or convulsions, and feelings of choking due to the rise of an "hysterical ball" from the womb to the throat. In the 1700s and 1800s, other symptoms indicative of an hysteric were added, such as the "vapors" (fainting, dizziness), paralysis of the limbs, loss of sensation in the skin (anesthesias), a deep suggestibility or gullibility and dissociative "trance-like" states of *absences* (as it was termed in France). The symptoms were often very changeable, alternating or appearing and disappearing without warning. Sometimes hysterics would also develop psychotic symptoms such as hallucinations, delusions, and poor REALITY TESTING, leading 20th-century psychiatric manuals to refer to this as "hysterical psychosis."

"Hysteria" was generally an uncommon diagnosis in psychiatric institutions until the last quarter of the 19th century. The explosion of interest in this disorder was perhaps first evident in France, but soon spread to Germany, England, and the United States. In a book on the French psychiatric profession in the 19th century, historian Jan Goldstein reports that at the SALPÊTRIÈRE asylum for women in Paris, only 1 percent of the admissions for the two-year period 1841–42 were given "hysteria" as a diagnosis, but in the period 1882–83 a full 20.5 percent received that diagnosis. Also in this later period, two males were admitted to the Bicêtre asylum for men with this diagnosis, revealing a change in thinking about this "female malady."

The work of J. M. Charcot at the Salpêtrière in the 1870s legitimized hysteria as a distinct diagnostic category, and he identified four successive stages or "periods" that marked the fundamental nature of a "grand" hysterical attack *(grande hystèrie)*: developing from physical rigidity, to spasmodic movements *(grands mouvements)*, to a vividly dramatic, almost theatrical acting out of intense emotional states *(attitudes passionnelles)*, and then to a final delirious period in which the afflicted person laughed, cried, and was otherwise highly labile until he or she returned to a more reasonable state. Charcot eventually recognized that hysteria was not a form of severe insanity *(aliéne)* but was instead a mental disorder that fell into a borderline area of partial normality *(demi-fou)*. This also reflects the distinction, largely coming into vogue at about this time, between a PSYCHOSIS and a NEUROSIS. Sigmund FREUD studied with Charcot in Paris in the winter of 1885–86, and as a result of his exposure to Charcot's hypnotic treatment of hysterics he and his mentor Joseph Breuer began to treat "hysterical neurosis" in

their private practice patients in Vienna. In 1895 they published their famous book of such case histories, *Studien Über Hysterie (Studies on Hysteria)*. Freud's theories about the causes of hysteria in sexuality formed the basis of his "psychoanalysis" in the decades to come.

Due to the sometime psychosis-like symptoms in hysteria (disturbances in attention, "dreamy" or "indifferent" quality in interactions with others, delusions, and hallucinations), there was much discussion at the turn of the century as to how it was related to KRAEPELIN's dementia praecox. One of the most important contributions made by Swiss psychiatrist and psychoanalyst C. G. JUNG was his detailed analysis of the similarities and differences between these two disorders in his 1907 monograph, *Über die Psychologie der Dementia praecox: Ein Versuch (The Psychology of Dementia Praecox)*, particularly in his chapter on "Dementia Praecox and Hysteria." He pictured dementia praecox as the far more serious disorder and the one that was probably organic in origin.

In the 20th century, "hysteria" survived as a diagnosis as one of the "neurotic disorders" of the World Health Organization's *ICD-9* (1978); and in *DSM-III-R* (1987) it was split up into no less than four different types of somatoform disorders.

Goldstein, J. *Console and Classify: The French Psychiatric Profession in the Nineteenth Century.* Cambridge: Cambridge University Press, 1987.

Micale, M. S. "On the Disappearance of Hysteria: A Study in the Clinical Deconstruction of a Diagnosis," *Isis* 84 (1993): 496–526.

I

ICD-10 This is the acronym for the periodically revised manual produced by the WORLD HEALTH ORGANIZATION entitled: *The International Statistical Classification of Disease, Injuries, and Causes of Death.* It is usually revised at 10-year intervals; the very first edition appeared in 1900 and the most recent—*ICD-10*—in 1992. A more detailed revision of *ICD-10* by major medical organizations in the United States, to make it more useful to clinicians, researchers, epidemiologists, and others, is the *Clinical Modification* (or *ICD-10-CM*). With the growing importance of mental disorders, WHO produced in 1978 a special publication that included the chapter on mental disorders from *ICD-9* and a glossary and classification guide; it is perhaps the most useful summary of the *ICD-9* position on mental disorders.

Although *DSM-IV* may be more widely used in clinical practice and research around the world, together with *ICD-10* these two manuals have become the standard classification systems for mental disorders in the 20th century.

Commission on Professional and Hospital Activities. *The International Classification of Disease, 10th Revision, Clinical Modification.* Ann Arbor, Mich.: Commission on Professional and Hospital Activities, 1992.

World Health Organization. *Mental Disorders: Glossary and Guide to their Classification in Accordance with the 10th Revision of the International Classification of Diseases.* Geneva: World Health Organization, 1992.

id The Freudian "unconscious." Sigmund FREUD borrowed the term Das Es from a colleague, Georg Groddeck. Psychosis was viewed by Freud as the result of the ego's inadequate defenses against the id, thereby resulting in a flood of irrational, instinctually based "primary process" material—as appears, for example, in dreams. *Id* is Latin for "IT" (Das Es).

ideas of reference One of the most common symptoms of the psychotic disorders. It is an idea that certain events or people in a person's immediate environment have a magical "special meaning" for that person. For example, a song heard on the radio may be interpreted by a psychotic person as having been specifically played at that time to convey a special message to him or her. Ideas of reference are not as strong as DELUSIONS, nor are they as long-lasting. They tend to be transient and specific to the immediate situation the psychotic person finds him- or herself in at the moment.

idiot savant See AUTISTIC SAVANTS.

idiot's cage The name for an iron cage used to confine severely mentally ill and mentally retarded people for public display, usually as entertainment. Such cages were used well into the 1700s and had variations such as the BELGIAN CAGE that were used in the 1800s.

illusion This is a mistaken perception of an *actual* object or event in the environment. Illusions are different from HALLUCINATIONS, which do not have actual external stimuli for the sensory experience.

illusion des sosies See CAPGRAS SYNDROME.

illusion of intermetamorphosis See INTERMETAMORPHOSIS SYNDROME.

illusion of negative doubles See CAPGRAS SYNDROME.

illusion of positive doubles See FREGOLI'S SYNDROME.

immediacy hypothesis This is the hypothesis that the behavior of people with schizophrenia is controlled primarily by stimuli immediate in their environment. "Normal" people are "controlled" by much wider and less immediate (i.e., not in the immediate environment) stimuli, according to this hypothesis, which is largely based on a radical behavioral interpretation of COGNITIVE STUDIES OF SCHIZOPHRENIA. This hypothesis was first put forth by Kurt Salzinger in 1966.

See also ATTENTION, DISORDERS IN.

Salzinger, K. *Schizophrenia: Behavioral Aspects*. New York: Wiley, 1973.

immersion therapy See BATHS; HYDROTHERAPY.

immune system alterations in schizophrenia Research on mental disorders such as schizophrenia has always been directly influenced by new concepts and technologies that have emerged in other medical sciences. By the end of the 19th century, a time when most physicians had little or no formal training in medical schools, a "laboratory revolution" in medicine was well underway that would change the practice of medicine forever. Instead of relying on the training of apprentice physicians by master physicians through the relating of clinical anecdotes and the shadowing of the day-to-day medical practicing of the master by the apprentice, many physicians in Europe and North America called for the application of new knowledge gained through basic research in laboratories to everyday medical practice. Laboratory-based knowledge of human physiology and especially the potential causes of disease were especially valued. This revolution in medicine was eventually won by the physicians who sought to make medicine a science based on objective, quantitative, and replicable laboratory findings, and less an art based on subjective personal experiences.

The discovery of "microbes" or "bacteria" and the demonstration that these "germs" either directly caused disease or were secondarily involved in the deteriorating effects of disease was an idea finally accepted by the medical elites by 1880. The "germ theory of disease" led to the medical science of bacteriology, and many diseases that were thought to be caused by heredity, such as tuberculosis and syphilis, were found to be caused by bacteria. The rise of bacteriology (starting in the 1880s), and the emergence of endocrinology from general physiology (starting in earnest after 1890), led to various theories of AUTOINTOXICATION AS A CAUSE OF DEMENTIA PRAECOX (SCHIZOPHRENIA).

The immune response (the 1890s) By 1890 the discovery of "reactions" in the blood to foreign organisms or substances ("antigens", as evidenced by the production of detectable "antitoxins," "defensive ferments," or "antibodies," led to the rise of immunology in medicine. Originally, immunology was named immunochemistry in 1904 by the noted Swedish chemist and physicist Svante Arrhenius (1859–1927). The focus on the identification and investigation of the antigen-antibody reaction dominated early research in immunology from 1890 to 1910, as historian A. M. Silverstein has documented. From about 1910 to about 1940 knowledge of the "immune response" was applied to the development of *serum therapy* (the production of vaccines and other therapies to prevent or cure various diseases, based on antibodies present in the blood of ill persons). Starting in 1940, immunology was revitalized by the introduction of techniques and concepts from molecular biology, and a great deal of attention was focused on the lymphocytes (white blood cells produced in the lymph glands) as an important aspect of the immune response. In 1949 the Australian researcher MacFarlane Burnet (1899–1965) added an important dimension to the definition of immunity when he proposed that animal bodies had some sort of mechanism of

biological memory for distinguishing "self" from "not-self." Antigens present in the body before birth were accepted as "self." No antibodies were made in response to them.

The immune system (the mid-1960s) Theories of immune reactions, how such reactions may relate to one another, and their connection to the nervous system and endocrine system, were not viewed as comprising aspects of a comprehensive functional system until the mid-1960s. The first reference to the immune system was to the lymphoid system in 1963. As historian of science Anne Marie Moulin has documented, it was only during that decade that the first modern concept of an integrated "immune system" came into being in connection with the development of *cellular immunology.* Cellular immunology arose as a reaction to purely chemical interpretations of immune reactions (*humoral immunology*) that became popular in the mid-20th century. The immune system was conceptualized in terms of its function, not its structure, and focused on a set of autonomous cells involved in all immune reactions. These cells were imagined as freely wandering throughout the whole body, unrestricted by any internal organ.

All that had been known for most of the 20th century was that immune responses (such as the activation of lymphocytes, the production of antibodies, the development of immunity to a disease through exposure to it, allergic reactions, and so on) defended the body against infectious organisms such as bacteria and viruses as well as against toxins manufactured within the body, or entering from outside the body. Each immunity response came from a separate place in the body (the bone marrow produced granulocytes and macrophages, plasma cells produced antibodies, and the lymph nodes produced lymphocytes), but how all these different places in the body were connected, if at all, was not understood. Nor were the presumed connections between immune responses, the endocrine system, and the nervous system. The new concept of a "system" of "restless cells" roaming the entire body at all times took the focus away from immunity being localized only in specific areas of the body (such as in "central" organs like the spleen versus "peripheral" organs like the lymph nodes).

Historian of science Anne Marie Moulin identified four essential main features of the immune system concept that emerged from the mid-1960s to the mid-1970s:

(1) Immunity is a permanent function of the entire body.
(2) The representation of immunity requires anatomical and histological knowledge of its parts.
(3) Knowledge of immunity, beyond this morphological description, refers to a logical category—the so-called immunocompetence of cells—whatever their localization.
(4) All immunological phenomena can be described and explained in terms of the immune system.

The rise of psychoneuroimmunology in the 1970s, led by the work of Robert Ader, focused attention on the interconnections of the immune, endocrine, and nervous systems and their possible relevance to mental disorders such as schizophrenia.

Immunology and the understanding of neurosyphilis The success story of the linkage of the clinical symptoms, cellular pathology, and etiology (underlying cause) of syphilis in an astonishingly brief six-year period had a major impact on biological psychiatrists looking for the cause of schizophrenia in the early 20th century. This story is told in detail in classic books on the Wasserman reaction test by Ludwig Fleck (1935) and Felix Plaut (1911). In 1905 the spiral-shaped bacterium that caused syphilis was discovered by two German researchers. By the following year, antibodies created as a defense against the syphilis bacterium were identified, leading directly to the development of the famous Wasserman blood test for syphilis in 1906. Finally, in 1913, the syphilis bacterium was found in the brain tissue of persons in asylums suffering from the degenerating psychotic disorder known as GENERAL PARALYSIS OF THE INSANE (GPI). GPI, which accounted for more than 20 percent of the inpatients committed to asylums, was thereby proven to be a syndrome caused by the tertiary stage of syphilis and was therefore soon renamed neurosyphilis. Hopes were raised for the discovery of similar bacterial organisms that may be involved in dementia praecox (schizophrenia). If specific infectious

organisms could be found for the psychotic disorders, then antibodies could be located in the blood or cerebral spinal fluid and a diagnostic BLOOD TEST FOR SCHIZOPHRENIA could be developed. As a result, starting in the first decade of the 20th century, a great deal of research—all ultimately fruitless—was aimed at finding immune system alterations in dementia praecox (schizophrenia).

Immunological studies of dementia praecox Changes in the numbers of white blood cells in "lunatics" or "insane persons" had been observed through primitive microscopic examinations throughout the latter half of the 19th century. We now know that such changes in white blood cells—leukocytes—might be an indication of altered immune functions, although the linkage of immune response and white blood cell count did not become apparent until the early 20th century.

One of the first promising immunity findings involved injecting persons with dementia praecox and manic depression with cobra venom and looking for the antibodies created as an immune response. In 1909 two German researchers from Eppendorf created a minor sensation when they injected patients with cobra venom and found that all the dementia praecox patients and a portion of the manic-depressive subjects invariably reacted to the toxin (by producing antibodies to fight it that were detectable in the blood), while other psychiatric patients and normals did not. The excitement over the "Much-Holzmann psycho-reaction" was over within two years. Although the "Much-Holzmann psycho-reaction" was quickly discredited by other researchers, it was the first promising immune response finding for dementia praecox and manic-depressive insanity.

In an era in which autointoxication theory influenced medical and psychiatric cognition, researchers posited that bacteria in the intestines spread throughout the body and caused damage to internal organs. These damaged organs would release debris such as "toxic albumins" into the bloodstream, which would then be carried to the brain and cause the symptoms of insanity. Immune responses to such foreign materials were eagerly sought in countless laboratory studies. Such theories were many and varied, as were the hypothetical substances that could be detected in the blood or cerebral spinal fluid of the insane. Between 1912 and 1918 several prominent dementia praecox researchers relied heavily on a test known as the Abderhalden defensive ferments reaction test, first developed in 1909 by Swiss biochemist Emil Abderhalden as a pregnancy test. It was thought that this blood test could differentially diagnose dementia praecox from other mental disorders and from the blood of persons with no mental disorders. The problem with this test, as many researchers discovered by 1914, was that Abderhalden's reaction test was highly subjective and not quantitative (the identification of a particular deep blue or violet color was evidence of a "reaction"—not a measurement of any sort), resulting in enormous experimenter bias and error. Furthermore, there was no other corroborating evidence of an immunity response such as "defensive ferments," and soon it was apparent that Abderhalden's defensive ferments simply did not exist.

Throughout the 20th century, searches for specific and replicable evidence for immune system abnormalities or dysfunction in dementia praecox (schizophrenia) produced wildly conflicting results. Most of the research focused on lymphocytes and immunogobulins, yielding confusing and contradictory results. Diagnostic criteria for identifying subjects with dementia praecox or schizophrenia were not standardized, so the comparison of groups across studies and the generalizing of findings were not possible with any degree of accuracy. Also, much of the confusion regarding immunity was due to a general lack of knowledge about the complexities of the immune system (until the 1960s) and the lack of powerful computer-aided technologies to study them properly (until the 1980s). Even well into the 1990s very few researchers were looking into the role of the immune system in schizophrenia, and chapters reviewing this area of research disappeared from major volumes on the disease. For example, not only is there no chapter on immune system functioning in schizophrenia in the important 2003 volume *Schizophrenia*, 2nd ed., by Steven Hirsch and Daniel Weinberger, nowhere in the volume is such a research literature even acknowledged as existing. However, with further advances in technology and a more sophisticated view of the "immune

system," the latter half of the 1990s brought new researchers to this very old problem in schizophrenia research. The most prominent of the new generation of researchers on the role of immune function in schizophrenia—Norbert Mueller and his colleagues, Markus Schwarz, Manfred Ackenheil, and Michael Riedel—are located at the Psychological Clinic at Ludwig Maximilian University in Munich, Germany.

The concept of the immune system in the early 21st century At the beginning of the 21st century, the relatively primitive "immune system" concept of the 1960s had given way to a highly complex and still somewhat mysterious notion of a mechanism of involving at least two functionally different immune systems. The first, sometimes called the innate immune system, is a more primitive and, assumedly, older immune system in terms of the evolutionary development of life on this planet. This "phylogenetically older" immune system is the first line of defense in many organisms, including humans. The second immune system, assumed to be of more recent origin in the evolution of life on this planet, is known as the adaptive immune system. It is found in "higher" organisms, including humans. This second line of defense includes higher functions such as "memory" and can be conditioned. It is the adaptive immune system's mysterious memory ability that can "recognize" an enemy (e.g., a virus) upon re-exposure to it (that is, a second exposure to the antigen of the intruder), and it can initiate a specific immune response.

The innate and adaptive immune systems are further broken down into two other components. The first, known as cellular immunity, refers to the direct actions of immune cells (such as lymphocytes, macrophages, and leukocytes) and the products they secrete (cytokines) on substances recognized as foreign ("not-self"). In the older innate immune system, cellular immune structures include monocytes, macrophages, granulocytes, and NK (natural killer) cells. In the more recent adaptive immune system, cellular immune structures are T (thumus) and B (bone marrow) cells.

The second, known as humoral immunity, refers to the production of proteins known as antibodies or immunoglobulins that act on some of the other cells in the immune system. Humoral productions of the innate immune system include complement, APP, and mannose binding lectin (MBL). Humoral productions of the phylogenetically more-recent adaptive immune system are the antibodies. A special class of antibodies, known generally as autoantibodies, directs its actions against the body, mistaking "self" for "not-self" and thereby causing the inflammation of cells and eventually disease (cellular pathology). Such diseases are known as autoimmune diseases.

Although the findings of immune system alterations in schizophrenia are varied, inconsistent, and difficult to interpret, two patterns of immune system alterations have been repeatedly noted. The first involves elevated interleukin-6 (IL-6) production. IL-6 is an important cytokine that initiates the immune system response to foreign intruders and especially activates the B-cell system, activating B-cells to synthesize antibodies. IL-6 is released from different cell types in the blood (macrophages, monocytes, and T and B cells). IL-6 may be involved in the exacerbation of symptoms in autoimmune disorders in the central nervous system (brain and spinal cord). IL-6 has also been shown, in vitro, to stimulate neurons to secrete neurotransmitters such as dopamine and probably other catecholamines as well. Several studies have found elevated levels of IL-6 in schizophrenia, perhaps indicating an activation of the innate immune system in schizophrenia. One possible mechanism for this is the activation of the monocyte/macrophage system, leading to an overproduction of IL-6 by the innate immune system. IL-6 levels also increase when the T-Helper-2 cell system is activated (see below). Some studies have found that treatment with ANTIPSYCHOTIC DRUGS significantly lowers levels of IL-6. Hence, at present, the role of IL-6 in the pathophysiology of schizophrenia is suggestive.

A second finding in several studies indicates T-Helper-2 cell activation in schizophrenia. There is a functional balance between the TH-1 system and TH-2 system in the body. In schizophrenia, the activation of the TH-2 system has been coupled with evidence of a lack of activation of the TH-1 system. A lack of activation of the TH-1-related cellular immune system blunts immune system response to exposure to various antigens. In schizophrenia, additional suggestive evidence that there may be

a blunted answer of the cellular mediated (TH-1) response is found in publications prior to the introduction of antipsychotic drugs. Antipsychotic drugs mainly stimulate the TH-1 system to action.

It has been noted for decades that there may be an increased antibody production in persons with schizophrenia. This observation led to the theoretical speculation that schizophrenia is an autoimmune disease. However, although about 20 to 35 percent of persons with schizophrenia were estimated in these studies to show evidence of an autoimmune response, the effect of antipsychotic drugs in producing this effect was not taken into account. It has been known since at least the late 1970s that treatment with phenothiazines increases the production of antibodies that can be detected in the blood and cerebral spinal fluid of persons with schizophrenia. We now know that antipsychotic medications may activate not only TH-1 cell production but also the production of antibodies by activating B cells. Activated B cells produce antibody cells.

The immune system alterations associated with treatment with antipsychotic drugs indicate that both arms of the more recent adaptive immune system may be activated. The cellular immunity arm of the adaptive immune system evidences alterations in the activity of the TH-1 system and the activation of the B cell system. The activation of B cells produces a humoral immunity response, the production of antibodies. This is the second arm of the adaptive immune system. Future studies of the phylogenetically older innate immune system—which is still not well understood—may indicate this system is activated in persons with schizophrenia who are not medicated. Such a definitive finding may demonstrate that such innate immune system alterations may be part of the underlying natural disease processes of schizophrenia and may give us a better idea of the involvement of the immune system in this disorder. Immune system alterations in schizophrenia may therefore be found to be due to a dysfunction in the oldest part of the immune system, the phylogenetically-older innate immune system.

At present, the elevations of IL-6 and the shift from TH-1 blunting to TH-2 activation—the firmest findings of immune system alterations in schizophrenia—may be artifacts of treatment with antipsychotic drugs and have little or no connection to any involvement of the immune system in the etiology (cause) or the pathophysiology of the disease. The theory that schizophrenia may be an autoimmune disease is therefore based on evidence tainted by the effect of antipsychotic drugs on persons with schizophrenia and has little to support it. This situation may change. In a review of the autoimmune hypothesis by Amanda Jones and colleagues published in *Immunology and Cell Biology* in 2005, the discovery that some autoantibodies are directed specifically against neurotransmitter receptors in the brain may give a new perspective on the cause of schizophrenia. The first to propose a similar theory, that schizophrenia is caused by autoantibodies attacking dopamine receptor sites in the brain, was first put forth by J. G. Knight in 1982. The first study to report the detection of "anti-brain antibodies" in persons with schizophrenia was published by Lehmann-Facius in 1939.

Currently, the interdependence of the immune system, the nervous system, and the endocrine system is not well understood in human beings. All three are highly complex systems in the body, each ancient and mysterious in its own right. Nonetheless, the search for immune system alterations continues to this day in schizophrenia research, with not only the blood but also the cerebral spinal fluid examined for antibodies to possible pathogens. Evidence connecting schizophrenia to allergic reactions to foods, viruses transmitted from cats to humans (toxoplasmosis), and a lengthy list of other possible pathogens is still rather weak. Maternal exposure to viruses early in pregnancy has long been suspected to be a RISK FACTOR involved in the etiology of some forms of schizophrenia and bipolar disorder, although no confirmatory antibodies have yet been detected (Yolken and Torrey, 1995). Thus, at present, neither of the two main theories of immunological involvement in the cause and pathophysiology of schizophrenia—the autoimmune hypothesis and the viral infection hypothesis—have much scientific support.

Lymphocytes as a neutral probe into brain functioning and gene expression In 2004 a research group from Groningen, The Netherlands, led by Anatoliy Gladkevich proposed the hypothesis that

lymphocytes—which make up about 20 percent of all white blood cells—might carry information that reflects the metabolism of brain cells and might be utilized as an indirect probe of a limited number of cellular functions, including gene expression. They proposed focusing on the T (thymus-derived) cell, B (bone marrow–derived) cell, and NK cell subpopulations of lymphocytes. This suggestion was recently put into practice by noted schizophrenia researcher Ming T. Tsuang and colleagues and used to develop a genetic diagnostic blood test for schizophrenia and bipolar disorder. Lymphocytes were used to extract mitochondrial RNA from the blood of persons with schizophrenia and bipolar disorder for the purpose of genetic microarray analysis. The assumption was that the switching on of certain genes would leave identifiable mRNA traces in lymphocytes, thus giving an indication of brain functioning. Eight candidate genes were identified as possible biomarkers that could differentially diagnose schizophrenia from bipolar disorder and from normal controls. Both schizophrenia and bipolar disorder were found to have unique blood-based gene expression profiles. The procedure had an overall estimated accuracy of 95 to 97 percent. The preliminary report appeared in the *American Journal of Medical Genetics* in January 2005. However, this study has not yet been replicated, and the results remain tentative.

Fitzgerald, J. G. "Immunity in Relation to Psychiatry," *American Journal of Insanity* 67 (1911): 687–703.

Fleck, L. *Genesis and Development of a Scientific Fact.* 1935 (German). Reprint, Chicago: University of Chicago Press, 1979.

Gladkevich, A., H. F. Kauffmann, and J. Korf. "Lymphocytes as a Neural Probe: Potential for Studying Psychiatric Disorders," *Progress in Neuro-Psychopharmacology and Biological Psychiatry* 28 (2004): 559–76.

Jones, Amanda, et al. "Immune Dysregulation and Self-reactivity in Schizophrenia: Do Some Cases of Schizophrenia Have an Autoimmune Basis?" *Immunology and Cell Biology* 83 (2005): 9–17.

Knight, J. G. "Dopamine-receptorstimulating Antibodies: A Possible Cause of Schizophrenia," *Lancet* 2 (1982): 1073–1076.

———. "Is Schizophrenia an Autoimmune Disorder? A Review," *Methods and Findings of Experimental Clinical Pharmacology* 6 (1984): 395–403.

Lehmann-Facius, H. "Serologisch-analytische versuche mutliquoren und seren von schizophrenien," *Allgemeine Zeitschrift fuer Psychiatrie* 110 (1939): 232–243.

Moulin, A. M. "The Immune System: A Key Concept for the History of Immunology," *History and Philosophy of the Life Sciences* 11 (1989): 13–28.

Much, H., and W. Holzmann. "Eine Reaktion im Blute von Geisteskranken," *Munchener mediziner Wochenschrift,* 56 (1909): 1,001–1,009.

Mueller, N., M. Riedel, M. Ackenheil, and M. J. Schwarz. "The Role of Immune Function in Schizophrenia: An Overview," *European Archives of Psychiatry and Clinical Neuroscience,* 249 (1999): 62–68.

Plaut, F. *The Wasserman Sero-Diagnosis of Syphilis in Its Application to Psychiatry.* Translated by S. E. Jelliffe and L. Casamajor. New York: Journal of Nervous and Mental Disease Publishing Company, 1911.

Silverstein, A. M. "History of Immunology: A History of Theories of Antibody Formation," *Cellular Immunology,* 91 (1985): 263–283.

Tsuang, M. T., N. Nossova, T. Yager, M. M. Tsuang, S. C. Guo, K. G. Shyu, S. J. Glatt, and C. C. Liew. "Assessing the Validity of Blood-based Gene Expression Profiles for the Classification of Schizophrenia and Bipolar Disorder: A Preliminary Report," *American Journal of Medical Genetics Part B: Neuropsychiatric Genetics,* 133B (January 2005): 1–5.

impulsive character See BORDERLINE SCHIZOPHRENIA.

incidence of schizophrenia See EPIDEMIOLOGY.

incipient schizophrenia An older term for that phase of the schizophrenic disease process when signs of the impending disorder first clearly make their appearance. This usually involves a clear deterioration in functioning before the active phase of the disorder. This is now called the PRODROMAL PHASE.

incoherence Uncomprehensible speech. This term is applied when a person's speech is marked by ILLOGICAL THINKING, excessive use of incomplete sentences, tangential or irrelevant

statements, or abrupt changes in the topic of conversation. Grammar may be distorted and word usage may be bizarre or idiosyncratic. Incoherence may be a sign of FORMAL THOUGHT DISORDER. It is commonly found in schizophrenia (particularly the DISORGANIZED TYPE) and in the atypical PSYCHOSES. Incoherence does not apply to an identifiable speech or language disorder such as an aphasia.

incomplete penetrance In GENETICS STUDIES, the likelihood that a particular genetically transmitted abnormality (such as a disease) will be expressed depends on the degree of penetrance of that disorder. For example, with SCHIZOPHRENIA it may be that close biological relatives (such as MONOZYGOTIC TWINS) will carry the genetic predisposition to developing the disease, but the genetic abnormalities that may produce the disease may not be expressed equally in the psychological and physiological development of these persons. For example, although the CONCORDANCE RATE for schizophrenia between monozygotic or "identical" twins is suggestively high, nonetheless one twin will often develop schizophrenia and the other will not, rendering them discordant for schizophrenia. This is an example of incomplete penetrance—the genetic defect does not fully "penetrate" or influence later "expressed" psychological and physiological development (in this case, in the genetically "identical" twin that does not develop schizophrenia). Because the modes of GENETIC TRANSMISSION for mental disorders are presently unknown, incomplete penetrance continues to be a major problem in genetics studies of these disorders.

Inderal See PROPRANOLOL.

index case In GENETICS STUDIES of schizophrenia, particularly the "family studies" using the CONSANGUINITY METHOD, the index case is the person who is diagnosed with the disorder. Such information as the possible risk for SCHIZOPHRENIA in relatives of a schizophrenic person are made by analyzing the relationships between the index case and other family members. Another term for the index case is the PROBAND.

India The prevalence rates for schizophrenia in India have been found to range from 2.2 to 5.6 per 1,000. India is unusual in that the greater rates for schizophrenia have been found in the higher socioeconomic groups, which is unlike the pattern for most of the rest of the world, in which the higher rates are found in the lowest socioeconomic strata of society.

Torrey, E. F. "Prevalence Studies of Schizophrenia," *British Journal of Psychiatry* 150 (1987): 598–608.

indolamines A group of biogenic amines including the NEUROTRANSMITTER SEROTONIN. The biogenic amines are implicated in the development of certain mental disorders, including SCHIZOPHRENIA, BIPOLAR DISORDER, and DEPRESSION.

See also BIOGENIC AMINE HYPOTHESIS.

induced delusional disorder See FOLIE À DEUX.

infantile autism See AUTISM, INFANTILE.

infectious agent hypothesis See FOCAL INFECTION AS CAUSE OF PSYCHOTIC DISORDERS; VIRAL THEORIES OF SCHIZOPHRENIA.

infectious insanity See FOLIE À DEUX.

influenced psychosis See FOLIE À DEUX.

information processing in schizophrenia By employing metaphors and concepts derived from the computer sciences, COGNITIVE STUDIES OF SCHIZOPHRENIA have attempted to demonstrate the differences in the processes of thinking between

people who are diagnosed with schizophrenia and those who are not. These studies examine the stages of information processing—essentially defined as the encoding, transformation, storage, and retrieval of information for the purpose of regulating behavior—to determine at what stage or stages defects occur in schizophrenics that are unlike those found in most normals.

A comprehensive review of the literature of schizophrenia studies, conducted from an information-processing approach and compiled and analyzed by Canadian psychologists Leonard George and Richard Neufeld, appeared in *Schizophrenia Bulletin* in 1985. They conclude that the following traditional schizophrenic symptoms have the accompanying interpretations according to information processing theory.

Sensory and perceptual anomalies Hallucinations may occur in conjunction with an interaction of several defects in information processing: a disruption in sensory processing, leading to the spontaneous retrieval of information in long-term memory; a predisposition toward representing this information as mental imagery; and the misattribution of these products of internal processing to external sources.

Body-image distortions These may be misperceptions based on the result of a general sensory analysis dysfunction.

Loosening of associations This anomaly may be related to studies that show a schizophrenic deficit in the implementation of the network of semantic relations in long-term memory.

Delusions A large body of evidence indicates cognitive and perceptual differences between paranoid and nonparanoid schizophrenics, with the paranoid characterized by a "premature judgment" or "jump to conclusions" response set.

Movement abnormalities These may be due to inadequate or inaccurate feedback information, or may reflect strategies for coping with attentional dysfunction.

See also ATTENTION, DISORDERS IN; NEUROPSYCHOLOGICAL STUDIES.

George, L., and R. W. J. Neufeld. "Cognition and Symptomatology in Schizophrenia," *Schizophrenia Bulletin* 11 (1985): 264–285.

informed consent Before any medical procedure is performed, physicians must legally obtain the informed consent of the patient to perform the procedure. This involves an explanation of the purpose of the procedure, how it is done, and the potential risks involved for the patient that may result from the procedure. If the patient agrees, the consent is then given in writing. Although obtaining informed consent usually presents no problem in most people who are about to undergo a medical procedure or treatment (e.g., surgery), for individuals who are suffering from a psychotic disorder there are dilemmas. Can a person who is having problems remaining in contact with "reality" and is unable to think clearly and comprehend difficult information truly give informed consent?

This is an ethical and legal issue that is continually debated not only in the psychiatric profession but also in the legal system. For example, all the present medical treatments for the psychotic disorders (ANTIPSYCHOTIC DRUGS, electroconvulsive therapy, etc.) have side effects that effect either the immediate functioning of the individual (e.g., loss of memory after ECT) or his or her long-term health (e.g., TARDIVE DYSKINESIA caused by years of treatment with antipsychotic drugs). Most studies confirm the obvious: psychotic patients may say that they understand what is being explained to them, but in fact when they are given an objective examination afterward, they reveal that they did not. The "lack of informed consent" before administering treatment to patients is one of the most common causes of legal action against psychiatrists.

Cohen, R. J., and W. E. Mariano. *Legal Guidebook in Mental Health.* New York: Free Press, 1982.

Irwin, M., et al. "Psychotic Patients' Understanding of Informed Consent," *American Journal of Psychiatry* 142 (1985): 1,351–1,354.

inheritance, modes of See GENETIC TRANSMISSION.

input dysfunction hypothesis This is one of the early "cognitive" interpretations of the behavior of schizophrenics that was put forth to explain defi-

cits in attention. In 1964, British psychologist Peter Venables proposed that schizophrenics suffer from an "input dysfunction" in their ability to focus attention. Essentially, he postulated that the ability to focus attention was related to levels of internal "arousal" in the nervous system. It is a well-known fact that for most of us, when we are nervous about performing some activity (such as public speaking, a job interview, or taking a test), our ability to focus our attention may be affected. Venables proposes that in chronic nonparanoid schizophrenics there is a heightened arousal of the brain and nervous system (termed "cortical arousal"), which leads to an oversensitivity. Thus, when stimuli from the outside confronts the schizophrenic (even simple social interactions, for example), the person finds this to be "too intense," and he or she "shuts down." They may withdraw, become apathetic, and feel a restriction in their range of feelings (these are now called NEGATIVE SYMPTOMS). The field of attention is then narrowed in these people. In contrast, acute schizophrenics suffer from a lowered level of cortical arousal when compared to normals, resulting in an expansion of attention that is so broad that they feel that they cannot shut anything out of awareness. Everything hits them at once, and they report feeling "flooded."

Venable's "input dysfunction theory" is only one of the many theories put forth in the 1960s about deficits in the ability of schizophrenics to focus attention. An excellent summary of these detailed theories, and of the research on all areas of "schizophrenic cognition," can be found in a classic volume by Loren J. and Jean P. Chapman, *Disordered Thought in Schizophrenia.*

See also ATTENTION, DISORDERS IN.

Chapman, L. J., and J. P. Chapman. *Disordered Thought in Schizophrenia.* Englewood Cliffs, N.J.: Prentice Hall, 1973.

Venables, P. H. "Input Dysfunction in Schizophrenia." In *Progress in Experimental Personality Research.* Vol. 1, edited by B. A. Maher. New York: Academic Press, 1964.

insane A word derived from the Latin *insanus,* for "unsound (in mind)."

insanity Originally termed "insanity of mind," this refers to the state of being insane. Presently, it has only a legal meaning (not a psychiatric one) relating to the soundness of mind of a person when involved in actions that have legal consequences. More generally, it has come to mean that a psychosis was present when a person committed such a legally consequent act. Throughout most of the 18th and 19th centuries, "insanity" was a generic term for all mental illnesses and was used in the same way that we rely on the term "mental disorders" today. Until the latter part of the last century, "lunacy" was a synonym also used by the psychiatric and legal professions to refer to mental illness. In 19th-century France, the distinction made was between *aliéne* and *demi-fou,* roughly our present distinction between a "psychosis" and "neurosis." Although a vast literature has existed since the early 1800s on the legal issues raised by acts committed by mentally ill offenders ("insane" offenders), the word "insanity" was still being used in a quasi-psychiatric sense (at least in the United States) in the 1920s. In 1923 William Alanson White, the superintendent of St. Elizabeth's Hospital in Washington, D.C., and the foremost forensic psychiatrist in the country, argued forcefully in a book that the word "insanity" was entirely to be considered a legal term and had no medical meaning. White, as the president of the AMERICAN PSYCHIATRIC ASSOCIATION at that time, was also instrumental in changing the name of the *American Journal of Insanity* to the *American Journal of Psychiatry* in 1922.

See also FEIGNED INSANITY; M'NAUGHTEN RULES.

Hughes, J. S. *In the Law's Darkness: Isaac Ray and the Medical Jurisprudence of Insanity in Nineteenth-Century America.* New York: Oceana Publications, 1986.

Quen, J. M. "Isaac Ray and the Development of American Psychiatry and the Law," *Psychiatric Clinics of North America* 6 (1983): 527–537.

White, W. A. *Insanity and the Criminal Law.* New York: Macmillan, 1923.

insanity by contagion See FOLIE À DEUX.

insanity defense This is the legal defense in which a person may plead that he or she is not

guilty for committing an alleged crime by reason of insanity. It apparently dates back to 13th-century English constitutional law, when it was popularly known as the "wild beast test," i.e., if people act like wild beasts they cannot be held accountable for their actions. Over the centuries the concept that a person could not be responsible for criminal acts because he or she was *non compos mentis* (mentally incompetent), usually due to being an "idiot" since birth or a "lunatic" thereafter, has undergone many changes. Our modern concepts of the insanity defense date back to the famous trial of Daniel M'Naughten in England in 1843 in which he was acquitted of a criminal act on the grounds of insanity. The judges in that trial relied primarily on the opinions in a book by American physician Isaac RAY, *A Treatise on the Medical Jurisprudence of Insanity* (1838), in which he advocated many reforms in the then-standard criminal laws and in the incompetency and commitment laws. The famous M'NAUGHTEN RULES, which later resulted from the trial, became the established criterion of "knowing right from wrong" for judging insanity.

The insanity defense has been disputed in the 1980s due to the "not guilty by reason of insanity" verdict against John Hinckley Jr., who attempted to assassinate President Ronald Reagan. Some states have abolished it completely, and many others have instituted major modifications that restrict its use. Some states have passed legislation allowing a variation on the verdict in the form of "guilty but insane."

Lewinstein, S. R. "The Historical Development of Insanity as a Defense in Criminal Actions," *Journal of Forensic Science* 14 (1969): 275–293, 469–500.

Oppenheimer, H. *The Criminal Responsibility of Lunatics: A Study in Comparative Law.* London: Sweet & Maxwell, 1909.

insight Family members of persons with schizophrenia insist that the worst symptom of their loved one's disease is "lack of insight" or "poor insight" into their own illness and the need for medication to treat it. Lack of insight is one of the most common features of psychotic disorders. Many persons simply are not aware, or do not acknowledge, that they are "delusional" due to an illness that needs treatment. The very meaning of the term "insanity" since antiquity is bound to this notion. Throughout the history of PSYCHIATRY, lack of insight has been viewed as a willful act of opposition requiring that a person be "flogged into reason," or as an unconscious psychological defense mechanism (Freudian PSYCHOANALYSIS), an adaptive coping strategy to avoid a painful awareness of truths about oneself, or—the current view—as the result of a neurocognitive deficit caused by abnormal brain functioning. This last interpretation was perhaps first proposed by the noted British psychiatrist Aubrey Lewis (1900–75) in 1934.

It has only been relatively recently, since the early 1990s, that correlational and experimental studies of insight in PSYCHOSIS have been conducted. Poor insight or unawareness of illness is directly correlated with medication noncompliance, making this a vital issue of concern for the treatment of BIPOLAR DISORDER, SCHIZOPHRENIA, and the other psychotic disorders. In studies conducted by Xavier Amador and colleagues, lack of insight in schizophrenia has not been found to be highly correlated to the severity of symptoms but instead is related to the type of symptoms. Poor insight is associated with the presence of NEGATIVE SYMPTOMS. Lack of insight is far more common in schizophrenia than in any other psychotic disorder. It is speculated that this may tie in with BRAIN ABNORMALITIES IN SCHIZOPHRENIA associated with the frontal lobe. Second in severity to schizophrenia, however, is the lack of insight manifested by persons experiencing a MANIC EPISODE.

See also BIPOLAR DISORDER; NEUROPSYCHOLOGICAL STUDIES OF SCHIZOPHRENIA.

Amador, X. F. *I Am Not Sick I Don't Need Help! Helping the Seriously Mentally Ill Accept Treatment.* Peconic, New York: Vida Press, 2000.

Amador, X. F., and A. S. David. *Insight and Psychosis: Awareness of Illness in Schizophrenia and Related Disorders.* 2nd ed. Oxford: Oxford University Press, 2004.

Lewis, A. J. "The Psychopathology of Insight," *British Journal of Medical Psychology* 14 (1934): 332–348.

institutionalization It has long been observed that many people who are diagnosed with SCHIZO-

PHRENIA and spend most of their time in institutions tend to get worse as the years go on. Patients become apathetic, submissive, resigned, emotionally flat, and lose their sense of appropriateness in social behavior. But is this due to the disease process or is it due to the experience of being involuntarily (usually) hospitalized in an institution?

There have been many theories about the effects of hospitalization on the course of schizophrenia, and the ACUTE-CHRONIC DISTINCTION in schizophrenia research is partly designed to "control" for such institutionalization effects. For example, Erving GOFFMAN pictures the "inmates" of "total institutions" (mental hospitals, prisons, etc.) as undergoing a degrading devaluation of any sense of self-worth or identity, as being, essentially, brainwashed into the "role" of career mental patient. Others have viewed a hospitalized schizophrenic patient as holding a unique privilege—not responsible for his actions. Therefore, there may be every incentive to be sexually or aggressively inappropriate with others and to abdicate responsibility for self-care (feeding oneself, hygiene, etc.). Therefore, according to this view, patients are "rewarded" for acting "crazy" and manipulatable and remaining in the hospital—which may be more like a vacation resort than anything else. This latter position reflects the "impression management" theory of the effects of the institution on schizophrenics proposed by Braginsky and Braginsky in the late 1960s.

Controlled studies of the effects of institutionalization (chronicity) on schizophrenic patients have generally found that there is little evidence of intellectual deterioration that cannot be attributed to the disease process. Furthermore, the "zombie-like" appearance of some severe schizophrenics in institutions cannot entirely be attributed to the influence of ANTIPSYCHOTIC DRUGS, since these behaviors match clinical descriptions of schizophrenics in institutions before the advent of this form of treatment. Some early studies of these effects, as well as a summary of the above theories, can be found in a 1973 book by Chapman and Chapman. However, given the often emotionally intense, noisy, and frequently violent "holding-tank" environments of most large psychiatric institutions, it is difficult to see how living in such a setting could not have a negative effect on the mental health of the patient.

See also HOSPITALISM.

Braginsky, B. M., and D. D. Braginsky. *Methods of Madness: The Mental Hospital as a Last Resort.* New York: Holt, Rinehart & Winston, 1969.

Chapman, L. J., and J. P. Chapman. *Disordered Thought in Schizophrenia.* Englewood Cliffs, N.J.: Prentice Hall, 1973.

insulin coma (or shock) therapy This was the most popular—and most consistently effective—form of treatment for ACUTE SCHIZOPHRENIA from 1933 to the late 1950s, when treatment with ANTIPSYCHOTIC DRUGS became dominant. This technique was invented by an Austrian psychiatrist, Manfred Joshua Sakel (1906–1957), who was working at the Lichterfield Hospital in Berlin with patients recovering from morphine addiction, between 1927 and 1933. To diminish the agitation and psychotic symptoms due to withdrawal, Sakel began giving them experimental doses of insulin, a relatively new drug—isolated and used for the treatment of diabetes only in 1922—whose full range of effects were not yet well known. He discovered that the higher doses did indeed relieve the agitative withdrawal symptoms. When he found that high doses would induce a coma in patients—particularly in those patients who were also diagnosed with SCHIZOPHRENIA—he began to experiment in 1933 with induced insulin comas as a treatment for schizophrenia.

This therapy essentially regarded the induction of a hypoglycemic (abnormally low blood sugar) coma as a form of "shock" to the system of a schizophrenic patient. The modified procedure, which eventually came into use after Sakel published his results in 1934, required several months of treatments on an inpatient unit with a highly trained staff, since inattentiveness could lead to the death of the patient. In his book, *Interpretation of Schizophrenia* (1974), Silvano Arieti described the usual procedure for insulin treatment:

> It consists of administration of insulin in progressively larger doses. One starts initially with 10 to 15 units and increases the dosage until the patient

undergoes severe hypoglycemic shocks, which are characterized by comas and, less frequently, by epileptic seizures. The average coma producing dose is 100 to 150 units. The state of coma used to be terminated in the fourth or fifth hour by administration of an adequate amount of carbohydrates. Sugar was given orally if the patient was able to drink, or through tube feeding, or through an intravenous injection of a glucose solution. Now termination is obtained through the use of glucagon, in doses of 0.33 to 1 mg intravenously or intramuscularly. Small amounts generally awaken the patient, who is then able to drink a sugar solution. From a minimum of twenty to a maximum of eighty comas are generally produced, usually at a frequency of at least three times a week.

Sakel's theoretical explanation for why insulin coma therapy worked with acute schizophrenics was never considered adequate and was rejected by most. Nonetheless, the treatment seemed to be the first one that was consistently successful with people who were undergoing their very first episodes of psychosis. Chronic schizophrenics did not benefit at all from the treatment. Critics of this method have pointed out that most people undergoing their very first schizophrenic episodes respond to just about any form of treatment (or go into spontaneous remission anyway). Sakel immigrated to the United States in 1937, where insulin coma therapy became a prominent treatment for schizophrenia for the next two decades.

Sakel, M. "New Treatment of Schizophrenia," *American Journal of Psychiatry* 93 (1937), 829–841.

———. *The Pharmacological Shock Treatment of Schizophrenia.* New York: Nervous and Mental Diseases Monographs, 1936.

intermetamorphosis syndrome One of the rarest of the psychotic MISIDENTIFICATION SYNDROMES, the intermetamorphosis syndrome involves the delusional belief that certain persons or objects have been interchanged. Rather than insisting that related persons are alien "impostors" (as in CAPGRAS SYNDROME), or that these strangers are, in reality, known persecutors who are inhabiting their bodies (FREGOLI'S SYNDROME), this delusion involves the belief that known persons have been interchanged or replaced by other known persons. For example, such a delusional person may insist that one's mother has been replaced by one's first-grade teacher, and so on. In the very first published case of the intermetamorphosis syndrome—by French psychiatrists P. Courboun and J. Tusques in 1932—a depressed woman with paranoid delusions of persecution insisted that her new coat had been replaced by a shabby, older one; that her two young hens had been replaced by older ones; and that various women had been metamorphosed into men, and the young into old. As with the other misidentification syndromes, intermetamorphosis syndrome may be the result of an ORGANIC MENTAL DISORDER or be found within the delusional systems of those diagnosed with the paranoid subtype of schizophrenia.

Courbon, P., and J. Tusques. "L'illusion d'intermétamorphose et de charmes," *Annales Medico-Psychologique* 90 (1932): 401.

interpersonal functioning In any of the psychotic disorders, but particularly in SCHIZOPHRENIA, there is a marked deterioration in the ability to sustain relationships with other people. In fact, social withdrawal, emotional detachment, and occupational problems often mark the beginning of the first full onset of schizophrenia. Since psychotic disorders, by their very definition, involve a disturbed relationship with the external demands of reality, this invariably leads to problems with others. Sometimes people may find themselves becoming preoccupied with bizarre ideas and fantasies and will therefore shut out relationships. Other afflicted people may instead do the opposite: They may begin to cling to others, becoming almost child-like in their dependence on them. Or they may begin to intrude upon strangers in public, demanding their attention and becoming physically too close to them, obviously making the strangers uncomfortable. These "inappropriate behaviors"—as the phrase is so often used in the psychiatric institutions of today—are often quite troublesome for the family members of schizophrenics and people with other psychotic

disorders, and often leads the family finally to seek help for the individual.

introversion A term coined by Swiss psychiatrist and psychoanalyst C. G. JUNG for a pervasive "attitude" toward the world in which one's "psychic energy" or "libido" is primarily directed inward toward the self and the internal world of one's own fantasies. Jung believed all people fit along a continuum from introversion to extroversion with, usually, one or the other as a dominant mode of approaching the world. Although introverted people were often very individualistic and were supposed to have a close relationship with the unconscious, they were often uncomfortable in groups or in social situations. In its extreme pathological form, introversion was thought to describe the withdrawal of many schizophrenic patients from the external world.

involuntary commitment See COMMITMENT.

involutional psychosis Also referred to as "involutional melancholia," this is a severe depression that has developed into a psychosis. Agitation, delusions, mood-congruent hallucinations, and somatic preoccupations characterize this disorder. It is also characterized by a loss of interest in activities, early morning awakenings, worse depression in the morning, significant weight loss or anorexia, and psychomotor retardation or agitation.

ipsity disorder See SUBJECTIVE EXPERIENCE IN SCHIZOPHRENIA.

Ireland Along with parts of Croatia and northern Sweden, western Ireland has one of the highest prevalence rates of SCHIZOPHRENIA in the world. Proportionately, Ireland has three times more people diagnosed with schizophrenia in psychiatric hospitals and three times more first admissions for schizophrenia than England. The schizophrenia first-admission rate is even three times that of the United States. Western and southwestern Ireland, which contain the poorer counties, have the highest schizophrenia rates. In these areas there is a one in 25 chance that a person will be hospitalized for schizophrenia at some point in their lives, making these rates the highest in the world. The counties most affected are Mayo, Kerry, Sligo, Roscommon, Galway, Clare, Cork, and Waterford. Northern Ireland, which is part of the United Kingdom, has always maintained a lower rate of schizophrenia than in the south. Studies in the United States and Canada have consistently found that immigrants from Ireland have very high first-admission rates to psychiatric hospitals when compared to other ethnic groups.

Torrey, E. F. "Prevalence Studies of Schizophrenia," *British Journal of Psychiatry* 150 (1987): 598–608.

isolation Isolating agitated or violent people who are psychotic has long been a method of preventing them from harming themselves or others. It has been considered by many, over the centuries, as a more humane form of restraint than either physical or chemical methods. The famous "padded rooms" invented by the German physician Ferdinand AUTENREITH (1772–1835), which were lined with cork and rubber, were widely copied throughout European asylums in the 19th century as places to isolate patients. Many institutions today still have isolation or "time-out rooms" for their more active patients.

In his 1838 classic, *Des Maladies Mentale,* ESQUIROL devotes many pages to a discussion of "isolation," but he uses the word in much the same way we use "hospitalization" today. His use of the term was to denote the isolating of the mentally ill person from his family by commitment in an institution for the "insane." Esquirol felt that the novelty of the new situation would have therapeutic value: "The first effect of isolation is, to produce new sensations, to change and break up the chain of ideas, from which the patient could not free himself. New and unexpected impressions strike, arrest, and excite his attention, and render him more accessible to those councils, that ought to bring him back to reason." Yet, after listing more virtues of commitment to an

asylum for the insane, Esquirol also expresses some words of caution about "isolation":

> But, it may be said, that there are insane persons who are cured at home. This is true. These cures, however, are rare, and cannot impair the general rule. They prove only, that isolation, like all other curative means, ought always to be prescribed by a physician. I will say more, – that isolation has been fatal to some persons. And what shall we conclude from this? That we should recommend it with caution; especially when it is to be prolonged; and also, that it is the nature of the best and most useful things, not to be always exempt from inconveniences. To the wise, judicious and experienced physician does it belong, to foresee and prevent them.

A more commonly used term in the 20th century for isolating patients in separate rooms is *seclusion.*

Esquirol, J. E. D. *Mental Maladies, A Treatise on Insanity.* Translated by E. K. Hunt. 1838. Reprint, Philadelphia: Lea & Blanchard, 1845.

Israel Israel is a nation of immigrants. Since studies of SCHIZOPHRENIA prevalence rates in immigrant groups are subject to errors in statistical measurement because of the large number of variables to take into consideration, it has been difficult to determine reliable prevalence rates for schizophrenia in Israel.

Torrey, E. F. *Schizophrenia and Civilization.* New York: Jason Aronson, 1980.

Italy It has been noted at least since 1862, when W. Charles Hood published his book *Statistics of Insanity,* that the rates of "insanity" in southern European countries were much lower than those in northern European countries. In fact, Hood found Italy to have the lowest rates in all of Europe. Although no conclusive prevalence rates have been calculated for Italy, it has been noted that, well into the 20th century, Italy had low hospitalization rates for SCHIZOPHRENIA as compared to other countries. Also, it has been found that the first-admission hospitalization rates for Italian immigrants in England and the United States are far lower than for other ethnic groups.

Torrey, E. F. *Schizophrenia and Civilization.* New York: Jason Aronson, 1980.

J

Janet, Pierre (1859–1947) A French philosopher and psychiatrist whose research on the nature of the unconscious mind and on psychotherapy makes him one of the most important figures in the history of psychology and PSYCHIATRY. He was appointed to teach philosophy at the Liceum of Le Havre in 1881 (at the age of 22) and did volunteer work at the local asylum, where he conducted research for his doctoral dissertation. His studies of the highly hypnotizable hysterical female patients there led to observations about the workings of the unconscious mind, which he incorporated into his dissertation and his classic book *L'Automatisme Psychologique (Psychological Automatisms)* (1889). He is best remembered for his descriptions of the psychological process known as DISSOCIATION and how it worked in people under hypnosis, in those with hysteria, and in those with multiple personalities. About 1980, when multiple personality disorder once again began to attract serious interest, the work of Janet likewise found new students. Janet wrote voluminously (in French) on a wide range of psychiatric, psychological, and philosophical topics, but only a few of these works have ever been translated into English. There are many papers on paranoid schizophrenia that Janet produced in the 1930s and 1940s that still await translation.

Janet, P. *L'Automatisme psychologique.* Paris: Félix Alcan, 1889.

Perry, C., and J. R. Laurence. "Mental Processing Outside of Awareness: The Contributions of Freud and Janet." In *The Unconscious Reconsidered,* edited by K. S. Bowers and D. Meichenbaum. New York: John Wiley, 1984.

Van der Hart, O., and B. Friedman. "A Reader's Guide to Pierre Janet on Dissociation: A Neglected Intellectual Heritage," *Dissociation* 2 (1989): 3–16.

Japan Japan and Sweden are the two countries in which the best data on the prevalence rates for SCHIZOPHRENIA have been collected. In Japan, the prevalence rates for schizophrenia have ranged from 2.1 to 2.3 per 1,000. The lowest socioeconomic level in Japan has been found to have prevalence rates for psychotic disorders that are three to five times higher than the highest socioeconomic levels.

Torrey, E. F. *Schizophrenia and Civilization.* New York: Jason Aronson, 1980.

jealous type One of the variants of delusional disorder as listed in *DSM-IV* (1994). It is a persistent, usually "nonbizarre" DELUSION in which a person is convinced that his or her spouse is being unfaithful—without any rational grounds for the suspicion. As this delusion can take on psychotic dimensions, such a person may take extraordinary measures to intervene and dissolve the fantasized relationship. He or she may keep the spouse locked in the house or may restrict that person's activities in other ways. The person with the delusional jealousy may secretly follow the spouse or have that person followed. In some cases the person with the psychotic delusion may physically harm the spouse. Although the delusion itself is so out of line with reality that it renders the person psychotic at times, no other FORMAL THOUGHT DISORDER or other sign of a psychosis is present. In its pure form, this delusion of jealousy has been called the OTHELLO SYNDROME.

jealousy, delusional See DELUSIONAL JEALOUSY.

Jung, Carl Gustav (1875–1961) A Swiss psychiatrist and psychoanalyst who formulated his own unique "analytical psychology" (first called "complex psychology") after breaking with his mentor, Sigmund FREUD, in 1913. The son of a Protestant pastor in Basel, Switzerland, the young Jung originally wanted to become an archaeologist. After a vividly symbolic dream, he decided instead to pursue medicine, which was an offshoot of his fascination with the natural sciences. During his medical school years (specifically, in 1896), Jung became interested in the unusual trances and hypnotic phenomena of his 15-year-old cousin, who was a medium. In an attempt to analyze her behavior, he read widely in philosophy and spiritualism. In 1902, he based his doctoral dissertation on this work with her. In 1900, during his final examinations, he came across a PSYCHIATRY textbook written by German psychiatrist and neurologist Richard von Krafft-Ebing that convinced him he should study psychiatry—commonly regarded at the time as an "inferior" medical discipline. Jung passed his medical examinations and won a position at the BURGHÖLZI HOSPITAL under the direction of Eugen BLEULER in 1900.

From the beginning, Jung was interested in pursuing the psychological and symbolic meaning behind the psychotic disorders and not just their classification, which was the traditional occupation of psychiatry in those days. As Jung tells it in a lecture given in 1925:

> I told nobody that I intended to work out the unconscious phenomena of the psychoses, but that was my determination. I wanted to catch the intruders in the mind—the intruders that make people laugh when they should not laugh, and cry when they should not cry.

Jung remained at the Burghölzi for nine years. During this time he developed a worldwide scientific reputation for his famous "word-association test" experiments and for his 1907 monograph on the psychological processes involved in dementia praecox (*Über die Psychologie der Dementia Praeçox*). It was likewise during these years that Bleuler was developing his ideas on "schizophrenia" (a term Bleuler first used in print in 1908), and Bleuler acknowledges the contributions of his assistant Jung in the preface to his famous book, *Dementia Praecox, Or the Group of Schizophrenias* (1911). Jung's later psychology was based largely on the dissociative experiences of his mediumistic cousin and his nine years of daily clinical work with institutionalized psychotic patients. He was particularly interested in the story-motifs and structures of schizophrenic hallucinations and delusions and how they seemed to correspond to the myths and fairy tales of centuries past. These organizing structural dominants of all psychological life, conscious and unconscious, he called "archetypes." In contrast, Freud (whom Jung was associated with from 1907 to 1913) based his theories of the structure and dynamics of the psyche on the neurotic patients he saw in the Viennese consulting room of his home and had only minimal contact with institutionalized patients.

Jung is famous for proposing that a "toxin" may be the actual cause of many of the seriously debilitating psychological symptoms of SCHIZOPHRENIA, although this toxin was first produced by the intense emotions of a psychological disturbance (i.e., a complex). He is also remembered for being perhaps the first to conduct individual psychotherapy with institutionalized schizophrenics; in his descriptions of his pre-psychoanalytic-period cases, he revealed a psychoeducational and rehabilitative approach rather than an insight-oriented one—an approach that is recommended for use with schizophrenics today. Although in his writings Jung sometimes refers to the successful treatment of "dementia praecox" in some patients, he later admitted that these were BORDERLINE CASES that did not develop into the full picture of this disorder. In a September 24, 1926, letter to an American psychiatrist who had asked about Jung's successful treatment of dementia praecox, Jung admits the limitations of his success:

> I suppose the news you heard of my successes in the treatment of Dementia praecox is greatly exaggerated. As a matter of fact I only treated a limited number of cases, and these were all what one might call in a liquid condition, that is, not yet congealed. I avoid the treatment of such cases as much as possible. It is true they can be treated,

> and even with the most obvious success, but such a success costs almost your own life. You have to make the most stupendous effort to reintegrate the dissociated psychic entities, and it is by no means a neat and simple technique which you can apply, but a creative effort with a vast knowledge of the unconscious mind.

Even in the face of the growing evidence for the organic basis of schizophrenia, until the end of his life Jung maintained that it may have an equally important psychological cause. His final statement on the issue was a letter sent to the chairman of a Symposium on Chemical Concepts of Psychosis (held in September 1957), clarifying his views on the issue; it was published in 1958. Jung asserts that the cause of schizophrenia is a "dual one: namely, up to a certain point psychology is indispensable in explaining the nature and the causes of the initial emotions which give rise to metabolic alterations. These emotions seem to be accompanied by chemical processes that cause specific temporary or chronic disturbances or lesions."

See also ABAISSEMENT DU NIVEAU MENTAL; BIOCHEMICAL THEORIES OF SCHIZOPHRENIA; BIBLIOTHERAPY; COMPLEX; DISSOCIATION.

Jung, C. G. *Letters. 1:1906–1950.* Princeton, N.J.: Princeton University Press, 1973.

———. *The Collected Works of C. G. Jung.* 20 vols. Princeton, N.J.: Princeton University Press, 1953–1979.

———. *Analytical Psychology: Notes of the Seminar Given in 1925.* Princeton, N.J.: Princeton University Press, 1989.

K

Kahlbaum, Karl Ludwig (1828–1899) In 1863 German psychiatrist Karl Kahlbaum of Prussia published his Habilitation (the equivalent of a second doctoral dissertation in Germany, necessary for becoming a university professor), *Die Gruppirung der psychischen Krankheiten* (*The Classification of Psychiatric Diseases*). In this book, Kahlbaum described a class of progressively degenerating psychotic disorders that he grouped under the term *Vesania typica* (typical insanity). This example, and numerous others in his textbook, indicated Kahlbaum's distate for those advocating that all the insanities were really manifestations of one underlying insanity (a concept termed the *EINHEITSPSYCHOSE* or "unitary psychosis"). In 1866 Kahlbaum became the director of a private psychiatric clinic in Goerlitz, Prussia, a small town near Dresden. He was accompanied by his younger assistant, Ewald Hecker (1843–1909), and together they conducted a series of research studies on young psychotic patients that would eventuate in a major influence on the development of modern psychiatry. Kahlbaum and Hecker were the first to describe and name such syndromes as dysthymia, cyclothymia, PARANOIA, CATATONIA and HEBEPHRENIA. These are just the diagnostic labels that survived into history. In an attempt to overthrow the confusion of the past, including the inclination of physicians since pagan antiquity to group all mental disorders as forms of either "MANIA" or "MELANCHOLIA" (terms that were not distilled down to their present meanings until the period between 1850 and 1900), Kahlbaum made the mistake of coining new names for just about every syndrome. Though acknowledged as a major psychiatric thinker in the 19th century, perhaps second only to Emil KRAEPELIN, his classification system was too novel and idiosyncratic to be widely adopted, and thus Kahlbaum receded into the shadows of history.

Perhaps their most lasting contribution to psychiatry was the introduction of the "clinical method" from medicine to the study of mental diseases, a method which is now known as psychopathology. Other than Benedict-Augustin MOREL's claims about mental illness in his DEGENERATION THEORY, the element of time had largely been missing from definitions of mental disorders. Psychiatrists made pronouncements about prognosis that were not based on careful observations of the changing symptoms of patients over time. MAD-DOCTORS, ALIENISTS, and other physicians who wrote about the insane arbitrarily invented names for insanities and described their characteristic signs and symptoms based on a short-term, cross-sectional observation period of their lunatic patients. When the element of time was added to the concept of diagnosis, a diagnosis became more than just a description of a collection of symptoms: diagnosis now also defined prognosis (course and outcome). An additional feature of the clinical method was that the characteristic symptoms that define syndromes should be described without any prior assumption of brain pathology (although such links could be made later as scientific knowledge progressed). Karl Kahlbaum first made his appeal for the adoption of the clinical method in PSYCHIATRY in his 1874 book on catatonia. Without Kahlbaum and Hecker there would be no dementia praecox.

See also DEMENTIA PRAECOX; NOSOLOGY.

Kahlbaum, K. *Die Gruppierung der psychischen Krankheiten und die Eintheilung der Seelenstorungen.* Danzig: 1863.

———. "The Relationships of the New Groupings to Old Classification and to a General Pathology of Mental Disorder," *History of Psychiatry* 7 (1999): 167–181.

Lanczik, M. "Karl Ludwig Kahlbaum and the Emergence of Psychopathological and Nosological Research in German Psychiatry," *History of Psychiatry* 3 (1992): 53–58.

Kallman, Franz J. (1897–1965) Kallman was a German-Jewish psychiatrist and researcher who, from 1928, directed neuropathology laboratories for psychiatric hospitals in Berlin. In 1936 he immigrated to the United States and brought his research on the genetics of MENTAL DISORDERS with him. A translated version of his manuscript was published in 1938, and it is considered by many contemporary scholars to be the first true starting point for the GENETICS STUDIES of schizophrenia. He also later became interested in the genetics of manic-depressive psychosis.

Kallman, F. J. *The Genetics of Schizophrenia.* New York: J. S. Augustin, 1938.

Kandinsky-Clérambault syndrome This is the type of delusional experience in which a person feels his or her mind is being controlled or influenced in some way by outside forces. It is a commonly reported experience in people diagnosed with SCHIZOPHRENIA. It was first described in 1890 by Viktor Chrisanfovich Kandinsky (1825–89) and Gaétan Gaitian de Clérambault (1872–1934).

Kanner, Leo (1894–1981) An Austrian-born psychiatrist who immigrated to the United States and became the "father of child psychiatry." He did research on INFANTILE AUTISM and CHILDHOOD SCHIZOPHRENIA, which he thought, based on psychoanalytic theory, were caused by disturbances in early mother and child relationships. Kanner separated infantile autism from childhood schizophrenia in 1943, believing them to be two separate types of childhood disorder. Because of his pioneering work in this area, infantile autism is also called Kanner's syndrome.

Kanner, L. *Child Psychiatry.* Springfield, Ill.: Charles Thomas, 1942.

Kanner's syndrome See AUTISM, INFANTILE.

karyotype This is a chromosome that has been stained with a special substance and prepared so that it can be identified. Only since the early 1960s, when it was developed, has the process of karyotyping chromosomes made it possible to identify and study specific chromosomes.

katatonia See CATATONIA.

Kirkbride, Thomas Story (1809–1883) An American physician from Philadelphia and one of the original 13 founders of the AMERICAN PSYCHIATRIC ASSOCIATION. Kirkbride was the superintendent of the psychiatric section of the Pennsylvania Hospital for more than four decades (from 1840 until his death)—so long, in fact, that the institution became known by Philadelphia locals as simply "Kirkbride's." He became interested in the effects on the patients of the institutional environment's construction and of staff management styles; he firmly believed that, by designing and building pragmatic institutions, mental illness could be cured. His 1847 textbook on this issue (second edition, 1880), considered one of the most important American psychiatric textbooks of the 19th century, is divided into two primary parts: the first concerning the physical details of the ideal institution and the second detailing administrative procedures.

Kirkbride, T. *On the Construction, Organization, and General Arrangements of Hospitals for the Insane, with some Remarks on Insanity and its Treatment.* Philadelphia: Blakiston, 1880.
Tomes, N. *A Generous Confidence: Thomas Story Kirkbride and the Art of Asylum Keeping, 1840–1883.* Cambridge: Cambridge University Press, 1984.

Kitsune-Tsuki psychosis This is an unusual psychotic disorder native to Japan in which a person maintains the DELUSION that he or she has been possessed by a fox. Kitsune-Tsuki psychosis is an

example of a "culture-bound syndrome." A European variation of this is LYCANTHROPY, in which a person believes he or she has been transformed into a wolf. Some psychiatric authorities on this syndrome have likened it to an atypical psychotic disorder marked by the "fox" delusion, and others have noted that it is similar to a POSSESSION SYNDROME.

Furukawa, F., and M. Bourgeois. "Délires de possession par le renard au Japon (ou délire de Kitsune-Tsuke)," *Annales Médico-Psychologiques* 142 (1984): 677–687.

Korsakov's psychosis More commonly known as Korsakov's syndrome, this syndrome of amnesia is due to the deficiency of thiamine in the body caused by chronic alcoholism. In *DSM-IV* (1994) it is called alcohol amnestic disorder. Once it appears, this syndrome follows a chronic course, and impairment may be so severe as to require lifelong custodial care. When thiamine is administered during a detoxification process before the syndrome is evident, it does not develop. Prior to the discovery that thiamine could reverse some of the other neurological signs that precede the amnesia of this syndrome, it routinely developed into its most severe forms. The syndrome is named after Sergei Sergeievich Korsakov (1853–1900), who was largely responsible for founding the discipline of psychiatry in Russia. He first described this syndrome in 1887 but called it *cerebropathia psychica toxemica*.

Kraepelin, Emil (1856–1926) Emil Kraepelin is now universally recognized as the most important figure in the history of psychiatry in the 20th century. Certainly he is the most important figure in the history of research on schizophrenia and the other psychotic disorders. Kraepelin was a German neurologist, psychiatrist, professor, and experimental researcher who understood (a) that mental disorders were caused by biological processes affecting the brain and (b) that heredity (genetics) played a significant role in the origins and development of DEMENTIA PRAECOX (SCHIZOPHRENIA). Kraepelin's biological outlook and his diagnostic classification of mental disorders remain the foundation of our understanding of schizophrenia today. Contemporary biological psychiatry and the diagnostic criteria for the psychotic disorders found in *ICD-10* (1992) and *DSM-IV* (1994) are thoroughly Kraepelinian.

Biographical history Kraepelin was described by one observer in 1916 as "a small stocky man with yellowish skin and a full, dark beard." He was an intense, driven man who characterized himself as having a "firm and persevering will." He was first and foremost a scientist and had no religious creed, although he was tolerant of other faiths. Like many German scientists in the 19th and early 20th centuries, he had a fascination with the religions of India and an attraction for pantheism. Kraepelin was a well-known activist with strong political views (monarchist and German nationalist, anti-socialist) and strong social views on a variety of issues (criminality, alcoholism, syphilis, mental illness, eugenics). Kraepelin also strongly opposed the anti-hereditarian, anti-laboratory science views of psychoanalysts Sigmund FREUD and Carl JUNG. Because of his utter disregard for the pseudoscience of psychoanalysis, throughout most of the 20th century Kraepelin has not been treated kindly by historians of psychiatry, as many of them were psychoanalytically trained American psychiatrists and uncritical disciples of Sigmund Freud. It is only now, with psychiatry's return to its biological and experimental roots, that Kraepelin is receiving the recognition that is his due.

Kraepelin's hereditary roots were in the Mecklenberg region of Germany. After earning his medical degree, Kraepelin taught medicine in the Baltic region of the Russian Empire at the university in Dorpat from 1866 to 1891. At Dorpat, Kraepelin conducted research on the effects of drugs on intellectual capacity and motor functions, examining the psychological effects of tea, alcohol, and other drugs. It was during this time that Kraepelin began his lifelong interest in conducting psychological experimentation on both normal and psychiatric populations, often using variations of the word-association test. During his tenure in Dorpat, Kraepelin wrote and published the very first edition of his famous textbook, *Psychiatrie* (1883),

which would undergo multiple revisions as he defined his ideas until the four-volume eighth and final edition (1909–15).

After sharpening his expertise in neurological and psychiatric problems, he moved to the University of Heidelberg, Germany, in 1891 and occupied himself with both clinical and research duties. Horrified by high percentage of alcoholism-related admissions to the psychiatric clinic at the university, in 1895 Kraepelin himself became abstinent and remained so for the rest of his life. Like August FOREL, Eugen BLEULER and many other major figures in medicine at the end of the 1800s, Kraepelin became an activist in the anti-alcohol movement. It was believed that chronic alcoholism caused hereditary DEGENERATION and therefore future generations would be permanently damaged (biologically) by the "sins of the fathers [and mothers]." During his tenure in Heidelberg, Kraepelin continued the psychological experiments he had learned in Leipzig from his beloved master Wilhelm WUNDT (1832–1920) and began the serious neuropathological search for the causes of psychotic disorders with colleagues Franz NISSL (1860–1919) and Alois ALZHEIMER.

In 1903 Kraepelin moved to Munich and became director of the Institute of Hygiene at the University of Munich. Alzheimer accompanied him. Together they continued their brain dissections and neurohistological research to find the cause of neurodegenerative and psychotic disorders. Besides his continuing efforts to refine his classification system of mental disorders, which was quickly becoming the world standard, Kraepelin continued the neuropathological, psychological, and serological research on the psychotic disorders and continued to compile statistics on the familial inheritance of mental disorders. His anthropological interests led him to do fieldwork in such places as India and Java. He visited the United States twice, in 1908 and 1925, both times as a consultant to the wealthy McCormick family of Chicago, who wanted his assessment of Stanley McCormick (1874–1947). On both occasions Kraepelin found him to be suffering from the catatonic subtype of dementia praecox. Kraepelin remained in Munich until his death at age 70 in 1926, although in his later years he often vacationed at a villa he and his wife owned in Italy.

Dementia praecox and manic-depressive psychosis Kraepelin first described and coined the terms for the two major FUNCTIONAL PSYCHOSES in successive revisions of his textbook: DEMENTIA PRAECOX was first discussed in the fourth edition (1893), and manic-depressive psychosis in the sixth edition (1899). He separated the two based on their outcomes: manic-depressive psychosis had a relatively good outcome, with many patients experiencing remissions; dementia praecox had a poor prognosis, following a chronic, degenerating course. In his fifth edition he puts forth the idea that it is a brain disease that is perhaps metabolic in origin, one in which the brain "autointoxicates" itself.

Kraepelin's influence on the practice of psychiatry was felt everywhere, as his classification system helped to unify the profession. In his memoirs, William Alanson White, one of the major figures in American psychiatry in the first third of the 20th century, tells of the confusing state of affairs in psychiatry in the 1890s prior to Kraepelin's work:

> Of course we systematically labeled each patient according to the diagnosis that we thought best fitted him, but I am quite sure that nobody felt that he had accomplished much in so doing. The fact that whenever a physician from another institution visited the hospital one of the first questions was "What classification do you use?" indicates to my mind the very serious discontent with this state of affairs . . . When, therefore, Kraepelin's classification, based upon a new descriptive symptomatology and the course and outcome of the disease process, came to be known, it was hailed everywhere with joy. Here was a new lease on life for all of us, a new interest in psychiatry, new points of view. The whole subject was revivified and made more alive, and the patients correspondingly became more interesting.

German Research Institute for Psychiatry As early as 1911 Kraepelin had official support from the Kaiser-Wilhelm Gesellschaft for his vision of a single, multidisciplinary institute where laboratory research could be conducted to find the causes and cures of mental illness. Funds were raised through donations by two Americans of German descent, Dr.

James Loeb and Alfred Heinsheimer, and in April 1918 the Deutsche Forschungsanstalt fuer Psychiatrie, or German Research Institute for Psychiatry, was officially opened within one of the buildings of the Munich University Psychiatric Clinic. With the end of World War I in November, riots on the streets of Munich, and a socialist revolution in Bavaria in 1919, the German economy collapsed. The donated money for the institute quickly evaporated during a period of extraordinary inflation. Kraepelin's institute survived from 1920 until 1927 on yearly donations from Dr. Loeb. In the last years of his life much of Kraepelin's energy was taken up with the search for funds. Finally, in 1927, the year after Kraepelin's death, a sizable grant from the Rockefeller Foundation allowed for the construction of a four-story-high building "with decorations in bright red and green" (according to a report in a Cologne newspaper) near the Schwabing Hospital in Munich. On June 13, 1928, the dedication ceremony to mark the opening of the Forschungsanstalt fuer Psychiatrie, Kaiser-Wilhelm-Institut took place. A marble bust of the late Kraepelin (a gift of Dr. Loeb) was placed in the lobby near the grand staircase. The street outside the institute was named after Kraepelin, as it still is today. However, the building itself was destroyed by American bombs during World War II, but the site on *Kraepelinstrasse* is now the home of the Max Planck Institute for Psychiatry.

During the years that Kraepelin was alive, the institute could manage only four divisions: laboratories for anatomy, serology, and psychology, and a fourth division for the collection of statistics on the hereditary transmission of dementia praecox and other mental disorders. Upon rededication in 1928, the institute housed six independent research divisions under one roof, adding a clinic archives division to keep track of the patients in the psychiatric wards at the nearby Schwabing Hospital, and a chemistry division.

The NATIONAL INSTITUTE OF MENTAL HEALTH (NIMH) in the United States was directly modeled on Kraepelin's institute when the National Institutes of Health was created after World War II. NIMH is now where most of the world's cutting-edge research on the biological causes of schizophrenia takes place. Kraepelin's vision lives on.

Brink, L., and S. E. Jelliffe. "Emil Kraepelin—Psychiatrist and Poet," *Journal of Nervous and Mental Diseases* 77 (1933): 277–288.

Engstrom, E. "Emil Kraepelin: Psychiatry and Public Affairs in Wilhelmine Germany," *History of Psychiatry* 2 (1991): 111–132.

Kraepelin, E. *Memoirs.* Berlin: Springer-Verlag, 1987.

———. *One Hundred Years of Psychiatry.* New York: Philosophical Library, 1962; first published, 1917.

———. "The Manifestations of Insanity (1920)." Translated by Dominic Beer. *History of Psychiatry* 3 (1992): 509–529.

Noll, R. "Styles of Psychiatric Practice, 1906–1925: Clinical Evaluations of the Same Patient by James Jackson Putnam, Adolf Meyer, August Hoch, Emil Kraepelin, and Smith Ely Jelliffe," *History of Psychiatry* 10 (1999): 145–189.

Rüdin, E. R. "Historical Record. Forschungsanstalt für Psychiatrie, Munich, (Institute for Psychiatric Research), 1925–1928," (1928). Unpublished manuscript in the files of the Rockefeller Archives Center, New Tarrytown, New York.

White, W. A. *William Alanson White: The Autobiography of a Purpose.* Garden City, N.Y.: Doubleday, 1938.

L

lactation psychoses It was commonly believed by the ancients and by physicians well into the 1800s that the severe mental disorders suffered by women shortly preceding and especially directly following childbirth were related to the production (or lack of production) of milk. It had been thought for centuries that milk was diverted from the breasts to other areas of the body, especially the brain, causing these MENTAL DISORDERS. This process was sometimes called lacteal metastasis. J. E. D. ESQUIROL found these disorders to be so common that he devoted an entire chapter to them in his *Des Maladies Mentales* (1838), entitled "Mental Alienation of Those Recently Confined, and of Nursing Women." "Confinement" or "to be confined" is an 18th-century term for the period during which a woman was "confined" to her "child-bed" before and after giving birth. "The number of women who become insane after confinement, and during or after lactation, is much more considerable than commonly supposed," according to Esquirol. He noted that he was not talking about the much more common "milk fever," the transient delirium that takes place after confinement, but instead the more serious postpartum depressions and psychotic episodes that can occur.

Esquirol, after observations made during autopsies, asserted that no milk was ever found in the brain tissue of deceased women who suffered from postpartum psychoses. Although it was commonly observed that the suppression or diminution of milk production after birth was sometimes associated with the onset of the psychosis, Esquirol denied that the cause was related to milk being diverted to the brain. "Finally, it would be strange to find milk in the brain after confinement or lactation, when there was suppression of this secretion, as to find menstrual blood in the cavity of the cranium, in females who have become insane after the suppression of the menses." Esquirol admitted, however, that many of these women responded well to treatment, particularly when it was designed to reestablish lactation or menstruation following childbirth. He recommended enemas, emetics, warm hip-baths, and, in the more extreme cases, to restore menstruation, the application of leeches to the vulva and cupping glasses to the thighs.

By the 20th century, however, the idea that psychoses occurring in women at about the time of birth were related to the lack of production of milk had been disregarded. Instead, the stress of pregnancy, and childbirth in particular, was thought to exacerbate an already existing underlying mental disorder such as schizophrenia or manic-depressive psychosis. This is the argument made by Eugen BLEULER in the fourth edition (1923) of his famous textbook *Lehrbuch der Psychiatrie* (first edition, 1916), in the section "Causes of Mental Diseases" in the English translation of 1924. Bleuler thus concludes: "The *lactation psychoses* have little practical significance."

See also BLEEDING; POSTPARTUM PSYCHOSIS; PUERPERAL INSANITY.

Bleuler, E. *Textbook of Psychiatry.* 4th ed. Translated by A. A. Brill. 1916. Reprint, New York: Macmillan, 1924.

Esquirol, J. E. D. *Mental Maladies: A Treatise on Insanity.* Translated by E. K. Hunt. 1838. Reprint, Philadelphia: Lea & Blakiston, 1845.

Laing, Ronald David (1927–1989) One of the most controversial psychiatrists of the 20th century, R. D. Laing, is best remembered as a critic of the profession of psychiatry and a strong advocate of the often-neglected human rights of psychotic

people. He was born and educated in Glasgow, Scotland, where he trained as a physician and a psychiatrist and served at the Glasgow Royal Mental Hospital. In 1957 he joined the famous Tavistock Clinic in London. However, by this time he had developed serious doubts about the profession of psychiatry. He felt there was a large gap between physicians and patients, and the meaning of people's lives was lost in dehumanizing clinical terms that placed them in an inferior position. Laing believed that society gave psychiatrists special powers over others that often led to abuse. His many books, starting with *The Divided Self* (1960), are thoughtful and provocative critiques of the present state of psychiatry. Beginning in June 1965 at Kingsley Hall, a community center in London, Laing and his colleagues began an experiment in which they lived with severely disturbed psychotics who would otherwise be locked up in mental institutions. There was no staff per se, no locked doors, no psychiatric treatment—just a group of people living together and trying to come to terms with one another. The atmosphere was described as being more like a "hippie commune" than a mental hospital ward. The Philadelphia Association, as this charitable organization was called, ended its experimental program at Kingsley Hall in May 1970.

Laing was often more criticized than applauded during his lifetime. His views were often regarded as mystical or downright dangerous for schizophrenics and others who, it was felt, might be led astray by Laing's antimedical, overly optimistic view of psychosis and its successful outcome. However, many of those sympathetic to his work introduced his radical ideas into practice and were collectively known as the "anti-psychiatry movement," a term that Laing says in his 1985 memories he never approved of. It was, however, invented by a colleague of Laing's, psychiatrist David Cooper, who set up an "anti-psychiatry ward" in a large mental hospital near London in 1962. Laing, however, was obviously sympathetic to the thesis of antipsychiatry, namely, that the role of psychiatry is to exclude and repress those persons that society wants excluded and repressed.

Boyers, R., and R. Orrill, eds. *R. D. Laing and Anti-Psychiatry.* New York: Harper & Row, 1971.
Cooper, D. *Psychiatry and Anti-Psychiatry.* London: Tavistock Publications, 1967.
Laing, R. D. *Wisdom, Madness, and Folly: The Making of a Psychiatrist.* New York: McGraw-Hill, 1985.

language abnormalities in schizophrenia One of the most distinctive signs of schizophrenia is a disturbance in language. Odd phrasing, loosening of associations, bizarre content of speech and the use of nonexistent words ("word salad") can all mark the person suffering from schizophrenia. To the extent that our spoken language reflects our thought processes, most studies of schizophrenic language are incorporated in research on FORMAL THOUGHT DISORDER, usually in the form of COGNITIVE STUDIES OF SCHIZOPHRENIA. One of the first books to appear on the subject of language abnormalities in schizophrenia was edited by J. S. Kasanin and published in 1944. Although abnormalities in language occur as a result of many mental disorders, studies by researcher Nancy Andreasen and colleagues at the University of Iowa suggest that alogia, the diminished capacity to think or express thoughts (also known as the NEGATIVE SYMPTOM of schizophrenia called poverty of speech), may be an especially important identifying indicator of schizophrenia and may also point to a poor prognosis. Because language ability is largely governed by the left hemisphere of the brain, there has been much speculation that schizophrenia may be the result of abnormalities in this area of the brain.

See also BRAIN ABNORMALITIES IN SCHIZOPHRENIA; LATERALITY AND SCHIZOPHRENIA.

Andreasen, N. C., R. E. Hoffman, and W. M. Grove. "Language Abnormalities in Schizophrenia." In *New Perspectives in Schizophrenia,* edited by M. N. Menuck and M. V. Seeman. New York: Macmillan, 1985.
Kasanin, J. S., ed. *Language and Thought in Schizophrenia.* Berkeley: University of California Press, 1944.

Lasègue's disease A rarely used 19th-century term for "persecution mania," the paranoid delusion that one is being deliberately persecuted by others when in fact there is no evidence to support this. It was initially described by Ernest Charles

Lasègue (1816–83) in 1852. Lasègue is more commonly remembered, however, for an article he published with J. P. J. FALRET in 1877 that identified another psychotic delusional syndrome—FOLIE À DEUX.

lashing See FLOGGING.

latent psychosis This terms refers to the idea that a person has an underlying psychotic process that can break out into a full overt psychosis under the right circumstances. References to latent psychoses are found in the older psychiatric literature, but the idea is now generally subsumed under such terms as the *incipient* or *prodromal phases* of a psychotic disorder, particularly schizophrenia.

latent schizophrenia This term refers to people who exhibit odd or eccentric behavior, perhaps even with transient hallucinations and delusions, but who never develop the full symptomatology of schizophrenia. In *DSM-IV-TR* (2000), latent schizophrenia is called SCHIZOTYPAL PERSONALITY DISORDER—one of the "schizophrenia spectrum" disorders (including, for example, SCHIZOID PERSONALITY DISORDER and SCHIZOPHRENIFORM DISORDER) that seem to be related in some way to schizophrenia. "Latent schizophrenia" is still a valid diagnostic category in *ICD-10* (1992), but it is not recommended for general use. *ICD-9* suggested that this label replace such previously used terms as *latent schizophrenic reaction, borderline schizophrenia, prepsychotic schizophrenia, prodromal schizophrenia, pseudoneurotic schizophrenia,* and *pseudopsychopathic schizophrenia.* The pre-1980 psychiatric literature speaks of "prepsychotic symptoms," which are summarized in a review by Docherty et al. (1978).

Eugen BLEULER, who coined and first used the term *schizophrenia* in a publication in 1908, also refers to "latent schizophrenia" for the first time in this same seminal classic. In his 1911 classic, *Dementia Praecox, Or the Group of Schizophrenias,* Bleuler notes in the introduction to his discussion of the "symptomatology" of schizophrenia that the symptoms can only be described when defining the clear-cut cases of the disorder and that "the milder cases, latent schizophrenics with far less manifest symptoms, are many times more common than the overt, manifest cases." He later emphasizes just how important the "subgroup" of schizophrenia known as latent schizophrenia is when compared with the other "schizophrenias":

> There is also a latent schizophrenia, and I am convinced that this is the most frequent form, although admittedly these people hardly ever come for treatment. It is not necessary to give a detailed description of the various manifestations of latent schizophrenia. In this form, we can see in *nuce* all the symptoms and all the combinations of symptoms which are present in the manifest types of the disease. Irritable, odd, moody, withdrawn or exaggeratedly punctual people arouse, among other things, the suspicion of being schizophrenic.

People with latent schizophrenia may very well be those who are genetically predisposed for developing schizophrenia but never manifest the full symptoms of the disorder.

See also BORDERLINE CASES; BORDERLINE SCHIZOPHRENIA; INCOMPLETE PENETRANCE.

Bleuler, E. *Dementia Praecox, Or the Group of Schizophrenias.* Translated by Joseph Zinkin. 1911. Reprint, New York: International Universities Press, 1950.

———. "Die Prognose der Dementia Praecox—Schizophreniegruppe," *Allgemeine Zeitschrift für Psychiatrie* 65 (1908): 436–464.

Docherty, J. P., et al. "Stages of Onset of Schizophrenic Psychosis," *American Journal of Psychiatry* 135 (1978): 420–426.

late-onset schizophrenia Since the time of Emil KRAEPELIN, who relied on Ewald Hecker's description of the youthful age of onset of HEBEPHRENIA to help define his concept of DEMENTIA PRAECOX, schizophrenia has often been regarded as a disease that shows its first serious signs in late adolescence or early adulthood. Cases of persons developing schizophrenia after the age of 40, for

example, were considered relatively uncommon. However, a comprehensive review of the research on this issue by M. J. Harris and D. V. Jeste suggested that late-onset schizophrenia may be more common than originally thought. Although they were careful to point out the possible faults in the more than 30 studies (mainly from Europe) they review, they nonetheless found that persons who develop late-onset schizophrenia (that is, after age 40) have the following characteristics: (1) they tend to have predominant paranoid symptoms, (2) 66 to 87 percent are female, (3) more instances of hearing loss or eye disease seem to occur among this group, (4) prior to the full outbreak of the active phase of schizophrenia, these persons tend to have personalities that have strong "paranoid" or "schizoid" traits, (5) the disease tends to follow a chronic course, and (6) there is some alleviation of symptoms with ANTIPSYCHOTIC DRUGS.

Harris, M. J., and D. V. Jeste. "Late-Onset Schizophrenia: An Overview," *Schizophrenia Bulletin* 14 (1988): 39–55.

laterality and schizophrenia Most people are familiar with the media versions of the popular-psychology interpretations of "right brain" versus "left brain" functioning. It is roughly true that the left hemisphere of the brain is responsible for performing the more analytic, sequential, verbal, and temporal sequencing functions, whereas the right hemisphere tends to serve more visual and spatial functions. The term *laterality* refers to the scientific evidence for this phenomenon. Since the 1960s, researchers have found that the two hemispheres of the human brain are not identical in many areas: Their respective structures (morphology) and biochemistry (proportions of various neurotransmitters) are not alike, and the two sides of the brain seem to serve different psychological functions. Laterality is found not only in humans but also in other primates and mammals (such as rats).

Since Paul Broca (1824–80) published his famous report in 1861 of the autopsy of a male patient from the BICÊTRE asylum in Paris that localized the speech center of humans in the left hemisphere (now called "Broca's area"), language ability has commonly been assumed to be in this area of the brain. Furthermore, because approximately 93 percent of humans are right-handed, and speech has long been observed to be controlled by areas located in the hemisphere of the brain that is contralateral ("opposite-sided") to the dominant hand—the left hemisphere—it was thought that the language center could always be determined by handedness. However, although in the vast majority of cases expressive language is largely centered in Broca's area in the left hemisphere, this is not always the case, particularly for left-handed people who prove to be right-hemisphere dominant. Many people seem to have functions such as language and handedness distributed in unique patterns between the two hemispheres, and language and handedness may not even be related at all in some people. There are many differences in laterality between the sexes as well, with females appearing to be more like left-handed people in general, with more functions such as speech distributed in areas in both hemispheres. This is why it is thought that women and left-handed people in general can recover more completely from strokes (cerebral vascular accidents) than right-handed men.

Given the hypothesis that schizophrenia and, perhaps, the other psychotic disorders are brain diseases, is there evidence that they can be localized according to laterality in the brain?

The first evidence that laterality may be a factor in the psychotic disorders was found by neurologist P. Flor-Henry in 1969. Flor-Henry noticed in a study of temporal-lobe epilepsy (which can have many psychotic symptoms) that when the focal point of the seizure was in the left hemisphere, schizophrenia-like psychotic features would appear, whereas when the seizure focus was in the right hemisphere, the psychotic symptoms resembled those found in affective psychoses. When the epileptic patient had "bilateral foci," the psychotic symptoms seemed to be "schizo-affective" in nature. Based on Flor-Henry's initial study, there have been many other such neurophysiological studies of the psychotic disorders trying to link schizophrenia with the left hemisphere and bipolar disorder with the right hemisphere.

There have been many published reviews of the evidence suggesting that laterality may be related to schizophrenia, although not all the evidence points conclusively to the left hemisphere as the source of dysfunction. This may be due to the fact that much of the research does not take schizophrenic subtype differences or gender differences into account. For example, paranoid schizophrenics are often distinguished from schizophrenics diagnosed with one of the nonparanoid subtypes on the basis of many perceptual and cognitive tasks in tests, but few studies take these subtype differences into account in laterality studies, generally only comparing generic "schizophrenics" with "normals" or other groups. This is true in the many neuropsychological studies, as well as those neurophysiological studies using measurements with the EEG and evoked potentials, regional cerebral blood flow (rCBF), position emission tomography (PET SCANS), and measurements of neurochemical differences to detect asymmetry between the hemispheres in the activity of certain NEUROTRANSMITTERS such as DOPAMINE. However, an informed review of the major research into the issue of laterality and schizophrenia by psychiatric researcher Henry A. Nasrallah in 1986 provides the following cautious conclusion: "Overall the evidence for left hemisphere dysfunction and over-activation appears to be relatively better documented than other types of dysfunction, although it is by no means definitive."

Because schizophrenia seems to be characterized by language abnormalities, the left hemisphere is thought to be a prime candidate for the localization of the disease process. However, a number of studies point to the possibility that schizophrenia may be related to an "interhemispheric dysfunction," that is, it may be the result of disturbances in the way messages are passed and interpreted between the two hemispheres of the brain. A minority of studies even point to the right hemisphere as the source of dysfunctions in schizophrenia. Until more is understood about the importance of laterality in the functioning of the human brain, it may be difficult to conclusively resolve the question of laterality in the psychotic disorders.

Broca, R. "Remarques sur la siège de la faculté du langue articule," *Bull. Soc. Anat.* 6 (1861): 330–357.

Flor-Henry, P. "Psychosis and Temporal Lobe Epilepsy: A Controlled Investigation," *Epilepsia* 10 (1969): 363–395.

Nasrallah, H. A. "Is Schizophrenia a Left Hemisphere Disease? In *Can Schizophrenia Be Localized in the Brain?* edited by N. C. Andreasen. Washington, D.C.: American Psychiatric Press, 1986.

Wexler, B. E. "Cerebral Laterality and Psychiatry: A Review of the Literature," *American Journal of Psychiatry* 137 (1980): 279–291.

lazar house (lazaretto) See LEPER HOUSES.

leeches and leeching See BLEEDING.

legal issues in schizophrenia See COMMITMENT; CONFIDENTIALITY; INFORMED CONSENT; INSANITY DEFENSE; RIGHT TO REFUSE TREATMENT; RIGHT TO TREATMENT.

leg-locks A form of MECHANICAL RESTRAINT used in Europe until the mid-19th century. These were heavy iron clasps around each ankle or shin, linked by a chain or a thick metal ring.

leper houses Also known as lazar houses or lazarettos (particularly in Italy), these were asylums for lepers. After a drop in the incidence of leprosy in the 1500s, these places were used to contain the poor, the sick, and the mentally ill—in other words, they were places of exile for all society's undesirable elements. Many European asylums arose out of these former places of banishment for the lepers. According to French historian Michael Foucault, until about 1650 the mentally ill were not considered a "threat" to the existing "sane" society in Europe. After that time, the Age of Reason was on the rise, and for the first time the mentally ill were rounded up into institutions called hospitals to contain the socially displaced: the mentally ill, the poor, the disabled, the elderly, criminals, those with venereal diseases, and political dissidents. These "hospitals" largely had no medical function but were essentially places of confinement. Foucault argues

that the creation of these institutions was inspired by the older tradition of banishing lepers to leper houses and colonies.

Foucault, M. *Madness and Civilization: A History of Insanity in the Age of Reason*. New York: Random House, 1965.

Jones, K. *Lunacy, Law, and Conscience, 1744–1845: The Social History of the Care of the Insane*. London: Routledge & Kegan Paul, 1955.

Parry-Jones, W. *The Trade in Lunacy: A Study of Private Madhouses in England in the Eighteenth and Nineteenth Centuries*. London: Routledge & Kegan Paul, 1972.

leucotomy The name given by Portuguese neurologist António EGAS MONIZ for his intrusive PSYCHOSURGERY procedure in which the skull of a person is opened and the white fibers connecting the frontal lobe to the rest of the brain are severed. It is derived from two Greek words meaning "white" and "to cut." Egas Moniz performed the first leucotomy on a human subject (a chronically depressed female patient from a local mental hospital in Portugal) on November 15, 1935. The first leucotomy performed in the United States was completed on September 14, 1936, in Washington, D.C., by American neurologists Walter FREEMAN and James Watts. In 1936, Freeman began to refer to the procedure as a "lobotomy" to separate himself from the shadow of Egas Moniz and create an international reputation of his own. A leucotomy was a form of major surgery that involved opening the skull, whereas a technique devised by Freeman in 1946, the "trans-orbital lobotomy," only involved the penetration of an "ice pick" or similar instrument into the eye socket (the "orbit of the eye"), behind the eye and into the brain.

licensed houses A 19th-century British term for those "private madhouses" that had obtained a license to house and provide limited care to the mentally ill. Licenses were obtained by petitioning the College of Physicians. These private madhouses generated a hefty profit for their operators, for their overhead could be kept quite low by providing the absolute minimum in food and custodial care for their mentally ill residents. This brisk and lucrative "trade in lunacy" finally degenerated to such inhumane conditions that a regulative body, the COMMISSIONERS IN LUNACY, was established in 1845 to monitor the private madhouses and ensure that they met minimum standards.

See also HOXTON MADHOUSES.

life expectancy of schizophrenics See MORTALITY.

limbic system In most research on the areas of the brain that seem to be implicated in the disease process in SCHIZOPHRENIA, the one characteristic that does seem to unite them (even more than laterality) is the fact that most of these areas are interconnected in the brain according to what has been identified as the "limbic system." The limbic system (also sometimes called the visceral brain), which involves a number of structures that lie deep below the surface of the brain (the cortex), was long considered to be one of the oldest parts of the brain and the one that governs many of the primitive, instinctual functions. Recent neurological research now considers the limbic system to be a major integrative system, where raw sensations are selected and integrated and sent to sites throughout the brain. The limbic system is composed of such subcortical structures as the hippocampus, amygdala, hypothalamus, mammillary bodies, the olfactory area, and bordering areas of the frontal and temporal lobes. Much of the work that identified the role of the limbic system as this large integrated network was conducted by neurologist Paul MacLean in the 1940s.

The evidence that schizophrenia involves abnormalities in the limbic system and its connections come from a wide variety of areas. EEG studies have shown abnormalities in the limbic areas of the brain, and brain structure abnormalities and neurochemical disturbances have been found in these areas. Because there is still much more to be learned about the functions of the brain as a whole, more research needs to be conducted to understand exactly how the limbic system is involved in the organic disease process of schizophrenia and to determine the meaning of these disparate research findings from many different areas when taken as a whole.

In his 1988 book, psychiatrist E. Fuller Torrey writes that one of the "four established facts" about the causes of schizophrenia is that "the limbic system and its connections are primarily affected."

MacLean, P. D. "Psychosomatic Disease and the 'Visceral Brain,'" *Psychosomatic Medicine* 11 (1949): 338–353.

Torrey, E. F. *Surviving Schizophrenia: A Family Manual.* 2nd ed. New York: Harper & Row, 1988.

Torrey, E. F., and Peterson, M. R. "Schizophrenia and the Limbic system," *Lancet* 2 (1974): 942–946.

linkage In genetics, "linkage" refers to the tendency of two ALLELES at different places (loci) on the same CHROMOSOME to be inherited together. The closer they are together, the lesser the chances of a genetic recombination occurring between them. Therefore, there is a greater probability that they will be inherited together. For example, in the search for the gene or genes that predispose to schizophrenia, it may well be that the abnormal gene responsible for a BIOLOGICAL MARKER OF SCHIZOPHRENIA (for example, eye movement abnormalities) may be "linked"—because of its physical closeness—to the actual disease gene that produces schizophrenia.

linkage analysis See GENETICS STUDIES.

linked markers See GENETIC MARKERS OF VULNERABILITY; MOLECULAR MARKERS.

lithium Lithium is the most commonly used drug for the treatment of recurrent affective (or mood) disorders such as BIPOLAR DISORDER or recurrent unipolar depression, MANIC EPISODES or acute HYPOMANIC EPISODES. A naturally occurring salt, lithium was discovered in 1817 by Swedish chemist John A. Arfvedson (1792–1841). Medical uses began to be applied in 1858 for the treatment of such conditions as gout and urinary calculi. It was later combined with bromides and used as a sedative. In 1940 lithium chloride was administered to cardiac patients as a salt substitute, but the severe toxic reactions they developed strongly discouraged researchers from conducting further studies on this drug. However, psychopharmacologist J. F. J. Cade continued research with lithium and in 1949 published the first scientific report of the antimanic effects of lithium. In a study of agitated psychotic patients, Cade found that 10 manic patients responded favorably to lithium, six schizophrenic and chronically depressed psychotic patients did not, and one patient's symptoms reappeared after the lithium was stopped. Its use for the treatment of affective disorders was not approved in the United States until 1970.

It is not clearly understood how lithium works to produce its results in behavioral changes. However, it is estimated that between 70 percent and 80 percent of people with "typical" bipolar disorder respond favorably to lithium therapy. This means, however, that 20 percent to 30 percent of people experiencing mania do not respond to lithium. Lithium may take one to two weeks to be fully effective, but after the acute symptoms of a disorder lessen, lithium maintenance therapy can reduce the number, severity, and frequency of episodes. The side effects of long-term lithium therapy may cause various endocrine abnormalities (thyroid problems, diabetes mellitus), kidney damage, cardiac reactions, skin problems, gastrointestinal problems, and some central nervous system problems such as fine hand tremors and other neuromuscular problems. Because lithium can be lethal at toxic levels, blood levels of the substance must be assessed regularly to avoid dangerous concentrations.

Baldessarini, R. J. *Chemotherapy in Psychiatry: Principles and Practice.* Cambridge, Mass.: Harvard University Press, 1985.

Cade, J. F. J. "Lithium—Past, Present, and Future." In *Lithium in Medical Practice,* edited by F. N. Johnson and S. Johnson. Baltimore: University Park Press, 1978.

———. "Lithium Salts in the Treatment of Psychotic Excitement," *Medical Journal of Australia* 11 (1949): 349–352.

lobectomy A form of extreme surgery in which an entire lobe of the brain is removed. Although this procedure was sometimes performed to remove tumors and halt their spread in the brain, in the 1930s it was suggested that it might be an effective

form of PSYCHOSURGERY for some mentally ill persons, specifically if the frontal lobe of the brain was removed. A full lobectomy was first performed on the chimpanzees Becky and Lucy in June 1934 at the Yale primate research laboratory by John Fulton and Carlyle Jacobsen. The entire frontal mass of the brain was extracted and a cottonoid (a sterile, oil-soaked cotton wad) was put in its place to fill in the space left in the skull and to support the remaining sections of the brain. At an international conference in London in August 1935, Fulton and Jacobsen reported on the behavioral changes that were observed in these animals as a result of the lobectomy. They inspired Portuguese neurologist António EGAS MONIZ to suggest at their presentation that lobectomies be performed on humans. The horrified response of most of the participants caused him to modify his views, but on his return to Portugal after the conference he devised a less radical procedure, the LEUCOTOMY, which merely severed the connections of the frontal lobe to the rest of the brain, and performed the first psychosurgery on a human subject in November 1935.

See also FREEMAN, WALTER; TRANSORBITAL LOBOTOMY.

lobotomy The term that American neurologist Walter FREEMAN invented to replace LEUCOTOMY, the name given by Portuguese neurologist António EGAS MONIZ for his famous psychosurgical procedure that severed the white fibers connecting the frontal lobe to the rest of the brain. Freeman suggested the name change at a meeting of the Southern Medical Association in Baltimore in November 1936, and it was first used in a published article in 1937. Because leucotomy referred to the severing of specific fibers, "lobotomy" was suggested as a more general term for any psychosurgical procedure that involved the cutting of the nerve fibers of a lobe of the brain.

Freeman, W. J., and J. Watts. "Prefrontal Lobotomy in the Treatment of Mental Disorders," *Southern Medical Journal* 30 (1937): 23–31.

lock hospitals A term popular in England for LEPER HOUSES and later asylums for the mentally ill in which persons would be involuntarily "locked in."

locus In genetics research, the word *locus* (plural, *loci*) is often used to refer to the place where a particular gene (or genes) is located.

lod score See LINKAGE ANALYSIS.

longitudinal studies These are also known as "long-term follow-up" studies. Particular groups of patients, or cohorts, are identified and followed throughout the course of their lives. The best studies follow patients from childhood (such as the HIGH-RISK STUDIES), although most have simply followed patients diagnosed with a particular illness. The purpose of these studies is to provide a picture of the natural course of a disease, identifying its characteristics throughout the life cycle of an individual. A special issue of *Schizophrenia Bulletin* devoted to a comprehensive review of such studies appeared in 1988 (vol. 14, no. 4).

See also COURSE AND OUTCOME OF SCHIZOPHRENIA.

loosening of associations This is one of the primary symptoms of the major psychotic disorders, particularly schizophrenia. It is considered a sign of FORMAL THOUGHT DISORDER. Loosening of associations refers to the verbal expression of thoughts that are disjointed and jump from one subject to another without any relationship whatsoever; in addition, the speaker demonstrates no awareness of the disconnection of these thoughts. When loosening of associations is severe, the person may be perceived as speaking nonsense or gibberish and may be incoherent.

Eugen BLEULER thought that such ASSOCIATION DISTURBANCES were one of the "primary symptoms" of schizophrenia that uniquely characterized it when compared with other mental disorders. He recognized the importance of loosening of associations in his first publication (1908) that introduced the concept of schizophrenia and its divergence

from Kraepelin's notion of DEMENTIA PRAECOX. Bleuler writes:

> On the psychological side the most fundamental disorder appears to be a change in associations. In schizophrenia it is as if the physiological inhibitions and pathways have lost their significance. The usual paths are no longer preferred, the thread of ideas very easily becomes lost in unfamiliar and incorrect pathways. Associations are then guided by random influences, particularly by emotions, and this amounts to a partial or total loss of logical function. In the acute stages associations are broken up into little fragments, so that in spite of constant psychomotor excitement, no kind of action is possible because no thought is followed through, and because a variety of contradictory drives exist side by side and cannot be synthesized under one unitary or affective point of view.

Disturbances in associations are also related to disturbances in attention and are more commonly found in the nonparanoid subtypes of schizophrenia that are characterized by such NEGATIVE SYMPTOMS. However, loosening of associations can also sometimes appear in MANIC EPISODES or in the ACUTE AND TRANSIENT PSYCHOTIC DISORDERS.

See also PRIMARY SYMPTOMS OF SCHIZOPHRENIA; the FOUR A'S.

Bleuler, E. "The Prognosis of Dementia Praecox: The Group of Schizophrenias" (1908). In *The Clinical Roots of the Schizophrenia Concept: Translations of Seminal European Contributions On Schizophrenia,* edited by J. Cutting and M. Shepherd. Cambridge: Cambridge University Press, 1987.

loxapine See ANTIPSYCHOTIC DRUGS.

Loxitane See ANTIPSYCHOTIC DRUGS.

lunacy, lunatic Derived from the Latin word for moon—*luna*—these terms were used for centuries to reflect the belief that mental disorders were caused by the influence of the moon. Both terms were in common usage until the mid- to late 19th century, when the term *INSANITY* replaced them as a generic reference to "mental illness" or "mental disorders," as we would term them today. The mentally ill were called lunatics, and the physicians who administered aid to them were sometimes called lunatic-doctors. Whereas *lunacy* was a term used in medical and legal texts and organizations (e.g., COMMISSIONERS IN LUNACY), the popular term *madness* was not used in these official capacities.

lunacy trials Beginning with Illinois in 1867, many states passed "jury trial commitment" laws that entitled a person to be judged insane by a body of his or her peers before being involuntarily committed to an institution. These began as the result of the influence of Elizabeth Packard, whose husband had her committed to the Illinois State Asylum at Jacksonville for three years simply for disagreeing with him on philosophical issues. Although Illinois repealed its "lunacy trial" bill in 1892, many states still had such laws on the books well into the 20th century. There were many critics of the lunacy trials, who felt that they caused unnecessary public embarrassment to the patient and that they cast the mentally ill person into the role of a criminal. The First International Congress of Mental Hygiene, a congregation of the organizations of the Mental Hygiene Movement founded by Clifford BEERS, condemned the practice of lunacy trials in 1930. A long transcript of such a lunacy trial and a description of the events that transpired, including the incarceration of a Philadelphia businessman who was eventually set free by the jury, can be found in the 1869 autobiographical account by Ebenezer Haskell.

See also COMMITMENT.

Haskell, E. *The Trial of Ebenezer Haskell, in Lunacy and His Acquittal before Judge Brewster, in November, 1868, together with a Brief Sketch of the Mode of Treatment of Lunatics in Different Asylums in This Country and in England, with Illustrations, including a Copy of Hogarth's Celebrated Painting of a Scene of Old Bedlam, in London, 1635.* Philadelphia: E. Haskell, 1869.

lycanthropy Described since ancient times as a form of "MELANCHOLIA," lycanthropy is a mental disorder in which an individual believes that he or she has been transformed into an animal, especially a wolf. This disorder has also been referred to as "werewolfism," in reference to the Anglo-Saxon term (literally, a "man-wolf"). Lycanthropy was long thought to be an extinct disorder, but at least 18 individual cases have been reported since 1975. Most of these cases concern people who have been diagnosed with one of the psychotic disorders, usually PARANOID SCHIZOPHRENIA, DEPRESSION with psychotic features, or BIPOLAR DISORDER. In the past century, such terms as *insania zoanthropica, zoanthropy* and *cyanthropy* have been used occasionally in psychiatric texts to refer to this exotic disease of the mind.

Jackson, S. W. *Melancholia and Depression: From Hippocratic Times to Modern Times.* New Haven, Conn.: Yale University Press, 1986.

Keck, P. E., et al. "Lycanthropy: Alive and Well in the Twentieth Century," *Psychological Medicine* 18 (1988): 113–120.

Noll, R. *Vampires, Werewolves and Demons: Twentieth Century Reports in the Psychiatric Literature.* New York: Brunner/Mazel, 1991.

Verdoux, H., et al. "La Lycanthropie: Une pathologie contemporaine?" *Annales de Psychiatrie* 4, no. 2 (1989): 178–179.

lypemania This is J. E. D. ESQUIROL'S term for MELANCHOLIA, a group of disorders that we now refer to as depression. Depressed or "melancholic" persons were referred to as "lypemaniacs."

M

mad-business This was the 17th- and 18th-century term used for any profession that dealt with "mad-people" or "madmen." This included physicians, apothecaries, and others who were responsible for the custodial care of the mentally ill, as well as the entire system of private "mad-houses" (after 1845 called LICENSED HOUSES) in England.

mad-doctor Also known as lunatic doctors, mad-doctors were physicians who provided medical care to the mentally ill. This term was popular in the late 1600s and colloquially, into the 1800s. Our current usage of the term is different, referring instead to representations of psychotic scientists or physicians in literature and in motion pictures. For example, the profane experiments of the grandiose Dr. Victor Frankenstein, as described in the book *Frankenstein, Or, the Modern Prometheus* by Mary Shelley in 1816, may be the first such depiction of this image, and it has been carried into this century in many films, notably in the many roles played with such zeal by actor Lionel Atwill in the 1930s and 1940s.

Mad Hatter, mad as a hatter The "Mad Hatter" was a popular character in Lewis Carroll's *Alice in Wonderland* (1865), and it is because of this book that we are familiar with this term today. However, the expression "mad as a hatter" predates this book, although there are conflicting views as to how it originated. Some have argued (namely William Hazlitt) that the expression comes from a 17th-century eccentric named John Hatter. Another view is that a 17th-century hatter by the name of Robert Crab is the original "mad hatter," since he developed grandiose religious delusions and proclaimed himself a prophet after receiving head wounds in 1642 during the English civil war. However, modern interpretations suggest that the profession of hatmakers may have had more than its share of psychotic individuals due to the toxic effect of a substance they all commonly employed in making felt hats—mercuric nitrate—which may have induced an ORGANIC MENTAL DISORDER that included such psychotic symptoms as delusions and hallucinations.

Spalding, K. "Poisoning from Mercurous Nitrate Used in the Making of Felt Hats," *Modern Language Review* 46 (1951): 442.

madness An Old English word first appearing in the 1300s, "mad" or "madness" has always referred to mental disorder, extreme foolishness or folly or an insane rage or fury. It has always been used as part of everyday conversation, but with the rise of the profession of PSYCHIATRY in the 1800s the terms *lunacy* and then *insanity* were almost exclusively used in the official sense. Hence, there were more often commissions on "lunacy" or journals of "insanity," but no such uses seem to have been made of the coarser term *madness*. The word is still used today (as is its 16th-century synonym, *crazy*, which is derived from a French word meaning "cracked") in this coarse sense.

Dalby, J. T. "Terms of Madness: Historical Linguistics," *Comprehensive Psychiatry* 34 (1993): 392–395.

mad-shirt A sacklike garment that was used as a form of mechanical restraint for unmanageable patients. It is described as a close-fitting cylindrical garment, usually made of canvas or other

strong material, which was pulled down over the head of the individual and fastened tightly below the knees. It is reported to have been in use at the Pennsylvania Hospital in Philadelphia in the early 19th century.

See also HORN'S SACK; STRAITJACKET.

magical thinking This refers to the unusual belief that some people may have in which they feel that their thoughts, words, or actions can influence other people or events in the physical world in such a way that defies our known physical laws of cause and effect. Sometimes this can reach delusional proportions and become a fixture of the person's belief system about him- or herself and the world. For example, a person with grandiose paranoid delusions may insist that he or she personally caused the 1989 San Francisco earthquake and will do so again if he or she is not immediately released from involuntary commitment to a hospital. Loren J. Chapman and Jean P. Chapman, two noted schizophrenia researchers from the University of Wisconsin in Madison, theorize that magical ideation in undiagnosed people in the general population is a strong indicator of "psychosis-proneness," particularly to schizophrenia. They have developed a 30-item Magical Ideation Scale with such items as "I think I could learn to read other people's minds if I wanted to" (keyed true), and "The hand motions that strangers make seem to influence me at times" (keyed true). They are conducting long-term studies to test their hypothesis that magical thinking in undiagnosed persons may be a sign of later schizophrenia. These persons may in fact be the type referred to with the labels LATENT SCHIZOPHRENIA, SCHIZOTYPAL PERSONALITY DISORDER, OR BORDERLINE SCHIZOPHRENIA.

Chapman, L. J., and J. P. Chapman. "Psychosis-Proneness." In *Controversies in Schizophrenia,* edited by M. Alpert. New York: Guilford Press, 1985.

magnetic resonance imaging One of the BRAIN IMAGING TECHNIQUES currently used in research on the psychotic disorders, particularly schizophrenia. In MRI (its common acronym), a high-strength magnetic field works on the hydrogen atoms located in the brain. Once "oriented," radio frequency pulses are bounced off the hydrogen atoms. The resonant echoes are detected and, with the aid of computer analysis, can be constructed into an image of the inner structure of the brain. MRI has advantages over the use of the CT SCAN in that it can better identify the differences between gray matter and white matter in the brain. The first published study of schizophrenia using MRI was reported by R. C. Smith and colleagues in 1984.

A comprehensive review (by R. W. McCarley and colleagues) of 118 MRI studies of schizophrenia published between 1987 and May 1998 reported BRAIN ABNORMALITIES that tended to be supported by other neuropathological, neuroimaging, and neuropsychological evidence. The authors of the study also argue that the MRI studies suggest that structural abnormalities differ in bipolar (manic-depressive) psychosis and in schizophrenia—just as Kraepelin predicted in the beginning of the 20th century.

McCarley, R. W., et al. "MRI Anatomy of Schizophrenia," *Biological Psychiatry* 45 (1999): 1,099–1,119.

Smith, R. C. "Nuclear Magnetic Resonance in Schizophrenia: A Preliminary Study," *Psychiatry Research* 12 (1984): 137–147.

magnetic resonance spectroscopy imaging (MRSI) A BRAIN IMAGING technique that measures certain chemical characteristics in living brains to determine the integrity of specific populations of nerve cells. This is one of the new technologies for studying NEURAL CIRCUITRY IN SCHIZOPHRENIA. Many MRSI studies use the technique of proton magnetic resonance spectroscopic imaging (abbreviated as 1H-MRSI in the scientific literature). MRSI has largely focused on one potential BIOLOGICAL MARKER of schizophrenia, N-acetylaspartate, or NAA. NAA is a measure of the health of certain populations of nerve cells. When compared to healthy, non-schizophrenia controls, NAA has been found to be reduced in certain areas of the brain in persons with schizophrenia and in their family members. Children with CHILDHOOD-ONSET SCHIZOPHRENIA also seem to have

NAA reductions, lending support to the neurodevelopmental model of schizophrenia that claims a continuity of disease process from childhood into adulthood. Although promising, one drawback to this form of neuroimaging is that the spatial resolution of MRSI is poor compared with either magnetic resonance imaging and position emission tomography scans, and therefore it is more difficult to pinpoint exact locations in the brain that may be dysfunctional.

Bertolino, A., et al. "Reproducibility of Proton Magnetic Resonance Spectroscopic Imaging in Patients with Schizophrenia," *Neuropsychopharmacology* 18 (1998), 1–9.

Brooks, W. M., et al. "Frontal Lobe of Children with Schizophrenia Spectrum Disorders: A Proton Magnetic Resonance Spectroscopic Study," *Biological Psychiatry* 43 (1998): 263–269.

Mahler's syndrome See SYMBIOTIC PSYCHOSIS.

malaria therapy See FEVER THERAPY.

malingering The intentional faking of psychological or physical symptoms for some ulterior motive (e.g., to receive worker compensation instead of returning to work, or to avoid military duty). It is quite common for many relatives and friends of mentally ill persons—particularly those with schizophrenia or severe depression—to unjustly accuse them of malingering to avoid the responsibilities of life. Strongly expressed sentiments of this sort by family members of schizophrenics can actually worsen the person's very real condition and increase the probability of relapse. However, with more education about mental illness, such misconceptions will hopefully diminish.

See also FEIGNED INSANITY.

malvaria A new subtype of schizophrenia proposed by psychedelic researcher Abram Hoffer in 1963 that was supposedly characterized by a "mauve factor." The idea never took hold and was never seriously considered by mainstream psychiatry.

See also TRANSMETHYLATION HYPOTHESIS.

Hoffer, A. "Malvaria: A New Psychiatric Disease," *Acta Psychiatrica Scandinavica* 39 (1963): 335–366.

mania One of the two ancient categories of insanity (along with MELANCHOLIA). *Mania* was the term used by the ancient Greeks for "madness." From ancient times until the second half of the 19th century, all forms of mental illness were interpreted as either forms of melancholia or mania, and these terms had a variety of meanings that do not correspond to our contemporary psychiatric definitions of the clinical syndromes of mania and depression. From the time of the Greeks, mania referred to states in which a person was highly energized, excitable, euphoric, "possessed," talkative, frenzied, enraged, irritable, grandiose, and hallucinating. In ancient times as now, "maniacs" sometimes went through periods were they did not sleep for days or weeks at a time. Until the late 19th century, "mania" almost always referred to an elevation or an increase in intensity of moods, thoughts, and behaviors (as opposed to melancholy, where there was a decrease in intensity in these areas). From antiquity until the time of KRAEPELIN, perhaps hundreds of different forms of insanity were labeled as special forms of mania, sometimes with a single symptom dominating the picture (e.g., kleptomania).

Starting in the 1850s with the proposal that states of mania and melancholy (depression) could alternate in the same person as aspects of a single underlying disease process (the CIRCULAR INSANITY of French psychiatry), attention was turned to carving out the core clinical concepts of mania and melancholia (depression) and thereby separating them from their ancient, varied, and confusing meanings. All the confusing forms of mania (and melancholia, except one form, involutional melancholia) were grouped under the concept of MANIC-DEPRESSIVE ILLNESS (*das manisch-depressive Irrsein*) by Emil Kraepelin in 1899. The two great and ancient insanities of mania and melancholia were now replaced by manic-depressive illness and dementia praecox. By the end of the 20th century,

manic-depressive illness became the AFFECTIVE DISORDERS or mood disorders, and dementia praecox became schizophrenia and other psychotic disorders.

Although Kraepelin identified numerous forms of mania and "mixed states" (dysphoric states in which depression and mania were mixed), and changed these diagnostic categories until his death, for the rest of the 20th century mania was still largely viewed as a state of euphoric intensity that, over time, might devolve into irritability, rage, and psychotic delusions. Prior to 1980, when the diagnostic concept BIPOLAR DISORDER was introduced to replace manic-depressive illness, anyone experiencing depressive episodes with no history of mania was often labeled manic-depressive. After 1980, a person must experience at least one MANIC EPISODE to be diagnosed as bipolar.

Current research on mania indicates there are three primary forms: the classical form of euphoric mania, dysphoric mania (known as MIXED STATES), and psychotic mania. Only the first, euphoric mania, responds well to treatment with LITHIUM. The other dysphoric (or mixed) mania responds to treatment with ANTIPSYCHOTIC DRUGS, particularly olanzapine (Zyprexa). Psychotic mania may respond to either lithium or olanzapine (Zyprexa). In clinical practice, without knowing the medical history of a patient, a person experiencing mania with psychotic features (particularly delusions) is indistinguishable from someone experiencing an acute episode of schizophrenia (particularly paranoid schizophrenia).

See also FUNDAMENTAL STATES OF MANIC DEPRESSIVE INSANITY.

Cassidy, F., et al. "Signs and Symptoms of Mania in Pure and Mixed Episodes," *Journal of Affective Disorders* 50 (1998): 187–201.

Diethelm, O. "Mania: A Clinical Study of Dissertations Before 1750," *Confina Psychiatrica* 13 (1970): 26–49.

Suppes, T., et al. "Report of the Texas Consensus Conference Panel on Medication Treatment of Bipolar Disorder 2000," *Journal of Clinical Psychiatry* 63 (April 2002): 288–299.

mania sine delirio Literally, "mania without delirium." This refers to a MANIC EPISODE in which the consciousness of the afflicted person is not clouded (see DELIRIUM), nor is thinking permanently impaired. This is perhaps the most ancient definition of MANIA that exists. Sometimes in the older psychiatric literature, the word *delirium* means a disturbance in the rational thinking processes (e.g., delusions) and may not refer specifically to our modern concept of delirium as an organic disease of the brain. Philippe PINEL devoted an entire section to this "species of mental derangement" in his 1801 classic textbook, *Traite médico-philosophique sur l'aliénation mentale, ou la manie,* in which he referred to it in French as *manie sans délire.* According to Pinel, this type of mania "may be either continued or intermittent. No sensible change in the functions of the understanding; but perversion of the active faculties, marked by abstract and sanguinary fury, with a blind propensity to acts of violence." Due to the problems in institutional management created by such agitated "maniacs," it is not surprising that they frequently received the more extreme "treatments," such as extensive BLEEDING, the CAUTERY TREATMENT, the BATH OF SURPRISE, and DOUCHING with cold water. J. E. D. ESQUIROL describes the treatment of a typical maniac in the following passage from his 1838 textbook:

> A maniac becomes furious during the night, and utters frightful howls. At two o'clock in the morning, I order the douche, and whilst the cold water is falling upon his head, inundating his body, he appears to be greatly pleased and thanks us for the kindness we have shown him; becomes composed; and sleeps remarkably well the rest of the night.

Esquirol, J. E. D. *Mental Maladies: A Treatise on Insanity.* Translated by E. K. Hunt. 1838. Reprint, Philadelphia: Lea and Blanchard, 1845.

Pinel, P. *A Treatise on Insanity.* Translated by D. D. Davis. 1801. Reprint, Sheffield, England: W. Todd, 1806.

manic-depressive illness One of the two comprehensive categories of insanity that have dominated psychiatry since 1899. Throughout the 20th century, and into the 21st century, all disorders of emotion, affect, or mood have been defined

under, or in relation to, manic-depressive illness or its successor, BIPOLAR DISORDER (1980). All major psychotic disturbances of intellectual functioning, on the other hand, have been subsumed under, or related to DEMENTIA PRAECOX (1893) or SCHIZOPHRENIA (1908). Manic-depressive illness and schizophrenia have been the two anchors of modern psychiatric diagnostic manuals since 1899.

Historical background From Greek and Roman antiquity until the latter half of the 1800s, the two great forms of insanity were mania and melancholia. Hundreds of various manias or forms of melancholy (including syndromes we might term delusional or paranoid) were defined in terms of these two anchors. Much of the times these disorders were seen to be mutually exclusive, but by the 1800s some "mad-doctors" or "alienists" began to see certain disorders as first starting off as a form of melancholy then morphing into a form of mania, or vice versa. Mania and depression in their modern sense were not defined until the late 1800s.

Descriptions of persons who suffered from bouts of recurring and alternating depression and mania have existed since the first century A.D. The clearest description of what may have been manic-depressive illness can be found in the second-century A.D. works of Aretaeus of Cappadocia. The description of euphoric mania turning into irritable mixed states with psychotic features is a familiar one to clinicians even today:

> If mania is associated with joy, the patient may laugh, play, dance night and day, and go to the market crowned as if a victor in some contest of skill. . . . The ideas the patient has are infinite . . . believing they are experts in astronomy, philosophy or poetry. . . . The patient may become excitable, suspicious, and irritable . . . his hearing may become sharp . . . some get noises and buzzing in the ears . . . or may have visions . . . bad dreams and his sexual desires may get uncontrollable . . . if aroused to anger, he may become wholly mad and run unrestrainedly, roar aloud . . . kill his keepers, and lay violent hands upon himself.

It was not until 1854 that French *alienists* Jean-Pierre Falret and Jules-Gabriel-François Baillarger independently described CIRCULAR INSANITY (Falret) or "double formed insanity" (Baillarger). This is the first time that the two very distinct phases were viewed as expression of one underlying chronic illness. In Prussia, German psychiatrist Karl Kahlbaum coined the term *cyclothymia* for a less severe form of circular insanity that was primarily a disorder of emotion and not intellectual functioning and that did not progress into terminal dementia, unlike the more severe form of circular insanity that affects cognitive functioning and the will and that leads to mental confusion, dementia, and "complete mental degeneration." Kahlbaum's distinction between cyclothymia and what we now call bipolar disorder is still reflected today in *DSM-IV-TR* (2002). Kahlbaum is perhaps second only to Kraepelin in terms of his influence on our current methods and categories of mental disorder classification.

manic episode According to *DSM-IV-TR* (2000), the experience of a diagnosable manic episode, whether currently or in the past, is the essential criterion of being given a diagnosis of BIPOLAR DISORDER (technically, Bipolar I Disorder). However, as clinicians well know, the idea that someone who is "bipolar" or "manic-depressive" alternates between manic episodes and depressive episodes is simply untrue. In fact, manic-depression in its classic form is rare. Indeed, there are many persons who experience manic episodes and/or MIXED EPISODES who never experience an episode of major depression. Whether the presence of a manic episode really means a "bipolar" disorder is present remains doubtful.

In *DSM-IV-TR*, a manic episode is defined in the following way:

(1) There is a distinct period of abnormality and persistently elevated, expansive, or irritable mood, lasting at least one week (or any duration if hospitalization is necessary).
(2) During the period of mood disturbance, three or more of the following symptoms must have persisted (four if the mood is only irritable):
   (a) inflated self-esteem or grandiosity
   (b) decreased need for sleep

(c) more talkative then usual or pressure to keep talking
(d) flight of ideas or subjective experience that thoughts are racing
(e) distractibility (attention too easily drawn to unimportant or irrelevant external stimuli)
(f) increase in goal-directed activity (either socially, at work or school, or sexually) or psychomotor agitation
(g) excessive involvement in pleasurable activities that have a high potential for painful consequences (e.g., engaging in unrestrained buying sprees, sexual indiscretions, or foolish business investments)

Emil Kraepelin first proposed the "nosological dichotomy" of the endogenous psychoses manic-depressive illness (*manisch-depressive Irresein*) and the so-called *"Dementia-praecox Gruppe"* in a public lecture delivered in Heidelberg, Germany, on November 27, 1898. These ideas were reflected in print a few months later, beginning the process that would change psychiatric classification up to the present day. In 1899 the 6th edition of Emil Kraepelin's book, *Psychiatrie,* grouped all the affective disorders described by previous generations of psychiatrists (all the simple manias, periodic or circular insanities and their mixed forms, and the affective melancholias, except involutional melancholia) and grouped them under a major class of insanity, manic-depressive illness (*das manisch-depressive Irresein*).

> ". . . we are definitely in a position to class within the large framework of manic-depressive insanity even the smallest fragment of a pathological process belonging here; there are no bridges leading over to the other groups of mental disorders, except perhaps for degenerative psychosis. For all of these reasons, I feel bound to take the clinical circle of forms of manic-depressive insanity as a homogenous whole, and to depict the individual pictures and types of course as special forms of the one, common, pathological process.
>
> As its name suggests, manic-depressive insanity takes place in single attacks which present either the signs of so-called *manic excitation,* flight of ideas, elated mood, and urge to be active, or those of a particular *psychic depression with psychomotor inhibition,* or finally a *mixture of the two states* (p. 273).

The "attacks" of manic-depressive illness (or insanity) were relatively short-lived (days or weeks at the most, sometimes months in the case of depressive attacks) but always eventually remitted. Patients between episodes returned to full normal functioning without any deterioration or degeneration of cognitive functioning (which was, instead, the essential feature of diseases like dementia praecox). In the short term, therefore, prognosis was good. However, Kraepelin noted that this disorder lasted a lifetime in most people. The number of attacks, the type of attack (manic, depressive, or mixed states), and the period of relative health between attacks were variable. Kraepelin also noted that some persons experienced only manic attacks, or periodic mania, and some only bouts of depression or periodic melancholia (both of which would be termed *unipolar* today), but that both were still aspects of the same disease and should be diagnosed as manic-depressive (*bipolar* in our terms today). Kraepelin noted that in about 60 percent of the cases the disease started with a depressive episode. Two-thirds of all his patients with manic-depressive disorder were female. In two-thirds of the total cases (both men and women), the age of onset was before age 25. The attacks come and go without external causes (hence, they are endogenous, or generated from within).

Delusions, illusions, and hallucinations are common during attacks, particularly in manic attacks. In "mixed forms," the manic excitement and irritability are combined with the low spirits and negative thoughts of depression. The identification of mixed states was an important element in linking mania and depression together as two aspects of the same underlying disease, and Kraepelin's descriptions of such states came from the work of one of his assistants at the University of Heidelberg, Wilhelm Weygandt. Weygandt's monograph on this topic, *Uber die Mischzustande des manisch-depressive Irreseins (On the Mixed States of Manic-Depressive Insanity)* also appeared in 1899.

In 1899 Kraepelin was clear on the distinction between manic-depressive illness and dementia

praecox. The clinical pictures were distinct and, he believed, they were caused by very different underlying disease processes (dementia praecox being a degenerative disorder). However, by the end of his career, he was not so sure that these two great insanities were so distinct. In 1920 he wrote: "We must, then, accustom ourselves to the idea that the phenomena of illness which we have hitherto used are not sufficient to enable us to distinguish reliably between manic-depressive illness and schizophrenia in all cases." This lack of clarity between the two great psychotic disorders resulted in geographical and national differences in diagnosis. Books and articles appearing in the 1970s reported that schizophrenia was overdiagnosed in the United States and manic-depression underdiagnosed compared to Europe, particularly the United Kingdom, where the reverse was true. As schizophrenia researcher Nancy Andreasen (1938–) pointed out in a 1994 article examining this issue, such evidence of cultural style differences in diagnosis cast doubt on the idea of dementia praecox or schizophrenia as an "ahistorical" disease entity like physical diseases such as cancer or diabetes. History, tradition, and culture have always played an important role in shaping our concepts of mental disorders. Manic-depression and schizophrenia are no exceptions.

Cause "We are completely in the dark about the nature of manic-depressive insanity," Kraepelin wrote in 1899 when addressing the issue of etiology (cause). He devoted exactly two paragraphs to this topic, stressing the "periodic" nature of the illness and how such cycling resembles metabolic processes and epileptic attacks. "This could indicate a chemical theory, all the more so as we now seem to be coming close to postulating an autointoxication in the case of epilepsy too, which likewise is periodic. . . . Still, we can probably expect this matter to be clarified some day by metabolic investigations" (p. 309). At this time Kraepelin held to the theory of AUTOINTOXICATION AS A CAUSE OF DEMENTIA PRAECOX, and so it was a natural speculation on his part that autointoxication may also play a role in manic-depressive insanity. In later writings on manic-depression, Kraepelin stressed the fact that heredity may be involved, noting that the disease ran in families.

Research Manic-depressive illness never captured the attention of biological psychiatrists the way that dementia praecox did. Volumes reviewing the experimental literature on dementia praecox and schizophrenia have appeared with great regularity since the 1920s, with Leopold Bellak editing such compilations each decade from the late 1940s to the late 1970s. The most recent series seems to be the successive editions of *Schizophrenia* by Steven R. Hirsch and Daniel Weinberger (2nd ed., 2003). However, only two such comprehensive reviews of manic-depressive illness have appeared in the last 50 years—*Manic-Depressive Disease: Clinical and Psychiatric Significance* (1953) by John D. Campbell, and *Manic-Depressive Illness* (1990) by Frederick K. Goodwin and Kay Redfield Jamison. This relative inattention by researchers to manic-depressive insanity since 1899 reflects the fact that persons with this disorder undergo long periods of normal functioning with only cyclic episodes that may require institutionalization and hence is not as disabling a disease as schizophrenia. Additionally, pharmacological treatments for bipolar disorder have been effective in controlling the illness and allow most persons to live productive lives, whereas the medications for schizophrenia have been far less successful in restoring social and occupational functioning. Research conducted since the introduction of the RESEARCH DIAGNOSTIC CRITERIA (1978) and *DSM-III* (1980) have studied this mental disorder according to the criteria given to it under its new name, BIPOLAR DISORDER.

Andreasen, N. "Changing Concepts of Schizophrenia and the Ahistorical Fallacy," *American Journal of Psychiatry* 1 (1994): 355–362.

Campbell, J. D. *Manic-Depressive Disease: Clinical and Psychiatric Significance.* Philadelphia: JB Lippincott, 1953.

Goodwin, F. K., and K. R. Jamison. *Manic-Depressive Illness.* Oxford: Oxford University Press, 1990.

Kraepelin, E. *Psychiatry: A Textbook for Students and Physicians,* Volume 2*: Clinical Psychiatry,* translated by Sabine Ayed, edited by Jacques Quen. Canton, Mass.: Science History Publications, 1990. [Originally published in two volumes in 1899 as the sixth edition of *Psychiatrie: Ein Lehrbuch für Studirende und Aerzte.* Leipzing: Verlag von Johann Ambrosius Barth.]

Salvatore, P., et al. "Weygandt's *On the Mixed States of Manic-Depressive Insanity:* A Translation and Commentary on

Its Significance in the Evolution of the Concept of Bipolar Disorder," *Harvard Review of Psychiatry* 10 (2002): 255–275.

Weygandt, W. *Uber die Mischzustande des manisch-depressiven Irreseins.* Munich: Verlag von J. F. Lehmann, 1899.

MAO activity See ENZYME DISORDER HYPOTHESIS.

marital schism See FAMILY INTERACTION THEORIES.

marital skew See FAMILY INTERACTION THEORIES.

marital status of schizophrenics It has long been observed that most people with severe mental disorders that are admitted to psychiatric hospitals are unmarried. For example, even in 1812, American physician Benjamin RUSH could conclude, based on the patient statistics of the Pennsylvania Hospital in Philadelphia, "Single persons are more predisposed to madness than married people." Almost all studies of the first admission rates of psychiatric hospitals in recent decades have likewise shown that more unmarried than married people have serious psychiatric illnesses, and that this unmarried rate is consistently higher among males than females. In schizophrenia, these high rates are related to the age of onset of illness (it is generally earlier than in bipolar illness) and the subtype of schizophrenia (the unmarried rate is higher for the nonparanoid subtypes). According to a comprehensive review by Letten Saugstad of Norway published in 1989, the single to married ratio in SCHIZOPHRENIA is 7.7:1 for males, and 4.5:1 for females, and for manic-depressive psychosis (bipolar disorder) the ratios were a far lower 1.5:1 for males and 1.3:1 for females. The likelihood of a schizophrenic person remaining married is directly related to the severity and course of illness, with those people with the worst prognosis obviously having the greater marital disruptions and divorces. Thus, in schizophrenia, being single or divorced is associated with a poor prognosis for the illness.

Eaton, W. W. "Marital Status and Schizophrenia," *Acta Psychiatrica Scandinavica* 52 (1975): 320–329.

Saugstad, L. F. "Social Class, Marriage, and Fertility in Schizophrenia," *Schizophrenia Bulletin* 15 (1989): 9–43.

masturbation Masturbation (also known as self-pollution, onanism, or chiromania) was first proposed as a cause of physical and mental disease in a pamphlet published in England in 1710 entitled *ONANIA, or the Heinous Sin of Self-Pollution and All Its Frightful Consequences in Both Sexes, Considered.* The author was anonymous, but it is suspected to be the work of a clergyman. Although masturbation had long been known as a sin since biblical times, this pamphlet is the first place where direct biological effects are connected with this practice. With the rise of DEGENERATION THEORY in the mid-1800s, the direct mental and physical weaknesses caused by this practice were not only harmful to its practitioners, but also to future generations. Seminal loss in men depleted the vitality and the potentially good heredity of males. The shocks to the "spinal marrow" produced by masturbation in both men and women also led to hereditary taint that could be passed on to the next generation. Physical diseases like tuberculosis and insanities such as epilepsy might also result from such practices.

In French alienist J. E. D. ESQUIROL's 1838 textbook, *Mental Maladies,* a chart of the "physical causes" of MANIA in males and females in separate asylums in Paris lists masturbation as the cause of insanity in 16 cases. As he put it later in his book, "Masturbation, that scourge of human kind, is more frequently than is supposed, the cause of insanity, especially among the rich." Treatments for chronic masturbation included the application of ice or leeches to the scrotum or vulva, cold sitz baths, cold enemas, or confinement in MECHANICAL RESTRAINTS such as STRAITJACKETS or MUFFS. Major medical authorities continued to link masturbation with the development of "neurasthenia" and even psychotic disorders at least until the 1930s.

Englehart, H. T. "The Disease of Masturbation: Values and the Concept of Disease," *Bulletin of the History of Medicine* 48 (1974): 239–248.

Gilbert, A. N. "Doctor, Patient, and Onanist Diseases in the Nineteenth Century," *Journal of the History of Medicine,* July 1975, pp. 217–234.

Hare, E. H. "Masturbation and Insanity," *Journal of Mental Science* 108 (1962): 16.
Macdonald, R. "The Frightful Consequences of Onanism: Notes on the History of a Delusion," *Journal of the History of Ideas* 28 (1967): 423–431.

Maudsley, Henry (1835–1918) A British psychiatrist, editor of the *Journal of Mental Science* and the benefactor and founder of the famous Maudsley Hospital in London, Henry Maudsley was perhaps the most important figure in British psychiatry from the 1870s until his death. He was married to the daughter of the man who had previously dominated psychiatry in Britain, John CONOLLY, the leader of the NONRESTRAINT MOVEMENT. Like his contemporary Wilhelm GRIESINGER in Germany, Maudsley believed in the physiological basis of all mental disorders and particularly emphasized the role of heredity in transmitting these disorders. His first book, *The Physiology and Pathology of Mind* (1867), was considered a turning point in British psychiatry due to this biological perspective. In this book he proposed that there were "two great divisions" in the "varieties of insanity," namely *"Affective* and *Ideational,"* and these were distinguished on the basis of whether or not a person had delusions (delusions being a sign of an ideational insanity). He was much criticized for his chapter in that book entitled "Insanity in Early Life," because it was not generally accepted in those times that children could develop psychotic disorders. Although he recommended the earliest possible treatment of people with mental disorders in settings that removed them from their families, he also believed that the most chronic mental patients should be discharged from asylums and cared for at home. As treatment, Maudsley recommended baths, emetics, and purgatives, a good diet and the use of opium.

Unlike his cheerful and emphatic father-in-law, John Connolly, Maudsley was often described as arrogant, aloof, somewhat mean-spirited, and bitter. In 1896, at the age of 60, Maudsley's rather pessimistic view of life was reflected in this confessional passage about his career:

> A physician who had spent his life in administering to diseased minds might be excused if, asking at the end of it whether he had spent his life well, he accused the fortune of an evil hour which threw him on that track of work. He could not well help feeling something of bitterness in the certitude that one-half the diseased he had dealt with never could get well, and something of the misgiving in the reflection whether he had done real service to his kind by restoring the other half to do reproductive work. Nor would the scientific interest of his studies compensate entirely for the practical uncertainties, since their revelation of the structure of human nature might inspire a doubt whether, notwithstanding impassioned aims, paeans of progress, endless pageants of self-illusions, its capacity of degeneration did not equal, and might someday exceed, its capacity of development.

Maudsley, H. "Insanity in Relation to Criminal Responsibility," *Alienist and Neurologist,* April 17, 1896.
———. *The Physiology and Pathology of Mind.* New York: D. Appleton, 1867.

mechanical restraint Throughout history, the mentally ill have been abused and generally mistreated, both before and after the rise of institutional care in the late 1700s and especially during the early 1800s. More often than not, the human needs of the mentally ill (who were viewed as wild, like beasts) were met with FLOGGINGS and lashings, placement in cages, or restraint by chains. Masks and gags that would keep talkative patients silent were perfected by Ferdinand AUTENREITH in Germany in the late 1700s. Various machines based on the CIRCULATING SWING or the GYRATOR were used to spin patients into obedience, as would the "hollow wheel" (HAYNER'S WHEEL) treadmill. Another 17th-century invention, by MacBride in England, was the "straight-waistcoat," later known as the STRAITJACKET, and this in turn inspired other variations by other asylum keepers, including the sacklike mechanical restraints known as HORN'S SACK or the MAD-SHIRT that would be placed over the unmanageable patient's head in order to subdue him or her. Despite the widespread influence of the NONRESTRAINT MOVEMENT in Europe beginning in the 1840s, many such inhumane devices

of mechanical restraint as the straitjacket, MUFFS or the BED SADDLE survived into the 20th century.

Part of the reason that the use of mechanical restraints was so common in the treatment of the mentally ill was due to the prevailing belief in those days that mental illness was incurable. According to Emil KRAEPELIN in his book *One Hundred Years of Psychiatry* (which is actually an excellent history of the use of mechanical restraints), it was only about 1820 that the idea took hold in Europe (and presumably the United States) that some cases of mental illness might be treatable and that some patients could be rehabilitated. Mechanical restraints, although often portrayed as "treatments" that led to "cures," were in fact merely coercive methods to subdue difficult patients during periods of crisis. Philippe PINEL made the first steps to correct the torturous treatment of the mentally ill by freeing dozens of patients from their chains on May 24, 1789 (with his male nurse, Pussin), and by advocating the practice of "moral medicine." Yet rehabilitative treatment for these patients was not begun until two decades later.

When Emil Kraepelin served at the Heidelberg Clinic from 1891–1903, he used no coercion with his patients—a standard philosophy of the time that was not everywhere practiced to the letter. To demonstrate to his medical students how much had changed in the institutional treatment of the mentally ill, he set up a small museum of mechanical restraints. Kraepelin relates in his memoirs:

> The revolution caused by the systematical introduction of bed rest, the frequent use of baths, and finally the newer narcoleptics and tranquilizers was striking. To give the students an idea of these advances, I began collecting means of mechanical restraint, for example, straightjackets, chairs, footcuffs, muffs, gloves, and so on with corresponding illustrations from the old asylums and made a little museum, which I showed the students during the semester. I managed to get some chains, which had once been used to chain a patient.

Perhaps the only form of mechanical restraint still in use today is the FOUR-POINT RESTRAINT or FIVE-POINT RESTRAINT used for brief, supervised periods. Seclusion or isolation rooms are still used in some institutions as well. However, many patients and patient advocates charge that the modern equivalent of these mechanical restraints is in reality the use of ANTIPSYCHOTIC DRUGS as a form of CHEMICAL RESTRAINT to keep patients manageable in an institutional setting.

Illustrations of almost all the forms of mechanical restraint ever used are reproduced in a useful book by A. A. Roback and Thomas Kiernan.

Kraepelin, E. *One Hundred Years of Psychiatry.* 1917. Reprint, New York: Philosophical Library, 1962.

Roback, A. A., and T. Kiernan. *Pictorial History of Psychology and Psychiatry.* New York: Philosophical Press, 1969.

medical disorders that mimic psychotic disorders It has long been known that some physical illnesses can have serious effects on the mental health of an individual. Some of the more serious diseases can actually produce symptoms that, upon first presentation, may look like one of the psychotic disorders. A person may be disoriented and confused, act bizarrely and experience hallucinations and delusions, but then be found to be suffering only from a treatable physical ailment. The following medical disorders are those most likely to resemble a psychotic disorder, particularly schizophrenia:

Viral encephalitis This is literally a "viral infection of the brain." Such brain infections can resemble schizophrenia in their earliest stages of infection. The most commonly reported viruses implicated are cytomegalovirus, measles, coxsackie, herpes simplex, Epstein-Barr, and equine encephalitis. As we know from the history of the disorder that used to be called the GENERAL PARALYSIS OF THE INSANE, cerebral syphilis can resemble schizophrenia in its most advanced stages, though it is rarely encountered today. The suspected viral cause of the psychosis can be confirmed with a spinal tap (lumbar puncture). The human immunodeficiency virus (HIV) can cause mental deterioration (dementia), and individuals who are seropositive for HIV and manifest the AIDS DEMENTIA COMPLEX may be diagnosed with AIDS solely on the basis of this dementia.

Temporal lobe epilepsy This type of epilepsy has long been reported to include psychotic symptoms (delusions and hallucinations) in some people.

Thyroid disease Any disease process involving the hormones and their role in the nervous system of human beings (neuroendocrinopathy) can cause psychosis-mimicking symptoms. Primary hypothyroidism is perhaps the most commonly misdiagnosed medical disorder that mimics a psychiatric disorder, because it involves so many symptoms that resemble a severe depression (depressed mood, weight change, sleep disturbances, and, in its most extreme forms, delusions and hallucinations). Thyroid disease can be mistaken for the mood disorders and, in some cases, schizophrenia.

Huntington's disease A genetically transmitted disease that strikes in midlife, Huntington's disease in its earliest stages is perhaps more persistently misdiagnosed as schizophrenia than is any other medical disorder. When the characteristic abnormal movements begin later in the disease ("choreiform movements"), the actual diagnosis is usually made without difficulty.

Multiple sclerosis Multiple sclerosis has much in common with schizophrenia. Like schizophrenia, it often begins in people between the ages of 18 and 40. In its earliest stages, patients may report feeling "tired" or "weak" a lot of the time, may become depressed, and may undergo a certain amount of intellectual deterioration. Multiple sclerosis is commonly misdiagnosed in its early stages, but as the disease progresses the characteristic symptoms become obvious.

Brain tumors Brain tumors may cause psychotic symptoms that resemble schizophrenia. Although "psychosis secondary to brain tumor" is rare, it is easily misdiagnosed. Elderly persons are more likely to have psychotic symptoms from brain tumors. The most likely place for a brain tumor to cause schizophrenia-like symptoms is on the pituitary gland, although some temporal lobe tumors may also cause psychosis. The correct diagnosis is easily made with neuroimaging scans using magnetic resonance imaging or computed tomography.

Traumatic injury to the brain Psychotic syndromes occur more frequently in individuals who have had a traumatic brain injury than in the general population. Sometimes a chronic, schizophrenia-like syndrome can develop after a serious head injury. People diagnosed with schizophrenia have a higher frequency of traumatic brain injury than individuals diagnosed with other psychiatric disorders.

Parkinson's disease PD is a degenerative neurological disease caused by the arteriosclerotic changes in the part of the brain that controls smooth movement, the basal ganglia. It is often a crippling disease, characterized by muscular tremors, rigidity of movement, droopy posture, and masklike facial grimaces. In the latter stages of the disease, hallucinations and other psychotic symptoms develop in about 40 percent of all persons who have PD.

There are a number of other medical disorders that may produce symptoms resembling schizophrenia, though less commonly. These may include the following medical disorders: stroke (cerebral vascular accident, or CVA); metal poisoning (e.g., mercury, lead); insecticide poisoning (e.g., organo-phosphorous compounds); Wilson's disease; tropical infections; acute intermittent porphyria, metachromatic leukodystrophy; lupus erythematosus; normal pressure hydrocephalus; hepatic encephalopathy; pellagra; pernicious anemia; leptospirosis, and sarcoidosis.

Extein, I., and M. S. Gold. *Medical Mimics of Psychiatric Disorders.* Washington, D.C.: American Psychiatric Press, 1986.

Lisanby, S. H., et al. "Psychosis Secondary to Brain Tumor," *Seminars in Clinical Neuropathology* 3 (1998): 12–22.

McAllister, T. W. "Traumatic Brain Injury and Psychosis: What Is the Connection?" *Seminars in Clinical Neuropsychiatry* 3 (1998): 211–223.

Peyser, C. E., et al. "Psychoses in Parkinson's Disease," *Seminars in Clinical Neuropsychiatry* 3 (1998): 41–50.

medical model of mental disorders This is the prevailing philosophical position in our culture on the nature of mental disorders. Mental disorders are viewed as equivalent to physical "illnesses," which can be "diagnosed" and "treated." Critics of the medical model, such as American psychiatrist Thomas Szaz, believe the "myth of mental illness" has outlived its usefulness as a way to conceptualize the social and psychological phenomena we label "sick." Other models of mental disorder can be based on other premises. For example, in other

cultures (or subcultures within our own society), supernatural models may be more accepted, with mental disorders viewed as the result of spirits or demons that must be exorcised.

The psychotic disorders have been assumed to be brain diseases since the 19th century. However, due to the great influence in American psychiatry of psychoanalysis and FAMILY INTERACTION THEORIES throughout most of the 20th century, which emphasized the social and cultural causes of schizophrenia, the medical model did not really gain prominence again in schizophrenia research until the 1970s with the advent of new BRAIN IMAGING TECHNIQUES and other technological advances in the field of biochemistry genetics, and psychopharmacology.

Siegler, M., and H. Osmond. *Models of Madness, Models of Medicine.* New York: Macmillan, 1974.

medical restraint See CHEMICAL RESTRAINT.

médicine mentale Literally "mental medicine." This was one of the earliest terms used in France for the professional discipline of psychiatry. By the 1820s, the status of *médicine mentale* was debated in many circles. During this time J. E. D. ESQUIROL argued that former methods of studying human nature, particularly "metaphysical philosophy," completely ignored the "physical man." *Médicine mentale* was thus based on a physiological foundation, as evidenced by the methodology used by Esquirol and Philippe PINEL in their investigations of the causes of mental illness: namely, autopsies.

Meduna, Ladislaus von (1896–1964) The originator of chemically induced convulsive therapy for schizophrenia. Meduna was a neuropathologist in Budapest, Hungary, who also worked at a prominent asylum in that city. Meduna had observed that persons with schizophrenia rarely suffered from epilepsy. Using his microscopic skills as a neuropathologist, Meduna began to look for differences between the brain cells of epileptics and schizophrenics. To his eye, glial cells were quite different in the two disorders, thus verifying his clinical observation. From these two basic observations he created a theory that schizophrenia and epilepsy were somehow "in opposition" to one another. Therefore, he reasoned (somewhat poorly), if he could bring about an epilepsy-like seizure in schizophrenics it would cure them. He first used camphor to induce seizures, then switched to a cardiac stimulant, pentylenetetrazol, which was marketed in the United States as Metrazol and in Europe as Cardiazol. In his first series of 26 schizophrenics, 10 showed remarkable improvement after their chemically induced seizures. Meduna's published report of this study in the *Zeitschrift fuer die gesamte Neurologie und Psychiatrie* in 1935 attracted wide attention in central Europe but did not attract the attention of American psychiatrists until mid–1937. In that year Meduna published a book on his new therapy, *Die Konvulsionstherapie der Schizohrenie* (*The Convulsion Therapy of Schizophrenia*), and two years later he immigrated to the United States and took a position as professor of psychiatry at Loyola University in Chicago.

METRAZOL SHOCK THERAPY, as it was also called, did not have a long history in psychiatric therapeutics. ELECTROSHOCK THERAPY and INSULIN COMA THERAPY soon overshadowed it.

megavitamin therapy Megavitamin therapy for schizophrenia was first reported in a publication by psychiatrist Abram Hoffer and his colleagues in 1957. On the basis of the TRANSMETHYLATION HYPOTHESIS, a BIOCHEMICAL THEORY OF SCHIZOPHRENIA, they reasoned that a toxic substance was created when the NEUROTRANSMITTER epinephrine was metabolized in the brain. This toxic metabolite—adrenochrome—was thought to be responsible for producing the symptoms of schizophrenia. To block the production of adrenochrome, schizophrenic patients were administered high doses of niacin (vitamin B_{-3}). In later studies, the doses of niacin were raised even higher and combined with ECT and other somatic treatments. The literature on megavitamin therapy is voluminous, and highly controversial, with most knowledgeable assessments of this area of research tending to

discount the claims of lasting therapeutic success with megavitamin therapy.

In 1968 Linus Pauling, a Nobel laureate in chemistry, coined the term *orthomolecular psychiatry* to refer to the treatment of mental disorders through nutritional changes. Pauling argues in his first paper on the subject that mental illness is the result of chemical imbalances in the brain that could be corrected through a proper diet and nutritional supplements. Pauling speaks of creating an "orthomolecular environment of the mind" that eliminates the altered subjective experiences of PSYCHOSIS (which in orthomolecular psychiatry is called metabolic dysperception). Orthomolecular therapy grew in the 1970s among its adherents, and a wide variety of vitamins and minerals have been used in the treatment of SCHIZOPHRENIA and other disorders. These research reports have been reported in such publications as the *Journal of Orthomolecular Psychiatry.*

Although it is entirely possible—and even probable—that nutrition may affect the development and the course of schizophrenia and other psychotic disorders, due to its lack of conclusive evidence, orthomolecular treatment is considered at present to be outside the mainstream of psychiatry.

See also FOOD ALLERGIES AS A CAUSE OF PSYCHOSIS; TRANSMETHYLATION HYPOTHESIS.

Hawkins, D., and L. Pauling. *Orthomolecular Psychiatry: Treatment of Schizophrenia.* San Francisco: Freeman, 1973.

Hoffer, A., et al. "Treatment of Schizophrenia with Nicotinic Acid and Nicotinamide." *Journal of Clinical and Experimental Psychopathology* 18 (1957): 131–158.

Pauling, L. "Orthomolecular Psychiatry," *Science* 160 (1968): 265–271.

melancholia Along with MANIA, melancholia is one of the two great ancient categories of madness or insanity. In humoral medicine, melancholy was thought to be caused by an excess of "black bile" (which is the exact meaning of melancholy). From antiquity to the mid-1800s, mania and melancholia were prime organizing categories for all other insanities. Originally, melancholia had nothing to do with what we think of today as DEPRESSION. Instead the term was used as a general designation for the types of madness characterized by fixed DELUSIONS (such as found in PARANOIA). Mania was a broad category for any disorder that involved hallucinations. A second meaning for melancholia was any sort of lessening in intensity or weakness in mood, intellectual functioning, or "will." The multitude of various maladies and weakened states of mind that were grouped under this old term can be found in Robert Burton's (1577–1640) huge volume, *The Anatomy of Melancholy* (1621). Burton himself clearly suffered from both anxiety and depression (which we now know are often combined). The connection of melancholia with ancient humoral theories of health and illness was first severed by British physician William Cullen in his book *First Lines of the Practice of Physic* (1777).

Although some sort of mood disorder or anxiety disorder was always present in ancient descriptions of melancholy, melancholy was finally distilled down to something that resembles modern concepts of depression after 1850, and certainly by the last two decades of the 19th century. In 1980 *DSM-III* introduced the diagnosis of "major depression," and this concept has had a profound impact on psychiatric practice as well as on the public imagination, setting the state for the acceptance of ANTIDEPRESSANT DRUGS such as Prozac (1988) as the desired remedy for everyday psychic ills. The most comprehensive description of the millennia-old history of melancholia can be found in an excellent book on the subject by Yale University historian of psychiatry Stanley W. Jackson.

Jackson, S. W. *Melancholia and Depression: From Hippocratic Times to Modern Times.* New Haven, Conn.: Yale University Press, 1986.

Mellaril See ANTIPSYCHOTIC DRUGS.

Mendelian transmission The modern science of genetics is based upon the work of an Austrian biologist and Augustinian monk, Gregor Johann Mendel (1822–84). In his experiments with peas grown in the garden of the monastery at Brünn,

he discovered lawful patterns of heredity in the ways certain characteristics, or traits, were transmitted from generation to generation in the plants. Classical Mendelian transmission is monogenetic transmission—that is, a single gene with dominant and recessive ALLELES distributes certain traits (called Mendelian traits) in a typical fashion: Three offspring have the dominant characteristic for every individual with a recessive trait. It has long been known that the genetic predisposition to the psychotic disorders is passed on from generation to generation in a NON-MENDELIAN PATTERN OF TRANSMISSION that is, as yet, not well understood.

See also GENETIC TRANSMISSION.

mental alienation Mental illness. Although used in a different context for centuries, it was not until the 1800s that mental alienation (*aliénation mentale*) became a medical term. With legislative reforms in France in 1838, the term began to refer to the legal status of insanity (*folie*). At about this time it became popular with physicians who treated the mentally ill as a term for severe mental illness. The term "mental alienation" first began appearing in English medical texts about 1860, and it was at about this time that the term "ALIENIST" began to be popularly used to describe a physician who specialized in the treatment of the mentally ill. In English, "mental alienation" referred to mental disorders that were not diseases of the brain (as was delirium). Along with the concepts of "insanity" and "dementia," the old concept of mental alienation helped to form the concept of PSYCHOSIS in the latter half of the 19th century.

Berrios, G. E. "Historical Aspects of Psychoses: 19th-Century Issues," *British Medical Bulletin* 43 (1987): 484–498.

mental disorder This is now the officially accepted term for what has been called in the past mental illness, psychiatric disorder, or mental diseases. The word *disorder* is used to make the concept more neutral and specifically to downplay the causal assumptions of a medical model of madness that is communicated with the words *illness* or *disease*.

mental hospitals See ASYLUMS.

mental hygiene movement Since the reform era of the mid-1800s, in the United States and Europe there was a growing concern surrounding the treatment and possibly even the prevention of mental disorders. The term that came to be used for this concept—mental hygiene—was coined and first used in a book in 1843 by William C. Sweetwater, an American physician. It was later also used by Isaac RAY as the title of a book on this subject published in 1863. However, in this century the term *mental hygiene* has come to be associated with an American reformer, Clifford BEERS.

At the turn of the century, American businessman Clifford Beers suffered a mental disorder that led to his hospitalization in private and then in public institutions. The horrors of his treatment led him to seek reforms in the treatment of the mentally ill once he had recovered. The first step was the publication of his vivid autobiography, *A Mind That Found Itself,* in March 1908. On May 6, 1908, Clifford Beers met with 13 other interested men and women in New Haven and founded the Connecticut Society for Mental Hygiene. The objectives they agreed upon that day have influenced all other mental health organizations since that time and have remained a vital plan of action for community responses to mental illness in society:

> The chief purpose of the Society shall be to work for the conservation of mental health; to help prevent nervous and mental disorders and mental defects; to help raise the standards of care for those suffering from any of these disorders or defects; to secure and disseminate reliable information on these subjects; to cooperate with federal state, and local agencies or officials and with public and private agencies whose work in any way relates to that of a society for mental hygiene.

The public response to this new organization was impressive (helped, no doubt, by Beers's shocking book), and groups began to spring up in other areas of the country and, later, in other countries. By 1909 Beers formed the National Committee for Mental Hygiene and had the sup-

port of such prominent figures as psychologist and philosopher William James and psychiatrist Adolf MEYER. In 1930 the First International Congress on Mental Hygiene met in Washington, D.C. Later, this organization once again changed its name to the National Council for Mental Hygiene. It is now known as the National Mental Health Association.

Historical essays on the Mental Hygiene Movement and its influence can be found in the supplement included in later editions (starting in 1953) of Beers's book.

Beers, C. *A Mind That Found Itself: An Autobiography.* New York: Longman, Green, 1908.

mesoridazine See ANTIPSYCHOTIC DRUGS.

Messiah complex See AMENOMANIA; MONOMANIA.

metabolic disorder hypothesis In biological terms, the word *metabolism* refers to the chemical processes within the body in which new substances are synthesized (catabolism) or broken down (anabolism) in order to bring about growth, regulation (homeostasis), tissue repair, and energy supply. Although the notion of the physical basis of metabolism (conversion of organic matter from one form into another) dated from the time of the ancient Greeks, the rise in experimental biology in the mid-1830s led to a primary focus on the processes of metabolism. "Soluable ferments" (enzymes) were known and studied in the 19th century, but the importance of enzymes in metabolism was not recognized. It was not until 1926 that technological advances allowed for the identification and study of individual enzymes. However, by the 1890s it was certainly clear that "internal secretions" from glands with and without ducts were involved in metabolism, leading to the modern concept of the hormone (1905) and the rise of modern endocrinology. After 1930, the rise of MOLECULAR BIOLOGY deepened understanding of the hormones, enzymes, and other biological processes involved in metabolism. Since 1902 it had been hypothesized that hereditary transmission played a role in enzyme formation, leading to the "one-gene, one-enzyme" idea until the 1960s, when this notion was replaced with a "one-gene, one-polypeptide" hypothesis. Molecular biology research has focused on the genes linked to the formation of these chemicals involved in metabolism.

Mental disorders as metabolic disorders By the 1890s it was clear that some diseases—such as diabetes—were related to metabolism. As is the usual pattern in the history of medicine, the excitement caused by the discovery of a new mechanism for the cause of disease often leads to speculation that the new mechanism causes many, if not all, diseases. In the 21st century it is the assertion that genetics plays a role in the cause of most mental and physical disorders that has become popular. By the mid-1890s microbes (bacteria) and imbalances in the production of "internal secretions" by the glands, leading to "metabolic disorders," were two medical theories that were quickly extended as explanations of the cause of most physical and mental diseases. Together these were known under the general term *autointoxication.*

When Emil KRAEPELIN first introduced his concept of dementia praecox in 1896, he included it under a broad category of mental disorders that he believed were "metabolic disorders" (*Stoffwechselerkrankungen*) in the fifth edition of his famous textbook, *Psychiatrie.* In subsequent editions of *Psychiatrie,* he eventually dropped this broad assertion. However, for at least the first two decades after introducing dementia praecox as a diagnostic entity, Kraepelin held firm to the belief that this disease was caused by a poisoning of the brain arising from the "sex organs," since the disease most commonly appeared in the years directly following puberty. Heredity did, of course, play a role, but he claimed that it merely made one vulnerable to developing this abnormal functioning of the sex glands and did not directly cause dementia praecox. AUTOINTOXICATION AS A CAUSE OF DEMENTIA PRAECOX (SCHIZOPHRENIA) was an influential hypothesis that led to many theories of etiology (and radical forms of treatment) until the 1930s. Following Kraepelin and advances in endocrinology, ENDOCRINE ALTERATIONS IN SCHIZOPHRENIA

were studied throughout the 20th century, but relatively few publications have appeared on this subject in the 21st century.

Metabolism and heredity The role of heredity (or genetics) in the development of metabolic diseases was documented convincingly by A. E. Garrod (1857–1936) in 1909 in his book *Inborn Errors of Metabolism.* Modern GENETICS STUDIES have found links between endocrine disorders and genes for some forms of diabetes and other disorders, but no such connection between genes and metabolic or endocrine disorders has been found for schizophrenia.

The return of metabolic studies in the 1950s Research on the "psychosis-causing" or psychotogenic effects of hallucinogenic drugs such as LSD-25 led to speculation that there may be a similar chemical process at work in the bodies of persons who suffer from schizophrenia. In 1952 Humphrey Osmond and J. R. Smythies proposed a new theory about the cause of schizophrenic symptoms based on this premise, the TRANSMETHYLATION HYPOTHESIS. The assumption was that if such a psychotogenic process was happening in the body, metabolic products of it should be detectable in the blood or urine. The search for such metabolites and the enzymes that led to their creation dominated psychiatric research from 1957 to 1967, an era that psychiatrist and historian David Healy characterized as "the flourishing of metabolic psychiatry." Ultimately no such endogenous psychotogenic substance was found in persons with schizophrenia, and by 1979 the transmethylation hypothesis no longer guided schizophrenia research. Findings were numerous, contradictory, and not directly applicable to the design of new antipsychotic drugs. Instead it was replaced by the DOPAMINE HYPOTHESIS and the search for neurotransmitters involved in the pathophysiology and possible etiology of schizophrenia. Basic research on neurotransmitters was directly relevant to the creation of new antipsychotic drugs and attracted significant funding by pharmaceutical companies. Despite a few promising leads, the pharmaceutical industry was far less interested in funding large scale research on the transmethylation hypothesis because drug development seemed less promising.

Problems in studying metabolism in schizophrenia Although endocrine and immune system alterations have been documented, though inconsistently, in schizophrenia, it is not possible to determine if these findings are due to the effect of ANTIPSYCHOTIC DRUGS or to the underlying disease process of schizophrenia. Antipsychotic drugs are known to affect both endocrine and immune functions. Another further problem lies in the difficulty in knowing if metabolic or immune disturbances cause schizophrenia, or if they are caused by schizophrenia. Although tighter links have been forged between AFFECTIVE DISORDERS and metabolic disorders, there is no convincing evidence that schizophrenia is a metabolic disorder.

See also ENDOCRINE ALTERATIONS IN SCHIZOPHRENIA; IMMUNE SYSTEM ALTERATIONS IN SCHIZOPHRENIA.

Healy, D. *The Creation of Psychopharmacology.* Cambridge, Mass.: Harvard University Press, 2002.

Yao, J. K., and R. D. Reddy. "Metabolic Investigations in Psychiatric Disorders," *Molecular Neurobiology* 31 (2005): 193–203.

Metrazol shock therapy One of the chemically induced forms of the CONVULSIVE THERAPIES of schizophrenia, invented by Hungarian psychiatrist Ladislas von MEDUNA (1896–1964) in the early 1930s. Believing that SCHIZOPHRENIA and epilepsy were physiologically incompatible, Meduna reasoned that the artificial induction of seizures in schizophrenic patients would alleviate their symptoms. First he used camphor. He then set out to do this through chemical means by administering an initial intravenous dose of 3 c.c. of pentylenetetrazol (Metrazol) with an increase of 1 c.c. if a convulsion was not induced in the patient. Achieving what he interpreted as a convincing success, he published his results in 1935. The treatment spread quickly, and by 1940 literally thousands of schizophrenic patients in Europe and the United States had been treated with Metrazol shock therapy, both in institutions and in private practice. Metrazol shock therapy was much easier to administer than the INSULIN COMA (OR SHOCK) THERAPY of Manfred Sakel (1900–57), which required a highly trained staff to administer and monitor the potentially life-threatening treatments.

Metrazol is a derivative of camphor, a substance used since the 18th century on institutionalized

mentally ill patients. In fact, the earliest use of a chemically induced convulsion therapy for mental illness was reported by British physician William Oliver in 1785. Oliver administered a high dose of camphor to a patient experiencing a manic episode in order to sedate him, but instead the patient experienced a convulsion. However, his manic symptoms seemed to miraculously disappear. But when the same patient was suffering from depression two years later, the same treatment had no effect. Oliver's report of convulsive treatment was cited occasionally in early psychiatric manuals, but it does not seem that it inspired others to apply the method as a formal treatment for mental disorders until Meduna's work in the 1930s.

In a 1938 article that reviewed the research on Metrazol shock therapy to date and gave a report on the treatment of 35 patients in a private practice setting, Philadelphia psychiatrist N. W. Winkleman of the University of Pennsylvania Medical School gives the following vivid description of what Metrazol shock therapy was like:

> The technic of the therapy as advised by von Meduna consists of two injections per week. Within a few seconds to minutes after the intravenous injection of 3 c.c. to 10 c.c. of metrazol, the patients usually give a short cough. This is followed in rapid succession by generalized body twitching, opening of the mouth, frequently with a cry, generalized convulsive seizures of the entire body, intense rigidity, gradual closing of the mouth with such vigor that frequently the patients have bitten through a wooden tongue depressor. Then cyanosis, dyspnea, apnea occur until finally after a few seconds of cessation of breathing the patient suddenly inspires and relaxes. The mouth gag is usually kept in the mouth rather tightly until the patient returns to full consciousness and frequently the patient makes sucking movements on the mouth gag. The patients are frequently in a confused state which lasts for a variable period after the convulsion is at an end. They may struggle to get out of bed or they may talk in an incoherent manner. Frequently they are confused for a period up to two hours and are then able to be up and around and are then given their food after three or four hours.

The convulsions (sometimes called "Metrazol storms") were often so severe that some patients experienced shoulder and jaw dislocations, with reports that sometimes teeth would actually break in the process. To prevent shoulder dislocations, Winkleman and A. M. Rechtman, a Philadelphia orthopedic surgeon, invented a leather "belt" or "restraining device" that fastened the wrists of a person to the hips so that the arms would be immobile during convulsions. A picture of this device, which resembles MECHANICAL RESTRAINTS used in the 18th and 19th centuries, can be found in Winkleman's article.

The primary drawback to Metrazol shock therapy was that the convulsion did not occur immediately after the injection of the drug, during which time the patient was conscious and experiencing feelings of intense fear and terror that were a side effect of the drug. Furthermore, sometimes convulsions could not be produced, and these patients would remain in an agitated state for days until another treatment could be applied. ELECTROSHOCK THERAPY replaced Metrazol shock therapy after 1940 because it induced immediate unconsciousness and convulsions and was therefore considered more humane.

See also MEDUNA, LADISLAS JOSEPH VON.

Oliver, W. "Account of the Effects of Camphor in a Case of Insanity," *London Medical Journal* 6 (1785): 120–130.

von Meduna, L. *Konvulsionstherapie der Schizophrenie*. Halle: Marhold, 1937.

———. "Versuche über die biologische Beeinflüssung des ablaufes der Schizophrenie. I. Campher- und Cardazolkampfe," *Zeitschrift für Neurologie und Psychiatrie* 152 (1935): 235–262.

Winkleman, N. W. "Metrazol Treatment in Schizophrenia: A Study of Thirty-five Cases in Private Practice, Complications and Their Prevention," *American Journal of Psychiatry* 95 (1938): 303–316.

Meyer, Adolf (1866–1950) A Swiss neurologist and psychiatrist who immigrated to the United States in 1892 after completing his medical studies, Adolf Meyer was perhaps the single most influential figure in American psychiatry from about 1895 to the 1920s. He established many links between

American and European psychiatrists, and he was instrumental in modernizing the medical school teaching of psychiatry. He became a professor of psychiatry at the Johns Hopkins Hospital in Baltimore, Maryland, in 1910 and director of the famous Henry Phipps Psychiatric Clinic in 1913.

He coined the term *psychobiology* to describe his approach to psychiatry, which emphasized that a person's mental state was influenced by biological and environmental factors. Meyer liked to emphasize the lifelong history of a person and his or her subjective experience of a disease. His influence can be seen in the first standard American diagnostic manual for mental disorders, *DSM-I* (1952), in which many of the disorders were labeled as various types of "reactions"—a reflection of Meyer's philosophy that all mental disorders were psychological responses (reactions) to the environment, past experience, or biological processes.

Meyer attempted to replace traditional terms for mental disorders and other psychiatric terms with his own idiosyncratic vocabulary (for example, *parergasia* for schizophrenia, *thymergasia reactions* for manic-depressive psychosis, *holergasic disorders* for the psychotic disorders, *ergasiology* for psychobiology, and *ergasiatry* for psychiatry). None of these terms, however, ever gained wide acceptance.

Meyer resisted the theories of Emil KRAEPELIN and those who believed in the strict biological causes of mental disorders. Meyer and his "Meyerians" (like the Freudians and psychoanalysts after them) refused to believe in heredity (genetics) as the primary cause of mental disorders. It is therefore not surprising that these "mind twist men" (the Meyerians and psychoanalysts) were hostile to the "brain spot men" (the Krapelinians).

Meyer's main contribution to the history of dementia praecox and schizophrenia was a monograph he coauthored in 1911. It reinterprets the causes and symptoms of dementia praecox as "reactions" to psychosocial stressors. Meyer was one of a long list of famous figures in early 20th-century psychiatry who treated the same psychotic patient, Stanley McCormick (1874–1947), of the prominent Chicago family. However, neither he nor any of the others could cure this patient.

Meyer has not fared well in histories of psychiatry. Meyer was seen as ruminative and vague even by his own contemporaries, and it is said he never met a theory or new treatment in psychiatry that he did not like. His vague and virtually useless concept of "psychobiology" seemingly welcomed biological research on dementia praecox and schizophrenia, psychoanalysis, psychological research, autointoxication and focal infection theories of the cause of insanity, dental and abdominal surgery as a treatment for psychosis, the convulsive therapies (Metrazol, insulin, and electroshock), and a whole host of other theories and techniques. Logical contradictions, inconsistencies, and potential dangers of treatments (for example, abdominal surgery as a treatment for schizophrenia) did not seem to bother him. Although it is true his notion of mental disorders as "reactions" was a corrective to those who believed in the influence of heredity, including Kraepelin, he also did not totally reject Kraepelin.

Meyer was the first psychiatrist in the United States to critique Kraepelin's concept of dementia praecox. In an 1896 book review of the fifth edition of *Psychiatrie,* he criticizes Kraepelin's view of dementia praecox as a "metabolic disorder" and criticizes Kraepelin's speculation that dementia praecox is caused by an autointoxication. However, by 1918, Meyer was willing to support Henry A. Cotton of the New Jersey State Hospital at Trenton when he began the first of thousands of surgical procedures to cut out infected tissues in the body that were causing autointoxications of the brain and producing mental illness.

Lidz, T. "Adolf Meyer and the Development of American Psychiatry," *American Journal of Psychiatry* 123 (1966): 320–332.

Meyer, A., S. E. Jelliffe, and A. Hoch. *Dementia Praecox: A Monograph.* Boston: R. G. Badger, 1911.

Noll, R. "Styles of Psychiatric Practice, 1906–1925: Clinical Evaluations of the Same Patient by James Jackson Putnam, Adolf Meyer, August Hoch, Emil Kraepelin and Smith Ely Jelliffe," *History of Psychiatry* 10 (1999): 145–189.

milieu therapy The idea behind milieu therapy is that by creating a specially designed "therapeutic environment" for patients with severe mental ill-

ness, the course of the disease can be affected in a positive way. This idea is as old as those of the earliest pioneers of reform in the MORAL TREATMENT of mental illness, namely Philippe PINEL in France, Vincenzo CHIARUGI in Italy, and especially William Tuke in England, whose YORK RETREAT may have been the first true attempt at such a therapeutic environment. Since the early 19th century there have always been small private institutions that have attempted to provide such environments, but it was not until the 1930s and 1940s that the concept of constructing special wards or buildings for the purpose of milieu therapy came about.

American psychiatrist Harry Stack Sullivan may be given credit for stimulating the use of milieu therapy with his 1931 publication describing his special unit for young males with acute schizophrenia. However, it was the work of T. F. Main with neurotics at the Cassel Hospital in England that popularized the notion of the "therapeutic community," a term coined by Main in a 1946 paper. This approach demanded a more active participation by the patients in the management of the environment and emphasized three elements: (1) a flattening of the hierarchical structure of authority, (2) the blurring of role differentiations between staff and patients, and (3) the cultivation of open communication in order to minimize differences between the social life within the institution and that of the world outside. Many such experimental wards and units for the treatment of schizophrenia were initiated using this approach.

The environments of many psychiatric institutions have undergone extensive transformations since the 1950s in order to make them more "therapeutic." However, as a specific mode of treatment for schizophrenia and the psychotic disorders, the measurable positive effects of such an environment have been small in research studies. Hence milieu therapy has been criticized by researchers Van Putten and May in a 1976 review of the research literature: "Milieu therapy has increasingly become an ideology rather than a defined method of treatment sustained to a large extent not by scientific evaluation but by a steady flow of rhetoric and by humanitarian and emotional justifications." Nonetheless, in conjunction with other forms of treatment, it seems incontrovertible that a more humane environment can only help those who are suffering from severe mental disorders.

Main, T. F. "The Hospital as a Therapeutic Institution," *Bulletin of the Menninger Clinic* 19 (1946): 66–70.

Sullivan, H. S. "Socio-Psychiatric Research: Its Implication for the Schizophrenia Problem and for Mental Hygiene," *American Journal of Psychiatry* 10 (1931): 977–991.

Van Putten, T., and P. R. A. May. "Milieu Therapy of the Schizophrenias." In *Treatment of Schizophrenia: Progress and Prospects*, edited by L. J. West and D. E. Flinn. New York: Grune & Stratton, 1976.

misidentification syndromes These are a group of syndromes characterized by delusions that persons or objects in the environment are something other than what their true nature is. Familiar persons can be regarded as impostors (as in CAPGRAS SYNDROME), strange persons can become known persons who are believed to be persecuting the delusional person (FREGOLI'S SYNDROME), or persons in the delusional individual's immediate environment can become other known individuals (such as in the INTERMETAMORPHOSIS SYNDROME, in which a doctor, for example, can be mistaken for a first grade teacher). All of the misidentification syndromes are generally part of one of the psychotic disorders and are not diagnostic categories themselves.

"The Delusional Misidentification Syndromes," *Biblioteca Psychiatrica* 164 (1986): 1–153.

mixed states When Emil KRAEPELIN introduced MANIC-DEPRESSIVE ILLNESS in 1899 as one of the two main categories of insanity (the other being DEMENTIA PRAECOX), he described a disorder in which mania, depression, and psychotic states that were a combination of the two alternated over the course of the life span of afflicted persons. The presence of these "mixed states" (*Mischzustande*) led Kraeplin to believe that mania and depression were indeed two aspects of the same pathological process. The primary study of these mixed states was conducted by an assistant physician working

under Kraepelin at the Psychiatric Clinic of Heidelberg University, Wilhelm Weygandt (1870–1939). In the same year that Kraepelin published his first description of manic-depressive illness, Weygandt also published his dissertation as a monograph describing these mixed states in detail, providing 16 case history examples of patients who were manifesting symptoms of both mania and depression at the same time. Such mixed states were not uncommon in manic-depression. In addition to pure mania and pure depression, Weygandt described six separate mixed states, many of which Kraepelin later included in subsequent editions of his textbook, *Psychiatrie*. Weygandt summarized his main conclusions thus:

> In summary, cases of circular or manic-depressive insanity, a mixture of the cardinal symptoms of each of the two typical phases commonly occurs. Those combinations are usually brief, although sometimes the mixed state marks the entire course of a single episode, or most of it. Later episodes with mixed features show a longer course than do pure depressive or manic episodes, yet the prognosis is favorable in any kind of episode. This clinical approach has achieved good results both diagnostically and prognostically in the Clinic of Heidelberg, where fewer than one-third of [manic-depressive] patients have shown no mixed states at all, and over 20 percent of patients have had one or more episodes in which mixed features predominate.

Since 1899, "mixed states" have been acknowledged by psychiatry but have been little understood. Following the pattern set by the reconceptualizing of manic-depression as BIPOLAR DISORDER in *DSM-III* in 1980, *DSM-IV-TR* (2000) merely defines a "mixed episode" as one in which "criteria are met for both a manic episode and for a Major Depressive Episode (except for duration) nearly every day during at least a 1-week period." Because these criteria have been so vague, in the 1990s researchers began to investigate the nature of "mixed states" and have attempted to develop better diagnostic criteria that could be included in future editions of the *DSM* series. In the early 21st century the trend is to view mixed states as primarily a form of mania, dysphoric mania, separate from the classical idea of mania as euphoric mania and a newly proposed form, psychotic mania.

Mixed mania (dysphoric mania) is found mostly in females. It is associated with a higher rate of suicidal thoughts than in those persons suffering other forms of mania. Dysphoric mania also does not respond well to treatment with LITHIUM but does seem to respond better to the ANTIPSYCHOTIC DRUG OLANZAPINE (Zyprexa). Persons with bipolar disorder who experience mixed states are much less stable between episodes and are more likely to be "rapid cyclers" (four or more episodes of mania or major depression in a 12-month period) or "continuous cyclers" (those for whom there is no clear break between episodes). Thus, the presence of multiple mixed episodes (dysphoric mania) is a feature of the most disabling and severe courses of bipolar disorder.

Marneros, A. "Origin and Development of Concepts of Bipolar Mixed States," *Journal of Affective Disorders* 67 (2001): 228–240.

Salvatore, P., et al. "Weygandt's *On the Mixed States of Manic-Depressive Insanity:* A Translation and Commentary on Its Significance in the Evolution of the Concept of Bipolar Disorder," *Harvard Review of Psychiatry* 10 (2002): 255–275.

Weygandt, W. *Uber die Mischzustande des manisch-depressive Irreseins*. Munich: Verlag von J. F. Lehmann, 1899.

M'Naughten Rules A legal interpretation named after Daniel M'Naughten (?–1865), the man whose celebrated trial legitimized the legal verdict "not guilty by reason of insanity," also referred to as the M'Naughten Rules. M'Naughten (also spelled McNaughton) was a British joiner who apparently led a solitary existence for most of his life. As an adult, he developed paranoid delusions that he had enemies who were trying to kill him. He also complained of violent headaches, which leaves open the possibility that he may have been suffering from one of the MEDICAL DISORDERS THAT MIMIC PSYCHOTIC DISORDERS. In any event, his paranoid delusions also began to take on a political nature. He became convinced that the members of the Tory party were the persecutors who were

out to get him, and to fight back he attempted to assassinate British prime minister Sir Robert Peel (1788–1850) but instead mistakenly shot Edward Drummond, the prime minister's secretary. In his subsequent trial in 1843 he was found not guilty by reason of insanity—a historic judicial decision that caused considerable public outrage. The House of Lords then required the judges in the M'Naughten trial to provide a written explanation of how they reached their controversial decision. Their criteria for judging a criminal not guilty by reason of insanity have been referred to as the M'Naughten Rules and have greatly influenced legislation in Great Britain and in the United States.

M'Naughten himself was involuntarily committed to the BETHLEM ROYAL HOSPITAL, where he was incarcerated for the remainder of his life. The attempted assassination of President Ronald Reagan in 1981 by John Hinckley Jr. caused a similar public outcry when he too was found not guilty by reason of insanity—based, in part, on the more than a century of legislation influenced by the M'Naughten Rules.

See also INSANITY DEFENSE.

Quen, J. M. "An Historical View of the M'Naughten Trial," *Bulletin of the History of Medicine* 42 (1968): 43–51.

West, D. J., and A. Walk, eds. *Daniel McNaughton: His Trial and the Aftermath.* Ashford, Kent: Headley Brothers for the British Journal of Psychiatry, 1977.

Moban See ANTIPSYCHOTIC DRUGS.

mode of inheritance In GENETICS STUDIES, the pattern of inheritance (e.g., dominant or recessive) of a particular ALLELE.

molecular biology Molecular biology is an interdisciplinary field of research that investigates the role of molecules in the form, function, and evolutionary descent of living things. The methods used are from organic chemistry, structural chemistry, and genetics. The term *molecular biology* was first used in 1938, but the field itself dates from about 1930. After the discovery of the structure of the DNA molecule in 1953 by Watson and Crick, molecular genetics became an important area of research.

Molecular biology has come to dominate research and treatment in psychiatry. Many psychiatrists openly admit they would like to see psychiatry disappear into molecular biology. In the last 30 years, many articles in the top psychiatric journals are about molecules rather than the mentally ill as individual persons. The rise in power of the pharmaceutical industry has fueled this revolution in the perspective of what constitutes a mentally ill person. New drugs are developed through basic molecular biological research. Molecular biology has strikingly redefined our culture's concept of what it means to be a human being, whether in health or illness.

molecular markers These are certain biochemical substances, identified by their molecules, that can be traced throughout a family to see if they are "markers" that are genetically transmitted along with the disease genes of a particular medical or mental disorder. If the disease and the marker are found to be inherited together in a family, it can be inferred that the disease gene lies very near (is linked to) the marker gene.

molindone See ANTIPSYCHOTIC DRUGS.

monasteries For many centuries in Europe, monasteries served as hospitals for the sick and the poor. Although the Roman Catholic church banned the practice of medicine by the clergy (particularly such treatments as BLEEDING) in the early 13th century, monks were still allowed to provide food and shelter to the needy. The mentally ill were among those cared for by the various religious institutions, and some of them later became asylums for the mentally ill (as was the case for the BETHLEM ROYAL HOSPITAL).

See also ALMSHOUSES; BASKET MEN.

monoamine oxidase (MAO) An enzyme that breaks down NEUROTRANSMITTERS such as norepinephrine and serotonin. The inhibition of this

enzyme in the functioning of the brain produces an antidepressant effect, and the MAO inhibitors were therefore the first drugs to be used in the treatment of depression.

monomania A term for a very popular psychiatric diagnosis in France in the 1830s and 1840s, monomania referred to a type of mental disorder in which a person would have fixed, and often grandiose, ideas that did not correspond to reality. Although the person maintained these delusions, no other sign of mental deterioration was present. Save for these pockets of delusions in their thought pattern, the persons affected were otherwise considered rational. After J. E. D. ESQUIROL introduced the term around 1810, "monomania" quickly caught on with intellectuals as a cultural metaphor for political, religious, and other social extremism. In his 1838 book, *Des Maladies Mentales,* Esquirol identified several subtypes of monomania, generally depending upon the content of the primary delusions, the cause of the disorder, or its behavioral consequences: for example, theomania (religious delusions), erotic monomania, or erotomania (erotic delusions), monomania resulting from drunkenness, incendiary monomania (pyromania) and homicidal monomania.

Although monomania was the most popular diagnosis given in French asylums in the 1830s and 1840s (rivaled only by the GENERAL PARALYSIS OF THE INSANE), the condition was criticized by many alienists for being too general and thus virtually disappeared by the end of the century. Perhaps the most specific modern equivalent to monomania is the delusional (paranoid) disorders listed in *DSM-IV,* particularly the "grandiose type." However, the category was so broad that it might have also included cases of what we may now term paranoid schizophrenia or bipolar disorder.

The best and only English-language history of this 19th-century psychotic disorder is the chapter entitled "Monomania" in a 1987 book by Jan Goldstein on the French psychiatric profession in the 19th century.

Goldstein, J. *Console and Classify: The French Psychiatric Profession in the Nineteenth Century.* Cambridge: Cambridge University Press, 1987.

monosymptomatic hypochondriacal psychosis A proposed psychotic disorder, especially in Europe, in which a person maintains a psychotic hypochondriacal delusional system that is distinct from the rest of the personality. The single delusion usually contains one of the three following themes: FORMICATION (a tactile hallucination in which the person feels that bugs are crawling under his or her skin); dysmorphophobia (the delusional belief that one is misshapen and unattractive); or the "olfactory reference syndrome" (the delusion that one emits a foul body odor).

Munro, A., and J. Chamara. "Monosymptomatic Hypochondriacal Psychosis: A Diagnostic Check List Based on 50 Cases of the Disorder," *Canadian Journal of Psychiatry* 27 (1982): 374–376.

monozygotic twins "Identical twins." Monozygotic twins share all of their genes in common, whereas "fraternal twins" share only half of their genetic heritage. Therefore, the CONCORDANCE RATE for genetically transmitted disorders is much higher in monozygotic twins than in fraternal, or dizygotic, twins.

The study of monozygotic and dizygotic twins has provided some of the strongest evidence of the significant role that genes play in the predisposition to developing schizophrenia. The median monozygotic (MZ) concordance rate for schizophrenia is 46 percent. This is three times the corresponding concordance rate for dizygotic (DZ) twins, which is 14 percent. Two conclusions can be drawn from this: (1) The MZ:DZ ratio of more than 3:1 strongly indicates that genes play a role in the development of schizophrenia, and (2) since the MZ concordance rate is significantly less than 100 percent, this means that schizophrenia is not caused 100 percent by genetic factors. Therefore, nongenetic factors of unknown origin also play a significant role in schizophrenia.

Prescott, C. A., and I. I. Gottesman. "Genetically Mediated Vulnerability to Schizophrenia," *Psychiatric Clinics of North America,* 16 (1993): 245–267.

mood This term refers to a pervasive and long-lasting emotion that seems to color a person's

perception of the world and of the self. The most commonly experienced moods are anxiety, elation (elevated mood), depression (dysphoric mood), anger (irritable mood), and euphoria (euphoric mood). In an expansive mood, a person may just blurt out whatever emotions he or she may be feeling at the time, and this often includes grandiose overevaluations of self-importance. When a person is not experiencing an elevated or a depressed mood, the term for this is euthymic mood, that is, mood in the "normal" range of experience.

mood disorders An umbrella term introduced in *DSM-III-R* in 1987 to apply to the group of disorders previously termed the AFFECTIVE DISORDERS. These include the BIPOLAR DISORDERS (cyclothymia, and the three types of bipolar disorders: mixed, manic, and depressed) and the depressive disorders (formerly called unipolar depression). The mood disorders have been found to have seasonal patterns in which the mood disorder returns during a particular 60-day period every year.

Moon, influence of on madness Since classical times it was thought that the Moon caused madness or made it worse, and the idea of "lunacy" in the ancient sense of the word did not really die out until the 1800s. Although many of the 18th-century authors of the earliest psychiatric texts (such as John HASLAM) expressed their skepticism of this theory of the cause of mental illness, American physician Benjamin RUSH did not dismiss it outright. Instead, he concocted a pseudoscientific theory that mental illness gives some people a "sixth sense" that renders them more sensitive to moonlight and to the changes in the temperature and density of the air when the moon was full. In his 1812 book on the diseases of the mind, Rush writes:

> The moon, when full, increases the rarity of the air and the quantity of light, each of which I believe acts upon sick people in various diseases, and, among others, in madness ... The inference from these facts is, that the cases are few in which mad people feel the influence of the moon, and that when they do, it is derived chiefly from an increase of its light ... It is possible, further, that in the few cases in which the light of the moon, or the rarity of the air, is felt by deranged persons in a hospital, that their noise, by keeping a number of patients in neighboring cells awake, and in a state of inquietude from the want of sleep, may have contributed to establish that general belief in the influence of the moon upon madness, which has so long obtained among physicians.

Oliver, J. F. "Moonlight and Nervous Disorders: A Historical Study," *American Journal of Psychiatry* 99 (1943): 579–584.

Rush, B. *Medical Inquiries and Observations upon the Diseases of the Mind.* Philadelphia: Kimber & Richardson, 1812.

moral insanity A term introduced in English by psychiatrist and anthropologist James Cowles Prichard in 1835 to refer to a type of mental illness in which a person would exhibit severe disturbances in emotions or engage in highly pathological or self-destructive behaviors but would not have any intellectual impairment (i.e., no FORMAL THOUGHT DISORDER). Thus, a person had the ability to reason yet would engage in irrational behaviors. Unlike another popular diagnosis in Europe at that time, MONOMANIA, there were no delusions in a particular subject area or any hallucinations relating to those specific delusions.

In his book *A Treatise on Insanity and Other Disorders Affecting the Mind,* Prichard defines "moral insanity" in the following way:

> . . . a morbid perversion of the natural feelings, affections, inclinations, temper, habits, moral dispositions, and natural impulses, without any remarkable disorder or defect of the intellect or knowing and reasoning faculties, and particularly without any insane illusion or hallucination . . . The individual is found to be incapable, not of talking or reasoning upon any subject proposed to him, for this he will often do with great shrewdness and volubility, but of conducting himself with decency and propriety in the business of life.

Although Prichard based his idea of a moral insanity on many similar ideas proposed perhaps

as early as the 17th century, his concept that there was no intellectual impairment came under attack by other medical authorities. However, by 1850 the debate had shifted from the intellectual versus emotional issue to the irrational behavior of such persons, specifically on how "moral insanity" was related to immoral and criminal actions. Thus, by the 20th century, the original meaning of Prichard's "moral insanity" as essentially a synonym for an "emotional illness" was eliminated from the psychiatric vocabulary and was reduced to our modern notions of sociopathic personalities, psychopathic personalities, and, as they are now called, antisocial personalities—that is, persons who repeatedly engage in acts destructive to themselves or others (e.g., criminal activities) without any realization of the consequences of their actions or any seeming ability to feel empathy for those persons who become the "victims" of their antisocial behaviors.

The term *moral insanity* was first used in German (*moralische Insanie*) in 1819 by J. C. A. Grohmann (1769–1847) to describe a particular symptom.

Carlson, E. T., and N. Dain. "The Meaning of Moral Insanity," *Bulletin of the History of Medicine,* 1962, pp. 130–140.
Prichard, J. C. *A Treatise on Insanity and Other Disorders Affecting the Mind.* London: Sherwood, Gilbert & Piper, 1835.

moral treatment The treatment of mental illness through means other than physical ones (e.g., bleeding, bathing and purging). Perhaps the best modern translation of the meaning of "moral treatment" is a broad interpretation of our word *psychotherapy* but also may refer to modern ideas of MILIEU THERAPY. *Traitement moral* is the name for the revolutionary philosophy for the treatment of the mentally ill proposed by the great French reformer and physician Philippe PINEL in his 1801 book, *Traite médicophilosophique sur l'aliénation mentale, ou la manie* (English translation of 1806 entitled *A Treatise on Insanity*).

Moral treatment, as prescribed by Pinel, did not solely mean an ethical approach to treating the mentally ill, nor did it mean a method of treatment that instructed patients in ethics. Since the early 1800s the French word *moral* had several meanings, especially referring to that which was psychological in nature and not physical. Thus, Pinel could talk of the "passions" (emotions) as a "moral cause" of mental illness.

In his book, Pinel advocates an understanding of the character of the patient and his or her humane treatment. Coercion and mechanical restraints were to be banned except in extreme circumstances. Pinel also thought that by improving the physical environment of asylums that patients would improve, and so he advocated the supervised daily cleaning of the patients' cells. Certain physical activities were recommended as beneficial to patients, such as exercise, work, experiencing beautiful scenery and listening to soft, melodious music. Although these ideas seem quaint and rather obvious today, in Pinel's time the mentally ill were thought to have brain lesions that rendered them to a bestial level, and were therefore incurable. Hence, treatment to improve or rehabilitate the mentally ill in any permanent sense was not considered a rational idea.

Thus, the trend toward "moral medicine," as it was sometimes called, began with Pinel and finally culminated in a general interest throughout Europe in rehabilitating treatments about the year 1820. The NONRESTRAINT MOVEMENT that began in the 1830s in England was directly inspired by Pinel in France (and at about the same time by Chiarugi in Italy and Tuke in England). Our continuing efforts today to improve the daily life of the mentally ill person and to discover new methods of treatment and rehabilitation are a continuation of the *traitement moral* of Pinel.

Bockoven, J. S. *Moral Treatment in American Psychiatry.* New York: Springer, 1963.
Carlson, E. T., and N. Dain. "The Psychotherapy That Was Moral Treatment," *American Journal of Psychiatry* 117 (1960): 519–524.
Riese, W. "An Outline of a History of Ideas in Psychotherapy," *Bulletin of the History of Medicine* 25 (1951): 442–456.

morbid jealousy See OTHELLO SYNDROME.

Moreau de Tours, Jacques-Joseph (1804–1884) A French alienist who was part of the "Esquirol Cir-

cle." He wrote his 1830 doctoral thesis on MONOMANIA under the supervision of J. E. D. ESQUIROL. He is best remembered for his self-experimentation with hashish and cannabis to produce ALTERED STATES OF CONSCIOUSNESS that helped him gain insight into mental illness. In his 1845 book on these experiments, he introduced the concept of DISSOCIATION for the first time. Moreau de Tours is considered the first medical researcher to use drugs to produce an "artificial psychosis," although reports of the creation of an "artificial insanity" through the use of chemical substances date from at least the experiments of the Paracelsian iatrochemist Jan Baptista van Helmont (1577–1644).

See also PSYCHOTOMIMETIC.

Moreau de Tours, J.-J. *Du hachisch et de l'aliénation mentale: Etudes psychologiques.* Paris: Fortin, Masson, & Cie, 1845.

Morel, Bénédict-Augustin (1809–1873) A French psychiatrist who worked under Jules FALRET at the SALPÊTRIÈRE hospital in Paris. He wrote several important psychiatric texts during his career, but he is best remembered for his 1857 theory that many mental diseases were the result of physical, intellectual, and moral (emotional) DEGENERATION. Morel coined the term *démence précoce* in 1852 to refer to rapid degeneration, and this concept was later borrowed by Emil KRAEPELIN when describing DEMENTIA PRAECOX in 1896.

Morel, B. A. *Etudes cliniques: Traité théorique et pratique des maladies mentales.* Nancy: Grimblot: Paris: J.-B. Baillière, 1852.

mortality in schizophrenia Since the first mortality studies of people with schizophrenia were published in 1934, it has been known that schizophrenia is a life-shortening disease. In fact, in a major review of the mortality research on schizophrenia that was published in 1989, researcher Peter Allebeck of Huddinge, Sweden, concludes that the overall death rate is about twice that of the general population. In the studies of institutionalized schizophrenic patients prior to the invention of ANTIPSYCHOTIC DRUGS, tuberculosis was the major cause of death. However, starting in the 1950s, most patients were treated with antipsychotic medication and were returned to the community through DEINSTITUTIONALIZATION. As these patients are no longer monitored on a daily basis by medical staff, and often cast into the community with little or no social support, it is not surprising that suicide has become the leading cause of death for persons with schizophrenia. In fact, some estimates are so high that it is estimated that perhaps 10 percent to 13 percent of schizophrenics commit suicide. A second major cause of death is accidents. Young white schizophrenic men with high levels of premorbid functioning and high expectations are particularly at risk.

Other studies have been conducted to see if the high mortality rates in schizophrenics are due solely to suicides and accidental deaths. It has been found that the death rate due to "natural" cardiovascular disorders is also higher in schizophrenics than in the general population. Other studies have shown that institutionalized psychiatric patients (regardless of diagnosis) have a higher mortality as a whole than the general population.

Currently it is estimated that persons with schizophrenia live, on average, 10 to 15 years less than persons in the general population.

Allebeck, P. "Schizophrenia: A Life-Shortening Disease," *Schizophrenia Bulletin* 15 (1989): 81–89.

Caldwell, C. B., and I. I. Gottesman. "Schizophrenics Kill Themselves Too: A Review of Risk Factors for Suicide." *Schizophrenia Bulletin* 4 (1990): 571–589.

Malzberg, B. *Mortality among Patients with Mental Disease.* New York: State Hospital Press, 1934.

mosaicism A term used in GENETICS STUDIES that refers to the condition of having a mixture of normal and abnormal chromosomes. A person who has mosaicism has various amounts of normal cells and trisomies (cells with three chromosomes), resulting in varying degrees of illness.

motion pictures, depictions of psychosis in Persons with psychotic disorders have been portrayed

in Greek classical tragedy, Elizabethan and Jacobean plays, stage melodramas, and Gothic novels of the 18th and 19th centuries and 20th-century feature films. Perhaps the first extensive portrayal of the interior world of psychosis in motion pictures is the famous German expressionist film of 1919 *The Cabinet of Dr. Caligari.* In the surprise ending to this dreamlike film the audience learns that the entire story was merely the delusion of an institutionalized psychotic patient.

In a book on the portrayal of insanity in the feature film, authors Michael Fleming and Roger Manvell identify several major "themes of madness" that have often reflected prevailing societal attitudes toward mental illness and the psychiatric profession. These are

(1) the family and madness (*A Woman under the Influence,* 1974)
(2) institutionalization of the mad (*The Snake Pit,* 1948; *One Flew over the Cuckoo's Nest,* 1975)
(3) possession as madness (*The Exorcist,* 1973; *Three Faces of Eve,* 1957)
(4) the struggle between love and aggression (*Bad Timing: A Sensual Obsession,* 1980)
(5) the love of aggression (*M,* 1931; *Straw Dogs,* 1971)
(6) violence against women (*Psycho,* 1960)
(7) murder and madness (*White Heat,* 1949; *Badlands,* 1974)
(8) war and madness (*The Deer Hunter,* 1978)
(9) drugs and madness (*The Lost Weekend,* 1945)
(10) paranoia and madness (*The Caine Mutiny,* 1954; *Repulsion,* 1965)
(11) sanity as madness, madness as sanity (*Harvey,* 1950; *The King of Hearts,* 1966)
(12) madness and the psychiatrist (*Dressed to Kill,* 1980)

Fleming and Manvell's book also provides a synopsis of 150 films dealing in one way or another with the problems of mental illness.

Prior to *The Cabinet of Dr. Caligari,* many shorter films appeared that depicted psychiatric patients, asylums, and psychiatrists. Perhaps the earliest American film to depict a psychotic individual is the 1904 one-reeler *The Escaped Lunatic.* The Biograph publicity bulletin for this film reveals that it is about

> the escapades of an insane man who imagines himself to be Napoleon I. He escapes from the asylum by a miraculous jump from a third story window, and is pursued across the country by the keepers through a series of ludicrous adventures, until finally disgusted at the chase, he jumps back into the window of the asylum, and is very comfortably reading a newspaper when the tired and mud-spattered keepers enter.

A subsequent one-reel film made in 1906, *Dr. Dippy's Sanitarium,* is the first American film to depict a mental health professional other than an attendant (a "keeper"). The first motion picture image of a psychiatrist is the one we still often see depicted in comedies and cartoons today: bearded (often with a goatee), wearing pince-nez glasses, and somewhat portly with a distinctive formal continental European bearing. As in *The Escaped Lunatic,* there is a psychotic individual who grandiosely believes he is Napoleon, but there is also a depiction of a woman with HYSTERIA who resembles a somnambulist, gliding about in a flowing white gown with her extended arm holding a candle in its holder. Whereas *Dr. Dippy's Sanitarium* appears to be the first film portrayal of a psychiatrist, the first literary appearances of the figure of the alienist can be found at least as early as 1861 in the novels of Oliver Wendell Holmes.

As with the mentally ill, psychiatrists have been depicted in films in a number of different ways. In their book *Psychiatry and the Cinema,* Krin Gabbard and Glen O. Gabbard propose that psychiatrists have been portrayed in three primary ways: as the "alienist," the "quack," or the "oracle."

Recent trends in motion pictures and television have unjustly overemphasized the "homicidal maniac" stereotype of people suffering from psychotic disorders—particularly in films in the horror genre. Many advocacy groups for the mentally ill have formally objected to these unrealistic portrayals and have attempted to counter these negative stereotypes with factual information about mental illness for the general public.

Fleming, M., and R. Manvell. *Images of Madness: The Portrayal of Insanity in the Feature Film.* Cranbury, N.J.: Associated University Presses, 1985.

Gabbard, K., and G. O. Gabbard. *Psychiatry and the Cinema.* Chicago: University of Chicago Press, 1987.

moxa See CAUTERY TREATMENT.

MRI See MAGNETIC RESONANCE IMAGING.

muffs A form of MECHANICAL RESTRAINT in which a patient's hands were bound together at the wrists in a thick, tubular canvas casing. In his autobiography, Clifford BEERS describes his experience of being forced to wear muffs every night during his first few weeks in a "sanitarium" while the attendant who watched over him slept:

> . . . I was subjected to a detestable form of restraint that amounted to torture. To guard me at night while the remaining attendant slept, my hands were imprisoned in what is known as a "muff." A muff, innocent enough to the eyes of those who have never worn one, is in reality a relic of the Inquisition. It is an instrument of restraint which has been in use for centuries and even in many of our public and private institutions is still in use. The muff I wore was made of canvas, and differed in construction from a muff designed for the hands of fashion only in the inner partition, also of canvas, which separated my hands, but allowed them to overlap. At either end was a strap which buckled tightly around the wrist and was locked.

Beers, C. *A Mind That Found Itself: An Autobiography.* New York: Longman, Greens, 1908.

multifactorial threshold model of genetic transmission This is the hypothetical model of the genetic transmission of schizophrenia first proposed in detail by I. I. Gottesman and J. Shields in 1967. Essentially, the multifactorial threshold model suggests that schizophrenia is caused primarily by the additive effect of a large numberof genes of small effect, in addition to certain environmental (but somewhat less powerful) influences. This is a type of polygenetic model of transmission and is sometimes called complex development (as opposed to another type of polygenetic model, GENETIC HETEROGENEITY). Genetic influences are assumed to account for 80 percent of the development of schizophrenia, and environmental factors 20 percent. This is a more complex revision of older DIATHESIS-STRESS THEORIES of the cause (etiology) of schizophrenia. In the multifactorial model, it is assumed that schizophrenia only becomes fully developed in those persons in whom a critical threshold of liability is exceeded (i.e., in those persons in whom enough of the disease-causing genes have added together, plus enough of the right environmental causes have been introduced—thus pushing the person's nervous system "over the edge," as it were, to provoke the onset of the illness).

In this model, the chance of developing this disorder is normally distributed throughout the population. On the average, relatives of schizophrenics are at greater risk than the general population, and therefore a greater proportion of these people have a liability that exceeds the threshold. This model predicts that those schizophrenic persons who have the most severe manifestations of the disorder (i.e., those with the highest liability) will have the greatest proportions of relatives who will be affected. This is a feature of the model that corresponds to the findings of twin studies and consanguinity studies of schizophrenia. This model also makes the prediction that a person is at greater risk for developing schizophrenia if two or more persons in the family are affected.

There have been several criticisms of this model. One is that the specific environmental causes of schizophrenia are hard to pin down. Second, all of the genes that combine their effects may not be of equal importance, for there may be a single major gene that has a far greater effect upon the risk for schizophrenia than the other "polygenes." This second idea is the basis for a "mixed model" of genetic transmission, first proposed as a possible mode of GENETIC TRANSMISSION for schizophrenia by Paul Meehl in 1972.

Gottesman, I. I., and J. A. Shields. "A Polygenic Theory of Schizophrenia," *Proceedings of the National Academy of Sciences of the United States of America* 58 (1967): 199–205.

McGue, M., et al. "The Transmission of Schizophrenia under a Multifactorial Threshold Model," *American Journal of Human Genetics* 35 (1983): 1,161–1,178.
Meehl, P. E. "A Critical Afterward." In I. I. Gottesman and J. A. Shields, *Schizophrenia and Genetics: A Twin Study Vantage Point.* New York: Academic Press, 1972.

multiple insanity See FOLIE À DEUX.

multiple personality and schizophrenia Many people often confuse schizophrenia with having "split personalities." Although schizophrenia literally means "split-mind," schizophrenia is a very distinct disorder from multiple personality disorder. An expanded definition of multiple personality disorder (MPD) made its first appearance in *DSM-III* in 1980 as one of the new category of mental disorders known as the DISSOCIATIVE DISORDERS. Prior to 1980, multiple personality was considered to be rare, with only about 200 cases reported in the psychiatric literature. However, since that time it is estimated that more than 6,000 cases have been diagnosed. In *DSM-IV* (1994) MPD was renamed "dissociative identity disorder."

Multiple personality was far more commonly recognized prior to 1910, and reports of this disorder virtually disappeared between 1910 and 1975. It has been suggested that this was due to the fact that most people with MPD were misdiagnosed with schizophrenia, the then-new diagnosis that Bleuler was popularizing at that time as a much more inclusive disorder than Emil Kraepelin's DEMENTIA PRAECOX. In 1988 a major study by Canadian psychiatrist Colin Ross found that in a sample of 236 persons diagnosed with MPD, almost 41 percent had once previously been diagnosed with schizophrenia. It was found that many FIRST-RANK SYMPTOMS that are thought to characterize schizophrenia also characterize MPD. People with multiple personality disorder experience delusions, experiences of being influenced, feeling that their thoughts were being broadcast from their heads, feeling that their thoughts were being withdrawn from their heads, and they also report auditory hallucinations (which are thought to be the "alternate personalities" talking to one another inside the person's body). All these are also commonly reported in schizophrenia.

Rosenbaum, M. "The Role of the Term Schizophrenia in the Decline of the Diagnosis of Multiple Personality," *Archives of General Psychiatry* 37 (1980): 1,383–1,385.
Ross, C., and G. R. Norton. "Multiple Personality Disorder Patients with a Prior Diagnosis of Schizophrenia," *Dissociation* 1 (1988): 39–42.

multiple sclerosis and schizophrenia Multiple sclerosis (MS) is a neurological disease primarily of body musculature and movement but with certain psychological effects as well. Although it is quite distinct from schizophrenia in its total picture, there are nonetheless many similarities between the two disorders that may point to a common type of cause for them. For example, the age of onset in both MS and schizophrenia is at its peak in the early to mid-20s, with a range between ages 15 and 45. The course of the two diseases is very similar, with periods in which the symptoms are very active (exacerbations) often interspersed, at least in the earlier stages, with partial or total disappearance of the symptoms for short periods (remissions). The highest pockets of the disease seem to be distributed in the Northern Hemisphere, particularly in Europe and North America. All these points of correspondence were discussed in a 1988 paper on this topic by psychiatrist J. R. Stevens that was published in *Schizophrenia Bulletin.* Her interpretation of the similarities between MS and schizophrenia is that they both may be neurological disorders that are caused by viruses.

See also VIRAL THEORIES OF SCHIZOPHRENIA.

Stevens, J. R. "Schizophrenia and Multiple Sclerosis," *Schizophrenia Bulletin* 14 (1988): 231–241.

Munchausen's syndrome This is a type of mental disorder in which the person fakes a serious physical illness, constructs an elaborate system of lies to account for it, and then must wander until finally a physician "catches on" to the pathological lying of the patient, who then repeatedly enacts the same scenario for other physicians. In *DSM-III-R*

(1987) this is known as a factitious ("not genuine") disorder with physical symptoms. Other proposed names for this syndrome have been hospital addicts and hospital hoboes. In 1951 R. Asher published the first description of this disorder and named it after an 18th-century German baron, Hieronymus Carl Friedrich von Münchausen (1720–97), who became famous for telling tall tales of exotic adventures to his friends. There have been cases on record of such persons even faking psychotic disorders such as schizophrenia just to be admitted to a psychiatric hospital. Although these persons are not found to be out of touch with reality, no one theory has been put forth that adequately explains their behavior.

Asher, R. "Munchausen's Syndrome," *Lancet* 1 (1951): 339.

museums, psychiatric In the United States there are several small museums that contain items relating to the treatment of institutionalized people with psychotic disorders. The better collections can be found in the Midwest. The museum at the Menninger Institute in Topeka, Kansas, maintains a collection of restraining devices, including straitjackets and photographs from old asylums from around the world. The Medical History Museum in Indianapolis, Indiana, is notable for the exquisite architectural detailing from psychiatric wards. The St. Joseph's State Hospital Museum in Kirksville, Missouri, has a collection of restraining devices and other items, which chronicle the history of psychiatric treatment from the 15th century to the present. This museum also contains a unique exhibit featuring 1,446 objects that were surgically removed from a psychiatric patient's gastrointestinal tract, including nuts, bolts, spoon handles, nails, stones, pins, pieces of glass, and a thimble.

Lipp, M. *Medical Landmarks USA.* New York: McGraw-Hill, 1990.

music therapy The act of listening to or playing music as a treatment for mental illness. In 1727 the first book devoted to music therapy appeared in print, *Medicina Musica* (the shortened title of the expanded 1729 edition), written by an English apothecary named Richard Browne. He recommended its use in calming "maniacal" patients. Philippe Pinel in France recommended it as a form of his MORAL TREATMENT of mental illness, and this suggestion was repeated by many other authors of psychiatric books. Music therapy remains a part of most psychiatric institutions today and helps to make them more humane places to live.

mustard pack A form of treatment developed in the late 1800s that involved adding "crude mustard" to wet sheets in which agitated patients were packed. It is said that the technique of packing agitated mentally ill people in wet sheets was invented in 1840 by a Silesian peasant named Priessnitz who gained a reputation for favorably treating disease by packing people in cold, wet sheets. It was apparently first used to treat mental illness in 1860 by an English physician, Lockhart Robinson, at the Sussex County Asylum in England.

In the traditional wet pack, a cold, wet sheet is wrapped around the naked body of a patient, who is then rolled up in two or three blankets. In the mustard pack (apparently first used on the mentally ill by another English physician, S. Newington), two handfuls of crude mustard are tied in a cloth, put in hot water and then squeezed, then wrapped around the abdomen or legs, with a blanket then wrapped around this. Because the mustard acted as an irritant to the skin, this was quite an unpleasant procedure to experience. Packing in wet sheets was a technique that continued to be used until well into the 20th century and probably did not disappear until the advent of ANTIPSYCHOTIC DRUGS in the 1950s.

Williams, D. "Baths." In *A Dictionary of Psychological Medicine,* edited by D. H. Tuke. London: J. & A. Churchill, 1892.

mystic paranoia See FOLIE À DEUX.

myth of mental illness In 1960 American psychiatrist Thomas Szaz published a paper in which

he argues that the concept of mental illness is, in reality, a myth. Szaz insists that the term is used to stigmatize anyone who deviates from certain psychological, ethical, or legal norms. "We call people physically ill when their body-functioning violates certain anatomical and physiological norms; similarly, we call people mentally ill when their personal conduct violates certain ethical, political and social norms." Furthermore, since (at that time) there was very little evidence for the physiological basis of the various mental disorders, they are not medical disorders that should be treated with medical procedures. Hence, there is no such thing in reality as a purely "mental illness."

Szaz gained notoriety for his notion of the "myth of mental illness," and his many publications that question the standard operating procedure of psychiatrists and the mental health system created much animosity toward him. Nonetheless, the value in his writing is that he dared to "question authority," and his works stimulated a good deal of discussion about psychiatric procedures, patients' right to refuse treatment, and other significant issues with medical and legal implications.

Szaz, T. "The Myth of Mental Illness," *American Psychologist* 15 (1960): 113–118.

N

National Institute of Mental Health The primary research and information organization in the United States devoted to the study of mental disorders. It was established by the National Mental Health Act passed by the U.S. Congress in 1946 but did not formally begin operation until 1949. NIMH distributes federally mandated grant money to states and institutions for research on mental disorders. Since 1954, NIMH has devoted a major effort to schizophrenia research with the establishment of the NIMH Laboratory of Psychology and Psychopathology at the NIMH campus in Bethesda, Maryland. From 1955 to 1966 the laboratory carried out a program of research on the nature of the behavioral deficits in schizophrenia, initiated by David Shakow, who was then Chief of the Laboratory. David Rosenthal (who succeeded Shakow as chief in 1977) and Seymour Kety conducted other studies on the genetics of schizophrenia, the most famous of which is the case of the GENAIN QUADRUPLETS. Rosenthal's work on the genetic factors in the development of schizophrenia helped to define the nature of the transmission of schizophrenia. In 1989, NIMH launched a program to find the genes involved in schizophrenia, bipolar disorder, and Alzheimer's disease. Interestingly, all three of these disorders were first described by Emil KRAEPELIN and his research group in Heidelberg, Germany, in the late 1890s, but their search for the patterns of hereditary transmission was unsuccessful. The NIMH Genetics Initiative has taken up Kraepelin's unfinished task. The goal is to create a national resource of demographic, clinical, and diagnostic data that would be available to the world scientific community. DNA extracted from immortalized cell lines is also available to researchers for genetics work.

Mirsky, A. F. "Research on Schizophrenia in the NIMH Laboratory of Psychology and Psychopathology, 1954–1987," *Schizophrenia Bulletin* 14 (1988): 151–156.

Navane See ANTIPSYCHOTIC DRUGS.

negative symptoms The symptoms of schizophrenia that are best conceptualized as "defects"—that is, as something "taken away" from the personality of the afflicted person. The negative symptoms seem to most resemble those types of symptoms found in people with brain damage due to other causes, and as such, negative symptoms have been correlated to structural BRAIN ABNORMALITIES IN SCHIZOPHRENIA. Prominent negative symptoms are: (1) poverty of speech (alogia), (2) restricted affect and diminished emotional range, (3) diminished interest in the environment and a reduction in curiosity, (4) diminished sense of purpose, and (5) a diminished interest in social interaction with others. POSITIVE SYMPTOMS, on the other hand, are those symptoms that seem to be "added to" the personality, such as hallucinations and delusions.

The distinction between negative and positive symptoms has its origins in 19th-century neurology. Perhaps the first use of these terms was by the British neurologist J. R. Reynolds in 1858. They became popularized, although not in a sense directly appropriate to schizophrenia, by the famous British neurologist John Hughlins Jackson, who discussed them in 1894 as part of the FACTORS OF INSANITIES. The explicit application of these concepts to schizophrenia can be credited to a paper published in 1974 by J. S. Strauss, W. T. Carpenter, and J. J. Bartko.

Negative symptoms characterize the most chronic forms of schizophrenia, and their early signs indicate a poor prognosis. ANTIPSYCHOTIC DRUGS have a minimal effect in diminishing or reversing negative symptoms. At present, there is no fully effective treatment for these symptoms.

See also CROW'S HYPOTHESIS; DEFICIT SYMPTOMS/SYNDROME.

Berrios, G. E. "Positive and Negative Symptoms and Jackson: A Conceptual History," *Archives of General Psychiatry* 42 (1985): 95–97.

Reynolds, J. R. "On the Pathology of Convulsions, with Special Reference to Those of Children," *Liverpool Medico-Chirurgical Journal* 2 (1858): 1–14.

Strauss, J. S., W. T. Carpenter, and J. J. Bartko. "The Diagnosis and Understanding of Schizophrenia: III. Speculations on the Processes That Underlie Schizophrenic Symptoms and Signs," *Schizophrenia Bulletin* 1, Experimental Issue 11 (1974): 61–69.

negativism, schizophrenic A concept put forth in 1910 by Eugen BLEULER to account for the baffling and often frustrating "contrary" or "oppositional" behavior of people with schizophrenia. Such reactions often infuriate those responsible for the care of people with schizophrenia, who may frequently forget that such actions are expressions of the disease itself. The best example of this is the primary schizophrenic symptom of AMBIVALENCE, in which an impulse is balanced by contrary ones, thus paralyzing the willful activity of the schizophrenic. In his 1911 book, Bleuler notes that in "negativism," "the patients cannot or will not do what is expected of them (passive negativism); or they do just the very opposite or, at least, something else than what is expected (active or contrary negativism)." Bleuler largely attributed this negativism to the nature of the disease rather than to the intentions of the patient. Bleuler's concept of negativism was criticized in 1911 by his former assistant, C. G. JUNG, who was then a disciple of Sigmund FREUD's and who thus interpreted such "negativism" according to the psychoanalytic concept of an unconscious (but meaningful) resistance. Negativism is no longer discussed in the modern literature of schizophrenia.

Bleuler, E. *Dementia Praecox, Or the Group of Schizophrenias*, tr. J. Zinkin. 1911. Reprint, New York: International Universities Press, 1950.

———. "Zur Theorie des schizophrenen Negativismus," *Psychiatrisch-neurologische Wochenschrift* (Halle) 12 (1910–11): 171–195.

Jung, C. G. "A Criticism of Bleuler's Theory of Schizophrenic Negativism." In *The Collected Works of C. G. Jung*. Vol. 3. Princeton, N.J.: Princeton, University Press, 1960.

negligent release In the United States, there have been many legal suits brought against institutions and responsible psychiatrists for releasing patients who then go on to do harm to themselves or others. In such "negligent release" suits, the charge is that psychiatric authorities released individuals to the community who were still dangerous and in need of commitment.

neologisms The expression of neologisms (literally meaning "new words") by people with psychotic disorders (particularly schizophrenia) is a clear sign of FORMAL THOUGHT DISORDER. A person may create entirely new words, distort actual words, or give new and unusual meanings to words that already have an accepted meaning.

neural circuits in schizophrenia Neural circuits are the information superhighways of the brain. It has long been known that information is processed by the human brain in "cell assemblies" or "neural networks" that cut across the lobes of the cortex, as well as involved subcortical structures of the brain (such as the thalamus, a major relay center, and the hippocampus, a major center for turning short-term memories into long-term memories). These pathways of nervous tissue use electrical impulses and chemicals (NEUROTRANSMITTERS) to excite or inhibit neighboring clusters of neurons as messages are sent and received. Information from the external senses (sight, hearing, touch, taste, scent) and from internal sources (the autonomic nervous system, for example) is processed along certain discrete pathways or neural networks that crisscross several major "functional centers" of the brain.

For years there have been computer models of neural networks in cognitive neuroscience research that have been used to understand the functioning of the normal human brain. With advances in computing power and software innovations, the trend in the schizophrenia research of the 1990s was to develop complex, interactive models of the neural circuits that seem to dysfunction in the brains of people who suffer from schizophrenia (and those of close biological relatives, who often have some of the same dysfunctions).

In recent years, inferences about the location and function of such neural circuits in schizophrenia have come from (1) postmortem neuropathological studies, (2) neuropsychological test data, (3) structural neuroimaging studies, particularly those employing positron magnetic resonance spectroscopy, and (4) functional neuroimaging studies (rCBF, PET, fMRI), which actually allow us to see the pathways in the brain "light up" as the brain of a person with schizophrenia performs a particular task.

There is much that still needs to be resolved in the definition of the neural circuits involved in schizophrenia, but some of the most promising neural circuits are (1) the temporolimbic cortex, (2) the prefrontal cortex, and (3) the thalamus. Imbalances in the functioning between these regions or neural circuits is the basis of DISCONNECTION THEORIES OF SCHIZOPHRENIA.

Bogerts, B. "The Temporolimbic System Theory of Positive Schizophrenic Symptoms," *Schizophrenia Bulletin* 23 (1997): 423–435.

Jones, E. G. "Cortical Development and Thalamic Pathology in Schizophrenia," *Schizophrenia Bulletin* 23 (1997): 483–501.

McCarley, R. W., et al. "Neural Circuits in Schizophrenia," *Archives of General Psychiatry* 51 (1994): 515.

neurasthenia A word coined by New York neurologist George Miller Beard in 1869 for a type of "nervousness" disorder that could be treated by HYDROTHERAPY, weak electrical currents, and rest. It was considered a uniquely American neurotic disorder, for "nervous exhaustion" was brought about by the "wear and tear" on the nervous system induced by overwork. In the upper classes, MASTURBATION was also thought by Beard to be a significant cause of neurasthenia, although among members of the lower classes, as Beard points out in his 1884 book *Sexual Neurasthenia,* this was not the case because, for example, "Strong, phlegmatic Irish servant-girls may begin early the habit of abusing themselves and keep it up for years, but with little apparent harm." Whereas Beard thought many of the vague and mild symptoms were part of an actual nervous disease, many of his contemporaries rejected them as mild and easily reversible symptoms of tiredness or out-and-out signs of malingering and attention seeking. Special private sanitariums, retreats, spas, and hydropathic institutions were set up in the late 1800s to treat individuals, largely female and from the upper classes of society, who suffered from "nervousness" or neurasthenia.

Neurasthenia is still included as a diagnostic category in the World Health Organization's *ICD-10* (1992). It is defined as "a neurotic disorder characterized by fatigue, irritability, headaches, depression, insomnia, difficulty in concentration, and a lack of capacity for enjoyment (anhedonia). It may follow or accompany an infection or exhaustion, or arise from continued emotional stress."

Beard, G. M. *American Nervousness.* New York: Putnam's, 1881.

———. *Sexual Neurasthenia: Its Hygiene, Causes, Symptoms, and Treatment.* Edited by A. D. Rockwell. New York: Treat, 1884.

Drinka, G. F. *The Birth of Neurosis: Myth, Malady, and the Victorians.* New York: Simon & Schuster, 1984.

neurochemistry of schizophrenia See BIOCHEMICAL THEORIES OF SCHIZOPHRENIA.

neurodevelopmental model of schizophrenia At the beginning of the 21st century, this is the dominant explanatory paradigm in schizophrenia research. Rather than assuming that the causes of schizophrenia are to be found around the time the first symptoms usually appear in late adolescence or early adulthood, the neurodevelopmental model assumes that the underlying disease process

must begin during fetal development along with the development of the nervous system.

Proposals for a similar model of certain psychotic disorders had been made by Thomas Clouston in 1873 for a syndrome he called ADOLESCENT INSANITY, Emil KRAEPELIN in 1896 for DEMENTIA PRAECOX, and Eugen BLEULER in 1908 for SCHIZOPHRENIA. The neurodevelopmental model of schizophrenia was first articulated in its modern form in the work of R. M. Murray in 1985 and Daniel R. Weinberger in 1986. It became influential as a paradigm almost immediately. The neurodevelopmental model has proven to be a useful organizational concept for a wide range of studies in neuropathology, neuroimaging, genetics, neuropsychology, epidemiology, and developmental biology. One criticism of the neurodevelopmental model of schizophrenia is that it may concern only one subtype or syndrome of schizophrenia and may ignore others with a later onset.

The primary argument in favor of a neurodevelopmental model is the evidence that has accumulated that schizophrenia is probably not a neurodegenerative disease. Circumstantial evidence pointing to causes that happen during fetal neural development, during gestation, or around the time of birth all lend support to a neurodevelopmental model. However, strong evidence in favor of the neurodevelopmental model is lacking. Some aspects of the model as proposed by Daniel Weinberger of the National Institute of Mental Health in Bethesda, Maryland, are based on speculative models of the role of dopamine and on connections between the frontal lobe and subcortical structures. However, the neurodevelopmental model has directed basic research into new areas and will probably be a very difficult model to reject or falsify conclusively.

See also BRAIN ABNORMALITIES; CHILDHOOD-ONSET SCHIZOPHRENIA; FETAL NEURAL DEVELOPMENT.

Murray, R. M. "Neurodevelopmental Schizophrenia: The Rediscovery of Dementia Praecox," *British Journal of Psychiatry* 165 (1994): 6–12.

Weinberger, D. R. "The Pathogenesis of Schizophrenia: A Neurodevelopmental Theory." In *The Neurology of Schizophrenia*, edited by H. A. Nasrallah and D. R. Weinberger, 397–406. Amsterdam: Elsiever, 1986.

neurohistological studies of schizophrenia See BRAIN ABNORMALITIES IN SCHIZOPHRENIA.

neuroimaging studies of schizophrenia See BRAIN IMAGING STUDIES OF SCHIZOPHRENIA.

neuroleptic This is another word for any drug that changes the mental state of anyone who ingests it. It is often used synonymously with the term *psychotropic*. The term *neuroleptics* is sometimes used as an alternative name for ANTIPSYCHOTIC DRUGS as well, although technically it can refer to antianxiety or antidepressant drugs.

neuroleptic malignant syndrome This is a rare but serious disorder that may be a side effect from the use of ANTIPSYCHOTIC DRUGS. The symptoms of this disorder are fever, muscular rigidity, stupor, autonomic dysfunction (increased pulse, sweating, and respiration), and, occasionally, death. NLMS, as it is sometimes abbreviated, develops suddenly over a 24- to 72-hour period anywhere from hours to months after the initiation of therapy with antipsychotic drugs. At present, it is difficult to predict who will or will not develop NLMS, because a person who had previously undergone a period of treatment without developing the syndrome may suddenly develop it during other treatment periods. Neuroleptic malignant syndrome is often associated with the use of high-potency antipsychotic drugs. It is more common in young adult males with psychotic disorders and in persons with organic mental disorders. The use of antipsychotic drugs must be discontinued immediately if NLMS occurs, for about 15 percent to 20 percent of the patients who develop this disorder die. The exact cause of the disorder is unknown.

Caroff, S. N. "The Neuroleptic Malignant Syndrome," *Journal of Clinical Psychiatry* 41 (1980): 79–83.

Levinson, J. L. "Neuroleptic Malignant Syndrome," *American Journal of Psychiatry* 142 (1985): 1,137–1,145.

neuropathology of schizophrenia See BRAIN ABNORMALITIES IN SCHIZOPHRENIA.

neuropsychological studies of schizophrenia In the 1970s, special batteries of psychological tests were devised to assess brain functioning in persons suspected of having an organic brain dysfunction. These "neuropsychological tests" targeted such processes as memory, perception, concept formation, visual-spatial ability, attention span and intelligence to see if they were disrupted in ways that were characteristic of brain-damaged individuals who took such tests. Perhaps the two most famous of these batteries are the Halstead-Reitan battery and the Luria-Nebraska battery. Major reviews of the more than 100 studies of the performance of persons with schizophrenia on neuropsychological tests have confirmed that "chronic" and "nonparanoid" schizophrenics are indistinguishable from persons who have known brain damage that is diffuse rather than focal (i.e., spread throughout the brain rather than localized damage in one place).

In the 1980s and 1990s, neurological studies of schizophrenia were often correlated with neuropathological findings and with neuroimaging findings to develop new models of how the schizophrenia disease process works in the brain. The studies of C. D. Frith of the cognitive neuropsychology of schizophrenia have been highly influential.

In schizophrenia the following cognitive functions have been consistently found to be impaired: attention, working memory (a form of short-term memory associated with the functioning of the frontal lobe of the brain), episodic or autobiographical memory, and executive functioning (the overall organization of various goal-oriented cognitive functions). Additionally, as we now know from long-term follow-up studies of children of schizophrenic parents who later went on to develop schizophrenia, all these cognitive deficits have been found to be present in the prodromal phase of schizophrenia, years before the first psychotic episode. Furthermore, most of the cognitive impairment in schizophrenia happens early in the disease process. Very little decline in cognitive functioning is found after the first episode of psychosis. This contradicts the view of schizophrenia as a progressive neurodegenerative disease. Antipsychotic drugs do not improve cognitive functioning in schizophrenia.

It has long been known that many of the problems people with schizophrenia face every day stem from these severe problems in cognition. To address the treatment implications of this issue, including the development of new drugs that may enhance cognitive performance in schizophrenia, the NATIONAL INSTITUTE OF MENTAL HEALTH began a new research initiative in April 2003, the NIMH-Measurement and Treatment Research to Improve Cognition in Schizophrenia (MATRICS). There are two goals: one, to develop a standard "consensus battery" of neuropsychological tests that can measure cognition in schizophrenia in a valid and reliable way; and two, to develop a consensus among experts in the field as to which molecules should be targeted for the development of new drugs that can improve the cognitive performance of people with schizophrenia as measured in drug trials by this new test battery. Seven cognitive deficits in schizophrenia are being targeted:

(1) speed of information processing
(2) attention or vigilance
(3) working memory
(4) verbal learning and memory
(5) reasoning and problem solving
(6) verbal comprehension
(7) social cognition

David, A. S., and J. C. Cutting. *The Neuropsychology of Schizophrenia*. East Sussex, England: Lawrence Erlbaum Associates, 1994.

Frith, C. D. *The Cognitive Neuropsychology of Schizophrenia*. Hove, England: Lawrence Erlbaum, 1992.

neurosis In contemporary usage, the term *neurosis* refers to a wide variety of mental disorders that do not involve a break with reality (as in PSYCHOSIS) and do not have an apparent organic basis. However, this term has changed its meaning over the past two centuries, and even now there is some controversy about the actual meaning of the word.

The word *neurosis* was first used by English physician William Cullen in 1776 in his book *Synopsis Nosologiae Methodical*. Following Cullen, throughout most of the 19th century neuroses referred

to a large class of diseases that included present-day neurotic and psychotic disorders, neurological disorders, and many other medical disorders. The defining characteristics of the neuroses were a disorder of the "general" functions of the central nervous system and the lack of fever in an individual. Thus, throughout the 19th century, a neurosis was a disease of the brain and nervous system, whereas a psychosis (particularly in Germany) originally referred to the psychological aspects of a mental state.

However, by the year 1900, the term *neurosis* began to take on more of the meaning of a "psychological disorder" without reference to its organic nature, and thus the types and number of neuroses were greatly reduced. *Psychosis* began to be used instead to refer to the growing number of mental disorders that were organic in nature (e.g., dementia praecox). At about this time Sigmund FREUD began to redefine the neuroses (which he also termed *psychoneuroses*) according to psychoanalytic theory—specifically, that the neuroses were mental disorders that were caused by an unconscious conflict. This latter meaning of neuroses became the standard during much of the 20th century, and the "neurotic disorders" were a common part of most diagnostic manuals. However, in 1980, the AMERICAN PSYCHIATRIC ASSOCIATION'S *DSM-III* eliminated the term *neurosis* because of its theoretical assumptions based on psychoanalysis and instead introduced a largely atheoretical and neutral descriptive terminology, using various classifications of "mental disorders" to account for the more traditional neuroses.

The WORLD HEALTH ORGANIZATION'S *ICD-9* (1978), however, used the category termed "neurotic disorders" and defined them in the following way:

> The distinction between neurosis and psychosis is difficult and remains subject to debate. However, it has been retained in view of its wide use.
>
> Neurotic disorders are mental disorders without any demonstrable organic basis in which the patient may have considerable insight and has unimpaired reality testing, in that he usually does not confuse his morbid subjective experiences and fantasies with external reality. Behavior may be greatly affected although usually remaining within socially acceptable limits, but personality is not disorganized. The principal manifestations include excessive anxiety, hysterical symptoms, phobias, obsessional and compulsive symptoms, and depression.

López Piñero, J. M. *Historical Origins of the Concept of Neuroses,* trans. G. Berrios. Cambridge: Cambridge University Press, 1983.

neurotransmitter Any specific chemical agent released by one brain cell or neuron (the pre-synaptic cell) when it is stimulated that crosses the gap between neurons (the synapse) to stimulate or inhibit a neighboring brain cell (the post-synaptic cell). More than 100 such neurotransmitters are currently known.

The rise of endocrinology as a new medical science in the early 20th century provided a direct and important analogical bridge that led to the discovery of neurotransmitters in the brain. Following the 1921 discovery by Otto Loewi (1873–1961) of a substance in the brain later identified as acetylcholine, neurotransmitters were referred to as neurohormones or neurohumors. Indeed, the term *neurotransmitter* did not come into use until the 1960s. It is important to remember that neurotransmitters have been conclusively demonstrated to be part of the pathophysiology of mental disorders and have been related to certain symptoms (such as dopamine for hallucinations and delusions in some persons with schizophrenia). Neurotransmitters have never been found to cause any mental disorder, whether it is schizophrenia or depression.

See also ANTIDEPRESSANT DRUGS; ANTIPSYCHOTIC DRUGS; DOPAMINE HYPOTHESIS .

neurotransmitter disorder as a cause of schizophrenia The first theory of the cause of schizophrenia that is based on the hypothesis of a neurotransmitter disorder was put forth by biochemists D. W. Wooley and E. Shaw in 1954. They proposed that a decrease in the (then) newly discovered transmitter serotonin (5HT) may be related to the development of schizophrenia. Part

of the reason for this was that LSD was thought to be a powerful serotonin agonist, and at that time the "psychedelic model" of psychosis was in vogue, which suggested that schizophrenic experience was related to the experiences of those who ingested hallucinogenic substances. This hypothesis was not seriously considered for very long and was largely replaced by the DOPAMINE HYPOTHESIS in 1976. Other neurotransmitters that have been implicated as possible causes of schizophrenia are norepinephrine, GABA, the endorphins, and glutamate.

Wooley, D. W., and E. Shaw. "A Biochemical and Pharmacological Suggestion about Certain Mental Disorders," *Proceedings of the National Academy of Sciences of the United States of America* 40 (1954): 228–231.

———. "A Biochemical and Pharmacological Suggestion about Certain Mental Disorders," *Science* 119 (1957): 587–588.

night attendant service Until 1829, it was customary for patients in almost all asylums throughout Europe and the United States to be locked in their cells or strapped or chained to their beds for the night without supervision. The death of such a restrained patient in that year at the Lincoln Asylum in England led to the eventual adoption of "night attendants" who would keep watch over such mechanically restrained patients. However, this policy was not adopted in every British asylum nor throughout Europe on a large scale for many years. Even in the 20th century, reports of unsupervised patients in restraints continue to surface from time to time. However, the general policy in psychiatric institutions today is that physically restrained patients must be continually supervised by at least one staff member.

NIMH See NATIONAL INSTITUTE OF MENTAL HEALTH.

nitrogen inhalation therapy This is one of the forms of COMA THERAPY that were developed in the 1930s as a type of treatment for schizophrenia. Introduced by Franz A. Alexander and colleagues in 1939, this form of treatment involved having schizophrenic patients breathe in pure nitrogen to reduce the amount of oxygen in the brain (cerebral hypoxia) in order to induce a comatose state. It never became popular, for ELECTROSHOCK THERAPY and INSULIN COMA (OR SHOCK) THERAPY, introduced just prior to the invention of nitrogen inhalation therapy, had already taken root and were considered much more successful in the treatment of schizophrenia.

Alexander, F. A. D., and H. E. Himwich. "Nitrogen Inhalation Therapy for Schizophrenia," *American Journal of Psychiatry* 94 (1939): 643–655.

nitrogen metabolism disorder hypothesis This is the hypothesis put forth by the Norwegian psychiatric researcher Rolf Gjessing (1889–1959) in 1938 that the catatonic subtype of schizophrenia is caused by a primary disturbance of nitrogen metabolism that causes a shift back and forth from positive to negative balances of nitrogen in the body of a catatonic. Gjessing discovered that by administering the drug thyroxin, these metabolic shifts could be prevented with therapeutic results. Unfortunately, the nitrogen metabolism disorder hypothesis as a cause of schizophrenia was found to apply only to the very small group of persons suffering from periodic catatonia, and thus Gjessing's findings were not generalizable to the other subtypes of schizophrenia.

Gjessing, R. "Disturbances of Somatic Functions in Catatonia with a Periodic Course and Their Compensation," *Journal of Mental Science* 84 (1938): 608–621.

nonallelic genetic heterogeneity Because many mental disorders—in particular, schizophrenia and bipolar disorder—seem to constitute a spectrum of disorders rather than a single disease entity, it has been thought that there are different genetic causes of these disorders that nevertheless manifest similar symptoms when they are evident in a person. This has been called ETIOLOGIC HETEROGENEITY. One reason for etiologic heterogeneity may be nonallelic genetic heterogeneity, which refers to

the fact that although two or more persons may manifest the same symptoms of a particular disease, and therefore may have the same diagnosis, nonetheless different genes may be affected in different individuals to cause the disorder. In other words, the differences are not caused by alternate forms of the same gene (alleles). Nonallelic genetic transmission has been hypothesized for the psychotic disorders.

noninjurious torture This is the self-explanatory term used by German physician Johann Christian Reil (1759–1813) to refer to his philosophy of the treatment of institutionalized patients with mental disorders. Although Reil was more of a philosopher than a clinician and had no extensive experience in treating the mentally ill, he nonetheless wrote a 500-page volume in 1803 outlining his suggestions for the psychological treatment of such patients. He advocated the use of fear and intimidation to shock patients back into rationality, as well as the BATH OF SURPRISE, sudden loud noises, FLOGGING with a whip, the use of the straitjacket, and a whole host of other "treatments."

Reil, J. C. *Rhapsodien über die Anwendung der psychischen Curmethode auf Geisteszerruttungen.* Leipzig: 1803.

non-Mendelian patterns of transmission This term is used as an umbrella for a wide variety of theories of genetic transmission that do not fit strict "single gene" patterns that are known to characterize classical MENDELIAN TRANSMISSION. The psychotic disorders follow non-Mendelian patterns of genetic transmission. All theories that resort to the hypothesis that more than one gene is implicated in the transmission and development of a particular disorder (i.e., polygenetic theories) can be referred to as non-Mendelian.

nonparanoid schizophrenia In 1911 schizophrenia was divided into a paranoid subtype and three nonparanoid subtypes, which are currently known as the disorganized type, the catatonic type and simple schizophrenia. It has long been observed that those schizophrenics with nonparanoid diagnoses tended to be more disorganized and have more FORMAL THOUGHT DISORDER than the paranoid subtype; they were believed to have an earlier onset and a poorer prognosis than the paranoid subtype; and they tended to exhibit a more diffuse set of symptoms than the paranoid subtype. Starting in the 1970s and 1980s, research psychologists conducted numerous studies that found significant differences between paranoid and nonparanoid schizophrenics in many areas. On cognitive, perceptual, and problem-solving tests, paranoids and nonparanoids have shown consistent differences. Nonparanoids tend to exhibit a more conservative response style than paranoids, who often "jump to conclusions" without having enough of the relevant information to make a logical decision on tasks presented on various tests.

Many of these differences between nonparanoid and paranoid schizophrenics that have been found in COGNITIVE STUDIES OF SCHIZOPHRENIA support the notion that schizophrenia is not a unitary disorder but may instead be several different disorders.

A major issue of *Schizophrenia Bulletin* devoted to reviewing the research on the differences between nonparanoid and paranoid cognition was published in 1981 (vol. 7, no. 4).

Kendler, K. S., and K. L. Davis. "The Genetics and Biochemistry of Paranoid Schizophrenia and Other Paranoid Psychoses," *Schizophrenia Bulletin* 7 (1981): 698–709.

Magaro, P. A. "The Paranoid and the Schizophrenic: The Case for Distinct Cognitive Style," *Schizophrenia Bulletin* 7 (1981): 632–661.

nonrestraint movement This term was used by English physician John CONOLLY to describe the great shift in the philosophy and treatment of the institutionalized mentally ill in the 19th century that advocated the absolute minimum use of MECHANICAL RESTRAINTS. Although the philosophy of MORAL TREATMENT and moral medicine had been given lip service since the time of Philippe PINEL around 1801, a truly humane approach to

the institutionalized mentally ill was not adopted by the vast majority of European asylums that still restrained most patients whether they were violent or not. First-person descriptions of conditions in asylums in the early 1800s attest to these terrible abuses. Considered incurable by most, and no better than animals, the mentally ill were feared by many. Although some institutions began experimenting with nonrestraint policies, it was not until John Conolly successfully adopted such policies at the Hanwell Asylum in England between 1839 and 1843 that the issue was discussed in earnest around the world. His ideas caught the imagination of the public, due largely to strong support from publications such as the *Lancet* and the *Times* of London.

When Conolly first arrived at the Hanwell Asylum, he found the following items and immediately abolished them: 51 leather straps, 10 leather muffs, two screw-gags, two extra-strong chain leg-locks, 353 handcuffs and leg-locks, 49 restraint-chairs (similar to the American physician Benjamin RUSH'S TRANQUILLIZER), and 78 leather-and-ticking restraint-sleeves. Despite loud cries of criticism, Conolly implemented his experimental program with great success. His methods were copied by most English asylums and then by European and American institutions in the years that followed. Our modern policies of nonrestraint except in the most extreme circumstances is directly due to the influence of John Conolly and his nonrestraint movement.

Marx, O. M. "Descriptions of Psychiatric Care in Some Hospitals during the First Half of the 19th Century," *Bulletin of the History of Medicine,* 1967, pp. 208–214.

Zilboorg, G. *A History of Medical Psychology.* New York: W. W. Norton, 1941.

nonsense syndrome See GANSER'S SYNDROME.

norepinephrine and schizophrenia The neurotransmitter norepinephrine (or "noradrenaline"), a CATECHOLAMINE (like DOPAMINE), has been studied for a possible link to schizophrenia. Some studies have found increased levels of norepinephrine (NE) in the brain, blood and cerebro-spinal fluid of schizophrenics. Some studies have even connected these increased blood plasma levels of NE with POSITIVE SYMPTOMS and the paranoid subtype of schizophrenia. However, further studies that replicate these findings need to be done before any firm conclusions can be reached.

Hornykiewicz, O. "Brain Catecholamines in Schizophrenia—A Good Case for Noradrenaline," *Nature* 299 (1982): 484–486.

Norway See SCANDINAVIA.

nosology The science of the classification of diseases. Nosology involves, more specifically, the underlying theory behind the grouping of diseases. In psychiatry there are no "diseases" in the sense that they can be found in the rest of the medical sciences, because no distinctive cellular pathology (disease at the level of cells), nor distinct biological etiologies (causes), nor, therefore, any objective diagnostic tests (such as a blood test) exist that enable us to identify any mental disorder as a disease. Instead, mental disorders are syndromes (distinctive clusters of symptoms and signs linked to particular courses and outcomes). The nosological approach in psychiatry starts with the premise of an underlying disease process (e.g., in the brain) that exists before the production of symptoms. The disease determines the symptoms.

A contrasting approach, also influential in psychiatry, is that of psychopathology. The assumption since at least Karl Ludwig Kahlbaum's 1874 book on catatonia is that the objective identification and classification of symptoms of mental illness led to their grouping into syndromes. Concepts of disease were constructed from symptoms identified in this way. The symptoms determine the disease.

Classification systems reflect the cognitive categories of the cultural and scientific beliefs of their historical eras. As a result, in psychiatry there are fundamental differences in certain diagnostic categories that are due to national traditions and histories. Differences between North American,

German, and French classifications for certain mental disorders persist to this day. However, most of our current diagnostic concepts for mental disorders found in *DSM-IV-TR* (2000) and *ICD-10* (1992) were first established by German and French psychiatrists between 1860 and 1920. However, the original classification systems differed widely in their nosologies.

O

obsession A persistent, intrusive, generally undesirable idea, mental image, or impulse that cannot be wilfully eliminated through logical or rational thought. Although obsessions are the hallmark of obsessive-compulsive disorder, which is not one of the psychotic disorders, obsessions may nonetheless be found in psychotic disorders such as schizophrenia. The term was first used in its modern psychiatric sense by the French alienist Benedict Augustin MOREL in 1860.

obstetric complications and schizophrenia See PERINATAL FACTORS AND SCHIZOPHRENIA.

occupational therapy Perhaps the earliest form of therapy for the mentally ill. Since the days of ancient Egypt, afflicted persons have traditionally been given physical activities or manual labor to perform. This "occupational therapy" has probably derived from the observation that persons with debilitating mental illnesses just seem to get worse if they are left alone to vegetate without becoming involved in meaningful activities. With the rise of the philosophy of "moral treatment" in the early 1800s, many institutions for the insane developed work programs involving their residents. In his 1801 *A Treatise on Insanity*, Philippe PINEL noted that his patients at the BICÊTRE in Paris "were supplied by the tradesmen of Paris with employments which fixed their attention." By the 20th century, the term *occupational therapy* came into vogue and developed a professional status, with occupational therapists now part of practically every inpatient psychiatric unit or hospital. The current focus has shifted to more of a rehabilitation model, so that activities are designed to (ideally) teach skills that enable the patient to find employment when he or she is discharged and returned to the community. For the most chronic forms of mental illness (such as schizophrenia), this goal is not so realistic; nonetheless, anyone who has ever been employed in a psychiatric inpatient facility would no doubt agree with the observation made by C. G. JUNG in 1939 that "the results of occupational therapy in mental hospitals have clearly shown that the status of the hopeless cases can be enormously improved."

See also FARMING AS TREATMENT.

Jung, C. G. "On the Psychogenesis of Schizophrenia," *Journal of Mental Science* 85 (1939): 999–1011.

odor of the insane For centuries it was believed that mentally ill people may have a particular odor that distinguishes them from others. This idea was given a certain shortlived credibility in a book by English physician George Man Burrows (1771–1846), who ran his own private asylum known as the Clapham Retreat. In his 1828 *Commentaries on Causes, Forms, Symptoms and Treatment of Insanity* he asserted that "mania" could be diagnosed by a particular odor, that of fermenting henbane. Needless to say, there is no scientific validation of this idea. However, in modern times, persons under treatment for a psychotic disorder are often characterized by the strong odor of "THORAZINE breath" that is part of the olfactory environment of many psychiatric inpatient units.

olanzapine See ANTIPSYCHOTIC DRUGS.

olfactory hallucinations These are hallucinations of smell. Olfactory hallucinations are not

commonly reported among people with psychotic disorders, but they can occur. More commonly they occur along with such neurological disorders as convulsive disorders, especially those due to temporal lobe lesions (temporal lobe epilepsy) or uncinate gyrus fits. They have also been reported in person's suffering from migraines or Parkinson's disease.

Asaad, G., and B. Shapiro. "Hallucinations: Theoretical and Clinical Overview," *American Journal of Psychiatry* 143 (1986): 1,088–1,097.

olfactory reference syndrome This is the delusion in which a person is convinced (falsely) that he or she is emitting a strong, foul body odor, such as a fecal or rotting-flesh stench. It is a delusion and not an OLFACTORY HALLUCINATION. It can be a part of a psychotic disorder, or it can be a part of a less serious disorder known as the monosymptomatic hypochondriacal syndrome.

oligophrenia See PROPFSCHIZOPHRENIA.

oligosymptomatic types A term coined by psychiatrist Silvano ARIETI in 1959 to describe "very mild" cases of schizophrenia. Arieti distinguishes the oligosymptomatic forms of the four subtypes of schizophrenia from BORDERLINE CASES by noting that the latter are not psychotic, whereas the mild cases of schizophrenia are psychotic. Arieti's term never gained prominence in psychiatric terminology.

Arieti, S. *Interpretation of Schizophrenia.* 2nd ed. New York: Basic Books, 1974.

onset of psychosis See AGE AT ONSET.

opium Opiates were commonly used in the 18th and 19th centuries as a form of CHEMICAL RESTRAINT to quell the agitation of certain persons confined to asylums. In the 20th century, the search for other somatic treatments eventually led to the discovery of ANTIPSYCHOTIC DRUGS, thus finally eliminating the use of opiates for persons with psychotic disorders.

Orap See ANTIPSYCHOTIC DRUGS.

organicity in schizophrenia See BRAIN ABNORMALITIES IN SCHIZOPHRENIA.

organic mental disorders This is the generic name for a group of mental disorders that have a known or presumed organic cause. For example, such disorders as alcohol withdrawal delirium or multi-infarct dementia would be classified as organic mental disorders.

organic mental syndromes This term refers to a cluster of psychological or behavioral signs and symptoms whose cause is unknown. These signs and symptoms are those that have long been identified by physicians as due to the dysfunctioning of the brain. For example, an individual who enters a hospital may exhibit the signs and symptoms of delirium or dementia, but the exact cause may be unknown. Such behavior may be due to the influence of a stroke, substance abuse, or other toxicity, or perhaps even a brain tumor or other neurological disease. In this case, a tentative diagnosis of an organic mental syndrome is given until the source of brain dysfunction is known, at which time it is rediagnosed as an organic mental disorder.

organic psychosis See FUNCTIONAL PSYCHOSIS.

orthomolecular psychiatry See MEGAVITAMIN THERAPY.

Othello syndrome This is a delusional syndrome in which the dominant delusion is that one's spouse or sexual partner is secretly unfaithful.

When this delusion of infidelity occurs in its purest form, it is often called the Othello syndrome after the Shakespearean character whose jealousy was the central delusion that led to his madness. Other names that have been given to this delusional syndrome are sexual jealousy, the erotic jealousy syndrome, morbid jealousy, and psychotic jealousy. In all these cases the jealous person maintains a psychotic delusion that accompanies a significant break from reality. However, there are persons who are generally not suffering from a psychotic disorder who may be jealously obsessed with the past sexual activity of their mates, but there is no delusion about any current infidelity. In this case the syndrome is called retrospective ruminative jealousy. In DSM-IV (1994), the Othello syndrome was included under the label "delusional disorder, jealous type."

Enoch, M. D., and W. H. Trethowan. *Uncommon Psychiatric Syndromes.* 2nd ed. Bristol, England: John Wright & Sons, 1979.

oubliettes A term popular in the 19th and early 20th centuries for the primitive seclusion cells that were used to contain agitated or violent patients in mental hospitals. They were usually cylindrical pits large enough for only one person that were dug into the basement floor and covered with a heavy metal grate. Such oubliettes once existed in the basement of the Center Building of St. Elizabeth's Hospital in Washington, D.C. The word is derived from the French verb *oublier,* meaning "to forget." Such inhumane forms of seclusion were also more commonly called "strong rooms."

outpatient care The concept that mentally ill persons could still live in the community and yet come to a clinic or hospital for outpatient treatment was first put into practice by the Pennsylvania Hospital in Philadelphia (at its Pine Street location) in November 1885. Although "nerve clinics" offering primarily HYDROTHERAPY and various tonics were established almost two decades earlier in Philadelphia (1867) and Boston (1873) for what would later be called NEURASTHENIA, Pennsylvania Hospital was the first mental hospital to offer an outpatient department. The clinic was operated by the medical staff of the Department for the Insane of the Philadelphia Hospital. The concept that such a clinic could be used for preventing the development of more serious mental illness was quite revolutionary for its time. Historian of the Pennsylvania Hospital Thomas G. Morton writes in 1897 that

> . . . the service was regarded at that time as experimental. . . . It was undertaken under a conviction that in a city of one million inhabitants, a large number were suffering from premonitory symptoms of insanity as nervous prostration and depression, who might receive timely advice and treatment, and that a further development of mental disorder might thus be arrested.

In England the first outpatient departments were opened at Saint Thomas' Hospital in London, and at the Wakefield Asylum, in 1890.

Morton, T. G. *History of the Pennsylvania Hospital.* Philadelphia: 1897.

outpatient commitment This is a legal procedure allowed in about two-thirds of the United States in which a person is committed to treatment in an outpatient program rather than a psychiatric hospital. This differs from "conditional release," in which a person who is already committed and residing in a psychiatric hospital is released to the community on the condition that he or she follows through with an outpatient treatment program. Outpatient commitment has been used infrequently due to the extra responsibility it places on psychiatrists, who must first initiate a legal proceeding and go to court to testify. Psychiatrist E. Fuller Torrey is an advocate of outpatient commitment.

Torrey, E. F. *Surviving Schizophrenia.* 2nd ed. New York: Harper & Row, 1988.

ovariotomy The surgical removal of the ovaries in a woman was thought to be a cure for severe

mental disorders. French surgeon Jules-Émile Péan (1830–98) performed the first ovariotomy in France in 1864 and performed what may have been the first such operation for the treatment of hysteria in 1882. In the late 19th century, it was performed on women suffering from HYSTERIA following the theory of Jean Martin Charcot that the disorder had a sexual basis. Hysterectomies and ovariotomies were also considered a cure for schizophrenia according to the focal theory of infection of American psychiatrist Henry Cotton, who performed such operations on patients with schizophrenia at the Trenton State Hospital in New Jersey around 1920.

See also FOCAL INFECTION AS CAUSE OF PSYCHOTIC DISORDERS.

P

P300 event-related potential One of the proposed BIOLOGICAL MARKERS OF SCHIZOPHRENIA found in EEG STUDIES.

pacifick medicines The 18th-century term for drugs given to the mentally ill to "calm" or perhaps "subdue" them. They were commonly derivatives of OPIUM. The modern term for such drugs might be "tranquilizers."

See also ANTIPSYCHOTIC DRUGS.

Packard, Elizabeth Parsons Ware See COMMITMENT.

packing (as treatment) Until well into the 20th century, a common method for treating agitated persons with mental disorders. It involved packing the patients in wet sheets, usually cold, and then wrapping them further in several blankets. Sometimes these sheets were saturated with mustard, which acted as an irritant and thus caused such agony in patients that they eventually succumbed to exhaustion. This practice is said to have been invented in 1840 by a Silesian peasant named Priessnitz, who gained a reputation for treating physical illness by applying cold-water wet packs. This technique was first used on the mentally ill in 1860 in the Sussex County Asylum in England by Dr. Lockhart Robinson. It was finally judged an inhumane form of treatment and abandoned in the 20th century.

Williams, D. "Baths." In *A Dictionary of Psychological Medicine.* Vol. 1., edited by D. H. Tuke. London: J. & A. Churchill, 1892.

padded room A single-person room lined with rubber and cork in which agitated mental patients were incarcerated. The first padded room was invented by Ferdinand AUTENREITH (1772–1835) for use in German asylums. Throughout the 19th century and into the 20th, practically every large institution for the care of the mentally ill possessed such a room for the seclusion of violent or agitated patients.

paleologic thought A term coined by Silvano ARIETI for the type of primitive logic that underlies the thought processes of all schizophrenics. It is the particular laws of this type of logic that Arieti proposes lead to delusions. Arieti also argues that the thought processes of very young children and people in primitive societies also manifest this type of logic. Paleologic thought was believed to be a developmentally earlier type of thinking than Aristotelian logic, which Arieti says is the "usual logic of the normal human being."

Arieti, S. *Interpretation of Schizophrenia.* 2nd ed. New York: Basic Books, 1974.

Papua New Guinea In 1929 physician and anthropologist C. G. Seligman reported that he found no cases of psychotic disorders in Papua New Guinea native villages living a traditional life-style but found several cases among those "natives" who were in close contact with Europeans. A major study conducted by E. Fuller Torrey, B. G. Burton-Bradley, and colleagues in the early 1970s found that the prevalence rates for schizophrenia differed greatly across the country. However, Torrey concludes: "Papua New Guinea provides another case

study in which schizophrenia appears to be more common in areas with longer contact with Western civilization and rare in areas with little such contact."

Torrey, E. F. *Schizophrenia and Civilization.* New York: Jason Aronson, 1980.

paralytic insanity See GENERAL PARALYSIS OF THE INSANE.

paranoia A psychotic disorder described since antiquity in which a person has a fixed false belief about reality. This has been the traditional meaning of the word *DELUSIONS* in English, the word *délire* in French, and *Wahn* in German since at least the 16th century. Insanity has often been defined by the presence of delusion, and so these two terms were used interchangeably. These false beliefs are the result of faulty logical reasoning, and although they may dominate the person's mental life, usually their intellectual ability and general global level of functioning remain intact. This has traditionally distinguished paranoia from either DEMENTIA PRAECOX (SCHIZOPHRENIA) or manic depressive illness. Paranoia thus has been regarding as a third class of psychotic disorders that fall in-between these two major insanities identified by Emil KRAEPELIN in the sixth edition of his textbook, *Psychiatrie,* in 1899.

Throughout most of the 19th century psychiatrists did not use the word *paranoia* for these delusional disorders. Delusion, insanity, *délire,* and *Verrücktheit* (in German) were most often the terms used for paranoia. Starting in the 1850s, French psychiatrists began to identify and classify specific delusions (such as "delusions of persecution," identified by Ernest-Charles Lasegue in 1852, the later the identification and classification of "systematized" delusions in the work of Valentin Magnan and his colleagues starting in the 1880s). Likewise, in German psychiatry there was a growing acknowledgement that some persons could have fixed delusions and not undergo intellectual impairment or further deterioration in functioning. In 1863 Karl KAHLBAUM called delusions "diastrephia" and distinguished them from the major forms of psychosis, the *"Vesania typica,"* which were chronic and deteriorating. In 1893, in the fourth edition of *Psychiatrie,* Emil Kraepelin introduced the concept of *"Verrückheit* (Paranoia)" which was a "durable delusional system in the presence of an intact personality." In this edition of his textbook, in which he introduced the term *dementia praecox* for the first time, he identified a chronic degenerative psychotic disorder which he calls "dementia paranoides." In the sixth edition of *Psychiatrie* (1899), dementia paranoides would become the paranoid subtype of dementia praecox. In this edition he distinguishes between dementia praecox and paranoia:

> The delusions in dementia praecox are extremely fantastic, changing beyond all reason, with an absence of system and a failure to harmonize them with events of their past life; while in paranoia the delusions are largely confined to morbid interpretations of real events, are woven together into a coherent whole, gradually becoming extended to include even events of recent date, and contradictions and objections are apprehended and explained.

By the end of the 1800s, paranoia referred to a whole class of fixed delusions that dominated a person who did not deteriorate further into dementia praecox or MANIC-DEPRESSIVE ILLNESS, as in the CHRONIC DELUSIONAL STATES IN FRENCH PSYCHIATRY. These could be delusions of persecution, jealousy, grandiosity, erotomania, hypochondria, litiginous, and so on. Today, such a broad class of delusions is seen as "types" of a larger "delusional disorder" in *DSM-IV-TR* (2000) or "persistent delusional disorders" in *ICD-10* (1992). Paranoia is no longer viewed as an independent class of psychotic disorders in its own right, and *paranoid* now referring to delusions of persecution specifically. In the early 1980s, literature reviews by noted schizophrenia researcher Kenneth Kendler concluded that the available evidence indicates that paranoia is not a subtype of manic-depressive illness and that "paranoia and schizophrenia are distinct syndromes."

Since the 1913 volume of the eighth edition of Kraepelin's *Psychiatrie,* there has been a continuum

of paranoid disorders from paranoia to PARAPHRENIA (a deteriorating form of paranoia resembling dementia praecox, in that hallucinations may be present, but the delusions remain systematic and there is no intellectual deterioration), then finally the dementia paranoides subtype of dementia praecox. In *DSM-IV-TR* this continuum is reflected in the increasing severity of paranoid personality disorder to delusional disorder (paranoid type) to schizophrenia (paranoid type).

Kendler, K. S. "Nosology of Paranoid Schizophrenia and Other Paranoid Psychoses," *Schizophrenia Bulletin* 7 (1981): 594–610.

paranoia erotica A now-defunct term for EROTOMANIA, it was coined and first described by psychiatrist L. Bianchi in 1906. He felt that this type of delusional syndrome could sometimes occur alone without any other evidence of a psychotic disorder and that it "occurred often in individuals of defective sexual life, not much inclined to copulation, sometimes in old maids who have never had an opportunity of marrying."

Bianchi, L. *A Textbook of Psychiatry,* trans. J. H. MacDonald. London: Baillière, Tindall & Cox, 1906.

paranoid cognitive style A concept derived from COGNITIVE STUDIES OF SCHIZOPHRENIA, it refers to the fact that people diagnosed with paranoid schizophrenia have a unique way of responding to perceptual, cognitive, and behavioral tasks in experiments. Paranoid cognitive style is characterized by a "jump to conclusions" strategy—that is, such persons give a response to an ambiguous stimulus (for example) without really having enough information in the first place to make a reasonable correct response. Paranoid cognitive style is also marked by a certain rigidity of thought processes and a reliance on verbal information processing.

Magaro, P. A. "The Paranoid and the Schizophrenic: The Case for Distinct Cognitive Style," *Schizophrenia Bulletin* 7 (1981): 632–661.

paranoid-nonparanoid distinction, the It has become clear after decades of research that there are some fundamental differences between the paranoid subtype of schizophrenia and the three nonparanoid subtypes. Persons with the nonparanoid forms of this disorder tend to be more disorganized and to have more formal thought disorder, more overall cognitive deterioration, an earlier age of onset, and a poorer prognosis than those persons diagnosed with the paranoid subtype. In cognitive, perceptual and behavioral studies of schizophrenia, many differences have been demonstrated to exist between these two major divisions of schizophrenia. Much of this research has been summarized in the special 1981 issue of *Schizophrenia Bulletin* (vol. 7, no. 4) devoted to paranoia.

paranoid personality disorder This is nonpsychotic disorder in which a person maintains a pervasive and unwarranted tendency, beginning before early adulthood, to interpret the words and actions of people as deliberately demeaning or threatening. These sorts of persons often expect to be hurt or exploited in some ways by others, read "hidden meanings" into the harmless remarks or actions of others, and are generally hypersensitive and easy to anger. They usually bear grudges forever, are generally somewhat humorless and are often interested in mechanical devices or electronics. Such persons are often sensitive to rank and often are jealous of those in positions of power and disdain those persons of lower rank. It is not exactly known how this personality disorder is related to schizophrenia, paranoid type, or to the delusional (paranoid) disorders.

paranoid schizophrenia, or paranoid type One of the classic forms of DEMENTIA PRAECOX and SCHIZOPHRENIA. In *DSM-IV-TR* (2000) the "paranoid type" is defined as "preoccupation with one or more delusions or frequent auditory hallucinations" and the absence of "disorganized speech, disorganized or catatonic behavior, or flat or inappropriate affect." The classic AUDITORY HALLUCINATIONS are of voices. The delusions are "bizarre" and do not seem to be based on a faulty logical premise, as is the case

in DELUSIONAL DISORDER. Delusions of persecution ("The pope is turning my family against me and stealing my money") and grandiosity ("I am Christ") are common.

The current paranoid type of schizophrenia is a descendant of the syndrome named and described by Emil KRAEPELIN in the 1893 fourth edition of his textbook, *Psychiatrie*. In that edition, Kraepelin introduced DEMENTIA PRAECOX for the first time (which was essentially the same syndrome as HEBEPHRENIA, identified in 1871 by Ewald Hecker), and placed it alongside CATAONIA and DEMENTIA PARANOIDES as forms of "psychic degenerative processes." Dementia paranoides differed from an earlier description of PARANOIA by Karl KAHLBAUM in terms of its sudden onset and its deteriorating course, resulting in "feeble-minded confusion." In 1899 dementia praecox became a comprehensive category of degenerative psychoses, and the "paranoid form" was subsumed under it along with catatonic and hebephrenia. In 1911 Eugen BLEULER kept the paranoid type as one of his forms of schizophrenia. This subtype has remained relatively unchanged up to the current time. However, although subtypes of schizophrenia have been a part of clinical lore, at present there is no hard scientific evidence from biological, genetic, or longitudinal studies that the various subtypes of schizophrenia are independent disorders. In the course of the life of a person with schizophrenia it is not unusual for them to have symptoms from one or more of the classic subtypes, thus blurring the vision we have of the variants of this tragic disorder.

Kendler, K. S., and M. T. Tsuang. "Nosology of Paranoid Schizophrenia and Other Paranoid Psychoses," *Schizophrenia Bulletin* 7 (1981): 594–610.

paraphrenia The term, no longer in use, for a type of paranoid MENTAL DISORDER that was introduced by Emil KRAEPELIN in the 8th edition of his *Psychiatrie*, which was published in four volumes between 1909 and 1913. Paraphrenia is a paranoid psychotic disorder in which people may present fantastic or bizarre delusions that are somewhat organized and accompanied by hallucinations; but, unlike the paranoid form of DEMENTIA PRAECOX, FORMAL THOUGHT DISORDER is usually absent, and there is little or no deterioration of the rest of the personality. Like dementia praecox, Kraepelin thought that paraphrenia was a chronic disorder, but that unlike dementia praecox it did not lead to dementia. Kraepelin identified four subtypes of paraphrenia: systematica (the most common type), expansive, confabulans, and phantastica. In terms of the severity of the paranoid psychotic disorders described by Kraepelin, paraphrenia occupies a midpoint between paranoid dementia praecox (the most severe disorder) and paranoia (the least severe of the three).

Kendler, K. S., and M. T. Tsuang. "Nosology of Paranoid Schizophrenia and Other Paranoid Psychoses," *Schizophrenia Bulletin* 7 (1981): 594–610.

parataxic distortion A term used by American psychiatrist and psychoanalyst Harry Stack Sullivan (1892–1949) to identify one of the three developmental modes of experience through which all humans pass: the prototaxic, the parataxic, and the syntaxic. Experiences in the parataxic mode are often fragmented, momentary states of being that have no logical connections or relationship between them. Sullivan thought that this mode of experience, usually found only in very young children, characterized many schizophrenic adults, leading to distorted interpretations of interpersonal situations. This happens by incorrectly inferring casual relationships between events that are actually independent. If parataxic distortions are not corrected, Sullivan felt that the schizophrenic would then receive less and less "consensual validation" and that this lack of respect and validation for the thoughts and feeling of the afflicted person would only serve to increase problems in his or her day-to-day interpersonal relationships.

Sullivan, H. S. In *The Interpersonal Theory of Psychiatry*, edited by H. S. Perry and M. L. Gawel. New York: W. W. Norton, 1953.

parergasia A term coined by Adolf MEYER for schizophrenia. Meyer attempted to rename all the

major mental disorders based on concepts from his own theory of "psychobiology." None of his proposed terms—including this one—were ever adopted by mainstream psychiatry.

paresis See GENERAL PARALYSIS OF THE INSANE.

Parkinsonism The cluster of Parkinsonian symptoms that is induced as a side effect of treatment with ANTIPSYCHOTIC DRUGS. The signs and symptoms are very much like those found in Parkinson's disease, which was first described by British physician and surgeon James Parkinson (1755–1824) in 1817 in his treatise *Essay on the Shaking Palsy.* However, Parkinson's disease is caused by an unknown pathological process of the nervous system, whereas Parkinson's syndrome is a drug-induced disorder.

Parkinson's syndrome is characterized by a triad of signs: tremor, rigidity, and AKINESIA (also called BRADYKINESIA). The tremor is worse when the person's afflicted body part is at rest, and it is usually found in the hands, often with the thumb rubbing against the pad of the index finger to produce a "pill-rolling" movement. However, the wrists, elbows, head, or almost any other body part can experience tremor. Rigidity is the increase in the normal resting tone of a body part and is usually only detectable upon physical examination. Akinesia (an absence of motion) or bradykinesia (a slowness of motion) are more commonly found earlier in Parkinson's syndrome than in Parkinson's disease. The bradykinetic person may have a masklike face, with diminished expressiveness and less frequent eye blinking. The body is turned "en bloc," as if the person were a solid mass without joints. The slowed movements may make the person seem apathetic or "zombie-like," and drooling can often occur.

Parkinson's syndrome can develop in persons who are taking antipsychotic drugs within weeks to months after the beginning of therapy. Women and elderly persons are the most commonly affected. Treatment for this syndrome may include lowering the dosage of antipsychotic drugs, switching to a less potent drug and/or introducing an antiparkinsonian agent such as AMANTADINE (trade name Symmetrel), BENZTROPINE (Cogentin), biperiden (Akineton), DIPHENHYDRAMINE (Benadryl), or trihexyphenidyl (Artane).

Gelenberg, A. J. "Psychoses." In *The Practitioner's Guide to Psychoactive Drugs.* 2nd ed., edited by E. L. Bassuk, S. C. Schoonover, and A. J. Gelenberg. New York: Plenum, 1983.

Parkinson's disease and psychosis See MEDICAL DISORDERS THAT MIMIC PSYCHIATRIC DISORDERS.

pathogen Something that causes a disease process.

pathognomonic Certain signs and symptoms are said to be pathognomonic of a particular disease if they alone can identify the presence of that particular disease. Although this may be true for many medical disorders whose physiological basis is quite well known and can be diagnosed through physical measurements, such is not the case for mental disorders. For example, because DELUSIONS and HALLUCINATIONS can occur in many disorders (and sometimes in normal persons), they would not be considered pathognomonic of SCHIZOPHRENIA. No single symptom alone is pathognomonic of schizophrenia.

See also FIRST-RANK SYMPTOMS.

pathognomy A 19th-century pseudoscience that, like phrenology and PHYSIOGNOMY, influenced the development of psychiatry as a science. Pathognomy (also called "movable physiognomy") was the study of the various expressions of the human face as they reflect different emotions and underlying musculature, and particularly as they reflect the inner emotional states of the mentally ill. The internationally acclaimed Scottish anatomist, physiologist, and neurologist Sir Charles Bell (1774–1842) of Edinburgh was one of the earliest to take a scientific interest in the expressions of mentally ill persons, and in his 1806 book, *Essays on the Anatomy of Expressions in Painting,* he compares the expres-

sions of "madness" with those found in "lower animals" and attributed them to fear and terror. Bell was a gifted illustrator and included a sketch of a typical "outrageous maniac" that he observed on a visit to the ROYAL BETHLEM HOSPITAL ("Bedlam") in July 1805. In his book he gives advice to painters on "what ought to be represented as the prevailing character and physiognomy of a madman," and in doing so, Bell sets the following scene:

> You see him lying in his cell regardless of every thing, with a death-like fixed gloom upon his countenance. When I say it is a death-like gloom, I mean a heaviness of the features without knitting of the brows or actions of the muscles.
>
> If you watch him in his paroxysm you may see the blood working to his head; his face acquires a darker red; he becomes restless; then rising from his couch he paces his cell and tugs his chains. Now his inflamed eye is fixed upon you, and his features lighten up into an inexpressible wildness and ferocity.

The famous Scottish physician Alexander Morison (1779–1866), who in 1822 delivered the first formal lectures in psychiatry in Great Britain, published a textbook in several editions that discussed the pathognomy of mental illness and included a series of relevant illustrations of patients who represented various diagnostic categories. In his *Outlines of Lectures on Mental Diseases* (1826), Morison writes: "The appearance of the face, it is well known, is intimately connected with, and dependent upon, the state of mind." He continued his research on the pathognomy of mental disorders and in 1840 published a textbook with 108 original drawings of the facial expressions of the mentally ill, *The Physiognomy of Mental Diseases.* Many of the expressions depicted would be similar to those seen on the faces of persons with psychotic disorders in the psychiatric hospitals and wards of today.

Gilman, S. L. *Seeing the Insane.* New York: Wiley, 1982.

pauper lunatics A term especially popular in the 19th century for the destitute mentally ill. An analogous term today might be the "homeless mentally ill."

Pavlov's theory of schizophrenia The famous Russian physiologist Ivan Pavlov (1849–1936), who influenced the field of learning by establishing the importance of the autonomic nervous system in the phenomenon known as "conditioned reflexes" (the discovery of which led to a Nobel Prize in 1904), became interested in SCHIZOPHRENIA after several visits to a Russian psychiatric hospital in 1918. Pavlov was particularly interested in catatonic patients and in his writings compared them to animals that had been experimentally conditioned. In early articles (1919), he interpreted the behavior of catatonic schizophrenics as resulting from an inhibition of the cerebral cortex of the brain, specifically a motor inhibition (inhibition of voluntary movement). Later (1930) Pavlov theorized that schizophrenia was a chronic state of hypnosis caused by hereditary and learned weakness of the cells of the cerebral cortex. Pavlov felt that the disease might begin as a learned response but later becomes organic in nature.

Pavlov, I. P. "Last Communications on the Physiology and Pathology of the Superior Nervous Activity," *Journal of Mental Science* 80 (1934): 187–197.

peas therapy Yet another of the bizarre somatic treatments for psychotic disorders and other MENTAL DISORDERS in the 18th and 19th centuries, peas therapy involved the creation of a head wound into which strings of dried peas would be inserted. It was thought that this would work as a counterirritant to the irritation of the brain within the skull that was causing the insanity. It was reportedly used by the famous Scottish physician James Cowles Prichard (1786–1848), who in his day was one of the most eminent alienists in Britain.

pedigree A diagrammed ancestral line of descent (a "family tree") that is used in GENETICS STUDIES to analyze the inheritance of psychiatric disorders

or other associated characteristics. It is often more difficult to determine correct pedigree information for genetics studies of psychiatric disorders than for studies of other types of illnesses. Often family members may be inaccessible or uncooperative, or, as in the case of people with schizophrenia, who tend to produce fewer children than normals, the families may simply be too small to do a thorough study. Researchers often try to minimize the limitations to pedigree studies by locating and studying "geographical isolates," that is, communities that have been in one place for many generations and have not interbred very much with groups from other areas. The geographical isolation itself, as well as consanguineous marriages (marriages within the same bloodlines), helps to minimize the probability that the illness that is being studied for its possible genetic transmission is due to more than one genetic variant.

Pardes, H., et al. "Genetics and Psychiatry: Past Discoveries, Current Dilemmas, and Future Directions," *American Journal of Psychiatry,* 146 (1989): 435–443.

pediluvia One of the inhumane somatic treatments for mental illness used in the 19th century in which the legs of patients were plunged into vast amounts of water containing an irritating substance.

pellagrous insanity Pellagra is a disease caused by a deficiency of niacin. The term is derived from two Italian words meaning "skin" and "rough." Pellagra was first described in the 1730s in Spain, and its symptoms include diarrhea, dermatitis, and in its latter stages, mental disorders such as DEPRESSION and DEMENTIA. Thus, many persons who survived into the final stages of this disorder needed institutional care, usually in psychiatric hospitals. Although cases of pellagra are relatively uncommon today, it was estimated that in 1917 there were 125,000 cases of pellagra in the United States, primarily in the southeastern states. However, it was estimated that only 4 percent to 10 percent of persons with pellagra ("pellagrins") went on to develop the psychotic disorder known as "pellagrous insanity."

Copper, T. C. "Pellagrous Insanity," *American Journal of Insanity,* 1928, pp. 945–952.

penetrance In GENETICS STUDIES, the proportion of persons with a given GENOTYPE that actually manifest a particular PHENOTYPE.

peptides and schizophrenia A peptide is an intermediate level of biochemical synthesis between amino acids and proteins. A protein is composed of one or more peptides. Some of these protein particles have been demonstrated to have significant effects on behavior. Neuropeptides have been demonstrated to act as NEUROTRANSMITTERS, and therefore it has been suggested that a neuropeptide abnormality in the brain might be a possible contributing cause of SCHIZOPHRENIA. However, an informed review of the existing studies thus far by Herbert Meltzer in 1987 concludes, "It should be clear from this brief review that there is as yet no clear evidence for a neuropeptidergic mechanism in schizophrenia." Nonetheless, he recommends the exploration of the relationship between neuropeptides and schizophrenia as a possibly fruitful area of research for the future.

Meltzer, H. Y. "Biological Studies in Schizophrenia," *Schizophrenia Bulletin* 13 (1987): 77–111.

perceptual anomalies in schizophrenia It has long been known that persons who are undergoing a brief psychotic episode or who have a chronic psychotic disorder have quite a different sensory experience of the world than those who are not psychotic. Although many attempts have been made by clinical observers (as well as by writers in fictional treatments of madness) to understand and describe this "other worldliness" of psychosis, it was not until the 1960s that the first scientific studies attempted to find a measure that could quantify the phenomenology of the ALTERED STATES OF CONSCIOUSNESS found in psychosis, and specifically in SCHIZOPHRENIA. The perceptual anomalies caused by the ingestion of hallucinogenic substances such as peyote or LSD led to their early label as "psychotomimetic"

or "psychosis-mimicking" drugs. Disorders of attention in schizophrenia have often suggested that a "filtering" mechanism that separates out meaningful from peripheral information is dysfunctional in persons with schizophrenia, and so along these lines some theorists have suggested that "perceptual dyscontrol" may be a useful way of attempting to describe and understand the mysterious symptoms of this psychotic disorder.

In a 1976 paper published in *Schizophrenia Bulletin*, psychiatrist Lionel Corbett lists the following perceptual anomalies found in people with schizophrenia:

1. Changes in stimulus intensity control:
   - Enhancement; increased vividness of sounds, colors, appetite, even to the point of pain.
   - Diminution; sensations become muted; awareness is deadened.
2. Shifts in quality: Objects change size, faces swell, printed words rearrange themselves and zigzag; sudden changes in gestalts occur.
3. Abnormal concomitant perceptions: Each true stimulus is accompanied by a second sensation; for example, every word heard is associated with a pain in the head.
4. Abnormal perceptual alienation: Things and people look strangely different; voices sound unreal; the world looks fresh, exciting, and overpoweringly beautiful or uncanny and menacing. Sometimes perceptions lose their meaning, so that sounds, faces, and speech do not make any sense.
5. Splitting of perceptions: For example, a bird is heard chirping, but the bird and its song seem separated as though they do not belong together.
6. Loss of perceptual constancy: Depth perception and perspective are lost, so that everything looks two-dimensional and flat. Buildings seem to be crumbling, the steepness of stairs cannot be judged, the edges of rooms curve.
7. Failure of gating: The perceptual world is flooded with uncontrolled images, originating both internally and externally.
8. Abnormal time perception: Time speeds, slows, stands still, or the moment expands into eternity. Events become discontinuous, or time sensation becomes erratic.
9. Abnormal space perception: For example, micropsia, dysmegalopsia; space expands.
10. Distortion of bodily perception: The limbs feel light or heavy, or as though they are coming apart. The nose, hands, face, feet, or hips seem to have changed size. The skin texture or body odor seems different, the head feels odd or numb.
11. Hallucinations, including hallucinatory memory.
12. Changes in the perception of emotion: The experience of having lost all feelings; changes in the feeling tone of perceptions—for example, the touch of normal objects becomes charged with unpleasant affect. Sometimes percepts become unduly imbued with ecstatic, wonderful feelings.

See also ATTENTION, DISORDERS IN; PSYCHEDELIC EXPERIENCES IN SCHIZOPHRENIA; SUBJECTIVE EXPERIENCES IN SCHIZOPHRENIA.

Corbett, L. "Perceptual Dyscontrol: A Possible Organizing Principle for Schizophrenia Research," *Schizophrenia Bulletin* 2 (1976), 249–265.

perceptual delusions See DELUSIONAL PERCEPTION.

perinatal factors hypothesis Because genetics cannot account for 100 percent of the causes of SCHIZOPHRENIA, many theorists have postulated that there may be environmental causes of this brain disease. One possibility that has attracted attention is that certain factors surrounding the birth of the person who later develops schizophrenia may contribute to or actually cause the disease itself. Among the first to investigate these perinatal factors was researcher W. Pollin and colleagues in the mid-1960s. Many other investigators have followed suit and have examined a variety of possible factors in the development of schizophrenia. For example, in examining birth weight as a perinatal factor, it has been found that in those pairs of MONOZYGOTIC TWINS ("identical twins") discordant for schizophrenia (that is, one has it and the other doesn't),

the "normal" twin is usually the one who weighed more at birth and is usually born first. Other studies (conducted in the 1970s by Sweden's Thomas F. McNeil and colleagues) indicate that birth complications are more likely to have occurred in the ill twin of monozygotic twins discordant for schizophrenia, thus suggesting that given identical genes, environmentally induced injuries may influence the later expression of the illness.

Perhaps the most important study of the role of pregnancy complications and the risk of schizophrenia was conducted by Christiana Dalman and colleagues in Sweden and published in 1999. In this longitudinal cohort study, Sweden's National Birth Register was linked to the National Inpatient Register. The researchers followed up on the lives of 507,516 children born between 1973 and 1977 with regard to a diagnosis of schizophrenia between 1987 and 1995. They found 238 cases that matched. Using Sweden's detailed central medical databases, they also had access to data on physical and psychiatric illnesses in the mothers. Risk factors that increased the risk of schizophrenia in a newborn were (1) preeclampsia (hypertension in the mother that is also an indicator of fetal malnutrition), which was the only statistically significant risk factor, (2) vacuum extraction from the womb during birth, and (3) minor physical abnormalities in the fetus. These problems are caused by (1) malnutrition during fetal development, (2) extreme prematurity, and (3) hypoxia or ischemia around the time of birth.

Other perinatal factors that have been investigated in schizophrenia research are the mother's nutritional status at the time of the birth of the child, complications arising during the delivery of the child, possible hypoxia due to postnatal apnea in the newborn, intracranial hemorrhages, the immediate postnatal living environment of the newborn, and possible exposure to infectious diseases. Currently, new research on perinatal factors is being conducted in the area of fetal neural development.

See also FETAL NEURAL DEVELOPMENT AND SCHIZOPHRENIA; RISK FACTORS.

Dalman, C., et al. "Obstetric Complications and the Risk of Schizophrenia," *Archives of General Psychiatry* 56 (1999): 234–240.

McNeil, T. F. "Perinatal Factors in the Development of Schizophrenia." In *Biological Perspectives of Schizophrenia,* edited by H. Helmschen and F. Henn. Chichester, England: John Wiley & Sons, 1987.

Pollin W., et al. "Life History Differences in Identical Twins Discordant for Schizophrenia," *American Journal of Orthopsychiatry* 36 (1966): 492–509.

perphenazine See ANTIPSYCHOTIC DRUGS.

persecutory delirium See DELUSIONS, PERSECUTORY.

persecutory type According to *DSM-IV* (1994), the variant of delusional disorder in which the predominant theme of the person's delusion is that the afflicted person (or someone that he or she is close to) is being deliberately mistreated or threatened in some way. Persons with this disorder may continually complain to landlords, the police, or the FBI, for example, about being mistreated. Persons with this disorder are often resentful and angry and may become violent toward those they believe are persecuting them. This is the most common subtype of delusional disorder.

See also PARANOIA.

perseveration The tendency to continue to repeat particular behavior long after it is necessary to perform it. Persons with brain damage often perseverate, since it seems that the ability to inhibit an impulse to perform an action once it has started is impaired, thus causing the organically impaired person to repeat ritually the same activity over and over again. Due to the evidence for the underlying organic basis of schizophrenia, it is not surprising to at times find such behaviors in people with this disorder.

persistent delusional disorders See DELUSIONAL DISORDERS.

pervasive developmental disorders See CHILDHOOD SCHIZOPHRENIA.

PET scan A type of BRAIN IMAGING TECHNIQUE or neuroimaging technique that measures regional brain metabolism. The acronym stands for positron emission tomography, and the first published report of its use was in a paper by L. Sokoloff in 1977. PET scans examine functional changes in the brain, specifically: (a) biochemical changes such as oxygen metabolism, glucose metabolism, and changes in neurotransmitter receptor numbers, and (b) changes in physiological parameters, such as regional blood flow and blood volume.

PET uses computer-generated images, displayed as if they were slices of the brain. These images serve to map and quantify metabolic changes throughout the brain. Through either intravenous or inhaled means, the subject is administered "tracer agents" that have been tagged with a short-lived (usually two to four hours) positron-emitting isotope. A variety of brain functions can be studied with PET since hundreds of different tracer agents can be tagged with positron-emitting isotopes. The PET scanner follows the course of the positron emissions and translates these signals into pictures.

The first published report of the use of PET in schizophrenia research was a preliminary report on a single chronic schizophrenic subject by T. Farkas and colleagues in 1980. The first published controlled study of PET using schizophrenics and normal control subjects was produced by M. S. Buchsbaum and colleagues in 1982.

Farkas, T., et al. "The Application of [18F] 2-deoxy-2-fluoro-D-glucose and Positron Emission Tomography in a Study of Psychiatric Conditions." In *Cerebral Metabolism and Neural Function*, edited by J. V. Passonneau et al. Baltimore: Williams & Wilkins, 1980.

pharmacologic challenge A method employed in GENETICS STUDIES to search for markers of vulnerability by administering drugs in subclinical doses for a limited period of time. A selected drug is given both to persons who are thought to be genetically vulnerable to the later development of a disease and to normals. If the two groups respond differently, then the difference in response is attributed to genetic differences. At that point, response differences to a particular drug can be used as a useful marker of vulnerability. No such marker has yet been discovered for schizophrenia using a pharmacologic challenge.

pharmacotherapy of the psychotic disorders See ANTIPSYCHOTIC DRUGS.

phenocopy An individual who exhibits a trait that is due to nongenetic factors.

phenomenology of schizophrenic experience See ALTERED STATE OF CONSCIOUSNESS; PERCEPTUAL ANOMALIES IN SCHIZOPHRENIA; SUBJECTIVE EXPERIENCES OF SCHIZOPHRENIA.

phenothiazine Technically, the parent chemical compound for the synthesis of a large number of ANTIPSYCHOTIC DRUGS, including promethazine and CHLORPROMAZINE. By the late 1940s, researchers had discovered all the major chemical groups that are currently used in psychopharmacology. At about this time it was discovered that promethazine, a phenothiazine derivative, effectively potentiated the sedative properties of barbiturates (the type of drugs primarily used for mental illness for the first half of the 20th century) when used together but was useless when used alone. Therefore, researchers sought to develop other phenothiazines that might have a stronger effect. This was achieved in 1949 when Charpentier synthesized chlorpromazine (trade name: THORAZINE). By 1952 the antipsychotic effect of this drug had been documented in published reports, and it was approved for use with persons with psychotic disorders in the United States in 1954.

phenotype An observable trait in a person, physical or behavioral, surmised to be due genetics.

Philadelphia Association, the See LAING, RONALD DAVID.

photophilia in schizophrenia It has been reported by many observers of people with psychotic disorders that they sometimes exhibit photophilic (sun-loving) or photophobic (sun-avoiding) tendencies. Schizophrenics in particular have been observed in sun-gazing activities, sometimes resulting in damage to the retina. Psychiatrist Hector Gerbaldo suspects that people with schizophrenia have a decreased sensitivity to light, and that this may be important later in understanding the relationship between SCHIZOPHRENIA and photosensitive neuroendocrine processes (neural and hormonal processes that are stimulated by sunlight). It has been hypothesized that psychotic symptoms may be tied in with natural biological rhythms, and therefore the study of photophilia in schizophrenia may shed light on chronobiological studies of the psychotic disorders.

Gerbaldo, H., B. Thaker, and S. Cassady. "Sun Gazing and Photophilia in Schizophrenia," *American Journal of Psychiatry* 148 (1991): 693.

physical abnormalities in schizophrenia Many investigators looking for "biological markers" of schizophrenia have found minor physical abnormalities in schizophrenia, confirming, somewhat, the approach of the study of PHYSIOGNOMY. Minor physical anomalies (PAs) are often defined in research studies as slight defects of the head, hands, mouth, hair, eyes, ears, and feet. Generally, most researchers believe that these anomalies are due to perinatal factors and are associated with injury or unusual development during the first trimester of pregnancy, since this is the most critical period for the development of the epidermis, hair, ears, nose, and eyes. Between 1967 and 1989 the only five studies of PAs in schizophrenics that have ever been conducted have all found positive results. In a 1989 study by M. F. Green and colleagues at the UCLA Research Center in Camarillo, California, schizophrenic patients had significantly more physical anomalies than the normal control group subjects. They also found that the most common anomalies in schizophrenics were anomalies of the mouth and unusual head circumference, especially in women. In addition, the more prevalent physical anomalies were found in those persons, especially males, who had an earlier age of onset for schizophrenia. None of these anomalies, particularly the head circumference anomalies, were found to be related to cognitive performance, confirming a conclusion that Philippe PINEL made in 1801: "I have also taken, by means of a caliber compass, the dimensions of the heads of different persons of both sexes, who had been, or who were at the time in a state of insanity. I generally observed that the two most striking varieties, the elongated and the spheroidal skulls are found indifferently and bearing, at least, no evident relation to the extent of the intellectual faculties."

See also PERINATAL FACTORS HYPOTHESIS.

Green, M. F. "Minor Physical Anomalies in Schizophrenia," *Schizophrenia Bulletin* 15 (1989): 91–99.

Pinel, P. *A Treatise on Insanity,* trans. D. D. Davis Shefield. 1801. Reprint, England: W. Todd, 1806.

physical disease and schizophrenia The belief in the existence of a relationship between physical and mental illness has a long history. Indeed, throughout the centuries it has been reported that severe physical illnesses can sometimes alleviate the symptoms of mental illness, as was the basis for the rationale for FEVER THERAPY. Many studies have examined the risk factors for specific physical illnesses to which persons with SCHIZOPHRENIA may or may not be susceptible. A 1988 review of this vast area of research by psychologist Anne Harris of Arizona State University has concluded that: (a) persons with schizophrenia may be at increased risk for breast cancer and possibly for cardiovascular disease, (b) persons with schizophrenia seem to have a decreased risk for developing rheumatoid arthritis or lung cancer (even in light of the fact that so many of them are heavy smokers), and (c) the overall risk for cancer is, however, greater in persons with PARANOID SCHIZOPHRENIA than in those diagnosed with the other subtypes. The problem with these studies, however, is that the risk factors for particular disease may one day be found to have nothing to do with the schizophrenic disease process per se in individuals but instead may be determined by the effects of antipsychotic medication or other as yet unknown confounding factors.

Harris, A. H. "Physical Disease and Schizophrenia," *Schizophrenia Bulletin* 14 (1988): 85–96.

physiognomy The attempt to gain insight into a person's character or personality based on his or her physical characteristics (particularly facial expressions) dates from at least Aristotle, who, in the *Physiognomica* (a book attributed to him), suggested that people have the temperament of animals they may resemble. In 1775 J. K. Lavater published his *Physiognomische Fragmente,* which attempted to construct a classification system of character based on facial expressions. In a later work published in Paris, *L'Art de connaitre les hommes par la physionomie* (1806), Lavater explains that "physiognomy is the science or knowledge of the correspondence between the internal and external man, the visible superficies and the invisible contents." Franz Joseph Gall's (1758–1828) influential pseudoscience of phrenology (which dominated psychiatric thought between the 1820s and 1840s) likewise drew attention to the relationship between physiology and mental faculties, with the structure of the skull allegedly related to structural characteristics of the brain that were correlated with specific mental functions. Phrenology had a profound effect on the history of psychiatry, since it conclusively introduced the (then) controversial notion that the mind had a primarily physiological basis in the brain.

It has long been proposed that specific psychotic disorders could be diagnosed in part through the physical characteristics of a particular individual. This early protoscientific attempt to understand the "biological markers" of mental illness involved the study and classification of the physiognomy of the "insane." Philippe PINEL devoted considerable effort to measuring the size and shapes of the heads of many of his institutionalized patients as well as "a great number of skulls in different museums," finding only a relationship between skull size and shape and mental retardation. He devotes a whole section to the topic—"Of Malconformation of the Skulls of Maniacs and Idiots"—in his 1801 *A Treatise on Insanity.* Pinel's pupil, J. E. D. ESQUIROL (1772–1840) maintained a large collection of plaster casts of the faces of institutionalized patients at the Salpêtrière in Paris. During the early 1820s, another member of the "Esquirol Circle," Etienne-Jean Georget (1795–1828), commissioned the painter Géricault to paint 10 studies of "lunatics," all of which were "monomaniacs." Later in the 19th century, Cesare Lombroso (1836–1909) studied criminal behavior and believed that certain physical characteristics in a person were "stigmata of degeneracy" that could identify the "criminal type."

In the 20th century, German psychiatrist Ernst Kretschmer (1888–1964) correlated body type and constitution with specific mental disorders in his famous book *Körperbau und charakter* (1921). The ASTHENIC TYPE was thought to characterize schizophrenics. In the United States, American psychologist William H. Sheldon (1899–1977) correlated various psychotic disorders with body types and proposed that certain very thin individuals called ectomorphs would be more likely to develop schizophrenia than endomorphs, who were heavier and more likely to develop manic-depressive psychosis. Similarly, American psychiatrist Alexander Lowen, a disciple of Wilhelm Reich's "bioenergetics analysis," combined physiognomy and psychoanalytic thought by identifying the "schizophrenic character" and the "schizoid character" in his writings of the 1950s.

Cooter, R. "Phrenology and the British Alienists, ca. 1825–1845." In *Madhouses, Mad-Doctors, and Madmen: The Social History of Psychiatry in the Victorian Era,* edited by A. Scull. London: Athlone Press, 1981.

Goldstein, J. *Console and Classify: The French Psychiatric Profession in the Nineteenth Century.* Chicago: Chicago University Press, 1987.

Lowen, A. *Physical Dynamics of Character Structure: Bodily Form and Movement in Analytic Therapy.* New York: Grune & Stratton, 1958.

Sheldon, W. H. *The Varieties of Human Physique.* New York: Harper Brothers, 1940.

pica The eating of nonfood substances (e.g., dirt, paint chips, hair, cloth). Pica can sometimes be the result of a person's psychotic disorder, particularly in severe cases of chronic schizophrenia.

pimozide See ANTIPSYCHOTIC DRUGS.

Pinel, Philippe (1745–1826) A French ALIENIST and one of the most important figures in the development of modern psychiatry. In 1793, following the French Revolution, Pinel was appointed chief physician at the BICÊTRE asylum in Paris, where he became famous for freeing more than 50 male patients from their chains. (Although the action was initiated by Jean-Baptiste Pussin, not Pinel.) In 1795 he became the head of the other major asylum in Paris at that time, the Salpêtrière, where he was also known for his humane philosophy of treatment, which he later called the MORAL TREATMENT. His 1801 textbook, *Traité médico-philosophique sur l'alienation mental ou la maine,* is one of the long-standing classics of psychiatry and had a profound effect on the classification and treatment of the mentally ill worldwide. He is credited (along with John HASLAM of England) with providing the first complete description of a case of schizophrenia in 1809.

Goldstein, J. *Console and Classify: The French Psychiatric Profession in the Nineteenth Century.* Chicago: Chicago University Press, 1987.

Riese, W. *The Legacy of Philippe Pinel: An Inquiry into Thought on Mental Alienation.* New York: Springer, 1969.

Pinel-Haslam syndrome, the The proposed name for the type of schizophrenia that according to CROW'S HYPOTHESIS is called "Type II" schizophrenia—the type that is characterized by NEGATIVE SYMPTOMS, is more organically based, and has an earlier onset and a more chronic course. This term was first proposed by M. Altschule in 1967 as a replacement for the term *schizophrenia.*

See also HISTORICAL EVIDENCE OF SCHIZOPHRENIA.

Altschule, M. D. "Whichophrenia, or the Confused Past, Ambiguous Present, and Dubious Future of the Schizophrenia Concept," *Journal of Schizophrenia* 1 (1967): 8–17.

placebo A harmless, impotent substance that can be given to a patient and affects that person through suggestion. Placebos are important in testing the efficacy of new drugs, since control groups given the placebo should not show any difference in affect, behavior, or other areas, whereas those persons in the experimental group who are given an actual drug should indeed show such differences. The word is derived from a liturgical hymn from the Roman Catholic church, specifically, the first antiphon of the vespers for the dead: "Placebo Domino in regione vivorum" ("I shall be pleasing to the Lord in the land of the living").

platelet MAO activity hypothesis See ENZYME DISORDER HYPOTHESIS.

Poland Although no conclusive studies have been conducted in Poland, the prevalence rate for schizophrenia is estimated to be higher than in most countries. This is based on data from Australia, England, and the United States, which concludes that Polish immigrants (as well as Russian and, in some studies, Swedish immigrants) have very high rates of first admission to psychiatric hospitals when compared with other ethnic groups.

Torrey, E. F. *Schizophrenia and Civilization.* New York: Jason Aronson, 1980.

polydipsia This is a medical term for frequent drinking because of excessive thirst. Polydipsia is a commonly observed behavior in people with psychotic disorders. Although studies have indicated that 6 percent to 17 percent of all chronically ill psychiatric patients manifest this behavior, 69 percent to 83 percent of people diagnosed with SCHIZOPHRENIA do so. Both relatives and institutional caretakers of people with schizophrenia can acknowledge that this is a very common activity, but the reason for it still remains a matter of conjecture. Irrational or psychotic thoughts that encourage drinking, the mouth dryness caused by ANTIPSYCHOTIC DRUGS, and the hyperactivity of the thirst centers in the hypothalamus in the brain have all been posited as contributing to this behavior. However, polydipsia can be dangerous, as it can lead to abnormally low concentrations of

sodium ions in the circulating blood, which is a condition known as hyponatremia. The constant drinking of water can lead to water intoxication, with such symptoms as confusion, lethargy, the worsening of psychotic symptoms, and even death. Perhaps the earliest case report of a person with schizophrenia engaging in dangerous polydipsia was reported in 1938 by Barahal, who described an example "in which a female dementia praecox patient drank excessive quantities of tap water resulting in edema, coma, convulsions, with subsequent recovery." Other terms for this syndrome have been *compulsive water drinking, self-induced water intoxication and psychosis, psychogenic polydipsia, primary polydipsia,* and *psychosis-intermittent hyponatremia-polydipsia (PIP) syndrome.* The primary treatment remains fluid restriction and the removal of exacerbating factors.

Barahal, H. S. "Water Intoxication in a Mental Case," *Psychiatric Quarterly* 12 (1938): 767–771.

Illowsky, B. P., and D. G. Kirch. "Polydipsia and Hyponatremia in Psychiatric Patients," *American Journal of Psychiatry* 145 (1988): 675–683.

polygenetic theory See DIATHESIS-STRESS THEORIES.

polymorphic psychotic symptoms A term used in *ICD-10* (1992) to distinguish a syndrome of psychotic symptoms found in ACUTE AND TRANSIENT PSYCHOTIC DISORDERS that are not characteristic of the longer-term symptoms found in SCHIZOPHRENIA. Polymorphic symptoms are rapidly changing and variable, changing from hour to hour or day to day. These symptoms include HALLUCINATIONS, DELUSIONS, perceptual disturbances, and emotional turmoil (irritability and anxiety, although sometimes alternating with feeling of ecstasy and happiness).

polypharmacy The mixing of several drugs in one prescription. Psychiatrists are often cautious about the possible dangers of such a practice, since care must be taken when prescribing, for example, an antipsychotic, an antidepressant, and an ANTIPARKINSONIAN DRUG all at the same time.

poor houses See ALMSHOUSES.

portmanteau word This is a word that has two separate meanings "packed" into it in a forced fit. Persons with psychotic disorders, particularly schizophrenia, can sometimes create such NEOLOGISMS that are usually quite meaningless. For example, the "pillfill" might be a word for the little plastic cup in which a nurse hands a patient his or her medication. Author Lewis Carroll coined the term in his novel *Through the Looking Glass* (1872).

positive symptoms Specifically, DELUSIONS and HALLUCINATIONS. Positive symptoms have been postulated to be the characteristic symptoms of "Type I" schizophrenia by British researcher Timothy Crow and are thought to be related to increased dopamine receptors in the brain. However, CROW'S HYPOTHESIS has been challenged by prominent schizophrenia researcher Herbert Meltzer of Case Western Reserve University, who argues that the connection between increased DOPAMINE activity and positive symptoms is not clear-cut, and indeed dopamine activity may be related to NEGATIVE SYMPTOMS as well.

See also FACTORS OF INSANITIES, THE; NEGATIVE SYMPTOMS.

Berrios, G. E. "Positive and Negative Symptoms and Jackson: A Conceptual History," *Archives of General Psychiatry* 42 (1985): 95–97.

Meltzer, H. Y. "Dopamine and Negative Symptoms in Schizophrenia: A Critique of the Type I-II Hypothesis." In *Controversies in Schizophrenia,* edited by M. Apert. New York: Guilford Press, 1985.

possession syndrome Since antiquity there have been numerous reports of persons who claim to be "possessed" by evil spirits. French ALIENIST J. E. D. ESQUIROL referred to this syndrome in the 19th century as CACODEMONOMANIA. Case histories of such persons continue to appear from time to time in modern psychiatric literature. More than likely, such persons are experiencing a DISSOCIATIVE DISORDER in which a person's consciousness, memory, and

identity are split into two or more separate personality states or personalities. Many persons who were thought to be "possessed" over the centuries may have instead been afflicted with multiple personality disorder, with the switching of alternate personalities leading to a supernatural explanation. However, in persons with schizoprenia, it is not uncommon to encounter reports that the person feels "possessed" or has delusions about being possessed by evil spirits, malevolent family members, and so on.

The belief in possession is so widespread that an exhaustive study of 488 randomly selected societies in 1968 by cultural anthropologist Erika Bourguignon of Ohio State University found that 74 percent of them had some sort of belief in possession, and many had ritualized forms of "possession trance" that were accepted among religious practitioners. Due to the influx of many immigrants into the United States and Canada from South America and the Carribean, where there are many cultures that promote such beliefs and religious practices, clinicians are encountering more and more examples of such cases.

Bourguignon, E. *Possession.* San Francisco: Chandler & Sharp, 1976.

Goodman, F. D. *How about Demons? Possession and Exorcism in the Modern World.* Bloomington: Indiana University Press, 1988.

McAll, R. K. "Demonosis or the Possession Syndrome," *International Journal of Social Psychiatry* 17 (1971): 150–158.

Noll, R. *Vampires, Werewolves and Demons: Twentieth Century Case Reports in the Psychiatric Literature.* New York: Brunner/Mazel, 1991.

postpartum psychosis The phenomenon that still occurs from time to time in which a psychotic episode (usually a psychotic depression) or more serious psychotic disorder (such as schizophrenia or bipolar disorder) seems to be induced by the stress of childbirth. It was first described by the French physician Charles Lepois (1563–1633), who thought it was due to an excess (*plethora*) of dark humors (see HUMORAL THEORY OF MENTAL ILLNESS). Well into the 1800s some physicians believed that the severe mental disorders suffered by women shortly preceding and especially directly following childbirth were related to the production (or lack of production) of milk (see LACTATION PSYCHOSES). In 1838 French alienist J. E. D. ESQUIROL observed that fully one-twelfth of the women admitted to the SALPÊTRIÈRE in Paris became psychotic after giving birth.

Research into the types of psychotic disorders that are brought on by childbirth has resulted in conflicting conclusions over the years. In a major study published in 1969 by Protheroe in England, almost twice as many cases of manic-depressive psychosis were reported as cases of schizophrenia. In some previous studies, more cases of schizophrenia were reported as postpartum or puerperal insanity. One of the best sources of information on postpartum psychotic disorders is the chapter titled "Postpartum Schizophrenic Psychoses" in Silvano ARIETI's book *Interpretation of Schizophrenia* (1974). Today, with the use of synthetic hormones, ANTIPSYCHOTIC DRUGS and psychotherapy, such psychotic episodes in women rarely become chronic illnesses.

Arieti, S. *Interpretation of Schizophrenia.* 2nd ed. New York: Basic Books, 1974.

Protheroe, C. "Puerperal Psychoses: A Long-Term Study, 1927–1961," *British Journal of Psychiatry* 115 (1969): 9–30.

postpsychotic depression See DEPRESSION.

poverty of content of speech Also known as Alogia, one of the NEGATIVE SYMPTOMS of schizophrenia. According to *DSM-III-R* (1987), this is "speech that is adequate in amount but conveys little information because of vagueness, empty repetitions, or use of stereotyped or obscure phrases."

poverty of speech One of the NEGATIVE SYMPTOMS of schizophrenia, it is reduction in the amount and frequency of speech.

predisposing factors Any fact of a person's life, whether genetic or environmental, that may increase the likelihood that that person will

develop a specific disease. For example, in both schizophrenia and bipolar disorder, a family history that includes several afflicted persons with the same psychotic disorder is a strong predisposing factor to the possible development of the disease.

See also HIGH-RISK STUDIES; RISK FACTORS.

Enoch, M. D., and W. H. Trethowan. *Uncommon Psychiatric Syndromes*. 2nd ed. Bristol, England: John Wright & Sons, 1979. (The chapter on the *couvade* syndrome is an exemplary resource.)

Small, G. W. "Pseudocyesis: An Overview," *Canadian Journal of Psychiatry* 31 (1986): 452–457.

prefrontal lobotomy See LOBOTOMY.

pregnancy complications and schizophrenia See PERINATAL FACTORS HYPOTHESIS.

pregnancy delusions A commonly encountered type of delusion found in both women and men with severe psychotic disorders, usually schizophrenia. A man may claim, for example, that he has been pregnant for nine years.

In persons who may not have psychotic disorders, there have been many cases on record of women who have developed a psychosomatic syndrome in which they may fully believe they are pregnant and at times mysteriously manifest many of the symptoms of pregnancy but may not actually be so. With this mysterious syndrome—called pseudocyesis (a term coined by John Mason Good in his *Physiological System of Nosology* in 1823)—women may report morning sickness or feeling fetal movements, and, incredibly, the abdomen may enlarge and the breasts may enlarge and actually begin to produce milk. This psychosomatic disorder has been reported since 300 B.C. when Hippocrates, the father of medicine, wrote about women "who imagined they were pregnant, seeing the menses suppressed and the matrices swollen," treating 12 such cases himself. Although modern technology has allowed the early detection of pregnancy and has eliminated most cases of pseudocyesis, the continued rare occurrence of such cases has led to a new scientific name for the syndrome: the galactorrhea-amenorrhea hyperprolactinemia syndrome, or GAHS. A related syndrome in men is *couvade,* from the French for to "brood" or "hatch," and it essentially refers to what is conventionally known as "sympathetic labor pains."

premorbid functioning The physical, psychological and interpersonal level of functioning of a person before the first clear signs of a mental disease process are apparent. Another, older term for this is "premorbid personality." In schizophrenia it has generally been found that persons with the paranoid subtype have a higher level of premorbid functioning than those with the nonparanoid subtypes. Premorbid functioning is a factor in the PROCESS-REACTIVE DISTINCTION IN SCHIZOPHRENIA, with "process" schizophrenics being characterized by poor premorbid history and "reactive" schizophrenics having a much better premorbid level of functioning.

See also AGE AT ONSET; COURSE AND OUTCOME OF SCHIZOPHRENIA.

prenatal factors See FETAL NEURAL DEVELOPMENT AND SCHIZOPHRENIA; PERINATAL FACTORS HYPOTHESIS; RISK FACTORS.

prepsychotic panic A commonly reported phenomenon by people who later develop a full psychotic episode or disorder. It is the crucial point in the person's life when he or she realizes that his or her experiences of the world are aberrant, and this engenders a sense of isolation and loneliness. Fear, terror and sheer panic are experienced by the individual who experiences the world as splitting or crumbling. It may very well be the point at which the person realizes he or she is losing control and will soon no longer be able to function in a healthy way. Many people enter treatment at this point and can be helped with pharmacotherapy and psychotherapy, although many still go on to develop a psychosis. American psychiatrist Harry Stack Sullivan described just such a "schizophrenic panic," which he thought was the

result of an extreme injury to self-esteem or sense of self. Silvano ARIETI describes this initial stage of "prepsychotic panic" in the development of a full case of schizophrenia as follows: "when the patient starts to perceive things in a different way, is frightened on account of it, appears confused, and does not know how to explain 'the strange things that are happening.'"

Arieti, S. *Interpretation of Schizophrenia.* 2nd ed. New York: Basic Books, 1974.
Sullivan, H. S. *Conceptions of Modern Psychiatry.* New York: Norton, 1953.

prepsychotic personality See LATENT SCHIZOPHRENIA.

pressured speech This is one of the hallmarks of a MANIC EPISODE. It occurs when a person is rapidly talking in great bursts and is difficult, if not impossible, to interrupt. Often the person is speaking very loudly and emphatically and without any prompting from anyone else. Indeed, such persons may continue to speak even though no one is listening. Beside manic episodes, pressured speech may occur in persons who are diagnosed with schizophrenia, an organic mental disorder, major depression with psychomotor agitation, other psychotic disorder, or in short-term reactions to stress.

prevalence of schizophrenia See EPIDEMIOLOGY.

primary process According to Sigmund FREUD, this is the type of psychological process that is characteristic of the unconscious. From the point of view of psychoanalysis, primary process is the most primitive and infantile form of psychological activity, and it is most evident in dreams, fantasies, and hallucinations. A psychotic episode or psychotic disorder would then be considered the eruption or intrusion of this primitive and infantile mode of experience into consciousness. Primary process is to be distinguished from secondary process, which is the more logical, sequential, and rational form of thought that typifies normal waking consciousness. The principal drive behind primary process, according to Freud, is the pleasure principle, whereas the primary motivation behind secondary process is the reality principle. Freud developed the distinction between primary and secondary process as early as 1895 in his "Project for a Scientific Psychology" but developed these ideas in more detail in his book, *The Interpretation of Dreams*.

Laplanche, J., and J. B. Pontalis. *The Language of Psycho-Analysis,* trans. D. Nicholson-Smith. New York: W. W. Norton, 1973.

primary symptoms of schizophrenia See FUNDAMENTAL SYMPTOMS OF SCHIZOPHRENIA.

primitive thinking See MAGICAL THINKING.

prison psychosis See GANSER'S SYNDROME.

private madhouses Common in France, Germany, and especially Britain in the 18th and 19th centuries, these were privately owned "madhouses" for mentally ill people with money. Those without money—the "pauper lunatics"—sometimes had their costs paid by local church parishes. The earliest of the private madhouses were developed in England in 1615 (the Kingsdown house at Box, closed finally in 1940), but they did not become a popular practice until the next century. Most were owned by businessmen, not medical professionals, and many were run by women—usually the wives, widows, and daughters of the owners. Some of these private madhouses were passed on for many generations within the same family.

Private madhouses were a profit-making enterprise, and scandals and abuses were frequent. In 1706 British author Daniel Defoe wrote an essay calling for the abolition of private madhouses because of the inhumane treatment prevalent in so many of them. It was finally a novel, *Hard Cash,*

by British author Charles Reade (1814–84), that ignited the movement for reform in the 1860s. *Hard Cash* (first published in England in 1863, and then in the United States in 1864 under the title *Very Hard Cash*) is the story of a sane young man who is diabolically committed to a private asylum by his business associates who covet the young hero's wealth. Reade based the novel on an actual incident in his own life in which he was instrumental in gaining the release of a young man who was wrongfully committed to a private madhouse. Prior to being released as a novel, Reade's *Hard Cash* was first serialized in a periodical edited by Charles Dickens, *All the Year Round*, and both of these men were attacked by the *British Medical Journal* for being irresponsible in making "diabolical charges upon the character of all medical men connected with the management of lunatics."

Ackerknecht, E. H. "Private Institutions in the Genesis of Psychiatry," *Bulletin of the History of Medicine* 60 (1986): 387–399.

Parry-Jones, W. L. *The Trade in Lunacy: A Study of Private Madhouses in England in the Eighteenth and Nineteenth Centuries.* London: Routledge & Kegan Paul, 1972.

proband In GENETICS STUDIES, the proband is the person in a given PEDIGREE diagnosed with the disease. Relationships between that person and others in the family are then studied to determine possible patterns of genetic transmission. Another name for proband is INDEX CASE or "propositus" (plural: probands or propositi).

process-reactive distinction in schizophrenia, the This distinction is one attempt to further differentiate the possible subtypes of schizophrenia. The process-reactive distinction divides persons with schizophrenia into two groups based on differences in premorbid personality, the course of the disease, and its PROGNOSIS. The idea is that the premorbid history of a person who develops schizophrenia and the rapidity with which the first symptoms appear are related to how well or ill the person eventually becomes in the course of his or her lifetime. Therefore, it is also sometimes referred to as the "poor premorbid/good premorbid" distinction, or, by some, the "poor prognosis/good prognosis" distinction (see PREMORBID FUNCTIONING).

Eugen BLEULER first discussed the differences between psychotic disorders that were based on a "morbid reaction to an affective experience" (such as an emotional shock or stressor), which he called reactive psychoses or situation psychoses, and those psychoses based on a "morbid process in the brain," which he termed process psychoses or progressive psychoses. However, as Bleuler notes in the fourth edition (1923) of his *Textbook of Psychiatry*, "no (diagnostic) division can be based on these classes because the two symptomatologies intermingle."

However, based on Bleuler's observation about psychotic disorders in general, the idea was further developed by others that some persons with schizophrenia could have a variety of the disease caused by an organic disease of the brain and another variety that seemed to be induced as a reaction to stress or other environmental factors. Revising some proposals for studying the problem of prognosis in schizophrenia first put forth in a 1937 article, in 1956 Gabriel Langfeldt (1895–1983) of Norway proposed that schizophrenics who had a poor premorbid history (that is, a long-term history of poor social, occupational, and psychological functioning perhaps dating from childhood) be called process schizophrenics. Furthermore, Langfeldt also argued that these persons generally had a poor prognosis and a lifelong history of long-term institutionalization. Langfeldt noticed that there was another type of schizophrenia characterized by persons who may have had a generally good premorbid history and who develop an acute onset of symptoms rather than the slow, insidious development of symptoms found in process schizophrenics. Furthermore, these persons had a better chance of recovery than those with process schizophrenia. Langfeldt called this reactive disorder schizophreniform psychosis.

Throughout the years, the process-reactive distinction has been given many other names as well. These clinical dichotomies have been termed true

schizophrenia/schizophreniform, demential praecox/schizophrenia, typical schizophrenia/atypical schizophrenia, chronic schizophrenia/episodic schizophrenia, and degenerative schizophrenia/psychogenic schizophrenia.

Decades of research that has divided schizophrenia into these two forms has proven useful, for significant differences have been found between the two types of persons with schizophrenia. Process schizophrenics tend to perform more poorly on cognitive, perceptual, and behavioral tasks in experiments. Reactives perform closer to normals on these tasks. Process schizophrenics are also more likely to have NEGATIVE SYMPTOMS, which is to be expected if this is a form of the disorder that seems to be the most organic and genetically based. Reactive schizophrenics tend to demonstrate a fuller range of affect and have shorter hospitalizations and fewer admissions than process schizophrenics. The paranoid subtype of schizophrenia tends to be more common among those in the reactive category, whereas the nonparanoid subtypes tend to be found among those considered process schizophrenics.

The process-reactive distinction has been important for understanding schizophrenia. One of the most consistent research findings is that the premorbid level of social functioning is an important factor in determining the prognosis of cases of schizophrenia, although it is not 100 percent predictive and must be considered with other factors. This vast literature is reviewed by J. Higgins in a 1969 article, and in 1977 an entire issue of *Schizophrenia Bulletin* (vol. 3, no. 2) was devoted to the issue of the premorbid adjustment aspect of the process-reactive distinction.

Bleuler, E. *Lehrbuch der Psychiatrie.* 4th ed. Berlin: Springer, 1923. (English translation, 1924.)

Higgins, J. "Process-Reactive Schizophrenia," *Journal of Nervous and Mental Disease* 149 (1969): 450–465.

Langfeldt, G. "The Prognosis in Schizophrenia and the Factors Influencing the Course of the Disease," *Acta Psychiatrica et Neurologica Scandinavica Supplementum* no. 13 (1937).

———. "The Prognosis in Schizophrenia," *Acta Psychiatrica et Neurologica Scandinavica Supplementum* no. 110 (1956).

prochlorperazine See ANTIPSYCHOTIC DRUGS.

prodromal phase The prodromal phase is the period prior to the full expression of psychotic symptoms (DELUSIONS, HALLUCINATIONS, etc.) in which there is a clear deterioration in a person's previous level of functioning. Often during this period the person will tend to withdraw from social situations, perhaps begin to exhibit poor grooming and hygiene or express odd or bizarre ideas. Often the person's affect will become rather blunted, or he or she may express it inappropriately (e.g., laughing to him- or herself in the middle of a serious discussion). Sometimes he or she will have perceptual abnormalities and may seem to have lost a zest for life by developing a lack of initiative or energy. Insensitive family members or friends may accuse the person of being "lazy" when in fact this is not really the case. Often those who know the person who is undergoing the prodromal phase of schizophrenia will comment on that fact that he or she "is no longer the same person." The length of the prodromal phase is extremely variable, perhaps weeks in some cases to many years in others. The poor premorbid adjustment of "process schizophrenics" (see the PROCESS-REACTIVE DISTINCTION IN SCHIZOPHRENIA) may be due to the presence of the prodromal phase of the illness.

See also AGE AT ONSET.

prognosis The foretelling of the probable course and outcome of a disease. Even after more than a century of scientific research on schizophrenia, it is impossible to predict with any certainty the course and outcome of any individual case of schizophrenia.

Much attention has been paid to the prognosis of schizophrenia. Indeed, Emil KRAEPELIN's classification of the psychotic disorders was based on prognosis, with dementia praecox representing the types of psychosis that follow a chronic degenerating course, and MANIC-DEPRESSIVE PSYCHOSIS being the type of psychotic disorder that has a better outcome. Within the field of schizophrenia research specifically, the concept of "poor prognosis/good prognosis" types of schizophrenia has been examined in depth.

In *Surviving Schizophrenia: A Family Manual,* psychiatrist E. Fuller Torrey lists the following factors, which, when considered together in an individual's unique history, help to determine whether that person fits in the good prognosis or the poor prognosis group:

1. *History of adjustment prior to onset of illness.* This has often been regarded as perhaps the most important factor. If the person seemed relatively normal prior to the obvious onset of schizophrenia, then the chances for a better outcome are greater than for those who may have seemed "odd," withdrawn, or delinquent since childhood.
2. *Gender.* Women have a much better prognosis for schizophrenia than men. Women have a later AGE AT ONSET than men, shorter hospital stays, and fewer relapses.
3. *Family history.* A family history of schizophrenia often indicates a poor prognosis, especially if the blood relationship is close between the INDEX CASE and the affected relatives. A good outcome is suggested by no family history of schizophrenia or psychiatric disorders, or, as it turns out, if there is a history of depression or bipolar illness in the family.
4. *Age of onset.* The earlier schizophrenia develops and is diagnosed in a person, the worse the potential outcome will be. Alternatively, those persons who develop schizophrenia relatively late (especially after age 30) have a much better prognosis.
5. *Suddenness of onset.* If the first symptoms come on rapidly, then the prognosis is much better than if the symptoms developed over a period of months or years.
6. *Precipitating events.* If there is a definite stressful situation or event that is pointed to as the starting point for the onset of the schizophrenic symptoms, the prognosis is good. This corresponds to the "reactive schizophrenia" notion of a subtype that may be more environmentally induced and less genetically and organically based.
7. *CT scan findings.* If a person who is diagnosed with schizophrenia is given a CT scan and the ventricles of the brain are found to be enlarged, this is an indication of poor prognosis. If the CT scan results are normal, then the prognosis is much better.
8. *Response to medication.* One of the strongest indicators of prognosis is response to ANTIPSYCHOTIC DRUGS. If the initial response to antipsychotic medication is weak, then the prognosis is far worse, especially since these drugs are the first line of defense against the debilitating effects of schizophrenia.
9. *Clinical symptoms.* Torrey lists a number of symptoms that may appear during the first schizophrenic episode that he states "can be used as predictive factors." Initial symptoms that indicate a good outcome are the presence of (a) paranoid symptoms, (b) catatonic symptoms, (c) depression or other emotions, (d) a previous diagnosis of schizoaffective disorder, (e) symptoms that are not typical of schizophrenia, and (f) confusion ("I don't understand what is happening to me!" is an example Torrey gives). Initial symptoms that indicate a poor outcome are the presence of (a) NEGATIVE SYMPTOMS such as flat or blunted affect, apathy, extreme social withdrawal, poverty of speech, blocking, etc., and (b) obsessive and compulsive symptoms.

See also COURSE AND OUTCOME OF SCHIZOPHRENIA; GENDER DIFFERENCES IN SCHIZOPHRENIA; HIGH-RISK STUDIES; LONGITUDINAL STUDIES; PROCESS-REACTIVE DISTINCTION IN SCHIZOPHRENIA, THE.

Stephens, J. H. "Long Term Prognosis and Follow-up in Schizophrenia," *Schizophrenia Bulletin* 4 (1978): 25–47.

Torrey, E. F. *Surviving Schizophrenia: A Family Manual.* 2nd ed. New York: Harper & Row, 1988.

projection In Sigmund FREUD's psychoanalysis, projection is a defense mechanism in which feelings, qualities, or wishes that the person refuses to recognize or are rejected in him- or herself are expelled ("projected") from the self and located in another person, group, or thing. Projection is one of the most primitive of the defense mechanisms and is prevalent in the psychotic disorders,

particularly those involving PARANOIA or paranoid delusions. In fact, Freud first became aware of the phenomenon of projection in 1895–96 when studying the mental processes involved in paranoia.

projective tests Psychological tests that attempt to infer qualities of an individual's personality by analyzing the free responses he or she gives to selected stimuli. The idea is based on FREUD's concept of PROJECTION. The answers given on a projective test are thought to contain information about the unconscious wishes, fears, and desires within a person, as well as give an idea of how, at a more conscious level, the person constructs reality and how approaches are taken to problem solving. Projective tests give a good idea of how strong a person's defense mechanisms are, thereby indicating how strong the ego is and how well the person can deal with the demands of life and of reality. Projective tests can use structured stimuli (such as words for the Word Association Test, or charcoal drawings for the Thematic Apperception Test) or unstructured stimuli (such as the various inkblot tests, especially the Rorschach). What is interesting about the history of projective tests is that they were first developed by clinicians using institutionalized people with dementia praecox (schizophrenia) and other serious mental disorders.

C. G. JUNG (1875–1961), the Swiss psychiatrist and psychoanalyst, was the first to use a projective test for diagnostic purposes with people with mental disorders. Even though the Word Association Test had been used by others in previous studies to study the way the "normal," rational, conscious mind works, Jung used the association test to discover the unconscious feelings, wishes, fears, and desires that revealed something about the deeper aspects of the human personality. He experimentally demonstrated the phenomenon of COMPLEXES using these tests, and his published research (which appeared in journals between 1904 and 1910) made him world famous.

Swiss psychiatrist Hermann Rorschach (1884–1922) initially invented an inkblot test to examine the fantasy capacity of successful art students versus less talented ones. Although Rorschach conducted his initial experiments with the inkblots in 1911, over the years he experimented with more than 300 psychiatric patients in asylums and clinics in Switzerland as well as normal persons. Many of the institutionalized patients had psychotic disorders, such as schizophrenia and manic-depressive psychosis, and so it is with these types of patients that Rorschach fine-tuned his famous test. He finally published the results of his studies in 1921 in his famous book *Psychodiagnostik* (Psychodiagnostics).

Projective tests for the purposes of diagnosing schizophrenia (or other mental disorders) has fallen into disrepute. From a scientific standpoint, they are unreliable.

Jung, C. G. *Experimental Researches: The Collected Works of C. G. Jung.* Vol. 2. Princeton, N.J.: Princeton University Press, 1973.

Rabin, A. I. "Projective Methods: A Historical Introduction." In *Assessment with Projective Techniques: A Concise Introduction,* edited by A. I. Rubin. New York: Springer, 1981.

Rorschach, H. *Psychodiagnostik.* Bern und Leipzig: Ernst Bircher Verlag, 1921.

Weiner, I. B. *Psychodiagnosis in Schizophrenia.* New York: Wiley, 1966.

prolonged sleep therapy See SLEEP TREATMENT.

Prolixin See ANTIPSYCHOTIC DRUGS.

propfschizophrenia A now-defunct term for a type of schizophrenia that was only thought to be found in a small number of persons who were mentally retarded. It was considered to have an onset after puberty and was characterized by paranoid episodes with delusions and hallucinations. *Propfhebephrenia* is another term formerly used for the same concept. *Oligophrenia* was a term used for "mental defective" or "idiots" (as the mentally retarded were termed earlier in this century), and propfschizophrenia was often referred to as a variety of this class of disorders.

propositus See PROBAND.

protein factors hypothesis Since the time of Emil KRAEPELIN, the search for a toxin or other substance that was to be found in the blood of schizophrenics has been reported from time to time. In many studies the blood or urine of schizophrenics has been analyzed, and substances that were assumed to be protein factors have been singled out as being possibly related to the cause of the disorder, or at least to the expression of its symptoms. Often these substances were isolated and then injected into other organisms (e.g., cells, plants, animals), which then changed their usual behavior, thus indicating that quite possibly these substances were affecting the behavior of humans.

See also AUTOINTOXICATION; TRANSMETHYLATION HYPOTHESIS.

Frohman, C. E., et al. "Evidence of a Plasma Factor in Schizophrenia," *Archives of General Psychiatry* 2 (1960): 255–262.

pseudoabstraction A characteristic of the thought and language of some schizophrenics who begin to use polysyllabic, highly abstract words, perhaps taken from philosophy or the sciences, but without using them meaningfully or in the proper context. Silvano ARIETI remarks that in a patient who is exhibiting pseudoabstraction, "If we ask him to explain what he means with these big words, he will be unable to do so. He will use other big words to accentuate the feeling of confusion. . . . Various German authors have very appropriately called this characteristic 'talking on stilts.'"

Arieti, S. *Interpretation of Schizophrenia.* 2nd ed. New York: Basic Books, 1974.

pseudocyesis See PREGNANCY DELUSIONS.

pseudodementia Sometimes a person may exhibit signs and symptoms of an ORGANIC MENTAL SYNDROME such as dementia without having any underlying brain disease process. Sometimes persons who are experiencing a major depressive episode may appear to have DEMENTIA due to the seriousness of the vegetative signs. In rarer cases, the PRODROMAL PHASE of schizophrenia may resemble dementia in extreme instances.

pseudodementia syndrome See GANSER'S SYNDROME.

pseudologia fantastica The clinical term for "pathological lying." The term is coined from two Greek words meaning "elaborate false speech."

pseudoneurotic schizophrenia See BORDERLINE SCHIZOPHRENIA.

pseudoschizophrenia syndrome A type of epilepsy that resembles schizophrenia and is supposedly characterized by its "hypnoid states." This concept has never gained wide usage. Although the relationship between convulsive disorders such as epilepsy and schizophrenia have been investigated, no support has ever been found for a pseudoschizophrenia syndrome.

Zec, N. R. "Pseudoschizophrenic Syndrome," *Psychiat. et Neurol.* 149 (1965): 197–209.

psychedelic experiences in schizophrenia With the advent of the "psychedelic revolution" in the mid-1960s, the metaphors supplied by the types of experiences reported by persons who had ingested hallucinogenic substances (e.g., LSD, mescaline) came to be applied to numerous areas of human experience. In particular, the psychedelic metaphors were applied to the subjective experience of psychosis. Because many persons in the PRODROMAL PHASE of schizophrenia and other psychotic disorders report perceptual anomalies and other phenomena related to ALTERED STATES OF CONSCIOUSNESS, many investigators during this period

began to turn their attention to the similarities between drug-induced hallucinatory states of consciousness and psychotic experience (see PERCEPTUAL ANOMALIES IN SCHIZOPHRENIA). The most notable attempt at such a comparison was published by Malcom Bowers and Daniel X. Freedman in 1966.

Due to a long-standing tradition of romanticizing "madness," psychotic experiences were compared with psychedelic experiences as possible "transcendent" experiences, notably by R. D. LAING. However, in a sharp critique of Laing's "psychedelic model" of schizophrenia, Miriam Siegler, Humphrey Osmond, and Harriet Mann constructed a detailed comparison of the subjective experiences of psychedelic experiences with those of schizophrenia and found many disturbing differences. They make the analogy of the difference between good dreams, bad dreams, and nightmares, with psychosis represented by the latter and psychedelic experiences by the first two. With the metaphoric fad of the 1960s no longer in fashion, the psychedelic model of schizophrenia is no longer discussed in the literature on this disorder.

See also SUBJECTIVE EXPERIENCES IN SCHIZOPHRENIA.

Bowers, M., and D. X. Freedman. "Psychedelic Experiences in Acute Psychosis," *Archives of General Psychiatry* 15 (1966): 240–248.

Laing, R. D. "Transcendental Experience in Relation to Religion and Psychosis," *Psychedelic Review* 6 (1965): 7–15.

Siegler, M., and H. Osmond. *Models of Madness, Models of Medicine*. New York: Macmillan, 1974.

Siegler, M., H. Osmond, and H. Mann. "Laing's Models of Madness." In *R. D. Laing and Anti-Psychiatry*, edited by R. Boyers and R. Orrill. New York: Harper & Row, 1971.

psychesthenia A disorder caused by the "exhaustion" of the nervous system. It is related to the concept of NEURASTHENIA in that the "wear and tear" of the "nerves" was thought to lead to a "nervous breakdown," which may result in some cases in more serious disorders such as schizophrenia or one of the other psychotic disorders. Pierre JANET introduced the term in 1903 in his book *Les obsessions et la psychasthénie.*

psychiatric social work In many instances, it is the nonmedical professionals such as social workers who are in the "frontlines" of the battle against the inhumane treatment of the mentally ill. It was only in the 1920s that the specialization of psychiatric social work came into existence, largely through the proliferation of "child guidance clinics" in the United States and England. In the decades since, psychiatric social workers have provided critical services for people with mental disorders in virtually every aspect of community care.

psychiatry The medical profession devoted to the study and treatment of mental disorders. The word *psychiatry* was first used in English in 1846 to refer to this profession. Other terms have been *medical psychologist* or *alienist,* and in an earlier age these physicians were also known as mad-doctors or lunatic doctors. The word is derived from the German term *psychiaterie,* which was first used in 1803 by the physician and student of mental illness Johannes Christian Reil (1759–1813) in a book entitled *Rhapsodies in the Application of Psychic Methods in the Treatment of Mental Disturbances.* The word *psychiatrie* was first used by Johann Christian Heinroth (1773–1843), and Ernst von Feuchtersleben (1806–1849) used the term *psychiatrics* for the profession in 1845.

Hunter, R. A., and I. Macalpine, eds. *Three Hundred Years of Psychiatry, 1535–1860: A History Presented in Selected English Texts.* Oxford: Oxford University Press, 1963.

psychoanalysis See DIRECT ANALYSIS.

psychoanalytic theories of schizophrenia Sigmund FREUD coined the term *psychoanalysis* in 1896 to refer to his philosophy and system of therapy that was based on a careful analysis of internal unconscious processes. Although Freud did treat some

manic-depressives, he never treated schizophrenic patients (unlike his colleague, C. G. JUNG, who held a position in a psychiatric hospital for nine years). Freud was very pessimistic about the treatment of schizophrenia with psychoanalysis and tended to discourage it. He left few writings on the subject, but this gap was filled by those psychoanalysts who came after him, notably Karl Abraham, Paul Federn, Melanie Klein, Frieda FROMM-REICHMANN, Leland Hinsie, John Rosen, Otto Fenichel, and Harold Searles.

According to Freud, schizophrenia involves a withdrawal of libido from the objects of the external world and into the self. This withdrawal of energy into the self was termed by Freud a regression into a state of primary narcissism similar to that found in infants in a period before there is any differentiation between ego, superego, or id and before there is any discriminative ability between the inner and outer worlds. Because of this, Freud believed no transference could take place between the schizophrenic patient and the analyst, and therefore no treatment could be possible. Because the regression to a state of primary narcissism characterized psychoses, he called them narcissistic neuroses (as opposed to transference neuroses, which were the usual phenomenon in psychoanalysis). Freud wrote in 1924 that in the narcissistic neuroses "the resistance is unconquerable" and that psychoanalytic techniques therefore "must be replaced by others; and we do not know yet whether we shall succeed in finding a substitute."

The central aspect of the schizophrenic experience, according to most psychoanalytic theorists, is the initial break with reality, after which the ego returns to its original infantile, undifferentiated state in which it is submerged or dissolved wholly or partially into the id. Although such regressions may be found in normals, the schizophrenic regresses to a fixation point in development that is further back than any encountered in the neuroses.

Psychoanalytic theories of schizophrenia dominated American psychiatry from the 1920s until the 1960s. Since biological research had turned up no definite cause of schizophrenia, psychoanalysts argued that this failure was in fact a confirmation of their anti-biological, anti-genetics, anti-laboratory science biases. Psychoanalysis continued to emphasize the exclusive master-apprentice model of medical training that had been challenged circa 1900 by those physicians who wanted to base medical therapeutics on laboratory findings, not general clinical "impressions" or vivid anecdotes. However, by 1980s it had become resoundingly clear that there was absolutely no empirical support from cognitive neuroscience research for any of the claims made by Freud, Jung, Adler, and their followers.

Historians of science now view psychoanalysis as a pseudoscience, not a scientific discipline. Psychoanalysis is to the 20th century what phrenology was to the 19th century and animal magnetism was to the 18th century.

Cioffi, F. *Freud and the Question of Pseudoscience.* Chicago: Open Court, 1998.

Crews, F. *Unauthorized Freud: Doubters Confront a Legend.* New York: Viking, 1998.

Dolnick, E. *Madness on the Couch: Blaming the Victim in the Heyday of Psychoanalysis.* New York: Simon & Schuster, 1998.

Gellner, E. *The Psychoanalytic Movement: The Cunning of Unreason.* Evanston, Ill.: Northwest University Press, 1996.

psychogenic psychoses See REACTIVE PSYCHOSES.

psychological research Although the search for the biological basis for schizophrenia and the psychotic disorders has been a primary focus of investigation since the 18th century (see ABLATION STUDIES), psychological experiments have given us much useful information on cognition, perception, learning, language, memory, and behavior in these disorders. The current trend is to correlate the overall findings of these studies and match this knowledge with the new discoveries gained by biochemical techniques, brain imaging, and other areas of scientific inquiry.

Francis Galton founded the first psychological laboratory in England in 1884, and his Anthropometric Laboratory collected data on more than 9,000 subjects. Galton charged his subjects a fee

for providing them with their test results. However, the first laboratory designated solely for the application of the experimental method to psychology was founded in Leipzig, Germany, by Wilhelm Wundt in 1879. In the 1880s, many Americans flocked to Germany to learn the experimental method (generally from Wundt), and subsequently between 1888 and 1895 many universities and hospitals set up "psychological laboratories" to conduct research. Harvard University was probably the first to do so in the United States, but the eminent American philosopher and psychologist William James (1842–1910), who taught at Harvard, was not impressed with the experimental method. Ridiculing the stereotypical obsessive-compulsive style of the Germans, James snidely remarks in the first volume of his landmark *Principles of Psychology* (1890), "This method taxes patience to the utmost, and could hardly have arisen in a country whose natives could be *bored*. Such Germans as Weber, Fechner, Vierordt and Wundt obviously cannot ..."

Emil KRAEPELIN was an admiring disciple of Wilhelm Wundt and learned the techniques of psychological research from him. Kraepelin was one of the first to conduct psychological association experiments on subjects who were given various drugs. Since Kraepelin defined DEMENTIA PRAECOX, he was arguably the first to conduct experimental research on this disorder.

A useful summary of the psychological research on schizophrenia can be found in a review article by A. I. Rabin, Stuart Doneson, and Ricky Jentons in L. Bellak's *Disorders of the Schizophrenic Syndrome*.

Boring, E. G. *A History of Experimental Psychology.* New York: Century Company, 1929.

James, W. *The Principles of Psychology.* 2 vols. New York: Henry Holt, 1890.

Rabin, A. I., et al. "Studies of Psychological Functions in Schizophrenia." In *Disorders of the Schizophrenic Syndrome,* edited by L. Bellak. New York: Basic Books, 1979.

psychomotor agitation Excessive movement that is associated with inner tension. Often the activity is repetitious and nonproductive. When the agitation is at a high level, some persons may scream, shout, or complain loudly. People with psychomotor agitation can be seen pacing, pulling at their clothes or hair, wringing their hands, being unable to sit in one place for more than a few seconds, etc. When this type of behavior is a side effect of ANTIPSYCHOTIC DRUGS, the behavior is called AKATHISIA.

psychoneurosis A nonpsychotic mental disorder of a purely psychological (and not organic) origin. The word was introduced by Swiss neuropathologist Paul Charles Dubois (1848–1918) and was often used by Sigmund FREUD.

psychopathology The study of mental disorders. Despite the fact that mental disorders have been reported since antiquity, the clinical and descriptive categories now in use were only developed in the 19th century.

See also KAHLBAUM, KARL; NOSOLOGY.

Berrios, G. E. "Descriptive Psychopathology: Conceptual and Historical Aspects," *Psychological Medicine* 11 (1984): 677–688.

psychose passionelle See EROTOMANIA.

psychosis The term *psychosis* was coined by the Austrian physician and poet Ernst von FEUCHTERSLEBEN in 1845. Today psychosis refers to a MENTAL DISORDER in which there is gross impairment in reality testing (a "break with reality") and the creation of a new reality. Although the word *psychoses* first appeared in the early part of the 19th century, it has only been used in this sense since the end of that century, encompassing phenomena that were formerly described by the terms *insanity, alienation,* and *DEMENTIA*. Throughout most of the 19th century the word *neuroses* referred to an enormous class of diseases that included all the insanities, most neurological conditions, all the present-day neuroses, and some medical disorders—thus, they

were considered "organic" in origin. The word *psychoses* instead referred to psychological or experiential states, and the terms *neuroses* and *psychoses* were not dichotomous and did not depend upon one another for definition. By the end of the 1800s the new classificatory systems of Karl KAHLBAUM and especially Emil KRAEPELIN introduced the modern concept of psychosis and drastically reduced the number of the "insanities."

Two classification dichotomies that were popular in the late 19th century and survived into the early part of the 20th are (a) functional versus organic psychoses (see FUNCTIONAL PSYCHOSES), and (b) exogenous (in neurology, diseases due to toxins and infections) versus endogenous psychoses (due to inner or constitutional factors).

Beer, M. D. "The Importance of the Social and Intellectual Contexts in a Discussion of the History of the Concept of Psychosis," *Psychological Medicine* 25 (1995): 317–325.

Berrios, G. E. "Historical Aspects of Psychoses: 19th-century Issues," *British Medical Bulletin* 43 (1987): 484–498.

Feuchtersleben, E. von. *Lehrbuch der aerztlichen Seelenkunde.* Vienna: Carl Gerold, 1845.

psychosis gene See GENETICS STUDIES.

psychosis of association See FOLIE À DEUX.

psychosocial stressors Psychological or social sources of stress that can exacerbate mental disorders, including psychotic disorders. Severe tragedies (the death of loved ones) can even lead to the development of such disorders, as can the developmental phases of life (e.g., the stresses of adolescence, childbirth). The types of psychosocial stressors that clinicians are advised to document by severity are (a) conjugal (marital and nonmarital), for example, engagement, marriage, discord, separation, divorce, death of a spouse; (b) parenting; (c) other interpersonal problems; (d) occupational; (e) financial; (f) living circumstances, for example, change in residence; (g) developmental phases of life; (h) physical illness or injury; and (i) family factors.

psychosurgery The history of psychiatry can only be understood in the context of the history of medicine. As new biological discoveries, theories of disease, or treatments for disease were introduced into the practice of medicine, it was only natural that they be applied to the most mysterious class of diseases of all—the insanities. The advance of surgery as a technique for treating or curing disease began in earnest after the introduction of anesthesias (starting in 1846 with ether) and the general adoption of techniques of antisepsis (in the 1860s and 1870s) such as hand washing or the treating of the surgeon's hands with "Listerizing" preparations (the mouthwash Listerine is a descendant of these substances, bearing the name of Joseph Lister, a pioneer of antiseptic surgery). It was only natural that advances in surgical procedure would be applied to solving the problems of psychiatry. The three areas of the body that were the focus of psychosurgery were the brain, the mouth (dentistry), and the abdomen.

Brain surgery Although ancient peoples performed operations on the skulls and perhaps the brains of ill individuals (a phenomenon known as TREPHINING), the very first brain operation that specifically intended to treat or cure psychotic disorders was performed in Marin, Switzerland, in December 1888. Gottlieb Burckhardt (1836–1907), a Swiss psychiatrist and director of a private psychiatric clinic, operated (unsuccessfully) on the brains of six persons with psychotic disorders. He published his findings in an article in the *Allgemeine Zeitschrift für Psychiatrie* in 1891. No more brain operations to treat or cure mental disorders were performed for 47 years. It was not until November 1935 that neurologist EGAS MONIZ (1874–1955), working with neurosurgeon Almeida Lima, performed the first LEUCOTOMY on an asylum patient in Lisbon, Portugal. The following year, neuropathologist Walter FREEMAN (1895–1972) and neurosurgeon James Watts (1904–94) performed the first LOBOTOMY on a patient at George Washington University Hospital in Washington, D.C. After 1942, "psychosurgery" gained in prominence and was widely practiced in

the United States and Canada by the late 1940s. The development of the "icepick technique" of TRANSORBITAL LOBOTOMY by Freeman in 1946 led to the rapid spread of psychosurgical treatments for schizophrenia and other mental illnesses (including depression, anxiety, and other less severe conditions). Whereas major surgery in an operating room was required for traditional lobotomies, leucotomies, or TOPECTOMIES, a transorbital lobotomy only required a local anesthetic and could be performed in outpatient settings (which was where Freeman first tried it out). As historian Jack Pressman documented in his book, *Last Resort: Psychosurgery and the Limits of Medicine* (1998), psychosurgery "made sense" in the context of its era and was supported by some of the most important figures in medicine and psychiatry. Egas Moniz won the Nobel Prize in Medicine in 1949 for his leucotomy treatment. After the widespread introduction of ANTIPSYCHOTIC DRUGS in asylums after 1954, psychosurgery and other "somatic" treatments such as INSULIN COMA THERAPY and ELECTROSHOCK THERAPY began to decline in use. By the 1960s, brain operations to alleviate mental disorders had virtually disappeared (except for the treatment of severe seizure disorders).

Ovariotomies (oophorectomies) In 1872 an American surgeon, Robert Battey, published an article on "normal ovariotomy" in the *Atlanta Medical and Surgical Journal* that inspired the surgical removal of the ovaries in perhaps as many as 150,000 women in America, Britain, and Germany by 1906. These operations were much less welcome in France. Known as "Battey's operation," it was performed on otherwise normal, healthy women as a method of preventing later "incurable diseases." It was quickly adopted by psychiatrists who applied it to incurably insane women in asylums.

In 1893 the first large-scale experimental surgical program for the treatment of insanity was approved for a clinical trial at the Norristown Insane Asylum in Pennsylvania. The plan, proposed by Dr. Joseph Price, was to perform "oophorectomies" on "fifty patients selected as being cases likely to be benefited with this operation." However, when the fifth patient to be operated on died during surgery, the program was halted. The suspended program quickly became a political issue in Pennsylvania, leading to an investigation by the Lunacy Committee of the State Board of Charities. A member of the committee called the procedures "illegal . . . brutal and inhuman, and not excusable on any reasonable ground . . . it is regarded by the best medical authorities as a useless and improper expedient for the cure or relief of insanity, and the operation of oophorectomy in a public hospital upon indigent insane women must be regarded as largely experimental, and for that reason bound to reflect upon hospital authorities now boasting of modern humane methods."

The collapse of the clinical trial in Pennsylvania did not deter individual asylum superintendents from approving such surgeries on a limited case-by-case basis in their own institutions. In the mid-1890s ovariotomies, hysterectomies, and male castrations had been performed on asylum patients at a great many institutions, but by the end of that decade critics of the procedure slowed the spread of these experimental procedures. In the early 1900s such surgeries were still performed but as part of the eugenics program to halt DEGENERATION. This was especially true in the United States, where new state laws advocating forced sterilization for the "morally insane," the mentally ill, the mentally retarded, and criminals were in effect after 1907. After July 1918 Henry A. COTTON (1877–1933) of the New Jersey State Hospital at Trenton resumed this procedure along with a whole host of other forms of surgery to eliminate sites of FOCAL INFECTION AS A CAUSE OF MENTAL DISORDER.

Thyroid surgery Following the classic AUTOINTOXICATION theory that an overproduction of "internal secretions" from glands poisoned the brain and caused mental illness, Newdigate M. Owensby (1882–1952), chief physician at the Bay View Asylum in Baltimore, Maryland, hypothesized that the symptoms of DEMENTIA PRAECOX were caused by an oversecretion of the thyroid gland. The oversecretion was thought to be caused by diseased blood vessels in the gland. According to the December 20, 1907, edition of the *New York Times*, in July 1907 Owensby chose "the worst patient in the asylum," and cut away the diseased portion of the thyroid, "giving opportunity for new blood vessels to form." In October 1907 the man was discharged, symptom free. By December 1907 Owensby had operated on at least four

other patients, reporting therapeutic success in all of them. There is no indication that Owensby continued these experiments after 1907. Owensby later become one of the first psychiatrists in Georgia, achieving notoriety in 1940 for using metrazol convulsive therapy to attempt to reverse homosexuality in five male and one female patient.

Dental surgery In the very first years of the 20th century, reports that psychotic symptoms were reduced or eliminated after rotting or impacted teeth were pulled led to an increase in such procedures. As a site of focal infections that could spread from the mouth to the brain, the logic of removing teeth as a treatment method for the mentally ill "made sense" within an era dazzled by the "germ theory of disease." At Trenton, Henry Cotton installed a dental operating clinic in 1919 and routinely had all the teeth of newly admitted patients removed. He also convinced his wife and his two sons to have all their teeth removed as a preventive measure. The removal of teeth was also a major focus of treatment for psychiatrist Thomas C. Graves in Birmingham, England, in the 1920s and 1930s.

Abdominal surgery In May 1916, Chicago medical professor and specialist in the surgery of the abdomen and head, Bayard Taylor HOLMES, was the first to perform abdominal surgery specifically for the treatment and cure of dementia praecox (schizophrenia). The patient was his own son, Ralph Loring Holmes, who had developed dementia praecox in 1905 at the age of 17 as a first-year medical student. The previous year, Holmes had devised an AUTOINTOXICATION theory of the cause of dementia praecox based on the idea that fecal stasis in the colon led to the production of toxic amines (histamine) that was carried to the brain by the bloodstream and caused psychosis. Holmes or his associates performed a series of cecostomies on at least 22 persons diagnosed with dementia praecox, leaving a hole (stoma) open near the appendix through which a hose was inserted daily for constant irrigations. His son Ralph, the first to receive this experimental surgery for dementia praecox, died four days after the operation at Lakeside Hospital in Chicago. Abdominal surgeries involving the whole or partial removal of the colon, stomach, rectum, cervix, testes, and so on were performed on more than 2,000 patients at the New Jersey State Hospital at Trenton between 1918 and 1933. Hundreds died from postoperative infections and other complications. In England, Thomas Graves continued to perform such operations well into the 1930s.

Surgery on the brain, reproductive organs, mouth, and abdomen is no longer performed for the treatment of schizophrenia or any other mental disorder.

Anonymous. "An Experiment in Castration," *Medical Record* 43 (1893): 433–434.

Dally, A. *Fantasy Surgery 1880–1930.* Atlanta and Amsterdam: Rodopi, 1996.

Pressman, J. *Last Resort: Psychosurgery and the Limits of Medicine.* Cambridge: Cambridge University Press, 1998.

Reilly, P. R. *The Surgical Solution: A History of Involuntary Sterilization in the United States.* Baltimore: Johns Hopkins University Press, 1991.

Scull, A. *Madhouse: A Tragic Tale of Megalomania and Modern Medicine.* New Haven, Conn.: Yale University Press, 2005.

Stone, J. L. "Dr. Gottlieb Burckhardt—the Pioneer of Psychosurgery," *Journal of the History of the Neurosciences* 10 (2001): 79–92.

psychotherapy of schizophrenia Because people with schizophrenia have so many personal problems associated with daily living, most find themselves in some form of psychotherapy at some point in their lives, and this can be supportive for them. The earliest recorded cases of individual psychotherapy with schizophrenic persons can be attributed to Swiss psychiatrist and psychoanalyst C. G. JUNG at the BURGHÖLZI HOSPITAL in Switzerland. There is a vast literature on the psychotherapy of schizophrenia, and the various therapeutic modalities that have been tried include individual, group, family, and a whole host of "brand name" psychotherapeutic orientations.

Throughout most of the century the emphasis has been on the alleviation of the disease process itself with psychotherapy, but with the new emphasis on the organic basis of schizophrenia (and the discouraging results of psychotherapy on the disease itself), this goal is no longer deemed

justified. Instead, the focus has shifted to improving the psychosocial adaptation of individuals with schizophrenia, their vocational functioning, and the subjective well-being of these persons. Also, family therapy approaches have shifted away from viewing family dynamics as the cause of schizophrenia and now focuses instead on the potential influence of the family on the course of the illness and how family members may be taught strategies to make that influence more positive and reduce relapses (see EXPRESSED EMOTION).

In general, the well-controlled scientific research on the influence of psychotherapy on schizophrenics has tended to conclude that insight-oriented individual or group psychotherapy may be too intense for such individuals and perhaps worsen symptoms. Indeed, E. Fuller Torrey goes so far as to label psychoanalysis, insight-oriented therapy, and group psychotherapy as "ineffective treatments" in his book *Surviving Schizophrenia: A Family Manual* (1988). It is now generally recommended that psychotherapeutic treatments be psychoeducational and supportive in nature and used as an adjunct to treatment with ANTIPSYCHOTIC DRUGS.

See also FAMILY INTERACTION THEORIES; GROUP PSYCHOTHERAPY.

Mueser, K. T., and A. S. Bellack. "Psychotherapy for Schizophrenia." In *Schizophrenia,* edited by S. R. Hirsch and D. R. Weinberge. London: Blackwell Science, 1995, pp. 626–648.

psychotic disorders in *DSM-IV-TR* According to the most recent revision of the most widely used diagnostic manual for mental disorders in North America, *DSM-IV-TR* (2000), the disorders listed below are considered to be characterized by "psychosis" (a clear break with reality, often characterized by delusions, hallucinations, disorganized thought processes, bizarre and/or disorganized behavior, and a decline in social and occupational functioning). Entries for each can be found in this book.

- Schizophrenia (paranoid type, disorganized type, catatonic type, undifferentiated type, residual type)
- Schizophreniform Disorder
- Schizoaffective Disorder (bipolar type, depressive type)
- Delusional Disorder (erotomanic types, grandiose type, jealous type, persecutory type, somatic type, mixed type, unspecified type)
- Brief Psychotic Disorder (with marked stressors [brief reactive psychosis], without marked stressors, with postpartum onset)
- Shared Psychotic Disorder (Folie à Deux)
- Psychotic Disorder Due to a General Medical Condition
- Substance-induced Psychotic Disorder
- Psychotic Disorder Not Otherwise Specified

There may also be a primary diagnosis of a mood disorder that includes psychotic features. Psychotic features may be specified for Major Depressive Disorder, Single Episode; Major Depressive Disorder, Recurrent; Bipolar I Disorder, Single Manic Episode; Bipolar I Disorder, Most Recent Episode Manic; Bipolar I Disorder, Most Recent Episode Mixed; Bipolar I Disorder, Most Recent Episode Depressed; and Bipolar II Disorder, Depressed.

psychotic disorders in *ICD-10* According to the WORLD HEALTH ORGANIZATION, the following psychotic disorders included in *ICD-10* (1992) can be found in all countries of the world. Although this manual strives to be culture-free, it still reflects the major traditions of European PSYCHIATRY of the past 150 years. Entries for the major disorders below are included in this book.

- Schizophrenia (paranoid, catatonic, hebephrenic, residual, undifferentiated, simple, postschizophrenic depression)
- Schizotypal Disorder
- Persistent Delusional Disorder
- Acute and Transient Psychotic Disorders
- Induced Delusional Disorders
- Schizoaffective Disorder
- Other Non-organic Psychotic Disorders
- Unspecified Non-organic Psychosis

psychotic jealousy See OTHELLO SYNDROME.

psychotogenic drugs Literally, "psychosis-causing drugs." With the severe and widespread substance-abuse epidemic following the "psychedelic revolution" of the 1960s, psychiatric facilities around the world have been flooded with individuals, many of them young (see YOUNG ADULT CHRONIC PATIENTS), whose substance abuse has led to permanent psychotic disorders. Such persons with a psychotic disorder and a history of chronic substance abuse are called dually diagnosed patients. Current research studies are beginning to find that premorbid psychotogenic drug use (e.g., cocaine, PCP, LSD, marijuana) contributes to the development of psychotic disorders and may hinder the effectiveness of ANTIPSYCHOTIC DRUGS (a phenomenon called neuroleptic refractoriness), especially at the beginning of the illness.

Bowers, M. B., Jr., et al. "Psychotogenic Drug Use and Neuroleptic Response," *Schizophrenia Bulletin* 16 (1990): 81–87.

psychotomimetic Literally "psychosis-mimicking." Hallucinogenic (psychedelic) drugs were for a time referred to as "psychotomimetic drugs" because it was thought they could mimic the subjective experience of psychosis in anyone who ingested them. Prior to the banning of research using psychedelic drugs in the 1960s, some investigators administered such drugs to research subjects so as to better understand various dimensions of the psychotic disorders (see PSYCHOTOGENIC DRUGS). This sort of research has a long history dating from the 17th century. In Immanuel Kant's published lectures on "anthropology" (what we would now call empirical psychology), he cites the efforts of researchers to induce an "artificial insanity" through psychotomimetic drugs:

> On the other hand, attempts to observe oneself in a condition which approaches derangement, produced in oneself voluntarily and by physical means, in order to better understand the involuntary through such observations, indicate that one has understanding enough to investigate the sources of the phenomenon. But it is dangerous to perform experiments with the mind, and to make it disordered to a certain extent, for the sake of observing it and investigating its nature by means of the features which may be discovered in such experiments. Thus Helmont reports, after consuming a certain dose of *napell* (a poisonous root), having the unmistakable feeling as if he thought in his stomach. Another doctor increased his consumption of camphor, little by little, until it appeared to him as if everything along the street were in a great tumult. Still others have experimented on themselves with opium so long that they felt a weakening of the mind whenever they stopped using more of this brain-stimulant. An artificial insanity can easily become a real one.

See also TRANSMETHYLATION HYPOTHESIS.

Kant, I. *The Classification of Mental Disorders,* trans. C. T. Sullivan. Doylestown, Pa.: The Doylestown Foundation, 1964 [1798].

psychotropic See NEUROLEPTIC.

puerperal insanity Another name for POSTPARTUM PSYCHOSIS.

pulse Since the days of ancient Greece and Rome and well into the 19th century, it was commonly believed that a physician could diagnose mental disorders simply by taking the afflicted person's pulse and determining the heartbeat rate. In his famous textbook of 1812, American physician Benjamin RUSH of Philadelphia reports that: ". . . seven-eighths of all the deranged patients in the Pennsylvania Hospital in the year 1811 had frequent pulses, and that a pardon was granted to a criminal by the President of the United States, in the year 1794, who was suspected of counterfeiting madness, in consequence of its having been declared by three physicians that that symptom constituted an unequivocal mark of intellectual derangement."

The diagnostic importance of the pulse was still so highly regarded at the end of the last century that 20 columns were given to it in Daniel Hack Tuke's famous *Dictionary of Psychological Medicine.*

Rush, B. *Medical Inquiries and Observations upon the Diseases of the Mind.* Philadelphia: Kimber & Richardson, 1812.
Tuke, D. H. "Pulse." In *A Dictionary of Psychological Medicine,* edited by D. H. Tuke. London: Churchill, 1892.

purging One of Pinel's three USUAL TREATMENTS for MENTAL DISORDERS around 1800, purgatives were given to patients to help them expel bad humors or other bodily toxins that were thought to be the cause of mental illness. Purgatives have been used for thousands of years for the treatment of mental illness, and the herb *hellbore* was used for this purpose until the end of the 19th century.

pyknic type One of the four physiological types identified by Ernst Kretschmer in the 1920s. It was a thick-torsoed type with rounded shoulders that tended to resemble an orangutan. Most pyknic types were thought by Kretschmer to be "circulars" (manic-depressives).

See also ASTHENIC TYPE; ATHLETIC TYPE.

Q,R

quetiapine See ANTIPSYCHOTIC DRUGS.

race and schizophrenia In the United States, blacks have a higher rate of schizophrenia than do whites. This conclusion has been confirmed across many studies. However, psychiatrist E. Fuller Torrey argues in his book *Surviving Schizophrenia: A Family Manual* that this may have more to do with geography and socioeconomic status than with racial differences or racism. Most of the studies that have found a higher rate in blacks have been conducted in dense urban areas, but those studies done in rural areas find that the schizophrenia rates in whites and blacks are the same. Therefore, Torrey concludes, "This argues strongly against race as being the cause of the difference. Rather it suggests that it is because blacks live in the inner city, and not because they are black, that they have a higher schizophrenia rate."

Torrey, E. F. *Surviving Schizophrenia: A Family Manual.* New York: Harper & Row, 1988.

Ray, Isaac (1807–1881) An American physician and legal scholar, Ray was one of the original 13 founders of the AMERICAN PSYCHIATRIC ASSOCIATION. His classic textbook, *Treatise on the Medical Jurisprudence of Insanity* (1838), is considered to be perhaps the most influential American psychiatric text of the 19th century.

Hughes, J. S. *In the Law's Darkness: Isaac Ray and the Medical Jurisprudence of Insanity in Nineteenth Century America.* New York: Oceana Publications, 1986.

rCBF The acronym for regional cerebral blood flow, a measurement used to study the relationship between cerebral metabolism and psychiatric disorders.

See also BRAIN IMAGING STUDIES.

reactive psychoses It has long been noted that BRIEF PSYCHOTIC EPISODES sometimes result from the experience of trauma or extreme and prolonged stress. Conditions that produce such "reactions" include combat, imprisonment, and involuntary commitment to a mental hospital. Based on his study of the psychology of prisoners, August Wimmer (1872–1937), director of the St. Hans Psychiatric Hospital near Roskilde, Denmark, published a study on psychotic disorders that arose in reaction to stress and that were "psychogenic" rather than the result of hereditary DEGENERATION (as proposed by French psychiatrist Valentin Magnan) or a combination of heredity predisposition and glandular AUTOINTOXICATION AS A CAUSE OF DEMENTIA PRAECOX (as believed by Emil KRAEPELIN and Wilhelm Weygandt). The title of Wimmer's 1916 study was *Psykogene Sindssygdomsformer* (Psychogenic Forms of Mental Disease). Following Wimmer, these psychotic disorders were originally called psychogenic, but they were more often called reactive throughout the 20th century, with the two terms being used interchangeably. The term *reactive* gained ascendancy after 1927 when the German psychiatrist Kurt Schneider proposed three "abnormal psychic reactions":

(1) emotional syndromes
(2) paranoid states
(3) syndromes with a disturbance of conscience

According to Wimmer, psychogenic (reactive) psychoses are independent of schizophrenia and

MANIC-DEPRESSIVE ILLNESS, develop in a person with a "predisposed foundation," are caused by psychosocial stressors, and end in full recovery with no lasting deficit. A similar diagnostic concept was added to *DSM-IV* in 1980 under the label "Brief Reactive Psychosis," but this changed to "Brief Psychotic Disorder" in 1992 in *DSM-IV.* Under the *DSM-IV* definition, a triggering stressor or trauma is not necessary, as there are causes of postpartum psychosis and other psychotic disorders that have no apparent trigger.

Pillman, F., and A. Marneros. "Brief and Acute Psychoses: The Development of Concepts," *History of Psychiatry* 14 (2003): 161–177.

Wimmer, A. "Psykogene Sindssygdomsformer." In *Jubilee Publication, St. Hans Hospital 1816–1916,* edited by A. Wimmer, 85–216. Copenhagen: Gad, 1916.

reactive schizophrenia See PROCESS-REACTIVE DISTINCTION IN SCHIZOPHRENIA, THE.

reality testing The ability to "test" or evaluate the external world ("reality") objectively and to distinguish it from the internal psychological state. It is also the ability to discriminate ego boundaries between what is the self and what is nonself (the "I" versus the "not-I"). The term was coined by Sigmund FREUD in 1911 as *Realitätsprüfung.* The hallmark of PSYCHOSIS is that reality testing is impaired.

recessive In GENETICS STUDIES, the opposite of DOMINANT.

recombination The process by which a pair of homologous chromosomes exchange sections yielding a new combination of genes.

recoverable psychosis According to the classification system of Emil KRAEPELIN, the group of recoverable psychoses was characterized by its primary entity, MANIC-DEPRESSIVE ILLNESS. These were psychotic disorders that had exacerbations and remissions but did not lead to the gross cognitive deterioration of chronic, progressively worsening disorders such as dementia praecox.

recovery with defect The term describes those persons whose basic personality is permanently altered after recovery from their primary mental disorder. Today, such a condition in schizophrenia might be termed the RESIDUAL PHASE. This term was coined by the German physician K. G. Neumann (1744–1850).

reference, ideas of See IDEAS OF REFERENCE.

refrigerator mother The name for the cold, rejecting mother who would thereby induce autism in her child.

See also AUTISM, INFANTILE.

regression A concept introduced by Sigmund FREUD in 1900 in his classic book *The Interpretation of Dreams,* although he did not use the word until much later. Essentially, regression means a reversion to earlier forms of thought, object-relationships, or behavior that the individual had previously experienced. Thus, according to PSYCHOANALYSIS, persons with psychotic disorders are "regressed" because they show signs of returning to infantile modes of thought, behavior and experience. In DEGENERATION THEORY, "reversions to type" were found in the physical stigmata of criminals, idiots, and the insane.

See also PSYCHOANALYTIC THEORIES OF SCHIZOPHRENIA.

relapse, signs of Those people with schizophrenia who seem to fare the best are those who are aware of the signs of an impending relapse of an active phase of the illness and who therefore seek help. In a useful study of relapse by Marvin Herz and Charles Melville published in 1980, they found the following signs and symptoms of relapse to be the most frequently reported by patients and their families:

Patients Reported	Percent
being tense and nervous	80
eating less	72
trouble concentrating	70
trouble sleeping	67
enjoying things less	65
restlessness	63
not able to remember things	63
depression	61
being preoccupied with one or two things	60
seeing friends less	60
being laughed at, talked about	60

Families Reported	Percent
being tense and nervous	83
restlessness	79
trouble concentrating	76
depression	76
talking in a nonsensical way	76
loss of interest in things	76
trouble sleeping	69
enjoying things less	68
being preoccupied with one or two things	65
not able to remember things	60
hearing voices, seeing things	60

It is extremely important for family members and persons with schizophrenia to recognize these signs of relapse and to seek medical help immediately.

Herz, M. "Prodromal Symptoms and the Prevention of Relapse in Schizophrenia," *Journal of Clinical Psychiatry* 46 (1985): 22–25.

Herz, M. I., and C. Melville. "Relapse in Schizophrenia," *American Journal of Psychiatry* 137 (1980): 801–805.

religious delusions Religious delusions are quite common in the psychotic disorders. Persons may believe, for example, that they are God, Jesus Christ, or a prophet who relates messages from God to the world. Many of these delusions are also grandiose in nature.

remission The abatement of an illness. In schizophrenia, the period after a remission may still evidence residual deficits from the illness. Full remissions from schizophrenia apparently do occur, but they are extremely rare, and the few that are on record are an issue of controversy. A return to full premorbid functioning is also rare in schizophrenia.

See also RESIDUAL PHASE.

Renfield's syndrome A term first used by Richard Noll (1991) to refer to CLINICAL VAMPIRISM, since contemporary reports of people with this delusional disorder seem to develop the same sequence of symptoms as the human vampire Renfield in Bram Stoker's novel *Dracula* (1897).

Noll, R. *Vampires, Werewolves and Demons: Twentieth Century Case Reports in the Psychiatric Literature.* New York: Brunner/Mazel, 1991.

repression A term used by Sigmund FREUD (*Verdrängung* in the original German) for a psychological operation in which a person attempts to push away, expel, or keep in the unconscious representations (thoughts, images, memories) that are connected to an instinct. Repression occurs when it is determined that the expression of an instinctual urge, which is probably in itself pleasurable (e.g., sex), may have painful consequences. Repression is considered one of the most basic defense mechanisms for keeping threatening materials out of conscious awareness. Freud once wrote that "the theory of repression is the cornerstone on which the whole structure of psychoanalysis rests." According to psychoanalytic theory, the failure of repression in the psychotic disorders leads to HALLUCINATIONS and bizarre and inappropriate behavior.

See also PSYCHOANALYTIC THEORIES OF SCHIZOPHRENIA.

Laplanche, J., and J. B. Pontalis. *The Language of Psycho-Analysis,* trans. D. Nicholson-Smith. New York: Norton, 1973.

research diagnostic criteria (RDC) In an effort to ensure that diagnostic groups of persons with

mental disorders have the same characteristics across different studies performed in different settings, several attempts have been made to set standard guidelines for selecting subjects for research. An early system was the FEIGHNER RESEARCH CRITERIA, but currently the most widely accepted criteria is the Research Diagnostic Criteria developed at the New York Psychiatric Institute. When research studies refer to "RDC schizophrenics," they are referring to schizophrenic subjects that fit the RDC definitional guidelines.

Endicott, J., et al. "Diagnostic Criteria for Schizophrenia: Reliabilities and Agreement between Systems," *Archives of General Psychiatry* 39 (1982): 864–889.

Spitzer, R. L., J. Endicott, and E. Robins. "Research Diagnostic Criteria: Rationale and Reliability," *Archives of General Psychiatry* 35 (1978): 773–782.

Reserpine See antipsychotic drugs.

residual phase The residual phase follows the active phase of the illness. In many ways, the clinical picture of the residual phase resembles many of the signs and symptoms of the initial PRODROMAL PHASE, except that the blunting or flattening of affect and a marked impairment in social and occupational functioning are found. Some DELUSIONS and HALLUCINATIONS may persist in the residual phase, but they may not be accompanied any longer by strong affect (e.g., a strong screaming reaction to the hearing of voices may not be found in the residual phase). The most common course of schizophrenia is a disease process characterized by acute exacerbations of symptoms followed by periods of residual impairment between active phases of the illness. During the first years of the disorder (some say five to 10 years), the residual impairment between episodes increases and then seems to plateau at some point for the remainder of the person's life. Depression is often present in the residual phase.

restraints See CHEMICAL RESTRAINTS; MECHANICAL RESTRAINTS.

retrospective ruminative jealousy A (usually) nonpsychotic delusional disorder related to the OTHELLO SYNDROME in which a person is obsessed with the past sexual activities of the current sexual partner or spouse. However, there is no delusion about present infidelity.

RFLP See MOLECULAR MARKERS.

right to refuse treatment In the United States, the legal principle has developed over a series of cases since 1975 that holds that no one admitted to a psychiatric facility for treatment, whether the commitment was voluntary or involuntary, can be forced to submit to any form of treatment against his or her will unless it is determined that a life-and-death emergency exists.

Applebaum, P. S. "The Right to Refuse Treatment with Antipsychotic Medications: Retrospect and Prospect," *American Journal of Psychiatry* 145 (1988): 413–419.

right to treatment In the United States, the legal principle has developed that when a psychiatric facility has assumed the responsibility of providing treatment for a person, that facility is then legally obligated to provide adequate treatment for that individual.

risk factors Most of what we have learned about the potential causes, courses, and outcomes of schizophrenia comes from epidemiological studies. In current epidemiological research in medicine, a distinction is being made between risk indicators or proxy markers and risk modifying factors. Risk indicators are any variables that precede an outcome (e.g., the first episode of schizophrenia) but are not causally related to that outcome (e.g., season of birth). *Risk modifying factors* is a term reserved for factors that appear to contribute to the cause of the outcome. Risk modifying factors can be fixed (for example, gender) or variable (e.g., amount and frequency of cannibis use), endogenous (e.g., genetics) or exogenous

(e.g., obstetric complications, maternal exposure to infections).

Family history/genetics The strongest risk factor correlated to developing schizophrenia is family history. Being biologically related to a person with schizophrenia has been found to be the greatest risk factor in developing schizophrenia in the future. Genetic relatedness is a key factor: the closer the blood relationship, the greater the risk for developing schizophrenia. Having a biological parent with schizophrenia is the strongest predictor of outcome for adult psychiatric disorders. This is one of the very few firm facts we know about schizophrenia.

Environment There is no single environmental factor that predicts a higher risk of developing schizophrenia. In persons who are biologically related to someone with schizophrenia, certain environmental or nongenetic risk factors have been identified as possible risk indicators or risk modifying factors. These are as follows:

Age and sex The vast majority of people who develop schizophrenia have their first episode somewhere between 15 and 24 years of age. For the vast majority of males the peak age of onset is 20 to 24 years old, then the rate remains at a constant low rate. In contrast, there is a small peak for females between 20 and 24 years old, followed by a constant low rate until age 35, after which it begins rising. Cases of late-onset schizophrenia are predominantly women.

Perinatal factors (maternal obstetric complications) Birth complications have been correlated with the later development of schizophrenia in studies dating back to the mid-1960s. The strongest findings are, in order:

(1) perinatal brain damage (any cause)
(2) brain damage due to hypoxia (lack of oxygen)
(3) Rh incompatibility
(4) pre-eclampsia
(5) low birth weight

Prenatal factors The strongest prenatal risk factor found thus far, ranking third behind family history and perinatal brain damage, is maternal bereavement. Unwantedness, famine, flood, and maternal depression are much lesser factors.

Infection Exposure to various infections during pregnancy have been linked to the later development of schizophrenia in the unborn child. Of the various infectious agents studied, rubella (German measles) carries the strongest risk, followed by influenza, respiratory infections, and the polio virus. More recent research has focused on exposure to toxoplasmosis (a virus transmitted from cats to humans) as a possible viral risk factor.

Premorbid intelligence Low IQ and the risk of developing schizophrenia have been linked in several studies.

Place and time of birth Being born in urban environments confers a higher risk than being born in a rural setting. Also, the SEASONALITY OF BIRTHS effect for persons born in the Northern Hemisphere confers a greater risk for developing schizophrenia if one is born in the winter and spring months (particularly February to May). Both findings have been linked to the greater presence of viruses, but no one really knows what causes this effect. Interestingly, season of birth effects have also been found for bipolar disorder, autism, attention deficit disorder, alcoholism, stillbirths, diabetes, Alzheimer's disease, and Down's syndrome. No one knows how to interpret these facts either.

Migrant status and ethnic minorities In some groups (such as African-Caribbean immigrants to the United Kingdom), being an immigrant and ethnic minority confers a higher risk for developing schizophrenia.

Epidemiological research into the risk factors associated with the development of schizophrenia will continue to be a vital area of research. Genetics alone cannot explain schizophrenia, and it is only through the clues revealed through the study of correlated environmental factors that new hypotheses about the causes of schizophrenia will emerge.

Murray, R. M., et al. *The Epidemiology of Schizophrenia*. Cambridge: Cambridge University Press, 2003.

Risperdal See ANTIPSYCHOTIC DRUGS.

risperidone See ANTIPSYCHOTIC DRUGS.

ritualistic behavior Sometimes people with schizophrenia are described as engaging in ritualistic behavior—that is, they repeat stereotyped actions based, perhaps, on MAGICAL THINKING. For example, such a person may repeatedly take off all his or her clothes, crouch down on the floor in a praying position, and then get up and put the clothes back on, only to repeat continually these actions over and over again for long periods of time.

Rorschach test See PROJECTIVE TESTS.

rotatory machines See CIRCULATING SWING; GYRATOR.

Rush, Benjamin (1746–1813) The first American physician to specialize in mental disorders. In fact, his profile appears in the logo of the AMERICAN PSYCHIATRIC ASSOCIATION. He graduated from the Presbyterian College of New Jersey (later renamed Princeton) when he was 15 years old and later went to Edinburgh and received a medical degree from the university there in 1768. During his stay in Scotland and England, Rush visited the major psychiatric hospitals of his day, including the BETHLEM ROYAL HOSPITAL, and was influenced by English physician William Cullen's ideas on the classification and treatment of mental disorders. Rush was a signer of the Declaration of Independence, and as physician at the Pennsylvania Hospital in Philadelphia (starting in 1783), he was the leading American physician of his day. Rush's own son John became insane at the age of 30 and was admitted to the Pennsylvania Hospital as a "lunatic," and he remained there until his death 27 years later.

Besides conducting an abundance of research on all aspects of medicine, Rush took a particular interest in diseases of the human mind. Rush's treatments covered a wide range from the "moral treatment" (influenced in Philadelphia, no doubt, by the Quakers) of institutionalized patients to some fairly terrifying methods of BLEEDING and MECHANICAL RESTRAINT, including his famous invention the stationary "coercion-chair" or TRANQUILLIZER and the GYRATOR. His 1812 textbook was the only American textbook on psychiatry for more than 70 years.

Goodman, N. G. *Benjamin Rush: Physician and Citizen, 1746–1813*. Philadelphia: University of Pennsylvania Press, 1934.

Rush, B. *Medical Inquiries and Observations on the Diseases of the Mind*. Philadelphia: Kimber & Richardson, 1812.

S

Sakel, Manfred Joshua (1906–1957) The inventor of INSULIN COMA THERAPY for schizophrenia.

Salpêtrière, la The famous Paris asylum for insane females. Although it was a place of incarceration for socially undesirable females since 1656, following the French Revolution of the early 1790s it became primarily a hospital for mentally ill women. The Salpêtrière played an important role in the history of psychiatry, for Philippe PINEL made many of his clinical observations as head of the institution in the 1790s and Jean Martin Charcot established a neurological clinic there in 1878. It was there that Charcot developed an interest in hypnotism and HYSTERIA.

Scandinavia The Scandinavian countries contain areas with some of the highest prevalence rates of schizophrenia in the world. This fact was observed as early as 1862 in a book by W. Charles Hood, *Statistics of Insanity,* in which he reported that the northern European countries had the highest rates of insanity and the southern European countries had the lowest. The Scandinavian countries, particularly Sweden, have been found to have prevalence rates for schizophrenia that are two to three times that of the United States. The highest prevalence rates for any area of the world have been found in northern Sweden in two studies that were conducted 25 years apart by J. A. Böök and colleagues. The rural area of Sweden that was north of the Arctic Circle was found by Bvvk to have a prevalence rate of 9.5 per 1,000. Other Swedish studies have found lower rates, but these are still quite high when compared with other areas of the world. High rates have also been found in areas of Norway and Finland, but somewhat less so for Denmark.

Böök, J. A. "Schizophrenia in a Northern Swedish Population, 1900–1975," *Clinical Genetics* 14 (1978): 373–394.

Torrey, E. F. "Prevalence Studies of Schizophrenia," *British Journal of Psychiatry* 150 (1987): 598–608.

schizoaffective disorder The term *schizoaffective* was coined by Jacob S. Kasanin (1897–1946) in 1933 to describe cases of BORDERLINE SCHIZOPHRENIA. Kasanin's concept was accepted for a time as a possible fifth subtype of schizophrenia. It is now a psychotic disorder that has symptoms of both a schizophrenic and a mood disturbance, and at other times with psychotic symptoms but without mood symptoms. The diagnosis is made only if the criteria for schizophrenia or for a mood disorder cannot be met and if it cannot be determined if an organic factor is responsible for this confusing mixture of symptoms. Family studies indicate that schizoaffective disorder is distinct from BIPOLAR DISORDER but that it may bear a closer relationship to schizophrenia. There are two subtypes of schizoaffective disorder: schizoaffective disorder, bipolar type, which, with its current or previous manic episode, makes it more closely related to a mood disorder than to schizophrenia; and schizoaffective disorder, depressive type, which does seem to be more closely related to schizophrenia.

The typical age of onset for schizoaffective disorder is early adulthood. The course of the disorder tends to be chronic, but the prognosis is better than that for schizophrenia and worse than that for a mood disorder. It is not known how prevalent this disorder is, but it is less common than schizo-

phrenia. Some family studies have indicated that there is an increased risk of schizophrenia in the first-degree biological relatives of people with this disorder.

See also ATYPICAL PSYCHOTIC DISORDERS.

Bertelsen, A., and I. I. Gottesman. "Schizoaffective Psychoses: Genetical Clues to Classification," *American Journal of Medical Genetics* 60 (1995): 7–11.

Kasanin, J. "The Acute Schizo-affective Psychoses," *American Journal of Psychiatry* 97 (1933): 97–106.

schizoid personality disorder According to *DSM-IV-R* (1994), the defining characteristic of this nonpsychotic mental disorder is "a pervasive pattern of indifference to social relationships and a restricted range of emotional experience and expression, beginning in early adulthood and present in a variety of contexts." These people appear to be cold and aloof, and they do not seem to desire or enjoy close relationships with other people. They almost always choose solitary activities and occupations, and they express little desire for sexual relationships with others. A person who meets the criteria for schizoid personality disorder must have demonstrated a lifelong course, and even though many of the signs and symptoms may resemble the PRODROMAL PHASE of schizophrenia, it is not thought that persons with this personality disorder go on to develop schizophrenia.

See also SCHIZOTYPAL PERSONALITY DISORDER.

schizomimetic Behavior in a person that mimics or resembles the signs and symptoms of schizophrenia but in fact is not due to the presence of that disorder.

schizophrene An obsolete term for persons with schizophrenia. We now call them schizophrenics. An analogous outmoded term for persons with bipolar disorder is *circulars.*

schizophrenia A term coined by Swiss psychiatrist Eugen BLEULER to replace the term *DEMENTIA PRAECOX* for the most prevalent group of the psychotic disorders. In 1899 Emil KRAEPELIN had unified what were previously separate disorders—hebephrenia, catatonia, and paranoia (of a specific type)—under the general heading of dementia praecox, which he regarded as all chronic and progressively degenerative diseases. Thus, the basis of Kraepelin's classification was the *prognosis* of these disorders.

Bleuler disagreed with the overtly negative prognosis as the defining characteristic of this disorder and instead renamed it schizophrenia (from two Greek words meaning "to split" and "mind") to stress what for him was the fundamental nature of these psychotic disorders: the splitting or dissociation of psychic functions (for which Bleuler used the German word *Spaltung*).

Although Bleuler had been using the word *schizophrenia* in clinical presentations and lectures at the BURGHÖLZI HOSPITAL in Zurich, Switzerland, where he was the chief physician, he introduced the concept in print in a 1908 article titled "The Prognosis of Dementia Praecox: The Group of Schizophrenias" (*Die Prognose der Dementia Praecox—Schizophreniegruppe*). In the first paragraph of that historic article, in which he questions the importance of Kraepelin's idea of prognosis, Bleuler writes:

> In using the term dementia praecox I would like it to mean what the creator of the concept meant it to mean. To treat the subject from any other point of view would serve no purpose, but I would like to emphasize that Kraepelin's dementia praecox is not necessarily either a form of dementia or a disorder of early onset. For this reason, and because there is no adjective or noun that can be derived from the term dementia praecox, I am taking the liberty of using the word *schizophrenia* to denote Kraepelin's concept. I believe that the tearing apart or splitting of psychic functions is a prominent symptom of the whole group and I will give my reasons for this elsewhere.

So what is "split" (*Spaltung*) in schizophrenia? Bleuler argues that it is primarily encountered in the disturbance of associations that characterize normal trains of thought, although there are

also splits in the normal functions of affect and of behavior (especially relating to the external world). Thus, the FOUR A'S (associations disturbances, autism, ambivalence, affective disturbances) that constitute the FUNDAMENTAL SYMPTOMS OF SCHIZOPHRENIA according to Bleuler are all manifestations of the splitting of psychic functions.

In 1911 Bleuler published his classic book that still influences our current thinking about schizophrenia: *Dementia Praecox oder die Gruppe der Schizophrenien (Dementia Praecox, or the Group of Schizophrenias)*. In it, Bleuler defines his conception of the disease in the following way:

> By the term "dementia praecox" or "schizophrenia" we designate a group of psychoses whose course is at times chronic, at times marked by intermittent attacks, and which can stop or retrograde at any stage, but does not permit a full *restitutio ad integrum*. The disease is characterized by a specific type of alteration of thinking, feeling, and relation to the external world which appears nowhere else in this particular fashion.

Bleuler divided the clinical picture of schizophrenia into its "fundamental symptoms" (*Grundsymptome*), which were caused directly by the disease process itself, and its accessory symptoms (*akzessorische Symptome*). The fundamental symptoms (the "four A's") are present to some degree during the entire course of the illness, whereas the secondary symptoms (delusions, hallucinations, transient catatonic episodes, behavioral disturbances) come and go throughout the course of the illness and are found in other mental disorders as well. In addition, Bleuler added a fourth subtype of the disease—"simple schizophrenia"—that had been proposed by Otto Diem in 1904.

Bleuler's dementia praecox Bleuler had believed he was further developing Kraepelin's concepts of dementia praecox rather than inventing an entirely new disorder. Bleuler's objections to Kraepelin's dementia praecox were many, however. He objected (as many others did, particularly British psychiatrists) that there was no dementia in the classical, organic sense of the term (for example, as in today's Alzheimer's disease), but instead an intellectual deterioration that may or may not end up looking like dementia. He noted the deterioration was not progressive, with episodes of partial remission or complete recovery occurring in some cases. The term *praecox* was also objectionable to Bleuler since he had encountered cases of schizophrenia that occurred during midlife (currently named LATE-ONSET SCHIZOPHRENIA). There were also cases of LATENT SCHIZOPHRENIA, according to Bleuler, in which the psychotic disorder was not triggered by an endogenous disease process but by personal experiences, such as trauma. Bleuler went so far as to believe that cases of latent schizophrenia were more common than cases of manifest schizophrenia. Bleuer also noted the existence of people with paranoid personality disorders who resembled cases of dementia praecox. Bleuler widened Kraepelin's concept of dementia praecox by arguing that these cases, too, should be considered part of the disease (an idea that has taken hold in our current notions of schizophrenia spectrum disorders, especially SCHIZOTYPAL PERSONALITY DISORDER). Influenced by his associate Carl Gustav Jung (1875–1961) and by Freud and the psychoanalytic movement, Bleuler believed in the possibility of psychogenic or reactive triggers for schizophrenia, which Kraepelin did not allow.

In sum, Bleuler greatly widened the circumference of persons whom he considered should be diagnosed with dementia praecox. He also left open the possibilities for various courses and outcomes, and better prognoses, than Kraepelin did. He emphasized the heterogeneous nature of schizophrenia, with the possibility that multiple disease processes may underlie it, whereas Kraepelin held to the conviction that dementia praecox was one disease with at least three forms. It was therefore Bleuler's wider concept of schizophrenia that took hold, especially in America, and dominated psychiatry until 1980. In that year, the narrower diagnostic criteria and pessimistic prognosis for schizophrenia became the official diagnosis of this disorder in *DSM-III*. This narrower, "neo-Krapelinian" definition of schizophrenia persists today.

Symptoms and Diagnostic Path

Schizophrenia remains a disease of unknown cause, with no single identifiable pathophysiol-

ogy, no truly effective treatment for most, and no known cure. There is no objective medical test for diagnosing this disorder. No blood test or brain scan can confirm a diagnosis. The current diagnostic criteria for this book from both the North American *DSM-IV-TR* (2000) and the European *ICD-10* (1992) can be found in an appendix to this book. Sometimes schizophrenia may resemble other psychotic disorders, especially MANIC-DEPRESSIVE ILLNESS or BIPOLAR DISORDER.

Reviews of the significant epidemiological, biological, and clinical features of this disease can be found in the following entries in this book: COURSE AND OUTCOME OF SCHIZOPHRENIA; PRODROMAL PHASE; RESIDUAL PHASE; RISK FACTORS; BRAIN ABNORMALITIES IN SCHIZOPHRENIA; NEUROPSYCHOLOGICAL STUDIES OF SCHIZOPHRENIA; SUBJECTIVE EXPERIENCES IN SCHIZOPHRENIA.

Treatment Options and Outlook

The treatment of schizophrenia is primarily based on the administration of ANTIPSYCHOTIC DRUGS. Severe side effects of these drugs, such as TARDIVE DYSKINESIA, PARKINSONISM, or NEUROLEPTIC MALIGNANT SYNDROME are also discussed in detailed entries. Other than programs that educate family members about the disease, and how to alter their own behavior to prevent relapse in their relative with schizophrenia (see EXPRESSED EMOTION), there is no form of psychotherapy that has been shown to be effective for the long term for people with schizophrenia. Antipsychotic drugs do not seem to delay or reverse the natural course of the schizophrenia disease process. Antipsychotic drugs do not improve NEGATIVE SYMPTOMS or cognitive deficits (for example, attention, working memory, and goal-directed thinking).

No one knows the cause or pathophysiology of schizophrenia. However, the most prominent theory generating research at present is the NEURODEVELOPMENTAL MODEL OF SCHIZOPHRENIA. Schizophrenia does not seem to follow the pattern of being a neurodegenerative disease like Alzheimer's disease, so neurodevelopmental theories are prominent almost by default. The strongest evidence for a biological cause for schizophrenia seems to lie in the evidence provided in GENETICS STUDIES. There is no single environmental factor that has been strongly linked to the cause and development of schizophrenia.

Risk Factors and Preventive Measures

There are no known preventive measures for schizophrenia.

See also RISK FACTORS.

Bleuler, E. *Dementia Praecox oder die Gruppe der Schizophrenien.* A volume in *Handbuch der Geisteskrankheiten,* edited by G. Aschaffenburg. Leipzig: F. Deuticke, 1911.

———. "Die Prognose der Dementia Praecox—Schizophreniengruppe," *Allgemeine Zeitschrift für Psychiatrie* 65 (1908): 436–464.

Cutting, J., and M. Shepherd, eds. *The Clinical Roots of the Schizophrenia Concept: Translations of Seminal European Contributions on Schizophrenia.* Cambridge: Cambridge University Press, 1987. (Contains an almost complete translation of Bleuler's 1908 article.)

schizophrenia spectrum disorders See SCHIZOTYPAL PERSONALITY DISORDER.

schizophreniform disorder According to *DSM-IV-TR* (2000), a person must be given the diagnosis of schizophreniform disorder if they manifest the characteristic symptoms of the active phase of schizophrenia for a period of one month but not more than six months and there is a full recovery. If symptoms persist after six months, they are given the diagnosis of schizophrenia. Schizophreniform disorder is perhaps nothing more than a conceptual bridge, based on duration of symptoms, between BRIEF PSYCHOTIC DISORDER and schizophrenia. Although it is in *DSM-IV-TR,* there is no scientific evidence to support schizophreniform disorder as a distinct diagnostic category. For this reason it does not appear in the WORLD HEALTH ORGANIZATION'S *ICD-10* (1992).

schizophreniform psychoses A term for persons with an ATYPICAL PSYCHOTIC DISORDER with a good prognosis that was often misdiagnosed as "genuine" or "process" schizophrenia, another syndrome that had a chronic and deteriorating

course. Persons who developed schizophreniform psychoses were well-adjusted prior to becoming ill. The onset of psychotic symptoms was sudden, and in response to identifiable causes such as stress or trauma. Although the psychotic symptoms resembled those of schizophrenia, there were also elements of an AFFECTIVE DISORDER such as manic-depression and a clouding of consciousness. Unlike persons with true schizophrenia, persons with a schizophreniform psychosis were responsive to treatments such as electroshock therapy. The concept was introduced into psychiatry by Gabriel Langfeldt (1895–1983), a psychiatrist in Vinderen, Norway, in his 1939 book, *The Schizophreniform States*. From the 1940s to the 1980s Langfeldt's concept of schizophreniform psychoses was popular in psychiatry, particularly in Europe and Scandinavia. Langfeldt's term lives on as SCHIZOPHRENIFORM DISORDER in *DSM-IV-TR*, although the clinical picture differs sharply from his suggested symptoms for the disorder. Reanalyses of the 100 case histories documented by Langfeldt as schizophreniform have found that his cases more closely match affective or mood disorders with psychotic features.

Langfeldt, G. *The Schizophreniform Disorders*. Copenhagen: Munsksgaard; Oxford: Oxford University Press, 1939.

schizophrenogenic mother Due to the influence of psychoanalysis and, later, FAMILY INTERACTION THEORIES, it was thought that the behavior of certain family members—particularly the mother—was responsible for causing a schizophrenic breakdown in children. The term *schizophrenogenic mother* (although previously used in a paper by Frieda FROMM-REICHMANN) was introduced into the mainstream by psychoanalytic psychiatrist Trude Tietze in a 1949 published study of 25 mothers of schizophrenic patients. They were all seen as "domineering" and with "warped psychosexual development" that psychologically injured their children. In the 1950s and early 1960s medical students training in psychiatry were routinely taught that mothers were "pathogens." One of the most prominent figures in clinical psychology, Paul Meehl, likewise believed in this. A useful review of the long and tragic course of the idea of the schizophrenogenic mother in American culture and psychiatry was published by C. E. Hartwell in 1996. Today, it is clear that there is no scientific evidence to support the notion of the schizophrenogenic mother.

Hartwell, C. E. "The Schizophrenogenic Mother Concept in American Psychiatry," *Psychiatry* 59 (1996): 274–279.

Tietze, T. "A Study of Mothers of Schizophrenic Patients," *Psychiatry* 12 (1949): 55–65.

schizotaxia A term coined by psychologist Paul Meehl in 1962 to refer to the genetically transmitted "neural integrative defect" that predisposes a whole class of individuals to develop SCHIZOTYPY or SCHIZOPHRENIA. Schizotaxia, according to Meehl, is the only thing that is inherited in schizophrenics, and it does not necessarily lead to the development of this disorder unless there are certain environmental factors that also push the individual in the direction of psychopathology. Schizotypy refers to the unusual personality organization that these environmental influences may cause, but persons who are schizotypes still may not necessarily develop schizophrenia. Instead, Meehl suggests: "It seems likely that the most important causal influence pushing the schizotype toward schizophrenic decompensation is the schizophrenogenic mother."

Meehl first proposed these ideas in a Presidential Address to the AMERICAN PSYCHOLOGICAL ASSOCIATION in September 1962, and the idea of "schizotaxia, schizotypy, schizophrenia" was important in developing later diathesis stress models of schizophrenia and of the role of genetics in SPECTRUM DISORDERS.

Meehl, P. "Schizotaxia, Schizotypy, Schizophrenia," *American Psychologist* 17 (1962): 827–838.

schizotypal personality disorder This type of personality disorder best exemplifies what Paul Meehl meant by "SCHIZOTYPY" (see SCHIZOTAXIA). The person with schizotypal personality disorder displays a "pervasive pattern of peculiarities of

ideation, appearance, and behavior and deficits in interpersonal relatedness, beginning by early adulthood and present in a variety of contexts, that are not severe enough to meet the criteria for schizophrenia." These persons may exhibit IDEAS OF REFERENCE, be extremely uncomfortable in social situations, exhibit extremely odd beliefs or engage in magical thinking, may look odd or unkempt, talk to themselves, speak oddly, have no close friends, have silly or inappropriate affect, or perhaps even be a little suspicious or paranoid. It is estimated that approximately 3 percent of the population of the United States has this disorder and that it is more common among the FIRST-DEGREE RELATIVES of persons with schizophrenia.

Historical Background

When Eugen BLEULER proposed his concept of SCHIZOPHREHNIA in 1908, he widened the circumference of the definition DEMENTIA PRAECOX to include persons who had dementia praecox–like symptoms that were much less severe and who had a much better prognosis than those identified by Emil KRAEPELIN. He also referred to persons who had "latent dementia praecox" that might worsen into cases of full, active schizophrenia under stress or the experience of trauma. Later, in 1911, he would add a fourth form of dementia praecox that loosely corresponded to this group, SIMPLE SCHIZOPHRENIA. The New York psychoanalyst Sandor Rado was the first to use the term *SCHIZOTYPAL DISORDERS* in the *American Journal of Psychiatry* in 1953 to refer to persons who were genetically predisposed to schizophrenia but who did not go on to develop the full disorder. These persons appeared to have stable if bizarre personality traits rather than a psychotic disorder, therefore beginning with *DSM-III* in 1980, this diagnostic group was renamed Schizotypal Personality Disorder and included in a "cluster" with two other similar personality disorders: Paranoid Personality Disorder and Schizoid Personality Disorder. Schizoid personality disorder and schizotypal personality disorder are part of what was termed *schizophrenia spectrum disorders* by Seymour Kety and David Rosenthal of the NATIONAL INSTITUTE OF MENTAL HEALTH in Bethesda, Maryland, in the early 1970s. A significant finding of their initial 1968 report of the Danish adoption studies was that some relatives of persons with schizophrenia who did not have the disorder nonetheless exhibited symptoms or traits of a "borderline state" of schizophrenia. GENETICS STUDIES of schizophrenia that have followed Kety and Rosenthal's work have replicated this finding, indicating that close biological relatives of persons with schizophrenia may share the same genes underlying the predisposition to the disorder ("schizotaxia") but may express watered-down or less severe symptoms or traits of schizophrenia ("schizotypy"). Although the current assumption in modern genetics studies is that schizotypal personality disorder is a form of "subthreshold" schizophrenia," similarities between the symptoms of the two disorders do not necessarily mean they have a common etiology (cause). However, as a recent survey of the experimental research on schizotypal personality disorder (SPD) by O'Flynn, et al., concluded in 2003, "Studies of the phenomenology, genetics, biology, cognition, outcome and treatment response of SPD have consistently supported a close relationship of SPD to schizophrenia."

In clinical practice as well as research studies, the "cluster A" personality disorders (paranoid, schizoid, and schizotypal) are highly overlapping and often difficult to distinguish in practice. The high comorbidity of these disorders is interpreted by some schizophrenia researchers as an indication that there may be gradations along the schizophrenia spectrum rather than distinct disorders. From least in severity to worst, the gradation would go from schizoid to paranoid to schizotypal personality disorders to schizophrenia.

The terms *schizotypal, schizotypy,* and *schizophrenia spectrum disorders* are all used interchangeably in the literature on schizophrenia research.

In *ICD-10* (1992), schizotypal disorder is not a personality disorder but is one of the five categories of ATYPICAL PSYCHOTIC DISORDERS.

See also BORDERLINE CASES; BORDERLINE SCHIZOPHRENIA; LATENT SCHIZOPHRENIA.

O'Flynn, K. O., J. Gruzelier, A. Bergman, and L. J. Siever. "The Schizophrenia Spectrum Personality Disorders." *Schizophrenia.* 2nd ed., edited by S. R. Hirsch and D. Weinberger. Cambridge: Blackwell, 2003.

schizotypy See SCHIZOTYPAL PERSONALITY DISORDER.

schizovirus According to the VIRAL THEORIES OF SCHIZOPHRENIA, there is a possibility that some individuals with schizophrenia develop the disorder due to a chronic infectious agent of the nervous system. Although such a possibility had been noted by Emil KRAEPELIN at the turn of the century, the hypothesis was not investigated seriously until E. Fuller Torrey resurrected this notion with a series of studies at the NATIONAL INSTITUTE OF MENTAL HEALTH in the 1970s. In a 1988 article, he reports, "My psychiatric research colleagues regarded the efforts whimsically as the search for the 'schizovirus' or 'schizococcus.'" However, as Torrey admits, there is yet very little direct evidence to link viruses with schizophrenia. Yet, he writes, "The search for the putative 'schizovirus' continues. Whether the quest will eventually lead to Jason's fabled Golden Fleece, or merely be another blind alley down which schizophrenia research has wandered, remains to be seen."

Torrey, E. F. "Stalking the Schizovirus," *Schizophrenia Bulletin* 14 (1988): 223–229.

Torrey, E. F., and M. R. Peterson. "Slow and Latent Viruses in Schizophrenia," *Lancet* 2 (1973): 22–24.

Schnauzkrampf Interest in the PHYSIOGNOMY of mental illness was a major concern in the 19th century. In schizophrenic people with CATATONIA, it was reported by German psychiatrist Karl KAHLBAUM that they tended to exhibit a protrusion of the lips that resembled an animal snout (*Schnauzkrampf*).

Scotland Scotland has a higher prevalence rate for schizophrenia than England, its neighbor to the south. The observation that there has always been more "insanity" among the Scottish dates at least from the mid-19th century. A schizophrenia prevalence study by Mayer-Gross in Scotland, in which 56,231 persons were surveyed, found a prevalence rate of 4.2 per 1,000.

Torrey, E. F. *Schizophrenia and Civilization*. New York: Jason Aronson, 1980.

seasonal affective disorder The observation that DEPRESSION and MANIA are sensitive to seasonal and environmental influences has been reported for at least 2,000 years. Hippocrates noted in the fourth century B.C. that "it is chiefly in the changes of season which produce diseases, and in the seasons the great changes are from cold or heat." As early as 1801, French ALIENIST Philippe PINEL noted winter and summer onsets for mood disorders. *DSM-III-R* (1987) included criteria for "seasonal pattern" in mood disorders such as BIPOLAR DISORDER or recurrent major depression in which it must be established that, through the years, there has been a regular appearance of an episode of the disorder in a given 60-day period of the year. In a 1989 review of all the research studies that link seasonal patterns to mood disorders, it was found that there are two primary, opposite seasonal patterns of annual mood disorders, namely depression: those with winter depression (onset during September, October, and November) and summer depression (onset during March, April, and May). It is estimated that seasonal affective disorder has been found to occur in about 16 percent to 38 percent of all persons who experience recurrent depression. The vast majority of persons (83 percent) who develop SAD (the apt acronym for seasonal affective disorder) are females in their 30s. It is generally important to identify those persons who suffer from recurrent winter depression because they have been found to respond to a novel form of treatment—phototherapy (bright light administered to such persons for varying lengths of time and intensity of brightness).

Rosenthal, N. E., and M. C. Blehar, eds. *Seasonal Affective Disorder and Phototherapy*. New York: Guilford, 1989.

Rosenthal, N. E., and T. A. Wehr. "Seasonal Affective Disorders," *Psychiatric Annals* 17 (1987): 670–674.

Wehr, T. A., and N. E. Rosenthal. "Seasonality and Affective Illness," *American Journal of Psychiatry* 146 (1989): 829–839.

seasonality of births in the psychotic disorders One of the most consistent findings in the epidemiology of the psychotic disorders is that there is a seasonal excess of births in the winter and early spring months (roughly December through May) of people

who go on to develop schizophrenia and/or bipolar disorder later in life. The very first published study to document this remarkable phenomenon appeared in 1929. In it, a Swiss psychiatrist named Tramer analyzed birth data for 3,100 patients with psychotic disorders institutionalized in Swiss clinics.

Since then, the most vigorous proponent of this hypothetical risk factor for schizophrenia is E. Fuller Torrey. In a comprehensive review article on this issue published in *Schizophrenia Research* in 1997, Torrey and his colleagues analyzed more than 250 studies on seasonality of birth that covered 29 Northern and five Southern Hemisphere countries. A consistent finding across studies was a 5 percent to 8 percent winter-spring excess of births of people who later went on to develop schizophrenia or bipolar disorder. Of the 86 studies dealing specifically with schizophrenia, a total of 437,710 individuals with schizophrenia were analyzed. According to Torrey et al., "The schizophrenia birth excess, therefore, may be said to be predominantly from December to May, with its maximum peak in January and February." In BIPOLAR DISORDER, those with mania have a December to March peak, and those with major depression have a March to May peak.

This birth-excess effect was also found for persons diagnosed with SCHIZOAFFECTIVE DISORDER (December–March), major depression (March–May), and autism (March). However, no other major psychiatric disorders seemed to be related to the season of a person's birth.

The seasonality of birth effect is not correlated with gender, social class, race, measurable pregnancy and birth complications, clinical subtypes, or neurological, neuropsychological, or neuroimaging measures.

What, then, causes this remarkable effect? Torrey and colleagues offer the following hypotheses: seasonal effects of genes, subtle pregnancy and birth complications, sunlight's effect on the internal chemistry of the body, toxins, nutrition, temperature/weather, infectious agents (such as viruses), or a combination of any number of these environmental and genetic factors.

Torrey, E. F., et al. "Seasonality of Births in Schizophrenia and Bipolar Disorder: A Review of the Literature," *Schizophrenia Research* 28 (1997): 1–38.

Tramer, M. "Uber die biologische Bedeutung des Geburtsmonates, insbesondere für die Psychoseerkrankung," *Schweitzer Archiv für Neurologie and Psychiatrie* 24 (1929): 17–24.

secondary process See PRIMARY PROCESS.

secondary symptoms of schizophrenia See ACCESSORY SYMPTOMS.

segregation analysis This is a major statistical method used in population genetics research that compares the observed frequency of an illness in a pedigree with a pattern that would occur if a hypothesized mode of genetic inheritance (e.g., one of the patterns of monogenetic transmission or polygenetic transmission) were accurate. Although there are limitations to segregation analyses, such analyses on diverse phenotypes in relevant pedigrees have been able to reject the "single-locus model" (that is, the idea that all cases of schizophrenia have a common single cause and that no familial resemblance is environmentally determined). It has also ruled out the strict polygenetic inheritance model (that is, that schizophrenia is caused by the additive effect of many genes in all cases).

Garver, D. L., et al. "Schizophrenia and the Question of Genetic Heterogeneity," *Schizophrenia Bulletin* 15 (1989): 421–430.

seleniasmus Yet another synonym for lunacy. The word is derived from the name for the Greek goddess of the moon, Selene.

self-image in schizophrenia According to Silvano ARIETI, a person's self-image consists of three components: body image, self-identity, and self-esteem. In schizophrenia, all three of these components are disrupted. There are body image distortions and perceptual anomalies, GENDER-IDENTITY CONFUSION, and a loss of self-esteem

that can be so severe that it may precipitate the PREPSYCHOTIC PANIC that may then lead to a psychosis. American psychiatrist Harry Stack Sullivan devoted considerable work to exploring the development of self and self-image, which he felt originated in the child's passive incorporation of reflected appraisals from significant adults. Several papers on the transformation of self-image in the person stricken with schizophrenia were published in a special issue of *Schizophrenia Bulletin* (vol. 15, no. 2) in 1989 devoted to the theme "Subjective Experiences of Schizophrenia and Related Disorders."

Estroff, S. E. "Self, Identity, and Subjective Experiences of Schizophrenia," *Schizophrenia Bulletin* 15 (1989): 189–198.

self-injurious behavior, or self-mutilation The deliberate cutting, scratching, burning, tearing, or other action performed against one's own body. Self-mutilation is a serious sign of extreme internal distress in many of the persons who do it. It is a side effect of many psychiatric disorders, especially in the psychotic disorders, the DISSOCIATIVE DISORDERS, BORDERLINE PERSONALITY DISORDER, sexual masochism, and the eating disorders bulimia and anorexia nervosa. Self-injurious behavior (SIB) is also quite commonly seen in the mentally retarded, and studies have reported that as many as 40 percent of the institutionalized mentally retarded, especially those with a rare enzyme deficiency known as Lesch-Nyhan syndrome, bang their heads; chew their fingers, lips, or the skin of other parts of their body; and abuse themselves in a multitude of other ways.

Favazza, A. *Bodies under Siege: Self-Mutilation in Culture and Psychiatry.* Baltimore: Johns Hopkins University Press, 1990.

sensorimotor gating This is one of the oldest theories in studies of schizophrenic cognition but has been given new life under a new name with the neuropathological and neuroimaging studies of the 1980s and 1990s. The idea is that the brain of a person with schizophrenia cannot screen out relevant from irrelevant sensations. The metaphorical "gate" that lets sensory and motor messages in and out of the cortex is broken. This failure in "gating" to "screen out" irrelevant stimuli leads to a disruption in the ability of a person with schizophrenia to willfully focus his or her ATTENTION. The person feels flooded by irrelevant sensations, feelings, and thoughts and, in an effort to cope, can "shut down" and become unresponsive. Genes that seem to be linked to sensorimotor gating have been found in mice (in 1998) and are suspected to exist in humans as well.

Swerdlow, N. R., and M. A. Geyer. "Using an Animal Model of Deficient Sensorimotor Gating to Study the Pathophysiology and New Treatments of Schizophrenia," *Schizophrenia Bulletin* 24 (1998): 285–301.

Serentil See ANTIPSYCHOTIC DRUGS.

Seroquel See ANTIPSYCHOTIC DRUGS.

serotonin hypothesis Serotonin is a neurotransmitter that functions in both the central and the peripheral nervous systems. In the peripheral nervous system (PNS) it functions as a vasoconstrictor. In the central nervous system (CNS) it has many functions, primarily the inhibition of certain brain areas during sleep.

The chemical name for serotonin is 5-hydroxytryptamine, or 5HT. Serotonin was the basis for the first theory of a NEUROTRANSMITTER DISORDER AS A CAUSE OF SCHIZOPHRENIA, which was proposed in a paper by biochemists D. W. Wooley and E. Shaw in 1954.

Many of the ATYPICAL ANTIPSYCHOTICS introduced in the 1990s act on serotonergic pathways in the brain to alleviate the symptoms of schizophrenia. However, given that more than 100 different neurotransmitters in the brain have now been found, it is no longer argued by schizophrenia researchers that serotonin (or dopamine or norepinepherine or glutamine) can act alone in the disease processes of schizophrenia.

Baumeister, A. A., and M. F. Hawkins. "The Serotonin Hypothesis of Schizophrenia: A Historical Case Study on the Heuristic Value of Theory in Clinical Neuroscience," *Journal of the History of the Neurosciences* 13 (September 2004): 277–291.

Wolley, D. W., and E. Shaw. "A Biochemical and Pharmacological Suggestion about Certain Mental Disorders," *Proceedings of the National Academy of Sciences of the United States of America* 40 (1954): 228–231.

sertindole See ATYPICAL ANTIPSYCHOTICS.

sex differences in schizophrenia See GENDER DIFFERENCES IN SCHIZOPHRENIA.

sexual jealousy See OTHELLO SYNDROME.

shamanism and schizophrenia Shamanism is a magico-religious tradition that has been reported for centuries in simple societies that are based on hunting, gathering, and fishing. The shaman is an individual who deliberately enters an altered state of consciousness (through drugs, drumming, dancing, fasting) in order to induce visionary states in which he performs certain culturally prescribed actions, usually either healing or divination. Unfortunately, especially prior to the "psychedelic era" of the 1960s, the only frame of reference most anthropologists possessed for understanding the unusual experiences these people had during their visions was psychiatric diagnostic manuals. Thus, such experiences were long interpreted as signs of psychosis, and the myth grew that shamans were nothing more than severely disturbed individuals who may even be psychotic but whose society has a role for them and therefore they are accepted and "healed" to some extent.

A widely cited 1967 paper by Julian Silverman did much to promote this pathologizing of shamans by comparing the experiences of the altered states of consciousness in the early training of the shaman with the symptoms of acute schizophrenia. Unfortunately, Silverman's paper was taken as the final word on the issue for almost two decades. However, a 1983 paper by clinical psychologist Richard Noll strongly criticized this assumption on phenomenological grounds, and now anthropological studies of religion no longer view the experiences of shamans as "schizophrenic" or "psychotic."

Noll, R. "Shamanism and Schizophrenia: A State-Specific Approach to the 'Schizophrenia Metaphor' of Shamanic States," *American Ethnologist* 10 (1983): 443–459.

———. "What Have We Really Learned about Shamanism?" *Journal of Psychoactive Drugs* 21 (1989): 47–50.

Silverman, J. "Shamanism and Acute Schizophrenia," *American Anthropologist* 69 (1967): 21–31.

shared delusional (or paranoid) disorder See FOLIE À DEUX.

shared psychotic disorder See FOLIE À DEUX.

shock therapy See ELECTROSHOCK THERAPY.

sibship The group of all siblings of the afflicted person and their parents.

sign The sign of an illness is an objective indicator of a pathological condition. This differs from a SYMPTOM in that the sign of a disorder is observed by an examiner and is not a subjective report by the individual. For example, a runny nose is the sign of the common cold, whereas the feeling of discomfort or fever are symptoms of this illness.

silly dementia See HEBEPHRENIA.

simple schizophrenia The fourth subtype of schizophrenia added by Eugen BLEULER to the original three of paranoia, hebephrenia, and catatonia grouped together in 1899 by Emil KRAEPELIN as DEMENTIA PRAECOX. This subtype was outlined by Swiss psychiatrist Otto Diem in 1903. Diem

worked under Bleuler at the BURGHÖLZI HOSPITAL, and the idea for his article may have been suggested by Bleuler as an elaboration of an earlier idea by Czech psychiatrist Arnold Pick (1851–1924). In the English translation (in Cutting and Shepard's book) of his original article, Diem acknowledges the "characteristic mental debility" of Kraepelin's dementia praecox in the three original subtypes and then proposes that "there is one further condition which leads to the same end state, to the same disorder of intelligence and affect." Diem calls this *dementia simplex,* or "simple schizophrenia." Diem notes that, after puberty, "the onset of this particular form of the illness is habitually simple, insidious, and without warning signs, and the illness progresses without acute progressive attacks and remissions. There are no definite affective disturbances of a manic or a melancholic nature, no hallucinations or delusional ideas, and none of the other characteristic symptoms of the other forms of dementia praecox . . . such as catalepsy, affectations, mannerisms, stereotypies, negativism and mutism." The term *simple schizophrenia* entered the official psychiatric diagnostic manuals and remained there for many years. In *DSM-IV-TR* (2000), it is no longer considered one of the four main subtypes of schizophrenia and is instead currently referred to as schizotypal personality disorder. Simple schizophrenia still exists as a subtype in *ICD-10* (1992).

Black, D. W., and T. J. Boffeli. "Simple Schizophrenia: Past, Present, Future," *American Journal of Psychiatry* 146 (1989): 1,267–1,273.

Diem, O. "The Simple Dementing Form of Dementia Praecox," ("Die einfach demente Form der Dementia praecox"), *Archiv Für Psychiatrie und Neruenkrankheiten* 37 (1903): 111–187. Translated and reprinted in J. Cutting and M. Shepherd, eds. *The Clinical Roots of the Schizophrenia Concept.* Cambridge: Cambridge University Press, 1987.

simulated insanity See FEIGNED INSANITY.

sleep studies It has often been remarked how "dreamlike" the hallucinatory and confusional states of some persons with schizophrenia seem to be. This has led researchers to explore the psychophysiology of sleep and to see if people with schizophrenia manifest any significant differences in the normal stages of sleep or in REM (rapid eye movement) sleep that is associated with dreaming. A 1977 review of this vast experimental literature by Mendelson et al. concluded that investigators "have failed to establish any unique or even consistent abnormalities in the sleep of schizophrenic patients." However, a later reassessment of this conclusion by Buchsbaum in 1979 suggests that the highly contradictory results of the study of sleep in persons with schizophrenia may simply indicate the great diversity in the sleep neurophysiology of persons with psychotic disorders and perhaps warrants more carefully controlled studies with larger sample sizes of schizophrenic subjects. Although the issue of REM sleep differences in schizophrenics when compared with normals is still controversial, Buchsbaum does suggest that one fairly consistent finding is that people with schizophrenia have much lower amounts of delta, or stage IV, sleep than do people without this disorder.

Buchsbaum, M. S. "Neurophysiological Aspects of the Schizophrenic Syndrome." In *Disorders of the Schizophrenic Syndrome,* edited by L. Bellak. New York: Basic Books, 1979.

Mendelson, W. B., J. C. Gillin, and R. J. Wyatt. *Human Sleep and Its Disorders.* New York: Plenum, 1977.

Reich, L., et al. "Sleep Disturbance in Schizophrenia," *Archives of General Psychiatry,* 32 (1975): 51–55.

sleep treatment In 1922 Swiss psychiatrist Jakob Kläsi (1883–1980) introduced the first somatic treatment specifically for schizophrenia. It was referred to as "prolonged sleep therapy." He used barbiturates to induce continuous periods of sleep of one week or longer in persons with schizophrenia. They were only allowed to be awakened for eating and performing other bodily functions. Kläsi reported good results with his sleep treatment, but it never became an accepted treatment. The strong sedatives he used were rather toxic and would result in respiratory complications, espe-

cially pneumonia. This form of treatment was used until the 1950s.

Kläsi, J. "Ober die therapeutische Anwendung per 'Dauernarkose' mittels sominifens bei Schizophrenen," *Z. Neurol. Psychiatr.* 74 (1922): 557–592.

sluggish schizophrenia In the former Soviet Union, perhaps 40 percent of all persons labeled with schizophrenia are within the form of the disorder identified as "sluggish schizophrenia." In many ways this concept is compatible with Eugen BLEULER'S concept of LATENT SCHIZOPHRENIA, which he presented in 1911. In Soviet psychiatry, there is a long-established tradition of studying "soft" forms of schizophrenia. In 1969 A. V. Snezhnevsky and colleagues published an influential book that introduced a new classification system for the various schizophrenias, including the new concept of "sluggish schizophrenia." Sluggish schizophrenia is not viewed as an initial or PRODROMAL PHASE of schizophrenia, but instead it is an independent diagnostic category characterized by a slowly progressive course, subclinical manifestations in the latent period, overt psychopathological symptoms in the active period. Then follows a period in which the POSITIVE SYMPTOMS decrease and the NEGATIVE SYMPTOMS predominate the clinical presentation during the stabilization of the patient. In the United States, "sluggish schizophrenia" may have been called SIMPLE SCHIZOPHRENIA or by its currently accepted name, SCHIZOTYPAL PERSONALITY DISORDER.

The diagnosis of "sluggish schizophrenia" has long been claimed by Soviet dissidents to be the excuse for putting countless political prisoners into Soviet mental hospitals for punishment. During the week of June 30, 1989, the Reuters news agency reported from Moscow that the current issue of an influential Moscow journal, the *Literary Gazette,* published an article by writer Leonid Zagalsky that for the first time publicly named and condemned the two top Soviet psychiatric authorities and their mentor, A. V. Snezhnevsky, for condoning the imprisonment in mental hospitals of otherwise healthy persons under the label "sluggish schizophrenia."

See also ABUSE OF PSYCHIATRIC PATIENTS; BORDERLINE SCHIZOPHRENIA.

Smulevich, A. B. "Sluggish Schizophrenia in the Modern Classification of Mental Illness," *Schizophrenia Bulletin* 15 (1989): 533–539.

Snezhnevsky, A. V., ed. *Shizofrenia: Klinika i Patogenez.* Moscow: Meditsina, 1969.

smoking and schizophrenia As anyone who has ever visited or worked in a psychiatric hospital will know, persons with schizophrenia tend to smoke a great deal. Some have even been seen to smoke two or more cigarettes at a time, and many persons chain-smoke so much that their lips and fingers are stained with nicotine. Cigarettes are the currency of the psychiatric hospital, and all sorts of economic transactions (including prostitution) are based on them. One study of outpatients with schizophrenia found that 88 percent of them were regular smokers, a number three times higher than the nonpsychiatric control group subjects in the study and still far higher than persons who are diagnosed with other psychiatric disorders. It is not known why nicotine addiction is so prevalent in persons with schizophrenia, nor is it known why, paradoxically, lung cancer does not seem to be a major cause of death among schizophrenics despite their years of heavy daily smoking.

See also PHYSICAL DISEASE AND SCHIZOPHRENIA; RISK FACTORS.

Hughes, J. R., et al. "Prevalence of Smoking among Psychiatric Outpatients," *American Journal of Psychiatry* 143 (1986): 993–997.

social drift theory See SOCIOECONOMIC STATUS AND SCHIZOPHRENIA.

social skills training The poor social interactions of people who develop schizophrenia adds considerably to the often terrible quality of their lives and alienates them from other members of the community. Social adjustment has repeatedly been found to be a relatively strong predictor of

relapse, rehospitalization, and long-term outcome. Therefore, since the 1970s and 1980s in particular, there has been a strong emphasis on teaching persons with schizophrenia certain "social skills" that may help prevent relapse or rehospitalization as they continue to adjust to life with such a chronic and debilitating disease. Social skills that are often trained are learned abilities such as making eye contact, the content of speech, voice inflection, and facial expression. The training techniques often include modeling new behaviors, role playing, homework and even training in social perception in order to help keep such persons from misinterpreting the expressions and actions of others.

Many studies have indicated that social skills training procedures are effective in teaching some persons with schizophrenia new skills, and that such newly learned behaviors can be maintained for varying periods of time. Some studies have even associated some forms of social skills training with reduced rates of relapse. However, due to the organic nature of the disease, it is difficult to maintain such learned skills once the person with schizophrenia is no longer monitored and trained consistently within a structured program, and therefore those persons who would most benefit from such training are strongly encouraged to be involved in such programs as often as possible.

Bellak, A. S., ed. *Schizophrenia: Treatment, Management, Rehabilitation.* New York: Grune & Stratton, 1984.

Penn, D. L., and K. T. Mueser. "Research Update on the Psychosocial Treatment of Schizophrenia," *American Journal of Psychiatry* 153 (1996): 607–617.

socioeconomic status and schizophrenia One of the most overwhelming pieces of evidence that we have about schizophrenia is that it occurs at an unusually high rate in the lowest socioeconomic strata of urban communities. However, there are several different interpretations of this finding. One of them is the famous "social drift" explanation—that is, that persons who develop schizophrenia tend not to be able to function very well in the social or occupational spheres and therefore tend to "drift" downward to the lower socioeconomic layers of society. An alternative hypothesis asserts that it is the unhealthful and stressful living conditions of persons of low socioeconomic levels (e.g., living in a ghetto) that produces the disorder.

Perhaps another explanation may involve a mixture of these two theories, in that if schizophrenia is a genetic disease, then previous generations have gotten sick and have already drifted downward in socioeconomic status over the generations, and therefore a higher concentration of persons with this disorder should be found at these lower levels of society.

Faris and Dunham published the first major study of the relationship between schizophrenia and socioeconomic status in 1939 and gave the first evidence for the inverse relationship between class and schizophrenia. Their research was corroborated by Hollingshead and Redlich in 1958, in their famous book *Social Class and Mental Illness,* in which they present the "social drift" hypothesis. In 1980 epidemiologist W. W. Eaton published a review of 17 studies conducted throughout the world and found that 15 of them confirmed the same conclusion that Faris and Dunham reached in 1939: that schizophrenia forms a concentric pattern, with the highest admission rates for schizophrenia in the central slum areas of the city with the lowest socioeconomic status and then diminishing rates as one looks farther and farther from the inner-city slums to the higher-status suburbs.

It is not likely that one's socioeconomic class actually causes schizophrenia, and this is a conclusion reached in 1992 in a major review of the issue in *Science.*

Dohrenwald, B. P., et al. "Socioeconomic Status and Psychiatric Disorders: The Causation-selection Issue," *Science* 255 (1992): 946–952.

Faris, R. E. L., and H. W. Dunham. *Mental Disorders in Urban Areas.* Chicago: Chicago University Press, 1939.

Hollingshead, A. B., and F. C. Redlich. *Social Class and Mental Illness: A Community Study.* New York: Wiley, 1958.

Solian See ANTIPSYCHOTIC DRUGS.

somatic delusions Delusions involving the body. An example is the delusion that one has a hole in the middle of one's body through which the wind is blowing. Another type may be a PREGNANCY DELUSION.

See also DELUSIONAL DISORDER.

somatic type One of the subtypes of the psychotic disorder known as DELUSIONAL DISORDER in which a person may have the delusion that he or she has some physical defect, disorder or disease.

spectrum disorders Influenced by Paul Meehl's DIATHESIS-STRESS THEORY of "schizotaxia, schizotypy, schizophrenia" and by the later GENETICS STUDIES of David Rosenthal and Seymour Kety, it has been suggested that many persons may inherit a genetic defect (schizotaxia, in Meehl's words) that may then give rise to a spectrum of disorders, all the way from a schizoid personality disorder to schizotypal personality disorder to schizophrenia. In other words, a spectrum of related disorders from the least serious to the most serious may be due to similar or related genetic factors. The evidence supporting a spectrum concept of schizophrenia is that first-degree biological relatives of persons with schizophrenia have a greater risk of developing schizotypal personality disorder or paranoid personality disorder or other schizophrenia-spectrum disorders.

See also SCHIZOTAXIA; SCHIZOTYPAL PERSONALITY DISORDER.

spinning chair See CIRCULATING SWING.

Spitzer, Robert (1932–) An American psychiatrist from New York who is perhaps second only to Emil KRAEPELIN in changing the language and classification systems of psychiatry. Spitzer led the task force that produced *DSM-III* in 1980. This revision of the diagnostic manual completely changed clinical research and practice and is regarded as the most influential psychiatric text of the 20th century. Many of the changes were either proposed or personally approved by him.

Spiegel, A. "The Dictionary of Disorder: How One Man Revolutionized Psychiatry," *New Yorker*, January 3, 2005, pp. 56–63.

spontaneous remission Although many clinicians have reported rare cases of spontaneous remission in cases of schizophrenia, *DSM-IV* (1994) cautions that "a return to full premorbid functioning in this disorder is not common. Full remissions do occur, but their frequency is currently a subject of controversy."

spread eagle cure In 19th-century America, this was a technique used in all asylums and prisons for agitated patients or inmates. The procedure involved stripping the violent patient of all clothes and throwing him flat on his back. Four men would take hold of each of the limbs and spread them out at right angles from the body. A physician or an attendant would then stand up on a chair or a table and pour buckets of ice-cold water on the restrained person's face until he was completely subdued. In some instances, the shock was so great that death resulted. A picture of this torturous procedure appears in Emil KRAEPELIN's book *One Hundred Years of Psychiatry*.

Kraepelin, E. *One Hundred Years of Psychiatry*, trans. W. Baskin. 1917. Reprint, New York: Philosophical Library, 1962.

stadium melancholicum This is the 19th-century term for the depression that sometimes precedes the onset of a psychotic disorder. German psychiatrist Wilhelm GRIESINGER writes in his 1861 book, *Mental Pathology and Therapeutics*: "The *stadium melancholicum* which precedes insanity is by some physicians designated as the period of incubation, or prodromal stadium . . . (that) the stage of incubation has almost always a depressive character is interesting and of great importance."

See also PRODROMAL PHASE.

Griesinger, W. *Mental Pathology and Therapeutics*. 2nd ed., trans. C. L. Robertson. New York: William Wood, 1882.

State Care Act of 1890 This was the legislative act passed by Congress that divided each of the United States into districts and mandated a state hospital for each of the districts. With this act, the term *asylum* was replaced by the term *hospital* in reference to these institutions.

Stelazine See ANTIPSYCHOTIC DRUGS.

stereotypy Long observed to be a behavioral sign of psychotic disorders, particularly schizophrenia, stereotypy refers to seemingly meaningless repetitive acts that are rigidly performed over and over again, as if engaged in an idiosyncratic ritual. One of the first psychiatrists to find a symbolic meaning in the stereotypies of psychotic individuals was C. G. JUNG, who, in his autobiography, *Memories, Dreams, Reflections* (1962), relates the story of a quiet old woman who made strange repetitive sewing motions with her hands. In trying to understand what possible meaning the action could have had for her, he investigated her past and found out that many years previously, the woman had suffered the onset of her psychosis after losing a lover who happened to make shoes—hence the source of her sewing motions. Psychoanalyst Frieda FROMM-REICHMANN writes in a 1942 paper that "the seemingly meaningless and inappropriate stereotyped actions of schizophrenics are meaningful, as are the rest of their communications. They serve to screen the appropriate emotional reactions that are at their bottom. . . . They are a means of defense against non-acceptance and rebuff."

Fromm-Reichmann, F. "A Preliminary Note on the Emotional Significance of Stereotypes in Schizophrenics" (1942). In *Psychoanalysis and Psychotherapy: Selected Papers of Frieda Fromm-Reichmann,* edited by D. M. Bullard. Chicago: Chicago University Press, 1959.

Storch's theory of schizophrenic cognition Alfred Storch was a German psychologist who published one of the first comprehensive studies of the peculiarities of thought and language in schizophrenia. Storch was a pupil of the comparative psychologist Heinz Werner. In his 1922 book (published in an English translation in 1924), Storch compared the similarities between the thought processes of schizophrenics and those of persons in primitive societies. He compared the magical worlds of persons living in such societies and the delusional worlds of schizophrenics, especially their preoccupations with religious and mystical issues. Such comparisons are today considered invalid due to the ethnocentrism that colors them. Persons who live in preliterate societies are as "normal" in their thought processes as "normal" persons are in our own, and mental illness is known in these societies and is recognized as such.

Storch, A. *The Primitive Archaic Forms of Inner Experiences and Thought in Schizophrenics.* New York and Washington, D.C.: Nervous and Mental Disease Publishing Company, 1924.

straitjacket, or straight-waistcoat A form of MECHANICAL RESTRAINT invented by a man named MacBride in England in the 1700s for restraining agitated patients in asylums. The heavy canvas coat had sleeves that wrapped around the body and could be tied in the back. Such forms of restraint were used well into the 20th century and may still be in use in some places even today.

See also CAMISOLE.

street drug psychosis A psychotic disorder whose onset is related to the use of PSYCHOTOGENIC DRUGS.

See also SUBSTANCE ABUSE; SUBSTANCE-INDUCED PSYCHOTIC DISORDER.

street people A term for vagrants of all sorts, but especially the homeless mentally ill persons who live on the streets. It is an American term that came into vogue in the 1980s. A 19th-century term for the same class of individuals was PAUPER LUNATICS.

stress It is clear that stress is related to the onset and relapse of many mental and physical disorders.

However, a direct connection between stressful life events and the development of schizophrenia has not been demonstrated. Given that about 80 percent of the vulnerability to schizophrenia is now estimated to be from genetic factors (see GENETICS STUDIES), it is probably true that part of the remaining 20 percent may be related to physically or emotionally stressful environmental influences that contribute to the exacerbation of the disease process. However, a major review of the stress issue in schizophrenia published in 1985 has concluded that "there is no good evidence that life stress is causally related to episodes of schizophrenia."

Gruen, R., and M. Biron. "Stressful Life Events and Schizophrenia," *Neuropsychobiology* 12 (1984): 206–208.

Tennant, C. C. "Stress and Schizophrenia: A Review," *Integrative Psychiatry* (1985): 248–261.

strong rooms See OUBLIETTES.

subjective experiences of schizophrenia With its emphasis on biological and biochemical factors in the development of mental disorders (and the psychotic disorders in particular), psychiatry has been criticized for ignoring the actual experience of an illness by the afflicted person. Indeed, psychiatry has been accused of viewing the notion of the "self" as perhaps a bit mystical, and most professional psychiatric journals today have less and less space for detailed "case histories" of individual experiences. Most studies of the subjective experience of schizophrenia agree on the alterations in the sense of "self" that the disease process produces. Hearing voices, perceptual anomalies, odd beliefs, intrusive thoughts, strange feelings (or lack thereof)—all these highly self-threatening phenomena have been documented in the various reports of persons with psychotic disorders (see PERCEPTUAL ANOMALIES IN SCHIZOPHRENIA). By understanding what actually goes on inside the thoughts and emotions of a person with schizophrenia, we can all develop a deeper empathy for the afflicted person and interact with him or her in a much more genuinely supportive manner.

Based on their work in the United Kingdom, McGhie and Chapman's 1961 paper on attention disturbances is an exemplary study of the inner experiences of schizophrenics and what these reports may mean from a theoretical point of view. The "psychedelic era" generated new interest in purported PSYCHEDELIC EXPERIENCES IN SCHIZOPHRENIA, which then led to a series of studies comparing drug-induced states with psychotic states of consciousness. In the United States, psychiatrist Malcom Bowers's book, *Retreat from Sanity: The Structure of Emerging Psychosis*, published in 1974, provided clinicians and the general public with a series of vivid case histories of what it must be like to undergo a psychotic episode. An excellent collection of historical accounts of the subjective experience of mental illness, particularly of institu- tionalization, was published by Dale Peterson in 1982, containing a comprehensive bibliography of first-person accounts of experiences with "madness." Indeed, most of the major attempts to study the subjective experiences of people with schizophrenia were published in the 1960s and 1970s—prior to the revolution in BRAIN IMAGING TECHNIQUES and GENETICS STUDIES that have shifted the focus to the purely organic view of this disease. In an effort to resurrect interest in the more human and experiential side, in 1989 *Schizophrenia Bulletin* (vol. 15, no. 2) devoted an entire special issue to the theme "Subjective Experiences of Schizophrenia and Related Disorders."

Historical Background

Beginning at least with German psychiatrist Karl Ludwig Kahlbaum's 1874 book on catatonia, psychiatry has been concerned with psychopathology in a very specific way: the objective identification and classification of symptoms of mental illness that could then be grouped into syndromes. A disease was constructed from its symptoms. A second approach in psychiatry, that of nosology, assumed that there are underlying disease processes that exist prior to the appearance of symptoms, and the disease determines the symptoms. Both approaches are still quite influential in psychiatry. However, the subjective human experience of being a particular mentally ill person is lost in these approaches. Both emphasize what is common and

universal across persons (symptoms) and not how a particular form of a symptom (e.g., an auditory hallucination of voices) is actually experienced by a particular person in the course of his or her life. Individual patients are thus objectified, reduced to collections of interchangeable modular components of mental illness stripped of any connection to the meaning of one's personal history.

In 1913 the German psychiatrist Karl Jaspers (1883–1969) transformed the psychopathology approach by applying the philosophical methods of phenomenology to psychiatry in his book *Allgemeine Psychopathologie.* Jaspers was interested in the ways in which patients experienced their consciousness of themselves, the meaning they attached to their symptoms and their illness as a whole, and their feelings. From 1908 to 1915 Jaspers was associated with the psychiatric clinic at the University of Heidelberg in Germany and later was appointed a professor of philosophy there. His work inspired a "phenomenology" movement in psychiatry that was centered in Heidelberg and included such prominent German psychiatrists as Karl Wilmanns (1873–1945); Hans Walther Gruhle (1880–1958); Wilhelm Mayer-Gross (1889–1961), who wrote his paper on "the phenomenology of abnormal feelings of happiness"; Kurt Beringer (1893–1949), who wrote a 1924 monograph on the "dream-like (oneiroid)" forms of experience in psychotic disorders; and Hans Prinzhorn (1886–1933), who compiled a vast collection of the "art of the insane" as evidence of the inner, subjective world of madness, and published an influential book on the subject (see ART, SCHIZOPHRENIC). From 1945 to 1955, Kurt Schneider (1887–1967) became chair of the department. Schneider's FIRST-RANK SYMPTOMS of schizophrenia are a product of this phenomenological tradition at Heidelberg that started with Jaspers.

In the 1950s the subjective experiences of persons with schizophrenia again became a focus of understanding by psychiatrists influenced by the philosophy of existentialism. Prominent among this group was Ludwig Binswanger (1881–1966), who developed a method of psychotherapy based on existential principles, *DASEINANALYSE.* This work influenced British psychiatrist R. D. LAING and the antipsychiatry movement.

Phenomenological and existential approaches to the inner experiences of persons with schizophrenia were always more popular in Europe and the rest of the world than in the United States, where there is a traditional aversion among psychiatrists to any philosophical tradition other than its homegrown pragmatism of William James and John Dewey. Other than its 70-year (1910–80) flirtation with Freudian psychoanalysis and its murky metaphysical ideas, abstract European philosophical concepts have generally been avoided like cholera by anti-intellectual Americans.

Beginning in the 1990s, clinical psychologist Louis Sass of Rutgers University in New Jersey and psychiatrist Josef Parnas of Denmark have been promoting a return to the study of the inner world of schizophrenia by redefining it as a "self-disorder" or an "ipseity disorder" from the Latin, *ipse,* for "self" or "itself." Relying on European phenomenological psychiatry, cognitive science, and phenomenological philosophy, they argue that schizophrenia is characterized by "complementary distortions of the act of awareness: hyperreflexity and diminished self-affection." *Ipseity* is defined as "the experiential sense of being a vital and self-identical *subject* of experience or *first person perspective* on the world." Whether the reframing of schizophrenia as an ipseity disorder proves to have direct application in clinical practice and research remains to be seen.

Bowers, M. *Retreat from Sanity: The Structure of Emerging Psychosis.* New York: Human Sciences Press, 1974.

Freedman, B. J. "The Subjective Experience of Perceptual and Cognitive Disturbances in Schizophrenia," *Archives of General Psychiatry* 30 (1974): 333–340.

Freedman, B. J., and L. J. Chapman. "Early Subjective Experience in Schizophrenia Episodes," *Journal of Abnormal Psychology* 82 (1973): 46–54.

Kleinman, J. E., et al. "A Comparison of the Phenomenology of Hallucinogens and Schizophrenia from Some Autobiographical Accounts," *Schizophrenia Bulletin* 3 (1977): 560–586.

McGhie, A., and J. Chapman. "Disorders of Attention and Perception in Early Schizophrenia," *British Journal of Medical Psychology* 34 (1961): 103–115.

Peterson, D., ed. *A Mad People's History of Madness.* Pittsburgh: University of Pittsburgh Press, 1982.

Sass, L. A., and J. Parnas. "Schizophrenia, Consciousness, and the Self," *Schizophrenia Bulletin* 29 (2003): 427–444.

substance abuse Psychiatric facilities the world over have been deluged since the 1960s with a new type of patient—the "dual diagnosis" patient who is often young, a substance abuser, and perhaps even schizophrenic. Considering the prevalence of illicit drug use in our society by adolescents, and given the fact that it is usually in late adolescence or early adulthood that the first serious onset of schizophrenia has been documented for almost a century, the combination ("comorbidity") of schizophrenia and substance abuse is perhaps the rule and not the exception in today's treatment centers. The issues that are often raised are whether certain drugs actually do initiate the onset of schizophrenia, how they affect its course, and how a history of substance abuse with PSYCHOTOGENIC DRUGS may affect treatment, especially with antipsychotic drugs.

In a major review of the impact of substance abuse on schizophrenia, researchers Winston Turner and Ming T. Tsuang arrived at the following conclusions regarding the present state of scientific knowledge about this relationship:

1. It is evident that substance abuse may profoundly affect the course and outcome of schizophrenia, but the true impact remains largely undefined.
2. There is some evidence that drugs tend to hasten the age of onset of psychosis, but it is unclear whether the effect is to precipitate latent or subliminal psychotic behavior or to initiate psychosis in persons who would not have had a psychotic episode if they did not abuse drugs.
3. Drug abuse just before hospitalization is fairly common, and the drugs of choice do not appear to be random, but it has yet to be determined whether the specific benefits the schizophrenic patients are receiving from the drugs differ from those experienced by persons who do not have schizophrenia.
4. The relationship between characteristics of drug abuse (drug type, quantity, and frequency of drug abuse) and the degree of psychopathology, manifestations of the disease, and long-term outcome has yet to be addressed.
5. Drugs may be precipitating relapse and subsequent rehospitalization among those persons with schizophrenia who are in remission and who would otherwise remain outside of the hospital.

At the end of the 20th century, one of the greatest obstacles to the effective treatment of schizophrenia was the fact that so many young patients used drugs and alcohol. An estimate by Lisa Dixon speculates that half of persons in the United States with schizophrenia may also be battling a diagnosable drug or alcohol disorder. Those persons with schizophrenia at greater risk for addiction tend to be of younger age, of male gender, and have a lower grade of completed education. It is clear now from research studies that persons with schizophrenia who also have a substance abuse problem have poorer outcomes. Furthermore, when compared to other persons diagnosed with schizophrenia, they have more psychotic symptoms, poorer treatment compliance, they tend to be more violent, they are more likely to be homeless, and they are more likely to have medical problems (including HIV infection). Integrating substance abuse treatment (AA, etc.) with mental health services is currently the only viable treatment option.

In the early 1990s the WORLD HEALTH ORGANIZATION conducted a 10-country study of the comorbidity of substance abuse and schizophrenia. It was found that 57 percent of males with schizophrenia abused alcohol. Illegal drugs, primarily cannabis (marijuana) and cocaine, were found to be in use by 24 to 41 percent of all persons with schizophrenia surveyed in the study. In a two-year follow-up study the WHO found that cannabis use was a major risk factor for relapse in schizophrenia. In clinical practice it is not unusual to meet young persons who experienced their first episode of schizophrenia after smoking marijuana, and this connection has long been part of the anecdotal lore of mental health professionals. There is no strong evidence as to whether smoking marijuana is actually a causal factor in the onset of schizophrenia, but the evidence concerning its correlation to increased rates of relapse suggests this may be a precipitating factor in the illness of some young persons.

See also COMORBIDITY.

Dixon, Lisa. "Dual Diagnosis of Substance Abuse in Schizophrenia: Prevalence and Impact on Outcomes," *Schizophrenia Research* 35 (1999): 93–100.

Turner, W. M., and M. T. Tsuang. "Impact of Substance Abuse on the Course and Outcome of Schizophrenia," *Schizophrenia Bulletin* 16 (1990): 87–95.

substance-induced psychotic disorder A *DSM-IV-TR* diagnostic category for persons who develop a psychotic disorder during, or within a month of, substance intoxication or withdrawal. The symptoms must be severe and in excess of what would normally be expected from intoxication or withdrawal. To receive this diagnosis there can be no evidence of a preexisting psychotic disorder.

subtype An identifiable variant of a particular disease.

suicide and schizophrenia Persons with schizophrenia live, on average, 10 to 15 years less than persons in the general population. The main causes of this are deaths due to suicide and to accidents. The single most common cause of death in persons with schizophrenia is suicide. Current estimates place the suicide rate in schizophrenia as equal to, or greater than, the risk of suicide in persons suffering from major depression. In 1995 a study conducted in Scotland found that the suicide rate for persons with schizophrenia was increasing, with the most dangerous period being the first year following discharge from the hospital.

See also COMORBIDITY; MORTALITY IN SCHIZOPHRENIA; RISK FACTORS.

Geddes, J. R., and E. Juszczak. "Period Trends in Rate of Suicide in First 28 Days after Discharge from Psychiatric Hospitals in Scotland, 1968–1992," *British Medical Journal* 311 (1995): 357–360.

surgery See AUTOINTOXICATION AS A CAUSE OF DEMENTIA PRAECOX, COLUMBIA-GREYSTONE PROJECT; FOCAL INFECTION A CAUSE OF SCHIZOPHRENIA; LEUCOTOMY; LOBECTOMY; LOBOTOMY; PSYCHOSURGERY; TOPECTOMY; TRANSORBITAL LOBOTOMY.

Sweden See SCANDINAVIA.

swinging chair See CIRCULATING SWING.

symbiotic psychosis This was a syndrome proposed by child psychoanalyst Margaret Mahler to describe a psychotic disorder of childhood that may resemble schizophrenia. It has also been called the "Mahler syndrome." According to Mahler, it occurs in children who have reached a level of development in which they are able to differentiate and individualize from the mother (usually ages two to four) but cannot proceed to a full separation. Whenever separation is attempted, panic ("separation anxiety") sets in. Mahler writes: "The symbiotic psychotic syndrome is aimed at restoring the symbiotic-parasitic delusion of oneness with the mother and thus serves a function diametrically opposite to that of the autistic mechanism." Mahler says that the psychosis may be insidious and may not be detected until school age. The primary symptoms of REGRESSION are catatonia-like temper tantrums and states of panic.

Mahler, M. S. *On Human Symbiosis and the Vicissitudes of Individuation.* Vol. 1, *Infantile Psychosis.* New York: International Universities Press, 1968.

symptom Generally, a symptom is any manifestation of a pathological condition. Although a strict interpretation of this word is that it refers only to subjective complaints of distress, it may, in some instances, also refer to objective pathological conditions.

See also SIGN.

syndrome A cluster of symptoms that commonly appear together and constitute a recognizable condition. The term *syndrome* is often less specific than the words *disease* or *disorder. Disease* is used when

a specific etiology (cause) of an illness is known, or if its specific organic disease process is known. Most mental disorders therefore are in fact syndromes rather than diseases.

synesthesia A condition in which a sensory experience normally associated with one modality occurs when another modality is stimulated. For example, a loud, sudden sound might produce visual images of lights flashing or swirling colors. Such experiences have been reported with the use of hallucinogens and in acute psychotic episodes.

See also PSYCHEDELIC EXPERIENCES IN SCHIZOPHRENIA.

syphilitic psychosis See GENERAL PARALYSIS OF THE INSANE.

T

tactile hallucinations A hallucination of "touch." Often a tactile hallucination involves something that is felt on or under the skin, and a delusional interpretation of the sensory experience usually accompanies a tactile hallucination. FORMICATION is a specific type of tactile hallucination in which something (usually "bugs") is felt to be crawling just below the surface of the skin. Formication is commonly reported in alcohol withdrawal delirium and in withdrawal from cocaine intoxication.

Taiwan The prevalence rate for schizophrenia in Taiwan has been found to be 2.2 per 1,000. Studies of prevalence rates for schizophrenia among the aboriginal population has been found to be among the lowest rates in the world—0.9 per 1,000.

Torrey, E. F. *Schizophrenia and Civilization.* New York: Jason Aronson, 1980.

tangentiality A feature of the peculiar thought processes found in schizophrenia and in schizotypal personality disorder in which a person does not stick to one topic when speaking but gets pulled off into tangential currents of thought. Usually these are topics that are unrelated to the main point of the conversation, but the person seems unable to focus attention enough to stay consistent with the main topic.

taraxein hypothesis In 1957 a research study by Heath and coworkers announced that they had isolated an abnormal blood protein in the serum of people with schizophrenia that they called taraxein. When they injected this protein into monkeys, it apparently produced abnormal behavior. Furthermore, when injected into normal human subjects, Heath claimed that this substance induced a temporary psychotic disorder that mimicked schizophrenia. It was claimed that taraxein was in the gamma immunoglobulin (IgG) of persons with schizophrenia and that it acted as an antibody against antigens that were present in the person's own limbic system in the brain. Therefore, since it interfered with brain functioning, it was argued that taraxein was a probable cause of schizophrenia, making it an autoimmune disease. Heath's findings have not been replicated by other laboratories.

See also IMMUNE SYSTEM ALTERATION IN SCHIZOPHRENIA.

Heath, R. G., and I. M. Krupp. "Schizophrenia as an Immunologic Disorder: Demonstration of Antibrain Globulins by Fluorescent Antibody Techniques," *Archives of General Psychiatry* 16 (1967): 1–9.

Heath, R. G., et al. "Effect on Behavior in Humans with the Administration of Taraxein," *American Journal of Psychiatry* 114 (1957): 14–24.

tardive dyskinesia This is an involuntary movement disorder directly caused by brain changes resulting from the long-term use of ANTIPSYCHOTIC DRUGS. It appears either during treatment with antipsychotic drugs or shortly (four to eight weeks) after terminating such treatment.

Symptoms and Diagnostic Path

The TD syndrome is characterized by abnormal movements in the following areas of the body, as summarized by M. Marsalek in an article published in 2000:

- Tongue: rolling, arrhythmic tongue protrusions (fly catching sign), tongue producing a bulge in the cheek (the bon-bon sign)
- Lips: pouting, smacking, puckering, sucking
- Mouth: chewing movements
- Face: grimacing, paroxysms of rapid eye-blinking
- Neck: arrhythmic head nodding
- Trunk: irregular rocking movements of the upper torso
- Upper extremities: abnormal stereotypic movements in the fingers may look as though the patient is playing an invisible guitar (also formerly known as the "pill-rolling" movement)
- Lower extremeties: flexing, rotation of the ankles, involuntary stamping movements, retroflexion of the toes

Treatment Options and Outlook

Tardive dyskinesia is a chronic disorder. At present there are no uniformly safe and effective treatments for it.

Marsalek, M. "Tardive Drug-induced Extrapyramidal Syndromes," *Pharmacopsychiatry* 33 (2000): 14–33.

temperament See FUNDAMENTAL STATES OF MANIC-DEPRESSIVE INSANITY.

temporary psychosis See ATYPICAL PSYCHOTIC DISORDERS.

theomania A type of MONOMANIA identified by J. E. D. ESQUIROL in 1938 for the category of persons with a psychotic disorder that includes those "who believe that they are God, who imagine that they have conversations and intimate communications with the Holy Spirit, angels and saints, and who pretend to be inspired, and to have received a commission from heaven to convert men." This disorder is in distinction to CACODEMONOMANIA, which involves the delusional belief of contact with "evil" forces.

Esquirol, J. E. D. *Mental Maladies: A Treatise on Insanity,* trans. E. K. Hunt. 1838. Reprint, Philadelphia: Lea and Blanchard, 1945.

therapeutic community See MILIEU THERAPY.

thioridazine See ANTIPSYCHOTIC DRUGS.

thiothixene See ANTIPSYCHOTIC DRUGS.

thioxanthenes See ANTIPSYCHOTIC DRUGS.

Thorazine The trade name for CHLORPROMAZINE. It is named after the Norse god of Thunder, Thor.

See also ANTIPSYCHOTIC DRUGS.

thought broadcasting A delusion common in schizophrenia in which the person believes or experiences his or her own internal thoughts as being broadcast from one's head as they are occurring so that others can hear them.

thought disorder See FORMAL THOUGHT DISORDER.

thought insertion Another common delusion found in persons in schizophrenia, it is the delusion that thoughts belonging to other persons or entities are being inserted into one's mind.

thought withdrawal One of the most common delusions found in schizophrenia, "thought withdrawal" is the belief that thoughts have been removed from one's head.

thrashing See FLOGGING.

Three Christs of Ypsilanti Social psychologist Milton Rokeach published his famous study of the impact that three paranoid schizophrenic men, who all believed they were Jesus Christ, had on one another when they were placed together in the same bedroom, same workplace, and same cafeteria table at Ypsilanti State Hospital in Michigan

from July 1959 to August 1961. The purpose was to record the changes in each of the men, who all claimed the same delusional identity. Although no one improved in any overall sense, two of the Christs modified their self-identities a bit to avoid conflict, whereas the third ended up becoming more firmly entrenched in his identity, even to the point of denying that the other two were alive (see COTARD'S SYNDROME). Rokeach concludes in the final sentence of his books: "And, finally, we have learned that even when a summit of three is composed of paranoid men, deadlocked over the ultimate in human contradiction, they prefer to seek ways to live with one another in peace rather than destroy one another."

Rokeach, M. *The Three Christs of Ypsilanti: A Psychological Study.* New York: Alfred A. Knopf, 1964.

thyroid disease masking as psychosis See MEDICAL DISORDERS THAT MIMIC PSYCHOTIC DISORDERS.

token economy See BEHAVIOR THERAPY.

topectomy A PSYCHOSURGERY procedure invented by J. Lawrence Pool, a research assistant in the Department of Neurology at Columbia University in 1947. The term is derived from two Greek words meaning "place" and "excision." An attempt to create a more conservative form of psychosurgery, topectomy involved destroying parts of the frontal cortex itself rather than severing the white fibers below (as in a LEUCOTOMY). It considerably reduced the chances of hemorrhaging and therefore the likelihood that a patient would become a zombie-like vegetable, as was the case in many psychosurgical patients of Walter FREEMAN. The topectomy was one of the forms of psychosurgery studied by the COLUMBIA-GREYSTONE PROJECT in 1947 and was performed on patients of the New Jersey State Hospital in Greystone Park.

Tory rot An 18th- and early 19th-century American psychotic disorder identified by Benjamin RUSH to refer to those "insane" persons who did not believe in the value of the American Revolution. Rush was convinced that these people were mentally ill and that they died from their insanity. It is not known if Rush involuntarily committed any of these people to the Pennsylvania Hospital in Philadelphia, which would have made them political prisoners.

Lloyd, J. H. "Benjamin Rush and His Critics," *Annals of Medical History* 2 (1930): 470–475.

toxin theory See AUTOINTOXICATION AS A CAUSE OF DEMENTIA PRAECOX (SCHIZOPHRENIA).

tranquillizer A form of MECHANICAL RESTRAINT invented by American physician Benjamin RUSH in 1808. Also called a "coercion chair," it was designed to restrain agitated or violent patients. The device was an instrument of torture in which a person would sit upright in a chair, arms shackled to the arms of the chair and feet clasped by the ankles in a device at the bottom of the chair; it had a wooden block that could be raised or lowered and would fit over the head of the person, making him or her completely immobile. In his 1812 treatise, Rush extols the virtues of the use of the "tranquillizer" for violent patients:

> Confinement by means of a strait waistcoat or of a chair which I have called a tranquillizer. He submits to them both with less difficulty than to human force, and struggles less to disengage himself from them. The tranquillizer has several advantages over the straight waistcoat or mad shirt. It opposes the impetus of blood towards the brain, it lessens muscular actions every where, it reduces the force and the frequency of the pulse, it favours the application of cold water and ice to the head, and warm water to the feet, both of which I shall say presently are excellent remedies in this disease; it enables the physician to feel the pulse and to bleed without any trouble, or altering the erect position of the patient's body; and, lastly, it relieves him, by means of a close stool, half filled with water, over which he con-

stantly sits, from the festor and filth of his alvine evacuations.

Since Rush's time, the word *tranquillizer* has been part of the slang of asylums and mental hospitals, referring to just about any method that quiets an agitated patient. It is thought that this is the source of our use of the word *tranquilizer* for sedative medications. A graphic reproduction of the famous illustration of Rush's device appears on the cover of the book cited below by Sander Gilman.

Gilman, S. L. *Seeing the Insane.* New York: Wiley, 1982.

Rush, B. *Medical Inquiries and Observations upon the Diseases of the Mind.* Philadelphia: Kimber & Richardson, 1812.

transcultural studies of schizophrenia See CROSS-CULTURAL STUDIES.

transmethylation hypothesis Based on studies of how hallucinogenic drugs, particularly LSD-25, worked on the brain to produce "psychotogenic" (psychosis-causing) effects, from at least 1957 to the mid-1970s the dominant theories of schizophrenia were based on various "inappropriate methylation" or transmethylation hypotheses. The term *transmethylation* was coined by the organic chemist John Harley-Mason of Cambridge University in England in 1951. The first publication advocating this hypothesis was published in 1952 in the *Journal of Mental Science* and coauthored by Humphrey Osmond (1917–2004) and John Smythies. They suggested that schizophrenia was caused by a toxic hallucinogenic substance, produced in the brain, through the faulty methylation of adrenaline. Throughout the 1950s Osmond was joined by Abram Hoffer (1917–) in this research at the mental hospital in Weyburn, Saskatchewan, Canada. Osmond coined the term *psychedelic* in 1957 for hallucinogenic drugs such as LSD-25 and mescaline, which he had personally introduced to the British author Aldous Huxley (1894–1963) in 1953. In 1959 Osmond and Hoffer revised their transmethylation theory, claiming the toxic substance was adrenochrome. Replication attempts by others could not find adrenochrome in the bodily fluids of persons with schizophrenia. However, Hoffer's suggestion that the production of adrenochrome could be blocked by administering high doses of niacin (vitamin B_3) led to the fad of MEGAVITAMIN THERAPY for schizophrenia and a new but marginal discipline known as orthomolecular psychiatry.

The assumption was that if the body of a person with schizophrenia was producing LSD-like or mescaline-like substances, then metabolites of these chemicals should be detectable in the blood or urine. For two decades schizophrenia researchers searched for enzymes that converted one biochemical molecule into another less-active substance or its detectable metabolite after breakdown. A prominent proponent of this line of research during this era of "metabolic psychiatry" was Seymour Kety (1915–2000), the head of the neuroscience laboratories at the National Institute of Mental Health.

No endogenous psychotogen or psychosis-causing metabolite was ever found in persons with schizophrenia. However, the basic research conducted within the framework of the transmethylation hypotheses led to many useful discoveries, including the metabolites of dopamine and serotonin, which had applications to other fields of research, such as psychopharmacology. By the late 1960s the focus of research had shifted from the search for toxic metabolites to instabilities of the methylation process itself. By the late 1970s, the TRANSMETHYLATION HYPOTHESIS had been replaced by a new one: the DOPAMINE HYPOTHESIS. Research into the various transmethylation hypotheses slowed to a trickle and had virtually disappeared by the 21st century. The last such publication in this tradition appeared in 1999, reporting the "experimental psychosis" induced by the ingestion of Ayahoasca, a South American hallucinogenic beverage prepared by boiling two plants found in the Amazon region.

See also BIOCHEMICAL STUDIES OF SCHIZOPHRENIA; METABOLIC DISORDER HYPOTHESIS.

Hoffer, A., and H. Osmond. "The Adrenochrome Model and Schizophrenia," *Journal of Nervous and Mental Disease* 123 (1959): 18–35.

Luchins, D., et al. "A Review of Nicotinic Acid, N-methylated Indoleamines and Schizophrenia," *International Pharmacopsychiatry* 13 (1978): 16–33.

Osmond, H., and J. R. Smythies. "Schizophrenia: A New Approach," *Journal of Mental Science* 98 (1952): 309–315.

Pomilio, A. B., et al. "Ayahoasca: An Experimental Psychosis That Mirrors the Transmethylation Hypothesis of Schizophrenia," *Journal of Ethnopharmacology* 65 (April 1999): 29–51.

transorbital lobotomy The famous "ice-pick technique" of PSYCHOSURGERY invented by psychiatrist Walter FREEMAN in 1946 as an alternative to the formal surgical procedures that involved the opening of the skull. Transorbital lobotomies avoided this by lodging an ice pick–type instrument behind the orbit of the eye and into the frontal lobes, where a few quick strokes could damage enough of the brain tissue to achieve the desired tranquilizing effect. Freeman first used this technique on outpatients in his Washington, D.C., office in 1946 against the advice of his associate, James Watts, who refused to cooperate with him. For these first patients Freeman did use an actual ice pick from his kitchen drawer at home, and this historic kitchen utensil is in the collection of the James W. Watts and Himmelfarb Health Sciences Library of George Washington University in Washington, D.C. The development of the transorbital lobotomy technique led to the mass brain damaging of thousands of institutionalized psychiatric patients in the 1940s and 1950s.

treatment-resistant schizophrenia Despite the many positive reports about the beneficial effects of treating people with schizophrenia with ANTIPSYCHOTIC DRUGS, there are still patients who are refractory to this form of therapy. Those who are not helped by antipsychotic drugs range in estimates from 20 to 33 percent of schizophrenics. These estimates do not include the 15 percent or so of schizophrenic patients who improve with just placebo treatment in double-blind studies of antipsychotic drugs.

Research on persons who develop treatment-resistant schizophrenia have found the following characteristics:

(1) there is no clear relationship between initial symptoms, positive or negative, and outcome (a fact that rejects the claims of CROW'S HYPOTHESIS regarding Type II schizophrenia)
(2) poor premorbid functioning
(3) early age of onset of illness
(4) male gender
(5) presence of neurological "soft signs" in males
(6) early cognitive impairment

The duration of time during which the illness was left untreated has no apparent relationship to being treatment-resistant. Research on the new atypical ANTIPSYCHOTIC DRUGS indicates many of them may be as useful as clozapine as a form of maintenance therapy. All in all, the reasons why so many persons with schizophrenia simply do not respond to current medication remain a mystery.

Barnes, T. R. E., P. Buckley, and S. C. Schulz. "Treatment-resistant Schizophrenia." In *Schizophrenia. 2nd ed.*, edited by S. R. Hirsch and D. Weinberger. Cambridge: Blackwell, 2003.

trepanation (or trephination) Perhaps the earliest form of PSYCHOSURGERY for epilepsy and mental disorders, this technique involved the removal of a (usually) circular piece of the skull for the purposes of surgical treatment of the brain. Trephined skulls dating from Neolithic times have been found in Europe and among the ruins of the great civilizations of the world, including the ancient Incas. During the Middle Ages trepanning continued as a treatment and was done by using carpenters' drills. Sir William Osler (1848–1919) writes in a 1921 book, *The Evolution of Modern Medicine,* that "the operation was done for epilepsy, infantile convulsions, headache and various cerebral disease believed caused by confined demons, to whom the hole gave a ready method of escape."

Horrax, G. *Neurosurgery—An Historical Sketch.* Springfield, Ill.: Charles C. Thomas, 1952.

trichtillomania An infrequently observed but not uncommon behavior observed in people with psychotic disorders (and with other types of mental disorders) is the compulsive pulling out of one's

hair, resulting in bald patches on the scalp or on other parts of the body. In *DSM-III-R* trichtillomania is included among the impulse control disorders. Trichtillomania was first described by the French physician Hallopeau in 1889. Most studies of trichtillomania have concluded that it is (1) a chronic disorder that (2) frequently involves multiple hair sites, and (3) that is highly correlated with the presence of another mental disorder (for example, major depression, the mental disorder with which trichtillomania is most closely correlated).

Christenson, G. A., et al. "Characteristics of 60 Adult Chronic Hair Pullers," *American Journal of Psychiatry* 148 (1991): 365–370.

Hallopeau, M. "Alopcie par grattage (trichomanie ou trichtillomanie)," *Annales Dermatol. Venerol.* 10 (1889): 440–441.

trifluoperazine See ANTIPSYCHOTIC DRUGS.

Trilafon See ANTIPSYCHOTIC DRUGS.

tuberculosis and psychosis The idea has often been put forth that certain diseases are incompatible and cannot be found in the same person. This was the untested hypothesis behind the CONVULSIVE THERAPY idea in the 20th century that epilepsy and schizophrenia could not be found together in the same person. In the 18th and 19th centuries, it was believed that those persons who developed pulmonary tuberculosis were not likely to develop a psychotic disorder. No scientific support for this theory has ever been put forth.

However, in the 1930s the opposite hypothesis was put forth: namely, that tuberculosis might be the cause of certain mental diseases, including schizophrenia. In 1933 Austrian researcher E. Löwenstein published a paper describing a new and more sensitive technique for the detection of Koch's bacillus (the cause of tuberculosis) and suggested that he could establish a diagnosis of tuberculosis in cases that may not, on first appearance, look like tuberculosis. Included among these were some mental disorders, including schizophrenia. For a few years following this announcement, the hypothesis was discussed that schizophrenia and tuberculosis may be related after all, but no confirming evidence was ever put forth.

See also PHYSICAL DISEASE; SCHIZOPHRENIA.

Hunter, R. A., and J. G. Widdicombe. "Tuberculosis and Insanity: Historical and Experimental Observations on the Straight-waistcoat as Collapse Therapy," *St. Bart's Hospital Journal* 61 (1957): 113–119.

Löwenstein, E. "Über Tuberkelbasillämie bei Nervenkrankheiten," *Wein. Klin. Wchschr.* 46 (1933): 228–231.

twins method and studies Studying pairs of twins in which one or both members have schizophrenia or bipolar disorder has been an important area in GENETICS STUDIES of these psychotic disorders. Indeed, they have been so fruitful that NIMH genetics researcher David Rosenthal has concluded that "the twins studies probably have contributed our most reliable data regarding the inheritance of schizophrenia."

Twins studies compare the CONCORDANCE RATE for schizophrenia in pairs of MONOZYGOTIC ("identical") TWINS with the rate found in DIZYGOTIC ("fraternal") TWINS. In fact, it was Rosenthal himself who pioneered the scientific study of schizophrenic twins for their possible information regarding genetic transmission, publishing the first study using the strategy of comparing the concordance rate of monozygotic twins in 1962. In some later studies, the rate in first-degree biological relatives is also compared.

There are two major assumptions behind the twins studies: (a) that monozygotic twins share all the same genes, whereas dizygotic twins only have about half of their genes in common, and (b) that both varieties of twin pairs are exposed to the same prenatal and postnatal environmental influences. Therefore, given these two assumptions, it would be expected that monozygotic twins would show a greater concordance for genetically transmitted diseases of all types than dizygotic twins—which is, indeed, the case.

According to a review of genetics studies of schizophrenia by K. S. Kendler in 1986, the twins studies of schizophrenia have fairly consistently

reported a three-times greater risk for developing schizophrenia in the monozygotic twins of persons with schizophrenia than in the dizygotic twins of afflicted persons. Furthermore, the risk for developing schizophrenia is 40 percent to 60 percent greater in these monozygotic twins than in the general population. Other studies have demonstrated that monozygotic twins reared apart from each other are concordant for schizophrenia (that is, both twins have it) at about the same rate as those who are raised together, thus strongly confirming the role of genetics over the environment. Still, there are monozygotic twins who are discordant for schizophrenia, and future research must determine why this is so if schizophrenia is a genetically transmitted disease.

For bipolar disorder, twins studies also point to a strong genetic component for the transmission of the illness. A famous Danish twins study of manic-depressive disorders published in 1977 found that there was a 79 percent concordance rate for bipolar illness in the monozygotic twins of persons diagnosed with this disorder, in contrast to a concordance rate of only 19 percent in the dizygotic twins of persons diagnosed with bipolar disorder. Reanalysis of the Danish data by others found these rates to be too high. Other studies of bipolar disorder find the rates for MZ twins to be closer to 44 percent.

One of the most intriguing studies using the twins method was conducted by E. Fuller Torrey and his colleagues. Finding large numbers of pairs of twins that were discordant (one twin had the disease, the other didn't) for schizophrenia or bipolar disease, Torrey and his colleagues conducted a series of neuropsychological, neurophysiological, genetic, and neuroimaging studies to answer the age-old question: "Why is one twin sick and the other one isn't if X is a genetic disease?" Although they did not find the answer to this question, the data they collected will be a valuable contribution to solving that riddle in the 21st century.

See also GENETICS STUDIES.

Bertelsen, A., et al. "A Danish Twin Study of Manic-Depressive Disorders," *British Journal of Psychiatry* 130 (1997): 330–351.

Kendler, K. S. "Genetics of Schizophrenia." In *Psychiatry Update: American Psychiatric Association Annual Review.* Vol. 5, edited by A. J. Frances and R. J. Hales. Washington, D.C.: American Psychiatric Press, 1986.

Rosenthal, D. "Problems of Sampling and Diagnosis in the Major Twin Studies of Schizophrenia," *Journal of Psychiatric Research* 1 (1962): 116–134.

Torrey, E. F., A. E. Bowler, E. H. Taylor, and I. I. Gottesman. *Schizophrenia and Manic-Depressive Disorder: The Biological Roots of Mental Illness as Revealed by the Landmark Study of Identical Twins.* New York: Basic Books, 1994.

two-syndrome concept of schizophrenia See CROW'S HYPOTHESIS.

Type I/Type II schizophrenia See CROW'S HYPOTHESIS.

U

undifferentiated type This is one of the four subtypes of schizophrenia currently recognized by *DSM-IV* (1994), and it is probably the most common diagnosis given to people with schizophrenia (with the paranoid subtype close behind). The essential features of this subtype are prominent psychotic features such as delusions, hallucinations, formal thought disorder, incoherence, or grossly disorganized behavior, but it may combine features of two or more of the other subtypes, or features that simply cannot fit into the diagnostic descriptions of the other subtypes. Hence, "undifferentiated type" is a garbage pail diagnosis.

unitary psychosis See *EINHEITSPSYCHOSE*.

United States Worldwide prevalence rates for schizophrenia have been found to range from less than 1 to 17 per 1,000 persons. However, most studies conducted worldwide—including those in the United States—fall within the 2 to 5 per 1,000 range. In the United States, specific prevalence rates from research studies have ranged from 1.1 (among the rural Hutterites, a closed religious community) to 4.7 (if age corrected, from 2.1 to 6.4) per 1,000. The highest rates of schizophrenia are found in the urban areas and among the lowest socioeconomic strata of American society. E. Fuller Torrey has suggested that preliminary evidence shows that the prevalence rate for schizophrenia in the United States may have risen since 1950 and recommends that more comprehensive research be carried out to investigate this possibility.

Torrey, E. F. "Prevalence Studies of Schizophrenia," *British Journal of Psychiatry* 150 (1987): 598–608.

"usual treatment, the" Philippe Pinel's phrase that he used several times in his 1801 book, *A Treatise on Insanity,* to describe the treatment of institutionalized persons with mental disorders in the 18th and early 19th centuries—namely, "bleeding, bathing and purging."

Utica crib A form of mechanical restraint originally developed in France by a physician named Aubanel in 1845 but first used in the United States at the Utica State Hospital in New York State upon the recommendation of its superintendent, Amariah Brigham, one of the original 13 founders of the AMERICAN PSYCHIATRIC ASSOCIATION. It was a crib bed but with a hinged lid that could be locked, keeping the patient confined in a horizontal position.

V

V.A. hospitals Hospitals in the United States for veterans of military service. They are managed under the auspices of the Veterans Administration, and their psychiatric wards serve as an adjunct to the state hospital system for the mentally ill.

vampirism, clinical Although it is quite rare, there have been actual case reports of people with psychotic disorders engaging in clinical vampirism—that is, the ingestion of blood, whether one's own or the blood of others. Clinical vampirism is actually a "blood fetish" that often develops in childhood, when the child finds the taste of his own blood enjoyable. Then, after puberty, these pleasurable feelings become associated with sexual activities, usually masturbation. The typical course starts with autovampirism, causing bleeding from one's own body through simple cuts or scrapes, to then opening major blood vessels to drink one's own blood. In some people, the fetish graduates to true clinical vampirism—the desire to drink the blood of others. Psychologist Richard Noll has suggested this delusional syndrome be named RENFIELD'S SYNDROME, after the character in Bram Stoker's *Dracula*. People with schizophrenia have been reported to have engaged in clinical vampirism, but this is an extremely rare occurrence.

Benezech, M., et al. "Cannibalism and Vampirism in Paranoid Schizophrenia," *Journal of Clinical Psychiatry* 42 (1981): 7.

Noll, R. *Vampires, Werewolves and Demons: Twentieth Century Case Reports in the Psychiatric Literature*. New York: Brunner/Mazel, 1991.

Prins, H. "Vampirism—A Clinical Condition," *British Journal of Psychiatry* 146 (1985): 666–668.

variable expressivity In GENETICS STUDIES, if the same genetically transmitted abnormality produces different manifestations for either genetic or nongenetic reasons, it is said that this abnormality is characterized by variable expressivity. For example, the finding in schizophrenia research that smooth-pursuit eye movement abnormalities have been found in 60 percent of persons with schizophrenia and in 55 percent of their first-degree biological relatives might be an example of variable expressivity, because in many instances there are persons with schizophrenia who do not have abnormal smooth-pursuit eye movement but their nonschizophrenic relatives do (see EYE MOVEMENT ABNORMALITIES IN SCHIZOPHRENIA). All this may really mean is that an underlying process (or "latent trait," perhaps) may induce a disorder in the brain that produces either schizophrenia, smooth-pursuit eye movement abnormalities, or both. These three possibilities illustrate the variable expressivity of this underlying process or trait.

Holzman, P. S. "Eye Movement Dysfunction and Psychosis," *International Review of Neurobiology* 27 (1985): 179–205.

vascular-inflammatory theory of schizophrenia See BLOOD VESSEL ALTERATIONS IN SCHIZOPHRENIA.

ventriculomegaly Literally, "enlarged ventricles," a common characteristic of some persons with schizophrenia. Ventricle size in the majority of schizophrenics is within the normal range.

See also BRAIN ABNORMALITIES IN SCHIZOPHRENIA.

verbigeration A term for the repetitious, meaningless speech of persons with psychotic disorders. It was first introduced by German psychiatrist Karl KAHLBAUM in 1874. In the English translation of the fourth edition of Eugen BLEULER's famous textbook on psychiatry, he defines this psychotic behavior in the following way: "The stereotype of speech, or *verbigeration,* always repeats the same words or sentences, often entirely senseless ones."

violence and schizophrenia Contrary to the popular negative stereotype of the mentally ill as "psycho killers," it is probably not true that persons with schizophrenia are more violent toward others than those persons who do not have this disease. It is true that those persons with schizophrenia that do tend to be violent toward others are of the paranoid subtype or have transient paranoid delusions, are undermedicated or have ingested street drugs of some sort. It is also true that persons with schizophrenia have a higher rate of crimes against property than persons in the general population. In addition, persons with schizophrenia have higher rates of violence against themselves in the form of suicide when compared with the general population, and perhaps even for acts of self-mutilation, although there are no statistics for this latter observation. Although a prior history of violence is the best predictor of future violence in individual cases, it is still next to impossible for clinicians to accurately predict future acts of "dangerousness" or of violence.

McNiel, D. E., and R. L. Binder. "Predictive Validity of Judgments of Dangerous in Emergency Civil Commitment," *American Journal of Psychiatry* 144 (1987): 197–200.

Rada, R. T. "The Violent Patient: Rapid Assessment and Management," *Psychosomatics* 22 (1981): 101–109.

Weaver, K. E. "Increasing the Dose of Antipsychotic Medication to Control Violence," *American Journal of Psychiatry* 140 (1983): 1,274.

Yesavage, J. A. "Inpatient Violence and the Schizophrenic Patient: An Inverse Correlation between Danger-Related Events and Neuroleptic Levels," *Biological Psychiatry* 17 (1982): 1,331–1,337.

viral theories of schizophrenia Since the turn of the century, it has often been suggested that infectious agents might be the cause of schizophrenia. Both Emil KRAEPELIN and Eugen BLEULER commented on the fact that infectious processes might play a role in the development of schizophrenia. When it was discovered conclusively at around that time that the syndrome known as the GENERAL PARALYSIS OF THE INSANE was caused by tertiary syphilis, similar infectious agents were sought for dementia praecox (schizophrenia). Most of the research centered on bacteria (see FOCAL INFECTION AS CAUSE OF PSYCHOTIC DISORDERS and TUBERCULOSIS AND PSYCHOSIS), since viruses were not well understood at the time.

After the First World War, worldwide outbreaks of influenza and Von Economo's encephalitis drew attention once again to this hypothesis, since post-encephalitic patients seem to have the same signs and symptoms of schizophrenia. However, after the 1920s, the rise of psychoanalytic, psychosocial, and family interaction theories of the causes of schizophrenia drew attention away from possible organic causes, such as viruses. It wasn't until the 1950s that interest once again briefly revived, only to subside until the 1970s, when research on the role of infectious agents in the development of many physical diseases began to uncover some promising results.

E. Fuller Torrey is responsible for drawing attention once again to the viral hypothesis of schizophrenia, after he became aware of some research that demonstrated that "slow" or latent viruses could cause central nervous system diseases after remaining latent in the body for perhaps 20 years or more. Such research continues into the possible viral causes of multiple sclerosis and many other diseases of the central nervous system. Torrey began research at the National Institute of Mental Health in the early 1970s by collecting the blood and cerebral spinal fluid (CSF) from persons with schizophrenia and then analyzing these fluids to detect evidence of a viral presence. His first publication on this viral hypothesis appeared in 1973.

Although other infectious agents such as bacteria, rickettsiae, and fungi cannot be ruled out, viruses are prime suspects in schizophrenia for

several reasons: (1) their frequent neurotropism, that is, their affinity for neural tissue, (2) their ability to remain latent in brain tissue for many years, perhaps even decades, (3) they can attack very specific areas of the brain (often the limbic system, which is implicated in schizophrenia) and leave others untouched, (4) their propensity to produce relapses and remissions, and (5) their ability to alter the enzymatic functions of brain cells without causing visible structural damage to the cells that could be picked up, for example, by BRAIN IMAGING TECHNIQUES or neuropathological methods. They have even been found to cause changes in the neurotransmitters of the brain, perhaps even producing the biochemical changes that produce the symptoms of schizophrenia.

There are several viral models as possible causes of schizophrenia. Some of them are based on the idea that an *in utero* infection of the fetus may affect fetal neural development and therefore result in schizophrenia later in life. This theory fits in with the research on perinatal factors as contributing causes to schizophrenia. Other theories propose that the mother or even the father may be an asymptomatic carrier that transmits the virus across the placenta during pregnancy. The SEASONALITY OF BIRTHS of persons who develop schizophrenia also fits well with a viral theory, since many viral infections are seasonal, and the excess of schizophrenic births in late winter to spring may be a reflection of prenatal infection. The fact that schizophrenia runs in families may be attributed to viral theories as well, since persons may be inheriting a genetic predisposition to being affected by a particular virus, or the virus may actually be transmitted on the gene itself (as is the case in retroviruses).

However, despite the logic of viral theories of schizophrenia, the research has not been very fruitful. In 1988 E. Fuller Torrey concluded in his review of the issue: "Despite the theoretical attractiveness of infectious agents as etiologic models, there is as yet little direct evidence with which to link them to schizophrenia. This may be because laboratory technology is not yet sensitive enough, we have not yet looked for the correct infectious agent, or the infectious hypothesis is simply wrong. In addition, adoption studies suggest that if infectious agents are involved in such cases, transmission of the agent must occur in utero or at birth."

Throughout the 1990s the search for a virus that may be related to schizophrenia continued to fail. Using the long latency period of the human immunodeficiency virus (HIV) as a model (since it takes so many years for symptoms to appear in infected persons), schizophrenia researchers used the new tools of genetics research to find evidence of the presence of a retrovirus in persons with schizophrenia. In one major study, DNA and RNA was extracted from the brain tissue of deceased persons with schizophrenia and also from controls. The new PCR (polymerase chain reaction) procedure was used because it can allow for the detection of small amount of genetic material from viruses present in the blood, urine, or tissue of humans. The researchers used PCR with primers from 12 different viruses, some of them retroviruses, all of them speculated to be involved in schizophrenia at one time or another. Absolutely no trace of any genes from any of these viruses were found. The search for the "schizovirus" continues.

See also CATS AND SCHIZOPHRENIA.

Taller, A. M., et al. "Search for Viral Nucleic Acid Sequences in Brain Tissues of Patients with Schizophrenia Using Nested Polymerase Chain Reaction," *Archives of General Psychiatry* 53 (1996): 32–40.

Torrey, E. F. "Stalking the Schizovirus," *Schizophrenia Bulletin*, 14 (1988): 223–229.

Torrey, E. F., and M. R. Peterson. "Slow and Latent Viruses in Schizophrenia," *Lancet* 2 (1973): 22–24.

visual hallucinations Hallucinations of sight. These may include formed images (such as people or alligators) or unformed images (such as flashes of light). Visual hallucinations have often been attributed to an organic cause, such as the presence of drugs in the person's system, or perhaps a metabolic disorder or an infection. In schizophrenia, auditory hallucinations have been the most commonly reported type. However, a 1989 study found that visual hallucinations may occur in 32 percent to 56 percent of persons with schizophrenia at some point in their illness, and that they are usually associated with auditory hallucinations,

delusions, and thought disorder. They found that visual hallucinations were slightly more prevalent in the nonparanoid forms of schizophrenia than in the paranoid forms but that this difference was not statistically significant in the study. They suggest that most clinicians do not ask about visual hallucinations (the most common interview question is often, "Do you hear voices?"), and that probably accounts for why they are so infrequently discussed in the literature of schizophrenia.

Bracha, H. S., et al. "High Prevalence of Visual Hallucinations in Research Subjects with Chronic Schizophrenia," *American Journal of Psychiatry* 146 (1989): 526–528.

vorbeireden See GANSER'S SYNDROME.

vulnerability model of schizophrenia What do all the various theories of schizophrenia (genetic, environmental, developmental, learning, neurophysiological) have in common? Can they be unified in some way? These were the questions asked by researchers Joseph Zubin and Bonnie Spring, who propose in a 1977 paper that the concept of vulnerability is the common link between all these theories. They write: "The vulnerability model proposes that each of us is endowed with a degree of vulnerability that under suitable circumstances will express itself in an episode of schizophrenia illness." However, the researchers "distinguish between *vulnerability* to schizophrenia, which we regard as a relatively permanent, enduring trait, and *episodes* of schizophrenic disorder, which are waxing and waning states." Thus, they suggest that both vulnerability and episodic "markers" (biological, genetic, environmental) must be found. Since the publication of this article, the concept of vulnerability in this wider, more general sense is often referred to in the literature of schizophrenia.

Zubin, J., and B. Spring. "Vulnerability—A New View of Schizophrenia," *Journal of Abnormal Psychology* 86 (1977): 103–126.

W

water drinking, excessive, in persons with schizophrenia See POLYDIPSIA.

water therapy See HYDROTHERAPY.

wet sheets See PACKING (AS TREATMENT).

whipping See FLOGGING.

Williamsburg Eastern Lunatic Asylum The first official asylum for the mentally ill to be founded in the United States. It was established in Williamsburg, Virginia, in 1773, and was open to all levels of society except slaves.

witchcraft It has often been reported, especially in psychiatric textbooks, that the most prevalent theory of the causes of mental illness (and particularly the psychotic disorders) was a supernatural one based on "demons" or malevolent "spirits." Furthermore, it has often been reported that most of those people who died during the Great Witch Hunt in Europe, between about 1500 and 1650, were mentally ill. However, research by psychologist Thomas Schoeneman has demonstrated that these assertions, despite wide report in psychiatric textbooks, are untrue and that the evidence shows that most of the people who were executed for witchcraft were poor women with a sharp tongue and a bad temper, or old and unmarried—or that, in some areas, just about anyone was suspect.

Schoeneman, T. J. "The Mentally Ill Witch in Textbooks of Abnormal Psychology: Current Status and Implications of a Fallacy," *Professional Psychology: Research and Practice* 15 (1984): 299–314.

withdrawal, social This is one of the most commonly reported signs of schizophrenia and is present long before the definite outbreak of a psychosis in many persons. Social withdrawal is therefore part of the PRODROMAL PHASE of schizophrenia and can later develop into one of the chronic NEGATIVE SYMPTOMS of this disorder. Such persons may shun contact with others, for example, or be unable to interact or make eye contact when in the presence of others.

word salad A very descriptive term for an abnormality of language that can be found in some persons with schizophrenia or with certain types of aphasias. A person speaking word salad just seems to toss out words without regard to their meaning, making unusual and meaningless combinations and perhaps even creating NEOLOGISMS.

work (as therapy) See FARMING (AS TREATMENT); OCCUPATIONAL THERAPY.

World Health Organization One of the semi-autonomous organizations created by the United Nations, the World Health Organization (WHO) has been instrumental in sponsoring epidemiological and CROSS-CULTURAL STUDIES of schizophrenia and other mental disorders.

World Psychiatric Association An international association made up of national associations of psychiatrists from various countries. It was founded in 1961.

Y, Z

York Retreat The famous humane institution for the insane founded in 1792 by the Religious Society of Friends in York, England. Founded by William Tuke (1732–1822), it helped to put into practice the MORAL TREATMENT of the institutionalized mentally ill in England, as was shortly thereafter the case in Philippe PINEL's France and Vincenzo CHIARUGI's Italy. The emphasis was on occupational therapy and good food and sanitary conditions, with MECHANICAL RESTRAINTS used rarely, if at all. William Tuke's grandson, Samuel Tuke (1784–1857), wrote a glowing description of the treatment of the mentally ill at the Retreat, and after its publication in 1813 it helped influence Parliament to investigate conditions in British asylums.

Daniel Hack Tuke (1827–95), one of the leading psychiatrists in England in the 19th century, was the son of Samuel and the grandson of William Tuke.

Tuke, S. *Description of the Retreat.* London: 1813.

young adult chronic patient With the ever-increasing problem of patients presenting with the dual diagnosis of a traditional psychotic disorder (schizophrenia, bipolar disorder, schizoaffective disorder) and a history of substance abuse since the 1960s, more and more young persons who are nonetheless following a chronic course of illness have made up a large percentage of the admissions to psychiatric facilities. This person has been labeled by psychiatrist Bert Pepper as the "young adult chronic patient." A young adult chronic patient is defined as one who is between 18 and 35 years old, abuses alcohol and drugs, is sexually active, has unpredictable and sometimes violent behavior, has frequent suicidal thoughts, often has children with whom there is little or no relationship, often has been arrested, cannot seem to hold down a job, and is attention-seeking but also tends to reject treatment.

See also SUBSTANCE ABUSE.

Pepper, B. "The Young Adult Chronic Patient: Population Overview," *Journal of Clinical Psychopharmacology* 5 (1985): 3S to 7S.

ziprasidone See ANTIPSYCHOTIC DRUGS.

Zyprexa See ANTIPSYCHOTIC DRUGS.

APPENDIXES

APPENDIX I

NORTH AMERICAN DIAGNOSTIC CRITERIA FOR SCHIZOPHRENIA

DSM-IV-TR (2000)

Source: American Psychiatric Association. *Diagnostic and Statistical Manual of Mental Disorders, Fourth Edition Text Revision.* Washington, D.C.: American Psychiatric Press, 2000.

DIAGNOSTIC CRITERIA

A. *Characteristic symptoms:* Two (or more) of the following, each present for a significant portion of time during a 1-month period (or less if successfully treated):

1. delusions
2. hallucinations
3. disorganized speech (e.g., frequent derailment or incoherence)
4. grossly disorganized or catatonic behavior
5. negative symptoms, i.e., affective flattening, alogia, or avolition

Note: Only one Criterion A symptom is required if delusions are bizarre or hallucinations consist of a voice keeping up a running commentary on the person's behavior or thoughts, or two or more voices conversing with each other.

B. *Social/occupational dysfunction:* For a significant portion of the time since the onset of the disturbance, one or more major areas of functioning such as work, interpersonal relations, or self-care are markedly below the level achieved prior to the onset (or when the onset is in childhood or adolescence, failure to achieve expected level of interpersonal, academic, or occupational achievement).

C. *Duration:* Continuous signs of the disturbance persist for at least 6 months. This 6-month period must include at least 1 month of symptoms (or less if successfully treated) that meet Criterion A (i.e., active-phase symptoms) and may include periods of prodromal or residual symptoms. During these prodromal or residual periods, the signs of the disturbance may be manifested by only negative symptoms or two or more symptoms listed in Criterion A present in an attenuated form (e.g., odd beliefs, unusual perceptual experiences).

D. *Schizoaffective and mood disorder exclusion:* Schizoaffective Disorder and Mood Disorder With Psychotic Features have been ruled out because either (1) no Major Depressive, Manic, or Mixed Episodes have occurred concurrently with the active-phase symptoms; or (2) if mood episodes have occurred during active-phase symptoms, their total duration has been brief relative to the duration of the active and residual periods.

E. *Substance/general medical condition exclusion:* The disturbance is not due to the direct physiological effects of a substance (e.g., a drug of abuse, a medication) or a general medical condition.

F. *Relationship to a pervasive developmental disorder:* If there is a history of Autistic Disorder or another Pervasive Developmental Disorder, the additional diagnosis of Schizophrenia is made only

if prominent delusions or hallucinations are also present for at least a month (or less if successfully treated).

PARANOID TYPE

A type of Schizophrenia in which the following criteria are met:

A. Preoccupation with one or more delusions or frequent auditory hallucinations.
B. None of the following is prominent: disorganized speech, disorganized or catatonic behavior, or flat or inappropriate affect.

CATATONIC TYPE

A type of Schizophrenia in which the clinical picture is dominated by at least two of the following:

1. motoric immobility as evidenced by catalepsy (including waxy flexibility) or stupor
2. excessive motor activity (that is apparently purposeless and not influenced by external stimuli)
3. extreme negativism (an apparently motiveless resistance to all instructions or maintenance of a rigid posture against attempts to be moved) or mutism
4. peculiarities of voluntary movement as evidenced by posturing (voluntary assumption of inappropriate or bizarre postures), stereotyped movements, prominent mannerisms, or prominent grimacing
5. echolalia or echopraxia

DISORGANIZED TYPE

A type of Schizophrenia in which the following criteria are met:

A. All of the following are prominent:
   1. disorganized speech
   2. disorganized behavior
   3. flat or inappropriate affect
B. The criteria are not met for Catatonic Type.

UNDIFFERENTIATED TYPE

A type of Schizophrenia in which symptoms that meet Criterion A are present, but the criteria are not met for the Paranoid, Disorganized, or Catatonic Type.

RESIDUAL TYPE

A type of Schizophrenia in which the following criteria are met:

A Absence of prominent delusions, hallucinations, disorganized speech, and grossly disorganized or catatonic behavior.
B. There is continuing evidence of the disturbance, as indicated by the presence of negative symptoms or two or more symptoms listed in criterion A for Schizophrenia, present in an attenuated form (e.g., odd beliefs, unusual perceptual experiences).

APPENDIX II

EUROPEAN DIAGNOSTIC CRITERIA FOR SCHIZOPHRENIA

ICD-10

Source: World Health Organization. *International Classification of Diseases, Tenth Edition (ICD-10).* Geneva: WHO, 1992.

F20 SCHIZOPHRENIA

The schizophrenic disorders are characterized in general by fundamental and characteristic distortions of thinking and perception, and by inappropriate or blunted affect. Clear consciousness and intellectual capacity are usually maintained, although certain cognitive deficits may evolve in the course of time. The disturbance involves the most basic functions that give the normal person a feeling of individuality, uniqueness, and self-direction. The most intimate thoughts, feelings, and acts are often felt to be known to or shared by others, and explanatory delusions may develop, to the effect that natural or supernatural forces are at work to influence the afflicted individual's thoughts and actions in ways that are often bizarre. The individual may see himself or herself as the pivot of all that happens. Hallucinations, especially auditory, are common and may comment on the individual's behaviour or thoughts. Perception is frequently disturbed in other ways: colours or sounds may seem unduly vivid or altered in quality, and irrelevant features of ordinary things may appear more important than the whole object or situation. Perplexity is also common early on and frequently leads to a belief that everyday situations possess a special, usually sinister, meaning intended uniquely for the individual. In the characteristic schizophrenic disturbance of thinking, peripheral and irrelevant features of a total concept, which are inhibited in normal directed mental activity, are brought to the fore and utilized in place of those that are relevant and appropriate to the situation. Thus thinking becomes vague, elliptical, and obscure, and its expression in speech sometimes incomprehensible. Breaks and interpolations in the train of thought are frequent, and thoughts may seem to be withdrawn by some outside agency. Mood is characteristically shallow, capricious, or incongruous. Ambivalence and disturbance of volition may appear as inertia, negativism, or stupor. Catatonia may be present. The onset may be acute, with seriously disturbed behaviour, or insidious, with a gradual development of odd ideas and conduct. The course of the disorder shows equally great variation and is by no means inevitably chronic or deteriorating (the course is specified by five-character categories). In a proportion of cases, which may vary in different cultures and populations, the outcome is complete, or nearly complete, recovery. The sexes are approximately equally affected but the onset tends to be later in women.

Although no strictly pathognomonic symptoms can be identified, for practical purposes it is useful to divide the above symptoms into groups that have special importance for the diagnosis and often occur together, such as:

(a) thought echo, thought insertion or withdrawal, and thought broadcasting;
(b) delusions of control, influence, or passivity, clearly referred to body or limb movements or specific thoughts, actions, or sensations; delusional perception;
(c) hallucinatory voices giving a running commentary on the patient's behaviour, or discussing the patient among themselves, or other types of hallucinatory voices coming from some part of the body;
(d) persistent delusions of other kinds that are culturally inappropriate and completely impossible, such as religious or political identity, or superhuman powers and abilities (e.g. being able to control the weather, or being in communication with aliens from another world);
(e) persistent hallucinations in any modality, when accompanied either by fleeting or half-formed delusions without clear affective content, or by persistent over-valued ideas, or when occurring every day for weeks or months on end;
(f) breaks or interpolations in the train of thought, resulting in incoherence or irrelevant speech, or neologisms;
(g) catatonic behaviour, such as excitement, posturing, or waxy flexibility, negativism, mutism, and stupor;
(h) "negative" symptoms such as marked apathy, paucity of speech, and blunting or incongruity of emotional responses, usually resulting in social withdrawal and lowering of social performance; it must be clear that these are not due to depression or to neuroleptic medication;
(i) a significant and consistent change in the overall quality of some aspects of personal behaviour, manifest as loss of interest, aimlessness, idleness, a self-absorbed attitude, and social withdrawal.

DIAGNOSTIC GUIDELINES

The normal requirement for a diagnosis of schizophrenia is that a minimum of one very clear symptom (and usually two or more if less clear-cut) belonging to any one of the groups listed as (a) to (d) above, or symptoms from at least two of the groups referred to as (e) to (h), should have been clearly present for most of the time during a period of 1 month or more. Conditions meeting such symptomatic requirements but of duration less than 1 month (whether treated or not) should be diagnosed in the first instance as acute schizophrenia-like psychotic disorder and are classified as schizophrenia if the symptoms persist for longer periods.

Viewed retrospectively, it may be clear that a prodromal phase in which symptoms and behaviour, such as loss of interest in work, social activities, and personal appearance and hygiene, together with generalized anxiety and mild degrees of depression and preoccupation, preceded the onset of psychotic symptoms by weeks or even months. Because of the difficulty in timing onset, the 1-month duration criterion applies only to the specific symptoms listed above and not to any prodromal nonpsychotic phase.

The diagnosis of schizophrenia should not be made in the presence of extensive depressive or manic symptoms unless it is clear that schizophrenic symptoms antedated the affective disturbance. If both schizophrenic and affective symptoms develop together and are evenly balanced, the diagnosis of schizoaffective disorder should be made, even if the schizophrenic symptoms by themselves would have justified the diagnosis of schizophrenia. Schizophrenia should not be diagnosed in the presence of overt brain disease or during states of drug intoxication or withdrawal.

F20.0 PARANOID SCHIZOPHRENIA

This is the commonest type of schizophrenia in most parts of the world. The clinical picture is dominated by relatively stable, often paranoid, delusions, usually accompanied by hallucinations, particularly of the auditory variety, and perceptual disturbances. Disturbances of affect, volition, and speech, and catatonic symptoms, are not prominent.

Examples of the most common paranoid symptoms are:

(a) delusions of persecution, reference, exalted birth, special mission, bodily change, or jealousy;
(b) hallucinatory voices that threaten the patient or give commands, or auditory hallucinations

without verbal form, such as whistling, humming, or laughing;

(c) hallucinations of smell or taste, or of sexual or other bodily sensations; visual hallucinations may occur but are rarely predominant.

Thought disorder may be obvious in acute states, but if so it does not prevent the typical delusions or hallucinations from being described clearly. Affect is usually less blunted than in other varieties of schizophrenia, but a minor degree of incongruity is common, as are mood disturbances such as irritability, sudden anger, fearfulness, and suspicion. "Negative" symptoms such as blunting of affect and impaired volition are often present but do not dominate the clinical picture.

The course of paranoid schizophrenia may be episodic, with partial or complete remissions, or chronic. In chronic cases, the florid symptoms persist over years and it is difficult to distinguish discrete episodes. The onset tends to be later than in the hebephrenic and catatonic forms.

DIAGNOSTIC GUIDELINES

The general criteria for a diagnosis of schizophrenia (see introduction to F20 above) must be satisfied. In addition, hallucinations and/or delusions must be prominent, and disturbances of affect, volition and speech, and catatonic symptoms must be relatively inconspicuous. The hallucinations will usually be of the kind described in (b) and (c) above. Delusions can be of almost any kind of delusions of control, influence, or passivity, and persecutory beliefs of various kinds are the most characteristic.

Includes:

- paraphrenic schizophrenia

Differential diagnosis It is important to exclude epileptic and drug-induced psychoses, and to remember that persecutory delusions might carry little diagnostic weight in people from certain countries or cultures.

Excludes:

- involutional paranoid state (F22.8)
- paranoia (F22.0)

F20.1 HEBEPHRENIC SCHIZOPHRENIA

A form of schizophrenia in which affective changes are prominent, delusions and hallucinations fleeting and fragmentary, behaviour irresponsible and unpredictable, and mannerisms common. The mood is shallow and inappropriate and often accompanied by giggling or self-satisfied, self-absorbed smiling, or by a lofty manner, grimaces, mannerisms, pranks, hypochondriacal complaints, and reiterated phrases. Thought is disorganized and speech rambling and incoherent. There is a tendency to remain solitary, and behaviour seems empty of purpose and feeling. This form of schizophrenia usually starts between the ages of 15 and 25 years and tends to have a poor prognosis because of the rapid development of "negative" symptoms, particularly flattening of affect and loss of volition.

In addition, disturbances of affect and volition, and thought disorder are usually prominent. Hallucinations and delusions may be present but are not usually prominent. Drive and determination are lost and goals abandoned, so that the patient's behaviour becomes characteristically aimless and empty of purpose. A superficial and manneristic preoccupation with religion, philosophy, and other abstract themes may add to the listener's difficulty in following the train of thought.

DIAGNOSTIC GUIDELINES

The general criteria for a diagnosis of schizophrenia (see introduction to F20 above) must be satisfied. Hebephrenia should normally be diagnosed for the first time only in adolescents or young adults. The premorbid personality is characteristically, but not necessarily, rather shy and solitary. For a confident diagnosis of hebephrenia, a period of 2 or 3 months of continuous observation is usually necessary, in order to ensure that the characteristic behaviours described above are sustained.

Includes:

- disorganized schizophrenia
- hebephrenia

F20.2 CATATONIC SCHIZOPHRENIA

Prominent psychomotor disturbances are essential and dominant features and may alternate between

extremes such as hyperkinesis and stupor, or automatic obedience and negativism. Constrained attitudes and postures may be maintained for long periods. Episodes of violent excitement may be a striking feature of the condition.

For reasons that are poorly understood, catatonic schizophrenia is now rarely seen in industrial countries though it remains common elsewhere. These catatonic phenomena may be combined with a dream-like (oneiroid) state with vivid scenic hallucinations.

DIAGNOSTIC GUIDELINES

The general criteria for a diagnosis of schizophrenia (see introduction to F20 above) must be satisfied. Transitory and isolated catatonic symptoms may occur in the context of any other subtype of schizophrenia, but for a diagnosis of catatonic schizophrenia one or more of the following behaviours should dominate the clinical picture:

(a) stupor (marked decrease in reactivity to the environment and in spontaneous movements and activity) or mutism;
(b) excitement (apparently purposeless motor activity, not influenced by external stimuli);
(c) posturing (voluntary assumption and maintenance of inappropriate or bizarre postures);
(d) negativism (an apparently motiveless resistance to all instructions or attempts to be moved, or movement in opposite direction);
(e) rigidity (maintenance of a rigid posture against efforts to be moved);
(f) waxy flexibility (maintenance of limbs and body in externally imposed positions); and
(g) other symptoms such as command automatism (automatic compliance with instructions), and perseveration of words and phrases.

In uncommunicative patients with behavioural manifestations of catatonic disorder, the diagnosis of schizophrenia may have to be provisional until adequate evidence of the presence of other symptoms is obtained. It is also vital to appreciate that catatonic symptoms are not diagnostic of schizophrenia. A catatonic symptom or symptoms may also be provoked by brain disease, metabolic disturbances, or alcohol and drugs, and may also occur in mood disorders.

Includes:

1. catatonic stupor
2. schizophrenic catalepsy
3. schizophrenic catatonia
4. schizophrenic flexibilitas cerea

F20.3 UNDIFFERENTIATED SCHIZOPHRENIA

Conditions meeting the general diagnostic criteria for schizophrenia (see introduction to F20 above) but not conforming to any of the above subtypes, or exhibiting the features of more than one of them without a clear predominance of a particular set of diagnostic characteristics. This rubric should be used only for psychotic conditions (i.e. residual schizophrenia and post-schizophrenic depression are excluded) and after an attempt has been made to classify the condition into one of the three preceding categories.

DIAGNOSTIC GUIDELINES

This category should be reserved for disorders that:

(a) meet the diagnostic criteria for schizophrenia;
(b) do not satisfy the criteria for the paranoid, hebephrenic, or catatonic subtypes;
(c) do not satisfy the criteria for residual schizophrenia or post-schizophrenic depression.

Includes:

- atypical schizophrenia

F20.4 POST-SCHIZOPHRENIC DEPRESSION

A depressive episode, which may be prolonged, arising in the aftermath of a schizophrenic illness. Some schizophrenic symptoms must still be present but no longer dominate the clinical picture. These persisting schizophrenic symptoms may be "positive" or "negative," though the latter are more common. It is uncertain, and immaterial to the diagnosis, to what extent the depressive symptoms have merely been uncovered by the resolution of earlier psychotic symptoms (rather than being a new development)

or are an intrinsic part of schizophrenia rather than a psychological reaction to it. They are rarely sufficiently severe or extensive to meet criteria for a severe depressive episode, and it is often difficult to decide which of the patient's symptoms are due to depression and which to neuroleptic medication or to the impaired volition and affective flattening of schizophrenia itself. This depressive disorder is associated with an increased risk of suicide.

DIAGNOSTIC GUIDELINES

The diagnosis should be made only if:

(a) the patient has had a schizophrenic illness meeting the general criteria for schizophrenia (see introduction to F20 above) within the past 12 months;
(b) some schizophrenic symptoms are still present; and
(c) the depressive symptoms are prominent and distressing, fulfilling at least the criteria for a depressive episode, and have been present for at least 2 weeks.

If the patient no longer has any schizophrenic symptoms, a depressive episode should be diagnosed. If schizophrenic symptoms are still florid and prominent, the diagnosis should remain that of the appropriate schizophrenic subtype.

F20.5 RESIDUAL SCHIZOPHRENIA

A chronic stage in the development of a schizophrenic disorder in which there has been a clear progression from an early stage (comprising one or more episodes with psychotic symptoms meeting the general criteria for schizophrenia described above) to a later stage characterized by long-term, though not necessarily irreversible, "negative" symptoms.

DIAGNOSTIC GUIDELINES

For a confident diagnosis, the following requirements should be met:

(a) prominent "negative" schizophrenic symptoms, i.e. psychomotor slowing, underactivity, blunting of affect, passivity and lack of initiative, poverty of quantity or content of speech, poor nonverbal communication by facial expression, eye contact, voice modulation, and posture, poor self-care and social performance;
(b) evidence in the past of at least one clear-cut psychotic episode meeting the diagnostic criteria for schizophrenia;
(c) a period of at least 1 year during which the intensity and frequency of florid symptoms such as delusions and hallucinations have been minimal or substantially reduced and the "negative" schizophrenic syndrome has been present;
(d) absence of dementia or other organic brain disease or disorder, and of chronic depression or institutionalism sufficient to explain the negative impairments.

If adequate information about the patient's previous history cannot be obtained, and it therefore cannot be established that criteria for schizophrenia have been met at some time in the past, it may be necessary to make a provisional diagnosis of residual schizophrenia.

Includes:

- chronic undifferentiated schizophrenia
- "Restzustand"
- schizophrenic residual state

F20.6 SIMPLE SCHIZOPHRENIA

An uncommon disorder in which there is an insidious but progressive development of oddities of conduct, inability to meet the demands of society, and decline in total performance. Delusions and hallucinations are not evident, and the disorder is less obviously psychotic than the hebephrenic, paranoid, and catatonic subtypes of schizophrenia. The characteristic "negative" features of residual schizophrenia (e.g. blunting of affect, loss of volition) develop without being preceded by any overt psychotic symptoms. With increasing social impoverishment, vagrancy may ensue and the individual may then become self-absorbed, idle, and aimless.

DIAGNOSTIC GUIDELINES

Simple schizophrenia is a difficult diagnosis to make with any confidence because it depends on

establishing the slowly progressive development of the characteristic "negative" symptoms of residual schizophrenia without any history of hallucinations, delusions, or other manifestations of an earlier psychotic episode, and with significant changes in personal behaviour, manifest as a marked loss of interest, idleness, and social withdrawal.

Includes:

- schizophrenia simplex

APPENDIX III

SOURCES OF INFORMATION CONCERNING SCHIZOPHRENIA

INFORMATION, SUPPORT, AND ADVOCACY ORGANIZATIONS

Since information on schizophrenia and its treatments changes rapidly, please check the Web sites of these organizations to get the most up-to-date information. Some of these organizations maintain Web sites that are tremendously rich sources of current information.

NAMI (Formerly called THE NATIONAL ALLIANCE FOR THE MENTALLY ILL)

NAMI is the national umbrella organization for more than 1,100 local support and advocacy groups for families and individuals affected by serious mental illnesses. NAMI is the first place for families to turn when a loved one has been diagnosed with schizophrenia or another serious mental disorder. All local chapters are listed on NAMI's Web site.

NAMI
2107 Wilson Boulevard
Suite 300
Arlington, VA 22201-3042
(800) 950-NAMI (6264)
http://www.nami.org

STANLEY RESEARCH FOUNDATION / NAMI RESEARCH INSTITUTE
5430 Grosvenor Lane
Suite 200
Bethesda, MD 20814
(301) 571-0770
http://www.stanleyresearch.org

NATIONAL ALLIANCE FOR RESEARCH ON SCHIZOPHRENIA AND AFFECTIVE DISORDERS (NARSAD)
60 Cutter Mill Road
Suite 404
Great Neck, NY 11021
(516) 829-0091
http://www.mhsource.com

NATIONAL INSTITUTE OF MENTAL HEALTH (NIMH)
Office of Communication and Public Liaison
Information Resources and Inquiries Branch
6001 Executive Boulevard
Room 8184, MSC 9663
Bethesda, MD 20892-9663
(301) 443-4279
http://www.nimh.nih.gov

NIMH SCHIZOPHRENIA GENETICS INITIATIVE

For the latest information on the genetics of schizophrenia, regularly check out the Web site of the NIMH Schizophrenia Initiative, as they gather data from large numbers of families of people with the illness. http://www.grb.nimh.nih.gov/gi.html

WORLD WIDE WEB SOURCES OF INFORMATION

http://www.schizophrenia.com

By far the best Web site devoted solely to schizophrenia. Besides basic information for families and persons who have schizophrenia,

there are multiple links to other schizophrenia-related Web sites and discussion and chat areas.

www.ncbi.nlm.nih.gov/pubmed

PubMed is a search service provided by the National Library of Medicine in Bethesda, Maryland, as part of its MEDLINE medical Web site. Scientific and medical journals that publish articles on schizophrenia or the other psychotic disorders are added to the PubMed data base daily. This is the best place to look for (literally) up-to-the-minute scientific research on schizophrenia and the psychotic disorders. One must first register to use the service, but there is no registration fee. One can order copies of scientific and medical articles and have them sent via the mail, but there is a rather steep fee for this service.

http://www.mentalhealth.com

An information source and a search engine maintained by Internet Mental Health. Quite useful.

OTHER ONLINE RESOURCES

British Columbia Schizophrenia Society
http://www.bcss.org

The Experience of Schizophrenia
http://www.chovil.com

Mental Health Infosource
http://www.mhsource.com/narsad.html

Public Citizen: eLetter on Drugs for Severe Psychiatric Illness
http://www.citizen.org/eletter

Schizophrenia Society of Canada
http://www.schizophrenia.ca

Treatment Advocacy Center
http://www.psychlaws.org

APPENDIX IV
DIRECTORY

Academy for Eating Disorders
60 Revere Drive
Suite 500
Northbrook, IL 60062-1577
(847) 498-4274
http://www.aedweb.org

Academy of Psychosomatic Medicine
5272 River Road
Bethesda, MD 20816
(301) 718-6520
http://www.apm.org

American Academy of Addiction Psychiatry
1010 Vermont Avenue, NW
Suite 710
Washington, DC 20005
(202) 393-4484
(202) 393-4419 (fax)
http://www.aaap.org

American Academy of Child and Adolescent Psychiatry
3615 Wisconsin Avenue, NW
Washington, DC 20016-3007
(202) 966-7300
(202) 966-2891 (fax)
http://www.aacap.org

American Academy of Family Physicians
P.O. Box 11210
Shawnee Mission, KS 66207-1210
(800) 274-2237
http://www.aafp.org

American Academy of Neurology
1080 Montreal Avenue
Saint Paul, MN 55116
(651) 695-2717
(800) 879-1960
(651) 695-2791 (fax)
http://www.aan.com

American Academy of Pediatrics
141 Northwest Point Boulevard
Elk Grove Village, IL 60007
(847) 434-4000
http://www.aap.org

American Academy of Physician and Patient
16020 Swingley Ridge Road
Suite 300
Chesterfield, MO 63017
(636) 449-5080
(636) 449-5051 (fax)
http://www.physicianpatient.org

American Association for Geriatric Psychiatry
7910 Woodmont Avenue
Suite 1050
Bethesda, MD 20814-3004
(301) 654-7850
(301) 654-4137 (fax)
http://www.aagpgpa.org

American Association for the Advancement of Science
1200 New York Avenue, NW
Washington, DC 20005

(202) 326-6450
http://www.aaas.org

American Association for Social Psychiatry
Medical College of Wisconsin
Froedtert Behavioral Center
9200 West Wisconsin Avenue
Milwaukee, WI 53226
(414) 257-5070

American Association for the History of Medicine
Department of Medical Humanities
East Carolina University
School of Medicine
Greenville, NC 27834
http://www.histmed.org

American Association of Community Psychiatrists
AACP c/o Frances M. Roton
P.O. Box 570218
Dallas, TX 75228-0218
(972) 613-0985
(972) 613-5532 (fax)
http://www.comm.psych.pitt.edu

American Association of General Hospital Psychiatrists
Mt. Auburn Hospital
Wyman 2
Cambridge, MA 02238
(617) 499-5008

American Association of Neuropathologists
Department of Pathology
Case Western Reserve University
2103 Cornell Road, WRB, 5-101
Cleveland, OH 44106-7288
(216) 368-2488
(216) 368-8964 (fax)
http://www.aanp-jnen.com

American Association of Psychiatric Administrators
P.O. Box 570218
Dallas, TX 75357-0218
(800) 650-5888
(972) 613-5532 (fax)
http://www.psychiatricadministrators.org

American Association on Mental Retardation
444 North Capitol Street, NW
Suite 846
Washington, DC 20001-1512
(800) 424-3688 or (202) 387-1968
(202) 387-2193 (fax)
http://www.aamr.org

American Board of Medical Specialties
1007 Church Street
Suite 404
Evanston, IL 60201-5913
(847) 491-9091
(847) 328-3596 (fax)
http://www.abms.org

American Board of Psychiatry and Neurology
500 Lake Cook Road
Suite 335
Deerfield, IL 60015
(847) 945-7900
http://www.abpn.com

American College of Mental Health Administration
7804 Loma del Norte Road, NE
Albuquerque, NM 87109-5419
(505) 822-5038
http://www.acmha.org

American College of Neuropsychopharmacology
545 Mainstream Drive
Suite 110
Nashville, TN 37228
(615) 324-2360
(615) 324-2361 (fax)
http://www.acnp.org

American College of Psychiatrists
732 Addison Street
Suite C
Berkeley, CA 94710
(510) 704-8020
(510) 704-0113 (fax)
http://www.acpsych.org

American Hospital Association
One North Franklin
Chicago, IL 60606

(312) 422-3000
http://www.hospitalconnect.com

American Managed Behavioral Healthcare Association
AMBHA
1101 Pennsylvania Avenue, NW
Sixth Floor
Washington, DC 20004
(202) 756-7308 (fax)
http://www.ambha.org

American Medical Association
515 North State Street
Chicago, IL 60616
(312) 464-5000
http://www.ama.org

American Neurological Association
5841 Cedar Lake Road
Suite 204
Minneapolis, MN 55416
(952) 545-6284
(952) 545-6073 (fax)
http://www.aneuroa.org

American Neuropsychiatric Association
700 Ackerman Road
Suite 625
Columbus, OH 43202
(614) 447-2077
http://www.anpaonline.org

American Nurses Association
8515 Georgia Avenue
Suite 400
Silver Spring, MD 20910
(800) 274-4ANA
http://www.nursingworld.org

American Orthopsychiatric Association
Department of Psychology, Box 1104
Arizona State University
Tempe, AZ 85287-1104
(480) 727-7518
(480) 965-8544 (fax)
http://www.amerortho.org

American Pediatric Society
3400 Research Forest Drive
Suite B-7
The Woodlands, TX 77381
(281) 419-0052
(281)419-0082
http://www.aps-spr.org

American Psychiatric Association
1000 Wilson Boulevard
Suite 1825
Arlington, VA 22209-3901
(703) 907-7300
http://www.psych.org

American Psychiatric Nurses Association
1555 Wilson Boulevard
Suite 515
Arlington, VA 22209
(703) 243-2443
http:llwww.apna.org

American Psychological Association
750 First Street, NE
Washington, DC 20002-4242
(202) 336-5500
(800) 374-2721
http://www.apa.org

American Psychosomatic Society
6728 Old McLean Village Drive
McLean, VA 22101-3906
(703) 556-9222
(703) 556-8729 (fax)
http://www.psychosomatic.org

American Society for Adolescent Psychiatry
P.O. Box 570218
Dallas, TX 75357-02 18
(972) 686-6166
http://www.adolpsych.org

American Society of Addiction Medicine
4601 North Park Avenue
Upper Arcade #101
Chevy Chase, MD 20815
(301) 656-3920
(301) 656-3815 (fax)
http://www.asam.org

American Society of Clinical Hypnosis
140 North Bloomingdale Road
Bloomingdale, IL 60108-1017
(630) 980-4740
http://www.asch.net

American Society of Clinical Psychopharmacology
P.O. Box 40395
Glen Oaks, NY 11004
(718) 470-4007
http://www.ascpp.org

American Society of Law, Medicine and Ethics
765 Commonwealth Avenue
Suite 1634
Boston, MA 02215
(617) 262-4990
(617) 437-7596 (fax)
http://www.aslme.org

Association for Academic Psychiatry
AAP Executive Office
464 Common Street, #147
Belmont, MA 02478
(617) 393-3935
(617) 393-1808 (fax)
http://www.hsc.wvu.edu/aapl

Association for Ambulatory Behavioral Healthcare
247 Douglas Avenue
Portsmouth, VA 23707
(757) 673-3741
http:llwww.aabh.org

Association for Psychological Science
1010 Vermont Avenue, NW, 11th Floor
Washington, DC 20005-4918
(202) 783-2077
(202) 783-2083 (fax)
http://www.psychologicalscience.org

Association for the Advancement of Philosophy and Psychiatry
Department of Psychiatry
UT Southwestern Medical Center at Dallas
5323 Harry Hines Boulevard
Dallas, TX 75390-9070
http://www3.utsouthwestern.edu/aapp/

Association of American Indian Physicians
1225 Sovereign Row
Suite 103
Oklahoma City, OK 73108
(405) 946-7072
(405) 946-7651 (fax)
http://www.aaip.org

Association of Behavioral Healthcare Management
12300 Twinbrook Parkway
Suite 320
Rockville, MD 20852
(301) 984-6200
(301) 881-7159 (fax)
http://www.nccbh.org/abhm/

Association of Directors of Medical Student Education in Psychiatry
Department of Psychiatry & Behavioral Sciences
University of Louisville School of Medicine
501 East Broadway
Suite 340
Louisville, KY 40202
(502) 852-5431
(502) 852-3971 (fax)
http://www.admsep.org

Association of Gay and Lesbian Psychiatrists
4514 Chester Avenue
Philadelphia, PA 19143-3707
(215) 222-2800
http://www.aglp.org

Bazelon Center for Mental Health Law
Judge David L. Bazelon Center for Mental Health Law
11011 5th Street, NW
Suite 1212
Washington, DC 20005
(202) 467-5730
(202) 223-0409 (fax)
http://www.bazelon.org

Black Psychiatrists of America
640 Temple 8th Floor
Detroit, MI 48201
(313) 833-2421
(313) 833-4281 (fax)

Canadian Medical Association
1867 Alta Vista Drive
Ottawa, ON K1G 3Y6
(800) 457-4205
http://www.cma.ca

Canadian Mental Health Association
Canadian Mental Health Association
8 King Street East
Suite 810
Toronto, ON M5C lBS
(416) 484-7750
http://www.cmha.ca

The Canadian Psychiatric Association
141 Laurier Avenue West
Suite 701
Ottawa, ON K1P 5J3
(613) 234-2815
http://www.cpa-apc.ca

The Center for Behavioral Health, Justice, and Public Policy
8490 Dorsey Run Road
Jessup, MD 20794
(410) 724-5007
http://www.umaryland.edu/behavioraljustice

Center for Mental Health Services
P.O. Box 42557
Washington, DC 20015
(800) 789-2647
http://www.mentalhealth.samhsa.gov/aboutken/contact.asp

Center for Psychiatric Rehabilitation
Boston University
940 Commonwealth Avenue West
Boston, MA 02215
(617) 353-3549
(617) 353-7700 (fax)
http://www.bu.edu/cpr

Criminal Justice/Mental Health Consensus Project
Project Coordinator:
Council of State Governments / Eastern Regional Conference
40 Broad Street
Suite 2050
New York, NY 10004
(212) 482-2320
(212) 482-2344 (fax)
http://www.csgeast.org

Epilepsy Foundation
4351 Garden City Drive
Landover, MD 20785-7223
(800) 332-1000
http://www.efa.org

Federation of Families for Children's Mental Health
9605 Medical Center Drive
Suite 280
Rockville, MD 20850
(240) 403-1901
(240) 403-1909 (fax)
http://www.ffcmh.org

Frontier Mental Health Services Resource Network
Western Interstate Commission for Higher Education
Mental Health
P.O. Box 9752
Boulder, CO 80301
(303) 541-0256
(303) 541-0291 (fax)
http://www.wiche.edu/Mentalhealth/Frontier/frontier.asp

Group for the Advancement of Psychiatry
P.O. Box 570218
Dallas, TX 75357-02 18
(972) 613-3044
http://www.groupadpsych.org

HSRI–The Evaluation Center
The Evaluation Center @HSRI
2269 Massachusetts Avenue
Cambridge, MA 02140
(617) 876-0426, Ext. 4
http://www.tecathsri.org/contact.asp?frm=gen

Indo-American Psychiatric Association
107 Chesley Drive
Unit #4
Media, PA 19063
(610) 891-9024, ext. 115
http://www.myiapa.org

Institute of Medicine–National Academy of Sciences
500 Fifth Street, NW
Washington, DC 20005

(202) 334-2352
http://www.iom.edu

International Academy of Law and Mental Health
Académie internationale de droit et de santé mentale
c/o Chaire de psychiatrie légale et d'éthique biomédicale Philippe Pinel
Faculté de médecine, Université de Montréal
C.P. 6128, Succ. Centre-Ville,
Montréal, QC, H3C 3J7
Canada
+1(514) 343-5938
+1(514) 343-2452 (fax)
http://www.ialmh.org

International Society for the Study of Bipolar Disorders
P.O. Box 7168
Pittsburgh, PA 15213
(412) 605-1412
http://www.isbd.org

International Society for the Study of Dissociation
60 Revere Drive
Suite 500
Northbrook, IL 60062
(847) 480-0899
(847) 480-9282 (fax)
http://www.issd.org

Mental Health Liaison Group (MHLG)
http://www.mhlg.org

Mental Health Part D
http://www.mentalhealthpartd.org/

Mental Health Statistics Improvement Program Online
http://www.mhsip.org

NAMI/National Alliance on Mental Illness
Colonial Place Three
2107 Wilson Boulevard
Suite 300
Arlington, VA 22201-3042
(703) 524-7600
(703) 524-9094 (fax)
http://www.nami.org

NARSAD, The Mental Health Research Association
60 Cutter Mill Road
Suite 404
Great Neck, NY 11021
(516) 829-0091
(800) 829-8289
http://www.narsad.org

Nathan S. Kline Institute for Psychiatric Research
140 Old Orangeburg Road
Orangeburg, NY 10962
(845) 398-5500
(845) 398-5510 (fax)
http://www.rfmh.org/nkil

National Alliance of Multi-Ethnic Behavioral Health Associations
1875 I Street, NW
Suite 5009
Washington, DC 20006
(202) 429-5520
(202) 429-9574 (fax)
http://www.nambha.org

National Asian American Pacific Islander Mental Health Association (NAAPIMHA)
1215 19th Street
Suite A
Denver, CO 80202
http://www.naapimha.org

National Association of Psychiatric Health Systems (NAPHS)
701 13th Street, NW
Suite 950
Washington, DC 20005-3903
(202) 393-6700
http://www.naphs.org

National Association of Social Workers
750 First Street, SW
Suite 700
Washington, DC 20002-424 1
(202) 408-8600
http://www.naswdc.org

National Association of State Mental Health Program Directors
66 Canal Center Plaza
Suite 302
Alexandria, VA 22314

(703) 739-9333
http://www.nasmhpd.org

National Empowerment Center
599 Canal Street
Lawrence, MA 01840
(800) 769-3728
(978) 681-6426 (fax)
http://www.power2u.org/contact.html

National Institute of Mental Health (NIMH)
6001 Executive Boulevard
Room 8184, MSC 9663
Bethesda, MD 20892-9663
(301) 443-4513
(866) 615-6464
(301) 443-4279 (fax)
http://www.nimh.nih.gov

National Latino Behavioral Health Association (NLBHA)
P.O. Box 387
506 Welch Street, Unit B
Berthoud, CO 80513
(970) 532-7210
(970) 532-7209 (fax)
http://nlbha.org

National Leadership Council on African American Behavioral Health, Inc.
http://www.nlcouncil.org

National Mental Health Association (NMHA)
2001 North Beauregard Street
12th Floor
Alexandria, VA 22311
(703) 684-7722
(703) 684-5968
http://www.nmha.org

National Mental Health Consumer's Self-Help Clearinghouse
1211 Chestnut Street
Suite 1207
Philadelphia, PA 19107
(800) 553-4539
http://www.mhselthelp.org

National Resource and Training Center on Homelessness and the Mentally Ill
(800) 444-7415
http://www.nrchmi.samhsa.gov

National Research and Training Center on Psychiatric Disability
104 South Michigan Avenue
Suite 900
Chicago, IL 60603
(312) 422-8180
(312) 422-0740 (fax)
(312) 422-0706 (TDD)
http://www.psych.uic.edu/uicnrtc

Network of Care for Mental Health
Trilogy Integrated Resources LLC
1101 Fifth Avenue
Suite 250
San Rafael, CA 94901
(415) 256-9036 (fax)
http://networkofcare.org

Schizophrenia International Research Society
P.O. Box 212
Piermont, NY 10968
http://www.schizophreniasirs.org

Society of Behavioral Medicine
555 East Wells Street
Suite 1100
Milwaukee, WI 53202-3823
(414) 918-3156
http://www.sbm.org

Society of Biological Psychiatry
c/o Mayo Clinic Jacksonville
Research—Birdsall 310
4500 San Pablo Road
Jacksonville, FL 32224
(904) 953-2842
953-7117 (fax)
http://www.sobp.org

Society for Neuroscience
11 Dupont Circle, NW
Suite 500
Washington, DC 20036
(202) 462-6688
(202) 462-9740 (fax)
http://web.sfn.org

Southern Psychiatric Association
35 Lakeshore Drive
Birmingham, AL 35209

(205) 945-1840
(800) 423-4992
http://www.smaservicesinc.com

Treatment Advocacy Center
The Treatment Advocacy Center
200 North Glebe Road
Suite 730
Arlington, VA 22203
(703) 294-6001 or 6002
(703) 294-6010 (fax)
http://www.psychlaws.org

World Federation for Mental Health
P.O. Box 16810
Alexandria, VA 22302-0810
(703) 519-7648
http://www.wfmh.com

World Health Organization
20 Avenue Appia
CH-1211 Geneva 27
Switzerland
http://www.who.int/en

World Psychiatric Association
WPA Secretariat
Psychiatric Hospital
2, ch. du Petit-Bel-Air
1225 Chêne-Bourg
Switzerland
+41 22 305 57 30
http://www.wpanet.org

INDEX

Page numbers in **boldface** indicate major treatment of a topic.

C

D

M

N

ABOUT THE AUTHOR

Richard Noll, Ph.D., is a clinical psychologist, a historian of science, and an award-winning author. From 1994 to 1998 he was a postdoctoral fellow and lecturer in the history of science at Harvard University. He is a former Resident Fellow of the Dibner Institute for the History of Science and Technology as well as Visiting Scholar at the Massachusetts Institute of Technology. Noll is the author of dozens of scholarly articles and seven books on the history of psychiatry, unusual psychiatric syndromes, and anthropology. His book *The Jung Cult: Origins of a Charismatic Movement* (Princeton University Press, 1994) was chosen by the Association of American Publishers as the Best Book in Psychology published that year, and Princeton University Press submitted it as one of its entries for the Pulitzer Prize competition. Noll's scholarship has been translated into 13 foreign languages, and he has taught courses or delivered invited lectures in 14 foreign countries on five continents.

Currently, Noll is associate professor of psychology at DeSales University in Center Valley, Pennsylvania.